VINCENT E. PETRUCCI

UNITED STATES
DEPARTMENT OF AGRICULTURE

W. M. JARDINE
Secretary

YEARBOOK OF
AGRICULTURE
1928

MILTON S. EISENHOWER
Editor

ARTHUR P. CHEW
Associate Editor

UNITED STATES
GOVERNMENT PRINTING OFFICE
WASHINGTON : 1929

Organization of the United States Department of Agriculture

Corrected to January 1, 1929

Secretary of Agriculture.............................. W. M. Jardine.
Assistant Secretary................................. R. W. Dunlap.
Director of Scientific Work........................... A. F. Woods.
Director of Regulatory Work.......................... Walter G. Campbell.
Director of Extension Work........................... C. W. Warburton.
Director of Personnel and Business Administration.......... W. W. Stockberger.
Director of Information.............................. Milton S. Eisenhower.
Solicitor.. R. W. Williams.
Weather Bureau.................................... Charles F. Marvin, Chief.
Bureau of Animal Industry........................... John R. Mohler, Chief.
Bureau of Dairy Industry............................ O. E. Reed, Chief.
Bureau of Plant Industry............................ William A. Taylor, Chief.
Forest Service..................................... R. Y. Stuart, Chief.
Bureau of Chemistry and Soils........................ H. G. Knight, Chief.
Bureau of Entomology............................... C. L. Marlatt, Chief.
Bureau of Biological Survey.......................... Paul G. Redington, Chief.
Bureau of Public Roads.............................. Thomas H. MacDonald, Chief.
Bureau of Agricultural Economics...................... Nils A. Olsen, Chief.
Bureau of Home Economics........................... Louise Stanley, Chief.
Plant Quarantine and Control Administration............. C. L. Marlatt, Chief.
Grain Futures Administration......................... J. W. T. Duvel, Chief.
Food, Drug, and Insecticide Administration .... Walter G. Campbell, Director of Regulatory Work, in Charge.

Office of Experiment Stations......................... E. W. Allen, Chief.
Office of Cooperative Extension Work.................... C. B. Smith, Chief.
Library... Claribel R. Barnett, Librarian.

FOREWORD

THIS is the third in a series of Yearbooks intended primarily to inform the practical farmer about what is new in agriculture. Like the preceding volumes, it contains numerous short articles dealing with the research and regulatory work of the Department of Agriculture, and chronicles other developments in agricultural science and practice. This feature of the Yearbooks for 1926 and 1927 has been widely commended. ℂ Effort has been exerted to make the book as nearly up to date as possible, so that it may be properly entitled a yearbook. It is meant for the general reader rather than for the technician or the student. Hence popular presentation and variety of interest have seemed more desirable than exhaustiveness in the selection of material. Its wide scope has necessarily involved some sacrifice of detail; but this has not entailed a sacrifice of accuracy or of scientific significance. Each article has the indorsement of a consensus of experts, and many of the articles announce important discoveries. Thus the work should have reference value as well as popular interest. ℂ I know of no other equally comprehensive and authoritative book treating current agricultural problems. All aspects of farming, from the first steps in the preparation of the soil to the last steps in placing finished products in the consumer's hands, are discussed by specialists. New knowledge about animal and plant breeding, the control of diseases and pests, the conservation of soil resources, and so forth, is brought into relationship with research in marketing, and into the problem of adjusting output to demand, so that science may be applied equally to the production and to the sale of farm commodities. In short, the book stresses the fact that progress in agriculture calls for simultaneous action in many directions. By the collaboration of many writers it gains rather than loses in unity of emphasis, because each is alive to the interrelations of seemingly distinct problems. By indicating diverse means of agricultural advancement, it shows the impossibility of solving all the farmer's problems at one stroke. ℂ In addition to the articles, the book contains the annual report of the Secretary of Agriculture and a large compilation of agricultural statistics. These features include material for the last dates that could be covered before the copy had to be sent to the printer. Some of the statistical tables, for example, give figures for the entire calendar year 1928. A full index with cross references is provided and, in addition, the articles are arranged alphabetically. (I need scarcely add that the department will be glad to give additional information about any of the matters discussed. It is the department's function to disseminate as well as to discover useful knowledge. The Yearbook can advance this object substantially by acquainting farmers and the general public with the character, the extent, and the value of the department's work. In so far as this is accomplished, the volume should contribute to the prosperity and the well-being of all our people.

W. M. JARDINE,
Secretary of Agriculture.

CONTENTS

	Page
The Year in Agriculture	1
What's New in Agriculture	117
Department Publications	637
Agricultural Maps	640
Agricultural Statistics	666
Statistics of Grains	669
Statistics of Fruits and Vegetables	759
Statistics of Field Crops Other than Grain	828
Statistics of Farm Animals and Animal Products	902
Statistics of Dairy and Poultry	973
Foreign Trade of the United States in Agricultural Products	1015
Miscellaneous Agricultural Statistics	1036
Index to Articles	1121
Index to Statistics	1139

(v)

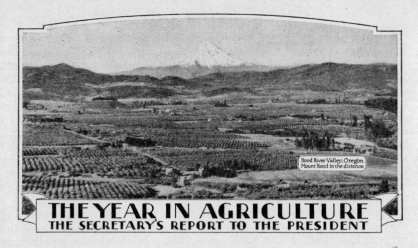

Hood River Valley, Oregon. Mount Hood in the distance.

THE YEAR IN AGRICULTURE
THE SECRETARY'S REPORT TO THE PRESIDENT

WASHINGTON, D. C., *November 5, 1928.*

To the PRESIDENT:

Although conditions are never uniform in an agricultural industry as large and varied as that of the United States, the situation this year is perhaps less uneven than in any year since 1920. Certainly there are fewer distress areas. As usual, the situation has bright spots, and spots that are not so bright. Nevertheless, the bright spots predominate. The livestock industries have prospered conspicuously. Substantially larger returns than those of the preceding year will be earned by dairymen, beef producers, and poultrymen. Hog raisers have grounds for optimism. In the early part of 1928 hog prices were unsatisfactory, but the later months brought great improvement. Returns will be smaller, however, from cash grains, hay, tobacco, and potatoes. Present indications are that the gross income of agriculture as a whole will be larger than that of the crop year 1927–28. In all probability this improvement will be reflected in at least a proportionate increase in net income, for the best available evidence indicates that production costs have not been larger than a year ago and may have been somewhat smaller.

As the current marketing season still has some months to run, it is not yet possible to estimate its probable financial results in detail. But it is clear that the year will carry forward the story of recovery from the effects of the postwar depression. This is demonstrated not only by definite assurance of an increased gross income for agriculture, as a whole, but also by numerous signs of progress in an adjustment of farm enterprises to market requirements. Many branches of the agricultural industry have made new gains in the efficiency of production, and likewise in the adjustment of supply to demand. It is beyond question that 1928 will go down in American agricultural history as a year of achievement.

Season's Production Heavy

The season was one of heavy production despite hampering weather conditions in some areas. Yields per acre were about 3 per cent above the average for the last 10 years and about 1.7 per cent above those of last year.   Good yields were harvested except in the eastern and central parts of the Cotton Belt, in parts of the eastern Corn Belt, and in an area affected by drought, comprising most of South Dakota, western Nebraska, eastern Colorado, New Mexico, and southern Texas.   Sharp changes in temperature in the spring destroyed the winter wheat seeded on fully 10,000,000 acres and thinned the stand on a large additional acreage.   Reseeding was complicated by a cold and wet June.   In the late summer and fall the South Atlantic States had torrential rains that set new precipitation records at many stations.   These adverse conditions, however, were largely offset by generally favorable harvesting weather in the more important agricultural States, and the upward trend recorded in farm production in the last few years continued.

Acreage of crops harvested was the largest on record, exceeding that of 1927 by 8,000,000 acres, or 2.4 per cent, the increase being larger than that of any year since 1918.   It should be recalled, of course, that the area harvested last year was diminished by the Mississippi floods.   Expansion of acreage is not always desirable, and the expansion this year in the case of certain crops—notably potatoes— was definitely undesirable.   Expansion of acreage, however, is at least a mark of confidence in the future of agriculture.   The increase was pretty well distributed throughout the country and was divided among cotton, spring wheat, potatoes, and other leading crops.   A decline representing a shift to more intensive crops took place in the acreage previously devoted to hay.

Cotton Acreage Increased

Cotton was planted on about 46,700,000 acres, an increase of 11.4 per cent over the acreage planted last year.   As a result, the area in cotton was only 4 per cent below the record acreage of 1926.   Losses from the boll weevil, however, were the heaviest since the first few years after that pest spread through the Cotton Belt.   Weather conditions were unfavorable for cotton.   In consequence the cotton crop in October was estimated at less than 14,000,000 bales, compared with 17,977,000 bales in 1926.   Last year's small crop of 12,955,000 bales was held down by acreage reduction, boll-weevil damage, and the Mississippi floods.   Although cotton prices now are lower than those prevailing in October, 1927, the market has showed strength recently. Since the production is greater than last year, the outlook for cotton incomes is encouraging.

Our wheat production exceeded 900,000,000 bushels for the first time since 1919.   The increase was mostly in hard winter and in durum wheat.   Indications are that the world's supply of wheat for the 1928–29 marketing season will be about 5 per cent greater than that of the 1927–28 season.   Canada, our most important competitor in wheat, has a record crop, although a part has been reduced in quality by frosts.   Europe, outside of Russia, has a crop somewhat larger and of better quality than that of last year.   But the increase in the world's supply will be considerably offset by an increase in the demand.   In Europe the consumption of wheat will probably be stimulated by its relatively low price, and by the fact that the corn crop in southern Europe is short.   Moreover, Russia's rye crop is short, and that country will probably import more wheat than it did in 1927–28. Turkey and northern China have short wheat crops. The prospect is for consumption of this season's large wheat production to an extent that should leave only a comparatively small increase in the carry-over.

Effect of Early Marketing

In the last two months wheat prices in the United States have averaged about 23 per cent lower than those of the corresponding period in 1927. This depression is doubtless to some degree a result of the increase in the world's production of wheat, but the decline was greater than supply and demand conditions seem to justify. It is well known that heavy marketings at the beginning of a season tend to depress prices too much, as was strikingly demonstrated in 1923–24. The present season resembles 1923–24 in its wheat-supply position, and may resemble it also in its wheat-price movements. In 1923–24 wheat prices fell during the early marketing, but advanced as the season progressed. Wheat moved to market in heavy volume during August of this year. The price depression was manifestly attributable in part to a glutted domestic market. Our share in the world's output of wheat does not give us a determining influence on the price of the crop, which depends on total world production. This is shown by the fact that in some years recently big crops in the United States have sold at high prices, whereas in other years small crops have sold at low prices. Yet marketing is important as well as production. This season's experience strongly emphasizes the need of marketing machinery to feed the wheat supply into trade channels as it is required, so that gluts may be avoided and prices kept reasonably stable.

In the long run the final governing influence on prices is the law of supply and demand. Sometimes, however, the market fails correctly to appraise these factors, and it seems of late to have given insufficient importance to the demand side of the equation. The world's demand for wheat has increased at the rate of about 4 per cent a year in recent years. In the 1927–28 season, for example, the world's wheat supply was about the same as it was in 1923–24. Yet the prices of all classes of wheat in the United States were considerably higher. The average price of No. 2 hard red winter wheat at Kansas City in the 1927–28 season was about $1.41 a bushel, or 36 cents a bushel higher than the average for 1923–24. This is a clear indication that the demand for wheat has increased. Many factors tend to enlarge the world's consumption of wheat, among which the more important are increases in population, recovery in the purchasing power of consumers, and a shift from other breadstuffs to wheat. These factors will be influential this season.

Utility of Economic Information

Production power, however, tends to run ahead of the increase in consumer requirements, and the adjustment of production plans on the basis of economic information becomes yearly more imperative. As evidence of the use that might be made of this department's economic services I may perhaps draw attention to the statement entitled " Outlook for Winter Wheat," which was issued August 23,

1927. This statement said that "with normal yields in important producing countries the world market situation next year may not be as favorable for marketing our export surplus as it is now." In January, 1928, the spring-wheat growers were advised that "the present indications are that with average or better than average yields another large world crop of wheat will be harvested in 1928," and that "they should hesitate to increase their acreage." It was further stated that "the outlook for durum is quite unsatisfactory * * * it appears that unless there are crop failures in some of the competing countries even stronger competition may be expected in the next season than in 1927–28." Farmers make far more use of economic information in planning their work than they formerly did, but the practice might be greatly increased with advantage.

Corn Crop Largest Since 1923

Corn production is estimated at about 2,900,000,000 bushels, the largest crop since 1923. In proportion to the number of livestock on farms the output is fairly large and will undoubtedly stimulate livestock production. Corn, which furnishes about half our grain supply, was grown this year on an acreage a little larger than that harvested last year, and the yields, although uneven, averaged a little better. Iowa had a record crop and good yields were raised also in Illinois, Missouri, Kansas, Oklahoma, and Texas. Indiana's crop was about equal to the average of the last 10 years and Wisconsin's crop slightly above the 10-year average. In other important corn-raising States the yields were disappointing. This is a season of abundant feed grains, since oats as well as corn were a plentiful crop, but opportunities exist to feed considerable grain profitably to hogs, cattle, and poultry.

A scarcity of corn and other feedstuffs in Europe has been a factor in maintaining relatively good prices for corn through the past season and is likely to be a factor in the situation for the coming season. The 1927 corn crop of Europe was considerably short of the good crop in 1926. This year's crop is still smaller. Some of the south European countries will have no export surplus and may import some corn to meet their domestic requirements. North Europe will have to depend upon South Africa, Argentina, and the United States for corn.

Argentina's Corn Position

Argentina is our greatest competitor in corn markets, selling not only in Europe but in the port markets of the United tSates. Production in Argentina amounted to 306,000,000 bushels last year, compared with a pre-war average of 192,000,000. Argentina places nearly all of her corn crop on the market. Of the 306,000,000 bushels she will probably export 250,000,000 bushels. More than 180,000,000 bushels were moved out between April 1 and October 13 of this season. Fortunately Europe took nearly all of this and only a few million bushels have come to the United States. Supplies of old corn remaining in Argentina and South Africa for export during the remainder of this year are no greater and may be less than on the corresponding date of last year, but the new crop in Argentina is being planted under excellent conditions.

Estimates for our buckwheat, rice, and bean crops all show a production less than last year, although sufficient for current needs. Fruit production was heavier than last year but less than in 1926. Potato production made a record. Possibly 15 per cent of the potato supply will either be utilized as feed for livestock or wasted. Sweet potatoes were a light crop, acreage having been reduced following the excessive production of 1927, and yields held down by unfavorable weather. Other vegetables were grown on an increased acreage but gave rather light yields. Tobacco, planted on an increased acreage, was harvested in rather low yields, so that the crop in weight is not above normal requirements. Considerable differences exist among the various types from the standpoint of quality and stocks on hand.

Exports of Agricultural Products

Exports of agricultural products in the 1927–28 season declined as compared with those of the preceding year. Shipments of pork products, wheat, and cotton dropped by an amount that more than outweighed increased shipments of certain less important export items. In value our agricultural exports for the year were 4 per cent less than those of the preceding year and were the smallest in the last five years. The proportion borne by our agricultural exports to our total exports of all commodities amounted only to 38 per cent. This percentage, with the exception of the figures recorded for 1916 and 1917, is the lowest on record.

Our cotton exports declined 30 per cent in volume, although in value the decline amounted to only about 5 per cent. This is a reflection of the higher price level prevailing in 1927–28. When the season opened foreign cotton-consuming countries, which had bought heavily of our 1926 crop, had considerable stocks on hand, which reduced their import requirements. Takings by Great Britain and Japan, where the textile industries have been seriously depressed, show the greatest reduction. Shipments to continental Europe declined less, and cotton consumption there, particularly in Germany, continued high. Foreign stocks of cotton have now been considerably reduced and the American cotton export outlook is consequently somewhat improved, although the textile industries in many of our leading markets remain depressed.

Our wheat exports declined about 6 per cent as compared with the previous year. The principal factors contributing to this decline were larger bread-grain crops in European importing countries and increased production in Canada and Argentina. On the other hand, the European market for feed grains was better, and our exports of barley and corn increased. Rice shipments to Latin American and European markets increased, although at lower prices, but exports of California rice fell materially. Our exports of flue-cured tobacco increased 14 per cent over those of the preceding year. The United Kingdom and China, our leading markets for this type of tobacco, took substantially larger quantities, and our exports of cigarettes to China increased. American flue-cured tobacco has been put in a favorable position by increased use of cigarettes and by limited foreign production of similar tobacco. But exports of this type were offset by reduced shipments of the darker pipe and chewing tobaccos, which are meeting increased foreign competition.

Apples, the leading item in our fruit exports, were exported in a reduced volume, but encouraging gains were recorded in the exports of a number of other fruits, including grapefruit, prunes, and raisins. Exports of prunes and raisins were the largest on record and were 48 and 28 per cent, respectively, larger than in the preceding year. Better quality and better packing have put American fruit in a more favorable position in foreign markets. Lower exports of pork products reflected increased competition from the Netherlands, Denmark, and the Irish Free State in the British bacon trade, and also increased hog raising in European countries. Shipments of bacon and ham were considerably smaller. Our lard exports increased 6 per cent in volume but declined slightly in value. Hog production in continental Europe, although smaller this year than last, seems likely to continue more nearly adequate to meet domestic requirements than it was in the years immediately following the war. This fact has an important bearing on the outlook for our export trade in pork products.

GROSS INCOME OF AGRICULTURE

Comparison of this year's expected results with those of other recent years is necessary to place the current situation in its proper historical setting. This comparison will show us where agriculture is moving, as well as where it stands. Latest comprehensive figures available relate to the crop year 1927–28. In that period the gross income of American agriculture from all products amounted to $12,253,000,000, compared with $12,127,000,000 in the crop year 1926–27 and $12,670,000,000 in the crop year 1925–26. The total for 1925–26 was the highest since 1919–20. Agriculture's gross income in 1919–20, in which year the postwar boom reached its peak, was estimated at $15,700,000,000. It dropped to $9,200,000,000 in 1921–22, then gradually recovered until 1925–26. From that point it dropped about 4 per cent the following year, and in 1927–28 regained 1 per cent from the previous year's recession. Gross-income figures, though not a measure of agricultural prosperity, indicate trends and therefore have an important place in the financial record.

In the last two years the gross income of agriculture has changed but little, but important fluctuations have taken place in its distribution. In 1926–27, for example, the income from grains, cotton, fruits, and vegetables was materially below that of 1925–26. In 1927–28, grain and cotton growers made considerably better earnings, but returns from hogs, fruits, vegetables, and poultry were relatively low. Regional variations in returns characterize the present year. As I have already noted, increased returns from the livestock industries will be materially offset by reduced returns from certain field crops, though the gross income of agriculture as a whole promises to be larger than last year.

The net income of agriculture, or the balance available to farm operators for their labor, capital, and management after deducting expenses of production, is a complex item difficult to express briefly. It may be said, however, that viewed either from the standpoint of labor income or from the standpoint of investment returns the net income of agriculture, like the gross income, reached its highest point since the postwar depression in 1925–26, fell somewhat in 1926–27, and increased again in 1927–28, though not sufficiently to put it back to the 1925–26 level.

National Responsibility for Farm Welfare

This does not mean that agricultural grievances are insubstantial, nor does it mean that the remedy for these very real difficulties should be left to the free play of economic forces. During the World War, largely because of appeals for increased farm production, agriculture underwent abnormal and unbalanced expansion. The postwar agricultural price depression was brought about by world conditions, for which the chief responsibility rests elsewhere than upon the farmers. The situation from which agriculture is still suffering has complex economic, social, and other roots. For these the Nation can not escape its just share of responsibility in that its officials advocated overwhelming expansion of production during the war. In like manner the Nation must accept its share of responsibility in seeking and applying sound and adequate relief. In short, agriculture is entitled to practical governmental help in rebuilding its fortunes on a firm and permanent foundation. Failure to extend such help not only would stamp the United States as ungrateful for the response of farmers to its appeals but would materially weaken the social and economic fabric of the Nation.

The Price Situation

The price situation has changed in ways important to farmers during the last year. From June, 1927, to June, 1928, the average level of the prices of farm commodities advanced, whereas the average level of the prices of things bought by farmers remained practically unchanged. Much of the rise that took place in farm-commodity prices, however, came after most of the 1927–28 products had been marketed. Farmers therefore did not get the full benefit of the rise. Cotton and cattle contributed to the rise of the farm-commodity price average in the first half of the 1927–28 season. In the second half the greatest contribution was made by hogs and wheat.

As a measure of the purchasing power of farm products the department recently began using for comparisons the retail prices that farmers pay for what they buy instead of the wholesale prices of nonagricultural goods. Farmers, of course, obtain most of their supplies at retail rather than at wholesale, and a retail index is therefore more appropriate as a measure of the exchange value of farm commodities. Moreover, many of the articles included in the wholesale-price index formerly used enter only slightly or not at all into the expenditures of the average farmer. At the present time (September) the new index of retail prices paid by farmers stands at approximately 157, compared with 100 before the war. Prices received by farmers on September 15 were 141 per cent of the pre-war average. These two price levels as of September 15 indicate a relative purchasing power of farm products of 90.

FARM-COMMODITY PURCHASING POWER

It should be noted that the new index numbers do not measure the purchasing power of farmers, but merely that of a fixed quantity of farm products. They show the power of a given amount of agricultural commodities to purchase certain kinds of other goods, compared with pre-war exchange ratios. The index numbers do not measure changes in farm receipts or in farm expenses nor do they take into account variations in the quantities of farm products sold or of goods purchased. Since these factors influence the buying power of the farmer as an individual, their exclusion from the basis for calculating index numbers makes the latter a measure of the exchange value per unit of goods rather than a measure of the buying power of the producers. Unless this is borne in mind, the index-number system may be misinterpreted.

Under the new system the department uses the prices of commodities purchased by farmers for the family living and for operating the farm. Indexes of these prices are constructed with practically the same base period (1910–1914), and as nearly as possible in the same manner, as the index of prices received by farmers for the commodities they sell. The prices paid are weighted by estimates of quantities purchased for the average farm in the period 1920–1925. Thus an attempt is made to measure the purchasing power of farm commodities in terms of the usual things that farmers actually buy. But the list includes only commodities; it does not include certain very important services for which farm income is disbursed, such as payments of interest on mortgages and loans, rents, and railroad fares.

The New as Compared with the Old Index

Measurement of farm-commodity purchasing power on a basis of retail instead of wholesale price comparisons tells a slightly different story from that told by the index numbers previously in use. Retail prices commonly lag behind wholesale prices in readjustment periods. When prices are advancing it is usual for wholesale prices to advance more quickly and more steeply than retail prices. The opposite happens in periods of falling prices. In consequence the new index-number system shows, for the early years of the post-war depression period, a somewhat smaller disparity between the prices of farm products and the prices of other goods than was shown by the old system. On the other hand, when prices are advancing the tendency is for the retail comparison to show less advance than would be shown by the wholesale comparison. For example, in June, 1928, the last month for which the purchasing-power index was compiled by the old method, farm commodities had a relative exchange value of 95 in terms of the wholesale prices of nonagricultural goods. By the new method, using retail prices as the basis for comparisons, the index number computed for June was 93.

The purchasing power attained by farm products at the present time, as already mentioned, is expressed by the index number 90, with 100 representing the base period 1910–1914. Corresponding annual figures, expressing the average farm-commodity purchasing power since 1920, in terms of this mode of reckoning, are 99 for 1920, 75 for 1921, 81 for 1922, 88 for 1923, 87 for 1924, 92 for 1925, 87 for 1926, and 85 for 1927.

Taxes and farm wages, which do not figure in the index number, remain relatively high. Farm taxes are about 250 per cent of the pre-war level and farm wages 170 per cent of that level. The prices of commodities purchased by farmers for use in production are lower than the prices of commodities entering into the family living, the figures being respectively, about 148 per cent, and about 162 per cent of the pre-war level. Among the items contributing to the high cost of living on the farm are furniture and furnishings at 208 per cent of the pre-war level, clothing at 179 per cent of the pre-war level, and building materials for the home at 171 per cent of the pre-war level. Food prices are about on the same level as commodity prices generally. Some production items are relatively low, notably feed and fertilizer prices. The prices of farm machinery are close to the general price level.

READJUSTMENT IN CAPITAL VALUES

Indexes of prices and purchasing power, however, tell the story of the agricultural situation only in part. They do not indicate the effects of the tremendous readjustment in capital values which agriculture has undergone in recent years. Although the purchasing power of farm commodities increased from 1921 to 1928, farm real-estate values continued to fall. A survey made in March, 1928, showed that farm real-estate values were only 17 per cent above the pre-war level, compared with 57 per cent above that level in 1921. These figures make no allowance for recent changes in the value of the dollar. In terms of a dollar of constant purchasing power farm real-estate values last March for the United States as a whole were about 20 per cent below the position they held 15 years before.

This decline in farm real-estate values has been a more important factor in the depression than may have been recognized, especially in the case of those who purchased land at the high valuations of the boom period. Real estate comprises more than four-fifths of the average farmer's capital investment. It provides the security for most of his borrowings, the assessment basis for most of his taxes, and a depository for his savings. In the first 20 years of the present century increases in land values were the usual form in which farmers accumulated their wealth. It is therefore encouraging to note that the downward movement is slackening. The drop in 1927 was less than in the immediately preceding years, and a tendency toward comparative steadiness appeared in areas where the decline had been especially prolonged and severe. This was the case in Iowa, Montana, and the Dakotas. Average values per acre in Iowa declined less in 1927 than in any year since the beginning of the postwar depression.

Changes in Tenure Status

Readjustment of land values has been accompanied by changes in the tenure status of farmers. As here used the term "tenure status" includes both variations in the percentage of tenants and variations in the farm owner's equity in his farm. From 1921 to 1925 the percentage of tenants in the country increased from 38.1 to 38.6. In this period tenants migrated in such large numbers from most of the old Cotton Belt as to leave much of the poorer land unfarmed. Tenancy increased in the new Cotton Belt, in the West North Central States, and in the mountain divisions. Areas near industrial centers, on the other hand, showed an increase in owner-operator farmers. This movement was most noticeable in the North Atlantic States, where many influences promote it. Cheap automobiles and good roads solve the transportation problem and the progress of invention makes city conveniences available to farm homes near cities. Moreover, a small land holding may contribute toward living expenses. But the output of such truck-gardening farms adds comparatively little to the Nation's commercial agricultural production. Such evidence as is available indicates that since the census of 1925 tenancy has continued to increase in some regions, and that taking the country as a whole there has been no increase in owner-operator farmers.

Much involuntary farm ownership has resulted from the postwar decline in farm values, and this involuntary ownership has created new problems. Tenant operation pending disposal is not considered wholly satisfactory. Owners report difficulty in getting good tenants and the satisfactory handling of foreclosed properties is often a complex problem. In certain cut-over regions, where postwar commodity prices will not sustain production, much tax delinquency exists.

It is well to bear in mind, however, that the story of land utilization in the United States during the last few years has another aspect. Though in some districts land that perhaps never should have been farmed may eventually go back to grass or timber, in other regions farm acreage has expanded and is still expanding. This is unmistakable evidence that American agriculture is vigorous and progressive, and through efficiency can occasionally turn even a bad economic situation to good account. In southern portions of the Great Plains region the recent expansion of the cultivated area has been notable. This growth, which had its start in war-time needs for increased production, has been sustained by improved mechanical methods in the raising of cotton and grain.

Expansion in Great Plains

While the cultivated area in some other sections has receded, that of the six principal Great Plains States—the Dakotas, Nebraska, Kansas, Oklahoma, and Texas—has increased. The average acreage of the principal crops in these States for the 3-year period, 1925–1927, was more than 8,000,000 acres greater than in the 3-year period, 1919–1921. Texas contributed nearly 5,000,000 acres to this expansion, North Dakota and Nebraska about 1,000,000 acres each, and Kansas, South Dakota, and Oklahoma the remaining million acres. Strong stimulus was exerted by technical progress in cotton growing and in wheat growing by the eastward and northward march of the combined harvester and thresher. Technical progress enabled Montana, part of which is in the Great Plains area, to expand its cultivated area about 1,000,000 acres. Colorado had an expansion of some half a million acres. Minnesota increased its cultivated area by more than 1,000,000 acres. In most of these States the tendency toward acreage expansion was also in evidence in 1928 and seems likely to continue into 1929.

In Texas the expansion in acreage was chiefly in the west and northwest sections, where comparative absence of the boll weevil stimulated cotton growing. Considerable gains also took place in the acreage devoted to small grains. Throughout the Great Plains the increase in the cultivated area has been largely at the expense of grazing land. Minnesota's expansion can be attributed in part to increased efficiency in crop production and in part to steady growth in the dairy industry. In Wisconsin cultivated acreages showed little change in the 6-year period mentioned. This stability was probably due in part to small increases on the newer farms in the northern portions of that State and in part to the fact that returns from dairying were relatively favorable. In most other States east of the Mississippi River the area in cultivated crops declined.

Significance of Tenancy Trend

In appraising the present situation as to farm-land values, it should not be assumed that the above-noted growth of tenancy is necessarily an unfavorable sign. In many regions productive farm land can be rented more cheaply than it can be owned when terms of cost, including taxes, depreciation, and repairs, are taken into consideration. Ownership has many advantages. Nevertheless, it may be better to be a renter on good land than an owner on poor land for which too much has been paid. After all, the farmer's problem is to lay out his available capital in the most economical and productive manner. It is not by any means always best to invest heavily in land. Many inquiries come to the department from city dwellers and farmers living in areas where land is still relatively high in price as to the desirability of purchasing presumably run-down farms or abandoned land. Bargains can doubtless be obtained by men who know land values. Prospective buyers should bear in mind, however, that not all land obtainable at a low price per acre is truly cheap.

Such figures as are available on recent tenancy changes indicate that many farmers are unwilling to pay too much for the privilege of owning. In the first 20 years of this century farm-land values in certain important Western States rose faster than land incomes. The net rate of return upon the farm real-estate investment declined steadily until it reached a level materially below the prevailing rate of return on such investments as first mortgages. A change has come about in recent years with the decline in farm-land values. At present valuations the return obtainable on an investment in farm land is somewhat more in line with the prevailing rate of return on other investments. Undoubtedly, however, the problem of tenancy is in part a reflection of unwillingness among farm operators to pay interest charges exceeding the returns obtainable on land investments. Those who supply mortgage-investment money may see in the present relationship of land values to current and prospective earning power a promise of an increased margin of safety. Purchasers will find their returns more adequate to meet their capital charges.

COTTON SITUATION AND PROBLEMS

Conditions for cotton growers were not unsatisfactory during the 1927–28 season. In the months of heaviest movement from the farm cotton prices were the best of the year. The average price at the farm in September, 1927, was 22.5 cents a pound. For the entire season the average price of Middling spot cotton in 10 spot markets was 19.72 cents a pound, compared with 14.4 cents in 1926–27. As finally estimated our total cotton production in 1927 was 12,955,000 500-pound bales, compared with 17,800,000 in 1926. Though 5,000,000 bales smaller, the crop exceeded that of 1926 in value by more than $325,000,000. Many growers were consequently enabled to overcome the financial handicaps left by the preceding unfortunate season.

Our cotton supply quickly moved into consumption. In the 12 months ended July 31 last the world's consumption of American cotton was about 15,400,000 bales. This was only about 300,000 bales less than the record consumption of the preceding year. Our cotton exports during the year 1927–28, although amounting to only 7,500,000 bales, compared with 10,900,000 bales in 1926–27, represented a value of $821,000,000. In the preceding season the much larger volume of our cotton exports realized a value estimated at only $855,000,000. In the first half of the season mill activity was at the highest rate ever recorded, and at the end of the year the world's supply of American cotton was about 2,700,000 bales less than that on hand at the end of the 1926–27 season. On June 30 last the world's carry-over of American-grown cotton was estimated at the modest amount of 5,000,000 bales.

As is usually the case when the supply of cotton is large, the last three years have produced much discussion as to the factors influencing value and price. Although such discussion normally centers around the quality of the cotton in the annual carry-over, it is generally extended to include the quality of the new crop. In the winter of 1926–27 many persons contended that the cotton carry-over was low and inferior in grade and staple length, and that when counted as so many bales in the supply it exerted an unduly depressing influence on prices. Many growers asserted that the country was probably producing cotton averaging lower in both grade and staple value than it did in earlier times, when more attention was paid to cleanliness in harvesting, and the special influences that have since contributed to shorten the average length of the staple had not been set in operation.

Demand for Data as to Quality

It was felt, in short, that the supply of good cotton was probably not as large as a mere enumeration of the number of bales in the carry-over and the crop might indicate. Accordingly a demand arose for better information as to the quality of the cotton supply, and Congress passed legislation (the Mayfield-Jones Act) and provided funds for this purpose. Thus began an important new branch of the department's work, the main object of which is to furnish regular reports as to the supply of cotton, including both the crop and the carry-over in terms of grade, staple length, and tenderability. Substantial benefits to both producers and consumers of cotton should result.

Cotton prices are affected, of course, by the quality as well as by the quantity of the crop. With a given supply, the lower the quality the lower the price; and conversely, the higher the quality, within limits, the higher the price. Heretofore, however, information as to the quality of the cotton supply has not been generally available, and consequently the principle that quality goods should bring a premium has been overlooked in cotton buying as far as the average farmer is concerned. Growers selling cotton in small lots in country markets often can not get a better price for medium than for very short-staple cotton. Unquestionably, this condition has discouraged the production of good-quality, long-staple cotton. Information obtained under the Mayfield-Jones Act will show cotton buyers and spinners where superior fiber is grown and will tend to bring about a better local price differentiation as to different quality cottons.

In 1927 grade and staple estimates were issued experimentally, covering part of Georgia and another area comprising 6 counties in the southwestern corner of Oklahoma and 21 adjacent counties in Texas. These reports proved of such value and interest that Congress made funds available to extend the work throughout the Cotton Belt. This year all interested persons were enabled to judge market prospects and transact business in cotton on the basis of information concerning the quality as well as the quantity of the supply. The first official canvass of the quality of carry-over cotton was made August 1 and published shortly thereafter. The necessary facts were obtained from owners of cotton, who furnished reports as to the number of bales and the staple length of the cotton in their possession. Information was gathered covering the actual cotton in public and private storage warehouses and compresses, in consuming establishments, on farms, and in transit from merchants to domestic spinners. Data as to the current crop were obtained from gins scattered throughout the cotton States.

Hearty Cooperation Received

In assembling this information the department received the hearty cooperation of growers, spinners, and merchants, and the undertaking aroused wide interest. It drew attention forcibly to the importance of adjusting staple lengths upward in keeping with the demand for better cotton, and promised to exercise a sensible influence in keeping grade differences and staple premiums more strictly in line with the demand for the different grades and staple lengths.

Facts disclosed by the grade and staple reports made in 1927 illustrate the value of the new work. It was found in Georgia that the growers were producing far too much cotton under fifteen-sixteenths of an inch in staple length. No less than 78 per cent of Georgia's cotton production in 1927 was seven-eighths inch or less. On the other hand, the amount of untenderable-length cotton grown in Georgia—namely, cotton thirteen-sixteenths of an inch or less in staple length—proved to be less than 2½ per cent of the State's total production. The survey demonstrated, in short, that Georgia, although producing only a small percentage of actually untenderable-length cotton, nevertheless produces far less cotton of the greater lengths than she might. Evidence was furnished that Georgia, with encouragement in the form of price differentials, could produce cotton from fifteen-sixteenths of an inch to 1 inch in length of staple in most of her counties. Indeed, a fractional percentage of the crop ran from 1 1/16 to 1¼ inches in length.

In the Texas-Oklahoma area staple lengths both better and worse than those of Georgia were grown. About 18 per cent of the crop in the Texas-Oklahoma area was thirteen-sixteenths of an inch. On the other hand, only approximately 44 per cent of its output was seven-eighths inch or less, compared with 78 per cent in the Georgia area. The Texas-Oklahoma area surpassed Georgia in the production of $\frac{15}{16}$-inch cotton. About 25½ per cent of its production was of that length, compared with only 15½ per cent in Georgia. In the grade lengths the Texas-Oklahoma area had a marked superiority. Nearly 11 per cent of its crop was $1\frac{1}{32}$ inch in length of staple, whereas in the Georgia area only 2.64 per cent of the crop attained that length. Of cotton $1\frac{1}{8}$ of an inch and above, the Texas-Oklahoma area had only a slightly better percentage than Georgia. In general the survey showed that the Texas-Oklahoma area is producing short untenderable lengths to a greater extent than Georgia. In both regions it was evident that a larger proportion of cotton 1 inch or more in staple length could be grown. There is a limit to the length of staple that can be profitably grown, determined largely by the fertility of the soil and by the degree to which the variety planted is adapted to its local conditions. In many regions, however, the present tendency is to prefer yield to quality. Longer staples could be produced on numerous farms with no increase in production costs. The problem is to get that combination of yield and staple length which will bring the best net return.

In view of the complaint that American cotton is not meeting the world's demand for good staple lengths as satisfactorily as it formerly did, the evidence furnished by the grade and staple estimates that improvement is possible has obvious importance. These estimates, moreover, should have a beneficial influence in addition to their mere demonstration that more good cotton might be grown. They should facilitate the payment of adequate premiums for superior fiber. Heretofore the practice has been to assemble cotton in even running lots at central points rather than at points of origin. This has entailed the payment of flat prices at country markets, with the result that the grower of superior cotton has been penalized unjustly.

Premiums at Country Markets

Spinners and merchants realize the desirability and justice of reflecting premiums for quality in prices at country markets. With the Cotton Belt adequately mapped from a quality standpoint, growers who produce good cotton will have a better chance to cooperate with neighboring growers in assembling even running lots in commercially significant quantities. Indeed, some of the cooperative organizations have already taken effective steps in this direction. Thus the grade and staple reports should have the doubly salutary effect of indicating opportunities for improvement and facilitating the payment of rewards for improvements accomplished. In the 1927–28 season the premiums paid for the different staple lengths were not as high as they would have been had the supply of staple cotton not accumulated to an appreciable extent from the two preceding years. Normally the premiums paid for superior fiber, if fairly reflected in prices to the individual producers, would constitute a substantial encouragement to the efficient and progressive grower.

Another important departmental activity relating to cotton seeks to promote increased use of the fiber. This object may be attained by extending old and finding new uses for cotton. From the years 1905–6 to 1913–14 the world's consumption of cotton increased annually by a little more than half a million bales. About 240,000 bales of this increase was apparently due to growth of population and the remainder was attributable to increased per capita use of the fiber, either in familiar or in new ways. In the last five years the average increase in the consumption of cotton has been approximately a million bales a year. This exceptionally large gain seems to involve the consumption of approximately three-fourths of a million bales a year in new uses and in the extension of old uses.

Early in 1926 the department concentrated increased attention on the problem of finding additional uses for cotton. Results of preliminary research were published in a report entitled "A Partial List of Uses of American Raw Cotton." Subsequently Congress appropriated funds for expanding this research program and directed the Departments of Agriculture and Commerce to pursue it jointly. A committee composed of members of the Department of Agriculture, members of the Department of Commerce, and representatives of the Cotton Textile Institute (Inc.) was formed to correlate all studies and prevent duplication of work. Under the direction of this committee research is under way in two principal directions: (1) Analysis of the consumption of American cotton by grade and staple, and (2) search for possibilities of enlarging old uses and finding new uses for cotton. This year information was assembled concerning the operation of more than 11,000,000 out of the 34,000,000 active consuming spindles in the United States, and important conclusions have been derived therefrom.

Little Competition in Longer Staples

It has been established that most American mills require cotton better than the average of the grades and staples produced in the United States. Growers have therefore at least a potential opportunity to increase their income by producing cotton of higher spinning value. In the United States and probably throughout the cotton-consuming world the strongest demand is for Middling to Strict Middling cotton from fifteen-sixteenths to $1\frac{1}{16}$ inches in length of staple. Foreign competition in the production of these lengths is practically nonexistent. Clearly, the American cotton industry has here an opportunity which ought not to be neglected.

As already mentioned, our cotton growers produce a large excess of cotton seven-eighths of an inch or less in length. Their output of such cotton is far beyond American mill requirements. In producing excessive quantities of short-staple cotton, United States growers compete with growers of the short cottons of the Orient, and fail to take advantage of their ability to produce the better staples which other countries have not succeeded in growing in important commercial quantities.

Studies of the use of cotton bags in the wholesale grocery trade have disclosed the existence of a large field in which cotton bags might be substituted for jute bags or bagging. Cotton bagging can be made from the lowest grades and staple lengths of American cotton and can be manufactured from high-grade cotton waste. It is true that such bagging ordinarily costs more than jute bagging. In

1926, however, owing to special economic conditions, cotton bagging was cheaper than jute bagging, and cotton could certainly be more often used for bagging.

Many advantages should accrue from increased use of cotton bagging. In the first place, a lighter weight bagging would effect a saving in transportation costs. Then, too, a strong, lightweight cotton bagging of standard construction and weight would help to obviate the practice, much complained of by the American cotton trade, of challenging and taring American cotton in spinners' markets at home and abroad. Moreover, cotton lint does not adhere to cotton bagging as tenaciously as it does to jute bagging.

It should be possible to manufacture a lightweight cotton bagging that could be sold in competition with jute bagging. Four different weights of cotton bagging have been tested in the department's research program. Even the lightest is superior to 2-pound jute bagging and to burlap covering. The use of cotton bagging for cotton must depend largely on its cost as compared with jute bagging. It would probably be necessary also to establish the sale of cotton on the basis of its net weight in all markets, both local and foreign. Settlements made on the basis of gross weights would involve loss if lightweight bagging were used.

Cotton Uses on Farms

Investigation of the present uses of cotton products on the farm showed that 150 articles other than clothing and household furnishings are made of cotton products. More than 100 articles not now made of cotton might, in the opinion of many farmers, be made of that product. Among these suggested new uses for cotton is the use of cotton bags for fertilizer. This alone would afford an outlet annually for approximately 170,000 bales of low-grade cotton. Experiments are under way to determine the practicability of cotton bags as containers for wool.

But the development of new uses for cotton involves economic as well as physical factors. It is not sufficient to decide that cotton might be substituted for other materials in various uses. The question arises, At what price can the substitution be made? In a year of large production and low cotton prices the opportunity to substitute cotton for jute, for example, would be much greater than in a year of low cotton production and high cotton prices. Permanent substitution of cotton for other fabrics is possible only if the increased demand for cotton thus created still leaves a price differential in favor of the use of cotton.

Accordingly, the department is studying price relationships among different bagging materials in order to determine at just what price cotton would have to sell to compete with bags made from other materials. Final results of this investigation will be available shortly and should exercise an important influence on manufacturers' plans. The first results are now being published in the form of a report on cotton bags and other containers in the wholesale grocery trade. Another report is in preparation relating to the use of bags in the fertilizer industry. It is impossible at this stage to predict how far the competitive use of cotton may be extended, but it can safely be declared that substantial progress in that direction is practicable.

PREMIUMS FOR HIGH-PROTEIN WHEAT

Work similar in principle is going forward in connection with wheat. For several years protein has played an important part in the prices paid for bread wheats and also in the prices paid for certain of the durum wheats. It has not been a price factor to any considerable extent in the case of soft red winter wheat, which is used mostly for pastry, biscuits, crackers, etc. In fact, a high-protein content is not desired in that class of wheat. In the case of the bread wheats, however, high protein commands premiums. Wheat buyers have long distinguished between strong and weak wheats. Strong wheat is characterized by quantity and quality of protein. Not until recent years, however, has the demand for high-protein wheat been sufficient to make protein a definite price factor. To-day the baker demands from the miller flour with a guaranteed quantity of protein. This is made necessary by modern bakery methods whereby the dough is mixed by electric-power machinery. Such methods require a stronger flour than is required by the house-wife's methods of hand kneading and mixing.

When the Government released its war-time control over the price and the marketing of wheat, the movement of the crop passed again into the hands of commercial dealers. Thereupon protein became an important market factor. The crops of 1920–1924, inclusive, were marketed with increasing requirements of protein content as a price factor. In this period private and commercial laboratories determined the protein content of considerable wheat. Since 1925 practically all the wheat received at the principal terminal hard-winter and spring-wheat markets in the central West has been tested for protein content, besides being inspected for certification as to its commercial grade. At Kansas City, Minneapolis, Duluth, and Superior laboratories for wheat-protein testing are operated by the State authorities. In States that have no grain-inspection department, official protein tests are made by commercial grain-inspection organizations. Protein testing is also done in several markets by private commercial laboratories. In addition, protein-testing service has been established at points more accessible to the country shipper and to the farmer. This is the case in the central Northwest spring-wheat States and to a more limited extent in the hard-winter wheat territory of the Southwest. Service is given in some places by State institutions and in others by commercial agencies.

Generally speaking, the bread-wheat crops average year in and year out from about 11 to 12.5 per cent protein. Premiums paid for protein vary from year to year, and even within a given crop movement, in accordance with changes in supply and demand. In general it may be said that the amount of premiums paid at any particular time depends not only on the average portein content of the hard red spring and hard red winter wheat crops, but also on the range of protein within the wheat crop as a whole. Terminal market premiums, however, are not always reflected to the individual grower, except when he ships his own wheat direct to the terminals. This phase of the situation urgently demands a remedy, and the department has studied the problem accordingly.

Protein Problem at Country Points

Many reasons prevent individual growers under present conditions from receiving the full terminal-market value for their high-protein wheat. Lack of understanding on the part of farmers as to what protein is and how it affects prices at terminal markets is quite general. Moreover, neither the farmer nor the country buyer usually knows the protein content of the wheat when it is hauled to the country station. Then, too, facilities are lacking for determining the protein content at the time of its sale at the country points. It would not help greatly if the protein content were known to both buyer and seller, for the country elevator, which is merely the channel through which the producer's grain flows to the terminals, can not be conveniently used by the country-elevator operator for handling and storing separately each individual lot of wheat.

Yet the grower is entitled to the full market value of his wheat. He can to a certain extent influence the protein content of his product. If he selects his seed carefully, properly prepares and cultivates his soil, and uses sound methods of crop rotation, his wheat will have a higher protein content than it would otherwise have. Growers who exercise these precautions should have the cash reward represented by the premium obtainable at terminal markets for high-protein wheat. In short, premiums for protein should be reflected in dollars and cents at country markets to the individual who has the premium wheat. In an effort to bring this about the department held conferences this year with State agricultural colleges in several Wheat Belt States where protein is a factor in marketing and prices. These conferences were attended by wheat growers, country grain buyers, millers, farm-bureau officials, and officials of State departments of agriculture. Intense interest was shown in the problem and the department was assured cooperation in its efforts to find a solution. It is too early as yet to forecast what the outcome of these conferences will be. But the problem does not appear to be insoluble and there is ground for hope that ways and means will be devised in the near future for reflecting more completely protein values in the prices paid to individual growers at country points.

IMPROVEMENT IN LIVESTOCK INDUSTRY

General improvement in the livestock industry, in which all its branches shared, was the most outstanding development in the 1928 agricultural situation. Cattle prices continued the advance which started late in 1926, and by last midsummer reached the highest average level ever recorded in peace time. Hog prices early in the year touched the bottom of a long decline which had started 18 months previously and are now in the upward swing of a new price cycle. Lamb prices were well maintained notwithstanding increased production. Wool prices were higher. Range conditions generally were fair to good throughout the year; all sections were free from serious droughts. Abundant supplies of corn, hay, and other feedstuffs were harvested.

In short, the livestock industry is now in the best-balanced condition it has held for many years. Production of cattle, hogs, and sheep has been adjusted more nearly in line with consumer demand for meats at prices assuring reasonable profits to the livestock producers. Total production of meats from inspected slaughter for the calendar year 1928 will probably be slightly larger than in either 1927 or 1926. Total gross income from livestock sales will be larger than last year, and will be almost equal to that of 1926, which was the highest in recent years as a result of that year's high level of hog prices. This year the proportion of the gross income distributed to cattlemen will more nearly equal that going to hog producers. Sheepmen also will receive a larger share.

Prosperity was brought to the livestock industry through readjustments in production, whereby producers reduced their breeding herds and disposed of burdensome surpluses. This readjustment was completed first in the sheep industry about 1922. It was not until 1927 that market supplies of cattle were reduced sufficiently to cause a material rise in the general level of cattle prices. The production cycle of hogs is of much shorter duration than that of cattle and sheep. Hence the swine industry within the last six years has experienced two periods of surplus production and low prices, and one period of small supplies and high prices. It has now entered its second period of reduced production. An upward swing of prices is in progress, which assures hog producers a favorable outlook for the coming year.

Follows Six Years of Depression

Recovery of the cattle industry follows six years of acute depression, during which period cattlemen were forced to liquidate the herds built up during war time. Between January 1, 1918, and January 1, 1928, production was curtailed to such an extent that the number of cattle in the country was reduced by 15,500,000 head, or about 22 per cent. At the present time the number is about the same as in 1913, but the Nation has 23,000,000 more consumers. Reduction in market supplies first developed in the latter half of 1927. Prices responded by advancing sharply. Supplies continued to fall off in 1928, and average prices advanced still higher. In September, 1928, the price level was the highest since 1919. The advance was particularly marked in the prices of the lower-grade cattle. From the standpoint of purchasing power, cattle are at the highest point on record. Margins on cattle feeding this year exceeded all expectations, and the demand for range cattle was never better.

Records of the last 28 years show that under normal business conditions the prosperity of cattlemen in this country varies inversely with the per capita supply of beef available for consumption. A yearly supply in excess of 61 pounds per person tends to depress cattle prices to such levels as to force liquidation. On the other hand, a per capita supply maintained at or below that amount will bring about a rise in prices. In 1926 the per capita supply of beef amounted to 63.3 pounds. In 1927 it dropped to 58 pounds, and average cattle prices advanced 18 per cent. For the current year the per capita supply will probably not exceed 54 pounds and will be the smallest for any year for which records are available. As a result, average prices of cattle during the first eight months were 27 per cent higher than in 1927 and 44 per cent above those in 1926.

In High Phase of Price Cycle

The cattle industry has a definite cycle averaging from 14 to 16 years. Apparently it is now near the low point of the production cycle and the high point of the price cycle. Previous similar points occurred in 1912 and 1898. It requires three to four years to increase beef supplies through restocking and herd expansion. Since the population of the country is increasing at the rate of more than 1,500,000 annually, the general outlook for the cattle industry is extremely favorable.

The world beef-cattle situation is somewhat similar to that in the United States. Supplies have been reduced and prices are relatively high. The number of cattle in Argentina, the greatest surplus-producing country, has declined materially. Slaughter in Argentine freezing and chilling plants in the first seven months of this year was 14 per cent less than in the corresponding months of 1927. The number of cattle in Australia has also been reduced. Exports from Australia in 1927 were reduced to nearly one-half of the exports of 1926. Exports in the first seven months of 1928 ran a little higher than in the corresponding period of 1927, but the total for the year will probably be less. Decreases in production in Argentina and Australia are partly offset by increases elsewhere. The production of both cattle and hogs has recovered in Europe, and this has had a tendency to reduce the European demand for overseas beef. Canada and New Zealand are increasing their beef production and turning to the United States as an outlet, but the quantities received from these countries are not sufficient to materially affect the market.

Swine producers enjoyed favorable conditions as the year advanced, largely as a result of readjustments effected in production. A high level of hog prices in 1925 and 1926 caused hog producers to expand their output in 1927. When the increased supplies began to reach the market prices started downward. The decline was accelerated by a falling off in both the foreign and the domestic demand for pork products and by an unusually large seasonal movement of hogs to market last winter and last spring. But as soon as these heavy market supplies showed a tendency to fall off prices moved sharply upward. By mid-September the hog-price level was fully 50 per cent above that prevailing early in the year.

Present conditions in the hog industry indicate a very favorable outlook for 1929. The June, 1928, pig survey showed a decrease of about 7 per cent in the spring-pig crop compared with that of 1927 and indicated the probability of a reduction in the fall-pig crop. Thus a smaller supply of hogs for next year's market is practically assured, although average weights will probably be heavier. A larger and more evenly distributed corn crop is expected to lower production costs, and both the foreign and the domestic demand show improvement. This is good evidence that better times are in prospect for hog producers.

Third Largest Hog Slaughter

Inspected slaughter of about 47,800,000 hogs was recorded for the hog-crop year ended October 31, 1928. This was a result of the large increase in the 1927 pig crop over that of 1926. It was the third largest slaughter on record, being 11 per cent larger than that of 1927 and 17 per cent larger than that of 1926, although much smaller than the slaughter in 1923 and 1924. The total market value of the hogs slaughtered under Federal inspection in 1928 will probably be about $1,000,000,000, or about 6 per cent less than in 1927 and 16 per cent less than in 1926. It is worth pondering that 48,000,000 hogs sold this year for almost $200,000,000 less than the amount received for 41,000,000 hogs in 1926. Leaders in the hog industry are working on plans for stabilizing production on a more profitable basis and reducing the extent of the periodic price swings.

Hog production is being reduced in some foreign countries, and foreign demand for the hog products of the United States is increasing. The number of hogs in Denmark is 10 per cent less than last year. The number of brood sows in the United Kingdom has been reduced 5 per cent, in Germany 2 per cent, and in the Netherlands 20 per cent. These are the most important foreign producing countries. Foreign demand for hog products from the United States has been weak in the past year, but it is improving. The demand for hog products should be considerably better in the coming year than it has been in the past year. It seems probable, however, that hog production in Europe will be larger in the next decade than during the decade now ending.

Sheep Industry Continues Prosperous

The high degree of prosperity which the sheep industry has enjoyed since 1922 continues. Lamb prices during the first eight months of 1928 averaged higher than at any time since 1925 and have since been fairly well maintained, notwithstanding increased production and larger market supplies. Demand for wool improved during the year. The crop of western-fed lambs was marketed in an orderly manner, which strikingly demonstrated the value of organized marketing. At the beginning of the marketing season the outlook did not promise remunerative returns. Yet in the face of apparently increased supplies prices advanced sharply and were well maintained until the last of the crop had been sold. The strength of the market apparently was due to three factors: (1) Higher pelt values, reflecting higher wool prices; (2) a decrease in the number of lambs fed in the eastern Corn Belt, which more or less offset large increases in the West; (3) orderly marketing of western lambs, which prevented gluts in the eastern cities where lamb prices are largely made.

The sheep industry is on the upward swing of a production cycle. The number of sheep in the country has been expanding since the low point reached in 1922. At the beginning of 1928 the number was 23 per cent larger than at the 1922 low point, and the lamb crop this year showed an increase of 8 per cent over that of 1927. Consumer demand for lamb also has shown a definite upward trend, but has not kept pace with the growth in sheep numbers. So far, however, the increase in production has been well absorbed, owing to an increasing demand for lambs for flock expansion. During the period of depression in the cattle industry many cattlemen switched to sheep. Now that the cattle industry is again on a profitable basis there may be a tendency to switch back. There is consequently a possibility that the demand for sheep for flock expansion may diminish. Sheep producers would be well advised to give more attention to increasing the demand for their product.

World's Sheep Numbers Increase

The number of sheep in the world is increasing. The number in seven countries, including the United States, New Zealand, the United Kingdom, France, and three other European countries, increased from 125,700,000 in 1927 to 128,300,000 in 1928. Most of this increase was in the United States. In several European countries the upward tendency seemed to have been checked. In Australia the number declined from 104,300,000 to 96,000,000, owing to drought. But with a good lambing season and improved pasture conditions the Australian reduction will be nearly recovered by the end of another year. Sheep are increasing in Argentina and in the Union of South Africa.

Increases in the number of sheep in the United States, Canada, and the United Kingdom have increased wool production, but the gains in these countries are partly offset by decreases in France, Germany, and elsewhere. It is reported that improved range and pasture conditions in Australia are producing more wool from the 96,000,000 sheep in 1928 than from the 104,000,000 in 1927. The world's wool clip outside of Russia and China for 1928 seems likely to be somewhat larger than that for 1927 and about equal to or a little larger than the clip of 1926. The world's demand for wool seems likely to be as good as or better than in 1928.

DAIRY SITUATION FAVORABLE

Generally favorable conditions prevailed this year for the dairy industry. Prices were good and the returns to producers relatively better than those of some other leading farm enterprises. Supplies of roughage and hay were large, and this fact, despite high prices for concentrated feeds, gave dairymen a margin of returns over feed costs as wide as or wider than that of several recent years. Although total milk production was about the same as in 1927, output of cheese, dry milk, and ice cream increased, while that of condensed and evaporated milk and butter decreased. A steady upward trend in the consumption of market milk and cream was recorded, but data are not yet available to show whether this increase sufficed to offset the indicated decrease in the consumption of butter and condensed and evaporated milk.

The consumption of dairy products increases annually. Part of the gain is attributable to the normal growth of population and part to an increase in per capita consumption. Nevertheless, the consumption is not yet up to the level most desirable from a public-health standpoint. Additional increases may be expected from continued effort to improve the quality of dairy products and from educational work to acquaint the public with the reasons for according a larger place for dairy products in the diet. As a matter of fact, there is room for an increase in both the production and the consumption of dairy products in the United States. This country is not entirely self-sufficient in the production of dairy products. For several years it has had an annual import balance equivalent to about 1,000,000,000 pounds of fluid milk, due largely to the importation of certain varieties of cheese from Switzerland, France, and Italy. There has also been a small import balance of butter and dry milk.

Dairy products have brought remunerative prices throughout the entire period of the postwar agricultural depression, and significant regional developments have taken place. Long-distance shipments of fluid milk and cream have affected the demand for cream in areas near large consuming markets. Shipments of sweet cream now appear in the Atlantic seaboard markets from the western North Central States. A notable shift in dairy-producing areas has taken place toward the South, where new creameries, cheese factories, and condensaries have been established. This is in part a result of the fact that market milk commands a price above what can be obtained for milk sold in the form of manufactured products. Such developments, with the changed competitive conditions which they involve, are natural in a progressive and growing industry. In general, the dairy situation remains one of the brightest spots in the agricultural picture.

Foreign Dairy Production

Foreign dairy production appears to be increasing more rapidly than production in the United States, but the recovery of European buying power and increases in our import tariff rates have held imports in check and have maintained prices in the United States above foreign-market prices. Dairy production has developed very rapidly in the Southern Hemisphere in recent years. In the 1927–28 season exports of butter from Australia, New Zealand, and Argentina amounted to 284,000,000 pounds and exports of cheese to 177,000,000 pounds, compared with a pre-war average of 124,000,000 pounds of butter and 57,000,000 pounds of cheese. Conditions are now reported to be favorable for a considerable increase in production over last year. Russia is recovering from the effects of the war. Exports from Siberia now amount to about one-half of the pre-war exports of all Russia, and exports from Baltic countries which have separated from Russia have increased, so that the total exports from Russia and former territory are now equal to pre-war. In the meantime Denmark and the Netherlands continue to expand production. The 1927 butter exports of Denmark amounted to 316,000,000 pounds as compared with a pre-war average of 196,000,000, and the butter exports of the Netherlands amounted to 106,000,000 pounds compared with 75,000,000. The Netherlands has also increased exports of cheese from a pre-war average of 127,000,000 to 205,000,000 pounds.

Fortunately, the economic recovery of Germany has provided an expanding market for these dairy products. The United Kingdom has also continued to buy large quantities. Nevertheless, New Zealand and Denmark continue to ship butter to the United States in the high-price season, and Canadian cheese producers, meeting hard competition from New Zealand and the Netherlands in Europe, are turning to the United States as a market for their products. Switzerland has also been increasing cheese shipments to the United States.

Imports Checked by Tariff

Increases in the tariff rates on butter, cheese, and milk have checked but not stopped imports of dairy products. In 1920 the United States imported 37,000,000 pounds of butter. Following the enactment of the tariff, imports dropped to 7,000,000 in 1922, but this was only a temporary decline, as in 1923 imports amounted to 24,000,000 pounds. The increase in the tariff on butter from 8 to 12 cents per pound, effective March 6, 1926, did not eliminate imports but has held them to about 8,000,000 pounds per year in the past two years. The increase in the import duty on Swiss cheese from 25 to 37½ per cent ad valorem, effective July 8, 1927, had a temporary effect in the checking of imports of cheese from Switzerland, but in the past few months imports have again recovered to about the same level as before the tariff went into effect. Imports of milk and cream from Canada have increased from 2,590,000 gallons in 1919 to 7,479,000 gallons in 1926. Sanitary regulations, effective May 15, 1927, temporarily reduced imports; but a quick recovery from this reduction is to be expected.

IMPROVEMENT IN POULTRY INDUSTRY

The poultry industry has done considerably better this year than it did in 1927. In the fall of 1927 stocks of eggs in storage were heavy and prices low, and poultry also was relatively low in price. Stocks were reduced rapidly as the season advanced, however, and toward the end of the year were small. This year the prices of both poultry and eggs have averaged higher than in 1927, and the outlook for the remainder of the season is for prices at least equal to those of the corresponding period in 1927. Egg production this fall and next winter promises to be no greater and prices should be fairly well maintained.

A trend toward greater specialization, strongly marked in the poultry industry during the last few years, continues, particularly in egg farming. In this branch of the industry the size of the average individual farm is increasing, as well as the number of specialized farms. Accordingly, egg production on specialized farms grows steadily in importance and market influence, though the farm flocks of the Middle West still furnish the bulk of the eggs and poultry entering into commercial channels. Specialization in the poultry industry is promoted by such developments as the recent improvement of the mammoth incubator, the use of coal-stove brooders whereby chick rearing on a large scale at a low cost is possible, the systematic breeding of poultry for increased egg production, the use of electric lights to induce out-of-season laying, and better knowledge of nutrition.

Poultrymen are emphasizing breeding improvement to produce flocks with higher laying capacity and greater freedom from disease. Great possibilities have been opened by methods for rearing chicks closely confined or semiconfined. This system has merits both as a labor saver and as a means of controlling diseases and parasites, and realization of its present promise would introduce profound changes into the poultry industry. Similar methods applied to the raising of turkeys have created hope that the turkey industry may be reestablished in sections from which it has largely disappeared. Effort to acquaint the public with the food value of poultry and eggs is not as well maintained as it might be with advantage.

FRUIT AND VEGETABLE INDUSTRY

Our fruit and vegetable industry continues to progress in specialization, in the technic and efficiency of production, in the standardization, quality, and pack of its products, and in the breadth of its marketing program. Little has yet been done, however, to stabilize production or to prevent the recurrent glutting of markets. On the Pacific coast fruit production is increasing. It is increasing also in the citrus areas of the South and in many of the best fruit sections in the East. On general farms where fruit is raised as a side line the trend seems to be downward. Fruit consumption per capita is increasing, although the rate of increase is difficult to measure, owing to the rapid change that is taking place in fruit-consumption habits.

The variety offered for sale, coupled with increased per capita purchasing power, has shaken the preferred position of some favorite fruits. Lunch boxes contain fewer apples and more oranges and bananas. Fewer pies are made with dried apples and more with other dried, canned, or cold-pack fruits. Prunes and raisins have gained greatly in popularity. Northern peaches feel the competition of southern peaches, and southern peaches feel the competition of western cantaloupes. Juice grapes encroach upon the market for cider apples. Hawaiian canned pineapples compete with western canned peaches. Oranges and grapefruit have replaced other products. Fresh, dried, and canned fruit has become available in steadily increasing variety and quantity and on a constantly rising level of quality.

Naturally, however, this development has been accompanied by steadily increasing competition among the producers. In areas where crops are irregular or not of the best quality, many growers have been crowded out. Yet the volume of production continues to increase. When high prices for any kind of tree fruit prevail for several years in succession the result is usually a great expansion of the acreage set to young trees. Production continues to expand as the new trees come into bearing and grow larger and may exceed the requirements. Finally correction is brought about, but in a costly and discouraging manner, by the neglect or removal of trees and the bankruptcy of many producers. Partial relief is obtained by a constant struggle for a wider distribution and a continuous effort to improve the quality of the offering. This policy, unquestionably sound and effective as far as it goes, needs, however, to be supplemented by a more far-sighted adjustment of production plans to market needs.

Expansion Effect Is Long Continued

Apple growers still feel the effects of the undue expansion of apple orchards that took place 15 or 20 years ago. Peach production in the Southeast seems to be passing a peak, and unless prices improve the production may decline too rapidly, until the stage is set for another wave of overplanting. The production of certain fruits in California has exceeded requirements. California growers this year had particular difficulty in marketing clingstone canning peaches, and trouble is expected with grapes. Some relief can doubtless be obtained by skillful marketing, but the really effective remedy, that of curtailing production, is difficult, painful, and time consuming.

Vegetable growers face similar problems. Our national food habits are changing rapidly, and the trend can not be predicted. Shipments of vegetables have been greatly expanded in recent years. Production of asparagus, lettuce, and spinach for shipment has approximately doubled during the last six years, but the production of some of the cheaper vegetables has hardly been maintained. People are spending more money for vegetables, but this is chiefly due to a shift from the old staples to the more costly kinds. If we include potatoes, there is little to indicate that the pounds of vegetables consumed per capita have materially increased.

Improved transportation and the development of new producing areas in the South and the Southwest have extended the season for most kinds and made larger supplies of fresh vegetables available during the winter. On the other hand, fewer cellars are stocked with a winter supply of potatoes, onions, beets, carrots, turnips, etc. Tremendous unmeasured expansion in long-distance shipments of vegetables by motor truck has taken place. The indicated increase in consumption, however, is partly offset by a reduction in the proportion of our population on farms and in rural areas. Moreover, long-distance shipment of vegetables has reduced the relative importance of the market gardens near cities.

Constant Shifts Involved

Shifting of the demand from one season to another and from one vegetable to another entails constant shifts in producing sections. Areas but recently desert or swamp now ship trainloads of produce daily, whereas other areas, left behind in the struggle for the shifting market, have dropped vegetable production and gone back to staple crops. Nevertheless, the output has been maintained close to market requirements, and in years when the acreage is large or the weather exceptionally favorable to production prices are carried below the cost of producing and shipping. Losses thus incurred run into big figures.

Under average weather conditions 3,500,000 acres planted to potatoes will produce about 400,000,000 bushels. This is as large a quantity as can usually be marketed. Greater production is economic waste. This year the potato acreage was expanded about 10 per cent beyond normal requirements. Indications are that the bulk of the excess area, amounting to possible 350,000 acres, will either not be dug or will be dug only to furnish feed for livestock. In this country the value of potatoes as feed for livestock is only about one-fifth of their usual cost of production.

This excessive production was predicted by the Department of Agriculture in January and March. The warning was repeated in May. More confidence on the part of producers in the value of economic data would certainly have kept the production down somewhat. However, such mistakes can not be entirely prevented until more adequate statistical information is available and the forecasting of acreages is a demonstrated possibility. The department hopes eventually to be in a position to keep a careful watch on plantings, both of fruit and vegetables, so that growers may have warning of undue expansion. As in the case of other farm enterprises, the best remedy for maladjustment in fruit and vegetable production is the collection and intelligent use of production statistics.

Necessity of Production Statistics

Economic information becomes more important to the fruit and vegetable industry with each new development in its transportation facilities, and in its technic for preventing the deterioration of perishables. These agencies of progress, as is well known, have enormously extended the distribution area of the fruit and vegetable growers. They have made available the year round such formerly seasonal products as lettuce and celery, citrus and core fruits. Such products are now commercially grown thousands of miles from leading consuming markets. New possibilities have been opened up by the motor truck, which is developing specialized fruit and vegetable areas within overnight hauling distance of market centers. But the growth of the market has been accompanied by corresponding or greater growth in production. If production is to be kept in a satisfactory relationship to market requirements adequate statistics of supply and demand are indispensable. When production outruns consumption the producer suffers materially, but it does not follow that the consumer benefits. Studies made by the department show that overproduction results in ruinously low returns to growers without necessarily affecting retail prices proportionately. Consumers as well as producers would benefit from a better adjustment of supply to demand based on statistical interpretation of market tendencies.

In another part of this report I have mentioned the new produce agency act, which is designed to improve business practice in the fruit and vegetable industry. Another recent law, providing for the standardization of baskets and hampers, promises additional benefit. Advantage should also result from present tendencies toward the better coordination of marketing activities. Within the last few years organizations roughly corresponding to that of the clearing house in the banking industry have been set up in some sections for the purpose of tabulating and exchanging information about shipments and supplies. These organizations, which attempt to deal with the whole industry of a district rather than with the problems of a restricted locality, have found the services of the department very useful. The fruit and vegetable industries are in a state of development and transition. Their present difficulties result from a superabundance rather than from a deficiency of energy and enterprise, and we may confidently expect these difficulties to be overcome.

AGRICULTURAL RELIEF

The betterment of agriculture necessitates a combination of individual efficiency, cooperative enterprise, and wise public policy. Many of the fundamental principles that make for success in industry and trade can be applied to agriculture. It is necessary to reduce wastes in production and distribution, to expand markets, to find new uses for agricultural products, to organize producers for greater bargaining power, and to invoke Government aid in research and in the maintenance or creation of favorable market conditions. Legislation should be enacted for the control of recurring surpluses of farm products so as to minimize price fluctuations. On this subject I presented my views in detail last year. On this occasion it will suffice to outline them briefly.

The surplus problem is of vital importance not only to agriculture but to the Nation as a whole. It is therefore proper to make the solution of it in some measure a governmental responsibility. This need not involve going further than the Government has gone in aid of other economic interests, although legislation dealing with the agricultural surplus necessarily must be sufficiently different from other legislation to meet the peculiarities of the problem. No law dealing with this question would be entirely adequate at first. Changes in a surplus-control program probably would be necessary in the light of experience. As an initial step it should suffice to create a Federal farm board with adequate authority to finance the handling of surpluses through central stabilization corporations, for which purpose a revolving fund should be provided. Advisory councils responsible to the farmers should be created to assist the board. In this way the surplus problem would, I am convinced, be brought nearer to a solution.

Much can be done for agriculture through indirect Government assistance. Farmers and business men interested in agriculture may cooperate in promoting standardization on the basis of grades and inspection facilities made available through administrative services. Advantage can be taken of the extensive economic data regularly published by the Department of Agriculture. This information is indispensable to a satisfactory adjustment of production to market requirements. Its interpretation and practical application necessitate action by the farmers themselves, individually and through their organizations. The indirect assistance given by the Government to agriculture through its efforts to reflect premiums for quality goods in prices at the farm can scarcely be overestimated. I have already given details concerning work done to encourage the production of high-protein wheat and better staple cotton. In the long run help of permanent value to agriculture will result from just such activities as these, whereby facilities are created for encouraging quality production by cash rewards.

Farmer's Share of Consumer's Dollar

Vigorous efforts should be made to reduce costs and risks in marketing. The prices paid by consumers for farm commodities are in many cases adequate to insure satisfactory returns to the farmer provided high distribution costs can be reduced. In other words, the task is to increase the farmer's share of the consumer's dollar. On this problem much scattered information is available from which I might cite numerous striking examples. I refrain, however, because the whole problem has not been adequately studied, and a just estimate of it can not be made without much more comprehensive information than we at present possess. Accordingly, I repeat my previous indorsement of the proposed census of distribution, which should go a long way toward disclosing the weak links in our distribution system and indicating opportunity for specific improvements. Wide spreads between farm prices and consumers' prices are usually the result not of excessive charges by middlemen and others but of excessive service costs. The remedy is not necessarily to eliminate the middleman, but rather to discover means of speeding up and cheapening the distribution process.

RECENT AGRICULTURAL LEGISLATION

In the heat of discussion about general farm-relief legislation we may perhaps fail to appreciate the substantial aid given to agriculture in recent years by the enactment of laws intended to meet various specific requirements. Among the most important of these laws is the cooperative marketing act of July 2, 1926. This measure enables the department to carry on extensive research and other work in the field of marketing. It is not enough to assist the farmer by introducing improved field crops and livestock and by waging war on animal and plant diseases and pests. Assistance must also be given in developing an improved technic of selling and distribution. Under the cooperative marketing act the department is given the authority and the means to encourage farmers' cooperative activities, not by regulation but by research and practical services of various kinds. The scope of this work extends beyond marketing. It also includes effort to eliminate waste in distribution and to effect a better adjustment of production to consumption. Thus it is closely associated with the work done by the department for many years in the grading and standardization of farm products.

In short, the cooperative marketing act authorizes and enables the department to assist the cooperative movement in solving its problems of organization, management, sales policy, financing, and membership relations. As the movement is still in its infancy, the solution of these problems necessitates research as well as education and help in giving effect to principles and methods of demonstrated utility. An important feature of the act permits farmers and farmers' associations to exchange crop and market information directly or through a common agent, an essential practice in efforts to adjust supply to demand. This valuable right was not definitely established prior to the passage of the cooperative act, for the Supreme Court of the United States had decided that certain uses of information by trade associations violated the antitrust law. Under the cooperative law and other legislation of a similar remedial character, cooperative associations are practically exempted from the Federal antitrust laws.

Laws Affecting Collective Bargaining

It may be interesting briefly to mention the steps by which farmers' business organizations have been granted the necessary scope for collective bargaining, because their freedom of action in this respect has often been challenged. To-day there is little room for the application of Federal antitrust laws to farmers so long as they do not unduly enhance the prices of the commodities dealt in and do not resort to violence or other unlawful means in the conduct of their business. Cooperative marketing necessarily involves concerted action. It was therefore essential at the outset to protect farmers against the Sherman antitrust law, since that measure is broad enough to apply to cooperative activities that affect interstate or foreign commerce. It denounces every contract, combination, or conspiracy in restraint of interstate or foreign commerce and makes violation of its provisions a misdemeanor punishable by fine or imprisonment. Congress as long ago as June, 1913, undertook to free farmers from the risk of such punishment by declaring that no part of the appropriation for the enforcement of the antitrust laws should be "expended for the prosecution of producers of farm products or associations of farmers who cooperate or organize in an effort to obtain and maintain a fair and reasonable price for their products."

This saving provision was reenacted annually, and in the Clayton antitrust law of October 15, 1914, a section was included dealing specifically with labor organizations and with agricultural and horticultural organizations. This section declared that nothing in the antitrust laws should be construed to forbid the existence and operation of such organizations when instituted for purposes of mutual help, without capital stock and conducted for mutual profit. The Clayton law further provided that neither such organizations nor their members should be held or construed to be illegal combinations or conspiracies in the restraint of trade.

These provisions, however, were not entirely sufficient for the purposes of the cooperative movement, because they involved the restriction that organizations desiring the benefits of the Clayton Act should not have capital stock. Such restrictions made it impossible for cooperative bodies to do business on equal terms with commercial organizations. Accordingly they were removed by the Capper-Volstead Act of February 18, 1922, which gave cooperative associations the right to incorporate and to possess capital stock and also authorized necessary contracts between associations and their members. The Capper-Volstead Act retains the provision that cooperative associations must be conducted for the mutual benefit of their members, and it limits dealing in the products of nonmembers to an amount not greater in value than that of the products handled for members. Associations may restrict each member to one vote regardless of the stock he holds and may limit their dividends to 8 per cent a year. They are required to comply with one of these restrictions and may comply with both.

States Have Cooperative Laws

All but two of the States now have statutes authorizing the formation of cooperative associations. In 28 States these statutes have been upheld by their supreme courts, and contracts made by associations with their members likewise have been declared valid. Moreover, the Supreme Court of the United States has passed on the validity of a State cooperative statute and has held that it does not violate either the State or the Federal Constitution. This important decision was rendered February 20, 1928, in the case of the Liberty Warehouse Co. v. The Burley Tobacco Growers (48 Sup. Ct. Rept. 291). It may therefore be confidently concluded that the cooperative movement is now on a sound legal basis. As already intimated, cooperation must not be employed for the purpose of unduly enhancing the price of agricultural commodities. Under the Capper-Volstead Act the Secretary of Agriculture is authorized to take corrective action when such a practice seems to exist. I have previously observed, however, that agriculture does not lend itself to monopoly practices, and it is very unlikely that cooperative activity will develop antisocial characteristics.

Another important phase of recent cooperative legislation forbids discrimination against farmers' organizations by grain exchanges, boards of trade, and similar institutions. Such discrimination is prohibited in the act of March 4, 1927 (44 Stat. 1423), which declares that no board whose members deal in farm products in interstate commerce shall exclude from its membership privileges any representative of a farmers' cooperative association or group of associations. It is provided that farmers' organizations desiring membership in grain exchanges or boards of trade must have adequate financial responsibility and must agree to comply with the conditions lawfully imposed on other members. An important feature of the act declares that no board of trade may forbid an association represented thereon from making returns to its members on a patronage basis. This act follows a similar provision in the grain futures act of September 21, 1922, applying to terminal grain markets. The United States Supreme Court has pronounced the grain futures act constitutional. The right to return patronage dividends had previously been given to cooperative organizations of livestock producers under the packers and stockyards act of 1921, which act likewise has been upheld by the Supreme Court of the United States.

Agricultural Credit Legislation

Important legislation affecting agricultural credit has been enacted in recent years. A law passed February 8, 1927, amended the agricultural credits act of 1923 by authorizing national agricultural credit corporations to make loans on farm crops being grown for market. Another important piece of recent financial legislation was the act passed February 25, 1927, amending section 24 of the Federal reserve act so as to authorize any national banking association to make loans upon real estate, including farm lands situated within the bank's Federal reserve district, or within a radius of 100 miles of the bank irrespective of district lines. Loans thus made may be for as much as 50 per cent of the value of the land and may run for as long as five years.

Substantial benefits to the fruit and vegetable industry seem likely to accrue from the produce agency act of March 3, 1927. This measure is intended to obviate complaints by farmers against the manner in which commission merchants handling farm produce conduct their business. Such complaints formerly were not infrequent. Returns were often made to farmers indicating that the produce shipped by them proved unsalable due to its low grade or deterioration. Occasionally handling charges were represented as exceeding the sale price of the goods. In the case of egg shipments heavy deductions were sometimes made for breakage. Investigation showed that sometimes the returns were false and that the commission merchant had profited at the expense of the shipper. The produce agency act is intended to obviate such fraudulent practices. It makes it unlawful for a commission merchant receiving perishable farm produce in behalf of another person to destroy, abandon, discard as refuse, or dump the produce without sufficient cause. False reports made with intent to defraud are forbidden, and the Secretary of Agriculture is authorized to provide an inspection service certifying to the condition of the produce upon application by any financially interested person. Inspection certificates thus issued are prima facie evidence in the Federal courts of the truth of the statements contained therein.

Many other examples of helpful legislation enacted in recent years could be cited. Those I have given, however, should suffice to show that considerable constructive work has been done by Congress in the interest of agriculture since 1924, the benefits of which will be felt long after the postwar agricultural depression has passed away.

THE TARIFF AND AGRICULTURE

In my report last year and also in 1926 I discussed the relationship of the tariff to agriculture. I pointed out that since agriculture is becoming less and industry more dependent on the foreign market the tendency is for our tariff system to grow relatively more valuable to the farmer than to the manufacturer. It is a gross error to declare, as is often done, that the tariff benefits only the industrial branch of our national business. About one-third of our total agricultural production meets the products of foreign competitors in our own markets. In the calendar year 1924 no less than 45 per cent of our imports of dutiable articles consisted of essentially competitive agricultural products. It need scarcely be emphasized that tariff protection on farm commodities of which we import considerable amounts is valuable to our farmers.

Those who deny the present and prospective value of the tariff to agriculture can not have considered how much of our farm production meets foreign competition within the United States. Vegetable oils, imported as such or extracted from imported oil-bearing materials, afford a good example of this competition. Many of these oils compete directly with certain of our domestic oils and fats, such as lard, butter, and cottonseed oil. The diversity of the oil-bearing materials makes it difficult to estimate the power of this foreign competition. It is significant, however, that a definite tendency toward increased foreign production of vegetable-oil materials has been accompanied in recent years by greatly increased imports of these products into the United States. In 1927, for example, imports of vegetable oil-bearing materials alone, not including substantial imports of extracted oil, totaled almost 1,000,000 tons, an increase of more than 300 per cent over the average imports during the five years immediately preceding the war. Obviously, this is a field in which tariff duties may benefit our producers.

Production of several of our important crops, such as beef, mutton, spring wheat, corn, and dairy products closely approximates our domestic requirements. Our output of such commodities fluctuates close to the margin between an export and an import basis. Tariff duties on such articles do not necessarily exclude foreign supplies when our own output is insufficient, but before imports begin domestic prices must rise above world prices by the amount of the tariff and the cost of transportation from abroad to our markets. Corn is a good example. In July and August, 1927, the price of corn in Chicago was from 26 to 37 cents a bushel above the price of corn in Buenos Aires. This margin attracted shipments of Argentine corn to United States ports, and in August, 1927, total United States corn imports amounted to 1,176,651 bushels. The duty on corn is 15 cents a bushel. Unquestionably, but for that duty our imports of corn last year would have been much larger.

Dairy Industry Protected

Our dairy industry enjoys effective tariff protection, although its output as a whole practically equals domestic consumption. Estimates of the milk equivalent of the total quantity of milk and milk products consumed in the United States indicate that approximately 1 per cent is imported. Under our tariff the American price of butter is usually higher than in the important foreign dairy markets. It is true that imports narrow the margin when it becomes wide, but only after leaping the tariff barrier. American dairymen, if deprived of tariff protection, would be subject much more frequently to foreign competition in the domestic market. Duty-free imports would enter the United States whenever the difference between American and foreign prices sufficed to cover transportation costs, whereas under present conditions the margin must cover those costs plus the tariff.

Our beef producers enjoy tariff protection, as do producers of spring wheat. Since the war beef production and spring-wheat production have fluctuated between an export and import basis. As our population increases these products probably will tend to rest regularly on an import basis. We usually import 80 per cent of our sugar, 50 to 55 per cent of our wool, 50 per cent of our flaxseed, 40 per cent of our edible nuts, 30 per cent or more of the cattle hides we use, and more than 50 per cent of the calf, sheep, and lamb skins. These commodities are important items in our agricultural business. It would be unwise to deprive the producers of tariff protection merely because some of our farm crops are not yet in position to profit from the tariff. Yet that is practically what would be involved in a campaign for lower tariff duties in the supposed interests of agriculture, because farmers could hardly obtain lower duties on the commodities they purchase without accepting lower duties on the commodities they sell.

Relationship to World Markets

We should recognize that the relationship of our agriculture to world markets to-day is different from what it formerly was. Only 30 years ago about 27 per cent of the total value of our agricultural output entered the export trade as against about 15 per cent during recent years. In the earlier period the farmer had more reason to talk about the small value of the tariff to him, since his commodities, which were largely exported, had their prices determined, not in the domestic but in the world market. At present, with our agricultural exports decreasing in proportion to our total exports as well as to our total agricultural output, and with imports of agricultural products offering increased competition in the home market, the position of the farmer in respect to the tariff is greatly altered. It would be unwise to forget this fundamental tendency in shaping our tariff structure.

Ultimately we must either balance our domestic structure so that the country will maintain within itself a prosperous agriculture

capable of making us self-sufficient in food and fibers or we must
follow the way that leads to dependence on foreign food supplies,
with our own agriculture relegated to a secondary place in our
national life. The second course is not desirable. It is one thing
to import commodities which we can not ourselves produce and
another to depend on foreign countries for cereals, meats, and dairy
products. Tariff protection will tend to prevent that undesirable
condition. The United States was formerly the world's chief food-
exporting country. That it may one day become dependent on outside sources for agricultural commodities that might be produced
at home is suggested by the decline that took place in our farm
production per capita of the population between 1897 and 1921. In
that period, owing mainly to a retarded increase in our production
of wheat, beef, mutton, and wool, our farm output failed to keep
pace with the increase in our population. Since 1922 our farm
production per capita has increased at a rate exceeding the rate of
growth in our population. This condition, however, may be only
temporary.

Competition Becoming Keener

Provided technical progress is maintained and our farmers are
encouraged with suitable rewards, no apprehension need be felt at
present as to our domestic food production. These conditions, however, can not be preserved without forethought. Agricultural competition is becoming more intense throughout the world. Immense
new areas have recently been brought into cultivation in Canada,
South America, and Australia. These countries, under present conditions, must find their principal market in Europe, where they are
already giving our farmers keen competition. It behooves us to
see that the battle ground is not transferred to the United States,
as it would be transferred by tariff reductions on agricultural
products.

Some advocates of tariff reduction in the supposed interests of
agriculture believe the result would be to increase our imports of
nonagricultural goods. It might rather increase our imports of agricultural goods. Our manufacturing industries seem well able to
resist foreign competition, as is shown by their increasing sales in
foreign markets. Since the beginning of the century the proportion
of manufactured goods entering export trade has more than held its
own, despite a fivefold increase in our annual creation of values by
manufacturing processes. Agriculture, on the other hand, is losing
ground in the foreign market and is moving into a position in which
its chief care will be not to lose ground in the home market as well.
In all probability the time is not distant when the home market will
be the chief preoccupation of our farmers.

It may be argued, from the fact that our agricultural production
has increased greatly in recent years, that American agriculture
stands in little need of tariff protection. But the postwar increase
in farm output was not a response to satisfactory prices. It was
rather the result of war-time stimulation and, to some extent at any
rate, of an effort, not entirely logical perhaps, to compensate for low
prices by increased production. Certainly the present rate of increase in American farm production will not be maintained indefinitely without better compensation than agriculture has received

since the war. Hereafter it will be increasingly evident, I think, that the maintenance of adequate agricultural production in the United States necessitates a tariff policy calculated to maintain the home market for the home producer. The United States, unlike certain other countries, is not in imminent danger of becoming dependent on food imports owing to lack of domestic agricultural resources. Such dependence may conceivably arise, however, if we fail to encourage proper utilization of our resources.

FARM TAXATION LITTLE CHANGED

Little change in farm taxation has taken place in the last year. Fortunately the problem is getting increased attention and a start has been made not only toward greater economy in expenditure but also toward a better adjustment of tax levels for State and local purposes. The drastic upward trend in State and local taxes which was especially marked from 1915 to 1923 has been checked. The recorded increase in farm taxes from 1924 to 1927 amounted to only about 3½ per cent. This evidence of progress may be attributed in part to reassessments on account of the reduced value of farm land, but more particularly to economy, a diminished rate of expansion in public expenditures, and to the tapping of new sources of revenue to supplement the general property tax. Improvement in farm income has made farm taxes less onerous in many sections, but this should not cause a diminution in efforts for greater economy and for improvement in the system of taxation.

The farmer's tax problem is essentially a State and local rather than a Federal problem. Comparatively few farmers are subject to the Federal income tax levy, since personal exemptions have been increased materially in the downward revision of Federal taxes in recent years. Moreover, in States where an inheritance tax is imposed, the deduction up to 80 per cent of the Federal estates tax relieves estates of most of the contribution to the Federal Government that otherwise would be necessary on the death of the owners. Minor Federal excise taxes affecting farmers have been repealed recently, including the automobile tax. Additional relief has come through continued Federal aid for roads and for various agricultural purposes. Such contributions have improved the roads greatly while imposing only a part of the total cost on State and local sources of revenue, and have enhanced the educational opportunities of the rural population.

Notwithstanding tax reductions and subventions by the Federal Government, the crux of the farm-tax problem lies within the sphere of State policy. In recent years the trend in the fiscal policy of the States has been toward securing a greater share of the necessary revenue from sources other than tangible property. Gasoline taxes yielded the States nearly $259,000,000 in 1927, thus aiding greatly in placing the cost of road construction and maintenance more on those who use the roads and less on the adjacent farm property. Even with the gasoline tax, levies for roads constitute one of the principal burdens on farm real estate.

The Search for New Revenue Sources

It is not easy to discover new and appropriate sources of revenue to supplement existing ones. When new sources are found, care is necessary to prevent the new revenues from becoming mere additions to present expenditures, rather than a means of relief to overburdened taxpayers. The gasoline tax worked so well from its inception that many States soon increased the rate. In some States it has reached 4 or 5 cents a gallon. Although such a rate may not be excessive for the States concerned, it suggests that a tax which serves its purpose exceptionally well may be overworked. Some States are attempting to raise additional revenues by excise taxes on certain commodities of wide use, but not of first necessity. Several are levying income or business taxes of one kind or another. These taxes indicate a desire to reach taxable capacity other than that represented by tangible property such as farm real estate, livestock, implements, etc.

Encouraging effort to improve the prevailing system of State and local taxation has followed a demonstration by farmers, and especially by research agencies, that taxes on agricultural property generally are greater in proportion to income than on other property. As a result many States have given some relief to their poorer agricultural sections by widening the base of taxation for school and road purposes. In States with large industrial and other urban development increased State contributions for schools and roads tend to reduce the tax load on agriculture without handicapping the rural schools. Justification for this may be found in the fact that the importance of every school extends beyond the district in which it is located. This is especially true of rural schools since through migration to the cities many rural pupils become citizens of urban communities.

Research in farm taxation by the Department of Agriculture and by agricultural experiment stations in many States is of comparatively recent origin. Already, however, it has yielded results that have been received with a high degree of favorable public interest, especially on the part of farmers. Effective work also is being done by taxpayers' leagues in the Western States and in some of the Central States, where such organizations investigate and help to control State and local expenditures. The same function might be undertaken with advantage by farm groups, for intelligent scrutiny of public expenditure is necessary to economical use of public funds.

CREDIT FACILITIES OF AGRICULTURE

The availability and cost of credit are of much importance to farmers. In proportion to the output the capital and investment requirements of agriculture are large. Rarely does a farmer on starting to farm have capital enough to pay for his farm, with necessary improvements and equipment. Even after these have been provided the production of crops and livestock requires a substantial investment in capital and labor. Furthermore, the period required for production is mainly fixed by nature and exceeds the production period involved in most other industries. Hence many years of accumulation and saving are necessary before the average farmer can finance his farm plant and his production program without the aid of borrowed capital. Farm-mortgage credit, as well as production and marketing credit, are destined to remain important questions.

The importance of the Federal farm loan system as a source of credit to the farmer is increasing. Net mortgage loans of the Federal and joint-stock land banks outstanding on December 31 increased from $1,192,235,609 in 1923 to $1,825,441,964 in 1927, or 53 per cent. Since Federal farm loans constitute one of the cheapest sources of farm-mortgage credit, their rapid increase in proportion to the total volume of credit reduces the average rate of interest on long-term loans. Moreover, their amortization feature distributes the burden of repayment over a long period and lessens total interest payments each year by reducing the principal outstanding. Life-insurance companies are another source of long-term credit offering favorable terms to farmers. Between 1923 and 1927 the farm-mortgage loans of life-insurance companies increased approximately 25 per cent and in 1927 totaled nearly $2,000,000,000. The department hopes in the near future to show annual changes in the volume and cost of the total farm debt.

Rates of interest on loans by the Federal and joint-stock land banks have declined in recent years. In July, 1925, the rate of the Federal land banks was uniformly 5½ per cent, except in one land-bank district where a 5¼ per cent rate prevailed. By July, 1926, 3 of the 12 banks had lowered their charge from 5½ to 5 per cent. In July, 1927, 8 land banks charged 5 per cent, 3 had a rate of 5¼ per cent, and 1 had a rate of 5½ per cent. In July, 1928, the rate was 5 per cent in all but the Spokane and Columbia districts, where 5¼ per cent was charged. Nearly a score of the joint-stock land banks have reduced their interest rates from the 6 per cent which prevailed in 1924 to 5¼ and 5½ per cent. It seems probable, however, that—temporarily, at any rate—somewhat higher interest rates will become necessary on farm-mortgage loans by the land banks. A few of the joint-stock land banks have already announced fractional increases. A probable rise in the rates of the Federal land banks has been indicated in recent statements by some of those banks.

Intermediate Credit Banks

The services rendered to farmers and farmers' cooperative organizations by the Federal intermediate credit banks are of growing importance. Total direct loans and rediscounts of these banks, which began operations in 1923, increased from approximately $90,000,000 in 1924 to more than $142,000,000 in 1927. From 1923 to December 31, 1927, 77 cooperative marketing associations, with a combined membership of more than a million persons, borrowed from them. Their facilities have enabled the cooperative associations to make advances to growers covering a substantial part of the value of their crop. Since their organization the intermediate credit banks also have rediscounted farmers' notes for 615 financial institutions, chiefly agricultural-credit corporations and livestock-loan companies. Live-stock-loan companies that rediscount with the intermediate credit banks have been serviceable in meeting the needs of ranchmen who want loans larger than local banks can handle. In the case of loans on dairy cows, notes are sometimes made for 18 or 20 months and are repaid on an amortization plan whereby an agreed amount is deducted monthly from cream checks.

The intermediate credit banks helped to restore confidence in the areas stricken by floods in 1927. Credit corporations with large capital were organized in Arkansas and Mississippi, and the intermediate credit banks stood ready to discount their paper. The knowledge that the resources of these banks were available improved the situation, though the amount of credit actually called for from this source was relatively small.

Early this year the 12 Federal intermediate credit banks were making loans to farmers' cooperative associations at 4½ per cent and were for the most part discounting agricultural-credit paper for local banks and agricultural-credit corporations at the same low rate. Later, when money rates tightened in credit and investments centers, several of the intermediate credit banks found it necessary to increase their interest charges. At this writing two of the banks charge 5½ per cent on discounts of farmers' notes.

Local Banking Difficulties

Many serious farm-credit problems still remain. One such problem arises out of local banking difficulties. In the fiscal year ended June 30, 1927, there were 831 bank failures in the United States, more than three times as many as in 1923 and nearly 50 per cent than in 1926. The increase occurred chiefly in rural districts, reaching a maximum in the last half of 1926. Since then the number of bank failures has shown a marked reduction. Many bank failures may be traced to the period of inflation after the war and the ensuing collapse of prices. The fall in the price of cotton and wheat in 1926 also contributed to the failure of many country banks.

In some parts of the country the problem of merchant credit, discussed at some length in my 1927 report, remains serious. Merchant credit is costly chiefly because of bad bills. Also it tends to discourage thrift, especially where credit is freely granted. The farmer should seek every means of establishing such contacts with banks or credit corporations as will enable him to dispense with merchant credit.

Much has been done in recent years to improve agriculture's credit facilities, but much remains to be done. Research is necessary to determine how our banking and credit structure might be improved, and governmental action, both State and National, is required to give effect to principles of demonstrated value. Local banking should be improved to give greater stability, to diminish the depositors' risk, and to furnish more stable and dependable service to stronger and better-managed institutions. This is to a large degree a matter of State action.

COOPERATIVE ORGANIZATION OF FARMERS

Cooperative organization among the farmers of the United States, as is well known, has developed greatly in recent years. Naturally its progress has not been uniform. Setbacks as well as advances have been recorded. But there remains a remarkable net gain, the value of which can not be estimated wholly in terms of business done, membership gained, or savings effected. It includes also such important, if not easily measurable, results as a widespread realization among farmers that success in agriculture requires efficient selling as well as efficient production. Hereafter this realization will play an increasing part in the adjustment of output to market requirements, which must play a large part in any rational program for the solution of the surplus problem.

Agricultural cooperation is sometimes charged with responsibilities that do not belong to it. When markets are depressed by overproduction it is difficult even for the most efficient cooperative organization to obtain satisfactory prices. This difficulty is sometimes considered evidence that cooperation does not work. But such an attitude is unjustified. Cooperation can not correct all the basic difficulties of agriculture and is not designed to do so. It may influence the volume of production. But the control of conditions such as exist in the California dried-fruit industry and in the marketing of potatoes this year does not fall directly within the sphere of cooperative responsibilities. The remedy for the surplus problem will necessarily transcend the powers of the cooperative associations. For the present our cooperative organizations must be judged as marketing concerns operating sometimes under favorable, and sometimes under unfavorable, conditions. Cooperative marketing aims to give the farmer an efficient and economical marketing system, while at the same time promoting the adjustment of production to market needs. It emphasizes quality output, and is perhaps the chief influence in the standardization, handling, packing, and processing of farm commodities. It sometimes favorably modifies the purchasing practices of commercial agencies. These and similar activities are the true standards by which cooperative marketing should be judged.

Problems of Cotton Cooperatives

Cooperative organizations must be adapted to varying conditions of production and marketing, and their services and problems vary correspondingly. Cotton cooperatives have exceptional obstacles. Cotton is produced by a large number of scattered farmers whose credit needs often make cooperation difficult. Yet the cooperative marketing of cotton has made considerable progress in the seven years that have elapsed since the first of the present large-scale associations was organized. Probably the most fundamental service rendered, not only to association members but to cotton farmers generally, is the development of a system of payment for cotton on the basis of its grade and staple. This development, besides modifying dealers' practices, has encouraged the production of better cotton. Savings to their members in interest, storage, and insurance costs have also been effected by the cotton cooperatives. Sales direct to mills, recent plans to centralize sales in regional offices, and economic research carried on for the past two years by the American Cotton Growers Exchange have increased the efficiency of the associations as sales agencies. The establishment of affiliated local gins in some States has provided improved ginning service for members.

After from five to seven years' experience, the cotton-marketing associations are better able than ever before to give their members efficient marketing services. They have contributed to the improvement of marketing conditions and are now prepared to extend and strengthen their services. These associations were obviously on trial during their earlier years. They now appear to have the support of a sufficient number of the growers to assure the permanency of cooperative cotton marketing.

Cooperative organization among grain farmers has been chiefly characterized by the formation of local elevator associations which have corrected local abuses in grain marketing, reduced local handling margins, and improved local services. The organization of State-wide wheat-marketing associations, or wheat pools, has been undertaken, but the quantity of grain handled by such pools has so far been comparatively small. However, they constitute an important experiment in the centralized marketing of grain. Whether such marketing will develop chiefly through extension of the scope of the pooling organizations or through the formation of central organizations by farmers' elevators remains to be seen. Farmer-elevator groups have taken steps to set up terminal-market sales agencies, while the pools are attempting to acquire country as well as terminal facilities and to improve local contracts with their members.

The Livestock Associations

In the cooperative marketing of livestock the most outstanding development has been the formation of cooperative terminal-market agencies. Twenty-five such agencies operated during 1927 in 19 terminal livestock markets. Their business for the year reached the impressive total of $267,200,000, compared with $95,969,000 in 1922.

These agencies have greatly strengthened the marketing position of livestock producers. The associations have rendered efficient selling service and made substantial savings in marketing costs for stockmen. The purchase of feeder cattle and lambs and the financing of purchasing and feeding operations are among their services. In addition, they help the producers in dealing with the general problems of the industry. Marketing, legislation, or transportation questions can be handled more adequately when producers are organized. The organizations also influence the supply of livestock and the rate of its movement to market. They help to coordinate production and marketing, and thus to stabilize prices. Livestock shipping associations, by the use of motor trucks, are developing larger units which may serve several communities.

Producers of dairy products have set up and operated some of the most effective cooperative organizations in this country. In the marketing of butter Land o' Lakes Creameries has materially increased the production of high-grade, sweet-cream butter, which is sold under the trade-mark of the cooperative and has created an extensive market for butter of this quality. In 1927 the business of this organization exceeded $46,000,000. The Challenge Cream and Butter Association, which in 1927 sold 52 per cent of the butter consumed in Los Angeles, has likewise developed a demand for a product of high, uniform quality. Associations marketing milk have made a noteworthy improvement in the handling and marketing of this product. Inspections to improve sanitary conditions in dairies and milk plants, supplemented by continuous laboratory tests of milk delivered by members, have improved and safeguarded the quality and wholesomeness of the product. The associations have increased the consumption of milk by advertising and educational campaigns and by insisting on quality production.

Handling Milk Surpluses

Milk-marketing associations have made notable progress in the control and handling of surpluses. Their price policies have tended to maintain a level of price which is profitable to the efficient dairyman, but which does not encourage expansion within the market area or the shipment of milk from distant regions. Seasonal surpluses are reduced by methods of payment that encourage increased production during the fall and in general tend to uniform production throughout the year. Production thus stabilized results in stabilized, profitable prices. This service can be performed only by producers' organizations, because the voluntary informed cooperation of the producer is necessary to carry out any program looking toward adjustment of production.

Cooperative marketing of fruits and vegetables has been distinguished by the development of a large number of local associations, which render important local services. In many sections, however, the coordination of selling and other functions by the development of federations or a similar type of central organization is necessary. A number of large-scale associations marketing fruits and vegetables are nationally known for their success in this field. These organizations have improved handling practices and standardized grades, and where they control a major percentage of the crop have improved distribution materially. The California Fruit Growers Exchange has improved methods of selling and distributing California citrus fruit and has increased consumption by advertising and by service to retail dealers and also through special merchandizing devices, such as the manufacture and sale at cost of an electrically driven juice extractor for the use of soda fountains. In July last, 46,000 such extractors were in use, each having an estimated consuming capacity of 50 boxes of citrus fruits a year. The work of the Florida Citrus Exchange, the American Cranberry Exchange, and several other organizations of the same type indicates that material progress is being made. No spectacular developments have taken place recently in the cooperative marketing of fruits and vegetables, but the associations concerned have made steady progress. Their leaders are giving thought to the consolidation of existing organizations through the formation of overhead sales agencies, particularly for commodities not now handled by large-scale cooperatives.

Unnecessary Costs Eliminated

The growth of large cooperative-marketing associations tends to eliminate unnecessary agencies and facilities, whose maintenance adds to the marketing costs that the farmer must pay. Savings which corporations seek through consolidation are obtained, in part, for agriculture by the centralization of handling and marketing in large-scale cooperatives. Cooperative associations handle and market the products of their members at cost. Thus all savings effected go to the producers. Moreover, in regions where strong cooperatives are active, marketing services are performed better and at comparatively less expense than formerly, as a result in part of the influence of the cooperatives on the charges and services of privately owned agencies.

An idea of the present status of large-scale cooperative marketing in the United States can be gained from the fact that more than 150 farmers' marketing associations each transact an annual business exceeding $1,000,000. Five or six associations have an annual business approximating $50,000,000 each. Two have passed the $80,000,000 mark. This development of large-scale cooperative business appears, when we recall that only about one-third of our farmers are members of cooperative associations, as a very striking proof that magnitude of operations may be as profitable for agriculture as for other businesses. As a group our large cooperative associations do a conspicuously efficient job.

One of the most significant recent developments in agricultural cooperation is the attention given by the cooperatives to research. Twenty or more cooperative associations have research departments which assemble data on which to base price and sales policies. The use of crop and market information by these organizations is placing them in the forefront among merchandising concerns. Knowledge gained by research has frequently demonstrated the advisability of centralized action. As a result many local associations, while retaining control of local functions, have turned selling and distribution over to central agencies. Recently, for example, most of the state-wide cotton-marketing associations placed the sale of their cotton in the hands of regional officers of the American Cotton Growers' Exchange. Economic studies have given impetus also to further coordination of the activities of the livestock, dairy, and poultry handling cooperatives.

Suspension of Operations

A few large organizations have been forced to suspend operations in recent years. Several others have been more or less disorganized by low prices for the products they handle. In the last two years five large-scale tobacco-marketing associations have ceased business. The principal reasons for their failure include overproduction, changes in the demand for certain types of tobacco, mistakes in management, and the failure or inability of members to support their organizations. These failures, however, do not justify discouragement about cooperative marketing in general, or even about the cooperative marketing of tobacco.

The experiments in question have taught some important lessons. Growers have learned much about the marketing of their products and about the relation of supply and quality to prices. Moreover, the price policies followed by the tobacco associations, though perhaps unwise from the standpoint of the continuance of the cooperative concerns, probably increased returns to their members for two or three years. Nonmembers also benefited. The brief existence of these associations has left a nucleus of growers who understand and appreciate cooperative marketing.

Cooperative buying of supplies by farmers has become an important part of the cooperative movement. In the East associations for the purchase of dairy feed, seeds, fertilizers, and other bulk supplies are well established. The Cooperative Grange League Federation Exchange, Ithaca, N. Y., and the Eastern States Farmers' Exchange, Springfield, Mass., each purchased approximately $10,000,000 worth of supplies for their members in 1927. Their activities have resulted in substantial savings to their members, and what is equally important have given them goods of known, standard quality. Cooperative purchase of bulk supplies by marketing associations has been for many years an important feature of their services. Fertilizer, feed, seeds, fuel, and fencing are some of the items purchased extensively by marketing associations. Approximately 50 per cent of all such associations reporting to the department in 1925 stated that they bought supplies for their members.

Another type of cooperative purchasing is that carried on by subsidiaries of large marketing associations. Organizations of this kind are engaged principally in the purchase of marketing and processing supplies, such as containers and machinery. They also buy farm supplies for members of the associations with which they are affiliated.

THE HUMAN FACTOR IN AGRICULTURE

In discussing agricultural problems it is not enough to consider products, values, and profits. The human element—the men, women, and children on the farm—must also be taken into the reckoning. The human factor in agriculture is too often thought of as uniform and unchanging. In reality it is extremely variable and its characteristics are less known than those relating to land, field crops, and livestock. In recent years the public mind has been disquieted, and rightly so, by a rapid decrease in our farm population. Though the postwar loss of population from the country to the towns and cities should not be considered as wholly the result of unfavorable farm conditions, it is unquestionably due to that cause in some degree. It is therefore encouraging to note that the rate of movement is declining. In this, as in other important phases of agriculture, an approach to greater stability can be discerned.

Estimates based on surveys started in 1922 indicate that since that year a gross movement of persons leaving farms for urban centers has taken place to the number of 2,000,000 a year. Simultaneously an opposite movement of population to the farm has taken place amounting to from 1,000,000 to 1,400,000 persons a year. In other words, the net annual loss of farm population has ranged from 1,000,000 to 600,000 persons. Increase of births over deaths has partly counteracted the downward tendency. Nevertheless there remains an estimated absolute annual loss ranging from 650,000 to 200,000 persons. Our total net loss of farm population between the census enumeration of 1920 and that of 1925 was 2,000,000 persons; the estimated loss from 1925 to January 1, 1928, was 1,283,000 persons. In eight years, therefore, the farm population has diminished 3,283,000 persons, or an average of 400,000 a year.

But in 1927 the situation changed materially. That year saw a smaller gross movement of population away from the farms and a larger gross movement to the farms, so that the net loss was only 192,000, the smallest of any year in the period under review. The exodus was losing momentum rapidly. Some relative loss of population from the country to the town is apparently a normal characteristic of our agriculture by reason of the comparatively high natural rate of increase in the country and because of the progressive substitution of mechanical power for man power. A readjustment of farm personnel to a diminishing labor requirement need give us no concern. It is an evidence of health and progress rather than of deterioration in agriculture. Continuance of present tendencies in the movement of farm population may bring us within a few years to a point at which the annual loss will not exceed the proportion necessary to allow for draining off the excess in natural increase and for the drop in labor requirements.

Persons Leaving the Farms

In the flow of population away from the farms we can distinguish a stream of young adults just ready to enter various occupations, a considerable number of older persons seeking better earnings or jobs more interesting to them than farming, a fair sprinkling of prosperous adults desiring the comforts of urban life, and a group forced to leave agriculture through the disabilities of age. This normal movement involves a perpetual turnover of agricultural personnel, and in periods of agricultural difficulty its volume may be considerably increased. Young people leave the farms for a twofold reason: (1) More children are born and reared on farms than can find a suitable place in farming. The census of 1920 showed that 4,000,000 more persons under 21 years of age were living on farms than there were in any urban group of our population equal in size to the farm group. When we bear in mind the constantly increasing power of agriculture to produce more food and fibers with a given amount of labor, it is obvious that this excess of young people on the farms must be drawn away. (2) Many young people born on farms do not take to farm life. It is natural for such persons to seek other occupations and the fact is not necessarily evidence that farming is without attractions for those adapted to it. American farm people have always been more mobile than those of some other nations, although it is true that some of them are not mobile enough and cling to farm life under unsatisfactory conditions. The normal movement of adolescents away from the farm is quite compatible with the well-being, both of agriculture and of the Nation.

Remedy Not Identical for All

Naturally in a country of such diverse resources, corresponding diversity exists in farm living standards. Farmers occupying extremely small or poor farms need certain assistance that farmers on rich, large farms do not need. The problem of the latter group is not so much how to increase production, or even how to decrease costs, as it is how to cope with economic conditions that too often deprive them of due reward for their efforts. In the first group the problem mainly involves farm organization and management and the size of farms. In the second it is primarily a question of adjusting production to market requirements and effecting economies in distribution and selling. The distinction, in other words, is between farms lacking and farms possessing facilities for doing efficient work.

These differences in basic farming conditions naturally have their counterpart in differences in living standards. City dwellers often think of the farmer and talk of farm life as if there were only one type of farmer and one type of farming. The truth is, of course, that farm conditions vary in all parts of the country to such a degree that no single formula can be invented for the solution of all farm problems. Measures taken for the relief of agriculture must reckon with differences of farming technic in various sections, and differences in the human factor engaged in agriculture. In one district the chief need may be further scientific research; in another it may be more important for the moment to encourage a more general application of well-established scientific practice. Though all farmers may profit by improving their technic, the opportunity for progress in that direction is greater in some localities than in others. In like manner the opportunity to benefit agriculture by improvements in marketing is greater for some regions and for some crops than for others. If we forget these facts and fall into the habit of lumping all farm difficulties together under the general name of the "farm problem," we shall waste much time in discovering the true path of progress.

Rural Governmental Institutions

More attention might perhaps be given to the improvement of rural governmental institutions. In our pioneer epoch the American farm dwelling came inevitably to be situated not in a village but on the farm. American farm homes, except in some localities in New England and in parts of the West, are scattered. Under such conditions adequate governmental organization does not easily spring up. Distances between farms tend to prevent the formation of governmental units capable of undertaking all the usual functions of local collective welfare. The tendency instead, when the need arises for a particular institution, such as a school, a road, or a court district, is to create an organization to discharge that one function. In recent years rural governmental organization has become more complex and comprehensive. Farmers are still handicapped, however, by inadequate civic institutions, and it might sometimes be possible to remedy the trouble by establishing alliances between rural institutions and the urban centers that serve farm needs.

Some few farmers, of course, live within the corporate limits of cities and share their advantages. Others live so close to cities that they can use the church, school, library, and other urban facilities almost as freely as if they dwelt within the city limits. It is estimated that about 8,000,000 of our farm population live within 5 miles of cities having a population of more than 2,500. Approximately 20,000,000 other farm people, however, do not live near cities. These people maintain trade and social contacts with some 13,000 corporate villages ranging in population from 100 to 2,500 and with some 26,000 smaller villages or hamlets not incorporated. Though automobiles and good roads have lessened the farmer's isolation they have not abolished it. Hence many farmers are without good hospital, library, and school facilities. It would seem that public bodies might do something toward making better provision for these wants.

But the improvement of rural life is not wholly, and perhaps not even largely, a governmental problem. Much can be done by making various modern appliances more easily available in the farm home and better adapted to it. The farmer's house is often too far from other houses to admit of city methods of bringing to the farm family the convenience of running water, gas for cooking, electricity for light and power, and sewers. Kitchen facilities, heating plants, lighting equipment, sewage-disposal facilities, etc., must be produced in a form especially adapted for farm use. In this field the inventor and the manufacturer must come to the farmer's aid. The market is waiting for the industrial pioneer.

Census Figures on Farm-Home Equipment

Only a comparatively small percentage of our more fortunately situated farm homes are well equipped with modern appliances. The last census reported that 10 per cent of our farms had water piped in; 7 per cent had gas or electric lighting; approximately 38 per cent had telephones. In certain favored situations the percentage ran higher. In New England, for example, 48 per cent of the farms had water piped in, and nearly 25 per cent enjoyed the same advantage in New York, New Jersey, and Pennsylvania. Twenty-eight per cent of the farms in Massachusetts were equipped with gas or electric lights. In Utah, where many farmers live in villages after the European manner, 43 per cent of the farmers' homes had gas or electric lights, and in California 26 per cent. In telephone installation the percentage of farms enjoying this great advantage ran up to 86 per cent in Iowa, 78 per cent in Kansas, 76 per cent in Nebraska, 73 per cent in Illinois, 66 per cent in Indiana, and 62 per cent in Minnesota and in Missouri. It is evident from these figures that farmers will have improved household facilities when the opportunity exists.

The architecture of the farm house needs study. Houses built to fit farm wants need not lack either beauty or convenience. Part of the money provided for the farm home should be set aside for shrubbery and other adornments. It should be easy to plant the lesson of beauty in the minds and hearts of rural young people, so that when they become farmers their desires will not be limited to the attainment of economic security, but will include also the provision of beauty and harmony in the home and its surroundings. Instruction given to the young people of the farm in home decoration will return its cost a thousandfold. It should be emphasized, however, that the problem is not merely to transplant to the farm what has already been worked out by the city, but rather to adapt improved appliances to the special needs of the farm home.

CHANGES IN DEPARTMENT ORGANIZATION

During my term of office the improvement of the department's organization has been sought by carrying out, as far as practicable, the principle of segregating research and regulatory work into separate administrative units. The purpose of this separation is twofold: To free the scientists from regulatory duties which invariably distract their attention from research work; and to provide for more effective administration by grouping within a single organization the work of enforcing all the statutes dealing with the same industries or operating within the same general field.

This reorganization has been effected by increasing the duties of some units and by creating new units for the administration of specific statutes. There has been consolidated in one unit, known as the Bureau of Chemistry and Soils, the work conducted by the former Bureau of Soils and the Fixed Nitrogen Laboratory and some of the chemical work conducted by the former Bureau of Chemistry and the Bureau of Plant Industry. All the regulatory work formerly administered by the then Bureau of Chemistry and the Insecticide and Fungicide Board is now under a unit known as the Food, Drug, and Insecticide Administration.

The Packers and Stockyards Administration has been abolished and responsibility for the enforcement of the packers and stockyards act of 1921 transferred to the Bureau of Animal Industry. Since several other laws relating to the livestock industry are enforced by the same bureau, this change in organization has provided for centralized administrative authority in the enforcement of statutes relating to traffic in livestock and has reduced the number of independent subdivisions dealing with a single industry.

A new unit, designated as the Plant Quarantine and Control Administration, has recently been established, and has taken over the work of preventing the entry of insect pests and plant diseases into the United States, and of controlling the spread of pests already established in the country. These functions were previously discharged by the former Federal Horticultural Board, the Bureau of Entomology, and to a limited extent by the Bureau of Plant Industry. I am convinced that the new arrangement will insure better protection for our crops, and will permit more effective research work by the units that have been relieved of responsibility for regulatory work.

The Personnel Administration

A little more than three years ago nine separate offices concerned with the business administration of the department were consolidated into one organization, known as the Office of Personnel and Business Administration. Responsibility for the supervision and coordination of the general business activities of the department was delegated to the Director of Personnel and Business Administration. This organization has expedited work, eliminated confusion and waste by establishing a more orderly and efficient business procedure and effected greater uniformity in the organization of the business offices in the department.

Independent points of contact have been reduced in number and executive leadership has been focussed on a smaller number of administrative units. The personnel has developed a greater sense of responsibility and a keener spirit of organization, loyalty, and pride in accomplishment. Separation of regulatory from research and service functions has improved the department's relations with the public. When these duties are administered by the same bureau, the enforcement of regulatory statutes may interfere with the cordial and sympathetic relations necessary for advantageously carrying on research. Research workers are now able to maintain effective contacts with outside agencies without being embarrassed by possible differences arising between those agencies and the regulatory units of the department.

Enlargement of scientific knowledge may be impeded by the administrative responsibilities frequently imposed upon outstanding investigators. After years of meritorious service devoted to administrative work it seems fitting that members of the department who have attained distinction in science should be relieved of executive responsibilities, so that they may devote all their energies to research. Accordingly, at their own request, I have relieved from further administrative duties the former chief of the Bureau of Biological Survey, E. W. Nelson, an internationally recognized leader in the study and conservation of wild life; the former chief of the Bureau of Entomology, L. O. Howard, long recognized as a distinguished investigator in entomology; and the head of the office of foreign-plant introduction of the Bureau of Plant Industry, David Fairchild, eminent agricultural explorer and authority on foreign-plant introduction.

On June 30, 1928, the department had on its rolls 22,189 employees, of whom 4,902 were located in the District of Columbia and 17,287 stationed in the field service. This was an increase of 111 in the District of Columbia and of 417 in the field service over the number of employees in the department on June 30, 1927.

Decline in Turnover

The turnover in the personnel during the fiscal year 1928 was 9.5 per cent, or 1.19 per cent less than for the preceding year and 4.31 per cent less than for the fiscal year 1924. The lower classification grades continue to show the higher turnover. In the Washington force 60 per cent of the total turnover occurred in the first three grades of the clerical and custodial services. The turnover of scientific employees was 5.8 per cent of their number, 69 per cent of this turnover occurring among employees receiving $3,600 or less. Sixty-four per cent of the scientific employees who resigned during the year left the service to accept positions which afforded either a higher salary or a better opportunity for advancement.

The employment situation in the department shows marked improvement, both in a steady decline of turnover in personnel and in increased loyalty, cooperation, and devotion to duty. Some of the factors which have contributed to this gratifying condition are a rise in the average of salaries, a reduction of inequalities in compensation for positions involving like duties and responsibilities, greater opportunity for advancement afforded under the personnel classification act, consistent promotion from within the ranks, and the prospect for better housing conditions which will be afforded by the new buildings for which Congress has made provision.

The policy of the department is to give adequate recognition of meritorious service by providing more responsible employment and suitable financial rewards. I want every employee to feel that he shares in the responsibility for the welfare of the department and for the service which it renders. That this feeling prevails is apparent from the esprit de corps which now exists among department workers.

Increases in Salaries

Attractive opportunities for workers now exist in all the department's activities. On July 1, 1924, following the increases due to the classification act, the average salary of permanent employees in Washington was $2,052. On July 1, 1928, including the increases provided under the Welch Act, the average salary had risen to $2,292, an increase of $240. Similarly, on July 1, 1924, the average salary of permanent field employees was $2,091, and on July 1, 1928, it had risen to $2.411, an increase of $321. During the last four years there has been a marked improvement especially in the salaries of workers in the professional and scientific grades. On July 1, 1928, the average salary of Washington employees in these grades was $3,894, which represents an average increase of more than $500 over the average salary in these grades on July 1, 1924. In consequence of this improved situation the department is in a more favorable position than ever before to offer substantial inducements to qualified research men to enter the service.

During the fiscal year ended June 30, 1928, 101 employees were retired on an average annuity of $807.45. Of these, 76 were retired on account of age, 23 on account of disability, and 2 on account of reduction in force. Notwithstanding the increased annuity provided by the retirement law as amended in 1926, many employees who have reached the age of retirement prefer to continue in the service, since the present retirement pay is insufficient for the needs of those who have dependents.

The numbers and average annuities of former employees of the department retired since the enactment of the general civil service retirement act are shown in Table 1.

TABLE 1.—*Number and average annuities of former employees of the Department of Agriculture retired since 1921*

Fiscal year	Retired on account of age		Retired on account of disability		Retired on account of reduction in force		Total	
	Number	Average annuity	Number	Average annuity	Number	Average annuity	Number	Average annuity
1921	102	$574.08	28	$528.94			130	$564.35
1922	8	482.18	13	491.27			21	487.81
1923	16	620.56	22	496.05			38	548.48
1924	21	596.45	10	457.56			31	551.65
1925	26	597.52	15	482.78			41	555.55
1926	17	727.02	17	571.88	1	$527.44	35	643.96
1927	34	755.39	33	716.96	1	821.16	68	737.71
1928	76	825.77	23	769.89	2	543.30	101	807.45

Sick-Leave Regulations

There is a widespread but mistaken impression that employees regularly take the full allowance of annual and sick leave which may be granted in accordance with the law. A survey of the leave situation in the department covering the calendar years 1921 to 1927, inclusive, shows that for employees in the District of Columbia the average number of days of annual leave was 26.9, and that only 54 per cent of the employees took the full allowance of 30 days of annual leave. For the same period the average number of days of sick leave was 7.4; only 5.1 per cent of the employees took the full allowance of 30 days of sick leave and 28 per cent of the employees took no sick leave. On an average 9.5 per cent of the employees took the full allowance of both annual and sick leave.

The leave allowance of employees outside of the District of Columbia is governed by a special law, which provides that the Secretary of Agriculture may grant leaves of absence not to exceed 15 days in any one year and an additional 15 days in cases where an employee is ill. For the 7-year period 1921 to 1927 the average number of days of annual leave of employees outside of the District of Columbia was 12 and the full allowance of 15 days was taken by only 49 per cent of the field employees. The average number of days of sick leave was 3; only 6.8 per cent took the full allowance of 15 days of sick leave and 53 per cent of the field employees took no sick leave. Both in Washington and in the field the average amount of sick leave taken by men is approximately one-half that taken by women.

Although 30 days sick leave is far in excess of the requirement of the average employee, cases of protracted illness, in which the allowable 30 days is exhausted before the employee is able to return to duty, are not infrequent, and the additional time required for recovery must be taken as leave without pay. During the calendar year 1927 2½ per cent of the department's employees in Washington found it necessary to take leave without pay in addition to the 30 days sick leave with pay. As a measure of relief from this situation I favor legislation which will recognize cumulative sick leave as a means of mitigating the hardships suffered by deserving employees who may occasionally need an unusual amount of sick leave.

HOUSING SITUATION OF THE DEPARTMENT

During recent years the housing situation of the department in Washington has become deplorable. The 19 major units of the department occupy about 40 buildings, some of them in widely scattered locations. Units of some bureaus are scattered in as many as 8 or 10 buildings. It would be difficult to overestimate the loss to the Government in impaired efficiency of administration and operation caused by this unsatisfactory situation. Congested offices and overcrowded laboratories are found in practically every branch, thus making impossible maximum efficiency of the staff of the department. Delays and confusion are encountered in the transaction of public business, intercommunication is made difficult instead of convenient, and the task of coordinating the work of the department is greatly complicated. Persons who call at the department, many of them from out of Washington, frequently find upon reaching the administration building, which is in a location somewhat remote from the business section of the city, that the particular office with which their business is to be transacted is in another part of the city. A number of the offices have been assigned space in the unsatisfactory temporary buildings erected as an emergency measure to house war activities. Not only are valuable records in these buildings exposed to undue hazard but the efficiency of the work is greatly reduced. While many of the buildings, such as the temporary war buildings, are Government owned, it has been necessary for Congress to appropriate more than $1,500,000 to meet the rent bill of the department during the past 10 years.

Any program contemplating the full measure of constructive public service from the funds invested in the Department of Agriculture must have among its first objects the remedying of this fundamental difficulty under which the department labors. All the offices and laboratories in Washington should be concentrated as rapidly as possible in buildings on or adjacent to the departmental reservation on the Mall. Bureaus whose work is closely related should be located in proximity to each other, and all units of each separate bureau should be under the same roof. Such a plan would permit much more effective organization of the work, better and more economical business operation, and closer administrative supervision.

Provision for Growth Needed

An essential part of a permanent program to meet the need for adequate housing is provision for growth. The development of the department since 1908, when the present east and west wings were completed, has been so great that the space estimated at that time as sufficient to house the entire department is now insufficient to house adequately two of the larger bureaus. With the increased growth of the United States and accompanying changes in our systems of marketing and distributing agricultural products, continued development of the Department of Agriculture may be expected. Housing for these activities should be planned now and not left haphazardly to the future.

Legislative provision has recently been made to relieve this unsatisfactory situation. Congress has authorized an appropriation of $2,000,000 for the construction of a central administration building to connect the east and west wings completed in 1908, and good progress has been made on this unit during the past year. This building, which should be completed by the spring of 1930, will permit the concentration of all general administrative and business units of the department. The administration building is monumental in design and with the connecting wings will contribute much to the beauty of the Mall. It will be one of the finest Government buildings in Washington and will represent agriculture in a fitting manner. However, completion of the administration building will not in itself add to the amount of floor space available to the department, because the group of unsightly structures which have been erected on the Mall from time to time during the past 50 years will have to be removed.

Additional Buildings to Be Erected

The need for additional space will be met by the acquisition of land adjoining the department's reservation on the Mall, and the erection of large modern office and laboratory buildings. Congress has authorized an appropriation of $5,750,000 for this purpose, of which $2,200,000 already has been appropriated. These new buildings, while not of the same character as that of the buildings to be erected on the Mall proper, will be of attractive design and substantial construction, and well adapted to the department's needs. Present plans contemplate construction of the first unit, which will contain 321,000 square fleet of floor space, as soon as title to the land can be acquired. The buildings south of the Mall will be of the extensible type, to provide for future growth. This should prevent recurrence of the present unsatisfactory situation.

In viewing the developments of the department during the past four years, it is difficult to select any one of greater importance than the progress now being made in meeting the housing situation. The splendid cooperation of the Public Buildings Commission and of the Office of the Supervising Architect of the Treasury Department, which are charged with the actual planning and construction of the buildings, is an important and much appreciated factor.

REGULATORY WORK WINS COOPERATION

Important developments have taken place in the department's regulatory work during the last few years. Fifteen or more principal regulatory laws, and a larger number of subordinate ones, are administered by the department, in a spirit which I believe tends to obtain a maximum of compliance with a minimum of difficulty and resistance. This is accomplished by emphasizing service features rather than penal clauses, and by making it clear that producers and consumers alike have an interest in impartial law enforcement. It is characteristic of all the regulatory laws, in a varying degree, that they involve the control of commercial agencies. The department seeks to protect the public in the manner contemplated by the statutes by a policy of education and of cooperation with the commercial agencies concerned. I can not describe the regulatory activities of the department in detail, but their nature may be illustrated by a typical example. In this way the general policy and purpose of the department's regulatory work can be indicated, while at the same time an account is given of certain developments of great practical importance and value to agriculture and also to the Nation.

Criticism of the Federal grain standards act has long since dwindled to insignificant proportions. It is now generally recognized that the penal provisions of this law have no other purpose than to promote a uniform method of grading in the general interest. Occasionally some section of the country, where smut or other damage has been extensive, may agitate for an indulgent application of the Federal grades. This feeling, however, generally gives place to a realization that the ultimate results of any such relaxed application of the standard would be harmful. Precedents of that sort would inevitably lead to the destruction of the grading system, and would not benefit the favored region more than temporarily. As soon as it became known that the bars had been let down by the grain inspectors, the market would reflect the fact in falling prices. Farmers would thus be no better off than had they allowed their grain to be graded strictly in accordance with the law.

In judging the utility of the Federal grain standards act, which became a law in August, 1916, it should be remembered that prior to its passage there was a total lack of uniformity in the standards for grades of grain throughout the United States. Commercial grades were established either by commercial boards of trade or chambers of commerce except in about half a dozen States which had enacted laws providing for grain grades and grain inspection. Under that system, or rather lack of system, grade terms meant different things in different places. With grain marketing on an interstate and foreign commerce basis, State or local control of grades and inspection services was hopelessly inefficient. Foreign buyers complained that they could not buy grain intelligently under a multiplicity of grades and under conditions which inevitably created lack of confidence in grade certificates.

Immense Improvement Effected

Accordingly the way was paved for the Federal Government to enter the field, and official standards under the grain standards act were promulgated for shelled corn in 1916, for wheat in 1917, for oats in 1919, for rye in 1923, for grain sorghums in 1924, for feed oats and mixed feed oats in 1925, and for barley in 1926. The result was an immense improvement in the facilities for doing business in grain. As is usually the case with new and complex legislation, the law was often violated in the early days of its enforcement. To-day, however, its requirements and prohibitions are generally known and infractions of the statute have largely ceased.

How uniform standards correctly applied in all markets promote the interests of all concerned is shown by the results following the establishment of Federal standards for barley in 1926. Barley grown east of the Rocky Mountains has been almost wholly on an export basis since the enactment of the Volstead Act. It has moved to the United Kingdom and continental Europe, where it is used almost exclusively for feed. Yet prior to the establishment of Federal standards American barley was sold to foreign buyers as " 48-pound malting barley." It was inspected and graded into ocean carriers under that name. But 48-pound malting barley did not mean the same thing at any two markets, either at inland points or along the seaboard. This situation led domestic dealers, exporters, and foreign buyers to unite in a request for the establishment of Federal barley standards, and since that request was granted no major difficulties in the merchandising of barley have arisen.

True to its policy of administering the grain standards act as essentially a service statute the department takes frequent counsel with the grain trade on problems involving policy and procedure. This is done so that the law may be administered in the light of what is considered good commercial practice, good business ethics, and well-recognized trade custom. In consequence, a high degree of cooperation in the enforcement of the law has been developed between Federal officials and the grain trade. Evidence of the satisfactory manner in which grain standardization is effected appears in the marked degree of uniformity that has been established in the application of the grades. About 450 inspectors apply the Federal grain standards in 150 markets. These inspectors perform something like 1,500,000 inspections a year. It might be supposed that the grading work done by so many different men at so many different points would show considerable variation. This is not the case, as can be seen from the following illustration showing grading at two markets in the same State during July, 1928. Each market received approximately 25,000 cars of wheat, the bulk of which was shipped direct from country stations. Both markets drew the wheat from the same general territory. Although the grain was inspected and graded in the two markets by many different inspectors, the receipts for the month fell closely into the same numerical grades, as Table 2 illustrates.

TABLE 2.—*Grading of wheat in two markets in the same State during July, 1928*

Grade	Market A (25,499 cars)	Market B (22,268 cars)	Grade	Market A (25,499 cars)	Market B (22,268 cars)
	Per cent	*Per cent*		*Per cent*	*Per cent*
1	43.2	48.8	4	8.5	7.6
2	31.4	30.3	5	.8	.6
3	12.0	11.2	Sample	6.3	3.4

Disputes as to Inspections

Sometimes disputes arise as to the accuracy of grain inspections. Since grading is not an exact science, provision is made for appeals from the judgment of licensed inspectors. In one case recently, for example, a large volume of grain moving in carload lots was certificated as No. 2 hard winter wheat at the shipping point. On arriving at its destination, this grain was certificated by another inspector as No. 3 and No. 4 hard winter wheat. Accordingly an appeal was taken to the Federal supervisor. The supervisor sustained the grading given at the destination point. Another appeal was taken to the Federal Grain Supervision Board of Review at Chicago. This board likewise decided that the grain should be graded No. 3 and No. 4, whereupon the shipper carried a final appeal to the Secretary of Agriculture. The case afforded an opportunity to learn whether the Federal grain supervisors were interpreting the wheat standards in line with good commercial practice. I, therefore, called upon each of the presidents of the five principal grain exchanges handling hard winter wheat to appoint from their membership a committee of experts to examine and report on the samples of wheat in question. Each of the committees found that the wheat had been properly graded as No. 3 and No. 4 and that it would not meet the requirements for grade No. 2.

Grain Futures Administration

Closely connected with the United States grain standards act is the United States grain futures act of September 1, 1922. At the beginning of my administration the enforcement of the grain futures act was still in an experimental stage. Since then much progress has been made in eliminating faulty practices and in promoting better understanding among the general public as to the functions and operations of the grain futures markets.

Valuable results have come from formal cooperative agreements entered into in 1925 with the principal grain exchanges. These agreements recognize that the grain trade is willing and anxious to keep within Federal laws, and is in a position, through the grain exchanges, to cooperate with the department in preventing infractions. In making these agreements the department has not divested itself of any responsibilities or ceased to recognize its exclusive obligations to enforce the laws which it is required to administer. Prevention, however, is better than correction, and this end can be promoted by invoking the influence and disciplinary power of the grain exchanges in the maintenance of approved trade practices.

It is believed, in other words, that faulty trade practices can be more effectively prevented through cooperation with the grain exchanges than by arbitrary procedure. Accordingly the Chicago Board of Trade and other contract markets have set up business-conduct committees with broad powers over the business conduct of members and power also to limit daily fluctuations in grain prices during emergency periods. These committees cooperate closely with the grain futures administration. They have accomplished results that fully demonstrate the value of this means of handling critical market conditions. Workable plans are being put in operation for dealing with the many disturbing factors which unduly influence prices in the grain futures markets.

It has been demonstrated by investigations made in connection with the enforcement of the grain futures act that large-scale speculative practices by a few individuals often play an important part in price movements, with but little regard for supply and demand conditions. In some instances individuals have accumulated long or short lines of 5,000,000 bushels or more.

Speculative holdings by individuals have occasionally exceeded 10,000,000 bushels. There have also been days when the volume of trading by a single person has exceeded 10 per cent of the business done during that day in the principal grain future. Such large-scale operations may be a very disturbing element in the market; in fact domination of the market by a few large-scale speculators always results in abnormal price changes. Although the grain futures act enables the department to obtain information about individual commitments in the various futures, it does not provide authority to prevent excessive trading. I believe the act should be amended so as to prohibit excessive trading for purely speculative purposes, and legislation contemplating this change was introduced at the last session of Congress. Such an amendment should contribute greatly toward the prevention of abuses in grain trading, without imposing any unnecessary or harmful restrictions on legitimate trading.

Regular Publication of Futures Data

One of the greatest benefits resulting to the public from the enforcement of the grain futures act is the regular publication of information pertaining to trading in grain futures markets. Previously no reliable information of this character was available. Lack of it possibly facilitated abuses on the one hand and on the other hand gave rise to extreme views as to the influence exercised by grain traders on grain prices. Under present conditions information as to the volume of trading in grain futures and also as to open commitments is made available to all persons interested. In August of this year the information service was extended to include daily releases showing both the volume of trading and the aggregate open commitments by futures. This information should help to eliminate "squeezes" and "corners" in the closing days of an expiring future, an advantage that no one familiar with the grain trade will underestimate.

When the grain futures act was first put in effect some grain traders predicted its effect would be to discourage trading in futures, and thereby to narrow the grain market and increase price fluctuations. But the volume of trading in futures has increased instead of diminishing. Last year, for example, the volume of trading in grain futures was no less than 18.4 per cent greater than the average for the two years immediately prior to the enforcement of the act. Total sales for future delivery on all contract markets aggregated 20,903,549,000 bushels compared with 19,964,384,000 bushels in the preceding year. This increase, which amounts to 4.7 per cent, is conclusive evidence that the grain futures act is entirely without the discouraging influence on trading in grain futures which its opponents predicted it would exercise. As in former years, trading in wheat continues to constitute more than half the business done in grain futures. Last year 53.6 per cent of the total volume of trading was in wheat, 37.4 per cent was in corn, and 6.1 per cent was in oats. The remaining 2.9 per cent represented trading in rye, barley, and flax futures. The Chicago Board of Trade handled 86 per cent of all the trading done in grain futures.

Other Regulatory Laws

The problems presented in the enforcement of the laws relating to grain have their counterpart in the administration of other important regulatory statutes, such as the plant quarantine act, the meat inspection act, the food and drugs act, and the insecticide and fungicide act. These laws are not all equally characterized by what have been termed "service features." All, however, are intended for the protection of agriculture and the welfare of the Nation. It is invariably helpful to enlist the hearty and intelligent cooperation of the interests subject to the laws, so that voluntary action may be substituted for the compulsive correction of improper practices. Most violations of the regulatory laws result from lack of information about their requirements. This obstacle is progressively lessened by the contacts which the department must establish with trade agencies. The department's policy of an advisory rather than an arbitrary attitude has been abundantly justified by results not only in the shape of more easy discharge of necessary administrative functions but in substantial advantages to manufacturers, shippers, and others.

Packers and Stockyards Act

In the enforcement of the packers and stockyards act by the Bureau of Animal Industry a valuable activity has been the preparation of data on the larger stockyards in the Middle West for use in the valuation of stockyard properties and the study of stockyard rates. This work was carried on at 10 markets, and comprises the valuation of stockyard properties, of the financial results of stockyard operations, of the competitive relationship of various markets, and of the services rendered. This information is required as a basis for determining and prescribing just and reasonable rates and charges for stockyards' services.

Informal adjustments of numerous complaints are made, especially with respect to price, quality, and weight of feed, shortages in count and loss of animals in the yards, errors in accounting, and the handling and sale of crippled livestock. In more serious cases formal proceedings are instituted. But the number of such cases is relatively small, and every effort is made to press hearings to a conclusion so that final decisions can be rendered with minimum delay. In a few exceptional cases resort to the criminal provisions of the act is necessary. In the last year a few persons were indicted, pleaded guilty, and were fined. Practically all market agencies and traders have complied with the provisions of the act requiring them to furnish bonds. This action, accomplished largely by informal procedure, greatly increases the protection of producers and shippers.

The interests of livestock shippers are safeguarded by constant supervision of the operation and maintenance of scales at public stockyards, and, on the whole, conditions in the weighing of livestock have been materially improved. A number of yards have installed small scales for weighing small drafts.

ANIMAL INDUSTRY PROBLEMS

The campaign against tuberculosis of livestock, which the department is conducting in cooperation with State and local officials, has made excellent progress in the volume of tuberculin testing and in the extent of territory in which systematic testing has been completed. In some months during the fiscal year 1928 the number of cattle tested exceeded a million head, and the total number during the year was approximately 11,300,000. The progress of the work has been marked by a decline in the percentage of reactors found, showing gradual eradication of the disease. The estimated extent of bovine tuberculosis in the United States is now officially estimated at about 2 per cent, compared with 4 per cent shortly after the cooperative tuberculosis-eradication work began about a decade ago.

The testing of individual herds is supplemented by efforts to eliminate the disease from entire communities, counties, and States, as well as from individual farms. The number of counties engaged in this work exceeds 1,100 and is rapidly increasing. Similar public interest is revealed in the increasing number of cities and towns requiring the tuberculin testing of cattle that contribute to urban milk supplies. A survey of milk ordinances shows that fully 2,100 municipalities require either the tuberculin testing of cattle or the pasteurization of milk. In about three-fourths of these cities and towns the tuberculin test is compulsory. The remainder permit a choice between pasteurization and tuberculin testing. There has also been a decline in tuberculosis among swine, as shown by records of the Federal meat-inspection service. Considering the magnitude of the livestock industry and the task of detecting and eradicating so insidious a germ disease, the present status of the campaign against tuberculosis is gratifying.

Hog-Cholera Prevention

Owing to the effectiveness and wide use of the preventive-serum treatment, hog cholera, which at one time caused heavy losses and disheartened swine growers, is no longer a limiting factor in hog production. The department maintains a corps of trained veterinarians who investigate outbreaks, hold demonstrations of control methods, conduct educational work for the prevention of the disease, and aid State and local authorities in keeping it under control. The preventive-serum treatment continues to undergo various refinements, including the increasing use of improved types of serum. Records of the Bureau of Animal Industry, which supervises the manufacture of veterinary biological products, show continued increase in the exports of such products. The exports consist chiefly of antihog-cholera serum, indicating that foreign countries find the preventive-serum treatment of economic value.

Despite various obstacles the systematic eradication of cattle ticks from the Southern States goes forward, and each year more territory is reclaimed from this pest. The tick-infested area has been reduced to about 25 per cent of its original size. South Carolina and Virginia were released last year from the Federal quarantine against cattle ticks, and Oklahoma has nearly completed its tick-eradication program. Many southern communities which recently completed the eradication of cattle ticks are already benefiting from the introduction of improved cattle for breeding. In a part of eastern Georgia, where purebred beef bulls were introduced two years ago, livestock owners now are furnishing feeder cattle in carload lots. Two counties in western Florida recently received their fourth carload of purebred breeding stock for the establishment of improved herds. Similar activities are in progress in tick-free areas in Oklahoma. Commercial dairy and beef development, such as the establishment of creameries, ice-cream factories, and meat-packing establishments, have followed closely in the wake of tick eradication. The Southern States have been untiring in supporting this campaign.

Inroads of Animal Parasites

Developments in research and regulatory work have directed attention to the serious inroads which many animal parasites make among domestic livestock. Although certain well-known pests, such as cattle ticks, scab mites, and roundworms of swine, are being reduced, hordes of other parasites continue to take enormous toll. The attacks of these pests explain why many young animals die or become unthrifty. Some parasites, notably liver flukes, are invading new territory. The economic losses caused by animal parasites are without question greatly underestimated, since they not only reduce vitality and delay maturity, but also invade tissues and organs and cause a loss of meat. The identity of parasites affecting domestic animals is readily determined in most cases, but effective control measures for many parasites are yet to be developed.

To cope more fully with this situation, the department is extending its research activities. Work thus far conducted has yielded excellent dividends in practical benefits to stock owners. The cooperation of the public in reporting losses and aiding the department's investigators is requested.

Inspection services conducted by the Bureau of Animal Industry give valuable results. Federal meat inspection was conducted during the fiscal year 1928 at 829 establishments in 255 cities and towns throughout the country. Department inspectors supervised the conversion of 75,000,000 head of livestock into more than 13,000,000,000 pounds of dressed meat and lard to supply interstate and foreign demand. During the year 1,155,710,000 pounds were exported under official certification. This efficient service detects infectious centers where diseased animals originate, eliminates unfit meat from the food supply, insures wholesomeness, clean handling, and truthful labeling, and stimulates foreign purchase of our meat. The meat-inspection service covers about two-thirds of the meat supply of the entire country and is conducted at a cost of only one twenty-sixth of a cent a pound for dressed meat and lard.

Another important and extensive branch of livestock work is the enforcement of animal quarantine and transportation laws and of regulations governing the importation and exportation of livestock. In supervising the interstate transportation of livestock in the fiscal year 1928, department employees at market centers inspected approximately 19,000,000 cattle, 21,000,000 sheep, and 43,000,000 hogs. Large numbers of these animals were dipped so that they might be handled in interstate commerce. Department employees supervised the immunization and disinfection, against hog cholera, of more than half a million swine.

Inspections of Cars

The scrutiny of animals for the purpose of preventing the spread of diseases and parasites is supplemented by inspections of cars, of which more than 33,000 were found during the fiscal year 1928 to have carried animals affected with communicable diseases. These cars were cleaned and disinfected under Federal supervision. About 40,000 additional cars were cleaned and disinfected to comply with department regulations or at the request of State officials and transportation companies.

The department's supervision over establishments licensed under the virus serum toxin act has shown a general compliance with that law and with supplementary regulations to insure purity and potency in biological products. The need of such supervision may be seen in occasional violations which have resulted in the revocation or suspension of licenses. Recent causes have included improper methods, false records, insanitary conditions, and other irregularities. Strict enforcement of this act is necessary to provide the livestock industry with pure and potent biological products which may be used with confidence in preserving the health of animals.

Many problems in the breeding, feeding,, and management of domestic livestock and poultry are under investigation. Each year adds new results for the guidance of stock owners. Recent surveys of ranch organization and methods of production in several typical areas of the West should benefit cattle, sheep, and goat producers. The results enable a ranch owner to compare his methods, investment, and returns with those of typical ranches. Wide variation in ranch methods and financial returns exists, and many stock owners may profit by studying the management of the most successful ranches.

Cooperation with Experiment Stations

In response to the need for more information concerning factors influencing the quality of meat, the department is cooperating with 20 State experiment stations and other agencies in seeking the causes of tenderness, color, palatability, and other characteristics of this food.

The investigations extend from the breeding of the animals to the cooking of the meat. In beef, tenderness apparently depends on the quantity and character of connective tissue and on the length and arrangement of fibers. There appears to be no close relation between dark color and either tenderness or palatability.

Experimentation is contributing useful new knowledge of the most profitable methods of beef production. The feeding of supplemental grain rations to steers fattened on grass has materially increased the quantity, quality, and profitableness of the beef produced.

Nutrition studies conducted by the department with hogs at several farms have shown the economy of finishing hogs for market at early ages. In view of the market's growing preference for lighter-weight hogs, the selection of types which develop early is of greater importance than formerly.

Results of Sheep Investigations

Sheep investigations have shown the influence of many factors, such as age, fineness of staple, and face covering, on the yield of wool. Objections to so-called wool blindness resulting from extreme covering of wool on the face appear to be well founded. This condition is associated with a lighter total fleece weight compared with similar sheep having less wool on the face. Studies of this character throw new light on the desirability of having show-ring standards conform with the practical utility of domestic animals.

The department's efforts toward improving its stud of Morgan horses, maintained at Middlebury, Vt., have resulted in increases in weight and height and in the development of stamina and other desirable qualities. Morgan horses bred and developed by the department have performed creditably in recent endurance rides and have won prizes at expositions. A promising new branch of the department's horse investigations is a series of feeding experiments now in progress in cooperation with the War Department. Cavalry and artillery horses are used in tests to determine the possibility of variations from the standard ration used in the Army, with the aim of reducing the cost of feed.

Investigations in poultry production have shown that for best growth and egg production the rations should contain approximately 18 per cent protein. Whether the source of the protein be meat scraps or dry skim milk seems to make little difference. The rations for both growing chicks and laying hens should be properly balanced in minerals, especially calcium and phosphorus. The addition of sulphur in certain forms has proved beneficial in increasing egg production and promoting the growth of feathers. Systematic breeding methods have led to an increase in average egg production per bird in the flocks of Barred Plymouth Rocks, Rhode Island Reds, and White Leghorns on the department's farm at Beltsville, Md. Close inbreeding has resulted in increased embryo mortality during incubation and has retarded the rate of maturity of the chicks that hatch.

Betterment of Animal Types

As in the past, the department has supported various extension efforts to improve domestic animals. An interesting world survey on the subject reveals a keen interest in the betterment of animal types in the principal livestock countries. There is universal reliance on the use of selected purebred sires to bring about improvement in animal types. Many countries are fostering educational methods, breeding centers, and various forms of direct assistance to livestock owners, to improve the quality of products and win a larger proportion of world trade. Improvement of livestock in the United States is essential to the future welfare of the industry, since competition in the production of better animals is developing throughout the world.

Investigations regarding the bacilli of tuberculosis have resulted in the production of an artificial medium capable of yielding a more abundant growth of the bacteria than ever before. This discovery is of value in the making of tuberculin, the diagnostic agent used in the campaign against tuberculosis in cattle, swine, and poultry. An efficient disinfectant for sausage casings, which serves as a cleaning and purifying agent and removes practically all bacteria, has been developed. Investigations have confirmed earlier work which indicated that pork is a food relatively rich in the antineuritic vitamin.

Increasing losses caused by that baffling disease, infectious abortion, have necessitated an active program of research to develop better prevention and control measures. Investigations have shown new facts concerning both natural and artificial immunity. These studies will be energetically pursued, for the toll of the disease probably exceeds $50,000,000 annually, and a pressing need exists for more effective means for its control. Meantime, cattlemen can do much to control the disease by reducing the amount of infection that comes near susceptible animals. Indiscriminate mingling of healthy and diseased animals contributes greatly to the spread of the malady.

A special research committee of the department is studying bacillary white diarrhea of young chickens. This disease causes heavy losses, and a pressing need exists for improved control measures. The first problem is the effect of incubators on the spread of the disease. This portion of the work is nearly completed. Other intensive research on the disease is in progress.

Foot-and-Mouth Disease

A comprehensive report prepared by the department's foot-and-mouth disease commission, which studied that disease in Europe, is now available. This valuable document shows that the greatest danger of spreading the disease occurs in its early stages. The experiences of European countries in attempting to control the malady confirm the methods of eradication which have proved successful in the United States. Under conditions prevailing in this country prompt diagnosis of the disease followed by the slaughter and the burning or burying of affected or exposed animals is especially desirable.

The danger of a shortage of trained veterinarians, mentioned in my last report, has been somewhat lessened by a larger attendance in accredited veterinary colleges whose graduates are eligible to take civil-service examinations for veterinary positions in the department. The registration for the college year 1927–28 was 723, compared with 666 for the preceding year. This increase took place largely in the freshman class. Evidently more young men are being attracted to the veterinary profession. The situation is further helped by the higher salaries the department is now paying veterinarians. An average increase of $153 was made possible by the recognition by the Bureau of the Budget and Congress of the need for reducing the discrepancy between salaries paid veterinarians and other scientific workers in the department.

RESEARCH IN PLANT INDUSTRIES

The progressive farmer, from the very nature of his profession and regardless of nationality or region, must have an alert and inquiring mind and constantly must utilize his new observations or the new information he may have obtained from others, in order to raise, to protect, and to improve his crops. The great wealth of information upon which our modern agriculture is based teems with ideas developed or at least partially originated by thoughtful men actually cultivating their own land, and endeavoring better to understand and to improve their crop production. In the United States the stimulating influence of our farmer pioneers, with their genius for overcoming the diverse and unusual obstacles to a successful agriculture in a new country, has played a large part in making our Nation a leader in agricultural investigation.

The present era requires group action rather than individual action. In research as in other lines of endeavor the need for more complete and new information to meet the new and important problems constantly arising with our more complex crop production is too urgent to permit us to wait for the gradual accumulation of individual experience. The resources of our agricultural colleges as well as of this department are now supplementing and enormously enlarging the experimental activities formerly left to the progressive landholder, but now clearly recognized as a paramount national responsibility.

The rapid centralization and specialization of agricultural research during the last few years have made possible greater accuracy and also greater speed in obtaining reliable results. It is not too much to hope that future years will lead to more and more effective organization for solving important agricultural questions, and we may accordingly expect steadily increasing benefits to American agriculture and to the Nation as a whole.

Research Cost Returned Manyfold

Attempts to reckon the money value of scientific research are never very successful. Discoveries that seem unimportant at first may turn out to have immense significance later. It is difficult to measure the economic results even of achievements the practical utility of which is obvious, since their effect may be felt in diverse ways by many industries simultaneously. Unquestionably, however, the work done by the Bureau of Plant Industry in the last few years has saved immense sums, not only to farmers but to the Nation as a whole.

This can be demonstrated without trying to give an accurate monetary expression of the economic gains realized. Whatever reduces the cost of production or leads to the creation of new use values helps to solve our economic problems. Judged by this criterion, the work of the Bureau of Plant Industry is abundantly justified. It has promoted national progress in agriculture by the interpretation of facts and by the discovery and application of scientific principles to crop production and plant growth.

Space limitations oblige me to cite only a few of the bureau's recent contributions to farm efficiency. These citations should be regarded as typical rather than exceptional cases. In a brief review it is impossible to mention all the many complex and important research results for which credit may be claimed. I hope the examples given will lead to a better appreciation of the essentially practical aspects of the bureau's scientific investigations, and of the manner in which those investigations touch the lives of individual farmers.

The work of foreign plant introduction is of increasing importance to our country. Through such activity new plant material is supplied from the world's varied array of plant possibilities, not only for the improvement and extension of established plant industries but also for the development of new-crop enterprises adapted to the requirements and needs of America.

Nine months of exploration in British East Africa, ended in February, 1928, resulted in the collection of more than 160 kinds of seeds of different grasses and other forage-crop plants adapted for trial both as pastures and meadows in the North and South. Extensive studies were made of the regions visited, with a view to determining their agricultural aspects as a probable factor in the future development of the economics of world agriculture.

A large collection of interesting and valuable Chinese bamboos, seeds, and other propagating material of new plant possibilities were received from Canton, China, before the development of the domestic conditions there forced the Department of Agriculture's explorer to suspend operations and return home.

From the agricultural exploration work in Madagascar, inaugurated just before the close of the present fiscal year, the department hopes to secure seeds and other plant propagation material of a wide range of potentially promising rubber-producing plants for trial in this country.

Precautions Against Pests

The Bureau of Plant Industry is exercising every precaution to guard against the introduction and dissemination of new plant diseases, insects, and other pests. All its foreign-plant introductions are carefully inspected and subjected to fumigation or other protective treatment upon receipt in Washington. As a result of this practice, supplemented by the sanitary means and improved practices in operation at our plant-introduction gardens, in connection with the propagation, growing, handling, and testing of new plant immigrants, the bureau is able to distribute its foreign-plant introductions with the assurance that the precautionary methods employed have guarded against the introduction of any new plant pests or the dissemination of pests already established.

In many sections land brought into cultivation by irrigation has become unproductive after a few years. Large investments of capital and labor are required to provide irrigation water and to develop irrigated land. It is therefore essential that such land should be highly and continuously productive. Some irrigated lands are highly productive and others are not. If knowledge as to the reason for these differences is not available, it is obvious that the development of irrigated lands must continue to be a speculative enterprise. Here, perhaps, is the principal reason for the fact that credit for operations on irrigated land is relatively costly.

Agronomic work has been conducted by the bureau at field stations with a view to determining the factors responsible for the productivity of irrigated land. This work has yielded important practical results. It has shown that the chief hazards in irrigation farming, aside from those common to ordinary farming, may be grouped into three classes: The accumulation in the subsoil of excessive quantities of water, the accumulation in the soil of the root zone of excessive quantities of soluble salts, and changes in the physical condition of the soil by which it becomes impermeable to the movement of water and consequently unproductive. These three difficulties may occur together, but any one of them occurring alone eventually may cause disaster. Understanding of the nature and causes of these difficulties makes it possible to anticipate injury before it becomes serious.

Two Sources of Injury

Our investigators have found that the accumulation of soluble salts in the surplus zone, or root zone, to the point of injury to crop plants may come about in either of two ways. Where the subsoil is saturated with moisture so that the surplus soil is kept moist from below, continued evaporation results in concentrating the soil solution past the limit of tolerance of crop plants. A similar condition may result where the subsoil is not saturated. When irrigation water is used so sparingly that all the water applied is held within the root zone, to be absorbed by plants or lost by evaporation, the salts carried in solution in the irrigation water remain in the root zone and in time make the soil solution too concentrated.

Changes in the physical condition of the soil, in the direction of permeability, result from reactions that take place between the soil and the salts in the soil solution. When the salts in the soil solution are chiefly salts of sodium, the reaction with the soil is in the direction of replacing calcium from combination with the soil. The sodium passes into soil combination and the replaced calcium passes into solution, and accordingly may be more or less rapidly leached. Soil containing appreciable quantities of combined sodium, as a result of such replacement reactions, become dispersed and gelatinous when wet, do not absorb water readily, and become hard or " bake " upon drying.

As for the other principal cause of difficulty (the accumulation of injurious quantities of subsoil water) it has been found that this is often due to percolation losses from canals and ditches. It was formerly attributed chiefly to the excessive use of irrigation water by farmers. In any particular case the first need is to decide what is the chief source of the water causing the trouble. A correct diagnosis may point to preventive measures less expensive and more effective than drainage. Loss of productivity in irrigated soils is a difficulty better dealt with by prevention than by cure. Recent research work by this department throws a flood of light on how prevention may be accomplished.

Homesteads in Dry Regions

Maintenance of homesteads in the so-called dry-land regions is another subject to which the bureau has devoted considerable attention. It has been demonstrated that homes can be established and families maintained from the returns of fruits and vegetables on farms in the Great Plains area, which comprises more than 400,000 square miles. In this region agricultural difficulties resulting from the unusual climatic conditions prevailing are substantial, and progress must of necessity be slow. Patient scientific work, however, is discovering solutions to various problems.

Shelter-belt trees have been found to prevent soil blowing, often a serious problem. Protection afforded to crops by shelter belts, supplemented by proper cultural treatment of the soil, has proved very valuable. Years of experiment at the United States Northern Great Plains Field Station, Mandan, N. Dak., have produced shelter trees that can be grown successfully in the region, and the demand for such trees now exceeds the supply. As a result of this and similar work attractive farmsteads are beginning to dot the prairies in the plains region. This is a favorable augury, for it is well known that any permanent agriculture must plant its roots around the farm home. Sufficient vegetables can be grown to support a family of five on a 1-acre plat in the dry-land region. With this fruit and vegetable output, and also with a cow or two, a litter of pigs, and a flock of poultry, a competent farm economy can be established.

Important investigations are under way to develop wheat varieties resistant to smut and rust. Stinking smut has always been a problem in wheat production. It is especially prevalent in the Pacific coast region and in recent years has been increasing east of the Rockies. To-day it is an important commercial problem in most of our wheat markets. As yet no smut-resistant variety of wheat has been demonstrated as suitable for general culture in the regions growing hard red spring, hard red winter, and soft red winter wheat. Until resistant strains suited to these areas are devolped it will be necessary to continue seed treatment to prevent smut. In the last season all the smut-resistant varieties under experimental observation showed more or less smut infection, and the reason for this susceptibility is being sought.

Smut-Resistant Strains Developed

A number of strains comparatively resistant to stinking smut have, however, been developed. Some of these have been distributed to growers in the Pacific Northwest, where they are increasing in acreage. Other resistant strains have been developed but not distributed, either because they are not adapted to general culture or because seed is not yet available. The resistant strains that have been distributed have a limited adaptation and can be profitably grown only on a small part of the present wheat acreage of the country. Extensive cooperative breeding programs on hard spring wheats and durum wheats are under way with the State experiment stations, and several varieties resistant to leaf rust and more or less resistant to stem rust have become of commercial significance. These require adequate testing over the entire spring-wheat area. Commercial development of some promising resistant strains is probable within the near future.

One of the most striking recent discoveries of the Bureau of Plant Industry is the influence of pollen on the development of the fruit of the date palm. This discovery, which has been fully confirmed with every precaution to prevent error, has shown that different kinds of pollen yield different qualities of dates differing widely in important commercial attributes. Pollen from certain male trees causes the production of small seeds and small fruits that ripen early. Pollen from other trees causes the production of large seeds and large fruits that ripen late.

As the difference in time of ripening often amounts to several weeks, it is occasionally sufficient to decide whether the crop can be ripened properly, cured, and sold, or will be lost completely as the summer rains begin. All date palms must be pollinated artificially in order to cause them to produce fruit crops. Since it is as easy to use one kind of pollen as another, the bureau's discovery gives the date grower power to influence the time of ripening of his crop, and to a certain extent, the power also to influence the size of the fruit. These, of course, are matters of vital importance in successful commercial date growing.

In all probability the scientific importance of this discovery will be very great. It is, so far as is known, the first definitely proved instance of the effects of pollen on the development of fruit. Similar effects may be observed in plants other than the date palm, and studies of this character are under consideration. This is bound to be a subject of great scientific as well as of great practical importance.

Rubber-Production Possibilities

Investigation of rubber-production possibilities in the United States is under way on the basis of a recently developed principle or method of procedure. Attention is given first to the cultural character of the plants, so as to determine which species are best adapted for our conditions. Intensive investigation of special processes of extraction and utilization of rubber or of rubber by-products is then concentrated on the more promising species This work is not restricted to the plants that have heretofore been considered as commercial sources of rubber, for the agricultural possibilities of a plant do not depend upon its abundance in the wild state.

It has been found that tropical rubber trees will grow to normal maturity and produce seeds in Florida. This is indicated by the behavior of all the principal types. Accordingly, experiments in selection, adaptation, and cultural behavior are in progress. Tolerance to frost and cold weather in southern Florida has been demonstrated for the Hevea or Para rubber tree of Brazil, and for several other tropical rubber trees. This has been shown through the repeated cold spells of the last few years, and particularly in the winter of 1927–28 when a minimum temperature of 28° F. was experienced. Study of seedling adaptations of the Hevea rubber tree indicates a wide range of possible cultivation, not limited to the equatorial belt of South America but including the West Indies and Central America. In California the cultivation of guayule is being increased to the scale of commercial production by a private company, and the department is studying other native rubber plants.

Constructive changes in the cotton industry are projected by the department, their practicability having been demonstrated. These improvements require the cooperation of entire communities of cotton growers. Popular understanding and leadership must, therefore, be developed before substantial progress can be expected. Interest in the subject has been aroused, however, and many demands are made for assistance in putting improved methods in operation. Community cooperation makes it possible to change the basis of production from the usual conditions of mixed and mongrelized seed stocks to regular supplies of pure seed. Thus all the farmers in an organized community or district can produce fiber of the same character, and with production thus unified the way is open for utilization of improved varieties and methods.

Cotton in Atlantic Coast Section

In the Atlantic coast section the outlook for continued cotton production seems to lie in the possibility of a return to longer staples, either sea-island or long-staple upland varieties. In recent years short-staple upland varieties have replaced the former production of sea-island cotton in this region. This replacement is perhaps only a temporary expedient. A return to long-staple cotton may be feasible if communities can unite on a single variety. It is difficult, however, to avoid weevil injury to the long staples if earlier short-staple varieties are to continue to be grown in the same district.

Many additional problems have been created for the cotton industry by the recent development of an extensive new area of production in the plateau region of northwestern Texas, where the crop can be grown more cheaply than in many of the older producing districts. This extension involves increased competition and has already seriously threatened production in some of the more humid districts of the former Cotton Belt. In other parts of the old South the outlook will depend largely on the extent to which better facilities and improved methods are employed. In districts where conditions favor the production of fiber of premium quality and length of staple, the prospect is not discouraging. The best assurance of a favorable market status for any community of cotton growers is to be found in the regular production of fiber of good quality. Present conditions tend to impress that principle on the minds of the growers and to promote compliance with it. In the Texas plateau region a limited rainfall involves hazard and difficulty in production, but the rainfall requirement is less than at lower altitudes and the boll weevil is not present. Unquestionably, therefore, we may expect significant changes in the cotton-growing industry.

Great benefit to the citrus industry has resulted from work done by the department in bud selection for nursery propagation. This work, which is based upon tree-performance records, promotes the elimination of nonproductive and nonpaying trees through top-working them with productive strains of high quality. It also promotes the planting of new orchards with trees propagated only from highly productive parent stock. Total production as well as quality has thus been increased materially, with a relatively small increase in the acreage devoted to citrus fruits. It is conservative to estimate that several millions of dollars have been contributed to the citrus industry of California by the elimination of nonproductive trees through the principles of fruit improvement by bud selection. Some important conclusions have been developed from bud-selection research. In the early stages of the work propagations were made from various strains. The progeny trees, planted in orchard form, have now been producing fruit long enough to justify the conclusion that in tree and fruiting characteristics they reproduce the qualities of the parent stock with remarkable consistency.

Problem of Arsenical Sprays

In recent years the presence of arsenical spray residues on fruit has created a problem in both export and domestic markets. The necessity of removing such residues, so that the quantity remaining will be within a specified tolerance, has been urgently projected into the business of handling and marketing apples and pears. It has been felt particularly with respect to fruits grown in arid or semi-arid regions. In such regions larger spray residues are likely to remain on fruit than in humid sections, where more or less frequent rains tend to wash them off. Wiping the fruit, either mechanically or by hand, has proved an insufficient remedy. It has therefore been necessary to resort to washing with dilute solutions of either hydrochloric acid or alkalies, and fairly effective methods for so doing have been developed.

Many thousands of strawberry seedlings resulting from hand-made crosses have been under careful observation and several promising seedlings have been placed for testing with experiment stations, nurserymen, and others to determine their range of adaptability. A larger selection has been reserved for further study. As a result of these experiments, up to the present time four varieties of strawberries have been selected as definitely superior to the commercial varieties now used for making preserves and crushed fruit. Some selections have also shown superior merit in color, firmness, productivity, and high flavor. About 11,000 raspberry seedlings, likewise the result of hand-made crosses, have been under observation. The raspberry-breeding work is relatively less advanced than the strawberry work; one hybrid raspberry variety, however, has been selected as superior for the canning trade. These selections are being propagated with the object of giving them wide commercial tests. Canners, preservers, and commercial growers believe that with both these fruits substantial progress has been made.

Phony Disease of Peaches

Diligent study has not yet disclosed the nature of the phony disease of peaches, which is prevalent in Georgia and is increasing in severity. At its present rate of progress this disease may reach other States in a few years. All experiments to control it have yielded astonishingly negative results. The trouble stands out distinctly as the least understood of all fruit diseases, if not of all plant diseases. A tree once affected remains diseased always. No beneficial effect has yet been observed from the use of fertilizers, soil treatment, or other attempted remedial measures. This fact suggests that the disease is not physiological or nutritional. Attempts to transmit the disease by the injection of the juice expressed from various parts of phony trees have failed. Nor is the disease transmitted when buds or scions from phony trees are budded on nursery trees or on normal peach trees. Growth following such budding is invariably normal. On the other hand, when normal buds or scions are budded on phony roots the resulting growth is always typical of the disease.

The phony disease has been found growing naturally only in the peach tree. It attacks seedling trees and trees of all commercial varieties grown in Georgia. It has never been observed in wild plums, although wild plums are abundant near commercial peach orchards. It seems not impossible, however, that the disease may attack fruits closely related to the peach if it is introduced into districts where such fruits are grown. A small percentage of trees in badly diseased orchards appear to be resistant to the phony disease. This behavior suggests the possibility of selecting resistant stocks. Vigorous effort to control the trouble is urgently necessary. Although the communicability of the phony disease has not been definitely established, it has already traveled 200 miles from Marshallville, Ga., where it was first observed. It has increased from commercially unimportant numbers 30 years ago to a degree that threatens a great industry.

Results of Control Efforts

Recent attemps to control the virus of mosaic diseases, which cause very destructive losses on a wide variety of crops, including beans, tomatoes, potatoes, sugar beets and sugar cane, corn, wheat, and tobacco, have given a measure of success. Promising results have been obtained in efforts to develop resistant varieties, and by the roguing out of diseased specimens of susceptible crops in the early stage of the growing season. Infection tests have been carried on with mild mosaic, rogose mosaic, leaf roll, and spindle tuber on some of the most important commercial varieties of potatoes. None of the varieties or seedlings tested is immune to all of these diseases. Nevertheless, considerable variation in susceptibility has been observed, especially in the case of mild mosaic and spindle tuber. The Irish Cobbler variety has not manifested the mild-mosaic symptoms characteristic of the Green Mountain variety. Similar responses to mild mosaic have been noted with some seedlings. Field inspection during five seasons, combined with roguing the diseased plants from tuber-unit isolated seed plots, have eliminated certain virus diseases and retained other types within relatively low percentages under northern Maine conditions. Disease-free potatoes propagated in tuber-unit plots surrounded by forests have been maintained free from disease for several seasons. This indicates that no infection was contracted from noncultivated plants. Certain commercial growers, by conducting isolated field or seed plots, have developed and maintained potatoes sufficiently free from the virus diseases to qualify for certification of seed stocks.

Valuable results have been obtained in a study of the winter cover-crop problem in the South. In most sections of the South the use of winter legumes should extend the grazing season so that cattle might be kept outdoors the year around. An outstanding need is an adequate seed supply of hairy vetch, Monantha vetch, Austrian winter pea, and bur clovers. Several years ago a source of winter-pea seed was discovered in Europe, and a supply was imported under the name "Austrian winter pea." In seven years of continuous testing in Georgia this winter pea has never failed to make a good growth. It is now grown on small acreages over most of Georgia and to a less extent in Alabama and South Carolina. It will withstand low temperatures as well as hairy vetch, and is ready to plow under earlier in the spring. This is of great importance, because the foundation of all permanent improvement in agriculture in the South consists in the adoption of a sound system of rotations involving the use of legumes which either by means of their residues or by means of the entire crop turned under add nitrogen and organic matter to the soil.

New Sugar-Beet Varieties

Encouraging progress has been made in the development of sugar-beet varieties resistant to the curly-top disease. It is expected that it will be possible, after a few more trials, to put several of the newly developed strains on the market. In experimental tests they have shown decided superiority to the commercial varieties, not only in resistance to curly top but in sugar production. It has been discovered also that partial shading offers an important means of controlling the disease, which is transmitted by the sugar-beet leaf hopper. This disease has assumed increased importance from the discovery that it may also attack tomatoes, beans, summer squash, peppers, horse-radish, and spinach. Relationship of light to the control of the disease will, it is hoped, develop further indirect methods for eliminating injury.

New varieties of sugar cane introduced into the United States in recent years have proved of great value. The cultivation of these varieties has rehabilitated the sugar-cane industry in Louisiana. An imperative need exists, however, for the breeding and development of varieties more resistant to disease and more specifically adapted to culture in the United States. Accordingly, the department's plant explorers are searching for promising strains in New Guinea and other islands of Melanesia, where the sugar-cane plant has reproduced itself by seed through countless generations. Under such conditions it is reasonable to expect that natural selection will have eliminated seedlings susceptible to mosaic and similar destructive diseases. Sugar cane indigenous to this region belongs to the thick-stemmed or " noble " type, which planters everywhere esteem. It has been found that the disease-resistant varieties that have been introduced improve in vigor and in resistant qualities when crossed with primitive types. Although this proceeding gives smaller and more slender hybrid varieties, the superior performance of such varieties under present tests makes them acceptable to planters. It is hoped, however, that high-yielding, thick-stemmed varieties immune to disease may be found in Melanesia or may be developed by breeding from varieties obtained there.

Influencing Plant Ripening

Some years ago an extraordinarily important discovery was made in the Bureau of Plant Industry relating to the influence of the length of day on plant growth, which opened an almost unlimited field of research. It was demonstrated that the change in the length of day which comes with changes in the seasons and in latitudes controls or affects features of plant behavior of fundamental importance to agriculture. Subsequent investigation has revealed something about the significance of length of day under practical growing conditions. Information has been sought which may indicate how the time of flowering and fruiting of certain types of plants and their adaptability to different latitudes can be favorably influenced.

Clearly this discovery opens up new possibilities in the control of plant life. An example of its significance in the case of soy beans has been very strikingly furnished in the vicinity of Washington, D. C. In this locality the Biloxi variety regularly flowers in the early fall rather than in midsummer, because the summer days are too long. On the other hand, the Peking variety regularly flowers late in July because it responds to a somewhat longer day. But it is prevented from flowering by the longest days of early summer. In the case of both varieties the time of flowering is delayed by a higher latitude and hastened by a lower latitude. It has been found, on the other hand, that some of the very late varieties are not particularly sensitive to changes in the length of day. In the case of these strains the length of the vegetative period is not greatly affected by the date of planting. More effective use of the different varieties may be expected from the clearer understanding of these differences in behavior.

ECONOMIC SERVICES AND RESEARCH

In the last few years the work of the Bureau of Agricultural Economics has been greatly enlarged, and at the same time farmers and the public generally have become better acquainted with its value. Demands are constantly made on the bureau for new services and for the extension of services already well established. The inspection of fruits and vegetables, which not many years ago covered only a few thousand cars at terminal markets, last year was applied to 243,262 cars at shipping and receiving points. This was an increase of approximately 17,000 cars over the number inspected the preceding year and more than 50 per cent over the number inspected four years ago. An increase took place also in the inspection of dairy and poultry products, hay, grain, and other commodities. Much commodity-inspection work was done for other departments of the Federal Government. Meat grading and stamping, a service begun as an experiment, proved highly successful and was put on a fee basis. By this service beef carcasses are stamped so that the grade appears on retail cuts. A seed verification service has been inaugurated. This requires the maintenance of records and accounts by seed dealers under the supervision of the department. As yet the service is limited to alfalfa seed, a product whose point of origin is very important. Eventually the service will probably be extended to include other seeds. The service is conducted on a voluntary basis by means of cooperative agreements between seed dealers and the department. A great increase has taken place in the demand for copies of the official cotton standards which are prepared and sold by the bureau.

The scope of standardization has been widened by the use of standardized grades as a basis for price quotations in the bureau's market news services. Shipping and receiving point inspection likewise promotes standardization, since it is conducted on the basis of official grades. Standardization facilitates the interpretation as well as the improvement of market conditions. It is easier to analyze supply and demand information when it comes from many sources in a common language, so to speak. A recent development in standardization was the enactment at the last session of Congress of a measure authorizing the Secretary of Agriculture to use certain funds for studies covering all phases of the marketing of wool, as a step toward the establishment of wool standards. This work is under way.

Much of the bureau's work involves the administration of various Federal laws. In this task the officials charged with administrative functions receive general cooperation and support from the agricultural and trade interests particularly concerned. As a result the regulatory work has become largely a service function. The licensing and supervision of warehouses under the United States warehouse act, for example, insures the safe storage of the farmer's crop until it can be marketed advantageously and at the same time makes the warehouse receipt better collateral for bank loans. Thus the farmer's business is facilitated, while at the same time the stabilization of markets is promoted. Further progress under the United States warehouse act was taken last year when tentative standards were drafted for canned vegetables destined for storage in federally licensed warehouses. Regulations were also promulgated for the storage of cold-pack fruit.

Demand Growing for Market News

Crop and livestock information is in steadily increasing demand. In the last fiscal year the call for statistical information was practically double that of the previous year, with farmers particularly showing increased interest in economic information. The departments crop and livestock reporting service now issues regular reports on 80 field crops and 10 livestock commodities. In the last few years the information gathered has gained tremendously in variety and comprehensiveness. I referred last year and the year before to recent improvements made in the technic of crop reporting, and this useful progress continues. Crop statistics for past years have been reviewed, the revision in the case of livestock numbers and values going back to 1900. Facts are now gathered also as to the disposition of crops. Acreage statistics are being revised in the light of recent changes in the sources of information and in the methods of obtaining data.

Among the more recent developments in the crop-reporting field is the publication of monthly reports on the production of eggs and of milk on farms whose operators cooperate with the crop-reporting service. These reports form the basis of monthly indexes of egg production and milk production. The country is constantly demanding more information on marketing as well as on production. Accordingly, the bureau's market news service endeavors to publish the desired information in the most useful form. Its leased-wire telegraph service, connecting many of the principal markets, is the mainstay of the service. Branch offices serve as bases for gathering and transmitting information and also for distributing data locally required. Additional distribution is given to the bureau's economic information by radio, telephone, and commercial telegraph, as well as by mimeographed bulletins and press releases.

Underlying the service and regulatory work of the bureau is the research work of the entire department. Much of the work done by other bureaus is utilized by the Bureau of Agricultural Economics, and a high degree of cooperation between the bureau's economists and the other scientific workers of the department has been brought about. In this way duplication of effort has been reduced and related studies have been coordinated. Problems presenting a complex intermixture of economic, agronomic, biological, or chemical factors are thus brought more easily within the scope of scientific investigation. Cooperation in scientific inquiries is not limited to divisions of the Department of Agriculture. It exists among all the departments of the Government. Important information is constantly made available to the Bureau of Agricultural Economics by research workers in the Department of Commerce, the Department of the Interior, the Post Office Department, and the State, Army, Navy, and Labor Departments. Thus aided the bureau has won international recognition as the leading organization in its field.

Farm-Management Work Reorganized

The bureau's farm-management work has been reorganized so as to give the most practical assistance possible to farmers in solving the question of what to produce and how to produce it so as to obtain the greatest profit. All data available in the bureau, such as information on prospective market requirements and prices, production trends in competing regions, and production costs are interpreted in the light of conditions governing successful farming in particular regions in such a way as to assist individual farmers in determining sound production programs for their farms. This work is carried on in practically all cases in cooperation with State and local agencies. A more profitable system of farming on tobacco farms of south-central Virginia is being brought about through the work of this department and the Virginia Polytechnic Institute. Farmers are reorganizing their farms so that tobacco plays a less important part in their income. Poultry, dairy, and hay enterprises have been expanded and in general only the better fields planted to tobacco. The same type of work is carried on in many other sections.

Special studies are under way in the area affected by the corn borer to determine the most economical methods of controlling the pest and the adjustment it will necessitate in farm activities. The results of these studies have been published, and should assist farmers in adopting methods which will be successful in meeting the emergency. A new project, known as farm budgeting, has been inaugurated in several States under which definite farm plans are worked out with farmers who agree to put them into operation. These plans are the result of farm budgets for different systems carefully worked out and compared. The farmers keep accounts during the year and the results obtained are compared with the results that might have been obtained with other systems as shown by the budget statements. Much progress has been made in promoting the use of records and accounts of farm activities.

Assistance is being given American farmers through the work of the foreign offices of the department. The department's specialists abroad explain to foreign buyers the standards for American farm products, and advise American producers and shippers with regard to foreign marketing conditions. Much information is received in the department from its foreign offices, from the consular service, from commercial attachés, and from the International Institute of Agriculture, which is summarized and published. This information is supplemented by special reports on the economic situation in foreign countries as it affects the demand for American agricultural products. Surveys are made of production and trends of production in foreign countries for the purpose of informing American producers with regard to the competition they must expect. The information received is necessary for consideration in connection with statistics covering the situation in the United States.

Foreign competition in either the domestic or the foreign market or in both directly affects about 90 per cent of the agricultural products of the United States which enter into market channels. In a normal season, more than 50 per cent of the cotton crop, 30 per cent of the tobacco crop, and 20 per cent of the wheat crop are exported. About 34 per cent of the average production of lard and 8 per cent of other hog products are exported annually. Knowledge of production outside of the United States and also of foreign market conditions is essential in planning the production and marketing of these products. Knowledge of foreign production and markets is equally necessary in the case of products of less importance. In some cases, indeed, such knowledge is more important than knowledge of the situation in the United States.

Many serious marketing difficulties have their origin in irregularities of production, resulting from variations in acreage, yields, or both. Farmers have comparatively little control over yields each year, but acreage is more amenable to adjustment. Studies have shown in the case of some crops that annual variations in acreage are an important factor in variations in production. In other words, farmers are not entirely without power to influence the volume of their output. Too often, however, high prices stimulate increased planting or breeding without due consideration of market prospects. Thus production becomes unstable and unbalanced, and the farming industry suffers from extreme price fluctuations. It is to the interest not only of the farmer but of the entire community that agriculture should not be periodically depressed by overproduction and low prices.

As a means of promoting orderly production and orderly marketing, the Bureau of Agricultural Economics gathers information to show the probable trend of production and demand. Research of this type has been in progress for six years. Bulletins have been published dealing with factors affecting the prices of hogs, oats, and cotton; the prices of lambs, wheat, wool, and apples have been discussed in special articles. In these price studies the first step is to discover and measure the influence of the principal price-determining factors. Then the influence of these factors is traced by comparisons with prices reconstructed over a series of past years. In this way the past is studied to throw light on the future. Forecasts of supply and demand thus obtained have been about 90 per cent accurate.

Timely forecasts issued with due caution help farmers to decide what to produce and when to sell their products. Analysis of the past relation of price to supply and demand conditions discloses the value of crops on the basis of current supply and demand conditions, and thus gives farmers an invaluable guide both in marketing and in future production. On the supply side, information is regularly furnished by crop forecasts. Information about demand is less abundant and exact, but is constantly growing in volume and reliability. Each month the Bureau of Agricultural Economics issues a price-situation statement in which current market conditions are examined and supply and demand prospects indicated.

Five years ago the department began issuing outlook reports annually as an aid to farmers in adjusting their production. Simultaneously a system of reports was inaugurated giving information as to the intentions of farmers to plant crops or to breed and feed animals. The intentions-to-plant reports inform individual farmers what the farmers of the country as a whole are planning. Such information, when furnished in time to influence planting or breeding, may help greatly in forestalling maladjustments in production.

Commercial agencies often are able to supply themselves with information on supply and demand conditions affecting the prices of products handled by them, but individual farmers are unable to do so because of the complexity of the problem. Timely information of this character is essential to balanced production and orderly marketing, and is helpful not only to farmers but also to the general public. Therefore it is a proper function of governmental agencies to compile and publish information of this character as a guide to private effort.

It is worth noting that the major farm relief proposals discussed within the past few years were predicated on price analysis and market forecasting. In fact, the measure which attracted most attention would have demanded considerably more price analysis than the department is at present in a position to furnish. This is a recognition of the obvious truth that modern agriculture can not prosper without economic information as a guide to production and marketing.

Blind competition leads inevitably to disastrous extremes in output, and therefore to destructive price fluctuations. When the department's outlook and intentions-to-plant reports are better understood and more generally used by farmers, an important step will have been taken toward the stabilization of agriculture. I have mentioned the fact that accurate forecasts of excessive potato production this year failed to influence planting materially. Similar examples might be cited in regard to other crops. Each year, however, farmers become more aware of the utility of economic information and better skilled in applying it to their business.

Extension of Economic Information

Attention is given by the department and by the cooperative extension agencies of the various States to extension activities designed to furnish more complete economic information to farmers. Research results are not realized in full until they are communicated to farmers through extension activities. Farmers are relying more and more on the extension agencies for economic counsel. It is imperative to provide them with essential facts about farm management and about the proper adjustment of farm enterprises to probable market requirements. This can be done without giving less attention to the technical problems of production. Knowledge gained by the study of prices and price trends becomes of practical value to agriculture only when it influences the production plans of individual farmers or groups of farmers.

Farmers highly value extension work of an economic character. This is shown by the widespread interest taken in the department's outlook work and in that of the cooperative State agencies. In some districts farmers have taken the lead in late years in calling conferences to discuss economic questions. Interest in economic questions is not confined to prices and market prospects. It includes also such broader aspects of the agricultural problems as are involved in the taxation of land, reclamation and reforestation, and other land problems. Facts gathered by research workers on these problems gain increased practical significance when presented to farmers through extension agencies or in other ways. Constructive and permanent means of improving agricultural conditions depend in the last resort on an appreciation by farmers and by the general public of the complex nature of agricultural problems. Economic extension work is among the most powerful influences in producing this frame of mind.

Crop-Insurance Studies

The uncontrolled hazards of agriculture are a serious problem. Whatever the farmer may do to safeguard his production, the dangers of loss from storm and flood are ever present. In industry, systems of insurance have been developed to provide safeguards against unexpected losses. Agriculture needs similar protection in crop and livestock insurance. Our experience with crop insurance is limited, and research is required to show the way toward better methods. Crop insurance has received the consideration of Congress in response to a resolution of the Senate. A report on the problem is being prepared.

CHEMISTRY AND SOILS WORK

In 1927 the department's Bureau of Chemistry, its Bureau of Soils, and its Fixed Nitrogen Research Laboratory were consolidated in a single research unit called the Bureau of Chemistry and Soils. I wish to refer in this report to work done during the entire period of my administration. Some of the accomplishments I am about to mention were launched or completed before the above-mentioned consolidation was effected. It will be convenient, however, to speak of them as activities of the Bureau of Chemistry and Soils since the department units concerned are now merged therein. The record is singularly rich in cash results achieved for farmers.

A typical example is a service rendered to some 400,000 farmers who produce cane and sorghum sirups. These commodities are annually produced to the amount of about 80,000,000 gallons. It has been difficult to find a market for these products, owing to their lack of uniformity and to the poor keeping quality of some sirups put up in retail packages. A remedy for the trouble has been found in a method of blending, standardizing, and treating sirup, so as to produce an article of standard and sustained character. This method, the result of prolonged research in the Bureau of Chemistry and Soils, will probably permit the establishment of cooperative blending and canning plants. Another recent achievement of the bureau which promises substantial benefit to cane-sugar producers is a method of making a creamed sugar residue which has been named "cane cream," and put on the market by one large producer in Louisiana.

Instances of similar contributions by the Bureau of Chemistry and Soils to agricultural welfare could be multiplied indefinitely. Its research work has shown how losses in refining cottonseed oil, which amount to some 7 or 8 per cent of the crop, may be materially reduced. As our vegetable-oil crop has an average annual value of about $500,000,000, this discovery promises to effect large savings. Studies are under way which may develop means of reducing losses in the curing of hides and tanning materials and in other branches of the leather-goods industry. Such losses are estimated to exceed $250,000,000 annually. The turpentine and rosin industry has been benefited by improved stills, devised and patented in the department, which are expected to save producers $1,000,000 annually and to yield better and cleaner turpentine and rosin. Processes have been worked out that triple the life of the shade cloth used by tobacco growers in their plant beds, their annual bill for which exceeds $2,000,000.

Insecticides and Fungicides Improved

Much has been done to improve and cheapen insecticides and fungicides. About the only available material which can be used as a contact insecticide in the fight against sucking insects is nicotine. But nicotine costs as much as $3 a pound. In view of the quantity necessary in the war on insect pests, this price often makes its use impracticable. In the last few years the Bureau of Chemistry and Soils has synthesized and produced two new chemical compounds obtained as a by-product from the manufacture of illuminating gas. These compounds have insecticidal properties nearly as great as those of nicotine and can be produced, it is believed, at a cost of only a few cents a pound. Their appearance in chemical markets is expected shortly.

Still another extremely important recent discovery by the bureau is that of a new fumigant which may be substituted for the highly inflammable carbon bisulphide and the hazardous hydrocyanic acid. This fumigant, ethylene dichloride-carbon tetrachloride mixture, although discovered only within the last two years, is now produced in large commercial quantities.

In the fight against the boll weevil the odorous principle of the cotton plant has been studied. This principle, which is believed to furnish the attraction to the weevil, has been isolated and the compound can probably be made synthetically. Here is a possible means of furnishing bait for boll weevils which may have considerable importance in the fight against the pest.

With a small appropriation provided by Congress, a campaign was begun in 1927 to reduce the loss from farm fires, which amounts annually to more than $150,000,000, in addition to the loss of about 3,500 lives. Although the work has barely started, it has already indicated the likelihood that within the next few years the farm fire loss may be reduced as much as 10 per cent. Dust explosions as a source of loss in many localities have been materially reduced by methods developed by the Bureau of Chemistry and Soils. Equipment developed in the bureau has been widely adopted and methods of threshing and grain handling have been put in effect. It has been estimated, indeed, that savings thus made may in a single year equal the entire cost of the bureau's research work.

Soil Survey Extended

Soil investigations and particularly the department's soil survey have proved extremely valuable in recent years. Field parties have mapped 21,838 square miles in detail and have made reconnaissance surveys of more than 17,000 square miles during the past fiscal year. These surveys, added to the area previously covered, give a grand total of approximately 754,000 square miles of detailed surveys and 598,000 square miles of reconnaissance work. Knowledge of our soil resources has thus been made greater than that of any other country. Indeed, it may exceed that of all other countries combined. From field studies of the major groups of soils in the United States and Central and South America much information has been gained that should aid in solving fundamental problems of soil classification.

In recent years the department's soil-survey work has been utilized by other agencies of the Government. A typical example was the appointment recently by the Secretary of the Interior of a fact-finding committee to investigate the present status and determine the future policies of the Reclamation Service. This committee took into consideration the results of soil-survey work by the Department of Agriculture on reclamation projects completed and pending. It was so strongly impressed by the value of soil surveys that it recommended that no additional engineering work should be done on old or new reclamation projects until the soils included had been studied and their suitability for agriculture determined. Accordingly the department is now frequently called on to make detailed soil surveys of areas within contemplated reclamation and colonization districts.

In like manner it is requested by the Indian Service to examine agricultural-development projects before engineering expense is incurred. The Department of Commerce has obtained from the Department of Agriculture information about the soils of American countries to the south, with particular reference to rubber production in the West Indies and Central America. Within the department the Bureau of Public Roads makes use of the soil survey in its highway-engineering work.

In growing soil-improving crops such as clover, alfalfa, and soy beans, soil and seed inoculation with nitrogen-fixing bacteria is desirable. This has stimulated the production, by both public and private agencies, of cultures for inoculation purposes. The department, while encouraging such work, inspects cultures offered for sale to farmers, a service rendered necessary by the fact that soil " cure-alls " and other nostrums are sometimes sold. In general the quality of the cultures offered is good. Occasionally, however, brands fail to show the merits claimed for them and steps are then taken to prevent possible purchase. Studies now in progress may reveal means whereby some of the little-known members of the invisible soil population may be made more efficient by selection, by adjustment of crops, or by addition of fertilizers and soil amendments. For the present, however, the nodule bacteria of legumes remain the only ones that can be satisfactorily utilized in trade.

Developments in Fertilizer Industry

Important developments have lately taken place in the fertilizer industry. The Bureau of Chemistry and Soils has contributed materially to the progress effected. Much research work has been done to increase the supply of fertilizer ingredients from our own great natural resources. Studies have also been conducted to improve the technic of fertilizer production and to cheapen and improve the finished product. To-day the fertilizer industry is in a rapid transition to a chemical basis, largely as a result of the development of methods for fixing atmospheric nitrogen.

The department's fixed-nitrogen laboratory has made noteworthy contributions to the science of fertilizer synthesis. It has established and interpreted some of the fundamental chemical, physical, and engineering data involved. The information has been put at the disposal of American fixed-nitrogen plants and men trained in the department's laboratory have been in constant demand by the fixed-nitrogen industry. Some idea of the progress made can be gained from the fact that the production of fixed nitrogen in the United States now exceeds 36,000 tons a year, compared with only 6,000 tons in 1923, and plants now under construction will double the present output. In comparison with Germany's output of fixed nitrogen, however, ours is small. Germany's annual production of 660,000 tons indicates the need for energetic development of the American industry.

American farmers are, of course, still heavily dependent on foreign materials for nitrates and potash. Exploitation by foreign agencies not subject to American control can only be terminated by the development of American production, at least to the point where the prices of these essential commodities will be dictated at home and not abroad. Research in the Bureau of Chemistry and Soils is conducted to assist in developing an American potash industry, the necessary raw materials of which exist here in abundance. Gratifying progress is being made. Four years ago our annual production was 20,000 tons actual potash (K_2O). Last year the output amounted to 44,000 tons.

Concentrated Fertilizer Mixtures

Another important branch of the department's fertilizer studies indicates the economy of concentrated fertilizer mixtures. Fertilizers should be marketed in a high state of concentration. Four or five years ago commercial fertilizer mixtures seldom contained more than 15 per cent plant food. Sale of such mixtures entailed the sacking, transportation, and handling of 85 per cent of materials from which the farmer obtained little, if any, benefit. The freight bill paid annually by the American farmer for the delivery of the 7,000,000 tons of fertilizer which he purchases amounts to approximately $20,000,000. If the concentration of fertilizers should be increased twofold, the freight bill would be cut in two and the annual bill of $12,000,000 paid for sacks would likewise be halved.

Research in the bureau has shown that higher concentration is practicable. Methods have been devised whereby the diluents found in fertilizer ingredients as formerly prepared may be largely eliminated. Salts containing two and even three elements of plant food and representing a concentration as high as 85 per cent have been developed as a substitute for salts containing only one plant-food element. The fitness of these materials both for the fertilizer trade and in the field has been demonstrated. As a result, fertilizer mixtures containing as high as 60 per cent plant food are now being successfully marketed at a lower price and a greater profit. Means of utilizing American raw materials of nitrogen, phosphate, and potash in manufacturing processes have been demonstrated and opportunities have been pointed out for the development of additional resources.

These results indicate the value of chemistry to agriculture. Nevertheless, there is need for a wider application of chemical research to agriculture, for the problems awaiting solution are complex. Our knowledge of the chemistry of cellulose, lignin, starch, proteins, vitamins, and other constituents of crops and animals is very incomplete. Comparatively little is known as yet about some of the common processes of animal life, such as the production of milk in the lacteal gland. Operations of plant and animal life are chemical processes upon the control and stimulation of which agriculture is coming increasingly to depend. Every farm is a chemical factory. Agricultural chemistry treats of the composition of soils, crops, and farm animals, and of the mutual chemical relations of these in so far as they concern the production of food and fibers. Its contributions to human welfare in the past, great though they have been, are undoubtedly little more than a hint of what will be achieved in the future.

Recently the Bureau of Chemistry and Soils sent a questionnaire to agricultural chemists asking what they considered the 12 most important contributions made by chemical research to national prosperity. The replies indicated a belief that the work leading up to the passage of the Federal food and drugs act, the development of accurate methods for analyzing agricultural products, food studies made possible by the use of the respiration calorimeter, research into the chemical composition, properties, and nutritive values of various crops, and the experimental use of lime to correct the sterility of acid soils stand in the forefront of the chemical services most highly valued. Other highly regarded technical developments are: Tests of fertilizers for farm crops, studies of vitamins, reclamation of alkali soils, development of the cane and beet sugar industries, investigations of the chemistry of soils, and work on the utilization of wastes and by-products in agriculture.

Prevention of Spoilage

Research by the Bureau of Chemistry and Soils is of value to farmers not merely in facilitating their production but in enabling them to prevent their products from spoiling. Moreover, agricultural marketing is becoming more and more dependent on the application of chemistry to the demands of popular taste. Markets for particular varieties of fruits and vegetables have been widened by chemical analyses such as those used in tests in the breeding of new strains rich in sugars, starches, acids, or essential oils. Chemical tests determine when fruits are ready to pick. The ripe orange with a green skin can be colored without injury to its food properties by exposing it to ethylene gas. Scientific tests of the maturity of fruits have saved millions to horticulturists by enabling them to pick their crops at the most advantageous time. Some farming industries like fruit and dairy enterprises, when sufficiently organized, find it profitable to employ agricultural chemists just as do many highly capitalized manufacturing industries. An indication of the part played by chemistry in agriculture is the fact that no fewer than one-fifth of the chemists listed in American Men of Science are engaged in work of an agricultural-chemical nature.

RESEARCH IN DAIRYING

Research conducted by the department's Bureau of Dairy Industry is throwing invaluable light on many practical problems. An example is its work on the mineral constituents of a ration, particularly calcium and phosphorus, which shows their importance in maintaining a normal milk flow and probably also in bringing about successful reproduction. The bureau has demonstrated that a large milk yield can not be kept up without drawing on the reserve mineral supply in the animal's skeleton if calcium and phosphorus are not available in the feed. These minerals are much more readily available in properly cured legume hay, particularly alfalfa, than in the inorganic form. The practical significance of these facts is obvious.

Important facts have also been learned recently about the cow's udder. It had been generally believed that the milk-storing capacity of the cow's udder is not more than half a pint to each quarter, and that the greater part of the milk obtained at milking is secreted during the milking process. That this is incorrect was demonstrated by slaughtering cows just previous to the usual milking time. The udders were amputated and the milk drawn. In one experiment the quantity obtained averaged 61.1 per cent of the normal yield by the same cows. In another test the quantity obtained was 76 per cent of that given by the cows when alive. It was shown that milk secretion is largely a continuous process and that the capacity of the secretory system is much greater than had been supposed. This knowledge should help to lay a more scientific foundation for the selection of dairy cattle.

The sterility of cattle, or their failure to reproduce, is one of the greatest sources of loss to the dairy industry. Experiments by the bureau have shown that some forms of sterility in cows can be overcome by feeding sprouted oats. Sprouted grains, together with regular exercise, are effective also in prolonging the active service of valuable sires. Other experiments show that when roughages of

the proper quality are available, cows of more than average producing capacity obtain sufficient nutrients from a ration consisting
entirely of roughage. Cows with a producing capacity considerably
above the average utilize grain profitably when fed at the rate
of 1 pound to each 6 pounds of milk produced per day. They can
not do so, however, when fed grain at the rate of 1 pound to each 3
pounds of milk produced.

Breeding projects undertaken by the bureau continue with favorable results. Bulls are provided from its experimental breeding herds
for other Federal institutional herds and for State universities and
agricultural colleges. Two daughters of two of these bulls, one in
the herd of the University of California and the other in the herd
of the New Jersey Agricultural College, made world's records for
their respective age classes last year.

Records Prove Value of Work

Some 200 young bulls are used on the herds of farmers in the
vicinity of the bureau's experimental herds, chiefly for the purpose
of determining their hereditary make-up for milk and butterfat
producing capacity. In the vicinity of the experiment station at
Huntley, Mont., 94 daughters of the bureau's bulls have completed a
year's production record. This shows an increase per cow per year
of 77.4 pounds of butterfat over the record of their dams, when both
records are computed to a mature basis. The increased fat production
had a local value of not less than $34.06 per cow per year. The
farmers living near the Huntley station herd have some 425 heifers
sired by the bureau's bulls. If the increased production shown by
the 94 already mentioned is maintained by the other 331 heifers,
the annual value of the increased output will aggregate some $14,475.
The bulls found to have an inheritance for a high level of production will be used in the bureau's experimental herds or in the herds
of cooperating agricultural colleges.

That the average production of dairy cows in the United States
might be greatly increased is a matter of common observation. The
average dairy cow produces about 4,500 pounds of milk and 180
pounds of butterfat a year. Contrast this showing with the performance of the cows in dairy herd-improvement associations. Records
of the production of such cows are regularly tabulated by the Bureau
of Dairy Industry on the basis of information representing dairy
herd-improvement associations in 43 States. In 1927 the average
production of cows owned by members of these associations was 7,410
pounds of milk and 293 pounds of butterfat. This showing is considerably greater than that made by the dairy herd-improvement
associations in 1920. In that year the average production of association cows was only 5,989 pounds of milk and 247 pounds of butterfat. Each year since 1920 has seen a gain in the average production. The Bureau of Dairy Industry cooperates with a majority
of the States in the dairy herd-improvement work, which takes
rank among the most effective means of increasing the efficiency
of American dairying.

Studies of Dairy Sanitation

Valuable results have come from studies of dairy sanitation by the bureau. How to handle milking machines so as to produce milk of low bacterial count is a problem on dairy farms. The bureau has evolved a simple, inexpensive method of cleaning and sterilizing such machines. This method, which can be used on any farm, enables the dairyman under average farm conditions to produce milk even in the summer with an average bacterial count as low as 2,000 or 3,000 per cubic centimeter.

Another recent contribution to dairy sanitation made by the bureau is the demonstration of economical methods for producing steam on the small dairy farm for the sterilization of utensils. City health departments often require steam sterilization of all dairy utensils, because the unsterilized utensil is the greatest source of bacterial contamination in fresh milk. Tests made by the bureau cover sterilizing cabinets constructed of wood, concrete, and galvanized iron. Other tests were made with a small galvanized water heater and steamer. The first device mentioned requires a steam boiler for its operation and the second does not. When the tests were completed blue prints of approved types of sterilizers were drawn up and sent to dairymen, milk inspectors, and other interested persons. The tests showed the bacteriological efficiency of the different appliances examined and also the cost of operation of each type.

Milk dealers, as well as milk producers, are confronted with bacteriological problems. One such problem is how to obtain milk of a low bacterial count, and another is how to handle milk so that it will not become recontaminated. In order to learn where and how recontamination of milk chiefly occurs, studies were made at 97 milk plants of varying size and type. These studies showed that the management and proper cleaning of equipment in the milk plant are of vital importance, and indicated also that the importance of proper distribution of refrigeration in cold-storage rooms is not always recognized. Variations in temperature amounting to as much as 15° F. sometimes exist in different parts of a cold-storage room. This knowledge has led to further studies in methods of air circulation and in the arrangement of refrigerator rooms.

It is well known, of course, that the conservation of milk in a condensed, evaporated, or desiccated form is based on the destruction of bacteria or on the creation of conditions tending to prevent the development of bacteria. It is also a matter of common knowledge that the flavor of butter and cheese depends greatly on the encouragement of bacteria producing desirable effects and on the suppression of bacteria tending to cause spoilage.

Bacteria Growth Rate

Accordingly the bureau has studied conditions governing the rate of growth of bacteria, the effects of growth of one species on another species, and various other bacterial problems. It has been discovered that the cells in passing through different stages of normal growth undergo physiological changes which exercise a marked effect on the resistence of the bacteria to heat and other unfavorable conditions. Bacteria in the rapidly growing stage, for example, can be more easily destroyed than is possible after they reach a more dormant condition. This knowledge has a practical application in the preparation of " starters." It has also been successfully applied in the development of methods to suppress abnormal fermentations in cheese.

Some of the bureau's recent contributions to our knowledge about dairying, while of the highest practical value, involve more technical description than can be given in this report. The examples cited are intended merely to give an idea of the character and value of the work done. An easily grasped instance is the application of an investigation recently made on the viscosity of milk and cream. Viscosity is important commercially because it affects the whipping quality of cream and the appearance of table cream. Cream with a poor viscosity, even though containing the requisite amount of butterfat, appears thin to the consumer. A dealer selling such cream is consequently at a disadvantage when competing with another selling cream having the same butterfat content but greater viscosity. The department's researches into this problem led to the development of several methods for increasing the viscosity of cream. Methods have also been developed whereby the destruction of viscosity by different practices in milk-handling plants may be prevented. In the same connection valuable data have been obtained regarding the effects on milk and cream of temperature, aging, acidity, heating, and other factors. Methods have also been developed by which strongly flavored feeds may be given to dairy animals without tainting their milk. This is of great importance, because losses from off-flavored milk amount to many million dollars annually.

Better Cheese Making Facilitated

More efficient methods of cheese making have been developed as the result of investigations conducted in the dairy bureau. These investigations have sought, first, means of encouraging the domestic production of kinds of cheese now largely imported; and, second, means of controlling the abnormal fermentations that cause losses by lowering the quality of cheese. It is estimated that gassy fermentations decrease, by from 3 to 10 cents a pound, the value of a considerable proportion of our domestic production of Swiss cheese. In both these directions progress has been made. Better methods have been demonstrated for making Swiss cheese equal in appearance and flavor to the best imported product, and pure cultures have been introduced for the control of abnormal fermentations. These have come into general and successful use, with the result that the average quality of domestic Swiss cheese has been decidedly improved. Two characteristic defects—pressler and niszler—appear in the abnormal gassy fermentations of cheese. Studies have shown that these defects are caused by the same organism and that the time and character of the fermentation are determined by the physiological condition of the cells when the cheese is made. This knowledge has made it possible to obtain a maximum development of the corrective cultures at the stage when they are most effective in suppressing undesirable gas formers. Great success has attended the application of these methods in our domestic cheese factories and they are now widely applied.

One of the most serious difficulties met with in the evaporation of milk is coagulation during the sterilizing process. Accordingly, investigations have been conducted to determine the conditions under which milk is stable or unstable under the action of heat. Within certain limits there is no reaction under which milk will invariably be stable. The optimum reaction varies with the milk of individual cows, and a very small change from the reaction giving certain milk its maximum stability will produce a great change in the temperature of coagulation. From this discovery to its practical application is only a step. The amount of heat treatment which the milk receives before its concentration is an important factor in controlling the coagulation temperature. A relatively low temperature at that stage gives a low stability but a heavy body. As the temperature approaches the boiling point, the product gains in stability while losing in body. In making sweetened condensed milk these conditions are reversed. In that process a low " forewarming " temperature tends to prevent the thickening that usually develops in the product sooner or later. It has also been demonstrated by the bureau that the heat treatment of milk is an important factor in making dried skim milk, which finds a profitable outlet in bread making. When the dried product is made from preheated milk, its use in bread gives remarkable values. The loaf is improved in nutritive value, in color, in texture, and in flavor. Moreover, a larger loaf is obtained, so that under favorable conditions the increased output offsets the cost of the dried milk.

Ice-Cream Making Studies

Studies of ice-cream making have given important results, particularly in explaining and preventing the phenomenon known as sandiness. Valuable knowledge has also been gained regarding the preference of the consumer for certain combinations of ingredients. Methods of incorporating fruit in ice cream affect markedly the consumer's choice. The bureau is promoting the use of dry skim milk in ice cream and other food products, and the manufacture of dry skim milk is already an important industry. Other studies now under way are directed to solving the problem of converting the proteins of skim milk, buttermilk, and whey into acceptable forms of human food. There is a decided shrinkage of food value when these products are converted into pork, veal, or poultry. Great financial loss results from total failure to turn milk by-products into marketable commodities.

The department's by-product studies have developed a process of converting dry skim milk into a nonperishable poultry food, by a technic well adapted to factories handling only a relatively small supply or those not in a position to buy equipment for making dry skim milk. By this means large quantities of skim milk are now conserved. More difficult is the problem of utilizing whey. Only a limited use exists for lactose, the chief ingredient of whey, and no product has yet been made from lactose which can not be made from a cheaper sugar. Further investigations on this problem, however, will doubtless bring results of practical importance.

PROGRESS OF ECONOMIC ENTOMOLOGY

The conditions which man finds best for his progress and prosperity are unfortunately exactly those which are most favorable to insects. The cultivation of enormous areas of cotton in the South, of corn and wheat in the Middle West, and of citrus groves in Florida and California, permits the insects that feed on these crops to multiply in destructive numbers. Losses from insect pests in the United States amount to probably not less than $2,000,000,000 annually. But applied entomology keeps the losses down. Were it not for control methods developed by entomologists, the yearly toll would probably be as large again. New methods of control are constantly being found and old ones improved. Growth of economic entomology has been very great in recent years, largely as a result of increased understanding on the part of the public of the necessity for insect control in successful agriculture and in human affairs generally.

During the last two or three decades the number of scientists engaged in entomological work in the Federal Bureau of Entomology and at the agricultural colleges and experiment stations, and the funds devoted to this work, have materially increased. In the Federal Bureau of Entomology the number of entomologists employed this year was 320, compared with 80 in 1905, and funds appropriated for research and control operations this year were thirty-six times the sum appropriated in 1905. Insect problems have been pressing in the period mentioned, and this fact has naturally contributed to increased appreciation of the work of the entomologist. The establishment in the United States of such pests as the San José scale, the cotton-boll weevil, the gipsy moth, the Japanese beetle, and the European corn borer has necessitated vastly increased activity in the war against our insect enemies.

Much of the work of the Federal bureau is in cooperation with State workers, especially on projects of interstate interest. Most of the bureau's operations, however, are conducted at some 80 field stations located where different pests are troublesome. Some work, particularly the importation of beneficial insects to prey on different introduced insect pests, is carried out in foreign countries in cooperation with foreign governments. Entomologists are convinced that the control of insects by the utilization of their natural enemies offers great possibilities. Accordingly, steps are being taken to effect an exchange among various countries of the beneficial insects that live at the expense of other insects.

Japanese-Beetle Control

Improvements continue to be made in methods and materials used for the control of the Japanese beetle. A miscible carbon disulphide has been perfected for use in the control of larvæ in the soil. It is much superior to the various types of carbon disulphide emulsion previously used, since it can be applied effectively even when the soil temperature is as low as 35° F. Serious difficulties arose in the commercial production of oleate, or coated lead arsenate. Successful investigations leading to certain changes in methods of its manufacture have made available a standardized and improved product. This material more than any other is used in the control of the Japanese beetle.

Traps baited with the attractant geraniol are coming into more general use. Under certain conditions these play an extremely useful part in facilitating the capture of large numbers of the beetles. Their use thus far has been restricted, however, and does not take the place of timely and thorough spraying. The pyrethrum-soap spray, developed for use against the Japanese beetle, has proved a useful contact insecticide against other insects as well. It has been found effective against the striped cucumber beetle, the squash bug, and other insects heretofore difficult to kill. By incorporating a small percentage of sodium silicate in this soap its toxicity has been greatly increased.

The value of community effort in the control of the Japanese beetle has been officially recognized by the States of New Jersey and Pennsylvania. During the past year 12 communities in New Jersey and 3 in Pennsylvania conducted community spraying campaigns, and twice as many communities are planning similar campaigns for next year. Five species of oriental parasites of the Japanese beetle are now established in New Jersey and Pennsylvania. In one locality near Riverton, N. J., 25 per cent of the beetles were found parasitized during the year 1927.

Recognizing the impossibility of the eradication of the European corn borer and its inevitable spread into the middle Corn Belt, the department in cooperation with the States concerned has developed a definite and comprehensive program to retard the spread of the borer, and prevent as far as possible its increase. The department proposes to finance scouting to determine the further spread of the borer as a basis for quarantine measures. Quarantine enforcement within States will of course be done under delegated State authority. Responsibility for scouting and quarantine enforcement is accepted by the department to release State funds and personnel hitherto used in such work. In this way State departments of agriculture will be enabled to give their undivided attention and resources to the problem of holding the increase in the number of borers below serious commercial damage. The department's program also provides for research work in all fields related to the borer problem. It welcomes the fullest cooperation on the part of the States in coordinated research activity and practical control measures. The department and the State agricultural colleges will continue an intensive educational campaign now being conducted by their cooperating extension service in the infested territory.

Insect Infestation of Flour

It became increasingly evident several years ago that if American flour is to be exported to Europe and elsewhere in competition with other flours some way must be found to reduce insect infestations. Serious losses had been suffered by exporters; it seemed probable that unless improved conditions could be brought about our export trade in flour would be jeopardized. The export market absorbs a large quantity of flour, and any contraction of the outlet would have a serious effect on the entire milling industry. In locally consumed flour, insects can be easily dealt with provided interested parties will apply available control methods. Export flour, however, must run the gantlet of the home milling plant, railroad freight cars, storage at docks and ship terminals, and finally ship transportation. Hence the problem of protecting it from destructive insects is complicated by factors beyond the control of the exporter.

The immediate crisis in insect infestation in export flour has been met and the danger greatly reduced by the cooperation of flour-mill owners, railroads, ship terminals, and steamship lines. Mills exporting flour are systematically fumigated or heated for the destruction of insects at the point of origin of the flour. Railroad freight cars are fumigated to lessen the likelihood that flour will become infested en route between factory and ship terminals. Inspections are made of flour on arrival at the exporting point. Dock terminals are kept as sanitary as possible. Ships carrying export flour are inspected before each shipment is loaded, and fumigated by approved methods if insects are found present. Combined official and unofficial effort has accomplished notable results.

In order to prevent the spread of the gipsy moth farther west than the area of infestation in the New England States, a barrier zone was established in 1923 extending from the Canadian border on the north to Long Island Sound on the south, a distance of some 250 miles. The zone, which is 30 miles wide, is flanked on the west by the Hudson River and farther north by a tier of towns in New York State west of Lake Champlain. It is located along the shortest possible line that could be drawn to cut off the area infested with the gipsy moth from the rest of the United States. This strip of territory avoids the rugged Catskill and Adirondack Mountain regions in New York State and the Green Mountain range in Vermont, but considerable difficult country is included in the Berkshire Hills region in Massachusetts and northwestern Connecticut.

Strenuous efforts are being made to clean up existing colonies and keep the zone free from the gipsy moth. The number of colonies of this insect has been reduced and some of the towns on the western side have been released from continuous inspection. At one time three small colonies of the insect were found west of the Hudson River, but two of these have already been exterminated. Thus far the work in the zone has made satisfactory progress and the westward spread of the pest has been checked. However, at the present time these substantial results are threatened by the rapidly increasing abundance of the pest in the region adjoining it to the east and special efforts will be necessary to maintain the benefit which has already been secured.

Insect Carries Curly-Top Disease

From the fact that the sugar-beet leaf hopper, a small insignificant insect, is the carrier of the so-called curly top of the sugar beet, it is proving to be the limiting factor in the extension of the sugar-beet industry in the intermountain region. Where factories are situated close to the natural breeding grounds of the insect, as in the Twin Falls-Burley district in Idaho, the disastrous season of 1926 brought the industry in those places to the lowest ebb in its history. Fortunately, studies of the insect in its desert breeding grounds and the relation of the insect to weather conditions had progressed to the point where the information could be made available to farmers. Available data indicated prospects for a favorable beet year in 1927 in the Twin Falls-Burley district. A prediction to that effect by the Bureau of Entomology encouraged growers and led to the planting of a large acreage, which proved the most profitable on record.

This year applied entomology rendered beet growers an equally unmistakable, though different, service. The situation prior to planting indicated that beet growing would be attended by serious hazards. With the hearty cooperation of the sugar-beet industry, a prediction was issued to that effect. It is conservatively estimated that in one factory district alone 10,000 acres of beets would have been planted had it not been for this prediction. The desirability of avoiding plantings in years of serious outbreak, and conversely, of heavy plantings of sugar beets in years when prospects are good has thus been demonstrated, and the prediction service is rapidly becoming established as an essential part of the agricultural program in a large and highly developed irrigated area.

Cattle Grubs Cause Heavy Loss

Livestock raisers in the United States suffer heavy loss from the effects of two closely related grubs that attack cattle. Though distributed among many different livestock enterprises, this loss falls heaviest on dairymen and cattle feeders. It is of such a nature, moreover, as not to be entirely apparent to stock owners, and the seriousness of the situation is not fully appreciated. In an effort to cut down the damage inflicted by cattle grubs, the department has embarked on an extensive research program and has initiated control undertakings in various parts of the country. It is hoped that in time the pests can be eradicated. Losses resulting from the infestation of cattle by grubs include reduced milk flow, impaired flesh condition, and sometimes the death or injury of animals. Serious damage is also done to hides, with the result that manufacturers have established a rather definite system of dockage for all grubby hides and leather produced therefrom. Carcasses of animals slaughtered during the season of grub infestation must be trimmed. This results in loss of time, wastage of 1 or 2 pounds of meat per animal, and a lower sale value due to the unsightliness of the trimmed meat. Some estimates of the damage caused annually by cattle grubs run as high as $100,000,000.

WILD-LIFE ADMINISTRATION

The need for taking measures to improve the wild-life situation continues. The increasing utilization of lands for agricultural and industrial operations and for the extension of urban conditions is not favorable to the continuance of some forms of wild life. It even threatens local extermination of many game and other species that are dependent upon marsh and water areas. Remedial measures are being taken by the department in a conservation program. The Bureau of Biological Survey is continuing wild-life research, the administration of wild-life refuges, cooperative work to curb the destructiveness of injurious species, and the administration of protective laws, with a view to the adoption of a broad policy in the conservation, utilization, and control of the wild-life resources of the country.

A forward step in wild-life conservation during the year was the congressional enactment of a measure to establish the Bear River Migratory Bird Refuge at the mouth of Bear River, Utah, authorizing an appropriation of $350,000, of which $200,000 was made available to begin the work and carry it through the fiscal year 1929. This will permit diking and ditching in the Bear River marshes and the impounding of fresh waters covering approximately 45,000 acres, thereby creating a good feeding, resting, and breeding ground for wild fowl. Besides providing a great bird refuge, the work will help to prevent loss of birds through alkali poisoning. Difficulty experienced in securing land for the extensive upper Mississippi River Wild Life and Fish Refuge has been lessened by another Federal enactment authorizing the department to increase from $5 to $10 an acre the average price that may be paid for the land needed. This will result in the acquisition during the coming year of a large additional area. Wild life has increased on that part of the refuge now under the control of the department.

Accurate knowledge concerning the food habits of various species is necessary in appraising the economic value of American bird life. For more than 40 years the Department of Agriculture has played a leading part in this important field of research. Its work is invaluable in helping to solve problems arising from the varied relations of bird life to agriculture, horticulture, and forestry. Excellent codes of laws, both Federal and State, affording legal protection to beneficial species throughout the country, have been enacted largely as a result of knowledge gained in field and laboratory research. Methods of attracting beneficial insectivorous species about farm and home grounds have been evolved from the study of the food habits of such birds, and areas suitable for wild fowl have been improved. Facts helpful in the development of control measures for the comparatively few species requiring control have been disclosed. During the past fiscal year the food of some 1,555 birds was studied, bringing to nearly 99,000 the total number of bird stomachs examined by the Bureau of Biological Survey since this work was first undertaken.

Censuses Taken of Waterfowl

In order to obtain more comprehensive and reliable information regarding the abundance, distribution, and movements of waterfowl as a basis for adequate regulations under the migratory bird treaty act, a series of censuses was begun during the year in cooperation with the Office of National Parks of Canada. At more than 3,000 stations in important breeding, migration, and concentration areas of the birds, observations and reports are made by volunteer cooperators each month. State and provincial departments of game and conservation and National, State, and provincial organizations, of sportsmen and conservationists, as well as several bureaus of other Federal departments, have participated in organizing the work. Reports received totaling many thousands give far more detailed and complete information than has heretofore been available. Information from the first year's reports has been mapped to show in a graphic way conditions that must be considered in programs to insure the maintenance of waterfowl in satisfactory numbers.

Good progress has also been made in research work on the seasonal movements of birds. Reliable information is obtained through field observations and the application of the bird-banding methods of investigation by representatives of the department and cooperating organizations and individuals. More than 1,400 banding stations are established throughout the country, reports from which showed approximately 127,000 birds banded during the year, with return records totaling about 7,000 from more than 400,000 banded since 1920.

Cooperation of State game authorities and others with the Federal game protectors has brought about a better observance of the migratory bird treaty act, with a corresponding improvement in conditions affecting migratory birds. The problem of providing further protection to the woodcock has given the department considerable concern. Many persons, believing these valuable games birds are decreasing throughout the range, have urged a closed season of from three to five years. Others, particularly in the New England States, say the birds are increasing, and protest against further restrictions on hunting. After consultation with the migratory bird treaty act advisory board, State game authorities, and others, the open season on woodcock throughout its entire range was shortened to one month.

Conservation of Elk, Buffalo, Etc.

The solution of serious problems concerned with the care of large numbers of buffalo, elk, deer, and antelope on reservations maintained by the department is complicated by lack of funds for proper administration. On some ranges interior fencing is needed to protect the grass by rotation grazing. It has been and will continue to be necessary to dispose of the annual surplus of buffalo and elk on some preserves in order to insure sufficient forage for herds of even the present size. If any of the herds are to be permitted to increase in size, additional grazing space must be provided.

The problems on the elk refuge maintained by the department near Jackson, Wyo., detailed in my report last year, are still serious. Following recommendations made by a commission appointed by the President's Committee on Outdoor Recreation, a biologist familiar with big-game animals has been engaged in studying the Jackson Hole elk herd and all conditions affecting their welfare, including their breeding and feeding habits, seasonal movements, range and food requirements in relation to livestock, and the diseases, parasites, and other factors involved in depleting their numbers. The program calls for one of the most complete and systematic studies ever undertaken of any species of big-game animal in the United States. Results already obtained indicate that necrotic stomatitis induced by eating hay containing wild barley is one of the most serious causes of loss on the winter feeding ground.

A maximum of 9,000 elk were fed at the elk refuge during the past winter, and when feeding ended very little hay was left on hand. If the coming winter is mild the available supply of hay will probably suffice, but if the season is severe the crop raised at the refuge, even though supplemented by hay purchased by the State of Wyoming, will be insufficient and there will be great mortality among the elk. The refuge area should be further enlarged by the inclusion of suitable adjacent hay and grazing lands so as to provide a crop of hay ample to meet requirements under all conditions.

At the request of the board of game commissioners of Pennsylvania, a field naturalist of the Bureau of Biological Survey was detailed to investigate conditions attending heavy losses of deer in certain sections of that State. His studies revealed overstocking and overgrazing and the consequent starvation of thousands of young deer. The analysis thus made affords a sound basis for adoption of corrective measures in Pennsylvania, and is proving exceedingly helpful to Federal and State officials in appraising conditions detrimental to deer in other regions.

Forest Life Studied

Investigations of the activities and habits of wild mammals and birds that inhabit forested areas have been undertaken and efforts made to determine their relation to forest production. In these studies forest wild life has been viewed not only as a source of food, fur, or other products, but also as an agency in the control of insects, rodents, or other species destructive to forests. The investigations cover the beneficial activities of forest animals, such as their distribution of seeds, their injurious habits, such as the eating of seeds or seedlings, the killing or deforming of trees, and their competing with livestock in the consumption of forage. Information of much value has been obtained bearing on the desirability of conserving and increasing the number of beneficial or valuable species and on the need for control measures where undue damage is done. Work on this project will be continued.

Fox farming in the Northern States and the raising of fur bearers in captivity throughout the country have increased the calls upon the department for aid in solving numerous problems. The fur-animal experiment station at Saratoga Springs, N. Y., and the rabbit experiment station at Fontana, Calif., both maintained by the department, are operated for the purpose of studying the habits of fur animals in captivity, and problems in feeding, housing, sanitation, and parasite control. To supplement work at the experiment stations, diseases of fur animals are studied in cooperation with the University of Minnesota with a view to controlling losses which on many fur farms are extensive. Investigations also are made in cooperation with the Alaska Game Commission for the improvement of conditions on fur farms in the Territory.

The pelts of fur animals raised in captivity are coming to be more in demand on the market from the fact that, taken at the season when they have reached their maximum quality, they are usually of uniform texture. The demand for attractive and durable furs for wearing apparel has greatly stimulated the fur-farming industry. Incidentally, species of valuable forms of wild life are preserved, though the industry can not take the place of natural conditions in perpetuating fur-bearing animals.

Losses from Predatory Animals

The depredations of such predatory wild animals as coyotes, wolves, mountain lions, bobcats, and lynxes have caused millions of dollars loss in livestock in the range States. Likewise, such injurious small mammals as prairie dogs, ground squirrels, jack rabbits, field mice, pocket gophers, rats, woodchucks, and porcupines have destroyed millions of dollars' worth of agricultural crops. The policy of the department in control operations against injurious mammals and birds, as definitely stated recently, is to reduce losses through the local eradication of stock and crop pests where agricultural and other economic activities demand such action. It does not contemplate the general extermination of harmful species, even if that were possible. This policy is being made known by field leaders of the Bureau of Biological Survey to their cooperators in order to clear up misapprehensions that have been entertained by many who are working for the conservation of wild life.

In control campaigns directed by the department against predatory animals during the year the skins or scalps of 35,709 coyotes, 9 large gray wolves, 716 red wolves, 219 mountain lions, 40 lynxes, 4,838 bobcats, and 226 predatory bears were taken in 13 Western States, thereby effecting an estimated saving of more than $5,000,000 in livestock. This was done in cooperation with State and county agencies, livestock associations, and individuals. Congress has authorized an investigation by the department of the feasibility of a cooperative program to extend over five or more years for the eradication, suppression, or bringing under control of predatory animals, and of the estimated cost as compared with present methods. A report will be made to the next regular session of Congress, based in part on field operations and on research work that has been in progress for several years at the department laboratory at Denver, Colo.

Organized rodent-control operations were carried on by the department during the year in cooperation with agricultural colleges, county agents, State departments of agriculture, county officials, farmers' and stockmen's associations, and other Federal departments in 18 States, and educational work on the subject was undertaken in 10 others. In the field campaigns 1,653 tons of poisoned bait, and approximately 71 tons of calcium cyanide, and 313 tons of carbon disulphide were used to destroy rodent pests on 14,545,591 acres of Federal, State, and private lands. This resulted in savings in crops conservatively estimated at $5,800,000.

Protecting Reindeer Against Pests

Investigations conducted at the reindeer experiment station of the Bureau of Biological Survey, at Fairbanks, Alaska, and on typical grazing areas throughout the Territory continue to yield valuable information regarding the nutritive qualities of lichens and supplementary foods, the carrying capacity of lichen range, and the recovery period following grazing. Information also is being obtained there regarding the warble and nose flies, which are among the most serious pests of reindeer and caribou in Alaska. Studies of the life history of these flies, including the collection and rearing of grubs, indicate that a large measure of protection can be had by concentrating the herds at fawning time, when also the grubs are dropped, and then moving them to an area about 20 miles distant.

Assistance also was given reindeer owners in Alaska at the round-ups in demonstrating improved methods of counting, marking, and ownership distribution of animals, and information was given regarding improved methods of breeding and feeding. Studies were made at Washington, D. C., in cooperation with the Bureau of Education of the Department of the Interior regarding the most satisfactory market cuts of reindeer carcasses, the chemical and nutritive properties of the meat, and methods of dressing, handling, storing, and cooking. Experiments in cross-breeding reindeer and caribou have been successful in producing young weighing approximately 5 pounds more than reindeer fawns at birth. Plans for fencing pastures and corrals contemplate handling about 75 reindeer and caribou for use in the experimental investigations.

FEDERAL EXPENDITURE FOR RESEARCH

This report, although citing only a few of the results achieved by the department through scientific research, presents so formidable an array of accomplishments that research activities may seem to be adequately manned and financed. That is not the case. Federal expenditure for research in agriculture is not large considering the magnitude of the problems awaiting solution. Much less money is expended in the United States for agricultural than for industrial research. The department's research program should be expanded. I need not emphasize the fact that expenditure for wisely directed scientific research is a sound investment. Every dollar expended by this country heretofore in agricultural research has been returned many thousandfold in savings to farmers and to the Nation. Examples already cited in this report give some inkling of the dividends paid on funds invested in scientific investigations.

Yet many problems of the greatest importance lie practically untouched, and the department's research units are inadequately financed. Funds already provided are fully absorbed by the necessity of dealing with problems of pressing importance. It has been necessary to postpone work of a broad and fundamental character in order to tackle immediate problems. This is probably not the most economical procedure, for some of the greatest achievements in agricultural science have resulted from investigations undertaken primarily to reveal scientific truths, rather than to win immediate economic returns. Until a few years ago the funds available for research in the department were not increased sufficiently to offset the declining purchasing power of the research dollar. As a result agriculture lagged, while business and industry made great forward strides in the application of research to their practical concerns. Although funds were provided to meet other needs such as the eradication and control of insect pests and the enforcement and control of regulatory laws, research funds remained about stationary or showed only a slight increase here and there to meet specific requirements.

Expenditure by the department for research during each of the fiscal years 1921, 1922, and 1923 was about $9,000,000. This is a rough estimate, because expenditures made by the department in those years were not classified in detail. In 1924 classification of expenditures showed a total of $9,700,000 devoted to research. This sum was increased in 1925 to $10,100,000, in 1926 to $10,300,000, and in 1927 to $10,600,000. In the fiscal year 1928 the total was $11,300,000. In the same years expenditures for other activities also were increased.

In consequence the proportion expended for research, although fluctuating somewhat from year to year, remained about 6 per cent of the department's total expenditures, and about 23 per cent of what may be called the department's expenditures for ordinary activities. In the total expenditures there are included outlays for roads and various other forms of Federal aid to the States.

Work Is Inadequately Financed

This relationship between expenditure for research and for other department activities shows, I think, that research is inadequately financed. I believe we can safely expect increased expenditure for research to bring returns equal to those accruing from similar expenditure heretofore. In view of the needs of the agricultural industry, which represents a capitalization of nearly $60,000,000,000, the present Federal allocation of funds for agricultural research is modest, to say the least. As a matter of fact, the Federal Government and the States together expend scarcely $20,000,000 annually for research activities, compared with probably $180,000,000 expended annually by private industries for a similar purpose. Additional funds might be advantageously provided regularly to increase research activities and to maintain existing studies on a sound footing.

Funds for research must, of course, be provided largely through taxation, and the expenditure of such funds should therefore be managed with care and economy. This principle is sedulously kept in mind by the department. A business policy has been put into effect which takes into account the necessity of making no expenditure except on a definite prospect of a full return. This principle, however, does not exclude, but rather encourages, the support of research work. It would be false economy to restrict our national investment in agricultural science. Scientists should have adequate funds to do their work and adequate pay. Money provided to satisfy these requirements may generally, if care is taken to see that it is used for its proper objects, be set down on the credit side of the ledger.

The figures I have given show that up to the fiscal year 1928 only moderate increases were provided in the department's research appropriations. In the appropriation bill for the fiscal year 1929, however, Congress granted a material advance. Increases were provided for research projects involving an additional expenditure of $1,800,000. This substantial encouragement, the longest forward stride in a number of years, may, I hope, be considered the beginning of a program which will result in materially increased assistance to scientific work. The increased appropriations provided for the current fiscal year will help greatly in dealing with various urgent problems.

Endowment of Experiment Stations

In addition to the increased appropriations made available directly for the department's work, Congress has enlarged the Federal endowment of the State agricultural experiment stations. This has been done under the Purnell Act, approved February 24, 1925, under which measure the State agricultural experiment stations are enabled to inaugurate many new lines of research as well as to strengthen research projects already going forward. Special provision is made for research in marketing and in other phases of agricultural economics, and also in home economics. Great stimulus to agricultural research has resulted already from the passage of the Purnell Act, and the ultimate good which will be derived therefrom can not be estimated.

Prior to the passage of the Purnell Act each State received $30,000 annually for research from the Federal Government under the Hatch and Adams Acts. The Purnell Act authorized increases to each State in annual increments of $10,000 each for the fiscal years 1926 to 1930, and $60,000 annually thereafter. Thus the Federal grant to each State for agricultural research will be brought, in 1930, up to $90,000 annually. Funds thus authorized are provided annually in the appropriation act of the Department of Agriculture and are paid to the States upon approval of proposed research projects. In this way the cooperation of research agencies for the efficient coordination of research is promoted. Congress this year extended the provisions of the Purnell Act to the Territory of Hawaii, beginning with the fiscal year 1930.

All told, therefore, the increased research funds provided by Congress for the fiscal year 1929 amount to $2,280,000—$1,800,000 for the department's research program and $480,000 for payments to the States under the Purnell Act. This is very satisfactory progress. Further evidence of the interest taken by Congress in agricultural research was furnished by the enactment, at the last session, of the McNary-McSweeney Forestry Research Act, authorizing appropriations for research in all phases of forestry, including the production of timber, the utilization of forest products, and forest economics. Appropriations authorized by the act involve fixed annual amounts for various phases of forestry research over a 10-year period. A new chapter in the history of our forest management and conservation is thus started.

FORESTRY AND AGRICULTURE

The importance of wood as a farm product is seldom realized. Data on the forest products derived from farms of the United States are gathered only once in 10 years by the census. In 1919 the reported value of such products totaled nearly $395,000,000, as against slightly more than $195,000,000 in 1909 and less than $110,000,000 in 1899. What change from the 1919 figures those for 1929 may show is, of course, wholly uncertain, especially since 1919 was a year of abnormally high prices. Nevertheless, in the long run undoubtedly wood will constitute an increasingly valuable farm crop.

It makes possible the productive use of much farm land that otherwise could earn nothing and adds to the value of considerably more. It is a crop which does not have to be harvested and disposed of irrespective of market conditions each season, but on the contrary can be left in place to accumulate like money in a savings bank. It is both a cash crop and a means of supplying economically farm requirements that would otherwise necessitate cash outlays; 55.2 per cent of the reported 1919 farm-forest products value represented products sold or cut and held for sale and 44.8 per cent products for use on the farm as building material, fence posts, poles, etc., and as fuel—the latter the chief item. In total value the farm-forest products of 1919 came to more than three times that of sugar beets and sugar cane combined, nine-tenths that of all orchard fruits, approximately three times that of all citrus fruits, not very far behind that of tobacco, and more than four-fifths that of spring wheat.

Relatively little of this value was obtained through forest culture. The 1920 census reported approximately 168,000,000 acres as the area of woodland included in farms. Only 21 per cent of this was classed as timberland; that is, with trees mostly of saw-log size. In part this timberland is land still under virgin forest. Other portions are under second growth, that has succeeded the original stand not as a result of any practice of forestry but as a gift of nature. In small part only do the saw-log stands represent a deliberate purpose to grow timber. In some part they doubtless occupy land which the owner expects to clear. Likewise the 79 per cent of our farm woodlands that does not have trees mostly of saw-log size is largely in a wild-land condition.

More and Better Farm Forestry Needed

Of the total farm area of more than 950,000,000 acres at the time of the last decennial census more than 1 acre out of every 6 was farm woodlands, and in the naturally forested regions the proportion is of course much greater. While a certain amount of this land will in time be brought under tillage, other land not now occupied by tree growth will be reforested, naturally or artificially. In my report of two years ago I pointed out how in some parts of the East the amount of improved farm land began to lessen well before the end of the last century, declining between 1880 and 1920 in the North and Middle Atlantic States by some 13,700,000 acres. The reversion of once-cleared pasture and of lands formerly cultivated to forest growth is a part of the process of adjustment of land use to economic conditions—an adjustment which, as I took occasion to say in the earlier report, should be hastened rather than delayed, in the interest of greater agricultural stability. Farm forestry affords a means in the timber-producing regions of putting to its best use much of the poorer land which if cultivated swells the crop surpluses without giving the farmer a fair return. The present acreage of farm woodlands is approximately twice that of the productive timberland in all the national forests, and acre for acre can on the average grow more wood. From every standpoint there are strong reasons for developing and making known to our farmers the methods whereby this great aggregate of potentially timber-producing land may be used most effectively and most profitably to them.

This will be a very large task. Most farm woodlands are in bad condition. Generally speaking, the make-up of the forest growth has been so altered through fires, through overgrazing, and through cutting without regard for, or knowledge of, the consequences—through prolonged treatment as wild lands, in other words, and through lack of proper protection and care—that many years of well-directed, skillful handling will be necessary to rejuvenate them and convert them into thrifty, well-stocked stands of the best kinds of trees. They are much like ill-tended gardens full mostly of weeds.

But though largely run down, they can be built up and restored through use. Forestry is applied chiefly in the process of cutting—by taking out what is not wanted in the future forest and giving what is left the best conditions for growth and reproduction. There is no reason why the farm woodlands should not keep on providing fuel, fence posts, construction and repair material, and salable products essentially as they are now doing and yet improve steadily in value and growing power.

Markets for Wood-Lot Products

Along with the process of working over the wild-land farm wood lots into well-conditioned little forests will have to go the process of developing suitable markets for their products. There are cases in which the market is developing first and leading the way for the farmer. A New England box manufacturer, for example, employs a forester whose advice can be obtained free of charge by farmers in the territory from which the factory draws its raw material; and a North Carolina paper mill is endeavoring to build up a source of sustained supply of the pulp wood which it consumes by interesting farmers in its neighborhood in continuously growing suitable wood, and in cutting yearly the equivalent of the annual increment.

There is, however, for most wood-lot owners as yet no ready means for selling to advantage a small yearly output of material for industrial use; and this is doubtless one reason why the wood lots do not produce relatively more of such material as against firewood and other products of scrub forests.

Public Encouragement Necessary

The only way that the latent possibilities of timber growing as a means of utilizing the portions of farms better suited to wood crops than field crops or pasturage can be developed within a reasonable time is through public encouragement. For this there is ample ground. There is greater danger of a shortage of timber supplies within the next 50 years than there is of a shortage of food supplies; and both from the standpoint of the promotion of general prosperity and from that of the promotion of rural welfare, intelligent, skillful use of the enormous total acreage which should be utilized for timber growing is of prime importance.

For such public encouragement the way is already blazed. The Clarke-McNary law, passed in 1924, authorized and directed the Secretary of Agriculture to cooperate with the various States in producing and distributing material for planting portions of farms needing artificial forestation or reforestation. It also authorized and directed cooperation with State officials or other suitable agencies in assisting farmers to establish, improve, grow, and renew useful timber crops, windbreaks, and shelter belts. And the McSweeney-McNary law, enacted last spring, authorized the inauguration of a far-reaching program of Federal research in forestry which for the first time affords the prospect that the basic knowledge essential for skillful timber growing will be progressively obtained at a rate commensurate with its importance.

The cooperative work designed to assist farmers to grow timber crops is organized as a part of the agricultural extension work of the department. It is indeed fortunate that this great educational agency for disseminating knowledge of desirable practices as they are worked out and for promoting their adoption is available to hasten progress. The educational task to be performed, however, is greater than any single agency can be expected to carry out entirely. It must enlist all the agencies that can be utilized to incorporate forestry in the practice and transmitted lore of agriculture. It must give us forest-minded farmers, must develop for their observation and instruction multitudinous practical examples of applied silviculture, and must permeate our agricultural colleges and high schools, our agricultural press and literature, and our agricultural leadership, national and local, with sound conceptions.

A Field for Cooperative Effort

It is the duty of the Department of Agriculture to do all that it can not only through the Extension Service but through every means at its command to build up farm forestry. The field is preeminently one for cooperative effort, since there are involved both a national interest in permanent supplies of forest products and in efficient land use and to no less degree State and local interests in the same matters. As rapidly as is feasible the cooperative activities under the Clarke-McNary law for the promotion of farm forestry should be enlarged. Most of the States now have at least started State forestry work, and some have seasoned strong organizations. The State forestry departments should play an important part in the educational movement for familiarizing the public generally with good timber-growing practices.

In spite of all the public attention that forestry has received and all the public interest that forest preservation has aroused, the true nature of the problem to be worked out is seldom fully grasped. It is thought of in too narrow terms. There is much anxiety—and with reason—over the question of adequate future timber. There is widespread recognition of the necessity to prevent forest fires. There is a general desire to keep the country well supplied with forest growth as a protection to stream flow and for other indirect benefits, including scenic protection and recreational enjoyment. There is what can perhaps best be described as a sort of instinctive dislike and disapproval of deforestation that is not promptly followed by agricultural development, as a public loss and injury. All these things are embraced in the forest problem, but they are merely single aspects of it and do not go to its heart.

Forest Administration Misunderstood

Similarly, the true nature of the undertaking involved in public forest administration frequently fails to be recognized. It is in danger of being thought of as essentially the business of disposing of forest products, dealing with applicants for privileges of land occupancy, constructing and maintaining improvements, and handling personnel, including on occasion the large bodies of fire fighters that are recruited to meet emergency conditions. While all these things have to be done in connection with public forest administration and must be done in a businesslike way, they are subordinate or incidental to the technical task involved in forest-crop production and forest-soil use.

Although nearly a quarter of a century has passed since, in recognition of the technical character of the work, the national forests were placed in charge of the Department of Agriculture, it is still not an uncommon popular supposition that the Department of the Interior administers the forests; and it is sometimes assumed that, were the work of the executive departments more logically organized, the forests would be assigned again to the Department of the Interior, or to a department of public works. Such a viewpoint simply illustrates the failure of the public to grasp the real nature of our forest problem and the true character of forestry as an applied branch of scientific agriculture and a part of agricultural economics.

Yet the public mind is moving toward a practical realization that to use aright the most fundamental, extensive, and valuable of all our material resources, the soil of the country, farming, and forestry must not be separated, but must be coordinated in sound, comprehensive plans of regional development. Perhaps the most significant evidence of this trend just now is to be found in the Lake States, where lumbering and fire have worked together to convert very extensive areas of originally superb forests into almost valueless land. The agricultural development which it was long supposed would follow removal of the timber has taken place only in part, and when attempted on the poorer soils has largely failed. It is now plain that substantial parts of the three Lake States must either grow timber or be waste land, at least for a long time. A general awakening to this, and to its significance from the standpoint of local and State prosperity, is under way. Hence has arisen the idea of land economic surveys to get at the facts, as a basis for wiser public policies in matters affecting the form of land use.

Forestry an Agricultural Problem

One outcome of such surveys, it seems certain, will be to disclose clearly that in natural forest regions where a considerable part of the land is not best suited to field crops the public welfare calls for measures that will systematically promote tillage where success can be expected, and timber growing or pasturage, or both uses judiciously combined, on the rest of the land. And the whole thing is fundamentally an agricultural problem—a problem of determining in some better way than that of trial and failure, with all its economically and socially wasteful sequels, how best to utilize the soil resources. Large-scale timber growing on nonfarming land instead of impeding the development of farms actually increases both the opportunity to farm profitably and the numbers of the farm population. It furnishes local markets, additional employment, and greater local resources. Forestry and agriculture should be developed not independently and separately but jointly and with a common purpose—to obtain the utmost benefit from the land.

The extensive abandonment of tilling and the consequent decline in wealth and population in many rural districts of the Northeast are bringing a somewhat similar recognition there of what the true nature of the forest problem is and how it integrates with agriculture. In the South, with its more than 100,000,000 acres of pine land of which relatively little promises conversion into farms and from which most of the virgin timber has been removed, like conditions are bound to develop on an even broader scale. Some of the West, too, is approaching a real problem of idle cut-over lands and land abandonment after lumbering. Throughout it will become increasingly evident that public forest policies must be shaped in close connection with the protection and advancement of agricultural interests.

Forest Experiment Stations

An important and, indeed, essential agency for making possible the best land use through forestry and agriculture, each in its right place and both working together, is forest research. Timber growing under practices that seek to obtain the best yield in quality and quantity is too new in the United States to have back of it the kind of knowledge applied by the farmer in tilling his fields. Therefore a series of forest experiment stations is being built up, one for each of the principal forest regions. Their purpose is, in a word, to do for forestry what the agricultural experiment stations have done for farming, except that they must start further back in the development of the science of forest use than was necessary for the agricultural experiment stations in their part of the field.

The establishment of forest experiment stations that fit into the series has been under way for some years. Under the terms of the McSweeney-McNary law, passed last spring, the completion of the series to a total number of 14 was authorized, and appropriations to provide and maintain the stations were authorized up to a maximum of $1,000,000 annually. The process of building up these stations will be gradual, so that the funds required to maintain them on an adequate basis will not be needed up to the maximum authorized for a number of years; and it, of course, remains for Congress to fix the pace through actual appropriations at which the contemplated work shall go forward. Nevertheless, the prospect for the development of the art of timber growing to a point where it will compare not unfavorably with our knowledge of the best practices for growing other soil crops is greatly brightened by the new law.

Scope of McSweeney-McNary Law

The McSweeney-McNary law did much more than lay down a program for forest experiment stations. It recognized the necessity for a broad development of research under a comprehensive plan, with the cooperation of many agencies, including other bureaus of the Department of Agriculture, to the end that our knowledge of the country's forest resources, our probable requirements, and the best methods of meeting them may be commensurate with the importance of the forest in our national economic and social life. Research in methods of utilizing forest products, for example, is as essential as research in methods of production, and should be conducted in close coordination with the studies that directly concern forest conditions. In fact, no line of separation between the two fields can be drawn; the work now being done by the Forest Service at the Forest

Products Laboratory is leading back to the conditions under which wood is grown, and is aiding in the development of logging practices through which forestry can be successfully applied.

Primarily because of a relatively easy fire season in the summer of 1927, the expenditures for national-forest administration, protection, and improvement during the fiscal year 1928 were more than $2,000,000 under those for the previous year. The receipts, on the other hand, were approximately $275,000 greater. Broadly speaking, the national-forest receipts substantially balance the outlay for the administration of current business on the forests, including the business arising from forms of public use that do not yield revenue as well as those that do; while outlays for development and improvements, including those for maintaining as well as for constructing improvements, and the fluctuating but always large cost of protecting the forest resources against destruction or impairment by fire, are what the Nation puts into the national forests annually as beneficial public enterprises and properties that are being developed and safeguarded to meet the future needs.

When the forests were established they were almost entirely without facilities for their administration, protection, or use. Like any undeveloped wilderness property they necessitated extensive expenditures to develop and equip them. Protection was at a high cost in comparison with what could be accomplished, and the public got out of the forests relatively little in comparison with their value. While the expenditures made in the past have done much to remedy this condition, much remains to be done. In particular there is urgent need for a larger investment in the improvements which make possible more efficient and more economical protection.

PREVENTING THE SPREAD OF PLANT PESTS

The maintenance of plant quarantines and the control and prevention of spread of dangerous insect pests and plant diseases is one of the most important functions of the Government as related to the agricultural industry and to the public generally. The department's activities in this line have been administered by three bureaus, namely, the Federal Horticultural Board, the Bureau of Entomology, and the Bureau of Plant Industry. Prompted by the same considerations which caused me to reorganize the work in the Bureau of Chemistry, and continuing the policy of separating the regulatory and research work, I requested Congress to establish a new unit in the department, to be known as the Plant Quarantine and Control Administration, to take charge of all functions concerned with plant quarantines and the control and prevention of spread of plant pests. This recommendation was approved and the change became effective with the fiscal year beginning July 1, 1928.

This reorganization in itself will not require any increase in expenditures and it is believed that the centralization of responsibility will result in increased efficiency in the administration of the quarantines and control operations. Under this arrangement the Federal Horticultural Board is abolished and all its functions are transferred to the new administration, together with the regulatory and control operations directed against the gipsy and brown-tail moths, Japanese and Asiatic beetles, the European corn borer, and the Mediterranean fruit fly which have been conducted by the Bureau of Entomology, and also the enforcement of the white-pine blister-rust quarantine, the detailed administration of which has been under the Bureau of Plant Industry. In order not to lose the advantages of having matters pertaining to quarantines and their establishment considered by a group, an advisory Federal Plant Quarantine Board composed of five members, four of whom will be selected from existing bureaus in the department, has been established.

Additional Authority to Enforce Quarantines

The protection of the agricultural interests of the country through the more effective enforcement of plant quarantines has been strengthened by an important amendment to the plant quarantine act. This amendment authorizes agents of the department, when they have reason to believe that articles are moving in violation of any of the Federal plant quarantines or restrictive orders, to stop and without warrant to inspect, search, and examine persons, vehicles, receptacles, boats, ships, or vessels, and to seize, destroy, or otherwise dispose of articles found to be moving or to have moved in interstate commerce or to have been brought into the United States in violation of any quarantine order promulgated under the plant quarantine act. Such authority has been greatly needed, and its addition to the powers of port inspectors and road station officers will enable them more effectively to prevent the importation and dissemination of plants or plant products infested with pests and diseases.

Mexican Fruit Worm Eradication

One of the most important accomplishments of the year was the apparent elimination of the Mexican fruit worm from the lower Rio Grand Valley of Texas.

The pest concerned has been responsible for heavy losses in Mexico, and similar fruit flies have proven disastrous to citrus-fruit production in Hawaii and other fruit-growing sections of the world. The discovery of the insect in Texas in 1927, therefore, caused the greatest concern. Energetic clean-up measures were immediately instituted under the leadership of the specialists of the department and of the State of Texas, and these appear to have been successful in eliminating it from the area. No specimens have been taken since June, 1927, and the crop of the season of 1927–28 is apparently entirely free from infestation.

The eradication method employed was outlined in my report of last year. It consisted (1) of the destruction during the summer of 1927 of all susceptible ripe and ripening fruit throughout the two counties infested; (2) of the maintenance of a starvation period from June to September, inclusive, in which no such ripe fruit was permitted to exist in the region; and (3) of a plan of continuous inspection of the local citrus groves and fruit, carried out under the authority of Federal and State quarantines during the shipping period from October to February. This program was followed in March, 1928, by another starvation period during the spring and summer of 1928, when host fruits ripening at this time were eliminated. It is expected to continue these means of eradication for the permanent protection of the fruit industry of the United States.

The Texas counties involved have become, in recent years, one of the leading grapefruit and orange-producing areas of the country According to a survey by department inspectors, 3,419,157 citrus trees are growing there, of which 477,202 have reached bearing age. The shipments of citrus fruits from this region are increasing rapidly and, for the fiscal year 1928, totaled more than 1,700 carloads, distributed to all parts of the United States. The permanent establishment of the Mexican fruit worm would, therefore, have constituted a menace, not only to an important local horticultural industry, but to all other fruit-growing sections, especially of the South, which might be reached by commercial shipments of the fruits attacked.

The apparent eradication of the pest is an achievement which demonstrates the tremendous advantage of a prompt attack on newly introduced insects and plant and animal diseases. If elimination from the area proves to be complete, duplicating similar accomplishments with respect to the foot-and-mouth disease, the pink bollworm in eastern Texas and Louisiana, and the citrus canker in Florida and adjoining States, encouragement will be given to such efforts in similar emergencies in the future.

Unfortunately, in this case, the dangers of reintroduction and reestablishment are so great that controls over the production and distribution of citrus in the region must be continued in future years, at least until the insect is eradicated on the Mexican side of the river and infested fruit from the interior is prevented from reaching the Mexican towns along the border. Much has already been accomplished along these lines, due to the active and hearty cooperation of the Mexican officials and the local residents.

Cotton Pink Bollworm

In December, 1927, the pink bollworm of cotton, which had been eradicated from extensive areas of eastern Texas and Louisiana some years ago, was discovered to have been reintroduced into the main Cotton Belt at a different point, namely, the western extension of continuous cotton culture in west-central Texas.

The serious nature of this discovery was at once appreciated and every available resource was employed to meet the situation. Scouting crews assigned to determine the limits of the infestation found seven Texas counties involved, namely, Andrews, Dawson, Ector, Glasscock, Howard, Midland, and Martin, growing nearly 400,000 acres of cotton. State and Federal quarantines were promptly extended to cover the region to prevent such spread as might otherwise occur with shipments of cottonseed and other products. Preliminary eradication measures were at once instituted, including sterilization of all seed before planting, clean-up operations around oil mills and cotton gins, tracing the movement of seed and lint for the past three years, and destroying such seed as had been moved out of the area and was still obtainable.

The most effective feature of the program which resulted in the total eradication of this insect from eastern Texas and Louisiana during the energetic campaign waged from 1917 to 1921 was the establishment of noncotton zones. The raising of cotton in the regions found infested at that time was prohibited for a period of from one to three years, the growers' losses being reimbursed from

State and Federal funds. This plan proved completely successful and was recommended by the department for adoption in the present instance. The State of Texas was, however, without funds, could not participate in meeting such costs for the crop of 1928, and could make no provision therefor until the next meeting of her legislature in 1929. In view of the gravity of the situation, Congress, by a joint resolution passed in May, authorized for this crop year full compensation from Federal funds to cover cotton growers' actual and necessary losses due to prohibition of the growth of cotton in such zones. The appropriation which followed this authorization measure was included in the second deficiency act for the fiscal year 1928 and provided that the funds appropriated would not be available for the crop of 1928 unless the State contributed one-half of the cost.

FEDERAL-AID ROAD CONSTRUCTION

The Federal-aid road work of the year resulted in the initial improvement of 8,184 miles and the completion of advanced stages of improvement on 2,014 miles, the latter including the surfacing of roads previously graded and drained, the elimination of grade crossings, and other work designed to improve the quality of the service afforded.

Since the beginning of Federal cooperation in 1916 the work done, including that of the past year, has resulted in the improvement of 72,394 miles, all of which, except a limited mileage built prior to 1921, is in the Federal-aid highway system. A portion of this improved mileage is now undergoing further improvement by the process of stage construction, and such subsequent improvements have effected reductions in distance of 34 miles. For these reasons the improvements classified as completed at the close of the year aggregated 71,074 miles.

At the close of the fiscal year initial improvement was under way on 9,494 miles and stage construction was in progress on 1,285 miles.

The 8,184 miles of initial improvement completed during the year included 8,130 miles of roads and 54 miles of major bridges ranging in length of span and approaches from 20 feet to over 3 miles.

The initial road improvements consist of the construction of 2,182 miles of graded and drained earth roads, 844 miles of sand-clay roads, 1,836 miles of gravel roads, 92 miles of water-bound macadam roads, 464 miles of bituminous macadam roads, 136 miles of bituminous concrete pavement, 2,533 miles of Portland cement concrete pavement, and 42 miles paved with brick.

For each project the type of improvement is chosen to meet the present and probable future demands of traffic, modified to a certain extent by the desirability of extending some degree of improvement as rapidly as possible with the funds available to the entire system.

The latter consideration accounts for the extensive mileage of graded earth and sand-clay roads built as initial improvement. As these roads develop in traffic importance, they are further improved by stage construction. During the past year nearly 1,500 miles of previously constructed earth roads have been surfaced in this manner, so that although the year's initial construction of earth roads was 2,182 miles, the mileage of this lowest type was increased during the year by only 685 miles.

The large mileage of bridges completed is an especially gratifying feature of the year's work. With their approaches, the new bridges have an aggregate length of 54 miles, and there have now been built with Federal aid bridge structures and approaches of an aggregate length of 222.5 miles.

Construction of Toll Bridges

The use of Federal funds for payment of half the cost of large bridges offers a partial solution of the difficult problem presented by the urgent need of many such structures on the important highways and the limited State and local revenues available for their construction. Deficiency of public revenues for this purpose has resulted during the past several years in the construction of numerous important bridges by private builders under franchises authorizing the collection of tolls. Many such private toll bridges have already been built or authorized on the Federal aid highway system, thus defeating in a measure the clear intent of Congress, as manifested by the Federal highway legislation, that the roads upon which Federal funds are expended should thereafter be freely opened to public use.

The department has done everything in its power to discourage the erection of these private toll structures and, as an alternative measure, it has urged the use of the available Federal funds to an increasing degree for this purpose; and it is distinctly gratifying, therefore, to report a very substantial increase in the number of Federal-aid bridges planned and completed.

Roads in the National Forests and Parks

The work of road construction in the national forests has two principal objects. The first is the improvement of the main highways that cross the forest areas and connect communities within and adjacent to them. The second is the building of roads and trails required for the administration, protection, and development of the forests.

Toward the attainment of the first object a definite program of construction has been agreed upon following conferences with State and local officials. The program involves the ultimate improvement of a system of forest highways, including 13,911 miles, correlated with the Federal-aid and State highway systems, and work is progressing as rapidly as the somewhat limited funds will permit.

Up to the close of the fiscal year 3,775 miles of these main highways had been improved, 281 during the last year.

The improvement of these roads is an obligation the Government owes to the States in which the forests are located and to the increasing numbers of interstate travelers. The forest areas are large and numerous. They are not taxable by the States; and, especially in the Western States, they are so located that they must be traversed by all who travel any appreciable distance.

In providing for the improvement of the main transforest arteries with Federal funds the Government has recognized this obligation and has made very considerable progress in discharging it, although it is not keeping pace with the improvement of connecting roads outside the forest areas.

It so happens that many of the national parks are completely surrounded by national forests, or practically so. Access to the parks by highway is furnished in many cases only by forest roads, and the greatly increased volume of motor travel to the parks will not be accommodated adequately until these roads are satisfactorily improved.

This need has been recognized and the utilization of the park areas is being facilitated by the correlated improvement of the approach highways and the interior park roads. By an advantageous interdepartmental agreement the Bureau of Public Roads of this department has undertaken to advise and assist the National Park Service of the Department of the Interior in surveying, planning, and constructing roads in the parks. As the same bureau also supervises the Federal-aid and forest road work it is able to effect a desirable correlation of all improvement projects.

Highway Research

Encouraging progress has been made in the development of methods of improving light-traffic earth and gravel roads with asphaltic oils, and thus producing at low cost road surfaces capable of carrying traffic the year round with a minimum of mud and dust. The methods, which have been tried and improved by the Bureau of Public Roads in cooperation with the highway departments of California and South Carolina, are applicable to the thousands of miles of rural roads on which traffic is so light as to preclude the construction of more expensive surfaces, and on this account are of special importance to agriculture.

When applied to crushed-gravel roads, of which there are thousands of miles in the Western States, these methods not only eliminate the dust which has become an intolerable nuisance, but effectively prevent the wearing down of the surface, which in some cases has amounted to 1½ inches a year. The annual loss from this cause has amounted to as much as $1,000 a mile. The cost of the treatment which accomplishes these results rarely exceeds $1,700 a mile and the treatment will apparently be effective for several years.

Other current highway researches deal with the classification of soils according to their suitability for road foundations and methods of treating unsuitable soils to improve their supporting capacity; with the qualities of road-surfacing materials and the design of the various types of surfaces; and with the economics and efficiency of construction methods.

Economies in method and material shown to be possible by these investigations are repeated time after time on the thousands of miles of road constructed each year and, thus multiplied, return to the public a large saving out of all proportion to the comparatively small expense of the research which makes them possible.

Corn-Borer Control

One of the most promising methods of controlling the European corn borer is the destruction of the borer by mechanical means. A relatively simple low-cutting attachment for corn binders has been developed which cuts the stalk off at the surface of the ground.

When the binder so equipped is used to harvest corn for silage or fodder very good control of the borer is obtained. In collaboration with the manufacturers, improvements have been worked out on attachments for plows which make possible the covering of cornstalks much more effectively than can be done with plows without such attachments. Much study has been given to the problem of removing cornstalks from the fields that are to be planted to small grain, better devices for cutting stalks have been worked out, and in collaboration with the manufacturers, rakes more efficient than those now in common use are being developed. Considerable progress has been made in the design of a mobile burner for destroying the borer in stalk fields. Apparently this device may have considerable application in controlling other insect pests.

Crop Machinery

The cost of harvesting grain and other crops with the combined harvester-thresher depends in considerable measure upon the design of the mechanical parts and their adjustment in operation according to the kind and the condition of the crop, to conserve power, prevent breakage, and reduce losses of the grain; and upon the care given to the machine when not in use. Studies of these features previously made in harvesting wheat in the Great Plains States have been supplemented in the past year by studies of the harvesting of soy beans and grain sorghums in the middle Western and Eastern States.

The common practice of ginning cotton as picked results in considerable losses from ginning wet cotton, which causes injury to the lint. After studies had shown that moisture amounting to $2\frac{1}{2}$ to 5 per cent of the weight of the raw cotton should be removed, various experimental units for artificial drying were made and tested. One full-sized unit was constructed and it dried some 60 bales in 1927. The results obtained indicate that the dryer is practicable and that its common use would make possible more rapid harvesting of cotton.

Drainage Investigations

Foreknowledge of the approximate results that farm drains will give in any particular soil depends as yet upon experience in similar soils in the same locality, for some of the influential factors have not been determined and evaluated. Therefore, studies have been begun of the effects of the various physical characteristics of soils in their relation to the movement of soil water in order that correct methods of drainage may be determined without tedious and costly experimentation in each new locality.

Measurements of the amount of erosion from experimental plots on moderately sloping hillsides show a measureable depth of soil removed by each storm, and that the rate of erosion varies greatly with the kind of crop and method of cultivation. The extension workers of many State agricultural colleges are using the results of the department's studies on design and construction of terraces.

Irrigation Investigations

The irrigation requirements of arid and semiarid lands in the Missouri and Arkansas River Basins are set forth in a late publication by the department.

Duty-of-water studies are being prosecuted in southern California in cooperation with State and local interests. Comparative measurements of evaporation losses from standard experimental tanks and one of 85 feet diameter show that the rate of evaporation from a small tank is greater than from a large reservoir. Studies on delivery of irrigation water and canal management have been made, and the results published during the last year. The control of gravel and silt in irrigation channels and reservoirs, the reclamation of alkali land, and the economic problems of pumping for irrigation are other subjects that have been studied.

STATE EXPERIMENT STATIONS

Cordial relationships are maintained with the State experiment stations through the department's administration of the Federal acts appropriating funds for research at these stations. In this work the department seeks to develop cooperation and community of interest. It refrains from arbitrary supervision of the work, but scrutinizes the research as regards definiteness of purpose, the relation of new projects to established knowledge, the essentials of procedure, and the adaptation of studies to the ends in view. Care is taken to guard against duplication of effort and the collection of scattered information without adequate consideration of the requirements.

Three years' work at the State experiment stations under the Purnell Act has revealed certain favorable tendencies in research in this field. One is a stimulus given to cooperation among the stations and with the Department of Agriculture. Another gain is improvement in the planning of research. There is greater definiteness of plan and also more care in selecting manageable subject matter. More emphasis is placed on improved technique in analyzing data. This is particularly noticeable in studies in which the department and the stations cooperate.

Cooperation between the department and the State experiment stations in the study of common problems has resulted in a comprehensive national system of agricultural research. These cooperative enterprises are under the general charge of joint committees from the department and the stations. Every station is represented in this cooperative work, there being nearly 900 definite agreements, besides a number of less formal cooperative understandings. The work covers a wide range, but is especially active in the study of the distribution and marketing of farm produce, rural social organizations, rural home management, vitamins in relation to human nutrition, and quality and palatability of meat.

EXTENSION SERVICE

Funds for cooperative extension work from all sources for 1928 amounted to $20,952,560, an increase of about $800,000 over the previous year and of $1,800,000 over 1924. The increase for the most part was from State and county funds, indicating an increasing local appreciation of extension activities. Of the 5,161 persons employed on the cooperative extension staffs of the 48 States on June 30, 1928, 3,675 were resident county workers, an increase during the past four years of 248. Of these, 2,318 were county agricultural agents or assistant agents, 941 were home demonstration agents, 145 were engaged in boys' and girls' club work, and 271 in negro extension work. The staff of full-time and part-time specialists numbered 1,004, an increase of 134 over 1924. Of this increase 31 were extension foresters. The employment of extension foresters by the States has developed largely because of Federal cooperation under the terms of the Clarke-McNary Act, approved June 7, 1924. As more than one-third of the total land in farms in the United States is woodland or woodland pasture, the importance of farm-forestry extension in assisting farmers to develop these lands most profitably is readily apparent.

Public appreciation of and interest in the further development of extension work was evidenced during the year by the passage of several acts by the Seventieth Congress. Foremost of these is the Capper-Ketcham Act, approved May 22, 1928, which authorized an additional annual appropriation of $20,000 to each of the States and to Hawaii for cooperative extension work, this total of $980,000 to be increased by $500,000 the succeeding year. The additional $500,000 is to be divided among the States and Hawaii, in the ratio that the rural population of each bears to the total rural population of the United States and Hawaii, on condition that an equal amount of funds from within the State be expended for extension work. The primary purpose of the Capper-Ketcham Act is to provide funds for the employment of additional county extension agents, particularly for the further development of home demonstration and boys' and girls' club work. The initial appropriation of $980,000 for the fiscal year 1929 was included in the second deficiency act.

In the agricultural appropriation act for 1929, the supplemental Smith-Lever appropriation was increased from $1,300,000 to $1,580,000. This act also contained an appropriation of $400,000 to assist States and counties flooded in 1927 to employ extension agents to aid in the more rapid rehabilitation of these areas. An act approved May 16, 1928, extended the provisions of the Smith-Lever extension act and the several experiment station acts to Hawaii, and extension work will be begun there during the coming year, in cooperation with the University of Hawaii.

Twenty-two Educational Films Made

During the year, 22 new educational motion-picture films on agricultural subjects were completed, totaling 30 reels and representing work of nine of the bureaus of the department. Notable among the new films were those on the cooperative marketing of livestock, the agricultural outlook, the use of airplanes in boll-weevil control, terracing, boys' and girls' club work, control of rats and pocket gophers, and two entitled "The Forest—and Health" and "The Forest—and Wealth." The department now has more than 2,000 copies of its films available for circulation, from which more than 8,000 loan shipments were made during the year. Colleges, farm organizations, foreign governments, and other agencies have purchased at least an equal number of copies. It is estimated that during the year 10,000,000 people saw one or more of these films.

Department exhibits were presented at 65 fairs and expositions, in many cases these exhibits consisting of a carload or two carloads of specially prepared material. The showings included 33 State and interstate fairs and the Third World's Poultry Congress. At this congress, which was held in Ottawa, Canada, July 27 to August 4, 1927, two carloads of exhibits were shown, portraying the importance of the poultry industry in the United States and illustrating some of the major findings of the poultry experiments of the department and the State experiment stations. An exhibit is now in preparation for showing at the Ibero-American Exposition, to be held in Seville, Spain, in 1929.

Rehabilitating Flood Areas

Rehabilitation of the lower Mississippi Valley flood area proceeded rapidly during the year, material for reconstruction and refurnishing of homes and seed and feed necessary for crop production being furnished by the American National Red Cross to those who were unable to finance expenditures for these purposes from their own resources. Agricultural extension agents employed by this department and the State colleges of agriculture cooperated with Red Cross relief officials and with local committees in working out agricultural programs for the flooded area. They located suitable supplies of seed, urged the planting of truck crops in certain areas to provide quick returns, aided in the marketing of these crops, and otherwise assisted greatly in the prompt recovery of this region. Wherever land emerged from the flood early enough for planting and was not reflooded in 1927, satisfactory crops were produced. The Red Cross furnished planting seed in the spring of 1928 to farmers who were unable to produce crops the previous year because of late planting or repeated flooding. Assistance was also given to farmers in the area flooded by the White and St. Francis Rivers in Arkansas in 1928.

Everywhere throughout the area attention was given to the use of improved seed of adapted varieties, to the growing of forage crops, to increasing the acreage of legumes to the introduction of improved livestock, including poultry, to the planting of home gardens, and to the preservation of surplus fruits and vegetables for use when fresh supplies are not available. Many thousands of packages of garden seeds of varieties suitable for a family garden were distributed by the American Red Cross both in 1927 and 1928. The result of these activities is that the lower Mississippi Valley now is planted to better seed and has more gardens than ever before, while in other respects its farms, except such as have been subject to later overflows, are nearly back to normal. This prompt recovery is due primarily to the resolute spirit of the people, to the prompt and effective aid given by the American Red Cross, and to the planning, supervision, and untiring service of men and women extension workers throughout the area. A special appropriation by the Congress available in May, 1928, provides for the continuance of extension agents throughout the flooded area during the fiscal year 1929, where such agents can not be maintained by local agencies, and for the employment of additional agents to aid in rehabilitation.

On November 3 and 4, 1927, torrential rains over New England and eastern New York caused unprecedented floods there, especially in Vermont and in the Connecticut Valley. While the property damage was largely to factories, mercantile establishments, railroads, roads and bridges, farmers in the fertile valleys suffered heavily, particularly along the Winooski, Missisquoi, and Lamoille Rivers in Vermont. The sudden rush of flood waters down these narrow valleys carried everything before it. Known loss of life in New England was 88, of whom 48 perished in the Winooski Valley. Property damage was estimated at upwards of $32,000,000, with $1,500,000 agricultural loss and $7,500,000 damage to roads and bridges in Vermont alone. The American people promptly responded to the appeal of the Red Cross for aid, and assistance was quickly rendered by that organization.

WORK OF THE WEATHER BUREAU

Among the major activities of the department, the benefits of the well-known weather service extend to almost every industry and activity of the Nation. Every year adds to the number of persons who learn how to use the weather forecasts, crop reports, and warnings of frosts, cold waves, storms, floods, and hurricanes to their personal advantage or the better management of their industries or business operations. This is particularly true of the farmer. A dozen years or more ago his rural location cut him off to a large extent from the immediate receipt of useful weather advices and bulletins. Radio, however, now changes all this and "listening in" two or more times daily the farmer is able to get practically all the current weather news as readily and completely as his city neighbors.

One of the first lines of work organized by the Weather Bureau at the time of its creation in 1871 was the systematic collection of observations from the rural and farming communities for establishing the climate of the United States. It now has more than 50 years' observations of this character from many stations, as distinguished from the observations made in the cities by the relatively small number of commissioned employees. These 50 years and more of observations from the rural communities are of inestimable value in establishing the climatic characteristics of the different sections of the United States, either for agricultural, industrial, hygienic, or resort purposes. The country at large is indebted to the farmer and to rural residents for the contributions they have made in the form of daily meteorological observations furnished to the Weather Bureau. The Government supplies a few simple instruments and instructions, and day by day the farmer, without compensation, systematically makes and records the simple observations required. For many years the number of these public-spirited citizens of the rural communities has exceeded 3,000 and at times even 4,000.

These observations over the continental United States, and like observations by citizens of other nations provide very complete climatic data for much of the land area of the world. A somewhat similar service has existed through the cooperation of shipmasters sailing the oceans of the globe, who every day on each voyage make certain weather observations at sea, and mail copies of their reports to the Weather Bureau on reaching port, necessarily a long time after the observations have been taken.

International Action Taken

During the past year, owing to the possibilities afforded by radio, a concerted international action has been taken to effectively organize the making of simultaneous observations over the oceans of the globe, such reports to be furnished coastal stations in the best position to receive them and thus make almost instantly available simultaneous observations from all parts of the world, such observations being coordinated with like telegraphic reports received from continental stations. These reports, like the mail reports and the cooperative reports from the rural observers, are in the main made without cost except for telegraphic transmission, and it is not too much to say that the extensive world-wide cooperation between all nations concerning meteorological matters promises to be one of the agencies by which the peoples of the earth are being brought closer and closer into co-operation and acquaintance, without rivalry and with the ultimate result of greater harmony and mutual appreciation.

The extension of the work of the Weather Bureau to serve aviation and transoceanic flights was very great during the past fiscal year, and the department is exerting itself to the utmost limit of funds available to cooperate with the increasing number of air-transport organizations and supply the most complete and effective meteorological service possible.

PROGRESS IN HOME ECONOMICS

Signally useful work has been done in the last few years by the department's Bureau of Home Economics. Both producers and consumers have obtained from the bureau vital information concerning the utilization of agricultural products, the relation of many kinds of foods and textiles to health and standards of living, and the possibility of introducing improvements in producing, selling, and buying. The research program of the bureau, although not yet covering all requirements, is extensive and constantly being made more practical.

One of the principal branches of the bureau's work is the study of family dietaries. An analysis of approximately 3,000 family dietaries is now under way and should yield valuable data. Dietary scales and standards used by various investigators have been revised and a new double scale proposed. In addition a short-cut method for calculating the energy, protein, and mineral value of diets has been developed. The final results of these studies, in addition to showing kinds and quantities of food consumed, will indicate their value in terms of energy and nutrients needed for health and well being. During the last year new figures on the chemical composition of fresh fruits have been published. These figures, besides being generally useful to producers and consumers, furnish dietitians and physicians with more accurate data for calculating special diets.

Improved household methods of cooking beef and lamb have been presented in popular form. Wide attention has been drawn by the bureau to the use of the meat thermometer. This aid to scientific cooking has aroused interest among hotel and restaurant managers as well as among home makers because it insures uniform results, and prevents overcooking and loss of weight and flavor.

Effective ways of using cotton textiles for clothing and household purposes have been described and illustrated. Designs developed for various types of children's clothing, research on starches and other materials for fabric finishing, and the study of washing temperatures have furnished much-needed facts for home makers.

Study of textiles has thrown light on the possibility of finding new uses for cotton. Osnaburg, a fabric made of low-grade cotton hitherto utilized chiefly for industrial purposes, was found suitable for window curtains, bed covers, and other household furnishings. A survey showing the extent to which cotton and other textiles have been used proved valuable to the cotton trade as well as to consumers. Another survey on trends in home sewing showed the number and types of garments made at home and analyzed the main problems of the home seamstress. Studies on the use of time by home makers have thrown light on the need for home labor-saving equipment and indicated other ways of saving the home-maker's time. These studies, together with those demonstrating the value of household budgets, should promote substantial progress in the technic of home making.

THE PRESS SERVICE

Extensive publicity is obtained for the department's work through the press. In the last year requests from newspapers and newspaper syndicates for the regular and special information services issued by the department's press service increased materially. During the fiscal year ended June 30, 1928, the press service issued 934 regular mimeographed releases, 33 special articles, 125 bulletin reviews, 37 statements by the Secretary, and numerous statements by department officials. Agricultural feature articles were also furnished to the large press associations as well as to many farm publications. These articles, many of them illustrated, constitute a valuable means of communication with the public. A special effort has been made in recent months to make news photographs of department work, and excellent results have been obtained in the press. Graphs and maps prepared in the press service are also being supplied to newspapers. Through the foreign-language information service the department places much information in the foreign-language press. In 1927 the foreign-language information service issued 234 of the department's releases, which were printed 2,057 times. One specially prepared article was used by 117 foreign-language publications. Three thousand country weeklies and semiweeklies received a weekly release called "Page, Line, and Paragraph," which is extensively used. Agricultural college editors publish much material sent them by the press service. Press correspondents and press associations in Washington demand increasing commodity information. Such information is furnished through the press service on the basis of cable reports and statistical and economic studies done in the Bureau of Agricultural Economics. This material is distributed largely by messenger to the press associations and correspondents.

RADIO SERVICE EXPANDED

The radio service of the department has passed its experimental stage and become an established and valuable part of the department's facilities for carrying the results of its work to the Nation. During the last year educational programs of the department reached the listening public from 149 broadcasting stations. These stations devoted in the aggregate more than 1,000 hours each month to broadcasting of information from the department. At prevailing commercial rates this broadcasting time would command more than $500,000. Forty-six broadcasting stations cooperated in transmitting a special series of nine weekly releases on corn-borer control, thereby affording a good demonstration of the value of radio service in emergency educational campaigns.

Development of broadcasting networks during the year brought new opportunities of speaking direct from Washington to the farm audience. Approximately 300,000 members and leaders of boys and girls' 4–H Clubs, in addition to the usual audience of broadcast listeners, heard an evening program of the National 4–H Club camp. This program, by arrangement with the National Broadcasting Co., was transmitted through 23 stations. That company has just placed at the department's disposal a network of 15 stations which sends a 15-minute program of important current information spoken by members of the department staff to a potential audience of some 400,000 farm families each week day (noontime) except Saturday.

Evidence of growth in the number of listeners to the department's radio releases is given by an increasing demand for printed matter supplementing spoken facts. Aunt Sammy's Radio Recipes, a cook book, compiling recipes and menus sent by radio in the Housekeepers' Chat, prepared by the Bureau of Home Economics, was sent on request to 185,000 homes in the last fiscal year. Forty-five thousand booklets containing the agricultural economic lessons of the United States Radio Farm School were issued. So that listeners may set down for reference broadcast information, arrangements have been made for publication of Aunt Sammy's Radio Record for hearers of the Housekeepers' Chat, and of the United States Farm Radio Record for listeners to the farm broadcasts.

The cordial cooperation of broadcasters played an essential part in the expansion and stabilization of the radio service which took place during the last year. With a continuation of this cooperation, and with the rapid progress of the radio art generally, growth in the usefulness of radio as a means of placing facts before farmers is certain.

DEPARTMENT PUBLICATIONS

Publications to the number of 33,716,481 were distributed to the public during the year. Of this number, 13,152,367 were farmers' bulletins and 20,564,214 were miscellaneous publications—bulletins, circulars, leaflets, and bulletin lists. Compared with the distribution the previous year there was an increase of 6,000,000 copies. By far the greater part of this increase was in the distribution of farmers' bulletins and lists of farmers' bulletins.

The distribution of farmers' bulletins was greater than that for any year since 1923. Members of Congress sent out 9,065,441 copies of farmers' bulletins, the largest distribution by them since 1922. There was an increase of 1,214,013 copies as compared with the fiscal year preceding.

Substantial progress was made during the year in the indexing work of the publications of the department. To meet the needs of libraries, investigators, students, and others who require information as to what the department has published along various lines, a complete analytical index of the publications of the department for the last 25 years is in preparation. The first part of this report was embodied in the list of publications of the United States Department of Agriculture from January, 1901, to December, 1925, inclusive, which was published during the year as a miscellaneous publication.

In addition to the information available to the public in the form of printed publications there are numerous items of interest and value in the material that is mimeographed or multigraphed and distributed to those best served by this service. Thus during the year over 51,000,000 duplicated impressions or pages of this material were made available in the Division of Publications.

ADDITIONS TO LIBRARY

Additions to the department's library in the last year included 15,800 books, pamphlets, and bound volumes, and the current issues of more than 3,400 periodicals. The library now contains about 205,000 volumes. As its resources become better known outside the department, scientific workers make increasing use of its facilities. Last year 2,432 books were lent by the library to scientific workers outside of Washington. Efficient catalogues, indexes, and bibliographies make the resources practically available.

W. M. JARDINE,
Secretary of Agriculture.

WHAT'S NEW IN AGRICULTURE

AIRPLANE Dusting of Cotton Fields Proves Effective, Economical — About eight years ago a couple of hardy pioneers up in Ohio had the temerity to risk confinement in an insane asylum by suggesting that the airplane might have value as a farm implement. They could see no reason why it could not be used as a means of dusting poisons over crops needing protection from the depredations of insects or the ravages of disease. They even made a preliminary test of the idea and continued to insist that it was feasible. Out of this small beginning has grown a new industry, that of insecticide and fungicide dusting by airplane. (Fig. 1.)

This preliminary test was conducted in 1921, and by 1922 arrangements had been perfected for tentative experiments on dusting calcium arsenate for the boll weevil. Poisoning the weevil was then in its infancy but growing rapidly, and the problem of machinery for dusting was an acute one. To the surprise of almost everyone concerned, these preliminary experiments with the airplane yielded successful results, and it was soon seen that cotton could be dusted just as efficiently with the airplane as with the best of machinery on the ground, and much better than with some types of the latter. Furthermore, a study of the operation showed that here was apparently one use for the airplane in which it could compete with existing equipment on a basis of comparative cost, and show at least as good results, at no more cost to the farmer, and still pay a profit to the operator of the airplane. Commercial companies then became interested, and by 1924 the first commercial airplane dusters were in operation. Since then there has been a steady increase in airplane dusting of cotton in spite of the fact that the succeeding years were marked by comparatively light damage by the weevil and correspondingly little need for poisoning. By 1927 the industry had developed to the point where approximately 500,000 acres of cotton was treated by airplanes in the United States, and the season of 1928 will show still further increase.

In addition to this activity in the United States, various foreign countries have become interested in the possibilities of utilizing the airplane as an aid in their work of dusting infested crops, and at the present time at least eight foreign countries are making more or less use of this device.

Airplanes Used for Many Crops

Naturally, its use has not been confined to cotton. Applications of dust have been made by airplane to such crops as peaches, pecans, walnuts, wheat, alfalfa, tomatoes, cantaloupes, and peppers, besides numerous others. Such applications have been made to various types of forest areas, and airplanes are now being used for the distribution of poison to control the malarial mosquito. This is especially applicable to swamp lands inaccessible to any other type of machine.

The first question of the individual farmer is naturally, just how does all this concern him, inasmuch as he can not afford to buy an airplane? Airplane dusting is not done on this basis, as the capacity of a plane is so great that very few farms are big enough to require one. Airplane dusting is sold by contract. The operating company provides

FIGURE 1.—Filling hopper of dusting airplane with poison

the planes, pilots, poison, and everything else needed for making the applications, and the farmer merely contracts for such applications as he needs on his crops, whether the acreage is 10 or 10,000. An idea commonly encountered is that airplane dusting is of value only for the "big man" with large acreage, but this is a mistake. The service is just as useful for the small farmer with a small acreage; the only problem is to get enough people in any community to subscribe for the service to make it worth while to maintain an airplane there for local use. Furthermore, the airplane is so mobile that this acreage can be scattered over a distance of 25 to 50 miles from the center of activities, and still be reached very promptly. The general price of airplane dusting has been no more than it would cost a farmer to make the applications himself with machinery on the ground, and it is to be expected that prices can be lowered as the industry develops.

Airplane dusting, of course, has its limitations, and can be used only in areas where conditions are suitable. Reasonably level land is absolutely essential (fig. 2) and fairly treeless areas are highly desirable. The planes can be flown into small fields surrounded by obstructions, but the maneuvering necessary so reduces the dusting capacity of the plane that such operations are not profitable; it is frequently possible, however, to remove some of these obstructions at comparatively little cost and thus make suitable a field which was previously totally unfitted for airplane dusting. On all places where the fields are reasonably free from obstructions the farmer merely contracts for the applications, tells the operating company when and where he wants them made, and the company does the rest. In some instances dusting companies employ entomologists who are available to act as advisers to the farmers and assist them in deciding just when and where applications are needed.

Advantages of the Method

Airplane dusting has many advantages under conditions where it is thus recommended. In the first place, the use of the plane tends to

FIGURE 2.—Airplane treating cotton field with calcium arsenate for control of the boll weevil

induce more general poisoning in a community; and, of course, any tendency toward community action in poisoning the boll weevil immediately results in greater ease of control and increased profits to the farmer. When the farmer contracts for airplane dusting it is not necessary for him to have available either mules or labor for operating machinery on the ground and he has no investment tied up in such equipment. The fact that his organization is not called upon for any work whatever makes it possible to carry out a full program of poisoning without the slightest interference with the usual farm operations. Above everything else, the greatest advantage of the airplane is the fact that it can be operated regardless of conditions of the soil, and a muddy field is no handicap to airplane dusting. Boll weevils are most active in rainy weather, and poisoning is then most urgently needed; but cotton fields then become so boggy that machinery on the ground can not be operated, or only under great difficulty. The plane, on the other hand, can be started in as soon as the rain stops and can quickly poison the endangered field. The mobility of the plane is especially valuable in permitting immediate application to the most seriously infested areas, regardless of how scattered they may be. The pilot has such control of his dust cloud that he can dart in and out of various fields and quickly cover exactly those spots where poisoning is most urgently needed.

From a business viewpoint airplane dusting is especially valuable in stabilizing crop loans. Any one of the more reliable operators can furnish a bond guaranteeing performance of contract, and thus the banker, in making a crop loan, is assured that the crop concerned will be protected against weevils whenever and wherever such protection is needed; and this assurance constitutes the best guarantee of the safety of the loan.

Active Season is Short

One of the primary problems confronting organizations for dusting cotton is the fact that the active season is limited to only a few months in the year, and they thus have the problem of carrying the overhead of their organization for the remainder of the year. For this reason they are especially interested in extending their operations to any other use which can be found at other seasons, and many of them are becoming quite successful in thus extending their period of activity. The largest such organization in the United States, for example, sends its equipment and personnel to South America for work during the northern winter season, when it is summer there, and thus gets two full seasons of operation every year. Undoubtedly, as time goes on, more and more uses will be found for this equipment, and each new use will be reflected in further reduction in the cost of dusting to the farmer.

B. R. Coad.

ALASKAN Forests to Supply Paper While Maintaining Growth — With one or more newspapers going into almost every home in the land, the United States is the world's greatest user of newsprint, and the yearly consumption now equals 58 pounds per capita. This paper is largely made from the wood of those northern conifers, the spruces, hemlocks, and true firs, which extend across the continent along and on both sides of the line dividing the United States and Canada. There is a constant reaching out into more remote sections of this broad forest area to supply the large and increasing demand for newsprint. Our own portions of this forest have finally proved unable to meet the increases, and the expanding industry has crossed the line into Canada, which is now the center of production for our newsprint requirements

The reaching out for print paper into regions more and more remote from the principal markets has progressed to the point where the extensive spruce and hemlock forests on the coast of Alaska have come within the zone of economic production. The principal pulp-wood forests of Alaska occur in the panhandle extending down from the main body of the Territory along the west side of British Columbia for a distance of 350 miles. This region, known as southeastern Alaska, consists of a narrow strip of mainland and a paralleling chain of many islands penetrated and separated by an intricate system of narrow, navigable waterways. Its southern limits are about 600 miles northwest of Seattle, from which it is reached by the protected waterway known as the inside passage. The Japan current of the Pacific Ocean gives it a mild winter climate so that a zero temperature is seldom experienced, the snowfall at the coast line is not excessive, and the waterways are not icebound. There are numerous water-power sites that can be developed for paper-mill use, the pulp timber is readily accessible to the many protected waterways, and the cheap transportation which water affords is available for moving the wood to the mills and the paper to the ports of eastern and western United States.

For Timber Production Indefinitely

This region is to be devoted indefinitely to timber production. It has good timber-growing possibilities but is not well adapted to exten-

FIGURE 3.—Extensive forests of spruce and hemlock suitable for paper making are found along the heavily indented coast line of southeastern Alaska. They are owned by the Federal Government and are dedicated to the continuous production of timber crops. They will supply in perpetuity a large annual yield of pulp timber that will help materially in meeting the Nation's demand for newsprint paper

sive agriculture or stock raising. The Federal Government, which owns the timber lands, has placed them in the national-forest system, where they will be managed primarily for the production of timber crops and on a basis of supplying a sustained yearly output of raw material to the local paper-making and other wood-using industries. The growing of timber will thus constitute the foundation of a permanent regional development.

Within the national forests the timber alone is sold, the land being retained for further timber production. All woods operations are conducted under the supervision of forest officers to insure satisfactory utilization of the timber on the logging areas and the application of the proper forestry measures to keep the lands productive. Large blocks of timber can be placed under long-term contracts by paper manufacturers, with provision that payments for the timber shall be made as cutting proceeds and that the rates shall be subject to readjustment at stated intervals during the life of the contract.

The present volume of standing timber on the national forests of Alaska has been conservatively estimated after extensive field work to be 78,500,000,000 board feet, of which 74 per cent is western hemlock and 20 per cent Sitka spruce, both good pulp woods for newsprint paper. Studies by the Forest Service indicate that under a proper system of forest management the timberlands of this region can produce 1,500,000 cords of pulp wood yearly in perpetuity. In other words, timber to that amount can be removed from the forest each year and will be fully replaced by tree growth. Converted into newsprint, this represents a production of 1,000,000 tons, or more than 25 per cent of the entire present annual consumption of the United States.

Policy Beneficial to All

The Forest Service policy of limiting the development of paper mills in this region to a total capacity commensurate with the growing power of the forest will prevent a repetition of the overdevelopment and inevitable subsequent collapse through timber exhaustion that has characterized the industry in other sections of the United States. Everyone will be benefited by managing the forests according to this policy, which is made possible by the fact that all the available timber in the region is controlled by one agency, the Federal Government. It is highly important to the paper-manufacturing companies because the heavy capital investments for an efficient modern plant can only be justified by assurance of a long operating life; it provides for a permanent local industry and hence fosters a permanent general development of the region; and it gives the United States an unfailing source of supply for a large quantity of newsprint paper.

The Government has recently made awards of sufficient timber and water power for the development of two large newsprint projects in this region, and within the near future the news of the world will be brought to our homes on paper made from spruce and hemlock trees now growing on the far-off Alaskan hills.

B. F. HEINTZLEMAN.

ALFALFA and Red-Clover Seed, If Imported, are Colored Artificially   The United States does not produce sufficient seed of the two staple forage crops, alfalfa and red clover, to meet the domestic seed requirements. In certain years from one-fourth to one-third of the red-clover seed sown in the United States has been imported, while the proportion of alfalfa seed imported has been somewhat less.

Comparative tests have been made by the United States Department of Agriculture and State agricultural experiment stations through a series of years to determine the relative crop-producing value in the United States of alfalfa and red-clover seed grown in the United States and in the principal countries of the world producing seed for export. These comparative tests show that seed grown in certain countries does not produce well when seeded in the regions of the

United States where those crops are important. As this difference in adaptability became generally recognized United States grown seed commanded a higher price than imported seed. In the case of red-clover seed this difference in price, following the demand for United States grown seed, was so great that domestic seed at times brought a premium of 50 per cent over imported seed. Then followed a period when imported seed was substituted for and sold as United States grown seed.

In order to remedy this condition the Federal seed act was amended by requiring that all seed of alfalfa and red clover imported into the United States be colored. Previous to the coloring provision of the act there was no practical way in which information as to foreign and domestic origin could be carried to the farmer who sowed the seed.

Different Types of Coloring

As the comparative tests showed a marked difference in adaptability of seed grown in different countries the Federal seed act provides different types of coloring for imported seeds. When, after comparative tests, it has been found that seed of alfalfa or red clover grown in any particular country is not adapted to general agricultural use in the United States, seed grown in such country must be colored 10 per cent red before it can be imported into the United States.

Red-clover seed grown in Italy and alfalfa seed grown in Africa and Turkestan are colored 10 per cent red. Alfalfa seed grown in South America is colored 10 per cent orange-red, and seed of both alfalfa and red clover of unknown origin 10 per cent red. Alfalfa and red-clover seed from Canada are colored 1 per cent violet. Both alfalfa and red-clover seed of known origin from other countries are colored 1 per cent green.

This coloring requirement of the Federal seed act makes it possible for every farmer buying seed of alfalfa and red clover to know whether he is buying domestic or foreign-grown seed, and in the case of foreign-grown seed, if it is colored 10 per cent red, to know that it is of unknown origin or has been found to be unadapted to general agricultural use in the United States.

Doubtless the most important result of the coloring of imported seed is that a country-wide agronomic test is now being made with foreign and domestic-grown seed, as every farmer knows which he is sowing. It is not without interest to note that this country-wide test is being carried on without expense other than the actual cost of coloring the imported seed.

E. BROWN.

ALFALFA and Red Clover Yellowed By Leaf-hopper Attack During the summer months alfalfa and red-clover plants often turn yellow and are decidedly dwarfed. In alfalfa this unthrifty condition has been known for years as yellows or yellow top. In clover it has often been referred to as sunburn.

Recent work has shown that this damage is caused by the potato leaf hopper, the same insect that is responsible for the serious disease of potatoes, known as hopper burn. This tiny green leaf hopper is extremely agile and easily escapes detection by moving underneath leaves or in back of stems when the plant is examined. The infestation in some instances is so heavy that the hoppers arise in swarms in front of an individual walking through the fields.

The injury to alfalfa appears as a yellowing and bronzing of the leaves together with extreme dwarfing of leaves, petioles, and stems. Often the tips of the affected leaves have a reddish tinge, or they may become brown and curled. The yellowing and dwarfing are usually most noticeable on the younger tips of the branches, which has led to the descriptive common name "yellow top." This condition apparently is not transferred from plant to plant without the presence of these insects. Experiments have shown that one part of a plant may be severely damaged whereas another branch of the same plant may escape attack and develop in a normal manner. (Fig. 4.) Likewise, alfalfa stands which are so badly dwarfed with yellow top as not to justify the expense of mowing may later in the season recover entirely and produce heavy crops the following season. Seedling and even older alfalfa plants may at times be so severely damaged that they fail to recover.

FIGURE 4.—Yellow top on alfalfa. Right half of plant caged and infested with leaf hoppers; left half caged and kept free from leaf hoppers. Note extreme dwarfing of part exposed to these insects

Similar Effects on Red Clover

In red clover the same yellowing and dwarfing of the leaves and stems are common. On this crop a conspicuous reddening of leaves develops, especially near the tips or along the veins. The leaf tips, and often the entire leaf, may wither and turn brown without any preliminary discoloration. On seedlings this wilting of leaves is most serious, for the new leaves may be attacked and destroyed as rapidly as they are produced until the young plant is killed. On mature plants the damage by these insects may often weaken the plants so that they succumb after the first cutting and before a second crop can be harvested.

It has been observed that leaf-hopper injury is worse on varieties of legumes that have smooth stems and petioles, whereas those that are extremely hairy are likely to be avoided by the insects. There is a marked difference in hairiness between American-grown red clovers and plants raised from seed grown in foreign countries. The imported, smooth strains are most severely damaged. Most of our native-grown red clover is sufficiently resistant to avoid serious losses from leaf hoppers during any average season.

Alfalfa and other legumes also show differences in varietal susceptibility. The development of varieties more resistant to hopper attack
offers a likely method for controlling the pest; the time of cutting may
in some cases serve to modify the damage by leaf hoppers. Often it is
observed that there are striking differences in the extent of damage on
adjacent fields which have been cut not more than a week apart.
Fields of alfalfa or red clover badly dwarfed by leaf hoppers should
be harvested as soon as practicable.

JOHN MONTEITH, Jr., and
E. A. HOLLOWELL.

**ANIMAL Husbandry
Research Yields
Dividends to All** A flock of Government-owned sheep is
allowed to feed each summer on lush,
palatable forage in the Targhee National
Forest, about 40 miles west of Yellow-
stone National Park. During the fall and early winter they are
grazed in the deep canyons of the Lemhi National Forest, about 40

FIGURE 5.—Rambouillet ewes and lambs on the United States Sheep Experiment Station range,
where they were handled under practical conditions while being used in wool experiments

miles southwest of Dubois, Idaho, until snowstorms make it necessary to drive them back toward the headquarters of the United States
Sheep Experiment Station (fig. 5), near Dubois, Idaho. They are
wintered in an irrigated valley 10 miles west of Dubois. At lambing
time they are moved to the lambing sheds of the station, 6 miles north
of Dubois. During the first week in June the sheep are sheared.
The fleeces and the sheep are weighed and scored for many of the
important characteristics which sheep and wool are known to possess.
This procedure is repeated year after year. A detailed history of
each sheep is recorded and compared year after year. This record
constitutes, however, but the preliminary of an exhaustive study of
the wool of these sheep. Here are some of the steps that follow:
A 1-pound sample of wool is taken from the side of each fleece at
shearing, after being measured for length of staple. The samples are
placed in individual moisture-proof containers and shipped to the

wool laboratory near Washington, where a 250-gram portion of each is used in laboratory determinations of moisture, grease, dirt, and clean wool per fleece. The wool is first dried in an electric conditioning oven. The grease is then removed with carbon tetrachloride, after which the fleece sample is again dried. Finally the wool is scoured in a solution of water and neutral soap and again dried, to determine the amount of dirt which it contained.

All these processes require careful technique and a high degree of accuracy. Most of them would appear to the average sheep producer as a waste of time and money. "What has all this evaporating and hot-air drying and careful weighing to do with the wool which my sheep grow?" he might well inquire.

Research Replaces Theories with Facts

Here is the answer: Every sheepman who is in business for profit is interested in obtaining from his flock the greatest possible quantity of high-quality wool. Flocks vary greatly with respect both to amount and character of the wool grown per sheep. There are many theories as to the cause of this variation. What are the facts? It is to obtain the facts that such minute weighings and measurements as those described briefly above are undertaken.

Many facts of practical value to sheepmen and of ultimate benefit to all who buy, sell, or use wool and products made of wool, are being obtained. For example, the timeworn theory that the best sheep have a covering of wool over their faces is being disproved. The department's studies to date show that ewes of the Rambouillet breed which are free from heavy face covering yield the heaviest fleeces, both unscoured and scoured. Knowledge of this exploded theory is also of value because of the fact that some breeders have developed sheep with so much face covering that many individuals of the flock have been troubled with "wool blindness."

That folds around the neck and shoulders of a sheep are indicative of a more valuable fleece has also been disproved. Although ewes free from folds yielded slightly less wool, their fleeces showed greater length of staple, slightly greater fineness of fiber, less grease and dirt, and a little higher character.

Seasonal variations have always been given by many as the cause of fluctuations in the yield of wool. Mild or severe winters, periods of drought, and scanty feed have been blamed for light or heavy shearings. The department has proved that there is some justification for these traditions, but that a far greater cause of variation in wool production is to be found in the wide variation during any one season in the amount and quality of wool produced by each sheep. One ewe may be the same age and receive exactly the same feed and care during the year as another, and yet produce twice as much wool of equal or higher quality. Here, then, is a golden opportunity for the farmer to profit by the teachings of research. Seasonal variations can not be controlled. Variations in the wool-producing ability of a flock of sheep can be controlled, owing to the fact that there are often such great variations among the individual sheep as to make a great difference in the total output of a band.

Rigid culling of those sheep which are low producers and retention for breeding of those which are yielding each year a heavy fleece of good quality is the lesson to be learned.

In 1840 the average weight of fleece sheared from American sheep was less than 2 pounds. By 1900 it had increased to nearly 5½ pounds. To-day it is approaching 8 pounds. In other words, an average sheep to-day grows wool enough each year to make approximately one suit of clothes. In 1840 it took the wool of four sheep to make a suit of equal weight and quality. There is still room for improvement. By "weeding out" the poor producers and breeding from the heavily fleeced sheep, flock owners can raise the average.

Size of Eggs

Last year a White Leghorn hen on the department's experiment farm at Beltsville, Md., completed the three hundred and sixty-fifth day of her pullet-laying year with the enviable record of 306 eggs laid. Yet she was culled from the flock and sold for meat. None of her eggs were kept for hatching. The only reason, in fact, that she was not marketed earlier was because it was important to get her record with that of her sisters and other hens in a study of the inheritance of egg production. Her year's performance may mislead some, and she may have been fooling herself, but not Uncle Sam's poultry experts. Her eggs were undersized, poorly shaped, and altogether below the standards which have been set in the department's breeding project. They might not have hatched well had an effort been made to reproduce her kind. When marketed, her 306 eggs contained less food value than 18 or 20 dozen of standard-sized eggs.

"But," someone may reason, "306 eggs in one year is a splendid record. Wouldn't the great number make up for their small size?" The reply to that is that this hen did lay a greater total weight of eggs than the average of many of the highest-producing flocks of the country, but that the Government's breeding specialists have learned that it is very much more difficult to breed into a flock of chickens the factors which are responsible for size and quality of eggs than it is to breed for greater numbers of eggs. Therefore, in the interests of the future of the industry, a minimum standard of 2 ounces per egg and 24 ounces to the dozen has been adopted as a basis for culling the department's flocks of breeding hens.

There was a time when nearly all our eggs were laid during a few months in the spring and summer. Most hens went on a complete strike during the greater part of the other two seasons. But now, as a result of studies of egg production, inheritance, and scientific systems of culling those hens which are not good layers, we all can enjoy strictly fresh eggs the year round. Poultry research workers are still not satisfied. They are now searching for means of further increasing the fall and winter egg production of chickens so that the poultry keeper's income may be more nearly uniform and the American housewife may be able to buy eggs at a fairly uniform price throughout the year.

Goat's Milk

The value of goat's milk for infants and invalids is being studied in connection with the breeding of milk goats. The evidence shows that the mortality of infants fed substitutes for mother's milk is about three times that of breast-fed infants. With the increased tendency toward artificial feeding, it seems timely that research be instituted for a more satisfactory substitute for human milk. A study of the chemical, bacteriological, and nutritional work which has been done by scientists on this subject is fragmentary and lacks uniformity. Certainly here is a field of animal-husbandry research which challenges the interest of all and calls for the highest type of carefully controlled laboratory work.

Supplementing Grass to Produce Better Beef

One of the major lines of animal-husbandry investigation to-day is the study of the factors which influence the quality of meats in which 24 State experiment stations are cooperating with the department. How may we breed our cattle so that when fattened they will yield tender, juicy steaks and roasts? To what extent does feeding influence the final result? Can a steer of plain breeding be made to produce a steak as tender and palatable as that from a purebred, if he is fattened on the same raton? Can both kinds of cattle be fed principally on grass and make choice carcasses?

These are some of the questions we expect to answer. The last one, concerning grass, contains many possibilities and is of interest to city people and farmers alike. Grass is the farmer's cheapest feed. Beef grown from it costs the farmer only a fraction of that produced with corn. There are 600,000,000 acres of land in the United States which will grow well no other crop but grass. Beef has been grown on grass alone since the beginning of the cattle industry. But that beef has not been of the proper weight and age and has scarcely been of the right quality to satisfy the discriminating demands of to-day. The problem is to discover methods of husbandry by which high-quality yearlings and 2-year-old cattle may be marketed directly off grass, with a minimum of high-priced, supplementary feeds and therefore at a minimum cost to both producer and consumer.

E. W. Sheets.

A PHIDS' Life History Differs Greatly From That of Most Insects Plant lice, or aphids, constitute one of our most remarkable groups of insects. They may be seen abundantly on any of our fruit trees, as well as on almost every plant that grows. The injury caused by them is often severe, since they suck up the sap through a long slender beak which is inserted into the plant tissues.

If we examine a branch of a tree or other plant which is infested we will see the aphids, in most species grouped together in colonies, usually either on the under side of a leaf or along the twig. They may be greenish, brownish, black, or of other color, depending on the species, or even covered with mealy powder or long, waxlike filaments. (Fig. 6.)

These insects have a very unusual life history; one differing from those of almost all other insects. The egg is laid in the fall of the year, usually on the bark of the twig. With the coming of warm weather in the spring this egg hatches into what is known as the stem mother. There are no males until the next fall. The stem mother gives birth to living young, without the necessity of fertilization. These young are all females, and, when mature, give birth to other living young. This continues throughout the summer, there being numerous generations. In each generation there are usually some which are winged (fig. 7) and others which are wingless, each form being fully mature.

As the spring advances the number of winged forms increases, until, in the case of many species, they fly away to an entirely different kind of plant. Plants so chosen are known as summer hosts; on them new colonies are started, and there may be several generations on them before the return migration to the winter host. On the latter the true sexes which have been produced mate and the eggs are laid.

Thus we see that there are several forms of aphids, such as the stem mother, the wingless viviparous female, the winged viviparous female, the male, and the egg-laying female. These may vary considerably

FIGURE 6.—Green apple aphids on apple twigs. Injury to foliage is shown. Approximately natural size

in appearance from each other and have often been described as distinct species.

Some Species Live Underground

In the case of some species the aphids may be on the roots, concealed from sight, as well as above ground. This is true of the common woolly aphid of the apple. On certain of the annual plants there are species which live only on the roots, and their presence is usually not detected until the plants begin to die.

Leaves infested with aphids are usually more or less curled. Sometimes they are so badly curled that they almost form galls. True galls are also formed by certain aphids either on the leaves or petioles, or sometimes on the roots. If the galls are cut open the aphids may be seen within. These galls are of various types and sizes, depending upon the species of aphid causing them. They open up when it is time for the aphids to migrate. Of course not all species of aphids produce galls; in fact, among the fruit aphids there are practically no gall-forming species. Simple leaf curling, however, is very com-

mon. The fruit also is often very gnarled and knotted and remains very small, failing to thin out in the clusters.

One of the most interesting facts about aphids is their association with ants. The latter are very fond of the excrement of the aphids, which is a sweetish substance known as honey dew. They will attend the aphids very carefully, carrying them from place to place

FIGURE 7.—Apple-grain aphid winged migrants. Enlarged about 25 diameters. From a painting

where the "pasturage" may be better. In the case of underground aphids, the ants carry them from the roots of one plant to the roots of other plants and occasionally build a "shed" of soil over a colony of aphids above ground, as a protection to the colony. Ants do not usually injure the tree themselves, but they indicate the presence of aphids.

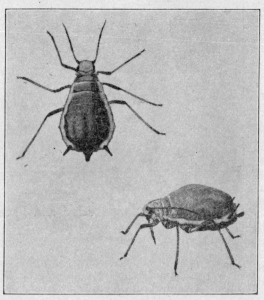

The honey dew, or excrement, is often produced in such enormous quantities that it rains down on automobiles which are parked under the trees. It is a sticky substance, coating the leaves, and dripping off when present in excessive quantities. A black, sooty fungus grows on it, often covering the leaves and fruit as if the tree had been dusted with a black powder; the fungus is not especially injurious in itself, but mars the appearance of the foliage and fruit.

FIGURE 8.—Green apple aphid. Enlarged about 15 diameters. From a painting

Like all other insects, aphids have their enemies, being preyed upon by many different kinds. Perhaps the most conspicuous and most important are the lady-bird beetles, which devour enormous numbers of aphids, often cleaning up entire colonies. Another type of enemy is parasites, which lay usually a single egg to an aphid. The young parasite hatching from the egg feeds within the body of the aphid, carefully avoiding the vital organs.   Thus the aphid continues to live until the parasite matures, but as a rule it does not produce young.

In addition to these parasites and predators, aphids are attacked by diseases, which sometimes spread very rapidly and destroy large numbers of the aphids.

Influenced By Weather Conditions

To a very great extent weather conditions influence the number of aphids, this influence acting both on the aphids and on their enemies.   Often the enemies are held back by adverse weather, and the aphids are permitted to multiply to enormous numbers.   Usually cool, moist weather brings on a large outbreak of aphids, but with certain species, such as the melon louse, the reverse is true.   When there is a large outbreak a sudden change in weather will often quickly reduce the numbers present.

The group as a whole being indigenous to the northern, temperate climates, there are a large number of species on our deciduous fruit trees.   We can name but a few of the more important, such as the rosy apple aphid, green apple aphid (fig. 9), apple-grain aphid, woolly aphid, rusty plum aphid, mealy plum aphid, water-lily aphid of plum, black cherry aphid, green peach aphid, and black peach aphid. Each of these lives and works in its own way, but in general conforms to the outline here discussed.

P. W. MASON.

ANTS That Invade Houses Are Easily Killed by Poison   There are a number of species of ants that invade our houses, getting into food supplies and annoying us by their presence. (Fig. 9.)   Some of them build their nests in the walls or under the floors, while others may live outdoors under stones in the yard or in nests in the lawn.   Some feed upon sweets, while others prefer grease and meats.   When the nests can be found the simplest method of destroying them is to inject a few teaspoonfuls of carbon disulphide or ethylene dichloride into the opening from which the ants are seen to emerge.   The fumes given

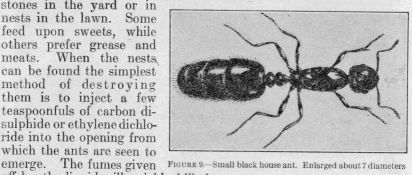

FIGURE 9.—Small black house ant. Enlarged about 7 diameters

off by the liquid will quickly kill the occupants of the nest.

Dusting with sodium fluoride wherever the ants are troublesome in the house is a simple remedy, and often so effective that other methods of prevention need not be resorted to.

When other methods fail, the use of poison baits will usually solve the problem.

One of the best is prepared as follows:

Boil together for 30 minutes—

Granulated sugar	pounds	1¼
Water	pints	1¼
Tartaric acid (crystallized)	gram	1
Benzoate of soda	do	1

Dissolve one-eighth ounce of sodium arsenite (c. p.) in 1 fluid ounce of hot water. Cool both solutions and then mix them well. Add two-thirds pound of strained honey and stir the mixture well.

The bait should be placed around the house where the ants are troublesome, by the use of small pieces of sponge soaked in the poison. The sponges may be placed on saucers or concealed in small, perforated cans.

Another excellent bait is prepared by mixing 1 pint of water, 1 pound of sugar, 27 grams of thallium sulphate, and 3 ounces of honey. The whole should be brought to a boil, mixed thoroughly, and allowed to cool. Thallium sulphate is a dangerous poison and should be handled with great care.

Less complicated baits can be made by dissolving 4 ounces of sugar in a quart of water and adding one-half ounce of tartar emetic, or by working small quantities of tartar emetic in grease or pieces of bacon rind.

E. A. Back and
R. T. Cotton.

Figure 10.—A narrow-ridge farm in the Appalachian uplands

APPALACHIAN Land Uses Affected By Aftermath of War The aftermath of the war has had its effect on agriculture in the Appalachians as it has elsewhere. The rugged topography of much of the Appalachian farm land is not suited to large farm machinery, particularly of the automotive type. Farmers on the rough and stony uplands of the eastern mountain States have found it well-nigh impossible to compete effectively in the markets for agricultural staples.

A rapid, almost revolutionary, readjustment of land utilization has been in progress recently in the Appalachians. The United States

Department of Agriculture, in cooperation with the West Virginia, Pennsylvania, and Kentucky Agricultural Experiment Stations, undertook in 1928 to study the nature of the necessary readjustment and to determine what could be done to facilitate it.

Field studies indicate that the necessary readjustment of population to resources is taking place. With the higher wages farm laborers now require, it is uneconomical to farm the rougher portions of land so intensively as before. This means that in the central Appalachians rough land with a slope of 16 degrees or more (equivalent to a rise of 29 feet in 100) is going back to woodland. Slopes less steep can be left in pasture advantageously (1) if farms are favorably situated with reference to roads and markets, (2) if the land is smooth enough to permit cutting brush with horse-driven mowers, and (3) if the farms have sufficient crop land to furnish concentrates for winter feeding. Brushcutting by hand is not practicable so long as the present level of wages prevails.

In the central Appalachians it has been determined that farms on the very narrow ridges (fig. 10) and in the very narrow V-shaped val-

FIGURE 11.—Broad-valley farms yield good incomes

leys can not ordinarily be depended upon to yield a satisfactory living. Broad-valley farms (fig. 11) and smooth uplands are adapted to machine farming and yield a living comparable with the living obtained from good farm lands elsewhere. A classification of 175 farms in the rougher farming section of the southern Appalachians shows that farm income is closely related to topography. (Table 1.)

TABLE 1.—*Relationship of farm income to topography*

Topography	Number of farms	Income
Narrow valley	57	$322
Narrow ridge	57	433
Broad ridge	16	735
Gently rolling upland	36	750
Broad valley	16	790

"Income" as used here does not include the value of the food products contributed to the family living by the farms. The value of
food products supplied by the farms ranged from $250 to $500, depending largely on the size of the farm family.

Farms on Uplands and in Valleys

In the central Appalachians the studies indicate that the gently
rolling upland, the broad-valley farms, and the broad-ridge farms all
yield some balance of income over that required to support a reasonable standard of living. The narrow V-shaped valleys and the narrow-
ridge farms yield less income and ordinarily do not attract progressive
farmers. The ratio between these two types of farms and all the farms
varies from county to county. In many of the rugged counties in the
Appalachians 25 to 50 per cent of the farms are narrow-valley or narrow-ridge farms. The reforestation of these two types of farms will
mean a considerable increase in woodland but a proportionate decrease
in the number of farm homes. The central Appalachians are especially well adapted to the growing of superior hardwood timber.

By utilizing the narrow-ridge and narrow-valley farms for growing
timber and the broad-valley bottom lands and smooth uplands for
farm crops and pasture, the Appalachian land resources will yield larger
farm incomes and will support higher standards of farm living.

MILLARD PECK.

AVOCADO Culls May Prove Source of Oil and Livestock Feed   The commercial production of avocados
is rapidly increasing in both California
and Florida. The extension of the market caused by the increase in production
naturally necessitates more rigid grading of the fruit than formerly.
This grading results in increasing quantities of culls, which consist very
largely of blemished, misshaped, and undersized fruit. At present
most of the culls are allowed to go to waste, but before long there
will be a sufficient quantity of cull fruit for utilization on a small
commercial scale.

One possible use for this fruit is the production of oil and press cake.
The oil could be used for edible purposes or for making soap, depending
upon the quality; the press cake could be utilized for feeding poultry
and stock. The oil, which is in the fleshy or edible part of the fruit,
can be satisfactorily expressed only after partial dehydration of the
fruit. After the removal of the seed the fruit is sliced, and the slices
are dried in a current of air at room temperature. The oil is then
expressed by means of a hydraulic press of cage type. The cold-
pressed oil has but little odor, a pleasant fruity flavor, and good
keeping properties when obtained from sound fruit.

The oil content ranges from 14 to about 30 per cent of the edible
portion of the fruit. The oil expressed from a sample of avocado of the
Fuerte variety was dark green, but after the oil had stood for about
six months in a gallon glass bottle in subdued light the green color
largely disappeared. It is probable that avocados of some varieties
would yield a yellow oil. Like olive and peanut oils, avocado oil
belongs to the nondrying class.

G. S. JAMIESON.

AVOCADO Industry Is The avocado is rapidly taking its place Rapidly Developing in as a standard salad fruit and is no Florida and California longer an expensive and rare luxury. Its high nutritive value warrants its more extensive use in the dietary. In oil content, ranging from 10 to 30 per cent, it far exceeds any other fruit eaten in the fresh state; while its 2 per cent of protein is more than double the protein in the commonly grown edible fruits. It possesses practically 75 per cent of the fuel value of cereals and has far more than that of lean meat or eggs. It possesses twice the amount of mineral matter contained in any other fresh fruit and yields an excess of base-forming elements.

The avocado is a native of tropical America, where it occurs principally as a dooryard fruit tree growing as a seedling. Three distinct races are recognized—West Indian, Guatemalan, and Mexican.

The West Indian race, native of the moist lowlands, is the most tender. Despite its lack of hardiness it thrives in the warmer parts of southern Florida and constitutes the larger part of Florida plantings. The fruits mature in the summer and fall months. While lower in oil content than the more hardy Guatemalan and Mexican varieties, its fruits are usually glossy green, of good size and attractive appearance, and meet a ready sale.

Some Varieties Resist a Little Frost

The Guatemalan and Mexican varieties, derived from higher altitudes of Central America, are able to stand a few degrees of frost. They are chiefly grown in California, although a few varieties and hybrids of these races are now being grown in Florida for the late fall and winter market. Owing to soil and climatic differences, few if any of the varieties succeeding in California have proved to be well adapted to Florida, and the converse is also true.

For winter production in Florida, new varieties have had to be originated, the best of which are hybrids, the Winslowson and Collinson, showing evidence of both West Indian and Guatemalan stock. The Fuerte variety, a Mexican-Guatemalan hybrid, has proved to be the preeminent variety for California planting, but it has been a practical failure in Florida. The result of these limitations is in the main fortunate, the production for market in Florida being heaviest in the fall and early winter months, while the bulk of the California shipping crop matures in the winter, spring, and early summer months.

Between 4,000 and 5,000 acres are now set to avocados in California, with about 75 per cent of this acreage yet to come into bearing. About 1,000 acres are planted in Florida, and the prospect is that this acreage will be rapidly extended. Only budded trees are planted, the Mexican stock being used in California and the West Indian in Florida. Despite the fact that avocados have been grown for 50 years or more both in California and in Florida, it is only through decades of expensive failures that enough has been learned as to methods of propagation, cultivation, and the best varieties and stocks to warrant the present commercial expansion of the industry. There is still much to be learned, but a few limiting factors are recognized as vital.

All Varieties Need Frost Protection

(1) *Frost protection.*—Even the so-called hardy varieties, such as the Fuerte, suffer from freezing weather and are about as tender as lemon trees.   Sites must be chosen favored by latitude or topography to avoid cold injury, and in addition some form of grove heating is generally a paying investment.

(2) *In Florida drainage is next in importance.*—No fruit tree is more easily injured by a high water table than the avocado.   At the same

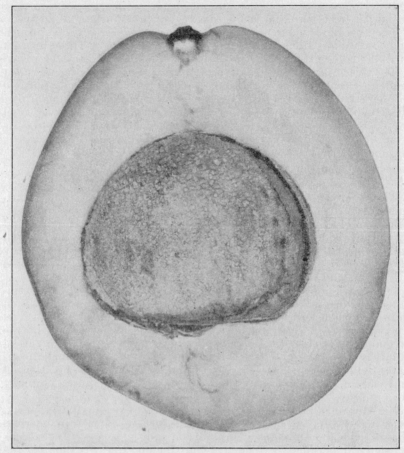

FIGURE 12.—Trapp avocado, the first named variety to be propagated by budding and grafting. Selected and propagated by George B. Cellon, of Miami, Fla., in 1901

time the tree must have ample soil moisture to draw on all the time. In California irrigation is universally practiced, and provision for irrigation would pay well during most seasons in Florida.   Even with irrigation the avocado will not thrive in hot, arid regions, as it prefers a fairly humid, equable climate.

(3) *Varieties for planting.*—Scores of varieties at one time considered promising have been discarded, and the process is still going on. For California, the leading commercial varieties are Fuerte, Puebla, Nabal, Queen, and Taft.   In Florida, Pollock, Trapp, Winslowson,

Collinson, and Lula are now most commonly planted. Interplanting of varieties to facilitate cross-pollination increases the chances for fruit setting, especially with certain varieties more or less self-sterile particularly when they are grown in regions having warm sunshiny weather during the avocado flowering season. This self-sterility in the avocado is of a unique type, due to the synchronous opening and closing of the flowers, pollen not being shed until the second flower opening. Some varieties are morning pollenizers, and others shed pollen in the afternoon. By interplanting such reciprocating varieties, pollination is rendered more certain.

The rapid expansion of the avocado industry now taking place will necessitate the development of hitherto untouched markets through a cooperative program of advertising and education to make known the remarkable qualities of this truly American fruit. To this end cooperative associations are already functioning both in California and in Florida, thus affording a reasonable hope of financial success in the effort to add this unique fruit to our national menu. As a step toward diversification through the planting of noncompetitive special crops, this effort deserves encouragement and success.

T. RALPH ROBINSON.

BAGASSE From Sugar Cane, Once Waste, Now Is Valuable in Industry — Bagasse is that part of sugar-cane stalks remaining after the sugar-bearing juice has been removed. It consists largely of fiber and pith, and as it emerges from the mill it carries from 45 to 52 per cent of water. After partial drying, the material affords a satisfactory fuel for sugar-factory use, and until comparatively recent years this was the only purpose for which it was used. However, the quantity produced in the United States was greatly in excess of the quantity used for fuel, and the remaining portion represented a purely waste product, the disposal of which was a constant problem that was usually solved by wasteful burning.

Numerous attempts had been made to utilize this material, but it was not until about 1921 that a process was developed for successfully utilizing it for the manufacture of a lumber substitute. The rapid expansion of this industry created a demand for bagasse that resulted in this hitherto waste product becoming a valuable raw material. In fact, during 1925 to 1927 the low yields of sugar cane in Louisiana resulted in such limited production of bagasse that its use for fuel was largely discontinued, many of the factories turning to the use of other fuels and selling all of their bagasse at a profitable price.

Still Much Used for Fuel

The introduction of new, disease-resistant varieties of sugar cane has greatly stimulated the industry, these new varieties being grown on approximately 135,000 acres in 1927–28, while the acreage for 1928–29 may reach 250,000. Production of bagasse varies, depending upon production of cane and other factors; but a conservative estimate of the bagasse that may be produced from 250,000 acres is 1,125,000 tons of wet or 563,000 tons of dry material. The production of this huge quantity will undoubtedly result in the resumption of its use for fuel, but it is hardly probable that the part not so used will again become a worthless waste product.

In addition to the above-mentioned uses, bagasse may be used as an ingredient of cattle feeds, as an absorbent in the manufacture of explosives, and for the manufacture of a coarse grade of paper, while suggested commercial possibilities include its use in the manufacture of artificial silk and in the production of alcohol.

SIDNEY F. SHERWOOD.

BEDBUGS are Quickly Exterminated by the Fumigation Method — In these days of extensive travel it is scarcely surprising that bedbugs are occasionally encountered and accidentally carried into many homes. (Fig. 13.) The problem of eradicating them after they have become established is a very vexing one for the housekeeper.

To exterminate them quickly and completely nothing is more effective than a thorough fumigation with either hydrocyanic-acid gas or sulphur fumes. As the fumes of hydrocyanic-acid gas are deadly to human life this gas should be used only by a professional fumigator. Sulphur fumes can be used with safety by the average housekeeper, but it should be remembered that the fumes tarnish polished metals and have a tendency to bleach highly colored furnishings and wall paper.

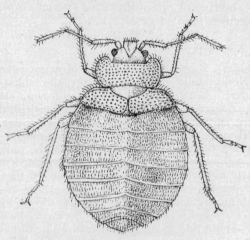

FIGURE 13.—Adult bedbug. Enlarged about 7 diameters

Although other remedies are not so quickly effective, complete relief can be obtained by the painstaking use of sprays, such as gasoline, kerosene, benzene, or a mixture of 1 ounce of bichloride of mercury dissolved in 1 pint of denatured alcohol, to which is added one-fourth pint of turpentine. If desirable the bichloride of mercury can be dissolved in water and used alone in a 1 to 1,000 solution. Since bichloride of mercury is a deadly poison it must be handled with great care.

The sprays should be injected into the cracks and crevices of the bed and woodwork of the room where the bedbugs are concealed.

E. A. BACK and
R. T. COTTON.

BEE BREEDING By Artificial Insemination Done Experimentally — Relatively little progress has been made by queen breeders and beekeepers in improving the races of honeybees, primarily because of the difficulty encountered in controlling the mating of queens. In nature the mating takes place only during flight, and never within the hive. Many attempts have been made to control mating. Enormous wire inclosures in which queens and drones were liberated have been used in efforts to secure controlled matings, but because of the limited range of flight to which the queens and drones were necessarily restricted, and the natural confusion and loss of direction experienced by the bees when thus inclosed, this means has not proved successful. Unsuccessful attempts have also followed the use of large greenhouses in which queens and drones were allowed to fly A number of experimenters have also tried to inseminate queens artificially in various ways by the use of instruments, but such attempts until recently have invariably been followed by failure.

Queen breeders, however, have had to find some means for keeping the races of bees as pure as possible. The races of bees found in this country differ considerably in their characteristics. The common black bee, also known as the German bee, readily succumbs to European foulbrood, a contagious disease of the brood of bees. Caucasian bees have a characteristic of using propolis, or bee glue, rather freely. This is a resinous substance gathered from the buds of trees and shrubs, and the habit of Caucasian bees of fastening the frames and movable parts of the hive securely with propolis is objected to by many practical beekeepers. Carniolan bees have a great propensity for swarming. Each race has its rather pronounced characteristics. It is easy, therefore, to understand why it has been necessary for queen breeders to take every precaution possible to prevent crossing of the various races.

A queen breeder who specializes in the production of high-grade Italian queens is forced to take precautions to prevent virgin queens from mating with drones of the German, Caucasian, or any other race, and also with hybrid bees, which may be present in the immediate vicinity; and similarly with breeders of queens of other races. Some accomplish this purpose by rearing an excess of drones of the desired race, thus minimizing the chances of cross mating; others go further and supply all beekeepers within a radius of 2 or 3 miles of the queen-rearing yards with purely mated queens of the desired stock, thus surrounding the queen-rearing yards with a preponderance of drones of the desired stock. The application of this method usually results in a relatively small percentage of mismated queens.

Experiments in Isolated Localities

Breeding experiments have also been attempted in isolated localities in which no bees were found. This method of controlling mating, however, is expensive and can not be used by the average queen breeder. Even when this method is used it is not possible to select an individual drone to mate with a selected virgin queen, and so the best that can be done under such circumstances is to secure mating from the drones of any one colony.

The United States Department of Agriculture has been using at its experimental apiary at Somerset, Md., a method of artificial insemination of queen bees devised by L. R. Watson, of Cornell University. It consists essentially in filling a very delicate microsyringe with mucus taken from the mucus gland of a living drone, together with a requisite amount of semen. The virgin queen bee to be inseminated is securely fastened to a small operating table and, with the aid of a binocular microscope of wide field, the vagina is held open and the syringe inserted. In unloading the syringe the sperm fluid, or semen, is first injected; this is followed immediately by the mucus, so that when the syringe is withdrawn the mucus is left in the vagina. The mucus hardens upon contact with the air, leaving a sort of plug which prevents the loss of semen. This same process occurs essentially in nature, for ·

when a drone mates with a queen the drone organs are torn from the body in such a manner that a mucus plug is left inserted in the queen. The mucus is later either absorbed by the queen or removed by the bees, so that the oviduct is not in any way obstructed after the spermatozoa have all found their way into the spermatheca of the queen. The spermatheca is a small sacklike organ in which the spermatozoa are stored and nourished during the life of the queen. Figure 14 illustrates the process and the apparatus employed.

Specialists at the bee culture laboratory of the Bureau of Entomology have been using the Watson method with an encouraging degree of success, although the method still leaves much to be desired. However, it is quite obvious that artificial insemination will permit the performance in a scientific way of experiments on the breeding of honey-

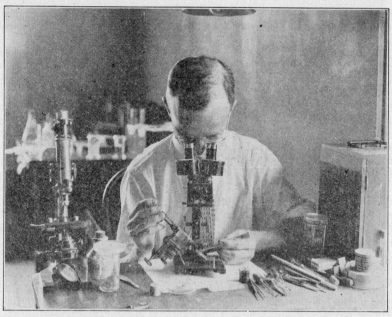

FIGURE 14.—Artificial insemination of queen bees

bees. It is also quite apparent that more simplified methods of artificially inseminating queen bees may be developed, as already one of the veteran queen breeders of the South is reported to have met with considerable success in artificially inseminating queen bees without the use of a syringe.

Method is Costly and Difficult

Because of the cost of the instruments employed in the Watson method and the great care that must be exercised in using them, the method will in all probability never be available for beekeepers, or even for queen breeders. In the present development of controlled mating, breeding experiments on honeybees should logically be carried on by State experiment stations or by the Federal Government. For this reason specialists at the bee culture laboratory are planning extensive experiments which will be conducted primarily at the southern bee culture field laboratory, recently established at Baton Rouge, La. It is felt that as much progress can be made in the development of desirable strains of bees through scientific breeding as has been made in the breeding of livestock and plants.

JAS. I. HAMBLETON.

BEEKEEPING Studies to be Made in South in Field Laboratory A study of the census figures on bees and honey, judging at least from the number of colonies reported on farms, would lead one to believe that the Southern States, particularly those in the eastern half of the United States, were of importance in the production of honey. Commercial production of that commodity in the South, however, has not been developed to any great extent, and few of the Southern States export much of it, the great majority of them having to buy honey from some of the Northern and Western States to supply the demands of the local market. There is every reason to believe, however, that in practically all of the Southern States beekeeping can be developed as a profitable and distinct agricultural industry.

The scarcity of accurate information about the floral sources of honey is probably one of the principal reasons for the lack of development of commercial beekeeping in this section. In the Southern States, nevertheless, are found many nectar-secreting plants which occur in abundance over wide areas. It is an indication of the lack of knowledge of southern honey flora that beekeepers there often report the production of surplus honey from unknown sources. A study of the honey plants of the South, with a general mapping of the areas in which they occur, together with the application of sound beekeeping practice, will be one of the objectives of the new Southern States bee culture field laboratory which has recently been established at Baton Rouge, La.

During the last 20 years, and particularly during the last decade, the production of package bees, shipped either on combs or combless, has been developed as a definite industry, and at the present time many beekeepers in the South manage their apiaries almost exclusively for producing package bees. These packages are shipped into the Northern States and into Canada to replace the heavy winter losses annually sustained there. Package bees are also now being largely used in establishing new apiaries throughout the United States. To a great extent the Northern States are already depending upon southern beekeepers for package bees. In connection with the production of package bees many problems must be solved before this specialized industry can be placed upon a firm financial basis. The package producer must learn how to produce young bees in great numbers at a specified time, as package bees must be received by northern beekeepers within an interval of two or three weeks in the early spring. Old bees for this purpose are practically worthless. Methods must also be worked out to prevent losses sustained in the transportation of bees in package form. These, and many other problems connected with the package industry, will be given consideration by the new field laboratory.

Queen Rearing in the South

The queen-rearing industry is likewise largely confined to the Southern States. The season in the South is long, and the secretion of nectar is such that it lends itself excellently to the production of queen bees. Most of the so-called commercial queen breeders, however, should really be classed as queen raisers, as very little real systematic work along breeding lines is being conducted by the large producers. Several classes of queen bees are regularly offered for sale—untested, tested, select tested, and breeding. Queens are also largely designated by color, such as leather-colored Italians, golden Italians, three-banded Italians, etc. None of these designations, however, have been clearly defined, and there is no uniformity of opinion as to what constitutes, for example, a three-banded tested Italian queen. The southern bee culture field laboratory will undertake to define, if possible, the various classes of queens now offered for sale and will devote considerable time to studying the advisability of having United States standards for queens and for package bees.

JAS. I. HAMBLETON.

BEESWAX Goes Largely Into Candles But Has Numerous Other Uses Candle making takes more beeswax than any other one industry. The principal demand for beeswax candles comes from the Catholic Church. In the early days of the church, when other waxes were little known, canon law decreed that candles for mass and benediction should

FIGURE 15.—Making beeswax candles by hand-dipping process. Cotton wicks suspended on a revolving frame are dipped into melted beeswax and after the wax has hardened are dipped again and again until the required diameter is reached

contain a majority of beeswax, and this decree still holds. Some candles for church purposes contain only 51 per cent of beeswax, while in others there is up to 100 per cent of pure beeswax. Some manufacturers stamp on each candle the percentage of beeswax it contains.

Most beeswax candles are still made by hand dipping. The wicks are suspended from a frame, and a number are dipped at the same time into a vat of the liquid beeswax mixture. After the wax has hardened somewhat on the wicks, the candles are dipped again and again until the required diameter is reached. Finally, the candles are made smooth, and fluted ends are pressed on by machinery. In some factories modern molding machines are used to permit a larger output of candles.

The next most important use of beeswax is for comb foundation. This is sheeted wax about one-eighth of an inch thick, embossed on both sides with indentations having the exact shape and form of the bottom of honeycomb cells. When the foundation is placed in the hive the bees build it out into full-length comb. Its purpose is to save work on the part of the bees and thus permit them to put more of their energy into the gathering of nectar. As a preliminary step,

FIGURE 16.—Beeswax being sheeted and rolled into strips preparatory to being stamped into comb foundation

the beeswax as it comes from the beekeeper is refined by careful heating and slow cooling to separate the wax completely from all foreign matter.

The use of beeswax in the manufacture of cosmetics is growing. White or bleached beeswax is desired for face creams and lip sticks, as it is said to be less oily than the yellow, and the bleaching process makes it harder. In the manufacture of cold creams and other toilet creams, beeswax is usually mixed with mineral oil, petrolatums, or other fatty bases.

Beeswax is incorporated in some ointments and salves, and old-style porous plasters are coated with a preparation containing beeswax, because it forms a protecting film over the surfaces to which it is applied.

Large quantities of light-colored beeswax, often mixed with paraffin, are used in making impressions for false teeth and bridge work. Pure beeswax is put up in thin sheets for building bites and contours on trial plates, and in cake form for taking impressions.   In combination with paraffin and color it is sold for impression work.   Base plate wax, used in setting up artificial teeth when a whole plate is made, contains from one-third to one-half of pure beeswax.

Beeswax is used extensively in shoe polish. Manufacturers of leather dressings take some, while a large volume is used in floor polishes.

As beeswax is not attacked by acids, it is used in linings of carboys for holding acids, and electrotypers use it for modeling purposes. Beeswax is used in making dull varnishes and as a basis for embossing. Interior-wood finishers add turpentine to beeswax to give a high polish to furniture. Wax figures for displaying wearing apparel and headdresses require considerable wax. Tailors and thread makers take some beeswax for waxing threads, and small cakes are sold to needleworkers. Laundry supply houses and cleaning establishments use beeswax for cleaning irons.

Sailmakers mix beeswax with rosin and paraffin for preserving their twine, for use between each seam that is sewed together in a sail, and for making the wire rope in the sails sufficiently rough so that the canvass will not slip when it is sewed around it. Beeswax is mixed with rosin and linseed oil to make the grafting wax used by fruit growers.

These are only some of the more important uses of beeswax; it is employed in many other ways.

HAROLD J. CLAY.

BEEF Grading and Stamping Protects Consumer's Interest   The question "Why is it I can't get good quality beef?" is asked on every side. The frequency with which it is repeated tends to illustrate the seriousness of the situation and demonstrates the need for some preventive measures.

Investigations have shown that the majority of consumers do not know how to select beef on the basis of quality. Many do not know that there is a wide range of quality in beef.   Some expect to purchase tender and appetizing beef that is all lean meat and do not know that a percentage of fat is essential to tenderness and a high degree of palatability.   Others when questioned as to the points on which they base their selections say they look for beef with yellow fat.   These erroneous ideas have been handed down for generations with the result that skepticism concerning beef quality has tended to increase. Hence the frequency of the question "Why is it I can't get good quality beef?"

Beef of quality that will satisfy the average person is generally available. But beef without some fat will not make satisfactory roasts and steaks because it lacks the essential elements which contribute to tenderness and palatability, and beef with yellow fat does not give satisfaction to those who appreciate quality, for yellow fat in beef is usually associated with beef from dairy cows. Generally these are not slaughtered until after they have ceased to be economical milk producers and have passed the age when it might have been possible to convert them into satisfactory meat cuts for the table.

Beef possesses a wide range of quality, but this fact has not been generally known, especially by housewives.

It was because of these conditions and the uncertainties which accompanied the consumers' beef purchases that the Government beef grading and stamping service was inaugurated in May, 1927, at 10 of the larger slaughtering centers as an experiment to determine its practicability. Results have shown that such a service is not only practicable but that it is valuable to both consumers and livestock producers.

Means of Identifying Quality

It is valuable to consumers in that it provides a means of identifying the grade or quality of the beef they purchase. They no longer are compelled to rely on the advice of the market man. The Government grade stamp on the beef is the Government's guaranty of quality to the consumer. That consumers generally are willing to pay for quality in beef when they have authoritative assurance of quality has been forcefully demonstrated since the grading service

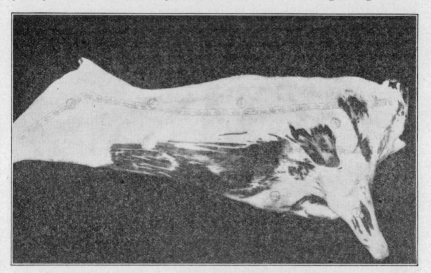

FIGURE 17.—Graded and stamped side of beef. The ribbon stamp shows that the beef is of Choice grade and that it is steer beef rather than cow or bull beef. The round inspection stamp guarantees the soundness and wholesomeness of the meat

has been in effect. The Government's grade stamp on the beef provides this assurance.

The grading and stamping service is valuable to livestock producers because it eliminates possible substitution and misrepresentation in the sale of products to consumers. Choice grade beef, when marked with the Government's stamp, is sold as Choice grade beef. The same is true with Prime grade beef, Good grade beef, and all other grades. Those who produce the better grades do not have to compete with those who produce the poorer grades; their product is sold for exactly what it is because the grade stamp guarantees its quality.

Furthermore, the quality represented by a given grade is uniform the country over, and from season to season, for the factors by which the grade of a carcass is determined are not influenced by environment, location, or season.

Consumers should become familiar with the grade names and should understand their significance. Prime grade represents the highest quality, Choice grade the next highest, followed by Good grade, Medium grade, and Common grade.

Beef carcasses and cuts are graded and stamped at the packing plant by official Government beef graders, many of whom have qualified for this work by a lifetime experience.

Each Retail Cut Bears Stamp Mark

After the grader determines the proper grade of a given carcass of beef, he applies the stamp. Beginning at the hind shank with a continuous rolling motion to the neck, the stamp leaves a ribbonlike imprint on each side of the carcass. The stamp is so placed that at least a portion of its imprint is left on each retail cut. The stamp is for the benefit of consumers, that they may select the particular grade of beef desired. The ink used in this process of stamping is made of harmless vegetable compounds, and the stamp's impression on the beef does not detract from its appearance. This service benefits consumers because the grade is stamped on the beef, and, as the grades represent rather definite degrees of quality, price ranges can be adjusted to quality. The Government grade stamp is the consumers' guaranty of quality.

W. C. DAVIS.

BEEF Should Be Bought and Cooked According to Both Quality and Cut his; it is the housewife's. Meat use to which it can best be put.

Much is heard about the butcher's method of cutting beef. In reality, the meat retailer has no method of his own. He uses one, but it is not Meat is selected and cut according to the The various cooking methods devel-

oped by the women-folk are the basis for the butcher's cutting methods. The most tender kinds and cuts of meat can be broiled and fried successfully. The less tender parts should be "swissed" or pot roasted. Those that are still less tender must be cooked as

FIGURE 18.—Roast beef. It takes well-bred, well-fattened animals to produce tender, juicy roasts and steaks

brown stews, and still other parts are used for soup stock.

The housewife who appreciates these natural differences in the various kinds and cuts of meat will select the kind best suited to her needs from the standpoint of her table and her pocketbook. She will understand that most cuts can be made into palatable meat dishes, if properly prepared, and she will decide the use to which her meat purchase is to be put before she makes her purchase. (Figs. 18, 19, 20.)

Guides in Purchasing Meat

There are several guides available for the meat purchasers who desire to select the more tender cuts. The higher grades are usually well finished, or, in plainer words, they show considerable fat. Although

it is true that many people do not care for fat, the fact remains
that a liberal covering on the outside of the meat and a mixing or

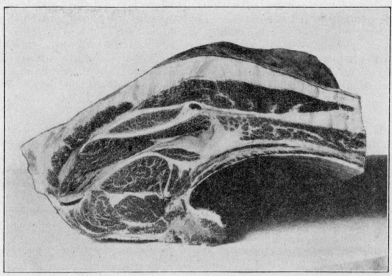

FIGURE 19.—A Prime beef chuck. This chuck has such high quality that it would yield some
excellent steaks and oven roasts

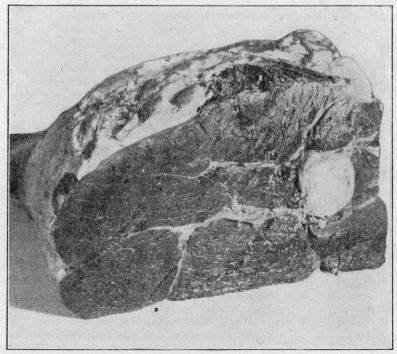

FIGURE 20.—Medium round, too deficient in fat, marbling, and fineness of grain to make a tender
steak. It should be braised or pot roasted

marbling of fat flakes throughout the lean are a normal part of choice
meat. Perhaps some would call it waste, but it has served its purpose

and been worth the money in the increased quality of the lean. Choice beef is normally a bright or cherry red and the fat a white or cream color as contrasted with the yellow fat and dark-red lean of the meat from plainer cattle. There are several exceptions to these color guides, however, and they should not be followed too closely. The backbone of a young animal is soft and red in contrast to the harder, whiter bone of an older one. Parts of the animal's carcass that have been most freely exercised, such as the neck, shank, and flank, contain tougher meat than the larger, less-used muscles of the ribs and loin.

Knowledge of Cuts Aids in Cooking Them

It is not difficult to learn the characteristic bone and muscle shapes of the various cuts of meat, but it requires practice. Those who are interested in learning meat facts can always make more progress under the guidance of an experienced and reliable meat merchant, one who learns his customers' needs and is interested in satisfying them.

All butchers are not alike, either in their knowledge of meat or in their willingness to aid their patrons, but many are more than glad to assist in the proper recognition and identification of the kind of meat that patrons wish to buy.

Quality meat costs more than other meat for the same reason that quality products of all kinds are in higher demand. But if the consumer is familiar with the quality and cut of meat which he is buying and with the cooking methods best adapted to that particular piece of meat, appetizing and nourishing meat dishes can be prepared, regardless of the cost, whether the piece is steak, roast, or stew.

H. K. WARNER.

BEEF Steers Produced on Range Should Show Maximum Weight for Age Weight for age is a factor of prime importance to producers of range cattle whether the feeders are sold by weight or by the head. While at the present time many feeders are sold by the head, the practice of selling by weight is gaining favor, and it is still more advantageous to the cattleman who has produced the maximum weight for a certain age. The man who has produced a growthy, thrifty, uniform drove of cattle which are carrying all the weight reasonably expected for their age is in a position to profit by selling by weight. If these cattle are to be shipped they offer an advantage over inferior or stunted cattle, since the net return per head is considerably larger.

Although a Corn Belt farmer who is an experienced feeder has learned to reject "dogies," or feeders which are not up to standard in size and weight for their age, it is nevertheless a fact that a considerable number of feeder cattle are bought on the market each year by inexperienced feeders who are unable to recognize the stunted cattle. This is particularly true when they have been cut out of a number of loads of better stock and grouped together so as to be sold, very likely, by a smooth-talking scalper. These farmers may be feeding cattle for the first time, and an unprofitable experience with cattle they do not know have been stunted will very likely discourage them so that they will discontinue the cattle-feeding business. It is true that any appreciable reduction in the number of men feeding cattle adversely affects the rangeman's market, for it lessens the competition between feeders and packer buyers. The sale of inferior animals brings a lower immediate return per head to the producer and eventually tends to reduce profits still more by bringing about a lessened demand for feeders.

Better Livestock Methods Pay

It is likewise true that an improvement in cattle-raising methods under which low-grade, stunted, or otherwise undesirable cattle are no longer raised, but only thrifty, uniform cattle of good quality are put on the market, is a substantial means of obtaining a larger return per head to the cattleman. Moreover, cattle feeders who are pleased at the progress their cattle make in the feed lot, and a consuming public which regularly obtains only good-quality beef, tend in the long run to keep the range cattleman's business on a profitable basis.

Greater weight for age, then, which will mean greater return to the producer may be accomplished by using better bulls, practicing more careful selection of female stock for replacement of cows in the breeding herd (fig. 21), more careful management of the range to insure ade-

FIGURE 21.—A breeding herd of the type that puts the weight on the offspring

quate grazing, and providing adequate water so that stock will not be forced to travel long distances to drink or be compelled to get along with less than is needed for most favorable growth. Seasonal dipping controls parasites which keep cattle from making normal gains.

A point seldom carefully considered by the rangeman is his operating cost in terms of pounds of beef produced. It may appear to be the easiest way out at times to let the breeding herd and even the young cattle get along on the range the best way they can—to compel them to rustle for their feed and water—but a smaller animal with less weight than normal results from such a practice. This means fewer pounds of beef turned off at the end of the year and greater operating cost per pound, since the expense of branding, herding, gathering, salting, vaccinating, dehorning, grazing, and shipping has not been reduced. Moreover, these stunted cattle bring less per pound and may even cause a reduction in price per pound of the better cattle with which they are sold. Hence the producer has reduced his chance for profit in two directions.

This factor of maximum weight for age can result only from breeding the right type of cattle and from proper feeding. Early maturity is essential, but this factor is not necessarily associated with a compact, small-type individual.

In the range country it is essential to have a certain amount of ruggedness and ranginess in the cattle for them to utilize the range to best advantage. The breeders who are supplying the top-feeder cattle to-day have developed breeding herds with these characters combined with early maturity.

Feeding is as important as breeding. Though beef calves can not be developed properly unless they possess beefy characteristics resulting from the breeding of real, beef-type ancestry they must be given the feed sufficient to meet their needs.

Feeding Bulls on the Range

In the range country it is not always practical to do much feeding, except during the months when the herd is in winter quarters. A few

FIGURE 22.—A satisfactory method of increasing the weight of calves is by feeding them grain within a creep before weaning

breeders, however, who depend on year-round range, make a practice of feeding their herd bulls out on the range. This may not appear to be practical, yet if the ranch is well organized it can be done without much difficulty. The benefits of such a practice are easily observed in the offspring. On ranches, where some fattening is done and the herd is easily accessible, it is often desirable to give the calves a little feed while they are running with their dams. A creep (fig. 22) is useful in this connection. A mixture of grain and cake can be placed in troughs within the creep, so as to be accessible to the calves at almost any time. It will be necessary, perhaps, to spend a little time in getting the calves used to entering the creep, but they soon become accustomed to it, and little difficulty should be experienced.

W. H. BLACK.

BELT Failure Often   A belt is a vital link in many operations.
Caused By Neglect   Belt failure causes inconvenience and
or Faulty Installation   delay, which is often more expensive
than the cost of the belt. Faulty
installation, neglect, and mistreatment are responsible for most belt
failures.

Leather belts should be selected and installed according to the advice
of reputable belting manufacturers, most of whom maintain a department for advising their customers regarding installation requirements.
A leather belt of first quality, adapted to the work, properly installed,
and kept in condition will run from 10 to 25 years, or even longer.
(Fig. 23.)

First-quality belting is cut from a definite part of the hide, extending
from 15 to 18 inches on each side of the backbone and from the root of
the tail for about 48 to 50 inches toward the shoulder. This part,
known as center stock, commands the highest price. It is more

FIGURE 23.—The result of proper care. This belt, which has been kept in good condition, has run
every day for 27 years in a country mill. Even now, the breaks are usually where it has been riv-
eted and not where laced or glued

uniform in texture and strength than the rest of the hide, and consequently is less prone to stretch unevenly. In wide first-quality belting
the backbone line can be plainly seen in the center of the strip. Narrow
first-quality belting is also cut from center stock, but on one side of the
backbone line. A lower grade is cut from side stock.

Close inspection affords the buyer some protection against low-
grade belting. A belt should be uniform in texture, thickness, and
width, and should feel uniformly pliable and firm, without soft spots,
hard spots, or limp places. A belt should not have defects, such as
cuts, holes, or brand marks. The grain should show hair holes of a
uniform distribution and size but should not show wrinkles; wrinkles
indicate that the leather is from shoulder or neck stock. When the
leather is bent grain side out over a round pole or pipe from 2 to 4
inches in diameter, depending upon the thickness of the leather, the
grain should not crack. When similarly bent, flesh side out, there
should be no wrinkling or lifting of the grain, which is known as piping
and indicates either side or belly leather, or poor hides or tannage.

Laps should all run in the same direction and should be well made,
with perfect overlapping and tightly glued edges, and without inserted
shims or thin pieces of leather to build up false thickness. Likewise,

there should be no shims between the plies of double or triple belting. The wider the belt the longer the lap, but no lap should be less than 3 inches. Laps should not open on bending the belt. Gluing or cementing laps is preferable to other methods of fastening, as the holes for laces or other fasteners weaken the leather.

A dull, oil finish, of a soft grippy nature, is desirable. A high, glossy finish, until worn off, promotes slipping and heating. For the sake of a light color and glossy finish many belts are deprived of a final touch that would make them more pliable and would keep them longer in prime condition.

Operating conditions are sometimes severe, the belting being exposed to water, steam, oil, heat, dirt, and fumes. As all leather belting is not alike in withstanding such adverse conditions, it is advisable to use belting that has been specially tanned or treated for the particular condition existing.

Overloading Shortens Life

It is false economy to select a belt that is too narrow or too light for the work. In addition to lowered operating efficiency, a belt constantly overloaded is under a strain that shortens its life. Often it is cheaper in the end to use a narrow 2-ply belt than a wider single belt. As a general rule it is best not to use a single belt wider than 8 inches.

A new leather belt stretches from one-eighth to one-fourth of an inch per foot. This is not a sign of poor quality. On the contrary, it indicates that the manufacturer has not taken out all the life of the leather by overstraining it. If this stretch is not allowed for in making the belt, it should be promptly taken up as it develops.

When making a lap or joint, cut the ends of the belt square. Do not trust the eye; use a try-square. If the ends are not cut square with the edges, a crooked belt, which will not stay on the pulleys, results. If laces or other fasteners are used the holes should not be punched too close together or too near the ends and edges. The holes in one end of the belt should be exactly opposite and correspond to those in the other end, for even tension on the belt.

Belts should not be run over needlessly small pulleys or on drives unnecessarily short. It is advisable not to run a double belt over a pulley less than 10 inches in diameter. Pulleys should always be wider than the belt. Vertical drives should be avoided if possible. For smooth, continuous running, shafts must be true and pulleys accurately adjusted. A leather belt works better with the grain side against the pulley.

Belts should be put on so that the feather edge of the laps on the outer surface of the belt does not run "into the wind"—that is, so that the pressure of the air or contact with objects while running will not lift the lap.

The tension of a belt is important; if the belt is either too tight or too loose it will slip, and the result will be both loss of power and a burned belt. A belt should be run slack rather than tight, and the slack should be on the high side so that the sag of the belt is toward the pulleys.

Guides should not be used to keep the belt on the pulleys. If it will not stay on without guides the installation is faulty. The constant rubbing against the guides tends to turn up the edge of the belt and to open laps.

Belt Needs Nourishment

A belt needs care and nourishment as it gradually loses some of its lubricating constituents. In time, if this loss is not replaced, the belt becomes dry and harsh, and the leather begins to rot, resulting in loss of strength and elasticity, and finally failure. (Fig. 24.) An effort should be made to keep a good belt in its original condition. Once a belt loses its original good properties no amount of artificial dressing can fully restore them.

When a belt is slipping there is a temptation to put on it anything that is sticky and will make the belt take hold. Instead the trouble should be located and corrected. Most sticky materials, such as rosin, pitch, asphalt, and tar, temporarily make the belt cling, but they do more harm than good, as they have no belt lubricating

FIGURE 24.—The result of poor installation and neglect. Unless kept clean, mellow, and in good condition with suitable belt dressings, a belt will soon look like this

properties and "gum" or glaze the surface of the belt, or "cake" on the belt and pulleys.

A suitable dressing penetrates and lubricates the leather, thus affording protection to the fibers and imparting flexibility so that the belt hugs the pulleys. Neat's-foot oil is considered very good, as is also castor oil. Among the best belt dressings are mixtures of cod and neat's-foot oils with tallow and wool grease free from mineral acids. Most belting manufacturers make belt dressings.

Belts should be kept clean. Dust and dirt should be frequently wiped off. Mixtures of dirt and oil can be removed with gasoline or naphtha, but precautions should be taken against explosion and fire. Oil-soaked belts should be sent to a manufacturer to be degreased.

Belts can often be cleaned by washing with warm water and a neutral soap, such as castile or white toilet soap. The washing should be rapid. Under no circumstances should the belt become wet, as it will then stretch and slip, and laps may become loose. Dressings or other materials that have caked on the belt injure it and cause uneven running. They should be completely removed. After the belt is clean apply the dressing to the outside while the belt is at rest, and let

it soak in over night.   The dressing should be applied evenly and
rubbed in with waste, felt, or some similar material.   If necessary a
light dressing may be applied to the pulley side, with waste or felt.
Even distribution and penetration should be obtained.   Belts should
be dressed to the extent that the leather feels mellow or pliant, but
not so that it feels greasy and soggy.   Because a little dressing is good
for belts, it does not follow that more is better.

Repair belts in time.   Prompt attention is cheaper and safer in the
end.   Joints especially must be periodically inspected and at the first
signs of weakening should be repaired.   A weakened fastener may
break but part way, and, as a result, the belt may be badly ripped,
even from end to end.

Belt stock and belts not in use should be stored on open shelves in
a well-ventilated room of even temperature and humidity, and not
where it is either dark and damp or exceedingly hot and dry.   A belt
that is not to be used for some time should not be left on the pulleys.

R. W. Frey and
F. P. Veitch.

BERMUDA-GRASS Pastures
Can be Made Profitable
By the Proper Methods
Bermuda grass is a plant immigrant which has added greatly to
the cultivator's task in the
Southern States, but it is in the
main a decided blessing.   It is a turf-forming grass, possessing both
surface and underground stolons or stems.   This character enables
it to spread and persist in the soil under heavy grazing, much as
Kentucky bluegrass does in the Northern States.   On the alluvial or
silt soils and the better clay soils of the uplands it is the most valuable
pasture grass of the Gulf States.   On the poorer soils, especially those
of a sandy nature, Bermuda grass is not productive.   Carpet grass is
better on sandy soils and will grow well on rather poor soils if they
are moist.

Bermuda grass has several characteristics which make it popular as
a pasture grass.   (1) It grows well in combination with white clover
and lespedeza, and these legumes enhance the nutritive value of the
herbage and lengthen the grazing season.   (2) Bermuda grass withstands excessive drought and thrives in wet seasons also.   (3) It is
widely distributed over the entire Cotton Belt and usually comes in
spontaneously when cultivated fields are turned into pasture.   Where
necessary it can be propagated easily by the vegetative method or by
seeding.

Many claim that Bermuda grass is less palatable and not so nutritious as other standard pasture grasses.   Such conclusions are largely
the result of poor management of the pasture.   After they approach
maturity and become stemmy, very few grasses are relished by livestock.   In this condition they contain a high percentage of crude
fiber, largely indigestible, and have a very low protein content.   It is
more necessary to keep a Bermuda-grass pasture closely grazed or
mowed at intervals than it is bluegrass pastures.

Three Methods of Improvement

The treatment that makes for success in managing Bermuda-grass
pastures is threefold.   (1) Seed legumes with it.   Common lespedeza
grows well in the Cotton Belt and in the summer adds greatly to the

value of the pasture. Like Bermuda grass, it starts growth late in the spring and stops with the first frost in the fall. To extend the grazing period of such pastures, therefore, it is necessary to mix with the Bermuda grass some winter-growing legumes such as white clover, hop clover, and black medic. These legumes are rather partial to limestone soils, but where they thrive cattle benefit greatly from the longer grazing season.

(2) The grass should not be allowed to get too large and stemmy. If at any time the animals fail to keep the herbage grazed off rather closely, the pasture should be mowed. Mowing removes the clumps of grass that have become too mature for the cattle to eat and stimulates the production of new shoots and new leaves.

(3) Light applications of fertilizer such as cottonseed meal or superphosphate will do much to keep the grass in a growing condi-

FIGURE 25.—Cattle find a good Bermuda pasture such as this palatable and make consistently good gains while grazing it

tion and are usually profitable. In 1928 an application of 150 pounds per acre of superphosphate to the Bermuda-grass pastures on the Iberia Livestock Experiment Farm at Jeanerette, La., resulted in an increase of approximately 40 per cent in their carrying capacity.

It is claimed that some of the best pastures in the Black Prairie Belt of Mississippi and Alabama will carry from two to three animal units per acre for 10 months of the year. These pastures consist in the main of Bermuda grass, Dallis grass, lespedeza, black medic, and white clover. Sweet clover and bur clover are also found in some pastures. Bermuda grass and lespedeza furnish grazing from May or June until frost in the fall, while black medic and white clover begin their growth in the fall and furnish grazing from January or February to June.

On old Bermuda-grass pastures the turf sometimes becomes so thick and sod-bound that the growth is slow and the legumes are crowded out. To restore a proper balance of legumes and stimulate the growth of the grass, such a pasture should be plowed in the late winter or early spring and seeded to lespedeza. In plowing the furrow, slices ought to be left on edge as much as possible. In this way the grass will begin growth along the edge of each furrow and quickly restore the turf. Before seeding to lespedeza the plowing should be disked and harrowed. Seeding on this 12 to 16 pounds·of lespedeza seed per acre in early spring will provide grazing for the animals during the summer while the Bermuda grass is reestablishing itself. A pasture renovated in this way may be improved still further by seeding 3 to 4 pounds per acre of white clover, hop clover, or black medic in the fall or early winter following the spring plowing.

Experiment Farm Results

Some striking results have been obtained in grazing Bermuda-grass pastures on the Iberia Livestock Experiment Farm. In 1927 a 25-acre pasture was grazed with 30 steers and 5 head of horses and mules. During August the steers made an average daily gain of over 2 pounds per head. In 1928 a mixed lot of cows and calves showed an average daily gain of 1 to 1.35 pounds per head. Two-year-old heifers gained 1.35 pounds and yearling heifers 0.85 pound daily. Such results are indicative of what may be expected of Bermuda-grass pastures when they are properly managed. Frequent use of the mowing machine keeps these pastures on the Iberia Livestock Experiment Farm in vigorous productive condition, and no difficulty is ever experienced in getting the animals to eat the grass.

H. N. Vinall and
W. T. Cobb.

BIBLIOGRAPHICAL Aids to the Use of Recent Agricultural Bulletins   A full and complete list of even the current sources of information regarding new publications on agriculture and the related sciences is obviously quite beyond the scope of a brief article, but it may be of some service to call attention to a few of the current bibliographical aids issued by the United States Department of Agriculture and other Government departments which contain references to these subjects.

First in importance is the Experiment Station Record, issued by the Office of Experiment Stations of the United States Department of Agriculture. This is an abstract journal covering both American and foreign literature on the following subjects: Agricultural and biological chemistry, meteorology, soils and fertilizers, agriculture and botany, genetics, field crops, horticulture, forestry, diseases of plants, economic zoology and entomology, animal production, dairying, veterinary medicine, agricultural engineering, rural economics and sociology, foods and human nutrition. Two volumes a year are published. It is an invaluable bibliographical aid for all research workers in the subjects covered. Another recent valuable bibliographical aid issued by the Office of Experiment Stations is the List of Bulletins of Agricultural Experiment Stations in the United States from their Establishment to the End of 1920, which is United States Department of Agriculture Bulletin 1199–D. There have been three biennial supplements to this list, the last one covering the years 1925 and 1926. The fourth, covering the years 1927 and 1928, is in preparation. The main list and the first supplement are merely check lists, but the second and third supplements contain both author and subject indexes.

Various Lists of Publications

Among other bibliographical aids issued by the Department of Agriculture mention should perhaps be made first of a List of Publications of the United States Department of Agriculture from January, 1901, to December, 1925, Inclusive, which was issued as Miscellaneous Publication No. 9–M of the department. This lists the publications chronologically by the various series. A combined index to Farmers' Bulletins Nos. 1 to 1000 was issued by the Division of Publications of the department in 1920. This index is now out of print. Leaflets giving lists of available Farmers' Bulletins, arranged numerically and by subject, can always be obtained on request from the Department of Agriculture. The Office of Information of the department issued in 1927 a handy list of all the available Publications of the United States Department of Agriculture. The former monthly list of publications of the department was discontinued some years ago. Announcements of new publications are now sent out in post-card form. A list of new publications of the department is also contained in The Official Record, the weekly organ of the Department of Agriculture. The Official Record contains in addition other bibliographical lists—namely, lists of new State experiment station publications, lists of articles and written addresses by department people issued in publications outside of the department, and finally, the list of principal library accessions received each week by the library of the department. While The Official Record is distributed free only to department workers and persons cooperating with the department, it is possible to subscribe for it from the Superintendent of Documents, Government Printing Office, at 50 cents a year.

Various price lists of agricultural publications are issued by the Superintendent of Documents, Government Printing Office. Among the subject lists of Government documents which that office keeps regularly in print, the following numbers are of particular interest to agricultural workers: 11, Foods and Cooking; 16, Farmers' Bulletins, Department Bulletins, Circulars, Agricultural Yearbooks, Statistical Bulletins, Leaflets, and Technical Bulletins; 38, Animal Industry; 39, Birds and Wild Animals; 41, Insects; 42, Irrigation, Drainage, and Water Power; 43, Forestry; 44, Plants; 45, Roads; 46, Agricultural Chemistry and Soils and Fertilizers; 48, Weather, Astronomy, and Meteorology; and 68, Farm Management. Copies of these various lists are sent free on application. Information in regard to the new publications of all the Government offices, as issued, is contained in the Monthly Catalogue, United States Public Documents, issued by the Superintendent of Documents. Since July that office has also been issuing a brief Weekly List of Selected Government Publications, the publications being grouped by subject in the alphabetical order of the subjects. Two other series issued by the Office of the Superintendent of Documents which are of great value and importance for reference purposes in libraries are, first, the Catalogue of Public Documents, of which 14 large, bound volumes have thus far been issued, covering the period from March 4, 1893, to June 30, 1919, and second, the Document Index, which lists the documents and reports issued by direct order of Congress.

State Publications Listed

State publications are listed currently in the Monthly Catalogue of State Publications, which has been issued by the Library of Congress since 1910. The publications are listed in each monthly issue by States only, but there is a subject and author index in each yearly volume.

Though a list of quite a different character, it may be of interest to mention here a 16-page leaflet issued by the Bureau of Education, Department of the Interior, entitled "Agriculture and Country Life, a Reading Course on the Problems of the Farmer." This leaflet is a helpful annotated list of 57 recent books on the various branches of agriculture.

Supplementing the printed lists which have been mentioned are various mimeographed lists issued by the library of the Department of Agriculture and its branches. A brief description of these follows: Agricultural Economics Literature, a monthly publication issued by the library of the Bureau of Agricultural Economics, contains reviews of important articles and books on agricultural economics as well as abstracts, notes of new publications, etc. It is described in more detail in another article in this issue of the Yearbook, on page 266. Agronomy Current Literature and Botany Current Literature, prepared in the library of the Bureau of Plant Industry, list the periodical articles on agronomy and botany appearing in current periodicals and bulletins and also some of the more important new books on these subjects. These lists are issued every two weeks. As the entries in both of these lists are printed on one side of the sheet, some workers make a practice of cutting up the sheets and mounting on cards the references of especial interest in their own work. Highways and Agricultural Engineering Current Literature, issued each week by the Bureau of Public Roads Library, lists the periodical articles and bulletins on the subject of highways and engineering. The library of the Forest Service issues every two months a list of current literature on forestry indexed in the Forest Service Library. The library of the Bureau of Entomology includes in each number of the Monthly Letter of the Bureau of Entomology the new books and bulletins on entomology. The Office of Cooperative Extension Work issues a monthly mimeographed list of new agricultural extension publications of the various States and the Office of Experiment Stations issues a monthly list of the State experiment station publications. The library of the department issues a monthly mimeographed publication entitled "Agricultural Library Notes," regular features of which are notes on some of the new and more popular agricultural books received by the library and lists of the new mimeographed publications of the department. Notes of bibliographies are also included.

Two Series of Bibliographies

In addition to these various mimeographed lists of current material, mention should also be made of two series of mimeographed bibliographies—namely, Bibliographical Contributions of the Library of the United States Department of Agriculture, and Agricultural Economics Bibliographies, issued by the Bureau of Agricultural Economics. The three most recent numbers in the series of Bibliographical Contributions are No. 17, Bibliography on Ice Cream up to and Including the

Year 1926, prepared in the Bureau of Dairy Industry Library; No. 18, Agricultural and Home Economics Extension in the United States, a Selected List of References, prepared in the Office of Experiment Stations Library; and No. 19, Cattle, Sheep, and Goat Production in the Range Country, prepared in the library of the department. The latest number in the series of Agricultural Economics Bibliographies is No. 25, Taxation and the Farmer; a Selected and Annotated Bibliography. Full lists of both series can be obtained on application to the librarian of the Department of Agriculture.

In conclusion it seems desirable to refer to one other bibliographical publication (which is not a Government publication) inasmuch as its particular field is agriculture—namely the Agricultural Index. This has been published since 1916. It indexes not only United States Government and State publications on agriculture, but also the publications of various agricultural organizations and a select list of approximately 120 periodicals. Nine numbers are issued each year. At the end of the year an annual bound volume is issued. Every three years the annual volumes are cumulated into a single volume.

The investigator and librarian having occasion to use agricultural literature will find it helpful to be familiar with the various bibliographical aids which have been mentioned.

CLARIBEL R. BARNETT.

BIRD Refuges Play Indispensable Part in Saving Wild Life — In utilizing native wild life for food and pleasure and in occupying for his own purposes lands and waters necessary for its maintenance, man has reduced the numbers of almost all species of native birds and mammals, and some he has exterminated. Corrective measures were at first taken by the enactment of protective laws, but long ago it became apparent that mere protection is insufficient to perpetuate the various species. To provide sanctuaries where certain wild mammals and birds may propagate, feed, and rest without molestation is fully as important as are other conservation measures.

Refuge areas are being established by the Federal Government, by the several States, by conservation organizations, and by private individuals, and so great is the need for such resorts that there is a large field of work for all agencies. The Federal Government has created refuges on suitable public lands from the Arctic to Porto Rico and from the Atlantic coast to the Hawaiian Islands. At present there are approximately 80 of these administered by the Bureau of Biological Survey to accommodate to some degree practically all the important species of birds and many of the valuable mammals found in North America. Congress also has enacted suitable legislation for the protection of animals and property on Federal reservations. Furthermore, to fulfill its obligations under treaty with Great Britain Congress passed the migratory-bird treaty act in 1918, and now it is generally conceded that the migratory birds that regularly cross the boundary between Canada and the United States are proper subjects for special protection by the Federal Government. On February 18, 1929, President Coolidge approved the migratory-bird conservation act, which authorizes Federal appropriations for the establishment of large areas throughout the entire country to be maintained as inviolate sanctuaries—feeding, nesting, and resting grounds where forever the migrating species of birds may enjoy complete protection. The entrance of the Federal Government into migratory-bird protection, supplementary to that afforded by the States, has meant the saving of many of the forms from extinction and the numerical increase of others.

Reservations Along Coasts

Many of the reservations administered by the Biological Survey are islands along ocean and lake coasts, and these serve as nesting grounds for sea birds.   (Fig. 26.)   The great need now is for additional marshland areas for ducks, geese, and shore birds.   The drainage of areas formerly frequented by such birds has forced the survivors to concentrate on the marshes remaining and in some instances to resort to marshland or alkali lakes where they have contracted disease and died

FIGURE 26.—A colony of California murres on a bird reservation on the Pacific coast

by millions. North American wild fowl can not long withstand such losses in addition to the thinning of their ranks by hunters. It is therefore of the utmost importance to the welfare of marsh-loving birds that numerous additional areas be set aside in suitable places throughout the United States where the former haunts of the birds have been reduced or where private holdings and extensive utilization of marshlands for hunting clubs have reduced the number of places where the birds may find sanctuary.

The few reservations now maintained by the Biological Survey that are primarily adapted for ducks, geese, swans, and shore birds are serving admirably their chief purpose. An example of this is the Lake Malheur Bird Refuge in southeastern Oregon, a marsh about 5 by 20 miles in extent, where large numbers of ducks and geese nest during the summer and where in spring and fall myriads of waterfowl stop on their flights north and south. (Fig. 27.) This area produces food in the form of wild fowl of very great economic importance, and in addition the birds produced afford healthful recreation to great numbers of western sportsmen.

Reservations in the Interior

Big Lake Reservation, in Arkansas, is primarily a wintering ground for immense numbers of ducks, which congregate there from large areas farther north. During the summer, when most of the ducks have returned northward, wood ducks nest there in considerable numbers, and this refuge has undoubtedly been an important factor in the restoration of these birds in that region, where a few years ago they were seriously in danger of extermination.

The Upper Mississippi River Wild Life and Fish Refuge consists of areas of overflowed bottom land extending in a narrow strip about 300

FIGURE 27.—A flock of snow geese that makes its headquarters at Malheur Lake Bird Refuge in southeastern Oregon

miles down the river from Wabasha, Minn., to Rock Island, Ill. In fall and spring these areas are frequented by great numbers of ducks and geese on their migrations through the Mississippi Valley, and a limited number of waterfowl nest within its boundaries.

The Savannah River Bird Refuge, near Charleston, S. C., consists of about 2,300 acres of lands that were formerly used for rice growing and were flooded in the course of work on the river channel. This refuge is frequented during fall and winter by many thousands of ducks from the north and during summer by great numbers of wood ducks.

The creation of a large fresh-water marsh at Bear River Bay, an arm of Great Salt Lake, Utah, on lands that are now mainly barren mud flats, was authorized by the Seventieth Congress. Engineering operations are under way for flooding the area and thus provide important nesting, feeding, and resting grounds for large numbers of waterfowl and other birds of many surrounding States.

While most of the reservations administered by the Bureau of Biological Survey are primarily for birds, all forms of wild life except a few injurious species are given protection on them. Some are favorite recreational areas, and their enjoyment by the public is permitted and encouraged to the fullest extent consistent with the purposes for which they were established. As wild-life lovers come to appreciate the wonderful benefits from such reservations, they insist that means be provided to increase the number and thus remedy in some degree the excessive losses that the wild fowl have suffered by reason of the destruction of their former haunts.

ERNEST P. WALKER.

BIRDS Can Be Attracted to Wood Lots by Various Measures and Practices — Bird conservation in the United States has no question marks attached to it. It is a profound conviction of the people that has been written into the best code of State and Federal protective laws in the world. Originally, the basis of much of this legislation was the demonstrated practical value of birds in controlling injurious insects, but later widespread appreciation of birds' esthetic worth has developed into a country-wide bird-protection sentiment. In addition to this fine public spirit, it is important that the human friends of the birds give practical attention to special local needs for their welfare.

The fundamentals of helping birds are to protect them as thoroughly as possible, to see that they have a continuous supply of water, to provide nest boxes for the hole-nesting species, and, when necessary, to supplement their natural food. As applied to wood lots, bird protection and attraction methods must be simplified. It is not feasible, as a rule, to adopt special protective measures, but vagrant cats can be eliminated from the farm, and occasionally a sharp-shinned or Cooper hawk or a red squirrel can be done away with. The more thoroughly protective measures can be applied, however, the better will be the results.

If a wood lot contains no small streams, it will probably be impracticable in most cases to remedy this defect. If there is a water supply not far away, some birds no doubt will nest in the wood lot, but if there is none within easy flying range, the other woodland attractions will go for naught.

Necessary to Provide Nest Boxes

The provision of nest boxes is an obligation nowadays upon all who would help birds. No longer is there the profusion of decaying or dead trees containing cavities which once formed the natural homes of a whole series of valuable birds. Unless nest boxes are provided for these species, all but the most expert drillers among the woodpeckers, and the few birds that fall heir to their abandoned nest cavities, will become greatly reduced in numbers. These hole-inhabiting birds, as the woodpeckers, crested flycatcher, tree swallow, house wren, nuthatches, titmice, chickadee, and bluebird, are among the most valuable bird friends of the forest, and action should be taken in every wood lot to furnish them places to rear their young (fig. 28).

Besides protection, water, and nest boxes, the birds' food supply should receive some attention. It is easy, for instance, in clearing woodlands to spare, here and there, a Juneberry, raspberry, blackberry, elderberry, or mulberry bush. The presence of their favorite wild fruits will induce more birds to nest in the wood lot and will help them with their food problems.   If wild berries are not already present, it will be well to plant some of the most favored kinds about the woodland margins.   The names of these fruits and the seasons when they are in bearing are given in Farmers' Bulletins of the Department of Agriculture, which also treat other phases of bird attraction.

Winter is Birds' Time of Need

Winter is the time of the birds' greatest need for artificial provision of food.   The foods commonly used for winter feeding include suet or other fat, pork rinds, bones with shreds of meat, various seeds, and the like.   The methods of making these supplies available to birds are as varied as the dietary itself.   They are described in Farmers' Bulletins of the department that can be had for the asking.

Feeding places for game birds and sparrows may be provided by erecting low hutches or making wigwamlike shocks of corn or grain sheaves under which food may be scattered.   The opening should be to the south.   These shelters should be inspected about once a week to see that they are not covered or blocked with snow, and to renew the food supply.   If predatory animals are attracted to such spots discontinue feeding there, scatter the food in a different place each time, and take steps to eliminate the predators.

In pruning trees it would be well also to allow for entertaining some of the seed-eating birds.   Alders and birches bear in their numerous cones a supply of seeds eagerly sought for by redpolls, siskins, and goldfinches during the winter.   The winged fruits of ashes and box elders are opened and the seeds eaten by pine and evening grosbeaks. Larches, pines, and other conifers attract crossbills, as well as some of the species just mentioned.

FIGURE 28.—The flicker, a wood-lot species that appreciates bird houses

A fundamental of forest protection everywhere is prevention of fires, which not only directly kill trees, especially those of the younger generation, but consume the humus so necessary to healthy forest growth and to water conservation.   Fire also damages trees not killed, by rendering them more subject to attacks of insects and to decay.   Prevention of fires is for the good of birds as well as of trees.   The measures that are recommended to minimize damage by fire, such as cleaning out old roads and trails as fire barriers and breaking up large woodlands into blocks by open fire lanes, also encourage the presence of birds. Birds are much more numerous around the margins and in openings of woodlands than in extensive dense forests.

Care of Wood Lot Aids Birds

Another good wood-lot policy, with regard to undergrowth, benefits the birds, for to them such growth is of importance in furnishing nesting sites and food and, together with the leaf mold, in maintaining a sufficient degree of humidity. Although it is contrary to general practice, foresters advise against grazing in wood lots. A closely pastured wood lot is recognizable at a glance; the ground is bare, puddled, and hard, and the undergrowth and limbs of the trees as high as the cattle can conveniently reach have been destroyed. The old trees are injured (stag-headed) by the compacting of the soil around their roots and by destruction of the humus layer, and reproduction is entirely prevented. Grazing and the continuous forest reproduction that is so necessary for wood lots are incompatible.

Gradual rather than widespread cutting of wood lots is recommended, as it interferes less with general conditions favorable to trees and always leaves some of the older seed-bearing individuals to provide for reproduction. This policy also is favorable to birds, for it permits most of them to resort to the same area year after year instead of seeking new homes, and in general involves the least change in the essential conditions of the environment. Indeed, practically everything that is good for maintaining the wood lot is good for birds.

W. L. McATEE.

BLACKBERRIES of Four English Varieties Are Introduced Into U. S. Two European varieties of blackberries have become important in the United States—the Evergreen (known also as the Oregon Evergreen, Black Diamond, Star, Wonder, etc.) and the Himalaya. The Evergreen was introduced from England into Oregon and Washington about 75 years ago and into New Jersey more than 25 years ago. It has become important in both regions because of its healthy plant, enormous yield, and firm fruit. The Himalaya is apparently identical with the Theodor Reimer, a German variety, and was introduced into this country between 1890 and 1900. It is prized on the Pacific coast for its vigor and productiveness and the delicious flavor of its fruit.

Because of the value of these two varieties in this country, all new English varieties are of interest. The United States Department of Agriculture has introduced three such varieties—Pollock, Sherlock jr., and Edward Langley. A fourth variety, Common British, was introduced by the Ohio Agricultural Experiment Station, and plants were sent to the United States Department of Agriculture for testing. The Common British resembles the broad-leaved type of the Evergreen found in New Jersey, Oregon, and Washington. Its leaves are not so finely divided, and the berries ripen several days earlier and seem slightly larger. In other fruit and plant characteristics, including vigor and type of growth, it is not easily distinguished from the Evergreen. It should be tested in comparison with the Evergreen, especially because it ripens somewhat earlier and may extend the marketing season.

Two Vigorous and Productive Varieties

The Pollock and Sherlock jr. resemble each other closely, and it is not certain that more than one should be grown. The Sherlock jr. does not seem to be quite so hardy as the Evergreen, hence it may be of most value in the milder portions of the regions where the Evergreen is grown and in those with still milder climates. The plants are as vigorous as the Evergreen, healthy and productive, and the crop ripens several days before that variety. The hairy canes are biennial at Washington, D. C., but are perennial, like those of the Himalaya, in California, where they bear year after year on the same canes. The berries are of fair size, firm like those of the Evergreen, with excellent flavor, and are easily picked from the long lateral fruit branches.

FIGURE 29.—The Evergreen blackberry, an important commercial variety

The Edward Langley does not produce quite as vigorous canes as the others; it is earlier than Himalaya; its leaves are mostly trifoliate, although some have five leaflets; its clusters are much more compact than the other European sorts; its berries are fully as soft as the Himalaya, but its seeds are much smaller, and its flavor is excellent. It is productive, but in California the berries are reported to separate with difficulty from the stems. In Maryland no such difficulty has been encountered. If it does not prove generally difficult to pick, its high quality and small seeds commend it. It seems more promising for Pacific coast conditions than for the eastern United States.

Sherlock jr., Pollock, and Edward Langley should probably all be trained as is the Evergreen in regions where the latter is grown. They are not adapted to the colder sections, but are recommended for trial in regions where temperatures below zero are rarely encountered.

GEORGE M. DARROW.

BLISTER-RUST Control in Western States is Aided By Nature   Control of white-pine blister rust is effected by the eradication of currant and gooseberry plants in and near white-pine forests, thus preventing the spread of the rust to the pines. This eradication is, in many cases, necessarily done by artificial means. The bushes are pulled or grubbed out or, where they grow in great profusion along streams, they are killed with chemicals. In the western white-pine forests of northern Idaho, nature is actively assisting man in this work.

Every kind of plant has special conditions most favorable for its growth, and changes in these conditions make it more difficult for the plant to live. The struggle for existence among plants is often very

FIGURE 30.—Idaho white-pine forest in which currants and gooseberries have been suppressed by forest competition

keen, and many of them die because of their inability to withstand the competition of their neighbors. This is frequently true of shrubs in forested areas. They grow vigorously when the new forest trees are very young, but as the trees become older many of them find the competition too keen and are gradually killed. The final result is that only those that are particularly adapted to growth in dense forests can survive. Currants and gooseberries are among the plants that are unable to withstand such competition in the denser forest types of northern Idaho, and nature in thus suppressing them is aiding man in the control of white-pine blister rust.

These facts make it possible to divide the forest land on which blister-rust control is to be established into temporary and permanent sites for growth of currants and gooseberries. The slopes back from the streams, where the forests can develop the densest growth, are termed temporary sites, because the formation of a normally dense forest will in time naturally suppress most of the currants and gooseberries. On these sites the artificial eradication of currants and gooseberries is unnecessary or at least can be delayed until the disease is near.

In places where the rust is already present, artificial eradication is necessary in order that the young pines may not be killed by the disease before they can form sufficient competition to suppress the currant and gooseberry bushes from which the infection comes. In such cases this same natural suppression is of distinct advantage in maintaining control of the disease, because it prevents the growth of new bushes following eradication.

Scattered through the western white-pine forests are local areas that can be considered only as permanent sites for currant and gooseberry growth. They consist principally of stream bottoms and swampy spots or rock outcroppings, where the competition of the forest is less severe, permitting uninterrupted growth of currant and gooseberry plants. These areas, particularly the stream bottoms, constitute the greatest danger of heavy infection of the pines by blister rust, because the opening in the forest is permanent and the kinds of currants and gooseberries growing there are highly susceptible. White pines growing near such areas must be protected from blister rust by artificial eradication of the infecting bushes, and the conditions thus set up must be maintained.

Over large areas of western white-pine forest nature has now accomplished the suppression of these dangerous currant and gooseberry plants. However, because of the recent spread of the disease in the western white-pine region, many areas of young pine growth containing unsuppressed currants and gooseberries require the systematic eradication of these bushes to prevent severe and rapid damage from blister rust.

STEPHEN N. WYCKOFF.

BLISTER-RUST Control Proves Feasible in the Eastern States — The destructiveness of white-pine blister rust in regions where it is present necessitates the application of control measures by forest owners to protect their white-pine stands from serious damage. The development of control measures in the United States began experimentally in 1917, when it became apparent the disease could not be exterminated. At that time nothing was known about control of the disease except that it lived alternately on white pines and currant and gooseberry plants, and that separation of these host plants should prevent its spread. Methods of eradicating wild currants and gooseberries, the cost of doing such work, and the distance which must separate the host plants to prevent severe infection of white pine were unknown. These problems had to be worked out to determine whether control of the disease was practicable. Investigations demonstrated that the eradication of currants and gooseberries within 900 feet of white-pine stands gave adequate local control of the disease under ordinary eastern forest conditions. This fact, combined with the experimental development of efficient methods of finding and eradicating the bushes at low cost, made local control of the disease feasible in the eastern United States.

Meanwhile, blister rust had spread rapidly and was causing severe damage to white pine in New England and New York. White pine not only makes this region attractive to those seeking recreation but also is one of the most important forest trees. It is highly valued and extensively used for timber production, reforestation, and ornamental planting. In order to protect existing white pine and to make possible its continued production in this region, it was necessary to secure the prompt and general application of control measures. The department in cooperation with the New England States and New York met this emergency situation by undertaking a joint program in 1922 to establish control of the blister rust on white-pine areas. This is accom-

FIGURE 31.—A, Unprotected; B, protected

plished by securing the systematic and general eradication of currants and gooseberries by pine owners. If these bushes are allowed to remain in the vicinity of white pine, the trees ultimately are killed by the blister rust.

The white-pine area of New England and New York is estimated at 8,221,167 acres. Wild currant and gooseberry bushes have been removed for the first time on 6,832,498 acres, thus bringing the disease under control on more than three-fourths of the white-pine acreage. More than 67,500,000 currant and gooseberry bushes have been up-rooted at an average eradication cost of 21 cents an acre. The initial removal of these bushes will be completed in this region within the next few years and control of the disease effectively established on protected areas. In order to keep the disease under continuous control, re-eradication of currants and gooseberries will be necessary over considerable areas at intervals of seven or more years, depending upon local conditions. At the present time control measures are being applied on more than 800,000 acres of land annually.

The affected States, towns, and individuals have cooperated effectively in the control work. More than 16,000 individuals and a large number of towns have cooperated in the application of control measures. Also hundreds of citizens who do not own white pine have voluntarily destroyed their cultivated currants and gooseberries to help protect this valuable species. This commendable public interest has made possible rapid progress in establishing control of this disease in the white-pine forests of New England and New York.

J. F. MARTIN.

BROOMCORN Harvesting at the Milk Stage Produces Best Brush — Though broomcorn is one of the minor crops produced in the United States, yet in certain localities in Oklahoma, Kansas, Texas, Colorado, and New Mexico it constitutes the most important cash crop for many farmers. If there are methods of handling and caring for a crop either to increase its yield or to better the quality, and incidentally to increase the cash returns, they are worth knowing.

The factors that determine the price of broomcorn are length and quality of brush. During nine years of experimenting at the United States Dry-Land Field Station, Woodward, Okla., Western Dwarf broomcorn has been harvested at three successive stages of development. The average length of brush varied, however, by only one-tenth of an inch after harvesting when the seed was in the milk stage, in the stiff dough stage, or fully ripe. Hence, the influence of time of harvesting on length of brush is negative.

It often has been stated that broomcorn brush will increase in weight as it becomes riper. In order to determine the facts, broomcorn has been harvested at three stages of development for nine years. The average number of heads in a pound of cured brush was 32.38 for brush harvested when the seed was in the milk stage, 31.87 when harvested in the stiff dough stage, and 32.12 when harvested when the seed was ripe. This very slight difference is not enough to determine when the brush should be harvested.

More Fine Fiber at Milk Stage

As the stage of harvesting does not significantly affect the length or weight of brush, any difference caused by time of harvesting or stage of development at harvest will be in quality of brush. This is expressed in terms of quality and color of fiber. Brush harvested at different stages of development shows practically no difference except that the more mature or riper brush loses more of the fine terminal fibers than does less mature brush, when the seed is knocked off in threshing. The difference in proportion of fine fiber is considerably in favor of harvesting at the milk stage, especially when compared with the ripe stage.

It is in the color of brush that the greatest difference is found when broomcorn is harvested at various stages of development (fig. 32). Broomcorn harvested when the seed is in the milk stage and properly

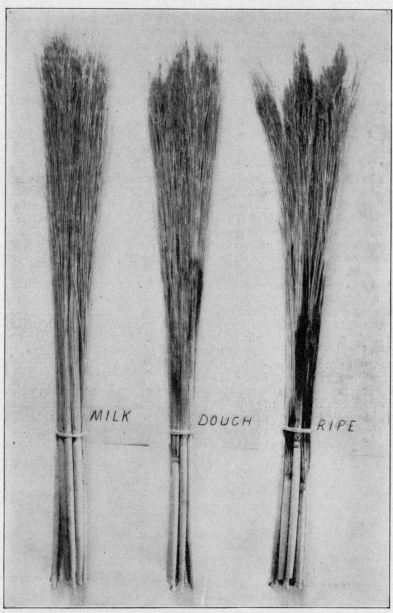

FIGURE 32.—Samples of Dwarf broomcorn brush harvested at three different stages of development; namely, when the seed was in the milk, in the dough, and ripe. That harvested at milk
stage is green, that at dough stage is somewhat discolored, that from ripe stage is badly discolored
and tips are warped. All crop of 1927, Woodward, Okla.

cured thereafter is pea green and of grade A for color. Broomcorn harvested when the seed is in the dough stage, about one week or 10 days later than the milk stage, shows some red "boot," or reddish discoloration toward the base of the brush. The tips also may be bleached or slightly red, and the grade for color probably will be only B. The brush harvested when the seed is ripe will show much red discoloration throughout the length of the brush and the basic color will be straw yellow instead of pea green.

Samples Appraised in Five Years

To determine the value of the brush from the three different stages of development, a sample from each was submitted for appraisal during each of the last five years. In Table 2 are given the comparative appraisal values in dollars per ton for each year and also the average value for the 5-year period.

TABLE 2.—*Appraised value (per ton) of samples of broomcorn brush*

Stage of seed development when harvested	1923	1924	1925	1926	1927	Average
Milk	$95.00	$90.00	$175	$100	$140	$120.00
Dough	70.00	67.50	125	70	120	90.50
Ripe	47.50	45.00	90	50	100	66.50

Broomcorn producers can determine the best stage at which to harvest the crop by looking at the color of the brush. In this experiment the development of seed was used, as it gives a definite stage of maturity.

No increase in weight of brush is obtained by letting the brush develop beyond the time the seed is in the milk stage or when the straws immediately above the knuckle are green. Brush of good color can not be produced if harvesting is delayed. The difference in price of brush harvested at the right time and that harvested later varies from $30 to $60 a ton, which often means the difference between profit and loss on the crop.

J. B. SIEGLINGER.

BULLETINS From U. S. and State Agencies Valued By Farmers Hundreds of bulletins and circulars covering a wide range of subjects are published each year by the United States Department of Agriculture and the State agricultural colleges and experiment stations. Do farmers read these bulletins and make practical use of the information in their farm operations? This is a question farmers can best answer for themselves.

Answers have been given by 1,676 nonselected farmers in representative areas of Minnesota, Wisconsin, and Ohio who were interviewed during 1927 by representatives of the Federal or State extension services.

Bulletins had been received from the United States Department of Agriculture or the State college of agriculture by 61.8 per cent of all the farmers interviewed. That one or more of the bulletins had been read was reported by 86.1 per cent of the farmers receiving them.

Information in the bulletins was found to be practical as indicated by the fact that 61.8 per cent of the farmers obtaining bulletins mentioned specific instances where use had been made of the bulletin information in connection with the operation of the farm or the management of the home. Of all the farmers interviewed, nearly 38 per cent were making practical use of information from Department of Agriculture or college and experiment station bulletins.

Information from Other Areas

It is interesting to compare the replies of these 1,676 farmers in three North Central States with similar information obtained from nearly 3,700 farmers in four sections of the country in 1912, or two years prior to the beginning of the nation-wide system of cooperative extension work as provided by the Smith-Lever Act. Of the 3,698 farmers interviewed in 1912, 43.3 per cent had received bulletins, as compared to 62 per cent of the farmers interviewed in 1927.

FIGURE 33.—Bulletin rack in the office of a county agricultural agent from which farmers select publications in which they are interested

Of those receiving bulletins in 1912, 84.2 per cent read them, as compared to the 86 per cent reading them in 1927. But 48 per cent of the farmers who had obtained bulletins in 1912 reported practical use of the information in contrast to nearly 62 per cent in 1927. The wider distribution of bulletins and their more extended use in 1927 as compared to 1912 is doubtless largely due to the development of the nation-wide system of cooperative extension work and the use of bulletins to supplement the other activities of extension workers such as meetings, result demonstrations, circular letters, and farm calls.

In order to understand better the value of bulletins from the farmers' point of view information was obtained in 1927 regarding other forms of printed information on agriculture and home economics available to the farm families included in the study. Approximately 93 per cent of the farm families took farm papers. More than 58 per cent of the farm homes received women's magazines regularly. Daily newspapers came to 79 per cent of the homes, and local weekly newspapers to 50 per cent of them.

Preferred Sources of Information

When asked to indicate the source of printed information preferred, one-third of the farmers mentioned farm papers and home magazines. Nearly one-sixth stated that bulletins from the agricultural college and the United States Department of Agriculture were most relied upon. Only a negligible number placed other forms of the printed

FIGURE 34.—Farm woman receiving from her county home demonstration agent a farmers' bulletin which contains information that will help her to solve some of her home problems

page first. That bulletins should yield first place in importance to farm papers and women's magazines in the farmers' estimation would seem but natural. The farm papers and women's magazines arrive in the home regularly each week or each month. Each issue contains a wide range of subject matter, and much of the material presented relates to the research and extension activities of the State colleges and of the United States Department of Agriculture. Much space is also devoted to the experiences of practical farmers and farm women in handling problems of current importance.

An effort was made to obtain suggestions from the farmers interviewed for improvements in bulletins, but those engaged in the study were impressed with the fact that farmers are little interested in the style of the cover page, character of the illustrations, exact length, and similar editorial refinements. They do desire a straightforward, interesting presentation of the subject matter published in a reasonably attractive and easily readable form.

According to their own statements farmers do obtain and make extensive use of the bulletins published by the United States Department of Agriculture and the State agricultural colleges.

M. C. WILSON.

BUSINESS Men Demand and Get Increasing Fund of Agricultural Information   With the growing realization of the interrelation between agriculture and business there has been in recent years an unprecedented demand from business men and economists for agricultural information. The postwar depression quickened a realization that had been more or less dormant before, but the interest has not abated as agriculture has climbed slowly back toward recovery.

The business man is not contented with theories and discussions; he wants authoritative facts. For these the industries have turned to the Department of Agriculture. The department is now placing the facts before the leaders of these industries through their official organs and trade papers.

The interrelation of agriculture and business is well illustrated in the case of bankers. Taking country bankers as an example, as agricultural conditions in their communities became acute the bankers called for more and more information for their farm clients; then as distressed farms came on the bankers' hands, they needed the information for themselves. Bankers' journals the country over are now meeting these needs and have been supplied with useful information by the Department of Agriculture.

Certain economists formerly contended that there was no such thing as agricultural economics. Now economists generally are vitally interested in agricultural matters, and all economic journals are reflecting this interest in full discussions of many pressing agricultural problems. The department's economists furnish some of the discussions as well as many of the facts upon which other discussions are based.

Interest in farm matters is not limited to those whose business is affected by agriculture. Scarcely any class of reader is uninterested. The best literary magazines are publishing essays and sketches on agricultural subjects, as are the best educational, historical, sociological, professional, and religious magazines. The Department of Agriculture has aided in supplying authors with many of the facts on which these articles are built and has helped the magazines in finding the authors and the articles.

Foreign magazines are now applying to the department in much the same way. An increasing number of requests is being received from them for agricultural material or for contacts with authors. These requests come largely from journals that are not strictly agricultural.

C. B. SHERMAN.

BUTTER Certified as Quality in butter is an object sought by to Quality Brings both producers and consumers. The Profit, Pleases Buyer producer seeks it in order to have a product which merits the top market price. The consumer seeks it because he desires the quality which will give him the greatest satisfaction and is willing to pay the price. How to obtain for the producer a top price and for the consumer a top quality has been a problem in the marketing of butter.

In 1917 Congress first authorized the Secretary of Agriculture to investigate and certify the quality and condition of butter. But it was not until 1924 that a marketing organization attempted to use the services of the Department of Agriculture to carry back to the producer definite information regarding the quality of each churning of butter produced and to carry on to the consumer similar information regarding the butter sold.

The grading certificate issued by the Government grader on each churning of butter produced by the 400 creameries who were members of this marketing association showed the quality of each churning. A copy sent to the buttermaker in the creamery showed him the quality of each churning of butter; when a defect was found in any churning he was advised how to remedy it. This daily grading of the product and the advisory service on methods of manufacture enabled the buttermaker to correct his methods promptly and thus to obtain a very high degree of excellence in his product. Since the marketing association paid the member creameries for each churning a different price for each score, each creamery always obtained top price for all of its butter which was of top quality.

Certificate in Each Carton

The Government grading certificate issued on each churning which scored 93 or higher was used by the marketing association as the basis for a certificate of quality which it placed in each carton of butter marketed under its own brand. This use of such a certificate of quality is authorized by the rules and regulations of the Secretary of Agriculture and the Chief of the Bureau of Agricultural Economics in the following rule:

An applicant for grading, or a vendor of butter previously graded by authorized official grader, may issue certificates of quality of substantially the following form, which is hereby approved:

CERTIFICATE OF QUALITY

Issued by authority of the United States Department of Agriculture.
This is to certify that the churning of butter from which the butter contained in this package was taken was graded by an official grader of the United States Department of Agriculture and that the date of said grading and number of the grading certificate issued are perforated (or stamped) hereon and that the quality (class or grade) was (_____) or higher.

Name of firm or applicant

Obviously such certificates of quality, stamped or perforated with the date of grading and evidencing the fact that the butter on that date was 93 score or higher is not only valuable and useful information to the consumer who wishes to buy a high quality product, but it is also valuable to the marketing association and butter distributor who wishes to capitalize the quality of the product and the fact that it has been officially graded 93 score or higher.

The use of quality certification of butter has been worth many hundreds of thousands of dollars to the producers as a basis for improvement of the quality of their product, and as an advertising medium it has probably been worth fully as much to the marketing agency. Finally, the consumer who demands best quality and is willing to pay the top price has reasonable assurance through the certificate of quality, backed by an official grading certificate, that he gets what he pays for.

Roy C. Potts.

CAKE of Different Kinds Needs Flour of Different Kinds The value of cake made annually by the commercial baker is estimated to be approximately $300,000,000. The baking industry consumes yearly for all purposes about 40,000,000 barrels of flour, 1,500,000 barrels of which is made into cake. From three to four times this quantity of flour is made into cake outside the bakeshop—in the home, and in restaurants, hotels, and institutions.

Cake may be divided into three general classes; angel food or sponge cake, loaf cake, and pound cake, each of which requires a different kind of flour. Angel food should be made with a short patent soft wheat flour. If a stronger flour is used it may be specially treated, or it may be mixed with starch. Good loaf cake is made with a somewhat longer patent flour, and the heavy cakes, such as pound cake, are made with the stronger flours.

Flour from soft wheat is the best kind for cake, but good cake may be made from the harder wheat flour either by separating the finer from the coarser particles and using only the finer part, or by mixing with the hard wheat flour from 20 to 30 per cent of the various starches or nonwheat flours. Starch from corn, wheat, potatoes, cassava, sago, rice, and even white corn flour will serve for this purpose with equal success. In some cakes, finely ground corn meal, partly gelatinized cornstarch and corn flour, or potato flour may be mixed with the wheat flour to the extent of 15 per cent without resulting in inferior products. Whatever kind of flour is used, if it is high-grade flour the part that consists of the finest particles is generally preferable for cake

Other Ingredients Used

In addition to flour, approximately $150,000,000 worth of other food products are made into cake each year. Shortening, for example, although used to a very slight extent, if at all, in foam cakes, that is, angel cake and sponge cake, and only in moderate quantities in loaf cake, forms about 20 per cent of the ingredients of pound cake.

Cake made in the home is much richer and consequently more expensive than that made by the baker. In pound cake, for instance, the housewife uses from 40 to 50 per cent more eggs, the most expensive ingredient, than does the baker. On the other hand, the baker uses a relatively larger quantity of both sugar and flour, the cheapest ingredients. As a rule the cost of the eggs is from 60 to 75 per cent of the total cost of the ingredients, whereas the flour costs about 7 per cent.

The quantity of cake made commercially is increasing rapidly, however, and unlimited possibilities are still ahead for the baker, provided he can make cake as good as that made in the home.

J. A. Le Clerc.

CALENDAR Has Played Great Part in History and Success of Farming Hunting, fishing, and agriculture were the chief occupations of primitive man, except when he was involved in conflict and warfare with neighboring tribes for either conquest or defense.

Success in farm operations depends very greatly upon the calendar employed to fix the times for planting, etc. Primitive man began, of course, without a calendar of any kind to guide him. First, he discerned the regular and frequent recurrence of day and night; then he learned that the moon went through its changes in sometimes 29, sometimes 30 days. Discovering these two calendar units, the day and the lunar month was a comparatively easy matter, but these units did not help him much in learning the time to plant and sow. Many centuries of time certainly elapsed before the number of days and months in a solar year was found out even approximately. Man's only guides to the cycle of a year were the slow seasonal changes from heat to cold; the high and low sun at noon, or its northern and southern points of sunrise and sunset, and especially the seemingly mysterious return of nature's growing season, seed time, and harvests. These were so irregular and indefinite that early man could not successfully tally the days, and even within historical times we find that thousands of years passed before anyone learned that the solar year contains very nearly 12$\frac{7}{19}$ lunar months, a fractional relation which even to-day baffles man's ingenuity to utilize in any practical calendar.

The moon has no influence of any kind upon the growth of vegetation or farm operations, many proverbs to the contrary notwithstanding. On the other hand, the sun alone is the ultimate source and control of all life on earth and the changing phases of vegetation are nature's true calendar, which varies little and never fails.

Egyptian Priests the Pioneers

These great calendar truths, including knowledge of the number of days and fractions in a solar year, were learned by the priests and astronomers of Egypt long before they became known elsewhere. Thus the Egyptian calendar ignored the lunar month and was composed of 12 months of 30 days each, the year being rounded out with a festival of 5 additional days. By watching and measuring the shadows cast by the great pyramids at noonday the priests were able to fix the exact dates of the equinoxes, a thing impossible and unknown to all others in those days. Aided by this vital information, and favored by the annual inundations of the Nile, the priests proclaimed from their temples the necessary instructions to the populace and tillers of the soil as to the best times to plant and gather their crops, mate their stock, and, in fact, gave Egypt the unrivaled prosperity and power it enjoyed in the days of its prime. The superior calendar knowledge of Egypt's priests and rulers was jealously guarded and kept secret from all other nations, and unquestionably was a very important factor which assured abundant crops, and explains and proves the truth of the old saying "There was always corn in Egypt." Babylonia and other competing nations were using crude forms of lunar calendars. Even the best of these which the ingenuity of modern man can devise causes wide calendar variation of the date of the equinox, that is, in the dates of seed times and harvests, ranging irregularly from 1 to 28 days, which variations repeat themselves in a cycle of 19 years, known as the Metonic cycle.

Moses the Greatest of All Calendar Reformers

Reared in the palace of Pharoah, learned in all the wisdom of the Egyptians, Moses, while leading his people to freedom from Egyptian bondage, set up, as is proven by an interpretation of the Bible, the first perpetual solar calendar recorded anywhere in history. By perpetual is meant that year after year the first day of the year was always the same day of the week. The calendar year began on or very near the day of the vernal equinox. The first five months contained exactly 30 days each. To commemorate the great events of the exodus which were enacted at the base of Mount Sinai on the forty-ninth and fiftieth days after leaving Egypt, when the Ten Commandments and many other laws were proclaimed to the Israelites, Moses joined these two days, the fourth and fifth (afterwards called the Pentacost) of the third month, into a prolonged double Sabbath and rest day. This made his calendar perpetual. The sixth month contained 33 days, and the first half year 183 days. The nearly equal second half year of 182 days, like the first of the year, began with a Sabbath which was on or near the autumnal equinox. Its first five months without the double Sabbath were almost exact duplicates of the five 30-day months of the first half year. The twelfth month, with 32 days, ended the year, and the new year began again on a Sabbath.

Although a definite leap-year rule is absolutely essential to the prolonged maintenance of any calendar, in order to take account of the fraction, 0.242 day by which the solar year is longer than 365 days, Moses, like the Egyptians, probably kept this knowledge secret among the high priests, and it seems probable that a complete week of seven days was interpolated in the middle of each cycle of 28 years.

In the vicissitudes of the life of the Hebrew nation the Mosaic calendar fell into confusion, or failed possibly from loss or misapplication of the leap-year rule. At any rate, we find that an imperfect lunar calendar replaced the solar calendar of Moses after the Jews returned from the Babylonian captivity.

Superstitious Reverence for the Calendar

In ancient times the calendar was made and controlled entirely by imperial or priestly authority, with which the common people had nothing at all to do. Out of this a superstitious belief has come down and is held by a few even to the present day, that the calendar is a sort of God-given institution which it is sacrilegious to alter or change. It is a fact, however, almost everywhere recognized to-day, that the calendar belongs to the people and can be changed whenever good and sufficient reasons for doing so are shown. Moreover, history shows that change after change has been made in the calendars of every nation, nearly always to suit the business, industrial, or religious needs of the people, but in some few instances to cater to the innocent vanity of some mighty ruler.

The Gregorian calendar now in use by every important nation of the world is itself less than 350 years old, and it has been in use in England and America less than 200 years. Even since the World War, Russia first, then the Greek orthodox churches, and still more recently the Mohammedan nations, have all taken over, in part or in whole, this sytem of reckoning time, and the evolution of the calendar is still going on.

Our present calendar comes down to us from the 10-month calendar Romulus gave to his new city, Rome. Less than 30 years later Numa added February to follow December, and January to precede March which it replaced as the first month of the year. The reckoning was on a lunar basis, which failed more or less in the next 300 years, and the Decemvirs shifted February from its place as the last month of the year to become the second month. Thus December, originally the last and tenth month of the year, became the eleventh month by Numa's change, and later (452 B. C.) was made the twelfth month by the Decembirs, as it still remains.

Again the calendar got into great confusion by the time of Julius Cæsar, who rejected the whole principal of lunar reckoning, acted on the advice of Sosigenes from Egypt, and gave alternate months 30 and 31 days, except February with 29 in common and 30 in leap years, which were to occur every four years. The month Quintilus was renamed July. A few years after the death of Cæsar, Augustus, to rival Julius and gratify his vanity, renamed the month Sextilius August in his own honor, increased October and December from 30 to 31 day months, reduced September and November to 30-day months, and made August a 31-day month by taking a day from February. This lawless arrangement is what inspired some poet to pen the lines—

> Thirty days hath September
> April, June, and November.
> --------------------------
> --------------------------

An Effort to Restore Mosaic Plan

The present-day movement to simplify the calendar is in reality an effort to restore the ancient and lost Mosaic plan to begin every year on the same day of the week. The last day of the year will be called "year day." In leap years another day called "leap day" will be inserted in midsummer as a holiday. Other changes plan to make the year consist of 13 equal 28-day months of exactly four weeks each, thus:

ALL MONTHS LIKE FEBRUARY						
WITH DAY-NAMES FIXED TO DATES						
Sun.	Mon.	Tue.	Wed.	Thu.	Fri.	Sat.
1	2	3	4	5	6	7
8	9	10	11	12	13	14
15	16	17	18	19	20	21
22	23	24	25	26	27	28

After a special study of the question by the League of Nations, all countries were requested to form so-called national committees to study and report upon the question of the public sentiment for or against calendar improvement. The committee for the United States is unofficial, but a number of Government departments are represented. George Eastman is chairman of the committee, and the writer is vice chairman and will be glad to give further information or correspond with any readers who may have questions to ask.

C. F. MARVIN.

CANNING of Vegetables By New Steam Process Holds Flavors Better — Recent investigations in canning technology have resulted in a new method of preserving vegetables which yields products far superior in flavor to those canned by the old methods. Peas, string beans, sweet corn, and Lima beans have been preserved by "waterless processing" in both tin and glass containers. The principle of the new method is the sterilization of vegetables in an atmosphere of steam instead of in water, brine, or sirup, as now generally used. The method has been used in a few homes, but, until recently, has not been followed in commercial practice. A small quantity of vegetables, however, were canned commercially by this method in the season of 1928.

The new method of canning is based upon the fact that steam sterilizes food more rapidly than does brine or sirup and at the same time does not remove those substances apparently necessary to the flavor. The steam within the container may be produced in either of two ways. First, the unclosed container, filled with solid food but without added liquid, is exhausted in flowing steam until the air is driven out, and then quickly sealed. Thus, when heated, the vegetable is cooked in steam. The second consists in producing steam within the container after it has been sealed. A small quantity of water is added to the vegetable in the container, after which most of the air is removed by a pump. The container is then sealed, a partial vacuum being maintained within. In the subsequent cooking the added water is readily converted to steam in the partial vacuum. The latter, known as the vacuum method, requires machinery in addition to that already in use in canneries, whereas the former requires only an exhaust box regulated to expose the open cans to flowing steam for the desired length of time.

When canned by the new method, string beans, for example, are graded as to size, the ends are cut off, all traces of dirt are washed off in running cold water, and the beans are sectioned. They are then blanched in boiling salt water for a few minutes, drained, and packed immediately into the containers. The filled cans are exhausted and sealed, or a small quantity of water is added, part of the air is withdrawn, and then the cans are sealed. The sealed cans are processed under pressure as usual. During the cooking positive pressure is developed within the container.

After the cooking, the containers are cooled immediately, whereupon the steam condenses, forming a partial vacuum which is considerably greater than that found in cans put up by the old method.

The new method is excellent for canning sweet corn. The corn is husked and washed, and the uncut ear is blanched in boiling salt water, after which the kernels are removed in "shoepeg" style and packed into containers without added sirup.   The corn is then treated according to either of the two procedures described for string beans.

The outstanding advantages of this method of canning as compared with the old method are marked improvement in retaining the flavor of various vegetables and lower cost of transportation owing to lighter weight.

LAWRENCE H. JAMES.

CATTLE-GRUB Damage Reduced By Various Methods of Control   It has been asserted by many that the cattle grub and its parent, the heel fly, cost cattle owners, dairymen, feeders, butchers, and tanners the enormous sum of $50,000,000 each year.   Although it has not been possible to verify these figures fully, the evidence is sufficiently strong to convince those who have studied the problem that the statement is not far from correct.   Yet, with the knowledge that this startling loss is being subtracted from the profits of the stock owners, little effort toward control of the cause is being put forth.   This inertia is probably chargeable partly to a lack of appreciation of the damage done, partly to familiarity with the insects, which has tended to breed contempt, and partly to a lack of simple, inexpensive control measures.

Stock owners are naturally interested in knowing how their animals are affected by these parasitic insects.   This information can best be presented by giving the essential facts regarding the life history and habits of the common cattle grub, and by indicating the many different types of injury produced as the different phases of the cycle are passed through.

When the heel flies appear on the first sunny days of spring, they begin at once to attach their eggs, whitish in color, to the hairs of the legs or lower parts of the bodies of the cattle.   Although the flies do not sting, their presence throws the animals into a state of uncontrollable fear, resulting in violent running of individuals and frequently the stampede of entire herds.   This violent agitation of the animals results in marked reduction of the milk flow in dairy cattle, lowered flesh condition in all animals, and, not infrequently, in death due to injury or to miring down in boggy ground.   The eggs hatch in three to four days and the tiny maggots, which are covered with spines, begin burrowing through the skin at the base of the hair where the eggs are attached.   This penetration causes much local irritation, resulting in stamping, and kicking, and in licking of the affected parts, and later, in a rough or scabby condition of the skin where the maggots enter.

Grubs Migrate Between the Muscles.

Upon passing through the skin the young grubs begin to migrate between the muscles, and in the course of two or three months are to be found on the surface of various organs in the abdomen and the chest.   Their presence is easily detected by the yellowish or greenish color of the inflamed tissues.

After several months of wandering through the body the grubs, which now have become about two-thirds of an inch in length, work their way upward toward the back of the host.   They often enter the spinal canal, and some evidence is at hand that certain forms of paralysis may be caused by their presence along the spinal cord. When the connective tissue of the back is reached, not infrequently large swollen and tender areas develop. Some of the grubs make an opening through the skin, and later a pocket or cyst is formed around each grub, in which the larval development is completed. The grubs become mature at the end of from 5 to 12 weeks, and are then about three-fourths of an inch in length and nearly one-half of an inch in thickness, dark brown to black in color, and well provided with rows of sharp spines. The grubs then work out through the holes in the skin, fall to the ground, and change into heel flies 20 to 60 days later, thus completing the life cycle, which has lasted about one year.

During the period of development in the region of the back the grubs often cause local abscesses which may discharge pus for several weeks. The carcasses of cattle slaughtered during the period when the grubs are present along the back are more or less damaged. Not only is it necessary to trim from 1 to 3 pounds of meat from such infested carcasses, but they are also rendered unsightly and so less salable.

It has not been the general practice of buyers of beef cattle to call the attention of the cattle raisers and feeders to the lowered value of animals heavily infested with grubs, nor is the fact brought directly to the attention of the producers that the hides are discounted on an average of about 1 cent per pound because of the presence of grub holes. Nevertheless such discounts are the rule and the producer must bear the loss.

Many Stockmen Neglectful

Although many observant and progressive dairymen and feeders and raisers of beef cattle recognize the serious hindrance to their business caused by the presence of these insects, unfortunately the rank and file of stock owners pay little attention to this important matter. It presents a problem with which the farmers and stockmen of every State of the Union are confronted, and recently acquired information clearly shows that it is becoming more serious, owing to the spread of a second species of grub known as the northern, or European, cattle grub.

Investigations that have been conducted thus far clearly indicate that the tremendous losses from cattle grubs can be greatly reduced by the employment of methods of control which are at present available, though they are certain to be improved.

As an addition to the old method of extraction by hand, which itself is not impractical under certain conditions, the Department of Agriculture has developed and is recommending other treatments which are satisfactory for conditions on the farm and about the dairy. To make measures for control or eradication successful it is necessary, however, that stock owners in general awaken to the fact that these insects are placing a heavy tax upon them; further, that they become familiar with the various methods of control which the department is recommending.

F. C. BISHOPP.

C ATTLE Malady Called More than 20 years ago Johne's dis-
Johne's Disease to Be ease, also called chronic bacterial
Fought Cooperatively dysentery, chronic bacterial enteritis,
and other names, was reported as
having appeared in the United States. Since that time considerable
study has been given the disease looking to methods of control and
eradication. For the benefit of cattle owners, the following description
of the symptoms of Johne's disease is given.

Affected animals show a loss in condition, despite good appetite and
proper food, followed by at first a moderate diarrhea which soon
becomes excessive, particularly after calving periods; and in numerous
cases death ensues. In some instances apparent improvement is
noted, only to be followed by a repetition of the symptoms at a
succeeding calving period. Apparently, methods of treating Johne's
disease by medication bring no improvement. Losses from the
disease in a badly infected herd are severe, although the progress of
the malady is very slow.

Diagnosis and Control Measures

Realizing the necessity for control measures, Congress, in its
appropriation bill for the fiscal year 1928, authorized the Department
of Agriculture to cooperate with the livestock owners, State livestock
sanitary officials, and others along the same lines as those on which
the work of tuberculosis eradication is conducted. Indemnity can be
paid for diseased cattle under the plan. This authority resulted in
some work being conducted in a number of States during the past year.

Methods pursued generally include the placing of the herd under a
cooperative agreement looking particularly to the proper cleaning and
disinfection of infected premises and the disposition of animals
classified as diseased.

A determination of the disease in a herd is made by the injection of
a product known as johnin, which is prepared in a manner somewhat
similar to tuberculin. The reaction consists in a rise in temperature
recorded as a result of regular temperature readings following the
injection. Diagnosis is also made by physical examination in cases
where the disease is known to exist in a herd. Avian tuberculin is
sometimes used as a diagnostic agent.

The results of the test have been fairly satisfactory, although the
production of johnin has not been actually standardized. Results in
one extremely badly infected herd, twice tested with johnin, have
indicated that practically 100 per cent of the animals condemned as a
result of the test were infected.

Recommendation to Cattle Owners

It is recommended that where livestock owners have any reason to
suspect the presence of Johne's disease in their herds by reason of the
symptoms indicated above, they confer with their local practicing
veterinarian and their State livestock sanitary officials. The disease
is not believed to exist to any such extent as to be unduly alarming.
However, it probably exists to a greater degree than is commonly
realized. Accordingly, attention should be given to this condition
so that the spread of the disease in a herd or community may be
prevented.

L. B. ERNEST.

CATTLE Tick Passes From Oklahoma After Battle of 22 Years The passing of the cattle tick in Oklahoma was marked by the release from quarantine December 1, 1928, of McCurtain and contiguous portions of Choctaw, Pushmataha, and Le Flore Counties. The eradication of cattle ticks from Oklahoma has been a strenuous struggle lasting 22 years. On July 1, 1906, the work of exterminating the cattle tick, scientifically known as *Boophilus annulatus*, was begun in Oklahoma, then a Territory embracing about half of the present State. Of the existing 77 counties, 61 were under Federal quarantine on account of fever ticks and 16 counties were free or nearly free.

At that time no better method than rotating pastures and the hand dressing of each animal with crude petroleum was known. Of the two methods, the latter, crude as it was, was the more nearly practicable. It may now well arouse wonder that with so impotent a weapon of offense a war of extermination was declared on the tick which was well entrenched in the whole of eight States and portions of seven others, embracing an area of one-fifth of the United States and involving no less than 17,000,000 cattle and 7,000,000 horse stock, which were required to be treated every 14 days for a period of from 9 to 12 months. At that time the dipping vat, as a means of destroying ticks, had not met with favorable consideration from the national directors of the project. Moreover, the construction of 100 or more dipping vats in each of the nearly 1,000 quarantined counties in the South would then have appeared highly preposterous. But the impracticability of applying the crude petroleum to individual animals with a grease rag, except a few cattle on the northern fringe of the quarantined area, soon became apparent. Necessity forced the use of the vat, and a reasonably safe and highly effective and cheap bath was gradually evolved. The arsenical solution and the dipping vat, neither of which was seriously contemplated in 1906, made tick eradication possible, and with their coming into use in Oklahoma and other States in about 1910, tick eradication really had its beginning.

Obstacles Were Overcome

The war waged by the Federal Bureau of Animal Industry and the State board of agriculture in Oklahoma against the tick progressed with varying degrees of success and rapidity, depending on the closeness of the cooperation of the two forces and the degree of interest shown by the stock owners and county authorities, upon whom the work depended for a considerable amount of the funds and for all enforcement measures. This task of eradicating ticks was not free from the inhibiting influence of small-caliber politicians, who, disregarding public interests, sought to encourage, create, and capitalize, to their political ambition, discontent among the stock owners. This, conceivably, required little effort, especially among small owners and renters, to whom the benefits seemed uncertain and remote.

Regardless of the character of the obstacles, they were met and overcome, though at great additional expense of time and money. Expensive, however, as the work has been, the benefits already derived have many times justified it, and those benefits will be continuous and cumulative and will increase in volume as time goes on. Already, even in the 16 counties in the southeastern part of the State, which were cleaned during the last 10 years of the 22-year fight, the number of cream stations has increased from 14 to 144 between the years 1923 and 1928. The improved quality of cattle found now in the released area, as compared with those when ticks held sway and prevented the introduction of blooded stock, is impressively apparent to those who have followed the progress of the work. Moreover, the degree of improvement is found in very much the order of the length of time the various counties have been free of ticks.

Better and More Milk and Beef

The average production of milk per cow increased from 234 gallons to 337 gallons in the period 1919 to 1925. Annual sales of butterfat increased more than tenfold during the progress of tick eradication.

FIGURE 35.—Purebred Shorthorn cattle, typical of the stock now raised in areas formerly ticky

While not all the increase in dairy production is due to tick eradication, nevertheless the growth commenced with and accompanied the progress of this work. Had not tick eradication been undertaken, any material increase in dairy production would necessarily have been confined to the 16 originally free or nearly free counties.

The quality of beef cattle (fig. 35) also has improved, in the various counties, to a degree comparable to the length of time they have been free from the cattle ticks. Recently plans were made to place at least 125 registered bulls of the beef type in McCurtain County—the last county to be released from quarantine—on the strength of assurance from Federal and State authorities that that county is now safe for good cattle from whatever area. A number of such bulls already have been introduced.

L. J. ALLEN.

CATTLE Tuberculosis Reduced 50 Per Cent By Testing Campaign It was a little more than 10 years ago that the cooperative plan of eradicating bovine tuberculosis was put into operation as an independent project. At that time only a limited amount of the work was being done, but during the year 1922 more extensive operations came into effect. A general survey of the extent of bovine tuberculosis was made that year by the various local, State, and Federal officials engaged in the campaign. Their estimates, based upon general knowledge of conditions, indicated that approximately 4 per cent of all the cattle were affected with bovine tuberculosis.

The area plan, which consists in the tuberculin testing of all cattle in any given area, such as a county, was taken up on rather a large scale in 1922, although during that year about three times as many

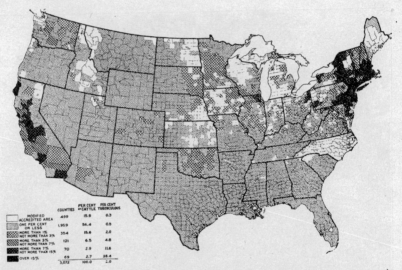

	COUNTIES	PER CENT OF CATTLE	PER CENT TUBERCULOUS
MODIFIED ACCREDITED AREA	499	15.9	0.3
ONE PER CENT OR LESS	1,959	56.4	0.5
MORE THAN 1% NOT MORE THAN 3%	354	18.6	2.0
MORE THAN 3% NOT MORE THAN 7%	121	6.5	4.8
MORE THAN 7% NOT MORE THAN 15%	70	2.9	11.6
OVER 15%	69	2.7	26.4
	3,072	100.0	2.0

FIGURE 36.—Note the predominance of the white and lightly shaded areas. Many economic benefits have resulted from tuberculosis eradication, especially in the modified accredited areas, shown in white on the map. Surveys show that infection decreased 4 per cent in 1922; 3.3 per cent in 1924; 2.8 per cent in 1926; and 2 per cent in 1928

cattle were tuberculin tested under the individual-herd plan as under the area plan. After two years had expired another survey revealed the fact that the approximate extent of tuberculosis in cattle had been reduced 0.7 per cent. In 1924 about twice as many cattle were tested under the area plan as were tested under the individual accredited-herd plan, showing that the area plan was meeting with favor throughout the country. The next survey of this kind was made in 1926; it showed a further reduction of 0.5 per cent, or that the infection of bovine tuberculosis among cattle was 2.8 per cent.

Extent of the Disease Reduced to 2 Per Cent

In 1926 about 8,650,000 tuberculin tests were made by the cooperative veterinarians, and 323,000 tuberculous cattle were removed from the herds in which they had been kept. More testing was done in 1927 than in 1926, and in 1928 the total number of tuberculin tests amounted to 11,281,000, while the number of tuberculous cattle found was 2.3 per cent. In the spring of 1928 a fourth survey was made and the result indicated that the infection had been further reduced; so that it had been brought down to 2 per cent or just one-half of what it had been six years before.

The accompanying map (fig. 36) shows the extent of bovine infection as of May 1, 1928. It also discloses the fact that in a limited number of counties there still remains a heavy infection of bovine tuberculosis.

The plan of placing counties in what is known as modified accredited areas was adopted in 1923. This plan provides that, when bovine tuberculosis among cattle in a certain area has been reduced to not more than 0.5 per cent of the total cattle population, that area, either county or district, is designated as a modified accredited area. In these areas the cattle industry can be conducted in a much safer manner. As indicated on the map this work has been in progress in many different States in practically all parts of the United States. In addition to 620 counties that are now in the modified accredited status the work is being conducted in about 600 other counties. On October 1, 1928, the last four counties in the State of North Carolina were placed in the modified accredited area, making 100 modified counties in that State.

Financial Benefits Follow Tuberculin Testing

The benefits of this campaign to the people of a county largely depend upon the extent of the livestock industry conducted. For instance, the State of Iowa produces large numbers of hogs, and it has been the practice during the last few years for some of the packers voluntarily to pay a premium of 10 cents per hundredweight for hogs originating in modified accredited counties. This has amounted to thousands of dollars in extra money paid for hogs. In counties where dairy cattle are raised and are for sale the price has increased from $25 to $50 per head for such cattle, according to quality.

Many owners of cattle in these counties, as well as in other parts of the country, maintain accredited herds of cattle. These herds are free from bovine tuberculosis as indicated by two or more annual tuberculin tests.

The work of tuberculosis eradication is cooperative in every respect and operates under the regulations and authority of the State wherein it is conducted.

A. E. Wight.

_____

CEMETERY Neatness and Beauty are Enhanced by Parklike Arrangement   Love ties bind us to the last resting place of those whom we hold most dear. As the years pass the significance of these areas is realized more and more, until they become invested with a feeling of reverence, almost of sacredness. This feeling is so widespread that legislatures have passed laws protecting grounds used for burial purposes, and the courts jealously guard them.

The early settlers buried their dead in the churchyard or in plots set apart on their own farms or plantations. Later, communities took the responsibility for providing appropriate places either by town, township, or parish governments owning burial grounds, or by private companies forming to meet the community needs. In the beginning graves were made in rows, the place in the row showing the date of burial as compared with adjoining graves. Subsequently, families had special areas set apart so that they might be laid near together, which eventually resulted in family competition in lot decoration, especially in the ostentation of markers.

While relatives continue living in the community these resting places are usually neatly kept, but on the death or removal of the remaining members of the family neglect is likely to follow. Usually this neglect occurs only here and there in a cemetery where burials are frequent, but gradually it spreads as the lots become filled.

Endowment Funds for Upkeep

To prevent such a condition endowment funds should provide an adequate annual income for the care of all lots. In modern cemeteries—even small ones—this is obtained by including in the cost of a lot a sum to be set aside for its perpetual care. Where this has not been done it is frequently possible to obtain such a fund by an appeal to those having relatives buried in the cemetery. Occasionally community pride will aid in securing adequate endowment funds for the upkeep of the grounds.

Neatness is the first essential of a cemetery. The most important factors contributing to this are a good turf kept reasonably short and carefully trimmed, especially close to the markers; graves kept filled, preferably level with the general surface; and markers kept straight and otherwise in repair.

Most cemeteries are overloaded with monuments. Modern practice limits the size of markers and the location of monuments, only a few of the latter being permitted, and these in locations that will add to the appearance of the cemetery as a whole.

The most attractive cemetery is one that is laid out with parklike characteristics, having winding roads, good lawns, and tree and shrubbery groups well located to make pleasing pictures in all directions. Lots are located in the lawns, being reached from the roadways over turf spaces between them. In such a cemetery lot markers are level with the ground. The most pleasing results are obtained when the grave markers are likewise level with the ground, although those from 6 to 12 inches high are far less objectionable than shafts and other large monuments.

In a cemetery thus restricted it is possible economically to keep the lawn in good condition, as the lawn mower can be run over lots and paths without interruption, and there are no lot plantings to add to the care and distract the attention. The shrubbery groups require less attention than the same number of shrubs scattered over the lots and are much more attractive.

Task Harder in Cemeteries Without Restrictions

In cemeteries without these restrictions the task is difficult. (Fig. 37.) Where all the lots are endowed for perpetual care the problem is simplified. If, in addition, lot owners will permit the removal of railings and copings, much will be gained. The substitution of turf walks for gravel or stone reduces the expense of upkeep and greatly improves the appearance. Graves level with the general surface are more likely to be kept neat than those that are raised. Trimming grass about stones is expensive, so that when it is possible to have but one marker

FIGURE 37.—A cemetery without turf, with raised graves and oversize grave markers

FIGURE 38.—A cemetery with good turf, well kept, level graves and moderate-size grave markers

for a grave instead of two the needed attention is less and the expense of unbroken greensward is increased.

In old cemeteries it is frequently difficult to find land suitably located for decorative plantings, because the whole area has been devoted to burial purposes. Sometimes unoccupied portions of lots are available, or where there are too many roads the closing of some of them may provide an occasional site that is suitable for such planting.

The essentials for an attractive cemetery are neatness, bringing into prominence lawns (fig. 38) and a limited amount of tree and shrub planting and the subordination of markers of all kinds. The entire cemetery rather than the individual lots should be considered as the unit.

FURMAN LLOYD MULFORD.

CHICK-REARING Methods Often Greatly Improved By Extension Campaigns When it is realized that the poultry industry has doubled in size within the last 20 years, one can appreciate why more time and attention are given to poultry extension problems. More farmers are interested financially in chickens than in any other kind of livestock. Any new methods that will increase the efficiency of the hen have a very wide appeal. This was especially true of the system, commonly called culling, for selecting low-egg-producing hens.

The thinking farmer, who culled his flock year after year, began to wonder why, with a high-producing strain of birds, he produced so many culls. When his attention was turned to the methods followed in raising the young stock, the source of the trouble was located. Surveys showed that where an unusually high percentage of mortality existed in young stock, the egg production the following year was not up to expectations. The death of young chicks also caused a great financial loss to the industry. In one county in Connecticut a survey showed that one-fourth of the baby chicks did not live to maturity, while in Indiana the death loss was estimated at one-third.

The solution to this problem was worked out by experiment stations and practical poultrymen, and poultry extension staffs undertook the task of getting these practices into general use. This was done with what were called "Grow-Healthy-Chick" campaigns. With different sections of the country presenting different problems, the rules or points to be followed in the campaign varied somewhat, but all embodied the principle of vigorous, healthy chicks, raised under sanitary conditions. In New Hampshire, for example, they emphasized clean chicks, raised on clean ground, with clean feed and clean management. In New Haven County, Conn., after a spirited contest, the slogan "Health Sticks to Clean Chicks" was adopted.

Fewer Death Losses and Greater Egg Production

Press articles and slogans are examples of the extension methods used to tell the story of "Growing Healthy Chicks." Meetings, tours to visit successful poultrymen, letters, bulletins, enrollment and record cards, and exhibits (fig. 39) were other means and agencies utilized. According to reports from eight States, 6,000 farmers, raising approximately 4,000,000 chicks, enrolled in the 1928 campaign to grow better chicks. Seventeen States have organized programs of this type under way, and several other large poultry-producing States are planning to launch similar campaigns.

The results obtained by the flock owners who followed the clean-chick campaign have been shown by a decrease in chick mortality and an increased egg production the following year. In Connecticut, considering data from more than one-half million chicks, the cooperators who followed all eight points in the campaign had an average chick mortality of 7.9 per cent, whereas those who failed to observe the rules for clean chicks and clean land lost 22.3 per cent. The cooperators just mentioned also averaged 40 more eggs per bird than the other poultrymen.

The eight points of the Connecticut "Grow-Healthy-Chick" campaign are as follows:

1. Clean chicks.
2. Clean incubators.
3. Clean brooder houses.
4. Clean ground.

5. Clean litter.
6. Clean feed in hoppers.
7. Clean management.
8. Clean laying houses.

In South Dakota the data from 50 farms showed 13 per cent less chick mortality in flocks on clean ground on which chicks or old hens

FIGURE 39.—A portable exhibit prepared by the United States Department of Agriculture to assist in the "Grow-Healthy-Chick" campaigns

had not been ranged the preceding year, than in flocks in which old ground was used for the baby-chick runs.

H. L. SHRADER.

C HILDREN'S Sun Suits Benefit Health and Promote Happy Play   Sunshine makes the garden grow, and we are just finding out that, if properly applied, it makes Johnnie grow, too. However, this information has so startled many mothers that there has been a tendency to sun bathe him a little too much. In the case of young children such baths should be given for only a very short period at first and with only a small part of the body bare. As the baby gets accustomed to the sun, the amount of the body exposed and the time allowed for the bath can be increased. We have all had cases of sunburn and know what a disagreeable and painful experience it is.

For the older child also, gradual exposure is important, and unless he is ill and the doctor has ordered special treatment, it is not necessary that he should shock the neighbors by playing in his birthday suit. The Bureau of Home Economics has recently devised some suits which are attractive enough to please the most fastidious and still allow a great deal of sun and air to reach the body. Sleeveless, low-necked, and short-legged rompers are suggested for the child who is not accustomed to much direct sunlight. When cut in one piece, these are the easiest kind of play suits to make and launder. A binding of contrasting color adds a great deal to their attractiveness.

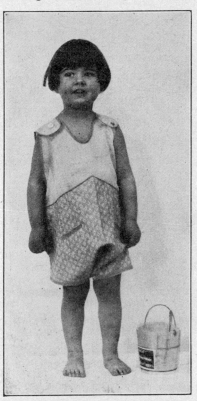

FIGURE 40.—Loosely-woven cotton fabrics make effective and durable sun suits

FIGURE 41.—Sun hats protect the head and add to the attractiveness of sun suits

After the skin has put on a protective layer of tan more open garments can be used. Those with sleeveless waists of net have proved popular. Cable net, marquisette, or a fabric of leno weave may be used. If desired, overalls may be worn as sun suits, but it is well to see that the legs are cut short and the straps are wide and well fitted up on the shoulders. Much needless annoyance has been patiently borne by the American boy who wears that time-honored piece of apparel. Have you ever noticed that he spends much time pulling up shoulder straps that have fallen down over his arms or hitching up his trousers in order to relieve the strain of straps that cut into his shoulders?

Best Fabrics for Sun Suits

Many questions have been asked concerning the best fabrics to use for sun suits. These have been answered by studies made at the Bureau of Standards, of the United States Department of Commerce. The results show that, comparing fabrics of the same weight, there is practically no difference in the amount of ultra-violet light transmitted through bleached samples of cotton, linen, and the two kinds of rayon tested. If any preference can be given to the kind of fiber, bleached white cotton and one kind of rayon (regenerated-cellulose rayon) is somewhat better than most of the other fibers. Whatever the kind of fabric, if it is dyed or yellowed with age or wear, the ultra-violet transmission is greatly reduced. Since it is not very practical to dress a child in all white for his play hours, and since sun suits made entirely of loosely woven fabrics would not answer the purpose, a compromise has been struck in the two suits illustrated. These have open-mesh white cotton tops and the lower parts are fast-colored cottons heavy enough to be serviceable but probably allowing some transmission of the health-giving rays.

In planning all of these suits it is important to see that they fit well and are so comfortable that children soon forget they have them on. It is especially desirable that the sun suit be made so as to encourage good toilet habits and that it is not so designed that the child is tempted to step out of it and go on his way in "nature's own."

RUTH O'BRIEN.

CHIMNEY Cleaning Without Sweep's Aid Requires Only Salt — Soot-coated chimneys can be readily cleaned without the aid of a chimney sweep. If when the fire is started in the fall the flues fail to draw properly because of an accumulation of soot, one of the following remedies will generally prove effective.

Common salt is one of the simplest materials to use. Before being applied the salt should be dried and the fire put into good condition with a substantial bed of hot fuel on top. Sprinkle about a pound of salt on the fire close to the furnace door, shut the door, and open all dampers so the fire will burn as rapidly as the drafts will permit. Keep the dampers wide open until the fumes have disappeared, or approximately half an hour. The soot is acted upon by the sodium and chlorine, which are dissociated when the salt is heated, and disappears as a gas or falls from the flue lining as scales. Additional charges of salt may be needed to remove heavy deposits of soot. Occasional applications of salt throughout the heating season will keep the flues clean.

A material sometimes used instead of salt is metallic zinc; a sheet about 6 to 8 inches square is generally effective. The jacket on a dry-cell battery is composed of zinc, and for this reason beneficial results are secured by the common practice of burning old batteries on a hot bed of coal.

Another method of cleaning a chimney flue is to fire a revolver, loaded with a blank cartridge, up the chimney. The flue opening, or fireplace, should be draped with an old blanket or burlap to prevent soot from falling back into the room. Fires should be extinguished before this method is used.

When wood is used as a fuel, especially green wood, creosote is likely to form. This is a sticky, tarry deposit which may be removed with salt, though the burning of salt in a wood fire is rather difficult. Salt or other chemicals will not remove the fine ash that collects on top of the fire box of boilers; this must be brushed out.

T. A. H. MILLER.

CHRYSANTHEMUM Flowering Season Varies According to Daily Exposure to Light Many of the finer late varieties of chrysanthemums appear to await the autumn days to flower. Do they really await timely conditions of coolness, as some have surmised, or does some other factor harmonize their flowering with the waning days of autumn? The plants themselves shall answer. Unquestionably, many plants have definite temperature requirements to thrive with foliage and flowers. The chrysanthemum, however, is not awaiting cooler temperatures, as it would seem, but shortening days. The later flowering varieties are typical short-day types of plants, like the poinsettia. This was first shown in a conclusive series of experiments by workers in the Bureau of Plant Industry of the United States Department of Agriculture. Cuttings of a late variety made in winter were brought through the necessary intermediate steps of pottings to large buckets or boxes in March and grown to bushy plants by May. These were then given exposures of 10 hours of daylight daily from 5.30 a. m to 3.30 p. m., light being excluded during the remainder of the day by placing the plants in suitable ventilated dark houses. Plants given this treatment have consistently flowered as early as July 15, or in early August, while plants receiving the full daylight did not flower until the middle of October.

Part of Plant Given Short Exposure

In other tests plants were so arranged that only a portion of an individual plant was given the same short daily exposure, while the rest of the plant was exposed to the full length of day. In these tests a small ventilated case capable of being closed to exclude light was used. Early flowering was always induced in that portion of the plant which was given the short exposures, while the outside portions flowered at the same time that control plants of that variety usually flowered out of doors.

It is evident that the chrysanthemum flowers because the autumnal days initiate flowering, not because they are cool. Flowering is quite as circumstantially associated with the heat of midsummer provided short daylight exposures are offered the plants.

These tests would appear to have certain practical interests to growers. For the breeder who would desire to synchronize the flowering of very early and very late sorts for crossing purposes, this behavior should offer helpful suggestions. For the practical grower who would hasten delayed conditions of flowering, it would seem that practical methods of timely darkening the plants for certain periods each day could sometimes be employed to advantage.

H. A. ALLARD.

FIGURE 42.—A, Plant at left given 10 hours of daylight daily beginning May 10, flowered August 8. Control plant of the same age at right exposed to the full length of
day did not flower until October; B, branches of an individual plant exposed to the
full length of day flowered October 18. Branch of the same plant given only 10
hours of daylight daily beginning May 21, by means of a light-proof case, flowered
July 15

CICADA Appearing at 17-Year and 13-Year Intervals is Not a Serious Pest

Of the many misinterpreted passages of Scripture, probably none is more universally misunderstood in this country than Exodus, chapter 10, verses 13, 14, and 15. "The plague of locusts" fills our newspapers almost annually as the successive broods of the periodical cicada appear in one section or another of the country. The name 17-year locust is most unfortunate and undoubtedly arose in the very earliest colonial days when the first brood was heard by the Plymouth colonies in the year 1634. The colonists, being entirely unfamiliar with the true migratory locust, mistook the swarms of this insect as a demonstration of the hand of Providence brought down by a second Moses. The locusts of Egypt and those of the early pioneer times in our Western States were true grasshoppers and not even distantly related to the misnamed 17-year locust or periodical cidada.

The cicada is probably one of the most fascinating insects that have attracted the attention of man. Its apparently spontaneous appearance, its strident and incessant roar, its disappearance for 17 years, or, in the extreme Southern States, 13 years, and its emergence again at an equal interval in almost identically the same spots, have always been a source of wonder around which naturally are woven most fantastic fables. With each appearance the newspapers cry "alarm," the communities become panic stricken, and the entomologists are swamped with correspondence. This misunderstanding is very unfortunate, as the insect is really not a serious pest at all, occasionally doing slight damage by slitting the young branches of shrubs and trees, but, for the most part, merely lightly pruning the plant in which it lays its eggs. The rapid settlement of large areas formerly frequented by this insect has undoubtedly restricted many of the important broods, and should the process finally result in the extermination of the cicada, one of the entomological wonders of the world will have followed the dodo and the great auk. The establishment of permanent colonies of this insect in public parks has even been suggested, and in one case attempted. A further attempt might be advisable in parts of the great national parks now being established in the regions of the Shenandoah Valley and the Great Smoky Mountains, to which future generations could make pilgrimages to see this marvelous phenomenon.

Second Brood Appeared in 1928

During the year 1928 the second large brood of this insect put in its appearance along the Atlantic seaboard. This brood extends from west central North Carolina along the Appalachian foothills and the Piedmont and coastal plains section across eastern Maryland, southeastern Pennsylvania, New Jersey, southeastern New York, and western Connecticut. A few doubtful records of the appearance of this brood have been made in the past outside of the territory named, one in Posey County, Ind., one in Kalamazoo County, Mich., and three from as many localities in Illinois. Not one of these scattered records has been verified by appearance in 1928, and it is highly probable that they are either the result of misdetermination or of the appearance of accelerated individuals of Brood III, which appears in the Middle West the year after Brood II appears in the East.

Over the lower Mississippi Valley, occupying almost exactly the territory not occupied by the 17-year race of the periodical cicada, occurs a 13-year race. The appearance of this race every 13 years led to very considerable confusion of the broods in the early studies of the insect, made when all the broods were thought to be of 17-year occurrence. Of this 13-year race a very small and doubtful Brood XXVII is recorded by C. L. Marlatt (Bul. 71, Bur. Ent. p. 75) from Franklin County, Miss. This brood was first observed in 1902, and again in 1915 in the same county. In each case but few specimens were seen. In the latter year a few specimens were observed at Lake Chicot, Chicot County, and Helena, Phillips County, Ark. This year the only report received of this brood was a single specimen taken in a boll-weevil emergence cage at Yazoo City, Yazoo County, Miss.

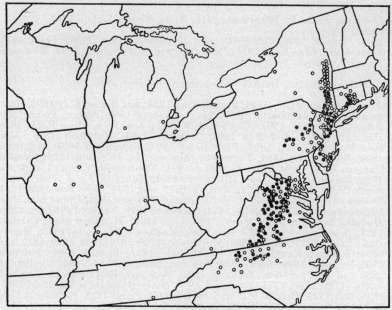

FIGURE 43.—Known distribution of Brood II up to and including its appearance in 1928. Black dots indicate 1928 records

The only brood of any size from which this specimen could have been retarded is Brood XXIII, which occurred in 1924. A retardation of four years is hardly in keeping with our general theory as to the appearance of these broods. These emergences are more easily accounted for by assuming that they are the last survivors of a disappearing brood that once flourished in that region before the advent of white men.

Record of Brood II

The following list of localities, arranged by States and counties, is intended to be a complete record of all observations on the appearance of Brood II.

Connecticut.

Fairfield;[1] *Hartford,* Avon 1911, Berlin 1911, Bristol 1894, East Berlin 1894, Farmington 1877, 1894, and 1911, *Hartford,* 1894, New Britain 1894, 1911, and 1928, Plainville 1894 and 1911, Rocky Hill 1911, Southington 1911 and 1928, West Hartford 1911, Windsor 1894; *Litchfield; Middlesex,* Cromwell 1911, Durham 1860, 1877, 1894, and 1911, Higganum 1894, Killingworth 1911, Middlefield 1894 and 1911, Middletown 1894 and 1911, Westfield 1894; *New Haven,* Branford 1894, 1911, and 1928, Cheshire 1911 and 1928, East Haven 1894 and 1911, Guilford 1894, 1911, and 1928, Hamden 1911 and 1928, Meriden 1877, 1894, 1911, and 1928, Mount Carmel 1894, New Haven 1894, 1911, and 1928, North Branford 1894, 1911, and 1928, North Guilford 1894, North Haven 1911 and 1928; Reeds Gap 1894, Wallingford 1894, 1911, and 1928, Woodbridge 1928.

District of Columbia.

Hope Hill 1894, Naval Observatory 1894, Zoological Park 1894.

Illinois.

De Witt, Clinton 1911; *Livingston,* Fairbury 1894; *Mason* 1877.

Indiana.

Dearborn; Fountain, Silverwood 1911; *Posey,* Mount Vernon 1894.

Maryland.

Anne Arundel 1894; *Calvert; Charles,* Hughesville 1911, Popes Creek 1911; *Montgomery,* Glen Echo 1911; *Prince Georges,* Seat Pleasant 1894, Westwood 1894; *St. Marys.*

Michigan.

Kalamazoo; Wayne, Detroit (Woodmere Cemetery) 1894.

New Jersey.

Atlantic, Atlantic City 1894, Bargaintown 1928, Egg Harbor City 1894, Hammonton 1894, Landisville 1877, Mays Landing 1860, Somers Point 1860; *Bergen,* Allendale 1894, Closter 1928, Fort Lee 1911, Glen Rock 1928, Highwood 1911, Hohokus 1894, Mahwah 1894, Maywood 1894, Midland Park 1877 and 1894, Park Ridge 1894, Ridgewood 1894, Waldwick 1894, Wortendyke 1894; *Burlington,* Moorestown 1894 and 1928; *Camden,* Camden 1894; *Cape May,* Woodbine 1894; *Cumberland,* Vineland 1894 and 1928; *Essex,* Avendale 1894, Bloomfield 1894, Hilton 1877 and 1894, Maplewood 1928, Montclair 1894, Newark 1877 and 1894, New Brooklyn 1894, Orange 1877, 1894, and 1911, South Orange 1877 and 1894, Upper Montclair 1928; *Gloucester,* Franklinville 1894, Glassboro 1928, Newfield 1877 and 1894; *Hudson,* Bayonne 1894; *Mercer,* Princeton 1928; *Middlesex* 1894, Carteret 1928, New Brunswick 1877 and 1928; *Monmouth,* Matawan 1860; *Morris,* Budd Lake 1894, Gillette 1894, Morristown 1809, 1826, 1843, 1860, 1877, and 1894; *Passaic,* Hawthorne 1894, Midvale 1894, Passaic 1894, Paterson 1894, Pompton 1894; *Salem* 1894; *Somerset,* Basking Ridge 1894, Middlebush 1860 and 1877; *Sussex,* Franklin 1894, Hamburg 1894; *Union,* Elizabeth (town) 1741, 1758, 1775, 1792, and 1877, Netherwood 1894, Plainfield 1860, 1894, and 1928, Roselle 1877 and 1894, Scotch Plains 1928, Springfield 1894 and 1928, Summit 1911, Westfield 1894 and 1928.

New York.

Albany, Albany 1860, Berne 1894, Bethlem Center 1894, Clarksville 1911, Coeymans 1911, Dunnsville 1911, Feura Bush 1911, Kenwood 1911, Menands 1911, New Scotland 1894, Normansville 1911, Ravena 1911, Voorheesville 1894; *Bronx,* West Farms 1860, 1877, and 1894; *Chenango,* Greene 1894; *Columbia* 1928, Claverack 1911, Ghent 1911, Hillsdale (Kopake Falls) 1911, Kinderhook 1911, Niverville 1911, North Chatham 1911, North Germantown 1911, Steuyvesant Falls 1911, Stockport 1911, West Taghkanic 1911; *Dutchess,* Annandale 1911 and 1928, Arlington 1911 and 1928, Bangall 1911, Barrytown 1894, 1911, and 1928, Camelot 1911, Chelsea 1911, Dutchess Junction 1911, Fishkill Landing 1911, Hyde Park 1911, New Hamburg 1911 and 1928, Poughkeepsie 1911 and 1928, Pleasant Valley 1928, Red Hook 1911, Rhinebeck 1928, Rhinecliff 1911, Staatsburg 1911, Tivoli 1894, 1911, and 1928; *Greene* 1928, Alsen 1911, Athens 1911, Cairo 1911, Catskill 1894, East Durham 1894, Greenville 1843, Leeds 1911, Morrison Hill 1911, New Baltimore Station 1911, West Athens 1911, West Coxsackie 1911; *Kings,* Brooklyn (Prospect Park) 1894, Flatbush 1928; *Montgomery,* Fonda 1877, 1894, and 1911; *Nassau,* Garden City 1911; *New York,* Bronx 1911, Central Park 1894, Fort Schuyler 1911, Morris Park 1894; *Orange,* Balmville 1911 and 1928, Bear Mountain Park 1928, Bellvale 1928, Bodine's Bridge 1911, Campbell Hall 1894, Cornwall

---

[1] Counties in italics.

1894, 1911, and 1928, Craigsville 1928, Crystal Run 1928, East Valley 1928, Edenville 1928, Fort Montgomery 1911, Goshen 1911 and 1928, Greenwood Lake 1928, Hamptonburg 1928, Highland Falls 1911 and 1928, Leptondale 1911, Little Britain 1928, Middlehope 1911 and 1928, Middletown 1894 and 1911, Monroe 1928, Mountainville 1911 and 1928, Newburgh 1911 and 1928, New Windsor 1843, 1860, 1877, 1894, and 1928, Pine Hill 1928, Pine Island 1928, Rock Tavern 1928, Roseton 1928, Sloatsburg 1928, Sugar Loaf 1928, Tuxedo Park 1928, Vail Gate 1928, Walden 1928, Warwick 1894, 1911, and 1928, Washingtonville 1928, West Point 1877, 1894, 1911, and 1928, Woodbury 1928; *Oswego,* Oswego 1894; *Putnam,* Cold Spring 1860, 1877, and 1911, Garrison 1911, Storm King 1911; *Queens,* 1758 and 1894; *Rensselaer,* Bath-on-the-Hudson 1894, Castleton 1911, East Greenbush 1877 and 1911, East Schodack 1911, Elliot's Station 1877, 1894, and 1911, Lansingburgh 1911, Maple Beach Park 1911, Nassau 1911, Reynolds 1911, Schaghticoke 1911, Schodack Center 1911, Troy 1894; *Richmond* 1877, Greatkills 1911 and 1928, Rossville 1911, South Beach 1894, Tottenville 1928, West New Brighton 1911; *Rockland,* Haverstraw 1911 and 1928, Iona Island 1911, Nyack 1894, 1911, and 1928, Spring Valley 1877 and 1894, Suffern 1911, Tallman 1894, Valley Cottage 1928; *Saratoga,* Mechanicville 1911, Schuylerville 1911, Stillwater 1911; *Suffolk,* Huntington 1894, Wyandanch 1911; *Sullivan,* Livingston Manor 1877; *Ulster,* Clintondale 1911, Ellenville 1894 and 1911, Esopus 1911, Highland 1911 and 1928, Kingston 1894 and 1928, Lake Minnewaska 1894, Malden 1911, Marlboro 1911 and 1928, Milton 1894, 1911, and 1928, New Paltz 1911 and 1928, Port Ewen 1911, Saugerties 1843, 1860, 1877, 1894, and 1911, Wallkill 1911, West Camp 1911; *Washington,* Easton 1894, Thomson 1877 and 1911; *Westchester* 1877, Baychester 1894, Bronxville 1894, Croton 1911, Dobbs Ferry 1911, Katonah 1911, Lowerre Summit 1911, Mount Vernon 1911, New Rochelle 1894, 1911, and 1928, Ossining 1911, Park Hill 1911, Peekskill 1894 and 1911, Pelham 1894 and 1911, Pelhamville? 1894, Scarborough 1894 and 1911, Tarrytown 1911.

North Carolina.

Alamance, Burlington 1894 and 1928, Haw River 1928; *Bertie?; Burke,* Morganton 1894; *Caldwell,* Yadkin Valley 1877; *Caswell* 1894; *Davie,* Farmington 1894; *Forsyth* 1928, Salem Chapel 1894, Craters 1894; *Granville* 1843, 1860, and (northeastern part) 1894; *Guilford,* Greensboro 1928, Guilford 1928, Guilford College 1894, New Gorden? 1877; *Iredell,* Elmwood 1894; *Orange,* Hillsboro 1928, Rock Spring 1894; *Rockingham,* Leaksville 1894, Wentworth 1928; *Rowan,* Salisbury 1894; *Stokes,* Saxon 1877 and 1894; *Surry,* Boyden 1894, Copeland 1928, Dobson 1894 and 1928, Fairview 1928, Pilot Mountain 1928, Rockford 1928; *Wake?; Warren* (southeastern corner) 1894; *Yadkin* 1894 and 1928.

Pennsylvania.

Berks, Hamburg 1894; *Bucks; Carbon* 1877 and 1928, Palmerton 1928; *Chester; Dauphin,* Dauphin 1928, Williamstown 1928; *Delaware; Lancaster; Lebanon; Lehigh,* New Tripoli 1928; *Luzerne,* Hazleton 1928; *Monroe* 1877, Saylorsburg 1928, Stroudsburg 1911; *Montgomery; Northampton,* Windgap 1928, Youngs 1894; *Philadelphia; Pike* 1877; *Potter,* Shinglehouse 1894; *Schuylkill,* Minersville 1860, 1877, and 1894, Pine Grove 1894 and 1928, Pitman 1928; *Wyoming.*

Tennessee.

Hamilton, Chattanooga 1860 and 1894.

Virginia.

Alexandria (Ind. City) 1928; *Albemarle* 1911, Charlottesville 1894, Ivy 1894 and 1928, Moormans River 1928, Proffit 1928, Rio 1894; *Arlington,* Barcroft 1911, Cherrydale 1928, Clarendon 1911 and 1928, Fort Myer 1928, Four Mile Run 1894, Halls Hill 1894, Lyon Park 1928, Rosslyn 1928; *Amherst* 1809, 1826, 1843, 1860, 1877, and 1911, Madison Heights 1928, Sandidges 1894; *Appomattox* 1911 Evergreen 1928; *Bedford,* Big Island 1894 and 1928; *Buckingham,* Buckingham 1894 and 1928, Dillwyn 1928, New Canton 1928; *Campbell,* Altavista 1928, Brookneal 1928, Concord Depot 1928, Fairview Station 1928, Kew 1894, Lawyers 1928, Lynchburg 1911 and 1928; *Caroline,* Golansville 1894; *Charlotte,* Charlotte 1928, Redoak 1911; *Chesterfield,* Bon Air 1911; *Culpeper,* Carlin (Spring) 1894, Culpeper 1894 and 1928; *Cumberland* 1877, Cartersville 1928, Tally 1911; *Fairfax,* Accotink 1928, Fairfax 1928, Mount Vernon 1860; *Fauquier,* Catlett 1860, 1877, and 1894, Markham 1928, The Plains 1928, Warrenton 1911 and 1928; *Fluvanna,* 1894, Bremo Bluff 1928; *Goochland* 1860, 1877, and 1894, Sandy Hook 1928; *Hanover,* Ashland 1928, Hewlett 1894, Montpelier 1928, Oliver 1894; *Henrico* 1911, Richmond 1877, 1894, and 1928; *Henry* 1894, Axton 1928, Martinsville 1928, Preston 1860 and 1877; *James City*, Toana 1877 and 1894; *Loudoun*, Aldie 1928, Hamilton 1928, Leesburg 1877 and 1894; *Louisa*, Buckner 1928, Louisa 1894 and 1928; *Lunenburg*, Kenbridge 1928, Meherrin 1928, Oral Oaks 1826, 1843, 1860, 1877, and 1894; *Madison*, Brightwood 1928, Madison 1928, Nethers 1928, Pratts 1928; *Mecklenburg*, Boydton 1911 and 1928, Chase City 1911 and 1928; *Nelson*, Afton 1928, Faber 1928; *Orange*, Gordonsville 1911 and 1928, Montpelier 1928, Orange 1911 and 1928, Somerset 1928; *Page*, Kimball 1928, Luray 1928, Massanutton 1843, 1860, 1877, and 1894, Rileyville 1928; *Pittsylvania*, Chatham 1928, Danville 1860, 1877, and 1911, Elba 1894, Galveston 1860, 1877, and 1894, Gretna 1928, Pittston 1843, 1860, 1877, and 1894, Whitmell 1928; *Powhatan*, Jefferson 1894 and 1928, Powhatan 1928, Subletts 1877 and 1894; *Prince Edward* 1843, 1860, 1877, and 1894, Hampden Sidney 1928, Rice 1928; *Prince William*, Quantico 1928, *Rappahannock*, Flint Hill 1928, Woodville 1894; *Shenandoah*, Seven Fountains 1911; *Spotsylvania*, Chancellor 1928, Fredericksburg 1928, Massaponax 1928, Spotsylvania 1860, 1877, 1894, and 1928; *Stafford*, Berea 1894, Falmouth 1911 and 1928, Leeland 1911, Tackett Mills 1860, 1877, and 1894; *Sussex*, Wakefield 1928; *Washington*, Abingdon 1894.

West Virginia.
Brooke, Wellsburg 1894.

J. A. HYSLOP.

CITRUS Decay Less if Care Used by Grower, Dealer, and Consumer   With reasonable care, oranges, grapefruits, and lemons can be kept in good condition for several weeks after removal from the tree. This is longer than most fresh fruits can be kept after becoming fully ripe. Like other perishable products, citrus fruits are subject to several forms of decay that often shorten the natural life expectancy.

The most common form of citrus fruit decay is blue-mold rot, of which there are two types, one olive green and the other blue green in advanced stages. Each of these rots starts at breaks in the protective skin of the fruit where the way is open for the causative fungus to gain entrance and start development. Such development is very rapid at ordinary temperatures, requiring only two or three days for the appearance of the characteristic soft decayed spots.

Sometimes the fungus causing a particular rot becomes established in the fruit while it is still on the tree; then the first protection is in the hands of the grower. Citrus brown rot, black rot, and the two forms of stem-end rot are examples of this class. Such forms of decay are usually slow in their development and their occurrence depends on special climatic or seasonal conditions.

Deadwood Should Be Removed

Beginning in the orchard, much can be done to improve the keeping quality of citrus fruit by pruning out deadwood that may harbor certain of the rot fungi, by spraying the young fruit with suitable fungicides to protect from early infection, by protecting against insect injuries and frost or wind damage, and by proper fertilizing, cultivating, and irrigating to insure production of fruit that is physiologically strong.

In picking and packing the fruit every practicable precaution must be taken to prevent injuries that may open the way for blue mold rots. Some of the main things to be avoided are clipper cuts, protruding stems that will stab other fruit, splinters, nails or grit in the field boxes, and rough handling or bruising of the fruit in any way.   It should be picked dry and kept as dry as possible afterwards.

In the packing house certain of the rots can be reduced by washing the fruit in warm water at about 115° to 120° F., or by using certain antiseptic chemicals in the wash water, or by a combination of these measures.   After being washed the fruit must be well dried before it is wrapped and packed.

Reducing the temperature of citrus fruits retards the development of all rots, varying in degree for the several types.   The more promptly the fruit is cooled after picking the better the results.   Precooling the packed fruit before loading in the car, followed by sufficient icing to keep the fruit cool, is the most effective way of using refrigeration in transit.   At terminal markets sudden changes in temperature that will cause sweating should be avoided.   Most of the citrus fruit moves into retail channels without prolonged storage.   If held for any length of time, cool and fairly dry storage at about 40° F., with reasonable ventilation, is desirable.

Handling in Stores and Homes

In retail stores and in homes the fruit should be kept cool and as dry as may be without causing shrinkage.   The temperature of an ordinary household refrigerator is very effective against stem-end rot but is less effective against blue mold rot.   Any fruits showing incipient decay should be sorted out and discarded.   At all stages of handling the fruit should move promptly, especially if temperatures are high.

H. R. FULTON.

———————

CITRUS Specialists Find New Methods of Propagation   The stock problem in the growing of citrus fruits has come to be recognized generally as one of capital importance, and the experimental work of the last few years has shown that the commonly used seedling stocks, such as sour orange, rough lemon, sweet orange, and grapefruit, are often exceedingly variable.

Now that selected bud wood of the best varieties of citrus fruits is available for nursery use, it becomes vitally important to have uniform, high-grade stocks, well adapted to the varieties propagated and well fitted to the soil where the orchard is to be planted, as well as resistant to root rot and other stock diseases.

The amount of variation exhibited by seedlings of the common sour orange, one of the most commonly used root stocks for oranges and lemons, has been shown by H. J. Webber's experiments at the Citrus Experiment Station at Riverside, Calif., to be very great; and he has likewise demonstrated that the growth and the yield of standard varieties of oranges budded on such variable stocks is also extremely variable, even when selected buds are used.   Abnormal stocks produce abnormal trees even when uniform buds are used.

For some years past the Office of Horticultural Crops and Diseases in the Bureau of Plant Industry has been giving especial attention to the vegetative propagation of citrus fruits and their wild relatives.   During these investigations new methods have been worked out which give surprisingly good results with almost all forms of citrus fruits and all of the wild relatives that have been tested.

The simplest of these new methods is the rooting of cuttings with leaves attached, in a propagating bed, the air above the cuttings being kept moist and the soil below kept about 10° F. hotter than the moist air above.

Terminal Twigs Best

Terminal twigs are best for making such cuttings; they must have reached a certain degree of maturity so that they are no longer soft, i. e., they can not be pinched off easily with the fingers, but on the other hand they do not need to be round and thoroughly hard. Such cuttings, watered freely, with little or no ventilation, will usually begin to strike roots within two to four weeks, and by a month or six weeks after being put in the frame they will usually be so well rooted that they can be removed and planted out in nursery rows or put into pots for culture under glass or in a lath house. The sour orange, the rough lemon, and citranges (hybrids of the common sweet orange and the trifoliate orange), all of them excellent stocks for citrus fruits, root freely by this method. Such cuttings develop much faster than young seedlings because of their greater leaf area, and if rooted during winter or early spring and set out in the nursery, by the time warm weather begins they will often grow large enough to be dormant budded by fall, thus saving a year over seedlings.

It is not necessary to have a greenhouse to do this kind of propagation. By using a solar propagating frame, described in detail in Department of Agriculture Circular No. 310–C, it is possible to get fairly good results, especially in the citrus-growing States of the Gulf coast. This solar propagating frame differs from the ordinary cold-frame chiefly in being elevated from the ground, providing a closed-in air space underneath the rooting bed which is warmed by the sun's rays through a glass window on the south side. There is also another closed-in air space above the rooting bed, kept very moist to prevent wilting of the leafy cuttings before they form roots, and shaded if necessary to prevent excessive heating from the sun's rays.

Use of Solar Propagating Frame

In the Gulf States such a solar propagating frame may be used for six to nine months of the year without artificial heat. Farther north its use is restricted to the warmer summer months unless some auxiliary heat is provided. Where electric current is available it is easy to arrange a small electric heater controlled by an automatic thermostat.

Observations made in Florida by one of the writers and in South Africa by H. J. Webber have proved conclusively that healthy citrus trees can be grown to great age and continue to produce heavy crops of fruit when grafted on stocks grown from cuttings.

Where for any reason especially well-developed tap roots are needed, there is another possibility of securing uniform citrus stocks by planting the seeds of the Rusk citrange and other sterile hybrids which often produce a fair crop of seed which reproduces the hybrid without any variation, because instead of a true embryo in the seed its place is taken in such hybrids by a mass of cells from the mother plant growing into the developing seed.

Another method of obtaining uniform citrus stocks is by making root cuttings. Vigorous young roots of the sour orange, rough lemon, and some other citrus stocks can be propagated fairly easily from root cuttings.   Roots taken from older trees do not seem to propagate so rapidly, but F. F. Halma, of the Citrus Experiment Station at Riverside, Calif., has shown that if scions of lemon or some other of the vigorous growing citrus species are inserted into such root cuttings growth starts very quickly in both root and scion and vigorous grafted plants are produced in a short time.   By making sure that well-nourished roots are taken from cuttings, it will probably be possible to reproduce the sour orange, rough lemon, and other citrus stocks on a commercial scale from ungrafted root cuttings.   Such cuttings would, of course, reproduce exactly the particular individual plant from which they were cut.

During the last few months a new discovery has been made that makes possible the rooting of all citrus fruit trees and almost, if not

FIGURE 44.—Cuttings of eight kinds of citrus root stocks rooted in a solar propagating frame. Left to right: Cleopatra mandarin, Thomasville citrangequat, Rusk citrange, Cuban shaddock hybrid, citron, Yuzu, sour orange, sweet lemon

quite, all of the wild relatives of citrus fruits, even those that up to now have resisted all efforts at vegetative propagation by known methods.   By using this new method the Satsuma orange, a variety hard to propagate vegetatively, and other citrus fruit trees grown in regions subject to very severe cold weather can be grown literally "on their own roots," so that if frozen to the ground they will sprout up again, and the sprouts from the base of the trunk or from the roots will not need to be budded or grafted to reproduce the variety originally planted.   By this same method stocks hard to propagate vegetatively by ordinary methods can be propagated from a single superior individual plant and perfectly uniform rootstocks secured.

New Method of Getting Root Stocks

This new method consists in approach-grafting a small seedling or a vigorously growing rooted cutting to one branch of a Y-shaped twig of the tree to be propagated, the nurse graft having its roots inclosed in rooting or sphagnum moss wrapped in waxed paper to prevent drying out, or in a special marcottage box, the free use of which to the public is guaranteed by Government patent No. 1655731.

As the nurse graft after about two weeks begins to unite with one of the side branches of the Y, the twig is "ringed" or girdled at the base of the Y about 6 inches below the fork. Finally, after about six to eight weeks, when the nurse graft is thoroughly united to one side of the twig, the Y is cut off at the girdled base and the whole Y cutting together with its nurse graft is plunged into a propagating bed or solar propagating frame having bottom heat and a relatively cool humid chamber above. The roots of the nurse graft are at this time taken out of the moss and spread carefully in the soil.

After the nurse graft gets well established, in a fortnight or so, the twig to which it is grafted is "nicked," i. e., given a shallow cut just below the graft union. Every few days this nick is deepened, and after six to ten weeks, when the roots have developed well on the base of the Y cutting, the grafted twig is severed entirely below the union, leaving a well-rooted cutting.

This Y nurse-graft cutting method produces, therefore, two well-rooted plants by one operation; the one a rooted cutting, the other a graft on the seedling or rooted cutting used as a nurse graft. Both plants can be utilized if the nurse graft selected is a suitable stock for the variety propagated. In actual tests of this method for propagating the Wase Satsuma orange, each Y cutting yielded one Wase Satsuma cutting on its own roots and one Satsuma plant grafted on Rusk citrange or Yuzu stock.

WALTER T. SWINGLE and
T. RALPH ROBINSON.

COD-LIVER Oil in Feeds Requires Care to Preserve Vitamin That the health of human beings and of some domestic animals is influenced by a substance obtained from the liver of a salt-water fish seems almost incredible, but this fact has been established by scientific research. Millions of dollars are spent annually in this country for the purchase of cod-liver oil, which is in demand because it is an excellent source of vitamins A and D.

Commercial practices deterimental to the vitamin A of cod-liver oil may be employed unwittingly by the commercial feed producer. For example, much of the cod-liver oil for animal consumption is sold mixed with a feed or a proprietary preparation, and although it may be possible to handle some of these products in such a way as to preserve the vitamin A, as yet this has not been adequately demonstrated. When used as a source of vitamin A in laboratories engaged in nutrition studies, cod-liver oil is either fed separately or mixed with small quantities of the other food, since vitamin A disappears rapidly from cod-liver oil spread over large surfaces, particularly when exposed to light and air. Vitamin D, on the other hand, is comparatively stable under the same conditions. Whether the benefits derived from cod-liver oil supplements to feeds are due to vitamin A or D, or both, it is not always possible to judge, but the full benefit of both vitamins is not assured unless the cod-liver oil is properly handled.

If the diet must be fortified with vitamin A and the feed dealer can not guarantee that the vitamin A of his cod-liver oil product is stable, it is advisable to buy cod-liver oil of a good grade and either give it separately or mix it with the other food shortly before feeding.

E. M. Nelson.

C OCKROACHES Can Be Quickly Eradicated by Sodium Fluoride

Few insects are more unwelcome in the house than the cockroaches, their only redeeming trait being that they occasionally eat bedbugs. They usually hide themselves during the day in dark crevices around the house, and emerge at night to feed upon anything edible that can be found. In addition to all types of foodstuffs, they will attack soiled fabrics, bookbindings, gummed labels, and will even nibble the finger nails and eyelashes of sleeping people.

Many people do not really know that the common waterbug (fig. 45), which is about half an inch long, belongs to the same family as the large, dark brown, winged or wingless cockroaches that may measure as much as 2 inches.

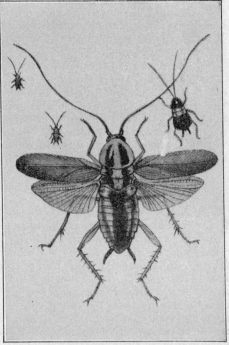

Figure 45.—German cockroach, or common waterbug, adult and immature stages. Enlarged about 2½ diameters

Fortunately, cockroaches are easy to kill. The liberal use of powdered sodium fluoride or sodium fluosilicate, dusted wherever the cockroaches are troublesome, will quickly eradicate them. In extreme cases, where instant relief is desired, fumigation with hydrocyanic-acid gas may be resorted to.

E. A. Back and
R. T. Cotton.

C OLORING of Mature Fruit by Ethylene Gas Unobjectionable   For many years the coloring of bananas, oranges, lemons, and grapefruit was hastened by storing them in a closed room in which an oil or gas stove was burning. To prevent the fruit from drying out, a pan of water was kept on the stove. It was at first thought that the heat caused the rapid coloring of the fruit, but this explanation was found to be incorrect, for rooms heated by steam failed to bring about the change.

After a long investigation chemists in the Bureau of Chemistry and Soils discovered that a gas contained in minute quantities in the vapors given off by burning oil, gasoline, commercial gas, and similar substances, is the agent causing the rapid change of color. This gas, known as ethylene, if used in extremely high dilutions will color some fruits in about 10 per cent of the time required for the normal coloring of fruits in storage. In dilutions as high as 1 part in 5,000 parts of air, it will color oranges and lemons in from three to five days. As ethylene was used during the World War in the manufacture of munitions it is available in commercial quantities, and the method is rapidly coming into use for coloring citrus fruits and Japanese persimmons. When used on persimmons, it not only colors but also softens them and removes the astringent taste.

As far as known, the method does not injure the fruit in any way. It is thought that the ethylene merely hastens the natural processes of coloring; therefore, no objection is offered to its use on fruit provided the fruit is mature. Its use on immature fruit or vegetables in such a way as to deceive the purchaser regarding their quality or maturity would be punishable under the State food laws, and if such fruit or vegetables were sold in interstate commerce, under the Federal food and drugs act.

E. M. CHACE.

COLOR Measurement of Farm Products is a Factor in Grading — Color measurement seems at first thought a far cry from the practical everyday life of the farmer. But the farmer watches his crops, whether they be fruits, vegetables, or grains, and decides when to harvest largely on a basis of color. No good farmer allows his bright, green alfalfa to lie in the fields and become bleached or brown when by prompt curing and storing methods the green color, essential to high-grade hay, can be preserved. Nor should a cotton farmer allow his bright, bloomy cotton to remain unpicked in the fields and thus lose grade by becoming dark and dirty from weather.

Color is an important factor in standards established by the Federal Government for many agricultural products. Hay, for example, is graded on color, foreign material, and condition, with the factor of leafiness added for alfalfa. The grade factors in cotton consist of color, leaf and trash, and preparation or ginning. Color is an important element in grading fruits and vegetables; it is a part of the specifications for cotton linters standards; it plays a part in grading rice, barley, and other grains, in honey, meat, breads, mayonnaise, and many other products which are grown on the farm or made from farm products. Often the color shows direct correlation with protein content, diastatic activity, or money value.

Because color is a grade factor, it is important that it be accurately measured. Thus standards may be kept constant from year to year and studies may be made of the relations which exist between grades.

Comparative Adjectives Inaccurate

Color descriptions made by the use of comparative adjectives are neither definite nor accurate. Hay that is called "pea-green" means one thing to one man and something different to another. What may be "good" color to one man may be but "fair" color to the next. The comparison depends largely upon the individual and his recent grading experience. To avoid such discrepancies, and to establish definite standards for grade color, measurements and comparison of color are being made by means of color units which are far superior to the descriptive terms. Color may be measured as simply as a solid, by substituting for length, breadth, and depth measurements those of hue, brilliance, and chroma.

Not all colors exhibit the quality of hue. Blacks, whites, and grays, when they are entirely neutral in color, have no hue. All other colors may be classified as reds, yellows, greens, blues, and purples. Some reds are more yellow than others, some yellows are more red than others. For this reason colors are compared to a scale of hues, the scale being based on 10 hues—those named, with 5 intermediate

FIGURE 46.—Latest development in instrument for measuring the color of hay. Approximately one-half of the area of hay exposed may be measured at one time. A similar instrument has been developed for cotton

hues added—which may be in turn subdivided into 100 hues or as many as it is possible for the eye to detect.

All colors—blacks, whites, and grays included—may be classified according to a scale of brilliance. Brilliance is the light-to-dark element in color. White is as light a color as one can see. Black is as dark a color as one can see. If black, absolute black, be placed at the bottom of the brilliance scale as 0, and white, absolute white, be placed at the top of the scale as 10, we have a decimal scale which may be divided into as many equal dark-to-light steps as the eye can see. Every color may then be compared to a definite step on this scale. Hay colors will, for the most part, compare with the middle and below-middle steps on this scale, from 3 to 5, whereas cotton colors, most of which are very light, will be higher up on the scale, from 7 to 9.

Chroma is Third Color Attribute

Chroma, the third color attribute, is the one by which the strength or weakness of a color is indicated. If a color is neutral gray, it has no chroma; if it is a very weak color it will be low in chroma when measured on a scale extending from 0, or gray, in equal steps from the low chromas, 1 and 2, out to the strongest that may be obtained, perhaps to 10 or even 12. Tomatoes which have been measured show chromas ranging from 8 to 13 and 14. Corn has less chroma, about 3.5 to 6; white cotton ranges from 1 to 3 or 3.5.

A complete color description consists of a notation for hue, brilliance, and chroma.

Enough samples of hay have been measured for color to allow the establishment of tables for alfalfa, timothy, prairie, Johnson, clover, and soy-bean hay by means of which it is possible to measure the color of a sample of hay and convert the measurement not only into grade factors but into what is known to inspectors and to the trade as "per cent green color." Measurements of a similar nature are being made of cotton colors.

DOROTHY NICKERSON.

COMBINE Harvester is Improved by Invention of New Attachments The combined harvester-thresher, generally known as the combine, has been the basis for practically all recent development in grain-harvesting machinery. The combine itself has not been changed materially in recent years, except for refinements in design and construction, but numerous attachments have been devised to meet adverse harvesting conditions and to make the combine adaptable to a greater variety of crops and crop conditions. In areas comparatively free from weeds, and for crops that ripen uniformly, the direct method of combining has been successful.

Two of the most recent developments are the windrow harvester and the pick-up. With these attachments grain may be cut and piled in windrows, picked up when dry and threshed with the combine. This method of harvesting has been practiced in some sections where conditions are not suitable for cutting and threshing the standing grain at one operation. Grain fields badly infested with weeds and crops which do not ripen uniformly have thus been harvested successfully. Under ordinary conditions the weeds and green grain dry out in four to eight days when windrowed, thus enabling the combine to do a better job of threshing and cleaning. By the use of such equipment harvesting may be started several days earlier than is customary with the combine alone. The windrow method has the disadvantage, however, of increasing the number of operations as well as the cost of harvesting machinery.

Figure 47 shows a windrower in operation. On some makes of combine the regular header platform is disconnected and used as a windrower, while in other cases the windrowers are separate and complete units. The windrows are formed by conveying the swath either to one side or to the center of the header platform. When deposited at the center, two platform canvases are used which run in opposite directions and convey the cut grain to the center of the header platform, sufficient space being provided between the canvases for depositing the cut grain. Power for operating the working parts on the windrower is usually taken from the ground or bull wheel, though some machines are operated by a power take-off from the tractor.

How the Pick-Up Machine Works

In Figure 48 a combine is shown operating with a pick-up attachment. The pick-up shown is attached directly to the combine in lieu

FIGURE 47.—Windrow harvester

FIGURE 48.—Windrow pick-up

of the regular header platform. On some machines, however, the pick-up is attached to the header platform. The pick-up operates in a manner similar to that of a hay loader. Tines or finger-like prongs lift the straw and deposit it on a canvas which conveys it to the combine. With either type of windrower and pick-up, the pick-up may be attached and the combine started before windrowing is completed, provided power units are available for both operations.

Some trouble has been experienced with the windrows settling down on the ground in fields where the stubble is thin and light, or where the straw was cut too short to form a sufficient mat for the stubble to support. Under such conditions a side-delivery rake may be used to turn the windrow in order to prevent the grain from sprouting on the ground and to facilitate picking up.

Tests have shown that the windrower and pick-up will do the work for which they have been designed, but it has not been shown that the expense of this auxiliary equipment and the cost of operation are always justified.

W. M. HURST.

COMBINED Wheat May Be Cleaned for Safe Storage in Two Ways   One of the principal difficulties in successfully harvesting and threshing grain in the spring-wheat area with a combine in its present design is occasioned by the prevalence of weeds in the grain fields. Some weeds, like wild oats, ripen before harvest and do not cause much

FIGURE 49.—Special grain cleaner attached to threshing machine

trouble in combining. Other weeds, like lamb's-quarters, pigeon grass, Russian thistle, and sweet clover ripen after the wheat is ready to harvest. They cause trouble in threshing, and because of the high moisture content of these weed seeds the threshed wheat containing such green seeds is usually not safe for storage.

Seeds of most of these latter weeds are smaller than wheat kernels. The percentage of such seeds is higher in the eastern and central part of the spring wheat area than in Montana. In the central part in 1928 the small weed seeds threshed with the grain often amounted to from 6 per cent to 10 per cent of the weight of the grain.

Most of these weed seeds contain from 20 per cent to 50 per cent moisture at the beginning of the combine harvest; if stored with the wheat their excess moisture is rapidly transferred to the wheat kernels, often increasing the moisture content of the wheat so much that the wheat begins to heat and becomes damaged in storage.

Manufacturers have placed several grain-cleaning devices on the market for removing these green weed seeds from the grain. Some of these devices are attached directly to the combine so that the green weed seeds are automatically removed as a part of the combining operation.   Some of these types of cleaning devices are only partly effective in removing the weed seeds; the less efficient remove only those weed seeds which contain the least moisture.   The green seeds containing high percentages of moisture are usually too large to pass through the standard screens provided in most of the cleaning attachments for combines.   Several special types of grain-cleaning attachments were used by combine operators in 1928 who cooperated with the United States Department of Agriculture and grain-cleaner manufacturers in an attempt to remove these larger seeds with the high percentages of moisture.

One device which was found to be effective in removing high-moisture weed seeds was operated on 60 lots of wheat in the central part of the area.   Average seed dockage in these lots was 7.5 per cent; of this the fine seed dockage ranged in the lots from 2 to 17 per cent. Average moisture content in the 60 lots, including the weed seed before cleaning, was 15.6 per cent which would cause the wheat to grade No. 4.   Such wheat would not be safe for storage.   Average moisture content of the wheat after passing through the cleaner was 14.4 per cent, which would permit the wheat to grade No. 2.   On the basis of prices for wheat at local elevators at that time, this would make the wheat worth 8 cents per bushel more after cleaning than before, because of lower moisture content and improvement in the grade as a result of the cleaning.   The lower moisture content would also permit safer storage.   Moisture content in weed seeds removed from the grain averaged 31 per cent.   At the beginning of the harvest period weed seeds removed from the grain had an average moisture content of 40 per cent.   At the end of the season, after the first frosts, the moisture content had diminished to an average of 19 per cent but was still much too high.

The new windrow and pick-up method used in connection with combine harvesting offers a method of drying the weed seed before the grain is threshed.   Extra cleaning attachments furnished by several of the combine manufacturers readily remove weed seed which has dried in the windrow.

Another method of removing the seeds, practiced by many farmers in the area, is to clean the wheat and other grains with a fanning mill or other grain-cleaning device within a few hours after harvest. Excess moisture in the weed seeds transfers rapidly to the grain kernels when the weed seeds remain with the grain in storage.   Even when cleaning is delayed overnight some moisture in the weed seeds passes to the wheat.   Complete transference of excess moisture does not usually occur for about one week after cutting, although one-half of the moisture usually transfers during the first 12 to 24 hours.

If wheat has stood for a few hours, say overnight, Russian thistle heads and spines shrivel and can be blown out of the wheat by the air blast in the fanning mill; then the wheat can be stored safely, if the grain itself is sufficiently low in moisture content.   None of the grain-cleaning devices that were tried out on combines in 1928 were satisfactory for removing green Russian thistle from the grain.

R. H. Black.

COMBINING Enterprises Properly May Increase Income From the Farm — Proper combinations of crops and livestock sometimes may be the means of reducing the amount of unused products on the farm or of increasing the production without an equal increase of expenses. For a group of farms with similar conditions, records will show a wide variation in the amout of the various cost items which enter into production. In each group a few careful feeders produce livestock with less than the average amount of feed; others use much more than the average in obtaining the same production. Similarly, a wide range is shown in the amount of labor used in growing crops on farms with similar conditions. A part of the difference in the relation between the amount of cost factors used in production and the amount of product obtained is due to different combinations of the enterprises.

Often by-products or joint products can be combined profitably with other lines of production. New enterprises may be introduced to give profitable employment to available labor. Cropping systems can sometimes be revised to obtain a greater production from the land. Some idle land may be put into use. The tendency toward specialization in producing one thing for sale often leaves unused products which might be used to advantage.

By drawing up plans for the operation of the farm or in budgeting the farm resources, economy through the combination of enterprises may be foreseen.

An example is drawn from the hill sections of Mississippi. Here, as a general rule, the farms are small, and the earnings of each farm are low compared with those in other farming sections. The size of a one-man business is limited by the acreage of cotton which he and his family can care for. The farm earnings, however, may be frequently increased by including additional lines of production.

A budget of expenses and income was worked out for a farm as operated in 1926, and for a farm of the same size with crops and livestock which would use more of the available resources and which would include some minor sources of income along with cotton.

In comparing earnings of the two systems, equal applications of fertilizer and yields were assumed. The typical farm had 12 acres of wage cotton and 6 acres of cropper cotton; the suggested system has merely 12 acres of wage cotton.

Hay and Small-Grain Acreage

The typical farm had 2 acres of hay and no small grain; the suggested system has 3 acres of hay and 6 acres of small grain, followed either by a second crop of hay or by pasture. The corn acreage is the same for both systems. The second budget included a charge for seeding cotton and corn land to a winter cover crop.

The typical farm had poultry, hogs, and cows for products used in the home. The suggested system called for 50 more hens and 3 more cows, with some products for sale.

Heavy applications of fertilizer are necessary if good cotton yields are to be obtained. A part of this fertilizer, not used by the first crop, remains in the soil. The winter cover crop uses this fertility and furnishes pasture for the livestock. The small grain and hay use land that would probably lie out and they provide feed for the livestock at little additional cost. If cows are kept and cream is sold, the remaining skim milk reduces the grain needed to produce each 100 pounds of pork.

The minor enterprises help to use the available resources more efficiently. The extra work on the suggested farm would not require additional hired labor, and the salable products would be increased. The budget, worked out with normal conditions for both systems, indicates that the suggested system would increase the farmer's earnings by more than 25 per cent, or from about $435 to $550.

Other uses of the resources could be made. A budget with sheep substituted for dairy cows indicates that, where sheep can be handled, they would normally increase the earnings of the farm. Not all joint products or available resources can be put to a profitable use, but by budgeting the expenses and income as shown the chances of increasing the farm earnings with a given combination of enterprises can be closely approximated.

R. S. KIFER.

CONTAINER Act Sets Standard Sizes for Hampers and Baskets   The standard container act of 1928 was passed by the Seventieth Congress and was signed by the President on May 21, 1928. This act establishes standard capacities for hampers, round stave baskets, and splint baskets for fruits and vegetables. It is a weights and measures law and as such is

FIGURE 50.—Types of baskets for which sizes have been established by the standard container act of 1928

applicable to intrastate as well as interstate commerce and supersedes all State laws or city ordinances in conflict therewith.

The standard sizes or capacities established for hamper or round stave baskets are as follows: One-eighth, one-fourth, one-half, five-eighths, three-fourths, 1, 1¼, 1½, and 2 bushel.

For splint baskets the standard sizes are 4, 8, 16, 24, and 32 quarts.

This act completes the standardization of baskets used for fruits and vegetables. The other three types, Climax baskets, berry boxes, and till baskets, were standardized by the standard container act of 1916.

The new law also standardizes the straight-side or tub baskets, which have come into common use during the past few years. These are not a separate type of basket but are considered as either hampers or round-stave baskets, depending upon the mode of construction. Included under the term "splint basket" are all types of splint and market baskets used for fruits and vegetables, whether of the square weave, diamond weave, or sheet-veneer type.

A departure in this law is a section requiring the manufacturers of hampers, round-stave baskets, and splint baskets to submit specifications for their baskets to the Secretary of Agriculture for his approval.

It is provided that specifications shall be approved if they provide for a basket of one of the standard capacities established in the law and for a basket which is not deceptive in appearance. It is believed that this provision will result in the adoption of more nearly uniform specifications than have been used in the past.

Penalty provisions of the law do not become effective until November 1, 1929, thus giving all parties concerned ample time to prepare for any changes necessary. The application of the law will result in economies in manufacture, will provide the shipper with a definite basis of sale, and will relieve him of unfair competition through use by his competitor of a "short" package.

H. A. SPILMAN.

COOPERATIVE Associations Practice Pooling to Cut Costs and Spread Risks — Pooling is that practice in a co-operative-marketing association which is concerned with determining the individual member-patron's share in sales returns, expenses, marketing, and other business risks. Pooling, in its relation to cooperative marketing, has been subject to various interpretations. There has been a tendency in some quarters to group cooperative marketing associations in two divisions—associations which pool sales returns or sales returns and expenses, and those which pool only sales expenses. Associations in the first group have been considered pooling organizations, whereas those in the second group have not. Certain cooperative leaders, as far back as 1919 and 1920, advanced a theory of cooperative marketing which linked pooling definitely with control of large quantities of the commodity. Others have believed that only associations engaged in marketing a single commodity were actually engaged in pooling. Hence the rather common use of the term "pool" to describe an association that handles only one product. The author believes, however, that a definition of pooling should cover the practice as it concerns not only sales returns, but also operating expenses, marketing, and other business risks or any combination of these.

The aim of pooling is to distribute equitably to all member patrons the results which accrue from group effort. Some of the economic advantages of group effort which are facilitated by pooling are the following: Improvement of the bargaining position of individual growers, through coordination of their efforts; elimination of waste; spreading of marketing risks among all members; and possibility of effective market expansion through control of the time, place, and form in which the commodity is sold.

Benefits of Large-Scale Operations

The combination of large quantities of agricultural commodities under the control of one organization facilitates better adaptation of the commodity to actual demand conditions. The mingling by growers of certain marketing functions, under the control of efficient management, permits an effective marketing and distribution program.

The average farmer does not have a sufficient quantity of product available for market at any one time to enable him to take advantage of the most economical ways of getting his product to market. The assembling, grading, and preparation for market of small lots of produce by numerous individuals at a local point costs more than the combination and handling of many small lots as a few large units under a common administration.

Any organization engaged in the marketing of agricultural commodities must always reckon with a number of marketing risks, such as price fluctuations, physical deterioration of product, and financial losses. Some of these risks are at times too great for a single farmer to bear. Pooling facilitates the spreading of these marketing risks among all members.

Only a few farmers, as individuals, can afford to undertake market development because of the expense involved and the lack of sufficient supplies to make the exploitation policy permanent. Here, again, the pooling by a large number of growers of the expense, risks, and other features involved in market expansion makes possible a program for widening the market for their product which is of benefit to the grower but which would be prohibitive if undertaken by an individual.

Chris L. Christensen.

COOPERATIVE Handling of Grain on Large Scale is Now Making Headway   Considerable information has been obtained during the last year from farmers' elevators and large-scale grain-marketing agencies regarding their methods of organization, operating practices, volume of business, and financial condition. Many significant facts were brought out.

From data obtained in the survey and from other sources it may be concluded that the farmers' elevator movement has passed its peak of rapid expansion. A number of associations passed out of existence during and immediately following the business depression of 1920–21, but in recent years the number of active associations has remained about constant. It is estimated that there are now approximately 4,000 local elevator associations operating one or more local elevator plants. In 1926–27 the number of stockholders of these associations was estimated at 450,000 and the number of patrons at 900,000. About 62 per cent of these farmers' elevators are operating with limitation of dividends payable on capital stock and about 73 per cent with provision for the payment of patronage dividends.

The volume of grain handled by farmers' elevators in 1926–27 was estimated at about 560,000,000 bushels, with a sales value of about $500,000,000. In addition, they handled supplies for farmers valued at $160,000,000. Nearly half of the farmers' companies do not handle sufficient grain to permit profitable operation, but nearly all of them have supplemented their incomes by handling side lines and performing other services such as feed grinding and seed cleaning.

From a financial standpoint the majority of the associations own their plants and equipment clear of debt and have surpluses which may be used for operating purposes. Although competition has been keen, more than one-half of the companies paid dividends on capital stock and about one-fourth returned patronage refunds to patrons during the 1926–27 season. More than 16 per cent reported being in debt, but this includes companies which have been recently organized.

On the whole, it may be said that farmers' elevators are in fairly satisfactory condition. New problems and conditions are constantly arising, however, which will need careful consideration if the present status of the movement is to be maintained.

Large-Scale Grain-Marketing Associations

Several types of large-scale cooperative grain-marketing associations are now operating. The combination of local cooperative elevators into what are commonly referred to as "line systems" represents one type. A number of such organizations have been in operation for 10 to 20 years. Certain advantages in costs, plus greater stability which

FIGURE 51.—Terminal elevator owned and operated by the Southwest Cooperative Wheat Growers Association. A number of the large-scale cooperative grain-marketing agencies are now acquiring country and terminal elevator facilities

comes from diversification and experienced supervision, are credited to this type.

Cooperative grain commission agencies form the second group of large-scale grain-marketing associations. These organizations are owned and controlled by farmers and farmers' elevators. They charge the usual commission rates and return their surplus earnings to members. Eight commission associations operating in 1927 represented over 900 local elevators and handled 34,000,000 bushels of grain. These associations have made substantial gains in recent years.

State-wide marketing associations, known as wheat pools, represent the third group. Over 70,000 farmers have signed contracts with eight of these agencies to deliver their grain to their association for a period of years. An advance payment is made at time of delivery and later payments are made as the grain is sold. The pool thus takes control of the grain and endeavors to regulate its sale according to supply and demand conditions. The volume handled by the pools has varied between 12,000,000 and 17,000,000 bushels in recent years, depending on the size of the crop. The expiration of the original contracts of several pools, during 1927 and 1928, was followed by the adoption of new contracts. These associations are now operating in their second contract period. A number of the pools are now acquiring elevator facilities or are strengthening their contacts with associations that operate such facilities. (Fig. 51.)

J. F. Booth and
W. J. Kuhrt.

COOPERATIVE Marketing of California Eggs is Promoted by Grading A detailed study of the Poultry Producers of Central California was completed during the year. This organization began business in 1917 and operates in 29 counties grouped around San Francisco Bay.

During the 11 years of operation members have delivered to the association nearly 200,000,000 dozens of eggs, starting with 6,405,960 dozen in 1917 and reaching 29,313,540 dozen in 1927. No data are available to show what percentage of the production has been received each year, but it is interesting to note that the average annual rate of increase in the association's receipts has been approximately 41 per cent, whereas census data indicate that production in the area in which the association operates has increased, between 1909 and 1924, at an average annual rate of 10.2 per cent. Apparently the growth of the association is more than keeping pace with that of the industry in the area. The association's growth has been practically uninterrupted; there were only two years in which the volume fell below that of the previous year.

Inasmuch as the grading practice has an important bearing on the merchandising program of a cooperative, it is interesting to follow the way in which this organization has changed its practice to meet market needs. From 1917 until July 1, 1926, eggs were "surface" graded on the basis of the accepted and more or less indefinite classifications current in the trade. Size, shape, shell texture, and color determined the sorting into extras, standards, mediums, etc. For part of this time, until about 1922 or 1923, much of the product was accepted and sold on the basis of members' grading with the exception of the share which was sold to the local retail trade, a considerable part of which was candled.

Grading Becomes More Discriminating

As the association was constantly attempting to improve the trade opinion of its product, the grading became more discriminating, and eventually all eggs were regraded, although still on the basis of outside appearance. Increasing competition, together with the desire to establish more definitely its product in eastern markets, led to the adoption of a program, on July 1, 1926, of complete grading on the basis of both appearance and interior quality by the candling process, which has unquestionably improved the quality of the pack and its reputation in the trade.

The present grading policy is aimed toward producing a pack for each of the association's brands of as nearly unvarying quality as possible. Nothing is gained by placing a brand on a product if the quality is shifted up and down in response to changes in the relative strength of the market, for such practice creates an uncertainty in the mind of the buyer and tends to depress the price he is willing to pay for the brand. If this association's grading policy is strictly adhered to, it will tend toward the creation of a trade preference for its brands.

A. V. SWARTHOUT.

COOPERATIVE Marketing Contracts Established on a Firm Legal Basis — Cooperative marketing contracts now have a standing and status equivalent to that of commercial contracts. It is a mistake to think of cooperative-marketing contracts as being in a peculiar class or as possessing characteristics different from those of other contracts. Every element in a cooperative contract has a counterpart in contracts of a noncooperative character. It is true that there was a time when the courts looked askance at cooperative-marketing contracts and in some instances held that they were void. This illegality arose from the fact that the farmers, by acting together through the instrumentality of contracts, were deemed to restrain trade.

Principally during the last 10 years, or earlier in some States, statutes have been enacted which expressly provide for the formation of cooperative associations. Many contain provisions stating that the associations formed thereunder are not to be deemed monopolies or as acting in restraint of trade. Furthermore, there has been a change in the attitude of the public toward large-scale organizations. Such organizations are not now generally viewed with disfavor. These factors, singly or in combination, have caused the supreme courts of 28 States to hold cooperative marketing contracts valid. In doing so the courts have recognized the lack of bargaining power possessed by individual farmers in marketing their products, the economies that may be effected through efficient large-scale associations, and the need for allowing farmers to unite for marketing their products and to improve and equalize their economic position.

On February 20, 1928, the Supreme Court of the United States decided the case of the Liberty Warehouse Co. *v.* Burley Tobacco Growers Cooperative Marketing Association. This is the first case directly involving a cooperative association and the cooperative marketing act under which it was formed that has been passed upon by the Supreme Court of the United States. That court found the cooperative-marketing act constitutional and the contracts of the association valid. Cooperative-marketing contracts may now be regarded as an integral part of our business life and as an established part of agricultural cooperation.

L. S. HULBERT.

COOPERATIVE Marketing of Dressed Turkeys is Means of Added Profit — Farmers who market their turkeys alive often fail to realize a large part of the profit from them. Very satisfactory returns have been obtained by growers who have dressed their turkeys on the farms and sold them cooperatively in car lots. Marketing dressed turkeys in car lots is one of the most practical of cooperative-marketing projects. The growers in a county or district, through their local organization, determine approximately the number of turkeys available for sale. Representatives of the growers get in touch with prospective buyers and receive from them sealed bids which are opened at a stated time. The entire number is then sold to the highest bidder, who then states the dates on which he wishes the dressed birds delivered. The farmers dress the turkeys the day before delivery and cool them overnight on the farms. The birds are weighed, graded, and paid for as they are delivered. The purchaser bears all expenses and assumes all responsibility after the birds are received.

Marketing on the North Platte Irrigation Project

On the North Platte irrigation project in western Nebraska and eastern Wyoming 500 farmers in 1927 dressed and delivered 12 carloads of turkeys, totaling approximately 24,400 birds, for which they received $96,000. Cooperative marketing of turkeys on the project was started in 1924, when 219 farmers marketed five carloads for

FIGURE 52.—Farm-dressed turkeys on a cooling rack in the North Platte Valley

$27,682. The volume has gradually increased each year as the project has grown in popularity.

Turkeys dress away about 12 per cent. In a flock of average weight the owner realizes from 50 cents to $1 a bird for the labor of dressing. The average gain is about 75 cents a bird. This increased price which the grower receives by dressing his turkeys represents 15 to 20 per cent of the value of the average-sized live turkey and is fully three-fifths as much as the entire feed cost of raising and fattening the bird on the North Platte project. For the time spent in dressing, the grower realizes for his labor many times more per hour than for any other equal amount of time he has devoted to growing his turkeys.

Estimating that the growers of the North Platte Valley received for their dressed turkeys 75 cents a bird more than they would have received had the turkeys been marketed alive, they sold the 24,400 turkeys marketed from the 1927 crop for $18,300 more than the same turkeys would have brought alive. By dressing the turkeys on the farms the growers keep the shrink at a minimum. Practically all the dressing is done by family help. The turkeys, therefore, are dressed on the farm with less expense than in any other way.

This Method of Marketing is Educational

Marketing turkeys dressed and selling cooperatively not only nets the farmers more money for their birds, but the plan is educational. The growers learn much about grading and soon develop an appreciation of the value of quality. When farmers learn to dress their own turkeys they do much better work than they can hire done, and the quality of dressing done on the farms is far superior to that ordinarily done by hired help in commercial plants. Buyers who handle dressed turkeys in car lots realize this fact and prefer turkeys dressed by farmers and their families.

In the North Platte Valley most of the turkey growers exchange work with their neighbors, two or three families working together at the job of dressing. Two rough pickers and three or four women removing pin feathers make good time with the work, and the job is finished before it becomes too tiresome.

When the marketing project was first started, it was necessary to give dressing demonstrations in each community. Now practically every experienced turkey grower knows how to dress his birds. New growers who join the association are requested either to see a dressing demonstration or to work with a neighbor who knows how to dress before they attempt to kill and dress turkeys for cooperative shipment.

D. H. PROPPS.

COOPERATIVE Marketing Hampered by Lapses Into Former Practices   Maintenance of a loyal membership in a cooperative marketing association is difficult at best. In time of acute price depression the strain upon its members becomes intense. Many of them may become panicky. Losing much of their restraint and forgetting their pledges to the cooperative association, they tend to drop back into unorganized and haphazard marketing. Each member seems obsessed with the idea that he must get rid of his own crop before the price drops yet further. The result is a scramble to move the crop to market at top speed. Glutted markets and still lower prices generally follow. The cooperative-marketing association and its members are left "holding the bag" and are frequently the heaviest losers. The story might have been vastly different had all the members stayed with their organization instead of some breaking away, flooding the markets, and demoralizing prices for all. The more highly perishable the commodity, the greater appears to be the organization's liability to such desertions in periods of falling prices.

Such a cycle of events was well illustrated in the summer of 1928 during the marketing of the potato crop from one of the heavy producing sections in which a research project on membership relations in cooperative marketing happened to be under way. In this section the less-informed members—tenants and operators of smaller farms—most frequently succumbed to their fears. On the other hand, a few large producers, seemingly from highly individualistic motives, joined the stampede to move their crops. For all of these groups the habit of cooperation with its accompanying restraint upon acts injurious to group welfare had not become sufficiently established to overcome older habits of single-handed action built up in the past when heavy price declines were even more severe and more frequent.

Habits of Cooperative Action

Every cooperative-marketing association, but especially those associations handling perishable or semiperishable commodities, will soon seek to develop strong habits of cooperative action among its members—first, by keeping the members thoroughly informed concerning the association's work, so as to create greater confidence in the organization; second, by holding local group meetings that the members may get better acquainted with and feel more responsibility toward each other and to the association leaders; third, by encouraging every member actively to participate in some phase of work of the association. Something has already been done in this direction. Generally speaking, preventive educational measures are much more

FIGURE 53.—Waiting for freight cars to arrive. More than 40 truck loads of potatoes were lined up before the freight cars came in. The 20 cars put on the siding (all it would hold) were filled in two hours. Falling prices caused the farmers to rush shipments to market

fundamental and effective than are court injunctions, law suits, or other forms of compulsion used to enforce delivery contracts after the crisis has arrived. The latter methods, if resorted to, usually leave the association in a weakened condition and cause a lingering resentment in the minds of the members who were punished for deviating from their path of duty. Successful cooperation in the United States is developed as an habitual way of doing things, working almost unconsciously. Members thus are fully fortified against the temptation to slip back at times into the old path of each for himself.

T. B. MANNY.

COOPERATIVE Marketing Schools for Farmers Held in Three Commonwealths Ten-day schools in cooperative marketing, designed primarily for farm people, were held in Colorado, Arizona, and Tennessee during 1928. The schools were conducted under the auspices of the State department for vocational education in each State; 11 schools were held in Colorado, 4 in Arizona, and 6 in Tennessee. The instructor for all but two of the schools was a man with both academic and practical training in agricultural cooperation. The first two schools in Colorado were conducted by a representative of the Division of Cooperative Marketing, and a second representative of the division assisted in four or five of the later schools in that State. Assistance in some phases of the work was also given by State extension officials, county agents, and representatives of cooperative associations. Two schools, as a rule, were carried on simultaneously in adjoining communities, one being held during the afternoon and the other at night.

It was the purpose of these schools to bring to the farmers unbiased information with regard to marketing and the place and accomplishments of cooperative organizations in providing improved marketing facilities. An important feature of the schools was the fact that they furnished a forum for the discussion of community problems, and in more than one instance they led to the adoption of plans for meeting these problems.

Definite Program Followed

The schools followed a fairly definite program which began with an outline of the status of cooperation, a discussion of marketing functions, and the services which cooperative associations can perform. This was followed by discussion of pooling, financial problems, the responsibilities of members, directors, and managers, and a frank analysis of the advantages and limitations of cooperation. The program was sufficiently flexible to allow ample time for consideration of the special interests and problems of those in attendance. Since each school was conducted by one man throughout the 10-day period, each group became sufficiently well acquainted with the instructor to overcome the disinclination to ask questions or participate in discussion which is so often apparent in farmers' meetings. After the first two or three sessions each school was conducted largely by the conference method.

Attendance at the schools was satisfactory from the point of view of interest and numbers. At many night sessions 70 to 80 farm men and women were present. Schools held in the afternoon did not attract so many people, but, on the average, about 30 were in attendance at these sessions. Other educational activities of the Division of Cooperative Marketing are described in the Yearbooks for 1926 and 1927.

A. W. McKay.

C ORN-BORER Control by Mechanical Means is Advanced a Stage. Among the various methods being advocated for the control of the European corn borer are those by mechanical means, one of which is the cutting of corn low, or within 2 inches of the ground surface. Investigations by entomologists indicate that corn cut at ground level contains over 99 per cent of the borers in the whole plant. Proper treatment, therefore, of the resulting fodder—such as ensiling or effective shredding—would result in practically complete destruction of the borers.

The standard corn binder leaves stubble from 4 to 6 inches high. The borers left in this stubble may greatly increase the intensity of infestation the following year. Entomologists have found 10 per cent of all the borers in the whole plant located within 6 inches of the ground.

Efforts during the past two or three years toward devising a satisfactory, yet economical, method of low-cutting corn have resulted in the development of the stationary low-cutting attachment for corn binders. This consists essentially of a flat, stationary knife, an elevating shield, extension butt gatherer chains, and extra throat springs.

FIGURE 54.—Cutting corn with binder equipped with stationary knife, low-cutting attachment. Corn on left of macnine cut with standard binder

FIGURE 55.—Two rows cut with standard binder; balance with stationary knife, low-cutting attachment

The flat knife, sharpened on a 2-inch taper on the under forward edge and mounted 4 inches below the gatherer angles for clearance, cuts the stalks at ground level as the binder is pulled along. A slight outward curvature (51-inch radius) is given to the knife to insure better cutting and clearing of trash.   The side knives are slightly cut away to permit the installation of the shield which elevates the stalks and prevents them from being cut a second time.   Sufficient throat space is left at the side of the elevating shield for weeds to pass to the reciprocating knife and be cut so as to prevent clogging.

Extension butt gatherer chains pull the butts up the shield so as to maintain the vertical position of the stalk.   If the butts were retarded, as would otherwise occur, throat clogging with stalks would result. Extra throat springs press the stalks positively against the chains so their lugs will more effectively elevate them.   The butt throat spring keeps the butts on the elevating shield and prevents their getting into the weed throat where second cutting would occur.

Satisfactory Performance in Tests

Repeated tests on cornstalks growing in a wide variety of soil conditions, in foul soil rank with weeds, and in fact in any soil which would support a stalk and where any other binder would be used, have shown satisfactory performance.   Binders fitted with these attachments, operated by farmers and pulled by either horses or tractors, have proved effective.   (Figs. 54 and 55.)

To date, these attachments have been worked out for only two of the well-known makes of binders.   Attachments for others are in the process of development.   As the farmer can make these devices himself, or will shortly be able to obtain them from the respective binder manufacturers, an important step has been made in controlling the corn borer by mechanical means.

R. B. GRAY.

CORN-BORER Research Lays Foundation for Control of the Pest   When, in the fall of 1917, it was discovered that a dangerous alien insect enemy of that wonderful giant grass which Americans value highly as corn but which the rest of the world calls maize or mealies, had silently deployed its ravaging ranks throughout the fertile fields of the market gardens of suburban Boston, the announcement caused not a single ripple of interest on the surface of the ocean of finance.   Now, however, after the lapse of a decade, and the expenditure of fully $15,000,-000 in combat against this same pest, the financiers of agriculture, and indeed the whole business organization of the Corn Belt, stand on the qui vive for news regarding the progress of the fight against the European corn borer.

The story of that fight has been published; the actual weapons of combat and the telling way in which they are being employed have been abundantly described both in the daily press and in popular periodicals throughout the country, but the story of how these weapons were forged, and from whence came the basic knowledge which has since given corn growers the right to regard the corn borer as a foe that can be conquered, remains to be related.

After this intruder was discovered by Stuart Vinal, who died in 1918 as the direct result of his devotion to this problem, it was dispatched to Washington for identification; and, at the very moment that its dangerous character was confirmed, plans began evolving in the

Bureau of Entomology of the Department of Agriculture for the laying of that foundation of research which constitutes the indispensable basis for all efficient insect-control work.

Tiny Laboratory Building Obtained

As a nucleus for such work, a tiny laboratory building was rented at Arlington, Mass., in the spring of 1918. Here began the first serious studies of the corn borer made in this country, and from this humble beginning has grown that fine research organization which since has become responsible for the accumulation of the vast array of tabulated information regarding the corn borer that even now points the way to ascendency over the pest.

Soon it was ascertained that the insect had come to America both from Italy and from Hungary, hidden away in broom corn imported from these countries for manufacture. A search of their literature revealed that it was known there as a pest of maize, but the publications regarding it were of rather fragmentary character. No complete account was extant, and some of the published information seemed contradictory and confused in character. Through L. O. Howard, then chief of the Bureau of Entomology, the services of J. Jablonowski, official entomologist for the Kingdom of Hungary, were engaged to write a full account of the corn borer and its habits in his country and adjacent territory. This he did in a very competent manner; and his manuscript, which later was abstracted and mimeographed, proved invaluable as a source of suggestive information.

In 1919, after public interest in the pest had partially awakened and funds for more adequate research had become available, it was determined to attempt to introduce the parasitic enemies of the corn borer from Europe, as an aid to active control work. Since that time the collection and shipment to this country of many thousands of the beneficial insect parasites of the corn borer, comprising at least 12 species, has been accomplished.

Research in Massachusetts

Although the corn borer was discovered to be present in the east-central and western parts of New York in 1919, the major research studies of it were conducted for several years in eastern Massachusetts because the insect was very abundant there, not only in corn but in many other host plants which it did not attack in the more western regions. This condition afforded facilities for research which were not available elsewhere.

A branch laboratory was, however, established, first at Scotia, N. Y., near the location of the first infestation found in that State, but afterwards transferred to Silver Creek, in the corn-canning section of the same State, where it has since remained.

The small laboratory at Arlington soon became inadequate, and more spacious quarters were obtained in the same town. Here, during the period from 1920 to 1925, inclusive, the pioneer, basic, research work on this insect was accomplished. The reactions of the insect to heat, cold, and humidity were determined for the egg, larval, and pupal stages. The degree of fecundity of the adult was observed, and its powers of flight were demonstrated over the waters of Cape Cod Bay for a distance of some 20 miles. The ability of the borers to survive while submerged in either fresh or salt water for days at a time was shown, and their almost complete immunity from the effects of frost was demonstrated by freezing them and afterwards thawing them out and observing the erstwhile frozen corpses transform into healthy moths which laid eggs that produced voracious progeny.

Most important investigations to determine the plants affording potential food and shelter to the insect were conducted on a plat of ground donated for that purpose by a public-spirited citizen of the near-by town of Medford. Among the plants thus tested were many standard varieties of corn, sorghum, including the sweet, grain, and broom varieties, cotton, sugar cane, small grains, including rice and millets, tobacco, garden vegetables, and flowering plants, and weeds almost without number.

Experiments With Forage

The forage legumes were experimented with in great variety, including the clovers, alfalfa, soy beans, cowpeas, velvet beans, and many others.

Another line of research followed at this time was the testing of lights of various colors and intensities, to determine whether the moths could be lured to them and trapped. The results of this work were negative in all cases, but they furnished information that has proved invaluable in the last several years, when inventors and others, literally by hundreds, have approached the department with proposals to utilize trap lights in this impracticable way.

Various poisonous chemicals were tested as insecticides for the pest, including practically all of the standard arsenicals and many other poisons, but without any substantial success. In point of fact, much of the work of these years along all lines had negative results, but these served to clear the ground for subsequent work which gave results of the utmost utility.

It was in these years, too, that the first efforts toward mechanical and cultural control were initiated. The first experiments were undertaken to determine the effects of both spring and fall plowing on the corn borer, hidden at these seasons in the stalks, cobs, and stubble of corn. The first tests of the burying of stalks in compost or manure were made, and many futile attempts were made, with various apparatus, to dig out and burn the stubble above the surface of the ground.

The lines of promising procedure indicated by the research work of these early years are the ones which now are being followed successfully in the fight against the corn borer in the Corn Belt. As the insect grew more numerous in the region of the Great Lakes, it became possible to test in a large and practical way such simple methods of control as the plowing under of cornstalks, stubble, and débris, the breaking over of standing stalks with a pole or iron rail and the subsequent raking and burning of them. The last-named method, followed by the plowing under of the remaining débris, gave a control that was entirely satisfactory.

Beneficial Parasites Established

In the meantime additional field laboratories had been established at Sandusky, Ohio, and at Monroe, Mich., where the reaction of the corn borer to these environments was studied, and its parasites were reared and liberated to prey upon it, and thus eventually to aid the corn growers in their fight against the pest. Seven of these parasites have now been recovered from the field, a fact indicating that they have become successfully established; and although many years must elapse before material benefit can be expected from them, substantial aid may be hoped for in the end.

In order that this serious problem shall have the benefit of the most highly trained minds in the land, the department for the last three years has called annual conferences of eminent entomologists, agronomists, and other scientists, in Washington, to consider the complete program of corn-borer research for the ensuing year. Such meetings have been the source of material aid in obtaining complete cooperation of the States interested, and have elicited suggestions for supplementary lines of research that may prove of great value. One such development is the building in the summer of 1928 of two field cages, each of one acre in extent. These cages were erected over fields that had been treated for control by cultural methods, to ascertain how many moths would escape death in the clean-up process. The results in both cases indicate the substantial success of the treatments, and serve to clinch the argument in favor of plowing and other simple farm operations as the logical method of control now at hand.

Research is the foundation upon which is built the structure of all efficient insect-control work.

W. R. WALTON.

———————

CORN Breeding for Resistance to Cold Yields Good Results   Frost before corn is fully matured is one of the great hazards of the corn crop. The Corn Belt is subjected to wide variations in temperature in the early fall. Almost every year there is a period varying from a few days to more than two weeks when the night temperatures drop below 50° F. This cool period usually is ended by still colder nights, the effects of which are described popularly as light frost, heavy frost, or killing frost. Frequently the colder period is followed by several days or weeks of warmer weather, favorable for normal ripening of uninjured corn.

Recent studies indicate that corn plants may be injured by temperatures above those at which frosts occur. Some strains are injured by a succession of cool nights during which the temperature drops only to 50° or 45° F. Other strains are killed by a few hours of exposure to temperatures around 40°. Although some strains may not actually be killed by such temperatures, their maturing often may be slowed down sufficiently to reduce the quality of the grain. Corn from plants killed prematurely by cold not only is inferior in quality but also is more susceptible to ear rots. Thus there frequently is much commercial damage to the crop when the temperature falls below 40° for a few hours, even if there is no actual frost.

Differences in Cold Resistance

It has been found also that commercial open-pollinated varieties and recombinations of inbred strains vary greatly in their resistance to injury from cold, including so-called light and killing frosts. Many of these have been injured or killed by a succession of cold nights with temperatures above freezing. Other recombinations and small percentages of plants in some commercial varieties have withstood temperatures below 32° F. for as much as six hours. A few hybrids apparently have not been injured by exposure to a temperature of 28° for several hours. These differences have been observed under natural conditions during the last five years at widely separated points in the Corn Belt, and some of these differences were demonstrated

FIGURE 56.—Portable refrigeration chamber used in the field study of cold resistance and susceptibility. The desired temperature is obtained by an automatically controlled mechanical refrigeration unit mounted on the side of the chamber

under accurately controlled artificial conditions in the field in 1928. (Fig. 56.)

Some cold-resistant and cold-susceptible strains have remained so from year to year. Open-pollinated varieties have been improved in cold resistance by the continuous selection of well-matured seed from vigorous plants, the stalks and some leaves of which have remained green after exposure to several cool nights. However, the greatest improvement in cold resistance probably will come from selection within inbred lines. Recombinations of cold-resistant inbreds, possessing other necessary qualities, not only have given higher yields of better corn but also have been more resistant to stalk breaking and stalk rotting after maturity.

Seed From Cold-Resistant Plants Superior

Seed from cold-resistant plants has proved superior to that from plants of the same inbreds and recombinations killed prematurely by cold, even when both lots of seed apparently were equal in visible characters and in laboratory germination. This superiority of matured seed from cold-resistant plants expresses itself in increased seedling resistance to disease, in greater cold resistance in the fall, and in greater resistance to lodging and stalk breaking after maturity.

J. R. HOLBERT, and
W. L. BURLISON.

CORN Plants Dying Early May Reveal Potash Lack in Soil The premature dying of corn plants in black sandy soils is due to soil conditions characterized by a failure to supply these plants with sufficient potassium salts to complete the development and maturing of the ears. The plants may develop vigorously during the seedling and early growth periods and

FIGURE 57.—These corn plants were starved for potash at the roasting-ear stage of ear development. Such plants die prematurely and the ears remain starchy and chaffy with unfilled tips

attain normal size for the variety, yet before killing frosts occur they break over, the leaves die suddenly, and the ears remain incompletely developed, with soft cobs and chaffy grains. Such ears are subjected to further losses in quality through weathering and subsequent invasion by ear rots. Local areas in individual fields of corn, entire fields, or entire localities may suffer from this general failure of the corn plants to utilize the full growing season, even when the best locally adapted strains of corn are grown.

Cooperative experiments conducted in areas where premature dying is prevalent in Indiana indicate an unbalanced condition of soil fertility. A thorough examination of the cropping history on these areas generally reveals the continued removal of crop residues and a fertilizer practice confined to the application of phosphates. This trouble is encountered frequently on these soils even when available potash is supplied in small quantities either in farm manures or as mineral salts. Under these conditions the supplies of available potash are exhausted by the corn crop just at the roasting-ear stage of ear development when the plants seem to have the greatest demand for potassium salts.

Usually Have Enough Nitrate

The tests on corn plants in the first phases of premature dying show that they usually are amply supplied with nitrates. The silk emergence is not delayed, yet the plants are checked in development while the grains are still in the milk. When these plants are split lengthwise the nodal tissues are found to be disorganized. Chemical tests show this internal symptom to be associated with the accumulation of iron compounds in these tissues. Some strains of corn are more affected by the nodal accumulations and the subsequent premature ripening than others. When adequate potassium salts are supplied to these corn plants the nodal tissues remain clear and free from iron accumulations and, unless frost occurs, the leaves remain green until the grains are completely filled.

Accordingly, the control measures for premature ripening include a

FIGURE 58.—These corn plants supplied with adequate potash maintained green leaves until the ears were mature

more careful selection of seed for local adaptation, together with changes in crop-residue disposal and fertilizer practices to supply the needed potassium salts to carry the plants through the season to complete maturity. JOHN F. TROST.

CORN-STOVER Shredding Pays if Supply of Hay and Straw is Short   Use of shredded corn stover is rather common in the eastern part of the Corn Belt. In parts of western Ohio and southeastern Michigan the fodder grown on about 25 per cent of the 1927 corn acreage was shredded. In the western part of the Corn Belt the number of acres shredded and the percentage of the total acreage shredded were relatively small.

Shredding is most important in those districts and on those farms where there is a shortage of hay or straw for roughage. Farmers who have too few cattle to make a silo practicable often shred to provide sufficient roughage, as do those with large herds of dairy cows, which require a large quantity of roughage not only for feed but for bedding. Over a large area in southwestern Ohio corn is cut so that winter

FIGURE 59.—About one-half as much man labor is required by the use of a husker-shredder in harvesting corn as is necessary for husking out of the shock by hand and hauling the ear corn and stover to the barn

wheat can be drilled, and it is shredded principally to get the corn husked.

Shredded stover has about the same feeding value as unshredded stover that is in equally good condition. If the shredded stover keeps well it usually has a greater feeding value than shock fodder that has been left in the field all winter. It is a better roughage than oat straw or timothy hay for cattle and better than straw for horses. It is best suited to wintering mature animals like idle horses and dry beef cows.

An important reason for shredding on many farms is to get an extra supply of good bedding. Ordinarily from one-third to one-half of the stover fed to livestock is refused; this is taken out of the manger for bedding purposes. It is more readily absorbent than straw and does not work back in the stall so freely.

The shredded material makes much better bedding than unshredded stover and the manure is more easily handled. The greater ease in handling this material when cleaning barns and feed lots is generally recognized by those who have used shredded stover.

About 19 hours of man labor per acre of corn yielding 40 bushels is necessary to husk corn out of the shock by hand, put it in the crib, and haul the stover to the barn. Only 10 man hours per acre are necessary for husking and shredding corn with the same yield per acre.

Space Requirements Halved

Besides saving labor in harvesting the shredded stover requires not more than half as much storage space as the long fodder. Most barns are not built to store unshredded stover conveniently; the husker-shredder can blow the material into a hay loft or other space difficult of access. Shredded stover is easier to handle and handier to feed than unshredded stover. Bundles of unshredded stover are often pulled out of the rack and tramped in the manure.

Considering all the advantages of shredded stover, the use of the husker-shredder is entirely justified on farms where corn is now husked out of the shock by hand unless a farmer is willing to expend his own labor at much less than the usual rate for hired labor to avoid the cash outlay for the use of a machine.

With increased corn-borer infestation in prospect, the husker-shredder has another advantage in the disposal of stalks. It is difficult to burn long stalks that have been partly tramped in the manure; it is often unfeasible to bury them deeply enough to prevent the emergence of the corn borer in the spring; and if the unshredded stover is fed to livestock on pastures the remaining stalks must be raked and burned, or plowed under. This extra work is obviated by shredding, since from 85 to 95 per cent of the borers in the stalks are killed in the shredding process.

GEORGE W. COLLIER.

C. S. A. 2-26

UNITED STATES DEPARTMENT OF AGRICULTURE
BUREAU OF AGRICULTURAL ECONOMICS
BOARD OF COTTON EXAMINERS

147

FORM A
SAMPLE CLASSIFICATION MEMORANDUM

Request ....

Marks	No. B/C

Location of cotton ....

MARKS—TAG NOS.	GRADE :	REDUCED FROM—	: a/c	STAPLE	REMARKS	MARKS—TAG NOS.	GRADE :	REDUCED FROM—	: a/c	STAPLE	REMARKS

...., ..., 19......

Pursuant to Section 4 of the U. S. Cotton Standards Act and the regulations of the Secretary of Agriculture thereunder, we certify that we have examined the samples of cotton described herein and find the classification of such samples, according to the official cotton standards of the United States, to be as shown above.

This classification applies only to the samples as and when submitted, and may or may not be the true classification of the cotton which said samples purport to represent.

BOARD OF COTTON EXAMINERS,

By...
Chairman.

U. S. GOVERNMENT PRINTING OFFICE

FIGURE 60.—Memorandum used in submitting cotton samples for classification by United States boards of cotton examiners at various cotton markets

COTTON Classification Service is Maintained Under Standards Act

A cotton classification service is now maintained by the Division of Cotton Marketing under the United States cotton standards act which should prove of much value to cotton farmers as well as to dealers and handlers in general. Any grower or owner of cotton may send representative samples of it, for classification, to the United States boards of cotton examiners at New Orleans, Houston, Galveston, or New York, or to the appeal board of review examiners at Washington. Suitable forms for requesting this service may be secured, upon request, from any of these boards.

Persons submitting samples for classification in this way are given a memorandum of classification on a form such as that illustrated in Figure 60, on page 232. The cotton farmer who wants direct evidence of the quality of his commodity may easily avail himself of this service for the small charge of 40 cents for each sample submitted.

Other forms of classification service are provided for the settlement of disputes between buyers and sellers and for the determination of the grade of bales of cotton which are stored in approved warehouses and sampled under official supervision.

C. L. FINCH.

COTTON Fabrics Again in Fashion's Favor for Women's Summer Wear

The cycle of fashion has again whirled around and brought cotton back into its own. This is fortunate for American producers and manufacturers, both of whom have suffered financially during the past few years. It is well for them that Dame Fashion is again looking with favor upon their products, but it is especially fortunate for the American woman who for several summers has also suffered—not financially, but for want of cool, washable dresses, of this serviceable material.

Those of us who have lived through the hot summer months have longed for the old-fashioned dimities and prints in which we used to be so comfortable. Now they are back in overwhelming array, together with cotton piqués and broadcloths of every description. There has never been such a wide variety of artistically designed cotton fabrics, and never have the dress manufacturers and stylists showed such an interest in the possibilities of cotton as a dress material.

All of this has not come about by accident. Home economics and other clothing specialists have long been advocating that, during certain seasons, cotton has advantages for both clothing and household purposes which can not be excelled by other fabrics. Of course, like anything else, the particular fabric chosen must be appropriate for the specific use to which it is to be put. All cotton fabrics are not suitable for all purposes, and attempts to use them where other fibers are more appropriate only brings dissatisfaction.

Cotton is suitable for summer, street, house, and party frocks if correct designs and colors are chosen. It is not suitable for elaborate evening gowns. If the correct textures are chosen, it is one of the best materials for underwear. Cotton is also preeminently the children's fiber, for in their clothing washability counts above all else.

In many instances cotton is the fabric that should be chosen for household textiles. Fads for other materials may come and go, but eventually the home maker who is sincerely trying to get her money's worth comes back to cotton for most of her curtains and bedding.

FIGURE 61.—Osnaburg, a fabric made of low-grade cotton and hitherto used for industrial purposes, has artistic possibilities in interior decoration

Possibilities of Industrial Cloths

Recently she has been learning of the many possibilities among the so-called industrial cloths. These fabrics are made primarily for use in certain kinds of manufacturing processes, but most of them are of that coarse, open construction which is now so popular for use in interior decoration. Many of them are inexpensive, and all are very durable. Osnaburg, sometimes called almanac and Greenville cloth, is one of these. It can be obtained in a great variety of finishes, but the type with irregular yarns which add to the "craftsman" appearance of the fabric is perhaps more desirable for most purposes.

Osnaburg makes excellent coverlets, pillows, bags, curtains, and draperies for the all-year-around house, and in the camp or summer cottage it is one of those materials that look well on almost every piece of makeshift furniture. Attractive pillows for the boat or canoe can be made of it if contrasting colors are used for decoration. In addition to its utility it has the great advantage of being very inexpensive. Since it is manufactured from a grade of cotton which is not satisfactory for finer goods, it helps the American producer by increasing the use of the less salable part of the cotton supply.

These are just a few of the examples of the cotton fabrics which are now available. If they are chosen wisely, their use will bring great comfort as well as the satisfaction of knowing that a product of American industry is being utilized to good advantage right at home.

RUTH O'BRIEN.

COTTON-FIBER Research Points Way to Better Marketing Practices In the efforts which have been made in recent years to improve cotton marketing methods, emphasis has been given to the importance of recognizing and rewarding quality. That quality in production is most encouraged when better quality is given a better price and poorer cotton is given a just discount has been repeatedly pointed out. Quality deserves and receives special consideration in the marketing of such a crop as cotton. The crop embraces a wide range of unassorted qualities. At the same time nearly all of the crop must undergo manufacture before it can be used. The properties of the raw cotton fibers, individually and in mass, affect both the manner of behavior of the material in the processes of manufacture and the qualities of the finished product.

To meet the requirements of delicate machinery, to insure the correct behavior of the material in manufacture, and to effect the production of textile goods of specified qualities, it is necessary that at some point in the marketing operations the raw cotton be selected out of the crop and be accumulated according to a system of quality classification for the particular purpose for which it is needed.

Accordingly, official standards for grade and length of staple have been established to facilitate and give stability to these operations in marketing. The grade standards embrace factors of quality—color, foreign matter, and ginning "preparation." The staple standards consider only length of fiber. Thirty-seven grades and something over 34 lengths of staple are officially recognized.

These standards have been developed by use of the best methods as yet available. They permit of fine distinctions in the classification and selection of cotton and fulfill to a large degree the requirements of the markets and the mills. The relationships, however, between the qualities represented in the established standards and the qualities of manufactured products have not yet been determined. The usefulness of the standards will be materially enhanced when these relationships can be established. To bridge this gap is a long task in which research workers are now engaged.

33023°—29——16

Cotton fibers possess certain properties, other than those recognized and graduated in the standards, which may affect both their behavior in manufacturing processes and the quality of the manufactured product. Preliminary studies have shown that fiber strength, cross-section area, and shape, flexibility, and conformation are influential. Relative uniformity of length is important, as is the distribution of shorter and longer fibers about the predominant or modal length.

Existence of differences in these properties is clearly indicated by results obtained from different cottons in manufacture. It is here that differences in the utility of cottons appear, though often from hidden causes. These differences in utility may and often do account for differences in price amounting to several cents a pound in addition to the price differences attributable to grade and staple length. Differences in these characteristics affect the appearance and "feel" of the sample so that in discriminating markets, where these properties are referred to by the general term "character," variations are roughly

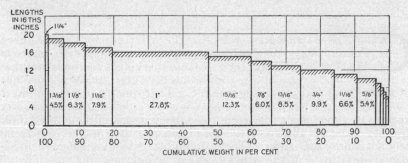

Weight distribution of fiber lengths in a relatively uniform cotton classed as one-inch staple. Variation of fiber lengths is an important factor of cotton quality. Different cottons vary greatly in this respect

FIGURE 62.—Weight distribution of fiber lengths in a relatively uniform cotton classed as 1-inch staple. Variation of fiber lengths is an important factor of cotton quality. Different cottons vary greatly in this respect

distinguished both in classification and in price. The lack, however, of practical and well-defined standards for character is a serious drawback in cotton marketing.

In establishing standards for character, all these properties need to be scientifically described and measured and then, through special spinning tests under controlled conditions, to be correlated to the spinning behavior and to the measurable qualities of the product. With this done, their influence upon spinning behavior of the fiber and upon the quality of the product may be understood, and the relative importance of the principal fiber characteristics and properties established. Beginnings in this work fortunately have been made.

Such an evaluation of the properties of cotton fibers is the key to the extension of the standards system and to further simplification and refinement of existing standards; and the results should have wider application, particularly in indicating quality objectives to agronomists and commercial cotton breeders and in affording criteria of progress. Precise measures of the properties of cotton fibers are useful in any study of the factors of heredity and environment which influence their development.

ARTHUR W. PALMER.

COTTON Cooperatives Liberalize Contracts and Extend Services — Cooperative cotton marketing began during the economic depression of 1920 and 1921, when the price of cotton fell from more than 40 cents per pound to less than 15 cents. By 1923, cotton cooperatives had been formed in every important cotton-producing State. Most of the original cooperative marketing contracts, which were for five years, contained no withdrawal provision and provided for only seasonal pools. Toward the end of this period, it was evident that the new contracts would have to be so drawn as to take into consideration the credit conditions which confront many cotton growers and that they should also confer upon grower members the right to withdraw at stated periods. One or two associations liberalized their contracts after the first three or four years and, by the 1928 season, all of the 15 large-scale cotton cooperatives were operating under contracts which were different in many respects from the original ones.

In these new contracts an annual withdrawal clause is provided so that dissatisfied members can terminate their membership during stated periods, and a part of the sales responsibility is left in the hands of the grower by provision for short-time pools. Under these agreements the grower has the choice of four alternatives when he ships cotton to his association: (1) The daily pool, under which he may select the day on which his cotton shall be sold; (2) the monthly pool, under which the grower may select the month in which his cotton shall be sold; (3) the seasonal pool, under which the time of sale is fixed by the association, and which is similar to the pool provided for in the old contract; and (4) what is known as a suspense pool. Cotton may be shipped to the suspense pool and held there pending a final decision as to which of the other three pools the grower wishes to use.

Futures Market Used for Hedging

In the daily and monthly pools, the futures market is used by the association to hedge the members' cotton until such time as the spot cotton is sold. This is done by selling on the cotton futures exchanges futures contracts equal in quantity to the number of bales owned by the member. When the spot cotton is sold, an equal number of futures contracts are bought, thereby removing the hedge. A member who ships to a short-time pool receives the usual initial advance at time of shipment, generally about 60 per cent of the market value, and, in addition, when he orders his cotton "fixed" on the futures market, he receives a second advance which brings his total advance up to 85 to 90 per cent of the market value of his cotton. The remaining amount, less association operating expenses, is given to him at the end of the marketing season. The use of the futures markets for hedging purposes enables the association to liquidate the member's cotton at his option, and for this reason these pools appeal to a large group of producers who need their money as promptly as possible.

The cotton cooperatives, in addition to adjusting their form of organization and contracts to suit the growers' needs, have made great progress in adjusting their practices and policies to meet mill needs. They are planning their operations with the thought of rendering maximum service to both growers and spinners.

At a conference of cotton cooperatives, held in Memphis, Tenn., in September, 1928, the representatives present subscribed to the following economic services as those which cotton cooperatives can render advantageously to the grower:

Accurate grading and stapling by licensed classers, under Government supervision.

Making returns to growers on the basis of grade and staple.

Selling direct to mills.

Providing an efficient selling agency for members who use short-time pools.

Obtaining highest possible average seasonal pool prices through (1) use of a trained sales force and (2) by sales based on scientific analysis of market conditions.

Reduction of market risks by pooling.

Storage and insurance at minimum rates.

Obtaining funds for commodity financing at low rates of interest.

Stimulation of interest in better ginning.

Encouragement of the production of better staple.

J. S. HATHCOCK.

COTTON Progress in Irrigated Valleys a Community Problem Farmers will grow good cotton if they can sell it for more than poor cotton. Selling at "flat prices" is the commercial millstone that keeps the cotton farmers submerged and hopeless. How they are to get more for producing the better cotton is the crucial question of cotton improvement. Without this inducement, it is useless to bewail the production of inferior fiber or to expect that production will be improved in the direction of better quality. Improved varieties and methods are at hand but can not be used effectively unless the issue of better prices for better cotton can be definitely determined and brought home to the farmers. The individual farmer has no prospect of changing the commercial system, but communities of producers acting together can obtain better treatment.

Greater progress has been made in community production and marketing of cotton in the irrigated valleys of the Southwestern States than in the older cotton centers. The farmers of the irrigated districts are more familiar with ideas of community cooperation and standardized products than are farmers in the eastern Cotton Belt. In California especially, where highly organized fruit industries have been developed, many of the cotton growers are aware that a standardized product is necessary for establishing better marketing systems, as they also have recognized the need of community organization in order to maintain pure stocks of seed. A one-variety organization of cotton growers has maintained itself in the Coachella Valley of southern California since 1920, and many other communities in the irrigated valleys are now planting only one variety of cotton.

Struggling Under Double Handicap

Some of the irrigated valleys are still struggling under the double handicap of mixed stocks of seed and irregular conditions of production, while other communities have established the production and use of good seed but have still to recognize adequately the requirements of uniform conditions in the fields, in order to produce regular, uniform fiber. Where the cotton is grown on heavy impervious soils and periods of extreme temperatures are encountered, great irregularity of the fiber may result, even in purebred varieties. The damage to the plants is easily seen by inspection of the fields, in wilting of the leaves, blasting of the buds, and stunted, misshapen bolls that fail to open properly. The damaged bolls have many abortive seeds, and the fiber is much shorter and weaker than in well-developed bolls. All varieties of cotton are affected, the Pima cotton less than upland varieties, and the Acala cotton less than the eastern upland sorts; but no variety produces good cotton under the extreme conditions or uniform cotton in "spotted" fields.

The farmers, of course, are aware of the injury to their cotton, but as long as it all brings the same price there is no definite inducement to take the precautions that are necessary to produce uniform fiber or to place the damaged cotton in separate bales. Where cotton is irregular in the fields, the usual commercial classing of samples from

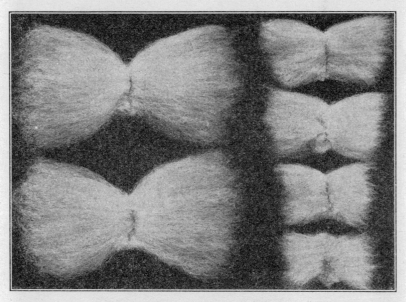

FIGURE 63.—Effects of extreme conditions on length of staple. Good fiber of Acala cotton compared with short, weak fiber produced under severe stress conditions in the Salt River Valley, Ariz. (Natural size.)

the bales does not establish a satisfactory condition of uniformity in the fiber. The lack of necessary discrimination of fiber quality under the present commercial system has become especially plain in the southwestern districts, because the conditions of production in many localities are very irregular.

Difficulties in Marketing

When the effects of irregular conditions of production are considered, it is no wonder that difficulties have been encountered in the marketing of the irrigated cotton. The buyers as well as the growers are being forced to a clearer recognition of the need of uniform conditions in the fields, in order to produce uniform fiber. Classing the cotton in the field is easier and much more effective than classing the fiber from the bales. Some of the more progressive buyers already are adopting the precaution of going into the fields to determine the uniformity of the cotton, and this practice may become general as the facts are better known. There is no way to be assured of the uniformity of the bales except by seeing the cotton in the field. Separation of the good and bad cotton probably is the only effective way of discouraging the production of inferior fiber, which on the present basis tends to depreciate the value of all of the irrigated cotton.

Where the community production of one variety of cotton has been established, the classing of the cotton in the field becomes a practical possibility and opens the way to a just discrimination of fiber quality in primary markets, of which there is little prospect where many varieties are grown and the seed is mixed and mongrelized. With production based on one variety, the crop can be standardized by

FIGURE 64.—Effects of extreme conditions in reducing size of bolls. Full-size boll of Mebane cotton in comparison with small bolls produced under severe stress conditions in the Imperial Valley, Calif. (Natural size.)

reference to the conditions of growth. Working out these relations in the irrigated districts may be to the great advantage of the entire Cotton Belt, as leading to more general use of good varieties and to the production of uniform, standardized fiber.

O. F. COOK.

COTTON Quality Studies Show Opportunities to Adjust Staple Production Cotton prices are affected by the quality as well as by the quantity of cotton produced. In the research program of the Bureau of Agricultural Economics the research on cotton marketing embodies two types of study—technological, to determine the elementary physical properties of cotton fiber; and economic, dealing with supply and consumption in terms of quality and with the markets and marketing processes.

Data obtained in Georgia and a Texas-Oklahoma area, compared with results of a study of American mill consumption, indicate that these areas produce too much cotton seven-eighths of an inch and under, and too little cotton fifteen-sixteenths of an inch and above, in length. This situation may be attributed to the custom of local buyers of paying flat prices for all qualities in a given market. This serves as a rather effective discouragement to quality and an encouragement to quantity production.

In these areas the yields of cotton the past year of 1 inch and above in length suggest the possibility of producing satisfactory crops of cotton from fifteen-sixteenths of an inch to $1\frac{1}{16}$ inches in the uplands and from $1\frac{1}{8}$ to $1\frac{1}{4}$ inches in the more fertile valleys.

In several of the States practical programs are already under way in which the information gathered last year is being used to encourage production of cotton of better quality.

The studies have the enthusiastic support of the spinners, merchants and farmers, and the agricultural colleges of the Cotton Belt.

B. YOUNGBLOOD.

COTTONSEED'S Kernel Content and Components Are Basis for Grading Cottonseed crushers produce two major and two minor products from the seed. The major products are cottonseed oil and protein and the minor products are linters and hulls. Apparently if these variable major products could be grouped in order of increasing quantities, the grading of cottonseed would be simplified.

The oil and protein are contained within the kernel and the kernel is confined within the hull. But kernels and hulls may have variable moisture contents, and the hulls may be thick or thin, dense or light. The kernels may be well developed and full or poorly developed and shriveled. The season and the soil may be good or bad, conducive to high or to low oil development, the oil content of the kernels actually varying from 25 to 42 per cent or more. The same or other conditions may affect the protein development, and it actually varies in the kernels from below 25 to above 46 per cent. The kernels may vary from about 45 to 65 per cent of the total weight of the seed and the net kernel content of seed as received at the oil mills has been found to be as low as 35 per cent. In other words, some tons of cottonseed, as they arrive at the oil mills, contain only 700 pounds of kernels, whereas other lots may have over 1,300 pounds of kernels to the ton.

The value of a ton of seed may be measured by its kernel content even though a pound of oil is worth many pounds of protein, for nature has set up a natural correlation between the amount of oil and the amount of protein in the same seed. This relation is so consistent that it may be considered a rule that as the percentage of oil goes down the percentage of protein goes up, the values tending to balance one another. The net kernel content of the seed is believed to be the most accurate physical indicator of the quantitative value of cottonseed. It is difficult to make a perfect separation of kernels from hulls. Mechanical engineers are working on the problem, and when a machine is made by which the net kernel content of a representative sample of cottonseed can be discovered it will be possible for every seller and buyer of cottonseed to determine its quantitative value.

Determining Oil and Protein Content

Percentages of oil and protein can be determined chemically in a sample of cottonseed and the pounds of oil and protein in any lot of seed can be calculated provided the amount of moisture and dirt or trash in the lot of seed is known. Since the values of the oil and protein respond to the same influences, there is a correlation of values of a unit of oil and of a unit of protein. The ratio, 1 to 5, is so constant as to be almost fixed. The unit of protein used is a pound of cake or meal analyzing 41.13 per cent protein and known as 8 per cent ammonia cake.

With this relation the number of pounds of protein indicated by chemical analyses may be converted into terms of oil, which if added to the indicated pounds of oil will give, in effect, an oil cake reciprocal. In analyses of approximately 400,000 tons of seed originating in all parts of the Cotton Belt the average oil-cake reciprocal has been found to be 555.

Suppose we assume as a standard ton one having an oil-cake reciprocal of 555, then each 1 per cent of this reciprocal, either greater or less than the standard, would be equivalent to 1 per cent of the basis value. For example, if a ton of seed with a reciprocal of 555 is worth $50, then a ton of seed with a reciprocal of 555 plus 5.55, or 560.55, would be worth 1 per cent premium, or $50.50, and conversely a ton with a reciprocal of 549.45 would be worth a discount of 1 per cent, or $49.50.

Table Prepared for Grading

Almost all analytical chemists report the percentage of oil, ammonia, moisture, and foreign matter. With such data, if we make a further assumption, that of a standard analysis of 19 per cent oil, 3½ per cent ammonia, and 11 per cent moisture and foreign matter, repetends for oil, ammonia, or protein, and foreign matter, each equivalent to 1 per cent of value are readily determined. A table has been prepared which will assist in determining quickly the relative value of any seed as compared with the value of the standard ton. A copy of the table will be supplied on request. In this table it is assumed that the percentage of oil and of ammonia are calculated on the basis of the standard tolerance 11 per cent of foreign matter, including moisture, and that the actual percentage of foreign matter, including moisture, as found in the seed is given in the report of the chemist.

G. S. MELOY.

CROP Reports Lessen Price Swings; Assist Farmer to Plan Work That farmers are making increasing use of the crop reports issued by the Department of Agriculture is evidenced by the increasing number of letters received from farmers telling how they have benefited by using the information contained in these reports. Some of the farmers who write to the department have figured out in dollars and cents the cash value of certain reports to them, and are strong believers in the reports. However, many farmers still believe that the crop reports are compiled and published for the benefit of trade interests and that they are harmful to the farmers' interest. Sometimes farmers, in response to an invitation to become voluntary crop correspondents, refuse, saying they would feel they were hurting themselves and their neighbors and playing into the hands of the speculators.

The idea seems to be rather widespread in some sections that the Government crop reports hurt the farmers by placing information in the hands of the speculators. This feeling probably grows out of the experience of years of large crops when the reports are associated with falling prices. Many farmers, without thinking the problem through, blame the Government reports for the reduced prices, instead of placing the blame, where it belongs, on the fact of the big crop. The big buyers have their own sources of information. Through trade channels and trained observers sent out to study crop and livestock conditions, they obtain the facts, and if they can keep these facts to themselves they have an advantage over the producers. A farmer is often badly misled by judging the whole crop by conditions in his locality. The farmer who refuses to furnish such crop information and wants to have the Government reports abolished is deluding himself with the idea that by refusing to furnish information he will prevent the facts from getting to those interested in buying his crops. As long as crops are grown in the open and the roads are free, experienced crop observers can form rather close estimates of the condition and yield of various crops. If the crop-reporting system were abolished, the farmers would be the principal losers.

Farmers Made the First Request

It was the farmers themselves who insisted that the Government crop-reporting system be started. In 1855 the president of the Maryland Agricultural Society sent a circular to the presidents of the other State societies, in which he said:

For the promotion of the farming interest of the country, we are anxious to procure the earliest possible information of the crops that the same may be laid before the farmer to guide him in the selection of the best time to dispose of the fruits of his labors. The duty should properly be imposed upon an agricultural department of the General Government, but in the absence of such provision, and in view of the artful practices of speculators and others, operating most disastrously through the base venality of the public press, upon this leading interest, the obligation is devolved upon us.

Many farmers think the Government has a tendency to overestimate crop production. A study of past reports indicates that crops have been more often underestimated than overestimated. Trade interests believe that the Government reports tend to be too conservative. The crop-reporting board is constantly striving for accuracy, knowing that in the end farmers and all other interests will be best served by the truth. If it should continually underestimate the crop, then trade interests would soon learn to discount the Government reports by the amount the estimates were usually below the actual facts. The margin required by dealers between cost and selling prices is less than if they were uncertain as to the size of the crop. This is particularly true of crops which do not have a futures market, such as apples and potatoes.

How the Individual Farmer Benefits

Just how do crop reports benefit the individual farmer? Undoubtedly their greatest value is indirect. Crop reports help to keep a proper relation between supply and price and enable farmers, because of competition between buyers, to obtain the largest possible return.

But the individual farmer can use the reports to govern his own activities. Supply, the principal factor affecting the prices of many products, is made known to the farmer through these reports. By studying the relation of supply to price, which can be learned from Government publications, he can arrive at a fair idea as to what time of the year would be the most profitable for marketing his products.

When the total potato crop, for example, falls below a certain amount it has usually indicated rising prices throughout the marketing season, unless, as sometimes happens, competition among buyers makes the price high at harvesting season. Potato growers who study these things make more money than their neighbors. One large grower, who has made a study of the relation of supply and price, states that he has only once in the last 10 years failed to sell his crop at the top of the market.

The intention-to-plant-and-breed reports issued by the department are probably more useful to the average farmer than are the regular reports issued during the growing season, as this information is gathered and published before planting begins. Farmers, by observing the trend and by studying the agricultural outlook report issued by the department every January, can sometimes make changes in planting and breeding programs which will increase their net returns. The pig surveys are an example. These surveys, made as of June 1 and December 1, not only show the number of pigs born and saved in the fall and spring, from which the changes in the number to be marketed for six months to a year in advance can be determined, but also give the intentions-to-breed reports, which are published in time to enable the farmers to increase or decrease the number of sows to be marketed or bred.

Letters are received from farmers asking why they should give information as to their production when other lines of business do not furnish such information. As a matter of fact, industrial concerns furnish much more information to the public, through Government reports, than do farmers. Information as to unfilled orders, quantities manufactured, stocks, shipments, etc., are regularly furnished to the Department of Commerce by the steel industry, by cotton mills, by lumber mills, and by many other industries. Some of this information is published weekly and some monthly. Farmers furnish less information as to production, stocks, etc., than almost any other business group. The compilation of data for industrial concerns was started at the insistence of these industries, just as the crop reports were begun at the insistence of the farmers.

Misleading Reports Discouraged

The publication of unbiased reports by the Federal Government tends to prevent the issuance of, or to prevent great harm from, incomplete and misleading reports by private agencies. Speculation results from uncertainty, and to the extent that the official crop reports eliminate uncertainty, speculation is discouraged and investment encouraged.

Transportation companies use the crop reports in estimating the number of cars that will be required to move the crops. Improved distribution of cars means better service to the farmers. Bankers and financial institutions use the crop reports as an indication of the amount of capital that will be required to finance the growing and marketing of crops. Insurance companies that deal in crop insurance use the reports and statistics as a basis for establishing fair premium rates. Merchants and manufacturers use crop reports as an index of the buying power of farmers and as a guide to the production, distribution, and sale of farm machinery, equipment, and supplies. From 6 to 12 months are required for the cycle of operations involved in buying raw materials, converting them into manufactured products, and distributing them to the country merchants for sale. It is a great convenience for farmers to be able to secure their machinery and supplies when needed. And to the extent that farmers and merchants can better estimate the demand for their wares and avoid losses from overproduction and bad distribution, they can afford to charge less for the risks involved and supply farmers at lower prices.

W. F. CALLANDER.

CROP-YIELD Forecasts Demand Study of Many Complex Relationships The major function of the crop-reporting board is the recording of the annual production of crops, livestock, and livestock products. But because those functions which are tinged with prophecy are usually more outstanding, the crop forecasts of the board probably attract more attention than its more staid and routine activities. Forecasting of yield per acre and probable production was a natural outgrowth of the function of recording production. If the department's statements of production are valuable to the farmer in planning his marketing program it naturally follows that its statements of probable production are more valuable, since the former are made after he has marketed a portion of his crop whereas the latter are made before he begins to market.

Forecasting of yields per acre had its beginning in the reports of crop progress or condition, the collection of which was begun soon after the Civil War. These related to the progress of the crop as viewed by the farmer who made the reports. If the report was made just at harvest and reported the crop as excellent it followed that a high yield was indicated. If made just after a crop had been practically ruined beyond recovery it followed that a low yield was indicated. Between these two extremes was a vast middle ground wherein the indication of condition in terms of yield per acre was obscure, particularly in the case of early season reports.

The interpretation of condition in terms of probable yield per acre was begun by the department in 1912 for a few major crops, and in 1915 for the principal crops. In general, the interpretation was made on the assumption that the effect of weather and other influences subsequent to the date of the condition report would be average and that probable yield would vary directly in proportion to condition. This practice forms the backbone of the present practice, although modifications have been introduced, based upon studies of the relationship of condition and yield, upon the effect of various factors upon the relationship of condition and yield, and upon the relationship of weather directly to final yield. It is the policy of the department to include in its interpretations the results of these other studies as rapidly as the results prove trustworthy.

The Boll Weevil and Cotton Reports

Such studies are available for an increasing number of crops and in an increasing number of States. Results of studies of the variation in the relationship of condition and yield of cotton due to the boll weevil have played an important part in the cotton crop forecasts. Direct relationships of certain weather factors to the final yield of winter wheat in a number of States have been incorporated. Similar studies in a few States on weather and final potato yields have been used. Studies have been made for all major crops to determine the validity of the assumption that probable yield varies proportionally with condition. In many instances it has been found that some ratio other than a one-to-one ratio has existed in the past. For all major crops, data on probable yield reported by correspondents at the date of the last condition report of the season are now utilized in arriving at indicated final yield.

The necessity for a departure from the original policy and practice in interpreting yield from condition is illustrated by studies in connection with the cotton crop. Almost coincident with the inauguration of the statements of yield and production indicated by condition, the boll weevil spread rapidly over practically the remainder of the Cotton Belt proper. It at once assumed the dominating rôle in the relationship of condition (particularly early in the season) and final yield per acre. Variation in the damage by the boll weevil was so pronounced that new averages or relationships of condition to final yield were established each year. If the board should continue to interpret probable yield per acre in years of heavy damage on the basis of averages established during years of negligible weevil damage and vice versa, statements of indicated production early in the crop season would likely be more misleading than helpful. The board, therefore, considered it necessary to devise methods of discounting for probable weevil damage.

Study Made of Past Damage

A study has been made of the extent of boll-weevil damage in past years. The department has asked its crop correspondents in February of each year since 1909 their judgment of the yield per acre in per cent of normal of each important crop and the reduction from a normal or full yield due to stated causes. For cotton, one of these causes was the boll weevil. An analysis of the returns showed that damage due to the boll weevil exceeded that due to any other single factor in the variation in amount of damage from year to year and that damage imputed to the weevil in general assumed a cyclical tendency of recurring light and heavy damage periods six to eight years in length.

In these series of data the board has a basis for an interpretation of probable yield per acre which makes an approximate allowance for the departure of probable weevil damage in the current season from the average damage which is reflected in the average relationship of condition and yield. It is necessary to judge of the probable position of the current year in a cycle and to study other years in relatively similar positions in the cycle to determine the extent to which subsequent changes were due to unanticipated weevil damage. This has been supplemented by a study of the relationship of winter weather and spring temperatures and rainfall in determining the probable extent of weevil damage in the current year.

In addition the board has, for a few years, gathered data during the early months of crop growth which give indications of the extent of weevil infestation. Special inquiries have been made concerning the number of weevils as compared with the number on the same date the preceding year, and in a usual year, and concerning infestation as a percentage of full infestation. Field statisticians of the board, assisted by selected reporters, have made counts of weevils found in fields and of punctured and unpunctured squares, which are measurements of infestation. Such evidence has been used to gauge the probability of relatively light or heavy unanticipated damage from the boll weevil in the current season.

The board is directed by Congress to issue "reports on the condition and probable ginnings (production) of cotton." To the extent that measurable bases exist for an interpretation varying from a proportional interpretation, the board feels that its plain duty requires the use of all such measurable data. The present policy of the board represents a progressive step intended to render the crop-reporting service of increasing assistance to farmers in planting and marketing their crops.

Joseph A. Becker.

D AIRY Cows Help in Developing Nevada Reclamation Project   The Newlands Reclamation Project in western Nevada has a soil especially adapted to the growing of alfalfa. Because of the ease with which this crop is grown on new land and the universal success obtained with it, alfalfa is the principal crop on the project. Dairying has followed closely the development of the alfalfa acreage, the abundant alfalfa crops now finding a ready market through dairy cattle in the form of butterfat and in the sale of surplus cows.

Crops Without a Market

At the close of the year 1914 the farmers on the Newlands project found themselves facing a very discouraging situation. Two years' alfalfa crops were on the farms with little prospect of a market. The price offered was not sufficient to pay the cost of production. The low price locally was due in large part to the cost of moving the hay to market, freight charges sometimes equaling the value of the hay on the farm. The reclamation of additional land pointed to a still greater surplus of alfalfa hay in the near future.

To remedy this situation, the office of demonstrations on reclamation projects recommended the development of dairying on the project to furnish a market for the surplus alfalfa. The dairy project has been an important part of the organized extension effort since that time.

Butterfat is a highly condensed product which commands a high price in comparison to transportation cost. It did not take the dairymen long to realize that a carload of hay shipped at a transportation cost of $80 could be converted into butter through good dairy cows and transported to the same market for $7.50, thus saving $72.50 in freight charges. At the same time a home livestock industry would be built up which would provide profitable employment during the entire year and which would aid in retaining the soil fertility.

In 1914 there were 1,500 dairy cows on the project. Small importations during the next eight years and the natural increase resulted, at the end of 1927, in a dairy-cattle population of 5,200 high-quality milking cows and 4,000 high grade and registered heifers.

The increase in the number of dairy cattle has been accomplished by increased interest in higher production. Herd-testing work in 1915 showed the average production to be about 180 pounds of butterfat per cow annually. Through culling, as a result of dairy herd testing work and the general use of purebred sires, the production per cow has been increased to 275 pounds. This increase is due to improvement in quality of the cows, as the records were made on a straight alfalfa-hay ration.

Dairy Cattle Sales Add to Income

The strict supervision under which dairy cattle were brought on to the Newlands project has proved of great value in the later develop-

FIGURE 65.—Typical dairy herd on the Newlands Irrigation Project

ment. The aim has always been to maintain a tuberculosis-free area. Other dairy districts which have not realized the importance of disease-free dairy cattle are now looking toward this isolated community for foundation herds. The income from the sale of mature dairy cows is now approximately $25,000 per month, with a steady demand. These surplus dairy cattle go largely to California. An abundance of alfalfa hay of high feeding value marketed through dairy cattle provides a sure and profitable income for this agricultural community where many other types of farming dependent on distant markets would prove hazardous.

L. E. CLINE.

DAIRY Cows' Persistency in Production of Milk Is Subject of Studies   The quantity of milk which a dairy cow produces during a given period depends on her maximum daily yield and the length of time that she maintains her production at or near this maximum. The same quantity of milk may be produced during a year if a cow reaches a high daily average, maintains that average for a short time, and then gradually declines in production until the end of the year (lactation curve A in fig. 66); as if she has a lower maximum daily production and maintains that level for a longer period before the decline begins (lactation curve B).

It has often been assumed that persistency, or the ability to prolong the period of high production, is a heritable characteristic in dairy cattle. If the assumption is true, it should assert itself to the same degree in each lactation period, provided the environmental conditions are favorable. Milk-production records of animals in the herd of the Bureau of Dairy Industry at Beltsville, Md., indicated some difference in the persistency shown by cows with increasing age. A study was made, therefore, of the records of 15 cows to test the validity of the assumption.

All the cows in this herd are tested under conditions which are maintained as nearly uniform as possible, in order that the results may not be affected by a difference in environment. The animals are kept in box stalls, milked three times a day, fed a uniform ration according to production, and have no pasture during the test year. They are put

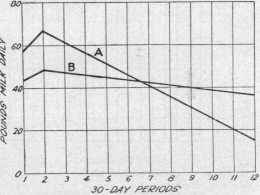

FIGURE 66.—Comparison of lactation curves of dairy cow for one year: A, high daily average at the beginning, but poorly maintained; B, lower average at the start with less decline in production

on official yearly test after freshening with first calf and again when they have passed the age of 5 years.

Records for Two Periods

Fifteen Holstein cows in the herd have completed two normal lactation periods under these conditions, making a total of 30 records. Averages were made for the fifteen 2-year-old or first-calf records and the 15 mature records. The lactation periods were divided into 12 periods of 30 days each to insure uniformity throughout. In finding the percentage of milk produced during each of the twelve 30-day periods, the 360-day production was considered as the total. This method was followed in order to overcome the differences in the actual milk figures and put all records on a parity. The results are shown in Table 3 and Figure 67.

If persistency is inherited and asserts itself to the same degree in each lactation period, the percentage of milk produced during the corresponding 30-day periods would be the same for these 15 animals as heifers and as mature cows. As a matter of fact, however, there is a characteristic difference in the two average lactation periods. Table 3 shows that these 15 animals were more persistent during their heifer lactation periods than during the periods at maturity. In the first six periods they produced 53 per cent of the total as heifers and 58.4 per cent of the total as mature cows. Although as mature cows they reached a maximum of nearly 11 per cent during the second period, their maximum as heifers was only 9.4 per cent during this period.

FIGURE 67.—Comparison of the 2-year-old records and mature records of 15 cows at Beltsville in respect to percentage of total production for each of twelve 30-day periods

TABLE 3.—*Comparison of the 2-year-old records and mature records of 15 cows at Beltsville in respect to percentage of total production for each of twelve 30-day periods*

30-day period	2-year-old records	Mature records	30-day period	2-year-old records	Mature records
	Per cent	*Per cent*		*Per cent*	*Per cent*
1	8.53	9.70	7	8.28	8.35
2	9.44	10.96	8	8.11	7.97
3	9.37	10.28	9	8.05	7.43
4	8.76	9.60	10	7.90	6.97
5	8.51	9.19	11	7.59	5.95
6	8.43	8.61	12	7.03	4.90

Persistency Characteristics Variable

Assuming that a 2-year-old heifer is capable of averaging 35 pounds of milk per day during her period of maximum production, her yield for the second 30-day period would be 1,050 pounds of milk, and on a basis of normal persistency for 2-year-olds her yearly record would be 11,170 pounds of milk. Normally the 2-year-old record is approximately 70 per cent of the mature record. This animal when mature, therefore, is theoretically capable of 15,957 pounds of milk per year. According to Table 3 she would produce 10.96 per cent of the total, or 1,749 pounds, during her 30-day period of maximum production, or an average of 58.3 pounds a day, which is 23.3 pounds, or 66.6 per cent, higher than her maximum daily average as a 2-year-old.

Although there are individual variations in this group of cows, only 2 of the 15 animals show a higher percentage maximum for a 30-day period as 2-year-olds than as mature cows. It is evident from the table, therefore, that the characteristic of persistency is variable throughout the life of the animal, and that on the average it is greater during the first lactation period than after the age of 5 years.

The observations recorded in this article represent only preliminary aspects of a broader study being undertaken in the department on the subject of persistency of milk production.

M. H. FOHRMAN.

D AIRY-FARM Labor Saved by Utilizing Latest Implements At the dairy experiment farm of the Bureau of Dairy Industry at Beltsville, Md., the use of a tractor-drawn corn harvester equipped with an elevator to deliver the bundles of corn on a wagon driven alongside (fig. 68) enabled a crew of 8 men and 4 teams to cut and place in the silo 57 tons of corn in 8 hours. Two days thereafter a crew of 9 men and 4 teams placed

FIGURE 68.—A tractor-drawn corn harvester and elevator which delivers bundles of corn on wagon

60 tons of corn in the silo in 8 hours. The labor was distributed as follows: 1 man to drive the tractor, 1 man on the harvester, 1 man to drive the teams when loading, 4 teamsters, 1 man at the cutter, and on the second day 1 man to help the teamsters unload.

The use of a side-delivery rake, a hay loader, two hay slings on each wagon, and a motor-driven hoist enabled a crew of 5 men and 2 teams to place in the haymow of a barn from the windrow 23 tons of alfalfa hay in 7 hours. The labor was distributed as follows: 1 man to drive the team when loading, 1 man to help the teamsters load, 2 teamsters, and 1 man to operate the hoist.

T. E. WOODWARD.

DAIRY Experiments at Beltsville Find Corn and Alfalfa Most Profitable The most profitable crops grown at the dairy experiment farm of the Bureau of Dairy Industry at Beltsville, Md., are corn (fig. 69), alfalfa, and pasture grass. A six-year rotation is followed, consisting of corn three years and alfalfa three years. The pasture, being more permanent, does not enter into the rotation.

In changing from corn to alfalfa the ground is manured in the fall after the corn is removed for silage. The land is then plowed; and since the soil is a rather heavy clay, it is left in the rough during the winter to allow a greater pulverization from freezing. The alfalfa is sown about the first of April, and two small cuttings are obtained the first year. If the corn during the previous year has not been kept free of weeds, the first cutting of alfalfa will contain many weeds. In this case after it is made into hay, instead of being put in the barn it is stacked in the pasture and fenced in such a way that the cows can eat it through the fence when the pastures become short or dry. The result is that nearly all the material is consumed.

FIGURE 69.—Corn, 51 days old, grown at Beltsville, Md. (Height of man about 5 feet 10 inches)

In changing from alfalfa to corn, the first cutting of alfalfa is removed the latter part of May or the first of June, the ground is plowed, and the corn is planted for silage. This practice has been uniformly successful. A tractor is used for plowing; and in case the ground is too dry and hard for the plows to penetrate, it is double disked and allowed to stand for a few days, when sufficient moisture will have accumulated to permit the use of the ordinary type of moldboard plow.

Manure is applied before each crop of corn except the one following the alfalfa, and in the summer when it can not be used on the corn or alfalfa it is placed on the pastures. Lime is applied every six years previous to sowing the alfalfa.

Pastures are usually sown in the spring on ground that has been fall plowed and manured. The kinds of seed and the quantities per acre are as follows: Orchard grass, 6 pounds; timothy, 4 pounds; redtop, 3 pounds; bluegrass, 4 pounds; red clover, 4 pounds; alsike clover, 2 pounds. If sown about the first of April the grass will be ready for grazing in June.

T. E. WOODWARD.

DAIRY-HERD Improve-ment Associations Formed in All Leading Countries Organizations for testing cows for milk and butterfat production and feed consumption have been created in all the leading countries of the world. In the United States these organizations are known as dairy-herd improvement associations; in Germany, Denmark, and the Scandinavian countries, as control societies; in Great Britain, as milk-recording societies; and in New Zealand and Australia, as group testing or cow-testing associations. They are, however, all intended for the same purpose—to develop higher producing and more efficient dairy herds.

Many dairy herds are not so efficient in the production of milk and butterfat as they should be. Studies of the records of thousands of individual cows have shown that on the average the high producing cows are the most efficient ones. By keeping records of milk and butterfat production and feed consumption through the medium of a trained tester, the factors of feeding, culling, and breeding, which affect dairy-herd improvement, can be brought into play.

Table 4 shows the latest available information for 22 countries carrying on work for the improvement of the dairy herds.

TABLE 4.—*Development of dairy-herd improvement work in 22 countries*

Country	Year of establishment of first organization	Number of organizations	Year of latest available information	Number of cows regularly tested
Denmark	1895	1,083	1923–24	412,022
Netherlands	1896	482	1921	155,900
Germany	1897	2,612	1928	924,484
Sweden	1898	507	1921–22	162,986
Norway	1898	204	1923	45,181
Finland	1898	543	1926	159,250
Scotland	1903	40	1922	28,000
United States	1906	947	1928	414,891
New Zealand	1909	77	1922	78,578
France	1910	30	1920	5,000
Ireland	1911	178	1924	43,230
England and Wales	1914	55	1923	104,000
Canada			1922	47,895
Australia:				
New South Wales	1908	32	1922	35,000
Victoria	1913		1921–22	1,183
South Australia			1922–23	650
Belgium			1922	273
Czechoslovakia	1905	35	1922	10,000
Switzerland			1922	4,000
Japan	1911	15	1922	463
Italy	1922	1	1922	692
Union of South Africa			1922	540
Latvia	1904	149	1922	20,535
Estonia		182	1927	34,003
Total		7,172		2,688,756

Denmark is the fatherland of the dairy-herd-improvement work. The first association was organized in that country in 1895. In percentage of cows on test Denmark still leads. In 1923–24 more than 30 per cent of all the cows in that country were under regular test. Germany, closely following the lead set by Denmark, organized its first association in 1897. The work there has developed rapidly except during the World War. At the present time Germany has by far the largest number of associations and of herds and cows on test of any country in the world, although the number of cows on test represents only 9.8 per cent of the total number in the country, as compared with the 30 per cent in Denmark.

The United States operated its first association, then known as a cow-testing association, in 1906. Although this country was late in starting the work, it has made fairly rapid strides. On January 1, 1928, it had 947 associations, with 414,891 cows on test. This represents, however, only 2 per cent of the total dairy cow population of the country.

These 22 countries have more than 7,172 associations, testing well over 2,500,000 dairy cows. Dairy-herd improvement therefore is not simply a State project or a national project, but an international one.

JOSEPH B. PARKER.

————

DAIRYING in Eastern Corn Belt Has Field for Continued Growth Extending from Kansas to the Atlantic coast, including roughly the States of Maryland, Delaware, Virginia, Kentucky, most of Tennessee, and the southern part of Missouri, is an area in which three of the five major farm crops (cotton, corn, wheat, oats, and hay) are either limited in acreage or occur only in a few localities. Oats occupies less than 5 per cent of the crop area. Wheat is an important crop in northern Virginia and parts of Maryland, but it is not generally grown in other parts of the area except in a few localities where the soil is suitable. Cotton occurs in southeast Missouri, west Tennessee, and southeast Virginia. Tobacco, peanuts, fruit, and truck are important in certain localities well adapted to their production. This leaves corn and hay to occupy by far the greater part of the crop area.

In Virginia, Kentucky, and Tennessee there are large groups of counties in which corn occupies from 50 to 70 per cent of the crop area, with small acreages of other crops, including hay. Even with this large percentage of land in corn, the production as a whole is usually below the quantity needed for feed, mainly on account of yield, making this a deficit corn-producing region. Therefore dairying is about the only livestock enterprise that can be materially increased. The production of hogs much beyond the present numbers is limited by the corn crop. The beef cattle business can not expand to any great extent for the same reason. The sheep enterprise can increase where pastures are available, but much of an increase in the number of sheep would reduce the pasture area for other animals, especially beef cattle.

Well Adapted for Forage Crops

Most of this area is well adapted to the production of forage crops, including many of the legumes. A slight rearrangement of the cropping system to include more legumes would be a distinct benefit in building up soil fertility and at the same time would supply feed for dairy animals. Dairying has for many years been an important enterprise near cities and larger towns where there is a market for whole milk. More recently dairying has increased in localities where there are facilities for shipping cream and where creameries have been established, giving the farmer with a few cows an opportunity to derive some income from the sale of cream.

The sale of butterfat during the five-year period, 1919 to 1924, is an indication of the trend in the dairy business in this area. In Maryland the sale of butterfat has increased from 448,000 pounds in 1919 to 2,000,000 pounds in 1924; Delaware 76,000 to 181,000 pounds; Kentucky 4,000,000 to 9,000,000 pounds; Tennessee 2,000,000 to 5,000,000 pounds; Missouri 17,000,000 to 31,000,000 pounds. The sale of whole milk has increased about 40 per cent during this period.

H. A. MILLER.

DAIRY Studies Show That Within Breeds the Bigger Cows Win A study carried on by the Bureau of Dairy Industry of the yearly individual records of more than 139,000 cows on test in dairy-herd-improvement associations in this country showed that within the breed the big cows win on the average in production of milk and butterfat and in income over cost of feed per cow. This study included both purebreds and grades of every age for each of the dairy breeds. Table 5 shows a comparison of the production and the income over cost of feed of cows of different sizes within a breed for which the largest number of individual records have been obtained.

TABLE 5.—*Comparison of production and income over cost of feed of cows of different sizes within one breed*

Group No.	Cows [1]	Estimated average weight	Yearly milk production per cow	Butterfat test	Yearly butterfat production per cow	Price of butterfat per pound	Cost of feed per cow	Income over cost of feed per cow
	Number	Pounds	Pounds	Per cent	Pounds			
1	803	800	6,895	3.8	262	$0.60	$62	$93
2	1,657	900	7,368	3.7	275	.58	64	95
3	8,756	1,000	7,920	3.7	290	.57	65	101
4	6,610	1,100	8,435	3.6	302	.58	68	107
5	8,678	1,200	8,932	3.5	315	.58	72	112
6	1,986	1,300	9,383	3.5	328	.58	74	115
7	1,169	1,400	9,734	3.5	341	.60	79	127
8	140	1,500	10,194	3.5	360	.59	82	136

[1] Total number, 29,799.

On an average the largest cows (Group 8) exceeded the smallest cows (Group 1) by 98 pounds of butterfat per cow. Their cost of feed was $20 higher, but they returned $43 more per cow in yearly income over cost of feed. The table shows that the price received per pound for butterfat was about the same for the different groups. The higher income over cost of feed for the large cows, therefore, was not the result of a higher price paid for butterfat. Only one conclusion appears to be possible: The income above feed cost advanced with size of cow because of greater production per cow.

An analysis of the figures in Table 5 shows that as size of cow advanced 100 pounds per cow for each group there was a fairly uniform gain in production of milk and of butterfat, in cost of feed per cow, and in income above feed cost. On the other hand there was a slight decrease in the butterfat test. Results similar to these were obtained from a study of the figures for the other breeds. All told the same story: Within the breed the big cows win.

Though the group figures always favored the large cows, it was found that many individuals among the large cows in each breed were unprofitable producers and that many small cows in each breed were profitable producers. Therefore, in selecting dairy cows of any breed it is not wise to select on the basis of size alone. Size, however, is a factor of great importance.

Figure 70 shows the world's record butterfat producer for the Jersey breed, Darling's Jollie Lassie, 435948. She produced 16,425

FIGURE 70.—Darling's Jollie Lassie, 435948, a world's record butterfat producer for Jerseys and a large cow of her breed

pounds of milk and 1,141.28 pounds of butterfat in one year. This cow weighed 150 pounds above the average of her breed.

                                                    J. C. McDOWELL.

DATE Varieties at All Growth Stages Shown by Vegetative Characters   The introduction of date culture into the United States has involved the importation of offshoots of many Old World varieties of the date palm and the growing of numerous seedlings in this country, some few of which are proving to be worth retaining and propagating as fruit-bearing varieties. Positive identification of these varieties is of vital importance for the development of the industry and for the protection of purchasers of offshoots, especially of rare varieties that command fancy prices. Identification by the fruit characters is the most obvious method and one as old as the industry itself. Yet confusion of varieties bearing a close resemblance in size, form, color of fruit, texture, and flavor is a frequent embarrassment to the American date grower.

Field study of details of the fruiting organs, of the size and length of the fruiting stalk, length of the fruiting head, and of the strands or shamruk, furnishes additional means of distinction which the gathered fruit does not afford. Add to the fruit characters those of the palms bearing the fruit, and we have means of positive identification of date varieties never before available. Features to be observed are the appearance of the trunk, the breadth and thickness of the leaf bases, the comparative length and stiffness or flexibility of the leaves, along with the broad outlines of the top, and its mass color, from a blue-gray on one to a yellow-green on another. The details of the foliage should be observed next. Is the rachis or midrib stout and rigid, maintaining much of this character clear to the tip? Or with a broad, thick petiole, does the rib taper to a slender apex, giving the long sweeping curve, with strength and grace combined, which characterizes the famous Menakher date of Tunis, one of the rarest of the varieties now growing in America? In sharp contrast is the Hayany variety of Egypt, with slender trunk, narrow leaf bases, slender and feathery rachis, and long, pendulous pinnæ.

Further Details of Leaf

Studying the leaf in greater detail, the tubular sheath of finer or coarser fiber is noted, then the spine area, longer or shorter, where the suppressed basal pinnæ appear as belligerent protective spines, stout and acute or slender, but sharp as needles. The spines change abruptly to pinnæ widely spaced or closely set on the rachis, which if long are usually slender and weak; if shorter, often broad, stiff, and acute.

In attachment to the rachis the folded pinnæ may turn the channel directly inward (introrse), toward the top (antrorse), or toward the base (retrorse). There is a definite grouping of these three pinnæ classes. The simplest and most frequent group is the double group, with an antrorse pinna below and a retrorse above. Triple groups have an introrse pinna between the antrorse and the retrorse, and the unusual quadruple groups have two inserted introrse pinnæ. All three groups are regarded as normal, and the proportion of each in all the pinnæ on the leaf is highly characteristic of the different varieties of the date palm.

The size of the angles at which the different classes of pinnæ are attached to the blade is another important character and gives a very distinct aspect to the leaves of different varieties. If most of the pinnæ of a leaf are set at from 60° to 90° from the axis of the leaf and lie nearly in the plane of the blade, this is the broad, smooth, 2-ranked blade. Some varieties with strongly diverse angles show rough, ragged blades and formidable spines.

In final analysis, each date variety may be distinguished from its fellows with reasonable certainty by its vegetative characters independently of its fruits.

Silas C. Mason.

DIET of College Students Ample, Analysis Shows — After the boys and girls go off to college questions about students' habits of living arise to worry the parents who are left behind. Food is a matter of particular concern. Are the children, now that they have left home, getting the right food? And in order to be sure that her child is not going hungry, many a mother straightway fixes up and sends off a box of her son's or daughter's favorite cakes and cookies.

Not only the parents but the institutions that have assumed responsibility for the further education of the young men and women of the country are becoming interested in the food habits of the students in our colleges and universities. Because of this interest, and in order to answer the questions that arise, the Bureau of Home Economics has been studying the food consumed by this group.

In 1918 the office of home economics collected information from 192 dining halls for college students, and in 1926 the Bureau of Home Economics collected 44 records suitable for analysis. These included dormitories, sorority and fraternity houses, and practice houses in all parts of the United States. This material was analyzed to see what the food was yielding in the way of nutrients.

The analysis of such material usually involves the calculation of the total energy, protein, calcium, phosphorus, and iron yielded by the diet, for these are the food constituents necessary for health and well-being that are in the most danger of being furnished in insufficient amounts. The results of such inadequacies are, on the whole, fairly definite. Eating inadequate amounts of energy-yielding foods results in loss of body weight and if continued over a long period of time there may be real emaciation. Insufficient amounts of protein also lead to a general breaking down of body tissue. If calcium and phosphorus are inadequate to meet the young person's need the trouble usually shows up in defective teeth. The blood is affected when the food yields an insufficient amount of iron, resulting oftentimes in anemia.

Comparisons With Standard

The studies that have been collected were analyzed for these five food constituents and compared not only with similar studies made by other investigators but by a standard accepted by nutritionists.

The results shown by the 234 studies collected in the Bureau of Home Economics are, on the whole, in agreement with those shown by other investigators. Altogether, these studies of the food consumed by college students show that the diet on the average is more than adequate to meet their needs. About 15 per cent more energy, calcium, and iron is yielded by the food than is estimated as needed. The phosphorus need is met by the food only somewhat less abundantly than is the case with the energy, calcium, and iron. The protein of the diet, on the other hand, is greatly in excess of the estimated need of the students. Sixty per cent more of this nutrient is yielded by the diet than is actually needed.

These figures would indicate that college students should be taught to demand more fruits and vegetables and less of the foods high in protein. In making such an adjustment, however, care should be taken that the minerals of the diet are not reduced.

EDITH HAWLEY.

D OCKAGE Removal at Thresher is Aided by Self-Cleaning Screen Dockage has greatly increased the cost of producing and handling grain in the spring wheat area. Dockage in threshed spring wheat has increased from approximately 1½ per cent average dockage in the 5-year period, 1894–1898, to over 6 per cent average dockage in the 5-year period ended with the 1928 crop.

Thirty years ago nearly every threshing machine was equipped with a screen for removing the small weed seeds. Before wild oats became so prevalent these sieves were effective, but in recent years the oats, filling the screen openings, prevented the screen from cleaning effectually and seriously retarded the flow of grain over the screen. Most threshermen discarded the lower cleaning sieve. Weed seeds

FIGURE 71.—One type of recleaner mounted on the deck of a threshing machine. The tank beside the thresher receives the small weed seeds; the wild oats are discharged from the opposite side of the cleaner into wagons or sacks. The clean grain in this illustration is being spouted directly into a temporary field storage bin

remained with the grain and were hauled with the grain to the elevator and dockage equal the weight of the weed seed was assessed against the grain when it was sold.

The average annual feeding value of dockage produced in the spring wheat area in its wheat, flax, and rye, is approximately $10,000,000. If this dockage can be removed as part of the threshing operation farmers will have this material for their own use as feed for livestock, and the handling charges for it will be saved. The advantages of cleaning grain at the thresher have been recognized for several years, and manufacturers have been cooperating with the Department of Agriculture in the development of various kinds of cleaning machines designed effectively to remove the dockage as part of the threshing operation.

Screens Can Again be Used

Screens that were in use before the increase of wild oats can now again be used through the development of a self-cleaning attachment to be used with the screens. This self-cleaning screen consists of a series of agitating racks rubbing on the under side of the screen which prevents the screen from clogging. Over 800 of these self-cleaning screens were successfully operated in the spring wheat area in 1928. They removed from the grain large quantities of small weed seeds and a part of the wild oats.

Several types of portable grain cleaners designed for cleaning grain at the threshing machine have been used experimentally by specialists of the department, and although 15 of these cleaners have been used successfully during the past four years their cost and the work involved in moving them from one thresher setting to another and placing them in position at the thresher have combined to prevent their being placed on the market.

Several types of cleaners mounted on the decks of threshing machines were also used in the experimental work. In 1928, approximately 100 threshing machines were equipped with special cleaners purchased by thresher operators. Most of the deck recleaners now in operation make separations according to the length of the kernels and employ either discs with pockets in them or indented cylinders for this purpose.

The deck type of recleaners removes nearly all of the dockage from the grain. The dockage is usually reduced to less than 1 per cent even when 10 per cent or 15 per cent dockage is present in the threshed grain before it reaches the cleaners.

Combines operating in the spring wheat area require a recleaner device for removing the fine seeds, which are usually high in moisture content. Approximately 1,000 of the combines sold in this area in 1928 were equipped with cylindrical woven-wire recleaners.

R. H. BLACK.

DOUGLAS Fir Cut-Over Land's Fire Hazard is Minimized by Grazing

In the Douglas fir region west of the Cascade Range in Oregon and Washington, enormous areas of virgin timberland have been cut over and are now in various stages of natural reforestation or reburning.

Providing adequate protection from fire to permit natural reforestation and to prevent cut-over lands from becoming a fire menace to adjoining uncut timber is an exceedingly difficult problem. Any measure which gives promise of reduction of the forest-fire hazard is worthy of careful consideration.

The use of livestock of the natural forage crop produced on Douglas fir cut-over areas offers one important means of reducing fire hazard through the removal of inflammable vegetation. On cut-over lands to be devoted to agricultural development, grazing is usually the first step in the subjection of land to the plow. On lands suited only to the growing of timber, if grazing is to be used in reducing fire hazard, it is essentially good business to develop the type of management that will neither delay nor prevent reforestation.

Will grazing produce a return from the land sufficient to meet the ever-increasing tax burden and interest charge? Can the area be grazed in a manner that will reduce the fire risk of a heavy stand of fire-weed and other transitory species without seriously injuring the future forest crop? Can livestock be moved from one area as it grows up to timber to other areas recently cut over, and a cycle of grazing use thereby developed somewhat comparable to the timber-cutting cycle? Practical tests with sheep on the Columbia National Forest in southwestern Washington are being made in an effort to answer these questions. Use by cattle of this type of range in western Oregon is likewise being studied.

Profitably Grazed by Sheep

Results of these studies indicate that Douglas fir cut-over lands can be grazed profitably by sheep in reasonably large bands during the summer period, where costs of transportation from winter range and feed are not excessive. Use of such lands by small farm flocks from adjacent ranches likewise gives promise of success. Also cattle have been grazed at a profit on Douglas fir cut-over lands seeded to grass.

Seeding of Douglas fir cut-over areas to cultivated forage species has proved practicable, materially increasing the grazing capacity and the

FIGURE 72.—Douglas fir cut-over areas in Oregon. Seeded to grass on the left; unseeded to the right. Uncut timber in the background

grazing value of the lands. A good cover of forage that lasts from 8 to 15 years is secured. Costs of seeding vary from 50 cents to $3.75 per acre, depending on the kind and amount of seed used and the type of country seeded. Seeding early in the fall in the ashes of the slash burn or the following winter on the snow has produced the best stands. A preponderance of weeds, largely unpalatable to cattle, makes grass seeding necessary where that class of stock is grazed. Seeding of cut-over areas by airplane in Southwest Oregon has recently proved a practical and economical method.

The season from May 1 to October 15 was found most desirable for sheep. Fullest use of the natural forage and greatest reduction in fire hazard are secured during that period. Yearlong use of unseeded ranges by either sheep or cattle is unprofitable from a grazing standpoint, and, moreover, is injurious to the range and to tree seedlings.

Grazing Capacity Variable

Grazing capacity is extremely variable. Satisfactory lamb gains of 6½ pounds per head per month have been made on a third of an acre of unseeded range, the capacity varying from one-fourth to 5 acres per head per month. Capacities of one-half acre per head per season for sheep and 6 acres for cattle are not uncommon on seeded areas.

The number of years that grazing use is profitable varies widely as a result of differences in site and in treatment following the slash burn. A limit of from 15 to 18 years is considered usual where there is single-burn, careful management, and the closest utilization. The relation of longer periods of use to ultimate reforestation has not yet been

FIGURE 73.—A band of sheep contentedly grazing on area cut over in 1917 on Columbia National Forest, Wash. Unseeded to grass. Note the young tree seedlings coming in

determined. Efforts, mainly in reburning, have been made to prolong this period of grazing usefulness. In the Coos Bay region where heavy burning and grass seeding are practiced on private land for the express purpose of producing pasture, the forage crop "plays out" in from 9 to 10 years. Palatable forage grasses and weeds are replaced by unpalatable plants and shrubs. Shrub and conifer encroachment preclude further profitable grazing use.

A Soil-Impoverishing Custom

Year-long grazing is undoubtedly a factor in shortening the period of grazing use. To lengthen this period, reburning is resorted to, followed by grass reseeding, and the process repeated. Needless to say, this practice, if long continued, retards and finally eliminates reforestation. A rather futile hope that the brush species also will be eliminated is responsible largely for this soil-impoverishing custom. The practice has brought grass seeding into evil repute among forest-ers, when as a matter of fact careful analysis would seem to indicate that repeated reburning and yearlong use are to blame. Examination of a number of areas repeatedly reburned has failed to show where the brush species have been finally eliminated by the seeding-reburning practice alone. On the contrary, among the outstanding indications which general study of the problem have developed are the following: (1) Douglas fir lands, short of intensive tillage practice, seldom remain permanently as forage-producing areas; (2) if the lands are given freedom from reburning, regardless of grazing use, reforestation is certain.

D. C. INGRAM.

DUST-EXPLOSION Hazard Exists in Nearly All Manufacturing Plants One of the earliest grain dust explosions in the United States occurred in the Washburn flour mills in Minneapolis on May 2, 1878. As the result of this explosion of flour dust 18 men were killed, and 3 mill buildings were destroyed.

Since the explosion in 1878 so many explosions have occurred in the manufacturing plants of the United States that dust explosions are now recognized as a definite industrial hazard. The Bureau of Chemistry and Soils has found that a dust explosion is similar to a gas explosion and that combustible dusts of practically all types, when mixed with air in proper proportions, can be ignited by an external source of heat or flame. A recent census shows that at least 28,000 industrial plants in the United States are subject to the hazard of dust explosions. These plants employ approximately 1,324,000 persons, and annually manufacture products valued at more than $10,000,000,000. Dust-explosion prevention is therefore a national economic problem.

Although the earliest dust explosions occurred in grain handling and milling plants, explosions have taken place in recent years in industries handling the following products: Starch, sugar, powdered milk, chocolate and cocoa, spice, rice, cottonseed meal, wood, hard rubber, paper, fertilizer, sulphur, zinc, aluminum and magnesium powders, pyroxylin lacquers, cork, dye materials, coal-tar pitch, and leather.

New Equipment Causes Risk

The dust-explosion hazard exists in practically all the manufacturing processes in industrial plants. The installation of new mechanical equipment has introduced additional hazards, and the use of electricity and electrical appliances has played a prominent part in many recent disastrous explosions. Definite progress has been made in obtaining scientific data on the causes of dust explosions in industrial plants and in the development of methods for their control and prevention, but it is apparent that the dust-explosion problem is extending into many new lines of industry, and the hazard must be recognized.

The Department of Agriculture is receiving the aid of many national organizations in reducing the loss of both life and property that results from dust explosions. In cooperation with the dust explosion hazards committee of the National Fire Protection Association, safety codes have been developed for dust-explosion prevention in the following industries: Flour and feed mills, sugar and cocoa pulverizing systems, terminal grain elevators, pulverized-fuel systems, and starch factories. These codes have been adopted by the National Board of

FIGURE 74.—What remained of the Washburn flour mills in Minneapolis after flour dust explosion on May 2, 1878

FIGURE 75.—The world's largest grain elevator, 10,000,000 bushels capacity, located at South Chicago, Ill., wrecked by a grain-dust explosion. The explosion killed six men and resulted in $4,500,000 property damage

Fire Underwriters and have been approved as American standard by the American Engineering Standards Committee. The chemical engineering division of the Bureau of Chemistry and Soils is desirous

FIGURE 76.—Effects of an explosion of cornstarch dust in a Middle West factory in which 42 men were killed and many others injured

of continuing to cooperate with the industries and other interested agencies in obtaining further information regarding the dust-explosion problem and in rendering all possible assistance in the development and application of effective methods of control and prevention.

DAVID J. PRICE.

DYES Important Both in Diagnosis of Disease and as Medicinal Agents Much of our knowledge of disease, especially that caused by microorganisms, has been acquired with the aid of dyes. Suitable dyes for this purpose, known as biological stains, are of vital importance to the medical profession. The diphtheria bacillus mycobaderium tuberculosis and the malaria parasite, for example, as well as numerous other pathogenic organisms, can be detected and identified after being stained with a dye that differentiates them from surrounding substances. Thousands of staining tests are carried out daily upon cultures taken from milk and water and from diseased persons. They indicate the presence and the identity of disease-producing organisms, thereby enabling the doctor to diagnose the disease.

When stained with dye solutions, the tissue of malignant tumor may be distinguished from that of harmless tumors by microscopical examination.

Many dyes render even more direct service to health, in that they destroy or paralyze pathogenic organisms without injuring the normal body tissues, when used as antiseptics against surface bacterial infection. The importance of dyes in medicine increases every year, and there are grounds for the belief that they may be used eventually to control many of the diseases caused by microorganisms.

W. C. HOLMES.

E CONOMICS Literature Monthly Review Aids the Extension Worker
Taking statistics to the farmer is an important part of the work of the county agents and other extension workers, who can often clinch an argument as to a better practice by showing statistically the proportion of cases in which it has succeeded in bringing the farmer a better return for his labor. The only way, however, in which the field worker can be prepared with the information necessary to make this sort of demonstration is to have a reservoir of general and specific information at his command.

This is not easy to provide in the busy life extension workers lead, with its minimum of time for reading and its maximum opportunity for applying the fruits of such reading to the problems which confront farmers. The monthly periodical entitled "Agricultural Economics Literature," prepared in the library of the Bureau of Agricultural Economics, is designed to help in the problem of keeping extension workers informed of useful publications. It is also designed to help the investigator, the professor, or the student in the field of agricultural economics to keep up with the literature of the particular subject with which he deals. This is increasingly difficult as research increases, but, unless an investigator does it, he may fail to apply to a piece of work in hand the findings of another investigator, or he may undertake work already adequately performed.

In Agricultural Economics Literature the material received in the library during the previous month is reviewed, described, or listed, and if the publication is systematically used it should save much time to workers in the field of agricultural economics as well as call to their attention information on their subjects which might otherwise escape their attention.

Contents of the Publication

Agricultural Economics Literature contains each month (1) a few careful reviews of new books relating to some phase of agricultural economics, written and signed by specialists in the bureau; (2) a section of descriptive notes and abstracts of books, pamphlets, reports and serials of special interest; (3) notes of bibliographies prepared in the library the previous month for distribution; (4) a list of the publications of the State departments of agriculture, State colleges, experiment stations, and extension divisions, the titles for which are obtained by examining the publications of all these agencies during the previous month and choosing those which are of economic significance; (5) publications of the United States Department of Agriculture, both printed and mimeographed, which are economic in character—those of the Bureau of Agricultural Economics and of other bureaus; (6) annotated list of periodical articles obtained by the reading of 111 domestic and 75 foreign periodicals by the staff to find the important articles in the field of agricultural economics; and (7) notes of other accessions to the library which are of more or less related interest but for which space is not available for fuller description. The address of the agency which issues a publication is given to aid the extension worker or other user in acquiring as easily as possible what is needed for his files.

MARY G. LACY.

EGG Standardization Facilitates Recognition of Quality in Prices   The system of paying all producers of eggs a flat price based on their average quality offers no incentive to produce eggs of best quality. In actual practice it penalizes the producer of good eggs and offers a premium to the producer of poor eggs.

Eggs vary in interior quality and other factors which affect their market value. Because of this, egg dealers have recognized the need of definite standards for measuring in a practical way the quality of eggs. To be of greatest value, these standards must be adequate, and

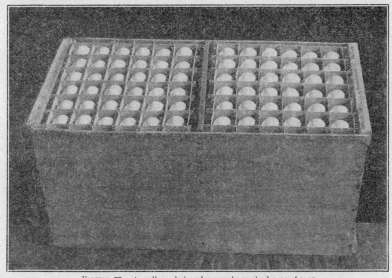

FIGURE 77.—A well graded and properly packed case of eggs

readily and universally applicable as a measure of egg quality. This means egg standardization. Standardization makes it possible to furnish the consumer with the quality of eggs he demands and to pay the producer for his eggs on a quality or graded basis.

In 1921 the Bureau of Agricultural Economics began to study this problem for the purpose of establishing national quality standards for eggs. In 1924 these standards were submitted to the egg trade for comment and criticism and were adopted at a meeting of the trade held in Chicago under the auspices of the National Poultry, Butter and Egg Association. These standards are known as the United States standards of quality for individual eggs.

Determining Quality in Eggs

Quality in eggs is commercially determined by candling. The factors considered in determining egg quality are the condition of the shell, air

33023°—29——18

cell, yolk, white, and germ. Table 6 shows the specifications for these factors in each of the four qualities of eggs of clean, sound shell as provided in the United States Standards.

TABLE 6.—*United States standards of quality for individual eggs*

Quality factors	Specification of each quality factor for—			
	United States Special	United States Extra	United States Standard	United States Trade
Shell____	Clean, sound_____	Clean, sound_____	Clean, sound_____	Clean, sound.
Air cell_	One-eighth inch or less, localized, regular.	Two-eighths inch or less, localized, regular.	Three-eighths inch or less, localized, may be slightly tremulous.	May be over three-eighths inch, may be bubbly or freely mobile.
Yolk____	May be dimly visible_	May be visible_____	May be visible, mobile.	May be plainly visible, dark in color, freely mobile.
White___	Firm, clear_____	Firm, clear_____	Reasonably firm_____	May be weak and watery.
Germ___	No visible development.	No visible development.	Development may be slightly visible.	Development may be clearly visible but no blood showing.

In addition to the standards for eggs of clean shell, two standards for eggs with dirty shells, United States Standard Dirties and United States Trade Dirties, have been defined. These are the same as those for United States Standards and United States Trades except for the dirty shells.

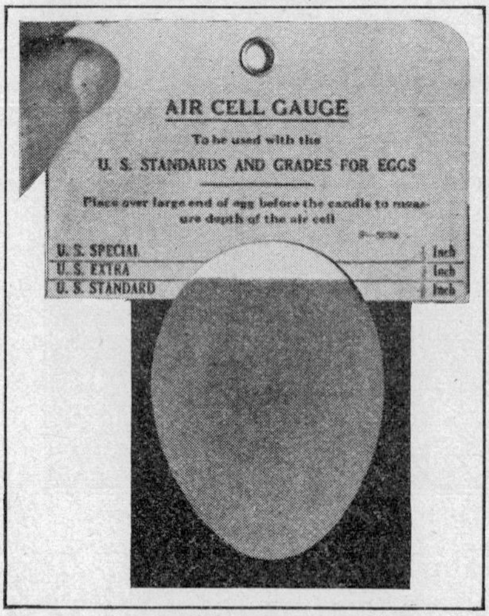

The standards of quality for individual eggs are used as a basis for formulating grades. The factors which determine the grade of a lot of eggs are quality, size and weight, package and style of packing, and uniformity. Uniformity in quality, size, and color of the eggs in a case or in a carton is an important factor in grading, but the prime factor in grading is quality. Market men usually look for quality first and then consider the other factors.

FIGURE 78.—The depth of the air cell may be measured by an air cell gauge as the egg is held before the candle. In regular candling the use of the gauge is necessary only on "line eggs." The egg in the illustration is a U. S. Extra

Candling Record Shows Grade

In applying the United States standards of quality to a lot of eggs to determine its grade, the eggs are candled, and the percentage of eggs conforming to each quality standard is determined. Since the United States grades consist of specified percentages of the various standards of quality, it is a simple matter to determine from the candling record the United States grade into which the lot falls.

The United States standards of quality for individual eggs are used as a basis for grading eggs by a number of the leading exchanges, several farmers' cooperative marketing associations and shippers, and some retail organizations. They are the basis of the mandatory New York State retail grades for eggs and of permissive grades for eggs in several States. They are coming into more general use every year.

Egg standardization, to be of greatest benefit to the egg industry, must begin with the producer and carry through to the consumer. Under these circumstances it permits a more enlightened marketing program to be effected, which results in the buying and selling of eggs on an equitable quality basis. Producers of eggs are encouraged to produce and market better-quality eggs because standardization provides a basis on which they can be rewarded for their extra effort by an increased price for the better quality. Dealers can handle a standardized product of known quality at lower cost and with greater satisfaction to the outlets which they supply. Consumers will purchase eggs with more confidence and in greater quantity when they are sure of being able to buy a dependable product at all times. Standardization means dependability, which is essential in developing consumer confidence with its increased consumption of eggs, which will make possible a more extensive and more stable poultry industry.

GEORGE H. POWERS.

E XHIBITS That Talk Prove an Effective Educational Device A cow 6 feet high that moves and talks in stentorian tones, a sow 8 feet long that snorts like a foghorn, and Tom and Henry, the talking manikins, are the beginnings of a new series of educational displays that add interest and punch to the exhibits program of the United States Department of Agriculture.

Formerly exhibits were largely thought of as things to be looked at, such as objects, models, live animals, illustrations, and mechanical devices, but these new exhibits have many of these features plus something more—sound. Other things being equal, the more senses to which you can appeal the greater the impression you can leave in the minds of the observers. Now we add one more channel to the observer's mind, namely, the ear.

The first talking exhibit put out by the department was the simplest of the new series. This exhibit, first shown at the National Dairy Exposition in 1927, consisted of two manikins or dummies built in full size and in three dimensions and dressed in typical farm clothes. These two farmers, Tom and Henry (fig. 79), were shown in a barnyard, and between them was a basket of feed in which a loud speaker was concealed. The operator of the exhibit was in the rear of the exhibit background. The two farmers discussed four different subjects namely, dairy-cattle breeding, better feeding, production of clean milk, and marketing.

The operator started the action by placing a specially made record containing the dialogue on a phonograph which was hooked up to a powerful amplifying device, which in turn actuated the power loud speaker concealed in the basket. The operator, by watching the two men through a hole in the background and listening to the dialogue, could synchronize proper gestures by the manikins with their apparent utterances. When it was time for Tom to speak the operator turned

a switch which made Tom's arm move up and down as though emphasizing an important point. In like manner when Henry replied a
second switch was turned, and Henry's arm waved a stick up and
down by way of emphasis. After several trials the operator became
skilled in sychronizing the movements of the farmers with their words.

When this exhibit was first shown it was planned to draw a crowd
in front of it by playing a piece of music, and having obtained an
audience, to present the four educational dialogues. Experience,
however, showed that it was the dialogues between the animated
farmers that drew and held the crowds. During the musical number
the crowd would start to drift away, and the only way they could be
held was to have Henry occasionally beat time to the music with his
stick. When the departing crowd saw this action starting they would
stop, many of them would come back to see if something more was

FIGURE 79.—Tom and Henry, the talking, moving manikins, at the National Dairy Exposition, 1927

going to happen, and a large number were held for further educational
dialogues. After the first trials the music was played very rarely, and
the four educational records were used almost entirely.

The Talking Cow

The success of the talking farmers at the 1927 National Dairy
Exposition led the department to use the talking exhibit idea in the
central feature in another exhibit in 1928. Belle, the talking cow
(fig. 80), a creature 6 feet high from hoof to shoulder and with a very
loud voice, then came into being. Belle was so constructed that her
various stomachs, intestines, udder, heart, and other important organs
could be seen. Belle told the visitors just what happened in her body
in transforming feed into milk and used the process as an explanation
of the fact that a cow must have certain ingredients in her feed if she
is to produce large quantities of milk economically. In accomplishing
this purpose she compared her body to a milk factory.

"In the first stomach the ground-up feed is mixed with digestive juices," said Belle, and at that moment the first stomach lighted up electrically, and a small man made of wire could be seen stirring vigorously a big vat of feed and digestive juices. "Next the feed goes to the second stomach," said Belle, "where certain compounds are broken up into simpler compounds and elements." Just as she mentioned her second stomach that portion of her anatomy lighted up, and a small man started hammering away with a sledge hammer at several pieces of material representing compounds. Belle then explained how the useless materials were sifted out in the next room of the factory and discarded and how the useful materials got into the blood stream and were conveyed to the udder, where certain compounds such as proteins, carbohydrates, fats, lime, and vitamins were taken out in very definite proportions to form milk. As Belle pointed out, if these compounds or elements were not in the feed when it reached her mouth they could not arrive at the udder or "mixing

FIGURE 80.—This is Belle, the talking cow

and assembling" room. In a similar manner Belle showed by means of her body why breeding was an important factor in building up a profitable herd.

The rear of this exhibit (fig. 81) was almost as interesting as the front because there were 12 controls for operating the cow centralized at one point where the operator could manipulate them. Six of these controls were switches for turning on lights and motors, five consisted of cords which operated the cow's tail, the dairyman's arm, and the three small men shown in the cow's stomach and intestines. Then there was a lever for moving the cow's head up and down and sideways and finally there was the electrola with an additional amplifier for producing the sound. The man who operated the cow was the busiest person on the fairgrounds, and after two or three hours of this kind of work he was glad to yield this position to another operator.

The Brood Sow's Rebellion

After the encouraging success of the talking cow in stopping and holding the attention of the people at the National Dairy Exposition, it was decided that an exhibit along similar lines should be prepared

for the 1928 International Livestock Exposition at Chicago.   Several
subjects were given careful study to determine their adaptability to
this type of exhibit, and it was finally decided that swine sanitation
and particularly the subject of how to avoid round worms in pigs was
most suitable.   This exhibit is much like a short playlet or "act"
(fig. 82) and has the following characters:

> Mr. Henry, a farmer.
> A brood sow, 4½ feet high.
> Betsy, a pig.
> Percy, another pig.

During the course of the playlet Mr. Henry scolds the sow for
attempting to push over a fence which bars the way to a fine pasture.

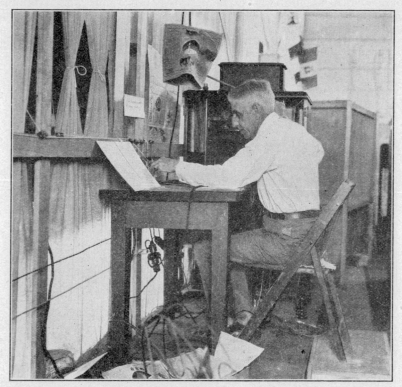

FIGURE 81.—In the rear of the talking cow the operator was kept very busy with the 12 control
cords and switches

The sow then explains, by tracing the history of the round worm
through her body, why she and her pigs should be on clean pasture
instead of the old worm-infested hog lot.   During the course of her
explanation as to the dangers to her pigs, little Betsy starts squealing
and gradually shrinks from a nice fat pig to a thing of skin and bones,
finally falling on the ground.   The sow blames the sad fate of little
Betsy on the farmer, and during the discussion her second pig Percy
starts squealing and shrinking, finally meeting the fate of Betsy.
The farmer then sees the error of his ways and promises that next time
the pigs shall have the finest pasture in the county.

The conversation is produced by means of a special record made for
the department, but a new force has been brought into use to operate

the dying, shrinking pigs—namely, air. Before the act opens the pigs are inflated by means of compressed air. By means of 3-way valves and a compression tank operated from the rear of the exhibit, air can be turned into the pigs, held at a certain pressure, or released. Sections of large inner tubes are used as the means of inflating the pigs. Levers and springs are used to make the pigs fall down after they have been deflated. At the end of each act the operator pulls a string which causes curtains to conceal the stage, thus affording an opportunity to set up the pigs and inflate them before the act starts over again.

Sound Alone Will Not Hold Attention

Experience has shown that sound alone will not hold the attention of the visitors, and that along with the speaking there must be some form

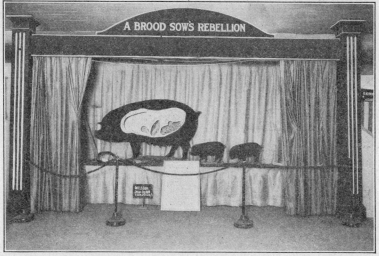

FIGURE 82.—The talking hog and shrinking pigs in this exhibit were of unusual interest to the crowds at the 1928 International Livestock Exposition

of interpretative action, the more the better. Since the first talking exhibit was made, the talking farmers, the manikins, have been remade to incorporate more action and to make them lighter and easier to ship about the country. The new manikins are cut out of flat boards, but have actual clothes fitted to them. Their jaws are now movable as well as their arms, sheet rubber being used on their faces to allow their jaws to move up and down without making wrinkles in their cheeks. The first set of rubber faces failed, as the cheeks and lips cracked with the motion, the oil in the paint used to color the faces having softened the rubber. No oil paints are now used on the rubber surfaces.

Each new exhibit of this type brings with it special problems to be solved, but inasmuch as the talking exhibits seem to attract more attention and hold the interest longer than any other so far developed, the extra effort required is well worth while.

H. T. BALDWIN.

E XTENSION Agents Get   Cooperative agricultural extension
Invaluable Help From   as conducted by the Extension Serv-
Local Volunteer Leaders   ice of the Department of Agriculture consists in giving instruction
and practical demonstrations in agriculture and home economics to
persons not attending or resident in the various State colleges of agriculture. The imparting of agricultural information and the teaching
of these subjects are done "through field demonstrations, publications,
and otherwise" in conjunction with the various State colleges of
agriculture.

The organization in charge of this work consists of a directing office
in Washington, a department in each State agricultural college known
as the extension department, and an organization in the county consisting of the county extension agents. During 1927, 3,603 county
extension agents were employed in the United States. Of this number
2,427 were county agricultural agents, 1,020 were county home demonstration agents, and 156 were county club agents. Two hundred and
seventy-seven of these agents were negroes, both men and women,
engaged in work with their own people.

As the agricultural program of a county is broad and complicated,
the agent finds it necessary to obtain additional help to accomplish the
aims of the program. Generally this assistance is termed "local leadership" and consists of aid given voluntarily by men and women community residents in building up the rural prosperity of the county. It is
with the development and use of this volunteer local leadership, so
important to the success of any county program, that we are concerned.

There are about 250,000 of these voluntary leaders in extension
work at the present time; 185,000 of them are aiding in adult work
while 65,000 are engaged in boys' and girls' 4-H club work. These
local leaders devote an average of three days' time a year to extension
activities, making a total of 750,000 days per year. This total is
the equivalent of 2,500 people working one year of 300 days each. It
is easily seen that the help given the paid extension agent by these
local leaders increases the value of his work many fold. In fact, the
amount of work a county agent can do in his county will be determined
largely by the number of local leaders he is able to enlist in the work
and the amount of training and direction he can give them.

Local leaders are in reality demonstrators who must be able to do
the work involved and who must also be able to show someone else
how to do it. They should be rural men and women capable of
learning worth-while tasks themselves and imbued with a spirit of
rural leadership that will help others in their community to progress.

The Selection of Leaders

The selecting of suitable leaders is, therefore, one of the most
important things an agent has to do if he is to depend upon local help
in carrying forward a county program. The ways by which leaders
are chosen vary greatly in different parts of the county or within a
State. In some instances selection is made by the county agent,
often in consultation with specialists, farm bureau workers, or community organizations. Where the farm bureau is especially strong
and active, its officials sometimes choose the local leaders. Frequently a man or woman who feels an urge to help in community

work volunteers to act as a local leader. Some leaders are chosen by community extension organizations or even by a part of such an organization, such as a group concerned with the development of a particular project. Most selections, however, are made with the advice and consent of the county extension agent. According to a recent study of local-leadership training made by the Office of Cooperative Extension Work, extension agents base their selection of leaders upon the following characteristics arranged in the order of importance: Personality, confidence of community, knowledge required, teaching ability, tact, adaptability, and willingness to serve.

The county extension agent may use the leaders individually or organize them into a county agricultural committee consisting of leading farmers, bankers, business men, and home makers who are especially interested in certain lines of agricultural work. The latter way has been found advantageous in many counties, as it gives greater permanence to the work and creates a feeling of unified procedure. The committee usually consists of two or three persons who are interested in poultry, the same number, perhaps, in dairying, certain crops, marketing, transportation, and similar enterprises. When such an organization is in force the committee meeting as a whole can take a comprehensive view of the county or community needs. The committee functions in groups, each group calling upon some other group whenever coordinating help is needed.

At the beginning of the year the agent calls a general meeting of the local leaders and lays before them his suggested plan for the annual county drive. He presents to them all the available statistics of county conditions to aid them in forming decisions and outlines for them his method of procedure. These may be discussed for several days. Amendments are made and a final program is decided upon. Frequently the agent calls in outside help for suggestions and generally meets with a ready response from the public-spirited citizens of his county. One of the first requisites to a successful program is local cooperation, and local leaders have taken an important part in the formulation of programs.

Supervision is Delegated to Groups

After a general program of county work for the year has been decided upon the agent delegates supervision of parts of it to groups in his committee that are especially interested in certain enterprises. To the dairy group he assigns the plans dealing with dairy work, to the crop groups the plans in which they are interested, and so on through his committee until each leader has some responsibility. Some of the duties within the general committee are to attend all general meetings and assist in planning work, to help organize communities to carry on the work, and to supply necessary material to communities for furthering the work.

Whenever the development of certain projects is to be attempted in a community, the local leader living in the community is generally placed in charge. Although this leader may be an adept in the line he is supervising, and may be an excellent farmer, or an expert dairyman, he may be unable to lead his neighbors or impart his knowledge to them. Method of presentation in extension work is, therefore, as important as abundant knowledge of subject matter. To overcome any difficulty the agent may find in this regard he establishes certain forms of training.

The training of local leaders varies with conditions in the county, with the needs of the leaders, and with the wishes of the agent.   If the State college of agriculture is not too far distant, leaders may attend college short courses, conferences, and similar functions.   When this is impracticable, the agent may call extension specialists into his county and hold short training schools or conferences for the local leaders. When neither of these methods is feasible, the agent trains his leaders by personal teaching or directing.   Leaders imbued with the proper spirit show no hesitancy in availing themselves of whatever opportunity is offered to improve their teaching ability.

Many of the details of procedure in local demonstrations, conferences, or field work of all kinds are left to the local leader.   Sometimes local leaders conduct their farms as demonstration fields under the supervision of the extension agent.   Such demonstration farms are scattered about over the country and exert a marked beneficial influence upon community agricultural development.

Functions of Its Leaders

A few of the more important ways in which local leaders function in extension work have been enumerated by C. B. Smith, Chief of the Office of Cooperative Extension Work, as follows:

They are carriers of instruction from the county agents and extension specialists to the group they represent.

They are demonstrators.

They call together groups of people to get information direct from extension agents.

They help in getting up educational exhibits at fairs.

They help in securing financial support for extension work.

They report extension news items for the local press.

They keep records and make extension reports.

In club work, they enroll members, organize clubs, call meetings, give instruction, train demonstration teams, hold achievement days, promote club camps, report accomplishments, and like matters.

With a nation-wide program of agricultural improvement, and a rather limited full-time force to direct its movement, the need of intelligent volunteer local leadership is becoming more apparent.   Much depends upon local initiative to carry forward rural development. For these reasons extension workers have found that it is very important that there be a wide recognition of the possibilities of using local leaders, careful selection of such leaders, and more emphasis upon local leader training schools for their intensive instruction.

F. A. MERRILL.

EXTENSION Workers Need General and Vocational Training   The nation-wide system of cooperative extension work was made possible through enactment of the Smith-Lever Act in 1914.   According to this act:

Cooperative agricultural extension work shall consist of the giving of instruction and practical demonstrations in agriculture and home economics to persons not attending or resident in said colleges in the several communities and imparting to such persons information on said subjects through field demonstrations, publications, and otherwise.

The act made no provision for the special training of extension workers.   From the beginning some State extension administrators and deans of agricultural colleges have believed that special training should be provided for those wishing to enter extension work, but only a few institutions have given such training.

Apparently the prevailing opinion has been that the general agricultural-college curricula, which are planned for the training of agricultural and home-economics students for various pursuits, should serve for the training of extension workers. The courses in the agricultural colleges were formerly concerned chiefly with the productive side of agriculture. Little or no consideration was given to problems of management, of distribution, and of the social aspect of farm life. Only within comparatively recent years have the agricultural-college curricula been broadened to include courses in agricultural economics, farm management, marketing, rural sociology, and related subjects. The colleges now offer broader training for extension workers, teachers, farmers, and research workers.

New Problems Constantly Arising

The agricultural industry is marked by change rather than by stability. Old problems of vital importance to the farmer continue to require attention; new ones are arising constantly. During the last six or eight years increased emphasis has been placed on the difficulties encountered by the farmer in deriving a reasonable income from his business. The numerous and complex agricultural problems of the farmers of the Nation are of much concern to the agricultural colleges and to the Federal Department of Agriculture. The State and Federal Governments spend large sums of money annually to improve agricultural conditions, a large amount being used in scientific investigations. To make the results of these investigations of greatest value, properly trained leaders with a vision of farm needs are necessary to serve as interpreters between the investigator and the farmer or the farm home-maker.

Extension work aims to aid farmers to solve their individual problems and to give guidance along all lines. The extension agent can render the greatest service by having carefully defined programs based upon the needs of individual farms and homes.

Successful farming requires more than ever before the exercise of sound business principles. In planning his work the farmer draws upon his experience and education to determine the necessary adjustments. As a business man he adjusts his plans to suit conditions, and in this phase of his business he frequently needs counsel. County agents need training that will enable them to understand the management of farming or of farm home making, so that if called upon they can assist in making decisions. It is the responsibility of the extension worker as a public servant and teacher to anticipate errors in both production and distribution, and to give instruction in the methods recommended by the agricultural experiment stations and the Federal Department of Agriculture.

Economic Problems Fundamental

Although the problems with which extension workers have to deal are not limited to the field of economics, the economic aspect of farming is fundamental and of far-reaching importance to the welfare of the farm family. Reduction in income means a lower standard of living, which effects changes in social conditions generally. Such conditions breed unrest, and farm families migrate to the city in search of employment. Tenancy increases, and problems of serious concern to rural progress arise.

Well-trained county extension workers, who have a thorough technical training and a broad understanding of the economic, social, and educational needs of farm people are constantly required to meet new problems in agriculture. Instruction and practical demonstrations dealing with many problems relating to the improvement of the farm and home are given by extension agents through individual and through group methods of instruction. Extension workers are essentially teachers, and the training required should be on a parity with that of other vocational teachers. The agents should have the ability to lead rural people in the development of a wholesome, happy, and contented farm life. To be successful, extension agents should have a pleasing personality, tact, and good judgment in dealing with people.

Requirements of Extension Work

Extension workers should have a broad educational foundation and technical training in college, with vocational experience in their particular field. Perhaps the training for extension workers can best be determined by the workers who have had practical experience with problems ordinarily found in county extension work. The results of a survey [1] made in 1927 of 300 county agents widely distributed in various States show that 89.6 per cent of the agents believe that professional training is essential. Some replies placed as much emphasis upon professional as upon technical courses. The following were listed as being the professional subjects of greatest value in training extension workers: Agricultural economics, marketing, extension methods, rural sociology, psychology, public speaking, English, pedagogy and practice teaching, and business methods. Public speaking and journalism also were included.

Special courses for extension workers are favored by deans of agriculture and of home economics and by directors and State leaders of extension work in 39 of 42 States that reported on the subject.[2] Over 90 per cent of those responsible for extension work in the States say that special courses are essential. The majority of those in charge of teacher-training divisions in land-grant institutions believe that extension workers should be as well prepared in professional subjects as are those who teach vocational agriculture or home economics in high schools under the Smith-Hughes Act. The same administrative officers suggest the following courses to supplement the technical subjects in training extension workers: Sociology, extension methods, psychology, agricultural economics, public speaking, agricultural journalism, and education. It is interesting to note the close correlation between the subjects suggested by administrative officers and those suggested by the agents.

---

[1] See U. S. Dept. Agr. Ext. Serv. Circ. 55, Special courses for preparation of agricultural and home economics extension workers. (Mimeographed.) E. H. Shinn and F. A. Merrill, September, 1927.

[2] See U. S. Dept. Agr. Ext. Serv. Circ. 59, A study of land-grant college curricula with reference to special courses for the preparation of agricultural and home-economics extension teachers without considering agricultural, home-economics, and closely related science subjects. (Mimeographed.) E. H. Shinn and F. A. Merrill, October, 1927.

Wide Variety of Courses

Of the total number of replies received from administrative officers in 42 States regarding the procedure institutions were following to attain these ends, 23 reported some form of training for extension work in agriculture and home economics. Wide variation is noted in the character and frequency of courses offered. The data show that few institutions have definite plans for such training, but the general feeling is that the training should be on a more definite basis. The course most frequently mentioned is extension methods, 19 of the 23 institutions reporting that a course of this kind is offered. In some institutions the course is offered by extension directors; in others by the division of teacher training. The courses are elective. In the small group of institutions that offer courses for extension workers students generally elect the courses desired from the regular subject-matter departments.

To provide the best curricula for extension workers it may be necessary in certain instances to omit some of the technical courses to allow time for professional courses. Technical training in agriculture or home economics should not be too highly specialized, as county extension workers are not specialists. Their duties lie in a wide field of activity and their training should be broad.

Extension workers should be encouraged to pursue graduate courses and to specialize along lines of most value to their work. Opportunity should be provided for leave of absence by some plan comparable to that offered to regular members of the agricultural college staffs.

In any program for the improvement of agriculture county extension workers are of far-reaching importance. They are making definite contributions in developing successful, happy, and contented farm people. What is most needed is definite training in both technical and professional subjects, that will give a broad vision of the work to be accomplished, with ability to determine the aims and to analyze the best procedure in accomplishing them. To provide suitable training for extension workers is a challenge to the best the agricultural colleges have to offer.

E. H. SHINN.

FABRICS' Stiffness is Measurable by Device Made for the Purpose As a part of the study on starches and other sizing agents for finishing new fabrics and restoring the finish to laundered materials, a quantitative method of measuring stiffness in fabrics has been developed in the Bureau of Home Economics. Heretofore stiffness had been judged principally by the "feel" of the fabric, which allowed great variation because of the personal judgment of different individuals.

As a first step it was necessary to define stiffness in such a way that physical methods could be applied for its measurement. One investigator had considered stiffness to be the ability of a strip of fabric to support its own weight. Thus, if a strip of fabric were to be clamped horizontally at one end and the other end allowed to swing free, as in the case of a cantilever beam, the more horizontal the strip remained the greater would be its stiffness; or, in other words, the greater the length of the strip supporting itself above a given angle of deformation the greater the stiffness.

Physical methods, based upon the natural laws governing the properties of elastic bodies, have been devised for testing the amount of flexure or bending in cantilever beams of such materials as wood or metal. Because of the great elasticity of fabrics, their bending is much greater than these wooden or metal beams although the cases are similar. By a modification of the formulas governing more rigid bodies, it has been possible to develop an expression for the elastic behavior of such flexible materials as textile fabrics.

The Apparatus Described

Upon such a theoretical basis a device has been constructed for measuring quantitatively the stiffness of fabrics and related materials such as paper. The apparatus consists of a vertical board upon which is mounted a clamp consisting of two rubber rolls through which the fabric is passed. A metal shelf slightly wider than the fabric extends from the clamp across the vertical board at a given angle. The shelf serves as a support for the projected fabric until the strip has been sufficiently shortened, by turning through the rolls, to support its own weight at the given angle. The angle chosen depends on the material to be tested. A 45° angle was used to test the stiffness of variously starched fabrics. A reading is taken at that point where the free end of the strip leaves the shelf.

The scale is so calibrated that it reads stiffness directly as the product of the length of the strip in millimeters capable of supporting itself and a certain factor which depends upon the angle of deformation of the strip. This factor remains constant for any given deformation, and the product of the fabric length supporting itself at any angle by the corresponding factor for that angle will always remain constant for a given fabric. This affords a very simple and direct procedure for measuring quantitatively the stiffness property of fabrics and related materials.

ESTHER C. PETERSON and
TOBIAS DANTZIG.

FAMILY Living Needs Studied in Relation to Income of Farms The manufacturer assumes that his activities must provide a profit sufficient to pay expenses and interest on investment. The laboring man considers that he should receive a living wage. Most farm families have not set for themselves any tangible ideal as to what the farm should furnish to provide a satisfactory living.

Groups of farm women in the far West have been asked what would be the minimum amount of money necessary to pay for food, clothing, education, fuel, light, and doctor's bills, for a family of five in order that they might give their children the kind of a home and training that would make them better able to meet life problems. It was decided that $1,200 was the minimum amount of cash necessary to provide the family with these living requirements and that at least $600 worth of fuel, food, and shelter must be furnished by the farm.

From this $1,200 cash income, $360 would be set aside to purchase the meats and groceries, assuming that the farm would furnish all the poultry and eggs, most of the meat and dairy products, and practically all the fruit and vegetables. A similar amount would be set

aside for clothing.   This $360 would enable the father to have a new
suit of clothes once in three years and an overcoat once in four years,
and the mother to have one new coat every three years.   With this
standard, the farm family would be at least respectably clothed.

The $1,200 also would provide at least $100 for the accumulation of
an educational fund, about $125 for fuel and light, $50 for doctor's
bills, and similar amounts for church and for amusement.   In addition
there would be available about $100 for the care of the house and
replacement of furniture, table linen, and dishes.

Estimating What is Required

If we assume that the farm should first supply the family with the
necessities of life, we have a way of arriving at what the farm must
produce in order to provide the family with sufficient income to
maintain a just standard of living.   The farmer's living then becomes
the first charge against the products that are sold.   If the farmer is
selling the products from only 12 milk cows and considers the $1,200
mentioned above as the first charge against the cash returns from his

FIGURE 83.—Farm home of a typical farm family having an income of less than $1,200 for living
expenses.   Attractive dwellings, adequate farm buildings, and reasonable living standards can not
be provided on an income which is sufficient only for the bare necessities of life

cows, he has an overhead living wage charge of $100 per cow.   If to
this is added an amount necessary to pay for other expenses in
connection with the cows, a fair index is given of what each cow must
earn in order to provide this living wage.

If the farmer has 40 acres of cropped land from which he sells
agricultural products and considers $1,200 for family living expenses
as his first charge against his crops, each acre would have an overhead
living wage charge of $30.   If there were added to this taxes, insur-
ance, interest, and cash cost of crop production, it is at once seen
which crops are likely to meet this requirement and which ones can
not.   On some farms the only product sold may be wheat.   If the
farmer has only 2,400 bushels to sell each year and still makes the
$1,200 his first charge against the wheat, he has an overhead living-
wage charge of 50 cents a bushel in addition to all of his cash-crop
production costs.

In Cache County, Utah, the farmers in the irrigated area were asked what system of farming would furnish at least $1,200 after all farm expenses were paid. They reported that a man must have 80 acres and produce better than average yields in order to obtain a yearly cash return of $1,200. On an 80-acre farm with only an average yield he must have the same crops and livestock, and in addition 400 to 600 laying hens. However, in this same area there were many 40-acre farms from which families were trying to make livings. Only the exceptional man was meeting the situation successfully. He had to have a very large portion of his farm in sugar beets, and a large-size

FIGURE 84.—Home of a typical farm family that has more than $1,500 to spend annually for living. The size of the farm business and the increased efficiency of production per unit are the factors that enable this type of farm family to maintain the standards of living to which all farming people are entitled

poultry unit in addition to his dairy, and do his utmost to keep cash expenses to the minimum.

Below-Standard Farms

These data point out the significance of the relationship between the farm income and the money available for living. A survey of 14,000 farms indicated that for the United States as a whole the average amount of cash available for family expenses was only $800; less than 25 per cent had $1,200 or more to spend for family living; 25 per cent between $800 and $1,200; and 50 per cent less than $800. The above figures seem to show that three-fourths of the farms in the United States do not have a large enough farm income to provide the farm family with the standard of living proposed.

EUGENE MERRITT.

FAMILY Living Supplied by Farm Recorded in Maryland Home Study The city home maker has to purchase with money practically all articles needed for the family living. The farm home maker, on the other hand, obtains housing, much of the food and fuel, and in some localities ice, directly from the farm. From her point of view what are these furnished items worth? What amount of the various goods does the farm furnish, and what would it cost the family to buy their equivalents?

To provide a very exact answer to these questions, 22 home makers of Frederick County, Md., cooperated in a study being made by the Bureau of Home Economics. Each one kept a careful and detailed record of all the money spent for the family living, and also of all food, fuel, and ice that the farm supplied for the family's use, from August 1, 1926, to July 31, 1927.

A hanging scale was placed in a convenient spot in each kitchen. Whenever articles of food were brought in from the garden or storeroom they were weighed, and the name of the item and the weight written on the wall card hanging near the scales. Quantities of furnished ice were recorded as used, and each week the amount of furnished fuel burned was noted. The complete record of all cash expenditures and of furnished articles used by the family was mailed to the bureau once a week. The records were edited immediately, and if any item seemed questionable a letter was sent to the home maker and the matter cleared up while the situation was still fresh in her mind. In this manner an exact listing of the kind, quantity, and price or value of all articles purchased or furnished by the farm for the family living during the 12-month period was made possible.

Workers from the bureau visited the shops where the home makers did their purchasing and obtained prices for the articles furnished by the farm. These were the retail prices that the home maker would have paid had she purchased the food, fuel, or ice from a regular dealer. Care was taken to price the same quality as that furnished by the farm. Prices quoted were, of course, for the season during which the article was used. The whole object was to find the value of the furnished articles in terms of the price that would have been paid had the article been purchased and not furnished by the farm.

Money Value of Things Got From Farm

Now, what did these furnished items amount to in money value and what proportion of the total family living was represented by them? Naturally, no general conclusion can be drawn from the records of 22 families. They are, however, a good sample of the situation in the county over which they were scattered, some on large and some on small farms.

In actual cash these families spent on the average $1,712.70 during the year. This varied from $737.70 for one family to $3,734.50 for the family spending the greatest sum. But if we consider the total value of the family living—that is, include the cash expenditures, 6 per cent of the equity in the house, and the value of all food, fuel, and ice furnished by the farm—these 22 families show a total value of family living ranging from $1,217.71 to $4,942.18, the average being $2,701.63. Just as many families reported a total value of family living less than $2,694.09 as reported a total value of family living greater than that sum. The average cash expenditure of the 22 families was 63.3 per cent of the total value of the average family living. Or, in other words, 36.7 per cent of the average total value of family living was furnished by the farm.

The largest single item in these family budgets was furnished food. The average value of this item amounted to $651.44, or 24.1 per cent of the total value of family living. The average family purchased $263.20 worth of food. Thus 69.2 per cent of the value of the food consumed was provided by the farm.

Housing was the next important item among the furnished goods. The average value of the 22 farmhouses was $4,677.27. The dwellings varied all the way from a small, rather old house worth about $1,000 to a modern, well-built house valued at $12,000. If the housing furnished by the farm is figured as 6 per cent of the value of the house, this item was worth, on the average, $280.64. This is not an attempt to place a rental value on the house. The sum merely represents the amount of income that the family would have had if the money invested in the house had been invested in an income-yielding security paying 6 per cent.

The value of the fuel furnished by the farm varied widely, ranging from $5 in the case of one family whose farm provided practically no fuel to $116.50 for a family living in a good house and using much fuel for heating.

Ten families did not have ice from the farm. The others had ice in amounts varying in value from less than a dollar to $35.10. For the entire group the average value of the ice furnished by the farm was $5.28.

Briefly stated, these families received, on the average, articles furnished by the farm to the value of $973.15 per family. This was made up of food valued at $651.44, fuel at $35.79, ice at $5.28, and housing at $280.64. In other words, through the facilities provided by the farm an average of nearly $1,000 was added to the value of the living of these 22 families during the year.

CHASE G. WOODHOUSE.

FARM Living Standards Widely Divergent on Good and on Poor U. S. Farms There are two widely divergent standards of living on the farms of the United States—a higher standard on high-value farms, a lower standard on low-value farms. This fact, which is quite obvious— since the income on low-value farms is in the long run lower than on high-value farms—gains national importance from three circumstances. The first circumstance is that when the per acre value of farm land and buildings is averaged by counties (fig. 85) nearly 40 per cent of the farm population of the United States is found living on land whose value is less than $40 per acre—that is, on relatively poor land; land whose soil is deficient or whose topography is difficult for farming. The second circumstance is this: when the value per farm of farm land and buildings is averaged by counties (fig. 86) 42.5 per cent of the farm population of the United States is found living on farms whose value is less than $4,000—that is, on relatively low-value farms; farms of such small acreage or of such poor land per acre that the value per farm is low. The third circumstance is (compare figs. 85 and 86) that the bulk of the farm population living on the poor, difficult, and low-per-acre-value land is virtually identical with the bulk of the farm population living on the low-value farms. In other words, on the

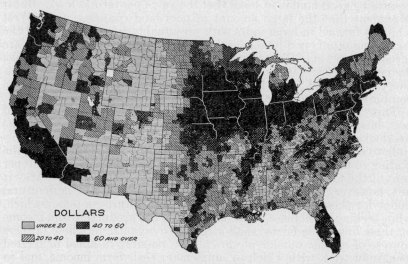

FIGURE 85.—Average value per acre of farm land and buildings by counties. The light-colored land is poor, occupied by 38.5 per cent of the farm population. The dark-colored land is middling and good, the darkest being middling. The less dark is good and is occupied by 40.5 per cent of the farm population

whole, the bulk of the counties having a low average value per farm for land and buildings are counties whose average value per acre of farm land and buildings is also low.

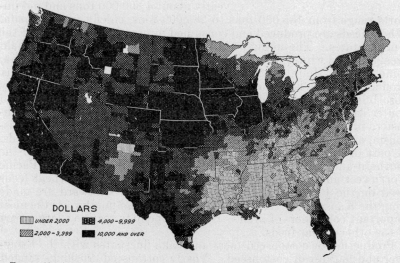

FIGURE 86.—Average value of land and buildings per farm by counties. The light-colored land is made up of low-value farms, occupied by 42.2 per cent of the farm population. The dark-colored land is made up of middling-value farms and high-value farms, the darkest being middling-value farms. The less dark is high-value farms and is occupied by 24.9 per cent of the farm population

It will be observed that the poor land of the western mountain region is in such large holdings that the per-farm value rises to an equality with the farms of the better-land areas. It will also be noticed that, in some other sections, the average acreage per farm of a few counties possessing good land is so small that the value per farm is low. But it is evident that the large amount of poor-land counties in the West which is farmed in large units with presumably fair incomes, and the small amount of good-land counties scattered here and there which are farmed in very small units with presumably low incomes on the whole, do not change the outstanding fact that 40 per cent of the farm population of the United States have a low standard of living, due chiefly to a combination of two facts, poor land and small acreage of farms.

This classification of farm population, according to good-land and poor-land farms, presents a national problem which can scarcely be overlooked much longer. Baldly stated the problem is this: Is it possible to organize agriculture on the low-value, poor-land farms of the Nation so that the occupation of farming alone shall return to 40 per cent of the farm population an adequate standard of living? May it not, however, be necessary to establish an entirely new agricultural policy for these people at the bottom of agriculture—a policy which, while seeking to increase, so far as possible, the production and income on these low-value farms, shall attempt to organize for these farmers sources of income outside of agriculture, possibly in allied or related local industries, with which to supplement their farm income, and so provide them with an adequate standard of living?

C. J. GALPIN.

FEEDS Commercially Produced Have Wide Distribution in U. S. About 5,000,000 tons of wheat mill feeds are consumed yearly in this country. Estimated wheat feed output averages yearly about 4,800,000 tons and net imports range from 185,000 tons to 285,000 tons, chiefly from Canada. Wheat feeds are produced and consumed in practically all parts of the United States. The spring wheat mills in the Minneapolis and Buffalo area, the hard winter wheat mills in and near Kansas City and Omaha, some mills in Mountain States and in Pacific Northwest, are surplus producers. New England, New York, Pennsylvania, and New Jersey absorb large quantities of the surplus of wheat feeds from spring and winter wheat mills and Canadian imports. Production of the southeastern mills is chiefly taken locally. Dairy sections of Minnesota, Wisconsin, and Michigan are heavy consumers of spring-wheat mill feeds. A part of the surplus from the Kansas City territory moves to the southern and the southeastern consuming areas. Mills in the Pacific Northwest and Mountain States supply the bulk of the wheat feeds used on the Pacific coast; occasional shipments westward are made from the Kansas City territory. Dairy cows and poultry are the most important consumers of bran. Hogs and poultry receive a larger part of the other wheat feeds.

Production of cottonseed meal and cake fluctuates with the carryover and harvest of cottonseed. Yearly cottonseed crushings ranged from about 3,000,000 tons to 6,305,000 tons in the years 1918–1927. The average output of cake and meal obtained per ton of seed crushed ranged from 878 to 972 pounds during that period. Exports of cake and meal have recently ranged from about 10 to 20 per cent of the yearly output and totaled about 500,000 tons in 1926–27 and 309,000 tons in 1927–28. Considering the mill stocks on hand at the beginning and end of the season, production during the year, exports, and consumption of meal as fertilizer, the consumption of cottonseed cake and meal as feed totaled nearly 2,000,000 tons in 1926 and 1927, and about 1,500,000 tons in 1927–28.

East and South Buy Concentrates

Eastern and Southern States buy much of their roughage and the prairie States relatively small amounts, but both sections purchase large quantities of concentrate feeds. The heaviest feeding of cottonseed meal occurs in the Cotton Belt, where other feeds are relatively scarce and high priced. A fair amount is taken by the dairy industry of New England, New Jersey, Pennsylvania, and Ohio; limited amounts crushed in California are largely consumed there.

About 700,000 tons of linseed cake and meal have been produced annually in recent years, and with yearly exports about 300,000 tons a domestic consumption of about 400,000 tons is indicated. The bulk of the output is centered at Minneapolis, St. Paul, Chicago, Milwaukee, and Superior, where crushers use domestic seed, and at Buffalo, Edgewater, N. J., and other eastern points, where Canadian and Argentine seed is crushed. Smaller amounts are produced in Ohio, Iowa, Kansas, California, and Oregon.

The heaviest feeding of linseed cake and meal is found in the Northeast and North Central States where the bulk of this feed is produced. Smaller amounts are fed in other sections of the northern United States; practically none is consumed in the South. Dairy cows received by far the largest amount. Cows on farms studied in New York were fed an average of 87 pounds per year. From this, the amounts ranged downward to 57 pounds per year fed in Minnesota and 15 pounds in some dairies in Colorado, to 2 pounds per year in South Dakota.

Between 500,000 and 625,000 tons of gluten meal and feed and 25,000 tons of corn oil cake were reported as being produced annually by the Associated Corn Products Manufacturers in 1925 to 1927 from operations of cornstarch and corn-sirup plants. Their production represents a large percentage of the United States output. The greater portion of this output was produced in the Corn Belt and consumed in the dairy sections of the Northwest. About 485 pounds per cow were consumed yearly on the limited number of farms studied in New York where, as on Wisconsin farms, cows averaged about 5 pounds per year.

Production of Dried Beet Pulp

Annual production of dried beet pulp in recent years has totaled about 150,000 tons. The wet and dried beet pulp is consumed largely in the central and far West with the Northeast supplied generally by Canada and the East by foreign imports.

About 325,000 tons of alfalfa meal were ground during 1927, principally in California, Colorado, and Missouri. Most of this meal was sold to manufacturers of mixed feeds.

The bulk of the commercial feeding-tankage output is produced and consumed in the Corn Belt. Tankage is fed principally to hogs; considerable quantities are consumed by poultry. Feeding requirements of important poultry sections in the Northeast and on the Pacific coast increase the demand for this feed.

In considering the demand for commercial feeds the condition of of pastures, meadows, and grazing lands is an important factor. Better-than-average condition enables the farmers to carry their stock into cold winter months with smaller expenditure for commercial feeds. The supply of cereal grains, hay, straws, other fodders, and silage tend to similarly affect the consumption of manufactured feeds.

FLOYD J. HOSKING.

F ENCE-POST Treatment Economizes Timber From Custer Forest   The timber resources of the Custer National Forest in southeastern Montana and northeastern South Dakota are being administered to supply the needs of a prairie region in which the majority of the settlers are located at distances of 60 to 100 miles from a railroad. The local market readily consumes the natural yield that can be cut in the form of saw timber from the partly timbered hills within the national-forest boundaries.

The Black Hills variety of western yellow pine is the only native wood found in commercial quantities. It forms stands 100 per cent pure except for occasional relatively small patches of aspen, Rocky Mountain red cedar, green ash, box elder, lance-leaf cottonwood, and, in rare instances, paper birch.

With the limited local supply and constant demand for lumber one of the chief problems in the management of this forest is to make the present supply of mature timber last until the more extensive stands of small sapling and pole timber grow to saw-timber size. There are many overstocked stands of this young growth in which thinnings would increase the rate of growth of the remaining trees and reduce the period of time required to produce the final product. The material which would be removed in thinning such stands is of the right size for making fence posts. It is part of the forest working plan to produce through thinnings enough small round posts to supply the local needs. When properly treated such posts give very satisfactory service.

As stock farming is the principal industry in the surrounding region, large quantities of fence posts are required annually for use on homesteads, farms, and ranches. In the past, large durable split posts could be readily obtained from dead western yellow pine timber thoroughly impregnated with pitch and known as "pitch pine," but the supply of this material is now practically exhausted. Consequently, within a very short time the demand for fence posts must be filled with round posts cut from the young pine stands and given a preservative treatment, or with material imported from the timber-producing regions farther west.

The small open-tank wood-preservation plant shown in the accompanying photograph was installed in the Long Pines district of the Custer National Forest in 1923. In 1926 the capacity of the plant was doubled through the addition of two more treating tanks.

Treating Posts With Creosote

A large number of round western yellow pine posts from thinnings in the 20 to 40 year age classes have been treated with coal-tar creosote and with a creosote-petroleum mixture consisting of 40 per cent coal-tar creosote and 60 per cent fuel oil. The posts treated for demonstration purposes have been used in the construction of about 6 miles of range division fences and 1 mile of administrative fence.

With this treated timber it is not necessary to use the large-sized line posts commonly cut and used in the past. By using a post from 3 to 4 inches in top diameter and long enough to allow a few inches above the top wire, the cost of creosote and handling is reduced. The treated pine post of this size will last at least twice as long as the small untreated split posts shipped in from other regions and affords ample strength for the fence line.

These round sap-pine posts are very easily treated. Penetrations of 1 to 2 inches with the preservative are obtained by submerging the butts of the posts in a creosote-petroleum mixture heated to about

FIGURE 87.—Creosoting western yellow pine posts

190° F. for one to two hours, followed immediately by a cold bath for about the same period of time. After the butt treatment has been completed, the tops of the posts are given a shallow treatment by placing them in the hot tank for about 30 minutes.

Fence posts from thinnings in the young pine stands are sold at a very low stumpage price, and those who may desire to use the Long Pines treating plant on a cooperative basis will be allowed to do so free of charge. Under such conditions it is estimated that farmers contributing their own labor and preservative can purchase and treat western yellow pine posts 3 to 4 inches in top diameter at a total cash outlay of about 15 cents per post. Detailed cost records also have been worked up for the benefit of others who may find it necessary to have all of the work done by contract.

C. N. WHITNEY.

FENCE Posts Properly Treated Have Greatly Increased Durability Fence posts that rot quickly are a continual source of trouble and expense. Posts that give long years of satisfactory service without renewal keep fencing costs low. Farmers who do not have a supply of durable fence-post timber on their own land may be able to purchase naturally durable wood posts or commercially creosoted posts from their local dealers. Well-creosoted posts can be relied upon for an average life of 20 to 30 years or more, and several creosoting companies are now specializing in the treatment of fence posts and their distribution through retail dealers.

If durable posts are not readily available at a reasonable cost, the farmer can use posts of nondurable species of wood and, by giving them a good preservative treatment, make them give very long and satisfactory service.

Pressure processes, such as those used by commercial creosoting companies, are most thorough and effective for applying wood preservatives but the apparatus is too expensive for farm use. A hot and cold bath open-tank process is the most thorough method of treatment that is practicable on the farm. It consists of heating the posts for one or more hours in a metal tank containing preservative (usually coal-tar creosote) at a temperature ranging from 180° to 220° F. The posts are then quickly transferred to a tank of preservative having a temperature of about 100°, and are left there for one hour or more. Instead of a separate tank being used for the "cool" bath, the heating of the oil in the hot bath may be stopped, and the wood and preservative allowed to cool together.

Treatments Prove Very Effective

Such treatments prove very effective and will give to posts of very low natural durability a life of 20 years or more. Sap pine posts, for example, which may last only 2 or 3 years untreated, can be so thoroughly creosoted by the hot and cold bath process that a life of at least 30 years may well be expected. The length of life obtained will depend upon the preservative used and the thoroughness of the treatment, deep penetration with a good preservative being necessary for the best results. Some species of wood are more resistant to treatment than others. Practically all species, however, except those of great natural durability, can be treated so effectively that the increase in durability will more than repay the cost of treatment.

Preservative treatment is also very effective for stable floors, bridges, hog houses, and any other constructions used on the farm under conditions that favor the early decay of wood.

Applying the preservative with a brush or dipping the wood in the preservative are simpler and less expensive methods than the hot and cold bath treatment, but generally they are much less effective and not so useful. Farmers' Bulletin No. 744–F contains detailed instructions on the preservative treatment of farm timber.

GEORGE M. HUNT.

FERTILIZER Concentration   The materials used in fertilizer
Need Not Increase the   mixtures may be conveniently
Risk of Burning Plants   divided into two classes according as they are quickly or slowly
soluble in soil water. To the first class belong such inorganic products
as Chilean nitrate, sulphate of ammonia, and the various potash salts.
Examples of the second class are cottonseed meal, tankage, basic slag,
and superphosphate.

In the early history of the fertilizer industry slowly soluble materials
were relatively cheap. They therefore constituted the bulk of fertilizer mixtures and danger from burning in the use of such mixtures
was relatively slight. Recent developments in fertilizer manufacture
have somewhat reversed this situation. Soluble fertilizer materials
such as those produced by nitrogen fixation are now being placed on
the market at a much lower price per unit of plant food than the slowly
soluble materials. Danger from burning in the use of mixtures prepared from such materials must therefore be greater than in the mixtures formerly used unless a method is found for reducing the quantity
of fertilizer applied to the soil without reducing its fertilizing value.
Fortunately such a method has been devised. It consists of simply
increasing the proportion or concentration of the plant food elements
in the fertilizer. Thus by combining both nitrogen and potash in a
compound known as nitrate of potash a product is obtained which
contains 4.4 times as much plant food as the same weight of an equivalent mixture of kainite and nitrate of soda. The plant food in an
application of 100 pounds of the latter mixture may be duplicated by
the addition of only 23 pounds of nitrate of potash to the same soil
area. Danger from burning or from detrimental salt action must
therefore be greatly reduced when a mixture of this kind is replaced
by the equivalent amount of the higher grade material.

Plant Food in Ammonium Phosphate

Ammonium phosphate in the same way contains approximately as
much plant food as three times the weight of either sulphate of
ammonia or nitrate of soda. This new fertilizer salt has the further
advantage that it is more easily distributed and shows less tendency to
concentrate locally in the soil than most soluble salts.

TABLE 7.—*Fertilizer formulas for a 3–9–3 commercial mixture and for equivalent
quantities of concentrated mixtures*

Item	Commercial fertilizer 3-9-3	Concentrated fertilizer	
		A 3.4 (3–9–3)	B 2.7 (3–9–3)
	Pounds	*Pounds*	*Pounds*
Superphosphate	1,125		
Double superphosphate		141	50
Monoammonium phosphate		128	263
Diammonium phosphate		80	
Ammonium sulphate	72		
Sodium nitrate	95		123
Potassium nitrate		96	
Potassium sulphate		36	
Manure salts	138		300
Kainit	270		
Cottonseed meal	150	55	
Sewage sludge	150	55	
Total	2,000	591	736
Total readily soluble salts	575	340	686
Soluble salts per unit of plant food	38	23	46

In Table 7 are given fertilizer formulas for an ordinary 3–9–3 fertilizer and for equivalent quantities of two concentrated mixtures. The total readily soluble salts in a ton of the ordinary fertilizer amounts to 38 pounds per unit of plant food and in the equivalent quantities of the concentrated mixtures A and B to 23 and 46 pounds, respectively. Although fertilizer A is more concentrated as regards its plant food content than either of the other two, it contains the least proportion of readily soluble salts. Concentrated fertilizer B on the other hand contains relatively more soluble salts than the ordinary fertilizer. Danger from burning in the use of concentrated fertilizers A and B would therefore be expected to be less and greater, respectively, than in the case of the ordinary fertilizer.

The Danger from Burning

It may be concluded that the relative danger from burning in the use of concentrated and low-grade mixtures will in general depend on their relative content of soluble salts per unit of plant food. If concentrated mixtures are prepared in such a way that the ratio of their soluble salts to plant food content is greater than in certain low-grade mixtures, then danger from burning may be greater with the concentrated fertilizer. The present tendency, however, is toward the use of larger proportions of soluble salts in ordinary fertilizers, and concentrated mixtures may now be prepared which contain a much lower ratio of soluble salts and which can therefore be used with less danger from burning than the average mixture of ordinary grade.

WILLIAM H. ROSS and
ALBERT R. MERZ.

FERTILIZER Consumption in Cotton Area Varies With Return From Crop The cotton crop receives a larger total quantity of fertilizer than any other one crop in the United States. Considering the extent to which the Cotton Belt specializes on one crop and the fact that (except in bottom lands like those of the Mississippi Delta and in the dry regions of the West) cotton is typically a fertilized crop, it is not surprising that the quantity of fertilizer consumed in the cotton States is largely determined by the economics of the cotton-growing industry.

The price of cotton prevailing during the selling season and up to planting time is the outstanding factor in determining the quantity of fertilizer sold in these States during any one year. For example, following the low prices received for the 1914 crop, fertilizer consumption in seven of the cotton States decreased approximately 40 per cent; again, following the price depression of 1920, consumption fell almost 50 per cent. Similar, but less extreme, examples of the effect of cotton prices on fertilizer consumption are given from year to year. This adjusting of production practices to prices received for the previous crop tends to result in a poor balance between the production and demand for cotton; but it is the price during this period which determines the amount of money cotton farmers have to spend, and, for want of a better criterion, it has been accepted by them as indicating the price during the succeeding marketing period.

Yield of cotton is the second most important factor. Its significance is most clearly seen in States like Georgia where the weevil took its heaviest toll. Low yields caused less fertilizer to be used the following year; first, because farmers had less money to invest and, second, because they were fearful that the weevil would again wipe out crop and profits.   On the other hand, the large yield in 1926 did much to diminish the effect of the low cotton prices in reducing farmers' fertilizer purchases in these States during 1927.   In North Carolina, where the weevil damage has been less, the trend of consumption has continued upward, interrupted only by unsatisfactory price conditions.

Scale of Production Important

The scale of cotton production, as denoted by the acreage of the crop the preceding year, also affects fertilizer consumption. · When produc-

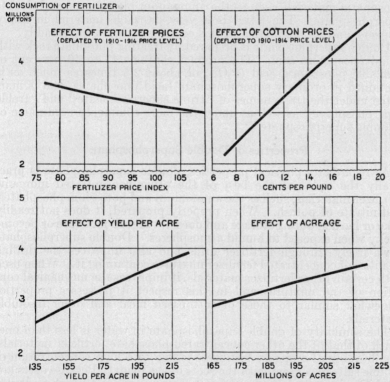

FIGURE 88.—These curves show the average effect of fertilizer prices at planting time, cotton prices during the fall and winter prior to planting time, and yield per acre and acreage of the previous year's cotton crop, upon the annual consumption of fertilizers in the Cotton States

tion is on a large scale, favorable conditions of price and yield have more effect on increasing purchases than when it is on a small scale.

The price of fertilizer influences the quantity purchased, since the higher the price the greater is the tendency to economize on it.   The importance of this factor is about equal to the importance of the yield of cotton in determining purchases.

Locally, the condition of the tobacco, fruit, or truck crop producers is significant.   Nevertheless, the combined effect of the price, yield, and acreage of cotton for one year determines largely the quantity of fertilizer purchased for use on the following crop.

LAWRENCE MYERS.

FERTILIZER Known as Double Superphosphate Has Useful Properties

For many years superphosphate (acid phosphate) has been the principal phosphate fertilizer used in this country. This material is a mixture of phosphate and gypsum, and it contains 17 to 20 per cent of available phosphoric acid (P_2O_5).

In preparing many of the high-analysis fertilizer mixtures which are being used in increasing quantities, the manufacturer finds it necessary to use, in addition to superphosphate (acid phosphate), certain quantities of more concentrated phosphate materials in order to obtain the desired percentage of available phosphoric acid (P_2O_5) in the final product. There are available for this purpose several concentrated phosphatic materials such as the ammonium phosphates, and double superphosphate. The latter is a very desirable material in many respects, and its production in this country is increasing steadily.

Double superphosphate is prepared by treating phosphate rock with liquid phosphoric acid. The product contains 43 to 46 per cent of available phosphoric acid (P_2O_5), or about 2.5 times as much as is contained in ordinary superphosphate (acid phosphate), and is marketed under the trade names of "triple superphosphate" and "treble superphosphate" as well as under the more commonly used name of "double superphosphate."

Properties of Double Superphosphate

As regards its physical properties, double superphosphate is practically the equal of the best of the other concentrated inorganic fertilizer materials, such as the ammonium and potassium phosphates, and nitrate of potash. When properly prepared, it does not readily cake or harden during storage and does not absorb moisture or become sticky when exposed to humid atmospheres. Double superphosphate flows freely through fertilizer drills and also improves the drilling qualities of concentrated fertilizer mixtures containing it. When used with certain other fertilizer materials, it improves the mechanical condition of the mixtures and in this respect it possesses properties somewhat similar to those of cottonseed meal and other insoluble materials.

The solubility of double superphosphate in water is less than one-tenth of that of the other concentrated phosphate fertilizer materials. The burning of crops by fertilizers is due to a high concentration of soluble salts in contact with the roots of the plant. Because of its low solubility in water the danger of burning is much less when double superphosphate and superphosphate are used as fertilizers than when equivalent quantities of phosphoric acid (P_2O_5) are applied in the form of the more soluble phosphate materials.

Double superphosphate may replace superphosphate (acid phosphate) in fertilizer mixtures in which the latter is generally used, without undergoing undesirable changes in physical or mechanical condition. As is the case with superphosphate, it should not be mixed with excessive quantities of cyanamid, ground limestone, hydrated lime, and other materials containing high percentages of active lime. Mixtures with the sulphates of ammonia and potash and other soluble sulphates, cake soon after preparation owing to a chemical reaction. This reaction is, however, soon completed, and when the mixtures are pulverized they do not cake a second time.

K. D. JACOB.

FIRE Risk in Country Grain Elevators Not Recognized Enough The isolated country grain elevator located along the railroad or in a small settlement is a serious fire hazard. This is due both to the nature of the business and to the fact that available fire-fighting facilities are totally inadequate to cope with a fire in such a large building.

FIGURE 89.—Fire in such an isolated plant is soon beyond control

FIGURE 90.—All that remains after a fire in a well-filled country elevator

An analysis of fire losses in country elevators shows that practically all are preventable. It is a case where precaution, care, and attention to fire-prevention practices by the elevator operator are of greater value than fire-fighting equipment. Unfortunately, when the operator is hired by a company in some distant terminal market there is an absence of direct responsibility, and the care and protection of the plant are often neglected.

What precautions should the elevator owner take to protect his property? The most important is to obtain a reliable manager who will take an interest in fire protection and cooperate with him in eliminating the hazards usually found in such plants. A thorough inspection of the plant before closing at night should be required, and sufficient help should be provided so that the care and repair of machinery are not neglected during the rush periods.

Hot bearings are responsible for many elevator fires. An automatic hot bearing alarm is a good investment.

Stones, scrap iron, shotgun shells, matches, and other material capable of starting a fire in machinery have been found in grain brought to country elevators. Screens to eliminate such material before it enters the house should be provided.

Idlers frequently smoke around the elevator. Smoking should be prohibited and idlers kept out of the plant.

Lightning is a frequent cause of fires in country elevators. The plant should be protected with properly installed lightning rods.

Accumulated dust may cause the destruction of the elevator by a dust explosion. High weeds and rubbish around the plant may become ignited, and the flames spread to the elevator. The grounds should be kept clean.

Buildings should be as fire resistant as possible. Fire extinguishers and water barrels should be placed at convenient points about the plant, and a loud alarm or some means of calling assistance in case of fire should be provided. A small fire in a country elevator, if not checked promptly, is soon beyond control.

HYLTON R. BROWN.

FLAX Resistant to Wilt Developed at Experiment Stations Flax wilt is caused by a fungus (*Fusarium lini*). Seed treatment is not effective because this soil-borne fungus may infect a susceptible flax plant at any time after the roots come in contact with the soil. The use of wilt-resistant varieties, therefore, is the only safe insurance against loss.

The State agricultural experiment stations of North Dakota and Minnesota have developed several new wilt-resistant varieties of flax. Linota, Buda, Bison, and Rio are improved varieties distributed by the North Dakota station. The Minnesota station has developed and distributed three varieties—Chippewa, Redwing, and Winona.

The Linota and Buda varieties are well adapted to the heavy soils of the Red River Valley in North Dakota and adjoining Minnesota. Both are highly wilt resistant and more or less resistant to rust. The plants are midhigh (28 to 36 inches), the flowers blue, and the seeds small. The Chippewa variety, a Minnesota selection from Primost (Minn. No. 25), is similar in type of plant to Linota. It also has given satisfactory yields in the Red River Valley. Winona is wilt resistant, but quite susceptible to rust. Bison flax, recently distributed in North Dakota, has larger seeds than those of Linota and Buda. The plants are of medium height, and the flowers are the slightly deeper wisteria blue. This variety has not yet been tested widely, but, if found satisfactory, its large seeds will make it popular with linseed crushers.

Rio Selected from Argentine Type

Rio is a selection of the Argentine type of flax. It is earlier and more uniform in ripening than the commercial Argentine variety and therefore more desirable. The plants are short to midhigh (18 to 24 inches) and somewhat later in maturing than common flax. It has large blue flowers and large, tightly closed bolls. The large seeds usually yield a somewhat higher percentage of oil than common flaxseed. Besides being highly wilt resistant, this variety is entirely immune from rust, which makes it valuable to the plant breeder. Unfortunately, it is very susceptible to pasmo, another injurious flax disease.

The Redwing variety, recently developed by the Minnesota station, is not yet available for commercial sowing. This valuable early variety can be distinguished from most varieties by its light blue flowers. It is resistant to both wilt and rust and has strong stems which rarely lodge when grown on rich soils.

A. C. DILLMAN.

FLEAS Controlled By Creosote Oil Sprays and Other Insecticides The widespread and serious annoyance caused by fleas in practically all parts of the United States during 1928 has greatly stimulated interest in methods of fighting them. All fleas must have blood to enable them to reproduce, and infestations by fleas are always connected either directly or indirectly with the sleeping places of dogs, cats, hogs, or chickens. The eggs are laid by the fleas while on the host. These fall among the débris, mainly in the sleeping places of the animals, and soon hatch into slender maggots which live in the dust and produce another brood of adults in from two weeks to three months later. The adult fleas can live for several weeks without food, a fact which explains how hordes of hungry fleas may greet one in his home upon his return from a vacation.

To combat fleas the breeding places should be located and sprayed lightly but thoroughly with creosote oil, by means of a good force pump. If handled carefully, creosote oil may be used in basements and outbuildings, although it stains considerably. The same treatment is applicable to chicken houses and runs which become infested with the hen flea or sticktight flea. If fleas are found to be breeding under rugs, or in the cracks of floors, the rugs should be removed, hung up in the sun and thoroughly beaten, and the floors wiped up with gasoline. Flaked naphthalene, scattered over the floor at the rate of 5 pounds to a room and left in the closed room for 8 to 10 hours, is also effective in killing the adults and young.

At the same time that the breeding places are treated the infested cats and dogs should be dusted with fresh pyrethrum powder, or better with powdered derris root.

F. C. BISHOPP.

FLOWERS May Disappoint Unless Effort Made to Check Fungous Disease The serious study of flower-garden pests is of recent origin. For many years plant pathologists have been fully occupied with the numerous diseases of cereals and fruit and vegetable crops, the economic importance of garden flowers not being deemed sufficient to warrant the great amount of careful work requisite for the study of a plant disease and the development of effective control measures. But decorative plants are becoming increasingly important in our present scale of living. Much more than formerly people have the means and leisure to gratify the desire for beautiful surroundings by growing flowers.

There are also new diseases of garden flowers to contend with. Snapdragon rust has become a pest of country-wide distribution within the last two decades; hollyhock rust is spreading similarly, probably through dissemination of contaminated seed. The rise in popularity of gladioli has been attended by a great increase in the number of spotted and scabby bulbs offered for sale.

In the present brief article it is possible to mention only a few of the principal diseases of garden flowers and give a bare outline of the essentials of disease control.

Some fungous diseases affect only plants weakened by unfavorable cultural conditions, chief among which are water-soaked soil and shade or crowding, which are likely to result in root rot and mildew. Lily bulbs and the fleshy roots of dahlias and peonies are injured by contact with fresh manure and later succumb to rot. Excessive heating and drying of the surface soil causes the lower leaves of perennial phlox and asters to wither, suggestive of a fungous blight. The first essential in avoiding troublesome diseases is to provide the most favorable cultural conditions possible in respect to site, exposure, soil composition, moisture supply, and fertility. What is best for each different kind of plant must be learned by experience, but disease control begins with good culture.

Healthy Start Desirable

A healthy start often means a thrifty plant; on the other hand, weak or sickly seedlings seldom recover. Many fungous diseases of garden flowers are seed borne, notably aster wilt, sweet-pea streak, and anthracnose. Seed disinfection often insures a healthy start. Although no one fungicide can be used safely and effectively to disinfect all kinds of seeds, mercury bichloride (corrosive sublimate) is a good general-purpose disinfectant. From tablets of this chemical, procurable at drug stores, one can easily prepare the 1-to-1,000 solution in common use. Most flower seeds should be treated in this solution not over 15 to 30 minutes, then rinsed in water. Proprietary mercuric seed disinfectants, known as organic mercuries, are now in commerce. In numerous tests these have been shown to be about as effective as corrosive sublimate and safer to use with flower seeds; they are also available in convenient dust forms for dry treatment of seeds that are injured by soaking. They can also be used to treat such plant parts as bulbs, tubers, and roots, which are often the means of introducing disease.

Some fungous diseases do not appear until plants are well started, often coming during the period of bloom and causing destructive blights. Although uncleanly garden conditions, such as the presence of weeds and diseased remnants of other flowers, are conducive to these foliage diseases, healthy plants also may be attacked. Protection against such diseases must be sought through the maintenance of sanitary conditions throughout the garden and by the application of fungicides at the first sign of trouble. Very little is accomplished by fungicides which are not applied till disease becomes rampant. For garden flowers dust fungicides are preferable to sprays, being more convenient to apply and causing no spotting of the foliage. A good general-purpose fungicide is a dust containing copper sulphate and lime in finely ground form. It should be applied when the plants are moist with dew and the air still, using a hand duster. This is specially recommended to prevent peony blight, delphinium black spot, and similar diseases. Against rust diseases, such as hollyhock and snapdragon rust, sulphur is more effective than copper fungicides. The very finely ground dusting sulphur is essential and should be applied on warm, still days. These fungicides may be combined with arsenical poisons to destroy leaf-eating insects.

The Virus Diseases

One other group of plant diseases, known as the virus diseases, also appear on garden flowers. Aster yellows is a conspicuous example. Annual asters and many plants belonging to the aster and other plant families become diseased following the bite of an insect which has previously fed on diseased plants. The disease is transmitted only through the bite of this insect, and affected plants never recover. Yellows is carried over winter on perennial plants such as certain daisies, sow thistles, and plantains. Control depends on the early

FIGURE 91.—Aster yellows, a virus disease. This disease develops in annual asters following the bite of a certain insect which has fed on other plants affected with yellows and has become a disease carrier. Prevention depends on keeping these insects away from asters and on destroying weeds which carry the disease over winter

eradication of all perennial weeds and garden flowers showing yellow symptoms and on protecting susceptible plants from visits by disease-carrying insects. Asters which show symptoms early in the season should be pulled out at once.

FREEMAN WEISS.

33023°—29——20

FLY-CONTROL Methods in Use at Beltsville Can Be Used on All Dairy Farms — The first warm days of spring bring forth a host of insects which rapidly increase in numbers and remain until the coming of cold weather. Of these insects none give so much trouble to the dairy farmer as the fly. It not only mars the appearance of equipment, ceilings, walls, and windows but is of constant annoyance to animals and caretakers. It carries on its feet and body thousands of undesirable bacteria which contaminate milk with various organisms.

Of the many species of flies three cause the most trouble to the dairy farmer: The house fly, a nonpiercing-mouth insect breeding in decaying vegetable matter; the stable fly, a piercing-mouth insect breeding in decaying vegetable matter; and the horn fly, another piercing-mouth species, which breeds in the fresh droppings of cattle.

Since 1924 the Bureau of Dairy Industry, in cooperation with the Bureau of Entomology, has conducted a systematic fly campaign at its dairy experiment farm at Beltsville, Md. Three methods of suppression have been employed, all of which are generally applicable to dairy farms. These methods are control of breeding places, trapping, and spraying. The control effected at the farm by following this plan is indicated by the reduction in the quantity of flies caught in traps from 86 gallons in 1925 to 30 gallons in 1928.

Control of Breeding Places

The big problem in the control of breeding places is the removal of the manure. In the case of the milking herd, if the manure is piled in the open, it should be removed at least once a week or more frequently in warm weather. It has been observed at Beltsville that flies breed more freely in the manure from calves receiving milk in any form than in the manure of the milking herd or the remainder of the calf herd receiving a ration free of milk. In large breeding establishments or on large dairy farms where many calves are raised and their manure piled separately, it is necessary, therefore, to remove it at least twice a week. If the manure from calves receiving milk and that from the rest of the herd are mixed, it should be disposed of oftener than once a week. It is best to store manure under a covered shed. If this is not available piling it on a concrete surface is of help in preventing the escape of mature larvae. If the manure is piled directly on the ground, clay soil is preferable to gravel, as the open spaces in the gravel soil are favorable for the larvae to pupate.

Regardless of the frequency with which the manure is removed, some larvae will mature and enter the ground. Treatment of the soil every few weeks with fuel-oil distillate at the rate of 5 gallons to every 100 square feet of ground will kill larvae which have entered and serves as a repellent for some time after its application. This distillate should not be applied directly to the manure as it tends to impair the value of the latter for soil improvement.

Control by Trapping

The flies themselves may be destroyed in two ways—by trapping and by spraying. Trapping is very effective for the house fly. Farmers' Bulletin 734–F, Fly Traps and Their Operation, describes various types of traps which may be used. In order that the traps may be of the greatest usefulness certain points should be given careful attention. Location is of prime importance. The traps should be placed at the natural congregating place of the flies, preferably on the floor in a sheltered spot and where there is good light. Choice of bait is also important. In the control work at Beltsville it has been found that either blackstrap molasses or corn sirup mixed with water in the proportion of 1 part to 4 parts water is a lasting and attractive bait. Other substances, such as watermelon rinds, crushed fruit, skim milk, and certain grain feeds may be used, but these require more attention. The molasses and sirup baits should be replenished at least twice each week during hot weather, and the bait pans should be cleaned and new bait placed in them every two weeks. When adding bait it is advisable to examine the cone of the trap for spiders, as they are apt to weave their web across the narrow opening, thus preventing the flies from entering the trap.

Traps should be emptied regularly even though they are not so full as desired, as this lessens the odor which emanates from the dead flies and which is undesirable around dairy buildings. At the time of emptying the traps should be cleaned, as flies will not enter dirty traps readily. Steam has been found to be very effective for cleaning and leaves the traps very nearly free of odors.

FIGURE 92.—Type of heavy duty sprayer used in fly control work at Beltsville, Md.

If steam is not available the traps should be washed with water and allowed to dry in the sun before being placed over the bait pans.

Control by Spraying

Spraying the cows directly is of advantage mainly in controlling the horn fly. With other kinds of flies the better plan is to spray them thoroughly with a killing spray while they are settled on various parts of the stable. The sprayer used should be capable of withstanding a pressure of from 35 to 45 pounds, and the spray nozzle should throw a finely atomized spray covering considerable area. The number of flies killed depends upon the time of day that the spray is used. As a general rule, flies are congregated on the ceilings and walls in the early morning and are somewhat sluggish in their movements. This is one of the best times to spray. By late afternoon the flies begin to gather at certain points in the buildings for the night. This is again a good time to spray. It is also a good plan to spray the feeding places of flies when a large number of them have gathered. If the manure is properly hauled, thorough spraying need be done but three times per week. Figure 92 shows a heavy duty sprayer from which good results have been obtained. An 8-foot bamboo extension pole is used to replace the nozzle in the illustration and is useful to reach out-of-the-way places where flies congregate.

An effective spray can be made by soaking 5 pounds of unground, half-closed pyrethrum flowers contained in a double-thickness cheese-cloth bag in 10 gallons of kerosene and 5 quarts of fuel oil of gravity 28–32 according to American Petroleum Institute scale. This mixture should stand 24 hours before being used. In spraying horn flies with this mixture care should be taken not to spray directly on the animal but parallel with it so that the spray comes in contact with the flies as they rise from the animal. The animal should not be brushed for some time after being sprayed, as this forces the oil next to the skin and may cause a loss of hair.

R. P. HOTIS.

FOOD Colors Certified by the Department are Both Harmless and Pure — Three senses are preeminent in nature's testing of foods—taste, smell, and sight. Of these, taste is the most important for human beings, but sight and smell are almost equally valuable. Through generations of training we have grown to associate certain colors with certain food products, and our impulse is to turn away from articles exhibiting unaccustomed variations. In short, a change of color is a danger signal, ranking with a bad taste or a disagreeable odor in its indication that something is wrong. In the early days, when the producer and consumer of food were one, every vegetable or fruit was personally conducted from the field to the table, so that loss of color could frequently be accounted for and discounted by a knowledge of the cause. But nowadays, when we do our gardening in the grocery or delicatessen, and must usually make our first judgment by appearance alone, we depend more than ever on our eyes to guide us in our choice.

This fact was recognized many years ago, and the first use of artificial color in foods was for the purpose of covering up a change of shade due to damage or adulteration. Mineral salts of all kinds were freely employed, and brilliant compounds of lead, mercury, and copper found their way into materials intended for human consumption. Naturally, the results were very serious, and the prejudice against artificial colors in foods, which still exists, dates back to the revelations of the early investigators in this field.

Legitimate Use of Color in Foods

There are, however, certain conditions under which artificial color may be legitimately added to foods. A dye, harmless in itself and containing no harmful impurities, may be used without objection if it does not result in concealing damage or inferiority, provided appropriate label declarations are made. Our soft drinks, for example, are tinted artificially, for the amount of flavoring extracts in the average beverage of this type is never sufficient to give the liquid the brilliant pink or green that the consumer has learned to expect.

The first artificial colors used were mineral pigments, which are usually unsatisfactory and frequently poisonous, and vegetable colors, which are generally harmless and often unsatisfactory. As a result, upon the introduction of the coal-tar dyes, with their intensity and variety of shades, a wide demand arose for their use. There are thousands of these colors, some of which are harmless and a few of which are poisonous, while little is known about the great majority. When the Department of Agriculture took over the regulation of their use, about 20 years ago, 7 colors, offering a wide variety of shades, were selected as permissible for use in foods. Since that time additions to the list of permitted coal-tar food dyes have been made, until it now includes 14 colors.

The work has not ended there, however. The fact that these dyes are on the permitted list is not a guarantee of their harmlessness, for harmful impurities may be introduced in the course of manufacture. To assure the public of pure and harmless colors, the Food, Drug, and Insecticide Administration of the Department of Agriculture issues certificates to all manufacturers who submit samples of each batch of dye for examination, if these batches meet the very high standards of purity that have been established. Such dyes are known as "certified colors," and the name "certified" has become widely recognized as the Government's guarantee of purity and harmlessness in coal-tar food colors.

H. T. HERRICK.

———

FOOD, Drug, Insecticide Administration Protects Farmers in Many Ways The Federal food and drugs act provides protection in several ways to those engaged in agricultural pursuits. In raising stock enormous quantities of manufactured feeds are fed each year. The farmers who buy these products are vitally interested in what they are made of and what their guaranteed analyses are. Practically all feeds bear labels showing, among other things, the percentage of protein and a list of the ingredients. A feed which is high in protein and is made from whole grains is, of course, more expensive than one low in protein and containing less valuable by-products, such as oat hulls. As statements appearing upon the label guide purchasers in buying feed for their stock, it is imperative that these statements be true. While most manufacturers undoubtedly would honestly market their goods regardless of legal restrictions, there are always some who would not, and it is against this class that farmers need protection. The food and drugs act affords this protection.

An interesting example of a frustrated attempt to cheat stock raisers was the case of a manufacturer whose plant was visited by a Federal inspector in the course of his routine inspection of feed factories. The inspector noted that, although all of the horse and dairy feeds were being packed in bags labeled "100 Lbs. Net," the bags were being filled with only 97 to 98 pounds of feed. The poultry feeds, although labeled as containing barley, did not contain any full barley grains, but instead were "filled" with barley skimmings, the light grains and hulls obtained in cleaning barley.   In many other products in this factory cheap fillers were being substituted for the higher priced grains mentioned on the labels.   After this information had been obtained the inspectors of the Food, Drug, and Insecticide Administration throughout the territory where the firm's products were distributed were notified to collect samples and submit them to the Government laboratories for examination.   Some 30 samples were then collected from different interstate shipments.   Upon analysis these samples were found not only to be short weight and misbranded as to ingredients, but the guaranteed analysis was not true.   The percentage of protein actually present ran from 2 to 5 per cent less than was stated on the labels.   A large number of these consignments were then seized and citation was issued with the intention of instituting criminal proceedings against the firm.   As a result of these actions and the accompanying loss of patronage, the firm went into bankruptcy and later entirely out of business.

Microscope Aids Detection

At first it was difficult to detect adulteration in feeds where the material had been finely ground, but this problem has been largely solved by use of the microscope, which in most instances readily shows the difference between the cell structure of the product stated on the label to be present and that of the adulterant.

The price paid for cottonseed meal depends upon the percentage of protein it contains.   Every year enough samples are collected from each cottonseed meal mill to indicate their practices, and when shipments are found labeled as containing more protein than they actually do contain they are removed from the market for relabeling.

The food and drugs act also prohibits the sale of drug products bearing labels that are false and fraudulent.   Farm animals are subject to many diseases, and proper treatment of these ailments is necessary if the farmer is to be protected from serious losses.   Many stock medicines have been found so labeled as to create the impression that they will cure or prevent many serious animal diseases, when, as a matter of fact, they are of little or no value.   Manufacturers who are honestly selling veterinary remedies that are competent treatments for the diseases mentioned need, of course, have no fear of difficulties with the food and drugs act, but many cases against misbranded preparations are inaugurated each year.

An outstanding example of such a case was a product labeled as a treatment for contagious abortion in cattle.   Every farmer knows what large financial losses may result from this disease, once it gets started in a herd.   No competent treatment for this disease has been discovered and the stock raiser's losses from it are so great as to make the additional expenditure for a worthless remedy particularly undesirable.   Examination of samples of the alleged remedy in question showed that it consisted essentially of brown sugar, bran, and water.   A 9½-pound treatment, costing less than 40 cents, was sold for $5.   Interstate shipments throughout the United States were then seized, and the misbranded article was thus removed from the channels of commerce.   The firm stated that before the Government stopped the sale of the product its monthly sales were about $15,000.

Protection Under Insecticide Act

The insecticide act affords the same protection against misbranded insecticides and fungicides that the food and drugs act does against misbranded foods and drugs. Farmers use large quantities of insecticides and fungicides to keep their crops, farm animals, and poultry free from insect pests and fungous diseases. The Food, Drug, and Insecticide Administration systematically tests these articles and compares the actual results produced by using them as directed with the claims made upon the labels. Where misrepresentations are found appropriate steps are taken to effect a correction.

An interesting case on record is one where a manufacturer labeled and represented his product as composed of lead arsenate, sulphur, and lime. The analysis of the product showed it to consist of lime only. He had left out the two effective ingredients and was selling a small quantity of lime at a fancy profit. To add insult to injury, the following statement appeared upon his labels, "If you want a cheaper insecticide, mix one part of the contents of this package with three parts lime."

GEORGE P. LARRICK.

FOOD Spoilage, Which Causes Heavy Losses, Due to Many Causes It has been estimated that the losses sustained by American agriculture and by the industries which utilize agricultural products, as a result of the deterioration of foodstuffs, amount each year to several hundred millions of dollars. The destructive agencies that produce these enormous losses are exceedingly complex, but they may be classified, for the most part, under the following four general subdivisions: (1) Enzymes, (2) microorganisms, (3) atmospheric influences, and (4) internal chemical changes. Illustrations will be given of the deteriorative changes produced in foods by each of the four factors mentioned.

Action of Enzymes

When apples, bananas, or other starch-containing fruits of hard texture are stored for a few days in a warm place a gradual softening of the tissues is observed. In this so-called process of after-ripening, which is necessary for improving the edible qualities and sweetness of the fruit, part of the starch is converted into sugar, a change brought about by a ferment or enzyme known as amylase that occurs naturally in the cells of many fruits and vegetables. The activity of this enzyme may exceed, however, the stage which is necessary for obtaining the optimum degree of flavor and palatability. Too much of the starch is converted into sugar, this and the partial solution of the cellular tissues by cytases and other enzymes causing the fruit to become soft and acquire a condition known as overripe. Deterioration has set in and the market value of the fruit begins to decline. A similar condition exists in certain vegetables, such as the sweet potato, whose agreeable flavor is due to the conversion of a part of its starch into sugar by means of an amylolytic or starch-dissolving enzyme. If sweet potatoes are stored too long in a warm place the excessive conversion of their starch into sugar causes a softening of the tissues which then become very susceptible to decay.

Another vegetable enzyme which produces the deterioration of agricultural products is invertase. When sugar cane is stored in the factory yard after cutting there is a gradual daily loss in its sugar content (more rapid in warm weather than in cold) which is due to a splitting of the cane sugar by the naturally occurring enzyme, invertase, into its simple constituents, glucose and fructose. The losses from this cause, which are very great in tropical countries, can be reduced by grinding the sugar cane as rapidly as possible after it is cut.

A third type of deterioration which is produced by vegetable enzymes results from the splitting of the neutral oil that is contained in the germ of cereal grains and other seeds into free-fatty acids which impart to the food products (such as germ-containing meal) that are made therefrom a diagreeable rancid taste. The action of this fat-splitting enzyme, called lipase, is very rapid when the oil-bearing tissues of plants are exposed to the air. For this reason edible oils should be expressed as rapidly as possible after the seeds or other plant organs are crushed. Any prolonged delay between the time of crushing and pressing will greatly diminish the market value of the resultant oil.

In the drying of many fruits, potatoes, and other vegetable products, an objectionable darkening of the dehydrated product, which greatly injures its market value, is produced. This darkening is produced by an oxidizing enzyme, called oxidase, and it is for the prevention of its action that fruits and vegetables before dehydration are exposed to the fumes of burning sulphur. Owing to disadvantages connected with the sulphuring process chemists are now in search of other methods for preventing the enzymic darkening of fruits and vegetables during dehydration.

Microorganisms

The most deleterious agents concerned in the deterioration of food products are microorganisms. The souring of milk, the molding of bread and pastry, the heating of grain, the swelling of canned goods, the decay of fruits and vegetables, and the putrefaction of meat products are all familiar examples of the destructive changes which are produced by the activity of yeasts, molds, bacteria, and other forms of microorganic life. The monetary losses from this cause, which are almost incalculable, affect every class of the public—the farmer, the manufacturer, the distributor, and the consumer. An excessive rainfall, an unexpected period of hot weather, a delayed shipment, a neglectful employee, a break down in a refrigerating plant, and a multitude of other causes create conditions that result each year in many millions of dollars loss from the spoilage of food. There are five general methods for reducing the losses from the deterioration of foods by microorganisms. The first of these is selection of sound raw material and cleanliness in surroundings and in the methods of handling foods. Improved sanitary measures that remove the sources of pollution by which bacteria gain access to milk and other foods is one of the most effective means of counteracting the attacks of microorganisms. A second method is the destruction, by means of heat, of the organisms which produce the spoilage of foods. The sterilization may be only partial, as in the pasteurization of milk, or it may be practically complete, as in the processing of canned goods at high temperature and pressure, the particular type of treatment depending on the nature of the product and the probable length of time before it will be consumed.

Preservation by Refrigeration

A third method of reducing the spoilage of foods by microorganisms, employed especially in the case of such products as fruits, vegetables, and meat which it is desired to keep in the raw condition, is artificial refrigeration. This does not destroy microorganic life but simply retards its growth and multiplication. It is, therefore, not so effective a method as sterilization, but it has the advantage of preserving the natural flavor and other qualities which are affected or destroyed by heat. A fourth method of protecting foods against the destructive action of microorganisms is dehydration. A definite percentage of moisture is necessary for the growth of yeasts, molds, and bacteria, and if the quantity of water in fruits, vegetables, grains, meat, flour, and sugar is reduced to the necessary minimum the product can be preserved under ordinary conditions of temperature and humidity for an indefinite time. A fifth method for preventing the deterioration of food products by microorganisms consists in the use of preservative agents, such as sugar, vinegar, and salt, which inhibit the growth of yeasts and bacteria. The use of sugar in the canning of fruits and that of salt in the pickling of meats are examples of this method of preservation. Chemical preservatives, such as sulphur dioxide and benzoic acid, which have no nutritive or condimental value, are sometimes used for this purpose, but their employment is not usually necessary and furthermore is not to be recommended because of their deleterious physiological effects upon susceptible people.

Atmospheric Influences

The two most important atmospheric influences which are involved in the deterioration of foods are moisture and oxygen. Food products of a hygroscopic or water-attracting character may absorb so much moisture from the air as to become easily subject to the attacks of molds and bacteria. Edible fats, such as lard, which contain unsaturated fatty acids, absorb oxygen from the air, with the production of objectionable rancid flavors that greatly impair the market value of the product. The sealing of foods in durable air-tight containers is the most general method for preventing the deleterious effects of atmospheric influences. Maintenance of a vacuum in the container, and the replacement of the air which surrounds the food by an inert gas, such as carbon dioxide, have been employed in special cases.

Food products which are perfectly protected against the destructive action of enzymes, microorganisms, and atmospheric influences may yet undergo deterioration as a result of internal chemical changes caused by the interreaction of substances contained within the product itself. Amino acids, sugars, aldehydes, organic acids, and other ingredients of the food may interreact chemically, resulting in a darkening of color, production of gas, and the formation of objectionable flavors which impair the value of the product.

Interaction of Causes

In most cases of deterioration of food products, not one but several of the major causes that have been mentioned are involved. Plant enzymes decompose the food product into substances that are easily attacked by microorganisms, which in turn secrete enzymes that further decompose the food. Many substances of enzymic origin, such as invert sugar, attract atmospheric moisture, which in turn favors the growth of microorganisms. The amino acids, sugars, aldehydes, and other compounds of enzymic and microbic origin react with one another with the production of substances which further impair the value of the commodity. The cycles of deteriorative changes are thus seen to be exceedingly complex. The chemist must study carefully the peculiar characteristics of each individual article of food and summon to his aid that method which is most effective in preventing deterioration and at the same time least detrimental to the appearance, flavor, aroma, palatability, and nutritive value of the product.

C. A. BROWNE.

FOOT-AND-MOUTH Disease Eradication By Slaughter Proved Cheapest for U. S. Two methods of controlling foot-and-mouth disease are recognized, one being the stamping out or slaughter method, and the other the isolation and quarantine method. The first method consists in the slaughter of all infected and exposed animals as soon as possible after the establishment of the disease, the disposal of the carcasses by deep burial or burning, the cleaning and disinfection of the infected premises, and the adoption of certain quarantine measures.

This is the method used in the United States in eradicating the disease when outbreaks occur. It is also the method used in England and to a limited extent in several of the continental European countries.

The second method consists in the isolation of the affected and exposed animals, allowing the disease to run its course, and by quarantine measures attempting to limit or prevent its spread. This is the method used in many of the countries of Europe. The adoption of one or the other of these two methods is not made arbitrarily but is dependent on the conditions existing in a country.

Slaughter Method Is Most Effective

The slaughter, or stamping-out method, has for its object the complete eradication of the disease in the shortest possible time. Its practical use is limited to outbreaks of disease in countries like the United States and England, which are normally free from the disease and are protected from its ready introduction by geographical location and quarantine measures.

Thus, when outbreaks have occurred in the United States, the prompt use of the stamping-out method has resulted in complete eradication of the disease within a comparatively short time, as a consequence of which the country has been entirely free of foot-and-mouth disease except during the time required for eradication.

However, when foot-and-mouth disease is once firmly established in a country over a wide area and in addition is subject to frequent introductions of the diseases from other countries, the use of the stamping-out method is either restricted, or it must be abandoned for economic reasons.

This is the condition in which many countries of Europe find themselves, and as a consequence they are compelled to resort to the quarantine and isolation method. That this method fails to eradicate the disease completely is shown by its continued presence in those countries.   The best that can be expected of this method is to limit the spread of the disease as much as possible.

Heavy Toll of the Disease Abroad

Though the cost of eradicating foot-and-mouth disease from the United States has been considerable, the amount is very small compared to the economic loss that would result if the disease should become established here.   Statistics on the losses resulting from the epizootic of foot-and-mouth disease that swept over a large portion of Europe between 1918 and 1921 show the toll that the disease may exact in countries where it is enzootic.   The direct loss to the livestock industry in Germany in the years 1920 and 1921 has been estimated to be about $119,000,000, which does not include losses caused by disruption of business because of quarantine restrictions.

In Switzerland the losses from this epizootic, for the period from 1919 to 1921, were reported to be about $70,000,000.   These figures are especially significant in view of the fact that the number of susceptible animals in Switzerland at that time was less than one-fiftieth of the number in the United States and that the area of that country is only about one-tenth that of the State of California.

Importance of Excluding the Malady

Some idea of the losses that the disease would cause in this country if it once became established can be gathered from the foregoing figures. Foot-and-mouth disease has appeared in the United States on eight different occasions; each time it was eradicated by means of the stamping-out method.   The cost of eradication work for all these outbreaks was about $20,000,000.   When this amount, spread over a period of more than 50 years, is compared to the losses caused by the disease in Germany and Switzerland over a period of only 2 years, the economy of the slaughter method is readily appreciated and the importance of preventing the disease from gaining a foothold in the country is realized.

Until science supplies new methods of combating this scourge, the stamping-out or slaughter method is the one that the United States must rely on in eradicating any future outbreaks of the disease, with the knowledge that it is the surest and most economical method known to-day.

This is the opinion of all having expert knowledge on the subject and is concurred in by the United States Department of Agriculture foot-and-mouth-disease commission after an extensive study of the disease and methods for its control in European countries.

H. W. Schoening.

FORECLOSURE Rate in Farm Realty Still Heavy in 1927–28   The last farm real estate survey made by the Bureau of Agricultural Economics shows encouraging declines in "forced" sales of land during the 12 months ended March 15, 1928.   Chief among these declines were lower rates recorded in the Dakotas and Montana, where losses had been among the highest in the country.   The improvement extended

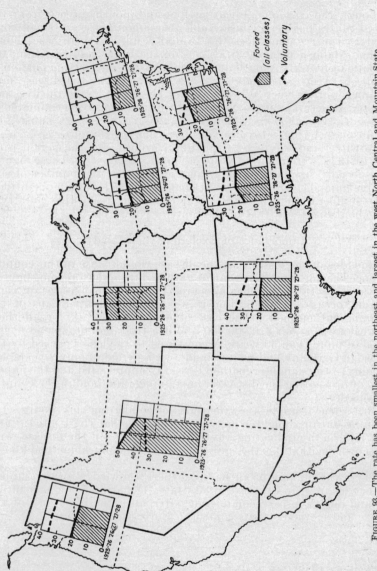

FIGURE 93.—The rate has been smallest in the northeast and largest in the west North Central and Mountain State

to virtually all the States of the far West. A downward tendency was likewise evident among some, but not all, of the nine Northeast States. In the States of the South and Middle West, forced sales did not show any general declining tendency over the 3-year period for which information is available. Here and there they have even crept upward, as for example, in Indiana, Illinois, and Iowa. Involuntary transactions of all kinds, including "deeding back," are included.

Generally speaking, the forced-sale rate remains high. For the last three surveys it has averaged 23 farms per thousand for the United States. About a third of all transfers have been forced sales. The rate has been smallest in the Northeast, with approximately 8 to 9 farms per 1,000, and largest in the West North Central States, with almost 32 per 1,000, and in the mountain section, with almost 45 (fig. 93). How far above pre-war these rates are can not be told for lack of comparable data. The number of farm bankruptcy cases concluded in the courts during the last few years has averaged from seven to nine times the pre-war rate.

Voluntary Buying Low

Voluntary buying remains generally low, and during the three years even dropped somewhat for the country as a whole, from 30 farms per thousand in 1925–26 to 28 in 1926–27 and to only 26 in 1927–28. The only area of much improvement was in the Dakotas, Montana, Wyoming, and Idaho, where voluntary buying increased while forced sales declined, and an encouraging tendency developed toward steadiness in values. How far below normal voluntary buying is, is uncertain, but a rate of about 17 per thousand for 1927–28 in Iowa, compares with an estimate of 60 once made as the pre-war Iowa normal. Disparity is also indicated by the fact that the States of the Middle West which ordinarily enjoy land markets among the most active in the country have, in recent years, shown rates much below other sections which ordinarily have less active markets. Iowa, for example, had a rate of 17 farms per thousand, Minnesota and Wisconsin had 18, and Illinois had 20, but in 1927–28 only four other States in the entire country fell as low as 20.

A complete table of the results of these surveys is given in this Yearbook.

E. H. WIECKING.

F OREST-FIRE Fighting With a Power Pump Is Found Effective   Are gasoline motor-driven pumps effective in controlling forest fires? A small woods fire in southern Massachusetts on a 1928 May day brought under control by the use of such a pump was convincing evidence of their effectiveness under the conditions encountered. The fire occurred at the height of the spring forest-fire season, which means warm cloudless days and a low relative humidity. Given a good start, spring fires in this portion of New England have covered 1,000 to 3,000 acres of land in the course of an afternoon. The area in which the fire occurred was grown up to chestnut and oak sprouts, gray birch, northern white pine, and pitch pine. There was also some meadow covered with dry grass.

A Massachusetts district forest warden got a call for this fire just as he had finished another job a mile or so distant. He had good equipment in the shape of a powerful 1½-ton truck which carried his pump and about 5,000 feet of 1-inch fabric hose. Collecting a crew of several men, he drove rapidly to the fire, where he found he could drive his truck to a brook within 50 yards of one point of the fire. In the spring it is nearly always possible in Massachusetts to find water enough for operating a motor-driven pump. Four men unloaded the pump and set it down beside the brook. The other men coupled the hose to the engine, strung out and coupled together several 50-foot lengths, and everything was set to go. In the meantime the mechanic at the pump had coupled on one end of the intake hose and thrown the other end in the brook.

Half a Mile of Fire Line

At this time there was fully a half mile of blazing fire line, which a number of men from the neighborhood were attempting to extinguish with shovels, brooms, and pails of water carried from the brook. The chut, chut, chut, of the pump was a welcome sound, and the 25 or 30 gallon stream of water which soon came from the nozzle of the hose was an even more welcome sight. The man handling the nozzle knew his business. Coming up to the line of fire, he turned left and, walking rapidly, sprayed the edge of the fire as far as it was burning on that side and part way around its end. He then retraced his steps to his starting point and sprayed the right-hand edge of the fire. He again retraced his steps to the starting point and walked directly through the area already burned over until he reached the far edge of the fire. Here he repeated his tactics of first turning left and spraying the left wing of the fire, then coming back and going around the right wing. Thirty minutes after the fire truck arrived on the scene the running fire was stopped. A patrol was put on, but the fire did not break out again.

Let anyone who wishes compare this with the time it would have taken a crew of 10 to 20 men to build a fire line around and control a fire which was one-half mile in periphery when the crew arrived. Are these pumps effective? They certainly are where there is water and where they can be transported within a reasonable distance of the fire. That is generally possible in the Northeastern States. Further, they are fully as effective for direct attack on fires as they are for mopping-up purposes.

C. R. TILLOTSON.

FOREST-FIRE Patrol by Airplane Greatly Helps Ground Force The first experiments with airplanes for forest-fire patrol in the United States were made in California in 1920. The work was conducted for the Forest Service by the Army Air Service and was sufficiently promising to warrant its continuation in the two succeeding seasons. It was then discontinued until 1925. In that year Congress appropriated $50,000 for renewed cooperation between the Forest Service and the Army Air Corps in aerial forest-fire control.

Beginning July 1, 1925, the Forest Service hired civilian pilots and mechanics. The pilots were Army reserve officers with pilot's training and operated its own patrol in the national forests and adjacent forest areas in California, Oregon, Washington, Idaho, and Montana. An Army officer was detailed for technical inspection of equipment. Liberty-motored Army DeHaviland planes were loaned by the Army for the project. In some instances Forest Service officers experienced in fire-control work were detailed to direct the work and fly with the planes as observers. The patrol was maintained during the seasons of 1925, 1926, and 1927. Regular beats were not flown in any instance, but planes were sent out to scout rough and remote mountain areas immediately after such areas had been visited by the severe and often rainless electrical storms which start many forest fires in the mountain regions of the western United States. In areas not readily seen by the fire-control forces on the ground many small fires were promptly discovered and reported by the planes, with the result that the fire-suppression crews were able to reach the fires while they were still small and to control them with a minimum of expense and loss.

Used for Mapping Large Fires

Planes were also used for scouting and mapping large fires. The information so obtained was furnished to the ground forces for use in planning control work.

During the year 1927 forest-patrol planes made 247 flights and flew 547 hours on fire-control work. In competition with a highly organized fire-detection force on the ground they furnished first report on 35

FIGURE 94.—Scouting lightning fires in the Kaniksu National Forest, Idaho, by airplane

fires and made scouting trips and reports on 82 going fires. During the three years 1925 to 1927, inclusive, the forest-patrol flights over rough mountain areas remote from landing fields were made without injury to personnel and with only minor and repairable damage to equipment.

Some experiments were made in the use of airplanes in forest mapping, both by sketching and by photographic methods and in scouting for forest insect damage. The results obtained were encouraging and seem to warrant further work of this kind.

The use of the airplane in the United States Forest Service is still in a more or less experimental stage, but it promises to be a very valuable supplement to the ground forces in fire control and in some other lines of forest work. Its future depends largely on further perfection of the airplane, on cheaper operation, and on the skill, resourcefulness, and persistence with which foresters make use of it.

HOWARD R. FLINT.

FOREST-FIRE Prevention is an Individual and Social Responsibility About 140,000,000 acres of land in this country is in farm woodlands, and many additional millions of acres of forest land lie adjacent to farms and villages. Much of this land is swept by the forest fires which occur each year in many parts of the country. As a result soil values are destroyed, timber growth is greatly diminished or stopped, and timber-destroying fungous diseases and insects follow to take their toll from the forest growth. Moreover, great injury is done to quail and other game. The spring fires destroy the nests, and the fall fires seriously reduce the food supply of the creatures of the woods.

A feeling of helplessness in regard to forest fires prevails among many owners of farm woodlands and timber holdings. Forest fires are so common that their occurrence is accepted as inevitable, like the coming of the seasons. However, forest fires do not simply happen. A few are caused by lightning, but most of them are set by man—some deliberately, others through carelessness. Fires spread to adjoining forests from brush burnings on new ground clearings; they run to woods from fires set on pastures or fields to burn off rank vegetation; they are set to protect fences against wood fires on other property; and for many other reasons. Many forest fires which could be easily controlled in their earlier stages are allowed to smolder for a day or more without attention, and eventually, fanned by rising winds, they race into large conflagrations. These are examples of the real causes of the fires which annually lick up the landowner's profits in annual growth of timber, sweep away his capital stock of trees, destroy game, ruin the fertility of forest soils, hasten erosion and the rise of flood waters during storms, and upset the flow of springs and streams.

The Landowner's Responsibility

What can be done about this waste? It depends on individual and community interest in forest-fire control and on acceptance by individual landowners of responsibility for the protection of their forest property.

A fire sighted in a building usually stirs to immediate action the man who discovers it. No man will sit and watch someone build a fire which threatens a shed, a home, or a place of business, nor will he allow an incipient blaze on the roof of a building to burn without making an effort to extinguish it. Neither an officer of the law nor a property owner will permit a man to set fire to a building or cause that to be done without attempting to identify and bring the culprit to justice.

What a different attitude exists in many sections of the United States with regard to forest fires and the men responsible for setting them! The forest supplies the raw material from which homes are built and towns constructed. Yet the forests are being gradually destroyed, chiefly because of the inaction of the men who own them and of the communities dependent upon them. This destruction can be prevented by the application of the same principles and practices by which homes and villages are protected against fires. Where the right attitude prevails the woods fire is as rare as the fire in the town.

Some Fire-Prevention Rules

Some of these principles and practices are as follows:

That individual and mass opinion consider the man an outlaw who willfully or through gross carelessness sets fire to woods or allows it to be set.

That the law be brought to bear on him.

That it be realized that fires in the woods start from causes as definite as those which start fires in the home or the town.

That it be every property owner's business to prevent woods fires originating from his act or from that of others.

That every fire set near woods for a legitimate purpose be completely extinguished by the one who sets it.

That the same care be used in discarding a match, cigarette, cigar stub, or pipe "heel" in the woods as in the home.

That when a man sees smoke in the neighboring woods he immediately investigate it and make preparations to fight the fire, as he would in the case of fire in a building.

That persons try to extinguish fires in woods as promptly and completely as those threatening homes or other buildings.

That cooperative fire-fighting units be organized to attack and handle large forest fires, and that such organizations seek the advice and assistance of the State forester in those States having State forestry laws.

That the owners of woodlands and the law-enforcement officers of a community be as persistent in bringing the law to bear on the man who sets fire to the woods and damages the property of another, as they are in the case of the offender who sets fire, or causes it to be set, to a barn or shed, a garage or store.

EVAN W. KELLEY.

FOREST Fires Destroy Deer, Grouse, Bear, and Other Wild Life — Few sportsmen realize how birds and animals are killed by forest fires, how coverts and nests are destroyed, and how the food upon which wild life depends goes up in smoke when the forest burns.

Forest and brush fires not only destroy the forage upon which big game live, but so scorch and burn many of the animals that they die. A fire creeping across the nesting grounds of grouse and other game birds often destroys the eggs and young birds and drives the parent birds from their home. Fire also spoils fishing, for good fishing depends on clear water, and when the forest is destroyed the resulting erosion fills the streams and lakes with ashes and mud and puts an end to good sport.

Many fires are started each year in the woods by careless hunters and fishermen. Realizing this fact, the leading sportsmen's associations and outdoor clubs of the country are joining with Federal and State forestry authorities in a wide-spread educational campaign looking to the preservation of wild life by the prevention of man-caused fires. Man-caused fires are a disgrace to civilization and should be made a thing of the past.

Deer, Grouse, and Squirrels Are Victims

Forest Supervisor Humphrey, of the Manti National Forest, says:

In August, 1926, I was detailed to the Lost Johnny Creek fire on the Flathead Forest in Idaho. * * * Along the edge of the fire, where we were trenching, we saw a number of pine squirrels that apparently had their feet so badly burned that they could not climb trees. The deer in this locality are of the whitetail species. I found two deer on the creek below the fire fighters' camp that were burned to a crisp. Two other deer—one a large buck and the other a yearling—

died near the Riverside pasture gate. Another old buck, with the hair over his hind quarters badly singed and his feet so burned he could hardly walk, was seen by the entire crew a number of times between Riverside and Murray Creeks. I also saw a fawn in the vicinity of Spring Meadows that had evidently lost its mother. The feet of this fawn were badly burned.

A great many grouse that had died from the effects of the fire were also found. In fact, the fire fighters reported finding dead grouse almost daily.

This fire did not travel fast enough to overtake either the game or the birds. It is my opinion that both, after the fire had died down, drifted back to their old range through the smoldering ashes. After getting in where the ashes were extremely hot and burning their feet they would become bewildered, and probably they ran on and on until they were so badly burned that, even though they got out of the fire, they would die later from the effects of the burns. Both deer and grouse appeared very reluctant to move away from their home grounds which had been destroyed by the fire and returned immediately after the fire had quieted down, before the ground had time to cool. Nearly every day we would see deer wandering through the burn, especially on the meadows, even though the forage was practically all destroyed.

Ranger E. E. Stock, of the Minidoka National Forest, reports:

While I was on the Loon Creek fire, Challis National Forest, in late August, 1924, I saw the carcasses of two bucks which had been killed by the fire. It appeared that they had been trapped by the fire, and were within 100 or 150 feet of each other. One was badly burned, with nearly half the hide gone and the flesh gone from the top half. There were no tracks or any signs of any animal or bird having been there. The other deer seemed to have been caught in a less heated spot, and its whole body was in a natural position, except that the hair was burned off to the hide almost as slick as if it had been shaved.

Heaps of Charred Bones

Supervisor Guy B. Mains, of the Boise National Forest, says:

In 1905 I saw a covey of young blue grouse caught in burning brush and killed by a forest fire. I have seen two nests of grouse eggs on Middle Fork Payette roasted in early spring fires.

Logging Engineer U. S. Swartz, of the Forest Service, Ogden, Utah, states:

After the fires of 1894, known in history as the Hinckley fires, in northern Minnesota, I spent three months estimating damage to timber. Hundreds, and, I dare say, thousands of heaps of charred bones bore mute evidence of the destruction of wild life by fire. Most of these charred bones were those of rabbits or pheasants, but many were those of deer and bear; also three of the animals called "timber cruisers."

Ranger David Laing, of the Boise National Forest, says:

In May, 1919, Ranger John R. Smith reported to me that he found thousands of dead cutthroat trout in the creek above Smith Lake after a hot forest fire had burned over the area. The trout were spawning in the creek at the time and as there was heavy brush along the creek, making a hot fire, I believe the fire killed the fish.

Harvey H. Steed, of Auburn, Wyo., told Ranger Bruce, of the Caribou National Forest that—

while he was fighting fire on Stump Creek several years ago he came across a covey of blue grouse almost completely surrounded by fire. As they attempted to fly away their wings were singed and they dropped into the fire and were destroyed—not one escaped.

R. H. RUTLEDGE.

FOREST Fires Fought   The 14 national forests in the State of
in Oregon by Settlers   Oregon contain 13,238,092 acres of land.
Aiding U. S. Foresters   To protect this large acreage of forest
land during the hot, dry summers, there
are 580 rangers, lookouts, and patrolmen.   These men are the first line
of defense in the battle against forest fires.   In the second line are an
additional 795 men working on forest roads and trails who, when the
fire call comes, drop trail tools, grab fire tools, and go to the fire.   The
total of 580 first-line men provides one man for each 22,825 acres—a
pretty large order for
even an experienced
woodsman, as most of
them are.

The Forest Service
has long realized the
seriousness of this
insufficiency of man
power.   Annual appro-
priations would permit
of no increase.   Addi-
tional men could be
drafted during an emer-
gency—that is, to fight
a fire—but like many
emergency troops, such
men are the day-laborer
type, largely unskilled,
and therefore expensive
in the long run.

Forest officers con-
ceived the idea of using
the ranchers and settlers
in the many small towns
and communities near
the national forests.
The plan was tried out
on the Mount Hood
National Forest, in
Oregon.   The forest
rangers called the
ranchers together, told
them of the dilemma of

FIGURE 95.—Fighting a forest fire is hard and often dangerous
work

the service, the need for a voluntary fire-fighting force, the willingness
of the service to instruct the men in the rudiments of fire fighting,
use of a compass and maps, and the special fire tools and equipment,
and the great need for immediate action when a fire started.

Ranchers Agree to Help

The ranchers saw the point, realized the need, realized also their
"stake" in the near-by national forests, and agreed very willingly to
join cooperative fire-fighting units.   The forest rangers then proceeded
to organize these units.   A fire chief, assistant fire chief, foreman, time
keepers, camp superintendent, straw bosses, emergency lookouts,

truck drivers and packers, cooks and laborers, and plain fire fighters, were selected, and each given some instruction in his job, this instruction being carried on by the rangers mostly at night meetings, on Sundays, or holidays during the winter months. Many of the men welcomed the chance to learn how to run a compass, read a map, pace correctly, run a portable gasoline pump, and fight different kinds of forest fires. Considerable good-natured rivalry sprang up between different communities.

Not only were fire fighters selected, but the ranches where tools, trucks, horses, and pack outfits could be furnished were listed, as well as country stores where food supplies were obtainable, and each merchant was furnished with check lists of supplies for 5, 10, and 20-man fire crews.

FIGURE 96.—The path of a forest fire

The men in these cooperative units are paid the going fire wages only when actually fighting a forest fire. The Government would have to pay them in any case if they were hired to fight fire. Under the cooperative unit plan, however, the Forest Service gets not only organized and partly trained men but men who are interested in reaching the fire and putting it out quickly. As with the Organized Reserves of the United States Army, in a war emergency each man has a place, knows where he fits in, and knows what he has to do. Not only do the members of these units drop their own work and go to a forest fire when the call comes, but if any member sees or hears of a fire he immediately gets in touch with his fire chief, and the unit literally springs into action without waiting for a call from the forest ranger. In fact, it is a matter of great pride if some unit can spot a forest fire and get on it before the local forest ranger can call on them.

A large forest fire usually means days, sometimes weeks, of the hardest kind of work, both day and night, sometimes work of a highly dangerous character. The district ranger or some of his regular summer protective force will go to every fire of any appreciable size just as soon as possible. But with an immense area to cover, and oftentimes many lightning fires springing up after a dry storm, the regular force can not get to all fires quickly. In such an emergency the central dispatcher runs over the list of cooperative units, picks out the one nearest the fire, calls its fire chief, gives him the location of the fire, its approximate size and some directions on how best to reach it, how many men to take—and that particular unit goes into action.

How the Units Work

In 1927 large forest fires were burning on the north side of the Columbia River. The air was thick with smoke and firebrands. Many of these brands were blown across the Columbia River to the Mount Hood National Forest. An unlucky dry and dead standing tree received one of these firebrands and was set on fire. This fire passed from one snag to another, and soon a large fire was raging up the steep slopes through an old burned area.

The call for help came to the central dispatcher, who referred to his list of cooperative units. The nearest unit was the Crag Rats in Hood River, 18 miles away. This was an organization of peppy young mountain climbers who had become enthusiastic forest-fire fighters. A call went out to them, and in about one hour 27 trained men were on the fire and ready for action. They were assigned to one side of the fire and held their line like veterans. At that time no timekeepers,

FIGURE 97.—A forest fire on the Mount Hood National Forest

camp superintendents, or gas-pumper men were available from the regular protective force, so these positions were taken over by men listed in the unit organization plan for such positions. There was no delay. The quick arrival and effective hard work of the Crag Rats unit unquestionably prevented this fire from becoming a very large one.

The Mount Hood National Forest, where this cooperative unit idea started, has a year-long force of 12 forest rangers and lumber scalers, a summer protective force of 50 men, and 200 men on road and trail work; these are its first and second lines of defense. It has now organized and given some training to about 250 additional men in 20 different communities surrounding the six ranger districts of that forest of 1,159,730 acres. This forest has therefore available 512 men for fire fighting. The voluntary cooperative unit of 250 men are the forest reserve corps of the Mount Hood Forest, a most valuable third line of defense.

JOHN D. GUTHRIE.

FOREST Grazing Permits Largely Influenced by Proximity of Ranches
Livestock use of the national forests has had, in the main, a direct relation to ranch property. Over 4,500,000 acres of improved ranch land and 22,000,000 acres of grazing land are used by 27,000 owners in connection with their livestock operations on the national forests. The proximity of these ranch lands to the forest ranges has been a prominent factor in the allotment or distribution of grazing privileges. In the nature of things lands within or close to the outer boundaries of the forests have been considered most dependent upon national forest ranges.

On the other hand, more or less extensive use of these ranges has been made by livestock owners who have had no appreciable land holdings or whose base of operation has been at a distance. This was more frequently the case some 20 years ago when large areas of unappropriated public domain were available outside the forest boundaries for the use of local settlers. As these outside lands have been absorbed under the different land laws, the near-by demands for

FIGURE 98.—This mountain ranch supplies fall and spring pasture and winter hay for cattle grazed on the adjacent national forest in summer

national-forest range have been intensified, and stockmen from a distance have had to compete with this newer demand.

Cattle and sheep are pastured upon the national forests to the number of 12 or 13 millions, depending upon the natural increase which goes with the parent stock to the ranges. Of older animals under formal permit, 1,403,192 cattle and 6,376,838 sheep were grazed during the calendar year 1927 on all the national forests. These are large numbers and naturally mean much to land settlements; but total livestock ownership throughout the Western States represents several times these numbers. This fact has given rise to the establishment of lines or dependency zones around those national forests where competition is keenest, and close decisions become necessary in the allotment of privileges. These lines undertake to mark a boundary beyond which lands are considered less dependent. New demands or applications from lands beyond such boundaries are not permitted to compete with applications from holdings within them.

Carrying Capacity of Different Land

The commensurability of dependent lands—their ability to feed stock in the colder seasons of the year—is also used in the nature of a measuring stick by which to determine the extent of use or the numbers of stock different applicants are entitled to on a regular production basis. The "economic herd" in connection with the applicant's investments also constitutes an important consideration in the permanency of his business. Different classes of lands, therefore, have different values in providing feed or range for livestock during the period of the year in which the summer pastures in the mountains can not be used. Seasons are necessarily short at high altitudes, and from five to nine months of the year livestock must be provided for outside the national-forest boundaries on public, leased, or owned land.

To get at the pasturage and feeding values of lands on which grazing applications may be based or permits issued, so-called converting factors have been developed. These naturally differ somewhat for different localities according to the feeding or range customs and the most economic practices that may be applicable. No hard and fast commensurability standards would be practicable for all situations. Only general standards can, therefore, be used. However, a fair idea of working principles is obtained from the following, which have been developed in central Colorado in cooperation with the stockmen themselves. The figures have been built up from the average use of lands in the average successful instances in management of livestock for the locality where farm and range lands form an intimate part of the livestock enterprise:

Winter feeding requirement: Cattle and horses, 500 pounds of hay per month of actual feeding period; sheep, 80 pounds of hay per month of actual feeding period.

Converting factors:

Irrigated seeded pasture (not used during summer), 1 acre = 1 ton hay.

Dry seeded pasture (not used during summer), 5 acres = 1 ton hay.

Hay meadow stubble, 3 to 6 acres (depending on growth after last cutting) = 1 ton hay.

Grain stubble, 20 acres = 1 ton hay.

Native pasture, 5 to 15 acres (depending on character and whether used in summer) = 1 ton hay.

Straw, 5 tons = 1 ton hay.

JOHN H HATTON.

FOREST Lands in Lake States to be Bought by U. S. Government   The Clarke-McNary law, enacted June 7, 1924, authorizes the purchase of land for national forests on the watersheds of navigable streams for timber production. Under this law the National Forest Reservation Commission has already approved the establishment of three purchase units in Michigan and one in Minnesota which may involve the acquisition of approximately 1,900,000 acres. The ultimate plans, including the consideration of a similar area for Wisconsin, call for the purchase of approximately 2,500,000 acres in the three States.

Congress in authorizing and the National Forest Reservation Commission in approving the purchase plan for the Lake States give definite recognition to the interstate character of the problem created by these devasted forest lands and the part the Federal Government, through the Forest Service, should play in hastening their reclamation.

It is estimated that there is a total of approximately 33,000,000 acres of timberland in the three Lake States once covered with magnificent forests but now so badly devasted and burned that they are producing little of merchantable value. This is a matter of grave concern to the farmers and industries not only in the Lake States themselves but in the entire Middle West, since it materially affects the supply of timber available within a short distance. Between the years 1905 and 1919 the transportation charge on lumber in the country retail trade in southern Minnesota increased about $9 per thousand board feet. The reestablishment of forests on nonagricultural land in the northern Lake States will provide homegrown timber in those States and will help to supply near-by markets of the Middle West generally.

Encouragement to Private Owners

It is the hope of the National Forest Reservation Commission and the Forest Service that, through the practice of intensive forestry methods within the units established, private owners, as well as local

FIGURE 99.—Cut-over forest land in St. Louis County, Minn. Such land purchased by the Federal Government for addition to national forests can be restored to productiveness in a reasonable time only by intensive protection, management, and reforestation

political units, will be encouraged to reestablish the forest on similar lands under their control.

After purchases have brought under Government ownership a sufficient acreage in each unit, intensive systems of fire protection will be set up, existing forest stands will be subject to improvement cuttings in order that maximum growth may be obtained, devastated lands will be replanted, and the areas developed so that they will serve their highest purpose socially and economically. Aside from the production of a maximum amount of wood per acre and the demonstration of the practice of forestry, the purchase areas will be used for research and experimentation on a large scale, the encouragement and development by demonstration of effective efforts toward fire prevention and suppression, protection of watersheds of navigable streams, recreation, and the protection and cultivation of wild life.

Planting of forests will be one of the major activities. Within the Huron National Forest in Michigan this work has already attained considerable proportions, 20,727 acres having been planted. Similar work will be carried on in other units as sufficient consolidated acreage is obtained and money is available.

Only True Forest Land Purchased

Only true forest land is being acquired. No agricultural land is desired. Most of the tracts involved are tax-delinquent lands, the owners seeing no profit in them. Under present laws the projects become in fact cooperative enterprises of the States, the counties, and the Federal Government. The Federal Government acquires the land, pays the cost of bringing it back to a productive condition, protecting it while the timber crops are maturing, and when the timber is harvested returns 25 per cent of the gross receipts to the counties in which it is located and expends another 10 per cent in addition to special appropriations for the construction of roads.

E. W. TINKER.

FOREST-LECTURE Tour of Schools Conducted in Pacific Northwest The States of Oregon and Washington have almost a third of the remaining merchantable forest in the United States, and the basic industry of the two States is the cutting and manufacturing of this timber. The young people of the region need to know what forestry is, for they will soon have the handling of the forest crop and will have to decide how to handle it so that it may always contribute to the welfare of the Pacific Northwest.

To meet a demand on the part of both teachers and pupils for specific information about the Pacific coast forests, the species and their characteristics, the uses made of the local woods, how they grow, and the details of fire prevention and suppression methods, and to bring to the school child a realization of the all-important fact that in this region forests would largely reproduce themselves if given a chance—that the young trees, the tiny seedlings hid in the brake fern and salal, are the forests of to-morrow and must be protected from the all-devouring fire—a lecture tour was organized to carry forestry and forest-fire prevention to the schools. The project was on a cooperative basis, with the State, the Federal Government, and the private forest protective associations sharing the cost. This fact is important, for it is impressed on each audience addressed that the task is one in which the three agencies are equally interested and that the educational work is made possible by the three agencies working together to protect from fire the rich forest resources of the region.

The main objective was to reach the country school, the small, outlying group which is so often overlooked in educational campaigns, although high schools and academies and city schools were not omitted.

How the Lecture Service Works

A truck, fully equipped and in charge of two men representing the State forester's office and the United States Forest Service, drives up to a country school about 11 in the morning, for example. One of the men knocks on the door, and when answered by the teacher tells her the who and why of the call. In every case an invitation is immediately given to enter and put on the lecture. Within a few minutes the screen is put up, the windows darkened, and on the wall of the school-room flash lantern-slide projections of forest scenes; of forest activities; of how tiny Douglas firs start from even tinier seeds; of how they are hidden beneath shrubs and weeds until they establish themselves; of how they grow amazingly fast; of how they are utilized for lumber in homes, tables, and desks; of how many million feet go out each month to distant peoples; of how timber is a crop, to be grown, harvested, and new crops grown on the same land.   Then there are shown on the screen forest camp grounds; wild life at home in the forest; clear, pure water in waterfall and lake, behind waterpower and irrigation dam, and in city reservoir, all coming from the forests back in the mountains. The story of the forest-fire lookout is shown the children—how he guards the forests throughout the long, hot days of summer and why he does this; how fires are fought; how camp fires must be totally extinguished before breaking camp; and always how to keep fires from starting in the forest and how to fight them if they do get started.

FIGURE 100.—A forest ranger bringing forestry to the school children

Then a motion picture or two is shown, the half-hour or hour is up, the light is let in, the teacher thanked, and the truck is ready to go to the next school.

Contacts are made with county school superintendents, city super-intendents, and principals before talks are given within their areas, and always their consent is forthcoming.

Equipment Includes Truck

The truck used is a ¾-ton truck, with spare tires and with chains, for rough mountain roads to be traveled during the fall, winter, or early spring months.   Shelves and chests are built inside the truck to hold the equipment in order and safety.   The equipment includes balopticons, motion-picture projectors, lantern slides, screens, portable lighting plant, canvas for darkening windows, an extra motion-picture reel or two for rewind, hand-power rewind, film-repair outfit, shears, film cement, film-repair clamp, 100 to 150 feet of extension cord, fuse plugs, extra connection plugs, repair tape, extra lamps for balopticon and projector, surveyor's tripod with detachable table top for holding lanterns in a small space, and signal cord for use in large halls.

The lecture can be adapted to fit a 20-minute, half-hour, or hour period—whatever time the teacher feels can be spared—or it can be expanded into a 2-hour evening's program in a high-school auditorium or town hall.

During the past two years some 700 of these school lectures have been given practically throughout the State of Oregon, and a similar campaign is to be started shortly in the State of Washington.

JOHN D. GUTHRIE.

FOREST Litter a Good Fertilizer of Farm as Well as Tree Crops About a ton of leaves, or needles, and other organic matter falls yearly to the ground in an acre of well-stocked pine woods. In some of the hardwoods like the oaks, the yearly cast-off of such leaves, twigs, flowers, and fruit probably amounts to about 2 tons. This material goes to make up

FIGURE 101.—Fertilizer and fuel—valuable by-products of the farm woods

nature's protective blanket over the forest floor. It is well known that the woods litter, if not destroyed by fire, gradually changes to humus, or decomposed organic matter, rich in plant food.

We know that trees grow faster with a deep accumulation of leaves and humus. A pure, even-aged loblolly pine stand in eastern Maryland was raked for many years on one side of a dividing road. The growth of the trees was measured on 2 acres lying on opposite sides of the road. Each had the same number of trees. The acre raked yearly had a stand of 18,600 board-feet, while the other with its accumulated straw had 24,800 board-feet. The trees were 55 years old, and the blanket of organic matter had added over $1 an acre yearly in the value of the growth.

Unburned woods of short-leaf and loblolly pines in central and eastern North Carolina were found to have on the ground an average of a pound of dry organic matter per square foot, or a total per acre, eliminating area occupied by tree trunks and a few bushes, of not less than 18 tons. A chemical analysis of samples consisting of both the fresh and the decomposed forest organic matter revealed the fact that each ton contained about 12.1 pounds of ammonia (NH_4), 2.8 pounds of phosphoric acid (P_2O_4), and 3.9 pounds of potash (K_2O). At prevailing wholesale prices, this is the equivalent per acre of $39.20 for the ammonia, $2.52 for the phosphoric acid, and $4.21 for the potash, a total value per acre of $45.93.

An Example in Tennessee

A farmer raked all the litter from beneath the trees on a measured acre of heavy oak woods in Gibson County, Tenn., and plowed it under on an acre of field crop land. For three years he measured the yields of corn and cotton on the treated and on adjacent untreated acres, with some interesting results. The first year his crops on the treated acre were worth $20.65 more than on the untreated land, the second year $14.80, and the third year $13 more. Although a marked effect was shown at the end of the third year, the farmer was unable to take more records, so the story of the value of the woods fertilizer is incomplete, at a total, however, for the first three years of $45.45 per acre.

The high water-holding value of woods mold when applied to the soil should be considered along with the value of its chemical fertilizing materials. In the Southern States large amounts of pine straw, or litter, are raked for stable bedding, for mulching strawberries, and as a general crop fertilizer. In the opinion of forestry experts the value of woods litter as a crop fertilizer is greater than its value as a means of stimulating increased growth of forest trees if it is allowed to remain undisturbed in the woods.

W. R. Mattoon.

FOREST Litter Aids in Conserving Water for California Farms — Water is the limiting factor in the development and growth of California. The summer flow of streams is now appropriated; ground-water supplies have been steadily lowering in response to the heavy draft of pumping for irrigation. Imported waters such as those of the Colorado River are being sought, but the chief reliance of the State must be placed in the storage of native waters of winter precipitation for irrigation in the dry summers.

Seasonal distribution of precipitation is unequal. The year's water supply falls during three winter months, on high and abrupt mountains. Water drains rapidly through steep canyons across low, narrow agricultural plains, until three-fourths of it escapes to the ocean before the growing season begins. The geographical distribution is no better; three-fourths of the water falls in the north half of the State, where lies one-fourth of the arable land. Southern California, which includes one-fifth of the agricultural land, comprising the rich "citrus empire," has but 1 per cent of the State's water supply. Three to eight square miles of watershed in this region are needed to produce the water, in addition to overhead rainfall, required for 1 square mile of agricultural or urban land.

Artificial storage must be increased. Nevertheless the principal source of supply will continue to be underground water basins of California valleys filled with deep porous outwash deposits. More than 70 per cent of the irrigation waters of southern California are pumped from these basins.

Forest Litter's Function Demonstrated

Controlled experiments conducted by the California Forest Experiment Station of the Forest Service have demonstrated that the accumulated litter of fallen leaves and twigs on the soil performs the important function of keeping open the pores and seepage channels into the mountain soils. The absorption capacity of mountain areas is controlled at the soil surface. The experiments show that forest soils burned bare of litter lose ten to thirty fold more surface run-off than soils mantled with a complete cover of litter. The reason appears to be that the forest litter prevents the beating rain drops from picking up soil particles which, on being rearranged, would clog up the pores and seepage channels into the soil. In other words, the rain water is kept clear. This function of forest litter is emphasized in the results of comparative erosion, which is greater by one hundred to five thousand fold from bared soils than from litter-covered soils. Experiment as well as experience demonstrates that clear water sinks more rapidly into the soil than muddy water. The preservation of the forest litter, whether derived from trees, or from shrubs such as compose the chaparral forests of California, is therefore of the highest importance in the absorption of rain by mountain slopes.

More important than this, however, is the rôle which forest litter plays in the artificial spreading of flood waters over porous outwash fans to sink and store such waters in deep underground basins for subsequent pumping. Waters for sinking must be regulated and clear. Rainfall may intermittently exceed the absorption capacity of the catchment basins and cause floods. Engineering flood control and detention and desilting works are required as protection against such floods, as well as for handling normal rainfall, if the vegetative cover of the watershed is inadequate. High flood stages can not be handled in spreading operations; on the other hand quieter but muddy flood waters are not suitable for sinking into the outwash fans. Mud clogs the soil surface and renders the fan less and less pervious and finally useless for storing purposes. Experience dictates that muddy waters as well as excessive flood stages must pass to the ocean as lost waters.

The loss of litter layers as a result of forest fires or whatever other cause not only reduces the storable water but also leaves the soils exposed to excessive erosion, products of which are carried by the resultant high stages to silt up and destroy the storage capacity of flood-control reservoirs, or to cover and damage valley orchards and farm lands with sterile outwashed sands. Keeping run-off waters clear, whether for temporary detention storage in mountain slopes, for sinking into underground basins of outwash-filled valleys, or for reservoir storage, is the important function of ground litter alike from forests and from the chaparral and brush fields of California.

W. C. LOWDERMILK.

FOREST Planting on Huron Forest Both Efficient and Cheap   Fifty years ago Michigan was the largest lumber-producing State in the Union. To-day it has within its boundaries the largest forest-planting project. Wasteful methods of logging, followed by forest fires, have stripped most of the 19,000,000 acres of timber land in the State of their forests, and to-day there are 12,000,000 acres of nonproductive cut-over lands. The Federal Government owns about 170,000 acres, mostly of this type of land, located in two national forests—the Huron in Iosco, Alcona, and Oscoda Counties in the eastern part of the lower peninsula, and the Michigan in the eastern part of the Upper Peninsula. Both of these forests are located in the plains on barrens—gently rolling hills having a very fine sand of lake wash and glacial formation which is almost entirely free from clay and gravel.

The forests consist of a scattered growth of scrubby jack pine and oak of little merchantable value. The spring rains encourage a luxuriant growth of grass and weeds. This is usually dried up by the droughts in July and August, and creates a high fire hazard. Cattle and sheep can be grazed on this vegetation in early spring, but after the grass dries it has small nutritive value.

Agriculture on the sand plains has been a failure because of the poor soil, the irregular character of the precipitation, and the frosts which are likely to occur at any time during the season. As a result the region is thinly settled. For example, Oscoda County has only 63 families, widely scattered, within its boundaries.

In 1911 the Forest Service started to plant trees on the Huron National Forest, the first plantation consisting of 114 acres. It was found that small coniferous seedlings could be established if planted in furrows. The furrows break up the natural vegetation and make basins for the accumulation of moisture so that the little trees have a chance to survive during the midsummer droughts.

Efficient System Developed

Since the first planting in 1911 a system has been developed by which the work is done efficiently and cheaply. The plowing of furrows is usually started in June. Farmers and their teams are hired. They plow across a section with sulky plows, weaving through the brush as best they can. About 10 miles of plowing in this type of country constitutes a good day's work.

Planting is started early in September or after the first fall of rain. Each man uses a bar 42 inches long with a cutting blade 12 inches long and 4 inches wide. With this bar a slit is made into which the roots of the tree are inserted, and the hole is closed with another thrust of the bar several inches beyond the tree. The trees are set 8 feet apart in the furrows, which are about 8 feet apart, so that approximately 700 trees are planted to the acre.

An average of about 2,800 trees, or 4 acres, is planted per man day. Two-year old Norway pine seedlings about 3 or 4 inches in height are used. The trees are raised in the Forest Service nursery at East Tawas, Mich. They cost about $1.40 a thousand or about $1 an acre. The cost of plowing, planting, equipment, supervision, and other items brings the total cost of the planting acre up to an average of $3.44.

From 50 to 75 men are used during the planting season and they are housed in tents and sheds. The operation is usually completed before cold weather sets in, but if this is impossible, planting is resumed the following spring. Good results are secured from planting in either season but the fall work usually produces a higher survival.

Area of Sand Plains Planted

In 1927, 4,246 acres of sand plains in the Huron National Forest were planted, making a total of 20,727 acres that have been reforested. Trees are now being raised to increase this program, and starting in 1930, an area of 10,000 acres will be planted annually on the Huron Forest. At present there are about 140,000 acres to plant, but additional land is being purchased by the Forest Service to add to this forest until its ultimate size will be about 550,000 acres. As most of

FIGURE 102.—Norway pine on the Michigan National Forest four years after planting

the land that is being purchased is barren, it is evident that planting will be continued here for many years to come.

To protect these planted forests from fires which burn through them so easily, plowed fire lines are located at intervals. Towers, from which the entire forest can be seen, have been erected, and lookout men are on the alert so that quick and accurate reports of fires can be telephoned to the forest rangers. Each ranger station is completely equipped with trucks, plows, shovels, and other tools needed to put out forest fires. With this system it has been possible to keep all but a few small fires out, so that now a magnificent young forest of Norway pine is fast changing the appearance of the sand barrens.

FRED R. JOHNSON.

FOREST Purchases by U. S. Help Solve Farm Problem in the East — The eastern national forests are making a definite contribution to the solution of the farm problem of the Eastern States. Under the act of March 1, 1911, and its amendment, there has been acquired or is in the process of being acquired, as a part of the system of eastern national forests, more than 3,000,000 acres of land in the Southern States, in north-western Pennsylvania, and in the mountains of New England.   These national forest lands are located in the mountains or in the rough portions of these various regions.   In making purchases the larger tracts are first acquired.   These usually consist of forested wild land on the higher mountains.   Adjoining or near the large tracts are smaller tracts lying in the foothills or along the small streams.   Such tracts often contain areas of marginal farming lands or lands of higher quality but in units too small to support a family.

There has been acquired a total of 72,535 acres of marginal farming land which at one time or another has been tilled.   Of the 3,172 tracts acquired, 1,472, or 46 per cent, contained land that at some time had been in cultivation.   Of 1,293 tracts in the Southern Appalachians the average area of the cleared land was only 28 acres, and on 55 tracts in the White Mountains and in Pennsylvania it was less than 44 acres.   Considering the rough character of the land and the large proportion that must be devoted exclusively to grazing, units of such size are too small adequately to support a family.   Doubtless many of the larger tracts with more than 100 acres of cleared land included in their aggregate a number of these small farms.   It is known that a few large tracts offered by a single owner were entirely built up by the assemblage of small marginal farms.

Many Clearings Date from Pioneer Days

These little marginal farms sometimes mark a period in the progress of the settlement of the country; sometimes they indicate merely a stage in an agricultural and economic development.   Many of the clearings date back to pioneer days.   Families pushed forward and were halted by the mountains; they made a stand and perhaps later moved onward to the wider west, which at that time was Ohio and Kentucky, with its richer opportunities, leaving behind them the hillside fields and the cabin to mark their passing.   But most of the farms were the homes of those who lacked either the means or the incentive to push on toward the setting sun.   They were content to stop and to stay.

So long as a pioneer existence was sufficient; so long as game was abundant; so long as the native range for cattle was ample, under-stocked, and free; so long as timber of high quality was plentiful and the winter months could be devoted to marketing high-grade logs—these men and their families found that a living not too much below the prevailing simple standard could be secured.   Pioneer conditions passed, however, and as they passed other changes took place.   There was a general raising of living standards and a general introduction of machinery into farming.

The marginal and submarginal farms of the Appalachian and New England mountains no longer afforded more than a bare existence.   They offered homes but not the facilities for industrial farming.   They did not yield the income which would enable the owner to meet present living standards.   The rough, hilly lands which made up most of the fields and the very small amount of level lands were not suffi-cient to justify the use of modern labor-saving farm machinery.

The hillside farms, with the soil depleted and often badly gullied, were sold—when there was a purchaser.   Otherwise they were left—

the owners sometimes let them revert to the State for taxes, gave up farming, and lost the fruits of years of preparation, hard work, and struggle.

Area of Low-Grade Farm Land Reduced

The purchase of more than 1,500 of these farms with the 72,000 acres of marginal land has reduced the area of low-grade farming lands by this amount. It has done more. These farms, instead of being abandoned and a total loss to the owners, have been paid for at a price that represents their value for growing timber—often low, compared with the value at some past time when the land was fresh. Frequently this payment was sufficient to enable the owner, if so inclined, to make a modest start on more level and fertile lands under conditions that promised a reasonable reward for his efforts.

Another and perhaps more important service is being performed by these forests in demonstrating to private owners of woodland methods of management that will make their own lands more productive. Considerably more than half of the total area in farms in the hilly region of the Eastern States is not being cultivated but is woodland or potential woodland. To make this woodland area productive—relatively as productive as other parts of the farm—would be to add in the aggregate many millions of dollars to the farmers' incomes. To assist in securing this added value is one of the functions of the national forests of the East. Private owners note the beneficial results of fire prevention work on the nearby forests and the principles of preparedness and suppression which are employed, and they adopt them. They note the methods of cutting timber, the care exercised to protect young growth, the leaving of an abundance of middle-sized trees for an early second cut, and the leaving of seed trees. They are realizing the beneficial results and adopting the methods, and thus adding materially to the earning value of their farms.

The eastern national forests are thus being of direct benefit to the farmers of these regions, in assisting in solving the farm problem and making farming more profitable by reducing the area of low-grade farming land, and by showing farmers methods of handling the wooded portions of their farms in a more profitable manner.

W. W. Ashe.

FOREST-RANGE Fencing is Proceeding Rapidly in Arizona and New Mexico   The fencing of the national forest ranges is taking place at a rapid rate in Arizona and New Mexico. In the past it has been the practice on many forests to graze cattle and sheep on the same ranges.

Under this method of dual use it was impossible to place the responsibility for any damage that might occur to the range or to the forest. The stockman who operates upon an individual fenced range takes a greater personal interest in building up the range and in protecting the forest. He becomes interested also in the quality of animals grazed rather than mere numbers and wants to see real feed that will make fat animals and large calf and lamb crops.

Accordingly from a range protection standpoint, as well as in the interest of livestock production, it has been found advisable to allow but one class of stock to graze on a specific allotment and where practicable to allot separate ranges to individual owners. In order to confine stock within these range divisions the construction of many miles of fences was necessary. With funds appropriated by Congress and with the help of the stockmen, more than 1,700 miles of fences have been constructed since 1926. Specifications provide for a four-wire fence with the top wire 48 inches and the bottom wire 18 inches above ground; wooden posts at least 4 inches at top diameter set 2 feet in the ground; sound oak, pitch pine, or juniper is used; all four wires are stapled to the posts with 1¾-inch or 2-inch staples; three stays 52 inches in length, so placed that they will rest on the ground, are used between two posts, and are tied on to each wire with tie wire. The corner posts must be at least 8 feet long, and must be set in the ground 3½ feet and must be well braced.

The completion of these fences has made it possible to regulate the number of livestock using a particular range unit at any time of the

FIGURE 103.—Range fences on the national forests of the Southwest facilitate the protection of forage and timber reproduction against damage from overgrazing

year. Lightly grazed areas thus can be grazed fully; overgrazed spots, where stock naturally concentrate, can be given the necessary protection, and damage to timber reproduction which is apt to result from too severe grazing of an area can be kept within reasonable control.

E. G. MILLER.

FOREST Tree Seedlings Kept From Damping-Off by Aluminum Sulphate —— Damping-off is the name commonly used for a group of fungous diseases that kill and rot germinating seeds and seedlings in the first growing season. The uncertainty introduced into production by the sporadic character of damping-off epidemics is a more serious matter than the size of the average losses.

Everyone who remembers his barefoot days knows how the surface soil heats in the sun. If seed beds become too dry and are not well shaded, the soil is sometimes so hot that the stems of seedlings are shriveled and killed just above the ground level. Nurserymen often mistake this condition for damping-off. In heat-killed seedlings the shriveled base of the stem is light colored, and at first the shriveling is entirely above the ground line. Shriveling due to damping-off, on the other hand, is usually just an extension of the decay which has worked up from some point below the ground line, and the color is darker. Heat is an important source of loss of natural seedlings in the forest, but in most nurseries the losses are mainly due to damping-off.

Methods of Preventing Damping-Off

Where damping-off is troublesome, dense seed sowing should be avoided. Very early spring sowing, or still better fall sowing, in most northern nurseries is less liable to result in loss than late spring sowing. Heavy or excessively wet soil should be avoided, and the beds should be well ventilated; but heat or drought injury may be caused by keeping the beds too dry. At some nurseries it may prove profitable to use surface soil from the forest for the top 2 inches of the seed bed. Coniferous nurseries should be located on slightly acid soils, and lime or wood ashes should not be used in the beds. Poorly rotted manure and dried blood also are likely to increase disease.

In a large proportion of the nurseries damping-off causes considerable loss despite the best care, and chemical treatment of the soil is advisable. Sulphuric acid has been used successfully in many places. However, its corrosive qualities are inconvenient and its effects are not as lasting as might be desired.

FIGURE 104.—Beds of Douglas fir at the Forest Service nursery at Monument, Colo., which have been protected from damping-off and root sickness by treatment with aluminum sulphate. The two thinly stocked plots near the center of the picture were left untreated for comparison, and nearly all of the seedlings on them were killed or dwarfed

For the last five years a new acidifying material, aluminum sulphate, previously employed in growing azaleas and their relatives, has been under investigation as a substitute. While the powder is irritating if it gets into the nose, it is not corrosive. For conifers it is applied at the time of sowing, at the rate of one-half ounce per square foot; it may be dissolved in water, or put on the beds dry and then washed in by sprinkling. The commercial material has been purchased in small lots at 4 cents a pound. In tests at a number of places it has proved equal or superior to acid in controlling damping-off. It has also been found very effective against the root sickness which occurs during the second year in one of the important forest nurseries. Its value in controlling damping-off is strikingly shown in Figure 104. Aluminum sulphate is expected to be successful at any nursery where sulphuric acid is successful, and is likely to displace acid as the most popular treatment for conifers. Like sulphuric acid, it helps to control weeds and at many nurseries will more than pay for itself in this way.

Because of differences between nurseries, both in the character of the soil and in the kinds of damping-off fungi that have to be controlled there is no one treatment that is sure to succeed everywhere. On some soils the standard treatment is too weak, while in others it results in injury to the germinating seed and smaller amounts should be employed or the beds must be allowed to rest a week or two between treatment and sowing. In some places neither acid nor aluminum sulphate will be satisfactory in any strength. Formaldehyde, at the rate of three-eighths fluid ounce per square foot, dissolved in water and applied 10 days before sowing, gives excellent results at some nurseries where the acid materials are not successful. Mercury and zinc compounds and Bordeaux mixture have also been used successfully against damping-off in some places, but the data so far available on them do not represent enough nurseries to justify general recommendations. To determine whether any treatment is good for a particular soil, it is necessary at first to test it on small plots with near-by untreated plots for comparison. Each plot should get the same amount of seed, so that the number of seedlings living at the end of the season will indicate the value of the treatment.

CARL HARTLEY.

FREIGHT-RATE Charges Under Hoch-Smith Law Help in Farm Relief Reductions in the charges for the transportation of agricultural products have long been looked upon as a likely means of improving the financial condition of farmers. This possibility of relief has been embodied in the Federal statute known as the Hoch-Smith resolution, which became law January 30, 1925. It directs the Interstate Commerce Commission to establish for agricultural products affected by depression "the lowest possible lawful rates compatible with the maintenance of adequate transportation service."

In outlining the circumstances affecting a number of its decisions the commission has mentioned this provision of the law. At present it is conducting a special comprehensive investigation into the rates on grain, cotton, cottonseed, livestock, hay, and certain nonagricultural products, thereby accumulating evidence on which to base further action under the resolution.

Any attempt to effect rate relief makes it necessary, for constitutional and economic reasons, to consider the cost of transportation. The commission has said that even under the resolution the rates on any part of the traffic must "be high enough to cover all of the cost that may fairly be allocated to the service." For example, the rates on milk should cover part of the cost of furnishing and operating baggage cars, in which milk is to some extent transported. In most cases no method has been agreed upon for deciding what costs "may fairly be allocated" to the cost of handling any particular commodity. But in 1927 the commission felt compelled to allow some increases in the New England milk rates, because it doubted whether the rates prevailing were compensatory. On the other hand, the commission felt more free to reduce rates on California deciduous fruit because the increasing volume of traffic had presumably reduced the unit cost of handling. It recognizes, however, that not all the cost of transportation can "fairly be allocated"; every part of the traffic, therefore, must yield "some margin of profit" above its allocable share of the expenses.

Shifting of Burdens

The effect of the resolution is that in this respect "agricultural commodities affected by depression shall * * * be included in the class of most-favored commodities." Part of the burden of transportation costs may, therefore, be shifted from depressed agricultural industries to others which have been faring better. Decreases in agricultural rates do not necessarily involve actual increases in others. Reductions may leave the carriers still earning a return which the commission and the courts will consider adequate, especially if the volume of business handled by the roads increases or if operating costs per unit of traffic are reduced. The commission said in 1926, however, that in the country northwest of Chicago to the Rockies the roads were not earning a fair return on any reasonable valuation. Railway income there has shown some improvement since that time.

Should increases prove necessary not all other industries can appropriately be chosen to bear them. Some, like the coal industry, are themselves depressed; others might turn to other forms of transportation; still others, like milling and packing, are closely affiliated with agriculture. But it should be possible to find comparatively prosperous industries such that the effects of increases in their rates will be either absorbed by them or more or less generally diffused. The examiner in charge of the part of the inquiry which deals with products of the iron and steel industry has found the latter "reasonably" prosperous, although he recommends reductions. The commission has refused to order reductions in the rates on products of the zinc industry, holding that the latter was on the way to prosperity, and that it was necessary to conserve revenues for agricultural relief.

Relief to Depressed Farm Enterprises

Meanwhile relief or protection has already been afforded to depressed agricultural industries. In 1926 a request of the western railroads for a general increase of 5 per cent was refused on the grounds that it failed to discriminate between the products of depressed agriculture and those of more prosperous industries. In the same year the New England railroads proposed to increase their milk rates by 20 per cent. Evidence in behalf of producers indicated that Vermont farmers were losing $3.22 per cow per year. The commission refused to allow the whole amount of the increases requested, although granting them in part. In another case the California deciduous fruit growers' association introduced evidence to show that prices, having risen to 90 per cent above their 1917 level in 1920, had fallen back again, while freight rates remained 50 per cent above their level of the earlier year, and that mortgages were increasing, taxes were becoming delinquent, and bankers were taking over farms. The commission in 1927 ordered a reduction of about $7\frac{1}{2}$ per cent in the rates from California to east of the Rockies. In February, 1928, it adopted a nominally reduced general level on southern peaches, finding that the prospects of the industry were "far from encouraging." In July it concluded that the grape growers of the Chautauqua Belt in New York were suffering "substantial" losses, which they could not well avoid by turning to the growing of other products, and reduced their rates from second to third class, or lower in some cases. Two weeks later it refused to allow the carriers of hay moving between the North and the South to increase their rates to the full extent demanded, naming among its reasons the steady fall in hay prices since 1920 and the failure of recent prices to cover estimated costs of production.

Readjustment of freight rates alone may not bring the return of farmers on their labor and investment up to the level considered normal in other industries, but rate readjustment can make a welcome contribution.

THOR HULTGREN.

FRUIT and Vegetable Inspection at Shipping Points Is Increasing   All plans recently proposed for the more efficient marketing of fresh fruits and vegetables have one point in common—improved standardization of quality and condition of the products and of the containers in which they are marketed.   All agree that this is one of the most practical

FIGURE 105.—Federal market inspector examining car of bunched carrots

means of securing the greatest possible returns alike in years of moderate production and in years when a surplus reduces the price out of all proportion to its size. Not all agree as to how this can best be accomplished. Some favor arbitrary governmental control not only of grading but of selling, as is practiced in New Zealand and Queensland, South Africa; others believe that the individual grower, growers' organization, or shipper can do his own grading. Our States vary widely in their legislation regarding this question. Variations in local conditions account for these differences even though they do not always warrant them.

The Federal Department of Agriculture, naturally looked to as an agency for securing coordination of various efforts, has endeavored to unify the fruit and vegetable standardization work of the States (1) by recommending grade specifications for these products and (2) by making it easier for growers, shippers, and receivers to use these grades in a practical way by offering an inspection service. Upon application, disinterested inspectors will certify the compliance of individual carlots with the recommended grades.

Work Has Grown Rapidly

Begun in 1917 in receiving markets, this work grew so rapidly that by 1922 approximately 30,000 cars yearly were being inspected. But shippers were not satisfied to be told of their failures in grading after their products had reached the terminal markets. They demanded a similar service at shipping points, so that they might start their cars to destinations with evidence that they had complied with the quality specifications of their sales contract.

This extension of the service, granted by Congress in 1922, in cooperation with the States, has reached a point where 41 States cooperate with the department in a service which covers all the principal fruits and vegetables; 210,832 cars were certified at shipping point in 1928.

This shipping-point service, while giving to its users the many immediate advantages which come from having official evidence of quality and condition of products which are particularly difficult to market because of their perishable nature, has exerted its greatest influence through the encouragement it has given to the more general use of uniform standards throughout the United States. When this service was begun, Federal grades were available only for potatoes, among the perishables. State grades for apples were in use in two or three States. Federal grades have now been promulgated for 35 fruits and vegetables, and it is estimated that two-thirds of our shipments of these products are now being marketed under well-recognized grades.

F. G. Robb.

FRUITS and Vegetables for Canning Are Sold Increasingly by Grade — United States grades for fresh fruits and vegetables have long been recognized by growers, shippers, and buyers, but it was not until 1923 that the Department of Agriculture undertook to formulate grades with definite specifications for fruits and vegetables used for commercial canning purposes. After three seasons' investigations, grades were recommended for cannery tomatoes. Since that time there has been increased interest on the part of both growers and canners in the idea of contracting on the basis of these grades and of having impartial inspectors determine the percentage of various grades in each load as it is delivered to the cannery.

Last season 15 canners of tomatoes contracted with their growers on the basis of the United States grades, and approximately 12,000 loads were inspected by licensed inspectors who determined the percentage of U. S. No. 1, U. S. No. 2, and cull tomatoes in the loads.

Canners paid a certain price for U. S. No. 2, a premium for U. S. No. 1, and nothing for cull tomatoes. Progressive growers of high-quality tomatoes are recognizing the advantage of contracting with a canner on a basis which gives proper recognition to variations in quality. Canners are also finding that the system of buying on grades results in an improvement in the quality of pack of their tomatoes as well as in the amount packed out.

Growers and canners of apples and cabbage are also interested in United States grades for these commodities when used for canning

FIGURE 106.—Inspecting tomatoes at a cannery

purposes, and the department hopes to have investigations completed so that grades can be recommended for use in the 1929 season.

R. R. PAILTHORP.

FRUIT Washes and Their Relation to Storage Diseases Washing fruit as an adjunct to ordinary harvesting operations has developed from the necessity of removing spray residue from apples and pears in compliance with pure-food laws in both the United States and foreign countries. After considering the capacity of any washing method to remove spray residue, the question most frequently asked is, What effect will it have upon the fruit, and especially upon its keeping quality? In order to obtain definite information of this character a large number of experiments and observations have been conducted at the United States Fruit Disease Field Laboratory, Wenatchee, Wash.

It has been found that certain methods cause injury and an increased loss from storage rots, but it is now possible to point out the hazards involved in washing and, in most cases also, methods of avoiding them. Direct injury from chemical solvents is more frequently encountered on pears than on apples. This is largely due to the fact that pears are often picked immature when the lenticels are incapable of excluding chemical solutions. Pears are particularly susceptible to injury from the use of alkaline washes, which produce a blackening at the lenticels. Provided thorough rinsing is given, similar injury from hydrochloric acid washes does not ordinarily occur on pears unless the concentration is above 1 per cent (actual hydrochloric acid) and the exposure longer than three minutes.

Washing Damage Seldom Direct

In commercial washing, apples are seldom directly injured by either the alkaline or acid chemicals now used, damage resulting only when the fruit is left in the solutions too long or when it is not thoroughly rinsed. The principal hazard in washing apples, aside from increases in rots due to punctures resulting from extra handling, is caused by soluble arsenic, derived from the spray residue itself. This injury is usually localized in the calyx region (fig. 107), although it sometimes occurs also at the base of the stem. It consists of a black or brownish area which in advanced stages may be depressed and extend one-eighth of an inch or more into the flesh, the affected tissues becoming brown and dry. This injury usually appears within two weeks after washing and opens the way for storage rots, particularly if the fruit is stored wet.

The association of this injury with hydrochloric-acid washing at first led to a popular assumption that it was due to acid burning. However, it is equally associated with alkaline washes and sometimes is found also on unwashed and heavily sprayed apples after rainy fall weather. Experiments conducted at the Wenatchee laboratory proved that the injury may result from the accumulation of dissolved arsenic in the washing solutions. These washes should be changed after the equivalent of about 500 bushels of apples has been treated in each 100 gallons of chemical solvent.

Chemical Reaction During Washing

When spray residue is incompletely removed from the deeper portion of the calyx, as is frequently the case, arsenical injury may result from the chemical reaction initiated during the washing process and continued under the influence of moisture retained on the apples. An effort should, therefore, be made to dry the apples as quickly as possible.

Arsenical injury is increased by submersion methods which subject the fruit to chemical action for a period of several minutes and by the application of the solvent in solid jets under considerable pressure. In these methods of washing the solution penetrates deeply into the calyx, from where it can be removed only with difficulty in rinsing operations. Some of the washing devices either submerge the apples in boxes or cause the fruit to float through long tanks with occasional submersion under paddle wheels. These methods sometimes result in excessive losses from core rots due to the penetration of cleaning solutions through open calyx tubes.

Certain varieties of apples—notably Jonathan, Spitzenburg, Stayman Winesap, and sometimes Delicious—are often characterized by a considerable proportion of open calyx tubes. These should preferably be cleaned by devices which apply the washing solution as a spray. On the other hand, other varieties, such as the Rome Beauty, Winesap, Ben Davis, Arkansas Black, and Yellow Newtown, seldom have enough open calyx tubes to give serious trouble, and these can be washed by submersion without influencing core rots.

Infective Material in Rotted Apples

Hundreds of spores of rot-producing organisms are commonly found on a single sound apple as it comes from the orchard, while a rotted apple may bear enough infective material to destroy several carloads.

Rotted fruit, therefore, should be sorted out before washing to reduce to a minimum the accumulation of spores in the washing solutions. It has been found that more spores are removed from apples where they are washed under sprays than by either submergence or floating in the cleaning solutions.

If no injury to the skin were produced in the process, the removal of spores in this manner should reduce the chances for storage rots to develop. However, the increased handling incident to washing usually produces more stem punctures and other abrasions from which rots may start. The results of work at the Wenatchee laboratory indicate that under good commercial practice this increase in loss is not sufficient to offset the advantages of washing.

Much work has been done to find or develop a disinfectant to kill the spores of rot organisms during the washing process. However, no economical method has been found of accomplishing this during the short time that the apples are exposed to washing solutions.

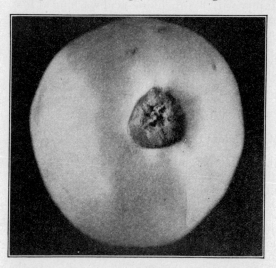

FIGURE 107.—Arsenical injury at the calyx of Winter Banana apple

It should be emphasized that the difficulties and dangers pointed out above are a matter of concern only under improper operation. The washing treatment has now had two years' test on a large commercial scale. Comprehensive studies and surveys covering important shipping points and all the larger marketing centers have shown conclusively that both in storage and on the market washed fruit holds up as well as or better than that which is unwashed, and in addition it usually offers a more attractive appearance.

D. F. FISHER.

FRUITS' Composition Given in Tables for Reckoning Nutrients New tables on the proximate composition of fresh fruits have been issued by the Bureau of Home Economics for use in calculating the nutritive value of diets. These contain data on most of the common fruits of our markets and some of the less familiar kinds. In the past the diet specialist or the patient on a diet for diabetes or other abnormal condition has had no convenient reference to turn to for reliable average figures on such fruits as avocados, grapefruit, limes, Japanese persimmons, or oranges of the Mandarin type.

Many of the foods now in daily use were not important enough 30 years ago, when the tables of Atwater and Bryant were published, to be included in that study, and no tables issued since then have filled these gaps satisfactorily. More than 40 fruits and juices have been added to the early list.

The new data on most of the common fruits are, for the most part, in fairly good agreement with those in the earlier study; but a few significant differences stand out. Grapes and certain kinds of plums, according to the new tables, are somewhat lower in total carbohydrates and in fuel value, and peaches, pineapples, and fresh prunes are higher than they have been calculated formerly.

Furthermore, the difference in composition between fresh prunes and other plums is brought out in the new tables, whereas the old figures failed to show any real distinction. There is, of course, no very sharp line of demarcation between these types of plums, but prunes, which are plums suitable for drying, are higher in sugar and total solids than other plums. The new average figures on European and on Japanese types of plums indicate that these run appreciably lower in nutrients than the fresh prunes.

Grapefruit is often figured in diabetic diets as containing only about 5 per cent total carbohydrates, and in other calculations as much as 12 per cent, a difference that may be important in strict diets. The new figure on Florida-grown grapefruit is just under 9 per cent.

CHARLOTTE CHATFIELD.

FUR Farmers Aided by Research in Combating Outbreaks of Disease Throughout the entire country, but especially in the Northern States, where the propagation of fur bearers in captivity has been extensively developed during recent years, frequent outbreaks of disease among the animals cause heavy losses. Certain fur farmers consider that carefully planned sanitary measures and the right kinds and quantities of food are enough to prevent these outbreaks of infections. It has been found, however, that even on well-regulated ranches several infectious diseases, commonly referred to by fox breeders as distemper, may gain entrance and assume devastating proportions, some causing losses as high as 50 per cent of the stock on the ranch. Hygienic procedure and quarantine restrictions are important in checking the spread of epizootics, but they are valueless in the cure of infected animals. In order to obtain more complete knowledge of the nature of the ailments and to work out practical methods of protecting or curing the animals, extensive experiments are being conducted by the Bureau of Biological Survey in a program of cooperative research with the medical college of the University of Minnesota.

Red foxes and low-grade silver foxes are being used in large numbers for tests in transmitting infection and for studying diseases under controlled conditions. The responsible organisms can thus be isolated and the exact nature of the injury caused in the various organs can be recognized by gross and microscopic examinations of fresh specimens. The ultimate object of these investigations is to develop a means of curing animals that are affected and of protecting others from infection. Greater success appears to be possible in measures of prevention than of cure. Certain advances have been made, and a number of animals have been vaccinated experimentally in tests under ranch conditions. Dogs and certain other fur animals apparently are susceptible to the diseases of foxes or to some that are similar. Fur farmers would do well not to introduce new animals on a ranch without quarantining them for at least one month. Such stock should be carefully watched for symptoms of disease.

Control of Intestinal Parasites

Intestinal parasites are being controlled on fur ranches by the administration of suitable anthelmintics. Lungworm trouble in foxes, however, continues to be a serious menace in some places. Removing animals that show symptoms of this form of parasitism to noncontaminated premises will frequently prevent loss. Worms can be removed from the trachea by means of a specially designed brush, but skill is required in the operation.

On rabbitries, also, infectious diseases sometimes become serious. Prompt disposal of sick animals and the disinfection of their hutches are the best-known methods of controlling the more common diseases of rabbits. Tularemia, a disease frequently encountered in wild rabbits, which is communicable to man, has not been detected in animals raised in domestic rabbitries, although it has been produced in rabbits in laboratory experiments. Since domestic rabbits are thus susceptible to the disease, it is believed that their usual freedom from infection in rabbitries is due to the methods under which they are kept. Conditions in commercial rabbitries are such that animals are seldom exposed to the natural insect carriers of tularemia.

Raising fur bearers in captivity is a highly specialized industry, and combating the ailments of the animals requires a familiarity with all their characteristics and a knowledge of the fundamental principles of nutrition and of the treatment of disease. Extended research in this field is necessary to solve the many new problems.

J. E. SHILLINGER.

GIPSY-MOTH and Brown-Tail Moth Campaign Status — Two entirely opposite conditions are evident in a review of the gipsy-moth situation for the summer of 1928. The enormous increase of this insect in the older infested territory is alarming, but the success that has accompanied the Federal campaign to prevent the spread of this insect and to clean up the infestation in New Jersey is gratifying.

A larger extent of severe defoliation of forest, shade, and fruit trees in eastern New England was caused in the summer of 1928 by the gipsy moth than has previously occurred for many years. Over 260,000 acres of trees were severely and partially defoliated, whereas only 142,000 acres were defoliated in 1927, 82,000 acres in 1926, and about 50,000 acres in the previous year.

The principal function of the Federal work in opposing the gipsy moth and the brown-tail moth is to prevent the infested areas from becoming larger; as this is actually being accomplished, such success leads to the hope that the time may come when it will be practicable to begin to reduce the size of the infested areas. Although such a campaign would be enormous and costly, its possibility should not be lost sight of.

The losses which have occurred in the older infested area are inestimable. Many oaks and pines have already been destroyed, and many of the trees which have withstood the attacks of these insects have been retarded in their growth and are in a weakened condition.

To prevent the occurrence of similar and even greater losses to the timber, shade trees, and ornamental plantings in the States west of New England, the Federal Government has for nearly 25 years vigorously resisted a further advance of these insects. For many years the spread of the insects was greatly retarded, but owing to the extremely heavy infestation by the gipsy moth this insect continued to advance little by little until it crossed the Connecticut River in Connecticut, Massachusetts, and Vermont, journeyed over the Berkshire Hills in Massachusetts and Connecticut and the Green Mountains of Vermont, even making its way into the edge of New York State and Canada. The beautiful forests of the Catskills and Adirondacks were threatened.

Determined Stand Made in 1923

A final, determined stand was made in 1923, when a new campaign was launched with the Federal forces placed well beyond the most advanced points which the insect had reached. At this time New York and Canada joined the Federal forces, since they were vitally concerned in preventing this insect from gaining a foothold in their territory. The new battlefield, consisting of more than 8,000 square miles, was termed the barrier zone. It lies in an open, rolling country, approximately 30 miles wide and 250 miles long, running north and south from Canada to Long Island Sound. In this section the open country, the tree growth, and the topography are advantageous to the workers and less favorable for the establishment of new colonies of the gipsy moth. Gradually every town in this area was examined, and the work disclosed many isolated infestations consisting of from one cluster to several thousand clusters of gipsy-moth eggs. The most modern methods of combating these insects were vigorously applied to every infestation, and gradually they have been exterminated.

A severe gipsy-moth infestation which was found by the forces of the Canadian Government in Canada, a few miles northwest of Lake Champlain, has been eradicated by them, and great inroads have been made in the territory occupied by the gipsy moth, resulting in the freeing from the pest of large areas within the barrier zone. Intensive work must continue, especially in that part of the zone which lies in southwestern Massachusetts, northwestern Connecticut, and the region west of this section in New York State. This area is particularly difficult to work and seems to be very favorable for the gipsy moth. New infestations are being discovered there, but persistent searching and the application of the most practical methods of extermination will finally rid this area of the insect enemy.

The gipsy moth is steadily losing ground against the forces of the State of New Jersey and of the Federal Government in the infested area in that State. A separate invasion of the gipsy moth was discovered there in 1920. When first found it had spread over 400 square miles, and the infestation consisted of more than 3,000,000 egg clusters. More than half of this territory has now been freed from the insect, and the infestation in the remaining portion has been reduced to less than 100 egg clusters.

Another phase of the condition is serious. In New England, east of the barrier zone, the gipsy moth is increasing rapidly in abundance, and the area of the generally infested territory (fig. 108) has been increased. Severe infestations have already developed near the eastern edge of the zone. Unless the most dangerous infestations in this area are eradicated, the moth will inevitably spread through the

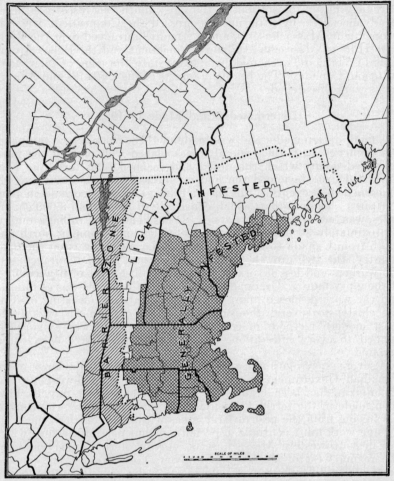

FIGURE 108.—Map showing the portion of New England infested by the gipsy moth and the barrier zone to the westward

zone and the ground that has already been freed of this pest will become reinfested.

Brown-Tail Moth's Spread Checked

The brown-tail moth has not advanced over such an extensive area as has the gipsy moth. Its winter webs are conspicuous and easily collected and destroyed. During the last few years it has not been as serious a pest as the gipsy moth, and for several years there has been practically no spread of it.

While the chief struggles against the gipsy moth have been raging successfully in the barrier zone and in New Jersey, they have been supplemented by a vigorous enforcement of quarantine regulations to prevent the insect escaping from the infested area.

Continual improvements are being made in the equipment and the methods used in carrying on the warfare in the field. These improvements are reflected in lowered costs of operation and in more efficient work. Total reliance has not been placed upon man to combat successfully these pests; throughout the campaign the introduction of their insect enemies to aid in this conflict has been intensively carried on. Several very beneficial forms are now established and are in constant combat with the gipsy and brown-tail moths. Parasites and predators rarely exterminate a colony of the gipsy moth or of the brown-tail moth, but many records have been obtained which prove that they are, at times, of inestimable value in aiding in the reduction of the numbers of these and many other injurious insects.

The formerly continuous dispersion of the gipsy moth has been stopped since the establishment of the barrier zone in 1923. The eradication of the gipsy moth in New Jersey, although not completed, is progressing extraordinarily well, and the end seems to be in sight. The most serious condition at the end of the summer of 1928 is the increasing abundance of the gipsy moth in the older infested territory, where large areas have been completely defoliated. From this territory heavy infestations have developed toward the west; the generally infested area has increased, and the presence of colonies of the gipsy moth west of the Connecticut River are a constant threat and a source of danger to the barrier zone.

A. F. Burgess.

GRAIN Drying on Farm Awaits Development of Suitable Equipment Much grain is damaged annually because of excessive moisture when stored or when shipped to market. As a result, requests have been received by the department for information regarding drying units suitable for use on farms and at local elevators. Practically all of the grain driers now in use are in large elevators or mills. Drying units suitable in capacity and price for farm use have not as yet been developed. However, there is considerable interest in the development of such equipment by manufacturers and some experimental work has been done by the department as well as by certain State agricultural experimental stations.

Available information on artificial drying of grain is limited. Consequently, practically all of the experimental work has been for the purpose of determining fundamental principles involved in drying grain rather than for the development of grain driers.

The moisture content of cereal grain under natural conditions varies with the temperature and relative humidity of the surrounding air. When the relative humidity is high, moisture may be absorbed; whereas if it is low, moisture may be evaporated from the grain. The rate at which this change takes place depends largely upon the atmospheric conditions, the moisture content of the grain, and the extent to which the grain is exposed to the air. The drying process is necessarily slow, because the moisture is distributed throughout the kernels and must be brought to the surface of each kernel before it can be evaporated.

With laboratory equipment and under the most favorable drying conditions secured by forced ventilation with heated air, from 20 to 45 minutes is required to reduce the moisture content of wheat from about 20 to $13\frac{1}{2}$ per cent. With equipment suitable for commercial use it takes about one hour to accomplish the same results. The exact time required to dry grain depends in part upon the temperature, relative humidity and velocity of the drying air, and upon the quantity of water to be evaporated.

Drying With Heated Air

Tests have shown that the grain must be in thin layers for uniform drying when heated air is used. When the air is forced through 12 inches or more of damp grain, drying is not uniform throughout the mass. The heated air dries out the grain quickly at first, but as it moves through the grain moisture is absorbed and the temperature reduced to the point that it is no longer effective. Under certain conditions moisture may be evaporated from the grain and again deposited before the air has reached the outer surface of the layer.

The weight per bushel (generally referred to as the test weight) of wheat increases, as it is dried, to a maximum test weight when the moisture content reaches about 12 per cent. The rate at which the grain is dried apparently does not affect the maximum test weight. Tests have shown that the weight per bushel of different samples of the same grain were approximately the same at about 12 per cent of moisture, whether dried artifically in about 40 minutes or dried under atmospheric conditions for several days.

Heating air for drying is the most expensive item in the artificial drying of grain. When exhaust steam can be used or when steam is available for use in steam coils for heating, the cost per bushel may be very low. Where a special boiler is maintained primarily for grain drying the cost per bushel of grain dried may be very high. This is especially true if it is necessary to dry small quantities of grain intermittently, as so much heat is then lost in starting and stopping. The exact cost, under any set of conditions, depends upon a variety of factors, such as the quantity of moisture to be evaporated, the quantity of grain to be dried, the kind of grain, the efficiency of the heating units, atmospheric conditions, and depreciation of the equipment.

Driers which use direct heat from a furnace are being tried out. Such driers will doubtless require less fuel, as the heat may be utilized efficiently.

W. M. Hurst.

GRAIN Quality Affected by Time of Harvesting With Combine Machine   Moisture content, test weight per bushel, protein content, and respiration activities are four factors that are always present in grain. These factors signify quality and condition according to the degree present. They are influenced by the time at which the grain is harvested and threshed.

Harvesting and threshing too early is detrimental to quality. At that time the natural moisture in the grain is high, the test weight per bushel is low, the protein is not fully developed, and respiration activities are enormous. The time to cut and thresh wheat for best quality is when it has reached the ripe stage and the moisture in the grain has come down to from 12 to 14 per cent. Then the test weight will be at its height, the protein will be fully developed, and the respiration activities will be such that the grain is in a reasonably safe storage condition.

Experiments conducted at the Arlington Experiment Farm, Rosslyn, Va., by the Bureau of Agricultural Economics showed that wheat when ripe enough to be harvested with a binder had to be left standing in the field during clear weather for about eight days longer before the natural moisture decreased to around 13 per cent, which is considered a safe moisture content for harvesting and threshing the grain in one operation   At that stage the test weight was at its height, the protein had reached a near-constant point, and the respiration activities had all but ceased. (Fig. 109.)

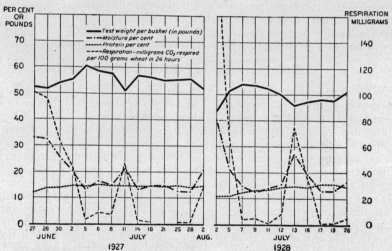

FIGURE 109.—Test weight per bushel, moisture content, respiration activities, and protein content of wheat harvested and threshed at the Arlington Experiment Farm, Rosslyn, Va., at intervals during the seasons of 1927 and 1928

Later rain on the standing grain increases its moisture content and respiration activities and lowers its test weight, but has no effect on protein content. The moisture increase depends on the moisture content of the grain before the rain comes and on the amount of rain that falls. The time required for the grain to dry after a rain varies. It depends partially on the amount of moisture increase and weather conditions following the rain. Under favorable drying weather the moisture may go from 17 per cent down to 13 per cent in one day. Heavy dew at night tends to increase the moisture in dry grain and retards the drying of damp grain.

After dry grain is made wet by rain the test weight per bushel is lowered. Then as the grain dries the test weight increases, but it never goes back to where it was. Test weight lost between naturally dry grain and grain wetted after becoming ripe, whether before or after cutting from the stalk, may amount to as much as 6 pounds per bushel. Such losses are likely to occur more often in a humid than in a semihumid climate. But in either climate they are likely to occur if grain is left standing in the field until it is long overripe.

B. E. ROTHGEB.

GRAZING Too Early in Season Is Harmful to Livestock and Range   After a long winter, during which all the trees and shrubs have been bare and dormant and the herbaceous vegetation has been covered with snow, the appearance of bare ground and of growing plants is a welcome sight. Small stems and leaves are seen pushing upward from the ground, daily growing larger and longer. Some of these are biennial and perennial plants that are growing from the old bases of plants of the past year. Others are plants freshly germinated from seeds that have lain dormant during the winter. Catkins and leaves appear upon the trees and shrubs, and by close observation one can see that the twigs and stems are beginning to grow.

The food necessary for this initial spring growth is stored in the seeds of annual plants and in the roots of perennials. Nature has provided this reserve of prepared food in order that early spring growth may be carried on until new leaves have developed enough to manufacture food. Nature, however, did not provide protection against heavy grazing by hungry livestock during this critical period.

Too Early Grazing Retards Plants

What happens when a cow or sheep nips off the plant, or a large portion of it, in the early spring? Much of the stored food has already been used to make the growth the sheep or cow consumes. Not many, sometimes none, of the leaves are left to make more food. Even if some leaves remain on the plant, these can not always make appreciable amounts of food because the temperature is not high enough. The plant is greatly handicapped and does not recover its normal vigor during the entire summer. At the Great Basin Range Experiment Station in the mountains east of Ephraim, Utah, very careful studies were made to determine the effect of such early grazing upon plants. It was found that the plants grazed too early produce 25 per cent less growth over the season than do plants that are not grazed until they have a good start. Moreover, in the early spring it is necessary for livestock to consume a much greater number of small and very succulent plants, containing as much as 85 per cent water, than is necessary to secure the same nourishment if the plants are allowed to reach maturity. It is not uncommon for range animals to starve after plant growth has started just enough to lure them away from old dry feed on an eager search over a wide area for new, luscious, but inadequate forage.

That plants are injured by trampling when the ground is wet is self-evident. It is not so evident that they are injured indirectly because the ground is packed. The roots need air. The air enters the soil through the air spaces between the soil particles. When the soil is packed these air spaces are more limited and air is more or less excluded. Water evaporates more rapidly from packed soil because, for one reason, in packed soil there is a continuous passageway from soil particle to soil particle so the soil water can travel to the surface where evaporation is going on. In unpacked soils the air spaces between particles check the current to the surface and the soil moisture is held more as thin films around the soil particles. As water is one of the main factors affecting forage production, any condition that lessens the amount of it in the soil should be avoided if possible. For these reasons ranges should not be grazed in the spring while the soils are wet from the melting snow.

Poisonous Plants Appear Early

Several poisonous plants, especially larkspur and death camas, are among the very earliest plants on the ranges. They make a luxuriant growth, where they appear, before many of the other plants are well started. When stock are on the ranges too early, they eat many of these poisonous plants and die as the result.

In order to insure conservative and economical use of the forage, due consideration must be given the growth requirements of plants and their food value at different stages of development. In handling grazing on the national forests it is necessary to regulate the period of use so that livestock will not enter the ranges until the forage has developed far enough to permit grazing with safety. Much observation and considerable experimentation have been carried on to determine when plants have reached this stage, and the information gained has been pretty well confirmed in actual range practice. On the basis of this information, the following standards have been set up by the Forest Service as general guides in deciding when ranges are ready for grazing:

The important browse plants, such as chokecherry, service berry, rose, birchleaf mahogany, snowberry, and bitter brush, should be in full leaf or nearly so.

The grasses should be from 6 to 10 inches high, and many of the earliest ones in boot.

The important herbs (other than grasses) should be well leafed out and well started in growth.

Generally ranges are ready for grazing about three or four weeks after active plant growth has begun.

Forage Development Not Uniform

The development of forage on the ranges is far from uniform. Often the grasses develop faster and are ready for grazing earlier than the other herbs and browse. Naturally the plants on the more southerly exposures develop earlier than those on the more northerly exposures. Generally every 1,000-foot rise in elevation makes a difference of from 10 days to two weeks in the development of the vegetation, other conditions being the same, and consequently plants may be on a south exposure but still be late developing if they are at a high altitude. There is much variation in the development of plants in different years. The plants may develop as much as three weeks earlier during an early spring than during a late spring.

ARNOLD R. STANDING and
ERNEST WINKLER.

GRUBSTAKE Stage of Settlers in Northern Lake States Measured   The grubstake stage in land settlement represents the length of time the average settler, in developing a new farm, is dependent upon outside financial assistance. During this period the land-selling agency, or other agencies financially interested in his welfare, advance him funds to protect their investment in his land or in other community enterprises.

In 1925 a survey of 386 settlers on cut-over land in northern Wisconsin was made to ascertain the length of time required for a settler to pass through the grubstake stage. No settler was considered to have passed through this period unless he had an income-producing unit of at least 15 cultivated acres and indebtedness not in excess of the sum of one-half the value of the land and one-fifth the value of the buildings. Loans to settlers having less than these minimum requirements are not usually considered safe investments.

Of those settlers who purchased farms larger than 120 acres not one passed through the grubstake period in less than 12 years, and only half of those included in the survey who had owned farms larger than 120 acres for more than 12 years had passed beyond that stage. Twelve years, therefore, is apparently the minimum period required for the average settler who purchases more than 120 acres of cut-over land to pass through the grubstake period.

All settlers who had been on farms containing from 41 to 120 acres less than 11 years were still in the grubstake stage. From this it would appear that the average settler who purchases more than 40 acres of cut-over land has little prospect of developing his farm beyond the grubstake stage in less than 11 years. It is interesting to note that every settler who had purchased only 40 acres of cut-over land passed through this stage within 5 to 11 years. This indicates that the average grubstake period is shorter for those farmers who buy small tracts. A small tract can be cleared rather quickly, and in the meantime the settler is not burdened with large expenditures for interest and taxes on idle acres.

WILLIAM A. HARTMAN.

HAIL-OCCURRENCE Data for the United States Gathered and Analyzed — The occurrence of hail, like other weather events, is the result of natural physical laws, and since no means exist at the present whereby such phenomena can be controlled or their destructive effects materially modified, they must be endured.

The only recourse of the agriculturist or horticulturist who happens to be located in a region subject to destructive hailstorms, and these may occur locally over wide areas, is to either change his crop methods, that is, raise crops not usually materially affected by the occurrence of hail, or protect his financial interests by proper crop insurance. The first plan may be adopted to some extent, but usually it is found safer to provide adequate insurance.

No important parts of the United States proper, particularly the portions devoted to the main crops, appear entirely immune from at least occasional visits of this character, and while they may frequently bring no material loss, there is no evidence to indicate they may not also assume violent proportions at any time, though the probabilities of such vary greatly in different sections.

Hail Data Summarized

Data on the occurrence of hail in the United States have been collected to some extent for many years, and these have been summarized in various ways, the most recent discussion being by A. J. Henry, in the Monthly Weather Review of March, 1917. However, the data heretofore presented have been obtained mainly from the regular telegraphic-reporting stations of the Weather Bureau, which are too widely separated to afford a clear estimate of the probable conditions existing over the extensive areas lying between these stations, nor have the figures indicated in any way the character of these storms, whether causing or not causing material damage. Furthermore, individual hailstorms usually cover small areas only, and observing stations, though lying in a region of possible frequent hail occurrence, may escape actual visitations for many years and thereby fail to indicate properly the probability of occurrence in their vicinities.

Since 1915 the Weather Bureau has collected as fully as possible from the large corps of regular and cooperative observers and from press dispatches which are carefully scrutinized and investigated, reports on the occurrence of hail during the period of principal crop growth, April to September, inclusive, for all parts of the country. These data have been presented in the reports of the Chief of Weather Bureau yearly since that time, in the form of dotted charts, each dot representing the location of a hailstorm. Two charts have been published annually, one showing the locations of moderately heavy hailstorms, or those doing no important damage, and the other showing the occurrence of damaging hail, or at least hail in such quantity that it would have been destructive to growing crops, though at the time no crop may have been in a state of growth whereby material damage could have occurred.

Probability of Storms Indicated

The 12 seasonal charts of damaging hail were carefully divided into squares of equal area, 10,000 square miles each, and the number of dots in each of the squares determined for every year of this period, the means of these for the full 12 years showing for all parts of the country the probable number of hailstorms causing material damage liable to occur in each square per year. It may be stated, however, that the various parts of the country do not all possess equal facilities for gathering reports of such storms, due to differences in the density of the population or otherwise.

This combined 12-year chart shows that hail occurred in each of these squares at some time during the 12-year period in practically all parts of the country, save for a small area in southern California and near-by portions of Nevada, and over a few other small areas.

Damaging hailstorms appear most frequent in the middle Plains, where over considerable areas, including most of Kansas and Iowa, and the near-by portions of surrounding States, an average of from 2 to 4 damaging hailstorms may be expected to occur per season in each 10,000 square miles of area. Of course, the individual separate storms usually cover only small areas, a characteristic that is also associated with the violent rotary winds known as tornadoes, and are usually associated with them. They frequently occur in connection with thunderstorms. The total area of all damaging hailstorms in a single square per season would usually amount to but a few square miles, so that at the worst the yearly possibility of any particular section lying in the path of a damaging hailstorm would be exceedingly small, even in the areas of most frequent occurrence.

Risk Less Outside Middle Plains

Outside the area referred to above, the probability of hail damage decreases in all directions, except over a limited area from central Kentucky northward over eastern Indiana and the eastern half of the lower Michigan peninsula, over much of Ohio, and into western Pennsylvania. A similar area, though less extensive, appears over eastern Pennsylvania, central Maryland, and northern Virginia.

The average number of hailstorms diminishes rapidly with approach to the Great Lakes, save in eastern Michigan, and is comparatively small in all southern and far western districts, though damaging hailstorms may occur at long intervals as far south as extreme southern Florida, and in the Rio Grande Valley of Texas.

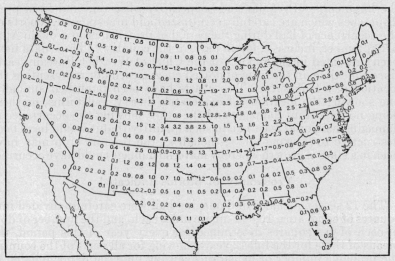

FIGURE 110.—Average annual number of hailstorms in the United States causing material damage per each 10,000 miles, 1916–1927, inclusive, April 1 to September 30

Figure 110 shows the average distribution of damaging hailstorms during the 12-year period referred to, and should give valuable assistance both to the companies issuing insurance and to the individuals seeking protection, in arriving at a fair basis for estimating the approximate cost of the risk.

P. C. DAY.

HARNESS Life Can Be Doubled or Trebled by Cleaning and Repairing Discriminative buying, prompt repair, and proper care of leather harness pay big dividends. When the usual life of a harness is doubled the cost is cut in two. Some farmers get excellent service from their harness for 25 years or longer (fig. 111); unfortunately many others are unable to use theirs longer than from 2 to 5 years. The life of a harness depends to a great extent upon its quality and workmanship, and the care that it receives.

Harness too heavy for the work is more economical than harness that is too light. Especially should lines, breeching, holdback straps, tugs or traces, belly bands, and yoke straps be sufficiently heavy and strong for the work required. Weak tugs and weak straps will not stand heavy work, nor can a runaway team be stopped with weak lines.

The leather should be carefully examined to see that it has no cuts, holes, brands, thin places, or other physical imperfections that impair its strength. New harness leather that shows cracks on the grain side when it is sharply bent is practically worthless, and the presence of cracks in old harness shows that it is deteriorating. Harness leather should be pliable, not stiff. It should not feel harsh and dry. It should contain from 20 to 25 per cent grease, for protection, preservation, and strength. More than 25 per cent grease is not necessary. The grease should be thoroughly incorporated into the leather; it should not be simply on the surface. Because "strong" acids, or mineral acids, rot leather in time, a guaranty by the maker that they have not been used is advisable.

Since harness, as a rule, is made up of many different pieces and parts, the quality of the workmanship should receive consideration. The sewing should be consistent with the weight and type of the harness. It should be done with sufficiently heavy thread and sufficient rows of stitches to stand the strain. The needle holes especially should not be so close together that the thread will readily cut through the leather. The riveting and fastening of buckles, rings, snaps, and

FIGURE 111.—Harness 40 years old, of good quality, selected for the work, and not neglected. It has been kept clean, promptly repaired, and frequently oiled

other metal parts should be secure, so that they will remain solidly in place.

Neglect of harness is costly. Breaks and rips should be promptly and properly repaired. Makeshift jobs are but temporary and go from bad to worse. Harness should be kept clean, especially the leather parts, which should be washed and oiled from two to four times a year, depending upon the conditions of use. The useful life of harness can be doubled and quadrupled by such treatment.

Clean the harness with tepid water and neutral soap, such as castile or white toilet soap, using a sponge or fairly stiff brush. Scrape off cakes of hardened grease or foreign matter with a dull knife. Rinse in clean, tepid water, and hang the harness in a warm room until it is no longer wet, but is still damp. Then oil the harness and leave it in a warm place for 24 hours before using it. Harness should be oiled or greased while still damp; otherwise it may absorb so much oil that it will pull out of shape or take up sand and grit, thereby injuring the leather as well as spoiling its appearance. Harness should never look or feel greasy.

Neat's-foot oil or castor oil, or a mixture of these with wool grease, is a good dressing for driving harness. For heavy harness a mixture of tallow and cod oil, neat's-foot oil and tallow, or any or all of these with wool grease, in a paste of about the consistency of butter, is beneficial. Apply the grease lightly to driving harness and liberally to work harness. Rub the oil or grease, warm to the hand, thoroughly into the leather while it is still damp from the washing. After the harness has hung in a warm place over night remove with a clean, dry cloth any oil that the leather has not absorbed.

F. V. VEITCH and
R. W. FREY.

HAY Marketing Is Much Improved by Federal Inspection Increased use of United States hay standards and the Federal hay-inspection service last year had a considerable influence on the improvement of marketing conditions in the hay industry. During the year ended June 30, 1928, 29,343 inspections were made, an increase of 71 per cent over

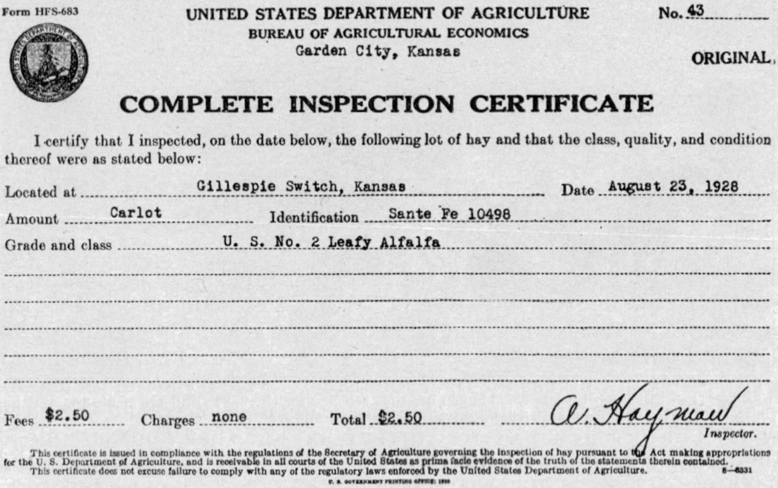

Form HFS-683

UNITED STATES DEPARTMENT OF AGRICULTURE
BUREAU OF AGRICULTURAL ECONOMICS
Garden City, Kansas

No. 43

ORIGINAL.

COMPLETE INSPECTION CERTIFICATE

I certify that I inspected, on the date below, the following lot of hay and that the class, quality, and condition thereof were as stated below:

Located at .... Gillespie Switch, Kansas .... Date August 23, 1928

Amount ...... Carlot ...... Identification ...... Sante Fe 10498

Grade and class ...... U. S. No. 2 Leafy Alfalfa

Fees $2.50   Charges none   Total $2.50   *A. Hayman*
Inspector.

This certificate is issued in compliance with the regulations of the Secretary of Agriculture governing the inspection of hay pursuant to the Act making appropriations for the U. S. Department of Agriculture, and is receivable in all courts of the United States as prima facie evidence of the truth of the statements therein contained. This certificate does not excuse failure to comply with any of the regulatory laws enforced by the United States Department of Agriculture.

FIGURE 112.—Federal certificate for a complete inspection of a car lot of hay

the previous year. The full benefit of these facilities can not be obtained, however, unless their use is combined with sound business practices.

No set of standards nor any method of inspection can prevent business disputes or losses if sales contracts are loosely or improperly drawn or parties to the contracts are not careful to comply fully with all their terms. Sometimes parties to inadequate contracts call upon the Department of Agriculture for assistance in obtaining settlements. Usually the department can not be of much service in such cases, as it has authority only to promulgate standards of quality and condition for hay and to provide an impartial and disinterested application of these standards through the Federal inspection service.

The United States hay standards provide definite quality descriptions for most of the commercial classes and grades of hay. The addition of indefinite qualifying terms or statements should be avoided. Such qualifications are often susceptible of several interpretations, depending on the viewpoint of the individual. Contracts containing them are frequently little better than those made on the basis of indefinite descriptive terms such as "pea-green leafy alfalfa" or "good feeding hay." Federal hay inspectors certificate the class and grade of lots of hay only according to the United States standards when such standards apply. Consequently a Federal hay-inspection certificate can not be of greatest value in settlement of disputes in connection with contracts if qualifying terms are added to the United States standards any more than when sales are,made on the basis of descriptive terms.

Necessity of Precision in Contracts

The place at which the grade of a lot of hay is to be determined should always be stated clearly in the sales contract. Too often the contract merely calls for a certain grade of hay, without specifying the point at which the hay is to meet the requirements of that grade. Sometimes in such cases the shipper obtains and furnishes the buyer a Federal certificate of complete inspection at shipping point or at some point en route showing the hay to be of contract grade at the time the inspection was made, but when the hay reaches destination it is found to be of some other grade because it is musty or hot or for other reasons. Such cases usually result in controversies which are difficult of settlement because the contract fails to state where the grade was to be determined.

If the buyer is willing to accept shipping-point grades and assume the risk of a change of grade in transit, the contract should state that it is made on the basis of Federal inspection at shipping point or on shipping-point grades. If destination grades or inspection are to govern, the contract should be worded accordingly.

Railroad trackage conditions at many terminal markets and other consuming points are such that only partial or car-door inspections can be made of hay received. Partial inspections are of little value unless shippers load cars uniformly throughout. Unevenly loaded cars usually result in unpleasant recriminations. When partial inspection of a car of hay indicates that it is of the grade purchased and the buyer accepts it or forwards it to some other point and then finds on unloading that the hay in the ends of the car is of a lower grade than that in the doorway, he is inclined to feel that he has been imposed upon by the shipper regardless of whether the car was intentionally loaded in that way.

Complete Inspection Preferable

If hay is sold on the basis of shipping-point inspection, contracts should state that Federal certificates of complete inspection are to be furnished, unless both parties are willing to accept partial inspections. Failure to have a clear understanding on this subject often leads to trouble, and sometimes the buyer is compelled to accept hay, some of which is not at all what he wanted, on the basis of a partial inspection.

It is always best, if possible, to obtain Federal inspection on hay sold on the basis of United States standards, but sales can be made on the basis of United States standards without obtaining inspection. On September 1, 1928, there were 74 licensed Federal hay inspectors, stationed at important central hay markets, shipping points, and United States Army posts. Thus Federal inspection is available in connection with a large portion of the hay commerce of the country, but hay is shipped between many points where inspection service can not now be readily obtained. If such sales are made on the basis of United

States standards, the parties to such contracts have a clear, easily interpreted description of the quality of hay sold. Then, if any question is raised of whether the hay fills the requirements of the designated grade, the nearest Federal hay inspector may be called in at relatively small expense to inspect the hay and settle the controversy. Lists of Federal hay inspectors may be obtained from the Bureau of Agricultural Economics at Washington or from Federal supervising hay inspectors in Atlanta, Chicago, Kansas City, San Antonio, Salt Lake City, or Los Angeles.

K. B. SEEDS.

HIDES and Skins to Be Classed and Graded Under U. S. Standards — The simplest way to realize the reasons for standardized market classes and grades of hides and skins is to consider the present methods and practices of marketing these commodities. An established trade practice in marketing hides and skins is to attempt to describe them by naming their points of origin. This system involves the use of such terms as "big packer," "small packer," "city packer," "country packer," "city butcher," "wholesale butcher," "retail butcher," and "country." These and many other names in common usage can be combined under three general designations—(1) packer, (2) butcher, and (3) country hides and skins.

Packer hides and skins are taken off in establishments where the slaughtering is of a wholesale character. Men are usually employed exclusively to remove hides and skins; each worker has a specified task to perform, in which he becomes proficient. The resulting hides and skins are practically free from cuts and scores, are usually perfect in pattern (excepting those which are koshered or have the throat cut crosswise), are allowed the proper time for curing and are delivered out of the first salt in good condition, with a liberal tare allowance for moisture and manure.

Packer hides and skins are seldom allowed to freeze or to be exposed to excessive heat. Causes for decomposition are thereby reduced or minimized. They are salted a short time after their removal from the animals. These hides and skins can be procured in any desired weight and grade selections, which fact makes them attractive to the tanner. They form a superior product in dependable supply.

Butcher and country hides and skins are taken off by small butchers or by farmers in slaughterhouses and on farms. These men are usually not very proficient in skinning animals, so the hides and skins are frequently cut or scored and of an imperfect pattern. They are not likely to give the proper care and attention to the matter of cure or to have the proper facilities, and they frequently allow the commodities to be exposed to excessive cold or heat, which practice invites decomposition. Skulls, horns, tail bones, udders, sinews, dewclaws, and switches are not always removed. Dirty salt is often employed. Such hides and skins must be resalted and regraded by men engaged in the hide industry. This expense, as a rule, falls on the producer. As the relation of the raw hide or skin to the finished product is what determines its real value, the utmost care should be exercised by farmers and ranchmen in the process of skinning animals even at the expense of much time. Butcher and country hides and skins can seldom be procured in a variety of weight and grade selections unless the buyer goes to considerable trouble.

The Bureau of Agricultural Economics is about to formulate grade standards for these three major groups. Attention will be paid to the characteristics which each group or lot of hides and skins possesses rather than to names and points of origin. Every factor having an important bearing on the value of the commodities will be considered.

Hides in the Grubby Season

Many cattle hides taken from animals during the "grubby season" (December to May), are not suitable for harness, belting, upholstering, bag, case, and strap leather because of the holes caused by the grubs in the middle of the back, the most valuable part of the hide. Such hides can be used for sole leather, although there is some waste because of grub damage. Leather made from heavy calfskins is not suitable for women's shoes, but is adapted to men's and boys' shoes. Mens' heavy working shoes are made from cattle hides that weigh from 25 to 45 pounds. When leather with a clear grain is desired, butcher

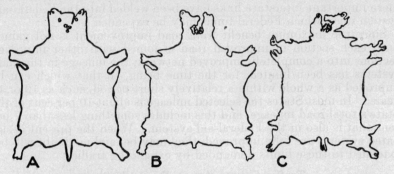

FIGURE 113.—Note the difference in pattern in the three hides. Because of the straighter edges and squarer shape the hide represented in A will produce a greater quantity of leather than B and considerably more than C

and country hides and skins are preferred, because they are not scratched or branded as much as packer hides.

Exact knowledge of the kind and grade of a lot of hides and skins offered for marketing is necessary to successful trading. There are two ways of obtaining such information—through personal inspection or through a reliable market news service. Personal inspection is expensive. No reliable news service can be maintained unless each group name stands for a definite thing at all times and places, and under all circumstances. This can be accomplished through standardization of grades.

Surveys of existing conditions in the hide-and-skin industry are under way. This work is in its infancy, but steady progress has been made. A tentative schedule of market groups is being subjected to various tests to determine its practicability. Through such work the Bureau of Agricultural Economics hopes to eliminate existing confusion by establishing uniform methods of grading, selecting, marketing and receiving all kinds, classes, and grades of hides and skins.

M. C. ROMBERGER.

HIGHWAY Needs Are At the crossroads on main highways of almost any State motorists are likely to find, these days, khaki-clad youngsters, pencil and pad in hand, whose duty it is, apparently, to count the vehicles as they pass. Occasionally they halt the drivers to ask, often with more good nature than diction, "Whereja from, and whereja goin'?"

In answering the questions operators of motor vehicles are helping materially to make road building more efficient and businesslike. They are taking part in a traffic census; and the traffic census is the indispensable first step in the orderly process of modern highway planning and improvement.

In all States the highway funds of the State are now expended by competent highway departments under expert engineering supervision; and definite systems of connected main highways have been designated for improvement, so that the taxpayer may know where his taxes will be spent. These are known as the State highway systems; and their more important interstate links have been welded into the Federal-aid system upon which Federal funds may be expended.

Since the maximum benefit from road improvement is not gained until each section of improved road is joined with other improved sections into a completely improved network, the mileage in the main systems has been limited, for the time being, to that which can be improved as a whole within a relatively short period, such as 10 or 15 years. In most States the selected mileage is about 10 per cent of the State's total road mileage, and this includes something less than 7 per cent that is also in the Federal-aid system. When the present designated systems are fully improved, they may be, and no doubt will be, extended to those limits demanded by expanding traffic.

Traffic Counts Attest Roads' Utility

How carefully these systems have been chosen, and how well they serve the needs of the large majority of people, is shown by the traffic counts. In Maine, for instance, the principal system includes 1,630 miles on which the traffic census shows there is an average daily travel of 1,044 vehicles. The remaining 21,474 miles in the State serve an average of only 70 vehicles a day. These figures demonstrate that the State's main highway systems, which include only 7 per cent of the total road mileage, accommodates more than half the entire movement of vehicles.

The rate at which the highway systems can be improved is fixed by the amount of money appropriated annually for the purpose. The first concern of the modern highway official is that there shall be set aside from each annual appropriation an amount sufficient to maintain the roads already built.

His next problem is to decide upon the order in which the various sections of the system shall be improved. In this he is guided by traffic maps which the census has enabled him to prepare. As the illustration shows (fig. 114), the roads on such a map are indicated by bands of varying width, and the width at any point represents, to a convenient scale, the average daily traffic at the particular point.

The maps show the order in which the roads should be improved according to their traffic importance and are an intelligent, indisputable, and businesslike answer to Tom, Dick, and Harry, each of whom asks that his particular road be improved before all others.

Traffic counts also indicate the type of pavement to be used on the various highways. According to highway engineers, there is "no best type of pavement." Each of the several types of surfaces has a proper place in the improvement of a system of highways. Even in the main systems of some of the States there are roads which serve a traffic that is not too great in volume or weight to be supported by a sand-clay surface, the lowest type surface. There are many roads which need no surfacing better than gravel, and many others which are adequately improved if surfaced with bituminous macadam.

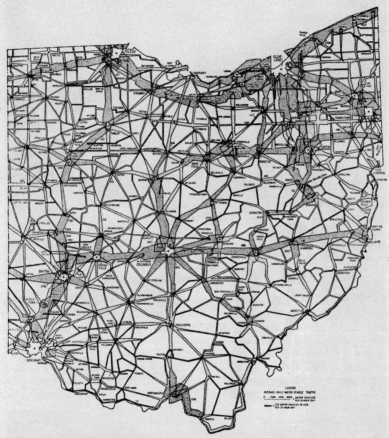

FIGURE 114.—Traffic map of Ohio. The width of the bands shows clearly the order in which the roads should be improved

However, the roads that serve the greatest traffic volume must be hard surfaced or paved with brick, concrete, sheet asphalt, or asphaltic concrete to enable them to withstand the pounding of the thousands of vehicles that ply over them.

Operating Savings Should Repay Investment

Businesslike road building, according to the engineer, is based on the principle that the money invested in the improvement of a road shall be repaid by the savings in the cost of operating vehicles which the improvement makes possible.

Careful experiments show that the cost of operating a motor vehicle varies according to the character of the surface over which it is driven —the harder and smoother the surface the lower the operating cost. The experiments show that gasoline consumption, vehicular wear and tear, and the wear of tires are greatest on unimproved roads. They are less when the road is surfaced with gravel or sand-clay or macadam, and least when a hard smooth pavement is provided. Between the cost of operating a passenger automobile over an unimproved earth

FIGURE 115.—Traffic counting on a main road in Connecticut. The traffic census enables the engineer to make a traffic map for his guidance in the work of improvement

road and over a smooth pavement the differential may be as high as 2½ cents a mile. Between the unimproved road and the macadam surface the operating cost differential is smaller, and the softer sand-clay surface affords a still smaller yet quite appreciable saving.

Multiplied by the number of vehicles that use the road in the course of a year, these small savings reach suprisingly large totals which, on the time-honored principle that a penny saved is a penny earned, are the highway's earnings turned back to the public which built it.

In the course of a year a mile of paved road that carries a traffic of 10,000 vehicles a day will earn about $90,000 which is more than twice its cost of construction and many times its annual cost of about $4,500—a remarkably good investment.   Reduce the daily traffic to 1,000 vehicles, and the annual earnings are still about twice the annual cost; but lay the same pavement on a road that carries only 400 vehicles a day, and its annual earnings will not amount to as much as the annual cost.   Under this traffic the pavement becomes a losing investment.

Roads Where Traffic Is Light

There are thousands of miles of roads, even of those included in the main highway systems, that serve no more than 400 vehicles a

FIGURE 116.—Businesslike road building pays. On the heavily traveled highways motorists may save more than the cost of the most expensive pavement in a single year

day.   For these roads, paved surfaces are not justified.   For them it can readily be shown that the smaller savings made possible by a gravel surface will produce in a year a total in excess of the smaller annual cost of the road; and so, for them, the businesslike engineer says the gravel surface is best.

By such methods, employed by the State highway departments and the Federal Bureau of Public Roads, the main highways of the country are now built with businesslike precision; and the results are quite different from those obtained by the old haphazard, happy-go-lucky methods.

H. S. FAIRBANK.

HOG-CHOLERA Losses Can Be Much Reduced by Sanitary Measures   No one is so vitally interested in the prevention of losses from hog cholera as the farmer who raises hogs for the market, for every hog that dies of cholera reduces his income.   Naturally the farmer is interested in protecting the health of his herd, and the majority of farmers do so, as far as they know.   However, there is a lack of uniformity in the methods employed by different hog growers and many do not seem to have any fixed plan.

Some fail to attain success in maintaining the health of their animals, through inexperience in hog raising. Many have inherited faulty notions concerning the nature of the hog, its habits, feed, and care. These individuals do not accept advice readily. Others do not seem to comprehend that the word "sanitation" is applicable in any way to a hog. One of the most deplorable and prolific causes for losses from cholera is carelessness on the part of hog owners or failure to apply the knowledge which they have acquired through reading, observation, and experience. The development of the immunization treatment against hog cholera by the Bureau of Animal Industry was a boon to the swine industry, but too many hog growers expect this treatment to save their hogs regardless of the condition of the animals when treated; they do not seem to realize that anti-hog-cholera serum and hog-cholera virus must be used under favorable conditions to be efficacious.

Sanitation Is Aid to Health

As a general rule the farmer should do all that he reasonably can to maintain the health of his herd through breeding, feeding, and sanitary measures, and apply the immunization treatment as a reserve measure when danger of cholera threatens. Of course, it is realized that there are densely hog-populated sections of the country where hog cholera appears every year, which makes it necessary to apply the immunization treatment systematically each year.

A healthy hog is better able to resist disease or the reaction of the hog-cholera virus administered with serum than the hog whose vitality has been lowered through faulty feeding, bad care, disease, or parasitic infestation. During the last year there was reported from different sections of the country an increased prevalence of mange, necrotic enteritis, hog flu, pneumonia, rickets, and parasitic infestation. The complaints were usually associated with faults of environment which could be corrected. Most farmers of the North know that from the health standpoint there are advantages in late farrowing. They know that clean, dry, properly ventilated, and well-lighted sleeping quarters are conducive to health, and they appreciate the importance of an abundant, constant supply of clean drinking water and a balanced ration. Much valuable information has been accumulated on the importance of a balanced ration, but there is yet much to learn concerning the reaction of the hog's system to different feeds, especially the relation of this reaction to disease, and the immunization treatment against hog cholera.

Diseases Sometimes Mistaken for Hog Cholera

Frequently growing hogs are affected with preventable diseases which produce a sufficient decline in resistance to make the use of virus in the simultaneous treatment hazardous. It is worthy of note that necrotic enteritis has been reported in a large proportion of the herds where the results from immunization had not been satisfactory. Necrotic enteritis is regarded as a filth-borne disease, as it is found most frequently among swine that are confined to insanitary quarters. The information we have on the subject suggests the importance of providing decent living conditions for hogs. Medicinal treatment for necrotic enteritis is unsatisfactory. A change of feed and the removal of the animals to clean uncontaminated quarters, preferably a suitable pasture, is the most satisfactory way of treating this disease.

Hog flu is an infectious herd disease which appears most frequently among swine that have been exposed to cold, stormy weather in the late fall or early winter. The exposure may result from excluding the animals from shelter, allowing them to nest in manure piles, under the barn, or failure to control drafts in hog houses that are otherwise suitable for the purposes intended. These conditions are favorable also for producing pneumonia. Necrotic enteritis, hog flu, and pneumonia are examples of diseases which frequently result from carelessness on the part of hog owners in not providing reasonably sanitary living conditions for their animals. These and other diseases have sometimes been mistaken for hog cholera. When the simultaneous treatment is administered to swine thus affected, losses from cholera may occur, as the conditions are not favorable for the establishment of immunity. The farmer's mistake is in allowing conditions to exist that are responsible for the appearance of diseases, among his hogs, which might be mistaken for hog cholera.

Heavy infestation with parasites, especially internal parasites, lowers the vitality of hogs and renders them less favorable subjects for immunization. Losses from hog cholera may result through breaks in immunity in hogs treated by the simultaneous method when their vitality is thus lowered. What is known as the McLean County system of swine sanitation has shown a practical way to reduce to a minimum the injurious effects of parasites.

Delay in Immunizing May Be Costly

A valuable help in the control of hog cholera is to maintain the health of hogs so that they are in fit condition to receive anti-hog-cholera serum and hog-cholera virus when it becomes necessary to immunize them.

It is important that hogs be immunized promptly when immunization seems advisable. One day's delay may result in the spread of infection, resulting in the ultimate loss of more than enough hogs to pay for treating the entire herd. Anti-hog-cholera serum is a preventive for hog cholera, not a cure, and it is of no value in the prevention or treatment of any other disease. Frequently losses are increased through administering virus in connection with serum to pigs affected with diseases other than cholera. This suggests the advisability of employing a competent veterinarian immediately when disease appears in a herd, as he is qualified by education and experience to diagnose the diseases of swine and to prescribe proper treatment.

The farmer may help reduce losses from hog cholera by raising healthy herds, by avoiding the known modes of spreading hog cholera, by following professional advice, and by giving special attention to his herd for at least two weeks immediately following immunization. Farmers' Bulletin 834-F, Hog Cholera, contains information in regard to the nature of hog cholera, the ways by which it is spread, the immunization treatment, care of herds following immunization, and other helpful information.

U. G. HOUCK.

HOG Profits Greatly Affected by Heavy Death Rate of Pigs   The infant mortality among pigs is high. About 40 per cent of the pigs which are farrowed die before they reach the time of marketing. Most of these deaths occur during the suckling period, when the pigs are small. However, the cost of the feed consumed by the breeding herd during the gestation and suckling periods must be borne proportionately by the surviving members of the litter. Thus, weanling pigs from large litters begin their fattening period handicapped by a smaller initial cost than similar pigs weaned from small litters. While the deaths after weaning are relatively few, they represent a direct loss of the feed which the pigs have consumed. It should be clear that the profits of hog production are affected greatly by the deaths which occur between the time of farrowing and marketing.

Interesting facts concerning pigs in the Corn Belt are shown in the table. Spring pigs and fall pigs have about equal chances of reaching the consumer—60 out of 100. About 40 per cent of the pigs farrowed die at some stage of the process of production. Deaths among spring pigs before weaning are greater than among fall-farrowed pigs, but deaths after weaning are greater among the fall pigs. Explanation of this difference is largely a question of weather. The suckling period of spring pigs comes during the spring, when the weather is cold and wet. The fall litters suckle during the more favorable weather of August, September, and October. However, after weaning, the spring pigs enjoy the fine summer and autumn weather, whereas the fall pigs must fatten during the cold of winter.

Differences in Death Rates

Some interesting differences in death rates for spring pigs farrowed during the four principal farrowing months are also shown. There are fewer deaths before weaning among late-spring than early-spring pigs and the reverse is true for deaths after weaning, largely because of weather. The wet weather of late spring apparently is not as hazardous for late-spring pigs as the cold weather of early spring. After weaning the fattening period of late-spring pigs usually extends into the following winter, when deaths from cholera, pneumonia, and "piling up" in quarters tend to increase.

The percentage of pigs raised to maturity is influenced by the size of litter farrowed. Table 8 shows that the number of pigs farrowed per litter decreases as the time of farrowing becomes later. The breeding herds farrowing late-spring pigs usually have a much larger proportion of gilts to old sows. Losses are less for late-spring pigs, but the number of pigs raised per litter is greater for early-spring pigs because of the larger litters farrowed. Young gilts can hardly be expected to farrow as large litters as old sows, but their selection from large litters will tend to increase their ability to farrow large litters.

The time of farrowing is largely determined by the system used in the production of hogs. If the two-litter system is used, the spring pigs should be farrowed in February and March so the fall pigs can be farrowed and weaned before too late in the fall. If the one-litter system is used the pigs may be farrowed in late spring. The control of deaths among pigs depends largely upon housing and care. The problem differs somewhat for different classes of pigs and in the various stages of the pork-production process. The reduction of death losses is a factor in cost of production which will repay every hog producer for his effort.

TABLE 8.—*Farrowing and death records of spring and fall litters of pigs* [1]

Farrowing date	Number of records	Average number litters per farm	Number of pigs per litter					Per cent		
			Farrowed	Weaned	Deaths		Raised	Deaths		Raised
					Before weaning	After weaning		Before weaning	After weaning	
February	39	9.92	8.92	5.57	3.35	0.28	5.29	37.6	3.1	59.3
March	194	12.65	8.32	5.23	3.09	.38	4.85	37.1	4.6	58.3
April	179	14.47	7.70	5.21	2.49	.52	4.69	32.3	6.8	60.9
May	60	19.37	7.22	5.24	1.98	.48	4.76	27.4	6.7	65.9
Average of spring litters	472	13.97	7.91	5.25	2.66	.45	4.80	33.6	5.7	60.7
August	52	9.42	8.42	5.66	2.76	.50	5.16	32.8	5.9	61.3
September	108	8.21	8.24	5.66	2.58	.84	4.82	31.3	10.2	58.5
October	31	6.42	7.90	5.89	2.01	.73	5.16	25.4	9.3	65.3
Average of fall litters	191	8.25	8.26	5.69	2.57	.72	4.97	31.1	8.7	60.2

[1] Henry County, Iowa, and Warren County, Ill _____ 2 years.
McLean and Woodford Counties, Ill _____ 2 years.
Humboldt County, Iowa _____ 3 years.
West central Indiana _____ 5 years.

OSCAR STEANSON.

HOG Profits Increased by Proper Selection of Foundation Animals — Success in the hog business depends not only on the use of approved methods of feeding and management, but to a large extent on the ability of hogs to utilize feeds for the most profitable and economical gains.

There is no one best breed; in fact more difference often occurs among individuals within the breed than among breeds themselves. In the selection of a breed, consideration should be given to the one most common in the neighborhood. Such a selection helps to insure a near-by market for the exchange or sale of breeding animals. When a locality is noted for outstanding animals of a certain breed it becomes an attraction for prospective buyers for both breeding animals and fat hogs. The question of personal likes and dislikes for a breed may also be a controlling factor. A person will take more interest in the care, feeding, and management of a breed that strikes his fancy than in one which he dislikes because of some prejudice.

Qualities Desirable in Breeding Animals

It is desirable to purchase purebred hogs when founding a herd rather than buy grade hogs and expect to improve the herd by the use of purebred boars. The fact that hogs multiply rapidly makes it possible to purchase a few good, purebred sows at little additional cost and within a few years have a uniform herd of considerable size.

The breeding of purebred livestock has tended to establish definite characteristics. The fact that pure breeding is in itself a selective mating of individuals of known ancestry tends to eliminate the less meritorious animals. Breeders of purebred hogs have developed their herds not only from the standpoint of type, size of litter, early maturity, and similar qualities, but also from the standpoint of their ability to produce rapid and economical gains.

The question whether the sow or boar has the greater influence on the offspring is still open for discussion. Equal attention should be given to the selection of the sow and boar.

Points of a Good Sow

The sows should be of uniform type and conformation for the breed. (Fig. 117.) Above all she should show refinement, femininity, and docility. She should possess a neat-appearing head, rather thin

FIGURE 117.—A good foundation sow that embodies the qualities desirable in a breeding animal

neck, good, clear eyes with plenty of width between them, and ears of fair size but not obstructing the vision. She should be upstanding, with sufficient daylight underneath the body to prevent the udder from dragging during the suckling period. The legs should be well placed under the four corners of the body. They should have good-quality bone, enabling her to support her weight at all ages and move about freely and easily. The pasterns should be short and straight. There should be plenty of width between the front legs, indicating chest capacity. The back should be well arched to furnish strength. She should be well muscled over the loin with full, well-rounded hams. The body should be uniform in width, carrying back evenly from the shoulders to the hams. There should be good depth of body, indicated by a large heart girth. The udder should be well developed, with at least six well-developed teats in each of the two rows.

Selection of the Boar

When possible, final selection of the boar should not be made until he is at least 6 months of age. Any serious defects that may develop should be in evidence at that age. It is often advisable to purchase a

FIGURE 118.—A tried boar of desirable type with a record of transmitting uniformity to his offspring

tried boar (fig. 118) of the right type and conformation, if one can be obtained at a reasonable price. Be sure that the boar is particularly strong in those characters in which the sows are weak in order that

FIGURE 119.—Sow (left) and three of her daughters, showing uniformity of type and conformation

their faults may be less likely to be transmitted to the offspring. Type, quality, and masculinity are three essentials necessary for a herd boar. He should possess the same general type as that of the sows in the herd.

Quality is indicated by a smooth covering of flesh, hair that has life to it as indicated by a glossy appearance, pasterns that are straight and show strength, a bone that is strong and of sufficient size to carry the weight at all ages, and a hide that is mellow and pliable, with freedom from wrinkles or creases in the sides or shoulders.

Masculinity is the character that distinguishes the boar from the sow in appearance. The head should be massive in size, with plenty of width between the eyes. The neck should be short, thick, and well crested. He should be snugly made over the shoulders, and smooth through the shield. The back should be well arched, the width carried back uniformly. The hams should be well rounded and full to the hocks. Constitution is indicated by heart girth as measured back of the shoulders. Chest capacity is indicated by the width between the front legs as viewed when one stands directly in front of the boar.

Attention should also be given to the disposition of the boar. A cross boar—that is, one inclined to fight, one difficult to manage, or hard to keep in a pen or pasture—is a dangerous animal to have in the herd. He should have a good disposition, and be easily handled and driven. Never trust a quiet boar at any time, as he may strike when least expected.

Finally after selection of the sows and boar which have met the desired standards of conformation and type as individuals, a study should be made of the record of their ancestors, through the pedigree, with special emphasis on the size of the litter. When possible, one should see the sire and dam of the animal to be purchased and note whether they are desirable in type and have uniformly transmitted that character to the offspring. (Fig. 119.)

J. H. Zeller.

HOGS Can Be Produced Profitably in Parts of Northern Great Plains
A comparison of the number of hogs in the northern Great Plains area with those in Corn Belt centers of production might easily lead a person unacquainted with conditions in the former region to believe that hog production there is unprofitable. As a matter of fact there are probably few sections of the country where pork production has yielded more profitable returns than in some sections of the northern Great Plains. Necessarily, the number of hogs there will always be comparatively small, owing to the fact that large areas of the land are better adapted to sheep and cattle ranges than to crop production. However, in many localities, especially along the eastern border of the area, and up the creek and river valleys to the westward, where corn and small grains are easily grown, conditions are peculiarly suitable for profitable pork production.

There has been a steady increase in the number of hogs in this general region for the last 20 years, and nothing indicates a change in this trend in the near future. The most important factor responsible for the increased number of hogs in the Northwestern States has been a trend away from the one-crop system of wheat farming to a more diversified agricultural system. Continuous cropping with wheat had caused loss of fertility, decreased yields, and the appearance of weed pests, and resulted in a trend toward larger acreages of corn and barley, and alfalfa and other pastures. An increased number of hogs on the farms has followed these changes in the cropping system, and has led many farmers to the discovery that they had overlooked many natural advantages for profitable swine production.

Since 1920 the corn acreage in North Dakota, Montana, and Wyoming has practically doubled, and the yield has been found to compare favorably with average yields for the entire country. During the same period the barley acreage in those States has increased about 50 per cent, so that an increasing quantity of feeding grains has been available. The small grains produced are usually of excellent quality and high feeding value. Barley grown there commonly weighs 50 pounds to the measured bushel, and oats often 36 or even 40 pounds a bushel.

Area Is Healthful for Hogs

The northern great plains area has been found to be a very healthful place to raise hogs. As the region is largely semiarid the cold, damp weather and frequent storms experienced in humid climates are unusual, with the result that losses from hog flu or pneumonia are light. The summer days are long, with a maximum of 16 or 17 hours of sunshine, a condition which is very desirable in swine production and especially advantageous for the young pigs. The isolation of one farm from another in the more sparsely settled localities is also an important factor affecting the healthfulness of the hogs, as parasites and infectious diseases are not so prevalent where there is little or no contact with herds of adjoining farms. At three Federal experiment stations in the area it has been found that the death losses in hogs, especially in suckling pigs, are considerably smaller than at experiment stations in the more humid regions.

Pastures play an important part in hog raising everywhere and alfalfa grows luxuriantly in the area described. Where there is sufficient moisture from either rainfall or irrigation, the alfalfa pastures are unsurpassed in carrying capacity, palatability, and in high-protein content. Alfalfa hay also is used to a considerable extent in winter feeding, so that only small quantities of high-priced protein feeds are needed. Sweet clover, field peas, and rye also are used as hog pastures to a lesser extent.

While it is true that hog raisers in the area are a long way from the central markets, this drawback is partially offset by the competitive nature of the available markets. The rapid increase in population on the Pacific coast in recent years has created a stable demand for hogs at the coast markets, whose attractive prices draw many hogs from the Northwestern States.

R. E. HUTTON.

_____

HONEY Has Valuable Food Properties But Is Low in Vitamins Honey is a wholesome natural food of great value in the diet, chiefly because of its high sugar content. Foods furnishing carbohydrates or sugars are essential as a source of energy in the body. A large proportion of carbohydrates or sugars present in food products are highly complex in character. When these foods are eaten the sugars must be broken up into the so-called simple sugars before they can be absorbed from the digestive tract and taken up by the blood stream. This is accomplished by the various ferments or enzymes of the digestive system.

The sugars found in honey are unlike those occurring in most other foods in that they are already in the form of simple sugars that can be easily digested and absorbed. For this reason honey is an excellent form of sweet for use in the diet of infants and those whose digestion is impaired because of illness or disease. Honey also contains a rather high percentage of minerals that are so necessary for health and well being. Most honeys contain a small amount of protein which seems to be of good quality.

With all of these valuable food properties to its credit honey would naturally be considered as a most excellent food. However, at the present time no statement concerning a food is complete unless some mention is made of vitamins.

The presence or absence of vitamins in foods is determined by feeding tests with small animals such as white rats and guinea pigs. Methods have been worked out that make it possible to determine the relative amounts of vitamins A, B, C, and D which a food may contain when a large number of tests are made. Rats are used to make the tests for vitamins A, B, and D, but are unsatisfactory for vitamin C, as they show no effects of a lack of this vitamin in their diet. Guinea pigs may be used for the vitamin C determination.

Vitamin Tests Negative

A total of about 350 rats and 26 guinea pigs were used in the course of this study on three samples of honey and one sample of honeycomb. The samples of honey represented the extremes of color variation— two being light-colored honeys and the other a very dark buckwheat honey. All of the tests made for each of the four vitamins were consistently negative. This was so even when the honey made up a large proportion of the diet.

The only conclusions that could be drawn from such results were that none of the honeys nor the honeycomb examined contained any trace of vitamins A, B, C, or D. The honeys came from widely separated localities and were very different in colors so that although only three samples were examined it seems safe to assume that a honey containing any appreciable amount of vitamins A, B, C, or D would be the exception rather than the rule.

HAZEL E. MUNSELL.

HORSE Malady Called Dourine Yielding to Eradication Program The eradication of dourine in horses of the several Navajo Indian reservations in the northeastern part of Arizona is being definitely accomplished. The area includes approximately 20,000 square miles of open or unfenced range territory on which there are fully 50,000 head of horses owned by Navajo and Hopi Indians. It is believed to be the last remaining area in the United States containing the disease.

The extensive, unfenced and scantily watered desert range areas of northeastern Arizona give ample opportunity for horses to travel long distances, which would permit the rather wide dissemination of this communicable disease of breeding horses and asses were it not for effective control measures.

Nature of the Disease

The character of dourine, the vast, unfenced ranges, the wild nature of the animals, and the great distances from points where eradication work is in progress to railway shipping stations present adverse conditions of the greatest magnitude. Dourine is a disease caused by the presence in the subject of a specific, microscopic, animal parasite. It is solely a disease of breeding horses and asses, manifesting itself, in the primary stage, as a local infection and in the secondary stage as a constitutional trouble with skin lesions, nervous disturbances, and extreme emaciation. It is always spread through the act of breeding. As the disease is chronic in nature and often very difficult to diagnose by clinical observation, it becomes necessary to resort to the laboratory method of detection to avoid overlooking cases that may possibly not show physical symptoms at the time of examination.

The general method of eradication of dourine in areas of the Navajo Indian reservation in northeastern Arizona consists in the following

FIGURE 120.—An improvised corral in a box canyon

procedure: The gathering of the animals from the open ranges and their confinement in corrals until such time as a laboratory blood specimen can be procured from each animal; the immediate destruction of animals manifesting clinical symptoms of the disease, together with positive reactors which have been so designated by the laboratory test as being affected with dourine; and the castration of all uncontrolled stallions.

Gathering the Horses a Difficult Problem

The complete gathering of horses from the vast, unfenced range areas such as exist in northeastern Arizona presented a difficult problem, but is being accomplished. For the gathering of the horses, range outfits consisting of from 6 to 10 Indians, mounted on horses, are used as round-up crews. These outfits, which are provided with the necessary camping equipment and supervised by experienced veterinarians, are located at designated points, usually at or near some permanent corral, watering place, or other convenient concentration point. On each drive or round-up, which requires from one to three days to complete, the riders cover certain designated areas, usually a locality within a radius of from 15 to 20 miles of camp, driving all horses in the territory covered by the ride toward the testing corral where they are confined upon arrival. When permanent corrals are not available, it becomes necessary to locate temporary, improvised inclosures for confining a herd of horses while blood samples are being drawn. When possible, under such circumstances, a deep canyon may be selected. When horses are so confined, the sides of the canyon must be sufficiently abrupt so as not to permit the escape of the horses. (Fig. 120.)

Lariat ropes are stretched across the canyon at distances, allowing sufficient space between the ropes to confine the herd of horses to be tested. Strips of burlap sacking material or the highly colored

FIGURE 121.—A desert refrigerator for blood samples. Evaporation from cloths and wet sand cools the bottles

Navajo blankets are suspended from the ropes stretched across the canyon; wild or untamed range horses will seldom attempt to pass through or over these man-made obstructions. It may be necessary at times, in addition to these improvised obstructions, to station mounted Indians to assist in confining the herd of horses within the inclosures. Canyons having a sandy bottom are preferred, as they help to prevent injuring the horses, when the animals are cast and tied or bound for the branding and securing of the blood samples.

Taking the Samples

After being confined in the corral the animals are usually lassoed or roped, cast, and tied, when a veterinarian secures approximately 3 ounces of blood from the jugular vein through an aspirating needle into a previously sterilized bottle. The bottles containing the blood are immediately placed in a shaded and protected place (fig. 121) just outside the corral and the blood is there allowed to coagulate or clot under as low a temperature as is possible to obtain through a rapid water evaporation process. The reduction in temperature is satisfactorily accomplished through placing the bottles containing the blood in wet sand, shaded with a large piece of burlap sacking material kept constantly saturated with water and suspended just above the bottles, thus allowing the moistened air to pass around the bottles and cooling them by evaporation. From this blood, after coagulation, about one-half ounce of the liquid portion or serum is poured into a small bottle; a suitable preservative is added and the bottle then tightly corked, properly labeled, and packed for shipment to the pathological laboratory of the Bureau of Animal Industry at Washington, where the serum receives the blood test for dourine. Telegraphic reports are received from the bureau laboratory at Washington concerning the results of the tests as rapidly as they are completed, and animals designated as positive reactors, and hence as being affected with dourine, are thereafter destroyed as soon as possible.

In the outlying districts where the serum samples are obtained it is not unusual for boxes of serum samples to be transported a distance as great as 200 or more miles before finally reaching the railway shipping point from which the material is shipped to the laboratory. Some of the districts are, in fact, as much as 50 miles from the nearest mail-stage route. This distance must be traveled with a team and wagon and the boxes of serum further continued over as many as two different mail-stage routes before they finally reach the nearest railway shipping point. Such difficulties are overcome through the utmost care in packing the serum samples to withstand the long inland transportation hauls, and advance arrangements must be made for the transfer of boxes in order to avoid any unnecessary delay in the samples reaching the railway shipping station.

During the testing of horses each horse is fire-branded with a permanent mark of identification to act as a check on animals tested and as a definite means of determining that no horses remain unexamined. At the time the blood samples are drawn from the horses in the corral all stallions of the age of 2 years or over, which are not being kept under definite quarantine control, are castrated. Since dourine is a disease of breeding horses, the gelding of stallions constitutes a very important factor in preventing the further dissemination of the disease on open ranges, such as are found in the Navajo Indian Reservation.

Affected Herds Are Retested

The examination and testing of horses for dourine on the Navajo Indian Reservation in Arizona is almost exclusively accomplished during the spring and summer months when the weather and range feeding conditions and the physical state of the livestock permit the work to be done to best advantage. Herds of horses in which dourine is found to exist are retested within a period of from 30 to 60 days in order that no affected animals, which did not show a positive reaction to the test when first applied, possibly because of recent infection, may escape discovery. Usually a second test is sufficient to effect positive designation of all diseased horses, though in some instances a third and fourth test become necessary. It frequently also becomes essential to make repeated search of ranges to determine definitely that all horses have been brought in for examination and testing, since in some instances the Indian owners do not fully realize the importance of testing all horses, especially if some of them should perchance be considered favorite animals. In certain cases the cunning instinct of a few old, untamed horses, particularly range stallions, makes it very difficult or nearly impossible to get the horses into a round-up drive. After repeated unsuccessful attempts to drive such animals into a round-up herd, it may become necessary to resort to catching them by a method of relay riding or through the use of a specially devised trap corral at watering places or at salt licks.

Dourine-affected Indian horses are eliminated by slaughter. The Federal Government pays Indian owners an indemnity, based on appraised value, for all horses destroyed on account of the disease.

With the complete eradication of dourine in horses on the Navajo Indian reservations and the elimination of many otherwise worthless breeding horses, through the castration of stallions, the Indians are aided in breeding better, though perhaps fewer, horses. The reduction in numbers of worthless horses likewise serves a further useful purpose—that of permitting the utilization of the ranges for more profitable enterprises, such as the raising of sheep and cattle, which have heretofore proved to be highly remunerative to these Indians.

F. L. SCHNEIDER and
H. E. KEMPER.

HORSES of United States Supply Foreign Demand for Edible Horse Meat   An adequate supply of horses is an asset of inestimable value to any nation. It is an indispensable service which these animals furnish in the everyday activities of agriculture, commerce, and recreation and through the utilization, in the arts, of their by-products and of

FIGURE 122.—Semiwild horses collected for conversion into wholesome horse meat

their flesh as food. In some of the foreign countries where the supply of beef, pork, and mutton is limited, horse meat is consumed by the people, who regard it as an acceptable substitute for other meat. This practice has long prevailed, and while horses have contributed somewhat liberally to the meat supply in parts of Europe, yet practically no horse meat has been consumed as human food in the United States.

During two periods the United States has been called upon to supplement the foreign demand for horse meat. The first period covered the years 1898–1904, when horses and ponies in the Northwest were slaughtered under Federal control in one plant at Linton, Oreg. During that period 12,700 of these animals were slaughtered, and 984,700 pounds of horse meat were exported for food. Since then a number of plants in various parts of the United States have operated intermittently under local control, with a view to encouraging the

FIGURE 123.—Fresh horse meat which has received Government inspection and been found to be fit for human food

domestic consumption of horse meat. The price of choice cuts ranged as low as 10 cents a pound; yet this inducement proved insufficient to maintain the business when the cost of beef, pork, and lamb receded. In the absence of competent inspection, the freedom from tuberculosis has placed the raw meat of horses in a commanding position as feed for carnivorous animals.

Federal Inspection Again Authorized in 1919

Again, during and immediately following the World War, it was represented through various channels that great numbers of horses in the West were worthless for the usual purposes and were consuming range grasses which should be utilized by other livestock. At that time there was an urgent demand in the United States for meat at a reduced price. There was also prospect of supplying horse meat for European markets.   In response to these representations, Congress enacted legislation in July, 1919, providing for Federal inspection of equine meat under conditions similar to those prescribed for the meat of other animals.   The law, which is still in force, is construed to apply only to horses (fig. 122) and not to mules, burros, or other solipeds.

Under the provisions of the law, the transportation of undenatured horse meat involving interstate or foreign commerce, whether the product is intended for human consumption or for feeding animals, is not permitted without Federal inspection.   (Fig. 123.)   On account of the existence of certain diseases and abnormal conditions peculiar to horses, the inspection, both ante mortem and post mortem, differs somewhat from that of other meat-producing animals.   The veterinary inspectors must be ever on the alert for glanders, dourine, strangles, and azoturia, as well as other diseases and inflammatory conditions. Fresh horse meat which has received Government inspection and been

FIGURE 124.—Horse meat in tierces bearing the export stamp which is the Government's guaranty that the product was derived from healthy animals and prepared under sanitary conditions

found to be fit for human food is marked by the application of a harmless green fluid with a hexagonal brand.   The export containers bear Government stamps and are accompanied with official certificates of distinctive wording, all of which are green in color, readily to distinguish horse meat from other meat.

Production of Horse Meat Increasing

During the nine years since the enactment of the law 211,447 head of horses have been slaughtered under Federal inspection, and 24,190,894 pounds of horse meat have been exported.   As evidence of the growing importance of the industry it is of interest to note that more than

100,000 horses were collected and converted into wholesome horse meat last year. The foreign demand for this commodity is practically limited to horse meat in tierces (fig. 124) bearing the export stamp, which is the Government's guaranty that the product was derived from healthy animals and prepared under sanitary conditions. A substantial business has been developed through canning horse meat with other ingredients for dog and fox feed in this country, but such products must be prepared under Federal inspection or in a manner to make them unsuitable for human food before they are permitted to enter interstate or foreign commerce.

R. P. STEDDOM.

HOUSE-FLY Control Is Best Accomplished by Preventing Breeding The common house fly has come to be looked upon almost universally as a dangerous carrier of disease as well as an annoying pest. Unfortunately, many efforts toward control of this insect are misdirected, with corresponding disappointment in results.

The keynote to control of the house fly is prevention. Of what avail are fly-swatting campaigns in which hundreds of flies may be killed, when tens of thousands of flies are bred in uncared-for manure piles, hog pens, open privies, and cesspools? Although thorough screening of houses and places where food is handled and sold is essential until there has been more general adoption of sound sanitary practices, the screening only partially and ineffectually guards the individual against these germ-laden insects. Fly paper, fly poison, and swatters aid, but their application is rather limited. Fly sprays, such as kerosene extract of pyrethrum, are very useful for killing flies in buildings. Conical fly traps, properly placed and baited, are also valuable in cutting down the number of flies about premises. However, all of these are secondary to the elimination and treatment of breeding places.

Treatment of Breeding Places

All accumulations of fermenting vegetation and manure, especially horse, pig, and calf manure, should be disposed of by thinly scattering on fields at intervals of not to exceed three days. When this is impractical the material should be stored in fly-tight boxes or pits, fitted with fly traps to capture the flies which may hatch out. The application of borax or hellebore to the manure at regular intervals in comparatively small quantities is effective in destroying the fly larvae. Where large quantities of manure are produced daily it may be piled up in a long, compact rick, with vertical sides. The heat of the manure drives the larvae to the surfaces, where they can be destroyed with borax or crude petroleum.

Frequent search for breeding places, and their prompt elimination, coupled with spraying, trapping, and other measures here mentioned, will reduce trouble from house flies to a minimum, especially if the work is carried out on a community basis.

F. C. BISHOPP.

ICE Chest for Small Family May Be of Simple Construction   Frequently the farmer has need of an ice box to store quantities of household provisions for short periods of time or to hold several blocks of ice as supply for a small refrigerator. Figure 125 shows the essential points of construction. The inside dimensions will depend upon the size of box required. A 300-pound block of ice measures about 11 by 22 by 44 inches, and 4 inches more should be allowed to permit placing blocks of this size in the box. A box 26 inches wide, 48 inches long, and 36 inches deep, inside dimensions, will hold three blocks laid flat. If three half blocks

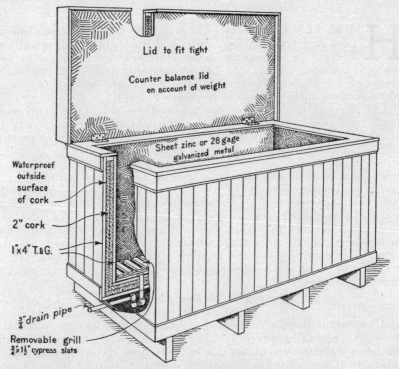

Lid to fit tight

Counter balance lid
on account of weight

Sheet zinc or 28 gage
galvanized metal

Waterproof
outside
surface
of cork

2" cork

1"x4" T.&G.

¾" drain pipe

Removable grill
¾x1½" cypress slats

FIGURE 125.—Ice chest for family use

are piled on top of each other and one half block is stood on edge, there will be space for two blocks of ice and 15 inches at one end for storage shelves. When several cans of milk are to be stored, a 36-inch width will be needed. The height will depend upon the size of the cans.

Insulation equivalent to 2 inches of sheet cork should be provided. When sheet cork is not available, other types of board insulation or granulated cork may be used by allowing for their thicknesses in the space indicated for 2-inch cork in the illustration.

T. A. H. MILLER.

IMMIGRANT Plants   About 30 years ago the department took
Hold Large Place   the first steps toward systematizing the
Among U. S. Crops   work of foreign-plant introduction. An office was established and charged with the
duty of searching the world for new plant immigrants, bringing them
in, testing them, and, if they were found worthy, propagating and distributing them in the United States. Other offices of the Bureau of
Plant Industry have also been active in plant-introduction work, particularly the follow-up phases involving the testing and extension of
crops. Since the day the first plant immigrant arrived under the system established 30 years ago, a record or sort of pedigree has been kept
of each and every entrant. The numbers now reach over 77,000 and
are increasing at the rate of 3,000 to 4,000 a year.

Many of the immigrants have their little day or hour and are never
again heard from. Others sink out of sight for a time and later achieve
great prominence.

Cereals, including our great grain crops, wheat, barley, oats, rye,
and rice, were naturally among the first crop plants to attract attention in the matter of improvement through the introduction of new
forms. During more than a quarter of a century of systematic
foreign introduction approximately 3,500 wheats have been introduced. Russia has yielded the largest number of wheats, but nearly
every country in the temperate regions of the earth has yielded its
store of worth-while things.

Introduction of Kharkof Wheat

Looking through our records we find, under F. P. I. No. 5641, a
wheat introduced in 1900 from Starobelsk, Kharkof, Russia. This
wheat was called "Kharkof," and was a bearded hard red winter wheat,
but came from a region much farther north than Turkey wheat, and
was therefore extremely hardy. Especially resistant to piercing, dry,
winter winds, where there is little snowfall, it was admirably adapted
for trial as a winter wheat in Minnesota, South Dakota, Iowa, northern Nebraska, Wisconsin, and perhaps southern North Dakota. The
Kharkof wheat was distributed widely in Kansas and other hard winter wheat States and later in Montana. It has made a place for itself
in our scheme of agricultural production, and from the evidence at
hand it appears that our farmers are now growing in excess of 2,000,000
acres of this wheat annually.

A Sample from the Crimea

About the same time that the Kharkof wheat was introduced, a
small sample of another wheat was sent in from the Crimea in Russia
under F. P. I. No. 6015. This was described as a very hard red winter
wheat. Nothing was heard from this wheat for a long time, and no
special distribution of it was undertaken by the department. A
small sample was sent to the workers at the Kansas Agricultural
Experiment Station, and selections were made from the progeny of
this sample. From these selections a promising wheat was secured
which was named Kanred. The popularity of the Kanred is due to
its high-yielding qualities and its resistance to rust. The area sown
to it is more than 4,000,000 acres.

33023°—29——25+

One of the largest introductions of wheats was of the so-called hard Russian or durums. There are more than 4,000,000 acres annually devoted to the production of these hard spring wheats at the present time, yielding around 50,000,000 to 85,000,000 bushels annually. The two outstanding varieties of the durum wheats are those introduced under the names of Arnautka and Kubanka.

Early Baart wheat (F. P. I. No. 5078) is another important wheat introduction, this time Australia being the country from which the immigrant came. It was first distributed to experiment stations, and most of this wheat now grown is the product of seed supplied to the Arizona Agricultural Experiment Station by this department. This wheat is found to be valuable for irrigated sections of Arizona and California, but it is also adapted to dry lands in Washington. Upward of one-half million acres are planted annually.

Of some of the more recent wheats, Federation (F. P. I. No. 38347) was introduced from Australia in 1914. It is a valuable spring wheat for southern Idaho and southeastern Oregon. About half a million acres of this wheat are annually grown. Hard Federation is another valuable wheat, introduced from Australia in 1915. This was first distributed in 1919, and about 50,000 acres now are grown annually. It is a high-yielding variety on dry lands. It has also produced very high yields in central Montana, where red wheat is now grown almost exclusively.

Such are a few of the wheats which owe their chief value to the fact that they, one and all, possess certain characteristics not possessed by older wheats we already had—characteristics which have added many millions of dollars each year to the wealth of our country.

Oats, Rye, and Barley Introductions

Other grain crops, such as oats, rye, and barley, while not of the same economic importance as wheat, nevertheless play a very vital part in American husbandry. One of the first important numbers of the oat family was introduced in 1901. This was the Sixty-Day oat (F. P. I. No. 5938), another Russian contribution. The Sixty-Day oat is now one of the most important varieties in the United States, particularly in the Corn Belt. Five million acres would probably be a fair estimate of the area annually sown to this variety and to varieties selected from it. Then there is the Swedish Select (F. P. I. No. 2788), introduced from Russia in 1899, and the Victory (F. P. I. No. 22306), introduced in 1908. From the first there is estimated to be approximately 4,000,000 acres annually planted, while of the second probably about 200,000 acres were grown.

Of barleys, six or eight varieties have found a place worthy of being classed in our list of Who's Who celebrities. The Club Mariout (F. P. I. No. 9877) came from Egypt in 1903. Beldi (F. P. I. No. 7583) is an Algerian barley. It came in in 1901. Hannchen (F. P. I. No. 10585) was introduced from Sweden in 1904. The Chevalier (F. P. I. No. 5473) was introduced in 1901. These several barleys have become permanently established in our American agriculture and are annually planted to the extent of 400,000 to 500,000 acres.

Practically the whole of our rice industry, largely developed in the last 25 years, is based upon introduced varieties. Some of the most important of these rices did not come in in the usual way, but are introductions nevertheless.

Grasses and Forage Crops

In shaping our abbreviated Who's Who in plant immigrants we must mention a few of the outstanding grasses and forage crops. More than 600 alfalfas have been brought in, and of these but 2 that are outstanding can be mentioned—namely, the Peruvian alfalfa (F. P. I. No. 3075), introduced from Peru in 1899, and the variegated alfalfa introduced a few years later. The Peruvian alfalfa has attained great popularity in certain parts of Arizona and in the interior valleys of California. It is also being grown extensively in New Mexico and in southern Texas.

Of other important forage crops, mention can be made of only a few. Sudan grass, a very valuable annual hay plant, was introduced from northern Africa in 1909. This plant immigrant almost immediately sprang into prominence, particularly in the southern Great Plains area. It is drought-resistant, hence has proved valuable in the drier sections of the Southwest. Probably no less than 100,000 acres are devoted to this crop, with an annual value of something like $10,000,000. Another spectacular group of immigrants in forage crops are the soy beans. Hundreds of varieties of soy beans have been brought in from many parts of the world. Manchuria has furnished a long list. Probably the annual aggregate value of the soy bean and its products in the United States will run close to $25,000,000.

No Who's Who of plant introductions would be complete without some reference to the crop plants that enter into our great textile industries. Cotton is the outstanding crop of this nature. Cottons have been introduced from many lands, but Egypt and Mexico have furnished varieties of great value. Acala cotton, discovered in southern Mexico something over 20 years ago, is now the predominant crop in the irrigated valleys of the Southwestern States, including the Imperial Valley of California and the adjacent cotton-growing districts in Mexico. The annual value of this introduction now exceeds $50,000,000. Egyptian cottons or selections from them also enter into our picture of valuable industries. Arizona has been enriched to the extent of many millions of dollars by these cottons during the last eight or nine years.

Fruit and Shade Trees

And now we come to a larger group of plant immigrants, whose impress on our daily lives is difficult to measure, and yet whose intangible benefits are worthy of careful consideration. These are the fruits, both tree and small fruits; shade trees, trees for shelter belts and windbreaks; and ornamental plants of many kinds. Just by way of indicating the numbers of some of these things—that is, the individual introductions—our records show 700 pears, over 600 apples, more than 500 peaches, approximately 450 plums, fifty-odd nectarines, over 600 oriental persimmons, more than 225 jujubes, 353 avocados, 498 mangoes, about 400 strawberries, and nearly 100 blackberries, with a long list of less important things.

B. T. GALLOWAY.

INSECT Control in National Parks Is Many-Sided Problem

Magnificent forests are one of the greatest attractions offered by most of our national parks. Glaciers, rivers, lakes, canyons, geysers, and other natural phenomena may be the main attraction that lures the sightseer, but he would not linger long if it were not for the surrounding forest that provides an appropriate setting for nature's objects of wonder or beauty. Forests form a living ground for the remnants of our once abundant wild life. They also conserve the water supply which produces the streams, falls, and lakes that make the wilderness areas so attractive to most people.

FIGURE 126.—Western yellow pine killed by the western pine beetle in Yosemite National Park

National-park forests differ from national forests, other Government forests, many State forests, and most private forests because they are not established for the value of the timber, forage, or water power that they produce, but because of their value for purposes related to recreation, wild life, natural history, and education. For this reason their value is greater, and more intensive and costly methods of protection are justified.

Damage by Insects

Among the greatest enemies of our national-park forests are destructive insects. The mountain pine beetle has killed large areas of lodgepole pine in Yosemite and Crater Lake Parks. It has killed many sugar pine trees in the Yosemite and Sequoia Parks, many western white pines in the Ranier and Glacier Parks, and many white-bark pines in the Glacier and Yellowstone Parks. The Black Hills beetle killed an average of 100,000 yellow pine trees per year in the Grand Canyon Park and the adjacent Kaibab National Forest during the period from 1919 to 1925. A less extensive though potentially as dangerous epidemic in the Rocky Mountain Park was put under control during the summer of 1928. Other species of bark beetles, such as the western pine beetle (fig. 126), the Douglas-fir beetle, and the Engelmann spruce beetle, have killed great numbers of trees in several of the parks. The spruce budworm defoliated and killed several thousand acres of Douglas-fir forest in the Roosevelt Canyon section of the Yellowstone Park between 1920 and 1925. During the same period the lodgepole sawfly and the lodgepole needle-tyer killed 12,000 acres of lodgepole pine in the west Yellowstone section of the Yellowstone Park. (Fig. 127.) Various engraver beetles have killed numerous lodgepole pines around camp sites and areas of geyser formation in the Yellowstone, and piñon pine on the Mesa Verde. Borers of several species have caused trouble in the Yellowstone to lodges built of unbarked logs.

FIGURE 127.—Spraying to control infestation of lodgepole pine needle-tyer in Yellowstone National Park

Forest-insect problems in the national parks naturally fall into four classes or general problems.

First is the problem of perpetuating the forest as a whole. In this case the individual tree is not important. We do not care if one tree dies, so long as another takes its place. A forest with many scattering dead trees appears perfectly normal when viewed as a whole. We do care, however, if an entire forest is devastated. Every effort should be made to prevent such epidemics as those of the Black Hills beetle in the Kaibab section of the Grand Canyon Park and of the needle-tyer and sawfly defoliators in the Yellowstone.

Forest Growth on Camp Sites

The second problem is one of keeping a forest growth, or at least some trees, on special areas, such as camp and administrative sites and along the highways. This is an important problem in all the parks. Camp sites in particular are nearly always chosen because of an attractive growth of trees. Soon, however, the continual packing of the soil and other unnatural results of intensive use by many more or less irresponsible human beings bring about an unhealthy condition which attracts insects and favors diseases that may cause the death of many trees. Camps with their buildings and other improvements represent large investments, and it is therefore important that the trees surrounding them be kept in as attractive a condition as possible. If the trees die, the camps must be moved, with consequent loss in investment and further destruction of natural resources, or else new trees must be grown to take the places of those lost. Trees along the highways are growing under more adverse conditions than those in the undisturbed forest. They are also more valuable, because they are viewed at closer range by the traveling public. Any poor condition of such trees is immediately noted and creates an unfavorable impression.

Third is the problem of protecting the individual tree, especially valuable because of its aesthetic, educational, or historical interest. Examples of this class are the giant sequoias of the Yosemite, General Grant, and Sequoia National Parks, and the best specimens of sugar pine and yellow pine in the Yosemite. These are irreplaceable and should be kept as they are as long as possible without regard to the cost. The more valuable the tree the greater the interest in it and the more it is apt to be injured unintentionally by its many admirers. Once harmed in any way it becomes more liable to attack by insects and must be watched closely so that preventive measures may be taken before it is too late.

Protection of Buildings

Fourth, we have the problem of protecting buildings constructed of forest trees felled and cut into logs. Many camps and administrative buildings are now made of logs, and this will probably always be the case. Where timber is plentiful, it is more economical to construct log buildings. Then, too, this type of construction is more appropriate, fitting, and attractive in a national park, where the glorification of nature is the main object. The great drawback, however, where buildings are made of unbarked and untreated logs, is the damage caused by various species of bark-boring and wood-boring grubs. These mine through the inner bark and outer wood until much of that part of the log is destroyed. The buildings themselves become unsightly when the bark becomes riddled with wormholes and falls off, and the dust from the boring continually falling down into rooms, especially dining rooms, is particularly annoying and disagreeable.

Conditions involving forest insects being as they are in the national parks, the only logical way to face the problem is to control the insects. Known methods of control should be introduced where feasible and new methods developed where the circumstances demand them. Values and conditions being different in national-park forests from those in forests primarily valuable for their timber, it is logical to suppose that correspondingly different methods of control can be used to advantage.

As with all insects, the method used to control a destructive forest insect depends upon its life history and habits. An insect that kills the tree by feeding on and destroying the foliage is usually fought by applying poison to the foliage or by applying some smothering or corrosive substance to the insect while it is on the foliage. An insect that kills the tree by boring through and destroying the living inner bark and outer wood, thus girdling it, is fought by destroying the insect while it is developing under the bark of an infested, dying tree. The insect may be destroyed by felling and burning the infested tree, or by felling it and turning it in the hot sun for several days, or by felling and barking it. This destruction of the insect prevents it from reaching full development, emerging, and attacking a living tree.

Interdepartmental Cooperation to Protect Parks

Forest-insect problems in the national parks are handled through interdepartmental cooperation. Forest entomologists of the Department of Agriculture investigate infestations by destructive insects and recommend feasible methods of protection; park administrators carry out these recommendations. Investigations of various infestations by insects have been made in the Sequoia, Yosemite, Crater Lake, Rainier, Glacier, Yellowstone, Grand Canyon, Mesa Verde, and Rocky Mountain Parks. Control work has been carried on in the Sequoia, Yosemite, Crater Lake, Yellowstone, Grand Canyon, and Rocky Mountain Parks.

Speaking generally, we may say that destructive infestations by insects in park forests may be expected at any time and that forest insects play about the same rôle in national-park forests as in other forests. The more intensive use of the trees, however, and their greater value for recreational, educational, and historical purposes, makes it both possible and justifiable to use more intensive and costly methods of control. This situation gives reasonable assurance that the national-park forests will be kept in as natural a condition as possible, thus fulfilling the main purpose of the creation and existence of the national parks.

H. E. Burke.

INSECT-PEST Survey Assembles Data from All Parts of Country

Unfortunately in one sense, fortunately in another, the great accumulation of data in the enormous field of entomology has led to a finer and still finer subdivision of the subject and to specialization on the part of those engaged in its investigation. This specialization has materially refined the methods employed and has made much more accurate the recorded observations on separate phases of the subject; it has, however, inhibited to a certain extent that broader viewpoint which looks upon the separate phenomenon as but a demonstration of the forces that are generally prevalent.

One of the various phases of this broader study of insects in their complete environment is that phase known as geographical distribution. Studies of distribution of the old type were usually compilations of the records of collections. This method of study resulted in a conception of geographical distribution which removed from that subject practically all its biological significance. A particular instance might be cited as an illustration. Distribution of the chinch bug was accepted as covering the entire North American continent east of the one hundredth meridian and south of the Great Lakes and the St. Lawrence River. However, an examination of the recorded data for the last 50 years on outbreaks of this insect of such magnitude as to attract the attention of entomologists and growers demonstrates very clearly that the normal chinch-bug association is located in a more or less elliptical area extending from the eastern third of Kansas diagonally in a northeasterly direction across central Missouri, southern Illinois, and southern and central Indiana to eastern Ohio, with a few isolated islands in the Carolinas, Florida, and elsewhere, where this insect again figures as a major component of a limited association.

In the case of insects of economic importance, these records of appearances in such numbers as to attract the attention of entomologists and growers are of decided usefulness in survey work. They probably constitute the best type of records of abundance that we are able to obtain with present methods and personnel.

Much Valuable Information Lost

It has been the custom in the past for the entomologists throughout the country to record these occurrences in their private notes or in the records of the institution with which they were connected. With changing conditions at the institutions and the dispersal of the observer's personal effects, the great mass of these data have been lost.

Realizing this, the entomologists of the country and the Federal Bureau of Entomology organized in 1921 the insect pest survey as a medium through which all workers could keep more closely in touch with current conditions as to the abundance of insects in the various parts of the country and as a repository for the miscellaneous field observations, which up to that time were available to but a limited few.

The object of the insect pest survey is to collect accurate and detailed information on the occurrence, distribution, ecology, and relative abundance of the insect pests throughout the States and to study these data from month to month and year to year with relation to the several factors that influence the degree of abundance of insects. The useful results to be obtained from a survey of this nature, maintained for a series of years, are manifold; we should be able to throw light on the reason of the cyclic and sporadic appearances of insect pests, the gradual shift of regions of destructive abundance, the limiting barriers to normal dispersal, and the directive influences that determine the paths of diffusion.

The survey, in its work of collecting scientific data on entomological conditions throughout the country, is voluntarily assisted by the entomological agencies now existing in the several States, including the entomologists of the State agricultural experiment stations, the agricultural colleges, State universities, plant boards, and entomological commissions, as well as the entomologists in the field laboratories of the several divisions of the Bureau of Entomology. The survey now has representatives in every State of the Union, and, by informal cooperative arrangements, is also receiving monthly summary notes of entomological conditions from the Dominion of Canada and occasional notes from Mexico, Hawaii, Haiti, and Porto Rico.

Representatives Report Monthly

These representatives report monthly to the survey on the conditions as to insect pests prevailing in their respective territories. The survey assembles these reports and issues a monthly bulletin of the conditions throughout the United States and Canada. These bulletins are distributed to the collaborators of the survey and to practically all of the educational institutions offering instruction in entomology, public libraries in many of the large cities, agricultural experiment stations, and other agencies that might make them available to those interested in such matters. Seven volumes of these bulletins have been issued up to the current year, making available more than 2,000 pages of data. This output, however, is but a small part of the total accumulation of data received by the survey, now consisting of considerably more than 71,000 separate records, covering 3,000 genera and 6,000 species of insects. These data are filed so that they are readily available for the use of any investigator working in a field covered by the activities of the survey.

For workers interested in the insects affecting particular plants, the survey maintains a cross-reference index to all of the insects known to affect any given plant.

Data Not Adequate for All Purposes

The data now being received are of value for broad general correlations, but, of course, for finer analysis of cause and effect a much more refined type of data will be necessary. The survey has realized this, but it has also realized the fact that its collaborators were not in a position to give detailed reports of the most desirable type. That these data, fragmentary as they are, are of value is indicated by the enormous number of requests that the survey received from commercial houses manufacturing or distributing insecticides and insecticidal apparatus, produce agencies dealing in commodities the production of which is affected by insects, and commercial entomological agencies interested in extending their activities into profitable fields. That it is of use to the official entomologist in forewarning him of insect troubles likely to develop in his own territory is evident from a statement in the annual report of the extension entomologist of New York State for 1926. Early in the spring of that year reports from certain Southern States, published in the survey bulletin, indicated clearly that the year was one of low abundance of aphids. With this warning in advance, he organized a survey of the fruit belt of New York and found that similar conditions prevailed in that State, and through the spray service conducted by his office he recommended that the insecticide for the control of aphids be eliminated from the usual list of materials for spraying in the spring, thus saving $250,000 in that year for the fruit growers ordinarily using this spray service.

One of the most spectacular phases of economic entomology in the last quarter of a century has been the terrific devastation wrought by insects recently introduced into this country from various parts of the world and the monumental efforts put forth for their suppression and the prevention of additional introductions. This work has broadened the scope of economic entomology in this country to include the insects of the world.

Classifying Scattered Observations

Observations have been made and are still being made by a large army of entomological workers scattered throughout the world and are recorded in a multitude of scattered publications. The insect pest survey is now bringing together these observations and classifying them in such a manner that in the near future it will be possible to make promptly available all of the survey data obtainable on any insect that might be introduced into the United States or intercepted at a port of entry, thus placing the entomologists of this country in a much better position to formulate a method of procedure.

With the gradual perfection of organization and the development of more accurate methods of survey in this country, the insect pest survey should become the repository of the most complete record ever assembled of insect conditions that have prevailed and are prevailing in the United States and to a great extent elsewhere in the world.

J. A. HYSLOP.

INSECT Poison Called Rotenone Highly Toxic But Costly at Present
Man has always been obliged to share his crops with worms and insects. In order to control these pests he has had to resort to the use of insect poisons.

The ideal insecticide kills all insects but is neither injurious to plants nor toxic to animals. Substances which are very effective as insecticides and not injurious to plants are found in the plant world. Among these are the pyrethrins, two similar but highly complicated chemical compounds found in the flower of a species of pyrethrum. Unfortunately they are too expensive to use on a large scale and there is little hope of preparing these or related substances artificially.

The root of a vine (*Derris elliptica*) that grows in the East Indies contains a substance called rotenone, which may be easily extracted and purified and which is extremely toxic to fish and to some insects. It has long been a practice in Borneo to throw the crushed roots of the Derris plant into rivers and then pick up the fish that it has killed or stunned.

Preparations of rotenone have lately appeared on the market in the form of a semisolid solution in fish oil. For use as an insecticide this is emulsified with soap and sprayed on plants or trees. In a few days, in contact with the soap and air, according to Japanese investigations the rotenone is completely decomposed, but in the meantime it destroys most soft-bodied insects with which it comes in contact or insects which eat the sprayed foliage or fruit, for rotenone is both a contact and a stomach poison. Its toxicity seems to be of about the same order as that of the pyrethrins or nicotine. Unlike arsenic and other mineral poisons, the toxic effect of which can not be destroyed and which are removed with difficulty, this natural organic insecticide automatically disappears.

Rotenone at present is too expensive for wide use, but there is some hope of producing it artificially or at least of developing a similar chemical product.

F. B. LA FORGE.

INSECTICIDE Research Develops a Promising Substitute for Nicotine
The insecticides of value in common use are made from poisonous plants, from suitable extracts of these, and from combinations of common mineral poisons. Pyrethrum, Derris, tobacco, sulphur, arsenic, fluorides, and a few other less commonly used insecticides fall into these classes.

Considerable effort has been put forth in testing a large number of substances used in the dye and pharmaceutical industries and in other industries in which chemistry elaborates new compounds. It was found in this way that paradichlorobenzene, naphthalene, carbon tetrachloride, and other products have insecticidal properties, but the haphazard experimentation has given meager results and must give way to a more scientific study of insect poisons.

Nature has indeed given us effective poisons in pyrethrum, tobacco, and Derris, and in other members of the plant kingdom which, as we might expect, are harmless to plant hosts although occasionally harmful to animals. The principal disadvantage of these poisons is their cost, for an insecticide must be cheap to permit its general use. Can the chemist synthesize these active poisons in the laboratory? Even in this age of synthetic rubber, camphor, dyes, and plastics the economic synthesis of these naturally occurring insect poisons presents great difficulties. Nicotine, it is true, has been synthesized at great cost in effort and material, but its economic synthesis is a problem for future accomplishment.

If the chemist can not duplicate nature's organic insecticides, he may still have the chance of imitating them. With this idea in mind, neonicotine, a substance almost identical in chemical structure with nicotine, has been prepared. Laboratory tests have shown it to be equivalent to nicotine for many purposes in its toxicity to certain insects. The full estimate of its usefulness naturally awaits the production of sufficient material for tests in the field.

Neonicotine can be changed to other forms, such as methyl, ethyl, and other derivatives not possible with nicotine, with physical properties better adapted to some purposes but with no loss in toxicity. The series of neonicotine insecticides offers interesting possibilities.

Can neonicotine be produced cheaply? The answer to this can not be given at this time. Its synthesis from benzol is now being studied, with a view to preparing it more economically. The unsolved problems do not appear to be unduly formidable.

C. R. Smith.

INSECTICIDE Residues Removed from Fruit by Various Washes — Lead arsenate is the only dependable stomach insecticide for the control of codling moth and various other chewing insects that attack apple, pear, peach, and other fruit trees. In some parts of the country, notably Colorado and Washington, the codling moth is less susceptible to control by lead arsenate than in other parts of the country. This may be due to a resistance on the part of the insect that has been developed by years of arsenical spraying. Owing to the great difficulty in controlling this insect it has become necessary to apply 8 or 10 sprays of lead arsenate in order to produce marketable apples. This heavy spraying results in the accumulation upon the fruit of quantities of arsenic exceeding 0.01 grain arsenic trioxide per pound, the maximum quantity permitted under the regulations of the British Government, and consequently the fruit must be washed or wiped in order that it may be marketed.

Various chemicals have been proposed for apple-washing solutions, but the commercial washes now in use are either hydrochloric acid or a dilute alkali. The acid process is more generally used. This process consists in first subjecting the fruit to a bath of dilute hydrochloric acid (1 to 3 gallons acid to 100 gallons water) by passing the fruit on conveyors under or through sprays of acidulated water, then rinsing thoroughly in clear water, and removing the excess moisture either with an air blast or with towels.

The insecticide division of the Bureau of Chemistry and Soils has recently found that certain salts, notably Glauber's salt, common salt, copperas, and ferric chloride, enhance the effectiveness of the hydrochloric acid in removing arsenical spray residue from apples and pears. The use of some of these salts, combined with cleaning solution, materially reduces injury to fruit that may be caused by the stronger acid and diminishes the damage to machinery caused by the acid. The practicability of using these salts in commercial washing machines is being investigated.

If an effective nonarsenical stomach insecticide could be found to take the place of lead arsenate the spray-residue problem would be solved, provided the new material was not poisonous to man.

R. C. ROARK.

INSURANCE Against Trifling Losses Is Wasteful Generally — Purchase of insurance against serious losses that may occur to a farmer is not only wise; it is necessary in order to guard against possible financial embarrassment or disaster. But to have the insurance cover minor losses, as well as the more serious, is decidedly wasteful and adds unnecessarily and disproportionately to the cost of protection.

Unfortunately this uneconomic practice of covering small and trifling losses as well as those against which protection is really needed is becoming common with all classes of insurance companies, including the farmers' mutuals. Too frequently losses amounting to only a few dollars, or even less than a dollar, are covered by the insurance policies and are reported, investigated, approved, paid, and recorded at an expense to the company that often exceeds the indemnity to the insured. This practice, which has resulted mainly from competition for business, tends to make the insurance company a clumsy and expensive agency for handling minor repair items, as well as an agency for worthwhile protection against individual disaster.

The practice of covering trifling losses is also usually unfair to the more broad-minded and public-spirited among the insured, who often attend to the minor repairs made necessary by a windstorm or other hazard insured against, at their own expense, because they recognize the waste involved in shifting trifling losses to the insurance company. The more selfish and thoughtless, on the other hand, make claim for all such losses, and thereby unduly raise the cost of insurance protection not only to themselves but to the entire group of insured.

All persons interested in insurance protection, and particularly those who are entitled to a voice as members of a mutual company, should endeavor to hold the organization to its real purpose of furnishing worth-while protection at a minimum of cost. Where the unsound practice now prevails of covering and paying trifling losses, it should be remedied by proper amendment to the by-laws or policy forms and by firm adherence to a more sound practice.

V. N. VALGREN.

INTENTIONS-TO-PLANT Reports Aid Farmer to Plan Production Farmers everywhere are attempting to adjust their crop rotations and crop acreages to secure the maximum returns, but the best-laid plans are often upset by the marked variations from year to year in the production and prices of the various crops. These variations are mostly due either to the changes in yields that result from unusual weather conditions or to changes in the acreages harvested. The unusual weather conditions can not as yet be foretold, and the same is true of those changes in acreage that are caused by unexpected weather conditions at planting time, but it is becoming increasingly evident that any general tendency to increase or decrease the acreage of a given crop can be determined and measured before the crop is planted and before it is too late for farmers to revise their plans.

Each March since 1923 some 50,000 farmers in all parts of the country have been reporting to the United States Department of Agriculture, or to some cooperating State agency, the number of acres that they expect to devote to each crop and, for comparison, the number of acres of the same crops harvested the preceding season. Each August similar reports have been made on fall-seeded wheat and rye. These acreages are summarized in the March and August intentions-to-plant reports.

Reports Have Proved Reliable

A review of the acreage intentions in comparison with the acreages finally harvested shows that for most crops the reported intentions are an accurate indication of farmers' plans at the time they report. Of course, there are always some sections in which the weather is either too wet or too dry for planting, and there are always some farmers who are prevented by sickness or other obstacle from planting their crops, or who lose part of their crops from hail, overflow, drought, insects, or diseases.

The reliability of the intentions reports as an indication of farmers' plans is demonstrated by the reports on potatoes, for of all the important crops the acreage planted to potatoes is probably the least dependent on weather conditions at planting time. To the extent that we can judge by the experience of the last six years, the intentions reports appear to be not only a reliable indication of the acreage of potatoes which farmers as a whole intend to plant, but if allowance is made for usual failure to plant and for the acreage lost they are a reliable indication of the acreage to be planted and of the acreage to be harvested, except in so far as an intentions report itself demonstrates to farmers that a change in plan is necessary.

The purpose of the intentions report is to show to individual producers the acreage intended on other farms before it is too late for the individual producers to change their plans. Each year an increasing number of farmers are using the reports in this way.

Tobacco Growers Benefited

There are many illustrations of how practical they are or can be to farmers. In 1926 Maryland tobacco growers indicated an intention to increase their acreage 20 per cent. The danger of such an increase was pointed out to them and they increased acreage only 3 per cent, with the result that the favorable prices of 1925 were maintained through 1926. In 1927 tobacco growers in the Connecticut Valley indicated an intention to increase acreage by 12 per cent. Reasons why so large an increase was inadvisable were explained and acreage was increased only 8 per cent, resulting in slightly improved prices. In the same year growers of cigar tobacco in the Miami Valley of Ohio and Indiana reported an intention to decrease acreage 8 per cent. Their situation was such as to call for an even greater reduction, and the reasons were stated in the supplementary outlook report. The result was that acreage was reduced 27 per cent, thus rectifying the unfavorable supply situation in which they were placed. Because of this and because of the excellent quality of their 1927 crop they received prices nearly double those of the previous year.

On the other hand, in regard to the potato crop, farmers were warned in January, 1928, that the indications were for a substantial increase in acreage and those who were planning to expand their acreage because of profits secured during the preceding three years, were asked to bear in mind the unfavorable returns during the three years 1922 to 1924. But the intentions-to-plant report showed an intention to increase acreage 7 per cent over the previous year. The warning was repeated. As a matter of fact, acreage was increased 9 per cent over the 1927 total, the yields were unusually heavy, and we had a total crop of 463,000,000 bushels—the largest potato crop ever grown. The average price of $1.04 per hundred pounds in Chicago during September, 1928, was the lowest September average in that market in 15 years.

JOHN B. SHEPARD.

INVESTMENT of Farm Savings Not Diverse Enough, Records Show — Farmers should invest their savings after a consideration of all investment opportunities rather than merely those directly connected with the farm. Studies in several States show that the amount of farmers' investments is a very small proportion of the farmers' property and that the vast majority of farmers have no outside holdings whatever. Analysis of farmers' records in nine areas showed that in each of four Southern States less than 2 per cent of the farmers' property was in the form of investments which might serve as an emergency reserve and provide income independent of the farm. Such investments as are found are chiefly mortgages or stock in local enterprises. Holdings in other property outside the farm are likewise of small amount. This concentration of farmers' resources in farm property appears to be typical of other areas.

TABLE 9.—*Average outside investments and total assets of farm owners in four States January 1, 1926*

	Number of farms included	Average investments in bonds, stocks, and mortgages per farm	Average total assets per farm	Percentage outside investments are of total assets
		Dollars	*Dollars*	*Per cent*
Arkansas (January, 1927)	42	18	7,923	0.2
Georgia	45	98	7,500	1.3
North Carolina	96	84	12,523	0.7
South Carolina	130	195	11,276	1.7

In recent years, reduced farm returns, increased debt, increased foreclosures and farm bankruptcies, have directed attention to low rates of return on farm property. In 1925, 36 per cent of the owner-operated farms were mortgaged with an indebtedness representing about 42 per cent of the value of the mortgaged property.

This situation has caused some lenders to ask whether the farm industry in the better-developed sections has not, under present conditions, about all the funded indebtedness it can profitably use. Certainly many individual mortgaged farms are not earning more than, or as much as, their interest charges, but nearly two-thirds of the farms of the country are not mortgaged and therefore could provide ample security to lenders.

Prospective Use of Borrowed Capital

Whether such loans would be profitable for farmers must depend upon the use made of the proceeds, but whenever existing capital invested in agriculture is not yielding the current rate of interest, the farmer should assure himself that use of borrowed or owned capital will improve the situation before further capital is employed. This fact is of the same importance to a farmer with respect to capital he may have to invest as it is for other capital seeking investment. More attention to rates of return by those farmers who have funds to invest would tend to reduce the amount of capital in the agricultural industry and should aid in placing the farming industry on a better-paying basis.

A mortgage on farm land is often a better investment than is the land itself at market price, because of larger and more regular returns, because of less necessity for supervision, and because it constitutes a prior lien on the land and its income. A rate of 6 per cent for a loan of half the market value of a farm whose production yields only 3 per cent of that value can result only in continued payment of interest without any reduction of the debt itself. Such instances are not uncommon. Hence, when farm mortgage lenders consider restricting loans in a given field, farmers may do well to consider carefully before putting additional capital into farm property.

The generally low net earnings in agriculture since 1920 have not made it possible for most farmers to invest any funds outside the farm. This low return from farm property is evidence of the need of diversifying the farmer's holdings whenever capital becomes available. With recognition of the fact that farm returns since 1920 have not justified the expectation formerly held of higher land values, there has come the realization that many other forms of capital have not so suffered, and that such investments when properly selected are not only safe, but are readily sold.

Employing Earnings as Needs Dictate

Each farmer must use his earnings in the light of his particular needs. Those farmers who are in debt and whose farms are already equipped for most profitable production will often find best employment of their surplus earnings by reducing obligations and decreasing the interest charges. If increased acreage or improved equipment will result in a satisfactory production unit, the farmer should employ his capital for the most profitable use. The important point is that there should be a free flow of available capital both to and from agriculture prompted by the relative returns to be derived, a movement of capital in which farmers' liquid funds should participate.

The farmer should exercise great care in selecting his investments. Whenever he considers the purchase of securities, he should, if possible, get the advice of an experienced investment banker, a specialist in helping investors to determine not only what to shun but also what to invest in with reasonable safety and profit. Often the farmer could, by consulting his local banker, avoid fraudulent or other unsound "investment" schemes.

Just as diversity of crops and livestock contributes to regularity of farm receipts, so it is often desirable that all funds shall not be invested on the farm, nor even where they might be subject to the same uncertainties which affect the farm. This principle of diversity is followed in many lines of business. For instance, other things being equal, those banks that distribute their loans among many borrowers and types of business are considered the safest; insurance companies distribute their investments and limit their liabilities on single risks. The rapid growth of investment trusts is largely due to their distribution of investors' funds among many diversified holdings selected for yield and safety.

The annual income from individual farms is notoriously irregular. Weather, pests, storms, and surplus production in competing areas of the world are some of the factors over which the farmer has no control and which are frequently the cause of reduction in the year's receipts. In such years, expenses for feed are often greater than usual, whereas taxes, labor, and living costs remain nearly constant; hence, a source of income outside the farm is needed. In years of good returns, and whenever there are funds available for investment, farmers may therefore well devote more attention to rates of returns from alternative uses of capital and to the policy of not putting all the eggs into one basket.

DAVID L. WICKENS.

IODINE Survey Planned in Studies of Minor Constituents of Food That the chemical elements present in plants in relatively large quantities, such as calcium, carbon, hydrogen, nitrogen, oxygen, phosphorus, and sulphur, are the only ones of significance in nutrition has long been believed. For some time, however, evidence has been accumulating which indicates that certain minor constituents may be of great importance.

It is now known, for example, that a disease of the thyroid gland, generally termed goiter, is caused by a deficiency of iodine in the diet. The use of this element in the form of its salts has been only partly successful in the prevention of goiter, and apparently to obtain the full benefit, foodstuffs containing iodine in an organic combination must be consumed.

Iodine Survey Planned

As yet but few data are available on the iodine content of ordinary food plants and its variation with the region where a crop is grown. The crop chemistry laboratory of the Bureau of Chemistry and Soils is accordingly planning to carry out an iodine survey of the United States with the object of ascertaining what crops contain the most iodine, in various parts of the country, and thus making it possible for everyone to obtain a sufficient quantity of this substance.

Other minor constituents may prove equally important. It has been suggested, for example, that there is a connection between manganese and the vitamins, those mysterious factors which are so necessary to physical well-being. Nickel and cobalt are reported to be present in insulin, used in the treatment of diabetes, and copper is said to be contained in liver, used in the treatment of anemia of certain types. It seems probable that surveys of food plants with respect to these and other minor elements may yield information of value in improving health through modifications of the diet.

E. T. WHERRY.

IRRIGATION Pipes of Concrete Economical Under Some Conditions — Where economic conditions justify its use, concrete pipe is replacing the earthen ditch on irrigated farms of the West. By this substitution the farmer saves valuable water, spreads it more uniformly over the surfaces of fields, lessens the work of applying it, prevents the growth of weeds on ditch banks, removes a barrier to transportation, prevents the waterlogging of soils, and salvages fertile land for cropping. A California prune grower replaced earthen ditches with concrete pipes and thereby added 5 acres to his orchard. He claims that the products derived from this acreage when the trees reach the bearing stage will pay for the concrete pipe.

Earth ditches can not be replaced economically by concrete pipes on all irrigated farms. Where land and water are reasonably cheap or the average profits from farming low, the cheaper methods of distributing water must of necessity be followed; but where land and water are valuable, labor scarce and expensive, and gross annual profits more than about $70 an acre per annum, the advantages gained by permanent farm structures usually prove worth the investment. This applies to intensively cultivated orchards and vineyards, many truck farms, and the more profitable diversified farms.

In 1919 there were under irrigation in southern California, exclusive of Imperial County, over 750,000 acres chiefly devoted to fruit and nut production. In that territory nearly all the water used for agricultural purposes is conveyed and distributed through concrete pipe or other impervious conduits. This practice, coupled with economy in applying water to crops and an extended use of pumped well water, has safeguarded the fertile soils from the injurious effects of water-logging and saved the orchardists the expense of installing drainage systems. Here it was that concrete pipe became part of the common equipment of irrigated farms and orchards and its use has spread in recent years to other parts of California and to Oregon, Washington, and Arizona.

During the earlier stages of the industry, it was quite generally believed that farmers could satisfactorily make and lay concrete pipe. Many small factories were also established. Some, which had suitable materials and exercised skill and care in making and laying their products, attained a reasonable measure of success; but the majority used unsuitable material and mixtures, and through ignorance or carelessness failed to make pipe in accordance with engineering requirements. Many failures resulted and farmers and their advisors became skeptical of the utility of all concrete pipe.

Comprehensive Tests Made

It was at this stage of the industry that the engineers of the Department of Agriculture began to investigate the subject. By testing the strength and other properties of concrete pipe; by collecting samples of the materials used from widely separated localities and grading and proportioning these in many combinations; and by determining the effect on strength produced in different mixtures by light and heavy tamping, variations of cement and water content, and differences in reinforcing, manufacturing, and curing, a foundation was laid in accordance with technical and scientific standards upon which it was possible to build a permanent industry to benefit thousands of western farmers. The principal fact disclosed by the investigation was that high-grade concrete pipe of uniform quality could not be made with inadequate equipment, unskilled labor, and faulty materials; hence the gradual elimination of the smaller and less successful plants and the enlargement of the better plants, the products of which are tested and guaranteed.

One characteristic of concrete-pipe lines requires further investigation. Concrete expands and contracts under climatic influences in about the same degree as steel, and when no expansion joints are inserted in pipe lines failure may result. Pipes laid in cool weather may subsequently expand and rupture under high temperatures. The reversal of the process must likewise be guarded against. When cold water enters a pipe laid at a higher temperature contraction takes place and may cause leaks. The remedy for this defect lies in the insertion, at proper intervals, of expansion and contraction joints so designed that they will be both efficient and cheap.

The purchaser of concrete pipe should exercise his privilege of requiring the manufacturer to make it conform in all respects to the standard specifications now in use; and if the maker contracts to lay the pipe, he should guarantee to repair all leaks or ruptures for two successive irrigation periods.

Where concrete pipe is subject to water hammer caused by the operation of pumps or the inclusion of air, a standpipe is a more reliable and effective preventive than safety valves or other mechanical devices.

SAMUEL FORTIER.

JAPANESE Beetle in Narrow Range Meets Variety of Conditions — During the last several years data have been gathered bearing on fluctuation in concentration of the Japanese beetle from year to year in various parts of the earlier infested territory, and on the successive stages represented in the extension of its range to its present dimensions. The facts show clearly that, even within the limits of a narrowly circumscribed area, environmental conditions may be encountered sufficiently diverse in character or intensity to markedly influence the insect's rate both of increase and of spread.

Certain of the results are represented on the map (fig. 128) accompanying this article. In this figure the heavy broken line, of alternating dots and dashes, outlines approximately that portion of the present range of the Japanese beetle within which the insect is represented everywhere in sufficient numbers to enable it to be found without detailed or arduous scouting. It is true that the beetle has been found at a considerable number of stations situated far beyond these limits, but such occurrences represent localized infestations consequent upon the artificial conveyance of beetles from the central (or normal) infested district to localities more or less remote from it.

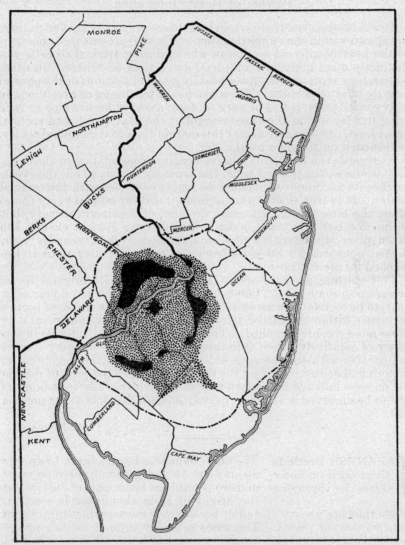

FIGURE 128.—Map of New Jersey and a portion of Pennsylvania showing the distribution of the principal infestation by the Japanese beetle

The original center of this district, where the Japanese beetle was first found, and from which it began its dispersal over its present range, is indicated on the map by a black star situated within the heavily stippled section. That section includes the part of the normal area of distribution in which the beetle is abundant enough to be of economic significance owing to its depredations on useful or ornamental plants, and is therefore termed the heavily infested section. Outside of this, in all the section represented in the unshaded portion of the distribution area the beetle is present, but, in 1928, not in large enough numbers to be seriously injurious.

Patches of Heavy Infestation

It will be observed that certain solid black or heavily shaded patches are shown within the stippled section. These represent those portions of the heavily infested section in which, during 1928, the beetle was distinctly more abundant and destructive than elsewhere. In other words, they represent the most heavily infested portions of the general heavily infested section. These patches of maximum or exceptionally heavy infestation, it will be noticed, form a sort of broken ring or zone lying not far within the outer margin of the heavily infested section, or, at least, considerably nearer this margin than to the original center, represented on the map by the star.

As regards the matter of relative density of population of the Japanese beetle at the present time, the territory within which the beetle reaches its maximum abundance no longer coincides with the original center. It is true that at the beginning, and for several years thereafter, the latter actually formed the area of maximum density, but within the last few years, most evidently since 1925, a change has taken place; the territory of maximum density has, year by year, shifted outwards on all sides from the original center until it has reached its present position.

This shifting of the heaviest infestation from its original to its present position has been shown by field surveys, conducted year after year, to be correlated with an actual reduction in the number of beetles occurring within the earlier infested districts and a rapid increase in those more recently invaded. This rapid increase of the beetle in territory of relatively recent infestation appears to be in every respect comparable with the increase which took place at the beginning in the original center. During the first few years of the present decade the damage inflicted in the latter by the insect was fully as striking as any to be observed in the most heavily infested districts at the present day.

HENRY FOX.

JAPANESE Beetle Is Controlled on Some Trees by Spraying   The adult Japanese beetles begin to appear about June 15 and gradually become more numerous until the latter part of July, when the height of their abundance is reached. While they are present the adult beetles may cause serious injury to a wide variety of plants. The more seriously injured include apple, peach, grape, cherry, plum, quince, corn, and bean. The most serious damage to ornamental plants has occurred on elm, linden, horsechestnut, sugar maple, Norway maple, white oak, Lombardy poplar, rose, althea, hollyhock, dahlia, hibiscus, and zinnia. The beetles feed on the foliage, fruit, and blossoms.

Experience has shown that it is much easier to prevent infestation than it is to drive the insects away after they have once become numerous on the plants. The point underlying success in preventing injury by the Japanese beetle is to maintain, on the foliage and fruit, a coating of some material which the insects do not like. This coating must be maintained throughout the time when the adult beetles are present. Lead arsenate has been found one of the most useful materials for this purpose.

To obtain the most successful results it is necessary that all portions of the foliage should be thoroughly covered by a coating of the spray. Good spray equipment should be used capable of throwing a mist over the tops and sides of the plants, thus covering the upper and lower surfaces of the leaves. The spray should be applied between June 25 and July 1. In case rains should remove portions of the deposit on the plants, it may be necessary to repeat the spraying two or three weeks later.

The Protection of Apples

Trees bearing late-ripening varieties of apple, beginning with the Wealthy, may be protected by a thorough application of a mixture composed of powdered lead arsenate 6 pounds, wheat flour 4 pounds, and water to make 100 gallons. The flour and lead arsenate should be thoroughly mixed in a dry state, and sufficient water may then be added to form a thin paste. Stir until no lumps remain, dilute with more water, and strain into the spray tank.

Early-ripening varieties of apple, including Yellow Transparent, Williams, Starr, and others, may be protected by the use of the spray formula recommended for later varieties, provided that all residue is removed from the fruit when harvested. This is satisfactorily done by thoroughly washing it in a bath of dilute hydrochloric acid. In case washing is impracticable, early varieties of apples may be protected by a thorough spraying with a lime wash prepared by slaking 16 pounds of stone lime in a small quantity of water, to which is added sufficient water to make 100 gallons. The lime sprays should be applied before the beetles appear in any considerable numbers and must be repeated as often as it becomes necessary to maintain the coating of the lime on the fruit and foliage. Any residue remaining on the fruit may be removed by wiping or by washing.

Lead Arsenate for Young Peach Trees

Young and nonbearing peach trees may be protected by a thorough spraying with a mixture composed of 3 pounds of powdered lead arsenate, 8 pounds of a good grade of hydrated lime high in calcium content, and sufficient water to make 100 gallons. It may be necessary to repeat this treatment in order to protect new growth. Late-ripening varieties (including Elberta and those ripening later) may be protected by the use of the materials recommended for nonbearing peach trees, provided that the application is made not later than June 25. Early-ripening varieties of peaches can not be adequately protected from the Japanese beetle by the use of arsenical sprays. Some protection for them can be obtained by placing canvas beneath infested trees and jarring the beetles off the plants early in the morning. The collected beetles may be killed by being placed in barrels containing kerosene oil.

Grapevines may be protected by a thorough spraying with a mixture composed of 6 pounds of powdered lead arsenate, 5 pounds of cheap wheat flour, and water to make 100 gallons. The Japanese beetles feed only on the grape foliage, and cause no damage to the fruit. Every effort should be made to coat the foliage thoroughly, getting the least possible residue on the berries. The spray should be a fine mist directed downward on the foliage. It is usually necessary when the first spraying is made during the last week in June to repeat the application three or four weeks later in order to cover new growth.

Ornamental shrubs and shade trees should be sprayed in the last week in June with a mixture of 8 pounds of oleate-coated lead

FIGURE 129.—Japanese beetle trap. The beetles are captured by falling in the funnel placed in the top of the trap

arsenate and 100 gallons of water. For preparing smaller quantities use 2 heaping tablespoonfuls of coated lead arsenate to each gallon of water. The spray should be applied not later than July 1, and all portions of the foliage should be thoroughly covered. In the case of plants making considerable growth during July and August it may be necessary to repeat the application in the latter part of July in order to protect the new foliage.

Japanese Beetle Traps

Very efficient traps, one of which is illustrated in Figure 129, have been devised for capturing the adult Japanese beetles. Many types of these traps have been tested, and most of them have been found efficient for this purpose. The traps should be used in connection with spraying, since the use of the traps alone does not protect fruit, flowers, or foliage. The efficiency of the traps is materially increased when the surrounding foliage has been sprayed with lead arsenate. It is recommended that on the average suburban lot, approximately 60 by 100 feet in size, three to six standard traps can be used to good advantage. Geraniol bait must be maintained in a fresh condition and replenished frequently. To obtain the best results the trap should be suspended from a post extending from 5 to 7 feet above the ground in the open sunlight and at a distance of not less than 5 feet from the nearest tree or shrub.

Loren B. Smith.

J**APANESE Higan Cherries Gain in Favor for the Adornment of Parks** Every year the Japanese flowering cherries, with their numerous varieties differing in color, size, and degree of doubleness, are becoming more popular as their peculiar beauty is appreciated. An ever-increasing

Figure 130.—The compact, bushy form of the spring cherry as it grows at the Arnold Arboretum, Jamaica Plain, Mass.

number of inquiries gives evidence of the growing interest in these immigrants from the Orient, and already a number of cities are planning definitely to utilize them in beautifying their parks.

At the present time probably the most popular forms are those with large double flowers. But there is a relatively little-known group of Japanese flowering cherries, mostly single, which are quite as attractive in their way as are the large double varieties. Collectively these are known as the Japanese Higan cherries (*Prunus subhirtella*) because of their early-flowering habit. Very early in the spring, about the time the forsythias begin to show yellow, the leafless limbs of these trees suddenly clothe themselves with masses of pink.

Several Varieties in the Group

Several varieties are included in this group. One of these, the Benihiganzakura (*P. subhirtella ascendens*), a large, thick-branched tree, grows spontaneously in parts of Japan and is generally considered to be the wild ancestor of the other early Japanese flowering cherries. It is of no particular horticultural merit. The only double-flowering variety is the Jugatsuzakura (*P. subhirtella autumnalis*). This low, bushy tree has small, semidouble pink flowers, borne not only in the spring but also in the autumn. Jugatsu means October and zakura

FIGURE 131.—The innumerable flowers of the Higanzakura form a dense mass of beauty

means flowering cherry. Either the autumn crop of flowers is small and the spring crop large, or vice versa. The Jugatsuzakura is grown extensively in the vicinity of Tokyo.

The two remaining varieties deserve special mention. One, the Higanzakura (*P. subhirtella*), is cultivated extensively in western Japan, but it is not known in the wild state. It is probably the most floriferous of all the Japanese flowering cherries, not even excepting the deservedly popular Yoshino, which adorns the banks of the Tidal Basin in Washington, D. C. It is a rather small, bushy tree, growing to about 25 feet in height, in general habit resembling the Japanese plum. (Fig. 130.) The flowers, somewhat larger and paler pink than those of the other forms, appear very early in the spring in such vast numbers as to hide completely most of the branches. (Fig. 131.) In older trees the outer ends of the branches nearly touch the ground, so that the trunk itself often is not visible. The literal meaning of higan is equinox. As applied to the flowering cherries of Japan, it means early.

The Weeping Variety

The other variety which should be more widely grown is the weeping or pendulous form (*P. subhirtella pendula*), considered by many horticulturists to be the finest of the group. Known to the Japanese as the Shidarehiganzakura (drooping early flowering cherry), it is cultivated all over that country in courtyards, temple grounds, and cemeteries. Individual trees often attain a great age and large size. One tree near the town of Hachioji is reported to be nearly 70 feet tall, with a trunk 10 feet in circumference. The degree of pendulousness varies greatly. While the typical form resembles in habit the weeping willow, all gradations from this to the ascending form are to be found.

In using the Japanese names of these varieties of cherries, the name zakura (flowering cherry) may properly be omitted, leaving the four variety names in the following forms: Higan, Benihigan, Shidarehigan, and Jugatsu. It should be understood that all these are varieties of Japanese flowering cherries and that when the names are written in full the word zakura should be added.

Seed Crops Usually Abundant

All the early Japanese Higan cherries except the Jugatsuzakura usually bear abundant crops of seeds, and among the seedlings all forms are likely to appear. In order to perpetuate a desired variety, propagation by budding or grafting on seedlings of *P. subhirtella* is recommended. If other stocks are used, the tree is not likely to be as long lived. So far, no great success has been attained in this country in propagating the cherries of this group by cuttings.

The Higan cherries of Japan are comparatively hardy and probably can be grown in the same general areas as the peach, and possibly even farther north.

PAUL RUSSELL.

KAPOK and Like Fibers Used for Pillows, Life Preservers, Insulation — Kapok is a light, buoyant down. It is composed of fine white or usually light colored, smooth, hairlike fibers about an inch long. These fibers are single cells with thin walls completely closed around a central cavity. Each individual fiber is therefore a miniature gas bag. Unlike nearly all other fibers and plant tissues, the cell walls do not absorb moisture. Water can not enter the cells unless the walls are broken.

The allied fibers, pochote, semul, samohu, paina, samauma, and others from other trees of the same family as kapok, are all of similar structure, varying in length, luster, and the thickness of the cell walls.

All of these fibers are produced in the seed pods of trees belonging to the Bombax family. They grow on certain portions of the inner walls of the seed pods and to a less extent on the seeds, but in most species at maturity both seeds and down are entirely free from any attachment.

Practically all of the fiber or down of this class entering commerce heretofore has consisted of kapok from the randoe tree, *Ceiba pentandra indica*, of Java and the Philippines, and semul from the red semul tree, *Gossampinus heptaphylla*, of India. There are 54 different species of trees belonging to 4 genera of the Bombax family now known to yield fiber of this class, and others are being discovered as new areas are explored. These now known include 11 species of the genus Ceiba, ranging from northern Mexico to Brazil, with *Ceiba pentandra*, cultivated for the production of kapok, widely distributed in the tropics of both hemispheres; 25 species of Bombax, chiefly in Brazil, but some extending to southern Mexico and 1 in tropical Africa; 7 of Chorisia, confined chiefly to the La Plata region in South America, and 11 of Gossampinus, in southern Asia and tropical Africa. All are native in tropical or subtropical countries. Some are known to yield down fully equal in quality to the kapok now on the market. Kapok has been produced most extensively and with the greatest care in Java; but with the same care in picking the seed pods, cleaning the down, and in grading, inspecting, and marketing, just as good down may be produced in other tropical countries.

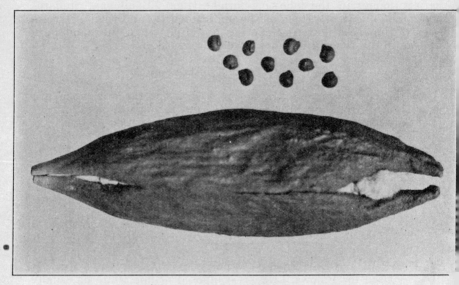

FIGURE 132.—Kapok seed pod and seeds. The down grows on the inner walls of the seed pods and less on the seeds, but when mature and dry neither down nor seeds have any attachment

Not Textile Fibers

These are not textile fibers, for they do not cling together so as to make a strong yarn. Their valuable properties are resiliency, buoyancy, and resistance to transmission of heat. In each of these properties their value is diminished if the fibers are crushed or broken.

Because of their resiliency they are used in mattresses, pillows, and upholstery. Because of their buoyancy, greater than that of cork, they are used in life preservers. Because of their resistance (kapok now heading the list of tested temperature insulators) their use is increasing in refrigerators, refrigerator cars, trucks for distributing ice cream, and for many purposes where efficient heat insulation is required.

LYSTER H. DEWEY.

LABELS on Packages   American housewives have good reason
of Foodstuffs Mean   to put their faith in the veracity of the
Much to Alert Buyer   declarations of quality and quantity
borne on the packages of food they
buy each day, now that manufacturers and packers show such a very
general disposition to meet the demands for truthful labeling made
by Federal, State, and city pure-food laws. But labels are of infinite
variety, and the fact that they are for the most part truthful profits
us little unless we give them enough intelligent consideration to
learn the message they have for us. Many labels show at a glance
what kind of material, and how much, the package contains. Others,
however, are so ornate, or the containers on which they appear are
so designed to appeal to our sense of the aesthetic rather than to our
common sense, that a
close scrutiny of the
printed matter is neces-
sary to prevent disap-
pointment when the
packages are opened at
home.

For instance, the dol-
lars and cents value of
the statement of the
quantity of contents re-
quired by the Federal
food and drugs act to
be plainly given on all
but very small packages
of food is often disre-
garded. Take, by way
of illustration, the two
bottles of vanilla ex-
tract shown in Figure
133.   Assuming that
the quality is the same
in each case and each
bottle retails at the
same price, which is the
better buy? Offhand,
we should probably
select the taller bottle.

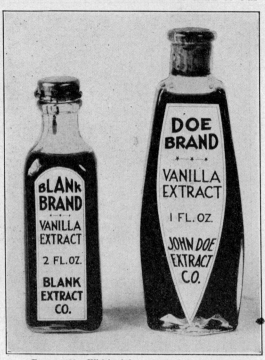

FIGURE 133.—Which of these two is the better buy?

But another look at the label shows us that it contains exactly half
as much as the shorter one. If then we are out after flavoring material, not bottles, we shall undoubtedly buy the plain bottle, leaving
the fancier one, with its false sides, to decorate the shelves of the
shop. Without this one short line on the label declaring the quantity we might easily have been deceived into paying flavoring extract
prices for a bottle soon to be thrown away. (Fig. 134.)

Misleading Oil Containers

Another kind of container that may blind the eye to the real facts
in the case is well illustrated by the cans of salad oil shown in Figures
136 and 137. Before the enactment of food-control legislation corn

oil, cottonseed oil, and other vegetable oils, all excellent in themselves, were flagrantly misbranded as pure olive oil, which is the most expensive of the salad oils and is considered particularly desirable by many because of its characteristic flavor. Twenty years ago a can bearing the label shown in Figure 135 might have contained real olive oil from Italy, and, then again, it might not. To-day it is pretty safe to assume that such a can does contain olive oil. Cans bearing misleading labels like the one in Figure 136 are also fast disappearing from the market, but they have not yet gone entirely. Here is a case where sharp eyes will prove a distinct advantage to the buyer. The packer who sent out the can labeled as shown in Figure 137 may have thought he was complying with the letter of the law, but he was most certainly

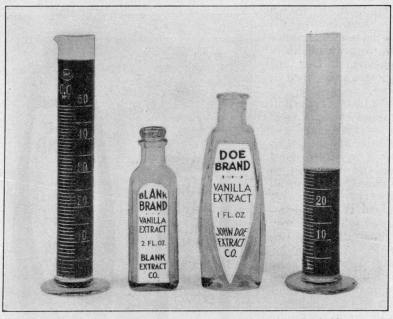

FIGURE 134.—This is the way the contents of the two bottles looked after they had been poured out into glass cylinders of the same size

seeking to evade its spirit. Labels like the one in Figure 138 tell their story plainly and accurately.

It seems reasonable to expect that, through the enforcement of the various pure-food laws designed to protect consumers against substitute and short-weight or short-volume food products and honest manufacturers from unfair competition with such goods, labels will become increasingly reliable. Human nature being what it is, however, we shall probably always have to contend with some dishonest vendors. In any case an intelligent consideration of the labels is bound to be an advantage to the housewife, for the statements on truthful labels enable her to get just what she wants at a price commensurate with her means, and any joker in labels that are on the borderline between fact and fancy usually becomes apparent upon careful reading.

KATHARINE A. SMITH.

FIGURE 135.—The Federal food and drugs act
demands that a can bearing such a label as this
shall contain only pure olive oil from Italy

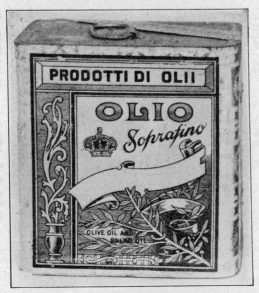

FIGURE 136.—A cursory glance at this label might lead one to
suppose that the can contained pure olive oil

FIGURE 138.—No one could be deceived by such a label as this

FIGURE 137.—Although the statements in this label ar perfectly true, the arrangement and sizes of type used might convey a wrong idea

L AMBING Loss Declines   The lambing of range ewes in the
in the National Forests   mountains and foothills of the West,
as Shelter Is Provided   extensively followed before the establishment of the national forests, and
quite generally permitted in the earlier years of national-forest admin-

FIGURE 139.—Part of the day's lamb drop on a ranch where feed, running water, sheds, and shelter are provided

istration, is rapidly becoming history.   Like many other of the earlier
practices in livestock management, range lambing has given way to
improved methods.

FIGURE 140.—Docking and marking ewes on a ranch 29 miles southwest of Pueblo.   The ewes and lambs were summer-grazed on the Rio Grande National Forest

It was recognized from the beginning as one of the more destructive
uses of the forest ranges because of its injury to early plant growth,
and the policy of the Forest Service has been to discourage it.   Also
there has been a growing realization that open range, high altitude

lambing practices are not as profitable as other methods.   As this fact
has become known, the eliminating process has been greatly simplified.

Open-range lambing practices had been followed for 50 years or
more in many places in the Rocky Mountain district.   The Forest
Service did not undertake to make radical adjustments at first.   It
realized that old-time customs were hard to change.   Grazing practices were, therefore, contained pretty much in status quo for some
years, with concentration principally on reducing or alleviating overgrazing.   The stockmen, having adjusted themselves to certain investments and practices and to certain ranges, were entitled to reasonable
advance notice.   Besides, demonstrations and figures were necessary.
Experiments were conducted with sheds and pastures, with significant
results.   Principal of these were the shed and pasture lambing experiments on the Cochetopa National Forest in Colorado.   Fortified with

Figure 141.—Flushed ewes showing good fleshing and an alert, thrifty appearance
as a result of extra feed

figures, the Forest Service was in position to bring about the change
more rapidly.   In some localities five years' advance notice was considered sufficient to enable stockmen to make provision for changing
their methods.   Now in many sections range lambing has been completely discontinued, and the lambing has been transferred to ranches,
fields, and shelters.

An illustration of these changes is shown in the following figures for
Colorado and Wyoming: In 1915, 106,560 range ewes were lambed on
8 Colorado national forests.   In 1927, 23,393 were lambed on 3 forests.
Lambing on Wyoming and Colorado forests in 1915 showed a total of
180,910.   In 1927, for both States, it was but 40,503, a reduction of
more than 77 per cent in the 12-year period.   The practice will be
practically discontinued in the national forests of the Rocky Mountain
district in the next 2 or 3 years.

Reductions in losses, improved forage and range conditions, and the
increased revenues which have resulted from the improved methods
have rapidly made permanent converts of the sheep growers.

J. H. HATTON.

LAMB Twinning Can Be Increased by Extra Feed at Breeding Season   For the last 12 years investigators of the United States Department of Agriculture have been conducting experimental work to determine the effect of different methods of feeding ewes at breeding time on the number of twin lambs produced. The results have been that a highly nourished condition of the ewes resulting from extra feed during a period commencing two weeks before and continuing throughout the breeding season, commonly known as "flushing," has shown an increase in twin lambs. (Fig. 141.) While the percentage of increase has varied from year to year, the average has been 16 more lambs per 100 ewes for the flushed ewes than for the check lots which did not receive this liberal feeding.

A study has been made of the comparative value of a supplementary grain ration and of extra-quality pasture for furnishing this extra feed. Very little difference was found in the lambing percentage of ewes flushed by these two methods; but since extra-quality pasture can usually be more cheaply and readily supplied, this method seems advisable in most instances.

The pasture should be sufficiently luxuriant to cause the ewes to gain rapidly. Seasons sometimes occur, however, in which pastures are too short for this purpose. In such seasons it is advisable for farmers to give the flock a supplementary grain allowance of from one-half to 1½ pounds per head daily, the amount depending on the size of the sheep and the amount and quality of green feed available.

A mixed-grain ration consisting of equal parts by weight of corn and oats has been found to be a satisfactory ration for this purpose. Forage crops, such as soy beans, cowpeas, sweet clover, and alfalfa, in sections where they can be safely used for pasture, make satisfactory pasture crops on which to flush ewes, but it is questionable whether there is anything better than fresh, sweet bluegrass when it is available. Although ewes gain readily on young tender clover, much difficulty has been experienced in getting them with lamb while on this type of pasture.   C. G. POTTS.

LAWN Grass Aided, Weeds Checked by Ammonium Sulphate   There are two principal ways of applying fertilizers to the lawn. One method involves direct soil treatment, in which case fertilizers like well-rotted manure or compost, bone meal, commercial fertilizer, and similar plant-food materials are incorporated with the soil before sowing the grass seed. The second method represents broadcast applications of fertilizer materials to the established lawn. With reference to the second method, it has been found that top dressing with highly soluble nitrogen salts exerts a stimulating influence on the lawn grasses and one that is being more generally practiced in recent years.

Investigations have shown that ammonium sulphate is particularly well adapted for this purpose. This fertilizer salt is a combination of ammonia, an alkaline compound, and sulphuric acid. It is obtained in large quantities in the United States as a by-product material of the coke and illuminating gas industries. Ammonium sulphate is quite soluble in water, possesses a good mechanical condition, and is, moreover, quickly available to plants, particularly to members of the grass family.

Aside from the stimulating effect this fertilizer salt has on lawn grasses, it has a tendency to gradually impart a degree of acidity to the soil that checks the growth of weeds in the lawn. This has been found to be noticeably true in the case of some of the common lawn-infesting weeds such as chick weed, dandelion, and plantain. To anyone who has attempted the back-breaking and knee-stiffening job of getting rid of these lawn pests through the laborious efforts of hand eradication, any substitute method will be appreciated.

May Be Broadcast

Ammonium sulphate may be applied broadcast to the established lawn at the rate of 3 to 4 pounds to 1,000 square feet, preferably mixed with 10 to 15 pounds of some diluting material like sand or fine dry soil, which enables one to distribute the fertilizer salt more uniformly. In applying the fertilizer salt it will be well to apply one-half of it in one direction, the balance in the other. This is the rate of application to be made in the early spring and after this initial top-dressing further applications may be made at monthly intervals, but the quantity to use will depend on soil and weather conditions. If the soil has begun to dry out, as it may during the summer months, the rate should be cut down to 1 or 2 pounds to 1,000 square feet. In all cases the fertilizer should be washed in thoroughly with the hose immediately after it goes on the lawn or applied during rainy weather. This will prevent the grass from "burning," as may easily happen if no precaution is taken.

A good way to apply ammonium sulphate to the lawn is to mix it with two or three times its weight of cottonseed meal, the latter furnishing not only some nitrogen in an organic form but a fair amount of slowly available phosphoric acid and potash. This mixture is practically odorless and is easy to apply, the color of the cottonseed meal being an aid to this. Nine to twelve pounds of the mixture will be sufficient for 1,000 square feet of lawn surface. If any difficulty is experienced in distributing this quantity uniformly some sand can be mixed with it. The quantity suggested represents the early spring application. Later on the quantity should be reduced to 3 or 4 pounds to the same area. Good results have been secured by the Department of Agriculture with the ammonium sulphate-cottonseed meal mixture on bent grasses.

For Grasses Tolerant of Acidity

Ammonium sulphate has been found to be particularly desirable for lawn grasses which show a preference for, or are tolerant of, acid soils. Such grasses are chiefly the bents and fescues. Kentucky bluegrass, however, while able to withstand a fair degree of acidity, will probably require some additional treatment to prevent too great a degree of soil acidity from developing. For Kentucky bluegrass lawns a light application of sodium nitrate may be needed from time to time. This can be applied in the following mixture to 1,000 square feet of lawn surface: Ammonium sulphate, 2 pounds; sodium nitrate, 1 pound; and cottonseed meal, 6 pounds. This treatment will be better to apply than lime alone, which is not a fertilizer and is of little value as a top dressing for grass unless used in connection with a nitrogen fertilizer.

The use of ammonium sulphate or a mixture of this salt and cottonseed meal on golf courses, principally the putting greens, which are generally composed of one of the varieties of bent grass, has been found to be particularly desirable for keeping down weed growth, although seasonal conditions with respect to rainfall appear to play a part in determining how effective such treatment will be.

B. E. BROWN.

L AWN Growing Requires   The standard of excellence for the lawn
      Good Seed, Fertilizer,   is high.   The incentive to make good
      and Persistent Work   lawns is great, but the necessary effort
                                             is usually not forthcoming; hence the
preponderance of failures.   While it is possible to succeed in some parts of the country with relatively little labor, in most cases much labor is

FIGURE 142.—Some handwork is essential to keep a lawn free from weeds

required; yet there are but few sections where conditions are so adverse that passably good lawns can not be made if sufficient attention is given them.   Generally speaking, the price of a good lawn is intelligent effort and lots of it.

Misdirected efforts of one kind or another pursue the lawn from its inception, and to discuss them adequately would require a lengthy treatise.   But some errors or neglects are more general and important than others, and a brief discussion of them may focus attention on what is necessary if success is to be achieved.

It is a fact generally accepted, although not fully understood, that the desire to indulge in gardening activities comes to the point of action in the average individual in the spring, and usually only then.   The result is that the sowing of seed of northern lawn grasses at that time of year is a very common practice.   This is a fundamental error.   For the purpose of illustration, northern turf grasses may be likened to winter wheat in certain vegetative habits of growth.   Winter wheat, as is well known, requires for its best production fall sowing in order that it may stool out before the severe weather of winter arrives and be ready for the business of making a crop the following spring.   A careful study of the northern lawn grasses shows that they should be sown in the late summer or early fall if they are to compete successfully with the noxious lawn weeds the next spring and subsequently.

Seed of most southern lawn grasses should be sown in the spring; consequently southern lawns usually escape the error in making that so badly handicaps many northern lawns.

Frequent Close Mowing Required

Good lawns without frequent and fairly close mowing are well-nigh impossible. It is difficult to specify the frequency of cutting that is necessary, but since the height of the grass is the criterion, no one need make a serious mistake in this respect. It is the nature of turf

FIGURE 143.—A broad sweep of lawn is a thing of beauty

grasses, with very few exceptions, that the quality of turf they produce is poor nearly in proportion to their approach to maturity—that is, to seed production—and in the case of Kentucky bluegrass, the king of all northern lawn grasses, seed setting interferes so seriously with turf making that it is usually long in getting back to good turf conditions after it has been allowed to set seed. In the meantime weeds take advantage of the situation. Another point in favor of close mowing is that the growth of many important lawn weeds is impaired by it. The urgent recommendation is that the lawn be kept closely cut at all times. This applies to southern as well as to northern lawn grasses.

A question very commonly asked is whether clippings should be allowed to remain on the lawn or be removed. Briefly, the answer is, "Remove them." In some cases they may be of slight benefit when left lying where they fall, but generally they are more likely to be detrimental.

Insufficient Watering Common

Failure to water lawns is a very important cause of poor quality. Although they may suffer from poor drainage, it is uncommon indeed for lawns to be injured by overwatering. There is much theory, some of it supported, in part at least, by facts, regarding root development, the effect on the leaves when water is applied during hot sunshiny times, and the time of day that water should be applied. There is need for investigation of these and other points, but for the present the layman may well satisfy himself with the practice of watering plentifully and when necessary and also at the time of day when it can be done conveniently. Heavy sprinkling is almost always indicated, but the mistake should not be made of regarding it as

FIGURE 144.—To have a good lawn keep the grass cut

unnecessary to water to-day because the lawn was watered heavily two days ago.

Conditions of atmosphere, texture of soil, exposure, and other factors influence the need for watering, so that it is practically futile to lay down a regimen for it. But the grass sends out the call which the veriest amateur may interpret unmistakably. Always this rule should be in mind, "When in doubt, water." The fear of developing shallow roots or of scalding the grass when water is applied during a hot sunshiny time may be dismissed. Nevertheless, heavy watering is preferable to light sprinkling, and morning and evening are the best times of the day to water, largely because of better conservation. Lawns should not be allowed to become dry, for many troublesome lawn weeds withstand drought better than do the lawn grasses.

Most lawns could be much improved by the proper use of fertilizers. This feature of lawn maintenance is much neglected. A great deal remains to be learned regarding the reaction of turf grasses to fertilizers, but sufficient information is available upon which to base some fairly definite recommendations.

In times past it was a common practice to topdress lawns in the late fall or winter with stable manure. While such manure is a good fertilizer, the practice of applying it in a coarse form frequently results in injury rather than benefit by killing the grass in patches, thereby allowing ample opportunity for the invasion of weeds. In fact, the covering of the lawn by any material for winter protection is rarely advisable. But the day for available supplies of stable manure in cities and towns is past; so attention must be directed to other turf fertilizers. Many are on the market, but some are better than others.

Nitrogen Principally Required

In making a selection the element to which chief consideration should be given is nitrogen. Experience and experiment indicate that most lawns require very little added potassium or phosphorus for their

FIGURE 145.—A neat lawn adds to the attractiveness of the home

successful development. At the Rothamsted station, England, on a soil not greatly different from many of our lawn soils, plots fertilized annually with only ammonium sulphate for more than half a century are supporting an excellent growth of turf grasses. There is another point to be considered. Fertilizers tending to produce an acid reaction in the soil when applied to lawns usually cause a depression of growth of many of the important lawn weeds. Results of investigations here and abroad amply warrant this conclusion. The use of ammonium sulphate is commended because of its high nitrogen content and its acid tendency.

Where the soil is not already acid, ammonium sulphate can be used advantageously on the lawn even where the dominant grass is Kentucky bluegrass. It is a quick-acting fertilizer and must be put on with care to avoid burning the grass. Two to three pounds to 1,000 square feet of lawn, applied in a water solution or mixed with sand or loam and then well watered in after application, is suggested for the spring treatment; then from 1 to 2 pounds similarly applied in the late spring or early summer, and a similar quantity in early fall—not late fall. This treatment, if consistently followed, should benefit the lawn greatly.

Ammonium phosphate is likewise a good nitrogenous acid-reacting fertilizer. It may be used in the manner suggested for ammonium sulphate. It is well to remember, however, that either of these fertilizers used to excess, particularly where the soil is already acid, may bring about a condition unfavorable to Kentucky bluegrass. There are other nitrogenous fertilizers that will give good results when properly used. Cottonseed meal and soy-bean meal are examples. These, however, are not classed among the acid-reacting fertilizers. If used they should be applied at the rate of approximately 10 to 15 pounds for 1,000 square feet at the times of the year indicated for the application of ammonium sulphate. Even distribution is important. Bone meal is commonly recommended, but its action is relatively slow, and the use of prepared animal manures is almost invariably uneconomical.

The use of lime alone as a top-dressing should be avoided, even on Kentucky bluegrass. There is strong evidence that when used in this manner it encourages the growth of weeds, and its benefit to the turf grasses is, to say the least, negligible unless used in combination with a nitrogen-carrying fertilizer.

Inattention to Weeds

Weeds seem to be ready at all times to take advantage of mistakes or neglect in lawn making or maintenance. In fact, with the best care it is impossible to prevent their incursion to some extent. The proper selection of turf grasses and the following of proper methods from the beginning, including the use of so-called acid-reacting fertilizers, help to control weeds, but with the most intelligent efforts there remains much old-fashioned weeding to be done if the lawn is to be kept clean. Chemical sprays are useful, but they do not eliminate weeds, and in many cases they are ineffective.

Lawn failures from weed invasion usually can be averted only by the very best methods and a large amount of strenuous hand labor. Furthermore, the labor must be timely. Attention to summer weeds in the fall and to winter weeds in the spring, as is often the case, results in little else than physical exercise for the worker. The time to remove most weeds, for economy of effort and the welfare of the turf, is when they appear.

Verily, the way of the lawn maker is hard.

RUSSEL A. OAKLEY.

LIGHT Rays a Factor in Helping to Solve Many Farm Problems Every farmer has noticed that most plants do not develop normally or produce good yields when grown in the shade. The family, as well as the animal life about the farm, is equally dependent upon sunlight for healthy growth and development, although this is not ordinarily so vividly brought to our attention. This growth is the result of chemical reactions occurring within the plant or animal, and is hastened by the energy derived from the sun. Sunlight consists of a mixture of colors, as seen in the rainbow, each of which represents a different range of wave lengths of light. In addition to the visible there are the invisible rays, some of which are shorter than the violet and others longer than the red. The short rays are known to be especially active in the stimulation of chemical reactions and life processes.

Studies are now in progress in an attempt to make use of the stimulating property of light to find out how nitrogen is fixed, in order to improve the present commercial methods of nitrogen fixation and fertilizer development. Some of these methods depend upon the use of iron mixtures called catalysts which speed up chemical reactions to a point sometimes hundreds of times greater than would be the case without them. The effect of some of the shorter light rays on these catalysts and in turn on nitrogen fixation is being investigated.

Another form of very short and invisible radiation now being applied is X rays, commonly used by physicians and dentists to locate defects or foreign materials. Examinations and photographs can be made of catalyst materials, soils, fertilizer materials, nitrogen compounds, and many agricultural products, such as cotton and leather. In many cases the X-ray method is the only one whereby the structure of the material or other desired information can be obtained. Thus the various radiations serve as an additional tool for helping to solve some of the farmer's problems.

C. H. KUNSMAN.

LILY Breeding Is Fertile Field for Plant Improvement Considering the admiration man has for the lily, it is rather remarkable that the genus still persists in a state of nature to a larger extent than almost any other. The hybrids are few, and the recognized horticultural varieties of any origin are confined to a small number of species. It is maintained by some that this results from incompatibility, from parthenogenetic tendencies, or other causes, and that we must ever depend mostly on native species in the lily instead of on man-made improvements such as exist in other genera of admired and domesticated plants.

Few authentic hybrids have been made, and still fewer have persisted beyond the human generation that produced them. But are we justified in the view that such will always be the case? The writer sees no reason for assuming that the lilies are any more resistant to improvements than any other group of plants. While it is true that there is little improvement to show for the large amount of effort that has been expended in lily culture, recent tendencies point to improved forms with greater beauty, greater vigor, and greater adaptability to cultural requirements.

The lily throughout its history, except in one or two spots, has not been handled with the commercial acumen that has characterized the development of other bulbous genera. Seldom has the newly developed variety been propagated to commercial quantity before being placed on the market. The beautiful Backhouse hybrids, for example, are sold in pea sizes, and no one is working up a large stock to insure perpetuation. The same thing obtains with some of the rare species. No stocks have been accumulated, and the few bulbs existing are likely to disappear.

But conditions are changing. There are among the lilies, as in most genera, species which have good parental qualities. There are those which have excellent seed habits and those which are receptive to a wide range of pollens.   Some of the results of these discoveries are the Backhouse hybrids of delicate pastel shades.   More recent is the group of more brilliantly colored west-coast hybrids, which are being produced in quantity at Bellingham, Wash.; while the recently commercialized *Lilium longiflorum erabu* from Japan is another result.

Receptive to Wide Range of Pollens

Recent experiences indicate that *Lilium superbum* is receptive to a wide range of pollens.   *L. regale* has the same characteristic, although the resulting seedlings are predominantly Regal.   But what the second generation may bring forth no one has progressed far enough to predict.   This lily takes the pollen of *L. leucanthum chloraster*, *L. sargentiae*, *L. browni colchesteri*, etc. Such crosses should yield results of great interest.

Lilium columbianum reacts to pollens of a wide range of Martagon lilies of both hemispheres.   The European group of *L. martagon* is known to be amenable; so are the West coast species, as abundantly proved at Bellingham, Wash.   The splitting up in the latter comes in the first generation, and the second generation is a riot of brilliantly colored lilies, no two of which are alike.   *L. pardalinum*, *L. parryi*, and the *L. humboldtii* group produce very remarkable hybrids which are desirable garden lilies. (Fig. 146.)

Doctor Stout has shown that even our old *Lilium tigrinum*, which seldom seeds in this country, can be made to seed with foreign pollen. Results have been obtained with pollen of both *L. pseudotigrinum* and *L. superbum*, the latter in reciprocation.

Persistency is indispensable when one undertakes to hybridize lilies. The fact that a cross has been tried without success augurs little.

FIGURE 146.—A yellow first-generation hybrid lily produced by crossing two west American species. The shape of the flower is that of *Lilium humboldtii magnificum*, but the position on the stem and color simulate *L. parryi*

Walter Van Fleet tried for 10 years to cross *L. tenuifolium* and *L. concolor* by reciprocally pollinating them.   The seed from the last reciprocal cross he made was entrusted to the writer the fall before he died. Fully 1,000 plants were grown.   Only one was an undoubted hybrid. There was no appreciable variation in the others, and there has been no breaking up in the second generation of the general progeny.   The hybrid has produced no seed thus far.

Large Progenies Necessary

To improve lilies by hybridization it is necessary to deal in large progenies. When a cross has been effected and the seedlings grown to maturity, it is imperative that the basis for the establishment of the new variety be a single seedling. Vegetative propagation of this seedling will constitute the variety, which should be propagated into a large stock to insure its perpetuity before dissemination.

All this takes time. Basing judgment on experience with our West coast Martagons, it takes four or five years before the first seedling can safely be picked out. After that the matter becomes a long grind of careful propagation and culture to work up the stock to a commercial status by vegetative means. It looks now as if a seedling selected at 5 years of age in 1924 will yield enough material to start a progeny of 25,000 in 1930. It will take at least two years longer to grow these to a size fit for marketing. This is considered quick work.

Breeding lilies promises good results. In the writer's opinion there is no more fertile field for plant improvement to-day than the lily. Enough has been accomplished by breeders in the last few years to justify the prediction that present activity will lead inevitably to the production of new and better plants. It seems safe to predict that in the future we may look upon the wild lily with much the same sort of appreciation that we now view the native species of tulips.

DAVID GRIFFITHS.

LIVESTOCK Betterment Registers Advancement Throughout the World   A survey of livestock improvement in 33 important stock-raising countries has resulted in information of interest to stock owners in the United States. Since the quality of domestic livestock extends to meat and other products derived from the animals, the betterment of herds and flocks has an important bearing on competition among nations in the sale of surplus livestock products. The information was obtained through the Consular Service and the foreign offices of the United States Department of Agriculture, with the State Department cooperating. Reports were received from Canada and Mexico, 5 countries in South America, 18 in Europe, 3 in Africa, 2 in Asia, and 2 in Oceania.

The numbers and kinds of animals vary greatly in the different countries. Some export large quantities of livestock products; others produce less than is needed for home consumption. In many countries plans for improving livestock are largely in the hands of stockmen and dairymen. In others the Government has endeavored to bring about livestock betterment through legislation, distribution of improved breeding stock, subsidies, prizes, and other inducements.

Purebred Sires a Dominant Influence

Although the conditions of production are extremely varied, the use of carefully selected purebred sires is the dominating influence underlying all plans for improvement. This applies to all classes of livestock and to both governmental and private activities. The reports show universal agreement that the use of purebred males is an economical and effective means of improving all kinds of farm animals.

The study indicates that the business of importing high-quality breeding animals is extensive. Importations are especially conspicuous in South American countries and others producing meat for export. There is a desire among livestock breeders for animals of the highest type and also a willingness to pay high prices for such animals. In Argentina, already widely known for its beef cattle, marked improvement in swine has taken place during the last 10 years.

Extensive Interest in Dairying

The reports show wide interest in dairying. The dairy cow and industries that utilize milk have entrenched themselves strongly throughout the civilized world. Great attention has been devoted to the development of herds having high average milk production. In southeastern Australia, where official cow testing of dairy herds began in 1913, the yearly average butterfat production has been raised from 275 to 560 pounds.

In several countries, notably those of the British Empire, there are comprehensive "schemes for livestock improvement," inaugurated and fostered by the Government in cooperation with county and local authorities.

The establishment and maintenance of experiment stations and animal-breeding centers has been an important factor in the improvement of livestock in most countries. This feature is noticeable among the newer countries formed since the World War. The Government of Yugoslavia is seeking to increase the use of improved sires. It maintains five animal-breeding farms at various points throughout the kingdom. It has six stations for stallions and three for bulls, boars, and rams.

In many countries poultry raising is receiving much official attention, and the production of domestic fowls is increasing. In the Union of South Africa poultry raisers have the assistance of three poultry officials in each province. These experts conduct extension work, including lectures, demonstrations, and visits to farms. They also act as judges at poultry shows.

Importance of Disease Control

The survey, though dealing chiefly with breeding questions, shows a close relation between the control of animal diseases and the establishment of profitable livestock industries. In some instances the establishment of a veterinary service marked the beginning of livestock improvement and of production on a commercial basis.

Throughout most of the countries there has been an increasing tendency toward greater uniformity in breed characteristics and toward standardization of breeds. Such a policy naturally produces more desirable market animals.

Other methods for livestock betterment in various countries include educational literature, official awards at shows, purebred-sire legislation and subsidies, demonstrations and exhibits.

Results Are Available to Public

The reports have been summarized in a mimeographed pamphlet, copies of which may be obtained, without cost, from the Bureau of

Animal Industry. Familiarity with animal breeding in other countries should be helpful to livestock breeders in America. Such information shows where the greatest competition exists now and is likely to exist in the future, and is a reminder that continued efforts are needed to retain the present prestige of the United States in animal breeding and world trade in livestock products.

D. S. BURCH.

LIVESTOCK Cooperative Association Efficient, Intensive Study Shows The sales efficiency of a cooperative marketing association is a question of first importance to its members. Attempts to discredit the sales organizations of cooperatives have been numerous. It has even been stated that at times of heavy receipts the sales organizations have been unable to meet the demands of the peak loads placed upon them and have found

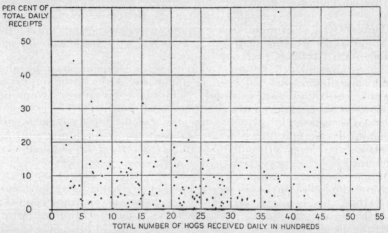

FIGURE 147.—The wide scattering of the dots indicates that there was no tendency as volume of business increased for the association to sell larger quantities of hogs to operators who sometimes functioned in the capacity of traders. Agencies functioning as order buyers, traders, or brokers, or in all three capacities, were included. Exclusive order buyers were not included. Data for 141 trading days in 1925 are shown

it necessary to increase the relative quantities of animals sold to traders or speculators.

The Division of Cooperative Marketing recently has had an opportunity to make an intensive study of the sales operations of an important cooperative livestock commission association. Sales records for 141 trading days during the year 1925 were examined and analyzed. The principal phase of this analysis was directed toward the determination of the relative quantities of animals sold to traders or speculators under variations in the daily volume of the association's receipts. No evidence was found of any tendency on the part of the sales organization of the association to sell relatively more of its receipts of cattle, calves, and hogs to traders or speculators on days of heavy receipts than on days of lighter receipts.

In the accompanying chart (fig. 147) the daily hog sales to traders or speculators, or to operators who sometimes functioned in these capacities, are plotted as percentages of the total sales for each day. Had there been any relationship between the volume of total daily sales of hogs by the association and the relative amount sold to the trader and speculator group, the dots would have been so grouped as to exhibit a definite trend. The wide scattering disproves in this instance the assertion that the sales organization found it necessary to sell greater numbers of hogs to traders or speculators on days of heavy receipts.

A study of the number of buyers of hogs indicated that, as the number of hogs received by the association increased, the number of buyers patronizing the association increased. The larger number of hogs attracted more buyers to the association's pens.

As a result of the department's study of this sales organization, including prices obtained for hogs sold by it, there appeared to be definite grounds for the conclusion that the association's sales organization was competent to meet the demands placed upon it by large volumes of business. It was apparent that under peak loads of business the sales organization functioned satisfactorily and efficiently.

KELSEY B. GARDNER.

LIVESTOCK Farmers Can Obtain Better Profits With Better Husbandry Animal husbandry has been described as the science which Noah founded as an art. True, Noah did not specialize in domestic animals. Yet he must have known how to take good care of them, for he brought the ancestors of our cattle, horses, sheep, and hogs safely through the flood. He protected them from the predatory animals that were also in the Ark. He must have made wise provision for feeding and caring for them during their stay in his big boat. He was not a scientist according to our modern understanding of the term, but he must have been highly skilled nevertheless.

Many modern stockmen would do well to profit by Noah's example and use more care in their business. Three ingredients go into every animal grown and marketed. They are breeding, feeding, and care. Care, the least expensive of the three, is the part most often neglected; feed, the most expensive item, is often grossly wasted through a lack of care; and breeding, though it may be of the highest quality, can not prevail against carelessness. Disease germs and parasites, for example, which result from slipshod husbandry and neglect, are no respecters of pedigree.

Lack of Care May Be Costly

A few examples will serve to illustrate the relative cheapness of care and its importance. In a study of the cost of raising and fattening hogs on 51 farms in Iowa and Illinois, the department learned that feed made up 64 per cent of the total cost of the hogs when marketed. The labor of the farmers represented but 8 per cent of the total. Thus the feed given those hogs cost the farmers eight times as much as the care. Much of the feed, however, was wasted, for 340 of every 1,000 pigs farrowed were lost before weaning time. Let us look into the causes of the deaths.

More than 90 of the pigs in each 1,000 were lain on and crushed or smothered by the sows. Care would have avoided most of this loss— care in the shape of a simple guardrail around the inside of the farrowing house, the cost of which would have been insignificant when spread over a period of years.

Exactly 50 of the 1,000 pigs were born dead. Lack of proper handling and management of the sows were directly responsible for most of that. Seventeen of them were chilled to death. Greater watchfulness or a warmer house was needed. Fourteen of them were eaten by the sows. A poorly balanced ration in the breeding herds was the brand of mismanagement to blame. (Fig. 148.)

The Determining Factor

As the cost of feeding and caring for a sow throughout the year has to be paid by her pigs, it is clear that those sows whose litters are large at marketing time, in both numbers and total weight, are the sows which produce the cheapest pork. Good breeding is desirable. Well-balanced and nourishing feeds also are important. The item of care, however, is the great determining factor responsible for the number of

FIGURE 148.—The results of two extremes in feeding. These hogs are litter mates. The large one was raised by a Louisiana pig-club boy, and it shows the results of overfeeding, probably of an unbalanced ration. The other was raised by the boy's father and evidently neglected

pigs which get to market. The farmer who remembers this and practices good husbandry gets well paid for his pains.

The same is true in other lines of livestock production. A 5-year study of the cost of fattening beef cattle in the Corn Belt showed that feed constituted from 75 to 85 per cent of the total cost (depending on the season) and that the value of the farmer's time in feeding and caring for the cattle was but one-twentieth to one-fifteenth as great as the value of the feed which the steers consumed.

That there was great variation in the degree of skill with which these cattle were fed—or, in other words, the quality of the husbandry which these various farmers practiced—is shown by the fact that the rate of gain made by the heavy steers varied from 0.4 to 4.4 pounds a day, while the cost of a pound of gain made by the medium-weight cattle during one winter ranged from 2 to 58 cents.

Not all farmers have available the ideal feeds in exactly the proper balance for their various flocks and herds. A great many farmers are unable to afford the immediate purchase of high-quality breeding stock. But there is no farmer in the country who can not afford to

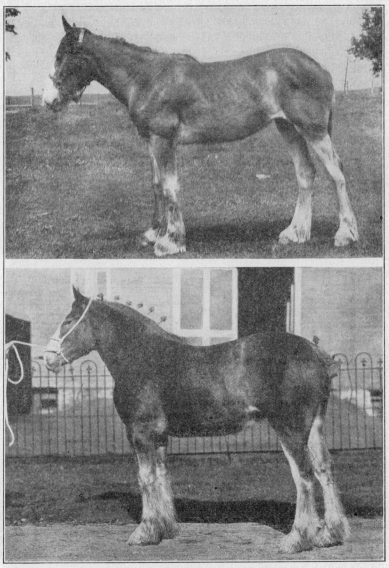

FIGURE 149.—Clydesdale filly, Lady Footprint, in run-down condition in the late summer of 1918, and later in good condition, after proper feeding, in December of the same year, when she won fourth prize at the International Live Stock Exposition

mix large quantities of careful husbandry into his daily work with his stock. (Fig. 149.) This better husbandry inevitably will be followed by greater profits and better animals.

WILLIAM JACKSON.

LIVESTOCK Feeder Who   With our knowledge of breeding, of
      Knows Feed Nutrients   differences among feeds, of the pro-
      Can Cut Down Costs   cesses of animal nutrition, and of
                            sanitation, we have become accus-
tomed to 1,000-pound beef yearlings, ton-litters of pigs at 6 months of
age, and cows producing 1,000 pounds of butterfat in one year. As
the engineer becomes familiar with the chemical composition, the
tensile strength, the coefficients of expansion, the absorptive capacity,
and the rusting and corrosive qualities of the materials with which he
works, so the feeder needs to know the composition, the palatability,
the digestibility, and the growth, reproductive, maintenance, and
fattening qualities of the feeds which are available for his livestock.

How Chemistry Aids Farmers

Chemical analyses as they are used commercially give the percentages of water, ash, or mineral matter, crude protein, crude fiber, starch
and sugar (nitrogen-free extract), and fat or oil (ether extract) which
a feed contains. These analyses require expensive and elaborate
chemical apparatus and the services of an experienced chemist.
All of these five substances—mineral matter, crude protein, crude
fiber, nitrogen-free extract, and ether extract—are in reality names
for groups of chemical compounds. What differences do variations
in these substances make? For instance, while water is a very
necessary nutrient, any excess of it in feeds is objectionable, for two
important reasons. First, one does not want to pay a dollar a bushel
or $40 a ton for water when it can be obtained free wherever there is
rain. Second, the drier feeds are, except extreme dryness, the longer
and better they keep.

Another nutrient—crude protein—is absolutely essential for the
growth, repair, and reproduction of animal tissue, and nothing else
will take its place. Protein can be used in the body to produce heat
and energy, but in most instances crude fiber, starch, sugar, and fat
or oil are much cheaper fuels. Although crude fiber is used similarly
to starch and sugar, it is much bulkier and harder to digest, hence
less valuable and oftentimes objectionable when present in large
quantities. Cattle wintered on straw, which is largely crude fiber,
lose heavily in weight, although they are getting as much as they can
eat. Oats, however, having 11 per cent of crude fiber, are an excellent
feed for horses.

Fat also is a very valuable component of animal feed in spite of the
fact that animals can produce fat from protein, crude fiber, starch,
and sugar. Fat is a very concentrated feed, as a pound of it will
produce about two and one-fourth times as much heat or energy when
it is oxidized or burned as crude fiber, sugar, or starch. Food for
human consumption is often spoken of as rich when it has a high
content of fat or oil. Fat has another important quality in animal
feeding when it contains essential fat-soluble vitamins.

Minerals Also Are Essential

Ash or mineral matter, like protein, is absolutely essential in the
structure of animal tissue. The bones especially are rich in mineral
elements, the principal ones being calcium and phosphorus. Hogs
fed on corn alone, a ration deficient in ash, develop leg weakness and

their bones break very easily. Either the sun's rays or a vitamin abundant in the leaves of plants and the livers of fish are essential for the utilization of calcium as found in plants and inorganic forms. To be effective, the sun's rays must strike the body directly and not pass through ordinary glass.

In general, the feeds usually raised on a farm supply adequate mineral matter. There are notable exceptions, however, in certain localities where there are shortages of certain mineral elements, such as calcium and iodine. Such deficiencies may be corrected by adding minerals containing these essential elements to the common salt which should be always available to all livestock. Unfortunately, analyses for mineral matter obtained by burning and weighing the residue or ash do not show a deficiency of any particular element. The same is true of protein. There is a considerable number of proteins; some are essential for certain vital processes, such as growth and reproduction, and can not be replaced by any of the others. Generally speaking, the proteins of animal origin are superior to those of vegetable origin, and those found in leguminous plants, such as alfalfa, are superior to those found in cereals, such as corn.

In addition to the nutrients shown by chemical analyses there are several factors essential to proper animal nutrition, such as certain rays from the sun, vitamins, and the oxygen of the air. Vitamins are present in feeds in such minute quantities that they can not be separated and weighed. A shortage of certain vitamins causes deficiency diseases, such as rickets, scurvy, and beriberi. Other vitamins are essential for such vital processes as growth and reproduction. In the plant world the leaves and the germ of the seed are generally richest in vitamins, while in the animal body the digestive organs are richest in vitamins.

Planning Well-Balanced Rations

Farmers who are accustomed to feed their livestock exclusively on home-grown feeds, which do not contain an adequate quantity of all the necessary nutrients, may lower their costs of production by marketing a part of the grain or hay which they raise and buying some feed which makes a better balanced ration of the resultant supply of feed. For instance, should corn, oats, and timothy be the crops raised the rations fed to the livestock would be seriously deficient in the character of the protein and ash. Both fattening and maintenance costs in pounds of feed could be reduced considerably by selling a part of the grain, hay, or both, and purchasing some meal rich in protein, some legume hay, or both.

A much better solution, however, for obtaining a properly balanced ration would be to grow a sufficient quantity of some legume, such as alfalfa, clover, soy beans, or cowpeas. Legume hay alone, or legume hay and oat straw or corn stover, make a satisfactory maintenance or wintering ration, whereas a full-feed ration of two parts grain and one part legume hay by weight makes a satisfactory fattening ration. For fattening young hogs it takes about 50 per cent more corn when they are fattened on corn alone than when they are fattened on corn balanced by some feed rich in protein, such as soy-bean meal or tankage. Such a difference indicates clearly how a decided loss in feeding hogs can be turned into a substantial profit.

33023°—29——28

Exact Analysis Usually Unnecessary

Fortunately it is not necessary, for practical purposes, to know the exact analysis of each feed as it is raised and fed on the farm. In general, the grains, such as corn, are rich in carbohydrates, especially starch; the cereal products, such as bran, are fairly rich in protein; the packing-house products, such as tankage and the cake or meal left from extracting oil from cottonseed, flaxseed, and soy beans, are very rich in protein; the straws, stovers, and coarse hays are high in crude fiber; the legume hays are fairly rich in proteins and the more important minerals; the oil-bearing seeds are rich in oil; the green feeds, grasses, legumes, roots, and silage are very high in water and are well supplied with vitamins.

With a few exceptions, each of the feeds of these general classes contains some appreciable if not adequate quantity of each of the necessary nutrients. Consequently, in the feeding of livestock generally there should be no unthriftiness from malnutrition if they are fed liberally with a variety of feeds well supplied with the necessary nutrients. It is important that they receive in addition an abundant supply of the most plentiful and the cheapest factors in nutrition— good water, fresh air, and the direct rays of the sun.

ARTHUR T. SEMPLE.

LIVESTOCK Improvement Can Be Accomplished by Selective Breeding   Probably in no group of artisans is an ideal more firmly established than among breeders whose aim is to develop superior strains of livestock. Ever since the pioneer breeders of more than a century ago laid the foundations of our breeding methods, painstaking breeders have been devoting a lifetime of untiring energy to the improvement of conformation and the increase of production in order that the livestock industry might enjoy a higher position than it has in the past.

How can this good work be continued and further improvement be effected? How can the farmer increase his milk yields, produce better beef, shear more wool, and raise more and better swine by the application of breeding principles?

Strange as it may appear, the basic methods are essentially the same as those which were used a century ago. The material available for selection at the present time is, however, vastly greater in numbers and possibly superior in quality to that which existed in England during the eighteenth century, when Robert Bakewell was fixing types in English breeds of cattle and sheep by breeding methods.

Variation is the real basis of improvement. The selection and the combination of the desirable variations are the keynotes to success in animal breeding. In most cases the desire is not to produce something radically new, but rather to improve the herd or flock which is at hand. Particularly is this true of the average livestock producer, whose primary interest lies in market animals rather than in breeding stock as such.

To him the problem is not how to produce something better than the best which existed before, but rather to raise the average of his stock more nearly to that of the best. Then the problem reduces itself largely to the introduction of new blood. Since this can best be done by the medium of improved sires, the question becomes one of selecting these sires.

Considerations in Selection of Sire

In selecting a sire there are three main considerations to be kept in mind—(1) the individuality of the animal, (2) his pedigree, (3) the performance of his progeny.

Individuality is important, but we must keep distinctly and clearly in mind the fact that what we see as the animal stands before us is controlled, so far as breeding is concerned, by a multitude of factors found in the germ cells. How these factors will be sorted out and recombined in the next generation can not be ascertained accurately by a mere examination of the various points of conformation. Consequently, selection based on individuality sometimes brings great disappointment because of the failure of the animal to "breed on."

In regard to the points of individuality which should receive particular attention it is well to have in mind the ideal type toward which one is working as well as the good and bad points of the females with which the sire is to be used. It is particularly important that the sire should be as good as the females in average conformational characters and distinctly superior in those particular respects which he is selected to improve.

The pedigree is an item of considerable guidance value. Much careful study, together with a detailed knowledge of breed history and the approximate utility value of the various family names, is necessary for a proper evaluation of the pedigree. The character and relationships of the animals in the pedigree indicate the probable type which the sire will produce. If there is evidence of extensive line breeding to prepotent individuals of the same type, the chances are increased that this type will predominate among the offspring. If, on the other hand, the ancestry contains a variety of types, there is little chance of predicting correctly what the sire will produce, even though the individual ancestors are the best of their kind. Another important point is the degree of relationship. A prepotent sire or dam is particularly important. The dam's sire has only about half as much prediction value as the sire himself. Ancestors further back than the fourth generation need hardly be considered as individuals. Inferior ancestors, as well as the superior ones, are important and must receive careful consideration.

Progeny Performance a Valuable Test

The most important test that a breeder can use in making his selection is that of progeny performance. No matter how excellent in appearance a sire may be and no matter how many noted animals may appear in his pedigree, unless his progeny are of the desired type and show high production he is not a desirable sire. Thus the progeny performance test is of great value, particularly among dairy cattle. There it has been clearly shown that a milk record for even a 7-day period is worth about twice as much as the score on conformation made by the best judge. In beef cattle there is, of course, a somewhat different situation, since meat instead of milk is the market product, and we have not yet perfected a means of measuring efficiency in beef production in advance of slaughter. In the absence of more definite measures, knowledge of the important current sires in the breed and a careful study of the pedigree, therefore, become very important as a means of estimating the probable prepotency.

Only a small part of the total livestock population of this country consists of registered purebreds, and the grading up of the heterogenous native stock which exist in certain sections by the use of the proved purebred sire offers the greatest opportunity for improvement. Much has been written about the scrub sire, and many such animals have been replaced by purebreds, but there are still thousands of scrub sires which could be profitably replaced by more desirable and prepotent individuals. There must be a careful culling of purebreds as well as of grades. There is no particular reason why a herd of grades will not produce as much as or more than a herd of purebreds, but the grades tend to show breeding segregation into the good, medium, and poor, while the purebreds tend to "breed on."

Choose the Best Among the Purebreds

A fact of considerable importance, and one which is frequently overlooked, is that inferior sires occur among registered purebreds. These individuals carry more potential harm than a grade of similar quality because they are more nearly pure and will tend to "breed on" the undesirable qualities. It is important, therefore, that careful culling be practiced among purebred cattle.

In dealing with sheep, swine, poultry, and other classes of animals, the fundamentals of improvement are the same as in the case of cattle. In sheep there is the dual condition of conformation and wool production to be considered. In poultry, among the egg breeds the annual egg production is the main item, while among the meat breeds the situation may be compared with that existing among the beef breeds of cattle. Swine offer an added factor in number of young. In this case the number of pigs farrowed has not been determined definitely as due to inheritance, although inherited factors are undoubtedly concerned. Hence, not much weight can be given to number of young at a single farrowing period as an indicator of what the number will be at the next period, even if the same sire is used.

Briefly, the ideal in improving a herd or flock of the character found on the average farm is to use a proved sire which shows superior individuality and breeding ability for his class and breed.

HUGH C. McPHEE.

LIVESTOCK Improvement Greatly Influenced by Educational Exhibits

"I built a hog trough like the one you showed here two years ago," said a farmer smiling at the man in charge of the department's livestock exhibit. "Did it work?"

"It's the only good trough I have on the place," replied the farmer. "I had one old sow, though, that didn't take to it at first."

"What was the trouble?"

"Well, she couldn't get her feet in it, and she couldn't root it over. I'd like another copy of the bulletin telling how to make that trough. I want to send it to my boy down in Missouri."

The foregoing is typical of comments heard at the department's educational exhibits at State fairs and important livestock events. The exhibit in question did not tell the farmer how to construct the trough, nor did it urge him to do so. Instead, it merely showed the trough in a well-arranged hog lot, containing well-fed, sleek hogs.

Bulletins or blue prints showing the details of construction were obtainable at a near-by information booth.

The exhibit merely conveyed the idea to the farmer. Details of construction and measurements were of no use to him at the moment. Had the exhibit attempted to cover all this information it probably would have failed even to convince the farmer of the desirability of duplicating the trough on his own farm. This particular exhibit has been found to be so attractive to farmers that it is repeated every few years at some of the larger fairs.

Other successful exhibits showing new ideas in modern hog-lot equipment have created much interest among hog raisers. One of them is a "creep" which enables young pigs to obtain a special growing ration, unmolested by the sows. Another is a hayrack for hogs. A farmer who adopted this innovation—perhaps the first seen in his neighborhood—furnished an example of how such exhibits benefit the farming community generally. When this one farmer placed in his hog lot a "new-fangled" item of equipment that kept his hogs from wasting hay, he created interest and set an example for an entire neighborhood. Other farmers see the hayrack and build racks like it. Many of them probably did not know the value of legume hay for furnishing cheap protein for swine during winter, when pasture is not available. Some of them may not even have realized that hogs would eat hay. And those who had previously fed hay to hogs will probably keep it before them more constantly with this convenient and inexpensive item of equipment.

Results Are Encouraging

It is only through voluntary testimony of the kind described and by noting the number of requests for more information that the value of exhibits as teaching agencies has been appraised. At a recent exhibit at one of this country's great stock shows there were offered to the visitors blue prints of drawings, specifications for the construction of certain farm buildings and livestock equipment, and an educational poster on the subject of quality in meat. All that was required of the visitor who wished any of these was that he write his name and home address in a book for that purpose. The farmers were not urged to use this service, and no attendants were present to assist with the registration. The aim was principally to aid only those who were sufficiently interested in the blue prints or posters.

In this particular case visitors from 32 States and 2 foreign countries availed themselves of the service offered. A total of 470 people from the State in which the exhibit was shown registered in the book, and 49, 35, 25, and 22, respectively, from four of the nearest States.

Swine-Sanitation Exhibit Is Popular

One of the department's most widely known exhibits portrays the high points of the McLean County system of swine sanitation. In this display two pens of live pigs of the same age and breed are used. The pigs in one pen had been kept free of worms by means of the system, while the pigs in the other were wormy. The difference in size and condition of the pigs told the story. This exhibit was first shown in 1921 and has been in continual demand ever since, having been shown in one form or another in nearly every State. This system of swine raising is now used in practically every section of the United States where hogs are raised, and it is believed that the exhibit can be credited with a large share of this noteworthy result.

FIGURE 150.—An example of the interest that farmers take in studying livestock exhibits

Railroad Exhibits Are Valuable

The fact that railroads and other commercial concerns are using exhibits as a visual demonstration to livestock farmers of the desirability of improved practices is additional evidence of the value of this means of extension teaching. Elaborate displays have been used

FIGURE 151.—An exhibit in which live steers (a feeder steer on the left and a finished steer on the right) are shown with measured quantities of feeds to illustrate the results of steer-feeding practices

on many of the special trains run by railroads to encourage the adoption, by farmers, of purebred sires. Two or more carloads of exhibits are used in conjunction with a series of lectures on the subject of better sires to convince those who visit the train. Then, as a rule, a purebred bull, or boar, or ram is left at each stop in exchange for a scrub animal. Thus a nucleus is begun in each community for furnishing a practical demonstration of the soundness of the principles presented by the exhibit and the lecturers.

The Farmer is Shown "Why" Rather Than "How"

Successful exhibits do not attempt to portray more than the outstanding facts concerning an improved practice. Sometimes the aim is merely to arouse interest. (Fig. 150.) A good rule to follow in building exhibits is to present the information so that "he who runs may read." If the farmer can be convinced of the desirability of a thing he will take steps to learn how to do it and to put it into practice on his farm. (Fig. 151.) He will not stand much urging, however, and he has no time for details. He wants to know, not "how" but "why." If he is merely told "how" by an exhibit he will perhaps forget all about it by the time he reaches home and may even resent the entire experience. But if he is convinced of the soundness of the teaching and can carry home in his pocket the detailed directions, thus having the "why" in his head and the "how" in his pocket, the chances are that his poultry plant or his hog lots or his breeding herds or flocks will in due time contain object lessons for his neighbors.

R. S. ALLEN.

LIVESTOCK Industry Suffers Heavy Loss By Abortion Disease About 10 years ago, infectious abortion and tuberculosis rivaled each other for the distinction of being the greatest plague of livestock in the United States. Since that time, tuberculosis has declined materially as the result of systematic eradication, but the abortion disease is a more conspicuous cause than ever of livestock losses. This malady threatens the source of the Nation's cattle supply and affects the very organ, the udder, on which the entire dairy industry depends.

Abortion disease is responsible for an estimated economic loss of more than $50,000,000 annually. Losses take the form of calf mortality, reduced milk flow, temporary or permanent sterility, and various breeding troubles. The bacillus which causes infectious abortion has been under investigation in the United States and abroad for the last 20 years. During that time much has been learned concerning the organism, its behavior under various circumstances, its long life in dead animal tissue, and the symptoms and lesions it causes in live animals.

Two different blood tests provide the means of detecting the disease in animals. Such medicinal remedies as have been tried thus far have shown no curative value, but the germs of abortion disease succumb quickly to the action of ordinary disinfectants and of direct sunlight. Pasteurization also destroys any bacilli of the disease in milk.

The practical value of the information which follows depends on its application by cattle owners. Methods of excluding infection from healthy herds and of suppressing the disease in herds already infected are discussed in Farmers' Bulletin 1536-F. Veterinarians have rendered valuable service in aiding cattle owners, particularly dairymen, in the prevention and eradication of infectious abortion.

Methods of Combating the Disease

Success in combating the disease, especially in badly infected herds, requires detailed precautions as well as great care in disposing of infected material from aborting cows. Owing to the practical difficulties involved in the control by these methods of a disease so widespread and so serious, there is need for continued research to develop simpler and more effective control measures.

The Federal Goverament has appropriated $92,500 for the investigation of infectious abortion during the next fiscal year. Plans include technical research and experiments on farms to determine the most effective means of utilizing present knowledge. Research on other animal diseases in the past has resulted in material benefits year after year. Losses have been greatly reduced, and the knowledge that a disease has been conquered has given stock owners a feeling of greater security.

Lines of Research in Progress

Experimental work now in progress on infectious abortion involves many phases of the problem, most of them closely related. It extends to the following main subjects: Abortion vaccines; duration of immunity given by vaccination; best age at which to vaccinate; feasibility of combating the disease by removing affected animals as determined by the agglutination test; practicability of building a clean herd from an infected one by protecting the progeny from infection; methods of keeping losses at a minimum while herd immunity is developing; methods of excluding the disease from abortion-free herds; influence of other infections and factors in the abortion problem; effect of nutrition on the susceptibility of animals to bacillus-abortion infection; possible channels of infection other than those now known; effect of the disease on milk production of cows; and virulence and other characteristics of various strains of the abortion bacillus.

The technical nature of the work and the need for studying the disease for a series of years in the same herds require that such experiments be conducted by trained investigators under closely controlled conditions at well-equipped experiment stations. Because of the need of repeating promising lines of study to verify results, there must be great patience on the part of all concerned.

This brief discussion of the abortion-disease problem is presented to acquaint stock owners with the comprehensive program of work now in progress and with the department's appreciation of the need for improved means of suppressing the malady.

JOHN R. MOHLER.

LIVESTOCK Weighed Under Improved Conditions at Many Public Stockyards — A scale is an instrument of precision. When properly chosen and used, it is capable of giving weights with a high degree of accuracy. This fact is of particular value to the livestock industry, as livestock is one of the highest-priced food commodities produced on the farm and is sold in quantity on the basis of weight. A large portion of the livestock marketed is sold at stockyards which come under the provisions of the packers and stockyards act. This gives the United States Department of Agriculture a special interest in the weighing of livestock and the equipment and methods employed. (Fig. 152.)

Small scales should be used for weighing small drafts and single animals. Large scales were introduced originally when livestock shipped to the stockyards were generally sold in carload lots or greater numbers. Nowadays, the average number of head per draft is small, and many single animals are weighed. The natural tendency has been to continue old equipment and methods under the new conditions and weigh single animals on carload scales.

Cooperating with the Department of Agriculture, the stockyards in several instances have installed small scales for weighing small drafts of livestock. The greater sensitiveness and the smaller graduations provided on the beams, enabling the weighings to be made in smaller steps, increase the accuracy of the weights. In some instances,

FIGURE 152.—Typical weighing scene at one of the smaller stockyards. The weight obtained is just as much a factor as the price in determining the money a farmer receives for his livestock

2-pound intervals are now used where previously 10-pound steps were employed. On many of the larger scales the 10-pound steps have been cut to 5 pounds, which makes more accurate weighing possible in the case of the larger scales.

An improved scale arrangement, facilitating the weighing of the miscellaneous mixture of large and small drafts which reach the scales, has been worked out and is now in use at some of the stockyards. It consists of a large and a small scale built alongside each other. The small scale is between the large scale and the scale house. The weigher sits in a bay window on an elevated floor with both beams before him, and facing both scales he commands a view of the scale platforms, gates, and approaches. The two scales comprise a weighing unit. The alleys and gates are arranged so that at the last moment the animals can be delivered to either scale without back tracking, delay, or confusion.

Deep Pits Safeguard Scales

The conditions which give a scale the valuable properties of accuracy and precision make it vulnerable to disturbing influences, and the accuracy may be impaired by derangements and interferences in the parts which are generally out of sight in the pit below the platform. When provision is not made for the frequent and convenient examination of scale parts, obstructions may occur and remain undiscovered, causing errors in the weights. Experience has shown that frequent inspections of scale parts are necessary to safeguard the scale against such conditions. Accumulations of dirt, rust, and ice and the presence of rats are among the common causes of error.

Many stockyards in recent scale installations have followed the suggestions of the department, and have installed the scales in deep, well-drained, concrete pits equipped with electric lights. Such pits are sometimes as clean as the stockyards office. (Fig. 153.) It takes

FIGURE 153.—View of a roomy scale pit that enables the scale to be examined without difficulty. A deep, clean, dry pit facilitates inspection and care and safeguards accuracy

but a moment to turn an electric switch, flooding the pit with light, and to enter the pit and examine the scale parts in proper detail. This is a great safeguard to the weights obtained over the scale.

Such pits also make the scales last longer. A scale, many months after being installed in a deep, dry pit, was recently visited, and, contrary to prior experience with the scale installed in a shallow pit, the knife-edges and bearings which determine the accuracy of the scale, and the other parts, were free from rust or visible deterioration.

Scale Accuracy Established By Test Weights

Regular tests are necessary if scales are to be reliable. (Fig. 154.) The accuracy of a scale should be determined by the use of standard-test weights up to the capacity at which it is used, and the test weights should be applied in different positions on the scale platform. Experience shows that the accuracy of a scale at a heavy load can not be safely deduced from tests made at lighter loads and that a scale may be accurate for a load in one position or corner and inaccurate when the load is placed at some other point on the scale platform.

Many stockyards have followed the department's recommendations and have provided themselves with scale-testing equipment consisting of 1,000 or 2,000 pounds of 50-pound weights, 50 or 60 pounds of assorted small weights, and a sufficient number of 1,000-pound, cast-iron, standard, test weights to test the scales up to the capacity at which they are used.

The present testing equipment has the advantage that it has passed through a form of evolution resulting in a simple and satisfactory form of 1,000-pound weight and a simple, 2-wheeled cart for handling it. (Fig. 155.) The weight recommended consists of a cast-iron, cubical

FIGURE 154.—A test of a livestock scale with thirty 1,000-pound weights and twenty 50-pound weights, making a total of 31,000 pounds. The determination of accuracy involves testing at various loads, usually at 1,000-pound steps, up to the maximum load at which the scale is used

weight about 16 inches on a side. Some of the carts most recently made have pneumatic tires which facilitate moving the loaded cart over rough surfaces. The weight is picked up by the simple method of elevating the handle of the cart, inserting a hook which is near the center of the axis of the cart under the handle of the weight, and then lifting the weight by bearing down on the handle. With good design, it was found possible to reduce the length of the handle to 5 feet and have sufficient leverage for lifting the 1,000-pound weight satisfactorily, and the short handle facilitates the handling of the weights in crowded or narrow places. The weight of the cart has been reduced to a minimum, and one man can load the cart and handle it onto and off the scale. With this equipment, the scales can be tested for the various loads and positions of the loads, and the accuracy of the scale established. If the scale is found to be inaccurate, the testing equipment provides a means for selecting any load for testing and adjusting the inaccurate scale part.

The introduction of this type of testing equipment has often been followed very soon by the discovery and elimination of defects not

FIGURE 155.—A 1,000-pound, cast-iron, test weight loaded on simple, rubber-tired, 2-wheeled cart. One man readily handles a 1,000-pound weight

previously discovered, resulting in a material improvement in the condition and accuracy of the scales.

C. A. BRIGGS.

LOGGING With Tractors Has Many Advantages Over Older Methods In logging operations in Arizona and New Mexico the gasoline tractor has recently taken the place of the horse or bull team. In the early days bull teams and 4-wheeled logging trucks were used in transporting the logs from the woods to the railroads or to the mills. Later the bull teams were supplanted by horses. The 4-wheeled trucks gave way to the so-called big wheels or carts, which were developed in the Lake States pineries. The two wheels were from 10 to 11 feet in diameter, and the logs were suspended from the lower part of the single axle. This style of logging was the standard method used on the larger western yellow-pine operations for almost 20 years.

Within the past five years experiments with the gasoline tractor of the crawler type in moving logs from the stump to the logging spurs have convinced lumbermen that the tractor has many advantages over the older methods, and most of the logging is now done by this type of machine. In most cases the logs, which are cut double length, are skidded on the ground direct from the stump to the track. Some experimental work has been done also with so-called hydraulic big wheels hauled by a tractor. These wheels are constructed of metal instead of wood, as formerly, and are capable of carrying from 1,500 to 3,000 feet of logs. This method is used only on long hauls.

Some work has been done with tractors in pulling one or more 8-wheeled wagons on which logs 1,500 to 2,000 board feet are loaded. Since there is considerable friction in skidding logs on the ground, this method reduces the power required and a smaller machine can be used.

Damage to the forest from tractor logging is now being studied. The tractors are thought to be slightly more destructive than horses and big wheels, but with certain restrictions and as the drivers become more expert the machines can, no doubt, be operated with a minimum of damage and are less destructive than steam skidders.

FIGURE 156.—Big wheels and tractor in logging work

The tractors have proved their value in fire suppression. They can be used to excellent advantage in building fire lines by dragging one or more logs along the route of the proposed fire line. This opens a line which can be completed rapidly by a few men with hand tools.

QUINCY RANDLES.

LUMBER Grades Suited for Various Kinds of Buildings on the Farm — To buy lumber economically consideration must be given to the exact properties required and how they occur in the various lumber grades. Experience and judgment determine which properties are important; a knowledge of characteristic defects provides information on which grade to select. The characteristics of the grades in this article apply only to yard lumber conforming with American lumber standards— namely, A, B, C, and D Select and Nos. 1, 2, 3, 4, and 5 Common, all of which are familiar to local dealers. The qualities of lumber important to farm uses are found in the grades as follows:

Strength

For many construction purposes commonly thought of as requiring strength, other qualities, such as adequate bearing and nailing surfaces and stiffness, are of as much importance as strength. Under such requirements No. 1 Common is a satisfactory grade for large and permanent farm structures. The size and character of the knots are limited in this grade, so that the lumber, in addition to stiffness, gives fair strength in bending. Decay is prohibited, and shake (lengthwise separation of the wood) is narrowly limited. No. 2 Common is suited for less-exacting construction and No. 3 for small structures where it is possible to saw out the large defects.

Where resistance to breaking is of importance the clearer grades of yard lumber or timber of the structural grades should be used. Where the requirement is limited as to size and species of wood, C Select specifies as many defects as are permissible for good strength. The fact that C Select lumber is generally drier than the lower grades assures relatively high strength qualities.

Where the construction is designed to eliminate vibration and deflection as far as possible, as in most house floors and walls, stiffness becomes the controlling factor. All grades above No. 2 Common are similar in stiffness, and No. 2 Common has but slightly less stiffness than the higher grades.

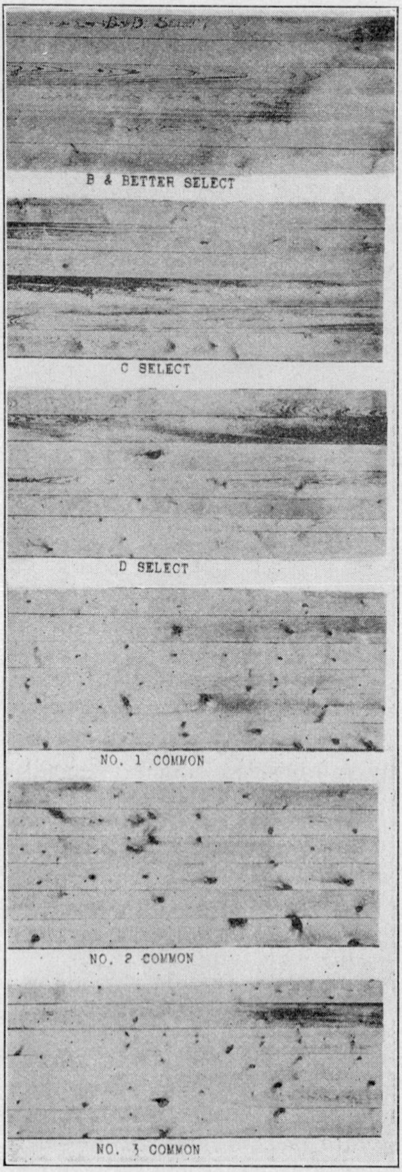

Varnish or Natural Finishing

B Select (commonly sold as B and Better) assures the best appearance with natural or varnish finishes. Where the smoothest appearance is not required, C Select gives reasonable satisfaction. Decorative effects are sometimes produced in panels for residences with knotty lumber from No. 1 Common and No. 2 Common.

Where wood is not exposed to weather, the defects allowed in C Select are such that they can be covered if the priming is properly done. D Select, with some cutting, gives almost as good quality as C Select. Where smooth appearance is required under exposure to the weather, B Select gives the best results. C Select and D Select give reasonably good results where the best appearance is not required.

For painted surfaces that do not receive close inspection and where protection against the weather is as important as appearance No. 1 Common and No. 2 Common are satisfactory. The large knots and pitch pockets in No. 2 Common do not result in so smooth and lasting a painted surface as in No. 1 Common, but the general utility is good.

FIGURE 157.—Approximate range in quality in some of the standard grades of yard lumber as represented by the grades of one item and one species

Protection Against Leakage

For protection against liquids seeping or beating through wooden construction, No. 1 Common is suitable. This grade and the select grades are usually drier than the lower grades and therefore shrink and open less at the joints. Where tightness against leakage of grain is required, No. 2 Common, with a small amount of cutting to eliminate occasional knot holes, may be used. For temporary protection against the weather, No. 3 Common is satisfactory even though knot holes and other open defects occur.

Clear wood wears more evenly than that containing knots. A Select is the only grade entirely free of knots, but B Select, although containing a few small knots, withstands wear excellently. C Select has sufficient limitations on defects to assure good results. D Select and No. 1 Common limit the size and character although not the number of knots, and are satisfactory where uniformity of wear is not required.

Resistance to Decay

Except in the "all heart" grades, the lower grades are more resistant to decay than the higher grades. This is because the decay-resistant heartwood and the larger and more numerous knots occur in the same portion of the log. The lower grades, however, include more pieces containing original decay, which sometimes counteracts the effect of the larger heartwood content. So small an amount of advanced decay is allowed in No. 2 Common that the probable resistance to further decay of lumber of this grade is greater than that of the higher grades from the same species and producing region.

C. V. SWEET.

M ACHINERY Plays a Vital Rôle in Making Agriculture Efficient — Development and use of improved farm machinery in the United States closely followed the opening of large fertile tracts for settlement. This development has come about largely since the middle of the last century; during the last 60 years production per farm worker has more than doubled. The practice of planting grain by hand, cutting with the cradle, and threshing with the flail has given way to improved methods with the introduction of seeder and drill, the reaper, the binder, the mechanical power-driven thresher, the header, and the combined harvester-thresher. Production of other farm commodities has been similarly speeded up by the development of large units of motive power and large tillage, planting, and harvesting machines.

No measure is available of how much of the increase in production per farm worker is due to the use of more power, to the working of larger areas of land, and to general improvements in the technique of production. It is a fact, however, that from 1870 to 1925, the average acreage of improved land per farm worker increased from about 32 acres to approximately 49 acres, an increase of more than one-half. At the same time the value of machinery on farms in terms of the 1913 price level increased nearly ten times, or from $270,000,000 in 1870 to more than $2,666,000,000 in 1925. The number of agricultural workers increased also, but, the value of machinery on farms (in terms of the

1913 price level) increased from $36 per farm worker in 1870 to more than $200 per worker in 1925. In less than 60 years the value of farm machinery per worker increased five and one-half times.

Production Per Farm Worker

The American farm worker produces from two to five times as much as do similar workers in the important European countries. His high production capacity may largely be attributed to the use of large units of machinery and power and to the relatively small amount of field work done by hand.

Even with these increases in the value of machinery, and in acreage handled and physical production per worker, there is room for a further increase in the efficiency of labor on many farms through the extended use of larger machines and units of power and improved methods of production. But not all farms are suited to the use of the largest or even the larger machines and units of power. One man and two horses operating a 2-section harrow will cover only 12 to 15 acres per day whereas the same man with a 4-section harrow and tractor will cover 40 to 45 acres per day; but the saving of labor and the performance of operations on time do not alone determine the wisdom of using the larger outfit. The lay of the land, the cost of the machinery, and the amount of work done each year must be considered. Small farmers have nothing to gain and much to lose in buying expensive machinery larger than is needed. Where the saving of labor is practicable, the following examples of machine performance for operations common to most farms may be used as a guide. The indicated machine performances are only approximate, because wide variations exist in the physical and climatic characteristics of different sections of the country.

The usual day's work for a 12-inch walking plow drawn by two horses is 1½ to 2 acres; for a two 14-inch bottom gang plow drawn by four horses, 3½ to 4 acres; and for a three 14-inch bottom gang drawn by tractor, about 8 acres. The two larger outfits require from one-fourth to one-half as much labor to plow a given acreage as is required by the 12-inch walking plow.

One man and four horses with a 1-row lister can normally list 6 acres in a day, whereas the same man with a 2-row lister drawn by tractor will list 16 acres a day, an actual saving in labor of over 60 per cent.

The Performance of Cultivators

The performance of cultivators varies widely depending upon the number of rows cultivated and unit of power used. In cultivating corn and cotton under usual conditions, a fair day's work for a 1-horse cultivator making two trips to the row is 4 acres; for a 2-horse 1-row cultivator, 8 acres; and for a 4-horse 2-row cultivator about 15 or 16 acres. Two-row and 4-row cultivators drawn by general-purpose tractors cover daily around 20 and 40 acres, respectively, under favorable conditions. Each of these cultivators is operated by one man. Ten days of one man's time are required with the 1-horse outfit to cultivate the same acreage that the 4-row outfit cultivates in one day; with the 1-row machine a man cultivates in one week what he can cultivate with the 1-horse cultivator in two weeks.

There are so many sizes of harrows, drills, planters, mowers, rakes and other machines that the farmer needs only to study his requirements and farm organization to determine and install the size best suited to his purpose.

The use of different sizes of machines and units of power is only partly responsible for variations in the amount of labor devoted to the production of each farm commodity.   Some soils need more work than others.   Production methods differ under different geographic and economic conditions.   Introduction of new types of machines for performing certain operations and combinations of operations has resulted in a distinct saving of labor.   About 1830 the farmer used a crude plow, seeded his wheat by hand, cut it with a sickle, and threshed it with a flail.   From 30 to 35 hours of labor were then used in producing 10 bushels of wheat.   In recent years, those farmers in the central Great Plains States who cut their wheat with a binder and thresh from the shock use about 8 or 9 hours of labor for producing and hauling to elevator or shipping point 10 bushels of wheat.   Farmers of the Northwest who grow wheat on land that was summer fallowed the previous year and harvest with a combine use only 3 hours for each 10 bushels.

Variations in Requirements

Different practices and labor requirements prevail even in the same region.   In the Great Plains wheat region, the total labor for harvesting and threshing is reduced from about 4.6 hours per acre for cutting with a binder and threshing with a stationary thresher to about 3.8 hours for cutting with a header and threshing with a stationary thresher, and further to about three-fourths of an hour per acre for harvesting with a combine.   In Illinois wheat harvested with the binder and the stationary thresher requires about 6.5 man hours per acre.   If it is harvested with the combine only 1.5 hours are required.

The husking and cribbing of corn from the standing stalk requires from 6 to 8 hours of labor per acre, compared with 25 to 35 hours when cut by hand, shocked, husked by hand, and the corn and stover hauled to the crib and feed lot.

Hay cut with two 6-foot mowers drawn by a tractor and stacked with push rakes and stacking equipment is handled with about one-half the labor required when it is mowed with one 5½-foot mower, raked, loaded from the windrow with a hay loader, hauled to the barn, and unloaded with a mechanical fork or sling; and with one-third of the labor required when cut with a 5½-foot mower, raked, cocked, and loaded and unloaded by hand.

Economical labor-saving equipment and practices are increasing in all lines of crop and livestock production, and the point of maximum efficiency is still distant.   Continued improvement is expected, and any changes made by the individual farmer should be made with a full understanding that a corresponding change must be made in the organization of the business.   Labor is only one of the numerous items of cost, and the saving of labor is but one of many ways of increasing the income from the farm.   The farmer's task is to select wisely the equipment and method of production best suited to his conditions after considering probable expenses and returns incident to contemplated changes.

M. R. Cooper.

33023°—29——29

MEASURING Changes in Prices Paid and Prices Received by Farmers The agricultural depression during recent years has caused an increasing demand for a method of measuring the disparity between the value of farm products and the value of commodities bought by farmers. During the World War years the prices received for farm products advanced more rapidly than retail prices paid by farmers, and the value of farm products when exchanged for other commodities was somewhat higher than during the pre-war years. By 1919 retail prices had advanced to approximately the same level as the price of farm products, and during the sharp decline in prices in 1920–21 the price of farm products fell considerably below retail prices. Since 1921 retail prices have ranged from 152 per cent of pre-war prices in 1922 to 159 per cent in 1925. Farm prices since 1921 have fluctuated much more than retail prices, ranging from 124 in 1922 to 147 in 1925. In 1928 farm prices averaged 140 per cent of pre-war prices, whereas retail prices averaged 155 per cent of pre-war prices.

Changes in price are usually measured by index numbers which are calculated by letting the prices of a certain group of commodities during a given period be equal to 100 and then showing prices of those commodities at other periods as a percentage of the price in the base period. The index numbers shown here have been constructed to measure changes in the prices of commodities which farmers buy, as compared with prices paid for these commodities in the years 1910–1914. Therefore, the index for any period of time shows the relationship of prices at that time to prices during 1910–1914. Commodities included in making the index number are usually weighted according to their importance. In measuring the changes in prices paid by farmers for commodities bought, the index numbers are weighted according to the amount of the different commodities the average farmer usually buys in a year.

The retail prices used in constructing this index number were collected by the department from country and small-town merchants and dealers who sell directly to farmers. They are asked to report the price for that grade or quality which farmers usually buy. Several hundred, in some cases several thousand, separate reports are averaged to make the United States average price for a given commodity. The inquiry was made annually from 1909 to 1922; beginning with 1923 it has been made quarterly.

Classification of Items Purchased

Farmers buy commodities for consumption by their families and for use in production. Commodities bought are divided into items for family living and items to be used in production. An index number is calculated for each, in order that changes in prices for each group of commodities may be shown. Commodities bought for family maintenance are subdivided into the following groups: Food, clothing, household operating expenses (fuel, laundry supplies, and automobile expenses for the family), furniture and furnishings, and building materials for the house. In Figure 158 (division A) are shown the changes in the prices of commodities bought for family maintenance, and price changes in food, clothing, and operating expenses. In June, 1928, the index of all commodities bought for family maintenance was 163. The index of furniture and furnishings at 208, clothing at

179, and building materials for the house at 173, were materially above the combined index for family maintenance, whereas food at 160 and operating expenses at 131 were somewhat below.

Commodities bought for use in production were subdivided into items of feed, machinery, building materials for outbuildings and

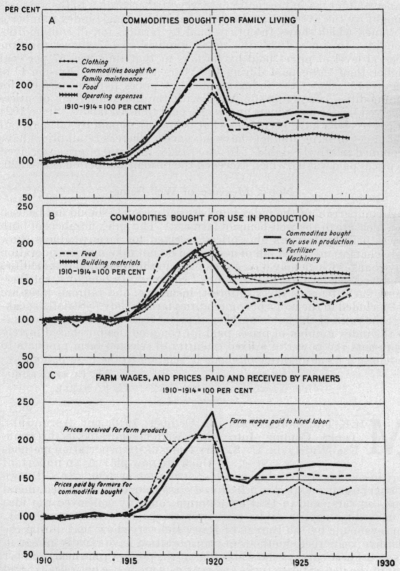

FIGURE 158.—Prices paid by farmers for commodities bought from 1910 to 1928

fences, fertilizer, equipment and supplies (tools, harness, binder twine, oil, gasoline, etc.), and seed. Division B of the figure shows the trend of the index numbers of all commodities bought for use in production, as compared with the index of feed, machinery, building materials, and fertilizer. In June, 1928, the index of all commodities bought for use in production was 148. Seed at 181, building materials at 161, and machinery at 156, were somewhat higher than the all-commodities index, whereas equipment and supplies at 130, fertilizer at 133, and feed at 143, were somewhat below the level of all commodities.

When the index numbers of commodities bought for family maintenance and for use in production are weighted according to the amounts bought by the average family and combined, a single index number is obtained which shows the prices paid by farmers for all commodities bought. In June, 1928, the index number at 157 shows that the general level of prices paid by farmers at that time was 57 per cent higher than those paid during the years 1910–1914. Division C of Figure 158 shows the index numbers of prices paid by farmers for commodities bought as compared with the index numbers of prices received for farm products and wages paid to hired labor. Since 1921 prices received have been somewhat below prices paid by farmers, but the prices of farm products have advanced, whereas retail prices have remained relatively stable. In June, 1928, the ratio of prices received to prices paid was 93, which exceeded the ratio in any period since 1920.

Not a Measure of Well-Being

A comparison of the index numbers in division C should not be used as a measure of the well-being of farmers. The index numbers of both prices paid by farmers and prices received for farm products show only changes in a fixed bill of goods and do not take into consideration any changes which may have taken place in the amount of commodities produced per farm or the amount of commodities bought. Furthermore, such items as taxes, interest, insurance, and railroad fares are not included in the index of commodities farmers buy. Strictly speaking, the ratio of the index number of prices received for farm products to the index number of prices paid for commodities purchased merely represents the power of a fixed quantity of selected farm products to purchase a fixed quantity of goods in relation to the base period.

C. M. Purves and
C. F. Sarle.

MILK Transportation in Tanks Coming Into Use Widely in U. S. In October, 1910, and April, 1914, there were inaugurated in this country two milk-transportation methods which are now playing an important part in our highly developed milk-distribution system. In 1910 two Massachusetts companies introduced glass-enameled, insulated, metal tanks on cars; and in 1914 a California company conceived the idea of mounting copper tanks on motor trucks for transporting milk. Surveys made by the Bureau of Dairy Industry show that during the past five years these methods of transportation have rapidly gained in favor. These surveys show also that at the present time nearly 80 per cent of the motor-tank trucks and tank cars are in use between 37° and 43° north latitude.

All tanks mounted in cars included in the survey are of glass-lined steel. The tanks mounted on motor trucks are constructed of glass-lined steel, nickel, copper, tin-lined steel, or stainless steel. A survey made in 1927 of 300 motor-tank trucks showed that 70 per cent of the tanks were insulated. This insulation consists of cork, felt, wood, and canvas pads over mineral wool. The type of chassis upon which the tanks are mounted depends upon the capacity of the tank and the road laws of the State in which operated. Most tanks up to 1,250 gallons capacity are mounted on regular motor chassis. Where the load to be carried is larger than this, the tank is usually mounted on a semitrailer (fig. 159); or in some cases two medium-size tanks, generally of 1,000 gallons capacity each or 1,250 gallons each, are mounted on a six-wheel chassis. The semitrailer type is harder to handle and requires a longer time to get into position, especially if the truck must be backed. The most popular size used on trucks is the 1,250-gallon tank.

An analysis of 103 motor routes throughout the country showed the average haul to be approximately 20 miles, with a return trip of the same distance, and the average speed to be 15 miles per hour. The

FIGURE 159.—A 2,000-gallon milk tank mounted on a semitrailer type truck equipped with air brakes

consensus of opinion of truck users is that 120 to 130 miles round trip is the economical limit of motor-tank truck transportation.

Methods of Hiring

The following methods of hiring hauling by motor-tank trucks are employed: (1) The company furnishes the tank and hires a hauler at either a specified rate per 100 pounds of milk hauled or by the day. In this case the company uses the tank for the display of its name and trade slogan; (2) the hauler furnishes the entire equipment and contracts for the hauling for a period of years at a stated rate per 100 pounds or per day; and (3) the hauler furnishes the tank and truck and receives railroad rates for hauling. Milk companies located some distance from railroad sidings save the hauling charge from the terminal to their plant by the use of the motor-tank truck.

Where road and weather conditions are favorable, substations and city milk plants may be established at favorable points. Milk delivery requires regularity. Therefore roads must be of such a nature that the daily delivery trip can be made on schedule time. The amount of snow that falls and the methods employed to clear it must be taken into consideration. In localities where snowfall is very heavy and power equipment for opening the road quickly and regularly is not employed, the motor-tank truck can not be used satisfactorily during the winter.

The standard railroad milk-tank car is of the express-car type, wired for electricity, with a thoroughly insulated body, an acid-resisting waterproof floor, and a patented removable one-piece roof. A tank is mounted in a special asphalt bed at each end of the car. The standard size of tanks is 3,000 gallons each, although recently tanks have been used holding 3,820 gallons each. These tanks are equipped with a 4-inch inlet with nonfoam device, 20-inch manhole, a mechanical agitator driven by a 2-speed motor, angle-stem thermometer, and standard 4-inch outlet. Accessory equipment in the car may consist of a stationary milk pump or air-pressure system, a water reservoir for washing the tanks, and a brine system for cooling, although the last feature has not come into general use. Cars of this type are either owned by the milk companies or leased to them by the car company at a daily rate.

A survey of 20 routes throughout the country shows that the average haul of milk-tank cars is 117 miles with a return trip of the same distance. The number of cars necessary for any route depends upon

FIGURE 160.—The interior arrangement of a modern milk-tank car

the railroad schedule, service on connecting lines, and the distance hauled. For 100 to 400 mile hauls three cars are usually needed.

Where conditions warrant it, milk transportation tanks reduce labor expense at country and city plants, eliminate the cost of ice and icing, reduce can investment, and result in milk reaching the plant in good condition with little or no waste en route.

An Early Milk-Train Route

It is interesting to compare the route and loading of a modern milk-tank car train with that of a milk-train route in the early part of the present century. The following extracts are from Department Bulletin No. 81, published in 1905:

The station at Northampton, Mass., is the starting place; time 5.50 in the morning. The train consists of a combination baggage car and smoker, a common passenger car, and a milk car with a few cans of cream and milk that came down from Keene, N. H., the previous afternoon. In 14 minutes we stop at Amherst to take on 20 cans of milk and to leave a cake of ice and a few empty cans. In 8 minutes more the train draws up at a flag station where 15 cans are loaded from the station platform and several empties thrown out. The next stop is at Belchertown. Here eight 1-horse wagons are hitched promiscuously to all kinds of available objects about the station; and 120 cans of milk are loaded, while the passengers are increased by one. Two or three miles farther on the train draws up at a highway crossing where there is a small platform and the usual shelter. Here nine single teams with common wagons are hitched to near-by fences and bushes while the farmers quickly transfer 150 cans of milk from the platform to the car. It is now 6.35, and we have reached Bondville, where there is a repetition of the scenes at the previous station and about the same amount of milk loaded.

After describing several other stops, the author says:

As the train has been moving on, the men on the car have had all the work they could do between the stations in stowing the cans into the closets and packing broken ice about them. The little rooms have been filled and some cans have been stacked on the floor of the car with boards between the tiers of cans, while broken ice has been packed about them. The car is full.

He continues his description of the confusion and bustle which takes place until the train reaches Boston, a distance of 105 miles.

A Modern Tank-Car Train

At the present time our tank-car train route starts at Harrington, Del. The morning train carrying four tank cars has spotted them at Mount Pleasant, Del., Kennedyville, Md., Harrington, Del., and has transferred one car to be spotted at Chestertown, Md. During the morning milk has arrived at the receiving stations located at these places, and has been sampled and cooled to 40° F. As soon as the tanks are thoroughly washed, the milk received is pumped into them and the car awaits the return train. At 1.48 the engine connects with the car at Harrington, one tank being full, and a few hundred pounds in the other. At 2.12 p. m. the train has reached Felton. The car is backed to the milk-receiving station, doors are opened, and the pipes are attached by three men in two minutes. In 10 minutes 20,033 pounds of milk at a temperature of 40° has been loaded and at 2.27 the car has been sealed and is on its way. The next stop is at Townsend, Del. Here a full car from Chestertown, Md., is attached to the train; another car from Kennedyville, Md., with one tank containing 10,000 pounds is picked up and switched to the receiving station. Three men require 1 minute to attach the pipes, and in 11 minutes 23,442 pounds of milk is loaded into the other tank. By 4.22 the car has been sealed and is on its way. At Mount Pleasant, Del., the last car is picked up and its load completed at Kirkwood, Del. By 7 p. m. the cars have been spotted in the city and are ready to unload. The whole route of 101 miles has been covered with no confusion, a minimum of labor, and the milk has reached its destination in as good condition as when it left the country receiving stations.

R. P. HOTIS.

MEAT Combines High Nutritive Value With Great Palatability To be satisfying, a meal must be both nutritious and palatable. The necessity for adequate nutrition is of course of primary concern when one measures the value of any food. If a hungry man were forced to choose between a meal which would delight his taste but would not adequately nourish him and another which would be balanced in sustenance but lacking in piquancy, he would choose the latter, particularly if he did not know where his next meal was coming from. We are not a nation of hungry men, however, and the factor of palatability, though not absolutely essential, is the deciding element in the majority of our homes. Meat has a place in both phases of a satisfactory meal.

Although present-day research workers believe that there is still much to learn concerning the kinds and significance of accessory food substances and vitamins, the rôle of certain of the inorganic constituents, and the relative values of the various groups of foodstuffs, modern science lists a great many facts indicating the nutritive value of meat.

Meat is an efficient source of protein. Containing, as it does, all the essential amino acids, it has the ability of supplementing the less efficient plant proteins. The fact that meat is a concentrated source of protein adds to its efficiency in this respect. Moreover, the protein found in meat is highly digestible; from 90 to 98 per cent of it is digestible.

The fat of meat is a source of concentrated energy and heat for the human body; it contains more than twice as much per pound as is furnished by the carbohydrates and proteins.

Meat contains valuable inorganic constituents or mineral matter, being rich in potassium, phosphorus, and iron. The normal development of teeth and bones requires, within certain limits, that there be a definite relation between the calcium and phosphorus present. Since meat is relatively rich in phosphorus and lacking in calcium, to furnish a well-balanced diet a supply of calcium must be provided in the form of vegetables, milk, or even calcium salts. Iron is another inorganic element of importance present in meat. Iron alone is not sufficient. Some unknown factor is needed to effect the regeneration of the hemoglobin of the red blood corpuscles. Meat and vegetables contain this factor.

Of the vitamins, the growth-promoting complex, vitamin B, is supplied in good quantities by muscle meat. This complex is composed of at least two vitamins. One, vitamin F, prevents or cures polyneuritis; the other, vitamin G, is possibly the pellagra-preventive factor. Meat is low in the antineuritic factor F but relatively rich in the pellagra-preventive factor. Meat is a fair source of vitamin A, the growth-promoting, fat-soluble factor, and of the antisterility factor, vitamin E. It is a fairly poor source of the antiscorbutic vitamin C. The abundance of vitamin D, the antirachitic factor, is somewhat indefinitely known. The quantities of the vitamins in meat are influenced to a considerable extent by the nature of the diet received by the animal from which the meat is obtained.

Even the most ardent advocates of the use of liberal quantities of meat in the human diet would have to admit that other foods may be used as sources of protein, fats, salts, and vitamins. It is when we consider some of the special characteristics of meat, peculiar to it alone, that we are able to account for its popularity in the diet of man.

Chief among these factors is its palatability. Meat possesses a flavor and a texture which are attractive to the palate and to the sight. Housewives and clever cooks take advantage of this fact in planning attractive meals. The substantial appearance of a juicy steak, a well-browned roast, crisp bacon, or bright, delicately cured ham makes an ideal setting around which to build an appetizing meal. The flavor and aroma of meat enhance those of other foods and stimulate their consumption, thereby often reducing the total cost of a meal. These characteristics are factors not easily measured but none the less potent on that account. It seems a happy circumstance that such a variety of nutriment and enjoyment should be obtainable from a single food.

PAUL E. HOWE.

MEAT Handling Needs to be Safeguarded by Constant Cleanliness — Meat is a perishable food; dirt or insanitary conditions promote its spoilage, whereas cleanliness in processing and handling preserves its maximum value and wholesomeness. It may deteriorate rapidly when exposed to unfavorable conditions, which may result in lowering both the food and commercial value, or in producing an unwholesome condition. To preserve its value it is necessary that, throughout its handling from the dressing of the carcass to the time it is to be served as food, cleanliness be observed.

To make sure that cleanliness will prevail it is necessary that proper facilities for conducting the work be provided, that operations be performed in a neat and careful manner, that proper protection be given to the meat at all times, and that no deleterious substances are used.

Desirable Meat-Handling Equipment

The facilities need not be elaborate. Especially where a small volume of product is handled they may be simple and comparatively inexpensive. The rooms in which operations are conducted should have impervious floors of suitable material and well-constructed, impervious walls, adequate drainage facilities, abundant supply of pure water, both hot and cold, sufficient natural light, and good ventilating and heating equipment. Refrigerated compartments need not be provided with natural light but must have sufficient artificial light. The utensils, tables, and other equipment with which meat is handled should be of such material and construction that they can be readily and thoroughly cleaned. Tables, trucks, containers, shelves, and other equipment must be of ample size to hold and retain the meat.

With proper facilities available the most important item in cleanliness presents itself, and that is the manner in which the meat is prepared and handled. This phase of the subject is ever present, from the time that the dressing of the animal is begun until the product is consumed. The dressing of the animal requires that the hide be removed or the carcass be freed of bristles, scurf, or dirt in a manner that will produce a clean carcass. If the carcass is to be dressed without removing the hide, all parts of the outer covering of the animal should be washed clean. The entrails must be removed with great care, so that no contamination occurs by soiling the meat or fat with the contents of such organs as the stomach, intestines, or bladder.

All subsequent handling of the carcass or its meat likewise should be done in such a manner that the meat will not be soiled by improper handling or be subjected to contact with objectionable substances. This requires care of the carcass or its meat, sanitary operating compartments, and thorough and frequent cleaning of the equipment and utensils.

Other Important Safeguards

The persons who handle the meat should have clean hands, be free of infectious or contagious disease, wear clean, washable, outer garments, and use care to prevent the meat from falling to the floor or rubbing against objects which will soil or stain it. They should not hold in the mouth a knife, skewer, or similar article used in dressing the carcass or preparing the meat.

The water used on the meat or to clean the establishment compartments or utensils should be pure enough to drink; otherwise it may unfavorably affect the meat. All ingredients, such as curing materials, added to the meat or used in its preparation should be free of deleterious substances. The meat and places where it is kept should be protected from rats, mice, flies, roaches, and other vermin, as they may contaminate the meat and thereby lower its marketability and its fitness for food.

When meat is transferred from one location to another it should be protected from dirt, dust, flies, and other contamination. Trucks or receptacles should be clean, and in addition the meats should be suitably wrapped or completely covered. Unless these precautions are strictly observed, dirt added here and there soon accumulates until the meat becomes decidedly dirty.

Cleanliness aids in producing a product that is uniform in flavor, color, and appearance, and such a product is preferred by the careful and discriminating consumer. Whether the meat is for sale or home consumption the care outlined should be essentially the same.

A. J. Pistor.

MEAT Labels Must Be Informative and Not False or Misleading — In the early days of regulational activities there were encountered many forms of misrepresentation. These included the application of the terms "ham," "California ham," "picnic ham," and "cottage ham" to products prepared from pork shoulders. It was common practice to use the terms "potted ham," "deviled ham," and "ham sausage" in labeling products which contained little or no ham, but which frequently consisted largely of meat by-products comprising organs and parts other than flesh. The term "veal loaf" was loosely applied to all forms of loaves irrespective of constituents. Lard containing little or no rendered leaf fat was branded "leaf lard." Fresh link sausage was designated "pork sausage" notwithstanding the fact that it may have consisted largely of substances other than pork, with an abundance of cereal and added water.

Such unqualified terms as "roast meat" and "roast beef" were applied to products which were not roasted but merely subjected to other cooking processes. The term "lard" was applied to mixtures and compounds containing beef or mutton fat and vegetable oils, and the term "potted chicken" was applied to canned tripe or other products containing little or no chicken. Therefore, the need for truth in meat labels is obvious.

Official Approval Required

Keen commercial competition prompts the manufacturer or distributor to seek every possible advantage in boosting his product and promoting its sale, and as a result extravagant claims and statements are apt to be made. Happily, however, for the protection of the purchaser and consumer of meat the Federal law and regulations require that labels, brands, and other marking devices applied to meat and meat food products or their containers must have official approval before their use is permitted. The specific terms of the law clearly do not countenance the use of labels which are false or misleading, and therefore their official disapproval in recent years has occasioned less opposition.

However, the highly developed field of advertising furnishes attractive means of arresting the attention of prospective consumers, and even yet there is need for firm insistence upon truth in meat labels to cope with the strong tendency of manufacturers to use labels which are unique in statement or design, and which, although technically correct, are cleverly prepared in a manner conducive to misconstruction. Meat labels demand the most careful study and analysis as well as knowledge of the ingredients of the articles labeled in order to preclude encroachment upon established procedure for the protection of consumers against deception.

Labels Affected by New Processes

In the present era of invention there are constantly being devised new equipment and processes of manufacture which render old terms of long and common usage inapplicable. Particularly is this true where such terms include a direct reference to equipment or process differing from that actually employed. Furthermore, there is a tendency on the part of manufacturers to employ names which are either meaningless or so broad in their scope as to obscure identity of inferior constituents and conceal the true characteristics of the meat or product. New meat products are constantly being prepared and new formulas adopted on account of the demand of the trade or the availability of ingredients used. It is, of course, desirable that such names be informative to the consumer. These new products and variations in standard products necessitate the adoption of new and revised labels which continually require vigilance to insure their truthfulness.

F. W. MEYST.

MEAT Market Reports Help Cattle Men to Suit Consumer Demand "The bunch grass levels where the cattle graze" may seem remote from the great consuming centers of the East, but in reality a relationship as intimate as that of a next-door neighbor actually exists. The metropolitan area around New York contains about one-tenth of the Nation's population. As the cow and the hen are barred by health regulations from its limits and the farms near it are devoted largely to dairying and truck farming, western ranges and midwestern feed lots must be largely depended upon for Sunday roasts and week-day stews.

New York and its environs consume about 10 per cent of all meats produced in this country. New York State, New Jersey, and Pennsylvania are important producing sections for lamb, veal, and slaughter dairy cows; Virginia, West Virginia, Tennessee, and Kentucky furnish lamb and beef cattle during their shipping seasons, and other Eastern States market their seasonal quotas of livestock. Nevertheless, the range country of the West and the central western feed lots are the sections depended upon for a steady, year-round supply. Hence, it is advisable that livestock producers and feeders everywhere maintain the closest possible relations with current supply, demand, and price conditions prevailing at big consuming centers.

The Bureau of Agricultural Economics maintains a daily meat market reporting service at New York, Chicago, Boston, and Philadelphia as a part of its national market news service. Timely information on conditions prevailing at the wholesale meat markets released daily by radio, telegraph, mimeographed reports, distributed through the mails, and in other ways is available without cost to those who need and request it. Special reports and reviews are released containing important information relating to the national supply of and future prospects for various kinds of livestock and meats. But many livestock producers fail to utilize the available information.

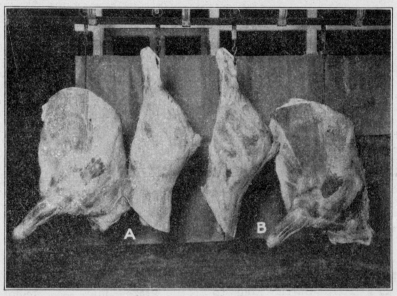

FIGURE 161.—Two sides of steer beef. A, Choice grade and sold on the New York market for 27 cents a pound wholesale; B, medium grade and sold for 19 cents a pound wholesale. This illustrates the penalty which frequently attaches to lower-grade beef

Farmers should not force their livestock into glutted markets or be slow to sell their stock when both animals and markets are right.

Characteristics in Highest Demand

Highest prices and quickest sales to-day usually go with chunky, well-finished carcasses, not overfat, and showing at least moderately high quality in the meat. Excessive fat means loss to dealers and consumers and such meat is discounted no matter how high the quality. Poorly conformed, underfed, thin carcasses lacking quality sell near the low end of the price scale. Weight is a matter of growing importance and in the New York market, for instance, a difference of 25 pounds above or below the carcass weight desired often adversely affects the sale $1 or more per 100 pounds. During the late fall, and winter and spring seasons heavy lamb carcasses and cuts frequently sell several cents a pound lower than similar quality in lighter weights.

Conversely, there are periods when quality and weights which are not usually in demand sell well.

The Government information regarding livestock markets can not be expected to reflect consumers' demands and what they are willing to pay for, except in an indirect way. National and local supply influences prices in wholesale markets everywhere, but other influences are often first noted in consuming centers and reflected back through livestock markets to sources of production. These include Jewish and other fasting periods; seasons of heavy poultry consumption; supplies and prices of fruits, vegetables, cereals, and dairy products; general and sectional working conditions; imports and exports; weather changes; and vacation periods.

Among the factors to be studied by livestock producers and feeders are demands and prices according to classes, weights, and grades; when shipments are likely to be profitable and when they are likely to contribute to an overloaded and weak market; at what seasons certain classes, grades, weights, and types are likely to bring best returns; the probable advantage of increasing or decreasing production; and changing quality produced. In short, meat-trade reports (especially when supplies and prices are

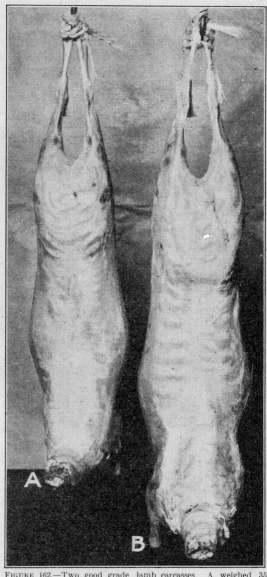

FIGURE 162.—Two good grade lamb carcasses. A weighed 35 pounds and sold on the New York market for 26 cents a pound wholesale. B weighed 57 pounds and sold for 20 cents a pound wholesale. This illustrates the penalty which usually attaches to undesirable weights

compiled and compared over long periods) may provide many advantages readily translated into dollars. Market stability tends to make livestock production a reasonably safe business and the meat market reports, if acted upon, assist stabilization.

B. F. McCARTHY.

Meat-Packing Plants Under Federal Control Use Pure Water Supply — The operations of meat-packing establishments require enormous quantities of water. An ample supply of pure, clean water is thus an essential part of every establishment of that kind.

Before Federal meat inspection is granted any establishment, a satisfactory water supply must be provided. To be acceptable, the supply must be ample in volume and distribution so that no operation need be slighted or neglected for lack of potable water. The standard of purity applied is the same as that for drinking water intended for human consumption. (Fig. 163.)

It should be remembered that infective bacteria have unlimited powers of multiplication and that meat furnishes an ideal medium

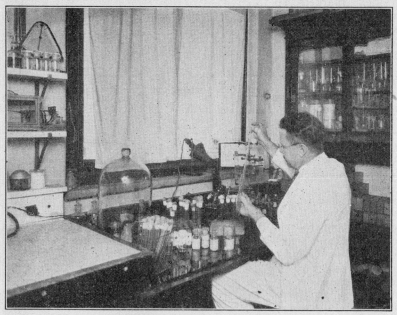

FIGURE 163.—Testing water for purity. Water used in establishments operating under Federal meat inspection must be as pure as drinking water intended for human use

for their development. A very minute infection with the causative organism of any disease capable of being carried by polluted water might, therefore, attain dangerous proportions before the meat reached the consumer. There is also to be considered the possibility that bacteria capable of causing food poisoning might gain access to meat and products through polluted water, develop on them, and render them unwholesome. Finally, infection of the meat with putrefactive organisms through impure water would inevitably cause spoilage and loss as well as endanger human health.

Sources, Distribution, and Purification

Establishments operating under Federal meat inspection derive their water supplies from a variety of sources, both public and private. A large proportion of them use, either wholly or in part, the public supply of the locality in which they are operated. In some of them the public supply is supplemented by water from private sources, and numerous establishments are wholly dependent upon private systems. Public water supplies are in general of acceptable purity, though, occasionally, they do not conform to the Government standard of purity. In such cases, further treatment within the establishment is required. When there is need for purification, standard methods are used, and official supervision consists in seeing that the treating plant is properly designed and equipped and is operated so as to purify the water. Wells constitute the principal source of private supply. Many of the wells are deep and the water-bearing strata well protected by overlying beds of rock or clay. Under such conditions, proper construction and protection of the well is all that is necessary to assure the purity of the supply. In many cases, however, the natural protection of the water-bearing strata is insufficient, and it becomes necessary to sterilize the water or prohibit its use. If the well water is clear, clean, and free from excess of soluble organic matter, its use is permitted after sterilization with chlorine or by other approved methods.

The distribution of water throughout the establishment involves possible opportunities for contamination which must be guarded against. This is particularly true where water is stored in reservoirs or is used over condensers and subsequently for other purposes. Protection of the distribution system is, therefore, quite as essential as assuring purity at the source.

Water Used for Nonpotable Purposes

Many establishments are so located as to have readily available a source of water which is unfit for use in connection with food products. There is, of course, no objection to the use of such water in boilers, in inedible-product departments, over condensers, in flushing stock pens, and for similar purposes. Under such circumstances it is necessary that an entirely separate system of pumps, pipes, tanks, and reservoirs, which has no connection whatever with the pure water supply and has no outlet in any department where edible products are prepared or handled, be provided for its distribution.

Supervision of water supplies in meat plants involves inspection of the source, constant observation, and regular laboratory examination of samples. Before meat inspection is granted, a thorough survey is made to determine conformity with the requirements of the meat-inspection act and regulations. When an establishment has been found acceptable and meat inspection is inaugurated, the water supply is kept under constant supervision. The necessity for continuous supervision is self-evident. Increasing volume of operations may render a once ample supply inadequate; wells once yielding pure water may become polluted under excessive pumping, through increasing surface pollution, or deterioration of protective structures; purification systems may be improperly or carelessly operated or may be operated beyond capacity in order to supply an increasing demand; public supplies may be outgrown by the community or become unsatisfactory through other causes. All water supplies, both public and private are therefore kept under continuous supervision. This supervision is not confined to the source of supply but also covers the use and distribution of water within establishments.

Collection and Laboratory Inspection of Samples

Finally, samples for bacteriological examination are collected regularly from the supplies of each inspected establishment. Samples are taken at the source and at points of use within the establishment. On account of the nature of the operations conducted and character of the surroundings, collection of representative samples is often a matter of considerable difficulty. Inspectors have, however, successfully mastered the problems involved so that the number of samples accidentally contaminated in collection is exceedingly small. After collection, the samples are forwarded to the meat-inspection laboratories and are there examined by the standard methods regularly used for determining the purity of water.

Whenever a sample is found to show evidence of pollution, additional samples are collected and the test repeated. In the event that the findings of pollution are confirmed, the source of pollution is traced and correction required. By the means outlined, the continued purity of the water supplies of federally inspected meat-packing establishments is assured.

ROBERT H. KERR.

MEATS for Export Are Required to Undergo Special Supervision   The Federal meat-inspection service of the Bureau of Animal Industry is of great assistance to farmers in obtaining satisfactory returns for livestock products by encouraging and facilitating the exportation of meats. This assistance consists in a careful study of the meat-

FIGURE 164.—Carcass inspection of pork

inspection laws and regulations of foreign countries, and seeing to it that all meat and meat food products are inspected, handled, and certified as required by the regulations of the country to which the products are destined. (Fig. 164.)

Fresh Pork Is Specially Certified

In order to establish and maintain a market for fresh-pork cuts in certain foreign countries it was necessary that the method of handling such cuts in the United States be changed to comply with the regulations of those countries. As fresh-pork cuts of the United States were refused admission into Great Britain prior to 1922 on account of the rigid inspection requirements of the Government of that country, arrangements were made by the United States Department of Agriculture, through diplomatic channels, whereby Great Britain agreed to receive from the United States fresh-pork cuts from selected carcasses when accompanied by special certification. As a consequence 11,724,497 pounds of fresh pork were certified for export to Great Britain during the fiscal year 1928. This special inspection is not required under the United States meat-inspection regulations for fresh pork intended for consumption in the United States or for export to other countries, but is conducted exclusively for the purpose of marketing our fresh pork in Great Britain.

FIGURE 165.—Inspection of animal casings

The meat-inspection regulations of the Netherlands prohibit the entry of fresh pork for the reason that it might be eaten without first being cooked or otherwise treated in a manner to destroy any live trichinae which might be present. Arrangements were made in 1923 whereby the Netherlands agreed to accept fresh pork from the United States provided it had been refrigerated at least three weeks at a temperature of $-15°$ C. ($5°$ F.), and was accompanied by special certification to that effect. Accordingly the Federal meat-inspection service supervises the freezing of fresh pork for the Netherlands and issues a special certificate showing that the product complies with the regulations of that country.

Special certificates in both English and French are issued for meat and meat food products exported to France, Switzerland, and Algeria.

Requirements for Preservatives and Animal Casings

In order to meet the demands of certain countries which do not object to meats being treated with preservatives, the use of which is prohibited in meats intended for consumption in the United States, the Federal meat-inspection service sees that the meats for those countries are segregated for treatment and are appropriately marked to show the presence of the preservative. Care is also taken to see that meats so treated are shipped direct to the country for which they are intended and are not disposed of in the United States.

As animal casings (fig. 165) are not classed as meat food products under the United States meat-inspection regulations, animal casings produced in the United States are not inspected except when presented for use as sausage containers in establishments operating under Federal meat inspection. However, in order to comply with the requirements of certain countries, including Australia, Austria, Poland, Canada, and New Zealand, a special inspection of animal casings is made. Only such casings are certified for exportation to those countries as are derived from animals which received ante-mortem and post-mortem veterinary inspection at the time of slaughter, and are sound, healthful, wholesome, and otherwise fit for human food. The casings must not have been treated with or contain any preservative, coloring, or other substance not permitted by the United States meat-inspection regulations, and must have been handled only in a sanitary manner.

WM. H. SMITH, Jr.

MEXICAN Bean Beetle Continues Destructive Spread in Eastern U. S. (Fig. 166.) Few insects have ever invaded so large an area of new territory in so short a time as has the Mexican bean beetle in the last eight years. After a remarkable increase in distribution in 1927 the beetle continued to spread in 1928. It has now reached the Atlantic from northeastern North Carolina to Monmouth County, N. J., having crossed Chesapeake Bay just as it apparently crossed Lake Erie to Canada in 1927.

The insect has also spread 65 miles westward in Michigan and is now present in the vicinity of Lansing and of Coldwater. In the fall of 1927 it reached De Kalb and Steuben Counties in northeastern Indiana, and it reached Whitley County in 1928. No records have been obtained of an appreciable spread westward in the States of Indiana, Kentucky, Tennessee, and Mississippi. Only a limited spread has taken place in western New York into the counties of Ontario, Yates, Schuyler, and Chemung, about 40 miles east of the 1927 line of distribution, but it is supposed to be present in south-central New York and in much of eastern Pennsylvania, since it has been found in Orange and Rockland Counties, N. Y., near the New Jersey line. No doubt practically the whole State of New Jersey is infested.

In South Carolina, Florence and Clarendon Counties are now reported to be infested, and considerable spread to the east has taken place in northeastern North Carolina, Bertie, Washington, and Pasquotank Counties being included in new territory. In the southern portion of North Carolina the beetle has been found as far east as Pender County.

The outstanding events of the season of 1928 were the heavy infestations of the beetle in sections of eastern Virginia and Maryland, where the beetle was either unknown or not numerous in 1927. These early initial outbreaks of the pest were probably due to the high winter survival of the beetle in the near-by infested territory, together with

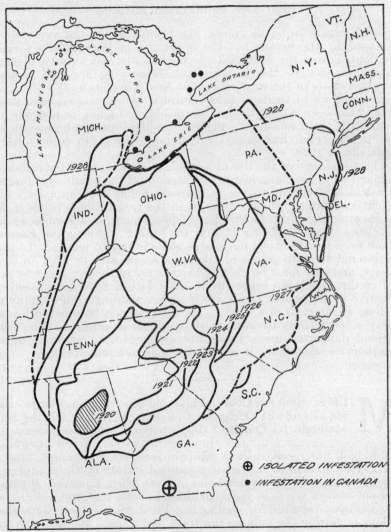

FIGURE 166.—Map showing known distribution of the Mexican bean beetle in the eastern part of the United States in the years 1920 to 1928

favorable conditions for maximum dispersal and reproduction early in the season of 1928.

Heavy infestations were also reported from North Carolina, northern Georgia, and northern Alabama. The survival of the pest over the winter was lower than usual in Alabama, but the beetle reproduced rapidly, so that considerable damage was done by midsummer. In southern Ohio the percentage of survival in the spring of 1928 was low, and conditions early in the spring were unfavorable for multiplication; but the second brood of beetles did considerable damage in some localities. In the vicinity of Columbus the beetle is becoming more numerous each year.

Bean Area in Michigan Menaced

In Michigan, so far as known, the bean crop has not as yet been damaged by the beetle, but the insect has become more generally distributed over the southeastern counties and may prove to be a serious menace to this important bean-growing area. A similar situation exists in the western part of New York State.

Research on methods of field control is being stressed even more than it has been during the last few years, and many tests are being made with nonarsenical insecticides. Sodium fluosilicate, one of the insecticides tried, has caused considerable injury to bean foliage, especially in 1928.

The advantage of the use of a stomach poison, such, for instance, as magnesium arsenate, is great on account of the continuous protection which it affords to the foliage which has been sprayed. Excellent results are usually obtained in the case of bush beans if the plants are sprayed up to the time of blossoming, in accordance with directions given in Farmers' Bulletin 1407–F. Along the Eastern Shore even this arsenical may cause some injury to foliage. In that section only certain grades of calcium arsenate may be used on bean foliage, and care must be exercised in the use of those.

Pyrethrum extract, especially if made with a light oil solvent, is effective in controlling the insect if a very thorough job of spraying is done at intervals of a week. The insects must be touched by the spray since it kills by contact only. This material may be used without danger on green beans after the pods have set, since, in the dilutions recommended, it is not poisonous to human beings.

NEALE F. HOWARD.

MILK Stations For Cooling Product Help Maintain Its Quality — The rapid growth of our large cities has made it necessary for the milk supply to be received from increasingly greater distances. When cities were small, milk was received from comparatively short distances; after it had been delivered to the country railroad station by the producer, it reached the city within a few hours. Even then, however, the milk did not always arrive in good condition because the producer did not have proper facilities for cooling it. Furthermore, there were often delays in getting the milk on the train and transferring it to the city plant from the railroad station. When milk stands for some time at a shipping point and then is transported for a long distance before being cooled, it will not arrive in good condition.

To provide a means of cooling the milk before shipment, country milk receiving and cooling stations have been established either by the producers or by the city distributors of milk at points in the country varying from 40 to more than 300 miles from the city. These stations are located in good milk-producing sections where a supply sufficient to insure the economical operation of a plant can be obtained from comparatively short distances. They are also usually located on the railroad so that the milk can be loaded directly from the plant to the shipping car. An adequate water supply and proper sewage disposal are important factors to consider when selecting the location for a milk-receiving station.

Method of Handling Shipments

The milk is brought to the station from the farm in the early morning, usually between 6 and 9 a. m., and in some cases it must all be in by 8 a. m. If the morning's milk reaches the plant within a short time after milking, it need not be cooled by the producer. In some sections of the South where the producer does not have proper facilities for cooling and storing the milk overnight, it is brought to the station twice a day. As the milk is received from the producer it is removed at once from his cans, weighed, and a sample taken for the purpose of determining the quality. The producer's cans are immediately washed and sterilized and returned to him. The milk flows from the weigh can to a mixing vat, whence it goes over a cooler which reduces the temperature of the milk to from 36° to 40° F. It is then drawn into shipping cans, which have been previously washed and sterilized, and loaded on the shipping car, which is an insulated milk-refrigerator car that has been set off at the station several hours previously and will be picked up when the milk train arrives. If the quantity of milk handled at a station is too small to fill a car, the car will not be set off but the milk must be held in the plant until the arrival of the train. In that case a cold-storage room will be necessary.

The building for the country milk-receiving station should be simple in construction. A frame structure with concrete floors and side walls of concrete to a height of about 3 feet is usually satisfactory. The floors must be well drained and the building well lighted and ventilated. The equipment for a country station should be as simple as possible so that it can be easily operated and cleaned. Equipment for mechanical refrigeration is usually provided, though in the northern part of the country enough natural ice is often harvested during the winter to supply the requirements for refrigeration throughout the year. Other equipment necessary are scales and weigh can, receiving vat, and milk cooler. A can washer and sterilizer must be provided for cleaning the producers' cans and the shipping cans. A steam boiler is needed to produce hot water for cleaning purposes and steam for power where electricity is not available.

During recent years much milk has been transported from the country to the city in glass-lined tanks mounted on railroad cars or on automobile trucks where conditions are favorable for truck transportation. Where this is done, no shipping cans are required. Instead, an insulated storage tank must usually be provided to store the milk after it has been cooled. At some such stations the transporting system is so arranged that the milk may be pumped directly from the cooler to the tank truck or tank car and no storage tank need be provided except as an emergency measure.

Various Functions Performed

During recent years, because of the building of automobile roads, it has been possible to bring the milk from the farm direct to the city plant by motor truck. When this can be done, a country receiving plant is not needed. This applies, however, only where milk is received from distances within the radius of the economical truck haul, which is not over 75 miles. As the supply for our large cities usually comes from considerably greater distances—often 300 miles or more—the country station will no doubt continue to perform an important function. Furthermore, where milk is brought to the city in tank trucks even from short distances from the city, the country station is required to serve as a concentrating point for receiving the milk from the producers and for cooling it before it is shipped.

Thus country milk plants serve a very useful purpose. They furnish a place for receiving the milk from the producers and for cooling it, thereby permitting it to arrive in the city in good condition. They also permit the producers to keep in closer touch with the person who weighs and samples the milk than would be possible if the milk were shipped direct to the city plant. The station operator keeps a close check on the quality of the milk that is received from each producer and can often assist him in improving the quality of his product by helpful advice. Furthermore, the country plant may serve as an equalizing agent for the uneven quantities of milk produced at different seasons of the year. During the season of surplus production the milk not needed in the city may be held in the country at a station equipped for manufacturing milk into by-products, with resulting savings in freight charges.

C. E. CLEMENT.

MOLDS Pressed Into Service in Utilizing Some Farm Products

Molds are known to most people as a pest. They invade the household, attacking foodstuffs in general and growing readily on damp clothing, paper, and leather. They seriously damage stored fruits, tubers, and grains. Science long ago declared war upon them and has been somewhat successful in combating their destructiveness.

Centuries ago, however, mankind learned that molds could be made to do useful work. Oriental peoples have used them for hundreds of years in the preparation of various foodstuffs and beverages, and in Europe it was found that some species are valuable agents in the ripening of cheese. In recent years molds of various species have been systematically studied with the view of utilizing some of their characteristic properties. In France they have been put to work to break down starchy materials in various alcoholic-fermentation processes. In the manufacture of gallic acid, an important dye intermediate made from tannin, the destructive characteristics of a mold have been employed; the process is based on a mold fermentation. A mold is now being used to manufacture citric acid from cane sugar, an acid that formerly was obtained exclusively from citrus fruits. It is also possible by mold fermentation to make citric acid from corn sugar. Recently a process has been developed in the United States Department of Agriculture whereby corn sugar is turned into gluconic acid through mold fermentation, thus at once producing an acid with possible industrial uses and opening up a new outlet for corn sugar.

There is a large field for investigation in the action of molds on farm wastes. Xylose, the one almost universal component of these wastes, is attacked by molds, but nothing is known of the products formed. It has been suggested that in the production of power, alcohol from vegetable material molds be used as a means of making the material available to the alcohol-producing yeasts that can not attack the raw vegetation. A mold cell is a veritable chemical factory, the product of which depends on the species of mold and on the nature of the material on which it is growing. Since the selective growth of these organisms on definite materials can be controlled, the possibilities of what they may accomplish are limited only by our knowledge of what reactions they may be able to bring about. A study of these reactions necessitates a great deal of time and work, and consequently our knowledge of them is very slowly being built up. As more is learned regarding the chemical actions brought about by these small plants, their usefulness to man will increase.

H. T. HERRICK and
O. E. MAY.

MOVIE Audiences in Many Countries See Department's Films To be precise, 99,601 is the tally of days of use of Department of Agriculture educational films during the past year, as reported to the office of motion pictures by borrowers. In that time department films have been shown in thousands of rural communities scattered throughout every State in the Union, as well as in the Canal Zone, in island possessions, and in many foreign countries. This service, which is free, except that the borrower pays transportation charges on the films he uses, has grown within the past decade until it now ranks among the more important of the channels through which the department reaches the public.

Extension workers, largely county agricultural agents, make more use of department films than any other class of borrowers, the total days of extension use being 35,000, as against 63,000 for all other groups. Among the latter, graded schools rank highest in number of pictures used, though comparatively low in days of use, as shipments to schools are usually for very short loan periods. Other important users are colleges, State officials, churches, Y. M. C. A. workers, and the field men of the United States Department of Agriculture.

In general, as the distance from Washington, D. C., increases, the fewer the pictures used by borrowers and the longer the period that each picture is used. The accompanying map (fig. 167) shows that shipments of films to far Western States are far fewer than shipments to Eastern States within easy reach of the source of supply. For example, 291 shipments were made to Ohio, as compared with 64 to California, the most populous of the Western States, and 8 to Arizona, the State getting the fewest shipments. Figure 168, a dot map based on days of use, shows that western borrowers seek to offset the long-haul cost of transportation by making more extended use of the pictures they get than do eastern borrowers. In other words, the western borrower's tendency is to show the same picture or pictures night after night, each night to a new community, while the eastern borrower tends to offer more frequent changes of programs. In this regard the West is at a marked disadvantage because the source of supply of department films is located on the Atlantic seaboard.

Distribution by States

Considering distribution by States, on the basis of shipments, number of pictures used, and number of days of use, the leading 10 States

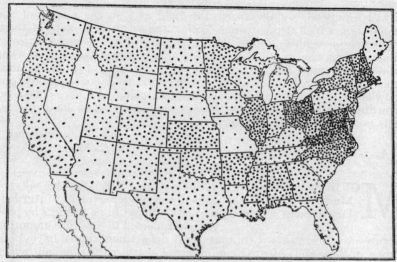

FIGURE 167.—Use of United States Department of Agriculture motion pictures during the fiscal year 1927–28.   Each dot represents 50 days use of a picture

in use of department films are: Ohio, New York, Illinois, Virginia, Minnesota, Colorado, District of Columbia, Michigan, Pennsylvania, and Texas.

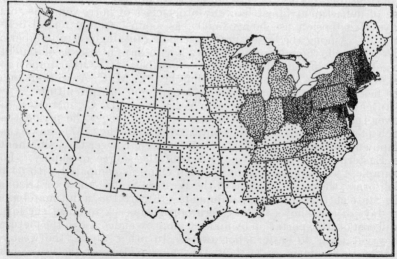

FIGURE 168.—Distribution of United States Department of Agriculture motion pictures for fiscal year 1927–28.   Each dot represents one shipment

These 10 States get 50 per cent of all shipments, and 49 per cent of all pictures used, and are credited with 38 per cent of the 99,000 days of use of department films.   In marked contrast with this showing is that of the 10 States, Nebraska, Connecticut, North Dakota, Louisiana, Maine, Arizona, Nevada, Idaho, Delaware, and Rhode Island, the use in which constitutes less than 5 per cent of the total.

Distribution of department films tends to concentrate in those sections of the country where the Federal Department of Agriculture or State agricultural colleges or departments of agriculture are waging special campaigns against insect pests, animal diseases, or bad practices by farmers. Ohio ranks first as a user of the department's educational pictures largely because of the intensive campaign that is being waged against the corn borer in that State and the heavy use of cornborer films by the workers engaged in that campaign. Arkansas ranks among the leading 10 States because Forest Service field men are making intensive use of motion pictures in the educational campaign they are conducting against the destructive practice of "woods burning" followed by the people of the Ozark country under the delusion that such burning improves pasture. A similar campaign is

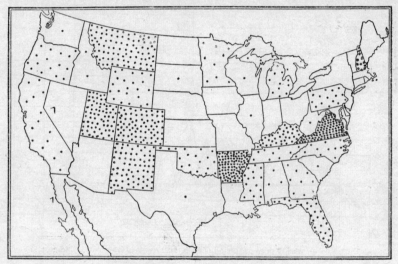

FIGURE 169.—Use of motion pictures by Forest Service field men during the fiscal year 1927–28. Each dot represents 25 days or less use of a picture

being conducted in Virginia. In each of these States the Forest Service maintains a peripetatic motion-picture show, a truck carrying a motion-picture projector and an electrical generator, which goes from schoolhouse to schoolhouse showing the department's film Trees of Righteousness, and other films designed to discourage "woods burning." (Fig. 169.)

Judging from fairly complete reports on actual attendance at showings of department films, as submitted by borrowers, between 5,000,000 and 6,000,000 persons saw one or more of these pictures during the year. Since outside agencies, such as State colleges, schools, cooperative associations, and foreign governments have bought and are circulating fully as many copies of department films as is the department itself, it is believed that the total attendance at showings of these films runs well above 10 million.

RAYMOND EVANS and
H. B. McCLURE.

MUSHROOM Culture in the United States Is a Growing Industry Few people realize that millions of pounds of cultivated mushrooms are grown and consumed in the United States annually. It has been estimated that more than 15,000,000 pounds were grown in this country in 1927. Fresh cultivated mushrooms are now a staple food in most of our large cities. The New York City market is the largest. It is not unusual for this market to consume 30 tons of fresh mushrooms in a single day. More than 300 growers have joined forces in the Mushroom Growers' Cooperative Association of Pennsylvania to convince the American public that there is absolutely no danger from eating cultivated mushrooms. Contrary to the general opinion, fresh mushrooms are reasonably low in price throughout most of the year.

The principal center of production is in eastern Pennsylvania, but there are also large commercial mushroom plants in the Hudson River

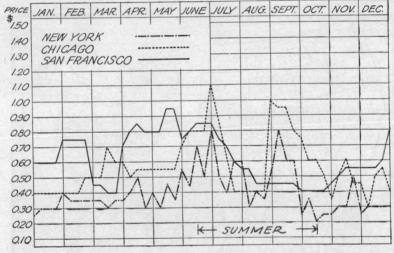

FIGURE 170.—Average weekly price per pound of fresh mushrooms in New York, Chicago, and San Francisco in 1927

Valley of New York, in Ohio, Illinois, Minnesota, Missouri, and on the Pacific coast. There are numerous growers who raise more than 50 tons of mushrooms a year and at least two who are said to produce more than 1,000,000 pounds a year. That there is a widespread interest in the industry is shown by the fact that in 1927 the Department of Agriculture answered more than 2,000 inquiries regarding mushroom culture from practically every State in the Union. Table 10 shows the average prices for 1927 in three cities.

TABLE 10.—*Average price in cents per pound of mushrooms at New York, Chicago, and San Francisco, 1927*

Market	Summer	Winter	Yearly
New York	48	35	40
Chicago	52	55	53
San Francisco	55	66	62

Several growers are canning mushrooms on an extensive scale, and American canned mushrooms may be found on the shelves of chain stores in almost every locality. However, this industry must meet foreign competition. According to the statistics of the Department of Commerce, the imports into the United States of prepared and preserved mushrooms have been rapidly increasing in spite of a 45 per cent ad valorem tariff rate. In 1924 there were imported 3,902,786 pounds of canned mushrooms, principally from France, and in 1927 imports reached 6,152,815 pounds.

Aside from foreign competition and the lethargic public demand, the chief limitations of the industry are the increase of parasites and the growing scarcity of horse manure. With the development of large centers of mushroom growing the problem of controlling fungous diseases and insect pests is becoming more and more acute. The Mycogone disease and plaster mold apparently are the principal fungous menaces of cultivated mushrooms. Mushroom flies, mites, and springtails are the chief offenders among the pests. In January, 1928, projects for the solution of these and allied problems were organized in the Bureau of Entomology and the Bureau of Plant Industry.

E. B. LAMBERT.

MUSKRAT Farming in Marsh Areas Becomes a Profitable Industry — Many persons now living can remember the good old days of muskrat trapping, when in early youth they made a good profit in selling the skins for as little as 15 to 25 cents apiece. Now muskrat pelts have advanced practically tenfold in price, the carcasses are sold

FIGURE 171.—Woven-wire fence in process of construction to inclose an area devoted to muskrat farming. The strip of metal at the top prevents muskrats from leaving the premises and lessens losses from natural enemies

as meat for as much as the pelts formerly brought, and the annual catch in the United States has reached the 14,000,000 mark. The earliest use for muskrat fur was in the manufacture of an excellent imitation of beaver hats. Modern fur dressers and dyers now imitate also many of the more costly furs with that of the muskrat. This practice, together with the multiplicity of designs decreed by fashion for women's apparel, has created a continuous demand for the pelts.

The increased demand and the rise in prices for pelts have developed the industry of muskrat farming. The value of the skins warrants commercial attempts to produce muskrats on large preserves and justifies efforts to prevent poaching. Many of the marsh areas bordering on the Great Lakes and the tidewater marshes of New Jersey, Delaware, Maryland, and Louisiana, and some of the more desirable inland marsh areas in the northern tier of States that formerly were considered useless, are now being utilized for muskrat farming. Because of the increased value of furs, these areas are yielding steady and profitable returns and when sold bring more than do adjacent cultivated lands.

The Chief Requirements

The chief requirements in muskrat farming are to maintain a food supply for the animals and to guard against depleting their numbers by too close trapping. In some localities muskrats are kept on definite premises by the erection of suitable fences (fig. 171), and these also aid in preventing poaching and lessening depredations by natural enemies.

Muskrats multiply rapidly. Their aquatic retreats and general habits assist them in protecting themselves. Though injurious to crops in some localities, muskrats generally inhabit places unsuited to agriculture. The areas adapted to the needs of muskrats are extensive in many States, and doubtless suitable marshland could be utilized for the industry in some sections where the animals do not now occur. As trapping is done in winter, muskrat farming appeals especially to farm men and boys. The commercial importance of the muskrat makes it desirable to conserve the marshlands in which it is found naturally. Owners of such areas should manage them intelligently so that a fair annual profit may be made while a sufficient stock of breeding animals is left for propagation.

FRANK G. ASHBROOK.

N ARCISSUS Bulbs Attacked by Flies May Be Fumigated — Narcissus bulbs are subject to attack by the larvae of two flies, the daffodil fly, *Merodon equestris* Fab. (fig. 172), and the lesser bulb fly, a term which includes several species of Eumerus.

In some sections of the United States these insects have become established and occasionally cause considerable loss. Which of the two should be considered the more serious is a debatable question. Growers generally believe that the daffodil fly causes more losses, but they do not belittle the activities of the lesser bulb flies. A single grub of the former can and usually does ruin the bulb which it infests, whereas the latter has to work in mass formation to accomplish its devastation; and 20, 40, or sometimes 100 or more larvae of the lesser bulb fly are found in single bulbs. Records show frequent losses of 10 to 15 per cent of bulb stocks, and in a few individual cases the damage has amounted to as much as 50 per cent.

For two reasons practical and satisfactory means of controlling these pests has been desired. In the first place, the growers in sections where these insects are established wish to avoid losses, and, second,

growers in uninfested localities wish to prevent the introduction there
of bulbs infested with these economic enemies.   Two kinds of treatment have heretofore been used to aid in reducing the menace of the
bulb fly and to insure the cleanliness of bulbs in commerce.   One of
these is known as the hot-water method and consists in the immersion
of the bulbs in water at a temperature of 110° to 111.5° F. for a period
of at least one hour.   Growers consider this method unsatisfactory for
bulbs they wish to ship, because of the extra cost and the difficulty
involved in drying them after the treatment.   This objection would
apply to any "wet" treatment.   Fumigation has been considered the
most practical dry
method.   In 1926,
when the Federal Hor-
ticultural Board pro-
mulgated quarantine
62, regulating the in-
terstate movement of
narcissus bulbs, a vac-
uum method employ-
ing carbon disulphide
was permitted.   The
high cost of the me-
chanical equipment
necessary for this
treatment has tended
to prevent its general
use, and such fumiga-
tions of bulbs have
been performed only
in localities where vac-
uum plants were in
operation for other
purposes.

Fumigation With Calcium Cyanide

A few trials in 1926,
and more extensive ex-
perimentation in 1927
and 1928, of fumiga-

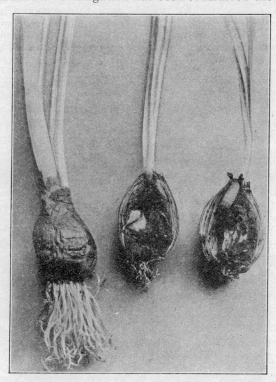

FIGURE 172.—Injury to narcissus bulbs by the daffodil fly.   At left,
a sound bulb; the others have been injured by the fly

tion with calcium cyanide at Santa Cruz, Calif., and Puyallup,
Wash., have justified the recommendation of this material for the
treatment of bulbs in storage (fig. 173) either for shipment or for
local planting.   With a dosage of 12 ounces of calcium cyanide for
each 100 cubic feet of space and an exposure of four hours or longer,
entirely successful results were obtained not only against the larvae
of both flies, but their eggs as well, and the pupae of the lesser bulb
flies.   No vacuum is needed.   After placing the bulbs in the fumigation box the calcium cyanide is placed on shallow pans which are then
pushed under the bulbs.   A type of calcium cyanide in the form of a
coarse dust is used which slowly evolves the needed hydrocyanic-acid
gas.   No detrimental effects on the bulbs have been observed, even

when the fumigations have been much heavier than that recommended, provided that the bulbs were thoroughly dormant. Freshly sprouted roots or tips of bulbs are injured by the gas, but they are not to be found where the bulbs are handled properly. The most noticeable effect of this treatment on bulbs grown in the field on the Pacific coast has been an advancement of the blooming for five to eight days. Under conditions prevailing on the Pacific coast this treatment has been so successful that it is now being tested in a commercial way in some of the principal bulb-growing districts of the United States.

Construction of Fumigation Chambers

The development of this method of treatment has necessitated a corresponding study of the construction of fumigation chambers. Tightness is the most important factor to be considered. The heavy

FIGURE 173.—Interior of a cooperative bulb warehouse in the Pacific northwest. Bulbs are delivered to the warehouse graded in trays, are fumigated, and then counted and packed

dosage used is necessary to insure sufficient gas to penetrate into the almost inaccessible cavities where the grubs are located. Tightness is essential to maintain the gas concentration by which complete effectiveness may be obtained. The department had previously developed a fumigation box for use with greenhouse plants, and published plans for it.[4] This type of box was remodeled to meet the needs of bulb growers by reducing the height and widening the door, so that the whole front could be opened. In details of construction the previous plans were followed. Two layers of tongue-and-groove flooring, with building paper between them, are used for walls, floor, top, and door, the boards of one layer extending at right angles to those of the other. For tightness and sturdiness this type of construction is considered the best. Among the details of construction it is

---

[4] WEIGEL, C. A., and SASSCER, E. R. INSECTS INJURIOUS TO ORNAMENTAL GREENHOUSE PLANTS. U. S. Dept. Agr. Farmers' Bul. 1362-F. 81 p., illus., 1926. (See p. 19.)

most highly essential to have the door fitted very accurately and the edges seated with felt, or rubber padding. Some fumigation boxes have been built with a single wall of knot-free "car-decking" (a tongue-and-groove board 1¼ inches thick by 4 inches wide), the grooves of which have been filled with a puttylike gum, used extensively for greenhouse glazing, before the parts were assembled. These boxes appear very satisfactory when the gum is carefully and thoroughly applied, and when the corners and edges and other places where leaks might occur are thoroughly protected by this means.

The calcium cyanide is spread thinly on wooden pans which are slipped under a skeleton frame or false floor supporting the trays of bulbs. Three square feet of surface of the pan should be allowed for each pound of the fumigating material. Slots in the side of the box should be provided through which these pans may be pushed under the bulbs. For ventilation it is advisable to have a trap door on the

FIGURE 174.—A fumigation box having a capacity of 150 cubic feet used in experimental work in the field laboratory of the Bureau of Entomology at Puyallup, Wash.

top of the box, and if the chamber is inside a building it is essential for safety to have a suction fan and a flue leading to the outside, so that the interior of the building will not be filled with the poisonous gas after a fumigation. In boxes of 150 cubic feet and larger it is also necessary to have a fan to keep in circulation the gas evolved and insure a uniform concentration of it in all parts of the fumigator.

Capacities of Boxes

Capacities of boxes in practical use range up to 560 cubic feet. A box used extensively in experimental work at Puyallup, Wash. (fig. 174), had a capacity of 150 cubic feet, and when full held slightly more than a ton of bulbs. This size would be practical for any grower having not more than 5 acres of bulbs. Two or three such units might be used by a grower having from 5 to 10 acres. For growers with more acreage a larger size may be necessary to handle the bulbs effectively, but 500 cubic feet has been found to be the approximate limit for individual boxes under the conditions that prevail in the Pacific Northwest when the expense and time of loading and unloading are considered. To care for the stock on very large acreage two or more of the larger units might be employed. A box with a capacity of 500 cubic feet should hold at one time between 3½ and 5 tons of bulbs. Experiments are now under way looking toward the possibility of fumigation in large units and in packing crates.

The growers in some sections are very well satisfied with this method of treating their bulbs. They find it simple in operation and low in cost in comparison with other measures, and feel satisfied with its efficiency. Many are fumigating all of their planting stock as an insurance against carrying infestation back to their fields. Some are planning to use fumigation and the hot-water treatment in alternate years for their planting and propagating stock.

CHARLES F. DOUCETTE.

NEGRO Extension Work Promoted by Local Organization Activity When negro farmers and home makers become interested in improving agricultural conditions a meeting is often called and a community agricultural organization formed. It may be called a community club, advisory board, executive board, advisory council, or auxiliary farm bureau, depending upon the State in which it is located. However named, such groups are all organized in about the same way and function alike. They meet with the county agents, study the needs of the community, select the important problems to be solved, and build a program of work intended to provide the solution of the problems.

The community organization brings accepted extension practices closer to the farmer than is possible in larger groups. After the election of officers its first activity is usually the selection of progressive negro farmers and farm women to act as local leaders for the extension work in the county. Local leaders are unpaid volunteer workers who help the county extension agents to organize a community for extension work. They arrange meetings, conduct farm and home tours, help in carrying on demonstration campaigns, and the like.

County supervisory boards or councils of agriculture are composed of presidents or elected representatives of community agricultural organizations. Their meetings are usually held monthly, the county agent participating in the discussion of plans and the progress which has been made in carrying them out. The county organization also assists in conducting county fairs, campaigns, picnics, farm and home tours, and other extension activities.

State supervisory boards or councils of agriculture are composed of delegates from the county organization. These also cooperate with the extension service in carrying to successful conclusion programs approved by the director of extension work.

Organization Activities Are Numerous

These different groups or organizations work for the needed county and State funds to be used in paying salaries to extension workers, aid in the development of successful local leaders, promote cooperative organizations for buying and selling agricultural products, and in many other ways assist the negro extension service in bettering farm production and marketing and living conditions.

A few examples of accomplishments are cited to show the influence that community, county, and State organizations have on improved farm and home practices.

A community club in Rowan County, N. C., repaired a bad piece of road cooperatively. The work was so well done that the county commissioners added this side road to the county system.

When extension work was introduced in Amherst County, Va., the people of Amherst community thought it a good thing for children but could not see where it would benefit the adults. The agent put forth special effort to make the work popular among the young people. The girls were organized into a 4-H club which met twice a month in different homes for club work. The mothers took as much interest as did the girls in tidying up the homes and serving refreshments. One

FIGURE 175.—Modern negro home which was built and beautified as a result of extension work. Hundreds of negro farmers have profited from the increased efficiency of negro extension work brought about by community, county, and State extension organizations

of the women, seeing the value of the work, offered to serve as a leader and invited the girls to meet in her home at any time they wished. A year later 10 of the women of that community were organized into a home demonstration club which grew to 19 members. This club has not missed holding a monthly meeting during the three years of its existence. The following are some of the things it has accomplished: Six houses painted, 4 houses remodeled, 4 kitchens improved and arranged for convenience, 2 yards graded, 2 sanitary toilets built, and some general improvements made in each home represented in the club.

The advisory board of Powhatan County, Va., purchased 22 acres of land and erected buildings on it for community and county activities. The advisory board of Robeson County, N. C., obtained from the county tax funds an annual appropriation of $500 toward the salary of a home demonstration agent to work with the women and girls of the county.

The Virginia State Advisory Board represents the negro farm families of the State and cooperates with the State Advisory Council (white) in bringing about better farming conditions.   At one of its annual meetings 79 farm men and women delegates from 28 counties represented 23,348 farm families.   The delegates alone owned 11,495 acres of land having a total valuation, including buildings, livestock, and machinery, of over a half million dollars.

The following stories of Albert Lee and Sam Glover illustrate the type of person who is selected as a local leader.   The results which they obtained through following the teachings of the negro extension agent have furnished inspiration to many others in their community.

FIGURE 176.—Negro home demonstration club learning how to cull poultry

Albert Lee of Nansemond County, Va., in getting ready for the annual inspection tour made by the farmers, painted his house, whitewashed his outbuildings, remodeled his barn, made his well sanitary and built a house over it, put a force pump on the back porch, and built a shed for housing his farm implements—all of which was done in one year.   He is a leader in his community.

Sam Glover of Orangeburg County, S. C., began demonstration work in 1916 on a farm of 25 acres of land in a low state of cultivation. He had one horse and no livestock of any consequence and lived in a house worth about $300.   His first demonstration was the growing of 3 acres of corn and cowpeas; the results were very gratifying.   The following year he grew 10 acres of cotton, 5 acres of corn, and 5 acres of small grain; the yields were good.   The third year he added through purchase, 25 acres to his farm, and the combined farms were worked according to demonstration methods.

Obtains Help from Extension Workers

He received constant advice and assistance from the extension workers on soil building, crop rotation, good seed, good livestock, and proper feeding. In 1928 he owned 125 acres of land in a high state of cultivation, a modern house worth $3,000, 2 Jersey cows, 15 head of hogs including 2 brood sows and a purebred boar, 3 head of horses, improved farm implements, an automobile, 450 bushels of corn, and wheat sufficient for the year. He sold 18 bales of cotton and had 8 tons of hay for sale above what was necessary to carry him through 1928. His wife and daughter sold $330 worth of vegetables, chickens, eggs, and butter in 1927. The entire farm with modern improvements

FIGURE 177.—Negro explaining to farmers the good points of a purebred bull owned by the community. Organization has helped negro farmers to improve their herds through the introduction of purebred sires and the elimination of grade animals from the head of the herd

is valued at $8,000. He has a life insurance policy for $3,000 and a bank account.

One of his daughters was graduated from the negro State college at Orangeburg and teaches in the rural schools of Orangeburg County, where she carries out the lessons learned in developing rural people. Three of the Glover children are in the State college at present. Sam Glover is a leader in his community club and in county-wide extension activities, and field meetings are often held on his farm.

J. B. PIERCE.

NEMAS Carry Bacterial and Fungous Diseases from Plant to Plant Few know that nemas—also called nematodes, roundworms, threadworms—living free in the soil or parasitic on plants, are disease carriers and as such sometimes play an important rôle in the dissemination of bacterial and fungous pests of plants. These little animals, much smaller than earthworms and very different in structure, move about in the soil, often from plant to plant. Their method of entering the host plant varies. Some enter the roots, some climb the stems and enter the leaves and the flowers and thence the seed.

The small size of the nemas, most forms reaching a length of only one-sixtieth to one-eighth of an inch, excludes their traveling long distances. A few yards is all they are likely to cover in a lifetime. But this is enough to enable them to carry germs from an originally diseased plant to neighboring plants. Often hundreds, even thousands upon thousands, of these nemas may be present at a disease center, from which they may carry the germs in all directions. A common feature of such nema-carried diseases is the appearance in the growing crop of small diseased areas which become larger and larger.

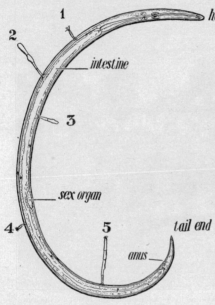

FIGURE 178.—A larval gall nema, *Tylenchus tritici*, of wheat carrying various spores (1–5) of the fungus *Dilophospora alopecuri* (partly after Atanasoff). The sexual organs of the nema are still undeveloped. Two kinds of spores are seen, so-called pycnospores 1 and 4 and secondary spores 2, 3, and 5. The spores are drawn on a somewhat larger scale than the nema

However, nemas themselves often are carried long distances by other agents, such as water, wind, and animals, or by man himself, who may transport them with soil on footwear, tools, and other articles, or may inadvertently ship them on or in seeds, seedlings, or other agricultural products. Such passively transported nemas may carry disease germs; such instances are known. It is claimed that the pseudomonas disease of wheat was brought from East India to Egypt associated with the gall nema of wheat.

Nemas, as a rule, have a smooth surface, apparently unfit for the attachment of another organism; yet it has been observed that bacteria as well as fungous spores may become attached to them, sometimes on account of the "stickiness" of either the nemas or the other organism.

Nemas disseminate spores and bacteria by another method. Just as birds feeding upon berries pass the seeds through their intestinal tract unimpaired and often bring them to favorable new locations where they may germinate and grow, so the nemas spread fungi and bacteria. Bacteria may pass uninjured through the intestine, the nema digesting only the slimy mass that often surrounds the bacteria. Or a nema feeding on fungi may digest the mycelium but not the spores, which often have a thick protective covering. These spores are later voided with the feces, and if the nema meanwhile has moved to a new location the spores may find it a suitable place for development.

Many nemas have their optimum development in association with rot and decay, which usually means an accumulation of bacteria and fungi. Such a rot on a plant may be the result of an attack by a noxious fungus or bacterium. The nemas moving through this mass will very probably carry some of these germs away to neighboring plants. Because of this kind of association, these nemas are called saprophytic (that is, living on decaying plants).

In the soil nemas play somewhat the rôle that the fly plays in the spread of human diseases. It has been observed, for instance, that a disease of red clover caused by a fungus, *Fusarium trifolii*, is spread by such nemas from an originally infested plant to neighboring ones. But more remarkable cases of dissemination by nemas of bacterial and fungous plant diseases are known. In one instance the nema, itself a parasite, carries the disease germs not only right to the host plant, but even to a specific part where alone the disease can develop. The gall nema of wheat is claimed to be the carrier of the pseudomonas disease of wheat, a bacterial malady, and also of the dilophospora disease, due to a fungus. Both diseases are always associated with this gall nema, and it is asserted that neither can develop unless the young wheat plant is attacked by this nema. Seemingly the germs attach themselves to the nema (fig. 178) as it moves about in soil water containing them.

G. Steiner.

NITROGEN Loss from Soil by Leaching Is Largely Preventable Nitrogen is lost from soils in the drainage water almost entirely in the form of nitrates under average farming conditions. These nitrates are produced in soil by bacterial action from the various organic and inorganic forms of nitrogen set free through decay processes. Nitrate formation is almost negligible during the winter months, proceeds slowly in the early spring, and is usually at its maximum during the hot summer months.

It is obvious, therefore, that in the prevention of nitrogen losses from soils by leaching we must modify farm practices so as to prevent the accumulation of nitrates during the late summer. This may be accomplished by planning the rotation so that a crop in an active growing condition is present, preferably at the time nitrate formation is proceeding most rapidly, or at least shortly thereafter. The ordinary rotation may do this; if not, an extra crop may be added to insure that the soil is not left barren and subject to severe leaching. Various types of crops may be used; cowpeas and soy beans are good hot weather crops, while rye is an excellent fall and winter cover crop. The planting of these crops need not be limited to areas that would otherwise be barren; they may be planted in other crops. For instance, cowpeas, soy beans, velvet beans, wheat, or rye may be drilled or sown between rows of corn after the final cultivation. An actively growing secondary crop is thus provided at a time when the main crop is reaching maturity. If the crop chosen is a legume, then not only are the soil nitrates utilized, but in most cases there is a considerable fixation of nitrogen from the atmosphere, thus adding to the value of the crop. These catch or cover crops, while grown primarily for the purpose of protecting the soil from erosion and leaching, may at the same time serve as important links in the cropping system. They may be cut for hay, be used for pasture, serve as green manure crops, or merely be allowed to remain as a protection for the soil.

The net result of the system recommended is that the nitrogen which would otherwise be lost is used to produce a crop which either has an immediate money value or else becomes a source of humus if returned to the soil. In the latter case the nitrogen is no longer in the nitrate form, but is present as a part of the plant tissues in an ideal condition to be converted into nitrates again when needed in the spring.

F. E. Allison.

NITROGEN Supply of United States Much Dependent on Imports In this country an adequate supply of fixed nitrogen is essential both in time of war and in time of peace. The United States is a consumer of great quantities of nitrogen used in a variety of forms by several industries. Agriculture is by far the largest user. The chemical industry, the explosives industry, and refrigeration rank next, in the order of quantity used. Agriculture leads also in the variety of forms in which nitrogen is used. While other industries must have nitrogen in the form of ammonia or sodium nitrate, agriculture can use these inorganic materials and also organic materials including all sorts of animal and vegetable waste. All but about 320,000 out of several million tons of nitrogen going annually into the soils of the United States is produced on the farm as manure, or is carried down by the rain, or is fixed from the atmosphere by bacteria of the soil and legumes.

However, agriculture demands an auxiliary supply in the form of commercial fertilizers. This is supplied partly by such materials as dried blood and tankage, fish scrap and cottonseed meal, but mainly by Chilean nitrate, by-product sulphate of ammonia and cyanamide, and other products of the fixation plants. This last class is of special interest on account of the fact that its production is capable of unlimited expansion and can be made to supply the demands of all nitrogen-using industries.

The annual inorganic nitrogen supply of the United States is approximately as follows—700,000 tons ammonium sulphate equivalent containing 154,000 tons of nitrogen from the coke ovens and gas works; 50,000 tons of ammonia containing 40,000 tons of nitrogen from fixation plants; 1,000,000 tons of Chilean nitrate containing 155,000 tons of nitrogen; other imports, including cyanamide, amounting to about 50,000 tons of nitrogen. These figures, totaling about 400,000 tons, vary from year to year, the tendency being toward steady growth in coke-oven production and more rapid growth in air fixation output and marked fluctuation in imports. It will be noted that the United States is still dependent in a large measure upon imports for its nitrogen supply.

This country will use increasing quantities of nitrogen in the future and agriculture will demand the major part of the supply. Aside from that produced on the farm it will come mainly from three sources—(1) the coke ovens, with production limited by the demand for coke; (2) imports from Chile, Germany, and Norway, and possibly other countries; (3) our own growing fixation industry, with unlimited possibilities for expansion.

For years the discussion has centered around the Government plant at Muscle Shoals. Ten years have passed since their construction and rapid progress has been made in the industry, with the result that these plants are out of date and of questionable value. Only 40,000 tons of nitrogen could be obtained from this source and would fall far short of supplying the demand, which requires the importation of some 200,000 tons annually. Evidently there is need of expansion in nitrogen-fixation capacity, and this situation is bringing about the development of an industry of the usual American type, assisted by the Government through its research activities.

P. E. HOWARD.

OAT Varieties That Resist Smut Grown by Experimentation In each of the three years 1924, 1925, and 1926 the oat smuts took a toll of about 50,000,000 bushels in the United States. In 1927 and 1928 oat smut appeared in epidemic form in various sections of the country. The annual losses in these last two years doubtless exceeded those of the three years noted above.

Oat smut may be controlled by treating the seed with formaldehyde, a treatment that is cheap, easy to apply, and very effective. However, in view of the heavy annual losses, it is evident that seed treatment is not practiced as extensively as it should be. Because of this fact the possibilities of discovering or developing satisfactory varieties highly resistant to the smuts of oats is receiving increased attention by agronomists and pathologists of the United States Department of Agriculture and the State agricultural experiment stations. The necessity for seed treatment with formaldehyde or other fungicides to control smut thus would be eliminated or reduced.

After extensive smut-inoculation studies by various investigators three varieties belonging to the common-oat group (*Avena sativa* L.) have been found which are highly resistant to or immune from the forms of both smuts now known. They are the Markton, Black Mesdag, and Navarro (Ferguson Navarro) varieties. Of these only the Markton has become of commercial importance. So far the distribution of Markton has been limited to Washington, Oregon, Idaho, and adjacent Montana, owing to its marked susceptibility to the rusts of oats. The Black Mesdag variety never has become of economic value owing to its poor yield and black kernels. The Navarro, a comparatively new and distinct oat, likewise appears to be poorly adapted and as yet is of no economic importance.

Value for Breeding

The Black Mesdag and Navarro both have potential value for breeding purposes in spite of their agronomic disadvantages. With Markton, they now are being used by plant breeders in hybridization experiments as resistant parents for the development of new varieties. In a few years, therefore, numerous strains of oats highly resistant to both smuts should be available unless new physiological forms of smut appear in the meantime that prove capable of infecting the parent and hybrid sorts.

For many years the Red Rustproof, Fulghum, and Burt, the so-called red-oat varieties of the South, have been considered highly resistant to the smuts of oats. However, during the last few years the occurrence of smut in these varieties, especially in Fulghum and its strains, has been decidedly on the increase. This apparent breaking down of resistance is explained by the occurrence of new physiological forms of the oat smuts. These varieties, therefore, no longer can be classed as smut resistant.

T. R. STANTON,
F. A. COFFMAN, and
V. F. TAPKE.

ORGANIC Materials May Hurt Crops If Applied Undecayed Most soils which are constantly under cultivation have a tendency to become low in organic matter or humus content unless farm practices are planned so as to make provision for the regular return of crop residues, stable manure, green crops, or other forms of organic materials. The necessity for maintenance of the humus supply in the soil is well understood, but the best method of doing this is not so obvious. However, many recent studies have given us the information needed for making practical recommendations.

Whenever readily decomposable organic materials are incorporated with the soil a rapid multiplication of bacteria and fungi occurs. These microorganisms are the agents of decay primarily responsible for the conversion of plant proteins into ammonia and nitrates, and the sugars, starch cellulose, and other carbohydrate materials into carbon dioxide. The more resistant portions of the plant substances remain to form a part of the soil humus. The growth requirements of the organisms which produce these changes are similar to those of higher plants, except that they obtain their energy from the residues of higher plants rather than directly from sunlight. They require adequate moisture, mineral matter, usually good aeration, and available forms of nitrogen.

It is this last requirement that needs most consideration. If a green-plant material is added to the soil it usually contains more nitrogen than needed by the decay organisms. There occurs a marked formation of ammonia, a considerable portion of which is later converted into nitrates. The bacteria and fungi assimilate a portion of the available nitrogen, but there remains a surplus for the crop. On the other hand, if straw, corn stalks, fresh stable manure, or other materials which are rather easily decomposed but which contain a very low percentage of nitrogen, are applied, they may not furnish enough nitrogen to meet the needs of the microorganisms. Unless the soil is especially high in nitrogen there is likely to be a temporary deficiency and the crop may suffer partial nitrogen starvation, often evidenced by a rather pale, yellowish-green color, and a stunted growth. Later, a return to normal may take place, but usually not in time to avoid crop injury if the planting was done at the time of the application of the organic materials.

The procedure to be followed in applying materials which are likely to produce crop injuries must vary with the existing conditions. The plant substances may be allowed to decay partially before application, preferably in a compost heap, they may be used as bedding for livestock, or they may be applied several weeks before planting. If application must be made immediately before planting, the quantity used should be very limited and the crop grown should be one that thrives on decaying organic matter. The efficient utilization of crop residues may require modifications of farm practices, but such changes usually prove profitable. Not only is the soil organic matter content maintained, but the energy supplied is partly utilized by bacteria which grow independent of higher plants and fix atmospheric nitrogen.

F. E. ALLISON.

PAPER-MULCH Trials Center About Three Lines of Usefulness   The experimental trial of paper mulch as an aid to crop production in the United States is centering about three lines of usefulness—(1) The development and trial of papers suitable for field culture of annual crops, (2) the improvement and trial of papers suitable for perennial crops and home-garden use, and (3) the development and trial of papers suitable as a winter mulch. The papers utilized for these purposes

FIGURE 179.—The effect of asphalt paper as applied only to the plant row. Potatoes and tomatoes in the foreground. Arlington Experiment Farm, 1928

have been designated arbitrarily as type A, type B, and type C, respectively. Present prices range from $30 to $200 an acre, varying both with the type of paper and the system of adapting it to the requirements of any specified crop plant. There are substantial indications that some of these papers will be of economic value, and with improvement in the papers and the methods of their application paper mulch appears to have a fair prospect of becoming an asset in agricultural practice.

Type A Papers

While the maximum effect of mulch paper appears to accompany complete soil coverage, confining paper to the planting row has practical advantages with many crops, reducing costs and permitting use of spray apparatus. This system is being tried with papers of type A in the field culture of annual crops of low per acre value, and its effectiveness is indicated by the results of some trials at the Arlington Experiment Farm as shown in Figure 179.

Type B Papers

The use of durable papers for perennial plants (type B) appears to be of promise in trials with small fruits, young fruit trees set in permanent orchard plantings, flowering plants, young evergreens, and nursery stock, as well as for home-garden use. The stimulation characteristic of the use of paper mulch with crop plants, moreover, may be made available to an appreciable extent with ornamental plantings by covering the paper with pine straw or other material simulating natural conditions. The heat-absorbing value of the black surface is necessarily sacrificed for the sake of appearances, but substantial advantages of increased moisture and weed suppression remain.

Type C Papers

The experimental trial of type C papers for winter mulching is developing (1) as a soil-conditioning mulch designed to insure a drier and warmer soil leading to earlier spring growth of crop plants such as asparagus and (2) as a protective mulch designed to insure a

FIGURE 180.—Asparagus grown in California in 1927 with and without type C winter mulch. A, Early pickings from rows 1,350 feet long (mulched, left and right center); B, size of stalks in mulched (left) and unmulched shoots

measure of frost protection with crop plants such as strawberries. Differences characterizing type C papers in asparagus trials in California are indicated in Figure 180.

Eradication of Weeds and Control of Diseases

In general, the measure of weed control afforded by paper mulch is of secondary importance to its stimulation of the mulched plant. In the case of particularly persistent and obnoxious weeds such as wire grass, witch grass, Bermuda grass, poison ivy, etc., however, the use of paper may become of first importance as a means of weed eradication.

From the crop-production standpoint paper mulch favors the plant over many diseases simply because hastened maturity shortens the period of susceptibility. From the disease standpoint paper mulch affords control of many soil-borne organisms either through the prevention of emergence or through the destruction of host tissues sustaining parasites.

L. H. FLINT.

PEACH Rots and How Temperature Affects Their Development High temperatures favor the development of peach rots, yet summer weather may be too hot for the greatest growth, and the effect of a particular temperature will vary with the rot organism and with its stage of development.

Practically all peach rots are caused by one or the other of two decay organisms, Monilia and Rhizopus. Monilia causes the brown rot so common in orchards and on the market, and Rhizopus a soft watery rot of the ripe harvested fruit. Monilia grows best at 70° to 80° F. and makes practically no growth as the temperature approaches 90°, while Rhizopus grows best at 90° to 95°. Monilia rots can start and grow at as low a temperature as 32°, while Rhizopus rots that are already started can barely enlarge at 40°, and their early stages of development are almost completely inhibited at 50°.

At 41° Monilia rots develop about four times as fast as at 32°; at 50° about two and two-tenths times as fast as at 41° and practically nine times as fast as at 32°; at 59° about one and six-tenths times as fast as at 50°, three and five-tenths times as fast as at 41°, and fourteen times as fast as at 32°; at 68° about one and six-tenths times as fast as at 50°, two and five-tenths times as fast as at 50°, five and five-tenths times as fast as at 41°, and twenty-two times as fast as at 32°. They develop slightly faster at 77° than at 68°, but at higher temperatures the growth soon begins to fall off.

Rhizopus rots rarely make a start at 50° F., but can grow fairly well at that temperature when once established. They develop about three times as fast at 59° as at 50°, about one and eight-tenths times as fast at 68° as at 59°, about one and five-tenths times as fast at 77° as at 68°, and about one and two-tenths times as fast at 86° as at 77°.

These various ratios apply approximately both to the number of rots appearing at the different temperatures and to the rate of development of a particular rot. They are quite significant in a study of the spoilage of harvested fruit. Peaches held in an ordinary refrigerator at 55° F. will develop less than half the Monilia rot that they would develop if exposed to the usual summer temperatures of 70° to 85°, and if held in a refrigerator at 40° they develop only about one-sixth as much rot as if exposed to outside temperature. Similar cooling of peaches to 55° reduces the Rhizopus rot to about one-fourth or one-fifth of what it would be at the usual summer temperatures, and holding at 40° entirely prevents its start.

Peaches held over in the packing house for the large part of a day before loading for shipment may develop as much tendency to rot in that time as during the whole period of transit under refrigeration.

Conditions in Refrigerator Cars

If loaded warm, the fruit in the top of a four-layer refrigerator car is usually 12° to 25° F. warmer than that in the bottom of the car during the first 24 to 36 hours after loading, and during this time the Monilia rots in the top of the car are developing three to four times as fast as those in the bottom of the car, and the contrast with the Rhizopus rots is several times greater than this. The result is that the fruit in the bottom of the car may arrive at the destination practically free from rot, while that in the top of the car is often badly specked at unloading and ready for further rot development with any delay on the market or in the home.

CHARLES BROOKS.

PEAT Deposits Under Some Conditions Are Serious Fire Hazard

The large peat deposits in the United States constitute, under some conditions, a fire hazard which may result in a disastrous fire.

Peat, a substance consisting of partly carbonized vegetable material, the result of the decomposition of various plants in the presence of water, when dry burns readily. The hazard of peat fires becomes serious in periods of drought and excessive evaporation, especially if the soil is drained.

In recent years a number of serious peat fires have occurred. In May, 1928, fires in piles of dry peat in northeastern Netherlands were reported to have caused an extensive loss of property. Similar fires occurred in the Netherlands in 1880 and 1917. Considerable areas have been burned over in other foreign countries, as, for example, in Yugoslavia in 1920.

Serious fires broke out in peat soil in the Everglades of Florida during the winter and spring of 1928. Specialists of the Department of Agriculture who were sent to the affected territory to make a survey of the situation found that approximately 1,250,000 acres of peat had been burned over, the depth ranging from a mere surface burning in some sections to severe burning several feet deep in others. So far as could be ascertained no lives were lost, and only a few buildings were destroyed.

Apparently the peat fires in Florida were caused indirectly by drought, evaporation, and drainage, and directly by clearing-off operations and by careless hunters, trappers, and smokers. Although press reports had ascribed most of these fires to spontaneous combustion of the peat soil, the survey did not bring out any confirmatory evidence that spontaneous ignition caused any of the fires. Whether peat soil or peat in storage is capable of igniting spontaneously, however, is a question that can be settled only by experimentation.

FIGURE 181.—Peat soil cracked by severe drying in section southeast of Lake Okeechobee, Fla.

HARRY E. ROETHE.

PECAN Shelling Plants Increase With Demand for Cracked Kernels

The demand for pecan kernels during recent years has grown steadily with the development of the pecan industry as a whole. By far the largest portion of the product is absorbed by the confectionery and bakery trade. This growing taste on the part of the consuming public for food products containing the cracked kernels has been the means of promoting the comparatively new industry of pecan cracking.

The extreme difficulty that the few big operators had in quickly absorbing the supply at going prices during years of maximum production has led to a wide expansion of the industry. In 1926, when the total production of unshelled pecans in the United States was estimated at 64,000,000 pounds, in comparison with 30,000,000 in 1925 and 20,500,000 in 1924, these large companies bought and placed in cold storage immense quantities of the unshelled product. At the end of the season hundreds of thousands of pounds still remained in the hands of producers and local merchants. Prices dropped to the extreme low level of the decade of about 8 cents a pound.

The result was that during that year dozens of small cracking establishments sprang up. Such a notable overflow of the cracking industry into the producing districts has taken place that in the important centers of production there is now to be found scarcely a town of 3,000 inhabitants or more without from one to several cracking establishments. Many of these are extremely small plants operated by street vendors, who each day crack only enough nuts to supply their immediate needs and whose total capacity for an entire season probably does not average more than 2 or 3 tons. Others are individuals who find it advantageous to dispose of their own crops by cracking the nuts and marketing the kernels, chiefly by parcel post. Still others are independent operators who crack a carload or more a season, especially during years of large production, but a good many of such plants are branches of the large companies that long have been in business outside the centers of production.

Small Operators Handicapped

As the small operators, however, usually lack the financial resources and facilities of cold storage necessary to acquire and hold in fit condition a sufficient quantity of nuts for more than a few months, and also lack the business connections essential to extensive sales, they are at a great disadvantage in competition with the large operators. Eventtually consolidation of the small operators and the elimination of the weakest is to be expected.

Regardless of competition between the large and small crackers, development of the industry in centers of production is of material advantage to the industry as a whole, in that it saves freight charges on the shells and forms an outlet for the cheaper labor that may be had in the small towns of the South, and by holding the larger part of the crop income in the producing areas prices are stabilized and the producer shares in the increased values. Local communities are also brought into closer contact with the industry, which necessarily has a direct result on community welfare.

Pecan cracking, in fact, has become of great importance to the industry as a means of getting the product to the consumer, for in spite of the high quality of the kernels, consumers will not buy as many pecans when the only way of getting at the kernels is by hand-cracking and extraction.

C. A. REED.

PECANS Respond to Commercial Fertilizer When Rightly Applied   Experimental work with pecans has demonstrated that tree growth and nut yield can be stimulated by the proper use of commercial fertilizer, and successful pecan growers of the southeast now realize that the southern soils need fertilization to produce successful crops of pecans as much as for the growth of successful crops of any farm produce. The correct fertilization of pecans is as important to crop quality and profitable yields as the correct fertilization of any crop.

Experiments have been conducted by the Department of Agriculture since 1918 to determine the proper fertilizer formulas and sources of fertilizers for the various soil types used in pecan growing in the South. The proper ratio of nitrogen, phosphoric acid, and potash in the fertilizer for best results varies according to the soil type and orchard management. The department's experiments have shown that for pecan growing on loams and clay loams a liberal supply of nitrogen and phosphoric acid is needed. On these soils potash has but little

FIGURE 182.—A well-tilled pecan orchard, where clean cultivation was practiced in the spring and early summer, and planted to a leguminous cover crop for green manure

effect on tree growth and nut yield. Orchards on sandy soils and very sandy loams require more potash, and fertilizers for these soil types should contain a good proportion of potash, for this and nitrogen have about equal value in nut production.

All Fertilizer Constituents Needed

The fertilizer for the pecan orchard on most soils should contain all three of the fertilizer constituents—nitrogen, phosphate, and potash. Phosphate and nitrogen influence tree growth, and the yield, filling qualities, and size of the nut; and potash the fat content, color, and plumpness of the kernel. Where leguminous cover crops are grown and turned under for manure, which supplies a considerable amount of nitrogen, fertilizers analyzing 4 to 5 per cent ammonia, 8 to 10 per cent phosphoric acid, and 3 to 4 per cent potash have given good results on bearing trees. For soils high in organic matter and nitrogen, a fertilizer containing 4 per cent ammonia, 10 per cent phosphoric acid, and 3 per cent potash could be used with good results, but for most soils a mixture containing 5 per cent ammonia is preferable. For young orchards from time of setting until they are 7 to 8 years old it is advisable to fertilize with a mixture containing even more nitrogen. A fertilizer containing 6 per cent ammonia, 8 per cent phosphoric acid, and 4 per cent potash has been used generally by nurserymen and orchard growers with success.

In preparing a fertilizer mixture for pecans, consideration should be given to the materials used. Superphosphate is used principally in

FIGURE 183.—Pecan orchard growing a green-manure crop of oats. Row of trees on left received no commercial fertilizer. Row on right had annual application of a complete fertilizer since the orchard was set

mixed fertilizers and is the most available source of phosphorus. The potash materials do not seem to vary widely in their effects, the sulphate and muriate being most widely used. The fertilizer mixture should contain several sources of nitrogen and should be derived partly from quickly available materials, such as nitrate of soda, sulphate of

FIGURE 184.—Row of trees on left were fertilized with a mixture of phosphate and potash. The row on right were fertilized with nitrogen, phosphate, and potash

ammonia, or synthetic nitrogen, and partly from slowly available sources, as fish scrap, tankage, blood, or cottonseed meal.

A fertilizer containing approximately 5 per cent ammonia, 10 per cent phosphoric acid, and 3 per cent potash can be prepared by mixing the materials in the following proportions:

	Pounds
Superphosphate (16 per cent P_2O_5)	1, 250
Muriate or sulphate of potash (50 per cent K_2O)	125
Nitrate of soda (18 per cent NH_3)	225
Sulphate of ammonia (25 per cent NH_3)	160
Organic source (fish scrap, tankage, or cottonseed meal) (9 per cent NH_3)	240
Total	2, 000

A 6-8-4 mixture suitable for young trees can be prepared as follows:

	Pounds
Superphosphate (16 per cent P_2O_5)	1, 000
Muriate or sulphate of potash (50 per cent K_2O)	160
Nitrate of soda (18 per cent NH_3)	220
Sulphate of ammonia (25 per cent NH_3)	160
Organic source (fish scrap, tankage, or cottonseed meal) (9 per cent NH_3)	460
Total	2, 000

In these fertilizers the nitrogen is derived partly from quickly available and partly from slowly available materials which is desirable in pecan fertilizers.

Organic Matter Required

The fertility of the soil in pecan orchards can not be maintained by the use of commercial fertilizers alone. Of equal importance are cultivation and the incorporation of organic matter. In the years before the trees begin to bear, the soil fertility and organic-matter content should be built up. Before the tree roots have spread widely, summer and winter cover crops should be grown over the entire area, and the vegetation produced turned under. When trees come to the bearing age deep plowing of the land becomes injurious and disking or shallow plowing is required. Cultivation of the orchard in spring and early summer, followed by the planting of a leguminous cover crop for green manuring, together with the use of commercial fertilizers should maintain the fertility of the soil sufficiently to support a successful orchard.

J. J. SKINNER.

PLANT Immigrants Pass Numerous Tests Before Becoming Established While the story of American agriculture has been marked by the phenomenal success of many introduced crops, it is not generally understood by what steps this success has been brought about, nor have the time and patient care necessary been generally appreciated.

The finding of plants in foreign lands and their forwarding across great distances by porter, caravan, rail, sea, and air, and their final arrival at an American port form a sequence that is colorful in its story of risk, sacrifice, humor, hardship, and patience. The journey from the port of arrival to the final place in farm and garden is also one marked by patience, effort, and sometimes disappointment, and usually covers a much longer period, unmarked by what is glamorous or bizarre, but equally important. A brief excursion into the mechanics and methods of this phase of plant introduction will shed some light on the naturalization process of new plant immigrants.

The introduction of new plants is attended by risks as well as benefits. In foreign countries plant diseases and pests at present nonexistent here abound. From the disastrous experiences of the past, the importance of the exclusion of new pests and diseases is apparent; hence a rigid quarantine system has been erected to safeguard the American plant industry. This requires exacting methods of handling all incoming plant material before it can be safely released for experimental work.

Assuming arrival at a port in the United States, all incoming introductions are subjected to careful inspection immediately, and all are then forwarded to Washington. Here special inspection and quarantine facilities are provided to cover the needs of all manner of plant forms.

Pathologists and entomologists carefully inspect each shipment for pests and signs of disease. A general fumigation is given all seeds regardless of their origin; bulbs are treated with hot water to kill nematodes. Seeds or plants coming from countries where especially dangerous pests or diseases occur are given additional treatment to insure safety. Quarantine houses are maintained where the plants may be grown under detention and observation over a period of time sufficient to permit the detection of any condition not discovered on arrival. In order to avoid the possible reintroduction of the dreaded citrus canker, special quarantine and propagation facilities have been developed, and only buds that have been produced on new wood developed after arrival at the quarantine house are used.

Proper Identification Necessary

While most of the material coming from abroad is received under its name, explorers often work in regions far from the beaten track where new or little-known plant forms occur; hence much material may arrive incompletely named or even nameless. Notes, photographs, herbarium specimens, and seeds are all used by specialists of the department for proper identification, and frequently the aid of botanists in other institutions and even in other countries is required to classify properly the newcomer.

Each new arrival is assigned a number which becomes its permanent attribute. These numbers now have passed F. P. I. 77,260, and give some indication of the vast number of introductions that have been made since the system was instituted more than a quarter of a century ago. Full description, notes, field data as to location, occurrence, economic importance, soil and climatic requirements, and the explorer's observations are recorded for each introduction. No "quota" is enforced as to the countries of origin, but, as is the case with human immigrants, certain plant groups are much more desirable than others. The past history, family connections and relations, and information on desirable or undesirable behavior are as expressly sought by officials responsible for plant immigration as is the case with persons desiring entrance to this country.

The list of new introductions, together with descriptive notes, is published quarterly in a Foreign Plant Introduction Inventory, so that plant experimenters in the United States as well as abroad can know what new plants have been received for trial to be made available for distribution later after propagation in quantity.

Propagation and Trial at Introduction Gardens

Unless detained for growth under quarantine, seeds and plants, after release from inspection and treatment, are sent to one or more of the four different plant-introduction gardens. These are located in Maryland, Georgia, Florida, and California. Material for propagation is allocated according to its climatic needs in so far as possible. Certain groups of seeds, such as those of cereal and forage crops, requiring larger areas for field testing, are turned over direct to the various specialists in those fields, who are best prepared to carry on studies and trial tests. Permanent plantings of trees and fruits are also made at the plant-introduction gardens, both to provide a basis for observation on behavior and a future supply of propagating material. These plantings are carefully labeled, mapped, and checked for a permanent record.

When a sufficient quantity of stock has been acquired through propagating, it is again inspected for insects and plant diseases, and if necessary given a precautionary treatment after which it is distributed under Federal certificate to plant experimenters. Workers in Federal and State experiment stations, botanical gardens, parks, arboretums, and similar institutions have first call on new introductions. It is because of their special needs that much of the foreign exploration is conducted. In addition to these specialists, there exists a large group of plant lovers and experimenters who are working with plants either commercially or as a hobby. From this group many interesting contributions have been made to the plant world. The ability and facilities of those desiring new plants for trial are determined before these names are placed on the distribution list. The demand for plants is far greater than the supply, and it is only when there is some assurance that a fair trial is possible and adequate records can be furnished that new names are accepted.

Lists Issued Annually

Annual lists of seeds and plants available are issued for experimenters. They give the number and descriptive information of each immigrant ready for trial. Such information is included on the identification tag which accompanies all plants forwarded from plant-introduction gardens.

The placing of well-grown plants in the hands of experimenters is but the beginning of another phase. A complete picture of the reaction of a foreign plant can be made only where adequate and full records are kept and notes taken over a period of time. These are obtained in various ways. Written reports are requested from experimenters, both station and individual. Representatives of the department visit these plantings, and the behavior of introductions is checked. Photographs play an important part in the record. Where a new fruit is involved, its tree habit is carefully noted and its suitability for commercial exploitation, fresh, canned, or otherwise preserved, is tested. Disease resistance as well as yield is an important factor with orchard and field crops. Hardiness in an otherwise ordinary variety may indicate value for breeding purposes. Careful records of detailed behavior are a vital part of the plant-introduction program.

Trial Period Long

New introductions make their way slowly. Innovations in the plant world do not become established over night. There has been smooth sailing indeed when a plant is established in our agriculture within 10 years after its arrival in this country, and it is more likely to be 20 years before its behavior can be known with certainty. The behavior of a plant in one part of the world is a guide, but by no means a reliable indicator of its behavior in another country, even under climatic conditions generally considered similar. A wide range of tests under various conditions is necessary.

The new plant, having been found in the far corners of the world, transported to our shores, rendered harmless as a source of new pests or diseases, properly identified and classified, propagated and distributed, is equipped to begin its fight for a place in American agriculture. The story of trials, successes, and failures is another chapter.

KNOWLES A. RYERSON.

POTASH Production in U. S. Increasing Though Still Far Below Needs
Potash production within the United States in 1927 underwent a marked increase, the continuation of that steady progress in production capacity and excellence of product which has been observed since 1921. In that year, which was characterized by the deflation of the war-time industry, the production was only 10,000 tons of actual potash, the output of 19 plants. In 1927 the production was approximately 44,000 tons of actual potash, the output of two major and four minor plants. This represents an increase of 86 per cent in actual potash production over 1926. Sales by producers amounted to 94,722 tons of salts containing 49,500 tons of actual potash and valued at $2,448,146 f. o. b. plants. Increase in sales of potash salts over the preceding year amounted to 84 per cent, which on the basis of potash content is equivalent to 98 per cent and on the basis of value, to 126 per cent.

As in 1926, this output was the product of the two major potash industries, utilizing respectively the saline brines of Searles Lake, with an output of 67,000 tons of potash salts of 98 per cent purity and 37,000 tons of borax as a by-product; and distillery waste, a by-product of alcohol manufacture, with an output of 12,000 tons of salts (ash) of 33 per cent purity and with ammonium sulphate and power as by-products.

During the year 1927 importations of potash from Germany and France amounted to 225,000 tons actual potash, for which the American farmer paid $13,000,000, the price he paid for 271,000 tons in 1913, which shows that while the amount purchased from abroad has decreased, the price has increased.

American production equals 20 per cent of foreign importations. American agriculture is still dependent on Europe for 80 per cent of its potash requirements. If 20 per cent of this required amount can be produced from two minor domestic sources it would appear entirely logical to conclude that from the many other greater potash resources still unexploited we should be able to proceed to the further development of our potash industry to the point at least where foreign dependence is terminated and American potash is available to supply the present and future demands of American agriculture. Inexhaustible supplies exist in our natural deposits of greensand, leucite, alunite, potash shales, and feldspars and quantities exceeding our current requirements are annually lost as industrial wastes. The profitable recovery of potash from these materials depends on by-products to share manufacturing costs, for which chemical processes are required. These are under development by both governmental and private agencies and a foundation of fundamental information, chemical and economic, is being laid whereon to build a potash industry commensurate with our national requirements and aspirations.

J. W. TURRENTINE.

POULTRY Breeders Can Increase Profits by Controlling Production According to the best estimates available the average egg production for all domestic chickens of laying age in the United States is about 70 eggs a year. It is estimated also that the number of eggs produced in the four months of March, April, May, and June approximates 75 per cent of the total production for the year. The correct basis for determining the worth of any hen as a layer should be not only the total number of eggs produced but also the time of production. (Fig. 185.) Ten eggs laid in November or December are worth approximately 20 laid in April or May. The average farm hen lays principally from March to June, the season of lowest prices, and consequently the season of relatively lower profits than at other times of the year.

A study of the trend in the average monthly farm prices for a period of years shows that lowest wholesale-egg prices prevail in April, and that there is a slight increase in July and August, with a more perceptible increase beginning in September. The highest price

FIGURE 185.—These full-sister Rhode Island Reds demonstrate the possibility of obtaining good egg production, especially during the period of high prices. The hen on the left laid 226 eggs in her pullet year, 88 of which were produced during the fall and winter. Corresponding figures for the other hen are 236 and 120 eggs, respectively

is reached in December, which is also the season of highest profits, provided there is good egg production. Moreover, if there is good egg production during the fall and winter, the average price per dozen for the year is increased.

Four Primary Factors Influence Returns

In actual practice there are four primary factors which affect economic returns in the production of eggs for market. These four factors are: (1) The quantity of feed consumed, (2) the price of feed from time to time, (3) the number of eggs produced, (4) the prevailing price of eggs at the time of production. The poultryman has little or no control over the price of feed or the price of eggs. Under ordinary conditions of practice the average quantity of feed consumed per bird from month to month is fairly stable. He can control the rate of egg production at different times of the year, and it is this particular aspect that deserves special mention. There is some variation in feed prices from season to season throughout the year but not nearly to the same extent as pertains to egg prices.

Breeding practice to increase egg production should take into consideration the constitutional vigor of both males and females, earliness of maturity in the pullets, intensity of production, non-broodiness, and persistency of production.

Proper selection of the breeding stock is the keynote in any improvement plan. Whether trap nesting is being practiced or not, considerable progress in the development of a high-laying strain can be made by selecting breeders based on their performance, but if trap nesting is practiced then the progeny test also should be applied. Then, again, breed type and standardbred quality should be given consideration, especially if hatching eggs, baby chicks, or breeders are to be sold.

Vigor, An Important Goal in Breeding

That constitutional vigor is of paramount importance in laying stock is shown by the fact that a 4-pound Leghorn and a 6-pound Rhode Island Red laying 216 eggs of standard size, 2 ounces each, would produce a weight in eggs equivalent to six times the weight of the Leghorn and four times the weight of the Red. High egg production constitutes a heavy drain on the birds' digestive and reproductive systems. A female must possess abundance of constitutional vigor to stand the strain of continuous production. Since constitutional vigor is inherited, the males should also possess it in abundance in order to transmit it to their progeny.

The selection of breeders based on their performance is a matter of easy application whether one is trap nesting or not. Where trap nesting is practiced it is an easy matter to determine and record the pullets that commence laying early in life, those that have a high intensity of production, those that do not go broody or that exhibit very little broodiness, those that show no winter pause in production, and those that lay well during the summer and fall months before terminating the first-year production.

A Convenient Banding System

Where trap nesting is not practiced, the matter of selecting the bets annual layers for future breeding purposes is not quite so simple but is still easily done. In the fall of the year as the pullets commence laying they should be banded with a numbered aluminum or colored, celluloid band. A very easy way of determining the approximate time that pullets commence to lay is by noting carefully the development of the comb and wattles and the width between the pelvic bones. From practical experience it has been found that birds of the lighter breeds, such as Anconas and Leghorns, should commence laying when about 180 days old and birds of the heavier breeds, such as Plymouth Rocks and Wyandottes, should commence laying when about 200 days old.

Pullets that lay at a high rate can be detected by the degree of bleaching of the yellow pigment, in normally yellow-pigmented breeds, such as Leghorns and Plymouth Rocks. During January and February the layers should be examined and those with the whitest beaks and shanks should be banded with a numbered aluminum or colored, celluloid band. The banding of birds according to the number of times they go broody should be a very simple matter.

The identification of birds that show no winter pause is a more difficult matter and may be dispensed with. Persistent layers during the summer and fall months may be banded readily. Such a system of banding is entirely practical and should do a great deal to improve the laying qualities of the flock if practiced from year to year. The banding of the birds should follow a definite method so that at the end of the year the best layers may be identified at a glance. If numbered aluminum bands are used, the numbers may be recorded under the four headings, earliness of maturity, intensity of production, broodiness, and persistency of production. Numbers recorded under the first two and the last headings indicate desirable birds, while numbers recorded under broodiness would indicate undesirable birds.

If colored, celluloid bands are used, one color, such as red, should be placed on the left leg of each bird to denote earliness of maturity, another color, such as white, should be placed on the right leg of each bird to denote intensity of production, a black band should be used every time a hen goes broody, and a blue band should be used to identify the persistent layers. At the end of the year the best layers would each have a red, white, and a blue band. But the real value of the measure of an animal as a breeder is the kind of progeny it produces. What the poultry breeder desires above all else is a method of selecting male and female breeders that can be relied on with a considerable degree of assurance to bring about an increase in egg production. This is desired particularly in the case of males, since the offspring of each male are much more numerous than the offspring of any female and the male constitutes one-half of the heritage given to all the offspring.

M. A. JULL.

POULTRY (Dressed) Is Covered in Tentative Grades and Standards Study and experimentation of the proper methods of hatching, rearing, and marketing poultry have been made by the Department of Agriculture for many years, covering every phase of the poultry industry from the selection of breeding stock, incubation of the egg, brooding, rearing, and feeding of the baby chick, and preparing it for market, to its final purchase by the consumer.

One important step in this marketing cycle has received little attention—the standardization and uniform grading of the dressed poultry product as it is prepared for market. Realizing the need of some such standard in the poultry industry, the Bureau of Agricultural Economics has endeavored to supply this need, and has drawn up in tentative form the United States standard grades for dressed poultry.

These standards have been formulated, not on ideals and theories but on the natural characteristics of the different poultry classes. Practical poultrymen have been consulted, the opinions of experienced market men have been obtained, and trade practice has been considered.

Four Grades Established

Four distinct grades have been made in the more important poultry classes: U. S. Prime is the highest grade poultry that can be marketed in commercial quantities; U. S. No. 1, U. S. No. 2, and U. S. No. 3 are grades of lesser quality.

The most important factor considered in placing a bird in any of these grades is the fleshing condition of the carcass. In order to grade U. S. Prime, birds must be full fleshed, of uniform pack, and free from deformities or dressing imperfections.

U. S. No. 1 birds must be well fleshed, of uniform pack, and free from deformities or dressing imperfections, or they may be full-fleshed birds that would grade U. S. Prime as to fleshing condition but be barred from that grade because of slight dressing defects or deformities.

U. S. No. 2 birds are poorly fleshed birds that have been well dressed, or they may be full or well fleshed birds with too great deformities or dressing imperfections to class as a U. S. Prime or a U. S. No. 1.

FIGURE 186.—Graders from the Bureau of Agricultural Economics grading a car of turkeys for the 1927 Christmas trade in Washington, D. C. Each turkey was stamped and tagged with its grade designation

U. S. No. 3 birds are not only poorly fleshed but have considerable dressing defects or deformities. All birds must be wholesome and, from external appearance, free of disease.

In addition to the four grades, the United States standards provide for different classes, based principally on age and weight. Young birds that weigh 2½ pounds or less are classed as broilers; those weighing more than 2½ pounds to those weighing 3½ pounds are classed as fryers; and those weighing more than 3½ pounds are classed as roasters. Male birds that are hard meated and well developed are classed as stags regardless of weight, and if fully matured are classed as cocks.

Other Poultry Graded Also

Distinct classes and grades are also made of the other varieties of poultry, such as ducks, geese, turkeys, guineas, capons, and squabs, and each grade and class is distinctly defined. A 5-letter code denoting grade and size is provided in the standards, which if used will not only simplify trading in the various classes and poultry grades, but will be a medium of lowering expense when trading is done by telegraph.

Standard sizes and dimensions of packing boxes have also been worked out and a uniform-size package made possible.

A demonstration to determine the practicability of these poultry grades and to ascertain the response of the consumer to "Government-graded poultry" was made in one of the eastern cities for the Christmas trade last year. A car of turkeys for one of the large chain stores was graded and the grade was stamped on the back of each bird. (Fig. 186.) So great was the demand for these turkeys that the original lot was exhausted soon after being placed on sale, and the graders from the department were called a second and a third time to grade additional quantities. The company for whom the grading work was done was so pleased with the result that it immediately applied for the service for the next year.

The cooperation and support that members of the poultry industry have given in promoting these poultry standards have been very encouraging. A universal language whereby each dealer may understand the quality of poultry being offered for sale without the necessity and delay of inspection, and the increased poultry consumption which should result from improved and uniform quality, are factors that will impress the members of the industry.

THOMAS W. HEITZ.

POULTRY (Dressed) Now Included in Federal Inspection Service Inspection of dressed poultry for condition and wholesomeness is a new activity of the Department of Agriculture undertaken for the first time in the spring of 1928. This service is authorized by the agricultural appropriation act.

Demand for this service came originally from a canning concern that wanted to export its poultry product to Canada. Under the Canadian regulations no canned poultry products can be brought into that country unless the poultry used in its manufacture has been properly inspected for soundness and wholesomeness as evidenced by a certificate accompanying the shipment, issued by the Federal Government of the country of origin. Because of these regulations, poultry products canned in the United States had been excluded from the Canadian market for about seven years.

Since such a service presented an opportunity to assist in opening up a foreign market for United States products, it was decided to undertake the work. The Secretary of Agriculture promulgated regulations, effective January 23, 1928, governing the inspection of dressed poultry for condition and wholesomeness, and the Chief of the Bureau of Agricultural Economics issued instructions governing the disposal of diseased poultry carcasses. Inspection is conducted under the supervision of the Bureau of Agricultural Economics which already had available a corps of competent licensed inspectors employed in the inspection of live poultry unloaded for use in New York City. Requests for the service were soon received by other concerns; by September, 1928, it was in effect at one canning plant in connection with its export product only and at three other plants in connection with their entire output, all of which is used in the United States.

Inspection of dressed poultry for condition and wholesomeness is, so far as the Department of Agriculture is concerned, a permissive service, not a compulsory one. Before the service is extended to a plant the establishment must be remodeled, if necessary, to meet the sanitary requirements of the Bureau of Agricultural Economics. The actual work of inspection must be performed by competent veterinarians in order to conform to the regulations of the Secretary. Since the department has no funds to defray the cost of the work, each plant bears the cost of the service rendered to it. If these costs were paid by the plants to the department the money would have to be deposited in the Treasury of the United States and would not be available to defray the further expenses of the service. Consequently the department has

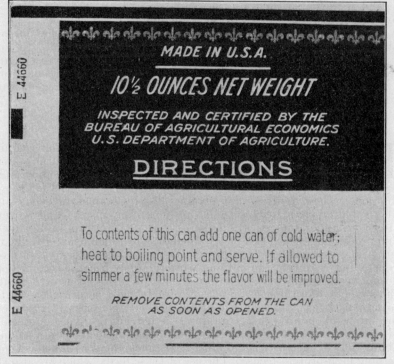

FIGURE 187.—The inspection legend of the Bureau of Agricultural Economics is permitted on labels of canned poultry products prepared from inspected and certified poultry

entered into cooperation with other agencies which employ the inspectors, collect the money from plants, and utilize it to pay the inspection salaries and other expenses. These inspectors are licensed by the department and work under the direct supervision of a responsible representative of the Bureau of Agricultural Economics.

Examining Poultry for Canning

The poultry used in canning is usually in a frozen condition. To render it suitable for inspection and evisceration it must be thawed, by placing it in tanks of water until thoroughly defrosted. The carcasses are then opened in such a manner as to disclose completely the viscera and the body cavity. Each carcass (with head, feet, and viscera intact) is placed on a metal moving-top table and this table top passed before the inspector. As it passes, the inspector gives each carcass a rapid but careful examination. If he finds that the carcass is decomposed, diseased, or otherwise unfit for human consumption, it is removed, thrown into the reject can, and denatured. If the carcass is sound and wholesome, it passes on to a point where the head and feet are chopped off. It is then placed upon another moving-table top where it is eviscerated and washed, ready for cooking. The top of this table is automatically cleaned as it travels back beneath the table.

Canned poultry products from poultry passed by licensed inspectors of the department, and prepared in plants operating under the supervision of the Bureau of Agricultural Economics, bear the inspection legend of the department on the can labels: "Inspected and Certified by the Bureau of Agricultural Economics, U. S. Department of Agriculture." Under certain conditions approved by the bureau, abbreviated forms may be used. This legend is a guaranty to consumers that the product was prepared under sanitary conditions and from poultry which was sound and wholesome. Consumers may buy and use canned poultry products bearing this inspection legend with complete confidence.

Rob R. Slocum.

POULTRY Need Protein for Their Best Growth and Egg Production — Chickens under wild conditions require only feed enough for natural growth and maintenance and to produce a few eggs in the spring months for reproduction. Their needs are largely supplied by grains and seeds supplemented by a little additional protein from insects and worms. However, under domestication, poultry are kept for profitable growth and production, which can be obtained only by much heavier feed consumption, especially of high-protein feeds. Eggs are scarce on most general farms, during the fall and winter, largely because the chickens do not receive sufficient protein in the ration for rapid growth during the summer, and the hens do not get protein enough during the winter to produce eggs. An egg, aside from the shell, contains 13.4 per cent protein, while poultry flesh contains 21.5 per cent protein. A mixture of corn, wheat, and other grains used for feeding hens, contains only about 10 per cent protein and must be supplemented with a mash containing high-protein feeds. The use of these feeds, which are also the highest-priced in the ration, not only greatly increases egg production but materially lowers the cost of production.

Sources of Animal Protein

The kinds and quantities of protein best suited for feeding chickens are now being studied and considerable information has been obtained, although, so far, this field has been only slightly investigated. Experiments have shown clearly that proteins from animal sources are generally better for feeding poultry than those of vegetable origin.

Meat scrap, fish meal, milk, and tankage are good sources of animal protein. They all supply valuable mineral in addition to their protein. Good quality is very essential in these high-protein feeds. Protein in a good grade of fish meal is probably equal to the same amount of protein in meat scrap. Tankage is not so good as these other proteins for poultry, and needs to be supplemented with mineral. Milk is one of the best sources of animal protein and has a relatively greater feeding value than its actual protein content. Milk is used in the ration to help prevent mortality of baby chicks, to increase the rate of gain of growing chicks, and to increase the feed consumption and egg production of laying stock. The relative value of the various milk products is based largely on their total milk solids. Milk is used in the poultry ration mainly as a supplement to the other protein feeds, because of the relatively high cost of its protein. The animal proteins, especially milk and meat scrap, are highly digestible.

Some Common Vegetable Protein Feeds

The high-vegetable-protein feeds do not give so good results as the animal-protein feeds. However, they have a place in the poultry diet but must be supplemented with additional minerals for good results. Soy-bean meal, cottonseed meal, peanut meal, and gluten meal are of value for this purpose. The use of considerable cottonseed meal in the ration may affect the quality of the eggs by discoloring the yolk. Eggs produced on cottonseed-meal rations which appear all right when fresh may develop discolored yolks when placed in cold storage. The mash should not contain more than 10 per cent of cottonseed meal.

The quality of the proteins materially affects the results in feeding poultry. However, information on this phase of poultry feeding is very limited. It is known that at least three of the amino acids which make up the proteins are essential in the ration. These are trypto-phane, lysine, and cystine. Meat scraps and all the high-protein feeds may vary materially in the quality of their proteins.

The protein analyses of these high-protein feeds vary greatly and their analyses should be given more attention in mixing rations. The protein content of meat scraps may vary from 40 to 75 per cent, which may make a difference of nearly 10 per cent in the total protein content of two mash mixtures made by the same formula but containing two different samples of meat scraps.

The proportion of mash and of scratch feed used in the ration greatly affects the amount of proteins supplied. Ready-mixed laying mashes usually contain about 21 per cent of protein whereas scratch feeds contain only about 9 per cent protein. As a general rule, about equal parts of mash and scratch should be fed as the average for the year, but the proportions are varied at different seasons. All-mash rations are used somewhat but do not appear to have any marked advantage for average conditions over the feeding of scratch and mash.

Proportions to Feed

The general practice is to use rations with less protein for young chicks than for partly grown chicks or for laying hens. Apparently, the protein requirements for young chicks are at least as great as for laying hens. Protein makes up 35 per cent, and fat 10 per cent, of the unabsorbed yolk of the chick at hatching time. Recent experiments indicate that somewhat higher protein rations than are commonly used for young chicks can be fed to advantage. Very high protein rations tend toward lack of uniformity in the growth of the chicks; moderate variations in protein content do not appear to have any effect on the mortality either of chicks or of hens.

The department has conducted a number of tests (fig. 188) on the effect of various amounts of protein from dried skim milk and from high-grade meat meal both on growth of chicks and on egg production. The best growth and the lowest feed consumption per pound of gain in young chicks was obtained in the dried-milk rations containing from 13.9 to 17.5 per cent of protein, and in the meat-meal rations containing from 19.5 to 21.5 per cent protein. The best results with laying hens were obtained from the skim-milk rations containing about 15 per cent protein and from the meat-meal rations containing about 20 per cent protein. The best amount of protein to use in a ration from one product does not necessarily represent the best amount of protein from other products. These rations consisted only of corn meal and minerals with either meat meal or dried milk, and just as good growth and egg production were obtained on less protein from rations which contained a greater variety of proteins and of other feeds.

FIGURE 188.—Two groups of chickens of the same age; the larger chickens received plenty of protein, whereas the smaller ones were fed a low-protein ration

A. R. LEE.

POULTRY'S Mineral Requirements Vary at Different Ages The inorganic compounds required by a growing chick, a laying pullet, and a hen are the same in kind but quite different in quantity. In other words, the mineral requirements of chickens vary with age. So long as a chick is actively growing, the inorganic materials required are chiefly those which are used in the formation of bone. Elements other than those commonly found in bone are necessary but the amounts are relatively small. Therefore, by far the greater part of the inorganic material required by the growing chick is calcium and phosphorus. In addition, the chick needs at least some sodium, potassium, magnesium, chlorine, iodine, fluorine, iron, sulphur, and silicon; also, possibly, some manganese, copper, and zinc. Just what other elements may be needed, except, of course, carbon, hydrogen, oxygen, and nitrogen, are not definitely known.

Sources of Calcium and Phosphorus

Usually sufficient amounts of all the elements except calcium, and occasionally phosphorus, are present in the feed. To insure an adequate supply of these two elements some source of calcium phosphate may be added to the ration. The best source of calcium and phosphorus, at the present time, is undoubtedly some form of bone or bone ash. If raw phosphate rock is used, it should not contain more than the very smallest traces of fluorine. When the feed consumed by the chicks contains a sufficient amount of phosphorus but not enough calcium, the latter may be supplied by adding calcium carbonate, in the form of either oyster shells or natural limestone. If limestone is used, it should not contain more than 1 or 2 per cent of magnesium compounds; the less magnesium the better.

When the calcium and phosphorus in a ration that is being fed to growing chicks are not in the proper proportions, a condition known as rickets may result, especially if the chicks receive but little direct sunlight. The effects produced by feeding such a ration may be corrected by adding a small amount of cod-liver oil to the feed. Since the efficacy of cod-liver oil, for this purpose, is due to its vitamin D content, only oils tested biologically for that vitamin should be used.

Caution in Use of Salt

A possible deficiency of sodium and chlorine may be guarded against easily by adding a small amount of ordinary salt to the feed. Although many of the published rations contain as much as 1 per cent of added salt, it is quite probable that 0.5 per cent is enough. The salt should always be well mixed with the feed because when it is fed alone it is appreciably toxic; as little as one-quarter of an ounce has been known to be fatal.

In the so-called goiterous sections of the country where the water and soil contain extremely small amounts of iodine, the ordinary salt used in compounding the ration should be replaced by "iodized" salt.

Although the need of growing chicks for mineral substances has been pointed out, there is also the possibility of feeding too much mineral matter. In such cases the growth of the chicks is usually very poor and uneven. When the feed contains as much as 5 or 6 per cent of total ash it is doubtful whether further additions are of value, especially if the constituents of the ash are reasonably well balanced to begin with.

When a pullet begins laying she is usually still growing, although the rate of growth is relatively much less than it has been. For that reason she still needs some calcium and phosphorus for growth. As soon as egg production begins the pullet requires relatively large amounts of calcium for the formation of eggshells. This additional requirement of calcium probably is best supplied in the form of oyster shells or limestone.

Effect of Feed on Shell Texture

As the pullet approaches full body maturity her need of calcium and phosphorus for growth becomes less and less but the amount of calcium required for eggshells is still great and is roughly proportional to the number of eggs produced. This being so, it is perhaps best to feed the mature hen somewhat less calcium phosphate than is fed to the growing, but egg-producing, pullet.

When the amount of available calcium in the feed of the egg-producing chicken is insufficient, a decrease in egg production usually follows and at the same time there is a tendency for the shells of the eggs to become thinner and poorer in texture. As soon as the amount of available calcium in the feed is increased there is a marked tendency for the shells to approach normal thickness and texture. Just because there is an abundance of calcium compounds in the feed, it does not follow that the chicken has at its disposal sufficient available calcium for the formation of eggshells, because the various compounds of calcium are not equally assimilated. Of the several calcium compounds usually fed to the egg-producing chicken, calcium carbonate is one of the most suitable.

So far as it is now known it is not likely that a poultry ration will be deficient in iron, magnesium, potassium, fluorine, or silicon, but there is a possibility of sulphur deficiency.

Varying Need of Chickens for Sulphur

Sulphur is an important constituent of feathers and eggs. Since feather growth is slower in chicks than in molting hens and since an appreciable amount of sulphur is found in eggs, the ration of the molting or egg-producing chicken is more likely to be deficient in sulphur than is the ration of the growing chick. Experiments conducted at the United States Animal Husbandry Experiment Farm, Beltsville, Md., have shown that the annual egg production of pullets and hens may be appreciably increased by feeding certain inorganic compounds of sulphur.

The practical significance of the foregoing information may be summarized as follows. The inorganic materials required by the growing chick are chiefly those used for bone formation, particularly calcium and phosphorus. Any form of bone or bone ash is a good source of calcium and phosphorus. Under certain conditions there may be a deficiency of calcium, phosphorus, sodium, chlorine, or iodine. If the calcium alone is insufficient more calcium carbonate, such as crushed oyster shells or ground limestone, should be fed. To guard against a deficiency of sodium and chlorine, small amounts of salt may be added to the ration; and in the so-called goiterous regions "iodized" salt is recommended. When producing eggs chickens require a large amount of calcium for the eggshells; this probably is best supplied by calcium carbonate. Sulphur is required for feather growth and egg production and at times the ration fed may be deficient in this element unless sulphur compounds are supplied.

H. W. TITUS.

PRODUCE Agency Act Protects Consignor in Interstate Trade When a farmer consigns his produce to a market to be sold for him on commission he must rely on the consignee to look after his interests faithfully in obtaining as large returns as possible. The consignee commission merchant becomes his agent or personal representative.

Many safeguards are available to a shipper to protect him against receiving unsatisfactory returns. Some are improved business practices, others are provided by the Government through recent legislation.

High quotations do not insure high returns. Before consigning, the shipper should investigate the reputation of the prospective consignee by consulting a rating book of produce dealers or by having his banker inquire as to the dealer's standing.

Reliable information can be obtained daily, without charge, from the United States Department of Agriculture as to movement, market prices, and demand for fruits and vegetables. This information, published in market news reports issued at Washington and at branch offices throughout the country, will aid the shipper in consigning his produce to the best advantage.

In case a dealer in a market undertakes to refuse a car which has been sold to him, and offers to handle the car for the shipper's account, thereby changing the transaction into a consignment, the shipper should call for Government inspection. It is also to the shipper's advantage to secure Government inspection at shipping point, if it is available.

It is highly important that produce be of good quality and condition at time of shipment, and placed under proper refrigeration, especially if it is to be rolled over a long distance. The amount of freight charges, the perishability of the commodity and the condition of the markets of the country should all be taken into consideration in determining when and where to ship. Produce should be carefully graded and attractively packed. Cars should be loaded uniformly throughout.

In making less-than-carload shipments care should be taken to mark all packages so that the consignee can determine by whom the shipment was made. A manifest of the goods shipped should be sent promptly to the consignee.

All correspondence, telegrams, and other papers relating to a shipment should be retained until a satisfactory settlement has been reached. In case of dispute these papers will be needed.

False Returns Forbidden

Congress has undertaken to safeguard the consignor of perishable farm produce through the passage in the early part of 1927 of the produce agency act. This act (44 Stat. 1355) forbids the making of false returns or statements to the shipper concerning the handling or disposition of the consignment, knowingly and with intent to defraud, or the dumping of consigned produce without sufficient cause. When returns show any considerable quantity of produce dumped the shipper should demand the certificate provided for in this act. This law relates only to perishable farm products received on consignment in interstate commerce.

Complaints by consignors relating to apparent violations of this act may be filed with the Bureau of Agricultural Economics in Washington for investigation with a view to prosecution. Copies of the law, regulations for its enforcement, and complaint blanks may be obtained from the Bureau of Agricultural Economics. All papers relating to the consignment must accompany complaints.

The Consignee's Obligations

In accepting a consignment of perishable farm produce a consignee owes his first duty to the consignor and must not allow goods which he has purchased to interfere with the sale of the consignment at the highest possible price. The consignee accepts the responsibility of placing the produce on the market promptly and selling it to the best advantage. He should sort or recondition the goods if such action will increase the net returns. He should issue and retain a sales slip to cover every sale and keep sufficiently complete records to show all important facts relating to the consignment in order to furnish any further information which his principal, the consignor, may wish at a later date. The consignee has no right, under the law, to buy in any part of the consignment to his own account, or to intermingle several lots and average the returns, without the consent of the consignor. If he grants credit to his customers the possibility of deductions or losses must be assumed by himself. His compensation is only the commission charged at the rate agreed upon between himself and the consignor. Prompt returns should be made to the shipper by furnishing a true and correct summary of the actual sales made. All expenses and other deductions should be itemized. The consignor is entitled to this as the owner of the goods.

H. A. Spilman and
W. L. Evans.

PRODUCE Clearing House Operation Necessitates Full Market Information — Comprehensive market information is essential in the operation of a fruit or vegetable clearing house. This information may be divided into two classes—market conditions and prices and car-lot shipments and receipts. While the first is essential in the marketing of any perishable crop, the latter is the more important because the basic purpose of a clearing house is to accomplish better distribution. Both kinds of information are available through the market news service of the Bureau of Agricultural Economics. When needed for clearing-house work, special arrangements are made with the originating public carriers for daily telegraphic reports of the movement of fresh fruits and vegetables giving carload forwardings, passings at important gateways, and diversions accomplished at specified points. The delivering railroads furnish daily reports showing the arrivals, number of cars on track, number diverted, and number unloaded in the important markets of the country. These records normally cover 80 per cent or more of the total tonnage moved to market and give a practically complete picture of the distribution of the crop.

These data are retabulated by the clearing house, incorporated into special reports, and used in planning daily car-lot distribution. The daily record of cars shipped gives the volume moving to market and to a great extent enables the shippers to maintain a steady flow to market. Passings reported at the principal gateways cover all cars concentrated into through trains. This record also includes primary destinations of shipments. The diversions at principal diversion points give amended destinations. The foregoing, when combined into one record, enables shippers to regulate the flow and avoid either glutting or undersupplying markets, since the reports are received in ample time to permit further diversions if the records indicate certain markets are likely to receive too many or too few carloads.

Daily car-lot arrivals on the principal markets, the number of cars on track, the number unloaded and number diverted, are also available. The clearing house can thus keep an accurate check on the daily supply in each market, the rate of movement into consumption, and in general effect a quicker handling of the product and a more prompt release of refrigerator cars than was formerly possible.

B. C. Boree.

PRUNE BUD Variations Have Varietal and Trade Significance   Most of the prunes grown in the United States are produced in the Pacific Coast States. In California the Agen, commonly known as the French or Petit, is the variety most widely cultivated, while the Imperial Epineuse, Sugar, and Sergeant varieties are also grown to a lesser extent. In Oregon and Washington the Italian prune is the most important cultivated variety.

In a study carried on during the last 15 years by the writer and his associates with individual Agen prune trees and their fruits in some of the Banning and Santa Clara Valley prune orchards of California, bud variations were found to be rather frequent. These are believed to be highly significant, especially when considered from the standpoint of maintaining both quantity and quality of the crops of the trees of this

FIGURE 189.—Branches from a tree of the common Agen prune showing large fruited forms occurring as bud variations. Morgan Hill, Calif.

variety. The variations found in trees of the Agen variety are similar in many respects and may be considered as typical of those which have been observed in trees of the other commercial prune varieties.

The bud variations found and studied in this variety may be classified as entire trees, limbs, and individual fruit variations. The entire tree variations are those in which the tree and its fruits as a whole differ in one or more marked characteristics from the normal for the variety. It is apparent that many, if not all, such variations arise from the unintentional propagation of buds from a limb or other entire tree bud variation in commercial nursery practice. The limb variations are those where one or more limbs in an otherwise normal tree vary in one or more characters from the normal limbs of the same trees. The individual fruit variations include those where a single fruit on a brancn varies in some one or more clearly definable characteristics from the normal ones on the same branch.

Characters Perpetuated by Budding

The experimental progeny propagations of the entire tree and the limb bud variations indicate that the characteristics of the parent trees or limbs have been generally perpetuated through budding. The individual fruit variations resemble closely the fruit characteristics of the limb and entire tree variations for the most part.

The prune bud variations studied may be further classified as to the quantity and the commercial quality of the fruit which they produce. In some instances trees and limbs in otherwise normal trees bear few if any fruits. This condition is very rare, but many trees have been found which characteristically bear light crops while in other instances much larger quantities of fruit than the normal are produced over a period of years. In other cases entire tree and limb variations have been found which bear fruits maturing two or three weeks earlier than the normal, while in other instances trees and limbs have been found which produce fruits ripening from two to four weeks later than the normal. Some of the tree and bud variations in Agen prune trees bear fruits which are more acid, while others produce characteristically sweeter fruits than the normal.

Large-fruiting, as well as abnormally small-fruiting, tree and limb variations have been found which have proved to be inherent ones through systematic progeny tests. Inasmuch as the commercial value of the crop of a given variety is dependent to a large degree upon the size of the fruits, these variations are of great importance to the industry, from the fact that they indicate the possibility of isolating strains in those varieties in which the trees tend to produce a large proportion of their crops of the most valuable commercial sizes.

Bud variations provide the basis for the isolation of superior strains by the systematic selection and propagation of the most desirable ones.

A. D. Shamel.

PUBLICATIONS for Farmers Distributed in Millions by Federal Government — The American farmer appreciates the importance of agricultural publications. Because of the growing complexity of his work and problems he requires the latest information as to ways and means of producing his crops and livestock, of combating diseases and insect pests, and of marketing his surplus. He therefore finds it necessary to read farm papers, to obtain bulletins pertaining to his work, and to seek advice from the county agricultural agent, the agricultural college and experiment station in his State, and the United States Department of Agriculture.

During the fiscal year ended June 30, 1928, more than 33,000,000 copies of bulletins, circulars, bulletin lists, and other publications of the United States Department of Agriculture were distributed free of charge. In addition to this distribution, the Superintendent of Documents sold more than a million copies during the year, for which he received approximately $75,000. Now just what is the relation between the free distribution and the distribution by sale? Briefly, the situation is this: On account of limited printing funds it is not possible to furnish everyone free copies of all the publications desired. As many free copies are published as are considered justified, and they are then distributed to those requesting them as long as the supply lasts. When this free supply is exhausted those desiring copies may purchase them from the Superintendent of Documents of the Government Printing Office. (Fig. 190.) And they may be purchased for a very small sum which represents practically the cost

FIGURE 190.—The United States Government Printing Office in Washington, D. C., the largest printing plant in the world. In the lower picture the buildings on the right are used by the Superintendent of Documents for the sale and distribution of Government publications

of printing. In the case of Farmers' Bulletins it frequently happens that although the department's supply is exhausted they may be obtained free from Members of Congress, who receive an allotment of four-fifths of all copies of Farmers' Bulletins. Last year the distribution of Farmers' Bulletins by Members of Congress amounted to more than 9,000,000 copies. In general, therefore, free copies of agricultural publications, if available, are obtained from the Department of Agriculture or Members of Congress, and sale copies are purchased from the Superintendent of Documents.

Duties of the Superintendent of Documents

Now just who is the Superintendent of Documents and what is his function in relation to publications? The title of that position is probably not clearly explanatory, for many suppose that that official has the responsibility of watching over the archives of the Government and safeguarding such important documents as the original copies of the Declaration of Independence, the Constitution, and other priceless State papers. It may, therefore, be a surprise to them to learn that the Superintendent of Documents does not have charge of such papers, but that he does have the important function of selling all Government publications that are for sale, and that he is the only official authorized by law to sell them. Hence it should be clear that all remittances for publications should be sent direct to him and not

FIGURE 191.—A stage in the printing and binding of the Yearbook of the Department of Agriculture for 1927 at the Government Printing Office

to the department which prepares the material. Surely that procedure seems simple and direct enough, and yet the Department of Agriculture annually receives thousands of letters containing remittances for publications, and in numerous cases the money is attached directly to a card received from the department on which specific directions are given that no money should be sent to the department but to the Superintendent of Documents, who is an official of the Government Printing Office and not of the Department of Agriculture.

In former years it was the practice to send publications to those whose names were on certain mailing lists regardless of any indicated desire on their part for such matter. This proved to be a very wasteful practice, and in these days of economical administration of Government that wastage has been eliminated. Instead of sending the publication direct, therefore, the plan is now followed of sending lists of publications, or announcements that certain manuscripts are being printed, and the suggestion is made that those desiring these publications may obtain them free of charge as long as the supply lasts and may thereafter buy them from the Superintendent of Documents. One great advantage of this practice is that in the main those who have special need for the printed information get it and make use of it, and that publications are not sent to those who have no need for them.

The Preparation of Publications

Those who thus receive Department of Agriculture publications may be interested to learn of the conscientious care exercised in preparing them in order to make them accurate, readable, properly organized, clear, and effective. The information is assembled after infinite pains have been taken in research work to ascertain the facts. Then a job equally as important as obtaining the facts is that of making them available to those who can use them. But it is apparent that if the manuscript is not well organized, if the statements are not clear and readable, if the information is not presented effectively, there is a very definite public loss.

In order to get the material published in the best possible way the department has provided a series of checks and safeguards for the benefit of the reader as well as for the one preparing the material. The author is required to go over his material very painstakingly and write and rewrite it until he gets it into what seems to him satisfactory shape. Then coworkers in the same subject review the manuscript to determine if the subject matter is technically sound. The manuscript is next presented to editors who review the work from the dual standpoint of the author and his research and the public which is going to make use of the material. The editor is free to make suggestions which seem desirable concerning revision, condensation of the material, or improved arrangement. If any tables are given the data are very carefully checked and rechecked to make sure that the figures are correct. The illustrations and their legends are critically examined in order that they may be published in the best possible shape. All this careful work on manuscripts may at times seem unnecessary, but when it is remembered that it is not only the writer who is thus addressing the public but that the Department of Agriculture is held responsible for the material in its publications, the wisdom of having the material carefully prepared can be very readily appreciated.

Readers of department publications are especially invited to offer criticisms concerning their content at any time. Furthermore, if those who obtain these publications either free or by purchase can suggest better methods of distribution, such suggestions will be very welcome. The aim of the Department of Agriculture is to render the maximum service to the agricultural industry of America and to those engaged in it, and any suggestions which will tend toward the accomplishment of this end will be of value.

M. C. Merrill.

QUARANTINED Nursery Stock May Be Shipped If Infestation Removed Quarantines promulgated by the United States Department of Agriculture and by the States infested by the Japanese beetle prohibit the shipment of nursery stock, farm produce, fruit, and other agricultural products to points outside the infested area unless the products are free of all stages of the beetle. Within this regulated area there are approximately 5,000 dealers in nursery stock, among them being several large nurseries doing a national and international business. The policy was therefore adopted that, if satisfactory methods were found for preventing, removing, or destroying the infestations on nursery products, the nurseryman could export his products from the

FIGURE 192.—Preparing dilute carbon disulphide emulsion for application to evergreen nursery stock, to destroy infestations of the Japanese beetle

regulated area after the proper treatment had been applied and the danger of disseminating the beetle in them had been removed.

The problem was therefore presented of devising satisfactory methods for handling the thousands of varieties of nursery stock so as to satisfy these requirements. It has been found possible to prevent the infestation of greenhouse stock by covering all ventilators and doors of the greenhouse with cloth, and by permitting only uninfested soil, plants, and other needed articles to be taken into the protected greenhouse. The potting soil can be freed of infestation by fumigating with carbon disulphide in a sealed chamber for a period of 48 hours. The stock should be obtained from uninfested territory, or should be treated to free it of possible infestation before being taken into the greenhouse.

Deciduous trees and shrubs can usually be shipped free from soil. Infestations on this type of stock can be removed by washing all the soil from the roots.

Cleaning Herbaceous Plants

Many of the perennial herbaceous plants can be cleaned in a satis-factory manner by washing the soil from their roots. Some varieties of these plants have roots so matted or so filled with cavities that it is impossible to remove all larvæ by washing without causing appreciable injury to the roots. The larvae can be destroyed in the roots of these nonwashable varieties by submerging the roots for 24 hours in dilute emulsion of carbon disulphide, or by submerging the roots for the same period of time in a dilute emulsion of American wormseed oil. Submerging the infested roots in water at 112° F. for 70 minutes has recently been found an even more satisfactory method of destroying the larvae of the beetle.

Conifers, broad-leaved flowering evergreens, and other evergreens have to be dug with a mass of soil about their roots to facilitate suc-cessful transplanting. The soil can not be washed from the roots without causing serious injury. The infestation in the soil of this type of stock can be destroyed by applying a dilute emulsion of carbon disulphide before the tree is dug. (Fig. 192.) The method of treat-ment consists in forming about the base of the tree a circular basin with a galvanized iron collar, of such a size that it is from 12 to 18 inches larger in diameter than the prospective ball of soil. The collar is sunk into the ground to a depth of 3 inches, and soil is banked up on the outside. Dilute carbon disulphide emulsion is then poured into the basin, using 2.5 gallons to each square foot of area inclosed, and allowed to percolate through the soil about the roots of the plant. The soil is allowed to remain undisturbed for a period of 48 hours, at the end of which the evergreen is dug, wrapped, and shipped.

It has not been possible, thus far, to devise methods for freeing all varieties of nursery plants from infestation without injuring the plants. The methods which have been worked out have enabled the nursery industry within the regulated area to export a large number of its products and at the same time have prevented the artificial dis-semination of the Japanese beetle in those products.

WALTER E. FLEMING.

RADIO Audience Gets Housekeepers' Chats Five Days Each Week A personal representative of the United States Department of Agri-culture in the households of thou-sands of city, town, and farm women. That is what "Aunt Sammy" means to members of the radio audience who listen to the housekeepers' chats, a 5-day-a-week, 15-minute pro-gram syndicated to approximately 90 stations in the United States, and devoted exclusively to authentic information on subjects of inter-est to women. Thousands of letters from interested listeners leave no doubt as to the efficacy of radio as a means of disseminating scientific information of a practical nature. In four months more than 25,000 letters were received from women who sought advice on every phase of homemaking.

It is Aunt Sammy's duty to assemble material bearing on household economics from the various bureaus in the department and to compile this material so that it can be effectively presented by the women who actually broadcast the programs. These women are also known as "Aunt Sammy."

Using fan letters as a guide to what household information is most needed and desired, Aunt Sammy discusses nutrition, meal planning, cooking, clothing, health, house furnishing, gardening, and other kindred subjects. The letters indicate that planning and cooking three meals a day continue to be the biggest and most puzzling tasks of the average housewife.

The Bureau of Home Economics is the main source of information for the housekeepers' chats, and the success of the talks is due in large measure to the work of the bureau specialists in planning practical, well-balanced menus, calling for foods which are in season, and in furnishing recipes so nearly "fool proof" that they seem never to fail, even in the hands of inexperienced cooks. Great care is taken in writing the menus and recipes, so that they will be clearly understood over the air. Lists of ingredients are repeated and methods of cooking explained logically and simply.

Answers to Questions

Another important contribution of the Bureau of Home Economics is its answers to the hundreds of questions received as a result of the housekeepers' programs. If the answers are of general interest, they are incorporated into the programs; otherwise a personal answer is mailed.

Anticipating a demand for the radio recipes, the department had 50,000 loose-leaf cookbooks printed in 1926. Menus and recipes were furnished in loose-leaf form with a binder, and supplements were sent out from time to time. The loose-leaf cookbook was followed by Aunt Sammy's Radio Recipes, a bound book containing 70 menus and about 300 recipes developed by the Bureau of Home Economics and broadcast in the housekeepers' chats from October, 1926, to June, 1927. Two hundred and five thousand copies of Aunt Sammy's Radio Recipes have been distributed in response to individual requests from women listeners.

In order to put the home radio information service on a more systematic basis, Aunt Sammy's Radio Record was provided for listeners of the 1928–29 season. Aunt Sammy's Radio Record is a 48-page book. It contains directions for planning balanced meals and for setting the table, and space for taking down the menus and recipes which are being given in the broadcasts this season.

JOSEPHINE F. HEMPHILL.

RADIO Service of the Department Expands Educational Program — In common with other activities connected with the radio art, the general educational radio programs of the Department of Agriculture recently have been expanded in scope and have found a firmer place in the daily life of a million and a half farm families who regard their radio receiving sets as indispensable business equipment.

In addition to continuing the manuscript service containing programs for farmers, home makers, farm boys and girls, and all listeners interested in the broad problems of conservation and use of our plant and animal resources, the department radio service began this year a daily noon-hour broadcast direct from Washington through a network of 15 stations in the great central farming area. This service was established at the invitation of the National Broadcasting Co. and associated radio stations in October, 1928. It comprises a 15-minute program each weekday except Saturday, sent at 12.15 to 12.30 p. m. central standard time, direct from Washington through the cooperating stations. In this service members of the department staff give a variety of economic and production information bearing upon the problems of farmers in the area from the Alleghenies to the Rockies and from the Canadian to the Mexican borders.

The manuscript service is broadcast by 142 stations located in 41 States, the District of Columbia, and Hawaii. The service for home makers is elsewhere described in this Yearbook. Two 10-minute programs for farmers are broadcast five days each week. Four other 10-minute programs are sent on a weekly schedule, and two monthly releases are provided. The weekly features include one especially designed for farm boys and girls, giving a view of the activities throughout the Nation of 4-H clubs.

Broadcasting Corn-Borer Information

The usefulness of radio in agricultural emergencies was again demonstrated last year when 46 stations joined with the Department of Agriculture in sending a series of nine weekly broadcasts fully describing the corn-borer situation and giving information on methods of control. Other emergency broadcasts were supplied as need arose in farming localities. One broadcast, for example, was said by farmers and extension workers to have been of assistance in halting a cutworm invasion in a northwestern region.

The radio service is writing programs for five different farming regions of the Nation in order to provide information applicable to the conditions on the farms of listeners. To systematize the reception of information given in the broadcasts a United States Farm Radio Record has been provided for the use of listeners.

Along with other broadcasting agencies, the department's radio service found during 1928 that listeners have definitely passed the stage in which radio was chiefly interesting because of its novelty and are looking for quality entertainment and sound information programs. Consequently listeners no longer write large numbers of merely appreciative letters. They carry on correspondence chiefly to obtain further information regarding points mentioned in programs. Requests from listeners for publications of the department, aside from the special compilation of recipes and menus, average in the neighborhood of 5,000 per month and are increasing.

The experience of the department and the utterances of leaders of the radio industry indicate that the farmers' special need for a radio service is recognized by the industry. The reallocation plan put into effect by the Federal Radio Commission late in 1928 was said by members of the commission to be especially designed to maintain better listening conditions for farmer radio owners. It is apparent that radio broadcasting now is firmly established as an essential service to farmers and townsmen alike.

MORSE SALISBURY.

RAINFALL Distribution Is Compared at Near-by Measurement Stations Every farmer has observed that at times the rainfall on his neighbor's farm has been greater than on his own, and doubtless ponders at the way of Nature in distributing rain, particularly when lack of moisture spells disaster.

No other weather element is so uneven in its horizontal distribution as the rainfall—a fact not so widely known as it might be, because but few persons outside of those dwelling on mountains or high hills have the opportunity of seeing a summer shower travel deliberately over the lowlands wetting farmer A's land, but giving only a sprinkle to that of farmer B.

Because of the greater scatter of rainfall stations the statistics of rainfall give little useful information on differences of catch at relatively near-by stations except in a few cases. In the United States there is in actual use one rain gauge for each 595 square miles, whereas it is estimated that a single gauge to each quarter section of land would be required to give accurate figures on the amount of rain that falls each year.

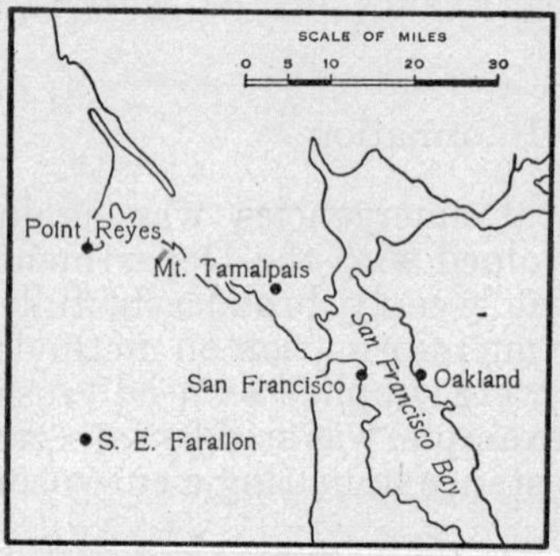

FIGURE 193.—Sketch map of San Francisco Bay region

The closest network of rainfall stations in the world so far as known is maintained on the island of Barbados, which has about 200 stations for its 166 square miles of area. Among the larger countries that maintain rainfall stations, Great Britain leads with one gauge for each 19 square miles of territory. There are, of course, limited areas in the British Isles, where the network is much closer, say near to a single gauge for each square mile.

Rainfall Gauges Near Each Other

The United States Weather Bureau network of rainfall stations contains a few cases of gauges being exposed within a relatively short distance of each other, Minneapolis and St. Paul, Minn., for example, where the distance between the gauges is but 10 miles. The San Francisco Bay region contains five gauges located as shown in Figure 193. The shortest distance between any two of these gauges—San Francisco and Oakland—is about 14 miles, the gauge at the last-named place is some distance from the center of the city, and the greatest distance is, say, 35 miles between Point Reyes and San Francisco.

The rainfall records of the pair of Minnesota stations above named are concurrent for 30 years, 1891–1920; they have been examined with a view to determining what, in the long run, are the differences in catch between the two places, assuming a standard exposure for each. The 30-year mean of the two stations for Minneapolis is 28.86 inches per annum; for St. Paul, 28.29 inches, or an average difference of but 0.57 inch per year. This means that at times the differences are greater and at times less than that amount. The differences in catch between the two stations, expressed as a percentage of the average annual rainfall, range from zero in two years to as much as 21 per cent in a single year, St. Paul receiving that amount less than Minneapolis. As a general rule, Minneapolis received a little more rain than St. Paul. The annual variations are shown graphically in Figure 194.

Comparing a pair of near-by stations in the more humid east, Washington and Baltimore, 40 miles apart, it appears that the yearly differences in rainfall increase with increase in distance apart, as might be expected. Washington rainfall expressed as a percentage of the mean equaled that of Baltimore in one year out of 30, was in excess in 13, and was deficient in 16 years. The annual variation is graphically shown in Figure 194.

The San Francisco Bay Stations

The San Francisco Bay group of stations yields results largely in accord with the foregoing. In this group the rainfall records for San Francisco, Oakland, and Point Reyes are concurrent and for the same

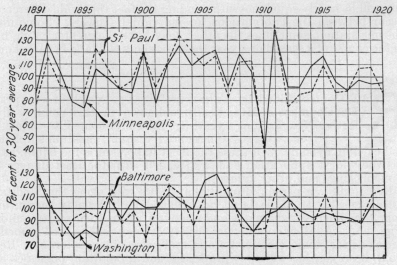

FIGURE 194.—Annual variation in precipitation at near-by places. (Variations in per cent of 30-year average)

period of years used in the Minnesota stations. The record for southeast Farallon, a rocky island in the Pacific off the Golden Gate, covers but 20 years, and that of Mount Tamalpais, altitude 2,375 feet, 22 years.

The 30-year mean annual rainfall for the first-named group is as follows:

San Francisco_____inches__ 20. 35
Oakland_____do____ 23. 73
Point Reyes_____do____ 21. 21

Thus slightly more rain is measured at Oakland across the bay from San Francisco than at the last-named place. There does not seem to be any physical reason for this difference and the writer is inclined to attribute it to possible differences in the exposure of the rain gauge at the two stations. The Point Reyes gauge, the most distant from San Francisco, was exposed on the side of a steep slope facing the ocean and about 500 feet above the water surface. The San Francisco gauge, prior to the earthquake of 1906, was exposed on top of an office building 157 feet above the ground, and subsequent to that year at an elevation of 191 feet above the ground, hence a little lower than the Point Reyes gauge.   The total rainfall of the two stations, although 35 miles apart, is nearly the same, although it might be expected that Point Reyes by reason of its direct oceanic exposure and greater altitude would have the larger rainfall.   The exposure of the rain gauge on southeast Farallon is practically at sea level, and the annual rainfall is a little less than at the immediate shore station, San Francisco. The gauge on the top of Mount Tamalpais catches, on the average, 27.25 inches of rainfall per annum, or 6.61 inches more than at San Francisco for identical years.   This may be attributed to the greater altitude of the former as compared with the latter, 2,375 feet against 191 feet.

The conclusion seems unavoidable that for two adjoining rainfall stations in the same climatic region the amount of rainfall in the long run will be nearly equal, notwithstanding the fact that wide differences occur between the two stations for individual showers.   Sometimes the one station, sometimes the other, may have the greater catch, but in the course of a season or a year the differences will largely cancel out.

Alfred J. Henry.

RAT Control Aided by Development of Effective New Poisons — Three useful rat poisons that were practically unknown in this country five years ago have now come into wide use. These are red squill, thallium sulphate, and calcium cyanide.   Of these the most important is red squill, as it has the widest application and is attended with the least danger to human beings and other animal life.

Red squill is a perennial plant that grows wild along the Mediterranean coast.   It has a large pear-shaped bulb, usually measuring from 3 to 6 inches in diameter and weighing up to 10 or more pounds. (Fig. 195.)   Another commercial variety, white squill, is used in medicine as a heart tonic, emetic, diuretic, and nauseant expectorant.   Red squill, however, has all these properties and in addition possesses an active principle not yet definitely isolated and identified, but found to be very poisonous to rats.

Red squill has been used as a rat poison in Europe for many centuries, but the variability in poisonous action (toxicity) and the uncertain results attending its use have kept it from becoming popular.   An investigation started in 1923 by this department, however, resulted in the perfection of a process for manufacturing a red-squill powder of high and uniform toxicity.   Commercial manufacturers of rat poisons have been quick to place red-squill products on sale in practically every State in the Union, and these are being used in large quantities, with results fully up to first expectations.

Unique Qualities of Red Squill

Experiments with red squill indicate that it is efficient, economical, and safer than any other rat poison.   Its chief appeal and value lie in the fact that it approaches the unique position of being a poison specific for rats.   In laboratory experiments red squill was fed to cats, dogs, poultry, pigeons, a pig, and to several native rodents with no apparent ill effect, although similar doses were uniformly fatal to rats. Field experiments on baby chicks from 5 to 18 days old indicated that they are not likely to eat in two consecutive days enough feed containing 10 per cent of red-squill powder to cause death, even when it is given to the exclusion of other feeds. Two hens that were given feed containing 10 per cent of red squill during a period of two weeks apparently thrived as well as others fed on untreated mash. These reactions to the poison may be explained by the highly acrid taste of squill, which is objectionable to most mammals other than rats, and by its strong emetic action, which causes most mammals promptly to vomit it. Rats can not vomit and are, therefore, unable to escape the effects of the squill. Chickens and other birds seem highly resistant to it. For these reasons red-squill baits are recommended in preference to other stronger poisons commonly used,

FIGURE 195.—Red-squill bulb (*Urginea maritima*). About one-fourth natural size

particularly on farms and in places where poultry, livestock, and other domestic animals would be endangered, or where food supplies are stored.

The toxicity of red-squill powders now on the American market ranges between 250 and 500 milligrams of dry squill for each kilogram the rat weighs (about 1.5 to 3 grains for each adult rat). This toxicity to rats is approximately twice as great as in barium carbonate. Squill is used in baits in concentrations ranging between 5 and 10 per cent. It is advisable to expose first a variety of unpoisoned baits, which will serve both to overcome the natural suspicion of the rats and to indicate the foods for which the rats show a preference. Such prebaiting, followed by a liberal application of squill baits, will usually result in the destruction of all the rats on any premises.

Properties of Thallium Sulphate

Thallium sulphate, which first came into use as a rat poison in Germany about 1920, has properties indicating that it might solve some of the difficult rodent-control problems in this country. Experiments conducted with it since 1924 have shown its value and resulted in its adoption to a limited extent. Thallium sulphate is a heavy mineral poison belonging to the lead group. It is more toxic than arsenic, is both tasteless and odorless, and is slow and cumulative in action. These properties make it exceptionally effective as a rat poison, but at the same time unfortunately render its use much more dangerous than many others. Most of the common poisons have

FIGURE 196.—Fumigation with calcium-cyanide dust, an effective means of destroying rats in their burrows

properties that quickly identify them, such as the intense bitterness of strychnine or the smoke, odor, or luminousness of phosphorus. If these are lacking, there may be an effective antidote, as with barium carbonate, but thallium sulphate has no warning property and, so far as known, no antidote. There is also danger of absorption through the skin, attended by impairment of the sexual glands, loss of hair, and the possibility of death. Furthermore, the bodies of rodents killed with thallium are a menace to the lives of other animals that may feed upon them. These factors render its use by the general public inadvisable, but in the hands of specialists it has been thoroughly demonstrated to be an effective poison against rodent pests. Thallium has been used most extensively in combating the California ground squirrel and species of prairie dogs that are especially difficult to control.

The minimum lethal does of thallium sulphate has been found to be approximately 25 milligrams to 1 kilogram of white rat (or 0.13 grain to one adult rat). An effective proportion of thallium sulphate is about 1 ounce to 12½ pounds of suitable rat bait.

Calcium-Cyanide Fumigation

Experiments with calcium cyanide in fumigating rodent burrows were probably first conducted in 1921. To-day vast quantities of it are being used throughout the United States for that purpose. It is a highly volatile chemical that rapidly gives off hydrocyanic-acid or prussic acid gas when acted upon by atmospheric moisture. That this gas is quick acting and deadly when present in lethal concentration renders it an effective means of destroying any of the deep-burrowing rodents. Because of its danger to human beings, it should be used carefully and the hands washed afterward. None should be taken into the mouth, and operators should stand to windward so as not to inhale the fumes.

Fumigation with calcium cyanide presents the most practicable means of destroying rats in their burrows, which are usually shallow, extensive, and with numerous openings that allow the rats to escape or retreat if any slow-acting gas is used. When calcium cyanide is forced through their runways, however, rats are usually overcome before they can make any successful move toward self preservation. This method may be used successfully in fields, along ditch banks, in refuse and garbage dumps, under tight floors, and, when the air is quiet, even in piles of lumber or trash and in corncribs. (Fig. 196.)

There is little danger attending the use of calcium cyanide in corn or other edible products if these are not fed for several days after the fumigation, for after the gas has entirely been given off the residue is nonpoisonous.

JAMES SILVER.

RED Clover's Hairiness in American Types Is Due to the Leaf Hopper The red clover grown in the United States and Canada is rough hairy and differs in this respect from the European, which is either quite smooth, like the Italian and some Russian varieties, or in which the hairs are closely appressed to the stem so that the stem seems to be smooth. (Fig. 197.) There is considerable variation in the degree of hairiness of American red clover, but whether the hairs are many or few they always stand out at right angles to the stem. Some American red-clover plants are very hairy, some less so, and plants with all degrees of hairiness can be found in the same field. Whatever the variations may be, however, there is seldom any uncertainty as to whether a given plant is of the American or of a European type. The characteristic hairiness is best seen on the stem just below the flower head.

This hairy characteristic of American red clover has been known for a long time, and there has been some speculation as to its cause, for it must be borne in mind that there was no red clover in America when the white man came and that our original stock came from England in the latter part of the seventeenth century. The English clover in turn came from Flanders, and both of these have closely appressed hairs. The difference is, after all, one of degree and of arrangement of the hairs, but it is so striking that some explanation as to how this difference came about is in order. The change from the European to the American type has come about so gradually that no one observed it while it was going on, and to-day when a solution

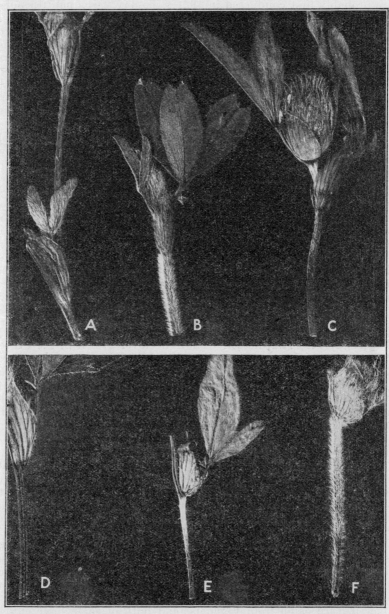

FIGURE 197.—Hairiness of various red clovers, magnified. A and B, wild red clover, A with appressed hairs, B with spreading hair; C, French; D and E, Russian, D showing the smooth form; F, American, with spreading hairs

is attempted it is possible only to bring together the pertinent facts
and offer a guess as to the cause of the change.

It is necessary first to turn to the wild red clover, the original species
which occurs wild in Britain and in Europe but which is a low-growing
plant of no great use except in pastures. The stems of this wild form
may have spreading hairs, hairs appressed to the stem, or the stem
may be smooth. (Fig. 197, A and B.) In other words, the natural
variations in the species cover the entire range found to-day in the various European and American clovers. The possibility of producing
rough hairy plants is therefore "in the blood," but the English clover
brought to America more than two centuries ago was relatively smooth,
as its Flemish ancestry shows.

When this English clover was brought to America it encountered
new conditions, among them a little insect not known in Europe and
called the potato leaf
hopper. This insect
damages red clover and
is especially hard on the
smooth forms. It also
does most of its harm on
the second, or seed, crop.
When very abundant it
may kill all the second
growth of the European
clovers grown in the
United States, and it al-
ways keeps down the
second growth so that
such plants do not seed
well. (Fig. 198.) The
hairy American type is
little affected, especially
when there are smooth
plants on which the leaf
hopper can feed. This
leaf hopper is native to
the United States and
without doubt turned
promptly to the new food

FIGURE 198.—The second growth of the smooth European red
clover (right) is kept down by leaf hoppers, while the hairy
American form (left) is little injured. Both plants grown under
cages in which leaf hoppers were confined

plant provided by the first red clover grown in America. With an
abundance of food the numbers of the leaf hoppers would naturally
increase, and in time they would be numerous enough to affect the
seed crop seriously.

Meanwhile there were probably a few rough hairy plants in a field,
as is the case to-day when seed from certain parts of England, such as
Kent, is sown. These plants would be less affected by the leaf hopper,
which also is true to-day, and would make relatively more seed than
the other plants in the field. It is not possible to estimate how many
years would be required for such a process to go on before the number
of rough hairy plants in a field would be a considerable proportion of
the whole, but it is certain that as the numbers of leaf hoppers increased with the new food supply the effect of the leaf-hopper damage
would become greater with the years. As this effect became greater

and the rough hairy plants each year produced relatively more seed than the relatively smooth ones, the proportion of rough hairy plants would increase; and so, gradually, under the attacks of a little green insect so small that it is seldom seen except by specialists, the type would be made over into the rough hairy form we have to-day.

Although it is not possible to look back 200 years and see what happened, a reasonable inference may be drawn from what is known to happen to-day, and from the known facts the most reasonable answer to the question of why American red clover is rough hairy is that the constant attacks of the leaf hopper carried on for more than 100 years gradually eliminated the smooth form by keeping down the production of seed, while the rough hairy form produced more seed than the other, and so constantly increased in numbers.

A. J. Pieters.

RED-CLOVER Seed Production Depends on Many Factors Red-clover seed production is influenced by a number of factors, biological and economic. The structure of the individual flower of a red-clover head is such that the pollen is liberated below the stigma, and without the help of insects to carry it upward to the stigma pollination can not be effected. Red-clover flowers are mainly self-sterile—that is, the pollen does not often fertilize the ovule of a flower on the same head or on any other head of the plant. For fertilization it is necessary that the pollen be carried to a stigma of another plant. In open flowers the stigma and anthers are inclosed in a structure that prevents free shedding of the pollen until the flowers are tripped; this is accomplished by insect visits. As the flower is tripped, the somewhat sticky pollen adheres to the mouth parts and body hairs of the insect, and thus it is carried from one flower to another. While many insects are seen visiting red-clover flowers, the different species of bumblebees are the chief cross-pollinators in the Eastern and Middle Western States.

In many localities there has been an alarming decrease in the amount of seed set from fields where large yields of seed were expected. This decline may be attributed to a decrease in the bumblebee population, brought about by extensive campaigns to clean up fence rows, the plowing of permanent meadows, and the clearing of wood lots, all of which measures tend to decrease the number of bumblebees' natural homes. A continual decrease in seed production in the future may be expected where such activities are carried on.

Various Insects Help Pollination

Various species of bees, moths, and butterflies also help in cross-pollinating red-clover flowers, but the activity of all of these, with the exception of the honeybee, is of minor importance except in certain restricted locations. In irrigated sections of the Western States large yields of clover seed are being produced; the honeybee is largely responsible for the cross-pollination. In the Western States the absence of flowering plants at the time that red clover blooms may be one reason for honeybees' visits to the red-clover flowers. In the Middle Western and Eastern States honeybees also sometimes act as cross-pollinators of red clover when dry environmental condition limit the number of flowers available for bee visitations. Therefore the factors which affect insect activity must be considered in a study of red-clover seed production.

That damp and rainy weather is detrimental to the setting of seed is a general conclusion of producers of red-clover seed. Recent experiments, however, indicate that large amounts of atmospheric and soil moisture do not limit the setting of seed so far as the plant itself is concerned, provided the pollen is successfully transferred from plant to plant. An excessive amount of moisture indirectly influences the setting of seed by affecting the activity of pollinating insects. Bumblebees caught visiting red-clover flowers, wet with dew and rain, have been examined, and apparently the pollen had been washed from their tongues and body parts, thus minimizing the chances for cross-pollination. Seed has been obtained, however, when red-clover flowers were artificially cross-pollinated under such moisture conditions. Under such conditions the flights of the bees are reduced and the health and increase of the colony impaired. After heavy rains followed by hot weather, pollen often disintegrates, and insects visiting the flowers do not secure sufficient quantities of viable pollen for cross-pollination. Bumblebees have a tendency to visit the older flowers rather than the young ones, even when the tissues of the former are browning. In such flowers the quantity of viable pollen for cross-pollination is reduced and in many cases it is likely that the ovules have become nonfunctional.

Seed Setting Depends on Insect Activity

The setting of seed depends upon the activity of pollinating insects, but destructive insects are also very numerous in some localities and in some seasons. These insects may limit the quantity of seed produced by destroying the ovules or the plants themselves before the seed is formed. The chalcid fly, the clover-flower midge, the clover-seed caterpillar, the lesser clover-leaf weevil, and the root borer are some of the more important destructive insects. A management practice whereby the first growth of clover is harvested for hay when the plants are in full bloom may help to control the midge and the seed caterpillar. Rotations where the occurrence of clover crops on the same soil are widely separated will aid in the control of the root borer.

Economic factors also are important in regulating the total volume of red-clover seed produced, but these factors can only be touched upon here. When the price of clover hay is high, the second growth clover may be used for that purpose instead of being saved for seed, or conditions may point to its profitable utilization as a green-manure crop. How much of the clover acreage is left for seed in any one year is largely determined by the requirements of the farm. At the present time it would appear that the harvesting of a seed crop should be a profitable enterprise, because of the high price and scarcity of adapted seed.

E. A. HOLLOWELL.

RESEARCH in Every Field Important to Progress of Mankind The public is familiar with such outstanding results of research as the telephone, radio, electric light, electric power, radium, X ray, the telescope and microscope, the discovery of the germs of disease, bacteria, protozoans like those causing malaria and yellow fever, and their carriers, the mosquito, the so-called filterable viruses and their carriers, the plant lice and leaf hoppers, and the hosts of other organisms that we must fight in order to live. We are conquering harmful organisms one by one as science learns the truth about them, but the fight has just begun. Enough has been accomplished, however, to stimulate us to greater effort, with the certainty of victory if we do not weary of the struggle. It is our duty to promote research in every possible way.

While my main purpose is to call attention to research in agriculture, I desire to emphasize the fundamental importance of research in every field. Research is the golden key that opens the doors to a better future.

Like pure gold, the research spirit is rare. It must be carefully sought and when found given every opportunity and freedom to develop. This is one of the outstanding problems of education and is receiving much thought to-day. It is of course a basic problem, because after all the investigator is the key to the solution of the problem. How shall we find him and develop him, or rather give him freedom to develop and then to live his life of research in the most productive possible way? The whole future of civilization depends on whether we arrive at the right solution.

The colleges and universities of the country are the social agencies responsible in large measure for doing this effectively. The division of educational relations of the National Research Council in cooperation with a number of the colleges and universities has been making a careful study of the best means available in finding, encouraging, and helping students who give unusual promise.

It is the aim of the Department of Agriculture to cooperate with all agencies with a special view to stimulating research in agriculture and rural life.

A. F. WOODS.

RICE Dried on Farm by Use of Machinery Imported from Italy — A longer growing season is required for rice in California than in the rice sections of the South because of the different varieties grown and perhaps to some extent also because of the coolness of the nights. Unfavorable conditions for early seeding may also at times cause the harvest to come late in the fall. Frequent occurrence of early fall showers or heavy fogs and dews may hold back rice harvesting and rice-threshing operations until the beginning of the winter rains.

Unharvested rice caught by the rains is likely to be a total loss for milling purposes. The character of the adobe soil upon which the rice is grown makes harvesting operations almost impossible during the winter. Rice that is threshed when wet with dew or threshed in a fog is sure to be damp. Damp rough rice is unsafe for storage and is not as marketable as dry rough rice. In the milling of damp rough rice many whole kernels are ground to powder, which throws an abnormal proportion of the rice into the bran or cheaper milling products. The milled products obtained from damp rough rice are also unsafe for storage.

During the 1927 harvest season the early rains caught a great quantity of unthreshed rice in the Sacramento and Northern San Joaquin Valleys, and much of the rice threshed that year after the rains came was too damp for safe storage.

Rice has long been considered one of the cereals difficult to dry; many of the early efforts to condition damp rice by artificial drying

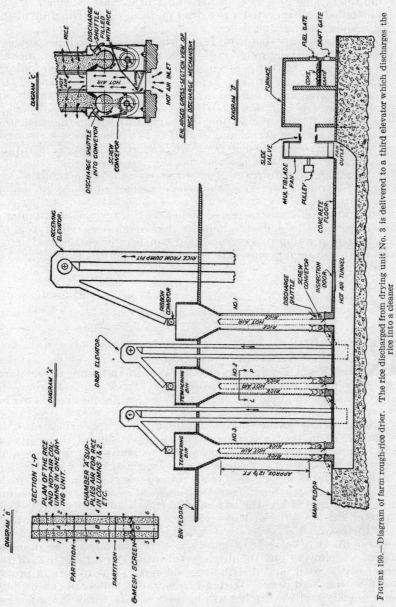

FIGURE 190.—Diagram of farm rough-rice drier. The rice discharged from drying unit No. 3 is delivered to a third elevator which discharges the rice into a cleaner

were not successful.   Damp rough rice that is dried too rapidly and with too high heat has a tendency to crack or check, which causes the kernels to break when they are being milled.   It was, therefore, with much interest that the Department of Agriculture observed in 1927 the drying operations of a rice farmer living near East Nicolaus, Calif., who installed and operated a rice drier on his farm.   (Diagram of this drier is shown in fig. 199.)

The drier was imported from Italy, where similar machines are used successfully for drying rough rice.   The unique factors which make it especially applicable to the drying of rough rice are (1) use of a large quantity of drying air at a comparatively low temperature, and (2) the fact that the rough rice is dried in three steps, and between the drying periods the rice is held in a relatively large bin for a time sufficient to allow a tempering or equalization of the moisture within the rice kernel and between the rice kernel and its hull.   Thus the excess moisture in wet rough rice is extracted so gradually and at such low temperatures that cracking or checking is avoided.

With a moisture decrease of about 7 per cent, as a result of this artificial drying of wet rice, the whole kernels obtained in milling as indicated by laboratory shelling tests increased about 46 per cent and the total hulled rice increased 29 per cent.   Such observations and tests as were made seemed to indicate that rough rice coming from the threshers in a damp or wet condition can be efficiently dried on the farm so it will be not only safe for storage but will also be improved in its milling quality.

E. N. Bates,
R. M. Gehl, and
G. P. Bodnar.

ROAD-WORK on Farm Outlets Needs Skill and Right Equipment — This article is intended to supply information which will be useful to farmers in maintaining their farm roads and those outlets from the farms to the more important highways which are sometimes cared for by farmers.

Before a road can be successfully maintained its surface must be so shaped as to shed water to ditches at each side of the road, the ditches must have sufficient slope so that no water will remain standing in them, and adequate culverts must be constructed where needed. Figure 200 shows a suggested shape of cross section for earth roads. The right-hand portion illustrates the most common case where a ditch is required, while the left-hand portion shows the correct shape where a fill is required or where the ground slopes sharply downward from the road.

Farm roads over level or gently sloping ground can be properly shaped by plowing out the ditches, throwing the furrow toward the center of the road, and distributing the earth so as to form a proper crown with a road drag.   With a blade grader, the work can be done more quickly and the ditches will be more satisfactorily shaped.   For a public highway it is desirable to use a tractor-drawn grader supplemented by other grading apparatus, such as drag scrapers (slips), fresnoes, wheelers, etc., where conditions require them.

These are construction rather than maintenance operations. Attempts to maintain a road which does not effectively shed water from its surface to ditches that will carry the water away from the road are largely wasted effort.

Where a mudhole forms during every wet spell, invariably the trouble is due to lack of drainage. Either the water is caught in ruts before it reaches the ditches or the ditches do not carry it away. Much time is spent in filling mudholes after they become impassable, when half as much labor during dry weather, directed toward drainage, would have prevented the difficulty.

Once a mudhole is formed, filling it with stone, gravel, or cinders is about the only satisfactory remedy while it remains wet. The use of brush, sod, and similar materials may make the place passable for the time being, but it is not recommended.

Road Drag Recommended for Maintenance

An earth road brought to the proper shape is not difficult to maintain under light traffic, unless the soil is particularly unfavorable.

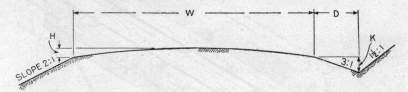

"W," width of road between ditches, not less than 20 feet, for a public highway.
"D," varies from 2 feet to 6 feet, depending on rainfall and grade.
"H," crown, varies from ½ inch to the foot for level grade to 1 inch to the foot for a grade of 5 per cent.
"K," usually varies from 12 to 18 inches and depends on width of road and amount of water to be carried.

FIGURE 200.—Typical cross section for earth road

The road drag is widely used for maintaining purposes and may be of the split-log, sawed-lumber, or steel type. Figure 201 shows a split-log drag and Figure 202 a design using sawed lumber. It can be drawn by two horses or by a truck.

The material required for the split-log drag shown in Figure 201 is as follows:

Metal—One steel plate with holes as shown, ¼ by 4 inches by 8 feet; two hook bolts with nuts and washers, ⅝ by 5 inches; one welded eyebolt with nuts and washers, ⅝ by 5 inches; six bolts with nuts and washers (countersunk), ⅜ by 5 inches; one-fourth pound wire nails, 8d.; one hitching link, ½ inch; one proof coil chain, 8 feet, ⅜-inch links, 6½-inch links; lumber—two half-round logs 8 inches by 8 feet; three cross pieces 3 inches by 3 feet 2 inches; one diagonal brace 2½ inches by 3 feet 6 inches; two boards 1 by 6 inches by 7 feet.

Properly used, and at the right time, the drag performs four distinct functions: (1) By moving at an angle with the traveled way, it tends to produce or preserve a crowned cross section; (2) if used when the surface is comparatively soft, it tends to reduce irregularities in the road by moving material from points which are relatively high to those which are relatively low; (3) when used after a rain, it accelerates the drying out of the road by spreading out puddles of water and thus exposing a greater area to evaporation; and (4) if the surface material is in a slightly plastic state, dragging smears over and partially seals the so-called pores of the earth and thus makes the road surface more nearly impervious to water.

To obtain the best results, dragging should be done only when the surface of the road is sufficiently moist for the material moved by the drag to compact readily after it is moved, but not sufficiently wet for traffic following the drag to produce mud.

The principal factor in successfully operating a properly constructed road drag, provided the condition of the road is favorable, is skill on the part of the operator. Such skill can be obtained only by intelligent experience, and no rules can be laid down which would enable an inexperienced operator to produce first-class results.

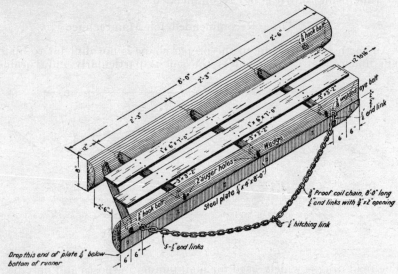

FIGURE 201.—Typical design of a split-log drag

The material required for the road drag shown in Figure 202 is as follows:

Metal—One steel plate with holes as shown, ¼ by 4 inches by 8 feet; eight bolts with nuts and washers (countersunk), ⅜ by 3 inches; one welded eyebolt with nuts and washers, ⅝ by 5 inches; two hook bolts with nuts and washers, ⅝ by 5 inches; one-third pound wire nails, 8d.; 3 pounds wire spikes, 30d.; one hitching link, ½ inch; one proof coil chain, 8 feet, ⅜-inch links, 6½-inch links; lumber—three 2 by 4 inches by 3 feet 2 inches; two 2½ by 2½ inches by 3 feet 2 inches; one 2 by 4 inches by 3 feet; two 1 by 6 inches by 7 feet; two 2 by 6 inches by 8 feet; two 2 by 10 inches by 8 feet.

The Position of the Hitching Link

Under ordinary circumstances, the position of the hitching link on the draw chain should be such that the runners will make an angle of 60° to 75° with the center line of the road, or, in other words, a skew angle of from 15° to 30°. But when dragging immediately over the ruts, or down the center of the road, after the sides have been dragged, it may be found advantageous to place the hitching link at the center of the chain and run the drag without skew. An intelligent operator will learn quickly to adjust such details as these, as well as to shift his

weight while riding upon the drag in order to make it cut where cutting
is desirable, and deposit material where material is needed.

Sometimes a few places are found on a road where, in spite of proper
drainage and dragging, bad ruts are formed.   In such places the soil
is almost always of a clayey nature and can be improved by spreading
over the surface any material of a granular nature, such as gravel,
sand, stone screenings, cinders, or ashes.   The mixing of this material
with the soil can be done by the traffic.   It can be applied in a rather
thin layer and successive layers applied as the need is demonstrated
until a stable surface is obtained.   This is the method sometimes used
in constructing a sand-clay road.   Proportions for a sand-clay mixture
vary, but generally from 60 to 70 per cent sand is used.   A smaller
percentage of sand mixed in a clay surface will be found to be decidedly
helpful.

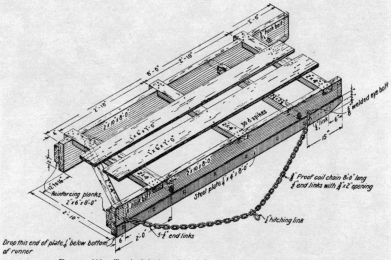

FIGURE 202.—Typical design of road drag constructed of sawed lumber

This method of treatment is particularly recommended for drives to
buildings and barns.

For the improvement of sandy roads, clay can be applied to the
surface as above described, only a smaller quantity of transported
material will produce satisfactory results.

Information is frequently requested as to how to prevent the dust
nuisance where a road passes near a dwelling.   Chemicals such as
common salt and calcium chloride, which will absorb moisture from
the atmosphere, may be scattered over road surfaces as dust layers.
They are effective for a time in humid climates but, since they are
soluble in water, they are eventually washed away.

In the vicinity of Washington, D. C., crank-case oil, drained from
automobiles, is used effectively as a dust layer.   It can usually be
obtained rather cheaply from garages.   The amount required depends
on the thickness of the layer of dust.   In one instance, on a road an
inch deep in dust about 75 gallons were used to treat a length of 100
feet and a width of 15 feet.   The oil was splashed on the surface with
buckets.   A treatment each spring is effective throughout the summer
and fall months.

R. E. ROYALL.

ROSES Developed for Dooryard Are Still Far From Well Known — Roses for the dooryard are rarely roses for the rose garden. In the latter place, where the plants are grown as an exhibition crop, for a show of flowers, or for the production of flowers for cutting, perhaps the most pampered crop the ornamental gardener handles, there is little place for the robust shrubs and climbers which will survive the less careful methods of the dooryard. The dooryard rose must grow luxuriously even without spraying and fertilizing, with rare or even no pruning, and provide at least one seasonal flowering, good foliage throughout the year, and handsome fruits, if possible. Before such requirements the ordinary hybrid tea rose goes down in defeat, and it is the approximation of this schedule that makes the Radiance

FIGURE 203.—The Mary Wallace rose, a popular new climber

variety and its red counterpart such popular favorites over large areas of the country.

From the wild roses which combine these qualities in largest measure, *Rosa rugosa*, *R. wichuraiana*, and *R. multiflora* have been evolved most of the hardiest roses of to-day, and it is from these that the late Doctor Van Fleet created some of the most successful roses he produced, combining them with various hybrid teas to secure finer and more continuous flowering. The earlier sorts are now well established in the trade, but his later creations which have been released by the Department of Agriculture for introduction with the cooperation of the American Rose Society are still far from well known.

The Mary Wallace variety (fig. 203), which is a complicated hybrid involving both *wichuraiana* and hybrid tea blood, has combined the vigor and hardiness of the wild species with the more elegant foliage and flowers of the hybrid tea ancestors. In addition it shows a tendency to autumn flowering which is not overcommon among the hardy climbing roses. In 1928 Mary Wallace was voted first place among the newer climbers by members of the American Rose Society, which shows that it is valued as well by more critical rosarians.

Heart of Gold is also a climber, but of more bushlike habit, and resembles somewhat in bloom the earlier American Pillar; but its single flowers are deep purplish crimson with a white center somewhat overshadowed by the center of golden stamens. In the autumn its huge panicles of scarlet hips are almost as attractive as the flowers.

FIGURE 204.—A cluster of blossoms of the Glenn Dale rose. The buds of lemon white fade to pure white as they open

Glenn Dale Another Strong Climber

Glenn Dale (fig. 204), the third of the trio of strong-growing climbers, is perhaps the most beautiful of them all, with admirable dark foliage and finely modeled buds of lemon-white color, fading to pure white as they open. This rose was awarded a certificate of merit at the Bagatelle Rose Garden in the summer of 1928, and it should supplant the admirable Silver Moon, which frequently is too rampant for ordinary quarters and which has lovely but very ragged flowers as compared to Glenn Dale.

A fourth climber, of very different habit and qualities, is Breeze Hill, which for all practical purposes should be considered a climbing Pernetiana. It is less rampant in habit but makes a sturdy bush when once established, and is useful in smaller quarters than the other climbers. The flowers are very fine, full double, and perfectly formed. In color they are a tender flesh pink stained with yellow and rose through the center. In addition they mature somewhat later than most climbers and so prolong the flowering season.

The two bush roses that the department has released for introduction are both hybrids of *Rosa rugosa*, one named Sarah Van Fleet for the originator's wife, and the other E. M. Mills for the distinguished rosarian. The first is a robust bush of typical *rugosa* character with abundant semidouble flowers of clear rose pink which are produced freely in the spring and sparingly through the remainder of the year. The original bush, now over 15 years old, still stands on the old Van Fleet place, a plant more than 8 feet high and almost as much in diameter, and flowers abundantly each year. This variety rarely fruits. The second is a very different type, although the foliage and stems are much like *rugosa*. The flowers, however, are borne singly on short lateral branches, all along the stems, so that one has long wreaths of bloom rather than terminal clusters. They are somewhat smaller than typical *rugosa*, semidouble, yellowish white tinted with rose on the edges. This variety also rarely fruits, but its abundant dark foliage makes this an admirable screen or low hedge plant.

B. Y. MORRISON.

ROSIN When Poorly Strained Is Much Reduced in Quality It is conservatively estimated that poorly strained rosin annually costs the producers half a million dollars and the users of rosin at least a million dollars for additional processing and loss of material, and in the decreased value of the rosin. The demand for brilliant, clean rosin, entirely free from dirt and specks of all kinds, is greater than ever before. The development and application of better methods of straining therefore is a real need of the naval stores industry.

Dirt in rosin is costly for several reasons. The presence of dirt makes rosin unfit for some purposes for which it would otherwise be suitable, and thus curtails the uses for rosin. The dirt must be removed to keep it out of the products made from rosin, and this cleansing process is expensive. But most important, dirt degrades the rosin, making it a grade lower than it would be had it been properly strained. It is not primarily the large, readily settled, and separated particles that cause the greatest loss, but rather the fine pieces of bark, sand, and clay that are hardly visible in the most critical examination that are most harmful and give the most trouble.

These facts have been fully established by the laboratory work in the naval stores section of the Bureau of Chemistry and Soils. Straining practices must be efficient before the naval stores industry can be on a sound basis. A study of the straining of the gum both before and after distilling is the first major problem to be worked out to a practical solution at the naval stores experiment station which it is planned to locate in the naval stores belt. The laboratory work has shown that the practical solution of this problem of long standing can be worked out only with the complete facilities afforded by a naval stores experiment station, where the problem can be attacked from all angles.

F. P. VEITCH.

RUST Epidemics of Local Areas Betray Barberries' Presence — The now well-recognized relation between the common barberry and the spread of black stem rust to wheat, oats, barley, and rye was not always a matter either of common or of scientific knowledge. Stem rust has been known as the most destructive disease of cereals for many hundreds of years. Common barberries also have been known for many centuries, their history tracing back to before 650 B. C. The relation of the two, however, was not noted until early in the seventeenth century, and no scientific explanation could be offered at that time. Farmers of that time had observed that, whatever was the cause of the rust on small grains, this rust was always severe near common barberry bushes and less severe as the distance from the barberry bushes increased.

These observations made repeatedly, year after year, were the basis of the demand by farmers for information as to exactly the relation between the barberry and the occurrence and spread of black stem rust. Scientific investigations were begun. As a result, in 1865 De Bary, a German scientist, discovered the true life cycle of the rust. He found that the rust grew on the leaves of barberries and that this rust was merely a different stage of the same rust that occurred on the stems and leaves of small grains. His experiments showed that the rust spores were spread from the barberry to the grains by the winds after which they reproduced on the grains and were able to spread during the growing season. Thus the observations made by the farmers nearly 300 years before were confirmed by scientific proof.

The Conclusion Often Corroborated

In the United States farmers and scientists have corroborated these conclusions many times. Each year local stem-rust epidemics betray the infected common barberries that have caused them. Since the campaign for the eradication of the common barberry from the 13 North-Central States was begun in 1918, more than 1,000 observations have been made of the spread of stem rust from barberries. Many of these rust spreads were local, having started late and having an opportunity to spread only a few miles from the bushes before the grain was harvested. In other cases infection from the barberries started on near-by grains and grasses early in the spring and spread like wildfire for many miles.

One of the most outstanding examples of the relation of stem rust to barberries was noted near Lake Preston, S. Dak. In 1904 farmers of the community had gathered and dug a hedge of barberries because stem rust was extremely destructive each year near the bushes and spread to the surrounding fields and finally over a great area. The bushes sprouted and rust again became destructive in this locality. In 1917, 27 farmers of that vicinity drew up and signed a statement condemning the local hedge of common barberries as a rust spreader and urged that a special barberry law be passed in South Dakota making it a crime to propagate, grow, or have growing any of the common rust-susceptible varieties of barberries on any public premises.

Large spreads of rust, as well as local ones, have betrayed the location of the bushes. In North Dakota in 1924 rust was discovered

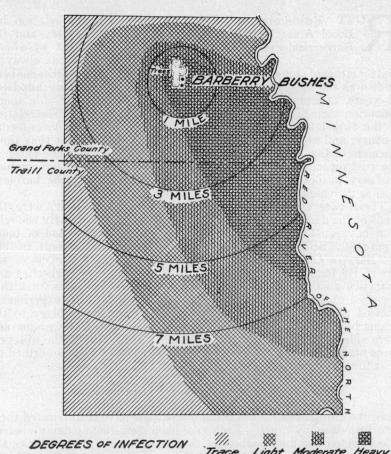

FIGURE 205.—Stem rust spreads from the common barberry to grains and grasses. Two infected common barberry bushes near Reynolds, N. Dak., were found in August, 1928, as a result of the stem-rust infection spread by these bushes. Map shows Grand Forks and Traill Counties, N. Dak., August, 1928

over a large area. The point of most severe damage was near Jamestown, and the epidemic gradually became less severe as the distance from Jamestown increased. This epidemic spread out in a fan shape to the north, northwest, and northeast for a distance of nearly 100 miles. No bushes were known to be located near Jamestown, but the severity of the rust in that locality indicated that barberries might be there. A search was made, and 86 large rusted barberry bushes were found. The effect produced by these bushes had led to their discovery.

Location of Focal Point Indicated

A study of the more general stem-rust epidemic of 1927 indicated that its focal point was located in southeastern Minnesota. In 1928 field agents of the Department of Agriculture surveyed approximately one-tenth of the area of the 30 counties in southeastern Minnesota and the adjacent portions of Iowa, Illinois, and Wisconsin, whence rust spores might have blown into this part of Minnesota. A total of more than 80,000 large barberry bushes and seedlings was found in these counties. These bushes had escaped from cultivation. They were found growing in dense timber, on steep hillsides, and along the stream banks, and therefore had not been found on the farmstead survey.

In this way the record obtained each year, showing localized or definite large areas of stem-rust infection, serves as a basis for finding the barberries in each community that have been missed in the systematic survey, or have grown from seed since the survey was made. By its tell-tale appearance, each local rust epidemic betrays the approximate location of the causative barberry bushes and leads to their discovery and destruction.

L. D. Hutton.

SEED-BORNE Diseases of Cereals Succumb to Dust Fungicides The chief seed-borne diseases of small grains in the United States are the loose and covered smuts of wheat, of oats, and of barley, and the stripe disease of barley. With the exception of loose smut of wheat, all of these diseases have been controlled fairly well for a number of years by immersing the seed in some fungicidal solution before sowing. Chief among these chemicals are formaldehyde and copper sulphate. In recent years organic mercury compounds have been used to a limited extent.

The outstanding disadvantages of these liquid treatments are:

They are disagreeable and cumbersome to apply.

The germination of the seed frequently is reduced because the chemical often impairs the viability of the seed, or the seed may be frozen or otherwise injured when unfavorable weather prevents immediate sowing after treatment.

The swelling of the treated seed interferes somewhat with drilling operations.

The first dust fungicide to be extensively used in this country was copper carbonate. This was found to be an effective preventive of bunt in wheat and in recent years has supplanted almost entirely the common liquid fungicides previously used for this purpose. It also controls certain diseases of sorghum. The success with copper carbonate led to the rapid development of dusts for combating other seed-borne cereal diseases more difficult to control. There are now on the market several such dusts which in recent experiments have proved satisfactory in preventing the smuts of oats and of barley and the stripe disease of barley.

These dust fungicides have such distinct advantages as:

They are easy to apply. The grain is mixed with the dust at the rate of 2 to 3 ounces per bushel in a barrel churn or other simple mechanical mixer.

Seed thus treated is not injured even when stored for months. Therefore, treating may be done during the slack season.

Dust fungicides protect stored grain from weevils and to a considerable extent from rats and mice.

Several disadvantages of dust fungicides may be mentioned:

They are poisonous and may cause physical discomfort when inhaled. A respirator should be worn while applying the dusts or handling dusted grain.

Dust fungicides are more expensive as a rule, although this objection may be largely outweighed by the smaller cost of application.

Dusted grain can not be used for animal or human consumption; therefore, only enough seed should be treated to suffice for sowing. This, however, applies also to some liquid fungicides.

Some dust fungicides interfere somewhat with the ready flow of the grain through the drill.

Germination of the seed in very dry soil is not conducive to good disease control by dust fungicides.

Despite these disadvantages, dust fungicides are being welcomed by farmers because of their advantages over the liquid fungicides hitherto used.

R. W. LEUKEL.

SEED Law Forbids the Interstate Shipment of Misbranded Seed
Forty-five States now have laws regulating the sale of agricultural seeds within their respective borders. These laws vary in their requirements, but are all intended to give the farmer information as to the quality of the seed he is buying. The individual States do not have control over interstate commerce and therefore can not prevent the shipment of agricultural seed into a State because it is misrepresented in any respect.

Section 6 of the Federal seed act prohibits the shipment in interstate commerce of misbranded seeds and is intended to supplement State laws. This legislation enables the United States Department of Agriculture to cooperate with the States in cases where gross misrepresentation occurs. This section of the act applies to false statements of all kinds, including origin, kind, and variety, as well as purity and vitality. Thus far the following types of cases have been prosecuted under this section:

The sale of mill-run cottonseed as pedigreed seed of a specific variety.

The sale of nonhardy alfalfa seed as seed of a hardy variety grown in a northern tier State.

The sale of soy beans that failed to germinate as of good germination.

The sale of common grain rye as rye of a particular variety.

E. BROWN.

SEED Samples of Introduced Plants Make Big Collection
Beginning with the first recorded introduction of Bronka cabbage from Moscow in 1898 and extending in a continuous stream since, the Office of Foreign Plant Introduction of the Bureau of Plant Industry, up to June 30, 1928, had numbered 77,260 plant importations. Since samples have been kept of practically all of these importations that were made

in the form of seeds, the collection of about 35,000 samples probably comprises the largest and most complete collection of economic foreign seeds in the United States, if not in the world. Of the 289 families of seed-bearing plants listed by Dalla Torre and Harms, 214 families are represented in the collection.

The samples vary in size from the almost impalpable dust of the orchid seeds to the double coconut of the Seychelle Islands, more than a foot in diameter and weighing up to 50 pounds. This variation in size has necessitated the working out of a series of vials of different diameters and adapting each size to a box that can be filed in the pigeonholes of a regulation herbarium case. These vials are in six sizes, ranging from five-eighths inch to $3\frac{1}{4}$ inches in diameter.

Besides these vials, there are a series of covered boxes for dried fruits and a series of fleshy-fruit samples preserved in formalin.

Among the interesting samples in the smallest-sized vials are two belonging to the banana family—the traveler's tree of Madagascar, with seeds the size of a kernel of coffee but covered with a silky fringed coat as bright a green as the brightest parrot; and the bird-of-paradise flower, with a black seed about the same size, more than half of which is covered with a brilliant scarlet plume.

Most of the 125 kinds of Australian eucalyptus so far introduced have small brownish seeds shaped like tiny boomerangs. One kind, however, has black seeds half an inch long that would do nicely for models of an Eskimo kayak, even to having a round light-colored spot on the top to mark the opening where the paddler sits.

Most Americans are familiar with pop corn, sweet corn, and field corn; but Cuzco corn, from Peru, whose kernels have to be turned sideways to get them into the $\frac{7}{8}$-inch vial, is not so well known. The bananas found in our markets are seedless; however, the Abyssinian banana and the Transvaal banana have dark-brown or nearly black seeds the size and shape of a wisdom tooth without the roots.

Seeds That Go in the 1¼-inch Vial

The $1\frac{1}{4}$-inch vial accommodates such seeds as those of the ginkgo of Japan with its ill-smelling, fleshy, plumlike, yellow fruits, each containing an edible seed like a large cherry pit, and not looking at all like its close relatives, the pines; the monkey-puzzle tree of Brazil, the seed of which is a chestnut-brown wedge 2 inches long; the familiar nutmeg from the Moluccas with its less familiar thin red lacework covering, which is mace; the cashew from tropical America, a short, thick, crescent-shaped nut with a white spot in the hollow of the crescent which gives the nut an odd monkeylike appearance; the cola nut from Africa, looking like a thick lobe of chicken's liver, and one of the flavoring ingredients in some of our numerous soft drinks; and the irregularly five-sided seeds of the chaulmoogra tree of Siam, from which is extracted an oil used in the treatment of leprosy.

The larger size vials are mostly filled with dried fruits the seeds of which are found in the smaller sizes. But there are some large seeds, such as the baby coconut from Chile, less than 2 inches in diameter; seeds of the mahogany tree of Honduras, which look like single maple keys but grow tightly packed in a large pod; the ivory nut palm of tropical America, from which most of our pearl buttons are made; and the seed of an Indian bamboo which is 5 inches long and 3 inches in diameter—and this is a grass seed.

Another interesting seed is the airplane seed from the East Indies, which grows in a large dry squash that is borne on a long vine climbing to the tree tops, where it opens when ripe and sets free the flat round seeds an inch across with a wing on each end 3 inches long and 1 inch wide, so placed that the seed in falling describes a spiral about 20 feet in diameter.

The history of each introduction is published in a quarterly Inventory of Plant Material Introduced, and there is also a file arranged alphabetically by the botanical names of the plants introduced. The identifying, bottling, labeling, and filing of all this mass of miscellaneous seeds and fruits might get to be exceedingly monotonous—but there is something new each day.

H. C. Skeels.

SHEEP of the Columbia Type Well Adapted to Intermountain Region
In the period between 1880 and 1890 the number of sheep in the United States reached its maximum. Transportation facilities were very poor in the West, and sheep were grown primarily for wool. Consequently the fine-wool type of sheep predominated. During recent years an increased demand for western lambs at the central markets has made the production of market lambs from Hampshire rams bred to crossbred ewes of the long wool, fine-wool type a very profitable practice in the intermountain region. This type of ewe is an excellent mother and the resulting lamb grown on the high summer ranges of our national forests reaches a marketable size and condition at an early age.

The black-faced ewe lamb is not desired, on the range, for breeding purposes; therefore it is a common practice to market both ewe and wether lambs. Under these conditions the producer is faced with the replacement problem. He must either maintain a flock of fine-wool ewes and raise his own crossbreds or he must purchase his replacement stock each year. Under normal conditions a crossbred ewe is a more economical producer than the fine wool, so that ewes of this type, breeding true, would readily find a place in the sheep industry. An attempt to solve these problems has resulted in the development of the Columbia type of sheep.

Origin and History of the Columbia

The Columbia is a crossbred type developed by the Bureau of Animal Industry, United States Department of Agriculture. The development work was begun at Laramie, Wyo., and since 1917 has been continued at the United States Sheep Experiment Station, Dubois, Idaho. The purpose of this work was to develop a crossbred sheep, suitable to western range conditions, that would breed true to type. Work was begun on this problem in 1912, using Lincoln, Leicester, Cotswold, and Romney rams and Rambouillet ewes. After careful study of the type and production of these various crosses, the Lincoln-Rambouillet was retained for further development and the others discarded. Since that time the Lincoln-Rambouillet crosses have been bred together without the introduction of new blood lines. Most of the Columbias in the bureau's flock trace back to a single outstanding Lincoln ram. Rigid culling has been practiced each year, eliminating all individuals that "throw back" to either of the original parent types, or show any other undesirable characteristics.

Characteristics of the Columbia

With only 15 years' development the Columbia breed is not absolutely fixed, but variation is becoming less each year.   The Columbia is a large, vigorous, heavy-boned animal, standing on rather long legs. (Fig. 206.)   As would be expected, it does not show quite the quality to be found in some of the older established breeds.   Ewes average about 135 pounds and rams up to 275 pounds under normal range condition.   Columbia ewes are very prolific and also consistently yield long-stapled fleeces of ¼-blood quality.   During a 3-year period the fleece weights of mature Columbia ewes, under strictly range conditions, averaged 11.27 pounds.   For the same period the average per cent of lambs produced and weaned by these ewes was 75.74.   These lambs averaged 78.02 pounds in weight at weaning time.

The farmer as well as the range man is interested in a sheep that will produce both a profitable fleece and lamb.   In many localities in the intermountain region, particularly on irrigated farms, a small flock of crossbred sheep of the Columbia or similar type should prove to be a paying venture.   The ewe lambs from this type are very desirable to

FIGURE 206.—Pen of yearling Columbia rams produced at the United States Sheep Experiment Station, Dubois, Idaho, and consigned to the national ram sale where they brought, on August 27, 1928, an average price of $145, a record for range rams

retain for breeding purposes, which is not the case when black-faced rams are used.   It is reasonable to assume that the demand for crossbred types will continue and increase.   In view of this probability the farmer may readily work up a sale for well-bred rams to neighboring range men, thus increasing the revenue from his flock.

J. M. COOPER.

SILO Filling Without a Man in the Silo Gives Good Results   In the fall of 1926 and of 1927 the four silos at the dairy experiment farm of the Bureau of Dairy Industry at Beltsville, Md., were filled without tramping and without keeping a man in the silo.   The cut corn was blown in at the top and allowed to fall where it would.   Many of the cobs rolled down the conical mass of cut corn and collected in one place.   As it was thought that enough air might be trapped around the cobs to allow spoiling to take place, it was considered advisable in 1926 to have a man enter the silo every hour or so and dig deeply enough into the side of the mass to give the cobs a new place to collect. This, however, was not done in 1927. During both years, when filling was almost finished it was necessary in every case to keep one or two men in the silo to level off the cut corn so that the silo could be completely filled. The silage kept in perfect condition both seasons.

It was noted that when silos are filled in this way the lighter portions of the corn plant collect at one side, whereas the heavier portions collect at the other side. Consequently, in feeding out the silage, to avoid getting a batch containing a preponderance of either leaves or the heavier portions of the corn plant, a layer should be taken off the entire surface. Although it is evident that neither tramping nor distributing is essential to proper preservation of the silage, it may be desirable in some cases to keep not more than one man in the silo for distributing the corn solely as a matter of convenience in feeding.

T. E. WOODWARD.

SMUT on Pacific Coast Wheat Can Profitably Be Removed by Washing — Wheat has been afflicted with stinking smut since the days of the Old Testament. Each year a surprising percentage of the wheat crop of our country is infected with this black, ill-smelling dust called smut. In the heads of growing wheat either clean normal wheat kernels or brownish-black smut balls are found; wheat kernels and smut balls seldom grow in the same head. The smut appears in threshed wheat as a mixture of whole smut balls and smut dust with the wheat. Smut dust is made up of millions of minute spores from the smut balls that are crushed in the thresher. Smutty wheat looks and smells very foul but the smut and its odor can be removed effectively by machinery designed for that purpose.

In the Pacific Northwest, where seed treatment as a smut-control practice is not entirely effective because of the dry-land method of farming, smut in wheat has reached the point where about half the wheat bought from the farmers is graded as "smutty." The presence of smut in wheat presents a serious handicap to efficient marketing, as all smutty wheat must be passed through the smut-removing machines.

For many years the only method of removing smut from wheat for export and the trade was by a dry scouring process. Pacific coast wheat is usually so dry and brittle that dry scouring damages the wheat by cracking many kernels. Pieces of finely cracked wheat mingle with the smut and are lost. The resulting loss in weight due to dry scouring often exceeds the percentage allowed by the State grain inspection department as "smut dockage." Scoured wheat, because of the injury to the germs, is unsuitable for seed.

Washers for removing smut from wheat have been in use in flour mills for many years, but until recently it was assumed that these washers could not be used for removing smut from wheat for commerce, as it was thought that washed wheat could not be safely stored without drying.

The Federal grain investigations office of the Pacific coast conducted a study of a wheat-washing process at the Portland, Oreg., municipal grain elevator on more than 5,000 tons of smutty wheat which was washed for export to determine the effect on the weight and grading factors. Washing was found to be effective and satisfactory in removing smut, the test weight of wheat was materially reduced immediately after washing, but the wheat tends to regain most of its original test weight, as the moisture penetrates the kernels.

The wheat gained weight during washing. There was over 2.5 per cent more weight of merchantable wheat after washing than before. The germination quality of the wheat was only slightly reduced. At present the washing method of removing smut from Pacific coast wheat is rapidly coming into use in preference to the dry-scouring methods.

E. N. Bates and
G. P. Bodnar.

FIGURE 207.—Double-cylinder wheat-washing machine located in a terminal grain elevator

SOIL Bacteria Useful to Farmers May Be Caused to Multiply The greatest scavengers on earth are the minute living organisms which inhabit the first few inches of agricultural soils. Although not visible to the naked eye, it has been demonstrated by the use of the microscope and other methods that they occur in enormous numbers when conditions are favorable. A rich soil may contain as many as 10 billions per ounce while a poor soil may only support about 15 millions per ounce. Many of these organisms are useful to agriculture in that they make plant food available out of the dead plant and animal remains that fall on or are put into the soil. Their most important contributions are a gradual supply of simple nitrogen compounds (nitrate and ammonia) and carbon-dioxide gas, two extremely essential materials for plant life. Not only do they alter material already in the soil but some of them actually add nitrogen compounds which they manufacture from the nitrogen of the air.

How can the farmer encourage the activities of beneficial soil organisms? Temperature and moisture usually can not be controlled except, of course, that water may be artificially applied and conserved by cultivation or mulching and excess water eliminated by drainage. Other factors more capable of being controlled are the food supply of the organisms and plants, cropping systems, tillage, and the reaction of the soil. Stable manure and composts contain large numbers of beneficial organisms and not only add to the soil population but stimulate the activity and growth of those already there. Green manures on the other hand only furnish food for those in the soil.

Abundant in Stable Manure

Since 1 ounce of good stable manure may hold 12 billion organisms, an enormous number may be added by applying even 2 or 3 tons per acre. Soils are usually inhabited by desirable organisms although under conditions of a depleted food or moisture supply or other adverse conditions, many undoubtedly perish. With the addition of manure or compost or the correction of the unfavorable circumstance the survivors multiply and start to work again. Mineral fertilizers, especially phosphate, exert a favorable influence on the activities of the beneficial soil organisms. Living legume roots apparently stimulate soil organisms while those of mustard and cereals depress them. Alternation of legumes with cereals is, therefore, one of the means to be used in assuring suitable conditions for the soil population. Plowing and cultivation will not only conserve moisture but will add air to the soil, thereby encouraging favorable bacterial action. Lime is an essential to legume nodule bacteria as well as to the plants on which they form nodules and it also favors the activities of most of the other unseen friends of agriculture.

Since most of the beneficial organisms are universally distributed in agricultural soils and may be augmented by common farm practices there is no reason for going much beyond the farm to secure them. The special preparations of these bacteria which have appeared for sale from time to time have not compared favorably with fertile soil and homemade compost. On the other hand, when a new legume is to be planted or the numbers of native nodule bacteria have been depleted by adverse conditions, it is necessary to introduce them artificially. This may be done by transferring field soil known to contain the proper organisms in abundance or by the application of artificially prepared cultures which are now easily procurable from commercial sources.

LEWIS T. LEONARD.

SOIL Deterioration by Sheet Erosion Lowers Fertility of Vast Area —— Farm and grazing lands throughout the United States are damaged by sheet erosion far beyond common belief. The accumulating result of this process of gradually working off the topsoil is seriously reduced soil productivity over many millions of acres, including our best cropping and grazing lands. Every rainfall heavy enough to cause water to flow downhill takes toll of the surface soil, the richest part of the land. Soil particles, together with humus and plant food, are picked up and transported to lower positions or swept into the streams and thence on out to sea; or else these particles are deposited in stream channels, irrigation ditches, and reservoirs where they restrict flowage and storage capacity to the great detriment of the users of water. They also increase overflows by choking channels and thus damage crops on alluvial plains. Much material is washed out over rich valley lands where it is not needed and where it may reduce productivity or even ruin the land. It often happens that only the coarser particles are left, the finer richer material being carried away in suspension.

The direct damage from sheet erosion is incalculably vast. Gullying and sliding cause much damage to fields and overgrazed and overburned watersheds and ranges. But this spectacular type of land impairment by unrestrained water is small in comparison with the never-ending process of soil wastage by sheets of rain water flowing down unprotected slopes. The process of planing off the surface is not conspicuous in most instances, because as a rule, only a thin layer

FIGURE 208.—Eroded hillside, Doniphan County, Kans., northwest of Troy. Alfalfa seeded in 1926 on the dark patches of middle ground, and grass on the associated light patches. The former is succeeding fairly well where from 5 to 7 inches of the original silt loam covering remains, but grass has driven out the alfalfa on those areas where all or nearly all the topsoil has washed away down to the silty clay loam sub-soil (Knox silty clay loam)

is taken off at one time thus affecting broad areas more or less equally. Attention is not attracted to the situation until the less-productive subsoil or barren bedrock begins to appear in patches. By this time it is often too late for remedial action. At this stage the surface layer that we call "the soil" is gone and the farmer or stockman must use what is left, or abandon the depleted area.

Many farmers are cultivating the subsoil and many stockmen are being forced to reduce the number of animals carried on private and public ranges because of forage depletion directly due to the removal of the more fertile surface material.

When the topsoil or humus layer is washed off, stiffer material or else rock or gravel is usually left in its place. Always the exposed material contains less humus; hence the soil, if it may be called such, is less retentive of moisture. The exposed material over a large part of the eroded lands consists of raw clay, which bakes and loses its moisture rapidly in dry weather, contains less available plant food, is more difficult to till, sheds the rains quickly and fills the streams with flood water and silt. This exposed material, with the spongelike, absorbent humus removed, often washes faster than the soil that formerly covered it. Thus erosion goes on faster as the surface covering is removed, until bedrock, or soft, rotten rock, or gravel and loose

FIGURE 209.—Prior to August, 1928, this slope in southern Utah was good grazing land. One rain swept away the surface soil from 80 per cent of the area to a depth ranging from 2 to 12 inches. All the surface soil practically was lost like a sheet stripped from the area, save where sagebrush, cedar, and pine held back islandlike patches of the topsoil. It will be a long time before grass will come back on such land, especially if grazing is permitted within the next four years

sublayer material is reached. Such loose material often gullies so rapidly and deeply that it is impracticable for the individual farmer or stockman to carry out corrective measures.

FIGURE 210.—This steep slope of one-time excellent soil has gradually lost its entire surface layer by sheet erosion. The 1928 corn crop in this eroded field was not worth harvesting, although it was an excellent corn season for the locality, west central Wisconsin. This land should either be turned over to permanent grass or restocked with timber

There is need for a national awakening to the grave dangers attending sheet erosion. Soil-saving and water-saving terraces should be built in thousands of fields; much steep land and highly erosive soil used for clean-cultivated crops should be devoted to permanent pasture or timber; overgrazed ranges should be regulated in accordance with the carrying capacity; and fire prevention on watersheds should be pushed. If a half million acres can be terraced in one year in a single State, as was done in Texas in 1927, it is evident that terracing might be extended rapidly over enormous areas now suffering from excessive washing. If costly floods can be prevented by taking sheep off overgrazed, badly eroded watersheds from which the soil-holding plants have been stripped, as has been done in the drainage basin of Manti Canyon, Utah, numerous other ranges can be saved or restored by similar restriction or regulation of grazing. Orange groves can be protected from damage by the overwash of erosional débris, following fires in the neighboring hills, by keeping the natural brush growth safe from fires, as has been done by many growers in parts of southern California. Other areas in many other parts of the country can be similarly protected and the normally stored ground-water conserved for irrigation and urban consumption.

In the near future the nation will have to deal with the erosion problem, just as Japan and other countries have been forced to deal with it. Remedies can be applied much more effectively now than later. The sooner the problem is attacked the greater will be the saving in farm and ranch land and in farm and ranch solvency.

HUGH H. BENNETT.

SOIL Particles That Glitter Are Often Mistaken for Gold — All is not gold that glitters; but we hesitate to take the chance of missing anything valuable, especially anything as valuable as gold. Therefore, when we see something that glitters we naturally want to investigate. One of the results of this very human tendency is that every year a large number of soil samples are received by the Bureau of Chemistry and Soils with the request that the bright, shiny particles in the soil be identified. Obviously the writers believe the particles to be gold. Often they say so. But unfortunately there are a great number of substances which glitter, many of them not even metals.

In soils perhaps mica and pyrite are the commonest and most deceptive of all these glittering substances. Both are found in numerous rocks, such as granites, schists, and gneisses; and in certain of these rocks, such as mica schists, the mica may be the most abundant mineral present. When these rocks are exposed for long ages to the action of the atmosphere they decompose or rot and form soils. During this process the oxygen and moisture of the air act upon the pyrite chemically and so change it that usually nothing visible is left except iron rust. But the mica continues to persist. In spite of all the time that has elapsed since the parent rock started to decompose, the mica can still be seen glittering in the soil about as brightly as ever. Owing to its flaky structure, it can be transported by water and wind more readily than can most other soil minerals and is therefore found in many soils which originated from rocks devoid of mica. In fact there are very few soils in which no mica can be found.

It is not gold; but neither is it altogether useless. Although it decomposes extremely slowly, yet it does decompose and yields a little potash to the soil. But even in this respect it may be deceptive, for it may still glitter after practically all of its potash has disappeared.

W. H. FRY.

SOIL Survey in 25 Years   During the past 25 years the depart-
    Maps More Than Half   ment has surveyed and mapped more
    Our Arable Land   than half of the total area of arable
land in the United States.

The finished work of the soil survey consists of a soil map showing in colors the location and extent of each type or kind of soil within the area, and a report which describes the soils and discusses briefly their suitability for particular crops and their productive capacity under proper systems of management. The reports also give a brief review of the economic and agricultural conditions within the area and furnish a foundation of facts upon which to develop a rational permanent agriculture.

Since this work touches so many lines of endeavor it is difficult to estimate the direct value to the individual farmer. In the more recently settled sections of the country the reports and maps have been used largely by new settlers in the selection of the farm lands best suited to their needs. In the older agricultural sections the surveys are utilized by farmers in the study of the soils of their farms and in the planning of soil-management practices to bring about increased acre crop production.

County agricultural agents use the surveys in the study of the soil conditions in their counties in order to be better able to advise specific farm practices suited to the various soil types and soil conditions.

Experiment Stations Use Soil Surveys

Experiment-station and agricultural-college workers use the reports and maps as a basis for the location of outlying experimental fields and in the application of these results to other areas of similar soils in other localities, thus giving a wide range of adaptation of their results to the soils of the county and State.

Other uses being made of soil survey reports are in connection with the location of new roads, the valuation of lands for loan purposes, and in the making of health and sanitary surveys.

Another phase of this work concerns the relation of soil types to the development and the spread of plant diseases. During the past field season a limited amount of work was undertaken for the purpose of studying the relationship of soil types to the root rot of cotton. As a result of this preliminary survey it seems certain that there is a very definite relation existing between certain soil types and the development and spread of this disease and it is hoped that a continuation of this line of soil study will be of material aid in indicating the soils in which the disease will develop and also indicate the characteristics of types and the particular field conditions which favor the spread of the organism responsible for this disease.

The total expense of making a detailed survey of a county is less than the cost of a quarter of a mile of modern concrete road. It is doubtful, therefore, if there is any other line of public work of such great economic value that can be done at so small a cost to the Government.

A. G. McCall.

SOLAR-RADIATION Study   The sun is a gaseous body having a
    Reveals Facts Highly   diameter of about 865,000 miles,
    Important to Farmers   which is more than 100 times the
                             diameter of the earth, and a tem-
perature at its outer radiating surface of about 6,000° on the absolute
centigrade scale. It is practically the only source of heat and light
for the planets of the solar system, and therefore the source of all forms
of life existing thereon.

The exact nature of the energy radiated from the sun is not certainly
known. It exhibits the characteristics of wave motion transverse to
its line of propagation. The energy radiated by a body as hot as the
sun includes a wide range of wave lengths. By passing it through a
prism of glass the energy will be arranged in the order of its wave
lengths. A visual examination will show the prismatic colors, with
violet at one end and red at the other. It is the combination of all
these colors that produces white daylight.

By means of a heat-measuring device it will be found that long-wave
radiation extends far beyond the red of the visible in what is known as
the infra-red spectrum, and that short-wave radiation extends beyond
the violet in what is known as the ultra-violet spectrum. Sensitive
photographic plates will detect the presence of ultra-violet radiation to
much shorter wave lengths than will the most delicate heat-measuring
instruments.

Characteristics of Different Parts of the Spectrum

Parts of the spectrum lying between different wave-length limits
have each their special rôle. Thus, the so-called visible spectrum, lying
between the extremes of the violet and the red, besides supplying us
with light is especially potent in promoting plant development, so
essential in the maintenance of animal life. The short-wave ultra-
violet light is a powerful germicide, and is therefore of great assistance
in combating disease. Also, by penetrating the skin to the capillary
blood vessels it produces certain changes in the composition of the
blood that stimulate physical development. Indeed, it seems to be
established that the higher forms of animal life, including domestic
animals as well as man himself, do not develop normally when deprived
of ultra-violet radiation. Hence the growing popularity of outdoor
sun baths, since ultra-violet rays can not pass through ordinary
window glass.

The infra-red includes approximately one-half the total energy
received from the sun. Its importance will be apparent when the total
energy is discussed.

In passing through the earth's atmosphere the solar rays are
depleted through absorption by atmospheric gases, principally water
vapor, and through scattering by the gas molecules and the solid and
liquid particles held in suspension. The loss through scattering is
much greater in short-wave than in long-wave radiation. In consequence, with increase in altitude the intensity of ultra-violet radiation
increases markedly. Also, skylight, which consists of the scattered
light that reaches the surface of the earth, is blue in color. The
purer the atmosphere the deeper the blue of the sky.

Daily Totals of Solar Radiation

The total solar radiant energy received on a horizontal surface has been termed "the fundamental basis of the science of meteorology." It is likewise of fundamental importance in climatological studies. The solar energy received diffusely from the sky is an important part of this total. At noon in summer it may be one-fifth of the whole, and the proportional part increases as the sun approaches the horizon.

Instruments have been devised for continuously registering the intensity of this total radiation, but published records are available from only about 21 stations, 7 of which are in the United States.

In Figure 211 abscissaes give the time scale in days of the year. The ordinates give the intensity scale, on the left-hand margin in units of energy, on the right-hand margin in units of heat. In the

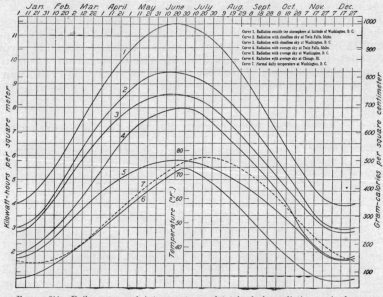

FIGURE 211.—Daily averages of air temperature and totals of solar radiation received on a horizontal surface

center is a temperature scale for curve 7. Curve 1 gives the daily totals of radiation that would be received at the latitude of Washington in the absence of an atmosphere, assuming the solar constant of radiation to be 1.937 gram-calories per minute per square centimeter, or 1.35 kilowatts per square meter. Curves 2 to 6 give measured daily totals of solar radiation received on a horizontal surface; curves 2 and 3 for cloudless sky conditions at Twin Falls, Idaho, latitude 42° 29' north, altitude 4,250 feet, and Washington, D. C., latitude 38° 56' north, altitude 414 feet, respectively; curves 4 to 6, for average sky conditions at Twin Falls, Wash., and the university station in Chicago, respectively. The latitude of the last-named station is 41° 47' north, the altitude 688 feet. Note the increase in daily totals at Twin Falls over the daily totals at lower altitudes. The effect upon vegetation of this increase, which is especially marked in the short-wave radiation, is a subject that is engaging the attention of plant physiologists. The marked deficiency at Chicago is due principally to the screening effect of city smoke.

On a cloudless day in midsummer at Twin Falls the daily receipt of solar energy per square mile of surface is equal to nearly 33,000,000 horsepower hours, and at Washington to nearly 30,000,000. On an average day in midsummer the daily total at Twin Falls is equal to about 27,500,000 and at Washington to about 20,000,000 horsepower hours.

If all this energy were absorbed by a layer of water 8 centimeters (3.15 inches) thick, and the water retained all the heat it received, the curves of Figure 211 tell us that on a clear day in June at Twin Falls its temperature would be increased about 100° C. (180° F.) and at Washington about 92° C. (166° F.). With average sky conditions the respective water temperature increases would be about 86° C. (155° F.) and 62° C. (113° F.).

What Solar Radiant Energy Does for Us

Solar radiation is the source of the power that keeps the atmosphere in circulation, including the secondary circulation in storms, which latter are sometimes appalling in their violence. It evaporates moisture from land and water surfaces, which is later precipitated in the form of rain or snow. In connection with the atmospheric circulation it controls weather and climate.

Its control of annual temperature changes is shown by a comparison of curves 5 and 7. The relation between the two curves is such that it may be expressed in a mathematical equation. Note that the annual march of temperature lags behind the annual march of radiation in the same way that diurnal temperature changes lag behind radiation changes.

In ages past solar radiation by stimulating plant growth has stored for our present use the supplies of coal and oil we are now spending so lavishly. If in the distant future these supplies become exhausted solar energy, the primary source, will still be unimpaired; and only man's ingenuity is required to make it directly available as power, heat, and light.

HERBERT H. KIMBALL.

SORGO Known As Atlas Yields Well and Resists Lodging Atlas is the name recently given to a new and promising variety of sorgo developed in cooperative sorghum-breeding experiments at the Kansas Agricultural Experiment Station. The name Atlas was chosen because of its strong stalks which resist lodging.

Atlas sorgo is a pedigree selection from a cross between Blackhull kafir and Sourless sorgo, made by I. N. Farr, a farmer and sorghum breeder of Stockton, Kans. Mr. Farr sent hybrid heads to the Kansas station. Headrows were grown, and in 1923 the strain recently named Atlas was selected as being the most promising.

Since 1923 this selection has been tested in varietal plots at the Manhattan and Hays stations and on the southeastern Kansas experimental fields. In 1927 and 1928 it was grown in direct comparison with other varieties by a number of Kansas farmers who cooperate with the Kansas station in conducting local varietal tests.

In nearly all of these tests Atlas has made good yields of both forage and grain, although the forage yields usually were not quite equal to those of Kansas Orange, the most popular variety of sorgo now grown in eastern Kansas. The tests indicate that in general Atlas sorgo may be expected to yield 80 to 90 per cent as much forage per acre as Kansas Orange. It is too tall and late for western Kansas.

The advantage of Atlas over Kansas Orange lies in two important characters, i. e., stiff stalks and white, palatable grain. Atlas has the stiff stalks and the white seed of its kafir parent and the sweet, juicy stalks and leafiness of the sorgo parent. Only one other sorghum variety, Sunrise kafir, that is grown on farms in the United States, has this particular combination of characters. Atlas sorgo has much stronger stalks than Sunrise kafir and produces higher yields of forage.

In 1927 and 1928 the dairy department of the Kansas station grew Atlas sorgo on a field scale for use as a silage crop. In both seasons the

FIGURE 212.—Atlas sorgo (left) standing erect, and Kansas Orange sorgo (right) badly lodged after fall rains. Agronomy farm plots, Kansas Agricultural Experiment Station, Manhattan, Kans., September, 1927

Atlas sorgo was lodged much less (fig. 212) than adjacent fields of Kansas Orange. The ability of Atlas sorgo to resist lodging has also been very clearly demonstrated in the varietal testing fields in southeastern Kansas.

Feeding trials with silage of these two varieties, conducted by the dairy department during the winter of 1927–28, indicated that silage of Atlas sorgo is about equal to that of Kansas Orange. During the same winter, grain of Atlas sorgo and of Dawn (Dwarf Blackhull) kafir, a standard commercial variety, was fed to hogs at the Hays station in self-feeders. The grain of Atlas sorgo was found to be just as palatable as that of Dawn kafir.

Atlas sorgo will grade as white kafir on the terminal markets. Thus the farmer in eastern Kansas and similar areas who grows Atlas sorgo either can feed the white, palatable grain to his livestock and obtain the same results as with kafir or he can market it and receive kafir prices for it. He can do neither of these things with the brown, bitter, unpalatable seed of the varieties of sweet sorghum now commonly grown.

JOHN H. PARKER.

SPRAY-RESIDUE Removal by Mechanical Methods Is Extensively Tested It is practically impossible to raise sound, clean apples or pears in any of the commercial fruit-growing regions of the United States without spraying with arsenical compounds to control the codling moth and other insect pests. In humid regions, or where only a few applications of the insecticide are necessary, most of it may be weathered off by the time the fruit is harvested. In localities where there is little rainfall during the growing season, or where numerous heavy applications of the insecticide are required, considerable residue may remain on the fruit at picking time. Numerous analyses by the Bureau of Chemistry of the Department of Agriculture in 1925 showed that apples and pears from some parts of the United States, particularly the western regions, carried arsenical spray residues in excess of the tolerance deemed safe for food products by health authorities of this country and of Great Britain, which is one of the principal export markets for American apples. Inasmuch as it was recognized as impossible to raise clean fruit without spraying, it was necessary to work out some method for removing this excess spray residue.

It was first thought that this residue could be removed by hand or machine wiping, and a number of machines were devised in which the fruit was passed through rapidly rotating disks of cloth or over or under brushes. This method, while effective under certain conditions and when only a small amount of spray residue in excess of the tolerance was present, would not remove heavy deposits. These dry-cleaning methods were used to some extent in the fall of 1925, rather extensively in 1926, and in some districts for the 1927 apple crop. Four types of machines were tested during the fall of 1927, analyses being made on the same lots of fruit before and after wiping. The results showed that from 22 to 33 per cent of the residue was removed. It is evident, then, that with arsenical residues running in excess of 0.015 arsenic as arsenic trioxide per pound of fruit (and where three or more cover sprays are applied, this is to be expected) it will be practically impossible to reduce them consistently to a tolerance of 0.01. In some sections dry wiping was more efficient, but it was evident that other methods were necessary where heavy spray schedules were employed.

Numerous Compounds Tested

Considerable work had been done toward developing a washing method with a solution that would dissolve the arsenate but would not injure the appearance or keeping quality of the fruit. Numerous compounds were tested, and some of them met the rather stringent requirements. Mineral acids and alkalies dissolve the residue, and of these hydrochloric acid and sodium carbonate, or mixtures of sodium carbonate and sodium hydroxide, are used most, the acid being used more than the alkalies. Hydrochloric acid was adopted rather than some of the other mineral acids because it was less dangerous to the operators and, when used properly, was not injurious to apples or pears. It was also cheap and efficient.

Various types of apparatus have been devised for applying this washing treatment to the fruit, ranging from the hand-dipping type, in which boxes or crates of fruit are placed in a small tank containing acid solution and pushed through by hand and then rinsed in another tank or in running water, to power washing machines in which the fruit is dumped on a conveyor and passes through the acid wash, then is rinsed, the excess moisture removed, and finally delivered to the grading and sizing machine automatically.

There are in use several types of power machines which wash the fruit satisfactorily, varying chiefly in the method by which the acid is applied and the way the fruit is rinsed and dried. The best results are apparently obtained with the types of machines that apply the acid to the fruit under very low pressure with a diffused or fanlike spray, or by pouring it over the fruit in large volume. Washers which submerge the fruit under the surface of the liquid or which direct a jet under high pressure on the apples are liable to cause injury to some varieties of apples.

It was found in 1927 that one type of machine which was well designed from an engineering standpoint was not at all adapted to the cleaning of apples. In this machine the fruit was forced 5 or 6 feet below the surface of the liquid and held there for several minutes. In some apples the calyx tube is open direct from the blossom end of the fruit to the core cavity, and when such fruit was submerged some of the acid solution was forced through the calyx tube into the core cavity, carrying with it any fungous spores that might be suspended therein. As there was considerable decay in fruit washed in this type of washer, it has been practically abandoned in the fruit districts of the West. Somewhat similar conditions occur when a jet under high pressure strikes the open calyx tube of an apple.

Importance of Thorough Rinsing

It is important also that the fruit be rinsed thoroughly after being washed with acid, (1) to remove the acid so that there will be no possibility of hydrochloric acid burning, and (2) because the acid solution dissolves the arsenical residue on the sprayed fruit and this arsenical solution is liable to cause injury, especially around the calyx end of the apple. In commercial operations acid injury is seldom found. Arsenical injury occurs somewhat more frequently. If the fruit is thoroughly rinsed after being treated, so that the acid and soluble arsenic are all removed, there is little danger of injury from either even if the fruit is packed wet, although drying or partial drying is recommended.

The concentrations of acid employed range from 0.32 to 1.30 per cent hydrochloric acid by weight, depending on the amount of spray residue present. The solution is usually not heated, although it may be heated to 100° F. without danger of injury to the late-season fruit.

As in all packing operations the fruit must be handled with care to avoid bruising, cutting, or stem punctures. It is possible that some little damage may occur in the extra handling caused by washing, and it is quite probable that some of the earlier machines did not handle the fruit with sufficient care. However, there has been surprisingly little injury to the fruit from washing, and the results obtained by various investigators in their experimental work, as well as surveys of fruit handled and stored commercially, indicate that this method of removing arsenical residue is safe and reliable.

This process of washing apples in preparation for market has been very generally adopted in the Pacific Northwest, California, New Jersey, Colorado, and Idaho, where the spray schedules are heavy, and in some of these localities for both Bartlett and late varieties of pears. It was estimated that between 20,000 and 30,000 carloads of the 1927 crop of apples and pears were washed

Other Products Carrying Spray Residue

In addition to apples and pears, there are a number of other fruits and vegetables sprayed with arsenicals and which at harvest time may bear a concentration of arsenic that would be considered deleterious to the health of the consumer. Chili peppers, grown in California, require heavy applications of arsenical sprays, and the excess residue must be removed before they can be marketed. Celery in some localities is sprayed heavily with arsenic and needs cleaning. With some of these crops the washing process has been used with considerable success.

LON A. HAWKINS.

STANDARD of Living May Be Improved by Use of Family Budget The popular method of raising the standard of living of farm families is, and justly so, an attempt by every means possible to increase the annual family income. A cash income of $1,000 in place of $800 may give, a small margin for items of comfort, health, pleasure, and culture, which will enable a farm family to hold a more self-respecting, desirable, and satisfying position in community life. In the midst of high endeavors to increase income, however, there is a second supporting line of attack to improve living conditions for the family—namely, through improved methods of turning income, such as it may be, into the goods, services, and facilities for family living which make up the family budget. This method, although not receiving much public attention—probably because everyone thinks the expenditures of the family which lives on narrow margins are pretty well determined by necessity on the one hand, and by the market price of goods, services, and facilities, on the other hand—still holds out several chances of improvement that merit serious consideration.

In a series of studies of the farmer's standard of family living (covering during the past six years more than 5,000 farm families in 15 States) it was found that broadly speaking there were two standards of living on farms: That of families living on good land on fair-sized farms, and that of families on poor land on undersized farms. For a household of 4.8 persons the average total living, including use of house and all food and other goods furnished by the farm, on good land, was in the neighborhood of $1,500; for five persons on poor land, in the neighborhood of $900. The percentage of the total amount which, in the first case, went for food was 41.2 per cent; for clothing, 14.7 per cent; for health, 3.8 per cent; for advancement (education, not including school taxes, church, reading, outings, etc.), 5.6 per cent; in the second instance, for food, 49 per cent; clothing, 6.7 per cent; health, 3.3 per cent; and advancement, 4.9 per cent.

Planning the Budget Pays

The first chance of improvement in living can not be said to be popular. It requires more painstaking care than many people will give the matter. The method is this: Planning the family budget in advance, year by year, distributing the expected income among the various needs so as to keep putting a larger percentage of income into the particular needs which mean a higher plane of living for members of the family than the hit-or-miss spending will provide. The wisdom of this procedure is borne out in the history of budget making. It invariably surprises a family, a firm, a corporation, or a nation to see the sum total of saving in expenditures by careful advance budgeting, and holding to the budget through the year.

The second line of improvement in turning income into goods is well known in theory, but in the United States falls far short of the

FIGURE 213.—Farmers' cooperative laundry, River Falls, Wis., erected in 1914; present value of plant, $15,646. Business of $491 done in 1914 had increased to $27,483 in 1927, of which $1,302 was profit

possible in practice. The farmers of several countries in Europe are especially proficient in this method, namely, collective turn of income into goods and services required—a species of consumers' cooperation. I do not refer here to cooperative stores for purchases, but rather to cooperative bargaining on the part of a group of families for various goods at regular trade establishments.

The third method of getting more value out of family income looks ahead a few years. It is still in the nature of collective consumers' effort, namely, wide collective effort of families to establish accessible facilities close to the farms for health, pleasure, comfort, advancement. This type of effort brings to pass a country hospital, a country playground, cooperative electric light and power, a rural laundry (fig. 213), a country library. This method requires considerable belief in the values to be obtained, on the part of the whole community; it requires unusually strong and consistent leadership; it requires a sustained support of the community clear through to ultimate working success; it requires a plan based on sound financial principles. Rare examples of this type of collective effort may be found in scattered farm communities in every State.

The wisdom, on the whole, of a scientifically planned income-spending program for farm families, as a line of economic tactics supporting the major strategy of the income-producing attack is so obvious that the wonder is that so little public attention has been given to it hitherto in the United States.

C. J. Galpin.

SUGAR-BEET Disease Control Progressing Toward Solution The sugar beet, in common with other agricultural crops, is subject in certain seasons to severe disease attack. The diseases vary somewhat with the geographical areas, and they vary in intensity from season to season. In the humid regions of eastern United States the chief diseases causing damage to the sugar-beet crop are seedling diseases of the damping-off type, root rot, and occasionally in seasons of abundant rainfall, Cercospora leaf spot. In the mid-west area Cercospora leaf spot and root rots are the most serious diseases, although nematode infestation of the soil has become increasingly important. In the far western areas curly top and nematode injury are of paramount importance.

Control measures for sugar-beet disease must take into consideration the local conditions, and the type of control must be adjusted to meet the situation.

For the eastern area the enormous loss caused by seedling diseases is a matter of grave concern. In certain seasons in Michigan, for example, as much as one-quarter of the acreage planted has had to be reseeded or has been abandoned because of failure to secure adequate stand. The stand on a considerable portion of the acreage left has been so poor as to make continuance of the crop in those fields a doubtful venture. The seedling diseases in the humid areas arise from common damping-off organisms such as *Pythium* spp., *Rhizoctonia* spp., and other soil-inhabiting organisms. *Phoma betae*, which is commonly introduced with the seed, is also an important pathogene.

Methods of seed treatment in which the seed is dusted with finely divided mercury and copper compounds have proved successful in protecting young seedlings not alone from the seed-borne organisms but also from the organisms of a soil source which attack the young seedling. The most promising dusts for this purpose have been some of the commercial organic mercury compounds, but excellent results have been obtained by use of mixtures of corrosive sublimate and copper carbonate. In areas where stands are likely to be injured by fungous attack if weather conditions are not favorable, the coating of the sugar-beet seed with some form of mercury compound, in strength not great enough to retard germination, promises to be extremely beneficial. Furthermore, the root rots which later in the season decimate stands of half-grown or nearly mature beets frequently arise from infection during the seedling stage. Seed treatment within certain limits will assist in general root-rot control.

May Cause Stunting

The Cercospora leaf spot may produce a marked stunting effect upon the crop if the attack takes on the form of an early epidemic. When the attack comes late in August and September, the continued loss of leaves which characterizes this disease depresses the sugar yield from 2 to 4 per cent. Direct control measures, consisting of four or five applications of Bordeaux mixture or the same number of applications of copper sulphate-lime dusts, have given successful control of leaf spot. In areas where leaf spot is a menace every season, spraying or dusting would be warranted, in the light of present results. For many regions, however, since the amount of leaf-spot damage varies from season to season, the practicability of spraying or dusting is still undetermined. In a year of severe attack the cost of treatment would be far exceeded by the gain in tonnage and in sugar percentage. In years of light attack the benefits would not be so marked, while in the absence of leaf spot there would be no returns from treatment. In

FIGURE 214.—Comparison of various sugar-beet seed treatments. Each lot of seed is planted in a single row, five times repeated in scattered locations in the plot. Rows 1, 4, 7, 10, and 13 were planted with untreated seed. These check rows run through the entire planting. Rows 5-A, 8-A, and 14-A were planted with seed treated with different commercial dusts containing organic mercury compounds. Rows 6-A and 9-A were planted with seed treated with specially devised mixtures of corrosive sublimate and copper carbonate. Seed used in rows 11-A and 12-A was treated with copper compounds. Seed used in rows 2-A and 3-A was pasteurized for a few minutes at 60° C., the 3-A material being subjected to weak formaldehyde fumes as well. All results in the other series, B, C, D, and E, were entirely consistent with what is shown in series A. (East Lansing, Mich., 1928.)

short, leaf spot can be controlled by applications of fungicide, but each year presents its own problems as to the advisability of such an additional expense.

For combating leaf spot and curly top, attempts are being made to develop resistant varieties of satisfactory commercial type. At the beginning of this work no commercial variety or strain was found showing any superiority to any other in resistance to either leaf spot or curly top. Among the many select lines of sugar beets produced by plant breeders of the Office of Sugar Plants, promising material from the standpoint of disease resistance was found. This material is being severely tested under epidemic conditions to eliminate the non-resistant forms and the forms of unsatisfactory commercial type. Many stocks of fairly resistant sugar beets which give promise of making a satisfactory crop in spite of diseases have now been obtained.

Primitive beet types of the species *Beta maritima* have been tested for curly top and Cercospora leaf-spot resistance, and some of these have been found which have far more resistance than any of the commercial strains of beets. It is noteworthy that these wild beets have a satisfactory sugar content but are lacking in size and in root type. These have been hybridized with commercial beets, and the progenies thus obtained showed much promise in the tests of 1928. It is possible that from these crosses resistant types of sugar beets may be obtained.

Responds to Good Treatment

In the control of the various diseases of the sugar beet, probably no factor is of more importance than good agricultural practice. Each season sees gains in this regard. Farmers are recognizing that the sugar beet responds promptly to good treatment. The wholesale disregard of crop rotation is a thing of the past, and farmers in the western areas are successfully avoiding nematode loss by long-time rotations. Similarly, the establishment of long-time crop rotations in place of the beet and grain alternations which have been the rule in many sections is doing much to reduce leaf-spot losses. Careful seed-bed preparation and improved drainage, together with selective thinning to leave the healthy, sturdy beet, are proving to be of great value in improving stands of sugar beets. The application of fertilizers in the row with the seed is pronounced in its effect on stand and vigor and in the avoidance of root rot. Prompt cultivation of fields, as soon as the rows can be followed, has proved efficacious in saving many stands from seedling diseases.

Viewing the disease situation as a whole, it may safely be said that many of the problems in sugar-beet growing are on the way to solution by the application of rational control measures and sound agricultural practice.

G. H. COONS.

SUGAR-BEET Leaf Hopper Studies Afford Basis for Damage Forecasts Direct methods of controlling the sugar-beet leaf hopper (*Eutettix tenellus* Baker) have often been tried, but without success. The failure has chiefly been due to two causes; (1) the insect is migratory in habit; (2) it is a virus carrier, and can leave seriously damaged beets behind it, even if it is destroyed shortly after reaching the beet fields.

Because this tiny leaf hopper has assumed such importance in influencing the development of the beet-sugar industry the attention of investigators has been turned to other and more indirect ways of escaping the heavy losses caused by it. The type of investigation now receiving most attention by entomologists deals with the study of the distribution and migration of the insect. The information thus obtained serves a twofold purpose. In the first place, it is possible to discover areas in which the insect is not known to occur and into which it migrates only at infrequent intervals; such areas give promise of being suitable for the production of sugar beets, at least in so far as the insect is concerned.

Secondly, a careful analysis of the results of studies of distribution and migration often enables the investigator to indicate years in which the insect may invade territory where it does not normally occur in destructive numbers. Information of this character is of great economic value. Under the normal method of planting sugar beets in the presence of the leaf hopper, heavy losses from it are generally followed by reduced acreages. As a result, in many cases small acreages are planted in years in which little injury is experienced. As the confidence of the industry returns, the acreage is increased until it is likely to reach a maximum just in time to suffer another heavy reverse. As a result of predicting the probable destructive presence of the insect it is possible to reduce acreages in years when the outlook for a favorable season is poor, and to encourage the planting of heavier acreages in years in which light losses should be experienced.

Fundamental Problems Studied

These investigations have been materially assisted by the vigorous prosecution of research of a fundamental nature into the relations existing between the insect and its environment. This research, initiated and carried on primarily as a purely academic phase of the problem, has proven to be the most fruitful source of data of great economic usefulness. Stations for observation have been set up in the breeding grounds of the insect in the desert, and the biology of the insect studied there throughout the year, so that progress has been made in determining the factors responsible for large populations of the pest, the relations between the insect, its host plants, and the virus carried by it, and the effect of climatic factors on all of these. These data have been used as a basis for predictions of outbreaks of the leaf hopper. Such advice as a guide to planting has necessarily been limited to a comparatively small area in southern Idaho which could be studied in sufficient detail to obtain the necessary data upon which it could be based.

The results of this work have enabled producers of sugar beets in the area under investigation to regulate their acreages according to the outlook, with the result that in 1927, after a favorable forecast, a large acreage was planted. The resulting crop was one of the greatest ever harvested in that area. In 1928, after a prediction of serious injury by the leaf hopper, the acreage of sugar beets was greatly reduced, thus enabling the growers to escape the heavy losses which would have followed such a general planting of sugar beets as has normally followed a good year. In each case the prediction included an accurate summary of insect conditions. It is hoped that a further study of the relationship of the leaf hopper to its environment will permit the extension of this service to other areas as required.

WALTER CARTER.

SUGAR-BEET Leaf Spot Controlled by Dusting from an Auto Truck Experiments at Rocky Ford, Colo., in cooperation with the American Beet Sugar Co., have shown that sugar-beet leaf spot can be successfully controlled even under epidemic conditions by applications of a dust containing dehydrated copper sulphate, 20 per cent, and hydrated lime, 80 per cent. Four or five applications made at 10-day intervals, beginning when the crop was about 2 months old, have sufficed to keep the foliage from showing any marked injury from leaf spot.

In order to extend the area and to increase the speed with which fields could be dusted, a commercial duster driven by a gasoline engine was mounted upon an automobile truck, and this outfit proved to be a very successful means of making dust applications.

Sugar beets in the Arkansas Valley districts are planted in 20-inch rows, with occasional fields using 22-inch and 24-inch spacing.   The truck has a tread of 56 inches and was found to run without injury to to the plants in fields with a 20-inch spacing, but it could not be used in fields where 22-inch spacing was used.   In fields spaced 24 inches to the row the truck could be used only when the beets were small.

For successful operation in the field the truck must start with the left wheels in what is called the "guess" row; that is, in the row between successive bouts of the 4-row planter.   With this arrangement the driver of the truck can adjust the movement of the truck to follow any deviations in the beet rows.   Irrigation furrows assist the driver in holding the truck in the proper place.   The truck can be driven from 7 to 10 miles an hour through the fields without injury to the plants, and the lateral ditches encountered in the larger fields have

FIGURE 215.—Auto truck equipped with duster for use in dusting sugar beets

not presented any difficulty so long as the footing was dry.   In some cases it has been necessary to employ planks to provide firm footing where the ditch banks were wet.   Injury to the plants at the ends of the field where the truck was turned was not greater than occurs with ordinary cultivations.

Wheel guards to turn back the beet leaves are an essential feature of the outfit.   These were made from 20-gauge galvanized sheet iron and were placed in front and at the sides of the wheels.   The duster was equipped with an apron of canvas which trailed behind and served to check the dissipation of the dust by the wind.   Eight rows were dusted at one time.

The speed of coverage together with the capacity for transport of materials would seem to make the truck duster serviceable for the protection of many crops.

GEORGE H. COONS and
DEWEY STEWART.

SUGAR-BEET Seed in
New Mexico Grown
by Rapid Method

The United States sugar-beet industry
has always been almost entirely dependent upon European producers for its
seed supply. This has been due pri-
marily to the fact that American sugar-beet growers have not been
able to produce the seed as cheaply as they could buy the imported
seed. The production of sugar-beet seed, therefore, has not been
established as an industry in this country. As a result of dependence
upon European seed, the sugar-beet industry was seriously handicapped during the World War. At that time the quality of European
seed deteriorated, and much of it was also found to be adulterated
with stock-beet seed. This situation resulted in attempts being made
by some of the American sugar-beet companies to produce their own
seed, but in recent years the industry has again become almost entirely
dependent upon European seed. The advantages of a domestic production of beet seed are obvious.

The New Mexico Agricultural Experiment Station, in cooperation
with the Office of Sugar Plants, Bureau of Plant Industry, United
States Department of Agriculture, has conducted experiments with
sugar-beet seed production from fall plantings by which the beets are
overwintered in the field. The beets make considerable growth in the
fall, and when the warm spring weather opens practically all of them
produce seed stalks. The tests have extended over a 6-year period,
and the results have been the same every year in that the beets
produced a good seed crop the following season. The crop in southern
New Mexico is harvested about July 1, and the time required for seed
production is reduced by about one-half over the time required by
ordinary methods.

Average Yields 1,500 Pounds an Acre

Average yields of approximately 1,500 pounds of seed to the acre
can be obtained, and in one instance a yield of 3,400 pounds was
obtained. The crop that was harvested in 1927 indicated that the
highest yields were obtained when the beets were planted at the rate
of 18 pounds of seed to the acre and left unthinned. The 1928 results
have been even more encouraging, and it was shown that the highest
yield of seed was obtained when the seed was planted broadcast with
a grain drill at the rate of 60 pounds to the acre. By planting in this
manner a yield of 2,186 pounds per acre was obtained. Tests have
shown that unthinned planting yields much more seed than when the
beets are spaced 12 or 24 inches apart. When the beets were planted
in 22-inch rows and spaced 12 inches apart the yield was 912 pounds
to the acre, but when unthinned the yield was 2,025 pounds. The
germination of the 1927 crop was low, but it is believed that this
difficulty has been overcome by proper irrigation during the pollination period. The seed produced in 1928 is apparently of good quality.

The great saving that can be made in time and labor indicates that
the production of sugar-beet seed in southern New Mexico may have
important commercial advantages.

JOHN C. OVERPECK.

S UGAR Beets With Only
One Viable Seed Would
Reduce Costs Greatly

Efforts have been made from time to time by plant breeders to develop a strain of sugar beets having only one viable seed in the cluster so as to reduce the expense of handwork in thinning. If this could be done an acre of beets could be produced at a fraction of the present cost, as nearly all the work of planting and cultivation could be done by machinery, cutting out the expensive hand labor.

The department worked on this problem for a number of years. Considerable progress was made by selection of plants showing the single-germ tendency. When the work began under C. O. Townsend and E. C. Rittue the average production of single germ seed was 1 in 2,000. The tendency was increased by selection to about 50 per cent single-germ seed. Progress beyond this point appeared to be difficult.

With increased knowledge of the science of genetics and new methods of causing variation through the use of radiation and the probability of inducing sports in this direction, plant breeders should be on the lookout for plants that show this tendency and renew the effort to make progress in this direction. It would be of great value to the beet-sugar industry.

. A. F. Woods.

S UGAR Cane Requires
Nitrogen As Chief
Plant-Food Element

The average results of preliminary study show that nitrogen is the plant-food element most essential to sugar cane, though phosphoric acid and potash may also be necessary for best results on certain soils. The immediate effects of an application of soluble nitrates are darker-green foliage and increased growth. Nitrates may also affect the ripening of the cane and thus the purity and percentage of sucrose in the juice at harvest. The amount of available nitrogen in the soil and fluctuations in temperature and moisture tend to complicate the problem of determining the effect of nitrogen as a fertilizer.

In Louisiana in 1922, 1923, and 1924 experiments were conducted under average plantation conditions on the older varieties of cane, D 74 and Louisiana Purple. Twenty-one mixtures, all containing different proportions of nitrogen, phosphoric acid, and potash, were used. Six mixtures, including one of nitrogen alone, two of nitrogen and phosphoric acid, two of nitrogen and potash, and one of all three elements, produced an average of 19.08 tons of cane to the acre. Similar mixtures, in which phosphoric acid predominated, gave an average yield of 16.96 tons, and mixtures in which potash predominated gave an average of 16.48 tons. The average yield of 26 unfertilized plots was 15.84 tons. The average percentage of sucrose for the fertilized groups was 10.72 per cent, 10.12 per cent, and 10.80 per cent, respectively, and for the unfertilized was 10.35 per cent.

Fertilizer Studies with Disease-Resistant Strains

Owing to the ravages of disease in the D 74 and Louisiana Purple varieties of sugar cane the experiment was shifted in 1925 to the new disease-resistant P. O. J. canes. In 1926 the P. O. J. 234 variety was used. The six mixtures highest in nitrogen gave an average of 23.3 tons to the acre, those in which phosphoric acid predominated gave an average of 20.5, and those highest in potash gave 19.8 tons. The average of 30 checks was 19 tons to the acre.

The experiment was repeated in 1927 with the new P. O. J. 213 variety of cane on land on which a heavy growth of soy beans had been turned under about two months prior to planting the cane. The six mixtures highest in nitrogen produced an average of 26.18 tons to the acre, those in which phosphoric acid predominated produced 23.39 tons, and those richest in potash produced 24.96 tons. The average of 16 unfertilized plots was 24.16 tons to the acre. No conclusions can be drawn from the analysis of the cane from the different plots, as it differed very slightly.

It was hoped that the preliminary studies described would yield readily available information for the guidance of sugar-cane planters in fertilizing the new varieties of sugar cane. A field station now being established in the heart of the sugar-cane belt has increased facilities for the study of soil-fertility problems affecting sugar cane. The effect of the different sources of nitrogen, of green manuring, moisture content, temperature, and liming, all of which may influence the effect of nitrogen as a fertilizer for sugar cane, are also to be studied.

Lewis A. Hurst.

SUGAR-CANE Varieties for Sirup Production Now Being Tried Out Nearly a decade ago the principal sirup-making sections of the eastern Gulf States began to experience a gradual falling off in the yields of sugar cane. The principal cause was the attack of the cane by the mosaic disease. Practically all varieties then in common use (except the Old Small Japanese) are highly susceptible to the disease and suffer serious reductions in yield when fully infected. The disease spread rapidly, until now there is apparently more or less infection in nearly all sections of the eastern Gulf States where sugar cane is grown.

Even before the farmers noticed a falling off in the yield measures were taken to find means of avoiding the losses due to this disease. As no remedy was known it became apparent at once that the best hope lay in the direction of immune or resistant varieties. Collecting and testing new varieties of cane, which had already been begun, were therefore pursued with increased vigor. Among imported varieties already on hand highly resistant or tolerant ones were found, and the supply of seed cane of the most promising one of these, the Cayana variety (originally designated Cayana-10), had been increased through distribution from a field station sufficient to supply all demands by the time the cane growers became aware of a decreasing yield and the need of a change of variety.

The Cayana was found to outyield greatly the old varieties, even when the old varieties did not suffer the handicap due to the disease. The old varieties now practically cease to produce paying stubble crops, while the Cayana makes from two to four successful stubble crops. It is a popular variety in the sirup-producing sections where it was early introduced.

The Cayana cane, however, has some serious disadvantages. The stalks are slender and the leaf sheathes adhere closely, thus greatly increasing the harvesting expenses. It is tough and fibrous, requiring strong mills and abundant power to grind. The sirup usually has more sediment, which the operator fails to remove by skimming during the boiling process, the common mode of clarification. The flavor of the sirup is pronounced by some consumers to be inferior to that from the old varieties, while others judge it equally good.

Other Kinds Resemble Cayana

Several other highly mosaic-resistant varieties, including Tekcha, Yontanzan, Kikaigashima, and Oshima, all from Japan, Uba from Natal, Khera from India, and Kavangire from Argentina, all closely resemble the Cayana, possessing the same advantages and disadvantages. There is no evidence, however, that any of these are superior to the Cayana, and there is evidence in the case of at least some of them that they are inferior in some respects. For these reasons none of them have been generally distributed among the farmers.

Many other varieties have been imported and tested, but most of them are inferior in yield to the Cayana. Among the newer importations are several Java seedlings. In yield, none of these are specially attractive for sirup canes, but P. O. J. 213 is the most promising. Each year, in addition to testing the imported varieties, from 100 to 500 promising new seedling varieties are selected and tested. While tests with these have not proceeded far enough to justify recommending any of them for general adoption in the sirup-producing sections, favorable results indicate that a few of them may be worthy of replacing the Cayana, as well as the old varieties.

P. A. YODER.

SUGAR Industry Saved in Louisiana by Using Disease-Resistant Varieties of Cane — Now that the reconstitution of the sugar industry in its traditional American home, Louisiana, seems well assured by the adoption of mosaic-tolerating cane varieties, it may be interesting to take stock of a few salient facts obtained by examining recorded statistics.

The year 1926 was the last in which the State's production of sugar was made from the "old" varieties D74, Ribbon, and Purple. From 127,916 acres of sugar cane harvested the yield was 6.7 tons per acre and the total production of sugar was 47,166 short tons, the lowest in half a century. A negligible proportion was made from the mosaic-tolerating varieties, as these were commercially grown on but part of a single plantation.

In 1927, due to the energetic activities of a thoroughly awakened minority of planters, one-fourth of the total acreage was planted in the mosaic-tolerating varieties. From the total of 72,987 acres harvested the yield of cane was 13.4 tons per acre and 70,792 short tons of sugar was produced.

This year, 1928, the Bureau of Agricultural Economics estimates that slightly over three-fourths of the total acreage has been planted to the mosaic-tolerating varieties. From 179,900 acres planted, of which it is estimated that the cane from 144,500 acres will be used for sugar, this bureau estimates a yield of 17.5 tons of cane per acre and a total production for the State of 171,000 short tons of sugar. As the yield of the old varieties, occupying still some 40,000 of the total of 179,900 acres, will not average much over 7 or 8 tons of cane per acre, it is obvious that the mosaic-tolerating varieties will yield well over 20 tons per acre. Although the grinding season has just started at this writing exceptionally high yields have already been reported for individual fields cut for seed. One planter reports 37 tons per acre of 213 P. O. J. and another 46 tons per acre of 36 P. O. J., both plant cane. The 1928 crop should be worth about $21,000,000, as compared with only $7,000,000 from a materially greater acreage in 1926.

Increased Use of Tolerant Varieties

The prospects are that the crop being planted for the harvest of 1929 will be almost entirely of the mosaic-tolerating varieties, and that practically a normal acreage will be planted to canes destined to outyield the old varieties even as they were in the days before mosaic had been introduced and become widespread.

It is perhaps too early to record a complete history of the sugar-cane mosaic epiphytotic in Louisiana. After the first crop made entirely of the mosaic-tolerating varieties has been crushed and converted into sugar, the writer, who introduced the original cuttings from which the present vast acreage has been propagated and who first commended them to the attention of Louisiana planters, hopes to assemble a fully documented record of this interesting period in the history of one of our oldest agricultural industries as another object lesson in the value to farming of modern scientific methods.

During the last decade this disease has attracted world-wide attention and has been the subject of investigations in 22 cane-producing countries. Some of these countries have adopted measures that have reduced the losses to a considerable extent. In other countries, including some of the leading exporters of sugar, such as Cuba, the losses have not yet reached the point where danger to the continued existence of the industry has forced the adoption of drastic measures on a large scale. In general, the means by which relief has been effected was the substitution of immune or tolerant varieties. The Province of Tucuman, Argentina, obtained relief in this way in complete ignorance of the fact that an infectious disease was being dealt with. Due to the fortuitous circumstance that a Dutch scientist employed to head the newly organized experiment station, had anticipated his arrival to report for duty at Tucuman by sending a miscellaneous collection of cane varieties, the station had at its disposal the means for a practical solution of the problem. The Dutch scientist failed to arrive, but his successor solicitously preserved the variety collection and started a series of carefully recorded plot tests with them in comparison with the commercially grown varieties. Fortunately, there were included the varieties later proved by the United States Department of Agriculture to be mosaic-tolerating, and their superiority in yield over the old varieties, whose failure was ascribed to degeneration or running out, was quickly demonstrated. This illustrates the value of careful observation and recording of the performance of crop plants even in the absence of exact knowledge of the biological facts involved.

Principal Facts About Mosaic

Practically all the fundamental biological facts concerned with sugar-cane mosaic have been elucidated by the Office of Sugar Plants of the Bureau of Plant Industry in this department, and with the hearty cooperation of a small group of enlightened planters they have been put to practical use in the rehabilitation of the Louisiana sugar industry. These facts, affirmed when knowledge of cane mosaic was practically all conjectural, include the following: That mosaic is caused by a virulent substance introduced into healthy plants; that the virus resides only in infected plants and nowhere else, except during the short period when it is transported from diseased to healthy plants; that the virus is transported from diseased to healthy plants by the medium of an insect vector, *Aphis maidis;* that the virus is injected by the insect into the phloem cells of the vascular bundles of leaves and is probably translocated to all parts of the plant through this system of tissues; that this identical virus attacks other genera of grasses, including many common weeds of the cane fields and cultivated crop plants and ornamental grasses, causing symptoms similar to those found in sugar cane; that inoculum derived from these other grasses is effective in causing the disease in sugar cane; that affected plants sometimes recover and give rise to healthy sprouts; that the insect vector responsible for the spread of the disease under natural conditions may be carried long distances by the wind; evidence of the existence of a considerable variation in severity of the disease among the different varieties of sugar cane susceptible to it; evidence of the existence of immune varieties of sugar cane; evidence that under different environmental conditions the same variety of cane will react differently to the disease.

These proved facts have been the basis of recommendations for control of mosaic announced by the United States Department of Agriculture, and although economic considerations have operated to make difficult the adoption in Louisiana of a rational system based wholly on biological facts, the practical solution of the problem of control is well advanced. Undiminished efforts are being continued to obtain varieties that may be more resistant to mosaic and to the other unfavorable conditions existing in parts of the sugar belt. A large collection of varieties has recently been brought to Washington from the heretofore unexplored interior of the island of New Guinea, obtained by the department's airplane expedition to that country, the original home of the "noble" type of sugar cane. These will shortly be tested for adaptation to conditions in Louisiana.

E. W. BRANDES.

SWEET Clover in Dry-Farming Belt, Once Started, Rarely Fails — Sweet clover, either alone or in combination with grasses, is rapidly increasing in popularity in the Great Plains States. Wherever the annual rainfall is 15 inches or more, sweet clover can be grown successfully with at least as much regularity as wheat. Like all cultivated crops under dry farming, sweet clover is subject to failures of the seeding, but when the crop is once started it rarely fails thereafter. Unlike other legumes, sweet clover is not often injured by drought, grasshoppers, rabbits, or even sand and hail storms, and it does not usually cause bloat when pastured. Because of its hardiness, sweet clover will probably become the standard leguminous pasture crop of the semiarid region.

Recent experiments have indicated several practices that increase the chances of obtaining a stand of sweet clover. Chief among these are early planting and a firm seed bed. The most reliable time for seeding is late winter.　Beginning in northern Texas about January 15, the most favorable planting date recedes northward until it becomes March 15 at the Canadian boundary.　Each week that planting is delayed after the most favorable date greatly lessens the chances of obtaining a stand and markedly reduces the size of the plants.

Sweet clover is even more sensitive to a loose, dry seed bed under dry farming than under humid farming.　A hard, compact seed bed is absolutely essential.　The most consistent success with sweet clover has been had from drilling unhulled or unscarified seed on sorghum, corn, or Sudan-grass stubble.　Complete failure usually follows seeding on freshly plowed land.　Planting later than April 15 on loose soil is simply inviting disaster.

Method of Planting Important

While not so imperative as date of planting, the method of planting is also important.　Drilled stands are nearly always better than seed-

FIGURE 216.—Second-year sweet clover yielding pasturage for two animals per acre in the Palouse district of Idaho

ings broadcast by hand, especially if a press drill or some means of firming the soil around the seed is used.　However, hand sowing on frozen ground in February is better than machine sowing in April or May.

The use or nonuse of a nurse crop depends chiefly on the weediness of the land.　Upon soil that is reasonably free of weed seeds, as good clean sorghum stubble, sweet clover may be seeded alone, and, in favorable years, a good crop of hay harvested in the fall.　If it is felt that a grain crop is necessary, a half seeding of wheat or barley will not injure the stand of clover, but the clover plants will not be large enough to cut for hay in the fall except in exceptional years.　A full seeding of grain eliminates the hay crop and may in dry years destroy the sweet-clover stand.

On weedy land there is nothing to do but use a nurse crop.　In dry years there will then be a poor crop of grain, a fair crop of weeds, and no clover.　In wet years there will be a good crop of grain and of weeds and a fair crop of clover.   Without the grain for a nurse crop, the weeds will outgrow the clover in both dry and wet years.   The best type of nurse crop varies in different localities, but in general is in the descending order of winter wheat, flax, spring wheat, barley, and oats.

Much interest is expressed in the possibility of getting sweet clover established in native sod.   The chances are against this, principally because the sweet-clover seed can not easily get down through the sod into the soil.   Some success has been had by drilling the seed into the sod during a thaw in February or March.   Others have obtained stands of sweet clover through sod land by plowing shallow furrows 3 feet apart across the field and sowing sweet clover in the fresh earth thus turned.   Still others sow the unhulled seed in the sod in late fall and have it tramped into the soil with sheep during the winter and early spring.

A better way to obtain the full value from sweet clover is to rotate it with Sudan grass.   The Sudan grass provides excellent grazing during the 6-weeks' gap that is likely to occur in midsummer between the time when the old sweet clover is finished and the new seeding of sweet clover is large enough for pasturing.   The Sudan-grass stubble then provides an excellent seed bed for the next sweet-clover seeding.

L. W. KEPHART.

SWEET Potatoes As Possible Source of Starch Investigated   Starches of various types and grades are used in a great variety of industries. Starch (principally corn) is also a raw material for the manufacture of modified starches, dextrins, corn sirup, and corn sugar.   The industrial value of starches used as such is based primarily upon adhesiveness, viscosity, penetrating power, and gloss.   These properties differ in starches of various types and sources, and this variation results in some difference in price and adaptability for various purposes.

Although starch can be obtained from many plants, the principal source of starch in this country is corn.   Production of starch from potatoes is practically confined to the State of Maine, where this industry serves as a means of utilization of cull potatoes.

The question whether starch can be recovered economically from cull sweet potatoes and satisfactorily used for industrial purposes has recently been raised.   Sweet potatoes constitute the second largest vegetable crop in the United States, the production for 1927 being 94,000,000 bushels.   A large quantity of culls results from the grading of sweet potatoes, averaging possibly 20 per cent of the total crop, and the production of starch is being considered as a possible means of using this waste.   At present there are no means of utilizing cull sweet potatoes other than as hog and cattle feed.

The recovery of starch from cull sweet potatoes is being investigated by the Bureau of Chemistry and Soils of this department.   A number of factors require careful consideration in order to determine whether such an undertaking is feasible.   Among these are deterioration during storage, cost of transportation, and price which can be paid to producers.   There are also a number of chemical and technological problems, such as production of a starch sufficiently light in color, determination of the characteristics of the starch and suitability for various purposes, and the utilization of other constituents of the sweet

FIGURE 217.—Starch plant at Arlington Experiment Farm, Va.

potato. In addition to the production of starch and by-products, other means of utilizing cull sweet potatoes are being investigated.

H. S. PAINE.

TAX Relief Sought Through Controlling Local Expenditures—Reduction in farm taxes may come through shifting the tax burden to other groups. It may also come through reduction in the expenditures of governmental units. Farmers and farm groups have taken a wide interest in the first method and some progress has been made in securing increased revenues from sources other than the general property tax. More attention should be devoted to the second method of reduction.

Tax money collected from farmers is spent largely by the counties and smaller governmental units. A recent report in South Dakota indicates that over an 8-year period 51 per cent of all taxes on farm

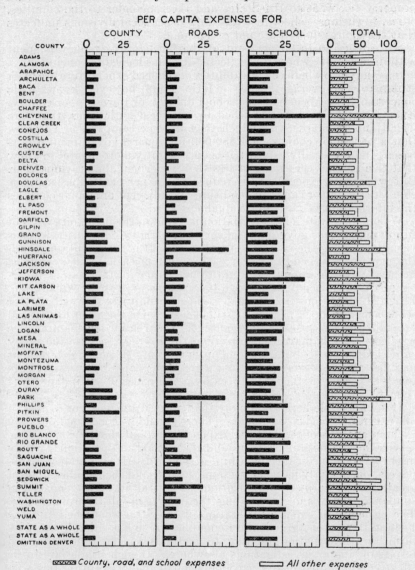

FIGURE 218.—Per capita annual county and local disbursements by counties, Colorado, 5-year average, 1921–1925. County expenses are those devoted to general governmental purposes in the counties. The school and road classifications are self-explanatory. All other expenses include irrigation district charges, city expense, and a miscellaneous group which amounts to about 3 per cent of the whole

property in the section studied was levied by the townships and the school districts, 33 per cent was levied by the counties, and only 16 per cent by the State. In Colorado about 15 per cent of the property tax is levied for the State and 85 per cent for the counties and smaller units.   In Arkansas the State takes 20 per cent of the total tax levied; the remaining 80 per cent goes to the smaller divisions.   The fact that in 1922 for the country as a whole only 10 per cent of the general property tax went to the States and the remainder to the counties, cities, townships, school districts, and other local divisions indicates that the figures quoted are not exceptional.

Since from 80 to 90 per cent of the farmers' tax money is spent within the county where it is collected it seems logical to conclude that here is the place where the possibilities of reduced expenditure are most striking.   The average farmer or farm group, however, knows little concerning the expenses of the school district, or township, or county. Even if the figures are published by the local authorities, there are usually no standards with which they may be compared.   To know that a particular county paid $80,000 for general governmental purposes is not especially helpful; it is only slightly more helpful to know that this is 5 per cent more or less than was spent the previous year. But when this expenditure is reduced to a per capita basis and is compared with per capita expenditures in adjacent or similar counties the information begins to be valuable.

Within any State a large variation is found in the per capita costs of supplying various governmental services.   Figure 218 illustrates this variation among the counties of Colorado.   It is not maintained that the per capita expenditures for each object in each county could be reduced to the minimum or even to the average for the State.   But it is urged that expenditures above the average need some explanation. Physical conditions may make road expenditures heavy.   Better schools may increase per capita school costs.   On the other hand, road expenditures may be high because of construction or maintenance wastes.   Schools may cost more than the average because too many small independent units are kept in operation.   County government may be taking an excessive amount from the people because there are too few people in the area to enjoy the luxury of an independent county.

It is impossible here to do more than suggest the need for studies of all features of local government.   These should be concerned not only with an analysis of receipts and expenditures, but should examine the services that the unit provides and its method of operation.   Study might well begin on the township or school district.   Groups of taxpayers, particularly in urban sections, have found such studies to be of great value.   Farmers' organizations in several States are engaged in similar research and are finding the results decidedly worth while. The agricultural experiment station of the State concerned and the Federal Bureau of Agricultural Economics are in a position to assist by furnishing information relating to methods and to objectives and results of similar investigations elsewhere.   If such studies are to be effective, they must have the cooperation of the local authorities, who are usually glad to help, and they must be undertaken with the idea of assisting the school district, the township, or the county to render greater service to the inhabitants and not with the sole purpose of reducing a few expenses.

WHITNEY COOMBS.

TEA, Coffee Standards   The Government annually buys large
    Save on Purchases by   quantities of tea for the use of the
    Government Agencies   Veterans' Bureau, the Navy Depart-
ment, the Department of Justice, and
other units. For years this buying was done by each department
through its own purchasing officer. This was very difficult for these
officers, as they had no expert knowledge of teas, which are bought
and sold in the importing and wholesale trade entirely by experts
familiar with the organoleptic tests. During the war, when the volume of purchases increased tremendously, the War Department
attached to the Quartermaster Corps a trained tea and coffee expert,
who did all of the purchasing of these commodities, and the Navy
Department engaged tea experts to make its purchases, paying these
experts a certain commission on each pound bought. At the same
time, many of the smaller departments, as well as the Marine Corps
and the Surgeon General's Office of the Army, were having their bid
samples and deliveries checked by the tea experts employed under the
tea act, which is now administered by the Department of Agriculture.

Although this method effected large savings in the Government's
annual purchase of teas, the system was not satisfactory until the tea
control laboratory of the Food, Drug, and Insecticide Administration
of this department established physical standards of quality to be
used by the several departments. In setting these standards a small
quantity of tea of the exact kind and quality desired by any one
department constitutes the control sample for that department for
one year, and a sample is sent along with each proposal for a new
supply. The companies competing for the contract submit teas of
the same kind and quality as the standards, at the price at which they
desire to sell. In this way the competition becomes very keen. All
bid samples received by the various departments are compared with
the control or standard sample "in blind" by one of the experts of the
Food, Drug, and Insecticide Administration, who advises the department which bidders have met the specifications. The lowest bidder
whose tea is up to the control sample receives the contract. After the
contract has been granted samples of all deliveries are forwarded to
these same experts to be compared with the control samples. Any
deliveries that fail to come up to the control samples are rejected.

Standard for Coffee Purchases

In furtherance of this system, the Veterans' Bureau recently set up
a standard for the purchase of all coffees, which are passed upon by
the tea control laboratory in cooperation with the food control laboratory of the Food, Drug, and Insecticide Administration. The coffee
for this bureau, however, must not only be up to the control sample in
quality but must exactly match it in all essential particulars, such as
acidity, flavor, and taste, thus assuring to the veterans a coffee of the
same "cup quality" all the year round. In purchasing both tea and
coffee for the veterans, control samples of very high quality have been
established.

The Government has saved many thousands of dollars in its purchases of tea and coffee during the two years that this system of buying
according to standards has been in effect.

G. F. MITCHELL.

TENANT Farming on Share Basis Usually Best for Beginners
Tenant farming offers one of the few remaining opportunities to work for oneself without investing a large amount of capital. The opportunity is open even to those whose only assets are ability and willingness to do farm work. But an inexperienced farmer who must go unknown and unrecommended to landlords is likely to obtain only a farm on which the chances of profit are small.

Parents may be in a position to rent land to a son or be of help in leasing land from others. If the opportunity they can furnish or procure offers a reasonable chance to get a living, the young man is likely to accept it in order to make a beginning. If the opportunity proves to be a poor one he may later, when better known and experienced, bargain successfully with other landlords for better farms. Nearly half of the tenant farmers of the United States get their first experience in farming for themselves on land leased from relatives.

An enterprising boy will want to do some farming for himself. A boy who earns his spending money out of enterprises which he considers his own, and which he is encouraged to expand out of earnings, develops in thrift and judgment more than a boy who is paid wages, or given spending money, without a chance to invest in something related to his daily life.

In starting to farm it is almost always best to do so as a share tenant. Experience is an asset in any calling and it is something that often costs a great deal to gain. On shares a farmer gains experience without bearing the entire cost, and the landlord's share interest invites his cooperation and supervision.

Beginners Usually Farm Reared

Beginners as tenant farmers are usually farm reared, newly married, and concerned in setting up new homes on the farms they have leased. To such a man the possibility of starting as a tenant is often contingent on the sacrifice of desired standards of living. This may be partly avoided by leasing on terms which throw the burden of furnishing the operating capital and farming expense upon the landlord.

The most extensive opportunity for a family without property to farm with something of tenant status exists in the South where, in 1925, more than a fifth of the farmers owned neither their land nor their work animals. These are the croppers; in number they approximate 279,000 white and 344,000 colored families. The majority of croppers in the South may be described as married laborers without capital of their own, hired to raise a cotton crop for a half share interest instead of wages. That they and their families may live while making the crop they commonly procure advances secured by their share interest in the crop. Each cropper is alloted a house in which his family may live by itself, a plot for gardening, and may keep a cow, hogs, and poultry. Each cropper family usually works by itself on land allotted to it and is not constantly under an overseer as would be the case if it were hired for wages.

To compete successfully in the North a prospective farm tenant must, in general, own the necessary work animals and implements. Occasionally a retiring farmer does not care to clear his farm of horses and implements and rent in the usual way. Promising young men of the neighborhood who have been doing farm work for wages often have the best chance of getting such farms as tenants. A third of the income has usually been considered adequate for furnishing the labor on a good general farm in the North—terms on which most northern tenants are unwilling to compete because they have their own work animals and implements.

Capital Required Varies Widely

A statement of the amount of money it takes to start as a tenant would need much qualification. Some men, even though their contracts require them to furnish the work animals and implements, begin with practically nothing. This they may do through agreements giving them the use of animals or implements in exchange for feed breeding, or care. Another way is to employ poor work animals and implements which other farmers are willing to give away or sell very cheaply. Handy persons willing to use time and sacrifice convenience can get along on surprisingly little.

Most farm tenants have good opportunities to increase their incomes and improve their status by adding to their capital. The advantages of increased capital are such that many tenants and their families use every opportunity to better their asset position. The whole adult family can help in this when it lives on a farm. The work to be done affords tasks for every able and willing person. The work affords exercise and training to those who do it, increases the family income, and reduces the expenditures for food and hired labor.

HOWARD A. TURNER.

TERRACING to Control Erosion If Well Done Is Paying Investment   Most of the worn-out farms scattered throughout the United States were not worn out by producing crops but because the owners did not take steps to prevent the washing away of the fertile topsoil. Many productive farms will join the worn-out class in a few years unless soil erosion is prevented. Some of the Federal farm loan banks realize this danger and now require that all rolling land upon which they make loans be terraced. They realize that unless erosion is controlled there is great danger that the security for their loan will be washed away.

Terraces, such as are meant in this connection, are not distinct steps, as is often believed, but are broad ridges of earth thrown up across the slopes. In constructing these ridges, broad shallow channels are formed along their upper sides; in these channels the water flows off at low velocity, so that its power to erode and carry off soil is destroyed.

The narrow-base terrace—that is, a terrace from 5 to 8 feet wide at the base and from 6 inches to 1 foot high—has been used extensively in the Piedmont section of the South. It is cheap to construct and easy to maintain. However, attempts to cultivate this type of terrace have not been successful generally; considerable land is lost to cultivation and the growth of weeds and grasses on the terrace is objectionable.

The broad-base terrace has been developed from attempts to render cultivable the narrow-base form. It has all the advantages of the latter form, with the added advantage that no land is lost to cultivation. Such a terrace has a base width of from 15 to 25 feet and is from 1½ to 2 feet high. When properly constructed it can not only be cultivated but it can be crossed at any angle with farm machinery. It is the type of terrace best adapted to general farming conditions and is especially suited for areas where modern farm machinery is employed.

The success or failure of a terrace system is largely a matter of properly locating the terrace lines. A very common cause of failure is the fact that the upper terrace in the field is made to drain too large an area. As a result the upper terrace breaks and a large volume of water rushes down the slope, breaking all terraces below. Frequently a farmer desires to terrace his farm, but his neighbor's farm lies at a higher elevation and the upper terrace would be required to handle run-off water from the higher land. In such cases an attempt should be made to induce the neighbor to terrace his farm also. If this can-

FIGURE 219.—A steel terrace grader in operation

not be done the water from above must be intercepted by a hillside ditch to carry it to the nearest drainage channel below.

Necessity for Drainage Outlets

Whenever possible terraces should end at natural drainage channels The absence of a suitable drainage outlet within the limits of the field often necessitates ending terraces at fence lines, depressions, or draws. The volume of water which is discharged from the ends of a system of terraces often erodes unsightly and objectionable ditches along the ends of the terrace to the foot of the slope. Erosion in such channels can be reduced greatly by seeding them with grass or placing soil-saving dams at frequent intervals along the ditch line.

In laying off terrace lines various kinds of homemade devices are employed, but unless the operator exercises special care in the use of them the results usually are poor. Many landowners realize the inefficiency of these devices and use as a substitute a farm level on a tripod that can be purchased for about $20. Such a level gives very satisfactory results in the hands of a careful operator. However, no attempt should be made to lay off a terrace system unless the operator has a thorough understanding of the terrace practices and the operation of the farm level. Both are simple and easily understood.

In construting terraces the work should begin invariably with the highest terrace in the field and each terrace should be completed before work is started on the one next below. If time cannot be spared to terrace the entire field it is better to construct well the first few terraces near the upper side of the field than to terrace the whole field poorly, for a break in a terrace near the upper side of a field is followed by breaks in all below.

Terraces are sometimes built with a plow alone. Several plowings are required to throw the terrace up to the desired height. A large 16-inch plow with an extra large wing attached to the moldboard is used very successfully. The disk plow and ordinary road grader are also effective. However the most commonly used and the cheapest implement for throwing up a terrace is a wooden V-shaped drag that can be made in the field with very little difficulty. Steel terrace graders costing from $60 to $125 are now on the market and give satisfactory results. (Fig. 219.) After the first three or four rounds have been plowed on each side of the center line of the terrace, the drag is used to push the loose earth toward the center and thus build the terrace higher. The plowing is resumed and the drag used again, and this is continued until the terrace has attained the desired width. If the terrace is not built sufficiently high the first time, the work is started again at the center and the plowing and dragging are repeated.

Slip-Scraper Work Required

In order to finish up terraces properly some work with the slip scraper is generally required. The top of the terrace should be tested with the level and rod to see that it conforms to the proper grade. Any low places detected should be filled with a shovel or scraper. All large embankments across draws and gullies should be built with slip scrapers, and it is necessary to build such embankments considerably higher than the rest of the terrace to allow for settling of the loose earth. Most breaks in terrace systems occur at crossings of gullies or draws, and it is therefore very important that high, broad, substantial banks be built across these places.

The terracing of farm lands requires considerable work, but the results obtained in increased productivity more than warrant the efforts expended.

LEWIS A. JONES.

TOBACCO Barns for Flue Curing Best If Made Fireproof Tobacco barns for flue curing have heretofore been constructed of logs or sawed boards. These materials are very inflammable when the temperature inside the barn reaches 180° or 200° F. To reduce the fire hazard various devices have been used, but not until recent years have fireproof materials been cheap enough in comparison with wooden construction to justify their use. Cement blocks made with cinders or stone, and hollow-tile blocks, are now being used in a small way in building fireproof barns for flue curing. The use of these materials reduces the fire hazard, and the walls offer greater resistance to outside changes in weather conditions, thereby enabling the grower to regulate the temperature better inside the barn. As the walls are tight, it is essential that adequate ventilation at the bottom and top of the barns be provided.

A barn 17 feet 8 inches square, inside dimensions, and 16 feet high, with seven tier poles, 20 inches apart on centers, will take care of 750 to 800 sticks of green tobacco and can be built at a cost not exceeding $450. If the cement blocks are made on the farm and farm labor used in the construction the cost can be reduced. Round tier poles, 5 inches in diameter at the small end, placed in the barn on steel strap hangers, are desirable and can usually be obtained from the farm wood lot at small cost.

The covering should be of some good fireproof material put on a skeleton roof of wooden construction. Should the tobacco catch fire

FIGURE 220.—Fireproof barns at North Carolina Tobacco Experiment Station, Oxford. Barn in foreground is built of cement cinder blocks; barn in background is built of hollow clay tile

and burn in a barn built of these materials, the walls should be left intact. A new top and set of tier poles can then be replaced in a very short time at a nominal cost. If a wooden structure were used a fire would result in total loss of the tobacco and the barn. By the use of fireproof materials duplex or even quadruplex barns may be built instead of building separate units, as at present.

E. G. Moss

TOBACCO Cooperative's Failure Attributed to Numerous Difficulties   Among the unsuccessful attempts to market tobacco cooperatively may be numbered the large growers' cooperative association that operated in Virginia, North Carolina, and South Carolina. This organization, composed of 96,000 tobacco growers, was placed in the hands of receivers in June, 1926, after four years of operation.

To determine, if possible, the reasons for the failure, the Division of Cooperative Marketing made a study of the association and of the environment in which it operated. It was found that failure was not due to any one cause, but to many causes. Some of these alone would, in time, have resulted in the downfall of the association; others merely hastened the time of failure. The causes of failure may be grouped under four broad headings—those connected with (1) the membership, (2) the management, and (3) the type of organization, and (4) causes outside of the association.

Disloyalty among the members was frequent from the beginning, and member defalcations accumulated as the years passed. This disloyalty may be attributed largely to the economic, social, educational, and psychological conditions of the growers in the Tri-State area. The percentage of tenancy is high; tobacco is often the only cash crop, and credit facilities are limited. Members were both whites and Negroes; many had low educational standards; and the percentage of illiteracy

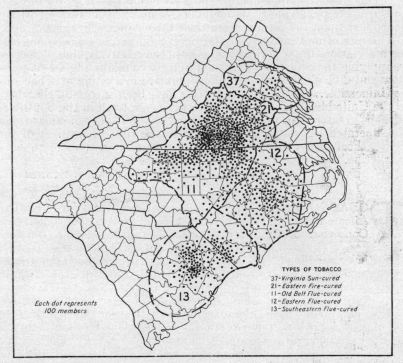

FIGURE 221.—Members of the Tobacco Growers Cooperative Association were distributed over three States in which five more or less distinct types of tobacco were grown. Lines of division by types are not distinct as necessarily shown, for the producing sections overlap and merge to some extent

was high. They were, with few exceptions, inexperienced in cooperative marketing and untaught as to its principles, possibilities, limitations, or difficulties. Many were easily influenced by interests which were not friendly to the association.

Mistakes in management were made from lack of experience with the cooperative form of business and lack of foresight rather than from dishonesty or insincerity. Extravagance in purchasing and operating warehouses and in salaries, secrecy as to the affairs of the association, lack of close contact with the members, and unwise policies in selling and redrying were among the factors which contributed to the failure through loss of the confidence of members.

The association was large and cumbersome. It covered three States in which five more or less distinct types of tobacco were grown. (Fig. 221.) Different problems existed in the different areas and in the selling and financing of each type of tobacco. The association was organized rapidly, with policy operations highly centralized and far removed from the growers; and in some localities questionable methods were used to obtain members—all of which added to the complexity and difficulty of management.

Strong, active, and organized opposition was encountered from those who would be eliminated from tobacco marketing if the cooperative should prove successful. Some of the large tobacco manufacturers were unfriendly to the farmers' organization and refused to buy from it. This made it impossible for the association to sell all its tobacco and to make payments to its members, many of whom were entirely dependent upon the returns from their tobacco for a livelihood.

The rate of mortality among farmers' cooperative tobacco marketing associations in the United States has been relatively high. Success in applying the cooperative method to tobacco marketing seems to be slow and difficult, but successful cooperative marketing of tobacco is not impossible. Tobacco cooperatives have been successful elsewhere in the United States. Difficulties to be encountered in the South are perhaps greater than those in other sections, but ably organized and well-operated associations can render to the tobacco growers of the South the benefits of an improved and efficient system of tobacco marketing.

J. J. SCANLAN.

TOBACCO Growth Much Affected by Care and Condition of Seed Bed — Though it may seem far-fetched to lay the blame of poor quality in tobacco on neglect of the seed bed, it can not be denied that healthy and stocky seedlings with ample root systems are essential to the production of a good crop of tobacco; a crop that will grow without interruptions caused by inferior root systems or disease. The losses annually resulting from wholly preventable diseases on tobacco seed beds would run into a considerable amount if delayed transplanting, the use of diseased plants, the reduction of acreage, and inferior quality of tobacco are taken into account.

Why do tobacco growers almost invariably sow their seed beds too thickly? Experience does not seem to teach them their mistake, as they persist in it every year. Thick seeding causes crowded plants with undeveloped root systems and a lack of resistance, so that diseases are developed and spread rapidly, especially wildfire, mosaic, root rot, and damping-off fungi. A covered seed bed, being humid and warm, affords an excellent medium for the development and transmittal of such diseases, especially when the young seedlings are crowded, unless precautionary measures are taken.

Sometimes the seedlings, when too thick, are thinned by hand, a very slow and laborious process; then again the excess seedlings are removed by raking the bed, which injures the tender leaves. Probably the best method is to reduce the average amount of seed sown by half, or preferably by two-thirds if it has been recleaned, so that all light, immature individuals are removed. If thoroughly recleaned, 1 ounce of tobacco seed contains approximately 300,000 viable seeds, so that by seeding at the rate of 1 ounce of seed to 700 square feet of seed bed a stand of three seedlings to the square inch should be obtained, or about 8,000 from 18 square feet. This rate of seeding affords plenty of space for the development of vigorous plants with healthy root systems and does not sacrifice space beyond reason.

Perhaps the most practical and economical method of controlling several of the diseases usually occurring in seed beds, notably root rot and damping-off, consists of a direct application of heat to the soil by means of an inverted pan. Soil sterilization by steam is practiced to some extent in most of the tobacco-producing sections in the country, but its effectiveness is greatly impaired by the short period of

FIGURE 222.—Tobacco seed beds should be steamed more thoroughly. By using four pans, connected in pairs, confining the steam under a pressure of 120 pounds to two of the pans for 30 to 40 minutes, then moving the steam connection to the second pair of pans, leaving the first pair undisturbed while the second pair are being steamed, each section of seed bed covered by the pans will be steamed for one hour and twenty minutes more efficiently and economically than if only one or two pans are used

application and the low steam pressure used. For maximum effectiveness in destroying diseases every section of the seed bed should be steamed for 30 to 40 minutes with a steam pressure of at least 120 pounds.

OTTO OLSON.

TOBACCO Wildfire Is Less Serious Menace Than It Once Seemed During the season of 1917 the tobacco crop of North Carolina was very generally affected with an apparently new disease which threatened to become a serious menace to tobacco production in the United States. On account of the rate at which the disease spread and of the serious injury to the leaves it came to be known as wildfire. In comparatively few years the same disease was found to occur in all the important tobacco-growing districts of the United States, as well as in several foreign countries. It may probably never be definitely known whether or not this disease was "new," or whether it had existed for some time prior to 1917, when it first attracted scientific attention and received satisfactory description. The disease, however, has not occurred again to a serious extent in North Carolina up to the present time. By 1922, however, extensive outbreaks had occurred in Tennessee, Kentucky, the Connecticut Valley, and in Wisconsin. The potential seriousness of the disease was generally admitted by all who observed it at its worst in individual fields. On the other hand many growers in all localities were more or less skeptical about its importance and slow to adopt any measures for its prevention or eradication.

In the meantime, scientific studies in various places repeatedly corroborated the results of the first investigators in North Carolina as to the bacterial nature of the disease, which is now recognized as due

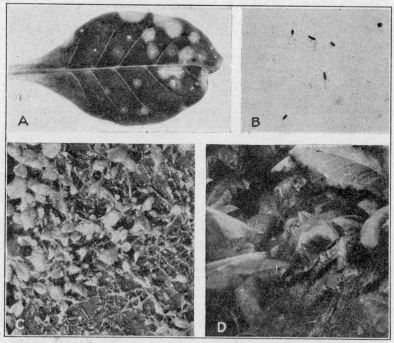

FIGURE 223.—Tobacco wildfire. A, The characteristic symptoms of the disease on leaf from tobacco seedling; B, *Bacterium tabacum*, the organism causing wildfire, magnified several hundred times; C, occasionally wildfire raises havoc with the young seedlings in the seed beds; D, the principal damage is done in the field as illustrated by this "close-up" between two rows

to *Bacterium tabacum* Wolf and Foster. It is also generally agreed that the disease originates in the seed bed in practically all cases, and that dashing rainstorms are responsible for much of the rapid spread in the field. While some minor disagreement exists in different districts as to the best methods of prevention or control, all are agreed that the transplanting of seedlings from infested seed beds should be avoided if possible.

Extensive field observations in the various districts have brought out the fact that wildfire is very sporadic in its occurrence, that general infection may exist in a field without causing any appreciable damage, and that crops apparently seriously affected in the early stages of growth often wholly or largely "recover."

After 10 years of experience with wildfire one is led to the conclusion that the disease is not likely to be as serious a menace to tobacco production as was at first feared. On the other hand, in certain districts, and particularly on individual farms in seasons favorable to the disease, heavy losses from it may be expected. In other words, as far as the individual grower is concerned, the potential danger is still large, although the likelihood of such wholesale and frequent crop injury as to make the culture of tobacco in any district hazardous on account of wildfire is very small. The situation is hopeful in that fairly reliable methods of prevention are available. These preventive measures are almost entirely based on adopting precautions to avoid seed-bed infection through exposure to any infective material from the preceding year's crop. This may involve attention especially to the location of seed beds, seed disinfection, and disinfection of any other material such as seed-bed frames or covers used on previously infected plant beds.

JAMES JOHNSON.

TOMATO-BLIGHT Control Effected by Destroying Remains of the Crop Early blight and Septoria leaf spot are two tomato diseases that defoliate the plants and greatly reduce the yield and quality of fruit. Sun scald and fruit rots usually follow in their wake. Early blight is common throughout the United States, but Septoria leaf spot is prevalent chiefly in the Middle East and Central West.

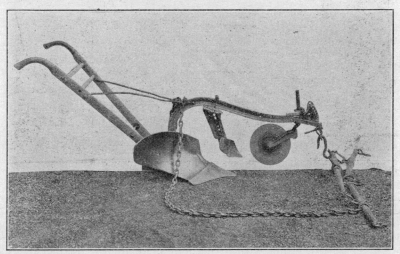

FIGURE 224.—Plow equipped for thorough plowing

These blights are caused by fungi—very minute organisms similar to the molds that grow on bread, meat, and other organic products. They live chiefly on dead plant materials, such as dead weeds and crop remains, and not infrequently subsist wholly upon these substances for several years in succession and meanwhile reproduce through small bodies called spores, the equivalents of seeds.

These spores germinate in warm, moist air and either perish for want of food or grow on dead organic matter or penetrate the tissues of live plants, such as tomatoes, Jimson weed, and horse nettle. When inside the plant they kill the tissues around the point of entrance, causing dark-colored spots. Death or blight of the foliage usually follows.

These blight fungi differ from numerous other fungi that are able to grow and reproduce only on dead organic matter, by their ability to attack live plants. When a tomato crop is planted in their midst they usually attack it. The amount of blight and damage produced depends largely upon the temperature and moisture and quantity of these fungi present. If the blight fungi are absent, these blights can not occur even under the most favorable conditions for their development.

Destruction of Crop Remains

Destruction of crop remains, such as wheat stubble, cornstalks, etc., and other plant débris robs these blight fungi of their food supply and

FIGURE 225.—Type of plowing done with plow illustrated in Figure 224

hence causes their deterioration and death. Complete burial of the dead organic matter lying on the surface of the soil by means of a properly equipped plow is the most economical means of depriving these fungi of this food material, as they do not thrive in soil; in fact, when so buried, either with or without plant débris, in the fall, they usually perish before spring. Much better control of these blights has been obtained in fields by fall plowing than by spraying or dusting. All dead plant material has to be thoroughly covered with soil, however, to obtain these results.

Thorough plowing can be done with a plow having a well-curved moldboard and a rolling colter, jointer, and chain attached, as shown in Figure 224. The rolling colter must be kept sharp, and a furrow 7 to 8 inches deep should be turned over in order to bury all trash. When properly regulated, this outfit will completely bury all crop remains, weeds, and vegetative growth, as shown in Figure 225.

The comparative effects of thorough fall plowing and combined fall and spring disking on the control of these blights were studied in field experiments at the Arlington Experiment Farm, Rosslyn, Va. Fall plowing gave excellent control of the blights in 1921 and 1924, when the fall-plowed and the disked fields were separated by half a mile. It also gave excellent results in 1926, but less favorable results in 1927, when the plots were separated only 200 to 250 feet. Although the blight fungi were probably carried into the fall-plowed plots from the disked plots in 1927, thus partly vitiating the effects of the fall-plowing, it is doubtful whether fall-plowed areas should be used for tomatoes when they are closer than one-fourth mile from tomatoes grown on disked or spring-plowed land. In all of our plowing experiments, the tomatoes grown on thoroughly fall-plowed land have been freer from blights than other tomatoes grown on spring-plowed land on the same farm.

W. S. Porte and
Fred J. Pritchard.

TOMATO Yellows Due to Virus That Causes Curly Top in Beets — Tomato yellows has long been known in the Pacific West, but it remained a mystery until recently. It was described a number of times under various synonyms, such as western blight, yellow blight, summer blight, and a few others. Tomato plants affected with yellows are distinguished by a general yellowish discoloration, upward rolling of their

FIGURE 226.—Two rows of tomato plants, one protected by a muslin cage until the end of June (on the left), the other unprotected (on the right). The protected plants were free from yellows and completely filled the row, while 87 per cent of the unprotected plants were either dead or dying from this disease. Shafter, Calif., July, 1927

leaves, and extreme rigidity. Internally, such plants reveal carbohydrate contents much higher than normal, likewise a higher percentage of soluble nitrogen.

It has been definitely established by the work of M. B. McKay, of the Oregon Agricultural Experiment Station, that tomato yellows is induced by the same virus that causes curly top of sugar beets and is transmitted by the beet leaf hopper (*Eutettix tenellus* Baker). However, the writer's work shows conclusively that the progress of the disease after the infection depends to a large extent on environmental conditions. The combined effect of these conditions may be measured roughly by evaporation. High rates of evaporation correlate with high percentages of the disease and with a greater severity of its symptoms. Light is the most important single factor. The yellows curve closely parallels the light curve when inoculated tomato plants are placed under a series of different light conditions.

Shading in the field has a doubly beneficial effect. It enables some plants to overcome the infection and also tends to repel the insects and thus to reduce the amount of infection. Knowledge of this fact has been put to practical use by the writer. Tomato plants were shaded in the field by means of muslin cages and certain tall-growing economic plants such as sunflower. In the southern San Joaquin Valley of California, in years when yellows reached 100 per cent in unprotected fields, less than 50 per cent of plants were affected in the rows interplanted with sunflower, still less under muslin tents, and none within insect-proof cages. The protective crops and the muslin covers could be removed about July 1 with very little danger of a later infection. Older plants do not contract the disease as readily as do younger plants.

Michael Shapovalov.

TREE Crops May Be Wind Sown at Distance From the Seed Trees The owner of a woodland who wants to make sure that a new crop of trees will be established on his land just as soon as possible after the mature crop has been harvested must give thought before he removes the old trees to the manner in which the new crop is to be started. Nearly all of the conifers or softwoods—pine, spruce, hemlock, etc.—depend upon the wind to scatter their seeds. With such species a satisfactory stand of young trees can safely be counted on within a reasonable time if the cutting is not too wide for the seeds to blow across from uncut timber to windward. If the area to be cut is too wide to depend upon seeding from the trees outside, or if there is no mature timber left on the windward side, it is necessary to leave enough seed trees scattered through the cutting to reseed the area. In either case it is necessary to know how far the seeds will be carried by the wind.

To find out what the distances are a series of tests has been conducted on the campus of the University of California. Ninety-eight lots of seeds were released 100 feet above the ground from a flag pole and the movements of the seeds measured with stop watch and tape. To check these tests in the free air against results in quiet air, 27 additional lots of seeds were dropped 160 feet down the concrete elevator shaft of the campanile—the 300-foot masonry bell tower that adorns the campus—early in the morning when temperature conditions within the tower were such that the air was perfectly at rest.

Wings Act As Parachutes

Tree seeds of the type adapted to distribution by wind have wings but they do not fly. Their wings merely act as parachutes which offer resistance to their fall through the air. While they are falling they drift with the wind. The distances they travel from the parent tree depend upon the length of time required for the seeds to drop from the trees to the ground and upon the distance the wind blows during this same time. Seeds are produced at different heights on the tree. Also, the seeds borne by one tree have shapes sufficiently different to produce some variation in their rates of fall. This is nature's arrangement for making sure that the seeds will be well scattered instead of all falling in one place. However, the seeds of any one species of forest tree are enough alike to have a rather definite average rate of fall.

Table 11 can be used to find the average distance to which seeds of some common western conifers are carried by winds of different velocities. This is done by multiplying the factor in the table by the elevation from which the seed is released and dividing by 100. For instance, the average Sitka spruce seeds released from a height of 150 feet in a wind blowing 15 miles per hour would be carried 7.12 times 150 feet or 1,068 feet, or $\dfrac{(\text{factor} \times \text{elevation})}{100} = \dfrac{712 \times 150}{100} = 1,068$.

TABLE 11.—*Factors to be used in estimating distance to which tree seeds of certain species will be carried by wind of stated velocities*

Species	Factors to be used with wind velocities at miles per hour—					
	5 miles	10 miles	15 miles	20 miles	25 miles	30 miles
	Factor	*Factor*	*Factor*	*Factor*	*Factor*	*Factor*
Sitka spruce	237	474	712	949	1,186	1,425
Western yellow pine	193	387	580	774	967	1,161
Douglas fir	167	334	501	668	836	1,002
White fir	139	277	416	555	693	832
California red fir	139	277	416	555	693	832
Lowland white fir	129	258	387	516	645	774
Incense cedar	125	249	374	498	623	747
Sugar pine	111	223	334	445	557	668
Redwood	85	171	256	342	427	513

The Quantity of Seed Required

One other point remains to be considered—namely, the quantity of seed required. Trees which depend upon the wind to scatter their seeds often produce these seeds in great quantities. Unfortunately the seeds are eaten greedily by birds, animals, and insects of various kinds. The rodents, especially, cause great losses. The forest owner must therefore plan to provide a seed supply large enough so that some seeds will be certain to survive until the time of germination. For this reason it is often necessary to leave from four to six seed trees per acre to insure prompt reproduction, even though the trees left are capable of sowing their seeds over a much larger area.

H. W. SIGGINS.

TREES of Small Size Unprofitable to Cut for Making Lumber — What size tree is the best for a farmer to cut from his woods for saw timber? The size for maximum profit clearly must vary with conditions and with the kind of timber, but there are several fixed and established relationships between trees of large and small diameters that should always be given careful consideration before cutting is begun.

It costs more than twice as much effort (in time and in labor) to manufacture 1 board foot of lumber from a tree 8 inches in diameter as from a tree 25 inches in diameter. Less than half as much salable lumber is obtained from a cubic foot of wood in the smaller-sized tree as from a cubic foot of wood in the larger-sized tree. Furthermore, the lumber obtained from the smaller tree has less than half the value per 1,000 feet of that from the larger tree.

The small tree is wasteful of wood. Even if sawed with the economical band saw, 71 per cent of the wood of a log 5 inches in diameter goes to waste in sawdust and slabs; but only 38 per cent of a log 20 inches in diameter is lost.

Small Logs Waste Time and Labor

In 5-inch logs 16 pounds of wood and bark must be handled for each foot of lumber obtained, while only 7½ pounds of wood and bark must be handled in 20-inch logs to get 1 foot of board. It clearly requires far more time and labor to handle a larger weight and number of logs in producing the same quantity of lumber. By timing the different steps—felling the trees and sawing them into logs, hauling the logs to a road, loading them on a wagon or truck, hauling to sawmill, and sawing into lumber—it is found that for each successive step far more time is required to handle enough small logs to produce 1,000 feet of lumber than to handle a sufficient number of larger logs to produce the same quantity.

TABLE 12.—*Number of board feet cut from 1 cubic foot of wood in logs of different diameters and proportion of wood not utilized for lumber*

Average diameter of logs at small end	Number of board feet to each cubic foot of wood (band saw)	Proportion of wood not utilized for lumber	Weight of wood (with bark) to each board foot of lumber	Average diameter of logs at small end	Number of board feet to each cubic foot of wood (band saw)	Proportion of wood not utilized for lumber	Weight of wood (with bark) to each board foot of lumber
Inches	Board feet	Per cent	Pounds	Inches	Board feet	Per cent	Pounds
5	3.5	71	16.0	14	6.9	41	8.3
6	5.2	54	11.0	16	7.1	40	8.0
10	6.0	48	9.6	18	7.3	39	7.7
12	6.5	44	8.9	20	7.4	38	7.5

But it is not logs that are to be considered; it is trees. The timing for logs has therefore been combined into trees of different diameters and the results given in Table 13. These data were obtained by following crews all day and noting separately the time required for each step in the operation they performed.

TABLE 13.—*Time in minutes per 1,000 feet of lumber sawed required for the different steps of logging and sawing into lumber trees of different diameters*

Diameter of trees (outside of bark) above ground (inches)	Time required for—				
	Felling and sawing into logs	Skidding and bunching	Loading and hauling to mill	Handling and sawing into lumber	All activities
8	345	143	411	312	1,211
10	290	94	380	248	1,012
15	202	54	312	143	714
20	151	48	280	112	591
25	109	43	255	102	509

Same Relative Result Under Varying Conditions

It is not material whether the sawyers in felling trees work fast or slowly; the relative time required remains the same. Likewise, in skidding it does not matter whether the team is a good team or a poor team; the relative skidding time remains essentially the same until a point is reached at which the team is overloaded. Nor does it matter whether, in hauling, all logs from small trees and all logs from large trees are hauled separately or mixed. Some methods of loading are more efficient than others, but it is essentially immaterial whether the logs are loaded by means of teams and rope and rolled up skids or by the most efficient type of steam loader. In either case far more time is required to load 1,000 board feet in small logs than in larger logs. When a team is used the logs are handled singly, and there is little difference in relative time until logs are handled which are so large as to overtax the capacity of the team.

Why logs from small trees reduce the output of a sawmill may be explained by referring to Table 14, which shows that in sawing up 8-inch trees 53 logs must be handled at the mill to produce 1,000 board feet of lumber, while with 20-inch trees only 4.7 logs must be handled.

TABLE 14.—*Number of logs from trees of different diameters and number of trees of different diameters required to produce 1,000 board feet of lumber, and the mill value of lumber per 1,000 feet produced from southern yellow pine trees of different diameters*

Diameter of trees (outside of bark) 4.5 feet above ground (inches)	Number of logs to produce 1,000 feet of lumber	Number of trees to produce 1,000 feet of lumber	Value of lumber per 1,000 board feet (southern yellow pine)
			Dollars
8	58.0	30.0	16.80
10	44.0	15.0	18.60
15	15.0	4.5	27.50
20	7.5	1.7	33.20
25	4.7	1.1	35.00

Money Costs Vary Also

The relative time required for all of these operations is summed up in column 6 of Table 13. To produce 1,000 board feet of lumber from trees 8 inches in diameter, including the work by sawyers, skidding time, and hauling, and the work by sawmill men, a total of 1,211 minutes is required; 714 minutes are required with 15-inch trees; but only 509 minutes are required with 25-inch trees. The actual costs in money will be in approximately the same relation. It is immaterial where the timber is located; the kind of timber does not change the relationship; the cost of wages does not affect it; some circular sawmills have a larger capacity than others, but the relative cost of handling is not greatly changed.

Table 13 gives relative time in minutes. The current local cost or rate of pay per hour can be computed and substituted for time, and the actual relative cost thus determined. Wages and the rental or use value of a team and the number of hours per day of work may vary, but regardless of these differences these costs can all be reduced to an hour-cost basis for any part of the United States and the actual relative cost per hour ascertained.

If the timber is sold either in the form of boards or of logs for sawmill use, the landowner sustains a loss in cutting small trees, because of securing lower grades of lumber or narrow widths and small sizes. Very knotty lumber, narrow widths, and small sizes of framing, as well as of finishing lumber, sell for less than lumber with fewer knots or of larger dimensions. Table 14 shows that in cutting southern yellow pine the value per 1,000 board feet of the lumber produced from trees 25 inches in diameter is more than twice that for the same amount of lumber sawed from trees 8 inches in diameter. Though the figures given are for southern yellow pine, the same principle applies to other kinds of trees if converted into lumber—to white pine, to oaks, to yellow poplar, and to the pines and firs of the Western States. The form and size in which such wood is marketed consequently largely determines its value.

Soil Capacity Is Lowered

Furthermore, the soil is capable of producing only a definite number of cubic feet of solid wood each year. This material may be cut in the form of the wasteful 8-inch trees or it may be cut in the form of larger trees. Cutting small trees for saw timber therefore actually has the result of lowering the capacity of the soil to produce this class of material.

The farmer, as a rule, is in an excellent position to take advantage of all of those factors which increase the earning value of his woodland. He can do his own logging or can closely supervise it. He has no investment in railroads, locomotives, or a large and costly mill, the construction costs of which must be paid for out of the timber cut and which is frequently given by the owners of large tracts of woodland as the motive inducing them to cut "clean," taking small as well as large trees. He can sell or cut a small amount of the largest or highest-grade trees at frequent intervals and can thus secure—

Low logging cost.

High quality of logs, selling at the best price or producing a high grade of lumber.

High producing capacity for his soil.

Frequent and regular returns; or he can carry the large timber as a reserve until a need or emergency makes it desirable to convert it into cash.

W. W. ASHE.

T REE Planting Goes Ahead in Nebraska With Federal Help   Nebraska has been known for years as the "Tree Planter's State." Arbor Day originated and was first observed in Nebraska in 1872, and on the first Arbor Day over a million trees were planted. For many years tree planting was practiced zealously by Nebraska farmers. During the dry years of the early nineties many trees died from lack of moisture and care. The windbreak or wood lot, opened up to the sun through the loss of some trees, gradually deteriorated. Grass came in and the tree roots became sod bound. Some farmers pulled out their trees because they wanted the ground for crops.

Farm planting was continued rather indifferently for a number of years, but now it has taken a new lease of life. In 1926 the extension service of the State agricultural college started to cooperate with the United States Forest Service under the Clarke-McNary law, which provides Federal aid to cooperating States to stimulate the planting of trees. The extension service purchases the broad-leafed trees from the commercial nurserymen of Nebraska, while the conifers are raised for the State at the Forest Service nursery at Halsey, Nebr. The trees are shipped in bulk to the agricultural college, where they are repacked and sent out to farmers. A charge of 1 cent each is made for the trees and a limit of 300 trees to the farm has been established.

As farmers found out that cheap trees could be purchased for windbreaks and wood lots the demand increased. The distribution of trees during the past three years was as shown in Table 15.

The governor of the State, the director of conservation and soil surveys, the chancellor of the State university, and the leading officials of the agricul-

FIGURE 227.—A western yellow pine plantation, Rock County, Nebr. This and similar early plantations demonstrate the feasibility of tree planting in Nebraska. After 30 years the average diameter of these trees was 10.1 inches, and the wood volume per acre 2,339 cubic feet

tural college have taken a great interest in this project and have done much to stimulate the revival of farm planting in Nebraska.

TABLE 15.—*Trees distributed to Nebraska farmers, 1926–1928*

Fiscal year (ended July 1)	Trees distributed	Number of farmers
1926	34, 000	104
1927	200, 000	1, 200
1928	682, 000	2, 600

Windbreaks for Farm Buildings

There should be a windbreak around the farm buildings, the feed lots, and the orchards on each farm. In addition, utilization of odd-shaped pieces of land for wood lots will provide fence posts, fuel, and other material for farm use.

The species recommended for planting vary according to the section of the State and the climatic and soil conditions. American elm, green ash, box elder, cottonwood, Russian olive, caragana, hackberry, western yellow, Scotch, and Austrian pine, and eastern red cedar are adapted to most parts of the State. Honey locust, catalpa, Russian mulberry, black walnut, western white spruce, northern white pine, and blue spruce will do well where the climatic conditions are not so severe. Jack pine is adapted to sandy soils only.

Trees must be planted in well-cultivated ground and the cultivation must be continued until the branches come together. The only exception to this rule is in the sand hills where cultivation would result in soil blowing. In sand, trees should be planted in furrows which are plowed through the grass, and no cultivation is advised after planting except in well-protected places.

FRED R. JOHNSON.

TREE Poisoning Tried for Clearing Land Is Found Effective During the past two years the Department of Agriculture has been experimenting with the use of poisons in killing trees as an aid in clearing farm land and in getting rid of trees that are, for any reason, objectionable. These experiments have not been completed, but they have been carried sufficiently far to demonstrate that poisons are effective in killing trees and in hastening the decay of trunks and stumps.

There are a number of poisons which may be used in varying degrees of strength. One which has given uniformly good results is composed of 1 pound of white powdered arsenic, 2 pounds of lye, and 2 gallons of water. To prepare the poison, first make a paste of the arsenic by adding a small quantity of water. Pour the lye into 1 gallon of water slowly and stir as the lye is added. The dissolving lye heats the water. While the solution is still hot, add the arsenic paste, a little at a time, and stir until all is dissolved; then add the second gallon of water. If it is desired to mark the trees which have been poisoned, add 1 pound of whiting to the solution. Care must be used not to inhale the fumes which are given off in making the solution, for they are poisonous.

Two gallons of poison will be sufficient for about 30 trees averaging 15 inches in diameter. The arsenic costs about 50 cents per pound in small lots and the lye costs about 20 cents per pound.

To apply the poison, cut a continuous ring of gashes around the tree, penetrating through the first and second barks and into the sap wood. The cuts should be made so that they will retain the liquid poison instead of permitting it to run down the outside of the trunk. Pour the poison into the cuts, using an old teakettle or coffee pot with a long spout for convenience in applying. The solution should be stirred frequently to prevent sedimentation. Three men can ring and poison about 200 trees in a day.

Experiments indicate that the best time to apply the poison is in the spring, just about the time the buds are forming. The poison seems to take effect more quickly on bright sunshiny days than on dark or rainy ones.

Effects of the Poison

The poison will generally cause the leaves of the trees to wither and fade within a couple of weeks, and from then on the process of decay goes on quite rapidly in some species of trees and more slowly in others. In the case of 208 trees of various species, poisoned in the spring, the trunks of 77 had fallen within one year. In another series of 46 trees, 27 had fallen within 15 months. It is probable that, under favorable conditions, the stumps of trees which remain two years after poisoning can be readily removed. Some of the trees which for experimental purposes were girdled but not poisoned died the fifteenth month after girdling, whereas others were still in full foliage at that time.

The formula recommended above seems to kill most species of trees except the pine, although the action is quicker with some species than

FIGURE 228.—Applying poison to a tree

with others. Of the species covered in the experimental work, the hackberry, elm, oak, ash, soft maple, willow, elder, persimmon, dogwood, hickory, and pecan seemed, after nine months, to be affected in about the order given. It is probable, however, that after a few more months all of these species will have died, for in another case where white, slippery, and red elm, sweet gum, hackberry, hickory, ash, redbud, Osage orange, and red locust had been poisoned 15 months, all were dead.

Utensils which have been used for holding the poison should be destroyed when the work is completed to prevent their use for other purposes which might be dangerous. Cattle should be kept out of the fields containing poisoned trees for a few days after poisoning, as there is a possibility of their licking the poison in the cuts on the trees. Chemical analyses of the withered leaves of poisoned trees show that there is no danger of poisoning cattle should they eat them. The wood of a poisoned tree is discolored and becomes soft and spongy, so that it is of no value as lumber.

There are a number of commercial tree poisons on the market which are used in the same manner as given above and with approximately the same results. They can be purchased ready to apply, or only require to be diluted with water before being used.

GEORGE R. BOYD.

TUBERCULOSIS of Fowls Can Be Eradicated by Using Simple Measures A survey made by the department in cooperation with the States has demonstrated that avian or fowl tuberculosis is prevalent over a much greater area than had been suspected. Because of the slow and insidious character of the disease, farmers and poultry raisers have often failed to recognize fowl tuberculosis until it was demonstrated by actual post-mortem examination. Much of this post-mortem work was done during the last year by veterinarians engaged in the work of

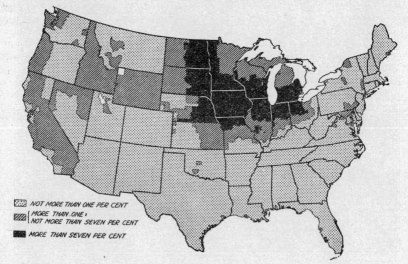

NOT MORE THAN ONE PER CENT

MORE THAN ONE, NOT MORE THAN SEVEN PER CENT

MORE THAN SEVEN PER CENT

FIGURE 229.—Extent of avian tuberculosis July 1, 1928. The intensity of shading shows the relative prevalence of avian tuberculosis in various parts of the United States

eradicating tuberculosis of cattle, and in many instances the results have been astonishing.

In many counties, particularly in the North Central States, fowl tuberculosis has been found to exist to a greater or less degree in from 60 to 75 per cent of the poultry flocks. The accompanying map (fig. 229) shows the extent of the disease, the dark area showing the States in which it has been found to be most prevalent. Fowl tuberculosis affects not only poultry but swine as well. Investigations have shown hogs to be very susceptible to the disease, becoming infected by eating dead birds or by the ingestion of droppings of poultry affected with the disease. Infection from this source has been found to be quite heavy.

The loss sustained by farmers and poultry raisers on account of fowl tuberculosis mounts into many thousands of dollars annually and will continue to increase each year unless efficient means for its control and eradication are put into effect. This loss is occasioned not only through an increasing death rate in infected flocks but also through loss in weight and through decreased egg production. The strength and vigor necessary for a normal egg production can not be maintained by birds affected with tuberculosis.

Practical Eradication Methods

That avian tuberculosis must be eradicated if the raising of poultry is to continue to be profitable is obvious. Eradication may be undertaken and carried through successfully by the average farmer, who should acquaint himself first with some of the physical symptoms manifested by affected birds. These are loss of vigor, progressive loss of flesh, lameness, swollen joints, drooping, and general unthriftiness. Positive diagnosis is made possible by the application of the tuberculin test, which should be undertaken only by a thoroughly competent veterinarian, or by a careful post-mortem examination. Lesions are usually most pronounced in the intestines, liver, and spleen, those in the liver being the more readily recognized by the layman. The intestines of a fowl affected with tuberculosis present nodules ranging in size from a grain of wheat to a pea, sometimes even larger, and when cut into will show a gritty substance. When the existence of tuberculosis in the flock has been established, immediate steps should be taken for its eradication. All diseased birds should be killed and burned. The remainder of fowls over 1 year old should be marketed. The chicken house should be moved to clean ground, if this is practicable, after it has been thoroughly cleaned and disinfected with an approved product. To undertake to eradicate tuberculosis by a perfunctory or careless job of cleaning and disinfecting is but a waste of time and energy as well as a useless expenditure of money. Lots and runways should be plowed up and seeded to some grain crop and a new start made on clean ground with young, healthy, vigorous birds of good breeding.

During the last fiscal year veterinarians engaged in eradicating tuberculosis in livestock under the cooperative plan inspected approximately 20,400,000 fowls and found more than 14,000 flocks affected with tuberculosis. Owners of these infected flocks were informed how to eradicate this disease, which in most cases has been done. A marked decline in the percentage of tuberculous swine has been noted in counties where successful efforts are being made to eradicate avian tuberculosis.

One Diseased Fowl May Cause a Large Loss

Fowl tuberculosis is not a self-limiting disease and will not eradicate itself, but is almost certain to bring disastrous results if not controlled. One tuberculous fowl will transmit the disease to other members of the flock, and through direct contact and contaminated premises a large per cent, if not the entire flock, will become diseased. If the farmer or poultryman fails to recognize these facts in connection with this disease, he is almost certain to be deprived of the income to which the exercise of a reasonable precaution would entitle him.

A 2-reel motion picture entitled "T. B. or not T. B." has been produced by the department, which deals with the eradication of tuberculosis in poultry and swine. This picture is used in educational work and may be obtained for this purpose through the Office of Motion Pictures of the department.

ELMER LASH.

TULIP "Breaking" Is Proved to Be Caused by Mosaic Infection A normal tulip flower containing anthocyanin pigment has the color uniformly diffused all over the surface of the segments except the base. When such a self-colored tulip is grown it sometimes undergoes, after a variable length of time, a remarkable change in which the anthocyanin pigment in the flower is segregated into irregular stripes up the middle of each segment or fine featherings upon its edges. Other changes in the plant are generally a distinct mottling in the green of the leaf, pigment markings in the stem, reduction in size, height, and vigor of the plant and diminution in offset production. This condition is known as "breaking" and has occurred almost as long as tulips have been grown. Pictures made as early as 1640–1650 are on record.

Generally in the past this condition has been considered as due to a reversion, a sport, a break, or some peculiar change in the bulb itself

FIGURE 230.—Tulip flowers from an experiment showing the transmission of mosaic or breaking by inoculation from Farncombe Sanders to Clara Butt and from Clara Butt to Farncombe Sanders. The flower at the left is Farncombe Sanders Rembrandt grown from a bulb as sold in commerce, and at the right Clara Butt Rembrandt. These represent the source of inoculum in each case. The upper flowers are Clara Butt control (left) and inoculated (right) with aphids transferred on April 27, 1927, from Farncombe Sanders Rembrandt. These are sister flowers—that is, they came from one plant two years previously, or in 1926. The lower flowers are Farncombe Sanders inoculated (left) by leaf mutilation on May 6, 1927, from Clara Butt, and control (right). Photographed April 21, 1928

that is "without parallel in the floral world." More recently the view that it is due to an infectious virus disease of the mosaic type has been gaining ground. None of the well-known details of the performance of this disorder are out of harmony with the view that it is a disease.

Experiments conducted recently show conclusively that the breaking of tulips is due to an infectious mosaic disease. The disease has been successfully transferred by inoculation from 15 varieties of broken tulips, including 4 commercial Rembrandts (broken Darwin) and 1 or more representatives of the cottage, breeder, and Darwin types, to a single variety, Clara Butt, which was used as a standard of comparison. It was transferred from Clara Butt to 17 other varieties. In all cases the flowers broke in a similar manner, which indicated that only one mosaic disease was involved. In the inoculation work suitable controls were maintained. This was usually done by taking for the experiment two bulbs from each clump produced by one plant. The plant from one of the bulbs was inoculated and the other maintained uninoculated as a control.

Three Methods of Inoculation

Infection was readily secured by three methods of inoculation— namely, leaf mutilation, which gave 30 per cent infection; tissue insertion, 33 per cent; and transfer of aphids, 12 per cent. The leaf-mutilation inoculations were made by applying juice pressed out of diseased plants to the leaves of the healthy plant mutilated by crushing between the thumb and finger. The tissue-insertion inoculations were made by inserting a wedge or slice of tissue cut from a diseased flower stalk into a slit cut in the healthy flower stalk and binding with moist raffia. The aphid-transfer inoculations were made by transferring aphids to healthy plants under cages after feeding them for some days on diseased plants. Three species of aphids, *Illinoia solanifolii* Ashmead, *Myzus persicae* Sulz, and *M. pelargonii* Sulz, were tested and found able to transmit the disease. *I. solanifolii* transmitted the disease readily and gave positive results in every case. The others gave relatively low percentages of transmission and failed entirely in some tests.

When handled from the standpoint of an infectious mosaic disease, the breaking of tulips can be controlled without question. Control practices involve the separation of stocks of mosaic and healthy tulips in planting, rigid roguing during the growing season to remove plants with broken flowers or mottled foliage, and possibly the use of aphid sprays or dusts under special conditions such as presence of the disease and abundance of aphids. The effectiveness of these methods in controlling the disease has been indicated by experience and experimental trials.

M. B. McKay,
Philip Brierley,
T. P. Dykstra.

U REA Demonstrated to Be Valuable As Nitrogen Fertilizer   The curiosity that prompts the small boy to take apart the family clock to find the "tick" has apparently not always been a characteristic of the human race. It was only a few centuries ago that man became curious in a practical way about the air, water, and minerals of the earth, and the attempts to satisfy this curiosity in an experimental way laid the foundations for the modern science of chemistry.

Early in the study of the composition of matter chemical compounds were classed either as organic or inorganic. In the former class were placed all compounds found in plants or animals, and it was assumed that they were formed there by a mysterious vital force and could be produced no other way. In 1773 urea, a rather simple compound containing carbon, oxygen, hydrogen, and nitrogen, was discovered in human urine and was of course classed as an organic compound. In 1828—just 100 years ago—Woehler, a German chemist, discovered that urea was formed on evaporating a solution of ammonium isocyanate. This compound had not been found in any plant or animal, and, moreover, could be made in the laboratory from its elements.

Dividing Line Swept Away

Thus at one stroke the barrier between organic and inorganic compounds was swept away. Since that time many plant and animal constituents have been made in the laboratory without the agency of any living matter, and there are few chemists who do not believe all plant and animal constituents can be artificially made.

From Woehler's time until recent years urea continued to be a compound of interest chiefly in the laboratory, where, because it was the form in which nitrogen is chiefly excreted from the human body, its properties were studied and methods for determining it devised. It was not difficult to make, but the demand was in ounces and it cost a dollar per pound or more.

During the development of fertilizer practice in the last half century suggestions were made from time to time that if the fertilizer elements could be supplied in more concentrated form there would be a material saving in the cost of transportation and handling, but it is only within the last decade that advance has been made in the use of concentrated fertilizer materials.

Plants Utilize Urea

Urea, a water-soluble compound containing 46 per cent nitrogen, naturally suggested itself as a concentrated form of nitrogen provided it proved to be readily utilized by plants and could be made cheaply enough. It has been demonstrated by several years' experimental field work that urea is changed in the soil so that it can be utilized by plants and that it ranks high among the sources of nitrogen for fertilizer purposes. The cost of manufacture, while it still makes urea cost somewhat more than other nitrogen carriers, is not now so excessive as formerly and increased demand and improvements in manufacture will undoubtedly help to lower this cost.

The interest in urea from a chemist's point of view is twofold: (1) Its preparation in the laboratory marks a milestone in the history of chemistry, and (2) it stands out as a simple chemical compound containing carbon, oxygen, hydrogen, and nitrogen that is made commercially from its elements. All the chemist needs is a lump of coal, some air and water. With the proper equipment and process, urea results.

EDMUND C. SHOREY.

VELVET Beans of a Bush Variety Developed With Distinguishable Seed. The original bush or bunch variety of velvet beans was first developed as a sport from the Alabama variety in 1914. The plant differed from all other cultivated varieties in being nontwining—that is, bush or bunch in habit. Unfortunately, the nearly spherical and grayish seeds marbled with brown were identical with the seed of the most widely grown twining varieties—the Georgia, the Alabama and the Florida.

In its place of origin it became abundantly established and soon replaced the other varieties. Its advantages were that it did not twine on the corn and therefore did not pull down the stalks, as was common with the twining sorts. It was found especially valuable as a green-manure crop in orange and other groves, where any variety that climbs the trees is decidedly objectionable, particularly while the trees are young. As a hay crop it has a particular advantage because the absence of twining stems does away with the common difficulty in mowing ordinary velvet beans, which make a tangled mass of vines. The principal objections to the bush variety are that the pods can not be gathered as rapidly as those of the twining varieties, and they lie so close to the ground that they become water-soaked in wet weather, causing many of them to decay.

With such advantages over the twining sorts, the demand greatly exceeded the supply of seed. With resulting high prices, unscrupulous growers and dealers took advantage of the similarity of seed of the twining and bush varieties and substituted cheaper seed of the former wholly or in part for the latter. This practice soon caused reliable

FIGURE 231.—A field of a new bush variety of velvet beans with gray seed developed by the United States Department of Agriculture

seedsmen to refuse to handle the bush variety, with the result that at the present time it has practically disappeared from the market.

Realizing the value of a bush variety of velvet beans, the United States Department of Agriculture attempted through selection and hybridization to develop bush varieties with seed easily distinguishable from that of twining sorts. Several very promising bush and semi-bush types have resulted from hybridizing black and gray colored varieties with the bush variety. Seeds of these types vary in color from gray to gray speckled with black, and there is also considerable variation in shape and size of the seed. All are quite distinct in color, shape, and size from the seed of the vining varieties. One of the most promising new types (fig. 231) is a sport with ash-colored seeds, selected from the original bush variety and, except for color of seed, identical with that variety. The department has no seed for distribution at the present time.

With seed easily distinguishable from the twining varieties, thereby eliminating the element of fraud, it is hoped that the new types of the bush variety will achieve the wide popularity which the bush variety previously held, and that they may become highly useful and particularly valuable for the special purposes indicated.

W. J. Morse.

WAGES of Farm Hands Augmented by Many Important Perquisites Wages of hired farm laborers properly include not only the cash payments commonly quoted but also the value of payments in kind and the value of privileges. These latter, except board, are commonly ignored in discussing wages, although they are of considerable aggregate value. Their inclusion with wage values makes real farm wages higher than they are commonly believed to be.

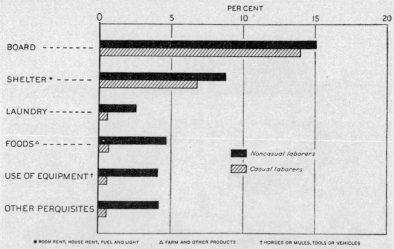

FIGURE 232.—Comparative percentages of total remuneration values received in perquisites by casual and noncasual farm hands

The Department of Agriculture has made two nation-wide studies of the perquisites of hired farm laborers, one of casuals, another of noncasuals. Noncasual laborers are permanent employees compared with casuals, being hired for the crop season or longer. Casuals are employed usually for short-time rush work, especially at harvest.

In the two studies the real wages of noncasual farm hands are made up of 60 per cent cash and 40 per cent perquisites. Similarly, casual laborers get 77 per cent of their remuneration in cash and 23 per cent in perquisites. The cash wages for their rush-time work average decidedly higher per day, and their perquisite values average slightly lower than for noncasuals. This sharply reduces the proportions of their total remuneration received as perquisites.

Board is the principal perquisite, both in frequency of occurrence and in value. Shelter, including room or house rent, fuel, and light, stands next. Other perquisites are of less frequency and smaller aggregate value.

Ninety-eight per cent of noncasual laborers were reported receiving perquisites, compared with 85 per cent of casual laborers. The latter

are on their employers' farms for only a short time, and, aside from
necessary board and lodging, have opportunity or desire for few perquisites. The former spend the season or longer on the same farms;
they receive perquisites in wider variety.

Board was reported furnished to 74 per cent of casual laborers but
to only 51 per cent of noncasual laborers; lodging (room or house rent)
to 62 per cent and 46 per cent, respectively; and washing was done for
23 per cent and 18 per cent, respectively. For the other perquisites
considered, the classifications in the two studies differed somewhat.

Principal Perquisites Other Than Board

The principal other perquisites and the percentages of casual farm
hands receiving them follow: Fuel, 18 per cent; light, 14 per cent;
foodstuffs other than table board, 9 per cent (the laborers receiving the
preceding were usually not lodged or boarded in the farm homes);
transportation between lodging and work, 13 per cent; use of farm
horses, mules, or vehicles (except for transportation), 12 per cent.

The principal perquisites, or groups of related perquisites, and the
percentages of noncasuals receiving them were: Dairy and poultry
products, 17 per cent; meats, 10 per cent; vegetables or fruits, 16 per
cent; keeping of livestock, 35 per cent; livestock feed, 17 per cent;
livestock pasturage, 18 per cent; garden, 30 per cent; garage, 37 per
cent; use of farm horses, mules, tools, or vehicles, 35 per cent.

There are striking differences in the proportions of single and married
noncasual farm hands receiving certain perquisites, as follows: Board
(and room and washing), single, 90 per cent, married, 10 per cent;
house rent, fuel and light, single, 0, married, 67 per cent; dairy and
poultry products, single, 0, married, 60 per cent; vegetables or fruits,
single, 0, married, 56 per cent; keeping livestock, single, 3 per cent,
married, 65 per cent; use of employers' horses or mules, single, 24 per
cent, married, 65 per cent; use of farm tools or vehicles, single, 29 per
cent, married, 69 per cent; garden space, single, 0, married, 63 per cent.

The comparative percentages of total remuneration values which
casual and noncasual farm hands received as perquisites are shown
in Figure 232.   J. C. FOLSOM.

WATERFOWL Breeding   With increase of population the
     a Necessary Adjunct   areas available for the natural pro-
     to Protective Measures duction of wild ducks and other
                             waterfowl are constantly being re-
duced. At the same time the numbers of hunters, with their destructive effect upon the abundance of these birds, are increasing. Thus
arises a problem in diminishing returns, and its only solution, if hunting is to be continued on the present scale, is to increase the production of waterfowl. Natural propagation may be aided both in unre-
served as well as in reserved waters by keeping the food supply adequate in variety and quantity and by controlling predatory enemies of
the birds. Creating refuges is in itself not sufficient. Left to themselves such areas may become paradises indeed, but more for the
vermin than for the creatures for which they were established. To
have their full effect, reservations must be thoughtfully administered
and efficiently patrolled. Their productivity can be increased several
fold by food planting and vermin control, and until this is accom-

plished it can not be claimed that the best is being done to encourage the natural propagation of waterfowl.

Propagation of game birds in confinement has its chief value as a protective measure in that it reduces the drain upon the wild stock. Some sportsmen and sporting clubs now produce or purchase from game farms all the birds needed for the season's sport, practices which if more widely followed would help lessen the menace to the wild supply. Such centers of propagation never reap the full harvest of the birds they produce, so that there is a steady overflow that not only increases the game-bird population of adjacent areas but in some degree contributes also to the main stream of waterfowl migration.

The inexperienced need not fear that waterfowl propagation is too difficult for them to attempt. Rather they should realize that successful methods already are well worked out. The propagation of one of the waterfowl species, the mallard, has been found to be fully as easy as that of any other game bird, lowland or upland. (Fig. 233.) Farmers' bulletins on the propagation of game birds are available.

FIGURE 233.—Mallards—aquatic game birds that are easy to propagate

Equipment for the propagation of waterfowl should include one or more ponds, hatching and rearing coops, broody hens, rearing fields for the young, and if the birds are to be used for sport a flight range, over which they can be trained to return to the home pond over high obstacles, so as to give difficult shots. Personnel employed should include at least one competent game breeder, but his assistants can be hired locally as needed and be sufficiently trained in a short time.

There must be, of course, some outlay of funds in waterfowl propagation, but the cost per bird should easily be kept far below the average cost of bringing to bag wild ducks from their natural haunts. Once this is realized, this economy alone should greatly increase interest in waterfowl propagation; but above all reasons looms one that must become evident to all in time: If sportsmen are to continue to reap their annual harvest in the hunting field, they certainly must sow.

W. L. McATEE.

WATER Supply of Rural Communities Frequently Requires Purification — Water in rural communities used for drinking and general household purposes is all too frequently excessively hard, highly mineralized with soluble sodium salts, loaded with iron compounds, turbid and cloudy, foul smelling and tasting, or polluted, whereas it should be lightly mineralized, practically free from iron, sparkling clear, and free from objectionable odor and taste and from microorganisms that may endanger health. Although all of the undesirable features enumerated are found in very few rural water supplies, one or more occur in a very large proportion of them. Fortunate indeed is the family possessing an abundant supply of water that is wholly acceptable for general use.

The hardness of water is due chiefly to salts of calcium and magnesium. The hardness that can be removed by boiling is called temporary hardness and that which remains after boiling is called permanent hardness. Temporary hardness is due in large part to limestone or magnesian limestone held in solution by carbon dioxide, and permanent hardness is due in large part to dissolved calcium sulphate or gypsum. Hardness in water is recognized by its harsh "feel," by the fact that a great deal of soap is required to produce a lather, and by the formation of deposits or incrustations in vessels in which the water is stored or heated. Temporary hardness can be reduced by treatment with minute quantities of limewater, followed by settling and filtering, and permanent hardness can be reduced by treatment with small quantities of washing-soda solution, followed by settling and filtering. These chemicals, however, should not be added by inexperienced persons to water to be used for drinking and they must be added in just the right quantities. As chemical analyses of water, as well as settling tanks, filters, and other equipment, are necessary for this work, it is preferable, when the outlay is warranted, to buy water-softening apparatus, several types of which are found on the market. The names of manufacturers of such apparatus can be obtained from a trade directory. It is usually not deemed practicable to install water softeners in the average rural household because of the expense. If the water is to be used only for cleansing purposes ammonia or borax may be used to soften it.

Distillation Generally Too Costly

The only way to render acceptable a water containing an excessively high proportion of sodium chloride, sodium sulphate, or sodium bicarbonate is to distill it. Distillation of water for general household use is generally held to be out of the question because of the expense.

Iron, when present even in small quantities, stains clothes and gives drinking water a very unpalatable appearance, due to the precipitation of the iron as insoluble oxides when the water is heated or allowed to stand. Frequently the iron can be removed by aerating, storing the water in tanks until most of the metal is precipitated, and then filtering. Sometimes, however, the iron is held in solution in organic combinations, and the addition of a very small quantity of limewater is necessary to precipitate it. As already indicated, it is inadvisable to add this or any other chemical if the water is intended for drinking.

Iron-removal apparatus can be bought on the market, but is rather too expensive for the average householder.

Water from newly dug wells is frequently turbid or cloudy, but it will usually become clear after a few months. The turbidity is almost always due to finely divided clay or siliceous matter that persists in staying in suspension. Water that becomes cloudy or turbid after rains is quite likely to be polluted and potentially dangerous to health. The usual method of removing turbidity is filtration through sand and gravel. Water filters can be bought on the market or they can be constructed at home from concrete, by following the directions in Farmers' Bulletin 1448–F.

Odors of water are described as fishy, aromatic, earthy, musty, rotten egg, etc. Many of these odors are due to microscopic organisms, as, for example, the fishy and oily odor of Uroglena, the aromatic or rose-geranium odor of Asterionella, the ripe-cucumber odor of Synura, and the green-corn odor of Anabaena. Others, such as the pig-pen odor of decaying Anabaena, are due to decomposition of microscopic organisms. A rotten-egg odor is usually due to hydrogen sulphide or other sulphur compounds, and an earthy odor is usually due to organic matter and clay. It is not generally believed that organisms such as Asterionella and Synura are injurious to health, but water containing them is objectionable from an aesthetic standpoint and it is possible that their presence in large numbers may cause temporary intestinal disorders. But odors may be caused by sewage or other pollution, in which case the water may contain pathogenic organisms, making it highly dangerous to health. Frequently filtration through sand or charcoal, or both, will remove or greatly reduce objectionable odors. This treatment, however, can not be depended upon to remove all disease-producing organisms.

Laboratory Analysis Required

There is no way of proving that a water is polluted with disease-producing organisms other than by laboratory analysis or by showing that a particular water supply is the direct cause of illness. Bad odor or taste, a cloudy or turbid appearance of the water after rains, and the development of intestinal disorders after drinking it sometimes indicate a polluted water supply. On the other hand, bad odor is often due to causes other than pollution, and a sparkling clear water may convey disease. Water believed to be polluted should not be used for drinking unless there is no other water available, in which case it should be heated until it boils vigorously. Other emergency methods of rendering polluted water safe for drinking can not be described here because of lack of space. Suspected water should always be analyzed as soon as possible and suitable remedial measures taken if pollution is proved. The United States Department of Agriculture can not analyze water for individuals, and many States are subject to similar restrictions. Specific inquiries regarding pollution of water, analyses, etc., can best be answered by State health officials, who are familiar with local conditions.

J. W. SALE.

WATERY Soft Rot Is Very Serious Market Disease of Vegetables Among the most serious diseases of vegetables are those caused by soil organisms. Watery soft rot is caused by a soil fungus (Sclerotinia) which is more or less common to all trucking regions and is especially destructive, because it can attack such a wide variety of crops. Lettuce, celery, carrots, turnips, cabbage, beans, peas, and practically all of the common vegetables are subject to this disease. A characteristic soft, watery decay is produced in all products and the plants are covered with a white cottony mold. (Fig. 234.) In transit, storage, and on the market badly decayed products actually leak, but there is no disagreeable odor like that produced by many other diseases.

As indicated, this disease originates in the field and is there known by a variety of names, the most common of which are foot rot, Sclerotinia rot, and drop. The fungus does not require wounds for infection and is therefore able to attack almost any part of a plant.

FIGURE 234.—Watery soft rot of carrots

Young plants often die, but if a plant is large and otherwise healthy when attacked, it may keep on growing and make a marketable product. It is these affected plants, however, that decay so badly during transit and marketing. The seriously decayed vegetables are discarded in the grading and packing process, but the products having small decayed spots are often overlooked. Unfortunately, even those with the smallest watery soft-rot spots are sure to suffer great loss before they reach the market. Wet field conditions favor the development of the fungus, and moist surfaces of the plants when packed favor its spread from one plant to another during transit. For example, in hampers of green beans and peas it is often found that the pods are overrun by a great abundance of white cottony mold and large numbers of them are joined together in "nests."

Conditions Influencing Fungus Growth

The fungus causing this disease grows very rapidly at ordinary temperatures and rather fast even at refrigeration temperatures.

Consequently watery soft rot is found causing damage in cars of produce under standard refrigeration. A cold-storage temperature of 32° F. will not entirely stop its development. The fact that watery soft rot continues to develop at low temperatures makes it one of the most serious of storage diseases; in fact, the greatest losses sustained in vegetable produce held in storage, particularly carrots and celery, are caused by it. Fortunately, two of the most valuable storage crops, onions and potatoes, are not affected by this disease. Fortunately, also, a large proportion of the shipments of vegetables susceptible to the disease originate in fields relatively free of it and move to market without serious loss.

The losses that do occur are serious enough, however, so that everything possible should be done to reduce or prevent them. In preparing produce for the market, care should be exercised to see that it is clean and free from disease. Such precautions, combined with careful handling during the harvesting and handling process and good refrigeration in transit, will do much to keep down loss from this disease, although its ability to develop at temperatures of 40° F. or below makes absolute control in transit very difficult if not impossible.

G. B. RAMSEY.

WEATHER Relationship to Yields Studied in Canada and Argentina — Studies are being conducted by the foreign service of the Bureau of Agricultural Economics to determine the relationship of weather and yields for certain foreign countries. Results obtained to date can not be regarded as final, but they give an indication of the value of such work, and afford a more definite objective basis for judging the current year's yield in certain countries, prior to the release of official estimates.

An analysis of temperature and rainfall data from April through July in its relation to wheat yields in the three western prairie Provinces of Canada—Manitoba, Saskatchewan, and Alberta—indicated a probable crop on the July acreage estimate between 476,000,000 and 552,000,000 bushels for 1928 in those Provinces, or, averaging the two extremes, about 515,000,000. This is based on a multiple correlation measuring the effect of temperatures for April, May, June, and July, and rainfall for the period April to July upon the yields of wheat from 1905–1927. Separate studies made for each Province gave somewhat different relationships between weather and yield in the different Provinces. For the three Provinces, the weather records of 19 stations were used.

A study of the relation of temperature and rainfall to the yield of wheat in Argentina indicates that there is a closer relationship between temperature changes and yield of wheat than between rainfall changes and yield of wheat. During the period 1890–1919, yield of wheat varied between 5 bushels per acre in 1896 and 18 bushels in 1893. Most of the wheat acreage of Argentina lies in the Provinces of Buenos Aires, Cordoba, Santa Fe, Entre Rios, and the Pampa territory. A small part lies outside this zone. In the northern part of Argentina, grain sowing begins in May, progresses southward, and continues as late as mid-August. June and July are the most important months for sowing. Harvest begins in the extreme north

(Tucuman) by the latter part of October and, progressing toward the south and into the mountains, continues as late as mid-January. The most important month is December, during which about 80 per cent of the wheat is harvested.

The rainfall data used covered the months of May to October, inclusive; temperature data covered August to October. The yield of wheat for 1927–28, based on the correlation of these factors with yield for the period, was about 11.5 bushels per acre, with a probable range of 0.94 bushel above or below. Including November temperatures with the other factors gave an indicated yield of 11.7 bushels, with a probable range of 0.9 bushel, plus or minus. Applying these yields to the official acreage reported for 1927–28, a production of 230,000,000 bushels was indicated, with a probable range of 18,000,000 bushels above or below. The Argentine Government's latest estimate on the 1927–28 crop is 239,000,000 bushels.

The above study treats the whole wheat area as a unit. In a later study of weather and wheat yield relationships in Argentina the wheat section is divided into northern and southern sections, because of the differences in the growing stages of the wheat crop for the two sections.

Corn Yields and Weather

Weather from October to February is shown to be closely related to yield of corn in Argentina. The earliest planting of corn is in September and the latest is in December. Corn harvest season is in March and April. The factors considered were temperatures in October, November, December, January, and February, and rainfall in October, November, and January. Monthly temperatures, averaging above 75° F. during the growing season, appear to be associated with lower yields. Although increased rainfall was usually associated with increased yields, rainfall changes do not appear to affect yield as markedly as do temperature changes. Weather during the corn season in Argentina for 1927–28, on the basis of the above correlation study on the official acreage, indicated a production of 314,000,000 bushels, with a probable range of 17,000,000 bushels. The last official estimate was 306,000,000 bushels.

Wheat Yields in Australia

A study of the relationship of weather to wheat yields in Victoria, Australia, shows the relative importance of certain rainfall and temperature data. Three stations in the Province were used and given weights. This study showed that rainfall was more important in determining the yield than was indicated in Argentina.

As more weather data from representative stations in the crop areas of foreign countries become available and with increasing accuracy in measuring yields, it should be possible to express the yields from the weather relationships with a fair degree of accuracy. At present these studies are a great aid in estimating yields early in the season for certain important countries; this enables the department to furnish producers timely information on foreign supply so the crop of the United States can be marketed to the best advantage.

O. L. DAWSON.

WILD Animals Affect Forest Production in Many Important Ways   Bits of information have been gathered here and there regarding the relation of wild animals to forests, studies of special problems have been made that throw some light on the intricate and important relationships that exist between them, and enough has been learned to show the urgent need for the application of modern research methods. Within the past year a far-reaching step was taken in this direction by congressional enactment of the McSweeney-McNary bill, which authorizes carefully planned attack upon forestry and wild-life problems. The measure contemplates that coordination and continuity of research necessary to obtain fundamental and permanent results.

In any program of forest administration knowledge of the numbers and activities of wild animals is of outstanding importance. Their interrelationships are intricate and vary greatly according to locality, season, and other factors, including the activities of man. Many animals are beneficial through their distribution and planting of seeds, working the soil, or destroying injurious insects and rodents.

Bats Valuable As Insect Killers

Bats stand out as examples of forest-inhabiting creatures that, so far as known, have no economically injurious habits but are of incalculable value as destroyers of nocturnal insects, including many that are injurious to forest trees. On the other hand, squirrels, chipmunks, and mice may in some areas prove of distinct value as natural distributors of acorns, nuts, and other tree seeds, but they may also at times consume practically the entire crop of seeds and thus prevent natural reproduction, or dig up and destroy all the seeds planted for reforestation purposes. Rabbits, wood rats, and porcupines have been known to destroy 50 per cent or more of the seedling trees on large planted areas. Where porcupines are abundant they may kill or deform a high percentage of the trees and thus ruin them for the market. Such burrowing animals as pocket gophers, by feeding on the root systems of plants or covering plants with dirt thrown out of burrows, may become seriously destructive. Secondary injury to the vegetation cover may occur by the trampling of grazing stock on areas undermined by burrowing species. The physical condition of the soil, however, may be improved for the germination of seeds of trees and forage plants and its water-storing capacity increased.

Prairie dogs, ground squirrels, and jack rabbits frequently consume or otherwise destroy 25 to 50 per cent or more of the yield over many millions of acres of forest land and compete with livestock for the most palatable and nutritious grasses. By consuming grass and destroying grass seed, these rodents interfere with improved grazing practices. Removal of the grass cover also makes conditions favorable for destructive erosion, which renders worthless great areas of otherwise valuable grazing land within forests.

Various kinds of predacious animals may cause heavy losses of livestock and game in forest areas, but may also help to repress such injurious species as rodents and to dispose of sick individuals of game birds and animals.

Game Animals Create Problems

Game animals constitute important products of forested areas. Their presence, however, involves problems of protection to forest trees, browse, and forage, as well as a proper adjustment in their numbers and range not only for their own well-being but in the interests of livestock production and other local or national industries. Excessive increase in numbers of deer in certain localities in recent years has afforded striking examples of starvation, suffering, and loss of animals, associated with serious damage to their food plants and to crops and orchards in adjacent agricultural areas. (Fig. 235.)

Game animals as a forest resource must be considered also from the standpoint of their recreational and their food values. A steadily increasing public interest in the recreational value of wild life is manifested not only by hunters but also by great numbers of persons who

FIGURE 235.—Deer in a forest area—a type of the wild life that may constitute an important financial and recreational asset in forest production

find enjoyment, mental stimulus, and physical recuperation in getting acquainted with the ways of the wild creatures of the forests. From the strictly economic standpoint, the more than 700,000 deer estimated to be on the national forests in 1927, reckoned at $20 a head, would give a total value of $14,000,000 in meat for human consumption, an item well deserving consideration.

Results obtained in the study by the Bureau of Biological Survey of the elk herd in Jackson Hole, Wyo., have demonstrated the value of research in obtaining information regarding their numbers, feeding and breeding habits, seasonal movements, diseases, parasites, and natural enemies as a foundation on which to establish permanent policies for the preservation of one of the most important herds of forest big-game animals in the United States. Conditions there are in many respects typical, and the results obtained and the methods of investigation that prove practicable there will be helpful elsewhere.

The Problem of the Fur Bearers

The place of fur-bearing animals in forest production is not yet adequately known, as no comprehensive studies have been made of their numbers, factors affecting their abundance, or of possibilities for local increase or for transplanting to other suitable regions. The establishment of beavers, muskrats, and other fur bearers in forested areas and on cut-over land affords prospect of important financial returns through the utilization of relatively worthless timber and other food supplies. Beaver dams should assist materially in the regulation of water run-off and stream flow, which are important in preventing floods and fires, conserving water for plant growth and emergency irrigation, and improving conditions for the production of fishes. The importance of fur-producing animals as a source of revenue from the forests is apparent, but more complete information is needed regarding their relationships and the conditions under which they may be made profitable without detriment to other forest interests.

The pioneer period of apparently inexhaustible resources of forest and wild life with its measureless waste and destruction of a priceless heritage is past. Depletion of this great reservoir of natural assets has reached a point where far-sighted and effective action based on a knowledge of the facts must be taken. Conditions are now ripe and the public mind is ready for constructive research that will lay a sure foundation on which wild-life production as an adjunct to forestry can be established and developed on a permanently sound and profitable footing.

W. B. BELL.

WILDERNESS Areas in the National Forests Are to Be Preserved Forty-two wilderness areas have recently been established by the Forest Service in the national forests of Colorado, Wyoming, South Dakota, and Minnesota, included in the Rocky Mountain district. Such action, involving 2,551,020 acres, indicates the recognition which is given in

FIGURE 236.—Big Water of Saganaga, Superior wilderness area, Minn.

planning the administration of these public properties, to the special suitability of certain areas for recreation and for scientific purposes.

In setting aside these units three classes have been specified. Class I is largely for scientific study and use. It comprises natural areas ranging from a few acres to one or more sections, set aside for observation and study in future years. The tracts are so located that they can be protected and exempted from every form of use, including grazing. European scientists have found that areas of this kind kept in their natural state are vital to the checking of observations of current conditions on lands being cultivated for the production of continuous forest crops.

The Class II wilderness areas are made up of rugged tracts difficult of access, the scenic beauty of which is dependent upon their retention in a primeval state. Here all commercial uses are prohibited. In laying out these areas an effort has been made to provide in so far as possible for the needs of big game.

The Class III wildernesses make up by far the larger part of the acreage and are predicated on the premise that the highest social values

FIGURE 237.—Typical wilderness country in the Rocky Mountains, Washakie National Forest, Wyo.

will be realized from these areas if no cultural developments are permitted. In these areas automobile roads will not be constructed, and resorts, summer homes, and improvements of a similar character will not be permitted. The utilization of the economic resources, such as timber, forage, and water, will be authorized and the improvements necessary to utilization will be permitted, every effort being made in their management to correlate the utilization plans with the controlling policies governing the wilderness areas.

Thirteen areas in Class I have been set aside; 1 area of 100,000 acres in Class II; and 28 areas involving 2,451,020 acres in Class III.

Pioneer Conditions for Recreation Seeker

There are certain types of recreation seekers who demand different conditions from those provided for in the usual resorts, automobile camps, or public camp grounds on intensively used highways. In order to enjoy his vacation period fully this type of recreation seeker must be surrounded by pioneer and primitive conditions that demand a display of his woodcraft and a certain amount of hardship accompanied by a marked degree of isolation. With the continuous forward march of intensive recreational development of one sort or another, the Forest Service has found that the wilderness type of recreation should be provided for this hardier type of recreation seeker. The setting aside of the wilderness areas of Class II and Class III was in recognition of his needs. It is believed the action taken by the Forest Service will satisfy a real and important want.

The whole wilderness area idea is an innovation in land economics and represents an attempt to set up barriers against the inroads of civilization and the usual type of recreational development, and to satisfy a demand for natural scientific laboratories and for recreational opportunities under pioneer conditions. E. W. TINKER.

WINDSTORM Insurance on Farm Property Is Highly Important

Windstorm insurance is of peculiar importance to farmers, whose buildings as a rule are of relatively light construction. Such insurance applies not only to buildings, however, but to household goods, equipment, and livestock, Although it is often called "tornado" or "cyclone" insurance, it covers loss from severe wind without distinction as to the kind of storm.

The most dangerous form of windstorm in the United States is the tornado. Such storms are most frequent, as well as most destructive, in the central part of the Mississippi Valley. Certain other areas suffer frequently from tornadoes, and no part of the country can claim complete exemption. In some of the South Atlantic States and those bordering on the Gulf of Mexico, another form of storm called a hurricane sometimes proves highly destructive. Local straight winds, usually though not always accompanied by thunder showers, may at times reach such intensity as to endanger buildings and other property.

Against property loss from windstorm, insurance is practically the only available safeguard. In the case of the fire hazard the danger can to a large extent be reduced by proper care. This is much less true of the danger from windstorm. The resistance of a building may be increased by proper construction and maintenance, but the storm itself can be neither avoided nor modified by human action. Insurance against windstorm may be said therefore to be fully as essential as insurance against fire, notwithstanding that the annual fire losses materially exceed the losses from windstorm.

Cost of Protection Varies

The cost of windstorm insurance varies for different parts of the country from about one-half to less than one-fourth the cost of fire insurance. The joint-stock fire insurance companies, as well as the larger general fire insurance mutuals, write windstorm insurance either through separate policies or through so-called combined policies, which cover both fire and windstorm. Farmers' mutual windstorm insurance, however, is written more largely by specialized mutual companies which limit themselves to insurance against this one hazard.

About 50 mutual windstorm insurance companies in the United States carry a total of risks approximating $2,000,000,000. The more successful of these operate in close affiliation with the numerous

farmers' mutual fire insurance companies. Examples of close cooperation between state-wide windstorm insurance mutuals and local
farmers' fire insurance mutuals are found in Iowa, Indiana, Ohio,
Missouri, and North Dakota. In a number of other States, district
windstorm mutuals are found which cooperate with the local fire
insurance mutuals in their respective territories.

About 13 per cent of the farmers' mutual fire insurance companies
also write combined protection covering windstorm as well as fire.
This practice is to be commended in so far as the larger farmers' fire
insurance mutuals are concerned. For the more local companies of
this kind which limit themselves to a county or less, or at most a few
counties, the practice of including windstorm in the hazards covered
is not wise. From the point of view of the fire hazard, each group of

FIGURE 238.—The result of a windstorm. This might happen in any part of the country

farm buildings, and in some measure each building in the group, is
a separate risk. A single tornado or other form of windstorm, on
the other hand, may destroy a large number of farm buildings in its
path.

The Problem for Local Mutuals

The local fire insurance mutuals that now include windstorm in
the hazards covered would greatly reduce the possibility of failure, or
serious embarrassment, by reinsuring or otherwise disposing of all
their windstorm risks. In States where farmers' mutual fire insurance
has been developed to a substantial extent on the local mutual basis,
and where no adequate facilities now exist for the insurance of farm
property against windstorm, the members of these companies would
do well to consider the example of Iowa, Missouri, and other States
by organizing a state-wide windstorm insurance company to be

managed and operated in close cooperation with the local fire insurance mutuals. Under efficient management, this plan makes possible reliable protection against windstorm as well as fire losses, at a minimum of cost.

V. N. VALGREN.

WINTER-WHEAT Seeding Date in Great Plains Varies With Locality — The best date for seeding winter wheat in the central Great Plains area depends on the locality. The date should be earlier the higher the altitude or the farther the distance north. The best time is influenced in this area, also, by the amount of available moisture at seeding time and the kind of seed bed, among other factors. Cooperative experiments conducted by the Bureau of Plant Industry and the Kansas Agricultural Experiment Station at the Fort Hays Branch Experiment Station, Hays, Kans., show that, when enough moisture is available in September to cause quick germination, early seeding usually results in slightly reduced yields. This is due in part to excessive fall growth which depletes the moisture supply, and in part to losses from Hessian fly infestation.

The best seeding time at Hays, Kans., is from September 25 to October 6. Wheat sown at this time usually becomes sufficiently well established to escape winter hazards to a large extent, and its emergence still is late enough to escape the Hessian fly. Wheat sown later than October 6 may produce weakened plants not able to survive low temperatures in the winter or soil blowing in the spring. Late seeding followed by cold wet weather also is favorable to smut infection, which reduces yields and quality.

Land that has been summer fallowed can be sown with good results at a somewhat later date than land that has been cropped. Sowing wheat in a dry, cloddy seed bed with little or no available subsoil moisture is a speculative risk, whatever the date, and often results in heavy financial losses to wheat growers. In exceptional years the yields obtained from seeding as late as October 20 have been higher than those from September seeding, but when this occurs the season generally has been characterized by a dry early fall followed by rains in late fall or early winter. The yield from late seeding usually does not exceed 15 bushels to the acre and is often much less. Yields as high as 25 bushels or more to the acre rarely are obtained unless there is an abundance of moisture stored in a well-prepared seed bed sown at the best seeding date.

A. F. SWANSON.

WOMEN Market 4-H Brand Products in Increasing Volume — Many thousands of women and girls who are developing the resources of their farms and farm communities, under the guidance of home demonstration agents, have profited much by learning to standardize and market their surplus home-grown and homemade products. In the beginning of this work the home demonstration agents assisted the girls and women in preparing and packing their products attractively and also in finding a market for their surplus. Business men and the home demonstration agents soon agreed that it was necessary to adopt a special trade name and label in order to identify these high-quality products when they were placed for sale in stores and markets.

The standardization and marketing of 4–H brand products began in 1910 and 1911, when farm girls enrolled in canning and poultry clubs first attempted to sell the surplus of fresh and canned produce from their tenth-acre tomato plots. A general-utility label showing a picture of a girl with a basket of fine tomatoes was first used on the tin cans which were packed for exhibit or sale. The use of a label that would certify the quality of these products resulted, at the request of

FIGURE 239.—The upper two labels were the first used in the United States on quality products packed in tin containers by 4–H club members. The lower label was adopted for 4–H brand products packed for sale in Texas

the home demonstration agents, in the adoption of a special brand name for all products which were prepared for market according to standard requirements. The 4–H brand label for tomatoes was generally used throughout the country. From that the 4–H brand name extended to other labels not only in girls' work but also in boys' work on boxes of seed corn, boxes of potatoes, top selected lambs, baby-beef sales, cotton, and many other products, as well as on farm-home products which were standardized for market by mothers and daughters jointly.

High Reputation Striven For

The pioneer agents worked systematically to raise and maintain standards of quality in order that the 4–H brand might establish a reputation for high quality. The numbers of mothers and daughters working together on the standardization of canned goods and poultry products for market increased rapidly. Many of the older and more successful club girls who had already established a reputation for high-quality products under the 4–H brand label would have lost much of the benefit derived from the publicity given to their products if when they advanced into the women's clubs they had been compelled to change the advertised name of their brand of homemade products. Consequently, for 14 years or more all individual demonstrators, both girl and woman members of home demonstration clubs, have continued

FIGURE 240.—Interior of the 4–H Basket Shop, Clay County, Ala., where more than $18,397 worth of pine-needle baskets have been sold

to use the 4–H brand labels on canned goods, baskets, rugs, and a great variety of articles which have been standardized for marketing. At first the same design on labels for a variety of products was used nationally. Later several home enterprises greatly increased their output, and special labels were designed in certain States. In other States individuals designed their own labels for special products.

The possibility of finding a good sale for farm-home products has encouraged farm women and girls to undertake larger and more important demonstrations with their home gardens and orchards, farm poultry flocks, and home dairies. Since so many women and girls have become interested in standardizing and marketing better farm butter, graded eggs, dressed poultry, improved varieties of fruits and vegetables, canned foods, home-cured meats, and other high-grade farm-home products, many thousands of dollars worth of farm surplus has been turned into farm-home conveniences. Living conditions have been improved in many parts of the country through this work.

Profits from Pine-Needle Baskets

In one county in Alabama 207 women shared in an $1,800 check which was the profit from one month's sale of standardized pine-needle baskets. Sales of baskets from this county in less than two years amounted to $18,397.05. Another story of a county commodity enterprise organized on a coopertive basis comes from a mountain county in Arkansas, where a group of women, organized as a county weavers' association, meet regularly to make braided and hooked rugs, hand-woven coverlets, and many other articles for sale in a rug shop which the group has established.

In Tennessee a group of women in Hamilton County and another group in Knox County have made progress in developing a profitable industry of making fine quality hooked rugs. Orders soon exhausted their supply of materials, and arrangements were made to obtain quantities of mill-end material and surplus waste from underwear manufacturers and hosiery mills. The women are now utilizing such mill by-products and are turning waste into wealth. In Apison community, Hamilton County, over $6,000 worth of fine hooked rugs of artistic design and standardized colors were sold last year, and the newer rug industry in Asbury community in Knox County continued to grow.

Organized Club Markets

The growth of organized club markets has been steady where quantities of improved varieties of fresh fruits and vegetables, better poultry, dairy, and meat products are sold. The home demonstration club market at Rocky Mount in Nash County, North Carolina, is a typical example. During the first seven months after the market opened in 1923, the sales aggregated $5,500. The next year they reached $10,358.84. In 1927, less than five years after the market opened, the total sales amounted to $31,015.77. The following products were sold at the Rocky Mount market during 1927:

Poultry	$6, 385. 33	Eggs	$2, 439. 38
Cakes	7, 246. 12	Fruit	1, 693. 70
Butter	2, 260. 43	Meats	1, 532. 00
Flowers	1, 302. 99	Canned goods	153. 28
Dressing	230. 00	Nuts	67. 56
Squabs	101. 93	Turkeys	49. 33
Honey	51. 13		
Miscellaneous	48. 34	Total	31, 015. 77
Vegetables	7, 454. 25		

Instructions were given the sellers in grading and standardizing by market specialists, the home demonstration agents, and various other specialists on the State extension staff. Through this marketing work groups of women have become intensely interested in learning how to produce the best quality in farm butter and other dairy, poultry, and meat products. They have in a very logical way come to appreciate the value of marketing homemade products in order to bring to the farm both the producers' and manufacturers' profits on many of the farm-grown products. Special butter cartons, egg boxes, and cottage cheese containers with 4–H brand labels printed on them have come into general use in many States. The 4-H brand stamp always signifies high-scoring products of quality, honest weight, and attractive pack.

In Alabama some outstanding results have been obtained from 25 club markets operated in the State. Nearly 3,000 different persons sold products at these markets and records show that the total sales made since these markets were opened to July 1, 1928, reached $648,-908.52. Many individual farm women sold more than $2,000 worth of produce in a year.

Marmalade Association in Texas

In 1926 a marmalade marketing association in Hidalgo County, Tex., was organized under the name of Home Demonstration Market-

FIGURE 241.—A 4–H club market in the public square, Charleston, Miss.

ing Organization of Rio Grande Valley. Its standardized products are now sold through the grocery stores and cafés in all towns in the county and are served on all Missouri Pacific dining cars running out of Houston. Orders have also been received from the Southern Pacific Railroad for individual jars to be served on their dining cars. Large quantities of small containers and gift packages have been sold at the holiday seasons. The farm women in this county have manifested much interest in other phases of home industries work like basketry, glove making, and the designing, tooling, and making of leather articles.

In Tarrant County, Tex., the marketing of 4–H quality household linens began in 1926 and has been continued by four women who make articles of quality in material, design, and workmanship. Among the articles sold have been towels, tablecloths, vanity sets, dresser scarfs, pillowcases, luncheon sets, and bedspreads.

FIGURE 242.—Labeling containers and preparing standardized 4-H brand gift packages for market in a home demonstration club in Florida

More than 20 women in Polk County, Fla., have met weekly in the county home demonstration agents' office to receive special instruction in the making of a variety of home industries articles. Hooked

FIGURE 243.—A farm home in Arkansas before and after improvements were made through profitable home enterprises fostered by the county home demonstration agent

rugs, leather articles, and repousse pewter have become remunerative sources of income for a number in this group.

Many women who before were not interested in home marketing have now become successful producers and sellers.

33023°—29——40

Results already obtained through profitable cooperative standardization work have proved that the fullest and finest development of our women and girls in the country comes through their interest and success in developing the resources of the farm home and the farm community, whether the products be for home use or for sale. Satisfaction and contentment are enjoyed by those who create useful and attractive food products and high-grade articles used for beautifying their homes. The best results have come when the ultimate aim has been not primarily a money profit, but means for making better and happier homes. Living conditions have been improved, family incomes have been increased, and homes have been beautified as a result of help received from home demonstration agents in the standardization and marketing of farm-home products. All this work had its beginning in many States with the adoption of a trade brand for quality products now widely known under the label of the 4-H brand.

OLA POWELL MALCOLM.

WOMEN on Farms Average 63 Hours' Work Weekly in Survey of 700 Homes There is much talk nowadays about the housewife with too much leisure. But as far as the farm woman is concerned, this is not yet a very troublesome problem. Of her the old saying still has significance: "Man works from sun to sun, but woman's work is never done."

Just how many hours may be considered a reasonable working week for the home maker? On this opinions differ. But few will deny that more than 60 hours a week means overwork. Yet by this easy test over half of the 700 farm women included in a recent study work too long. In industry the 8-hour day has been set as standard, with one day off in seven, and for many workers an additional half day on Saturday. Judged by this standard almost all of these farm women will be classed as overworked. But a 44-hour week is probably unduly short for the occupation of home making, where no time must be spent in going to and from work and where the strain and noise of modern industry is absent. Possibly a 50-hour week is a fair compromise—8 hours a day for six days with 2 hours on Sunday. Yet five-sixths of farm home makers are found to exceed even this liberal figure. No matter what standard we adopt, overwork appears to be the usual thing.

There is no reason to think that these 700 women were exceptionally industrious. If the facts were obtained for all of the 6,000,000 farm homes of the country the average would probably be even higher. For the women included in the study represent, on the whole, a superior group, with enough time, interest, and ability to keep careful records of how they spent their time for the seven days of a typical week. One hundred and twenty-nine of them live in the Middle West, 139 in New York, and the remaining 432 in three far Western States. On an average their records show 63 hours and 30 minutes of working time for the week.

Farm Woman Has Double Job

Not all of this time, of course, was spent in housekeeping and care of children. For the woman on the farm carries a double job; she is farmer as well as home maker. And in a few instances she adds a third paid job to the traditional two. It is this double or triple rôle which accounts for most of the overwork. For home making alone is still a full-time job for most farm women. According to these 700 records, it required an average of 52 hours and 17 minutes a week, and dairy work, care of poultry, gardening, and other jobs took an additional 11 hours and 13 minutes.

The term home making covers a multitude of tasks. How was this 52 hours a week distributed? Almost half of it was spent in feeding the family, and most of this in the preparation of meals and dish washing. The figures for the New York home makers may be taken as characteristic of the average situation. Of the 52 hours and 59 minutes which they spent during a week in home making, a total of 25 hours and 51 minutes was given to food—16 hours and 14 minutes to preparing meals, 8 hours and 30 minutes to clearing away meals, 53 minutes to food preservation, and 14 minutes to other food work.

Cleaning and straightening the house was the next highest item, requiring 8 hours and 15 minutes a week. The other items in the care of the house—care of fires, lights, water supply, repairing of furnishings, care of house surroundings—added another 2 hours and 17 minutes. Five hours and 21 minutes went to laundering, 4 hours and 11 minutes to sewing, 1 hour and 45 minutes to mending, and 13 minutes to other care of clothing.

Adding all of these items together, they give a total of 47 hours and 53 minutes devoted to housekeeping—to food, house, and clothing. Of the remaining 5 hours and 6 minutes which these New York farm women spent in home making, 2 hours and 26 minutes were given to care of children and other members of the family, 1 hour and 47 minutes to purchasing, planning, and other management, and 53 minutes to miscellaneous items.

Clearly this is a very different picture indeed from the one which is usually painted concerning the modern home maker. According to the current version, we should expect to find her housekeeping tasks reduced to a mere hour or so a day, with the care of children and the management of the family income absorbing the major part of her limited working time. For the city home maker this may be somewhat true. But for the farm woman it bears little resemblance to the actual situation.

Are we, then, to conclude that the farm home has not been touched by the industrial revolution? That ready-made clothing, ready-cooked foods, and better equipment and household conveniences have not cut down the time required in our grandmother's day for housekeeping? Such a conclusion would, of course, be unjustified. For though the working hours of the farm woman are still long, they were undoubtedly even longer 50 years ago. And much more help was given the home maker then than now by other members of the household. One-fifth of these New York housewives did all of their work themselves, and on the average they received only one hour a day of help.

Wide Variations in Different Homes

Averages, however, tell only part of the story. In some of these homes the time spent in home making by home maker and help together fell much above or below the average of 60 hours. What caused these variations?

The most important factor, of course, was difference in the size of the family. In the households with only two persons the routine tasks of preparing and clearing away meals, cleaning, laundering, and mending usually took less than 40 hours a week; whereas in the households with seven and more persons almost 60 hours was required. The size of the house and the conveniences and equipment also had their effect, and sometimes more time was spent just because there were plenty of people to do the work.

FIGURE 244.—Moisture-resistant coatings aid in preventing checking and weathering of wood. (See article on p. 623)

The influence of all these factors is clearly shown by the two New York households spending the lowest and highest time in home-making work. In the first of these the home maker had only herself and her husband to care for, with a 5-room house, running water in the kitchen, modern plumbing, electric lights, and a washing machine. Only 31 hours and 30 minutes were spent in home making during the week, and the home maker did all of the work except for the few minutes that her husband gave to looking after the fire.

In the other home there were four children, and the 9-room house could boast no modern improvements—no running water nor pump, no sink nor drain, and no electricity for light or power. But these factors in themselves were not enough to account for the enormous total of 117 hours spent in home-making work. The chief explanation lies in the fact that there were three daughters at home, all of them old enough and not too busy to share in the housework. Together they spent more time in home-making tasks than the home maker herself—57 hours compared with her 45. And even the husband and son contributed 15 hours. Clearly, when there are many hands to make the work light, there is little incentive to keep it down to a minimum.

HILDEGARDE KNEELAND.

WOOD Checking and Weathering Can Be Prevented by Paint   The checking and weathering of wood can be prevented to a large degree by keeping the wood well painted or by storing it under cover, or by both. Such care of wood prevents rapid changes in moisture content because wood is hygroscopic; that is, when wood dries it shrinks; when it absorbs moisture it swells. Shrinkage of a flat-sawed board is considerably more in the direction of the width than in the direction of thickness. The stresses and strains set up by this unequal shrinkage cause a lengthwise separation of the wood known as seasoning checks. By retarding rapid-surface drying the tendency to checking, especially at the ends of thick stock, is greatly reduced.

Wood exposed to damp weather or rain will absorb moisture on the surface and the surface layers will try to swell. This swelling is resisted by the dry interior of the wood, with the result that a squeezing action, which tends to give the surface layers a permanent

FIGURE 245.—Rapid changes in the dryness of lumber may be largely prevented by compact piling after seasoning

distortion, is set up. Later, when the surface dries out again, and attempts to shrink, a pulling action takes place, which may result in surface checks. If this process is repeated often enough weathering of the piece may take place. The injurious effects of changes in moisture content may be minimized, however, by retarding the rate of change. As already stated, this may be done by the use of paint or other moisture-resistant coatings, or by storing the wood under cover, or by both.

ROLF THELEN.

WOOD for Different Uses Needs Different Degrees of Dryness   Dry wood will absorb moisture from a damp atmosphere and wet wood will lose moisture to a dry atmosphere. These changes may take several weeks or longer to become complete, since daily fluctuations in atmospheric humidity have a slight effect upon the dryness of wood. However, wood in use changes in dryness from season to season, and as these changes take place they are accompanied by swelling and shrinking. Changes in dryness, particularly rapid changes in large timbers, are apt to damage the wood. Keeping wagons, implements, and other articles made wholly or partly of wood under cover will serve to hold the damage to a minimum.

Lumber to be used in a warm, dry place, like the inside of a house, should be correspondingly dry; if time permits, it can be brought to the proper dryness by leaving it in such a place for several months. Lumber to be used in barns or sheds need not be so dry. Posts and lumber for fences can often be rather green without detracting from their usefulness.

Lumber air dried during the summer may pick up moisture if left outdoors all winter, and it is becoming very common for lumber manufacturers and users to put dry stock under cover in the fall. If reasonably dry, it can be piled compactly and will then pick up moisture much more slowly than if piled in open stacks, and, of course, still more slowly than if left outdoors.

ROLF THELEN.

WOODLAND Thinning by Preserving Better Trees Often Profitable   Wherever farming has invaded formerly timbered areas, remnants of second-growth forests usually occupy the soil least suitable for cultivation. The value of these bits of woodland is often very high, but frequently their importance as shelter to crops and as sources of fuel, posts, poles, and other farm timbers is not fully realized. A little well-directed care in protection from fire, removal of insect-infested or diseased trees, prevention of injury to seedlings by overgrazing, and intelligent selection of trees in cutting to relieve crowding would mean more complete use of the soil and would improve the quality of the timber produced.

Beneficial thinnings can often be made at the time of ordinary utility cuttings by selecting the trees good enough for the purpose desired, rather than the best trees of the stand. The selection of the thriftier, more promising individuals for preservation is made easier by a simple classification universally used by foresters.

Largest Trees Called "Dominants"

When crowding begins in a stand of trees of the same age, some individuals secure an advantage in the competition for soil nutrients and light and become taller than the others with larger crowns and trunks. These largest trees are called dominants. They are the more rapid growers, the most vigorous of which would survive to maturity if natural competition proceeded undisturbed. The trees somewhat shorter than the dominants but still reaching into the upper crown canopy are called codominants. Such trees are declining in vigor and would become overtopped and die if unrelieved by cutting. Still lower in the scale of size and vigor are the intermediates, usually less than two-thirds the height of the dominants, with very small poorly developed crowns. Completely overtopped or understory trees are called suppressed. They have very small crowns and are on the verge of perishing. Still standing, or fallen to the ground, are the trees which have died from suppression.

In the natural struggle for existence the weaker dominants decline to codominants, these in turn become intermediates, the intermediates become suppressed, and the suppressed trees die. If the stand is undisturbed the understory trees never gain a place in the upper crown canopy. This unregulated competition often retards the growth of the entire stand.

The Thinning Process

The first thinning usually becomes necessary at an age of 30 to 40 years. First consideration should be given to removal of dead, diseased, broken, or poorly formed trees. When competition has not been too prolonged, thinning from above, or in the dominant stand, will greatly improve the vigor of the understory trees. If large material is needed and the dominants have attained suitable size, this method of cutting often coincides with practical necessity. Care should be taken in felling not to injure the smaller trees to be retained. If smaller material can be used and larger timber is desired later, the thinning should be made from below, removing enough of the weaker suppressed and intermediate, and perhaps some codominant trees to improve spacing and relieve the dominants from competition.

As a precaution against destruction of the entire stand by uncontrolled fires, slash from the cutting should be made into fuel or piled and burned in such a way as not to injure the remaining trees. This may also prevent development in the slash of insects, which under certain conditions emerge from the limbs and tops and attack standing trees. Care should be taken not to permit the fire to spread through the stand and destroy the litter and leaf mold. The feeding roots of trees are usually very near the surface and removal of the litter permits drying of the soil to a sufficient depth to kill the rootlets and retard growth.

DUNCAN DUNNING.

WOOD of Native Trees Compared Regarding Resistance to Decay   Wood kept constantly dry or continuously submerged in water does not decay, regardless of sapwood or species. A large proportion of the wood in use is kept so dry at all times that it lasts indefinitely. Moisture and temperature are the principal factors that affect the rate of decay; they vary greatly with the local conditions surrounding the wood in service. When exposed to conditions that favor decay, wood decays more rapidly in warm, humid areas of the United States than in cool or dry areas. High altitudes are as a rule less favorable to decay than low because the average temperatures are lower and the growing seasons for fungi are shorter.

The natural decay resistance of all common native species of wood is in the heartwood. When untreated, the sapwood of practically all species has low decay resistance and generally has short life under decay-producing conditions. The decay resistance or durability of heartwood in service is greatly influenced by differences in the character of the wood, the attacking fungus, and the conditions of exposure. Therefore great differences in length of life may be obtained from pieces of wood that are cut from the same species or even the same tree and used under apparently similar conditions.

Comparisons of Decay Resistance

General comparisons of the relative decay resistance of different species must at best be estimates. They can not be exact and they may be very misleading if considered as mathematically accurate and applicable to all cases. They may be very useful, however, if considered as approximate averages only, from which specific cases may vary considerably, and as having application only where the wood is used under conditions that favor decay. The following classification of common native species is subject to the limitations just mentioned.

On the basis of service records, supplemented by general experience, the heartwood of the following species may be classed as durable even when used under conditions that favor decay: The catalpas, practically all of the cedars, chestnut, southern cypress, the junipers, black locust, red mulberry, Osage orange, redwood, black walnut, and Pacific yew. On the other hand the heartwood of aspen, basswood, cottonwood, the true firs (not Douglas fir), and the willows when used under conditions that favor decay may be classed as low in decay resistance. The heartwood of Douglas fir, red gum, western larch, chestnut oak, southern yellow pine, and tamarack may be classed as intermediate. The heartwood of dense Douglas fir, honey locust, white oak, and dense southern yellow pine may also be classed as intermediate but nearly as durable as some of the species named in the high durability group. The heartwood of the ashes, beech, the birches, the hemlocks, sugar maple, the red oaks, and the spruces may be considered on the border line between the intermediate and nondurable groups and can not with assurance be placed wholly in either group.

GEORGE M. HUNT.

WOOD-SELECTION Rules Help But Should Not Be Followed Blindly The following rules for the selection of wood should be used only as rough guides and not as substitutes for specific information, such as may be obtained from the Forest Products Laboratory, Madison, Wis. Exceptions to most of them can be found, and if a large amount of material is involved or if the wood is to be used for some important purpose, dependence on these rules alone is inadvisable; additional information should be obtained.

Common Terms Used in Describing Wood

Sapwood is the outer portion and heartwood the center portion of a cross section of a log. The sapwood is usually lighter in color than the heartwood.

Springwood is the thin-walled, relatively weak, and usually light-colored portion and summerwood the thick-walled, heavy, and relatively strong portion of the ring that grows annually in the tree.

The term "softwoods" is applied to the group of trees that bear cones, examples of which are pine and spruce; "hardwoods" is applied to broad-leaved trees, such as oak and maple. Actually some softwoods are harder than some woods of the hardwood group.

Dense wood is heavy and hard; hickory is an example.

The term "heavy" is used in defining the actual wood substance apart from any moisture it may contain. Even a light wood may have much weight if it is saturated with water.

Heavy woods have high fuel value.

Seasoning wood increases its fuel value.

The heat value of 1 cord of heavy wood, 1½ cords of medium-heavy wood, or 2 cords of light wood is approximately equivalent to that of a ton of coal.

Softwoods generally burn more readily than hardwoods, light woods more readily than heavy woods.

Seasoning

Wood shrinks when it dries and expands when it takes up moisture.

Hardwoods shrink more than softwoods, heavy woods more than light woods.

Boards from small logs tend to warp more in drying than boards of the same width from large logs.

Properly kiln-dried wood is as strong as air-dried wood.

The amount of sap in trees does not vary with the season of the year.

Wood in contact with the ground or kept moist decays.

Wood continuously submerged in water or kept perfectly dry does not decay.

Green fence posts set in the ground last as long as seasoned posts.

Heartwood is generally more durable than sapwood of the same species.

Pitchy wood is more durable than nonpitchy wood of the same species.

Dark woods are usually more durable than light-colored woods.

Wood properly treated with a preservative is many times as durable as untreated wood.

The time of year when timbers are cut has no great effect upon their resistance to decay if they are properly cared for after cutting.

Wood is not effectively protected from decay by painting.

Posts or timbers with the bark on decay more rapidly than peeled posts or timbers.

Strength of Wood

Heavy wood is generally hard and strong, light wood soft and weak.

Heavy wood holds nails well, but tends to split in nailing.

Seasoned wood holds nails better than green wood.

Seasoned wood is stronger than green wood, except in shock resistence.

The growth change from sapwood to heartwood in the wood of the tree does not affect the strength.

Timber of the same species grown in widely different localities generally varies no more in strength than timber of the same species grown in one locality.

Woods of light weight are better temperature insulators than heavy woods.

Woods with prominent alternate annual growth rings of soft spring wood and hard summer wood are more difficult to work than woods either uniformly soft or hard.

Softwoods generally require less care in gluing than heavy woods.

A. O. Benson

WOODS on the Farm Like Saving Account If Rightly Handled

Timber trees on the farm are like money in a savings bank. They are an investment. The farm woods are increasingly being used as security for loans. In order to get the most out of the investment, the owner must give it good protection, as an element of risk is involved. Complete protection from fire comes as the first requisite, quite as much as protection from theft is a first essential in the case of money or other securities in a bank. Other forms of protection to timber are from damage by livestock, by insects, and by diseases.

The trees are the principal, and the new growth is the interest. Unlike the bank account, the better the care and the more complete the protection, the larger the rate of interest. There is a limit, however, to thus speeding up new growth.

FIGURE 246.—The farm woods, if rightly handled, is a savings bank paying a good rate of interest

The cutting of trees may be so regulated in amount as simply to remove the amount of new growth or the interest. This method of harvesting only as much as grows, known as a sustained yield, is a safe one to follow as a guide. If cutting is not properly regulated, it is an easy matter to over-cut the woods, and thus so reduce the principal in the woods bank that it will bring in but little interest. There is no more widespread and costly mistake being made than cutting that draws too heavily on the principal.

Often a Source of Profit

Farm woodlands have many times been the means of lifting a mortgage or of making the difference between loss and profit on the farm balance sheet. In the words of an Ozark Mountain farmer, "Timber is our legal tender." "Farm timber," says the head of the Federal land bank of Springfield, Mass., "furnishes an income from lands on many farms in New England that would otherwise be a liability because of the soil and rugged topography. The farm wood lot fills in the waste spaces, and wood and timber help out as part of the regular farm income." In the coastal-plain region of southern Georgia, a leading farmer recently said, "Young timber is the greatest investment of anything I know of. I'd rather have 300 or 400 young pines on an acre of my land than keep it in 25-cent tobacco." .

If the woods bank is used wisely and only the amount of the new growth is cut, the capital will be left untouched, and the land will be. kept growing timber at the maximum rate and will make the largest profit for the owner. In a nutshell, good woods practice is to cut only as much as grows, to use the ax and saw rightly, and to keep fires out at all times.

W. R. Mattoon.

WOOL Carelessly Packed Fails to Realize Its Full Value in Market Many growers apparently do not realize the effect that improper methods of packing have upon the prices received for wool.

Just a little more care in preparing wools for market would often mean better prices to growers. Sisal and jute twines are too widely used for tying fleeces. Paper twine is best as it contains no loose fibers to break off and mix with the wool. Since sisal and jute will

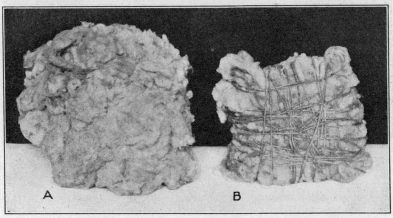

FIGURE 247.—Wool fleeces. A, Fleece neatly and securely tied with about 12 feet of paper twine; B, fleece tied with 110 feet of heavy jute twine weighing one-half pound. Jute or sisal twine is objectionable because fibers break off, become imbedded in the wool, and can not be removed without considerable expense and trouble

not take the wool dyes, wool containing these fibers make a defective cloth. Removal of fragments of sisal and jute from wool is an expensive operation; consequently wool containing these fibers can not command full market prices. As untied fleeces hamper grading and increase the cost of handling in central markets, buyers offer lower prices for them. Wool so put up that the individual fleeces are tied with the flesh side out, and with tags, dung locks, seedy, burry, and black wools packed separately, make the most favorable impression upon buyers. Even the best wool buyers can not accurately estimate the percentage of the various qualities when all kinds of wool are thrown together; therefore, under these conditions they can not accurately compute prices.

Instances of falsification in packing are relatively infrequent, but some unfortunate examples in the 1928 clip have appeared on the Boston market. In several large lots, a majority of the fleeces had concealed in them chunks of mud and dung weighing up to 2 pounds. Rocks, wet sand, and scrap iron packed with wool, and 100 feet of heavy twine used to tie fleeces were apparently intended to increase weights. A black list of growers known to have used such methods is doing much to eliminate such practices.

Packing wool while it is wet may cause serious damage. Excessive moisture, in conjunction with the dirt normally present, may cause wool to heat and become discolored and musty. This disqualifies it for worsted manufacture as weakened fibers break under the strain put upon them by worsted machinery and stains caused by heating can not be scoured out. Buyers avoid musty wools or offer extremely low prices for them. Usually, weak and stained wools can be sold only for woolen manufacture. Woolen wools of good color and strength usually average 10 cents per pound lower than corresponding

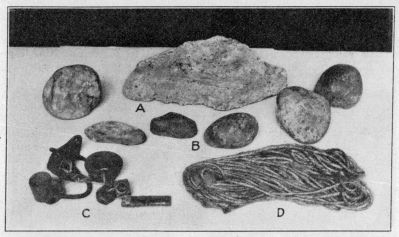

FIGURE 248.—Foreign materials found in wool fleeces. A, An 18-pound piece of concrete; B, stones; C, scrap iron (B and C had a combined weight of 20 pounds); D, hank of jute twine 110 feet long weighing one-half pound

grades of worsted wools, and stained, tender, or otherwise damaged woolen wools are often penalized another 10 to 15 cents per pound. These prices are all for scoured wool. It may be explained that woolen wools are comparatively short in fiber, whereas worsted wools are relatively long.

RUSSELL L. BURRUS and
JOHN P. ROBERTS.

WOOL Yields Can Be Increased by Rigid Culling and Selection The production of a heavier and better fleece per ewe is a matter of considerable concern to the sheep raiser, particularly on the western ranges and in other parts of the country such as the Ohio fine-wool region, where wool production is a specialty. Qualty as well as quantity is, of course, important if a good price is to be obtained for the clip. However, it is entirely possible to have high quality of wool in fleeces that have good length of staple and heavy weight of clean wool. In fact the investigations of the Bureau of Animal Industry show that length of staple and weight of clean wool per fleece are associated with superior quality.

While many factors are involved in the improvement of wool, the most vital are those which tend toward greater production. These in the main are weight of the scoured fleece and length of the staple. The inheritance of the sheep (fig. 249), its feed, management, and seasonal environment are important factors that influence both quantity and quality of the wool produced, but the most fundamental of them all is the inherent tendency of the individual sheep. The utilization of this last-mentioned factor for greater wool production is, of course, the most difficult. Whereas proper feeding and management may be accomplished in the flock as a whole, and seasonal variations may to a limited extent be controlled by management, the improvement of a flock by means of the natural characteristics of the sheep themselves must be handled through the selection or culling of

FIGURE 249.—Yearling daughters of a famous Rambouillet ram, Prince of Parowan, showing uniformity in type and wool of good combing length. The sire of these ewes has a record of having produced 31½ pounds of wool a year during the first seven years of his life

individuals. Successful sheep raisers have found that rigid culling of the aged ewes and light producers is a good practice for the immediate improvement of their flocks. They have found also that selective breeding is essential for future improvement.

Some Experimental Results

The fleeces of 100 Rambouillet ewes of the Government flock at the United States Sheep Experiment Station, Dubois, Idaho, which were grown in the years 1923, 1924, 1925, and 1926, were studied with respect to their yields of clean wool per fleece and the influence of their age and the season on these yields. Length of staple seemed but slightly affected by season. In 1923 it averaged 2.21 inches; in 1924, 2.14 inches; in 1925, 2.22 inches; and in 1926, 2.12 inches. There was a slight tendency for decrease in length with greater age.

A considerable difference in the average weights of clean wool was evident in each of these years. In 1923 the fleeces averaged 3.69

pounds of clean wool; in 1924, 4.05 pounds; in 1925, 4.20 pounds; and in 1926, 3.79 pounds. The variation can be attributed primarily to seasonal variation of feed, as the same ewes were considered throughout and otherwise their management was practically the same.

In spite of the above-mentioned irregular variation in the average yield of clean wool of these 100 ewes in the four different years—which must be attributed to seasonal effect—one influence remained stronger than that of season, the tendency of the ewes to produce light or heavy fleece weights, long or short staple, consistently. The ewes were divided, in 1923, into their four main fleece-length classes (averaging 1.3 inches, 1.8 inches, 2.3 inches, and 2.8 inches, respectively), and these classes were compared in the remaining three years. The results showed that, class for class, those ewes producing the shortest staple in 1923 continued to produce the shortest staple in the succeeding years, the next shortest class continued to produce the next shortest staple, and similarly for the other classes, so that, class for class, these ewes continued to produce staple of consistently comparative length in each succeeding year.

Similarly, when the ewes were divided into three main classes for clean weight of wool (averaging 2.5 pounds, 3.5 pounds, and 4.5 pounds, respectively, for 1923), the same condition existed. The classes producing lighter weights of clean wool in 1923 continued to produce lighter weights in the succeeding years, and those producing heavier weights continued to produce heavier weights in the succeeding years.

It is evident, therefore, that while season must be considered and every possible means used to offset adverse climatic conditions by proper feeding and management, if good wool yields are to be obtained, it is most important to select and maintain in the flock those ewes with heavier clean weight of fleece and greater length of staple, and to use rams which transmit these qualities.

MARY J. BRANDON.

WORLD'S Agriculture Much Changed by the War and Its Results The World War revealed in high light the basically vital significance of agricultural resources and greatly affected agriculture throughout the world. Many changes in world agriculture since 1914 are directly traceable to the war, while others are the results of forces only accelerated or retarded by the war. The war changed boundaries, which fact has affected international trade in farm products, caused or made possible agrarian reforms which have affected production in many countries, and stimulated the development of new agricultural areas in many other countries. An increase in the use of machinery, stimulated by the war but due mainly to the development of scientific inventions, and a greater application of science to production have encouraged the continuation of the expansion of production in many countries. The war, directly and indirectly, also affected the demand for farm products. The marked rapid changes in production and in the demand for farm products have given rise to serious agricultural problems in all parts of the world.

The immediate effect of the war was to eliminate Russia from the international trade in agricultural products, reduce the production of most European countries, and stimulate production in overseas countries from which supplies could be had most readily. Most European countries made strenuous efforts to continue and even increase agricultural production with but little success during the war. The end of the war found the cultivated area and the numbers of livestock reduced in many countries. It is estimated that the area of cereals, potatoes, and sugar beets cultivated in Europe, excluding Russia, in 1921 was about 11 per cent below the pre-war average. Production of butter and cheese in Europe outside of Russia had been cut about half and pork production was at least 15 per cent below the pre-war average. Russia, disorganized and with production greatly reduced, was not in position to resume exports to other European countries. Under normal conditions this situation would result in a great demand for products from surplus-producing countries other than in Europe.

Production Stimulated Outside Europe

Outside of Europe the immediate effect of the war was to stimulate production. The area devoted to cereals in Canada, United States, Argentina, and Australia in 1921 was 19 per cent greater than the pre-war average. The greatest development was in Canada where the area in wheat more than doubled. Livestock production was increased greatly. The production of pork in the United States, beef in Argentina, and butter and cheese in New Zealand and in Argetina was greatly stimulated. From the principal surplus-producing countries in 1921 the exports of butter were 204 per cent of the pre-war average, cheese 130 per cent, pork 180 per cent, and beef 163 per cent. Thus the surplus-producing countries outside of Europe were fully prepared to make up the European deficits at the end of the war.

At the end of the war the surplus-producing countries outside of Europe faced the prospect of recovery in the agricultural production of many European countries and had to sell to consumers whose purchasing power had been greatly curtailed. The great decline in prices which took place in 1920–21 was due largely to deflation, but it was due in part to the decline in the purchasing power of consumers.

Soon after the war the United States and all other surplus-producing countries began to feel the effect of the reduction in purchasing power of the European consumer. Italy began shipping larger supplies of lemons to the United States because few consumers in Germany and other north European countries could buy them. Some Danish and New Zealand butter, and Swiss and Canadian cheese began to be diverted to the United States because of the reduction in the purchasing power of European consumers.

European agriculture recovered rapidly. Recovery was most rapid in those countries, such as Denmark and the Netherlands, which were disturbed but not directly involved in the war. By 1925 many countries had recovered the pre-war acreage of crops and pre-war numbers of livestock. In 1927, the last year for which complete statistics, are available, the cultivated area of Europe outside of Russia had recovered to 97 per cent of the pre-war average, and the production of milk, butter, cheese, and pork was far above the pre-war average. Fortunately the recovery of production was accompanied by a recovery in purchasing power, so Europe has continued to take large quantities from surplus-producing countries. Market demand has been reduced for some commodities but for others the European market is to-day as good a market as it was before the war.

The Effect of Boundary Changes

Shifts in boundaries have had some effect upon the market for agricultural products of the United States in Europe. The creation of Poland has taken an agricultural surplus-producing area out of Germany and out of the protection of German tariffs. Separation of Austria and Hungary has made Austria a better market for our surplus products.

Agrarian reforms and unsettled political and social conditions have had some effect upon the agricultural situation. The Balkan countries have recovered from the war but slowly. Agrarian reforms in some areas have tended to reduce production and retard recovery of production of some commodities. This is particularly true of Rumania and Russia. These conditions will probably not persist indefinitely; it is to be expected that eventually production in these countries will recover from the effects of war and unsettled conditions following the war. Although they may not resume exports of wheat in so large a volume as before, it is to be expected that they may again export important quantities of wheat and many other products.

While agriculture in Europe has been recovering from the effects of the war, production in some countries outside of Europe has been readjusted to meet changing European conditions; in others production has continued to expand. The United States made some adjustments, reducing beef, dairy, and corn production to domestic requirements and making some reductions in the export surpluses of wheat and pork. Canada, Argentina, New Zealand, and Australia, on the other hand, continue to expand production and exports. Expansion of the wheat area in Canada was checked temporarily, but it is now greater than ever and is producing a record export surplus of wheat. From the point of view of the United States there is no prospect of curtailment of production or weakening in competition from these countries.

Before the war science was preparing for another "revolution" of agriculture. Agricultural and mechanical colleges in the United States have been long at work developing an agricultural science. Corresponding work was in progress in many other countries. Some great inventions just before the war were preparing the way for the application of more machinery to agriculture. The war stimulated the application of both machinery and science to agricultural production.

The Automobile and the Tractor

The automobile and the tractor now play an important part in the development of agricultural production in the United States and in many other countries. The automobile upon hard-surfaced roads is bringing remote areas closer to market, and the tractor makes it possible for a farmer to cultivate larger areas with a small amount of man labor. Both developments are contributing to the expansion of production in new and distant areas. Application of more machinery is also contributing to the shifting of population from farms to cities and to a rapid growth of industrial cities.

Science has shown how to produce more and better products with the same effort. For example, statistics show a great increase in the production per cow in Switzerland, in Denmark, and in the United States. This increase in production per cow, which is due to more scientific feeding and breeding, illustrates what is taking place with respect to many products in many countries.

Another significant development is a tendency to greater specialization in production. Use of machinery and of scientific knowledge encourages specialization. Improvement in transportation facilities and relatively cheap freight rates make it possible to specialize in production in distant areas most suitable for the product, and to market the product where there is the greatest demand.

Changes in markets and in demand for agricultural products are as significant as changes in production. The westernization of the Orient is increasing the oriental demand for the products of other countries. Japan is becoming a manufacturing country and the large coastal cities of China are importing large quantities of agricultural products from other parts of the world. Increase in demand from oriental markets has offset, in part, the reduction in European market demands. During the five years preceding the war only about 3 per cent of the agricultural exports of the United States went to Asia. In the past three years 11 per cent has been shipped to Asia. Peace in China now offers further opportunities for the development of the oriental market.

Changes in World Demand

There are some significant changes in the world's demand for agricultural products. Use of the automobile and the tractor is reducing the number of horses in the world, thereby reducing the demand for feed grains. Production of rayon has increased enormously as a substitute for or competitor with silk and wool. On the other hand, the demands for some commodities are increasing. It is apparent that the demand for wheat and sugar has increased rapidly in recent years. Although demand for wheat flour in the United States is now less than before the war, the demand has increased in many countries. In Europe wheat is taking the place of rye; in the Orient it is taking the place of rice and other grains as the bread grain of the people. The demand for tobacco, particularly of the cigarette type, has increased greatly. The enormous production and low prices of sugar have stimulated consumption in the United States and elsewhere. Another notable shift in demand is an increased use of vegetable oils as a substitute for, or in competition with, animal fats. There has been a tremendous growth in the use of vegetable oils both in the manufacture of soaps and as foodstuffs. These changes in demand must be taken into account in planning agricultural production.

O. C. STINE.

YELLOWS-RESISTANT Cabbages Developed by Plant Breeding The yellows disease, caused by a soil fungus (*Fusarium conglutinans*), is a decidedly limiting factor in cabbage production throughout the central belt of States from the Atlantic seaboard to the Rocky Mountains. It was first brought under control some 12 years ago when a resistant selection of storage cabbage, Wisconsin Hollander, was first introduced into general use in southern Wisconsin. Since that time breeding and selection work has been under way with the purpose of developing yellows-resistant strains of late, medium, and early varieties, so as to meet the needs of the various seasons throughout the infested area.

Two late flathead varieties particularly useful for sauerkraut manufacture, Wisconsin All Seasons and Wisconsin Brunswick, were introduced in 1922. Three midseason varieties suitable for shipping and sauerkraut manufacture were next perfected and introduced in 1927 as Marion Market (round head), Globe (round head), and All Head Select (flat head). (Fig. 250.)

During the earlier period of this investigation, lines were improved in resistance by mass selection of individuals surviving in succeeding generations on badly infested soil. This process yielded highly resistant strains within a few years but did not completely fix the resistant character. Later studies upon the inheritance of resistance showed it

FIGURE 250.—Cabbage variety trials on soil severely infested with the yellows organism at Racine, Wis., 1927. The two center rows, almost completely destroyed by yellows, are Commercial Hollander and Commercial Copenhagen Market. The row at the left is the resistant variety, All Head Select, a mid-season flat-head type; the one at the right is the resistant variety, Globe, a mid-season round-head type

to be a simple dominant Mendelian character. This fact having been ascertained, it has become a comparatively simple procedure to secure completely resistant strains by means of pure-line selection, while at the same time greater uniformity in other varietal characters may be attained. In this manner resistant strains have recently been developed from two of the earliest maturing varieties in use, the Early Copenhagen Market or Golden Acre and Jersey Wakefield. The new types are very close to the original varieties from which they were selected and have withstood the disease satisfactorily when planted upon infested soil in a number of States, including Wisconsin, Indiana, Ohio, Virginia, Kentucky, Mississippi, and Iowa. These will be introduced for general use as soon as seed can be multiplied.

J. C. WALKER.

DEPARTMENT PUBLICATIONS

List of new Farmers' Bulletins, Department Bulletins, Miscellaneous Circulars, Statistical Bulletins, Technical Bulletins, Circulars, Leaflets, and Miscellaneous Publications issued from January 1, 1928, to December 31, 1928, classified by general subject matter

[These different series of publications are indicated by the letters preceding each serial number]

BIRDS AND GAME:
The Spread of the European Starling in North America (to 1928)_____ Cir. 40
The European Starling in the United States_____ F. B. 1571
Game Laws for the Season 1928–29_____ F. B. 1575
Directory of Officials and Organizations Concerned with the Protection of Birds and Game, 1928_____ M. P. 30
Returns from Banded Birds 1923 to 1926_____ T. B. 32
Nematodes of Pathological Significance Found in Some Economically Important Birds in North America_____ T. B. 49
Wild Birds Introduced or Transplanted in North America_____ T. B. 61

CLOTHING:
Sun Suits for Children_____ Leaf. 24
Dresses for the Little Girl_____ Leaf. 26
The Changing uses of Textile Fibers in Clothing and Household Articles_____ M. P. 31

COTTON:
Standardized Cotton Tare in Egypt_____ Cir. 47
Factors Affecting the Price of Cotton_____ T. B. 50
The Irrigation of Cotton_____ T. B. 72
Marketing American Cotton on the Continent of Europe_____ T. B. 78

EXTENSION SERVICE:
Ten Years of Agronomy Extension 1915 to 1924_____ Cir. 22
Farm-Management Extension, 1914–1924_____ Cir. 30

FLOWERS:
A Score of Easily Propagated Lilies_____ Cir. 23
Japanese Flowering Cherries_____ Cir. 31
The Yellow Day Lilies_____ Cir. 42

FORAGE CROPS:
Johnson Grass as a Weed_____ F. B. 1537
Legume Hays for Milk Production_____ F. B. 1573
Preparing Johnson Hay for Market in the Black Prairie Belt of Alabama and Mississippi__ F. B. 1574
Sweet Clover_____ Leaf. 23
Save the Beans_____ M. P. 16

FORESTRY AND TREES:
Forests and Floods_____ Cir. 19
The Protection Forests of the Mississippi River Watershed and Their Part in Flood Prevention_____ Cir. 37
The Air Seasoning of Western Softwood Lumber_____ D. B. 1425
Timber Growing and Logging Practice in the Lake States_____ D. B. 1496
Bamboos and Bamboo Culture_____ Leaf. 18
The Farm Woods—A Savings Bank Paying Interest_____ Leaf. 29
Federal Legislation and Regulations Relating to the Improvement of Federal-Aid Roads and National-Forest Roads and Trails_____ M. C. 109
Management Plans with Special Reference to the National Forests_____ M. P. 11
National Forests of Colorado_____ M. P. 18
A Forest Fire Prevention Handbook for the Schools of Oregon_____ M. P. 20
Protect White Pine from Blister Rust_____ M. P. 22
Growing Pine Timber for Profit in the South_____ M. P. 24
Why Grow Timber?_____ M. P. 26
Measuring Forest-Fire Danger in Northern Idaho_____ M. P. 29
Experimental Tapping of Hevea Rubber Trees at Bayeux, Haiti, 1924–25_____ T. B. 65

FRUIT CROPS:
Marketing California Grapes_____ Cir. 44
Removal of Spray Residue from Apples and Pears in the Pacific Northwest_____ Cir. 59
Preparation of Eastern Grapes for Market_____ F. B. 1558
Preparing Strawberries for Market_____ F. B. 1560

FUR ANIMALS:
Fur Laws for the Season 1928–29_____ F. B. 1576
Chinchilla Rabbits for Food and Fur_____ Leaf. 22

GRAIN CROPS:
The Bates Laboratory Aspirator_____ Cir. 9
Chemical-Dust Seed Treatments for Dent Corn_____ Cir. 34
Improved Apparatus and Method for Making "Shellings" of Rough Rice_____ Cir. 48
Corn Breeding_____ D. B. 1489
Harvesting Grain Sorghums_____ F. B. 1577
The Husker-Shredder on Eastern Corn Belt Farms_____ F. B. 1589
Rate and Date of Seeding and Seed-Bed Preparation for Winter Wheat at Arlington Experiment Farm_____ T. B. 38
Inheritance of Awnedness, Yield and Quality in Crosses Between Bobs, Hard Federation, and Propo Wheats at Davis, Calif._____ T. B. 39
Broomcorn Experiments at the United States Dry-Land Field Station, Woodward, Okla__ T. B. 51
Relation of Kernel Density to Table and Canning Quality in Different Varieties of Maize__ T. B. 97
Respiration of Sorghum Grains_____ T. B. 100

INSECT PESTS:
Experimental Dissemination of the Tabanid Egg Parasite Phanurus Emersoni Girault and Biological Notes on the Species_____ Cir.   18
The Application of Sodium Fluosilicate by Airplane in an Attempt to Control the Sugar-Cane Moth Borer_____ Cir.   45
Insects Injurious to the Rice Crop_____ F. B. 1543
Insects Attacking the Peach in the South and How to Control Them _____ F. B. 1557
The Porto Rican Mole Cricket_____ F. B. 1561
Farm Practices Under Corn-Borer Conditions_____ F. B. 1562
The Sorghum Midge with Suggestions for Control_____ F. B. 1566
Mosquito Remedies and Preventives_____ F. B. 1570
The Striped Blister Beetle on Soy Beans_____ Leaf.   12
A Study of Phylloxera Infestation in California as Related to Types of Soils_____ T. B.   20
Experiments for the Control of the European Red Mite and Other Fruit-Tree Mites_____ T. B.   25
The Fall Army Worm_____ T. B.   34
The Sugar-Cane Moth Borer in the United States_____ T. B.   41
Life History of the Codling Moth in Delaware_____ T. B.   42
The Western Cedar Pole Borer or Powder Worm_____ T. B.   48
A Classification of the Higher Groups and Genera of the Coccid Family Margarodidae___ T. B.   52
Paradichlorobenzene Experiments in the South for Peach-Borer Control_____ T. B.   58
The European Corn Borer and Its Controlling Factors in Europe_____ T. B.   59
The Apple Maggot_____ T. B.   66
Tests of Blowfly Baits and Repellents During 1926_____ T. B.   80
The Hessian Fly in California_____ T. B.   81
IRRIGATION:
An Apparatus for Adding Gypsum to Irrigation Water_____ Cir.   33
Irrigation of Small Grain_____ F. B. 1556
Irrigation Requirements of the Arid and Semiarid Lands of the Missouri and Arkansas River Basins_____ T. B.   36
Delivery of Irrigation Water_____ T. B.   47
Silt in the Colorado River and Its Relation to Irrigation_____ T. B.   67
LIVESTOCK AND DAIRYING:
Dairy Work at the Woodward Field Station, Woodward, Okla., 1921 to 1926 _____ Cir.   12
Comparison of Purebred and Grade Dairy Cows_____ Cir.   26
The Regional Lymph Glands of Food Animals_____ Cir.   32
Some Results of Soft-Pork Investigations, II_____ D. B. 1492
Systems of Livestock Farming in the Black Prairie Belt of Alabama and Mississippi_____ F. B. 1546
Feeding Cattle for Beef_____ F. B. 1549
Care of the Dairy Cow at Calving Time_____ Leaf.   10
Sheep and Goat Lice and Methods of Control and Eradication_____ Leaf.   13
Raising the Dairy Heifer_____ Leaf.   14
Purebred Dairy Sires_____ Leaf.   16
Improving Dairy Herds_____ Leaf.   19
Care of the Dairy Calf_____ Leaf.   20
Preventing Feed Flavors and Odors in Milk_____ Leaf.   25
A Calendar of Livestock Parasites_____ M. P.   25
The Livestock Review for 1927_____ M. P.   28
Wild Tobaccos (Nicotiana Trigonophylla Dunal and Nicotiana Attenuata Torrey) as Stock-Poisoning Plants_____ T. B.   22
Sorgo Silage, Sorgo Fodder, and Cottonseed Hulls as Roughages in Rations for Fattening Calves in the Southwest_____ T. B.   43
The Swine Sanitation System as Developed by the Bureau of Animal Industry in McLean County, Ill_____ T. B.   44
A Study of Ranch Organization and Methods of Range-Cattle Production in the Northern Great Plains Region_____ T. B.   45
Ranch Organization and Methods of Livestock Production in the Southwest_____ T. B.   68
Some Factors Affecting the Demand for Milk and Cream in the Metropolitan Area of New York_____ T. B.   73
Report of the Foot-and-Mouth-Disease Commission of the United States Department of Agriculture_____ T. B.   76
Factors that Influence Wool Production with Range Rambouillet Sheep_____ T. B.   85
Four Species of Range Plants not Poisonous to Livestock _____ T. B.   93
MARKETING AND COOPERATION:
Joint Use of a Sales Organization by Two Cooperative Associations _____ Cir.   10
Market Classes and Grades of Calves and Vealers_____ Cir.   28
Marketing Farm Produce by Parcel Post_____ F. B. 1551
Car-lot Shipments and Unloads of Important Fruits and Vegetables, 1924–26_____ S. B.   23
Agricultural Cooperative Associations Marketing and Purchasing 1925_____ T. B.   40
Cooperative Marketing of Livestock in the United States by Terminal Associations_____ T. B.   57
Cooperative Marketing of Grain in Western Canada_____ T. B.   63
Marketing American Cotton in England_____ T. B.   69
Major Transactions in the 1926 December Wheat Future_____ T. B.   79
MISCELLANEOUS:
U. S. Grades, Color Standards, and Packing Requirements for Honey_____ Cir.   24
Soil Erosion: A National Menace_____ Cir.   33
Methods for Collecting and Preserving Pollen for Use in the Treatment of Hay Fever____ Cir.   46
A Seed Counter_____ Cir.   53
Developments and Problems in Farmers' Mutual Fire Insurance_____ Cir.   54
The Farm Real Estate Situation 1927–28_____ Cir.   60
Rural Libraries_____ F. B. 1559
Farm Budgeting_____ F. B. 1564
Shall I Buy a Combine?_____ F. B. 1565
Earthworms as Pests and Otherwise_____ F. B. 1569
Woodchuck Control in the Eastern States_____ Leaf.   21
Lamb as You Like It_____ Leaf.   28
List of Publications of the United States Department of Agriculture from January, 1901, to December, 1925, Inclusive_____ M. P.   9
Workers in Subjects Pertaining to Agriculture in State Agricultural Colleges and Experiment Stations 1927–1928_____ M. P.   12
Crop Report Regulations, 1928_____ M. P.   17
The Agricultural Outlook for 1928_____ M. P.   19

MISCELLANEOUS—Continued.
Research in Mechanical Farm Equipment_____ M. P.   38
Statistics of Fats, Oils, and Oleaginous Raw Materials_____ S. B.   24
Cold-Storage Holdings, Year Ended December 31, 1927_____ S. B.   26
Methods of Extracting Volatile Oils from Plant Material and the Production of Such Oils
  in the United States_____ T. B.   16
Coyotillo (Karwinskia Humboldtiana) as a Poisonous Plant_____ T. B.   29
Agricultural Survey of Europe—France_____ T. B.   37
Highway Bridge Surveys_____ T. B.   55
Bacteriology and Chemistry of Oysters, with Special Reference to Regulatory Control of
  Production, Handling, and Shipment_____ T. B.   64
The Combined Harvester-Thresher in the Great Plains_____ T. B.   70
The Value of Inert Gas as a Preventive of Dust Explosions in Grinding Equipment_____ T. B.   74
PLANT DISEASES:
Mushroom Diseases and Their Carriers_____ Cir.   27
Bacterial Wilt and Winter Injury of Alfalfa_____ Cir.   39
Rose Diseases, Their Causes and Control_____ F. B. 1547
Bread or Barberries_____ M. P.   7
Yellows: A Serious Disease of Tomatoes_____ M. P.   13
Formaldehyde Seed Treatment for Oat Smuts_____ M. P.   21
Black Currant Spreads White-Pine Blister Rust_____ M. P.   27
Clover Anthracnose Caused by Colletotrichum Trifolii_____ T. B.   28
Factors of Spread and Repression in Potato Wart_____ T. B.   56
Factors in the Inception and Development of Fusarium Rot in Stored Potatoes_____ T. B.   62
POULTRY AND EGGS:
Incubation and Brooding of Chickens_____ F. B. 1538
Poultry Houses and Fixtures_____ F. B. 1554
Ineffectiveness of Internal Medication of Poultry for the Control of External Parasites_____ T. B.   60
TRUCK CROPS:
Seed Production from Sugar Beets Over-Wintered in the Field_____ Cir.   20
The Commercial Production of Sauerkraut_____ Cir.   35
Sugar-Cane Variety Tests in Louisiana During the Crop Year, 1926–27_____ Cir.   36
Cucumber Growing_____ F. B. 1563
Vegetable Statistics Year Ended December 31, 1926, with Comparable Data for Earlier
  Years_____ S. B.   22
Source, Character, and Treatment of Potato Sets_____ T. B.   5

AGRICULTURAL MAPS

By O. E. Baker, Senior Agricultural Economist, Bureau of Agricultural Economics

This series of maps shows the approximate geographical distribution within the United States of the more important crops and farm animals. Impressions gained from these maps are essentially the same for most commodities as those that would be conveyed by maps made from 1928 data if such were available by counties. The census of 1925 is the latest comprehensive source of agricultural data for the counties of the United States, and county data are necessary in locating the dots on a map.

The map of agricultural regions (fig. 1) outlines areas characterized for the most part by a dominant crop or system of farming. As agriculture becomes more commercialized the trend is toward the concentration of production in those regions where physical conditions, including distance to market, are most favorable. This map may be helpful in keeping the major agricultural features of the country in mind.

The United States may be divided into an eastern and a western half. The transition zone which separates the East from the West lies, in general, along the one hundred and third meridian. The East is a region of humid-climate farming, based upon tilled crops, small grains, and tame hay and pasture; the West, with a few exceptions, is a region of wild hay and grazing, dry-farming, winter crops in certain localities, and irrigation farming, with only limited areas of ordinary farming such as characterize the East.

The East and West may then each be subdivided into regions. In the East the classification is based largely on temperature and the crops grown, whereas in the West rainfall and the native vegetation are the important factors. In the East the agricultural regions extend for the most part east and west, following parallels of latitude; in the West the regions are determined by the mountain ranges, and trend north and south. The average elevation of the eastern half of the United States is less than 1,000 feet; that of the western half, over 4,000 feet.

The contrast between the East and West is not as pronounced in livestock as in crops, except that hogs are largely confined to the East, while sheep are relatively much more important in the West. There is a marked distinction, however, in the manner of management, the livestock in the East being fed in the barnyards or fields, with shelter at night, while in the West much of the stock is grazed on the open range. In the East the hay and pasture region is primarily a dairy region, while the Corn Belt is the center of the beef-cattle and hog industry. In the West the sheep are generally located in the more arid and the cattle in the less arid areas. In the North Pacific region, with its cool, moist climate, similar to that of the hay and pasture region, dairying is again the dominant livestock industry.

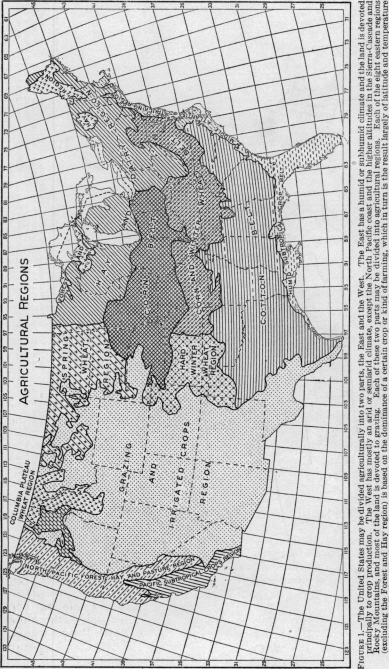

AGRICULTURAL REGIONS

FIGURE 1.—The United States may be divided agriculturally into two parts, the East and the West. The East has a humid or subhumid climate and the land is devoted principally to crop production. The West has mostly an arid or semiarid climate, except the North Pacific coast and the higher altitudes in the Sierra-Cascade and Rocky Mountains, and most of the land is devoted to grazing. Each of these two parts may be divided into agricultural regions. Each of the eight eastern regions (excluding the Forest and Hay region) is based on the dominance of a certain crop or kind of farming, which in turn is the result largely of latitude and temperature conditions. Each of the four western regions is based principally on the use of the land for crops, for pasture, or for forest, which in turn is determined largely by altitude and rainfall conditions

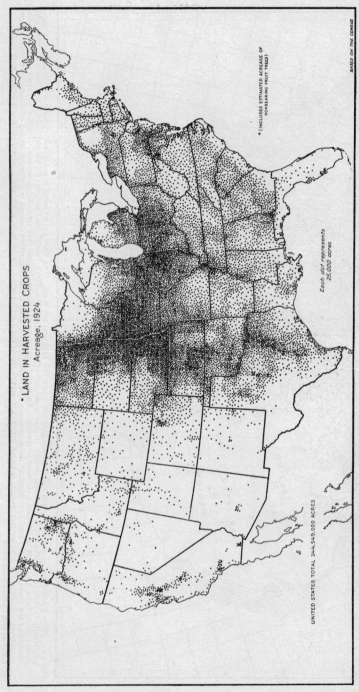

FIGURE 2.—Over five-sixths of the crop land is in the humid eastern half of the United States, and nearly two-thirds is concentrated in a triangular-shaped area, the points of which are located in western Pennsylvania, southern Texas, and northwestern North Dakota. In this area, which includes only about one-fourth of the land of the United States, are produced four-fifths of the corn, three-fourths of the wheat and oats, and three-fifths of the hay crop of the Nation. No region in the world of equal size affords natural conditions so favorable for the growth of corn, and few regions possess conditions so favorable for the culture of the small grain and hay crops

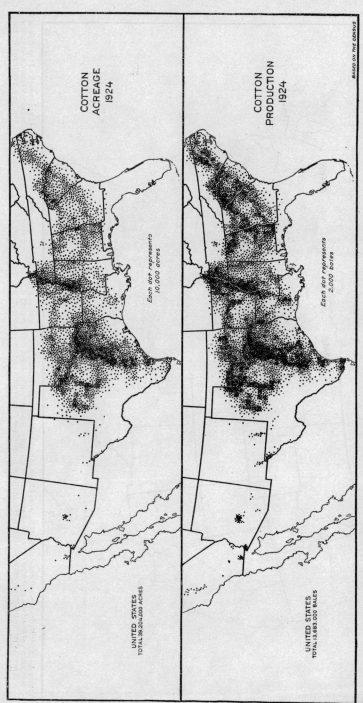

COTTON
ACREAGE
1924

Each dot represents
10,000 acres

UNITED STATES
TOTAL 39,204,000 ACRES

COTTON
PRODUCTION
1924

Each dot represents
2,000 bales

UNITED STATES
TOTAL 13,683,000 BALES

BASED ON THE CENSUS

FIGURE 3.—The northern boundary of the Cotton Belt is approximately the line of 200 days' average frost-free season and 77° mean summer temperature; the southern boundary is that of 10 inches autumn rainfall, because wet weather interferes with picking and damages the lint. The western boundary of cotton production without irrigation is approximately the line of 20 inches average annual rainfall. The densest areas on the map are districts of richer soils, notably the Black Prairie of Texas and the Yazoo Delta, or heavily fertilized soils, especially those of the Piedmont and Upper Coastal Plain

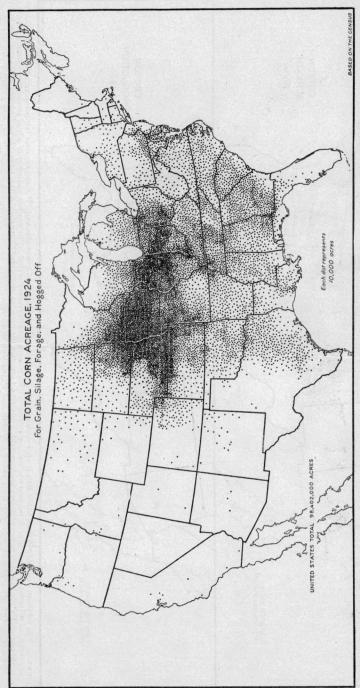

TOTAL CORN ACREAGE, 1924

For Grain, Silage, Forage, and Hogged Off

UNITED STATES TOTAL 98,402,000 ACRES

Each dot represents
10,000 acres

BASED ON THE CENSUS

FIGURE 4.—About 60 per cent of the corn of the world is produced in the United States, nearly all east of the line of 8 inches mean summer rainfall and south of the line of 66° mean summer temperature. Nearly 90 per cent of the corn production in the United States is in the Corn Belt, the Corn and Winter-wheat Region, and in the Cotton Belt. In the Corn Belt production exceeds 3,000 bushels per square mile and in some counties rises to 5,000 bushels. About half of the corn produced in the United States and nearly one-third of the world's crop is grown in the Corn Belt

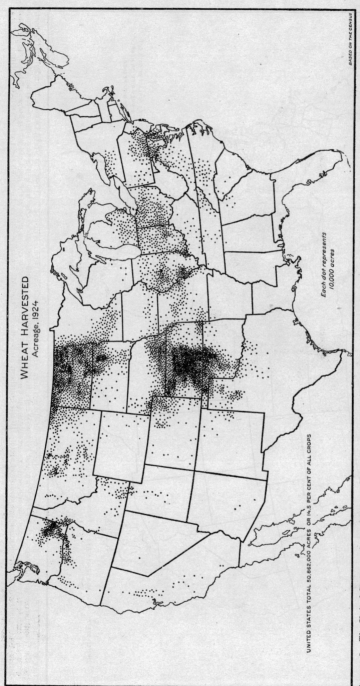

WHEAT HARVESTED
Acreage, 1924

Each dot represents
10,000 acres

BASED ON THE CENSUS

UNITED STATES TOTAL 50,862,000 ACRES OR 14.5 PER CENT OF ALL CROPS

FIGURE 5.—The United States produces about one-fifth of the world's wheat, as compared with three-fifths of the world's corn and cotton. The wheat crop of the United States, measured in bushels, is usually from one-fourth to one-third of the corn crop. Nearly three-fourths of the wheat crop was grown in nine States in 1924. Kansas was the leading State, as usual, with North Dakota second. The area extending eastward from Kansas to New York and Pennsylvania grows chiefly winter wheat, while in Minnesota, the Dakotas, and eastern Montana, the crop is practically all spring-sown wheat. In central Montana, Idaho, Washington, Oregon, and California both winter and spring varieties are grown

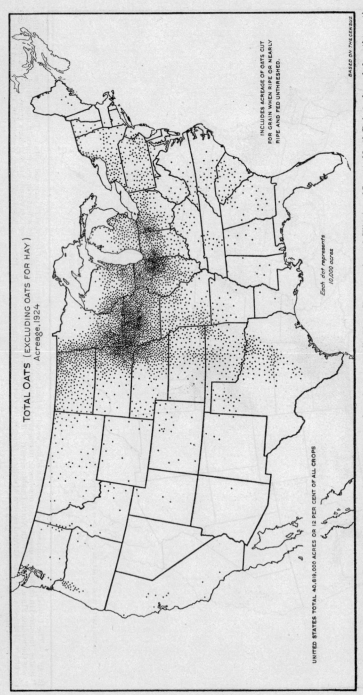

TOTAL OATS (EXCLUDING OATS FOR HAY)
Acreage, 1924

INCLUDES ACREAGE OF OATS CUT
FOR GRAIN WHEN RIPE OR NEARLY
RIPE AND FED UNTHRESHED.

BASED ON THE CENSUS

Each dot represents
10,000 acres

UNITED STATES TOTAL 40,619,000 ACRES OR 12 PER CENT OF ALL CROPS

FIGURE 6.—The Oat Belt of the United States consists of a crescent-shaped area extending from Vermont through Illinois and Iowa to North Dakota, bounded on the north by the Great Lakes and on the south by the Corn and Winter-Wheat Region. An arm extends southwestward from this belt across eastern Kansas and Oklahoma to central Texas. Oats prefer a cool, moist climate, and this acreage in the Corn Belt and to the southwest is owing more to the need of feed for horses and of a spring-grain nurse crop for clover than to particularly favorable climate. In the Southern States most of the oats are fall sown; in the North most are sown in the spring

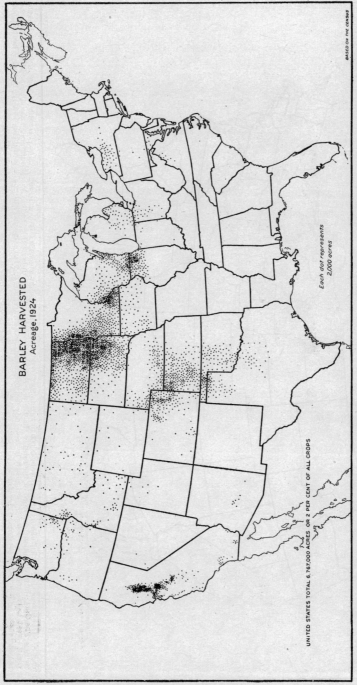

BARLEY HARVESTED
Acreage, 1924

Each dot represents 2,000 acres

UNITED STATES TOTAL 6,767,000 ACRES OR 2 PER CENT OF ALL CROPS

BASED ON THE CENSUS

FIGURE 7.—A dot on this map represents only one-fifth as much acreage as on the maps of corn, wheat, and oats. Barley is a minor crop in the United States compared with these crops, except in parts of Minnesota, the eastern portions of the Dakotas, and the valleys of California. In these four States three-fifths of the Nation's barley acreage is produced. Minor centers may be noted in western Kansas and adjacent States, in northern Illinois and Wisconsin, southeastern Michigan, and northwestern New York. These districts are characterized by a sunny climate and moderate to light rainfall

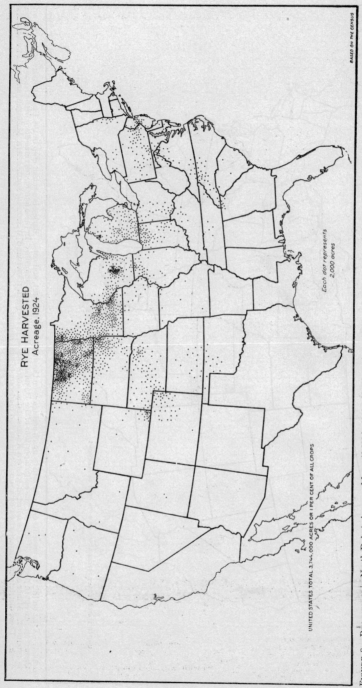

RYE HARVESTED
Acreage, 1924

UNITED STATES TOTAL 3,744,000 ACRES OR 1 PER CENT OF ALL CROPS

Each dot represents
2,000 acres

BASED ON THE CENSUS

FIGURE 8.—Rye acreage in North Dakota increased from 48,000 in 1909 to 2,422,000 in 1919, then declined to 1,468,000 acres in 1924. However, this acreage in North Dakota in 1924, as well as 1919, was about one-third of the total in the United States; although, owing to unfavorable seasons, the production was only one-fifth the national total. Prior to the World War rye was grown mostly in the sandy sections of the Lake States; this sudden extension into the subhumid lands of the Spring-Wheat Region is a significant and probably permanent development

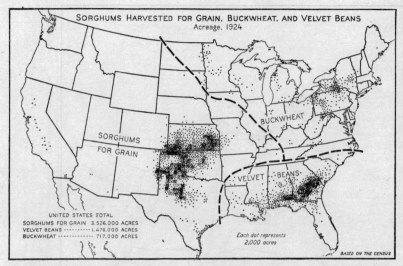

FIGURE 9.—The grain sorghums are, perhaps, our most drought-resistant crops. Expansion of acreage during the first two decades of the century in the southern Great Plains area was rapid. From 1899 to 1909 the acreage in the United States increased from 266,000 to 1,635,000, or sixfold, and between 1909 and 1919 it more than doubled. In 1924, acreage was about the same as in 1919, but there was a notable increase in Kansas and decline in parts of Texas. Buckwheat, practically confined to the Appalachian area and the Lake States, is peculiarly adapted to districts having cool, moist summers and sour soils. Acreage of the velvet bean, grown as a forage crop, has increased greatly in the Southeastern States, where the boll weevil has discouraged cotton growers and awakened interest in livestock production

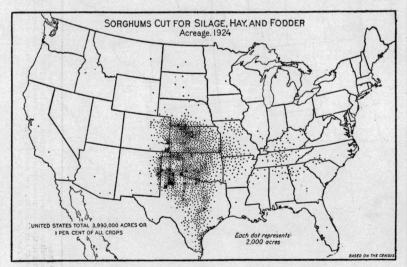

FIGURE 10.—Sorghums are grown for forage farther north, west, and south than for grain; sweet sorghums, which are not commonly grown for grain, are frequently used for forage far to the east in the Cotton Belt and the Corn and Winter Wheat Belt. Acreage of sorghums grown for forage is about the same as that grown for grain. The average yield per acre of sorghum forage was 1.7 tons in 1919 in the southwestern area, compared with less than 1 ton per acre for corn and 1.2 tons for corn in the entire United States. Yield-per-acre figures are not available for 1924

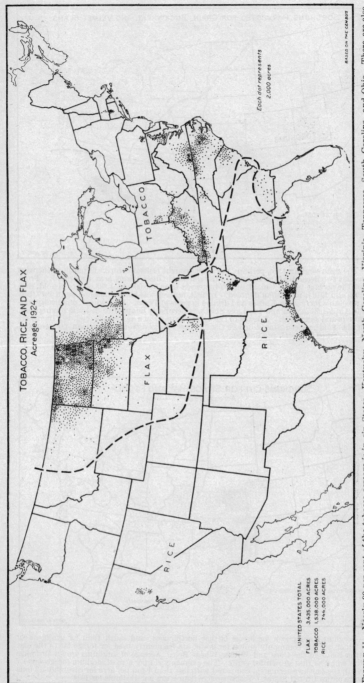

TOBACCO, RICE, AND FLAX
Acreage, 1924

Each dot represents
2,000 acres

BASED ON THE CENSUS

TOBACCO

RICE

FLAX

RICE

UNITED STATES TOTAL
FLAX   3,435,000 ACRES
TOBACCO 1,538,000 ACRES
RICE   744,000 ACRES

FIGURE 11.—Nearly 90 per cent of the tobacco acreage is in six States—Kentucky, North Carolina, Virginia, Tennessee, South Carolina, and Ohio. There are also important centers of production of certain types in southern Maryland, in Lancaster County, Pa., in the Connecticut Valley, and in southern Wisconsin. Tobacco is sensitive to soil conditions, but requirements vary with the different types. Rice production is now almost confined to the coastal prairies of Louisiana and Texas, the prairie district of eastern Arkansas, and the valley of the Sacramento in California, all areas of heavy subsoils which hold the irrigation water. Flax is grown in the Spring-Wheat Region

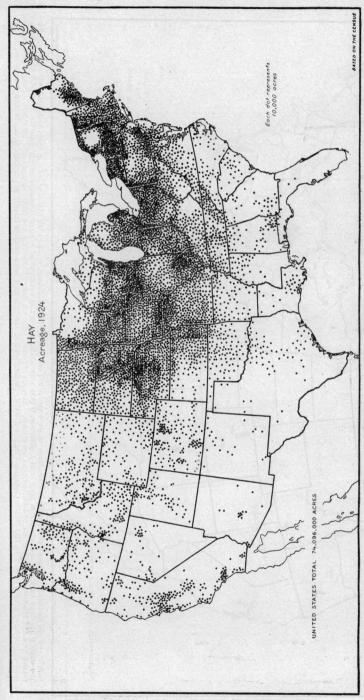

HAY
Acreage, 1924

UNITED STATES TOTAL. 74,096,000 ACRES

Each dot represents
10,000 acres

BASED ON THE CENSUS

FIGURE 12.—This map includes both wild and tame grasses and legumes cut for hay, including cowpeas, soy beans, and peanuts cut for hay, but not corn and the sorghums cut for silage or fodder, nor root crops used for forage. The hay crop is concentrated largely in the Hay and Dairy Region and around the margin of the Corn Belt. The greatest State acreage and production is found in New York; next come Wisconsin, Minnesota, Iowa, and Nebraska. Relative to acreage in crops, hay is most important in the Rocky Mountain region, where it occupies over half of the crop land

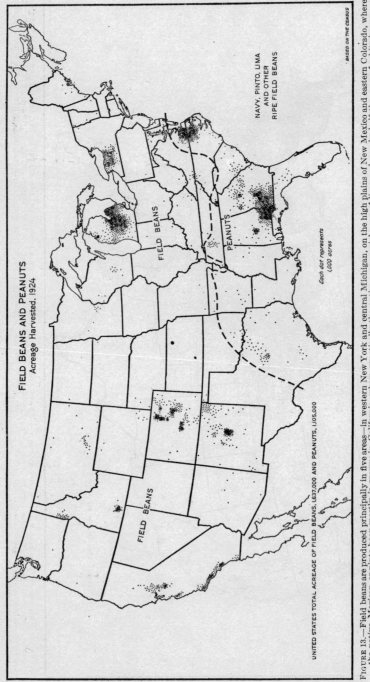

FIELD BEANS AND PEANUTS
Acreage Harvested, 1924

NAVY, PINTO, LIMA
AND OTHER
RIPE FIELD BEANS

· BASED ON THE CENSUS

Each dot represents
1,000 acres

UNITED STATES TOTAL ACREAGE OF FIELD BEANS, 1,637,000 AND PEANUTS, 1,105,000

FIGURE 13.—Field beans are produced principally in five areas—in western New York and central Michigan, on the high plains of New Mexico and eastern Colorado, where the native Mexican or pinto bean mostly is grown; in California, where practically the entire commercial crop of lima and nearly half the crop of white beans are raised; and in Idaho, where both white and pinto beans are grown. Acreage of peanuts shown does not include the crop "hogged off" by stock. Peanuts for human consumption are grown mostly in the North Carolina-Virginia district; those grown in Georgia and Alabama are largely fed to hogs or made into peanut butter

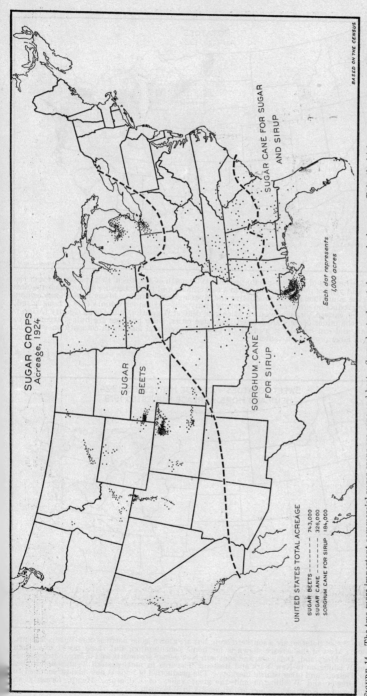

SUGAR CROPS
Acreage, 1924

SUGAR
BEETS

SORGHUM CANE
FOR SIRUP

SUGAR CANE FOR SUGAR
AND SIRUP

Each dot represents
1,000 acres

UNITED STATES TOTAL ACREAGE

SUGAR BEETS --------- 743,000
SUGAR CANE --------- 326,000
SORGHUM CANE FOR SIRUP 184,000

BASED ON THE CENSUS

FIGURE 14.—The two more important commercial sugar crops are cane and beet. Sugar beets do not, in general, show a sufficiently high sugar content to be manufactured profitably where the summer temperature is over 72°, and the beets must then compete with corn for the farmer's labor. Sugar cane is not grown in large amounts for sugar outside of the almost frost-free lower Mississippi Delta of Louisiana. The broad belt between the sugar-beet and sugar-cane areas is occupied by a thin, scattered acreage of sorghum cane. Acreage of sorghum cane in 1924 was less than half that in 1919. Sirup is mostly made from the sorghum on the farm; only a little enters into commerce

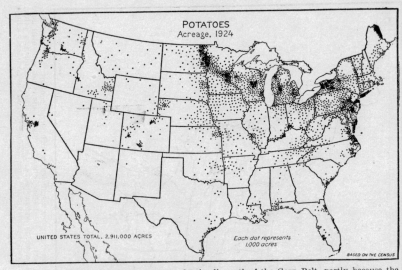

FIGURE 15.—Regions of heaviest potato production lie north of the Corn Belt, partly because the quality and yield of potatoes are better in a cool climate and partly because corn, which requires labor at the same time, is very productive and gives a greater return. Many of the large centers of potato production are in regions of sandy or loamy soils—Aroostook County (Me.), Long Island, New Jersey, eastern Virginia, western Michigan, central Wisconsin, and Anoka County (Minn.). Many of the minor centers are located near large cities, since potatoes are bulky, expensive to transport, and can be sold at a profit by local gardeners and farmers in competition with the crop from large production centers

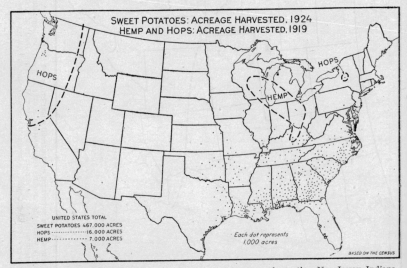

FIGURE 16.—Sweet potatoes are a southern crop, but are grown as far north as New Jersey, Indiana, and Iowa. Most of the acreage shown is for home consumption, but those raised in eastern Virginia and Maryland, Delaware, and southern New Jersey are mostly sold in large cities extending from Washington to New York and Boston. The area in northwestern Tennessee supplies Chicago, Detroit, and other central markets. The production of hops is now almost confined to western Oregon and Washington and the great valley of California. Hemp, formerly an important crop in Kentucky, is now grown mostly in Wisconsin

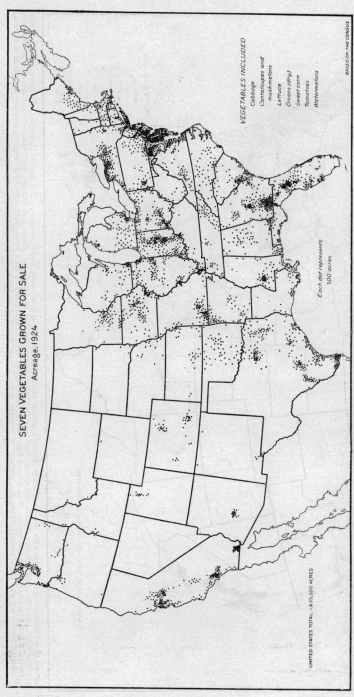

SEVEN VEGETABLES GROWN FOR SALE
Acreage, 1924

VEGETABLES INCLUDED

Cabbage
Cantaloupes and
  muskmelons
Lettuce
Onions (dry)
Sweet corn
Tomatoes
Watermelons

Each dot represents
500 acres

UNITED STATES TOTAL 1,635,000 ACRES

BASED ON THE CENSUS

FIGURE 17.—In the most important area of vegetable production, extending from New York City to Norfolk, Va., about one-fifth of our commercial crop is produced. A second important area extends from Utica, N. Y., west to Buffalo and Erie. Another belt surrounds the southern half of Lake Michigan and extends southward through Indiana. Florida and southern Georgia, where perhaps one-third of the winter vegetables are grown, constitute a fourth area. California has three important areas—the Sacramento-Stockton district, the Los Angeles district, and the Imperial Valley. Smaller centers of production adjoin most of the large cities

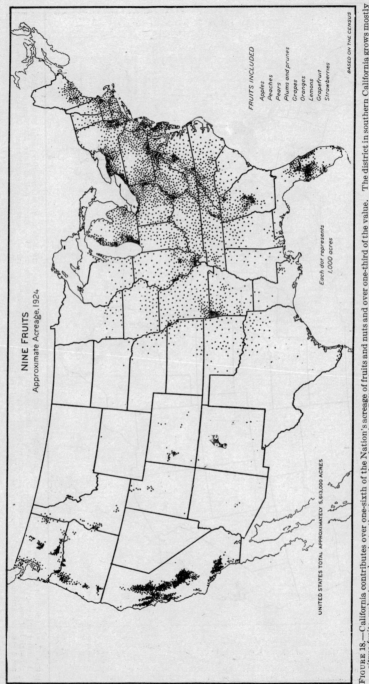

NINE FRUITS
Approximate Acreage, 1924

UNITED STATES TOTAL APPROXIMATELY 5,613,000 ACRES

Each dot represents
1,000 acres

FRUITS INCLUDED

Apples
Peaches
Pears
Plums and prunes
Grapes
Oranges
Lemons
Grapefruit
Strawberries

BASED ON THE CENSUS

FIGURE 18.—California contributes over one-sixth of the Nation's acreage of fruits and nuts and over one-third of the value.   The district in southern California grows mostly citrus fruits, walnuts, and apricots; that in central and northern California grapes, peaches, and apricots, plums and prunes, with some citrus fruits and pears in the foothills and apples near the cool coast.   The dots in Florida represent mostly citrus fruits; those in the Cotton Belt, especially Georgia, peaches; and those in extreme western New York and southwestern Michigan, grapes.   Elsewhere in the United States, with few exceptions the apple is dominant

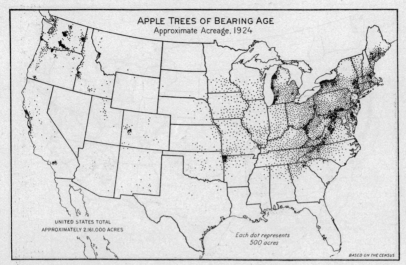

FIGURE 19.—About 14 per cent of the acreage of apple trees of bearing age was in the West in 1924, and nearly half of this western acreage was in the State of Washington. New York, Pennsylvania, Ohio, Michigan, and West Virginia, however, exceeded Washington in acreage. Most of the apple acreage is found in the Hay and Pasture Region from Maine to West Virginia and Michigan, where the climate is cool, but, owing either to lake or mountain protection, the winters are more moist and less severe than in the interior. The southern limit of the apple area extends only a little beyond the northern limit of cotton, and the western, or moisture limit, is about the same as that of timothy

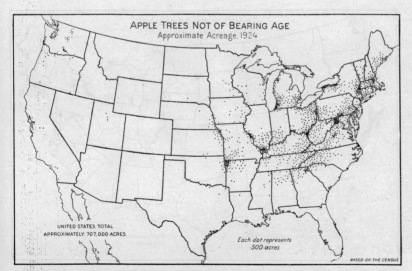

FIGURE 20.—There has been little planting of apple orchards in the West in recent years; the higher freight rates increase the difficulties of competition with eastern-grown fruit. Only 6 per cent of the apple trees not of bearing age were in the West in 1924. Most of the acreage of young trees is located along the shore of Lake Ontario in New York, in the Hudson Valley, in New England, along the Appalachians from Pennsylvania to Georgia, in the upper Ohio Valley, and along the Lake Michigan shore of Michigan. Trees not of bearing age numbered 34,000,000 in 1924 and 36,000,000 in 1920, as compared with nearly 66,000,000 in 1910

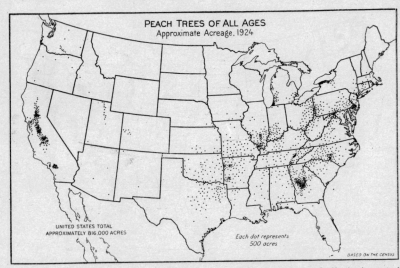

FIGURE 21.—Three major centers of peach acreage are shown—the early peach district in central Georgia, the late peach district along Lake Ontario in New York, and the canning and dried peach districts in California. An important district is rapidly developing in Moore County, N. C. Minor centers are in southern New Jersey, in southern Illinois, along the Michigan shore of Lake Michigan, and in Arkansas and Texas. Cold, dry winters prevent peaches being grown to the northwest of a line drawn from Chicago to Omaha, thence to Amarillo, Tex. The influence of the Great Lakes in tempering winter temperatures on their leeward shores and retarding growth in spring till danger of frost is past is evident

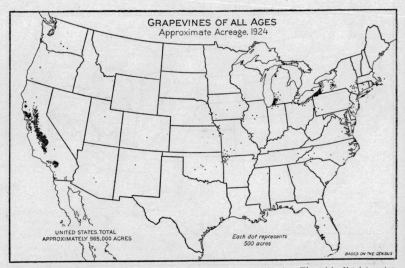

FIGURE 22.—Nearly three-fourths of the acreage of grapes is in California. The raisin district centers around Fresno, where the land is flat and the sunshine almost continuous. Juice grapes are grown mostly on the slopes of the valleys that open into San Francisco Bay. Table grapes are grown in both districts. A smaller center is found in southern California near San Bernardino. In the East the principal grape district extends along the southern shore of Lake Erie. Minor centers are in the Finger Lakes district of New York and in the southwestern corner of Michigan. These eastern grapes are mostly consumed fresh or made into grape juice

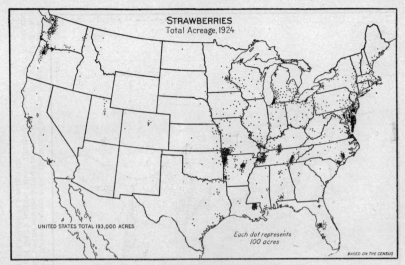

FIGURE 23.—Commercial production of strawberries has become concentrated in unusual degree in a few centers, notably in southern New Jersey, southern Delaware, and the "Eastern Shore" of Maryland and Virginia; in Hamilton and Rhea Counties, and in northwestern Tennessee; in southwestern Missouri and northwestern Arkansas; in White County, Ark.; in Tangipahoa Parish, La.; in Hillsborough County, Fla.; in Berrien County, Mich.; in Hood River County, Oreg.; and in the Willamette and Puget Sound Valleys. These districts contained one-third of the Nation's acreage of strawberries in 1924

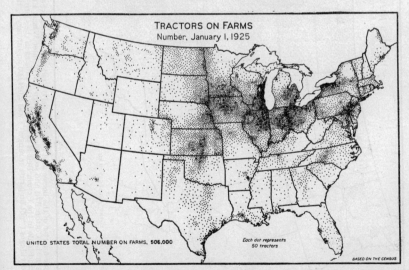

FIGURE 24.—Tractors are most numerous in the Corn Belt, in the southern portion of the Hay and Dairying Belt, in southeastern Pennsylvania, and in California—regions of fertile soils and of progressive agriculture. Increase in tractors since 1920 has been notable near large industrial centers, where wages are high, and less notable on large farms of the Central West, where larger tractors are used than in the East. Few tractors are found in the South, except in central North Carolina and in Texas. This is owing partly to the fact that the acreage of cotton on a farm is not limited by the area that can be plowed and cultivated but the area that can be picked. The coming of the tractor, truck, and automobile has caused the number of horses to decrease rapidly in the North and West; doubtless this has been an important factor in causing the decrease in the number of cattle and swine in the South

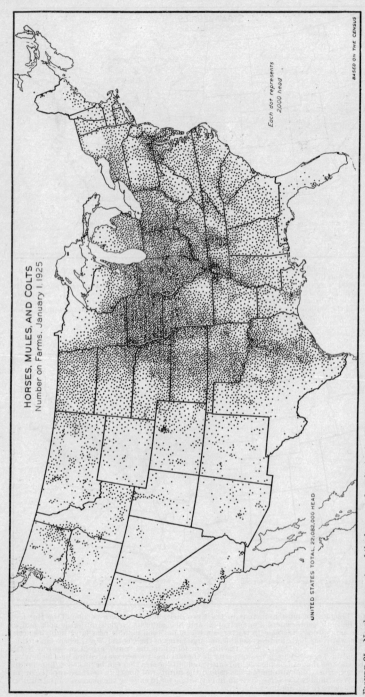

HORSES, MULES, AND COLTS
Number on Farms, January 1, 1925

Each dot represents
2,000 head

BASED ON THE CENSUS

UNITED STATES TOTAL, 22,082,000 HEAD

FIGURE 25.—Nearly one-quarter of the horses and mules in the United States are in the Corn Belt, and over three-quarters are in the humid eastern half of the country. The lesser density in the Cotton Belt and sections of the Corn and Winter-Wheat Region is owing chiefly to the smaller acreage in crops (fig. 2). The acreage of crops per mature horse and mule in the Cotton Belt is practically the same as in the Corn Belt or in the Hay and Dairy Region (about 19 acres). The number of horses and mules in cities and villages ("not on farms or ranges") was 2,084,000 on January 1, 1929, but probably only 1,400,000 or less in 1929

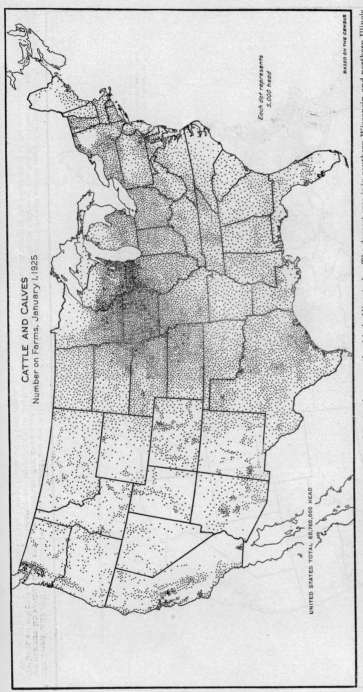

CATTLE AND CALVES
Number on Farms, January 1, 1925

Each dot represents
5,000 head

BASED ON THE CENSUS

UNITED STATES TOTAL 60,760,000 HEAD

FIGURE 26.—Cattle are more evenly distributed over the United States than any other kind of livestock. The densest area is in southern Wisconsin and northern Illinois, Iowa, northern Missouri, eastern Nebraska, southeastern South Dakota, and southern Minnesota. On January 1, 1925, there were about 13,000,000 cattle in the Corn Belt, or 55 to the square mile; 11,000,000 in the Hay and Pasture Region, or 34 to the square mile; 9,000,000 in the Corn and Winter-Wheat Region, or 30 to the square mile; 7,000,000 in the Cotton Belt, or 17 to the square mile; and 8,000,000 in the two wheat regions, or about 20 to the square mile. The western regions had about 11,000,000 cattle, an average of 9 to the square mile. In Iowa there were nearly 80 cattle to the square mile.

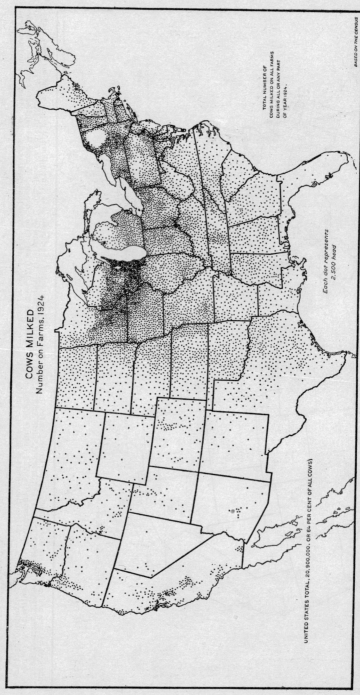

COWS MILKED
Number on Farms, 1924

TOTAL NUMBER OF
COWS MILKED ON ALL FARMS
DURING ALL OR ANY PART
OF YEAR 1924.

BASED ON THE CENSUS

Each dot represents
2,500 head

UNITED STATES TOTAL, 20,900,000, OR 64 PER CENT OF ALL COWS)

FIGURE 27.—Nearly half the cows milked in the United States are in the Hay and Dairy Region and adjacent northern and eastern margin of the Corn Belt. Most of these are dairy cows. Other dairy areas are in southeastern Pennsylvania, which is really Corn Belt country, in the valleys of the North and South Pacific regions, and in the irrigated districts of the interior Grazing and Irrigated Crops Region. Elsewhere in the West and in much of the South most of the cows milked are "beef cows." Over one-fifth of the cows milked in the United States are of beef breeds

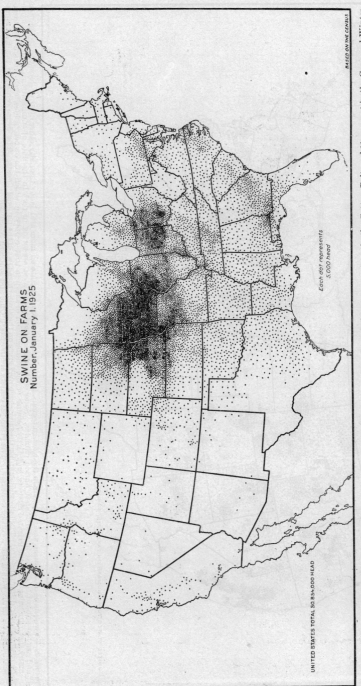

SWINE ON FARMS
Number, January 1, 1925

Each dot represents
5,000 head

BASED ON THE CENSUS

UNITED STATES TOTAL 50,854,000 HEAD

FIGURE 28.—Nearly 60 per cent of the hogs and pigs in the United States are in the Corn Belt, 14 per cent in the Cotton Belt, and 11 per cent in the Corn and Winter-Wheat Region. In 1919 there were on the average 108 swine per square mile in the Corn Belt, 18 in the Cotton Belt, 21 in the Corn and Winter-Wheat Region, 12 in the Hay and Dairy Region, and about 5 per square mile in the remainder of the United States. Just as the cool Hay and Dairy Region finds the best outlet for its crops in feeding dairy cows, so the warm, fertile Corn Belt finds the growing of corn and feeding of beef cattle and hogs its most profitable system of farming

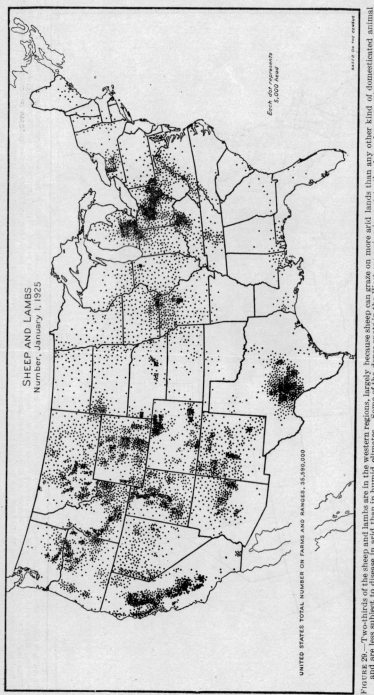

SHEEP AND LAMBS
Number, January 1, 1925

Each dot represents
5,000 head

BASED ON THE CENSUS

UNITED STATES TOTAL NUMBER ON FARMS AND RANGES, 35,590,000

FIGURE 29.—Two-thirds of the sheep and lambs are in the western regions, largely because sheep can graze on more arid lands than any other kind of domesticated animal and are less subject to disease in arid than in humid climates. Some of the dense spots in the West are owing in part to the date of enumeration, January 1, when many sheep are being fed in the irrigated districts, and partly because of the enumeration of sheep in that county in which the owner resides, even though the sheep be roaming over distant deserts. The following summer the same sheep may graze on the alpine meadows of the national forests. The dense centers in the East represent sheep on farms within the counties indicated. The principal centers are in eastern Ohio and southern Michigan

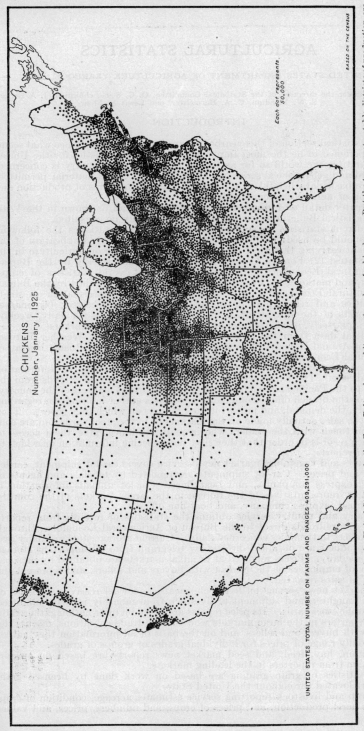

CHICKENS
Number, January 1, 1925

Each dot represents
50,000

BASED ON THE CENSUS

UNITED STATES TOTAL NUMBER ON FARMS AND RANGES 409,291,000

FIGURE 30.—Nearly half of the chickens in the United States are in the Corn Belt and around its margin, where feed is cheap. But the two most notable districts of production are the counties in southeastern Pennsylvania, near Philadelphia, and Sonoma County, Calif., especially the district around Petaluma. Six counties in southeastern Pennsylvania had over 5,000,000 chickens on January 1, 1925, or 1,150 to the square mile; in Sonoma County there were over 3,000,000 poultry, with a value of eggs and chickens produced amounting to over $11,000,000 in 1924. Los Angeles County, Calif., had 1,800,000 poultry. The California cities are supplied largely from these two counties; the eastern cities draw their supplies from a much wider territory

AGRICULTURAL STATISTICS

UNITED STATES DEPARTMENT OF AGRICULTURE YEARBOOK, 1928

Prepared under the direction of the Statistical Committee: O. C. Stine, chairman, J. A. Becker, S. W. Mendum, C. A. Burmeister, and Lewis B. Flohr

INTRODUCTION

The statistical section of this yearbook brings together in one place what seems from experience to be the most important agricultural statistics for the United States, and for the world so far as the agriculture of this country is concerned. Historical and geographical series have been given as far as material permitted. These are basic data helpful to the producer in his problems of production and marketing of agricultural commodities.

For greater detail on individual commodities than can be shown in the Yearbook, Statistical Bulletin series of the department may be consulted.

For current statistics to supplement the Yearbook statistics the following sources should be used: (1) Crops and Markets—a monthly publication of the department carrying the latest current statistics available on agriculture in the United States; (2) Foreign Crops and Markets—issued weekly by the Bureau of Agricultural Economics and devoted to current world statistics of crops, livestock, and markets; (3) Foreign Commodity News—published by the Bureau of Agricultural Economics and showing the latest world information on single commodities and released as important information is received; (4) market news reports of the Bureau of Agricultural Economics—issued daily, weekly, monthly, quarterly, or at irregular intervals, at the principal markets.

Statistical data from the following bureaus are included: Weather Bureau, Bureau of Animal Industry, Forest Service, Bureau of Public Roads, Bureau of Agricultural Economics, and Grain Futures Administration.

The Federal market news system supplies much price and market information presented here. The leased-wire system in use by the service extends from the Atlantic to the Pacific and reaches most of the important markets of the country. At each of the branch offices commodity specialists gather information regarding the supply, the demand, and prices for the products on which they report. They observe the sales actually made on the markets or in the stockyards and are constantly in touch with the traders who in many instances give them access to their office records in order that they may have specific information on which to base their reports.

The fruits and vegetables market news service covers car-lot shipment, car-lot unloads, and prices. Car-lot shipments are reported by officials and agents of railroads, express companies, and boat lines. Car-lot unloads information is obtained by representatives of the bureau in the larger markets of the country from railroad, express company, and boat-line officials.

The dairy and poultry service obtains the statistics of receipts from reports made by the railroads direct to the Bureau of Agricultural Economics, through its local offices in the cities concerned daily. Current storage stocks of dairy and poultry products are obtained directly by telegraph from all important storage warehouses daily. Prices reported at terminal markets are obtained by personal interview of employees of the bureau with buyers and sellers, and represent the majority of sales reported.

The market news service on livestock, meats, and wool receives statistics of receipts, slaughter, and shipment of livestock from monthly reports submitted by the public stockyards. Its price reports are based on information gathered by bureau reporters in the large markets who observe trade conditions, discuss the market with buyers and sellers, and on the basis of all information they gather quote a daily range of prices for individual grades or groups of grades.

The grain, hay, feed, and seed market news reports are based on current information from reporters in the leading markets.

The statistics of grain grading are based on work done by licensed grain inspectors located throughout the United States.

The crop and livestock reporting service estimates acreage, condition of crop, yield per acre, production, and prices of crops, and numbers, prices, and values

666

of livestock. The organization of this work outside of the crop-reporting board and the office force in Washington consists of 41 State field officers, with an agricultural statistician in charge. There is one field office for the New England States, one for Maryland and Delaware, and one for Utah and Nevada. There is a dual system of agricultural correspondents and reporters distributed over the country. One group sends their reports to the local State field office and the other group directly to the Bureau in Washington.

Acreages for the year 1909 are as reported by the Bureau of the Census; acreages in 1919 and in 1924 are based upon the census (preliminary for 1924 in some States), supplemented by State enumerations. In the intercensal years, from 1911 to 1915, estimated acreages were obtained by applying estimated percentages of decrease or increase to the published acreage in the preceding year. The estimates from 1915 to 1918, from 1919 to 1923, and for 1925 and 1926 are based upon acreage changes from year to year as shown by a sample of approximately 2 per cent of the crop acreages in each year, supplemented by State enumerations. Yields per acre are estimates based upon reports of one or more farmers in each agricultural township on the average yield per acre in their localities. Production is acreage times yield per acre.

Estimates of farm stocks, shipments, quality, crop condition, and miscellaneous information concerning crops are based either upon sample data or upon estimates of crop reporters for their localities. The sources of these data are indicated in the notes accompanying the tables.

Monthly estimated prices received by producers on the specified dates are based upon reports from special price reporters, who are mostly country dealers, on the average price paid to farmers and do not relate to any specified grade.

Farm value as shown is computed by applying the December 1 farm price to the total production. (The prices are reported by the crop reporters, who are mostly farmers.) The average price received for the portion of the crop sold may be greater or less than this price, depending upon the prices previous and subsequent to December 1 and the amount of the crop sold at the different prices.

Numbers of livestock on farms on January 1, 1920 and 1925, are based upon the census enumeration as of that date, supplemented by enumerations by State agencies, such as assessors and brand inspection boards, and by records of shipments during 1920 and 1925. In the intercensal years, from 1911 to 1916, the numbers of livestock were obtained by methods identical with those used for crop acreages. Estimates from 1917 to 1919, from 1920 to 1923, and for 1926 and 1927 are based upon a sample of approximately 2 per cent, supplemented by trends derived from assessors' enumerations, reports of brand inspection boards, market movements, and stockyard receipts. The census bases are not always comparable from one decade to another, because of changes of dates and classifications.

The average value per head on January 1 is estimated from reports of correspondents relating to livestock in their vicinity. These tend to reflect inventory values as distinguished from the monthly prices which relate to sales. The farm value on January 1 is computed by applying the average value per head to the number of head on farms.

Where a weighting factor was available market prices as shown are weighted averages, but in many cases a weighting factor was not available and the prices shown are usually the means of ranges of quotations without reference to quantity. The weighted price of wheat in Chicago is based on the number of carload sales reported, which range from 42 to 55 per cent of all receipts on that market. The weighted average price of hogs at Chicago is based on total sales of butcher and packer hogs to slaughterers.

Prices derived from different sources may not be strictly comparable, although for most general purposes they are satisfactory. The changes in the grade and weight groupings of many kinds of livestock which were made July 1, 1925, while not affecting certain price series, made others only fairly comparable and made comparison impossible in other cases. The data as to commercial stocks and movements of various commodities are as nearly complete as practicable and feasible, and are considered fairly representative.

Statistics of acreage and production in foreign countries are compiled as far as possible from official sources and are therefore subject to whatever errors may result from shortcomings in the reporting and statistical services of the various countries. Inaccuracies also result from differences in nomenclature and classification in foreign countries. Except where otherwise stated, pre-war data refer to pre-war boundaries. Yields per acre are calculated from acreage and production, both rounded to thousand units, and are therefore subject to a greater possibility of error when calculated for countries with small acreage.

The tables of international trade cover substantially the international trade of the world. The total imports and the total exports in any one year can not be expected to balance, although disagreements tend to be compensated over a series of years. Among the sources of disagreement are: The different periods covered by the "year" of various countries; imports received in the year subsequent to the year of export; lack of uniformity in classification of goods as among countries; different trade practices and varying degrees of failure in recording countries of origin and ultimate destination; different practices in recording reexported goods; and different methods of treating free ports. The exports given are domestic exports and the imports given are imports for consumption, whenever it is possible to distinguish such imports from general imports. While there are some inevitable omissions, there may be some duplication because of reshipments which do not appear as such in the official reports. In the trade tables, figures for the United States include Alaska, Porto Rico, and Hawaii, but not the Philippine Islands.

As an aid to the comprehension and use of these statistics, the following table of weights, measures, and conversion factors will be useful:

Weights, measures, and conversion factors used in the Department of Agriculture

Commodity	Unit [1]	Weight in pounds	Commodity	Unit [1]	Weight in pounds
Alfalfa seed	Bushel	60	Lemons	Box	[2] 74
Almonds	Short ton	2,000	Milk	Gallon	8.6
Apricots	do	2,000	Oats	Bushel	32
Do	Bushel	48	Oranges (Calif.)	Box	[2] 70
Asparagus	Short ton	2,000	Oranges (Fla.)	do	[2] 80
Barley	Bushel	48	Orchard grass	Bushel	14
Beans, snap	Short ton	2,000	Peanut oil	Gallon	7.5
Beans, dry	Bushel	60	Plums	Short ton	2,000
Beet sugar	Short ton	2,000	Potatoes	Bushel	60
Broomcorn	do	2,000	Prunes	Short ton	2,000
Buckwheat	Bushel	48	Rapeseed	Bushel	50
Cabbage	Short ton	2,000	Raisins	Short ton	2,000
Cane sugar	do	2,000	Rice, rough	Bushel	45
Clover seed	Bushel	60	Rice, cleaned	do	60
Corn, shelled	do	56	Rye	do	56
Corn, ear, husked	do	70	Rye flour	Barrel	196
Cottonseed	Short ton	2,000	Soy-bean oil	Gallon	7.5
Cotton, ginned	Bale	[2] 478	Spelt	Bushel	40
		[3] 500	Sugar	Short ton	2,000
Cottonseed oil	Gallon	7.5	Sugar beets	do	2,000
Flaxseed	Bushel	56	Sugar cane	do	2,000
Figs	Short ton	2,000	Timothy seed	Bushel	45
Grapefruit	Box	[2] 70	Tomatoes	do	56
Grapes	Short ton	2,000	Wheat	do	60
Hay	do	2,000	Wheat flour	Barrel	196
Hemp seed	Bushel	44	Walnuts	Short ton	2,000

Commodity	Equivalents
Almonds	1 pound shelled is equivalent to about 3⅓ pounds unshelled.
Apples	1 pound dried is equivalent to about 5 pounds of fresh.
Barley flour	1 barrel (196 pounds) is equivalent to about 9 bushels of barley.
Buckwheat flour	1 barrel (196 pounds) is equivalent to about 7 bushels of buckwheat.
Filberts	1 pound shelled is equivalent to about 2.22 pounds unshelled.
Malt	1.1 bushel (34 pounds) is equivalent to about 1 bushel of barley.
Oatmeal	1 barrel (196 pounds) is equivalent to about 10⅝ bushels of oats.
Do	18 pounds is equivalent to about 1 bushel of oats.
Peanuts	1 pound shelled is equivalent to about 1½ pounds unshelled.
Peaches (Calif.)	1 pound dried is equivalent to about 5½ pounds fresh.
Prunes	1 pound dried is equivalent to about 2½ pounds fresh.
Rye flour	1 barrel (196 pounds) is equivalent to about 6 bushels of rye.
Raisins	1 pound is equivalent to about 4 pounds of grapes.
Wheat flour	1 barrel (196 pounds) is equivalent to about 4.7 bushels of wheat.[4]
Walnuts (English)	1 pound shelled is equivalent to about 2.38 pounds unshelled.

[1] Standard bushel used in the United States contains 2,150.42 cubic inches; the gallon, 231 cubic inches.
[2] Net.
[3] Gross.
[4] Due to changes in milling processes equivalents have varied as follows: 1790–1879, 5; 1880–1908, 4.75; 1909–1917, 4.7; 1918–1919, 4.5; 1920, 4.6; 1921–1927, 4.7.

STATISTICS OF GRAINS

TABLE 1.—*Wheat: Acreage, production, value, exports, etc., United States, 1849, 1859, 1866–1928*

Year	Acreage harvested	Average yield per acre	Production	Price per bushel received by producers Dec. 1	Farm value Dec. 1	Spring wheat, price per bushel at Chicago, year beginning July 1	No. 2 red winter wheat, price per bushel at Chicago, year beginning July 1	Domestic exports	Imports	Net exports [6] Total	Percentage of production
	1,000 acres	*Bush.*	*1,000 bush.*	*Cts.*	*1,000 dolls.*	*Cts.*	*Cts.*	*1,000 bush.*	*1,000 bush.*	*1,000 bush.*	*Per cent*
1849			*100,486*			66		7,536	2,913	5,701	5.7
1859			*173,105*			90	82	17,213	[7] 4,493	[7] 12,720	7.3
1866	15,424	9.9	152,000	152.7	232,110	219	94	12,647	3,093	10,828	7.1
1867	18,322	11.6	212,441	145.2	308,387	198	145	26,323	2,014	24,550	11.6
1868	18,460	12.1	224,037	108.5	243,033	134	123	29,717	1,830	28,314	12.6
1869			*287,746*								
1869	19,181	13.6	260,147	76.5	199,025	98	84	53,901	1,286	53,126	20.4
1870	18,993	12.4	235,885	94.4	222,767	116	84	52,574	867	52,195	22.1
1871	19,944	11.6	230,722	114.5	264,076	124	109	38,996	2,411	37,587	16.3
1872	20,858	12.0	249,997	111.4	278,522	121	111	52,015	1,841	50,705	20.3
1873	22,172	12.7	281,255	106.9	300,670	116	103	91,510	2,117	90,418	32.1
1874	24,967	12.3	308,103	86.3	265,881	95	98	72,913	368	72,845	23.6
1875	26,382	11.1	292,136	89.5	261,397	106	86	74,751	1,664	74,508	25.5
1876	27,627	10.5	289,356	97.0	280,743	122	92	57,044	366	57,148	19.8
1877	26,278	13.9	364,194	105.7	385,089	111	121	92,142	1,391	92,028	25.3
1878	32,109	13.1	420,122	77.6	325,814	90	95	150,503	2,074	150,253	35.8
1879	*35,430*	*13.0*	*459,483*								
1879	35,430	14.1	499,893	110.6	552,884	110	99	181,807	487	181,951	36.4
1880	37,987	13.1	498,550	95.1	474,202	100	105	188,308	212	188,250	37.8
1881	37,709	10.2	383,280	119.2	456,880	128	115	123,371	867	123,211	32.1
1882	37,067	13.6	504,185	88.4	445,602	105	118	150,113	1,088	150,000	29.8
1883	36,456	11.6	421,086	91.1	383,649	93	102	113,822	33	113,892	27.0
1884	39,476	13.0	512,765	64.5	330,862	79	83	135,232	213	135,301	26.4
1885	34,189	10.4	357,112	77.1	275,320	81	88	96,611	389	96,569	27.0
1886	36,806	12.4	457,218	68.7	314,226	77	76	156,685	283	156,760	34.3
1887	37,642	12.1	456,329	68.1	310,613	75	75	122,616	596	122,524	26.8
1888	37,336	11.1	415,868	92.6	385,248	95	88	90,944	136	91,030	21.9
1889	*33,580*	*13.9*	*468,374*								
1889	33,580	12.9	434,383	69.5	301,869	81	86	112,488	163	112,507	25.9
1890	34,048	11.1	378,097	83.3	315,112	97	89	109,017	586	109,054	28.8
1891	37,826	11.5	584,504	83.4	487,463	89	96	229,465	2,463	228,841	39.2
1892	39,552	13.3	527,987	62.2	328,331	73	78	196,068	968	195,672	37.1
1893	37,934	11.3	427,553	53.5	228,599	60	68	168,498	1,183	167,531	39.2

Bureau of Agricultural Economics. Production figures are estimates of the crop-reporting board; italic figures are census returns.

[1] Spring wheat prices compiled as follows: 1839–1870, from Chicago newspapers, quoted; 1839–1849, spring wheat, contract grade; 1859, standard spring, contract grade; 1866–1870, No. 1 spring, contract grade; 1871–1884, annual reports of Chicago Board of Trade, quoted as No. 2 spring, contract grade; 1885–96, Bartel's Red Book, quoted as No. 2 spring; January, 1897–June, 1904, Chicago Daily Trade Bulletin, average of daily ranges; quotations used; January–October, 1897, No. 3 spring; November, 1897–June, 98, No. 3 spring, hard varieties; July, 1898–June, 1904, No. 1 spring; from February, 1897, "free on board" as used when available; July, 1904–December, 1918, Bartel's Red Book, average of daily ranges, quoted No. 1 northern. Subsequently from the Chicago Daily Trade Bulletin and are averages of the daily cash price per bushel weighted by car-lot sales.

[2] Prices, 1839–1898, are from the Price Current Grain Reporter 1924 Yearbook, p. 4, and are average cash prices for calendar years; subsequently from the Chicago Daily Trade Bulletin and are averages the daily cash price per bushel weighted by car-lot sales.

[3] Compiled from Commerce and Navigation of the United States, 1849, 1859, 1866–1917; Foreign Commerce and Navigation of the United States, 1918; Monthly Summary of Foreign Commerce of the United States, June issues, 1919–1926; January and June issues, 1927–28. Wheat flour converted to terms grain on the following basis: 1849, 1859, 1866–1879, 1 barrel is the product of 5 bushels of grain; 1880–1908, 5; 1909–1917, 4.7; 1918–1919, 4.5; 1920, 4.6.

[4] Includes flour milled from imported wheat.

[5] Includes wheat imported for milling in bond and export.

[6] Total exports (domestic plus foreign) minus total imports.

[7] Imports of flour estimated.

TABLE 1.—*Wheat: Acreage, production, value, exports, etc., United States, 1849, 1859, 1866–1928*—Continued

Year	Acreage harvested	Average yield per acre	Production	Price per bushel received by producers Dec. 1	Farm value Dec. 1	Spring wheat, price per bushel at Chicago, year beginning July 1	No. 2 red winter wheat, price per bushel at Chicago, year beginning July 1	Foreign trade, including flour, year beginning July 1			
								Domestic exports	Imports	Net exports	
										Total	Percentage of production
	1,000 acres	*Bush.*	*1,000 bush.*	*Cts.*	*1,000 dolls.*	*Cts.*	*Cts.*	*1,000 bush.*	*1,000 bush.*	*1,000 bush.*	*Per cent*
1894	39,425	13.1	516,485	48.9	252,709	57	57	148,630	1,439	147,740	28.6
1895	40,848	13.9	569,456	50.3	286,539	61	62	130,099	2,117	130,345	22.9
1896	43,916	12.4	544,193	71.7	390,346	70	67	148,767	1,545	148,725	27.3
1897	46,046	13.3	610,254	80.9	493,683	91	86	221,143	2,060	220,965	36.2
1898	51,007	15.1	772,163	58.2	449,022	71	90	227,240	1,875	227,300	29.4
1899	*52,589*	*12.5*	*658,534*								
1899	52,589	12.1	636,051	58.6	372,982	70	8 72	190,772	320	190,749	30.0
1900	51,387	11.7	602,708	62.0	373,578	75	76	220,653	603	220,723	36.6
1901	52,473	15.0	788,638	62.6	493,766	74	72	239,212	121	239,137	30.3
1902	49,649	14.6	724,808	63.0	456,851	77	75	207,835	1,080	208,016	28.7
1903	51,632	12.9	663,923	69.5	461,439	90	83	124,977	229	124,926	18.8
1904	47,825	12.5	596,911	92.4	551,788	114	9 100	46,319	3,296	43,612	7.3
1905	49,389	14.7	726,819	74.6	542,543	89	8 88	101,089	273	100,849	13.9
1906	47,800	15.8	756,775	66.2	501,316	84	77	150,597	602	150,594	19.9
1907	45,116	14.1	637,981	86.5	552,074	107	90	166,525	530	166,304	26.1
1908	45,970	14.0	644,656	92.2	594,128	116	96	116,373	475	115,901	18.0
1909	*44,263*	*15.4*	*683,379*								
1909	44,262	15.8	700,434	98.4	689,108	114	110	89,173	845	88,465	12.6
1910	45,681	13.9	635,121	88.3	561,051	107	102	71,338	1,175	70,164	11.0
1911	49,543	12.5	621,338	87.4	543,063	110	90	81,891	3,445	78,447	12.6
1912	45,814	15.9	730,267	76.0	555,280	94	103	145,159	1,304	143,938	19.7
1913	50,184	15.2	763,380	79.9	610,122	93	88	147,955	2,402	146,306	19.2
1914	53,541	16.6	891,017	98.6	878,680	132	108	335,702	728	335,162	37.6
1915	60,469	17.0	1,025,801	91.9	942,303	120	113	246,221	7,254	239,591	23.4
1916	52,316	12.2	636,318	160.3	1,019,968	196	168	205,962	24,960	181,067	28.5
1917	45,089	14.1	636,655	200.8	1,278,112	227	225	132,579	31,215	102,775	16.1
1918	59,181	15.6	921,438	204.2	1,881,826	234	222	287,402	11,289	276,615	30.0
1919	*73,099*	*12.9*	*945,403*								
1919	75,694	12.8	967,979	214.9	2,080,056	276	224	222,030	5,511	216,671	22.4
1920	61,143	13.6	833,027	143.7	1,197,263	198	223	369,313	57,682	312,625	37.5
1921	63,696	12.8	814,905	92.6	754,834	136	125	282,566	17,375	265,590	32.6
1922	62,317	13.9	867,598	100.7	873,412	122	114	224,900	20,031	205,079	23.6
1923	59,659	13.4	797,394	92.3	736,006	119	102	159,880	28,079	131,892	16.5
1924	*50,862*	*15.7*	*800,877*								
1924	52,535	16.5	864,428	129.9	1,123,086	155	158	260,803	6,201	254,695	29.5
1925	52,255	12.9	676,429	141.6	957,907	166	164	108,035	15,679	92,669	13.7
1926	56,337	14.8	831,040	119.8	995,954	140	138	219,160	13,264	205,994	24.8
1927	58,784	14.9	878,374	111.5	979,813	140	140	206,259	15,734	190,578	21.1
1928 10	57,724	15.6	902,749	97.2	877,193						

8 Weighted average for 11 months.
9 Weighted average for 10 months.
10 Preliminary.

TABLE 2.—*Wheat: Acreage harvested and production, by States, average 1921–1925, annual 1926–1928*

State and division	Acreage harvested				Production			
	Average, 1921–1925	1926	1927	1928 [1]	Average, 1921–1925	1926	1927	1928 [1]
	1,000 acres	1,000 acres	1,000 acres	1,000 acres	1,000 bushels	1,000 bushels	1,000 bushels	1,000 bushels
Maine	6	6	4	4	143	120	72	80
Vermont	4	2	1	1	71	40	20	16
New York	395	279	301	316	7,675	4,887	6,291	4,702
New Jersey	68	60	60	60	1,347	1,320	1,380	1,200
Pennsylvania	1,250	1,177	1,098	1,108	22,831	23,533	20,301	17,171
North Atlantic	1,723	1,524	1,464	1,489	32,068	29,900	28,064	23,169
Ohio	2,157	1,795	1,615	872	33,218	40,384	29,068	9,475
Indiana	1,913	1,703	1,790	910	28,408	34,048	27,749	9,590
Illinois	2,847	2,283	2,509	1,563	47,926	41,034	34,844	24,200
Michigan	928	984	897	887	16,086	17,998	19,270	14,202
Wisconsin	148	128	145	104	2,568	2,599	3,142	2,141
Minnesota	2,036	1,929	1,763	1,599	28,346	24,811	20,925	23,955
Iowa	571	378	441	428	11,080	8,078	8,236	8,270
Missouri	2,490	1,403	1,568	1,511	30,893	21,474	15,700	19,194
North Dakota	9,247	9,653	10,246	10,367	104,921	77,081	130,191	142,923
South Dakota	2,763	1,917	3,037	3,262	32,100	11,611	45,386	34,546
Nebraska	3,411	3,077	3,630	3,672	48,754	40,085	73,826	69,919
Kansas	9,405	10,147	9,946	10,473	114,542	150,084	111,327	177,833
North Central	37,916	35,397	37,587	35,648	498,842	469,287	519,664	536,248
Delaware	106	103	98	102	1,728	2,060	1,862	1,836
Maryland	553	520	525	530	9,522	11,960	9,188	8,745
Virginia	755	687	687	673	9,442	11,336	8,381	9,758
West Virginia	195	147	135	122	2,449	2,352	1,796	1,586
North Carolina	513	447	483	444	5,074	6,303	5,168	5,150
South Carolina	112	50	80	64	1,135	800	880	800
Georgia	138	104	125	94	1,294	1,560	1,150	1,034
South Atlantic	2,372	2,058	2,133	2,029	30,645	36,371	28,425	28,909
Kentucky	467	258	296	115	5,357	4,773	2,812	920
Tennessee	408	440	528	422	4,269	7,920	3,696	3,714
Alabama	14	7	7	4	143	94	74	44
Mississippi	5	4	6	3	71	68	102	60
Arkansas	63	30	28	22	702	405	322	253
Oklahoma	3,507	4,214	3,708	4,413	40,552	73,745	33,372	59,576
Texas	1,415	1,802	1,850	2,016	15,795	32,796	17,945	22,176
South Central	5,878	6,755	6,423	6,995	66,890	119,801	58,323	86,743
Montana	3,204	3,570	3,850	4,235	44,134	44,744	80,208	77,218
Idaho	1,010	1,045	1,171	1,160	24,689	24,633	32,374	28,792
Wyoming	169	198	226	243	2,694	3,714	4,186	4,098
Colorado	1,452	1,463	1,419	1,339	19,492	18,452	20,112	18,564
New Mexico	147	249	55	186	1,763	5,653	570	2,054
Arizona	39	38	58	47	923	950	1,450	1,269
Utah	255	237	242	257	5,591	5,505	5,678	6,861
Nevada	18	17	18	18	464	408	460	482
Washington	2,281	2,107	2,261	2,271	43,639	40,901	58,436	48,644
Oregon	1,028	1,026	1,065	1,027	20,931	18,706	26,782	23,318
California	599	653	812	780	11,386	12,015	13,642	16,380
Far Western	10,203	10,603	11,177	11,563	175,706	175,681	243,898	227,680
United States	58,092	56,337	58,784	57,724	804,151	831,040	878,374	902,749

Bureau of Agricultural Economics. Estimates of the crop-reporting board.

[1] Preliminary.

TABLE 3.—*Wheat, winter: Acreage harvested and production, by States, average 1921–1925, annual 1926–1928*

State and division	Acreage harvested				Production			
	Average, 1921–1925	1926	1927	1928 [1]	Average, 1921–1925	1926	1927	1928 [1]
	1,000 acres	*1,000 acres*	*1,000 acres*	*1,000 acres*	*1,000 bushels*	*1,000 bushels*	*1,000 bushels*	*1,000 bushels*
New York	380	270	289	306	7,436	4,725	6,069	4,529
New Jersey	68	60	60	60	1,347	1,320	1,380	1,200
Pennsylvania	1,242	1,170	1,090	1,101	22,710	23,400	20,165	17,066
North Atlantic	1,690	1,500	1,439	1,467	31,493	29,445	27,614	22,795
Ohio	2,144	1,789	1,610	864	33,021	40,252	28,980	9,331
Indiana	1,909	1,697	1,782	900	28,350	33,940	27,621	9,450
Illinois	2,735	2,163	2,293	1,261	46,127	38,934	30,956	18,915
Michigan	915	979	891	882	15,928	17,916	19,156	14,112
Wisconsin	76	65	73	42	1,453	1,339	1,716	777
Minnesota	121	146	155	165	2,181	2,555	3,317	2,640
Iowa	525	342	400	393	10,477	7,524	7,600	7,664
Missouri	2,484	1,391	1,558	1,496	30,804	21,282	15,580	18,999
South Dakota	101	75	105	105	1,418	638	1,890	1,260
Nebraska	3,177	2,881	3,457	3,492	46,097	37,165	70,868	66,697
Kansas	9,393	10,139	9,936	10,433	114,435	150,057	111,283	177,361
North Central	23,579	21,667	22,260	20,033	330,291	351,602	318,967	327,206
Delaware	106	103	98	102	1,728	2,060	1,862	1,836
Maryland	553	520	525	530	9,522	11,960	9,188	8,745
Virginia	755	687	687	673	9,442	11,336	8,381	9,758
West Virginia	195	147	135	122	2,449	2,352	1,796	1,586
North Carolina	513	447	483	444	5,074	6,303	5,168	5,150
South Carolina	112	50	80	64	1,135	800	880	800
Georgia	138	104	125	94	1,294	1,560	1,150	1,034
South Atlantic	2,372	2,058	2,133	2,029	30,645	36,371	28,425	28,909
Kentucky	467	258	296	115	5,357	4,773	2,812	920
Tennessee	408	440	528	422	4,269	7,920	3,696	3,714
Alabama	14	7	7	4	143	94	74	44
Mississippi	5	4	6	3	71	68	102	60
Arkansas	63	30	28	22	702	405	322	253
Oklahoma	3,507	4,214	3,708	4,413	40,552	73,745	33,372	59,576
Texas	1,415	1,802	1,850	2,016	15,795	32,796	17,945	22,176
South Central	5,878	6,755	6,423	6,995	66,890	119,801	58,323	86,743
Montana	532	521	648	810	8,416	7,294	14,256	12,150
Idaho	419	447	501	456	9,607	10,281	12,274	10,488
Wyoming	26	48	54	62	419	864	918	930
Colorado	1,137	1,207	1,086	923	14,342	14,484	14,118	11,076
New Mexico	99	212	25	150	1,094	4,876	150	1,500
Arizona	39	38	58	47	923	950	1,450	1,269
Utah	147	149	152	162	2,623	3,129	2,888	3,726
Nevada	3	5	4	4	75	120	96	104
Washington	1,179	847	1,228	1,424	26,545	19,481	36,226	35,600
Oregon	735	880	900	837	15,843	16,720	23,400	20,088
California	599	653	812	780	11,386	12,015	13,642	16,380
Far Western	4,915	5,007	5,468	5,655	91,274	90,214	119,418	113,311
United States	38,434	36,987	37,723	36,179	550,593	627,433	552,747	578,964

Bureau of Agricultural Economics.　Estimates of the crop reporting board.

[1] Preliminary.

TABLE 4.—*Wheat, spring other than durum:*[1] *Acreage harvested and production, by States, average 1921–1925, annual 1926–1928*

State and division	Acreage harvested				Production			
	Average, 1921–1925	1926	1927	1928 [2]	Average, 1921–1925	1926	1927	1928 [2]
	1,000 acres	1,000 acres	1,000 acres	1,000 acres	1,000 bushels	1,000 bushels	1,000 bushels	1,000 bushels
Maine	6	6	4	4	143	120	72	80
Vermont	4	2	1	1	71	40	20	16
New York	15	9	12	10	239	162	222	173
Pennsylvania	[3] 13	7	8	7	[3] 202	133	136	105
North Atlantic	33	24	25	22	575	455	450	374
Ohio	12	6	5	8	197	132	88	144
Indiana	4	6	8	10	58	108	128	140
Illinois	112	120	216	302	1,799	2,100	3,888	5,285
Michigan	13	5	6	5	158	82	114	90
Wisconsin	72	63	72	62	1,115	1,260	1,426	1,364
Minnesota	1,737	1,592	1,340	1,086	23,465	19,582	14,070	15,747
Iowa	47	36	41	35	603	554	636	606
Missouri	6	12	10	15	88	192	120	195
North Dakota	5,765	5,849	6,024	5,301	60,575	40,943	71,083	69,973
South Dakota	1,614	1,077	1,953	1,875	16,501	5,924	27,342	19,312
Nebraska	234	196	173	180	2,657	2,920	2,958	3,222
Kansas	13	8	10	40	107	27	44	472
North Central	9,629	8,970	9,858	8,919	107,324	73,824	121,897	116,550
Montana	2,486	3,035	3,187	3,410	33,375	37,330	65,652	64,790
Idaho	592	598	670	704	15,082	14,352	20,100	18,304
Wyoming	143	150	172	181	2,274	2,850	3,268	3,168
Colorado	316	256	333	416	5,150	3,968	5,994	7,488
New Mexico	48	37	30	36	669	777	420	554
Utah	108	88	90	95	2,968	2,376	2,790	3,135
Nevada	15	12	14	14	389	288	364	378
Washington	1,102	1,260	1,033	847	17,094	21,420	22,210	13,044
Oregon	293	146	165	190	5,089	1,986	3,382	3,230
Far Western	5,102	5,582	5,694	5,893	82,089	85,347	124,180	114,091
United States	14,765	14,576	15,577	14,834	189,988	159,626	246,527	231,015

Bureau of Agricultural Economics. Estimates of the crop-reporting board.

[1] For table on "Durum wheat" see page 674.
[2] Preliminary.
[3] 3-year average.

TABLE 5.—*Durum wheat: Acreage harvested, yield per acre, and production in four States, 1918–1928*

ACREAGE HARVESTED

State	1918	1919	1920	1921	1922	1923	1924	1925	1926	1927	1928 [1]
	1,000 acres	1,000 acres	1,000 acres	1,000 acres	1,000 acres	1,000 acres	1,000 acres	1,000 acres	1,000 acres	1,000 acres	1,000 acres
Minnesota	123	125	115	147	248	225	126	146	191	268	348
North Dakota	2,204	2,749	3,210	3,788	4,026	3,667	2,757	3,170	3,804	4,222	5,066
South Dakota	636	699	716	961	1,239	1,275	865	900	765	979	1,282
Montana	350	209	368	380	279	128	78	64	14	15	15
Total	3,313	3,782	4,409	5,276	5,792	5,295	3,826	4,280	4,774	5,484	6,711

YIELD PER ACRE

State	1918	1919	1920	1921	1922	1923	1924	1925	1926	1927	1928
	Bush.	Bush.	Bush.	Bush.	Bush.	Bush.	Bush.	Bush.	Bush.	Bush.	Bush.
Minnesota	20.0	11.9	12.0	11.9	16.0	12.7	21.5	15.2	14.0	13.2	16.0
North Dakota	14.0	7.9	10.5	9.7	15.0	9.1	16.3	14.6	9.5	14.0	14.4
South Dakota	19.5	9.8	12.4	11.0	15.5	12.0	15.4	13.9	6.6	16.5	10.9
Montana	12.9	4.5	11.5	11.2	14.7	10.2	18.0	10.0	8.6	20.0	18.5
Average	15.2	8.2	10.9	10.1	15.1	10.0	16.3	14.4	9.2	14.4	13.8

PRODUCTION

State	1918	1919	1920	1921	1922	1923	1924	1925	1926	1927	1928
	1,000 bush.	1,000 bush.	1,000 bush.	1,000 bush.	1,000 bush.	1,000 bush.	1,000 bush.	1,000 bush.	1,000 bush.	1,000 bush.	1,000 bush.
Minnesota	2,460	1,485	1,383	1,754	3,960	2,858	2,709	2,219	2,674	3,538	5,568
North Dakota	30,856	21,720	33,702	36,741	60,397	33,370	44,939	46,282	36,138	59,108	72,950
South Dakota	12,403	6,848	8,884	10,570	19,206	15,300	13,321	12,510	5,049	16,154	13,974
Montana	4,516	943	4,231	4,259	4,106	1,306	1,404	640	120	300	278
Total	50,235	30,996	48,200	53,324	87,669	52,834	62,373	61,651	43,981	79,100	92,770

Bureau of Agricultural Economics.   Estimates of the crop-reporting board.

[1] Preliminary.

TABLE 6.—*Wheat: Yield per acre and estimated price per bushel, December 1, by States, average 1914–1920, 1921–1925, annual 1924–1928*

State	Yield per acre							Estimated price per bushel						
	Av., 1914–1920	Av., 1921–1925	1924	1925	1926	1927	1928	Av., 1914–1920	Av., 1921–1925	1924	1925	1926	1927	1928
	Bush.	*Bush.*	*Bush.*	*Bush.*	*Bush.*	*Bush.*	*Bush.*	*Cts.*	*Cts.*	*Cts.*	*Cts.*	*Cts.*	*Cts.*	*Cts.*
Maine	22.7	24.4	26.0	28.0	20.0	18.0	20.0	190	161	170	170	175	175	165
Vermont	23.0	19.6	21.0	21.0	20.0	20.0	16.0	181	142	152	150	132	140	131
New York	21.5	19.4	18.7	19.5	17.5	20.9	14.9	170	126	144	152	132	125	137
New Jersey	18.3	19.7	18.5	21.0	22.0	23.0	20.0	176	127	157	143	132	125	124
Pennsylvania	17.7	18.3	16.5	20.0	20.0	18.5	15.5	168	121	144	147	129	127	129
Ohio	18.0	15.5	18.0	15.0	22.5	18.0	10.9	167	125	145	158	127	125	131
Indiana	16.1	14.9	17.0	14.5	20.0	15.5	10.5	166	123	142	155	124	124	124
Illinois	17.4	16.7	16.1	16.1	18.0	13.9	15.5	164	117	136	150	122	120	112
Michigan	17.8	17.5	24.0	•17.0	18.3	21.5	16.0	166	122	138	156	122	120	128
Wisconsin	19.2	18.2	24.0	20.1	20.3	21.7	20.6	162	112	128	136	126	117	106
Minnesota	13.3	14.3	22.1	13.4	12.9	11.9	15.0	163	112	130	137	123	110	96
Iowa	18.0	19.1	20.2	16.2	21.4	18.7	19.3	154	108	127	136	120	117	100
Missouri	13.8	12.6	13.3	13.2	15.3	10.0	12.7	161	117	133	150	124	122	121
North Dakota	10.3	11.5	15.7	11.7	8.0	12.7	13.8	159	104	126	131	117	103	81
South Dakota	11.9	11.7	14.6	11.8	6.1	14.9	10.6	154	103	125	128	118	106	85
Nebraska	16.0	14.2	19.1	12.8	13.0	20.3	19.0	152	105	122	140	117	109	94
Kansas	14.4	12.0	16.3	9.0	14.8	11.2	17.0	156	112	128	148	119	117	94
Delaware	15.6	16.4	17.8	18.5	20.0	19.0	18.0	171	119	144	145	130	125	125
Maryland	16.7	17.3	15.8	21.0	23.0	17.5	16.5	170	122	145	151	130	127	127
Virginia	12.9	12.6	13.4	14.2	16.5	12.2	14.5	174	131	148	161	131	132	135
West Virginia	14.1	12.7	13.0	13.5	16.0	13.3	13.0	175	132	147	158	135	137	137
North Carolina	10.0	10.1	12.0	•11.0	14.1	10.7	11.6	189	148	160	171	143	145	152
South Carolina	10.8	10.4	11.0	11.0	16.0	11.0	12.5	219	175	170	185	155	152	161
Georgia	10.5	9.5	9.5	10.5	15.0	9.2	11.0	215	165	169	182	150	155	167
Kentucky	11.9	11.6	10.3	14.0	18.5	9.5	8.0	172	129	143	160	133	135	138
Tennessee	10.5	10.5	10.5	12.5	18.0	7.0	8.8	176	134	147	166	136	139	143
Alabama	10.3	10.5	10.0	11.0	13.4	10.6	11.0	204	156	162	175	160	155	157
Mississippi	14.8	14.3	12.4	18.0	17.0	17.0	20.0	203	139	150	160	129	135	137
Arkansas	11.5	11.6	11.5	13.0	13.5	11.5	11.5	166	119	133	150	128	125	122
Oklahoma	13.5	11.4	16.0	8.2	17.5	9.0	13.5	155	110	124	147	118	120	100
Texas	13.0	11.0	18.5	8.0	18.2	9.7	11.0	168	119	129	155	120	121	110
Montana	14.6	13.7	16.4	10.8	12.5	20.8	18.2	154	104	124	139	112	96	83
Idaho	22.9	24.3	19.4	28.1	23.6	27.6	24.8	145	120	131	125	106	98	90
Wyoming	21.7	16.0	15.2	17.5	18.8	18.5	16.9	150	95	111	124	107	94	83
Colorado	19.2	13.4	14.4	12.7	12.6	14.2	13.9	149	100	118	136	107	104	85
New Mexico	18.8	10.9	14.2	6.2	22.7	10.4	11.0	156	122	125	150	110	119	107
Arizona	26.4	23.4	21.0	23.0	25.0	25.0	27.0	190	139	141	175	130	135	130
Utah	20.9	21.8	16.5	26.2	23.2	23.5	26.7	150	103	130	130	105	102	98
Nevada	26.4	25.6	22.6	30.4	24.0	25.6	26.8	159	132	150	146	116	125	122
Washington	19.4	18.9	14.3	19.4	19.4	25.8	21.4	152	107	130	130	116	108	100
Oregon	19.3	20.2	16.5	19.6	18.2	25.1	22.7	151	89	129	136	120	112	103
California	16.2	18.4	15.0	19.0	18.4	16.8	21.0	164	126	154	148	130	118	118
United States	14.6	13.9	16.5	12.9	14.8	14.9	15.6	159.2	111.4	129.9	141.6	119.8	111.5	97.2

Bureau of Agricultural Economics. Estimates of the crop-reporting board.

TABLE 7.—*Winter and spring wheat: Acreage sown and harvested, production, and farm value, United States, 1910–1928*

Year	Winter wheat						Spring wheat including durum				
	Acreage sown in preceding fall	Acreage harvested	Average yield per acre	Production	Price per bushel received by producers Dec. 1	Total farm value Dec. 1	Acreage harvested	Average yield per acre	Production	Price per bushel received by producers Dec. 1	Total farm value Dec. 1
	1,000 acres	1,000 acres	Bush.	1,000 bushels	Cents	1,000 dollars	1,000 acres	Bush.	1,000 bushels	Cents	1,000 dollars
1910	31,659	27,329	15.9	434,142	88.1	382,318	18,352	11.0	200,979	88.9	178,733
1911	32,648	29,162	14.8	430,656	88.0	379,151	20,381	9.4	190,682	86.0	163,912
1912	33,229	26,571	15.1	399,919	80.9	323,572	19,243	17.2	330,348	70.1	231,708
1913	33,274	31,699	16.5	523,561	82.9	433,995	18,485	13.0	239,819	73.4	176,127
1914	37,158	36,008	19.0	684,990	98.6	675,623	17,533	11.8	206,027	98.6	203,057
1915	42,431	41,308	16.3	673,947	94.7	638,149	19,161	18.4	351,854	86.4	304,154
1916	39,245	34,709	13.8	480,553	162.7	781,906	17,607	8.8	155,765	152.8	238,062
1917	38,359	27,257	15.1	412,901	202.8	837,237	17,832	12.5	223,754	197.0	440,875
1918	43,126	37,130	15.2	565,099	206.3	1,165,995	22,051	16.2	356,339	200.9	715,831
1919	51,483	50,494	15.1	760,377	210.5	1,600,805	25,200	8.2	207,602	230.9	479,251
1920	44,861	40,016	15.3	610,597	148.6	907,291	21,127	10.5	222,430	130.4	289,972
1921	45,625	43,414	13.8	600,316	95.1	571,044	20,282	10.6	214,589	85.6	183,790
1922	47,930	42,358	13.8	586,878	104.7	614,399	19,959	14.1	280,720	92.3	259,013
1923	46,091	39,508	14.5	571,777	95.1	543,530	20,151	11.2	225,617	85.3	192,476
1924	38,916	35,656	16.6	592,259	131.6	779,548	16,879	16.1	272,169	126.2	343,538
1925	39,848	31,234	12.9	401,734	147.9	594,289	21,021	13.1	274,695	132.4	363,618
1926	39,887	36,987	17.0	627,433	121.2	760,406	19,350	10.5	203,607	115.7	235,548
1927	43,373	37,723	14.7	552,747	116.7	645,326	21,061	15.5	325,627	102.7	334,487
1928 [1]	47,280	36,179	16.0	578,964	103.6	599,557	21,545	15.0	323,785	85.7	277,636

Bureau of Agricultural Economics. Estimates of the crop-reporting board.

[1] Preliminary.

TABLE 8.—*Winter wheat: Percentage of acreage abandoned, average 1914–1920, 1921–1925, annual 1925–1928* [1]

State	Av., 1914-1920	Av., 1921-1925	1925	1926	1927	1928	State	Av., 1914-1920	Av., 1921-1925	1925	1926	1927	1928
	P. ct.	P. ct.	P. ct.	P. ct.	P. ct.	P. ct.		P. ct.	P. ct.	P. ct.	P. ct.	P. ct.	P. ct.
N. Y.	3.5	2.8	2.5	8.0	1.0	6.0	Ky.	6.6	11.0	13.0	2.5	3.0	67.0
N. J.	4.9	2.8	2.0	3.0	1.0	5.0	Tenn.	8.8	5.7	6.0	1.7	5.0	28.0
Pa.	3.2	2.1	2.0	2.0	2.5	9.0	Ala.	8.1	10.4	6.0	3.0	10.0	15.0
Ohio	6.0	9.9	23.0	3.0	3.0	64.0	Miss.	10.9	26.4	40.0	20.0	10.0	40.0
Ind.	9.8	6.1	10.4	3.0	3.0	60.0	Ark.	3.3	5.3	10.0	3.0	20.0	30.0
Ill.	13.0	5.8	3.0	5.0	5.5	62.0	Okla.	8.4	10.6	20.0	2.0	20.0	7.0
Mich.	5.7	2.5	1.5	7.0	2.0	10.0	Tex.	17.4	20.2	54.0	3.0	24.0	23.0
Wis.	12.0	12.2	30.0	10.0	2.5	32.0	Mont.	20.9	28.2	70.0	20.0	12.0	18.0
Minn.	11.9	9.8	16.0	7.0	2.0	45.0	Idaho	5.4	7.5	15.0	6.0	4.0	5.0
Iowa	14.6	4.6	9.0	4.0	2.5	22.0	Wyo.	7.1	12.0	15.0	4.0	12.0	10.0
Mo.	7.8	4.6	4.0	5.5	11.0	32.0	Colo.	9.1	22.7	33.0	20.0	30.0	40.0
S. Dak.	13.9	17.7	25.0	20.0	10.0	40.0	N. Mex.	14.4	42.0	80.0	3.0	89.0	45.0
Nebr.	14.6	11.2	19.0	12.0	4.0	10.0	Ariz.	7.2	6.6	3.0	2.0	1.0	1.0
Kans.	15.3	16.1	20.0	11.0	20.0	15.2	Utah	3.7	3.1	2.0	2.0	3.0	2.0
Del.	3.6	2.9	1.5	2.0	1.0	1.0	Nev.	4.9	3.0	2.0		0	1.0
Md.	3.1	2.5	1.5	1.5	1.5	3.0	Wash.	12.8	21.8	70.0	4.0	6.0	6.0
Va.	2.5	2.7	2.0	1.5	6.0	6.0	Oreg.	3.4	16.2	65.0	3.0	1.0	3.0
W. Va.	2.1	4.9	10.0	1.0	1.5	15.0	Calif.	13.0	24.6	25.0	7.0	3.0	9.0
N. C.	3.3	2.4	1.5	2.0	3.0	7.0							
S. C.	5.8	4.7	4.0	2.5	6.0	12.0	U. S.	10.4	12.1	21.6	7.3	13.0	23.5
Ga.	10.3	12.9	5.0	3.0	8.0	15.0							

Bureau of Agricultural Economics. Estimates of the crop-reporting board.

[1] For entire season, planting to harvest. Includes winter abandonment, which is estimated on May of each season.

NOTE.—A table similar to Table 7, 1927 Yearbook, is omitted.

... y, and production in specified countries, average 1909-1913, 1921-1925, annual, 1926-1928

Country	Acreage — Average 1909-1913[1]	Average 1921-1925	1926	1927	1928 preliminary	Yield per acre — Average 1909-1913[1]	Average 1921-1925	1926	1927	1928 preliminary	Production — Average 1900-1913[1]	Average 1921-1925	1926	1927	1928 preliminary
	1,000 acres	*1,000 acres*	*1,000 acres*	*1,000 acres*	*1,000 acres*	*Bushels*	*Bushels*	*Bushels*	*Bushels*	*Bushels*	*1,000 bushels*	*1,000 bushels*	*1,000 bushels*	*1,000 bushels*	*1,000 bushels*
NORTHERN HEMISPHERE															
NORTH AMERICA															
Canada	9,945	22,063	22,896	22,460	24,119	19.8	16.6	17.8	21.4	22.1	197,119	366,483	407,136	479,665	533,572
United States	47,097	58,092	56,784	58,724	57,724	14.7	13.8	14.8	14.9	15.6	690,108	804,151	831,040	878,374	902,749
Mexico	[2]2,174	2,098	1,286	1,311	1,252	[2]5.3	5.0	8.0	9.1	9.1	[3]11,481	10,388	10,333	11,890	11,332
Guatemala		24	25	23			9.2	8.0	9.6			222	200	220	
Total countries reporting all years	59,216	82,273	80,519	82,555	83,095	15.2	14.4	15.5	16.6	17.4	898,708	1,181,022	1,248,509	1,369,929	1,447,653
EUROPE															
United Kingdom:															
England and Wales	1,787	1,746	1,592	1,636	1,395	31.2	32.9	30.6	32.5	33.9	55,770	57,524	48,683	53,116	47,264
Scotland	57	57	54	67	58	39.9	39.5	38.7	36.2	39.9	2,273	2,251	2,091	2,427	2,315
Northern Ireland	8	4	6	6	5	35.9	27.8	37.7	35.3	37.6	287	111	226	212	188
Irish Free State	35	34	29	34	31	37.4	33.3	39.8	41.8		1,310	637	1,155	1,421	
Norway	12	27	22	25	25	25.5	23.6	26.6	24.2	27.0	306	586	586	605	676
Sweden	255	352	381	404		31.8	30.1	31.9	28.0		8,103	10,602	12,153	11,298	
Denmark	154	202	252	274	252	41.1	44.4	40.8	34.3	48.1	6,322	8,973	8,767	9,408	12,125
Netherlands	138	147	132	150	148	36.1	42.5	41.6	41.0	51.1	4,976	6,243	5,487	6,156	7,569
Belgium	404	339	354	391	428	37.6	38.9	36.2	41.6	41.5	15,199	13,194	12,801	16,277	17,778
Luxemburg	27	23	32	36	36	22.8	17.0	19.4	19.5	22.2	615	392	622	702	799
France	16,500	13,507	12,971	13,065	12,795	19.7	21.5	17.9	21.1	21.7	325,644	290,875	231,767	276,128	277,657
Spain	9,547	10,457	10,775	10,826	10,571	13.7	13.6	13.6	13.4	12.3	130,446	142,420	146,599	144,825	129,591
Portugal	[4]1,211	1,078	1,063	1,082		[4]9.8	9.9	8.1	10.6		[4]11,850	10,626	8,560	11,447	
Italy	11,793	11,537	12,145	12,295	12,264	15.6	17.2	18.2	15.9	18.7	184,393	198,307	220,644	195,800	228,896
Switzerland	105	110	127	127	127	31.6	30.1	33.4	32.4	33.6	3,314	3,314	4,244	4,119	4,270
Germany	4,029	3,613	3,957	4,321	4,277	32.6	27.3	24.1	27.9	33.1	131,274	98,714	95,429	120,522	141,593
Austria	635	456	500	505	505	29.2	18.4	18.9	23.7	23.9	12,813	8,400	9,438	11,960	12,055
Czechoslovakia	1,718	1,523	1,552	1,579	1,609	23.6	23.6	22.8	25.6	25.8	37,879	36,015	34,130	40,385	41,434
Hungary	3,712	3,345	3,706	4,021	4,133	19.3	17.8	20.2	19.1	22.3	71,493	59,678	74,909	76,933	92,037
Yugoslavia	3,982	3,953	4,178	4,521	4,742	15.6	14.9	17.1	12.5	20.3	62,024	58,753	71,427	56,668	96,378
Greece	[3]1,134	1,075	1,304	1,233	1,313	[4]14.4	8.8	9.5	10.5	11.9	[4]16,273	9,417	12,403	12,970	15,676

[1] Where changes in boundary have occurred averages are estimates for territory within present boundaries. [2] 2-year average. [3] 4-year average. [4] 1 year only.

TABLE 9.—*Wheat: Acreage, yield per acre, and production in specified countries, average 1909–1913, 1921–1925, annual, 1926–1928*—Contd.

Country	Acreage					Yield per acre					Production				
	Average, 1909–1913	Average, 1921–1925	1926	1927	1928, preliminary	Average, 1909–1913	Average, 1921–1925	1926	1927	1928, preliminary	Average, 1909–1913	Average, 1921–1925	1926	1927	1928, preliminary
	1,000 acres	*1,000 acres*	*1,000 acres*	*1,000 acres*	*1,000 acres*	*Bushels*	*Bushels*	*Bushels*	*Bushels*	*Bushels*	*1,000 bushels*	*1,000 bushels*	*1,000 bushels*	*1,000 bushels*	*1,000 bushels*
NORTHERN HEMISPHERE—Con.															
EUROPE—continued															
Bulgaria	2,409	2,390	2,617	2,658	2,779	15.7	13.1	14.0	17.8	18.2	37,823	31,399	36,544	47,347	50,691
Rumania	³9,515	7,068	8,222	7,663	7,923	³16.7	12.7	13.5	12.6	14.6	³158,672	89,570	110,883	96,734	115,544
Poland	3,330	2,507	2,719	2,814	2,666	19.0	17.5	19.0	19.3	20.2	63,675	43,963	47,080	54,230	53,882
Lithuania	211	214	303	297	395	15.5	16.6	13.8	17.8	18.4	3,264	3,563	4,180	5,273	7,275
Latvia	85	89	122	145	164	17.4	16.0	15.2	18.2	15.2	1,475	1,426	1,860	2,636	2,499
Estonia	23	47	59	67	72	15.8	14.2	14.3	16.1	15.3	364	667	844	1,079	1,103
Finland	8	36	39	44	42	17.1	20.5	23.7	24.2	20.9	137	739	924	1,064	879
Russia	74,209	39,066	70,882	75,941	68,044	10.2	10.1	11.6	9.8	12.5	758,941	394,393	819,744	745,885	859,789
Total countries, excl. Russia, reporting all years	71,343	64,472	67,740	68,766	68,724	18.6	18.1	17.5	18.0	19.8	1,326,711	1,166,545	1,182,568	1,237,485	1,359,874
Estimated European total, excluding Russia	72,800	65,900	69,200	70,400	70,200						1,348,000	1,192,000	1,205,000	1,262,000	1,383,000
AFRICA															
Morocco	(1,700)	2,272	2,558	2,304	2,354		9.6	6.3	10.7	9.4	(17,000)	21,758	16,174	24,618	22,193
Algeria	3,521	3,416	3,741	3,469	3,593	10.0	7.8	6.3	8.2	8.7	35,161	25,647	23,551	28,323	31,415
Tunis	1,310	1,402	1,840	1,408	1,730	4.8	5.6	7.1	5.9	7.0	6,224	7,892	13,044	8,267	12,125
Egypt	1,314	1,462	1,532	1,655	1,590	25.6	25.2	24.3	26.8	23.5	33,662	36,806	37,207	44,347	37,296
Total	7,845	8,552	9,671	8,836	9,267	11.7	10.9	9.3	11.2	11.1	92,047	93,103	89,976	105,555	103,029
ASIA															
Cyprus	162	191	191	171		13.7	12.0	9.5	14.0		2,216	2,292	1,819	2,390	
India	29,224	29,560	30,471	31,303	32,211	12.0	11.4	10.7	13.7	9.0	351,841	336,289	324,651	334,992	289,781
Japanese Empire:															
Japan	1,179	1,197	1,146	1,161	1,198	21.3	23.9	26.3	26.7	27.5	25,088	28,553	30,188	31,018	33,000
Chosen	574	882	595	897	896	12.0	11.6	11.8	10.1	9.5	6,898	10,208	10,517	9,043	8,527
Formosa	15	7	4	4		11.3	9.1	13.0			169	64	13	39	
Kwantung	⁵4	4	4			⁵10.0	11.8	8.5	9.8		⁵40	47	34		
Total Asiatic countries reporting all years	30,977	31,639	32,512	33,361	34,305	12.4	11.9	11.2	11.2	9.7	383,827	375,030	365,356	375,053	331,308

Estimated Asiatic total, excluding Russia and China	37,600	37,900	37,700	38,300	39,100						419,000	447,000	434,000	442,000	370,000
Total Northern Hemisphere countries, excluding Russia, reporting all years	169,381	186,936	190,442	193,518	195,391	15.9	15.1	15.2	16.0	16.6	2,701,293	2,815,700	2,886,409	3,088,022	3,241,864
Estimated Northern Hemisphere total excluding Russia and China	177,500	195,000	197,300	200,200	201,900						2,759,000	2,914,000	2,979,000	3,181,000	3,305,000
SOUTHERN HEMISPHERE															
Brazil		[3] 224	240	330			21.9	20.7	12.7			4,908	4,960	4,203	
Chile	1,003	1,443	1,462	1,530	1,975	29.9	17.9	15.9	18.5		20,062	25,761	23,286	28,307	
Uruguay	[3] 791	867	988	1,051	1,233	[3] 8.2	11.2	10.4	14.6		[3] 6,517	9,680	10,238	15,397	
Argentina	16,051	16,935	19,274	19,714	20,899	9.2	12.0	11.5	12.1		147,059	203,388	220,827	239,162	
Union of South Africa	[4] 803	868	881	912	985	[4] 7.5	8.6	9.1	7.3	7.0	[4] 6,034	7,459	8,043	6,644	6,943
Southern Rhodesia		[5] 4	5				[5] 6.2	7.8				[5] 31	39		
Australia	7,603	10,010	11,688	12,264	14,000	11.9	12.8	13.8	9.5	11.0	90,497	128,520	160,762	116,737	154,000
New Zealand	241	224	222	262		28.7	29.6	35.8	36.4		6,925	6,640	7,952	9,541	
Total Southern Hemisphere countries reporting all years	8,406	10,878	12,569	13,176	14,985	11.5	12.5	13.4	9.4	10.7	96,531	135,979	168,805	123,381	160,943
Estimated Southern Hemisphere total	26,700	31,000	35,200	36,700	40,200						282,000	391,000	441,000	424,000	475,000
Total Northern and Southern Hemisphere countries, excluding Russia, reporting all years	177,787	197,814	203,011	206,694	210,376	15.7	14.9	15.0	15.5	16.2	2,797,824	2,951,679	3,055,214	3,211,403	3,402,800
Estimated world total excluding Russia and China	204,200	226,000	232,500	236,900	242,100						3,041,000	3,305,000	3,420,000	3,605,000	3,780,000

Bureau of Agricultural Economics. Official sources and International Institute of Agriculture. Figures in parentheses indicate unofficial estimates. For each year is shown the harvest during the calendar year in the Northern Hemisphere and the succeeding harvest in the Southern Hemisphere.

[3] 4-year average. [4] One year only. [5] 3-year average.

TABLE 10.—*Wheat: World production, 1890–1928*

Year	World production excluding Russia and China	Northern Hemisphere production excluding Russia and China	European production excluding Russia	Selected countries						
				Russia [1]	United States	Canada	India	Argentina	Australia	France
	1,000,000 bushels	1,000,000 bushels	1,000,000 bushels	1,000,000 bushels	1,000,000 bushels	1,000,000 bushels	1,000,000 bushels	1,000,000 bushels	1,000,000 bushels	1,000,000 bushels
1890	1,878	1,802	1,056	213	378	--------	229	31	27	330
1891	1,989	1,904	900	181	585	--------	257	36	26	215
1892	2,053	1,938	1,045	266	528	--------	227	59	33	311
1893	2,076	1,936	1,097	482	428	--------	286	82	37	278
1894	2,406	2,018	1,080	477	516	--------	271	61	28	344
1895	2,126	2,039	1,057	310	569	--------	261	46	18	340
1896	2,057	1,986	1,103	412	544	--------	201	32	21	340
1897	1,893	1,790	842	340	610	--------	200	53	28	242
1898	2,552	2,374	1,168	459	772	--------	269	105	41	365
1899	2,319	2,150	1,113	454	636	--------	255	102	40	365
1900	2,210	2,064	1,096	423	603	--------	200	75	48	326
1901	2,472	2,357	1,103	428	789	--------	265	56	39	311
1902	2,510	2,368	1,207	607	725	--------	227	104	12	328
1903	2,651	2,412	1,266	621	664	--------	298	130	74	363
1904	2,478	2,238	1,116	667	597	--------	360	151	55	300
1905	2,673	2,441	1,223	636	727	--------	283	135	69	335
1906	2,950	2,694	1,356	543	757	--------	320	156	66	329
1907	2,619	2,344	1,176	571	638	--------	317	192	45	381
1908	2,544	2,283	1,181	628	645	112	229	156	63	317
1909 [2]	2,819	2,554	1,240	846	700	167	285	131	90	359
1910 [2]	2,777	2,495	1,201	836	635	132	360	146	95	253
1911 [2]	3,043	2,758	1,347	563	621	231	376	166	72	322
1912 [2]	3,093	2,770	1,284	801	730	224	371	187	92	334
1913 [2]	3,098	2,853	1,301	1,028	763	232	368	105	103	319
1914	2,834	2,601	1,072	[3]834	891	161	312	169	25	283
1915	3,497	3,102	1,125	[4]827	1,026	394	377	169	179	223
1916	2,734	2,457	1,049	[5]531	636	263	323	84	152	205
1917	2,574	2,178	740	622	637	234	382	235	115	[6]135
1918	2,911	2,608	909	--------	921	189	280	217	46	182
1919	2,821	2,517	899	--------	968	193	378	156	146	237
1920	2,948	2,595	949	320	833	263	378	156	146	237
1921	3,169	2,787	1,216	205	815	301	250	191	129	323
1922	3,225	2,868	1,044	243	868	400	367	196	109	243
1923	3,551	3,119	1,257	249	797	474	372	248	125	276
1924	3,143	2,730	1,051	472	864	262	361	191	165	281
1925	3,435	3,067	1,391	730	676	395	331	191	115	330
1926 [7]	3,420	2,979	1,205	820	831	407	325	221	161	232
1927 [7]	3,605	3,181	1,262	746	878	480	335	239	117	276
1928 [7]	3,780	3,305	1,383	860	903	534	290	--------	154	278

Bureau of Agricultural Economics. For each year is shown the production during the calendar year in the Northern Hemisphere and the succeeding harvest in the Southern Hemisphere.

[1] Includes all Russian territory reporting for years named.
[2] The average production for the 1909–1913 period as computed from figures given here for estimated world total, Northern Hemisphere total, European total, and European countries whose boundaries were changed by the World War will not agree with estimates appearing elsewhere for present territory, due to changes in boundary.
[3] Total Russian Empire exclusive of the 10 Vistula Provinces of Russian Poland and the Province of Batum in Transcaucasia.
[4] Exclusive of Russian Poland, Lithuania, parts of present Latvia and Ukraine, and 2 Provinces of Transcaucasia.
[5] Beginning with this date estimated production is within present boundaries of the Union of Socialist Soviet Republics, excluding Turkestan, Transcaucasia, and the Far East, which regions in 1924 produced 51,706,000 bushels, and in 1925, 58,000,000 bushels.
[6] Beginning with this date production is within postwar boundaries and therefore not comparable with earlier years.
[7] Preliminary.

TABLE 11.—*Wheat: Stocks and shipments, United States, 1909–1928*

Year beginning July	Stocks of old wheat on farms July 1 [1]	Stocks of old wheat in mills and elevators July 1 [2]	Merchant mill stocks July 1 [3]	Commercial visible stocks end of week nearest July 1 [4]	Weight per measured bushel of new wheat [5]	Stocks of wheat on farms on Mar. 1 following [1]	Stocks of wheat in mills and elevators on Mar. 1 following [2]	Shipped out of country where grown [6]
	1,000 bush.	*1,000 bush.*	*1,000 bush.*	*1,000 bush.*	*Pounds*	*1,000 bush.*	*1,000 bush.*	*1,000 bush.*
1909	14,171				57.9	163,371		428,262
1910	36,725				58.5	162,705	98,597	352,906
1911	34,071				57.8	122,041	95,710	348,739
1912	23,876				58.3	156,471	118,400	449,881
1913	35,515				58.7	151,795	93,627	411,733
1914	32,236				58.0	152,903	85,955	541,198
1915	28,972				57.9	244,448	155,027	633,380
1916	74,731				57.1	100,650	89,173	361,088
1917	15,611				58.5	107,745	66,138	325,500
1918	8,063				58.8	128,703	107,037	541,666
1919	19,261	19,672			56.3	169,904	123,233	591,552
1920	49,546	37,304			57.4	217,037	87,075	491,035
1921	56,707	27,167			57.0	134,253	75,071	502,470
1922	32,359	28,756			57.7	156,087	102,908	584,089
1923	35,894	37,117			57.4	137,721	98,284	505,792
1924	30,981	36,626			58.9	112,095	67,673	630,819
1925	29,357	25,287			58.3	100,137	76,333	483,519
1926	20,973	29,501	22,447		59.1	130,230	85,907	580,112
1927	27,215	21,776	34,149	21,888	58.5	130,944	75,118	638,925
1928 [7]	23,555	18,856	29,782	[8] 39,315	58.5			

Bureau of Agricultural Economics.   Prior to 1918 stocks in mills and elevators not included.

[1] Based on percentage of crop on farms as estimated by crop reporters.
[2] Based on percentage of crop as estimated by about 3,500 mill and elevator operators
[3] Census.
[4] Domestic grain in store and afloat at United States markets.
[5] Based on estimates of crop reporters on Nov. 1.
[6] Based on percentage shipped out as estimated by crop reporters.
[7] Preliminary.
[8] Revised.

TABLE 12.—*Wheat: Receipts inspected, by markets, 1917–1927*

Market	Year beginning July										
	1917	1918	1919	1920	1921	1922	1923	1924	1925	1926	1927
	1,000 bushels	*1,000 bushels*	*1,000 bushels*	*1,000 bushels*	*1,000 bushels*	*1,000 bushels*	*1,000 bushels*	*1,000 bushels*	*1,000 bushels*	*1,000 bushels*	*1,000 bushels*
Minneapolis	90,311	123,119	127,145	119,107	109,461	126,508	99,366	76,960	118,730	85,466	129,966
Duluth	23,481	113,911	16,611	50,194	55,995	71,154	38,460	102,654	67,447	49,985	98,032
Kansas City	24,848	69,182	116,694	115,200	126,025	77,302	59,948	86,713	51,571	90,535	74,595
Chicago	12,146	73,446	62,244	22,190	45,483	39,207	43,017	59,831	19,058	30,811	34,592
St. Louis	17,120	43,001	43,685	27,109	32,262	27,254	26,859	26,909	25,148	26,247	24,423
Omaha	10,829	24,066	30,031	31,031	30,140	28,760	19,763	31,660	16,903	21,642	30,008
Wichita	7,000	15,332	21,100	16,363	25,186	21,185	22,151	29,559	18,972	28,166	21,191
Portland, Oreg	5,957	10,612	12,468	28,842	36,566	22,395	36,732	21,559	27,892	35,299	42,931
New York	22,950	49,990	28,821	52,750	33,136	27,368	9,186	21,978	6,334	33,855	45,096
Philadelphia	8,180	34,713	23,816	19,564	17,598	36,893	6,252	18,236	5,767	6,933	4,026
Baltimore	6,434	25,724	24,522	25,653	12,817	13,434	16,480	14,286	13,862	21,204	13,904
New Orleans	2,710	16,409	15,678	67,483	30,325	24,628	6,261	32,630	2,235	8,908	7,622
Galveston	1,996	10,128	26,042	73,334	44,126	17,400	7,055	33,953	2,769	44,781	11,332
All other inspection points	111,858	200,241	236,976	204,418	242,466	224,418	213,715	256,192	201,036	308,383	260,728
Total	345,820	809,874	785,833	853,238	841,586	757,906	605,245	813,120	577,724	792,215	798,446

Bureau of Agricultural Economics.   Compiled from reports of licensed inspectors through district offices Federal grain supervision.

TABLE 13.—*Wheat: Monthly marketings by farmers, as reported by about 3,500 mills and elevators, United States, 1917–1927*

Year beginning July	Percentage of year's receipts												
	July	Aug.	Sept.	Oct.	Nov.	Dec.	Jan.	Feb.	Mar.	Apr.	May	June	Season
1917	7.4	12.4	19.3	18.0	13.7	7.6	4.7	3.9	3.7	4.1	3.1	2.1	100.0
1918	17.6	19.9	18.0	13.8	8.7	7.3	4.6	3.1	2.0	1.6	1.9	1.5	100.0
1919	17.1	23.2	15.6	11.1	7.5	5.7	4.2	3.0	2.9	3.1	3.4	3.2	100.0
1920	12.1	14.3	15.9	10.6	6.9	6.2	5.5	5.3	4.9	5.0	6.4	6.9	100.0
1921	19.1	18.2	16.4	10.6	6.8	5.4	4.4	4.9	3.9	3.2	3.5	3.6	100.0
1922	14.8	17.3	14.2	12.0	8.6	7.4	5.5	5.1	4.3	3.7	3.4	3.7	100.0
1923	13.4	17.6	16.7	13.7	9.5	6.2	4.6	4.8	3.3	2.9	3.7	3.6	100.0
1924	13.6	19.8	17.5	14.5	8.6	5.6	5.3	4.2	2.5	1.6	3.1	3.7	100.0
1925	14.6	18.6	18.7	10.9	8.6	7.0	4.7	4.0	3.0	3.0	2.9	4.0	100.0
1926	21.8	20.3	13.2	10.0	5.8	5.0	4.6	4.6	3.6	2.4	3.2	5.5	100.0
1927	15.4	18.6	19.6	12.6	7.7	5.6	4.5	4.1	3.8	2.5	2.5	3.1	100.0

Bureau of Agricultural Economics.

TABLE 14.—*Wheat: Supply and distribution and per capita disappearance in the United States, averages 1899–1925, annual 1925–1928*

Item	Year beginning July							
	Average, 1899–1908	Average, 1909–1913	Average, 1914–1920	Average, 1921–1925	1925	1926	1927	1928
	1,000 bushels	*1,000 bushels*	*1,000 bushels*	*1,000 bushels*	*1,000 bushels*	*1,000 bushels*	*1,000 bushels*	*1,000 bushels*
Supply:								
Stocks on farms, July 1[1]	46,423	28,872	32,631	37,059	29,357	20,973	27,215	23,555
Stocks in country mills and elevators, July 1	27,000	29,000	26,997	30,991	25,287	29,501	21,776	18,856
Commercial visible (Bradstreet's July 1	31,817	24,168	19,290	25,519	29,285	16,484	25,516	42,208
Stocks of flour (in terms of wheat) July 1[2]	7,709	8,305	8,606	8,676	8,530	9,757	9,076	9,019
In merchant mills and elevators[3]					21,648	24,640	37,321	32,944
In transit to commercial mills[3]					9,000	7,390	11,535	11,241
New crop[4]	677,927	690,108	844,605	804,148	676,429	831,040	878,374	902,749
Imports (flour included) July 1 to June 30[5]	753	1,834	19,806	17,473	15,679	13,264	15,734	--------
Total supply	791,629	782,287	951,935	923,866	815,215	953,049	1,026,547	--------
Distribution:								
Exports (flour included) July 1 to June 30[5]	156,435	107,103	257,030	207,237	108,035	219,160	206,259	--------
Reexports July 1 to June 30[5]	399	195	562	221	313	98	53	--------
Shipments (flour included) to Alaska, Hawaii, and Porto Rico[5]	[6] 2,034	2,549	2,546	2,836	2,741	3,082	2,690	--------
Estimated seed requirements[7]	70,444	72,326	88,312	86,849	83,180	88,919	94,978	--------
Carry-over on June 30—								
On farms[1]	40,654	32,485	36,127	29,913	20,973	27,215	23,555	--------
In country mills and elevators[2]	25,400	31,600	26,449	31,457	29,501	21,776	18,856	--------
Commercial visible (Bradstreet's)	28,668	25,326	18,265	26,822	16,484	25,516	42,208	--------
Flour (in terms of wheat)[2]	7,374	8,935	8,290	9,240	9,757	9,076	9,019	--------
In merchant mills and elevators[3]					24,640	37,321	32,944	--------
In transit to commercial mills[3]					7,390	11,535	11,241	--------
Accounted-for distribution	331,408	280,519	437,581	394,575	303,014	443,698	441,803	--------
Disappearance including food and feed	460,221	501,768	514,354	529,291	512,201	509,351	584,744	--------
Population, Jan. 1 (thousands)[8]	82,614	94,378	102,880	112,696	116,257	117,882	119,320	--------
Per capita disappearance, including food and feed, bushels	5.6	5.3	5.0	4.7	4.4	4.3	4.9	--------

Bureau of Agricultural Economics. Compiled as follows:

[1] From returns to the bureau from crop reporters.
[2] From Chicago Daily Trade Bulletin. Stocks in country mills and elevators, from 1899–1918, are stock in second hands less visible supply on July 1, as given by Chicago Daily Trade Bulletin; subsequently same as Note 1.
[3] Bureau of the Census figures raised to represent all merchant mills.
[4] Based on returns to the bureau from crop reporters.
[5] From reports of Foreign and Domestic Commerce of the United States.
[6] 7 years' average.
[7] Amount of seed used per acre from returns to the bureau from inquiries sent to crop reporters.
[8] Bureau of the Census.

TABLE 15.—*Wheat: Receipts inspected, all inspection points, by classes, 1925–1927*

Class and year beginning July	No. 1	No. 2	No. 3	No. 4	No. 5	Sample	Total
	1,000 bushels	*1,000 bushels*	*1,000 bushels*	*1,000 bushels*	*1,000 bushels*	*1,000 bushels*	*1,000 bushels*
Hard red spring:							
1925	86,832	36,280	28,471	14,683	5,042	5,173	176,481
1926	51,160	29,373	23,823	17,677	4,114	10,706	136,853
1927	106,285	56,839	41,268	18,763	6,200	11,939	241,294
Durum:							
1925	9,733	28,610	7,975	4,272	686	1,568	52,844
1926	2,405	10,548	6,548	7,764	1,395	4,403	33,063
1927	11,331	31,170	9,692	5,567	2,147	2,414	62,321
Hard red winter:							
1925	51,498	92,972	33,812	9,239	3,918	3,143	194,582
1926	201,893	145,602	31,067	10,084	7,821	10,978	407,445
1927	100,264	123,475	41,434	19,331	11,127	14,664	310,295
Soft red winter:							
1925	8,309	30,939	10,273	2,877	1,249	1,463	55,110
1926	35,810	40,147	11,656	7,903	2,881	6,011	104,408
1927	10,563	25,795	13,659	7,942	2,305	3,371	63,635
White:							
1925	5,091	20,435	11,816	3,840	649	543	42,374
1926	10,981	25,696	8,215	1,999	423	659	47,973
1927	17,822	25,819	8,733	3,072	1,370	3,492	60,308
Mixed:							
1925	15,119	24,019	10,115	4,017	1,533	1,530	56,333
1926	15,877	20,626	10,011	7,340	2,597	6,022	62,473
1927	14,807	22,624	12,042	5,570	2,453	3,097	60,593
Total:							
1925	176,582	233,255	102,462	38,928	13,077	13,420	577,724
1926	318,126	271,992	91,320	52,767	19,231	38,779	792,215
1927	261,072	285,722	126,828	60,245	25,602	38,977	798,446

Bureau of Agricultural Economics. Compiled from reports of licensed inspectors through district offices of Federal grain supervision. See 1927 Yearbook for data for earlier years.

TABLE 16.—*Wheat: Visible supply in the United States,[1] 1909–1928*

Year beginning July	July	Aug.	Sept.	Oct.	Nov.	Dec.	Jan.	Feb.	Mar.	Apr.	May	June
	1,000 bush.	*1,000 bush.*	*1,000 bush.*	*1,000 bush.*	*1,000 bush.*	*1,000 bush.*	*1,000 bush.*	*1,000 bush.*	*1,000 bush.*	*1,000 bush.*	*1,000 bush.*	*1,000 bush.*
Average:												
1909–1913	24,168	28,569	37,458	48,202	56,838	63,908	66,229	62,228	58,419	53,802	43,857	34,183
1914–1920	19,290	24,822	38,946	56,235	69,877	76,250	75,530	69,586	60,014	49,475	35,591	27,728
1921–1925	25,519	34,513	52,612	64,541	66,786	67,445	68,605	62,988	59,746	52,365	43,975	35,777
1909	12,771	12,611	15,514	28,589	37,820	41,688	37,949	36,638	34,461	37,558	33,771	24,795
1910	16,396	17,053	38,352	48,437	53,420	57,002	59,369	56,357	50,566	42,697	34,656	32,769
1911	29,639	46,389	54,581	61,500	73,792	81,215	81,501	70,748	66,982	59,826	48,022	35,994
1912	27,615	23,595	26,862	40,998	52,494	67,575	77,471	76,131	73,895	69,000	53,508	43,697
1913	34,420	43,198	51,980	61,485	66,663	72,061	74,854	71,264	66,191	59,931	49,327	33,662
1914	17,136	36,456	39,964	61,784	76,262	86,332	85,957	81,776	58,923	46,287	31,407	22,871
1915	10,734	9,361	12,679	22,498	33,338	60,678	80,150	77,834	73,748	66,691	57,658	52,512
1916	50,515	49,591	65,754	70,420	75,455	76,191	73,584	59,477	54,160	48,525	32,831	34,876
1917	19,901	11,692	10,315	13,072	22,855	29,633	26,476	20,436	15,484	10,180	6,656	4,379
1918	2,465	20,462	54,236	98,155	131,852	131,584	129,627	140,607	127,207	100,505	55,247	27,626
1919	10,873	25,968	65,479	95,550	107,783	101,058	85,117	68,494	58,632	51,909	47,756	41,233
1920	23,404	20,226	24,195	32,169	41,596	48,273	47,797	38,475	31,945	22,229	17,584	10,598
1921	9,966	28,727	47,159	62,758	62,767	53,507	56,776	48,802	46,714	42,287	36,644	31,497
1922	20,342	23,077	32,479	38,025	39,023	39,764	43,856	53,823	54,562	51,862	49,521	37,203
1923	29,403	40,526	63,922	72,930	79,034	82,269	84,030	75,111	72,914	66,739	50,383	48,686
1924	38,597	46,193	79,700	92,353	100,712	108,997	99,121	84,476	76,437	62,766	49,529	38,328
1925	29,285	34,041	39,800	56,639	52,394	52,686	59,244	52,730	48,105	38,173	33,798	23,170
1926	16,486	34,575	72,884	84,724	81,175	78,910	70,811	62,317	61,271	53,827	42,402	31,115
1927	25,516	37,533	71,908	88,755	98,675	100,013	94,336	83,720	77,949	73,220	66,184	52,460
1928	42,208	66,762	96,798	118,327	143,003	145,234						

Bureau of Agricultural Economics. Compiled from Bradstreet's. Includes grain stored at approximately 50 interior and seaboard points of accumulation and grain in transit by canals and lakes; also Pacific coast stocks at Portland, Tacoma, and Seattle. Bureau of Agricultural Economics is now securing and compiling data to replace this table as soon as enough years are covered.

[1] Saturday nearest the 1st of each month.

TABLE 17.—*Wheat: Commercial stocks in store, 1926–27 to 1928–29*

DOMESTIC WHEAT IN UNITED STATES [1]

	July	Aug.	Sept.	Oct.	Nov.	Dec.	Jan.	Feb.	Mar.	Apr.	May	June
	1,000 bush.	*1,000 bush.*	*1,000 bush.*	*1,000 bush.*	*1,000 bush.*	*1,000 bush.*	*1,000 bush.*	*1,000 bush.*	*1,000 bush.*	*1,000 bush.*	*1,000 bush.*	*1,000 bush.*
1926–27							66,340	56,303	56,262	49,910	37,667	27,833
1927–28	21,052	33,677	62,042	78,811	89,684	91,589	88,581	79,152	72,858	68,791	61,957	48,286
1928–29	38,587	52,421	93,870	115,469	139,493	140,172						

UNITED STATES WHEAT IN CANADA

	July	Aug.	Sept.	Oct.	Nov.	Dec.	Jan.	Feb.	Mar.	Apr.	May	June
1926–27							1,067	549	437	378	746	1,344
1927–28	1,362	1,280	4,249	4,560	7,258	5,156	3,933	2,285	1,680	977	863	2,314
1928–29	2,506	2,258	2,546	3,295	8,602	8,280						

CANADIAN WHEAT IN UNITED STATES [2]

	July	Aug.	Sept.	Oct.	Nov.	Dec.	Jan.	Feb.	Mar.	Apr.	May	June
1926–27							23,394	14,500	9,532	6,650	10,724	16,749
1927–28	7,472	4,835	3,410	3,784	8,617	31,375	35,764	28,703	19,260	11,848	6,597	11,549
1928–29	11,132	13,605	3,789	7,548	18,291	33,902						

Bureau of Agricultural Economics. Compiled from weekly reports to the Grain, Hay and Feed Market News Service. Data are for stocks on the Saturday nearest the 1st day of the month.

[1] Includes wheat stored at 39 interior and seaboard points of accumulation, exclusive of wheat in transit on lakes and canals.

[2] Includes wheat stored at lake and seaboard ports, exclusive of wheat in transit on lakes and canals.

TABLE 18.—*Wheat: Inspection for export, by classes, United States, average 1921–1925, annual 1923–1927, and July–December, 1928*

Year beginning July	Hard red spring	Durum	Hard red winter	Soft red winter	White [1]	Mixed [2]	Flour as wheat	Other wheat [3]	Total
	1,000 bushels	*1,000 bushels*	*1,000 bushels*	*1,000 bushels*	*1,000 bushels*	*1,000 bushels*	*1,000 bushels*	*1,000 bushels*	*1,000 bushels*
Average, 1921–1925	9,997	7,198	49,594	11,776	11,998	12,955	67,088	36,631	207,237
1923	1,022	4,908	19,640	9,810	18,653	5,435	81,087	19,325	159,880
1924	16,760	5,945	90,840	6,944	10,063	9,386	65,313	55,552	260,803
1925	3,338	4,170	7,358	2,282	16,914	5,944	44,846	23,183	108,035
1926	1,829	611	66,874	29,980	26,615	1,398	62,910	28,943	219,160
1927	5,209	3,496	41,603	9,915	28,150	1,874	60,260	55,752	206,259
1928, July to December	1,086	865	24,191	1,642	9,193	805	28,750	34,984	101,516

Bureau of Agricultural Economics. Inspections of United States wheat for export data furnished monthly by Federal grain supervision officers at the export markets. Inspections are made at the ports of export.

[1] White wheat in the Pacific Northwest region consists of both spring and winter wheat; no attempt has been made to classify this wheat as other than white wheat, part of which is spring and part winter.

[2] Mixed wheat exported from Atlantic coast ports are estimated as approximately 70 per cent durum and the remainder as hard red spring; that exported from Gulf ports as approximately half and half hard and soft winter; and that exported from Pacific coast ports as approximately 90 per cent white and the remainder as winter wheats.

[3] Exports of wheat other than reported as "Federal inspected" including exports through Canada. These exports are not "Federal inspected" and are exported largely through the customs districts of Buffalo, Chicago, Duluth and Superior, Wisconsin, and Ohio.

NOTE.—A table, similar to table 19, 1927 Yearbook, is omitted.

TABLE 19.—*Wheat, including flour: International trade, average 1910–1914 annual 1925–1928*

Country	Average 1910–1914 Imports	Average 1910–1914 Exports	1925 Imports	1925 Exports	1926 Imports	1926 Exports	1927 Imports	1927 Exports	1928 preliminary Imports	1928 preliminary Exports
	1,000 bushels	1,000 bushels	1,000 bushels	1,000 bushels	1,000 bushels	1,000 bushels	1,000 bushels	1,000 bushels	1,000 bushels	1,000 bushels
PRINCIPAL EXPORTING COUNTRIES										
Canada	447	94,286	651	194,849	372	320,649	408	304,948	476	305,658
United States	1,808	104,967	6,201	260,802	15,679	108,035	13,264	219,160	15,734	206,259
Argentina	[1] 3	85,220	[2] 10	125,289	15	99,803	14	138,240	2	178,135
Australia	[1] 7	[1] 49,732	3	124,112	3	77,234	4	96,584		72,962
British India [3]	[4] 332	[4] 50,821	49	45,209	1,327	8,054	2,428	11,088	1,788	14,328
Hungary	[5] 7,214	[5] 49,116	1,029	15,630	34	19,345	1	21,143	2	22,135
Russia	[5] 556	[5] 164,862	0	301	0	27,085	0	49,202		
Yugoslavia [6]	0	0	0	9,570	0	11,549	0	10,034	[5] 0	[5] 1,156
Rumania	[5] 196	54,630	752	4,788	280	8,558	[5] 1	[5] 11,038	[5] 0	[5] 7,431
Algeria	[5] 639	[5] 5,936	[5] 2,702	1,892	[5] 1,182	6,007	[5] 3,584	2,182	[5] 1,597	6,351
Chile	[1] 170	[1] 2,593		8,822	731	1,696	758	516	622	585
Tunis	[5] 1,746	[5] 960	1,035	547	611	3,437	1,142	1,970	1,127	629
Bulgaria	[5] 0	[5] 11,182	[5] 1,943	323	[5] 5	4,128	[5] 1	2,236		
Spain	6,009	71		2	692	1,466	683	56	985	2,125
PRINCIPAL IMPORTING COUNTRIES										
United Kingdom	219,474	4,493	234,512	18,443	201,313	13,420	226,908	10,292	222,270	11,181
Italy	56,431	3,637	102,126	5,867	66,339	2,469	88,184	1,034	87,796	1,111
Germany	91,851	23,300	76,243	5,227	76,410	20,252	99,252	5,735	98,557	6,798
France	44,081	1,230	43,818	2,646	35,978	1,955	53,878	592	53,717	137
Belgium	72,877	21,965	45,135	5,791	42,722	3,701	41,236	1,378	44,607	2,651
Netherlands	[5] 80,702	[5] 58,435	30,623	4,507	29,150	1,699	29,060	867	31,534	586
Brazil [2]	20,495	0	28,592	17	27,452	22	31,143	38	[7] 32,216	
Japan	[5] 4,116	[5] 28	15,205	1,985	27,980	4,899	18,458	4,014	21,995	4,859
China [2]	6,691	5,401	31,569	793	10,162	1,343	22,354	374	15,464	1,464
Czechoslovakia	0	0	23,902	[5] 888	19,388	212	21,085	89	21,323	41
Austria	[5] 11,402	[5] 871	16,406	[5] 254	14,822	[7] 171	16,888	89	16,230	165
Switzerland	[5] 16,937	[5] 14	14,355	0	14,245	0	17,220	0	18,427	0
Greece	[1] 7,035	[1] 2	[6] 21,791	[6] 0	[5] 18,590	[5] 0	19,502	0		
Irish Free State	0	0	19,101	0	18,539	90	19,511	37	18,691	56
Sweden	[5] 7,080	[5] 23	11,461	107	6,677	639	8,484	2,576	10,391	1,660
Egypt	[5] 8,244	[5] 59	9,476	88	12,520	26	8,861	64	6,803	433
Denmark	[5] 7,155	[5] 597	7,265	796	6,886	897	7,695	1,085	10,704	220
Poland	0	0	[5] 16,571	[5] 23	3,460	5,080	8,331	833	7,840	225
Union of South Africa	[1] 6,274	[1] 253	6,773	16	6,063	15	4,110	8	8,212	8
Norway	[5] 3,674	[5] 0	5,489	[5] 16	6,346	[5] 5	5,944	[5] 4	6,862	[5] 4
Cuba	4,248	0	6,019	0	5,773	0				
Finland	[1] 4,912	[1] 0	4,212	0	4,879	0				
New Zealand	[1] 163	[1] 918	3,007	2	2,978	1	4,854	0	5,499	0
Syria and Lebanon [6]	0	0	2,065	0	3,168	0	2,769	1	1,032	1
Latvia	0	0	[6] 1,963	[5] 20	[6] 1,579	[5] 2	1,980	0		
French Indo-China [6]	0	0	1,089	0	1,094	0	[6] 1,690	[5] 50		
Estonia	0	0	849	0	952	0	1,143	0		
Ceylon [6]	0	0	791	0	896	0	902	0	1,062	0
Total, 42 countries	692,969	795,602	794,787	840,312	688,066	753,161	784,030	898,486	762,580	849,354

Bureau of Agricultural Economics. Official sources except where otherwise noted.

[1] Average of calendar years, 1909–13.
[2] Year ended December 31.
[3] Sea-borne trade only.
[4] Includes some land trade.
[5] Year ended July 31, International Yearbook of Agricultural Statistics.
[6] International Crop Report and Agricultural Statistics.
[7] International Yearbook of Agricultural Statistics.

TABLE 20.—*Wheat: Estimated production, by classes,[1] United States, average 1921–1925, annual 1923–1928*

Year beginning July	Hard red spring	Durum	Hard red winter	Soft red winter	White	Total
	1,000 bushels	*1,000 bushels*	*1,000 bushels*	*1,000 bushels*	*1,000 bushels*	*1,000 bushels*
Average, 1921–1925	155,192	66,834	276,464	223,228	82,432	804,151
1923	126,876	55,269	241,851	271,631	101,767	797,394
1924	192,341	66,105	364,662	189,441	51,879	864,428
1925	156,053	65,008	205,799	169,792	79,777	676,429
1926	120,834	47,478	360,440	228,886	73,402	831,040
1927	201,927	83,162	317,042	180,887	95,356	878,374
1928	195,106	97,833	384,176	139,788	85,846	902,749

Bureau of Agricultural Economics. Estimated production by classes based upon questionnaire surveys of local authorities; supplemented by judgments of cereal specialists.

[1] The spring and winter wheats listed do not include the spring and winter in the white wheats. Production estimates are based on the estimate of percentage classification by States as reported for 1920, 1923, and 1924; the percentages for 1921 and 1922 were interpolated from the 1920 and 1923 percentages. The estimated production for 1927 and 1928 is subject to revision.

TABLE 21.—*Wheat: Estimated price per bushel, received by producers, United States, 1909–1928*

Year beginning July	July 15	Aug. 15	Sept. 15	Oct. 15	Nov. 15	Dec. 15	Jan. 15	Feb. 15	Mar. 15	Apr. 15	May 15	June 15	Weighted av.
	Cts.	*Cts.*	*Cts.*	*Cts.*	*Cts.*	*Cts.*	*Cts.*	*Cts.*	*Cts.*	*Cts.*	*Cts.*	*Cts.*	*Cts.*
Average:													
1909–1913	93.6	89.5	87.7	88.1	87.3	86.7	88.4	89.2	88.9	89.3	90.3	89.0	88.7
1914–1920	167.4	166.6	165.0	164.8	162.2	161.7	167.9	170.6	170.0	177.1	183.8	178.8	165.1
1921–1925	108.8	109.8	108.4	110.9	113.8	117.1	123.3	126.9	126.4	121.2	123.0	120.1	113.7
1909	114.0	101.2	94.9	97.2	99.2	101.0	104.2	105.0	104.8	102.2	98.8	96.4	100.7
1910	97.1	97.4	94.8	92.1	89.4	88.4	89.2	87.6	84.6	84.2	85.4	85.3	91.7
1911	83.5	83.8	86.6	90.0	89.4	87.7	89.2	90.6	91.6	80.0	81.8	82.0	88.3
1912	94.4	87.8	84.6	83.6	79.7	76.1	78.0	80.2	79.8	80.0	81.8	80.6	83.3
1913	79.2	77.1	77.5	77.4	78.4	80.4	81.3	82.4	83.6	84.0	84.2	80.6	79.3
1914	76.7	84.9	93.4	95.4	97.9	103.2	118.8	131.8	132.6	135.6	135.6	117.2	99.4
1915	100.0	100.8	93.0	92.0	92.5	97.4	108.4	108.8	100.8	100.6	101.2	96.5	98.2
1916	100.0	119.2	133.8	147.4	159.4	155.3	157.6	164.6	172.2	213.0	247.2	234.3	144.4
1917	224.5	219.3	205.2	200.3	200.4	201.4	201.6	202.0	202.6	203.1	203.0	202.8	205.8
1918	203.8	205.0	205.7	205.9	205.1	204.5	206.2	207.8	211.1	222.6	229.8	225.2	206.3
1919	219.6	211.4	207.6	211.4	214.0	223.4	233.8	231.2	230.3	242.6	250.8	256.0	218.6
1920	242.9	225.4	216.5	201.2	165.8	146.4	149.2	148.2	140.4	122.1	119.0	119.8	182.9
1921	108.5	103.0	103.4	99.9	93.4	93.0	95.2	107.0	117.0	119.0	118.8	109.6	104.4
1922	99.8	92.6	89.2	94.1	99.4	103.2	104.6	104.4	106.0	108.4	108.2	100.8	98.0
1923	89.6	86.4	91.0	94.2	93.7	94.5	96.7	98.0	98.8	95.8	96.8	98.5	92.4
1924	105.8	116.8	114.2	129.7	133.6	141.1	162.1	169.8	164.0	140.5	149.1	152.7	127.8
1925	140.3	150.4	144.4	136.4	148.8	153.7	158.1	155.5	146.0	142.2	142.1	138.9	145.9
1926	127.7	125.1	117.7	121.4	123.6	122.8	122.2	122.8	120.9	117.2	123.2	130.1	123.8
1927	127.3	123.5	119.2	113.7	111.4	113.9	115.2	116.2	121.6	129.2	144.3	132.0	120.5
1928	118.1	95.2	94.4	98.7	97.1	98.2							

Bureau of Agricultural Economics. Based on returns from special price reporters. Mean of prices reported on 1st of month and 1st of succeeding month, July, 1909–December, 1923.

TABLE 22.—*Wheat: Weighted average price[1] per bushel of reported cash sales, 1909–1928*

NO. 1 NORTHERN SPRING, MINNEAPOLIS

Year beginning July	July	Aug.	Sept.	Oct.	Nov.	Dec.	Jan.	Feb.	Mar.	Apr.	May	June	Weighted av.[1]
	Cents	Cents	Cents	Cents	Cents	Cents	Cents	Cents	Cents	Cents	Cents	Cents	Cents
Average:													
1909–1913	110	102	100	99	97	97	100	100	100	99	102	101	99
1914–1920	199	197	189	187	188	189	197	192	196	207	217	207	190
1921–1925	145	134	132	133	133	141	148	150	146	145	148	144	139
1909	129	106	104	104	105	112	114	114	115	111	110	109	109
1910	121	113	109	108	104	103	106	102	98	96	99	97	105
1911	99	105	109	110	105	102	106	106	108	110	116	113	107
1912	109	98	89	90	84	82	89	87	85	88	91	92	87
1913	91	88	87	84	85	86	87	93	92	91	94	92	88
1914	92	110	112	111	118	120	138	152	149	158	158	135	120
1915	144	118	97	102	102	114	129	126	114	122	122	111	109
1916	121	164	164	179	195	179	193	186	203	238	296	273	176
1917	266	247	217	217	217	217	217	217	217	217	217	217	220
1918	217	223	223	219	222	222	221	224	236	256	259	248	225
1919	266	259	256	267	285	307	301	267	284	306	309	293	272
1920	288	256	254	216	179	166	179	172	166	153	157	169	207
1921	167	148	151	134	125	131	134	151	151	158	161	149	143
1922	149	111	110	115	123	125	123	126	124	130	128	117	120
1923	112	118	121	120	114	116	119	121	121	121	122	125	117
1924	137	131	130	146	148	166	189	187	171	150	167	164	156
1925	159	164	150	149	155	169	173	167	161	164	162	163	161
1926	172	149	143	149	146	146	143	142	139	138	147	149	146
1927	147	143	134	129	130	132	135	134	139	153	157	148	136
1928	138	119	119	116	116	115							

NO. 2 RED WINTER, ST. LOUIS

	July	Aug.	Sept.	Oct.	Nov.	Dec.	Jan.	Feb.	Mar.	Apr.	May	June	Weighted av.[1]
Average:													
1909–1913	98	99	101	105	102	105	108	106	105	104	106	97	100
1914–1920	183	182	185	184	183	188	200	196	195	206	215	198	183
1921–1925	125	128	134	138	139	147	156	156	150	148	146	139	137
1909	113	112	114	123	122	128	130	127	123	112	116	102	113
1910	107	102	102	100	96	98	103	96	93	90	94	88	99
1911	84	88	94	100	96	97	102	101	104	113	121	111	94
1912	103	104	103	109	104	107	111	109	108	109	104	99	105
1913	85	88	94	93	94	95	96	95	95	94	96	84	89
1914	87	93	110	110	111	118	140	157	150	154	150	119	110
1915	117	114	114	121	116	123	134	130	117	122	120	110	120
1916	125	145	160	173	187	183	196	188	205	266	304	265	163
1917	236	232	215	215	215	215	215	215	215	215	215	215	223
1918	221	221	219	222	222	232	241	238	255	271	260	241	223
1919	222	220	221	224	229	248	270	255	258	276	299	289	230
1920	273	251	258	226	202	199	202	190	166	141	158	150	213
1921	123	123	136	126	120	121	122	138	142	141	138	118	127
1922	112	109	114	123	129	136	137	139	136	139	133	123	121
1923	97	99	109	116	112	114	116	118	114	113	112	116	107
1924	135	138	140	156	163	179	210	202	186	177	186	189	159
1925	159	172	171	170	171	184	194	185	170	171	162	147	169
1926	142	134	136	140	136	137	138	135	130	129	142	150	138
1927	141	142	142	145	141	144	151	156	169	196	196	179	149
1928	147	138	145	144	145	139							

Average of daily prices weighted by car-lot sales.

Table 22.—*Wheat: Weighted average price per bushel of reported cash sales, 1909–1928*—Continued

NO. 2 HARD WINTER, KANSAS CITY

Year beginning July	July	Aug.	Sept.	Oct.	Nov.	Dec.	Jan.	Feb.	Mar.	Apr.	May	June	Weighted av.
Average:													
1909–1913	96	93	94	95	92	94	97	95	95	96	97	96	95
1914–1920	187	185	181	177	178	181	191	185	187	199	210		
1921–1925	120	121	123	126	128	134	140	141	138	134	135	128	127
1909	114	102	102	106	104	110	111	111	110	108	107	108	107
1910	104	100	99	95	91	93	95	90	88	88	90	88	98
1911	87	93	95	104	100	100	105	103	105	109	111	109	97
1912	92	89	88	88	83	84	87	86	86	88	87	88	88
1913	82	83	87	84	83	84	85	86	88	87	90	85	84
1914	78	91	104	102	108	113	134	154	149	154	150	121	105
1915	136	126	107	107	103	112	120	120	105	112	110	100	119
1916	114	141	157	167	185	172	189	182	197	243	301	274	171
1917	268	261	212	212	212	212	212	212	212	212	212		
1918	220	216	216	216	215	224	231	226	239	262	260	247	219
1919	225	218	224	230	246	263	282	242	249	275	293	276	242
1920	268	245	244	207	176	169	172	162	155	133	147	138	183
1921	118	115	122	110	109	109	113	129	134	135	134	117	120
1922	113	104	104	113	117	117	114	115	116	120	116	104	113
1923	96	101	109	112	109	109	113	111	109	104	106	108	105
1924	120	119	120	137	143	162	182	181	171	151	163	160	135
1925	154	164	158	158	163	172	178	171	161	159	155	153	163
1926	137	131	132	139	137	138	137	135	133	131	142	144	135
1927	136	135	131	128	131	132	133	133	138	152	160	147	135
1928	120	106	107	110	112	111							

Bureau of Agricultural Economics. Compiled from Minneapolis Daily Market Record, St. Louis Daily Market Reporter, and Kansas City Grain Market Review, formerly Daily Price Current. Data, 1899–1908 available in 1924 Yearbook, pp. 582–583, Table 32.

Table 23.—*Wheat: Weighted average price [1] per bushel of reported cash sales of all classes and grades, combined markets, 1918–1928*

FOUR MARKETS COMBINED [2]

Year beginning July	July	Aug.	Sept.	Oct.	Nov.	Dec.	Jan.	Feb.	Mar.	Apr.	May	June	Weighted av. [3]
	Cents	Cents	Cents	Cents	Cents	Cents	Cents	Cents	Cents	Cents	Cents	Cents	Cents
Av. 1921–1925	124.5	123.7	125.1	127.7	129.7	135.5	141.6	143.5	140.3	137.3	138.6	133.9	130.6
1918	221.2	219.9	218.5	218.3	219.4	220.6	220.7	221.3	232.4	249.2	251.7	238.2	221.7
1919	223.1	221.0	223.6	229.3	246.5	256.8	267.9	240.1	248.6	278.2	292.3	277.0	241.8
1920	270.6	247.3	246.6	205.8	175.1	167.2	172.4	163.2	154.3	135.3	147.6	144.1	193.3
1921	122.9	121.7	128.5	117.3	113.1	113.8	115.8	131.4	136.1	138.5	135.0	122.5	123.7
1922	117.1	107.6	108.6	113.4	120.0	121.3	118.3	120.0	120.4	125.0	122.2	112.6	116.0
1923	99.8	102.7	109.5	112.6	107.3	106.4	111.4	112.7	112.6	111.0	111.6	117.9	108.5
1924	126.2	124.6	128.3	145.0	148.9	166.4	189.5	185.9	174.0	153.4	167.4	163.7	145.6
1925	156.6	161.9	150.7	150.0	159.1	169.7	173.0	167.4	158.5	158.8	157.0	153.0	159.1
1926	142.1	135.9	137.7	142.2	138.5	139.0	138.2	135.8	133.3	133.4	144.6	148.8	139.0
1927	140.4	137.9	131.7	128.2	127.1	129.9	133.3	134.1	139.0	155.2	156.9	145.8	135.7
1928	127.1	111.8	114.0	111.4	112.6	110.4							

SIX MARKETS COMBINED [2]

Year beginning July	July	Aug.	Sept.	Oct.	Nov.	Dec.	Jan.	Feb.	Mar.	Apr.	May	June	Weighted av.
1923	99.0	101.8	106.8	110.4	105.7	105.0	110.3	111.8	111.6	109.9	110.5	116.6	107.0
1924	125.7	123.5	128.3	144.8	148.2	163.6	188.8	184.8	172.1	150.8	165.5	161.6	145.3
1925	155.7	160.5	144.8	143.3	153.5	165.7	170.3	164.8	154.9	156.0	153.8	151.6	155.0
1926	141.6	135.3	135.6	139.4	137.7	139.5	138.8	136.2	133.6	134.7	145.1	148.6	138.3
1927	138.7	136.4	128.7	125.1	125.6	'128.0	131.0	132.0	136.6	150.7	151.4	141.8	132.9
1928	126.0	109.4	108.9	107.0	109.1	107.4							

Bureau of Agricultural Economics. Compiled from daily trade papers of markets named.

[1] The prices in this table are comparable with prices paid to producers, in that the latter are averages of the several prices reported which cover all classes and grades sold by producers.

[2] Four markets are Chicago, Minneapolis, Kansas City, and St. Louis; 6 markets also include Omaha and Duluth.

[3] Average of daily prices weighted by car-lot sales.

TABLE 24.—*Wheat, No. 1, Manitoba Northern:*[1] *Average price per bushel of daily cash closing prices at Winnipeg, 1909–1928*

Year beginning July	July	Aug.	Sept.	Oct.	Nov.	Dec.	Jan.	Feb.	Mar.	Apr.	May	June	Average
Average:	Cents	Cents	Cents	Cents	Cents	Cents	Cents	Cents	Cents	Cents	Cents	Cents	Cents
1909–1913	108	106	99	93	91	89	92	93	93	95	97	97	96
1914–1920	178	184	188	184	185	180	185	184	185	192	200	191	186
1921–1925	140	139	123	118	123	127	132	138	133	134	140	136	132
1909	131	119	100	97	97	98	103	103	104	103	98	93	104
1910	108	107	103	98	92	90	94	93	90	90	95	97	96
1911	95	101	101	100	99	95	97	97	98	101	104	106	99
1912	107	106	100	91	85	80	82	84	85	89	93	96	92
1913	97	95	89	81	83	84	85	88	90	90	93	94	89
1914	90	108	113	111	118	118	136	153	149	157	161	132	129
1915	135	125	95	96	102	107	122	126	110	115	117	111	113
1916	118	149	159	172	193	176	180	168	185	233	275	249	188
1917	234	240	225	221	221	221	221	221	221	221	221	221	224
1918	221	221	224	224	224	224	224	224	224	224	224	224	224
1919	216	215	253	253	252	244	240	231	236	240	238	232	238
1920	233	233	245	211	184	167	171	166	168	157	167	169	189
1921	164	156	133	104	102	105	108	131	137	140	144	131	130
1922	135	117	99	101	110	108	107	110	110	119	115	112	112
1923	106	111	104	96	96	91	94	97	95	96	103	112	100
1924	135	142	142	160	164	173	196	197	176	156	182	171	166
1925	162	167	138	127	142	157	156	155	148	157	154	153	151
1926	159	151	144	143	141	134	136	140	143	145	155	161	146
1927	162	160	145	144	145	140	143	142	148	157	157	143	149
1928	131	119	117	124	121	117							

Bureau of Agricultural Economics. Compiled from Winnepeg Farmers' Advocate, July, 1909–September, 1923; November, 1923–December, 1927, from Minneapolis Daily Market Record.

[1] Reported as "No. 1 Northern" in the Minneapolis Daily Market Record. The two terms are used interchangeably in Canada.

TABLE 25.—*Wheat, good average quality, imported, red: Average spot price per bushel of 60 pounds at Liverpool, 1914–1928*

Year beginning July	July	Aug.	Sept.	Oct.	Nov.	Dec.	Jan.	Feb.	Mar.	Apr.	May	June	Average
	Cents	Cents	Cents	Cents	Cents	Cents	Cents	Cents	Cents	Cents	Cents	Cents	Cents
Average, 1914–1920	196	201	199	204	208	209	214	214	220	222	220	210	
1914	105	128	129	128	138	147	167	195	191	194	198	165	157
1915	163	161	167	171	159	173	194	190	200	193	171	155	175
1916	158	196	200	215	222	239	239	243	242	246	246	246	224
1917	250	250	238	226	226	226	232	232	239	232	232	232	235
1918	232	232	232	239	246	246	246	246	243	241	241	239	240
1919	229	221	216	216	211	195	190	175	211	237	234	240	215
1920	234	220	213	234	253	239	233	214	213	213	217	[1]196	223
1921	[1]171	[1]159	[1]156	[1]131	[1]126	[1]137	144	166	162	158	160	143	151
1922	152	137	132	148	148	148	148	143	140	145	149	138	144
1923	138	132	125	126	126	125	126	(2)	128	123	125	126	
1924	143	160	163	176	179	189	210	214	198	175	184	182	181
1925	176	188	180	166	171	189	183	181	164	167	173	172	176
1926	174	171	166	173	179	179	[3]169	[4]169	[4]164	[4]158	[4]168	[3]180	171
1927	[3]176	[4]166	[3]157	[3]155	[3]155	[3]156	[4]156	[4]154	[4]154	(2)	(2)	(2)	
1928	(2)	(2)	(2)	(2)	(2)	(2)							

Bureau of Agricultural Economics. Compiled from Broomhall's 1921, 1925, and 1927 Corn Trade Yearbooks for the periods July, 1914, to May, 1921, and January, 1922, to December, 1926; and from Corn Trade News for the other months. Conversions at par of exchange beginning with January, 1926. Prior to that date conversions were at monthly average rate of exchange as given in Federal Reserve Bulletins.

[1] No. 2 hard winter when available, otherwise No. 2 red winter.
[2] No quotations.
[3] No. 2 hard winter.
[4] No. 2 red winter.

TABLE 26.—*Wheat ground in United States mills, census years, 1879–1927*

Year	Merchant mills	Custom mills	All mills	Year	Merchant mills	Custom mills	All mills
	1,000 bush.	*1,000 bush.*	*1,000 bush.*		*1,000 bush.*	*1,000 bush.*	*1,000 bush.*
1879			304,776	1919	612,563	6,105	618,668
1889			385,750	1921	521,234	³ 6,105	527,339
1899	471,307	¹ 18,607	489,914	1923	538,312	³ 6,105	544,417
1904	494,095	² 6,988	501,083	1925	530,593	³ 6,105	536,698
1909	496,480	6,988	503,468	1927 ⁴	544,054	³ 6,105	550,159
1914	545,728	² 6,988	552,716				

Bureau of Agricultural Economics. Rearranged from reports of the Bureau of the Census, as follows: 1879 from 1880 Census of Manufactures, p. 451; 1889 from 1900 Census of Manufactures, Vol. IX, part 3, p. 365; 1899 and 1904 from 1910 Census of Manufactures, Vol. X, p. 415; 1909, 1914, and 1919 from 1919 Census of Manufactures, Vol. X, p. 110; 1921 from 1923 Biennial Census of Manufactures; 1923 and 1925 from 1925 Biennial Census of Manufactures; 1927 from release of Census of Manufactures, Mar. 6, 1929.

¹ Difference between all mills and merchant mills.
² 1909 custom mills.
³ 1919 custom mills.
⁴ Preliminary.

NOTE.—Tables similar to Tables 27 and 29, 1927 Yearbook, are omitted.

TABLE 27.—*Flour, wheat, spring patents: Average wholesale price per barrel, Minneapolis, 1909–1928*

Year beginning July	July	Aug.	Sept.	Oct.	Nov.	Dec.	Jan.	Feb.	Mar.	Apr.	May	June	Average
	Dolls.	*Dolls.*	*Dolls.*	*Dolls.*	*Dolls.*	*Dolls.*	*Dolls.*	*Dolls.*	*Dolls.*	*Dolls.*	*Dolls.*	*Dolls.*	*Dolls.*
Average:													
1909–1913	5.48	5.27	5.00	4.94	4.81	4.76	4.88	4.88	4.87	4.81	4.94	4.98	4.97
1914–1920	9.52	9.87	9.37	9.24	9.17	9.27	9.61	9.42	9.42	9.97	10.54	10.15	9.63
1921–1925	7.99	7.73	7.56	7.51	7.50	7.79	8.03	8.18	8.00	7.95	8.01	7.87	7.84
1909	6.21	5.89	5.14	5.29	5.22	5.48	5.58	5.45	5.52	5.38	5.42	5.33	5.49
1910	6.20	5.79	5.75	5.21	5.03	5.01	5.28	4.91	4.75	4.64	4.89	4.81	5.19
1911	4.88	4.88	4.98	5.25	5.05	5.05	5.00	5.10	5.10	5.10	5.43	5.60	5.12
1912	5.43	5.24	4.68	4.63	4.59	4.13	4.26	4.43	4.43	4.43	4.43	4.63	4.61
1913	4.66	4.57	4.45	4.33	4.18	4.15	4.26	4.52	4.54	4.51	4.51	4.51	4.43
1914	4.62	5.78	6.02	5.58	5.79	6.01	6.86	7.54	7.16	7.61	7.41	6.78	6.43
1915	6.78	6.42	5.13	5.23	5.28	5.98	6.23	6.13	5.70	5.90	5.79	5.29	5.82
1916	5.68	7.69	8.26	9.08	9.56	8.60	9.00	8.45	9.44	11.33	14.09	13.08	9.52
1917	12.86	13.22	11.15	10.84	10.24	10.07	9.85	10.05	9.89	9.90	9.42	9.89	10.62
1918	10.45	10.53	10.49	10.44	10.41	10.44	10.42	10.69	11.22	12.09	12.52	12.00	10.98
1919	12.15	12.13	11.54	12.03	13.20	14.48	14.97	13.73	13.41	14.69	15.49	14.64	13.54
1920	14.12	13.33	13.02	11.45	9.74	9.28	9.94	9.38	9.10	8.30	9.04	9.40	10.51
1921	9.27	8.34	8.62	7.67	7.39	7.26	7.33	8.17	8.27	8.46	8.32	7.71	8.07
1922	7.95	7.22	6.68	6.76	6.88	6.86	6.71	6.72	6.72	7.00	6.80	6.35	6.89
1923	6.21	6.37	6.45	6.43	6.21	6.30	6.44	6.51	6.49	6.56	6.83	7.12	6.49
1924	7.72	7.69	7.52	8.19	8.22	9.03	9.80	10.02	9.34	8.54	9.12	8.86	8.67
1925	8.78	9.04	8.52	8.52	8.81	9.52	9.85	9.46	9.19	9.20	9.00	9.32	9.10
1926	9.27	8.50	7.87	8.08	7.85	8.02	7.95	7.85	7.74	7.75	8.23	8.39	8.12
1927	8.26	7.98	7.52	7.43	7.38	7.37	7.48	7.47	7.88	8.48	8.68	8.36	7.86
1928	7.92	7.20	7.16	6.89	6.79	6.64							

Bureau of Agricultural Economics. Compiled from the Minneapolis Daily Market Record.

TABLE 28.—*Bread: Average retail price per pound (baked weight) in leading cities of the United States, 1913–1928*

Year beginning July 15	July 15	Aug. 15	Sept. 15	Oct. 15	Nov. 15	Dec. 15	Jan. 15	Feb. 15	Mar. 15	Apr. 15	May 15	June 15	Average
	Cents	*Cents*	*Cents*	*Cents*	*Cents*	*Cents*	*Cents*	*Cents*	*Cents*	*Cents*	*Cents*	*Cents*	*Cents*
Average:													
1914–1920	8.9	8.9	9.0	9.0	9.0	8.8	8.9	9.0	9.0	9.1	9.3	9.3	9.0
1921–1925	9.1	9.1	9.0	9.0	9.0	8.9	9.0	9.0	9.0	9.0	9.0	9.0	9.0
1913	5.6	5.6	5.6	5.6	5.6	5.6	6.2	6.2	6.2	6.2	6.2	6.2	5.9
1914	6.2	6.3	6.4	6.4	6.4	6.5	6.8	7.1	7.1	7.1	7.2	7.2	6.7
1915	7.1	7.1	7.0	7.0	6.9	6.9	6.9	7.0	7.0	7.0	7.0	7.0	7.0
1916	7.0	7.1	7.7	8.1	8.4	7.8	7.9	8.0	8.1	8.4	9.5	9.6	8.1
1917	9.9	10.2	9.9	9.9	9.9	9.3	9.4	9.5	9.6	9.8	9.9	10.0	9.8
1918	10.0	9.9	9.9	9.8	9.8	9.8	9.8	9.8	9.8	9.8	9.8	9.9	9.8
1919	10.0	10.1	10.1	10.1	10.2	10.2	10.9	11.1	11.2	11.2	11.5	11.8	10.7
1920	11.9	11.9	11.9	11.8	11.6	10.8	10.8	10.6	10.5	10.3	9.9	9.8	11.0
1921	9.7	9.7	9.6	9.5	9.3	9.1	8.8	8.6	8.7	8.7	8.8	8.8	9.1
1922	8.8	8.7	8.7	8.7	8.7	8.6	8.7	8.7	8.7	8.7	8.7	8.7	8.7
1923	8.8	8.7	8.7	8.7	8.9	8.9	9.2	9.5	9.4	9.4	9.4	9.4	9.1
1924	8.7	8.8	8.8	8.8	8.9	8.9	9.2	9.4	9.4	9.4	9.4	9.4	9.4
1925	9.4	9.4	9.4	9.4	9.4	9.4	9.4	9.4	9.4	9.4	9.3	9.3	9.4
1926	9.4	9.4	9.4	9.4	9.4	9.4	9.4	9.4	9.1	9.1	9.1	9.2	9.2
1927	9.3	9.3	9.3	9.3	9.3	9.2	9.2	9.1	9.1	9.1	9.2	9.2	9.2
1928	9.2	9.2	9.1	9.1	9.1	9.0							

Bureau of Agricultural Economics. Compiled from Bureau of Labor Statistics reports of retail prices, monthly.

TABLE 29.—*Bran: Average wholesale price per ton in 100-pound sacks, Minneapolis, 1909–1928*

PURE

Year beginning July	July	Aug.	Sept.	Oct.	Nov.	Dec.	Jan.	Feb.	Mar.	Apr.	May	June	Average
	Dolls.	Dolls.	Dolls.	Dolls.	Dolls.	Dolls.	Dolls.	Dolls.	Dolls.	Dolls.	Dolls.	Dolls.	Dolls.
Average: 1909–1913	19.48	20.19	19.92	19.47	19.78	20.68	21.89	21.85	21.54	20.73	20.28	18.68	20.37
1914–1920	28.55	29.64	28.26	26.99	28.40	29.60	31.23	30.29	30.61	31.41	30.26	27.99	29.44
1921–1925	19.64	20.82	21.58	22.68	24.38	25.92	26.29	25.50	24.74	24.54	23.79	21.23	23.43
1909	20.50	20.08	18.95	19.06	19.02	20.49	22.66	22.09	20.83	18.42	17.93	16.40	19.70
1910	19.62	19.89	18.54	17.99	19.23	21.17	21.73	21.25	20.82	21.43	21.48	19.62	20.23
1911	20.08	20.96	21.42	21.43	22.05	22.99	23.96	25.25	25.13	24.23	23.32	20.22	22.59
1912	20.82	19.25	19.13	19.01	18.48	18.51	19.53	18.03	17.21	16.25	16.58	16.94	18.31
1913	16.40	20.75	21.54	19.86	20.10	20.22	21.59	22.63	23.71	23.34	22.08	20.23	21.04
1914	18.36	22.21	21.71	19.69	20.89	21.54	22.31	22.69	21.17	22.45	19.86	19.62	21.04
1915	20.42	20.06	18.18	18.19	19.96	18.41	18.78	20.08	18.53	18.62	18.99	18.32	19.04
1916	17.67	20.00	21.95	24.45	27.07	25.93	28.75	28.64	34.17	38.57	34.20	26.65	27.34
1917	32.29	31.80	30.26	30.64	33.30	38.62	32.50	32.50	32.85	33.04	31.09	30.70	32.47
1918	26.00	29.31	29.06	28.46	27.80	32.94	47.26	42.83	38.09	39.56	37.88	34.36	34.46
1919	37.26	41.99	37.66	36.89	37.97	41.58	41.98	42.67	46.70	50.25	53.18	50.74	43.24
1920	47.83	42.09	39.03	30.62	31.81	28.20	27.05	22.63	22.73	17.39	16.62	15.52	28.46
1921	14.83	15.49	14.53	13.60	19.75	21.75	22.16	25.41	24.58	23.06	21.77	16.05	19.42
1922	15.90	14.77	17.62	22.48	23.37	24.89	26.67	27.96	28.72	28.41	27.30	21.18	23.27
1923	20.35	24.89	28.50	28.54	26.34	25.28	25.56	24.40	23.37	21.64	18.59	20.04	23.96
1924	23.07	24.29	23.62	25.23	26.14	30.94	30.52	25.14	23.89	23.94	27.33	26.85	25.91
1925	24.05	24.44	23.61	23.56	26.31	26.74	26.66	24.57	23.16	25.65	23.96	22.02	24.57
1926	22.50	22.59	22.27	21.21	24.17	26.99	27.61	28.41	27.99	27.83	28.91	27.11	25.63
1927	25.73	27.32	26.38	26.45	28.94	30.60	31.25	32.96	36.16	34.78	35.50	30.22	30.52
1928	27.90	24.71	25.99	28.66	31.35	32.21							

STANDARD

Year beginning July	July	Aug.	Sept.	Oct.	Nov.	Dec.	Jan.	Feb.	Mar.	Apr.	May	June	Average
Average: 1921–1925	19.01	19.84	20.74	21.90	22.89	25.25	25.65	24.78	23.95	23.88	23.09	20.59	22.80
1920	45.52	41.86	38.42	30.62	31.30	26.41	25.93	21.44	21.63	16.41	15.97	14.80	27.53
1921	14.06	13.91	12.95	12.15	14.79	20.63	20.98	24.75	23.85	22.29	20.91	15.35	18.05
1922	15.31	14.06	16.88	21.81	22.65	24.09	25.99	27.34	28.22	27.74	26.75	20.83	22.64
1923	19.84	23.62	27.79	28.07	25.65	24.77	24.98	23.66	22.00	20.84	17.66	19.12	23.17
1924	22.27	23.43	23.00	24.66	25.62	30.43	30.14	24.49	23.45	26.84	26.34	25.34	25.34
1925	23.58	24.20	23.09	22.83	25.73	26.34	26.17	23.68	22.24	25.05	23.30	21.31	23.96
1926	22.02	21.69	21.64	21.33	23.14	26.02	26.48	27.64	26.96	27.31	28.43	26.51	24.93
1927	25.13	26.85	25.88	25.96	28.41	30.09	30.66	32.47	35.68	34.28	35.03	29.68	30.01
1928	27.29	24.12	25.49	28.09	30.82	31.69							

Bureau of Agricultural Economics. Compiled from the Minneapolis Daily Market Record.

TABLE 30.—*Middlings, standard: Average price per ton, in 100-pound sacks, Minneapolis, 1909–1928*

Year beginning July	July	Aug.	Sept.	Oct.	Nov.	Dec.	Jan.	Feb.	Mar.	Apr.	May	June	Average
	Dolls.	Dolls.	Dolls.	Dolls.	Dolls.	Dolls.	Dolls.	Dolls.	Dolls.	Dolls.	Dolls.	Dolls.	Dolls.
Average: 1909–1913	21.53	22.11	21.80	20.93	20.58	20.87	21.75	21.86	21.26	20.67	20.40	20.44	21.21
1914–1920	35.65	38.86	32.73	29.78	29.63	30.09	31.73	31.95	31.65	32.61	32.85	31.76	32.44
1921–1925	21.24	21.88	22.29	22.97	23.62	25.00	26.19	25.15	24.19	24.09	23.78	22.80	23.60
1909	21.20	20.72	19.03	18.92	18.78	20.19	22.36	22.03	20.95	18.48	18.79	18.06	19.96
1910	21.59	21.94	19.76	19.40	20.84	22.10	21.94	21.30	20.34	20.92	21.40	20.79	21.03
1911	22.18	23.92	24.59	23.60	23.25	22.77	23.54	25.25	25.00	24.29	23.95	22.81	23.76
1912	23.90	22.88	22.28	20.51	18.37	18.60	19.65	18.96	17.39	16.62	17.04	18.73	19.58
1913	18.79	21.11	23.35	22.23	21.64	20.67	21.27	21.75	22.63	23.04	22.17	21.83	21.71
1914	21.20	24.27	23.25	20.52	20.90	21.88	22.67	23.10	22.67	23.12	22.69	22.68	22.29
1915	25.08	35.08	19.86	18.66	18.00	18.45	19.42	21.61	20.22	19.50	20.06	20.10	21.34
1916	32.25	34.50	22.59	27.19	30.81	27.88	28.83	32.55	34.20	39.56	36.09	33.24	31.64
1917	41.71	41.94	35.10	36.25	37.40	39.05	34.50	34.50	34.85	35.04	33.27	32.69	36.36
1918	27.91	31.00	30.89	30.77	30.09	36.27	48.84	44.14	38.58	40.74	44.81	42.92	37.25
1919	47.16	53.08	51.65	44.46	41.33	43.17	43.97	47.28	51.00	54.94	57.74	55.99	49.36
1920	54.22	52.12	45.79	30.58	28.86	23.94	23.47	20.91	20.87	15.38	15.29	14.83	28.86
1921	14.07	14.64	13.95	13.16	15.32	20.73	20.51	24.76	25.52	23.21	21.20	17.13	18.68
1922	17.30	16.24	18.03	23.06	23.23	23.73	25.81	27.26	28.11	27.79	28.85	25.69	23.76
1923	24.83	25.89	27.85	27.78	25.13	23.80	25.43	23.95	21.65	20.96	18.00	19.92	23.78
1924	24.46	25.68	25.27	26.64	27.99	31.44	33.08	26.09	23.62	24.28	29.07	29.68	27.28
1925	25.53	26.95	26.37	24.19	26.31	25.28	26.10	23.71	22.03	24.20	21.77	21.60	24.50
1926	22.96	23.01	22.67	22.31	24.16	27.38	27.35	28.61	28.46	27.79	29.13	29.10	26.08
1927	31.42	34.46	29.22	26.88	28.72	30.00	30.52	32.71	35.85	34.33	37.14	35.30	32.21
1928	32.18	24.31	27.44	28.61	31.01	31.21							

Bureau of Agricultural Economics. Compiled from the Minneapolis Daily Market Record.

TABLE 31.—*Wheat futures: Volume of trading in wheat futures in eight markets, by months, 1924–25 to 1927–28*

Year and market	1927					
	July	Aug.	Sept.	Oct.	Nov.	Dec.
	1,000 bush.	*1,000 bush.*	*1,000 bush.*	*1,000 bush.*	*1,000 bush.*	*1,000 bush.*
1924–25	1, 332, 893	1, 300, 002	1, 068, 406	1, 595, 688	1, 339, 778	1, 528, 039
1925–26	1, 459, 986	1, 560, 407	1, 474, 886	1, 572, 553	1, 500, 362	2, 349, 337
1926–27 [1]	1, 437, 933	1, 226, 296	1, 155, 606	1, 089, 614	1, 227, 071	972, 602
1927–28	1, 004, 220	1, 134, 405	918, 646	916, 988	837, 255	542, 758
Chicago Board of Trade	862, 988	958, 235	699, 249	722, 415	636, 816	436, 484
Chicago Open Board	28, 329	27, 901	23, 996	28, 224	26, 184	22, 578
Minneapolis	42, 560	66, 473	89, 184	91, 058	98, 167	46, 736
Kansas City	54, 487	57, 686	35, 664	28, 598	35, 318	21, 120
Duluth	7, 543	14, 834	63, 849	40, 222	35, 441	11, 550
St. Louis	5, 265	6, 285	3, 900	3, 570	3, 118	2, 533
Milwaukee	2, 378	2, 085	1, 719	2, 414	1, 527	1, 292
Seattle	670	906	1, 085	487	684	465

Year and market	1928						
	Jan.	Feb.	March	Apr.	May	June	Total
	1,000 bush.	*1,000 bush.*	*1,000 bush.*	*1,000 bush.*	*1,000 bush.*	*1,000 bush.*	*1,000 bush.*
1924–25	1, 908, 039	1, 780, 769	2, 273, 124	1, 482, 231	1, 507, 950	1, 759, 046	18, 875, 965
1925–26	1, 455, 699	1, 284, 398	1, 864, 396	1, 397, 092	1, 221, 903	1, 203, 900	18, 344, 919
1926–27 [1]	704, 208	580, 648	919, 808	846, 138	1, 260, 415	1, 163, 976	12, 584, 315
1927–28	384, 203	507, 925	922, 726	1, 590, 458	1, 471, 075	941, 234	11, 171, 893
Chicago Board of Trade	298, 582	407, 218	773, 908	1, 354, 075	1, 266, 452	786, 742	9, 203, 164
Chicago Open Board	20, 999	22, 490	30, 398	38, 156	39, 865	33, 243	342, 363
Minneapolis	40, 918	44, 118	58, 889	95, 560	81, 052	69, 540	824, 255
Kansas City	12, 953	18, 675	34, 424	61, 969	51, 274	29, 232	441, 400
Duluth	8, 566	11, 724	18, 098	24, 664	20, 157	15, 844	272, 492
St. Louis	1, 036	1, 746	4, 293	9, 932	7, 004	4, 553	53, 235
Milwaukee	903	1, 779	2, 106	5, 019	4, 747	1, 633	27, 602
Seattle	246	175	610	1, 083	524	447	7, 382

Grain Futures Administration.

[1] Trading in New York and Seattle included.

TABLE 32.—*Wheat futures: Open contracts in wheat futures on the Chicago Board of Trade by months, on the last day, during the crop year 1927–28*

1927	Bushels	1928	Bushels
July	74, 562, 000	January	84, 191, 000
August	78, 686, 000	February	88, 041, 000
September	84, 860, 000	March	94, 906, 000
October	89, 037, 000	April	121, 502, 000
November	83, 744, 000	May	93, 240, 000
December	74, 205, 000	June	87, 159, 000

Table 33.—*Rye: Acreage, production, value, exports, etc., United States, 1909-1928*

Year	Acreage harvested	Average yield per acre	Production	Price per bushel received by producers Dec. 1	Farm value Dec. 1	Price per bushel of No. 2 rye at Chicago year beginning July 1 [1]	Foreign trade, including flour, year beginning July 1 [2]			
							Domestic exports	Imports	Net exports [3]	
									Total	Percentage of production
	1,000 acres	*Bushels of 56 lbs.*	*1,000 bushels*	*Cents*	*1,000 dollars*	*Cents*	*1,000 bushels*	*1,000 bushels*	*1,000 bushels*	*Per cent*
1909	*2,196*	*13.4*	*29,520*							
1909	2,196	16.1	35,406	72.2	25,548	76	242	30	212	0.6
1910	2,185	16.0	34,897	71.5	24,953	84	40	227	4 187	.5
1911	2,127	15.6	33,119	83.2	27,557	91	31	134	4 103	.3
1912	2,117	16.8	35,664	66.3	23,636	65	1,855	1	1,854	5.2
1913	2,557	16.2	41,381	63.4	26,220	64	2,273	37	2,236	5.4
1914	2,541	16.8	42,779	86.5	37,018	105	13,027	147	12,880	30.1
1915	3,129	17.3	54,050	83.4	45,083	99	15,250	566	14,684	27.2
1916	3,213	15.2	48,862	122.1	59,676	154	13,703	428	13,275	27.2
1917	4,317	14.6	62,933	166.0	104,447	211	17,186	834	16,352	26.0
1918	6,391	14.2	91,041	151.6	138,038	161	36,467	638	35,829	39.4
1919	*7,679*	*9.9*	*75,992*							
1919	6,307	12.0	75,483	133.2	100,573	170	41,531	1,077	40,454	53.6
1920	4,409	13.7	60,490	126.8	76,693	162	47,337	452	46,885	77.5
1921	4,528	13.6	61,675	69.7	43,014	97	29,944	700	29,244	47.4
1922	6,672	15.5	103,362	68.5	70,841	81	51,663	99	51,564	49.9
1923	5,171	12.2	63,077	65.0	40,971	70	19,902	2	19,900	31.5
1924	*3,744*	*14.9*	*55,674*							
1924	4,150	15.8	65,466	106.5	69,696	125	50,242	1	50,241	76.7
1925	3,974	11.7	46,456	78.2	36,340	96	12,647		12,646	27.2
1926	3,578	11.4	40,795	83.4	34,024	101	21,698	1	21,697	53.2
1927	3,648	15.9	58,164	85.3	49,609	106	26,327	2	26,325	45.3
1928 [5]	3,444	12.1	41,766	86.4	36,067					

Bureau of Agricultural Economics. Production figures are estimates of the crop-reporting board; italic figures are census returns. See 1927 Yearbook, page 764, for data for earlier years.

[1] Prices are from Chicago Daily Trade Bulletin and are averages of daily prices weighted by car-lot sales.
[2] Compiled from Commerce and Navigation of the United States, 1909-1917; Foreign Commerce and Navigation of the United States, 1918; Monthly Summary of Foreign Commerce of the United States, June issues, 1919-1926; January and June issues, 1927-28, and official records of the Bureau of Foreign and Domestic Commerce. Rye—General imports, 1909; imports for consumption, 1910-1927. Rye flour—imports for consumption, 1909-1927. Rye flour converted to rye on the basis that 1 barrel of rye flour is the product of 6 bushels of grain.
[3] Total exports (domestic plus foreign) minus total imports.
[4] Net imports.
[5] Preliminary.

TABLE 34.—*Rye: Acreage and production, by States, average 1921–1925, annual 1926–1928*

State and division	Acreage				Production			
	Average, 1921–1925	1926	1927	1928 [1]	Average, 1921–1925	1926	1927	1928 [1]
	1,000 acres	*1,000 acres*	*1,000 acres*	*1,000 acres*	*1,000 bush.*	*1,000 bush.*	*1,000 bush.*	*1,000 bush.*
Connecticut	3				64			
New York	48	25	21	20	784	388	368	314
New Jersey	55	41	36	41	986	779	720	758
Pennsylvania	175	93	86	103	2, 903	1, 488	1, 462	1, 596
North Atlantic	283	159	143	164	4, 766	2, 655	2, 550	2, 668
Ohio	73	50	35	30	1, 064	875	560	399
Indiana	252	145	119	86	3, 238	2, 102	1, 618	946
Illinois	173	83	62	62	2, 690	1, 245	899	899
Michigan	441	173	178	182	5, 856	2, 336	2, 617	2, 366
Wisconsin	358	256	238	167	5, 336	3, 840	4, 046	2, 171
Minnesota	765	440	383	402	13, 196	5, 940	7, 009	5, 950
Iowa	42	31	43	54	755	542	645	972
Missouri	25	24	16	19	306	310	176	228
North Dakota	1, 401	1, 222	1, 381	1, 271	17, 179	9, 287	23, 063	12, 710
South Dakota	285	103	154	162	4, 154	639	2, 772	1, 458
Nebraska	173	253	274	249	2, 174	2, 606	4, 110	3, 486
Kansas	59	41	45	32	646	480	576	518
North Central	4, 047	2, 821	2, 928	2, 716	56, 595	30, 202	48, 091	32, 103
Delaware	5	4	3	3	69	60	45	45
Maryland	17	15	14	15	266	270	214	225
Virginia	38	43	42	46	446	580	496	621
West Virginia	10	12	8	7	116	156	104	94
North Carolina	65	104	94	89	618	1, 352	1, 128	1, 024
South Carolina	6	8	9	7	67	112	117	80
Georgia	18	22	26	22	166	264	260	220
South Atlantic	160	208	196	189	1, 748	2, 794	2, 364	2, 309
Kentucky	18	18	14	7	203	279	154	87
Tennessee	19	32	26	25	190	448	208	205
Arkansas	1	1	1	1	10	11	10	9
Oklahoma	35	36	22	26	423	558	198	312
Texas	15	20	14	15	161	380	98	180
South Central	89	107	77	74	993	1, 676	668	793
Montana	134	107	134	154	1, 699	1, 284	2, 412	2, 156
Idaho	9	3	3	3	153	46	48	48
Wyoming	37	51	54	40	486	714	675	440
Colorado	85	89	76	74	874	1, 024	798	814
New Mexico	2	1	1	1	28	18	6	12
Utah	9	4	4	3	90	36	40	2
Washington	18	18	22	18	218	216	352	270
Oregon	26	10	10	8	357	130	160	120
Far Western	321	283	304	301	3, 905	3, 468	4, 491	3, 894
United States	4, 899	3, 578	3, 648	3, 444	68, 007	40, 795	58, 164	41, 760

Bureau of Agricultural Economics. Estimates of the crop-reporting board.

[1] Preliminary.

TABLE 35.—*Rye: Yield per acre and estimated price per bushel, December 1, by States, average 1914–1920, 1921–1925, annual 1924–1928*

State and division	Yield per acre							Estimated price per bushel						
	Av., 1914–1920	Av., 1921–1925	1924	1925	1926	1927	1928	Av., 1914–1920	Av., 1921–1925	1924	1925	1926	1927	1928
	Bush.	*Bush.*	*Bush.*	*Bush.*	*Bush.*	*Bush.*	*Bush.*	*Cts.*	*Cts.*	*Cts.*	*Cts.*	*Cts.*	*Cts.*	*Cts.*
Connecticut	20.1	18.8	18.0	19.0				159	139	140	130			
New York	17.6	16.3	17.0	16.5	15.5	17.5	15.7	139	100	113	100	100	105	112
New Jersey	18.3	18.0	17.5	18.0	19.0	20.0	18.5	138	97	113	93	95	97	104
Pennsylvania	17.0	16.6	16.0	17.0	16.0	17.0	15.5	130	98	113	105	97	105	107
North Atlantic	17.4	16.8	16.5	17.1	16.7	17.8	16.3	134.6	99.0	113.1	101.4	96.8	102.7	106.7
Ohio	16.3	14.7	16.0	15.0	17.5	16.0	13.3	125	89	111	88	88	92	103
Indiana	15.1	12.8	13.5	11.4	14.5	13.6	11.0	124	83	106	85	85	88	94
Illinois	16.9	15.3	14.5	13.8	15.0	14.5	14.5	124	85	107	90	86	92	92
Michigan	14.6	13.4	14.5	12.5	13.5	14.7	13.0	126	78	106	78	78	89	93
Wisconsin	17.0	15.0	17.0	14.8	15.0	17.0	13.0	127	79	109	76	84	90	90
Minnesota	17.7	17.0	22.0	13.0	13.5	18.3	14.8	124	72	108	71	76	85	85
Iowa	17.8	17.6	18.0	16.4	17.5	15.0	18.0	118	78	102	80	82	86	86
Missouri	13.0	12.2	13.5	12.0	12.9	11.0	12.0	128	98	105	120	113	110	106
North Dakota	11.9	12.0	15.0	10.0	7.6	16.7	10.0	120	67	104	65	73	80	76
South Dakota	16.4	13.8	14.0	9.5	6.2	18.0	9.0	115	67	102	67	73	79	79
Nebraska	15.5	12.5	14.5	12.3	10.3	15.0	14.0	110	70	97	71	76	77	77
Kansas	14.7	10.8	14.2	8.9	11.7	12.8	16.2	121	82	98	98	94	92	82
North Central	14.9	13.8	16.4	11.4	10.7	16.4	11.8	122.0	73.7	105.4	71.6	78.3	82.7	82.0
Delaware	15.2	13.6	13.5	15.0	15.0	15.0	15.0	137	109	125	120	110	115	120
Maryland	15.6	15.8	15.0	19.0	18.0	15.3	15.0	134	107	122	114	105	110	115
Virginia	12.9	11.6	11.5	12.0	13.5	11.8	13.5	138	109	128	127	112	115	120
West Virginia	13.7	11.6	11.2	13.0	13.0	13.0	13.5	139	108	129	120	110	110	115
North Carolina	9.8	9.2	9.0	11.5	13.0	12.0	11.5	163	137	149	157	125	135	145
South Carolina	10.5	10.4	11.0	10.5	14.0	13.0	11.5	237	201	190	210	175	175	185
Georgia	9.1	9.2	9.2	9.3	12.0	10.0	10.0	202	173	183	180	160	165	175
South Atlantic	12.1	10.9	10.5	12.3	13.4	12.1	12.2	151.4	127.9	143.8	144.5	124.6	132.3	137.9
Kentucky	12.4	11.4	11.0	13.0	15.5	11.0	12.4	140	115	127	125	108	120	132
Tennessee	10.0	9.8	11.0	11.0	14.0	8.0	8.2	159	128	138	130	120	129	138
Arkansas	10.6	10.4	11.0	11.0	11.0	10.0	9.0	157	122	131	130	125	140	140
Oklahoma	12.8	12.0	14.0	12.0	15.5	9.0	12.0	129	89	101	110	90	99	92
Texas	12.9	10.6	16.0	4.0	19.0	7.0	12.0	153	111	111	120	97	95	103
South Central	12.2	11.2	13.2	10.6	15.7	8.7	10.7	140.6	105.8	113.7	119.2	102.9	113.2	111.3
Montana	14.2	12.5	14.0	12.5	12.0	18.0	14.0	119	65	91	74	75	73	69
Idaho	16.5	16.4	10.0	20.0	15.5	16.0	16.0	115	81	122	80	73	75	72
Wyoming	15.9	14.0	10.0	12.0	14.0	12.5	11.0	126	66	88	64	67	69	72
Colorado	13.2	10.3	9.0	10.0	11.5	10.5	11.0	109	67	85	67	71	70	70
New Mexico		10.2	16.0	4.0	18.0	6.0	12.0		92	100	100	85	75	80
Utah	11.6	9.7	6.6	11.0	9.0	10.0	8.0	131	85	107	100	80	82	87
Washington	13.8	11.7	7.9	11.0	12.0	16.0	15.5	142	98	133	125	100	90	90
Oregon	13.6	13.0	10.0	14.0	13.0	16.0	15.0	142	98	136	110	96	95	102
Far Western	13.3	12.1	11.0	11.6	12.3	14.8	12.9	122.1	70.0	92.5	74.7	74.6	74.1	72.3
United States	14.8	13.8	15.8	11.7	11.4	15.9	12.1	124.2	77.6	106.5	78.2	83.4	85.3	86.4

Bureau of Agricultural Economics. Estimates of the crop-reporting board.

TABLE 36.—Rye: Acreage, yield per acre, and production in specified countries, average 1909-1913, 1921-1925, annual 1926-1928

Country	Acreage (1,000 acres)					Yield per acre (Bushels)					Production (1,000 bushels)				
	Average 1909-1913[1]	Average 1921-1925	1926	1927	1928 preliminary	Average 1909-1913[1]	Average 1921-1925	1926	1927	1928 preliminary	Average 1909-1913[1]	Average 1921-1925	1926	1927	1928 preliminary
NORTHERN HEMISPHERE															
NORTH AMERICA															
Canada	117	1,386	754	743	840	17.9	14.4	16.2	20.1	17.4	2,094	19,994	12,179	14,951	14,618
United States	2,236	4,899	3,578	3,648	3,444	16.1	13.8	11.4	15.9	12.1	36,093	68,007	40,795	58,164	41,766
Total	2,353	6,285	4,332	4,391	4,284	16.2	14.0	12.2	16.7	13.2	38,187	88,001	52,974	73,115	56,384
EUROPE															
Norway	37	28	23	23	23	26.3	27.9	28.1	26.3	26.6	973	780	647	606	612
Sweden	977	836	838	849		24.7	26.2	27.6	22.1		24,100	21,911	23,094	18,726	
Denmark	636	535	514	453	361	30.0	24.6	24.3	22.9	27.3	19,104	13,162	12,480	10,364	9,842
Netherlands	557	499	488	487	483	29.5	31.5	39.4	27.7	35.3	16,422	15,731	19,216	13,489	17,047
Belgium	672	559	558	573	568	35.2	36.8	36.0	38.1	48.7	23,644	20,564	20,108	21,854	27,676
Luxemburg	26	18	17	17	15	25.0	19.4	20.8	20.8	23.6	651	349	353	354	354
France	3,095	2,196	1,865	1,921	1,954	17.0	15.4	15.4	17.7	18.1	52,501	40,645	30,076	33,955	35,362
Spain	1,988	1,802	1,865	1,818	1,535	13.9	15.4	12.6	14.6	15.9	27,636	27,721	23,504	26,515	24,407
Portugal	271	604	591	618		8.3	8.8	6.1	7.6		(2,300)	5,330	3,614	4,677	3,418
Italy	346	317	298	307	311	18.3	18.8	21.8	19.3	21.0	6,317	5,277	6,496	5,937	6,535
Switzerland	60	48	49	49	49	29.7	32.6	32.3	32.4	34.8	1,783	1,563	1,583	1,589	1,705
Germany	12,713	10,745	11,694	11,610	11,462	29.0	23.8	21.6	23.2	29.3	368,337	255,937	252,187	289,025	333,499
Austria	1,110	878	972	948	947	21.4	24.5	19.3	23.2	20.2	23,785	16,086	18,712	20,126	19,145
Czechoslovakia	2,605	2,128	2,008	2,012	2,048	24.4	18.5	22.2	24.5	25.7	63,538	52,200	45,908	49,296	52,677
Hungary	1,608	1,591	1,729	1,583	1,641	19.5	16.9	18.2	14.1	19.8	31,377	26,845	31,416	22,365	32,528
Yugoslavia	732	477	500	516	510	12.3	12.6	14.9	11.5	14.3	9,004	6,001	5,923	5,923	7,283
Greece	76	84	117	117	134	14.9	12.5	13.7	12.9	15.9	1,129	1,051	1,600	1,505	2,124
Bulgaria	542	443	462	464	479	16.4	12.5	15.4	17.8	19.2	8,345	5,831	7,133	8,242	9,220
Rumania	1,286	692	720	695	731	16.1	12.1	15.4	13.4	13.7	20,644	8,371	11,242	9,323	11,483
Poland	12,127	10,920	11,937	12,081	11,226	18.1	18.3	16.5	18.5	20.7	218,943	200,157	197,289	223,939	232,458
Lithuania	1,749	1,355	1,108	1,240	1,161	13.9	16.9	12.5	17.1	16.4	24,283	22,942	13,810	21,188	19,035
Latvia	888	624	621	633	637	14.7	15.3	9.9	16.1	13.3	13,061	9,535	6,119	10,188	8,459
Estonia	486	394	336	587	357	16.7	15.9	13.4	18.4	16.2	8,129	6,246	4,490	6,735	5,794
Finland	589	578	565	567	573	17.8	19.6	21.1	22.7	19.1	10,490	11,316	11,908	12,892	10,940
Russia	61,055	56,896	69,797	69,585	63,495	12.0	11.0	12.9	13.4	11.9	735,505	626,009	902,311	933,033	753,433

	Area					Yield per acre					Production				
Total European countries, excluding Russia, reporting all years	43,928	36,911	38,610	38,481	37,190	21.6	20.3	18.7	20.2	23.4	950,096	749,310	723,731	775,410	870,085
Estimated European total, excluding Russia	45,200	38,400	40,100	40,000	38,700						[5]978,000	779,000	752,000	800,000	890,000
Total Northern Hemisphere countries, excluding Russia, reporting all years	46,281	43,196	42,942	42,872	41,474	21.4	19.4	18.1	19.8	22.3	988,283	837,311	776,705	848,525	926,469
Estimated total excluding Russia and China	48,020	45,100	44,800	44,800	43,400						1,023,000	873,000	812,000	879,000	954,000
SOUTHERN HEMISPHERE															
Chile	5	4	6	6	9	22.2	16.0	9.5	19.5	—	111	64	57	117	---
Argentina	85	380	544	894	1,194	7.5	8.1	6.0	7.4	—	640	3,061	3,268	6,614	---
Union of South Africa	108	[2]164	138	---	---	6.7	[2]5.5	6.4	---	---	724	[2]909	886	---	---
Australia	[4]9	4	3	---	---	12.7	12.8	13.7	---	---	114	51	41	---	---
New Zealand	[4]4	1	1	---	---	[4]28.5	23.0	26.0	---	---	[4]114	23	26	---	---
Estimated world total, excluding Russia and China	48,300	45,700	45,500	45,900	44,800						[5]1,025,000	879,000	817,000	888,000	965,000

Bureau of Agricultural Economics. Official sources and International Institute of Agriculture. Figures are for crops harvested during the calendar year in the Northern Hemisphere and the succeeding harvest in the Southern Hemisphere.

[1] Where changes of boundary have occurred, averages are for territory within present boundaries.
[2] Three-year average.
[3] Four-year average.
[4] Two-year average.
[5] The estimate for the 5-year period, 1909–1913, given in this table, is somewhat larger than the figures obtained by averaging the five years in Table 37. This is because in this table estimates for warring countries are for postwar boundaries, whereas in Table 37 they are for pre-war territory. As a result, in excluding Russia, which country lost territory in the war, a smaller area is excluded in this table than in Table 37.

TABLE 37.—*Rye: World production, 1894–1928*

Year	World production excluding Russia and China	Northern Hemisphere production excluding Russia and China	European production excluding Russia	Selected countries						
				Russia[1]	United States	Germany	France	Poland	Hungary	Czechoslovakia
	1,000,000 bushels	1,000,000 bushels	1,000,000 bushels	1,000,000 bushels	1,000,000 bushels	1,000,000 bushels	1,000,000 bushels	1,000,000 bushels	1,000,000 bushels	1,000,000 bushels
1894	663	662	618	931	30	279	75	--------	80	--------
1895	620	618	573	773	31	260	72	--------	47	--------
1896	664	663	621	790	29	285	70	--------	37	--------
1897	599	598	551	654	33	273	48	--------	26	--------
1898	667	666	619	738	33	297	67	--------	33	--------
1899	710	708	664	912	30	342	67	--------	36	--------
1900	675	673	629	920	31	337	59	--------	31	--------
1901	690	688	644	755	31	321	58	--------	31	--------
1902	733	731	682	919	35	374	46	--------	38	--------
1903	768	767	721	912	32	391	58	--------	37	--------
1904	755	754	709	1,008	32	396	53	--------	33	--------
1905	782	781	732	737	35	378	59	--------	38	--------
1906	787	785	736	668	37	379	51	--------	39	--------
1907	751	749	700	815	35	384	56	--------	30	--------
1908	827	826	776	790	36	423	52	--------	34	--------
1909[2]	872	870	821	904	35	447	56	--------	47	--------
1910[2]	818	816	768	875	35	414	44	--------	52	--------
1911[2]	828	826	779	769	33	428	47	--------	54	--------
1912[2]	862	860	810	1,051	36	457	49	--------	57	--------
1913[2]	892	889	834	1,011	41	481	50	--------	56	--------
1914	766	763	707	[3] 870	43	347	44	--------	45	--------
1915	691	689	621	[4] 910	54	301	33	--------	48	--------
1916	663	661	598	[5] 771	49	287	33	--------	--------	--------
1917	548	545	466	614	63	[6] 228	25	--------	--------	--------
1918	590	588	476	--------	91	250	[6] 29	--------	--------	--------
1919	681	679	586	--------	75	238	29	103	--------	--------
1920	619	616	533	368	60	194	34	74	[6] 21	33
1921	853	850	760	401	62	268	44	168	23	54
1922	864	858	716	568	103	206	38	197	25	51
1923	925	919	826	549	63	263	37	235	31	53
1924	743	739	653	737	65	, 226	40	144	22	45
1925	1,008	1,001	938	878	46	317	44	257	33	58
1926[7]	817	812	752	902	41	252	30	197	31	46
1927[7]	888	879	800	933	58	269	34	224	22	49
1928[7]	965	954	890	783	42	335	35	232	33	53

Bureau of Agricultural Economics. For each year is shown the production during the calendar year in the Northern Hemisphere and the succeeding harvest in the Southern Hemisphere.

[1] Includes all Russian territory reporting for the years shown.

[2] The average production for the 1909–1913 period as computed from figures given here for estimated world total, Northern Hemisphere total, European total and European countries whose boundaries were changed by the World War, will not agree with estimates appearing elsewhere for present territory due to changes in boundary.

[3] Exclusive of the 10 Vistula Provinces of Russian Poland and the Province of Batum in Transcaucasia.

[4] Exclusive of Russian Poland, Lithuania, parts of Latvia and the Ukraine, and the two Provinces of Batum and Elizabetpol in Transcaucasia.

[5] Beginning with this year estimates for the present territory of the Union of Socialist Soviet Republics exclusive of Turkestan, Transcaucasia, and the Far East, which terrritory in 1924 produced 8,646,000 bushels.

[6] Beginning with this year postwar boundaries, therefore not comparable with earlier years.

[7] Preliminary.

TABLE 38.—*Rye: Monthly marketings by farmers, as reported by about 3,500 mills and elevators, United States, 1917–1927*

Year beginning July	Percentage of year's receipts												
	July	Aug.	Sept.	Oct.	Nov.	Dec.	Jan.	Feb.	Mar.	Apr.	May	June	Season
1917	2.8	14.8	20.5	17.1	11.3	7.6	5.8	6.4	7.6	3.4	1.7	1.0	100.0
1918	5.6	11.3	14.9	14.5	12.2	9.5	8.4	4.9	6.3	4.8	3.4	4.2	100.0
1919	8.2	15.0	13.3	12.4	7.8	9.1	8.5	4.7	6.2	6.4	4.3	4.1	100.0
1920	7.3	20.7	18.1	12.2	8.8	7.0	6.6	4.7	4.3	3.7	3.3	3.3	100.0
1921	13.9	20.8	17.6	10.6	6.3	5.9	4.5	4.8	4.9	4.0	4.2	2.5	100.0
1922	10.7	20.5	14.8	12.3	10.2	8.7	6.5	5.3	4.0	2.9	2.2	1.9	100.0
1923	5.3	18.8	19.2	14.2	9.4	8.5	5.4	5.9	3.5	2.5	3.0	4.3	100.0
1924	3.9	16.9	25.4	23.3	10.7	7.0	5.0	3.1	1.7	1.0	1.2	.8	100.0
1925	5.2	19.2	23.3	12.4	8.7	8.9	6.6	4.6	3.1	2.4	2.8	2.8	100.0
1926	8.0	20.1	19.7	13.0	8.5	6.0	6.0	6.0	3.7	2.6	3.0	3.4	100.0
1927	4.7	19.0	25.6	17.5	9.8	5.8	4.4	4.1	3.7	2.4	1.7	1.3	100.0

Bureau of Agricultural Economics.

TABLE 39.—*Rye: Classification of receipts graded by licensed inspectors, all inspection points, 1923–1927*

Year beginning July 1	Receipts of—						Shipments of—	
	No. 1	No. 2	No. 3	No. 4	Sample grade	Total	Sample grade	Total
1923–24: Cars	14,394	13,532	3,872	1,061	473	33,332	26	30,796
1924–25: Cars	27,977	24,251	8,841	2,957	876	64,902	69	70,946
1925–26: Cars	3,969	11,730	5,111	1,794	494	23,098	30	19,133
1926–27: Cars	3,892	9,921	5,794	3,597	1,445	24,649	123	31,285
1927–28: Cars	10,659	15,573	4,976	1,409	564	33,181	22	28,960

Bureau of Agricultural Economics.

TABLE 40.—*Rye: Receipts at markets named, averages by groups, 1909–1925; annual, 1921–1927*

Year beginning July	Minneapolis	Duluth	Chicago	Milwaukee	Omaha	Total, 5 markets	Fort William and Port Arthur [1]
	1,000 bushels	*1,000 bushels*	*1,000 bushels*	*1,000 bushels*	*1,000 bushels*	*1,000 bushels*	*1,000 bushels*
Average:							
1909–1913	3,579	1,039	2,213	1,950	----------	----------	----------
1914–1920	8,967	8,799	5,267	3,664	----------	----------	----------
1921–1925	9,904	25,285	5,957	2,116	1,360	44,622	6,856
1921	4,754	17,444	4,235	2,282	2,048	30,763	5,297
1922	15,111	42,744	7,585	3,241	1,916	70,597	11,552
1923	13,336	16,836	2,952	1,449	736	35,309	6,837
1924	8,447	38,496	12,586	2,733	1,207	63,469	5,265
1925	7,872	10,907	2,426	876	892	22,973	5,329
1926	4,123	13,351	2,355	1,268	941	22,038	7,763
1927 [2]	5,423	25,089	4,151	673	1,564	36,900	11,963

Bureau of Agricultural Economics. Compiled from reports of Minneapolis Chamber of Commerce, Duluth Board of Trade, Chicago Board of Trade, Milwaukee Chamber of Commerce, Omaha Grain Exchange, American Elevator and Grain Trade, and Canadian Grain Statistics.

[1] Crop year begins September.
[2] Beginning January, 1928, figures are subject to revision.

TABLE 41.—*Rye: Commercial stocks in store, 1926–27 to 1928–29*

DOMESTIC RYE IN UNITED STATES [1]

	July	Aug.	Sept.	Oct.	Nov.	Dec.	Jan.	Feb.	Mar.	Apr.	May	June
	1,000 bushels	*1,000 bushels*	*1,000 bushels*	*1,000 bushels*	*1,000 bushels*	*1,000 bushels*	*1,000 bushels*	*1,000 bushels*	*1,000 bushels*	*1,000 bushels*	*1,000 bushels*	*1,000 bushels*
1926–27							13,092	12,880	13,897	13,905	7,818	3,783
1927–28	1,018	1,454	2,091	2,608	2,077	2,970	3,281	4,027	4,321	5,090	5,544	2,662
1928–29	2,499	2,170	1,351	2,684	4,771	5,589						

UNITED STATES RYE IN CANADA

	July	Aug.	Sept.	Oct.	Nov.	Dec.	Jan.	Feb.	Mar.	Apr.	May	June
1926–27							1,658	1,704	1,583	1,384	3,379	869
1927–28	1,465	589	686	1,385	1,390	1,208	930	772	351	259	47	512
1928–29	750	449	357	838	1,248	1,478						

CANADIAN RYE IN UNITED STATES [2]

	July	Aug.	Sept.	Oct.	Nov.	Dec.	Jan.	Feb.	Mar.	Apr.	May	June
1926–27							2,266	1,922	1,631	494	689	792
1927–28	63	50	20	124	441	802	851	458	203	90	90	371
1928–29	248	255	12	83	205	258						

Bureau of Agricultural Economics. Data are for stocks on the Saturday nearest the 1st day of the month.

[1] Includes rye stored at 39 interior and seaboard points of accumulation, exclusive of rye in transit on lakes and canals.

[2] Includes rye stored at lake or seaboard ports, exclusive of rye in transit on lakes and canals.

TABLE 42.—*Rye, including flour: International trade, average 1910–1914, annual 1925–1928*

Country	Average 1910–1914		1925		1926		1927		1928 preliminary	
	Imports	Exports	Imports	Exports	Imports	Exports	Im- ports	Ex- ports	Im- ports	Ex- ports
PRINCIPAL EXPORTING COUNTRIES	*1,000 bushels*	*1,000 bushels*	*1,000 bushels*	*1,000 bushels*	*1,000 bushels*	*1,000 bushels*	*1,000 bushels*	*1,000 bushels*	*1,000 bushels*	*1,000 bushels*
United States	0	888	0	50,242	0	12,647	0	21,698	0	26,327
Russia	[1] 5,381	[3] 33,979	0	2,579	0	7,094	0	16,691		
Canada	65	58	28	5,875	23	5,768	47	8,229	114	10,379
Hungary	[1] 140	[1] 14,150	13	5,196	1	6,832	1	10,455	1	4,431
Argentina	0	[2] 273	0	1,693	0	1,812	0	5,902	0	7,060
Poland			[1] 2,582	[3] 2,211	2,334	11,983	4,273	5,063	4,832	375
Rumania	[1] [4] 26	[1] 2,992	0	477	51	105	[1] 0	[1] 1,503	[1] 0	[1] 2,189
Bulgaria	0	[1] 1,925	[1] 15	34	0	59	0	506		
Yugoslavia	0	0	0	[3] 246	0	[3] 231	0	[1] 506	0	[1] 13
Algeria	0	0	0	[3] 43	0	[3] 47	0	[3] 28	[1] 0	[1] 40
PRINCIPAL IMPORTING COUNTRIES										
Germany	16,226	43,936	22,057	5,413	9,149	15,963	22,797	7,876	24,861	10,199
Finland			6,310	13	6,471	7	5,296	10	4,932	10
Norway	[1] 10,644	[1] [5] 51	7,502	0	7,719	0	7,038	0	7,307	0
Denmark	[1] 8,753	[1] 288	7,002	532	8,610	425	6,550	445	7,401	417
Netherlands	[1] 29,557	[1] 17,889	6,376	2,913	6,046	434	4,037	840	4,148	629
Czechoslovakia	0	0	8,730	128	8,169	102	4,631	131	7,622	102
Austria	[1] 1,469	[1] 2	4,180		4,020	[6] 162	4,277	248	4,617	101
Sweden	[1] 3,940	[1] 59	4,815	28	1,455	98	633	1,645	4,177	636
Latvia	0	0	[3] 1,981	[1] 152	[3] 2,648	[1] 66	[3] 2,043	[1] 20		
France	3,316	26	1,306	479	894	128	5,016	1	768	8
United Kingdom [7]	2,120	7	1,559	76	1,167	165	792	173	717	83
Estonia	0	0	[3] 1,483	[1] 1	1,921	[1] 1	1,944	0	1,085	0
Belgium	5,755	830	1,117	847	1,913	84	3,484	18	756	66
Italy	654	2	24	357	493	24	538	2	107	17
Switzerland	[1] 728	[1] 1	35	1	85	0	15	0	53	0
Total 25 countries	88,774	117,356	77,115	79,536	63,169	64,237	73,412	81,990	73,498	63,082

Bureau of Agricultural Economics. Official sources except otherwise noted.

[1] Year ended July 31, International Yearbook of Agricultural Statistics.
[2] Average of calendar years, 1909–13.
[3] International Crop Report and Agricultural Statistics.
[4] Average for the seasons 1911–12 to 1913–14.
[5] Season 1913–14.
[6] Year ended June 30, International Yearbook of Agricultural Statistics.
[7] Year ended Dec. 31.

TABLE 43.—*Rye: Estimated price per bushel, received by producers, United States, 1909–1928*

Year beginning July	July 15	Aug. 15	Sept. 15	Oct. 15	Nov. 15	Dec. 15	Jan. 15	Feb. 15	Mar. 15	Apr. 15	May 15	June 15	Weighted av.
	Cents	Cents	Cents	Cents	Cents	Cents	Cents	Cents	Cents	Cents	Cents	Cents	Cents
Average:													
1909–1913	74.7	72.4	71.7	72.0	71.7	71.3	72.1	72.2	72.0	72.4	72.8	72.9	72.1
1914–1920	129.2	127.3	126.8	125.8	124.6	125.9	129.0	131.1	135.5	142.1	143.4	139.1	129.3
1921–1925	78.5	77.8	74.3	77.1	76.9	80.7	83.9	85.4	83.0	78.4	78.6	76.9	78.8
1909	80.1	75.4	72.6	73.2	72.7	73.3	75.4	76.3	76.6	75.8	74.8	74.7	74.6
1910	74.5	74.2	73.4	72.2	71.6	72.4	73.2	72.5	73.6	75.6	76.8	77.4	73.4
1911	76.2	76.2	78.3	81.4	83.2	83.0	83.6	84.2	84.6	84.8	85.4	84.8	81.0
1912	80.8	74.4	70.4	69.4	67.6	65.0	66.4	66.0	63.0	62.6	63.2	63.6	68.7
1913	62.0	61.8	63.9	64.0	63.3	63.0	62.1	61.8	62.4	63.0	63.6	63.8	62.9
1914	62.0	68.2	77.2	79.6	83.3	88.4	95.4	103.0	102.9	101.2	100.0	95.9	83.3
1915	91.4	87.2	83.6	83.7	84.6	84.4	86.8	87.0	84.6	83.6	83.8	83.6	85.0
1916	83.4	91.6	101.9	109.7	118.7	120.3	121.0	124.8	130.8	149.8	173.6	180.0	113.0
1917	177.6	170.0	165.8	169.3	167.4	168.2	172.6	187.9	218.0	228.1	204.4	178.8	176.4
1918	166.9	161.6	156.6	153.3	152.1	151.2	145.6	136.3	139.0	150.6	149.6	141.2	152.1
1919	144.2	144.0	137.0	132.8	131.5	142.8	153.4	149.8	150.6	169.6	183.5	186.4	146.9
1920	178.8	168.8	165.6	152.2	134.4	125.8	128.1	128.8	122.4	112.0	108.8	108.0	148.2
1921	101.0	94.0	89.2	81.6	72.2	69.6	70.0	77.0	83.8	85.9	87.8	82.8	86.9
1922	74.0	66.9	63.2	65.2	68.2	70.7	71.7	71.0	70.1	70.8	69.2	62.2	68.1
1923	56.3	55.3	57.2	58.8	62.1	63.9	63.5	64.5	62.8	60.4	60.1	61.6	59.4
1924	68.8	79.8	80.1	105.7	108.6	112.7	126.2	132.2	125.1	100.9	103.6	101.8	96.3
1925	92.3	92.8	81.9	74.1	73.4	86.8	88.2	82.5	73.4	73.8	72.5	76.0	83.1
1926	80.7	86.1	81.6	82.4	83.0	82.4	83.6	88.4	86.4	85.2	90.1	94.9	84.2
1927	91.2	80.6	81.4	81.0	84.0	87.8	88.0	89.5	96.0	99.8	111.5	106.8	84.7
1928	99.2	83.6	81.8	87.1	86.3	87.2							

Bureau of Agricultural Economics. Based on returns from special price reporters. Mean of prices reported on 1st of month and 1st of succeeding month, July, 1909–December, 1923.

TABLE 44.—*Rye No. 2: Weighted average price per bushel of reported cash sales, Minneapolis, 1909–1928*

Year beginning July	July	Aug.	Sept.	Oct.	Nov.	Dec.	Jan.	Feb.	Mar.	Apr.	May	June	Weighted average [1]
	Cts.	Cts.	Cts.	Cts.	Cts.	Cts.	Cts.	Cts.	Cts.	Cts.	Cts.	Cts.	Cts.
Average:													
1909–1913	71	69	69	70	69	69	72	71	72	73	75	70	70
1914–1920	146	139	138	136	138	142	147	145	159	165	167	159	143
1921–1925	86	83	82	83	84	91	95	97	89	86	87	84	87
1909	76	67	66	68	69	72	77	76	74	73	71	69	70
1910	73	73	71	72	74	77	79	78	84	88	101	87	77
1911	79	80	85	92	88	87	90	88	89	89	87	79	86
1912	69	64	62	63	58	56	58	57	55	57	57	56	60
1913	57	61	61	56	54	55	55	56	56	57	60	59	58
1914	58	80	89	87	101	106	115	124	112	111	116	112	98
1915	102	97	90	96	93	92	96	95	89	93	94	94	94
1916	93	115	120	126	144	138	142	142	158	180	226	237	135
1917	220	175	184	181	177	183	193	224	291	274	230	185	193
1918	184	168	160	158	162	157	154	134	154	171	155	145	158
1919	154	148	139	136	138	166	173	153	170	195	208	214	160
1920	209	192	185	166	148	149	158	144	142	128	137	126	161
1921	115	100	99	80	72	78	75	95	97	97	102	86	92
1922	76	69	66	71	81	83	82	80	76	81	72	64	75
1923	61	62	66	66	64	65	67	66	63	61	63	70	65
1924	83	86	95	121	123	133	154	154	130	106	114	111	114
1925	95	100	83	77	81	98	99	91	81	85	83	89	88
1926	102	97	93	95	94	94	99	102	99	99	109	111	98
1927	104	92	92	92	99	102	103	106	114	124	128	123	104
1928	111	94	94	94	98	97							

Bureau of Agricultural Economics. Compiled from Minneapolis Daily Market Record. Chicago prices, 1909–1927 appear in Table 46, 1927 Yearbook.

[1] Average of daily prices weighted by car-lot sales.

TABLE 45.—*Corn: Acreage, production, value, exports, etc., United States, 1890–1928*

Year	Acreage	Average yield per acre	Production	Price per bushel received by producers Dec. 1	Farm value Dec. 1	Price per bushel at Chicago [1]	Foreign trade, including meal, year beginning July 1 [2]			
							Domestic exports	Imports	Net exports [3]	
									Total	Percentage of production
	1,000 acres	*Bushels of 56 lbs. shelled*	*1,000 bushels*	*Cents*	*1,000 dollars*	*Cents*	*1,000 bushels*	*1,000 bushels*	*1,000 bushels*	*Per cent*
1890	70,390	20.7	1,460,406	50.0	729,647	58	32,042	2	32,039	2.2
1891	74,496	27.6	2,055,823	39.7	816,917	47	76,602	16	76,596	3.7
1892	72,610	23.6	1,713,688	38.8	664,390	41	47,122	2	47,120	2.7
1893	74,434	22.9	1,707,572	35.9	612,998	41	66,490	3	66,487	3.9
1894	69,396	19.3	1,339,680	45.1	604,523	44	28,585	17	28,569	2.1
1895	85,567	27.0	2,310,952	25.0	578,408	26	101,100	5	101,096	4.4
1896	86,560	28.9	2,503,484	21.3	532,884	25	178,817	7	178,811	7.1
1897	88,127	24.3	2,144,553	26.0	558,309	30	212,056	4	212,052	9.9
1898	88,304	25.6	2,261,119	28.4	642,747	34	177,255	4	177,252	7.8
1899	*94,914*	*28.1*	*2,666,324*							
1899	94,914	25.9	2,454,628	29.9	734,916	36	213,123	3	213,121	8.7
1900	95,042	26.4	2,505,148	35.1	878,243	43	181,405	5	181,400	7.2
1901	94,636	17.0	1,613,528	60.1	969,285	62	28,029	19	28,011	1.7
1902	95,517	27.4	2,619,499	40.1	1,049,791	47	76,639	41	76,598	2.9
1903	90,661	25.9	2,346,897	42.1	987,882	49	58,222	17	58,210	2.5
1904	93,340	27.1	2,528,662	43.7	1,105,690	48	90,293	16	90,278	3.6
1905	93,573	29.4	2,748,949	40.8	1,120,513	44	119,894	11	119,883	4.4
1906	93,643	30.9	2,897,662	39.3	1,138,053	50	86,368	11	86,358	3.0
1907	94,971	26.5	2,512,065	50.9	1,277,607	68	55,064	20	55,044	2.2
1908	95,603	26.6	2,544,957	60.0	1,527,679	65	37,665	258	37,437	1.5
1909	*98,383*	*25.9*	*2,552,190*							
1909	98,383	26.1	2,572,336	58.6	1,507,185	59	38,128	118	38,010	1.5
1910	104,035	27.7	2,886,260	48.0	1,384,817	53	65,615	53	65,562	2.3
1911	105,825	23.9	2,531,488	61.8	1,565,258	71	41,797	54	41,744	1.6
1912	107,083	29.2	3,124,746	48.7	1,520,454	53	50,780	903	49,913	1.6
1913	105,820	23.1	2,446,988	69.1	1,692,092	70	10,726	12,368	[4] 1,639	
1914	103,435	25.8	2,672,804	64.4	1,722,070	70	50,668	9,899	40,816	1.5
1915	106,197	28.2	2,994,793	57.5	1,722,680	79	39,897	5,211	34,761	1.2
1916	105,296	24.4	2,566,927	88.9	2,280,729	111	66,753	2,270	65,092	2.5
1917	116,730	26.3	3,065,233	127.9	3,920,228	163	49,073	3,197	45,950	1.5
1918	104,467	24.0	2,502,665	136.5	3,416,240	162	23,019	3,346	19,684	.8
1919 [5]	*87,772*	*26.7*	*2,345,833*							
1919	97,170	28.9	2,811,302	134.5	3,780,597	159	16,729	10,283	6,509	.2
1920	101,699	31.5	3,208,584	67.0	2,150,332	62	70,906	5,791	66,116	2.1
1921	103,740	29.6	3,068,569	42.3	1,297,213	55	179,490	142	179,374	5.8
1922	102,846	28.3	2,906,020	65.8	1,910,775	73	96,596	182	96,415	3.3
1923	104,324	29.3	3,053,557	72.6	2,217,229	88	23,135	240	22,896	.7
1924 [5]	*82,329*	*22.2*	*1,823,880*							
1924	100,863	22.9	2,309,414	98.2	2,266,771	106	9,791	4,618	5,348	.2
1925	101,359	28.8	2,916,961	67.4	1,966,761	75	24,783	637	24,150	.8
1926	99,713	27.0	2,692,217	64.2	1,729,457	87	19,819	1,098	18,731	.7
1927	98,393	28.1	2,763,093	72.3	1,997,759	101	19,389	5,463	14,344	.5
1928 [6]	100,761	28.2	2,839,959	75.1	2,132,991					

Bureau of Agricultural Economics. Production figures are estimates of the crop-reporting board and relate to equivalent production of grain on entire acreage grown for all purposes; italic figures are census returns. See 1927 Yearbook, page 774, for data for earlier years.

[1] Prices 1890–1898 are averages of the weekly quotations for No. 2 or better in annual reports of Chicago Board of Trade; subsequently prices are compiled from the Chicago Daily Trade Bulletin, average of daily prices weighted by car-lot sales, No. 3 yellow.

[2] Compiled from Commerce and Navigation of the United States, 1890–1917; Foreign Commerce and Navigation of the United States, 1918; Monthly Summary of Foreign Commerce of the United States, June issues, 1919–1926; January and June issues, 1927–28 and official records of the Bureau of Foreign and Domestic Commerce. Corn—General imports 1890–1909 and 1912–1927; imports for consumption 1910–11. Corn meal—imports for consumption, 1890–1927. Corn meal converted to terms of grain on the basis that 1 barrel is the product of 4 bushels of corn.

[3] Total exports (domestic plus foreign) minus total imports.

[4] Net imports.

[5] Corn harvested for grain; total acreage of corn in 1924 is 98,401,627 acres.

[6] Preliminary.

TABLE 46.—*Corn: Acreage and production, by States, average 1921–1925, annual 1926–1928*

State and division	Acreage				Production			
	Average, 1921–1925	1926	1927	1928 [1]	Average, 1921–1925	1926	1927	1928 [1]
	1,000 acres	*1,000 acres*	*1,000 acres*	*1,000 acres*	*1,000 bush.*	*1,000 bush.*	*1,000 bush.*	*1,000 bush.*
Maine	18	13	14	13	804	455	518	520
New Hampshire	21	15	15	14	979	645	615	560
Vermont	85	84	84	80	3,917	3,612	3,276	3,520
Massachusetts	55	45	46	45	2,453	1,980	1,886	1,890
Rhode Island	11	9	10	10	469	369	380	390
Connecticut	67	54	55	55	3,073	2,268	2,090	2,310
New York	744	670	663	650	27,498	23,450	22,542	22,100
New Jersey	220	188	179	181	9,489	8,648	7,160	6,968
Pennsylvania	1,485	1,394	1,270	1,283	65,393	57,154	50,165	50,037
North Atlantic	2,707	2,472	2,336	2,331	114,076	98,581	88,632	88,295
Ohio	3,736	3,591	3,376	3,646	146,588	147,231	109,720	136,725
Indiana	4,722	4,672	4,205	4,583	171,184	177,536	132,458	161,322
Illinois	9,030	9,205	8,469	9,570	329,215	322,175	254,070	367,488
Michigan	1,672	1,593	1,418	1,461	59,373	54,162	38,995	51,135
Wisconsin	2,188	2,119	2,100	2,121	87,511	73,106	68,250	91,203
Minnesota	4,165	4,343	4,172	4,089	143,116	147,662	127,246	143,115
Iowa	10,707	11,170	10,901	11,174	426,298	435,630	386,986	476,012
Missouri	6,390	6,471	5,796	6,260	181,585	176,011	168,084	181,540
North Dakota	924	1,009	959	997	24,043	18,162	23,975	24,426
South Dakota	4,257	4,630	4,655	4,469	112,350	83,340	134,995	93,849
Nebraska	8,155	8,994	8,805	8,937	218,107	139,407	291,446	212,701
Kansas	5,546	5,563	5,897	6,634	111,577	61,193	176,910	179,118
North Central	61,493	63,360	60,753	63,941	2,010,948	1,835,615	1,913,135	2,118,634
Delaware	166	138	135	136	5,440	4,278	4,725	4,488
Maryland	602	554	515	530	23,467	22,049	22,660	19,345
Virginia	1,773	1,694	1,626	1,642	44,763	46,585	47,967	45,155
West Virginia	558	485	441	459	18,510	16,005	14,774	16,524
North Carolina	2,490	2,376	2,352	2,305	49,094	52,272	53,626	42,642
South Carolina	1,860	1,426	1,497	1,422	26,841	22,103	25,449	17,064
Georgia	4,191	3,817	3,893	3,620	51,840	55,346	54,502	38,010
Florida	713	551	573	607	9,786	7,714	7,449	7,891
South Atlantic	12,352	11,041	11,032	10,721	229,740	226,352	231,152	191,119
Kentucky	3,187	3,069	2,885	3,029	85,216	101,277	75,010	66,638
Tennessee	3,215	3,099	2,944	2,915	73,997	85,222	70,656	56,842
Alabama	3,305	2,825	2,800	2,650	45,525	45,765	44,800	30,475
Mississippi	2,514	1,918	1,918	1,765	40,653	36,826	34,140	22,945
Arkansas	2,197	2,026	1,925	2,002	38,896	41,533	36,575	33,033
Louisiana	1,516	1,127	1,161	1,242	25,030	19,722	20,318	21,114
Oklahoma	2,992	2,353	3,177	3,050	49,125	61,178	84,190	70,150
Texas	4,771	3,844	5,189	4,722	90,444	106,863	119,347	99,162
South Central	23,698	20,261	21,999	21,375	448,886	498,386	485,036	400,359
Montana	320	359	305	274	6,595	3,949	7,168	5,206
Idaho	63	66	76	53	2,382	2,706	3,116	2,438
Wyoming	138	176	176	167	2,905	3,520	3,520	3,006
Colorado	1,334	1,496	1,284	1,438	21,686	10,472	19,902	18,694
New Mexico	228	221	166	199	4,065	4,420	2,490	3,482
Arizona	35	40	44	39	974	1,120	1,408	1,014
Utah	23	18	19	18	560	432	513	522
Nevada	1	2	2	2	34	48	50	44
Washington	61	49	43	46	2,273	1,715	1,591	1,794
Oregon	67	75	81	82	2,120	2,475	2,916	2,952
California	105	77	77	75	3,661	2,426	2,464	2,400
Far Western	2,377	2,579	2,273	2,393	47,255	33,283	45,138	41,552
United States	102,626	99,713	98,393	100,761	2,850,904	2,692,217	2,763,093	2,839,959

Bureau of Agricultural Economics. Estimates of the crop-reporting board.

[1] Preliminary.

Table 47.—*Corn: Utilization for grain, silage, hogging down, grazing, and forage, by States, 1927 and 1928*

State	1927					1928				
	For grain		For silage		Hogging down, grazing, and forage acreage	For grain		For silage		Hogging down, grazing, and forage acreage
	Acreage	Production	Acreage	Production		Acreage	Production	Acreage	Production	
	1,000 acres	*1,000 bushels*	*1,000 acres*	*1,000 tons*	*1,000 acres*	*1,000 acres*	*1,000 bushels*	*1,000 acres*	*1,000 tons*	*1,000 acres*
Maine	1	37	10	112	3	1	40	9	94	3
New Hampshire	3	123	10	107	2	3	120	9	104	2
Vermont	8	312	64	672	12	8	352	60	690	12
Massachusetts	11	451	28	322	7	11	462	27	310	7
Rhode Island	3	114	5	52	2	3	117	5	55	2
Connecticut	20	760	31	341	4	21	882	30	315	4
New York	160	5,440	366	3,367	137	165	5,610	348	3,062	137
New Jersey	142	5,680	29	290	8	143	5,506	29	270	9
Pennsylvania	953	37,644	200	1,500	117	982	38,298	184	1,380	117
Ohio	2,866	93,145	252	1,814	258	3,135	117,562	227	1,771	284
Indiana	3,450	113,160	190	1,235	565	3,810	137,160	180	1,260	593
Illinois	7,410	225,264	356	2,243	703	8,553	331,856	335	2,345	682
Michigan	720	19,800	380	2,280	318	794	27,790	365	2,592	302
Wisconsin	650	21,125	1,150	7,475	300	888	38,184	978	7,628	255
Minnesota	2,322	70,821	450	2,925	1,400	2,391	83,685	438	3,022	1,260
Iowa	9,026	320,423	289	2,312	1,586	9,345	398,097	275	2,255	1,554
Missouri	5,341	154,889	61	427	394	5,838	169,302	67	436	355
North Dakota	212	5,512	67	234	680	218	5,559	69	242	710
South Dakota	3,270	96,465	65	358	1,320	2,879	61,898	72	346	1,518
Nebraska	7,552	249,971	39	254	1,214	7,559	179,904	43	202	1,335
Kansas	5,463	163,890	80	512	354	6,141	165,807	104	582	389
Delaware	131	4,585	3	27	1	132	4,356	3	24	1
Maryland	473	20,812	27	197	15	487	17,776	27	189	16
Virginia	1,528	45,076	58	435	40	1,547	42,542	61	488	34
West Virginia	406	13,601	22	147	13	422	15,192	24	158	13
North Carolina	2,251	51,323	16	88	85	2,207	40,830	14	70	84
South Carolina	1,440	24,480	7	32	50	1,365	16,380	7	28	50
Georgia	3,805	53,270	9	32	79	3,534	37,107	9	32	77
Florida	561	7,293	2	11	10	594	7,722	2	11	11
Kentucky	2,695	70,070	40	260	150	2,820	62,040	44	308	165
Tennessee	2,787	66,888	31	146	126	2,760	53,820	30	150	125
Alabama	2,760	44,160	5	21	35	2,560	29,440	5	16	85
Mississippi	1,822	32,432	13	65	83	1,627	21,151	14	66	124
Arkansas	1,844	35,036	4	20	77	1,912	31,548	5	25	85
Louisiana	1,114	19,495	10	35	37	1,191	20,247	10	50	41
Oklahoma	3,113	82,494	10	65	54	2,986	68,678	10	55	54
Texas	5,049	116,127	10	40	130	4,626	97,146	9	36	87
Montana	93	2,186	9	36	203	84	1,596	9	34	181
Idaho	52	2,132	10	75	14	32	1,472	9	81	12
Wyoming	107	2,140	4	20	65	107	1,926	4	18	56
Colorado	941	15,056	51	291	292	1,007	13,594	57	342	374
New Mexico	138	2,208	5	20	23	165	2,970	7	28	27
Arizona	31	992	4	28	9	26	676	4	28	9
Utah	10	280	4	40	5	9	270	4	34	5
Nevada	1	28	1	7	0	1	23	1	7	0
Washington	19	703	15	150	9	20	780	16	144	10
Oregon	45	1,665	27	173	9	45	1,665	28	196	9
California	39	1,287	20	188	18	37	1,221	20	200	18
United States	82,838	2,300,845	4,539	31,481	11,016	85,191	2,360,359	4,287	31,779	11,283

Bureau of Agricultural Economics. Estimates of the crop-reporting board.

Table 48.—*Corn: Yield per acre and estimated price per bushel, December 1, by States, average 1914–1920, 1921–1925, annual 1924–1928*

State and division	Yield per acre							Estimated price per bushel						
	Av. 1914–1920	Av. 1921–1925	1924	1925	1926	1927	1928	Av. 1914–1920	Av. 1921–1925	1924	1925	1926	1927	1928
	Bush.	Bush.	Bush.	Bush.	Bush.	Bush.	Bush.	Cts.	Cts.	Cts.	Cts.	Cts.	Cts.	Cts.
Maine	44.6	43.4	43.0	45.0	35.0	37.0	40.0	144	107	136	112	100	110	115
New Hampshire	44.8	47.2	48.0	50.0	43.0	41.0	40.0	136	99	134	100	100	105	120
Vermont	44.6	46.2	47.0	48.0	43.0	39.0	44.0	137	99	118	100	95	105	110
Massachusetts	46.5	45.2	45.0	50.0	44.0	41.0	42.0	138	105	129	110	115	120	130
Rhode Island	41.0	41.8	40.0	45.0	41.0	38.0	39.0	160	121	140	120	115	120	135
Connecticut	47.0	46.2	43.0	50.0	42.0	38.0	42.0	143	105	120	110	115	120	130
New York	37.3	36.8	34.0	36.0	35.0	34.0	34.0	132	93	117	97	86	96	99
New Jersey	40.5	43.0	34.0	52.0	46.0	40.0	38.5	116	81	116	73	80	85	97
Pennsylvania	41.6	43.9	36.5	51.0	41.0	39.5	39.0	114	83	118	80	78	91	93
North Atlantic	40.6	42.0	36.3	46.8	39.9	37.9	37.9	120.8	87.3	118.2	85.3	82.7	93.9	97.7
Ohio	38.9	39.0	26.0	48.0	41.0	32.5	37.5	95	68	104	57	60	77	76
Indiana	35.9	36.1	25.6	43.5	38.0	31.5	35.2	89	61	94	55	50	68	69
Illinois	34.1	36.4	33.0	42.0	35.0	30.0	38.4	88	63	95	58	56	71	70
Michigan	31.9	35.5	28.5	40.0	34.0	27.5	35.0	109	75	106	75	73	85	84
Wisconsin	35.7	40.0	26.0	46.5	34.5	32.5	43.0	103	73	105	72	75	84	78
Minnesota	34.1	34.6	27.0	36.0	34.0	30.5	35.0	84	58	85	56	56	64	62
Iowa	37.9	39.9	28.0	43.9	39.0	35.5	42.6	83	59	93	56	56	69	67
Missouri	26.4	28.4	24.0	29.5	27.2	29.0	29.0	96	69	96	69	68	75	73
North Dakota	21.9	26.8	21.5	23.5	18.0	25.0	24.5	100	54	76	55	68	62	61
South Dakota	29.1	26.8	21.3	17.5	18.0	29.0	21.0	81	53	80	60	58	57	62
Nebraska	26.5	26.8	22.0	26.0	15.5	33.1	23.8	84	58	91	61	68	62	71
Kansas	17.3	20.3	21.7	16.6	11.0	30.0	27.0	95	62	87	66	70	61	65
North Central	31.2	32.7	25.8	34.4	29.0	31.5	33.1	88.3	62.0	92.7	59.9	59.7	68.0	69.3
Delaware	33.4	32.7	27.0	37.0	31.0	35.0	33.0	101	75	112	65	64	80	88
Maryland	37.8	38.9	31.0	45.0	39.8	44.0	36.5	102	76	111	70	64	80	88
Virginia	27.1	25.0	21.0	22.0	27.5	29.5	27.5	118	94	126	101	85	92	100
West Virginia	31.7	32.9	26.0	36.5	33.0	33.5	36.0	127	96	124	100	94	100	103
North Carolina	20.3	19.7	18.0	18.5	22.0	22.8	18.5	131	101	124	110	88	91	103
South Carolina	17.4	14.3	12.0	12.3	15.5	17.0	12.0	142	100	123	110	90	90	106
Georgia	15.0	12.3	11.5	10.7	14.5	14.0	10.5	122	92	112	100	76	81	105
Florida	15.1	13.8	13.5	15.0	14.0	13.0	13.0	109	90	112	100	92	97	109
South Atlantic	20.5	18.5	16.0	17.6	20.5	21.0	17.8	122.9	92.8	119.2	98.8	82.4	88.2	101.0
Kentucky	27.9	26.7	25.0	26.5	33.0	26.0	22.0	102	78	102	81	65	88	96
Tennessee	25.6	23.0	21.5	20.0	27.5	24.0	19.5	104	84	108	89	66	83	100
Alabama	15.3	13.7	12.5	13.5	16.2	16.0	11.5	112	96	122	100	76	92	110
Mississippi	17.1	16.0	12.0	18.0	19.2	17.8	13.0	112	94	126	94	82	93	102
Arkansas	19.5	17.4	16.0	14.0	20.5	19.0	16.5	118	89	107	97	80	87	91
Louisiana	18.8	16.3	11.5	18.0	17.5	17.5	17.0	111	92	115	94	90	90	94
Oklahoma	17.6	16.2	19.0	7.5	26.0	26.5	23.0	99	74	89	90	56	59	63
Texas	19.9	17.6	16.0	8.5	27.8	23.0	21.0	112	91	110	110	60	65	78
South Central	20.2	18.7	17.3	15.9	24.6	22.0	18.7	106.2	85.5	107.2	91.5	67.5	77.3	88.1
Montana	18.7	21.0	18.0	16.5	11.0	23.5	19.0	113	76	99	95	92	72	82
Idaho	34.3	37.3	30.7	41.0	41.0	41.0	46.0	120	79	113	75	90	82	92
Wyoming	22.4	21.6	12.0	23.0	20.0	20.0	18.0	109	69	94	70	72	74	75
Colorado	19.4	16.1	10.0	15.0	7.0	15.5	13.0	97	64	88	70	71	68	68
New Mexico	23.3	17.6	18.0	18.0	20.0	15.0	17.5	128	95	110	100	87	93	89
Arizona	29.0	27.4	22.0	26.0	28.0	32.0	26.0	164	118	125	130	120	115	125
Utah	28.0	23.6	20.0	24.0	24.0	27.0	29.0	132	100	145	100	115	110	120
Nevada	32.3	24.2	22.4	25.0	24.0	25.0	22.0	141	118	121	120	120	115	112
Washington	34.0	36.6	30.0	35.0	35.0	37.0	39.0	127	99	112	95	95	90	99
Oregon	31.0	31.5	30.5	29.0	33.0	36.0	32.0	121	99	121	107	100	95	100
California	34.4	34.9	33.5	35.1	31.5	32.0	32.0	139	108	138	118	106	108	105
Far Western	22.7	19.8	14.4	18.5	12.9	19.9	17.4	113.4	78.3	101.6	82.9	85.5	78.1	81.3
United States	27.0	27.8	22.9	28.8	27.0	28.1	28.2	96.7	69.3	98.2	67.4	64.2	72.3	75.1

Bureau of Agricultural Economics. Estimates of the crop-reporting board.

TABLE 49.—*Corn: Acreage, yield per acre, and production in specified countries, average 1909–1913, 1921–1925, annual 1926–1928*

Country	Acreage					Yield per acre					Production				
	Average 1909–1913[1]	Average 1921–1925	1926	1927	1928, preliminary	Average 1909–1913[1]	Average 1921–1925	1926	1927	1928, preliminary	Average 1909–1913	Average 1921–1925	1926	1927	1928, preliminary
	1,000 acres	*1,000 acres*	*1,000 acres*	*1,000 acres*	*1,000 acres*	*Bushels*	*Bushels*	*Bushels*	*Bushels*	*Bushels*	*1,000 bushels*	*1,000 bushels*	*1,000 bushels*	*1,000 bushels*	*1,000 bushels*
NORTHERN HEMISPHERE															
NORTH AMERICA															
Canada	309	293	210	132	139	56.0	44.3	37.2	32.3	37.7	17,297	12,974	7,813	4,262	5,241
United States	104,229	102,826	99,713	98,303	100,761	26.0	27.8	27.0	28.1	28.2	2,712,364	2,850,904	2,692,217	2,763,093	2,839,959
Mexico	[2]6,093	7,498	8,106	8,020	—	[2]13.5	11.3	10.7	10.1	—	133,362	84,406	86,578	81,165	—
Guatemala	—	390	253	278	—	—	11.8	14.1	15.5	—	[3]6,245	4,614	3,563	4,321	—
Total North American countries reporting area and production, all years	104,538	103,119	99,923	98,525	100,900	26.1	27.8	27.0	28.1	28.2	2,729,661	2,863,878	2,700,030	2,767,355	2,845,200
Estimated North American total	111,700	111,500	109,000	107,500	109,900	—	—	—	—	—	2,877,000	2,964,000	2,805,000	2,864,000	2,943,000
EUROPE															
France	1,160	830	834	861	844	19.4	17.8	15.2	24.1	17.2	22,467	14,754	12,686	20,721	14,558
Spain	1,134	1,167	1,006	1,143	—	23.4	22.2	17.1	22.8	—	26,548	25,933	17,186	26,104	23,877
Italy	4,090	3,802	3,769	3,540	3,485	25.1	24.9	31.3	23.7	18.6	102,676	94,800	118,088	83,938	64,991
Austria	190	140	153	147	146	23.8	26.7	25.0	33.7	26.5	4,530	3,739	3,825	4,948	3,862
Czechoslovakia	376	390	393	391	391	22.3	26.7	26.6	30.1	20.4	8,398	10,444	10,452	11,754	7,986
Hungary	2,192	2,437	2,631	2,625	2,637	27.7	23.9	29.1	26.0	16.4	60,813	58,354	76,544	68,347	43,324
Yugoslavia	4,786	4,759	4,929	5,106	5,696	23.4	23.0	27.2	16.5	14.3	111,897	109,399	134,249	83,007	81,212
Bulgaria	1,492	1,458	1,515	1,682	1,595	17.6	14.4	18.0	12.5	11.5	26,277	21,021	27,312	20,954	18,292
Rumania	[4]9,644	8,799	10,031	10,427	11,010	[4]20.0	15.9	23.9	13.3	9.8	[4]193,209	140,201	239,492	139,092	108,380
Poland	164	177	195	196	201	17.2	18.6	21.4	20.6	—	3,300	2,822	4,166	4,042	—
Russia, European and Asiatic	3,246	5,293	7,294	7,131	10,697	16.1	17.4	19.7	20.9	—	52,185	92,262	143,354	148,834	—
Total European countries reporting area and production, all years	23,930	22,615	24,255	24,779	25,804	22.2	20.0	25.7	17.5	13.3	530,267	452,712	622,648	432,761	342,605
Estimated European total, excluding Russia	26,400	25,200	26,800	27,400	28,500	—	—	—	—	—	[5]581,000	500,000	665,000	479,000	388,000
AFRICA															
Morocco	(438)	437	562	527	637	—	8.3	9.8	9.1	10.2	(3,500)	3,629	5,523	4,788	6,477
Egypt	[6]1,705	1,985	2,165	2,214	—	[6]37.7	34.8	37.2	—	—	[6]64,273	69,096	80,585	—	—
Estimated African total	2,600	3,100	3,400	3,700	3,800	—	—	—	—	—	75,000	84,000	99,000	96,000	99,000

	Acreage (1,000 acres)					Yield per acre (bushels)					Production (1,000 bushels)				
ASIA															
India	6,372	5,937	5,504	5,555	—	[3]13.9	13.9	13.6	13.8	—	[3]82,620	82,482	74,960	76,760	—
Japan	133	141	129	—	—	25.5	25.8	23.0	—	—	3,391	3,634	2,971	—	—
Chosen	156	231	246	251	—	14.3	12.2	11.4	11.3	—	2,236	2,819	2,804	2,827	—
Kwantung	99	162	196	191	—	17.5	17.1	14.1	17.7	—	[2]1,737	2,771	2,755	3,387	—
Philippines	[4]812	1,338	1,318	1,387	—	[4]9.2	12.5	13.7	13.8	—	[4]7,461	16,755	18,036	19,145	—
Estimated Asiatic total	9,800	10,500	9,700	10,000	9,900						148,000	183,000	205,000	210,000	206,000
Total Northern Hemisphere countries reporting area and production all years	128,906	126,171	124,740	123,831	—	25.3	26.3	26.7	25.9	—	3,263,428	3,320,219	3,328,201	3,204,904	—
Estimated Northern Hemisphere total excluding Russia	150,500	150,600	148,900	148,600	152,100						[5]3,681,000	3,731,000	3,774,000	3,649,000	3,636,000
SOUTHERN HEMISPHERE															
Brazil	(6,000)	6,980	6,919	7,831			25.4	20.1	20.4		(140,000)	177,338	138,808	160,075	
Chile	56	63	58	62		26.0	23.3	27.2	8.3		1,455	1,466	1,577	1,577	
Uruguay	589	492	494	598		10.4	11.3	6.8	28.5		6,120	5,577	3,344	4,956	
Argentina	8,710	8,688	10,599	10,739		22.0	25.2	30.3	14.3		191,698	218,969	320,853	305,691	
Union of South Africa	(2,300)	4,456	5,192	4,802			12.8	12.6	14.6		[4]33,517	56,890	65,203	68,463	
Southern Rhodesia	161	223	267	277		11.4	18.4	22.5			1,834	4,105	6,015	4,054	
Java and Madura	(3,000)	3,982	4,771	—			15.2	16.7			(42,000)	60,616	79,700	78,618	
Australia	353	326	286	—		28.5	26.5	24.4			10,057	8,641	6,970	9,750	
Total Southern Hemisphere countries reporting area and production all years through 1927	17,760	20,839	23,471	24,247		21.0	22.2	22.8	22.4		373,169	462,879	534,223	543,239	
Estimated Southern Hemisphere total	21,900	24,700	30,900	31,500							445,000	564,000	667,000	675,000	
Total Northern and Southern Hemisphere countries reporting area and production all years through 1927	146,666	147,010	148,211	148,078		24.8	25.7	26.1	25.3		3,636,597	3,783,098	3,862,424	3,748,143	
Estimated world total excluding Russia	172,400	177,300	179,800	180,100							[5]4,128,000	4,295,000	4,441,000	4,324,000	4,126,000

Bureau of Agricultural Economics. Official sources and International Institute of Agriculture. Figures refer to the crop harvested in the calendar year in the Northern Hemisphere and the succeeding harvest in the Southern Hemisphere.

[1] Where changes in boundary have occurred, the averages reported are estimates for the crop within present boundaries.

[2] 1 year only.

[3] 2-year average.

[4] 4-year average.

[5] The estimate for the 5-year period, 1909–1913 given in this table is somewhat larger than the figure obtained by averaging the same 5-year period in Table 50. This is because in this table estimates for warring countries are for postwar boundaries, whereas in Table 50 they are for pre-war territory. As a result in excluding Russia, which lost territory in the war, a smaller area is excluded in this table than in Table 50.

[6] Includes some sorghum.

TABLE 50.—*Corn: World production, 1900–1928*

Year	Estimated world production, excluding Russia	Estimated European production, excluding Russia	Selected countries						
			United States	Italy	Rumania	Argentina	Brazil	Yugoslavia	Russia[1]
	1,000,000 bushels	*1,000,000 bushels*	*1,000,000 bushels*	*1,000,000 bushels*	*1,000,000 bushels*	*1,000,000 bushels*	*1,000,000 bushels*	*1,000,000 bushels*	*1,000,000 bushels*
1900	3,582	440	2,505	88	85	99	----------	18	34
1901	2,745	497	1,614	100	117	84	----------	19	68
1902	3,683	392	2,616	71	68	149	----------	18	49
1903	3,551	459	2,347	89	80	175	----------	19	51
1904	3,502	279	2,529	91	20	141	----------	9	26
1905	3,902	404	2,749	97	59	195	----------	21	34
1906	4,088	533	2,898	93	131	72	----------	28	92
1907	3,768	441	2,512	88	58	136	----------	18	64
1908	3,830	465	2,545	96	79	177	----------	21	82
1909	3,858	499	2,572	99	70	175	----------	34	55
1910	4,060	564	2,886	102	104	28	----------	29	102
1911	3,908	501	2,531	94	111	296	----------	27	95
1912	4,451	547	3,125	99	104	197	----------	----------	94
1913	3,890	576	2,447	108	115	263	----------	----------	84
1914	4,186	559	2,673	105	103	325	----------	----------	[2]90
1915	4,352	520	2,995	122	86	161	----------	----------	[3]72
1916	3,770	389	2,567	82	----------	59	204	----------	[4]62
1917	4,178	351	3,065	83	----------	171	95	----------	----------
1918	3,579	299	2,503	77	31	224	87	----------	----------
1919	4,242	454	2,811	86	[5]141	259	197	----------	----------
1920	4,689	520	3,209	89	182	230	186	[5]101	46
1921	4,315	394	3,069	92	111	176	181	74	46
1922	4,240	425	2,906	77	120	176	202	90	81
1923	4,519	468	3,054	89	151	277	180	85	67
1924	3,872	589	2,309	106	155	186	162	149	91
1925	4,530	626	2,917	110	164	280	162	149	177
1926	4,441	665	2,692	118	239	321	139	134	143
1927	4,324	479	2,763	84	139	306	160	83	149
1928[6]	----------	389	2,840	65	108	----------	----------	81	----------

Bureau of Agricultural Economics. Official sources and International Institute of Agriculture. For each year is shown the production during the calendar year in the Northern Hemisphere and the succeeding harvest in the Southern Hemisphere.

[1] Includes all Russian territory reporting for the years shown.
[2] Total Russian Empire exclusive of the 10 Vistula Provinces of Russian Poland and the Province of Batum in Transcaucasia.
[3] Exclusive of Russian Poland, Lithuania, parts of present Latvia and the Ukraine, and the Provinces of Batum and Elizabetpol in Transcaucasia.
[4] Beginning this year estimates within present boundaries of the Union of Socialist Soviet Republics, exclusive of Turkestan, Transcaucasia, and the Far East, which territory in 1924 produced 26,048,000 bushels.
[5] Production in present boundaries beginning this year, therefore not comparable with earlier years.
[6] Preliminary.

TABLE 51.—*Corn: Monthly marketings by farmers, as reported by about 3,500 mills and elevators, United States, 1917–1927*

Year beginning July	Percentage of year's receipts												
	July	Aug.	Sept.	Oct.	Nov.	Dec.	Jan.	Feb.	Mar.	Apr.	May	June	Season
1917	5.3	4.0	3.4	3.8	8.8	12.2	14.2	16.1	13.7	7.1	5.6	5.8	100.0
1918	6.7	6.9	8.4	6.7	7.3	12.0	15.0	7.2	7.5	8.2	8.0	6.1	100.0
1919	4.5	5.6	4.9	5.6	9.2	15.0	12.9	9.5	8.7	5.9	7.6	10.6	100.0
1920	5.4	5.6	6.9	5.3	7.1	11.3	14.3	11.7	8.9	5.6	8.5	9.4	100.0
1921	4.9	7.3	8.6	6.7	6.6	12.4	13.8	12.4	7.5	4.7	7.6	7.5	100.0
1922	6.8	7.5	9.1	8.2	8.7	13.6	10.7	11.0	6.6	5.3	6.1	6.4	100.0
1923	6.8	7.2	6.1	5.6	10.4	12.3	12.9	13.3	7.4	6.1	5.9	6.0	100.0
1924	6.6	6.2	6.5	7.0	11.1	13.0	13.6	9.5	8.1	6.3	7.8	4.3	100.0
1925	5.1	7.6	5.9	9.3	9.3	14.6	12.1	10.4	8.5	5.3	7.1	8.2	100.0
1926	5.7	6.2	6.6	10.1	9.1	12.9	11.7	10.8	6.9	4.8	6.1	9.1	100.0
1927	5.1	6.5	6.3	6.2	8.6	15.5	13.8	11.7	8.9	5.4	6.6	5.4	100.0

Bureau of Agricultural Economics.

TABLE 52.—*Corn: Farm stocks, growing conditions, and shipments, United States, 1909–1928*

| Year beginning November | Stocks of old corn on farms Nov. 1 [1] | Condition of new crop | | | | Proportion merchantable [1] | Stocks of corn on farms on Mar. 1 following [1] | Shipped out of county where grown [1] |
		July 1	Aug. 1	Sept. 1	Oct. 1			
	1,000 bush.	*P. ct.*	*P. ct.*	*P. ct.*	*P. ct.*	*P. ct.*	*1,000 bush.*	*1,000 bush.*
1909	77,403	89.3	84.4	74.6	73.8	82.7	980,848	620,057
1910	113,919	85.4	79.3	78.2	80.3	86.4	1,165,378	661,777
1911	123,824	80.1	69.6	70.3	70.4	80.1	884,059	517,766
1912	64,764	81.5	80.0	82.1	82.2	85.0	1,290,642	680,831
1913	137,972	86.9	75.8	65.1	65.3	80.1	866,352	422,059
1914	80,046	85.8	74.8	71.7	72.9	84.5	910,894	498,285
1915	96,009	81.2	79.5	78.8	79.7	71.1	1,116,559	560,824
1916	87,908	82.0	75.3	71.3	71.5	83.9	782,303	450,589
1917	34,448	81.1	78.8	76.7	75.9	60.0	1,253,290	678,027
1918	114,678	87.1	78.5	67.4	68.6	82.4	855,269	362,589
1919	69,835	86.7	81.7	80.0	81.3	87.1	1,045,575	470,328
1920	139,083	84.6	86.7	86.4	89.1	86.9	1,564,832	705,481
1921	285,769	91.1	84.3	85.1	84.8	87.5	1,305,559	587,893
1922	177,287	85.1	85.6	78.6	78.4	88.3	1,093,306	518,779
1923	83,856	84.9	84.0	83.3	82.0	80.8	1,153,847	600,745
1924	102,429	72.0	70.7	66.4	65.3	66.0	757,890	417,780
1925	58,248	86.4	79.8	75.5	76.2	78.8	1,329,581	578,551
1926	183,015	77.9	72.5	73.8	72.4	71.1	1,134,370	447,102
1927	113,412	69.9	71.2	69.7	73.6	73.4	1,011,908	501,748
1928 [2]	53,753	78.1	83.3	78.4	77.7			

Bureau of Agricultural Economics. Estimates of the crop-reporting board.

[1] Based on reported percentages of entire crop on farms, proportion merchantable, and per cent shipped out of county where grown.
[2] Preliminary.

TABLE 53.—*Corn: Receipts at primary markets, averages by groups, 1909–1925, annual 1921–1927*

Year beginning November	Chicago	St. Louis	Kansas City	Peoria	Omaha	Indianapolis	Total 10 markets [1]
	1,000 bushels	*1,000 bushels*	*1,000 bushels*	*1,000 bushels*	*1,000 bushels*	*1,000 bushels*	*1,000 bushels*
Average:							
1909–1913	107,215	22,694	19,862	17,030	24,361	18,385	232,934
1914–1920	102,255	22,726	18,402	25,709	26,112	20,347	245,238
1921–1925	115,756	30,949	18,569	22,380	23,105	18,767	266,365
1921	187,884	34,055	16,031	24,960	31,115	21,291	375,409
1922	116,711	30,263	15,595	21,284	23,308	18,839	253,590
1923	101,200	39,289	21,105	17,744	27,679	17,728	274,128
1924	80,700	23,185	21,470	21,234	13,345	17,613	202,504
1925	92,283	27,952	18,643	26,678	20,076	18,363	226,192
1926	91,880	21,039	14,767	23,292	20,482	19,977	217,881
1927 [2]	105,134	34,943	47,603	23,434	31,019	22,712	290,442

Bureau of Agricultural Economics. Compiled from reports of Chicago Board of Trade, Duluth Board of Trade, Indianapolis Board of Trade, Kansas City Board of Trade, Omaha Grain Exchange, St. Louis Merchants Exchange, Milwaukee Chamber of Commerce, Minneapolis Chamber of Commerce, and American Elevator and Grain Trade.

[1] Includes also Milwaukee, Minneapolis, Duluth, and Toledo.
[2] Beginning January, 1928, figures are subject to revision.

TABLE 54.—*Shelled corn: Classification of receipts graded by licensed inspectors, all inspection points*

TOTAL OF ALL CLASSES AND SUBCLASSES UNDER EACH GRADE, BY CARS, ANNUAL, 1917–1927

Year and class	Receipts of—							
	No. 1	No. 2	No. 3	No. 4	No. 5	No. 6	Sample grade	Total
Year beginning Nov. 1—	*Cars*	*Cars*	*Cars*	*Cars*	*Cars*	*Cars*	*Cars*	*Cars*
1917	2, 281	18, 714	58, 562	56, 240	45, 610	44, 621	98, 844	324, 872
1918	12, 661	34, 727	40, 872	41, 491	28, 832	16, 061	19, 638	194, 262
1919	28, 517	47, 961	38, 774	56, 647	27, 313	9, 188	13, 058	221, 458
1920	68, 550	88, 875	64, 237	63, 081	21, 176	9, 420	8, 738	324, 077
1921	30, 970	197, 254	115, 207	42, 880	21, 963	15, 979	4, 951	429, 204
1922	21, 580	141, 563	98, 932	24, 262	4, 270	3, 526	3, 711	297, 844
1923	3, 038	59, 592	111, 932	69, 365	35, 905	15, 410	10, 742	305, 984
1924	7, 883	80, 883	56, 542	34, 431	31, 370	17, 252	12, 345	240, 706
1925	3, 358	59, 985	62, 757	51, 092	48, 348	40, 116	31, 473	297, 129
1926	1, 616	34, 390	57, 931	48, 217	50, 195	46, 180	31, 171	269, 700
1927	9, 682	87, 801	78, 352	47, 890	34, 638	27, 553	29, 006	314, 922

TOTAL INSPECTIONS BY GRADE AND CLASS, BY CARS, NOV. 1, 1927, TO OCT. 31, 1928

Class:								
White	3, 066	16, 854	14, 293	6, 638	3, 708	3, 279	3, 703	51, 541
Yellow	5, 186	43, 970	40, 988	30, 602	25, 818	20, 021	19, 559	186, 144
Mixed	1, 430	26, 977	23, 071	10, 650	5, 112	4, 253	5, 744	77, 237

Bureau of Agricultural Economics.

TABLE 55.—*Corn, including meal in terms of grain: International trade, average 1910–1914, annual 1925–1928*

Country	Year ended June 30									
	Average 1910–1914		1925		1926		1927		1928 preliminary	
	Imports	Exports	Imports	Exports	Imports	Exports	Imports	Exports	Imports	Exports
PRINCIPAL EXPORT-ING COUNTRIES	*1,000 bushels*	*1,000 bushels*	*1,000 bushels*	*1,000 bushels*	*1,000 bushels*	*1,000 bushels*	*1,000 bushels*	*1,000 bushels*	*1,000 bushels*	*1,000 bushels*
Argentina_____	[1] [2]	[1] 115,749	[2] 2	158,626	[2] 2	142,956	[2] 7	272,454	_____	279,455
United States_____	[3] 4,441	41,409	4,617	9,791	635	24,783	1,098	19,819	5,463	19,410
Rumania_____	[1][3] 364	[1][3] 46,998	12	24,631	21	21,239	0	[4] 59,037	0	_____
Yugoslavia [4]_____	0	0	0	37,713	0	41,122	0	[5] 14,496	0	[5] 671
Union of South Africa_____	[1] 143	[1] 3,952	[2] 23	6,992	[2] 20	38,332	[2] 23	1,430	[2] 23	17,620
Russia_____	[6] 299	[6] 28,354	0	6,836	0	7,867	0	8,170	_____	_____
Bulgaria_____	[1] 44	[6] 9,234	0	5,624	0	3,799	0	5,365	0	2,366
Hungary_____	0	0	116	[4] 3,296	46	8,752	330	2,524	688	2,028
Dutch East Indies [2]_	0	[1] 1,215	0	[4] 3,677	7	3,310	10	2,684	10	1,536
French Indo-China [4]_	0	0	0	1,578	0	2,374	0	2,604	_____	_____
British India_____	0	[1] 7 580	0	715	0	38	0	2	0	1,048
China [2]_____	[8] 38	[8] 148	89	545	0	758	0	983	0	490
PRINCIPAL IMPORT-ING COUNTRIES										
United Kingdom____	80,441	[1] 115	71,131	3,049	70,914	2,593	71,196	2,794	75,838	2,552
Netherlands_____	[6] 30,377	[6] 8,641	33,367	175	38,965	443	47,149	736	53,275	729
Germany_____	32,056	2	22,268	187	19,679	103	57,910	4	72,050	4
France_____	19,793	88	21,255	99	21,326	108	29,123	94	25,539	32
Belgium_____	25,818	8,238	19,199	537	22,588	655	26,873	1,501	33,325	1,117
Denmark_____	[6] 11,777	0	20,740	0	16,198	0	22,727	0	29,730	0
Irish Free State_____	0	0	15,227	125	14,127	92	15,679	172	16,847	152
Spain_____	2,023	49	13,260	1	18,547	1	11,540	1	_____	_____
Italy_____	14,829	265	6,406	708	14,232	119	16,134	23	21,135	24
Canada_____	10,678	27	7,735	33	9,325	62	14,924	56	15,151	41
Czechoslovakia_____	0	0	11,893	0	13,824	12	13,073	2	5,952	7
Austria_____	[6][9] 15,455	[6][9] 263	5,500	0	6,387	19	7,946	18	6,136	13
Switzerland_____	[6] 3,984	[6] 1	6,343	0	5,539	0	4,832	0	5,459	0
Norway_____	[6][10] 1,292	0	3,235	0	4,497	0	5,048	0	5,176	0
Sweden_____	[6] 1,656	[6] 26	4,040	0	3,771	0	4,652	0	7,752	0
Cuba_____	2,860	0	3,461	0	3,103	0	_____	_____	_____	_____
Australia_____	[1] 440	[1] 10	7	2,554	1,573	34	1,193	2	_____	_____
Mexico [2]_____	4,459	101	749	29	2,615	8	4,303	2	_____	_____
Poland_____	0	0	[2] 291	[2] 99	1,792	65	4,235	21	3,018	8
Greece_____	0	0	[4] 911	_____	_____	_____	1,270	0	_____	_____
Egypt_____	[6] 504	[6] 63	109	65	944	0	294	235	30	5,853
Japan [4]_____	0	0	198	0	558	0	1,511	0	_____	_____
Tunis_____	[6] 442	[6] 8	[4] 980	0	291	23	684	35	_____	_____
Algeria_____	[1] 231	[1] 1	390	77	65	10	600	12	240	25
Finland_____	[1] 260	0	101	0	44	0	148	0	206	0
Uruguay_____	[2] 5	[2] 201	[2] 103	[2] 33	[2] 97	43	_____	4	_____	_____
Latvia [4]_____	0	0	25	0	20	0	8	0	_____	_____
Estonia_____	0	0	[4] 26	[4] 0	[4] 16	[4] 0	0	0	23	0
Total 40 countries_	264,711	265,738	273,809	267,795	291,768	299,720	364,520	395,280	383,066	335,181

Bureau of Agricultural Economics. Official sources except where otherwise noted. Maicena or Maizena is included with "Corn and corn meal."

[1] Average of years ended Dec. 31. International Yearbook of Agricultural Statistics.
[2] Year ended Dec. 31.
[3] 3-year average.
[4] International Crop Report and Agricultural Statistics.
[5] Compiled from consular reports.
[6] Average of years ended July 31, from International Institute of Agricultural Statistics.
[7] 2-year average.
[8] 4-year average.
[9] Average for Austria-Hungary shown on Austria.
[10] 1 year only.

TABLE 56.—*Corn: Visible supply in United States,*[1] *1909-1928*

Year beginning November	Nov.	Dec.	Jan.	Feb.	Mar.	Apr.	May	June	July	Aug.	Sept.	Oct.
	1,000 bushels	1,000 bushels	1,000 bushels	1,000 bushels	1,000 bushels	1,000 bushels	1,000 bushels	1,000 bushels	1,000 bushels	1,000 bushels	1,000 bushels	1,000 bushels
Average:												
1909–1913	3,352	2,088	7,342	10,406	15,165	16,233	8,358	4,656	7,980	4,583	3,566	5,444
1914–1920	3,763	2,953	6,909	12,521	17,069	18,949	13,827	9,059	8,509	6,140	4,048	5,245
1921–1925	7,679	7,861	17,054	23,496	31,478	34,183	26,334	17,732	16,882	11,558	8,053	8,853
1909	2,653	3,289	8,465	9,764	13,480	13,778	10,603	5,940	5,146	3,770	2,750	5,011
1910	3,510	1,545	5,099	9,145	11,794	11,166	7,047	4,685	7,482	7,100	6,724	6,339
1911	1,703	2,054	5,140	6,900	14.257	15,914	7,490	5,699	8,204	2,451	1,823	3,101
1912	2,689	1,525	5,879	9,717	17,918	21,494	7,270	2,549	11,479	6,389	2,612	7,308
1913	6,206	2,026	12,126	16,505	18,374	18,812	9,380	4,409	7,589	3,203	3,923	5,461
1914	3,114	3,382	19,703	34,156	41,238	32,877	20,203	12,795	5,225	2,306	2,382	3,444
1915	3,288	4,387	8,919	14,773	24,605	27,697	21,004	14,505	6,870	5,167	3,330	5,093
1916	2,361	2,677	5,838	10,671	12,931	11,974	7,173	2,629	3,277	2,841	2,371	1,163
1917	1,277	1,932	3,155	4,623	8,939	19,016	16,111	13,038	11,487	9,466	5,232	5,503
1918	4,733	2,216	2,415	5,549	4,483	2,514	4,245	2,600	4,038	2,461	956	2,163
1919	1,484	1,477	2,921	3,575	4,951	5,669	5,035	2,740	4,364	6,152	2,564	7,587
1920	10,085	4,597	5,409	14,297	22,333	32,896	23,018	15,103	24,304	14,584	11,500	11,765
1921	18,891	15,518	23,279	30,778	44,792	46,889	35,564	27,046	29,337	19,509	7,314	12,206
1922	8,806	11,072	16,760	21,658	27,529	28,742	22,339	6,734	3,366	2,373	1,587	2,052
1923	809	2,690	8,799	9,379	18,898	26,074	17,978	12,288	8,279	4,887	5,070	7,154
1924	8,097	7,563	18,573	27,571	32,292	32,727	23,379	17,140	13,094	6,093	6,524	5,470
1925	1,790	2,461	17,861	28,092	33,878	36,485	32,408	25,453	30,333	24,930	19,771	17,381
1926	22,258	28,699	34,712	38,792	45,103	47,244	36,621	29,961	34,427	30,205	22,312	23,687
1927	20,574	19,216	27,034	31,849	40,998	43,856	33,556	25,496	16,008	13,267	9,516	6,791
1928	2,030	6,419										

Bureau of Agricultural Economics. Compiled from the Chicago Daily Trade Bulletin. Bureau of Agricultural Economics is now securing and compiling data to replace this table as soon as enough years are covered.

[1] Saturday nearest the 1st of each month.

TABLE 57.—*Corn: Commercial stocks in store, 1926–27 to 1928–29*

DOMESTIC CORN IN UNITED STATES[1]

	Nov.	Dec.	Jan.	Feb.	Mar.	Apr.	May	June	July	Aug.	Sept.	Oct.
	1,000 bushels	1,000 bushels	1,000 bushels	1,000 bushels	1,000 bushels	1,000 bushels	1,000 bushels	1,000 bushels	1,000 bushels	1,000 bushels	1,000 bushels	1,000 bushels
1926–27			36,019	40,670	47,515	49,759	39,010	31,224	36,268	31,782	23,324	24,913
1927–28	21,661	20,254	28,741	30,717	44,786	48,273	36,835	27,497	17,650	12,304	9,768	6,804
1928–29	2,032	6,353										

UNITED STATES CORN IN CANADA

	Nov.	Dec.	Jan.	Feb.	Mar.	Apr.	May	June	July	Aug.	Sept.	Oct.
1926–27			2,147	1,715	1,788	1,403	1,781	1,452	1,184	1,706	1,188	2,010
1927–28	1,994	2,263	1,891	1,598	1,312	976	626	1,634	1,337	818	510	534
1928–29	252	268										

Bureau of Agricultural Economics. Compiled from weekly reports to the Grain, Hay and Feed Market News Service. Data are for stocks on the Saturday nearest the 1st day of the month.

[1] Includes corn stored at 39 interior and seaboard points of accumulation, exclusive of corn in transit on lakes and canals.

TABLE 58.—*Corn: Stocks of old corn on farms November 1, by selected States and by geographic divisions, 1909–1928*

| Year | Principal producing States | | | | | | |
	Iowa	Illinois	Nebraska	Missouri	Indiana	Ohio	Total
	1,000,000 bushels	*1,000,000 bushels*	*1,000,000 bushels*	*1,000,000 bushels*	*1,000,000 bushels*	*1,000,000 bushels*	*1,000,000 bushels*
Average:							
1909–1913	16.9	17.3	8.4	10.5	7.9	5.8	66.8
1914–1920	15.7	12.1	7.7	6.3	6.7	4.3	52.9
1921–1925	28.5	14.1	19.7	9.7	9.6	7.4	89.0
1909	12.9	10.5	9.3	7.3	4.4	3.8	48.2
1910	20.5	21.9	14.1	6.9	10.9	8.0	82.3
1911	18.6	19.6	9.6	17.6	8.3	5.0	78.7
1912	8.9	10.4	2.5	4.6	4.9	4.2	35.5
1913	23.8	24.3	6.5	15.9	11.0	7.8	89.3
1914	14.2	9.0	2.9	5.2	6.3	5.4	43.0
1915	27.3	10.2	7.8	3.2	6.5	5.0	60.0
1916	5.4	10.1	7.0	6.7	6.7	5.4	41.3
1917	4.0	3.6	3.9	1.9	2.6	1.7	17.7
1918	14.4	16.7	15.0	16.9	7.9	2.2	73.1
1919	11.7	13.8	4.3	4.0	6.6	2.3	42.7
1920	33.2	21.6	12.9	6.4	10.5	8.1	92.7
1921	61.6	28.3	51.1	21.3	21.1	14.1	197.5
1922	38.8	15.9	24.9	11.0	10.2	9.3	110.1
1923	17.7	6.3	4.7	6.4	4.4	6.0	45.5
1924	18.3	11.8	10.3	5.1	9.7	5.8	61.0
1925	6.1	8.0	7.7	4.5	2.8	1.8	30.9
1926	34.5	35.5	20.1	10.7	20.3	16.2	137.3
1927	20.0	21.9	4.5	7.1	12.6	8.8	74.9
1928	5.0	2.8	11.7	3.2	2.0	1.4	26.1

Year	North Atlantic	East North Central	West North Central	South Atlantic	South Central	Far Western
	1,000,000 bushels	*1,000,000 bushels*	*1,000,000 bushels*	*1,000,000 bushels*	*1,000,000 bushels*	*1,000,000 bushels*
Average:						
1909–1913	3.0	34.3	46.3	6.2	14.4	9.2
1914–1920	2.9	25.9	37.5	8.2	13.9	.4
1921–1925	4.5	36.2	77.2	8.0	14.2	1.4
1909	2.0	21.8	37.0	5.3	13.6	.1
1910	2.4	44.1	53.6	4.7	10.6	.3
1911	3.6	36.0	58.5	7.4	18.1	.3
1912	3.5	22.3	21.5	6.5	10.8	.1
1913	3.7	47.1	60.8	7.2	18.7	.4
1914	2.6	24.9	28.0	9.4	14.9	.2
1915	2.9	26.7	47.9	7.7	10.2	.6
1916	2.9	24.2	33.5	9.5	17.4	.5
1917	1.8	9.1	12.6	4.6	6.2	.1
1918	2.8	27.2	52.4	10.4	21.5	.3
1919	2.4	24.3	26.0	7.6	9.2	.3
1920	5.0	44.6	62.4	8.3	17.9	.7
1921	6.1	71.3	167.9	13.2	24.0	3.3
1922	6.0	42.0	99.3	8.0	20.7	1.3
1923	4.4	22.9	38.3	6.4	11.3	.5
1924	3.7	30.9	50.7	8.3	7.2	1.6
1925	2.1	13.9	30.0	4.1	7.7	.5
1926	6.2	80.5	79.8	6.5	9.1	.9
1927	3.8	46.8	37.1	7.6	17.7	.4
1928	2.3	7.1	30.1	5.4	8.2	.6

Bureau of Agricultural Economics. Compiled from estimates which are based on percentages of crops on farms as estimated by crop reporters. Stocks as given here are comparable with United States totals in Table 25, except for 1909 and 1910, for which years revisions are not available by States and geographic regions to make them comparable with the latest revisions of the United States total.

TABLE 59.—*Corn: Estimated price per bushel, received by producers, United States, 1909–1928*

Year beginning November	Nov. 15	Dec. 15	Jan. 15	Feb. 15	Mar. 15	Apr. 15	May 15	June 15	July 15	Aug. 15	Sept. 15	Oct. 15	Weight-ed av.
	Cents	Cents	Cents	Cents	Cents	Cents	Cents	Cents	Cents	Cents	Cents	Cents	Cents
Average:													
1909–1913	59.4	57.7	58.9	60.1	61.3	63.4	66.2	68.4	70.0	72.1	71.7	66.7	62.8
1914–1920	100.1	98.7	101.9	105.0	109.5	116.5	123.7	127.1	130.5	130.8	122.4	107.7	110.7
1921–1925	71.7	71.8	74.0	76.5	77.4	77.1	79.6	81.6	84.9	88.8	86.6	82.7	78.1
1909	60.0	60.1	63.8	65.6	65.7	64.5	64.4	65.7	66.7	66.8	63.7	56.8	63.2
1910	50.3	48.1	48.6	49.0	49.3	50.8	53.4	57.6	62.9	65.8	65.8	65.2	53.5
1911	63.2	62.0	63.4	65.6	68.8	75.2	81.0	81.8	80.2	78.4	73.9	64.3	68.8
1912	53.6	48.8	49.8	51.4	53.0	55.2	58.7	61.9	64.3	70.4	75.4	73.0	56.7
1913	69.9	69.4	69.0	68.7	69.9	71.4	73.6	75.2	76.2	79.2	79.8	74.4	71.8
1914	67.5	65.3	69.5	74.0	75.1	76.4	77.8	77.8	78.3	78.1	73.9	66.2	71.4
1915	59.7	59.8	64.4	67.4	69.2	71.3	73.2	74.8	77.4	81.5	83.0	83.6	69.6
1916	87.0	89.4	92.9	98.4	107.2	132.0	155.4	162.4	180.6	186.0	175.3	160.6	119.0
1917	137.0	131.4	136.8	146.6	154.0	154.6	154.1	153.1	156.7	162.7	162.6	149.9	148.1
1918	138.4	140.6	141.4	137.6	143.4	156.1	166.9	173.8	183.8	188.3	169.6	143.6	153.1
1919	134.0	137.4	143.6	147.6	153.6	164.1	177.4	185.4	174.6	159.7	138.5	104.3	151.5
1920	77.2	66.8	64.6	63.4	63.8	61.2	61.0	62.4	62.0	59.0	53.6	46.0	62.1
1921	41.7	42.8	44.6	50.3	55.8	58.3	60.6	61.9	63.3	63.6	62.2	62.2	54.3
1922	64.3	67.6	70.2	72.5	75.3	79.6	84.0	85.8	87.0	87.0	86.2	84.8	76.7
1923	78.3	72.2	73.6	76.5	77.2	78.2	78.6	80.8	98.3	104.4	109.7	108.9	84.0
1924	99.6	105.6	112.0	114.5	112.1	103.8	107.5	111.0	104.4	106.5	98.8	83.0	105.8
1925	74.6	70.7	69.6	68.5	66.6	65.7	67.1	68.6	71.5	79.5	76.2	74.5	71.0
1926	66.0	64.5	64.3	66.5	65.2	65.6	73.0	88.9	92.4	97.7	95.3	87.6	74.9
1927	73.7	75.1	75.2	79.0	86.2	91.9	102.5	102.2	102.4	98.2	95.1	84.7	85.8
1928	75.4	76.1											

Bureau of Agricultural Economics. Based on returns from special price reporters. Mean of prices reported on 1st of month and 1st of succeeding month, November, 1909–December, 1923.

TABLE 60.—*Corn, No. 3, yellow: Weighted average price[1] per bushel of reported cash sales, Chicago, 1909–1928*

Year beginning November	Nov.	Dec.	Jan.	Feb.	Mar.	Apr.	May	June	July	Aug.	Sept.	Oct.	Weight-ed av.[1]
	Cents	Cents	Cents	Cents	Cents	Cents	Cents	Cents	Cents	Cents	Cents	Cents	Cents
Average:													
1909–1913	60	55	56	56	57	61	64	64	65	73	71	66	61
1914–1920	115	110	111	109	114	121	130	130	134	136	124	112	115
1921–1925	79	77	79	80	79	78	81	82	89	90	87	88	79
1909	59	59	64	63	61	57	60	59	62	64	58	50	59
1910	49	45	45	45	45	50	54	55	63	65	67	73	53
1911	68	61	62	64	68	78	79	75	68	79	74	65	71
1912	52	46	46	48	49	55	57	60	62	74	75	70	53
1913	72	66	62	62	64	67	70	72	71	82	79	73	70
1914	67	64	71	74	72	75	77	74	78	81	74	65	70
1915	63	69	74	74	73	76	75	74	81	85	86	96	79
1916	98	92	98	100	109	140	159	170	199	206	210	203	111
1917	221	177	177	181	170	165	160	162	170	172	158	141	163
1918	133	145	143	127	153	162	174	178	192	195	155	141	162
1919	146	147	151	146	158	169	202	189	158	158	131	91	159
1920	77	74	65	63	62	57	60	63	60	56	53	45	62
1921	47	47	48	55	57	58	62	61	64	62	64	69	55
1922	71	73	70	72	73	79	82	84	88	88	89	104	73
1923	82	71	76	78	77	77	77	82	109	117	114	110	88
1924	111	120	124	122	117	105	115	113	108	102	91	82	106
1925	83	76	79	75	72	71	71	70	78	80	79	77	75
1926	71	75	74	73	68	71	87	99	102	109	97	84	87
1927	84	86	89	95	99	106	108	103	106	102	100	96	101
1928	84	83											

Bureau of Agricultural Economics. Compiled from Chicago Daily Trade Bulletin. Data for 1899–1908 available in 1924 Yearbook, p. 612, Table 73.

[1] Average of daily prices weighted by car-lot sales.

TABLE 61.—*Corn: Weighted average price [1] per bushel of reported cash sales of all classes and grades, Chicago, and six markets combined, 1918–1928*

CHICAGO

Year beginning November	Nov.	Dec.	Jan.	Feb.	Mar.	Apr.	May	June	July	Aug.	Sept.	Oct.	Weighted av.[1]
	Cents	Cents	Cents	Cents	Cents	Cents	Cents	Cents	Cents	Cents	Cents	Cents	Cents
Av. 1921–1925	74.7	74.5	74.9	75.1	74.7	75.7	80.1	80.8	88.0	89.1	86.4	87.1	79.0
1918	118.6	138.6	131.4	122.0	144.2	160.1	174.0	173.7	191.8	193.2	156.6	140.0	150.4
1919	143.8	141.6	144.9	139.5	155.1	159.7	197.4	183.3	155.3	154.9	132.2	95.9	144.1
1920	78.8	72.5	62.1	59.9	60.7	54.5	61.2	59.1	59.4	56.2	53.2	46.2	56.6
1921	46.7	47.1	47.3	54.0	57.1	58.2	61.4	60.0	63.7	62.0	63.0	69.0	56.9
1922	71.1	72.4	70.1	72.5	72.8	79.3	81.8	84.0	87.1	88.2	88.8	102.4	78.1
1923	76.1	69.8	74.4	75.2	74.4	76.4	76.7	82.6	109.1	117.2	114.9	110.0	86.0
1924	109.3	115.3	113.1	110.8	103.8	99.1	113.4	111.6	106.1	101.8	89.4	80.9	105.7
1925	70.3	67.8	69.5	63.1	65.2	65.3	67.4	65.7	74.0	76.1	75.9	73.1	68.4
1926	66.5	65.3	64.5	62.1	59.4	66.5	81.5	91.2	96.1	105.2	92.1	79.5	74.9
1927	79.8	78.9	78.7	84.0	89.4	98.8	104.6	101.3	104.7	100.3	98.6	88.8	91.0
1928	80.7	79.8											

SIX MARKETS COMBINED [2]

Year beginning November	Nov.	Dec.	Jan.	Feb.	Mar.	Apr.	May	June	July	Aug.	Sept.	Oct.	Weighted av.[1]
Av. 1921–1925	74.1	73.5	74.1	74.1	73.7	75.1	79.4	80.3	87.2	88.1	86.0	86.6	78.2
1918	122.5	140.4	133.0	123.0	143.1	160.6	172.2	173.9	189.9	191.5	156.1	139.9	150.3
1919	143.2	140.4	143.2	137.9	153.1	163.8	191.7	181.0	154.8	153.2	130.1	94.3	146.5
1920	76.5	68.6	60.3	58.1	58.8	52.9	58.9	48.3	57.5	54.0	51.9	45.2	• 55.5
1921	45.6	45.7	46.0	53.3	55.4	56.5	59.6	59.3	62.1	60.1	62.3	69.4	55.7
1922	70.8	71.6	69.2	71.6	72.4	79.0	82.1	83.1	85.6	86.4	88.3	100.3	77.4
1923	74.9	67.5	72.8	73.7	72.7	74.7	75.4	82.7	106.6	114.4	113.7	109.2	83.0
1924	108.3	114.4	112.9	108.6	103.5	99.0	111.9	109.7	105.3	101.3	89.1	80.8	106.0
1925	71.0	68.3	69.5	63.2	64.6	66.4	68.0	66.9	76.3	78.3	76.5	73.2	69.0
1926	67.3	65.9	65.2	62.7	60.9	67.0	83.0	91.5	96.7	104.2	92.2	79.9	75.8
1927	78.7	77.0	78.6	84.1	89.6	98.2	104.0	100.8	102.7	96.8	97.5	89.3	89.2
1928	79.8	78.4											

Bureau of Agricultural Economics. Compiled from Chicago Daily Trade Bulletin, St. Louis Daily Market Reporter, Omaha Daily Price Current, Kansas City Grain Market Review, Minneapolis Daily Market Record, Cincinnati Daily Trade Bulletin. The prices in this table are comparable with prices paid to producers in that the latter are averages of the several prices reported which cover all classes and grades sold by producers.

[1] Average of daily prices weighted by car-lot sales.
[2] Markets are Chicago, St. Louis, Omaha, Kansas City, Minneapolis, and Cincinnati (not included from November, 1918, through December, 1919.)

TABLE 62.—*Corn, yellow, La Plata: Spot price per bushel of 56 pounds at Buenos Aires, 1912–1928*

Year beginning November	Nov.	Dec.	Jan.	Feb.	Mar.	Apr.	May	June	July	Aug.	Sept.	Oct.	Average
	Cents	Cents	Cents	Cents	Cents	Cents	Cents	Cents	Cents	Cents	Cents	Cents	Cents
1912	52	53	54	54	54	56	55	55	55	55	55	62	59	55
1913	58	58	55	56	56	54	59	55	57	1 56	55	49	56
1914	53	54	54	61	56	57	54	50	51	49	51	51	53
1915	54	52	56	60	56	51	45	43	45	51	55	70	53
1916	103	93	107	107	99	103	127	146	143	127	87	85	110
1917	95	88	79	79	74	59	53	57	64	68	65	63	70
1918	63	63	57	52	47	55	55	55	96	107	91	79	68
1919	74	71	70	71	83	103	113	110	96	90	92	83	88
1920	77	82	88	91	91	78	61	63	65	66	65	58	74
1921	61	63	63	73	79	77	75	71	78	78	76	74	72
1922	70	74	80	82	81	80	77	75	73	69	74	78	76
1923	81	79	78	82	77	67	65	57	68	85	93	105	78
1924	106	107	112	108	96	91	100	92	93	96	91	82	98
1925	84	86	78	73	66	70	68	68	68	70	65	60	71
1926	56	55	60	63	62	60	60	63	70	76	77	76	65
1927	75	83	86	97	102	95	90	91	90	86	91	94	91
1928	97	93											

Bureau of Agricultural Economics. Compiled from International Yearbook of Agricultural Statistics, 1912–1921. Subsequently Review of the River Plate. Average of weekly quotations. Conversions at monthly average rate of exchange as given in Federal Reserve Bulletins.

[1] Interpolation, no quotation.

33023°—29——46

TABLE 63.—*Corn, yellow, La Plata: Spot price per bushel of 56 pounds at Liverpool, 1912–1928*

Year beginning November	Nov.	Dec.	Jan.	Feb.	Mar.	Apr.	May	June	July	Aug.	Sept.	Oct.	Average
	Cents	Cents	Cents	Cents	Cents	Cents	Cents	Cents	Cents	Cents	Cents	Cents	Cents
1912	68	67	71	75	76	74	72	69	67	67	70	66	70
1913	63	67	65	66	68	68	74	76	78	97	93	83	75
1914	78	83	98	106	102	106	111	97	92	90	85	94	95
1915	106	119	140	144	142	143	147	133	145	154	139	148	138
1916	169	181	189	192	200	216	(¹)	217	217	217	217	217	203
1917	217	217	223	223	223	223	223	223	242	261	261	261	233
1918	261	261	204	175	174	174	174	172	165	166	169	168	191
1919	165	152	²149	³177	³196	197	181	167	153	143	160	149	166
1920	115	125	128	122	130	128	118	109	105	93	83	72	111
1921	78	88	92	108	108	103	106	101	110	110	109	108	102
1922	96	100	99	104	105	109	114	110	102	94	98	97	102
1923	96	102	103	115	111	107	112	100	94	104	114	124	107
1924	121	122	131	129	114	111	130	128	127	138	120	103	123
1925	107	110	97	91	89	94	89	87	100	98	90	93	95
1926	95	92	89	93	87	88	94	93	91	98	97	96	93
1927	97	104	110	119	127	129	127	125	123	119	107	116	117
1928	123	120											

Bureau of Agricultural Economics. Compiled from International Yearbook of Agricultural Statistics, 1912–1921. Subsequently Broomhall's Corn Trade News. Conversions at monthly average rate of exchange as given in Federal Reserve Bulletins to December, 1925, inclusive; subsequently at par of exchange.

¹ Not quoted.　　　²Afloat price.　　　³ Nominal.

TABLE 64.—*Corn futures: Volume of trading in corn futures in all markets where corn futures are traded in, by months, 1924–25 to 1927–28*

Year and market	1927		1928			
	Nov.	Dec.	Jan.	Feb.	Mar.	Apr.
	1,000 bushels	1,000 bushels	1,000 bushels	1,000 bushels	1,000 bushels	1,000 bushels
1924–25	557,304	706,562	709,377	677,274	810,362	669,751
1925–26	317,253	514,258	302,297	236,083	316,906	291,590
1926–27	383,247	394,929	261,079	287,881	428,858	312,646
1927–28	472,862	681,076	510,743	698,043	732,790	745,222
Chicago Board of Trade	439,685	630,561	470,789	649,031	675,642	691,036
Chicago Open Board	10,073	15,386	15,607	17,753	18,547	17,264
Kansas City	19,068	28,933	19,721	24,012	30,622	30,202
St. Louis	2,010	3,523	2,307	3,106	3,295	2,321
Milwaukee	2,026	2,673	2,319	4,141	4,684	4,399

Year and market	1928						Total 1927–28
	May	June	July	Aug.	Sept.	Oct.	
	1,000 bushels	1,000 bushels	1,000 bushels	1,000 bushels	1,000 bushels	1,000 bushels	1,000 bushels
1924–25	510,347	565,855	462,734	394,331	441,945	335,161	6,841,003
1925–26	237,152	342,491	448,305	438,929	367,625	340,191	4,153,080
1926–27	692,490	921,473	575,266	712,699	835,732	587,568	6,393,838
1927–28	699,564	566,913	553,604	615,550	371,784	466,957	7,115,108
Chicago Board of Trade	643,930	524,573	511,522	570,497	345,894	435,720	6,588,880
Chicago Open Board	17,299	15,126	14,070	12,637	8,013	13,121	174,896
Kansas City	31,378	23,015	24,075	28,789	15,153	15,155	290,123
St. Louis	1,731	848	993	938	568	897	22,537
Milwaukee	5,226	3,351	2,944	2,689	2,156	2,064	38,672

Grain Futures Administration.

TABLE 65.—*Oats: Acreage, production, value, exports, etc., United States, 1900–1928*

Year	Acreage harvested	Average yield per acre	Production	Price per bushel received by producers Dec. 1	Farm value Dec. 1	Price per bushel at Chicago, year beginning Aug. 1 [1]	Foreign trade, including meal, year beginning July 1 [2]			
							Domestic exports	Imports	Net exports [3]	
									Total	Percentage of production
	1,000 acres	*Bushel of 32 lbs.*	*1,000 bushels*	*Cents*	*1,000 dollars*	*Cents*	*1,000 bushels*	*1,000 bushels*	*1,000 bushels*	
1900	30,290	30.2	913,800	25.4	232,074	26	42,269	32	42,237	4.6
1901	29,894	26.0	778,392	39.7	308,796	43	13,278	39	13,240	1.7
1902	30,578	34.5	1,053,489	30.6	322,423	34	8,382	150	8,233	.8
1903	30,866	28.2	869,350	34.0	295,232	38	1,961	184	1,857	.2
1904	31,353	32.2	1,008,931	31.1	313,488	32	8,395	56	8,339	.8
1905	32,072	34.0	1,090,236	28.9	314,868	31	48,435	40	48,395	4.4
1906	33,353	31.0	1,035,576	31.9	329,853	37	6,386	91	6,379	.6
1907	33,641	23.9	805,108	44.5	358,421	50	2,519	383	2,195	.3
1908	34,006	25.0	850,540	47.3	402,010	52	2,334	6,692	[4] 4,252	
1909	*35,159*	*28.6*	*1,007,143*							
1909	35,159	30.4	1,068,289	40.6	433,869	42	2,549	1,063	1,704	.2
1910	37,548	31.6	1,186,341	34.4	408,388	33	3,846	140	3,707	.3
1911	37,763	24.4	922,298	45.0	414,663	50	2,678	2,660	30	([5])
1912	37,917	37.4	1,418,337	31.9	452,469	35	36,455	765	35,695	2.5
1913	38,399	29.2	1,121,768	39.2	439,596	40	2,749	22,333	[4] 18,858	
1914	38,442	29.7	1,141,060	43.8	499,431	50	100,609	670	100,158	8.8
1915	40,996	37.8	1,549,030	36.1	559,506	41	98,960	720	98,648	6.4
1916	41,527	30.1	1,251,837	52.4	655,928	54	95,106	841	94,348	7.5
1917	43,553	36.6	1,592,740	66.6	1,061,474	71	125,091	2,915	122,273	7.7
1918	44,349	34.7	1,538,124	70.9	1,090,322	70	109,005	838	108,167	7.0
1919	*37,991*	*27.8*	*1,055,183*							
1919	40,359	29.3	1,184,030	70.4	833,922	80	43,436	6,077	37,365	3.2
1920	42,491	35.2	1,496,281	46.0	688,311	51	9,391	3,827	5,831	.4
1921	45,495	23.7	1,078,341	30.2	325,954	35	21,237	1,824	19,422	1.8
1922	40,790	29.8	1,215,803	39.4	478,948	41	25,413	340	25,087	2.1
1923	40,981	31.9	1,305,883	41.4	541,137	45	8,796	4,271	4,550	.3
1924	*37,650*	*34.7*	*1,304,599*							
1924	42,110	35.7	1,502,529	47.7	717,189	50	16,777	3,067	13,926	.9
1925	44,872	33.2	1,487,550	38.0	565,506	41	39,687	212	39,565	2.7
1926	44,177	28.2	1,246,848	39.8	496,582	43	15,041	135	14,988	1.2
1927	41,941	28.2	1,182,594	45.0	531,762	55	9,823	233	9,611	.8
1928 [6]	41,733	34.7	1,449,531	40.9	592,674					

Bureau of Agricultural Economics.   Production figures are estimates of the crop-reporting board; italic figures are census returns.   See 1927 Yearbook, page 788, for data for earlier years.

[1] From Chicago Daily Trade Bulletin, averages of the daily cash quotations of No. 3 white oats weighted by car-lot sales.
[2] Compiled from Commerce and Navigation of the United States, 1900–1917; Foreign Commerce and Navigation of the United States, 1918; Monthly Summary of Foreign Commerce of the United States, June issues, 1919–1926; January and June issues, 1927–28, and official records of the Bureau of Foreign and Domestic Commerce.   Oats—general imports, 1900–1927; oatmeal—general imports, 1900–1909; imports or consumption, 1910–1927.
[3] Total exports (domestic plus foreign) minus total imports.
[4] Net imports.
[5] Less than 0.05 per cent.
[6] Preliminary.

TABLE 66.—*Oats: Acreage harvested and production, by States, average 1921–1925, annual 1926–1928*

State and division	Acreage harvested				Production			
	Average, 1921–1925	1926	1927	1928 [1]	Average, 1921–1925	1926	1927	1928 [1]
	1,000 acres	*1,000 acres*	*1,000 acres*	*1,000 acres*	*1,000 bushels*	*1,000 bushels*	*1,000 bushels*	*1,000 bushels*
Maine	126	136	124	120	4,870	5,168	4,588	4,200
New Hampshire	15	11	11	10	577	440	429	390
Vermont	82	82	83	79	2,944	3,116	3,237	2,686
Massachusetts	9	9	8	7	310	306	280	224
Rhode Island	1	3	2	2	43	96	64	56
Connecticut	12	15	15	15	347	480	480	405
New York	1,014	1,017	1,000	1,020	31,976	34,578	35,000	33,660
New Jersey	62	50	49	50	1,706	1,650	1,764	1,500
Pennsylvania	1,148	1,111	1,100	1,067	37,141	35,552	39,600	34,678
North Atlantic	2,469	2,434	2,392	2,370	79,914	81,386	85,442	77,799
Ohio	1,628	1,980	1,900	2,413	55,259	75,240	60,800	89,281
Indiana	1,834	2,050	1,948	2,532	51,089	61,500	48,700	93,684
Illinois	4,309	4,661	4,008	4,649	139,045	123,516	102,204	174,338
Michigan	1,540	1,570	1,617	1,633	47,688	51,810	54,170	58,461
Wisconsin	2,566	2,577	2,422	2,495	97,506	96,638	93,247	108,532
Minnesota	4,345	4,532	4,350	4,089	159,041	129,162	116,580	153,338
Iowa	6,013	6,218	6,001	6,001	216,311	195,867	192,032	240,040
Missouri	1,656	2,173	1,565	1,606	37,482	43,460	26,605	44,968
North Dakota	2,463	2,024	2,125	1,934	67,004	34,408	45,688	59,954
South Dakota	2,604	1,984	2,550	2,193	82,450	23,213	74,715	59,211
Nebraska	2,521	2,537	2,441	2,392	69,986	52,516	69,813	78,936
Kansas	1,561	1,626	1,301	1,301	34,998	35,122	30,574	37,729
North Central	33,039	33,932	32,228	33,238	1,057,859	922,452	915,128	1,198,472
Delaware	6	4	4	4	146	112	116	120
Maryland	56	52	51	54	1,702	1,706	1,708	1,701
Virginia	173	186	186	182	3,721	4,836	3,999	4,641
West Virginia	189	207	217	204	4,520	5,796	5,251	5,712
North Carolina	241	310	273	191	4,765	6,820	5,733	4,202
South Carolina	386	416	449	337	8,557	10,483	10,327	7,751
Georgia	419	475	442	265	7,569	10,925	9,282	5,300
Florida	27	12	11	11	348	200	121	191
South Atlantic	1,496	1,662	1,633	1,248	31,329	40,878	36,537	29,618
Kentucky	247	259	215	305	5,043	6,346	4,085	7,930
Tennessee	218	276	179	188	4,467	6,900	3,043	4,042
Alabama	224	107	101	70	4,225	2,354	1,768	1,225
Mississippi	110	41	48	41	2,082	902	912	820
Arkansas	270	243	207	155	5,615	5,346	4,140	3,410
Louisiana	44	30	35	44	975	798	612	1,078
Oklahoma	1,361	1,340	1,112	890	29,104	37,520	21,128	23,140
Texas	1,447	1,964	2,003	1,402	34,753	83,666	42,063	35,751
South Central	3,922	4,260	3,900	3,095	86,264	143,832	77,751	77,396
Montana	621	641	596	554	17,600	16,666	23,840	20,221
Idaho	167	119	143	137	7,125	4,760	6,721	6,439
Wyoming	146	120	120	132	4,690	4,200	4,320	4,092
Colorado	215	195	189	193	6,032	4,680	5,481	5,983
New Mexico	53	54	30	36	1,103	1,512	660	720
Arizona	16	15	17	14	492	525	612	532
Utah	72	54	51	55	2,783	2,160	2,142	2,475
Nevada	2	2	2	2	87	64	80	80
Washington	210	229	183	201	9,660	9,847	9,150	9,447
Oregon	282	304	310	304	8,862	8,816	10,540	10,944
California	138	156	147	154	4,220	5,070	4,190	5,313
Far Western	1,923	1,889	1,788	1,782	62,654	58,300	67,736	66,246
United States	42,850	44,177	41,941	41,733	1,318,021	1,246,848	1,182,594	1,449,531

Bureau of Agricultural Economics. Estimates of crop-reporting board.

[1] Preliminary.

TABLE 67.—*Oats: Yield per acre and estimated price per bushel, December 1, by States, average 1914–1920, 1921–1925, annual 1924–1928*

State	Yield per acre							Estimated price per bushel						
	Average, 1914–1920	Average, 1921–1925	1924	1925	1926	1927	1928	Average, 1914–1920	Average, 1921–1925	1924	1925	1926	1927	1928
	Bush.	*Bush.*	*Bush.*	*Bush.*	*Bush.*	*Bush.*	*Bush.*	*Cts.*	*Cts.*	*Cts.*	*Cts.*	*Cts.*	*Cts.*	*Cts.*
Maine	37.4	38.6	38.0	45.0	38.0	37.0	35.0	74	56	65	55	63	68	70
New Hampshire	37.3	37.7	39.0	39.0	40.0	39.0	39.0	73	64	73	64	65	70	65
Vermont	37.0	36.0	38.0	40.0	38.0	39.0	34.0	73	61	69	59	60	65	70
Massachusetts	35.6	34.4	34.0	38.0	34.0	35.0	32.0	74	64	70	65	70	70	70
Rhode Island	31.2	30.8	30.0	33.0	32.0	32.0	28.0	74	64	75	65	70	75	70
Connecticut	31.7	29.8	29.0	33.0	32.0	32.0	27.0	73	64	70	61	66	69	70
New York	34.0	31.6	36.0	36.0	34.0	35.0	33.0	67	53	62	52	50	55	54
New Jersey	32.5	27.8	30.0	30.0	33.0	36.0	30.0	67	55	64	54	50	53	53
Pennsylvania	34.7	32.5	36.0	35.0	32.0	36.0	32.5	64	52	62	51	49	54	53
Ohio	37.8	33.4	41.0	41.5	38.0	32.0	37.0	56	43	52	39	39	45	42
Indiana	36.5	27.6	37.0	28.0	30.0	25.0	37.0	53	39	48	37	35	43	37
Illinois	39.8	32.3	39.0	32.5	26.5	25.5	37.5	54	38	47	35	35	43	38
Michigan	35.2	31.0	38.8	32.0	33.0	33.5	35.8	55	42	48	40	40	48	43
Wisconsin	39.9	38.1	40.0	48.5	37.5	38.5	43.5	55	40	48	38	40	47	43
Minnesota	34.4	36.3	43.0	42.0	28.5	26.8	37.5	49	33	43	31	34	40	35
Iowa	38.9	36.1	42.0	39.2	31.5	32.0	40.0	50	34	44	32	35	42	37
Missouri	28.4	22.4	25.0	26.0	20.0	17.0	28.0	55	43	51	44	42	47	42
North Dakota	23.9	27.2	34.0	27.0	17.0	21.5	31.0	48	28	36	27	33	35	30
South Dakota	33.7	31.6	37.0	34.0	11.7	29.3	27.0	47	30	40	28	36	36	33
Nebraska	32.4	27.8	28.0	27.4	20.7	28.6	33.0	49	34	43	36	40	40	38
Kansas	27.9	22.6	25.0	23.0	21.6	23.5	29.0	55	40	47	44	44	45	42
Delaware	30.5	26.4	30.0	25.0	28.0	29.0	30.0	70	66	66	65	59	68	60
Maryland	30.7	30.6	34.0	32.0	32.8	33.5	31.5	68	53	64	53	50	54	56
Virginia	22.2	21.5	23.5	21.5	26.0	21.5	25.5	77	64	72	70	63	64	64
West Virginia	24.9	24.0	24.0	27.0	28.0	24.2	28.0	73	62	73	62	59	64	63
North Carolina	18.5	19.6	18.0	19.0	22.0	21.0	22.0	86	74	84	76	69	72	78
South Carolina	20.1	22.1	19.5	19.0	25.2	23.0	23.0	93	84	97	90	67	75	88
Georgia	19.4	17.9	15.5	17.0	23.0	21.0	20.0	96	81	95	87	69	75	85
Florida	16.7	13.1	13.5	14.0	16.7	11.0	17.4	86	80	90	90	65	80	88
Kentucky	23.4	20.5	23.2	21.0	24.5	19.0	26.0	70	57	67	59	53	60	57
Tennessee	22.4	20.5	21.0	22.0	25.0	17.0	21.5	73	59	69	64	55	60	60
Alabama	18.8	18.2	15.0	17.0	22.0	17.5	17.5	87	77	87	78	68	70	75
Mississippi	19.2	18.6	16.0	19.0	22.0	19.0	20.0	85	74	85	78	66	70	75
Arkansas	24.6	20.8	18.0	16.0	22.0	20.0	22.0	72	57	64	58	52	58	59
Louisiana	22.8	21.7	20.0	21.0	26.6	17.5	24.5	80	74	83	80	64	66	65
Oklahoma	25.6	21.6	25.0	23.0	28.0	19.0	26.0	58	46	53	51	37	44	47
Texas	27.7	23.9	34.0	12.3	42.6	21.0	25.5	65	55	59	63	38	47	51
Montana	29.0	28.2	29.5	22.5	26.0	40.0	36.5	60	42	47	53	53	44	41
Idaho	40.0	42.4	36.0	49.0	40.0	47.0	47.0	66	45	58	43	45	50	48
Wyoming	34.1	32.0	30.0	35.0	35.0	36.0	31.0	69	46	58	46	45	42	45
Colorado	34.0	28.0	25.0	27.0	24.0	29.0	31.0	65	46	58	50	44	48	45
New Mexico	30.8	20.7	20.0	20.0	28.0	22.0	20.0	73	60	60	64	56	56	60
Arizona	36.9	30.8	28.0	30.0	35.0	36.0	38.0	89	74	81	75	75	70	75
Utah	41.6	38.6	32.8	47.0	40.0	42.0	45.0	73	55	70	62	60	60	56
Nevada	40.1	36.1	30.0	40.0	32.0	40.0	40.0	88	74	72	65	62	65	65
Washington	43.0	45.7	38.5	44.0	43.0	50.0	47.0	68	52	59	52	53	56	55
Oregon	35.0	31.4	28.0	33.0	29.0	34.0	36.0	66	50	61	51	50	53	51
California	32.4	29.5	18.2	34.7	32.5	28.5	34.5	76	65	87	61	48	63	60
United States	33.3	30.9	35.7	33.2	28.2	28.2	34.7	55.3	39.3	47.7	38.0	39.8	45.0	40.9

Bureau of Agricultural Economics. Estimates of the crop-reporting board.

TABLE 68.—*Oats: Acreage, yield per acre, and production in specified countries, average 1909–1913, 1921–1925, annual 1926–1928*

Country	Acreage Average 1909–1913[1]	Acreage Average 1921–1925	Acreage 1926	Acreage 1927	Acreage 1928 prelim.	Yield Average 1909–1913[1]	Yield Average 1921–1925	Yield 1926	Yield 1927	Yield 1928 prelim.	Production Average 1909–1913[1]	Production Average 1921–1925	Production 1926	Production 1927	Production 1928 prelim.
	1,000 acres	*1,000 acres*	*1,000 acres*	*1,000 acres*	*1,000 acres*	*Bushels*	*Bushels*	*Bushels*	*Bushels*	*Bushels*	*1,000 bushels*	*1,000 bushels*	*1,000 bushels*	*1,000 bushels*	*1,000 bushels*
NORTHERN HEMISPHERE															
NORTH AMERICA															
Canada	9,597	14,585	12,741	13,240	13,137	36.6	31.4	30.1	33.2	34.4	351,690	457,948	383,416	439,713	452,153
United States	37,357	42,860	44,177	41,941	41,733	30.6	30.9	28.2	28.2	34.7	1,143,407	1,318,021	1,246,848	1,182,594	1,449,531
Total	46,954	57,435	56,918	55,181	54,870	31.8	30.9	28.6	29.4	34.7	1,495,097	1,775,969	1,630,264	1,622,307	1,901,684
EUROPE															
England and Wales	2,039	2,039	1,863	1,751	1,762	47.5	47.4	56.0	53.7	57.4	96,913	96,575	104,324	94,080	101,090
Scotland	952	970	940	897	878	46.8	49.0	55.9	48.4	56.1	44,507	47,563	52,500	43,400	49,280
Irish Free State	(692)	762	647	645	649		49.1	69.1	62.5	63.0	(45,866)	37,381	44,711	46,735	
Northern Ireland	(357)	362	320	310	307	38.9	53.8	64.0	62.3	47.2	(19,303)	19,488	20,491	19,303	19,356
Norway	264	274	241	240	246	43.9	41.6	55.3	52.8	48.4	10,276	11,406	13,332	12,665	11,608
Sweden	1,961	1,807	1,827	1,803	1,808	43.9	41.7	47.9	43.8	48.4	86,050	75,374	87,596	78,895	87,516
Denmark	1,161	1,119	1,048	1,012	997	52.2	54.1	57.6	60.1	72.6	60,557	60,542	60,333	60,863	72,338
Netherlands	346	380	380	365	374	51.4	51.4	59.3	57.5	67.8	18,070	19,531	22,530	21,144	25,353
Belgium	668	656	668	658	667	65.8	62.4	75.9	70.1	72.5	43,964	40,954	50,729	46,102	48,343
Luxemburg	77	70	71	70	70	43.9	30.4	45.8	39.5	44.7	3,382	2,130	3,249	2,763	3,131
France	10,084	8,521	8,677	8,544	8,572	36.5	35.3	42.0	40.2	39.2	368,462	390,569	364,120	343,279	336,255
Spain	1,276	1,623	1,863	1,909	1,956	22.8	22.1	20.2	20.5	18.2	29,110	35,900	37,688	39,216	35,609
Portugal	(600)	563	499	552	528	29.4	11.4	9.5	10.0		(7,000)	6,422	4,747	5,528	3,876
Italy	1,276	1,194	1,231	1,203	1,288	29.4	31.7	33.0	25.5	37.6	37,537	37,840	40,647	30,720	48,412
Switzerland	81	81	51	51	51	55.3	54.7	60.7	50.9	56.5	4,784	2,790	3,107	2,880	2,880
Germany	9,529	8,246	8,590	8,589	8,696	55.3	44.1	50.7	50.9	55.4	527,178	363,272	435,722	437,249	481,960
Austria	883	739	777	769	767	38.4	30.5	38.6	39.3	38.7	29,030	22,556	29,955	30,231	29,652
Czechoslovakia	2,506	2,044	2,120	2,108	2,120	33.5	28.8	44.8	47.9	42.7	96,147	82,029	95,072	101,000	90,500
Hungary	849	785	680	643	650	24.7	28.8	36.5	35.0	36.5	28,464	22,644	24,802	22,513	23,725
Yugoslavia	1,358	923	871	936	965	² 29.1	22.4	28.3	21.5	24.8	33,516	20,644	24,645	20,114	23,975
Greece	140	206	275	255	302	21.2	20.3	18.0	18.2	29.0	² 4,075	4,187	4,958	4,650	8,765
Bulgaria	408	362	320	326	294	² 28.2	20.1	21.0	19.8	24.5	8,651	7,100	6,725	6,446	7,210
Rumania	² 2,119	3,133	2,665	2,680	2,759	28.4	19.6	30.0	21.5	24.5	³ 59,776	62,819	79,850	59,810	67,546
Poland	6,666	5,933	6,437	6,474	6,663	29.4	32.5	32.6	28.3	39.2	195,825	192,564	210,110	233,550	261,119
Lithuania	961	842	1,240	766	638	23.8	27.4	37.3	21.9	29.4	22,910	23,078	30,182	16,741	18,739
Latvia	765	740	792	738	590	25.1	24.6	24.0	16.6	17.0	19,188	18,206	19,000	12,205	10,037
Estonia	394	390	362	360	342	24.9	³ 23.3	25.3	18.7	22.3	9,795	9,505	9,170	6,727	7,639
Finland	999	1,058	1,090	1,112	1,122	20.4	32.6	37.5	39.2	31.3	20,391	34,529	40,835	43,609	35,115
Russia, European and Asiatic	41,256	25,401	37,572	42,953	41,853	22.4	20.3	26.3	20.7	26.5	924,918	514,789	987,675	888,735	1,109,197

	Area harvested					Yield per acre					Production				
Total Europe, excluding Russia, reporting area and production all years	47,762	44,105	45,079	44,260	44,577	38.9	36.1	41.1	40.0	42.3	1,358,558	1,594,307	1,851,190	1,770,852	1,887,797
Estimated European total, excluding Russia	49,400	45,800	46,500	45,800	46,000						[4]1,931,000	1,658,000	1,921,000	1,842,000	1,956,000
AFRICA															
Morocco	25	35	56	63	75		18.4	13.7	22.1	30.6	(500)	645	765	1,395	2,297
Algeria	449	605	621	527	607	30.0	21.0	14.0	20.1	22.7	13,489	12,713	8,693	10,607	13,779
Tunis	133	124	95	96	91	27.4	19.7	22.5	20.4	24.6	3,642	2,439	2,136	1,963	2,239
Total	607	764	772	686	773	29.0	20.7	15.0	20.4	23.7	17,631	15,797	11,594	13,965	18,315
ASIA															
Turkey	[2]380	[5]206	222	65	—	[2]56.7	[2]55.3	24.7	18.7		[2]21,562	[2]11,391	1,481	1,215	
Syria and Lebanon	110	[3]26	60	302	26		[2]16.7	40.0	41.0		(175)	[3]435			
Japan		278	289			44.8	39.0	15.5	15.4		4,928	10,847	10,764	12,372	
Chosen	141	276	277	272		15.6	16.5				2,202	4,545	4,296	4,178	
Total Northern Hemisphere, excluding Russia, reporting area and production all years	95,323	102,304	102,769	100,127	100,220	35.4	33.1	34.0	34.0	38.0	3,371,286	3,386,073	3,493,048	3,407,124	3,807,796
Estimated Northern Hemisphere total excluding Russia and China	97,700	104,900	105,100	102,500	102,500						[4]3,474,000	3,478,000	3,592,000	3,509,000	3,906,000
SOUTHERN HEMISPHERE															
Brazil	78	16	14	138	243	42.7	30.1	23.4	46.3		3,333	482	328		1,851
Chile	66	105	136	138	150	19.5	37.7	35.9	23.9		1,285	3,954	4,878		6,395
Uruguay		120	102	160		22.6	18.1	14.1	16.5			2,166	1,443		3,293
Argentina	2,336	2,662	3,171	3,160	3,608	11.9	22.3	20.9	10.1	11.5	54,246	59,286	66,276		52,290
Union of South Africa	809	681	580	600	630	23.8	8.9	10.6			9,661	6,093	6,119		6,081
Australia	745	1,000	844			49.1	19.0	18.6			17,768	19,010	15,714		7,256
New Zealand	366	125	117	86	303		48.0	52.1	54.6		17,978	5,996	6,091		4,695
Total Northern and Southern Hemisphere countries, excluding Russia, reporting area and production all years	96,132	102,985	103,349	100,727	100,850	35.2	32.9	33.9	33.9	37.8	3,380,947	3,392,166	3,499,167	3,413,205	3,815,052
Estimated world total excluding Russia and China	102,200	109,700	110,200	107,800	108,600						[4]3,581,000	3,579,000	3,697,000	3,602,000	

Bureau of Agricultural Economics. Official sources and International Institute of Agriculture. Figures given are for crops harvested during the calendar year in the Northern Hemisphere and the succeeding harvest in the Southern Hemisphere.

1 Where changes in boundary have occurred the averages are estimates for territory within present boundaries.

2 1 year only.   3 4-year average.

4 The estimate for the 5-year period 1909–1913 given in this table is somewhat larger than the figure obtained by averaging the same 5 years in Table 69. This is because in this table estimates for warring countries are for postwar boundaries, whereas in Table 69 they are for pre-war territory. As a result, in excluding Russia, which lost territory in the war, a smaller area is excluded in this table than in Table 69.   5 2-year average.

TABLE 69.—*Oats: World production, 1894–1928*

Year	Estimated world production excluding Russia	Estimated European production excluding Russia	Selected countries							
			United States	Russia[1]	Germany	France	Canada	Poland	England and Wales	Argentina
	1,000,000 bushels	*1,000,000 bushels*	*1,000,000 bushels*	*1,000,000 bushels*	*1,000,000 bushels*	*1,000,000 bushels*	*1,000,000 bushels*	*1,000,000 bushels*	*1,000,000 bushels*	*1,000,000 bushels*
1894	2,303	1,451	716	744	453	294			119	
1895	2,503	1,432	886	717	430	306			105	
1896	2,320	1,376	780	800	411	296			93	
1897	2,232	1,282	791	664	394	253			99	1
1898	2,501	1,511	843	688	465	322			102	1
1899	2,633	1,462	926	995	474	308			99	2
1900	2,624	1,454	914	854	489	285			99	2
1901	2,344	1,415	778	624	486	255			91	2
1902	2,888	1,576	1,053	931	514	320			115	4
1903	2,829	1,649	869	800	542	344			109	3
1904	2,716	1,435	1,009	1,124	478	291			112	4
1905	2,823	1,460	1,090	937	451	306			99	6
1906	3,673	1,683	1,036	714	581	295			109	12
1907	2,861	1,768	805	921	630	353			121	34
1908	2,832	1,632	851	959	530	327	250		106	32
1909	3,415	1,863	1,068	1,163	629	383	353		104	36
1910	3,223	1,660	1,186	1,065	544	332	244		104	47
1911	3,135	1,683	922	876	531	349	365		96	69
1912	3,700	1,720	1,418	1,089	587	355	392		89	76
1913	3,580	1,909	1,122	1,251	669	357	405		91	43
1914	3,266	1,681	1,141	[2]915	623	318	313		93	49
1915	3,594	1,401	1,549	[3]897	412	339	465		101	75
1916	3,259	1,469	1,252	[4]845	484	277	410		102	32
1917	3,217	1,047	1,593	761	[5]250	[5]220	403		106	69
1918	3,215	1,117	1,538		302	181	426		140	34
1919	3,040	1,319	1,184		310	180	394	76	111	31
1920	3,647	1,478	1,496	486	332	291	531	129	105	51
1921	3,136	1,511	1,078	359	345	244	426	150	98	31
1922	3,384	1,545	1,216	409	277	288	491	176	91	56
1923	3,846	1,810	1,306	405	421	337	564	243	93	76
1924	3,683	1,630	1,503	603	390	306	406	166	105	53
1925	3,848	1,792	1,488	798	385	328	402	228	97	80
1926	3,697	1,921	1,247	988	436	364	383	210	104	66
1927	3,602	1,842	1,183	889	437	343	440	234	94	52
1928[6]		1,956	1,450	1,109	482	336	452	261	101	

Bureau of Agricultural Economics. Official sources and International Institute of Agriculture. For each year is shown the production during the calendar year in the Northern Hemisphere and the succeeding harvest in the Southern Hemisphere.

[1] Includes all Russian territory reporting for the years shown.

[2] Total Russian Empire exclusive of the 10 Vistula Provinces of Russian Poland and the Province of Batum in Transcaucasia.

[3] Exclusive of Russian Poland, Lithuania, parts of present Latvia and the Ukraine, and the provinces of Batum and Elizabetpol, in Transcaucasia.

[4] Beginning this year estimates for the present territory of the Union of Socialist Soviet Republics exclusive of Turkestan, Transcaucasia, and the Far East, which territory in 1924 produced 20,248,000 bushels.

[5] Beginning with this year postwar boundaries and therefore not comparable with earlier years.

[6] Preliminary.

TABLE 70.—*Oats: Monthly marketings by farmers, as reported by about 3,500 mills and elevators, United States, 1917–1927*

Year beginning July	Percentage of year's receipts												
	July	Aug.	Sept.	Oct.	Nov.	Dec.	Jan.	Feb.	Mar.	Apr.	May	June	Season
1917	4.7	16.4	13.5	11.1	7.7	7.8	8.3	8.0	7.1	6.5	4.0	4.9	100.0
1918	8.0	19.6	11.9	9.9	7.2	6.7	6.7	4.5	5.5	6.3	7.0	6.7	100.0
1919	14.4	18.4	10.1	9.2	5.8	8.3	8.2	6.6	4.9	4.3	5.2	4.6	100.0
1920	8.3	18.7	13.8	9.5	5.5	5.8	6.6	6.6	6.0	4.6	6.8	7.8	100.0
1921	15.1	16.5	11.8	7.9	5.3	6.1	7.3	6.9	5.6	4.3	7.2	6.0	100.0
1922	8.9	15.7	11.9	10.1	7.8	8.6	7.4	7.1	6.5	4.7	5.4	5.9	100.0
1923	7.0	17.7	14.1	11.5	6.8	7.6	7.7	7.9	5.2	4.8	4.8	4.9	100.0
1924	14.0	20.7	17.8	11.5	5.6	4.8	4.7	3.5	3.9	3.9	5.0	4.6	100.0
1925	10.4	22.2	13.2	9.3	6.3	6.8	6.1	6.2	5.2	4.2	4.5	5.6	100.0
1926	10.9	21.8	11.7	8.7	5.8	6.4	6.1	6.7	5.6	4.4	5.5	6.4	100.0
1927	9.3	22.7	13.8	9.7	5.7	6.7	6.3	6.3	6.2	3.8	4.1	5.4	100.0

Bureau of Agricultural Economics.

TABLE 71.—*Oats: Farm stocks, growing conditions, and shipments, United States, 1909–1928*

Year beginning August	Stocks of old oats on farms Aug. 1 [1]	Conditions of new crop				Weight per measured bushel of new oats [2]	Stocks of oats on farms on Mar. 1 following [1]	Shipped out of county where grown [1]
		June 1	July 1	Aug. 1	Sept. 1			
	1,000 bush.	*Per cent*	*Per cent*	*Per cent*	*Per cent*	*Pounds*	*1,000 bush.*	*1,000 bush.*
1909	27,478	88.7	88.3	85.5	83.8	32.7	385,705	343,968
1910	66,666	91.0	82.2	81.5	83.3	32.7	442,665	363,103
1911	67,801	85.7	68.8	65.7	64.5	31.1	289,989	265,944
1912	34,875	91.1	89.2	90.3	92.3	33.0	604,249	438,130
1913	103,916	87.0	76.3	73.8	74.0	32.1	419,481	297,365
1914	62,467	89.5	84.7	79.4	75.8	31.5	379,369	335,539
1915	55,607	92.2	93.9	91.6	91.1	33.0	598,148	465,823
1916	113,728	86.9	86.3	81.5	78.0	31.2	394,211	355,092
1917	47,834	88.8	89.4	87.2	90.4	33.4	599,208	514,117
1918	81,424	93.2	85.5	82.8	84.4	33.2	590,251	421,568
1919	93,045	93.2	87.0	76.5	73.0	31.1	409,730	312,364
1920	54,819	87.8	84.7	87.2	88.3	33.1	683,759	431,687
1921	161,108	85.7	77.6	64.5	61.1	28.3	411,934	258,259
1922	74,513	85.5	74.4	75.6	74.9	32.0	421,118	303,950
1923	70,965	85.6	83.5	81.9	80.3	32.1	447,366	322,971
1924	65,710	83.0	86.9	88.2	89.3	33.4	538,832	422,112
1925	90,179	79.6	76.3	79.1	82.1	32.9	571,248	364,407
1926	107,917	78.8	74.5	71.4	67.9	30.9	421,897	272,804
1927	61,237	79.9	79.9	74.8	70.3	30.4	373,167	229,089
1928 [3]	42,315	78.3	79.9	84.8	84.4	32.6		

Bureau of Agricultural Economics. Estimates of the crop-reporting board.

[1] Based on percentage of crop as reported by crop reporters.
[2] Average weight per measured bushel as reported by crop reporters.
[3] Preliminary.

TABLE 72.—*Oats: Receipts at primary markets, averages by groups, 1909–1925, annual 1921–1927*

Year beginning August	Chicago	Milwaukee	Minneapolis	St. Louis	Peoria	Omaha	Total, 10 markets [1]
	1,000 bushels	*1,000 bushels*	*1,000 bushels*	*1,000 bushels*	*1,000 bushels*	*1,000 bushels*	*1,000 bushels*
Average:							
1909–1913	107,484	14,044	17,313	22,457	10,329	12,330	208,920
1914–1920	121,551	30,540	31,722	27,601	12,366	15,780	273,759
1921–1925	71,694	20,319	35,908	31,711	12,750	14,676	225,815
1921	78,042	23,612	33,072	26,118	13,485	10,964	215,715
1922	85,169	22,780	25,706	33,261	15,947	14,886	224,104
1923	69,902	20,496	29,259	35,791	13,406	18,385	219,972
1924	74,698	20,542	54,886	34,724	11,164	16,023	261,562
1925	50,660	14,165	36,616	28,662	9,749	13,124	207,723
1926	49,420	14,857	18,170	19,746	8,256	6,636	140,031
1927 [2]	53,609	10,476	27,283	19,394	8,906	8,858	155,247

Bureau of Agricultural Economics. Compiled from reports of Chicago Board of Trade, Duluth Board of Trade, Indianapolis Board of Trade, Kansas City Board of Trade, Omaha Grain Exchange, St. Louis Merchants Exchange, Milwaukee Chamber of Commerce, Minneapolis Chamber of Commerce, and American Elevator and Grain Trade.

[1] Includes also Duluth, Toledo, Kansas City, and Indianapolis.
[2] Beginning January, 1928, figures are subject to revision.

Table 73.—*Oats: Classification of receipts graded by licensed inspectors, all inspection points*

TOTAL OF ALL CLASSES AND SUBCLASSES UNDER EACH GRADE, BY CARS, ANNUAL, 1919–1927

Year and class	Receipts of—					
	No. 1	No. 2	No. 3	No. 4	Sample grade	Total
Year beginning August 1—	*Cars*	*Cars*	*Cars*	*Cars*	*Cars*	*Cars*
1919	5,652	51,006	94,497	15,805	3,537	170,497
1920	8,803	60,169	73,072	14,766	6,831	163,641
1921	2,519	31,643	105,103	31,774	6,664	177,703
1922	2,548	47,348	95,984	17,004	4,640	167,524
1923	2,724	41,530	90,759	22,643	11,307	168,963
1924	1,489	33,631	110,377	24,580	14,853	184,930
1925	2,197	53,587	75,634	17,989	6,260	155,667
1926	1,465	19,692	49,581	28,548	17,695	116,981
1927	2,836	29,103	64,444	19,397	5,727	121,507

TOTAL INSPECTIONS BY GRADE AND CLASS, BY CARS, AUG. 1, 1927, TO JULY 31, 1928

Class:						
White	1,122	23,506	61,316	18,751	5,081	109,776
Red	327	3,546	2,103	498	187	6,661
Gray	27	35	32	14	11	119
Black	0	2	0	0	0	·2
Mixed	17	374	230	134	84	839
Feed	502	431	364	---------	192	1,489
Mixed feed	841	1,209	399	---------	172	2,621

Bureau of Agricultural Economics.

Table 74.—*Oats: Commercial stocks in store, 1926–27 to 1928–29*

DOMESTIC OATS IN UNITED STATES [1]

	Aug.	Sept.	Oct.	Nov.	Dec.	Jan.	Feb.	Mar.	Apr.	May	June	July
	1,000 bush.	*1,000 bush.*	*1,000 bush.*	*1,000 bush.*	*1,000 bush.*	*1,000 bush.*	*1,000 bush.*	*1,000 bush.*	*1,000 bush.*	*1,000 bush.*	*1,000 bush.*	*1,000 bush.*
1926–27						47,123	47,421	45,105	38,481	30,513	22,553	17,686
1927–28	11,886	23,224	26,513	25,682	24,784	23,815	20,006	21,127	16,803	11,667	7,171	3,338
1928–29	1,939	15,992	17,561	16,900	15,399							*

UNITED STATES OATS IN CANADA

1926–27						352	247	218	164	635	1,432	1,759
1927–28	1,253	1,238	1,435	1,110	825	670	563	438	216	57	239	60
1928–29	4	978	2,326	1,031	547							

CANADIAN OATS IN UNITED STATES [2]

1926–27						228	228	171	66	117	321	19
1927–28	24	26	0	139	296	609	312	247	117	21	199	122
1928–29	101	123	141	211	711							

Bureau of Agricultural Economics. From weekly reports to the Grain, Hay, and Feed Market News Service. Data are for stocks on the Saturday nearest the 1st day of the month.

[1] Includes oats stored at 39 interior and seaboard points of accumulation, exclusive of oats in transit on lakes and canals.
[2] Includes oats stored at lake and seaboard ports, exclusive of oats in transit on lakes and canals.

TABLE 75.—Oats: Visible supply in United States,[1] 1909-1928

Year beginning August	Aug.	Sept.	Oct.	Nov.	Dec.	Jan.	Feb.	Mar.	Apr.	May	June	July
	1,000 bush.	1,000 bush.	1,000 bush.	1,000 bush.	1,000 bush.	1,000 bush.	1,000 bush.	1,000 bush.	1,000 bush.	1,000 bush.	1,000 bush.	1,000 bush.
Average:												
1909-1913	7,185	13,460	18,525	19,024	17,969	16,286	14,857	14,521	13,869	10,748	7,866	7,894
1914-1920	7,879	14,984	23,791	26,613	28,498	28,660	26,513	25,203	23,404	20,717	17,141	13,698
1921-1925	21,818	34,206	47,372	51,211	50,468	51,075	50,611	49,063	43,706	36,706	28,498	25,539
1909	3,800	5,183	12,799	13,264	13,586	11,180	8,759	8,630	9,916	9,223	6,905	4,245
1910	2,761	12,551	18,802	17,022	15,505	16,129	15,997	15,769	13,129	10,559	8,125	9,570
1911	11,293	20,742	21,044	22,600	20,315	18,754	15,431	14,366	13,429	11,991	8,052	3,690
1912	1,031	4,160	9,260	10,552	10,774	8,457	9,646	12,343	13,115	8,704	8,105	14,756
1913	17,131	24,662	30,718	31,684	29,664	26,909	24,450	21,489	19,755	13,262	8,144	7,210
1914	6,482	20,124	27,285	31,866	32,471	32,956	33,173	33,258	27,284	23,022	12,623	4,345
1915	1,309	2,924	14,381	15,730	20,928	21,081	20,175	20,265	17,892	12,096	16,192	12,452
1916	8,537	27,691	38,866	45,580	47,467	48,823	42,675	36,740	34,191	28,933	17,454	9,741
1917	6,679	7,277	14,165	17,453	18,595	17,657	13,879	13,947	18,098	21,911	20,822	13,227
1918	7,876	19,309	24,689	22,050	29,143	34,828	30,505	27,666	22,882	21,507	15,827	18,094
1919	20,481	19,411	19,552	19,196	16,922	13,080	11,550	10,401	9,576	6,813	8,642	3,623
1920	3,786	8,149	27,602	34,414	33,961	32,194	33,632	34,142	33,903	30,740	28,426	34,401
1921	37,562	60,455	65,843	69,998	69,198	67,728	68,010	68,529	64,644	55,837	47,950	42,743
1922	36,667	38,355	35,968	34,077	32,940	32,391	30,861	27,683	24,044	21,932	13,514	8,523
1923	5,477	10,111	16,514	20,488	18,686	19,940	17,539	17,741	16,715	10,656	6,720	5,264
1924	3,086	11,403	52,715	66,564	67,265	72,128	73,570	72,386	61,104	48,082	35,331	33,263
1925	26,298	50,706	65,818	64,926	64,251	63,187	63,076	58,974	52,023	47,025	38,976	37,900
1926	33,772	43,671	48,450	48,097	48,288	44,927	45,422	43,454	37,145	29,573	20,502	17,790
1927	12,001	21,501	24,931	23,857	23,252	21,907	20,350	19,791	15,746	11,168	7,086	3,225
1928	2,377	13,376	15,193	14,472	13,295	--------	--------	--------	--------	--------	--------	-------

Bureau of Agricultural Economics. Compiled from the Chicago Daily Trade Bulletin. Bureau of Agricultural Economics is now securing and compiling data to replace this table as soon as enough years re covered.

[1] Saturday nearest the 1st of each month.

TABLE 76.—*Oats, including oatmeal: International trade, average, 1910–1914, annual 1925–1928*

Country	Average, 1910–1914		1925		1926		1927		1928 preliminary	
	Imports	Exports	Imports	Exports	Imports	Exports	Imports	Exports	Imports	Exports
PRINCIPAL EXPORTING COUNTRIES	*1,000 bushels*	*1,000 bushels*	*1,000 bushels*	*1,000 bushels*	*1,000 bushels*	*1,000 bushels*	*1,000 bushels*	*1,000 bushels*	*1,000 bushels*	*1,000 bushels*
Argentina	[1] 55	[1] 42,569	0	48,533	92	32,006	102	39,691	80	28,831
Canada	84	15,245	1,059	42,339	2,246	35,951	2,051	13,381	2,770	10,194
United States	5,352	9,655	3,041	16,777	185	39,686	99	15,041	202	9,823
Rumania	[2][3] 72	[2][3] 10,493	6	5,433	1	1,352	0	[4] 6,634		
Russia	[2] 1,206	[2] 70,466	0	113	0	1,354	0			
Algeria	[2] 79	[2] 4,102	795	642	68	2,595	1,560	102	498	1,565
Chile	[1] 2	[1] 2,469	0	3,810	0	4,093	0	6,087	0	4,021
Hungary	[2] 1,420	[2] 12,416	280	518	7	3,806	0	2,381	1	1,199
Tunis	[2] 2	[2] 2,875	[2] 116	[4] 742	28	1,462	92	1,047		
Yugoslavia [4]	0	0	0	470	0	1,056	0			
Australia	[1] 898	[1] 270	8	324	343	133	260	205		
British India	[2][5] 87	[2][3] 43	0	50	0	53	0	52	0	44
Bulgaria	0	[2] 178	0	10	0	4	0	14		
PRINCIPAL IMPORTING COUNTRIES										
United Kingdom	68,371	[1] 1,591	33,760	1,104	36,897	1,136	24,911	2,024	31,494	713
Germany	37,202	33,575	20,076	7,223	28,204	5,334	19,255	7,923	16,522	13,311
Switzerland	[2] 12,464	[2] 13	9,099	4	10,662	4	9,895	4	9,770	4
Belgium	8,420	62	8,285	113	9,618	25	6,576	120	6,607	32
France	29,846	122	4,068	960	14,110	388	3,309	488	2,489	1,735
Italy	8,158	65	8,731	128	7,743	42	7,723	0	9,064	
Netherlands	[2] 38,862	[2] 30,771	5,569	502	7,477	287	6,452	167	6,945	260
Austria	[2] 2,295	[2] 114	6,683	0	4,877	11	5,819	12	5,303	12
Sweden	[2] 6,468	[2] 1,899	3,229	715	2,908	329	1,631	2,429	2,215	530
Czechoslovakia	0	0	2,747	1,432	4,747	44	323	3,595	530	5,862
Irish Free State	0	0	3,351	2,344	2,862	3,485	1,824	2,756	875	5,740
Finland	[5] 1,150	[5] 356	1,297	15	1,529	17	1,279	4	990	92
Poland	0	0	[2] 5,505	[2] 10	1,283	5,926	2,870	1,048	1,619	659
Denmark	[2] 4,720	[2] 152	2,621	488	842	411	1,922	164	2,204	122
Norway	[2][6] 497	[2][6] 27	1,494	6	1,413	11	582	6	682	
Cuba	1,291	0	1,855	0	1,502	0		0		
Estonia	0	0	242	0	669	0	354	0	622	
Latvia [2]	0	0	480	416	513	27	705	6		
Japan [2]	5	42	237	0	153	0	144	0	7	
Greece	0	0	694	0			423	0		
Union of South Africa	[1] 366	[1] 434	252	515	231	125	191	69	126	7
Ceylon	[5] 90	0	0	0	[4] 61	0	[4] 69	0		
Total, 35 countries	229,462	240,004	125,580	135,736	141,271	141,153	100,421	105,450	101,615	84,83

Bureau of Agricultural Economics. Official sources except where otherwise noted.

[1] Average of calendar years, 1909–1913 from original source.
[2] Year ended July 31, International Yearbook of Agricultural Statistics.
[3] Average for the season 1911–12 to 1913–14.
[4] International Crop Report and Agricultural Statistics.
[5] Average for calendar years 1909–1913, International Yearbook of Agricultural Statistics.
[6] Season 1913–14.

TABLE 77.—*Oats: Estimated price per bushel, received by producers, United States, 1909–1928*

Year beginning August	Aug. 15	Sept. 15	Oct. 15	Nov. 15	Dec. 15	Jan. 15	Feb. 15	Mar. 15	Apr. 15	May 15	June 15	July 15	Weighted av.
	Cents	*Cents*	*Cents*	*Cents*	*Cents*	*Cents*	*Cents*	*Cents*	*Cents*	*Cents*	*Cents*	*Cents*	*Cents*
Average:													
1909–1913	40.9	38.8	38.4	38.2	38.3	39.0	39.8	40.3	40.9	41.5	41.8	40.9	39.9
1914–1920	58.8	55.9	54.6	54.8	56.4	58.7	60.3	62.1	64.3	65.2	64.0	61.9	58.5
1921–1925	38.6	37.4	38.4	38.9	40.6	42.2	43.0	43.0	42.5	42.9	43.1	41.8	40.4
1909	46.2	41.6	41.0	40.6	41.5	43.9	45.5	45.8	44.4	43.2	42.6	41.9	43.2
1910	40.0	37.3	35.6	34.6	33.8	33.2	33.0	32.8	32.8	34.0	36.1	38.8	36.2
1911	40.3	41.4	43.2	44.4	45.0	46.3	48.6	50.9	54.0	55.6	53.9	48.4	46.1
1912	39.6	34.3	33.6	32.8	32.0	32.3	32.8	33.1	33.6	35.1	36.8	37.6	34.9
1913	38.4	39.4	38.8	38.6	39.2	39.2	39.1	39.2	39.5	39.8	39.4	37.8	38.9
1914	39.5	42.8	43.1	43.4	44.4	47.6	51.1	52.8	53.4	52.4	49.0	46.0	44.9
1915	42.0	36.5	34.7	35.5	37.6	41.8	43.6	42.4	42.3	42.4	41.2	40.2	39.3
1916	41.6	43.8	46.8	50.7	51.9	53.3	56.0	59.2	66.2	70.4	69.4	71.3	51.4
1917	67.7	62.0	62.0	64.2	70.2	76.3	82.4	87.6	87.4	82.0	77.2	74.6	72.1
1918	71.6	70.6	69.6	69.6	70.8	67.6	63.4	64.2	68.4	71.0	71.0	73.1	70.1
1919	73.5	70.0	68.6	69.6	74.3	80.4	83.6	87.6	94.5	100.6	103.7	93.2	80.3
1920	76.0	65.4	57.6	50.2	45.8	43.7	41.8	40.6	38.0	37.4	36.8	34.7	51.1
1921	32.0	30.6	30.1	29.7	30.6	31.9	34.7	36.6	37.2	38.2	37.8	36.2	33.4
1922	33.6	33.4	36.4	38.8	40.3	41.5	42.4	43.5	44.8	45.3	43.7	40.2	39.0
1923	37.6	38.0	39.4	40.8	42.6	43.4	45.4	46.2	46.5	46.3	46.8	49.4	42.6
1924	49.1	47.1	48.9	47.4	50.6	54.0	53.4	49.7	44.7	45.4	48.3	45.3	48.3
1925	40.7	38.1	37.2	37.6	39.1	40.0	39.2	38.8	39.4	39.5	38.9	37.7	39.0
1926	37.9	35.6	39.0	39.8	41.1	42.6	43.4	43.4	43.2	45.4	48.0	46.3	41.2
1927	44.4	43.9	44.6	45.1	48.1	49.3	51.3	54.5	56.9	62.0	61.4	56.2	49.6
1928	38.4	36.7	39.0	39.8	42.5								

Bureau of Agricultural Economics. Based on returns from special price reporters. Mean of prices reported on 1st of month and 1st of succeeding month, August, 1909–December, 1923.

TABLE 78.—*Oats, No. 3 white: Weighted average price [1] per bushel of reported cash sales, Chicago, 1909–1928*

Year beginning August	Aug.	Sept.	Oct.	Nov.	Dec.	Jan.	Feb.	Mar.	Apr.	May	June	July	Weighted av.[1]
	Cents	*Cents*	*Cents*	*Cents*	*Cents*	*Cents*	*Cents*	*Cents*	*Cents*	*Cents*	*Cents*	*Cents*	*Cents*
Average:													
1909–1913	38	39	38	38	39	41	40	40	41	41	42	42	40
1914–1920	57	56	55	57	60	62	62	64	67	66	65	65	60
1921–1925	39	40	41	42	44	45	44	43	43	43	44	43	42
1909	38	39	40	40	44	48	47	44	42	40	38	41	42
1910	35	34	32	32	32	33	31	31	32	34	39	44	33
1911	41	45	47	48	47	50	52	53	57	55	53	49	50
1912	33	33	33	32	33	33	33	32	35	38	40	40	35
1913	42	43	40	40	40	39	39	39	39	40	40	37	40
1914	42	48	46	48	49	53	58	57	57	54	49	53	50
1915	41	34	36	36	42	48	45	42	44	43	39	41	41
1916	44	46	49	55	53	57	56	61	69	70	67	78	54
1917	61	60	60	65	77	82	89	93	89	77	77	77	71
1918	70	72	69	72	72	65	58	63	70	69	70	78	70
1919	73	68	70	73	82	86	86	93	101	109	113	91	80
1920	70	62	54	51	48	44	42	42	36	39	37	34	51
1921	32	35	31	33	34	34	36	36	38	38	37	36	35
1922	32	38	42	43	44	43	44	45	46	45	43	40	41
1923	38	40	43	43	44	46	48	47	48	48	51	54	45
1924	50	48	50	50	58	58	53	48	42	45	49	44	50
1925	41	39	39	40	42	42	41	40	42	41	40	42	41
1926	38	38	44	42	46	46	43	44	45	50	49	45	43
1927	47	47	48	49	54	55	56	59	63	67	68	56	55
1928	38	41	42	44	46								

Bureau of Agricultural Economics. Compiled from the Chicago Daily Trade Bulletin. Data for 1899–1908 available in 1924 Yearbook, p. 628, Table 94.

[1] Average of daily prices weighted by car-lot sales.

TABLE 79.—*Barley: Acreage, production, value, exports, etc., United States, 1900–1928*

Year	Acreage harvested	Average yield per acre	Production	Price per bushel received by producers Dec. 1	Farm value Dec. 1	Price per bushel at Chicago, year beginning August[1]	Foreign trade, including barley flour and malt, year beginning July 1[2]			
							Domestic exports	Imports	Net balance[3]	
									Total	Percentage of production
	1,000 acres	*Bushels of 48 lbs.*	*1,000 bushels*	*Cents*	*1,000 dollars*	*Cents*	*1,000 bushels*	*1,000 bushels*	*1,000 bushels*	
1900	4,545	21.1	96,041	40.5	38,896	[4] 56	6,619	175	+6,445	6.7
1901	4,742	25.7	121,784	45.2	55,068	64	9,079	60	+9,019	7.4
1902	5,126	29.1	149,389	45.5	67,944	56	8,745	59	+8,686	5.8
1903	5,568	26.4	146,864	45.4	66,700	56	11,280	94	+11,187	7.6
1904	5,912	27.4	162,105	41.6	67,427	49	11,105	84	+11,021	6.8
1905	6,250	27.2	170,089	39.4	66,959	50	18,431	20	+18,410	10.8
1906	6,730	28.6	192,270	41.6	80,069	61	8,616	41	+8,632	4.5
1907	6,941	24.5	170,008	66.3	112,675	84	4,554	202	+4,370	2.6
1908	7,294	25.3	184,857	55.2	102,037	67	6,729	4	+6,725	3.6
1909	*7,699*	*22.5*	*173,344*	----						
1909	7,699	24.4	187,973	54.8	102,947	67	4,454	5	+4,449	2.4
1910	7,743	22.5	173,832	57.8	100,426	92	9,507	187	+9,320	5.4
1911	7,627	21.0	160,240	86.9	139,182	122	1,655	2,772	−1,117	.7
1912	7,530	29.7	223,824	50.5	112,957	68	17,874	15	+17,859	8.0
1913	7,499	23.8	178,189	53.7	95,731	65	6,945	351	+6,594	3.7
1914	7,565	25.8	194,953	54.3	105,903	72	28,712	103	+28,609	14.7
1915	7,148	32.0	228,851	51.6	118,172	69	30,821	37	+30,783	13.5
1916	7,757	23.5	182,309	88.1	100,646	191	20,319	462	+19,857	10.9
1917	8,933	23.7	211,759	113.7	240,758	146	28,717	517	+28,200	13.3
1918	9,740	26.3	256,225	91.7	234,942	104	29,324	24	+29,301	11.4
1919	*6,473*	*18.9*	*122,025*							
1919	6,720	22.0	147,608	120.6	178,080	145	34,691	335	+34,356	23.3
1920	7,600	24.9	189,332	71.3	135,083	78	27,255	20	+27,234	14.4
1921	7,414	20.9	154,946	41.9	64,934	61	27,546	8	+27,538	17.8
1922	7,317	24.9	182,068	52.5	95,560	65	21,909	38	+21,871	12.0
1923	7,835	25.2	197,691	54.1	107,038	72	13,913	55	+13,858	7.0
1924	*6,767*	*23.5*	*159,139*							
1924	6,925	26.2	181,575	74.1	134,590	90	28,543	48	+28,495	15.7
1925	7,997	26.7	213,863	58.8	125,709	72	30,448	53	+30,395	14.2
1926	7,970	23.2	184,905	57.5	106,237	77	19,655	49	+19,605	10.6
1927	9,476	28.1	265,882	67.8	180,200	91	39,274	45	+39,230	14.8
1928 [5]	12,539	28.5	356,868	55.2	197,128	----				

Bureau of Agricultural Economics. Production figures are estimates of the crop-reporting board; italic figures are census returns. See 1927 Yearbook, page 799, for data for earlier years.

[1] From Bureau of Labor Statistics as follows: Bulletin No. 39, 1900–1901. August, 1900–December, 1901, choice to fancy malting, by samples. Wholesale price bulletins—monthly quotations, January, 1902–December, 1913, choice to fancy malting; January, 1914–September, 1927, fair to good malting. Beginning October, 1927, grade reported as feeding, but as grade remained unchanged, no change was made in comparative prices.

[2] Compiled from Commerce and Navigation of the United States 1900–1917; Foreign Commerce and Navigation of the United States, 1918; Monthly Summary of Foreign Commerce of the United States, June issues; 1919–1926; January and June issues, 1927–28, and official records of the Bureau of Foreign and Domestic Commerce. Malt converted to terms of barley on the basis that 1.1 bushels of malt is the product of 1 bushel of barley. Barley flour converted on the basis that 1 barrel of flour is the product of 9 bushels of barley. Exports of flour not reported prior to 1919. Barley—general imports, 1900–1909; imports for consumption, 1910–1927. Malt—general imports, 1900–1914; imports for consumption, 1915–1927. Imports of flour not reported prior to 1915; imports for consumption, 1915–1927.

[3] The difference between total exports (domestic exports plus reexports) and total imports. Net exports indicated by +; net imports indicated by −.

[4] Average for 11 months.

[5] Preliminary.

TABLE 80.—*Barley: Acreage harvested and production, by States, average 1921–1925, annual 1926–1928*

State and division	Acreage harvested				Production			
	Average, 1921–1925	1926	1927	1928 [1]	Average, 1921–1925	1926	1927	1928 [1]
	1,000 acres	1,000 acres	1,000 acres	1,000 acres	1,000 bushels	1,000 bushels	1,000 bushels	1,000 bushels
Maine	3	4	4	4	98	120	108	112
Vermont	8	6	6	6	219	180	174	150
New York	160	179	188	169	4,240	5,066	5,452	4,648
New Jersey	[2] 1	1	2	2	[2] 28	33	74	60
Pennsylvania	13	18	21	29	306	486	588	783
North Atlantic	184	208	221	210	4,890	5,885	6,396	5,753
Ohio	82	116	155	333	2,179	3,712	4,185	9,191
Indiana	35	23	35	94	730	575	833	2,256
Illinois	213	302	453	680	6,443	9,362	13,364	20,060
Michigan	147	133	186	270	3,446	3,790	5,301	8,100
Wisconsin	447	521	620	725	13,518	17,974	21,390	26,898
Minnesota	964	1,307	1,460	2,000	25,806	32,675	43,800	60,000
Iowa	153	268	454	808	4,400	8,174	14,256	27,068
Missouri	6	9	7	17	143	216	161	374
North Dakota	1,311	1,472	1,663	2,179	28,341	21,050	42,406	55,564
South Dakota	919	778	1,200	1,644	20,890	7,858	36,000	35,675
Nebraska	253	227	246	430	6,140	4,699	7,577	14,018
Kansas	711	266	452	633	13,422	3,032	5,695	17,661
North Central	5,240	5,422	6,931	9,813	125,458	113,117	194,968	276,865
Maryland	7	10	9	13	232	343	274	403
Virginia	12	14	13	14	309	434	338	406
North Carolina	[2] 8	15	20	32	[2] 196	390	480	736
South Atlantic	22	39	42	59	620	1,167	1,092	1,545
Kentucky	6	7	6	2	155	231	162	50
Tennessee	16	40	42	21	360	1,200	798	420
Oklahoma	143	110	36	23	2,857	2,970	594	506
Texas	112	174	195	156	2,243	6,090	3,120	3,276
South Central	278	331	279	202	5,616	10,491	4,674	4,252
Montana	101	150	195	209	2,369	3,600	6,435	6,374
Idaho	101	112	129	144	3,757	4,144	5,676	6,192
Wyoming	23	42	59	77	702	1,386	2,006	2,310
Colorado	285	380	410	547	6,366	6,080	9,020	13,128
New Mexico	8	8	8	12	152	208	144	228
Arizona	26	25	20	17	863	875	700	646
Utah	18	20	30	34	642	800	1,410	1,666
Nevada	6	7	9	11	222	280	405	440
Washington	80	64	58	55	2,656	2,176	2,436	1,952
Oregon	80	82	91	105	2,416	2,296	3,185	3,675
California	1,045	1,080	994	1,044	29,301	32,400	27,335	31,842
Far Western	1,774	1,970	2,003	2,255	49,445	54,245	58,752	68,453
United States	7,498	7,970	9,476	12,539	186,029	184,905	265,882	356,868

Bureau of Agricultural Economics. Estimates of the crop-reporting board.

[1] Preliminary.   [2] 2-year average.

TABLE 81.—Barley: Acreage, yield per acre, and production in specified countries, average 1909–1913, 1921–1925, annual 1926–1928

Country	Acreage (1,000 acres)					Yield per acre (Bushels)					Production (1,000 bushels)				
	Avg. 1909–1913[1]	Avg. 1921–1925	1926	1927	1928, prelim.	Avg. 1909–1913[1]	Avg. 1921–1925	1926	1927	1928, prelim.	Avg. 1909–1913[1]	Avg. 1921–1925	1926	1927	1928, prelim.
NORTHERN HEMISPHERE, NORTH AMERICA															
Canada	1,574	3,022	3,647	3,506	4,881	28.8	25.4	27.4	27.6	27.9	45,275	76,899	99,987	96,938	136,391
United States	7,620	7,498	7,970	9,476	12,539	24.3	24.8	23.2	28.1	28.5	184,812	186,029	184,905	265,882	356,868
Total	9,194	10,520	11,617	12,982	17,420	25.0	25.0	24.5	27.9	28.3	230,087	262,928	284,892	362,820	493,259
EUROPE															
England and Wales	1,488	1,352	1,148	1,049	1,185	34.0	32.8	37.2	38.3	40.1	50,658	44,379	42,761	40,227	47,549
Scotland	191	158	122	120	112	37.6	38.6	41.7	36.6	42.9	7,173	6,092	5,087	4,387	4,807
Irish Free State	(164)	159	141	121	149	---	38.2	47.5	52.0	37.6	(7,397)	6,074	6,692	6,295	5,600
Norway	89	137	143	150	---	32.2	32.0	35.8	31.1	---	2,867	4,383	5,125	4,672	---
Sweden	448	409	443	415	---	33.6	31.6	33.8	30.1	---	15,035	12,921	14,971	12,472	---
Denmark	639	605	770	822	873	42.0	46.4	42.0	43.9	58.4	26,860	28,072	32,415	36,082	50,981
Netherlands	68	63	67	66	70	48.1	52.4	53.1	51.8	65.0	3,270	3,302	3,558	3,416	4,547
Belgium	88	84	87	79	77	50.5	49.1	48.3	52.8	61.0	4,446	4,127	4,201	4,169	4,694
France	1,987	1,713	1,706	1,747	1,817	26.6	25.6	26.9	28.8	29.2	52,826	43,892	45,835	50,327	53,100
Spain	3,510	4,343	4,473	4,452	4,449	21.3	21.2	21.5	20.7	18.4	74,689	92,268	96,284	92,220	81,740
Portugal	(170)	182	185	193	---	---	11.3	8.0	10.3	---	(1,200)	2,053	1,485	1,982	---
Italy	647	576	587	583	560	16.4	17.9	18.8	16.2	19.7	10,638	10,283	11,023	9,443	11,024
Germany	3,464	3,198	3,671	3,653	3,753	38.6	31.3	30.8	34.4	41.0	133,787	100,182	113,102	125,750	153,721
Austria	421	320	362	366	366	23.9	22.1	25.1	29.9	32.0	10,065	7,072	9,074	10,935	11,730
Czechoslovakia	2,275	1,673	1,790	1,755	1,792	31.3	30.0	29.3	33.5	33.0	71,108	50,110	52,500	58,750	59,167
Hungary	1,322	1,096	1,049	1,002	1,014	24.5	20.3	24.3	23.6	27.5	32,369	22,198	25,509	23,684	27,871
Yugoslavia	1,058	902	867	966	970	19.1	15.6	19.9	15.0	18.2	20,229	14,027	17,274	14,449	17,637
Greece	[2]369	383	506	465	598	18.8	14.8	15.1	15.6	18.2	[2]6,953	5,676	7,620	7,271	10,858
Bulgaria	516	539	552	560	601	20.1	17.2	20.1	23.0	26.2	10,380	9,266	11,085	12,867	15,744
Rumania	[3]3,378	4,315	3,534	4,359	4,273	18.3	12.8	21.9	13.3	15.2	[3]61,677	55,295	77,388	57,950	64,808
Poland	3,048	2,855	3,048	3,063	3,164	22.7	22.7	23.4	24.5	28.1	69,055	64,865	71,401	75,059	89,053
Lithuania	536	451	487	487	408	16.5	15.5	17.8	17.7	20.3	8,820	6,979	8,662	8,630	8,282
Latvia	463	414	470	458	364	17.1	13.2	14.1	13.0	9.0	7,922	5,464	6,630	5,974	3,275
Estonia	329	307	532	295	282	18.8	18.8	16.2	14.7	14.9	6,201	5,782	8,630	4,335	4,200
Finland	278	273	300	267	268	17.8	18.5	23.9	24.6	22.0	4,947	5,046	7,170	6,571	5,889
Russia, European and Asiatic	26,193	14,804	18,217	17,479	17,159	16.0	12.8	13.9	12.3	15.3	418,030	190,072	253,010	215,472	261,804
Total Europe, excluding Russia, reporting area and production all years	26,164	25,847	26,356	26,764	27,143	25.9	23.1	25.3	24.6	27.1	676,940	597,131	665,562	657,168	736,262

Column groups (column headings for acreage / yield / production do not appear on this page; the first data row, "Estimated European total excluding Russia," carries the large round-number estimates). Each group spans five year-columns.

Country or region	Acreage (1,000 acres)					Yield per acre (bu.)					Production (1,000 bu.)				
Estimated European total excluding Russia.	27,000	26,600	27,200	27,500	27,900						[4]702,000	619,000	690,000	679,000	760,000
AFRICA															
Morocco	(3,000)	2,862	3,157	2,469	2,526		14.1	9.4	13.8	16.9	(38,000)	40,304	29,762	33,955	42,761
Algeria	3,395	3,017	3,543	3,360	3,430	13.5	10.2	6.5	10.3	11.1	45,974	30,779	23,002	34,554	38,100
Tunis	1,228	1,022	1,409	861	1,359	6.4	6.7	6.3	4.8	9.3	7,826	6,843	8,818	4,134	12,631
Egypt	398	381	333	376	366	29.8	30.0	30.3	31.8	29.5	11,867	11,427	10,097	11,961	10,799
Total	8,021	7,282	8,442	7,066	7,681	12.9	12.3	8.5	12.0	13.6	103,667	89,353	71,679	84,604	104,291
ASIA															
India	8,877	6,976	6,573	6,387		16.4	19.2	18.3	18.6		145,496	133,793	120,587	119,000	
Syria and Lebanon	(450)	[3]682	601	655	849		10.7	17.6	23.4	15.4	(5,000)	7,300	10,588	15,325	13,085
Japan	3,042	2,630	2,431	2,343	2,240	31.5	30.3	36.2	35.2	37.3	95,784	79,819	88,099	82,482	83,505
Chosen	1,623	2,139	2,185	2,190	2,210	19.9	17.1	17.5	16.1	15.3	32,243	36,607	38,307	35,312	33,879
Total Northern Hemisphere countries, excluding Russia, reporting area and production all years.	48,494	49,100	51,632	52,000	57,543	23.6	21.9	22.4	23.8	25.4	1,143,721	1,073,138	1,159,127	1,237,711	1,464,281
Estimated Northern Hemisphere total, excluding Russia and China.	64,200	62,700	64,300	62,900	68,500						[4]1,408,000	1,332,000	1,413,000	1,475,000	1,704,000
SOUTHERN HEMISPHERE															
Chile	111	160	155	168	221	36.8	33.4	29.2	40.3		4,090	5,347	4,523	6,765	
Argentina	[3]230	726	979	1,186	1,321	[3]19.1	13.7	18.8	12.3		[3]4,395	9,924	18,372	14,560	
Union of South Africa[5]	[2]109	99	69	68	85	[2]11.7	11.8	15.6	12.0	11.5	[2]1,274	1,172	1,075	814	974
Australia	154	307	371			19.6	19.7	3.5			3,021	6,048	1,295	903	
Estimated Southern Hemisphere total.	800	1,500	1,800	1,900	2,100						17,000	31,000	47,000	32,000	
Total Northern and Southern Hemisphere countries, excluding Russia, reporting area and production all years.	48,603	49,199	51,701	52,068	57,628	23.6	21.8	22.4	23.8	25.4	1,144,995	1,074,310	1,160,202	1,238,525	1,465,255
Estimated world total excluding Russia and China.	65,000	64,200	66,100	64,800	70,600						[4]1,425,000	1,363,000	1,460,000	1,507,000	

Bureau of Agricultural Economics. Official sources and International Institute of Agriculture. Estimates given are for crops harvested during the calendar year in the Northern Hemisphere and the succeeding harvest in the Southern Hemisphere.

[1] Where changes in boundary have occurred, averages are estimated for territory within present boundaries.
[2] 1 year only.
[3] 4-year average.
[4] The estimate for the 5-year period; 1909–1913, given in this table is somewhat larger than the figure obtained by averaging the same 5 years in Table 83. This is because in this table estimates for warring countries are for postwar boundaries, whereas in Table 83 they are for pre-war territory. As a result, in excluding Russia, which lost territory during the war, a smaller area is excluded in this table than in Table 83.
[5] Excludes native locations which produced 38,550 bushels in 1917–18 and 29,056 bushels in 1920–21.

TABLE 82.—*Barley: Yield per acre and estimated price per bushel, December 1, by States, average 1914–1920, 1921–1925, annual 1924–1928*

State	Yield per acre							Estimated price per bushel						
	Av., 1914–1920	Av., 1921–1925	1924	1925	1926	1927	1928	Av., 1914–1920	Av., 1921–1925	1924	1925	1926	1927	1928
	Bush.	*Bush.*	*Bush.*	*Bush.*	*Bush.*	*Bush.*	*Bush.*	*Cts.*	*Cts.*	*Cts.*	*Cts.*	*Cts.*	*Cts.*	*Cts.*
Maine	26.1	29.0	26.0	35.0	30.0	27.0	28.0	121	95	108	80	92	94	110
Vermont	30.0	29.2	31.0	32.0	30.0	29.0	25.0	116	92	103	83	85	95	110
New York	27.7	26.7	30.6	29.0	28.3	29.0	27.5	105	76	91	77	75	80	78
New Jersey		[1] 28.0	29.0	27.0	33.0	37.0	30.0		[1] 90	92	88	85	83	86
Pennsylvania	26.7	24.3	26.5	25.5	27.0	28.0	27.0	100	75	90	86	80	83	84
Ohio	28.4	26.3	28.0	31.0	32.0	27.0	27.6	87	67	85	70	62	72	60
Indiana	28.5	21.2	24.0	23.0	25.0	23.8	24.0	89	64	77	71	66	73	59
Illinois	32.3	30.0	32.0	33.0	31.0	29.5	29.5	91	60	75	63	58	73	53
Michigan	25.3	24.2	29.3	24.5	28.5	28.5	30.0	92	68	80	72	65	76	70
Wisconsin	31.2	30.4	32.0	36.8	34.5	34.5	37.1	92	63	78	66	65	75	65
Minnesota	25.1	26.7	32.0	30.0	25.0	30.0	30.0	80	49	69	52	51	65	50
Iowa	29.4	28.6	31.0	31.3	30.5	31.4	33.5	82	54	70	57	56	66	54
Missouri	25.3	25.6	25.0	31.0	24.0	23.0	22.0	94	78	82	95	80	95	80
North Dakota	18.6	21.4	26.0	22.5	14.3	25.5	25.5	72	42	62	43	46	59	43
South Dakota	25.9	23.1	27.0	26.0	10.1	30.0	21.7	76	44	64	47	52	58	48
Nebraska	25.7	24.0	25.0	24.3	20.7	30.8	32.6	71	47	63	54	58	55	51
Kansas	20.3	18.4	16.5	16.0	11.4	12.6	27.9	74	49	65	58	61	55	50
Maryland	30.8	32.6	35.0	33.0	34.3	30.5	31.0	99	80	93	87	80	87	85
Virginia	27.4	26.1	27.0	26.0	31.0	26.0	29.0	110	87	105	97	90	87	85
North Carolina		[1] 23.0	23.0	23.0	26.0	24.0	23.0		[1] 115	110	120	100	110	120
Kentucky	27.6	25.8	24.0	26.0	33.0	27.0	25.0	110	85	101	95	86	91	91
Tennessee	22.2	21.9	20.0	23.0	30.0	19.0	20.0	120	100	110	110	96	100	110
Oklahoma	21.9	19.6	23.0	14.0	27.0	16.5	22.0	96	63	70	75	58	65	65
Texas	23.6	19.8	25.0	7.2	35.0	16.0	21.0	96	69	76	90	53	70	73
Montana	21.9	23.4	25.0	21.0	24.0	33.0	30.5	84	60	69	72	64	60	56
Idaho	33.6	36.8	31.0	44.0	37.0	44.0	43.0	91	62	82	56	60	68	63
Wyoming	32.3	29.8	29.0	33.0	33.0	34.0	30.0	107	65	72	61	62	61	61
Colorado	28.7	22.2	20.0	21.6	16.0	22.0	24.0	85	56	72	58	55	56	54
New Mexico	28.3	18.0	15.0	17.0	26.0	18.0	19.0	97	76	60	85	65	70	75
Arizona	35.1	33.0	30.0	35.0	35.0	35.0	38.0	112	90	88	100	85	75	80
Utah	35.7	35.8	28.5	43.0	40.0	47.0	49.0	97	69	87	85	72	76	73
Nevada	37.4	34.7	39.5	48.0	40.0	45.0	40.0	117	91	110	82	85	80	80
Washington	33.0	32.6	22.6	34.0	34.0	42.0	35.5	94	68	85	68	65	77	70
Oregon	30.5	29.8	22.0	33.0	28.0	35.0	35.0	101	73	100	73	65	77	72
California	27.4	27.7	21.9	31.0	30.0	27.5	30.5	99	76	116	75	58	93	72
United States	25.5	24.8	26.2	26.7	23.2	28.1	28.5	84.5	56.3	74.1	58.8	57.5	67.8	55.2

Bureau of Agricultural Economics. Estimates of the crop-reporting board.

[1] 2-year average.

TABLE 83.—*Barley: World production, 1894-1923*

Year	Estimated world production excluding Russia	Estimated European production excluding Russia	United States	Russia [1]	Germany	Japan	Canada	India	Spain	Rumania
	1,000,000 bushels	1,000,000 bushels	1,000,000 bushels	1,000,000 bushels	1,000,000 bushels	1,000,000 bushels	1,000,000 bushels	1,000,000 bushels	1,000,000 bushels	1,000,000 bushels
1894	935	544	78	277	131	81			57	17
1895	1,008	527	115	226	128	80			47	22
1896	973	528	99	254	125	71			36	32
1897	907	481	103	239	118	73			46	21
1898	1,040	564	100	307	130	83			73	30
1899	1,017	533	117	227	137	77			54	5
1900	1,269	522	96	237	138	82			57	15
1901	1,085	570	122	240	153	83			80	24
1902	1,127	592	149	338	142	74			81	25
1903	1,099	589	147	357	153	60			64	30
1904	1,068	512	162	346	135	81			54	12
1905	1,067	532	170	347	134	77			46	26
1906	1,226	610	192	331	143	84			90	34
1907	1,161	569	170	377	161	90			54	20
1908	1,132	536	185	402	141	87	47		70	13
1909	1,338	621	188	502	161	87	55		79	20
1910	1,242	560	174	488	133	82	29		76	29
1911	1,326	606	160	437	145	86	44		87	26
1912	1,345	589	224	496	160	91	49		60	21
1913	1,400	637	178	600	169	101	48		69	27
1914	1,213	546	195	[2] 433	144	86	36	125	72	26
1915	1,244	477	229	[3] 429	114	95	54	143	84	29
1916	1,201	507	182	[4] 305	128	89	43	148	87	30
1917	1,170	427	212	325	[5] 90	89	55	156	78	
1918	1,273	420	256		94	88	77	156	90	[5] 5
1919	1,117	479	148		88	89	56	130	82	32
1920	1,249	552	189	216	82	85	63	150	90	68
1921	1,246	567	155	119	89	82	60	117	89	44
1922	1,312	599	182	176	74	81	72	146	78	94
1923	1,428	664	198	196	108	69	77	145	112	61
1924	1,324	577	182	181	110	[6] 75	89	137	84	31
1925	1,503	689	214	279	119	[6] 91	87	123	99	47
1926	1,460	690	185	253	113	[6] 83	100	121	96	77
1927	1,507	679	266	215	126	[6] 82	97	119	92	58
1928 [7]		760	357	262	154	[6] 84	136		82	65

Bureau of Agricultural Economics. Official sources and International Institute of Agriculture. For each year is shown the production during the calendar year in the Northern Hemisphere and the succeeding harvest in the Southern Hemisphere.

[1] Includes all Russian territory reporting for the years shown.
[2] Total Russian Empire exclusive of the 10 Vistula Provinces of Russian Poland and the Province of Batum in Transcaucasia.
[3] Exclusive of Russian Poland, Lithuania, parts of present Latvia and the Ukraine, and two Provinces of Transcaucasia.
[4] Beginning this year estimates within present boundaries of the Union of Socialist Soviet Republics excluding Turkestan, Transcaucasia, and the Far East, which regions in 1924 produced 20,897,000 bushels.
[5] Postwar boundaries beginning this year and therefore not comparable with earlier years.
[6] Weighed bushels, those reported for the earlier years being measured bushels.
[7] Preliminary.

TABLE 84.—*Barley: Monthly marketings by farmers, as reported by about 3,500 mills and elevators, United States, 1917-1927*

Year beginning July	Percentage of year's receipts												
	July	Aug.	Sept.	Oct.	Nov.	Dec.	Jan.	Feb.	Mar.	Apr.	May	June	Season
1917	2.2	15.0	23.4	16.5	8.5	8.6	6.5	7.5	6.1	2.9	1.8	1.0	100.0
1918	1.9	9.8	13.6	10.5	7.9	7.8	8.1	5.4	7.2	9.0	11.6	7.2	100.0
1919	18.5	19.2	14.3	9.9	6.4	7.5	5.4	3.1	3.7	3.4	3.0	5.6	100.0
1920	7.0	16.5	15.0	9.9	9.9	7.2	6.7	5.5	6.5	4.2	5.7	5.9	100.0
1921	35.0	14.0	10.5	7.8	4.4	4.2	3.9	4.3	4.2	3.0	4.4	4.3	100.0
1922	17.4	22.9	14.6	10.8	5.2	6.0	4.8	3.2	3.5	1.9	2.7	7.0	100.0
1923	10.3	23.7	15.1	9.9	7.8	6.5	4.1	3.5	3.1	2.6	2.3	11.1	100.0
1924	9.0	16.8	21.4	17.0	8.1	5.7	5.1	3.8	3.3	2.4	2.7	4.7	100.0
1925	16.4	19.1	18.4	11.7	6.6	5.1	4.0	3.4	3.1	2.0	3.3	6.9	100.0
1926	17.4	16.5	11.6	7.4	6.2	4.8	5.1	3.2	3.9	3.6	4.1	16.2	100.0
1927	9.1	17.4	18.7	12.2	8.0	5.7	4.7	4.5	4.5	2.1	2.7	10.4	100.0

Bureau of Agricultural Economics.

TABLE 85.—*Barley: Commercial stocks in store, 1926–27 to 1928–29*

DOMESTIC BARLEY IN UNITED STATES [1]

	Aug.	Sept.	Oct.	Nov.	Dec.	Jan.	Feb.	Mar.	Apr.	May	June	July
	1,000 bushels	*1,000 bushels*	*1,000 bushels*	*1,000 bushels*	*1,000 bushels*	*1,000 bushels*	*1,000 bushels*	*1,000 bushels*	*1,000 bushels*	*1,000 bushels*	*1,000 bushels*	*1,000 bushels*
1926–27						7,097	6,664	6,116	5,339	3,675	3,046	2,720
1927–28	3,108	5,041	6,549	5,957	5,769	4,825	4,423	4,273	4,588	3,890	2,410	2,801
1928–29	3,395	9,318	10,681	11,067	11,744							

UNITED STATES BARLEY IN CANADA

	Aug.	Sept.	Oct.	Nov.	Dec.	Jan.	Feb.	Mar.	Apr.	May	June	July
1926–27						272	300	64	70	59	0	13
1927–28	5	66	665	344	152	40	42	9	25	9	1	20
1928–29	0	767	4,171	5,599	2,319							

CANADIAN BARLEY IN UNITED STATES [2]

	Aug.	Sept.	Oct.	Nov.	Dec.	Jan.	Feb.	Mar.	Apr.	May	June	July
1926–27						2,942	2,246	1,677	608	2,401	1,573	175
1927–28	19	27	27	717	1,768	1,945	1,499	1,191	557	112	483	278
1928–29	300	249	1,751	2,959	4,778							

Bureau of Agricultural Economics. Compiled from weekly reports to the Grain, Hay and Feed Market News Service. Data are for stocks on the Saturday nearest the 1st day of the month.

[1] Includes barley stored at 39 interior and seaboard points of accumulation, exclusive of barley in transit on lakes and canals.
[2] Includes barley stored at lake and seaboard ports, exclusive of barley in transit on lakes and canals.

TABLE 86.—*Barley: Farm stocks, growing conditions, and shipments, United States, 1910–1928*

Year beginning August	Stocks of old barley on farms Aug. 1 [1]	Condition of new crop				Weight per measured bushel of new barley [2]	Stocks of barley on farms on Mar. 1 following [1]	Shipped out of county where grown [1]
		June 1	July 1	Aug. 1	Sept. 1			
	1,000 bushels	*Per cent*	*Per cent*	*Per cent*	*Per cent*	*Pounds*	*1,000 bushels*	*1,000 bushels*
1910	8,075	89.6	73.7	70.0	69.8	46.9	33,498	86,955
1911	5,763	90.2	72.1	66.2	65.5	46.0	24,754	91,620
1912	2,591	91.1	88.3	89.1	88.9	46.8	62,301	120,143
1913	11,252	87.1	76.6	74.9	73.4	46.5	44,126	86,262
1914	7,609	95.5	92.6	85.3	82.4	46.2	42,889	87,834
1915	6,336	94.6	94.1	93.8	94.2	47.4	58,301	98,965
1916	10,982	86.3	87.9	80.0	74.6	45.2	33,244	79,257
1917	3,775	89.3	85.4	77.9	76.3	46.6	44,419	84,056
1918	4,510	90.5	84.7	82.0	81.5	46.9	81,746	99,987
1919	11,897	91.7	87.4	73.6	69.2	45.2	33,820	50,471
1920	4,122	87.6	87.6	84.9	82.5	46.0	65,229	68,663
1921	13,487	87.1	81.4	71.4	68.4	44.4	42,294	55,738
1922	7,497	90.1	82.6	82.0	81.2	46.2	42,469	66,560
1923	6,805	89.0	86.1	82.6	79.5	45.3	44,930	68,190
1924	6,359	79.5	80.2	80.7	82.5	47.0	40,576	68,071
1925	5,728	83.1	81.2	79.5	80.3	45.9	52,915	80,547
1926	9,622	81.0	73.3	69.8	68.7	45.9	39,183	55,983
1927	3,754	81.5	84.2	83.3	82.9	46.8	61,972	87,975
1928 [3]	7,751	82.7	81.3	86.5	84.4	46.6		

Bureau of Agricultural Economics. Estimates of the crop-reporting board.

[1] Based on percentage of entire crop as reported by crop reporters.
[2] Average weight per measured bushel as reported by crop reporters.
[3] Preliminary.

TABLE 87.—*Barley: Receipts at markets named, averages by groups, 1909–1925, annual 1921–1927*

Year beginning August	Minne- apolis	Duluth	Chicago	Milwau- kee	Omaha	Total 5 markets	Fort William and Port Arthur [1]
	1,000 bushels	*1,000 bushels*	*1,000 bushels*	*1,000 bushels*	*1,000 bushels*	*1,000 bushels*	*1,000 bushels*
Average:							
1909–1913	25,204	10,267	24,872	15,636			5,769
1914–1920	30,067	8,230	22,476	15,674			8,094
1921–1925	17,594	8,084	9,661	10,226	885	46,451	21,594
1921	11,926	5,179	7,573	9,330	1,152	35,160	11,597
1922	14,244	3,844	10,103	8,922	801	37,914	15,756
1923	15,396	3,654	9,755	9,077	948	38,830	15,910
1924	23,158	14,501	11,336	13,127	796	62,918	28,045
1925	23,245	13,244	9,540	10,673	729	57,431	36,662
1926	12,086	6,667	8,386	8,440	594	36,173	35,784
1927 [2]	22,982	22,691	11,320	11,061	1,768	69,822	23,652

Bureau of Agricultural Economics. Compiled from reports of Minneapolis Chamber of Commerce, Duluth Board of Trade, Chicago Board of Trade, Milwaukee Chamber of Commerce, Omaha Grain Exchange, American Elevator and Grain Trade, and Canadian Grain Statistics.

[1] Crop year begins September.
[2] Beginning January, 1928, figures are subject to revision.

TABLE 88.—*Barley: Classification of receipts graded by licensed inspectors, all inspection points*

TOTAL OF ALL CLASSES AND SUBCLASSES UNDER EACH GRADE, BY CARS, ANNUAL, 1926–1927

Year and class	Choice No. 1	No. 1	Choice No. 2	Special No. 2	No. 2	Choice No. 3	No. 3	No. 4	No. 5	No. 1 Feed	Sample	Total
	Cars	*Cars*	*Cars*	*Cars*	*Cars*	*Cars*	*Cars*	*Cars*	*Cars*	*Cars*	*Cars*	*Cars*
Beginning July 1—												
1926 [1]	215	481	107	2,168	2,005	421	4,929	4,026	266	916	15,063	30,633
1927	262	2,199	90	14,913	12,151	274	16,299	6,197	183	2,875	10,923	66,366

TOTAL INSPECTIONS, BY GRADE AND CLASS, JULY 1, 1927, TO JUNE 30, 1928

Barley	34	1,850	20	14,906	11,792	36	15,923	5,820	45	2,874	10,725	64,025
Black	0	0	0	0	0	0	0	0	0	0	0	0
Bright Western	210	298	51	5	297	190	256	287	111	1	102	1,808
Western	12	42	16	1	55	44	116	88	27	0	93	494
Bright Two-Rowed	5	9	3	1	7	1	3	2	0	0	0	31
Two-Rowed	1	0	0	0	0	3	1	0	0	0	2	7
Mixed	0	0	0	0	0	0	0	0	0	0	1	1

Bureau of Agricultural Economics.

[1] Barley grades became effective August 24, 1926.

TABLE 89.—*Barley, excluding flour and malt: International trade, averages 1910–1914, annual 1925–1928*

Country	Average 1910–1914		1925		1926		1927		1928 preliminary	
	Imports	Exports	Imports	Exports	Imports	Exports	Imports	Exports	Imports	Exports
PRINCIPAL EXPORTING COUNTRIES	*1,000 bushels*	*1,000 bushels*	*1,000 bushels*	*1,000 bushels*	*1,000 bushels*	*1,000 bushels*	*1,000 bushels*	*1,000 bushels*	*1,000 bushels*	*1,000 bushels*
Canada	66	5,210	0	27,796	10	30,893	29	42,533	3	25,131
Rumania	[1][2] 63	[1][2] 16,804	0	7,743	0	12,675	0	[3] 31,936	0	[3] 24,509
United States	0	7,896	0	23,653	0	27,181	0	17,044	0	36,580
Russia	[1] 124	[1] 173,240	0	3,235	0	36,940	0	20,465		
Argentina	[4] 3	[4] 764	--------	4,229	--------	6,383		14,217	--------	11,598
British India	[1][5] 23	[1] 10,640	[1] 4	[6] 18,075	[6][7] 3	[6] 684	[6][7] 127	[6] 394	--------	[6] 8,275
Czechoslovakia	0	0	2,292	3,153	1,709	5,134	9	5,070	64	7,365
Poland	0	0	[1] 227	[3] 4,550	94	7,374	111	4,678	138	3,084
Chile	[4] 88	[4] 1,062	0	2,362	0	2,480	0	5,596	0	2,452
Algeria	[1] 213	[1] 5,482	1,964	957	282	4,504	2,736	388	166	6,672
Tunis	[1] 328	[1] 3,055	[1] 523	[3] 313	0	[3] 2,680	0	[3] 3,740	--------	--------
Australia	[4] 159	[4] 51	70	1,553	0	760	1	2,106	--------	--------
Hungary	[1] 229	[1] 11,836	199	385	2	2,264	3	2,323	5	2,221
Bulgaria	0	[1] 1,876	0	523	0	1,117	0	1,025	0	--------
Sweden	[1] 28	[1] 102	31	540	14	523	5	1,878	40	16
Yugoslavia	0	0	0	[3] 1,197	0	[3] 1,105	0	--------		
PRINCIPAL IMPORTING COUNTRIES										
Germany	148,297	136	31,018	2,849	53,090	525	97,886	75	85,765	199
United Kingdom	48,550	[4] 101	41,140	[8] 45	35,712	[8] 472	29,708	[8] 433	34,230	--------
Netherlands	[1] 38,039	[1] 26,975	9,293	782	14,905	425	13,603	590	10,181	711
Belgium	18,351	3,079	12,068	103	13,361	250	11,618	205	11,801	327
Denmark	[1] 2,994	[1] 2,906	5,128	3,071	2,914	2,909	3,109	2,635	2,294	3,291
Austria	[1] 716	[1] 8,123	3,890	--------	3,772		2,962	159	2,849	315
Switzerland	[1] 1,140	[1] 1	2,956	1	3,102	0	2,534	0	2,841	0
France	6,711	787	2,113	914	2,188	701	1,708	263	1,538	3,108
Norway	[1] 4,550	0	1,501	0	1,652	0	1,227	0	1,273	0
Greece	0	0	[3] 1,498	0			1,028	0		
Irish Free State	0	0	784	100	1,613	55	418	996	480	612
Spain	640	117	553	928	1,560	258	1	1,079	--------	--------
Cuba	255	0	542	0	536	0	--------			
Egypt	[1] 732	[1][9] 42	126	107	314	0	666	25	11	670
Italy	824	20	212	610	127	76	326	1	273	16
Syria and Lebanon	0	0	[3] 518	0	[3] 453	0	[3] 234	0	--------	--------
Estonia	0	0	[3] 140	0	[3] 273	0	81	0	195	0
Latvia	0	0	[3] 196	[1] 203	[3] 176	0	[3] 99	0		
Finland	0	0	42	0	39	0	17	0	30	0
Japan	15	0	48	0	42	0	14	0	26	0
Ceylon	0	0	[3] 12	0	[3] 13	0	[3] 15	0	--------	--------
Total, 37 countries	273,138	280,305	119,088	109,977	137,956	148,368	170,275	159,854	154,203	137,152

Bureau of Agricultural Economics. Official sources except where otherwise stated.

[1] Year ended July 31—International Yearbook of Agricultural Statistics.
[2] Average for season 1911–12 to 1913–14.
[3] International Crop Report and Agricultural Statistics.
[4] Average for calendar year 1909–13.
[5] Average for season 1909–10 to 1911–12.
[6] Sea trade only.
[7] Year ended Mar. 31.
[8] Year ended Dec. 31.
[9] Average for season 1912–13 to 1913–14.

Table 90.—*Barley: Estimated price per bushel, received by producers, United States, 1909–1928*

Year beginning August	Aug. 15	Sept. 15	Oct. 15	Nov. 15	Dec. 15	Jan. 15	Feb. 15	Mar. 15	Apr. 15	May 15	June 15	July 15	Weighted av.
	Cents	Cents	Cents	Cents	Cents	Cents	Cents	Cents	Cents	Cents	Cents	Cents	Cents
Average:													
1909–1913	60.1	60.0	60.5	60.5	60.9	62.4	63.3	63.6	64.6	64.7	63.0	59.4	60.8
1914–1920	88.1	85.7	84.3	84.4	85.7	88.5	91.9	95.6	98.8	99.1	94.8	90.8	87.2
1921–1925	58.2	56.1	57.3	57.3	58.1	59.8	60.5	61.1	61.2	61.8	61.1	60.7	58.6
1909	57.9	54.0	53.4	53.6	55.8	58.4	59.8	60.0	58.1	56.1	54.8	54.3	55.6
1910	56.0	56.6	55.7	56.6	58.8	62.0	63.6	66.0	71.6	73.9	72.0	69.7	60.8
1911	73.2	79.4	83.3	85.9	86.6	88.8	91.1	91.6	94.2	93.6	86.5	74.4	81.9
1912	60.2	54.2	54.3	52.2	50.2	50.6	50.2	48.8	48.4	50.5	53.2	52.2	52.7
1913	53.0	56.0	55.8	54.2	53.0	52.3	51.8	51.4	50.5	49.2	48.3	46.3	53.0
1914	48.8	52.2	51.8	53.0	54.3	58.6	65.3	66.2	64.2	62.9	58.9	56.2	54.8
1915	54.3	49.4	48.4	50.8	53.2	58.3	60.6	58.4	58.4	59.6	59.4	59.3	53.8
1916	66.1	74.7	79.8	85.6	87.6	89.9	94.8	99.6	111.2	119.7	113.0	110.6	83.4
1917	112.2	112.0	112.6	112.5	120.1	129.2	146.5	165.6	164.4	147.0	126.9	114.2	122.5
1918	105.4	98.2	95.2	93.3	91.5	89.0	86.1	89.0	98.3	106.6	108.8	113.6	100.0
1919	117.2	115.4	116.2	118.8	125.4	133.6	133.2	134.6	143.2	147.4	145.2	131.5	124.9
1920	113.0	98.1	86.4	76.5	67.8	60.8	57.0	55.6	51.8	50.4	51.1	50.0	70.7
1921	48.2	46.2	43.6	41.8	42.8	44.0	47.0	51.2	54.6	57.0	55.0	51.0	48.4
1922	47.7	46.2	49.2	52.0	55.6	56.8	56.2	58.0	59.6	60.8	58.3	54.7	51.8
1923	52.2	51.9	54.7	55.2	57.6	56.5	58.0	60.0	61.0	60.0	61.9	68.8	56.6
1924	75.7	75.6	81.4	79.7	76.2	82.4	84.8	81.5	76.1	75.9	76.4	73.5	77.4
1925	67.1	60.8	57.6	58.0	58.4	59.5	56.3	54.6	54.8	55.1	53.7	55.3	59.2
1926	55.0	52.9	54.4	56.0	56.4	58.0	61.3	62.2	64.1	68.4	76.3	71.4	61.9
1927	69.0	69.5	66.8	66.8	71.5	73.6	75.4	79.4	81.3	84.5	81.7	77.6	72.6
1928	58.9	54.1	55.2	54.5	55.0								

Bureau of Agricultural Economics. Based on returns from special price reporters. Mean of prices reported on 1st of month and 1st of succeeding month, August, 1909–December, 1923.

Table 91.—*Barley, No. 2: Weighted average price [1] per bushel of reported cash sales, Minneapolis, 1909–1928*

Year beginning August	Aug.	Sept.	Oct.	Nov.	Dec.	Jan.	Feb.	Mar.	Apr.	May	June	July	Weighted av.[1]
	Cents	Cents	Cents	Cents	Cents	Cents	Cents	Cents	Cents	Cents	Cents	Cents	Cents
Average:													
1909–1913	59	63	63	63	63	69	66	66	67	65	61	60	64
1914–1920	95	92	93	95	99	103	105	111	112	111	102	100	102
1921–1925	63	63	63	64	64	66	68	67	69	68	67	68	65
1909	45	48	49	52	57	61	60	58	54	54	53	60	54
1910	61	63	63	66	70	77	74	81	88	75	77	87	74
1911	85	94	95	98	91	105	100	95	101	99	76	60	92
1912	46	49	50	47	45	49	48	46	46	50	52	48	48
1913	58	61	56	53	50	52	50	48	47	48	47	45	51
1914	59	58	55	59	57	68	75	70	70	70	66	68	65
1915	59	48	51	56	61	70	66	65	68	70	68	69	63
1916	81	81	103	111	107	117	117	121	136	148	138	149	117
1917	131	133	128	127	149	156	188	212	182	146	123	118	149
1918	102	95	91	94	92	90	87	93	109	113	112	121	109
1919	133	127	129	133	152	152	137	151	160	174	149	116	143
1920	102	99	92	82	74	69	65	67	61	59	57	62	74
1921	58	55	50	54	47	51	56	58	61	62	56	56	55
1922	49	54	57	60	61	57	60	59	64	61	58	59	58
1923	56	58	60	61	62	62	68	70	75	70	73	76	63
1924	80	81	85	81	87	93	94	88	81	84	84	84	84
1925	72	66	65	63	65	65	62	62	63	65	64	67	67
1926	63	62	65	64	67	69	71	72	77	88	88	81	71
1927	77	72	73	77	83	84	87	90	92	93	94	85	84
1928	65	63	63	62	62								

Bureau of Agricultural Economics. Compiled from Minneapolis Daily Market Record.

[1] Average of daily prices weighted by car-lot sales.

Table 92.—*Flaxseed: Acreage, production, value, foreign trade, net supply, etc. United States, 1909–1928*

Year	Acreage	Average yield per acre	Production	Price per bushel received by producers Dec. 1	Farm value Dec. 1	Price per bushel of No. 1 flaxseed at Minneapolis, year beginning Sept. 1 [1]	Flaxseed, including linseed oil in terms of seed, year beginning July 1 [2]			Net supply [3]
							Imports	Exports, domestic and foreign	Net imports	
	1,000 acres	*Bushels of 56 lbs.*	*1,000 bushels*	*Cents*	*1,000 dollars*	*Cents*	*1,000 bushels*	*1,000 bushels*	*1,000 bushels*	*1,000 bushels*
1909	*2,083*	*9.4*	*19,513*							
1909	2,083	9.5	19,699	152.8	30,093	206	5,190	157	5,033	24,732
1910	2,467	5.2	12,718	231.7	29,472	249	12,083	71	12,012	24,730
1911	2,757	7.0	19,370	182.1	35,272	214	7,137	125	7,012	26,382
1912	2,851	9.8	28,073	114.7	32,202	138	5,364	711	4,653	32,726
1913	2,291	7.8	17,853	119.9	21,399	152	8,730	401	8,329	26,182
1914	1,645	8.4	13,749	126.0	17,318	170	10,880	552	10,328	24,077
1915	1,387	10.1	14,030	174.0	24,410	204	14,699	288	14,411	28,441
1916	1,474	9.7	14,296	248.6	35,541	291	12,438	482	11,956	26,252
1917	1,984	4.6	9,164	296.6	27,182	378	13,387	499	12,888	22,052
1918	1,910	7.0	13,369	340.1	45,470	419	8,823	455	8,368	21,732
1919	*1,261*	*5.3*	*6,653*							
1919	1,503	4.8	7,178	438.5	31,475	452	25,212	506	24,706	31,884
1920	1,757	6.1	10,752	176.7	18,999	209	16,969	226	16,743	27,495
1921	1,108	7.2	8,029	145.1	11,648	219	22,630	151	22,479	30,508
1922	1,113	9.3	10,375	211.5	21,941	258	28,033	166	27,867	38,242
1923	2,014	8.5	17,060	210.7	35,951	244	20,528	140	20,388	37,448
1924	*3,435*	*8.2*	*28,246*							
1924	3,469	9.1	31,547	227.4	71,728	263	14,677	128	14,549	46,096
1925	3,078	7.3	22,424	226.5	50,783	252	20,246	125	20,121	42,545
1926	2,907	6.7	19,335	194.0	37,510	224	24,295	146	24,149	43,484
1927	2,837	9.1	25,847	186.0	48,079	220	18,131	118	18,012	43,859
1928 [4]	2,721	7.1	19,321	201.1	38,857					

Bureau of Agricultural Economics. Production figures are estimates of the crop-reporting board; italic figures are census returns. See 1927 Yearbook, page 809, for data for earlier years.

[1] The figures shown, 1909–1920, are averages of daily closing prices compiled from annual reports of the Minneapolis Chamber of Commerce; 1921–1927, are averages of daily prices weighted by car-lot sales, compiled from Minneapolis Daily Market Record.

[2] Compiled from Commerce and Navigation of the United States, 1909–1917; Foreign Commerce and Navigation of the United States, 1918; Monthly Summary of Foreign Commerce of the United States, June issues, 1919–1926; January and June issues, 1927–28 and official records of the Bureau of Foreign and Domestic Commerce.

[3] Production minus net exports or plus net imports.

[4] Preliminary.

TABLE 93.—*Flaxseed: Acreage and production, by States, average 1921–1925, annual 1926–1928*

State	Acreage				Production			
	Average, 1921–1925	1926	1927	1928 [1]	Average, 1921–1925	1926	1927	1928 [1]
	1,000 acres	*1,000 acres*	*1,000 acres*	*1,000 acres*	*1,000 bushels*	*1,000 bushels*	*1,000 bushels*	*1,000 bushels*
Wisconsin	7	11	10	9	94	132	132	122
Minnesota	521	814	757	726	5,374	7,652	7,343	5,518
Iowa	8	15	19	19	82	174	228	198
Missouri	[2] 1	2	7	7	[2] 8	16	46	56
North Dakota	1,067	1,380	1,242	1,143	8,228	7,590	10,184	8,115
South Dakota	354	475	594	588	2,774	2,755	5,940	3,410
Nebraska	5	7	7	8	40	61	70	64
Kansas	33	38	31	25	222	262	170	172
Montana	159	165	170	196	1,059	693	1,734	1,666
United States	2,156	2,907	2,837	2,721	17,887	19,335	25,847	19,321

Bureau of Agricultural Economics. Estimates of the crop-reporting board.

[1] Preliminary.   [2] 2-year average.

TABLE 94.—*Flaxseed: Yield per acre and estimated price per bushel, December 1, by States, average 1914–1920, 1921–1925, annual 1924–1928*

State	Yield per acre							Estimated price per bushel						
	Av., 1914–1920	Av., 1921–1925	1924	1925	1926	1927	1928	Av., 1914–1920	Av., 1921–1925	1924	1925	1926	1927	1928
	Bush.	*Bush.*	*Bush.*	*Bush.*	*Bush.*	*Bush.*	*Bush.*	*Cts.*	*Cts.*	*Cts.*	*Cts.*	*Cts.*	*Cts.*	*Cts.*
Wisconsin		12.5	13.0	13.8	12.0	13.2	13.5		198	225	226	200	190	199
Minnesota	9.4	10.2	11.4	10.0	9.4	9.7	7.6	258	209	233	230	197	192	205
Iowa	10.0	10.1	11.7	10.5	11.6	12.0	10.4	240	199	225	220	195	195	198
Missouri	8.1	[1] 8.2	9.0	7.5	8.0	6.5	8.0		[1] 208	225	190	195	188	190
North Dakota	7.2	7.7	8.5	6.5	5.5	8.2	7.1	260	204	227	226	193	184	201
South Dakota	8.8	8.0	8.6	6.8	5.8	10.0	5.8	250	199	223	225	190	185	201
Nebraska	7.9	8.6	7.0	9.0	8.7	10.0	8.0	233	201	225	230	185	175	190
Kansas	6.1	6.7	6.5	6.8	6.9	5.5	6.9	241	190	215	200	200	185	185
Montana	5.4	6.7	8.7	4.5	4.2	10.2	8.5	255	194	221	220	185	175	192
United States	7.2	8.3	9.1	7.3	6.7	9.1	7.1	257.2	204.2	227.4	226.5	194.0	186.0	201.1

Bureau of Agricultural Economics. Estimates of crop-reporting board.

[1] 2-year average.

TABLE 95.—Flax: Acreage and production in specified countries, average 1909–1913 and 1921–1925, annual 1926–1928

Country	Acreage					Seed production					Fiber production				
	Average, 1909–1913 [1]	Average, 1921–1925	1926	1927	1928, preliminary	Average, 1909–1913 [1]	Average, 1921–1925	1926	1927	1928, preliminary	Average, 1909–1913 [1]	Average, 1921–1925	1926	1927	1928, preliminary
	Acres	Acres	Acres	Acres	Acres	1,000 bushels	1,000 bushels	1,000 bushels	1,000 bushels	1,000 bushels	1,000 pounds	1,000 pounds	1,000 pounds	1,000 pounds	1,000 pounds
NORTHERN HEMISPHERE															
NORTH AMERICA															
Canada	1,034,874	769,552	738,397	475,852	378,081	12,040	6,438	5,995	4,885	3,614					
United States	2,489,800	2,156,400	2,907,000	2,837,000	2,721,000	19,543	17,887	19,335	25,847	19,321					
Total North America	3,524,674	2,925,952	3,645,397	3,312,852	3,099,081	31,583	24,325	25,330	30,732	22,935					
EUROPE															
United Kingdom:															
England and Wales	486	7,801	3,515	3,504											
Northern Ireland	} 53,014	36,267	30,524	26,334	37,247						19,500	12,123	13,498	11,173	
Irish Free State		8,288	6,802	5,998	8,000						4,200	2,652	2,507	2,218	
Sweden [2]	[3] 4,016	5,651	5,357			[4] 14	6	3			[4] 1,128	685	456		
Netherlands	33,055	27,839	34,226	26,630	39,348	376	330	313	407	468	17,276	16,186	23,048	15,184	30,865
Belgium	48,930	47,290	58,508	52,116	88,820	[3] 472	410	465	502	702	[3] 51,888	40,004	76,895	72,789	81,342
France	61,666	45,508	66,383	60,384	78,484	534	363	590	19		40,732	29,123	48,962	41,016	82,244
Spain	[5] 7,349	[4] 3,856	3,378	3,000		[3] 26	[3] 48	18	298	315	[3] 1,995	[3] 1,278	1,573	1,649	
Italy	[3] 42,852	51,700	54,830	43,220	44,000	340	451	459	43	44	6,675	5,159	5,512	4,608	5,090
Austria	12,787	9,055	9,296	9,209	9,100	112	55	43	51		7,480	7,433	7,425	13,653	9,788
Czechoslovakia	61,404	56,438	54,135	53,697	54,000	435	349	331	371	353	39,143	28,397	24,339	25,386	24,465
Hungary	7,967	6,716	4,149	5,700		63	45	33	31		6,671	5,056	3,194	3,086	
Yugoslavia	32,274	33,179	30,196	30,267	33,000	161					22,277	18,465	18,999	18,551	
Bulgaria	756	635	472	628	608	6	3	2	3	3	382	188	146	108	294
Rumania	[4] 71,253	40,021	50,616	48,800	48,000	[4] 707	228	244	241		[4] 11,044	[4] 6,831	4,821	5,353	
Poland	191,710	242,006	268,100	270,589	274,000	1,703	2,000	2,814	3,041	3,050	47,336	104,905	131,311	148,798	164,906
Lithuania [2]	143,257	144,360	200,400	208,000	237,000	1,126	1,195	1,574	1,405	1,377	49,703	62,119	84,612	73,987	77,162
Latvia [2]	161,906	132,076	157,600	156,200	170,000	953	783	971	655	411	62,318	46,964	55,816	40,939	32,275
Estonia	135,193	75,365	83,433	88,086	91,000	733	387	475	368	334	49,518	22,187	20,425	21,267	20,338
Finland [2]	[6] 12,236	14,761	13,501	13,334	14,000						2,710	3,259	3,383	3,542	2,646
Russia, including Asiatic Russia	3,165,082	2,799,900	4,168,000	4,351,000	4,292,000	18,984	15,025	20,507	22,507	22,765	739,990	644,969	729,500	754,865	763,000
Total European countries reporting all years, including Asiatic Russia	4,227,375	3,764,688	5,287,022	5,444,492	5,488,607	25,398	21,081	28,231	29,608	29,842	1,115,141	1,010,853	1,211,374	1,216,092	1,294,415

	Area					Production					Yield				
Kenya	7,154					19				488				1,091	
Morocco	1,366	40,844	46,944	59,000	54,000	363	437	375		188				441	
Algeria	(8,000)	5,996	6,720	6,187	8,000	7	37	41		51					
Tunis	[5]4,628	3,181	1,695	1,695		30	37	19						2,090	
Egypt						31	69			[6]7,265				2,668	1,146
ASIA															
India [7]	3,824,880	3,481,600	3,331,000	3,352,000		20,578	18,680	16,240	14,040						
Japanese Empire:															
Japan	12,139	49,911	47,730			[4]98	304	266		30,003		61,241	70,642		
Chosen	3,000	3,386	3,889	3,905								1,142	1,287		1,185
Total Northern Hemisphere countries reporting all years	7,760,049	6,737,480	8,986,053	8,822,531	8,649,688	57,018	45,799	54,035	60,756	53,316	1,115,141	1,010,853	1,211,374	1,216,092	1,294,415
Estimated Northern Hemisphere total	11,626,000	10,307,000	12,389,000	12,250,000		79,091	65,497	71,231	75,669		1,219,400	1,124,000	1,331,600	1,331,500	
SOUTHERN HEMISPHERE															
Chile	[4]748	913				19	16					[4]127		[4]734	
Uruguay	[4]126,528	116,279	175,117	175,493	196,108	[4]951	1,197	1,970	1,954						
Argentina [8]	4,113,434	5,224,745	6,672,000	7,055,000	7,297,000	31,117	52,365	69,091	79,444						
Australia	[5]1,056	394	388	5,207		[5]9	[4]4					[5]128	33		
New Zealand	[6]2,565	8,693	4,933			121	77	98							
Total Southern Hemisphere countries reporting all years	4,289,962	5,341,024	6,847,117	7,230,493	7,493,108										
Total Northern and Southern Hemisphere countries reporting all years	12,000,011	12,078,504	15,833,200	16,053,024	16,142,796	57,018	45,799	54,035	60,756	53,316	1,115,141	1,010,853	1,211,374	1,216,092	1,294,415
Estimated world total [9]	15,870,000	15,658,000	19,243,000	19,487,000		111,187	119,200	142,389	157,183		1,219,700	1,124,700	1,331,600	1,331,500	

Bureau of Agricultural Economics. Official sources and International Institute of Agriculture. Estimates given are for crops harvested during the calendar year in the Northern Hemisphere and the succeeding harvest in the Southern Hemisphere with the exception of India. See note on India.

[1] Where changes in territory have occurred averages are estimates for territory within present boundaries.
[2] Flax and hemp.
[3] 3-year average.
[4] 4-year average.
[5] 2-year average.
[6] 1-year only.
[7] Figures are for crop sown in autumn of year given and harvested in spring of the succeeding year.
[8] Acreage figures are for area sown. Figures of area harvested are not available for all years but over a 16-year period the harvested area has averaged 10 per cent below the sown area.
[9] Excludes a few minor producing countries for which no statistics are available and which do not enter into world trade. No figures are included for Germany whose acreage in 1913 was 37,800 acres and has now fallen from 118,000 acres in 1921 to 36,000 acres in 1928. No production figures are available.

TABLE 96.—*Flaxseed: Monthly marketings by farmers, as reported by about 3,500 mills and elevators, United States, 1917–1927*

Year beginning July	Percentage of year's receipts												
	July	Aug.	Sept.	Oct.	Nov.	Dec.	Jan.	Feb.	Mar.	Apr.	May	June	Season
1917	1.8	3.6	21.5	28.1	17.6	7.6	4.7	4.0	4.8	1.8	1.6	2.9	100.0
1918	1.8	2.9	14.8	21.5	15.0	10.9	5.2	4.4	5.8	4.3	5.0	8.4	100.0
1919	3.6	8.0	20.6	22.2	11.1	7.4	5.0	6.3	3.1	3.1	2.6	7.0	100.0
1920	2.1	4.7	23.6	28.6	13.0	6.2	5.0	3.3	3.1	2.1	3.4	4.9	100.0
1921	6.4	10.9	20.7	25.7	12.0	6.9	4.3	2.8	3.0	2.4	2.1	2.8	100.0
1922	2.5	13.4	27.6	23.3	11.4	5.9	4.7	3.0	2.7	2.3	1.6	1.6	100.0
1923	1.1	10.0	30.7	27.3	12.1	6.0	2.6	2.3	2.0	1.5	2.1	2.3	100.0
1924	.5	5.3	23.0	34.5	17.8	6.7	3.8	2.7	1.8	1.4	1.2	1.3	100.0
1925	1.1	11.1	34.3	23.5	12.4	5.6	2.7	2.0	1.8	1.5	1.9	2.1	100.0
1926	1.4	12.0	25.5	32.5	11.2	6.3	2.4	2.3	1.7	.9	1.7	2.1	100.0
1927	1.0	6.1	32.9	33.4	10.5	5.3	3.0	1.9	1.9	1.2	1.7	1.1	100.0

Bureau of Agricultural Economics.

TABLE 97.—*Flaxseed: Commercial stocks in store, 1926–27 to 1928–29*

DOMESTIC FLAXSEED IN UNITED STATES [1]

	Sept.	Oct.	Nov.	Dec.	Jan.	Feb.	Mar.	Apr.	May	June	July	Aug.
	1,000 bushels	*1,000 bushels*	*1,000 bushels*	*1,000 bushels*	*1,000 bushels*	*1,000 bushels*	*1,000 bushels*	*1,000 bushels*	*1,000 bushels*	*1,000 bushels*	*1,000 bushels*	*1,000 bushels*
1926–27					2,684	2,328	2,089	2,014	1,834	1,396	1,445	909
1927–28	584	1,583	5,353	4,703	4,247	3,542	2,816	2,178	1,691	882	781	615
1928–29	317	704	2,721	1,343								

CANADIAN FLAXSEED IN UNITED STATES [2]

	Sept.	Oct.	Nov.	Dec.	Jan.	Feb.	Mar.	Apr.	May	June	July	Aug.
1926–27					14	14	17	17	17	57	11	13
1927–28	0	0	1	12	18	0	0	0	0	0	0	1
1928–29	1	1	0	0								

Bureau of Agricultural Economics. Compiled from weekly reports to the Grain, Hay, and Feed Market News Service. Data are for stocks on the Saturday nearest the 1st day of the month.

[1] Includes flaxseed stored at 5 points of accumulation, exclusive of flaxseed in transit on lakes and canals.
[2] Includes flaxseed stored at lake or seaboard ports, exclusive of flaxseed in transit on lakes and canals.

TABLE 98.—*Flaxseed: Receipts at Minneapolis, 1909–1928*

Year beginning September	Sept.	Oct.	Nov.	Dec.	Jan.	Feb.	Mar.	Apr.	May	June	July	Aug.	Total
	1,000 bush.	*1,000 bush.*	*1,000 bush.*	*1,000 bush.*	*1,000 bush.*	*1,000 bush.*	*1,000 bush.*	*1,000 bush.*	*1,000 bush.*	*1,000 bush.*	*1,000 bush.*	*1,000 bush.*	*1,000 bush.*
Average:													
1909–1913	774	1,661	1,556	1,246	799	631	621	406	314	280	282	177	8,745
1914–1920	528	1,317	1,121	824	456	421	538	332	348	537	392	183	6,998
1921–1925	1,932	2,088	1,230	781	546	345	359	323	366	360	272	700	9,301
1909	999	2,219	1,892	601	966	670	826	437	222	159	123	137	9,251
1910	854	1,530	1,292	535	338	300	232	112	118	122	133	191	5,757
1911	563	1,212	1,570	1,716	531	459	397	468	571	440	487	160	8,574
1912	700	1,657	1,520	2,245	1,450	1,246	1,057	742	518	514	432	281	12,362
1913	756	1,686	1,505	1,131	711	478	592	270	139	165	233	117	7,783
1914	901	1,890	1,247	1,016	599	443	384	142	77	146	239	115	7,199
1915	347	1,038	1,506	1,113	319	399	810	486	440	363	441	199	7,461
1916	316	2,380	1,694	1,045	544	442	441	384	263	565	325	92	8,491
1917	265	980	1,112	614	533	553	527	283	349	648	208	94	6,166
1918	536	915	857	788	558	473	829	439	436	942	642	196	7,611
1919	753	570	568	492	344	368	409	159	295	522	554	297	5,331
1920	580	1,444	861	699	298	269	364	434	578	572	338	289	6,726
1921	500	1,144	375	354	308	200	254	196	300	220	157	288	4,296
1922	909	1,121	580	577	447	249	319	476	401	481	359	1,019	6,938
1923	2,654	1,953	1,308	877	358	250	229	210	296	296	264	269	8,964
1924	2,265	3,475	2,781	1,375	1,244	750	671	374	402	442	286	1,094	15,159
1925	3,331	2,745	1,107	722	375	276	320	357	431	360	294	830	11,148
1926	1,539	2,905	1,103	669	415	318	273	169	257	277	145	441	8,511
1927	4,465	3,894	1,065	490	727	500	468	326	428	437	175	564	13,539
1928 [1]	3,206	3,973	1,333	601									

Bureau of Agricultural Economics. Compiled from annual reports of the Minneapolis Chamber of Commerce.

[1] Beginning January, 1928, figures are from the Minneapolis Daily Market Record, and are subject to revision.

TABLE 99.—*Flaxseed used in the production of oil in the United States, 1919–1928*

Year beginning Oct. 1	October–December	January–March	April–June	July–September	Total
	1,000 bushels	*1,000 bushels*	*1,000 bushels*	*1,000 bushels*	*1,000 bushels*
1919	7,684	6,336	6,407	6,542	26,969
1920	6,341	6,343	6,332	5,812	24,828
1921	7,539	6,713	3,441	5,583	23,276
1922	8,602	8,292	8,689	8,223	33,806
1923	8,970	9,575	9,434	7,550	35,529
1924	11,530	12,516	9,128	7,822	40,996
1925	11,798	10,651	7,767	9,500	39,716
1926	11,085	11,037	8,963	9,051	40,136
1927	12,699	11,885	9,608	7,603	41,795
1928 [1]	11,191				

Bureau of Agricultural Economics. Compiled from reports of the Bureau of the Census.
[1] Preliminary.

TABLE 100.—*Flaxseed, International trade, average 1911–1913, annual 1924–1927*

Country	Year ended Dec. 31									
	Average 1911–1913		1924		1925		1926		1927 preliminary	
	Imports	Exports	Imports	Exports	Imports	Exports	Imports	Exports	Imports	Exports
PRINCIPAL EXPORTING COUNTRIES	*1,000 bushels*	*1,000 bushels*	*1,000 bushels*	*1,000 bushels*	*1,000 bushels*	*1,000 bushels*	*1,000 bushels*	*1,000 bushels*	*1,000 bushels*	*1,000 bushels*
Argentina	1	25,562	1	53,453	0	37,821	1	65,866	0	74,585
British India	[1] 323	[1] 14,409	253	13,010	517	[2] 14,246	823	[2] 7,455	968	[2] 8,670
Canada	89	10,645	395	3,101	0	5,502	810	2,653	354	2,185
Uruguay	0	994	0	1,110	0	1,474	0	2,093	0	[2] 2,274
Russia	80	5,739	[3] 6	[3] 1,175	[3] 0	[3] 1,958	[3] 0	[3] 1,833	[3] 0	[3] 94
Lithuania	0	0	0	734	0	810	0	1,014	0	985
Latvia [3]	0	0	408	736	576	988	324	672	498	576
Morocco	0	338	0	283	0	304	0	296	0	476
Eritrea [3]	0	0	250	210	1	379	0	258	0	178
China	0	648	0	209	0	199	0	155	0	221
Poland	0	0	6	264	145	370	244	56	552	61
Estonia	0	0	101	111	11	36	0	196	24	69
Tunis	0	39	0	21	0	53	0	31	0	46
Rumania	19	120	0	2	1	25	0	100	[3] 0	[3] 107
PRINCIPAL IMPORTING COUNTRIES										
United States	7,298	101	16,589	0	16,510	0	22,550	0	21,821	0
United Kingdom	15,908	0	17,765	0	13,521	0	14,324	0	14,104	0
Netherlands	8,741	2,488	11,479	165	10,221	232	12,927	231	14,372	148
France	6,304	60	6,493	30	5,907	20	7,145	20	7,081	18
Germany	15,312	210	5,109	24	9,871	66	12,545	50	15,715	67
Belgium	9,313	5,965	3,694	245	3,153	284	3,662	300	3,935	214
Italy	1,698	1	2,288	1	1,836	2	2,272	1	2,878	0
Sweden	911	7	1,212	0	1,335	0	1,547	0	1,467	0
Australia	103	0	[3] 718	[3] 0	[3] 863	[3] 0	[3] 801	[3] 0	[3] 825	[3] 0
Denmark	1	0	865	0	574	0	916	0	557	0
Czechoslovakia	0	0	837	2	668	11	761	11	930	2
Norway	445	0	605	0	597	0	613	0	572	0
Spain	0	0	620	0	516	0	613	0		
Japan	[4] 27	[4] 27	406	1	362	0	288	1	363	0
Finland	110	0	177	0	192	0	165	0	197	0
Hungary	0	0	13	11	31	8	82	10	101	12
Austria	[5] 1,913	[5] 41	[3] 17	[3] 0	[3] 23	[3] 0	10	0	13	0
Total, 31 countries	68,596	67,394	70,307	74,898	67,431	64,788	83,423	83,302	87,327	90,988

Bureau of Agricultural Economics. Official sources except where otherwise noted.

[1] 2-year average.
[2] Sea trade only.
[3] International Yearbook of Agricultural Statistics.
[4] 1 year only.
[5] Average for Austria-Hungary.

TABLE 101.—*Flaxseed: Estimated price per bushel, received by producers, United States, 1909–1928*

Year beginning September	Sept. 15	Oct. 15	Nov. 15	Dec. 15	Jan. 15	Feb. 15	Mar. 15	Apr. 15	May 15	June 15	July 15	Aug. 15	Weighted av.
	Cents	*Cents*	*Cents*	*Cents*	*Cents*	*Cents*	*Cents*	*Cents*	*Cents*	*Cents*	*Cents*	*Cents*	*Cents*
Average:													
1909–1913	167.0	166.4	163.3	161.1	166.5	172.4	173.5	154.8	175.9	171.5	169.0	170.7	165.1
1914–1920	274.8	260.7	254.9	257.7	263.2	270.8	276.9	281.0	281.1	275.5	278.8	185.8	267.1
1921–1925	198.1	201.0	203.6	210.5	221.4	231.3	234.7	234.7	237.3	228.4	220.1	213.3	207.6
1909	123.0	131.3	146.4	162.0	182.0	193.0	193.5	201.7	202.5	189.5	196.6	214.8	148.6
1910	227.2	231.8	230.6	226.4	227.5	237.3	237.6	238.2	233.4	215.3	202.4	201.4	229.8
1911	204.3	207.8	196.4	184.6	189.0	187.4	187.6	186.2	193.0	201.7	186.8	168.9	195.8
1912	155.2	140.6	124.0	110.4	107.8	114.2	116.3	114.0	115.0	114.6	116.0	123.2	127.4
1913	125.2	120.6	119.3	122.0	126.0	130.2	132.6	133.8	135.8	136.4	143.4	145.0	123.9
1914	133.4	123.0	122.4	130.4	149.2	160.8	162.8	168.6	169.6	161.0	148.6	144.0	131.6
1915	145.8	155.5	168.4	180.0	198.4	206.7	202.3	197.0	184.2	169.8	170.6	184.2	169.6
1916	194.7	217.0	241.6	249.6	252.2	253.4	259.6	283.4	299.7	288.4	274.8	287.2	233.8
1917	305.6	302.2	296.2	303.7	318.8	338.2	364.8	376.5	368.4	356.4	379.9	395.8	315.9
1918	381.0	357.4	337.0	333.9	318.9	318.8	338.0	355.0	375.4	416.7	492.4	529.0	374.2
1919	477.8	410.2	410.3	436.0	445.0	464.6	464.2	452.0	434.6	390.4	331.6	297.0	427.0
1920	285.0	259.9	208.4	170.2	160.0	153.4	146.5	134.2	135.7	145.8	154.0	163.4	217.6
1921	163.8	154.0	145.0	148.1	162.1	194.6	217.4	224.6	233.8	230.0	217.2	200.8	171.0
1922	189.1	199.4	211.0	217.8	229.9	245.4	261.6	279.5	273.1	248.4	228.8	210.4	209.5
1923	208.4	212.1	211.4	218.8	218.8	224.9	223.7	217.7	222.6	213.1	218.1	210.2	212.3
1924	201.2	210.8	222.7	235.8	271.8	275.3	267.8	244.7	251.8	246.8	227.6	229.5	220.7
1925	227.9	228.9	228.1	232.1	224.5	216.4	202.9	207.0	205.4	203.9	208.7	215.7	224.6
1926	211.3	197.5	195.5	196.4	193.0	195.7	195.1	196.1	205.7	204.7	198.4	203.7	205.8
1927	197.1	191.2	184.2	185.3	188.4	189.9	194.8	198.4	210.5	209.0	195.5	181.7	189.1
1928	181.6	198.1	198.1	205.4									

Bureau of Agricultural Economics. Based on returns from special-price reporters. Mean of prices on 1st of month and 1st of succeeding month, September, 1909–December, 1923.

TABLE 102.—*Flaxseed, No. 1: Average price per bushel, Minneapolis, 1909–1928*

Year beginning September	Sept.	Oct.	Nov.	Dec.	Jan.	Feb.	Mar.	Apr.	May	June	July	Aug.	Average
	Cents	*Cents*	*Cents*	*Cents*	*Cents*	*Cents*	*Cents*	*Cents*	*Cents*	*Cents*	*Cents*	*Cents*	*Cents*
Average:													
1909–1913	195	190	182	182	194	196	195	198	196	189	189	196	192
1914–1920	299	280	291	292	302	301	310	307	309	302	319	326	303
1921–1925	231	233	237	248	262	273	268	274	266	255	254	240	247
1909	141	157	175	193	218	218	225	238	222	204	234	247	206
1910	266	262	261	242	260	268	260	256	247	224	210	234	249
1911	247	235	204	206	215	206	206	215	223	225	197	186	214
1912	176	160	135	125	129	134	126	129	130	131	138	147	138
1913	145	138	135	144	149	153	158	154	156	159	168	164	152
1914	151	133	145	154	183	186	191	193	195	176	167	167	170
1915	170	186	199	207	231	232	227	213	196	180	196	215	204
1916	211	254	278	284	289	281	290	318	333	311	301	346	291
1917	338	316	329	340	360	374	408	409	393	386	440	439	378
1918	409	359	377	354	341	345	375	388	412	486	594	587	419
1919	492	432	483	499	512	509	502	468	453	392	348	328	452
1920	323	283	227	206	196	182	178	158	184	186	189	201	209
1921	203	181	181	189	213	246	257	270	280	250	259	229	219
1922	228	238	248	262	280	304	307	340	294	280	270	234	258
1923	238	248	242	246	250	258	249	247	246	244	247	244	244
1924	226	240	258	284	315	312	297	279	280	268	249	254	263
1925	259	258	256	261	250	243	232	234	230	233	244	238	252
1926	233	221	222	224	223	225	222	224	234	225	223	222	224
1927	221	213	213	215	224	227	233	236	246	238	221	205	220
1928	209	228	235	239									

Bureau of Agricultural Economics. The figures shown for 1909–1920 are averages of daily closing prices compiled from annual reports of the Minneapolis Chamber of Commerce; 1921–1925 are average of daily prices weighted by car-lot sales, compiled from Minneapolis Daily Market Record. Data 1899–1908 available in 1924 Yearbook, p. 646, Table 125.

TABLE 103.—*Linseed oil: International trade, average 1909–1913, annual 1924–1927*

Country	Average 1909–1913		1924		1925		1926		1927 preliminary	
	Imports	Exports	Imports	Exports	Imports	Exports	Imports	Exports	Imports	Exports
PRINCIPAL EXPORTING COUNTRIES	*1,000 pounds*	*1,000 pounds*	*1,000 pounds*	*1,000 pounds*	*1,000 pounds*	*1,000 pounds*	*1,000 pounds*	*1,000 pounds*	*1,000 pounds*	*1,000 pounds*
Netherlands	457	73,634	599	142,548	164	146,519	914	164,911	579	150,621
United Kingdom	58,018	58,013	5,902	68,477	38,407	56,786	31,924	51,336	47,815	44,628
Belgium	10,233	26,790	1,184	19,489	1,659	27,101	4,054	15,114	759	20,952
PRINCIPAL IMPORTING COUNTRIES										
Germany	5,231	4,377	68,508	865	58,779	4,869	41,826	6,701	44,057	5,525
United States	2,605	4,105	13,247	2,387	13,607	2,487	15,041	2,567	946	2,525
France	3,382	10,931	13,731	5,062	9,250	3,311	15,480	4,122	6,150	4,783
Switzerland	7,825	16	12,471	11	11,047	5	13,033	25	14,234	4
Brazil	8,726	0	8,853	0	11,724	0	10,285	0		
Austria	[1] 16,367	[1] 6,542	8,355	[2] 110	7,635	[2] 347	8,807	437	8,956	591
Australia [2]	[3] 12,252	[3] 0	6,696	26	6,247	42	5,802	36	4,575	10
Finland	812	0	4,358	0	4,490	0	5,154	0	5,954	0
Union of South Africa	3,449	0	4,349	0	4,122	0	4,804	0	4,259	0
Egypt	3,647	0	4,122	3	4,901	3	5,211	4	4,825	2
Dutch East Indies	[4] 3,199	0	3,597	0	4,831	0	4,683	0	[5] 4,384	0
New Zealand	4,188	0	3,623	9	3,673	7	5,216	5	2,869	0
Hungary	0	0	3,649	205	3,757	53	3,841	16	6,398	15
Norway	1,609	[2] 31	3,065	[2] 55	2,328	6	3,591	[2] 27	3,148	[2] 18
Italy	1,042	165	4,378	272	1,139	460	1,604	400	4,227	427
Chile	2,854	15	2,603	0	2,113	0	[2] 2,802	[2] 0		
British India	3,430	1,967	2,161	545	2,139	842	2,168	414	1,885	547
Yugoslavia [2]	[6] 445	0	1,519	0	2,743	27	3,663	188	1,788	7
Czechoslovakia	0	0	1,015	298	2,032	72	2,227	6	1,098	40
Canada	2,279	0	964	98	341	66	937	56	738	53
Denmark			578	67	2,110	112	1,675	30	1,972	314
Philippine Islands	809	0	839	0	748	0	952	0	1,155	0
Greece	246	0	877	0	[2] 743	[2] 161	312	0	280	0
Argentina	886	[6] 2	739	1,108	1,015	503	715	391	587	238
Sweden	933	5	368	81	387	937	905	1,019	560	1,189
Total, 28 countries	154,924	186,593	182,350	241,716	202,131	244,716	197,626	247,805	174,198	232,480

Bureau of Agricultural Economics. Official sources except where otherwise noted. Conversions made on the basis of 7.5 pounds to the gallon.

[1] Average for Austria-Hungary.
[2] International Yearbook of Agricultural Statistics.
[3] From original source.
[4] 2-year average.
[5] Java and Madura only.
[6] 4-year average.

TABLE 104.—*Linseed oil: Average price per gallon, New York, 1910–1928*

Year beginning September	Sept.	Oct.	Nov.	Dec.	Jan.	Feb.	Mar.	Apr.	May	June	July	Aug.	Average
Average:	Cents	Cents	Cents	Cents	Cents	Cents	Cents	Cents	Cents	Cents	Cents	Cents	Cents
1914–1920	117	112	105	106	106	106	109	114	116	118	119	123	113
1921–1925	91	90	90	91	91	94	94	95	97	96	96	96	94
1910	90	90	95	95	95	96	96	91	91	89	87	80	91
1911	87	88	84	71	74	71	70	73	73	76	77	66	76
1912	66	62	56	43	42	46	45	44	46	45	47	49	49
1913	50	47	46	48	48	48	50	51	50	50	52	59	50
1914	57	49	44	45	48	56	55	58	62	63	54	50	53
1915	52	55	60	61	66	72	77	76	75	67	63	71	66
1916	70	82	90	92	94	95	94	107	121	121	112	118	100
1917	125	118	115	121	129	129	141	157	157	157	164	188	142
1918	190	183	155	158	150	145	148	154	161	181	210	222	171
1919	204	179	175	182	177	177	180	183	169	165	152	141	174
1920	122	120	98	82	78	66	66	61	70	75	75	74	82
1921	74	68	67	72	82	82	84	90	84	89	87		79
1922	88	89	88	89	92	95	102	116	115	112	104	97	99
1923	90	94	92	92	92	91	93	90	94	94	98	102	94
1924	102	102	108	110	117	116	111	104	105	106	98	102	107
1925	103	¹99	96	95	87	85	80	81	81	84	89	90	89
1926	83	81	81	80	79	78	80	84	87	87	83	83	82
1927	80	77	77	75	77	77	77	77	81	80	76	76	78
1928	77	80	80	80									

Bureau of Agricultural Economics. Figures for 1910–1915 from Monthly Labor Review; 1916–1918 from War Industries Board Price Bulletin; 1919–1928 from Oil, Paint, and Drug Reporter, average of weekly range.

¹ Beginning October, 1925, prices were quoted on pound basis and have been converted to price per gallon by multiplying by 7.5.

TABLE 105.—*Linseed meal: Average price per ton, Minneapolis, 1909–1928*

Year beginning September	Sept.	Oct.	Nov.	Dec.	Jan.	Feb.	Mar.	Apr.	May	June	July	Aug.	Average
Average:	Dolls.	Dolls.	Dolls.	Dolls.	Dolls.	Dolls.	Dolls.	Dolls.	Dolls.	Dolls.	Dolls.	Dolls.	Dolls.
1909–1913	33.43	32.88	32.21	32.22	33.15	33.27	32.00	31.12	31.08	30.30	30.77	32.71	32.10
1914–1920	53.43	52.01	52.03	52.96	54.47	52.60	51.56	50.00	48.77	48.29	50.15	52.07	51.53
1921–1925	46.85	47.86	48.43	50.19	51.27	50.89	49.11	48.14	48.24	47.13	47.62	48.61	48.69
1909	32.00	31.20	32.60	33.38	35.14	35.50	35.06	34.50	34.50	30.17	31.38	33.04	33.21
1910	33.50	33.04	32.15	32.77	33.90	34.45	32.48	31.13	32.00	32.00	32.00	35.24	32.89
1911	36.64	37.00	35.84	36.69	38.00	37.80	36.67	34.83	34.00	33.08	33.00	33.00	35.55
1912	33.00	31.89	31.22	29.26	28.73	28.36	27.04	26.15	25.50	25.50	25.98	30.75	28.62
1913	32.00	31.26	29.25	29.00	29.96	30.25	28.73	29.00	29.42	30.73	31.50	31.50	30.22
1914	31.02	29.22	32.70	34.00	37.52	38.07	35.08	32.22	31.50	32.50	34.54	25.51	32.82
1915	37.50	37.50	36.86	37.56	37.38	37.00	34.31	32.12	29.27	30.18	19.88	21.48	32.59
1916	37.50	39.02	43.96	46.40	45.12	44.45	43.50	45.46	47.81	45.92	49.71	54.62	45.29
1917	56.67	57.50	56.22	59.98	57.69	57.75	59.17	60.00	59.46	57.28	57.62	59.00	58.20
1918	59.00	59.96	60.00	62.40	76.56	67.71	65.12	68.00	69.36	70.25	80.83	93.23	69.37
1919	85.29	76.21	79.22	84.40	84.58	82.59	79.00	72.48	70.58	68.24	68.00	67.04	76.47
1920	67.00	64.69	55.25	46.00	42.42	40.64	44.77	39.69	33.38	33.65	40.50	43.59	45.96
1921	42.84	39.08	41.38	47.00	48.00	50.86	55.81	54.38	53.23	51.00	48.28	46.44	48.19
1922	43.32	50.46	53.65	54.88	57.62	55.23	49.19	47.00	45.81	41.88	43.84	49.28	49.35
1923	52.21	52.78	50.92	49.76	49.31	45.74	45.10	43.20	42.58	44.44	47.16	48.73	47.66
1924	48.08	50.00	48.86	50.58	51.31	49.91	45.08	43.68	45.96	47.63	47.98	49.08	48.18
1925	47.78	46.96	47.35	48.72	50.09	52.70	50.37	52.44	53.60	50.69	50.86	49.54	50.09
1926	47.83	46.56	46.11	46.91	47.76	48.12	52.00	53.30	54.06	57.44	55.33	52.82	48.59
1927	49.50	48.46	48.00	48.00	50.92	52.00	53.30	54.06	57.44	55.33	52.82	49.17	51.58
1928	49.75	57.33	59.00	61.43									

Bureau of Agricultural Economics. Compiled from the Minneapolis Daily Market Record.

NOTE.—Prices at New York, 1909–1927, appeared in Table 101, 1927 Yearbook.

TABLE 106.—*Rice, rough: Acreage, production, value, exports, etc., United States, 1909–1928*

Year	Acreage	Average yield per acre	Production	Price per bushel received by producers Dec. 1	Farm value Dec. 1	Foreign trade, mostly cleaned rice, but including rice bran, meal, and broken rice, year beginning July 1 [1]			
						Domestic exports	Shipments from United States to Alaska, Hawaii, and Porto Rico	Imports	Net balances [2]
	1,000 acres	Bushels of 45 lbs.	1,000 bushels	Cents	1,000 dollars	1,000 bushels	1,000 bushels	1,000 bushels	1,000 bushels
1909	*610*	*35.8*	*21,889*						
1909	610	33.8	20,607	79.5	16,392	964	4,276	8,114	−2,581
1910	723	33.9	24,510	67.8	16,624	1,082	4,606	7,516	−1,605
1911	696	32.9	22,934	79.7	18,274	1,420	4,890	6,842	−157
1912	723	34.7	25,054	93.5	23,423	1,401	4,806	7,996	−1,332
1913	827	31.1	25,744	85.8	22,090	807	5,244	10,447	−3,756
1914	694	34.1	23,649	92.4	21,849	2,789	4,640	9,979	−419
1915	803	36.1	28,947	90.6	26,212	4,391	5,191	9,516	+2,651
1916	869	47.0	40,861	88.9	36,311	6,529	5,818	7,778	+6,167
1917	981	35.4	34,739	189.6	65,879	7,069	4,878	16,418	−1,148
1918	1,119	34.5	38,606	191.8	74,042	6,953	5,995	13,094	+7,638
1919	*911*	*38.8*	*35,331*						
1919	1,063	39.5	41,985	266.6	111,913	17,402	5,547	6,477	+19,948
1920	1,336	39.0	52,066	119.1	62,036	15,871	6,614	3,485	+21,217
1921	921	40.8	37,612	95.2	35,802	19,494	7,179	2,650	+25,952
1922	1,055	39.2	41,405	93.1	38,562	13,344	8,290	2,503	+20,308
1923	895	37.7	33,717	110.2	37,150	8,199	9,094	1,376	+16,416
1924	*744*	*39.7*	*29,526*						
1924	850	38.2	32,498	138.5	45,009	4,033	8,152	2,076	+10,687
1925	889	37.5	33,309	153.8	51,232	1,734	8,049	4,679	+5,602
1926	1,034	40.4	41,730	109.6	45,722	10,957	8,743	2,558	+17,587
1927	1,012	44.2	44,774	92.9	41,616	11,153	9,184	1,588	+19,037
1928 [3]	965	43.4	41,881	88.5	37,077				

Bureau of Agricultural Economics. Production figures are estimates of the crop-reporting board; italic figures are census returns. See 1927 Yearbook, page 819, for data for earlier years.

[1] Compiled from Commerce and Navigation of the United States, 1909–1917; Foreign Commerce and Navigation of the United States, 1918; Monthly Summary of Foreign Commerce of the United States, June issues, 1919–1926; January and June issues, 1927–28, and official records of the Bureau of Foreign and Domestic Commerce.

[2] The difference between the total exports (domestic exports plus reexports plus shipments to Alaska, Hawaii, and Porto Rico) and total imports. Net exports indicated by +; net imports indicated by −.

[3] Preliminary.

TABLE 107.—*Rice, rough: Acreage and production, by States, average 1921–1925, annual 1926–1928*

State and division	Acreage				Production			
	Average, 1921–1925	1926	1927	1928 [1]	Average, 1921–1925	1926	1927	1928 [1]
	1,000 acres	1,000 acres	1,000 acres	1,000 acres	1,000 bush.	1,000 bush.	1,000 bush.	1,000 bush.
Missouri	[2] 2	10	3	10	[2] 175	610	75	400
South Carolina	7	5			147	85		
Georgia	3	3			64	60		
Mississippi	1	1			17	18		
Arkansas	151	199	175	164	6,765	10,547	7,700	7,708
Louisiana	480	501	500	484	16,677	16,282	20,000	18,392
Texas	163	166	174	174	5,962	6,142	8,039	7,308
United States except California	805	885	852	832	29,701	33,744	35,814	33,808
California	115	149	160	133	5,965	7,986	8,960	8,073
United States	922	1,034	1,012	965	35,708	41,730	44,774	41,881

Bureau of Agricultural Economics. Estimates of the crop-reporting board.

[1] Preliminary. [2] 2-year average.

TABLE 108.—*Rice, acreage, yield per acre, and production in specified countries, average 1909–1913, 1921–1925, annual 1926–1928*

Country	Acreage — Average 1909–1913	Acreage — Average 1921–1925	Acreage — 1926	Acreage — 1927	Acreage — 1928, preliminary	Yield per acre — Average 1909–1913	Yield per acre — Average 1921–1925	Yield per acre — 1926	Yield per acre — 1927	Yield per acre — 1928, preliminary	Production — Average 1909–1913	Production — Average 1921–1925	Production — 1926	Production — 1927	Production — 1928, preliminary
	1,000 acres	*1,000 acres*	*1,000 acres*	*1,000 acres*	*1,000 acres*	*Pounds*	*Pounds*	*Pounds*	*Pounds*	*Pounds*	*1,000,000 pounds*	*1,000,000 pounds*	*1,000,000 pounds*	*1,000,000 pounds*	*1,000,000 pounds*
NORTHERN HEMISPHERE															
United States	716	922	1,034	1,012	965	922	1,076	1,121	1,229	1,205	660	992	1,159	1,244	1,163
Mexico	[1]66	[2]110	118	112		[1]515	652	822	893		[1]34	75	97	100	
Hawaii	19	[2]4	3	4							[1]26				
Central and South America and West Indies:															
Guatemala		6	2	4									1	2	
Salvador	[1]7	[3]13									[2]2	[3]17			
Costa Rica	[5]15	[4]17									[1]9	[2]5			
Colombia		[2]42	44			[5]1,133	[2]294	500			[5]17	[2]21	22		
Ecuador							[2]500					[2]41			
British Guiana	36	44	49	50		1,500	1,182	1,347	1,560		54	52	66	78	
Dutch Guiana			28					607			2	14	17	15	
Porto Rico	[1]16		7	7		[1]250					[1]4	[3]3		2	
Trinidad and Tobago	[4]12	[3]8											[3]4	4	
Europe:															
Spain	94	115	122	120	113	3,191	3,270	3,366	3,508	3,407	300	376	435	421	385
Portugal	[5]17	28	28	31		[5]1,353	1,222	857	968		[5]23	22	24	30	
Italy	358	316	366	351	333	1,804	2,316	2,527	2,698	2,580	646	732	925	947	839
Yugoslavia	[6]5	4	3	4	4						[6]3	3	2	2	2
Bulgaria	7	11	17	12	18			1,176		1,111	9	14	20	15	20
French West Africa:															
French Guinea		[2]2,008	2,051	2,100			487	621	648			[4]978	1,274	1,361	
French Senegal		119	124	99			546	548	545			65	68	54	
Upper Volta		[3]44	20	20			[3]136		150			[3]6	1	3	
Sierra Leone	[7]250	390	400	400		[7]828	797	932	932		[7]207	311	373	373	
Egypt	257	192	237	436		2,132	1,536	1,696			548	295	402		
Asia:															
Turkey	[1]153		133			[1]1,118					[1]171				
India	67,004	81,400	79,223	77,790	79,258	957	863	838	805	791	64,144	70,225	66,385	62,657	
Andaman and Nicobar		3	3	4											
British North Borneo	[7]64	62	71	69		[7]594	677	648	870		[7]38	42	46	60	
Brunei		3	4					614	614			[4]2	2	1	
French Establishments in India	40	45	44	44		650	644	614	614		26	29	27	27	
Japanese Empire—															
Japan	7,300	7,705	7,740	7,777	7,825	2,163	2,350	2,236	2,509	2,397	15,787	18,107	17,462	19,509	18,756
Chosen (Korea)	2,905	3,824	3,802	3,927	3,716	1,134	1,191	1,235	1,384	1,186	3,293	4,556	4,807	5,435	4,220
Taiwan (Formosa)	1,193	1,283	1,402	1,446	1,456	1,184	2,476	1,392	1,563	1,447	1,413	3,177	1,952	2,174	2,107
Kwantung		4	7	7							1	3	2	3	

Country	Acreage					Yield per acre					Production				
French Indo-China	[2]8,550	11,953	12,805	7,319		[2]858	643	646	949		[2]7,332	7,682	8,276		6,946
Siam	[2]4,555	5,964	6,881			[2]935	1,017	1,042			4,258	6,065	7,169		
Federated Malay States	[2]124	107	166			[2]637	629	452			[2]79	124	75		
Unfederated Malay States		407	399				698	722				284	288		
Straits Settlements	93	72	70				914					75	64		
Philippine Islands	2,817	4,229	4,465			431	649	690			1,213	2,744	3,083		
Ceylon	695	799	830	835	834	587	589	634	653	644	408	471	526	545	537
SOUTHERN HEMISPHERE															
Brazil	[4]1,029	1,315	1,265			996	706	967			[1]90	1,025	929		1,223
Argentina	[2]8	16	10	11			1,312				[2]8	[4]21	12		10
Belgian Congo		27	40				222	200				6	8		
Madagascar	[3]1,009	[4]1,298	1,357	1,433		[3]888	[4]1,018	602	964		[3]896	[4]1,322	817		1,429
Java and Madura:															
Irrigated	5,953	7,135	7,289	7,551		1,005	927	975	971		5,983	6,615	7,108		7,331
Nonirrigated	[9]930	879	1,103	1,203		[9]474	494	538	563		[9]450	434	593		677
Total, Java and Madura	6,900	8,014	8,392	8,755	8,691	932	880	918	915	850	6,433	7,049	7,701	8,008	7,389
Fiji Islands	[3]12	11									[3]23	7			
Total, 9 countries reporting acreage and production all periods	20,168	22,989	23,795	24,235	23,951	1,435	1,543	1,470	1,580	1,480	28,949	35,474	34,987	38,298	35,496
Estimated world total, exclusive of China [10]											109,000	126,000	125,000	125,000	125,000

Bureau of Agricultural Economics. Official sources and International Institute of Agriculture. Yields have not been calculated when total acreage is below 15,000 acres. Acreage and production data, in most cases are for crops harvested in the calendar year in the Northern Hemisphere and the succeeding harvest in the Southern Hemisphere.

[1] 1-year only.
[2] 2-year average.
[3] 3-year average.
[4] 4-year average.
[5] Year 1915.
[6] Pre-war average.
[7] Year 1914.
[8] European Turkey included.
[9] Rough estimate for nonirrigated rice.
[10] Unofficial estimates of the Chinese crop are as follows: 70,219,000,000 pounds in 1917; 53,788,000,000 pounds in 1920; and 50,056,000,000 pounds in 1923

TABLE 109.—*Rice, rough: Yield per acre and estimated price per bushel, December 1, by States, average 1914–1920, 1921–1925, annual 1924–1928*

State	Yield per acre							Estimated price per bushel						
	Average 1914–1920	Average 1921–1925	1924	1925	1926	1927	1928	Average 1914–1920	Average 1921–1925	1924	1925	1926	1927	1928
	Bush.	*Bush.*	*Bush.*	*Bush.*	*Bush.*	*Bush.*	*Bush.*	*Cts.*	*Cts.*	*Cts.*	*Cts.*	*Cts.*	*Cts.*	*Cts.*
Missouri		[1] 62.5	50.0	75.0	61.0	25.0	40.0		[1] 140	140	140	110	90	90
South Carolina	23.0	21.2	14.0	16.0	17.0			179	119	140	125	120		
Georgia	26.2	21.4	17.0	17.0	20.0			162	125	140	145	110		
Mississippi	28.0	17.0	10.0	18.0	18.0			140	118	136	110	120		
Arkansas	44.7	45.2	42.0	43.0	53.0	44.0	47.0	146	116	138	150	100	90	86
Louisiana	34.8	34.7	34.6	33.3	32.5	40.0	38.0	148	114	136	153	105	87	90
Texas	33.9	36.9	40.0	37.0	37.0	46.2	42.0	153	116	125	149	110	86	88
California	60.5	51.5	48.5	46.6	53.6	56.0	60.7	146	135	166	170	131	115	88
U. S	37.9	38.7	38.2	37.5	40.4	44.2	43.4	148.4	118.2	138.5	153.8	109.6	92.9	88.5

Bureau of Agricultural Economics. Estimates of the crop-reporting board.

[1] 2-year average.

TABLE 110.—*Rice, in terms of cleaned rice: World production, 1909–1928*

Year	Estimated world production, exclusive of China	Production in chief producing countries [1]							
		India	Japan	Indo-China	Java and Madura [2]	Siam [3]	Chosen	Philippines	United States
	1,000,000 pounds	*1,000,000 pounds*	*1,000,000 pounds*	*1,000,000 pounds*	*1,000,000 pounds*	*1,000,000 pounds*	*1,000,000 pounds*	*1,000,000 pounds*	*1,000,000 pounds*
1909	107,000	63,869	16,474		5,723	3,734	2,343	1,164	572
1910	106,000	64,552	14,650		5,738	3,466	3,269	1,267	681
1911	109,000	63,943	16,246		6,170	4,533	3,634	717	637
1912	109,000	63,802	15,778	6,614	5,842	4,561	3,413	1,512	696
1913	113,000	64,555	15,789	8,051	6,440	4,994	3,804	1,404	715
1914	113,000	61,109	17,909	9,521	6,339	4,708	4,439	1,100	657
1915	124,000	73,315	17,569	7,921	6,451	4,786	4,036	1,289	804
1916	129,000	78,521	18,363	6,733	6,409	5,011	4,377	1,745	1,135
1917	132,000	80,559	17,143	6,313	6,742	5,133	4,261	2,210	965
1918	105,000	54,466	17,184	6,302	6,831	4,642	4,765	2,085	1,072
1919	123,000	71,734	19,107	6,532	7,435	3,114	3,974	2,243	1,166
1920	117,000	61,949	19,857	6,284	6,250	5,868	4,639	2,560	1,446
1921	127,000	74,240	17,335	7,931	5,624	5,806	4,500	2,681	1,045
1922	133,000	75,495	19,067	7,629	6,864	5,954	4,717	2,703	1,150
1923	118,000	63,164	17,418	7,206	6,832	6,034	4,767	2,566	937
1924	127,000	69,601	17,960	7,801	7,076	6,779	4,153	2,818	903
1925	126,000	68,627	18,756	7,841	6,677	5,752	4,641	2,949	925
1926 [4]	125,000	66,385	17,462	8,276	7,108	7,169	4,807	3,083	1,159
1927 [4]	125,000	62,657	19,509		7,331	6,946	5,435		1,244
1923 [4]			18,756		[5] 7,389		4,220		1,163

Bureau of Agricultural Economics. The figures for each year include the crop harvested in the Northern Hemisphere within the calendar year and the following harvest in the Southern Hemisphere. Estimates of world rice production for the period 1900–1909 appear in Agriculture Yearbook, 1924, p. 653.

[1] China is an important producing country, but official statistics are not available.
[2] Irrigated rice.
[3] Estimated figures obtained by multiplying acreage under rice as classified for revenue purposes up to 1912, and acreage as reported by the Department of Land and Agriculture from 1912 on by an average yield for the years 1920–1923, for which years official estimates have been published of acreage, yield, and total production.
[4] Preliminary.
[5] Total.

TABLE 111.—*Rice, rough: Receipts at New Orleans, 1909–1928*

Year beginning August	Aug.	Sept.	Oct.	Nov.	Dec.	Jan.	Feb.	Mar.	Apr.	May	June	July	Total
	1,000 lbs.	1,000 lbs.	1,000 lbs.	1,000 lbs.	1,000 lbs.	1,000 lbs.	1,000 lbs.	1,000 lbs.	1,000 lbs.	1,000 lbs.	1,000 lbs.	1,000 lbs.	1,000 lbs.
1909	46,004	52,219	35,185	19,112	12,556	24,583	13,812	10,170	5,661	13,239	10,545	1,428	244,514
1910	28,948	51,977	27,521	17,868	18,891	17,678	9,254	8,294	9,354	10,377	3,807	4,972	208,941
1911	18,470	37,853	37,781	31,091	13,203	21,995	17,439	4,652	953	627	83	3,235	187,382
1912	18,169	30,103	30,748	38,071	30,829	12,846	2,601	1,832	419	1,086	4,042	3,322	174,068
1913	33,577	25,420	18,910	31,763	23,714	24,147	17,166	7,301	7,957	4,253	1,728	1,223	197,159
1914	31,623	36,413	24,732	34,707	31,503	10,054	14,046	6,277	759	579	1,640	1,376	193,709
1915	27,210	48,168	32,322	40,948	14,217	20,335	11,830	13,744	7,639	1,850	234	158	218,655
1916	35,959	46,698	41,009	37,791	18,349	5,021	15,140	23,733	10,503	1,938	1,717	1,618	239,476
1917	26,057	41,326	40,425	28,849	9,662	5,531	9,528	21,534	9,081	4,917	305	733	197,948
1918	20,719	55,998	26,574	16,157	12,440	14,944	14,503	8,270	8,842	7,770	3,786	2,709	192,712
1919	18,766	43,507	33,548	18,097	24,829	20,983	9,820	7,459	8,440	7,255	8,838	5,339	206,881
1920	27,889	40,123	45,620	33,881	21,366	18,338	8,253	23,160	20,417	36,841	19,382	14,057	309,327
1921	35,893	28,138	23,169	13,598	31,345	16,987	16,463	37,710	13,859	3,926	3,397	2,653	227,138
1922	15,545	28,886	41,076	31,446	22,092	14,070	8,308	2,813	15,605	3,195	6,383	7,035	196,454
1923	7,008	16,021	19,400	19,015	17,523	14,069	5,163	6,294	1,549	995	109	120	107,266
1924	13,587	28,232	31,274	26,869	19,292	12,882	12,034	2,130	2,320	1,027	1,484	1,038	152,169
1925	20,910	20,840	14,115	12,790	22,898	19,758	11,077	6,442	6,009	2,774	1,238	1,828	140,679
1926	6,937	19,755	17,057	13,664	14,618	13,554	7,852	12,847	2,108	4,843	7,847	3,921	125,003
1927	23,399	14,604	19,357	7,213	7,299	3,447	3,217	2,421	1,168	561	38	-------	82,724
1928	4,172	7,847	13,234	8,910	5,162	-------	-------	-------	-------	-------	-------	-------	-------

Bureau of Agricultural Economics. Converted from quotations on 162-pound sacks as published in annual report of New Orleans Board of Trade.

TABLE 112.—*Rice, rough:* [1] *Wholesale price per 100 pounds, New Orleans, 1909–1927*

Year beginning August	Aug.	Sept.	Oct.	Nov.	Dec.	Jan.	Feb.	Mar.	Apr.	May	June	July	Average
	Dolls.	Dolls.	Dolls.	Dolls.	Dolls.	Dolls.	Dolls.	Dolls.	Dolls.	Dolls.	Dolls.	Dolls.	Dolls.
1909	2.16	1.84	1.73	1.70	1.62	1.88	1.70	1.54	1.79	1.77	1.57	2.41	1.81
1910	1.73	1.41	1.41	1.46	1.50	1.54	1.42	1.52	1.33	1.45	1.39	1.70	1.49
1911	1.74	1.54	1.65	1.72	1.64	1.80	2.04	2.17	2.42	2.36	2.19	2.64	1.99
1912	2.21	2.09	1.64	1.98	2.09	2.18	2.16	1.82	2.23	2.01	2.11		2.06
1913	2.31	2.10	1.95	2.47	1.70	1.91	1.67	1.36	1.62	1.93	1.90	2.09	1.92
1914	2.67	2.41	1.64	1.70	2.09	1.96	2.22	2.27	2.31	2.20	2.19	2.09	2.15
1915	1.98	1.77	1.64	1.93	1.74	1.72	2.07	2.20	2.23	1.69			1.91
1916	2.41	1.89	1.96	2.12	2.04	2.05	2.18	2.30	3.09	3.91	3.40	3.95	2.61
1917	4.09	4.01	3.70	4.25	4.38	4.48	4.71	5.13	4.75	5.27	4.86	4.40	4.50
1918	4.44	4.32	3.86	3.78	3.86	3.63				4.56		6.10	
1919	8.02	5.86	5.17	5.23	5.17	6.49			5.94	5.48	6.10		
1920	3.94	3.63	2.93	2.93			1.79	1.86		1.90	1.78	1.72	
1921	2.17	2.23	2.21	2.00		2.54	2.21	2.48	2.07	1.99	2.25	2.48	
1922	2.40	1.85	1.92	2.47	2.21	2.20	2.10	2.49		2.01	2.46		
1923	2.74	2.44	2.40	2.58	2.64	2.48	2.49	2.85		2.62			
1924	2.95	2.60	2.76	3.10	3.78	3.58			3.42	3.09	3.67	3.67	
1925	3.42	2.80	2.78	2.91	3.28	3.07	2.77	2.78	2.78	3.14	2.93		
1926		2.47	2.17	2.12		2.31	1.79			1.78	2.09		
1927	2.16	2.19	2.42										

Bureau of Agricultural Economics. Converted from price per 162 pounds, published in annual reports of the New Orleans Board of Trade.

[1] Price is average of range of all rough rice reported; includes Honduras, Japan, and Blue Rose.

TABLE 113.—*Rice, including flour, meal, and broken rice: International trade, average 1909–1913, annual 1924–1927*

Country	Average 1909–1913		1924		1925		1926		1927 preliminary	
	Imports	Exports	Imports	Exports	Imports	Exports	Imports	Exports	Imports	Exports
PRINCIPAL EXPORTING COUNTRIES	*Million pounds*	*Million pounds*	*Million pounds*	*Million pounds*	*Million pounds*	*Million pounds*	*Million pounds*	*Million pounds*	*Million pounds*	*Million pounds*
British India	278	5,338	391	5,120	35	5,539	148	5,272	147	5,065
Siam [1]	0	1,929	0	2,497	0	2,975	0	2,906	0	3,820
French Indo-China	0	2,288	0	2,623	0	3,250	0	3,503	0	3,619
Italy	4	142	4	379	1	354	1	401	2	579
United States	210	16	41	155	68	67	117	117	54	310
Madagascar [2]	0	[2] 14	0	175	0	92	0	48	0	23
Spain	5	18	0	116	1	100	0	142	[2] 0	[2] 117
Brazil	25	0	43	14	164	1	10	17	0	37
PRINCIPAL IMPORTING COUNTRIES										
China	705	0	1,760	6	1,685	5	2,493	4	2,812	12
British Malaya	[2] 2,000	[2] 1,299	1,308	420	1,465	547	1,696	629	1,887	660
Japan	656	62	1,089	8	1,714	29	768	14	1,300	12
Dutch East Indies	1,178	132	995	89	1,178	68	1,390	71	[3] 230	[3] 20
Ceylon	822	0	877	0	969	0	1,030	0	1,072	0
Germany	914	397	913	462	1,175	449	766	344	757	294
France	518	79	431	67	502	95	478	105	486	170
Cuba	262	0	445	0	424	0	477	0	----	----
United Kingdom	769	91	320	22	294	19	244	18	267	17
Netherlands	779	476	252	149	296	234	330	285	262	203
Philippine Islands	413	0	333	0	223	1	155	1	28	2
Mauritius	133	1	98	0	135	0	117	0	[2] 131	[2] 3
Argentina	93	6	98	1	149	1	127	0	154	0
Russia	250	6	[2] 124	[2] 3	[2] 195	[2] 0	[2] 83	[2] 0	[2] 149	[2] 0
Czechoslovakia	0	0	114	0	111	0	107	0	120	0
Belgium	181	100	82	2	85	3	83	4	100	4
Egypt	99	54	40	73	98	62	97	40	32	84
Austria	[5] 183	[5] 0	51	0	58	0	54	0	59	0
Canada	32	2	37	3	45	2	39	2	43	1
Hungary	0	0	44	0	32	1	12	4	7	5
Total, 28 countries	10,509	12,450	9,890	12,384	11,102	13,894	10,822	13,927	10,099	14,997

Bureau of Agricultural Economics. Official sources except where otherwise noted.

Mostly cleaned rice. Under rice is included paddy, unhulled, rough, cleaned, polished, broken, and cargo rice, in addition to rice flour and meal. Rice bran is not included. Rough rice, or paddy, where specifically reported, has been reduced to terms of cleaned rice at the ratio of 162 pounds of rough or unhulled to 100 pounds of cleaned. "Rice, other than whole or cleaned rice," in the returns of the United Kingdom is not considered paddy, since the chief sources of supply indicate that it is practically all hulled rice. Cargo rice, a mixture of hulled and unhulled, is included without being reduced to terms of cleaned. Broken rice and rice flour and meal are taken without being reduced to terms of whole cleaned rice.

[1] Fiscal year Apr. 1–Mar. 31.
[2] International Yearbook of Agricultural Statistics.
[3] Java and Madura only.
[4] 2-year average.
[5] Average for Austria-Hungary.

TABLE 114.—*Rice, Blue Rose, clean: Average wholesale price per 100 pounds, New Orleans, 1914–1928*

Year beginning August	Aug.	Sept.	Oct.	Nov.	Dec.	Jan.	Feb.	Mar.	Apr.	May	June	July	Average
	Dolls.	Dolls.	Dolls.	Dolls.	Dolls.	Dolls.	Dolls.	Dolls.	Dolls.	Dolls.	Dolls.	Dolls.	Dolls.
Average—													
1914–1920			5.20	5.04	4.85	4.95	5.03	5.27	5.54	5.72	6.01	6.34	
1921–1925	4.71	4.75	4.62	4.80	4.80	4.88	4.98	5.01	5.03	5.03	5.39	5.47	4.95
1914			3.62	3.06	3.16	3.56	3.75	3.50	4.10	4.06	3.47	3.88	
1915	3.88	3.38	3.06	2.87	2.97	2.75	3.06	3.38	3.56	3.68	3.81	3.40	3.32
1916	3.40	3.31	3.00	3.31	3.16	3.18	3.31	3.87	4.94	6.18	6.13	6.25	4.17
1917	4.75	6.81	6.32	6.56	5.94	6.41	6.64	7.56	8.19	8.94	8.90	8.94	7.15
1918	7.88	6.75	6.56	6.44	6.06	5.94	5.94	5.82	5.63	5.25	8.00	10.82	6.76
1919		9.00	8.44	8.44	9.25	9.81	10.19	10.38	10.12	9.50	9.19	8.00	
1920	7.25	6.25	5.38	4.62	3.44	3.00	2.50	2.38	2.25	2.40	2.56	3.06	3.76
1921	3.19	3.50	3.78	3.69	3.12	3.10	3.18	3.44	3.56	3.60	4.31	4.38	3.57
1922	4.10	4.25	3.62	3.82	4.00	4.06	3.94	3.91	4.00	3.56	3.75	3.94	3.91
1923	3.78	4.00	4.88	4.66	4.38	4.62	4.69	5.06	5.06	5.88	6.12	6.19	4.94
1924	5.88	5.69	5.12	5.50	6.10	6.30	6.50	6.38	6.34	6.50	6.81	6.88	6.17
1925	6.62	6.31	5.69	6.34	6.41	6.31	6.59	6.25	6.19	5.60	5.94	5.94	6.18
1926	4.94	5.62	4.81	4.44	4.38	4.50	4.19	4.34	4.06	4.12	4.52	4.22	4.51
1927	4.12	4.12	3.84	3.62	3.69	3.82	3.72	3.67	3.75	4.15	4.00	4.00	3.88
1928	4.00		3.87	3.92	3.82								

Bureau of Agricultural Economics. Compiled from annual reports of the New Orleans Board of Trade. Prices for 1928 are from the New Orleans Times Picayune and are subject to revision.

TABLE 115.—*Buckwheat: Acreage, production, value, exports, etc., United States, 1909–1928*

Year	Acreage	Average yield per acre	Production	Price per bushel received by producers Dec. 1	Farm value Dec. 1	Foreign trade, including flour, year beginning July 1 [1]		
						Domestic exports	Imports	Net balance [2]
	1,000 acres	Bushels of 48 lbs.	1,000 bushels	Cents	1,000 dollars	1,000 bushels	1,000 bushels	1,000 bushels
1909	878	16.9	14,849					
1909	878	20.5	17,983	70.2	12,628	158	11	+147
1910	860	20.5	17,598	66.1	11,636		92	−92
1911	833	21.1	17,549	72.6	12,735		21	−21
1912	841	22.9	19,249	66.1	12,720	1	64	−63
1913	805	17.2	13,833	75.5	10,445	1	206	−205
1914	792	21.3	16,881	76.4	12,892	414	259	+155
1915	769	19.6	15,056	78.7	11,843	515	402	+113
1916	828	14.1	11,662	112.7	13,147	260	266	−6
1917	924	17.3	16,022	160.0	25,631	6	510	−504
1918	1,027	16.5	16,905	166.5	28,142	119	413	−294
1919	743	17.1	12,690					
1919	700	20.6	14,399	146.1	21,032	245	160	+85
1920	701	18.7	13,142	128.3	16,863	399	336	+63
1921	680	20.9	14,207	81.2	11,540	485	113	+372
1922	764	19.1	14,564	88.5	12,889	172	286	−114
1923	739	18.9	13,965	93.3	13,029	92	322	−230
1924	717	16.8	12,004					
1924	745	17.9	13,357	102.6	13,708	191	546	−355
1925	747	18.7	13,994	88.8	12,423	79	88	−9
1926	694	18.3	12,676	88.2	11,183	66	86	−20
1927	810	19.5	15,755	83.5	13,155	554	74	+480
1928 [3]	750	17.6	13,163	87.6	11,525			

Bureau of Agricultural Economics. Production figures are estimates of the crop-reporting board; italic figures are census returns. See 1927 Yearbook, page 825, for data for earlier years.

[1] Compiled from Commerce and Navigation of the United States, 1909–1917; Foreign Commerce and Navigation of the United States, 1918; Monthly Summary of Foreign Commerce of the United States, June issues, 1919–1926; January and June issues, 1927–28, and official records of the Bureau of Foreign and Domestic Commerce. Buckwheat and buckwheat flour—imports for consumption, 1909–1928. Buckwheat flour converted to terms of grain on the basis that 1 barrel of flour is the product of 7 bushels of grain.
[2] The difference between total exports (domestic exports plus reexports) and total imports. Net exports indicated by +; net imports indicated by —.
[3] Preliminary.

TABLE 116.—*Buckwheat: Acreage harvested and production, by States, average 1921–1925, annual 1926–1928*

State and division	Acreage harvested				Production			
	Average 1921–1925	1926	1927	1928 [1]	Average 1921–1925	1926	1927	1928 [1]
	1,000 acres	*1,000 acres*	*1,000 acres*	*1,000 acres*	*1,000 bush.*	*1,000 bush.*	*1,000 bush.*	*1,000 bush.*
Maine	12	15	14	13	295	345	322	299
Vermont	3	3	2	2	73	69	52	48
New York	215	190	201	192	4,357	3,591	4,221	3,475
New Jersey	7	2	1	1	144	36	21	20
Pennsylvania	217	190	210	195	4,665	3,610	4,935	3,802
North Atlantic	457	400	428	403	9,580	7,651	9,551	7,644
Ohio	25	22	28	35	500	385	588	700
Indiana	11	20	15	15	159	320	255	225
Illinois	5	5	6	5	80	65	97	70
Michigan	51	50	53	48	731	765	689	720
Wisconsin	29	23	23	25	422	345	382	412
Minnesota	54	66	126	88	735	1,122	1,764	1,074
Iowa	5	5	15	7	80	90	195	102
Missouri	1	1	1	1	13	15	20	13
North Dakota	[2] 7	9	11	10	[2] 68	135	160	145
South Dakota	10	9	18	19	123	126	279	276
Nebraska	1	1	1	1	16	11	15	10
North Central	196	211	297	254	2,886	3,379	4,444	3,747
Delaware	6	2	2	2	99	32	37	34
Maryland	8	8	8	7	170	162	176	133
Virginia	17	16	14	17	318	352	294	326
West Virginia	32	36	39	40	635	684	858	800
North Carolina	8	10	10	10	149	220	200	190
South Atlantic	72	72	73	76	1,370	1,450	1,565	1,483
Kentucky	8	8	9	14	130	136	144	238
Tennessee	3	3	3	3	51	60	51	51
South Central	11	11	12	17	182	196	195	289
United States	735	694	810	750	14,017	12,676	15,755	13,163

Bureau of Agricultural Economics. Estimates of the crop-reporting board.

[1] Preliminary.   [2] 2-year average.

TABLE 117.—*Buckwheat: Yield per acre and estimated price per bushel, December 1, by States, average 1914–1920, 1921–1925, annual 1924–1928*

State	Yield per acre							Estimated price per bushel						
	Av., 1914–1920	Av., 1921–1925	1924	1925	1926	1927	1928	Av., 1914–1920	Av., 1921–1925	1924	1925	1926	1927	1928
	Bush.	Bush.	Bush.	Bush.	Bush.	Bush.	Bush.	Cts.	Cts.	Cts.	Cts.	Cts.	Cts.	Cts.
Maine	24.5	25.4	24.0	26.0	23.0	23.0	23.0	122	100	95	100	83	90	90
Vermont	22.4	21.6	22.0	22.0	23.0	26.0	24.0	126	95	105	90	85	96	105
New York	18.4	20.3	21.0	19.0	18.9	21.0	18.1	128	93	101	86	89	84	90
New Jersey	19.0	20.8	19.0	21.0	18.0	21.0	20.0	129	105	117	100	100	84	92
Pennsylvania	18.7	21.5	19.0	23.0	19.0	23.5	19.5	121	88	103	91	89	85	89
Ohio	20.3	20.1	16.0	19.7	17.5	21.0	20.0	119	94	103	86	95	86	87
Indiana	16.6	15.6	14.0	13.2	16.0	17.0	15.0	122	97	103	85	95	85	85
Illinois	17.8	14.9	14.0	14.0	13.0	16.2	14.0	140	103	120	100	92	85	90
Michigan	13.0	14.4	14.0	13.7	15.3	13.0	15.0	117	86	96	90	80	80	79
Wisconsin	15.0	14.5	13.0	16.0	15.0	16.6	16.5	126	87	103	79	87	82	83
Minnesota	16.5	13.8	12.0	14.0	17.0	14.0	12.2	114	83	102	75	75	70	76
Iowa	14.9	15.3	15.0	17.5	18.0	13.0	14.5	138	98	103	90	82	85	90
Missouri	14.8	13.4	13.0	14.0	15.0	20.0	13.0	140	·118	105	90	85	90	95
North Dakota	------	¹10.0	8.0	12.0	15.0	14.5	14.5	------	¹60	60	60	80	64	68
South Dakota	------	12.6	14.8	12.0	14.0	15.5	14.5	------	83	107	70	80	64	67
Nebraska	16.8	15.8	15.0	14.0	11.0	15.3	9.6	126	90	100	100	90	85	85
Delaware	19.0	16.8	16.8	16.0	16.0	18.5	17.0	120	88	102	92	90	95	95
Maryland	20.2	20.7	18.0	24.0	20.2	22.0	19.0	126	96	110	100	100	93	95
Virginia	20.2	18.6	17.3	16.0	22.0	21.0	19.2	124	95	106	110	95	93	95
West Virginia	20.3	19.6	17.0	18.0	19.0	22.0	20.0	131	95	112	100	100	97	97
North Carolina	18.7	18.2	18.0	14.0	22.0	20.0	19.0	111	104	119	110	100	100	100
Kentucky	------	16.1	14.0	12.5	17.0	16.0	17.0	------	102	119	100	84	86	86
Tennessee	17.9	17.1	19.0	15.0	20.0	17.0	17.0	118	105	125	115	100	90	100
United States	18.3	19.1	17.9	18.7	18.3	19.5	17.6	124.1	90.9	102.6	88.8	88.2	83.5	87.6

Bureau of Agricultural Economics. Estimates of the crop-reporting board.

¹ 2-year average.

TABLE 118.—*Buckwheat: Estimated price per bushel, received by producers, United States, 1909–1928*

Year beginning September	Sept. 15	Oct. 15	Nov. 15	Dec. 15	Jan. 15	Feb. 15	Mar. 15	Apr. 15	May 15	June 15	July 15	Aug. 15	Weighted av.
	Cents	Cents	Cents	Cents	Cents	Cents	Cents	Cents	Cents	Cents	Cents	Cents	Cents
Average:													
1909–1913	73.0	71.1	70.2	70.3	70.8	70.9	71.4	72.6	74.4	77.3	78.3	76.1	72.0
1914–1920	131.2	126.2	124.1	124.8	125.1	125.3	126.5	129.8	138.5	148.9	150.1	142.8	129.6
1921–1925	102.4	93.2	90.8	91.7	91.7	92.0	94.1	93.6	97.8	100.2	102.1	103.6	94.3
1909	76.0	73.3	70.8	70.0	71.0	71.3	72.0	72.2	72.4	75.8	76.4	73.7	72.1
1910	72.0	68.6	66.0	66.0	65.1	64.2	64.7	65.6	68.0	71.2	74.2	75.0	67.5
1911	71.8	71.3	72.8	73.2	73.6	75.2	76.9	78.4	82.4	85.5	84.9	80.1	75.4
1912	73.2	67.6	65.8	66.4	68.1	68.2	67.6	69.8	71.1	71.8	72.6	71.2	68.3
1913	72.0	74.8	75.5	76.0	76.1	75.4	76.0	77.1	78.2	82.2	83.4	80.5	76.6
1914	79.2	78.4	77.2	77.2	80.8	84.6	85.4	85.0	85.8	89.5	90.6	85.3	81.1
1915	77.6	76.1	78.6	80.1	81.1	82.0	83.2	84.0	86.0	90.0	91.0	87.7	81.5
1916	88.4	96.6	107.8	115.0	115.9	119.7	139.4	167.2	196.4	199.2	196.8	176.8	126.5
1917	159.4	154.3	157.1	161.4	162.3	165.0	169.2	173.0	183.5	195.9	196.8	191.5	167.1
1918	185.2	176.5	169.8	164.7	160.5	153.2	149.0	148.4	156.4	163.2	163.4	162.8	164.7
1919	160.9	156.5	148.6	148.4	152.8	155.3	159.4	166.0	174.5	191.4	192.0	178.8	159.2
1920	167.8	145.2	129.6	126.8	122.0	117.5	112.6	112.6	116.0	115.7	117.5	117.0	126.8
1921	110.2	95.0	82.6	82.4	84.4	85.6	89.2	93.0	95.4	100.0	99.2	91.0	89.1
1922	85.2	82.2	84.4	89.0	88.5	88.6	92.6	95.0	98.4	102.3	101.4	99.4	89.9
1923	96.6	94.2	93.4	94.7	92.7	92.5	94.7	93.6	97.0	96.5	104.5	123.9	96.3
1924	118.8	107.1	106.8	104.6	107.0	112.2	112.4	104.1	113.3	112.3	115.7	110.0	108.6
1925	101.2	87.6	86.7	87.9	85.7	80.9	81.7	82.5	85.0	90.1	89.9	93.7	87.5
1926	90.4	86.5	83.6	83.5	83.6	84.6	86.0	85.1	88.1	98.8	101.0	98.1	87.0
1927	92.3	82.9	79.4	81.0	82.0	85.2	90.2	94.8	102.3	109.0	108.0	98.1	87.6
1928	92.6	84.5	84.8	88.7	------	------	------	------	------	------	------	------	------

Bureau of Agricultural Economics. Based on returns from special price reporters. Mean of prices reported on 1st of month and 1st of succeeding month, September, 1909–December, 1923.

TABLE 119.—*Sorghums for grain, forage, and all purposes:*[1] *Acreage, production, value, United States, 1919–1928*

Year	For grain			For forage			For all purposes [2]			Price per bushel received by producers Dec. 1 [3]	Farm value Dec. 1
	Acreage	Yield per acre	Production	Acreage	Yield per acre	Production	Acreage	Equivalent yield per acre	Equivalent production on total acreage		
	1,000 acres	*Bushels*	*1,000 bushels*	*1,000 acres*	*Tons*	*1,000 tons*	*1,000 acres*	*Bushels*	*1,000 bushels*	*Cents*	*1,000 dollars*
1919	3,775	28.0	105,858	2,666	2.10	5,603	6,441	24.5	157,805	128.1	202,094
1920	4,232	28.6	120,848	2,562	2.16	5,539	6,794	25.7	174,790	93.7	163,860
1921	3,920	25.9	101,506	2,465	1.99	4,900	6,385	23.1	147,609	39.0	57,576
1922	3,566	19.1	68,154	2,212	1.63	3,601	5,778	17.0	98,158	88.1	86,517
1923	4,403	19.2	84,505	2,258	1.72	3,895	6,661	17.4	116,109	95.0	110,258
1924	3,778	21.1	79,890	2,311	1.80	4,157	6,089	19.2	117,057	85.2	99,765
1925	4,076	18.3	74,467	2,564	1.61	4,118	6,640	16.0	106,434	75.4	80,251
1926	4,367	22.9	100,044	2,323	1.75	4,061	6,690	20.6	137,515	53.9	74,065
1927	4,394	22.8	100,364	2,329	2.06	4,800	6,723	20.4	137,358	61.6	84,614
1928 [4]	4,281	23.2	99,172	2,216	2.14	4,740	6,497	21.9	142,533	62.1	88,471

Bureau of Agricultural Economics. Estimates of the crop-reporting board.

[1] Kafirs, milo, feterita, durra, etc.
[2] New series replacing old series which related to grain only.
[3] From 1919 to 1924, Nov. 15 price.
[4] Preliminary.

TABLE 120.—*Sorghums:*[1] *Acreage and production, by States, average 1921–1925, annual 1926–1928*

State	Acreage for all purposes [2]				Production for all purposes [2]			
	Average, 1921–1925	1926	1927	1928 [3]	Average, 1921–1925	1926	1927	1928 [3]
	1,000 acres	*1,000 acres*	*1,000 acres*	*1,000 acres*	*1,000 bush.*	*1,000 bush.*	*1,000 bush.*	*1,000 bush.*
Missouri	70	94	113	99	1,282	1,692	2,712	2,326
Nebraska	21	22	30	24	421	233	705	485
Kansas	1,289	1,345	1,547	1,284	23,431	20,175	32,487	28,633
Oklahoma	1,736	1,817	1,744	1,709	25,458	34,523	34,880	30,762
Texas	2,545	2,854	2,654	2,760	54,195	71,350	55,734	69,000
Colorado	262	227	284	256	3,447	1,135	2,840	2,560
New Mexico	218	195	171	188	3,751	4,095	2,394	3,384
Arizona	53	40	50	52	1,388	1,240	1,550	1,508
California	115	96	130	125	3,702	3,072	4,056	3,875
United States	6,311	6,690	6,723	6,497	117,073	137,515	137,358	142,533

Bureau of Agricultural Economics. Estimates of the crop-reporting board.

[1] Kafirs, milo, feterita, durra, etc.
[2] New series replacing old series which related to grain only.
[3] Preliminary.

TABLE 121.—*Sorghums:* [1] *Yield per acre and estimated price per bushel, December 1, by States, average 1921–1925, annual 1924–1928*

| State | Yield per acre [2] | | | | | | Estimated price per bushel | | | | | |
	Average 1921–1925	1924	1925	1926	1927	1928	Average, 1921–1925	1924 [3]	1925	1926	1927	1928
	Bush.	*Bush.*	*Bush.*	*Bush.*	*Bush.*	*Bush.*	*Cts.*	*Cts.*	*Cts.*	*Cts.*	*Cts.*	*Cts.*
Missouri	18.8	15.0	15.0	18.0	24.0	23.5	96	115	100	80	75	80
Nebraska	19.7	18.0	15.0	10.6	23.5	20.2	74	91	75	80	80	85
Kansas	18.5	18.8	16.0	15.0	21.0	22.3	68	80	71	60	60	61
Oklahoma	14.6	18.0	12.5	19.0	20.0	18.0	71	77	75	45	50	62
Texas	21.2	21.0	18.0	25.0	21.0	25.0	82	87	76	55	65	60
Colorado	12.8	8.0	11.0	5.0	10.0	10.0	73	90	71	60	65	60
New Mexico	17.2	20.0	18.0	21.0	14.0	18.0	75	100	65	40	80	60
Arizona	25.2	18.0	20.0	31.0	31.0	29.0	87	130	66	60	75	80
California	32.1	30.5	34.0	32.0	31.2	31.0	102	135	107	84	97	90
United States	18.5	19.2	16.0	20.6	20.4	21.9	76.5	85.2	75.4	53.9	61.6	62.1

Bureau of Agricultural Economics. Estimates of the crop-reporting board.

[1] Kafirs, milo, feterita, durra, etc.
[2] New series replacing old series which related to grain only.
[3] Nov. 15 price.

TABLE 122.—*Grain sorghums:* [1] *Receipts at Kansas City, by months, 1909–1928*

Year beginning November	Nov.	Dec.	Jan.	Feb.	Mar.	Apr.	May	June	July	Aug.	Sept.	Oct.	Total
	1,000 bush.	*1,000 bush.*	*1,000 bush.*	*1,000 bush.*	*1,000 bush.*	*1,000 bush.*	*1,000 bush.*	*1,000 bush.*	*1,000 bush.*	*1,000 bush.*	*1,000 bush.*	*1,000 bush.*	*1,000 bush.*
Average:													
1909–1913	177	272	269	229	115	92	87	87	42	22	26	47	1,464
1914–1920	147	480	628	509	475	371	318	302	231	134	83	83	3,762
1921–1925	310	585	491	455	343	264	228	287	170	100	64	72	3,371
1909	106	50	125	150	161	45	32	20	12	8	5	4	718
1910	107	287	224	179	86	52	71	56	30	42	19	62	1,215
1911	202	323	255	410	191	198	186	121	75	46	62	103	2,172
1912	446	645	610	333	111	151	129	223	90	11	33	26	2,808
1913	22	53	133	72	25	15	16	15	3	1	9	42	406
1914	311	719	661	618	189	486	252	186	206	204	112	130	4,074
1915	367	1,116	1,200	936	866	682	625	256	202	104	85	24	6,463
1916	79	199	192	274	72	45	38	9	8	8	6	6	936
1917	88	278	464	385	506	322	98	107	40	29	9	7	2,333
1918	51	163	153	168	384	329	375	95	160	65	87	80	2,110
1919	22	233	745	721	741	449	540	817	768	235	160	123	5,554
1920	112	654	980	463	569	287	301	644	234	293	120	209	4,866
1921	263	350	471	537	392	312	199	212	150	84	35	120	3,125
1922	168	444	420	233	169	139	76	50	69	35	19	18	1,840
1923	195	350	465	579	398	340	274	262	250	106	63	103	3,385
1924	647	1,152	683	636	497	320	301	440	221	183	68	24	5,172
1925	279	629	416	290	261	211	290	469	162	94	136	97	3,334
1926	397	493	626	442	293	216	192	241	249	285	79	112	3,625
1927	410	905											
1928													

Bureau of Agricultural Economics. Compiled from annual statistical reports of Kansas City Board of Trade.

[1] Includes kafir corn, milo maize, and feterita. Quoted as kafir in Table 117, 1927 Yearbook.

TABLE 123.—*Grain sorghums: Classification of receipts graded by licensed inspectors, all inspection points*

TOTAL OF ALL CLASSES AND SUBCLASSES UNDER EACH GRADE, 1925–1927; BY GRADE AND CLASS 1927–28

Year and class	Receipts of —					
	No. 1	No. 2	No. 3	No. 4	Sample grade	Total
Beginning July 1—	*Cars*	*Cars*	*Cars*	*Cars*	*Cars*	*Cars*
1925	312	4,158	5,796	1,639	495	12,40C
1926	878	7,180	6,674	1,792	691	17,215
1927	1,175	9,885	8,125	3,143	965	23,29

TOTAL INSPECTIONS, BY GRADE AND CLASS, JULY 1, 1927, TO JUNE 30, 1928

Kafir	458	4,212	2,239	1,308	333	8,55C
Milo	635	4,557	4,716	1,380	477	11,76
Durra	20	13	1	6	22	6
Feterita	1	5	11	1	0	1
Darso	2	22	62	75	6	16
Freed sorgo	0	1	3	1	1	
Brown kaoliang	0	0	0	0	0	
White hegari	0	1	0	0	0	
Schrock kafir	0	1	4	6	1	1
Shallu	0	0	0	0	0	
Mixed	25	473	484	140	71	1,19

Bureau of Agricultural Economics.

TABLE 124.—*Kafir, No. 2 White: Weighted average price* [1] *per bushel of reported cash sales, Kansas City, 1909–1928*

Year beginning November	Nov.	Dec.	Jan.	Feb.	Mar.	Apr.	May	June	July	Aug.	Sept	Oct	Weighted av. [1]
Average:	*Cents*	*Cents*	*Cents*	*Cents*	*Cents*	*Cents*	*Cents*	*Cents*	*Cents*	*Cents*	*Cents*	*Cents*	*Cents*
1909–1913	66	64	70		69		77						
1914–1920	118	114	113	114	115	117	124	123	132	142	130	120	12
1921–1925		77		81	79	80	80	86	93				
1909	67	73	86	80	77	74	82	84	86	101	100	67	8
1910	63	54	54	52	53	53	59	69	80	75	71	68	6
1911	59	55	67	(2)	72	80	81	70	91	94	76	63	7
1912	55	48	48	46	45	46	49	62	61	79	86	85	5
1913	88	91	96	96	99	(2)	112	(2)	(2)	(2)	(2)	(2)	
1914	58	64	74	77	72	66	64	67	65	61	58	59	6
1915	51	55	55	54	52	59	59	62	68	88	96	103	6
1916	131	118	136	139	149	178	212	188	224	251	243	207	18
1917	190	182	186	207	215	189	164	148	170	190	190	183	18
1918	166	146	146	151	143	150	166	192	197	202	135	131	16
1919	150	164	139	122	129	133	148	141	132	136	125	101	13
1920	78	66	55	51	48	45	58	63	68	63	63	57	5
1921	48	50	50	72	74	67	72	77	93	96	111	102	7
1922	100	91	89	90	93	96	99	94	84	83	(2)	(2)	
1923	(2)	71	(2)	68	67	73	62	85	94	(2)	113	89	
1924	88	98	109	103	93	92	97	105	113	116	107	100	10
1925	82	77	77	72	68	70	69	70	79	76	74	71	7
1926	64	64	63	63	65	69	79	102	110	97	(2)	70	
1927	69	71	74	81	88	90	92	91	92	83	89	83	8
1928	78	74											

Bureau of Agricultural Economics. Compiled from Kansas City Grain Market Review, formerl Daily Price Current. Quoted per 100 pounds; converted to bushels of 56 pounds.

[1] Average of daily prices weighted by car-lot sales.　　　[2] No quotations.

FRUITS AND VEGETABLES

TABLE 125.—*Apple trees, New York, Illinois, and Washington: Estimated number of trees, by age groups, in commercial orchards and in farm orchards, January 1, 1928* [1]

NEW YORK

Age groups (seasons of growth)	Years when planted	Commercial orchards		Farm orchards		Total	
		Number	Per cent	Number	Per cent	Number	Per cent
Years							
3 and under	1925 to 1927	889, 300	9. 8	148, 800	5. 6	1, 038, 100	8. 9
4 to 13	1915 to 1924	2, 338, 500	25. 8	456, 400	17. 1	2, 794, 900	23. 8
14 to 23	1905 to 1914	2, 764, 300	30. 6	475, 600	17. 8	3, 239, 900	27. 6
24 to 33	1895 to 1904	1, 006, 900	11. 1	454, 900	17. 0	1, 461, 800	12. 5
34 to 43	1885 to 1894	611, 800	6. 8	361, 500	13. 5	973, 300	8. 3
44 to 53	1875 to 1884	759, 400	8. 4	447, 400	16. 7	1, 206, 800	10. 3
54 to 63	1865 to 1874	441, 000	4. 9	178, 900	6. 7	619, 900	5. 3
64 to 73	1855 to 1864	144, 600	1. 6	64, 200	2. 4	208, 800	1. 8
74 and over	1854 and earlier	87, 200	1. 0	85, 100	3. 2	172, 300	1. 5
Total		9, 043, 000	100. 0	2, 672, 800	100. 0	11, 715, 800	100. 0
1	1927	145, 000	1. 6	26, 100	1. 0	171, 100	1. 5
2	1926	402, 100	4. 4	41, 400	1. 6	443, 500	3. 8
3	1925	342, 200	3. 8	81, 300	3. 0	423, 500	3. 6
4	1924	366, 900	4. 0	76, 700	2. 9	443, 600	3. 8
5	1923	356, 000	3. 9	41, 000	1. 5	397, 000	3. 4
6	1922	331, 800	3. 7	58, 400	2. 2	390, 200	3. 3
7	1921	176, 000	1. 9	23, 400	. 9	199, 400	1. 7
8	1920	268, 900	3. 0	66, 700	2. 5	335, 600	2. 8
9	1915 to 1919	838, 900	9. 3	190, 200	7. 1	1, 029, 100	8. 8
14 to 18	1910 to 1914	1, 754, 300	19. 4	300, 800	11. 3	2, 055, 100	17. 5
19 to 23	1905 to 1909	1, 010, 000	11. 2	174, 800	6. 5	1, 184, 800	10. 1

ILLINOIS

3 and under	1925 to 1927	380, 600	9. 4	109, 200	4. 9	489, 800	7. 8
4 to 13	1915 to 1924	2, 247, 600	55. 3	543, 900	24. 6	2, 791, 500	44. 5
14 to 23	1905 to 1914	525, 000	12. 9	381, 000	17. 2	906, 000	14. 4
24 to 33	1895 to 1904	714, 800	17. 6	653, 900	29. 6	1, 368, 700	21. 8
34 to 43	1885 to 1894	189, 700	4. 7	121, 700	5. 5	311, 400	5. 0
44 to 53	1875 to 1884	3, 200	. 1	402, 000	18. 2	405, 200	6. 5
54 and over	1874 and earlier	1, 700	(2)			1, 700	(2)
Total		4, 062, 600	100. 0	2, 211, 700	100. 0	6, 274, 300	100. 0
1	1927	98, 000	2. 4	50, 700	2. 3	148, 700	2. 4
2	1926	115, 500	2. 8	10, 700	. 5	126, 200	2. 0
3	1925	167, 100	4. 1	47, 800	2. 2	214, 900	3. 4
4	1924	204, 400	5. 0	39, 800	1. 8	244, 200	3. 9
5	1923	374, 700	9. 2	76, 200	3. 4	450, 900	7. 2
6	1922	298, 900	7. 4	222, 500	10. 1	521, 400	8. 3
7	1921	235, 100	5. 8	20, 000	. 9	255, 100	4. 1
8	1920	310, 800	7. 6	60, 500	2. 7	371, 300	5. 9
9 to 13	1915 to 1919	823, 700	20. 3	124, 900	5. 6	948, 600	15. 1
14 to 18	1910 to 1914	233, 700	5. 8	202, 000	9. 1	435, 700	6. 9
19 to 23	1905 to 1909	291, 300	7. 2	179, 000	8. 1	470, 300	7. 5

[1] In this study all orchards of 100 or more apple trees were classed as "commercial" orchards and all smaller orchards as "farm" orchards, irrespective of the age or productiveness of the trees. The numbers shown in Tables 125, 126, and 127 represent the totals reported on the apple-tree survey of 1927, adjusted to equal the estimated total number of trees in orchards of the sizes shown. The adjustments were made by counties, or by groups of counties. Trees for which the varieties were unknown or not reported were assumed to include the same proportion of each variety as orchards in the same area for which varieties were reported. The varieties for which the age was unknown or not reported were assumed to include the same proportion of trees in each age group as those varieties in the same area for which age was reported. The figures in Tables 125 and 126 have been rounded to avoid an appearance of accuracy which they do not possess. The unrounded figures in Table 127 represent merely the number indicated by this survey. Since the reports received did not distinguish between trees set in the spring and those set in the fall, it has been assumed that all were planted in the spring; that is, trees reported set in 1927 were assumed to be 1 year old on Jan. 1, 1928.

[2] Less than 0.1 per cent.

NOTE.—A table, similar to Table 120, 1927 Yearbook, number of apple trees, census years, is omitted.

TABLE 125.—*Apple trees, New York, Illinois, and Washington: Estimated number of trees, by age groups, in commercial orchards and in farm orchards, January 1, 1928—Continued*

WASHINGTON

Age groups (seasons of growth)	Years when planted	Commercial orchards		Farm orchards		Total	
Years		Number	Per cent	Number	Per cent	Number	Per cent
3 and under	1925 to 1927	318, 400	5. 0	22, 600	3. 4	341, 000	4. 9
4 to 13	1915 to 1924	1, 095, 700	17. 2	115, 200	17. 5	1, 210, 900	17. 3
14 to 23	1905 to 1914	4, 684, 900	73. 6	346, 600	52. 8	5, 031, 500	71. 6
24 to 33	1895 to 1904	226, 000	3. 6	106, 000	16. 1	332, 000	4. 7
34 to 43	1885 to 1894	34, 500	. 5	51, 700	7. 9	86, 200	1. 2
44 to 53	1875 to 1884	7, 800	. 1	14, 100	2. 2	21, 900	. 3
54 and over	1874 and earlier	200	(2)	400	. 1	600	(2)
Total		6, 367, 500	100. 0	656, 600	100. 0	7, 024, 100	100. 0
1	1927	44, 600	. 7	5, 300	. 8	49, 900	. 7
2	1926	186, 300	2. 9	10, 100	1. 5	196, 400	2. 8
3	1925	87, 500	1. 4	7, 200	1. 1	94, 700	1. 4
4	1924	171, 600	2. 7	8, 000	1. 2	179, 600	2. 6
5	1923	140, 900	2. 2	8, 400	1. 3	149, 300	2. 1
6	1922	221, 100	3. 5	9, 800	1. 5	230, 900	3. 3
7	1921	87, 900	1. 4	10, 900	1. 6	98, 800	1. 4
8	1920	165, 800	2. 6	11, 900	1. 8	177, 700	2. 5
9 to 13	1915 to 1919	308, 400	4. 8	66, 200	10. 1	374, 600	5. 4
14 to 18	1910 to 1914	3, 250, 600	51. 1	206, 200	31. 4	3, 456, 800	49. 2
19 to 23	1905 to 1909	1, 434, 300	22. 5	140, 400	21. 4	1, 574, 700	22. 4

Bureau of Agricultural Economics.
2 Less than 0.1 per cent.

TABLE 126.—*Apple trees, New York, Illinois, and Washington: Estimated number of trees of the principal varieties, all orchards, and number of young trees in commercial orchards, January 1, 1928* [1]

NEW YORK

Variety	Trees of all ages in—						Young trees (1 to 8 years of age) in commercial orchards in—			
	Commercial orchards		Farm orchards		Total		Lake Shore district[2]	Southern Hudson River district[3]	State	
	Number	P. ct.	Number	P. ct.	Number	P. ct.	Number	Number	Number	P. ct.
Baldwin	2, 383, 200	26. 3	486, 200	18. 2	2, 869, 400	24. 5	132, 100	67, 900	250, 000	10. 5
McIntosh	1, 264, 300	14. 0	125, 300	4. 7	1, 389, 600	11. 9	249, 400	216, 700	752, 900	31. 5
Rhode Island Greening	1, 097, 300	12. 1	269, 900	10. 1	1, 367, 200	11. 7	158, 000	33, 100	251, 800	10. 5
Northern Spy	526, 800	5. 8	325, 100	12. 2	851, 900	7. 3	14, 500	21, 200	125, 700	5. 3
Wealthy	519, 000	5. 7	34, 600	1. 3	553, 600	4. 7	60, 700	16, 900	110, 500	4. 6
Ben Davis	385, 200	4. 3	68, 200	2. 6	453, 400	3. 9	7, 000	3, 100	11, 200	. 5
Cortland	241, 000	2. 7	6, 700	. 2	247, 700	2. 1	73, 600	113, 700	228, 100	9. 5
Oldenburg (Duchess)	235, 300	2. 6	22, 700	. 8	258, 000	2. 2	19, 300	11, 800	35, 900	1. 5
Delicious	234, 000	2. 6	26, 900	1. 0	260, 900	2. 2	33, 800	112, 000	188, 900	7. 9
Tompkins King	187, 800	2. 1	59, 600	2. 2	247, 400	2. 1	9, 000	2, 500	14, 300	. 6
Rome Beauty	183, 100	2. 0	7, 100	. 3	190, 200	1. 6	9, 000	45, 000	84, 300	3. 5
Roxbury Russet	101, 300	1. 1	44, 000	1. 6	145, 300	1. 2	1, 000	400	1, 900	. 1
Twenty Ounce	98, 500	1. 1	13, 500	. 5	112, 000	. 9	8, 000	3, 000	13, 200	. 6
Hubbardston	97, 000	1. 1	12, 500	. 5	109, 500	. 9	3, 200	100	3, 700	. 2
Stark	86, 900	1. 0	11, 400	. 4	98, 300	. 8	2, 300	3, 300	10, 400	. 4
Jonathan	78, 700	. 9	10, 100	. 4	88, 800	. 8	9, 800	12, 500	25, 500	1. 1
Northwestern Greening	67, 600	. 7	4, 200	. 2	71, 800	. 6	8, 000	6, 800	19, 000	. 8
Wagener	63, 700	. 7	14, 500	. 5	78, 200	. 7	4, 100	1, 400	7, 800	. 3
Fameuse	62, 800	. 7	34, 800	1. 3	97, 600	. 8	100	(4)	25, 000	1. 0
Wolf River	62, 300	. 7	11, 000	. 4	73, 300	. 6	500	1, 800	5, 000	. 2
Maiden Blush	48, 800	. 5	7, 000	. 3	55, 800	. 5	2, 700	(4)	2, 700	. 1
Gano	47, 100	. 5	1, 800	. 1	48, 900	. 4	7, 300	100	7, 400	. 3
Yellow Transparent	41, 500	. 5	14, 600	. 5	56, 100	. 5	1, 300	14, 500	16, 700	. 7
Winter Banana	39, 000	. 4	9, 300	. 3	48, 300	. 4	4, 300	4, 300	9, 500	. 4
Golden Delicious	33, 000	. 4	6, 500	. 2	39, 500	. 4	5, 290	15, 000	31, 800	1. 3
Sutton	32, 300	. 4	1, 200	(5)	33, 500	. 3	(4)	800	900	(5)
Stayman Winesap	26, 200	. 3	1, 900	. 1	28, 100	. 2	2. 800	6, 000	11, 300	. 5
Gravenstein	26, 200	. 3	7, 000	. 3	33, 200	. 3	500	1, 400	1, 900	. 1
Yellow Newtown	18, 800	. 2	2, 400	. 1	21, 200	. 2	(4)	1, 900	1, 900	. 1
Esopus Spitzenburg	18, 600	. 2	14, 000	. 5	32, 600	. 3	1, 100	100	1, 300	. 1
Grimes Golden	7, 900	. 1	1, 600	. 1	9, 500	. 1	100	100	1, 200	. 1
All other varieties	727, 800	8. 0	1, 017, 200	38. 1	1, 745, 000	14. 9	30, 500	51, 200	137, 200	5. 7
Total	9, 043, 000	100. 0	2, 672, 800	100. 0	11, 715, 800	100. 0	858, 200	769, 400	2, 388, 900	100. 0

[1] See note 1, Table 125.
[2] Includes the counties of Niagara, Orleans, Monroe, and Wayne.
[3] Includes the counties of Columbia, Dutchess, Greene, Orange, Ulster, Rockland, Westchester, and Putnam. [4] No trees reported in survey. [5] Less than 0.1 per cent.

TABLE 126.—*Apple trees, New York, Illinois, and Washington: Estimated number of trees of the principal varieties, all orchards, and number of young trees in commercial orchards, January 1, 1928*—Continued

ILLINOIS

| Variety | Trees of all ages in— | | | | | | Young trees (1 to 8 years of age) in commercial orchards in— | | | |
| | Commercial orchards | | Farm orchards | | Total | | Western district [6] | Southern district [7] | State | |
	Number	P. ct.	Number	P. ct.	Number	P. ct.	Number	Number	Number	P. ct.
Jonathan	679,700	16.7	223,100	10.1	902,800	14.4	120,700	29,500	244,800	13.6
Yellow Transparent	517,400	12.7	60,400	2.7	577,800	9.2	14,800	305,400	342,900	19.0
Ben Davis	479,600	11.8	370,900	16.8	850,500	13.5	16,500	800	21,700	1.2
Winesap	452,200	11.1	174,300	7.9	626,500	10.0	33,000	194,200	254,000	14.1
Delicious	362,600	8.9	121,300	5.5	483,900	7.7	55,400	79,800	229,800	12.7
Grimes Golden	256,500	6.3	132,000	6.0	388,500	6.2	60,200	22,300	121,800	6.7
Willowtwig	168,900	4.2	11,400	.5	180,300	2.9	88,400	700	91,900	5.1
Stayman Winesap	114,800	2.8	24,000	1.1	138,800	2.2	7,700	5,400	78,800	4.4
Oldenburg (Duchess)	97,700	2.4	15,400	.7	113,100	1.8	5,500	10,600	23,100	1.3
Golden Delicious	92,800	2.3	52,500	2.4	145,300	2.3	26,200	15,600	89,500	5.0
Rome Beauty	81,700	2.0	36,300	1.6	118,000	1.9	10,900	5,000	46,600	2.6
York Imperial	70,800	1.7	15,200	.7	86,000	1.4	8,400	9,700	31,300	1.7
Wealthy	63,800	1.6	16,400	.7	79,400	1.3	15,300	4,400	23,300	1.3
Gano	55,500	1.4	37,000	1.7	92,500	1.5	3,400	600	5,700	.3
Arkansas (Mammoth Black Twig)	53,100	1.3	17,200	.8	70,300	1.1	10,200	1,700	14,300	.8
Benoni	42,900	1.1	2,300	.1	45,200	.7	600	1,700	3,000	.2
Black Ben	37,900	.9	55,600	2.5	93,500	1.5	4,500	100	7,100	.4
South Carolina Summer	33,800	.8	(4)		33,800	.5	(4)	28,300	28,300	1.6
Minkler	31,500	.8	44,500	2.0	76,000	1.2	1,000	500	2,800	.1
King David	28,500	.7	25,300	1.1	53,800	.8	10,700	600	12,200	.7
Kinnard	27,000	.7	(4)		27,000	.4	100	9,200	9,300	.5
Collins	19,500	.5	23,000	1.0	42,500	.7	6,000	(4)	6,400	.3
Ingram	17,200	.4	400	(5)	17,600	.3	600	4,100	5,100	.3
Maiden Blush	15,300	.4	18,600	.8	33,900	.5	4,100	100	4,300	.2
Starking	11,100	.3	1,600	.1	12,700	.2	3,100	2,500	11,100	.6
Oliver Red	10,900	.3	13,300	.6	24,200	.4	3,900	(4)	4,500	.2
Red June	10,100	.3	32,700	1.5	42,800	.7	(4)	5,600	5,900	.3
Ralls	10,100	.3	20,000	.9	30,100	.5	800	(4)	1,000	.1
Missouri Pippin	8,500	.2	1,700	.1	10,200	.2	300	(4)	400	(5)
Winter Banana	8,100	.2	33,800	1.5	41,900	.7	2,100	200	5,000	.3
Huntsman	6,000	.1	1,700	.1	7,700	.1	1,500	(4)	1,500	.1
Wolf River	5,500	.1	1,200	.1	6,700	.1	1,600	(4)	1,600	.1
All other varieties	192,400	4.7	628,600	28.4	821,000	13.1	29,700	22,100	75,500	4.2
Total	4,062,600	100.0	2,211,700	100.0	6,274,300	100.0	547,200	760,700	1,804,500	100.0

[4] No trees reported in survey.
[5] Less than 0.1 per cent.
[6] Includes the counties of Adams, Brown, Calhoun, Greene, Jersey, Macoupin, Madison, Pike, and Scott.
[7] Includes the counties of Gallatin, Jackson, Johnson, Pope, Saline, Williamson, Union, Alexander, Hardin, Massac, and Pulaski.

TABLE 126.—*Apple trees, New York, Illinois, and Washington: Estimated number of trees of the principal varieties, all orchards, and number of young trees in commercial orchards, January 1, 1928*—Continued

WASHINGTON

Variety	Trees of all ages in—						Young trees (1 to 8 years of age) in commercial orchards in—			
	Commercial orchards		Farm orchards		Total		Wenatchee Valley district [8]	Yakima Valley district [9]	State	
	Number	P. ct.	Number	P. ct.	Number	P. ct.	Number	Number	Number	P. ct.
Winesap	1,969,400	30.9	32,000	4.9	2,001,400	28.5	107,500	195,600	305,300	27.6
Delicious	1,268,800	19.9	46,700	7.1	1,315,500	18.7	245,100	245,000	549,300	49.7
Jonathan	1,034,500	16.2	44,000	6.7	1,078,500	15.4	14,000	20,000	39,600	3.6
Rome Beauty	734,500	11.5	35,500	5.4	770,000	11.0	16,700	50,800	100,100	9.1
Yellow Newtown	252,200	4.0	25,800	3.9	278,000	4.0	100	2,500	5,000	.4
Esopus Spitzenburg	234,300	3.7	21,800	3.3	256,100	3.6	100	2,600	3,900	.4
Stayman Winesap	186,200	2.9	4,200	.6	190,400	2.7	6,900	4,300	11,600	1.0
Winter Banana	96,500	1.5	22,800	3.5	119,300	1.7	19,300	6,500	28,400	2.6
Arkansas Black	60,300	1.0	7,600	1.2	67,900	1.0	200	500	1,900	.2
Gravenstein	45,500	.7	76,100	11.6	121,600	1.7	(4)	(4)	5,700	.5
King David	22,700	.4	1,800	.3	24,500	.3	(4)	(4)	(4)	
White Pearmain	22,700	.4	200	(5)	22,900	.3	300	(4)	300	(5)
Tompkins King	20,000	.3	36,000	5.5	56,000	.8	(4)	(4)	800	.1
Grimes Golden	18,700	.3	6,100	.9	24,800	.4	(4)	(4)	700	.1
Northern Spy	17,900	.3	32,300	4.9	50,200	.7	(4)	(4)	(4)	
Yellow Transparent	15,100	.2	27,200	4.1	42,300	.6	(4)	(4)	2,400	.2
Black Ben	14,900	.2	200	(5)	15,100	.2	100	(4)	100	(5)
Baldwin	14,900	.2	26,700	4.1	41,600	.6	(4)	(4)	(4)	
Ben Davis	13,300	.2	7,300	1.1	20,600	.3	(4)	(4)	100	(5)
Wagener	11,300	.2	20,300	3.1	31,600	.5	(4)	(4)	800	.1
Arkansas (Mammoth Black Twig)	10,500	.2	400	.1	10,900	.2	(4)	(4)	2,200	.2
McIntosh	7,600	.1	200	(5)	7,800	.1	1,300	(4)	2,300	.2
Starking	7,200	.1	400	.1	7,600	.1	5,300	(4)	7,200	.6
Red Astrachan	5,600	.1	10,200	1.6	15,800	.2	(4)	(4)	300	(5)
Rainier	5,500	.1	300	(5)	5,800	.1	1,900	2,100	5,500	.5
Richard	3,200	.1	(4)		3,200	(5)	3,200	(4)	3,200	.3
Golden Delicious	2,800	(5)	500	.1	3,300	(5)	(4)	(4)	2,000	.2
All other varieties	271,400	4.3	170,000	25.9	441,400	6.3	4,200	11,000	27,000	2.4
Total	6,367,500	100.0	656,600	100.0	7,024,100	100.0	426,200	540,900	1,105,700	100.0

Bureau of Agricultural Economics.

[4] No trees reported in survey.   [8] Includes the counties of Chelan, Douglas, Grant, and Okanogan.
[5] Less than 0.1 per cent.   [9] Includes the counties of Benton, Franklin, Kittitas, and Yakima.

TABLE 127.—*Apple trees, New York, Illinois, and Washington: Estimated number of trees of 16 leading varieties in commercial orchards, by age groups, Jan. 1, 1928* [1]

NEW YORK

Variety	Age groups and years when planted [2]								
	3 years and under, 1925 to 1927	4 to 13 years, 1915 to 1924	14 to 23 years, 1905 to 1914	24 to 33 years, 1895 to 1904	34 to 43 years, 1885 to 1894	44 to 53 years, 1875 to 1884	54 to 63 years, 1865 to 1874	64 to 73 years, 1855 to 1864	74 years and over, 1854 and earlier
	Number	Number	Number	Number	Number	Number	Number	Nymber	Number
Baldwin	59,272	330,010	636,762	316,054	310,809	402,252	221,830	66,205	40,006
McIntosh	324,667	592,601	321,237	22,316	2,262	577	640		
Rhode Island Greening	99,756	222,182	239,571	132,288	93,277	158,241	100,918	33,146	17,921
Northern Spy	49,927	128,780	169,614	82,738	39,744	31,437	14,433	6,028	4,099
Wealthy	16,246	183,396	270,479	44,385	3,688	369	349	25	63
Ben Davis	736	21,667	206,833	116,609	31,453	4,246	3,276	101	279
Cortland	170,081	64,085	6,666	63				105	
Oldenburg (Duchess)	2,616	60,405	150,598	15,539	3,405	2,244	302	143	48
Delicious	48,341	165,578	17,737	2,256	88				
Tompkins King	4,211	23,404	67,120	28,246	17,551	24,137	15,282	5,208	2,641
Rome Beauty	11,228	109,279	52,201	9,583	434	142	213		20
Roxbury Russet	490	1,890	2,522	7,296	13,721	35,896	26,193	9,134	4,158
Twenty Ounce	1,673	16,661	46,008	8,725	5,736	10,280	5,108	3,062	1,247
Hubbardston	395	11,046	47,876	22,487	6,566	5,503	2,366	236	525
Stark	1,878	21,469	43,398	18,303	1,645	96	111		
Jonathan	2,401	41,541	29,371	4,628	542	100	117		
All other varieties	95,382	344,506	456,307	175,384	80,879	83,880	49,862	21,207	16,193
Total	889,300	2,338,500	2,764,300	1,006,900	611,800	759,400	441,000	144,600	87,206

[1] See note 1, Table 125.   [2] Old trees shown for new varieties are mostly trees that have been top-worked.

TABLE 127.—*Apple trees, New York, Illinois, and Washington: Estimated number of trees of 16 leading varieties in commercial orchards, by age groups, January 1, 1928*—Continued

ILLINOIS

Variety	Age groups and years when planted [2]						
	3 years and under, 1925 to 1927	4 to 13 years, 1915 to 1924	14 to 23 years, 1905 to 1914	24 to 33 years, 1895 to 1904	34 to 43 years, 1885 to 1894	44 to 53 years, 1875 to 1884	54 years and over, 1874 and earlier
	Number	*Number*	*Number*	*Number*	*Number*	*Number*	*Number*
Jonathan	50,197	342,547	101,011	138,324	46,302	1,198	121
Yellow Transparent	29,075	409,289	63,643	14,056	1,337		
Ben Davis	2,584	43,038	65,283	298,279	70,267	149	
Winesap	40,207	323,135	48,102	31,357	9,220	90	89
Delicious	59,942	282,672	14,814	4,180	992		
Grimes Golden	30,517	134,584	41,899	42,342	7,083	75	
Willowtwig	25,176	117,567	11,166	8,155	6,431	405	
Stayman Winesap	51,783	46,412	8,501	8,104			
Oldenburg (Duchess)	5,447	58,978	24,195	6,524	2,556		
Golden Delicious	32,048	60,365	21	304	62		
Rome Beauty	10,895	53,657	2,687	11,904	2,413	144	
York Imperial	2,012	47,873	10,411	6,521	3,983		
Wealthy	1,137	37,095	17,271	6,010	1,113	374	
Gano	74	14,472	11,939	27,480	1,535		
Arkansas (Mammoth Black Twig)	2,497	28,448	8,009	9,810	4,336		
Benoni	52	10,335	24,503	4,066	3,915	29	
All other varieties	36,957	237,133	71,545	97,384	28,155	736	1,490
Total	380,600	2,247,600	525,000	714,800	189,700	3,200	1,700

WASHINGTON

Variety	Age groups and years when planted [2]						
	3 years and under, 1925 to 1927	4 to 13 years, 1915 to 1924	14 to 23 years, 1905 to 1914	24 to 33 years, 1895 to 1904	34 to 43 years, 1885 to 1894	44 to 53 years, 1875 to 1884	54 years and over, 1874 and earlier
	Number	*Number*	*Number*	*Number*	*Number*	*Number*	*Number*
Winesap	102,166	275,514	1,540,757	50,678	285		
Delicious	151,435	498,100	601,756	17,176	333		
Jonathan	5,209	64,234	940,804	24,105	148		
Rome Beauty	26,486	117,374	575,948	14,692			
Yellow Newtown	1,152	6,224	235,059	9,714	51		
Esopus Spitzenburg	406	5,302	212,019	15,112	1,203	258	
Stayman Winesap	542	14,752	165,837	5,069			
Winter Banana	2,717	42,048	49,265	2,369	101		
Arkansas Black	736	3,030	50,304	6,161	69		
Gravenstein	1,688	10,997	20,780	7,957	3,405	673	
King David		1,491	19,569	1,040	600		
White Pearmain	337	770	20,353	1,225	15		
Tompkins King	180	1,820	10,202	5,298	1,920	520	60
Grimes Golden	243	1,260	15,880	1,225	92		
Northern Spy		1,220	4,799	5,986	3,580	2,315	
All other varieties	25,103	51,564	221,568	58,193	22,698	4,034	140
Total	318,400	1,095,700	4,684,900	226,000	34,500	7,800	200

Bureau of Agricultural Economics.

[2] Old trees shown for new varieties are mostly trees that have been top-worked.

33023°—29——49

TABLE 128.—*Apples: Total production, foreign trade in the United States. and average price per barrel for Baldwin apples at Boston, 1889–1928*

Year	Production	Domestic exports year beginning July 1		Imports,[1] year beginning July 1, fresh and dried in terms of fresh	Average price of Baldwins at Boston, season November to April[2]	Year	Production	Domestic exports year beginning July 1		Imports,[1] year beginning July 1, fresh and dried in terms of fresh	Average price of Baldwins at Boston, season November to April[2]
		Green or ripe	Dried					Green or ripe	Dried		
	1,000 bushels	*1,000 barrels*	*1,000 pounds*	*1,000 barrels*	*Dollars*		*1,000 bushels*	*1,000 barrels*	*1,000 pounds*	*1,000 barrels*	*Dollars*
1889	*143,106*	454	20,861	[3]	3.24	1910	141,640	1,721	21,804	13	3.68
1890	80,142	135	6,973	[3]16	4.40	1911	214,020	1,456	53,665	9	2.56
1891	198,907	939	26,042	7	1.78	1912	235,220	2,150	41,575	8	2.28
1892	120,536	408	7,967	287	2.31	1913	145,410	1,507	33,566	20	3.95
1893	114,773	79	2,847	93	4.21	1914	253,200	2,352	42,589	22	2.08
1894	134,648	819	7,086	126	2.40	1915	230,011	1,466	16,219	5	2.36
1895	219,600	360	26,692	51	3.10	1916	193,905	1,740	10,358	7	3.44
1896	232,600	1,504	30,775	66	1.03	1917	166,749	635	2,603	15	4.40
1897	163,728	605	31,031	8	3.23	1918	169,625	1,576	18,909	16	5.94
1898	118,061	380	19,306	79	3.18	1919	*136,561*				
1899	*175,398*	527	34,964	26	2.94	1919	142,086	1,051	11,819	283	6.71
1900	*205,930*	884	28,309	19	2.28	1920	223,677	2,665	18,053	47	4.02
1901	135,500	460	15,664	14	4.07	1921	99,002	1,094	12,431	451	6.69
1902	212,330	1,656	39,646	5	1.93	1922	202,702	1,756	12,817	63	4.84
1903	195,680	2,018	48,302	13	2.40	1923	202,842	4,098	30,410	44	4.02
1904	233,630	1,500	39,273	6	1.96	1924	*152,967*	3,201			
1905	136,220	1,209	27,853	33	3.59	1924	171,725		19,225	35	4.78
1906	216,720	1,539	45,698	5	2.44	1925	172,389	3,672	24,833	25	3.92
1907	119,560	1,050	24,238	87	2.35	1926	246,524	7,097	32,670	28	[4]3.22
1908	148,940	896	33,475	15	3.99	1927	123,693	3,143	21,704	51	[5]
1909	*145,412*	922	25,077	32	2.99	1928[6]	184,920				

Bureau of Agricultural Economics. Production figures are estimates of the crop-reporting board; italic figures are census returns.

Compiled from Commerce and Navigation of the United States, 1889–1917; Foreign Commerce and Navigation of the United States, 1918; Monthly Summary of Foreign Commerce of the United States, June issues, 1919–1926; January and June issues, 1927–28 and official records of the Bureau of Foreign and Domestic Commerce.

[1] Fresh apples, imports for consumption 1890–1921; general imports 1922–1927. Dried apples, imports for consumption, 1890–1927. Dried apples converted to terms of fresh on the basis that dried apples equal 20 per cent of fresh and 144 pounds of fresh apples equal 1 barrel.
[2] Figures 1889–1922 from Boston Chamber of Commerce reports. Average of weekly quotations of price actually paid by wholesale dealers on days quoted. Figures, 1923–1926 from Bureau of Agricultural Economics. Average of l. c. l. price for United States No. 1, one day weekly.
[3] No imports reported prior to Oct. 6, 1890. Figure for 1890 represents imports Oct. 6, 1890, to June 30, 1891.
[4] Average does not include December.
[5] Only quotations for season were $6.88 in February and $8.46 in April, 1928.
[6] Preliminary.

TABLE 129.—*Apples: Production, by States, 1923–1928*

State and division	Total						Commercial [1]					
	1923	1924	1925	1926	1927	1928 [2]	1923	1924	1925	1926	1927	1928 [2]
	1,000 bush.	*1,000 bush.*	*1,000 bush.*	*1,000 bush.*	*1,000 bush.*	*1,000 bush.*	*1,000 bush.*	*1,000 bush.*	*1,000 bush.*	*1,000 bush.*	*1,000 bush.*	*1,000 bush.*
Maine	2,500	3,241	3,305	2,260	2,236	1,400	1,440	1,980	1,935	1,350	1,365	861
New Hampshire	935	1,462	1,230	1,240	1,100	1,000	450	876	711	762	690	615
Vermont	521	895	935	800	990	560	267	480	510	465	570	330
Massachusetts	3,300	3,360	3,160	4,100	2,520	2,700	1,800	2,025	1,965	2,640	1,590	1,734
Rhode Island	450	324	299	391	242	230	240	192	171	237	150	144
Connecticut	1,600	1,480	1,375	1,900	1,045	1,500	600	855	900	1,050	540	753
New York	25,000	22,000	32,500	40,375	13,600	21,900	12,600	11,214	18,750	18,000	8,163	12,690
New Jersey	2,208	2,800	2,660	4,310	2,697	3,290	1,410	1,836	1,821	2,832	1,833	2,238
Pennsylvania	10,855	7,800	7,300	17,000	6,300	8,460	3,798	2,340	3,033	5,388	2,550	3,129
North Atlantic	47,364	43,362	52,764	72,376	30,730	41,040	22,605	21,798	29,796	32,724	17,451	22,494
Ohio	12,395	6,350	6,300	11,900	5,600	5,880	3,099	2,082	2,034	3,018	1,623	1,647
Indiana	5,035	1,800	2,430	4,100	1,249	2,520	900	435	600	864	276	528
Illinois	7,500	6,400	7,300	9,000	4,450	7,150	4,200	3,300	3,645	3,870	2,250	3,720
Michigan	13,159	6,000	9,000	9,045	4,288	5,400	6,354	3,000	5,100	4,467	2,271	2,787
Wisconsin	2,340	1,378	2,106	2,158	1,200	2,160	408	294	471	465	270	477
Minnesota	1,520	850	820	1,263	854	1,230	183	114	114	171	111	114
Iowa	4,350	2,800	2,400	3,652	1,720	2,740	870	450	240	402	207	330
Missouri	7,072	4,300	4,100	5,015	2,104	3,380	2,550	1,764	1,938	1,857	870	1,422
South Dakota	212	150	62	169	200	230	9					
Nebraska	880	1,000	450	700	850	470	309	360	195	228	330	90
Kansas	2,166	2,200	1,600	1,428	1,925	820	1,200	1,032	855	930	1,347	540
North Central	56,629	33,228	36,568	48,430	24,440	31,980	20,082	12,831	15,192	16,272	9,555	11,655
Delaware	1,200	1,250	1,340	2,376	1,150	1,520	1,020	930	1,140	1,980	900	1,290
Maryland	2,300	1,850	1,900	3,500	1,700	2,190	1,380	942	972	1,800	1,200	1,326
Virginia	10,000	14,500	7,844	19,902	6,600	16,100	5,850	7,560	4,320	11,100	4,950	11,100
West Virginia	8,320	7,000	4,185	10,875	5,000	8,750	4,200	2,400	2,247	5,100	4,050	4,410
North Carolina	2,700	6,350	3,192	5,986	1,825	5,040	300	921	480	1,035	273	750
South Carolina	274	600	386	647	363	480						
Georgia	864	1,500	741	1,827	595	1,400	180	360	180	456	240	351
South Atlantic	25,658	33,050	19,588	45,113	17,233	35,480	12,930	13,113	9,339	21,471	11,613	19,227
Kentucky	2,625	5,700	2,625	6,408	720	5,700	210	486	210	501	75	456
Tennessee	1,311	4,800	1,984	5,360	1,152	3,790	90	318	123	375	81	264
Alabama	731	1,190	595	1,328	328	885	36					
Mississippi	120	270	221	324	152	250						
Arkansas	3,025	4,100	4,315	3,450	1,015	2,200	1,968	2,160	1,950	1,500	609	1,242
Louisiana	31	30	28	35	18	30						
Oklahoma	1,240	1,170	644	770	493	350	126	162	87	93	60	33
Texas	270	330	264	380	168	216	45					
South Central	9,353	17,590	10,676	18,055	4,046	13,421	2,475	3,126	2,370	2,469	825	1,995
Montana	990	290	80	325	295	516	390	210	42	282	153	471
Idaho	5,600	2,178	6,079	4,200	6,000	5,000	4,800	1,800	5,250	2,775	5,478	4,500
Wyoming	35	50	25	47	40	48						
Colorado	3,010	3,024	3,200	3,444	2,592	3,020	2,409	2,418	2,850	2,907	2,253	2,700
New Mexico	1,400	840	1,021	1,147	456	675	945	567	780	600	360	507
Arizona	128	70	98	112	62	76	42	21	30	33	30	24
Utah	1,119	600	1,300	817	660	880	780	360	900	480	450	570
Nevada	56	40	74	42	18	52						
Washington	33,000	22,000	29,550	34,030	25,343	33,500	28,800	18,825	26,010	25,950	22,302	30,000
Oregon	8,000	6,500	5,400	8,036	4,320	6,950	5,250	4,500	3,888	5,250	2,925	4,800
California	10,500	8,903	6,016	10,350	7,458	12,282	6,300	4,470	3,291	6,144	4,656	6,981
Far Western	63,838	44,495	52,793	62,550	47,244	62,999	49,716	33,171	43,041	44,421	38,607	50,553
United States	202,842	171,725	172,389	246,524	123,693	184,920	107,808	84,039	99,738	117,357	78,051	105,924

Bureau of Agricultural Economics. Estimates of the crop-reporting board.

[1] Included in "Total crop." By commercial crop is meant that portion of the total crop which is sold for consumption as fresh fruit.
[2] Preliminary.

TABLE 130.—*Apples: Car-lot shipments, by State of origin, 1927–1928*

State and year	June	July	Aug.	Sept.	Oct.	Nov.	Dec.	Jan.	Feb.	Mar.	Apr.	May	June	Total
	Cars	Cars	Cars	Cars	Cars	Cars	Cars	Cars	Cars	Cars	Cars	Cars	Cars	Cars
Eastern:														
New England—														
1927 [2]			3	194	1,085	793	67	54	45	29	10			2,280
1928 [2]			4	73	637	314	41							
New York—														
1927 [2]		14	204	981	2,473	1,799	862	870	1,023	830	646	274	54	10,030
1928 [2]		14	315	1,230	2,851	1,947	1,396							
Pennsylvania—														
1927 [2]		13	57	166	1,304	591	252	297	183	111	7	11	13	3,005
1928 [2]		8	43	128	1,002	328	243							
Illinois—														
1927 [2]	162	248	266	984	755	22	23	35	22	25	7	2	1	2,552
1928 [2]	118	693	316	1,599	1,718	125	27							
Michigan—														
1927 [2]		1	185	264	1,111	325	21	20	22	23	13	15	2	2,002
1928 [2]			231	374	1,209	470	40							
Missouri—														
1927 [2]		7	28	356	302	11	6	8	12	2		4		736
1928 [2]		24	46	583	605	54	36							
Delaware—														
1927 [2]	3	694	207	179	233	5	8	14	7	2				1,352
1928 [2]	2	490	271	201	327	14	7							
Maryland—														
1927 [2]	8	136	78	269	749	441	85	18	6	1	1			1,792
1928 [2]		173	131	291	727	206	63							
Virginia—														
1927 [2]		100	520	1,901	2,732	1,091	548	757	426	251	111	145	104	8,686
1928 [2]		149	759	3,759	8,011	3,018	1,138							
West Virginia—														
1927 [2]		92	204	1,263	3,068	1,565	353	198	131	83	40	43	14	7,054
1928 [2]		71	246	1,223	3,190	1,115	320							
Arkansas—														
1927 [2]	13	28	235	188	82	4	13	18	18	20	10			629
1928 [2]	9	11	210	424	406	33	15							
Other Eastern—														
1927 [2]	57	174	493	1,009	1,974	280	72	64	71	57	25	10	11	4,297
1928 [2]	67	225	266	962	1,302	312	77							
Total Eastern—														
1927 [2]	243	1,507	2,480	7,754	15,868	6,927	2,310	2,353	1,966	1,434	870	504	199	44,415
1928 [2]	196	1,858	2,838	10,847	21,985	7,936	3,403							
Western:														
Idaho—														
1927 [2]		1	10	673	4,000	1,730	595	364	152	113	43	27	1	7,709
1928 [2]		3		1,129	2,963	1,031	425							
Colorado—														
1927 [2]			6	114	1,224	615	137	69	41	22				2,228
1928 [2]			1	251	1,406	687	213							
Washington—														
1927 [2]		15	93	2,444	9,621	6,347	2,496	2,079	2,364	1,685	1,290	1,209	637	30,280
1928 [2]		128	230	4,346	13,260	7,747	3,345							
Oregon—														
1927 [2]		1	11	214	1,371	815	251	291	232	133	62	11	4	3,396
1928 [2]		4	63	471	2,530	1,311	576							
California—														
1927 [2]	10	291	853	665	933	532	149	151	143	112	90	68	23	4,020
1928 [2]	30	1,450	1,128	1,204	1,154	367	172							
Other Western—														
1927 [2]			86	242	539	143	25	8	2	1				1,046
1928 [2]			21	204	800	252	27							
Total Western—														
1927 [2]	10	308	1,059	4,352	17,688	10,182	3,653	2,962	2,934	2,066	1,485	1,315	665	48,679
1928 [2]	30	1,585	1,443	7,605	22,113	11,395	4,758							
Total—														
1923	153	3,360	4,122	16,689	49,876	26,571	8,061	8,298	8,213	6,370	3,469	2,295	707	138,184
1924	205	2,362	3,126	14,641	39,866	20,231	6,399	5,294	4,024	3,277	2,295	1,615	509	103,844
1925	433	2,895	4,330	20,953	44,941	20,096	7,372	6,253	6,855	6,228	4,114	2,494	945	127,909
1926	260	3,840	3,388	21,022	45,438	23,349	8,375	7,969	8,020	5,348	3,596	2,355	888	133,848
1927 [2]	253	1,815	3,539	12,106	33,556	17,109	5,963	5,315	4,900	3,500	2,355	1,819	864	93,094
1928 [2]	226	3,443	4,281	18,452	44,098	19,331	8,161							

Crop-movement season [1]

Bureau of Agricultural Economics. Compiled from daily and monthly reports received by the bureau from officials and local agents of common carriers throughout the country. Shipments as shown in car lots include those by boat reduced to car-lot basis. See preceding Yearbooks for data for earlier years.

[1] Crop-movement season extends from June 1 of one year through June of the following year.
[2] Preliminary.

TABLE 131.—*Apples: Cold-storage holdings, United States, average, 1916–1920, 1921–1925; annual, 1927–1928*

BARRELS [1]

Year	Jan. 1	Feb. 1	Mar. 1	Apr. 1	May 1	June 1	Oct. 1	Nov. 1	Dec. 1
	1,000 barrels	*1,000 barrels*	*1,000 barrels*	*1,000 barrels*	*1,000 barrels*	*1,000 barrels*	*1,000 barrels*	*1,000 barrels*	*1,000 barrels*
Average: 1916–1920	2,890	2,293	1,605	955	434	127	------	2,925	3,507
1921–1925	3,604	2,817	2,012	1,173	586	204	811	3,712	4,199
1927	4,901	3,857	2,682	1,603	828	295	690	2,967	3,357
1928	2,758	2,038	1,358	801	415	195	1,013	4,622	4,575

BOXES

	1,000 boxes	*1,000 boxes*	*1,000 boxes*	*1,000 boxes*	*1,000 boxes*	*1,000 boxes*	*1,000 boxes*	*1,000 boxes*	*1,000 boxes*
Average: 1916–1920	5,349	4,644	3,254	1,916	923	259	------	2,808	5,570
1921–1925	9,986	8,272	6,170	4,050	2,055	710	809	6,460	11,075
1927	13,365	10,435	7,298	4,613	2,312	717	1,043	9,074	13,423
1928	12,260	9,809	7,023	4,960	2,889	1,223	1,854	12,333	17,452

TOTAL, IN BUSHELS

	1,000 bushels	*1,000 bushels*	*1,000 bushels*	*1,000 bushels*	*1,000 bushels*	*1,000 bushels*	*1,000 bushels*	*1,000 bushels*	*1,000 bushels*
Average: 1916–1920	14,020	11,524	8,069	4,780	2,224	640	------	11,584	16,091
1921–1925	20,799	16,722	12,206	7,568	3,814	1,322	3,248	17,595	23,671
1927	28,068	22,005	15,342	9,423	4,794	1,602	3,114	17,976	23,493
1928	20,534	15,923	11,097	7,363	4,134	1,808	4,893	26,199	31,177

Bureau of Agricultural Economics. Compiled from reports from cold-storage establishments.

[1] All apples, except those packed in western-style boxes, are tabulated in terms of barrels, on the basis of 3 bushels to the barrel; since Oct. 1, 1923, apples packed in bushel baskets are also included in this tabulation. Three boxes are considered the equivalent of 1 barrel. See 1927 Yearbook, p. 835, for data for 1915–1926.

TABLE 132.—*Apples:* [1] *International trade, average 1909–1913, annual 1924–1927*

Country	Average 1911–1913		1924		1925		1926		1927 preliminary	
	Imports	Exports	Imports	Exports	Imports	Exports	Imports	Exports	Imports	Exports
PRINCIPAL EXPORTING COUNTRIES	*1,000 bushels*	*1,000 bushels*	*1,000 bushels*	*1,000 bushels*	*1,000 bushels*	*1,000 bushels*	*1,000 bushels*	*1,000 bushels*	*1,000 bushels*	*1,000 bushels*
United States	------	9,870	96	12,360	84	10,044	54	16,170	162	15,534
Canada	840	3,858	531	4,572	459	4,011	546	3,579	630	2,901
France [2]	267	7,140	189	5,427	261	4,266	324	2,115	546	1,722
Australia [3]	78	1,140	0	1,365	0	1,824	0	2,703	0	1,317
Netherlands	105	933	363	1,059	153	2,178	609	582	402	1,461
Belgium	792	936	312	984	300	1,299	180	1,098	360	1,290
Italy	39	660	0	999	0	1,137	0	1,875	0	1,659
Rumania	6	0	0	420	0	1,083	0	768	------	------
New Zealand	[2] 51	[2] 15	39	204	39	177	30	603	36	441
PRINCIPAL IMPORTING COUNTRIES										
United Kingdom	7,686	0	15,750	0	13,155	0	18,339	0	13,512	0
Germany	14,454	93	11,301	78	8,580	69	8,322	15	7,890	30
Sweden	132	3	648	0	537	0	603	0	1,035	0
Egypt [2]	------	------	486	3	336	0	357	0	369	3
Denmark	108	3	396	0	393	0	621	0	1,020	0
Irish Free State	------	------	441	0	489	0	525	0	450	0
Norway [2]	222	0	189	0	168	0	189	0	249	0
Finland	192	0	153	0	141	0	162	0	162	0
Brazil	81	0	108	0	141	0	204	0	------	------
Cuba	39	0	87	0	90	0	90	0	------	------
Poland	------	------	150	6	84	42	3	9	30	9
Total, 20 countries	25,092	24,651	31,239	27,477	25,410	26,130	31,158	29,517	26,853	26,367

Bureau of Agricultural Economics. Official sources.

[1] Foreign weights are converted to bushels on the basis of 48 pounds per bushel; domestic, 1 barrel equals 3 boxes (or bushels). [2] Includes pears. [3] Year ended June 30.

TABLE 133.—*Apples: Estimated price per bushel, received by producers, United States, 1910–1928*

Year beginning June—	June 15	July 15	Aug. 15	Sept. 15	Oct. 15	Nov. 15	Dec. 15	Jan. 15	Feb. 15	Mar. 15	Apr. 15	May 15	Weighted av.
	Cents	Cents	Cents	Cents	Cents	Cents	Cents	Cents	Cents	Cents	Cents	Cents	Cents
Average:													
1910–1913	114.2	85.0	72.4	70.6	72.5	80.1	90.6	98.3	104.7	109.9	119.0	127.2	81.1
1914–1920	156.3	127.3	105.7	99.8	105.8	113.3	126.1	126.9	134.0	142.2	150.7	165.1	113.6
1921–1925	185.2	162.7	127.8	119.2	128.0	135.8	142.5	145.5	154.2	155.1	156.4	175.8	134.2
1910	112.0	76.9	73.8	73.6	77.4	89.3	100.2	115.7	118.6	124.7	138.8	139.6	88.1
1911	135.4	94.8	73.0	70.2	65.8	73.1	86.1	92.7	98.8	103.5	114.9	128.8	76.6
1912	108.0	82.5	67.5	62.2	61.3	63.5	72.6	74.3	78.4	82.4	85.0	94.0	66.8
1913	101.2	86.0	75.2	76.5	85.6	94.4	103.6	110.6	123.0	128.9	137.1	146.4	93.0
1914	135.6	91.2	68.6	61.6	56.0	57.3	66.6	69.3	73.1	73.4	80.1	90.6	62.7
1915	90.3	78.4	61.8	58.0	66.1	72.4	77.0	86.1	90.5	91.2	94.8	97.5	71.0
1916	104.9	86.5	80.7	75.6	82.5	92.0	103.4	104.3	114.4	126.9	137.1	142.9	90.7
1917	146.5	125.1	100.6	96.6	105.1	116.8	127.4	132.9	138.5	142.6	143.9	155.8	113.6
1918	144.6	125.7	114.5	118.9	129.4	138.9	150.9	148.9	159.8	190.1	203.5	220.8	137.5
1919	223.4	187.6	161.4	153.2	175.6	184.9	213.9	215.9	229.2	236.7	253.5	285.8	186.1
1920	249.1	196.7	152.1	134.8	125.9	130.7	143.2	130.8	132.8	134.7	142.2	162.3	133.8
1921	173.9	165.3	165.1	171.4	196.4	215.7	224.5	183.5	206.7	206.2	194.5	241.4	195.2
1922	202.7	181.7	100.4	94.3	93.4	101.5	108.6	131.5	142.3	144.9	156.5	178.7	109.4
1923	188.6	166.7	121.4	108.0	114.0	114.6	114.0	121.3	125.0	129.1	129.4	131.3	117.4
1924	159.3	141.3	121.6	109.8	115.9	119.5	128.2	144.9	150.7	155.4	158.4	179.2	122.1
1925	201.4	158.7	130.7	112.5	120.5	127.7	137.4	146.3	146.3	139.8	143.2	148.2	127.0
1926	168.7	133.8	103.8	88.4	80.2	81.6	87.7	97.3	98.8	100.0	103.8	113.5	88.3
1927	140.0	144.4	135.8	130.7	134.7	141.8	152.4	161.7	168.3	177.0	183.3	190.6	141.7
1928	188.7	156.0	105.5	96.6	99.4	107.9	118.5						

Bureau of Agricultural Economics. Based upon returns from special price reporters.

TABLE 134.—*Apples: Average l. c. l. price to jobbers, 1927–1928* [1]

BARRELS [2]

Market, variety, and year	Sept.	Oct.	Nov.	Dec.	Jan.	Feb.	Mar.	Apr.	May
New York:									
Baldwin—	Dollars	Dollars	Dollars	Dollars	Dollars	Dollars	Dollars	Dollars	Dollars
1927			5.93	6.31	6.44	7.28	8.02	8.25	8.69
1928			5.16	[3] 5.19					
Rhode Island Greening—									
1927		6.48	7.80	8.00	8.50	9.75			
1928		5.12	5.42	5.22					
McIntosh—									
1927	7.31	7.72	8.86	9.24	9.94	10.31			
1928		7.77	10.08	10.03					
York Imperial—									
1927		[3] 5.32	5.73	6.13	6.79	7.36	8.03		
1928			4.25	4.64					
Chicago:									
Baldwin—									
1927			6.68	6.85	7.52	7.86	8.78	8.23	8.64
1928			4.75						
Ben Davis—									
1927								6.79	7.24
Rhode Island Greening—									
1927		7.37	8.76	9.64	9.96				
1928		5.96	6.14	6.49					
Jonathan—									
1927	7.83	7.63	8.53	8.78	8.65	9.86			
1928	5.70	5.81	6.08	6.57					
King (Tompkins)—									
1928			5.12	5.51					
Northern Spy—									
1927			9.35	9.98	9.83	10.00	9.78	9.66	9.54
1928				8.00					

[1] Commodity reports began Sept. 7, 1921; Sept. 1, 1922, 1923, 1925; Sept. 2, 1924; July 14, 1926; Aug. 29, 1927 and 1928. Last commodity report of season May 1, 1922; May 12, 1923; June 8, 1924; Apr. 15, 1925; May 29, 1926; May 28, 1927; May 26, 1928.
[2] Quotations on 2½-inch stock unless otherwise stated.
[3] Less than 10 quotations.

TABLE 134.—*Apples: Average l. c. l. price to jobbers, 1927–1928*—Continued

BOXES [4]

Market, variety, and year	Sept.	Oct.	Nov.	Dec.	Jan.	Feb.	Mar.	Apr.	May
Chicago:									
Delicious—	*Dollars*	*Dollars*	*Dollars*	*Dollars*	*Dollars*	*Dollars*	*Dollars*	*Dollars*	*Dollars*
1927	--------	[5] 3.86	[5] 3.88	4.35	4.43	4.60	4.80	--------	--------
1928	--------	3.02	[5] 3.05	3.20	--------	--------	--------	--------	--------
Jonathan—									
1927	--------	[5] 2.79	[5] 3.11	--------	--------	--------	--------	--------	--------
1928	2.51	2.07	[5] 2.16	[5] 2.42	--------	--------	--------	--------	--------
Rome Beauty—									
1927	--------	[5] 3.62	[5] 3.19	3.23	3.11	[5] 3.37	[5] 3.14	--------	--------
1928	--------	2.35	[5] 2.25	2.15	--------	--------	--------	--------	--------

Bureau of Agricultural Economics. Compiled from daily market reports from bureau representatives at these markets. Average prices as shown are based on stock of good merchantable quality and condition; they are simple averages of daily range of selling prices. See 1927 year book, p. 837, for data for 1921–1926.

[4] Quotations on medium-large stock unless otherwise stated.
[5] Quotations include very large stock.

NOTE.—Tables similar to Tables 128, 129, 1927 Yearbook, l. c. l. apple prices, New York and Baldwin apple prices, Boston, are omitted.

TABLE 135.—*Citrus fruit production, by States, 1899, 1909, 1919–1928* [1]

ORANGES [2]

State	1899 [3]	1909 [3]	1919	1920	1921	1922	1923	1924	1925	1926	1927	1928 [4]
	1,000 boxes	*1,000 boxes*	*1,000 boxes*	*1,000 boxes*	*1,000 boxes*	*1,000 boxes*	*1,000 boxes*	*1,000 boxes*	*1,000 boxes*	*1,000 boxes*	*1,000 boxes*	*1,000 boxes*
California	5,882	14,440	15,265	21,296	12,640	20,106	24,137	18,100	24,200	28,167	23,000	31,000
Florida [5]	273	4,888	--------	--------	--------	10,200	12,900	11,600	9,100	10,700	8,200	13,000
Arizona	11	33	80	60	80	81	86	60	86	75	54	54
Alabama	([6])	1	[7] 20	[7] 82	[7] 82	[7] 175	[7] 225	([6][7])	[7] 100	[7] 75	[7] 110	[7] 38
Louisiana	1	152	37	42	50	60	75	75	100	150	200	220
Mississippi	--------	5	31	25	30	45	55	0	27	42	--------	--------
Texas	--------	11	9	--------	--------	4	6	12	10	20	30	70

GRAPEFRUIT

California	18	123	263	304	360	394	363	387	600	650	720	800
Florida [5]	12	1,062				7,600	8,400	8,600	7,300	7,800	7,200	9,000
Mississippi		1	([6])	1	1	1	1	9	1	1	--------	--------
Arizona	1	1	29	34	35	44	65	67	90	75	176	186
Louisiana		2	([6])	--------	--------	--------	--------	--------	--------	--------	--------	--------
Texas	--------	([6])	3	--------	--------	35	65	211	200	340	490	750

LEMONS

California	874	2,756	3,499	4,955	4,050	3,400	6,732	5,125	7,136	7,712	6,000	7,100
Florida	2	12	32	--------	--------	--------	--------	--------	--------	--------	--------	--------
Arizona	([6])	1	2	--------	--------	--------	--------	--------	--------	--------	--------	--------

Bureau of Agricultural Economics.

[1] The figures in this table of production include fruit consumed on farms, sold locally, and used for manufacturing purposes, as well as that shipped. The figures do not include fruit which ripened on the trees, but which was destroyed by freezing or storms prior to picking. For California the figures relate to the crop produced from the bloom of the year shown, fruiting through the winter and through the spring and summer of the following year, being picked from Nov. 1 of the year shown to Oct. 31 of the following year. Fruit not picked until after the latter date is included with the crop of the following year. For all States except California the estimates include all fruit picked after about Sept. 1 of the year shown.
[2] Including tangerines.
[3] Census. Size of boxes not specified.
[4] As estimated from prospects on Dec. 1, except Florida revised to Feb. 1, 1929.
[5] From prospects on Dec. 1, commercial shipments of Florida citrus from the 1928 crop were estimated at 12,000,000 boxes of oranges, and 8,000,000 boxes of grapefruit, compared with 7,100,000 boxes of oranges and 6,500,000 boxes of grapefruit shipped from the 1927 crop.
[6] 500 boxes or less.
[7] Equivalent in standard boxes, each equal to about 2 of the "half-straps" commonly used.

TABLE 136.—*Citrus fruits: Car-lot shipments, by States of origin, 1920–1927*

ORANGES[1]

State	Crop-movement season [2]							
	1920	1921	1922	1923	1924	1925	1926	1927 [3]
	Cars	*Cars*	*Cars*	*Cars*	*Cars*	*Cars*	*Cars*	*Cars*
California	46,844	28,376	48,346	44,905	34,439	47,017	53,511	43,543
Florida	20,859	[4] 15,718	23,006	33,418	25,091	19,625	22,536	16,455
Alabama	87	145	476	600	2	338	179	312
Mississippi			9	13		8	4	15
Louisiana				3	2	1	1	250
Texas				3	3	6	9	26
Arizona	49	78	71	94	45	96	73	33
Total	67,839	[4] 44,317	71,908	79,036	59,582	67,091	76,313	60,634

GRAPEFRUIT

Florida	11,115	12,943	16,969	19,614	20,087	14,269	17,304	14,172
Texas		8	48	99	521	298	747	1,036
California	451	503	507	469	449	546	597	741
Arizona	48	62	103	155	159	218	210	211
Total	11,614	13,516	17,627	20,337	21,216	15,331	18,858	16,160

LEMONS

California	11,836	9,907	8,946	13,388	11,680	13,981	13,496	12,680
Texas				1	[5] 2			
Arizona			1	2	1	1		
Total	11,836	9,907	8,947	13,391	11,683	13,982	13,496	12,680

MIXED CITRUS [6]

Florida			2,631	3,608	4,226	3,565	5,313	6,227
California			1,033	1,461	1,148	1,605	1,639	1,610
Texas			18	1	18		22	92
Arizona			3		10	1	10	11
Louisiana								1
Total			3,685	5,070	5,402	5,171	6,984	7,941

Bureau of Agricultural Economics. Compiled from daily and monthly reports received by the bureau from officials and local agents of common carriers throughout the country. Shipments as shown in car lots include those by boat reduced to car-lot basis.

[1] Include tangerines.
[2] Crop movement season extends as follows: Oranges.—From Sept. 1 of one year through August of the following year, except in California, where the season extends from Nov. 1 through October of the following year. Grapefruit.—From Sept. 1 of one year through August of the following year. Lemons.—From Nov. 1 of one year through October of the following year. Mixed citrus.—From Sept. 1 of one year through August of the following year, except in California, where the season extends from Nov. 1 through October of the following year.
[3] Preliminary.
[4] Includes one car in August, 1921.
[5] Reported in October, 1924.
[6] No reports available before 1922.

TABLE 137.—*Lemons: International trade, average 1911–1913, annual 1924–1927*
[Boxes of 74 pounds]

Country	Average, 1911–1913		1924		1925		1926		1927, preliminary	
	Im- ports	Ex- ports	Im- ports	Ex- ports	Im- ports	Ex- ports	Im- ports	Ex- ports	Im- ports	Ex- ports
PRINCIPAL EXPORTING COUNTRIES	*1,000 boxes*	*1,000 boxes*	*1,000 boxes*	*1,000 boxes*	*1,000 boxes*	*1,000 boxes*	*q,000 boexs*	*1,000 boxes*	*1,000 boxes*	*1,000 boxes*
Italy	2	8,147	1	5,237	1	7,078	0	7,008	0	7,345
Spain	0	101	0	213	0	656	0	372		
PRINCIPAL IMPORTING COUNTRIES										
United Kingdom	[1]1,116	0	1,781	0	1,895	0	1,942	0	[1]1,869	0
United States	[2]1,750	[3]66	634	228	1,572	162	999	296	849	308
Germany	[2]1,107		1,201		1,531	[4]23	1,615	[4]18	1,741	[4]29
Belgium [4]	763	0	1,058	7	825	3	1,018	4	803	4
Czechoslovakia			295	0	408	0	450	0	483	0
Rumania	123	0	183	0	198	0	225	0		
Poland			248	1	293	0	244	0	308	0
Netherlands	94	3	178	18	179	18	187	19	187	29
Switzerland			120	0	140	0	146	0	153	0
Hungary	[5]1,032	[5]228	113	0	131	0	114	0	216	0
Total, 12 countries	5,987	8,545	5,812	5,704	7,173	7,940	6,940	7,717	6,609	7,715

Bureau of Agricultural Economics. Official sources.

[1] Includes "Other citrus fruits, n. e. s."   [4] Includes oranges and similar fruits.
[2] 2-year average.   [5] Average for Austria-Hungary.
[3] 1 year only.

TABLE 138.—*Oranges: International trade, average 1911–1913, annual 1924–1927*
[Boxes of 78 pounds]

Country	Average, 1911–1913		1924		1925		1926		1927, preliminary	
	Im- ports	Ex- ports	Im- ports	Ex- ports	Im- ports	Ex- ports	Im- ports	Ex- ports	Im- ports	Ex- ports
PRINCIPAL EXPORTING COUNTRIES	*1,000 boxes*	*1,000 boxes*	*1,000 boxes*	*1,000 boxes*	*1,000 boxes*	*1,000 boxes*	*1,000 boxes*	*1,000 boxes*	*1,000 boxes*	*1,000 boxes*
Spain	0	14,830	0	18,958	0	20,199	0	20,265		
Italy	3	3,476	0	3,488	1	4,077	1	3,835	0	4,410
United States	[1]73	1,154	15	2,564	14	1,981	12	2,692	19	3,562
Palestine			0	1,781	0	1,848	0	1,885	0	2,645
Union of South Africa	0		0	399	0	660	0	563	0	749
Brazil	0	2	0	448	0	499	0	258		
Japan	0	353	0	277	0	369	0	491	0	479
China			253	384	359	233	526	231	461	313
Cuba		111	0	270		245		322		
PRINCIPAL IMPORTING COUNTRIES										
United Kingdom	7,638	0	10,395	0	10,788	0	11,160	0	11,352	0
France [2]	3,198	38	4,186	152	3,872	122	3,967	102	3,699	57
Germany	3,935		4,425		5,899		5,375		5,941	
Netherlands	631	9	2,109	779	1,850	561	1,717	456	1,631	527
Egypt		0	502	4	501	3	315	3	393	4
Poland			635	0	638	0	177	1	210	0
Switzerland	372	0	367	0	374	0	437	0	419	0
Norway [2]	208	0	297	0	338	0	369	0	387	0
Sweden	166	0	231	0	265	0	320	0	360	0
Denmark	97	0	238	0	230	0	229	0	221	0
Czechoslovakia			120	0	430	0	460	0	417	0
Irish Free State			245	0	234	0	244	0	255	0
Hungary	[3]2,110	[3]102	52	0	236	0	220	0	350	0
Total, 22 countries	18,431	20,075	24,070	29,504	26,029	30,797	25,529	31,104	26,115	12,746

Bureau of Agricultural Economics. Official sources.

[1] 2-year average.   [2] Includes lemons.   [3] Average for Austria-Hungary.

TABLE 139.—*Grapefruit, Florida: Average auction price per box at New York, 1919–1928*

Season beginning October	Oct.	Nov.	Dec.	Jan.	Feb.	Mar.	Apr.	May	June	July	Average
	Dolls.	Dolls.	Dolls.	Dolls.	Dolls.	Dolls.	Dolls.	Dolls.	Dolls.	Dolls.	Dolls.
1919	3.72	3.67	3.29	3.16	3.28	3.60	4.05	5.02	[1] 2.61	[1] 6.20	[2] 3.70
1920	5.31	4.71	3.92	4.86	4.30	4.71	4.55	4.54	4.21	[1] 4.33	[2] 4.55
1921	3.37	3.52	3.86	3.47	3.78	3.91	4.46	5.20	6.18	[1] 5.22	[2] 4.03
1922	3.75	3.84	4.00	3.73	3.96	3.63	3.98	3.48	3.26	2.96	3.70
1923	2.89	2.80	2.91	3.00	2.86	3.15	3.02	3.45	2.72	3.06	2.98
1924	4.19	2.99	2.39	2.94	3.00	2.90	4.04	4.50	5.99		3.38
1925	4.93	3.95	4.03	4.05	4.07	4.78	5.37	5.07	4.85	6.06	4.50
1926	[1] 5.21	4.20	3.57	3.74	4.01	4.01	4.01	3.99	4.00	2.89	[2] 3.94
1927 [3]	4.72	4.93	4.99	5.42	5.63	6.33	6.33	5.75	4.16	[1] 4.27	[2] 5.55
1928	2.68	2.20	3.44								

Bureau of Agricultural Economics. Compiled from New York Daily Fruit Reporter.
Monthly average obtained by taking simple average of reported averages of all sales of "golden" grade.
Includes all sizes. Yearly average weighted by number of sales reported during each month.

[1] 10 sales or less during month.
[2] See footnotes to figures used in obtaining this average.
[3] Includes average for August, 1928, of $5.46.

TABLE 140.—*Lemons, California: Average auction price per box at New York, 1919–1928*

Season beginning October	Oct.	Nov.	Dec.	Jan.	Feb.	Mar.	Apr.	May	June	July	Aug.	Sept.	Average
	Dolls.	Dolls.	Dolls.	Dolls.	Dolls.	Dolls.	Dolls.	Dolls.	Dolls.	Dolls.	Dolls.	Dolls.	Dolls.
1919	7.33	3.79	2.45	2.25	6.00	3.81	3.76	3.12	2.60	1.87	3.18	2.61	3.59
1920	4.73	2.78	3.04	3.39	4.11	3.14	2.91	3.82	8.17	8.99	3.72	5.87	4.64
1921	4.96	3.40	4.34	4.79	4.68	4.15	3.84	4.95	4.50	3.45	4.37	8.52	4.38
1922	8.51	7.44	5.61	5.01	5.42	4.20	4.79	6.12	7.92	6.07	7.68	7.28	6.25
1923	4.40	3.31	3.42	3.01	3.37	3.37	3.51	3.18	3.40	2.80	4.80	4.65	3.56
1924	4.90	6.80	4.65	4.45	4.30	4.51	4.76	5.71	6.52	4.48	4.50	8.87	5.36
1925	6.73	4.10	4.37	3.86	4.10	5.45	4.14	4.79	3.76	4.70	4.17	3.60	4.51
1926	4.46	3.86	4.08	4.14	3.43	3.96	3.54	3.92	4.58	6.34	6.44	8.40	4.20
1927	8.88	6.81	6.07	6.34	5.90	5.02	5.42	6.24	5.72	6.59	6.06	5.40	6.28
1928	4.81	4.82	5.55										

Bureau of Agricultural Economics. Compiled from New York Daily Fruit Reporter.
Monthly average obtained by taking simple average of reported averages of all sales. Includes all sizes and grades. Yearly average weighted by number of sales reported during each month.

TABLE 141.—*Oranges, California navel: Average auction price per box of certain brands at New York, 1919–1928*

Season beginning December	December	January	February	March	April	May	June	Average
	Dollars	Dollars	Dollars	Dollars	Dollars	Dollars	Dollars	Dollars
1919	5.80	[1] 5.98	[1] 6.39	5.13	7.10	5.71	4.76	[2] 5.70
1920	5.79	4.96	3.56	4.20	4.41	5.71	5.03	4.63
1921	6.46	4.64	[1] 4.81	6.51	[1] 6.97	[1] 6.78		[2] 6.07
1922	5.00	4.34	4.17	3.91	4.60	4.61	4.67	4.45
1923	4.44	3.50	3.50	3.23	4.05'	3.49	[1] 4.35	[2] 3.67
1924	4.71	5.32	4.98	5.76	5.72	7.05	6.74	5.94
1925 [3]	4.67	[1] 5.08	4.69	4.77	5.74	4.98		[2] 5.23
1926	5.50	5.36	4.86	4.94	5.36	5.06		5.15
1927	6.16	5.28	5.55	5.80	6.49	7.89		6.46
1928 [4]	5.26							

Bureau of Agricultural Economics. Compiled from New York Daily Fruit Reporter.
Monthly average obtained by taking simple average of reported averages of all sales of the following-named brands: Paul Neyron, Golden Cross, Glendora Heights, Pinnacle, Earlibest, and Big Tree. Includes all sizes. Yearly average weighted by number of sales reported during each month.

[1] 10 sales or less during month.
[2] See footnotes to figures used in obtaining this average.
[3] In 1925 the season began in November, with an average price of $7.03.
[4] In 1928 the season began in November, with an average price of $6.25.

TABLE 142.—*Oranges, California Valencia: Average auction price per box of certain brands at New York, 1919–1928*

Season beginning May	May	June	July	August	September	October	November	December	Average
	Dollars	Dollars	Dollars	Dollars	Dollars	Dollars	Dollars	Dollars	Dollars
1919	[1] 6.03	5.56	5.49	5.90	5.91	6.63	5.56	5.24	[2] 5.69
1920	4.91	6.52	7.05	7.57	7.88	7.91	9.22	[1] 8.67	[2] 7.56
1921	5.08	5.76	5.35	6.24	6.23	6.82	6.31		6.09
1922	7.86	8.42	9.33	8.95	9.09	8.45	5.04	[1] 5.90	[2] 8.13
1923	4.81	5.65	4.77	4.45	5.56	5.87	6.89		5.36
1924	4.34	4.97	4.57	5.81	5.92	6.64	6.53	[1] 5.19	[2] 5.70
1925	7.36	8.28	7.41	7.51	8.55	9.58			8.12
1926	4.74	4.71	5.31	5.32	6.09	6.93	7.50		5.80
1927	4.41	5.15	6.08	6.70	7.78	7.93	7.90		6.39
1928	8.14	7.41	7.86	7.96	8.38	8.47	8.62		8.06

Bureau of Agricultural Economics. Compiled from New York Daily Fruit Reporter.
Monthly average obtained by taking simple average of reported averages of all sales of the following-named brands: Carmencita, Shamrock, Bird Rocks, Bowman, Advance, and Premium. Includes all sizes. Yearly average weighted by number of sales reported during each month.

[1] 10 sales or less during month.   [2] See footnotes to figures used in obtaining this average.

TABLE 143.—*Oranges, Florida: Average auction price per box at New York, 1919–1928*

Season beginning October	Oct.	Nov.	Dec.	Jan.	Feb.	Mar.	Apr.	May	June	July	Average
	Dolls.	Dolls.	Dolls.	Dolls.	Dolls.	Dolls.	Dolls.	Dolls.	Dolls.	Dolls.	Dolls.
1919	[1] 3.16	2.80	3.95	4.22	6.43	6.63	9.40	8.32			[2] 5.91
1920	[1] 5.47	4.65	3.17	4.37	3.94	4.20	4.82	5.56	[1] 4.88	[1] 3.51	[2] 4.17
1921	3.06	4.18	4.29	3.95	4.85	6.68	7.15	8.06	8.99	[1] 9.79	[2] 4.44
1922	3.69	3.88	4.08	4.53	4.34	4.72	5.67	5.47	4.45	3.90	4.65
1923	[1] 3.11	3.55	2.68	2.84	3.02	3.16	3.51	3.85	4.88	[1] 4.81	[2] 3.27
1924		3.63	3.57	3.68	4.43	5.87	6.43	7.76	8.44		4.89
1925	7.80	6.80	4.00	4.23	4.41	4.95	5.82	5.91	6.54	[1] 7.45	[2] 5.07
1926	[1] 3.51	4.78	3.49	3.87	4.04	4.39	5.21	4.89	4.62	[1] 3.18	[2] 4.47
1927	[1] 3.31	6.10	5.81	5.56	6.58	6.77	7.35	8.49	8.26		[2] 6.38
1928	3.99	3.37	3.77								

Bureau of Agricultural Economics. Compiled from New York Daily Fruit Reporter.
Monthly average obtained by taking simple average of reported averages of all sales of "golden" grade. Includes all sizes. Yearly average weighted by number of sales reported during each month.

[1] 10 sales or less during month.   [2] See footnotes to figures used in obtaining this average.

TABLE 144.—*Cherries: United States imports and exports, annual, 1923–1928*

Year ended June 30	Imports			Exports [1]
	Natural, in brine	Prepared or preserved	Total	Canned
	1,000 pounds	1,000 pounds	1,000 pounds	1,000 pounds
1923				2,251
1924	[2] 2,970	[2] 1,380	[2] 4,350	1,675
1925	4,937	9,175	14,112	1,612
1926	2,904	11,153	14,057	1,688
1927	5,733	15,974	21,707	2,111
1928	15,146	1,049	16,195	1,719

Bureau of Agricultural Economics. Compiled from Monthly Summary of Foreign Commerce of the United States, June issues.

[1] Fresh cherries not separately reported   [2] Beginning Jan. 1, 1924.

TABLE 145.—*Cranberries: Production and farm value, United States, 1914–1928*

Year	Production	Price per barrel received by producers, Dec. 1	Farm value	Year	Production	Price per barrel received by producers, Dec. 1	Farm value
	1,000 bbls.	*Dollars*	*1,000 dolls.*		*1,000 bbls.*	*Dollars*	*1,000 dolls.*
1914	697	3.97	2,766	1922	560	10.18	5,702
1915	441	6.59	2,908	1923	652	7.15	4,664
1916	471	7.32	3,449	1924	582	9.42	5,485
1917	249	10.24	2,550	1925	569	11.20	6,370
1918	352	10.77	3,791	1926	744	7.56	5,623
1919	549	8.37	4,597	1927	496	12.28	6,089
1920	449	12.28	5,514	1928 [1]	531	14.58	7,743
1921	384	16.99	6,526				

Bureau of Agricultural Economics. Production figures are estimates of the crop-reporting board. Prices are based upon returns from special price reporters.

[1] Preliminary.

TABLE 146.—*Cranberries: Production and December 1 price, by States, 1924–1928*

State	Production					Price per barrel received by producers Dec. 1				
	1924	1925	1926	1927	1928 [1]	1924	1925	1926	1927	1928
	Barrels	*Barrels*	*Barrels*	*Barrels*	*Barrels*	*Dollars*	*Dollars*	*Dollars*	*Dollars*	*Dollars*
Massachusetts	325,000	429,000	430,000	370,000	325,000	9.90	11.25	7.75	12.50	15.00
New Jersey	215,000	115,000	210,000	75,000	135,000	8.75	10.75	7.00	11.00	13.00
Wisconsin	42,000	25,000	80,000	24,000	50,000	9.20	12.32	8.00	13.50	16.00
Washington			16,600	21,000	15,000			7.80	12.00	15.50
Oregon			7,000	6,000	6,000			7.50	10.50	13.50
United States	582,000	569,000	743,600	496,000	531,000	9.42	11.20	7.56	12.28	14.58

Bureau of Agricultural Economics. Production figures are estimates of the crop-reporting board. Prices are based upon returns from special price reporters.

[1] Preliminary.

TABLE 147.—*Cranberries: Car-lot shipments, by State of origin, 1920–1927*

State	Crop movement season [1]							
	1920	1921	1922	1923	1924	1925	1926	1927 [2]
	Cars	*Cars*	*Cars*	*Cars*	*Cars*	*Cars*	*Cars*	*Cars*
Massachusetts	966	644	999	1,324	1,045	[3] 1,457	3,762	1,242
New Jersey	452	637	789	713	806	427	804	290
Wisconsin	82	68	223	140	150	73	309	80
Other States	2	4	5	6	12	40	34	116
Total	1,502	1,353	2,016	2,183	2,013	[3] 1,997	4,909	1,728

Bureau of Agricultural Economics. Compiled from monthly reports received by the bureau from local agents of common carriers throughout the country. Shipments as shown in car lots include those by boat reduced to car-lot basis.

[1] Crop movement season extends from Sept. 1 of one year through April of the following year.
[2] Preliminary.
[3] Includes 1 car in August.

TABLE 148.—*Grapes: Estimated production, by States, 1925–1928*

State and division	1925	1926	1927	1928 [1]	State and division	1925	1926	1927	1928 [1]
	Tons	Tons	Tons	Tons		Tons	Tons	Tons	Tons
Me	48	49	58	76	Ga	1,470	1,892	1,472	1,672
N. H	95	96	91	91	Fla		700	610	900
Vt	49	36	45	36					
Mass	473	616	555	476	South				
R. I	300	212	152	190	Atlantic	11,967	18,569	13,957	17,079
Conn	1,063	1,275	1,087	1,314					
N. Y	51,840	106,700	51,520	85,470	Ky	972	1,274	632	1,200
N. J	2,200	2,820	2,535	2,822	Tenn	1,278	1,672	950	1,368
Pa	11,180	25,110	14,850	22,680	Ala	880	913	627	759
					Miss	285	300	225	259
North					Ark	4,400	13,000	3,000	17,000
Atlantic	67,248	136,914	70,893	113,155	La	42	42	30	38
					Okla	1,750	1,800	1,732	2,100
Ohio	13,750	29,100	20,000	28,700	Tex	940	1,200	1,260	1,440
Ind	2,450	4,606	2,580	4,980					
Ill	3,360	6,532	3,440	6,800	South				
Mich	22,100	60,900	51,700	72,800	Central	10,547	20,201	8,456	24,164
Wis	248	409	250	495					
Minn	30	85	152	198	Idaho	270	300	304	298
Iowa	2,835	6,052	5,329	6,225	Colo	260	320	314	357
Mo	7,300	12,880	7,000	14,000	N. Mex	475	531	458	600
Nebr	770	1,584	1,955	1,920	Ariz	419	900	1,900	1,785
Kans	2,216	3,700	3,735	3,465	Utah	1,000	1,300	1,320	1,520
					Nev	240	230	270	210
North					Wash	3,100	2,500	3,200	4,300
Central	55,059	125,848	96,141	139,583	Oreg	1,500	1,800	2,025	2,025
					Calif	[2]2,050,000	[2]2,129,000	[2]2,406,000	[2]2,331,000
Del	1,275	1,536	1,207	1,600					
Md	781	1,330	1,225	1,200	Far				
Va	1,653	2,790	2,048	2,560	western	2,057,264	2,136,881	2,415,791	2,342,095
W. Va	760	1,696	720	1,422					
N. C	4,950	6,840	5,135	6,000	U. S	2,202,085	2,438,413	2,605,238	2,636,076
S. C	1,078	1,785	1,540	1,725					

Bureau of Agricultural Economics. Estimates of the crop-reporting board.

[1] Preliminary.

[2] The totals shown for California include 138,000 tons not harvested in 1925; 15,000 tons not harvested in 1926, 142,000 tons not harvested in 1927, and 153,000 tons not harvested in 1928.

TABLE 149.—*Grapes: Car-lot shipments, by State of origin, 1920–1928*

State	Crop movement season [1]								
	1920	1921	1922	1923	1924	1925	1926	1927	1928 [2]
	Cars	Cars	Cars	Cars	Cars	Cars	Cars	Cars	Cars
New York	5,904	2,535	7,720	4,312	5,641	3,763	7,242	3,050	3,606
Pennsylvania	1,223	390	1,558	847	1,166	589	1,350	689	1,077
Ohio	62	72	80	92	29	19	110	5	10
Michigan	5,046	1,292	6,020	4,202	4,680	398	3,081	2,023	1,575
Iowa	104	77	237	217	79	50	176	196	221
Missouri	27	4	128	58	101	166	686	108	422
Washington	8	64	47	62	83	191	125	167	239
California [3]	28,832	33,344	43,952	55,348	57,695	76,066	64,327	75,820	71,370
Other States	104	39	177	198	459	636	1,493	514	1,305
Total [3]	41,310	37,817	59,919	65,336	69,933	81,878	78,590	82,572	79,825

Bureau of Agricultural Economics. Compiled from daily and monthly reports received by the bureau from officials and local agents of common carriers throughout the country. Shipments as shown in car lots include those by boat reduced to car-lot basis.

[1] Crop-movement season extends from June 1 through December of a given year.

[2] Preliminary.

[3] Figures include shipments in succeeding year as follows: 1920, 1 car in January; 1921, 2 cars in January; 1922, 7 cars in January; 1923, 13 cars in January; 1924, 6 cars in January and 2 cars in February; 1925, 21 cars in January; 1926, 2 cars in January and 1 car in February; 1927, 7 cars in January and 2 cars in February; 1928, 20 cars in January.

NOTE.—Tables similar to tables 144, 145, and 146, 1927 Yearbook, are omitted.

TABLE 150.—*Grapes: Weighted seasonal averages of auction sales of California grapes in 11 markets* [1]

Variety	Unit	Packages				Average price per package			
		1925 [2]	1926 [3]	1927 [4]	1928 [5]	1925 [2]	1926 [3]	1927 [4]	1928 [5]
		Thou-sands	Thou-sands	Thou-sands	Thou-sands	Dollars	Dollars	Dollars	Dollars
Alicante Bouschet	Lug	2,611	3,167	4,475	4,966	2.02	1.65	1.59	1.22
Carignane	do	795	774	1,313	1,710	1.48	1.47	1.32	1.06
Cornichon	Crate	352	229	189	57	1.35	1.27	1.20	1.15
Do	Lug	401	396	386	499	1.23	1.20	1.15	1.04
Emperor	Crate	206	107	67	10	1.10	1.39	1.11	1.04
Do	Lug	239	226	169	92	.96	1.38	1.16	1.16
Malaga	Crate	1,872	1,544	1,214	517	1.36	1.28	1.28	1.24
Do	Lug	2,339	2,193	2,505	2,611	1.03	1.11	1.19	1.16
Mataro	do	340	193	299	319	1.68	1.37	1.30	.96
Mission	do	1,039	499	530	585	1.12	1.31	1.06	.88
Muscat (type)	do	3,117	2,429	4,660	4,888	.97	1.02	1.02	.81
Petit Syrah	do	220	244	316	365	1.41	1.27	1.35	.96
Sultanina (Thompson Seedless)	Crate	1,537	866	1,081	479	1.31	1.24	1.42	1.03
Do	Lug	2,488	886	1,450	2,003	1.04	1.09	1.31	1.05
Flame Tokay	Crate	881	726	678	241	1.37	1.50	1.46	1.51
Do	Lug	2,327	1,769	2,107	2,520	1.13	1.40	1.38	1.32
Zinfandel	do	1,385	1,017	1,592	1,679	1.54	1.22	1.30	1.00
Total	Packages	22,159	17,283	23,401	23,550				

Bureau of Agricultural Economics. Compiled from daily reports of the fruit and vegetable market news service. Principal varieties only shown.

[1] Baltimore, Boston, Chicago, Cincinnati, Cleveland, Detroit, Minneapolis, New York, Philadelphia, Pittsburgh, and St. Louis.
[2] Aug. 3 to Nov. 14.
[3] Aug. 5 to Nov. 6.
[4] Aug. 2 to Nov. 12.
[5] July 19 to Nov. 30.

TABLE 151.—*Grapes: Average l. c. l. price to jobbers, specified markets, 1924–1928*

NEW YORK CONCORD—12-QUART BASKETS

Year	Boston		New York		Philadelphia		Pittsburgh	
	October	Novem-ber	October	Novem-ber	October	Novem-ber	October	Novem-ber
	Cents	Cents	Cents	Cents	Cents	Cents	Cents	Cents
1924	91		84		90		85	
1925	102		114		104		109	
1926	61		62	45	56	43	60	44
1927	56		61	68	64	66	64	67
1928	60		54		49		51	

MICHIGAN CONCORD—4-QUART BASKETS

Year	Chicago		Minneapolis		St. Louis	
	Septem-ber	October	Septem-ber	October	Septem-ber	October
	Cents	Cents	Cents	Cents	Cents	Cents
1924		28				30
1925	38	43	49	46	44	39
1926	21	18		27		22
1927	25	25		30		27
1928	21	21	24	26		23

Bureau of Agricultural Economics. Compiled from daily market reports from bureau representatives in the various markets.

NOTE.—A table similar to Table 149, 1927 Yearbook, l. c. l. grape prices, Kansas City and Pittsburgh, is omitted.

TABLE 152.—*Olive oil (including inedible): International trade, average 1909–1913,* annual 1924–1927

Country		Year ended Dec. 31								
	Average, 1909–1913 [1]		1924		1925		1926		1927, preliminary	
	Imports	Exports	Imports	Exports	Imports	Exports	Imports	Exports	Imports	Exports
PRINCIPAL EXPORTING COUNTRIES	*1,000 pounds*	*1,000 pounds*	*1,000 pounds*	*1,000 pounds*	*1,000 pounds*	*1,000 pounds*	*1,000 pounds*	*1,000 pounds*	*1,000 pounds*	*1,000 pounds*
Spain	30	86,454	1	101,695	3	112,990	9	165,960		
Italy	[2] 6,643	75,130	335	93,742	662	94,901	3,141	52,044	1,220	76,527
Greece	0	22,272	165	19,649	[3] 181	[3] 53,480	0	6,644	0	17,962
Tunis	2,020	18,090	4,267	19,638	3,694	37,071	613	49,012	486	56,707
Algeria	[2] 974	[2] 11,566	167	28,654	153	25,254	139	27,288	85	13,190
Portugal	[2] 2,020	[2] 5,492	1,240	2,609	[3] 2,254	[3] 3,957	[3] 4,709	[3] 4,375		
Yugoslavia [3]	0	0	1,222	1,310	1,614	455	1,012	281	559	1,289
Morocco	267	375	300	5,633	219	57	279	3,656	[2] 306	[2] 142
PRINCIPAL IMPORTING COUNTRIES										
United States	39,903	0	108,104	0	142,133	0	128,731	0	124,151	0
Argentina	48,248	0	[3] 64,639	[3] 0	79,705	[3] 0	[3] 91,174	[3] 0	[3] 77,066	[3] 0
France	[2] 42,502	12,935	38,459	12,759	37,859	9,112	45,930	11,670	29,855	18,604
United Kingdom	22,950	823	18,872	302	17,270	291	17,983	325	18,980	392
Cuba	0	0	16,035	0	17,273	0	17,319	0		
Uruguay	4,249	0	10,640	0	12,738	0	13,618	0	[3] 10,326	[2] 0
Chile	7,255	0	8,733	0	9,222	0	[3] 14,590	[3] 0	[3] 13,998	[3] 0
Brazil	8,409	0	7,496	0	13,297	0	11,262	0	9,661	0
Macao (Portuguese China) [3]	0	0	4,732	4,470	10,275	3,191	5,302	3,437		
Norway	3,458	33	9,878	0	4,722	0	6,148	0	7,006	0
Palestine	0	0	3,126	236	5,039	248	3,627	325	4,421	2,140
Switzerland	4,138	71	3,295	0	3,542	0	3,355	1	2,881	7
Egypt	4,803	0	3,043	28	3,344	34	2,934	38	1,911	29
Bulgaria	4,003	7	2,096	0	2,576	0	1,397	0	1,021	0
Canada	1,593	0	2,528	0	2,378	0	3,532	0	4,448	0
Belgium	[2] 4,295	[2] 582	2,079	35	1,829	52	1,528	36	797	17
Germany	6,085	0	2,060	44	3,362	35	1,837	34	2,438	50
Rumania	7,328	0	1,549	1	2,016	0	1,901	1		
Australia	510	11	[3] 1,184	[3] 0	[3] 1,121	[3] 0	[3] 1,413	[3] 1	[3] 1,351	[3] 1
Peru	[2] 684	[2] 77	901	0	1,011	0	1,238	0	917	0
Czechoslovakia	0	0	801	76	721	17	966	36	913	62
Sweden	889	2	400	0	498	3	405	5	312	4
Japan	126	0	227	0	316	0	357	0	309	0
Philippine Islands	360	0	276	0	266	0	348	0	328	0
Netherlands	[2] 282	[2] 205	173	22	191	8	171	5	150	17
Denmark	146	0	135	10	150	6	101	5	209	4
New Zealand	68	0	136	0	150	0	136	0	141	0
Total 35 countries	224,238	234,125	319,294	290,913	381,784	341,162	387,205	325,179	316,246	187,144

Bureau of Agricultural Economics. Official sources, except where otherwise noted. Conversions made on the basis of 7.5 pounds to the gallon.

[1] International Institute of Agriculture, "Oleaginous products and vegetable oils."
[2] 4-year average.
[3] International Yearbook of Agricultural Statistics.

TABLE 153.—*Peaches: Total production, foreign trade in the United States, and average price per bushel, 1913–1928*

Year	Production	Price per bushel, received by producer [2]	Farm value	Domestic exports, year beginning July [1]			
				Fresh	Dried	Canned [3]	Total in terms of fresh
	1,000 bushels	*Dollars*	*1,000 dollars*	*1,000 pounds*	*1,000 pounds*	*1,000 pounds*	*1,000 bushels*
1913	39,707				6,712		736
1914	54,109				14,465		1,586
1915	64,097				13,739		1,507
1916	37,505				8,188		898
1917	48,765				5,863		643
1918	33,094	1.62	53,637		4,835		530
1919	*50,686*						
1919	53,178	1.89	100,485		12,756		1,399
1920	45,620	2.10	95,970		3,573		392
1921	32,602	1.59	51,739	[4]611	6,260		699
1922	55,852	1.34	74,717	13,170	5,586	54,624	3,163
1923	45,382	1.37	62,025	15,065	12,975	50,374	3,835
1924	*47,755*						
1924	53,848	1.26	68,084	16,172	4,668	57,390	3,240
1925	46,562	1.38	64,171	15,749	3,351	83,160	4,161
1926	[5]69,865	1.00	68,426	14,453	6,968	81,896	4,477
1927	[5]45,463	1.18	50,494	18,048	6,542	86,634	4,703
1928 [6]	[5]68,374	.99	63,649				

Bureau of Agricultural Economics. Production figures are estimates of the crop-reporting board; italic figures are census returns. Prices based upon returns from special price reporters.

[1] Dried peaches converted to terms of fresh on the basis that dried peaches equal 19 per cent of fresh and 48 pounds of fresh peaches equal 1 bushel. Canned peaches converted to terms of fresh on the basis that 25 pounds of fresh equal 1 dozen cans of 1 pound each, and 48 pounds equal 1 bushel.

[2] From 1918 to 1922, Sept. 15 price; 1923–1925, Sept. 15 price in North, August 15 price in South; 1926–1928, approximate average price for the season.

[3] Canned peaches were reported in value only prior to July 1, 1922.

[4] No exports reported prior to Jan. 1, 1922. Figures for 1921 represent exports Jan. 1, 1922, to June 30, 1922.

[5] For quantities not harvested in 1926, 1927, and 1928 see Table 154.

[6] Preliminary.

NOTE.—A table similar to Table 152, 1927 Yearbook, number of peach trees, by States, census years, is omitted.

TABLE 154.—*Peaches: Production, by States, 1923–1928*

State and division	1923	1924	1925	1926	1927	1928 [1]
	1,000 bushels	*1,000 bushels*	*1,000 bushels*	*1,000 bushels*	*1,000 bushels*	*1,000 bushels*
New Hampshire	40		34	29	26	25
Massachusetts	205	40	218	213	140	189
Rhode Island	31	29	30	37	23	27
Connecticut	232	220	210	255	186	239
New York	1,700	2,178	1,920	2,300	1,140	2,400
New Jersey	2,642	2,500	1,740	3,000	2,304	1,625
Pennsylvania	1,907	1,715	600	2,498	947	1,867
North Atlantic	6,757	6,682	4,752	8,332	4,766	6,372
Ohio	1,386	800	1,100	2,120	1,326	1,742
Indiana	445	240	320	900	242	605
Illinois	675	700	500	2,660	1,122	1,638
Michigan	1,125	464	592	1,564	578	1,156
Iowa	40	3	12	97	65	50
Missouri	1,040	860	870	1,722	340	655
Nebraska	45	2	33	50	82	6
Kansas	78	231	371	266	259	84
North Central	4,834	3,300	3,798	9,379	4,014	5,936
Delaware	225	400	155	450	287	155
Maryland	631	600	240	700	352	465
Virginia	504	1,500	362	1,176	400	880
West Virginia	526	1,000	100	1,000	202	810
North Carolina	260	2,500	1,500	2,250	1,300	2,590
South Carolina	550	800	740	1,054	615	1,363
Georgia	5,248	8,342	7,304	9,400	5,943	10,000
Florida	120	127	115	125	69	112
South Atlantic	8,064	15,269	10,516	16,155	9,168	16,375
Kentucky	450	1,250	570	1,110	180	1,035
Tennessee	460	2,450	1,415	1,860	638	2,190
Alabama	779	1,230	1,312	1,159	540	1,350
Mississippi	260	700	712	551	279	635
Arkansas	1,110	2,700	2,200	2,400	1,628	3,000
Louisiana	175	230	275	228	86	211
Oklahoma	1,032	1,861	950	180	760	480
Texas	1,700	1,900	1,750	2,310	800	1,612
South Central	5,966	12,321	9,184	9,798	4,911	10,513
Idaho	282	102	23	297	144	335
Colorado	750	920	450	976	892	600
New Mexico	189	62	156	131	40	46
Arizona	70	40	65	91	55	66
Utah	802	750	100	550	561	612
Nevada	5	2	8	8	2	5
Washington	1,333	460	870	1,222	250	1,470
Oregon	500	189	222	384	160	292
California	15,830	13,751	16,418	22,542	20,500	25,752
Far Western	19,761	16,276	18,312	26,201	22,604	29,178
United States	45,382	53,848	46,562	[2] 69,865	[3] 45,463	[2] 68,374

Bureau of Agricultural Economics. Estimates of the crop-reporting board.

[1] Preliminary.
[2] The production of peaches shown above includes some estimated quantities not harvested or not utilized as follows: 1926, 1,462,000 bushels in Georgia and Northern States; 1927, 2,708,000 bushels in California; 1928, 2,917,000 bushels in California and 1,000,000 bushels in Georgia.

33023°—29——50

TABLE 155.—*Peaches: Car-lot shipments by State of origin, 1927–1928*

State and year	Crop-movement season [1]						
	May	June	July	August	September	October	Total
	Cars	Cars	Cars	Cars	Cars	Cars	Cars
New York:							
1927				2	1,015	142	1,159
1928 [4]				5	1,395	352	1,752
New Jersey:							
1927			8	366	714	1	1,080
1928 [4]				15	26		41
Illinois:							
1927			55	1,532	4		1,591
1928 [4]			24	1,963	19		2,006
Michigan:							
1927				6	391		397
1928 [4]				1	470	18	489
North Carolina:							
1927	16	87	1,577	22			1,702
1928 [4]		58	986	2,095			3,139
Georgia:							
1927	249	5,420	6,207	6			11,882
1928 [4]	3	1,489	11,884	2,645			16,021
Tennessee:							
1927			501	2			503
1928 [4]			24	2,137			2,161
Arkansas:							
1927			1,778	2			1,780
1928 [4]		1	2,184	1,766			3,951
Texas:							
1927	2		47				49
1928 [4]			236	40			276
Colorado:							
1927				897	809	3	1,709
1928 [4]				498	578	1	1,077
Utah:							
1927		1	2	59	736		798
1928 [4]				26	680	1	707
Washington:							
1927			1	27	212	8	248
1928 [4]			6	694	1,028	22	1,750
California:							
1927		97	1,727	8,397	4,904	20	15,145
1928 [4]	9	115	6,589	9,460	3,233	6	19,412
Other States:							
1927		33	772	1,899	954	4	3,662
1928 [4]		91	667	1,605	1,405	46	3,814
Total:							
1921	1,325	4,005	9,544	7,381	5,035	44	27,334
1922	695	3,189	7,598	11,928	13,779	1,216	38,405
1923	1	2,384	10,963	9,757	9,654	766	33,525
1924	28	1,873	14,599	13,683	7,889	[2] 1,323	[2] 39,395
1925	328	4,951	17,926	9,914	7,420	306	40,845
1926	52	2,209	21,793	24,538	8,847	[3] 1,026	[3] 58,465
1927	267	5,638	12,675	13,217	9,739	178	41,714
1928 [4]	12	1,754	22,600	22,950	8,834	446	56,596

Bureau of Agricultural Economics.* Compiled from daily and monthly reports received by the bureau from officials and local agents of common carriers throughout the country. Shipments as shown in car lots include those by boat reduced to car-lot basis. See 1927 Yearbook, p. 855, for data for earlier years.

[1] Crop-movement season extends from May 1 through October of a given year.
[2] Includes 1 car in November.
[3] Includes 5 cars in November.
[4] Preliminary.

TABLE 156.—*Peaches: Average l. c. l. price to jobbers at eight markets, 1927–1928*

Market, and season beginning May	6-basket carrier			Bushel basket				
	June [1]	July	August [2]	June [1]	July	August [2]	September	October [2]
New York:	Dollars	Dollars	Dollars	Dollars	Dollars	Dollars	Dollars	Dollars
1927	3.22	2.59	2.65	3.10	2.80	2.94	2.19	2.59
1928	3.48	2.17	1.62	3.61	2.01	1.69	2.05	1.74
Chicago:								
1927	2.30	2.32	--------	2.35	2.66	2.81	2.30	--------
1928	3.40	2.09	1.44	--------	2.18	1.94	2.15	2.11
Philadelphia:								
1927	2.56	2.36	3.67	--------	2.41	3.72	--------	--------
1928	3.41	2.14	1.52	--------	1.98	1.46	1.76	1.54
Pittsburgh:								
1927	--------	2.24	--------	--------	2.71	3.09	2.04	2.38
1928	2.81	1.76	1.28	--------	1.87	1.68	2.04	1.75
St. Louis:								
1927	2.16	--------	--------	2.05	2.50	3.28	2.72	2.56
1928	3.20	1.94	1.43	--------	1.94	1.65	2.26	2.41
Cincinnati:								
1927	1.93	--------	--------	2.46	2.39	3.33	2.40	2.28
1928	2.20	--------	--------	2.23	1.78	1.56	2.18	1.87
Kansas City:								
1927	--------	--------	--------	--------	2.52	3.43	2.58	--------
1928	--------	2.39	--------	--------	1.86	1.77	2.34	2.92
Washington:								
1927	2.68	2.33	2.74	3.36	2.56	2.51	2.10	2.52
1928	3.14	2.09	1.42	3.36	2.01	1.49	2.09	1.88

Bureau of Agricultural Economics. Compiled from daily market reports from bureau representatives in the various markets.

Average prices as shown are based on stock of good merchantable quality and condition; they are simple averages of daily range of selling prices.

Earlier data are available in 1925 Yearbook, p. 882, Table 206, and 1927 Yearbook, p. 856.

[1] Quotations began June 3, 1921, May 25, 1922, June 5, 1923, June 3, 1924, June 1, 1925, June 7, 1926, June 11, 1927; June 20, 1928.
[2] Last reported quotations of season Aug. 9, 1921, Oct. 11, 1922; Oct. 13, 1923 and 1924, Oct. 3, 1925, Oct. 21, 1926, Oct. 12, 1927; Oct. 15, 1928.

TABLE 157.—*Pears: Total production, foreign trade of the United States, and average price per bushel, 1913–1928*

Year	Production	Price per bushel received by producer [2]	Farm value	Domestic exports, year beginning July 1 [1]		
				Fresh [3]	Canned [3]	Total in terms of fresh
	1,000 bushels	Dollars	1,000 dollars	1,000 pounds	1,000 pounds	1,000 bushels
1913	10, 108	----------	----------	----------	----------	----------
1914	12, 036	----------	----------	----------	----------	----------
1915	11, 216	----------	----------	----------	----------	----------
1916	11, 874	----------	----------	----------	----------	----------
1917	13, 281	----------	----------	----------	----------	----------
1918	13, 362	1.38	18, 419	----------	----------	----------
1919	14, 204	----------	----------	----------	----------	----------
1919	15, 006	1.84	27, 614	----------	----------	----------
1920	16, 805	1.66	27, 865	----------	----------	----------
1921	11, 297	1.71	19, 268	----------	----------	----------
1922	20, 705	1.06	21, 943	36, 785	49, 358	2, 823
1923	17, 845	1.21	21, 570	50, 237	38, 431	2, 648
1924	18, 866	1.42	26, 689	41, 452	53, 851	3, 107
1925	20, 720	1.40	29, 066	71, 205	75, 876	4, 645
1926	25, 249	.89	22, 393	73, 877	66, 104	4, 293
1927	18, 373	1.32	24, 298	51, 056	52, 671	3, 258
1928 [4]	23, 783	1.02	24, 246	----------	----------	----------

Bureau of Agricultural Economics. Production figures are estimates of the crop-reporting board; italic figures are census returns. Prices are based upon returns from special price reporters.

[1] Canned pears converted to terms of fresh on the basis, one pound canned fruit is equivalent to two pounds fresh. No imports of pears reported.
[2] From 1918 to 1925, Nov. 15 price; 1926 to 1928, approximate average price for the season.
[3] Exports were reported in value only, prior to July 1, 1922.
[4] Preliminary.

TABLE 158.—*Pears: Production, by States, 1923–1928*

State and division	1923	1924	1925	1926	1927	1928 [1]
	1,000 bushels	*1,000 bushels*	*1,000 bushels*	*1,000 bushels*	*1,000 bushels*	*1,000 bushels*
Maine	7	12	13	6	13	10
New Hampshire	12	17	19	10	14	9
Vermont	6	12	12	6	12	6
Massachusetts	58	84	90	60	81	56
Rhode Island	10	12	13	12	12	7
Connecticut	37	62	60	57	54	42
New York	1,000	2,100	3,045	2,088	1,872	1,800
New Jersey	662	624	512	645	420	502
Pennsylvania	612	629	468	748	400	620
North Atlantic	2,404	3,552	4,232	3,632	2,878	3,052
Ohio	332	326	354	430	250	395
Indiana	334	180	209	328	140	288
Illinois	307	500	540	818	312	540
Michigan	1,005	810	450	889	702	819
Wisconsin	16	15	15	----	----	----
Iowa	62	40	45	68	41	47
Missouri	475	375	342	473	270	171
Nebraska	24	30	18	29	36	12
Kansas	134	262	165	186	258	51
North Central	2,689	2,538	2,138	3,221	2,009	2,323
Delaware	370	328	180	388	128	108
Maryland	374	335	280	394	193	193
Virginia	200	430	135	410	130	230
West Virginia	41	84	34	100	12	63
North Carolina	65	273	158	270	100	234
South Carolina	88	114	87	133	68	133
Georgia	192	232	155	257	104	245
Florida	35	55	54	66	44	52
South Atlantic	1,365	1,851	1,083	2,018	779	1,258
Kentucky	70	117	85	144	34	116
Tennessee	83	250	148	266	125	255
Alabama	174	224	157	211	83	234
Mississippi	90	187	189	189	120	194
Arkansas	45	124	89	116	70	102
Louisiana	45	65	74	71	50	69
Oklahoma	100	235	146	81	130	72
Texas	340	483	386	580	345	390
South Central	947	1,685	1,274	1,658	957	1,432
Montana	8	----	----	----	----	----
Idaho	72	60	39	68	56	72
Colorado	400	550	510	564	480	185
New Mexico	49	28	56	42	28	27
Arizona	18	11	14	15	12	15
Utah	64	70	25	80	60	87
Nevada	7	4	7	6	2	6
Washington	2,700	1,750	2,300	3,220	1,670	3,500
Oregon	1,580	1,225	1,500	2,100	1,900	2,700
California	5,542	5,542	7,542	8,625	7,542	9,126
Far Western	10,440	9,240	11,993	14,720	11,750	15,718
United States	17,845	18,866	20,720	25,249	18,373	23,783

Bureau of Agricultural Economics. Estimates of the crop-reporting board.

[1] Preliminary.

NOTE.—A table similar to Table 158, 1927 Yearbook, number of pear trees, by States, census years, is omitted.

TABLE 159.—*Pears: Car-lot shipments, by State of origin, 1920–1927*

State	Crop-movement season [1]							
	1920	1921	1922	1923	1924	1925	1926	1927 [2]
	Cars	Cars	Cars	Cars	Cars	Cars	Cars	Cars
New York	3,979	2,893	5,461	1,701	2,978	4,510	2,263	1,694
New Jersey	74	23	40	76	60	52	47	19
Ohio	64	17	96	33	47	62	100	130
Indiana	71		44	39	61	59	44	39
Illinois	1,179	33	468	318	595	614	858	228
Michigan	1,264	653	1,860	543	394	151	457	536
Delaware	290		151	541	273	128	249	49
Maryland	54	3	36	63	30	29	33	32
Texas	98	115	50	99	129	121	144	213
Colorado	654	745	774	696	955	717	750	737
Utah	88	33	82	65	81	29	77	34
Washington	1,902	2,903	2,678	4,274	2,456	3,560	5,278	2,589
Oregon	1,006	985	1,862	2,575	1,483	2,225	2,909	2,977
California	5,016	4,500	6,465	7,143	6,312	8,718	11,673	9,215
Other States	202	150	314	423	392	282	327	252
Total	15,941	13,053	20,381	18,589	16,246	21,257	25,209	18,744

Bureau of Agricultural Economics. Compiled from daily and monthly reports received by the bureau from officials and local agents of common carriers throughout the country. Shipments as shown in car lots include those by boat reduced to car-lot basis.

[1] Crop movement season extends from June 1 of one year through May of the following year.
[2] Preliminary.

TABLE 160.—*Pears: Estimated price per bushel received by producers, United States, 1910–1928*

Year	Aug. 15	Sept. 15	Oct. 15	Nov. 15	Dec. 15	Weighted average	Year	Aug. 15	Sept. 15	Oct. 15	Nov. 15	Dec. 15	Weighted average
	Cents	Cents	Cents	Cents	Cents	Cents		Cents	Cents	Cents	Cents	Cents	Cents
1910		100.9	98.6	100.8	122.4	100.9	1920	195.5	197.9	184.2	170.1	164.5	194.1
1911	118.0	103.8	97.2	85.1	111.0	109.4	1921	165.2	175.1	186.4	194.9	198.7	172.2
1912	106.3	100.0	83.1	79.3	92.8	100.4	1922	147.1		116.2	119.8	118.7	139.7
1913	109.9	119.3	95.6	93.0	97.9	111.2	1923	168.3	172.5	165.1	150.2	133.0	165.5
1914	98.8	92.8	80.4	77.5	82.5	93.7	1924	175.2	157.8	155.0	141.0		165.4
1915	80.8	83.8	82.7	89.8	89.7	82.5	1925	172.6	165.2	164.2	149.7	162.6	168.2
1916	109.0	102.7	96.9	93.3	105.6	104.8	1926	137.5	119.2	117.2	105.6	97.1	127.0
1917	132.2	125.0	118.2	116.1		127.4	1927	141.3	140.5	150.9	156.6	163.1	142.7
1918	168.4	157.8	147.5	140.1	156.6	161.1	1928	128.6	124.6	134.0	125.2	146.7	126.4
1919	188.4	183.0	181.3	182.0	219.5	185.7							

Bureau of Agricultural Economics. Based upon returns from special price reporters.

TABLE 161.—*Strawberries, commercial crop: Acreage, production, and price per quart, by States, 1925–1928*

State	Acreage				Production				Price per quart [1]			
	1925	1926	1927	1928	1925	1926	1927	1928	1925	1926	1927	1928
Early:	*Acres*	*Acres*	*Acres*	*Acres*	*1,000 quarts*	*1,000 quarts*	*1,000 quarts*	*1,000 quarts*	*Dolls.*	*Dolls.*	*Dolls.*	*Dolls.*
Alabama	3,440	3,620	4,520	5,380	5,504	5,140	7,924	11,836	0.16	0.18	0.15	0.16
Florida	4,240	2,980	3,680	3,640	8,056	5,513	6,900	5,096	.26	.35	.29	.35
Louisiana	10,340	18,500	21,100	23,200	10,340	24,975	16,711	33,083	.33	.29	.23	.23
Mississippi	1,160	920	600	1,000	1,276	1,104	960	1,500	.19	.27	.20	.18
Texas	980	720	1,200	1,850	1,078	1,056	2,520	2,830	.18	.29	.22	.20
Total	20,160	26,740	31,100	35,070	26,254	37,788	35,015	54,345	.26	.28	.22	.22
Second early:												
Arkansas	14,940	14,140	17,000	21,600	12,908	22,058	19,958	21,773	.16	.19	.11	.10
California, southern district	1,150	820	1,620	1,600	5,060	3,317	8,664	8,320	.19	.18	.24	.17
Georgia			170	170			245	265			.13	.12
North Carolina	5,130	5,080	5,800	6,200	12,312	10,907	16,658	16,659	.14	.16	.16	.12
South Carolina	430	300	300	300	1,032	600	528	720	.15	.16	.15	.12
Tennessee	18,780	13,730	14,960	16,460	22,536	17,162	26,479	25,102	.14	.18	.11	.12
Virginia	8,600	8,000	9,420	9,980	24,080	19,360	22,796	23,453	.13	.15	.14	.13
Total	49,030	42,070	49,270	56,310	77,928	73,404	95,328	96,292	.14	.17	.14	.12
Intermediate:												
California, other	2,020	2,090	2,130	2,150	10,100	8,747	9,419	8,925	.23	.20	.22	.15
Delaware	2,600	3,200	4,000	4,640	4,160	6,656	9,600	12,528	.15	.13	.11	.08
Illinois	3,330	3,060	4,280	4,700	4,662	3,461	3,595	6,228	.17	.12	.12	.12
Indiana	1,540	1,650	1,650	1,680	1,848	3,135	2,053	3,276	.17	.13	.14	.10
Iowa	2,760	2,850	2,560	2,560	3,588	3,819	4,915	3,072	.20	.12	.18	.15
Kansas	950	960	960	960	1,140	1,435	2,304	461	.18	.17	.15	.14
Kentucky	4,260	4,790	8,420	8,720	3,408	8,167	9,952	11,476	.19	.13	.19	.09
Maryland	9,100	10,650	12,780	13,800	17,290	34,080	28,666	16,105	.16	.15	.12	.07
Missouri	11,960	15,170	27,000	26,490	25,116	22,027	25,758	28,212	.19	.12	.15	.11
New Jersey	5,500	5,500	6,600	7,000	5,280	10,560	14,784	15,232	.14	.15	.12	.10
Total	44,020	49,920	70,380	72,700	76,592	102,087	111,046	105,515	.18	.14	.14	.10
Late:												
Michigan	6,450	6,230	6,480	6,090	3,225	9,569	12,843	9,013	.18	.13	.15	.15
New York	4,400	4,570	4,570	4,480	13,640	11,361	13,308	7,840	.18	.19	.18	.17
Ohio	3,700	3,600	3,780	3,700	3,330	9,000	5,795	5,920	.24	.16	.16	.18
Oregon	5,930	7,320	8,400	10,000	13,046	12,766	14,280	15,000	.12	.11	.08	.07
Pennsylvania	3,100	3,100	3,260	3,190	3,720	4,650	6,650	8,358	.21	.18	.15	.14
Utah	1,000	1,000	1,300	1,400	1,400	2,400	2,544	2,800	.19	.16	.12	.12
Washington	5,430	6,090	7,670	7,900	7,602	11,327	17,411	16,866	.20	.16	.12	.17
Wisconsin	1,840	1,840	2,760	2,840	1,840	3,588	5,299	3,096	.18	.18	.15	.21
Total	31,850	33,750	38,220	39,600	47,803	64,661	78,130	68,893	.17	.15	.14	.14
Grand total	145,060	152,480	188,970	203,680	228,577	277,940	319,519	325,045	.18	.17	.15	.14

Bureau of Agricultural Economics. Estimates based upon returns from crop reporters.

[1] Average for season.

Table 162.—*Strawberries: Car-lot shipments, by State of origin, 1920–1928*

State	1920	1921	1922	1923	1924	1925	1926	1927	1928 [1]
Early:	Cars	Cars	Cars	Cars	Cars	Cars	Cars	Cars	Cars
Alabama	139	285	460	693	408	421	440	901	1,025
Florida [2]	182	150	322	1,035	580	678	251	618	541
Louisiana	626	1,525	1,576	1,678	1,865	1,076	2,342	1,659	2,853
Mississippi	16	38	89	141	108	54	53	65	88
Texas	2	2	9	59	76	21	45	126	146
Second early:									
Arkansas	650	1,087	2,165	1,342	1,613	993	1,375	2,049	2,047
California, southern district			20		7	5		35	18
North Carolina	363	503	1,101	1,668	2,046	1,634	1,253	2,202	2,151
South Carolina			8	60	70	44	22	33	71
Tennessee	1,150	1,839	3,634	3,279	2,902	1,637	1,253	2,425	2,201
Virginia	270	679	1,691	1,193	1,919	1,249	1,136	1,104	983
Other States			3	27	26	20	7	20	23
Intermediate:									
California, other	[3] 258	[3] 292	181	[3] 226	184	125	104	147	141
Delaware	652	866	940	924	1,307	472	671	915	620
Illinois	112	73	260	224	367	295	247	176	324
Indiana	65	25	51	26	24	29	52	44	126
Iowa	43	20	73	82	113	37	49	41	19
Kansas			8	19	40	20	1	57	2
Kentucky	265	395	772	827	467	312	581	976	1,073
Maryland	793	1,132	1,634	1,916	2,155	1,092	1,394	1,515	981
Missouri	245	451	1,963	872	990	1,497	1,435	1,986	2,672
New Jersey	363	363	274	187	402	126	207	134	186
Other States			14	3		2		33	46
Late:									
Michigan	446	454	640	408	554	39	155	114	74
New York	257	243	325	301	345	200	238	189	70
Ohio	5	19	25	8	11			2	
Oregon	103	116	141	115	39	57	39	110	99
Pennsylvania	18	5	9	9	27		9	5	
Utah		3	13	23					11
Washington	22	140	188	177	39	42	17	93	106
Wisconsin	80	52	84	151	183	27	41	31	36
Other States	74	108	88	128	99	52	111	88	55
Total	7,199	10,865	18,761	17,801	18,966	12,256	13,528	17,893	18,788

Bureau of Agricultural Economics. Compiled from daily and monthly reports received by the bureau from officials and local agents of common carriers throughout the country. Shipments as shown in car lots include those by boat reduced to car-lot basis.

[1] Preliminary.
[2] Figures for Florida include shipments in December of preceding year as follows: 1921, 8 cars; 1924, 3 cars; 1925, 10 cars; 1927, 2 cars.
[3] Not reported by separate divisions.

Table 163.—*Strawberries: Average l. c. l. price per quart to jobbers at nine markets, 1927–1928*

Market, and season beginning March	Mar. [1]	Apr.	May	June [2]	Market, and season beginning March	Mar. [1]	Apr.	May	June [2]
New York:	Cents	Cents	Cents	Cents	Cincinnati:	Cents	Cents	Cents	Cents
1927	40	37	18	17	1927	31	22	12	
1928	50	36	20	10	1928	51	26	16	10
Chicago:					Minneapolis:				
1927	37	32	16	19	1927	45	39	20	27
1928	51	35	27	12	1928		43	26	13
Philadelphia:					Kansas City:				
1927	38	31	16		1927	34	34	17	
1928	45	37	14	7	1928	55	38	23	12
Pittsburgh:					Washington:				
1927	41	35	18	18	1927	40	24	16	14
1928	54	37	23	12	1928	55	39	14	10
St. Louis:									
1927	38	35	15						
1928	56	36	21	11					

Bureau of Agricultural Economics. Compiled from daily market reports from bureau representatives in the various markets. See 1927 Yearbook, p. 860, for data for earlier years

Average prices as shown are based on stock of good merchantable quality and condition; they are simple averages of daily range of selling prices. In some cases conversions have been made from larger to smaller units or vice versa in order to obtain comparability.

[1] Quotations began Mar. 17, 1921; Mar. 23, 1922; Mar. 28, 1923; Mar. 31, 1924; Mar. 19, 1925; Mar. 29, 1926; Mar. 7, 1927; Feb. 27, 1928.
[2] Last reported quotations of season June 3, 1921; June 6, 1922; June 13, 1923; June 17, 1924; June 9, 1925; June 19, 1926; June 20, 1927; June 12, 1928.

TABLE 164.—*Miscellaneous fruits and nuts:*[1] *Production and value, 1927 and 1928*

Crop	1927			1928		
	Production	Seasonal price	Value	Production	Price Dec. 1[2]	Value
	1,000 boxes	*Dollars*	*1,000 dollars*	*1,000 boxes*	*Dollars*	*1,000 dollars*
Oranges:[3]						
California	23,000	[4]4.00	92,000	31,000	[4]3.30	102,300
Florida[5]	8,200	[6]4.00	32,800	13,000	[6]2.15	27,950
Alabama	110			38		
Louisiana	200	3.00	600	220	3.00	660
Texas	30			70	2.00	140
Arizona	54			54		
Grapefruit:[3]						
California	720	[4]3.80	2,736	800	[4]3.50	2,800
Florida[5]	7,200	[6]3.10	22,320	9,000	[6]2.55	22,950
Texas	490			750	2.00	1,500
Arizona	176			186		
Limes: Florida	0			6		
Pineapples: Florida	13	1.90	25	9		
Cherries:	*Tons*			*Tons*		
Washington	3,100			7,900	168.00	1,327
Wisconsin	2,812	240.00	675	9,500		
Montana	300	100.00	30	127		
Idaho	2,200			4,000		
Utah	3,800	150.00	570	4,600	150.00	690
Oregon	10,500	160.00	1,680	10,875	160.00	1,740
California	12,000	180.00	2,160	19,000	150.00	2,850
Dried prunes:						
California	203,000	70.00	14,210	193,000	100.00	19,300
Oregon	16,000	90.00	1,440	2,000	160.00	320
Washington	3,500	95.00	332	750	160.00	120
Prunes, marketed fresh:	22,000			22,000		
Idaho	17,600	20.00	352	16,000	25.00	400
Oregon	8,283	25.00	207	15,750	28.00	441
Washington						
Walnuts, English:						
California	51,000	330.00	16,830	25,000	420.00	10,500
Oregon	800	360.00	288	1,500	440.00	660
Figs, fresh:						
California, commercial	5,400	110.00	594	5,400	87.00	470
Texas, commercial canning	4,879	80.00	390	200		
Filberts: Oregon	60					

Bureau of Agricultural Economics.

[1] Incomplete. Estimates for some States are not available. See also Table 165.

[2] For products marketed prior to Dec. 1 the prices shown represent approximate averages for the season.

[3] The estimates of citrus production include all fruit actually picked, however utilized. The figures relate to the crop produced from the bloom of the year shown. In California the season is considered as beginning Nov. 1, picking continuing throughout the following season until Oct. 31 of the following year, fruit not picked until after Oct. 31 being included with the crop of the following year. In other States the season begins Sept. 1. The estimates make allowance for average losses from storms and freezing between Dec. 1 and the end of the season. The estimates for oranges include tangerines. The forecasts for 1928 are based on prospects on Dec 1, except Florida citrus fruit revised to Feb. 1, 1929.

[4] Approximate net price to California growers for naked fruit delivered at packing house, calculated on packed box basis.

[5] Forecasts of commercial shipments from Florida amount to 12,000,000 boxes of oranges and 8,000,000 boxes of grapefruit, compared with 7,100,000 boxes of oranges and 6,500,000 boxes of grapefruit shipped from the 1927 crop.

[6] Approximate price to Florida growers per packed box. About $1 per box should be deducted to calculate value of fruit sold on the tree. Sales f. o. b. average perhaps 20 cents per box higher. Sales of grapefruit for canning substantially lower.

Table 165.—*Fruits and nuts: Production and value in California, 1919–1928*

Crop and year	Production	Farm value, Dec. 1 Per unit	Farm value, Dec. 1 Total
	Tons	*Dollars*	*1,000 dollars*
Apricots:[1]			
1919	175,000	80.00	14,000
1920	110,000	85.00	9,350
1921	100,000	50.00	5,000
1922	145,000	70.00	10,150
1923	210,000	25.00	5,250
1924	142,000	46.00	6,532
1925	150,000	54.00	8,100
1926	176,000	63.00	11,088
1927	208,000	57.00	11,856
1928	171,000	50.00	8,550
Prunes:[2]			
1919	135,000	240.00	32,400
1920	97,250	130.00	12,643
1921	100,000	130.00	13,000
1922	110,000	140.00	15,400
1923	130,000	100.00	13,000
1924	139,000	110.00	15,290
1925	146,000	110.00	16,060
1926	150,000	100.00	15,000
1927	203,000	70.00	14,210
1928	193,000	100.00	19,300
Plums:[1][3]			
1919	42,000	60.00	2,520
1920	35,000	90.00	3,150
1921	42,000	53.00	2,226
1922	48,000	50.00	2,400
1923	69,000	30.00	2,070
1924	39,000	45.00	1,755
1925	51,000	40.00	2,040
1926	71,000	25.00	1,775
1927	57,000	45.00	2,565
1928	66,000	37.00	2,442
Cherries:			
1919	12,400	150.00	1,860
1920	17,500	200.00	3,500
1921	13,000	125.00	1,625
1922	14,000	180.00	2,520
1923	17,000	160.00	2,720
1924	13,500	140.00	1,890
1925	12,000	160.00	1,920
1926	20,000	180.00	3,600
1927	12,000	180.00	2,160
1928	19,000	150.00	2,850
Grapes (all):			
1923	2,030,000	26.00	52,780
1924	1,535,000	35.00	53,725
1925	[4]2,050,000	28.00	53,536
1926	[4]2,129,000	25.00	52,850
1927	[4]2,406,000	24.00	54,336
1928	[4]2,331,000	16.00	34,848
Raisins:[5]			
1919	182,500	210.00	38,325
1920	177,000	235.00	41,595
1921	145,000	190.00	27,550
1922	237,000	105.00	24,885
1923	290,000	45.00	13,050
1924	170,000	70.00	11,900

Crop and year	Production	Farm value, Dec. 1 Per unit	Farm value, Dec. 1 Total
	Tons	*Dollars*	*1,000 dollars*
Raisins—Contd.			
1925	200,000	80.00	16,000
1926	272,000	70.00	19,040
1927	285,000	60.00	17,100
1928	255,000	40.00	10,200
Grapes (raisin varieties marketed fresh):[6]			
1923	130,000	20.00	2,600
1924	180,000	20.00	3,600
1925	378,000	20.00	7,560
1926	229,000	20.00	4,580
1927	303,000	23.00	6,969
1928	361,000	10.00	3,010
Grapes (table):			
1919	200,000	75.00	15,000
1920	166,000	75.00	12,450
1921	163,000	80.00	13,040
1922	213,000	60.00	12,780
1923	312,000	40.00	12,480
1924	325,000	40.00	13,000
1925	477,000	20.00	6,780
1926	398,000	25.00	9,575
1927	490,000	26.00	9,048
1928	460,000	26.00	10,010
Grapes (juice):			
1919	400,000	50.00	20,000
1920	375,000	75.00	28,125
1921	310,000	82.00	25,420
1922	450,009	65.00	29,250
1923	428,000	40.00	17,120
1924	350,000	63.00	22,050
1925	395,000	60.00	23,700
1926	414,000	45.00	18,630
1927	473,000	45.00	21,285
1928	490,000	25.00	11,800
Oranges:[7]	*Boxes*		
1919	15,265,000	2.75	[8]42,702
1920	21,296,000	2.18	[8]47,088
1921	12,640,000	2.80	[8]36,400
1922	20,106,000	2.00	[8]41,000
1923	24,137,000	2.00	[8]49,000
1924	18,100,000	3.55	[8]65,629
1925	24,200,000	2.84	[8]70,432
1926	28,167,000	3.07	86,473
1927	23,000,000	4.00	92,000
1928	31,000,000	3.30	102,300
Grapefruit:			
1919	263,000	---	---
1920	304,000	---	---
1921	360,000	---	---
1922	394,000	---	---
1923	363,000	---	---
1924	387,000	---	---
1925	600,000	---	---
1926	650,000	2.35	1,528
1927	720,000	3.80	2,736
1928	800,000	3.50	2,800

Bureau of Agricultural Economics; California estimates in cooperation with California Department of Agriculture; 1928 estimates are preliminary.

[1] To calculate the production of apricots and plums in bushels, multiply the production in tons by 2,000 (the number of pounds in a ton) and divide by 48, the usual number of pounds in a bushel.

[2] Dried basis. To calculate in terms of fresh fruit multiply the quantity of dried prunes produced by 2½.

[3] The production shown includes a small quantity of prune varieties shipped fresh, but does not include prunes dried.

[4] The totals shown for California include 138,000 tons not harvested in 1925; 15,000 tons not harvested in 1926; 142,000 tons not harvested in 1927; and 153,000 tons not harvested in 1928. The grapes not harvested were of table varieties, except 60,000 tons of raisin grapes and 18,000 tons of wine grapes in 1928. The values shown are based on the quantity harvested.

[5] Dried basis. To calculate the approximate quantity of fresh grapes used for raisins multiply the production of raisins by 4.

[6] For years prior to 1923 the quantity of raisins marketed fresh was small and has been included with other table grapes.

[7] Representing the commercial crop year beginning Nov. 1 of the year shown; the numbers for 1928, for instance, represent the fruit that set during the season of 1928 and will be picked and marketed from Nov. 1, 1928, to Oct. 31, 1929.

[8] Includes value of grapefruit.

TABLE 165.—*Fruits and nuts: Production and value in California, 1919–1928*—
Continued

Crop and year	Production	Farm value, Dec. 1 Per unit	Total
Lemons:[7]	*Tons*	*Dollars*	*1,000 dollars*
1919	3,499,000	2.00	6,998
1920	4,955,000	2.92	14,469
1921	4,050,000	3.45	13,973
1922	3,400,000	3.30	11,220
1923	6,732,000	1.60	10,771
1924	5,125,000	3.48	17,835
1925	7,136,000	2.11	15,057
1926	7,712,000	2.81	21,671
1927	6,000,000	3.80	22,800
1928	7,100,000	3.20	22,720
Figs, dried:	*Tons*		
1919	12,000	150.00	1,800
1920	12,300	90.00	1,107
1921	9,600	145.00	1,392
1922	11,000	120.00	1,320
1923	9,500	90.00	855
1924	8,500	100.00	850
1925	9,600	110.00	1,056
1926	11,400	95.00	1,083
1927	12,000	45.00	540
1928	10,000	45.00	450
Olives:			
1919	8,800	160.00	1,408
1920	8,000	95.00	760
1921	8,200	90.00	738
1922	10,000	125.00	1,250
1923	17,000	65.00	1,105

Crop and year	Production	Farm value, Dec. 1 Per unit	Total
Olives—Contd.	*Tons*	*Dollars*	*1,000 dollars*
1924	6,500	92.00	598
1925	14,000	60.00	840
1926	12,000	80.00	960
1927	21,500	80.00	1,720
1928	21,000	80.00	1,680
Almonds:			
1919	7,250	440.00	3,190
1920	5,500	360.00	1,980
1921	6,000	320.00	1,920
1922	8,500	290.00	2,465
1923	11,000	260.00	2,860
1924	8,000	300.00	2,400
1925	7,500	400.00	3,000
1926	16,000	300.00	4,800
1927	12,000	320.00	3,840
1928	13,700	340.00	4,658
Walnuts, English:			
1919	28,100	550.00	15,455
1920	21,000	400.00	8,400
1921	19,500	400.00	7,800
1922	27,000	360.00	9,720
1923	25,000	400.00	10,000
1924	22,500	460.00	10,350
1925	36,000	440.00	15,840
1926	15,000	480.00	7,200
1927	51,000	330.00	16,830
1928	25,000	420.00	10,500

[7] Representing the commercial crop year beginning Nov. 1 of the year shown; the numbers for 1928, for instance, represent the fruit that set during the season of 1928 and will be picked and marketed from Nov. 1, 1928, to Oct. 31, 1929.

TABLE 166.—*Pecans: Estimated production and value, by States, 1925–1928*

PRODUCTION

State	Improved				Seedling				Total			
	1925	1926	1927	1928	1925	1926	1927	1928	1925	1926	1927	1928
	1,000 lbs.	*1,000 lbs.*	*1,000 lbs.*	*1,000 lbs.*	*1,000 lbs.*	*1,000 lbs.*	*1,000 lbs.*	*1,000 lbs.*	*1,000 lbs.*	*1,000 lbs.*	*1,000 lbs.*	*1,000 lbs.*
Illinois		3	1		23	277	89	18	23	280	90	18
Missouri	4	8	2	1	432	792	178	143	436	800	180	144
North Carolina	74	248	248	220	61	202	202	180	135	450	450	400
South Carolina	270	510	364	345	180	340	242	230	450	850	606	575
Georgia	4,329	5,251	2,413	5,382	1,221	1,481	681	1,518	5,550	6,732	3,094	6,900
Florida	670	530	400	700	670	530	400	700	1,340	1,060	800	1,400
Alabama	762	1,195	556	1,040	411	644	300	560	1,173	1,839	856	1,600
Mississippi	1,783	1,508	1,120	2,205	3,311	3,692	2,080	4,095	5,094	5,200	3,200	6,300
Arkansas	105	150	75	85	1,995	2,850	1,425	1,610	2,100	3,000	1,500	1,695
Louisiana	274	274	131	248	1,551	1,551	744	1,402	1,825	1,825	875	1,650
Oklahoma	68	100	46	43	6,736	9,910	4,504	4,247	6,804	10,010	4,550	4,290
Texas	45	320	60	170	4,455	31,680	5,940	16,830	4,500	32,000	6,000	17,000
United States	8,384	10,097	5,416	10,439	21,046	53,949	16,785	31,533	29,430	64,046	22,201	41,972

TABLE 166.—*Pecans: Estimated production and value, by States, 1925–1928*—Continued

PRICE

State	Improved				Seedling				Total			
	1925	1926	1927	1928	1925	1926	1927	1928	1925	1926	1927	1928
	Cents	*Cents*	*Cents*	*Cents*	*Cents*	*Cents*	*Cents*	*Cents*	*Cents*	*Cents*	*Cents*	*Cents*
Illinois	35	32	35	20	17	17	14	15.0	17.4	17.1	14.4	16.7
Missouri	35	32	48	45	18	16	20	16.0	18.1	16.2	20.6	16.0
North Carolina	45	44	40	32	30	25	27	22.0	37.8	35.3	34.2	27.5
South Carolina	45	28	35	31	30	21	23	19.0	39.1	25.2	30.2	26.3
Georgia	37	31	34	28	25	15	17	13.0	34.4	27.5	30.3	24.7
Florida	37	30	33	31	22	14	17	16.0	29.5	22.0	25.0	23.5
Alabama	40	34	37	29	25	19	20	14.0	34.8	28.7	31.1	23.8
Mississippi	39	37	38	31	23	18	19	16.0	28.6	23.5	25.7	21.3
Arkansas	34	35	35	32	18	15	15	16.0	18.8	16.0	16.0	16.8
Louisiana	32	32	38	29	17	14	16	12.5	19.3	16.7	19.3	15.0
Oklahoma	35	30	35	40	15	10	13	12.0	15.2	10.2	13.2	12.3
Texas	34	30	35	38	17	11	16	11.5	17.2	11.2	16.2	11.8
United States	37.8	32.4	35.5	29.4	18.3	12.0	15.9	12.8	23.9	15.3	20.7	16.9

VALUE

State	Improved				Seedling				Total			
	1925	1926	1927	1928	1925	1926	1927	1928	1925	1926	1927	1928
	1,000 dolls.	*1,000 dolls.*	*1,000 dolls.*	*1,000 dolls.*	*1,000 dolls.*	*1,000 dolls.*	*1,000 dolls.*	*1,000 dolls.*	*1,000 dolls.*	*1,000 dolls.*	*1,000 dolls.*	*1,000 dolls.*
Illinois		1			4	47	13	3	4	48	13	3
Missouri	1	3	1		78	127	36	23	79	130	37	23
North Carolina	33	109	99	70	18	50	55	40	51	159	154	110
South Carolina	122	143	127	107	54	71	56	44	176	214	183	151
Georgia	1,602	1,628	820	1,507	305	222	116	197	1,907	1,850	936	1,704
Florida	248	159	132	217	147	74	68	112	395	233	200	329
Alabama	305	406	206	302	103	122	60	78	408	528	266	380
Mississippi	695	558	426	684	762	665	395	655	1,457	1,223	821	1,339
Arkansas	36	52	26	27	359	428	214	258	395	480	240	285
Louisiana	88	88	50	72	264	217	119	175	352	305	169	247
Oklahoma	24	30	16	17	1,010	991	586	510	1,034	1,021	602	527
Texas	15	96	21	65	757	3,485	950	1,935	772	3,581	971	2,000
United States	3,169	3,273	1,924	3,068	3,861	6,499	2,668	4,030	7,030	9,772	4,592	7,098

Bureau of Agricultural Economics. Based upon inquiries and investigations of field agricultural statisticians.

TABLE 167.—*Asparagus for consumption fresh, commercial crop: Acreage, production, and price per crate, by States, 1925–1928*

State	Acreage				Production				Price per crate [1]			
	1925	1926	1927	1928	1925	1926	1927	1928	1925	1926	1927	1928
Early:	*Acres*	*Acres*	*Acres*	*Acres*	*1,000 crates[2]*	*1,000 crates[2]*	*1,000 crates[2]*	*1,000 crates[2]*	*Dollars*	*Dollars*	*Dollars*	*Dollars*
California	6,600	9,980	10,080	10,400	1,115	1,856	1,341	1,633	2.05	3.26	2.99	2.27
Georgia	2,820	4,380	4,900	5,640	54	70	118	130	3.70	3.42	3.82	2.75
South Carolina	4,500	5,300	6,400	7,000	166	307	288	280	3.46	3.08	4.01	2.91
Total	13,920	19,660	21,380	23,040	1,335	2,233	1,747	2,043	2.29	3.24	3.21	2.39
Late:												
Delaware	1,200	1,500	1,500	1,920	58	90	81	161	3.24	3.00	2.70	1.65
Illinois	2,700	3,050	3,360	3,700	224	201	286	303	1.90	1.66	1.50	1.56
Iowa	140	150	200	200	9	9	14	14	1.70	1.65	2.00	2.00
Maryland	1,600	1,920	2,120	2,336	115	121	208	252	3.19	2.00	3.44	2.37
Michigan	320	390	480	620	24	26	38	60	2.55	2.90	2.74	1.59
New Jersey	9,000	10,000	10,500	10,500	648	740	882	819	3.25	3.05	2.80	2.45
Oregon			160	180			13	16			1.75	2.00
Pennsylvania	1,000	1,000	1,000	1,200	55	68	45	46	3.53	2.74	3.22	2.27
Washington	720	860	1,300	1,740	58	75	130	171	2.64	2.36	1.60	1.97
Total	16,680	18,870	20,620	22,390	1,191	1,330	1,697	1,842	2.95	2.67	2.56	2.14
Grand total	30,600	38,530	42,000	45,430	2,526	3,563	3,444	3,885	2.60	3.03	2.89	2.27

Bureau of Agricultural Economics. Estimates based upon returns from crop reporters.

[1] Average for season. [2] Crates of 24 pounds.

TABLE 168.—*Asparagus for canning, commercial crop. Acreage, production, and price per ton, by States, 1925–1928*

State	Acreage				Production				Price per ton			
	1925	1926	1927	1928	1925	1926	1927	1928	1925	1926	1927	1928
	Acres	Acres	Acres	Acres	Tons	Tons	Tons	Tons	Dolls.	Dolls.	Dolls.	Dolls.
California	34,800	46,300	48,300	49,300	45,200	50,900	53,100	64,100	78.36	66.29	70.00	79.36
New York	130	150	200	200	100	100	100	100	249.00	224.00	225.00	220.00
Total or average	34,930	46,450	48,500	49,500	45,300	51,000	53,200	64,200	78.74	66.59	70.28	79.58

Bureau of Agricultural Economics. Estimates based upon returns from crop reporters.

TABLE 169.—*Asparagus: Car-lot shipments, by State of origin, 1920–1928*

State	Crop-movement season [1]								
	1920	1921	1922	1923	1924	1925	1926	1927	1928 [2]
	Cars	Cars	Cars	Cars	Cars	Cars	Cars	Cars	Cars
New Jersey	465	237	154	64	156	150	226	156	34
Illinois	164	170	161	93	157	165	144	158	213
South Carolina	89	129	143	154	185	263	364	447	463
Washington	1	2	5	10	10	31	111	93	127
California [3]	502	362	304	458	718	1,279	1,503	1,154	1,876
Other States	5	2		6	9	18	71	124	165
Total [3]	1,226	902	767	785	1,235	1,906	2,419	2,132	2,878

Bureau of Agricultural Economics. Compiled from daily and monthly reports received from officials and local agents of common carriers throughout the country. Shipments as shown in car lots include those by boat reduced to car-lot basis.

[1] Crop movement season extends from Mar. 1 through July of a given year.
[2] Preliminary.
[3] California includes shipments in other months as follows: 1924, 6 in February; 1925, 10 in February; 1926, 8 in October and 5 in November; 1927, 6 in October and 1 in November; 1928, 24 in October and 8 in November.

TABLE 170.—*Beans, snap, for consumption fresh, commercial crop: Acreage, production, and price per hamper, by States, 1925–1928*

State	Acreage				Production				Price per hamper [1]			
	1925	1926	1927	1928	1925	1926	1927	1928	1925	1926	1927	1928
	Acres	Acres	Acres	Acres	1,000 hampers [2]	1,000 hampers [2]	1,000 hampers [2]	1,000 hampers [2]	Dollars	Dollars	Dollars	Dollars
Early:												
Alabama	680	710	960	1,000	45	53	73	64	1.37	2.34	1.10	1.75
California	2,000	3,000	3,120	3,250	430	645	484	429	1.75	1.45	1.76	1.60
Florida [3]	20,530	16,000	19,690	28,810	1,663	1,184	1,418	1,440	2.52	3.38	2.70	2.29
Georgia	1,300	1,740	1,880	1,360	68	108	62	68	1.65	2.08	.97	1.76
Louisiana [3]	7,120	10,940	13,370	12,970	527	580	1,016	636	1.42	2.41	1.45	1.47
Mississippi [3]	3,160	3,460	5,260	6,080	212	239	268	249	1.80	2.44	1.34	2.11
North Carolina [3]	3,290	3,390	4,480	6,900	329	305	381	593	1.36	1.89	1.78	1.02
South Carolina [3]	3,560	4,500	5,670	5,720	295	360	312	383	2.10	2.55	1.10	1.74
Texas [3]	4,730	5,240	6,220	6,030	364	477	286	573	1.28	1.63	1.68	1.54
Virginia [3]	3,400	2,860	3,170	3,600	388	440	434	371	2.06	2.26	1.85	1.11
Total	49,770	51,840	63,820	75,720	4,321	4,391	4,734	4,806	2.01	2.56	1.89	1.71
Late:												
Arkansas	1,600	1,280	1,120	1,410	98	46	68	83	1.82	1.44	1.40	.96
Delaware		200	150	130		13	18	14		1.00	1.25	1.20
Illinois	550	330	530	660	37	24	29	39	1.64	1.08	2.27	1.14
Maryland	3,920	4,250	4,250	4,340	392	382	340	326	.80	1.06	1.75	1.00
New Jersey	11,000	11,000	11,300	12,000	1,265	1,320	1,469	1,440	1.08	1.00	1.45	1.47
Tennessee	1,400	1,670	1,000	1,650	147	134	65	124	1.55	1.41	3.19	.93
Total	18,470	18,730	18,350	20,190	1,939	1,919	1,989	2,026	1.11	1.05	1.57	1.33
Grand total	68,240	70,570	82,170	95,910	6,260	6,310	6,723	6,832	1.71	1.99	1.80	1.60

Bureau of Agricultural Economics. Estimates based upon returns from crop reporters.

[1] Average for season.   [2] 1-bushel hampers.   [3] Includes fall crop of previous year.

TABLE 171.—*Beans, snap, for canning, commercial crop: Acreage, production, and price per ton, by States, 1925–1928*

State	Acreage				Production				Price per ton			
	1925	1926	1927	1928	1925	1926	1927	1928	1925	1926	1927	1928
	Acres	*Acers*	*Acres*	*Acres*	*Tons*	*Tons*	*Tons*	*Tons*	*Dolls.*	*Dolls.*	*Dolls.*	*Dolls.*
Arkansas	1,020	630	880	1,790	2,400	900	1,700	2,000	50.00	50.00	50.00	51.29
California	700	700	450	480	1,400	3,200	2,000	2,200	80.00	81.00	85.00	80.00
Colorado	1,800	700	900	1,600	5,400	2,200	2,200	3,400	56.67	53.33	60.00	60.00
Delaware	1,150	800	400	670	1,700	700	700	600	52.50	47.00	48.75	43.33
Indiana	1,300	850	850	1,800	3,100	700	2,000	3,200	50.00	55.00	55.50	55.00
Louisiana	720	800	1,640	3,040	1,400	400	2,000	2,100	52.50	50.00	50.00	50.00
Maine	1,210	860	600	970	2,500	2,000	1,400	2,300	60.00	57.00	55.83	59.72
Maryland	5,200	3,310	3,300	4,360	7,800	3,000	5,000	6,500	59.91	51.91	54.92	57.53
Michigan	3,000	2,400	2,400	2,950	4,500	2,900	2,200	4,400	59.00	51.20	53.00	58.36
Mississippi	1,670	1,550	1,780	1,690	1,700	3,300	2,700	2,900	52.50	50.00	51.33	50.00
New York	6,370	5,220	5,530	6,840	15,900	6,800	7,700	10,900	85.46	76.86	83.71	75.93
Oregon	1,200	1,250	650	650	4,800	3,100	1,600	2,500	60.18	64.00	65.00	65.00
Pennsylvania	1,320	1,010	890	1,060	2,600	1,200	1,400	2,200	48.75	41.83	50.98	58.33
South Carolina	1,160	700	700	700	2,900	1,000	1,000	1,500	44.00	42.00	45.00	45.00
Tennessee	1,150	1,080	1,250	1,220	2,100	2,400	1,800	1,800	56.00	40.81	50.00	50.00
Utah	450	610	880	1,020	1,100	1,500	2,400	2,400	54.62	49.68	53.13	58.27
Washington	460	270	370	700	1,800	1,000	1,000	2,400	46.67	60.00	60.20	60.00
Wisconsin	4,000	3,460	3,910	4,600	8,000	4,200	5,100	7,400	73.19	73.83	75.00	67.83
Other States	2,430	1,350	1,540	3,010	3,600	1,100	2,200	4,200	52.17	57.50	53.98	52.80
Total or average	36,310	27,550	28,920	39,150	74,700	41,600	46,000	65,200	63.82	60.43	62.61	61.35

Bureau of Agricultural Economics.   Estimates based upon returns from crop reporters.

TABLE 172.—*Beans, snap: Car-lot shipments, by State of origin, 1920–1928*

State	1920	1921	1922	1923	1924	1925	1926	1927	1928 [1]
	Cars	*Cars*	*Cars*	*Cars*	*Cars*	*Cars*	*Cars*	*Cars*	*Cars*
New York	43	28	11	33	81	62	39	31	49
New Jersey	90	111	68	15	100	48	56	203	110
Maryland	159	22	149	49	136	127	197	235	246
Virginia	155	79	268	101	899	570	841	877	658
North Carolina	133	128	219	261	559	459	550	504	690
South Carolina	142	331	503	585	517	334	449	425	432
Florida	547	407	750	1,848	1,093	2,083	1,094	3,403	1,773
Tennessee	20	23	63	81	248	84	174	45	119
Mississippi	105	79	252	47	85	88	130	143	192
Louisiana	35	202	90	107	439	683	588	662	813
Texas	7	39	26	88	210	407	414	471	299
Other States	37	151	232	113	251	279	322	302	379
Total	1,473	1,600	2,631	3,328	4,618	5,224	4,854	7,301	5,760

Bureau of Agricultural Economics.   Compiled from daily and monthly reports received by the bureau from officials and local agents of common carriers throughout the country.   Shipments as shown in car lots include those by boat reduced to car-lot basis.

[1] Preliminary.

TABLE 173.—*Cabbage, commercial crop: Acreage, production, and price per ton, by States, 1925–1928*

State	Acreage				Production [1]				Price per ton [2]			
	1925	1926	1927	1928	1925	1926	1927	1928	1925	1926	1927	1928
Fall:	*Acres*	*Acres*	*Acres*	*Acres*	*Tons*	*Tons*	*Tons*	*Tons*	*Doll.*	*Doll.*	*Doll.*	*Doll.*
South Carolina___	400	250	300	600	2,700	1,800	1,700	2,400	33.28	34.70	22.70	36.03
Virginia_____	200	200	100	180	1,800	1,500	500	900	16.00	16.20	15.00	71.08
Total_____	600	450	400	780	4,500	3,300	2,200	3,300	26.44	26.06	21.36	45.45
Early:												
California_____	6,080	6,480	6,350	6,400	42,600	42,100	40,000	38,400	18.33	28.53	18.00	31.00
Florida_____	4,650	3,660	3,010	2,900	29,800	22,000	14,700	16,000	28.13	48.44	31.22	36.93
Louisiana_____	2,720	3,800	5,880	8,980	14,100	20,500	30,000	51,200	31.20	52.76	20.96	23.09
Texas_____	14,360	14,300	18,530	15,840	76,100	82,900	122,300	91,900	10.71	29.23	9.76	19.15
Total_____	27,810	28,240	33,770	34,120	162,600	167,500	207,000	197,500	17.68	34.46	14.50	23.91
Second early:												
Alabama_____	2,880	3,900	4,200	2,400	14,400	19,500	22,700	11,800	23.43	20.17	19.60	62.62
Georgia_____	440	320	200	100	2,500	1,100	1,300	300	23.51	38.88	20.89	30.60
Louisiana_____	1,820	5,770	8,600	7,150	10,990	27,100	39,600	37,200	20.50	30.83	22.31	42.54
Mississippi_____	2,760	1,880	2,110	2,590	10,800	13,500	10,600	13,800	31.51	26.95	44.75	45.50
North Carolina___	630	620	780	780	5,100	3,100	3,300	3,900	25.46	30.00	50.75	54.00
South Carolina___	3,150	3,300	2,300	2,500	30,900	28,700	21,600	15,500	20.67	28.11	40.28	49.02
Virginia (E. Shore and Norfolk)___	3,500	4,000	6,400	6,700	25,900	22,400	32,000	32,800	36.23	39.43	76.40	35.44
Total_____	15,180	19,790	24,590	22,130	100,500	115,400	131,100	115,300	26.53	29.62	40.51	44.15
Intermediate:												
Arkansas_____			560	1,040			4,500	4,700			42.00	14.00
Delaware_____		300	250	250		1,900	1,700	1,400		24.00	28.00	40.00
Illinois_____	820	900	940	1,030	4,900	5,800	6,200	9,300	47.72	20.57	14.37	8.00
Iowa_____	960	1,000	1,080	1,200	4,800	7,500	6,900	10,800	33.20	11.12	26.37	13.23
Kentucky_____	240	240	240	260	1,700	1,700	1,600	1,600	45.00	20.00	40.00	15.00
Maryland_____	1,870	1,650	1,270	1,400	11,200	8,700	7,900	9,000	23.33	52.65	52.48	22.40
Missouri_____	750	860	860	950	6,000	6,900	7,300	5,200	50.00	13.50	44.22	11.25
New Jersey_____	5,000	6,000	6,600	6,890	26,000	41,400	46,200	39,400	40.00	24.00	29.20	30.00
New Mexico_____	400	500	600	500	2,800	4,000	4,200	3,500	42.50	32.23	66.20	56.25
New York (L. I.)_	3,000	3,000	3,090	3,090	25,200	24,000	43,300	27,200	26.00	15.33	18.41	23.00
Ohio (Washington Co.)_____	670	600	850	850	5,400	3,600	7,600	8,500	75.93	37.30	38.25	24.10
Tennessee_____	980	1,560	1,750	2,120	5,900	7,800	10,500	12,900	44.00	27.20	40.88	14.66
Virginia (S. W.)__	3,000	3,660	2,450	2,200	15,600	18,300	17,200	22,000	46.95	11.86	17.29	18.02
Washington_____	1,420	1,240	1,340	1,340	15,600	12,400	13,400	9,400	43.83	28.25	60.37	19.00
Total_____	19,110	21,510	21,880	23,030	125,100	144,000	178,500	164,900	39.41	22.48	31.15	21.82
Late:												
Colorado_____	2,000	3,220	2,600	3,100	23,000	43,800	37,700	44,600	18.96	7.29	13.90	13.01
Indiana_____	1,320	1,990	1,190	1,510	9,200	17,500	11,900	15,100	7.54	9.10	16.60	12.78
Michigan_____	3,160	2,960	3,120	3,170	31,000	23,100	23,100	25,700	10.10	9.48	11.68	12.62
Minnesota_____	3,390	3,250	3,070	2,500	26,800	31,500	30,400	26,000	16.52	8.10	9.27	14.32
New York (except Long Island)_____	27,800	28,560	33,910	28,130	283,600	305,600	417,100	202,500	10.49	9.95	5.97	25.56
Ohio (except Washington Co.)___	2,470	2,620	3,510	3,040	22,200	23,600	26,300	25,800	7.33	7.09	7.05	23.00
Oregon_____	1,630	1,710	950	950	6,500	17,800	9,500	8,100	29.09	17.31	18.35	31.23
Pennsylvania_____	1,940	1,740	1,300	1,300	19,400	15,800	15,100	10,000	21.78	20.19	20.33	26.40
Wisconsin_____	13,560	13,290	13,500	13,090	132,900	127,600	114,800	137,400	8.93	9.32	8.98	15.74
Total_____	57,270	59,340	63,150	56,790	554,600	606,300	685,900	495,200	11.18	9.86	7.96	20.03
Grand total__	119,970	129,330	143,790	136,850	947,300	1,036,500	1,204,700	976,200	17.72	17.84	16.09	24.05

Bureau of Agricultural Economics. Estimates based upon returns from crop reporters.

[1] Includes sauerkraut.   [2] Average for season.

TABLE 174.—*Cabbage for sauerkraut, commercial crop: Acreage, production, and price per ton, by States 1925–1928*

State	Acreage				Production				Price per ton			
	1925	1926	1927	1928	1925	1926	1927	1928	1925	1926	1927	1928
	Acres	Acres	Acres	Acres	Tons	Tons	Tons	Tons	Dolls.	Dolls.	Dolls.	Dolls.
Colorado	100	100	300	500	1,300	1,600	4,000	7,000	8.00	6.38	7.00	10.00
Illinois	420	360	360	360	3,400	2,900	4,000	3,300	7.75	7.56	8.27	10.00
Indiana	220	1,000	360	730	1,500	8,000	3,200	7,300	7.00	7.00	8.67	8.40
Michigan	1,190	1,500	1,530	1,620	11,900	15,000	13,800	13,000	6.58	6.50	6.40	7.46
Minnesota	420	420	430	430	4,200	4,400	5,200	4,600	7.00	5.00	6.25	6.75
New York	2,170	3,000	3,960	4,120	26,700	37,800	63,400	30,900	6.45	6.12	6.00	9.00
Ohio	1,410	1,850	2,590	2,250	12,700	20,400	33,700	19,600	8.20	6.00	7.50	7.26
Washington	330	380	260	260	4,000	3,800	2,600	2,200	10.00	10.00	10.00	10.00
Wisconsin	1,970	1,790	2,090	2,510	19,700	16,100	20,100	25,900	6.75	6.47	6.56	8.24
Other States	460	1,760	1,920	2,110	4,400	14,100	15,700	18,100	13.24	9.97	7.03	10.00
Total or average	8,690	12,160	13,800	14,890	89,800	124,100	165,700	131,900	7.35	6.80	6.69	8.55

Bureau of Agricultural Economics. Estimates based upon returns from crop reporters.

TABLE 175.—*Cabbage: Car-lot shipments, by State of origin, 1920–1927*

State	Crop-movement season [1]							
	1920	1921	1922	1923	1924	1925	1926	1927 [2]
	Cars	Cars	Cars	Cars	Cars	Cars	Cars	Cars
New York	9,511	9,315	10,273	9,087	11,816	12,545	[3] 12,898	[4] 14,078
Pennsylvania	[5] 240	300	406	317	409	552	523	420
Ohio	524	318	589	538	658	414	544	765
Illinois	157	107	144	289	279	198	195	193
Michigan	598	477	908	732	644	573	287	[6] 375
Wisconsin	4,766	2,908	5,875	6,415	4,955	5,409	5,177	4,547
Minnesota	895	592	1,192	989	1,552	873	1,125	1,009
Iowa	373	150	566	390	541	265	459	435
Maryland	219	325	448	220	509	238	166	293
Virginia	1,546	3,537	2,952	3,343	3,390	2,220	1,805	2,742
North Carolina	49	251	222	364	275	356	341	292
South Carolina	1,215	3,419	3,340	4,183	1,409	3,164	2,719	1,933
Florida	4,581	1,617	2,998	1,172	3,842	1,936	1,667	1,051
Kentucky	112	103	73	85	107	45	17	24
Tennessee	136	181	563	270	348	317	609	667
Alabama	420	1,068	1,460	1,358	920	1,301	1,831	1,515
Mississippi	878	509	1,629	1,134	605	674	990	710
Louisiana	203	350	425	330	80	693	435	480
Texas [7]	5,180	1,847	4,049	1,356	7,281	4,048	6,093	5,546
Colorado	1,832	2,523	1,964	3,174	1,473	1,432	1,274	683
Washington	114	170	104	155	52	103	154	139
California	913	1,008	647	616	376	860	412	443
Other States	364	357	520	473	430	836	794	727
Total [7]	[5] 34,826	31,432	41,347	36,990	41,951	39,052	[3] 40,515	[8] 39,067

Bureau of Agricultural Economics. Compiled from daily and monthly reports received by the bureau from officials and local agents of common carriers throughout the country. Shipments as shown in car lots include those by boat reduced to car-lot basis.

[1] Crop-movement season covers 17 months; from December through the second following April; i. e., the 1920 season begins December, 1919, and ends April, 1921.
[2] Preliminary.
[3] Includes 3 cars in May, 1927.
[4] Included 24 cars in May, 1928.
[5] Includes 1 car in May, 1921.
[6] Includes 1 car in May, 1928.
[7] Figures include shipments in November of preceding crop year as follows: 1920, 2 cars; 1922, 4 cars; 1923, 22 cars; 1924, 9 cars; 1925, 12 cars.
[8] Includes 25 cars in May, 1928.

TABLE 176.—*Cabbage, Danish: Monthly average l. c. l. price per ton [1] to jobbers at eight markets, 1927–28*

Market, and season beginning October [2]	Oct.	Nov.	Dec.	Jan.	Feb.	Mar.	Market, and season beginning October [2]	Oct.	Nov.	Dec.	Jan.	Feb.	Mar.
	Dollars	Dollars	Dollars	Dollars	Dollars	Dollars		Dollars	Dollars	Dollars	Dollars	Dollars	Dollars
Chicago:							Philadelphia:						
1927 [3]	19. 80	19. 40	19. 40	17. 80	16. 20		1927	14. 54	12. 71	12. 27	12. 40	[5] 13. 07	18. 33
1928 [3]	25. 60	35. 60	46. 40				1928	39. 48	34. 56	41. 29			
New York:							Pittsburgh:						
1927	18. 42	15. 32	14. 90	15. 31	[3] 14. 40	20. 04	1927 [5]	15. 00	11. 50	[6] 10. 57	13. 00	12. 79	
1928	41. 46	36. 90	43. 88				1928 [5]	31. 06	33. 55	42. 82			
Cincinnati:							St. Louis:						
1927	23. 08	12. 62	14. 28	15. 69	14. 65	21. 93	1927	19. 93	16. 81	18. 17	17. 91	18. 12	25. 88
1928	36. 00	35. 60	45. 79	●			1928	26. 56	32. 72	41. 54			
Kansas City: [4]							Washington:						
1927		.99	1. 04	1. 01	1. 16	1. 02	1927 [3]	27. 60	21. 20	18. 60	21. 60	20. 00	23. 20
1928	1. 54	1. 84	2. 38				1928 [3]	45. 80	43. 60	53. 80			

Bureau of Agricultural Economics. Compiled from daily market reports from bureau representatives in the various markets. Average prices as shown are based on stock of good merchantable quality and condition; they are simple averages of daily range of selling prices. In some cases conversions have been made from larger to smaller units or vice versa, in order to obtain comparability.
Earlier data are available in 1925 Yearbook, p. 896, Table 230, and 1927 Yearbook, p. 870.

[1] Unless otherwise stated, quotations are on bulk per ton sales.
[2] The season during which Danish cabbage prices are obtainable usually runs from October to March of the following year.
[3] Converted from hundredweight price.
[4] Bulk per hundredweight.
[5] Car-lot sales.
[6] Less than 10 quotations.

TABLE 177.—*Cantaloupes, commercial crop: Acreage, production, and price per crate, by States, 1925–1928*

State	Acreage				Production				Price per crate [1]			
	1925	1926	1927	1928	1925	1926	1927	1928	1925	1926	1927	1928
	Acres	Acres	Acres	Acres	1,000 crates[2]	1,000 crates[2]	1,000 crates[2]	1,000 crates[2]	Dollars	Dollars	Dollars	Dollars
Early:												
California (Imperial)	27, 560	35, 300	37, 920	33, 460	4, 961	5, 048	6, 029	6, 224	2. 07	1. 29	1. 49	1. 60
Florida	370	380	420	920	28	30	34	37	1. 72	1. 30	2. 23	2. 00
Georgia	750	700	710	650	82	70	57	52	2. 35	1. 38	.76	1. 50
Texas, Lower Valley	750	350	180	230	26	35	21	26	2. 15	1. 00	1. 54	1. 20
Total	29, 430	36, 730	39, 230	35, 260	5, 097	5, 183	6, 141	6, 339	2. 07	1. 29	1. 49	1. 60
Intermediate:												
Arizona	6, 000	7, 000	10, 000	10, 000	1, 350	1, 400	1, 900	2, 160	1. 38	1. 32	1. 46	1. 34
Arkansas	7, 930	7, 310	5, 410	6, 170	460	439	406	580	1. 32	1. 36	2. 19	1. 02
California (except Imperial)	10, 620	8, 380	7, 800	10, 250	1, 699	1, 575	1, 513	2, 112	1. 16	1. 60	1. 80	1. 07
Delaware	2, 500	2, 000	2, 000	1, 940	362	240	220	225	1. 08	.90	1. 25	1. 00
Illinois	400	400	200	420	52	26	6	45	1. 22	1. 08	1. 90	1. 20
Indiana	4, 820	4, 340	4, 380	4, 640	627	490	504	524	1. 29	1. 41	1. 92	1. 23
Maryland	5, 570	6, 120	7, 100	6, 040	902	998	888	495	.92	1. 42	2. 20	1. 21
Nevada	270	160	100	250	36	20	19	.50	1. 50	1. 18	1. 00	.80
North Carolina	2, 010	2, 100	2, 310	2, 310	241	176	266	261	1. 14	.88	.97	.98
Oklahoma	560	630	330	500	66	41	30	34	1. 10	.80	1. 00	.89
South Carolina	400	620	750	640	37	65	68	56	1. 47	.72	.97	1. 31
Texas, other	2, 250	2, 030	2, 030	2, 070	158	162	152	186	1. 69	1. 91	.78	.50
Total	43, 330	41, 090	42, 410	45, 230	5, 990	5, 632	5, 972	6, 728	1. 21	1. 40	1. 69	1. 15
Late:												
Colorado	7, 900	11, 670	12, 100	9, 000	1, 430	1, 984	1, 537	1, 170	.91	1. 17	1. 05	.94
Iowa	1, 000	1, 120	1, 130	1, 410	88	134	120	130	1. 20	1. 50	1. 00	1. 06
Kansas	450	450	450	450	58	63	52	57	.90	1. 17	1. 25	.92
Michigan	1, 500	1, 280	1, 220	1, 630	250	134	168	101	1. 58	1. 30	1. 23	1. 35
Nevada	660	350	300	150	87	46	57	30	1. 20	1. 12	1. 10	1. 70
New Jersey	4, 320	4, 500	4, 000	3, 400	821	518	440	544	.93	.65	.75	.95
New Mexico	2, 600	2, 600	2, 500	1, 400	390	442	250	189	1. 24	1. 06	1. 00	1. 10
Tennessee	560	600	480	470	67	39	32	33	1. 10	1. 15	1. 35	1. 05
Washington	1, 510	1, 300	1, 960	2, 000	275	218	245	200	.62	1. 28	2. 12	.61
Total	20, 500	23, 870	24, 140	19, 910	3, 466	3, 578	2, 901	2, 454	1. 00	1. 10	1. 10	.96
Grand total	93, 260	101, 690	105, 780	100, 400	14, 553	14, 393	15, 014	15, 521	1. 46	1. 29	1. 49	1. 31

Bureau of Agricultural Economics, estimates based upon returns from crop reporters.
[1] Average for season.　　　　[2] Standard crate.

TABLE 178.—*Cantaloupes:* [1] *Car-lot shipments, by State of origin, 1920–1928*

State	Crop movement season [2]								
	1920	1921	1922	1923	1924	1925	1926	1927	1928 [3]
	Cars	Cars	Cars	Cars	Cars	Cars	Cars	Cars	Cars
Indiana	632	644	894	681	822	1,089	629	415	465
Michigan	209	232	465	306	114	146	84	77	18
Delaware	600	942	843	818	511	657	551	427	427
Maryland	781	1,153	1,233	1,270	699	1,116	1,283	1,159	993
North Carolina	358	894	700	620	401	655	401	606	301
South Carolina	131	281	270	70	116	33	173	179	94
Georgia	387	619	1,632	217	586	117	136	108	104
Arkansas	986	1,554	1,002	337	1,052	1,245	1,127	788	854
Texas	169	156	186	387	456	498	514	242	244
Colorado	2,482	3,288	4,420	2,306	3,229	3,837	5,108	3,980	2,785
New Mexico	968	508	275	364	518	574	640	415	366
Arizona	1,159	1,504	1,558	1,208	2,145	3,833	3,712	5,217	5,900
Washington	380	208	371	207	298	221	·145	252	255
California [4]	13,251	13,166	15,304	16,486	19,932	18,707	18,320	22,406	25,271
Other States	460	666	777	646	617	1,091	601	486	523
Total	22,953	25,815	29,930	25,923	31,496	33,819	33,424	36,757	38,600

Bureau of Agricultural Economics. Compiled from daily and monthly reports received by the bureau from officials and local agents of common carriers throughout the country. Shipments as shown in car lots include those by boat reduced to car-lot basis.

[1] Includes honeydews and other miscellaneous melons not separately reported until 1923. The shipments of melons, other than cantaloupes, amounted in 1923 to 1,152 cars; in 1924 to 2,565; in 1925 to 3,654; in 1926 to 6,484; in 1927 to 6,516; and in 1928 to 9,728.
[2] Crop-movement season extends from Apr. 1 through November of a given year.
[3] Preliminary.
[4] Figures for California include shipments in December as follows: 1920, 1 car; 1925, 18 cars; 1926, 3 cars; 1927, 4 cars; 1928, 2 cars.

TABLE 179.—*Carrots, commercial crop: Acreage, production, and price per bushel, by States, 1925–1928*

	Acreage				Production				Price per bushel [1]			
	1925	1926	1927	1928	1925	1926	1927	1928	1925	1926	1927	1928
	Acres	Acres	Acres	Acres	1,000 bush.	1,000 bush.	1,000 bush.	1,000 bush.	Dollars	Dollars	Dollars	Dollars
Early:												
California	1,000	1,800	3,050	4,860	570	967	1,525	2,401	0.92	0.72	0.72	0.80
Louisiana	2,360	7,330	11,600	8,010	573	1,261	2,448	1,370	.70	.70	.51	.51
Mississippi	2,400	1,500	2,040	1,750	442	300	551	413	.76	1.23	.56	.33
Texas	5,750	3,920	4,340	3,780	1,501	1,047	998	748	.34	.32	.43	.48
Total	11,510	14,550	21,030	18,400	3,086	3,575	5,522	4,932	.57	.64	.56	.63
Intermediate:												
New Jersey	1,200	1,400	1,400	1,300	252	350	336	260	1.04	1.00	.92	1.18
North Carolina			680	450			136	90			.55	.48
Virginia			250	540			75	138			.80	.75
Total	1,200	1,400	2,330	2,290	252	350	547	488	1.04	1.00	.81	.93
Late:												
Illinois	800	800	800	800	380	352	356	352	.55	.75	.66	.90
New York	2,250	2,250	2,140	2,120	1,082	1,246	1,338	856	.61	.51	.46	1.00
Total	3,050	3,050	2,940	2,920	1,462	1,598	1,694	1,208	.59	.56	.50	.97
Grand total	15,760	19,000	26,300	23,610	4,800	5,523	7,763	6,628	.60	.64	.56	.72

Bureau of Agricultural Economics. Estimates based upon returns from crop reporters.
[1] Average for season.

33023°—29——51

TABLE 180.—*Car-lot shipments of carrots, 1920–1928*

State	Crop-movement season [1]								
	1920	1921	1922	1923	1924	1925	1926	1927	1928 [2]
California	111	19	21	24	157	278	557	2,363	2,929
Illinois	53	62	82	24	3	23	2	13	74
Louisiana	28	43	62	58	32	106	70	177	99
Mississippi	77	81	304	142	266	197	209	496	229
New Jersey	32	32	26	34	18	48	44	85	67
New York	1,158	1,247	1,523	1,410	2,262	1,825	1,845	2,430	886
Texas	5	198	48	65	282	575	1,136	903	1,685
Others	138	157	190	199	295	375	439	385	664
Total	1,602	1,839	2,256	1,956	3,315	3,427	4,302	6,852	6,633

Bureau of Agricultural Economics.

[1] Crop-movement season begins in October of the previous year in such early shipping States as California, Texas, and Louisiana and extends through June of the following year in order to include shipments from storage in Northern States and to have totals comparable with acreage and production figures.
[2] Incomplete; includes shipments through December, 1928, only.

TABLE 181.—*Cauliflower, commercial, crop: Acreage, production, and price per crate, by States, 1925–1928*

State	Acreage				Production				Price per crate [1]			
	1925	1926	1927	1928	1925	1926	1927	1928	1925	1926	1927	1928
	Acres	*Acres*	*Acres*	*Acres*	*1,000 crates*	*1,000 crates*	*1,000 crates*	*1,000 crates*	*Dollars*	*Dollars*	*Dollars*	*Dollars*
California [2]	6,610	10,500	8,950	12,800	2,148	3,224	2,452	3,558	1.11	.88	1.00	0.84
Colorado	1,000	1,100	1,160	1,700	160	99	336	510	.71	1.15	1.78	2.25
New Jersey	400	300	300	200	52	44	45	26	1.38	1.15	1.50	1.50
New York	5,530	5,560	5,060	4,320	713	1,334	794	557	1.55	1.36	1.83	1.64
Oregon [2]	1,600	5,000	2,100	1,360	320	825	420	292	1.05	.69	1.18	1.19
Utah	40	60	180	270	10	12	49	44	2.50	2.00	2.00	1.66
Total	15,180	22,520	17,750	20,650	3,403	5,538	4,096	4,987	1.19	.98	1.26	1.10

Bureau of Agricultural Economics. Estimates based upon returns from crop reporters.

[1] Average for season.
[2] Season of California and Oregon begins in October of the previous year.

TABLE 182.—*Cauliflower: Car-lot shipments, by State of origin, 1920-1927*

State	Crop-movement season [1]							
	1920	1921	1922	1923	1924	1925	1926	1927 [2]
	Cars	Cars	Cars	Cars	Cars	Cars	Cars	Cars
New York	781	567	683	653	734	834	1,019	696
Colorado		3	4	101	61	[3] 191	220	411
Oregon	76	134	282	374	109	1,246	780	559
California	2,957	3,629	3,604	3,054	3,404	4,357	4,730	[4] 7,040
Other States	39	30	35	121	146	[5] 100	[6] 143	[7] 340
Total	3,853	4,363	4,608	4,303	4,454	[8] 6,728	[6] 6,892	[9] 9,046

Bureau of Agricultural Economics. Complied from daily and monthly reports received by the bureau from officials and local agents of common carriers throughout the country. Shipments as shown in car lots include those by boat reduced to car-lot basis.

[1] Crop movement season extends from July 1 through June of the following year.
[2] Preliminary.
[3] Includes 1 car in June, 1925.
[4] Includes 1 car in July, 1928.
[5] Includes 2 cars in July, 1926.
[6] Includes 1 car in May and 6 in June, 1926.
[7] Includes 12 cars in June, 1927.
[8] Includes 1 car in June, 1925, and 2 cars in July, 1926.
[9] Includes 12 cars in June, 1927, and 1 car in July, 1928.

TABLE 183.—*Celery, commercial crop: Acreage, production, and price per crate, by States, 1925-1928*

State	Acreage				Production				Price per crate [1]			
	1925	1926	1927	1928	1925	1926	1927	1928	1925	1926	1927	1928
Early:	Acres	Acres	Acres	Acres	1,000 crates [2]	1,000 crates [2]	1,000 crates [2]	1,000 crates [2]	Dollars	Dollars	Dollars	Dollars
California [3]	6,330	6,250	8,550	9,050	1,386	1,369	2,078	1,810	1.34	1.49	1.82	1.49
Florida	4,320	3,520	4,240	5,350	2,000	1,320	1,908	2,204	2.24	3.00	2.08	2.83
Total	10,650	9,770	12,790	14,400	3,386	2,689	3,986	4,014	1.87	2.23	1.94	2.23
Late:												
Colorado	920	940	940	900	386	282	282	270	3.16	1.22	1.70	2.60
Michigan	3,860	3,720	3,760	3,990	780	521	846	898	1.68	1.92	1.38	1.22
New Jersey	1,420	1,350	1,300	1,320	416	417	370	298	1.52	1.09	.82	1.05
New York	4,660	4,890	4,620	4,590	1,351	1,506	1,714	1,299	1.27	1.50	1.20	1.75
Ohio	680	540	450	520	160	120	128	139	1.68	1.68	2.43	2.05
Oregon	340	360	410	410	111	144	178	184	1.69	1.83	1.81	1.48
Pennsylvania	380	260	280	270	112	88	81	71	1.11	1.46	1.42	1.83
Total	12,260	12,060	11,760	12,000	3,316	3,078	3,599	3,159	1.65	1.51	1.32	1.61
Grand total	22,910	21,830	24,550	26,400	6,702	5,767	7,585	7,173	1.76	1.85	1.65	1.95

Bureau of Agricultural Economics. Estimates based upon returns from crop reporters.

[1] Average for season.
[2] New York (two-thirds size).
[3] Season in California begins in fall of previous year.

TABLE 184.—*Celery: Car-lot shipments, by State of origin, 1920–1927*

State	Crop-movement season [1]							
	1920	1921	1922	1923	1924	1925	1926	1927 [2]
	Cars	Cars	Cars	Cars	Cars	Cars	Cars	Cars
New York	3,110	3,047	3,247	3,742	4,529	4,492	4,898	5,907
New Jersey	94	219	115	219	177	149	138	106
Pennsylvania	186	224	212	223	225	208	194	169
Ohio	46	67	76	55	64	71	51	63
Michigan	954	1,031	1,626	1,486	1,332	2,224	1,880	1,996
Florida	2,652	4,218	4,954	6,398	7,219	7,952	5,504	7,499
Colorado	305	211	222	125	197	399	211	161
Oregon	16	53	82	205	363	398	511	625
California	3,472	2,617	4,334	4,631	4,240	5,953	7,565	7,837
Other States	24	19	52	76	83	67	48	108
Total	10,859	11,706	14,920	17,160	18,429	21,913	21,000	24,471

Bureau of Agricultural Economics. Compiled from daily and monthly reports received by the Bureau from officials and local agents of common carriers throughout the country. Shipments as shown in car lots include those by boat reduced to car-lot basis.

[1] Crop-movement season covers 19 months, from December through the second following June; i. e., the 1920 season begins December, 1919, and ends June, 1921. [2] Preliminary.

TABLE 185.—*Corn, sweet, for canning, commercial crop: Acreage, production, and price per ton, by States, 1925–1928*

State	Acreage				Production				Price per ton			
	1925	1926	1927	1928	1925	1926	1927	1928	1925	1926	1927	1928
	Acres	Acres	Acres	Acres	Tons	Tons	Tons	Tons	Dolls.	Dolls.	Dolls.	Dolls.
Delaware	5,000	3,000	3,500	4,060	13,500	7,200	8,400	7,300	18.00	13.35	10.60	12.00
Illinois	70,650	58,280	40,650	54,880	169,600	145,700	81,300	120,700	14.29	14.23	11.06	12.35
Indiana	36,990	30,380	17,010	27,390	88,800	88,100	23,800	38,300	14.83	10.18	10.41	12.54
Iowa	70,720	50,480	26,750	39,860	190,900	151,400	61,500	91,700	11.14	10.35	8.96	9.71
Maine	15,630	14,650	8,260	10,770	45,300	46,900	23,100	30,200	29.76	28.72	22.30	24.70
Maryland	42,820	33,850	27,500	30,800	115,600	74,500	49,500	37,000	17.67	14.08	11.78	13.92
Michigan	13,630	11,080	9,400	8,930	34,100	22,200	14,100	16,100	14.30	12.54	12.98	12.08
Minnesota	30,540	24,450	18,500	25,340	64,100	73,400	33,300	63,400	10.28	9.93	10.00	10.58
Nebraska	8,880	6,970	4,600	5,470	19,500	18,800	11,500	9,800	10.94	10.07	8.32	9.73
New Hampshire	1,470	1,050	780	1,110	3,800	2,400	1,800	2,600	25.00	23.65	21.60	23.70
New York	31,350	27,420	20,290	27,000	72,100	60,300	32,500	32,400	20.74	18.24	18.80	19.45
Ohio	34,520	26,380	18,730	27,910	110,500	71,200	30,000	36,300	13.61	10.14	10.00	10.72
Pennsylvania	6,850	4,840	2,800	3,640	24,700	9,700	3,600	3,600	18.93	13.00	12.00	13.76
Vermont	2,620	2,290	1,870	1,940	6,800	5,000	4,100	4,700	19.94	21.30	19.10	18.30
Wisconsin	17,740	17,350	10,410	14,780	44,400	29,500	13,500	29,600	12.33	11.81	10.66	11.18
Other States	4,500	4,840	4,380	5,300	10,400	9,700	7,000	12,700	14.00	12.00	13.40	14.00
Total or av	393,910	317,310	215,430	289,180	1,014,100	816,000	399,000	536,400	15.04	13.23	12.05	12.86

Bureau of Agricultural Economics. Estimates based upon returns from crop reporters.

TABLE 186.—*Corn, canned: Pack [1] in the United States, 1917–1928*

State	1917	1918	1919	1920	1921	1922	1923	1924	1925	1926	1927	1928
	1,000 cases	1,000 cases	1,000 cases	1,000 cases	1,000 cases	1,000 cases	1,000 cases	1,000 cases	1,000 cases	1,000 cases	1,000 cases	1,000 cases
Maine	567	1,113	1,652	1,588	911	1,066	923	1,294	1,693	1,347	806	966
New York	257	489	1,014	829	564	616	434	749	1,311	1,038	676	666
Ohio	1,200	1,584	1,360	1,544	850	1,073	1,390	787	2,375	1,735	846	1,138
Indiana	742	513	586	861	709	665	1,208	846	2,223	2,044	703	1,131
Illinois	2,422	2,199	2,225	2,271	1,711	1,939	2,833	2,310	4,030	3,053	1,961	3,017
Wisconsin	166	373	635	590	576	625	648	388	1,148	843	310	578
Minnesota	202	309	456	643	573	598	898	1,199	1,541	1,762	1,088	1,648
Iowa	2,280	2,300	2,496	3,246	1,190	1,959	2,382	1,764	4,105	3,361	1,377	2,541
Maryland	2,002	2,033	2,081	2,217	1,130	1,944	2,256	1,707	3,678	2,133	1,493	1,648
Other States	965	809	1,045	1,251	629	934	1,134	1,087	2,216	1,753	1,087	1,164
United States	10,803	11,722	13,550	15,040	8,843	11,419	14,106	12,131	24,320	19,069	10,347	14,497

Bureau of Agricultural Economics. Compiled from National Canners' Association data, 1917–1926; Census of Manufactures, 1927–1928.

[1] Stated in cases of 24 No. 2 cans.

TABLE 187.—*Cucumbers for consumption, fresh, commercial crop: Acreage, production, and price per hamper, by States, 1925–1928*

State	Acreage				Production				Price per hamper [1]			
	1925	1926	1927	1928	1925	1926	1927	1928	1925	1926	1927	1928
	Acres	*Acres*	*Acres*	*Acres*	*1,000 ham-pers* [2]	*1,000 ham-pers* [2]	*1,000 ham-pers* [2]	*1,000 ham-pers* [2]	*Dol-lars*	*Dol-lars*	*Dol-lars*	*Dol-lars*
Early:												
Alabama	2,240	2,880	3,830	2,680	417	472	582	364	1.48	0.56	0.97	1.01
Florida	10,830	7,590	7,720	9,420	1,256	1,108	1,042	622	2.36	2.51	1.92	3.01
Georgia	610	720	720	720	70	67	90	45	1.15	.85	1.26	1.18
Louisiana	1,800	3,040	2,760	2,360	139	316	317	189	1.96	1.59	.79	1.25
South Carolina	2,900	4,120	4,300	5,300	458	490	636	398	1.58	1.02	1.37	.71
Texas (S. dist.)	980	3,000	4,150	4,980	66	357	415	344	2.14	1.55	1.05	1.69
Total	19,360	21,350	23,480	25,460	2,406	2,810	3,082	1,962	1.99	1.66	1.37	1.73
Second early:												
Arkansas	1,410	1,760	1,760	1,970	151	150	176	177	1.04	1.01	1.51	.63
California			1,000	1,050			163	181			.97	1.06
North Carolina	5,310	4,570	4,340	4,340	860	530	764	573	.93	1.13	.90	.72
Virginia	1,560	1,640	1,650	1,730	257	205	214	164	.75	1.15	.91	1.00
Total	8,280	7,970	8,750	9,090	1,268	885	1,317	1,095	1.33	1.50	.99	.80
Intermediate:												
Delaware	1,400	1,500	1,120	1,210	158	255	202	127	.57	.56	.90	.40
Illinois (southern)	740	560	560	590	130	67	28	30	.80	.78	1.21	.71
Maryland	2,080	2,080	1,700	1,750	416	260	292	315	.53	.56	1.30	.53
New Jersey	2,500	2,100	2,000	2,040	500	420	370	357	.67	.95	1.25	1.00
Total	6,720	6,240	5,380	5,590	1,204	1,002	892	829	.62	.74	1.19	.72
Late: New York	4,490	3,950	3,950	4,110	516	490	585	600	.60	.91	.98	1.06
Grand total	38,850	39,510	41,560	44,250	5,394	5,187	5,876	4,486	1.30	1.32	1.22	1.23

Bureau of Agricultural Economics. Estimates based upon returns from crop reporters.

[1] Average for season.   [2] Bushel hamper.

TABLE 188.—*Cucumbers for pickles, commercial crop: Acreage, production, and price per bushel, by States, 1925–1928*

State	Acreage				Production				Price per bushel			
	1925	1926	1927	1928	1925	1926	1927	1928	1925	1926	1927	1928
	Acres	*Acres*	*Acres*	*Acres*	*1,000 bush.*	*1,000 bush.*	*1,000 bush.*	*1,000 bush.*	*Dolls. p. bu.*	*Dolls. p. bu.*	*Dolls. p. bu.*	*Dolls. p. bu.*
California	3,210	2,560	2,120	2,760	491	369	337	486	1.09	0.93	0.97	0.62
Colorado	3,500	2,900	3,130	2,300	357	177	156	202	1.00	.87	.75	.72
Illinois	1,630	940	960	1,560	114	47	34	90	1.39	1.22	1.24	1.15
Indiana	8,430	7,250	6,800	9,870	430	392	258	572	1.11	1.12	.93	.96
Iowa	2,850	800	270	470	177	34	12	31	1.09	1.11	.90	1.03
Michigan	36,810	25,030	17,350	22,840	2,025	1,051	520	1,256	1.11	.98	.90	.92
Minnesota	4,340	3,000	3,060	3,210	195	135	92	96	1.03	.90	.73	.89
Missouri	1,050	2,800	670	1,260	61	98	35	76	.91	.82	1.00	.75
New York	1,320	920	680	800	152	32	35	44	1.00	.88	1.27	.88
Ohio	2,250	1,600	1,750	2,200	162	88	61	143	1.26	.90	1.02	1.00
Washington	670	530	410	460	97	32	28	44	1.00	.90	.82	.88
Wisconsin	20,960	11,950	6,800	10,190	1,216	598	272	550	1.03	.92	1.08	.83
Other States	13,110	9,460	7,940	9,570	1,337	615	540	459	.78	.92	.96	.84
Total or average	100,130	69,740	51,940	67,490	6,814	3,668	2,380	4,049	1.02	.96	.94	.86

Bureau of Agricultural Economics. Estimates based upon returns from crop reporters.

TABLE 189.—*Cucumbers: Car-lot shipments by State of origin, 1920–1928*

State	1920	1921	1922	1923	1924	1925	1926	1927	1928 [1]
	Cars	Cars	Cars	Cars	Cars	Cars	Cars	Cars	Cars
New York	312	540	395	383	694	686	456	607	1,001
New Jersey	287	271	164	258	276	481	261	368	370
Ohio	52	118	124	68	111	91	187	203	191
Illinois	142	164	68	15	77	245	150	101	148
Delaware	256	137	191	225	240	302	304	366	214
Maryland	297	343	368	446	311	598	479	692	563
Virginia	83	19	221	84	387	448	200	339	229
North Carolina	408	641	687	1,175	1,639	1,562	869	935	812
South Carolina	525	664	887	720	918	794	687	916	663
Georgia	1	3	211	45	154	72	62	72	76
Florida	835	1,414	2,034	1,647	1,381	1,963	2,048	2,300	1,572
Alabama	259	109	702	367	576	706	684	583	606
Texas	95	64	119	46	147	72	316	178	382
California		89	68	125	23	125	86	63	49
Other States	137	256	110	96	248	347	483	457	592
Total	3,689	4,832	6,349	5,700	7,182	8,492	7,272	8,180	7,468

Bureau of Agricultural Economics. Compiled from daily and monthly reports received by the bureau from officials and local agents of common carriers throughout the country. Shipments as shown in car lots include those by boat reduced to car-lot basis.

[1] Preliminary.

TABLE 190.—*Eggplant, commercial crop: Acreage, production, and price per bushel, by States, 1925–1928*

State	Acreage				Production				Price per bushel [1]			
	1925	1926	1927	1928	1925	1926	1927	1928	1925	1926	1927	1928
	Acres	Acres	Acres	Acres	1,000 bush.	1,000 bush.	1,000 bush.	1,000 bush.	Dol-lars	Dol-lars	Dol-lars	Dol-lars
Florida	1,400	1,020	630	1,550	384	392	202	372	1.30	1.34	1.26	0.91
Louisiana	800	1,060	890	830	152	138	139	132	1.05	1.05	1.00	.90
New Jersey	1,100	1,000	1,100	1,210	330	220	330	302	.73	1.00	.80	.88
Texas	190	180	370	300	38	41	111	90	1.00	1.00	.45	.59
Total	3,490	3,260	2,990	3,890	904	791	782	896	1.04	1.18	.91	.87

Bureau of Agricultural Economics. Estimates based upon returns from crop reporters.

[1] Average for season.

TABLE 191.—*Lettuce, commercial crop: Acreage, production, and price per crate, by States, 1925–1928*

State	Acreage				Production				Price per crate [1]			
	1925	1926	1927	1928	1925	1926	1927	1928	1925	1926	1927	1928
	Acres	*Acres*	*Acres*	*Acres*	*1,000 crates*[2]	*1,000 crates*[2]	*1,000 crates*[2]	*1,000 crates*[2]	*Dollars*	*Dollars*	*Dollars*	*Dollars*
Early:												
Arizona [3]	6,400	8,500	14,800	28,700	1,440	1,912	3,034	3,272	1.06	1.90	1.35	1.42
California—												
Imperial [3]	23,000	28,000	34,400	22,000	4,600	4,900	5,229	3,740	1.71	1.95	1.34	1.62
Other	24,680	37,100	42,010	50,570	4,368	5,565	6,049	7,636	1.16	1.37	1.75	1.84
Florida [3]	3,400	1,500	1,840	1,850	765	252	294	314	1.41	2.21	1.62	1.61
North Carolina	1,730	1,420	1,490	1,490	467	379	207	216	1.98	2.00	1.87	1.60
South Carolina	1,480	780	700	750	247	133	158	112	1.69	1.81	1.59	2.11
Texas [3]	680	640	950	1,000	68	72	103	100	1.38	1.19	1.00	1.02
Virginia	300	300	300	300	39	38	50	60	2.07	1.70	1.50	1.45
Total	61,670	78,240	96,490	106,660	11,994	13,251	15,124	15,450	1.42	1.70	1.37	1.68
Late:												
Colorado	10,500	13,240	13,240	9,800	1,396	1,523	1,456	1,127	1.58	1.43	1.63	1.07
Idaho	1,500	1,200	1,120	900	180	157	218	101	1.86	1.47	.96	1.67
New Jersey	2,200	2,400	2,450	2,300	541	503	612	442	1.64	1.08	2.04	1.89
New Mexico	1,400	1,030	410	400	280	77	59	18	1.76	1.66	.75	1.32
New York	6,820	7,200	5,540	4,460	1,323	1,246	1,457	1,004	1.42	1.60	1.48	2.68
Oregon	300	360	300	100	45	18	15	7	1.92	1.42	1.25	1.25
Pennsylvania	70	80	80	80	11	12	10	9	2.50	1.24	1.50	2.70
Washington	1,450	1,600	2,050	2,040	290	336	410	428	2.50	1.30	1.48	1.25
Wyoming	110	210	200	40	16	27	22	3	1.50	1.40	1.20	1.82
Total	24,350	27,320	25,390	20,120	4,082	3,899	4,259	3,139	1.63	1.43	1.57	1.75
Grand total	86,020	105,560	121,880	126,780	16,076	17,150	19,383	18,589	1.48	1.64	1.42	1.70

Bureau of Agricultural economics. Estimates based upon returns from crops reporters.

[1] Average for season.
[2] Crates of 4 dozen heads each.
[3] Harvest of crops begins in fall of previous year.

TABLE 192.—*Lettuce: Car-lot shipments by State of origin, 1920–1928*

State	1920	1921	1922	1923	1924	1925	1926	1927	1928 [1]
	Cars	*Cars*	*Cars*	*Cars*	*Cars*	*Cars*	*Cars*	*Cars*	*Cars*
New York	1,775	3,240	3,167	3,817	3,698	3,821	3,019	3,496	3,138
New Jersey	208	469	571	456	417	463	303	308	144
North Carolina	207	445	622	718	714	537	540	447	477
South Carolina	121	716	987	577	423	736	372	369	241
Florida	2,940	2,267	3,323	3,146	2,257	1,519	987	929	813
Idaho	25	180	889	1,241	532	501	398	196	67
Colorado	129	234	812	1,436	1,036	3,096	2,795	2,848	2,368
Arizona	254	168	678	1,108	2,049	3,519	4,906	9,131	9,204
Washington	354	635	812	1,081	674	820	904	1,151	1,232
California	7,358	9,850	9,744	15,113	18,480	21,618	27,341	27,574	33,446
Other States	417	534	635	792	655	676	540	401	316
Total	13,788	18,738	22,240	29,485	30,935	37,306	42,105	46,850	51,446

Bureau of Agricultural Economics. Compiled from daily and monthly reports received by the bureau from officials and local agents of common carriers throughout the country. Shipments as shown in car lots include those by boat reduced to car-lot basis.

[1] Preliminary.

TABLE 193.—*Onions, commercial crop: Acreage, production, and price per bushel, by States, 1925–1928*

State	Acreage				Production				Price per bushel [1]			
	1925	1926	1927	1928	1925	1926	1927	1928	1925	1926	1927	1928
Early (Bermuda and Creole):	*Acres*	*Acres*	*Acres*	*Acres*	*1,000 bush.*	*1,000 bush.*	*1,000 bush.*	*1,000 bush.*	*Dollars*	*Dollars*	*Dollars*	*Dollars*
California	1,550	2,850	3,950	3,950	488	926	1,118	980	1.74	1.39	1.80	0.77
Louisiana	2,320	2,750	2,900	2,310	278	352	316	293	1.36	1.17	1.22	.89
Texas	9,580	12,510	11,220	16,780	2,203	2,552	2,199	3,322	1.40	1.36	1.69	1.10
Total	13,450	18,110	18,070	23,040	2,969	3,830	3,633	4,595	1.45	1.35	1.68	.99
Intermediate (domestic):												
Iowa	740	780	800	820	313	246	206	205	2.36	.94	1.35	.88
Kentucky	750	1,000	800	800	210	250	110	232	1.58	.50	1.00	1.00
New Jersey	2,400	2,900	2,900	3,000	432	580	696	780	1.70	1.00	1.25	1.00
Texas (Collin Co.)	1,300	1,500	1,050	1,950	214	262	131	351	.92	.84	1.89	.56
Virginia	800	900	600	400	100	90	89	64	2.00	.76	.75	.51
Washington	1,500	1,800	1,000	1,000	525	648	418	415	.75	.45	.63	.40
Total	7,490	8,880	7,150	7,970	1,794	2,076	1,650	2,047	1.45	.73	1.11	.78
Late (domestic):												
California	5,850	6,000	4,780	4,110	1,755	1,776	1,898	1,225	1.16	.64	.69	1.21
Colorado	3,520	3,700	4,300	3,700	1,144	1,018	1,376	1,147	.78	.50	.45	1.42
Idaho	1,400	950	1,900	1,000	637	276	902	700	.71	.48	.47	1.14
Illinois	840	670	670	740	218	168	201	169	.85	.98	.87	1.22
Indiana	8,100	8,440	8,100	8,510	2,308	2,726	2,738	2,042	.98	.56	.59	1.60
Iowa (late crop)	1,400	1,600	1,470	1,540	556	480	400	616	.99	.46	.67	1.15
Massachusetts	3,920	4,420	4,550	3,500	1,533	1,746	1,342	840	1.08	.62	.74	1.01
Michigan	2,680	3,370	3,200	4,000	713	1,284	1,360	1,100	.86	.63	.54	1.40
Minnesota	1,560	1,870	2,180	1,740	452	527	691	632	.91	.54	.51	1.28
New York	8,910	7,580	8,530	5,870	3,430	2,729	3,352	1,291	.97	.67	.59	1.35
Ohio	3,460	5,300	7,000	7,350	1,031	1,367	2,352	970	1.06	.65	.60	1.60
Oregon	1,050	1,130	1,200	950	398	358	420	280	.71	.51	.58	1.43
Pennsylvania	190	180	180	150	53	50	54	37	1.61	.95	.75	1.10
Utah	500	800	900	1,000	330	360	360	475	.70	.60	.50	.86
Washington (late crop)			860	710			359	411			.57	1.12
Wisconsin	960	1,200	1,600	1,600	341	348	507	448	.90	.51	.58	1.25
Total	44,340	47,210	51,420	46,470	14,899	15,213	18,312	12,383	.97	.61	.59	1.33
Total domestic	51,830	56,090	58,570	54,440	16,693	17,289	19,962	14,430	1.02	.62	.64	1.25
Grand total	65,280	74,200	76,640	77,480	19,662	21,119	23,595	19,025	1.08	.75	.80	1.19

Bureau of Agricultural Economics.   Estimates based upon returns from crop reporters.

[1] Average for season.

TABLE 194.—*Onions: Car-lot shipments, by State of origin, 1920–1927*

State	Crop-movement season [1]							
	1920	1921	1922	1923	1924	1925	1926	1927 [2]
	Cars	Cars	Cars	Cars	Cars	Cars	Cars	Cars
Massachusetts	3,914	2,244	1,912	2,454	2,481	2,856	3,586	2,495
New York	3,384	2,890	2,812	5,505	5,335	5,109	3,720	4,101
New Jersey	371	429	479	335	403	235	253	295
Ohio	3,239	1,749	4,493	2,714	4,492	1,856	2,287	4,070
Indiana	4,124	1,972	4,684	4,610	3,735	4,158	4,493	5,000
Illinois	409	251	487	378	241	291	158	142
Michigan	939	417	1,867	1,222	1,623	1,402	2,171	2,653
Wisconsin	409	90	330	273	212	361	270	279
Minnesota	287	169	500	189	487	674	684	1,289
Iowa	830	416	927	882	1,176	1,365	1,434	1,333
Virginia	139	280	371	274	345	138	178	131
Kentucky	304	382	258	263	266	152	134	145
Texas	4,957	4,209	4,630	3,027	3,918	3,941	5,317	4,028
Idaho	28	50	161	256	322	876	531	891
Colorado	150	447	651	928	1,064	1,809	1,758	1,460
Utah	9	54	170	177	216	599	662	654
Washington	810	702	765	1,126	1,016	1,000	1,200	1,302
Oregon	27	343	263	392	558	681	678	671
California	4,802	3,542	4,349	3,427	2,671	3,603	3,013	3,753
Other States	341	254	369	330	235	540	536	499
Total	29,473	20,890	30,478	28,762	30,796	31,646	33,063	35,191

Bureau of Agricultural Economics. Compiled from daily and monthly reports received by the bureau from officials and local agents of common carriers throughout the country. Shipments as shown in car lots include those by boat reduced to car-lot basis.

[1] Crop movement season extends from March 1 of one year through June of the following year.
[2] Preliminary.

TABLE 195.—*Onions: United States imports, by countries, annual, 1920–1928*

Year ended June 30	Netherlands	Spain	Italy	United Kingdom	Canada	Canary Islands	Bermuda	Mexico	Chile	Australia	Egypt	Other countries	Total
	1,000 bush.	1,000 bush.	1,000 bush.	1,000 bush.	1,000 bush.	1,000 bush.	1,000 bush.	1,000 bush.	1,000 bush.	1,000 bush.	1,000 bush.	1,000 bush.	1,000 bush.
Av., 1910–1914	1	471	15	337	1	31	105	41	0	[1] 23	110	41	1,176
1920	0	1,497	19	48	4	25	66	1	0	23	194	7	1,884
1921	2	575	8	43	8	14	28	[2]	0	3	6	2	689
1922	40	1,522	74	247	66	18	34	26	43	119	243	56	2,488
1923	33	990	11	157	42	13	18	20	1	3	447	48	1,783
1924	[2]	1,098	17	52	1	8	9	29	30	4	148	10	1,406
1925	60	1,090	19	71	29	7	9	18	79	8	618	67	2,075
1926	11	1,342	100	36	11	4	9	20	26	3	599	33	2,194
1927	48	1,084	65	59	9	2	9	1	76	8	912	25	2,298
1928	11	701	35	12	2	1	3	[2]	213	3	392	26	1,399

Bureau of Agricultural Economics. Compiled from official records of the Bureau of Foreign and Domestic Commerce, Department of Commerce.

[1] Includes Tasmania.   [2] Less than 500 bushels.

TABLE 196.—*Onions: Average l. c. l. price per 100 pounds to jobbers at five markets 1927–1928*

Market, and season beginning August	Various common varieties								Bermudas					
									Apr.		May [2]		June [2]	
	Aug.[1]	Sept.	Oct.	Nov.	Dec.	Jan.	Feb.	Mar.	Yellow	Crystal white wax	Yellow	Crystal white wax	Yellow	Crystal white wax
	Dollars	*Dollars*	*Dollars*	*Dollars*	*Dollars*	*Dollars*	*Dollars*	*Dollars*	*Dollars*	*Dollars*	*Dollars*	*Dollars*	*Dollars*	*Dollars*
New York:														
1927	2.17	1.72	1.60	1.72	2.18	2.60	2.89	4.25	5.38	6.17	3.14	3.33	2.37	2.00
1928	2.62	3.53	3.62	4.14	4.42									
Chicago:														
1927	2.57	1.74	1.68	1.65	2.02	2.77	2.78	4.04	4.57	5.23	3.04	3.17	2.31	2.64
1928	2.72	3.35	3.66	4.22	4.59									
Philadelphia:														
1927	2.02	1.67	1.54	1.49	1.68	2.38	2.58	4.01	5.12		3.46	3.59	2.69	2.37
1928	2.34	3.43	3.41	3.89	4.40									
St. Louis:														
1927	2.58	1.78	1.70	1.49	1.84	2.47	2.86	4.30	5.36	5.16	3.10	3.28	2.22	2.62
1928	2.31	3.17	3.60	3.98	4.51									
Boston:														
1927	1.98	1.82	1.70	1.69	2.16	2.65	2.82	4.14	5.76		3.53	3.51	2.80	
1928	2.26	3.72	3.79	3.90	4.86									

Bureau of Agricultural Economics. Compiled from daily market reports from bureau representatives in the various markets. See 1927 year book, p. 878, for data for earlier years.

Average prices as shown are based on stock of U. S. No. 1 grade; they are simple averages of daily range of selling prices. In some cases conversions have been made from larger to smaller units, or vice versa, in order to obtain comparability.

[1] Quotations began Aug. 23, 1920; Aug. 22, 1921; Aug. 7, 1922; Aug. 14, 1923; Aug. 22, 1924; July 22, 1925.
[2] Last reported quotations of season June 11, 1921; June 14, 1922; May 29, 1923 ; June 4, 1924; June 10, 1925.

TABLE 197.—*Peas, green, for consumption fresh; commercial crop; Acreage, production, and price per hamper, by States, 1925–1928*

State	Acreage				Production				Price per hamper [1]			
	1925	1926	1927	1928	1925	1926	1927	1928	1925	1926	1927	1928
	Acres	*Acres*	*Acres*	*Acres*	*1,000 hampers* [2]	*1,000 hampers* [2]	*1,000 hampers* [2]	*1,000 hampers* [2]	*Dollars*	*Dollars*	*Dollars*	*Dollars*
Early:												
Arizona	1,150	400	500	60	52	11	25	3	1.41	1.56	1.33	2.00
California (Imperial)	1,400	4,000	5,700	9,000	66	400	365	540	2.56	2.36	2.12	2.31
California (other [3])	5,100	11,950	21,110	16,810	224	598	2,132	1,967	2.76	4.56	1.98	2.04
Florida	2,250	760	700	980	86	40	34	54	2.84	2.67	3.50	2.50
Louisiana	530	760	1,600	1,330	26	37	78	77	1.32	1.94	1.67	1.68
Mississippi	2,000	2,050	2,250	2,200	104	195	169	156	2.16	1.81	1.58	1.78
North Carolina	3,840	3,880	3,960	4,390	415	213	277	351	1.42	1.32	1.92	.82
South Carolina	1,160	1,700	2,200	3,100	93	95	99	183	2.05	1.26	1.09	1.50
Virginia	2,300	2,440	3,000	3,000	184	117	291	264	2.07	.93	1.57	1.02
Total	19,730	27,940	41,020	40,870	1,250	1,706	3,470	3,595	2.02	2.77	1.91	1.85
Late:												
Colorado	2,560	1,940	4,000	6,500	256	120	200	357	3.07	1.94	2.84	1.60
Delaware		60	80	80		4	7	6		2.25	2.00	1.75
Maryland	450	450	450	560	29	27	35	36	1.75	1.19	1.32	1.12
New Jersey	3,500	3,800	4,000	4,800	192	323	360	384	1.56	2.20	2.13	1.40
New York	6,980	8,070	6,940	7,500	510	646	923	660	1.65	1.33	1.86	1.30
Tennessee	460	500	500	500	21	25	28	35	1.60	1.87	2.17	1.00
Utah		200	200	230		30	16	23		1.95	2.40	2.60
Total	13,950	15,020	16,170	20,170	1,008	1,175	1,569	1,501	2.00	1.66	2.05	1.41
Grand total	33,680	42,960	57,190	61,040	2,258	2,881	5,039	5,096	2.01	2.32	1.95	1.72

Bureau of Agricultural Economics. Estimates based upon returns from crop reporters.

[1] Average for season.
[2] 1-bushel hampers.
[3] Includes the fall crop moved in September, October, and November.

TABLE 198.—*Peas, green, for canning; commercial crop: Acreage, production, and price per pound, by States, 1925–1928*

State	Acreage				Production				Price per pound			
	1925	1926	1927	1928	1925	1926	1927	1928	1925	1926	1927	1928
	Acres	*Acres*	*Acres*	*Acres*	*1,000 pounds*	*1,000 pounds*	*1,000 pounds*	*1,000 pounds*	*Cents*	*Cents*	*Cents*	*Cents*
California	4,890	2,680	750	1,230	6,846	6,432	2,100	2,460	3.2	3.2	3.0	2.8
Colorado	3,520	2,570	1,900	3,000	6,336	4,626	3,420	5,700	3.0	3.0	3.0	2.5
Delaware	2,500	2,000	1,700	2,060	4,000	2,000	5,100	3,529	3.5	3.8	3.0	3.0
Illinois	8,050	9,200	8,830	10,240	11,270	16,560	12,362	17,992	3.5	3.2	3.0	2.0
Indiana	4,320	6,000	1,880	3,760	6,912	10,800	3,008	6,964	2.7	2.6	2.9	2.0
Maine	1,770	1,410	720	920	3,186	1,128	1,152	1,656	3.5	3.5	3.5	3.5
Maryland	11,600	8,800	8,000	8,720	20,880	17,600	22,400	16,306	3.3	3.0	3.0	3.0
Michigan	13,010	14,430	8,400	11,930	13,010	23,088	11,760	18,659	2.5	2.5	2.8	2.0
Minnesota	7,880	8,570	6,980	7,890	9,456	6,856	11,168	16,285	2.4	2.7	2.2	2.0
New Jersey	280	350	500	350	392	700	1,200	770	3.4	3.0	3.2	4.0
New York	33,310	34,990	25,540	31,970	53,296	62,982	40,864	48,467	3.2	3.0	3.0	3.0
Ohio	4,850	4,210	2,990	3,320	4,850	5,894	4,784	4,741	3.1	3.2	3.1	2.7
Pennsylvania	1,690	1,400	1,320	1,680	1,690	2,520	3,696	3,063	3.0	2.9	2.9	3.0
Utah	10,750	9,510	8,460	10,150	34,400	24,726	20,304	26,035	2.8	2.9	2.7	3.0
Wisconsin	111,710	106,120	80,000	101,000	223,420	233,464	160,000	203,616	2.9	2.9	2.8	3.0
Other States	6,500	6,640	5,840	8,350	13,000	10,624	14,016	14,696	2.6	2.8	2.4	3.0
Total or average	226,630	218,880	163,810	206,570	412,944	430,000	317,334	390,939	3.0	2.9	2.8	2.8

Bureau of Agricultural Economics. Estimates based upon returns from crop reporters.

TABLE 199.—*Peas: Car-lot shipments, by State of origin, 1925–1928*

State	1925	1926	1927	1928 [1]	State	1925	1926	1927	1928 [1]
	Cars	*Cars*	*Cars*	*Cars*		*Cars*	*Cars*	*Cars*	*Cars*
New York	885	1,110	975	838	Idaho	13	40	101	176
New Jersey	20	27	40	38	Colorado	35	58	149	348
Maryland	48	55	54	68	Washington	43	64	111	152
Virginia	303	288	259	280	California	569	803	1,361	1,636
North Carolina	491	596	570	685	Other States	47	130	116	68
South Carolina	104	167	207	246					
Mississippi	149	233	243	250	Total	2,707	3,571	4,186	4,785

Bureau of Agricultural Economics. Compiled from daily and monthly reports received by the bureau from officials and local agents of common carriers throughout the country. Shipments as shown in car lots include those by boat reduced to car-lot basis.

[1] Preliminary.

TABLE 200.—*Peas, canned: Pack [1] in the United States, 1917–1928*

State	1917	1918	1919	1920	1921	1922	1923	1924	1925	1926	1927	1928
	1,000 cases	*1,000 cases*	*1,000 cases*	*1,000 cases*	*1,000 cases*	*1,000 cases*	*1,000 cases*	*1,000 cases*	*1,000 cases*	*1,000 cases*	*1,000 cases*	*1,000 cases*
New York	1,394	2,000	1,040	2,381	1,382	2,137	2,541	2,931	2,385	2,624	1,668	2,222
New Jersey [2]	755	332	248	549	345	153	199	331	257	143	267	242
Ohio	322	442	306	282	241	225	384	430	232	278	205	336
Indiana	604	454	381	271	182	268	367	483	86	500	90	427
Illinois	576	978	433	460	331	516	586	697	357	680	563	617
Michigan	523	477	425	549	317	455	392	710	451	723	399	542
Wisconsin	3,569	4,520	4,317	5,804	4,063	7,042	6,961	10,390	10,003	9,287	6,549	9,248
Minnesota [3]							254	470	432	446	497	722
Maryland	721	683	509	696	533	489	591	873	956	840	986	1,030
Utah	421	527	395	595	376	751	918	830	1,346	1,029	802	1,154
California	350	253	205	328	84	496	239	282	271	222	(4)	(4)
Other States	594	397	426	402	353	510	516	888	1,040	937	910	1,403
United States	9,829	11,063	8,685	12,317	8,207	13,042	13,948	19,315	17,816	17,709	12,936	17,943

Bureau of Agricultural Economics. Compiled from National Canners' Association 1917–1926; Census of Manufactures 1927–28.

[1] Stated in cases of 24 No. 2 cans.   [3] Previous to 1923, included in "Other States."
[2] Includes Delaware.   [4] Included in "Other States."

TABLE 201.—*Peppers, commercial crop: Acreage, production, and price per bushel, by States, 1925–1928*

State	Acreage				Production				Price per bushel [1]			
	1925	1926	1927	1928	1925	1926	1927	1928	1925	1926	1927	1928
	Acres	*Acres*	*Acres*	*Acres*	*1,000 bushels*	*1,000 bushels*	*1,000 bushels*	*1,000 bushels*	*Dollars*	*Dollars*	*Dollars*	*Dollars*
California	200	250	380	410	59	74	111	123	2.50	0.85	0.60	1.23
Florida	3,560	3,370	2,700	6,410	1,168	1,348	891	1,949	1.64	2.20	1.45	1.22
Louisiana	1,870	2,860	3,020	2,220	299	289	616	309	1.18	1.38	1.21	.73
Mississippi		200	150	400		17	13	34		1.70	1.25	.75
New Jersey	7,000	7,500	7,000	7,500	1,715	1,950	1,680	1,725	1.00	.63	.75	.65
North Carolina	650	650	620	670	130	124	81	134	1.62	1.25	.75	.53
Texas	420	500	730	900	84	88	110	144	2.06	1.10	.80	.82
Total	13,700	15,330	14,600	18,510	3,455	3,890	3,502	4,418	1.31	1.27	1.01	.93

Bureau of Agricultural Economics. Estimates based upon returns from crop reporters.

[1] Average for season.

TABLE 202.—*Potatoes: Acreage, production, value, exports, etc., United States, 1909–1928*

Year	Acreage	Average yield per acre	Production	Price per bushel received by producers Dec. 1	Farm value Dec. 1	Wholesale price per bushel at New York [1]	Domestic exports, year beginning July 1 [2]	Imports year beginning July 1 [2]	Net balance, year beginning July 1 [2][3]
	1,000 acres	*Bushels*	*1,000 bushels*	*Cents*	*1,000 dollars*	*Cents*	*1,000 bushels*	*1,000 bushels*	*1,000 bushels*
1909	*3,669*	*106.1*	*389,195*						
1909	3,669	107.5	394,553	54.2	213,679	49	999	353	+646
1910	3,720	93.8	349,032	55.7	194,566	54	2,384	219	+2,177
1911	3,619	80.9	292,737	79.9	233,778	106	1,237	13,735	−12,283
1912	3,711	113.4	420,647	50.5	212,550	62	2,028	337	+1,693
1913	3,668	90.4	331,525	68.7	227,903	78	1,794	3,646	−1,823
1914	3,711	110.5	409,921	48.7	199,460	47	3,135	271	+2,866
1915	3,734	96.3	359,721	61.7	221,992	103	4,018	210	+3,810
1916	3,565	80.5	286,953	146.1	419,333	238	2,489	3,079	−558
1917	4,384	100.8	442,108	122.8	542,774	129	3,453	1,180	+2,273
1918	4,295	95.9	411,860	119.3	491,527	127	3,689	3,534	+205
1919	*3,252*	*89.3*	*290,428*						
1919	3,542	91.2	322,867	159.5	514,855	284	3,723	6,941	−3,212
1920	3,657	110.3	403,296	114.5	461,778	103	4,803	3,423	+1,399
1921	3,941	91.8	361,659	110.1	398,362	123	2,327	2,110	+222
1922	4,307	105.3	453,396	58.1	263,355	97	2,980	572	+2,408
1923	3,816	109.0	416,105	78.1	324,889	118	3,075	564	+2,512
1924	*2,911*	*121.1*	*352,462*						
1924	3,327	126.7	421,585	62.5	263,312	78	3,653	478	+3,187
1925	3,092	104.6	323,465	186.8	604,072	238	1,824	5,420	−3,575
1926	3,122	113.5	354,328	141.4	501,017	161	2,092	6,349	−4,205
1927	3,476	115.9	402,741	96.5	388,741	129	2,424	3,803	1,313
1928 [4]	3,825	121.0	462,943	54.0	250,043				

Bureau of Agricultural Economics. Acreage, yield, and production figures are estimates of the crop-reporting board; italic figures are census returns. Prices received by producers are based upon returns from special price reporters. See 1927 Yearbook, p. 881, for data for earlier years.

[1] Compiled from Producers Price Current. Prices 1909–1919 are averages of the high and low weekly quotation of New York potatoes, October–June, converted from dollars per 180 pounds to cents per bushel beginning 1920, season September–May.

[2] Compiled from Commerce and Navigation of the United States, 1909–1917; Foreign Commerce and Navigation of the United States, 1918; Monthly Summary of Foreign Commerce of the United States, June issues, 1919–1926, January and June issues, 1927–28.

[3] The difference between total exports (domestic exports plus reexports) and total imports; + indicates net exports, and − indicates net imports.

[4] Preliminary.

TABLE 203.—*Potatoes, early and second early, commercial crop: Acreage, production and price per bushel, by States, 1925–1928*

State	Acreage				Production				Price per bushel [1]			
	1925	1926	1927	1928	1925	1926	1927	1928	1925	1926	1927	1928
	Acres	*Acres*	*Acres*	*Acres*	*1,000 bush.*	*1,000 bush.*	*1,000 bush.*	*1,000 bush.*	*Dollars*	*Dollars*	*Dollars*	*Dollars*
Early:												
Alabama	8,940	12,750	13,200	17,700	715	982	1,109	1,504	1.20	1.78	1.37	.75
California	11,850	14,980	17,800	22,650	1,635	2,097	1,798	2,741	1.19	1.23	1.08	.74
Florida	21,920	23,070	28,000	30,350	2,718	2,722	2,940	3,794	1.74	3.04	1.84	1.49
Georgia	2,010	2,250	2,250	2,500	131	191	259	225	1.61	2.17	1.96	.80
Louisiana	15,630	20,000	21,860	21,800	1,047	1,200	1,421	1,526	1.24	2.06	1.69	1.00
Mississippi	1,240	1,300	1,700	1,950	68	104	136	176	1.54	1.77	1.27	1.12
North Carolina	22,100	29,000	36,000	46,400	2,144	3,480	4,320	6,403	1.28	1.68	1.91	.54
South Carolina	14,860	18,720	18,000	24,000	1,828	2,527	2,070	3,360	1.48	1.72	1.92	.56
Texas [2]	10,710	11,730	22,110	25,400	932	1,067	1,437	1,727	1.44	2.37	1.69	.93
Virginia	90,050	89,000	78,700	90,900	9,185	9,345	14,087	15,908	1.40	1.32	1.36	.41
Total	199,310	222,800	239,620	283,650	20,403	23,715	29,577	37,364	1.41	1.72	1.55	.65
Second Early:												
Arkansas	3,400	4,180	3,890	6,030	289	280	276	555	1.39	1.50	1.67	.53
Kansas (Kaw Valley)	16,500	15,800	17,300	18,160	1,700	2,481	2,508	3,505	1.26	.83	.85	.25
Kentucky	5,620	5,620	5,340	5,340	601	584	662	1,041	1.63	1.25	.94	.38
Maryland	13,150	14,800	15,400	17,240	1,131	1,421	2,156	2,620	1.43	.97	1.20	.33
Missouri (Orrick district)	4,800	5,000	5,180	6,400	480	1,000	648	1,280	1.41	.77	1.08	.38
Nebraska (Kearney district)	1,500	1,200	1,700	1,900	172	132	255	285	1.42	.75	.75	.50
New Jersey	44,000	40,000	44,800	45,000	4,664	5,600	7,213	7,290	1.35	1.37	.81	.45
Oklahoma	14,500	14,400	15,000	17,000	1,450	1,411	1,530	1,428	1.20	1.52	2.00	.37
Total	103,470	101,000	108,610	117,070	10,487	12,909	15,248	18,004	1.34	1.18	1.02	.38
Grand total	302,780	323,800	348,230	400,720	30,890	36,624	44,825	55,368	1.39	1.53	1.37	.56

Bureau of Agricultural Economics.   Estimates based upon returns from crop reporters.

[1] Average for season.   [2] Includes fall crop of previous year.

TABLE 204.—*Potatoes: Acreage and production, by States, average 1921–1925, annual 1926–1928*

State and division	Acreage				Production			
	Average, 1921–1925	1926	1927	1928 [1]	Average, 1921–1925	1926	1927	1928 [1]
	1,000 acres	*1,000 acres*	*1,000 acres*	*1,000 acres*	*1,000 bushels*	*1,000 bushels*	*1,000 bushels*	*1,000 bushels*
Maine	133	127	161	172	34, 895	36, 830	37, 352	37, 840
New Hampshire	13	11	12	12	1, 915	1, 815	1, 800	1, 656
Vermont	23	20	21	21	3, 425	3, 100	3, 255	2, 982
Massachusetts	22	13	14	15	2, 937	2, 015	1, 400	1, 620
Rhode Island	2	3	2	2	301	450	220	244
Connecticut	20	14	15	17	2, 645	2, 170	1, 635	2, 210
New York	313	248	270	284	35, 268	29, 016	28, 620	32, 376
New Jersey	78	50	57	57	9, 766	7, 250	9, 177	9, 120
Pennsylvania	233	198	220	246	24, 958	22, 176	26, 400	31, 980
North Atlantic	837	684	772	826	116, 109	104, 822	109, 859	120, 028
Ohio	119	107	116	123	10, 401	10, 058	12, 180	12, 054
Indiana	64	48	53	61	5, 273	3, 840	5, 035	6, 649
Illinois	97	61	64	70	7, 168	4, 880	5, 376	7, 700
Michigan	302	249	289	306	31, 810	29, 880	23, 120	35, 802
Wisconsin	274	230	260	278	28, 659	27, 140	23, 920	31, 970
Minnesota	386	298	328	354	37, 668	29, 800	33, 128	38, 940
Iowa	85	74	75	81	7, 166	5, 846	6, 150	10, 935
Missouri	85	81	68	85	6, 424	6, 480	5, 644	10, 285
North Dakota	144	94	113	141	12, 531	7, 520	11, 526	14, 805
South Dakota	84	55	60	67	6, 304	3, 300	6, 900	6, 080
Nebraska	105	73	84	105	8, 552	5, 329	8, 904	10, 080
Kansas	59	43	49	54	4, 360	3, 913	5, 390	7, 560
North Central	1, 803	1, 413	1, 559	1, 725	166, 316	137, 986	147, 273	192, 810
Delaware	9	6	6	7	655	516	714	658
Maryland	45	39	43	47	3, 639	3, 510	5, 246	5, 405
Virginia	145	124	130	151	15, 371	11, 656	19, 760	21, 593
West Virginia	48	47	52	60	4, 635	4, 982	5, 876	7, 500
North Carolina	53	67	72	95	4, 753	6, 325	7, 368	10, 545
South Carolina	30	29	29	36	2, 817	3, 219	3, 034	4, 068
Georgia	21	19	17	22	1, 448	1, 197	1, 304	1, 682
Florida	23	24	29	31	2, 315	2, 832	3, 045	3, 875
South Atlantic	373	355	378	449	35, 632	34, 237	46, 347	55, 326
Kentucky	54	47	52	57	4, 196	4, 512	4, 732	5, 985
Tennessee	34	35	39	43	2, 426	2, 730	3, 432	4, 085
Alabama	35	29	33	38	2, 741	2, 030	2, 475	2, 812
Mississippi	14	12	12	15	1, 053	852	936	1, 330
Arkansas	31	32	29	36	1, 949	1, 920	1, 972	2, 700
Louisiana	28	36	41	41	1, 781	2, 196	2, 665	2, 870
Oklahoma	38	43	45	63	2, 526	2, 860	2, 925	5, 040
Texas	32	30	35	39	1, 894	2, 100	2, 310	2, 691
South Central	266	264	286	332	18, 566	19, 200	21, 447	27, 513
Montana	38	35	36	37	4, 223	2, 975	4, 860	4, 255
Idaho	70	91	115	116	12, 849	16, 198	24, 380	19, 720
Wyoming	17	13	17	21	1, 789	1, 456	2, 329	2, 352
Colorado	107	84	96	110	14, 773	11, 760	14, 400	13, 420
New Mexico	3	2	2	2	169	166	150	132
Arizona	4	4	4	3	309	220	320	222
Utah	16	17	22	23	2, 712	2, 465	2, 970	3, 312
Nevada	4	5	6	6	707	700	780	840
Washington	57	67	79	67	8, 383	10, 720	13, 430	9, 045
Oregon	43	45	52	52	4, 239	4, 500	6, 240	6, 240
California	58	43	52	56	8, 466	6, 923	7, 956	7, 728
Far Western	417	406	481	493	58, 619	58, 083	77, 815	67, 266
United States	3, 697	3, 122	3, 476	3, 825	395, 242	354, 328	402, 741	462, 943

Bureau of Agricultural Economics. Estimates of the crop-reporting board.

[1] Preliminary.

TABLE 205.—*Potatoes: Yield per acre and estimated price per bushel, December 1, by States, average, 1914–1920, 1921–1925; annual, 1924–1928*

State and division	Yield per acre							Estimated price per bushel						
	Av., 1914–1920	Av., 1921–1925	1924	1925	1926	1927	1928	Av., 1914–1920	Av., 1921–1925	1924	1925	1926	1927	1928
	Bush.	Bush.	Bush.	Bush.	Bush.	Bush.	Bush.	Cts.	Cts.	Cts.	Cts.	Cts.	Cts.	Cts.
Maine	196	262	315	250	290	232	220	109	89	43	200	133	85	40
New Hampshire	121	153	170	145	165	150	138	138	135	84	235	170	140	80
Vermont	121	151	160	125	155	155	142	118	119	85	215	140	125	85
Massachusetts	118	135	150	140	155	100	108	146	145	96	245	180	155	90
Rhode Island	118	130	140	140	150	110	122	148	144	95	245	180	155	90
Connecticut	104	134	130	135	155	109	130	144	149	100	250	180	165	90
New York	101	112	140	86	117	106	114	114	107	57	215	160	125	65
New Jersey	117	124	150	106	145	161	160	128	124	67	230	155	110	50
Pennsylvania	91	108	118	123	112	120	130	121	117	80	194	170	120	65
North Atlantic	114.3	139.3	167.9	132.6	153.2	142.3	145.3	117.7	107.5	59.7	207.0	152.8	110.2	57.5
Ohio	79	88	88	106	94	105	98	132	127	89	200	170	120	75
Indiana	76	83	99	83	80	95	109	127	122	80	216	165	110	70
Illinois	72	76	110	60	80	84	110	134	126	75	235	175	115	65
Michigan	86	107	130	103	120	80	117	95	74	35	162	120	90	40
Wisconsin	98	106	130	112	118	92	115	88	76	36	170	120	85	40
Minnesota	98	99	132	97	100	101	110	86	69	27	154	115	60	30
Iowa	79	86	136	63	79	82	135	124	115	55	235	170	100	51
Missouri	73	75	98	57	80	83	121	134	124	82	225	170	115	60
North Dakota	82	86	90	72	80	102	105	94	65	39	150	120	50	30
South Dakota	87	75	82	65	60	115	90	101	85	48	180	159	55	40
Nebraska	83	81	87	75	73	106	96	112	96	62	180	160	75	50
Kansas	70	75	95	67	91	110	140	136	130	91	235	170	100	45
North Central	85.7	93.0	115.2	88.8	97.7	94.5	111.8	103.0	86.0	45.9	177.7	134.1	82.6	43.8
Delaware	91	76	90	64	86	119	94	109	112	80	200	140	80	75
Maryland	92	80	83	73	90	122	115	103	109	81	194	140	105	50
Virginia	107	106	131	90	94	152	143	110	108	82	195	140	130	50
West Virginia	96	97	95	87	106	113	125	129	129	98	193	167	125	80
North Carolina	85	90	105	78	94	102	111	127	131	112	180	160	150	65
South Carolina	87	94	111	96	111	105	113	171	159	145	210	170	190	65
Georgia	69	67	72	49	63	77	76	169	165	150	210	190	165	115
Florida	87	101	88	124	118	105	125	178	196	165	260	300	185	150
South Atlantic	96.0	95.3	108.4	86.0	96.4	122.6	123.2	122.5	125.8	101.2	200.3	165.4	137.5	67.3
Kentucky	85	78	100	60	96	91	105	135	137	102	200	155	130	80
Tennessee	75	72	80	56	78	88	95	132	139	112	195	157	135	90
Alabama	78	76	90	57	70	75	74	163	169	155	220	190	150	85
Mississippi	81	75	81	67	71	78	89	151	176	164	200	180	165	120
Arkansas	71	63	74	60	60	68	75	155	157	128	210	185	150	80
Louisiana	65	65	68	60	61	65	70	159	168	150	210	190	165	100
Oklahoma	66	67	70	72	67	65	80	161	158	130	225	170	180	75
Texas	59	59	67	53	70	66	66	177	184	170	240	200	165	100
South Central	72.8	69.8	80.5	60.6	72.7	75.0	82.9	149.9	156.9	130.7	212.2	174.3	151.4	87.1
Montana	117	109	88	108	85	135	115	97	86	87	160	120	65	55
Idaho	158	183	170	196	178	212	170	87	71	54	145	105	55	45
Wyoming	128	107	95	120	112	137	112	108	102	87	160	125	70	65
Colorado	137	142	140	183	140	150	122	97	76	60	155	130	55	45
New Mexico	93	57	52	75	83	75	66	156	158	104	200	175	120	95
Arizona	96	74	54	57	55	80	74	163	150	150	230	200	110	110
Utah	163	165	137	160	145	135	144	92	80	74	133	105	75	45
Nevada	163	159	131	170	140	130	140	117	116	106	190	130	85	85
Washington	138	148	150	155	160	170	135	91	93	85	165	95	60	50
Oregon	115	98	96	104	100	120	120	89	95	95	150	100	75	70
California	138	148	162	159	161	153	138	125	121	90	200	132	95	65
Far Western	135.0	140.9	136.8	157.7	143.1	161.8	136.4	101.0	88.0	73.5	159.3	113.2	64.0	52.4
United States	97.9	107.5	126.7	104.6	113.5	115.9	121.0	110.4	99.1	62.5	186.8	141.4	96.5	54.0

Bureau of Agricultural Economics. Yield figures are estimates of the crop-reporting board.
Prices are based upon returns from special price reporters.

TABLE 206.—*Potatoes: Acreage, yield per acre and production in specified countries, average 1909–1913, 1921–1925, annual 1926–1928*

Country	Acreage — Average 1909–1913[1]	Acreage — Average 1921–1925	Acreage — 1926	Acreage — 1927	Acreage — 1928 preliminary	Yield per acre — Average 1909–1913[1]	Yield per acre — Average 1921–1925	Yield per acre — 1926	Yield per acre — 1927	Yield per acre — 1928 preliminary	Production — Average 1909–1913[1]	Production — Average 1921–1925	Production — 1926	Production — 1927	Production — 1928 preliminary
	1,000 acres	*1,000 acres*	*1,000 acres*	*1,000 acres*	*1,000 acres*	*Bushels*	*Bushels*	*Bushels*	*Bushels*	*Bushels*	*1,000 bushels*	*1,000 bushels*	*1,000 bushels*	*1,000 bushels*	*1,000 bushels*
NORTHERN HEMISPHERE															
North America:															
Canada	483	606	523	572	599	161.2	149.9	149.6	135.4	144.5	77,843	90,838	78,228	77,430	86,575
United States	3,677	3,697	3,122	3,476	3,825	97.3	107.5	113.5	115.9	121.0	357,699	395,242	354,328	402,741	462,943
Total	4,160	4,303	3,645	4,048	4,424	104.7	113.0	118.7	118.6	124.2	435,542	486,080	432,556	480,171	549,518
Europe:															
United Kingdom	1,166	652	794	814	1,153	218.2	235.1	109.1	225.2	184.5	254,441	153,291	86,617	183,344	212,768
Irish Free State		398	375	365	123		170.0	192.3	249.9	281.3		67,666	72,121	91,212	34,606
Norway	102	121	119	123		242.9	229.7	276.2	183.7		24,780	27,796	32,870	22,589	
Sweden	377	387	396	390		152.7	167.9	181.2	100.6		57,581	64,966	71,748	39,252	
Denmark	161	196	189	177	154	202.7	224.9	157.8	117.2	303.0	32,642	44,071	29,827	20,746	46,664
Netherlands	411	430	421	425	436	253.2	276.7	259.5	211.8	313.5	104,051	118,990	109,255	90,021	136,684
Belgium	404	406	397	416	410	274.3	265.4	277.8	292.3	267.7	110,830	107,736	110,276	121,590	109,759
France	4,066	3,607	3,611	3,699	3,619	129.6	125.1	113.3	174.1	110.6	526,793	451,353	409,193	643,997	400,242
Spain	[2]642	[3]781	763	763	802	[2]176.0	[3]125.6	152.4	173.8	130.6	[2]112,997	[3]98,084	116,292	132,646	104,718
Italy	759	840	769	874	875	88.9	78.7	110.4	81.8	62.6	67,514	66,079	84,914	71,477	54,742
Switzerland	[4]115	111	118	118	118	[4]214.5	217.1	189.9	216.6	204.5	[3]24,664	24,103	22,413	25,554	24,129
Germany	6,775	6,753	6,816	6,954	7,033	202.7	193.2	161.8	198.4	215.6	1,373,609	1,304,447	1,103,428	1,379,716	1,516,373
Austria	436	390	439	453	454	122.4	138.9	108.6	216.3	164.9	53,373	54,183	47,685	97,973	74,864
Czechoslovakia	1,849	1,580	1,551	1,607	1,666	132.6	156.4	119.6	208.3	151.5	245,210	247,176	185,432	334,705	252,470
Hungary	619	639	620	641	655	114.9	89.1	111.1	114.9	72.2	71,118	56,936	68,879	73,667	47,280
Yugoslavia	458	537	548	558		101.1	68.0	63.0	66.4		46,288	36,528	34,539	37,063	
Rumania	[3]399	568	586	616	575	108.0	101.2	121.7	128.2	122.0	43,086	57,489	71,335	78,949	70,135
Poland	5,693	5,485	5,834	5,946	6,102	156.2	177.5	156.7	196.2	168.5	889,531	973,614	914,123	1,166,897	1,028,439
Lithuania	403	374	362	343	301	101.4	162.2	169.0	135.4	113.3	40,864	60,654	61,170	46,444	34,109
Latvia	209	178	203	211	193	120.7	138.4	183.4	124.9	59.8	25,217	24,644	37,238	26,358	11,539
Estonia	190	173	172	176	174	144.9	149.0	197.8	154.8	101.8	27,526	25,773	34,020	27,253	17,717
Finland	[5]181	167	171	174	173	101.9	130.6	182.9	160.1	139.9	18,443	21,809	31,269	27,852	24,195
Russia	7,225	8,508	12,916	13,680	14,446	102.5	127.1	140.9	146.9		740,728	1,081,187	1,819,871	2,009,149	
Total European countries reporting area and production, all years	24,181	22,883	23,459	23,914	24,441	165.6	168.7	148.6	187.9	169.0	4,003,603	3,860,739	3,484,901	4,492,829	4,131,289

Item	Area					Yield					Production				
Estimated European total, excluding Russia	25,470	25,100	25,560	26,030	23,865	156.6	159.9	144.5	177.8	162.2	4,165,000	4,142,000	3,843,000	4,759,000	4,680,816
Total Northern Hemisphere reporting area and production, all years	28,341	27,186	27,104	27,962	28,865						4,439,145	4,346,819	3,917,457	4,973,000	
Estimated Northern Hemisphere total, excluding Russia	30,100	30,120	29,950	30,890	30,890						4,647,000	4,702,000	4,343,000	5,306,000	
SOUTHERN HEMISPHERE															
Brazil	69	⁴104	122				⁴84.7	80.7				⁴8,806	9,847	9,922	
Chile		77	76	72		123.3	146.3	131.9	156.0		8,510	11,264	10,027	11,231	
Argentina	217	331	278	311		140.6	90.2	138.1	81.3		30,515	29,866	38,382	25,282	
Australia	114	139	139			100.5	97.2				14,469	13,511			
Estimated Southern Hemisphere total	700	1,080	1,500	1,460							76,000	84,000	101,000	87,000	
Estimated world total, excluding Russia and China	30,800	31,200	31,480	32,350							4,723,000	4,786,000	4,444,000	5,393,000	

Bureau of Agricultural Economics. Official sources and International Institute of Agriculture. Estimates given are for crops harvested in the calendar year in the Northern Hemisphere and the succeeding harvest in the Southern Hemisphere.

1 Averages for countries having changed boundaries are estimates for present boundaries. 2 2-year average. 3 4-year average. 4 3-year average. 5 1 year only.

TABLE 207.—Potatoes: Car-lot shipments, by State of origin, 1927–1928

State and year	April	May	June	July	August	September	October	November	December	January	February	March	April	May	June	July	Total
	Cars	Cars	Cars	Cars	Cars	Cars	Cars	Cars	Cars	Cars	Cars	Cars	Cars	Cars	Cars	Cars	Cars
Maine:																	
1927 [2]					467	3,051	6,759	4,207	3,948	4,901	4,624	3,993	3,903	4,080	986	26	40,945
1928 [2]					33	2,851	5,941	3,844	3,785								
New York:																	
1927 [2]				31	1,554	2,482	2,736	1,397	716	885	914	767	567	248	22		12,319
1928 [2]					588	1,455	2,443	1,662	1,005								
New Jersey:																	
1927 [2]				188	4,893	1,399	63	56	7	3	1	55	11				6,676
1928 [2]				5	2,615	2,038	509	71	10								
Pennsylvania:																	
1927 [2]					28	555	853	636	205	309	367	259	136	26	1		3,375
1928 [2]					42	434	961	940	561								
Michigan:																	
1927 [2]					27	331	846	918	784	931	1,029	1,390	1,124	893	291	3	8,567
1928 [2]					13	668	1,808	1,321	761								
Wisconsin:																	
1927 [2]					297	1,744	2,215	1,323	1,020	1,842	1,970	2,092	1,374	990	584	4	15,455
1928 [2]					326	1,758	1,816	1,210	1,097								
Minnesota:																	
1927 [2]				20	1,265	4,777	8,990	3,226	1,098	2,191	4,264	4,249	1,652	1,363	387		33,482
1928 [2]				119	699	1,723	4,050	1,642	559								
North Dakota:																	
1927 [2]					6	1,249	3,248	528	125	439	844	1,183	258	50	3		7,933
1928 [2]						387	2,489	411	152								
Nebraska:																	
1927 [2]					577	625	1,113	718	372	1,127	975	403	97	25	12	1	6,045
1928 [2]				5	189	507	501	522	402								
Kansas:																	
1927 [2]			11	2,081	1,459	686	66	29		4	5						4,341
1928 [2]			1	971	1,734	1,379	517	99	23								
Maryland:																	
1927 [2]			115	2,488	616	16	9	31	24	27	42	109	59	9			3,545
1928 [2]			27	1,973	920	85	8	8	1								
Virginia:																	
1927 [2]			8,752	13,241	1,466	88	53	46	6	1	16	29	15				23,713
1928 [2]			8,615	13,924	4,044	441	133	70	20								
North Carolina:																	
1927 [2]		219	6,781	438	39	60	10	4	1		1	2					7,555
1928 [2]		18	7,594	998	504	378	105	32	6								

Crop-movement season [1]

[illegible]																	
1927 [2]		3, 313	629	1													3, 943
1928 [2]		1, 161	3, 470	38	36	18		1									
Florida:[3]																	
1927 [2]	3, 747	1, 601	47	7	1	1		1	27								5, 432
1928 [2]	1, 447	5, 895	386	10				1	1								
Alabama:																	
1927 [2]	27	1, 833	228	10			2		1	1							2, 102
1928 [2]		934	2, 121	66	6	2											
Louisiana:																	
1927 [2]	[4] 36	679	157					19	7								1, 298
1928 [2]	[4] 35	1, 121	461	4	9	6			5								
Oklahoma:																	
1927 [2]		5	1, 981	105	2			6	3	14	14						2, 130
1928 [2]			1, 313	749	41	6	2	2									
Texas:[5]																	
1927 [2]	1, 224	1, 366	404	7		1	1	1	23	12	10						3, 049
1928 [2]	1, 094	1, 326	893	95	11			1	15								
Idaho:																	
1927 [2]				115	764	1, 782	2, 869	2, 792	2, 135	3, 423	3, 740	3, 492	3, 240	3, 257	696		28, 305
1928 [2]				51	233	834	1, 714	1, 824	1, 602								
Colorado:																	
1927 [2]				63	788	2, 748	3, 207	2, 173	1, 478	2, 140	1, 780	1, 253	847	713	138		17, 328
1928 [2]				77	525	1, 883	2, 174	1, 493	1, 267								
Washington:																	
1927 [2]				271	335	886	1, 326	1, 098	565	735	905	1, 909	802	618	162		9, 612
1928 [2]				398	525	915	963	788	502								
Oregon:																	
1927 [2]				26	64	40	197	381	243	191	244	606	259	82	6		2, 339
1928 [2]				11	45	83	288	295	155								
California:																	
1927 [2]	1	92	882	929	1, 173	1, 041	745	744	661	688	558	282	121	53			7, 970
1928 [2]	6	392	974	607	668	785	836	677	667								
Other States:																	
1927 [2]	3	467	689	965	2, 032	1, 441	3, 025	790	246	368	553	1, 361	586	300	37		12, 863
1928 [2]		140	509	1, 037	2, 094	1, 922	1, 717	679	276								

Bureau of Agricultural Economics. Compiled from daily and monthly reports received by the bureau from officials and local agents of common carriers throughout the country. Shipments as shown in car lots include those by boat reduced to car-lot basis. Figures for earlier years appear in 1927 and earlier Yearbooks.

[1] Crop movement season extends from Apr. 1 of one year through July of the following year, except in Florida, where the season begins in March.
[2] Preliminary.
[3] Includes cars moved earlier as follows: 36 in March, 1923; 109 in March, 1924; 28 in February and 373 in March, 1925; 2 in February and 37 in March, 1926; 6 in February and 547 in March, 1927; 46 in January, 57 in February, and 143 in March, 1928.
[4] Includes 1 car in March, 1928.
[5] Includes cars moved in March, as follows: 11 in 1925; 3 in 1926; 158 in 1927; 132 in March, 1928.

TABLE 208.—*Potatoes: Car-lot shipments by months, total for the United States, 1920–1928*

Origin and year	Jan.	Feb.	Mar.	Apr.	May	June	July	Aug.	Sept.	Oct.	Nov.	Dec.	Total
United States:	Cars	Cars	Cars	Cars	Cars	Cars	Cars	Cars	Cars	Cars	Cars	Cars	Cars
1920	13,752	9,471	14,612	9,297	7,043	14,042	15,317	14,119	18,875	32,170	26,067	10,411	185,176
1921	14,477	12,487	16,449	14,948	14,926	16,421	15,606	16,240	26,322	42,956	16,729	10,440	218,001
1922	16,721	13,722	22,334	20,059	20,284	22,104	18,833	18,239	24,420	35,193	21,050	12,448	245,407
1923	17,261	14,606	24,462	23,190	16,300	20,294	16,733	16,735	24,044	35,220	20,732	11,977	241,554
1924	19,762	20,716	22,940	19,461	18,736	20,845	23,624	16,394	21,387	34,141	20,852	13,237	252,095
1925	21,715	20,394	21,639	20,123	20,215	19,798	17,765	14,864	23,569	33,631	16,286	11,524	241,523
1926	16,185	14,834	19,974	14,238	16,903	23,587	20,310	15,327	22,978	36,180	18,419	13,487	232,422
1927	17,974	17,784	21,497	20,283	16,691	22,155	21,053	17,853	25,003	38,333	21,124	13,695	253,445
1928 [1]	20,278	22,913	23,710	17,250	23,740	29,648	21,077	16,081	20,652	29,058	17,586	12,874	254,867

Bureau of Agricultural Economics. Compiled from daily and monthly reports received by the bureau from officials and local agents of common carriers throughout the country. Shipments as shown in car lots include those by boat reduced to car-lot basis, 400 bushels to 700 bushels to a carload.

[1] Preliminary.

TABLE 209.—*Potatoes, white: International trade, average 1911–1913, annual 1924–1927*

Country	Year ended Dec. 31									
	Average, 1911–1913		1924		1925		1926		1927 preliminary	
	Imports	Exports	Imports	Exports	Imports	Exports	Imports	Exports	Imports	Exports
PRINCIPAL EXPORTING COUNTRIES	1,000 bushels	1,000 bushels	1,000 bushels	1,000 bushels	1,000 bushels	1,000 bushels	1,000 bushels	1,000 bushels	1,000 bushels	1,000 bushels
Netherland	1,952	16,451	506	15,344	434	15,552	494	18,387	748	16,988
France	7,143	8,683	5,841	10,289	6,795	10,350	14,449	8,186	9,796	9,342
Italy	242	3,975	69	6,801	212	7,731	461	9,524	505	8,295
Poland	0	0	33	10,972	35	3,535	4	4,468	8	5,103
Belgium	4,921	8,692	2,704	2,814	4,804	3,778	4,502	9,400	3,811	6,670
Canada	525	1,207	940	3,130	572	6,281	467	8,169	504	7,687
Argentina	1,337	543	55	2,557	281	1,252	226	2,234	8	2,966
Spain	0	1,835	481	1,429	1,248	1,321	218	2,227	---	---
Hungary	0	0	17	626	117	1,238	82	4,987	211	2,662
Czechoslovakia	0	0	146	122	574	179	1,708	46	1,497	2,717
Estonia	0	0	0	791	0	851	1	396	3	1,310
Japan	0	440	0	303	0	474	0	485	0	733
Denmark	40	928	175	334	357	90	217	117	741	47
China	36	288	0	320	0	169	0	175	0	124
Russia	309	7,762	[1]7	[1]61	[1]15	[1]29	[1]7	[1]35	[1]6	1,066
PRINCIPAL IMPORTING COUNTRIES										
United Kingdom	11,382	6,246	16,791	1,531	18,331	1,614	12,618	1,937	10,838	3,039
Germany	29,180	12,412	10,652	2,317	14,395	9,774	15,975	3,565	23,484	2,537
Cuba	2,001	2	4,860	3	4,827	9	3,570	49	---	---
Austria	[2]4,070	[2]1,451	1,666	[1]15	2,215	[4]33	3,873	129	2,424	194
Switzerland	3,172	42	2,930	4	2,264	6	2,615	4	1,887	3
Uruguay	[3]768	1	1,234	1	[1]1,536	0	[1]1,631	1	[1]1,251	[1]1
United States	5,707	1,814	452	3,862	2,433	2,323	5,728	2,033	5,272	2,379
Algeria	1,218	931	1,305	1,067	1,313	1,795	1,165	1,553	1,264	1,152
Portugal	273	500	661	[1]30	[1]1,398	[1]155	[1]1,178	[1]269	---	---
Finland	479	15	614	1	635	0	493	0	327	2
Egypt	599	[3]28	765	68	841	77	827	77	853	101
Irish Free State	0	0	842	547	707	741	880	636	566	1,018
Brazil	939	0	1,534	0	496	2	1,588	0	1,314	---
Tunis	[4]294	[4]2	365	3	361	3	357	3	436	2
Sweden	700	64	268	5	344	3	36	16	615	158
Philippine Islands	334	0	300	0	322	0	336	0	345	0
Norway	215	60	1	104	157	20	1	76	52	87
Total 32 countries	77,836	74,372	56,214	65,451	68,019	69,385	75,707	79,184	68,766	76,383

Bureau of Agricultural Economics. Official sources except where otherwise noted.

[1] International Yearbook of Agricultural Statistics.
[2] Average for Austria-Hungary.
[3] 1 year only.
[4] 2-year average.

TABLE 210.—*Potatoes: Estimated price per bushel, received by producers, United States, 1909–1928*

Year beginning July	July 15	Aug. 15	Sept. 15	Oct. 15	Nov. 15	Dec. 15	Jan. 15	Feb. 15	Mar. 15	Apr. 15	May 15	June 15	Weighted av.
Average:	Cents	Cents	Cents	Cents	Cents	Cents	Cents	Cents	Cents	Cents	Cents	Cents	Cents
1909–1913	82.2	84.0	74.4	65.0	61.4	62.3	64.2	66.3	67.5	68.8	69.5	71.8	69.0
1914–1920	152.8	138.7	120.3	111.8	110.6	111.5	117.9	128.9	135.3	145.5	156.7	156.5	128.4
1921–1925	110.0	128.3	108.7	96.5	104.3	103.1	110.2	113.4	113.8	123.7	118.0	111.7	109.9
1909	88.0	78.3	67.9	61.0	56.0	55.0	56.1	55.4	51.0	42.9	37.9	38.8	57.9
1910	52.5	68.9	70.4	61.8	55.7	54.9	54.6	55.2	55.4	59.0	62.9	79.8	61.3
1911	116.2	124.8	101.0	82.3	78.1	82.2	89.4	98.2	109.6	122.2	123.5	111.6	.99.6
1912	95.0	75.8	58.0	48.3	48.0	50.6	51.8	52.6	51.2	49.2	51.7	52.5	55.6
1913	59.5	72.2	74.6	71.8	69.2	68.6	69.0	70.2	70.4	70.7	71.4	76.4	70.6
1914	84.3	81.0	69.8	58.8	50.8	49.2	50.0	50.4	49.1	49.2	50.6	51.4	58.0
1915	54.2	53.4	49.6	54.8	61.2	66.2	79.3	91.2	96.0	96.2	96.8	100.6	70.8
1916	98.8	102.4	110.6	123.8	140.9	146.7	159.8	206.6	237.7	257.2	276.8	261.0	166.3
1917	209.4	155.0	130.6	125.0	125.3	121.9	122.0	121.6	106.4	86.4	77.8	85.2	122.5
1918	118.2	145.2	146.2	135.4	123.2	117.7	115.2	111.9	107.4	112.2	120.2	124.9	125.6
1919	160.6	190.2	175.8	158.5	156.2	169.0	198.1	230.6	269.6	344.6	407.4	403.6	223.8
1920	344.4	243.9	159.8	126.6	116.4	110.0	100.6	89.8	80.9	72.9	67.6	68.5	131.5
1921	103.4	152.8	153.1	130.6	116.8	109.4	112.0	116.6	115.7	109.0	104.2	103.7	121.3
1922	109.0	101.4	78.8	66.2	60.5	58.8	62.0	64.2	68.6	77.4	79.0	79.8	73.9
1923	102.9	120.8	109.6	91.4	82.5	81.5	86.4	88.1	87.8	91.1	91.3	100.7	94.2
1924	109.0	111.3	81.0	68.8	63.5	64.1	70.2	72.3	71.4	70.5	70.6	84.4	76.5
1925	125.5	155.4	121.1	125.6	198.4	201.5	220.5	226.0	225.6	270.5	244.8	190.1	183.5
1926	174.6	140.5	130.6	126.4	141.3	137.0	139.1	134.1	127.0	126.8	146.0	191.0	140.8
1927	183.1	146.3	107.4	97.9	95.4	94.1	93.6	96.2	113.1	116.8	103.3	83.6	108.4
1928	77.9	73.1	64.8	58.0	56.9	57.7							

Bureau of Agricultural Economics. Based upon returns from special price reporters. Mean of prices reported on 1st of month and 1st of succeeding month, July, 1909–December, 1923.

TABLE 211.—*Potatoes: Shipping-point price, per 100 pounds in car lots, Minneapolis, 1919–1928* [1]

Year	Aug.	Sept.	Oct.	Nov.	Dec.	Jan.	Feb.	Mar.	Apr.	May	June
	Dollars	Dollars	Dollars	Dollars	Dollars	Dollars	Dollars	Dollars	Dollars	Dollars	Dollars
1919	2.97	2.55	2.36	2.63	3.00	4.22	4.16	5.21	6.89	7.14	
1920	[2] 2.62	[2] 1.98	1.57	1.82	1.34	1.14	.95	1.14	.85	.79	
1921	[2] 2.20	1.95	1.72	1.47	1.45	1.73	1.58	1.43	1.32	1.41	1.62
1922	[2] .99	[2] .92	[2] .77	.69	.64	.62	.61	.86	1.08	.84	.69
1923	1.54	1.19	.86	.81	.85	1.12	1.08	1.04	1.15	1.09	1.48
1924		.77	.67	.68	.73	.90	.87	.84	.69	.99	1.28
1925	2.11	1.83	2.39	3.39	3.48	3.92	3.55	3.85	4.49	3.11	
1926		2.20	2.19	2.21	2.09	2.08	1.81	1.78	1.91	2.96	3.98
1927	1.42	1.32	1.26	1.30	1.32	1.36	1.58	1.98	1.58	1.22	.99
1928	.69	.76	.65	.68							

Bureau of Agricultural Economics. Compiled from daily market reports from bureau representatives. Average prices as shown are based on stock of U. S. No. 1 grade; they are simple averages of daily range of selling prices.

[1] Minneapolis-St. Paul freight rate.　　　　[2] Field run and partly graded.

TABLE 212.—*Potatoes: Average l. c. l. price per 100 pounds, to jobbers, at three markets, 1919–1928*

Market, and season beginning April [1]	Apr.	May	June	July	Aug.	Sept.	Oct.	Nov.	Dec.	Jan.	Feb.	Mar.	Apr.	May
New York:	Dolls.	Dolls.	Dolls.	Dolls.	Dolls.	Dolls.	Dolls.	Dolls.	Dolls.	Dolls.	Dolls.	Dolls.	Dolls.	Dolls.
1919	6.25	4.29	4.37	3.43	3.39	2.79	2.57	2.63	3.09	4.23	4.49	5.49	7.58	7.19
1920		9.03	6.93	5.54	2.56	1.83	1.93	1.96	1.82	1.80	1.31	1.51	1.28	1.22
1921	4.41	4.18	1.90	2.23	2.90	2.11	2.09	1.92	2.07	2.33	2.18	2.03	1.79	1.58
1922	4.07	3.27	3.03	1.81	1.04	.95	.96	1.22	1.36	1.39	1.44	1.87	2.09	1.76
1923	7.24	4.13	3.08	3.08	2.57	1.49	1.85	1.67	1.59	1.96	2.01	1.96	2.12	1.73
1924	5.92	4.12	2.34	1.48	1.41	1.37	1.33	1.22	1.26	1.46	1.56	1.21	1.20	1.36
1925	4.03	3.34	2.83	3.18	2.83	2.43	3.23	4.09	4.20	4.61	4.57	4.67	5.64	4.10
1926	8.84	6.29	3.78	2.29	2.38	2.57	2.89	2.99	2.92	2.80	2.48	2.45	2.46	3.64
1927	4.15	4.50	4.03	2.07	1.83	2.11	2.26	2.26	2.17	2.25	2.64	2.95	2.68	1.94
1928	6.32	2.89	1.54	1.02	1.24	1.34	1.37	1.32	1.41					
Chicago:														
1919	6.40	5.32	4.33	4.18	[2]3.99	[2]2.73	[2]2.40	[2]2.90	3.83	5.54	4.80	[2]6.00	[2]6.98	[2]7.40
1920		9.14	8.38	[2]6.44	[2]3.42	[2]2.40	[2]1.85	[2]2.13	[2]1.58	[2]1.29	[2]1.15	[2]1.25	[2].98	[2].87
1921	4.83	4.50	[2]2.42	[2]2.33	[2]3.11	[2]2.65	[2]2.00	[2]1.75	[2]1.83	[2]1.98	[2]1.96	[2]1.80	[2]1.69	[2]1.70
1922	4.16	3.57	[2]3.03	[2]2.29	[2]1.63	[2]1.17	[2]1.00	[2]1.05	[2].96	[2]1.02	[2]1.07	[2]1.35	[2]1.53	[2]1.13
1923		4.80	[2]3.15	[2]2.76	[2]2.18	[2]1.70	[2]1.14	[2]1.24	[2]1.27	[2]1.58	[2]1.71	[2]1.75	[2]1.79	[2]1.50
1924	5.68	4.69	2.65	[2]1.76	[2]1.40	[2]1.32	[2].97	[2]1.31	[2]1.36	[2]1.47	[2]1.63	[2]1.44	[2].84	[2]1.18
1925	4.75	3.90	[2]2.96	[2]3.28	[2]2.68	[2]2.00	[2]2.67	[2]3.47	[2]3.64	[2]4.08	[2]3.81	[2]4.04	[2]4.62	[2]3.23
1926	8.59	6.57	[2]3.91	[2]2.35	[2]2.22	[2]2.45	[2]2.49	[2]2.65	[2]2.47	[2]2.55	[2]2.37	[2]2.42	[2]2.68	[2]3.51
1927	4.52	[2]4.48	[2]4.65	[2]2.30	[2]2.02	[2]1.82	[2]1.60	[2]1.60	[2]1.55	[2]1.63	[2]1.84	[2]2.36	[2]1.88	[2]1.43
1928	5.95	[2]2.94	[2]1.74	[2]1.15	[2]1.06	[2]1.04	[2]1.16	[2]1.24	[2]1.24					
Boston:														
1919		5.00	4.64	4.19	3.76	2.54	2.26	2.67	3.06	4.12	4.39	5.23	6.25	7.08
1920		9.18	7.97	6.13	3.02	2.17	2.20	2.36	1.95	1.78	1.39	1.41	1.16	.94
1921	4.82	4.76	2.36	2.63	3.29	2.22	1.87	1.90	1.88	2.31	2.03	1.80	1.51	1.36
1922	4.80	3.86	3.54	2.33	1.48	1.20	1.20	1.38	1.31	1.44	1.47	1.76	2.18	1.98
1923		5.14	3.57	3.64	3.21	2.04	1.72	1.66	1.61	1.93	1.93	1.86	1.93	1.92
1924	6.03	5.37	2.72	1.90	1.59	1.41	1.12	1.09	1.12	1.28	1.47	1.12	.99	1.17
1925	4.46	3.81	3.21	3.68	3.60	2.01	3.04	4.12	4.17	4.66	4.46	4.62	5.79	4.13
1926	7.73	6.51	4.24	2.47	2.87	2.21	2.66	2.95	2.82	2.77	2.48	2.42	2.37	3.44
1927	4.43	4.80	4.53	2.28	2.11	2.46	1.94	2.03	1.93	2.02	2.36	2.83	2.49	1.80
1928		3.28	1.84	1.19	1.40	1.26	1.15	1.15	1.15					

Bureau of Agricultural Economics. Compiled from daily market reports from bureau representatives in the various markets. Average prices as shown are based on stock of U. S. No. 1 grade; they are simple averages of daily range of selling prices. In some cases conversions were made from larger to smaller units or vice versa, in order to obtain comparability.

[1] Crop movement season extends from April of one year through May of the following year, with irregular quotations continuing through June and July.
[2] Car-lot sales.

TABLE 213.—*Potatoes, Maine and New York State: Average l. c. l. price per bushel to jobbers at New York, 1909–1928*

Season beginning September	September	October	November	December	January	February	March	April	May
Average:	Cents	Cents	Cents	Cents	Cents	Cents	Cents	Cents	Cents
1909–1913	67	64	66	68	73	73	73	78	77
1914–1920		118	124	128	147	152	155	175	170
1921–1925	118	111	122	126	140	141	141	153	127
1909	65	56	56	56	58	54	49	40	39
1910	55	55	51	49	52	49	47	62	57
1911	81	79	90	95	112	114	128	138	125
1912	60	59	64	68	63	67	62	66	77
1913	74	69	71	70	80	83	81	85	85
1914	62	56	54	51	51	48	47	50	46
1915		78	76	90	122	121	123	114	112
1916	118	125	169	161	198	267	267	300	318
1917	120	162	137	139	166	147	114	111	82
1918	158	144	137	150	142	126	111	143	149
1919	151	137	157	179	231	264	333	428	417
1920		125	138	127	116	88	88	78	66
1921	137	116	125	123	143	135	125	112	90
1922	86	78	82	86	93	96	121	125	110
1923	146	113	106	105	120	120	117	119	117
1924	91	72	70	73	82	94	73	71	76
1925	128	176	228	242	261	262	268	338	241
1926	140	162	171	170	161	146	142	143	216
1927	111	120	121	118	124	139	166	148	114
1928	78	69	68	72					

Bureau of Agricultural Economics. Compiled from Friday or Saturday issues, New York Producers' Price Current, average of weekly range.

In earlier years New York "State" quotations were included in the general term "State and Western." Earlier data are available in 1925 Yearbook, p. 928, Table 276.

TABLE 214.—*Spinach for consumption, fresh, commercial crop: Acreage, production, price per bushel, by States, 1925–1928*

State	Acreage				Production				Price per bushel [1]			
	1924–25	1925–26	1926–27	1927–28	1924–25	1925–26	1926–27	1927–28	1924–25	1925–26	1926–27	1927–28
	Acres	*Acres*	*Acres*	*Acres*	*1,000 bushels*	*1,000 bushels*	*1,000 bushels*	*1,000 bushels*	*Dollars*	*Dollars*	*Dollars*	*Dollars*
Arkansas			450	960			68	182			0.70	0.80
California	1,810	2,290	1,900	1,000	905	1,832	1,520	753	0.29	0.27	.30	.52
Idaho		80				29					.50	
Louisiana	2,470	5,100	6,430	6,890	679	1,392	1,061	737	.42	.65	.34	.48
Maryland	2,300	2,130	2,130	2,130	1,150	479	1,108	852	.34	.63	.35	.31
Missouri	1,000	1,200	1,200	1,320	360	432	432	482	.53	.60	.68	.70
New Jersey	1,800	2,600	2,600	2,720	783	806	715	884	.87	.60	.78	.74
North Carolina			320	310			80	62			.67	.96
South Carolina	1,000	2,000	900	600	480	632	164	180	1.05	.72	.85	.99
Texas	14,440	16,820	19,450	25,000	4,751	5,130	6,457	5,000	.63	.48	.50	.45
Virginia	8,500	8,050	7,860	8,200	3,060	1,731	2,468	2,157	.67	.73	.61	.84
Washington			250	300			100	90			.30	.41
Total	33,320	40,270	43,490	49,430	12,168	12,463	14,173	11,379	.60	.53	.50	.57

Bureau of Agricultural Economics. Estimates based upon returns from crop reporters.

[1] Average for season year beginning October.

TABLE 215.—*Spinach for canning, commercial crop: Acreage, production, and price per ton, by States, 1925–1928*

State	Average				Production				Price per ton			
	1925	1926	1927	1928	1925	1926	1927	1928	1925	1926	1927	1928
	Acres	*Acres*	*Acres*	*Acres*	*Tons*	*Tons*	*Tons*	*Tons*	*Dolls.*	*Dolls.*	*Dolls.*	*Dolls.*
California	9,690	9,590	10,300	12,340	29,100	46,000	51,500	65,400	17.64	16.15	14.50	15.50
Maryland	1,500	1,720	1,420	1,500	4,500	3,600	4,500	4,500	37.50	30.62	32.80	34.38
Total or average	11,190	11,310	11,720	13,840	33,600	49,600	56,000	69,900	20.30	17.20	15.98	16.72

Bureau of Agricultural Economics. Estimates based upon returns from crop reporters.

TABLE 216.—*Spinach: Car-lot shipments, by State of origin, 1920–1928*

State	Crop-movement season [1]								
	1920	1921	1922	1923	1924	1925	1926	1927	1928 [2]
	Cars	*Cars*	*Cars*	*Cars*	*Cars*	*Cars*	*Cars*	*Cars*	*Cars*
Missouri	5	132	53	46	103	113	100	33	100
Maryland	292	393	[3] 603	[4] 798	725	619	846	670	749
Virginia	1,372	2,475	2,212	3,208	3,107	2,946	2,669	3,213	3,058
South Carolina			161	422	161	501	614	462	282
Texas	861	1,463	1,455	2,433	3,038	3,235	4,513	4,495	5,528
California	326	149	302	473	70	241	305	445	334
Washington	4	19	13	23	40	[5] 123	121	145	153
Other States	31	116	115	[6] 177	263	141	215	192	369
Total	2,891	4,747	[3] 4,914	[7] 7,580	7,507	[5] 7,919	9,383	9,655	10,573

Bureau of Agricultural Economics. Compiled from daily and monthly reports received by the bureau from officials and local agents of common carriers throughout the country. Shipments as shown in car lots include those by boat reduced to car-lot basis.

[1] Crop-movement season extends from October of one year through December of the following year.
[2] Preliminary.
[3] Includes 5 cars in January, 1923.

[4] Includes 4 cars in January, 1924.
[5] Includes 4 cars in January, 1926.
[6] Includes 1 car in January, 1924.
[7] Includes 5 cars in January, 1924.

TABLE 217.—*Sweet potatoes: Acreage, production, and value, United States, 1909–1928*

Year	Acreage	Average yield per acre	Production	Price per bushel received by producers Dec. 1	Farm value Dec. 1	Year	Acreage	Average yield per acre	Production	Price per bushel received by producers Dec. 1	Farm value Dec. 1
	1,000 acres	*Bushels*	*1,000 bushels*	Cents	*1,000 dollars*		*1,000 acres*	*Bushels*	*1,000 bushels*	Cents	*1,000 dollars*
1909	*641*	*92.4*	*59,232*			1919	941	103.2	97,126	134.4	130,514
1909	641	90.1	57,764	68.5	39,585	1920	992	104.8	103,925	113.4	117,834
1910	641	93.5	59,938	67.1	40,216	1921	1,066	92.5	98,654	88.1	86,894
1911	605	90.1	54,538	75.5	41,202	1922	1,117	97.9	109,394	77.1	84,295
1912	583	95.2	55,479	72.6	40,264	1923	993	97.9	97.177	97.9	95,091
1913	625	94.5	59,057	72.6	42,884	1924	*467*	*80.2*	*37,444*		
1914	603	93.8	56,574	73.0	41,294	1924	688	78.4	53,912	128.8	69,444
1915	731	103.5	75,639	62.1	46,980	1925	779	80.0	62,319	136.4	85,034
1916	774	91.7	70,955	84.8	60,141	1926	819	101.0	82,703	95.5	78,956
1917	919	91.2	83,822	110.8	92,916	1927	933	100.9	94,112	82.5	77,615
1918	940	93.5	87,924	135.2	118,863	1928 [1]	810	95.9	77,661	93.6	72,680
1919	*804*	*97.2*	*78,092*								

Bureau of Agricultural Economics. Acreage, yield, and production figures are estimates of the crop-reporting board; italic figures are census returns. Prices are based upon returns from special price reporters.

[1] Preliminary.

TABLE 218.—*Sweet potatoes: Acreage and production, by States, average 1921–1925, annual 1926–1928*

State	Acreage				Production			
	Average, 1921–1925	1926	1927	1928 [1]	Average, 1921–1925	1926	1927	1928 [1]
	1,000 acres	*1,000 acres*	*1,000 acres*	*1,000 acres*	*1,000 bushels*	*1,000 bushels*	*1,000 bushels*	*1,000 bushels*
New Jersey	17	17	15	15	2,308	2,465	1,890	2,175
Pennsylvania	2				204			
Ohio	3	3	3	3	329	315	399	360
Indiana	3	3	2	2	314	330	224	232
Illinois	9	13	10	10	929	1,430	1,030	980
Iowa	3	3	3	3	294	309	270	369
Missouri	12	10	12	11	1,218	1,120	1,344	1,155
Kansas	3	4	3	2	385	516	408	260
Delaware	9	9	8	7	1,083	1,251	880	980
Maryland	9	11	11	10	1,176	1,815	1,584	1,500
Virginia	41	43	43	44	4,773	5,375	5,805	6,336
West Virginia	3	3	2	2	349	330	220	204
North Carolina	94	84	89	80	9,526	7,560	10,146	7,840
South Carolina	77	47	53	49	6,566	3,760	5,300	4,214
Georgia	129	110	132	119	9,741	9,460	10,560	10,234
Florida	30	28	29	28	2,589	2,800	2,668	2,464
Kentucky	17	17	16	14	1,634	2,040	1,488	1,246
Tennessee	38	50	48	41	3,704	6,150	4,704	3,895
Alabama	103	65	78	70	9,264	6,500	7,644	6,510
Mississippi	86	55	69	55	7,681	5,720	7,728	6,050
Arkansas	41	34	38	28	3,695	3,672	4,408	2,520
Louisiana	77	79	99	74	6,374	7,110	9,702	6,660
Oklahoma	24	24	23	20	2,169	2,520	2,438	1,780
Texas	89	92	133	109	6,783	8,556	11,970	8,284
New Mexico	1	1	1	1	125	135	102	119
Arizona	2	2	1	1	255	300	120	142
California	7	12	12	12	820	1,164	1,080	1,152
United States	929	819	933	810	84,291	82,703	94,112	77,661

Bureau of Agricultural Economics. Estimates of the crop-reporting board.

[1] Preliminary.

TABLE 219.—*Sweet potatoes: Yield per acre and estimated price per bushel, December 1, by States, average 1914–1920, 1921–1925, annual 1924–1928*

State	Yield per acre							Estimated price per bushel						
	Av., 1914–1920	Av., 1921–1925	1924	1925	1926	1927	1928	Av., 1914–1920	Av., 1921–1925	1924	1925	1926	1927	1928
	Bush.	Bush.	Bush.	Bush.	Bush.	Bush.	Bush.	Cents	Cents	Cents	Cents	Cents	Cents	Cents
New Jersey	123	133	140	117	145	126	145	144	156	155	240	120	120	120
Pennsylvania	117	125	117	115	----	----	----	137	158	150	210	----	----	----
Ohio	100	110	95	115	105	133	120	155	167	163	210	150	140	135
Indiana	106	120	115	108	110	112	116	152	145	142	190	145	135	130
Illinois	94	102	108	88	110	103	98	134	127	139	190	135	115	110
Iowa	91	88	80	109	103	90	123	192	177	190	230	200	150	155
Missouri	96	100	100	95	112	112	105	142	121	125	165	130	120	105
Kansas	104	113	113	116	129	136	130	155	130	135	170	135	110	110
Delaware	125	122	130	110	139	110	140	95	118	126	190	65	70	80
Maryland	128	130	140	129	165	144	150	104	120	127	170	75	70	80
Virginia	118	116	120	108	125	135	144	105	111	110	130	100	85	95
West Virginia	117	116	110	92	110	110	102	146	162	141	200	160	140	140
North Carolina	103	100	92	88	90	114	98	98	100	104	120	100	80	85
South Carolina	94	81	68	55	80	100	86	104	100	104	147	100	80	85
Georgia	89	74	70	47	86	80	86	93	85	100	125	80	75	85
Florida	105	87	84	85	100	92	88	105	115	130	140	125	85	115
Kentucky	100	96	80	90	120	93	89	122	125	128	153	108	120	115
Tennessee	102	98	95	90	123	98	95	99	111	140	140	70	85	95
Alabama	91	86	73	70	100	98	93	88	96	125	125	85	85	90
Mississippi	94	86	51	96	104	112	110	86	101	173	100	95	80	90
Arkansas	103	89	81	85	108	116	90	97	103	127	125	95	80	90
Louisiana	88	81	50	80	90	98	90	89	99	158	115	90	70	85
Oklahoma	96	89	87	94	105	106	89	141	124	150	135	100	80	95
Texas	91	75	57	73	93	90	76	120	117	158	142	95	75	100
New Mexico	130	125	120	140	135	102	119	188	216	255	165	100	130	145
Arizona	153	140	125	130	150	120	142	204	203	238	210	155	200	200
California	150	110	94	112	97	90	96	129	149	218	170	110	115	110
United States	97.4	89.3	78.4	80.0	101.0	100.9	95.9	102.0	105.7	128.8	136.4	95.5	82.5	93.6

Bureau of Agricultural Economics. Yield figures are estimates of the crop-reporting board. Prices are based upon returns from special price reporters.

TABLE 220.—*Sweet potatoes: Car-lot shipments by State of origin, 1920–1927*

State	Crop-movement season [1]							
	1920	1921	1922	1923	1924	1925	1926	1927 [2]
	Cars	Cars	Cars	Cars	Cars	Cars	Cars	Cars
New Jersey [3]	2,392	2,196	2,858	1,528	1,894	1,355	1,770	1,225
Delaware	1,877	1,722	2,632	1,549	1,750	1,742	1,885	1,517
Maryland	1,363	1,286	1,750	1,123	1,155	1,520	2,283	2,256
Virginia	4,839	5,300	6,633	5,374	5,213	4,750	6,501	6,616
North Carolina [3]	823	1,022	679	563	816	1,510	1,683	1,692
South Carolina	56	135	235	155	120	231	162	276
Georgia [3]	1,030	1,400	781	610	1,018	674	678	667
Florida	95	110	[4] 128	59	175	241	185	159
Tennessee [3]	924	1,578	1,495	726	1,137	2,592	4,972	3,587
Alabama	579	591	537	382	649	663	515	574
Mississippi	93	181	116	61	36	156	79	211
Arkansas [3]	568	584	240	263	371	476	548	392
Louisiana [3]	772	893	1,033	463	558	2,342	1,285	1,147
Oklahoma	91	147	85	110	107	216	268	294
Texas	632	759	974	535	221	485	702	1,284
California	856	1,000	982	684	466	1,161	1,186	805
Other States [3]	216	479	408	345	381	745	1,053	700
Total [3]	17,206	19,383	[4] 21,566	14,530	16,067	20,859	25,755	23,402

Bureau of Agricultural Economics. Compiled from daily and monthly reports received by the bureau from officials and local agents of common carriers throughout the country. Shipments as shown in car lots include those by boat reduced to car-lot basis.

[1] Crop movement season extends from July 1 of one year through June of the following year.
[2] Preliminary.
[3] Figures for certain States include shipments in July of succeeding crop year as follows: New Jersey—1920, 15 cars; 1922, 4 cars. Arkansas—1921, 1 car; 1926, 1 car. Kentucky—1921, 1 car; 1926, 12 cars. New Mexico—1921, 5 cars. Tennessee—1921, 17 cars; 1924, 3 cars; 1925, 11 cars; 1926, 309 cars; 1927, 6 cars; North Carolina—1926, 3 cars; 1927, 10 cars; Georgia—1927, 2 cars; Indiana—1926, 1 car. Louisiana—1926, 1 car; and for August, Tennessee—19 cars in 1926.
[4] Florida includes 2 cars in June, 1922.

TABLE 221.—*Sweet potatoes: Estimated price per bushel received by producers, United States, 1910–1928*

Year beginning July	July 15	Aug. 15	Sept. 15	Oct. 15	Nov. 15	Dec. 15	Jan. 15	Feb. 15	Mar. 14	Apr. 15	May 15	June 15	Weighted av.
	Cents	Cents	Cents	Cents	Cents	Cents	Cents	Cents	Cents	Cents	Cents	Cents	Cents
Average:													
1910–1913	95.0	97.9	89.0	79.8	72.8	75.7	83.0	87.0	92.0	99.6	102.0	97.1	85.1
1914–1920	128.9	139.8	129.6	111.7	101.4	102.4	112.1	118.0	128.2	138.8	139.8	137.3	118.8
1921–1925	141.6	156.1	138.4	124.7	109.2	113.1	120.4	130.0	139.1	147.4	149.1	147.2	129.7
1910	73.5	82.9	79.5	75.7	67.8	70.9	79.1	81.6	87.3	95.0	103.6	93.8	78.7
1911	104.1	107.4	97.9	85.6	76.2	79.0	86.9	93.5	102.4	117.4	118.6	111.4	92.2
1912	113.0	102.5	88.9	79.9	73.7	77.2	83.7	87.0	90.8	94.3	93.2	90.8	85.6
1913	89.4	98.8	89.8	78.0	73.4	75.8	82.5	86.1	87.3	91.9	92.7	92.5	84.0
1914	94.5	98.4	90.1	79.3	72.3	74.9	81.0	85.0	90.8	100.8	98.1	97.6	84.6
1915	93.1	97.2	80.0	69.7	62.9	65.0	72.7	76.4	80.1	81.0	78.9	83.9	75.4
1916	87.5	99.0	88.1	80.3	80.3	86.4	92.9	100.0	115.5	126.0	132.6	135.8	92.9
1917	124.4	126.3	120.3	110.5	105.6	110.8	123.1	129.8	149.2	158.1	158.2	134.0	122.3
1918	142.1	151.6	164.3	152.4	137.4	131.8	137.8	149.2	157.2	176.2	174.4	162.7	150.0
1919	159.7	195.4	174.6	150.9	135.1	135.6	151.1	163.6	179.2	193.9	199.7	205.2	161.7
1920	200.7	210.8	190.0	138.7	116.5	112.3	126.3	122.1	125.5	135.7	136.8	141.9	144.8
1921	151.2	154.2	118.2	104.0	91.5	95.3	102.3	106.9	114.3	116.0	117.1	120.7	110.9
1922	125.3	127.5	106.0	90.4	79.0	84.8	92.5	96.9	100.1	103.8	107.9	107.4	97.4
1923	112.1	151.3	133.6	114.8	101.0	103.8	112.5	123.7	129.0	140.4	139.2	138.9	121.7
1924	130.7	151.4	157.0	145.1	130.3	140.1	145.5	160.2	180.8	196.2	189.1	170.2	152.4
1925	188.7	196.3	177.4	169.4	144.4	141.5	149.3	162.4	171.4	180.4	192.2	198.8	165.9
1926	185.6	189.0	153.9	110.6	88.5	94.0	97.8	109.0	112.3	112.8	118.9	136.0	120.3
1927	136.4	146.7	121.9	98.1	86.5	91.9	93.4	98.6	109.6	115.1	121.4	124.7	106.5
1928	119.5	131.0	120.9	111.2	100.2	101.8							

Bureau of Agricultural Economics.   Based upon returns from special price reporters.

TABLE 222.—*Sweet potatoes: Average l. c. l. price per bushel to jobbers at three markets, 1927–1928*

Market, and season beginning August	August [1]	September [1]	October	November	December	January	February	March	April [2]	May [2]
	Dollars	Dollars	Dollars	Dollars	Dollars	Dollars	Dollars	Dollars	Dollars	Dollars
New York:										
1927	1.31	1.13	.93	1.29	1.48	1.66	1.88	2.08	2.04	
1928	1.57	1.29	1.05	1.31	1.62					
Chicago:										
1927	1.54	1.55	1.39	1.44	[3] 1.68	[3] 2.16	[3] 2.51	[3] 2.09	[3] 2.22	
1928	2.01	1.69	1.46	1.92	[3] 2.30					
St. Louis:										
1927	1.06	.88	.87	1.21	1.18	1.27	1.42	1.70	1.68	
1928		1.07	1.50	1.57	1.66					

Bureau of Agricultural Economics.   Compiled from daily market reports from bureau representatives in the various markets.

Average prices as shown are based on stock of good merchantable quality and condition; they are simple averages of daily range of selling prices.   In some cases conversions have been made from larger to smaller units or vice versa, in order to obtain comparability.

[1] Commodity reports began Aug. 23, 1920 and 1921; Sept. 1, 1922; Sept. 18, 1923; Sept. 2, 1924; Aug. 25, 1925; Aug. 16, 1926; Aug. 19, 1927; Aug. 22, 1928.

[2] Last commodity report of season May 26, 1921 and 1922; May 4, 1923; Apr. 15, 1924; Apr. 3, 1925; Apr. 16, 1926; Apr. 19, 1927; Apr. 13, 1928.   Subsequent prices for 1927, taken from miscellaneous reports.

[3] Includes kiln-dried.

TABLE 223.—*Tomatoes for consumption fresh, commercial crop: Acreage production, and price per bushel, by States, 1925–1928*

State	Acreage				Production				Price per bushel [1]			
	1925	1926	1927	1928	1925	1926	1927	1928	1925	1926	1927	1928
Early:	*Acres*	*Acres*	*Acres*	*Acres*	*1,000 bush.*	*1,000 bush.*	*1,000 bush.*	*1,000 bush.*	*Dolls.*	*Dolls.*	*Dolls.*	*Dolls.*
California(Imperial)	860	1,000	1,300	1,200	64	113	95	122	3.04	3.05	2.00	2.06
Florida	33,470	20,700	29,800	29,250	2,811	1,946	3,606	3,071	3.15	4.35	2.02	3.56
Georgia	1,040	1,850	2,090	2,090	74	111	163	142	2.55	2.50	1.36	1.76
Louisiana	1,020	1,690	1,980	1,690	102	128	178	166	2.99	1.81	1.00	1.27
Mississippi	11,100	14,200	15,360	16,800	1,310	1,406	1,997	1,344	3.25	3.28	2.40	1.75
South Carolina	2,650	3,450	2,000	2,600	217	386	160	322	2.40	3.33	1.51	1.87
Texas [2]	10,780	13,930	16,880	18,190	884	1,337	1,604	1,874	2.74	2.86	1.76	2.00
Total	60,920	56,820	69,410	71,820	5,462	5,427	7,803	7,041	3.07	3.51	2.02	2.61
Intermediate:												
Arkansas	480	1,180	2,730	3,280	43	132	303	341	3.26	1.26	2.24	.94
Illinois (Union Co.)	2,000	1,300	940	1,010	168	65	150	91	1.74	1.18	2.04	1.31
New Jersey	14,000	12,000	11,400	11,500	3,500	2,520	2,508	2,012	.85	.95	1.10	1.18
Ohio (Wash. Co.)	810	920	920	970	188	166	222	174	3.54	1.69	1.35	1.75
Tennessee	5,000	8,000	6,600	9,000	635	936	825	1,098	2.88	1.99	2.76	1.17
Total	22,290	23,400	22,590	25,760	4,534	3,819	4,008	3,716	1.30	1.25	1.58	1.18
Late:												
California (except Imperial)	11,300	12,090	21,550	20,650	2,418	2,007	1,789	1,755	1.69	1.19	1.16	1.32
Colorado	580	410	800	600	176	110	160	144	1.20	.76	.85	.31
Delaware	390	200	180	160	74	20	36	14	.65	1.00	.75	.42
Illinois (except Union Co.)	3,280	2,260	2,750	2,750	797	396	432	336	2.46	.99	1.51	.69
Indiana	7,480	4,350	4,780	4,970	1,414	592	650	537	1.89	.67	.60	.44
Iowa	410	570	450	190	59	67	72	24	1.20	.50	.51	.45
Kentucky	4,090	1,040	1,630	1,710	585	115	186	130	1.37	1.39	1.18	.42
Maryland	3,180	3,220	7,050	6,700	566	206	1,107	643	.89	.91	.80	.84
Michigan	860	290	290	290	184	51	57	61	1.35	1.33	.91	1.10
Missouri	6,910	1,080	4,480	4,480	864	89	318	291	1.38	.86	.61	.71
New York	2,380	1,740	2,640	2,640	595	311	631	560	1.25	.85	.56	1.69
Ohio (except Wash. Co.)	2,850	890	1,110	840	712	152	179	176	1.26	1.16	.78	.69
Pennsylvania	2,570	370	420	450	550	40	75	58	.81	.59	.60	.92
Utah	400	700	500	600	140	105	100	138	1.20	.75	.78	.56
Virginia	3,930	1,500	1,200	1,360	491	188	150	196	.71	.63	2.25	1.93
Total	50,619	30,710	49,830	48,390	9,625	4,449	5,942	5,063	1.50	1.00	.95	.93
Grand total	133,820	110,930	141,830	145,970	19,621	13,695	17,753	15,820	1.89	2.07	1.56	1.74

Bureau of Agricultural Economics. Estimates based upon returns from crop reporters.

[1] Average for season. [2] Includes fall crop of previous year.

TABLE 224.—*Tomatoes for manufacture, commercial crop: Acreage, production, and price per ton, by States, 1925–1928*

State	Acreage				Production				Price per ton			
	1925	1926	1927	1928	1925	1926	1927	1928	1925	1926	1927	1928
	Acres	*Acres*	*Acres*	*Acres*	*Tons*	*Tons*	*Tons*	*Tons*	*Doll.*	*Doll.*	*Doll.*	*Doll.*
Arkansas	20,340	11,630	17,820	19,600	61,000	29,100	53,500	43,100	13.65	11.86	12.76	12.39
California	30,000	32,250	28,760	25,790	180,000	206,400	178,300	201,200	16.29	15.61	15.00	14.56
Colorado	3,040	2,350	2,000	1,600	25,800	17,600	14,000	11,800	11.50	12.00	12.00	11.00
Delaware	20,000	11,700	15,000	13,500	106,000	23,400	76,500	32,400	16.27	20.00	14.00	15.22
Illinois	7,650	5,270	5,110	5,130	29,100	21,100	22,500	17,400	12.33	13.44	13.98	12.46
Indiana	67,340	49,990	42,990	49,870	303,000	175,000	163,400	149,600	12.79	12.60	13.06	12.82
Iowa	3,660	3,850	4,080	4,810	13,500	12,700	18,400	16,800	14.55	12.88	14.29	12.90
Kentucky	9,550	6,950	6,530	8,030	38,200	20,800	20,900	16,900	13.46	12.25	13.08	12.25
Maryland	49,800	37,000	34,410	22,710	249,000	88,800	151,400	63,600	15.97	13.90	14.28	14.54
Michigan	2,000	1,800	1,800	1,660	13,600	9,000	9,900	9,600	11.91	11.80	12.13	11.00
Missouri	39,150	25,620	19,440	18,700	137,000	64,000	38,900	33,700	13.52	11.85	12.87	12.75
New Jersey	32,000	32,000	30,000	33,000	224,000	153,600	156,000	118,800	17.00	20.40	18.00	18.50
New York	13,550	9,850	10,540	11,170	92,100	49,200	70,600	65,900	16.31	15.30	14.92	14.73
Ohio	8,560	8,000	10,000	10,400	51,400	38,400	45,000	60,300	13.09	11.20	12.45	11.31
Pennsylvania	4,780	3,370	3,740	3,600	25,800	10,100	18,700	13,000	16.00	13.40	14.24	14.24
Tennessee	11,820	8,200	8,450	10,220	23,600	24,600	24,500	18,400	15.39	13.42	13.75	13.53
Utah	6,860	2,630	5,200	4,950	123,500	18,400	48,400	57,400	11.98	10.00	11.00	11.00
Virginia	15,730	6,000	6,420	6,000	55,100	21,000	25,700	14,400	16.19	12.73	13.75	13.28
Other States	4,100	3,040	3,310	4,070	20,500	9,100	7,600	14,200	15.24	13.60	14.43	13.18
Total or average	349,930	261,500	255,600	254,810	1,772,200	992,300	1,144,200	958,500	14.77	14.72	14.32	13.93

Bureau of Agricultural Economics. Estimates based upon returns from crop reporters.

TABLE 225.—*Tomatoes: Car-lot shipments by State of origin, 1920–1928*

State	1920	1921	1922	1923	1924	1925	1926	1927	1928 [1]
	Cars	Cars	Cars	Cars	Cars	Cars	Cars	Cars	Cars
New York	1,945	1,073	1,902	1,261	954	1,024	656	951	1,109
New Jersey	2,798	2,121	1,930	1,648	2,150	1,907	2,006	1,329	677
Ohio	450	411	558	956	1,035	1,286	1,065	1,125	926
Indiana	1,265	552	1,332	1,185	1,479	1,889	1,514	1,132	799
Illinois	450	155	229	250	230	539	422	270	232
Maryland	194	110	242	271	66	313	259	586	613
Virginia	188	91	83	43	167	379	454	360	277
South Carolina		59	145	431	421	568	449	187	161
Georgia	1	4	23	18	176	85	169	82	73
Florida [2]	4,192	5,785	10,245	9,760	9,140	7,188	4,351	9,737	8,491
Kentucky	468	341	153	121	546	498	300	203	42
Arkansas	11	23	47	9	38	104	281	240	388
Tennessee	805	370	920	501	985	1,393	2,374	2,016	2,759
Mississippi	1,393	1,945	3,441	2,144	3,776	3,149	3,492	4,849	3,230
Texas [3]	1,393	2,025	1,893	1,084	1,694	2,398	2,890	3,393	4,440
Utah	261	100	378	369	380	1,457	272	883	900
California [3]	2,004	1,819	2,349	3,293	2,789	2,961	4,443	4,620	4,423
Other States	576	431	847	620	804	1,116	674	701	796
Total [2][3]	18,394	17,415	26,717	23,964	26,830	28,254	26,071	32,664	30,336

Bureau of Agricultural Economics. Compiled from daily and monthly reports received by the bureau from officials and local agents of common carriers throughout the country. Shipments as shown in car lots include those by boat reduced to car-lot basis.

[1] Preliminary.

[2] Figures for Florida include cars moved in preceding calendar year as follows: 1920, 14 cars in November, 34 cars in December; 1922, 10 cars in December; 1923, 26 cars in December; 1924, 2 cars in November, 55 cars in December; 1925, 14 cars in November, 31 cars in December; 1926, 7 cars in November, 13 cars in December; 1927, 1 car in December; 1928, 28 cars in November, 291 cars in December.

[3] Figures include cars in following calendar year as follows: California, 1922, 3 cars in January; 1924, 1 car in January; 1925, 1 car in January; 1926, 3 cars in February. Texas, 1922, 5 cars in January, and 2 cars in February; 1925, 8 cars in January; 1926, 15 cars in January; 1927, 1 car in January; 1928, 2 cars in January.

TABLE 226.—*Tomatoes: United States imports and exports, annual, 1923–1928*

	Imports				Exports	
Year ended June 30	Fresh	Canned	Other-wise prepared	Paste	Canned	Catsup and sauces
	1,000 pounds	1,000 pounds	1,000 pounds	1,000 pounds	1,000 pounds	1,000 pounds
1923			[1] 20,166		8,917	
1924	[2] 50,838	30,946	[2] 1,341	[2] 4,164	9,152	[2] 3,560
1925	69,216	73,902	9,443	17,382	5,203	5,520
1926	82,448	84,897	([3])	18,179	5,794	5,006
1927	124,489	80,257		15,642	7,504	7,556
1928	115,336	107,750		12,064	6,725	8,584

Bureau of Agricultural Economics. Compiled from Monthly Summary of Foreign Commerce of the United States, June issues.

[1] Beginning Sept. 22, 1922.
[2] 6 months, January–June, 1924.
[3] From 1926 on included with "tomatoes, canned."

TABLE 227.—*Tomatoes, canned: Pack* [1] *in the United States, 1917-1928*

State	1917	1918	1919	1920	1921	1922	1923	1924	1925	1926	1927	1928
	1,000 cases	1,000 cases	1,000 cases	1,000 cases	1,000 cases	1,000 cases	1,000 cases	1,000 cases	1,000 cases	1,000 cases	1,000 cases	1,000 cases
New York	553	396	437	515	214	340	266	325	389	302	300	261
New Jersey	380	667	60	517	116	337	412	186	418	204	254	95
Pennsylvania	[2] 488	[2] 441	[2] 384	[2] 680	[2] 186	[2] 644	258	150	338	118	167	95
Ohio	107	357	172	142	71	179	174	133	179	120	189	124
Indiana	398	968	876	778	530	1,312	717	1,050	1,955	900	1,131	613
Missouri	704	353	439	715	136	775	839	871	1,836	895	605	396
Delaware	1,381	879	189	553	176	590	1,216	803	1,272	228	827	325
Maryland	5,934	6,649	2,529	3,347	1,656	3,205	5,722	3,825	6,175	1,901	3,671	1,720
Virginia [3]	1,170	1,547	953	1,162	217	891	963	1,116	1,138	572	1,059	466
Kentucky [2]							59	136	275	223	253	111
Tennessee [2]							176	386	382	280	368	160
Arkansas [4]							270	768	1,168	558	678	613
Colorado [5]	213	306	290	218	62	168	182	180	309	183	127	158
Utah	513	953	594	444	132	664	584	417	1,353	235	792	924
California	2,603	1,790	3,052	1,773	339	1,701	2,397	1,767	1,839	2,347	2,257	1,991
Other States	632	576	835	524	182	732	437	406	744	389	459	487
United States	15,076	15,882	10,810	11,368	4,017	11,538	14,672	12,519	19,770	9,455	13,137	8,539

Bureau of Agricultural Economics. Compiled from National Canners' Association, 1917-1926; Census of Manufactures 1927-1928.

[1] Stated in cases of 24 No. 3 cans.
[2] Previous to 1923, Pennsylvania, Kentucky, and Tennessee composed one group.
[3] Includes West Virginia.
[4] Previous to 1923, included in "Other States."
[5] Includes Washington.

TABLE 228.—*Watermelons, commercial crop: Acreage, production, and price per car, by States, 1925-1928*

State	Acreage				Production				Price per car [1]			
	1925	1926	1927	1928	1925	1926	1927	1928	1925	1926	1927	1928
	Acres	Acres	Acres	Acres	Cars [2]	Cars [2]	Cars [2]	Cars [2]	Dolls.	Dolls.	Dolls.	Dolls.
Early:												
Alabama	10,030	11,030	9,820	9,330	2,618	3,254	2,946	2,332	188	93	175	151
Arizona	1,100	1,200	1,200	1,150	352	402		391	200	156	287	250
California (Imperial)	4,000	6,000	5,500	8,000	3,000	4,560	3,597	3,776	250	100	120	180
Florida	22,100	24,150	29,420	37,840	8,288	10,843	8,826	10,406	408	255	286	299
Georgia	45,890	53,600	55,220	62,950	15,878	20,958	17,946	18,885	244	121	161	141
Mississippi	810	1,240	1,300	1,400	304	217	390	392	223	89	140	150
North Carolina	4,100	4,880	5,610	5,610	1,304	1,484	2,014	2,003	198	77	149	136
South Carolina	11,010	12,720	12,470	14,340	4,668	5,215	4,240	4,302	166	88	168	94
Texas	32,020	34,900	29,660	30,250	5,636	6,980	8,156	7,562	228	222	165	186
Total	131,060	149,720	150,200	170,870	42,048	53,913	48,535	50,049	260	153	183	181
Late:												
Arkansas	1,480	2,700	2,200	2,290	432	540	594	687	226	121	186	135
California (other)	6,370	6,820	4,280	4,400	2,548	3,008	1,644	2,600	197	112	139	173
Colorado	300	300	700	600	108	105		120	168	95	242	150
Delaware	1,900	2,000	980	930	697	800	98	140	116	105	105	158
Illinois	2,820	3,200	2,880	3,170	818	816	734	824	159	86	269	162
Indiana	3,440	3,440	2,720	3,240	1,204	980	778	1,134	172	118	350	146
Iowa	1,880	1,640	1,380	1,610	658	420	442	523	165	84	218	157
Maryland	1,920	1,800	1,240	1,180	691	648	446	401	120	76	200	125
Missouri	12,200	17,500	8,000	13,680	3,575	5,688	1,800	2,873	135	114	201	154
New Jersey	2,400	2,200	1,900	2,000	2,000	1,200	462	380	205	210	250	270
Oklahoma	4,000	4,000	3,000	3,270	1,260	1,300	1,146	818	185	186	175	155
Virginia	3,100	3,100	2,320	2,320	976	781	731	784	173	141	144	165
Washington	840	640	710	890	294	234	249	320	135	118	225	202
Total	42,650	49,340	32,310	39,580	14,450	15,785	9,147	11,724	167	120	202	163
Grand total	173,710	199,060	182,510	210,450	56,498	69,698	57,682	61,773	236	146	186	177

Bureau of Agricultural Economics. Estimates based upon returns from crop reporters.

[1] Average for season. [2] Car of 1,000 melons.

TABLE 229.—*Watermelons: Car-lot shipments by State of origin, 1927–1928*

State and year	April	May	June	July	August	September	October	November	December	Total
Missouri:	*Cars*	*Cars*	*Cars*	*Cars*	*Cars*	*Cars*	*Cars*	*Cars*	*Cars*	*Cars*
1927				1	293	237	2			533
1928 [2]					739	114				853
North Carolina:										
1927				103	1,040	1				1,144
1928 [2]				126	1,117					1,243
South Carolina:										
1927			75	3,538	417		1			4,031
1928 [2]				3,011	810	1				3,822
Georgia:										
1927			4,261	10,578	1,858	64	1			16,762
1928 [2]			81	12,587	4,823	70				17,561
Florida:										
1927	4	1,452	6,183	814	32					8,485
1928 [2]		272	5,964	2,942	17					9,195
Alabama:										
1927			340	760	214	65				1,379
1928 [2]			2	510	193	64				769
Texas:										
1927		207	2,581	2,283	502	43	3			5,619
1928 [2]			2,135	3,072	1,216	25	2			6,450
California:										
1927			53	1,683	2,474	808	170	33		5,221
1928 [2]			233	2,171	2,490	490	185	23	1	5,593
Other States:										
1927			1	132	347	1,098	681	27		2,286
1928 [2]			3	57	202	1,891	675	31	2	2,861
Total:										
1920		17	5,475	18,057	11,401	2,230	49	22	63	37,314
1921	7	1,133	11,061	19,229	12,256	1,983	80			45,749
1922	8	3,566	15,291	18,003	9,061	1,616	80			47,625
1923	3	762	6,129	15,346	8,583	2,045	159	2		33,029
1924		65	6,602	26,024	10,470	2,458	120	4		[3]45,745
1925		605	11,767	17,814	11,524	2,390	82	2		44,184
1926		443	11,424	29,873	11,497	1,861	28			55,126
1927	4	1,713	15,255	20,898	6,262	1,261	67			45,460
1928 [2]		508	10,410	24,940	11,296	1,134	56	3		48,347

Bureau of Agricultural Economics. Compiled from daily and monthly reports received by the bureau from officials and local agents of common carriers throughout the country. Shipments as shown in car lots include those by boat reduced to car-lot basis. See 1927 Yearbook, p. 901, for data for earlier years.

[1] Crop movement season extends from Apr. 1 through December of a given year.
[2] Preliminary.
[3] Includes 2 cars in January.

TABLE 230.—*Watermelons, Tom Watson: Price per car to jobbers at four markets, 1924–1928* [1]

Market and season [2]	June	July	August	Market and season [2]	June	July	August
Chicago:	*Dollars*	*Dollars*	*Dollars*	Philadelphia:	*Dollars*	*Dollars*	*Dollars*
1924	576.00	249.00	291.00	1924		223.00	254.00
1925	576.00	362.00	[3]211.00	1925		315.00	[3]212.00
1926	623.00	281.00	[3]202.00	1926		219.00	204.00
1927	471.00	289.00		1927	408.00	307.00	258.00
1928	445.00	301.00	252.00	1928		316.00	210.00
New York:				St. Louis:			
1924	474.00	[4]270.00	[4]273.00	1924	[5]2.76	253.00	
1925	[4]512.00	[4]311.00	202.00	1925	[5]2.88	363.00	[3]185.00
1926	460.00	248.00	180.00	1926	[5]2.71	256.00	[3]150.00
1927	435.00	289.00	237.00	1927	[5]2.36	305.00	
1928	378.00	262.00	216.00	1928	[5]3.04	336.00	249.00

Bureau of Agricultural Economics. Compiled from daily market reports from bureau representatives in the various markets. Average prices as shown are based on stock of good merchantable quality and condition; they are simple averages of daily range of selling prices.

[1] Quotations are for Southeastern, 22–26 pound average, except in St. Louis, where larger sizes are included.
[2] Quotations began June 6, 1924; May 28, 1925; May 28, 1926; May 16, 1927; May 21, 1928. Last reported quotations of season Aug. 30, 1924; Sept. 5, 1925; Sept. 1, 1926; Aug. 26, 1927; Aug. 24, 1928.
[3] Thurmond Gray.
[4] Auction sales.
[5] Bulk per hundredweight.

TABLE 231.—*Truck crops, commercial crop: Acreage and production, United States, 1922–1928*

ACREAGE

Crop	1922	1923	1924	1925	1926	1927	1928
	Acres	Acres	Acres	Acres	Acres	Acres	Acres
Asparagus	32, 860	42, 050	50, 560	65, 530	84, 980	90, 500	94, 930
Beans, snap	49, 550	61, 280	84, 600	104, 550	98, 120	111, 090	135, 060
Cabbage	133, 830	104, 880	119, 120	119, 970	129, 330	143, 790	136, 850
Cantaloupes	103, 300	84, 160	95, 250	93, 260	101, 690	105, 780	100, 400
Carrots		9, 770	11, 480	15, 760	19, 000	26, 300	23, 610
Cauliflower	9, 250	11, 580	13, 000	15, 180	22, 520	17, 750	20, 650
Celery	17, 230	20, 660	22, 550	22, 910	21, 830	24, 550	26, 400
Corn, sweet	197, 600	252, 590	302, 790	393, 910	317, 310	215, 430	289, 180
Cucumbers	82, 200	91, 960	121, 760	142, 190	111, 810	93, 500	111, 740
Eggplant	2, 210	2, 470	2, 690	3, 490	3, 260	2, 990	3, 890
Lettuce	44, 900	57, 990	68, 660	86, 020	105, 560	121, 880	126, 780
Onions	63, 290	61, 940	65, 090	65, 280	74, 200	76, 640	77, 480
Peas, green	171, 800	207, 210	254, 270	260, 310	261, 840	221, 000	267, 610
Peppers	7, 860	8, 030	11, 160	13, 700	15, 330	14, 600	18, 510
Potatoes, early	311, 930	281, 740	38, 250	302, 780	323, 800	348, 230	400, 720
Spinach	23, 760	30, 550	334, 390	44, 510	51, 580	55, 210	63, 270
Strawberries	132, 800	148, 360	176, 470	145, 060	152, 480	188, 970	203, 680
Tomatoes	345, 420	379, 280	441, 790	483, 750	372, 430	397, 430	400, 780
Watermelons	211, 060	157, 350	184, 830	173, 710	199, 060	182, 510	210, 450
Total	1, 940, 850	2, 013, 850	2, 398, 710	2, 551, 870	2, 466, 130	2, 438, 150	2, 711, 990

PRODUCTION

Crop	1922	1923	1924	1925	1926	1927	1928
Asparagus crates	4, 041, 000	5, 854, 000	5, 500, 000	6, 301, 000	7, 813, 000	7, 877, 000	9, 235, 000
Beans, snap tons	79, 600	100, 300	110, 700	149, 800	117, 300	126, 700	147, 200
Cabbage do	1, 089, 000	805, 700	1, 066, 300	947, 100	1, 034, 200	1, 204, 700	976, 200
Cantaloupes crates	12, 805, 000	11, 745, 000	13, 834, 000	14, 553, 000	14, 393, 000	15, 014, 000	15, 521, 000
Carrots bushels		3, 184, 000	4, 084, 000	4, 800, 000	5, 523, 000	7, 763, 000	6, 628, 000
Cauliflower crates	2, 589, 000	3, 322, 000	2, 741, 000	3, 403, 000	5, 538, 000	4, 096, 000	4, 987, 000
Celery do	4, 822, 000	5, 684, 000	6, 509, 000	6, 702, 000	5, 767, 000	7, 585, 000	7, 173, 000
Corn, sweet tons	474, 700	603, 300	527, 800	1, 014, 100	816, 000	399, 000	536, 400
Cucumbers bushels	8, 867, 000	7, 671, 000	7, 549, 000	12, 699, 000	9, 224, 000	8, 256, 000	8, 535, 000
Eggplant do	856, 000	850, 000	795, 000	904, 000	791, 000	782, 000	896, 000
Lettuce crates	8, 837, 000	11, 672, 000	13, 221, 000	16, 076, 000	17, 150, 000	19, 383, 000	18, 589, 000
Onions bushels	18, 763, 000	17, 306, 000	19, 190, 000	19, 662, 000	21, 119, 000	23, 595, 000	19, 025, 000
Peas, green tons	181, 700	180, 900	274, 400	242, 400	261, 100	239, 300	277, 000
Peppers bushels	2, 654, 000	2, 953, 000	3, 674, 000	3, 455, 000	3, 890, 000	3, 502, 000	4, 418, 000
Potatoes, early do	36, 198, 000	26, 245, 000	44, 103, 000	30, 890, 000	36, 624, 000	44, 825, 000	55, 368, 000
Spinach tons	67, 900	95, 800	108, 300	106, 600	124, 400	141, 000	138, 200
Strawberries quarts	260, 403, 000	256, 409, 000	318, 121, 000	228, 577, 000	277, 940, 000	319, 519, 000	325,045,000
Tomatoes tons	1, 658, 000	1, 609, 000	1, 687, 000	2, 321, 600	1, 375, 800	1, 641, 300	1, 401, 500
Watermelons number	71, 128, 000	42, 734, 000	57, 086, 000	56, 498, 000	69, 698, 000	57, 682, 000	61, 773, 000

Bureau of Agricultural Economics.   Estimates based upon returns from crop reporters.

TABLE 232.—*Vegetables: Imports into the United States, exclusive of imports from Canada, 1925–1928*

Commodity and country from which imported	Year ended June 30				Commodity and country from which imported	Year ended June 30			
	1925	1926	1927	1928		1925	1926	1927	1928
	1,000 pounds	*1,000 pounds*	*1,000 pounds*	*1,000 pounds*		*1,000 pounds*	*1,000 pounds*	*1,000 pounds*	*1,000 pounds*
Beans, Lima: Total	1,332	1,232	1,044	2,778	Eggplant: Total	2,925	5,178	6,587	7,061
Cuba	1,329	1,229	1,033	2,729	Cuba	2,767	4,708	6,085	6,216
Mexico		3	11	49	Mexico	149	469	495	796
Other countries	3				Other countries	9	1	7	49
Beans, string: Total	64	503	469	914	Endive: Total	1,075	1,552	1,680	2,391
Mexico	62	413	428	888	Belgium	1,063	1,536	1,651	2,391
Cuba	2	90	41	26	France	12	6		
					England		10	28	
Beets: Total	828	997	644	864	Netherlands			1	
Bermuda	674	739	414	552	Horse-radish: Total	2,252	2,057	767	690
Mexico	154	258	220	312					
Other countries			10		Germany	2,252	2,029	767	690
					Other countries		28		
Cabbage: Total	842	14,698	3,050	95	Kale: Bermuda	643	678	908	676
Netherlands	794	11,566	3,009	40	Okra:				
Denmark		2,573			Total	293	929	640	1,349
Cuba		524		20					
Mexico	28	34	41	34	Cuba	293	893	640	1,345
Other countries	20	1		1	Mexico		36		4
Carrots: Total	2,462	2,668	2,408	2,026	Parsley: Total	1,110	1,515	1,045	1,621
Mexico	271	383	471	652	Bermuda	1,095	1,493	1,020	1,593
Bermuda	2,191	2,285	1,887	1,374	Mexico	15	22	25	28
Netherlands			50						
Celery: Total	1,313	2,271	3,706	2,667	Peas: Total	3,331	9,095	14,278	14,443
Bermuda	1,312	2,270	3,705	2,665	Mexico	3,328	9,090	14,277	14,441
Other countries	1	1	1	2	Other countries	3	5	1	2
Cucumbers: Total	331	670	1,325	1,247	Peppers: Total	10,441	17,391	17,608	16,631
Cuba	170	460	1,015	1,030	Cuba	6,338	12,032	8,620	6,008
Mexico	161	200	310	216	Mexico	4,102	5,350	8,968	10,602
Other countries		10		1	Virgin Islands		1	15	15
					Other countries	1	8	5	6

Bureau of Agricultural Economics. Compiled from the annual reports of the Federal Horticultural Board, 1925–1928, as provided by quarantine 56, which became effective Nov. 1, 1923.

TABLE 233.—*Fruits and vegetables: Unloads of 13 commodities at 11 markets in car lots, 1926–1928*

Commodity and year	New York	Chicago	Philadelphia	Pittsburgh	St. Louis	Cincinnati	Minneapolis	Kansas City	Washington	Cleveland	Detroit	Total
Apples:	Cars	Cars	Cars	Cars	Cars	Cars	Cars	Cars	Cars	Cars	Cars	Cars
1926	14,606	7,834	2,622	2,628	2,097	1,179	939	924	615	6,754	2,086	37,284
1927	12,827	6,868	1,586	2,127	1,248	1,301	712	1,050	316	1,106	1,824	30,965
1928	12,923	7,428	2,211	1,932	1,325	1,153	748	1,104	483	1,640	2,415	33,362
Cabbage:												
1926	4,329	2,058	2,049	1,303	1,253	759	208	451	512	714	757	14,393
1927	4,240	1,878	2,039	1,228	1,237	675	147	448	431	728	670	13,721
1928	4,853	2,228	2,199	1,158	1,194	725	137	407	578	572	717	14,768
Cantaloupes:												
1926	7,390	2,960	1,712	1,230	711	652	229	390	357	1,062	877	17,570
1927	7,401	3,211	1,932	1,302	697	667	243	426	359	1,039	1,000	18,277
1928	8,930	3,263	1,937	1,403	710	650	225	430	429	991	988	19,956
Celery:												
1926	3,275	2,121	1,281	758	528	335	330	331	263	337	578	10,137
1927	4,463	2,378	1,512	817	566	412	321	368	346	423	712	12,318
1928	4,926	2,302	1,698	791	617	374	340	405	353	411	708	12,925
Grapes:												
1926	18,753	5,822	4,630	3,007	772	562	442	363	237	1,294	1,679	37,561
1927	18,587	7,029	4,369	2,498	921	595	370	385	291	1,743	1,746	38,534
1928	14,435	5,751	4,061	3,016	931	637	405	492	295	1,468	2,036	33,527
Lettuce:												
1926	8,341	4,293	2,708	1,008	1,109	514	513	602	539	968	1,160	21,755
1927	9,054	4,548	2,911	1,087	1,271	561	463	636	530	1,017	1,388	23,466
1928	9,098	4,491	2,762	1,198	1,238	548	532	698	559	916	1,406	23,446
Onions:												
1926	8,009	2,349	2,018	898	877	421	207	388	307	781	1,133	17,388
1927	9,421	2,327	2,018	858	964	423	156	455	276	748	1,130	18,776
1928	11,863	2,347	1,962	851	796	465	197	432	318	785	1,079	21,095
Peaches:												
1926	6,032	2,689	1,295	1,095	742	860	254	382	365	1,162	1,660	16,536
1927	4,773	2,158	959	769	608	641	266	305	293	863	1,243	12,878
1928	5,859	2,374	1,467	1,037	816	909	321	558	329	933	1,452	16,055
Potatoes:												
1926	20,978	14,856	8,156	3,609	3,947	3,243	1,265	2,941	1,691	3,669	4,468	68,823
1927	22,308	15,685	7,818	3,775	4,410	3,001	798	2,907	1,691	3,703	5,500	71,596
1928	22,029	16,311	6,653	3,565	3,647	2,970	524	2,603	1,753	3,699	5,508	69,262
Strawberries:												
1926	1,625	1,526	363	360	171	282	236	124	61	279	478	5,505
1927	2,181	1,701	447	484	296	364	235	225	85	426	718	7,162
1928	2,097	1,590	378	520	330	559	249	267	53	428	877	7,348
Sweet potatoes:												
1926	2,113	1,467	414	834	183	481	158	111	288	641	583	7,273
1927	2,707	1,859	422	1,014	318	603	184	180	251	655	781	8,974
1928	2,235	1,711	281	973	215	496	185	101	272	564	631	7,664
Tomatoes:												
1926	5,170	2,568	1,130	1,068	481	283	172	236	227	299	766	12,400
1927	7,158	3,314	1,726	1,488	655	505	256	314	387	377	1,186	17,366
1928	7,456	3,132	1,355	1,347	527	478	227	282	341	340	1,129	16,614
Watermelons:												
1926	3,835	2,517	1,743	868	1,343	938	363	627	693	953	1,284	15,164
1927	3,328	2,397	1,340	795	930	794	298	513	494	811	1,167	12,867
1928	3,663	2,371	1,351	895	1,001	942	268	558	502	956	1,418	13,925
Total (13 commodities):[1]												
1920	48,295	27,225	17,521	14,421	7,359	6,225	1,828	5,032	2,847	7,585	6,272	144,610
1921	59,107	32,467	19,430	15,130	9,083	8,217	2,122	5,650	3,131	7,818	6,193	168,348
1922	67,448	35,405	20,126	15,869	10,436	8,874	2,819	5,989	4,079	9,666	8,633	189,344
1923	89,906	45,025	25,734	18,827	11,057	9,604	3,049	7,173	4,607	11,110	10,744	236,836
1924	102,035	49,484	29,661	18,443	12,244	10,465	3,844	7,220	5,365	13,509	11,517	263,787
1925	105,285	51,015	30,437	18,480	13,300	10,197	4,402	8,587	5,909	13,248	15,539	276,399
1926	107,870	53,060	30,121	18,666	14,214	10,465	5,316	7,870	6,155	13,913	17,509	285,203
1927	110,906	55,353	29,079	18,242	14,121	10,542	4,449	8,212	5,750	13,639	19,065	289,438
1928	111,893	58,331	28,315	18,686	13,347	10,906	4,358	8,337	6,547	13,703	20,364	294,787

Bureau of Agricultural Economics. Compiled from daily reports made by common carriers to bureau representatives in the various markets. Unloads as shown in car lots include those by boat reduced to car-lot basis. See 1927 yearbook, p. 904, for data for earlier years

[1] The totals include l. c. l. unloads converted to car-lot equivalents as follows: New York—6,756 cars in 1920; 5,498 in 1921; 6,393 in 1922; 5,856 in 1923; 5,805 in 1924; 4,765 in 1925; 3,414 in 1926; 2,463 in 1927; 1,526 in 1928; Chicago—3,032 in 1928; Washington—282 in 1928.

FIELD CROPS OTHER THAN GRAIN

TABLE 234.—*Beans, dry:* [1] *Acreage, production, value, exports, etc., United States, 1899, 1909, 1914–1928*

Year	Acreage	Average yield per acre	Production	Price per bushel received by producers Dec. 1 [2]	Farm value	Wholesale price at Chicago [3]	Imports year beginning July 1 [4]	Domestic exports, year beginning July 1 [4][5]
	1,000 acres	Bushels	1,000 bushels	Dollars	1,000 dollars	Dollars	1,000 bushels	1,000 bushels
1899	454	11.2	5,064			1.23	(⁶)	
1909	803	14.0	11,251			2.27	1,015	
1914	875	13.2	11,585	2.26	26,213	1.33	906	
1915	928	11.1	10,321	2.59	26,771	1.91	663	
1916	1,107	9.7	10,715	5.10	54,686	2.54	3,748	
1917	1,821	8.8	16,045	6.50	104,350	5.45	4,146	1,517
1918	1,744	10.0	17,397	5.28	91,863	6.89	4,016	4,489
1919	1,162	12.1	14,079					
1919	1,065	12.6	13,399	4.26	57,046	4.75	3,806	1,993
1920	852	10.8	9,225	2.96	27,282	4.06	824	1,216
1921	782	11.7	9,185	2.67	24,515	2.77	520	1,100
1922	1,086	11.9	12,877	3.74	48,133	4.48	2,623	672
1923	1,344	12.1	16,308	3.67	59,782	4.22	886	695
1924	1,637							
1924	1,576	9.6	15,164	3.74	56,744	3.28	1,421	549
1925	1,606	12.4	19,928	3.28	65,376	3.70	1,271	576
1926	1,649	10.5	17,396	2.93	51,005	2.97	1,051	529
1927	1,571	10.3	16,181	2.88	46,612	⁷3.31	2,465	427
1928 [8]	1,577	10.5	16,598	4.17	69,294	5.40		

Bureau of Agricultural Economics. Italic figures are census returns; census figures include all States; other figures, estimates of crop-reporting board, principal producing States only.

[1] Table includes, besides the ordinary edible beans and Limas, the blackeye of California which is identical with the blackeyed pea of the South. Soy beans not included.
[2] Farm prices are as of Nov. 15, 1914–1924.
[3] Prices 1899 and 1909 from Chicago Board of Trade annual reports, quotations for navy, good to choice; 1914–1928 from Daily Trade Bulletin, pea beans (quoted per 100 pounds; converted to bushels of 60 pounds):
[4] Imports and exports compiled from Foreign Commerce and Navigation of the United States, 1910–1918, and Monthly Summaries of Foreign Commerce of the United States June issues, 1919–1927.
[5] Not separately reported prior to 1918.   [7] 11 months.
[6] Not separately reported.   [8] Preliminary.

TABLE 235.—*Beans, dry:* [1] *Acreage, production, and December 1 price, by States, 1925–1928*

State	Acreage				Average yield per acre				Production				Price per bushel received by producers Dec. 1—			
	1925	1926	1927	1928 [2]	1925	1926	1927	1928	1925	1926	1927	1928 [2]	1925	1926	1927	1928
	1,000 acres	1,000 acres	1,000 acres	1,000 acres	Bus.	Bus.	Bus.	Bus.	1,000 bus.	1,000 bus.	1,000 bus.	1,000 bus.	Dolls.	Dolls.	Dolls.	Dolls.
Me	5	5	6	6	14.0	16.0	16.0	15.0	70	85	96	90	5.00	5.50	4.00	5.10
Vt	5	5	5	5	11.0	10.0	14.0	14.0	55	50	70	70	4.50	5.00	4.10	5.15
N. Y.	135	97	75	80	10.8	11.8	13.0	14.5	1,458	1,145	975	1,160	4.60	3.70	3.70	4.70
Mich.	639	552	566	538	13.5	12.0	8.5	11.0	8,626	6,624	4,811	5,918	2.95	2.80	3.00	4.45
Wis.	12	9	6	6	11.0	7.5	6.7	9.0	132	68	40	54	3.20	3.00	3.30	3.90
Minn.	8	7	5	5	13.0	12.0	11.0	9.0	104	84	55	45	3.40	3.10	3.30	4.00
Nebr.	2	4	5	9	9.0	8.3	12.3	9.7	18	33	62	87	3.60	3.70	3.50	3.50
N. C.			2	2			5.0	4.5			10	9			3.70	3.70
Mont.	37	43	32	43	12.5	10.0	20.0	14.5	462	430	640	624	3.05	2.80	3.00	3.85
Idaho	72	54	72	82	22.0	18.5	23.7	18.0	1,584	999	1,706	1,476	2.70	2.60	2.50	3.60
Wyo.	12	16	17	22	15.0	12.5	18.0	16.0	180	200	306	352	3.00	3.00	2.90	3.40
Colo.	320	350	281	309	7.0	3.0	5.5	4.5	2,240	1,050	1,546	1,390	2.40	2.80	2.70	3.40
N. Mex.	114	195	195	214	3.5	4.3	5.0	4.0	399	838	975	856	3.30	2.60	2.90	3.15
Ariz.	5	7	8	6	8.0	8.0	8.0	7.0	40	56	64	42	4.20	3.50	3.60	3.70
Calif.	240	305	296	250	19.0	18.8	16.3	17.7	4,560	5,734	4,825	4,425	4.10	3.00	2.70	4.40
U. S.	1,606	1,649	1,571	1,577	12.4	10.5	10.3	10.5	19,928	17,396	16,181	16,598	3.28	2.93	2.88	4.17

Bureau of Agricultural Economics. Estimates of the crop-reporting board.

[1] Table includes, besides the ordinary edible beans and Limas, the blackeye of California which is identical with the blackeyed pea of the South. Soy beans not included.
[2] Preliminary.

TABLE 236.—*Beans, dry:* [1] *Production by varieties, leading States, 1925–1928*

State and year	White pea beans	Small white	Large white	Great Northern	Yellow eye	White kidney	Red kidney	Cranberry	Red Mexican	Pinto	Pinks	Limas [2]	Black eye	Other varieties [3]	Total
	1,000 bus.	*1,000 bus.*	*1,000 bus.*	*1,000 bus.*	*1,000 bus.*	*1,000 bus.*	*1,000 bus.*	*1,000 bus.*	*1,000 bus.*	*1,000 bus.*	*1,000 bus.*	*1,000 bus.*	*1,000 bus.*	*1,000 bus.*	*1,000 bus.*
Maine:															
1925	11		2		30	7	9							11	70
1926	17		7		37	8	8							8	85
1927	19		8		41	10	10							8	96
1928	18		5		38	6	16							7	90
Vermont:															
1925	12		3		23	3	3							11	55
1926	9		3		22	3	3							10	50
1927	14		5		29	4	4							14	70
1928	10		7		31	4	3							15	70
New York: [4]															
1925	437		365		146	· 87	365							58	1,458
1926	355		137		149	137	344							23	1,145
1927	350		132		125	76	262							30	975
1928	438		184		121	45	340							32	1,160
Michigan:															
1925	7,073		345				1,035							173	8,626
1926	5,630		199				729							66	6,624
1927	4,090		193				432							96	4,811
1928	4,900		150				660							208	5,918
Wisconsin:															
1925	112		16											4	132
1926	58		5											5	68
1927	30		3											7	40
1928	36		10											8	54
Minnesota:															
1925	104														104
1926	84														84
1927	55														55
1928	45														45
Nebraska:															
1925		7								11					18
1926		13								20					33
1927		25								37					62
1928		18		27						42					87
Montana:															
1925				407										55	462
1926				422										8	430
1927				608										32	640
1928		19		568					25					12	624
Idaho:															
1925		50	341	990										203	1,584
1926		35	35	760					43					126	999
1927				1,416					102					188	1,706
1928		82		1,024					230					140	1,476
Wyoming:															
1925				133						13				34	180
1926				162						22				16	200
1927				214						61				31	306
1928				300						11				41	352
Colorado:															
1925										2,128				112	2,240
1926		11		11						996				32	1,050
1927				10						1,500				36	1,546
1928				56						1,302				32	1,390
New Mexico:															
1925										375	8			16	399
1926										805	8			25	838
1927										917	29			29	975
1928										800	34			22	856
Arizona:															
1925										1	34			5	40
1926										1	48			7	56
1927										1	55			8	64
1928											35			7	42
California:															
1925		375	50				40	85	290		960	1,870	825	65	4,560
1926		287	57				115	172	115	1,032	3,039	802		115	5,734
1927		483	24				106	188	217	34	893	2,268	516	96	4,825
1928		570	30				65	120	130	35	750	2,210	470	45	4,425
Total 14 States:															
1925	7,749	432	1,122	1,530	199	97	1,452	85	290	2,528	1,002	1,870	825	747	19,928
1926	6,153	346	443	1,355	208	148	1,199	172	158	1,844	1,088	3,039	802	441	17,396
1927	4,558	508	365	2,248	195	90	814	188	319	2,550	977	2,268	516	575	[5]16,171
1928	5,447	689	386	1,975	190	55	1,084	120	385	2,190	819	2,210	470	569	[5]16,589

Bureau of Agricultural Economics. Based upon reports by growers on proportion of total production made up of each variety, supplemented by investigations of field statisticians.

[1] Table includes, besides the ordinary edible beans and Limas, the blackeye of California, which is identical with the blackeyed pea of the South. Soy beans not included.

[2] Limas include baby Limas: 1925, 500; 1926, 969; 1927, 542; 1928, 620.

[3] "Other" include Bayo: 1925, 40; 1926, 50; 1927, 56; 1928, 15.

[4] Large white in New York is the marrow.

[5] Not including the production in North Carolina of "Other varieties": 1927, 10,000; 1928, 9,000.

TABLE 237.—*Beans, dry: Car-lot shipments by State of origin, 1920–1928*

State	1920	1921	1922	1923	1924	1925	1926	1927	1928 [1]
	Cars	Cars	Cars	Cars	Cars	Cars	Cars	Cars	Cars
New York	656	1,327	1,599	1,775	1,917	1,527	987	899	758
Michigan	3,187	5,990	5,087	5,998	8,701	8,748	9,239	7,926	5,729
Montana	42	17	34	76	84	242	336	376	554
Idaho	185	146	395	604	1,095	1,788	1,542	1,878	1,896
Wyoming	44		1	8	20	66	126	253	339
Colorado	231	542	483	1,091	1,454	2,426	2,186	1,908	1,484
New Mexico	608	974	289	85	275	307	358	495	558
California	3,956	3,854	3,822	3,284	2,230	2,278	2,806	3,319	3,072
Other States	72	105	51	69	127	158	103	100	45
Total	8,981	12,955	11,761	12,990	15,903	17,540	17,683	17,154	14,435

Bureau of Agricultural Economics. Compiled from monthly reports received by the bureau from local agents of common carriers throughout the country. Shipments as shown in car lots include those by boat reduced to car-lot basis.

[1] Preliminary.

TABLE 238.—*Beans, dried: Wholesale price per 100 pounds, 1927 and 1928*

PEA, BOSTON

Year	Jan.	Feb.	Mar.	Apr.	May	June	July	Aug.	Sept.	Oct.	Nov.	Dec.	Average
	Dolls.	Dolls.	Dolls.	Dolls.	Dolls.	Dolls.	Dolls.	Dolls.	Dolls.	Dolls.	Dolls.	Dolls.	Dolls.
1927	5.86	5.66	5.38	5.28	5.46	6.29	6.48	6.62	6.34	6.18	6.12	6.16	5.99
1928	6.69	7.88	8.71	9.81	10.08	10.18	10.30	10.22	9.94	9.75	9.55	9.50	9.38

PEA, CHICAGO

1927	5.18	5.08	4.54	4.50	5.10		6.19	6.38	6.32		5.93	5.98	
1928	6.28	7.05	8.61	8.68	10.46	10.40	10.50	10.50	9.25	8.75	8.60	8.87	9.00

SMALL WHITE, SAN FRANCISCO

1927	5.83	5.85	5.86	6.34	7.17	8.26	8.57	8.58	7.75	5.60	5.88	5.80	6.79
1928	6.21	6.66	8.42	9.20	9.28	9.03	8.75	8.36	7.15	8.11	8.40	8.52	8.17

LIMA, CALIFORNIA, NEW YORK

1927	7.14	6.94	6.97	6.97	6.86	6.74	6.68	6.67	6.96	6.97	6.85	6.83	6.88
1928	7.00	7.87	8.33	9.06	9.69	9.75	9.90	10.17	9.90	9.76	10.56	12.01	9.50

Bureau of Agricultural Economics. Compiled from the Boston Produce Market Report, weekly 1927–1928; Chicago Daily Trade Bulletin; San Francisco Commercial News, daily; and New York, Producers Price Current, daily.

TABLE 239.—*Soy beans: Acreage, production, and value, by States, 1927 and 1928*

State	Total production — Total acres, except hay [1] (1,000 acres) 1927	1928	Yield per acre [2] (Bushels) 1927	1928	Total production, except hay [2] (1,000 bushels) 1927	1928	Beans gathered — Acres from which gathered [3] (1,000 acres) 1927	1928	Beans gathered per acre (Bushels) 1927	1928	Total quantity gathered (1,000 bushels) 1927	1928	Farm price Dec. 1 of beans gathered (Dolls. per bu.) 1927	1928	Total value of total production, except hay [4] (1,000 dollars) 1927	1928
Ohio	75	58	16.0	16.5	1,200	957	35	37	10.0	10.4	350	385	1.95	1.95	2,340	1,866
Indiana	100	121	13.0	14.5	1,300	1,754	68	88	13.0	14.5	884	1,276	1.65	1.60	2,145	2,806
Illinois	220	220	13.0	16.5	2,860	3,630	184	186	13.0	16.5	2,392	3,069	1.40	1.40	4,004	5,082
Michigan	3	3	8.0	15.0	24	45	2	2	8.0	15.0	16	30	2.05	2.05	49	92
Wisconsin	1	3	10.0	12.5	10	38	1	2	10.0	12.5	10	25	2.80	2.55	28	97
Iowa	49	46	12.0	18.0	588	828	23	23	12.0	18.0	276	414	2.00	1.78	1,176	1,474
Missouri	114	114	10.5	12.5	1,197	1,425	104	103	10.5	12.5	1,092	1,288	2.00	1.90	2,394	2,708
Kansas	6	8	12.0	10.2	72	82	6	8	12.0	10.2	72	82	1.40	1.95	144	160
Delaware	14	15	16.0	18.0	224	270	14	15	16.0	18.0	224	270	2.20	1.50	314	405
Maryland	6	5	16.0	14.8	96	74	3	3	12.0	14.8	36	44	2.00	2.25	211	166
Virginia	23	21	14.0	13.0	322	273	14	14	14.0	13.0	196	182	2.50	2.00	644	546
West Virginia	3	3	15.0	14.5	45	44	3	2	16.0	14.5	48	29	1.90	2.65	112	117
North Carolina	184	196	17.0	15.0	3,128	2,940	94	94	15.0	11.5	1,410	1,081	1.50	1.65	4,692	4,851
South Carolina	42	29	11.5	14.0	483	406	16	9	5.0	5.5	80	50	2.20	2.05	918	832
Georgia	25	11	11.0	12.0	275	132	7	5	6.0	6.0	42	30	1.95	2.70	742	356
Kentucky	10	7	14.0	14.0	140	98	3	3	8.0	7.8	24	23	2.10	2.25	308	220
Tennessee	138	114	13.0	11.0	1,794	1,254	9	23	8.0	6.3	72	145	2.25	2.15	3,498	2,696
Alabama	23	20	13.0	14.0	299	280	3	3	5.2	7.6	16	23	2.10	2.15	628	602
Mississippi	73	44	14.0	15.5	1,022	682	12	12	6.5	10.0	78	120	2.25	2.30	2,300	1,569
Arkansas	18	34	15.0	15.0	270	510	6	2	4.0	8.4	24	17	2.50	2.40	675	1,224
Louisiana	24	36	12.5	12.0	300	432	8	10	9.0	5.3	72	53	2.50	2.45	750	1,058
Oklahoma	11	14	11.0	10.8	121	151	6	7	7.5	7.5	45	52	2.50	2.35	302	355
United States	1,162	1,122	13.6	14.5	15,770	16,305	621	651	12.0	13.3	7,459	8,688	1.80	1.80	28,374	29,282

Bureau of Agricultural Economics. Estimates of the crop-reporting board.

[1] Including acres planted in corn reduced to equivalent solid acres as well as the acreage grown alone.
[2] Including beans grazed or otherwise utilized, as well as those gathered.
[3] Acres from which all or part of the beans grown were gathered.
[4] Total production (except hay) multiplied by price of gathered beans to give approximate total value.

TABLE 240.—Soy beans, and soy bean oil: International trade, years 1923–1927

Year ended Dec. 31—

SOY BEANS

Country	1923 Imports	1923 Exports	1924 Imports	1924 Exports	1925 Imports	1925 Exports	1926 Imports	1926 Exports	1927 Imports	1927 Exports
	1,000 pounds	1,000 pounds	1,000 pounds	1,000 pounds	1,000 pounds	1,000 pounds	1,000 pounds	1,000 pounds	1,000 pounds	1,000 pounds
PRINCIPAL EXPORTING COUNTRIES										
China [1]	0	2,097,500	0	2,820,144	0	2,424,490	0	2,605,554	0	3,376,789
PRINCIPAL IMPORTING COUNTRIES										
Denmark	284,221	0	345,167	0	250,149	0	385,051	0	348,406	0
Germany	195,348	---	302,761	---	741,171	---	815,787	---	1,270,062	---
Japan, including Chosen	930,040	5,541	947,697	5,254	956,461	4,942	936,136	4,955	884,710	6,524
Netherlands	36,558	68	41,906	1,364	80,463	1,861	41,694	2,610	21,907	539
United Kingdom	252,529	0	249,700	0	360,600	0	101,082	0	182,831	0
United States [2]	3,648	0	4,184	0	3,812	0	3,728	0	4,189	0
Total, 7 countries	1,722,344	2,103,109	1,891,415	2,826,762	2,392,656	2,431,293	2,283,478	2,613,119	2,712,105	3,383,852

SOY-BEAN OIL

Country	1923 Imports	1923 Exports	1924 Imports	1924 Exports	1925 Imports	1925 Exports	1926 Imports	1926 Exports	1927 Imports	1927 Exports
PRINCIPAL EXPORTING COUNTRIES										
China	0	283,590	0	282,863	0	265,240	0	355,631	0	329,298
Denmark	7,489	25,179	5,972	33,207	9,703	28,327	2,288	31,391	4,394	33,837
Japan, including Chosen	1,048	5,731	188	9,265	33	15,955	128	19,236	115	11,167
PRINCIPAL IMPORTING COUNTRIES										
Algeria	32	0	2,567	7	5,271	11	5,165	3	17,860	[3] 15
France	5,952	44	9,739	0	14,787	58	13,057	67	24,759	85
Germany	58,285	1,959	42,165	8,553	73,793	6,314	44,094	11,160	25,290	34,663
Netherlands	65,837	18,714	67,298	18,416	84,792	27,963	109,709	37,447	166,388	75,314
Sweden	11,428	2,578	8,926	6,462	9,871	7,545	12,714	9,763	7,874	14,572
United Kingdom	49,567	16,910	65,740	31,497	65,209	42,399	108,067	55,019	118,075	63,025
United States	41,679	1,356	9,125	2,264	19,493	520	30,712	1,567	14,915	5,444
Total, 10 countries	241,817	356,061	211,720	392,534	282,952	394,332	325,934	521,284	379,670	567,420

Bureau of Agricultural Economics. Compiled from official sources.

[1] These figures are for yellow beans only, as they include most all soy beans, according to Agricultural Commissioner Paul O. Nyhus.
[2] Imports for consumption.
[3] International Yearbook of Agricultural Statistics.

TABLE 241.—*Soy beans: Estimated price per bushel, received by producers, United States, 1913–1928*

Year beginning October—	Oct. 15	Nov. 15	Dec. 15	Jan. 15	Feb. 15	Weighted average
	Dollars	*Dollars*	*Dollars*	*Dollars*	*Dollars*	*Dollars*
1913	1.96	1.57	1.72	1.96	1.80	1.76
1914	2.08	2.15	2.24	2.35	2.26	2.18
1915	1.88	2.08	2.23	2.31	2.39	2.11
1916	2.13	2.13	2.18	2.20	2.45	2.16
1917	2.73	2.86	3.33	3.47	3.82	3.05
1918	3.36	3.20	3.29	3.00	3.00	3.23
1919	3.34	3.35	3.44	3.76	4.05	3.45
1920	3.41	3.00	2.'28	2.18	2.17	2.80
1921	2.20	2.22	2.08	2.11	2.16	2.17
1922	1.89	2.06	1.97	2.07	2.13	2.00
1923	2.09	2.11	2.11	2.23	2.26	2.12
1924	2.23	2.16	2.36	2.59	2.64	2.29
1925	2.27	2.18	2.17	2.38	2.33	2.23
1926	1.97	1.85	1.83	1.90	2.03	1.89
1927	1.86	1.70	1.61	1.70	1.69	1.72
1928	1.72	1.69	1.70			

Bureau of Agricultural Economics. Based upon returns from special price reporters.

TABLE 242.—*Soy beans for seed: Average wholesale selling price per 100 pounds at Baltimore and St. Louis, 1920–1928*

Year	Baltimore						St. Louis					
	Jan.	Feb.	Mar.	Apr.	May	Av.	Jan.	Feb.	Mar.	Apr.	May	Av.
	Dolls.	*Dolls.*	*Dolls.*	*Dolls.*	*Dolls.*	*Dolls.*	*Dolls.*	*Dolls.*	*Dolls.*	*Dolls.*	*Dolls.*	*Dolls.*
Average 1921–1925		3.98	4.05	4.10	4.14		4.40	4.57	4.63	4.36	4.62	4.52
1920	6.80	8.00	8.00	8.00	8.60	7.88	8.10	10.00	9.90	9.65	10.00	9.53
1921	3.15	3.50	3.50	3.75	4.70	3.72	4.30	5.40	5.75	5.00	5.40	5.17
1922	3.20	3.50	3.50	3.50	3.30	3.40	4.00	4.00	4.20	3.85	4.55	4.12
1923		4.00	4.00	3.80	3.75		5.00	4.75	4.50	4.50	4.95	4.74
1924	3.50	4.00	4.00	4.50	5.00	4.20	4.70	4.70	4.70	4.70	4.60	4.68
1925	5.10	4.90	5.25	4.95	3.95	4.83	4.00	4.00	4.00	3.75	3.60	3.87
1926	3.35	3.42	3.50	3.56	4.62	3.69	3.55	3.61	3.88	4.25	4.85	4.03
1927	3.00	3.00	3.00	3.00	3.12	3.02		4.50	4.00	4.19	4.50	
1928	3.25	3.22	3.25	3.32	3.55	3.32	3.00	3.00	3.12	3.31	3.75	3.24

Bureau of Agricultural Economics. Compiled from weekly reports to the bureau from seedsmen in the various markets. These prices are the average wholesale selling prices for high quality seed.

TABLE 243.—*Soy-bean oil, crude, in barrels: Wholesale price per pound, Saturday nearest the 15th of the month, New York, 1910–1928* [1]

Year	Jan.	Feb.	Mar.	Apr.	May	June	July	Aug.	Sept.	Oct.	Nov.	Dec.
	Cents	*Cents*	*Cents*	*Cents*	*Cents*	*Cents*	*Cents*	*Cents*	*Cents*	*Cents*	*Cents*	*Cents*
1910	6.90	6.75	7.12	7.44	7.44	6.75	6.94	7.50	7.75	8.00	7.81	7.44
1911	7.38	7.88	7.56	7.00	7.00	6.25	6.38	6.44	6.69	7.62	7.00	6.88
1912	6.88	6.60	6.81	6.62		6.40	6.62	6.56	6.56	6.62	6.50	6.00
1913	5.88	6.12	5.94	5.94	6.00	6.00	6.44	6.50	6.50	6.50	6.44	6.44
1914	6.44	6.62	6.38	6.38	6.38	6.25				6.75	6.25	
1915			6.31	6.50	6.62	6.38	6.19	5.88	5.88	6.88	7.00	7.56
1916	8.19	8.56	9.38	9.38	9.12	8.12	7.88	7.88	8.50	10.00	11.31	11.87
1917	12.12	13.00	13.50	13.75	14.62	15.00	14.38	14.25	14.62	15.88	16.75	17.62
1918	18.25	18.88	19.25	19.62	19.12	18.38	18.25	18.25	18.38	18.38	17.25	17.00
1919	14.50	13.50	12.75	14.75	17.00	18.88	19.88	18.50	17.00	17.38	17.62	17.50
1920	19.50	18.25	18.62	18.00	17.75	17.00	15.50	14.00	13.50	12.62	11.75	9.00
1921	8.25	6.50	6.25	7.00	7.75	7.94	8.25	8.50	8.38	8.88	8.88	9.25
1922	8.88	9.12	10.88	11.38						10.00	10.38	10.88
1923	11.19	11.69	12.62	13.12	13.12	12.62	11.88	11.62	11.62	10.88	11.00	11.38
1924	11.62	12.50	12.50	11.75	12.38	12.00	12.38	12.50	12.75	12.25	13.12	13.38
1925	13.25	13.25	13.25	13.38	13.38	13.38	13.38	13.38	13.38	13.38	13.38	13.38
1926	13.38	13.38	13.38	13.38	13.38	13.50	14.00	14.00	14.00	14.00	13.00	12.00
1927	12.00	12.12	12.12	12.12	12.38	12.12	12.12	12.12	12.12	13.25	12.12	12.12
1928	12.12	12.12	12.12	12.12	12.12	12.38	12.38	12.38	12.38	12.38	12.38	12.38

Bureau of Agricultural Economics. Compiled from the Oil, Paint, and Drug Reporter.

[1] Prices through April, 1916, quoted as English; May, 1916–December, 1918, as Manchuria spot; beginning January, 1919, as crude.

TABLE 244.—Coupeas: Acreage, production, and value, by States, 1927 and 1928

State	Total production — Total acres except hay [1] 1927	1928	Yield per acre [2] 1927	1928	Total production except hay [2] 1927	1928	Peas gathered — Acres from which gathered [3] 1927	1928	Peas gathered per acre 1927	1928	Total quantity gathered 1927	1928	Farm price Dec. 1 of peas gathered 1927	1928	Total value of total production except hay [4] 1927	1928
	1,000 acres	1,000 acres	Bushels	Bushels	1,000 bushels	1,000 bushels	1,000 acres	1,000 acres	Bushels	Bushels	1,000 bushels	1,000 bushels	Dollars per bu.	Dollars per bu.	1,000 dollars	1,000 dollars
Ohio	2	2	9.0	15.0	18	30	2	2	9.0	15.0	18	30	2.40	2.40	43	72
Indiana	37	21	8.0	9.0	296	189	20	6	5.3	5.6	106	34	2.10	2.10	622	397
Illinois	65	48	7.0	8.0	455	384	64	47	5.5	5.5	448	258	1.75	1.85	706	710
Missouri	45	28	8.5	11.0	382	308	43	25	7.5	11.0	366	275	2.20	2.30	840	647
Kansas	2	3	10.8	9.0	22	27	2	3	10.8	9.0	22	27	2.20	2.30	48	62
Delaware	4	4	13.0	15.0	52	60	4	3	13.0	15.0	52	60	1.60	1.70	83	102
Maryland	2	2	14.5	14.8	29	30	2	2	8.0	9.0	16	18	2.10	2.30	61	69
Virginia	28	22	10.0	7.0	280	154	9	7	7.0	6.0	63	42	2.10	2.10	588	323
West Virginia	1	0	16.0		16		1		16.0				2.35		38	
North Carolina	172	104	12.0	9.0	2,064	936	89	53	9.0	6.5	801	344	1.75	1.95	3,612	1,825
South Carolina	319	229	9.5	6.0	3,030	1,374	210	128	6.0	3.0	1,260	384	1.35	1.55	4,090	2,130
Georgia	244	172	10.0	9.5	2,440	1,634	195	108	5.0	5.0	975	540	1.45	1.63	3,538	2,696
Florida	25	19	11.0	10.0	275	190	7	4	7.5	5.0	52	20	2.50	2.50		475
Kentucky	55	31	11.5	13.0	632	403	14	6	6.0	4.7	84	28	1.95	2.45	1,485	987
Tennessee	90	86	12.0	10.5	1,080	860	25	27	6.0	5.0	150	135	1.90	1.90	2,106	1,849
Alabama	235	196	11.0	10.5	2,585	2,058	85	82	5.2	4.5	442	369	1.85	1.90	4,912	3,910
Mississippi	141	94	11.0	10.0	1,551	940	55	46	5.5	4.5	302	207	1.85	1.95	2,869	1,833
Arkansas	112	73	13.0	11.8	1,456	861	58	48	3.4	3.1	197	149	1.95	1.95	2,839	1,679
Louisiana	34	43	12.5	12.5	425	538	27	27	6.0	5.0	162	135	2.35	2.30	1,076	1,237
Oklahoma	39	49	12.0	13.0	468	637	11	26	8.0	9.0	88	234	2.30	2.25	999	1,433
Texas	174	162	12.0	11.0	2,088	1,782	60	55	8.0	8.0	480	440	1.90	1.90	3,967	3,386
United States	1,826	1,388	10.8	9.6	19,644	13,395	983	706	6.2	5.3	6,100	3,729	1.80	1.93	35,300	25,822

Bureau of Agricultural Economics. Estimates of the crop-reporting board.

[1] Including acres planted in corn reduced to equivalent solid acres as well as the acreage grown alone. Acreage cut for hay is included in table of legume hay.
[2] Including peas grazed or otherwise utilized as well as those gathered.
[3] Acres from which all or part of the peas grown were gathered.
[4] Total production (except hay) multiplied by price of gathered peas to give approximate total value.

TABLE 245.—*Cowpeas: Estimated price per bushel, received by producers, United States, 1915–1928*

Year beginning August—	Aug. 15	Sept. 15	Oct. 15	Nov. 15	Dec. 15	Jan. 15	Feb. 15	Mar. 15	Apr. 15	May 15	June 15	July 15	Weighted average
	Dolls.	Dolls.	Dolls.	Dolls.	Dolls.	Dolls.	Dolls.	Dolls.	Dolls.	Dolls.	Dolls.	Dolls.	Dolls.
1915	1.74	1.55	1.56	1.51	1.52	1.56	1.57	1.54	1.50	1.49	1.40	1.35	1.52
1916	1.41	1.42	1.48	1.62	1.77	1.92	2.10	2.32	2.53	2.93	3.09	3.03	1.90
1917	2.65	2.17	2.20	2.27	2.38	2.62	2.92	3.02	2.93	2.83	2.57	2.48	2.36
1918	2.41	2.26	2.34	2.31	2.38	2.39	2.52	2.49	2.68	2.92	3.44	3.43	2.54
1919	3.10	2.69	2.61	2.71	2.81	3.13	3.72	3.94	4.21	4.84	4.84	4.71	3.19
1920	4.23	3.69	2.74	2.43	2.29	1.97	2.04	2.05	2.16	2.43	2.65	2.87	2.74
1921	2.41	2.00	2.01	1.85	1.76	1.72	1.80	1.86	1.85	1.90	1.84	1.70	1.91
1922	1.66	1.57	1.54	1.64	1.67	1.87	1.98	1.98	2.08	2.08	2.17	2.21	1.73
1923	2.08	1.87	1.94	1.95	2.01	2.12	2.21	2.32	2.46	2.53	2.82	2.86	2.14
1924	2.56	2.41	2.32	2.34	2.56	2.82	3.16	3.43	3.67	3.70	3.84	3.67	2.73
1925	3.24	3.12	2.93	2.98	2.87	3.03	3.21	3.37	3.50	3.43	3.47	3.47	3.09
1926	3.22	2.79	2.34	2.05	1.95	1.94	1.94	1.89	1.93	1.90	1.90	1.93	2.21
1927	1.84	1.80	1.70	1.72	1.65	1.71	1.74	1.76	1.86	2.00	2.09	2.09	1.80
1928	2.01	1.82	1.84	1.83	2.02								

Bureau of Agricultural Economics. Based upon returns from special price reporters.

TABLE 246.—*Cowpeas for seed: Average wholesale selling price per 100 pounds at Baltimore and St. Louis, 1920–1928*

Year	Baltimore						St. Louis					
	Jan.	Feb.	Mar.	Apr.	May	Av.	Jan.	Feb.	Mar.	Apr.	May	Av.
	Dolls.	Dolls.	Dolls.	Dolls.	Dolls.	Dolls.	Dolls.	Dolls.	Dolls.	Dolls.	Dolls.	Dolls.
Average, 1921–1925	4.79	4.95	4.90	5.13	5.35	5.02	4.66	4.79	4.93	5.08	5.58	5.01
1920	7.20	9.00	9.00	9.00	9.60	8.76	10.50	12.75	11.25	10.65	11.00	11.23
1921	4.50	4.50	4.50	5.30	6.20	5.00	4.00	4.20	4.45	5.05	6.50	4.84
1922	3.70	4.00	4.00	4.00	4.00	3.94	3.20	3.15	3.65	3.75	3.75	3.50
1923	4.25	4.25	4.25	4.25	4.25	4.25	5.00	4.95	4.75	4.75	4.95	4.88
1924	5.00	5.25	5.25	5.60	5.75	5.42	4.60	4.95	5.00	5.05	5.90	5.10
1925	6.50	6.50	6.50	6.50	6.55	6.51	6.50	6.70	6.80	6.80	6.80	6.72
1926		7.08	7.10	7.05	7.02		7.50	7.38	7.00	6.81	6.75	7.09
1927	3.75	3.75	3.56	3.50	3.50	3.61		4.00	4.00	4.00	4.00	
1928	3.00	3.05	3.50	3.62	3.88	3.41	4.00	4.00	4.02	4.14	4.50	4.13

Bureau of Agricultural Economics. Compiled from weekly reports to the bureau from seedsmen in the various markets. These prices are the average wholesale selling prices for high quality seed.

TABLE 247.—*Velvet beans: Acreage, yield per acre, and production, by States, 1927 and 1928*

State	Total acres for all purposes		Yield per acre of beans in the hull [1]		Total production of beans in the hull [1]	
	1927	1928	1927	1928	1927	1928
	1,000 acres	1,000 acres	Pounds	Pounds	1,000 tons	1,000 tons
North Carolina	8	7	1,300	1,300	5	5
South Carolina	73	67	1,075	800	39	27
Georgia	993	947	900	900	447	426
Florida	107	98	1,000	900	54	44
Alabama	300	362	1,000	900	150	163
Mississippi	26	33	1,000	1,250	13	21
Louisiana	27	27	1,350	1,400	18	19
United States	1,534	1,541	946.6	915.0	726	705

Bureau of Agricultural Economics. Estimates of the crop-reporting board.

[1] The figures refer to the yield and entire production of velvet beans in the hull and not merely to those gathered. The pods are gathered from one-fourth to one-third of the acreage and most of these are ground for feed, only enough being shelled to supply seed. A large proportion of the crop is grazed.

TABLE 248.—*Broomcorn: Acreage, production, and November 15 price, United States, 1915–1928*

Year	Acreage	Average yield per acre	Production	Price per ton received by producers Nov. 15	Year	Acreage	Average yield per acre	Production	Price per ton received by producers Nov. 15
	Acres	Pounds	Tons	Dollars		Acres	Pounds	Tons	Dollars
1915	230,100	454.1	52,242	91.67	1922	275,000	271.3	37,300	219.46
1916	235,200	329.3	38,726	172.75	1923	536,000	302.8	81,153	160.06
1917	345,000	332.8	57,400	292.75	1924	451,000	346.8	78,200	95.63
1918	366,000	340.4	62,300	233.87	1925	214,000	275.7	29,500	[1] 143.02
1919	352,000	303.4	53,400*	154.57	1926	306,000	355.6	54,400	[2] 78.77
1920	275,500	265.0	36,500	126.16	1927	230,000	335.6	38,600	[2] 109.12
1921	222,000	344.2	38,200	72.20	1928 [3]	252,000	361.2	45,500	[2] 106.59

Bureau of Agricultural Economics. Estimates of the crop-reporting board.

[1] Weighted average of the season to Dec. 1.   [2] Dec. 1 price.   [3] Preliminary.

TABLE 249.—*Broomcorn: Acreage, production, and December 1 price, by States, 1925–1928*

State	Acreage				Average yield per acre				Production				Price per ton received by producers Dec. 1			
	1925	1926	1927	1928 [1]	1925	1926	1927	1928	1925	1926	1927	1928 [1]	1925 [2]	1926	1927	1928
	1,000 acres	1,000 acres	1,000 acres	1,000 acres	Lbs.	Lbs.	Lbs.	Lbs.	Tons	Tons	Tons	Tons	Dolls.	Dolls.	Dolls.	Dolls.
Ill	30	40	28	24	560	420	380	440	8,400	8,400	5,300	5,300	175	115	155	145
Mo	4	3	3	4	322	250	400	430	600	400	600	900	200	87	90	90
Kans	22	31	27	38	286	327	375	420	3,100	5,100	5,100	8,000	120	85	96	96
Okla	108	158	112	114	205	375	349	351	11,100	29,600	19,500	20,000	136	70	98	111
Tex	11	15	10	9	318	410	260	350	1,700	3,100	1,300	1,600	140	75	110	107
Colo	15	30	28	36	250	225	315	340	1,900	3,400	4,400	6,100	140	83	120	85
N. Mex	24	29	22	27	225	300	220	270	2,700	4,400	2,400	3,600	90	60	110	90
U. S.	214	306	230	252	275.7	355.6	335.6	361.2	29,500	54,400	38,600	45,500	143.02	78.77	109.12	106.59

Bureau of Agricultural Economics. Estimates of the crop reporting board.

[1] Preliminary.   [2] Weighted average of the season to Dec. 1.

TABLE 250.—*Cotton: Acreage, production, value, exports, etc., United States, 1849, 1859, 1866–1928*

Year	Acreage harvested	Average yield per acre	Production [1]	Price per pound received by producers, Dec. 1	Farm value, Dec. 1	Average price per pound, New York [2]	Domestic exports, year beginning Aug.1 [3][4][5]	Imports, year beginning Aug.1 [4][6]	Net exports, year beginning Aug.1 [3][4][6][7]
	1,000 acres	Lbs.	1,000 bales	Cents	1,000 dollars	Cents	1,000 bales	1,000 bales	1,000 bales
1849			2,469			12.34	[8] 1,271	[8] 1	[9] 1,270
1859			5,387			11.00	[8] 3,535	[8] 4	[8] 3,531
1866	7,599	129.0	1,750			31.59	[8] 1,323	[8] 2	[8] 1,324
1867	7,828	189.8	2,340			24.85	1,511	2	1,510
1868	6,799	192.2	2,380			29.01	1,288	[9] 6	1,284

[1] 500-pound gross weight bales, from 1899–1927.

[2] Compiled from Cotton Fluctuation, 1849–1888, and are averages for crop year beginning September. From New York Commercial and Financial Chronicle, 1889–1899, and from reports of New York Cotton Exchange since 1900. Since 1889 the averages are for crop year beginning August.

[3] Excluding linters from 1914 to 1927.

[4] Compiled from Commerce and Navigation of the United States, 1849–1917; Foreign Commerce and Navigation of the United States, 1918; Monthly Summary of Foreign Commerce of the United States, June and July, 1919–1928, and January, 1928.

[5] Bales of 500 pounds gross weight.

[6] Bales of 478 pounds net, which are equivalent to bales of 500 pounds gross weight.

[7] Total exports (domestic plus foreign) minus imports.

[8] Year beginning July 1.

[9] Estimated from value of imports. Average import price per pound calculated by assuming that the percentage change in import price from the previous year is equal to the percentage change in the export prices.

TABLE 250.—*Cotton: Acreage, production, value, exports, etc., United States, 1849, 1859, 1866–1928*—Continued

Year	Acreage harvested	Average yield per acre	Production	Price per pound received by producers, Dec. 1	Farm value, Dec. 1	Average price per pound, New York	Domestic exports, year beginning Aug. 1	Imports, year beginning Aug. 1	Net exports, year beginning Aug. 1
	1,000 acres	Lbs.	1,000 bales	Cents	1,000 dollars	Cents	1,000 bales	1,000 bales	1,000 bales
1869			*3,012*			23.98			
1869	7,743	196.9	*3,012*			23.98	1,980	4	1,977
1870	8,885	198.9	3,800			16.95	2,894	3°	2,893
1871	7,558	148.2	2,553			20.48	1,851	7	1,844
1872	8,483	188.7	3,920			18.15	2,437	11	2,426
1873	9,510	179.7	3,683			17.00	2,706	5	2,702
1874	11,764	147.5	3,941			15.00	2,523	5	2,520
1875	11,934	190.6	5,123			13.00	3,003	5	2,999
1876	11,677	167.8	4,438	9.0	174,724	11.73	2,869	6	2,864
1877	12,133	163.8	4,370			11.28	3,198	7	3,194
1878	12,344	191.2	5,244	8.2	192,515	10.83	3,265	6	3,259
1879	*14,480*	181.0	*5,755*	10.3	269,305	12.02	3,711	7	3,705
1880	15,951	184.5	6,343	9.8	289,083	11.34	4,409	9	4,403
1881	16,711	149.8	5,456			12.16	3,430	9	3,426
1882	16,277	185.7	6,957	9.1	275,513	10.63	4,582	9	4,577
1883	16,778	164.8	5,701	9.1	250,977	10.64	3,745	15	3,734
1884	17,440	153.8	5,682	9.2	246,575	10.54	3,740	10	3,733
1885	18,301	164.4	6,575	8.4	251,775	9.44	4,193	11	4,185
1886	18,455	169.5	6,446	8.1	251,856	10.25	4,274	9	4,266
1887	18,641	182.7	7,020	8.5	290,901	10.27	4,557	11	4,547
1888	19,059	180.4	6,941	8.5	292,139	10.71	4,720	17	4,704
1889	*20,175*	159.7	*7,473*	8.5	275,249	11.27	4,934	19	4,915
1890	19,512	187.0	8,674	8.6	313,360	9.48	5,859	45	5,815
1891	19,059	179.4	9,018	7.2	247,633	7.68	5,888	61	5,827
1892	15,911	209.2	6,664	8.3	277,194	8.45	4,456	90	4,367
1893	19,525	149.9	7,493	7.0	204,983	7.75	5,309	58	5,253
1894	23,688	195.3	9,476	4.6	212,335	6.38	7,010	104	6,908
1895	20,185	155.6	7,161	7.6	238,503	8.10	4,710	115	4,598
1896	23,273	184.9	8,533	6.7	286,169	7.71	6,172	119	6,055
1897	24,320	182.7	10,898	6.7	296,816	6.40	7,757	102	7,656
1898	24,967	220.6	11,189	5.7	315,449	6.00	7,662	105	7,557
1899	*24,275*		*9,345*						
1899	24,327	183.8	*9,345*	7.0	326,215	8.36	6,228	140	6,091
1900	24,933	194.4	*10,123*	9.2	463,310	9.38	6,800	109	6,692
1901	26,774	170.0	*9,510*	7.0	334,088	8.73	6,949	202	6,750
1902	27,175	187.3	*10,631*	7.6	403,718	9.96	7,084	151	6,936
1903	27,052	174.3	*9,851*	10.5	516,763	12.84	6,207	103	6,107
1904	31,215	205.9	*13,438*	9.0	603,438	9.09	8,908	129	8,781
1905	27,110	186.6	*10,575*	10.8	569,791	11.30	7,118	144	6,980
1906	31,374	202.5	*13,274*	9.6	635,534	11.24	8,943	227	8,741
1907	29,660	179.1	*11,107*	10.4	575,226	11.53	7,666	153	7,518
1908	32,444	194.9	*13,242*	8.7	575,092	10.23	8,955	181	8,778
1909	*32,044*		*10,005*						
1909	30,938	154.3	*10,005*	13.9	697,681	14.66	6,353	170	6,194
1910	32,403	170.7	11,609	14.1	820,407	14.87	8,027	245	7,787
1911	36,045	207.7	*15,693*	8.8	687,888	10.85	11,116	233	10,885
1912	34,283	190.9	13,703	11.9	817,055	12.29	9,146	249	8,899
1913	37,089	182.0	*14,156*	12.2	862,708	13.21	9,508	273	9,251
1914	36,832	209.2	*16,135*	6.8	549,036	[10] 8.89	8,702	400	8,322
1915	31,412	170.3	11,192	11.3	631,460	11.98	6,113	458	5,673
1916	34,985	156.6	*11,450*	19.6	1,122,295	19.28	5,525	311	5,219
1917	33,841	159.7	*11,302*	27.7	1,566,198	29.68	4,402	231	4,175
1918	36,008	159.6	*12,041*	27.6	1,663,633	31.01	5,774	211	5,568
1919	*33,740*		*11,421*						
1919	33,566	161.5	11,421	35.6	2,034,658	38.29	6,707	732	5,993
1920	35,878	178.4	*13,440*	13.9	933,658	17.89	5,973	237	5,753
1921	30,509	124.5	*7,954*	16.2	643,933	18.92	6,348	380	5,980
1922	33,036	141.2	[11] *9,755*	23.8	1,160,968	26.24	5,007	492	4,536
1923	37,123	130.6	*10,140*	31.0	1,571,829	31.11	5,815	306	5,530
1924	*39,204*		*13,628*						
1924	41,360	157.4	*13,628*	22.6	1,540,884	24.74	8,240	328	7,923
1925	46,053	167.2	*16,104*	18.2	1,464,032	20.53	8,267	340	7,939
1926	47,087	182.6	*17,977*	10.9	982,736	15.15	11,299	419	10,900
1927	40,138	154.5	12,955	19.6	1,269,885	20.42	7,857	354	7,522
1928 [12]	45,326	151.8	14,373	18.0	1,291,589				

Bureau of Agricultural Economics; italic figures are census returns; other acreage, yield, and production figures are estimates by the crop-reporting board; acreage revised on census basis.

[10] Average for nine months only. Exchange closed August–Nov. 17, on account of war.
[11] Cotton ginned in the United States. Prior census reports include undetermined quantities Lower California cotton ginned in the United States. In later years no Lower California cotton ginned in the United States.
[12] Preliminary.

TABLE 251.—*Cotton: Acreage harvested, by States, 1917–1928*

State	1917	1918	1919	1920	1921	1922	1923	1924	1925	1926	1927	1928[1]
	1,000 acres	1,000 acres	1,000 acres	1,000 acres	1,000 acres	1,000 acres	1,000 acres	1,000 acres	1,000 acres	1,000 acres	1,000 acres	1,000 acres
Missouri	153	148	125	136	103	198	355	493	520	434	291	349
Virginia	50	44	42	42	34	55	74	102	100	93	64	79
North Carolina	1,515	1,600	1,490	1,587	1,403	1,625	1,679	2,005	2,017	1,985	1,728	1,890
South Carolina	2,837	3,001	2,835	2,964	2,571	1,912	1,965	2,404	2,654	2,648	2,356	2,355
Georgia	5,195	5,341	5,220	4,900	4,172	3,418	3,421	3,046	3,589	3,965	3,413	3,719
Florida	183	167	103	100	65	118	147	80	101	105	64	95
Tennessee	882	902	758	840	634	985	1,172	996	1,173	1,143	965	1,086
Alabama	1,977	2,570	2,791	2,858	2,235	2,771	3,079	3,055	3,504	3,651	3,166	3,595
Mississippi	2,788	3,138	2,848	2,950	2,628	3,014	3,170	2,981	3,466	3,752	3,340	3,994
Arkansas	2,740	2,991	2,725	2,980	2,382	2,799	3,026	3,094	3,738	3,790	3,048	3,610
Louisiana	1,454	1,683	1,527	1,470	1,168	1,140	1,405	1,616	1,874	1,979	1,542	1,985
Oklahoma	2,783	2,998	2,424	2,749	2,206	2,915	3,197	3,861	5,214	4,676	3,601	4,249
Texas	11,092	11,233	10,476	11,898	10,745	11,874	14,150	17,175	17,608	18,374	16,176	17,766
New Mexico						28	60	101	107	120	95	108
Arizona	41	95	107	230	90	101	127	180	162	167	139	200
California	136	85	85	150	55	67	83	130	169	162	128	218
All other	15	12	10	24	18	16	13	41	57	43	22	28
United States	33,841	36,008	33,566	35,878	30,509	33,036	37,123	41,360	46,053	47,087	40,138	45,326
Lower California (old Mexico)		88	100	125	85	135	150	137	150	130	110	160

Bureau of Agricultural Economics. Estimates of the crop-reporting board.

[1] Preliminary.

TABLE 252.—*Cotton: Yield per acre and estimated price per pound, December 1, by States, average 1914–1920, 1921–1925, annual 1924–1928*

State	Yield per acre							Estimated price per pound						
	Av., 1914–1920	Av., 1921–1925	1924	1925	1926	1927	1928	Av., 1914–1920	Av., 1921–1925	1924	1925	1926	1927	1928
	Lbs.	Lbs.	Lbs.	Lbs.	Lbs.	Lbs.	Lbs.	Cts.	Cts.	Cts.	Cts.	Cts.	Cts.	Cts.
Missouri	237	263	185	275	240	188	200	19.8	20.8	23.0	12.0	10.0	20.5	18.0
Virginia	248	243	180	250	264	230	265	20.3	22.7	23.0	19.0	11.4	20.0	18.2
North Carolina	253	252	196	261	292	238	212	20.2	22.7	22.6	19.0	11.5	19.5	18.5
South Carolina	327	154	160	160	182	148	147	20.6	22.6	22.1	18.8	11.7	19.6	18.4
Georgia	178	117	157	155	180	154	131	20.8	22.8	22.4	19.0	11.1	19.4	18.2
Florida	106	106	130	180	145	126	100	30.1	22.2	22.5	18.8	10.2	19.1	17.9
Tennessee	183	178	170	210	188	178	185	19.7	22.4	23.2	16.2	10.0	19.0	18.0
Alabama	134	139	154	185	196	180	145	20.3	22.7	23.7	18.9	10.7	19.0	18.2
Mississippi	162	169	176	275	241	194	176	21.1	23.3	23.7	19.5	11.6	20.5	18.5
Arkansas	180	161	169	205	195	157	161	20.5	22.1	22.8	16.1	11.0	20.2	18.2
Louisiana	157	152	145	232	200	170	165	20.1	22.0	22.4	18.1	11.0	19.2	17.9
Oklahoma	173	129	187	155	181	138	133	19.2	21.4	22.2	17.0	9.7	19.8	17.2
Texas	150	125	138	113	147	129	139	20.1	22.2	22.4	18.5	10.8	19.3	17.5
New Mexico			266	298	299	352	310			25.0	20.0	12.3	19.8	19.5
Arizona		278	285	350	349	315	320		27.8	26.4	21.5	13.3	25.6	23.5
California	332	271	284	340	387	340	340	24.2	24.2	24.0	22.0	14.0	21.0	19.5
United States	170.8	145.5	157.4	167.2	182.6	154.5	151.8	20.4	22.4	22.6	18.2	10.9	19.6	18.0

Bureau of Agricultural Economics. Estimates of the crop-reporting board.

TABLE 253.—Cotton: Percentage of acreage abandoned after June 25, average 1918–1927, annual 1924–1928

State	Average, 1918–1927	1924	1925	1926	1927	1928 [1]
	Per cent	Per cent	Per cent	Per cent	Per cent	Per cent
Missouri	5.0	6.0	4.0	8.0	4.5	6.0
Virginia	2.1	4.7	1.0	2.0	2.0	2.0
North Carolina	1.6	4.5	1.0	1.5	1.2	1.5
South Carolina	2.3	3.5	2.0	2.5	4.0	5.0
Georgia	3.6	1.7	2.0	1.5	2.5	4.0
Florida	5.5	3.0	1.5	3.0	4.0	6.0
Tennessee	2.4	2.0	1.5	3.0	2.0	3.0
Alabama	1.8	1.9	1.0	1.3	1.5	3.0
Mississippi	2.8	2.5	1.0	1.5	2.0	3.5
Arkansas	2.4	2.5	2.0	2.0	3.0	4.0
Louisiana	3.5	3.0	1.5	2.0	2.7	3.0
Oklahoma	6.9	4.0	2.0	8.0	14.0	4.0
Texas	4.2	3.0	8.0	4.0	4.0	3.2
New Mexico	[2] 13.2	20.0	23.0	4.0	5.0	5.0
Arizona	2.4	1.6	0	0.6	0.7	1.0
California	2.2	0	1.0	3.0	1.5	2.2
All other		10.8	3.4	2.3	5.0	3.4
United States	3.6	3.0	4.2	3.4	4.2	3.4

Bureau of Agricultural Economics. Estimates of the crop-reporting board.

[1] Abandoned after July 1.   [2] 5-year average.

TABLE 254.—Cotton: Production of lint in 500-pound gross-weight bales, by States, and linters, United States, 1917–1928

State	1917	1918	1919	1920	1921	1922	1923	1924	1925	1926	1927	1928 [1]
	1,000 bales	1,000 bales	1,000 bales	1,000 bales	1,000 bales	1,000 bales	1,000 bales	1,000 bales	1,000 bales	1,000 bales	1,000 bales	1,000 bales
Missouri	61	62	64	79	70	[2]149	[2]127	[2]193	[2]299	218	115	146
Virginia	19	25	23	21	16	27	51	39	53	51	31	44
North Carolina	618	898	830	925	776	852	1,020	825	1,102	1,213	861	840
South Carolina	1,237	1,570	1,426	1,623	755	493	770	807	889	1,008	730	725
Georgia	1,884	2,122	1,660	1,415	787	715	588	[2]1,002	1,164	1,496	1,100	1,020
Florida	38	29	16	18	11	25	12	[2]22	38	32	[2]17	20
Tennessee	241	330	310	325	302	391	[2]226	[2]354	[2]515	[2]451	[2]359	420
Alabama	518	801	713	663	580	824	587	[2]985	1,357	1,498	[2]1,191	1,090
Mississippi	906	1,226	961	895	813	989	604	1,099	1,991	1,888	1,355	1,470
Arkansas	974	987	884	1,214	797	[2]1,011	[2]622	[2]1,094	[2]1,600	1,548	1,000	1,215
Louisiana	639	588	298	390	280	342	367	492	909	828	548	685
Oklahoma	959	577	1,016	1,336	481	627	656	1,511	1,691	1,773	1,037	1,180
Texas	3,125	2,697	3,099	4,345	2,198	3,222	[2]4,340	[2]4,949	[2]4,163	[2]5,628	[2]4,352	5,150
New Mexico				10	6	12	[2]30	[2]57	[2]66	[2]75	[2]70	70
Arizona	22	56	60	103	45	47	78	108	119	[2]122	[2]91	134
California	58	67	56	75	34	21	54	77	122	131	91	155
All other	6	6	5	3	3	7	[2]8	[2]14	[2]26	[2]17	[2]7	9
United States	11,302	12,041	11,421	13,440	7,954	9,755	10,140	13,628	16,104	17,977	12,955	14,373
United States (linters) [3]	1,126	930	608	440	398	608	669	897	1,115	1,158	1,016	

Bureau of Agricultural Economics. Compiled from reports of the Bureau of the Census.

[1] Preliminary estimate of the Department of Agriculture.
[2] Slight differences from census figures on ginnings are due to ginnings in one State of cotton grown in another.
[3] Year beginning Aug. 1.

TABLE 255.—*Cotton ginned to specified dates and total, by seasons, United States, 1909–1928*

Season beginning August—	Cotton ginned to—										Total ginned [1]
	Sept. 1	Sept. 25	Oct. 1	Oct. 18	Nov. 1	Nov. 14	Dec. 1	Dec. 13	Jan. 1	Jan. 16	
	1,000 bales	*1,000 bales*	*1,000 bales*	*1,000 bales*	*1,000 bales*	*1,000 bales*	*1,000 bales*	*1,000 bales*	*1,000 bales*	*1,000 bales*	*1,000 bales*
1909	388	2,568		5,531	7,018	8,112	8,877	9,358	9,647	9,788	10,073
1910	353	2,312		5,424	7,346	8,780	10,140	10,695	11,085	11,253	11,568
1911	771	3,677		7,759	9,971	11,313	12,817	13,771	14,317	14,516	15,553
1912	731	3,007		6,874	8,869	10,300	11,855	12,439	12,907	13,089	13,489
1913	799	3,247		6,974	8,830	10,445	12,088	12,927	13,348	13,582	13,983
1914	480	3,394		7,620	9,827	11,668	13,073	13,972	14,443	14,916	15,906
1915	464	2,904		5,709	7,379	8,771	9,704	10,306	10,637	10,752	11,068
1916	851	4,082		7,303	8,624	9,615	10,352	10,839	11,039	11,138	11,364
1917	615	2,512		5,574	7,185	8,571	9,714	10,132	10,435	10,571	11,248
1918	1,038	3,771		6,811	7,777	8,706	9,571	10,281	10,774	11,049	11,906
1919	143	1,835		4,929	6,305	7,604	8,844	9,397	10,009	10,307	11,326
1920	352	2,250		5,755	7,509	8,915	10,141	10,876	11,555	12,015	13,271
1921	486	2,920		5,497	6,646	7,274	7,640	7,791	7,882	7,912	7,978
1922	806	3,866		6,978	8,139	8,870	9,320	9,489	9,597	9,648	9,729
1923	1,143	3,232		6,409	7,556	8,369	9,243	9,549	9,805	9,944	10,171
1924	947	[2] 2,666	4,528	7,616	9,716	11,162	12,238	12,792		13,307	13,639
1925	1,886	[2] 4,282	7,126	9,519	11,207	12,260	13,871	14,832		15,500	16,123
1926	697	[2] 2,509	5,643	8,728	11,254	12,956	14,644	15,541		16,616	17,755
1927	1,534	[2] 3,505	5,945	8,118	9,921	10,895	11,738	12,073		12,501	12,783
1928 [3]	957	[2] 2,504	4,964	8,155	10,164	11,323	12,564	13,147		13,890	

Bureau of Agricultural Economics. Compiled from reports of Bureau of the Census; quantities are given in running bales, except that round bales are counted as half bales. Linters not included.

[1] Includes cotton ginned after Jan. 16 and estimated quantities not ginned on Mar. 1. Quantities in Table 260 converted from running bales, average weight, by deducting average weight of bagging and ties, by States.
[2] Sept. 16.
[3] Preliminary.

TABLE 256.—*Cotton: Acreage and yield of lint per acre in specified countries, average 1909–10 to 1913–14, 1921–22 to 1925–26, annual 1926–27 to 1928–29*

Country	Acreage					Yield of lint per acre				
	Average, 1909–10 to 1913–14	Average, 1921–22 to 1925–26	1926–27	1927–28	1928–29 preliminary	Average, 1909–10 to 1913–14	Average, 1921–22 to 1925–26	1926–27	1927–28	1928–29 preliminary
	1,000 acres	*1,000 acres*	*1,000 acres*	*1,000 acres*	*1,000 acres*	*Lbs.*	*Lbs.*	*Lbs.*	*Lbs.*	*Lbs.*
United States	34,152	37,616	47,087	40,138	45,326	182	146	183	155	152
India	22,503	23,818	24,822	24,722	24,992	76	91	81	95	96
Egypt	1,743	1,768	1,854	1,574	1,805	399	367	409	382	379
China		4,675	3,529							
Brazil	[1] 887	1,475	986	1,213		209	184	235	194	
Russia (Asiatic)	1,569	771	1,731	1,987	2,435	276	184	209	182	
Mexico	253	330	613	326	521	353	322	281	263	250
Chosen (Korea)	146	405	529	503	505	67	128	129	126	142
Uganda	58	420	570	533	698	169	122	92	100	
Peru	[2] 163	284					334			
Anglo Egyptian Sudan	[2] 44	134	225	240	278	158	163	279	221	234
Argentina	5	156	177	210		221	188	157	231	
Total countries reporting 1926–27 to 1927–28			78,594	71,446						
Estimated world total, excluding China	62,500	69,000	80,900	73,800						

Bureau of Agricultural Economics. Official sources and International Institute of Agriculture. Data for crop year as given at the head of the table are for crops harvested between Aug. 1 and July 31 of the following year. This applies to both Northern and Southern Hemispheres. For the United States prior to 1914 the figures apply to the harvest year begining Sept. 1.

[1] Average for 3 years. [2] Average 1914–15 to 1918–19.

TABLE 257.—*Cotton: Production of lint in specified countries, average 1909–10 to 1913–14, 1921–22 to 1925–26, annual 1924–25 to 1928–29*

Country	Year beginning Aug. 1						
	Average, 1909–10 to 1913–14	Average, 1921–22 to 1925–26	1924–25	1925–26	1926–27	1927–28	1928–29 preliminary
NORTH AMERICA	Bales [1]	Bales [1]	Bales [1]	Bales [1]	Bales [1]	Bales [1]	Bales [1]
United States [2]	13,033,000	11,516,000	13,628,000	16,104,000	17,977,000	12,955,000	14,373,000
Mexico	187,000	222,106	196,332	202,247	359,820	179,000	[3] 272,000
Total North American countries reporting 1924–25 to 1927–28			13,824,332	16,306,247	18,336,820	13,134,000	14,645,000
SOUTH AND CENTRAL AMERICA AND WEST INDIES							
Venezuela		[4] 32,000	32,000	32,000	32,000	32,000	
Colombia		[4] 14,184	12,456	15,912	24,906		
Peru	110,000	200,408	211,522	204,308	258,409	251,150	
Ecuador	[4] 297	7,320	[3] 11,500	[3] 6,100	[3] 6,340	[3] 5,800	
Brazil	387,000	567,931	605,134	601,520	484,237	492,000	
Paraguay	[5] 92	9,686	12,222	11,481	10,625		
Argentina	2,314	61,289	70,711	134,767	58,113	101,467	
Guatemala	[4] 75	847	1,549	1,600	260		
Haiti [6]	9,300	18,445	16,630	23,035	22,604	[3] 14,000	
Dominican Republic [6]	[7] 992	515	709	640	414		
Porto Rico	[8] 1,319	1,356	1,900	1,891		1,062	
Salvador [6]		[4] 6,529	10,597	2,461	229		
British West Indies	6,058	4,451	4,350	3,876	4,281	4,245	
Total South and Central American countries and West Indies reporting 1924–25 to 1927–28			951,847	1,005,606	865,984	900,662	
EUROPE							
Italy	5,212	[9] 4,707	4,520				
Yugoslavia	922	333	385	580	385	189	
Greece	16,770	10,746	14,420	14,609	17,759	[3] 30,000	
Bulgaria	842	1,686	1,247	2,068	2,309	4,377	4,000
Malta	433	377	480	654	424	287	
Spain		[7] 698	1,154	1,108	3,599	2,670	
Total European countries reporting 1924–25 to 1927–28			17,686	19,019	24,476	37,523	
AFRICA							
Algeria	[9] 1,370	1,917	2,387	5,583	7,642	4,086	8,000
Morocco (French)		[4] 275	134	415	738	369	
French West Africa:							
Dahomey	[6] 664	2,939	3,943	6,549	4,718	3,920	
Ivory Coast [6]	212	2,498	3,729	6,314	6,743		
French Guinea	[6] [8] 167	707	404	2,237	2,315	2,306	
Senegal		1,677	1,845	1,605	2,629	2,306	
French Sudan		[7] 4,843	7,462	6,065	1,753		
Upper Volta		[7] 6,948	10,972	11,978	6,379	15,681	
French Togo	[4] 2,312	5,254	7,615	7,387	5,677		
Nigeria	8,702	24,185	32,750	40,091	22,982	16,742	
French Equatorial Africa		[7] 1,170	1,408				
Egypt	1,453,000	1,356,000	1,507,000	1,629,000	1,586,000	1,257,000	1,491,000
Anglo-Egyptian Sudan	14,455	45,836	40,665	106,460	131,007	111,000	136,000
Italian Somaliland	[6] 510	1,576	2,305	2,537	2,767	3,828	
Eritrea	[6] 1,022	1,373	2,767	1,845	2,767	1,384	
Gold Coast	104	1,781	2,500	500	84	84	
Belgian Congo		11,459	13,836	16,142	22,539	27,557	
Kenya	552	1,347	1,883	1,712	1,031	1,500	
Uganda	20,338	107,419	164,046	151,344	110,231	112,015	
Tanganyika	[6] [7] 7,971	11,122	15,726	18,179	20,318	13,360	20,000

[1] Bales of 478 pounds net.
[2] Linters not included. Production of linters during this period has been: Average 1909–10 to 1913–14, 02,711 bales; 1922–23, 607,779 bales; 1923–24, 668,600 bales; 1924–25, 897,375 bales; 1925–26, 1,114,877 bales; 926–27, 1,157,861 bales; 1927–28, 1,016,375 bales.
[3] From an unofficial source.
[4] Average for 2 years.
[5] For season 1915–16.
[6] Exports.
[7] Average for 4 years.
[8] For 1 year only.
[9] Average for 3 years.

TABLE 257.—*Cotton: Production of lint in specified countries, average 1909–10 to 1913–14, 1921–22 to 1925–26, annual 1924–25 to 1928–29*—Continued

Country	Year beginning Aug. 1						
	Average, 1909–10 to 1913–14	Average, 1921–22 to 1925–26	1924–25	1925–26	1926–27	1927–28	1928–29 preliminary
	Bales [1]	Bales [1]	Bales [1]	Bales [1]	Bales [1]	Bales [1]	Bales [1]
Nyasaland	4, 603	4, 751	5, 538	6, 459	4, 165	2, 336	
Northern Rhodesia	[9] 307	274	409	80	40		
Southern Rhodesia		[7] 2, 007	4, 010	5, 160	461	630	
Mozambique	[6] 388	2, 645	2, 496	2, 230	[3] 2, 200		
Union of South Africa	76	9, 041	14, 172	17, 055	8, 571	11, 233	
Total African countries reporting 1924–25 to 1927–28			1, 827, 292	2, 025, 265	1, 937, 424	1, 587, 377	
ASIA							
Cyprus	1, 938	1, 994	2, 557	2, 556	3, 598	1, 801	
Turkey, Asiatic	[8] 102, 116	64, 280	78, 400	126, 000	97, 000	105, 000	
Syria and Lebanon		7, 301	9, 685	13, 421	7, 760	10, 700	
Russia, Asiatic	904, 900	296, 181	453, 281	732, 822	755, 468	755, 000	
Iraq		1, 071	2, 092	2, 080	2, 929	1, 384	
Persia [6]	[5] 136, 000	[4] 71, 402	59, 171	83, 632	84, 610		
India	3, 585, 000	4, 522, 600	5, 095, 000	5, 201, 000	4, 205, 000	4, 913, 000	5, 018, 000
China [10]	694, 600	2, 024, 000	2, 179, 000	2, 114, 000	1, 584, 000	2, 000, 000	
Japanese Empire:							
Japan	4, 704	2, 459	2, 088	1, 561	1, 123		
Chosen (Korea)	20, 392	108, 279	122, 562	123, 214	142, 694	133, 000	150, 000
French Indo-China	[6] 13, 800	[11] 9, 279	[11] 7, 746	[11] 5, 667	[11] 3, 285	[11] 3, 996	
Dutch East Indies [6] [12]	[4] 18, 242	6, 649	[13] 6, 421	[13] 5, 469	6, 285		
Siam	[6] 3, 653	4, 135	4, 336	4, 624	2, 747	[3] 4, 310	
Total Asiatic countries reporting 1924–25 to 1927–28			7, 954, 659	8, 325, 384	6, 804, 481	7, 928, 191	
OCEANIA							
Australia	75	7, 919	12, 277	5, 684	5, 073	5, 020	
New Hebrides	[9] 547	2, 424	2, 131	3, 760			
Total Oceania reporting 1924–25 to 1927–28			7, 919	12, 277	5, 684	5, 073	5, 020	
Total all countries reporting 1924–25 to 1927–28			24, 583, 743	27, 683, 329	28, 054, 597	23, 592, 773	
Estimated world total, including China	20, 900, 000	21, 500, 000	24, 800, 000	27, 900, 000	28, 300, 000	23, 800, 000	

Bureau of Agricultural Economics. Official sources and International Institute of Agriculture except as otherwise stated. Data for crop year as given at the head of the table are for crops harvested between Aug. 1 and July 31 of the following year. For the United States prior to 1914 the figures apply to the year beginning Sept. 1.

[1] Bales of 478 pounds net.
[3] From an unofficial source.
[4] Average for 2 years.
[6] Exports.
[7] Average for 4 years.
[8] For 1 year only.
[9] Average for 3 years.
[10] For 1921–22 to 1927–28, Chinese Economic Bulletin quoting the Chinese Mill Owners' Association. The figures represent the crop in the most important Provinces where the commercial crop is grown. The average 1909–10 to 1913–14 is the commercial crop of China as estimated by the United States Bureau of the Census.
[11] Annam, Cambodia, and Cochin-China only.
[12] Includes Java and Madura and the outer possessions.
[13] Java and Madura only.

TABLE 258.—*Cotton: World production of lint, 1909–10 to 1928–29*

Year	Estimated world total, excluding China	Estimated world total, including China	Principal producing countries						Estimated world total commercial crop [2]
			United States	India	Egypt	China [1]	Brazil	Russia (Asiatic)	
	1,000 bales [3]	*1,000 bales* [3]	*1,000 bales* [3]	*1,000 bales* [3]	*1,000 bales* [3]	*1,000 bales* [3]	*1,000 bales* [3]	*1,000 bales* [3]	*1,000 bales* [4]
1909–10	16,800	--------	10,005	3,998	1,036	--------	--------	817	20,859
1910–11	18,460	--------	11,609	3,254	1,555	--------	--------	1,006	18,856
1911–12	21,990	--------	15,693	2,730	1,530	--------	360	969	22,247
1912–13	21,190	--------	13,703	3,702	1,554	--------	418	946	21,550
1913–14	22,350	--------	14,156	4,239	1,588	--------	477	1,104	22,612
1914–15	24,270	--------	16,135	4,359	1,337	--------	465	1,270	24,964
1915–16	17,750	--------	11,192	3,128	989	--------	339	1,512	18,419
1916–17	18,370	19,910	11,450	3,759	1,048	1,534	337	1,199	18,924
1917–18	17,660	19,750	11,302	3,393	1,304	2,092	414	634	18,140
1918–19	17,790	20,850	12,041	3,328	999	3,059	406	161	18,755
1919–20	18,730	21,330	11,421	4,853	1,155	2,599	461	81	20,220
1920–21	19,110	20,990	13,440	3,013	1,251	1,883	476	58	19,665
1921–22	13,930	15,450	7,954	3,753	902	1,517	504	43	15,334
1922–23	16,980	19,300	9,755	4,247	1,391	2,318	553	55	17,959
1923–24	17,710	19,700	10,140	4,320	1,353	1,993	576	196	19,005
1924–25	22,620	24,800	13,628	5,095	1,507	2,179	605	453	23,825
1925–26	25,790	27,900	16,104	5,201	1,629	2,114	602	733	26,618
1926–27	26,720	28,300	17,977	4,205	1,586	1,584	484	755	27,813
1927–28	21,800	23,800	12,955	4,913	1,257	2,000	492	755	23,370
1928–29 [5]	--------	--------	14,373	5,018	1,491	--------	--------	--------	--------

Bureau of Agricultural Economics. Data for crop year as given are for crops harvested between Aug. 1 and July 31 of the following year. For the United States prior to 1914 the figures apply to the year beginning Sept. 1.

[1] Chinese Cotton Mill Owners' Association. Figures represent the crop in the most important cotton-producing Provinces where the commercial crop is grown. Most of the cotton produced in other Provinces is used for home hand-loom consumption.

[2] Figures as reported by the United States Bureau of the Census, including the cotton destined to enter commercial channels for factory purposes. Estimates of the commercial crop in China are included.

[3] Bales of 478 pounds net.

[4] American in running bales and foreign cotton in bales of 478 pounds net.

[5] Preliminary.

TABLE 259.—*Cotton: Estimated monthly marketings by farmers, 1916–1927*

Year beginning August	Percentage of year's sales [1]												
	Aug.	Sept.	Oct.	Nov.	Dec.	Jan.	Feb.	Mar.	Apr.	May	June	July	Season
1916	3.9	14.6	23.0	21.6	15.0	6.4	4.0	3.9	3.0	2.5	1.6	0.5	100.0
1917	2.5	11.3	23.0	22.7	16.2	8.2	5.8	4.5	2.6	1.3	1.0	0.9	100.0
1918	3.3	10.9	18.1	16.4	13.6	5.4	4.4	4.6	7.5	6.8	4.4	100.0
1919	1.4	9.5	21.0	22.2	17.4	8.8	5.6	4.9	3.2	2.7	1.7	1.6	100.0
1920	3.1	10.0	16.2	15.7	11.0	6.4	5.6	6.0	6.7	6.9	6.8	5.6	100.0
1921	3.6	14.0	22.3	17.1	12.1	5.9	4.3	4.6	4.6	5.9	3.0	2.6	100.0
1922	5.2	16.8	25.3	19.8	12.8	5.9	4.4	3.7	2.0	1.0	1.5	1.6	100.0
1923	4.1	16.3	24.6	24.9	13.3	5.8	3.1	2.4	1.7	1.3	0.9	1.6	100.0
1924	3.3	15.2	25.2	22.3	14.5	7.0	5.3	3.4	1.6	1.0	0.6	0.6	100.0
1925	6.5	19.3	23.1	17.6	12.0	6.5	4.2	3.1	2.3	1.7	2.1	1.6	100.0
1926	2.7	15.2	22.0	19.5	12.5	6.3	5.8	5.0	3.8	3.1	2.5	1.6	100.0
1927	6.6	20.0	23.8	17.3	9.7	4.2	4.0	4.2	3.1	2.7	2.3	2.1	100.0

Bureau of Agricultural Economics.

[1] As reported by about 7,500 cotton growers, supplemented by records of State weighers, cooperative associations, and cotton dealers.

33023°—29——54

TABLE 260.—*Cotton: Supply and distribution, United States, 1913–14 to 1927–28*

Year	Supply			Distribution		
	Production, running bales [1]	Carry-over from previous year	Imports, equivalent 500-pound bales	Exports, running bales [1]	Consumption, running bales [1]	Stocks on hand at end of year
1913–14	13, 659, 167	1, 510, 606	265, 646	8, 654, 958	5, 577, 408	1, 365, 864
1914–15	15, 905, 840	1, 365, 864	363, 595	8, 322, 688	5, 597, 362	3, 936, 104
1915–16	11, 068, 173	3, 936, 104	420, 995	5, 895, 672	6, 397, 613	3, 139, 709
1916–17	11, 363, 915	3, 139, 709	288, 486	5, 302, 848	6, 788, 505	2, 720, 173
1917–18	11, 248, 242	2, 720, 173	217, 381	4, 288, 420	6, 566, 489	3, 450, 188
1918–19	11, 906, 480	3, 450, 188	197, 201	5, 592, 386	5, 765, 936	4, 286, 785
1919–20	11, 325, 532	4, 286, 785	682, 911	6, 545, 326	6, 419, 734	3, 563, 162
1920–21	13, 270, 970	3, 563, 162	226, 321	5, 673, 452	4, 892, 672	6, 590, 359
1921–22	7, 977, 778	6, 590, 359	363, 465	6, 184, 094	5, 979, 820	2, 831, 553
1922–23	9, 729, 306	2, 831, 553	463, 598	4, 822, 589	6, 666, 092	2, 324, 999
1923–24	10, 170, 694	2, 324, 999	292, 288	5, 655, 856	5, 680, 554	1, 555, 514
1924–25	13, 639, 399	1, 555, 514	313, 328	7, 996, 500	6, 193, 417	1, 610, 455
1925–26	16, 122, 516	1, 610, 455	325, 511	8, 050, 291	6, 450, 987	3, 543, 183
1926–27	17, 755, 070	3, 543, 183	400, 993	10, 922, 652	7, 202, 724	3, 762, 367
1927–28	12, 783, 112	3, 762, 367	338, 226	7, 539, 945	6, 832, 689	2, 531, 582

Bureau of Agricultural Economics. Compiled from Bureau of Census Reports. Linters are excluded.
[1] Round bales counted as half bales.

TABLE 261.—*Cotton: Estimated grade and staple of carry-over, July 31, 1928*

ALL COTTON

Grade and number	Total	Staple in inches—							
		13/16 and under	7/8	15/16	1 and 1 1/32	1 1/16 and 1 3/32	1 1/8 and 1 5/32	1 3/16 and 1 7/32	1 1/4 and over
	Bales	Bales	Bales	Bales	Bales	Bales	Bales	Bales	Bales
Total [2]	2, 536, 472	126, 999	484, 821	426, 787	660, 419	269, 807	310, 674	159, 609	97, 356

UPLAND COTTON

Grade and number	Total	13/16 and under	7/8	15/16	1 and 1 1/32	1 1/16 and 1 3/32	1 1/8 and 1 5/32	1 3/16 and 1 7/32	1 1/4 and over
Extra white:									
3–G. M	5, 480	32		23	168	858	2, 588	1, 811	
4–S. M	5, 226		72	24	301	1, 464	2, 548	721	96
5–M	3, 807		50	1	120	1, 109	1, 640	822	65
6–S. L. M	187				26	90	58		13
7–L. M	216			48	98	70			
Total	14, 916	32	122	96	713	3, 591	6, 834	3, 354	174
White:									
1–M. F	24			1	23				
2–S. G. M	1, 727	55	435	506	438	74	103	55	61
3–G. M	173, 685	8, 868	32, 561	36, 988	31, 246	18, 254	21, 840	14, 930	8, 998
4–S. M	762, 638	17, 711	137, 542	128, 349	201, 801	81, 827	100, 664	67, 470	27, 274
5–M	753, 891	10, 673	124, 361	120, 882	256, 502	96, 309	90, 682	45, 711	8, 771
6–S. L. M	330, 797	5, 940	68, 809	52, 524	96, 524	34, 195	49, 738	21, 112	1, 955
7–L. M	78, 236	2, 829	20, 953	15, 790	19, 270	9, 397	7, 574	2, 242	181
8–S. G. O. [1]	37, 782	2, 245	8, 889	7, 596	8, 157	5, 961	3, 983	885	66
9–G. O. [1]	15, 918	422	2, 958	3, 251	5, 356	2, 239	1, 351	292	49
Total	2, 154, 698	48, 743	396, 508	365, 887	619, 317	248, 256	275, 935	152, 697	47, 355
Spotted:									
3–G. M	14, 370	525	6, 781	3, 347	2, 692	753	188	83	1
4–S. M	54, 862	1, 459	20, 655	15, 730	10, 534	5, 381	960	143	
5–M	51, 940	3, 101	18, 964	13, 723	8, 895	5, 290	1, 366	428	173
6–S. L. M. [1]	24, 808	3, 619	7, 800	6, 791	4, 791	1, 186	546	75	
7–L. M. [1]	14, 555	1, 760	2, 293	5, 926	3, 331	1, 113	116	16	
Total	160, 535	10, 464	56, 493	45, 517	30, 243	13, 723	3, 176	745	174

[1] Untenderable according to sec. 5, United States cotton futures act.

TABLE 261.—*Cotton: Estimated grade and staple of carry-over, July 31, 1928*—Con.

UPLAND COTTON—Continued

Grade and number	Total	Staple in inches—							
		$\frac{13}{16}$ and under	$\frac{7}{8}$	$\frac{15}{16}$	1 and $1\frac{1}{32}$	$1\frac{1}{16}$ and $1\frac{3}{32}$	$1\frac{1}{8}$ and $1\frac{5}{32}$	$1\frac{3}{16}$ and $1\frac{7}{32}$	$1\frac{1}{4}$ and over
	Bales	*Bales*	*Bales*	*Bales*	*Bales*	*Bales*	*Bales*	*Bales*	*Bales*
Yellow tinged:									
2–S. G. M	106		53	15	38				
3–G. M	2,074	124	758	384	749	59			
4–S. M	9,929	430	4,329	3,587	1,410	69	69	34	1
5–M.[1]	16,094	1,405	6,486	3,196	3,624	1,326	55	2	
6–S. L. M.[1]	16,556	2,899	8,060	3,865	1,430	181	121		
7–L. M.[1]	9,839	1,464	5,430	2,114	731	53	24	23	
Total	54,598	6,322	25,116	13,161	7,982	1,688	269	59	1
Light yellow stained:									
3–G. M	194		149	21	24				
4–S. M.[1]	894	39	461	307	87				
5–M.[1]	1,515	95	796	286	338				
Total	2,603	134	1,406	614	449				
Yellow stained:									
3–G. M	66		40	25	1				
4–S. M.[1]	1,402	68	1,171	123	40				
5–M.[1]	1,418	68	1,169	153	22	1	5		
Total	2,886	136	2,380	301	63	1	5		
Gray:									
3–G. M	110		9	5	96				
4–S. M	140		7	14	106		5	8	
5–M.[1]	297		58	8	45	70	103	2	11
Total	547		74	27	247	70	108	10	11
Blue stained:									
3–G. M.[1]	94		20	46		28			
4–S. M.[1]	82		60	22					
5–M.[1]	145		52	21	1	29	42		
Total	321		132	89	1	57	42		
No grade [3]	28,651	21,875	2,590	1,095	1,111	984	814	90	92
Total [2]	2,419,755	87,706	484,821	426,787	660,126	268,370	287,183	156,955	47,807

AMERICAN-EGYPTIAN [1]

Grade designation	Total [2]	Staple in inches—				
		Under $1\frac{1}{2}$	$1\frac{1}{2}$ and $1\frac{17}{32}$	$1\frac{9}{16}$ and $1\frac{19}{32}$	$1\frac{5}{8}$ to $1\frac{23}{32}$	$1\frac{3}{4}$ and over
No. 1	277		16	69	192	
No. 1½	1,047		214	671	162	
No. 2	657		337	80	233	7
No. 2½	495		263	32	200	
No. 3	1,697		237	804	656	
No. 3½	961		134	666	161	
No. 4	269	16	172	7	74	
No. 4½	131	35	98			
No. 5	64		23	7	34	
Below No. 5 [3]	185	9	176			
Total [2]	5,783	58	1,670	2,336	1,712	7

[1] Untenderable according to sec. 5, United States cotton futures act.
[2] Bureau of Census Bull. 146.
[3] Includes bales not otherwise classified above.

TABLE 261.—*Cotton: Estimated grade and staple of carry-over, July 31, 1928*—Con.

EGYPTIAN COTTON [1]

	Total	Staple in inches—							
		Under 1⅛	1⅛ and 1 5/32	1 3/16 1 7/32	1¼ to 1 11/32	1⅜ to 1 15/32	1½ to 1 19/32	1⅝ to 1 23/32	1¾ and over
Total [2]	65, 356	1, 437	23, 371	1, 734	7, 502	21, 335	6, 976	2, 558	443

FOREIGN COTTON OTHER THAN AMERICAN-EGYPTIAN AND EGYPTIAN [1]

Growth	Total	Staple in inches—							
		13/16 and under	⅞	15/16	1 1/32	1 1/16 and 1 3/32	1⅛ and 1 5/32	1 3/16 and 1 7/32	1¼ and over
Peruvian	5, 505						73	920	4, 512
Chinese	29, 937	29, 937							
British Indian	9, 356	9, 356							
Other	780				293		47		440
Total [2]	45, 578	39, 293			293		120	920	4, 952

Bureau of Agricultural Economics.

[1] Untenderable according to sec. 5, United States cotton futures act.
[2] Bureau of Census Bull. 146.

TABLE 262.—*Cotton: Estimated grade and staple consumed, United States, year ending July 31, 1928*

ALL COTTON

Number and grade	Total	Staple in inches—							
		13/16 and under [1]	⅞	15/16	1 and 1 1/32	1 1/16 and 1 3/32	1⅛ and 1 5/32	1 3/16 and 1 7/32	1¼ and over
	Bales	*Bales*	*Bales*	*Bales*	*Bales*	*Bales*	*Bales*	*Bales*	*Bales*
Total [2]	6, 834, 063	159, 269	1, 878, 201	1, 782, 817	1, 854, 915	372, 208	439, 272	269, 756	77, 625

UPLAND COTTON

Number and grade	Total	13/16 and under [1]	⅞	15/16	1 and 1 1/32	1 1/16 and 1 3/32	1⅛ and 1 5/32	1 3/16 and 1 7/32	1¼ and over
1-M. F									
2-S. G. M	7, 157		1, 128	5, 436					593
3-G. M	605, 242		146, 163	147, 173	105, 229	77, 619	65, 114	60, 805	3, 139
4-S. M	2, 044, 057	4, 107	564, 739	596, 015	555, 856	134, 688	113. 529	66, 124	8, 999
5-M	2, 061, 947	56, 495	757, 771	527, 059	527, 925	107, 034	52, 083	33, 580	
6-S. L. M	657, 952	11, 115	132, 476	180, 205	268, 620	26, 703	33, 235	5, 598	
7-L. M	301, 166		59, 467	31, 759	193, 649	6, 370	8, 994	927	
8-S. G. O.[1]	208, 785	353	8, 366	57, 483	62, 855	49		79, 679	
9-G. O.[1]	82, 039		41, 591	14, 923	6, 130	19, 395			
Spotted:									
3-G. M	38, 311		16, 178	17, 155				4, 978	
4-S. M	138, 532	8, 052	77, 445	52, 329	706				
5-M	193, 928	3, 357	23, 623	72, 489	93, 778	350	331		
6-S. L. M	45, 366	9, 382	11, 179	20, 050	4, 755				
7-L. M	7, 461		718	6, 743					
Total	423, 598	20, 791	129, 143	168, 766	99, 239	350	331	4, 978	
Colored cottons [3]	74, 017	981	26, 421	35, 841	10, 656		118		
No grade [1]	53, 849		10, 936	18, 157	24, 756				
Total [2]	6, 519, 809	93, 842	1, 878, 201	1, 782, 817	1, 854, 915	372, 208	273, 404	251, 691	12, 731

[1] Untenderable.
[2] Report of Bureau of the Census.
[3] Colored cotton of various grades includes Yellow Tinge, Yellow Stain, Gray, and Blue Stained Cotton.

TABLE 262.—*Cotton: Estimated grade and staple consumed, United States, year ending July 31, 1928*—Continued

AMERICAN-EGYPTIAN COTTON [1]

Grade designation and number	Total	Staple in inches—			
		Under 1½	1½ and 1¹⁷⁄₃₂	1⁹⁄₁₆ and 1¹⁹⁄₃₂	1⅝ and above
1 and 1½	5,018	597			4,421
2 and 2½	5,946			4,089	1,857
3 and 3½	3,400				3,400
4 and 4½	773				773
5					
Below 5					
Total [2]	15,137	597		4,089	10,451

FOREIGN COTTON [1]

Growth designation	Total	Staple in inches—						
		½ and ⅝	1⅛ and 1⁵⁄₃₂	1³⁄₁₆ and 1⁷⁄₃₂	1¼ and 1¹¹⁄₃₂	1⅜ and 1¹⁵⁄₃₂	1½ and 1¹⁹⁄₃₂	1⅝ and above
Egyptian	217,584		163,085	7,427	13,320	27,697	5,653	402
Other	81,533	65,427	2,783	10,638			2,473	212
Total [2]	299,117	65,427	165,868	18,065	13,320	27,697	8,126	614

Bureau of Agricultural Economics.

[1] Untenderable.
[2] Report of Bureau of the Census.

TABLE 263.—*Cotton: Estimated grade and staple ginned to January 16, 1929, season of 1928–29*

ALL COTTON [1]

Grade and number	Total	Staple in inches—							
		1³⁄₁₆ and under [2]	⅞	1⁵⁄₁₆	1 and 1¹⁄₃₂	1¹⁄₁₆ and 1³⁄₃₂	1⅛ and 1⁵⁄₃₂	1³⁄₁₆ and 1⁷⁄₃₂	1¼ and over
	Bales	Bales	Bales	Bales	Bales	Bales	Bales	Bales	Bales
Total	13,891,857	[3] 1,927,047	5,832,860	3,179,316	1,568,674	733,498	439,589	157,637	53,236

UPLAND COTTON

Extra white:									
3–G. M	157,270	2,980	24,275	32,944	41,985	44,916	10,108	37	25
4–S. M	134,128	1,491	9,364	15,685	43,508	55,963	8,063	50	4
5–M	86,479	1,408	4,065	4,909	18,816	48,451	8,830		
6–S. L. M	13,804	774	2,026	1,476	2,805	5,096	1,627		
7–L. M	5,424	1,091	1,250	851	1,279	811	133	9	
Total	397,105	7,744	40,980	55,865	108,393	155,237	28,761	96	29
White:									
1–M. F	704	234	186	145	65	63	11		
2–S. G. M	42,600	10,424	18,242	8,712	3,793	627	328	239	235
3–G. M	1,637,209	326,977	617,251	380,820	173,054	61,800	48,986	22,755	5,566
4–S. M	4,913,876	661,162	2,069,037	1,173,493	575,015	201,054	152,016	69,909	12,190
5–M	3,224,592	338,362	1,381,365	774,196	384,032	168,359	126,646	44,241	7,391
6–S. L. M	1,333,885	169,315	567,180	303,371	149,750	80,047	50,952	11,902	1,368
7–L. M	397,930	71,157	176,502	84,161	32,091	19,798	11,110	2,991	120
8–S. G. O. [2]	192,211	31,751	84,986	49,399	17,215	5,991	2,339	483	47
9–G. O. [2]	59,074	8,438	23,305	17,178	6,969	2,620	486	66	12
Total	11,802,081	1,617,820	4,938,054	2,791,475	1,341,984	540,359	392,874	152,586	26,929

[1] According to official cotton standards of the United States.
[2] Untenderable.
[3] According to report of Bureau of the Census of Jan. 23, 1929.

TABLE 263.—*Cotton: Estimated grade and staple ginned to January 16, 1929, season of 1928–29*—Continued

UPLAND COTTON—Continued

Grade and number	Total	Staple in inches—							
		13⁄16 and under	7⁄8	15⁄16	1 and 1⁄32	11⁄16 and 13⁄32	11⁄8 and 15⁄32	13⁄16 and 17⁄32	11⁄4 and over
Spotted:	*Bales*	*Bales*	*Bales*	*Bales*	*Bales*	*Bales*	*Bales*	*Bales*	*Bales*
3–G. M	156,392	19,086	81,143	39,517	12,708	2,585	752	498	103
4–S. M	756,847	92,741	431,998	147,447	56,345	17,275	7,956	2,540	545
5–M	425,364	69,374	220,206	86,289	31,242	11,413	5,391	1,267	182
6–S. L. M.[2]	138,634	39,112	58,173	29,180	7,717	2,762	1,367	312	11
7–L. M.[2]	66,368	11,993	30,309	18,433	4,390	830	379	34	
Total	1,543,605	232,306	821,829	320,866	112,402	34,865	15,845	4,651	841
Yellow tinged:									
2–S. G. M	407	67	231	77	20		12		
3–G. M	4,387	238	3,203	729	144	39	34		
4–S. M	10,343	824	6,489	1,687	861	219	241	22	
5–M.[2]	5,189	1,109	2,626	703	504	164	83		
6–L. M.[2]	4,994	1,778	1,819	944	408	34	11		
7–L. M.[2]	5,435	1,250	2,618	1,156	401	10			
Total	30,755	5,266	16,986	5,296	2,338	466	381	22	
Light yellow stained:									
3–G. M	381	58	208	60	11	23	11	10	
4–S. M.[2]	520	39	300	50	77	43	11		
5–M.[2]	804	105	389	103	156	19	32		
Total	1,705	202	897	213	244	85	54	10	
Yellow stained:									
3–G. M	197	9	157	31					
4–S. M.[2]	294		248	35			11		
5–M.[2]	315	44	181	69		11		10	
Total	806	53	586	135		11	11	10	
Gray:									
3–G. M	3,505	193	2,542	342	193	110	113	12	
4–S. M	12,327	723	6,891	1,564	1,339	1,203	560	47	
5–M.[2]	3,987	405	1,238	706	308	557	672	101	
Total	19,819	1,321	10,671	2,612	1,840	1,870	1,345	160	
Blue stained:									
3–G. M.[2]	122		110	12					
4–S. M.[2]	65		54	11					
5–M.[2]	12						12		
Total	199		164	23			12		
No grade [2][4]	70,356	[4] 62,335	2,693	2,831	1,473	605	306	102	11
Total	13,866,431	1,927,047	5,832,860	3,179,316	1,568,674	733,498	439,589	157,637	27,810

AMERICAN-EGYPTIAN COTTON [2]

Grade designation and number	Total	Staple, in inches—				
		Under 1½	1½ and 117⁄32	19⁄16 and 119⁄32	15⁄8 and 123⁄32, inclusive	13⁄4 and over
1 and 1½	5,910	237	2,316	2,892	452	13
2 and 2 ½	13,125	211	5,231	6,786	837	60
3 and 3½	5,939	102	2,551	2,864	399	23
4 and 4½	452		168	234	50	
Below 5 [4]		[4]				
Total	25,426	550	10,266	12,776	1,738	96

Bureau of Agricultural Economics.

[2] Untenderable.
[4] Includes all bales not otherwise classified above.

TABLE 264.—*Cotton: Consumption by domestic mills, 1918–19 to 1927–28, inclusive*

[Exclusive of linters]

Month	1918–19	1919–20	1920–21	1921–22	1922–23	1923–24	1924–25	1925–26	1926–27	1927–28
	Bales	Bales	Bales	Bales	Bales	Bales	Bales	Bales	Bales	Bales
August	534,971	497,319	483,560	467,059	526,380	493,029	357,380	451,236	500,253	634,520
September	489,962	491,069	457,967	484,718	494,013	485,400	438,373	483,082	570,570	627,784
October	440,354	556,041	401,325	494,317	533,744	543,725	534,283	544,097	568,361	613,520
November	455,611	491,250	332,712	527,940	579,190	533,470	495,182	543,488	583,746	626,742
December	472,908	511,711	295,292	510,925	529,342	464,232	532,047	576,216	602,986	538,786
January	556,883	591,921	366,463	526,698	610,306	579,813	589,725	582,315	603,242	586,142
February	433,295	515,699	395,115	472,336	566,805	510,201	550,132	565,118	589,513	572,875
March	433,485	575,789	438,218	519,761	624,264	486,013	582,674	635,896	693,081	581,325
April	475,875	566,914	409,247	443,509	576,514	481,631	597,104	577,678	618,279	524,765
May	487,934	541,377	440,714	495,337	620,854	413,649	531,471	516,376	629,948	577,384
June	474,330	555,155	461,917	509,218	542,026	350,277	493,765	518,607	659,841	510,399
July	510,328	525,489	410,142	458,002	462,654	346,671	483,898	461,743	569,765	439,821

Bureau of the Census.

TABLE 265.—*Cotton: International trade, average 1910–1914, annual 1925–1928*

Country	Average, 1910–1914		1925		1926		1927		1928, preliminary	
	Imports	Exports	Imports	Exports	Imports	Exports	Imports	Exports	Imports	Exports
PRINCIPAL EXPORTING COUNTRIES	1,000 bales	1,000 bales	1,000 bales	1,000 bales	1,000 bales	1,000 bales	1,000 bales	1,000 bales	1,000 bales	1,000 bales
United States	232	8,840	324	8,239	338	8,110	400	11,281	367	7,889
British India [1]	[2] 57	[2] 2,154	89	3,331	96	3,218	413	2,422	158	2,528
Egypt	0	1,444	0	1,504	0	1,409	0	1,595	0	1,377
Argentina	0	[3] 1	0	24	0	71	0	88	0	41
PRINCIPAL IMPORTING COUNTRIES										
United Kingdom	4,143	0	3,654	0	3,345	0	3,728	0	2,460	0
Japan	[3] 1,405	0	2,669	0	3,233	0	3,485	0	2,617	0
France	1,440	337	1,540	91	1,565	88	1,692	133	1,624	129
Germany	2,142	221	1,467	163	1,587	205	1,812	280	2,563	392
Italy	902	0	1,073	3	1,023	2	1,037	1	982	1
Czechoslovakia			578	26	581	13	540	2	629	2
Spain	388	1	430	1	418	3	339	9		
Belgium	[4] 663	[4] 278	333	15	407	2	362	6	375	17
Canada	155	0	230	0	274	0	296	0	261	0
Poland		0	225	0	199	0	327	0	353	0
Austria	[3][5] 906	[3][5] 12	139	1	160	2	142	2	175	0
Switzerland	[3] 113	0	137	0	138	0	157	0	134	0
Netherlands	[3] 277	[3] 145	148	2	160	2	186	3	193	1
Sweden	[3] 93	[3] 1	89	0	97	0	114	0	111	0
Finland	[3] 37	0	28	0	40	0	41	0	46	0
Denmark	[3] 26	0	21	0	21	0	15	0	24	0
Norway	[3] 18	0	14	0	10	0	11	0	9	0
Estonia		0	[6] 21	0	[6] 21	0	24	0	26	0
Hungary			11	0	20	0	28	0	33	0
Total, 23 countries	12,997	13,434	13,220	13,400	13,733	13,125	15,149	15,822	13,140	12,377

Bureau of Agricultural Economics. Official sources except where otherwise noted. Bales of 500 pounds gross weight or 478 pounds net. The figures for cotton refer to ginned and unginned cotton and linters but not to mill waste, cotton batting, and scarto (Egyptian and Sudan). Wherever unginned cotton. has been separately stated in the original reports it has been reduced to ginned cotton in this statement at the ratio of 3 pounds unginned to 1 pound ginned. Wherever linters are stated separately, they have been excluded from these figures.

[1] Sea trade only.
[2] Includes some land trade.
[3] Year ended Dec. 31.
[4] 3-year average.
[5] Average for Austria-Hungary.
[6] International Crop Report and Agricultural Statistics.

TABLE 266.—*Cotton: Estimated price per pound, received by producers, United States, 1909–1928*

Year beginning August	Aug. 15	Sept. 15	Oct. 15	Nov. 15	Dec. 15	Jan. 15	Feb. 15	Mar. 15	Apr. 15	May 15	June 15	July 15	Weighted av.
Average:	*Cts.*	*Cts.*	*Cts.*	*Cts.*	*Cts.*	*Cts.*	*Cts.*	*Cts.*	*Cts.*	*Cts.*	*Cts.*	*Cts.*	*Cts.*
1909–1913	12.3	12.2	12.1	12.1	12.2	12.2	12.3	12.4	12.4	12.7	12.7	12.7	12.2
1914–1920	21.7	21.1	21.1	20.8	20.2	19.9	19.5	19.7	20.1	20.4	21.2	21.8	20.4
1921–1925	21.4	21.4	22.5	22.1	22.4	22.7	22.9	22.5	22.5	22.1	22.5	22.3	22.2
1909	11.5	12.2	13.2	13.8	14.2	14.3	14.0	14.0	14.0	14.1	14.0	14.1	13.6
1910	14.4	13.8	13.6	14.0	14.2	14.4	14.1	13.9	14.0	14.4	14.5	13.8	14.0
1911	12.5	11.0	9.6	8.8	8.6	8.7	9.4	10.0	10.5	11.0	11.1	11.6	9.6
1912	11.6	11.2	11.0	11.4	12.0	12.0	11.8	11.8	11.7	11.6	11.6	11.6	11.5
1913	11.6	12.6	13.2	12.6	12.0	11.8	12.2	12.2	12.0	12.3	12.4	12.4	12.5
1914	10.6	8.2	7.0	6.6	6.7	7.0	7.4	7.8	8.6	8.8	8.6	8.4	7.4
1915	8.3	9.8	11.4	11.4	11.4	11.4	11.3	11.3	11.5	11.8	12.4	12.6	11.2
1916	13.6	15.0	16.8	18.8	18.4	17.0	16.4	17.0	18.4	19.6	22.4	24.5	17.3
1917	23.8	23.4	25.3	27.5	28.3	29.3	30.0	31.0	30.2	28.0	28.0	28.2	27.1
1918	30.0	32.0	30.6	28.4	28.2	26.8	24.4	24.2	25.2	27.8	30.3	31.8	28.8
1919	31.4	30.8	33.9	36.0	35.8	36.0	36.2	36.8	37.5	37.4	37.3	37.1	35.2
1920	34.0	28.3	22.4	16.6	12.7	11.6	11.0	9.8	9.4	9.6	9.7	9.7	15.8
1921	11.2	16.2	18.8	17.0	16.2	15.9	15.7	16.0	16.0	17.3	19.6	20.6	17.0
1922	20.9	20.6	21.2	23.1	24.2	25.2	26.8	28.0	27.6	26.2	25.9	24.8	22.8
1923	23.8	25.6	28.0	29.9	32.1	32.5	31.4	27.7	28.7	28.1	27.8	27.3	28.7
1924	27.8	22.2	23.1	22.5	22.2	22.7	23.0	24.5	23.7	23.0	23.0	23.4	22.9
1925	23.4	22.5	21.5	18.1	17.4	17.4	17.6	16.5	16.6	16.0	16.1	15.4	19.6
1926	16.1	16.8	11.7	11.0	10.0	10.6	11.5	12.5	12.3	13.9	14.8	15.5	12.5
1927	17.1	22.5	21.0	20.0	18.7	18.6	17.0	17.8	18.7	20.1	19.7	21.0	20.2
1928	18.8	17.6	18.1	17.8	18.0								

Bureau of Agricultural Economics. Based upon returns from special price reporters. Mean of prices reported on 1st of month and 1st of succeeding month, August, 1909–December, 1923.

TABLE 267.—*Cotton, middling: Average spot price per pound at 10 markets in stated years*

Year beginning August	Aug.	Sept.	Oct.	Nov.	Dec.	Jan.	Feb.	Mar.	Apr.	May	June	July	Average
	Cents	Cents	Cents	Cents	Cents	Cents	Cents	Cents	Cents	Cents	Cents	Cents	Cents
Norfolk:													
1927	19.46	21.50	20.95	20.25	19.43	18.91	18.15	19.32	20.29	20.96	21.19	21.64	20.17
1928	19.03	18.17	18.80	19.11	19.46								
Augusta:													
1927	19.37	21.55	20.60	20.08	19.28	18.82	18.05	19.12	20.05	20.90	21.44	21.77	20.09
1928	19.11	18.00	18.70	18.94	19.22								
Savannah:													
1927	19.32	21.52	20.58	20.04	19.33	18.79	18.00	19.23	20.15	20.90	21.19	21.71	20.06
1928	18.88	17.89	18.65	19.00	19.45								
Montgomery:													
1927	18.79	20.78	19.95	19.40	18.78	18.23	17.44	18.59	19.48	20.25	20.64	21.20	19.46
1928	18.97	17.39	18.14	18.33	18.62								
Memphis:													
1927	18.95	20.70	19.92	19.61	18.83	18.25	17.40	18.43	19.45	20.14	20.59	21.07	19.44
1928	18.62	17.57	18.10	18.24	18.70								
Little Rock:													
1927	18.85	20.73	20.12	19.35	18.70	18.15	17.07	18.17	19.30	20.11	20.26	20.91	19.31
1928	18.45	17.60	18.18	18.25	18.71								
Dallas:													
1927	18.51	20.56	19.59	18.97	18.15	17.59	16.92	18.12	19.25	20.12	20.26	20.48	19.04
1928	18.02	17.13	17.99	18.32	18.67								
Houston:													
1927	19.46	21.50	20.49	19.81	19.06	18.41	17.46	18.78	19.74	20.56	20.76	21.08	19.76
1928	18.54	17.69	18.50	18.90	19.24								
Galveston:													
1927	19.49	21.53	20.58	19.88	19.11	18.54	17.62	18.86	19.84	20.66	20.82	21.14	19.84
1928	18.60	17.85	18.71	19.04	19.31								
New Orleans:													
1909	12.28	12.66	13.48	14.40	14.96	15.23	14.88	14.74	14.64	14.89	14.85	14.93	14.33
1910	14.92	13.49	14.21	14.50	14.85	14.95	14.62	14.54	14.70	15.48	15.26	14.30	14.65
1911	11.96	11.29	9.61	9.35	9.17	9.53	10.31	10.65	11.61	11.72	12.07	12.93	10.85
1912	12.07	11.37	10.95	12.15	12.81	12.58	12.61	12.45	12.44	12.29	12.44	12.34	12.20
1913	12.02	13.11	13.73	13.26	12.98	12.93	12.90	12.95	13.11	13.36	13.79	13.34	13.12
1914	(1)	2 8.42	7.02	7.43	7.18	7.87	8.01	8.34	9.43	9.04	9.12	8.71	
1915	8.94	10.40	11.95	11.50	11.89	12.04	11.45	11.73	11.88	12.61	12.80	13.03	11.68
1916	14.26	15.27	17.24	19.45	18.34	17.33	17.14	17.94	19.51	20.06	24.18	25.41	18.84
1917	25.07	21.68	26.76	28.07	29.07	31.07	30.91	32.76	33.05	28.90	30.71	29.50	28.96
1918	30.23	33.22	31.18	29.75	29.44	28.84	26.97	26.84	26.70	29.22	32.09	33.93	29.87
1919	31.38	30.38	35.28	39.58	39.89	40.28	39.39	40.69	41.41	40.31	40.49	39.41	38.21
1920	34.03	27.48	20.95	17.65	14.59	14.53	12.85	11.08	11.17	11.80	11.03	11.49	16.55
1921	12.78	19.35	18.99	17.27	17.16	16.53	16.36	16.74	16.80	19.31	21.68	22.01	17.92
1922	21.55	20.74	22.05	25.34	25.48	27.51	28.78	30.43	28.42	26.63	28.61	25.73	25.94
1923	24.22	27.71	29.18	33.68	34.88	33.93	31.90	28.74	30.41	30.70	29.43	29.23	30.33
1924	26.65	22.79	23.48	23.95	23.66	23.66	24.61	25.52	24.52	23.54	24.07	24.05	24.21
1925	23.07	23.09	20.86	19.82	19.27	20.26	19.83	18.25	18.11	18.06	17.54	18.24	19.71
1926	18.01	16.14	12.68	12.52	12.22	13.17	13.82	14.10	14.42	15.68	16.47	17.63	14.74
1927	19.36	21.53	20.73	19.99	19.26	18.72	17.90	18.94	20.07	20.77	21.10	21.45	19.98
1928	19.00	17.94	18.79	19.00	19.36								
10 markets combined:													
1915	3 8.80	10.29	11.99	11.49	11.97	12.10	11.64	11.78	11.94	12.67	12.89	13.11	11.72
1916	14.32	15.31	17.38	19.54	18.44	17.70	4 16.54	18.29	19.72	20.15	24.33	25.45	18.96
1917	25.26	22.08	26.86	28.21	29.19	31.05	30.97	32.84	32.87	29.32	30.10	29.44	29.02
1918	31.05	33.38	31.11	29.27	29.22	28.51	26.55	26.40	26.84	29.21	31.84	33.80	29.76
1919	31.50	30.30	35.44	39.59	39.70	40.46	39.49	40.68	41.74	41.01	40.58	39.58	38.34
1920	34.78	28.24	21.38	17.83	14.63	14.42	12.93	11.19	11.01	11.55	10.77	11.13	16.66
1921	12.53	19.50	19.25	17.43	17.47	17.04	16.73	17.12	16.92	19.22	21.58	22.27	18.09
1922	21.33	20.72	22.11	25.20	25.40	27.39	28.62	30.21	28.28	26.47	28.20	25.87	25.83
1923	24.22	27.67	28.90	33.30	34.39	33.69	31.73	28.54	30.25	30.32	29.37	29.32	30.14
1924	27.16	22.74	23.29	23.63	23.40	23.53	24.51	25.51	24.56	23.61	24.19	24.55	24.22
1925	23.35	23.23	20.95	19.92	19.31	20.04	19.63	18.33	18.05	17.95	17.52	17.92	19.68
1926	17.65	15.96	12.40	12.17	11.81	12.72	13.45	13.74	14.08	15.38	16.10	17.34	14.40
1927	19.16	21.19	20.35	19.74	18.99	18.44	17.60	18.76	19.76	20.54	20.82	21.25	19.72
1928	18.72	17.72	18.46	18.70	19.07								

Bureau of Agricultural Economics. Prior to Aug. 16, 1915, compiled from quotations in Market Reports of the New York Cotton Exchange, except Sept. 23 to Nov. 16, 1914, when the exchange was closed, quotations for which time were taken from the New York Commercial and Financial Chronicle; from Aug. 16, 1915, compiled from daily reports to the bureau from the cotton exchanges of the various markets. Prices 1900–1908 for New Orleans and 1914–1926 for other markets are available in 1924 Yearbook, p. 756, Table 313, p. 757, Table 314, and 1927 Yearbook, Table 254, p. 920.

¹ Market closed.　　　　² No quotations prior to Sept. 23.　Average for 7 days' business.
³ Does not include New Orleans.　　⁴ Does not include Savannah.

TABLE 268.—*Cotton: Average monthly premiums for staple lengths, New Orleans, 1920–21 to 1927–28*

Year and month	Premiums shown in hundredths of cent			
	Staple 1 1/16 inches	Staple 1 1/8 inches	Staple 1 3/16 inches	Staple 1 1/4 inches
1920–21				
August	433	2,150		
September	400	2,000		
October	340	869	1,200	
November	275	744	762	
December	160	500	850	
January	125	400	612	800
February	100	300	600	800
March	100	300	600	800
April	100	275	512	
May	72	287	537	800
June	69	312	650	
July	75	330	575	1,000
Average	187	706	690	840
1921–22				
August	75	433	733	1,033
September	133	550	883	1,250
October	185	720	1,080	1,480
November	225	600	1,000	1,400
December	225	600	1,000	1,400
January	225	600	1,000	1,400
February	212	525	825	1,200
March	187	431	625	950
April	150	375	550	800
May	150	375	550	800
June	150	375	550	800
July	150	375	550	800
Average	172	497	779	1,109
1922–23				
August	150	375	550	800
September	150	375	550	800
October	150	375	550	800
November	150	375	550	800
December	140	350	520	730
January	100	250	400	450
February	100	250	400	450
March	65	130	195	270
April	50	100	150	225
May	50	100	150	225
June	50	100	150	225
July	50	100	150	225
Average	104	240	360	500
1923–24				
August	50	100	150	225
September	50	100	150	225
October	100	175	275	500
November	100	175	275	420
December	100	175	275	400
January	100	205	325	420
February	100	175	275	400
March	100	175	275	400
April	100	175	275	400
May	100	175	275	400
June	100	175	275	400
July	100	175	275	400
Average	92	163	258	380

Year and month	Premiums shown in hundredths of cent			
	Staple 1 1/16 inches	Staple 1 1/8 inches	Staple 1 3/16 inches	Staple 1 1/4 inches
1924–25				
August	100	175	275	400
September	106	175	281	412
October	125	175	300	450
November	125	225	375	525
December	125	250	400	550
January	160	360	530	820
February	175	400	650	1,000
March	175	400	650	1,000
April	250	550	800	1,150
May	250	530	800	1,150
June	250	550	800	1,150
July	250	550	800	1,150
Average	174	362	555	813
1925–26				
August	250	550	800	1,150
September	194	287	625	887
October	175	300	575	800
November	231	375	537	850
December	250	400	600	900
January	250	400	600	900
February	250	400	600	900
March	200	350	550	900
April	200	350	550	900
May	200	350	550	900
June	200	350	550	900
July	200	350	550	900
Average	217	372	591	907
1926–27				
August	200	350	550	900
September	200	350	550	900
October	105	235	410	670
November	138	238	450	800
December	150	250	450	840
January	150	250	450	875
February	150	250	450	900
March	150	250	450	900
April	150	250	450	900
May	200	300	500	900
June	200	300	513	900
July	200	300	590	900
Average	166	277	484	730
1927–28				
August	163	244	525	788
September	169	263	513	788
October	250	350	550	850
November	238	338	513	800
December	200	300	400	650
January	200	300	400	650
February	200	300	400	650
March	200	300	400	650
April	175	250	350	550
May	175	250	350	550
June	170	245	340	535
July	150	225	300	475
Average	191	280	420	661

Bureau of Agricultural Economics.
Based on weekly quotations for middling short staple.

TABLE 269.—*Cotton: Average spot price per pound in specified foreign markets, 1912–1928*

LIVERPOOL, AMERICAN MIDDLING [1]

Year	Aug.	Sept.	Oct.	Nov.	Dec.	Jan.	Feb.	Mar.	Apr.	May	June	July	Average
	Cts.	Cts.	Cts.	Cts.	Cts.	Cts.	Cts.	Cts.	Cts.	Cts.	Cts.	Cts.	Cts.
1912	13.83	13.55	12.59	13.82	14.31	14.06	13.97	13.97	14.00	13.58	13.67	13.61	13.75
1913	13.38	15.10	15.55	14.94	14.54	14.34	14.25	14.28	15.02	15.20	15.71	14.74	14.75
1914	13.23	12.22	10.53	9.25	8.93	9.77	10.06	10.46	11.37	10.42	10.47	10.32	10.50
1915	10.79	12.24	13.90	13.74	15.03	15.99	15.61	15.48	15.47	16.77	16.47	15.94	14.79
1916	17.54	18.99	20.69	23.05	22.16	21.76	21.34	24.07	25.23	26.17	34.07	37.65	24.39
1917	38.21	35.96	34.85	43.38	44.25	46.16	45.88	47.19	46.52	42.28	43.89	43.09	42.64
1918	45.26	48.44	46.46	43.97	42.30	37.66	34.53	30.39	33.24	35.70	38.25	38.33	39.54
1919	34.06	32.20	38.06	41.90	40.92	43.61	41.61	45.16	44.17	42.51	44.48	41.83	40.88
1920	38.31	31.33	24.41	19.18	14.74	15.32	12.71	11.78	12.07	12.53	11.66	11.94	18.00
1921	13.34	20.70	20.85	18.46	18.84	18.12	17.75	19.21	18.89	21.42	23.46	24.98	19.67
1922	24.90	23.98	24.55	27.96	28.26	30.64	30.93	31.42	30.29	28.43	31.53	29.28	28.51
1923	28.18	31.99	31.96	35.74	36.00	34.33	32.53	29.77	33.15	32.00	30.74	30.38	31.90
1924	31.62	25.06	26.13	26.09	25.73	25.90	27.17	27.95	26.85	25.83	27.34	27.76	26.12
1925	26.28	26.25	23.17	21.51	20.51	21.68	21.40	20.32	20.31	20.73	19.98	19.76	21.82
1926	19.69	19.35	14.51	14.08	13.34	14.55	15.56	15.65	16.24	17.90	18.55	19.42	16.57
1927	21.10	24.17	23.36	22.73	21.98	21.68	20.53	21.80	22.75	23.52	23.82	24.44	22.66
1928	21.39	20.87	21.85	21.62	21.57	-----	-----	-----	-----	-----	-----	-----	-----

LIVERPOOL, EGYPTIAN UPPERS, GOOD [2]

Year	Aug.	Sept.	Oct.	Nov.	Dec.	Jan.	Feb.	Mar.	Apr.	May	June	July	Average
	Cts.	Cts.	Cts.	Cts.	Cts.	Cts.	Cts.	Cts.	Cts.	Cts.	Cts.	Cts.	Cts.
1912	20.2	19.1	18.3	18.9	19.3	19.9	20.1	20.2	20.3	20.2	19.7	19.0	19.6
1913	18.8	20.0	20.2	20.0	19.5	18.9	17.9	17.3	17.9	18.1	18.2	17.6	18.7
1914	16.5	16.1	13.5	12.6	12.2	12.2	12.8	14.0	15.5	14.5	14.4	13.8	14.0
1915	14.1	15.4	18.1	17.9	18.6	21.9	22.5	22.4	21.6	22.4	23.5	23.7	20.2
1916	23.7	27.2	31.2	39.5	39.6	39.7	41.9	44.5	50.5	52.0	55.4	60.3	42.1
1917	60.9	52.0	46.7	51.6	54.4	53.8	51.5	54.9	56.3	54.0	52.6	54.4	53.6
1918	55.8	55.4	54.3	51.7	50.4	50.3	50.0	49.3	48.3	48.3	58.4	46.4	50.7
1919	48.8	48.8	53.4	67.0	76.3	94.0	105.0	108.7	107.6	97.1	81.3	71.6	80.0
1920	68.6	53.4	37.0	29.4	23.4	24.6	20.8	19.6	21.5	18.8	18.8	18.0	29.5
1921	18.6	29.3	33.3	28.3	29.4	28.8	27.4	28.4	26.8	28.1	29.7	29.4	28.1
1922	28.1	27.4	27.3	30.7	31.2	31.9	32.5	33.9	33.0	30.4	31.9	31.0	30.8
1923	31.5	33.4	33.5	39.6	41.5	39.7	39.0	37.5	41.2	43.9	43.3	43.6	39.0
1924	45.6	35.5	34.3	35.4	37.5	40.3	41.3	45.1	43.6	42.1	41.6	41.4	40.3
1925	39.5	37.1	35.0	32.6	30.8	29.9	28.5	26.2	25.9	27.3	26.2	25.2	30.4
1926	26.0	28.0	23.8	22.2	19.4	21.8	24.3	23.5	23.3	26.7	28.3	30.2	24.8
1927	32.0	33.2	31.8	31.3	29.9	28.3	27.6	30.0	32.7	33.3	31.3	30.4	31.0
1928	27.1	25.1	25.9	25.6	25.5	-----	-----	-----	-----	-----	-----	-----	-----

LIVERPOOL, NO. 1 OOMRAS, FULLY GOOD [2]

Year	Aug.	Sept.	Oct.	Nov.	Dec.	Jan.	Feb.	Mar.	Apr.	May	June	July	Average
1912	12.2	11.9	11.6	12.1	12.5	12.7	12.8	12.7	12.5	12.2	11.9	11.8	12.2
1913	11.6	12.9	12.9	12.8	12.5	12.0	11.5	11.5	11.5	11.4	11.0	10.6	11.8
1914	9.7	9.1	8.8	7.9	7.7	8.5	8.4	8.5	9.2	8.9	9.1	8.9	8.7
1915	9.1	9.7	10.9	10.7	11.9	12.6	12.4	12.1	11.9	13.0	12.8	12.9	10.7
1916	14.2	15.0	15.8	17.6	16.6	16.9	17.3	20.2	21.0	22.1	31.2	33.4	20.1
1917	34.2	31.9	36.9	37.6	37.2	38.2	37.6	38.2	38.2	35.2	36.8	36.8	36.6
1918	37.8	44.1	42.4	37.5	34.3	35.3	32.6	27.7	28.9	30.1	32.4	32.2	34.6
1919	30.7	29.0	30.5	32.1	32.0	32.6	30.0	32.3	31.8	30.2	29.1	26.1	30.5
1920	23.8	21.6	18.5	15.7	12.0	11.9	10.6	9.2	9.4	9.8	9.2	9.3	13.4
1921	10.5	16.0	16.9	15.3	15.4	15.3	14.9	15.4	16.0	15.7	18.9	19.7	15.8
1922	19.8	18.9	18.8	20.6	20.5	21.9	22.2	21.7	20.7	19.4	20.8	20.2	20.5
1923	19.6	21.8	22.0	25.9	27.7	26.1	25.2	22.4	24.0	22.9	22.6	22.0	23.5
1924	23.4	19.7	22.3	23.3	23.5	22.6	23.5	23.2	22.2	21.2	21.6	22.0	22.4
1925	21.5	22.0	19.9	18.1	16.8	17.4	16.8	15.4	15.1	15.6	15.0	15.2	17.4
1926	15.5	15.4	12.5	12.1	11.5	12.5	13.3	13.4	13.9	15.4	16.2	17.0	14.1
1927	17.8	20.1	19.3	17.7	17.6	17.4	16.5	17.5	17.9	18.3	18.6	18.5	18.1
1928	16.0	14.7	15.7	15.9	16.4	-----	-----	-----	-----	-----	-----	-----	-----

Bureau of Agricultural Economics. Conversions at monthly average rate of exchange as given in Federal Reserve Bulletins to December, 1925, inclusive; subsequently at par.

[1] International Yearbook of Agricultural Statistics, 1921, p. 443. London Economist, 1922 to date. Average of weekly quotations.

[2] London Economist, average of weekly quotations to August, 1925, inclusive. Subsequently from Liverpool Cotton Association Daily Report.

TABLE 270.—*Cottonseed: Production and estimated price per ton, December 1, by States, 1922–1928*

State	Production, year beginning August [1]—							Estimated price per ton						
	1922	1923	1924	1925	1926	1927	1928	1922	1923	1924	1925	1926	1927	1928
	1,000 short tons	1,000 short tons	1,000 short tons	1,000 short tons	1,000 short tons	1,000 short tons	1,000 short tons	Dollars	Dollars	Dollars	Dollars	Dollars	Dollars	Dollars
Missouri	66	57	86	133	97	51	65	36.30	38.60	32.40	36.00	16.80	36.90	35.00
Virginia	12	22	17	23	23	14	20	34.50	43.30	36.30	35.00	26.00	42.00	41.00
North Carolina	378	452	366	488	539	382	373	39.30	44.60	35.00	33.00	22.00	37.00	40.00
South Carolina	218	341	357	394	448	324	322	41.30	48.00	36.10	32.00	21.00	39.50	39.00
Georgia	317	261	445	516	664	488	453	39.70	47.90	34.10	33.00	21.00	38.50	37.00
Florida	12	6	10	17	14	8	9	35.30	43.20	32.10	34.00	19.00	30.50	36.00
Tennessee	174	101	157	229	200	159	186	41.40	49.70	35.20	25.50	19.00	37.00	38.00
Alabama	366	260	438	602	665	529	484	36.60	47.60	34.30	29.00	19.00	37.00	38.00
Mississippi	439	268	487	884	838	602	653	36.60	49.30	35.70	22.00	21.00	38.50	39.00
Arkansas	449	276	486	711	687	444	541	35.30	44.40	33.20	18.30	17.50	36.50	37.50
Louisiana	152	163	219	404	368	243	304	32.30	40.70	29.20	24.50	18.00	33.00	32.50
Oklahoma	279	291	671	751	787	461	525	29.70	37.70	28.60	26.50	15.40	37.00	34.00
Texas	1,433	1,927	2,197	1,849	2,499	1,938	2,292	33.50	40.10	31.10	28.50	17.50	36.00	35.00
New Mexico	5	14	25	30	33	31	31	30.00	40.50	30.00	28.00	18.00	30.00	32.00
Arizona	21	34	48	53	54	41	59	25.30	40.70	21.20	26.60	18.00	30.00	30.00
California	12	24	35	54	58	40	69	40.00	50.00	40.00	40.00	20.00	37.50	31.50
All other	3	4	6	11	8	4	4	35.67	48.00	34.00	36.00	20.00	37.25	37.27
United States	4,336	4,502	6,051	7,150	7,982	5,759	6,390	35.67	43.00	32.39	27.27	18.68	36.80	36.29

Bureau of Agricultural Economics.

[1] Compiled from reports of Bureau of the Census. Estimated production of lint, by States (December preliminary estimate for 1928), in rounded thousands of 500 pounds gross weight bales, adjusting for net weight and assuming 65 pounds of cottonseed for each 35 net pounds of lint.

TABLE 271.—*Cottonseed and cottonseed products: Production in the United States, 1909–1928*

Year beginning August	Cottonseed		Cottonseed products		
	Produced [1]	Crushed	Crude oil	Cake and meal	Hulls
	1,000 short tons	1,000 short tons	1,000 short tons	1,000 short tons	1,000 short tons
1909	4,462	3,269	491	1,326	1,289
1910	5,175	4,106	630	1,792	1,375
1911	6,997	4,921	756	2,151	1,642
1912	6,104	4,580	697	1,999	1,540
1913	6,305	4,848	725	2,220	1,400
1914	7,186	5,780	860	2,648	1,677
1915	4,992	4,202	627	1,923	1,220
1916	5,113	4,479	704	2,225	969
1917	5,040	4,252	656	2,068	996
1918	5,360	4,479	663	2,170	1,137
1919	5,074	4,013	606	1,817	1,143
1920	5,971	4,069	655	1,786	1,256
1921	3,531	3,008	465	1,355	937
1922	4,336	3,242	501	1,487	944
1923	4,502	3,308	490	1,518	941
1924	6,051	4,605	702	2,126	1,331
1925	7,150	5,558	809	2,597	1,547
1926	7,989	6,306	944	2,840	1,854
1927	5,758	4,654	738	2,093	1,320
1928, preliminary	6,390				

Bureau of Agricultural Economics. Compiled from reports of the Bureau of the Census. Production for cottonseed, 1928 estimate of the Department of Agriculture.

[1] Production of cottonseed relates to the preceding crop year.

TABLE 272.—*Cottonseed: Estimated price per ton, received by producers, United States, 1910–1928*

Year beginning August	Aug. 15	Sept. 15	Oct. 15	Nov. 15	Dec. 15	Jan. 15	Feb. 15	Mar. 15	Apr. 15	May 15	June 15	July 15	Weighted average
Average:	Dolls.	Dolls.	Dolls.	Dolls.	Dolls.	Dolls.	Dolls.	Dolls.	Dolls.	Dolls.	Dolls.	Dolls.	Dolls.
1910–1913	19.57	20.75	20.91	20.77	21.81	21.90	21.95	22.21	22.70	22.53	21.94	21.47	21.10
1914–1920	43.27	41.94	46.14	48.12	47.41	47.11	47.46	47.20	47.87	47.82	46.69	45.96	45.70
1921–1925	33.39	31.73	33.70	35.29	36.12	36.57	36.96	37.61	39.65	39.35	37.87	37.03	34.31
1910		26.23	26.86	25.36	25.65	26.35	25.61	25.49	26.12	25.46	23.38	22.70	25.82
1911	20.45	18.09	16.73	16.69	16.70	16.57	16.81	18.21	18.62	19.21	19.24	19.04	17.08
1912	18.02	17.61	18.04	18.57	21.42	21.98	22.01	21.55	21.89	21.88	21.54	21.37	19.10
1913	20.24	21.07	22.01	22.46	23.48	22.70	23.37	23.60	24.17	23.56	23.62	22.78	22.39
1914	20.16	13.88	15.28	14.01	17.73	19.14	23.33	22.32	22.69	22.07	20.82	20.05	16.50
1915	20.14	20.98	33.73	34.01	35.54	36.85	36.75	36.56	38.13	37.91	35.79	36.06	32.65
1916	35.22	41.13	47.19	55.82	56.35	52.53	51.43	53.18	55.94	55.61	57.19	56.90	49.13
1917	56.61	57.58	65.02	69.38	68.29	67.51	66.95	68.27	68.08	68.16	66.03	64.11	66.15
1918	61.34	67.90	65.85	64.97	65.05	64.93	64.65	64.00	64.28	63.83	63.80	64.24	65.23
1919	66.23	62.13	66.95	72.65	69.07	69.88	69.34	67.18	68.71	69.88	66.16	61.64	67.27
1920	43.22	29.96	28.94	26.00	19.83	18.96	19.76	18.92	17.23	17.28	17.06	18.75	22.95
1921	22.06	27.19	31.05	29.15	28.78	29.24	30.17	32.72	40.79	40.21	37.71	36.92	29.72
1922	32.44	25.37	31.79	40.18	42.93	43.35	45.16	46.32	47.60	46.58	43.14	41.42	34.70
1923	37.47	40.88	40.90	45.92	45.54	44.37	43.27	41.34	40.42	40.53	39.96	39.07	42.23
1924	38.44	31.74	31.95	33.57	35.48	37.50	37.14	38.21	37.94	38.61	36.66	36.41	34.08
1925	36.52	33.48	32.82	27.64	27.87	28.40	29.06	29.47	31.51	30.84	31.89	31.31	30.82
1926	29.73	27.38	20.06	18.66	18.05	18.55	22.39	25.43	25.80	26.05	26.27	26.59	21.55
1927	25.95	34.41	36.60	37.51	37.14	37.40	37.44	37.77	39.40	43.00	41.25	39.27	35.94
1928	36.87	30.98	34.08	37.17	37.74								

Bureau of Agricultural Economics. Based upon returns from special-price reporters.

TABLE 273.—*Cottonseed oil, prime summer yellow: Average spot price per pound (barrels), New York, 1920–1928*

Year beginning August	Aug.	Sept.	Oct.	Nov.	Dec.	Jan.	Feb.	Mar.	Apr.	May	June	July	Average
Average 1921–1925	Cents	Cents	Cents	Cents	Cents	Cents	Cents	Cents	Cents	Cents	Cents	Cents	Cents
	10.78	10.28	10.09	10.13	10.19	10.56	10.57	11.27	11.38	11.62	11.87	11.93	10.89
1920	12.32	13.48	11.43	10.14	8.91	8.59	7.34	6.26	6.24	7.22	7.46	8.57	9.00
1921	8.69	9.88	8.69	8.30	8.28	8.62	9.96	11.48	11.57	11.71	11.33	10.97	9.96
1922	9.96	8.54	8.88	9.51	9.81	10.77	10.90	11.78	11.76	11.60	11.48	10.35	10.44
1923	10.34	11.62	12.01	11.67	11.00	11.00	10.03	9.77	10.09	9.82	10.42	11.98	10.81
1924	13.83	10.54	11.00	10.86	11.41	11.10	10.69	11.10	11.08	10.51	10.75	11.38	11.19
1925	11.09	10.81	9.86	10.32	10.47	11.33	11.28	12.24	12.38	14.48	15.38	14.99	12.05
1926	12.99	11.42	8.82	8.20	8.22	8.50	9.31	9.39	8.78	9.09	9.19	9.57	9.46
1927	9.89	10.74	10.83	10.55	10.06	10.02	9.27	9.64	10.04	10.52	10.22	10.03	10.15
1928	9.44	10.03	9.84	9.69	10.21								

Bureau of Agricultural Economics. 1920–21, from annual reports of the New York Produce Exchange; subsequently compiled from Oil, Paint and Drug Reporter average of daily ranges. Data for 1890–1919 are available in 1924 Yearbook, p. 766, Table 323.

TABLE 274.—*Cottonseed meal, 41 per cent protein: Price per ton, Memphis, 1920–1928*

Year beginning August	Aug.	Sept.	Oct.	Nov.	Dec.	Jan.	Feb.	Mar.	Apr.	May	June	July	Average
	Dolls.	Dolls.	Dolls.	Dolls.	Dolls.	Dolls.	Dolls.	Dolls.	Dolls.	Dolls.	Dolls.	Dolls.	Dolls.
1920				36.30	30.80	30.20	29.20	27.00		29.00	32.80	35.00	
1921		38.20	35.70	35.00	36.30	37.10	39.30	45.10	47.60	49.25	47.50	44.75	
1922	35.30	34.30	40.25	46.00	45.40	45.75	45.00	43.10	43.10	42.40	40.80	41.40	41.94
1923	43.20	42.90	44.90	47.40	45.00	43.62	41.00	39.60	39.50	39.50	40.25	43.62	42.54
1924	43.60	41.38	40.75	38.75	39.25	37.70	35.75	35.85	38.31	38.35	38.81	41.50	39.04
1925	44.10	36.88	34.35	34.12	34.00	32.62	31.12	31.00	31.94	30.67	31.00	31.10	33.58
1926	32.12	28.88	23.90	23.67	24.50	30.10	33.50	32.40	32.50	34.00	37.35	36.00	30.74
1927		37.40	37.70	39.60	41.40	40.40	45.10	49.30	55.50	61.50		41.50	
1928		38.40	43.90	44.15	45.60								

Bureau of Agricultural Economics. Compiled from reports made to the bureau.

TABLE 275.—*Cottonseed oil: International trade, average 1909–1913, annual 1924–1927*

Country	Average 1909–1913 Imports	Average 1909–1913 Exports	1924 Imports	1924 Exports	1925 Imports	1925 Exports	1926 Imports	1926 Exports	1927, preliminary Imports	1927, preliminary Exports
PRINCIPAL EXPORTING COUNTRIES	*1,000 pounds*	*1,000 pounds*	*1,000 pounds*	*1,000 pounds*	*1,000 pounds*	*1,000 pounds*	*1,000 pounds*	*1,000 pounds*	*1,000 pounds*	*1,000 pounds*
United States	[1] 4,715	292,257	0	43,343	0	62,415	0	40,901	0	67,982
United Kingdom	44,246	53,920	16,524	50,180	11,198	44,092	24,940	50,082	17,315	47,044
Egypt	1,927	3,568	34	16,085	391	8,101	1	30,532	0	31,229
Peru	0	[2][3] 158	0	10,083	0	7,309	0	10,601	0	15,596
China	0	2,110	0	1,374	0	4,903	0	0	0	0
Brazil	4,680	[4] 12	6	463	69	1,639	25	97		
PRINCIPAL IMPORTING COUNTRIES										
Canada	21,131	0	20,495	0	30,136	0	29,939	0	54,118	0
Netherlands	40,141	392	21,162	5,604	22,643	5,016	20,985	6,472	24,370	9,838
Germany	51,884	0	14,204	0	30,652	38	13,298	164	25,897	34
France	24,666	2,509	7,225	92	7,910	35	8,189	28	8,258	60
Norway	11,284	0	5,552	0	5,102	0	6,239	0	5,582	0
Denmark	[3] 7,081	0	3,466	1,180	4,721	287	8,398	558	6,131	609
Belgium	16,884	8,143	2,166	0	2,689	0	1,984	7	3,918	5
Argentina	7,510	12	517	0	1,838	2	768	10	2,461	210
Sweden	5,220	[1] 20	1,555	0	1,545	184	3,490	432	3,294	1,097
Greece	0	0	1,735	0	[2] 1,300	0	1,078	0	3,315	0
Australia	1,062	0	[2] 1,005	[2] 121	[2] 800	[2] 0	[2] 1,489	[2] 0	[2] 1,709	[2] 3
Czechoslovakia	0	0	1,214	52	281	0	312	0	132	0
Uruguay	[2] 3,938	0	1,749	0	146	0	382	0	[2] 557	0
Italy	34,498	6	36	0	105	2	233	1	59	1
Algeria	2,728	1,177	85	17	3	46	53	68	[2] 85	[2] 26
Total 21 countries	283,595	364,284	98,730	128,594	121,529	134,069	121,803	139,953	157,201	173,734

Bureau of Agricultural Economics. Official sources except where otherwise noted.

[1] 3-year average.
[2] International Yearbook of Agricultural Statistics.
[3] 4-year average.
[4] 1 year only.

TABLE 276.—*Cottonseed oil, crude: Average price per pound f. o. b. mills, 1909–1928*

Year beginning August	Aug.	Sept.	Oct.	Nov.	Dec.	Jan.	Feb.	Mar.	Apr.	May	June	July	Average
	Cents	*Cents*	*Cents*	*Cents*	*Cents*	*Cents*	*Cents*	*Cents*	*Cents*	*Cents*	*Cents*	*Cents*	*Cents*
Average:													
1909–1913		5.55	5.45	5.52	5.55	5.60	5.59	5.67	6.07	6.23	6.21	6.01	
1914–1920	11.67	11.23	11.64	11.92	11.80	12.11	11.96	11.96	11.94	12.12	12.80	12.22	11.95
1921–1925	8.34	8.32	8.59	8.73	9.14	9.39	10.00	10.00	9.92				
1909	5.01	4.82	5.63	5.97	6.32	6.18	6.12	6.46	7.03	7.12	7.27	7.27	6.27
1910		7.00	6.44	6.17	6.20	6.14	5.80	5.55	5.20	5.43	5.47	4.88	
1911	4.27	4.80	4.38	4.40	4.15	4.36	4.52	4.60	5.48	6.22	5.80	5.30	4.86
1912	5.24	4.95	4.84	5.02	5.27	5.22	5.36	5.44	6.03	5.87	6.23	6.20	5.47
1913	6.10	6.18	5.94	6.06	5.83	6.10	6.16	6.30	6.60	6.53	6.26	6.40	6.20
1914	5.26	5.36	4.71	4.54	4.44	5.15	5.81	6.00	5.60	5.16	5.09	4.83	5.16
1915	4.40	5.41	6.67	6.64	7.31	7.71	7.67	8.72	9.18	9.61	9.54	9.20	7.67
1916	8.85	8.82	10.10	11.35	11.35	11.10	11.20	11.64	13.20	14.10	14.67	14.00	11.70
1917	13.92	13.86	15.93	17.40	17.33	17.50	17.50	17.50	17.50	17.50	17.50	17.50	16.74
1918	17.50	17.50	17.50	17.50	17.50	17.50	17.50	17.50	17.50	17.50	21.56	21.75	18.19
1919	21.75	17.38	16.25	18.95	18.46	19.74	18.25	17.69	16.19	15.62	15.50	11.50	17.27
1920	10.00	10.25	10.35	7.08	6.19	6.10	5.80	4.70	4.43	5.34	5.74	6.76	6.90
1921	6.75	7.81	7.26	7.00	7.02	7.16	8.28	10.15	9.80	10.00	9.75	8.88	8.32
1922	8.50	6.46	7.34	8.30	8.52	9.84	9.92	10.45	10.25	9.88	9.75	9.00	9.02
1923		9.94	9.44	9.88	9.45	9.46	8.84	8.46	8.74	8.20	8.78	10.06	
1924	11.30	8.34	9.03	8.85	9.69	9.48	9.20	9.95	10.00	9.34	9.75		
1925		9.14	8.55	8.90	8.98	9.75	10.71	11.00	11.22	12.17			
1926	10.88	8.19	7.44	6.64	6.36	6.94	8.20	7.73	7.33	7.74	8.04	(1)	
1927	8.70	9.45	9.05	8.72	8.48	7.75	8.44	8.75	8.88				
1928		8.16	8.14	8.24	8.38								

Bureau of Agricultural Economics. Prices 1909–1912 and 1919–1927 are averages of weekly quotations in the Oil, Paint, and Drug Reporter; 1913–1918 from War Industries Board Price Bulletin No. 15.

[1] Nominal.

TABLE 277.—*Cottonseed meal, 41 per cent protein, bagged: Average price per ton, at nine markets, 1928*

Market	Jan.	Feb.	Mar.	Apr.	May	June	July	Aug.	Sept.	Oct.	Nov.	Dec.
	Dolls.	*Dolls.*	*Dolls.*	*Dolls.*	*Dolls.*	*Dolls.*	*Dolls.*	*Dolls.*	*Dolls.*	*Dolls.*	*Dolls.*	*Dolls.*
Boston	53.20	53.40	57.45	63.20	68.90	65.70	59.75	54.15	48.80	52.70	53.00	54.45
Philadelphia	52.10	53.10	56.75	63.60	68.20	67.45	58.75	47.65	46.65	51.70	51.90	53.30
Buffalo	49.50	50.90	55.30	62.65	67.25	65.40	¹56.50	50.75	46.70	50.65	50.25	51.00
Pittsburgh			¹54.85						42.95	49.65	49.85	50.60
Cincinnati	48.80	49.50	52.55	60.30	65.40	64.20	55.75	42.75	43.35	48.05	48.50	49.65
Chicago	48.90	49.50	53.15	59.20	66.80	63.40	54.65	50.90	¹44.80	49.75	49.15	50.15
Milwaukee	48.20	49.00	49.50	57.90	63.75	62.00	55.75	45.65	42.60	48.00	48.25	48.20
Minneapolis	49.60	49.50	52.70	59.60	67.00	65.10	57.00	48.90	44.45	49.00	49.80	50.90
Los Angeles	44.50	44.00	46.00	47.75	51.60	52.00	51.00	49.25		43.00	44.00	44.00

Division of Statistical and Historical Research.   Compiled from Crops and Markets.   ¹ 1 week missing.

TABLE 278.—*Hay, tame: Acreage, production, value, exports, etc., United States, 1909–1928*

Year	Acreage	Average yield per acre	Production	Price per ton received by producers, Dec. 1	Farm value, Dec. 1	Domestic exports, year beginning July 1 [1]	Imports, year beginning July 1 [1]	Net balance, year beginning July 1 [1,2]
	1,000 acres	*Short tons*	*1,000 short tons*	*Dollars*	*1,000 dollars*	*1,000 short tons*	*1,000 short tons*	*1,000 short tons*
1909	*51,041*	*1.35*	*68,833*					
1909	51,041	1.46	74,384	10.58	786,722	62	108	−47
1910	51,015	1.36	69,378	12.14	842,252	62	377	−315
1911	48,240	1.14	54,916	14.29	784,926	67	783	−716
1912	49,530	1.47	72,691	11.79	856,695	68	175	−107
1913	48,954	1.31	64,116	12.43	797,077	56	191	−135
1914	49,145	1.43	70,071	11.12	779,068	118	23	+96
1915	51,108	1.68	85,920	10.63	913,644	200	48	+151
1916	55,721	1.64	91,192	11.22	1,022,930	96	65	+31
1917	55,203	1.51	83,308	17.09	1,423,766	34	460	−426
1918	55,755	1.37	76,660	20.13	1,543,494	32	311	−278
1919	*55,653*	*1.34*	*74,724*					
1919	56,888	1.53	86,997	20.05	1,744,547	67	252	−185
1920	58,101	1.55	89,785	17.66	1,585,355	55	126	−71
1921	58,769	1.40	82,458	12.10	998,069	61	5	+56
1922	61,159	1.57	95,748	12.55	1,202,063	53	35	+18
1923	59,868	1.49	89,250	14.13	1,261,486	24	403	−380
1924	*59,073*							
1924	60,907	1.60	97,224	13.76	1,337,733	25	119	−94
1925	58,013	1.47	85,431	13.93	1,190,103	18	431	−413
1926	58,558	1.47	86,144	14.10	1,214,372	15	209	−194
1927	60,885	1.74	106,001	11.35	1,202,953	17	84	−67
1928 [4]	57,775	1.61	93,031	12.34	1,148,283			

Bureau of Agricultural Economics. Italic figures are census returns; other acreage, production, and yield figures are estimates of the crop-reporting board. See 1927 Yearbook, p. 927, for date for earlier years.

[1] Compiled from 1909–1917 Commerce and Navigation of the United States, 1918 Foreign Commerce and Navigation of the United States; 1919–1927 Monthly Summary of Foreign Commerce of the United States, June issues.
[2] The difference between total exports (i. e., domestic exports plus reexports) and total imports; plus (+) indicates net exports and minus (−) indicates net imports.   [3] Preliminary.

TABLE 279.—*Hay, wild: Acreage, production, and December 1 price, United States, 1909–1928*

Year	Acreage	Yield per acre	Production	Price per ton received by producers Dec. 1	Year	Acreage	Yield per acre	Production	Price per ton received by producers Dec. 1
	1,000 acres	*Short tons*	*1,000 short tons*	*Dolls.*		*1,000 acres*	*Short tons*	*1,000 short tons*	*Dolls.*
1909	*17,187*	1.07	18,383		1919	17,150	1.07	18,401	16.50
1910	*17,187*	.77	13,151		1920	15,787	1.11	17,460	11.35
1911	*17,187*	.71	12,155		1921	15,632	.98	15,391	6.63
1912	17,427	1.04	18,043		1922	15,871	1.02	16,131	7.14
1913	16,341	.92	15,063		1923	15,556	1.12	17,361	7.88
1914	16,752	1.11	18,615	7.49	1924	15,205	.98	14,859	7.83
1915	16,796	1.27	21,343	6.80	1925	14,560	.87	12,724	8.53
1916	16,635	1.19	19,800	7.90	1926	12,911	.74	9,568	10.05
1917	16,212	.93	15,131	13.49	1927	14,813	1.17	17,326	6.59
1918	15,365	.94	14,479	15.23	1928 [1]	13,144	.98	12,922	7.36

Bureau of Agricultural Economics. Figures in italics are census returns, others are estimates of the crop-reporting board.   [1] Preliminary.

TABLE 280.—*Hay, tame: Acreage and production, by States, average 1921–1925, annual 1926–1928*

State and division	Acreage				Production			
	Average, 1921–1925	1926	1927	1928 [1]	Average, 1921–1925	1926	1927	1928 [1]
	1,000 acres	*1,000 acres*	*1,000 acres*	*1,000 acres*	*1,000 tons*	*1,000 tons*	*1,000 tons*	*1,000 tons*
Maine	1,253	1,272	1,247	1,235	1,419	1,428	1,526	1,583
New Hampshire	456	469	463	459	524	534	588	647
Vermont	917	926	922	914	1,265	1,461	1,407	1,480
Massachusetts	446	475	466	460	585	594	674	717
Rhode Island	46	45	44	43	58	58	59	67
Connecticut	335	363	359	354	435	424	525	570
New York	4,920	4,847	4,850	4,597	6,508	6,393	7,311	6,439
New Jersey	287	250	257	247	420	391	461	453
Pennsylvania	3,000	2,916	3,075	2,924	4,102	3,820	5,063	4,645
North Atlantic	11,662	11,563	11,683	11,233	15,316	15,103	17,614	16,601
Ohio	3,240	2,938	3,139	2,780	4,335	4,033	5,152	3,698
Indiana	2,306	1,941	2,027	1,808	2,869	2,477	2,980	2,481
Illinois	3,343	3,078	3,556	3,064	4,386	3,621	5,286	4,045
Michigan	2,998	2,913	3,036	2,832	3,778	4,150	4,745	4,277
Wisconsin	3,217	3,368	3,444	3,270	5,118	5,742	6,986	5,017
Minnesota	2,088	2,267	2,454	2,447	3,295	2,977	5,080	4,387
Iowa	3,211	3,112	3,135	2,786	4,902	3,805	5,197	4,203
Missouri	3,380	3,147	3,553	3,299	4,080	3,531	5,197	4,183
North Dakota	978	1,331	1,040	1,063	1,517	1,365	1,944	1,991
South Dakota	1,043	1,363	1,105	1,086	1,696	1,366	2,271	1,655
Nebraska	1,625	1,761	1,727	1,550	3,578	3,282	4,145	3,351
Kansas	1,619	1,565	1,678	1,496	3,335	2,707	4,245	3,539
North Central	29,048	28,784	29,894	27,481	42,888	39,056	53,228	42,827
Delaware	76	76	80	81	104	112	142	138
Maryland	405	396	443	430	578	516	733	754
Virginia	1,009	979	1,077	1,063	1,086	992	1,472	1,451
West Virginia	775	784	831	814	1,003	1,036	1,259	1,182
North Carolina	736	759	806	752	779	681	761	734
South Carolina	366	257	441	434	274	199	353	376
Georgia	692	522	803	792	459	400	565	506
Florida	107	82	95	88	89	57	64	64
South Atlantic	4,166	3,855	4,576	4,454	4,373	3,993	5,349	5,205
Kentucky	1,097	1,156	1,318	1,253	1,412	1,525	1,871	1,644
Tennessee	1,320	1,396	1,352	1,310	1,486	1,766	1,762	1,780
Alabama	713	523	615	615	579	499	517	473
Mississippi	422	406	491	451	473	483	595	566
Arkansas	591	575	643	625	668	667	730	683
Louisiana	231	233	278	297	256	276	356	424
Oklahoma	767	572	566	576	1,231	883	901	841
Texas	640	620	629	637	848	847	749	733
South Central	5,781	5,481	5,892	5,764	6,954	6,946	7,481	7,144
Montana	1,136	1,309	1,274	1,294	2,030	2,063	2,706	2,558
Idaho	1,045	1,025	1,014	1,047	2,773	2,768	3,151	2,645
Wyoming	689	682	685	681	1,291	1,326	1,219	1,224
Colorado	1,221	1,210	1,225	1,207	2,510	2,820	2,658	2,497
New Mexico	171	182	196	186	368	435	434	407
Arizona	159	176	192	185	544	641	672	697
Utah	524	562	567	570	1,397	1,724	1,474	1,400
Nevada	191	209	208	208	495	520	494	541
Washington	976	909	932	906	2,080	2,001	2,317	2,140
Oregon	964	912	898	905	1,903	1,764	2,048	2,041
California	2,011	1,699	1,649	1,654	5,099	4,984	5,156	5,104
Far Western	9,086	8,875	8,840	8,843	20,491	21,046	22,329	21,254
United States	59,743	58,558	60,885	57,775	90,022	86,144	106,001	93,031

Bureau of Agricultural Economics. Estimates of the crop-reporting board.

[1] Preliminary.

TABLE 281.—*Hay, wild: Acreage and production, by States, average 1921–1925, annual 1926–1928*

State and division	Acreage				Production			
	Average, 1921–1925	1926	1927	1928 [1]	Average, 1921–1925	1926	1927	1928 [1]
	1,000 acres	*1,000 acres*	*1,000 acres*	*1,000 acres*	*1,000 tons*	*1,000 tons*	*1,000 tons*	*1,000 tons*
Maine	14	13	13	13	14	12	12	14
New Hampshire	14	17	17	16	13	15	17	18
Vermont	13	13	13	13	13	14	14	17
Massachusetts	12	13	13	12	12	12	13	15
Rhode Island	1	2	2	2	1	2	2	2
Connecticut	10	11	11	10	11	11	13	13
New York	67	68	68	68	77	76	78	74
New Jersey	20	16	17	16	26	25	26	26
Pennsylvania	22	20	15	15	27	25	22	22
North Atlantic	174	173	169	165	196	192	197	201
Ohio	4	5	5	7	5	6	7	8
Indiana	22	21	21	20	24	24	26	23
Illinois	53	37	34	41	63	41	48	46
Michigan	50	38	42	38	58	44	56	50
Wisconsin	304	228	205	207	388	301	297	279
Minnesota	2,012	1,865	1,884	1,809	2,422	1,492	2,826	2,171
Iowa	381	300	281	270	439	252	357	313
Missouri	140	130	130	143	146	117	176	157
North Dakota	2,091	1,259	1,360	1,210	2,081	818	1,700	1,355
South Dakota	3,339	2,315	3,010	2,107	2,883	926	3,311	1,264
Nebraska	2,567	2,530	3,056	2,903	2,326	1,644	3,056	2,526
Kansas	928	902	947	900	991	640	1,231	1,107
North Central	11,891	9,630	10,975	9,655	11,825	6,305	13,091	9,299
Delaware	3	4	3	2	4	6	5	3
Maryland	4	4	3	3	5	5	4	5
Virginia	14	26	23	21	13	26	29	28
West Virginia	12	13	12	12	13	14	18	16
North Carolina	72	58	52	52	68	52	57	60
South Carolina	5	3	3	6	4	2	2	4
Georgia	17	18	22	19	13	14	17	15
Florida	5	4	4	4	4	4	3	3
South Atlantic	132	130	122	119	124	123	135	134
Kentucky	24	23	32	58	25	29	45	81
Tennessee	48	56	50	50	50	62	60	60
Alabama	24	22	22	22	17	18	16	16
Mississippi	39	35	35	35	37	33	36	35
Arkansas	133	133	146	131	124	133	146	111
Louisiana	17	18	18	18	20	20	18	25
Oklahoma	491	549	565	492	461	439	554	492
Texas	207	231	219	219	196	277	219	208
South Central	983	1,067	1,087	1,025	930	1,011	1,094	1,028
Montana	659	393	865	606	581	314	995	545
Idaho	119	101	101	101	148	121	162	121
Wyoming	337	372	409	401	321	372	450	421
Colorado	373	360	396	376	375	360	396	338
New Mexico	38	30	30	33	31	33	30	30
Arizona	9	5	10	10	8	6	10	5
Utah	96	75	77	77	131	94	100	100
Nevada	169	160	160	160	204	160	144	192
Washington	28	30	30	31	38	42	52	46
Oregon	208	235	235	235	221	270	294	232
California	148	150	147	150	161	165	176	180
Far Western	2,185	1,911	2,460	2,180	2,219	1,937	2,809	2,260
United States	15,365	12,911	14,813	13,144	15,293	9,568	17,326	12,922

Bureau of Agricultural Economics. Estimates of the crop-reporting board.

[1] Preliminary.

33023°—29——55

TABLE 282.—*Hay, tame and wild: Yield per acre, by States, average 1921–1925, annual 1925–1928*

State and division	Tame hay					Wild hay				
	Average, 1921–1925	1925	1926	1927	1928	Average, 1921–1925	1925	1926	1927	1928
	Short tons	*Short tons*	*Short tons*	*Short tons*	*Short tons*	*Short tons*	*Short tons*	*Short tons*	*Short tons*	*Short tons*
Maine	1.13	1.21	1.12	1.22	1.28	0.99	0.94	0.94	0.95	1.05
New Hampshire	1.15	1.22	1.14	1.27	1.41	.91	.85	.90	1.00	1.15
Vermont	1.38	1.57	1.58	1.53	1.62	1.03	1.05	1.05	1.10	1.30
Massachusetts	1.31	1.33	1.25	1.45	1.56	1.00	1.00	.95	1.00	1.25
Rhode Island	1.28	1.28	1.29	1.34	1.56	.89	.85	1.00	1.00	1.10
Connecticut	1.30	1.29	1.17	1.46	1.61	1.08	1.05	1.00	1.20	1.30
New York	1.32	1.38	1.32	1.51	1.40	1.15	1.12	1.12	1.14	1.09
New Jersey	1.47	1.56	1.56	1.79	1.83	1.35	1.60	1.55	1.50	1.65
Pennsylvania	1.36	1.39	1.31	1.65	1.59	1.23	1.24	1.25	1.45	1.45
North Atlantic	1.31	1.37	1.31	1.51	1.48	1.12	1.12	1.11	1.17	1.22
Ohio	1.33	1.09	1.37	1.64	1.33	1.27	1.14	1.22	1.45	1.13
Indiana	1.23	.99	1.28	1.47	1.37	1.05	.90	1.15	1.25	1.15
Illinois	1.30	1.09	1.18	1.49	1.32	1.19	1.00	1.10	1.40	1.12
Michigan	1.25	.99	1.42	1.56	1.51	1.16	.97	1.17	1.33	1.31
Wisconsin	1.58	1.63	1.70	2.03	1.53	1.28	1.30	1.32	1.45	1.35
Minnesota	1.55	1.77	1.31	2.07	1.79	1.20	1.20	.80	1.50	1.20
Iowa	1.52	1.37	1.22	1.66	1.51	1.15	.98	.84	1.27	1.16
Missouri	1.20	1.11	1.12	1.46	1.27	1.05	.86	.90	1.35	1.10
North Dakota	1.55	1.71	1.03	1.87	1.87	.99	.95	.65	1.25	1.12
South Dakota	1.63	1.33	1.00	2.06	1.52	.85	.62	.40	1.10	.60
Nebraska	2.20	2.17	1.86	2.40	2.16	.91	.75	.65	1.00	.87
Kansas	2.06	1.99	1.73	2.53	2.37	1.07	.84	.71	1.30	1.23
North Central	1.47	1.37	1.36	1.78	1.50	.99	.85	.65	1.19	.96
Delaware	1.37	1.41	1.47	1.78	1.70	1.27	1.50	1.50	1.60	1.60
Maryland	1.42	1.39	1.30	1.65	1.75	1.19	1.10	1.21	1.40	1.68
Virginia	1.07	.76	1.01	1.37	1.37	.93	.65	1.00	1.25	1.33
West Virginia	1.29	1.20	1.32	1.52	1.45	1.12	1.30	1.10	1.50	1.33
North Carolina	1.05	.68	.90	.94	.98	.92	.62	.90	1.10	1.15
South Carolina	.69	.27	.77	.80	.87	.72	.33	.65	.68	.60
Georgia	.65	.33	.77	.70	.64	.79	.51	.80	.78	.80
Florida	.82	.69	.70	.67	.73	.84	.75	.95	.75	.85
South Atlantic	1.05	.84	1.04	1●17	1.17	.93	.72	.95	1.11	1.13
Kentucky	1.28	1.14	1.32	1.42	1.31	1.06	1.05	1.25	1.40	1.40
Tennessee	1.12	.92	1.27	1.30	1.36	1.00	.65	1.10	1.20	1.20
Alabama	.79	.67	.95	.84	.77	.72	.62	.84	.75	.75
Mississippi	1.11	1.00	1.19	1.21	1.25	.93	.75	.95	1.02	1.00
Arkansas	1.13	.80	1.16	1.14	1.09	.94	.70	1.00	1.00	.85
Louisiana	1.14	.90	1.18	1.28	1.43	1.12	.70	1.10	1.00	1.38
Oklahoma	1.57	1.28	1.54	1.59	1.46	.93	.66	.80	.98	1.00
Texas	1.30	.89	1.37	1.19	1.15	.95	.45	1.20	1.00	.95
South Central	1.19	.96	1.27	1.27	1.24	.94	.63	.95	1.01	1.00
Montana	1.79	1.66	1.58	2.12	1.98	.88	.90	.80	1.15	.90
Idaho	2.66	3.28	2.70	3.11	2.53	1.23	1.50	1.20	1.60	1.20
Wyoming	1.85	1.81	1.94	1.78	1.80	.95	1.05	1.00	1.10	1.05
Colorado	2.06	2.09	2.33	2.17	2.07	1.00	1.00	1.00	1.00	.90
New Mexico	2.14	2.26	2.39	2.21	2.19	.81	.80	1.10	1.00	.90
Arizona	3.42	3.47	3.64	3.50	3.77	.80	.75	1.20	1.00	.50
Utah	2.66	3.30	3.07	2.60	2.46	1.35	1.70	1.25	1.30	1.30
Nevada	2.60	3.06	2.49	2.38	2.60	1.19	1.30	1.00	.90	1.20
Washington	2.13	2.26	2.20	2.49	2.36	1.35	1.55	1.40	1.75	1.50
Oregon	1.97	2.06	1.93	2.28	2.26	1.03	1.20	1.15	1.25	1.20
California	2.55	3.05	2.93	3.13	3.09	1.07	1.40	1.10	1.20	1.20
Far Western	2.26	2.49	2.37	2.53	2.40	1.01	1.10	1.01	1.14	1.04
United States	1.51	1.47	1.47	1.74	1.61	.99	.87	.74	1.17	.98

Bureau of Agricultural Economics.   Estimates of the crop-reporting board.

TABLE 283.—*Hay, by kinds: Acreage, yield per acre, and production, United States, 1919–1928*

ACREAGE

Year	Alfalfa	Clover (red, alsike, and crimson)	Sweet clover	Lespedeza (Japan clover)	Clover and timothy mixed	Timothy	Grains cut green	Annual legumes	Millet, Sudan grass and other
	1,000 acres	1,000 acres	1,000 acres	1,000 acres	1,000 acres	1,000 acres	1,000 acres	1,000 acres	1,000 acres
1919	8,750	[1] 7,434			14,739	11,398	5,266	2,619	6,682
1920	9,131	[1] 7,659			15,632	11,416	4,704	2,756	6,803
1921	9,228	[1] 7,637			15,430	11,489	4,925	3,048	7,012
1922	9,368	[1] 9,079			16,100	11,409	4,560	3,510	7,133
1923	9,816	[1] 8,091			15,596	11,104	4,295	3,828	7,138
1924	10,759	7,412	790	344	17,476	9,566	3,278	3,710	7,572
1925	10,852	6,927	921	300	16,684	8,783	3,319	3,053	7,174
1926	11,076	5,637	1,029	330	15,762	9,561	4,320	3,370	7,473
1927	11,401	6,689	1,128	361	16,825	9,116	3,133	4,344	7,888
1928 [2]	11,040	5,300	1,220	359	16,078	8,537	2,953	4,269	8,019

YIELD PER ACRE

Year	Tons	Tons	Tons	Tons	Tons	Tons	Tons	Tons	Tons
1919	2.56	[1] 1.48			1.44	1.34	1.12	0.99	1.28
1920	2.71	[1] 1.42			1.37	1.33	1.31	1.06	1.24
1921	2.57	[1] 1.21			1.17	1.17	1.31	.99	1.21
1922	2.61	[1] 1.50			1.47	1.33	1.25	1.09	1.31
1923	2.65	[1] 1.33			1.30	1.15	1.37	1.05	1.34
1924	2.49	1.61	1.80	.94	1.58	1.38	1.14	.88	1.20
1925	2.62	1.33	1.73	.88	1.27	1.07	1.46	.85	1.09
1926	2.48	1.38	1.53	1.18	1.30	1.16	1.18	1.09	1.14
1927	2.79	1.75	2.02	1.30	1.63	1.43	1.49	1.10	1.25
1928 [2]	2.63	1.59	2.03	1.38	1.43	1.26	1.44	1.14	1.22

PRODUCTION

Year	1,000 tons	1,000 tons	1,000 tons	1,000 tons	1,000 tons	1,000 tons	1,000 tons	1,000 tons	1,000 tons
1919	22,364	[1] 11,030			21,282	15,238	5,909	2,599	8,575
1920	24,758	[1] 10,864			21,407	15,211	6,177	2,925	8,443
1921	23,705	[1] 9,237			18,028	13,486	6,475	3,020	8,507
1922	24,434	[1] 13,603			23,649	15,176	5,715	3,813	9,358
1923	25,990	[1] 10,789			20,216	12,776	5,876	4,037	9,566
1924	26,786	11,935	1,420	325	27,528	13,179	3,734	3,267	9,050
1925	28,439	9,201	1,594	263	21,271	9,400	4,835	2,593	7,835
1926	27,505	7,769	1,574	390	20,520	11,073	5,107	3,669	8,537
1927	31,823	11,727	2,274	469	27,353	13,058	4,655	4,787	9,855
1928 [2]	29,054	8,436	2,476	495	22,976	10,720	4,253	4,866	9,755

Bureau of Agricultural Economics.   Estimates of the crop-reporting board.

[1] All clover hay.   [2] Preliminary.

NOTE.—Tables similar to Tables 269–275, 1927 Yearbook, are omitted.

TABLE 284.—*Hay, all: Stocks on farms, United States, May 1, 1910–1928*

Year	Production of all hay preceding year	Stocks on farms May 1		Price per ton May 1 [1]	Year	Production of all hay preceding year	Stocks on farms May 1		Price per ton May 1 [1]
		Per cent	Stocks				Per cent	Stocks	
	1,000 short tons		*1,000 short tons*	*Dollars*		*1,000 short tons*		*1,000 short tons*	*Dollars*
1910	92,767	11.6	10,745	11.08	1920	105,398	10.2	10,707	24.22
1911	82,529	12.4	10,222	11.69	1921	107,245	17.9	19,160	13.08
1912	67,071	8.5	5,732	16.31	1922	97,849	11.2	10,969	12.98
1913	90,734	14.9	13,523	10.42	1923	111,879	12.0	13,379	12.69
1914	79,179	12.2	9,631	11.63	1924	106,611	12.0	12,835	13.69
1915	88,686	12.2	10,797	11.03	1925	112,083	13.9	15,598	12.32
1916	107,263	13.5	14,452	11.27	1926	98,155	11.7	11,455	12.95
1917	110,992	11.4	12,659	13.94	1927	95,712	11.2	10,746	13.23
1918	98,439	11.7	11,476	17.97	1928	123,327	14.5	17,896	10.50
1919	91,139	9.4	8,559	22.31					

Bureau of Agricultural Economics. Production and stocks are estimates of the crop-reporting board; prices are based upon returns from special price reporters.

[1] Prices 1923–1928 are the mean of Apr. 15 and May 15.

TABLE 285.—*Hay: Receipts at 11 markets, 1908–1927*

Year beginning July	Balti-more	Bos-ton	Chi-cago	Kan-sas City	Mil-wau-kee	Min-neap-olis	New York	Peoria	Phila-del-phia	St. Louis	San Fran-cisco	Total
	Short tons	*Short tons*	*Short tons*	*Short tons*	*Short tons*	*Short tons*	*Short tons*	*Short tons*	*Short tons*	*Short tons*	*Short tons*	*Short tons*
Average:												
1909–1913	63,399	144,674	305,601	297,787	39,610	46,350	318,776	40,496	83,589	241,320	154,134	1,735,734
1914–1920	44,827	95,900	264,783	420,495	24,816	34,442	224,989	36,490	61,151	229,995	104,394	1,542,282
1921–1925	17,075	45,664	154,127	287,220	15,543	27,592	83,557	27,100	41,853	133,347	67,445	900,523
1908	56,151	129,450	277,746	179,928	29,618	31,880	338,153	36,011	92,304	208,025	164,648	1,543,914
1909	58,877	142,930	256,269	232,368	29,151	26,310	334,760	44,118	83,233	200,456	168,220	1,576,692
1910	68,273	162,420	272,104	308,940	39,934	66,300	338,860	37,048	81,529	253,932	184,594	1,813,934
1911	68,235	163,220	352,324	318,948	43,634	63,570	292,411	39,361	95,715	259,642	147,483	1,844,543
1912	59,785	139,370	276,187	343,392	47,756	37,290	309,322	39,800	81,853	229,713	141,224	1,705,692
1913	61,823	115,430	371,120	285,288	37,574	38,280	318,528	42,151	75,614	262,855	129,147	1,737,810
1914	55,623	116,020	320,071	398,604	45,698	45,513	329,686	38,305	78,583	299,550	161,739	1,889,392
1915	50,042	126,400	280,224	398,172	34,248	45,306	296,200	38,792	88,780	223,815	145,373	1,727,352
1916	50,794	123,580	239,062	359,316	19,748	35,652	214,064	47,594	79,006	209,902	108,455	1,487,173
1917	63,799	95,170	351,972	419,964	21,061	39,126	200,197	40,800	60,296	238,144	86,228	1,616,757
1918	42,249	70,660	287,217	386,460	15,778	29,769	217,300	35,400	31,487	202,812	80,233	1,399,365
1919	32,059	57,270	225,217	617,052	18,233	22,607	170,742	33,400	49,868	256,112	80,775	1,563,335
1920	19,223	82,200	149,718	363,900	18,943	23,118	146,734	21,140	40,036	179,633	67,953	1,112,598
1921	14,158	51,080	142,753	225,516	17,901	23,718	102,381	10,970	51,262	119,991	59,185	818,915
1922	16,081	49,190	150,342	261,684	17,381	25,956	98,841	33,060	42,246	138,961	60,017	893,159
1923	25,664	42,910	146,496	290,676	17,183	30,432	64,332	28,200	32,824	142,184	50,159	887,699
1924	13,635	46,710	155,158	316,932	9,472	28,093	64,332	34,370	33,199	127,060	54,629	933,430
1925	15,839	38,430	175,885	341,892	15,778	29,761	66,587	34,370	33,199	127,060	[2] 23,165	[2] 719,242
1926	11,547	30,680	130,665	277,020	8,092	38,187	54,363	30,140	29,539	85,844	41,869	602,158
1927	6,438	25,990	104,241	223,212	6,764	17,214	42,886	40,030	22,397	71,117		

Bureau of Agricultural Economics. Compiled as follows: Baltimore, Baltimore Chamber of Commerce annual reports; Boston, Boston Chamber of Commerce annual reports, 1909–1918; Chicago, Board of Trade annual reports; Kansas City, Board of Trade annual reports; Milwaukee, Chamber of Commerce annual reports, except 1923 and 1924; Minneapolis, Chamber of Commerce annual reports; New York, New York Produce Exchange; Peoria, Board of Trade annual reports, 1909–1918; St. Louis, Trade and Commerce of St. Louis, 1909–1923, subsequently Daily Market Reporter; San Francisco, Chamber of Commerce annual reports, 1909–1920; other data from Hay Trade Journal ,weekly.

[1] Total for 6 months; not reported July–December, 1926.
[2] Not including San Francisco, July–December, 1926.

TABLE 286.—*Hay, tame: Estimated price per ton, received by producers, December 1, averages 1909–1913, 1914–1920, 1921–1925, annual 1925–1928*

State	Av. 1909–1913	Av. 1914–1920	Av. 1921–1925	1925	1926	1927	1928	State	Av. 1909–1913	Av. 1914–1920	Av. 1921–1925	1925	1926	1927	1928
	Dols.	Dols.	Dols.	Dols.	Dols.	Dols.	Dols.		Dols.	Dols.	Dols.	Dols.	Dols.	Dols.	Dols.
Me	13.90	15.53	14.32	12.00	13.20	12.70	11.40	N. C	15.84	19.86	20.20	22.00	20.00	18.00	17.30
N. H	16.62	18.39	20.70	18.50	19.00	16.30	14.10	S. C	17.04	21.71	19.50	20.00	20.00	18.00	18.50
Vt	13.92	16.23	17.06	13.20	14.50	11.70	11.60	Ga	16.82	19.97	18.34	21.00	18.00	16.30	15.60
Mass	20.72	23.34	24.60	23.00	23.90	21.00	19.10	Fla	17.36	18.27	20.20	23.00	22.00	18.20	19.00
R. I	21.14	24.81	25.56	23.50	25.00	22.00	22.00	Ky	14.50	18.93	16.74	18.70	16.70	14.50	16.50
Conn	20.88	23.10	25.10	24.50	25.70	21.70	18.90	Tenn	14.98	19.53	18.48	22.00	16.60	15.00	16.90
N. Y	15.20	17.40	15.48	14.60	15.00	11.30	11.30	Ala	13.66	16.79	18.02	20.00	18.00	15.00	15.80
N. J	19.14	22.96	20.40	20.00	20.30	17.50	14.60	Miss	12.14	15.07	15.94	17.70	16.00	15.00	15.20
Pa	16.02	18.94	17.16	17.00	18.50	13.50	12.50	Ark	12.06	15.30	15.30	18.00	16.00	14.00	14.40
Ohio	13.62	17.03	13.40	15.20	14.00	9.20	11.70	La	11.88	15.40	15.82	19.00	14.50	13.80	14.40
Ind	12.94	16.49	13.56	15.50	14.00	10.40	12.00	Okla	8.30	11.86	12.86	16.00	12.00	10.70	12.70
Ill	13.12	17.07	14.04	15.90	16.00	11.40	12.90	Tex	11.60	14.93	14.60	18.80	12.00	11.80	13.20
Mich	13.56	17.04	13.24	16.50	13.80	11.00	11.60	Mont	10.08	14.34	9.32	10.00	10.50	8.40	8.90
Wis	12.70	15.77	14.20	14.00	15.00	12.50	14.40	Idaho	7.84	13.60	9.26	8.50	9.00	8.70	11.00
Minn	8.00	10.20	10.62	11.00	14.20	9.00	11.10	Wyo	9.40	13.33	8.86	8.90	8.50	9.00	10.10
Iowa	9.66	13.78	11.34	13.50	15.50	12.50	13.00	Colo	9.76	12.66	10.48	12.00	8.60	9.20	11.70
Mo	11.02	14.94	11.62	12.80	13.50	9.90	10.60	N. Mex	11.24	15.47	15.72	15.00	12.00	13.40	16.90
N. Dak	6.18	9.57	7.36	7.20	11.00	7.80	6.70	Ariz	12.16	18.67	15.86	17.00	13.00	14.40	18.00
S. Dak	6.66	8.43	8.38	11.00	13.00	7.60	8.20	Utah	8.82	13.96	8.86	9.00	8.00	9.20	11.70
Nebr	8.34	10.74	10.02	12.10	14.00	8.50	10.00	Nev	10.10	13.83	11.00	9.00	10.50	10.00	12.20
Kans	8.76	11.80	10.24	12.10	13.00	8.60	9.40	Wash	12.54	17.50	13.84	15.00	13.70	12.90	13.10
Del	16.60	20.84	18.90	20.00	18.50	16.50	16.40	Oreg	10.14	14.39	11.60	11.60	11.00	11.20	11.70
Md	16.36	20.17	18.52	19.00	20.20	15.40	13.50	Calif	11.84	15.49	15.14	14.00	12.30	12.50	14.50
Va	15.80	19.91	18.50	21.00	19.50	16.00	15.30								
W. Va	15.64	20.16	18.36	20.00	19.40	15.00	14.70	U. S	12.25	15.43	13.30	13.93	14.10	11.35	12.34

Bureau of Agricultural Economics. As reported by crop reporters.

TABLE 287.—*Hay, all (loose): Estimated price per ton, received by producers, United States, 1909–1928*

Year beginning July	July 15	Aug. 15	Sept. 15	Oct. 15	Nov. 15	Dec. 15	Jan. 15	Feb. 15	Mar. 15	Apr. 15	May 15	June 15	Weighted av.
	Dolls.	Dolls.	Dolls.	Dolls.	Dolls.	Dolls.	Dolls.	Dolls.	Dolls.	Dolls.	Dolls.	Dolls.	Dolls.
Average:													
1909–1913	11.60	11.35	11.39	11.49	11.89	11.99	11.87	12.02	12.06	12.16	12.28	12.16	11.83
1914–1920	14.95	14.47	14.52	14.53	14.69	14.99	15.32	15.51	15.63	15.99	16.35	16.07	15.26
1921–1925	12.27	11.94	11.91	11.93	12.25	12.47	12.58	12.62	12.64	12.83	12.92	12.63	12.39
1909	10.12	9.70	9.85	10.19	10.42	10.48	10.90	11.48	11.57	11.30	10.96	10.80	10.58
1910	10.75	10.98	11.16	11.16	11.67	11.92	11.74	11.68	11.46	11.52	12.04	12.78	11.54
1911	13.51	13.73	13.58	13.57	13.95	14.02	14.07	14.52	15.15	15.98	16.26	15.27	14.36
1912	13.18	11.62	11.12	11.05	11.44	11.45	10.98	10.74	10.52	10.42	10.48	10.51	11.17
1913	10.45	10.74	11.24	11.48	11.97	12.06	11.68	11.68	11.60	11.58	11.64	11.46	11.49
1914	11.02	10.93	11.03	10.87	10.95	10.80	10.65	10.86	10.94	11.00	11.10	11.00	10.92
1915	10.52	10.07	9.89	9.90	9.92	9.97	10.31	10.65	10.80	11.06	11.37	11.28	10.34
1916	10.50	9.80	9.68	9.82	10.74	10.74	11.10	11.44	12.04	13.24	14.31	14.32	11.21
1917	13.43	13.08	13.54	14.50	15.85	17.32	18.48	19.01	18.91	18.32	17.55	16.60	16.60
1918	16.00	16.67	17.94	18.86	19.31	19.64	19.86	19.80	20.17	21.42	22.80	22.52	19.88
1919	20.94	20.34	20.16	19.58	19.40	20.00	21.16	22.04	22.62	23.58	24.54	24.24	21.34
1920	22.26	20.38	19.41	18.20	17.08	16.43	15.70	14.76	13.94	13.34	12.80	12.56	16.51
1921	12.17	11.72	11.53	11.24	11.19	11.29	11.34	11.58	12.05	12.64	12.82	12.28	11.83
1922	11.44	10.78	10.68	10.87	11.38	11.82	11.98	12.04	12.18	12.54	12.82	12.32	11.68
1923	11.78	11.98	12.25	12.44	12.75	13.15	13.59	13.60	13.63	13.73	13.65	13.75	12.93
1924	13.49	12.95	12.68	12.64	12.88	12.69	12.70	12.83	12.39	12.48	12.17	11.82	12.76
1925	12.48	12.25	12.42	12.47	13.07	13.40	13.31	13.03	12.97	12.78	13.12	12.98	12.83
1926	12.96	13.04	12.88	13.08	13.22	13.47	13.38	13.64	13.48	13.26	13.20	13.10	13.23
1927	11.71	9.97	10.51	10.63	10.54	10.55	10.60	10.24	10.19	10.29	10.70	11.01	10.57
1928	10.86	10.39	10.59	10.60	10.89	11.23							

Bureau of Agricultural Economics. Based on returns from special price reporters. Mean of prices reported on 1st of month and 1st of succeeding month, July, 1909–December, 1923.

Table 288.—*Hay, alfalfa: Estimated price per ton received by producers, United States, 1914–1928*

Year beginning July	July 15	Aug. 15	Sept. 15	Oct. 15	Nov. 15	Dec. 15	Jan. 15	Feb. 15	Mar. 15	Apr. 15	May 15	June 15	Weighted av.
	Dolls.	Dolls.	Dolls.	Dolls.	Dolls.	Dolls.	Dolls.	Dolls.	Dolls.	Dolls.	Dolls.	Dolls.	Dolls.
1914	8.65	8.38	8.72	8.96	9.20	9.05	9.48	9.32	9.79	9.81	9.58	8.50	9.12
1915	8.28	8.28	8.22	8.14	8.72	9.52	9.89	10.35	10.74	10.73	10.56	10.49	9.39
1916	9.87	9.80	10.06	10.25	11.37	12.31	12.79	13.63	14.68	17.68	17.92	16.77	12.76
1917	14.13	15.28	16.33	17.59	19.19	20.39	21.27	21.38	20.82	18.97	17.84	16.71	18.42
1918	16.58	18.22	19.72	20.23	20.42	20.74	20.42	20.91	21.40	22.28	23.32	20.89	20.35
1919	20.15	20.72	20.89	20.56	21.63	22.95	24.13	24.41	24.68	24.57	25.68	24.20	22.70
1920	21.70	20.43	19.12	18.03	17.10	16.59	14.98	13.55	12.88	11.35	10.88	10.64	15.96
1921	9.85	9.66	9.86	9.82	9.67	10.46	10.55	11.04	11.80	12.39	12.28	10.98	10.58
1922	10.61	10.54	11.15	11.87	12.70	13.31	14.06	14.02	14.33	14.09	14.40	13.63	12.82
1923	12.45	12.01	12.78	13.37	13.59	14.39	13.99	14.08	13.98	14.09	14.12	13.70	13.54
1924	13.19	13.84	13.59	12.85	13.91	13.40	14.50	14.78	14.44	14.08	14.34	12.83	13.81
1925	13.02	13.00	12.91	13.41	13.74	14.14	13.90	14.24	13.50	13.53	13.17	13.33	13.52
1926	12.94	13.15	13.13	13.29	13.79	13.57	13.83	14.21	14.38	12.56	13.59	13.03	13.57
1927	11.73	11.47	11.34	11.52	11.75	12.02	12.09	11.84	12.46	12.56	12.90	12.42	11.96
1928	11.98	11.82	12.20	12.82	13.29	13.90							

Bureau of Agricultural Economics. Based on returns from special price reporters.

Table 289.—*Hay, clover: Estimated price per ton received by producers, United States, 1914–1928*

Year beginning July	July 15	Aug. 15	Sept. 15	Oct. 15	Nov. 15	Dec. 15	Jan. 15	Feb. 15	Mar. 15	Apr. 15	May 15	June 15	Weighted av.
	Dolls.	Dolls.	Dolls.	Dolls.	Dolls.	Dolls.	Dolls.	Dolls.	Dolls.	Dolls.	Dolls.	Dolls.	Dolls.
1014	11.85	12.09	12.44	12.47	12.70	12.76	13.07	13.36	13.41	13.65	13.79	12.78	12.83
1915	11.65	10.87	10.82	10.60	10.59	10.95	11.24	11.41	11.70	11.87	12.52	12.46	11.29
1916	10.84	9.93	10.01	10.08	10.46	10.86	11.38	11.65	11.90	13.06	13.94	14.22	11.33
1917	12.95	12.76	13.79	15.01	17.14	18.67	19.82	21.11	21.37	19.68	18.30	16.54	17.21
1918	15.73	17.18	19.27	20.60	21.13	21.26	21.69	21.11	21.25	23.36	25.33	25.48	20.93
1919	22.02	21.58	21.74	21.17	21.61	22.60	23.78	24.94	26.13	26.93	28.31	27.80	23.69
1920	24.62	22.82	22.57	21.29	20.60	19.96	19.17	17.39	16.44	15.47	14.90	14.52	19.48
1921	13.89	14.17	14.37	13.99	13.83	14.17	13.90	14.10	14.06	14.51	14.90	14.33	14.15
1922	12.82	12.66	12.54	12.51	12.67	13.03	13.39	13.35	13.24	13.47	13.58	13.70	13.03
1923	13.52	13.51	14.12	14.73	14.94	15.82	15.51	15.93	16.31	16.08	15.92	15.95	15.14
1924	15.45	14.00	13.75	13.65	13.64	13.45	13.25	13.30	12.52	12.41	12.67	12.26	13.43
1925	13.03	13.67	14.06	14.09	14.74	15.28	14.79	14.82	14.79	14.88	15.13	15.07	14.52
1926	14.40	14.25	14.60	14.71	14.76	15.24	15.71	16.16	15.64	15.51	15.21	14.65	15.06
1927	13.11	12.16	11.78	11.91	11.86	11.91	12.24	11.96	12.02	12.23	12.51	12.63	12.15
1928	12.52	12.25	12.50	12.58	13.01	13.05							

Bureau of Agricultural Economics. Based on returns from special price reporters.

Table 290.—*Hay, timothy: Estimated price per ton, received by producers, United States, 1914–1928*

Year beginning July	July 15	Aug. 15	Sept. 15	Oct. 15	Nov. 15	Dec. 15	Jan. 15	Feb. 15	Mar. 15	Apr. 15	May 15	June 15	Weighted av.
	Dolls.	Dolls.	Dolls.	Dolls.	Dolls.	Dolls.	Dolls.	Dolls.	Dolls.	Dolls.	Dolls.	Dolls.	Dolls.
1914	13.06	13.09	13.54	13.66	13.69	13.69	14.07	14.28	14.28	14.53	14.74	14.33	13.87
1915	13.43	12.39	12.32	12.14	12.24	12.73	13.11	13.39	13.61	14.00	14.50	14.71	13.09
1916	12.97	11.74	11.57	11.54	12.03	12.29	12.61	12.91	13.20	14.26	15.31	15.76	12.83
1917	14.68	14.11	14.89	16.23	18.33	20.31	21.37	22.25	22.53	21.47	20.47	18.55	18.67
1918	17.61	18.98	20.85	22.60	22.93	22.94	23.48	22.69	22.68	24.74	27.27	27.50	22.66
1919	24.22	23.89	23.65	23.04	22.90	23.71	24.59	25.49	26.75	27.99	29.92	30.05	25.13
1920	26.59	24.35	24.15	22.74	22.09	21.22	19.88	18.30	17.04	16.09	15.44	15.16	20.64
1921	14.51	15.01	14.83	14.39	14.22	14.31	14.51	14.77	15.06	15.52	16.10	15.75	14.82
1922	14.33	13.61	13.44	13.70	13.93	13.91	14.41	14.46	14.59	14.64	14.96	14.95	14.18
1923	14.86	14.68	15.13	16.22	16.78	16.95	16.96	17.25	17.53	17.53	17.48	17.52	16.53
1924	16.74	15.24	14.47	14.54	14.00	14.37	14.29	14.24	13.31	13.39	13.38	13.05	14.30
1925	13.89	14.06	14.98	15.11	15.38	15.87	15.82	15.79	15.59	15.81	16.31	16.64	15.40
1926	16.01	15.52	15.32	15.49	15.62	15.41	14.58	15.82	15.39	15.05	15.14	14.97	15.42
1927	13.29	12.03	11.70	11.58	11.67	11.31	11.34	11.03	11.14	11.17	11.75	11.82	11.64
1928	11.68	11.70	11.77	11.86	12.18	12.35							

Bureau of Agricultural Economics. Based on returns from special price reporters.

TABLE 291.—*Hay, prairie: Estimated price per ton, received by producers, United States, 1914–1928*

Year beginning July	July 15	Aug. 15	Sept. 15	Oct. 15	Nov. 15	Dec. 15	Jan. 15	Feb. 15	Mar. 15	Apr. 15	May 15	June 15	Weighted av.
	Dolls.	Dolls.	Dolls.	Dolls.	Dolls.	Dolls.	Dolls.	Dolls.	Dolls.	Dolls.	Dolls.	Dolls.	Dolls.
1914	7.49	7.29	7.33	7.59	7.49	7.37	7.65	7.86	8.03	8.58	8.29	7.72	7.69
1915	7.37	6.83	6.64	6.44	6.75	6.95	7.38	7.34	7.39	7.56	7.71	7.97	7.13
1916	7.25	6.96	7.21	7.26	7.85	8.14	8.58	8.60	9.32	10.94	12.02	11.84	8.61
1917	10.11	10.82	11.40	12.29	13.32	14.91	15.39	15.74	15.47	14.47	12.75	12.78	13.31
1918	12.51	13.26	14.35	15.06	15.47	16.30	16.33	16.35	17.38	18.85	20.22	18.71	16.03
1919	16.10	16.10	15.90	15.88	16.91	17.19	17.54	17.36	16.52	16.66	18.06	17.59	16.78
1920	15.38	13.74	12.93	11.83	11.47	10.80	10.20	9.46	8.70	8.43	8.05	8.02	10.94
1921	7.67	7.50	7.52	6.78	7.49	7.47	7.39	7.67	7.94	8.02	8.24	8.40	7.62
1922	7.68	7.76	7.54	7.74	8.13	8.98	9.44	9.52	9.61	9.74	10.64	10.07	8.79
1923	9.17	8.97	8.58	9.19	9.07	9.26	8.84	8.87	8.66	8.78	8.74	8.54	8.92
1924	8.35	8.60	8.49	8.25	8.25	8.62	9.14	9.08	9.05	9.11	9.27	8.55	8.70
1925	8.93	8.55	9.24	9.41	9.39	9.78	9.73	9.53	9.48	9.08	9.54	9.59	9.36
1926	9.63	10.55	10.52	10.78	10.76	10.98	11.28	11.76	11.50	10.70	11.51	10.77	10.87
1927	9.15	8.65	7.98	7.67	7.47	7.55	7.41	6.98	6.79	6.96	7.32	7.59	7.64
1928	7.80	7.34	7.62	7.71	7.72								

Bureau of Agricultural Economics. Based on returns from special price reporters.

TABLE 292.—*Hay, alfalfa No. 1: Average price per ton at Kansas City, 1910–1928*

Year beginning July	July	Aug.	Sept.	Oct.	Nov.	Dec.	Jan.	Feb.	Mar.	Apr.	May	June	Average
Average:	Dolls.	Dolls.	Dolls.	Dolls.	Dolls.	Dolls.	Dolls.	Dolls.	Dolls.	Dolls.	Dolls.	Dolls.	Dolls.
1914–1920	19.02	21.29	20.97	21.87	23.61	24.19	24.29	23.83	23.71	24.43	24.17	21.98	22.78
1921–1925	17.74	19.04	19.73	21.92	22.30	22.32	22.71	21.52	22.76	23.67	22.99	18.21	21.24
1910	12.08	13.50	13.89	14.25	14.25	14.23	13.51	12.93	13.07	13.67	13.29	12.38	13.42
1911	15.13	14.44	14.87	15.00	15.27	15.50	17.72	18.37	20.49	22.73	19.34	11.62	16.71
1912	12.59	13.00	13.58	15.11	15.11	15.00	14.79	12.86	14.06	13.75	13.28	10.70	13.65
1913	12.12	14.80	16.14	16.54	16.00	16.01	15.96	15.25	15.18	15.30	15.54	14.23	15.26
1914	12.38	13.42	13.33	12.51	13.21	13.79	13.75	13.73	14.75	15.11	13.73	13.42	13.59
1915	11.54	11.90	12.25	13.11	12.83	14.35	14.54	15.34	13.92	14.44	14.45	11.42	13.34
1916	11.29	13.40	13.58	15.68	18.50	19.33	19.81	20.25	21.10	24.33	24.52	21.87	18.64
1917	21.18	24.09	24.07	27.43	31.10	32.76	30.01	31.33	27.56	24.11	22.64	20.57	26.40
1918	22.60	29.08	31.45	30.14	31.21	31.01	32.85	31.01	34.56	37.90	36.20	36.43	32.04
1919	26.93	27.63	24.96	30.24	33.39	35.10	35.75	34.83	33.79	34.10	35.46	31.75	31.99
1920	27.21	29.49	27.22	23.95	25.05	23.01	23.30	20.30	20.30	21.00	22.20	18.40	23.45
1921	17.50	19.00	17.20	10.80	20.40	19.60	20.00	19.60	22.10	22.50	22.10	15.40	19.60
1922	15.50	15.80	18.30	22.60	23.80	23.00	23.40	23.70	24.60	26.25	25.90	22.90	22.15
1923	18.90	20.90	22.80	24.90	24.80	24.90	25.30	23.50	24.70	26.10	24.50	18.00	23.28
1924	18.60	20.00	20.25	20.80	21.25	22.70	22.70	19.25	19.60	18.90	19.20	17.50	20.06
1925	18.20	19.50	20.10	21.50	21.25	21.40	22.15	21.56	22.81	24.62	23.25	17.25	21.13
1926	17.80	18.25	19.38	19.90	20.67	20.40	20.00	19.25	18.75	19.00	19.00	15.00	18.95
1927	14.75	15.25	18.00	19.50	20.00	22.25	21.50	22.50	24.25	26.00	26.00	20.00	20.83
1928	20.00	20.50	21.00	23.25	25.00	26.00							

Bureau of Agricultural Economics. Compiled from Kansas City Daily Price Current and Kansas City Grain Market Review, average of daily range; 1925–1928 from reports made direct to the bureau.

TABLE 293.—*Hay, prairie No. 1: Average price per ton at Kansas City, 1910–1928*

Year beginning July	July	Aug.	Sept.	Oct.	Nov.	Dec.	Jan.	Feb.	Mar.	Apr.	May	June	Average
Average:	Dolls.	Dolls.	Dolls.	Dolls.	Dolls.	Dolls.	Dolls.	Dolls.	Dolls.	Dolls.	Dolls.	Dolls.	Dolls.
1914–1920	15.35	15.71	16.00	16.27	17.20	17.21	16.90	16.48	17.66	18.96	19.53	18.23	17.12
1921–1925	12.04	11.30	11.97	13.56	13.26	12.95	12.73	12.44	13.04	14.21	14.72	14.23	13.04
1910	10.83	10.82	11.67	11.34	11.16	10.86	11.07	10.95	10.84	11.31	11.55	13.61	11.33
1911	15.93	12.93	11.50	11.60	12.07	12.61	13.84	13.66	16.70	20.85	20.48	15.16	14.78
1912	8.79	7.96	8.39	8.96	8.91	9.39	10.45	9.37	9.19	9.56	9.53	9.97	9.21
1913	10.60	13.62	15.76	16.00	15.66	15.57	14.20	14.50	14.40	16.00	16.42	15.43	14.85
1914	12.10	9.96	11.58	11.35	10.94	10.98	11.25	10.89	11.26	11.41	11.02	11.03	11.15
1915	11.32	8.65	8.63	9.71	9.54	8.97	8.84	9.15	8.96	9.50	9.74	8.65	9.30
1916	8.50	8.06	9.36	9.47	10.74	11.15	10.57	10.92	12.92	18.68	19.74	20.57	12.56
1917	18.14	18.57	18.06	19.60	25.07	25.47	24.00	23.79	23.42	21.13	19.17	17.66	21.17
1918	19.26	25.25	26.57	27.58	26.84	24.04	28.25	26.82	32.35	36.63	38.91	37.34	29.15
1919	20.89	19.98	19.32	19.75	21.12	25.34	21.40	20.68	20.64	21.70	24.02	18.95	21.15
1920	17.21	19.52	18.47	16.45	16.13	14.49	14.00	13.10	14.10	13.70	14.10	13.40	15.39
1921	12.30	11.40	11.30	12.40	12.00	11.30	11.10	10.30	11.50	11.90	12.40	11.90	11.65
1922	12.90	10.70	11.00	14.00	14.20	12.70	12.60	13.25	14.60	19.10	19.10	18.60	14.40
1923	11.80	11.50	13.80	14.60	14.75	14.75	14.30	14.50	14.80	14.50	13.90	12.50	13.85
1924	11.60	11.60	11.00	12.40	11.60	11.90	11.00	10.40	10.50	10.30	10.60	10.75	11.14
1925	11.60	11.30	12.75	14.40	14.00	14.10	14.15	13.75	13.81	15.25	17.62	17.38	14.16
1926	14.12	13.38	14.25	15.40	16.00	15.80	15.50	15.00	14.25	13.75	13.75	13.00	14.52
1927	10.50	10.00	10.25	11.50	11.00	11.50	10.50	10.50	10.50	11.25	11.50	11.25	10.90
1928	10.75	9.50	9.75	10.50	11.50	12.00							

Bureau of Agricultural Economics. Compiled from Kansas City Daily Price Current and Kansas City Grain Market Review, average of daily range; 1925–1928 from reports made direct to the bureau.

TABLE 294.—*Hay, timothy No. 1: Average price per ton at Chicago, 1910–1928*

Year beginning July	July	Aug.	Sept.	Oct.	Nov.	Dec.	Jan.	Feb.	Mar.	Apr.	May	June	Average
	Dolls.	Dolls.	Dolls.	Dolls.	Dolls.	Dolls.	Dolls.	Dolls.	Dolls.	Dolls.	Dolls.	Dolls.	Dolls.
Average: 1914–1920	23.39	24.86	23.68	23.54	23.71	23.25	23.59	22.88	23.83	25.33	26.16	24.50	24.06
1921–1925	24.40	24.52	24.42	24.12	24.05	23.50	23.73	22.85	23.63	24.55	24.37	24.31	24.04
1920	18.75	19.50	17.25	17.25	17.50	17.50	18.00	16.25	16.25	17.75	21.00	21.75	18.23
1911	23.50	21.50	20.00	20.50	21.25	21.00	21.75	20.75	21.50	24.00	26.00	21.25	21.92
1912	19.75	18.50	18.50	18.00	17.00	15.50	15.75	14.25	14.75	15.50	15.25	14.25	16.42
1913	15.00	17.75	17.75	18.00	17.00	16.25	15.50	14.75	15.25	16.00	16.25	15.25	16.23
1914	16.25	16.75	15.50	15.25	15.50	15.50	16.25	15.50	15.25	16.25	17.00	17.50	16.04
1915	19.25	20.25	19.00	17.00	15.50	15.50	16.25	15.50	16.75	18.75	18.75	18.00	17.54
1916	16.00	16.00	15.50	16.25	16.25	16.25	15.50	15.75	15.75	18.00	20.50	18.75	16.71
1917	17.75	19.25	21.00	25.00	27.25	27.00	28.25	29.00	28.00	24.00	23.00	19.00	24.04
1918	21.50	26.50	32.00	31.00	30.00	30.00	29.50	26.00	30.50	33.50	35.50	33.00	29.92
1919	34.50	35.00	29.00	28.00	29.50	30.00	32.50	34.00	35.35	43.00	46.50	42.75	35.00
1920	38.50	40.25	33.75	32.25	32.00	28.50	26.90	24.40	25.30	23.80	21.90	22.50	29.17
1921	24.40	24.00	24.20	22.60	22.90	21.90	22.50	21.80	23.60	26.80	25.70	23.60	23.67
1922	24.50	22.00	20.90	22.40	23.00	21.10	21.75	21.50	23.00	23.00	24.00		22.52
1923	24.00	25.20	26.60	26.50	26.80	27.10	26.80	24.80	25.30	26.20	26.30	25.20	25.90
1924	25.00	25.40	24.40	22.90	22.80	23.00	23.30	22.75	23.00	22.75	21.75	24.00	23.42
1925	24.10	26.00	26.00	26.20	24.75	24.40	24.30	23.40	23.25	24.00	25.00	24.75	24.68
1926	24.40	24.75	23.40	22.50	21.10	22.50	*21.75	20.75	20.00	20.50	20.50	19.25	21.78
1927	18.25	19.75	18.25	18.00	18.25	18.00	17.75	16.75	17.50	18.50	21.00	21.50	18.62
1928	21.50	21.25	24.00	24.25	23.75	23.50							

Bureau of Agricultural Economics. Compiled from Chicago Board of Trade and Daily Trade Bulletin, average of daily range; 1925–1927 from reports made direct to the bureau.

TABLE 295.—*Alfalfa meal, No. 1 medium: Average price per ton, bagged, in car lots, at Kansas City, 1920–1928* [1]

Year beginning July	July	Aug.	Sept.	Oct.	Nov.	Dec.	Jan.	Feb.	Mar.	Apr.	May	June	Average
	Dolls.	Dolls.	Dolls.	Dolls.	Dolls.	Dolls.	Dolls.	Dolls.	Dolls.	Dolls.	Dolls.	Dolls.	Dolls.
1919							40.70	40.00	38.10	40.40	46.75	42.75	
1920	38.25	35.50	34.60	29.70	29.90	25.40	23.10	19.60	18.60	18.70	18.00	18.10	26.02
1921	19.00	18.75	17.75	16.90	16.50	16.70	16.75	17.50	19.75	19.40	20.90	21.90	18.48
1922	18.55	19.50	21.20	24.60	26.25	26.25	25.40	24.40	26.50	26.10	23.45		23.96
1923	21.50	22.40	25.50	25.70	26.90	25.20	26.25	23.90	23.20	20.90	21.20	21.75	23.27
1924	22.00	22.60	23.25	23.10	22.50	23.90	24.20	22.50	22.25	22.00	22.70	22.90	22.82
1925	23.00	24.00	24.25	24.45	24.10	14.40	24.80	24.00	23.10	23.90	25.40	23.90	24.18
1926	23.00	22.80	22.25	22.40	22.90	22.30	22.00	21.75	21.40	21.00	22.20	21.60	22.13
1927	21.75	22.40	23.40	23.10	22.75	23.30	24.40	26.25	29.40	33.50	34.25	31.70	26.35
1928	27.60	25.60	26.00	26.60	26.60	28.55							

Bureau of Agricultural Economics.

[1] Average of prices reported to grain, hay, and feed market news service on each Saturday of the month.

TABLE 296.—*Pasture:* [1] *Condition, 1st of month, United States, 1909–1928*

Year	May	June	July	Aug.	Sept.	Oct.	Year	May	June	July	Aug.	Sept.	Oct.
	P. ct.	P. ct.	P. ct.	P. ct.	P. ct.	P. ct.		P. ct.	P. ct.	P. ct.	P. ct.	P. ct.	P. ct.
1909	79.1	86.9	91.8	86.4			1919	91.1	97.4	95.8	85.3	81.6	78.9
1910	86.9	87.1	79.7	71.5			1920	79.3	90.2	91.4	87.7	88.1	86.9
1911	83.1	82.7	67.2	62.7			1921	90.0	89.4	84.4	78.3	82.1	84.8
1912	82.9	92.5	89.7	87.3			1922	85.9	94.6	88.5	86.7	78.7	72.7
1913	85.5	88.1	81.6	74.3			1923	79.4	86.1	87.2	79.4	80.2	85.0
1914	88.9	90.0	83.0	76.2			1924	82.4	83.2	87.2	82.0	76.6	78.6
1915	88.4	92.5	93.2	95.5	97.7	95.9	1925	82.2	75.7	73.0	69.5	67.4	72.9
1916	84.8	90.8	94.8	84.5	79.8	76.9	1926	74.6	77.0	77.0	69.9	78.2	83.7
1917	79.9	83.1	84.1	78.5	77.5	75.5	1927	87.0	88.3	92.8	86.9	84.2	80.1
1918	81.6	89.3	82.0	72.4	67.7	73.5	1928	71.3	78.6	84.4	85.6	83.3	77.7

Bureau of Agricultural Economics. Estimates of the crop-reporting board.

[1] For range States, condition given as reported. Probably relates largely to farm pasture i. e., range not included.

TABLE 297.—*Pasture:* [1] *Condition, 1st of month, by States, average 1918–1927, and for 1928*

State and division	May Average, 1918–1927	May 1928	June Average, 1918–1927	June 1928	July Average, 1918–1927	July 1928	August Average, 1918–1927	August 1928	September Average, 1918–1927	September 1928	October Average, 1918–1927	October 1928
	P. ct.	P. ct.	P. ct.	P. ct.	P. ct.	P. ct.	P. ct.	P. ct.	P. ct.	P. ct.	P. ct.	P. ct.
Maine	88	81	89	88	87	95	86	95	82	94	80	93
New Hampshire	88	80	90	90	87	99	89	102	85	104	83	97
Vermont	88	79	90	90	91	96	92	96	88	96	88	94
Massachusetts	86	75	90	90	86	97	86	101	86	96	85	88
Rhode Island	85	76	90	87	88	97	86	94	86	88	85	82
Connecticut	83	77	89	89	87	98	84	100	85	100	85	96
New York	83	72	87	80	86	90	83	91	81	89	82	82
New Jersey	82	76	86	86	79	92	78	93	85	94	81	92
Pennsylvania	81	75	87	82	85	92	82	94	84	92	83	86
North Atlantic	83.0	74.4	87.8	82.8	85.8	92.1	83.2	93.5	83.0	91.8	82.8	85.9
Ohio	82	61	89	66	85	82	81	90	82	81	85	61
Indiana	83	61	89	73	86	84	77	86	79	82	81	67
Illinois	85	65	87	72	86	80	76	81	78	80	81	74
Michigan	73	55	86	80	81	87	72	85	72	82	80	79
Wisconsin	78	65	87	76	87	71	78	80	74	86	78	85
Minnesota	79	71	84	74	87	72	79	80	74	86	76	83
Iowa	86	66	86	75	89	76	80	85	82	89	87	89
Missouri	84	72	88	71	87	86	78	83	78	90	82	78
North Dakota	76	68	82	65	86	73	79	91	74	87	73	78
South Dakota	80	70	84	67	86	66	81	72	78	70	77	68
Nebraska	86	64	88	82	87	90	80	90	78	70	78	70
Kansas	85	70	88	85	86	95	80	96	76	92	80	84
North Central	82.4	65.8	86.9	74.5	86.3	81.4	78.7	85.4	77.8	83.2	80.9	76.7
Delaware	82	79	84	85	74	86	75	84	81	92	77	84
Maryland	80	74	83	84	76	90	75	87	81	92	78	93
Virginia	82	71	86	80	81	87	82	85	85	95	79	93
West Virginia	82	71	88	76	88	89	88	92	88	94	86	92
North Carolina	84	80	85	87	85	90	84	88	83	91	76	90
South Carolina	82	77	78	82	80	83	80	86	75	85	70	81
Georgia	83	79	83	86	82	89	84	90	78	90	72	82
Florida	82	84	82	82	88	87	91	90	90	89	87	88
S. Atlantic	82.4	74.9	84.7	81.8	83.0	88.1	83.4	88.1	83.5	92.2	78.4	89.4
Kentucky	86	65	89	73	88	90	81	92	81	90	82	72
Tennessee	85	73	88	83	86	93	78	90	79	90	76	85
Alabama	85	75	86	79	83	85	81	89	78	86	71	78
Mississippi	86	76	87	82	86	88	80	88	79	83	74	73
Arkansas	84	77	88	84	86	91	78	87	74	82	78	74
Louisiana	86	80	88	82	89	86	82	87	82	80	78	76
Oklahoma	84	77	88	88	86	92	77	90	71	76	75	63
Texas	84	70	88	77	87	85	77	77	72	72	75	71
S. Central	84.6	72.1	87.8	79.7	86.5	87.8	78.2	83.9	74.4	78.4	75.9	72.1
Montana	81	84	89	75	86	71	79	90	77	86	76	84
Idaho	88	83	92	91	87	86	82	83	80	75	80	73
Wyoming	90	84	96	91	95	95	90	95	88	94	87	92
Colorado	87	80	89	93	89	96	86	91	87	81	84	78
New Mexico	74	74	80	90	80	77	79	64	83	80	80	75
Arizona	84	83	84	80	82	75	83	75	86	80	83	80
Utah	88	84	92	94	88	86	84	74	83	68	82	60
Nevada	88	75	92	90	90	84	87	80	84	79	84	76
Washington	87	90	90	90	84	86	72	79	71	70	74	66
Oregon	92	93	93	94	88	85	82	82	77	74	80	72
California	86	88	84	83	82	82	80	80	78	79	77	77
Far Western	85.2	84.1	87.9	86.3	85.5	83.0	81.5	82.5	80.6	80.3	79.8	77.6
United States	83.4	71.3	87.1	78.6	85.9	84.4	79.8	85.6	78.5	83.3	79.7	77.7

Bureau of Agricultural Economics. Estimates of the crop-reporting board.

[1] For range States, condition given as reported. Probably relates largely to farm pasture, i. e., range not included.

TABLE 298.—*Hops: Acreage, production, December 1 price, imports, exports, and consumption in the United States, 1910–1928*

Year beginning July	Acreage	Average yield per acre	Production	Price per pound received by producers Dec. 1	Imports	Domestic exports	Net exports	Consumption by brewers [1]
	Acres	*Pounds*	*1,000 pounds*	*Cents*	*1,000 pounds*	*1,000 pounds*	*1,000 pounds*	*1,000 pounds*
1910	(2)	(2)	(2)		8,558	13,105	4,565	45,069
1911	(2)	(2)	(2)		2,991	12,191	9,235	42,437
1912	(2)	(2)	(2)		8,494	17,591	9,133	44,238
1913	(2)	(2)	(2)		5,382	24,263	18,911	43,988
1914	(2)	(2)	(2)		11,651	16,210	4,576	38,839
1915	44,653	1,187	52,986	11.7	676	22,410	21,869	37,452
1916	43,900	1,153	50,595	12.0	237	4,875	4,664	41,949
1917	29,900	983	29,388	33.3	121	3,495	3,411	33,481
1918	25,900	829	21,481	19.3	(3)	7,467	7,472	13,925
1919	21,000	1,189	24,970	77.6	2,696	30,780	28,187	6,441
1920	28,000	1,224	34,280	35.7	4,808	22,206	18,226	5,989
1921	27,000	1,087	29,340	24.1	893	19,522	19,116	4,453
1922	23,400	1,186	27,744	8.6	1,295	13,497	12,401	4,556
1923	18,440	1,071	19,751	18.8	761	20,461	19,832	3,815
1924	20,350	1,360	27,670	10.3	439	16,122	15,737	4 3,256
1925	20,350	1,404	28,573	21.8	581	14,998	14,592	4 3,426
1926	20,800	1,516	31,522	23.1	470	13,369	12,936	4 3,149
1927	24,600	1,246	30,658	22.9	753	11,812	11,087	4 3,071
1928 [5]	26,100	1,254	32,742	19.3				

Bureau of Agricultural Economics. Compiled from reports of the Division of Crop and Livestock Estimates, Bureau of Foreign and Domestic Commerce, records of the Bureau of Internal Revenue, and annual reports of the Commissioner of Prohibition.

[1] Figures for 1919 and subsequent years represent hops used to make cereal beverages.
[2] Not available.
[3] Less than 500 pounds.
[4] Not including 57,936 pounds in 1924, 71,508 pounds in 1925, 960 pounds in 1926, and 6,294 pounds in 1927, used in the manufacture of distilled spirits.
[5] Preliminary.

TABLE 253.—Hops. Acreage, yield per acre and production in specified countries, average 1909-1913, annual 1925-1928

Country	Acreage, Average 1909-1913[1] (Acres)	Acreage 1925 (Acres)	Acreage 1926 (Acres)	Acreage 1927 (Acres)	Acreage 1928 preliminary (Acres)	Yield per acre, Average 1909-1913[1] (Pounds)	Yield 1925 (Pounds)	Yield 1926 (Pounds)	Yield 1927 (Pounds)	Yield 1928 preliminary (Pounds)	Production, Average 1909-1913[1] (1,000 pounds)	Production 1925 (1,000 pounds)	Production 1926 (1,000 pounds)	Production 1927 (1,000 pounds)	Production 1928 preliminary (1,000 pounds)
North America:															
Canada[2]	[8]718	507	594	[1]1,037	[4]1,369	[8]1,429	1,673	1,626	1,375		[8]1,026	848	966	1,426	
United States[5]	[6]45,000	20,350	20,800	24,600	26,100	[6]1,103	1,404	1,515	1,246	1,254	53,654	28,573	31,522	30,658	32,742
Total	45,718	20,857	21,394	25,637	27,469						54,680	29,421	32,488	32,084	
Europe:															
England and Wales	33,797	26,236	25,599	23,004	23,762	977	1,514	1,453	1,244	1,141	33,021	39,760	37,184	28,616	27,115
Belgium	5,313	3,155	3,501	3,744	3,652	1,319	1,778	1,432	1,529	1,268	7,008	5,609	5,012	5,724	4,630
France	17,072	10,267	10,939	11,883	11,886	788	1,078	812	940	681	13,459	11,069	8,881	11,168	8,089
Germany	[7]54,786	30,821	35,012	38,318	37,740	[7]422	345	159	413	489	[8]23,114	10,646	5,562	15,827	18,445
Austria	[8]6,210	277	773	773		[8]573	386	308	298		[8]3,560	107	238	230	
Czechoslovakia	38,385	22,343	25,911	39,000	40,000	[8]599	694	823	613	434	22,997	15,508	21,316	23,922	17,368
Hungary	[8]628	106	86	321		[8]814	623	523	336		[8]511	66	45	108	
Yugoslavia	3,749	5,019	10,210	21,863	22,000	725	486	370	381		2,718	2,439	3,781	8,324	
Rumania	[8]664					825					[8]548	207			
Poland	11,963	6,175	5,263	6,373		493	548	601	678		[8]5,897	3,383	3,164	4,318	
Russia											6,797			[9]6,753	
Total all countries reporting for all years	153,102	97,861	111,172	137,812	139,040						99,599	82,592	77,955	85,257	75,647
Oceania:															
Australia	1,251	1,732	1,572	[4]1,557		1,285	1,261	1,449			1,607	2,184	2,278		
New Zealand	[6]653	648	636			[10](1,455)	1,159	1,409			[10](950)	751	896		
Total countries reporting acreage and production for all years	194,353	113,192	121,762	140,549	143,140						153,253	111,165	109,477	115,915	108,389
Estimated world total, exclusive of Russia[11]	220,200	128,400	141,100	173,800							170,070	121,150	120,893	133,521	

Bureau of Agricultural Economics. Official sources and International Institute of Agriculture except as otherwise stated. Production figures are for the crop year harvested in the calendar year in the Northern Hemisphere and the succeeding harvest in the Southern Hemisphere.

[1] Figures for Europe are estimates for territory within present boundaries. [2] British Columbia. [3] 2-year average. [4] Unofficial estimate. [5] Principal producing States. [6] 1 year only. [7] 3-year average. [8] 4-year average. [9] Production in Ukraine, where the bulk of the crop is grown, as reported in Economic Life. [10] Rough estimate of production for one year based on acreage in that year and yield in later years. [11] Exclusive of acreage and production in minor producing countries for which no data are available.

TABLE 300.—*Hops: International trade, average 1909–1913, annual 1924–1927*

Country	Average 1909–1913		1924		1925		1926		1927, preliminary	
	Imports	Exports	Imports	Exports	Imports	Exports	Imports	Exports	Imports	Exports
PRINCIPAL EXPORTING COUNTRIES	*1,000 pounds*	*1,000 pounds*	*1,000 pounds*	*1,000 pounds*	*1,000 pounds*	*1,000 pounds*	*1,000 pounds*	*1,000 pounds*	*1,000 pounds*	*1,000 pounds*
United States	6,235	15,416	406	17,391	592	20,655	568	12,833	554	14,119
Czechoslovakia	0	0	2,665	19,317	1,787	12,389	1,195	16,222	1,140	17,904
France	5,436	335	4,081	8,108	4,015	9,114	3,931	6,159	5,337	5,679
Yugoslavia [1]	0	0	192	2,817	298	6,964	169	6,945	273	9,030
Poland	0	0	719	624	308	1,661	330	1,850	593	3,843
New Zealand	61	352	3	663	2	340	18	393	4	530
PRINCIPAL IMPORTING COUNTRIES										
Germany	7,688	17,564	14,003	2,217	12,388	1,666	15,953	1,156	10,722	3,825
Irish Free State	0	0	8,156	0	6,758	0	6,575	0	5,174	0
United Kingdom	21,028	2,162	10,039	4,963	10,114	4,989	3,924	8,800	10,855	6,119
Belgium	6,915	4,814	3,800	3,664	4,621	3,989	4,626	3,140	4,481	1,853
Canada	1,396	176	2,064	700	3,524	85	2,165	357	1,962	709
Austria	[2] 938	[2] 18,333	2,881	[1] 156	3,058	[1] 127	2,977	130	2,924	62
Netherlands	2,938	1,405	1,295	317	961	207	931	135	1,556	24
Japan	253	0	1,209	0	908	0	798	0	1,011	0
Sweden	987	1	947	12	978	0	971	2	1,287	1 0
Argentina	618	0	538	0	1,142	0	1,000	0	1,042	0
Switzerland	1,257	[3] 2	843	0	828	0	977	0	1,072	0
Denmark	1,027	[4] 1	755	5	674	1	812	1	811	0
Italy	529	10	669	52	732	14	816	13	626	0
Union of South Africa	487	0	304	0	466	0	577	0	709	0
Norway	289	0	384	0	407	0	355	0	346	0
Russia [1]	[5] 1,258	[5] 2,348	401	0	542	0	87	0	2	2
Hungary	0	0	412	103	275	82	356	123	444	146
British India	246	0	176	0	171	0	209	0	148	0
Australia [1]	[5] 1,106	[5] 22	265	295	318	69	299	129	145	397
Total, 25 countries	60,692	62,941	57,207	61,404	55,867	62,352	50,619	58,388	53,218	64,242

Bureau of Agricultural Economics. Official sources except where otherwise noted. Lupulin and hopfenmehl (hop meal) are not included.

[1] International Yearbook of Agricultural Statistics.
[2] Average for Austria-Hungary.
[3] 1 year only.
[4] 3-year average.
[5] From original source.

TABLE 301.—*Peanuts: Acreage, yield per acre, production, and December 1 price United States, 1916–1928*

Year	Total acreage, yield, and production			Nuts gathered			
	Total area [1]	Yield per acre	Total production [2]	Area	Yield per acre	Total quantity gathered	Farm price, Dec. 1 [3]
	1,000 acres	*Pounds*	*1,000 lbs.*	*1,000 acres*	*Pounds*	*1,000 lbs.*	*Cents*
1916				1,043	881.1	919,028	4.4
1917				1,842	777.7	1,432,581	6.8
1918				1,865	664.9	1,240,102	6.4
1919				1,132	691.9	783,273	9.3
1920				1,181	712.5	841,474	5.2
1921				1,214	683.1	829,307	3.9
1922				1,005	630.0	633,114	4.6
1923				896	722.9	647,762	6.7
1924				1,187	627.7	745,059	4.6
1925				958	729.1	698,475	3.6
1926	1,315	669.1	879,923	843	749.5	631,825	[4] 4.5
1927	1,786	735.0	1,312,643	1,142	757.0	864,549	[4] 3.9
1928 [5]	1,910	644.6	1,231,190	1,180	685.6	809,060	[4] 4.5

Bureau of Agricultural Economics. Estimates of the crop-reporting board.

[1] Including acres planted in corn reduced to equivalent solid acres as well as the acreage grown alone.
[2] Including peanuts grazed or otherwise utilized as well as those gathered.
[3] Farm prices are as of Nov. 15, 1916–1923; Dec. 1, 1924–1928.
[4] Average price weighted on total production.
[5] Preliminary.

TABLE 302.—*Peanuts: Acreage, yield per acre, production, and December 1 price by States, 1925–1928*

State	Area				Yield per acre				Production				Farm price, Dec. 1			
	1925	1926	1927	1928[1]	1925	1926	1927	1928	1925	1926	1927	1928 [1]	1925	1926	1927	1928
	1,000 acres	*1,000 acres*	*1,000 acres*	*1,000 acres*	*Lbs.*	*Lbs.*	*Lbs.*	*Lbs.*	*1,000 lbs.*	*1,000 lbs.*	*1,000 lbs.*	*1,000 lbs.*	*Cts.*	*Cts.*	*Cts.*	*Cts.*
Va	138	138	152	152	1,040	990	810	910	143,520	136,620	123,120	138,320	4.0	4.3	4.5	4.7
N. C	185	180	211	195	1,150	1,030	954	950	212,750	185,400	201,294	185,250	3.9	4.2	4.5	4.9
S. C	11	8	11	10	430	675	775	690	4,730	5,400	8,525	6,900	3.8	5.2	3.7	4.2
Ga	278	211	304	350	500	525	725	540	139,000	110,775	220,400	189,000	3.4	4.9	3.9	4.4
Fla	41	39	44	44	600	680	640	575	24,600	26,520	28,160	25,300	3.2	4.5	3.7	4.2
Tenn	20	20	20	18	815	900	850	800	16,300	18,000	17,000	14,400	3.4	3.5	4.2	4.7
Ala	180	140	230	210	560	570	680	560	100,800	79,800	156,400	117,600	3.2	4.5	3.4	3.9
Miss	14	8	9	10	595	650	725	500	8,330	5,200	6,525	5,000	3.0	5.7	6.0	6.5
Ark	10	10	11	12	496	675	800	720	4,960	6,750	8,800	8,640	3.1	6.0	6.0	6.4
La	9	10	13	12	640	552	625	450	5,760	5,520	8,125	5,400	3.5	6.2	6.1	6.6
Okla	7	8	20	47	700	800	800	750	4,900	6,400	16,000	35,250	3.2	4.5	3.5	5.4
Tex	65	71	117	120	505	640	600	650	32,825	45,440	70,200	78,000	3.4	4.5	3.5	5.0
U. S	958	843	1,142	1,180	729.1	749.5	757.0	685.6	698,475	631,825	864,549	809,060	3.64	[2]4.54	[2]3.98	[2]4.56

Bureau of Agricultural Economics.   Estimates of the crop-reporting board.

[1] Preliminary.
[2] Average price weighted on total production, which includes peanuts grazed or otherwise utilized as well as those gathered.

TABLE 303.—*Peanuts: Estimated price per pound, received by producers, United States, 1910–1928*

Year beginning November	Nov. 15	Dec. 15	Jan. 15	Feb. 15	Mar. 15	Apr. 15	May 15	June 15	July 15	Aug. 15	Sept. 15	Oct. 15	Weighted av.
	Cts.	*Cts.*	*Cts.*	*Cts.*	*Cts.*	*Cts.*	*Cts.*	*Cts.*	*Cts.*	*Cts.*	*Cts.*	*Cts.*	*Cts.*
Average:													
1910–1913	4.6	4.6	4.5	4.7	4.8	4.9	4.9	5.1	5.0	5.0	5.0	4.6	4.6
1914–1920	5.9	5.7	5.9	6.1	6.2	6.4	6.7	6.8	6.8	6.4	6.3	5.7	5.9
1921–1925	5.4	4.9	5.2	5.5	5.7	5.7	5.7	5.8	5.7	5.6	5.7	5.3	5.2
1910	4.7	4.5	4.4	5.0	4.8	4.9	4.8	5.2	5.0	5.3	5.1	4.6	4.6
1911	4.4	4.4	4.3	4.7	5.0	4.9	4.9	5.2	4.9	5.0	4.8	4.7	4.4
1912	4.7	4.6	4.6	4.5	4.7	4.8	4.7	5.0	5.1	4.9	4.9	4.8	4.6
1913	4.4	4.8	4.7	4.7	4.7	4.9	5.1	5.1	5.2	4.9	5.0	4.5	4.6
1914	4.4	4.3	4.5	4.4	4.2	4.5	4.8	4.8	4.7	4.5	4.4	4.3	4.4
1915	4.2	4.2	4.3	4.4	4.4	4.6	4.6	4.7	4.6	4.6	4.4	4.4	4.3
1916	4.4	4.7	4.9	5.3	5.5	6.2	7.2	7.7	7.6	7.2	6.6	6.1	4.8
1917	7.1	7.1	7.0	7.2	7.4	8.3	8.2	7.9	7.8	7.9	8.3	6.9	7.1
1918	6.6	6.1	6.0	6.9	7.0	6.9	7.2	7.7	8.2	8.1	8.3	8.1	6.5
1919	9.1	9.1	9.9	10.5	11.2	10.9	11.2	11.2	11.0	8.5	8.0	5.8	9.2
1920	5.3	4.7	4.4	4.1	4.0	3.5	3.4	3.8	3.8	3.9	4.0	4.0	4.7
1921	3.7	3.5	3.6	4.0	4.3	3.9	3.9	4.2	4.4	4.4	4.7	3.6	3.7
1922	5.2	5.0	5.9	6.5	6.7	7.1	7.1	7.3	6.9	6.7	6.7	7.0	5.5
1923	6.8	6.2	6.4	6.7	6.8	6.7	6.4	6.5	6.4	6.6	6.4	6.4	6.5
1924	6.3	5.6	5.4	5.5	5.9	5.7	6.2	6.2	5.4	5.2	5.7	4.7	5.7
1925	5.1	4.4	4.5	4.7	4.6	5.1	5.0	4.7	5.3	5.3	5.1	4.9	4.7
1926	4.6	4.7	4.9	5.4	5.6	5.7	5.9	6.6	6.4	6.4	6.0	4.9	4.8
1927	4.6	5.2	5.4	5.4	5.4	5.5	5.7	5.6	5.5	5.5	5.0	4.6	5.0
1928	4.8	5.1											

Bureau of Agricultural Economics.   Based on returns from special price reporters.

Table 304.—*Peanuts: Monthly average prices of cleaned and shelled peanuts, for prompt shipment f. o. b. important shipping points, 1927–28*

	Nov.	Dec.	Jan.	Feb.	Mar.	Apr.	May	June	July	Aug.	Sept.	Oct.
VIRGINIA-NORTH CAROLINA SECTION [1]												
	Cts.	*Cts.*	*Cts.*	*Cts.*	*Cts.*	*Cts.*	*Cts.*	*Cts.*	*Cts.*	*Cts.*	*Cts.*	*Cts.*
Cleaned Virginias, Jumbos	9¼	10⅝	11½	11½	11½	11½	11⅝	11⅞	12	11⅞	11¾	11
Fancy	7	7¾	7⅞	7½	7½	7⅜	7⅜	7½	7⅝	7	6⅞	6⅝
Extras	5⅞	6½	6⅞	6¾	6½	------	6½	6⅝	6⅝	6¼	6⅛	5¾
Shelled Virginias, Extra Large	11⅞	13¼	13⅝	12¼	11⅝	11½	11⅝	11¾	12	11¾	11¾	11
No. 1	6¾	8¼	8⅛	8	8	8¼	8⅜	8⅝	8½	7⅞	7½	7⅛
No. 2	5⅜	6⅛	6⅜	6	5⅞	6	5⅞	5⅞	5⅞	5⅝	5⅝	5⅜
SOUTHEAST SECTION: SOUTH CAROLINA, GEORGIA, ALABAMA, AND FLORIDA [2]												
Shelled Spanish, No. 1	6⅝	7¾	7⅞	7½	7½	7⅜	7	6⅞	6½	6⅜	6¾	6⅝
Spanish, No. 1	5¾	6⅛	6¼	5¾	5¾	6	6⅛	6⅛	5⅞	5⅝	5¾	5¾
Runners, No. 1	5¾	7	7	6⅝	6⅞	7	6⅞	6¾	7	6⅝	6½	6⅛
Runners, No. 2	5¼	5⅞	5⅞	5½	5½	5¾	5¾	5⅝	------	5⅝	5⅞	5½
TEXAS [3]												
Shelled Spanish, No. 1	6¾	8	8⅜	8	8	7⅞	7½	7⅜	7⅛	7	7	6¾
Spanish, No. 2	6	6½	6½	6⅛	6⅜	6½	6½	6⅝	6½	6⅛	6⅛	6⅛

Bureau of Agricultural Economics. Based on returns from cleaners, shellers, and brokers. Crop year extends from November to next October in the Virginia-North Carolina section; farther south it begins earlier. See 1927 Yearbook, p. 948, for data for earlier years.

[1] Important shipping points: Suffolk, Franklin, Petersburg, and Norfolk, Va., Edenton and Enfield, N. C.

[2] Important shipping points: Albany, Cordele, Donalsonville, Fort Gaines, and Savannah, Ga., Dothan, Enterprise, Montgomery, Samson, and Troy, Ala.

[3] Important shipping points: Fort Worth and De Leon, Tex.

Table 305.—*Peanuts used in the production of oil in the United States, 1919–1928*

Year beginning Oct. 1	October-December	January-March	April-June	July-September	Total
	1,000 pounds	*1,000 pounds*	*1,000 pounds*	*1,000 pounds*	*1,000 pounds*
1919	4,364	5,867	9,214	15,770	35,215
1920	27,414	27,962	32,923	23,480	111,779
1921	40,338	44,152	25,964	4,703	115,157
1922	13,169	9,081	8,436	941	31,627
1923	6,164	4,676	5,471	1,928	18,239
1924	17,668	24,678	16,893	9,096	68,335
1925	17,134	17,880	10,668	4,389	50,071
1926	10,576	11,143	6,321	6,966	35,006
1927, preliminary	21,810	24,168	8,177	6,661	60,816
1928, preliminary	14,740	----------	----------	----------	----------

Bureau of Agricultural Economics. Compiled from reports of the Bureau of the Census. Quantities reported in terms of hulled have been converted to "in the hull" basis by multiplying by 1.5.

TABLE 306.—*Peanuts: International trade, average 1909–1913, annual 1925–1927*

Country	Average, 1909–1913		1925		1926		1927, preliminary	
	Imports	Exports	Imports	Exports	Imports	Exports	Imports	Exports
PRINCIPAL EXPORTING COUNTRIES	*1,000 pounds*	*1,000 pounds*	*1,000 pounds*	*1,000 pounds*	*1,000 pounds*	*1,000 pounds*	*1,000 pounds*	*1,000 pounds*
Senegal	[1]168	425,937	[1]47	985,409	[1]114	[1]1,067,024	[1]19	[1]894,488
British India	0	503,448	0	1,036,670	0	994,900	1,063,736	0
China	32,882	138,472	22,800	530,227	6,577	534,488	17,510	430,002
Nigeria	0	17,163	[1]0	[1]284,983	[1]0	[1]284,027	([1])	[1]203,329
Gambia	0	131,912	[1]0	[1]109,087	[1]0	[1]136,800	[1]0	[1]155,096
French possessions in India	0	306,701	228,212	0	---------	---------	---------	---------
Dutch East Indies	612	60,282	518	43,848	664	40,976	[2]0	[2]54,661
Mozambique	[3]1,098	[3]15,907	5	24,525	20	47,472	8	73,240
Tanganyika	0	[1]9,275	0	20,283	0	35,542	0	31,689
Anglo-Egyptian Sudan	0	1,961	[1]1	26,021	0	22,122	0	3,665
Spain	0	9,205	0	4,574	0	3,665	---------	---------
Guinea (French)	1	4,863	[1]11	8,903	[1]0	[1]7,744	[1]0	[1]10,916
Brazil	0	274	0	195	0	18	---------	---------
PRINCIPAL IMPORTING COUNTRIES								
France	1,239,659	47,107	1,503,887	16,082	1,516,515	14,668	1,450,637	11,388
Germany	174,970	98	713,245	0	977,777	0	930,555	0
United Kingdom	0	0	335,004	0	252,187	0	132,268	0
Netherlands	122,862	32,863	229,544	2,005	235,275	3,278	186,034	4,364
United States	20,988	6,804	120,158	3,489	67,874	4,232	62,697	4,827
Italy	1,194	804	97,271	43	194,522	283	287,131	40
Japan	0	10,675	23,434	2,976	26,036	364	24,384	288
Denmark	5,236	0	27,853	0	32,346	0	27,558	0
Canada	7,302	0	23,793	0	28,946	0	29,808	0
British Malaya	[1]19,488	[1][5]10,839	23,737	6,259	19,536	3,927	25,868	6,492
Belgium	[3]68,422	[3]43,393	32,838	410	88,824	119	56,540	267
Egypt	4,664	1,637	13,863	3,925	9,858	3,660	3,627	2,029
Algeria	7,022	218	8,066	387	7,387	331	[1]9,491	414
Sweden	[3][6]20	0	10,065	0	11,934	1	20,435	0
Poland	0	0	5,439	3	369	0	1,029	0
Tunis	[3]1,459	0	3,836	0	4,577	0	4,765	0
Argentina	8,667	0	4,967	326	5,343	41	6	33
Philippine Islands	2,264	0	2,808	0	2,429	0	3,238	0
Union of South Africa	3,164	7	2,666	154	3,631	78	4,033	277
Total, 32 countries	1,722,142	1,779,845	3,434,068	3,110,784	3,498,741	3,205,760	4,341,377	1,887,505

Bureau of Agricultural Economics. Official sources except where otherwise noted. Includes shelled and unshelled, assuming the peanuts to be unshelled unless otherwise stated. When shelled nuts were reported they have been reduced to terms of unshelled at the ratio of 3 pounds unshelled to 2 pounds shelled.

[1] International Yearbook of Agricultural Statistics.
[2] Java and Madura only.
[3] 2-year average.
[4] 1 year only.
[5] 3-year average.
[6] International Institute of Agriculture, "Oleaginous Products and Vegetable Oils."

TABLE 307.—*Peanut oil: International trade, average 1909–1913, annual 1924–1927*

Country	Average 1909–1913 [1]		1924		1925		1926		1927 preliminary	
	Imports	Exports	Imports	Exports	Imports	Exports	Imports	Exports	Imports	Exports
PRINCIPAL EXPORT-ING COUNTRIES	*1,000 pounds*	*1,000 pounds*	*1,000 pounds*	*1,000 pounds*	*1,000 pounds*	*1,000 pounds*	*1,000 pounds*	*1,000 pounds*	*1,000 pounds*	*1,000 pounds*
China	0	[2]35,593	0	89,636	0	78,408	0	109,697	0	78,889
France	142	50,967	3,154	66,384	3,510	53,744	9,937	67,300	13,815	67,887
Netherlands	2,743	18,569	19,133	24,280	40,209	26,336	59,916	26,892	61,789	34,735
United Kingdom			10,980	21,784	25,148	25,431	29,678	22,100	46,411	9,354
PRINCIPAL IMPORT-ING COUNTRIES										
Algeria			30,248	539	23,542	460	21,802	402	[3]23,477	[3]251
Canada		0	26,424	0	16,134	0	38,794	0	4,811	0
Germany	1,602		13,792	6,141	23,016	20,551	4,109	24,217	5,861	52,507
United States	[4]7,295	0	15,395	39	3,027	0	8,281	0	2,847	0
Norway		0	7,261	0	8,433	0	8,104	0	7,124	0
Italy	8,867	[2]4	8,605	3	9,074	105	14,936	106	16,580	171
Sweden	2,459		6,251	333	6,755	667	8,178	1,141	4,701	4,299
Belgium	2,233	2,065	3,678	4,917	9,184	5,030	6,636	4,879	6,526	5,607
Philippine Islands	[3]976	0	3,754	0	3,286	0	4,030	0	5,483	0
Morocco		0	2,448	0	1,894	0	1,615	0	1,163	0
Dutch East Indies	[5]2,090	[5]45	1,518	192	1,315	1,648	1,601	878	[6]98	[6]1,966
Denmark	2,941	[2]156	828	2,019	1,889	1,743	1,086	1,829	1,399	2,743
Yugoslavia	[3]273	0	[3]257	[3]0	[3]6,991	[3]0	[3]7,290	[3]0	[3]7,305	[3]0
Czechoslovakia	0	0	1,407	0	1,512	0	1,433	55	3,510	82
Total, 18 countries	31,621	107,399	155,133	216,267	184,919	214,123	227,426	259,496	212,900	258,491

Bureau of Agricultural Economics. Official sources except where otherwise noted. Conversions made on the basis of 7.5 pounds to the gallon.

[1] International Institute of Agriculture, "Oleaginous Products and Vegetable Oils."
[2] 4-year average.
[3] International Yearbook of Agricultural Statistics.
[4] 3-year average.
[5] 2-year average.
[6] Java and Madura only.

TABLE 308.—*Peanut oil, refined: Average price per pound (in barrels), at New York, 1916–1928*

Year beginning September	Sept.	Oct.	Nov.	Dec.	Jan.	Feb.	Mar.	Apr.	May	June	July	Aug.	Average
Average: 1921–1925	*Cents* 14.09	*Cents* 14.25	*Cents* 14.29	*Cents* 14.30	*Cents* 14.93	*Cents* 15.15	*Cents* 15.52	*Cents* 15.68	*Cents* 15.13	*Cents* 15.05	*Cents* 14.95	*Cents* 15.04	*Cents* 14.86
1916	12.19	12.60	13.33	13.49	13.50	14.38	14.80	17.58	17.83	17.87	17.44	18.05	15.26
1917	18.61	20.12	21.67	22.67	22.49	22.98	22.33	22.41	21.70	21.15	21.47	21.78	21.62
1918	21.44	22.75	22.75	21.06	20.36	20.25	19.90	22.38	24.58	26.91	29.31	30.05	23.48
1919	26.25	25.25	26.68	26.69	27.50	26.43	27.12	25.00	23.10	20.88	19.00	17.19	24.26
1920	16.88	16.20	14.62	12.75	12.52	12.34	11.00	10.70	10.50	10.25	10.00	10.12	12.32
1921	10.62	11.75	11.59	11.22	11.25	11.38	12.25	13.15	13.00	13.00	12.48	12.62	12.03
1922	12.40	12.25	13.03	14.25	16.88	17.38	17.85	17.75	16.56	16.00	16.00	16.00	15.53
1923	16.00	16.00	15.59	14.80	14.75	14.75	14.75	14.75	14.88	15.25	15.25	15.56	15.19
1924	16.45	16.25	16.25	16.25	16.75	16.75	16.75	16.75	15.20	15.00	15.00	15.00	16.03
1925	15.00	15.00	15.00	15.00	15.00	15.50	16.00	16.00	16.00	16.00	16.00	16.00	15.54
1926	16.00	16.00	15.50	14.62	14.50	14.50	14.50	14.50	14.50	14.50	14.50	14.50	14.84
1927	14.50	14.50	14.30	13.50	13.50	13.50	13.50	13.50	13.50	13.50	13.50	13.50	13.73
1928	13.50	13.50	12.25	11.00									

Bureau of Agricultural Economics. Compiled from Oil, Paint, and Drug Reporter, average of weekly range.

TABLE 309.—*Sugar beets: Production, United States, 1911–1928* [1]

Year	Acreage	Yield	Production	Price per ton	Value	Year	Acreage	Yield	Production	Price per ton	Value
	1,000 acres	*Short tons*	*1,000 short tons*	*Dollars*	*1,000 dollars*		*1,000 acres*	*Short tons*	*1,000 short tons*	*Dollars*	*1,000 dollars*
1911	474	10.7	5,062	5.50	27,841	1920	872	9.8	8,538	11.63	99,324
1912	555	10.2	5,648	5.82	32,871	1921	815	9.6	7,782	6.35	49,392
1913	580	10.1	5,886	5.69	33,491	1922	530	9.8	5,183	7.91	41,017
1914	483	11.6	5,585	5.45	30,438	1923	657	10.7	7,006	8.99	62,965
1915	611	10.7	6,511	5.67	36,950	1924	815	9.2	7,489	7.99	59,838
1916	665	9.4	6,228	6.12	38,139	1925	647	11.4	7,381	6.39	47,147
1917	665	9.0	5,980	7.39	44,192	1926	677	10.7	7,223	7.61	54,964
1918	594	10.0	5,949	10.00	59,494	1927	721	10.8	7,753	7.67	59,455
1919	692	9.3	6,421	11.74	75,420	1928 [2]	646	10.9	7,040	7.18	50,525

Bureau of Agricultural Economics.

[1] Most years from 1911–1923 include a small unknown quantity of beets grown in Canada for Michigan factories.
[2] Preliminary.

TABLE 310.—*Sugar beets: Acreage, production, yield per acre, price per ton, and value by States, 1924–1928*

State	Acreage					Production				
	1924	1925	1926	1927	1928	1924	1925	1926	1927	1928
	1,000 acres	*1,000 acres*	*1,000 acres*	*1,000 acres*	*1,000 acres*	*1,000 short tons*	*1,000 short tons*	*1,000 short tons*	*1,000 short tons*	*1,000 short tons*
Ohio	50	43	35	37	38	377	427	340	325	281
Michigan	134	99	100	99	65	954	969	793	698	428
Wisconsin	21	15	17	11	8	147	168	158	90	74
Nebraska	64	60	79	82	88	754	933	923	1,036	1,023
Montana	31	30	32	32	29	327	309	348	364	262
Wyoming	25	29	36	37	45	269	364	388	431	487
Idaho	40	36	18	29	26	275	456	108	381	285
Colorado	222	130	211	218	179	2,511	1,640	2,912	2,774	2,322
Utah	80	69	51	55	53	560	1,064	415	677	623
California	84	76	46	59	52	785	488	369	476	633
Other States	64	60	52	62	63	530	563	469	501	622
United States	815	647	677	721	646	7,489	7,381	7,223	7,753	7,040
Canada, for United States factories	2	6	10	11	8	24	57	77	69	48

State	Yield					Price per ton received by producers					Value				
	1924	1925	1926	1927	1928	1924	1925	1926	1927	1928	1924	1925	1926	1927	1928
	Short tons	*Short tons*	*Short tons*	*Short tons*	*Short tons*	*Dollars*	*Dollars*	*Dollars*	*Dollars*		*1,000 dollars*	*1,000 dollars*	*1,000 dollars*	*1,000 dollars*	
Ohio	7.5	9.9	9.7	8.8	7.4	9.48	6.90	7.00	7.00		3,574	2,945	2,383	2,272	
Michigan	7.1	9.8	7.9	7.0	6.6	8.85	7.05	7.00	7.16		8,443	6,833	5,552	4,996	
Wisconsin	7.0	11.2	9.3	8.2	9.3	7.02	7.25	7.24	7.00		1,032	1,218	1,141	633	
Nebraska	11.8	15.6	11.7	12.6	11.6	7.53	5.97	7.89	7.96		5,678	5,574	7,274	8,241	
Montana	10.5	10.3	10.9	11.4	9.0	8.21	6.35	8.09	8.22		2,684	1,960	2,814	2,996	
Wyoming	10.8	12.6	10.5	11.6	10.8	8.13	6.18	7.06	7.67		2,187	2,253	2,743	3,303	
Idaho	6.9	12.7	6.0	13.1	11.0	7.19	6.24	6.91	7.50		1,977	2,846	744	2,854	
Colorado	11.3	12.6	13.8	12.7	13.0	7.59	5.98	7.92	7.84		19,058	9,815	23,050	21,758	
Utah	7.0	15.4	8.1	12.3	11.8	6.92	6.03	6.97	7.03		3,875	6,416	2,894	4,761	
California	9.3	6.4	8.0	8.1	12.2	9.14	8.21	9.25	9.28		7,175	4,005	3,411	4,418	
Other States	8.3	9.4	9.0	8.1	9.9	7.24	5.83	6.31	6.43		4,155	3,282	2,958	3,223	
United States	9.2	11.4	10.7	10.8	10.9	7.99	6.39	7.61	7.67		59,838	47,147	54,964	59,455	
Canada for United States factories	12.0	9.5	7.7	6.3	6.0										

Bureau of Agricultural Economics.

TABLE 311.—*Beet sugar: Production, United States, 1911–1928* [1]

Year [2]	Factories operating	Average length of campaign	Sugar produced (chiefly refined)	Beets sliced	Beets paid for by factories	Acreage from which beets were harvested	Analysis of beets		Recovery of sucrose from beets [5]	
							Purity coefficient [3]	Percentage of sucrose [4]	Sliced	Paid for
	No.	Days	Tons	Tons	Tons	Acres	Per cent	Per cent	Per cent	Per cent
1911	66	94	600,000	5,062,000		474,000	82.21	15.89	11.84	
1912	73	86	693,000	5,224,000		555,000	84.49	16.31	13.26	
1913	71	85	733,000	5,659,000	5,886,000	580,000	83.22	15.78	12.96	12.45
1914	60	85	722,000	5,288,000	5,585,000	483,000	83.89	16.38	13.65	12.93
1915	67	92	874,000	6,150,000	6,511,000	611,000	84.38	16.49	14.21	13.42
1916	74	80	821,000	5,920,000	6,228,000	665,000	84.74	16.30	13.86	13.18
1917	91	74	765,000	5,626,000	5,980,000	665,000	83.89	16.28	13.60	12.79
1918	89	81	761,000	5,578,000	5,949,000	594,000	84.70	16.18	13.64	12.79
1919	89	78	726,000	5,888,000	6,421,000	692,000	82.84	14.48	12.34	11.31
1920	97	91	1,089,000	7,991,000	8,538,000	872,000	83.96	15.99	13.63	12.75
1921	92	76	1,020,000	7,414,000	7,782,000	815,000	83.09	15.77	13.76	13.11
1922	81	58	675,000	4,963,000	5,183,000	530,000	83.76	15.44	13.61	13.02
1923	89	70	881,000	6,585,000	7,006,000	657,000	83.43	15.30	13.37	12.57
1924	90	66	1,090,000	7,075,000	7,513,000	817,000	85.03	17.19	15.41	14.51
1925	88	71	913,000	6,993,000	7,423,000	653,000	82.84	14.86	13.06	12.30
1926	78	67	897,000	6,782,000	7,300,000	687,000	84.03	14.94	13.23	12.29
1927	83	69	1,093,000	7,443,000	7,821,000	732,000	84.60	16.11	14.68	13.98
1928 [6]			1,036,000		,088,000	654,000		16.74		14.62

Bureau of Agricultural Economics. Estimates of the crop-reporting board.

[1] Figures for important States in recent years published in Crops and Markets.
[2] Year shown is that in which beets were grown. Sugar-making campaign extends into succeeding year.
[3] Percentage of sucrose (pure sugar) in the total soluble solids of the beets.
[4] Based upon weight of beets sliced, except possibly in a very few factories.
[5] Sucrose actually extracted by factories (as percentage of weight of beets).
[6] Preliminary.

TABLE 312.—*Cane sugar: Production in Louisiana, 1911–1928*

Year [1]	Factories in operation	Sugar production		Average sugar made per ton of cane	Cane used for sugar			Molasses made [3]	
		As made	Equivalent refined [2]		Acreage	Average per acre	Production	Total	Per ton of sugar
	Number	Short tons	Short tons	Pounds	Acres	Short tons	Short tons	Gallons	Gallons
1911	188	352,874	328,879	120	310,000	19	5,887,292	35,062,525	99
1912	126	153,573	143,130	142	197,000	11	2,162,574	14,302,169	93
1913	153	292,698	272,795	139	248,000	17	4,214,000	24,046,320	82
1914	149	242,700	226,200	152	213,000	15	3,199,000	17,177,443	71
1915	136	137,500	128,200	135	183,000	11	2,018,000	12,743,000	93
1916	150	303,900	283,200	149	221,000	18	4,072,000	26,154,000	86
1917	140	243,600	227,000	128	244,000	15.6	3,813,000	30,728,000	126
1918	134	280,900	261,800	135	231,200	18	4,170,000	28,049,000	100
1919	121	121,000	112,800	129	179,900	10.5	1,883,000	12,991,000	107
1920	122	169,127	157,626	136	182,843	13.6	2,492,524	16,856,867	100
1921	124	324,431	302,370	155	226,366	18.5	4,180,780	25,423,341	78
1922	112	295,095	275,029	156	241,433	15.6	3,778,110	22,718,640	77
1923	105	162,023	151,005	136	217,259	11.1	2,386,650	15,719,400	97
1924	82	88,000	82,000	144	163,000	7.6	1,228,000	9,590,000	109
1925	91	139,000	130,000	105	190,000	14.0	2,645,000	17,783,000	128
1926	54	47,000	44,000	109	128,000	6.8	864,000	6,614,000	141
1927	46	71,000	66,000	147	73,000	13.4	962,000	6,624,000	93
1928 [4]		165,000	154,000	147	138,000	16.3	2,244,000	14,601,000	88

Bureau of Agricultural Economics. Estimates of the crop-reporting board.

[1] Sugar campaign, usually not ended before February following season of growth of cane.
[2] One ton of sugar as made is assumed to be equivalent to 0.932 ton of refined as tentatively recommended by the joint committee on sugar statistics of the Department of Commerce and the Department of Agriculture.
[3] Figures for molasses, 1911–1914, are as reported by the Louisiana Sugar Planters' Association: figures for later years as reported by Division of Crop and Livestock Estimates.
[4] Preliminary.

TABLE 313.—*Cane sugar: Production of Hawaii, 1914–1928*

Year	Average length of campaign	Sugar production		Cane used for sugar			Total area in cane	Average extraction of sugar	
		As made	Equivalent refined [1]	Area harvested	Average yield per acre	Production		Percentage of cane	Per short ton of cane
	Days	Short tons	Short tons	Acres	Short tons	Short tons	Acres	Per cent	Pounds
1914	183	612,000	573,000	112,700	43	4,900,000		12.49	250
1915	195	646,000	605,000	113,200	46	5,185,000	239,800	12.46	249
1916	180	592,763	554,708	115,419	42	4,859,424	246,332	12.20	244
1917	190	644,663	603,276	123,900	42	5,220,000	245,100	12.35	247
1918	184	576,700	539,676	119,800	41	4,855,000	276,800	11.88	238
1919	178	600,312	561,772	119,700	40	4,744,000	239,900	12.65	253
1920	175	555,727	520,049	114,100	39	4,473,000	247,900	12.42	248
1921	202	521,579	488,094	113,100	41	4,657,000	236,500	11.20	224
1922	199	592,000	554,000	124,000	41	5,088,000	229,000	11.64	233
1923	167	537,000	503,000	114,000	40	4,560,000	235,000	11.77	235
1924	192	691,000	647,000	111,000	51	5,661,000	232,000	12.21	244
1925	154	769,000	720,000	122,000	52	6,297,000	241,000	12.21	244
1926 [2]	180	787,246	736,705	122,309	53	6,495,686	237,774	12.12	242
1927 [2]	209	811,333	759,245	124,542	56	6,992,082	234,809	11.60	232
1928 [2]		904,040							

Bureau of Agricultural Economics. Estimates of the crop-reporting board.

[1] 1 ton of sugar as made is assumed to be equivalent to 0.9358 tons of refined, as tentatively recommended by the joint committee on sugar statistics of the Department of Commerce and the Department of Agriculture.
[2] Data collected through the Hawaiian Sugar Planters' Association.

TABLE 314.—*Sugar: Production in the United States and its possessions, 1909–1928*

Year beginning July	Beet sugar (chiefly refined)	Cane sugar (chiefly raw)					Total
		Louisiana	Other States	Porto Rico	Hawaii	Philippine Islands [1]	
	Short tons	Short tons	Short tons	Short tons	Short tons	Short tons	Short tons
Average:							
1909–1913	609,620	292,478	9,672	363,474	567,495	252,781	2,095,519
1914–1920	822,651	214,104	3,699	452,549	591,106	466,033	2,550,143
1921–1925	915,898	201,883		499,744	675,249	584,894	2,879,009
1909	512,469	320,526	11,200	346,786	517,090	140,783	1,848,854
1910	510,172	342,720	12,320	349,840	566,821	164,658	1,946,531
1911	599,500	352,874	8,000	371,076	595,038	205,046	2,131,534
1912	692,556	153,573	9,000	398,004	546,524	345,077	2,144,734
1913	733,401	292,698	7,840	351,666	612,000	408,339	2,405,944
1914	722,054	242,700	3,920	346,490	646,000	421,192	2,382,356
1915	874,220	137,500	1,120	483,590	592,763	412,274	2,501,467
1916	820,657	303,900	7,000	503,081	644,663	425,266	2,704,567
1917	765,207	243,600	2,240	453,794	576,700	474,745	2,516,286
1918	760,950	280,900	3,500	406,002	600,312	453,346	2,505,010
1919	726,451	121,000	1,125	485,071	555,727	466,912	2,356,286
1920	1,089,021	169,127	6,987	489,818	521,579	608,499	2,885,031
1921	1,020,489	324,431	3,270	408,325	592,000	533,189	2,881,704
1922	675,000	295,095	640	379,172	537,000	475,325	2,362,232
1923	881,000	162,023	2,800	447,570	691,000	529,091	2,713,484
1924	1,090,000	88,483		660,411	769,000	779,510	3,387,404
1925	913,000	139,381		603,240	787,246	607,362	3,050,229
1926	897,000	47,166		629,134	811,333	766.902	3,151,535
1927	1,093,000	70,792		748,677	904,040	[2] 702,000	
1928 [4]	1,036,000	165,391		[3] 644,000	[3] 929,600	[2] 740,000	

Bureau of Agricultural Economics. Cane sugar production 1909–1910 from Willett & Gray; 1911 and subsequently from United States Department of Agriculture. Hawaiian production from Hawaiian Sugar Planters' Association. Figures for earlier years appear in previous issues of the Yearbook.

[1] Exports 1909–1911, production 1912 and subsequently.
[2] Unofficial estimate of commercial crop.
[3] Unofficial.
[4] Preliminary.

TABLE 315.—Sugar beets: Acreage, yield per acre and production in specified countries, average 1909–1913, annual 1925–1928

Country	Acreage (1,000 acres)					Yield per acre (short tons)					Production (1,000 short tons)				
	Average 1909–1913[1]	1925	1926	1927	1928 prelim.	Average 1909–1913[1]	1925	1926	1927	1928 prelim.	Average 1909–1913[1]	1925	1926	1927	1928 prelim.
Canada	17	43	47	44	51	9.4	10.6	11.2	8.9	8.5	160	458	525	391	433
United States	485	647	677	721	646	10.0	11.4	10.7	10.8	10.9	4,860	7,366	7,223	7,753	7,040
England and Wales	2	55	126	223	176	[2]7.3	8.7	9.7	8.5	9.1	[2]29	479	1,220	1,904	1,602
Scotland	(3)	1	4	10	4		3.0	7.8	6.0	5.2	(3)	3	31	60	21
Irish Free State	(3)	(3)	9	18	17			10.7	8.3	9.4	(3)	(3)	96	150	[4]159
Sweden	78	100	111	101	105	13.3	15.0	14.3	10.8	10.8	1,036	1,503	1,585	1,095	1,129
Denmark	80	93	74	105	113	10.9	14.3	14.7	11.4	12.0	871	1,333	1,085	1,207	1,356
Netherlands	144	163	152	173	161	13.7	15.0	15.3	11.6	15.7	1,977	2,451	2,327	2,013	2,535
Belgium	146	178	188	175	156	12.3	13.4	13.4	12.5	12.5	1,793	2,389	2,519	2,186	1,951
France	612	537	563	590	538	[5]10.2	11.0	9.5	11.2	11.0	6,544	5,921	5,357	6,616	5,917
Spain	[5]114	282	178	154	161	8.3	7.3	11.3	10.9	11.7	949	2,070	2,009	1,675	1,884
Italy	130	141	197	219	269	15.3	12.3	12.9	13.8	11.7	1,983	1,735	2,532	3,022	3,154
Switzerland	2	3	4	4	4	13.0	16.0	14.0	13.8	14.2	26	48	56	55	57
Germany	[6]1,075	996	996	1,073	1,121	[6]13.7	11.4	11.6	11.2	10.8	[6]14,679	11,382	11,569	11,964	12,137
Austria	57	50	49	60	70	9.8	10.9	10.8	13.3	11.1	561	543	530	797	778
Czechoslovakia	716	760	671	726	667	10.9	13.2	10.8	12.3	9.3	7,804	10,003	7,274	8,955	6,207
Hungary	131	163	156	159	164	10.2	10.3	10.2	10.1	7.4	1,338	1,684	1,592	1,604	1,213
Yugoslavia	35	82	86	102	142	8.9	6.9	7.6	6.5	6.1	312	563	652	660	[4]871
Bulgaria	7	71	36	36	42	10.7	[7]	6.9	7.4	4.5	75	[7]	248	267	[4]190
Rumania	[8]72	159	204	209	141	[8]9.3	6.8	6.9	6.6	7.4	[8]668	1,089	1,416	1,383	1,037
Poland	431	425	457	499	579	10.7	9.6	9.0	8.0	8.4	4,611	4,064	4,106	3,990	4,850
Latvia	(3)	(3)	1	5	6			7.0	2.5		(3)		7	12	
Finland	(3)	3	5	7	8		6.3	7.4	8.3	6.5	(3)	19	37	58	52
Russia	1,484	1,286	1,334	1,643	1,963	[8]7.2	5.9	5.3	6.6	5.3	10,636	7,618	7,042	10,872	10,465
Australia	[9]1	2	2	3		[8]7.0	12.0	5.5			[8]7	24	11		
Total countries reporting for all years	5,818	6,168	6,195	7,056	7,354						60,623	60,656	58,930	66,202	63,154
Estimated world total[10]	5,819	6,170	6,197	7,059	7,357						61,579	62,751	58,957	67,909	

Bureau of Agricultural Economics.   Official sources and International Institute of Agriculture.

[1] Figures for Europe are estimates for territory within present boundaries.   [2] 2-year average.   [3] No sugar beets grown.   [4] Unofficial estimate.   [5] 3-year average.

[6] 1 year only, 1912.   According to statistics of the German Sugar Association the 1912 sugar-beet acreage and production was greater than any other year with the exception of production in 1913.

[7] No sugar was produced in Bulgaria in 1925.   The beets grown were probably shipped to neighboring countries for sugar manufacture or used for other purposes.   [8] 4-year average.

[9] Less than 500 acres.   [10] Exclusive of acreage and production in minor producing countries for which no data are available.

TABLE 316.—*Sugar: Production in specified countries, average 1909–10 to 1913–14, annual 1925–26 to 1928–29*

BEET SUGAR IN TERMS OF RAW SUGAR

Country	Average 1909–10 to 1913–14 [1]	1925–26	1926–27	1927–28	1928–29 preliminary
NORTH AMERICA	Short tons	Short tons	Short tons	Short tons	Short tons
Canada [2]	11, 782	41, 375	39, 994	34, 653	[3] 42, 000
United States [2]	655, 000	981, 000	964, 000	1, 175, 000	1, 114, 000
Total	666, 782	1, 022, 375	1, 003, 994	1, 209, 653	1, 156, 000
EUROPE					
England and Wales	413, 084	62, 863	186, 758	231, 596	225, 095
Scotland	(⁵)	163	3, 264	8, 013	2, 650
Irish Free State	(⁵)	(⁵)	14, 907	22, 487	24, 800
Sweden	153, 739	225, 419	⁶ 23, 006	160, 204	179, 000
Denmark	127, 091	194, 225	166, 580	157, 408	182, 000
Netherlands [2]	246, 341	330, 277	309, 386	280, 190	314, 000
Belgium	278, 837	361, 034	253, 341	296, 234	299, 000
France [2]	807, 887	795, 702	752, 136	936, 892	973, 000
Spain	115, 727	268, 894	239, 097	214, 161	220, 000
Italy [2]	208, 675	174, 381	344, 048	304, 499	422, 300
Switzerland	3, 784	7, 165	8, 763	7, 578	7, 700
Germany	⁷ 2, 340, 268	1, 763, 051	1, 833, 728	1, 846, 658	2, 039, 645
Austria	79, 528	86, 172	87, 631	121, 257	116, 000
Czechoslovakia	1, 221, 274	1, 650, 148	1, 152, 807	1, 372, 197	1, 152, 978
Hungary	175, 783	183, 128	192, 998	205, 799	240, 000
Yugoslavia	41, 459	66, 818	85, 750	93, 269	³ 139, 700
Bulgaria	4, 376	(⁵)	36, 312	³ 46, 702	³ 32, 200
Rumania	⁸ 88, 245	114, 829	153, 213	158, 760	133, 000
Poland	702, 626	638, 274	633, 546	623, 628	804, 000
Latvia	(⁵)	(⁵)	718	1, 160	1, 200
Finland	(⁵)	2, 259	4, 368	6, 016	4, 000
Russia, European	1, 557, 114	1, 065, 315	960, 124	1, 477, 000	1, 353, 000
Total	8, 155, 838	7, 990, 117	7, 442, 481	8, 571, 648	8, 865, 268
OCEANIA					
Australia	⁹ 1, 030	2, 593	³ 1, 318	³ 2, 000	³ 2, 631
World total, beet sugar [10]	8, 823, 650	9, 015, 085	8, 447, 793	9, 783, 301	10, 023, 899

CANE SUGAR (RAW)

NORTH AND CENTRAL AMERICA AND WEST INDIES					
United States	302, 150	139, 381	47, 166	70, 793	165, 391
Hawaii	567, 495	787, 246	811, 333	904, 040	³ 929, 600
Porto Rico	361, 974	603, 240	629, 134	748, 677	609, 800
Virgin Islands	9, 613	6, 343	6, 860	11, 829	8, 400
Central America:					
Honduras		³ 16, 877	³ 30, 395		
Guatemala	8, 998	20, 247	27, 600	³ 32, 247	³ 36, 000
Nicaragua	3, 742	³ 17, 500	³ 11, 250	³ 14, 200	³ 15, 000
Salvador	10, 834	³ 20, 000			
Mexico	163, 388	214, 618	203, 399	³ 196, 240	³ 190, 000
West Indies (British):					
Antigua	12, 919	13, 660	³ 26, 321	³ 22, 188	³ 12, 000
Barbadoes	27, 788	53, 938	³ 65, 727	³ 66, 000	³ 62, 000
Jamaica	23, 856	50, 278	69, 593	³ 75, 432	³ 73, 000
St. Christopher	13, 252	18, 245	20, 235	21, 776	³ 20, 000
Trinidad and Tobago	51, 275	82, 388	58, 220	91, 337	³ 84, 000
Cuba	2, 287, 052	5, 523, 946	5, 049, 632	4, 526, 879	³ 5, 488, 000
Dominican Republic	⁸ 104, 664	387, 806	347, 743	412, 380	³ 382, 959
Haiti	(¹²)	³ 11, 249	³ 14, 071	³ 18, 331	³ 18, 000
West Indies (French):					
Guadeloupe	40, 810	38, 461	28, 988	³ 37, 477	³ 28, 000
Martinique	42, 782	49, 646	³ 44, 530	³ 43, 028	³ 45, 000
Total North and Central American countries and West Indies reporting, all years	4, 021, 758	8, 018, 192	7, 461, 802	7, 292, 854	8, 167, 150

[1] Figures for Europe are estimates for territory within present boundaries.
[2] Refined sugar in terms of raw.
[3] Unofficial estimate.
[4] 2-year average.
[5] No sugar produced.
[6] Production in 1926–27 was curtailed because sugar-beet growers and manufacturers failed to agree on sugar-beet prices.
[7] One year only, 1912–13. According to statistics of the German Sugar Association the 1912–13 production was greater than any other year.
[8] 4-year average.
[9] 1 year only.
[10] Exclusive of production in minor producing countries for which no data are available.
[11] 3-year average.
[12] To small to report.

TABLE 316.—*Sugar: Production in specified countries, average 1909–10 to 1913–14, annual 1925–26 to 1928–29*—Continued

CANE SUGAR (RAW)—Continued

Country	Average 1909–10 to 1913–14	1925–26	1926–27	1927–28	1928–29 preliminary
EUROPE AND ASIA	*Short tons*	*Short tons*	*Short tons*	*Short tons*	*Short tons*
Spain	17,059	[3] 9,748	[3] 7,525	[3] 10,000	
India [13]	2,649,480	3,334,000	3,646,000	3,602,000	3,063,000
Formosa	192,299	551,068	455,171	620,276	808,645
Japan	75,718	100,875	109,924	129,797	132,720
Java [14]	1,512,569	2,535,152	2,174,585	2,638,547	3,220,838
Philippine Islands	294,380	607,362	766,902	([15])	([15])
Total European and Asiatic countries reporting, all years	4,430,066	6,521,095	6,385,680	6,990,620	7,225,203
SOUTH AMERICA					
Argentina	193,853	433,968	522,772	456,933	413,725
Brazil	[11] 332,813	996,901	937,578	[3] 728,000	[3] 756,000
British Guiana	[11] 112,297	120,490	109,930	127,714	[3] 122,419
Dutch Guiana	13,235	[3] 13,969	18,669	[3] 15,120	[3] 17,000
Ecuador	[4] 6,289	[3] 19,013	[3] 22,760	[3] 22,500	[3] 25,100
Peru	202,518	414,536	[3] 399,519	[3] 419,834	[3] 386,000
Venezuela	3,187	23,880	22,658	22,305	22,000
Total South America	864,192	2,022,757	2,033,886	1,792,406	1,742,244
AFRICA					
Egypt	67,127	105,706	78,872	100,725	98,700
Mauritius	233,671	265,903	212,289	238,500	252,000
Union of South Africa	88,165	239,851	242,662	247,273	[3] 294,250
Portuguese East Africa	26,460	64,000	72,000	[3] 79,366	[3] 87,300
Reunion	41,653	66,229	59,779	55,084	58,000
Madagascar	([12])	3,970	[3] 3,527	[3] 3,858	[3] 4,894
Total Africa	457,076	745,659	669,129	724,806	795,144
OCEANIA					
Australia	216,331	580,126	465,781	579,000	[3] 608,944
Fiji	84,629	113,000	77,360	[3] 106,528	[3] 121,000
Total Oceania	300,960	693,126	543,141	685,528	729,944
Total cane-sugar producing countries reporting all years	10,074,052	18,000,829	17,093,638	17,486,214	18,659,685
Estimated world total cane sugar [10]	10,544,000	18,819,000	18,083,000	18,503,000	19,721,000
Total world cane and beet sugar production in countries reporting all years	18,897,700	27,015,914	25,541,431	27,269,515	28,683,584
Estimated world total, cane and beet sugar [10]	19,368,000	27,834,000	26,531,000	28,286,000	29,745,000

Bureau of Agricultural Economics. Official sources and International Institute of Agriculture except as otherwise stated. Figures are for the crop years 1909–10 to 1928–29 for the countries in which the sugar-harvesting season begins in the fall months and is completed during the following calendar year, except in certain cane-sugar producing countries where the season begins in May or June and is completed in the same calendar year. Production in these countries is for the calendar years 1909 to 1928.

[3] Unofficial estimate.

[4] 2-year average.

[10] Exclusive of production in minor producing countries for which no data are available.

[11] 3-year average.

[12] Too small to report.

[13] The figures quoted for India are for the production of gur a low grade of sugar polarizing between 50° and 60°. This sugar is mostly consumed by the natives.

[14] All grades of sugar reduced to terms of head sugar a grade of sugar which contains at least 96.5 per cent sucrose.

[15] Figures for the total crop are not yet available. Trade reports place the 1927–28 commercial crop at 701,980 short tons and that of 1928–29 at 740,000 short tons.

TABLE 317.—*Sugar: Production, trade, and supply available for consumption in continental United States, 1909–1928*

IN TERMS OF RAW SUGAR

Year beginning July 1	Production [1]	Brought in from insular possessions [2]	Imports as sugar [3]	Domestic exports as sugar [4]	Exports in other forms [5]	Available for consumption [6]	
						Total	Per capita
Average:	*Short tons*	*Short tons*	*Short tons*	*Short tons*	*Short tons*	*Short tons*	*Pounds*
1909–1913	957,491	1,004,493	2,068,427	45,502	17,317	3,967,591	84.0
1914–1920	1,102,153	1,072,288	2,847,575	547,406	46,538	4,428,072	86.0
1921–1925	1,187,797	1,495,517	3,854,633	449,940	23,203	6,064,804	108.0
1909	882,630	927,752	1,934,754	72,382	24,351	3,648,403	79.7
1910	903,475	943,701	1,845,279	36,597	15,966	3,639,891	78.3
1911	1,005,337	1,187,663	1,832,424	50,380	15,160	3,959,883	83.9
1912	907,070	1,026,972	2,266,426	30,963	19,217	4,150,288	86.6
1913	1,088,844	936,376	2,463,252	37,190	11,892	4,439,489	91.3
1914	1,022,828	1,098,314	2,529,963	302,641	13,585	4,334,878	87.9
1915	1,078,407	1,102,057	2,689,067	882,864	12,213	3,974,453	79.4
1916	1,193,107	1,203,938	2,527,984	676,752	29,211	4,219,066	83.2
1917	1,068,437	975,684	2,344,816	305,429	46,131	4,037,377	78.5
1918	1,102,421	1,073,944	2,799,962	568,566	36,747	4,371,013	83.8
1919	903,060	975,735	3,812,955	776,502	98,386	4,816,862	91.1
1920	1,346,811	1,076,342	3,228,279	319,589	89,491	5,242,852	97.6
1921	1,424,726	1,340,867	3,940,777	1,085,349	31,397	5,589,624	102.4
1922	1,021,360	1,235,049	4,068,205	412,196	12,568	5,899,849	106.5
1923	1,111,898	1,274,870	3,436,955	152,883	24,617	5,646,223	100.2
1924	1,260,000	1,645,319	3,931,282	273,470	22,436	6,540,695	114.2
1925	1,121,000	1,981,482	3,895,947	325,804	24,998	6,647,627	114.4
1926	1,011,000	1,689,347	3,968,880	124,555	26,303	6,518,369	110.6
1927	1,246,000	2,051,756	3,415,736	115,781	29,473	6,568,238	110.1
1928	1,279,000						

IN TERMS OF REFINED SUGAR [7]

1921	1,325,906	1,260,894	3,686,397	1,009,377	29,182	5,234,638	95.9
1922	950,625	1,161,351	3,805,745	383,439	11,682	5,522,600	99.7
1923	1,034,615	1,198,777	3,214,883	142,217	22,943	5,283,115	93.7
1924	1,172,000	1,547,587	3,674,563	254,391	20,911	6,118,848	106.8
1925	1,043,000	1,859,332	3,634,323	303,073	23,298	6,210,284	106.8
1926	941,000	1,588,981	3,714,054	115,865	24,514	6,103,656	103.6
1927	1,159,000	1,930,732	3,196,396	107,704	27,469	6,150,955	103.1
1928	1,190,000						

Bureau of Agricultural Economics. Trade figures compiled from Commerce and Navigation of the United States, 1909–1917; Foreign Commerce and Navigation of the U. S., 1918; Monthly Summary of Foreign Commerce of the U. S., June issues, 1913–1926, January and June issues, 1927–28, and official records of the Bureau of Foreign and Domestic Commerce.

[1] Beet and cane sugar only.
[2] Duty free, from Hawaii, Porto Rico, Philippine Islands, and Virgin Islands of the United States since 1916.
[3] No account taken of sugar imported in other forms. Imports from the Philippine Islands excluded. Reexports deducted.
[4] Shipments to Hawaii and Porto Rico included. Direct exports to foreign countries from Hawaii and Porto Rico excluded.
[5] Sugar used in the manufacture of other commodities for export on which drawback was paid.
[6] No account taken of stocks at the beginning or end of year.
[7] Raw sugar converted to refined by multiplying by the following factors: Cuba and Hawaii, 0.9358; Porto Rico, 0.9393; Philippines, 0.95; all others (Santo Domingo, British West Indies, Louisiana, etc.), 0.932.

TABLE 318.—*Sugar: International trade, average 1909–1913, annual 1924–1927*

Country	Year ended Dec. 31—							
	Average 1909–1913		1925		1926		1927 preliminary	
	Imports	Exports	Imports	Exports	Imports	Exports	Imports	Exports
PRINCIPAL EXPORTING COUNTRIES	*Short tons*	*Short tons*	*Short tons*	*Short tons*	*Short tons*	*Short tons*	*Short tons*	*Short tons*
Cuba	656	2, 009, 899	1, 492	5, 435, 097	595	5, 227, 219	(¹)	¹4, 647, 930
Dutch East Indies	3, 562	1, 412, 555	4, 199	2, 279, 229	3, 372	1, 914, 463	² 237	²2, 202, 095
Czechoslovakia	0	0	52	912, 547	68	1, 019, 467	2, 833	615, 595
Philippine Islands	3, 950	179, 432	1, 103	602, 773	1, 352	453, 301	2, 509	609, 929
Netherlands	82, 721	200, 490	361, 839	416, 064	433, 744	347, 451	293, 131	307, 733
Peru	726	146, 736	350	229, 432	22	364, 921	27	331, 166
Dominican Republic	³ 766	92, 351	578	331, 974	191	372, 195	189	326, 166
Mauritius	⁴ 2	226, 255	0	211, 976	1	199, 754	¹ 3	¹ 251, 313
Poland	0	0	206	216, 085	61	293, 973	64	222, 966
Belgium	7, 892	154, 476	66, 925	231, 056	56, 494	176, 594	93, 312	116, 243
Germany	3, 486	873, 161	125, 202	125, 868	46, 668	254, 125	121, 983	164, 174
British Guiana	⁴ 6, 112	106, 196	436	109, 455	446	94, 856	455	122, 770
Australia	76, 233	268	¹ 392	¹ 175, 563	¹ 4, 069	¹ 129, 708	¹ 32	¹ 143, 334
Hungary	⁵ 3, 942	⁵ 848, 830	163	93, 376	138	72, 986	327	74, 045
Fiji	⁶ 386	78, 817	121	102, 753	136	63, 830	134	81, 483
Trinidad and Tobago	522	43, 755	1, 129	67, 930	1, 408	73, 560	1, 618	46, 822
Reunion	⁶ 2	41, 658	0	49, 978	¹ 0	¹ 69, 790	¹ 0	¹ 69, 183
Jamaica	395	14, 494	¹ 1, 009	42, 242	¹ 750	¹ 53, 933	¹ 1, 120	¹ 55, 774
Union of South Africa	29, 694	675	5, 946	59, 970	4, 654	65, 289	3, 061	60, 163
Formosa	554	5, 744	23, 518	27, 458	¹ 31, 924	¹ 14, 362	¹ 25, 083	¹ 13, 199
Russia	3, 744	293, 514	¹ 247, 686	¹ 31, 093	¹ 2, 764	¹ 82, 788	¹ 8, 689	¹ 121, 173
PRINCIPAL IMPORTING COUNTRIES								
United States	2, 122, 517	39, 684	4, 459, 766	379, 358	4, 710, 099	106, 893	4, 215, 773	125, 323
United Kingdom	1, 853, 605	32, 603	2, 365, 653	73, 832	1, 972, 516	86, 979	1, 892, 705	94, 915
British India	715, 990	26, 611	⁷ 841, 497	27, 332	⁷ 875, 927	41, 993	⁷ 840, 224	43, 444
China	343, 622	14, 933	795, 323	4, 789	777, 000	819	668, 240	2, 544
Canada	297, 893	820	594, 397	155, 161	580, 234	144, 938	494, 397	101, 116
France	186, 198	206, 897	374, 765	194, 971	486, 188	214, 110	392, 316	234, 983
Japan	176, 942	60, 204	423, 478	163, 342	504, 588	204, 206	468, 188	179, 347
Switzerland	118, 201	0	142, 230	63	142, 015	66	137, 422	57
British Malaya			126, 488	43, 183	121, 969	32, 070	124, 038	26, 653
Austria	0	0	106, 113	1, 013	114, 124	636	108, 132	370
Chile	84, 965	90	116, 694	118	135, 962	¹ 88	96, 558	
Irish Free State	0	0	98, 408	0	101, 855	0	81, 506	0
Morocco	61, 402	0	110, 558	0	109, 088	0	113, 008	0
Finland	50, 077	0	122, 397	0	37, 469	0	73, 489	0
New Zealand	62, 962	⁴ 13, 478	78, 229	411	88, 999	713	70, 122	641
Norway	52, 326	0	73, 016	0	81, 797	0	78, 839	0
Persia	109, 352	⁴ 557	70, 582	355	¹ 77, 612	¹ 117		
Portugal	39, 631	0	¹ 86, 968	¹ 129	¹ 85, 488	¹ 85		
Italy	9, 240	302	100, 571	10, 752	22, 798	8, 058	77, 707	5, 073
Denmark	21, 814	22, 536	27, 628	1, 490	22, 482	1, 100	12, 632	11, 920
Greece	11, 718	0	¹ 67, 392	0	53, 065	0	66, 460	
Sweden	1, 672	1	49, 000	1	117, 078	4	124, 868	13
Egypt	43, 020	8, 086	91, 462	18, 708	61, 973	8, 670	57, 119	6, 367
Algeria	37, 908	0	54, 608	5	53, 578	145	62, 594	¹ 88
Argentina	51, 690	72	80, 744	115	1, 498	162	853	69, 045
Anglo-Egyptian Sudan	13, 764	0	15, 129	0	24, 631	0	19, 575	
Total, 47 countries	6, 691, 863	7, 156, 180	12, 315, 442	12, 827, 047	11, 949, 890	12, 196, 417	10, 831, 572	11, 485, 155

Bureau of Agricultural Economics. Official sources except where otherwise noted. The following kinds and grades have been included under the head of sugar: Brown, white, candied, caramel, chancaca (Peru), crystal cube, maple, muscovado, panela. The following have been excluded: "Candy" (meaning confectionery), confectionery, glucose, grape sugar, jaggery, molasses, and sirups.

¹ International Yearbook of Agricultural Statistics.
² Java and Madura only.
³ 1 year only.
⁴ 4-year average.
⁵ Average for Austria-Hungary.
⁶ 3-year average.
⁷ Sea trade only.

TABLE 319.—*Sugar, raw, cane, and beet: World production, 1909–10 to 1927–28*

Year [1]	Estimated world total	Total European beet sugar	Chief producing countries				
			Cuba	India [2]	Java [3]	Germany [4]	Czecho-slovakia
	Short tons	Short tons	Short tons	Short tons	Short tons	Short tons	Short tons
1909–10	16, 831, 000	6, 598, 712	2, 020, 871	2, 480, 700	1, 368, 755	2, 146, 817	
1910–11	18, 828, 000	8, 407, 415	1, 661, 465	2, 587, 100	1, 411, 275	2, 770, 000	
1911–12	17, 904, 000	6, 628, 923	2, 123, 502	2, 744, 900	1, 616, 599	1, 551, 797	
1912–13	20, 367, 000	8, 884, 675	2, 719, 961	2, 861, 500	1, 550, 274	2, 901, 564	
1913–14	21, 005, 000	8, 709, 590	2, 709, 460	2, 573, 200	1, 615, 944	2, 885, 752	
1914–15	20, 878, 000	8, 128, 018	2, 921, 984	2, 736, 000	1, 548, 668	2, 720, 635	
1915–16	18, 874, 000	5, 644, 337	3, 398, 385	2, 949, 000	1, 454, 030	1, 678, 402	
1916–17	18, 593, 000	4, 443, 528	3, 421, 597	3, 093, 000	1, 796, 558	1, 721, 250	
1917–18	20, 293, 000	4, 664, 962	3, 889, 966	3, 839, 000	2, 008, 521	1, 726, 483	
1918–19	18, 791, 000	3, 867, 311	4, 490, 902	2, 752, 000	1, 960, 118	1, 297, 050	[5] 714, 490
1919–20	17, 999, 000	2, 856, 507	4, 183, 676	3, 404, 000	1, 472, 796	773, 700	552, 713
1920–21	19, 563, 000	4, 115, 784	4, 406, 413	2, 825, 000	1, 681, 338	1, 194, 729	796, 957
1921–22	20, 577, 000	4, 348, 764	4, 517, 470	2, 928, 000	1, 853, 357	1, 433, 742	730, 745
1922–23	20, 861, 000	4, 991, 306	4, 083, 483	3, 410, 000	1, 989, 170	1, 603, 933	811, 323
1923–24	22, 833, 000	5, 544, 488	4, 606, 223	3, 715, 000	1, 980, 653	1, 263, 455	1, 114, 566
1924–25	26, 624, 000	7, 672, 623	5, 812, 068	2, 852, 000	2, 201, 368	1, 723, 601	1, 574, 494
1925–26	27, 834, 000	7, 990, 117	5, 523, 946	3, 334, 000	2, 535, 152	1, 763, 051	1, 650, 148
1926–27	26, 531, 000	7, 442, 481	5, 049, 632	3, 646, 000	2, 174, 585	1, 833, 728	1, 152, 807
1927–28	28, 286, 000	8, 571, 648	4, 526, 879	3, 602, 000	2, 638, 547	1, 846, 658	1, 372, 197
1928–29	29, 745, 000	8, 865, 268	[6] 5, 488, 000	3, 063, 000	3, 220, 838	2, 039, 645	1, 152, 978

Bureau of Agricultural Economics. Estimated world total sugar production for the period 1895-96 to 1908-9 in Agriculture Yearbook, 1924, p. 808.

[1] Figures are for the crop years 1909–10 to 1928–29 for the countries in which the sugar harvesting begins in the fall months and is completed during the following calendar year except in the cane-sugar-producing countries where the season begins in May or June and is completed in the same calendar year. Production in these countries is for the calendar years 1909 to 1928.
[2] The figures quoted are the production of gur, a low grade of sugar which is mostly consumed by the natives.
[3] All grades of sugar reduced to terms of head sugar.
[4] Figures for 1909–10 to 1917–18 are for pre-war boundaries.
[5] Bohemia, Moravia, and Silesia only.
[6] Unofficial estimate.

TABLE 320.—*Sugar, raw (96° centrifugal): Average wholesale price per pound New York, 1909–1928*

Year	Jan.	Feb.	Mar.	Apr.	May	June	July	Aug.	Sept.	Oct.	Nov.	Dec.	Av.[1]
	Cents	Cents	Cents	Cents	Cents	Cents	Cents	Cents	Cents	Cents	Cents	Cents	Cents
Average:													
1909–1913	3.9	3.9	4.0	3.9	3.9	3.8	4.0	4.2	4.5	4.3	4.2	4.1	4.1
1914–1920	6.2	6.1	6.3	7.3	7.8	7.6	7.4	7.2	6.8	6.4	6.2	6.2	6.8
1921–1925	5.1	5.4	5.8	5.6	5.4	5.1	5.2	5.2	5.3	5.4	5.4	5.2	5.3
1909	3.7	3.6	3.8	3.9	3.9	3.9	3.9	4.1	4.2	4.3	4.4	4.2	4.0
1910	4.1	4.2	4.4	4.3	4.3	4.2	4.3	4.4	4.3	3.9	3.9	4.0	4.2
1911	3.6	3.5	3.8	3.9	3.9	3.9	4.3	4.9	5.9	5.9	5.1	4.8	4.5
1912	4.4	4.6	4.5	4.1	4.0	3.9	3.9	4.1	4.3	4.1	4.0	4.0	4.2
1913	3.5	3.5	3.5	3.4	3.3	3.3	3.6	3.7	3.7	3.5	3.6	3.4	3.5
1914	3.3	3.4	3.0	3.0	3.2	3.3	3.3	5.7	5.8	4.4	3.9	3.9	3.8
1915	4.1	4.7	4.8	4.8	4.8	4.9	4.9	4.8	4.3	4.1	4.8	4.9	4.7
1916	4.6	4.9	5.6	6.2	6.4	6.3	6.3	5.6	5.6	6.3	6.2	5.3	5.8
1917	5.2	5.2	5.5	6.2	6.1	6.0	6.6	7.3	7.0	6.9	6.9	6.3	6.3
1918	6.0	6.0	6.0	6.0	6.0	6.0	6.1	6.1	7.0	7.3	7.3	7.3	6.4
1919	7.3	7.3	7.3	7.3	7.3	7.3	7.3	7.3	7.3	7.3	7.3	10.2	7.5
1920	13.0	11.4	11.9	17.7	20.8	19.7	17.6	13.4	10.7	8.3	6.8	5.3	13.0
1921	5.4	5.3	6.1	5.4	4.9	4.2	4.4	4.7	4.3	4.2	4.1	3.7	4.7
1922	3.6	3.8	3.9	4.0	4.1	4.6	5.2	5.2	4.8	5.4	5.6	5.7	4.7
1923	5.3	6.2	7.3	7.8	7.9	7.4	6.9	6.1	7.0	7.6	7.3	7.3	7.0
1924	6.7	7.2	6.9	6.4	5.6	5.1	5.1	5.4	6.0	6.0	5.8	5.3	6.0
1925	4.6	4.6	4.7	4.5	4.3	4.4	4.3	4.4	4.3	3.9	4.0	4.1	4.3
1926	4.2	4.2	4.0	4.1	4.2	4.1	4.2	4.2	4.4	4.6	4.7	5.1	4.3
1927	5.1	4.9	4.8	4.8	4.8	4.6	4.5	4.5	4.8	4.7	4.7	4.6	4.7
1928	4.5	4.3	4.5	4.5	4.5	4.3	4.2	4.1	4.2	3.9	3.9	3.9	4.2

Bureau of Agricultural Economics. Compiled from Bureau of Labor Statistics reports. Data for 1890-1908 are available in 1924 Yearbook, p. 810, Table 388.

[1] Derived from the figures upon which the monthly averages are based.

TABLE 321.—*Sugar, granulated: Average retail price per pound, United States, 1913–1928*

Year	Jan. 15	Feb. 15	Mar. 15	Apr. 15	May 15	June 15	July 15	Aug. 15	Sept. 15	Oct. 15	Nov. 15	Dec. 15	Average
	Cents	Cents	Cents	Cents	Cents	Cents	Cents	Cents	Cents	Cents	Cents	Cents	Cents
Average:													
1914–1920	9.1	9.5	9.5	9.9	10.8	10.9	11.0	10.9	10.1	9.6	9.6	9.5	10.0
1921–1925	8.5	8.4	8.9	8.9	8.5	8.3	8.1	8.1	8.1	8.2	8.1	8.1	8.4
1913	5.8	5.5	5.4	5.4	5.4	5.3	5.5	5.6	5.7	5.5	5.4	5.4	5.5
1914	5.2	5.2	5.1	5.0	5.0	5.1	5.2	7.9	8.0	7.2	6.2	6.1	5.9
1915	6.0	6.5	6.6	6.7	6.8	6.9	7.0	6.7	6.5	6.1	6.6	6.8	6.6
1916	6.7	6.9	7.5	8.0	8.6	8.7	8.8	8.5	7.7	8.2	8.6	8.3	8.0
1917	8.0	8.1	8.8	9.6	10.1	9.4	9.2	10.0	9.9	9.8	9.6	9.5	9.3
1918	9.5	10.6	9.2	9.1	9.1	9.1	9.2	9.3	9.6	10.6	10.8	10.8	9.7
1919	10.8	10.7	10.6	10.6	10.6	10.6	10.9	11.1	11.0	11.4	12.5	14.5	11.3
1920	17.8	18.8	18.7	20.2	25.4	26.7	26.5	22.9	18.3	13.9	12.8	10.5	19.4
1921	9.7	8.9	9.7	9.7	8.4	7.8	7.1	7.5	7.3	6.9	6.7	6.5	8.0
1922	6.2	6.4	6.5	6.7	6.6	7.1	7.6	8.1	7.9	7.9	8.1	8.3	7.3
1923	8.3	8.7	10.2	10.6	11.2	11.1	10.5	9.6	9.6	10.6	10.3	10.4	10.1
1924	10.2	10.3	10.4	9.9	9.2	8.3	8.4	8.2	8.6	8.8	8.8	8.8	9.2
1925	8.1	7.7	7.7	7.5	7.2	7.2	7.1	7.0	7.0	6.8	6.6	6.7	7.2
1926	6.7	6.7	6.7	6.6	6.7	6.9	6.9	7.0	7.0	7.1	7.1	7.3	6.9
1927	7.5	7.5	7.4	7.3	7.3	7.3	7.4	7.3	7.2	7.2	7.2	7.1	7.3
1928	7.1	7.1	7.1	7.1	7.2	7.3	7.3	7.1	7.0	6.9	------	------	------

Bureau of Agricultural Economics. Compiled from Bureau of Labor Statistics retail prices.

TABLE 322.—*Sorgo sirup: Acreage, production, and December 1 price, by States 1925–1928*

State	Acreage				Average yield per acre				Production				Price per gallon received by producers Dec. 1			
	1925	1926	1927	1928[1]	1925	1926	1927	1928	1925	1926	1927	1928[1]	1925	1926	1927	1928
	1,000 acres	1,000 acres	1,000 acres	1,000 acres	Gallons	Gallons	Gallons	Gallons	1,000 gallons	1,000 gallons	1,000 gallons	1,000 gallons	Cts.	Cts.	Cts.	Cts.
Ohio	4	4	4	4	72	72	76	72	288	288	304	288	125	120	115	125
Indiana	2	2	2	2	88	92	80	96	176	184	160	192	112	105	110	115
Illinois	12	12	10	9	77	78	65	72	924	936	650	648	110	105	110	110
Wisconsin	2	2	2	2	70	66	55	64	140	132	110	128	135	140	135	140
Minnesota	2	2	2	2	71	80	70	84	142	160	140	168	115	120	110	120
Iowa	5	6	2	2	79	77	70	90	395	462	140	180	115	110	115	115
Missouri	22	25	22	22	76	78	79	85	1,672	1,950	1,738	1,870	102	100	100	100
Nebraska	2	2	2	2	70	64	80	83	140	128	160	166	100	100	105	105
Kansas	5	3	2	2	50	58	65	75	250	174	130	150	102	95	100	100
Virginia	11	12	10	12	78	100	92	86	858	1,200	920	1,032	95	95	95	95
West Virginia	8	8	6	7	80	97	89	88	640	776	534	616	115	110	110	110
North Carolina	28	30	22	20	68	91	92	86	1,904	2,730	2,024	1,720	98	90	90	90
South Carolina	20	22	26	18	39	77	71	72	780	1,694	1,846	1,296	92	75	75	80
Georgia	19	23	25	24	45	90	82	80	855	2,070	2,050	1,920	95	70	75	90
Kentucky	39	51	38	42	80	95	81	72	3,120	4,845	3,078	3,024	96	80	85	95
Tennessee	28	32	29	29	68	93	86	78	1,904	2,976	2,494	2,262	94	80	85	90
Alabama	42	36	35	30	70	100	82	75	2,940	3,600	2,870	2,250	90	80	80	90
Mississippi	34	27	30	30	76	100	85	80	2,584	2,700	2,550	2,400	75	70	70	80
Arkansas	38	38	44	40	68	77	80	70	2,584	2,926	3,520	2,800	93	85	85	90
Louisiana	1	1	1	1	75	135	110	80	75	135	110	80	80	70	75	75
Oklahoma	14	14	17	15	76	83	85	70	1,064	1,162	1,445	1,050	93	85	85	85
Texas	31	34	34	32	46	95	95	83	1,426	3,230	3,230	2,656	93	80	80	80
New Mexico	1	1	1	1	65	80	65	76	65	80	65	76	110	100	105	95
United States	370	387	366	348	67.4	89.2	82.7	77.5	24,926	34,538	30,268	26,972	94.9	84.2	85.0	91.5

Bureau of Agricultural Economics. Estimates of the crop-reporting board.

[1] Preliminary.

TABLE 323.—*Sugar cane sirup: Acreage, production, and December 1 price, by States, 1925–1928*

State	Acreage used for sirup				Average yield per acre				Production				Price per gallon received by producers Dec. 1			
	1925	1926	1927	1928[1]	1925	1926	1927	1928	1925	1926	1927	1928[1]	1925	1926	1927	1928
	1,000 acres	*1,000 acres*	*1,000 acres*	*1,000 acres*	*Gals.*	*Gals.*	*Gals.*	*Gals.*	*1,000 gals.*	*1,000 gals.*	*1,000 gals.*	*1,000 gals.*	*Cts.*	*Cts.*	*Cts.*	*Cts.*
South Carolina___	8	5	7	6	72	140	140	125	576	700	980	750	100	90	90	90
Georgia_____	32	35	34	29	110	175	150	140	3,520	6,125	5,100	4,060	100	75	75	75
Florida_____	10	10	9	8	210	210	183	180	2,100	2,100	1,647	1,440	105	85	85	85
Alabama_____	22	20	18	16	140	165	135	117	3,080	3,300	2,430	1,872	110	90	95	95
Mississippi_____	14	14	17	18	172	205	215	200	2,408	2,870	3,655	3,600	105	95	95	90
Arkansas_____	3	3	2	2	120	135	100	120	360	405	200	240	120	105	110	110
Louisiana_____	25	34	15	23	262	133	309	346	6,541	4,516	4,787	8,061	72	60	55	55
Texas_____	11	11	12	11	165	196	170	160	1,815	2,156	2,040	1,760	130	95	110	110
United States__	125	132	114	113	163.2	168.0	182.8	192.8	20,400	22,172	20,839	21,783	96.7	80.7	81.5	76.2

Bureau of Agricultural Economics.   Estimates of the crop-reporting board.

[1] Preliminary.

TABLE 324.—*Maple sugar and sirup: Production in 10 important States, 1917–1928*[1]

Year	Trees tapped	Sugar made	Sirup made	Total product in terms of sugar[2]	Average total product per tree	
					As sugar[2]	As sirup[2]
	Thousand	*1,000 pounds*	*1,000 gallons*	*1,000 pounds*	*Pounds*	*Gallons*
1917_____	17,313	10,525	4,258	44,589	2.58	0.32
1918_____	19,132	12,944	4,863	51,848	2.71	.34
1919_____	18,799	9,787	3,804	40,219	2.14	.27
1920_____	18,895	7,324	3,580	35,964	1.90	.24
1921_____	15,114	4,730	2,386	23,818	1.58	.20
1922_____	16,274	5,147	3,640	34,267	2.11	.26
1923_____	15,291	4,685	3,605	33,525	2.19	.27
1924_____	15,407	4,078	3,903	35,302	2.29	.29
1925_____	15,313	3,236	3,089	27,946	1.82	.23
1926_____	14,712	3,569	3,737	33,465	2.27	.28
1927_____	14,603	3,236	3,672	32,612	2.23	.28
1928_____	14,388	2,388	3,013	26,492	1.84	.23

Bureau of Agricultural Economics.

[1] The data from 1917–1923 include 11 States: Maine, New Hampshire, Vermont, Massachusetts, Connecticut, New York, Pennsylvania, Ohio, Indiana, Michigan, and Wisconsin; data for 10 States, excluding Connecticut, are shown for 1924 and 1925; 9 States, excluding Indiana, for which data are shown from 1926–1928, produced about 97 per cent of the maple sugar and about 92 per cent of the maple sirup in the United States in 1919 as reported by the Bureau of the Census.

[2] 1 gallon of sirup taken as equivalent to 8 pounds of sugar.

TABLE 325.—*Maple sugar and sirup: Production, by States, 1926–1928*

State	Trees tapped			Sugar made			Sirup made		
	1926	1927	1928	1926	1927	1928	1926	1927	1928
	Thousand	*Thousand*	*Thousand*	*1,000 pounds*	*1,000 pounds*	*1,000 pounds*	*1,000 gallons*	*1,000 gallons*	*1,000 gallons*
Maine_____	304	310	304	29	15	3	61	60	38
New Hampshire____	790	822	806	233	289	274	198	164	137
Vermont_____	5,554	5,665	5,722	1,602	1,694	1,133	980	1,417	1,038
Massachusetts_____	272	277	280	128	132	134	86	75	67
New York_____	3,958	3,839	3,647	1,168	733	549	1,128	1,002	718
Pennsylvania_____	696	626	607	223	148	67	251	139	157
Ohio_____	1,700	1,666	1,583	68	134	129	578	489	486
Michigan_____	863	828	869	100	72	70	300	172	208
Wisconsin_____	575	570	570	18	19	29	155	154	164
Total, 9 States[1]_____	14,712	14,603	14,388	3,569	3,236	2,388	3,737	3,672	3,013

Bureau of Agricultural Economics.

[1] These 9 States produced about 97 per cent of the maple sugar and about 92 per cent of the maple sirup made in the United States in 1919 as reported by the Bureau of the Census.

TABLE 326.—*Clover seed: Receipts, Chicago, averages 1909–1925, annual 1920–1928*

Year beginning September	Sept.	Oct.	Nov.	Dec.	Jan.	Feb.	Mar.	Apr.	May	June	July	Aug.	Total
	1,000 lbs.	*1,000 lbs.*	*1,000 lbs.*	*1,000 lbs.*	*1,000 lbs.*	*1,000 lbs.*	*1,000 lbs.*	*1,000 lbs.*	*1,000 lbs.*	*1,000 lbs.*	*1,000 lbs.*	*1,000 lbs.*	*1,000 lbs.*
Average:													
1909–1913	622	652	549	426	422	513	677	328	180	320	180	455	5,325
1914–1920	1,231	1,307	1,323	1,241	1,558	1,690	1,590	746	221	97	83	355	11,442
1921–1925	695	1,209	1,803	1,698	1,357	1,706	2,158	964	277	75	52	401	12,394
1920	1,207	969	747	1,004	2,288	2,165	4,062	1,570	418	164	84	365	15,043
1921	739	1,235	2,040	1,833	1,628	2,674	2,448	1,009	279	169	77	997	15,128
1922	1,358	1,293	1,479	1,214	1,044	629	1,825	845	350	109	8	272	10,426
1923	641	1,681	1,176	1,039	630	1,641	2,054	1,352	259	41	1	40	10,555
1924	346	888	2,195	1,801	1,500	1,507	1,574	765	9	27	68	328	11,008
1925	393	946	2,125	2,603	1,984	2,079	2,888	849	487	28	107	366	14,855
1926	1,107	3,596	2,133	1,350	1,695	1,857	1,671	546	55	----	----	64	14,074
1927	575	2,285	4,689	1,544	1,557	1,313	848	268	40	165	168		14,974
1928	958	3,125	2,751	1,746	----	----	----	----	----	----	----	----	----

Bureau of Agricultural Economics. Compiled from annual reports of the Chicago Board of Trade.

TABLE 327.—*Clover seed (red and alsike): Acreage, yield per acre, production, and December 1 price, by States, 1925–1928*

State	Acreage				Average yield per acre			
	1925	1926	1927	1928 [1]	1925	1926	1927	1928
	Acres	*Acres*	*Acres*	*Acres*	*Bushels*	*Bushels*	*Bushels*	*Bushels*
New York	7,000	3,000	1,000	1,000	1.7	1.7	1.8	1.8
Pennsylvania	16,000	8,000	14,000	16,000	1.8	1.5	1.6	1.6
Ohio	168,000	67,000	268,000	161,000	1.1	.9	1.2	1.2
Indiana	115,000	70,000	210,000	105,000	.7	.5	1.2	1.2
Illinois	110,000	77,000	187,000	75,000	.9	1.1	1.1	1.1
Michigan	72,000	43,000	97,000	87,000	1.4	1.5	1.6	1.6
Wisconsin	122,000	92,000	138,000	41,000	1.9	1.7	1.9	1.6
Minnesota	43,000	42,000	80,000	64,000	2.0	2.3	2.0	2.0
Iowa	95,000	51,000	123,000	74,000	1.0	.75	.84	1.3
Missouri	20,000	22,000	33,000	23,000	1.5	1.7	1.7	1.5
North Dakota			3,000	3,000			2.0	2.0
Nebraska	10,000	17,000	12,000	11,000	1.9	1.4	1.7	1.9
Kansas	8,000	13,000	12,000	6,000	1.8	2.1	1.6	1.5
Tennessee	5,000	2,000	3,000	2,000	1.4	2.5	2.0	1.9
Idaho	13,000	16,000	18,000	21,000	5.0	3.8	4.7	4.7
Oregon	3,000	7,500	15,000	23,000	2.5	3.0	3.5	3.3
United States	807,000	530,500	1,214,000	713,000	1.32	1.37	1.42	1.55

State	Production				Price per bushel received by producers Dec. 1			
	1925	1926	1927	1928 [1]	1925	1926	1927	1928
	1,000 bushels	*1,000 bushels*	*1,000 bushels*	*1,000 bushels*	*Dollars*	*Dollars*	*Dollars*	*Dollars*
New York	12	5	2	2	14.30	20.00	19.00	19.70
Pennsylvania	29	12	22	26	15.70	18.50	17.75	17.75
Ohio	185	60	322	193	15.10	19.25	16.00	16.90
Indiana	80	35	252	126	15.40	18.25	15.00	16.70
Illinois	99	85	206	82	15.60	18.75	15.00	17.00
Michigan	101	64	155	139	15.00	18.00	14.70	16.10
Wisconsin	232	156	262	66	14.60	17.70	15.50	16.50
Minnesota	86	97	160	128	14.40	17.50	15.50	16.00
Iowa	95	38	103	96	16.00	18.00	16.10	18.00
Missouri	30	37	56	34	13.60	16.50	13.50	14.80
North Dakota			6	6			13.50	15.00
Nebraska	19	24	20	21	12.00	15.90	15.15	15.60
Kansas	14	27	19	9	12.20	15.00	13.10	13.60
Tennessee	7	5	6	4	16.00	16.48	18.00	17.10
Idaho	65	61	84	98	14.20	17.00	13.50	14.60
Oregon	8	22	52	76	15.00	17.00	14.25	14.90
United States	1,062	728	1,727	1,106	14.90	17.71	15.22	16.30

Bureau of Agricultural Economics. Estimates of the crop-reporting board.

[1] Preliminary.

TABLE 328.—*Sweet clover seed: Acreage, yield per acre, production, and December 1, price, by States, 1925–1928*

State	Acreage				Average yield per acre			
	1925	1926	1927	1928 [1]	1925	1926	1927	1928
	Acres	*Acres*	*Acres*	*Acres*	*Bushels*	*Bushels*	*Bushels*	*Bushels*
Ohio	5,000	7,000	10,000	6,000	3.5	3.5	3.8	3.5
Indiana	2,000	3,000	6,000	3,000	4.0	4.0	2.0	3.0
Illinois	7,000	15,000	20,000	13,000	4.0	4.0	3.7	4.0
Minnesota	50,000	45,000	50.000	45,000	4.0	4.5	4.0	4.1
Iowa	15,000	20,000	26,000	8,000	4.5	4.0	4.3	4.4
Missouri	6,000	5,000	5,000	6,000	4.0	3.5	3.5	3.0
North Dakota	56,000	60,000	55,000	38,000	5.2	5.0	4.2	3.7
South Dakota	45,000	40,000	45,000	54,000	3.3	3.5	4.2	4.3
Nebraska	25,000	28,000	33,000	41,000	3.7	4.1	3.9	4.0
Kansas	30,000	27,000	34,200	22,000	4.0	4.4	4.0	4.1
Montana	7,000	6,000	6,000	7,000	3.1	5.0	5.0	4.5
Colorado	8,000	8,000	10,000	7,000	5.0	5.0	5.5	5.0
United States	256,000	264,000	300,200	250,000	4.14	4.32	4.08	4.05

State	Production				Price per bushel received by producers Dec. 1			
	1925	1926	1927	1928 [1]	1925	1926	1927	1928
	Bushels	*Bushels*	*Bushels*	*Bushels*	*Dollars*	*Dollars*	*Dollars*	*Dollars*
Ohio	17,500	24,500	38,000	21,000	7.70	8.00	6.20	5.80
Indiana	8,000	12,000	12,000	9,000	8.00	8.30	6.50	5.80
Illinois	28,000	60,000	74,000	52,000	8.30	8.80	7.00	5.30
Minnesota	200,000	202,500	200,000	184,500	3.30	6.10	3.50	3.40
Iowa	67,500	80,000	111,800	35,200	7.10	8.00	5.70	5.30
Missouri	24,000	17,500	17,500	18,000	7.10	8.00	6.00	5.40
North Dakota	291,200	300,000	231,000	140,600	4.30	7.00	4.25	3.50
South Dakota	148,500	140,000	189,000	232,200	4.50	7.30	4.20	3.00
Nebraska	92,500	114,800	128,700	164,000	5.00	5.80	5.00	3.90
Kansas	120,000	118,800	136,800	90,200	5.50	6.70	4.35	3.30
Montana	21,700	30,000	30,000	31,500	6.70	8.60	6.00	4.30
Colorado	40,000	40,000	55,000	35,000	5.70	7.30	4.50	3.70
United States	1,058,900	1,140,100	1,223,800	1,013,200	4.87	6.99	4.67	3.70

Bureau of Agricultural Economics. Estimates of the crop-reporting board.

[1] Preliminary.

TABLE 329.—*Lespedeza (Japan clover) seed: Acreage, yield per acre, production, and December 1 price, by States, 1925–1928*

State	Acreage				Average yield per acre			
	1925	1926	1927	1928 [1]	1925	1926	1927	1928
	Acres	*Acres*	*Acres*	*Acres*	*Bushels*	*Bushels*	*Bushels*	*Bushels*
Mississippi	25,000	29,000	31,000	24,000	4.7	6.1	6.2	4.7
Louisiana	14,200	11,600	5,400	6,000	5.1	5.6	5.2	5.2
2 States	39,200	40,600	36,400	30,000	4.85	5.99	6.06	4.80

State	Production				Price per bushel received by producers Dec. 1			
	1925	1926	1927	1928[1]	1925	1926	1927	1928
	Bushels	*Bushels*	*Bushels*	*Bushels*	*Dollars*	*Dollars*	*Dollars*	*Dollars*
Mississippi	118,000	178,000	192,500	112,800	4.10	3.60	2.81	2.79
Louisiana	72,000	65,000	28,100	31,200	3.67	3.13	2.45	3.21
2 States	190,000	243,000	220,600	144,000	3.94	3.47	2.77	2.88

Bureau of Agricultural Economics. Estimates of the crop-reporting board. No estimate has been made for Alabama and Tennessee, in which States some quantities of this seed are also produced.

[1] Preliminary.

TABLE 330.—*Timothy seed: Acreage, yield per acre, production, and December 1 price, by States, 1925–1928*

State	Acreage				Average yield per acre			
	1925	1926	1927	1928 [1]	1925	1926	1927	1928
	Acres	*Acres*	*Acres*	*Acres*	*Bushels*	*Bushels*	*Bushels*	*Bushels*
New York	3,000	2,000	2,000	3,000	4.2	4.3	4.8	5.0
Pennsylvania	12,000	8,000	10,000	8,000	4.2	4.3	4.8	5.5
Ohio	55,000	85,000	90,000	40,000	4.0	4.5	4.4	4.3
Indiana	30,000	30,000	25,000	12,000	2.4	3.5	4.0	3.8
Illinois	73,000	90,000	130,000	65,000	2.6	3.6	4.4	3.5
Wisconsin	3,000	4,000	10,000	3,000	5.0	4.7	4.4	4.6
Minnesota	40,000	42,000	40,000	30,000	4.4	3.5	4.2	3.7
Iowa	228,000	261,000	256,000	141,000	3.6	4.0	4.2	4.2
Missouri	95,000	120,000	135,000	71,000	3.3	3.4	3.8	3.5
North Dakota	3,000	2,000	5,000	2,000	4.0	3.0	2.8	3.5
South Dakota	18,000	20,000	15,000	11,000	3.2	2.0	4.0	3.0
Kansas	3,000	3,000	2,000	2,000	3.7	3.6	3.6	3.6
United States	563,000	667,000	720,000	388,000	3.47	3.79	4.18	3.91

State	Production				Price per bushel received by producers Dec. 1			
	1925	1926	1927	1928 [1]	1925	1926	1927	1928
	Bushels	*Bushels*	*Bushels*	*Bushels*	*Dollars*	*Dollars*	*Dollars*	*Dollars*
New York	12,600	8,600	9,600	15,000	4.10	3.70	4.00	2.80
Pennsylvania	50,400	34,400	48,000	44,000	4.10	3.55	2.85	2.90
Ohio	220,000	382,500	396,000	172,000	3.45	2.80	2.10	2.20
Indiana	72,000	105,000	100,000	45,600	3.60	2.90	2.15	2.20
Illinois	189,800	324,000	572,000	227,500	3.70	2.80	1.85	2.20
Wisconsin	15,000	18,800	44,000	13,800	3.10	2.50	2.25	2.40
Minnesota	176,000	147,000	168,000	111,000	4.00	2.50	1.70	2.15
Iowa	820,800	1,044,000	1,075,200	592,200	3.20	2.50	1.65	2.15
Missouri	313,500	408,000	513,000	248,500	3.60	2.50	1.75	2.15
North Dakota	12,000	6,000	14,000	7,000	3.70	2.70	1.85	2.15
South Dakota	57,600	40,000	60,000	33,000	2.30	2.20	1.75	1.90
Kansas	11,100	10,800	7,200	7,200	3.20	3.00	1.90	1.90
United States	1,950,800	2,529,100	3,007,000	1,516,800	3.43	2.62	1.82	2.19

Bureau of Agricultural Economics. Estimates of the crop-reporting board.

[1] Preliminary.

TABLE 331.—*Alfalfa seed: Acreage, yield per acre, production, and December 1 price, by States, 1925–1928*

State	Acreage				Average yield per acre			
	1925	1926	1927	1928 [1]	1925	1926	1927	1928
	Acres	*Acres*	*Acres*	*Acres*	*Bushels*	*Bushels*	*Bushels*	*Bushels*
Minnesota		5,000	3,800	3,800		2.2	1.7	1.8
Missouri			3,000	3,000			3.5	3.0
North Dakota	7,500	6,800	4,000	4,000	2.0	2.0	1.8	1.9
South Dakota	44,000	40,000	18,000	22,000	2.0	2.0	1.6	2.0
Nebraska	25,000	27,000	19,000	29,000	2.4	2.4	2.2	2.6
Kansas	47,000	41,000	8,200	7,000	2.4	2.7	2.2	2.4
Oklahoma	6,000	20,000	12,000	10,000	3.0	2.5	3.0	2.6
Texas	1,800	5,000	7,200	2,700	2.5	2.5	4.0	1.5
Montana	28,000	23,000	11,000	16,500	2.8	2.7	1.8	2.4
Idaho	16,400	20,000	30,000	15,000	4.0	3.1	6.0	3.4
Wyoming	4,000	5,000	3,000	3,000	2.7	4.0	3.0	3.0
Colorado	5,400	4,800	2,900	2,000	4.0	3.0	3.5	3.0
New Mexico	4,000	6,000	6,500	5,500	3.0	4.5	4.5	3.0
Arizona	20,000	18,000	22,000	22,000	6.0	5.5	5.0	4.5
Utah	69,000	71,000	72,000	73,000	6.4	4.05	3.68	1.7
Oregon		1,000	1,000	3,000		4.0	4.0	3.5
California	16,000	14,400	13,300	14,000	3.7	2.75	3.5	3.3
United States	294,100	308,000	236,900	235,500	3.77	3.11	3.59	2.51

[1] Preliminary.

TABLE 331.—*Alfalfa seed: Acreage, yield per acre, production, and December 1 price, by States, 1925–1928*—Continued

State	Production				Price per bushel received by producers Dec. 1			
	1925	1926	1927	1928 [1]	1925	1926	1927	1928
	Bushels	*Bushels*	*Bushels*	*Bushels*	*Dollars*	*Dollars*	*Dollars*	*Dollars*
Minnesota		11,000	6,500	6,800		20.50	16.35	19.40
Missouri			10,500	9,000			13.95	15.50
North Dakota	15,000	13,600	7,200	7,600	16.00	17.10	17.10	19.00
South Dakota	88,000	80,000	28,800	44,000	13.70	12.50	13.00	13.45
Nebraska	60,000	64,800	41,800	75,400	11.35	11.00	11.50	12.35
Kansas	112,800	110,700	18,000	16,800	9.20	8.50	9.15	10.85
Oklahoma	18,000	50,000	36,000	26,000	9.65	8.55	8.45	9.30
Texas	4,500	12,500	28,800	4,000	15.50	8.35	8.25	9.00
Montana	78,400	62,100	19,800	39,600	12.65	13.25	13.00	13.90
Idaho	65,600	62,000	180,000	51,000	11.75	10.25	9.25	13.30
Wyoming	10,800	20,000	9,000	9,000	10.00	10.35	12.25	13.10
Colorado	21,600	14,400	10,200	6,000	10.80	9.20	10.75	11.80
New Mexico	12,000	27,000	29,200	16,500	9.70	8.60	8.20	10.15
Arizona	120,000	99,000	110,000	99,000	9.30	8.25	8.20	11.50
Utah	441,600	287,600	265,000	124,100	9.50	8.50	8.25	11.50
Oregon		4,000	4,000	10,500		8.50	8.25	11.50
California	59,200	39,600	46,600	46,200	11.30	8.25	11.75	12.75
						10.75	9.60	11.70
United States	1,107,500	958,300	851,400	591,500	10.48	9.80	9.28	12.21

Bureau of Agricultural Economics.   Estimates of the Crop Reporting Board.   [1] Preliminary.

TABLE 332.—*Timothy seed: Receipts, Chicago, averages 1909–1925, annual 1920–1928*

Year beginning August	Aug.	Sept.	Oct.	Nov.	Dec.	Jan.	Feb.	Mar.	Apr.	May	June	July	Total
	1,000 lbs.	*1,000 lbs.*	*1,000 lbs.*	*1,000 lbs.*	*1,000 lbs.*	*1,000 lbs.*	*1,000 lbs.*	*1,000 lbs.*	*1,000 lbs.*	*1,000 lbs.*	*1,000 lbs.*	*1,000 lbs.*	*1.000 lbs.*
Average:													
1909–1913	2,965	7,614	5,305	3,111	1,698	1,716	2,059	3,082	2,255	695	855	1,238	32,595
1914–1920	3,282	8,951	5,261	3,354	2,418	2,043	2,529	3,612	2,081	1,619	787	685	36,621
1921–1925	6,967	9,908	4,687	2,527	1,580	1,655	1,878	2,244	1,346	796	495	422	34,504
1920	2,347	8,075	5,676	4,009	2,951	1,706	2,076	4,056	2,601	2,368	1,088	579	37,532
1921	10,849	6,239	4,586	3,198	2,317	2,404	2,899	2,828	780	1,263	472	119	37,954
1922	8,967	9,593	4,577	2,048	1,050	570	1,352	1,697	1,243	398	355	124	31,974
1923	5,386	13,397	4,419	1,606	1,329	662	1,298	1,815	1,162	65	315	507	31,961
1924	3,698	12,714	4,845	3,736	1,552	2,138	2,038	2,566	1,809	1,240	664	687	37,687
1925	5,933	7,599	5,009	2,047	1,651	2,499	1,801	2,316	1,734	1,015	667	672	32,943
1926	5,907	7,981	3,368	2,113	1,158	1,588	1,780	2,601	1,481	980	779	516	30,252
1927	6,548	7,387	3,741	3,812	961	1,170	1,669	1,826	1,625	1,613	1,039	896	32,287
1928	1,652	5,664	3,164	956	921								

Bureau or Agricultural Economics.   Compiled from annual reports of the Chicago Board of Trade.

NOTE.—A table similar to Table 317, 1927 Yearbook, is omitted.

TABLE 333.—*Alfalfa seed: Estimated price per bushel, received by producers, United States, 1912–1928*

Year beginning August	Aug. 15	Sept. 15	Oct. 15	Nov. 15	Dec. 15	Jan. 15	Feb. 15	Mar. 15	Apr. 15	May 15	June 15	July 15	Weighted average [1]
	Dolls.	*Dolls.*	*Dolls.*	*Dolls.*	*Dolls.*	*Dolls.*	*Dolls.*	*Dolls.*	*Dolls.*	*Dolls.*	*Dolls.*	*Dolls.*	*Dolls.*
1912	8.58	9.02	7.87	8.23	7.86	7.66	8.15	8.19	8.36	8.21	8.08	8.20	8.21
1913	7.96	7.42	6.96	6.36	6.60	6.55	6.48	6.60	6.77	6.77	6.83	6.92	6.96
1914	6.81	7.21	7.29	7.29	7.57	7.61	7.86	7.92	8.45	8.38	8.31	8.51	7.52
1915	8.30	7.94	8.37	8.65	8.88	8.84	9.20	10.02	10.39	10.70	10.10	10.30	9.16
1916	9.33	9.27	8.61	8.30	8.56	7.97	7.75	8.53	9.03	8.85	8.61	8.71	8.76
1917	8.69	9.04	9.04	9.43	9.58	10.14	9.90	10.60	10.53	10.09	10.13	9.67	9.66
1918	9.88	10.04	9.91	9.38	9.65	10.07	10.48	10.64	11.18	12.13	11.79	10.88	10.40
1919	11.34	12.34	14.90	15.23	16.68	16.60	19.57	21.43	21.80	22.40	20.42	19.41	16.97
1920	16.03	14.89	13.35	12.25	10.24	9.95	9.01	9.31	8.71	8.97	8.73	7.89	11.74
1921	8.51	8.53	8.33	8.09	7.63	7.39	8.45	7.50	9.00	8.89	8.48	9.00	8.22
1922	7.74	8.00	7.94	8.50	9.45	9.58	9.96	10.56	10.44	10.59	10.57	10.25	9.36
1923	10.38	9.20	10.75	10.21	10.19	10.43	10.51	11.17	11.41	11.39	11.11	10.63	10.63
1924	10.99	10.74	10.39	10.16	10.33	10.52	11.05	11.72	12.73	12.00	10.99	11.41	10.62
1925	9.88	10.51	10.30	10.65	9.87	9.51	9.48	9.82	9.94	9.92	10.22	9.79	9.99
1926	9.37	9.17	8.94	9.42	9.48	10.12	10.33	10.50	11.04	10.63	10.62	10.17	9.45
1927	9.62	9.69	9.78	9.98	9.74	9.55	9.74	10.11	10.35	10.52	10.91	10.24	9.87
1928	10.38	10.25	10.71	11.96	12.69								

Bureau of Agricultural Economics.   Based on returns from special price reporters.

[1] Straight crop year average until 1924.   Weighted average based on monthly movement.

TABLE 334.—*Clover seed: Estimated price per bushel, received by producers, United States, 1910–1928*

Year beginning September	Sept. 15	Oct. 15	Nov. 15	Dec. 15	Jan. 15	Feb. 15	Mar. 15	Apr. 15	May 15	June 15	July 15	Aug. 15	Weighted av.
	Dolls.	Dolls.	Dolls.	Dolls.	Dolls.	Dolls.	Dolls.	Dolls.	Dolls.	Dolls.	Dolls.	Dolls.	Dolls.
Average:													
1910–1913	8.79	8.71	8.62	8.82	9.14	9.74	10.01	10.19	9.97	9.56	9.34	9.40	9.25
1914–1920	13.84	13.87	14.00	14.23	14.76	15.57	16.08	16.44	15.73	14.76	14.44	13.92	14.80
1921–1925	11.15	11.86	12.14	12.85	13.31	13.97	14.68	14.60	14.40	13.56	13.44	12.82	13.09
1910	8.27	8.13	7.70	7.94	8.27	8.37	8.56	8.79	8.74	8.80	8.83	9.65	8.30
1911	10.19	10.33	10.37	10.62	10.89	12.22	12.89	12.91	12.53	11.69	10.64	9.80	11.25
1912	9.39	9.37	9.06	9.00	9.41	10.28	10.42	11.00	10.74	9.77	9.78	9.37	9.71
1913	7.31	7.00	7.33	7.70	7.99	8.07	8.17	8.06	7.87	7.96	8.12	8.76	7.75
1914	9.10	8.24	8.02	8.12	8.51	8.60	8.55	8.36	8.14	7.90	7.96	7.94	8.41
1915	8.49	9.70	9.67	10.01	10.27	10.47	10.76	10.58	9.98	9.47	9.15	9.12	9.98
1916	8.65	8.54	9.20	9.40	9.69	9.87	10.32	10.41	10.40	10.29	10.50	10.53	9.54
1917	10.89	11.92	12.91	13.53	14.48	16.46	17.49	17.86	16.58	15.88	14.71	15.20	14.48
1918	16.61	19.01	20.03	20.67	21.55	21.79	22.61	24.81	24.48	23.37	23.25	24.33	21.01
1919	25.38	26.47	26.53	27.63	28.06	31.21	31.88	32.23	29.84	26.21	25.52	19.97	28.34
1920	17.77	13.18	11.64	10.28	10.82	10.61	10.98	10.80	10.71	10.20	10.00	10.37	11.81
1921	10.25	10.21	10.09	10.38	10.69	11.88	13.00	13.13	12.84	11.60	11.00	9.88	11.14
1922	8.85	9.66	10.18	10.88	11.16	11.52	11.71	11.48	11.20	10.84	10.94	10.46	10.71
1923	11.07	12.20	12.18	12.22	12.51	12.67	13.04	13.09	13.07	12.72	12.42	12.09	12.38
1924	12.15	12.80	13.42	15.31	16.17	16.95	18.19	17.40	16.82	15.48	15.67	16.83	15.35
1925	13.42	14.42	14.85	15.48	16.04	16.83	17.45	17.88	18.08	17.16	17.17	16.83	15.87
1926	16.63	17.21	17.85	17.89	19.07	20.18	21.16	22.75	22.45	22.07	20.69	17.94	19.06
1927	16.78	15.67	15.07	15.33	15.97	16.37	16.90	16.92	17.04	16.89	16.42	15.90	16.11
1928	16.26	16.49	16.68	16.81									

Bureau of Agricultural Economics. Based on returns from special price reporters.

TABLE 335.—*Timothy seed: Estimated price per bushel, received by producers, United States, 1910–1928*

Year beginning August	Aug. 15	Sept. 15	Oct. 15	Nov. 15	Dec. 15	Jan. 15	Feb. 15	Mar. 15	Apr. 15	May 15	June 15	July 15	Weighted av.
	Dolls.	Dolls.	Dolls.	Dolls.	Dolls.	Dolls.	Dolls.	Dolls.	Dolls.	Dolls.	Dolls.	Dolls.	Dolls.
Average:													
1910–1913	3.91	3.66	3.72	3.72	3.68	3.74	3.92	4.07	4.12	4.14	3.98	3.92	3.82
1914–1920	3.35	3.21	3.29	3.25	3.30	3.49	3.57	3.69	3.69	3.80	3.66	3.61	3.39
1921–1925	2.82	2.79	2.93	2.85	2.98	3.11	3.19	3.24	3.27	3.20	3.13	3.13	2.97
1910		3.77	4.03	4.08	4.11	4.12	4.51	4.93	5.17	5.24	5.24	5.48	4.28
1911	6.52	6.65	6.91	6.90	6.72	6.99	7.26	7.33	7.27	7.16	6.68	5.96	6.87
1912	3.20	2.09	1.95	1.82	1.79	1.79	1.78	1.72	1.74	1.76	1.77	1.94	2.01
1913	2.01	2.13	2.02	2.08	2.10	2.07	2.12	2.30	2.28	2.38	2.23	2.32	2.13
1914	2.43	2.46	2.34	2.34	2.18	2.63	2.66	2.78	2.69	2.75	2.65	2.57	2.49
1915	2.56	2.62	2.72	2.91	2.86	3.05	3.19	3.28	3.51	3.33	3.26	3.08	2.89
1916	2.36	2.22	2.27	2.25	2.31	2.44	2.46	2.70	2.76	3.09	3.09	3.04	2.42
1917	3.23	3.31	3.61	3.25	3.37	3.57	3.78	3.84	3.74	3.84	3.56	3.67	3.50
1918	3.87	3.79	4.08	4.26	4.21	4.34	4.51	4.54	4.69	5.05	4.63	4.49	4.19
1919	4.58	4.55	4.78	4.67	4.98	5.35	5.62	5.61	5.63	5.61	5.46	5.44	4.98
1920	4.44	3.52	3.25	3.09	3.16	3.04	2.75	2.97	2.84	2.90	2.99	2.98	3.29
1921	2.71	2.31	2.70	2.41	2.57	2.70	2.82	2.95	3.11	3.21	2.81	2.53	2.64
1922	2.20	2.28	2.48	2.49	2.69	3.06	3.08	3.00	2.99	2.87	2.92	3.16	2.60
1923	2.63	3.01	3.12	3.15	3.19	3.37	3.56	3.60	3.54	3.48	3.44	3.23	3.19
1924	3.20	3.12	3.16	2.88	3.03	3.04	3.15	3.24	3.10	3.05	3.47		3.33
1925	3.36	3.21	3.21	3.31	3.41	3.38	3.56	3.51	3.47	3.36	3.41	3.26	3.33
1926	2.68	2.55	2.61	2.46	2.58	2.62	2.70	2.69	2.76	2.69	2.76	2.58	2.61
1927	2.06	1.66	1.58	1.61	1.73	1.78	1.92	1.86	1.88	1.96	2.08	2.07	1.77
1928	1.86	1.91	2.08	2.20	2.20								

Bureau of Agricultural Economics. Based on returns from special price reporters.

NOTE.—A table similar to Table 321, 1927 Yearbook, is omitted.

TABLE 336.—*Alfalfa seed: Average wholesale selling price per 100 pounds at Kansas City and Minneapolis, 1920–1928*

Year	Kansas City						Minneapolis					
	Jan.	Feb.	Mar.	Apr.	May	Av.	Jan.	Feb.	Mar.	Apr.	May	Av.
	Dolls.	Dolls.	Dolls.	Dolls.	Dolls.	Dolls.	Dolls.	Dolls.	Dolls.	Dolls.	Dolls.	Dolls.
Av. 1921–1925	19.68	19.82	20.26	20.71	20.78	20.25	21.11	21.12	21.34	22.07	22.03	21.53
1920	42.00	42.00	40.25	39.00	37.60	40.17	45.60	46.00	44.90	41.65	38.30	43.29
1921	18.50	18.00	18.40	18.50	18.15	18.31	19.00	19.00	19.40	21.40	21.00	19.96
1922	16.90	18.00	18.50	17.90	18.50	17.96	19.00	19.50	19.50	19.80	20.25	19.61
1923	19.50	19.50	19.50	20.65	21.00	20.03	21.25	21.00	20.50	20.75	21.00	20.90
1924	21.50	21.50	23.30	23.00	23.00	22.26	22.50	22.50	23.90	24.90	24.80	23.72
1925	22.00	22.10	22.60	23.50	23.25	22.69	23.80	23.60	23.40	23.50	23.10	23.48
1926	20.00	20.00	20.00	21.00	21.00	20.40	19.00	19.62	20.50	20.50	20.50	20.02
1927	19.50	20.00	20.00	20.00	20.00	19.90	21.00	21.00	20.62	20.88	20.50	20.80
1928	21.50	22.00	21.50	22.00	22.00	21.80	21.62	22.00	21.62	21.50	21.50	21.65

Bureau of Agricultural Economics. Compiled from weekly reports to the bureau from seedsmen in the various markets. These prices are the average wholesale selling prices for high-quality seed.

TABLE 337.—*Red-clover seed: Average wholesale selling price per 100 pounds at Chicago and Toledo, 1920–1928*

Year	Chicago						Toledo					
	Jan.	Feb.	Mar.	Apr.	May	Av.	Jan.	Feb.	Mar.	Apr.	May	Av.
	Dolls.	Dolls.	Dolls.	Dolls.	Dolls.	Dolls.	Dolls.	Dolls.	Dolls.	Dolls.	Dolls.	Dolls.
Av. 1921–1925	24.66	24.52	24.45	23.20	22.17	23.80	24.42	23.58	23.46	22.24	21.81	23.10
1920	55.20	57.00	56.30	50.25	43.20	52.39	57.25	58.50	57.45	49.70	43.50	53.28
1921	21.25	18.05	20.80	19.95	18.55	19.72	21.20	18.30	20.90	21.20	22.80	20.88
1922	22.20	24.55	25.45	23.35	21.95	23.50	23.30	25.40	26.60	23.60	22.90	24.36
1923	22.55	22.45	20.60	19.70	19.35	20.93	22.45	22.30	20.85	19.65	18.80	20.81
1924	23.10	21.55	21.10	19.00	19.00	20.87	22.45	20.50	19.75	18.70	18.40	19.96
1925	34.20	36.00	34.30	33.40	32.00	33.98	32.70	31.40	29.20	28.05	26.15	29.50
1926	32.17	33.50	34.69	34.00	34.00	33.67	26.25	25.41	25.01	23.92	24.70	25.06
1927	38.60	42.31	45.00	44.25	42.38	42.51						
1928	32.50	30.65	30.08	30.22	29.70	30.63						

Bureau of Agricultural Economics. Compiled from weekly reports to the bureau from seedsmen in the various markets. These prices are the average wholesale selling prices for high-quality seed.

TABLE 338.—*Alsike-clover seed: Average wholesale selling price per 100 pounds at Chicago and Toledo, 1920–1928*

Year	Chicago						Toledo					
	Jan.	Feb.	Mar.	Apr.	May	Av.	Jan.	Feb.	Mar.	Apr.	May	Av.
	Dolls.	Dolls.	Dolls.	Dolls.	Dolls.	Dolls.	Dolls.	Dolls.	Dolls.	Dolls.	Dolls.	Dolls.
Av. 1921–1925	19.53	19.20	19.29	19.20	18.83	19.21	20.31	20.12	20.01	19.91	19.96	20.06
1920	55.80	57.50	58.00	53.25	43.20	53.55	57.70	58.60	59.30	52.60	42.50	54.14
1921	25.65	22.40	22.45	21.60	19.50	22.32	26.60	25.45	25.15	23.10	22.50	24.56
1922	18.20	19.25	19.00	17.30	17.30	18.21	19.35	20.70	19.90	18.80	18.95	19.54
1923	16.50	16.50	16.50	16.45	16.35	16.46	17.90	17.60	17.50	17.50	17.40	17.58
1924	15.55	15.45	15.45	15.90	16.00	15.67	15.55	15.40	14.80	15.25	16.15	15.43
1925	21.75	22.40	23.05	24.75	25.00	23.39	22.15	21.45	22.70	24.90	24.80	23.20
1926	26.08	27.25	27.88	28.19	28.38	27.56	27.22	27.82	28.35	28.35	28.35	28.02
1927	36.01	37.94	39.44	38.71	34.56	37.33						
1928	28.35	28.06	27.80	27.70	27.09	27.80						

Bureau of Agricultural Economics. Compiled from weekly reports to the bureau from seedsmen in the various markets. These prices are the average wholesale selling prices for high-quality seed.

TABLE 339.—*Timothy seed: Average wholesale selling price per 100 pounds at Chicago and St. Louis, 1920–1928*

Year	Chicago						St. Louis					
	Jan.	Feb.	Mar.	Apr.	May	Av.	Jan.	Feb.	Mar.	Apr.	May	Av.
	Dolls.	Dolls.	Dolls.	Dolls.	Dolls.	Dolls.	Dolls.	Dolls.	Dolls.	Dolls.	Dolls.	Dolls.
Av. 1921–1925__	7.25	7.15	7.07	6.93	6.94	7.07	7.54	7.42	7.18	7.15	7.13	7.28
1920_____	13.50	13.90	13.30	12.65	12.30	13.13	14.05	14.75	13.65	12.80	12.50	13.55
1921_____	7.10	6.50	6.40	6.40	6.45	6.57	7.50	7.00	6.60	6.95	7.15	7.04
1922_____	7.05	7.30	7.30	6.60	6.70	6.99	7.00	7.30	7.00	6.45	6.35	6.82
1923_____	7.00	7.00	7.05	7.05	7.00	7.02	7.50	7.30	7.15	7.25	7.25	7.29
1924_____	8.15	8.25	8.10	7.75	7.55	7.96	8.45	8.45	8.25	8.20	8.00	8.27
1925_____	6.95	6.70	6.50	6.85	7.00	6.80	7.25	7.05	6.90	6.90	6.90	7.00
1926_____	8.10	8.10	7.99	7.78	7.75	7.94	8.33	8.12	8.00	8.06	8.00	8.10
1927_____	6.08	6.08	5.86	5.98	5.98	6.00	6.30	6.00	6.00	6.00	6.00	6.05
1928_____	4.75	4.55	4.32	4.75	5.30	4.73	4.69	4.75	4.75	5.00	5.19	4.88

Bureau of Agricultural Economics. Compiled from weekly reports to the bureau from seedsmen in the various markets. These prices are the average wholesale selling prices for high-quality seed.

TABLE 340.—*Sweet-clover seed: Average wholesale price per 100 pounds at Chicago and Minneapolis, 1920–1928*

Year	Chicago						Minneapolis					
	Jan.	Feb.	Mar.	Apr.	May	Av.	Jan.	Feb.	Mar.	Apr.	May	Av.
	Dolls.	Dolls.	Dolls.	Dolls.	Dolls.	Dolls.	Dolls.	Dolls.	Dolls.	Dolls.	Dolls.	Dolls.
1920_____	31.80	34.75	34.70	30.00	25.00	31.25	33.30	36.25	36.50	32.25	29.00	33.46
1921_____	9.65	8.75	9.00	8.60	8.05	8.81	10.65	10.00	10.00	9.60	9.00	9.85
1922_____	7.80	8.40	8.50	8.20	8.25	8.23	8.00	8.25	8.50	8.90	9.00	8.53
1923_____	11.50	11.50	11.75	11.90	11.75	11.68	12.40	12.00	12.40	13.00	12.25	12.41
1924_____	14.50	14.40	14.40	15.45	15.75	14.90	15.00	15.00	15.40	15.90	15.10	15.28
1925_____	12.40	12.94	12.75	12.31	11.75	12.43	13.00	13.00	12.75	11.94	11.00	12.34
1926_____	9.13	9.68	10.04	10.12	10.25	9.84	9.00	9.46	9.89	9.96	10.00	9.66
1927_____	14.09	13.90	13.82	12.82	11.54	13.23	14.38	14.31	14.00	13.00	12.50	13.64
1928_____	8.66	8.72	8.35	8.34	8.31	8.48	8.75	8.65	8.44	8.46	8.38	8.54

Bureau of Agricultural Economics. Compiled from weekly reports to the bureau from seedsmen in the various markets. These prices are the average wholesale selling prices for high-quality seed.

TABLE 341.—*Tobacco, unmanufactured: Acreage, production, value, exports, etc., United States, 1890–1928*

Year	Acreage	Average yield per acre	Production	Price per pound received by producers Dec. 1	Farm value, Dec. 1	Domestic exports, year beginning July 1 [1]	Imports, year beginning July 1 [1]	Net exports, year beginning July 1 [1][2]
	Acres	*Lbs.*	*1,000 lbs.*	*Cts.*	*1,000 dolls.*	*1,000 lbs.*	*1,000 lbs.*	*1,000 lbs.*
1890	722,028	722.8	518,683	8.3	42,846	249,233	23,255	227,254
1891	738,216	747.4	551,777	8.5	47,074	255,432	21,989	234,587
1892	720,189	687.6	495,209	9.3	46,044	266,083	28,110	239,153
1893	702,952	687.1	483,024	8.1	39,155	290,685	19,663	272,983
1894	523,103	777.4	406,678	6.8	27,761	300,992	26,668	276,223
1895	633,950	775.4	491,544	7.2	35,574	295,539	32,925	266,317
1896	594,749	677.6	403,004	6.0	24,258	314,932	13,805	302,847
1897	[3] 945,604	646.0	610,860			263,020	10,477	254,907
1898	[3] 933,868	748.0	698,533			283,613	14,036	271,559
1899	*1,101,460*	*788.1*	*868,113*					
1899	1,101,500	728.5	802,397	7.1	57,273	344,656	19,620	326,939
1900	1,046,427	778.2	814,345	6.6	53,661	315,788	26,851	290,915
1901	1,039,199	788.0	818,953	7.1	58,283	301,007	29,429	273,770
1902	1,030,734	797.3	821,824	7.0	57,564	368,184	34,017	337,902
1903	1,037,735	786.3	815,972	6.8	55,515	311,972	31,163	286,335
1904	806,409	819.0	660,461	8.1	53,383	334,302	33,288	304,694
1905	776,112	815.6	633,034	8.5	53,519	312,227	41,126	273,912
1906	796,099	857.2	682,429	10.0	68,233	340,743	40,899	302,506
1907	820,800	850.5	698,126	10.2	71,411	330,813	35,005	297,657
1908	875,425	820.2	718,061	10.3	74,130	287,901	43,123	247,155
1909	*1,294,911*	*815.3*	*1,055,765*					
1909	1,294,900	814.8	1,055,133	10.1	106,374	357,196	46,838	313,085
1910	1,366,100	807.7	1,103,415	9.3	102,142	355,327	48,203	309,171
1911	1,013,000	893.7	905,109	9.4	85,210	379,845	54,740	327,199
1912	1,226,000	785.5	962,855	10.8	104,063	418,797	67,977	353,575
1913	1,216,160	784.3	953,734	12.8	122,481	449,750	61,175	391,196
1914	1,223,500	845.7	1,034,679	9.8	101,411	348,346	45,809	306,426
1915	1,369,900	775.4	1,062,237	9.1	96,281	443,293	48,078	400,624
1916	1,413,400	816.0	1,153,278	14.7	169,672	411,599	49,105	370,987
1917	1,517,800	823.1	1,249,276	24.0	300,449	289,171	86,991	211,962
1918	1,647,100	873.7	1,439,071	28.0	402,264	629,288	83,951	577,323
1919	*1,864,080*	*736.6*	*1,372,993*					
1919	1,951,000	751.1	1,465,481	39.0	570,868	648,038	94,005	570,858
1920	1,960,000	807.3	1,582,225	21.2	335,675	506,526	58,923	456,477
1921	1,427,000	749.6	1,069,693	19.9	212,728	463,389	65,225	403,492
1922	1,695,000	735.6	1,246,837	23.2	289,248	454,364	73,796	386,213
1923	1,877,000	807.2	1,515,110	19.9	301,096	597,630	52,380	550,404
1924	*1,537,843*	*719.4*	*1,106,340*					
1924	1,705,800	733.6	1,251,343	20.7	259,139	430,702	75,131	357,478
1925	1,757,300	783.3	1,376,628	18.2	250,774	537,240	68,281	470,651
1926	1,656,400	783.6	1,297,889	18.2	236,702	516,402	91,089	426,545
1927	1,584,900	764.7	1,211,909	21.2	2o6,882	489,982	79,172	413,225
1928 [4]	1,912,100	718.3	1,373,501	18.5	254,322			

Bureau of Agricultural Economics. Italic figures are census returns, other acreage, yield, and production figures are estimates by the crop-reporting board. See p. 970, 1927 Yearbook, for data for earlier years.

[1] Compiled from Commerce and Navigation of the United States, 1890–1917; Foreign Commerce and Navigation of the United States, 1918; Monthly Summary of Foreign Commerce of the United States, June issues 1919–1926, January and June issues, 1927–1928, and official records of the Bureau of Foreign and Domestic Commerce.
[2] Total exports (domestic exports plus foreign) minus reexports.
[3] Revised on basis of 1899.
[4] Preliminary.

TABLE 342.—*Tobacco by types: Acreage, yield per acre, production, and value, 1927 and 1928*

Class and type	United type No.	Acreage		Yield per acre		Production		Average price per pound		Farm value	
		1927	1928	1927	1928	1927	1928	1927	1928	1927	1928
		Acres	*Acres*	*Pounds*	*Pounds*	*1,000 pounds*	*1,000 pounds*	*Cents*	*Cents*	*1,000 dollars*	*1,000 dollars*
Flue-cured types:											
Virginia	11	134,300	143,300	693	560	93,100	80,240	20.2	19.5	18,805	15,647
North Carolina	11–13	657,000	727,000	737	651	484,183	473,230	22.0	19.5	106,520	92,280
South Carolina	13	104,000	148,000	737	556	76,648	82,288	20.5	12.7	15,713	10,451
Georgia	14	80,500	121,000	720	685	57,960	82,867	18.9	12.8	15,954	10,607
Florida	14	5,400	7,900	757	609	4,053	4,811	19.0	12.0	770	577
Total		981,200	1,147,200	730	631	715,944	723,436	21.3	17.9	152,763	129,562
Dark-fired types:											
Virginia	21	33,200	31,000	800	704	26,560	21,824	9.9	10.0	2,629	2,182
Clarksville and Hopkinsville, Ky	22	35,000	47,500	690	758	24,150	36,000	16.8	14.0	4,057	5,040
Clarksville and Hopkinsville, Tenn	22	50,800	61,000	765	760	38,850	46,300	19.5	15.5	7,576	7,176
Total, Clarksville and Hopkinsville	22	85,800	108,500	734	759	63,000	82,300	18.5	14.8	11,633	12,216
Paducah, Ky	23	21,200	34,400	750	756	15,900	26,000	12.2	12.3	1,940	3,198
Paducah, Tenn	23	3,000	6,400	700	735	2,100	4,700	12.2	12.2	256	573
Total	23	24,200	40,800	744	752	18,000	30,700	12.2	12.3	2,196	3,771
Henderson stemming	24	6,500	7,500	646	733	4,200	5,500	9.7	11.2	407	616
Total		149,700	187,800	747	747	111,760	140,324	15.1	13.4	16,865	18,785
Air-cured types:											
Burley—											
Virginia	31	2,800	4,000	1,004	1,000	2,811	4,000	23.9	29.0	672	1,160
West Virginia	31	4,500	6,800	775	750	3,488	5,100	24.5	27.0	855	1,377
North Carolina	31	2,000	3,000	750	667	1,500	2,000	22.0	25.0	330	500
Ohio	31	9,000	15,800	850	856	7,307	13,526	24.8	30.0	1,812	4,058
Indiana	31	7,300	11,200	760	820	5,548	9,184	24.0	28.0	1,332	2,572
Missouri	31	4,000	4,400	1,100	1,100	4,400	4,400	22.0	27.0	968	1,188
Kentucky	31	185,700	250,100	701	788	130,109	197,000	26.3	30.0	34,219	59,100
Tennessee	31	30,800	41,000	812	835	25,034	34,259	26.3	29.0	6,584	9,935
Total		246,100	335,900	732	802	180,197	269,469	26.0	29.6	46,772	79,890

	No.										
Export—											
Maryland	32	32,000	31,000	818	700	26,176	21,700	23.0	18.0	6,020	3,906
Ohio	32	800	1,000	1,063	1,000	850	1,000	18.0	16.0	153	160
Total		32,800	32,000	824	709	27,026	22,700	22.8	17.9	6,173	4,066
One Sucker—											
Indiana	35	1,000	2,300	756	820	756	1,886	8.0	11.0	60	207
Kentucky	35	13,900	22,000	705	773	9,800	17,000	11.0	13.2	1,078	2,244
Tennessee	35	3,200	4,000	781	800	2,500	3,200	9.8	14.0	245	448
Total		18,100	28,300	721	780	13,056	22,086	10.6	13.1	1,383	2,899
Green River	36	27,900	33,200	649	738	18,110	24,500	9.1	11.0	1,648	2,695
Virginia sun-cured	37	6,700	7,700	821	719	5,500	5,536	13.1	8.5	721	471
Total air-cured types		331,600	437,100	735	788	243,889	344,291	23.2	26.1	56,697	90,021
Miscellaneous, Louisiana		1,000	1,000	400	405	400	405	45.0	45.0	180	182
Cigar types:											
Filler types—											
Pennsylvania Seed Leaf	41	33,400	36,350	1,362	1,341	45,480	48,740	12.9	13.9	5,867	6,775
Miami Valley	42–44	20,400	25,200	812	757	16,575	19,078	15.6	17.0	2,586	3,240
Georgia-Florida Sumatra	45	1,600	1,600	1,203	1,062	1,925	1,700	20.0	20.0	385	340
Total		55,400	63,150	1,155	1,097	63,980	69,518	13.8	14.9	8,838	10,355
Binder types—											
Broadleaf	51	11,450	10,800	1,309	1,311	14,993	14,162	21.0	21.0	3,149	2,974
Havana Seed, Connecticut Valley	52	11,800	13,350	1,324	1,309	15,622	17,474	23.4	24.0	3,663	4,194
Havana Seed, New York	53	800	800	1,200	1,275	960	1,020	18.0	19.3	173	197
Havana Seed, Pennsylvania	53	600	650	1,287	1,292	760	840	18.0	19.3	137	162
Wisconsin, southern	54	18,800	22,000	1,060	1,342	19,745	29,525	14.0	17.0	2,764	5,019
Wisconsin, northern	55	12,200	15,000	1,100	1,300	13,425	19,500	19.0	20.0	2,551	3,900
Minnesota	55		1,000		1,200		1,200		12.0		144
Total		55,650	63,600	1,177	1,316	65,505	83,721	19.0	19.8	12,437	16,590
Wrapper types—											
Connecticut Valley shade	61	7,100	8,000	900	867	6,390	6,936	105.0	100.0	6,709	6,936
Georgia-Florida	62	2,800	3,800	1,206	1,113	3,378	4,230	65.0	55.0	2,196	2,326
Connecticut Valley primed Havana Seed	65	450	450	1,473	1,422	663	640	30.0	30.0	199	192
Total		10,350	12,250	1,008	964	10,431	11,806	87.3	80.1	9,104	9,454
Total, cigar types		121,400	139,000	1,153	1,185	139,916	165,045	21.7	22.1	30,379	36,399
Total, all types		1,584,900	1,912,100	764.7	718.3	1,211,909	1,373,501	21.2	20.0	256,884	274,949

Bureau of Agricultural Economics. Estimates of the crop-reporting board.

NOTE.—1928 figures subject to revision on basis of later information.

TABLE 343.—Tobacco: Acreage, yield per acre, and production in specified countries, average 1909–1913, annual 1925–1928

Country	Acreage (1,000 acres)					Yield per acre (Pounds)					Production (1,000 pounds)				
	Average 1909–13[1]	1925	1926	1927	1928	Average 1909–13[1]	1925	1926	1927	1928	Average 1909–13[1]	1925	1926	1927	1928
North America, Central America, and West Indies:															
Canada	[2]15	28	33	44	43	[2]1,004	1,045	873	998	952	[2]15,066	29,266	28,824	43,917	40,956
United States	1,223	1,757	1,656	1,585	1,912	814	783	784	765	718	996,087	1,376,628	1,297,889	1,211,909	1,373,501
Mexico		39	39	38			528	510	524		29,096	20,578	19,889	19,912	
Cuba											[3]73,666	54,720	85,440	57,360	[3]60,000
Dominican Republic[5]											[4]25,417	45,000	17,500	35,000	25,000
Porto Rico[6]	[6]19	34	50	85	40	[7]459	688	700	549	550	[7]10,828	23,402	35,000	46,664	22,000
Europe:															
Sweden	[2]1	1	1	1		[2]1,744	1,731	1,687	1,232		[2]1,744	1,731	1,687	1,232	
Belgium	10	8	7	8	7	2,077	2,116	1,879	2,004	1,910	20,767	16,925	13,153	16,035	13,389
France	41	40	39	39		1,307	1,733	1,480	1,625		53,598	69,308	57,733	63,380	
Italy	20	98	97	92		1,148	942	1,008	719		22,964	92,373	97,796	66,173	
Germany	32	20	16	23		2,004	2,095	1,986	1,914		64,116	41,902	31,769	44,013	
Czechoslovakia	8	13	14	13	15	1,183	1,166	1,038	1,293	955	9,467	15,160	14,532	16,805	14,330
Hungary	93	38	52	58		1,203	992	1,101	1,190		111,883	37,687	57,266	69,004	
Yugoslavia	35	37	36	27	21	912	719	908	543		31,920	26,590	32,681	14,671	
Greece	[7]76	199	201	228		[7]776	674	673	611		[7]58,987	134,099	135,319	139,367	
Bulgaria	36	127	78	60	63	651	694	768	797	366	23,435	88,115	59,941	47,829	125,662
Rumania	[6]53	91	75	76	68	[6]909	397	537	585		[6]48,174	36,089	40,306	44,430	23,038
Poland	8	2	4	7	10	1,091	938	1,282	1,507	1,389	8,725	1,875	5,129	10,550	13,890
Russia	167	212	213	228		1,378	1,789	1,814	1,529		230,142	379,191	386,466	348,547	
North Africa:															
Algeria	25	81	81	72	1	948	811	804	812	1,102	23,709	65,655	65,152	58,454	1,102
Tunis	(8)	1	1	1		1,209	1,212	863	1,197		266	1,212	863	1,197	
French West Africa		33	[9]44	[10]51	[13]6		301	[9]251	250			9,921	12,787	[11]12,743	
Asia:															
Turkey		151	159	194			885	799	765		[3][7]88,180	133,686	127,038	148,384	[8]80,000
Palestine		3	2	2			498	623	688			1,495	1,246	1,376	
Syria and Lebanon	[7][12]2	8	7	7	[13]6	[7][12]180	780	731	520	467	[7][12]360	6,239	5,114	3,638	[13]2,804
India	1,057	1,250	1,266	[13]1,171											
Ceylon	14	19	13	13					692					8,995	
Indo-China[14]			19	19					600			8,995	8,995	11,392	
Japan	72	91	90	91	92	1,302	1,576	1,539	1,626	1,600	93,717	143,425	138,482	147,986	147,159
Chosen (Korea)	51	31	34	41		500	723	649	882		25,510	22,423	22,050	36,147	
Taiwan (Formosa)	1	2	2			1,120	1,102	1,101			1,120	2,204	2,202		
Siam	26	23	22	22			810	722	440			18,631	15,885	9,686	
Philippine Islands	154	177	185	207		422	522	542	535			92,377	100,196	110,707	
South America:															
Colombia	[13]17	39	41			[15]842	708	694			[15]14,322	27,606	28,434		
Brazil		161	203	185			785	770	810		[7]110,000	126,411	156,386	149,913	

Country	Acreage, 1,000 acres					Production, 1,000 pounds				
Bolivia	[4]2	3	11	12	11	806	753	[6]4,493	8,862	9,039
Chile	[3]3	1	5	5	1	534	534	3,137	10,519	9,153
Uruguay		1	1	1	1	1,046	431	431	534	534
Argentina	27	22	13	23		956	1,845	12,635	21,030	23,979
South Africa:										
French Equatorial Africa	11	13	16	16		75	69	62	895	991
Belgian Congo [13]	1	1				573	573		573	573
Union of South Africa [16]	26	34	30	46		[7]787	588	618	[7]14,961	15,275	20,000	24,000
Southern Rhodesia [17]	14	30				[6]498	404	639	304	[6]1,992	5,660	19,175	14,000
Northern Rhodesia [17]	5	7					414	429		2,071	3,006
Nyasaland	39	44	44			[8]	281	416	3,017	10,978	18,292
Madagascar	14	15	16			[4]467	1,091	1,274	1,080	[4]4,203	15,278	19,114	17,275
Oceania:										
Dutch East Indies, Java, and Madura [18]	65	68	67			1,451	1,311	1,265	1,249	94,302	85,227	85,999	83,687
Sumatra (East coast) [19]	46	47	49			1,068	851	940	827	46,278	39,593	44,202	40,545
Australia	3	2					751	417		2,135	2,252	834	[3]41,958
Total all countries reporting acreage or production, all years	1,479	2,189	2,044	1,997	2,272	1,470,886	2,103,106	2,003,312	1,963,548	1,981,965
Estimated world total exclusive of India and China [20]	2,671,000					3,551,000	3,510,000	3,485,000		

Bureau of Agricultural Economics. Official sources and International Institute of Agriculture except as otherwise stated. Figures refer to the crop harvested in the calendar year in the Northern Hemisphere and the succeeding harvest in the Southern Hemisphere except in the Dutch East Indies, where the harvest is usually completed within the calendar year.

[1] Averages for European countries are estimates for territory within present boundaries.
[2] 2-year average.
[3] Unofficial source.
[4] 3-year average.
[5] Unofficial estimate of the export crop.
[6] 4-year average.
[7] 1-year only.
[8] Less than 500 acres.
[9] French Guinea only.
[10] About 4,000 acres additional in French Soudan.
[11] About 900,000 pounds additional in French Soudan.
[12] Greater Lebanon only.
[13] Incomplete. Not included in total.
[14] Exclusive of Tonking.
[15] Year 1915.
[16] Exclusive of native production which amounted to 1,240,000 pounds.
[17] European cultivation only.
[18] Estate production including some tobacco purchased from natives. Figures for native production not available. Total production of the islands is roughly estimated, on the basis of average yield of 311 pounds per acre for the native net production, at 192,000,000 pounds in 1925, 194,000,000 pounds in 1926, and 212,000,000 pounds in 1927.
[19] Estate production of wrapper-leaf tobacco. Small quantities of low-grade tobacco also produced.
[20] No data are available for the total production of India and China. The acreage devoted to tobacco in India would indicate a production next to that of the United States in the size of the crop. China is also of considerable importance.

TABLE 344.—*Tobacco: Acreage and production, by States, average 1921–1925, annual 1926–1928*

State	Acreage				Production			
	Average, 1921–1925	1926	1927	1928 [1]	Average, 1921–1925	1926	1927	1928 [1]
	Acres	Acres	Acres	Acres	1,000 lbs.	1,000 lbs.	1,000 lbs.	1,000 lbs.
Massachusetts	9,120	6,500	7,100	7,600	11,750	9,412	8,683	9,462
Connecticut	29,280	21,900	23,700	25,000	38,812	29,346	28,985	29,750
New York	2,000	1,200	800	800	2,304	1,320	960	1,020
Pennsylvania	43,400	33,000	34,000	37,000	58,386	43,560	46,240	49,580
Ohio	49,020	44,200	30,100	41,800	42,889	37,389	24,652	33,440
Indiana	19,200	14,700	8,400	13,700	17,054	12,995	6,384	11,234
Wisconsin	40,400	29,000	31,000	37,000	46,980	33,350	33,170	49,025
Minnesota				1,000				1,200
Missouri	4,800	5,000	4,000	4,000	4,442	4,750	4,400	4,400
Maryland	28,200	31,000	32,000	31,000	21,833	26,040	26,176	21,700
Virginia	198,000	189,000	177,000	186,000	133,092	137,032	127,971	111,600
West Virginia	8,600	10,000	4,500	6,800	6,868	8,500	3,488	5,100
North Carolina	516,800	565,000	659,000	730,000	316,277	386,460	485,683	475,230
South Carolina	91,400	85,000	104,000	148,000	59,178	56,780	76,648	82,288
Georgia	29,800	51,900	81,500	122,300	20,879	39,963	59,088	84,387
Florida	4,800	6,000	8,800	12,000	4,303	5,808	8,228	9,221
Kentucky	490,400	426,000	290,200	394,700	411,920	358,568	202,269	306,000
Tennessee	126,200	136,000	87,800	112,400	94,501	106,216	68,484	88,459
Louisiana	1,000	1,000	1,000	1,000	454	400	400	405
United States	1,692,420	1,656,400	1,584,900	1,912,100	1,291,922	1,297,889	1,211,909	1,373,501

Bureau of Agricultural Economics. Estimates of the crop-reporting board.

[1] Preliminary.

TABLE 345.—*Tobacco: Yield per acre and estimated price per pound, December 1, by States, average 1914–1920, 1921–1925, annual 1924–1928*

State	Yield per acre							Estimated price per pound						
	Av., 1914–1920	Av., 1921–1925	1924	1925	1926	1927	1928	Av., 1914–1920	Av., 1921–1925	1924	1925	1926	1927	1928
	Lbs.	Lbs.	Lbs.	Lbs.	Lbs.	Lbs.	Lbs.	Cts.	Cts.	Cts.	Cts.	Cts.	Cts.	Cts.
Massachusetts	1,500	1,286	1,340	1,243	1,448	1,223	1,245	31.8	32.1	26.8	16.0	35.0	35.7	34.1
Connecticut	1,528	1,322	1,370	1,352	1,340	1,223	1,190	32.3	35.8	32.3	19.0	35.6	36.6	37.2
New York	1,257	1,152	1,175	1,100	1,100	1,200	1,275	17.7	24.1	22.3	22.0	19.0	18.0	19.3
Pennsylvania	1,401	1,348	1,250	1,400	1,320	1,360	1,340	14.8	15.8	15.7	15.0	10.1	18.4	18.0
Ohio	930	882	705	974	846	819	800	17.4	16.6	19.4	15.0	10.5	13.0	14.0
Indiana	893	888	893	871	884	760	820	17.6	16.1	16.6	18.0	9.7	22.0	20.0
Wisconsin	1,171	1,166	940	1,375	1,150	1,070	1,325	16.7	14.6	13.0	16.5	13.8	16.0	18.0
Minnesota							1,200							12.0
Missouri	984	918	852	815	950	1,100	1,100	22.2	25.8	25.0	27.0	15.0	22.0	22.0
Maryland	783	773	765	823	840	818	700	29.2	22.1	26.9	19.0	23.7	23.0	18.0
Virginia	687	667	650	647	725	723	600	22.6	20.2	21.4	15.6	17.6	17.8	17.2
West Virginia	801	797	775	775	850	775	750	25.4	21.5	21.4	18.2	13.1	24.5	23.0
North Carolina	638	607	577	695	684	737	651	26.9	25.6	25.8	23.0	26.4	22.0	18.5
South Carolina	662	645	485	740	668	737	556	17.5	17.4	17.0	17.0	23.3	20.5	12.7
Georgia	856	652	777	720	770	725	690	33.8	24.7	26.6	15.0	24.0	19.4	13.2
Florida	1,026	931	750	832	968	935	768	41.2	41.3	37.6	31.0	37.8	34.8	29.1
Kentucky	876	839	836	810	842	697	775	18.7	16.9	17.1	16.0	10.6	21.4	19.1
Tennessee	789	749	795	726	781	780	787	15.3	18.4	18.6	17.0	10.5	21.4	22.0
Louisiana	425	454	400	504	400	400	405	42.6	54.0	55.0	55.0	45.0	45.0	45.0
United States	813.2	761.9	733.6	783.3	783.6	764.7	718.3	20.8	20.4	20.7	18.2	18.2	21.2	18.5

Bureau of Agricultural Economics. Estimates of the crop-reporting board.

TABLE 346.—*Tobacco, unmanufactured: United States exports by classes, 1924–1928*

Countries to which exported	Year ended Dec. 31				
	1924	1925	1926	1927	1928
	1,000 pounds	*1,000 pounds*	*1,000 pounds*	*1,000 pounds*	*1,000 pounds*
Bright flue-cured:					
United Kingdom	121,040	131,034	120,564	166,655	162,329
Irish Free State	(1)	481	851	1,266	2,778
China	58,509	78,824	82,669	45,436	159,664
Hong Kong	611	2,239	370	191	625
Australia	17,093	19,638	20,843	17,247	20,050
Canada	11,167	9,445	13,517	13,037	13,440
Japan	11,208	7,741	7,188	9,991	15,241
Germany	16,743	5,988	12,385	12,809	16,327
British India	6,044	4,597	4,445	3,832	6,454
Netherlands	10,968	4,086	6,558	7,189	9,235
Denmark [2]	2,182	3,256	2,081	2,863	1,906
Java and Madura	359	3,016	4,666	9,223	11,684
Poland and Danzig	1,407	2,508	446	4,739	1,498
Belgium	3,109	2,009	1,065	1,625	3,528
Norway	968	825	959	1,454	879
Other countries	4,107	2,592	8,728	4,868	9,260
Total	265,515	278,279	287,335	302,425	434,898
Burley:					
Belgium	1,045	2,295	3,450	5,697	1,924
France	1,096	----------	413	229	149
United Kingdom	1,844	1,399	306	431	833
Irish Free State	(1)	----------	2	----------	1
Portugal	1,396	1,248	1,094	2,362	1,238
Netherlands	795	200	136	3,332	60
Germany	443	33	197	1,618	185
Other countries	779	842	1,131	4,175	2,154
Total	7,398	6,017	6,729	17,844	6,544
Dark fired Kentucky and Tennessee:					
United Kingdom	17,925	22,023	15,734	9,149	6,547
Irish Free State	(1)	626	2,105	455	534
Spain	31,104	15,025	1,479	19,423	13,292
France	33,527	12,253	32,823	20,769	13,465
Germany	17,805	11,471	10,453	10,027	9,280
Italy	15,508	10,212	4,066	385	650
Netherlands	13,852	9,071	13,611	8,039	9,384
British West Africa	5,111	7,059	4,399	5,425	5,195
Poland and Danzig	991	7,015	----------	2,844	4,199
Belgium	12,858	6,639	14,411	13,956	6,079
Denmark [2]	1,098	2,113	1,562	1,735	867
Argentina	2,006	1,886	1,909	3,343	1,337
Switzerland	1,357	1,259	2,305	1,566	1,455
Haiti	1,037	1,235	1,092	254	248
Algeria and Tunis	2,535	1,059	1,600	1,667	1,910
Norway	1,589	1,058	731	684	460
Portugal	2,912	924	1,786	2,531	1,851
Sweden	1,385	532	3,610	2,448	1,171
Other countries	7,628	5,514	6,174	7,309	6,090
Total	170,228	116,974	119,847	112,008	84,014
Dark Virginia:					
United Kingdom	6,527	4,889	3,626	1,357	1,234
Irish Free State	(1)	34	----------	89	223
Germany	3,585	3,621	3,571	5,493	2,966
Netherlands	2,726	2,971	2,341	2,807	1,164
Australia	3,144	2,912	2,480	2,336	780
China	3,947	399	70	1,774	111
Norway	2,285	1,506	2,293	2,020	2,657
Belgium	655	101	528	1,295	1,693
Canada	1,828	363	20	283	356
Sweden	1,916	606	95	256	502
Denmark [2]	629	405	100	142	185
British West Africa	423	368	232	399	296
France	313	232	514	1,631	1,240
Other countries	3,093	1,936	2,520	4,394	5,288
Total	31,071	20,343	18,390	24,276	18,695

[1] Included with United Kingdom.   [2] Denmark and Faroe Islands beginning Jan. 1, 1926.

TABLE 346.—*Tobacco, unmanufactured: United States exports by classes,
1924–1928*—Continued

Countries to which exported	Year ended Dec. 31				
	1924	1925	1926	1927	1928
	1,000 pounds	*1,000 pounds*	*1,000 pounds*	*1,000 pounds*	*1,000 pounds*
Maryland and Ohio export:					
France	6,196	6,404	5,610	8,956	3,547
Netherlands	3,663	2,947	4,595	5,317	3,328
Belgium	618	1,693	528	885	694
Germany	591	297	578	942	426
Italy	645	755	547	1,075	85
Switzerland	365	581	946	1,369	1,487
Other countries	752	1,236	788	1,492	1,380
Total	12,830	13,913	13,592	20,036	10,947
Green River (Pryor) and one sucker leaf:					
United Kingdom	6,093	9,018	3,638	4,633	2,401
Irish Free State	(1)	308	122	135	444
British West Africa	446	2,798	3,122	3,434	2,511
China	2,568	2,286	2,663	1,025	214
Italy			4	52	37
Germany	672		191	84	391
Belgium	2,097	700	1,491	2,488	1,619
Netherlands	2,978	573	178	143	56
Algeria and Tunis	239			3	111
Other French Africa	298	1,032	1,173	812	650
Other countries	694	1,256	1,494	6,390	3,161
Total	16,085	17,971	14,076	19,199	11,595
Other, including cigar leaf and black fat water baler and dark African:					
China	6,641	1,089	302	47	(3)
United Kingdom	6,220	2,714	407	291	221
Irish Free State	(1)	2			2
Germany	4,324	123	383	413	572
Australia	390	7	7	2	34
Belgium	4,059	818	120	348	142
British West Africa	2,859	1,029	640	800	1,236
Netherlands	6,643	956	1,678	657	983
Canada	1,556	1,500	1,513	1,732	1,939
Spain	576			15	3
Mexico	713	1,329	758	179	58
Sweden	1,739		(3)	3	
British India	1,005	(3)	112		
Algeria and Tunis	365	274	59	11	54
Other French Africa	1,515	754	578	560	669
Poland and Danzig	54			83	40
Portugal	125		27		13
Japan	601	(3)	42	5	(3)
France	323	2,650	10,225	4,019	1,002
Argentina	13	385	9		
Philippine Islands	310	443	462	434	474
Other countries	3,397	901	1,478	864	1,272
Total	43,428	14,974	18,800	10,463	8,714
Stems, trimmings, and scrap:					
Germany	9,411	1,775	3,049	597	168
Netherlands	12,730	276	260	226	678
Spain	2,441	1,492		6	25
Sweden	520	1,781	279	1,846	1,931
Belgium	1,337	908	559	167	356
China	861	972	3,169	1,843	3,643
Rumania		595			
France	33	404		39	137
Other countries	1,510	814	993	892	1,505
Total	28,843	9,017	8,309	5,616	8,443
Total tobacco leaf	546,555	468,471	478,769	506,252	575,407

Compiled from Foreign Commerce and Navigation of the United States, 1924–1927 and official records of the Bureau of Foreign and Domestic Commerce, 1928.

¹ Included with United Kingdom.   ² Less than 500 pounds.

TABLE 347.—*Tobacco, unmanufactured: International trade, average 1909–1913 annual 1925–1927*

Country	Average, 1909–1913		Year ended Dec 31					
			1925		1926		1927 preliminary	
	Imports	Exports	Imports	Exports	Imports	Exports	Imports	Exports
PRINCIPAL EXPORTING COUNTRIES	*1,000 pounds*	*1,000 pounds*	*1,000 pounds*	*1,000 pounds*	*1,000 pounds*	*1,000 pounds*	*1,000 pounds*	*1,000 pounds*
United States	52,768	381,127	77,690	477,488	67,906	487,058	102,754	511,868
Dutch East Indies	8,074	163,823	6,148	202,646	10,798	162,729	[1] 14,293	[1] 122,067
Brazil	620	59,991	3,260	76,830	3,624	61,044		70,294
Bulgaria	0	4,310	0	74,179	0	60,546	0	59,391
Philippine Islands	45	26,018	531	38,420	785	33,164	732	53,912
Greece	12,024	18,113			0	120,552	0	116,231
British India	6,538	28,874	[2] 6,693	[2] 33,600	[2] 5,157	[2] 33,306	[2] 5,304	[2] 27,992
Dominican Republic	0	22,395	0	49,075	0	21,504	0	44,750
Cuba	141	38,035	0	33,628	0	40,234		
Algeria	4,776	11,681	6,994	24,625	9,945	39,668	11,283	28,696
Paraguay	0	11,361	0	18,883	0	10,920	0	10,138
Russia	1,084	23,283	0	[3] 3,419	0	[3] 3,131		
Hungary	0	0	4,602	4,664	10,433	3,240	7,886	8,757
Ceylon	0	4,093	2	2,852	3	1,973		1,554
PRINCIPAL IMPORTING COUNTRIES								
Germany	168,437	116	270,225	578	135,346	672	210,918	545
Netherlands	57,218	3,786	67,603	3,230	70,952	3,322	68,159	3,473
United Kingdom	117,956	4,603	176,598	5,011	186,190	3,853	212,538	8,166
Poland	0	0	49,042	31	27,434	2,487	33,663	506
France	63,914	26	119,014	551	98,090	695	87,000	141
Spain	51,026	0	56,448	0	25,758	0		
China	15,113	25,487	73,558	27,495	100,678	28,962	84,400	30,249
Belgium	22,094	33	43,471	105	41,934	49	44,872	140
Czechoslovakia	0	0	45,622	0	41,528	28	37,721	95
Italy	47,732	3,008	25,609	6,980	12,970	6,997	12,383	5,295
Austria	[4] 49,984	[4] 23,192	25,682	1,392	29,235	737	40,034	1,983
Argentina	14,988	41	20,131	279	24,137	356	23,314	588
Egypt	19,005	0	16,709	0	16,370	0	15,929	0
Norway	3,994	0	4,360	0	4,981	0	5,103	0
Canada	17,891	433	14,848	2,516	16,100	5,508	18,679	5,867
Australia[5]	[6] 13,740	0	19,111	36	22,040	0	22,141	0
Switzerland	17,949	47	9,854	1	12,795	0	13,634	214
Japan	1,707	696	9,920	3,684	10,284	1,445	14,120	8,536
Denmark	8,774	100	10,322	0	12,303	7	11,714	1
Sweden	9,772	1	9,022	157	12,830	22	12,794	185
Irish Free State	0	0	9,309	228	7,896	473	10,005	346
Finland	9,597	0	6,686	0	6,557	0	7,107	0
Total, 36 countries	796,961	854,673	1,189,064	1,092,583	1,025,059	1,134,682	1,128,480	1,121,980

Bureau of Agricultural Economics. Official sources. Tobacco comprises leaf, stems, and strippings, but not snuff.

[1] Java and Madura only.
[2] Sea trade only.
[3] Russia: L'Economic de l'Union des R. S. S. 1922–23 and 1923–24 European border only; 1924–25 to 1925–26 Statistical Summary, Russia, includes Europe and Asia, year beginning October.
[4] Average for Austria-Hungary.
[5] Year ended June 30.
[6] Average years ended Dec. 31.

FARM ANIMALS AND ANIMAL PRODUCTS

TABLE 348.—*All cattle and beef cattle: Number and value per head in the United States, 1840, 1850, 1860, 1867–1929*

Year	All cattle on farms[1]	All cattle other than milk cows On farms[2]	Value per head Jan. 1 Old series[3]	New series[3]	Beef cattle on farms and elsewhere	Year	All cattle on farms[1]	All cattle other than milk cows On farms[2]	Value per head Jan. 1 Old series[3]	New series[3]	Beef cattle on farms and elsewhere
	Thousands	*Thousands*	*Dollars*	*Dollars*	*Thousands*		*Thousands*	*Thousands*	*Dollars*	*Dollars*	*Thousands*
1840, June 1[4]	*14,972*					1898	45,105	29,264	20.92		38,000
1850, June 1[4]	*16,078*	*9,693*				1899	43,984	27,994	22.79		37,100
1860, June 1[4]	*23,365*	*14,779*				1900	[5]43,902	27,610	24.97	23.60	37,500
1867	20,080	11,731	15.79		12,600	1900, June 1[4]	*67,720*	*50,584*			
1868	20,634	11,942	15.06		13,600	1900	57,518	41,226			
1869	21,433	12,185	18.73		14,800	1901	60,544	43,710	19.93	18.83	37,700
1870, June 1[4]	*22,501*	*13,566*				1902	62,215	45,518	18.76	17.73	36,400
1870	25,484	15,388	18.87		20,000	1903	63,788	46,677	18.45	17.44	35,600
1871	26,235	16,212	20.78		21,000	1904	64,137	46,717	16.32	15.42	33,800
1872	26,694	16,390	18.12		21,100	1905	64,003	46,431	15.15	14.32	33,300
1873	26,990	16,414	18.06		20,900	1906	62,872	43,078	15.85	14.98	34,800
1874	26,923	16,218	17.55		20,500	1907	62,373	41,405	17.10	16.16	37,900
1875	27,220	16,313	16.91		20,400	1908	60,794	39,600	16.89	15.96	35,900
1876	27,870	16,785	17.00		20,800	1909	59,634	37,914	17.49	16.53	34,400
1877	29,217	17,956	15.99		22,200	1910, April 15[4]	*61,803*	*41,178*			
1878	30,523	19,223	16.72		23,800	1910	57,940	37,315	19.07	18.02	32,000
1879	33,234	21,408	15.38		26,400	1911	56,219	35,396	20.54	19.41	30,500
1880, June 1[4]	*34,932*	*22,489*				1912	55,022	34,323	21.20	20.03	28,300
1880	33,258	21,231	16.10		25,900	1913	55,833	35,336	26.36	24.91	27,400
1881	33,308	20,939	17.33		24,900	1914	58,737	38,000	31.13	29.42	27,200
1882	35,892	23,280	19.89		27,600	1915	62,532	41,270	33.38	31.54	28,300
1883	41,172	28,046	21.81		33,400	1916	66,394	44,286	33.53	31.69	30,900
1884	42,547	29,046	23.52		34,100	1917	69,533	46,639	35.88	33.91	32,600
1885	43,772	29,867	23.25		34,400	1918	71,229	47,919	40.88	38.63	35,100
1886	45,510	31,275	21.17		35,700	1919	70,261	46,984	44.22	41.79	36,200
1887	48,034	33,512	19.79		37,900	1920, Jan. 1[4]	*66,689*	*46,984*			
1888	49,234	34,378	17.79		38,300	1920	68,871	47,444	42.18	39.93	35,778
1889	50,331	35,032	17.05		38,300	1921	67,184	45,776	30.60	28.92	34,755
1890, June 1[4]	*50,246*	*33,734*				1922	67,264	45,476	23.15	21.87	34,805
1890	52,802	36,849	15.21		39,800	1923	66,156	44,093	24.81	23.44	32,291
1891	52,896	36,876	14.76		40,900	1924	64,507	42,252	24.44	23.07	30,972
1892	54,067	37,651	15.16		42,000	1925, Jan. 1	*60,760*	*43,115*			
1893	52,378	35,954	15.24		40,500	1925	61,996	39,515	23.94	22.58	29,418
1894	53,095	36,608	14.66		43,700	1926	59,122	36,934	27.50	26.42	27,267
1895	50,869	34,364	14.06		41,700	1927	56,832	35,031	29.87	28.28	25,167
1896	48,223	32,085	15.86		39,700	1928	55,681	33,857	38.95	36.38	23,939
1897	46,450	30,508	16.65		38,700	1929	[6]55,751	33,931		43.12	23,833

Data for cattle on farms and value per head, except as otherwise stated, from records of the Bureau o Agricultural Economics as of Jan. 1.

[1] Figures 1900–1919 are tentative revised estimates of the Bureau of Agricultural Economics as first published in 1927 yearbook. Prior to 1900 estimates for each 10-year period represent an index of anima changes applied to census as base on first report after census data were available.

[2] Figures for the period 1900–1929 are obtained by subtracting the estimates of "milk cows on farms" shown on Table — from the revised estimates of "all cattle on farms" shown on this table.

[3] For 1926–1929, new series is average value by age and sex classification weighted by numbers in each class 1900–1925 is old series adjusted on basis average relationship between two series, 1926–1928. Old serie was weighted average by age groups only.

[4] Italic figures for census years represent classification of cattle as follows: 1840 reported as "neat cattle," 1880 and 1890 exclude an estimated number of unenumerated cattle on ranges as follows: 1880, 3,750,02; 1890, 6,285,220. No estimate made prior to 1880. Figures for censuses prior to 1900 were nominally exclu sive of calves, though some calves may have been included. 1900, 1910, and 1920 include calves. 1850–189 exclude working oxen as follows: 1850, 1,700,744; 1860, 2,254,911; 1870, 1,319,271; 1880, 993,841; 1890, 1,117,49 Not separately reported after 1890.

[5] Original estimate of the Bureau of Agricultural Economics.

[6] Preliminary.

TABLE 349.—*All cattle and calves, including cows and heifers kept for milk: Estimated number on farms and value per head, by States, January 1, 1925–1929*

State and division	Number, Jan. 1					Value per head, Jan. 1 [1]				
	1925	1926	1927	1928	1929 [2]	1925	1926	1927	1928	1929 [2]
	Thousands	Thousands	Thousands	Thousands	Thousands	Dollars	Dollars	Dollars	Dollars	Dollars
Maine	241	235	233	224	228	40.70	50.40	51.20	57.80	66.60
New Hampshire	125	119	113	112	115	45.70	56.90	64.10	79.30	88.70
Vermont	403	401	403	412	422	44.10	53.80	60.70	76.70	78.60
Massachusetts	195	187	181	181	183	62.40	71.50	81.60	102.80	106.60
Rhode Island	27	27	27	27	28	71.00	76.50	89.30	109.30	118.50
Connecticut	160	151	144	142	144	64.00	74.20	82.70	109.90	118.30
New York	1,852	1,824	1,808	1,865	1,895	52.10	66.70	74.20	90.60	100.40
New Jersey	154	154	157	161	163	64.80	81.40	87.90	102.40	114.20
Pennsylvania	1,318	1,298	1,289	1,332	1,372	48.30	58.40	60.70	77.10	86.90
North Atlantic	4,475	4,396	4,355	4,456	4,550	50.89	62.99	68.63	85.00	93.76
Ohio	1,675	1,616	1,608	1,624	1,640	43.50	49.20	52.50	64.30	71.30
Indiana	1,282	1,282	1,320	1,294	1,307	42.50	46.00	48.90	59.00	67.00
Illinois	2,345	2,251	2,161	1,967	1,967	41.80	48.20	50.00	59.30	69.00
Michigan	1,406	1,420	1,406	1,406	1,406	45.20	49.90	54.00	66.50	77.00
Wisconsin	3,035	3,005	2,960	2,920	2,862	42.60	53.20	57.20	69.90	79.20
Minnesota	2,853	2,853	2,710	2,710	2,737	35.70	42.20	43.00	54.40	63.40
Iowa	4,372	4,241	4,029	3,720	3,845	37.50	42.40	44.00	54.20	61.90
Missouri	2,442	2,369	2,174	2,109	2,109	30.70	33.20	37.40	47.60	57.80
North Dakota	1,341	1,260	1,100	1,067	1,078	27.30	30.80	33.30	43.70	53.80
South Dakota	2,074	1,919	1,635	1,570	1,570	29.30	33.20	35.40	47.90	55.90
Nebraska	3,314	3,191	2,819	2,766	2,766	31.40	35.80	37.00	49.40	59.30
Kansas	3,068	2,853	2,568	2,696	2,831	29.50	34.40	35.70	45.20	53.70
North Central	29,207	28,260	26,490	25,849	26,118	35.98	41.47	44.10	55.13	63.95
Delaware	46	48	48	49	50	50.00	53.60	60.30	77.60	93.70
Maryland	273	270	265	275	283	48.30	54.30	54.70	69.90	79.50
Virginia	827	744	707	729	765	31.20	32.40	35.00	47.10	54.80
West Virginia	591	526	473	482	496	30.90	33.30	36.30	52.00	60.40
North Carolina	545	523	486	496	506	28.50	30.00	34.80	44.70	48.30
South Carolina	341	300	280	275	272	24.30	23.90	28.40	34.10	38.90
Georgia	938	854	854	837	820	17.30	19.10	20.50	27.00	31.10
Florida	656	630	592	533	480	16.50	17.50	17.00	17.60	23.40
South Atlantic	4,217	3,895	3,705	3,676	3,672	26.18	28.00	30.15	39.70	46.52
Kentucky	938	910	910	955	955	26.80	30.60	35.40	46.90	52.00
Tennessee	1,023	921	912	958	977	20.80	23.70	28.50	38.90	43.60
Alabama	840	739	746	709	702	16.10	17.70	20.50	27.80	32.40
Mississippi	938	845	853	879	835	14.20	18.20	18.90	25.80	30.10
Arkansas	837	795	795	772	772	15.20	17.90	20.60	29.90	34.20
Louisiana	720	648	616	579	585	17.80	19.20	20.70	23.70	31.90
Oklahoma	1,695	1,610	1,723	1,723	1,723	21.10	25.40	30.90	39.70	45.20
Texas	6,275	5,900	5,841	5,607	5,607	20.60	21.40	27.20	37.60	42.20
South Central	13,266	12,368	12,396	12,182	12,156	19.89	21.98	26.68	36.16	41.12
Montana	1,340	1,280	1,114	1,114	1,103	28.70	31.10	33.00	46.00	57.90
Idaho	650	624	605	588	570	28.50	36.90	41.00	48.60	57.20
Wyoming	795	787	771	764	764	27.90	34.40	37.60	49.00	62.10
Colorado	1,465	1,377	1,418	1,317	1,317	26.00	32.00	36.20	46.70	55.30
New Mexico	1,290	1,213	1,189	1,070	1,017	21.50	27.00	29.20	38.90	46.50
Arizona	1,069	863	794	675	540	24.30	31.50	32.70	40.00	48.80
Utah	507	482	472	460	460	26.40	35.90	37.30	45.60	57.50
Nevada	419	385	350	332	315	24.10	36.20	35.80	46.40	59.80
Washington	582	558	530	530	541	43.70	44.40	50.00	58.20	72.40
Oregon	796	716	687	673	673	34.40	38.60	40.00	49.50	60.10
California	1,918	1,918	1,956	1,995	1,955	41.90	46.80	47.70	53.70	64.50
Far Western	10,831	10,203	9,886	9,518	9,255	30.25	35.98	38.44	47.79	58.49
United States	61,996	59,122	56,832	55,681	55,751	31.95	37.16	40.29	51.10	59.35

Bureau of Agricultural Economics. Estimates of the crop-reporting board.

[1] Sum of total value of subgroups (classified by age and sex), divided by total number and rounded to nearest dime for States. Division and United States averages not rounded. State figures are new weighted value series not comparable to State figures previously published.
[2] Preliminary.

TABLE 350.—*Cattle: Number in countries having 150,000 or over, average 1909–1913 and 1921–1925, annual 1926–1928*

Country	Month of estimate	Average, 1909–1913 [1]	Average, 1921–1925 [1]	1926	1927	1928 Preliminary
NORTH AND CENTRAL AMERICA AND WEST INDIES		*Thousands*	*Thousands*	*Thousands*	*Thousands*	*Thousands*
Canada	June	6,551	9,588	8,571	9,172	8,793
United States	January	56,750	65,421	59,122	56,832	55,681
Mexico	June	[2] [3] 5,142	[4] 2,492	5,585		
Guatemala	July	557	268	564	310	
Honduras		411	[5] 466			
Salvador		350				
Nicaragua		[3] [6] 252	1,200			
Costa Rica		[3] 333	435			
Cuba	December [7]	2,917	4,841	3,783		4,584
Dominican Republic	May		640			
Porto Rico		[3] 316	279			
Estimated total [8]		74,900	86,600			
SOUTH AMERICA						
Colombia		4,000	7,468	6,500		
Venezuela		2,004	2,689			
Ecuador			[9] 1,500	1,280		
Peru	February		1,198			
Bolivia		734	2,145	2,320		
Chile		1,780	1,957			
Brazil [10]	September	30,705	[3] [11] 34,271			
Uruguay		[3] [6] 8,193	[3] 8,432			
Paraguay	December [7]	4,422	[9] 4,600			
Argentina	do. [7]	[3] [12] 25,867	[3] 37,065		[9] 30,000	
Estimated total [8]		80,300	101,500			
EUROPE						
England	June	5,843	5,824	6,253	6,275	6,026
Scotland	do	1,203	1,171	1,198	1,210	1,209
Ireland	do	4,847	4,996	4,614	4,744	4,863
Norway [13]	do	[14] 1,134	1,128	1,200	1,209	1,221
Sweden	do	3,069	2,418			
Denmark	July	2,717	2,613	2,838	2,913	3,021
Holland	(May–June)	[3] 2,062	[3] 2,063			
Belgium	December [7]	1,925	1,550	1,655	1,712	1,739
France	do. [7]	15,338	13,582	14,373	14,482	14,941
France	do. [7]	15,338	13,582	14,373	14,482	14,941
Spain	do. [7]	2,587	3,457	3,794	3,688	
Portugal		[3] [15] 703	754			
Italy [10]	March–April	6,590	6,812			
Switzerland	April	[3] 1,443	[3] 1,425	[3] 1,587		
Germany	December [7]	18,474	16,786	17,202	17,221	18,011
Austria	December–April	2,356	2,241			
Czechoslovakia	December [7]	4,596	4,377	4,690		
Hungary	April	2,150	1,866	1,847	1,805	1,812
Yugoslavia [10]	January	5,155	4,122	3,738	3,760	
Greece [10]	December [7]	665	742	890	964	947
Bulgaria [10]	do. [7]	2,048	1,928			
Rumania [10]	do. [7]	5,648	5,570	5,219	4,992	4,744
Poland	November	8,664	8,063		8,602	
Lithuania		918	1,149	1,396	1,128	
Latvia	June	912	867	955	967	
Estonia	July	528	508	599	634	
Finland	September	1,605	1,847	1,860	1,872	
Estimated total, excluding Russia [8]		103,300	98,000			
AFRICA						
Morocco		[16] 675	1,711	1,933	1,865	
Algeria	September	1,112	853	946	849	887
Tunis	December [7]	195	459	370	468	501
French West Africa			2,165	2,329	2,402	
French Sudan			1,086	1,030		

[1] Average for 5-year period, if available, otherwise for any year or years within this period except as otherwise stated. In countries having changed boundaries the pre-war figures are estimates for one year only of numbers within present boundaries. For the pre-war average the years immediately preceding the war have been used.

[2] Year 1902. [3] Census. [4] Incomplete. [5] Year 1918. [6] Year 1908.

[7] Estimates reported as of December have been considered as of Jan. 1 of the following year, i. e., figures for number of cattle in France as of Dec. 31, 1925, have been put in the 1926 column.

[8] This total includes interpolations for a few countries not reporting each year and rough estimates for some others.

[9] Unofficial. [10] Buffaloes included. [11] Year 1920. [12] June, 1914. [13] In rural communities only. [14] September. [15] Year 1906.

TABLE 350.—*Cattle: Number in countries having 150,000 or over, average 1909–1913 and 1921–1925, annual 1926–1928*—Continued

Country	Month of estimate	Average, 1909–1913	Average, 1921–1925	1926	1927	1928
		Thousands	*Thousands*	*Thousands*	*Thousands*	*Thousands*
Nigeria			2,805	3,162	2,997	
French Cameroon			354	332	342	
Egypt[10]	September	1,316	1,310	1,485	1,497	
Anglo-Egyptian Sudan			864	1,500	1,501	
Italian Somaliland	February					
Eritrea		[8][11]1,246				
Kenya Colony	March–June	517	553		748	
Uganda		754	3,038	3,413	3,476	
French Equatorial Africa		556	1,109	1,338	1,733	
Belgian Congo			815	881		
Ruanda and Urundi		500	495	465	495	
Portuguese East Africa			700	650	700	
British Southwest Africa			270			
Bechuanaland		206	561	621	585	
Union of South Africa	April–May	[3]5,797	9,342	10,337	10,412	
Basutoland		[3]324	482	518	598	
Rhodesia:		[3]437	604	645	659	
Northern	December[7]	255	289	382	363	416
Southern	do.[7]	509	1,794	2,102	2,189	2,300
Swaziland		60	232	300	320	
Tanganyika Territory		2,095	3,806	4,479	4,706	
Madagascar	February	4,890	7,708			
Estimated total[8]		30,700	46,400			
ASIA						
Turkey, European, and Asiatic[17]		6,438	4,265	5,017	5,135	
Persia			[9]1,000			
Syria and Lebanon			257	243	220	
India:[10]						
British	December–April	128,451	146,759	150,832	151,288	
Native States	do	13,258	33,982	33,276		
Ceylon[10]	December[7]	1,484	1,459	1,457	1,537	1,588
China, including Turkestan and Manchuria		21,997				
Japan	December[7]	1,385	1,440	1,460	1,465	
Chosen	do.[7]	966	1,567	1,591	1,595	1,586
Formosa[10]	do.[7]	473	407	379	381	
French Indo-China[18]		[18]4,616	3,474			
Siam[10]		4,501	6,701	8,230	8,495	
Philippine Islands[10]	December[7]	1,190	2,393	2,622	2,846	3,089
Dutch East Indies:						
Java and Madura[10]	do.[7]	5,091	5,287	5,721	5,680	5,781
Outer possessions[10]	do.[7]	1,640	1,872	1,965	1,952	1,983
Estimated total, excluding Russia[8]		195,100	235,000			
OCEANIA						
Australia	December[7]	11,535	13,789	13,280	11,963	
New Zealand	January	[3]2,020	3,393	3,452	3,258	3,274
Estimated total[8]		13,800	17,400			
Russia[19]	Summer	[18]60,280	57,278	64,439	67,327	
Total countries reported all periods, including Russia:						
Pre-war to 1927 (48)[20]		375,752	415,850	427,667	429,027	
Pre-war to 1928 (23)[20]		138,187	150,203	145,590	144,268	144,413
Estimated world total[8]		558,400	642,200			

Bureau of Agricultural Economics. Compiled from official sources and the International Institute of Agriculture unless otherwise stated.

[3] Census.

[7] Estimates reported as of December have been considered as of Jan. 1 of the following year, i. e., figures for number of cattle in France as of Dec. 31, 1925, have been put in the 1926 column.

[8] This total includes interpolations for a few countries not reporting each year and rough estimates for some others.

[9] Unofficial.   [10] Buffaloes included.   [11] Year 1920.   [16] Year 1915.

[17] In addition there were 832,163 buffaloes in pre-war times, 555,596 in 1926, and 555,433 in 1927.

[18] Year 1916.

[19] Years 1916, 1923–1927 from Soviet Union Review, April, 1928, p. 62.

[20] Comparable totals for the number of countries indicated. Russia is excluded from the totals for the period pre-war to 1928 as no 1928 figures are available for that country.

TABLE 351.—*Cattle and calves: Receipts at principal public stockyards and at all public stockyards, 1909–1928*

Year	Chicago	Denver	East St. Louis	Fort Worth	Kansas City	Omaha	St. Joseph	South St. Paul	Sioux City	Total 9 markets [1]	All other stockyards reporting [2]	Total all stockyards reporting [2]
	Thousands	Thousands	Thousands	Thousands	Thousands	Thousands	Thousands	Thousands	Thousands	Thousands	Thousands	Thousands
1909	3,340	426	1,241	1,197	2,660	1,125	592	497	426	11,504		
1910	3,553	399	1,208	1,071	2,507	1,224	565	604	439	11,570		
1911	3,453	298	1,072	884	2,370	1,174	513	539	487	10,790		
1912	3,158	416	1,200	1,039	2,147	1,017	494	524	431	10,426		
1913	2,888	499	1,100	1,185	2,319	962	450	532	394	10,329		
1914	2,601	443	1,041	1,176	1,957	939	356	585	368	9,466		
1915	2,685	424	992	944	1,963	1,218	441	856	534	10,057	4,496	14,553
1916	3,250	601	1,200	1,081	2,331	1,434	480	941	602	11,920	5,756	17,676
1917	3,820	653	1,405	1,960	2,902	1,720	670	1,197	707	15,034	8,032	23,066
1918	4,448	728	1,509	1,665	3,320	1,993	870	1,430	818	16,781	8,514	25,295
1919	4,253	824	1,473	1,267	3,085	1,975	750	1,491	814	15,932	8,697	24,629
1920	3,849	617	1,254	1,134	2,500	1,603	643	1,373	752	13,725	8,472	22,197
1921	3,540	482	1,077	984	2,469	1,435	558	985	620	12,150	7,637	19,787
1922	3,934	656	1,400	1,084	2,983	1,744	655	1,387	747	14,590	8,628	23,218
1923	3,918	620	1,399	1,258	3,208	1,793	709	1,349	759	15,013	8,198	23,211
1924	3,997	630	1,385	1,392	3,043	1,863	720	1,323	836	15,189	8,506	23,695
1925	3,871	587	1,444	1,370	2,958	1,709	734	1,636	897	15,206	8,861	24,067
1926	4,012	529	1,526	1,185	2,617	1,815	679	1,910	969	15,242	8,630	23,872
1927	3,583	640	1,448	1,286	2,470	1,561	641	1,582	809	14,020	8,743	22,763
1928	3,267	667	1,315	1,211	2,210	1,518	598	1,490	813	13,089	8,389	21,478

Bureau of Agricultural Economics. Prior to 1915 figures compiled from yearbooks of stockyard companies; subsequent figures compiled from data of the livestock and meat reporting service of the bureau. Receipts 1900–1908 are available in 1924 Yearbook, p. 840, Table 435.

[1] Total of the rounded detail figures.   [2] Totals for all stockyards not available prior to 1915.

TABLE 352.—*Cattle and calves: Receipts and stocker and feeder shipments at all public stockyards, 1915–1928*

RECEIPTS, CATTLE

Year	Jan.	Feb.	Mar.	Apr.	May	June	July	Aug.	Sept.	Oct.	Nov.	Dec.	Total
	Thousands	Thousands	Thousands	Thousands	Thousands	Thousands	Thousands	Thousands	Thousands	Thousands	Thousands	Thousands	Thousands
1915	906	664	849	766	875	897	858	1,083	1,355	1,630	1,535	1,024	12,442
1916	1,043	892	976	862	1,078	1,051	948	1,346	1,548	2,134	1,716	1,257	14,851
1917	1,456	1,092	1,069	1,205	1,581	1,454	1,415	1,513	2,044	2,657	2,308	1,670	19,464
1918	1,500	1,284	1,408	1,634	1,432	1,450	1,730	1,697	2,411	2,484	2,340	1,871	21,241
1919	1,795	1,208	1,179	1,318	1,382	1,195	1,511	1,618	1,978	2,526	2,293	1,816	19,819
1920	1,514	1,147	1,207	1,090	1,303	1,343	1,203	1,458	1,789	1,744	1,978	1,084	16,860
1921	1,256	871	1,114	1,043	1,065	1,095	893	1,375	1,361	1,754	1,447	1,036	14,310
1922	1,222	1,044	1,145	1,009	1,358	1,217	1,255	1,608	1,802	2,243	1,846	1,392	17,141
1923	1,395	1,038	1,044	1,159	1,305	1,138	1,357	1,622	1,782	2,141	1,650	1,368	16,999
1924	1,388	1,041	1,084	1,161	1,317	1,172	1,254	1,398	1,938	2,096	1,796	1,528	17,173
1925	1,353	1,056	1,273	1,201	1,139	1,160	1,398	1,632	1,592	2,126	1,717	1,470	17,117
1926	1,314	1,065	1,233	1,146	1,277	1,279	1,279	1,421	1,827	2,030	1,836	1,327	17,034
1927	1,327	1,080	1,172	1,107	1,348	1,185	1,089	1,494	1,482	2,008	1,749	1,217	16,258
1928	1,272	1,045	966	1,119	1,188	1,057	1,158	1,308	1,669	1,913	1,419	1,075	15,189

RECEIPTS, CALVES

1915	123	103	168	221	236	216	181	164	176	188	189	146	2,111
1916	159	162	225	289	307	269	206	238	230	275	261	203	2,824
1917	240	210	260	335	381	305	313	302	313	397	317	229	3,602
1918	228	214	305	411	431	365	398	327	415	381	308	271	4,054
1919	325	245	337	455	454	392	505	421	418	482	410	366	4,810
1920	366	333	456	467	475	536	467	504	506	466	450	311	5,337
1921	388	319	452	450	477	485	451	492	545	557	481	380	5,477
1922	406	372	477	461	520	542	456	541	595	693	581	433	6,077
1923	482	389	458	511	595	492	546	592	512	661	532	442	6,212
1924	500	415	472	590	574	502	544	536	628	640	567	555	6,523
1925	516	473	588	626	597	586	572	612	566	663	565	586	6,950
1926	526	486	578	564	616	592	541	576	570	644	625	519	6,837
1927	504	476	571	567	607	547	457	571	507	627	598	473	6,505
1928	499	471	499	566	610	501	492	521	522	629	544	435	6,289

STOCKER AND FEEDER SHIPMENTS, CATTLE

1915	144	81	129	139	91	73	86	164	349	440	350	195	2,241
1916	211	193	241	255	280	258	167	322	448	653	434	245	3,707
1917	255	207	237	297	393	344	254	323	576	750	709	338	4,683
1918	215	206	306	377	481	386	268	410	588	674	598	355	4,864
1919	353	256	265	378	431	264	227	384	598	815	703	456	5,130
1920	336	230	230	233	311	262	214	308	480	563	540	274	3,981
1921	200	162	228	232	207	203	119	341	375	580	449	230	3,326
1922	223	234	266	223	338	243	216	453	595	792	630	331	4,544
1923	262	199	186	221	288	220	212	459	608	734	577	338	4,304
1924	231	165	167	230	267	191	161	293	556	724	497	288	3,770
1925	194	163	213	254	198	143	234	347	409	681	449	308	3,593
1926	207	164	171	190	201	158	188	240	495	648	521	273	3,456
1927	187	162	182	184	215	157	123	252	385	626	548	278	3,304
1928	215	175	154	236	263	165	175	312	525	704	420	218	3,562

STOCKER AND FEEDER SHIPMENTS, CALVES

1915	3	1	2	3	3	3	2	4	8	14	11	6	60
1916	10	4	9	7	8	6	5	8	16	29	27	11	140
1917	5	6	12	9	8	9	7	8	12	21	20	6	123
1918	7	8	13	8	10	7	6	8	16	30	25	11	149
1919	11	8	12	12	12	8	9	12	14	24	20	14	156
1920	12	10	11	12	11	10	5	6	8	17	13	6	121
1921	5	4	8	6	7	6	3	14	19	42	48	16	178
1922	10	9	16	11	21	17	7	16	35	72	80	26	320
1923	19	12	13	11	12	14	11	21	23	51	47	15	249
1924	11	5	8	9	8	10	9	13	24	39	51	21	208
1925	12	13	17	17	18	11	9	13	18	37	40	25	230
1926	18	13	13	13	17	11	11	12	26	45	49	28	256
1927	18	13	18	20	21	13	10	19	22	49	67	41	311
1928	18	19	19	18	21	19	21	24	38	95	76	35	403

Bureau of Agricultural Economics. Compiled from data of the livestock and meat reporting service of the bureau.

TABLE 353.—*Cattle (excluding calves): Receipts, local slaughter, and stocker and feeder shipments from public stockyards, 1925–1928*

Market	Receipts				Local slaughter				Stocker and feeder shipments			
	1925	1926	1927	1928	1925	1926	1927	1928	1925	1926	1927	1928
	Thousands	Thousands	Thousands	Thousands	Thousands	Thousands	Thousands	Thousands	Thousands	Thousands	Thousands	Thousands
Albany, N. Y	7	9	5	6	1	1	1	1	(1)	(1)	(1)	(1)
Amarillo, Tex.[2]	163	120	172	173	(1)	1	(1)	0	131	87	138	146
Atlanta, Ga	48	43	73	68	26	26	30	26	1	0	(1)	0
Augusta, Ga	7	6	7	7	5	4	6	7	1	1	1	0
Baltimore, Md	163	157	167	142	107	107	103	88	7	7	4	5
Boston, Mass	52	45	40	43	(3)	(3)	(3)	(3)	(3)	(3)	(3)	(3)
Buffalo, N. Y	291	297	299	227	125	138	132	128	13	8	7	2
Chattanooga, Tenn	15	14	12	15	13	13	11	11	2	1	1	3
Cheyenne, Wyo	10	9	16	16	0	0	0	0	0	0	0	0
Chicago, Ill	3,023	3,257	2,872	2,505	2,080	2,244	1,971	1,769	231	240	169	164
Cincinnati, Ohio	260	249	251	231	168	170	170	166	21	19	19	18
Cleveland Ohio	132	117	105	97	120	108	99	94	2	(1)	(1)	(1)
Dallas, Tex	10	10	8	12	10	10	8	11	0	0	0	0
Dayton, Ohio	23	24	24	21	21	22	21	17	0	0	0	0
Denver, Colo	527	473	577	590	135	121	127	131	272	285	302	348
Detroit, Mich	137	134	128	131	121	122	118	116	6	5	3	4
East St. Louis, Ill	1,038	1,074	1,004	900	404	444	397	276	140	110	97	83
El Paso, Tex	123	125	103	197	24	23	24	20	60	82	76	173
Evansville, Ind	23	24	35	37	13	16	27	30	3	4	6	5
Fort Wayne, Ind	7	8	11	15	2	5	7	9	(1)	(1)	2	(1)
Fort Worth, Tex	1,060	944	956	886	509	457	460	381	140	175	201	254
Fostoria, Ohio	4	3	2	3	1	1	1	2	2	1	0	0
Indianapolis, Ind	299	295	285	250	190	231	213	195	45	39	25	27
Jacksonville, Fla	6	7	25	40	5	6	12	14	(1)	(1)	12	10
Jersey City, N. J	220	190	189	225	220	190	189	225	0	0	0	0
Kansas City, Mo	2,409	2,183	2,070	1,859	1,236	1,148	1,055	816	858	706	681	700
Knoxville, Tenn	25	18	21	16	14	15	15	14	4	3	6	2
La Fayette, Ind	8	9	8	6	5	6	5	4	(1)	(1)	1	1
Lancaster, Pa	211	204	195	203	47	50	64	78	82	74	79	72
Laredo, Tex	13	11	9	10	3	4	4	3	9	2	1	1
Los Angeles, Calif	170	198	194	190	160	188	180	178	8	9	13	12
Louisville, Ky	137	118	130	134	71	70	64	63	24	18	27	19
Marion, Ohio	2	2	2	1	1	1	1	(1)	(1)	(1)	(1)	(1)
Memphis, Tenn	19	35	87	61	13	17	22	25	4	11	13	11
Milwaukee, Wis	127	153	157	151	90	104	121	127	8	6	4	4
Montgomery, Ala	58	66	117	90	5	6	7	6	6	8	15	19
Moultrie, Ga	6	8	15	13	4	5	9	8	1	1	2	3
Muncie, Ind	6	6	7	7	4	4	5	5	1	1	1	1
Nashville, Tenn	66	56	52	49	36	36	36	36	11	9	8	3
Newark, N. J	22	22	23	20	18	19	20	18	4	3	3	2
New Orleans, La	88	81	70	74	85	75	53	41	10	12	11	23
New York, N. Y	65	71	52	46	64	71	52	45	0	0	0	0
North Salt Lake, Utah	95	86	60	49	35	35	14	11	12	4	5	6
Ogden, Utah	155	157	154	140	9	11	13	9	61	61	61	58
Oklahoma City, Okla	300	252	295	263	210	170	203	163	54	42	59	52
Omaha, Nebr	1,593	1,692	1,463	1,423	995	1,077	939	848	383	393	346	355
Pasco, Wash	7	4	5	6	0	0	0	0	(1)	0	0	0
Peoria, Ill	27	33	39	34	10	11	12	11	4	6	6	5
Philadelphia, Pa	70	74	68	66	68	72	66	63	0	0	0	0
Pittsburgh, Pa	464	448	405	345	81	80	75	62	0	0	0	0
Portland, Oreg	148	144	132	117	91	84	76	71	10	6	5	6
Pueblo, Colo	108	91	116	126	1	1	2	1	43	35	31	55
Richmond, Va	28	22	20	17	18	15	12	11	1	1	2	2
St. Joseph, Mo	609	563	541	511	425	398	391	306	107	95	98	106
San Antonio, Tex	93	94	98	95	26	38	38	38	45	20	33	37
Seattle, Wash	51	54	54	43	50	53	53	41	(1)	0	0	0
Sioux City, Iowa	845	885	747	750	443	483	421	378	250	278	220	250
Sioux Falls, S. Dak	21	30	30	47	9	11	14	22	10	16	15	23
South St. Paul, Minn	995	1,180	955	917	521	571	527	495	313	408	307	291
South San Francisco, Calif	(4)	(4)	66	71	(4)	(4)	48	42	(4)	(4)	(1)	1
Spokane, Wash	53	47	53	39	30	27	27	24	11	8	10	8
Springfield, Ill	(5)	(5)	4	2	(5)	(5)	1	1	(5)	(5)	(1)	(1)
Springfield, Mo	(5)	(5)	12	16	(5)	(5)	4	5	(5)	(5)	2	3
Springfield, Ohio	5	6	4	1	1	1	2	1	2	2	0	0
Toledo, Ohio	17	19	14	15	7	9	7	6	3	7	5	7
Washington, D. C	19	16	16	13	19	16	16	13	0	0	0	(1)
Wichita, Kans	334	262	326	316	98	86	98	89	177	147	167	182
Discontinued markets	(1)	0	6	0	(1)	0	1	0	0	0	4	0
Total	17,117	17,034	16,258	15,189	9,303	9,528	8,899	7,925	3,593	3,456	3,304	3,562

Bureau of Agricultural Economics. Compiled from data of the livestock and meat reporting service of the bureau. Early data on cattle and calves combined in 1925 Yearbook, pp. 1042–1044. Local slaughter represents number driven out from public stockyards for local slaughter.

[1] Less than 500.
[2] Calves included with cattle.
[3] Disposition of stock not reported.
[4] Not included in report prior to Mar. 1, 1927.
[5] Not included in report prior to Jan. 1, 1927.

TABLE 354.—*Calves (exclusive of cattle): Receipts, local slaughter, and stocker and feeder shipments from public stockyards, 1925–1928*

Market	Receipts				Local slaughter				Stocker and feeder shipments			
	1925	1926	1927	1928	1925	1926	1927	1928	1925	1926	1927	1928
	Thousands	Thousands	Thousands	Thousands	Thousands	Thousands	Thousands	Thousands	Thousands	Thousands	Thousands	Thousands
Atlanta, Ga	7	13	23	14	3	3	7	6	0	0	0	0
Baltimore, Md	83	90	74	56	62	65	44	37	0	(1)	0	0
Boston, Mass	75	64	66	70	(2)	(2)	(2)	(2)	(2)	(2)	(2)	(2)
Buffalo, N. Y	308	297	312	318	87	77	68	57	0	0	0	0
Chicago, Ill	848	755	710	762	789	707	673	735	0	0	0	0
Cincinnati, Ohio	172	164	153	134	78	78	70	74	0	0	(1)	0
Cleveland, Ohio	160	143	123	114	144	133	120	109	0	0	0	0
Denver, Colo	60	56	63	77	40	38	31	29	17	18	30	44
Detroit, Mich	166	172	168	167	142	141	127	129	(1)	(1)	(1)	(1)
East St. Louis, Ill	406	452	444	415	146	88	86	119	3	2	2	1
El Paso, Tex	54	41	33	52	8	6	9	7	26	31	22	44
Evansville, Ind	19	27	30	39	4	4	22	37	(1)	1	2	1
Fort Worth, Tex	310	241	330	325	478	304	382	345	51	47	58	65
Indianapolis, Ind	248	246	203	188	56	64	69	64	0	0	0	0
Jersey City, N. J	525	518	454	416	525	518	454	416	0	0	0	0
Kansas City, Mo	549	433	400	351	395	311	280	213	49	55	75	79
Lancaster, Pa	22	33	22	27	6	6	11	9	0	0	0	0
Los Angeles, Calif	77	69	64	57	75	67	61	54	3	2	3	3
Louisville, Ky	103	98	100	113	31	32	32	29	0	0	0	0
Memphis, Tenn	5	13	20	27	4	9	17	24	(1)	1	1	1
Milwaukee, Wis	461	488	465	421	457	483	462	417	3	4	3	4
Montgomery, Ala	15	29	37	44	1	2	2	2	(1)	(1)	(1)	(1)
Nashville, Tenn	50	53	39	42	20	21	20	18	0	(1)	(1)	0
Newark, N. J	19	19	18	15	19	19	18	15	(1)	0	0	0
New Orleans, La	117	120	114	97	88	91	100	87	0	0	3	9
New York, N. Y	157	156	172	227	157	156	172	227	0	0	0	0
Oklahoma City, Okla	104	88	88	100	96	78	71	82	4	6	7	8
Omaha, Nebr	116	123	98	94	85	88	73	59	0	0	0	29
Peoria, Ill	29	37	38	42	7	8	7	7	2	1	2	2
Philadelphia, Pa	118	109	92	90	117	109	91	89	0	0	0	0
Pittsburgh, Pa	423	470	433	346	98	95	90	75	0	0	0	0
Portland, Oreg	27	21	16	13	21	18	13	11	(1)	(1)	0	0
Richmond, Va	11	15	14	12	9	11	8	8	0	0	(1)	0
South St. Paul, Minn	641	730	627	573	631	723	616	567	9	10	9	7
San Antonio, Tex	73	51	60	52	31	29	30	33	8	3	9	11
Sioux City, Iowa	52	84	62	63	41	39	27	25	10	39	30	35
St. Joseph, Mo	125	116	99	87	104	97	85	73	11	8	9	10
Washington, D. C	17	16	13	12	17	16	13	12	0	0	0	0
Wichita, Kans	83	68	80	78	42	35	37	28	22	15	20	23
All others	115	119	148	159	45	53	53	62	12	13	26	27
Total	6,950	6,837	6,505	6,289	5,159	4,822	4,560	4,384	230	256	311	403

Bureau of Agricultural Economics. Compiled from data of the livestock and meat reporting service of the bureau. Early data on cattle and calves combined in 1925 Yearbook, pp. 1042–1044. Local slaughter represents number driven out from public stockyards for local slaughter.

¹ Less than 500.
² Disposition of stock not reported.

TABLE 355.—*Feeder cattle, inspected: Shipments from public stockyards, 1928*

Origin and destination	January	February	March	April	May	June	July	August	September	October	November	December	Total
	Number	*Number*	*Number*	*Number*	*Number*	*Number*	*Number*	*Number*	*Number*	*Number*	*Number*	*Number*	*Number*
Market origin:													
Chicago, Ill.	7,768	10,430	10,037	6,489	6,782	6,126	6,789	10,631	28,300	42,347	24,103	11,577	171,379
Denver, Colo.	33,101	16,435	12,671	27,867	49,615	15,575	10,472	11,241	32,246	96,113	68,415	28,866	402,617
East St. Louis, Ill.	3,072	3,353	3,750	3,440	3,565	5,054	5,623	12,654	16,835	13,413	11,846	6,959	89,564
Fort Worth, Tex.	10,712	13,348	13,714	28,540	28,390	19,907	21,184	22,028	32,719	40,932	34,935	18,852	285,261
Indianapolis, Ind.	2,074	1,895	2,203	1,471	2,213	2,531	3,369	5,770	3,971	110	3,126	2,156	30,889
Kansas City, Kans.	37,756	35,575	28,659	28,169	28,967	21,170	37,270	78,656	121,119	156,889	75,901	38,959	684,090
Louisville, Ky.	1,103	1,794	1,597	1,597	2,788	2,763	1,744	2,251	3,621	3,371	1,455	520	24,556
Oklahoma City, Okla.	6,008	4,784	6,234	7,865	4,393	3,441	6,132	9,313	10,659	9,421	6,492	5,499	79,841
Omaha, Nebr.	27,453	18,873	15,343	10,374	8,397	5,626	9,963	28,384	72,545	92,122	44,878	20,770	354,728
Sioux City, Iowa	21,054	13,678	12,168	8,224	9,579	10,690	11,716	25,094	55,284	68,921	23,721	14,063	274,192
South St. Joseph, Mo.	3,519	3,947	1,874	1,839	1,628	2,664	3,886	7,824	12,526	12,515	4,755	2,894	59,871
South St. Paul, Minn.	9,545	9,612	8,363	7,180	9,717	9,714	15,301	26,105	38,358	37,683	18,457	8,238	198,273
Wichita, Kans.	18,476	16,326	15,752	19,614	17,773	6,068	7,212	19,979	22,585	30,335	20,371	10,471	204,962
All other inspected	13,785	10,506	13,766	15,635	21,383	26,996	25,734	35,774	48,995	57,354	45,131	29,126	344,185
Total	195,401	160,156	146,108	168,284	190,220	138,325	166,395	295,704	499,763	661,526	383,586	198,940	3,204,408
State destination:													
Colorado	14,627	11,117	5,324	11,612	19,458	10,086	6,244	6,125	14,863	49,823	44,564	16,623	210,466
Illinois	13,258	14,190	9,673	9,668	9,657	11,610	14,251	37,142	61,899	67,909	41,814	18,736	309,807
Indiana	4,864	4,827	6,703	4,131	5,049	6,842	8,842	15,341	20,214	17,395	12,728	6,334	112,565
Iowa	37,268	20,618	17,885	15,129	16,685	17,868	21,297	52,223	110,352	121,576	46,754	21,355	499,010
Kansas	34,010	32,649	28,134	38,629	33,599	12,764	20,428	45,767	59,958	89,159	53,076	29,874	478,047
Kentucky	2,239	3,387	3,028	2,095	7,052	2,700	9,188	5,729	6,999	6,760	2,117	1,201	58,701
Michigan	1,103	1,121	1,895	967	3,841	3,820	3,156	3,303	4,489	8,995	5,069	2,293	41,180
Minnesota	687	1,010	1,589	3,301	1,950	1,342	1,656	3,215	4,312	6,141	4,229	2,305	29,403
Missouri	11,508	11,194	9,693	12,364	7,341	9,579	11,747	24,359	42,102	50,516	25,442	12,883	229,228
Nebraska	41,474	26,143	21,387	24,464	28,918	14,007	24,331	34,021	72,371	107,580	49,344	29,629	473,669
Ohio	2,439	3,721	4,057	2,219	2,407	3,770	6,535	8,725	10,634	13,906	8,360	2,890	69,663
Oklahoma	7,911	7,782	9,601	14,382	11,380	6,109	9,472	16,659	16,982	18,272	15,030	9,907	143,487
Pennsylvania	1,097	782	509	499	550	1,551	2,900	11,673	19,375	15,885	9,461	5,528	69,910
South Dakota	4,304	3,738	3,130	2,431	3,204	3,405	3,070	6,157	10,076	14,647	5,685	4,551	64,398
Texas	8,319	9,425	11,048	11,862	12,197	13,530	12,136	12,457	23,211	33,224	31,511	17,544	196,464
Wisconsin	272	545	634	591	1,448	357	258	328	2,096	2,489	1,943	654	11,615
All other	10,021	8,363	11,818	13,940	24,984	14,390	10,428	12,480	19,830	37,249	26,450	16,533	206,495
Total	195,401	160,156	146,108	168,284	190,220	138,325	166,395	295,704	499,763	661,526	383,586	198,940	3,204,408

Bureau of Agricultural Economics. Compiled from Bureau of Animal Industry inspection records.

TABLE 356.—*Feeder cattle, inspected: Shipments from public stockyards, 1920–1928*

Origin and destination	1920	1921	1922	1923	1924	1925	1926	1927	1928
	Thou-sands	Thou-sands	Thou-sands	Thou-sands	Thou-sands	Thou-sands	Thou-sands	Thou-sands	Thou-sands
Market origin:									
Chicago, Ill_____	339	331	332	275	246	230	245	167	171
Denver, Colo_____	350	237	344	347	346	281	288	328	403
East St. Louis, Ill_____	119	129	184	170	136	113	110	97	90
Fort Worth, Tex_____	309	153	209	162	160	196	233	273	285
Indianapolis, Ind_____	64	51	44	59	49	55	44	29	31
Kansas City, Kans_____	751	708	1,106	1,138	901	825	706	671	684
Louisville, Ky_____	28	37	42	33	21	27	19	34	24
Oklahoma City, Okla____	120	94	91	77	56	78	69	89	80
Omaha, Nebr_____	475	396	566	545	476	390	379	329	355
Sioux City, Iowa_____	219	214	289	281	249	247	300	237	274
South St. Joseph, Mo____	62	64	104	97	85	71	56	51	60
South St. Paul, Minn___	159	144	306	223	173	208	291	203	198
Wichita, Kans_____	109	128	198	198	193	200	152	198	205
All other inspected_____	181	141	224	194	185	177	195	268	344
Total_____	3,285	2,827	4,039	3,799	3,276	3,098	3,087	2,974	3,204
State destination:									
Colorado_____	141	96	126	159	166	131	169	180	210
Illinois_____	294	330	546	500	439	437	435	290	310
Indiana_____	133	136	151	149	137	150	167	136	113
Iowa_____	471	468	841	742	570	487	577	431	499
Kansas_____	440	336	511	511	473	468	378	423	478
Kentucky_____	44	60	54	49	25	41	43	86	59
Michigan_____	55	53	50	46	47	49	41	36	41
Minnesota_____	35	25	18	22	31	36	32	25	29
Missouri_____	310	312	395	418	285	277	255	267	229
Nebraska_____	360	378	659	648	565	427	374	386	474
Ohio_____	102	115	123	113	90	97	102	93	70
Oklahoma_____	186	152	151	115	108	168	159	170	143
Pennsylvania_____	36	39	41	27	24	31	30	31	70
South Dakota_____	54	48	63	70	57	38	32	50	64
Texas_____	307	105	111	95	128	116	151	160	196
Wisconsin_____	42	35	30	23	23	26	29	12	12
All other_____	275	139	169	112	108	119	113	198	207
Total [1]_____	3,285	2,827	4,039	3,799	3,276	3,098	3,087	2,974	3,204

Bureau of Agricultural Economics. Compiled from Bureau of Animal Industry inspection records.

[1] Includes 2 head shipped to Alaska in 1925 and 10 head in 1926.

TABLE 357.—*Cattle, beef: Estimated price per 100 pounds received by producers in the United States, 1910–1928*

Year	Jan.	Feb.	Mar.	Apr.	May	June	July	Aug.	Sept.	Oct.	Nov.	Dec.	Weight-ed av.
	Dolls.	Dolls.	Dolls.	Dolls.	Dolls.	Dolls.	Dolls.	Dolls.	Dolls.	Dolls.	Dolls.	Dolls.	Dolls.
Average:													
1910–1913____	4.79	4.84	5.04	5.30	5.30	5.22	5.07	5.08	5.09	5.09	5.01	5.03	5.07
1914–1920____	7.39	7.57	7.82	8.17	8.30	8.29	8.07	7.92	7.76	7.53	7.35	7.26	7.76
1921–1925____	5.52	5.56	5.85	5.95	5.97	5.91	5.82	5.75	5.58	5.52	5.36	5.34	5.66
1910_____	4.71	4.64	4.87	5.31	5.23	5.20	4.84	4.64	4.65	4.64	4.48	4.45	4.78
1911_____	4.58	4.57	4.66	4.67	4.59	4.43	4.28	4.39	4.43	4.32	4.36	4.37	4.46
1912_____	4.46	4.61	4.75	5.15	5.36	5.23	5.17	5.37	5.35	5.36	5.22	5.33	5.14
1913_____	5.40	5.55	5.88	6.08	6.01	6.02	5.98	5.91	5.92	6.05	5.99	5.96	5.91
1914_____	6.04	6.16	6.28	6.29	6.33	6.32	6.38	6.47	6.38	6.23	6.02	6.01	6.24
1915_____	5.99	5.93	5.92	5.96	6.13	6.20	6.07	6.18	6.06	6.04	5.85	5.75	6.01
1916_____	5.85	5.99	6.37	6.66	6.73	6.91	6.78	6.51	6.55	6.37	6.44	6.56	6.48
1917_____	6.86	7.36	7.91	8.57	8.70	8.65	8.30	8.17	8.40	8.35	8.21	8.24	8.17
1918_____	8.33	8.55	8.85	9.73	10.38	10.40	10.07	9.71	9.63	9.33	9.14	9.28	9.46
1919_____	9.65	10.02	10.34	10.81	10.84	10.20	9.96	9.82	9.02	8.65	8.65	8.63	9.61
1920_____	8.99	8.98	9.08	9.20	8.97	9.32	8.93	8.56	8.29	7.77	7.15	6.36	8.38
1921_____	6.32	6.02	6.36	6.08	5.98	5.65	5.40	5.39	4.98	4.81	4.69	4.62	5.44
1922_____	4.75	5.07	5.46	5.53	5.70	5.84	5.76	5.51	5.44	5.48	5.29	5.28	5.43
1923_____	5.51	5.55	5.62	5.78	5.77	5.82	5.72	5.60	5.70	5.48	5.23	5.26	5.57
1924_____	5.38	5.47	5.63	5.82	5.94	5.79	5.65	5.67	5.53	5.52	5.43	5.35	5.59
1925_____	5.63	5.69	6.18	6.55	6.48	6.46	6.55	6.58	6.27	6.29	6.14	6.18	6.26
1926_____	6.31	6.42	6.65	6.66	6.57	6.56	6.46	6.29	6.48	6.43	6.32	6.42	6.46
1927_____	6.45	6.60	6.82	7.13	7.17	7.08	7.13	7.21	7.42	7.55	8.00	8.32	7.54
1928_____	8.48	8.72	8.81	8.92	9.09	9.10	9.19	9.51	9.96	9.63	9.27	8.94	9.18

Bureau of Agricultural Economics. Based on reports of special price reporters, weighted by States by number of cattle Jan. 1, to secure monthly weighted United States price. United States price weighted by market receipts at principal markets to get yearly weighted price.

TABLE 358.—*Calves, veal: Estimated price per 100 pounds received by producers in the United States, 1910–1928*

Year	Jan.	Feb.	Mar.	Apr.	May	June	July	Aug.	Sept.	Oct.	Nov.	Dec.	Weighted av.
	Dolls.	Dolls.	Dolls.	Dolls.	Dolls.	Dolls.	Dolls.	Dolls.	Dolls.	Dolls.	Dolls.	Dolls.	Dolls.
Average:													
1910–1913	6.51	6.49	6.67	6.52	6.34	6.54	6.48	6.59	6.78	6.80	6.74	6.74	6.60
1914–1920	9.83	9.96	10.06	10.10	9.85	10.02	10.30	10.32	10.51	10.35	10.01	9.89	10.11
1921–1925	8.30	8.53	8.55	7.98	7.80	7.77	7.88	7.94	8.25	8.38	8.00	7.94	8.09
1910	6.41	6.28	6.59	6.54	6.30	6.57	6.37	6.29	6.43	6.41	6.39	5.98	6.42
1911	6.50	6.38	6.48	5.96	5.68	5.72	5.74	5.93	6.11	6.15	6.10	5.98	6.04
1912	6.06	6.07	6.11	6.22	6.23	6.33	6.33	6.62	6.83	6.90	6.77	6.88	6.45
1913	7.06	7.23	7.49	7.38	7.17	7.53	7.46	7.53	7.73	7.72	7.70	7.74	7.48
1914	7.89	7.90	7.92	7.68	7.59	7.69	7.80	8.08	8.06	7.97	7.78	7.61	7.83
1915	7.66	7.62	7.50	7.31	7.35	7.53	7.87	7.75	7.80	7.91	7.69	7.61	7.63
1916	7.67	7.87	8.11	8.00	8.08	8.39	8.54	8.59	8.77	8.59	8.60	8.79	8.35
1917	9.15	9.88	9.94	10.49	10.48	10.60	10.77	10.56	11.08	11.10	10.66	10.98	10.51
1918	11.16	11.17	11.33	11.71	11.62	11.88	12.33	12.22	12.57	12.35	11.94	12.31	11.91
1919	12.39	12.18	12.65	12.78	12.11	12.40	13.38	13.43	13.39	12.87	12.65	12.67	12.76
1920	12.89	13.12	12.98	12.72	11.69	11.68	11.44	11.64	11.88	11.64	10.77	9.27	11.80
1921	9.34	9.08	9.05	7.73	7.55	7.43	7.37	7.31	7.67	7.61	7.20	7.14	7.81
1922	7.23	7.84	7.85	7.26	7.28	7.67	7.49	7.67	8.10	8.17	7.92	7.78	7.68
1923	8.05	8.37	8.20	7.78	7.69	7.66	8.00	8.00	8.34	8.37	7.85	7.75	7.99
1924	8.36	8.51	8.43	8.33	8.14	7.91	7.87	7.88	7.94	8.09	8.22	7.89	8.12
1925	8.50	8.87	9.21	8.80	8.35	8.18	8.65	8.80	9.07	9.52	9.16	9.17	8.85
1926	9.44	9.86	9.75	9.45	8.92	9.65	9.47	9.54	10.06	10.29	9.44	9.44	9.61
1927	9.75	10.10	10.10	9.90	9.37	9.46	9.82	10.37	10.78	11.04	10.67	10.71	10.16
1928	10.88	11.30	11.34	11.18	11.18	11.56	11.87	12.32	13.05	12.62	11.99	11.82	11.79

Bureau of Agricultural Economics. Based on reports of special price reporters. United States annual average weighted by market receipts at principal markets.

TABLE 359.—*Cattle, choice steers for chilled beef: Average price per 100 pounds, by months, Buenos Aires, 1909–1928*

Year	Jan.	Feb.	Mar.	Apr.	May	June	July	Aug.	Sept.	Oct.	Nov.	Dec.	Average
	Dolls.	Dolls.	Dolls.	Dolls.	Dolls.	Dolls.	Dolls.	Dolls.	Dolls.	Dolls.	Dolls.	Dolls.	Dolls.
Averages:													
1909–1913	3.54	3.58	3.72	3.82	3.89	3.90	4.02	4.19	4.34	4.51	4.41	4.00	3.99
1914–1920	6.52	6.59	6.61	6.65	6.59	6.37	6.68	7.07	7.41	5.50	6.93	6.63	6.80
1921–1925	4.48	4.53	4.66	4.49	4.32	4.36	4.55	4.73	4.97	5.02	4.59	4.32	4.59
1909	3.00	3.03	3.07	3.00	3.07	3.20	3.41	3.64	3.95	4.38	4.21	3.81	3.48
1910	3.34	3.30	3.61	3.61	3.54	3.64	3.71	3.98	4.28	4.62	4.32	3.47	3.78
1911	3.57	3.61	3.84	3.81	3.84	3.95	4.15	4.18	4.21	4.18	4.01	3.47	3.90
1912	3.58	3.78	3.62	3.73	3.72	3.71	3.71	4.05	4.15	4.15	4.15	4.08	3.87
1913	4.22	4.19	4.44	4.93	5.26	5.02	5.10	5.12	5.12	5.22	5.35	5.18	4.93
1914	4.96	5.27	5.47	5.69	5.47	5.67	5.73	6.01	6.21	6.29	5.86	5.80	5.70
1915	5.72	5.61	5.56	5.65	5.44	5.54	5.97	6.71	7.45	7.52	7.11	6.59	6.24
1916	6.93	7.15	6.91	6.93	6.84	6.31	6.42	6.54	6.54	7.16	6.95	6.74	6.81
1917	6.69	6.56	6.49	6.31	6.46	6.34	6.37	6.40	6.16	6.54	6.03	5.55	6.32
1918	5.39	5.83	5.88	6.06	6.04	5.98	6.21	7.49	8.41	8.49	8.03	8.06	6.82
1919	7.96	7.75	7.74	7.85	8.03	7.21	8.60	8.92	9.63	9.20	8.25	7.72	8.24
1920	7.96	7.97	8.20	8.06	7.88	7.56	7.47	7.42	7.15	7.27	6.28	5.98	7.43
1921	5.93	5.95	5.71	5.41	4.40	4.10	3.69	4.12	4.74	4.96	4.90	4.39	4.86
1922	4.68	4.53	3.97	3.30	3.31	3.90	4.41	4.50	4.24	3.84	3.30	3.25	3.94
1923	3.08	3.25	3.82	4.06	3.83	3.56	3.62	3.36	3.82	4.10	3.48	3.23	3.60
1924	3.19	3.40	3.61	3.50	3.56	3.76	4.51	4.93	5.15	5.95	5.62	5.42	4.38
1925	5.54	5.54	6.20	6.20	6.51	6.48	6.54	6.72	6.91	6.25	5.66	5.32	6.16
1926	5.40	5.42	5.27	5.39	5.52	5.24	5.58	5.70	5.45	4.63	4.06	4.21	5.16
1927	4.21	4.73	4.63	5.03	4.81	5.15	5.95	6.55	6.84	7.13	6.34	5.81	5.52
1928	6.11	5.86	6.21	6.33	6.65	6.99	6.79	6.60	6.67	6.38	5.61	5.32	6.29

Bureau of Agricultural Economics. Calculated from quotations in the Review of the River Plate. Prices prior to May, 1924, originally quoted on basis of price per head supplemented from 1916 by price per pound of dressed carcass weight. Calculations assume average dressed weight of 730 pounds or live weight of 1,259 pounds. Live-weight quotations per pound from May, 1924. Converted at average monthly rate of exchange as given in Federal Reserve Bulletins.

Table 360.—*Cattle and calves: Monthly average price per 100 pounds, Chicago, 1900–1928*

BEEF STEERS [1]

Year	Jan.	Feb.	Mar.	Apr.	May	June	July	Aug.	Sept.	Oct.	Nov.	Dec.	Average
	Dolls.	Dolls.	Dolls.	Dolls.	Dolls.	Dolls.	Dolls.	Dolls.	Dolls.	Dolls.	Dolls.	Dolls.	Dolls.
1900	5.20	4.85	4.85	4.95	5.10	5.20	5.25	5.40	5.35	5.25	5.15	5.00	5.15
1901	4.85	4.80	4.95	5.15	5.30	5.55	5.10	5.10	5.50	5.45	5.50	5.65	5.25
1902	5.70	5.55	6.05	6.45	6.60	6.95	7.10	7.05	6.65	6.20	5.20	4.80	6.20
1903	4.80	4.60	4.75	4.90	4.80	4.90	4.95	5.00	4.95	4.70	4.45	4.55	4.80
1904	4.65	4.50	4.60	4.65	4.85	5.60	5.40	5.10	5.10	5.20	4.95	4.40	4.95
1905	4.65	4.75	5.00	5.75	5.45	5.25	4.95	5.00	5.05	4.80	4.65	4.75	5.05
1906	5.00	5.05	5.15	5.05	5.20	5.20	5.40	5.45	5.50	5.60	5.60	5.50	5.30
1907	5.60	5.55	5.55	5.65	5.65	6.20	6.40	6.25	6.10	6.10	5.40	5.10	5.80
1908	5.30	5.40	6.00	6.50	6.60	6.90	6.45	6.00	5.95	5.70	5.90	6.00	6.10
1909	6.00	5.85	6.10	6.10	6.45	6.45	6.45	6.70	6.75	6.60	6.45	6.20	6.35
1910	6.20	6.35	7.35	7.55	7.50	7.50	7.10	6.85	6.80	6.60	6.45	6.20	6.80
1911	6.15	6.15	6.20	6.10	5.95	6.05	6.30	6.95	6.80	6.60	6.20	6.00	6.40
1912	6.85	6.60	7.20	7.65	7.95	8.00	7.90	8.50	8.15	7.90	8.10	7.85	7.75
1913	7.80	8.25	8.30	8.15	8.00	8.15	8.25	8.30	8.50	8.15	7.90	8.10	7.85
1914	8.45	8.30	8.35	8.50	8.40	8.60	8.80	8.90	9.10	9.35	9.05	8.60	8.65
1915	8.05	7.50	7.65	7.70	8.35	8.80	9.20	9.05	8.95	8.80	8.70	8.45	8.40
1916	8.35	8.35	8.75	9.10	9.50	9.85	9.85	9.25	9.45	9.40	9.75	10.15	9.40
1917	10.15	10.50	11.25	11.75	11.90	12.15	12.35	12.70	13.10	11.70	11.10	11.40	11.60
1918	12.10	12.00	12.60	14.70	15.40	15.85	16.05	15.75	16.00	14.80	15.05	14.90	14.65
1919	15.80	15.95	16.05	15.85	15.00	13.55	15.60	16.45	16.00	14.80	15.10	14.35	15.50
1920	13.95	13.05	13.10	12.30	12.25	14.95	15.00	14.85	15.05	14.20	12.00	10.10	13.30
1921	8.70	8.20	9.05	8.15	8.25	8.00	8.10	8.50	8.00	8.10	7.40	7.00	8.20
1922	7.23	7.62	7.87	7.90	8.21	8.76	9.42	9.52	9.84	10.23	9.16	8.76	8.65
1923	8.88	8.62	8.70	8.81	9.28	9.74	9.71	10.36	10.18	9.94	9.46	8.96	9.40
1924	8.99	8.81	9.17	9.52	9.59	9.28	9.31	9.53	9.52	9.57	8.90	8.71	9.24
1925	8.97	9.15	9.93	9.99	9.90	9.90	10.34	11.28	11.10	11.04	10.80	10.16	10.16
1926	9.48	9.42	9.42	9.11	9.07	9.51	9.44	9.30	10.00	10.00	9.48	9.72	10.16
1927	9.70	9.81	10.20	10.51	10.68	11.12	11.78	12.02	12.63	13.43	13.57	13.08	11.36
1928	13.67	13.15	12.83	13.01	13.19	13.86	15.11	15.30	15.91	14.61	13.84	12.86	13.91

VEAL CALVES

Year	Jan.	Feb.	Mar.	Apr.	May	June	July	Aug.	Sept.	Oct.	Nov.	Dec.	Average
1901	5.85	5.95	5.75	5.15	5.25	6.00	5.75	5.25	5.85	5.90	5.60	5.00	5.65
1902	6.30	6.75	6.00	5.50	5.75	5.75	6.50	6.75	7.00	6.80	6.60	6.60	6.35
1903	7.10	7.15	6.50	5.75	5.60	6.20	5.65	6.40	6.65	6.40	5.75	4.95	6.20
1904	5.85	6.35	5.65	4.60	4.60	4.90	5.75	5.60	5.60	6.10	6.00	6.00	5.60
1905	6.15	6.50	5.70	5.10	5.25	5.85	5.75	5.90	6.10	6.00	6.00	6.00	5.75
1906	7.00	6.40	6.25	5.60	5.65	5.80	5.60	6.00	6.00	6.00	6.00	6.60	6.25
1907	7.00	6.50	6.60	6.00	6.35	6.15	6.40	6.35	6.50	6.25	7.00	6.00	6.40
1908	6.75	6.60	6.20	5.50	5.60	6.00	6.00	6.75	7.60	7.20	6.50	7.40	6.50
1909	7.60	6.85	7.00	6.30	6.35	6.50	7.00	7.50	7.60	8.10	7.40	8.25	7.10
1910	8.60	8.65	9.00	7.85	7.35	7.85	7.60	7.75	8.50	8.65	7.40	8.25	8.10
1911	8.75	8.40	7.40	6.60	7.25	7.60	7.40	8.00	8.75	8.75	8.35	7.85	7.60
1912	8.75	7.50	8.00	7.40	7.75	8.00	8.75	9.75	11.25	10.00	9.85	10.25	8.75
1913	9.75	9.85	10.50	8.50	9.25	9.75	10.40	11.50	11.25	10.00	9.85	10.25	10.10
1914	11.00	10.75	9.00	8.85	9.50	9.40	10.40	11.50	11.00	11.40	10.50	10.35	10.10
1915	9.85	10.35	10.00	8.40	9.15	9.60	10.25	11.25	11.40	10.65	10.35	8.65	9.90
1916	10.15	10.65	9.65	8.75	10.40	11.25	11.40	12.00	12.40	11.50	11.85	11.75	10.85
1917	13.40	12.65	13.40	12.50	13.25	13.40	13.00	15.15	15.00	14.85	13.50	15.25	13.75
1918	15.35	14.15	15.25	14.50	13.50	15.55	16.70	17.25	18.60	17.10	16.80	16.50	15.75
1919	15.62	15.75	15.01	14.31	14.66	16.37	17.88	17.88	19.62	20.52	18.05	17.60	16.83
1920	17.74	16.73	16.73	14.22	12.12	13.68	13.98	15.08	16.39	14.18	13.74	10.39	14.58
1921	11.49	11.02	10.33	8.12	8.66	8.72	9.73	9.39	10.71	8.68	7.70	7.81	9.36
1922	8.36	9.16	8.26	6.97	8.46	8.89	8.90	10.88	11.92	9.65	8.91	9.42	9.15
1923	10.08	10.63	9.32	8.68	9.51	9.31	10.14	10.36	10.57	9.82	8.15	9.31	9.66
1924	11.08	10.54	9.75	9.03	9.30	8.74	9.48	10.63	10.09	10.10	9.48	9.43	9.66
1925	10.72	11.94	11.24	9.49	9.42	9.56	10.91	11.94	12.18	11.19	10.10	9.02	9.86
1926	12.18	12.43	12.06	9.91	11.04	11.09	11.38	12.46	12.59	11.80	11.09	11.31	11.61
1927	12.20	12.40	11.54	10.90	11.07	11.68	13.32	14.75	15.94	14.42	13.48	13.09	12.90
1928	13.70	15.04	13.75	13.02	13.95	13.24	14.84	16.68	17.36	14.94	14.22	13.94	14.56

Bureau of Agricultural Economics. Prices of beef steers prior to January, 1922, compiled from the Chicago Drovers Journal Yearbook. Subsequent figures are the weighted average price of all grades of beef steers sold out of first hands at Chicago. Veal calf prices prior to January, 1919, compiled from Chicago Drovers Journal Yearbook, and later from data of the livestock and meat reporting service of the bureau.

[1] Western steers not included.

TABLE 361.—*Cattle and calves: Average price per 100 pounds at Chicago and Kansas City, by months, 1928*

CHICAGO

Month	Beef steers						Heifers, 850 pounds up		Cows		Vealers (milk-fed)		Feeder steers, 800 pounds up	
	1,300 to 1,500 pounds, choice	1,100 to 1,300 pounds, choice	950 to 1,100 pounds		800 pounds up									
			Choice	Good	Medium	Common	Choice	Good	Good	Common and medium	Good and choice	Medium	Good and choice	Common and medium
	Dolls.	Dolls.	Dolls.	Dolls.	Dolls.	Dolls.	Dolls.	Dolls.	Dolls.	Dolls.	Dolls.	Dolls.	Dolls.	Dolls.
January	18.02	17.68	17.24	15.18	12.81	10.12	12.66	11.62	9.79	7.59	13.70	11.86	11.42	9.41
February	16.78	16.42	16.01	14.47	12.32	9.99	12.30	11.46	9.41	7.63	15.04	13.24	11.76	9.89
March	15.09	14.86	14.66	13.66	12.27	9.96	12.13	11.12	9.40	7.46	13.75	11.81	11.77	9.99
April	14.62	14.56	14.32	13.53	12.24	10.06	12.36	11.58	9.60	8.24	13.02	10.79	12.04	10.19
May	14.36	14.37	14.40	13.53	12.22	10.49	12.78	11.89	10.06	8.31	13.95	11.69	12.17	10.42
June	14.50	14.63	14.70	13.96	12.72	10.98	13.30	12.17	10.19	8.42	13.24	11.26	12.38	10.62
July	15.86	15.90	15.98	15.03	13.41	10.78	14.18	13.19	10.52	8.37	14.84	12.88	12.51	10.62
August	16.27	16.39	16.48	15.34	13.24	10.52	14.68	13.67	10.67	8.45	16.68	14.27	12.74	10.62
September	17.76	17.78	17.75	16.09	13.77	10.96	15.26	14.18	10.70	8.47	17.36	15.43	13.08	10.72
October	17.18	17.25	17.36	15.58	13.01	10.38	14.35	13.52	10.08	8.05	14.94	13.47	12.16	10.06
November	16.97	17.02	17.17	15.11	12.64	10.22	13.54	12.44	9.71	7.82	14.22	12.51	11.61	10.02
December	16.11	16.15	16.36	14.34	12.16	10.12	12.54	11.62	9.06	7.44	13.94	12.10	11.41	9.86
Average	16.13	16.08	16.04	14.65	12.73	10.38	13.34	12.37	9.93	8.02	14.56	12.61	12.09	10.20

KANSAS CITY

Month														
January	17.37	17.16	16.83	14.74	11.80	8.70	12.24	10.91	9.20	7.41	11.00	9.02	11.27	8.94
February	16.05	15.61	15.34	13.68	11.63	8.86	11.75	10.61	9.09	7.37	12.48	9.69	11.49	9.35
March	14.30	14.06	13.92	12.79	11.35	8.86	11.58	10.55	9.12	7.38	11.34	8.45	11.59	9.37
April	14.00	13.84	13.67	12.82	11.62	9.58	11.72	10.84	9.26	7.68	10.99	8.01	11.61	9.42
May	13.70	13.69	13.77	12.85	11.72	9.97	12.15	11.37	9.54	8.12	12.00	9.00	11.74	9.69
June	13.86	13.96	14.28	13.28	12.02	10.13	12.66	11.70	9.48	8.18	11.69	9.05	11.91	9.91
July	15.35	15.39	15.48	14.47	12.54	10.00	13.67	12.66	9.73	8.02	12.12	9.40	12.38	10.06
August	15.10	15.38	15.75	14.50	12.35	9.66	13.75	12.69	9.64	7.90	12.84	9.75	12.58	10.12
September	16.56	16.69	16.82	14.85	12.33	9.85	14.05	12.94	9.72	8.02	14.12	10.52	12.62	10.07
October	15.99	16.08	16.29	14.11	11.54	9.23	13.69	12.56	9.18	7.66	12.20	9.19	11.87	9.64
November	15.66	15.67	15.92	13.70	11.28	9.02	13.28	12.04	9.25	7.59	12.19	9.58	11.26	9.34
December	15.10	15.22	15.58	13.32	10.88	8.98	12.41	11.34	8.82	7.30	11.85	9.36	11.05	9.17
Average	15.25	15.23	15.30	13.76	11.76	9.40	12.75	11.68	9.34	7.72	12.07	9.25	11.78	9.59

Bureau of Agricultural Economics. Compiled from data of the livestock and meat reporting service of the bureau. Earlier data in 1927 Yearbook, pp. 991–994.

TABLE 362.—*Cattle and calves: Monthly slaughter* [1] *under Federal inspection, 1907–1928*

CATTLE

Year	Jan.	Feb.	Mar.	Apr.	May	June	July	Aug.	Sept.	Oct.	Nov.	Dec.	Total
	Thousands	*Thousands*	*Thousands*	*Thousands*	*Thousands*	*Thousands*	*Thousands*	*Thousands*	*Thousands*	*Thousands*	*Thousands*	*Thousands*	*Thousands*
1907	718	570	555	635	620	588	641	668	696	801	596	546	7,633
1908	643	527	520	463	491	525	563	640	768	821	681	637	7,279
1909	587	490	551	508	536	544	608	652	782	892	799	765	7,714
1910	632	527	599	533	551	621	615	679	796	831	780	644	7,808
1911	626	536	562	499	599	614	591	720	692	828	746	605	7,619
1912	675	515	564	522	563	511	508	632	644	808	691	620	7,253
1913	622	490	484	555	547	556	593	582	656	701	602	590	6,978
1914	585	499	476	474	474	490	505	518	650	744	658	682	6,757
1915	573	466	552	507	534	574	596	590	641	736	702	681	7,153
1916	623	550	597	476	564	648	562	743	791	941	972	844	8,310
1917	823	663	647	654	815	844	784	866	957	1,196	1,099	1,003	10,350
1918	895	785	828	915	782	830	1,020	987	1,143	1,251	1,233	1,160	11,829
1919	1,119	701	640	622	721	644	855	859	855	1,073	1,040	960	10,091
1920	832	631	683	638	626	657	661	686	825	843	859	667	8,609
1921	690	526	621	591	570	640	579	680	689	750	686	586	7,608
1922	642	569	674	590	702	724	697	761	796	884	859	779	8,678
1923	745	634	688	697	762	727	725	821	810	953	846	756	9,163
1924	812	669	665	689	773	670	764	786	870	1,016	952	926	9,593
1925	855	656	736	731	749	732	862	811	866	1,067	861	927	9,853
1926	819	695	786	766	788	852	864	811	971	996	947	887	10,180
1927	786	700	761	742	785	799	743	838	828	895	881	761	9,520
1928	711	666	665	623	723	706	662	717	764	801	762	667	8,467

CALVES

Year	Jan.	Feb.	Mar.	Apr.	May	June	July	Aug.	Sept.	Oct.	Nov.	Dec.	Total
1907	128	99	122	205	224	204	221	206	198	187	126	104	2,024
1908	117	88	137	197	205	211	192	185	187	180	143	116	1,958
1909	135	95	149	200	228	236	213	196	205	205	171	155	2,189
1910	132	117	188	222	252	238	198	206	197	188	168	132	2,238
1911	135	121	180	218	243	232	198	207	184	180	155	128	2,184
1912	152	126	180	245	258	229	201	192	190	193	163	149	2,278
1913	139	118	142	212	205	195	182	149	159	157	124	122	1,902
1914	122	100	145	186	183	187	153	129	130	135	107	119	1,697
1915	109	96	156	199	205	197	162	141	139	148	141	125	1,819
1916	129	143	189	233	267	228	178	207	186	204	217	185	2,367
1917	203	182	212	286	345	277	277	255	272	339	281	216	3,143
1918	210	193	260	351	357	312	355	274	317	306	272	249	3,456
1919	295	210	295	383	391	327	400	319	318	375	344	312	3,969
1920	305	283	390	382	369	431	343	332	348	315	316	245	4,058
1921	282	254	360	366	367	370	324	304	321	309	292	259	3,808
1922	288	279	391	365	401	389	329	345	353	383	348	309	4,182
1923	352	297	368	400	467	388	379	403	338	416	370	324	4,500
1924	373	346	377	466	470	408	421	374	419	473	392	416	4,935
1925	394	378	466	496	481	473	473	439	422	486	398	445	5,353
1926	410	378	464	461	455	480	425	379	408	446	435	410	5,153
1927	397	377	457	454	462	430	355	389	357	413	411	376	4,877
1928	383	374	407	438	473	398	362	369	352	405	378	341	4,680

Bureau of Animal Industry.

[1] The figures include rejected carcasses.

TABLE 363.—*Cattle and calves, slaughter statistics: Source of supply, classification, slaughter costs, weights, and yields, 1923–1928*

CATTLE

Year and month	Source of supply		Sex classification			Average live cost per 100 pounds	Average live weight	Dressed weight as percentage of live weight	By-product yield (on basis of live weight)		
	Stockyards	Other	Bulls and stags	Cows and heifers	Steers				Edible fat [1]	Edible offal	Hides
	Per cent	Per cent	Per cent	Per cent	Per cent	Dollars	Pounds	Per cent	Per cent	Per cent	Per cent
1923	89.86	10.14	4.04	48.06	47.90	6.82	952.89	54.13	3.84	2.80	6.79
1924	90.77	9.23	4.10	49.42	46.48	6.64	949.64	53.50	3.86	2.85	6.80
1925	90.74	9.26	3.38	51.31	45.31	7.11	954.06	53.06	3.61	2.94	6.77
1926	89.80	10.20	3.39	49.73	46.88	7.32	964.06	53.77	3.89	3.05	6.79
1927	89.90	10.10	3.72	49.27	47.01	8.62	945.99	53.57	3.71	3.03	6.84
1928	89.90	10.10	3.88	50.78	45.34	10.59	947.93	53.54	3.92	3.15	6.63
January	90.24	9.76	3.49	57.42	39.09	10.04	941.04	52.92	3.81	3.08	6.96
February	91.42	8.58	2.94	51.14	45.92	10.17	947.87	53.46	3.99	3.15	6.80
March	88.79	11.21	3.16	47.58	49.26	10.38	956.15	54.30	4.19	3.06	6.73
April	89.42	10.58	3.25	44.15	52.60	10.93	954.92	54.96	4.43	3.04	6.72
May	89.24	10.76	4.32	41.14	54.54	11.20	954.99	55.48	4.46	3.10	6.69
June	87.37	12.63	4.71	43.17	52.12	11.41	949.91	55.28	4.36	3.19	6.74
July	89.43	10.57	4.84	44.69	50.47	11.49	952.11	53.95	4.10	3.23	6.52
August	90.45	9.55	4.60	49.09	46.31	11.15	942.05	53.24	3.72	3.20	6.48
September	90.50	9.50	4.27	52.46	43.27	11.06	944.17	52.82	3.58	3.31	6.49
October	90.64	9.36	4.33	59.89	35.78	9.88	939.08	51.87	3.43	3.09	6.52
November	90.74	9.26	3.52	59.48	37.00	9.70	944.27	51.91	3.37	3.19	6.41
December	90.05	9.95	3.14	54.97	41.89	9.78	952.48	52.85	3.68	3.17	6.61

CALVES

Year and month	Source of supply		Average live cost per 100 pounds	Average live weight	Dressed weight as percentage of live weight	By-product yield (on basis of live weight)	
	Stockyards	Other				Edible fat [1]	Edible offal
	Per cent	Per cent	Dollars	Pounds	Per cent	Per cent	Per cent
1923	86.24	13.76	7.86	172.82	57.13	0.75	3.57
1924	87.08	12.92	7.67	176.78	57.28	.75	3.61
1925	87.18	12.82	8.66	176.93	57.51	.71	3.68
1926	85.28	14.72	9.82	176.39	58.52	.66	3.66
1927	84.18	15.82	10.58	175.94	57.31	.75	3.78
1928	85.10	14.90	12.21	175.94	56.14	.79	3.83
January	88.03	11.97	11.42	168.63	56.36	.91	3.59
February	86.21	13.79	12.40	166.69	57.32	.95	3.83
March	84.84	15.16	12.09	151.80	58.04	.86	3.97
April	84.84	15.16	11.88	149.61	56.47	.80	4.08
May	85.31	14.69	12.49	159.35	56.54	.74	3.91
June	82.71	17.29	12.22	172.71	55.93	.73	3.96
July	85.23	14.77	12.44	190.90	54.75	.70	3.90
August	85.73	14.27	12.91	202.21	55.26	.69	3.70
September	85.01	14.99	13.11	207.32	55.58	.77	3.64
October	85.70	14.30	11.84	196.40	55.27	.85	3.60
November	84.60	15.40	11.64	187.91	56.56	.76	3.86
December	82.27	17.73	11.96	172.03	56.40	.93	3.99

Bureau of Agricultural Economics. Compiled from monthly reports to the bureau from packers and slaughterers, whose slaughterings equaled 75 to 85 per cent of total slaughter under Federal inspection.

[1] Unrendered.

TABLE 364.—*Cattle: Slaughter in specified countries, average pre-war, annual, 1914–1927*

Year	Argentina, including chilling, freezing, salting, and canned-meat works [1]	Uruguay, excluding farm [2]	Australia	New Zealand [3]	Canada
	Thousands	Thousands	Thousands	Thousands	Thousands
Average pre-war [4]	1,691	914	1,572	[5]277	1,218
1914	1,589	663	2,092	[5]299	----------
1915	1,641	807	1,578	----------	----------
1916	2,102	798	1,373	389	----------
1917	2,496	1,056	1,345	344	----------
1918	3,292	1,062	1,335	358	----------
1919	2,342	1,061	1,598	417	1,891
1920	1,715	759	1,538	371	1,776
1921	1,550	717	1,649	268	2,017
1922	2,231	1,109	1,907	359	1,899
1923	3,338	1,393	2,049	423	1,850
1924	4,321	1,173	2,505	501	1,864
1925	3,871	1,233	2,434	469	1,921
1926	3,510	1,293	----------	413	1,903
1927	3,718	1,239	----------	----------	2,003

Bureau of Agricultural Economics. Compiled from official sources and cabled reports from agricultural commissioners abroad.

[1] Including municipal and private slaughterhouses, the figures were as follows in thousands—averages, pre-war, 3,272; 1921–1925, 5,961. The numbers killed in freezing and chilling plants alone were as follows in thousands—1925, 3,333; 1926, 3,060; 1927, 3,234; 1928, 2,830.
[2] Slaughtering in freezing and chilling plants alone were as follows in thousands—1925, 651; 1926, 714; 1927, 689.
[3] For years ended March 31 following.
[4] Average for five years immediately preceding war if available, otherwise for any year or years within that period, unless otherwise stated.
[5] Excluding farm slaughter which averaged only 7,493 for the 10 years 1917–1926.

TABLE 365.—*Beef, frozen: Stocks in cold-storage warehouses and meat-packing establishments, United States, 1916–1928*

Year	Jan. 1	Feb. 1	Mar. 1	Apr. 1	May 1	June 1	July 1	Aug. 1	Sept. 1	Oct. 1	Nov. 1	Dec. 1
	1,000 pounds	1,000 pounds	1,000 pounds	1,000 pounds	1,000 pounds	1,000 pounds	1,000 pounds	1,000 pounds	1,000 pounds	1,000 pounds	1,000 pounds	1,000 pounds
Average:												
1916–1920	241,004	232,368	211,860	191,820	155,267	132,130	115,407	117,061	114,596	120,943	149,804	187,302
1921–1925	95,513	92,530	86,432	77,177	64,149	51,252	43,196	34,901	31,011	30,970	42,716	66,881
1916	126,374	132,266	124,954	118,279	90,176	73,025	55,109	58,867	58,303	66,319	92,815	158,148
1917	202,442	190,909	169,793	154,193	118,391	103,007	109,354	108,729	100,453	119,221	179,032	235,664
1918	315,572	292,114	276,114	268,015	212,725	190,084	154,638	180,962	185,144	194,469	224,312	229,668
1919	298,818	294,514	265,293	221,725	184,586	163,913	162,639	159,279	162,069	166,244	184,196	223,311
1920	261,812	252,037	223,145	196,890	170,455	130,619	95,297	77,469	67,010	58,461	68,663	89,718
1921	120,245	119,965	122,402	114,063	100,672	88,836	76,523	66,262	50,204	44,296	49,014	63,188
1922	68,495	61,522	55,785	50,772	45,341	37,548	31,593	27,727	28,210	34,611	47,929	73,027
1923	91,805	89,272	75,604	65,292	54,522	41,207	34,385	24,112	24,625	27,590	43,772	71,024
1924	82,984	79,944	76,769	68,075	52,941	41,784	37,028	29,435	29,135	28,599	45,857	76,731
1925	114,034	111,947	101,599	87,684	67,271	46,887	36,452	26,970	22,879	19,755	27,008	50,436
1926	59,850	55,705	51,498	43,528	32,372	26,649	23,997	23,509	21,311	25,267	38,079	59,603
1927	72,352	67,431	60,659	50,945	39,712	28,719	23,261	18,552	17,241	19,456	26,696	45,567
1928	54,968	50,673	44,017	37,625	28,253	20,654	17,256	18,896	17,603	22,463	41,635	60,189

Bureau of Agricultural Economics. Compiled from reports from cold-storage establishments.

TABLE 366.—*Beef, cured and in process of cure: Stocks in cold-storage warehouses and meat-packing establishments, United States, 1916–1928*

Year	Jan. 1	Feb. 1	Mar. 1	Apr. 1	May 1	June 1	July 1	Aug. 1	Sept. 1	Oct. 1	Nov. 1	Dec. 1
	1,000 pounds	*1,000 pounds*	*1,000 pounds*	*1,000 pounds*	*1,000 pounds*	*1,000 pounds*	*1,000 pounds*	*1,000 pounds*	*1,000 pounds*	*1,000 pounds*	*1,000 pounds*	*1,000 pounds*
Average:												
1916–1920	34,261	33,612	34,088	31,251	27,730	25,340	26,432	26,723	27,392	27,707	29,904	33,332
1921–1925	22,971	23,202	23,888	24,414	23,826	23,170	21,827	20,399	20,147	18,997	19,173	21,705
1916	21,443	20,852	26,959	25,811	21,869	17,324	18,915	18,589	18,450	21,653	30,013	37,958
1917	37,301	35,891	37,660	30,601	29,409	30,831	35,679	32,401	30,290	31,246	32,223	38,325
1918	39,243	38,793	37,575	34,106	29,217	24,804	21,968	28,065	29,981	28,713	29,339	32,381
1919	36,267	35,810	31,246	30,689	27,822	27,089	29,244	30,943	35,526	37,328	37,595	35,547
1920	37,052	36,715	37,002	35,047	30,333	26,653	26,355	23,617	22,711	19,594	20,352	22,448
1921	22,567	22,926	24,006	24,282	21,516	20,716	19,697	17,829	17,130	15,526	14,472	17,144
1922	16,313	16,774	17,997	18,744	19,166	19,304	19,113	19,304	20,081	18,961	19,884	22,602
1923	24,450	24,841	24,987	25,210	24,013	23,816	22,835	21,781	21,416	20,597	19,649	22,142
1924	22,593	22,711	23,238	25,199	25,482	24,285	22,390	20,377	19,771	18,939	21,387	23,508
1925	28,930	28,758	29,210	28,634	28,952	27,731	25,102	22,704	22,335	20,964	20,473	23,128
1926	25,146	24,833	26,192	27,253	27,606	25,930	24,691	22,539	20,386	20,983	23,119	26,374
1927	28,521	27,823	27,361	26,214	23,216	21,694	20,495	17,170	16,205	16,422	17,220	19,778
1928	21,979	20,978	19,732	19,631	17,941	16,558	14,982	13,546	13,462	14,760	16,401	19,444

Bureau of Agricultural Economics. Compiled from reports from cold-storage establishments.

TABLE 367.—*Beef and beef products: International trade, average 1911–1913, annual 1925–1927*

Country	Average, 1911–1913		1925		1926		1927, preliminary	
	Imports	Exports	Imports	Exports	Imports	Exports	Imports	Exports
PRINCIPAL EXPORTING COUNTRIES	*1,000 pounds*	*1,000 pounds*	*1,000 pounds*	*1,000 pounds*	*1,000 pounds*	*1,000 pounds*	*1,000 pounds*	*1,000 pounds*
Argentina	144	940,300	14	1,694,255	41	1,682,805	....	1,838,428
Uruguay	152	119,675	0	378,078	0	366,562	0	347,264
Australia[1]	[2]437	[2]301,882	1,930	381,233	1,567	308,042	847	206,356
Netherlands	256,296	326,176	211,157	248,405	170,463	248,114	170,819	250,270
United States	17,668	213,722	15,870	162,640	20,106	158,612	42,574	132,544
Brazil	48,989	171	11,512	135,063	7,329	20,833	....	10,556
New Zealand	398	80,543	577	138,672	565	97,742	588	105,300
Denmark	18,815	43,485	11,862	61,214	13,242	42,304	14,824	9,978
Canada	3,091	6,448	447	36,312	361	29,340	400	59,130
Rumania	4	2,566	437	13,492	568	16,659		
China	85	8,787	577	7,418	2,851	5,297	597	4,624
Hungary	[3]12,983	[3]3,762	833	8,508	79	6,010	35	3,247
PRINCIPAL IMPORTING COUNTRIES								
United Kingdom	1,252,292	27,595	1,854,596	39,689	1,899,726	34,029	1,834,663	45,387
Germany	212,150	942	249,993	3,090	440,883	2,138	464,089	2,563
France	41,318	62,361	249,865	37,026	186,325	24,051	175,752	31,187
Belgium	6,034	1,577	191,802	52,467	130,789	58,559	128,409	28,177
Japan	9,002	0	54,819	0	74,707	0	74,504	
Cuba	37,822	0	49,444	0	39,917	0	....	
Italy	131	....	26,767	574	24,152	278	26,243	27?
Norway	20,203	2,337	16,697	754	16,645	1,830	14,446	1,75?
Sweden	12,912	17,285	20,720	12,904	19,430	7,645	17,253	3,69?
Czechoslovakia	0	0	17,243	207	10,775	375	5,154	79?
Spain	966	38	18,413	0	12,821	0	....	
Union of South Africa	17,622	292	9,601	22,754	6,186	34,998	10,395	14,47?
Irish Free State	0	0	11,102	8,115	10,760	7,318	10,996	5,53?
British India	7,434	773	10,239	1,289	15,716	1,230	10,425	1,11?
Philippine Islands	15,837	0	10,377	0	12,052	0	11,465	
Switzerland	9,052	440	5,483	749	6,568	773	5,883	90?
British Malaya	....	....	6,103	608	6,669	630	6,913	65?
Egypt	476	....	3,801	10	4,302	4	4,330	?
Finland	14,755	9	3,499	101	5,209	55	6,010	12?
Chile	6,636	298	8,763	190	....		....	
Poland	0	0	3,235	14,166	775	31,668	2,234	16,28?
Total, 33 countries	2,023,704	2,161,464	3,270,778	3,459,983	3,141,579	3,187,901	3,039,848	3,120,58?

Bureau of Agricultural Economics. Official sources.

[1] Year ended June 30. [2] Average for year ended Dec. 31. [3] Average for Austria-Hungary.

TABLE 368.—*Beef: Wholesale price per pound in Chicago, and retail price of certain cuts at Chicago, New York, and leading cities, 1913–1928*

Year	Wholesale, good native steer, Chicago	Retail											
		Sirloin steak			Round steak			Chuck roast			Rib roast		
		Chicago	New York	Average leading cities	Chicago	New York	Average leading cities	Chicago	New York	Average leading cities	Chicago	New York	Average leading cities
	Cents	Cents	Cents	Cents	Cents	Cents	Cents	Cents	Cents	Cents	Cents	Cents	Cents
1913	13.0	23.2	25.9	25.4	20.2	25.0	22.3	15.4	16.0	16.0	19.5	21.8	19.8
1914	13.6	25.3	26.8	25.9	22.4	26.3	23.6	16.9	16.8	16.7	20.7	22.1	20.4
1915	12.9	25.7	26.8	25.7	22.1	26.0	23.0	16.7	16.5	16.1	21.3	22.2	20.1
1916	13.8	26.8	28.1	27.3	22.6	27.4	24.5	16.6	17.3	17.1	21.9	23.2	21.2
1917	16.7	29.3	32.6	31.5	25.8	32.6	29.0	20.3	21.3	20.9	24.1	27.4	24.9
1918	22.1	35.3	40.9	38.9	32.3	42.3	36.9	25.9	28.5	26.6	29.7	35.3	30.7
1919	23.3	38.3	43.9	41.7	34.3	45.7	38.9	26.7	29.9	27.0	31.4	39.1	32.5
1920	23.0	43.0	46.9	43.7	36.3	47.3	39.5	25.9	28.9	26.2	33.7	40.5	33.2
1921	16.3	38.0	42.1	38.8	31.0	41.4	34.4	20.7	23.1	21.2	30.2	36.4	29.1
1922	15.0	37.2	41.1	37.4	29.1	39.6	32.3	19.1	21.4	19.7	28.8	35.3	27.6
1923	15.8	39.8	42.5	39.1	30.7	40.8	33.5	19.9	22.4	20.2	30.2	36.3	28.4
1924	17.1	41.2	43.0	39.6	32.1	41.4	33.8	21.0	23.1	20.8	31.6	36.9	28.8
1925	18.0	43.7	45.4	40.6	34.2	43.1	34.7	23.1	24.4	21.6	33.6	38.8	29.6
1926	16.4	44.3	45.4	41.3	35.9	43.5	35.6	25.2	24.6	22.5	34.9	38.8	30.3
1927	18.6	46.2	47.6	42.6	37.2	45.2	37.1	26.2	26.4	23.7	35.6	40.4	31.3
1928	22.8	52.5	52.3	47.8	43.0	49.4	42.0	31.7	29.9	27.9	39.7	44.0	35.0

Bureau of Agricultural Economics. Compiled from Bureau of Labor Statistics Wholesale and Retail Price Bulletin.

TABLE 369.—*Cattle: Tick eradication progress and status of the work November 1, 1928*

State	Quarantined counties		Released counties June 30, 1928			Released counties, tick-free on—			Cattle inspected and dipped, year ended June 30, 1928	
	July 1, 1906	June 30, 1928	Tick free	With one or more infested herds	Total counties released	Nov. 1, 1926	Nov. 1, 1927	Nov. 1, 1928	Herds	Cattle
Alabama	67	4	57	6	63	49	57	59	212,572	1,381,271
Arkansas	75	22	44	9	53	41	44	45	203,329	1,005,681
California	15	0	15	0	15	15	15	15	0	0
Florida	67	49	14	4	18	12	14	22	178,527	2,021,954
Georgia	158	0	153	5	158	151	153	154	10,367	115,281
Kentucky	2	0	2	0	2	2	2	2	0	0
Louisiana	64	43	4	17	21	11	4	8	120,156	1,146,200
Mississippi	82	23	46	13	59	47	46	46	111,991	862,480
Missouri	4	0	4	0	4	4	4	4	0	0
North Carolina	73	0	71	2	73	73	71	73	1,759	12,520
Oklahoma	61	4	54	3	57	55	54	54	141,535	902,714
South Carolina	46	0	44	2	46	40	44	46	21,306	108,647
Texas	198	80	77	41	118	72	77	79	487,926	10,064,048
Virginia	31	0	26	5	31	27	26	29	1,517	6,464
Tennessee	42	0	42	0	42	42	42	42	0	0
Total	985	225	653	107	760	641	653	677	1,490,985	17,627,260

Bureau of Animal Industry. More than 15,000 vats were in use for official dipping during the year.

TABLE 370.—*Cattle and calves: Statement of livestock and meat situation, 1923–1928*

Item	Unit	1923	1924	1925	1926	1927	1928
Federally inspected slaughter:							
Cattle	Thousands	9,163	9,593	9,853	10,180	9,520	8,467
Calves	do	4,500	4,935	5,353	5,153	4,876	4,680
Average live weight:							
Cattle	Pounds	952.89	949.64	954.06	964.06	945.99	947.93
Calves	do	172.82	176.78	176.03	176.39	175.94	175.94
Total live weight:							
Cattle	1,000 pounds	8,730,870	9,109,968	9,400,390	9,814,272	9,005,923	8,026,415
Calves	do	777,746	872,415	942,211	908,865	857,867	823,385
Average live cost per 100 pounds:							
Cattle	Dollars	6.82	6.64	7.11	7.32	8.62	10.59
Calves	do	7.86	7.67	8.66	9.82	10.58	12.21
Total live cost:							
Cattle	1,000 dollars	595,445	604,902	668,368	718,405	776,311	849,997
Calves	do	61,131	66,914	81,596	89,251	90,762	100,535
Carcasses condemned:							
Cattle	Thousands	77	89	96	98	75	65
Calves	do	12	13	11	12	10	10
Number passed for food:							
Cattle	do	9,085	9,504	9,757	10,082	9,445	8,403
Calves	do	4,488	4,922	5,341	5,141	4,866	4,670
Average dressed weight:							
Cattle	Pounds	515.85	508.10	506.16	518.33	506.74	507.47
Calves	do	99.34	101.26	101.46	103.66	101.41	98.85
Total dressed weight: [1]							
Beef	1,000 pounds	4,685,704	4,829,474	4,938,948	5,225,909	4,784,563	4,265,056
Veal	do	443,182	498,588	540,769	530,603	492,563	461,952
Imports, beef and veal [2]	do	19,356	27,386	26,675	42,890	78,243	121,945
Storage Jan. 1	do	116,255	105,577	142,964	84,996	100,873	76,947
Total supply	do	5,264,498	5,461,024	5,649,355	5,884,399	5,456,242	4,925,900
Storage Dec. 31	do	105,577	142,964	84,996	100,873	76,947	98,913
Exports [3]	do	29,459	27,203	26,541	24,862	19,489	13,635
Apparent domestic consumption	do	5,129,462	5,290,857	5,537,819	5,758,664	5,359,806	4,813,352
Apparent per capita consumption	Pounds	45.92	46.52	48.00	49.16	45.18	40.11

Bureau of Agricultural Economics.

[1] Sum of monthly production.
[2] Beef imports included fresh beef and veal, only, until Jan. 1, 1924, when canned beef was added. Jan. 1, 1928, pickled or cured beef was also included. For 1921 and 1922 see Table 352, Yearbook 1927.
[3] Exports and reexports of fresh, cured, and canned beef and veal.

TABLE 371.—*Hogs: Numbers and value per head in the United States, 1840, 1850, 1860, 1867-1929*

Year	Hogs on farms [1]	Value per head, Jan. 1		Hogs on farms and else-where	Year	Hogs on farms [1]	Value per head, Jan. 1		Hogs on farms and else-where
		Old series [2]	New series [2]				Old series [2]	New series [2]	
	Thousands	*Dollars*	*Dollars*	*Thousands*		*Thousands*	*Dollars*	*Dollars*	*Thousands*
1840, June 1	*26,301*				1898	39,760	4.39		55,100
1850, June 1	*30,354*				1899	38,652	4.40		54,900
1860, June 1	*33,513*				1900	[4] *37,079*	5.00	5.28	53,900
1867	24,694	4.03		28,200	1900, June 1	*62,868*			
1868	24,317	3.29		28,300	1900	52,600			
1869	23,316	4.65		27,600	1901	53,200	6.20	6.55	55,700
1870, June 1	*25,135*				1902	46,800	7.03	7.43	48,700
1870	26,751	5.80		32,300	1903	47,200	7.78	[*] 8.22	48,000
1871	29,458	5.61		36,400	1904	49,500	6.15	6.50	49,200
1872	31,796	4.01		40,100	1905	52,000	5.99	6.33	50,600
1873	32,632	3.67		42,100	1906	54,600	6.18	6.53	57,000
1874	30,861	3.98		40,700	1907	57,300	7.62	8.05	61,300
1875	28,062	4.80		37,800	1908	61,300	6.05	6.39	64,200
1876	25,727	6.00		35,500	1909	57,000	6.55	6.92	63,400
1877	28,077	5.66		39,500	1910, Apr. 15	*58,186*			
1878	32,262	4.85		46,500	1910	49,300	9.17	9.69	57,200
1879	34,766	3.18		51,200	1911	55,700	9.37	9.90	63,700
1880, June 1 [3]	*47,682*				1912	55,700	8.00	8.46	62,700
1880	34,034	4.28		51,200	1913	54,000	9.86	10.42	57,900
1881	36,248	4.70		53,100	1914	51,800	10.40	10.99	55,000
1882	44,122	5.97		62,900	1915	57,000	9.87	10.43	59,600
1883	43,270	6.75		60,000	1916	59,700	8.40	8.88	61,700
1884	44,201	5.57		59,600	1917	56,700	11.75	12.42	60,700
1885	45,143	5.02		59,300	1918	61,200	19.54	20.65	63,000
1886	46,092	4.26		58,900	1919	63,800	22.02	23.28	65,300
1887	44,613	4.48		55,500	1920, Jan. 1	*59,346*			
1888	44,347	4.98		53,600	1920	59,959	19.08	20.00	62,451
1889	50,302	5.79		59,200	1921	58,602	12.98	13.65	61,300
1890, June 1 [3]	*57,410*				1922	59,559	10.06	10.59	61,973
1890	51,603	4.72		59,100	1923	69,044	11.58	12.31	71,466
1891	50,625	4.15		59,400	1924	66,361	9.72	10.30	68,845
1892	52,398	4.60		62,900	1925, Jan. 1	*50,854*			
1893	46,095	6.41		56,700	1925	55,568	12.38	13.20	58,228
1894	45,206	5.98		57,000	1926	52,148	15.21	15.80	54,448
1895	44,166	4.97		57,000	1927	54,788	15.97	17.25	56,807
1896	42,843	4.35		56,600	1928	60,420	12.03	13.16	63,109
1897	40,600	4.10		55,000	1929	[5] 54,956		13.01	57,402

Bureau of Agricultural Economics. Data for hogs on farms and value per head (except italic figures, which are from the census) from the Bureau of Agricultural Economics as of January 1.

[1] Figures 1900-1919 are tentative revised estimates of the Bureau of Agricultural Economics as first published in 1927 yearbook. Prior to 1900 estimates for each 10-year period represent an index of animal changes applied to census as base on first report after census data were available.

[2] For 1926-1929, new series is average of values by age and sex classification weighted by number in each class adjusted on basis average relationship between two series, 1926-1928. Old series was "all swine" value only.

[3] Figures for census years 1880 and 1890 exclude estimate of unenumerated swine on ranges as follows: 1880, 2,093,970; 1890, 17,276.

[4] Original estimate of the Bureau of Agricultural Economics.

[5] Preliminary.

TABLE 372.—*Hogs, including pigs: Estimated number on farms and value per head, by States, January 1, 1925–1929*

State and division	Number, Jan. 1					Value per head, Jan. 1 [1]				
	1925	1926	1927	1928	1929 [2]	1925	1926	1927	1928	1929 [2]
	Thousands	Thousands	Thousands	Thousands	Thousands	Dollars	Dollars	Dollars	Dollars	Dollars
Maine	56	60	67	70	60	16.30	17.30	16.80	15.00	14.00
New Hampshire	18	19	23	29	30	15.80	15.20	16.60	16.10	15.60
Vermont	45	44	53	56	50	13.30	17.00	15.90	14.90	14.10
Massachusetts	60	67	84	97	92	15.60	17.40	18.00	15.30	15.30
Rhode Island	4	4	4	5	5	18.20	17.80	19.20	18.60	18.00
Connecticut	18	18	21	24	22	20.90	19.30	20.50	20.20	19.60
New York	259	249	284	341	290	15.50	16.50	17.40	15.10	14.20
New Jersey	56	56	60	63	54	16.10	17.80	20.10	14.90	15.50
Pennsylvania	734	683	731	841	715	14.40	16.20	17.50	14.70	13.80
N. Atlantic	1,250	1,200	1,327	1,526	1,318	14.93	16.50	17.54	14.98	14.24
Ohio	2,440	2,489	2,439	2,439	2,146	12.60	15.90	17.10	12.60	11.50
Indiana	3,100	2,820	2,961	3,227	2,904	12.10	16.00	17.70	12.90	12.00
Illinois	4,725	4,442	4,709	5,133	4,671	15.10	18.30	19.20	13.70	14.00
Michigan	855	820	845	862	690	13.40	15.20	16.80	12.40	12.40
Wisconsin	1,580	1,660	1,826	1,720	1,462	12.90	16.70	17.00	12.90	14.20
Minnesota	3,600	3,456	3,786	3,710	3,302	15.50	19.00	20.30	15.10	16.00
Iowa	9,633	9,633	10,060	10,900	10,246	17.00	18.70	20.20	14.40	15.00
Missouri	3,864	3,671	3,991	4,270	4,070	10.00	14.40	16.10	11.70	12.20
North Dakota	784	682	572	652	587	13.10	15.90	17.40	13.80	15.00
South Dakota	2,760	2,300	2,183	2,882	2,536	14.50	16.60	19.40	14.70	14.60
Nebraska	4,818	4,700	4,597	5,492	4,888	14.50	17.60	19.50	15.30	15.10
Kansas	2,467	2,220	2,109	2,531	2,531	12.70	15.20	16.60	13.70	12.70
N. Central	40,626	38,893	40,078	43,818	40,033	14.30	17.25	18.75	13.83	14.04
Delaware	24	21	24	26	24	12.60	13.70	11.30	12.00	10.80
Maryland	188	179	192	221	199	12.30	14.00	15.20	12.40	10.80
Virginia	584	531	558	642	578	10.40	11.30	12.20	11.20	9.90
West Virginia	184	180	202	232	197	10.90	13.20	13.40	12.90	11.50
North Carolina	894	832	849	951	874	13.00	13.00	14.20	13.50	12.40
South Carolina	580	452	443	509	458	11.50	10.00	12.20	11.20	9.00
Georgia	1,275	1,109	1,187	1,365	1,228	9.80	9.40	10.10	9.40	8.20
Florida	498	458	485	543	516	6.80	7.50	7.50	7.60	8.10
S. Atlantic	4,227	3,762	3,940	4,489	4,074	10.61	10.73	11.60	10.86	9.72
Kentucky	932	839	965	1,032	826	9.40	12.40	14.40	9.80	8.40
Tennessee	1,035	880	968	1,026	872	8.60	10.60	13.20	9.70	8.00
Alabama	845	776	854	982	874	10.10	9.90	10.60	10.40	9.50
Mississippi	729	678	744	878	729	7.90	9.80	9.90	8.90	8.70
Arkansas	857	823	946	1,041	885	8.20	9.00	10.20	8.60	8.30
Louisiana	528	496	511	460	437	8.60	8.80	10.10	9.60	10.20
Oklahoma	969	736	883	1,104	994	9.20	10.90	14.10	11.10	9.60
Texas	1,250	1,000	1,250	1,375	1,210	9.40	10.40	14.90	11.50	9.70
S. Central	7,145	6,228	7,121	7,898	6,827	8.98	10.32	12.48	10.07	9.02
Montana	280	250	240	288	328	11.90	13.30	16.40	14.30	13.10
Idaho	325	276	318	353	318	10.40	14.00	15.20	12.90	11.70
Wyoming	102	90	110	138	149	10.30	14.60	15.40	13.50	12.30
Colorado	493	443	443	509	550	10.90	13.60	16.00	13.10	12.00
New Mexico	59	47	64	77	73	10.40	13.00	14.10	10.40	10.70
Arizona	19	18	18	19	19	10.70	13.10	13.70	13.00	13.30
Utah	64	60	75	98	98	10.50	12.70	13.50	11.50	10.20
Nevada	25	22	26	29	29	11.30	13.10	14.00	12.30	12.30
Washington	198	168	198	238	214	12.90	14.90	17.00	14.10	12.70
Oregon	223	223	245	270	256	10.20	13.00	14.20	12.20	10.60
California	532	468	585	670	670	9.70	14.60	15.00	13.60	12.60
Far Western	2,320	2,065	2,322	2,689	2,704	10.73	13.87	15.37	13.22	12.11
United States	55,568	52,148	54,788	60,420	54,956	13.20	15.80	17.25	13.16	13.01

Bureau of Agricultural Economics. Estimates of the crop-reporting board.

[1] Sum of total value of subgroups (classified by age and sex), divided by total number and rounded to nearest dime for States. Division and United States averages not rounded. State figures are new weighted value series not comparable to State figures previously published.
[2] Preliminary.

TABLE 373.—*Hogs: Numbers in countries having 150,000 and over, averages 1909–1913 and 1921–1925, annual 1926–1928*

Country	Month of estimate	Average 1909–1913 [1]	Average 1921–1925 [1]	1926	1927	1928 preliminary
NORTH AND CENTRAL AMERICA AND WEST INDIES		*Thousands*	*Thousands*	*Thousands*	*Thousands*	*Thousands*
Canada	June	3,350	4,344	4,360	4,695	4,497
United States	January	53,300	61,827	52,148	54,788	60,420
Mexico	June	[2] 811	[3] 1,125	2,903		
Guatemala		188	57	92	51	
Salvador		220				
Dominican Republic	May		866			
Haiti				170	185	
Estimated total [4]		59,200	69,200			
SOUTH AMERICA						
Colombia		[5] 711	1,352	1,400		
Venezuela		195	512			
Peru	February–April		449			
Bolivia		114	362	498		
Chile		172	255			
Brazil	September	18,401	[2 6] 16,169			
Uruguay		[2 7] 180	278			
Argentina	December [8]	[2 9] 2,901	[2 10] 1,437			
Estimated total [4]		23,200	20,900			
EUROPE						
England and Wales	June	2,390	2,658	2,200	2,692	2,967
Scotland	do	150	167	145	197	194
Ireland	do	1,261	1,067	1,043	1,414	1,412
Norway [11]	do	[12] 334	216	303	300	283
Sweden	do	1,023	1,056			
Denmark	July	2,715	2,314	3,122	3,731	3,360
Holland	May–June	1,305	1,519			
Belgium	December [8]	1,533	1,081	1,152	1,144	1,124
France	do [8]	7,529	5,302	5,793	5,777	6,019
Spain	do [8]	2,544	4,500	5,267	5,032	
Portugal		[2 13] 1,111	1,019			
Italy	March–April	2,685	2,630			
Switzerland	April	[2] 570	[2] 640	635		
Germany	December [8]	22,533	15,776	16,200	19,424	22,899
Austria	do [8]	1,932	1,399			
Czechoslovakia	do [8]	2,516	2,201	2,539		
Hungary	April	3,322	2,424	2,520	2,387	2,662
Yugoslavia	January	3,956	2,875	2,806	2,770	
Greece	December [8]	346	390	452	510	453
Bulgaria	do [8]	546	832			
Rumania	do [8]	3,262	2,976	3,088	3,168	3,076
Poland	November	5,487	5,287		6,333	
Lithuania	Spring	1,358	1,521	1,441	1,010	
Latvia	June	557	465	521	535	
Estonia	July	252	299	333	354	
Finland	September	422	378	391	418	
Estimated total, excluding Russia [4]		71,800	61,100			
AFRICA						
Union of South Africa	April–August	[2] 1,082	870	909	848	
Madagascar	February	600	369			
Estimated total [4]		2,200	1,900			

[1] Average for 5-year period if available, otherwise for any year or years within that period unless otherwise stated. In countries having changed boundaries, the figures are estimated for 1 year only for numbers within present boundaries.
[2] Nearest census figure. [3] Incomplete.
[4] These totals include interpolations for a few countries not reporting each year, and rough estimates for some others.
[5] Year 1915. [6] Year 1920. [7] Year 1908.
[8] Estimates reported as of December have been considered as of Jan. 1 of the following year, i. e., the figure for the number of swine in France as of Dec. 31, 1925, has been put in the 1926 column.
[9] June, 1914. [10] Year 1922. [11] Number in rural communities. [12] September. [13] Year 1906.

33023°—29——59

TABLE 373.—*Hogs: Numbers in countries having 150,000 and over, averages 1909–1913 and 1921–1925, annual 1926–1928*—Continued

Country	Month of estimate	Average 1909–1913	Average 1921–1925	1926	1927	1928 preliminary
ASIA		*Thousands*	*Thousands*	*Thousands*	*Thousands*	*Thousands*
China (includes Turkestan and Manchuria)		76,819				
Japan	December [8]	297	590	673	621	
Chosen	do.[8]	629	1,078	1,150	1,221	1,244
Formosa	do.[8]	1,293	1,302	1,435	1,543	
Siam	March	749	864			
Straits Settlements		139	267			
Philippine Islands	December [8]	1,763	5,768	8,885	9,298	10,568
Dutch East Indies: Outer possessions	do.[8]		783		833	
Estimated total, excluding Russia [4]		82,700	87,700			
OCEANIA						
Australia	December [8]	910	918	1,128	989	
New Zealand	January	[2] 349	396	473	520	587
Estimated total [4]		1,300	1,300			
Russia [14]	Summer	[15] 20,336	16,592	18,398	20,222	
Total, countries reporting all periods including Russia:						
Pre-war to 1927 (28) [16]		137,961	138,151	136,428	145,659	
Pre-war to 1928 (16) [16]		104,766	107,784	103,034	111,266	121,765
Estimated world total [4]		260,700	258,700			

Bureau of Agricultural Economics. Official estimates and International Institute of Agriculture unless otherwise stated.

[2] Nearest census figure.
[4] These totals include interpolations for a few countries not reporting each year, and rough estimates for some others.
[8] Estimates reported as of December have been considered as of Jan. 1 of the following year, i. e., the figure for the number of swine in France as of Dec. 31, 1925, has been put in the 1926 column.
[14] Years 1916, 1923–1927 from the Soviet Union Review, Apr. 1928, p. 62.
[15] Year 1916.
[16] Comparable totals for the number of countries indicated. Russia is excluded from the totals for the period pre-war to 1928 as no 1928 figures are available for that country.

TABLE 374.—*Hogs: Results of spring and fall pig surveys for the Corn Belt and the United States, 1923–1928*

Crop	June survey comparisons				December survey comparisons			
	Sows for farrow as compared to preceding spring		Pigs saved		Sows for farrow as compared to preceding fall		Pigs saved	
	Intended [1]	Actual	Compared to preceding spring	Per litter	Intended [1]	Actual	Compared to preceding fall	Per litter
	Per cent	*Per cent*	*Per cent*	*Number*	*Per cent*	*Per cent*	*Per cent*	*Number*
Corn Belt, 1923	115.9	108.3	105.0	4.88	125.4	93.9	96.2	5.02
United States, 1923	113.1	103.9	100.9	5.02	128.3	91.3	93.2	5.07
Corn Belt, 1924	94.6	79.7	82.9	5.02	88.6	69.4	76.6	5.47
United States, 1924	98.8	78.8	[8] 80.2	5.05	94.1	71.8	77.8	5.45
Corn Belt, 1925	89.6	80.1	89.4	5.78	100.9	85.4	87.8	5.72
United States, 1925	94.3	81.2	91.3	5.79	104.5	84.6	88.1	5.73
Corn Belt, 1926	111.1	103.5	99.5	5.54	136.4	104.8	104.3	5.68
United States, 1926	111.9	101.7	98.8	5.58	139.0	102.4	103.0	5.77
Corn Belt, 1927	108.9	101.8	101.8	5.55	123.1	109.3	111.3	5.80
United States, 1927	113.2	103.0	103.5	5.62	129.9	110.2	111.0	5.81
Corn Belt, 1928	101.3	91.0	93.0	5.65	109.1	96.0	98.6	6.04
United States, 1928	105.8	92.3	92.9	5.64	111.7	93.3	94.7	5.96
Corn Belt, 1929	103.3							
United States, 1929	105.4							

Bureau of Agricultural Economics. Estimates of the crop-reporting board.

[1] As shown by preceding survey.

Table 375.—*Hogs: Results of spring and fall pig surveys, by States, 1927–1928*

State and division	Sows farrowed				Pigs saved per litter				Intended farrowings			
	Spring, 1927, compared with spring, 1926	Fall, 1927, compared with fall, 1926	Spring, 1928, compared with spring, 1927	Fall, 1928, compared with fall, 1927	Spring, 1927	Fall, 1927	Spring, 1928	Fall, 1928	In fall, 1927, compared with actual, 1926	In spring, 1928, compared with actual, 1927	In fall, 1928, compared with actual, 1927	In spring, 1929, compared with actual, 1928
	Per cent	Per cent	Per cent	Per cent	No.	No.	No.	No.	Per cent	Per cent	Per cent	Per cent
Maine	103.1	101.0	75.3	79.1	6.7	7.1	6.2	6.8	140.4	115.0	94.6	92.1
New Hampshire	81.0	123.1	78.9	103.7	6.8	1 6.3	6.5	6.1	129.8	106.1	84.9	91.7
Vermont	107.6	97.2	84.5	89.5	7.5	7.0	7.1	7.2	110.4	112.5	93.6	81.2
Massachusetts	99.7	153.1	133.6	115.1	5.6	5.9	5.8	6.8	141.8	115.4	70.3	114.7
Rhode Island	122.2	163.2	133.3	89.0	6.1	1 6.0	6.3	6.5	150.0	125.0	244.4	91.4
Connecticut	102.6	110.2	118.3	61.7	6.4	1 6.6	6.4	7.8	88.0	95.2	112.5	77.2
New York	105.4	133.3	82.2	78.1	7.1	7.1	6.5	7.3	129.9	126.6	86.9	92.4
New Jersey	95.8	102.4	89.1	84.4	5.7	1 5.4	5.8	5.1	116.1	98.1	100.4	86.7
Pennsylvania	102.4	107.7	85.4	91.6	6.6	6.4	6.0	6.3	129.7	102.8	103.6	95.0
North Atlantic	102.0	115.0	85.0	91.1	6.60	6.57	6.00	6.75	129.7	109.7	95.2	95.2
Ohio	108.4	104.1	95.2	92.6	6.0	1 6.4	6.1	6.5	121.3	98.0	106.8	98.6
Indiana	106.8	102.3	91.7	92.9	6.0	1 6.1	6.0	6.3	119.3	99.8	109.7	98.6
Illinois	104.3	103.6	90.6	98.7	5.8	5.9	5.8	6.2	113.6	103.9	105.1	106.8
Michigan	104.3	99.9	77.9	83.7	6.6	6.6	6.6	6.7	125.3	93.3	97.8	92.7
Wisconsin	98.8	96.6	82.1	84.6	6.3	6.3	6.3	6.3	107.2	99.2	86.7	101.5
Minnesota	99.3	97.8	80.7	90.5	5.6	5.6	5.6	5.8	120.6	95.3	103.3	102.9
Iowa	103.0	120.6	88.8	107.4	5.3	5.5	5.5	5.8	118.2	94.8	112.4	105.0
Missouri	106.4	110.0	100.7	96.4	5.8	6.1	6.2	6.1	123.1	105.8	112.1	104.8
North Dakota	89.6	131.3	90.6	97.2	5.8	5.5	5.8	5.6	169.3	105.7	147.0	120.4
South Dakota	92.3	114.5	92.5	87.0	5.1	5.4	5.3	5.6	159.1	109.3	116.5	102.7
Nebraska	96.5	125.3	98.8	88.0	4.9	5.3	5.0	5.3	144.3	106.9	110.9	99.3
Kansas	102.6	113.2	97.4	101.4	5.8	5.8	5.8	6.0	133.0	122.3	123.9	110.2
North Central	101.7	109.6	93.4	96.0	5.58	5.80	5.66	6.04	123.8	101.4	109.5	103.8
Corn Belt	101.8	109.3	91.0	96.0	5.55	5.88	5.65	6.04	123.1	101.3	109.1	103.3
Delaware	102.2	103.3	86.1	98.1	6.9	6.2	6.5	6.1	132.3	113.9	117.3	107.1
Maryland	102.9	109.6	98.5	103.5	6.3	6.5	6.3	6.0	124.7	112.3	106.6	101.1
Virginia	105.3	116.5	96.6	88.0	6.3	6.6	6.2	6.6	133.1	109.9	102.3	98.2
West Virginia	107.1	109.5	78.3	85.4	6.6	6.8	6.9	6.9	133.3	104.0	98.7	90.9
North Carolina	108.5	103.0	100.0	96.4	6.1	1 5.8	5.8	5.4	125.8	119.2	115.8	112.2
South Carolina	102.5	131.0	97.8	79.7	5.9	5.3	5.2	5.2	145.1	150.4	127.3	107.1
Georgia	108.5	111.9	109.0	92.7	5.9	5.6	5.4	5.5	146.8	144.4	133.7	122.7
Florida	100.8	95.0	92.1	98.4	5.2	5.3	5.2	5.2	119.7	139.1	119.6	127.0
South Atlantic	106.0	111.1	100.7	91.4	5.91	5.90	5.57	5.71	135.2	130.3	118.7	114.4
Kentucky	112.2	99.9	82.2	67.9	6.0	6.2	6.2	6.4	137.4	102.4	96.9	89.0
Tennessee	116.4	114.9	89.5	89.4	6.1	6.1	5.9	6.2	147.5	102.8	103.6	99.0
Alabama	106.6	116.0	108.9	84.1	5.4	4.8	5.1	4.6	155.1	137.0	125.7	112.4
Mississippi	105.2	108.1	91.5	82.5	5.6	5.7	5.4	5.2	165.1	119.2	127.0	120.9
Arkansas	109.5	90.0	84.5	77.0	5.8	5.4	4.8	5.1	142.1	105.7	113.4	117.6
Louisiana	103.6	84.6	84.4	80.5	5.1	5.3	5.0	5.2	143.1	143.9	138.9	143.8
Oklahoma	105.4	112.0	93.6	88.9	5.6	5.8	5.4	5.6	148.9	125.9	129.0	100.9
Texas	110.1	115.9	99.5	78.1	5.7	5.5	5.4	5.7	160.0	118.5	138.1	106.2
South Central	109.8	107.1	92.3	80.8	5.74	5.67	5.43	5.64	150.0	117.8	119.0	108.9
Montana	100.4	136.4	107.6	121.1	5.8	5.1	5.7	5.7	170.6	94.8	151.0	121.1
Idaho	110.7	121.6	85.2	82.1	5.9	5.8	5.8	6.1	138.3	114.0	88.4	98.1
Wyoming	109.9	161.1	106.5	116.3	5.7	5.4	5.9	5.0	212.5	130.7	191.5	121.1
Colorado	116.6	112.2	109.8	124.6	5.6	5.5	5.6	5.5	123.0	107.3	141.8	129.8
New Mexico	137.0	105.8	114.7	103.0	5.2	6.3	4.4	5.2	156.8	87.0	178.5	119.2
Arizona	124.3	127.6	142.0	95.1	6.0	5.4	7.3	5.2	227.8	91.7	127.8	94.1
Utah	121.2	153.3	112.4	92.2	6.0	6.0	6.1	6.5	172.5	141.2	174.3	123.0
Nevada	84.2	123.2	116.3	101.0	5.7	5.4	7.0	6.6	112.5	141.2	150.0	155.4
Washington	102.3	130.2	117.6	105.3	6.0	6.5	6.5	6.5	151.2	118.6	124.0	93.5
Oregon	108.3	108.6	111.0	97.7	6.4	6.5	6.3	6.4	138.3	114.0	130.6	98.1
California	117.6	105.6	119.5	94.7	5.6	5.8	5.8	6.1	133.2	116.6	120.2	111.1
Far Western	115.3	122.9	105.8	103.7	5.70	5.64	6.00	5.92	138.2	113.4	112.6	113.7
United States	103.0	110.2	92.3	93.3	5.62	5.81	5.64	5.96	129.9	105.8	111.7	105.4

Bureau of Agricultural Economics.   Estimates of the crop-reporting board.

1 Revised December, 1928.

TABLE 376.—*Hogs: Receipts at principal public stockyards and all public stockyards, 1909–1928*

Year	Chicago	Denver	East St. Louis	Fort Worth	Kansas City	Omaha	St. Joseph	South St. Paul	Sioux City	Total 9 markets [1]	All other stockyards reporting	Total all stockyards reporting
	Thousands	*Thousands*	*Thousands*	*Thousands*	*Thousands*	*Thousands*	*Thousands*	*Thousands*	*Thousands*	*Thousands*	*Thousands*	*Thousands*
1909	6,619	242	2,473	868	3,093	2,135	1,694	725	1,077	18,926	(2)	(2)
1910	5,587	187	2,054	541	2,086	1,894	1,353	836	1,044	15,582	(2)	(2)
1911	7,103	220	3,124	556	3,168	2,367	1,922	911	1,349	20,720	(2)	(2)
1912	7,181	222	2,530	388	2,523	2,886	1,970	984	1,698	20,382	(2)	(2)
1913	7,571	247	2,584	404	2,568	2,543	1,869	1,257	1,533	20,576	(2)	(2)
1914	6,618	256	2,559	515	2,265	2,259	1,725	1,590	1,257	19,044	(2)	(2)
1915	7,652	344	2,592	464	2,531	2,643	1,698	2,155	1,761	21,840	14,373	36,213
1916	9,188	467	3,057	968	2,979	3,117	2,199	2,675	2,131	26,781	16,484	43,265
1917	7,169	352	2,706	1,062	2,277	2,797	1,920	1,928	2,149	22,360	15,682	38,042
1918	8,614	384	3,256	762	3,328	3,430	2,351	2,061	2,421	26,607	18,256	44,863
1919	8,672	368	3,651	588	3,141	3,179	2,126	2,190	2,322	26,237	18,232	44,469
1920	7,526	341	3,399	413	2,466	2,708	1,914	2,247	2,173	23,187	18,934	42,121
1921	8,148	334	3,330	382	2,205	2,665	1,785	2,210	1,739	22,798	18,303	41,101
1922	8,156	395	3,606	510	2,655	2,839	2,061	2,523	1,856	24,601	19,467	44,068
1923	10,460	495	4,831	486	3,615	3,649	2,457	3,338	2,989	32,320	23,010	55,330
1924	10,443	569	4,580	392	2,933	3,978	2,234	3,751	3,732	32,612	22,802	55,414
1925	7,996	467	3,512	312	2,067	3,355	1,673	3,637	3,396	26,415	17,514	43,929
1926	7,093	497	3,536	217	2,036	2,647	1,462	3,451	2,475	23,414	16,358	39,772
1927	7,724	457	3,710	338	1,904	2,631	1,425	3,105	2,322	23,616	17,795	41,411
1928	8,539	567	4,036	432	2,391	3,179	1,724	2,902	2,754	26,524	20,003	46,527

Bureau of Agricultural Economics. Prior to 1915 receipts compiled from yearbooks of stockyard companies; subsequent figures compiled from data of the livestock and meat reporting service of the bureau. Receipts, 1900–1908, are available in 1924 Yearbook, p. 902, Table 500.

[1] Total of the rounded detail figures.   [2] Figures not available prior to 1915.

TABLE 377.—*Hogs: Receipts at all public stockyards, 1915–1928*

Year	Jan.	Feb.	Mar.	Apr.	May	June	July	Aug.	Sept.	Oct.	Nov.	Dec.	Total
	Thousands	*Thousands*	*Thousands*	*Thousands*	*Thousands*	*Thousands*	*Thousands*	*Thousands*	*Thousands*	*Thousands*	*Thousands*	*Thousands*	*Thousands*
1915 [1]	3,959	3,449	3,199	2,487	2,768	2,874	2,368	2,024	1,966	2,457	3,728	4,934	36,213
1916 [1]	5,309	4,233	3,489	2,852	3,332	3,054	2,524	2,634	2,386	3,640	4,873	4,939	43,265
1917	5,084	3,933	3,369	2,961	3,264	2,791	2,563	1,853	1,615	2,676	3,941	3,992	38,042
1918	4,444	4,486	4,424	3,696	3,345	2,979	3,099	2,467	2,376	3,399	4,594	5,554	44,863
1919	5,855	4,412	3,643	3,648	3,831	3,773	2,974	2,095	2,397	3,121	3,740	4,980	44,469
1920	5,262	3,422	3,940	3,024	4,210	3,709	2,811	2,491	2,391	2,789	3,872	4,200	42,121
1921	4,700	4,009	3,386	3,229	3,328	3,579	2,727	2,656	2,655	3,214	3,687	3,931	41,101
1922	4,278	3,613	3,411	3,067	3,737	3,776	2,980	3,037	3,062	3,682	4,421	5,004	44,068
1923	5,306	4,492	4,927	4,318	4,524	4,204	4,181	3,714	3,607	4,816	5,416	5,825	55,330
1924	6,253	5,335	4,833	4,374	4,321	4,296	4,091	3,197	3,216	3,990	4,904	6,604	55,414
1925	6,105	4,558	3,528	3,247	3,283	3,507	2,798	2,549	2,741	3,390	3,843	4,380	43,929
1926	4,304	3,372	3,579	3,135	3,037	3,143	2,854	2,804	2,819	3,261	3,554	3,910	39,772
1927	4,252	3,308	3,754	3,142	3,613	3,775	3,046	3,042	2,565	3.039	3,666	4,209	41,411
1928	5,306	5,267	4,639	3,483	3,723	3,548	2,924	2,523	2,600	3,666	4,075	4,773	46,527

Bureau of Agricultural Economics. Compiled from data of the livestock and meat reporting service of the bureau.

[1] Complete information for 1915 and 1916, particularly on disposition of stock, is not obtainable from many of these markets.

TABLE 378.—*Hogs: Receipts, local slaughter and stocker and feeder shipments at public stockyards, 1925–1928*

Market	Receipts				Local slaughter				Stocker and feeder shipments			
	1925	1926	1927	1928	1925	1926	1927	1928	1925	1926	1927	1928
	Thousands	Thousands	Thousands	Thousands	Thousands	Thousands	Thousands	Thousands	Thousands	Thousands	Thousands	Thousands
Albany, N. Y	[1]	[1]	[1]	[1]	0	0	[1]	[1]	0	0	0	0
Amarillo, Tex	20	10	21	84	2	1	[1]	0	0	0	0	0
Atlanta, Ga	124	140	147	112	87	94	104	78	[1]	0	[1]	0
Augusta, Ga	4	3	6	5	4	3	6	5	[1]	[1]	0	0
Baltimore, Md	1,007	948	1,010	1,199	836	824	869	1,024	0	0	0	0
Boston, Mass	11	12	11	19	[2]	[2]	[2]	[2]	[2]	[2]	[2]	[2]
Buffalo, N. Y	1,131	969	1,067	1,026	539	401	496	490	[1]	[1]	[1]	[1]
Chattanooga, Tenn	20	19	21	27	20	19	20	27	0	0	0	0
Cheyenne, Wyo	196	239	194	181	0	0	0	0	0	0	0	0
Chicago, Ill	7,996	7,093	7,724	8,539	5,601	4,984	5,612	6,394	[1]	1	1	1
Cincinnati, Ohio	1,040	1,047	1,253	1,567	755	729	858	1,040	2	1	2	0
Cleveland, Ohio	785	701	776	754	547	525	597	565	0	0	0	0
Dallas, Tex	54	44	61	66	54	44	61	66	0	0	0	0
Dayton, Ohio	122	118	131	130	92	86	96	85	0	0	0	0
Denver, Colo	467	497	457	567	344	364	335	463	40	21	21	16
Detroit, Mich	439	427	518	472	311	299	308	306	1	1	[1]	[1]
East St. Louis, Ill	3,512	3,536	3,710	4,036	1,138	1,053	1,086	1,050	14	19	40	30
El Paso, Tex	26	34	43	43	23	25	31	38	2	3	4	2
Evansville, Ind	152	169	273	305	19	17	96	150	5	10	11	11
Fort Wayne, Ind	94	92	97	112	20	14	16	24	7	8	40	3
Fort Worth, Tex	312	217	338	432	295	204	317	392	11	4	6	2
Fostoria, Ohio	106	86	87	88	7	3	3	5	3	2	0	0
Indianapolis, Ind	2,067	1,771	1,841	2,261	1,131	1,054	1,139	1,206	13	23	15	14
Jacksonville, Fla	54	46	43	39	21	14	10	11	1	2	1	1
Jersey City, N. J	467	356	240	241	467	356	240	241	0	0	0	0
Kansas City, Mo	2,067	2,036	1,904	2,391	1,237	1,427	1,385	1,706	67	110	98	105
Knoxville, Tenn	38	24	29	34	25	24	29	34	0	0	0	[1]
La Fayette, Ind	122	110	114	130	60	62	57	57	2	4	3	3
Lancaster, Pa	66	80	69	84	29	29	38	52	0	0	0	0
Laredo, Tex	3	3	3	3	3	3	2	3	[1]	0	0	0
Los Angeles, Calif	217	199	220	299	211	197	218	296	6	2	2	3
Louisville, Ky	295	282	396	400	234	189	215	252	2	3	6	4
Marion, Ohio	54	57	50	49	16	10	3	[1]	1	4	2	3
Memphis, Tenn	66	55	55	72	56	42	38	51	7	9	14	17
Milwaukee, Wis	459	613	563	502	453	560	540	492	0	1	1	[1]
Montgomery, Ala	47	71	86	58	2	2	5	6	4	14	24	2
Moultrie, Ga	38	52	65	70	30	38	47	52	1	5	10	3
Muncie, Ind	74	88	94	125	31	28	29	40	2	6	4	3
Nashville, Tenn	243	219	206	235	154	116	60	60	1	[1]	0	0
Newark, N. J	533	460	570	603	533	460	570	603	0	[1]	[1]	[1]
New Orleans, La	30	33	42	49	25	27	33	38	4	4	5	8
New York, N. Y	928	924	1,115	1,202	928	924	1,115	1,202	0	0	0	0
North Salt Lake, Utah	380	337	328	369	50	36	51	57	2	[1]	[1]	0
Ogden, Utah	255	294	233	250	64	55	47	57	3	4	3	3
Oklahoma City, Okla	276	218	285	441	240	184	245	384	1	4	3	8
Omaha, Nebr	3,355	2,647	2,631	3,179	2,416	1,685	1,933	2,169	3	11	26	39
Pasco, Wash	9	4	7	14	0	[1]	0	0	0	0	[1]	0
Peoria, Ill	706	753	626	739	109	103	90	132	4	12	14	18
Philadelphia, Pa	278	252	269	289	265	237	257	275	0	0	0	0
Pittsburgh, Pa	2,312	2,059	2,136	2,202	520	432	488	519	0	0	0	0
Portland, Oreg	265	231	247	305	165	132	149	205	19	20	16	20
Pueblo, Colo	29	11	17	20	[1]	0	0	0	0	0	0	0
Richmond, Va	197	182	226	265	194	177	220	265	1	2	2	2
St. Joseph, Mo	1,673	1,462	1,425	1,724	1,196	1,151	1,129	1,281	30	28	29	38
San Antonio, Tex	56	39	55	77	41	33	46	65	9	3	4	4
Seattle, Wash	256	208	183	241	249	199	173	230	7	8	8	8
Sioux City, Iowa	3,396	2,475	2,322	2,754	2,076	1,547	1,629	1,630	66	163	115	94
Sioux Falls, S. Dak	191	288	273	364	59	87	81	99	1	2	3	7
South St. Paul, Minn	3,637	3,451	3,105	2,903	2,824	2,573	2,176	2,031	160	375	358	224
South San Francisco, Calif	[3]	[3]	157	254	[3]	[3]	132	196	[3]	[3]	3	1
Spokane, Wash	166	102	133	128	103	44	59	69	10	10	8	8
Springfield, Ill	[4]	[4]	75	103	[4]	[4]	4	4	[4]	[4]	3	4
Springfield, Mo	[4]	[4]	77	135	[4]	[4]	13	25	[4]	[4]	6	16
Springfield, Ohio	109	124	105	73	3	5	7	6	5	11	0	0
Toledo, Ohio	126	112	97	98	14	45	27	26	[1]	1	2	1
Washington, D. C	140	119	138	190	140	119	138	190	0	0	0	0
Wichita, Kans	631	524	606	799	597	485	567	764	15	6	7	9
Discontinued markets	[1]	0	5	0	[1]	0	2	0	0	0	2	0
Total	43,929	39,772	41,411	46,527	27,665	24,580	26,347	29,283	532	917	922	735

Bureau of Agricultural Economics. Compiled from data of the livestock and meat reporting service of the bureau. Earlier data in 1925 Yearbook, pp. 1120–1122.
Local slaughter represents number driven out from public stockyards for local slaughter.

[1] Not over 500.
[2] Disposition not reported.
[3] Not included in report prior to Mar. 1, 1927.
[4] Not included in report prior to Jan. 1, 1927.

TABLE 379.—*Hogs: Monthly average live weight, Chicago, 1909–1928*

Year	Jan.	Feb.	Mar.	Apr.	May	June	July	Aug.	Sept.	Oct.	Nov.	Dec.
	Lbs.	Lbs.	Lbs.	Lbs.	Lbs.	Lbs.	Lbs.	Lbs.	Lbs.	Lbs.	Lbs.	Lbs.
Average:												
1909–1913	215	219	224	230	234	235	237	240	234	225	219	217
1914–1920	217	223	228	231	232	233	240	244	241	225	214	214
1921–1925	230	232	240	242	240	242	252	258	258	242	228	226
1909	203	204	206	212	216	219	225	232	232	227	225	214
1910	210	213	218	227	239	242	246	255	259	253	232	224
1911	226	230	239	241	242	236	233	239	224	212	208	213
1912	212	217	218	227	232	235	239	240	235	226	222	223
1913	226	230	240	242	242	244	243	233	222	209	207	213
1914	216	224	233	233	236	237	244	248	242	229	218	226
1915	223	224	231	233	233	231	238	246	235	204	187	190
1916	195	204	214	219	220	226	231	232	223	210	195	193
1917	199	204	209	213	217	225	232	233	231	212	209	211
1918	216	231	238	242	238	235	243	243	247	233	226	223
1919	228	232	230	230	232	233	242	251	254	237	226	224
1920	239	239	244	248	245	243	252	258	258	247	234	230
1921	234	234	241	242	239	241	250	259	262	243	225	226
1922	231	236	244	246	244	247	259	268	265	243	231	234
1923	239	241	247	249	242	242	250	253	254	247	234	231
1924	227	229	237	239	239	241	251	255	254	235	220	214
1925	220	222	229	235	236	238	249	256	253	242	228	225
1926	231	235	245	244	247	255	271	281	267	232	217	220
1927	226	229	240	239	243	248	257	265	261	235	215	217
1928	225	230	235	233	234	239	251	257	251	247	238	231

Bureau of Agricultural Economics. Figures for 1909–1919 compiled from Chicago Drovers Journal Yearbook; subsequent figures from data of the livestock and meat reporting service of the bureau, which are the weighted average of packer and shipper purchases. Data for 1900–1908 are available in 1924 Yearbook, p. 909, Table 506.

TABLE 380.—*Feeder hogs, inspected: Shipments from public stockyards, 1920–1928*

Origin and destination	1920	1921	1922	1923	1924	1925	1926	1927	1928
	Thousands	Thousands	Thousands	Thousands	Thousands	Thousands	Thousands	Thousands	Thousands
Market origin:									
Denver, Colo	8	4	3	12	9	7	7	9	8
East St. Louis, Ill	40	30	41	33	22	24	27	37	30
Fort Worth, Tex	29	45	38	24	9	13	14	16	11
Indianapolis, Ind	17	18	17	16	15	14	22	14	14
Kansas City, Kans	148	78	151	265	119	55	97	86	95
Los Angeles, Calif			2	13	1	5	1	2	2
Louisville, Ky	10	11	18	2	2	2	3	6	4
Oklahoma City, Okla	32	10	20	28	10	10	10	10	16
Omaha, Nebr	12	7	7	15	21	15	15	36	38
Portland, Oreg	11	11	17	19	20	18	20	16	19
Sioux City, Iowa	22	12	7	10	5	5	13	6	3
South St. Joseph, Mo	5	1		2	2	15	23	20	26
South St. Paul, Minn	105	97	112	136	118	157	357	301	197
Wichita, Kans	25	11	16	31	27	14	5	7	7
All other inspected	66	36	44	36	34	42	53	70	70
Total	530	371	493	642	414	396	667	636	540
State destination:									
California			9	17	2	4	3	4	4
Colorado				10	6	7	6	7	7
Illinois	61	40	63	96	44	47	106	64	41
Indiana	29	28	47	25	20	34	101	62	31
Iowa	133	76	120	176	74	33	75	78	75
Kansas	44	32	29	26	17	18	16	28	55
Kentucky	6	11					11	24	5
Michigan			10	10	15	20	31	23	17
Minnesota	26	25	34	34	40	40	51	42	41
Missouri	64	36	46	70	37	32	46	56	47
Nebraska	24	15	23	63	34	24	20	85	87
Ohio	11	12	11	11	8	23	77	35	6
Oklahoma	37	24	24	14	11	10	10	13	14
Oregon	10	10	12	18	19	17	19	15	18
Tennessee				6	5	6	11	6	5
Texas	22	12	11	19	26	23	27	18	14
All other	63	50	54	47	56	58	57	76	73
Total [1]	530	371	493	642	414	396	667	636	540

Bureau of Agricultural Economics. Compiled from Bureau of Animal Industry inspection records.

[1] Includes other shipments as follows: To Alaska, 543 head in 1923; 785 head in 1924; 577 head in 1925; 713 head in 1926, and 869 head in 1927; to Hawaii, 412 head in 1923.

TABLE 381.—*Feeder hogs, inspected: Shipments from public stockyards, 1928*

Origin and destination	January	February	March	April	May	June	July	August	September	October	November	December	Total
	Number	*Number*	*Number*	*Number*	*Number*	*Number*	*Number*	*Number*	*Number*	*Number*	*Number*	*Number*	*Number*
Market origin:													
Denver, Colo.	919	543	294	720	571	461	346	368	331	1,058	1,164	1,080	7,855
East St. Louis, Ill.	2,072	1,147	1,799	1,667	3,085	2,951	3,743	2,757	3,735	2,591	2,246	1,837	29,630
Fort Worth, Tex.	1,054	1,036	1,615	1,092	1,304	838	702	1,152	639	556	839	185	11,012
Indianapolis, Ind.	1,327	751	1,091	1,332	2,443	2,668	1,039	642	461	500	1,050	500	13,804
Kansas City, Kans.	7,511	7,310	9,937	8,283	8,938	6,023	2,452	5,167	13,599	11,675	8,853	5,151	94,899
Los Angeles, Calif.	518	9	120	286	148	66	183	47	82	503	294	155	2,411
Oklahoma City, Okla.	1,570	1,249	1,773	1,251	1,834	949	783	1,454	2,385	1,437	913	644	16,242
Omaha, Nebr.	2,623	2,948	5,408	2,814	3,581	5,849	3,346	1,448	2,257	3,169	2,551	2,146	38,140
Portland, Oreg.	1,676	1,702	1,710	1,939	1,256	1,546	1,419	2,306	1,218	971	2,028	1,534	19,305
Sioux City, Iowa	86	109	297	111	594	169	56	82	161	178	322	330	2,495
South St. Joseph, Mo.	2,638	2,680	2,265	1,360	1,964	2,088	1,668	1,352	2,488	3,238	2,097	1,700	25,538
South St. Paul, Minn.	29,467	22,033	24,134	16,545	16,177	9,112	5,974	5,208	10,681	21,033	21,574	15,337	197,275
Wichita, Kans.	75	393	648	567	476	1,076	385	657	1,556	369	636	228	7,066
All other inspected	5,297	5,916	7,283	9,099	7,926	4,063	5,164	6,118	6,842	5,308	5,735	5,183	73,934
Total	56,833	47,826	58,374	47,066	50,297	37,859	27,260	28,758	46,435	52,586	50,302	36,010	539,606
State destination:													
California	518	9	388	562	148	66	417	47	330	503	294	417	3,699
Colorado	919	826	294	720	571	461	346	216	335	617	864	1,097	7,266
Illinois	3,040	2,346	2,970	1,912	2,233	3,869	3,500	3,289	4,309	5,968	3,616	4,079	41,131
Indiana	2,670	1,956	3,129	2,806	3,966	3,116	1,640	2,422	2,806	2,228	2,455	1,413	30,607
Iowa	8,590	5,831	6,828	5,936	6,235	5,876	2,419	3,371	10,852	9,844	6,568	2,408	74,778
Kansas	6,122	5,199	6,680	4,385	3,906	4,109	1,381	2,929	4,041	6,238	6,220	3,843	55,053
Michigan	1,180	1,452	734	1,860	2,764	1,458	1,186	540	906	2,025	1,452	1,061	16,618
Minnesota	3,939	1,765	3,036	2,195	2,448	2,702	2,273	1,968	3,088	5,631	7,811	4,465	41,321
Missouri	3,841	5,061	7,599	4,415	5,565	2,649	1,931	1,893	4,385	3,518	3,330	3,136	47,323
Nebraska	14,279	10,275	13,142	9,349	10,565	5,976	3,641	2,312	4,834	5,947	4,428	2,327	87,075
Ohio	609	745	978	254	667	170	147	158	462	423	324	1,332	6,269
Oklahoma	1,690	1,119	1,101	1,104	1,691	564	783	1,472	1,900	1,207	476	717	13,824
Oregon	1,607	1,623	1,524	1,694	1,066	1,401	1,271	2,087	1,218	938	1,650	1,341	17,420
Tennessee	522	452	391	624	243	294	457	538	323	491	306	414	5,065
Texas	1,072	1,180	1,284	888	1,422	1,133	1,183	1,455	1,168	757	996	804	13,342
All other	6,233	7,987	7,920	8,143	6,490	3,981	4,672	4,061	5,478	6,251	9,512	7,156	77,884
Total [1]	56,833	47,826	58,374	47,066	50,297	37,859	27,260	28,758	46,435	52,586	50,302	36,010	539,606

Bureau of Agricultural Economics. Compiled from Bureau of Animal Industry inspection records.

[1] Includes other shipments as follows: To Alaska, 2 head in January, 128 in March, 199 in April, 317 in May, 34 in June, and 13 in July; to Cuba, 248 head in March.

TABLE 382.—*Hogs: Estimated price per 100 pounds received by producers in the United States, 1910–1928*

Year	Jan.	Feb.	Mar.	Apr.	May	June	July	Aug.	Sept.	Oct.	Nov.	Dec.	Weighted av.
	Dolls.	Dolls.	Dolls.	Dolls.	Dolls.	Dolls.	Dolls.	Dolls.	Dolls.	Dolls.	Dolls.	Dolls.	Dolls.
Average:													
1910–1913	6.93	6.97	7.31	7.54	7.14	7.10	7.13	7.30	7.49	7.37	6.96	6.73	7.12
1914–1920	10.54	10.81	11.37	11.85	11.96	11.76	12.11	12.48	12.44	11.91	11.19	10.65	11.49
1921–1925	7.86	8.13	8.84	8.52	8.25	8.01	8.50	8.97	8.71	8.70	8.08	7.89	8.32
1910	7.76	7.87	8.93	9.26	8.59	8.46	8.15	7.78	8.27	8.08	7.61	7.16	8.10
1911	7.44	7.04	6.74	6.17	5.72	5.66	5.92	6.54	6.53	6.09	5.86	5.72	6.30
1912	5.74	5.79	5.94	6.78	6.79	6.65	6.64	7.11	7.47	7.70	7.05	6.89	6.66
1913	6.77	7.17	7.62	7.94	7.45	7.61	7.81	7.79	7.68	7.60	7.33	7.16	7.44
1914	7.45	7.75	7.80	7.80	7.60	7.43	7.72	8.11	8.11	7.43	7.00	6.67	7.52
1915	6.57	6.34	6.33	6.48	6.77	6.80	6.84	6.61	6.79	7.18	6.35	6.02	6.56
1916	6.32	7.07	7.86	8.21	8.37	8.21	8.40	8.61	9.22	8.67	8.74	8.76	8.13
1917	9.16	10.33	12.32	13.61	13.72	13.50	13.35	14.24	15.69	16.15	15.31	15.73	13.46
1918	15.26	15.03	15.58	15.76	15.84	15.37	15.58	16.89	17.50	1C.50	15.92	15.82	15.85
1919	15.69	15.53	16.13	17.39	18.00	17.80	19.22	19.30	15.81	13.88	13.36	12.66	16.02
1920	13.36	13.62	13.59	13.73	13.44	13.18	13.65	13.59	13.98	13.57	11.64	8.90	12.86
1921	8.72	8.58	9.13	7.96	7.62	7.22	8.09	8.73	7.51	7.31	6.66	6.52	7.81
1922	6.89	8.24	9.08	8.83	9.05	9.11	9.12	8.54	8.23	8.33	7.78	7.63	8.32
1923	7.77	7.65	7.52	7.45	7.13	6.37	6.68	6.85	7.81	7.23	6.66	6.39	7.11
1924	6.59	6.54	6.63	6.70	6.68	6.55	6.60	8.54	8.50	9.45	8.62	8.39	7.46
1925	9.31	9.62	11.83	11.64	10.78	10.82	12.02	12.19	11.50	11.16	10.66	10.51	10.88
1926	10.99	11.76	11.65	11.49	11.97	12.80	12.69	11.66	12.07	12.06	11.45	10.97	11.75
1927	10.97	11.19	10.89	10.41	9.41	8.40	8.58	9.24	9.78	10.16	8.99	8.14	9.67
1928	7.81	7.62	7.48	7.75	8.82	8.70	9.64	10.01	11.17	9.55	8.51	7.93	8.60

Bureau of Agricultural Economics. Based on returns from special price reporters.

TABLE 383.—*Hogs: Average price per 100 pounds at Chicago, by months, 1901–1928*

Year	Jan.	Feb.	Mar.	Apr.	May	June	July	Aug.	Sept.	Oct.	Nov.	Dec.	Weighted av.
	Dolls.	Dolls.	Dolls.	Dolls.	Dolls.	Dolls.	Dolls.	Dolls.	Dolls.	Dolls.	Dolls.	Dolls.	Dolls.
1901	5.25	5.35	5.85	5.90	5.80	5.90	5.90	5.95	6.60	6.10	5.65	5.95	5.85
1902	6.20	6.10	6.35	6.95	7.00	7.35	7.65	7.15	7.55	7.00	6.30	6.20	6.85
1903	6.40	6.75	7.30	7.20	6.45	6.00	5.55	5.45	5.85	5.55	4.65	4.45	6.00
1904	4.90	5.15	5.35	5.10	4.65	5.05	5.40	5.30	5.75	5.40	4.80	4.50	5.15
1905	4.65	4.85	5.15	5.45	5.40	5.35	5.65	5.95	5.95	5.50	5.25	4.85	5.25
1906	5.40	6.00	6.30	6.55	6.45	6.55	6.65	6.25	6.25	6.40	6.20	6.25	6.25
1907	6.60	7.05	6.65	6.65	6.40	6.10	6.05	6.00	6.00	6.15	4.90	4.70	6.10
1908	4.40	4.45	5.00	5.85	5.50	5.80	6.50	6.55	6.85	5.95	5.80	5.65	5.70
1909	6.10	6.35	6.70	7.20	7.30	7.65	7.85	7.75	8.20	7.75	8.00	8.35	7.35
1910	8.55	9.05	10.55	9.90	9.55	9.45	8.75	8.35	8.90	8.50	7.60	7.65	8.90
1911	7.95	7.40	6.85	6.25	6.00	6.25	6.70	7.30	6.90	6.45	6.30	6.40	6.70
1912	6.25	6.20	7.10	7.80	7.65	7.50	7.65	8.25	8.45	8.75	7.75	7.40	7.55
1913	7.45	8.15	8.90	9.05	8.55	8.65	9.05	8.35	8.30	8.20	7.75	7.70	8.35
1914	8.30	8.60	8.70	8.65	8.45	8.20	8.70	9.00	8.85	7.65	7.50	7.10	8.30
1915	6.90	6.80	6.75	7.30	7.60	7.60	7.25	6.90	7.25	7.90	6.65	6.40	7.10
1916	7.20	8.20	9.65	9.75	9.85	9.70	9.80	10.33	10.70	9.80	9.60	9.95	9.60
1917	10.90	12.45	14.80	15.75	15.90	15.50	15.20	16.90	18.20	17.15	17.40	16.85	15.10
1918	16.30	16.65	17.10	17.45	17.45	16.60	17.75	19.00	19.65	17.70	17.70	17.55	17.45
1919	17.60	17.65	19.10	20.40	20.60	20.40	21.85	20.00	17.45	14.35	14.20	13.60	17.85
1920	14.97	14.55	14.94	14.79	14.28	14.68	14.84	14.74	15.88	14.17	11.83	9.55	13.91
1921	9.41	9.42	10.00	8.50	8.35	8.19	9.69	9.26	7.61	7.72	7.01	6.92	8.51
1922	8.02	9.90	10.43	10.31	10.48	10.33	9.70	8.51	8.75	8.80	8.07	8.18	9.22
1923	8.29	8.02	8.18	8.08	7.53	6.92	7.04	7.65	8.35	7.42	6.85	6.87	7.55
1924	7.10	7.06	7.35	7.36	7.34	7.04	7.68	9.38	9.57	9.91	8.97	9.38	8.11
1925	10.38	11.06	13.55	12.55	12.06	12.57	13.46	12.66	12.52	11.31	11.28	10.97	11.81
1926	12.02	12.45	12.20	12.33	13.55	14.01	12.51	11.48	12.03	12.72	11.80	11.57	12.34
1927	11.96	11.73	11.28	10.69	9.59	8.78	9.05	9.03	10.22	10.39	8.92	8.32	9.95
1928	8.25	8.08	8.08	9.28	9.67	9.91	10.65	11.53	11.89	9.57	8.83	8.61	9.22

Bureau of Agricultural Economics. Figures prior to 1920 are general average hog prices as published in the Chicago Drovers Journal Yearbook; subsequent figures compiled from reports of packer and shipper purchases; such purchases do not include pigs, boars, stags, extremely rough sows or cripples.

NOTE.—A table similar to Table 364, 1927 Yearbook, corn-hog ratios, is omitted.

Table 384.—*Hogs: Average price per 100 pounds at Chicago and Omaha, by months, 1927–1928*

Year and month	Chicago						Omaha					
	Butcher, bacon, and shipper hogs				Packing sows, rough and smooth, all weights	Average cost, packer and shipper hogs	Butcher, bacon, and shipper hogs			Packing sows, rough and smooth, all weights	Feeder and stocker pigs, 70 to 130 pounds, medium to choice	Average cost, packer and shipper hogs
	Heavy weight, 250 to 350 pounds, medium to choice	Medium weight, 200 to 250 pounds, medium to choice	Light weight, 160 to 200 pounds, common to choice	Light lights, 130 to 160 pounds, common to choice			Heavy weight, 250 to 350 pounds, medium to choice	Medium weight, 200 to 250 pounds, medium to choice	Light weight, 160 to 200 pounds, common to choice			
1927	Dols.	Dols.	Dollars	Dollars	Dols.	Dols.	Dols.	Dols.	Dollars	Dols.	Dols.	Dols.
January	11.89	11.97	11.99	11.96	10.97	11.96	11.61	11.66	11.61	10.85	11.12	11.61
February	11.70	11.89	11.96	11.88	10.74	11.73	11.33	11.44	11.51	10.74	11.68	11.37
March	11.10	11.49	11.69	11.64	10.24	11.28	10.75	11.05	11.25	9.84	11.39	10.92
April	10.52	10.81	11.03	10.98	9.50	10.69	10.08	10.37	10.52	9.10	10.67	10.19
May	9.52	9.83	9.88	9.80	8.54	9.59	9.08	9.34	9.46	8.14	9.63	9.12
June	8.79	9.06	9.06	8.74	7.71	8.78	8.52	8.75	8.76	7.58	7.99	8.46
			Medium to choice	Medium to choice					Medium to choice			
July	9.16	9.80	9.94	9.68	7.83	9.05	8.89	9.61	9.72	7.70	7.92	8.60
August	9.32	10.14	10.25	9.90	7.83	9.03	8.99	9.75	10.08	7.81	8.45	8.45
September	10.88	11.39	11.21	10.42	9.56	10.22	10.59	10.90	10.79	9.68	9.21	10.03
October	11.12	11.22	10.86	9.98	9.51	10.39	10.46	10.73	10.32	9.42	9.78	9.97
November	9.45	9.33	8.90	8.32	8.00	8.92	8.86	9.04	8.65	7.75	8.93	8.62
December	8.53	8.47	8.17	7.87	7.56	8.32	8.21	8.21	7.93	7.29	7.57	8.12
Average	10.16	10.45	----	----	9.00	9.95	9.78	10.07	----	8.82	9.53	9.62
1928												
January	8.26	8.34	8.17	7.89	7.25	8.25	8.02	8.06	7.91	7.10	7.17	7.98
February	7.99	8.21	8.12	7.76	7.15	8.08	7.63	7.81	7.78	6.75	6.46	7.66
March	7.99	8.23	8.10	7.58	7.14	8.08	7.66	7.88	7.78	6.82	6.50	7.74
April	9.10	9.32	9.22	8.65	8.04	9.28	8.72	8.95	8.87	7.76	7.16	8.82
May	9.62	9.76	9.37	8.70	8.71	9.67	9.18	9.39	9.10	8.38	7.39	9.21
June	10.04	10.06	9.74	9.07	9.01	9.91	9.66	9.68	9.26	8.68	7.43	9.42
July	10.84	10.94	10.77	10.28	9.77	10.65	10.60	10.68	10.16	9.26	8.19	10.20
August	11.64	11.86	11.69	11.36	10.63	11.53	11.18	11.42	11.06	10.16	9.28	10.89
September	12.14	12.26	11.98	11.60	11.02	11.89	11.56	11.81	11.54	10.56	10.14	11.35
October	9.73	9.77	9.63	9.28	8.84	9.57	9.37	9.40	9.17	8.48	8.59	9.16
November	8.92	8.92	8.74	8.44	8.18	8.83	8.55	8.57	8.34	7.92	7.33	8.52
December	8.65	8.66	8.56	8.20	7.97	8.61	8.20	8.22	7.97	7.71	6.63	8.25
Average	9.58	9.69	9.51	9.07	8.64	9.22	9.19	9.32	9.08	8.30	7.69	8.87

Bureau of Agricultural Economics. Compiled from data of the livestock and meat reporting service of the bureau. Earlier data in 1927 Yearbook, pp. 1012–1014.

Table 385.—*Hogs: Monthly slaughter [1] under Federal inspection, 1907–1928*

Year	Jan.	Feb.	Mar.	Apr.	May	June	July	Aug.	Sept.	Oct.	Nov.	Dec.	Total
	Thousands	Thousands	Thousands	Thousands	Thousands	Thousands	Thousands	Thousands	Thousands	Thousands	Thousands	Thousands	Thousands
1907	3,410	2,921	2,665	2,667	3,317	3,241	2,929	2,301	1,988	2,219	2,135	3,094	32,885
1908	4,961	3,890	3,111	2,304	3,088	3,094	2,416	2,231	2,231	3,368	3,803	4,147	38,643
1909	3,876	2,653	3,013	2,343	2,629	2,719	2,097	1,822	1,955	2,397	2,800	3,090	31,395
1910	2,693	2,324	1,891	1,778	2,206	2,612	1,988	1,824	1,564	1,851	2,456	2,827	26,014
1911	2,742	2,633	2,973	2,589	3,008	3,462	2,560	2,032	2,172	2,720	3,639	3,603	34,133
1912	4,147	3,302	2,700	2,412	2,844	2,835	2,354	1,875	1,701	2,455	3,020	3,407	33,053
1913	3,708	2,844	2,334	2,487	3,046	3,057	2,557	2,268	2,133	2,681	3,165	3,919	34,199
1914	3,489	2,723	2,548	2,312	2,569	2,926	2,260	1,799	1,907	2,682	3,047	4,271	32,532
1915	4,274	3,885	3,446	2,563	2,869	3,246	2,493	2,041	1,890	2,494	3,739	5,442	38,381
1916	5,387	4,276	3,430	2,853	3,275	3,163	2,530	2,517	2,287	3,327	4,771	5,267	43,084
1917	4,629	3,484	2,985	2,645	3,084	2,685	2,411	1,705	1,322	2,195	3,043	3,723	33,910
1918	3,961	3,998	3,926	3,290	3,092	2,783	2,940	2,283	1,980	3,018	4,280	5,662	41,214
1919	5,846	4,266	3,443	3,208	3,743	3,728	2,884	1,949	1,997	2,686	3,270	4,790	41,812
1920	5,079	3,104	3,482	2,590	3,585	3,566	2,644	2,191	1,988	2,487	3,329	3,985	38,019
1921	4,347	3,799	3,047	3,003	3,274	3,618	2,821	2,530	2,422	2,866	3,447	3,807	38,982
1922	3,985	3,480	3,350	2,946	3,716	4,046	3,104	2,888	2,747	3,332	4,318	5,201	43,114
1923	5,134	4,231	4,884	4,179	4,325	4,303	3,983	3,556	3,212	4,328	5,341	5,904	53,334
1924	5,911	5,006	4,536	4,073	4,278	4,288	4,114	3,070	2,857	3,498	4,641	6,600	52,873
1925	5,979	4,447	3,299	3,037	3,186	3,732	2,819	2,452	2,598	3,314	3,646	4,533	43,043
1926	4,501	3,351	3,562	3,105	3,131	3,430	3,127	2,834	2,616	2,976	3,610	4,394	40,636
1927	4,514	3,395	3,837	3,330	3,766	4,253	3,431	3,050	2,534	2,969	3,688	4,869	43,633
1928	5,479	5,780	5,140	3,446	3,885	4,078	2,984	2,545	2,508	3,713	4,455	5,782	49,795

Bureau of Animal Industry.
[1] The figures include rejected carcasses.

TABLE 386.—*Hogs, slaughter statistics: Source of supply, classification, slaughter costs, weights, and yields, 1923–1928*

Year and month	Source of supply		Sex classification			Average live cost per 100 pounds	Average live weight	Dressed weight as percentage of live weight	By-product yield (on basis of live weight)			
	Stock-yards	Other	Sows	Bar-rows	Stags and boars				Lard (rendered)	Edible offal [1]	Trimmings	Inedible grease (unrendered)
	P. ct.	P. ct.	P. ct.	P. ct.	P. ct.	Dollars	Pounds	P. ct.	P. ct.	P. ct.	P. ct.	P. ct.
1923	76. 07	23. 93	52. 42	46. 86	0. 72	7. 59	225. 33	76. 72	16. 49	2. 14	4. 53	1. 37
1924	77. 95	22. 05	52. 34	46. 96	. 70	8. 04	222. 31	75. 33	16. 45	2. 18	4. 59	1. 35
1925	75. 99	24. 01	52. 73	46. 65	. 62	11. 79	225. 50	75. 67	15. 04	2. 49	5. 08	1. 29
1926	72. 85	27. 15	51. 58	47. 78	. 64	12. 47	235. 06	76. 42	15. 89	2. 69	5. 50	1. 31
1927	67. 63	32. 37	50. 31	49. 10	. 59	10. 06	233. 33	76. 27	15. 36	2. 73	5. 64	1. 22
1928	64. 56	35. 44	51. 38	48. 04	. 58	9. 20	229. 26	75. 41	15. 40	2. 98	5. 53	1. 19
1928												
January	66. 41	33. 59	46. 34	53. 11	. 55	8. 27	224. 96	76. 12	15. 50	2. 74	5. 60	1. 17
February	65. 60	34. 40	45. 64	53. 97	. 39	8. 00	230. 86	76. 47	16. 33	2. 67	5. 12	1. 17
March	63. 17	36. 83	46. 05	53 45	. 50	8. 08	229. 47	75. 72	16. 55	2. 80	4. 92	1. 20
April	65. 23	34. 77	47. 78	51. 55	. 67	8. 94	225. 51	75. 52	16. 40	2. 90	5. 68	1. 27
May	67. 39	32. 61	51. 02	48. 32	. 66	9. 59	230. 31	75. 42	15. 74	3. 06	5. 76	1. 25
June	63. 59	36. 41	54. 85	44. 21	. 94	9. 66	231. 90	74. 77	15. 54	3. 04	5. 86	1. 22
July	65. 45	34. 55	61. 98	37. 24	. 78	10. 64	241. 27	74. 91	15. 12	2. 98	6. 42	1. 21
August	64. 42	35. 58	63. 33	35. 84	. 83	11. 42	243. 27	75. 66	14. 98	3. 05	6. 63	1. 21
September	66. 34	33. 66	60. 18	39. 11	. 71	12. 00	233. 05	74. 60	13. 77	3. 28	6. 66	1. 21
October	66. 98	33. 02	55. 91	43. 49	. 60	9. 71	226. 56	74. 40	13. 59	3. 31	5. 61	1. 18
November	64. 28	35. 72	53. 47	46. 08	. 45	8. 86	223. 65	74. 62	14. 26	3. 23	5. 47	1. 10
December	58. 60	41. 40	49. 32	50. 33	. 35	8. 54	222. 88	75. 39	15. 29	3. 18	5. 54	1. 14

Bureau of Agricultural Economics. Compiled from monthly reports to the bureau from packers and slaughterers, whose slaughterings equalled 75 to 85 per cent of total slaughter under Federal inspection.

[1] Unrendered.

TABLE 387.—*Hogs: Slaughter in specified countries, average pre-war and annual, 1914–1927*

Year	Germany, inspected slaughter	Denmark, in export slaughter-houses	England and Wales, sold off farms for slaughter [1]	Scotland, sold off farms for slaughter [1]	Ireland, purchased by Irish bacon curers	Canada	Netherland receipts at 21 markets
	Thousands	Thousands	Thousands	Thousands	Thousands	Thousands	Thousands
Average pre-war [2]	16, 406	2, 503	3, 487		1, 282	4, 280	875
1914	(3)	2, 858					1, 085
1915	(3)	2, 594					842
1916	(3)	2, 542					850
1917	(3)	2, 479					600
1918	(3)	324					217
1919	1, 368	456			874	5, 526	422
1920	3, 024	930	2, 700	146	898	4, 834	648
1921	6, 825	1, 641	3, 471	173	1, 030	5, 297	1, 362
1922	6, 923	2, 215	3, 229	176	926	5, 382	865
1923	5, 830	3, 414	3, 691	245	955	6, 056	906
1924	10, 527	4, 024	4, 500	242	1, 110	6, 625	1, 068
1925	12, 090	3, 766	3, 588		911	5, 720	1, 045
1926	13, 072	3, 838	3, 074		910	5, 636	1, 025
1927	17, 215	5, 098	3, 683		1, 050	5, 965	

Bureau of Agricultural Economics. Compiled from official sources and cabled reports from agricultural commissioners abroad.

[1] For years ended May 31 following.
[2] Average for 5 years immediately preceding war period if available, otherwise for any year or years within that period unless otherwise stated. In countries having changed boundaries, the figures are estimates for 1 year only for numbers within present boundaries.
[3] Not available for present boundaries. For former boundaries, the numbers slaughtered are as follows in thousands—1914, 19,441; 1915, 13,293; 1916, 6,548; 1917, 5,795; 1918, 2,430.

TABLE 388.—*Hogs: Statement of livestock and meat situation, 1921–1928*

PORK, INCLUDING LARD

Item	Unit	1922	1923	1924	1925	1926	1927	1928
Federally inspected slaughter.	Thousands__	43, 114	53, 334	52, 873	43, 043	40, 636	43, 633	49, 795
Average live weight_	Pounds_____	225. 95	225. 33	222. 31	225. 50	235. 06	233. 33	229. 26
Total live weight____	1,000 pounds	9, 741, 524	12, 017, 684	11, 754, 115	9, 706, 167	9, 551, 947	10, 180, 995	11, 416, 095
Average live cost per 100 pounds.	Dollars_____	9. 31	7. 59	8. 04	11. 79	12. 47	10. 06	9. 20
Total live cost_____	1,000 dollars_	906, 936	912, 142	945, 031	1, 144, 357	1, 191, 128	1, 024, 208	1, 050, 281
Carcasses condemned.	Thousands__	175	228	203	159	169	151	150
Number passed for food.	_____do_____	42, 938	53, 106	52, 670	42, 884	40, 467	43, 482	49, 646
Average dressed weight.	Pounds_____	172. 76	172. 93	167. 30	170. 46	179. 51	177. 93	172. 85
Total dressed weight.[1]	1,000 pounds	7, 419, 311	9, 182, 135	8, 819, 555	7, 322, 710	7, 272, 534	7, 730, 761	8, 579, 288
Imports, pork [2]_____	_____do_____	818	1, 101	5, 683	7, 235	9, 156	14, 524	12, 866
Storage Jan. 1:								
Pork_____	_____do_____	415, 096	570, 510	708, 869	647, 364	472, 219	472, 757	523, 425
Lard_____	_____do_____	47, 541	48, 808	49, 340	61, 049	42, 478	49, 992	54, 855
Total supply_____	_____do_____	7, 882, 766	9, 802, 553	9, 583, 447	8, 038, 358	7, 796, 388	8, 268, 034	9, 170, 434
Storage Dec. 31:								
Pork_____	_____do_____	570, 510	708, 869	647, 364	472, 219	472, 757	523, 425	670, 039
Lard_____	_____do_____	48, 808	49, 340	61, 049	42, 478	49, 992	54, 855	85, 217
Exports:								
Pork [3]_____	_____do_____	699, 496	928, 224	702, 337	519, 435	402, 665	282, 500	301, 246
Lard [4]_____	_____do_____	787, 447	1, 059, 510	971, 460	707, 683	717, 077	701, 699	783, 472
Pork and lard:								
Apparent domestic consumption.	_____do_____	5, 776, 506	7, 056, 610	7, 201, 237	6, 296, 544	6, 153, 896	6, 705, 555	7, 330, 460
Apparent per capita consumption.	Pounds_____	52. 56	63. 18	63. 32	54. 57	52. 54	56. 53	61. 08

LARD, RENDERED

Item	Unit	1922	1923	1924	1925	1926	1927	1928
Average yield per 100 pounds live weight.	Pounds_____	16. 22	16. 49	16. 45	15. 02	15. 89	15. 36	15. 40
Total production from inspected slaughter.	1,000 pounds	1, 575, 137	1, 971, 245	1, 922, 629	1, 451, 743	1, 513, 385	1, 556, 747	1, 749, 749
Storage Jan. 1_____	_____do_____	47, 541	48, 808	49, 340	61, 049	42, 478	49, 992	54, 855
Total supply_____	_____do_____	1, 622, 678	2, 020, 053	1, 971, 969	1, 512, 792	1, 555, 863	1, 606, 739	1, 804, 604
Storage Dec. 31_____	_____do_____	48, 808	49, 340	61, 049	42, 478	49, 992	54, 855	85, 217
Exports, lard and neutral lard.	_____do_____	787, 447	1, 059, 510	971, 460	707, 683	717, 077	701, 699	783, 472
Apparent domestic consumption.	_____do_____	786, 423	911, 203	939, 460	762, 631	788, 794	850, 185	935, 915
Apparent per capita consumption.	Pounds_____	7. 16	8. 16	8. 26	6. 61	6. 73	7. 17	7. 80

Bureau of Agricultural Economics.

[1] Includes dressed pork and dressed lard, except killing fats.
[2] Pork imports consisted of fresh pork until Jan. 1, 1928, when pickled, salted, and preserved pork was added.
[3] Exports and reexports of fresh, cured, and canned pork.
[4] Exports and reexports of lard and neutral lard.

TABLE 389.—*Lard: Total stocks in cold-storage warehouses and meat-packing establishments, United States, 1916–1928* [1]

(In thousands)

Year	Jan. 1	Feb. 1	Mar. 1	Apr. 1	May 1	June 1	July 1	Aug. 1	Sept. 1	Oct. 1	Nov. 1	Dec. 1
Average:												
1916–1920	73,142	94,772	100,619	99,546	105,594	99,815	115,129	120,532	109,518	83,522	56,703	54,165
1921–1925	53,211	73,570	91,725	103,458	117,510	131,313	156,178	155,350	124,980	77,777	37,957	35,851
1916	63,304	92,342	111,897	97,237	108,731	85,113	87,127	95,991	82,028	71,570	56,929	58,950
1917	80,977	86,208	88,460	65,179	61,640	72,365	95,197	112,249	102,172	69,929	37,095	44,367
1918	54,539	59,310	65,355	89,854	103,373	106,194	107,871	102,411	104,668	90,398	76,124	81,676
1919	104,274	138,353	125,410	112,469	112,409	83,096	92,132	100,478	87,947	76,456	66,036	49,147
1920	62,614	97,649	111,975	132,993	141,819	152,307	193,316	191,531	170,774	109,258	47,329	36,683
1921	59,319	83,549	117,690	128,614	152,428	181,992	204,301	194,490	149,886	85,115	48,850	42,001
1922	47,541	61,202	61,297	86,031	96,055	123,798	154,254	143,084	119,755	75,338	36,750	32,506
1923	48,808	56,266	59,101	66,743	85,251	84,530	123,896	143,579	115,860	72,608	35,225	35,327
1924	49,340	54,130	68,610	85,722	102,317	127,949	152,520	149,672	124,676	84,198	31,706	35,713
1925	61,049	112,704	151,927	150,182	151,499	138,295	145,919	145,924	114,724	71,626	37,256	33,710
1926	42,478	64,187	76,145	93,108	98,365	106,824	120,527	153,572	151,233	105,558	72,355	46,744
1927	49,992	69,576	77,103	92,069	99,611	111,976	147,318	179,136	167,018	118,174	72,121	46,154
1928	54,855	84,007	121,082	164,506	173,088	186,073	214,479	204,939	177,888	126,890	83,474	67,257

Bureau of Agricultural Economics. Compiled from reports from cold-storage establishments.

[1] Lard includes all prime steam, kettle-rendered, neutral, and other pure lards. It does not include lard substitutes nor compounds.

TABLE 390.—*Pork: Stocks in cold-storage warehouses and meat-packing establishments, United States, 1916–1928*

DRY SALT CURED AND IN PROCESS OF CURE

(In thousands)

Year	Jan. 1	Feb. 1	Mar. 1	Apr. 1	May 1	June 1	July 1	Aug. 1	Sept. 1	Oct. 1	Nov. 1	Dec. 1
Average:												
1916–1920	243,893	313,699	345,319	355,433	356,364	349,408	323,973	311,047	273,409	226,795	181,909	186,673
1921–1925	128,806	158,231	179,655	188,577	190,726	192,211	206,048	200,015	178,070	136,806	98,121	93,238
1916	145,661	194,053	226,910	206,703	202,392	206,008	202,088	205,251	183,194	140,908	118,958	142,858
1917	200,998	228,424	259,059	234,396	219,819	213,802	224,813	231,905	195,678	143,319	110,652	150,882
1918	252,934	341,422	402,734	448,114	471,809	493,795	402,549	370,203	333,472	283,572	247,194	283,002
1919	357,254	471,747	435,661	430,205	425,411	402,652	381,736	366,547	338,270	332,786	281,930	242,224
1920	262,620	332,848	402,229	457,745	462,389	430,782	408,681	381,328	316,433	233,389	150,812	114,400
1921	144,997	202,909	251,893	255,390	246,443	240,610	250,752	231,511	200,291	149,974	108,611	96,731
1922	111,071	128,690	139,281	145,183	142,030	157,689	186,948	179,856	165,608	122,783	85,671	83,017
1923	121,125	155,922	178,024	206,429	227,728	214,453	217,862	221,716	191,711	146,974	108,850	110,824
1924	148,121	167,507	178,258	192,934	191,882	206,009	212,158	202,612	180,127	135,702	81,460	78,871
1925	118,718	136,125	150,819	142,950	145,548	142,292	162,518	164,374	152,555	128,599	106,011	96,746
1926	119,617	138,005	144,071	151,286	140,324	136,801	148,164	168,882	172,766	143,572	98,521	66,765
1927	68,203	86,135	101,156	124,676	129,637	143,143	173,256	185,920	178,107	140,420	100,922	77,240
1928	97,335	119,751	160,609	178,012	173,652	169,663	174,906	164,473	156,462	125,899	101,123	102,440

PICKLED,[1] CURED, AND IN PROCESS OF CURE

(In thousands)

Year	Jan. 1	Feb. 1	Mar. 1	Apr. 1	May 1	June 1	July 1	Aug. 1	Sept. 1	Oct. 1	Nov. 1	Dec. 1
Average:												
1916–1920	278,118	339,742	380,567	382,009	382,685	387,887	394,113	378,975	330,193	269,231	225,930	235,713
1921–1925	351,495	385,108	426,738	432,850	434,109	424,442	422,583	399,780	370,052	314,821	271,438	293,931
1916	230,881	298,939	350,750	351,051	337,464	326,183	359,300	350,570	303,399	251,004	209,061	251,519
1917	307,478	348,269	378,847	362,931	381,236	403,185	412,810	403,704	328,943	252,152	192,884	204,907
1918	269,003	322,004	369,014	402,377	406,191	397,486	372,347	365,941	315,517	249,827	223,148	242,976
1919	303,763	392,260	435,197	431,714	434,671	440,989	422,387	384,764	341,724	297,712	239,719	226,893
1920	279,467	337,238	369,026	361,973	353,864	371,593	403,719	389,896	361,381	295,460	254,838	252,270
1921	294,993	316,328	376,374	367,553	355,041	366,346	366,623		320,190	257,244	212,528	221,345
1922	252,822	284,487	321,950	347,276	348,305	363,395	391,474	385,692	369,187	313,517	278,812	302,708
1923	377,107	412,806	451,279	469,130	499,119	483,213	473,569	449,441	413,798	367,374	325,456	384,604
1924	434,030	468,892	500,784	512,190	500,683	483,372	473,914	443,918	408,928	351,485	283,710	299,868
1925	398,521	443,025	483,302	468,099	467,395	425,481	407,610	373,227	338,156	284,485	256,684	261,128
1926	294,642	319,726	351,346	349,938	346,049	338,448	330,328	320,326	293,106	257,726		266,222
1927	306,904	352,681	392,642	420,037	435,967	432,965	450,172	440,744	407,239	341,460	289,553	276,916
1928	320,436	370,916	461,264	496,322	480,069	459,878	454,826	408,994	351,936	285,309	265,988	292,626

[1] Pickled pork includes sweet-pickled, plain-brine, and barreled pork.

TABLE 390.—*Pork: Stocks in cold-storage warehouses and meat-packing establishments, United States, 1916–1928*—Continued

FROZEN

Year	Jan. 1	Feb. 1	Mar. 1	Apr. 1	May 1	June 1	July 1	Aug. 1	Sept. 1	Oct. 1	Nov. 1	Dec. 1
	Thousands	Thousands	Thousands	Thousands	Thousands	Thousands	Thousands	Thousands	Thousands	Thousands	Thousands	Thousands
Average:												
1916–1920___	50,702	80,496	103,516	112,200	110,797	116,101	123,485	116,731	85,360	54,844	40,144	39,028
1921–1925___	94,863	141,329	175,953	190,727	186,970	180,415	176,658	151,665	110,390	68,511	42,663	45,858
1916_____	44,194	63,376	88,604	88,344	77,812	83,195	82,571	85,845	63,420	38,851	23,988	32,015
1917_____	50,564	66,062	63,352	64,996	74,728	77,534	91,562	96,648	72,286	39,767	25,347	23,504
1918_____	41,663	61,659	104,630	116,548	117,786	118,601	117,976	108,220	71,385	46,593	36,968	34,750
1919_____	61,539	104,708	128,897	142,189	139,205	144,212	155,263	131,137	90,510	61,417	47,271	44,864
1920_____	55,551	106,677	132,095	148,922	144,453	156,963	170,054	161,804	129,197	87,592	67,148	60,007
1921_____	93,990	150,594	208,889	219,964	200,706	194,486	182,163	149,435	103,486	64,682	38,517	37,513
1922_____	51,203	71,722	86,219	98,765	103,907	114,571	128,962	117,903	84,815	46,796	30,688	33,774
1923_____	72,278	120,196	154,377	189,115	213,224	210,645	217,074	195,002	148,753	98,795	71,640	82,068
1924_____	126,718	164,491	199,044	227,284	215,767	201,728	186,566	164,049	121,816	77,986	42,561	48,781
1925_____	130,125	199,642	231,234	218,508	201,246	180,645	168,527	131,935	93,078	54,294	29,910	27,153
1926_____	57,960	98,311	120,115	129,259	124,569	117,366	120,707	133,104	119,994	77,673	49,376	55,241
1927_____	97,650	150,255	177,876	193,733	204,608	211,742	220,847	214,607	181,072	126,887	76,644	65,666
1928_____	105,654	164,971	264,043	323,403	306,951	289,825	285,628	245,714	173,617	103,879	66,049	66,696

Bureau of Agricultural Economics.   Compiled from reports from cold-storage establishments.

TABLE 391.—*Pork and pork products: International trade, average 1909–1913, annual 1925–1927*

Country	Year ended Dec. 31							
	Average 1909–1913		1925		1926		1927 preliminary	
	Imports	Exports	Imports	Exports	Imports	Exports	Imports	Exports
PRINCIPAL EXPORTING COUNTRIES	1,000 pounds	1,000 pounds	1,000 pounds	1,000 pounds	1,000 pounds	1,000 pounds	1,000 pounds	1,000 pounds
United States_____	171	1,019,561	7,235	1,241,209	9,156	1,130,323	14,524	993,188
Denmark_____	7,124	298,086	2,826	462,925	2,540	460,191	3,569	616,322
Netherlands_____	88,143	139,916	13,980	259,464	23,811	204,391	13,863	306,312
Canada_____	29,189	47,694	18,821	156,717	18,712	115,821	11,492	87,127
Irish Free State_____	0	0	63,316	78,280	59,676	78,224	52,976	95,045
Sweden_____	6,736	19,445	15,395	17,041	11,498	31,610	7,330	61,255
Poland_____	0	0	26,339	57,735	17,385	39,864	40,313	38,387
Brazil_____	3,767	278	9,746	312	1,281	594	_____	174
China_____	_____	7,679	378	16,717	307	14,492	595	10,801
Hungary_____	0	0	254	32,485	63	54,685	19	20,576
New Zealand_____	248	1,049	139	5,784	17	8,659	9	12,761
Australia [1]_____	[2] 923	[2] 6,294	1,397	3,249	1,220	3,720	1,683	3,631
Argentina_____	1,977	9	50	1,416	55	12,584	232	8,266
Chile_____	3,195	9	511	259	_____	_____	_____	_____
PRINCIPAL IMPORTING COUNTRIES								
United Kingdom_____	875,929	15,820	1,373,856	6,162	1,297,155	5,381	1,358,270	6,186
Germany_____	265,669	3,532	412,163	2,819	385,273	4,071	296,743	5,039
Cuba_____	85,973	0	137,214	0	131,104	0	_____	_____
France_____	59,824	24,668	57,277	3,334	60,785	3,638	162,579	3,734
Czechoslovakia_____	0	0	84,353	4,277	88,871	3,977	75,439	3,770
Austria_____	[3] 14,338	[3] 3,343	47,504	575	21,152	1,200	27,789	907
Belgium_____	22,232	16,254	21,602	3,043	15,755	12,034	17,333	9,763
Italy_____	74,861	_____	13,360	1,502	5,444	8,662	6,389	3,603
Norway_____	9,751	26	13,619	6	8,256	9	4,516	7
Finland_____	_____	_____	9,312	895	14,334	373	11,256	115
Peru_____	_____	_____	12,848	0	14,742	0	11,999	18
Switzerland_____	21,976	105	6,550	819	6,594	34	6,657	23
Philippine Islands_____	4,414	0	5,823	0	6,174	0	7,516	0
Spain_____	553	641	975	1,790	474	2,972	_____	_____
Union of South Africa_____	8,249	30	1,567	96	1,076	1,514	1,272	222
Total, 29 countries_____	1,585,242	1,604,439	2,358,410	2,358,911	2,202,910	2,199,023	2,134,363	2,287,532

Bureau of Agricultural Economics.   Official sources.

[1] Year ended June 30.   [2] Average for years ended December 31.   [3] Average for Austria-Hungary.

TABLE 392.—*Hog products: Wholesale and retail price per pound of certain products,*
1913–1928

Year	Hams		Bacon			Fresh pork		Lard	
	Whole-sale, smoked, Chicago	Retail,[1] average leading cities	Whole-sale, short clear sides, Chicago	Whole-sale, smoked, No. 1 sweet-pickle cure, 8 to 10 pounds, Chicago[2]	Retail, average leading cities	Whole-sale, loins, Chicago	Retail, chops, average leading cities	Whole-sale, prime contract, New York	Retail, average leading cities
	Cents	Cents	Cents	Cents	Cents	Cents	Cents	Cents	Cents
1913	16. 6	26. 9	12. 7		27. 0	14. 9	21. 0	11. 0	15. 8
1914	16. 7	27. 3	13. 2		27. 5	15. 4	22. 0	10. 4	15. 6
1915	15. 3	26. 1	11. 6		26. 9	14. 3	20. 3	9. 4	14. 8
1916	18. 5	29. 4	14. 9		28. 7	16. 2	22. 7	13. 5	17. 5
1917	25. 2	38. 2	24. 8		41. 0	24. 4	31. 9	21. 7	27. 6
1918	31. 8	47. 9	27. 9		52. 9	29. 5	39. 0	25. 5	33. 3
1919	34. 3	53. 4	29. 1		55. 4	31. 5	42. 3	29. 0	36. 9
1920	33. 4	55. 5	20. 7	36. 2	52. 3	30. 7	42. 3	20. 0	29. 5
1921	26. 8	48. 8	13. 5	25. 3	42. 7	22. 5	34. 9	11. 1	18. 0
1922	26. 5	48. 8	14. 1	25. 8	39. 8	21. 7	33. 0	11. 5	17. 0
1923	21. 2	45. 5	12. 0	22. 4	39. 1	18. 0	30. 4	12. 3	17. 7
1924	20. 2	45. 3	14. 4	20. 9	37. 7	19. 1	30. 8	13. 3	19. 0
1925	27. 1	52. 6	22. 3	32. 6	46. 7	25. 0	36. 6	16. 8	23. 3
1926	30. 8	57. 4	20. 1	37. 3	50. 3	27. 8	39. 5	15. 0	21. 9
1927	24. 6	55. 0	18. 7	25. 5	47. 2	[3] 23. 9	36. 8	12. 9	19. 3
1928	22. 8	52. 8	16. 3	23. 8	44. 0	[3] 22. 0	34. 8	12. 3	18. 6

Bureau of Agricultural Economics. Compiled from Bureau of Labor Statistics Wholesale and Retail
Price Bulletins, unless otherwise stated.

[1] Mostly on sliced ham.
[2] Bureau of Agricultural Economics.
[3] Quotations for loins, 8 to 10 pounds, as quoted by Bureau of Agricultural Economics.

TABLE 393.—*Lard, refined: Average price per 100 pounds, Chicago, by months,*
1920–1928

Year	Jan.	Feb.	Mar.	Apr.	May	June	July	Aug.	Sept.	Oct.	Nov.	Dec.	Av.
	Dolls.	Dolls.	Dolls.	Dolls.	Dolls.	Dolls.	Dolls.	Dolls.	Dolls.	Dolls.	Dolls.	Dolls.	Dolls.
1920		23. 14	22. 93	22. 71	22. 75	22. 98	21. 71	21. 16	22. 58	23. 28	22. 07	18. 15	22. 25
1921	16. 03	14. 91	14. 48	13. 07	11. 88	12. 03	13. 94	13. 65	13. 51	12. 16	11. 62	11. 25	13. 21
1922	11. 19	12. 59	13. 50	12. 62	13. 15	13. 22	13. 06	13. 30	13. 00	14. 12	13. 78	13. 31	13. 07
1923	13. 20	13. 25	13. 87	13. 42	13. 12	13. 18	12. 84	12. 83	15. 06	15. 22	15. 72	15. 04	13. 90
1924	14. 52	13. 03	12. 84	12. 50	12. 19	12. 13	13. 65	15. 94	16. 25	18. 05	16. 68	18. 00	14. 65
1925	17. 59	17. 03	18. 25	17. 07	16. 50	18. 13	18. 42	18. 94	18. 95	18. 75	18. 50	16. 67	17. 90
1926	16. 81	16. 44	16. 70	16. 75	17. 13	18. 48	18. 00	17. 38	17. 50	16. 75	15. 75	15. 25	16. 91
1927	13. 59	13. 72	14. 38	14. 32	14. 12	13. 35	12. 25	12. 54	14. 25	14. 50	13. 60	13. 25	13. 66
1928	12. 50	11. 60	11. 50	12. 50	13. 10	13. 50	14. 00	14. 70	15. 25	14. 40	13. 62	12. 88	13. 30

Bureau of Agricultural Economics. Compiled from data of the livestock and meat reporting service
of the bureau. Prices, 1905 to January, 1920, compiled from the National Provisioner, available in 1927
Yearbook, p. 1018.

TABLE 394.—*Lard, American prime western steam: Average price per pound in Liverpool, 1909–1928*

Year	Jan.	Feb.	Mar.	Apr.	May	June	July	Aug.	Sept.	Oct.	Nov.	Dec.	Av.
	Cents	Cents	Cents	Cents	Cents	Cents	Cents	Cents	Cents	Cents	Cents	Cents	Cents
Average:													
1909–1913	11.5	11.6	11.8	11.7	11.8	11.9	11.9	12.1	12.5	12.5	12.5	12.1	12.0
1921–1925	16.2	16.0	14.9	14.0	13.6	14.0	14.5	14.9	15.0	15.2	15.5	15.0	14.9
1909	10.7	10.6	11.2	11.4	11.8	12.7	12.8	12.8	13.4	13.6	14.7	14.9	12.6
1910	14.1	14.0	15.5	14.8	14.5	13.7	13.3	13.1	13.6	13.8	12.7	11.5	13.7
1911	11.5	11.4	10.0	9.1	9.2	9.1	9.1	9.9	10.4	9.9	10.2	10.1	10.0
1912	10.2	10.0	10.2	10.9	11.4	11.6	11.4	11.8	12.4	13.0	12.6	11.9	11.4
1913	11.2	11.8	12.2	12.4	12.3	12.2	12.7	12.7	12.6	12.1	12.2	12.1	12.2
1914	12.3	11.8	11.5	11.3	10.8	10.9	11.0	12.6	11.4	11.3	12.2	11.7	11.6
1915	12.0	11.6	11.1	11.2	11.1	10.6	9.3	8.3	8.9	10.2	10.8	11.7	10.6
1916	12.7	12.4	13.8	15.4	16.5	15.7	15.4	15.7	17.3	18.3	20.3	20.1	16.1
1917	20.4	¹24.8	29.3	27.7	26.3	23.8	23.8	25.0	²25.9	¹27.1	28.2	28.6	25.9
1918	28.6	____	____	____	31.7	31.7	____	____	____	33.2	33.0	____	____
1919	____	____	____	____	38.1	37.1	36.3	36.5	36.8	35.6	32.9	____	____
1920	32.0	29.5	32.9	27.2	____	27.4	26.7	____	____	____	23.8	24.2	____
1921	23.4	²23.3	15.7	13.2	11.7	12.1	13.6	13.4	13.2	12.2	12.6	11.7	14.7
1922	11.3	12.9	13.1	12.8	13.6	13.5	13.2	13.3	12.7	13.2	14.1	13.6	13.1
1923	13.3	13.0	13.7	13.6	12.9	13.0	12.7	12.7	14.0	14.5	15.7	15.1	13.7
1924	14.8	13.1	12.8	12.7	12.3	12.2	13.7	15.8	15.8	18.1	17.2	18.1	14.7
1925	18.0	17.5	18.7	17.8	17.6	19.1	19.3	19.2	19.2	17.9	17.8	16.6	18.2
1926	17.2	16.5	16.5	16.0	17.6	18.4	17.8	17.0	16.6	15.8	14.2	14.3	16.5
1927	14.3	14.4	14.4	14.3	14.1	14.4	14.3	13.8	14.6	14.4	14.0	13.5	14.2
1928	13.6	12.9	13.0	13.3	13.4	13.3	13.7	13.9	14.4	13.9	13.4	13.2	13.5

Bureau of Agricultural Economics. Compiled from Manchester Guardian. An average of Friday quotations. Converted at monthly average rate of exchange as given in Federal Reserve Bulletins to 1925, inclusive; subsequently at par of exchange.

¹ Interpolated.
² Government control of prices began Sept. 3, 1917, and ended on Feb. 28, 1921.

TABLE 395.—*Bacon, Wilshire sides,¹ green, firsts: Average price per pound at Bristol, England, 1909–1928*

Year and month	American	Canadian	Danish	Irish	British
	Cents	Cents	Cents	Cents	Cents
Average:					
1909–1913	14.2	14.8	15.6	16.1	17.0
1914–1920	27.1	____	____	____	30.1
1921–1925	20.0	23.3	27.0	29.1	30.0
1909	13.6	14.3	15.0	15.9	16.7
1910	15.2	15.6	15.9	16.6	17.8
1911	12.8	13.1	14.3	14.8	15.8
1912	13.8	14.5	15.9	15.8	16.3
1913	15.8	16.3	17.1	17.4	18.4
1914	15.5	15.7	16.4	17.6	18.2
1915	17.0	18.4	20.4	20.8	21.4
1916	19.8	22.0	24.0	24.7	26.0
1917	30.1	____	____	____	33.0
1918	38.5	____	____	____	30.3
1919	37.1	37.9	____	38.4	38.4
1920	31.6	33.1	34.2	41.7	42.8
1921	21.8	26.5	32.8	34.7	36.2
1922	21.2	25.2	29.7	32.5	33.3
1923	17.5	20.9	23.6	25.8	27.0
1924	16.6	19.2	21.3	22.8	23.5
1925	23.0	24.7	27.5	29.7	30.0
1926	____	____	27.8	30.6	32.3
1927	____	____	21.1	25.5	26.9
1928	17.9	____	21.2	23.7	25.8
1927					
January	____	²20.9	21.5	27.8	28.7
February	18.6	____	21.1	27.9	29.3
March	19.0	____	21.9	28.2	30.2
April	18.7	____	21.9	28.2	29.6
May	____	____	22.8	28.7	29.6
June	____	20.9	22.6	27.2	27.6
July	____	18.9	21.1	23.5	25.5
August	____	18.0	21.0	23.6	25.0
September	____	____	23.4	26.2	27.4
October	____	____	20.6	21.9	23.9
November	16.6	____	17.5	21.0	22.1
December	16.2	____	18.3	21.6	23.9
1928					
January	16.5	____	18.3	21.9	26.5
February	16.4	____	18.5	22.6	26.5
March	16.1	____	18.6	23.1	26.8
April	16.2	____	18.9	24.1	27.6
May	15.6	____	20.2	24.8	26.9
June	16.4	____	23.2	25.3	26.5
July	20.6	____	24.3	25.2	26.4
August	20.9	____	24.3	25.2	26.5
September	20.3	____	23.9	24.8	25.4
October	19.5	____	20.8	22.0	23.0
November	18.4	____	20.3	21.9	23.1
December	18.5	____	22.6	23.0	24.8

Bureau of Agricultural Economics. Compiled from Agricultural Market Report, Ministry of Agriculture and Fisheries, Great Britain. Average for the last week of each month 1909–1923. Average of weekly averages 1924–1928. Converted at monthly average rate of exchange as given in Federal Reserve Bulletins, to December, 1925, inclusive; subsequently at par of exchange.

¹ Entire half of hog in one piece, head off, backbone out, ribs in. ² January 5 quotation only.

TABLE 396.—*Pork carcass, first quality, fresh, British: Average price per pound in Great Britain, 1909–1928*

Year	Jan.	Feb.	Mar.	Apr.	May	June	July	Aug.	Sept.	Oct.	Nov.	Dec.	Av.
	Cents	Cents	Cents	Cents	Cents	Cents	Cents	Cents	Cents	Cents	Cents	Cents	Cents
Average:													
1909–1913	14.2	14.2	14.2	14.1	13.8	13.9	13.5	13.7	14.3	14.9	14.9	15.1	14.2
1914–1920	23.8	24.6	25.3	26.9	25.7	25.5	25.6	24.9	26.1	26.9	27.0	26.9	25.8
1921–1925	25.6	24.6	24.5	25.1	25.0	21.9	20.4	21.6	23.5	24.0	24.3	25.0	23.6
1909	12.8	12.8	12.9	13.0	12.7	12.9	13.2	13.2	13.5	14.2	14.8	15.2	13.5
1910	15.1	15.0	15.0	14.8	14.7	14.1	13.9	14.6	15.0	15.4	15.3	14.9	14.8
1911	14.5	14.2	14.2	14.0	13.2	14.6	12.2	12.2	12.7	13.2	12.8	12.5	13.2
1912	12.7	12.7	12.8	12.8	12.5	12.6	12.8	13.0	14.4	15.1	15.1	15.7	13.5
1913	16.1	16.3	16.3	16.1	15.8	15.5	15.5	15.6	16.0	16.4	16.7	17.1	16.1
1914	16.8	16.2	16.2	15.8	14.5	13.9	13.3	14.5	15.1	16.5	16.4	16.3	15.5
1915	15.8	15.9	16.4	17.2	17.0	16.8	16.7	16.9	18.8	20.0	21.4	21.4	17.9
1916	20.1	21.6	21.6	23.6	21.9	21.7	21.7	21.7	23.8	25.4	25.0	26.1	22.8
1917	26.9	27.2	27.7	28.2	26.4	27.2	28.6	25.5	29.1	28.2	28.2	28.2	27.6
1918	28.2	28.2	28.2	31.8	31.8	31.7	31.7	31.8	31.8	34.2	35.7	35.7	31.7
1919	32.1	31.8	31.2	31.0	31.1	30.8	29.5	28.5	27.9	27.8	27.2	26.3	29.6
1920	26.8	131.0	136.0	41.0	37.2	36.1	37.6	35.4	36.3	36.4	34.9	34.2	35.2
1921	32.5	29.7	29.7	30.5	29.0	24.9	22.9	23.5	24.5	22.8	22.5	23.2	26.3
1922	22.5	23.9	24.4	25.3	25.0	23.0	23.9	24.7	26.6	27.3	28.5	30.3	24.5
1923	29.6	28.0	27.0	26.8	30.7	24.5	20.7	20.4	22.4	23.0	22.3	21.5	24.7
1924	20.4	19.2	18.5	19.2	18.1	16.6	14.1	18.1	19.0	20.2	20.5	21.0	18.7
1925	23.0	22.0	22.9	23.6	22.3	20.4	20.6	21.4	24.8	26.5	27.3	28.9	23.6
1926	28.3	27.9	28.0	27.1	27.6	26.0	26.4	26.6	28.8	30.3	29.8	29.3	28.0
1927	28.5	27.8	27.6	27.5	24.3	23.2	21.5	21.2	22.7	22.5	21.3	22.2	24.2
1928	21.7	21.1	21.0	21.1	19.7	18.8	18.6	18.9	20.3	20.9	20.5	21.6	20.1

[1] Bureau of Agricultural Economics. Compiled from Agricultural Statistics 1909–1922, and Agricultural Market Report, 1923–1928, Ministry of Agriculture and Fisheries, Great Britain. Conversions at monthly average rate of exchange as given in Federal Reserve Bulletins to December, 1925, inclusive; subsequently at par.

TABLE 397.—*Hogs: Cholera-control work by Bureau of Animal Industry, 1919–1928*

Year ended June 30, and State	Bureau veterinarians engaged in work [1]	Premises investigated	Demonstrations		Autopsies performed	Farms quarantined or carded	Farms cleaned and disinfected	Outbreaks reported to bureau veterinarians
			Number	Hogs treated				
1919	180	93,512		233,987	53,586	9,564	4,382	12,336
1920	140	46,125	3,037	347,702	10,963	6,129	2,099	9,788
1921	54	29,433	3,420	67,295	3,888	2,268	656	7,951
1922	80	47,137	4,343	88,846	5,390	1,401	439	7,920
1923	71	52,348	5,234	108,562	5,247	1,772	741	7,204
1924	45	29,443	3,178	78,007	3,686	1,634	847	7,225
1925	34	24,060	2,353	51,331	2,383	886	470	3,437
1926	35	20,599	2,579	69,230	2,446	854	347	4,558
1927	36.96	25,004	4,863	97,917	3,741	1,832	744	11,555
1928								
Alabama	1	1,230	1,018	23,606	267			339
Arkansas	1.16	648	244	3,148	39			927
California	1	409	39	543	157			84
Colorado	.1	46			30			15
Florida	2.5	1,357	1,140	35,414	128		116	235
Georgia	1.3	702	300	5,865	39		1	216
Idaho	1	762	17	1,558	55	25		25
Illinois	2	2,189	79	1,943	501	258	357	647
Indiana	2	756	5	128	208	31		227
Iowa	2.16	779	6	229	231			585
Kansas	1.16	532			14			38
Kentucky	2	2,669	121	2,698	196		6	297
Louisiana	1	262	111	4,160	37			61
Maryland	2	3,087	26	674	208	476	2	602
Michigan	2	662	49	2,195	136	24	15	334
Mississippi	1.04	731	86	1,317	18		2	57
Missouri	1	710	42	968	134			244
Montana	.5	125			23	27	2	29
Nebraska	.45	369			267			78
North Carolina	1	508	162	4,939	86	41		62
Ohio	1	993	1	79	52	6		98
Oklahoma	2	1,646	15	853	80	125	10	180
South Carolina	1	796	790	12,783	14			311
South Dakota	1	218			82			45
Tennessee	.5	116	1	52	36	34		342
Texas	2	618			34	19	1	147
Utah	.05	13			9	3		3
Virginia	1	731	83	1,173	121			310
Washington	1.5	725	6	107	41	17	3	58
Oregon	.5	90	4	59	4	23	6	27
West Virginia	.5	136	5	50	12	8		211
Wisconsin	1	551	94	1,365	109		1	107
Total	38.42	25,156	4,444	106,906	3,368	1,117	522	6,941

[1] Bureau of Animal Industry. Fractions denote veterinarians devoting a part of their time to the work.

TABLE 398.—*Sheep: Number and value per head in the United States, 1840, 1850, 1860, 1867–1929*

Year	Sheep on farms [1]	Value per head, Jan. 1	Sheep on farms and elsewhere	Year	Sheep on farms [1]	Value per head, Jan. 1	Sheep on farms and elsewhere
	Thousands	*Dollars*	*Thousands*		*Thousands*	*Dollars*	*Thousands*
1840, June 1 [2]	*19,311*			1898	37,657	2.46	42,600
1850, June 1 [2]	*21,723*			1899	39,114	2.75	44,600
1860, June 1 [2]	*22,471*			1900	[3] 41,883	2.93	48,100
1867	39,385	2.50	38,100	1900, June 1	*61,504*		
1868	38,992	1.82	37,600	1900	44,573		
1869	37,724	1.64	36,200	1901	46,155	2.98	50,400
1870, June 1 [2]	*28,478*			1902	46,667	2.65	51,900
1870	40,853	1.96	39,000	1903	45,180	2.63	53,000
1871	31,851	2.14	38,900	1904	42,439	2.59	42,500
1872	31,679	2.61	38,600	1905	40,268	2.82	36,800
1873	33,002	2.71	40,100	1906	42,454	3.54	41,000
1874	33,938	2.43	41,100	1907	44,518	3.84	42,700
1875	33,784	2.55	40,800	1908	46,557	3.88	43,500
1876	35,935	2.37	43,300	1909	48,382	3.43	44,300
1877	35,804	2.13	43,000	1910, Apr. 15	*52,448*		
1878	35,740	2.21	42,800	1910	47,072	4.12	44,800
1879	38,124	2.07	*45,500*	1911	47,349	3.91	45,700
1880, June 1 [2]	*35,192*			1912	43,279	3.46	44,600
1880	40,766	2.21	48,500	1913	40,700	3.94	43,700
1881	43,570	2.39	51,200	1914	37,773	4.02	42,200
1882	45,016	2.37	52,300	1915	36,287	4.50	42,200
1883	49,237	2.53	56,600	1916	36,543	5.17	41,100
1884	50,627	2.37	57,500	1917	36,700	7.13	40,200
1885	50,360	2.14	56,500	1918	39,000	11.82	40,900
1886	48,322	1.91	53,600	1919	41,000	11.63	41,100
1887	44,759	2.01	49,100	1920, Jan. 1	*35,034*		
1888	43,545	2.05	47,200	1920	40,243	10.46	40,693
1889	42,599	2.13	45,700	1921	38,690	6.28	39,123
1890, June 1 [2]	*35,935*			1922	36,186	4.80	36,591
1890	44,336	2.27	47,000	1923	36,212	7.53	36,617
1891	43,431	2.50	46,400	1924	36,876	7.91	37,288
1892	44,938	2.58	48,400	1925, Jan. 1	*35,590*		
1893	47,274	2.66	51,300	1925	38,112	9.70	38,538
1894	45,048	1.98	49,300	1926	39,730	10.51	40,174
1895	42,294	1.58	46,700	1927	41,881	9.71	42,314
1896	38,299	1.70	42,600	1928	44,554	10.25	45,124
1897	36,819	1.82	41,300	1929	[4] 47,171	10.60	47,775

Bureau of Agricultural Economics. Data for sheep on farms and value per head (except italic figures from the census) from reports of the Bureau of Agricultural Economics as of Jan. 1.

[1] Figures 1900–1919 are tentative revised estimates of the Bureau of Agricultural Economics as first published in 1927 Yearbook. Prior to 1900 estimates for each 10-year period represent an index of animal changes applied to census as base on first report after census data were available.
[2] Figures for census years 1860, 1880, and 1890 exclude an estimated number of unenumerated sheep on ranges as follows: 1860, 1,505,810; 1880, 7,000,000; 1890, 4,940,948. Censuses prior to 1900 excluded lambs.
[3] Original estimate of the Bureau of Agricultural Economics.
[4] Preliminary.

33023°—29——60

TABLE 399.—*Sheep and lambs: Estimated number on farms and value per head, by States, January 1, 1925–1929*

State and division	Number, Jan. 1					Value per head, Jan. 1 [1]				
	1925	1926	1927	1928	1929 [2]	1925	1926	1927	1928	1929 [2]
	Thousands	Thousands	Thousands	Thousands	Thousands	Dollars	Dollars	Dollars	Dollars	Dollars
Maine	89	95	92	92	93	7.60	8.00	8.30	8.50	8.40
New Hampshire	18	19	20	21	21	8.10	8.60	9.00	9.50	9.60
Vermont	40	43	43	44	45	8.30	8.90	9.40	9.30	9.00
Massachusetts	12	11	11	11	11	9.70	9.40	9.80	10.60	10.00
Rhode Island	2	2	2	2	2	10.00	9.50	10.00	10.50	11.00
Connecticut	8	8	7	8	8	9.40	10.20	10.40	10.80	11.90
New York	473	497	477	491	452	10.60	11.60	10.80	11.10	11.50
New Jersey	6	6	6	6	6	9.50	10.80	11.80	12.20	11.50
Pennsylvania	415	415	400	437	441	8.80	9.70	9.40	9.50	9.60
North Atlantic	1,063	1,096	1,058	1,112	1,079	9.52	10.35	9.98	10.16	10.30
Ohio	1,941	2,000	2,133	2,133	2,154	8.90	9.50	8.50	8.90	9.00
Indiana	595	647	731	705	726	10.60	11.50	10.10	11.00	11.20
Illinois	556	710	800	630	664	10.40	11.30	10.00	10.60	10.80
Michigan	1,066	1,173	1,314	1,314	1,380	11.20	12.00	10.40	10.90	11.00
Wisconsin	360	401	469	430	450	10.20	11.00	9.60	10.20	10.40
Minnesota	462	540	628	666	686	10.60	11.20	9.70	10.50	10.80
Iowa	870	.913	1,047	939	1,096	11.20	11.80	10.20	10.80	11.00
Missouri	894	940	986	942	987	9.40	10.00	9.70	10.10	10.60
North Dakota	311	373	460	529	582	9.90	11.20	10.20	10.70	11.00
South Dakota	682	700	749	809	890	10.50	10.80	9.90	10.60	10.50
Nebraska	780	810	684	905	1,050	10.50	10.30	8.70	9.10	9.50
Kansas	384	452	475	512	538	9.10	9.80	9.40	9.40	9.20
North Central	8,901	9,659	10,476	10,514	11,203	10.10	10.71	9.59	10.09	10.27
Delaware	2	2	2	2	2	10.00	10.00	10.00	12.00	11.50
Maryland	92	96	98	101	108	9.50	10.40	10.30	11.60	11.50
Virginia	351	362	380	426	469	8.90	10.10	10.30	11.50	11.80
West Virginia	485	485	500	565	593	8.20	9.40	10.10	10.90	11.00
North Carolina	67	73	80	85	89	6.20	6.60	7.40	9.00	9.00
South Carolina	14	13	14	15	15	4.40	4.10	4.90	4.90	4.90
Georgia	51	51	51	46	48	3.40	3.20	3.60	3.80	4.00
Florida	60	59	59	59	59	3.30	3.00	3.20	3.60	4.30
South Atlantic	1,122	1,141	1,184	1,299	1,383	7.90	8.85	9.31	10.38	10.59
Kentucky	715	751	871	958	996	8.90	10.10	10.70	11.20	11.40
Tennessee	292	286	300	345	352	5.90	7.40	10.10	9.60	9.60
Alabama	57	48	53	66	79	4.30	3.90	3.70	4.40	4.20
Mississippi	114	108	76	45	38	2.90	3.00	3.30	3.40	3.30
Arkansas	52	49	54	54	50	3.90	4.80	5.80	6.10	6.50
Louisiana	109	105	102	107	110	3.20	3.00	3.00	3.00	3.30
Oklahoma	64	70	84	97	107	7.30	8.80	9.20	8.80	10.00
Texas	3,500	3,535	4,065	4,593	5,052	7.50	8.10	7.80	8.40	8.90
South Central	4,903	4,952	5,605	6,265	6,784	7.36	8.10	8.23	8.75	9.14
Montana	2,579	2,880	3,053	3,358	3,761	10.40	11.40	10.50	11.00	11.30
Idaho	1,960	1,880	1,974	2,110	2,216	10.90	11.80	10.80	11.40	11.90
Wyoming	2,700	2,870	3,100	3,193	3,448	10.80	11.50	10.20	10.60	11.60
Colorado	2,565	2,537	1,938	2,806	2,780	10.30	10.50	9.40	9.70	10.60
New Mexico	2,100	2,050	2,250	2,362	2,362	8.50	9.50	8.70	9.00	10.30
Arizona	1,164	1,220	1,230	1,132	1,109	8.20	8.90	9.10	9.50	9.70
Utah	2,355	2,472	2,650	2,730	2,866	11.30	12.00	10.80	11.20	11.50
Nevada	1,100	1,175	1,198	1,234	1,259	11.00	11.70	10.60	11.00	10.80
Washington	516	478	526	552	574	11.20	12.10	11.00	11.50	12.00
Oregon	2,039	2,120	2,247	2,359	2,501	10.40	11.50	10.40	11.20	11.50
California	3,045	3,200	3,392	3,528	3,846	9.20	10.60	10.00	11.40	10.80
Far Western	22,123	22,882	23,558	25,364	26,722	10.15	11.04	10.12	10.68	11.12
United States	38,112	39,730	41,881	44,554	47,171	9.70	10.51	9.71	10.25	10.60

Bureau of Agricultural Economics. Estimates of crop-reporting board.

[1] Sum of total value of classes divided by total number and rounded to nearest dime for States. Division and the United States averages not rounded.
[2] Preliminary.

TABLE 400.—*Sheep: Number in countries having 100,000 and over, average 1909–1913 and 1921–1925, annual 1925–1928*

Country	Month of estimate	Average 1909–1913 [1]	Average 1921–1925 [1]	1925	1926	1927	1928 pre-liminary
NORTH AND CENTRAL AMERICA AND WEST INDIES		*Thousands*	*Thousands*	*Thousands*	*Thousands*	*Thousands*	*Thousands*
Canada	July	2, 208	3, 027	2, 756	3, 142	3, 263	3, 416
United States	January	43, 235	37, 215	38, 112	39, 736	41, 881	44, 554
Mexico	June	[2] [3] 3, 424	[4] 1, 362	[4] 1, 162	2, 698		
Guatemala		514	153	114	148	155	
Dominican Republic		(134)	148				
Estimated total [5]		49, 800	42, 200				
SOUTH AMERICA							
Colombia		[6] 246	776	780	800		
Venezuela		177	113				
Ecuador			500		700		
Peru			11, 363			[7] 12,000	
Bolivia		1, 750	3, 436	3, 436	4, 220		
Chile		3, 477	4, 332	4, 094			
Brazil	September	10, 550	[2] [8] 7, 933				
Uruguay		[2] [9] 26, 286	[2] 14, 443			22, 500	
Paraguay	December [10]	[11] 600					
Argentina	do [10]	[2] [12] 43, 225	[2] [13] 36, 209				
Falkland Islands		711	649	631	606	607	
Estimated total [5]		93, 200	80, 400				
EUROPE							
Iceland		589	565	566			
England and Wales	June	18, 346	14, 385	15, 975	16, 859	17, 072	16, 386
Scotland	do	7, 028	6, 827	7, 119	7, 203	7, 536	7, 505
Ireland	do	3, 787	3, 453	3, 297	3, 533	3, 721	3, 888
Norway [14]	do	1, 398	1, 380	1, 529	1, 595	1, 608	
Sweden	do	1, 205	1, 384	[15] 1, 200			
Denmark	July	533	380	261	233		
Faroe Islands		112	66				
Holland	May–June	[2] 842	[2] 668				
Belgium	December [10]	189	126				
France	do [10]	16, 176	9, 777	10, 172	10, 537	10, 775	10, 693
Spain	do [10]	15, 778	19, 229	18, 460	20, 067	20, 529	
Portugal		[2] [16] 3, 073	3, 684	3, 684		[7] 4, 450	
Italy	March–April	11, 615	12, 014			[7] 12, 500	
Switzerland	April	161	245		169		
Germany	December [10]	4, 988	5, 889	5, 735	4, 753	4, 080	3, 819
Austria	do [10]	301	526				
Czechoslovakia	do [10]	1, 322	[2] [8] 986		861		
Hungary	April	2, 406	1, 661	1, 891	1, 804	1, 611	1, 566
Yugoslovia	January	10, 496	7, 728	7, 907	7, 933	7, 736	
Greece	December [10]	5, 884	5, 965	6, 623	6, 636	6, 951	6, 442
Bulgaria	do [10]	8, 551	8, 186	7, 450		8, 682	
Rumania	do [10]	11, 128	11, 660	13, 612	12, 950	13, 582	12, 941
Poland	November	4, 473	2, 193			1, 918	
Lithuania	Spring	1, 152	1, 314	1, 455	1, 573	1, 365	
Latvia	June	996	1, 240	1, 182	1, 153	1, 128	
Estonia	July	486	654	720	666	667	
Finland	September	1, 330	1, 526	1, 451	1, 414	1, 368	
Estimated total, excluding Russia. [5]		134, 400	123, 700				

[1] Average for 5-year period if available, otherwise for any year or years within this period except as otherwise stated. In countries having changed boundaries the pre-war figures are estimates for one year only of numbers within present boundaries.
[2] Nearest census figure.   [3] Year 1902.   [4] Incomplete.
[5] These totals include countries with less than 100,000, interpolations for a few countries not reporting each year, and rough estimates for some others.
[6] Year 1916.   [7] Unofficial.   [8] Year 1920.   [9] Year 1908.
[10] Estimates reported as of Dec. 31 are considered as of Jan. 1 of the following year, i. e. figures for number of sheep in France as of Dec. 31, 1924, has been placed in 1925 column.
[11] Year 1915.   [12] June, 1914.   [13] December, 1922.   [14] In rural communities only.
[15] Estimate forwarded by Assistant Trade Commissioner Wrenn.
[16] 1906.

TABLE 400.—Sheep: Number in countries having 100,000 and over, average 1909-1913 and 1921-1925, annual 1925-1928—Continued

Country	Month of estimate	Average 1909-1913	Average 1921-1925	1925	1926	1927	1928 preliminary
		Thousands	Thousands	Thousands	Thousands	Thousands	Thousands
AFRICA							
Morocco		3,175	7,533	9,278	9,250	7,712	
Algeria	September	8,757	5,943	6,171	6,786	5,083	5,614
Libia (Italian)		996	1,043		1,329	2,172	2,142
Tunis	December [10]	705	1,794	1,379	4,365	3,968	
French West Africa			3,742			2,400	
French Sudan			2,173				
Gold Coast		250	373	320	325		
Nigeria			1,681	1,479	1,809	1,827	
Egypt	September	816	1,013	1,091	1,144	1,232	
Anglo-Egyptian Sudan			1,638	1,639	2,000	2,010	
British Somaliland					2,000	2,000	2,000
Italian Somaliland			1,666				
Eritrea (Italian) [17]		1,585	1,701			1,842	
Kenya Colony	March–June	5,469	2,600	2,679	2,756	2,842	
French Cameroon [17]		(200)	287	325	410	456	
Uganda		612	386	604	866	911	
Belgian Congo		300	304	310	300	285	
British Southwest Africa		555	954	966	1,069	1,252	
Bechuanaland		358	125	129	132	152	
Union of South Africa	April–August	30,657	32,483	35,570	38,849	40,109	40,694
Basutoland		1,369	1,954	2,051	2,100	2,149	
Rhodesia, Southern	December [10]	300	333	340	349	332	347
Swaziland		164	62				
Tanganyika Territory [17]		3,596	3,893	4,333	4,462	4,779	
Madagascar		318	110	110	116		
Estimated total [5]		72,500	75,800				
ASIA							
Arabia						3,500	
Cyprus	March	279	237	244	207		
Turkey, European and Asiatic		19,713	10,451	11,469	12,872	13,512	
			5,270	4,892	5,055		
Iraq (Mesopotamia) [17]	February		271	291	291	243	
Palestine	March		4,000	4,000			
Persia			1,797	1,290	[1]1,400	1,334	
Syria and Lebanon			22,412	23,226	23,201	23,237	
India, British	December–April	23,164	12,299	13,682	11,848		
Native States	do	8,038					
China (including Turkestan and Manchuria)		25,951					
Philippines	December [10]	96	260	319	344	369	395
Dutch East Indies:							
Java and Madura	do [10]		915			1,292	
Outer possessions	do [10]		115			115	
Estimated total, excluding Russia [5]		99,700	94,300				
OCEANIA							
Australia	December [10]	89,008	[18]85,556	[18]93,155	[18]103,563	104,267	99,216
New Zealand	April	23,996	23,382	24,548	24,905	25,649	27,134
Estimated total [5]		113,000	108,900				
Russia [19]	Summer	[6]111,051	92,501	106,800	113,600	121,739	124,500
Total countries reporting all periods, including Russia—							
Pre-war to 1927 (39) [20]		471,233	427,247	462,853	489,983	503,267	
Pre-war to 1928 (18) [20]		379,756	342,111	373,574	396,872	410,192	411,252
Estimated world total [5]		673,700	617,800				

Bureau of Agricultural Economics. Official sources and International Institute of Agriculture unless otherwise stated. Figures in parentheses are interpolated.

[5] These totals include countries with less than 100,000, interpolations for a few countries not reporting each year, and rough estimates for some others.   [6] Year 1916.

[10] Estimates reported as of Dec. 31 are considered as of Jan. 1 of the following year, i. e. figures for number of sheep in France as of Dec. 31, 1924, has been placed in 2925 column.   [17] Goats included.

[18] Revised estimates. These are on the average about 5 per cent above the unrevised estimates.

[19] Years 1916, 1923-1927 from the Soviet Union Review, April, 1928, page 62. Year 1928 from Economic Life, Dec. 13, 1928, Supplement No. 12.   [20] Comparable totals for the number of countries indicated.

TABLE 401.—Sheep: Receipts at principal public stockyards and at all public stockyards, 1909-1928

Year	Chicago	Denver	East St. Louis	Fort Worth	Kansas City	Omaha	South St. Joseph	South St. Paul	Sioux City	Total nine markets [1]	All other stockyards reporting [2]	Total all stockyards reporting [2]
	Thousands	Thousands	Thousands	Thousands	Thousands	Thousands	Thousands	Thousands	Thousands	Thousands	Thousands	Thousands
1909	4,441	634	776	188	1,645	2,167	621	496	78	11,046		
1910	5,229	596	736	163	1,841	2,985	560	865	151	13,126		
1911	5,736	617	992	187	2,175	2,978	718	712	212	14,327		
1912	6,056	777	1,031	284	2,134	2,951	729	628	207	14,797		
1913	5,903	620	950	328	2,095	3,222	812	785	271	14,986		
1914	5,378	692	749	408	2,002	3,114	830	795	404	14,372		
1915	3,510	765	648	363	1,815	3,268	878	704	337	12,288	6,147	18,435
1916	4,291	1,409	671	431	1,758	3,171	804	623	321	13,479	7,213	20,692
1917	3,595	2,060	531	406	1,499	3,017	679	430	267	12,484	7,732	20,219
1918	4,630	1,652	536	335	1,667	3,386	827	630	387	14,050	8,435	22,485
1919	5,244	2,087	724	453	1,945	3,789	1,007	912	686	16,847	10,409	27,256
1920	4,005	2,079	605	394	1,687	2,891	843	729	358	13,591	9,947	23,538
1921	4,734	1,468	636	357	1,780	2,753	931	633	288	13,580	10,588	24,168
1922	3,874	1,867	628	325	1,574	2,533	730	499	223	12,253	10,111	22,364
1923	4,098	1,857	561	386	1,671	2,970	979	454	216	13,192	8,833	22,025
1924	4,192	2,040	489	373	1,569	2,844	1,089	476	310	13,382	8,819	22,201
1925	3,969	2,357	559	314	1,500	2,420	1,143	545	360	13,167	8,933	22,100
1926	4,405	1,826	636	445	1,762	2,780	1,303	773	449	14,379	9,489	23,868
1927	3,829	1,908	574	445	1,616	2,604	1,348	705	527	13,556	10,383	23,939
1928	3,868	2,295	510	458	1,767	3,037	1,580	891	568	14,974	10,623	25,597

Bureau of Agricultural Economics. Prior to 1915 receipts compiled from yearbooks of stockyard companies; subsequent figures compiled from data of the livestock and meat reporting service of the bureau. Receipts, 1900-1908, are available in 1924 Yearbook, p. 935, Table 542.

[1] Total of the rounded detail figures.   [2] Figures prior to 1915 not obtainable.

TABLE 402.—Sheep: Receipts and stocker and feeder shipments at all public stockyards, 1915-1928

RECEIPTS

Year	Jan.	Feb.	Mar.	Apr.	May	June	July	Aug.	Sept.	Oct.	Nov.	Dec.	Total
	Thousands	Thousands	Thousands	Thousands	Thousands	Thousands	Thousands	Thousands	Thousands	Thousands	Thousands	Thousands	Thousands
1915 [1]	1,517	1,257	1,248	1,019	1,050	1,080	1,264	1,725	2,501	2,359	2,042	1,373	18,435
1916 [1]	1,450	1,280	1,156	1,144	1,347	1,394	1,451	1,984	2,650	3,231	2,126	1,479	20,692
1917	1,578	1,384	1,256	1,152	1,059	1,240	1,353	1,763	2,554	3,195	2,102	1,583	20,219
1918	1,354	1,096	1,270	1,159	1,214	1,429	1,639	2,270	3,496	3,327	2,605	1,626	22,485
1919	1,594	1,157	1,268	1,438	1,468	1,775	2,287	3,360	3,854	3,754	2,845	2,456	27,256
1920	1,614	1,416	1,315	1,466	1,488	1,640	2,034	2,606	2,895	3,027	2,471	1,566	23,538
1921	1,792	1,516	1,750	1,677	1,916	1,849	1,776	2,500	2,618	3,042	2,058	1,664	24,168
1922	1,835	1,399	1,465	1,227	1,692	1,700	1,677	1,951	2,303	3,311	2,288	1,516	22,364
1923	1,636	1,366	1,430	1,447	1,794	1,426	1,661	1,800	2,659	3,464	1,816	1,526	22,025
1924	1,697	1,412	1,367	1,348	1,344	1,550	1,672	2,005	3,027	3,295	1,879	1,605	22,201
1925	1,467	1,388	1,504	1,541	1,689	1,603	1,699	2,064	2,627	3,198	1,712	1,608	22,100
1926	1,548	1,486	1,694	1,502	1,717	1,913	1,739	2,277	3,279	3,090	1,917	1,706	23,868
1927	1,740	1,501	1,558	1,486	2,013	1,816	1,676	2,209	2,848	3,587	1,896	1,609	23,939
1928	1,705	1,669	1,520	1,591	1,952	1,913	1,898	2,362	3,386	3,938	2,053	1,610	25,597

STOCKER AND FEEDER SHIPMENTS

Year	Jan.	Feb.	Mar.	Apr.	May	June	July	Aug.	Sept.	Oct.	Nov.	Dec.	Total
1916 [1]	73	77	62	58	67	83	100	340	661	1,065	546	145	3,277
1917	126	107	68	102	76	146	195	368	968	1,195	791	306	4,448
1918	128	122	124	221	161	242	212	525	1,105	1,245	763	360	5,208
1919	229	131	136	207	160	223	340	1,039	1,505	1,386	860	740	6,956
1920	311	140	135	269	234	227	325	568	796	1,059	857	259	5,180
1921	88	62	84	107	123	89	139	404	555	731	511	202	3,095
1922	183	169	143	97	145	191	204	350	534	1,138	757	256	4,167
1923	171	169	114	82	216	117	188	341	897	1,489	540	154	4,478
1924	149	106	83	105	118	152	226	444	973	1,438	676	206	4,676
1925	138	119	94	109	178	137	193	421	857	1,392	475	219	4,332
1926	155	· 107	83	124	130	238	260	567	1,093	1,150	493	223	4,623
1927	207	136	140	118	259	258	216	390	947	1,560	497	174	4,902
1928	116	101	96	134	205	278	234	564	1,080	1,466	544	193	5,011

Bureau of Agricultural Economics. Compiled from data of the livestock and meat reporting service of bureau.

[1] Complete information for 1915 and 1916, particularly on disposition of stock, is not obtainable.

TABLE 403.—*Sheep: Receipts, local slaughter, and stocker and feeder shipments at public stockyards, 1925–1928*

Market	Receipts				Local slaughter				Stocker and feeder shipments			
	1925	1926	1927	1928	1925	1926	1927	1928	1925	1926	1927	1928
	Thousands	Thousands	Thousands	Thousands	Thousands	Thousands	Thousands	Thousands	Thousands	Thousands	Thousands	Thousands
Albany, N. Y	0	0	(1)	0	0	0	0	0	0	0	0	0
Amarillo, Tex	148	95	157	115	0	0	0	0	96	42	138	75
Atlanta, Ga	6	2	6	3	1	1	2	1	0	0	0	0
Augusta, Ga	(1)	(1)	(1)	0	(1)	(1)	(1)	0	0	0	0	0
Baltimore, Md	307	292	360	374	104	105	112	108	(1)	2	1	2
Boston, Mass	3	3	3	8	(2)	(2)	(2)	(2)	(2)	(2)	(2)	(2)
Buffalo, N. Y	1,059	1,111	1,234	994	129	133	160	154	9	15	9	8
Chattanooga, Tenn	2	1	2	1	2	1	1	1	0	(1)	(1)	(1)
Cheyenne, Wyo	105	110	113	104	0	0	0	0	0	0	0	0
Chicago, Ill	3,969	4,405	3,829	3,868	2,860	2,962	2,791	2,740	597	791	503	436
Cincinnati, Ohio	370	329	319	211	53	57	60	66	18	22	17	5
Cleveland, Ohio	416	393	449	416	188	191	206	218	0	0	3	4
Dallas, Tex	(1)	(1)	(1)	2	(1)	(1)	(1)	2	0	0	0	0
Dayton, Ohio	8	8	8	10	5	5	6	6	0	0	0	0
Denver, Colo	2,357	1,826	1,908	2,295	167	192	189	214	1,115	787	1,156	1,047
Detroit, Mich	367	393	484	451	200	233	293	265	10	14	19	16
East St. Louis, Ill	559	636	574	510	338	371	369	319	12	6	6	5
El Paso, Tex	124	83	123	170	6	10	10	11	78	28	71	72
Evansville, Ind	7	10	19	25	1	2	15	23	(1)	1	1	1
Fort Wayne, Ind	20	22	24	26	1	2	1	1	3	3	11	4
Fort Worth, Tex	314	445	445	458	141	205	224	214	60	77	47	81
Fostoria, Ohio	14	12	14	15	(1)	(1)	(1)	(1)	(1)	0	0	0
Indianapolis, Ind	147	221	216	225	58	66	68	83	17	19	22	23
Jacksonville, Fla	(1)	3	2	(1)	(1)	(1)	(1)	(1)	0	2	2	(1)
Jersey City, N. J	1,213	1,269	1,254	1,426	1,213	1,269	1,245	1,426	0	0	0	0
Kansas City, Mo	1,500	1,762	1,616	1,767	1,046	1,202	1,125	1,270	319	359	354	351
Knoxville, Tenn	3	(1)	1	1	(1)	(1)	1	1	0	0	(1)	0
La Fayette, Ind	6	4	8	6	2	1	2	1	2	2	1	1
Lancaster, Pa	18	34	20	29	3	4	4	5	0	0	0	0
Laredo, Tex	3	3	11	11	3	2	6	7	(1)	(1)	(1)	0
Los Angeles, Calif	30	46	34	41	28	47	32	40	1	(1)	0	1
Louisville, Ky	229	231	219	199	22	26	29	30	26	61	48	42
Marion, Ohio	8	16	6	8	(1)	(1)	(1)	(1)	(1)	1	1	1
Memphis, Tenn	4	3	4	4	1	1	1	1	(1)	(1)	2	1
Milwaukee, Wis	45	51	50	54	34	40	42	44	0	2	1	(1)
Montgomery, Ala	3	11	8	7	(1)	(1)	1	(1)	(1)	2	1	1
Moultrie, Ga	(1)	0	0	0	0	0	0	0	0	0	0	0
Muncie, Ind	11	17	16	17	(1)	(1)	(1)	(1)	1	3	3	2
Nashville, Tenn	145	165	155	150	20	20	23	18	2	2	6	1
Newark, N. J	38	39	41	67	38	39	41	67	0	0	0	0
New Orleans, La	2	2	4	2	1	1	1	1	1	1	3	1
New York, N. Y	109	149	270	379	109	149	270	379	0	0	0	0
North Salt Lake, Utah	688	600	616	681	44	49	18	13	378	320	346	317
Ogden, Utah	884	1,034	1,177	1,526	4	5	4	3	306	371	344	629
Oklahoma City, Okla	10	14	19	17	6	7	9	10	2	2	6	3
Omaha, Nebr	2,420	2,780	2,604	3,037	1,522	1,643	1,489	1,740	593	910	895	934
Pasco, Wash	71	59	70	52	0	0	0	0	0	0	6	0
Peoria, Ill	6	17	10	19	1	1	1	1	4	13	3	10
Philadelphia, Pa	227	220	241	235	223	213	238	232	0	0	0	0
Pittsburgh, Pa	910	1,073	1,003	986	105	114	120	108	0	0	0	0
Portland, Oreg	179	182	150	140	94	97	80	80	6	6	9	9
Pueblo, Colo	713	810	903	850	0	0	0	0	299	232	344	315
Richmond, Va	8	10	10	12	6	6	7	8	1	2	2	1
St. Joseph, Mo	1,143	1,303	1,348	1,580	866	1,010	1,045	1,150	203	231	243	329
San Antonio, Tex	11	14	37	30	3	4	5	6	4	7	16	17
Seattle, Wash	78	88	75	72	75	86	73	70	0	0	0	(1)
Sioux City, Iowa	360	449	527	568	274	336	375	410	61	84	106	102
Sioux Falls, S. Dak	2	8	9	8	(1)	(1)	1	1	(1)	-1	1	1
South St. Paul, Minn	545	773	705	891	347	411	448	468	63	130	89	110
South San Francisco, Calif	(3)	(3)	180	211	(3)	(3)	141	145	(3)	(3)	1	3
Spokane, Wash	37	57	40	49	10	9	8	8	16	22	22	12
Springfield, Ill	(4)	(4)	2	2	(4)	(4)	1	(1)	(4)	(4)	(1)	(1)
Springfield, Mo	(4)	(4)	8	14	(4)	(4)	(1)	(1)	(4)	(4)	1	2
Springfield, Ohio	16	26	31	10	(1)	1	1	1	0	5	0	0
Toledo, Ohio	20	11	11	7	1	2	2	2	(1)	1	0	0
Washington, D. C	14	13	11	11	14	13	11	11	0	0	0	0
Wichita, Kans	89	125	146	140	30	43	52	70	29	44	42	36
Discontinued markets	0	0	(1)	0	0	0	0	0	0	0	(1)	0
Total	22,100	23,868	23,939	25,597	10,399	11,387	11,459	12,253	4,332	4,623	4,902	5,011

Bureau of Agricultural Economics. Compiled from data of the livestock and meat reporting service of the bureau. Early date in 1925 Yearbook, pp. 1153–1155.
Local slaughter represents number driven out from public stockyards for local slaughter.

[1] Not over 500.
[2] Disposition not reported.
[3] Not included in report prior to Mar. 1, 1927.
[4] Not included in report prior to Jan. 1, 1927.

TABLE 404.—*Feeder sheep, inspected: Shipments from public stockyards, 1928*

Origin and destination	January	February	March	April	May	June	July	August	September	October	November	December	Total
	Number	*Number*	*Number*	*Number*	*Number*	*Number*	*Number*	*Number*	*Number*	*Number*	*Number*	*Number*	*Number*
Market origin:													
Chicago, Ill	13,417	8,215	5,748	5,113	10,126	14,723	13,366	65,099	117,266	128,042	36,378	23,792	441,285
Denver, Colo	9,481	15,610	8,918	4,626	2,126	4,523	11,869	30,223	131,685	511,213	215,178	58,662	1,004,114
East St. Louis, Ill	122		19	15	334	2,851	2,899	2,379	2,898	850	472	45	12,884
Fort Worth, Tex	2,616	3,138	6,493	10,021	12,069	15,726	5,721	7,640	20,652	13,102	4,995	3,360	105,533
Kansas City, Kans	16,679	15,655	11,125	13,577	19,910	8,769	10,095	36,557	59,016	58,747	23,484	6,106	279,720
Louisville, Ky			73	1,032	1,088	11,078	17,758	7,373	2,728	1,093	137		42,360
Ogden, Utah				10	2,768	51	417	13,556	38,917	18,351	1,821	9,474	85,365
Omaha, Nebr	15,859	12,856	10,670	11,519	29,242	31,744	61,403	180,082	294,740	170,111	39,059	25,083	882,368
Salt Lake City, Utah				1,469		26,546	1,400	4,836	27,009	52,465	17,783		131,508
Sioux City, Iowa	6,928	3,022	1,938	1,206	465	1,497	3,797	5,936	16,474	37,164	11,230	7,965	97,622
South St. Joseph, Mo	1,877	821	390	345	2,970	4,592	10,578	30,707	37,994	22,647	7,510	9,267	129,698
South St. Paul, Minn	1,657	2,616	1,268	651		276	587	3,591	8,588	23,696	16,172	9,709	68,811
All other inspected	2,334	2,416	1,020	2,628	3,343	9,636	6,479	11,079	28,561	27,307	14,193	5,271	114,267
Total	70,970	64,349	47,662	52,212	84,441	132,012	146,369	399,058	786,528	1,064,788	388,412	158,734	3,395,535
State destination:													
Colorado	4,851	3,489	3,286	4,626	4,589	31,442	12,331	13,368	77,796	387,029	126,414	61,174	730,395
Illinois	1,425	400	2,638	2,541	4,346	5,255	7,054	43,611	75,809	50,393	14,005	8,381	215,858
Indiana	1,355	2,487	1,371	1,026	766	8,035	5,192	21,752	28,607	23,931	5,058	4,821	104,401
Iowa	6,895	3,247	2,513	1,218	2,864	15,643	39,312	120,351	142,083	96,618	19,415	7,202	457,361
Kansas	11,028	7,367	4,212	4,088	12,231	9,374	9,512	41,746	71,019	55,986	19,019	9,954	255,536
Kentucky	112		73	1,032	1,406	11,156	19,155	7,408	2,611	1,017	125		44,095
Michigan	7,175	4,989	2,180	2,738	4,043	6,684	5,610	13,345	34,468	56,386	22,293	12,500	172,411
Minnesota	862	1,057	268			340	41	1,866	3,998	5,734	6,750	3,507	24,423
Missouri	6,326	3,431	2,701	7,594	6,680	4,198	10,031	28,485	50,692	35,438	9,400	6,040	171,016
Nebraska	19,911	30,103	22,491	19,506	30,820	18,294	21,242	74,057	228,513	256,177	115,642	26,864	863,620
Ohio	126	259	75	131	1,250	330	371	2,015	6,054	8,766	1,861	467	21,705
South Dakota	939	384	781	65	28	202	2,333	8,613	12,204	9,597	3,836	3,441	42,423
Texas	2,359	2,145	2,191	2,935	11,097	10,076	4,541	4,957	7,135	7,872	4,762	3,360	63,430
Wisconsin	2,966	1,559	1,843	2,086	1,586	1,773	879	2,438	12,542	22,719	4,729	2,546	57,666
All other	4,640	3,432	1,039	2,626	2,735	9,210	8,765	15,046	32,997	47,125	35,103	8,477	171,195
Total	70,970	64,349	47,662	52,212	84,441	132,012	146,369	399,058	786,528	1,064,788	388,412	158,734	3,395,535

Bureau of Agricultural Economics. Compiled from Bureau of Animal Industry inspection records.

TABLE 405.—*Feeder sheep, inspected: Shipments from public stockyards, 1920–1928*

Origin and destination	1920	1921	1922	1923	1924	1925	1926	1927	1928
	Thousands	Thousands	Thousands	Thousands	Thousands	Thousands	Thousands	Thousands	Thousands
Market origin:									
Chicago, Ill	829	530	709	683	730	590	784	517	441
Denver, Colo	1,139	576	954	1,002	1,092	1,022	764	1,133	1,004
East St. Louis, Ill	36	13	21	18	18	27	43	20	13
Fort Worth, Tex	59	41	65	39	61	62	87	63	106
Kansas City, Kans	338	251	243	281	280	215	282	283	280
Louisville, Ky	20	25	42	34	18	27	61	51	42
Omaha, Nebr	1,157	722	768	863	867	611	894	885	882
Sioux City, Iowa	73	50	35	48	59	57	79	96	98
South St. Joseph, Mo	63	39	32	61	103	52	78	106	130
South St. Paul, Minn	87	66	46	73	52	49	62	57	69
All other inspected	132	67	96	75	75	72	120	130	331
Total	3,933	2,380	3,011	3,177	3,355	2,784	3,254	3,341	3,396
State destination:									
Colorado	728	325	679	727	715	610	358	722	730
Illinois	338	198	227	256	280	248	320	193	216
Indiana	125	135	104	150	166	186	270	162	104
Iowa	615	292	282	405	403	302	476	381	457
Kansas	182	93	141	120	183	179	189	234	256
Kentucky	32	32	56	39	23	33	63	58	44
Michigan	280	189	359	314	341	266	342	203	172
Minnesota	45	43	22	32	28	33	40	34	24
Missouri	237	181	172	190	198	138	172	177	171
Nebraska	734	639	692	736	780	608	705	909	864
Ohio	104	83	81	52	32	26	85	33	22
South Dakota	26	11	10	14	14	11	22	43	43
Texas	81	22	35	16	31	25	61	41	64
Wisconsin	83	43	31	40	55	41	50	34	58
All other	323	94	120	86	106	78	101	117	171
Total	3,933	2,380	3,011	3,177	¹3,355	2,784	3,254	3,341	3,396

Bureau of Agricultural Economics. Compiled from Bureau of Animal Industry inspection records.

¹ Includes 41 head shipped to Alaska.

TABLE 406.—*Farm prices of sheep, per head, by ages, United States, January 1, 1912–1929*

Jan. 1—	Under 1 year old	Ewes 1 year and over	Wethers 1 year and over	Rams	Jan. 1—	Under 1 year old	Ewes 1 year and over	Wethers 1 year and over	Rams
	Dollars	Dollars	Dollars	Dollars		Dollars	Dollars	Dollars	Dollars
1912	2.64	3.45	3.43	8.26	1921	5.33	6.38	5.94	15.13
1913	3.11	3.98	3.93	8.80	1922	4.25	4.83	4.05	11.31
1914	3.22	4.09	4.06	8.49	1923	6.80	7.67	5.90	14.30
1915	3.62	4.59	4.48	9.01	1924	6.97	8.10	5.98	15.55
1916	4.13	5.35	5.02	10.32	1925	8.53	10.02	7.13	16.91
1917	5.63	7.48	6.78	13.62	1926	9.04	11.01	7.32	18.45
1918	9.06	12.70	11.26	20.84	1927	7.91	10.32	6.60	18.73
1919	8.82	12.44	11.02	21.90	1928	8.44	10.85	7.36	19.61
1920	8.07	11.04	9.64	21.94	1929	8.81	11.19	7.79	20.19

Bureau of Agricultural Economics. Based on returns from special price reporters.

TABLE 407.—*Sheep: Estimated price per 100 pounds received by producers, United States, 1910–1928*

Year	Jan.	Feb.	Mar.	Apr.	May	June	July	Aug.	Sept.	Oct.	Nov.	Dec.	Weighted av.
	Dolls.	Dolls.	Dolls.	Dolls.	Dolls.	Dolls.	Dolls.	Dolls.	Dolls.	Dolls.	Dolls.	Dolls.	Dolls.
Average:													
1910–1913	4.58	4.52	4.80	5.10	4.99	4.76	4.52	4.31	4.26	4.18	4.15	4.23	4.55
1914–1920	7.43	7.79	8.26	8.69	8.69	8.22	7.75	7.60	7.55	7.41	7.30	7.30	7.84
1921–1925	6.26	6.56	6.85	6.92	6.71	6.28	6.13	6.04	5.99	5.97	5.99	6.28	6.35
1910	5.63	5.09	5.64	6.10	5.79	5.44	5.47	4.68	4.81	4.68	5.63	4.54	5.24
1911	4.47	4.34	4.45	4.55	4.51	4.24	4.19	3.98	3.91	3.68	3.65	3.71	4.16
1912	3.89	4.01	4.12	4.57	4.74	4.52	4.21	4.26	4.11	4.19	4.05	4.21	4.24
1913	4.35	4.63	4.97	5.16	4.91	4.84	4.20	4.32	4.23	4.16	4.27	4.46	4.55
1914	4.67	4.67	4.77	4.96	4.87	4.70	4.75	4.87	4.80	4.81	4.68	4.95	4.79
1915	4.95	5.14	5.36	5.60	5.54	5.43	5.35	5.16	5.06	5.18	5.18	5.38	5.27
1916	5.52	5.90	6.35	6.61	6.66	6.54	6.33	6.22	6.25	6.20	6.41	6.77	6.29
1917	7.33	8.17	9.21	9.69	10.15	9.84	9.32	9.33	10.05	10.24	10.20	10.44	9.45
1918	10.55	10.75	11.41	11.98	12.32	11.56	11.04	10.99	10.79	10.35	10.11	9.46	10.95
1919	9.68	9.95	10.45	11.33	10.93	10.34	9.25	9.06	8.69	8.46	8.35	8.53	9.63
1920	9.34	9.97	10.25	10.66	10.34	9.13	8.21	7.54	7.24	6.62	6.20	5.54	8.51
1921	5.30	5.01	5.27	5.11	5.11	4.74	4.34	4.38	4.11	3.96	3.84	4.10	4.65
1922	4.57	5.71	6.51	6.43	6.65	6.09	6.11	5.98	5.70	5.93	6.02	6.27	5.96
1923	6.88	6.83	7.06	7.20	6.92	6.43	6.43	6.22	6.57	6.33	6.20	6.39	6.65
1924	6.71	6.82	7.22	7.45	7.33	7.09	6.60	6.32	6.30	6.32	6.39	6.84	6.81
1925	7.86	8.41	8.20	8.42	7.53	7.04	7.17	7.32	7.27	7.31	7.51	7.79	7.70
1926	7.95	8.20	7.66	7.67	7.78	7.56	7.09	6.92	7.13	6.93	6.75	6.95	7.43
1927	6.87	7.16	7.41	7.40	7.68	7.27	7.16	7.13	7.06	7.05	7.42	7.38	7.26
1928	7.52	7.60	7.85	8.11	8.09	7.84	7.56	7.53	7.58	7.50	7.50	7.29	7.68

Bureau of Agricultural Economics. Based on returns from special price reporters.

TABLE 408.—*Lambs: Estimated price per 100 pounds received by producers, United States, 1910–1928*

Year beginning June	June	July	Aug.	Sept.	Oct.	Nov.	Dec.	Jan.	Feb.	Mar.	Apr.	May	Weighted av.
	Dolls.	Dolls.	Dolls.	Dolls.	Dolls.	Dolls.	Dolls.	Dolls.	Dolls.	Dolls.	Dolls.	Dolls.	Dolls.
Average:													
1910–1913	6.26	5.98	5.51	5.47	5.35	5.31	5.52	5.78	5.78	5.94	6.20	6.26	5.76
1914–1920	10.92	10.31	10.16	10.08	9.89	9.78	9.80	10.18	10.53	10.83	11.44	11.44	10.44
1921–1925	10.20	9.95	9.66	9.62	9.72	9.84	10.16	10.74	11.08	11.50	11.22	11.32	10.42
1910	7.13	6.71	5.70	5.85	5.78	5.54	5.60	5.71	5.44	5.49	5.77	5.74	5.79
1911	5.51	5.42	5.25	5.02	4.68	4.68	4.93	5.22	5.15	5.38	5.98	6.16	5.28
1912	6.02	5.74	5.60	5.49	5.42	5.37	5.70	6.03	6.34	6.56	6.59	6.66	5.96
1913	6.36	6.05	5.50	5.51	5.51	5.64	5.85	6.16	6.18	6.31	6.47	6.49	6.03
1914	6.47	6.55	6.26	6.27	6.09	6.14	6.33	6.47	6.67	6.06	7.35	7.32	6.49
1915	7.26	7.21	6.70	6.71	6.70	6.76	7.32	7.29	7.78	8.10	8.58	8.49	7.38
1916	8.36	8.16	8.15	8.22	8.02	8.41	8.72	9.59	10.51	11.46	12.03	12.51	9.50
1917	12.64	11.19	12.08	13.06	14.09	13.79	13.81	13.83	13.77	14.11	15.34	15.39	13.60
1918	14.98	14.20	14.20	13.73	13.20	12.54	12.44	12.71	13.17	14.03	14.61	14.34	13.65
1919	13.89	13.09	12.91	12.25	11.47	11.45	11.85	12.91	14.08	14.17	14.63	14.26	13.05
1920	12.82	11.79	10.84	10.31	9.65	9.37	8.46	8.44	7.76	7.90	7.55	7.78	9.41
1921	7.59	7.37	6.99	6.27	5.98	6.12	6.60	7.33	8.87	10.21	10.54	10.39	7.83
1922	9.87	9.55	9.39	9.43	10.06	10.30	10.49	10.69	10.83	11.01	10.69	11.00	10.30
1923	10.72	10.60	9.96	10.28	10.17	10.01	10.10	10.19	10.53	11.22	11.32	11.43	10.54
1924	11.21	10.50	10.15	10.18	10.35	10.55	10.96	12.69	13.13	13.48	12.22	11.99	11.45
1925	11.62	11.71	11.80	11.95	12.04	12.20	12.67	12.79	12.02	11.56	11.32	11.78	11.98
1926	12.07	11.52	11.12	11.32	11.31	11.11	10.92	10.65	10.84	11.55	11.97	11.92	11.36
1927	11.95	11.44	11.15	11.14	11.22	11.42	11.39	11.34	11.90	12.31	12.73	13.03	11.76
1928	13.18	12.25	11.88	11.97	11.57	11.50	11.41						

Bureau of Agricultural Economics. Based on returns from special price reporters.

TABLE 409.—*Sheep and lambs: Average price per 100 pounds Chicago, by months, 1905–1928*

SHEEP

Year	Jan.	Feb.	Mar.	Apr.	May	June	July	Aug.	Sept.	Oct.	Nov.	Dec.	Average[1]
	Dolls.	Dolls.	Dolls.	Dolls.	Dolls.	Dolls.	Dolls.	Dolls.	Dolls.	Dolls.	Dolls.	Dolls.	Dolls.
1905	5.15	5.55	5.50	5.08	4.75	4.72	5.10	4.95	5.10	5.10	5.25	5.08	
1906	5.40	5.12	5.28	5.35	5.55	5.45	5.25	4.98	5.15	4.90	5.05	5.08	5.21
1907	5.15	5.20	5.50	5.65	5.78	5.90	5.32	5.32	5.18	4.82	4.38	4.18	5.20
1908	4.80	5.10	5.90	5.70	5.40	4.65	4.05	3.80	3.75	4.05	4.20	4.30	4.64
1909	4.90	5.00	5.25	5.65	6.15	5.30	4.70	4.60	4.65	4.30	4.55	4.85	4.99
1910	5.55	6.50	7.60	7.60	6.55	5.10	4.20	4.20	4.25	3.95	3.70	3.90	5.26
1911	4.10	4.15	4.70	4.20	4.45	3.80	3.95	3.50	3.80	3.65	3.45	3.55	3.94
1912	4.30	4.15	5.30	5.90	6.15	4.50	4.25	4.05	4.15	4.00	4.05	4.45	4.60
1913	5.35	5.90	6.40	6.45	5.85	5.05	4.50	4.35	4.30	4.55	4.60	4.95	5.19
1914	5.50	5.70	5.95	6.25	5.65	5.10	5.40	5.55	5.30	5.20	5.65	5.40	5.56
1915	5.80	6.45	7.45	7.70	7.35	5.50	6.05	6.25	5.75	6.00	5.85	6.20	6.36
1916	7.20	7.75	8.25	8.15	8.20	7.35	7.25	7.35	7.80	7.50	8.00	9.00	7.82
1917	10.00	11.25	11.70	12.10	13.00	10.00	9.10	9.75	11.15	11.65	11.25	11.50	11.04
1918	12.20	12.35	13.60	15.65	14.75	13.40	12.65	13.15	11.80	10.45	9.85	9.40	12.44
1919	10.35	11.35	14.05	14.50	12.25	9.30	9.70	9.75	8.30	8.15	8.30	9.60	10.47
1920	11.80	13.35	13.40	14.25	12.25	8.50	8.90	7.70	6.85	6.45	5.75	4.70	9.49
1921	5.07	4.90	6.14	6.58	6.33	4.46	5.08	4.53	4.49	4.71	4.40	4.92	5.13
1922	7.26	8.28	9.17	9.33	7.35	5.59	6.12	5.63	6.05	6.25	7.48	7.28	7.15
1923	7.72	8.08	8.64	8.90	6.74	5.00	5.16	7.09	7.25	6.35	6.89	7.37	7.10
1924	8.16	9.12	10.50	10.21	8.11	5.82	5.66	6.18	5.46	6.60	6.62	8.45	7.57
1925	10.33	9.69	9.22	7.84	7.96	6.25	7.48	6.83	6.95	7.64	8.16	9.57	8.16
1926	9.72	9.18	8.82	8.87	7.97	5.85	5.97	6.50	6.25	6.12	5.88	5.86	7.25
1927	6.94	8.03	8.88	9.62	7.44	5.88	6.25	6.47	6.14	6.00	6.40	6.41	7.04
1928	7.03	8.96	9.47	10.16	8.53	6.12	6.28	6.72	6.34	6.18	5.84	7.03	7.39

LAMBS

Year	Jan.	Feb.	Mar.	Apr.	May	June	July	Aug.	Sept.	Oct.	Nov.	Dec.	Average[1]
1905	7.15	7.40	7.05	6.80	6.25	5.90	6.30	7.05	7.00	7.05	6.90	7.25	6.84
1906	7.25	6.75	6.40	6.20	6.65	6.75	6.90	7.00	7.15	6.95	6.90	7.10	6.83
1907	7.30	7.30	7.55	8.05	7.80	7.20	7.05	6.90	6.90	6.80	6.05	5.70	7.05
1908	6.80	6.70	7.20	7.25	6.65	5.75	6.20	6.05	5.35	5.50	5.85	6.70	6.33
1909	7.35	7.50	7.65	7.85	8.25	7.60	7.70	7.35	6.80	6.50	7.10	7.50	7.43
1910	8.30	8.65	9.40	9.10	8.40	7.60	7.10	6.70	6.80	6.65	6.25	6.10	7.59
1911	6.20	6.05	6.10	5.50	5.85	6.10	6.30	6.35	5.70	5.75	5.45	5.75	5.92
1912	6.50	6.15	7.30	7.95	8.30	6.90	7.25	7.10	7.00	6.75	7.15	7.75	7.18
1913	8.55	8.50	8.60	8.40	7.40	6.85	7.55	7.40	7.15	7.05	7.25	7.60	7.69
1914	7.90	7.60	7.65	7.60	8.10	7.95	8.45	8.15	7.80	7.60	8.75	8.30	7.99
1915	8.40	8.75	9.55	9.65	10.10	9.20	8.75	8.90	8.75	8.75	8.80	9.00	9.05
1916	10.30	10.90	11.10	10.45	10.75	9.55	10.55	10.75	10.60	10.15	11.40	12.70	10.77
1917	13.85	14.30	14.25	14.40	16.90	15.25	15.65	15.50	17.50	17.40	16.75	16.45	15.68
1918	17.20	16.60	17.55	19.20	18.00	16.85	18.50	17.50	17.25	15.35	15.10	14.60	16.98
1919	16.25	17.40	19.05	18.15	16.25	14.05	17.10	16.75	14.85	15.00	14.50	16.40	16.31
1920	19.50	19.95	18.80	18.80	17.40	14.25	15.55	13.20	13.30	12.35	11.70	11.20	15.50
1921	10.72	9.07	9.91	9.69	11.07	10.67	10.09	9.46	8.86	8.66	9.25	10.86	9.86
1922	12.67	14.49	15.39	14.10	12.95	12.42	13.04	12.51	13.53	13.94	14.17	14.93	13.68
1923	14.69	14.85	14.56	14.42	14.12	14.81	14.22	12.89	13.52	12.93	12.75	12.96	13.89
1924	13.53	14.95	16.06	16.22	15.23	14.12	13.79	13.57	13.38	13.52	14.03	16.47	14.57
1925	18.28	17.59	16.28	14.85	13.06	15.86	15.11	14.88	15.19	15.20	15.44	16.15	15.66
1926	15.28	13.78	13.48	14.38	15.30	16.66	14.31	14.20	14.05	13.88	13.25	12.57	14.26
1927	12.64	13.28	15.27	15.87	14.75	15.66	14.25	13.68	13.46	13.70	13.80	13.14	14.12
1928	13.16	15.39	16.26	16.81	16.10	16.84	15.61	14.72	14.29	13.12	13.31	14.31	14.99

Bureau of Agricultural Economics. Figures prior to 1921 for sheep and lambs, compiled from Chicago Drovers Journal Yearbook; subsequent figures are bulk of sales prices from data of the livestock and meat reporting service of the bureau. See 1927 Yearbook, p. 1031, for prices of lambs, 1901–1904·

[1] Simple average of monthly prices.

TABLE 410.—*Sheep and lambs: Average price per 100 pounds at Chicago and Omaha, by months, 1927–28*

Column headers are given in two forms: the first applies to January–June 1927; the second (after the slash) applies to July 1927 onward.

Year and month	Chicago — Lambs, 84 pounds down, medium to choice / Good and choice	Lambs, all weights, cull and common / 110 pounds down, medium to choice	Yearling wethers, medium to choice / 120 pounds down, medium to choice	Ewes, common to choice / Cull and common	Ewes, cull / Good and choice	Feeder lambs, medium to choice / Good and choice	(Feeder) Medium	Omaha — Lambs, 84 pounds down, medium to choice / Good and choice	Lambs, all weights, cull and common / 110 pounds down, medium to choice	Yearling wethers, medium to choice / 120 pounds down, medium to choice	Ewes, common to choice / Cull and common	Ewes, cull / Good and choice	Feeder lambs, medium to choice / Good and choice	(Feeder) Medium
1927	Dols.	Dols.	Dols.	Dols.	Dols.	Dollars		Dols.	Dols.	Dols.	Dols.	Dols.	Dollars	
January	12.10	10.10	10.07	6.34	3.44	12.20		11.53	9.23	8.99	5.66	3.01	12.10	
February	12.79	10.83	10.85	7.74	4.39	12.57		12.37	10.49	10.12	7.39	4.24	12.55	
March	14.82	12.45	12.50	8.44	4.90	13.94		14.25	12.12	11.82	8.27	4.78	13.97	
April	15.36	12.92	13.15	8.70	5.14	14.00		14.90	12.72	12.46	8.15	4.78	14.04	
May	14.49	12.25	12.87	6.87	3.82			14.01	11.90	11.98	6.31	3.52	12.78	
June	15.33	12.43	12.80	5.61	3.03	12.75		14.65	12.16	11.93	4.93	2.76	12.19	
July	14.18	10.79	10.83	5.97	3.25	12.94	11.85	13.66	10.17	10.18	5.73	3.16	12.83	11.87
August	13.49	10.27	10.42	5.90	3.12	13.02	11.90	13.07	9.91	9.59	5.75	3.16	13.13	12.15
September	13.38	10.46	10.25	5.06	2.56	13.40	12.38	12.94	9.96	9.09	5.36	2.88	13.16	12.06
October	13.68	11.01	10.98	5.60	3.04	14.04	13.26	13.09	10.34	9.25	5.38	3.00	13.31	12.22
November	13.88	11.38	11.16	5.93	3.35	14.03	13.30	13.27	10.92	9.59	5.52	3.05	13.45	12.45
December	13.38	10.68	10.49	6.04	3.40	13.35	12.56	12.81	10.15	9.45	5.88	3.15	12.46	11.74
1928														
January	13.35	10.81	10.78	6.49	3.74	12.88	12.04	12.85	10.22	9.24	6.28	3.47	12.45	11.58
February	15.39	12.88	13.23	8.43	5.17	14.68	13.94	14.93	12.18	11.56	7.81	4.65	14.21	12.89
March	16.36	13.88	14.32	8.87	5.46	15.45	14.47	15.80	13.36	12.28	8.60	5.21	15.02	13.70
April	16.78	14.04	14.21	9.78	6.06	16.01	14.88	16.20	13.76	12.90	8.80	5.26	15.38	14.12
May	16.19	12.87	13.42	8.26	4.72			15.49	13.02	12.71	7.70	4.16		
June	16.65	13.01	12.40	6.62	3.74			15.88	12.74	12.63	5.76	3.03	12.92	12.00
July	15.39	11.86	11.27	6.21	3.54	13.37	12.74	14.67	11.35	10.76	5.75	3.25	13.09	12.24
August	14.50	10.48	10.68	6.43	3.58	13.78	13.19	13.94	10.43	10.35	6.15	3.45	13.47	12.70
September	14.12	10.08	10.26	6.06	3.44	14.03	13.20	13.73	10.01	9.78	6.21	3.50	13.25	12.38
October	13.10	9.68	9.84	5.77	3.38	12.85	11.91	12.83	9.35	9.28	6.00	3.36	12.82	11.94
November	13.30	10.07	10.00	5.89	3.40	12.86	11.89	12.67	9.67	9.03	5.77	3.19	12.39	11.54
December	14.17	10.46	10.78	6.77	3.96	13.52	12.28	13.46	10.34	9.84	6.38	3.74	12.96	11.92
Average	14.94	11.68	11.77	7.13	4.18			14.37	11.37	10.86	6.77	3.86		

Bureau of Agricultural Economics. Compiled from data of the livestock and meat-reporting service of the bureau. Earlier data in 1927 Yearbook, pp. 1032–1034.

TABLE 411.—*Sheep and lambs: Monthly slaughter under Federal inspection, 1907–1928*

Year	Jan.	Feb.	Mar.	Apr.	May	June	July	Aug.	Sept.	Oct.	Nov.	Dec.	Total
	Thousands	Thousands	Thousands	Thousands	Thousands	Thousands	Thousands	Thousands	Thousands	Thousands	Thousands	Thousands	Thousands
1907	1,017	837	842	861	769	735	865	900	892	973	793	769	10,252
1908	872	725	677	664	732	842	891	932	1,064	1,048	928	930	10,305
1909	906	806	903	839	712	843	964	1,019	1,153	1,169	1,029	1,000	11,343
1910	903	771	727	693	796	927	967	1,095	1,154	1,206	1,125	1,044	11,408
1911	1,130	1,019	1,059	974	1,085	1,146	1,150	1,268	1,257	1,428	1,304	1,200	14,020
1912	1,383	1,151	1,106	971	963	1,028	1,181	1,390	1,440	1,723	1,424	1,220	14,979
1913	1,192	961	883	1,049	1,127	1,135	1,273	1,243	1,486	1,514	1,258	1,284	14,406
1914	1,297	1,113	1,143	1,150	1,085	1,113	1,171	1,169	1,379	1,331	1,112	1,167	14,229
1915	1,196	946	986	830	739	883	984	1,139	1,220	1,116	1,132	1,041	12,212
1916	976	904	861	769	854	990	930	1,173	1,158	1,172	1,121	1,033	11,941
1917	956	819	861	777	632	710	688	766	740	822	764	809	9,345
1918	780	655	736	614	659	737	869	937	1,029	1,194	1,139	971	10,320
1919	1,004	754	738	808	894	931	1,160	1,234	1,292	1,414	1,227	1,235	12,691
1920	955	828	788	714	671	818	1,048	1,042	1,151	1,068	968	932	13,005
1921	1,068	958	1,075	1,041	935	1,116	1,060	1,237	1,249	1,285	1,040	890	10,929
1922	954	776	837	739	872	1,028	964	1,024	1,013	981	882	858	11,520
1923	1,021	836	977	960	972	914	962	957	990	1,046	915	878	11,991
1924	1,083	912	868	860	959	975	1,051	1,063	1,150	1,148	950	972	12,001
1925	990	854	984	1,012	1,030	999	1,071	1,031	1,086	1,083	879	981	12,961
1926	1,039	988	1,163	994	959	1,081	1,042	1,093	1,224	1,167	1,039	1,172	12,882
1927	1,115	1,006	1,027	960	992	1,058	1,014	1,168	1,185	1,194	1,070	1,094	13,488
1928	1,151	1,048	1,016	918	1,016	1,109	1,076	1,196	1,307	1,409	1,189	1,053	

Bureau of Animal Industry.

TABLE 412.—*Sheep and lambs, slaughter statistics: Source of supply, classification, slaughter costs, weights, and yields, 1923–1928*

Year and month	Source of supply		Age classification			Average live cost per 100 pounds	Average live weight	Dressed weight as percentage of live weight	By-product yield (on basis of live weight)	
	Stockyards	Other	Sheep	Lambs and yearlings					Edible fat [1]	Edible offal
	Per cent	Per cent	Per cent	Per cent		Dollars	Pounds	Per cent	Per cent	Per cent
1923	85.97	14.03	13.16	86.84		12.03	80.80	48.07	2.85	1.94
1924	83.60	16.40	10.66	89.34		12.77	80.14	47.53	2.76	1.95
1925	82.44	17.56	10.30	89.70		14.22	81.58	47.82	2.74	2.24
1926	84.64	15.36	9.62	90.38		12.86	81.34	47.62	2.68	2.35
1927	85.42	14.58	8.91	91.09		12.97	81.66	47.74	2.64	2.44
1928	86.31	13.69	8.26	91.74		13.53	81.93	47.36	2.52	2.49
January	88.12	11.88	6.64	93.36		12.48	87.41	46.86	2.61	2.44
February	87.21	12.79	7.21	92.79		14.25	90.32	46.58	2.73	2.36
March	85.04	14.96	7.07	92.93		15.11	89.25	46.51	2.76	2.27
April	85.13	14.87	6.67	93.33		15.63	84.27	46.91	2.90	2.58
May	79.14	20.86	11.84	88.16		15.25	78.51	48.29	2.57	2.64
June	85.46	14.54	9.29	90.71		14.37	75.25	48.78	2.15	2.72
July	86.98	13.02	9.60	90.40		13.72	75.87	48.28	2.35	2.61
August	86.55	13.45	6.99	93.01		13.06	78.19	47.67	2.11	2.49
September	87.88	12.12	7.37	92.63		12.99	79.14	47.66	2.32	2.49
October	87.54	12.46	9.55	90.45		11.95	81.24	47.40	2.46	2.39
November	88.17	11.83	9.21	90.79		12.03	81.80	46.91	2.52	2.53
December	86.88	13.12	7.66	92.34		12.87	83.47	46.82	2.68	2.43

Bureau of Agricultural Economics. Compiled from monthly reports to the bureau from packers and slaughterers, whose slaughterings equaled 75 to 85 per cent of total slaughter under Federal inspection.

[1] Unrendered.

TABLE 413.—*Mutton and lamb, frozen: Cold-storage holdings, United States, 1916–1928*

Year	Jan. 1	Feb. 1	Mar. 1	Apr. 1	May 1	June 1	July 1	Aug. 1	Sept. 1	Oct. 1	Nov. 1	Dec. 1
	1,000 pounds	1,000 pounds	1,000 pounds	1,000 pounds	1,000 pounds	1,000 pounds	1,000 pounds	1,000 pounds	1,000 pounds	1,000 pounds	1,000 pounds	1,000 pounds
Average: 1916–1920	8,063	7,329	6,482	5,115	4,355	4,669	4,068	3,744	5,547	8,853	14,639	17,110
1921–1925	16,888	18,524	41,478	10,368	7,413	5,364	4,088	3,283	2,927	2,964	3,379	3,608
1916	4,976	5,286	5,812	5,084	3,858	2,525	1,939	2,098	2,135	2,579	3,465	5,000
1917	4,886	5,895	4,949	4,872	4,369	3,508	4,380	3,912	2,716	2,768	4,194	5,406
1918	7,403	6,315	7,855	5,599	3,348	3,860	2,429	3,150	5,046	5,275	8,645	9,035
1919	12,760	11,360	8,013	6,505	7,623	7,718	7,279	7,263	7,817	8,318	7,894	9,409
1920	10,290	7,787	5,781	3,517	2,579	5,735	4,311	2,299	11,021	25,325	48,997	56,702
1921	68,032	78,082	59,304	38,520	25,129	15,877	8,714	6,751	5,903	5,993	6,840	7,520
1922	6,444	3,914	2,863	2,878	2,071	2,310	3,720	3,308	3,376	3,473	3,458	3,633
1923	4,523	5,980	5,758	6,635	5,774	4,445	3,556	2,752	1,785	1,719	1,997	2,014
1924	2,493	2,306	2,173	1,719	2,093	2,273	2,917	2,257	2,230	2,525	3,166	3,326
1925	2,949	2,336	2,294	2,090	1,998	1,913	1,535	1,349	1,339	1,112	1,435	1,549
1926	1,820	2,354	3,346	3,289	2,393	1,697	1,871	1,813	1,929	2,234	2,814	3,166
1927	4,556	4,447	4,074	2,940	1,862	1,210	1,360	1,161	1,302	1,991	2,958	3,790
1928	4,408	4,404	4,020	3,252	1,828	1,276	1,947	1,822	1,691	2,113	4,321	5,472

Bureau of Agricultural Economics. Compiled from reports from cold-storage establishments.

TABLE 414.—*Sheep and lambs: Statement of livestock and meat situation, 1921–1928*

Item	Unit	1921	1922	1923	1924	1925	1926	1927	1928
Federally inspected slaughter.	Thousands	13,005	10,929	11,529	11,991	12,001	12,961	12,883	13,488
Average live weight	Pounds	79.68	79.99	80.80	80.14	81.58	81.34	81.66	81.93
Total live weight	1,000 pounds	1,036,231	874,206	931,507	960,945	979,041	1,054,238	1,052,029	1,105,086
Average live cost per 100 pounds.	Dollars	8.61	12.18	12.03	12.77	14.22	12.86	12.97	13.53
Total live cost	1,000 dollars	89,219	106,478	112,060	122,713	139,220	135,575	136,448	149,518
Carcasses condemned	Thousands	11	12	14	13	14	16	16	18
Number passed for food.	do	12,994	10,917	11,515	11,978	11,987	12,945	12,867	13,470
Average dressed weight	Pounds	37.92	38.34	38.83	38.10	39.00	38.74	38.99	38.81
Total dressed weight	1,000 pounds	493,154	417,842	446,260	456,357	467,316	500,888	501,746	522,549
Mutton and lamb:									
Imports	do	25,395	12,155	5,215	2,166	2,770	3,365	2,646	3,268
Storage Jan. 1	do	68,032	6,444	4,523	2,493	2,949	1,820	4,556	4,408
Total supply	do	586,581	436,441	455,998	461,016	473,035	506,073	508,947	530,225
Storage Dec. 31	do	6,444	4,523	2,493	2,949	1,820	4,556	4,408	5,623
Exports [1]	do	64,104	1,957	2,124	1,507	1,541	1,230	971	1,042
Apparent domestic consumption.	do	516,033	429,962	451,381	456,560	469,674	500,288	503,569	523,560
Apparent per capita consumption.	Pounds	4.76	3.91	4.04	4.01	4.07	4.27	4.24	4.36

Bureau of Agricultural Economics.

[1] Includes reexports.

TABLE 415.—*Mutton and lamb: International trade, average 1911–1913, annual 1924–1927*

Country	Year ended Dec. 31									
	Average, 1911–1913		1924		1925		1926		1927, preliminary	
	Imports	Exports	Imports	Exports	Imports	Exports	Imports	Exports	Imports	Exports
PRINCIPAL EXPORTING COUNTRIES	*1,000 pounds*	*1,000 pounds*	*1,000 pounds*	*1,000 pounds*	*1,000 pounds*	*1,000 pounds*	*1,000 pounds*	*1,000 pounds*	*1,000 pounds*	*1,000 pounds*
New Zealand	0	235,509	0	278,426	1	291,039	0	279,731	0	311,135
Argentina	0	148,457	0	184,311	0	202,576	0	148,213	0	183,260
Australia	7	149,958	¹ 37	¹ 39,805	¹ 47	¹ 50,271	¹ 2	¹ 85,682	¹ 6	¹ 93,520
Uruguay	0	3,262	0	34,417	0	22,658	0	50,358	0	52,096
Netherlands	76	17,212	1,347	17,566	1,069	17,082	1,472	14,308	1,255	16,084
Canada	4,717	48	1,367	922	1,321	2,641	1,673	1,274	1,946	1,889
Union of South Africa	1,914	75	46	176	1	184	--------	175	52	133
PRINCIPAL IMPORTING COUNTRIES										
United Kingdom	596,899	0	577,176	0	622,482	0	613,633	0	627,303	0
France	930	334	24,475	251	23,737	200	20,385	146	29,822	274
United States	185	4,146	2,166	1,445	2,770	1,464	3,365	1,171	2,646	937
Germany	1,046	350	3,156	711	2,002	2,122	8,217	361	10,083	622
Belgium	--------	--------	2,975	489	2,904	627	3,130	475	3,909	830
Denmark	3,828	344	1,106	61	1,328	35	2,214	2	2,232	5
Sweden	1,218	100	651	105	731	60	1,148	7	1,371	29
Total, 14 countries	610,820	559,795	614,502	558,685	658,393	590,959	655,239	581,903	680,625	660,814

Bureau of Agricultural Economics. Official sources.

¹ Year ended June 30.

TABLE 416.—*Wool, raw: Production, imports, exports, and apparent consumption, United States, 1910–1928*

Year	Production			Imports ¹	Reexports ¹	Exports of domestic wool	Net imports ²	Apparent consumption
	Fleece	Pulled	Total					
	1,000 pounds	*1,000 pounds*	*1,000 pounds*	*1,000 pounds*	*1,000 pounds*	*1,000 pounds*	*1,000 pounds*	*1,009 pounds*
1910	281,363	40,000	321,363	180,135	9,055	³ 48	171,032	492,395
1911	277,548	41,000	318,548	155,923	3,511	(⁴)	152,412	470,960
1912	262,543	41,500	304,043	238,118	1,816	(⁵)	236,302	540,345
1913	252,675	43,500	296,175	151,581	3,860	³ 77	147,644	443,819
1914	247,192	43,000	290,192	256,501	6,342	³ 335	249,823	540,015
1915	245,726	40,000	285,726	402,611	2,081	³ 8,158	392,372	678,098
1916	244,890	43,600	288,490	442,650	2,128	3,919	436,603	725,093
1917	241,892	40,000	281,892	416,137	1,272	1,827	413,038	694,930
1918	256,870	42,000	298,870	447,426	452	407	446,567	745,437
1919	249,958	48,300	298,258	438,782	5,134	2,840	430,807	729,065
1920	244,179	42,900	287,079	254,905	12,393	8,845	233,666	520,745
1921	235,129	48,500	283,629	316,605	1,552	1,927	313,126	596,755
1922	221,713	42,000	263,713	366,538	4,225	453	361,861	625,574
1923	225,696	42,500	268,196	388,345	23,557	535	364,253	632,449
1924	235,575	43,800	279,375	262,655	27,476	309	234,869	514,244
1925	245,562	46,800	292,362	336,646	7,087	273	329,286	621,648
1926	260,976	50,600	311,576	299,451	14,082	292	285,077	596,653
1927	281,914	50,100	332,014	264,507	10,710	323	253,474	585,488
1928 ⁶	299,113	51,900	351,013	240,360	4,435	485	235,440	586,453

Bureau of Agricultural Economics. Production figures 1910–1913 from the National Association of Wool Manufacturers; 1914–1928 from the bureau; imports and exports from the Bureau of Foreign and Domestic Commerce.

¹ Hair of Angora goat, alpaca, and other like animals included in imports and reexports prior to 1914 and in exports for all years. ² Total imports minus domestic exports and reexports.
³ Exports for fiscal years ended June 30 of the years shown. ⁴ Included in all other articles.
⁵ No transactions. ⁶ Preliminary.

TABLE 417.—*Wool, fleece: Estimated production, by States, 1925–1928*

State and division	Production				Weight per fleece [1]				Number of fleeces [2]			
	1925	1926	1927	1928	1925	1926	1927	1928	1925	1926	1927	1928
	1,000 pounds	*1,000 pounds*	*1,000 pounds*	*1,000 pounds*	*Lbs.*	*Lbs.*	*Lbs.*	*Lbs.*	*Thousands*	*Thousands*	*Thousands*	*Thousands*
Maine	526	559	546	542	6.5	6.5	6.5	6.3	81	86	84	86
New Hampshire	102	110	117	115	6.4	6.5	6.5	6.4	16	17	18	18
Vermont	252	277	285	280	7.2	7.3	7.3	7.0	35	38	39	40
Massachusetts	68	62	63	66	6.2	6.2	6.3	6.6	11	10	10	10
Rhode Island	12	12	12	13	6.2	6.2	6.2	6.4	2	2	2	2
Connecticut	41	43	36	42	5.9	6.1	6.0	6.0	7	7	6	7
New York	2,898	3,081	2,956	2,966	7.3	7.3	7.3	7.2	397	422	405	412
New Jersey	31	32	32	30	6.2	6.3	6.3	6.1	5	5	5	5
Pennsylvania	2,805	2,805	2,730	2,948	7.5	7.5	7.5	7.5	374	374	364	393
North Atlantic	6,735	6,981	6,777	7,002	7.3	7.3	7.3	7.2	928	961	933	973
Ohio	14,467	14,760	15,662	15,826	8.1	8.2	8.2	8.2	1,786	1,800	1,910	1,930
Indiana	3,562	3,715	4,088	4,307	7.3	7.4	7.3	7.3	488	502	560	590
Illinois	3,419	3,648	4,162	3,724	7.4	7.6	7.5	7.6	462	480	555	490
Michigan	7,416	7,920	8,272	8,520	8.0	8.0	8.0	8.0	927	990	1,034	1,065
Wisconsin	2,250	2,508	2,774	2,808	7.5	7.6	7.6	7.8	300	330	365	360
Minnesota	3,151	3,634	4,211	4,661	7.8	7.9	7.9	7.9	404	460	533	590
Iowa	5,360	5,440	5,896	5,960	8.0	8.0	8.0	8.0	670	680	737	745
Missouri	5,208	5,250	5,523	5,962	7.0	7.0	7.0	7.2	744	750	789	828
North Dakota	2,263	2,772	3,469	3,984	8.2	8.3	8.3	8.3	276	334	418	480
South Dakota	4,446	4,714	5,160	5,644	7.8	8.1	8.0	8.3	570	582	645	680
Nebraska	2,212	2,175	2,442	2,370	7.5	7.5	6.6	7.9	295	290	370	300
Kansas	1,656	1,679	1,986	2,442	7.2	7.3	7.3	7.4	230	230	272	330
North Central	55,410	58,215	63,645	66,208	7.7	7.8	7.8	7.9	7,152	7,428	8,188	8,388
Delaware	12	12	12	12	6.0	6.0	6.0	6.0	2	2	2	2
Maryland	439	472	504	518	6.1	6.3	6.3	6.1	72	75	80	85
Virginia	1,485	1,630	1,710	1,895	4.7	5.0	5.0	5.0	316	326	342	379
West Virginia	2,272	2,311	2,457	2,684	5.2	5.3	5.4	5.4	437	436	455	497
North Carolina	270	304	350	357	4.5	4.6	4.8	4.7	60	66	73	76
South Carolina	48	45	50	52	4.0	4.1	4.2	4.0	12	11	12	13
Georgia	131	139	148	126	3.2	3.4	3.6	3.4	41	41	41	37
Florida	147	144	144	153	3.0	3.0	3.0	3.0	49	48	48	51
South Atlantic	4,804	5,057	5,375	5,797	4.9	5.0	5.1	5.1	989	1,005	1,053	1,140
Kentucky	3,125	3,278	3,845	4,051	4.8	4.8	4.8	4.7	651	683	801	862
Tennessee	1,144	1,118	1,174	1,287	4.3	4.3	4.3	4.1	266	260	273	314
Alabama	155	136	155	184	3.3	3.5	3.6	3.4	47	39	43	54
Mississippi	304	288	198	115	3.2	3.2	3.2	3.1	95	90	62	37
Arkansas	202	201	220	207	4.7	4.9	4.9	4.6	43	41	45	45
Louisiana	294	275	286	282	3.3	3.2	3.4	3.2	89	86	84	88
Oklahoma	394	456	562	615	7.3	7.6	7.7	7.5	54	60	73	82
Texas	25,280	27,297	32,725	35,591	8.0	8.1	8.5	8.4	3,160	3,370	3,850	4,237
South Central	30,898	33,049	39,165	42,332	7.0	7.1	7.5	7.4	4,405	4,629	5,231	5,719
Montana	20,640	23,320	24,166	26,626	8.6	8.8	8.6	8.6	2,400	2,650	2,810	3,096
Idaho	14,309	14,507	15,840	17,885	8.2	8.9	8.8	9.2	1,745	1,630	1,800	1,944
Wyoming	21,362	22,338	25,317	26,488	8.6	8.5	8.7	8.8	2,484	2,628	2,910	3,010
Colorado	6,862	7,740	8,118	8,831	7.3	7.5	7.3	7.6	940	1,032	1,112	1,162
New Mexico	11,084	12,060	12,600	12,400	5.8	5.9	6.0	5.8	1,911	2,044	2,100	2,138
Arizona	6,458	6,758	6,240	5,760	6.3	6.2	6.0	6.0	1,025	1,090	1,040	960
Utah	18,010	19,430	19,975	22,072	8.4	8.8	8.5	8.9	2,144	2,208	2,350	2,480
Nevada	7,560	8,730	8,015	8,580	7.2	7.9	7.3	7.5	1,050	1,105	1,098	1,144
Washington	4,560	4,194	4,753	5,000	9.5	9.8	9.8	10.0	480	428	485	500
Oregon	16,958	18,321	18,128	20,332	8.8	9.3	8.8	9.2	1,927	1,970	2,060	2,210
California	19,912	20,276	23,800	23,800	7.5	7.4	7.0	6.8	2,655	2,740	3,400	3,500
Far Western	147,715	157,674	166,952	177,774	7.9	8.1	7.9	8.0	18,761	19,525	21,165	22,144
United States	245,562	260,976	281,914	299,113	7.6	7.8	7.7	7.8	32,235	33,548	36,570	38,364

Bureau of Agricultural Economics. Estimates of the crop-reporting board.

[1] In States where sheep are shorn twice a year, principally Texas and California, this figure covers wool per head of sheep shorn and not weight per fleece.

[2] Includes some fleeces taken at commercial feeding plants. California figure includes some fleeces taken from early lambs.

TABLE 418.—*Stocks of wool, tops, and noils held by dealers and manufacturers in United States, 1920–1928*[1]

Date	Held by dealers					Held by manufacturers				
	Grease	Scoured	Pulled	Tops	Noils	Grease	Scoured	Pulled	Tops	Noils
	1,000 pounds	*1,000 pounds*	*1,000 pounds*	*1,000 pounds*	*1,000 pounds*	*1,000 pounds*	*1,000 pounds*	*1,000 pounds*	*1,000 pounds*	*1,000 pounds*
1920										
Jan. 1	152,003	24,630	17,907	4,735	3,893	152,089	20,030	6,302	13,875	7,316
Apr. 1	123,247	26,279	17,710	3,646	4,305	139,333	24,412	9,339	14,328	8,670
July 1	144,837	27,963	15,207	4,487	6,041	112,434	23,078	6,762	15,439	9,002
Oct. 1	179,376	29,988	11,229	5,564	4,754	79,762	15,612	7,593	15,839	9,124
1921										
Jan. 1	188,822	27,814	14,352	6,616	5,434	119,766	17,291	6,895	18,851	9,991
Apr. 1	194,891	22,807	15,505	7,623	3,690	165,398	18,442	11,296	19,325	9,316
July 1	176,584	19,703	12,127	4,883	4,139	164,713	18,042	10,787	20,247	8,101
Oct. 1	181,574	19,480	11,201	4,005	3,009	180,727	19,736	10,484	23,184	7,463
1922										
Jan. 1	102,384	13,468	9,222	2,866	2,453	171,597	21,097	9,312	17,536	7,136
Apr. 1	70,415	10,995	6,969	2,296	1,373	171,026	25,406	10,419	18,029	7,176
July 1	156,523	13,447	6,988	2,627	1,619	165,810	22,201	9,642	20,720	6,709
Oct. 1	176,377	16,521	7,384	3,327	2,695	191,351	20,336	8,686	19,227	5,904
1923										
Jan. 1	134,644	22,150	11,106	3,658	6,158	193,492	20,596	8,824	20,211	7,644
Apr. 1	126,158	24,734	13,503	3,378	6,378	175,422	21,787	11,930	18,402	8,247
July 1	186,729	21,075	13,126	5,125	5,977	161,435	18,464	11,148	16,579	8,364
Oct. 1	175,843	21,679	10,531	3,136	5,675	130,935	15,992	8,960	16,998	7,511
1924										
Jan. 1	144,014	16,665	7,700	2,988	3,783	121,173	16,947	8,971	16,543	7,206
Apr. 1	100,846	16,239	9,561	4,172	1,806	124,345	15,310	7,669	17,141	6,828
July 1	154,931	12,840	8,829	4,461	983	126,985	13,987	6,140	16,323	5,659
Oct. 1	132,953	12,544	7,475	3,869	1,994	129,330	15,165	6,747	16,562	4,867
1925										
Jan. 1	98,712	18,380	9,799	3,285	2,583	113,026	15,315	7,368	16,258	6,729
Apr. 1	65,912	16,819	12,624	2,754	2,412	95,122	15,437	7,025	15,921	6,020
July 1	147,654	15,039	11,267	2,571	3,292	95,021	16,455	7,381	15,252	5,463
Oct. 1	136,043	15,809	9,715	2,240	2,704	102,261	13,621	6,623	15,880	6,207
1926										
Jan. 1	117,726	14,658	10,552	2,428	2,407	97,162	12,666	7,852	15,346	6,121
Apr. 1	97,552	15,053	12,360	2,692	2,641	95,102	14,358	7,468	15,188	6,184
July 1	182,685	12,204	10,141	2,438	3,090	91,852	12,640	6,877	14,104	5,633
Oct. 1	166,380	12,810	8,709	2,310	2,769	90,992	12,407	6,376	13,771	5,047
1927										
Jan. 1	114,680	13,176	9,029	2,282	3,392	90,494	11,699	6,322	13,653	5,266
Apr. 1	81,869	11,923	9,851	2,140	3,409	90,805	12,486	6,095	13,858	5,045
July 1	177,315	9,111	7,914	2,864	3,186	96,091	12,709	5,758	14,641	4,479
Oct. 1	147,079	9,390	5,075	1,677	2,846	103,886	12,937	6,170	14,581	4,144
1928										
Jan. 1	97,787	8,775	6,351	3,208	2,495	98,577	13,134	5,416	13,654	4,542
Apr. 1	50,989	7,907	7,761	2,056	2,305	99,319	14,632	7,902	13,447	4,932
July 1	171,077	10,133	8,393	1,769	2,889	105,117	13,363	5,734	12,559	4,475
Oct. 1	170,143	9,695	8,998	2,282	2,688	94,752	11,469	5,409	12,294	4,428

Bureau of Agricultural Economics. Compiled from wool stock reports issued quarterly by the Bureau of Agricultural Economics and the Bureau of the Census. Stocks held by the Government are not included.

[1] Not including estimates for firms not reporting nor wool actually reported but for which no grade was stated. Beginning with 1922 estimates for firms not reporting were discontinued. The information in this table is, therefore, not complete as some firms do not report.

TABLE 419.—*Wool: International trade, average 1909–1913, annual 1925–1927*

Country	Average 1909–1913		1925		1926		1927 preliminary	
	Imports	Exports	Imports	Exports	Imports	Exports	Imports	Exports
PRINCIPAL EXPORTING COUNTRIES	*1,000 pounds*	*1,000 pounds*	*1,000 pounds*	*1,000 pounds*	*1,000 pounds*	*1,000 pounds*	*1,000 pounds*	*1,000 pounds*
Australia	324	676,679	¹ 1,739	¹ 670,890	¹ 2,542	¹ 781,279	¹ 5,563	¹ 763,556
Argentina	214	328,204	194	249,777	208	318,302	417	346,010
New Zealand	168	194,801	116	205,727	201	213,154	35	220,501
Union of South Africa	7	164,635	156	220,176	514	222,836	563	271,016
Uruguay	0	139,178	0	89,442	0	118,762	0	¹ 151,789
China	0	42,685	859	68,472	725	34,584	391	59,700
British India	23,721	56,496	² 22,399	³ 49,775	25,812	³ 40,375	32,191	³ 47,292
Chile	1,247	28,223	297	28,635		24,695		27,200
Algeria	2,445	19,871	2,967	21,811	4,522	30,757	3,213	26,662
Morocco	0	8,607	0	13,245	0	17,174	0	¹ 17,163
Irish Free State	0	0	1,331	10,051	1,529	11,610	1,660	16,670
Spain	2,446	28,505	2,795	6,518	5,054	6,707	¹ 3,774	¹ 17,435
Peru	⁴ 3	9,333	0	10,563	0	9,200	0	11,057
Hungary	0	0	1,174	14,714	1,529	13,460	2,120	9,897
Persia ⁵	⁴ 2,753	10,023	1,998	12,243	1,364	13,490		
Brazil		⁶ 2,959		6,610		15,886		11,054
PRINCIPAL IMPORTING COUNTRIES								
France	601,628	84,973	539,872	36,297	639,786	46,241	685,932	59,462
United Kingdom	506,155	41,164	414,172	53,775	490,700	54,395	515,789	62,021
United States	203,298	⁷ 46	339,254	273	310,266	292	267,287	323
Germany	481,988	42,817	299,253	19,285	326,123	16,933	424,775	22,814
Belgium	300,367	196,440	101,275	24,363	115,320	22,663	37,938	159
Italy	30,145	3,933	76,999	5,307	102,760	8,190	88,744	7,775
Japan	17,921	0	82,328	0	81,920	0	105,557	0
Czechoslovakia	0	0	28,753	2,925	30,306	4,034	39,008	3,585
Poland	0	0	23,939	2,219	25,828	1,349	36,019	971
Russia	106,184	32,406	¹ 41,312	¹ 12,069	¹ 50,363	¹ 4,334	¹ 69,877	¹ 3,426
Canada	7,794	1,323	13,561	6,351	15,378	4,389	14,354	11,357
Austria	63,942	9,622	14,118	1,513	14,348	1,084	17,160	879
Switzerland	11,211	338	14,867	59	18,237	40	18,887	46
Netherlands	31,991	26,362	8,273	1,820	9,902	2,746	11,839	3,413
Yugoslavia	0	0	⁸ 10,485	¹ 29	⁸ 9,547	¹ 84	⁸ 9,283	⁸ 89
Sweden	7,267	149	8,251	158	9,870	85	11,573	310
Bulgaria	⁶ 1,485	⁶ 117	2,961	1	1,859		2,199	
Finland	1,794	30	1,748		2,628		3,465	
Norway	3,644	123	1,913	368	1,761	331	2,117	554
Denmark	2,337	1,124	1,980	286	2,388	306	3,286	380
Greece	281	294	¹ 2,123	¹ 602	2,055	599	2,066	862
Rumania	2,473	3,538	970	638	2,452	653		
Total 38 countries	2,415,233	2,154,998	2,064,432	1,846,987	2,307,797	2,041,019	2,417,082	2,175,428

Bureau of Agricultural Economics. Official sources except where otherwise noted.
"Wool" in this table includes: washed, unwashed, scoured, pulled wool, slipe, also hair—goat's, camel's, mohair, Angora goat, cashmere goat and alpaca, and all other animal fibers included in the United States classification of wool. The following items have been considered as not within this classification: Carded, combed and dyed wool, flocks, sheep, lamb and goat skins with hair on, mill waste, noils, and tops.

¹ International Yearbook of Agricultural Statistics.
² Includes 9 months land trade.
³ Sea trade only.
⁴ 3-year average.
⁵ Year ended Mar. 31.
⁶ 4-year average.
⁷ 1 year only.
⁸ Compiled from consular reports.

33023°—29——61

TABLE 420.—*Wool: Quantities used in manufactures in United States, by classes, 1918–1928* [1]

GREASE

Year	Combing			Clothing			Carpet			Total		
	Domestic	Foreign	Total	Domestic	Foreign	Total	Foreign combing	Foreign filling	Total	Domestic	Foreign	Total
	1,000 lbs.	1,000 lbs.	1,000 lbs.	1,000 lbs.	1,000 lbs.	1,000 lbs.	1,000 lbs.	1,000 lbs.	1,000 lbs.	1,000 lbs.	1,000 lbs.	1,000 lbs.
Average: 1921–1925	153,843	108,108	261,950	19,094	6,329	25,423	52,977	52,851	105,828	172,937	220,264	393,201
1918	164,878	217,571	382,449	17,845	17,350	35,195	16,414	15,703	32,117	182,723	267,038	449,761
1919	182,936	172,346	355,282	20,995	11,869	32,864	24,672	28,747	53,419	203,931	237,634	441,565
1920	134,824	172,546	307,370	17,914	11,997	29,911	28,356	28,364	56,720	152,738	241,263	394,001
1921	159,340	117,704	277,044	20,243	11,134	31,377	22,968	27,291	50,259	179,583	179,097	358,680
1922	210,142	87,061	297,203	26,750	8,344	35,094	58,797	51,664	110,461	236,892	205,866	442,758
1923	111,494	169,540	281,034	17,487	7,072	24,559	72,231	63,215	135,446	128,981	312,058	441,039
1924	152,960	81,635	234,595	15,483	3,508	18,991	54,042	60,047	114,089	168,443	199,232	367,675
1925	135,278	84,598	219,876	15,506	1,586	17,092	56,848	62,037	118,885	150,784	205,069	355,853
1926	126,559	99,746	226,305	15,750	1,631	17,381	45,605	56,205	101,810	142,309	203,187	345,496
1927	173,095	76,061	249,156	16,935	1,664	18,599	44,755	70,516	115,271	190,030	192,996	383,026
1928	185,044	44,584	229,628	18,715	1,643	20,358	43,677	77,760	121,437	203,759	167,664	371,423

SCOURED

Year	Combing			Clothing			Carpet			Total		
Average: 1921–1925	6,939	3,335	10,274	41,224	17,630	58,854	860	4,137	4,997	48,163	25,962	74,125
1918	11,033	16,623	27,656	30,466	64,846	95,312	1,177	2,777	3,954	41,499	85,423	126,922
1919	5,767	4,520	10,287	30,902	28,662	59,564	1,279	4,407	5,686	36,669	38,868	75,537
1920	5,906	5,492	11,398	30,263	22,828	53,091	1,359	5,643	7,002	36,169	35,322	71,491
1921	7,074	3,040	10,114	34,630	18,236	52,866	630	4,147	4,777	41,704	26,053	67,757
1922	8,374	2,753	11,127	47,547	19,347	66,894	1,285	5,410	6,695	55,921	28,795	84,716
1923	7,051	3,774	10,825	42,506	21,909	64,415	1,010	4,914	5,924	49,557	31,607	81,164
1924	5,804	3,409	9,213	40,718	16,089	56,807	533	3,122	3,655	46,522	23,153	69,675
1925	6,393	3,698	10,091	40,720	12,568	53,288	843	3,091	3,934	47,113	20,200	67,313
1926	5,191	3,647	8,838	37,432	10,512	47,944	558	3,745	4,303	42,623	18,462	61,085
1927	4,712	3,235	7,947	43,352	8,376	51,728	671	4,223	4,894	48,064	16,505	64,569
1928	5,608	3,327	8,935	41,456	6,735	48,191	757	5,324	6,081	47,064	16,143	63,207

PULLED

Year	Combing			Clothing			Carpet			Total		
Average: 1921–1925	7,825	1,285	9,110	9,552	1,350	10,902	1,940	4,570	6,510	17,376	9,146	26,522
1918	9,977	2,685	12,662	8,497	2,918	11,415	179	1,277	1,456	18,474	7,059	25,533
1919	9,707	537	10,244	8,809	944	9,753	321	2,224	2,545	18,516	4,026	22,542
1920	7,514	675	8,189	6,116	714	6,830	420	2,499	2,919	13,630	4,308	17,938
1921	9,445	1,125	10,570	11,024	1,052	12,076	1,149	2,680	3,829	20,469	6,006	26,475
1922	9,609	960	10,569	9,840	1,485	11,325	2,264	3,415	5,679	19,449	8,124	27,573
1923	8,052	1,923	9,975	8,315	2,080	10,395	2,884	5,409	8,293	16,367	12,296	28,663
1924	5,852	691	6,543	9,508	1,240	10,748	1,052	4,707	5,759	15,360	7,690	23,050
1925	6,165	1,728	7,893	9,071	895	9,966	2,351	6,640	8,991	15,236	11,614	26,850
1926	7,389	2,452	9,841	8,341	678	9,019	3,752	9,163	12,915	15,730	16,045	31,775
1927	9,006	1,186	10,192	10,004	574	10,578	1,904	6,849	8,753	19,010	10,513	29,523
1928	9,504	945	10,449	10,888	743	11,631	1,301	7,007	8,308	20,392	9,996	30,388

Bureau of Agricultural Economics. Compiled from wool-consumption reports issued monthly by the Bureau of Agricultural Economics, January, 1918–April, 1922; and by the Bureau of the Census, May, 1922–December, 1928.

[1] Not including estimates for firms not reporting nor wool actually reported but for which no grade was stated. Beginning with May, 1922, estimates for firms not reporting were discontinued. The information in this table is, therefore, not complete as some firms do not report.

TABLE 421.—*Wool: Estimated production, in the grease, average 1909–1913, annual 1924–1928*

Country	Average, 1909–1913	1924	1925	1926	1927	1928 preliminary
	1,000 pounds	*1,000 pounds*	*1,000 pounds*	*1,000 pounds*	*1,000 pounds*	*1,000 pounds*
United States:						
Fleece	272, 248	235, 575	245, 562	260, 976	281, 914	299, 113
Pulled	41, 400	43, 800	46, 800	49, 600	50, 100	51, 900
Total	313, 648	279, 375	292, 362	310, 576	332, 014	351, 013
Canada	13, 188	15, 112	15, 553	17, 960	18, 673	19, 611
United Kingdom and Irish Free State	136, 021	104, 668	109, 853	114, 567	118, 537	119, 690
France	81, 600	44, 092	44, 974	46, 517	[1] 47, 600	[1] 47, 000
Germany	43, 893	51, 960	50, 160	41, 825	35, 900	33, 500
Argentina	332, 321	316, 000	319, 000	363, 000	331, 000	343, 000
Uruguay	133, 101	97, 000	116, 000	129, 000	131, 000	139, 000
Australia	727, 709	773, 984	830, 460	924, 410	865, 000	950, 000
New Zealand	179, 942	208, 269	200, 205	202, 386	228, 960	[2] 238, 000
Union of South Africa	157, 690	185, 200	220, 000	245, 573	273, 000	285, 000
Total	2, 119, 113	2, 075, 660	2, 198, 567	2, 395, 814	2, 381, 684	2, 525, 814
Estimated world production excluding Russia and China [3]	2, 769, 780	2, 731, 790	2, 856, 650	3, 083, 770	3, 083, 720	
Soviet Russia [4]	[5] 330, 311	164, 700	261, 000	301, 800	329, 800	350, 250
China exports	37, 318	64, 709	56, 817	27, 791	48, 023	

Bureau of Agricultural Economics. For complete reference to original sources see Foreign Crops and Markets, Feb. 11, 1929, pp. 182–183. Includes wool shorn in the spring in the Northern Hemisphere and that shorn mostly in last few months of the same calendar year in the Southern Hemisphere.

[1] Estimate based on percentage increase or decrease in sheep numbers compared with preceding year.
[2] Estimate furnished by Consul Bernard Gotlieb, July 31, 1928. In converting bales to pounds have used average weight for 1927 as reported by Dalgety & Co., Annual Review, 1927–28.
[3] Comparatively few countries publish official estimates of their total wool production, i.e., fleece wool and wool pulled from skins. In arriving at these totals, therefore, in the absence of official figures for most countries various estimates have been used. Some are estimates furnished by United States Government representatives abroad based on estimates of Government agencies, or reliable commercial sources; others are estimates obtained by multiplying the number of sheep on hand at the date nearest the shearing season by an average yield per fleece as furnished by official sources, U. S. Government representatives abroad or other reliable sources. In the case of the principal exporting countries not publishing official estimates of total production, exports alone or exports, stocks and domestic consumption have been used as representing production. For some Asiatic countries where neither exports nor sheep figures are available rough commercial estimates have been used while in some cases the estimates are those of the U. S. Department of Commerce, or the National Association of Wool Manufacturers.
[4] For the years 1925–1927 coarse wool made up about 98 per cent of the total production.
[5] 1916.

TABLE 422.—*Wool (unwashed): Estimated price per pound, received by producers United States, 1910–1928*

Year	Jan.	Feb.	Mar.	Apr.	May	June	July	Aug.	Sept.	Oct.	Nov.	Dec.	Weighted av.
Average:	*Cents*	*Cents*	*Cents*	*Cents*	*Cents*	*Cents*	*Cents*	*Cents*	*Cents*	*Cents*	*Cents*	*Cents*	*Cents*
1910–1913	19. 2	19. 2	19. 2	18. 2	17. 9	17. 3	17. 3	17. 5	17. 0	16. 9	16. 9	17. 0	17. 6
1914–1920	36. 6	36. 2	37. 8	37. 2	38. 2	38. 2	37. 8	37. 7	37. 4	37. 2	36. 9	37. 2	37. 6
1921–1925	30. 5	31. 6	32. 5	32. 2	32. 2	32. 3	32. 0	31. 1	31. 5	31. 9	32. 6	34. 0	32. 1
1910	24. 5	24. 6	24. 9	22. 3	22. 8	19. 5	19. 0	19. 5	17. 7	18. 1	17. 9	17. 8	20. 5
1911	17. 3	17. 3	16. 8	15. 7	14. 7	15. 5	15. 4	16. 0	15. 6	15. 5	15. 6	15. 5	15. 6
1912	16. 2	16. 3	16. 9	17. 3	17. 8	18. 7	18. 9	18. 8	18. 7	18. 5	18. 6	18. 6	18. 1
1913	18. 6	18. 7	18. 4	17. 7	16. 3	15. 6	15. 9	15. 8	15. 8	15. 5	15. 6	16. 1	16. 4
1914	15. 7	15. 7	16. 4	16. 8	17. 2	18. 4	18. 5	18. 7	18. 6	18. 0	18. 1	18. 6	17. 7
1915	18. 6	20. 2	22. 8	22. 7	22. 0	23. 7	24. 2	23. 8	23. 3	22. 7	22. 7	23. 3	22. 8
1916	23. 3	24. 2	25. 9	26. 3	28. 7	28. 7	28. 6	29. 0	28. 4	28. 7	29. 4	30. 8	27. 9
1917	31. 8	32. 7	36. 7	38. 8	43. 7	49. 8	54. 3	54. 8	54. 2	55. 5	55. 9	58. 2	47. 8
1918	58. 1	57. 1	60. 0	60. 0	58. 2	57. 4	57. 5	57. 4	57. 7	57. 7	56. 4	56. 2	57. 9
1919	55. 2	51. 1	51. 3	47. 9	48. 0	50. 5	51. 8	52. 2	51. 3	50. 6	51. 0	51. 6	50. 3
1920	53. 3	52. 5	51. 5	51. 3	50. 3	38. 6	29. 5	28. 3	28. 0	27. 5	24. 9	21. 9	39. 1
1921	19. 6	19. 8	18. 9	17. 9	16. 0	15. 4	15. 5	15. 4	15. 5	15. 8	15. 6	16. 9	16. 4
1922	18. 0	22. 3	25. 0	24. 8	29. 0	32. 8	32. 5	31. 6	31. 6	32. 2	33. 2	35. 3	29. 8
1923	35. 3	35. 3	37. 3	39. 2	41. 7	41. 5	38. 3	37. 0	37. 1	36. 9	36. 4	36. 2	38. 9
1924	36. 6	37. 5	38. 2	38. 4	37. 4	36. 0	34. 3	33. 5	35. 5	37. 3	40. 1	42. 2	36. 9
1925	42. 8	43. 2	43. 0	40. 8	36. 9	35. 7	39. 4	38. 1	37. 8	37. 2	37. 8	39. 5	38. 5
1926	38. 9	37. 7	34. 7	33. 2	32. 0	31. 4	31. 9	31. 9	32. 6	31. 6	31. 6	3. 01	32. 5
1927	30. 9	31. 1	31. 3	30. 4	30. 1	30. 2	30. 7	31. 2	31. 2	30. 9	31. 1	32. 0	30. 7
1928	33. 2	34. 4	35. 4	35. 6	37. 0	38. 7	37. 6	37. 0	36. 5	36. 0	35. 9	35. 6	36. 7

Bureau of Agricultural Economics. Based on returns from special price reporters. United States annual average obtained by using estimates of the Division of Crop and Livestock Estimates and the Division of Statistical and Historical Research.

TABLE 423.—*Wool, scoured basis, territory, grades 64s, 70s, 80s (fine strictly combing): Average price per pound, Boston market, 1910–1928*

Year	Jan.	Feb.	Mar.	Apr.	May	June	July	Aug.	Sept.	Oct.	Nov.	Dec.	Average
	Cents	Cents	Cents	Cents	Cents	Cents	Cents	Cents	Cents	Cents	Cents	Cents	Cents
1910	74	73	71	68	63	61	61	62	63	63	63	63	65
1911	61	59	54	53	52	52	55	56	59	60	61	61	57
1912	61	61	61	61	61	61	63	68	68	68	67	67	64
1913	66	64	59	56	55	54	54	54	54	53	53	52	56
1914	52	56	57	59	60	61	61	63	61	59	61	61	59
1915	63	73	73	71	69	71	71	71	71	71	71	73	71
1916	74	77	77	79	79	81	82	85	89	89	97	105	84
1917	113	123	128	133	138	174	174	178	181	180	180	180	157
1918	180	180	183	185	180	180	185	180	180	185	180	180	182
1919	160	152	158	165	165	175	185	185	185	200	200	200	178
1920 [1]	200	205	205	200	200	175	160	145	130	120	95	90	160
1921	84	90	89	88	86	82	82	82	82	82	84	88	85
1922	97	110	110	109	127	134	135	131	130	134	139	140	125
1923	143	144	144	149	153	150	144	137	132	130	130	134	141
1924	139	139	142	138	135	129	130	137	142	147	154	164	141
1925	168	164	153	138	126	130	137	132	129	128	131	131	139
1926	127	124	118	116	112	110	116	116	116	116	114	110	116
1927	110	110	110	109	108	108	111	111	111	112	112	112	110
1928	116	116	116	117	119	120	120	115	112	112	113	114	116

Bureau of Agricultural Economics. 1910–1920 prices from quarterly reports of the National Association of Wool Manufacturers. 1921–1923 average of weekly range quotations from the Boston Commercial Bulletin and 1924–1928 from the livestock and meat reporting service of the bureau.

[1] Prices June–December, 1920, largely nominal.

TABLE 424.—*Wool, scoured basis, territory, grade 56s (⅜ blood strictly combing): Average price per pound, Boston market, 1910–1928*

Year	Jan.	Feb.	Mar.	Apr.	May	June	July	Aug.	Sept.	Oct.	Nov.	Dec.	Average
	Cents	Cents	Cents	Cents	Cents	Cents	Cents	Cents	Cents	Cents	Cents	Cents	Cents
1910	69	61	60	57	56	56	56	57	57	56	54	53	58
1911	54	54	52	49	49	50	50	52	52	48	46	48	50
1912	51	52	51	51	51	52	58	58	58	58	58	58	55
1913	58	58	55	50	49	48	48	48	48	47	46	45	50
1914	43	47	47	47	50	52	52	49	48	49	51	53	49
1915	56	63	66	66	66	66	66	68	68	68	67	69	66
1916	70	71	71	71	72	74	76	78	79	80	87	90	77
1917	91	100	102	110	118	132	132	138	146	148	148	148	126
1918	148	149	152	152	142	142	(1)	(1)	(1)	(1)	(1)	(1)	------
1919	126	121	121	110	118	120	128	137	138	127	130	135	126
1920	135	135	131	130	125	112	99	95	88	74	65	56	104
1921	53	55	55	54	53	50	51	52	52	52	54	58	53
1922	63	76	77	74	83	88	88	90	92	95	99	98	85
1923	100	103	105	107	111	111	109	105	103	101	104	108	106
1924	113	116	116	113	109	97	100	109	113	117	122	133	113
1925	136	136	125	109	96	99	105	101	102	102	108	109	111
1926	103	99	93	91	89	89	90	90	91	93	93	91	92
1927	90	90	90	90	88	88	90	91	91	94	94	94	91
1928	97	99	100	106	107	108	107	103	104	104	104	104	104

Bureau of Agricultural Economics. 1910–1923 compiled from weekly quotations in the Boston Commercial Bulletin. 1924–1928 from the livestock and meat reporting service of the bureau.

[1] No quotations. Prices fixed by Government.

TABLE 425.—*Wool, grease basis, Ohio and similar, grade 56s (⅜ blood strictly combing): Average price per pound, Boston market, 1900–1928*

Year	Jan.	Feb.	Mar.	Apr.	May	June	July	Aug.	Sept.	Oct.	Nov.	Dec.	Average
	Cents	Cents	Cents	Cents	Cents	Cents	Cents	Cents	Cents	Cents	Cents	Cents	Cents
1900	29	28	27	27	26	25	25	24	24	24	23	24	26
1901	24	23	23	23	22	20	20	20	21	21	21	22	22
1902	22	22	22	22	22	22	22	22	22	23	23	24	22
1903	25	25	25	23	23	24	24	24	26	26	26	26	25
1904	25	26	26	26	26	28	28	28	29	29	31	32	28
1905	32	31	30	31	35	36	36	35	35	35	35	34	34
1906	34	33	33	33	33	33	33	33	33	34	34	34	33
1907	34	34	34	33	32	32	32	33	33	33	31	30	33
1908	31	31	30	29	25	26	25	25	26	26	27	28	27
1909	29	30	31	33	34	35	36	36	37	37	37	37	34
1910	36	36	36	34	31	28	28	28	28	29	30	30	31
1911	30	29	28	25	25	25	25	25	25	25	25	25	26
1912	27	30	29	28	27	29	30	30	30	30	30	30	29
1913	31	31	30	26	24	24	24	24	24	24	23	24	26
1914	24	24	24	25	26	28	28	28	28	28	29	30	27
1915	31	35	37	37	36	36	38	38	37	36	37	38	36
1916	38	40	40	40	40	41	42	42	42	43	45	48	42
1917	49	54	56	59	63	70	74	75	76	76	76	77	67
1918	78	77	78	78	76	76	(¹)	(¹)	(¹)	(¹)	(¹)	(¹)	------
1919	70	65	65	61	61	63	70	71	70	68	69	70	67
1920	70	70	70	69	66	57	52	49	45	40	37	30	55
1921	29	30	30	30	29	26	26	26	26	26	28	32	28
1922	36	39	40	38	42	47	46	46	47	49	53	54	45
1923	55	56	56	56	56	57	56	54	53	52	53	54	55
1924	55	56	57	55	53	49	48	53	55	59	63	69	56
1925	70	69	66	55	46	49	53	52	50	52	54	54	56
1926	54	53	49	46	44	43	44	44	44	45	46	45	46
1927	45	45	45	44	42	42	43	44	45	46	47	48	45
1928	50	52	52	53	55	57	56	55	55	55	56	56	54

Bureau of Agricultural Economics. 1900–1909 from quarterly reports of the National Association of Wool Manufacturers on Ohio, Pennsylvania, and West Virginia ⅜ blood, 1910–1923 from Boston Commercial Bulletin, average of weekly range on Ohio and Pennsylvania ⅜ blood, and 1924–1928 from the livestock and meat reporting service of the Bureau.

¹ No quotations.

TABLE 426.—*Wool (Australian scoured): Average monthly price per pound at London, Queensland superior combing wool, 1921–1928*

Year	Jan.	Feb.	Mar.	Apr.	May	June	July	Aug.	Sept.	Oct.	Nov.	Dec.	Average
	Cents	Cents	Cents	Cents	Cents	Cents	Cents	Cents	Cents	Cents	Cents	Cents	Cents
1921	------	------	------	------	------	------	------	51.75	52.75	58.73	60.69	58.87	------
1922	66.90	74.07	73.38	74.65	79.19	79.76	79.66	79.98	83.81	88.30	93.33	99.87	81.08
1923	101.82	102.61	100.18	99.06	102.20	101.92	103.13	102.61	107.49	107.44	102.26	103.36	102.84
1924	102.47	113.53	113.34	117.85	118.11	116.09	116.54	121.39	127.31	129.47	134.40	136.95	120.62
1925	138.26	128.76	122.40	119.38	111.25	111.38	108.32	107.26	107.03	107.75	109.04	104.08	114.58
1926	99.35	88.21	89.23	91.25	91.25	91.25	91.25	91.25	92.78	93.08	91.25	91.25	91.83
1927	91.25	93.27	93.27	93.27	91.25	92.26	92.87	93.27	94.29	95.30	97.33	97.33	93.75
1928	97.37	97.33	97.33	97.33	97.33	97.33	92.77	93.27	91.65	87.70	87.70	89.22	93.86

Bureau of Agricultural Economics. Compiled from weekly quotations of the London Economist. Conversions at monthly average rate of exchange as given in Federal Reserve Bulletins to December, 1925, inclusive; subsequently at par.

TABLE 427.—*Goats and mohair: Estimates* [1] *of goats clipped, mohair clipped, and average clip per goat (principal producing States), 1920–1928*

GOATS CLIPPED

	1920	1921	1922	1923	1924	1925	1926	1927	1928
	Thousands	Thousands	Thousands	Thousands	Thousands	Thousands	Thousands	Thousands	Thousands
Texas [2]	1,834	1,984	1,750	1,797	2,008	1,857	2,367	2,579	2,800
New Mexico	124	128	110	110	127	120	135	165	170
Arizona [2]	145	145	152	160	165	162	165	185	185
California	72	74	59	57	57	58	56	52	45
Oregon	113	115	105	103	101	110	115	115	125
Missouri	58	60	55	53	60	67	61	63	66
Total	2,346	2,506	2,231	2,280	2,518	2,374	2,899	3,159	3,391

MOHAIR (INCLUDING KID HAIR) PRODUCED

	1,000 pounds	1,000 pounds	1,000 pounds	1,000 pounds	1,000 pounds	1,000 pounds	1,000 pounds	1,000 pounds	1,000 pounds
Texas	6,786	7,607	6,838	7,352	7,996	8,519	9,887	11,312	12,330
New Mexico	397	422	352	374	457	444	473	611	629
Arizona	464	479	517	560	611	599	578	685	684
California	230	244	207	211	217	220	207	203	176
Oregon	452	460	431	422	414	462	483	483	525
Missouri	145	150	143	148	162	188	171	176	178
Total	8,474	9,362	8,488	9,067	9,857	10,432	11,799	13,470	14,522

AVERAGE CLIP PER GOAT CLIPPED [3]

	Pounds	Pounds	Pounds	Pounds	Pounds	Pounds	Pounds	Pounds	Pounds
Texas	3.7	3.8	3.9	4.1	4.0	4.6	4.2	4.4	4.4
New Mexico	3.2	3.3	3.2	3.4	3.6	3.7	3.5	3.7	3.7
Arizona	3.2	3.3	3.4	3.5	3.7	3.7	3.5	3.7	3.7
California	3.2	3.3	3.5	3.7	3.8	3.8	3.7	3.9	3.9
Oregon	4.0	4.0	4.1	4.1	4.1	4.2	4.2	4.2	4.2
Missouri	2.5	2.5	2.6	2.8	2.7	2.8	2.8	2.8	2.7
Average, 6 States	3.6	3.7	3.8	4.0	3.9	4.4	4.1	4.3	4.3

Bureau of Agricultural Economics.

[1] Figures for 1923, 1924, and 1925 are revisions of department's estimates previously published.
[2] Most goats clipped twice a year. In Texas, kids are clipped in the fall of year of birth. Figures include both goats and kids clipped.
[3] In states where goats are clipped twice a year figures include both spring and fall clip.

TABLE 428.—*Livestock: Number of animals slaughtered at Federal-inspected plants and number of whole carcasses condemned, 1907–1928*

Year ended June 30—	Cattle Slaughter	Cattle Condemned	Calves Slaughter	Calves Condemned	Sheep Slaughter	Sheep Condemned	Goats Slaughter	Goats Condemned	Swine Slaughter	Swine Condemned	Horses Slaughter	Horses Condemned	Total slaughter
	Thousands	Thousands	Thousands	Thousands	Thousands	Thousands	Thousands	Thousands	Thousands	Thousands	Thousands	Thousands	Thousands
1907	7,622	27.933	1,764	6.414	9,682	9.524	52	0.042	31,816	105.879			50,935
1908	7,116	33.216	1,995	5.854	9,703	8.090	46	.033	35,113	127.933			53,973
1909	7,325	35.103	2,047	8.213	10,803	10.747	69	.082	35,428	86.912			55,672
1910	7,962	42.426	2,295	7.524	11,150	11.127	116	.226	27,656	52.439			49,179
1911	7,781	39.402	2,220	7.654	13,006	10.789	54	.061	29,916	59.477			52,977
1912	7,532	50.363	2,243	8.927	14,209	15.402	64	.084	34,966	129.002			59,014
1913	7,156	50.775	2,098	9.216	14,724	16.657	57	.076	32,288	173.937			56,323
1914	6,724	48.356	1,815	6.696	14,959	20.563	122	.746	33,290	204.942			56,909
1915	6,965	52.496	1,736	5.941	12,909	17.611	166	.653	36,248	213.905			58,023
1916	7,404	57.579	2,048	6.681	11,986	15.057	180	.663	40,483	195.107			62,101
1917	9,299	78.706	2,680	10.112	11,343	16.749	175	1.349	40,211	158.480			63,708
1918	10,938	68.156	3,323	8.109	8,769	12.564	150	.419	35,449	113.079			58,630
1919	11,242	59.549	3,674	9.202	11,268	14.371	126	.318	44,398	128.805			70,709
1920	9,710	58.602	4,228	13.820	12,335	20.028	77	.135	38,982	133.476	1	0.064	65,332
1921	8,180	46.854	3,896	7.703	12,452	12.666	20	.023	37,703	122.609	1	.019	62,252
1922	7,871	55.170	3,924	11.408	11,968	10.476	14	.030	39,416	160.133	2	.026	63,196
1923	9,030	73.300	4,338	11.815	11,404	13.317	25	.081	48,600	196.325	1	.013	73,398
1924	9,189	83.923	4,668	12.736	11,505	12.853	31	.321	54,416	232.670	5	.036	79,814
1925	9,774	92.055	5,185	11.088	12,203	12.701	27	.114	48,460	180.427	12	.040	75,660
1926	10,098	103.636	5,312	11.933	12,354	14.462	43	.085	40,443	143.026	40	.065	68,289
1927	10,050	83.460	5,080	10.609	12,894	16.414	30	.074	42,650	173.591	43	.168	70,747
1928	9,040	69.354	4,774	9.934	12,984	15.364	20	.062	48,347	154.175	107	.301	75,273

Bureau Animal Industry.

TABLE 429.—*Meats and lard: Quantity apparently available for consumption, 1900–1928*

Calendar year	Apparently available for consumption								Percentage of total apparently available for consumption					
	Beef	Veal	Total beef and veal	Lamb and mutton	Pork	Total meats[1]	Lard	Total meats and lard	Beef	Veal	Total beef and veal	Lamb and mutton	Pork	Total meats
	Million lbs.	Million lbs.	Million lbs.	Million lbs.	Million lbs.	Million lbs.	Million lbs.	Million lbs.	Per cent	Per cent	Per cent	Per cent	Per cent	Per cent
Average:														
1900–1908	5,969	423	6,392	552	5,109	12,053	1,012	13,065	49.4	3.5	52.9	4.7	42.4	100
1909–1913	6,279	589	6,868	685	5,744	13,297	1,065	14,362	47.2	4.4	51.6	5.2	43.2	100
1914–1920	6,081	636	6,719	588	5,854	13,159	1,303	14,462	46.2	4.8	51.0	4.5	44.5	100
1921–1925	6,765	724	7,489	589	7,754	15,832	1,552	17,384	42.7	4.6	47.3	3.7	49.0	100
1900	5,165	265	5,430	516	4,927	10,873	1,002	11,875	47.5	2.5	50.0	4.7	45.3	100
1901	5,362	305	5,667	538	4,896	11,101	1,002	12,103	48.3	2.8	51.1	4.8	44.1	100
1902	5,434	346	5,780	557	4,584	10,921	932	11,853	49.9	3.2	53.1	5.1	41.8	100
1903	6,156	384	6,540	579	4,801	11,920	955	12,875	51.6	3.2	54.8	4.9	40.3	100
1904	6,081	425	6,506	563	5,185	12,254	1,025	13,279	49.6	3.5	53.1	4.6	42.3	100
1905	6,144	455	6,599	544	4,950	12,093	843	12,936	50.8	3.8	54.6	4.5	40.9	100
1906	6,235	464	6,699	554	5,128	12,381	959	13,340	50.4	3.7	54.1	4.5	41.4	100
1907	6,779	589	7,368	558	5,628	13,554	1,183	14,737	50.0	4.3	54.3	4.2	41.5	100
1908	6,367	573	6,940	557	5,884	13,381	1,203	14,584	47.6	4.3	51.9	4.1	44.0	100
1909	6,835	628	7,463	601	5,455	13,519	1,042	14,561	50.6	4.6	55.2	4.4	40.4	100
1910	6,561	632	7,193	596	5,267	13,056	1,052	14,108	50.3	4.8	55.1	4.5	40.4	100
1911	6,342	597	6,939	729	6,046	13,714	1,063	14,777	46.2	4.4	50.6	5.3	44.1	100
1912	5,807	598	6,405	773	5,873	13,051	1,068	14,119	44.5	4.6	49.1	5.9	45.0	100
1913	5,852	491	6,343	725	6,077	13,145	1,100	14,245	44.5	3.7	48.2	5.5	46.3	100
1914	5,722	448	6,170	724	6,102	12,996	1,192	14,188	44.0	3.4	47.4	5.6	47.0	100
1915	5,414	428	5,842	622	5,908	12,372	1,281	13,653	43.8	3.4	47.2	5.0	47.8	100
1916	5,639	536	6,175	613	6,055	12,843	1,368	14,211	43.9	4.2	48.1	4.8	47.1	100
1917	6,083	662	6,745	473	5,037	12,255	1,195	13,450	49.6	5.4	55.0	3.9	41.1	100
1918	6,522	765	7,287	486	5,684	13,457	1,374	14,831	48.5	5.7	54.2	3.6	42.2	100
1919	6,474	808	7,282	607	5,755	13,644	1,292	14,936	47.5	5.9	53.4	4.4	42.2	100
1920	6,713	805	7,518	590	6,437	14,545	1,416	15,961	46.2	5.5	51.7	4.0	44.3	100
1921	6,171	751	6,922	639	6,886	14,447	1,223	15,670	42.7	5.2	47.9	4.4	47.7	100
1922	6,643	797	7,440	545	7,260	15,245	1,558	16,803	43.6	5.2	48.8	3.6	47.6	100
1923	6,858	865	7,723	576	8,338	16,637	1,707	18,344	41.2	5.2	46.4	3.5	50.1	100
1924	7,001	929	7,930	589	8,492	17,011	1,749	18,760	41.1	5.5	46.6	3.4	50.0	100
1925	7,175	1,004	8,179	597	7,794	16,570	1,522	18,092	43.9	5.5	49.5	3.6	46.9	100
1926	7,454	964	8,418	641	7,689	16,748	1,584	18,332	44.4	5.8	50.2	3.8	46.0	100
1927	6,926	874	7,800	645	8,122	16,567	1,634	18,201	41.7	5.3	47.0	3.9	49.1	100
1928	6,210	822	7,032	673	8,863	16,568	1,763	18,331	37.4	5.0	42.4	4.1	53.5	100

Bureau of Animal Industry. Quantities in this table are based on carcass weights at slaughter, which do not include the edible offal. The Federally inspected part of each kind of meat, also of lard, is as reported by the Bureau of Agricultural Economics. The remainder, which includes the farm consumption, is estimated from the basis of the latest census data. Allowance is made for imports, exports, and quantities in storage.

[1] Not including goat meat.

Table 430.—*Meats and lard: Quantity apparently available for consumption, per capita, per annum, 1900–1928*

Calendar year	Beef	Veal	Lamb and mutton	Pork, not including lard	Total meats [1]	Lard	Total meats and lard
	Pounds	*Pounds*	*Pounds*	*Pounds*	*Pounds*	*Pounds*	*Pounds*
Average:							
1900–1908	72.2	5.1	6.7	61.8	145.8	12.2	158.0
1909–1913	67.2	6.3	7.3	61.3	142.1	11.4	153.5
1914–1920	59.4	6.2	5.8	57.3	128.7	12.8	141.5
1921–1925	60.4	7.8	5.3	69.3	142.8	13.9	156.7
1900	67.8	3.5	6.8	64.7	142.8	13.2	156.0
1901	69.0	3.9	6.9	63.0	142.8	12.9	155.7
1902	68.5	4.4	7.0	57.8	137.7	11.7	149.4
1903	76.0	4.7	7.2	59.3	147.2	11.8	159.0
1904	73.6	5.1	6.8	62.8	148.3	12.4	160.7
1905	73.0	5.4	6.5	58.8	143.7	10.0	153.7
1906	72.6	5.4	6.5	59.7	144.2	11.2	155.4
1907	77.5	6.7	6.4	64.6	155.0	13.5	168.5
1908	71.5	6.4	6.3	66.1	150.3	13.5	163.8
1909	75.4	6.9	6.6	60.1	149.0	11.5	160.5
1910	71.1	6.8	6.4	57.1	141.4	11.4	152.8
1911	67.7	6.4	7.8	64.5	146.4	11.3	157.7
1912	61.1	6.3	8.1	61.8	137.3	11.2	148.5
1913	60.6	5.1	7.5	63.0	136.2	11.4	147.6
1914	58.5	4.6	7.4	62.3	132.8	12.2	145.0
1915	54.5	4.3	6.3	59.5	124.6	12.9	137.5
1916	56.0	5.3	6.1	60.1	127.5	13.6	141.1
1917	59.5	6.5	4.6	49.3	119.9	11.7	131.6
1918	63.0	7.4	4.7	54.8	129.9	13.3	143.2
1919	61.6	7.7	5.8	54.8	129.9	12.3	142.2
1920	63.1	7.6	5.5	60.5	136.7	13.3	150.0
1921	56.9	7.0	5.9	63.5	133.3	11.3	144.6
1922	60.4	7.3	5.0	66.1	138.8	14.2	153.0
1923	61.4	7.7	5.2	74.7	149.0	15.3	164.3
1924	61.6	8.2	5.2	74.7	149.7	15.4	165.1
1925	62.2	8.7	5.2	67.6	143.7	13.2	156.9
1926	63.6	8.2	5.5	65.7	143.0	13.5	156.5
1927	58.4	7.4	5.4	68.5	139.7	13.8	153.5
1928	51.7	6.8	5.6	73.9	138.0	14.7	152.7

Bureau of Animal Industry. Quantities based on carcass weights and do not include the edible offal. Population figures used in estimating per capita consumption are census estimates for July 1 each year.

[1] Not including goat meat.

Table 431.—*Meat and meat products prepared under Federal inspection, 1907–1928*

Year ended June 30—	Pork placed in cure	Sausage chopped	Canned meats	Lard	Lard compounds and substitutes	Oleo products	Oleo-margarine	All other products	Tota
	1,000 pounds	*1,000 pounds*	*1,000 pounds*	*1,000 pounds*	*1,000 pounds*	*1,000 pounds*	*1,000 pounds*	*1,000 pounds*	*1,000 pounds*
1907	2,248,886	267,760	105,196	1,003,602	353,549	283,971	55,694	145,554	4,464,213
1908	2,875,997	416,200	92,582	1,433,778	436,448	293,425	79,380	330,487	5,958,298
1909	2,686,051	457,095	123,810	1,308,986	488,249	295,889	91,068	1,340,289	6,791,437
1910	2,216,680	485,864	127,263	948,468	671,526	296,429	139,158	1,338,576	6,223,964
1911	2,568,149	488,814	144,942	1,185,503	672,845	330,688	117,848	1,425,444	6,934,233
1912	2,633,752	523,893	153,871	1,309,140	648,443	297,038	128,319	1,585,103	7,279,559
1913	2,545,358	531,626	115,237	1,222,857	670,802	264,705	145,356	1,598,869	7,094,810
1914	2,568,335	542,017	120,473	1,187,963	590,409	274,625	143,999	1,605,475	7,033,296
1915	2,913,328	502,675	235,963	1,277,734	520,899	287,047	152,388	1,663,491	7,533,070
1916	2,922,381	565,047	164,200	1,277,870	397,089	287,047	152,388	1,708,972	7,474,994
1917	2,918,211	635,860	283,319	1,119,315	466,198	279,197	225,074	1,736,459	7,663,633
1918	3,132,549	624,827	468,633	943,851	453,164	263,630	265,335	1,743,196	7,905,185
1919	3,717,838	667,602	632,259	1,256,043	469,732	266,808	251,170	1,907,590	9,169,042
1920	2,903,854	682,521	211,521	1,316,918	328,567	253,397	151,638	1,723,697	7,127,820
1921	2,501,885	583,777	86,240	1,487,820	339,366	268,034	118,197	1,666,402	7,427,116
1922	2,725,031	568,626	109,481	1,659,331	312,014	264,705	129,767	1,920,156	8,888,547
1923	3,366,258	679,315	160,132	2,017,939	336,843	278,137	142,881	2,136,254	9,404,840
1924	3,502,368	707,323	183,026	2,110,660	363,320	259,008	133,836	2,170,598	8,912,077
1925	3,176,714	736,877	214,330	1,733,933	458,518	287,271	148,331	2,008,004	8,411,082
1926	2,850,622	771,655	214,167	1,598,754	543,913	275,636	148,331	1,977,161	8,566,444
1927	2,920,206	765,074	248,459	1,691,344	535,175	280,641	148,384	2,201,132	8,974,319
1928	3,033,861	777,606	254,769	1,845,129	472,604	237,228	151,990		

Bureau of Animal Industry. The above figures do not represent production, as a product may be inspected more than once in course of further manufacture.

TABLE 432.—*Meat and meat products: International trade, average 1911–1913, annual 1925–1927*

Country	Average, 1911–1913		1925		1926		1927, preliminary	
	Imports	Exports	Imports	Exports	Imports	Exports	Imports	Exports
PRINCIPAL EXPORTING COUNTRIES	*1,000 pounds*	*1,000 pounds*	*1,000 pounds*	*1,000 pounds*	*1,000 pounds*	*1,000 pounds*	*1,000 pounds*	*1,000 pounds*
Argentina	3,487	1,173,461	350	2,168,222	424	2,087,359	477	2,280,405
Australia	1,967	507,143	¹5,760	¹458,134	¹5,506	¹422,134	¹5,349	¹321,643
Brazil	54,012	1,520	23,201	153,040	9,372	30,033	--------	89,401
Canada	43,327	60,242	23,378	206,455	25,247	157,473	18,289	159,297
Chile	11,738	19,728	9,447	42,205	--------	32,144	--------	36,107
China	85	64,684	2,374	55,454	4,560	53,844	3,040	47,348
Denmark	32,184	368,188	18,633	564,984	24,642	551,033	33,205	682,919
Hungary	0	0	5,193	42,835	6,140	62,623	9,476	25,768
Irish Free State	0	0	77,524	89,997	73,891	88,199	66,667	105,423
Netherlands	359,864	497,402	253,792	553,776	224,127	495,723	216,180	608,075
New Zealand	960	326,539	1,239	449,916	1,064	398,502	943	441,124
Sweden	24,215	39,768	41,068	36,185	38,009	46,333	31,635	73,202
Union of South Africa	31,103	404	16,569	23,264	10,786	37,122	18,040	15,253
United States	18,719	1,277,524	62,943	1,584,468	102,626	1,445,219	161,302	1,290,979
Uruguay	²702	196,911	77	425,749	0	447,200	0	420,318
Yugoslavia	0	0	56	29,407	27	52,688	--------	41,317
PRINCIPAL IMPORTING COUNTRIES								
Austria	³49,268	³12,420	129,560	3,008	120,383	8,245	118,728	7,721
Belgium	179,120	127,057	286,811	67,702	213,882	84,087	215,068	52,731
Cuba	128,362	0	196,380	0	179,365	0		
Czechoslovakia	0	0	114,825	8,627	113,617	9,358	94,463	10,054
Finland	14,973	2,081	13,200	8,078	20,021	7,728	19,917	3,905
France	111,496	98,281	377,018	55,788	310,163	47,366	404,155	58,535
Germany	559,752	19,525	982,581	34,980	937,666	34,937	899,275	37,320
Italy	104,619	15,708	318,656	15,591	205,120	35,575	198,453	18,312
Japan	11,727	0	54,858	0	74,779	0	74,539	0
Norway	42,416	3,365	52,278	2,284	38,686	3,096	29,542	2,644
Philippine Islands	21,902	0	17,531	0	19,574	0	20,578	0
Poland	0	0	33,638	78,807	22,857	79,412	48,872	⁶63,266
Russia	130,897	53,175						
Spain	37,974	3,200	27,203	7,046	26,332	70,952		
Switzerland	60,174	3,169	27,639	3,897	30,010	3,208	31,242	3,218
United Kingdom	2,843,605	117,226	3,878,850	136,718	3,839,985	126,400	3,854,368	148,826
Total	4,878,648	4,988,721	7,052,632	7,306,617	6,678,866	6,917,993	6,573,801	7,045,111
Totals by kinds of meat:								
Beef	2,023,704	2,161,464	3,270,778	3,459,983	3,141,579	3,187,901	3,039,848	3,120,583
Mutton	610,820	559,795	658,393	590,959	655,239	581,903	680,625	660,814
Pork	1,585,242	1,604,439	2,358,410	2,358,911	2,202,910	2,199,023	2,134,363	2,287,532
Other	658,882	663,023	765,051	896,764	679,138	949,166	718,965	976,182
Total	4,878,648	4,988,721	7,052,632	7,306,617	6,678,866	6,917,993	6,573,801	7,045,111

Bureau of Agricultural Economics.   Official sources.

¹ Year ending June 30.   ² 1 year only.   ³ Average for Austria-Hungary.

TABLE 433.—*Meats, western dressed, fresh, and smoked: Average wholesale price per 100 pounds at Chicago and New York, by months, 1927–1928*

BEEF AND VEAL

Year and month	Chicago							New York						
	Steer beef					Cow beef, good	Vealers,[1] good	Steer beef					Cow beef, good	Vealers,[1] good
	Choice		Good		Medium			Choice		Good		Medium		
	700 lbs. up	Under 700 lbs.	700 lbs. up	Under 700 lbs.				700 lbs. up	Under 700 lbs.	700 lbs. up	Under 700 lbs.			
1927	*Dols.*	*Dols.*	*Dols.*	*Dols.*	*Dols.*	*Dols.*	*Dols.*	*Dols.*	*Dols.*	*Dols.*	*Dols.*	*Dols.*	*Dols.*	*Dols.*
Jan	16. 50	19. 00	15. 50	17. 00	14. 45	13. 72	20. 05	17. 36	18. 76	15. 59	15. 91	13. 44	13. 00	20. 28
Feb	16. 28	18. 78	15. 05	16. 05	14. 05	14. 00	20. 05	17. 44	18. 56	15. 96	16. 21	14. 62	13. 56	22. 36
Mar	17. 91	18. 97	16. 46	16. 89	14. 91	14. 60	19. 68	18. 01	18. 30	16. 59	16. 43	15. 13	14. 09	20. 72
Apr	19. 18	19. 18	17. 60	17. 35	15. 66	15. 38	17. 90	19. 02	19. 06	*17. 64	17. 60	16. 35	15. 04	18. 58
May	19. 00	19. 09	17. 25	17. 14	15. 35	15. 08	17. 25	19. 00	19. 00	17. 75	17. 75	16. 50	15. 02	18. 35
June	19. 14	18. 56	17. 46	16. 84	14. 89	14. 86	17. 78	19. 25	19. 37	17. 84	17. 84	16. 00	15. 87	18. 66
July	20. 50	19. 45	18. 90	17. 88	16. 15	14. 69	19. 75	20. 82	20. 84	19. 36	19. 44	16. 80	16. 51	21. 62
Aug	20. 64	20. 25	18. 99	18. 04	15. 78	14. 37	22. 40	22. 09	21. 89	19. 47	19. 51	16. 11	15. 14	23. 80
Sept	21. 38	21. 20	19. 15	18. 40	15. 80	14. 59	23. 35	22. 76	22. 70	20. 20	19. 72	15. 80	15. 06	22. 80
Oct	22. 80	22. 75	20. 08	19. 48	15. 61	14. 65	22. 75	23. 86	23. 86	20. 20	21. 02	16. 92	15. 60	20. 22
Nov	23. 98	23. 84	21. 31	19. 99	16. 28	14. 44	18. 86	24. 75	24. 75	21. 02	21. 02	16. 92	15. 60	20. 22
Dec	23. 35	22. 28	20. 80	19. 28	16. 48	15. 50	18. 62	23. 61	23. 61	20. 51	20. 51	17. 28	16. 30	20. 42
Average	20. 06	20. 28	18. 21	17. 86	15. 45	14. 66	19. 87	20. 66	20. 89	18. 48	18. 47	15. 90	15. 02	21. 06
1928														
Jan	23. 50	21. 92	21. 00	19. 49	17. 02	15. 52	19. 30	22. 50	22. 42	19. 91	20. 00	17. 22	16. 72	20. 68
Feb	23. 07	21. 32	20. 58	19. 18	**17. 02**	16. 19	22. 68	22. 43	22. 10	20. 56	20. 22	17. 95	17. 17	24. 89
Mar	21. 75	21. 00	*19. 50	19. 00	17. 00	15. 75	19. 25	21. 54	21. 54	20. 31	20. 04	18. 41	16. 95	20. 35
Apr	21. 20	20. 99	19. 24	19. 19	17. 61	16. 12	19. 40	20. 95	21. 91	20. 66	20. 41	18. 60	17. 38	21. 00
May	20. 63	21. 23	19. 25	19. 75	18. 64	17. 59	20. 95	21. 22	21. 22	20. 39	20. 39	18. 41	18. 15	22. 70
June	21. 60	22. 60	20. 60	21. 49	20. 10	18. 58	21. 40	22. 30	22. 65	21. 58	21. 85	19. 68	19. 10	21. 92
		550 to 700 lbs.		550 to 700 lbs.	500 lbs. up				550 to 700 lbs.		550 to 700 lbs.	500 lbs. up		
July	23. 22	23. 71	22. 21	22. 67	20. 74	18. 85	22. 84	23. 50	23. 74	22. 71	22. 84	20. 03	19. 39	22. 42
Aug	23. 48	24. 33	22. 48	23. 13	20. 50	18. 50	25. 48	25. 41	25. 94	24. 41	24. 34	20. 46	19. 85	26. 00
Sept	25. 01	25. 90	24. 09	24. 48	21. 24	18. 62	26. 68	26. 99	27. 39	25. 26	25. 14	20. 65	19. 66	26. 89
Oct	24. 53	25. 30	23. 06	23. 30	18. 91	16. 52	23. 24	26. 34	26. 54	24. 12	23. 98	19. 78	17. 61	24. 65
Nov	23. 40	24. 44	21. 83	22. 49	19. 24	16. 74	21. 70	24. 64	25. 19	22. 41	22. 90	19. 70	17. 15	22. 96
Dec	22. 78	23. 55	20. 55	21. 21	18. 22	15. 85	20. 84	23. 68	24. 20	21. 26	21. 64	19. 01	17. 12	19. 95
Average	22. 85	-------	21. 20	-------	-------	17. 07	21. 98	23. 54	------	21. 96	------	------	18. 02	22. 87

[1] Hide on.

TABLE 433.—*Meats, western dressed, fresh, and smoked: Average wholesale price per 100 pounds at Chicago and New York, by month, 1927–1928*—Continued

PORK CUTS

Year and month	Chicago						New York					
	Fresh pork			Cured pork and lard			Fresh pork			Cured pork and lard		
	Hams, 10 to 14 lbs.	Loins, 12 to 15 lbs.	Shoulders, New York style, skinned	Hams, smoked, regular No. 2, 14 to 16 lbs.	Bacon, No. 1, smoked, 6 to 8 lbs.	Lard, refined (hardwood tubs)	Hams, 10 to 14 lbs.	Loins, 12 to 15 lbs.	Shoulders, New York style, skinned	Hams, smoked, regular, No. 2, 10 to 12 lbs.	Bacon, No. 2, smoked, 8 to 10 lbs.	Lard, refined (hardwood tubs)
1927	*Dolls.*	*Dolls.*	*Dolls.*	*Dolls.*	*Dolls.*	*Dolls.*	*Dolls.*	*Dolls.*	*Dolls.*	*Dolls.*	*Dolls.*	*Dolls.*
Jan	24.00	20.08	16.31	28.25	34.75	13.59	26.25	21.60	18.70	26.38	26.75	14.12
Feb	23.62	19.54	16.09	27.50	34.38	13.72	26.12	20.81	18.02	25.62	26.25	13.56
Mar	22.60	20.28	16.41	26.25	34.50	14.38	25.20	21.33	17.86	25.50	25.70	13.50
Apr	22.62	20.10	16.16	26.12	34.38	14.32	24.00	20.74	17.75	25.50	25.50	13.88
May	21.50	18.65	14.36	25.75	33.75	14.12	23.50	19.48	16.19	25.00	25.38	14.12
June	20.20	16.99	12.19	24.60	32.45	13.35	23.00	17.78	13.85	24.02	23.20	14.00
July	20.50	17.16	12.00	22.50	32.00	12.25	21.00	18.50	13.58	22.90	22.38	13.75
Aug	20.76	21.64	13.48	20.70	32.20	12.54	22.00	23.34	15.40	22.90	21.90	13.55
Sept	21.00	26.38	16.02	20.25	34.75	14.25	21.38	27.80	17.25	23.38	22.00	14.06
Oct	20.65	25.90	17.70	22.25	36.75	14.50	21.25	27.70	18.98	23.90	22.50	14.44
Nov	18.60	19.23	14.44	22.10	36.60	13.60	19.00	19.98	16.16	22.95	21.90	14.10
Dec	16.25	15.21	12.35	20.50	31.75	13.25	17.38	16.29	13.89	21.05	21.25	13.69
Av	21.02	20.10	14.79	23.90	34.02	13.66	22.51	21.28	16.47	24.09	23.73	13.90
1928												
Jan	16.75	15.02	11.92	19.00	30.50	12.50	17.12	15.29	12.90	20.12	20.06	13.44
Feb	17.00	13.54	11.04	19.00	30.00	11.60	18.00	14.40	12.57	20.00	20.00	13.45
Mar	16.50	13.58	11.10	19.00	30.00	11.50	17.00	14.02	12.56	20.00	19.90	12.88
Apr	17.00	20.14	13.10	19.00	29.50	12.50	19.75	19.19	13.21	20.00	19.00	13.12
May	16.20	20.19	13.98	19.90	30.00	13.10	20.40	20.11	14.75	20.25	19.45	13.85
June	17.88	18.15	13.98	20.38	30.00	13.50	19.50	18.34	14.31	20.59	19.79	13.56
			8 to 12 lbs.						8 to 12 lbs.			
July	20.25	22.42	16.36	23.50	30.75	14.00	20.75	21.49	17.18	22.94	20.75	13.97
					No. 1 smoked, dry cure, 6 to 8 lbs.						No. 1 smoked, sweet-pickle cure 8 to 10 lbs.	
Aug	23.60	25.56	19.55	26.00	31.00	14.70	23.70	25.28	20.34	25.00	22.30	14.77
Sept	23.80	27.69	22.64	26.00	31.75	15.25	25.00	28.02	22.32	25.44	24.25	14.81
Oct	20.20	20.58	17.96	24.86	31.40	14.40	22.90	21.94	20.80	25.60	25.30	15.00
Nov	18.21	19.14	15.16	24.00	29.10	13.62	20.00	20.58	16.32	24.47	22.27	14.00
Dec	18.85	15.19	12.82	23.88	28.00	12.88	19.00	15.75	14.25	23.64	20.55	13.50
Av	18.85	19.27	14.97	22.04	--------	13.30	20.26	19.53	15.96	22.34	--------	13.86

TABLE 433.—*Meats, western dressed, fresh, and smoked: Average wholesale price per 100 pounds at Chicago and New York, by months, 1927–1928*—Continued

LAMB AND MUTTON

Year and month	Chicago							New York						
	Lamb						Mutton, good	Lamb						Mutton, good
	Choice		Good		Medium	Common		Choice		Good		Medium	Common	
	30 to 42 lbs.	42 to 55 lbs.	30 to 42 lbs.	42 to 55 lbs.				30 to 42 lbs.	42 to 55 lbs.	30 to 42 lbs.	42 to 55 lbs.			
1927	Dols.	Dols.	Dols.	Dols.	Dols.	Dols.	Dols.	Dols.	Dols.	Dols.	Dols.	Dols.	Dols.	Dols.
Jan	24.90	21.28	23.30	19.90	21.45	19.48	14.50	24.40	22.75	22.92	21.65	20.75	19.25	14.45
Feb	25.40	21.82	23.55	19.92	21.70	19.62	16.15	24.80	23.46	23.31	22.74	22.14	19.96	15.25
Mar	29.72	26.08	27.72	24.90	25.76	23.64	17.60	29.10	28.04	27.48	27.14	26.12	23.84	17.10
Apr	31.58	29.00	30.05	27.30	28.35	26.82	20.10	31.98	30.50	30.12	29.32	28.00	26.82	18.10
May	32.20	31.12	30.40	29.58	28.32	26.25	17.80	32.82	31.60	31.45	29.88	29.08	28.20	17.95
June	31.13	¹31.62	28.99	¹29.62	26.49	23.77	15.16	30.95	29.02	28.96	27.82	26.14	22.96	14.28
July	29.35		27.40		24.25	20.95	14.00	29.38	27.39	27.25	26.25	24.39	20.28	16.10
Aug	27.30	26.33	25.52	24.87	22.98	19.72	14.38	26.36	25.10	24.62	23.86	22.10	18.64	15.26
Sept	25.81	24.61	23.90	23.40	21.90	18.90	13.70	25.60	24.80	24.30	23.39	21.42	18.42	12.42
Oct	24.82	22.92	23.00	21.92	21.00	18.50	13.00	24.80	23.82	23.80	22.85	20.92	18.52	12.28
Nov	25.23	23.11	23.63	22.11	21.61	19.61	13.00	24.10	23.06	23.10	22.06	20.94	18.48	12.95
Dec	24.81	22.70	23.64	21.70	21.56	19.82	13.60	24.91	22.52	23.29	20.62	19.60	18.08	13.29
Average	27.69		25.92		23.78	21.42	15.25	27.43	26.00	25.88	24.80	23.47	21.12	14.95
1928														
Jan	24.02	21.34	22.90	20.31	20.65	19.65	13.00	23.75	21.74	22.50	20.15	19.70	17.57	14.66
Feb	25.86	23.78	24.84	22.76	22.74	21.76	14.62	26.11	24.24	24.77	23.24	22.32	21.32	14.71
Mar	27.25	25.25	26.25	24.12	24.12	22.21	15.25	28.22	26.72	26.72	25.70	24.95	23.82	16.78
Apr	29.80	28.28	28.80	26.78	26.52		16.90	30.50	29.15	29.38	28.10	27.48		19.10
May	32.06	30.80	31.06	29.30	28.68		18.08	32.70	32.08	31.90	31.18	29.96		16.70
June	31.45	31.05	30.05	29.50	27.20	22.55	16.00	30.88	29.55	29.40	28.28	26.50	22.35	14.65
	38 lbs. down	39 to 45 lbs.	38 lbs. down	39 to 45 lbs.	38 pounds down		70 lbs. down	38 lbs. down	39 to 45 lbs.	38 lbs. down	39 to 45 lbs.	38 lbs. down		70 lbs. down
July	30.20	29.92	28.50	28.22	25.25	22.18	16.00	28.89	28.00	27.44	26.88	24.89	21.90	15.16
Aug	28.04	27.64	26.40	26.00	23.94	20.94	15.72	27.38	27.38	26.32	26.32	24.26	21.74	15.06
Sept	27.05	27.08	25.72	25.72	23.28	20.79	14.55	28.08	28.08	26.98	26.98	25.26	22.95	14.45
Oct	23.66	23.64	22.56	22.54	20.88	18.80	12.52	25.14	25.14	23.84	23.84	22.30	20.40	12.92
Nov	23.49	23.49	22.30	22.30	20.52	18.50	12.20	24.18	24.18	22.78	22.75	21.00	18.92	12.12
Dec	24.12	24.12	23.05	23.05	21.64	19.94	12.98	24.30	24.10	22.68	22.58	21.03	19.06	12.54

Bureau of Agricultural Economics. Compiled from data of the livestock and meat-reporting service of the bureau. Earlier data in 1927 Yearbook, pp. 1050–1055.

¹ 2-week average in 5-week month.

TABLE 434.—*Hides, packer: Average price per pound at Chicago, averages 1894–1925; annual, 1920–1928*

Year	Steers					Cows			Bulls	
	Heavy native	Heavy Texas	Light Texas	Butt branded	Colorados	Heavy native	Light native	Branded	Native	Branded
Average:	Cents	Cents	Cents	Cents	Cents	Cents	Cents	Cents	Cents	Cents
1894–1898	9.24	8.68	8.06	8.23	7.53	8.28	8.30	7.53	7.25	5.83
1899–1903	12.34	12.80	11.56	11.37	11.01	10.75	10.13	10.03	10.05	8.45
1904–1908	13.86	13.96	13.23	12.67	12.49	12.65	12.24	11.94	10.85	9.46
1909–1913	16.53	16.05	15.30	15.26	15.26	15.31	15.03	14.39	13.21	11.89
1914–1920	29.17	26.74	25.87	26.32	25.55	27.86	26.89	24.43	22.66	20.08
1921–1925	15.76	14.67	13.47	14.64	13.64	14.10	13.28	11.66	10.83	9.25
1920	31.65	27.52	26.38	27.25	26.02	31.08	29.23	24.93	24.97	22.28
1921	13.88	13.10	11.43	12.83	11.85	12.41	11.37	10.00	8.40	7.13
1922	17.83	16.57	15.29	16.51	15.59	16.10	15.16	13.47	11.96	10.15
1923	16.46	14.79	13.77	14.89	13.86	14.21	12.94	11.11	11.69	9.89
1924	14.67	13.82	12.80	13.80	12.79	12.95	12.29	10.41	10.14	8.79
1925	15.96	15.08	14.06	16.16	14.12	14.82	14.62	12.05	9.98	10.29
1926	14.08	13.38	12.67	13.34	12.82	12.71	13.11	17.26	9.98	8.50
1927	19.28	18.21	17.49	18.23	17.74	18.08	18.66	21.79	14.09	12.88
1928	23.85	22.91	22.26	22.95	22.26	22.96	22.63		17.64	16.62

Bureau of Agricultural Economics. Compiled from annual reports of the Chicago Board of Trade. Data 1893–1919 available in 1925 Yearbook, p. 1199, Table 610.

TABLE 435.—*Hides, country: Average price per pound at Chicago, averages 1894–1925; annual, 1920–1928*

Year	Ex-tremes	Heavy steers	Heavy cows	No. 1 buffs	No. 2 buffs	Bulls	Country packer brands	Country brands	No. 1 calf-skins	No. 1 kip-skins
Average:	Cents	Cents	Cents	Cents	Cents	Cents	Cents	Cents	Cents	Cents
1894–1898	8.06	8.11	7.56	7.54	7.05	6.43	7.15	6.84	10.55	8.94
1899–1903	9.28	10.46	9.35	9.05	8.20	8.33	9.31	8.65	12.12	10.06
1904–1908	11.21	11.80	11.05	10.97	9.95	9.29	10.67	9.91	14.56	11.88
1909–1913	13.67	13.64	13.11	13.06	12.07	10.99	12.20	11.36	17.21	14.42
1914–1920	23.35	23.07	21.05	21.03	19.88	18.14	21.48	17.82	38.79	29.23
1921–1925	11.96	11.40	9.90	10.06	8.89	7.98	10.48	8.24	19.39	16.61
1920	22.79	24.20	19.27	18.93	17.93	18.76	20.60	14.94	40.98	33.97
1921	8.95	9.35	7.32	7.10	5.77	5.43	7.43	5.33	18.57	15.58
1922	12.93	12.03	10.85	10.86	9.52	8.23	12.53	8.42	18.95	17.29
1923	11.65	11.39	10.43	10.45	9.26	8.93	10.12	8.70	17.18	15.42
1924	11.86	11.31	9.24	9.63	8.63	7.86	9.81	8.23	20.39	16.62
1925	14.41	12.94	11.64	12.26	11.25	9.46	12.52	10.54	21.88	18.12
1926	13.46	11.63	9.54	10.70	9.70	8.03	10.52	9.00	18.02	16.12
1927	18.60	16.02	14.85	16.26	15.26	11.49	15.54	13.89	20.47	19.96
1928	22.04	18.53	18.05	19.71	18.71	14.88	19.18	17.38	27.84	25.23

Bureau of Agricultural Economics. Compiled from annual reports of the Chicago Board of Trade. Data 1893–1919 available in 1925 Yearbook, p. 1199, Table 611.

TABLE 436.—*Horses and mules: Number and value on farms, United States, January 1, 1910–1929*

Jan. 1	Horses			Mules		
	Number	Value per head Jan. 1	Farm value Jan. 1	Number	Value per head Jan. 1	Farm value Jan. 1
	Thousands	Dollars	1,000 dollars	Thousands	Dollars	1,000 dollars
1910 (Apr. 15)	19,833	108.03	2,142,524	4,210	120.20	506,049
1911	20,277	111.46	2,259,981	4,323	125.92	544,359
1912	20,509	105.94	2,172,694	4,362	120.51	525,657
1913	20,567	110.77	2,278,222	4,386	124.31	545,245
1914	20,962	109.32	2,291,638	4,449	123.85	551,017
1915	21,195	103.33	2,190,102	4,479	112.36	503,271
1916	21,159	101.60	2,149,786	4,593	113.83	522,834
1917	21,210	102.89	2,182,307	4,723	118.15	558,006
1918	21,555	104.24	2,246,970	4,873	128.81	627,679
1919	21,482	98.45	2,114,897	4,954	135.83	672,922
1920	19,848	96.52	1,915,653	5,475	148.46	812,828
1921	19,134	84.57	1,618,120	5,586	117.52	656,455
1922	18,564	71.18	1,321,396	5,638	89.14	502,563
1923	17,943	70.65	1,267,624	5,702	87.17	497,044
1924	17,222	65.48	1,127,619	5,730	85.90	492,209
1925	16,470	64.29	1,058,912	5,725	82.73	473,646
1926	15,830	65.50	1,036,843	5,740	81.49	467,760
1927	15,133	64.14	970,703	5,652	74.57	421,467
1928	14,540	67.05	974,855	5,532	79.71	440,958
1929 [1]	14,029	69.95	981,331	5,447	82.20	447,727

Bureau of Agricultural Economics. Estimates of the crop-reporting board. Figures in italics are census returns.

[1] Preliminary.

TABLE 437.—*Horses and horse colts: Estimated number on farms and value per head, by States, January 1, 1925–1929*

State and division	Number Jan. 1					Value per head Jan. 1 [1]				
	1925	1926	1927	1928	1929 [2]	1925	1926	1927	1928	1929 [2]
	Thousands	Thousands	Thousands	Thousands	Thousands	Dollars	Dollars	Dollars	Dollars	Dollars
Maine	84	80	78	74	72	119.00	129.00	130.00	135.00	140.00
New Hampshire	32	30	28	26	24	105.00	100.00	105.00	120.00	121.00
Vermont	64	61	57	54	53	104.00	110.00	110.00	119.00	124.00
Massachusetts	45	41	39	37	35	124.00	119.00	119.00	135.00	130.00
Rhode Island	6	6	5	5	4	124.00	120.00	120.00	135.00	130.00
Connecticut	35	33	32	29	27	127.00	120.00	128.00	140.00	145.00
New York	440	418	401	389	382	108.00	111.00	109.00	116.00	124.00
New Jersey	57	54	54	52	50	109.00	107.00	109.00	109.00	114.00
Pennsylvania	410	390	374	359	349	96.00	103.00	99.00	112.00	116.00
North Atlantic	1,173	1,113	1,068	1,025	996	105.63	109.51	108.06	117.32	122.49
Ohio	630	598	568	542	520	85.00	91.00	95.00	101.00	105.00
Indiana	556	548	540	522	517	69.00	78.00	80.00	82.00	82.00
Illinois	1,030	978	929	874	839	69.00	74.00	74.00	74.00	77.00
Michigan	482	463	444	426	409	84.00	89.00	89.00	98.00	110.00
Wisconsin	604	591	579	567	544	88.00	93.00	95.00	98.00	102.00
Minnesota	835	827	819	803	787	77.00	81.00	77.00	79.00	82.00
Iowa	1,180	1,145	1,111	1,089	1,046	72.00	74.00	74.00	75.00	78.00
Missouri	708	670	636	604	574	48.00	49.00	48.00	50.00	53.00
North Dakota	731	708	673	633	589	56.00	56.00	53.00	53.00	52.00
South Dakota	720	684	643	611	593	48.00	49.00	47.00	53.00	57.00
Nebraska	862	840	815	788	764	58.00	61.00	56.00	59.00	60.00
Kansas	931	894	840	798	766	46.00	48.00	41.00	43.00	49.00
North Central	9,269	8,946	8,597	8,257	7,948	65.55	68.93	67.84	70.52	73.85
Delaware	23	22	21	20	19	74.00	79.00	69.00	79.00	88.00
Maryland	117	112	104	100	97	74.00	77.00	78.00	89.00	92.00
Virginia	261	238	224	206	198	71.00	66.00	66.00	70.00	78.00
West Virginia	147	140	133	128	124	76.00	75.00	74.00	84.00	89.00
North Carolina	130	120	112	105	98	99.00	86.00	83.00	87.00	86.00
South Carolina	55	49	45	42	40	97.00	89.00	76.00	81.00	82.00
Georgia	56	51	46	41	39	86.00	83.00	74.00	78.00	78.00
Florida	29	28	27	26	25	98.00	97.00	82.00	83.00	87.00
South Atlantic	818	760	712	668	640	80.60	76.66	73.51	80.27	84.46
Kentucky	314	305	293	284	278	50.00	50.00	47.00	53.00	56.00
Tennessee	243	231	219	210	202	61.00	53.00	54.00	60.00	60.00
Alabama	90	86	82	73	65	70.00	68.00	63.00	66.00	66.00
Mississippi	135	125	118	106	100	63.00	60.00	56.00	61.00	58.00
Arkansas	188	169	157	146	136	42.00	42.00	40.00	43.00	41.00
Louisiana	132	126	113	107	102	62.00	55.00	49.00	52.00	53.00
Oklahoma	614	589	565	537	516	41.00	37.00	35.00	38.00	39.00
Texas	857	848	788	780	780	54.00	48.00	44.00	45.00	46.00
South Central	2,573	2,479	2,335	2,243	2,179	51.54	47.57	44.41	47.42	48.20
Montana	596	576	547	531	515	32.00	29.00	30.00	31.00	31.00
Idaho	233	226	221	214	210	45.00	52.00	52.00	51.00	54.00
Wyoming	200	198	194	190	186	29.00	29.00	31.00	31.00	32.00
Colorado	367	352	331	324	308	43.00	47.00	44.00	43.00	47.00
New Mexico	188	175	170	168	163	38.00	37.00	33.00	31.00	36.00
Arizona	112	106	101	98	90	59.00	50.00	50.00	49.00	51.00
Utah	110	106	104	102	100	61.00	61.00	61.00	61.00	63.00
Nevada	50	47	44	42	41	56.00	53.00	53.00	59.00	58.00
Washington	242	230	218	209	205	63.00	62.00	62.00	65.00	67.00
Oregon	225	214	201	191	181	67.00	65.00	62.00	65.00	65.00
California	314	302	290	278	267	78.00	76.00	76.00	74.00	78.00
Far Western	2,637	2,532	2,421	2,347	2,266	48.90	48.24	47.94	47.86	49.99
United States	16,470	15,830	15,133	14,540	14,029	64.29	65.50	64.14	67.05	69.95

Bureau of Agricultural Economics. Estimates of the crop-reporting board.

[1] Sum of total value of subgroups (classified by age), divided by total number and rounded to nearest dollar for States. Division and United States averages not rounded.
[2] Preliminary.

TABLE 438.—*Mules and mule colts: Estimated number on farms and value per head, by States, January 1, 1925-1929*

State and division	Number, Jan. 1					Value per head, Jan. 1[1]				
	1925	1926	1927	1928	1929[2]	1925	1926	1927	1928	1929[2]
	Thousands	Thousands	Thousands	Thousands	Thousands	Dollars	Dollars	Dollars	Dollars	Dollars
New York	7	7	7	7	6	115	112.00	120.00	125.00	120.00
New Jersey	5	5	5	5	5	125.00	114.00	118.00	118.00	123.00
Pennsylvania	53	53	52	51	51	105.00	113.00	110.00	121.00	127.00
North Atlantic	65	65	64	63	62	107.74	113.08	111.77	120.98	125.71
Ohio	33	32	33	33	32	93.00	96.00	94.00	103.00	101.00
Indiana	101	99	101	101	101	76.00	86.00	86.00	86.00	87.00
Illinois	168	165	160	150	144	80.00	85.00	85.00	82.00	86.00
Michigan	7	7	8	8	7	83.00	86.00	86.00	93.00	102.00
Wisconsin	7	7	7	7	7	85.00	87.00	86.00	95.00	95.00
Minnesota	13	13	14	14	14	80.00	79.00	81.00	83.00	83.00
Iowa	97	98	100	98	93	83.00	85.00	83.00	84.00	86.00
Missouri	372	365	347	330	313	67.00	71.00	66.00	68.00	75.00
North Dakota	9	9	10	10	10	62.00	59.00	55.00	57.00	55.00
South Dakota	21	22	22	22	22	61.00	64.00	57.00	63.00	65.00
Nebraska	120	120	118	110	106	74.00	78.00	69.00	74.00	76.00
Kansas	260	252	237	213	198	63.00	66.00	57.00	60.00	65.00
North Central	1,208	1,189	1,157	1,096	1,047	71.50	75.75	71.37	73.52	77.52
Delaware	9	9	9	9	9	90.00	100.00	91.00	95.00	96.00
Maryland	31	31	30	29	28	94.00	104.00	101.00	113.00	111.00
Virginia	104	104	103	105	105	91.00	87.00	86.00	92.00	97.00
West Virginia	15	15	14	14	14	86.00	85.00	78.00	81.00	86.00
North Carolina	279	276	279	279	276	119.00	117.00	107.00	119.00	124.00
South Carolina	199	193	185	179	177	122.00	120.00	95.00	105.00	105.00
Georgia	338	347	347	347	347	115.00	112.00	95.00	105.00	109.00
Florida	43	43	43	43	42	139.00	134.00	117.00	119.00	124.00
South Atlantic	1,018	1,018	1,010	1,005	998	114.63	112.46	98.28	107.95	111.42
Kentucky	301	304	301	295	292	63.00	63.00	58.00	67.00	69.00
Tennessee	352	356	352	341	321	74.00	72.00	69.00	75.00	80.00
Alabama	309	312	315	321	327	90.00	95.00	84.00	95.00	95.00
Mississippi	330	336	343	336	336	89.00	86.00	79.00	87.00	85.00
Arkansas	339	346	329	332	339	64.00	63.00	59.00	64.00	65.00
Louisiana	174	176	169	167	167	90.00	90.00	79.00	85.00	89.00
Oklahoma	369	369	365	347	333	61.00	57.00	51.00	52.00	58.00
Texas	1,042	1,052	1,031	1,021	1,021	83.00	75.00	69.00	71.00	71.00
South Central	3,216	3,251	3,205	3,160	3,136	77.19	74.05	68.06	72.94	74.49
Montana	11	11	11	11	11	47.00	50.00	45.00	47.00	47.00
Idaho	8	8	8	7	7	52.00	61.00	60.00	55.00	60.00
Wyoming	6	6	6	5	7	49.00	49.00	49.00	52.00	55.00
Colorado	39	38	36	33	32	57.00	59.00	55.00	56.00	58.00
New Mexico	33	34	34	31	30	58.00	54.00	45.00	45.00	50.00
Arizona	12	12	12	12	12	85.00	87.00	77.00	77.00	82.00
Utah	4	4	4	4	4	62.00	64.00	62.00	61.00	67.00
Nevada	4	4	4	4	4	62.00	64.00	60.00	61.00	62.00
Washington	27	27	28	29	29	68.00	67.00	72.00	73.00	74.00
Oregon	18	19	20	20	19	72.00	73.00	70.00	72.00	71.00
California	56	54	53	52	51	95.00	92.00	89.00	85.00	87.00
Far Western	218	217	216	208	204	70.29	69.67	66.36	66.34	68.43
United States	5,725	5,740	5,652	5,532	5,447	82.73	81.49	74.57	79.71	82.20

Bureau of Agricultural Economics. Estimates of crop-reporting board.

[1] Sum of total value of subgroups (classified by age) divided by total number and rounded to nearest dollar for States. Division and United States averages not rounded.
[2] Preliminary.

TABLE 439.—*Horses and mules: Farm value per head, by age groups, United States, January 1, 1910–1929*

Jan. 1—	Horses			Mules		
	Under 1 year old	1 and under 2 years	2 years and over	Under 1 year old	1 and under 2 years	2 years and over
	Dollars	Dollars	Dollars	Dollras	Dollars	Dollars
1910	46. 05	72. 63	116. 57	56. 76	84. 53	128. 96
1911	48. 09	75. 68	120. 04	59. 89	88. 13	135. 11
1912	45. 75	71. 96	114. 24	56. 12	83. 00	129. 46
1913	43. 75	76. 54	121. 06	59. 31	86. 56	134. 05
1914	47. 95	74. 87	119. 77	57. 45	83. 87	133. 76
1915	45. 36	70. 62	113. 10	51. 80	76. 46	121. 46
1916	44. 30	69. 08	111. 34	51. 59	76. 82	123. 55
1917	45. 17	70. 21	112. 64	53. 98	80. 28	128. 17
1918	45. 20	70. 21	114. 30	57. 61	86. 32	139. 88
1919	42. 62	65. 94	108. 17	59. 14	89. 14	147. 65
1920	37. 22	58. 81	103. 52	60. 16	90. 14	160. 55
1921	31. 59	49. 66	90. 35	47. 55	71. 77	125. 85
1922	26. 50	41. 07	75. 61	35. 55	52. 82	94. 81
1923	26. 51	40. 48	74. 53	34. 35	50. 94	92. 14
1924	24. 68	37. 36	68. 64	31. 83	47. 06	90. 42
1925	23. 80	37. 09	66. 83	30. 65	46. 63	86. 20
1926	24. 82	37. 75	68. 18	31. 30	47. 88	84. 76
1927	23. 75	37. 37	66. 75	29. 41	43. 91	77. 36
1928	24. 96	39. 21	69. 81	31. 19	46. 55	82. 56
1929	26. 34	41. 11	72. 84	32. 72	48. 63	84. 89

Bureau of Agricultural Economics. Based on returns from special price reporters.

TABLE 440.—*Horses: Price per head received by producers, United States, 1910–1928*

Year	Jan. 15	Feb. 15	Mar. 15	Apr. 15	May 15	June 15	July 15	Aug. 15	Sept. 15	Oct. 15	Nov. 15	Dec. 15	Weight ed av.
	Dolls.	Dolls.	Dolls.	Dolls.	Dolls.	Dolls.	Dolls.	Dolls.	Dolls.	Dolls.	Dolls.	Dolls.	Dolls.
Average:													
1910–1913	139	144	145	148	146	147	143	143	142	140	138	137	142
1914–1920	127	130	132	133	134	133	132	130	127	125	122	121	128
1921–1925	81	84	86	86	87	86	85	83	82	80	78	76	82
1910	140	147	150	154	148	151	148	148	145	144	143	141	146
1911	143	144	145	147	146	145	139	141	139	137	136	134	141
1912	134	137	140	142	144	145	142	142	141	140	139	139	140
1913	140	146	146	148	145	146	143	141	141	138	136	135	142
1914	137	139	138	138	139	136	137	135	132	131	130	130	135
1915	130	132	132	132	133	132	134	131	131	129	127	126	130
1916	128	129	131	133	134	132	133	131	131	130	129	129	130
1917	129	131	133	136	138	137	135	132	132	130	129	129	132
1918	130	133	137	137	136	135	132	131	128	126	122	121	130
1919	120	121	124	127	129	127	127	125	119	114	113	113	121
1920	118	123	127	131	132	130	127	124	119	112	103	97	119
1921	96	98	101	100	98	98	94	93	89	85	82	81	92
1922	82	84	86	87	89	88	88	86	84	81	79	79	84
1923	81	85	85	86	88	87	85	83	82	80	78	75	82
1924	73	74	75	76	78	77	77	79	78	77	76	73	76
1925	73	78	81	83	82	81	81	80	77	76	75	74	78
1926	75	80	82	84	84	83	82	80	78	77	75	73	79
1927	73	77	79	80	81	80	80	80	78	76	75	75	77
1928	77	82	85	85	86	86	85	84	82	80	79	78	. 82

Bureau of Agricultural Economics. Based on returns from special price reporters.

TABLE 441.—*Horses and mules: Receipts at public stockyards, 1916–1928*

Market	1916	1917	1918	1919	1920	1921	1922	1923	1924	1925	1926	1927	1928
	Thousands	*Thousands*	*Thousands*	*Thousands*	*Thousands*	*Thousands*	*Thousands*	*Thousands*	*Thousands*	*Thousands*	*Thousands*	*Thousands*	*Thousands*
Amarillo, Tex	14	13	15	15	13	2	3	6	7	12	8	9	8
Atlanta, Ga	------	------	78	60	26	3	8	34	35	41	24	33	32
Augusta, Ga	------	23	33	22	7	1	(1)	(1)	(1)	(1)	(1)	------	------
Baltimore, Md	14	7	9	5	4	2	2	3	1	2	1	1	1
Buffalo, N. Y	56	17	10	19	23	24	21	18	12	11	12	11	17
Chicago, Ill	205	107	88	46	43	34	32	26	21	18	18	16	19
Cincinnati, Ohio	20	27	19	19	14	6	4	4	3	3	2	2	1
Cleveland, Ohio	------	9	4	5	6	2	2	1	(1)	(1)	(1)	(1)	(1)
Denver, Colo	53	20	15	23	18	10	13	23	37	44	29	27	24
Detroit, Mich	------	14	4	2	3	1	1	2	3	1	(1)	1	1
East St. Louis, Ill	267	280	242	250	141	68	95	102	64	65	53	69	70
El Paso, Tex	23	15	9	16	14	10	6	7	6	19	15	6	14
Fort Worth, Tex	79	115	79	60	45	13	29	58	46	34	27	43	43
Indianapolis, Ind	29	62	20	9	9	3	2	1	1	1	1	2	2
Jersey City, N. J	155	70	42	11	3	2	1	1	2	2	2	4	2
Kansas City, Mo	123	128	85	83	72	30	38	43	36	34	29	44	43
Knoxville, Tenn	7	8	6	7	4	2	4	9	6	6	2	3	2
Lancaster, Pa	1	8	11	2	3	1	2	3	1	1	1	(1)	1
Louisville, Ky	5	14	17	11	9	2	3	2	1	1	1	1	1
Memphis, Tenn	40	61	33	33	8	15	46	60	47	43	38	52	29
Montgomery, Ala	------	7	24	22	12	4	14	5	9	12	7	8	7
Nashville, Tenn	16	74	104	97	30	(1)	------	------	(1)	(1)	(1)	------	------
Ogden, Utah	------	25	19	6	6	1	1	2	2	2	2	3	3
Oklahoma City, Okla	47	62	13	10	6	2	5	8	10	9	5	7	7
Omaha, Nebr	27	33	22	25	19	7	9	17	12	15	17	16	18
Philadelphia, Pa	11	10	8	7	6	3	3	3	2	2	2	2	1
Pittsburgh, Pa	54	39	35	18	20	11	14	12	8	9	9	11	14
Pueblo, Colo	8	7	4	4	4	1	1	1	3	3	2	3	2
Richmond, Va	18	25	24	25	16	10	13	16	9	(1)	------	(1)	(1)
St. Joseph, Mo	27	34	39	43	30	12	16	15	11	9	9	8	9
San Antonio, Tex	41	32	30	30	25	6	9	11	14	8	7	3	4
Sioux City, Iowa	17	29	23	16	23	7	8	15	14	18	19	13	13
South St. Paul, Minn	12	10	7	11	10	5	2	3	4	5	10	11	11
Spokane, Wash	6	7	5	3	3	1	1	1	1	1	1	1	2
Wichita, Kans	17	19	11	17	25	11	18	23	21	19	17	24	23
All others	86	65	29	36	25	5	17	16	19	18	21	15	26
Total	1,478	1,476	1,216	1,068	725	317	443	551	468	468	391	449	450

[1] Less than 500.

TABLE 442.—*Beeswax: Monthly average price per pound of domestic beeswax at Chicago, 1920–1928*

	Jan.	Feb.	Mar.	Apr.	May	June	July	Aug.	Sept.	Oct.	Nov.	Dec.
Chicago:[1]												
Light—	*Cents*	*Cents*	*Cents*	*Cents*	*Cents*	*Cents*	*Cents*	*Cents*	*Cents*	*Cents*	*Cents*	*Cents*
1920	44	41½	42¾	43¾	45¾	44	43¼	41	40	40¼	37	34¾
1921	31½	31¼	30½	31	32¼	31½	31¾	29	29	30¼	30¼	31
1922	31	31	29¾	28¾	33	31¼	31½	30¾	31	31½	31½	30½
1923	30¾	31½	32	32½	32	32	31	29	30	30	29	29½
1924	29¼	28½	29	31¼	28¾	27½	27	27	29	32½	32¼	33¼
1925	35	35	38	41¾	38	35	33½	33½	34	37¾	38	38
1926	------	40	------	------	------	------	39½	38½	38½	39½	39	39
1927	39	39	40	40	40	40½	41	41	41	43	41½	41½
1928	41½	41	40½	40½	41½	41½	------	41	41	41	41½	42½
Dark—												
1920	38½	36¼	39	40¾	42	40½	39½	37	35½	36½	34½	32¼
1921	29¼	28½	27¾	25¾	25¼	27¾	26¼	25¾	26½	27	27¼	27½
1922	28½	28	24½	25½	29	28	29	28	27¼	28	27¾	27¾
1923	28	28½	28½	28¾	29	29¼	28½	25½	25¼	26	26	24
1924	26	26¼	26	27	25¼	25½	25½	24½	26	29	28	27½
1925	31	31	33¾	36¾	34	29½	29½	29¾	29½	34½	34	34
1926	------	------	------	------	------	------	33	33	------	------	------	------
1927	------	------	34½	34½	34½	35	35	35	35	37	38	38
1928	38	38	38	------	------	37	------	36½	------	------	------	------

Bureau of Agricultural Economics.

[1] Sales by original receivers to wholesalers, polish and laundry-supply manufacturers, etc.

TABLE 443.—*Honey: Monthly average prices in producing sections and at consuming markets, 1920–1928*

EXTRACTED HONEY, PER POUND

	Jan.	Feb.	Mar.	Apr.	May	June	July	Aug.	Sept.	Oct.	Nov.	Dec.
CALIFORNIA WHITE ORANGE												
F. o. b. Southern California shipping points: [1]	*Cents*	*Cents*	*Cents*	*Cents*	*Cents*	*Cents*	*Cents*	*Cents*	*Cents*	*Cents*	*Cents*	*Cents*
1920	18¼	18¼	17¾	17¼	21	19¾	19½	19¼	18½	18¼	17¾	16¾
1921	16¼	13¾	13	12	11¼	11¼	9¼	10½	11	11¾	12¼	11½
1922	11½	11½	11	------	8½	9	9½	9½	9½	10¼	10¾	10¾
1923	10¾	10½	10¼	10¼	11¾	------	12	------	------	------	------	13¼
1924	13	------	14	14½	11¾	13¼	12	12½	13	13¼	14½	14¼
1925	14¼	------	15	------	13½	13	11¾	11¾	------	14½	15½	------
1926	12¼	11¾	11½	10½	9½	8¾	8¾	------	------	8½	------	------
1927	------	7¾	9	8¾	8	8¼	8¾	9	9¼	9½	9½	10
1928	10	10	10	9½	8¾	8¾	9	9¼	9¼	9½	9¾	9¾
New York City: [2]												
1920	20¾	18¾	17½	19¼	20	21¾	18	17¼	18¾	17	17	16¼
1921	17½	14¾	12¼	11	11½	12	11½	11	12¼	12½	12¾	12¾
1922	13½	13	13¼	12½	13	12	11¾	11¾	11¾	12	12½	12¾
1923	12¾	12¾	12¾	12¾	13	13½	13¾	13¾	14½	14	15	16
1924	15½	16	15	15½	15½	13½	14½	14	------	13¾	13½	------
1925	------	------	------	------	------	14¼	------	14½	14¼	13½	14	14½
1926	15¼	15	14½	------	------	------	11¼	11	11½	11¾	11¾	12½
1927	12½	12½	11	------	11	11¼	11½	12¾	13	12¾	13	13
1928	------	------	------	------	12½	12½	12½	12½	12¾	13	12¾	12½
INTERMOUNTAIN WHITE SWEET CLOVER AND ALFALFA												
F. o. b. intermountain points: [3]												
1921	------	------	------	8¼	7¾	7½	7¼	7¾	7¾	7¾	8	8½
1922	8½	8½	8½	8½	8½	8¾	9¼	------	8	8	8	8
1923	7¾	8	7¼	7½	7½	7¾	8½	8¾	8	9	9	9
1924	9	9¼	9¼	9¼	9¼	9	8¾	9	9	9	9	9¼
1925	9½	9¼	9¼	9¼	9	------	8½	8½	8½	8½	8½	8½
1926	8	8¼	8	7¾	7½	7½	7½	7	6¾	6¾	6¾	6¾
1927	6¾	6½	6	5¾	5¾	6	6	6¾	7	7½	7¾	7¼
1928	7¼	7½	7¼	7¼	7¼	7	7¼	7	7¼	7¼	7	7
WHITE CLOVER												
F. o. b. New York and North Central States: [4]												
1921	------	------	------	------	------	------	------	------	9¾	9¾	9¾	10¾
1922	10½	10	10¾	10¾	10½	11¼	11½	11	11	11	10¾	11
1923	11	10¾	10	10	10½	11	11	11¾	11¼	10¾	10¾	10¾
1924	10¾	10¾	10¾	11	11	10¾	10½	11	10¾	10¾	11¼	11
1925	11¼	11¼	11¼	11¼	11½	11½	11½	10¾	11	11	10¾	10½
1926	9¾	10	9¼	9¾	9	9½	10¼	10	9½	9½	10	9½
1927	10¼	10	9½	9½	9¼	8¾	8½	9	8½	8½	8¾	8½
1928	8½	8¼	8	8	8	8½	9¼	9	8¾	8½	9	8½
NORTHEASTERN BUCKWHEAT												
F. o. b. New York and Pennsylvania points: [4]												
1921	------	------	------	------	------	------	------	------	9	8¼	7½	8
1922	7	8	7½	7½	------	8	8½	6½	7¾	8	8	8
1923	7¾	8	8½	------	------	8	------	9	9	9¼	9	9
1924	9	9	8½	8¾	8½	8½	8¼	------	9	9¼	9	9
1925	8¾	9	10	9	------	------	------	9¼	9	8½	8½	8¾
1926	8	7¾	7½	7	6½	6½	6	6½	7	7	7	8
1927	8¼	7	7¼	------	8½	------	------	8	7½	7¼	7¼	7½
1928	7¼	7¼	7¼	6¾	------	------	------	8	7¾	7½	7½	7¼

COMB HONEY, 24-SECTION CASES

	Jan.	Feb.	Mar.	Apr.	May	June	July	Aug.	Sept.	Oct.	Nov.	Dec.
WHITE CLOVER COMB, NO. 1 AND FANCY												
F. o. b. New York and North Central States: [4]	*Dolls.*	*Dolls.*	*Dolls.*	*Dolls.*	*Dolls.*	*Dolls.*	*Dolls.*	*Dolls.*	*Dolls.*	*Dolls.*	*Dolls.*	*Dolls.*
1921	------	------	------	------	------	------	------	------	5.10	5.00	5.10	4.65
1922	5.00	5.10	5.00	4.50	------	------	4.45	5.00	4.55	4.90	4.70	4.70
1923	4.75	4.75	------	------	4.00	------	5.00	5.00	5.25	5.10	4.75	5.15
1924	4.75	4.75	5.05	4.80	5.50	------	4.80	4.85	4.95	4.80	5.10	4.95
1925	4.95	4.95	4.75	4.90	5.25	4.50	5.10	5.20	5.00	5.00	4.65	4.45
1926	4.25	4.25	4.25	4.00	4.00	4.00	4.25	4.75	4.50	4.25	4.25	4.25
1927	4.50	5.25	5.25	5.25	------	5.00	5.00	4.75	4.25	4.75	4.50	4.80
1928	4.80	4.80	4.50	4.80	4.50	4.25	4.50	4.50	4.50	4.50	4.80	4.50

Bureau of Agricultural Economics.

[1] Price to beekeepers or other shippers in car lots to July, 1923; thereafter, price in large lots, mostly less than car lots.
[2] Sales by original receivers to bottlers, confectioners, bakers, and jobbers.
[3] Price to beekeepers and other shippers, in car lots.
[4] Price to beekeepers in large lots, mostly less than car lots.

DAIRY AND POULTRY

TABLE 444.—*Milk cows or dairy cattle: Numbers and value per head in the United States, 1850, 1860, 1867–1929*

Year	Milk cows On farms	Value per head, Jan. 1—old series [1]	Dairy cattle on farms and elsewhere	Year	Milk cows On farms	Value per head, Jan. 1 Old series [1]	Value per head, Jan. 1 New series [1]	Dairy cattle on farms and elsewhere
	Thousands	*Dollars*	*Thousands*		*Thousands*	*Dollars*	*Dollars*	*Thousands*
1850, June 1 [2]	6,385		10,100	1898	15,841	27.45		26,400
1860, June 1 [2]	8,586		13,500	1899	15,990	29.66		26,800
1867	8,349	28.74	12,000	1900, June 1 [2]	17,136			
1868	8,692	26.56	12,400	1900	16,292	31.60	30.18	27,400
1869	9,248	29.15	13,000	1901	16,834	30.00	28.65	26,800
1870, June 1 [2]	8,935			1902	16,697	29.23	27.91	26,100
1870	10,096	32.70	14,000	1903	17,111	30.21	28.85	26,300
1871	10,023	33.89	14,100	1904	17,420	29.21	27.90	26,400
1872	10,304	29.45	14,700	1905	17,572	27.44	26.21	26,200
1873	10,576	26.72	15,400	1906	19,794	29.44	28.12	29,100
1874	10,705	25.63	15,800	1907	20,968	31.00	29.60	30,300
1875	10,907	25.74	16,300	1908	21,194	30.67	29.29	30,100
1876	11,085	25.61	16,900	1909	21,720	32.36	30.90	30,400
1877	11,261	25.47	17,400	1910, Apr. 15 [2]	20,625			
1878	11,300	25.74	17,700	1910	20,625	35.29	33.70	30,000
1879	11,826	21.71	18,900	1911	20,823	39.97	38.17	30,200
1880, June 1 [2]	12,443			1912	20,699	39.39	37.62	29,900
1880	12,027	23.27	19,500	1913	20,497	45.02	42.99	29,400
1881	12,369	23.95	20,100	1914	20,737	53.94	51.51	29,600
1882	12,612	25.89	20,500	1915	21,262	55.33	52.84	30,300
1883	13,126	30.21	21,300	1916	22,108	53.92	51.49	31,300
1884	13,501	31.37	21,900	1917	22,894	59.63	56.95	32,300
1885	13,905	29.70	22,600	1918	23,310	70.54	67.37	32,700
1886	14,235	27.40	23,100	1919	23,475	78.20	74.68	32,800
1887	14,522	26.08	23,600	1920, Jan. 1 [2]	19,675			
1888	14,856	24.65	24,100	1920	[3]21,427	85.56	81.51	32,986
1889	15,299	23.94	24,900	1921	21,408	64.13	61.19	32,626
1890, June 1 [2]	16,512			1922	21,788	50.97	48.68	32,943
1890	15,953	22.14	25,900	1923	22,063	50.94	48.67	33,452
1891	16,020	21.62	26,100	1924	22,255	52.30	49.94	33,684
1892	16,416	21.40	26,900	1925, Jan. 1 [2]	20,900			
1893	16,424	21.75	27,000	1925	22,481	50.66	48.39	34,047
1894	16,487	21.77	27,100	1926	22,188	57.34	55.02	33,257
1895	16,505	21.97	27,300	1927	21,801	62.43	59.58	33,013
1896	16,138	22.55	26,800	1928	21,824	77.43	73.93	33,508
1897	15,942	23.16	26,500	1929	[4]21,820		84.59	33,685

Bureau of Agricultural Economics. Data for milk cows on farms and value per head, except as otherwise stated from reports of the Bureau of Agricultural Economics as of Jan. 1. The tentative revisions on "all cattle on farms" for 1900–1919, as shown in Table 348 have not been made on "milk cows on farms." The figures for these years are made currently.

[1] For 1926–1929, new series relates to "milk cows and heifers, 2 years old and over"; 1900–1925 is old series adjusted on basis average relationship between two series, 1926–1928. Old series related to "milk cows."

[2] Figures for census years 1850–1890 represent "milch cows"; 1900, "cows kept for milk 2 years and over"; 1910, "cows and heifers kept for milk, born before Jan. 1, 1909" (15½ months and over); 1920, "dairy cattle 2 years old and over kept mainly for milk production." For comparison with 1920 the number of dairy cows and heifers 2 years old and over on Jan. 1, 1910, has been estimated by the census as 17,125,471; 1925, number of cows milked.

[3] Beginning with 1920, heifers 1 to 2 years old being kept for milk cows were estimated as follows: 1920–1929, respectively, 4,418,000, 4,155,000, 3,968,000, 4,147,000, 4,137,000, 4,195,000, 3,923,000, 4,059,000, 4,201,000, 4,377,000.

[4] Preliminary.

TABLE 445.—*Milk cows and heifers: Estimated number on farms and value per head, by States, January 1, 1925–1929*

State and division	Cows and heifers 2 years old and over kept for milk									
	Jan. 1					Value per head Jan. 1 [1]				
	1925	1926	1927	1928	1929 [2]	1925	1926	1927	1928	1929 [2]
	Thousands	Thousands	Thousands	Thousands	Thousands	Dollars	Dollars	Dollars	Dollars	Dollars
Maine	156	150	146	139	139	50.00	64.00	66.00	76.00	87.00
New Hampshire	85	80	77	75	75	56.00	72.00	80.00	100.00	113.00
Vermont	287	288	286	286	286	54.00	66.00	75.00	97.00	100.00
Massachusetts	148	140	136	135	134	74.00	86.00	98.00	125.00	130.00
Rhode Island	22	22	21	20	21	80.00	86.00	105.00	132.00	142.00
Connecticut	118	116	110	108	109	75.00	87.00	97.00	130.00	140.00
New York	1,383	1,362	1,318	1,330	1,330	61.00	79.00	90.00	111.00	124.00
New Jersey	123	123	119	122	122	72.00	92.00	103.00	120.00	135.00
Pennsylvania	889	862	845	855	855	58.00	71.00	75.00	97.00	111.00
North Atlantic	3,211	3,143	3,058	3,070	3,071	60.54	75.89	84.27	105.72	117.59
Ohio	964	945	926	917	908	54.00	62.00	67.00	83.00	93.00
Indiana	679	672	679	679	693	55.00	58.00	63.00	75.00	85.00
Illinois	1,049	1,039	988	968	949	57.00	63.00	67.00	76.00	89.00
Michigan	850	858	841	841	841	58.00	64.00	70.00	87.00	99.00
Wisconsin	2,015	2,055	2,014	1,984	1,935	53.00	65.00	70.00	86.00	97.00
Minnesota	1,560	1,560	1,513	1,498	1,483	49.00	57.00	57.00	72.00	85.00
Iowa	1,341	1,341	1,314	1,314	1,314	56.00	61.00	64.00	76.00	86.00
Missouri	835	827	827	827	810	42.00	44.00	48.00	61.00	74.00
North Dakota	520	530	472	463	454	42.00	45.00	48.00	61.00	75.00
South Dakota	544	539	513	518	523	45.00	49.00	52.00	68.00	77.00
Nebraska	625	625	613	613	613	50.00	54.00	55.00	71.00	84.00
Kansas	760	730	715	701	701	46.00	50.00	51.00	62.00	75.00
North Central	11,742	11,721	11,415	11,323	11,224	51.48	57.94	61.36	75.33	86.97
Delaware	34	35	35	36	37	57.00	61.00	70.00	92.00	110.00
Maryland	184	182	178	185	187	57.00	65.00	65.00	85.00	97.00
Virginia	393	380	357	364	382	39.00	40.00	44.00	58.00	70.00
West Virginia	225	221	207	215	219	38.00	41.00	45.00	65.00	75.00
North Carolina	312	303	297	294	294	37.00	39.00	45.00	59.00	64.00
South Carolina	176	155	150	144	145	34.00	33.00	39.00	47.00	55.00
Georgia	354	340	343	343	343	27.00	29.00	32.00	42.00	49.00
Florida	70	74	78	78	74	46.00	42.00	38.00	37.00	46.00
South Atlantic	1,748	1,690	1,645	1,659	1,681	38.11	40.31	43.89	57.58	66.85
Kentucky	473	464	469	493	493	35.00	38.00	45.00	60.00	65.00
Tennessee	462	434	425	438	447	29.00	32.00	38.00	53.00	60.00
Alabama	365	340	350	350	354	24.00	26.00	30.00	40.00	46.00
Mississippi	411	379	379	390	390	22.00	27.00	28.00	40.00	45.00
Arkansas	382	374	375	375	382	23.00	25.00	30.00	42.00	48.00
Louisiana	206	200	210	204	208	34.00	31.00	33.00	36.00	49.00
Oklahoma	582	570	581	610	610	32.00	37.00	45.00	56.00	64.00
Texas	985	936	936	936	955	30.00	30.00	41.00	57.00	61.00
South Central	3,866	3,697	3,725	3,796	3,839	28.90	31.19	37.87	50.84	56.92
Montana	187	190	181	177	177	46.00	50.00	51.00	63.00	79.00
Idaho	160	165	168	170	172	49.00	60.00	67.00	75.00	86.00
Wyoming	66	69	70	72	72	47.00	54.00	57.00	70.00	86.00
Colorado	224	224	240	242	244	44.00	49.00	56.00	69.00	77.00
New Mexico	64	64	64	65	65	42.00	42.00	45.00	57.00	67.00
Arizona	37	32	35	35	36	68.00	70.00	75.00	85.00	95.00
Utah	87	88	89	92	97	53.00	63.00	59.00	73.00	87.00
Nevada	19	20	20	20	20	58.00	72.00	75.00	85.00	98.00
Washington	283	275	275	275	280	62.00	63.00	70.00	80.00	99.00
Oregon	225	214	214	214	216	58.00	60.00	61.00	72.00	88.00
California	579	596	602	614	626	70.00	73.00	75.00	80.00	94.00
Far Western	1,931	1,937	1,958	1,976	2,005	57.71	61.79	65.18	74.53	88.53
United States	22,498	22,188	21,801	21,824	21,820	48.39	55.02	59.58	73.93	84.59

Bureau of Agricultural Economics. Estimates of crop reporting board.

[1] Total value divided by total number and rounded to nearest dollar for States. Division and United States averages not rounded. State figures are new weighted value series not comparable to State figures previously published.

[2] Preliminary.

TABLE 446.—*Heifers and heifer calves: Estimated number on farms, January 1, 1927, 1928, and 1929*

State	Heifers 1 to 2 years old being kept for milk cows			Heifer calves under 1 year being kept for milk cows		
	1927	1928	1929[1]	1927	1928	1929[1]
	Thousands	*Thousands*	*Thousands*	*Thousands*	*Thousands*	*Thousands*
Maine	33	32	34	34	33	35
New Hampshire	14	14	15	14	15	17
Vermont	47	49	55	49	55	59
Massachusetts	17	17	18	17	18	20
Rhode Island	2	3	3	3	3	3
Connecticut	13	13	13	13	13	14
New York	178	197	222	207	232	237
New Jersey	15	16	17	15	15	16
Pennsylvania	124	136	149	138	152	175
North Atlantic	443	477	526	490	536	576
Ohio	160	165	188	170	193	212
Indiana	112	125	135	137	150	159
Illinois	184	175	180	200	207	213
Michigan	153	159	165	180	182	184
Wisconsin	345	360	364	405	399	387
Minnesota	312	324	337	340	354	376
Iowa	245	250	250	240	240	240
Missouri	177	172	169	180	180	180
North Dakota	98	97	105	100	98	100
South Dakota	112	112	123	140	130	130
Nebraska	124	124	126	120	120	120
Kansas	120	125	131	125	130	137
North Central	2,142	2,188	2,273	2,337	2,383	2,438
Delaware	5	5	5	4	4	4
Maryland	25	26	27	25	27	29
Virginia	48	51	56	52	55	61
West Virginia	27	30	35	28	36	39
North Carolina	47	50	52	52	55	57
South Carolina	29	28	28	31	31	31
Georgia	77	77	77	90	90	84
Florida	18	19	17	18	19	18
South Atlantic	276	286	297	300	317	323
Kentucky	61	65	69	75	80	85
Tennessee	103	127	134	108	122	130
Alabama	87	88	90	87	90	92
Mississippi	82	90	95	91	99	99
Arkansas	90	92	92	105	103	101
Louisiana	41	41	42	32	34	35
Oklahoma	112	116	116	180	200	200
Texas	194	184	184	220	210	220
South Central	770	803	822	898	938	962
Montana	36	35	37	38	38	41
Idaho	40	43	44	44	48	48
Wyoming	14	15	15	19	20	20
Colorado	48	50	51	64	61	63
New Mexico	14	14	14	18	14	14
Arizona	10	9	9	13	13	12
Utah	21	23	25	24	26	28
Nevada	6	6	6	6	6	6
Washington	53	58	60	65	67	68
Oregon	44	45	46	45	47	48
California	142	149	152	130	137	134
Far Western	428	447	459	466	477	482
United States	4,059	4,201	4,377	4,491	4,651	4,781

Bureau of Agricultural Economics.

[1] Preliminary.

TABLE 447.—*Purebred dairy cattle: Number registered, by breeds, United States, 1900–1928*

Year	Ayrshire			Guernsey			Holstein-Friesian			Jersey		
	Bulls	Cows	Total	Bulls	Cows	Total	Bulls	Cows	Total	Bulls	Cows	Total
1900	--------	--------	--------	608	896	1,504	1,365	3,381	4,746	2,798	8,750	11,548
1901	--------	--------	--------	647	1,172	1,819	1,460	3,648	5,108	2,567	8,045	10,612
1902	--------	--------	--------	726	1,267	1,993	1,738	4,252	5,990	2,471	7,580	10,051
1903	--------	--------	--------	746	1,289	2,035	2,088	4,753	6,841	2,370	7,240	9,610
1904	--------	--------	--------	737	1,261	1,998	2,477	5,567	8,044	2,373	7,464	9,837
1905	--------	--------	--------	847	1,612	2,459	3,226	6,547	9,773	2,640	7,735	10,375
1906	--------	--------	--------	950	1,964	2,914	3,842	7,918	11,760	3,019	8,652	11,671
1907	--------	--------	--------	1,118	1,966	3,084	4,841	9,809	14,650	3,752	9,383	13,135
1908	--------	--------	--------	1,291	2,191	3,482	5,684	10,850	16,534	4,148	10,135	14,283
1909	--------	--------	--------	1,841	3,836	5,677	7,021	12,570	19,591	5,249	12,513	17,762
1910	--------	--------	3,233	2,420	4,194	6,614	9,689	16,487	26,176	6,333	14,509	20,842
1911	--------	--------	4,798	2,402	4,001	6,403	12,472	20,417	32,889	7,229	16,282	23,511
1912	--------	--------	2,884	2,942	4,578	7,520	13,743	23,792	37,535	7,562	16,591	24,153
1913	--------	--------	3,950	3,653	5,642	9,295	16,364	26,951	43,315	9,147	19,481	28,628
1914	--------	--------	4,912	4,348	6,937	11,285	18,336	29,750	48,086	10,079	22,861	32,940
1915	--------	--------	4,439	4,765	6,535	11,300	25,617	42,063	67,680	9,475	22,957	32,432
1916	--------	--------	4,033	5,030	7,654	12,684	26,116	46,549	72,665	10,242	24,997	35,239
1917	--------	--------	4,944	6,167	9,366	15,533	24,749	49,098	73,847	14,446	33,960	48,406
1918	--------	--------	8,494	6,108	9,356	15,464	28,730	59,549	88,279	8,904	25,398	34,302
1919	--------	--------	6,148	7,648	11,781	19,429	30,298	60,589	90,887	10,906	30,424	41,330
1920	--------	--------	6,809	7,427	11,956	19,383	36,791	77,712	114,503	11,669	32,162	43,831
1921	--------	--------	5,874	8,036	13,971	22,007	39,585	88,265	127,850	11,213	31,123	42,336
1922	1,565	4,816	6,381	8,065	14,007	22,072	30,631	83,141	113,772	11,651	33,801	45,452
1923	1,578	5,975	7,553	9,758	16,976	26,734	29,089	86,043	115,132	12,291	38,159	50,450
1924	1,431	5,508	6,939	10,301	18,166	28,467	28,209	83,320	111,529	12,331	39,832	52,163
1925	1,561	5,972	7,533	11,299	20,742	32,041	26,935	82,659	109,594	12,131	41,725	53,856
1926	1,720	6,142	7,862	12,392	22,298	34,690	28,117	82,971	111,088	12,837	42,915	55,752
1927	1,847	6,554	8,401	12,777	22,694	35,471	28,817	81,146	109,963	15,666	48,411	64,077
1928	2,274	7,837	10,111	14,363	24,664	39,027	33,512	88,214	121,726	19,393	54,516	73,909

Bureau of Agricultural Economics. Obtained from registry associations.

TABLE 448.—*Cattle: Tuberculin testing under accredited-herd and area plans, 1917–1928*

Year ended June 30—	Cattle tested					Modified accredited counties	Herds accredited [1]	Herds passed 1 test [1]	Herds under supervision [1]
	Accredited-herd plan	Area plan	Total	Reactors found	Per cent of reactors				
	Number	*Number*	*Number*	*Number*		*Number*	*Number*	*Number*	*Number*
1917	20,101	----------	20,101	645	3.2	--------	--------	----------	--------
1918	134,143	----------	134,143	6,544	4.9	--------	204	883	--------
1919	329,878	----------	329,878	13,528	4.1	--------	578	5,652	--------
1920	700,670	----------	700,670	28,709	4.1	--------	2,588	10,064	--------
1921	1,366,358	----------	1,366,358	53,768	3.9	--------	4,831	33,215	71,806
1922	1,722,209	[2] 662,027	2,384,236	82,569	3.5	--------	8,015	111,719	140,376
1923	1,695,662	1,765,187	3,460,849	113,844	3.3	--------	12,310	150,748	187,915
1924	1,865,863	3,446,501	5,312,364	171,559	3.2	38	19,747	216,737	305,809
1925	2,008,526	4,991,502	7,000,028	214,491	3.1	51	24,110	392,740	414,620
1926	1,989,048	6,661,732	8,650,780	323,084	3.7	109	24,009	382,674	435,840
1927	2,522,791	7,177,385	9,700,176	285,361	2.9	149	34,084	229,086	261,148
1928	2,589,844	8,691,646	11,281,490	262,113	2.3	180	38,880	427,595	473,218
Total	16,945,193	33,395,980	50,341,073	1,556,215	3.1	527	169,356	1,961,113	2,290,732

Bureau of Animal Industry.

[1] The figures in these columns represent net increases at the close of each year.
[2] Testing during 6 months.

TABLE 449.—*Cattle: Status of tuberculosis-eradication work, by States, June 30, 1928*

State	Accredited-herd work			Eradication from areas [1]			Total tuberculin tests, 1917 to June 30, 1928		
	Herds accredited	Herds passed one test	Herds under supervision	Modified accredited counties	Counties completing one or more tests of all cattle [2]	Total counties engaged in testing [2]	Total cattle	Reactors Number	Reactors Per cent
Alabama	239	5,169	7,716	0	0	[3]3	335,564	2,195	0.7
Arizona	43	8,109	8,181	0	0	14	207,838	5,925	2.8
Arkansas	16	3,892	3,385	0	0	1	61,304	363	.6
California	137	5,911	6,047	2	2	6	410,786	4,360	1.1
Colorado	164	3,104	3,663	0	0	3	72,454	1,630	2.2
Connecticut	1,562	4,364	7,050	0	0	4	418,533	39,400	9.4
Delaware	1,793	3,006	5,595	0	[4]1	[4]1	124,644	11,278	9.0
District of Columbia	8	90	99	0	1	1	12,693	122	1.0
Florida	435	7,441	8,310	0	3	3	277,958	3,426	1.2
Georgia	35	10,156	10,193	2	4	7	256,002	3,002	1.2
Idaho	55	30,911	34,286	19	19	34	587,853	4,052	.7
Illinois	1,461	124,844	140,042	17	17	75	3,624,735	164,030	4.5
Indiana	37,021	101,551	145,006	40	47	67	1,839,624	26,322	1.4
Iowa	8,008	94,939	157,279	43	50	60	5,086,093	134,922	2.7
Kansas	885	69,462	70,615	35	35	37	1,117,118	10,969	1.0
Kentucky	67	72,017	74,259	9	43	52	572,262	5,745	1.0
Louisiana	19	7,120	7,447	0	0	0	289,514	6,557	2.3
Maine	4,812	34,533	39,933	12	12	16	589,755	6,929	1.2
Maryland	5,690	11,141	24,544	0	3	12	645,497	45,311	7.0
Massachusetts	850	1,623	3,001	0	0	0	248,521	32,759	13.2
Michigan	74	155,327	159,001	55	63	70	2,814,408	56,564	2.0
Minnesota	8,489	56,305	70,301	15	26	26	3,930,444	93,635	2.4
Mississippi	32	9,700	9,739	2	3	5	254,849	1,190	.5
Missouri	978	64,389	67,938	6	6	10	875,779	7,166	.8
Montana	95	30,160	30,704	[5]7	[5]8	11	774,468	6,522	.8
Nebraska	109	65,750	66,889	29	38	40	1,789,215	24,705	1.4
Nevada	11	1,064	1,376	0	0	13	122,159	1,880	1.5
New Hampshire	3,283	2,214	5,896	1	1	5	336,948	20,195	6.0
New Jersey	1,954	3,116	7,289	0	0	0	313,083	21,387	6.8
New Mexico	18	1,465	1,523	0	0	22	57,594	338	.6
New York	56,927	39,388	110,455	7	17	48	3,734,779	346,078	9.3
North Carolina	373	252,300	253,055	93	93	100	777,691	3,877	.5
North Dakota	4,983	42,877	53,226	26	26	39	1,449,595	19,679	1.4
Ohio	659	147,474	153,260	20	29	54	1,840,786	63,598	3.5
Oklahoma	287	122	430	0	0	0	193,446	3,703	1.9
Oregon	442	42,207	42,698	4	10	26	971,302	11,549	1.2
Pennsylvania	4,295	93,315	111,901	14	17	58	2,223,655	108,943	4.9
Rhode Island	60	172	399	0	0	0	30,772	4,406	14.3
South Carolina	116	45,434	45,617	7	7	9	229,347	1,467	.6
South Dakota	1,359	8,711	10,311	4	5	5	617,501	12,543	2.0
Tennessee	325	47,283	47,716	4	4	11	416,811	2,397	.6
Texas	185	103	434	0	0	0	264,199	3,525	1.3
Utah	79	10,724	11,548	1	2	28	426,072	4,240	1.0
Vermont	5,632	3,252	12,162	([6])	([6])	7	937,322	39,636	4.2
Virginia	2,257	18,624	21,169	11	12	19	565,673	11,799	2.1
Washington	37	38,481	41,546	[5]4	[5]7	35	939,457	26,131	2.8
West Virginia	1,145	35,284	37,022	11	13	20	342,450	4,556	1.3
Wisconsin	11,848	137,009	149,772	27	55	63	5,225,414	136,622	2.6
Wyoming	4	9,480	10,704	0	0	0	138,014	1,094	.8
Alaska	0	0	0	0	0	0	798	19	2.4
Hawaii	0	0	0	0	0	0	67,227	1,381	2.1
Interstate testing [7]	0	0	0	0	0	0	896,168	5,908	.7
Indian schools [8]	0	0	0	0	0	0	413	27	6.5
Purebred in United States [8]	0	0	0	0	0	0	4,486	157	3.5
Total	169,356	1,961,113	2,290,732	527	679	1,120	50,341,073	1,556,215	3.1

Bureau of Animal Industry.

[1] Accredited-herd work began in 1917: Area work, 1921.
[2] Including District of Columbia.
[3] Testing carried as accredited-herd work.
[4] No testing in 1928.
[5] Not including part of 1 county.
[6] Not including 21 towns.
[7] Represents testing during 1927 and 1928.
[8] Testing in United States before work organized by States.

TABLE 450.—*Growth of dairy-herd improvement associations, 1906–1929*

State	1906	1907	1908	1909	1910	1911	1912	1913	1914	1915	1916	1917	1918	1919	1920	1921	1922	1923	1925	1926	1927	1928	1929
Michigan	1	4	2	5	4	3	4	4	3	3	10	15	7	13	14	11	17	53	105	108	102	105	94
Maine			3	4	3	6	5	4	5	8	11	5	1	0	0	0	3	4	2	1	0	0	0
New York			1	1	3	9	18	21	29	35	47	43	19	25	28	24	31	27	24	28	36	42	54
Vermont				2	8	10	11	17	28	33	38	47	18	12	18	17	21	20	17	23	23	25	23
Iowa				2	5	4	8	7	8	13	23	30	15	11	14	17	22	47	56	61	77	86	101
California				1	3	2	4	4	5	7	9	15	16	14	18	21	21	27	20	30	35	32	32
Wisconsin				9	10	10	8	11	24	37	51	81	112	105	115	103	127	151	176	169	159	166	154
Nebraska				1	0	0	0	3	2	3	4	4	2	2	0	0	1	4	2	6	10	17	23
Colorado					1	1	2	1	1	0	0	3	5	5	5	4	6	6	7	6	5	9	14
Pennsylvania					1	1	2	2	7	14	19	24	21	35	64	46	45	36	42	43	49	65	76
Ohio					1	0	0	1	4	5	20	30	24	24	41	35	36	36	21	25	28	29	39
Washington					1	3	1	0	0	1	12	18	11	9	6	10	10	11	10	8	11	10	12
Maryland						1	3	3	2	4	7	8	4	2	6	7	6	4	9	10	8	7	8
Illinois						4	3	2	7	3	3	17	15	27	23	25	24	23	24	26	30	34	51
Minnesota						3	7	10	9	11	22	26	23	21	19	23	37	55	88	84	85	105	117
New Hampshire						1	1	1	4	8	11	12	8	9	10	10	11	10	5	4	2	4	7
Oregon						1	1	1	7	11	15	17	11	6	9	5	5	4	7	8	9	11	14
Utah						1	0	0	1	1	0	1	0	1	1	1	1	4	5	4	5	5	5
Massachusetts						2	2	2	3	0	4	4	0	0	1	5	6	6	3	6	7	9	11
Virginia						2	2	2	1	1	1	4	3	15	13	13	13	9	8	11	13	14	20
Kansas								2	2	3	7	9	7	10	5	10	5	10	17	25	31	34	41
Indiana								1	1	0	1	1	0	0	5	5	2	3	2	0	2	(1)	8
West Virginia								1	3	6	3	0	0	0	1	0	2	1	1	2	4	5	3
Kentucky									2	1	2	5	4	5	6	7	11	12	13	19	21	25	34
Missouri									2	3	4	8	9	9	12	8	6	6	6	9	11	17	18
New Jersey									1	1	3	1	1	1	3	5	5	6	3	3	3	4	6
Connecticut									2	0	0	0	0	0	2	2	0	0	2	5	5	5	8
North Carolina										1	0	0	0	0	0	1	0	0	0	0	1	2	2
Louisiana										1	1	3	3	0	0	0	0	4	11	9	10	8	14
South Dakota											1	0	1	0	0	1	1	4	3	1	3	0	1
Nevada											2	2	1	0	0	2	1	1	2	1	1	2	3
Arizona											2	2	0	0	4	4	4	3	0	0	0	0	1
Rhode Island											2	3	2	2	1	0	0	0	0	0	0	0	1
Delaware											2	1	1	4	5	6	4	8	8	8	9	12	13
Idaho											1	0	0	0	0	3	2	1	1	2	0	1	1
Mississippi												1	2	0	0	0	2	2	4	3	7	7	8
Montana											1	8	4	6	3	3	4	2	2	2	2	3	7
Tennessee												1	0	0	0	1	1	1	0	1	1	2	2
New Mexico												1	0	1	0	0	1	0	1	0	0	0	1
Wyoming													2	1	3	1	1	0	0	0	1	3	4
Alabama													1	0	0	0	0	0	0	0	1	1	2
Georgia													1	1	1	2	6	8	5	3	6	4	7
North Dakota														1	1	2	1	3	5	5	5	12	22
Oklahoma														1	1	1	0	0	0	0	0	0	1
South Carolina														3	0	0	0	0	0	0	1	3	6
Texas															1	2	2	2	0	0	0	2	(1)
Arkansas																							1
Florida																							
Total	1	4	6	25	40	64	82	100	163	211	346	459	353	385	468	452	513	627	732	777	837	947	1,090

Bureau of Dairy Industry. Up to and including 1923 data were collected on July 1. Beginning with 1924 reports are made by calendar years. Last 5 columns give data for January 1.

[1] No report.

TABLE 451.—*Milk cows: Estimated price [1] per head received by producers, 15th of month, United States, 1910–1928*

Year	Jan.	Feb.	Mar.	Apr.	May	June	July	Aug.	Sept.	Oct.	Nov.	Dec.	Average
	Dolls.	*Dolls.*	*Dolls.*	*Dolls.*	*Dolls.*	*Dolls.*	*Dolls.*	*Dolls.*	*Dolls.*	*Dolls.*	*Dolls.*	*Dolls.*	*Dolls.*
Average:													
1910–1913	44.57	44.91	46.32	46.88	46.84	47.09	46.38	46.48	46.87	47.42	47.78	47.98	47.99
1914–1920	70.75	71.54	72.71	74.12	74.86	75.15	75.08	74.60	74.48	74.43	72.73	72.30	73.56
1921–1925	56.81	56.28	57.52	57.54	57.51	57.07	56.08	55.59	55.49	55.25	55.21	56.11	56.29
1910	41.18	40.35	41.75	42.22	42.38	43.46	42.86	42.77	42.68	43.20	43.34	43.41	42.47
1911	44.70	44.48	45.42	44.81	44.54	43.86	42.44	42.26	42.22	42.69	42.70	42.72	43.57
1912	42.89	43.40	44.09	45.14	45.63	45.84	45.41	46.11	46.79	47.30	47.38	48.62	45.72
1913	49.51	51.42	54.02	55.34	54.80	55.20	54.80	54.78	55.78	56.47	57.71	57.19	54.75
1914	57.99	59.09	59.23	59.60	59.85	59.82	59.67	60.72	59.58	59.53	58.77	58.23	59.34
1915	58.47	57.99	58.00	57.78	58.29	58.59	60.31	58.34	58.38	58.76	57.35	56.79	58.25
1916	57.79	57.99	59.51	60.68	60.98	61.63	62.04	61.32	61.41	62.19	62.67	63.18	60.95
1917	63.92	65.93	68.46	72.09	72.78	72.87	72.81	72.53	73.93	75.79	75.00	76.16	71.86
1918	76.54	78.36	80.71	82.45	84.11	84.74	84.97	84.06	85.21	85.41	84.51	85.78	83.07
1919	86.10	86.15	88.15	90.91	93.43	93.84	94.51	94.72	93.42	93.43	93.27	95.54	91.96
1920	94.42	95.27	94.94	95.36	94.56	94.56	91.23	90.50	89.40	85.90	77.56	70.42	89.51
1921	66.82	63.44	65.37	64.35	62.63	59.89	56.55	55.85	54.33	53.39	53.28	53.30	59.10
1922	52.83	53.54	54.87	54.46	54.76	54.87	54.20	52.67	52.79	52.86	51.62	53.21	53.56
1923	54.01	54.15	55.29	56.14	55.91	56.34	56.22	55.45	56.13	55.51	55.39	54.66	55.43
1924	55.57	55.49	55.88	55.92	56.37	56.45	55.46	55.74	55.54	54.30	55.05	54.00	·55.48
1925	54.81	54.79	56.19	56.85	57.88	57.79	57.95	58.26	58.68	60.17	60.69	60.38	57.87
1926	62.06	63.41	63.17	65.65	66.63	66.74	66.68	65.37	66.12	66.26	66.91	66.74	65.51
1927	66.77	68.22	70.18	71.98	72.43	74.19	74.15	74.24	76.10	78.62	81.09	82.36	74.19
1928	83.11	86.34	87.95	88.55	89.00	89.90	90.37	90.43	92.56	92.86	93.05	92.87	89.75

Bureau of Agricultural Economics.

[1] As reported by county dealers.

TABLE 452.—*Dairy products: Quantity produced, 1922–1927 and monthly, 1927*

All figures in 1,000 pounds.

Product	1922	1923	1924	1925	1926	1927 Total	Jan.	Feb.	Mar.	Apr.	May	June	July	Aug.	Sept.	Oct.	Nov.	Dec.
Creamery butter	1,153,515	1,252,214	1,336,080	1,361,526	1,451,766	1,496,495	97,965	95,522	111,451	126,415	168,808	188,792	170,484	146,808	113,546	102,399	86,058	88,247
Whey butter (made from whey cream)	2,291	1,904	1,665	1,774	2,872	1,217	74	72	94	88	108	135	152	138	117	96	76	67
Renovated or process butter	4,448	2,802	2,813	2,519	2,505	4,286	396	505	699	175	345	330	280	350	343	280	246	337
American cheese: Whole milk	282,806	308,108	324,695	347,240	335,915	307,777	16,660	17,085	21,318	24,533	34,704	41,489	38,195	31,944	25,783	23,012	16,717	16,337
Part skim	2,164	2,145	2,470	2,793	2,927	3,390	223	215	234	351	505	481	287	221	165	199	228	281
Full skim	2,500	2,033	1,605	3,298	1,384	1,888	93	105	107	180	198	239	157	150	145	205	144	165
Swiss cheese (including block)	19,983	24,555	21,844	23,457	20,883	18,141	168	167	262	744	2,639	3,371	3,199	2,659	2,166	1,619	832	315
Brick and Munster cheese	37,194	33,250	32,052	34,101	31,048	31,546	2,348	2,167	2,665	3,240	3,393	3,306	2,722	2,474	2,057	2,464	2,443	2,267
Limburger cheese	7,383	7,100	9,734	9,163	9,639	8,842	434	406	571	672	947	1,088	1,149	961	800	777	568	469
Cream and Neufchatel cheese	9,936	10,334	14,945	17,575	18,192	25,962	1,738	1,782	2,127	2,248	2,468	2,378	1,957	1,926	1,870	2,363	2,521	2,584
All Italian varieties of cheese	2,627	2,132	1,973	1,562	2,425	3,377	237	261	326	326	322	342	295	277	268	271	226	226
All other varieties of cheese	5,387	5,040	4,622	4,325	5,003	5,763	421	377	426	474	521	594	445	432	437	544	575	517
Total cheese (not including cottage, pot, and baker's)	369,980	394,697	413,940	443,514	427,416	406,686	22,322	22,565	28,036	32,768	45,697	53,288	48,406	41,044	33,691	31,454	24,254	23,161
Cottage, pot, and baker's cheese	32,389	35,527	54,347	59,485	67,977	75,679	5,823	5,988	7,317	6,935	7,759	8,177	6,199	5,687	5,085	5,820	5,380	5,509
Condensed milk (sweetened): Case goods—Skimmed	3,915	2,748	2,044	3,135	1,298	1,623	146	159	166	85	70	58	139	197	162	233	41	167
Unskimmed	230,456	196,058	187,281	186,807	154,944	161,355	13,190	9,556	11,567	16,948	19,961	19,980	14,438	12,561	9,132	11,834	10,722	11,466
Bulk goods—Skimmed	76,049	102,236	96,581	114,198	147,473	143,722	9,556	9,871	12,277	13,943	19,323	20,005	13,904	11,939	9,237	8,016	7,154	8,497
Unskimmed	30,292	44,860	47,429	44,758	55,737	39,668	2,263	2,105	2,376	3,745	6,246	7,716	3,070	2,935	2,630	2,887	1,523	2,172
Evaporated milk (unsweetened): Case goods—Skimmed	3,574	7,035	11,555	5,994	11,985	8,100	181	278	184	1,682	2,765	3,009	1					
Unskimmed	949,909	1,252,520	1,189,755	1,202,456	1,158,476	1,273,815	81,440	85,261	110,988	126,522	166,522	178,070	139,686	111,660	76,206	73,341	58,172	65,596
Bulk goods—Skimmed	67,066	77,416	83,131	86,954	116,758	126,085	6,261	6,688	9,035	10,861	14,392	15,661	15,352	12,638	11,672	8,897	7,418	7,210
Unskimmed	70,088	92,008	82,772	113,556	86,833	101,354	4,713	5,850	7,304	9,266	12,433	14,391	13,486	10,945	8,755	5,759	4,120	4,332
Total condensed and evaporated milk	1,431,349	1,774,881	1,700,548	1,757,858	1,733,504	1,855,722	117,750	119,768	153,897	183,352	241,763	258,890	200,076	162,875	117,794	110,967	89,150	99,440

	1923	1924	1925	1926	1927	1928	January	February	March	April	May	June	July	August	September	October	November	December
Condensed or evaporated buttermilk	44,343	54,833	66,837	77,079	86,687	99,180	6,301	6,122	6,101	8,579	11,766	13,458	11,038	10,434	7,749	6,585	5,407	5,640
Dried or powdered buttermilk	9,007	13,032	18,058	20,246	31,378	38,435	2,524	2,590	3,006	3,228	4,278	4,661	4,340	3,636	2,784	2,631	2,267	2,490
Powdered whole milk	5,599	6,560	7,887	8,931	10,768	11,464	593	737	997	956	2,090	2,166	1,104	742	668	495	330	586
Powdered skimmed milk	40,617	62,251	69,219	73,317	91,718	118,123	6,064	6,219	8,382	10,398	12,984	13,994	12,992	11,317	9,473	9,268	7,884	9,148
Powdered cream	118	328	1,018	339	331	338	11	3	20	22	72	75	62	5		3	15	50
Dried casein (skim milk or buttermilk product)	6,927	14,548	20,759	16,660	16,953	18,033	1,219	1,326	1,639	1,736	2,352	2,765	1,820	1,420	1,052	905	797	1,002
Malted milk	13,659	15,331	15,889	18,050	20,673	22,116	1,689	1,650	1,958	2,026	2,168	2,420	2,012	1,678	1,526	1,597	1,606	1,786
Milk sugar (crude)	2,191	2,872	3,331	5,655	4,476	4,077	369	276	411	428	507	524	354	269	236	246	213	244
Ice cream of all kinds (gallons)	161,609	173,412	181,564	214,382	215,248	226,756	8,402	9,769	13,239	17,145	23,806	29,957	36,177	28,651	24,440	15,571	10,846	8,753

Bureau of Agricultural Economics. Compiled from reports of factories made direct to the bureau.

NOTE.—A table similar to Table 428, 1927 Yearbook, milk production and utilization, is omitted.

TABLE 453.—*Fluid milk: Receipts at New York, by State of origin, 1927, 1928, and monthly, 1928*

[40-quart units] [1]

State of origin	1927	1928	January	February	March	April	May	June	July	August	September	October	November	December
Connecticut	162,613	82,720	8,786	8,654	9,681	7,505	7,835	8,043	5,810	4,106	4,394	5,823	6,001	6,082
Massachusetts	131,577	126,443	7,397	7,742	9,862	11,486	12,770	14,037	10,771	11,307	10,513	11,035	9,928	9,595
Maryland	43,632	66,164	7,081	3,207	5,890	6,584	1,116		400	325	2,425	7,839	15,169	16,128
New Jersey	2,051,503	1,700,809	160,024	150,178	166,179	152,136	157,249	157,192	139,375	125,904	116,132	126,984	123,714	125,742
New York	27,521,242	27,098,784	2,226,496	2,121,026	2,311,227	2,233,123	2,382,897	2,348,746	2,501,816	2,394,272	2,216,700	2,257,992	2,044,837	2,060,652
Pennsylvania	3,652,306	4,408,705	358,538	321,155	345,023	330,219	348,265	343,340	353,077	383,045	391,229	401,289	411,353	422,172
Vermont	889,847	1,068,937	72,251	66,979	87,131	80,128	88,298	93,753	94,232	105,287	90,813	100,106	100,671	89,288
Other	1,396	2,229						162						2,067
Total	34,454,116	34,554,791	2,840,573	2,678,941	2,934,993	2,820,181	2,998,430	2,965,293	3,105,481	3,024,246	2,832,206	2,911,068	2,711,673	2,731,706

Bureau of Agricultural Economics.

[1] 40-quart units equal 10 gallons, or about 86 pounds.

TABLE 454.—Fluid cream: Receipts, at New York, by State of origin, 1927, 1928, and monthly, 1928

[40-quart units] [1]

State of origin	1927	1928	January	February	March	April	May	June	July	August	September	October	November	December
Connecticut	114	282	200	65	48	51	------	10	7	------	------	------	------	------
Delaware	------	99	------	------	------	------	------	------	------	------	------	------	------	------
Illinois	953	2,658	------	200	400	------	534	300	216	------	500	300	------	455
Indiana	2,935	7,794	------	800	------	800	685	1,938	800	700	------	------	1,454	800
Iowa	10,962	23,117	600	------	1,420	1,191	2,843	2,629	5,063	4,971	3,200	800	200	200
Kentucky	------	200	------	------	------	122	170	349	------	------	------	67	88	184
Massachusetts	2,510	2,434	457	436	351	------	------	------	66	36	108	------	23	20
Maryland	------	613	30	------	------	------	------	------	115	400	25	------	------	------
Michigan	4,813	2,920	------	------	------	------	------	------	1,250	400	200	------	200	870
Minnesota	7,568	11,599	1,400	200	------	------	------	------	2,223	2,200	1,000	1,200	1,376	1,200
Missouri	------	2,269	------	------	------	------	------	------	------	------	603	603	624	1,042
New Jersey	39,990	41,900	3,147	2,852	2,879	2,994	3,440	5,115	4,123	4,321	6,710	3,265	1,596	1,458
New York	1,192,527	1,285,635	84,729	85,169	109,970	113,980	151,107	149,874	127,029	105,001	105,317	94,579	77,355	81,525
Ohio	------	11,170	700	800	700	500	1,060	1,150	850	1,400	800	400	1,910	900
Pennsylvania	197,678	183,852	14,200	10,928	12,103	13,850	19,506	19,221	19,115	18,219	18,123	16,241	11,115	11,231
Tennessee	210	7,767	207	------	------	------	------	434	1,902	1,951	649	218	217	2,189
Virginia	------	33	------	------	------	------	------	------	------	------	------	------	------	33
Vermont	73,738	96,830	5,901	5,911	7,644	7,980	13,540	13,803	16,222	10,149	4,220	4,595	3,022	3,843
Wisconsin	24,720	16,549	400	600	1,200	400	1,000	721	2,094	1,400	1,193	1,841	2,700	3,000
Canada	10,857	4,908	290	253	------	124	------	------	401	1,049	561	1,223	712	295
Total	1,571,375	1,702,659	112,261	108,214	136,715	141,992	193,885	195,544	181,476	152,197	143,206	125,332	102,592	109,245

Bureau of Agricultural Economics.

[1] 40-quart units equal 10 gallons, or about 82.5 pounds.

TABLE 455.—*Condensed milk: International trade, average 1909–1913, annual 1924–1927*

Country	Average 1909-1913 Imports	Average 1909-1913 Exports	1924 Imports	1924 Exports	1925 Imports	1925 Exports	1926 Imports	1926 Exports	1927 preliminary Imports	1927 preliminary Exports
	1,000 pounds	*1,000 pounds*	*1,000 pounds*	*1,000 pounds*	*1,000 pounds*	*1,000 pounds*	*1,000 pounds*	*1,000 pounds*	*1,000 pounds*	*1,000 pounds*
PRINCIPAL EXPORTING COUNTRIES										
Netherlands	[1] 23	55	235	233,901	288	248,676	389	293,046	278	324,800
United States	0	[2] 16,200	6,452	206,280	4,621	147,763	1,663	114,549	2,623	103,028
Denmark	[1] [2] 5	[2] 4,724	34	71,198	56	58,762	2	56,734	14	55,304
Switzerland	201	80,539	120	58,225	68	67,555	71	73,940	11	81,234
Canada	259	4,575	155	40,251	119	40,614	152	24,775	125	33,680
Australia	4,463	727	[1] 79	[1] 15,857	[1] 42	[1] 19,951	[1] 130	[1] 31,217	[1] 96	[1] 16,025
Norway	3	32,106	685	13,311	1,173	16,848	1,055	24,483	747	16,698
Italy	806	5,913	855	13,560	771	17,322	715	11,073	1,336	8,904
Irish Free State	0	0	2,368	2,705	2,442	6,569	1,659	9,169	1,494	6,302
New Zealand	261	132	31	1,408	93	1,144	7	1,225	3	1,555
Lithuania	0	0	24	946	1	1,958	[1] 62	5,782	[1] 83	8,888
Czechoslovakia	0	0	2,141	665	759	1,138	421	640	141	315
PRINCIPAL IMPORTING COUNTRIES										
United Kingdom	121,175	48,221	245,486	11,113	250,572	14,497	269,682	14,287	283,789	27,771
Cuba	28,457	0	47,312	0	47,316	0	48,567	0	------	------
Germany [3]	66	12,080	26,753	570	28,372	1,428	12,036	1,681	13,434	980
France	2,458	4,140	20,168	4,916	17,369	4,803	13,551	7,607	13,044	10,252
Dutch East Indies	[4] 13,049	89	17,677	0	20,009	77	24,301	0	[5] 10,458	0
Philippine Islands	12,311	0	17,890	0	22,533	0	24,142	0	25,974	0
Japan	10,061	0	12,743	74	9,429	284	9,641	213	9,586	399
British India	11,236	0	10,029	362	[6] 14,124	0	[6] 18,980	0	[6] 24,933	0
Union of South Africa	21,227	0	10,029	1	9,922	16	11,122	16	11,330	20
China	4,484	0	9,461	0	10,117	0	11,994	0	11,095	0
Peru	[1] [2] 2,038	0	7,097	0	9,339	0	8,886	0	7,629	0
Austria	[1] [7] 323	[1] [7] 79	4,340	507	1,154	27	1,358	64	1,105	254
Greece	[1] 176	[1] 0	[1] 5,359	[1] 1	[1] 5,359	[1] 0	5,111	0	7,052	0
French Indo-China	[1] 2,437	[1] 72	4,484	158	4,388	191	5,995	252	5,955	174
Siam	0	0	[1] 3,283	[1] 0	4,833	0	4,788	0	6,617	0
Jamaica [1]	2,860	0	3,427	0	3,387	0	3,803	0	4,103	0
Belgium [3]	0	0	3,878	390	4,260	1,096	3,370	1,312	2,861	2,613
Trinidad and Tobago	[1] 37	0	2,146	0	2,383	0	2,836	0	3,132	0
Algeria	[1] 143	[1] 38	2,759	45	3,047	66	2,725	[1] 229	[1] 3,682	[1] 129
Tunis	[1] 21,334	0	1,950	0	1,844	0	1,828	0	2,644	0
Poland	0	0	2,972	31	442	128	79	2	263	22
Egypt	[8] 1,628	0	1,740	160	1,173	253	1,339	289	1,395	351
Argentina	742	0	946	13	1,187	5	1,524	13	1,446	28
Brazil	8,694	0	1,426	0	761	0	1,838	0	------	------
Total, 36 countries	250,957	209,690	476,534	676,648	483,753	651,171	495,822	672,598	458,478	699,726

Bureau of Agricultural Economics. Official sources, except where otherwise stated.

[1] International Yearbook of Agricultural Statistics.
[2] 4-year average.
[3] Includes some powdered milk.
[4] 3-year average.
[5] Java and Madura only.
[6] Sea trade only.
[7] Average for Austria-Hungary.
[8] 1 year only.

TABLE 456.—*Milk, wholesale: Estimated price per 100 pounds received by producers, United States, 1923–1928*

Year	Jan. 15	Feb. 15	Mar. 15	Apr. 15	May 15	June 15	July 15	Aug. 15	Sept. 15	Oct. 15	Nov. 15	Dec. 15
	Dolls.	*Dolls.*	*Dolls.*	*Dolls.*	*Dolls.*	*Dolls.*	*Dolls.*	*Dolls.*	*Dolls.*	*Dolls.*	*Dolls.*	*Dolls.*
1923									2.81	2.98	3.02	2.92
1924	2.86	2.84	2.75	2.50	2.40	2.40	2.29	2.18	2.35	2.43	2.45	2.55
1925	2.48	2.55	2.62	2.48	2.47	2.47	2.45	2.55	2.56	2.73	2.69	2.65
1926	2.74	2.68	2.56	2.46	2.39	2.35	2.40	2.37	2.47	2.46	2.60	2.61
1927	2.68	2.64	2.55	2.58	2.51	2.44	2.40	2.36	2.48	2.55	2.56	2.64
1928	2.67	2.69	2.61	2.51	2.49	2.45	2.45	2.46	2.56	2.60	2.63	2.65

Bureau of Agricultural Economics. Based on returns from special price reporters. Prices quoted are to dealers, factories, etc.

TABLE 457.—*Milk, standard or grade B: Retail price per quart, delivered to family trade, New York, Chicago, New Orleans, and San Francisco, 1920–1928*

Market and year	Jan.	Feb.	Mar.	Apr.	May	June	July	Aug.	Sept.	Oct.	Nov.	Dec.
New York:	Cents	Cents	Cents	Cents	Cents	Cents	Cents	Cents	Cents	Cents	Cents	Cents
1920	18	16½	16½	15	15	15	16	17	18	18	18	17
1921	17	16	15			14	14	15	15	15	15	15
1922	15	15	15		13	13	14	15	15	15	15	16
1923	16	15	15	15	14	14	14	14	15	15	16	15
1924	15	14	14	14	13	13	13	13	14	14	15	15
1925	15	15	15	15	15	14	14	15	15	15	15	15
1926	15	15	15	15	15	15	15	15	15	15	15	15
1927	15	15	15	15	15	15	15	15	16	16	16	16
1928	16	15	15	15	15	15	15	16	16	16	16	16
Chicago:												
1920	15	15	14	14	14	14	15	16	16	16	15	14
1921	14	14	14	14	14	14	14	14	12	12	12	12
1922	12	12	12	12	12	12	12	12	12	12	12	12
1923	12½	13	13	13	13	13	14	14	14	14	14	14
1924	14	14	14	14	14	14	14	14	14	14	14	14
1925	14	14	14	14	14	14	14	14	14	14	14	14
1926	14	14	14	14	14	14	14	14	14	14	14	14
1927	14	14	14	14	14	14	14	14	14	14	14	14
1928	14	14	14	14	14	14	14	14	14	14	14	14
New Orleans:												
1920	19	19	19	19	17	17	17	17	19	19	19	18
1921	17	17	16	16	16	16	16	16	16	16	14	14
1922	14	14	14	14	14	14	14			14	14	14
1923	14		14	14	14	14	14	14	14	15	15	
1924		15	15	15	14	14	14	14	14	14	14	14
1925	14	14	14	14	12	12	12	12	12	14	14	14
1926	14	14	14	14	14	14	14	14	14	14	14	14
1927	14	14	14	14	14	14	14	14	14	14	14	14
1928	14	14	14	14	14	14	14	14	14	14	14	14
San Francisco:												
1920	16	16	15½	15	16	16	15½	17	17	17	17	17
1921	15½	15½	15	15	15	14½	14½	14	14	13½	13½	13½
1922	13½	12½	12½	12½		12½	12½	12½	12½	12½	12½	13
1923	12½	12½	12½	12½	12½	12½		12½			14	14
1924	14	14	14	14	14	14	14	14	14	14	14	14
1925	14	14	14	14	14	14	14	14	14	14	14	14
1926	14	14	14	14	14	14	14	14	14	14	14	14
1927	14	14	14	14	14	14	14	14	14	14	14	14
1928	14	14	14	14	14	14	14	14	14	14	14 -	14	14

Bureau of Agricultural Economics. Compiled from reports of the bureau secured through the cooperation of milk distributors, producers' associations, and municipal officers.

TABLE 458.—*Milk, standard or grade B: Retail price per quart, delivered to family trade in cities, 1928*

Market	Jan.	Feb.	Mar.	Apr.	May	June	July	Aug.	Sept.	Oct.	Nov.	Dec.
	Cents	Cents	Cents	Cents	Cents	Cents	Cents	Cents	Cents	Cents	Cents	Cents
Boston	16	15½	15½	14½	14½	14½	14½	15½	15½	15½	15½	15½
New York	16	16	15	15	15	15	15	16	16	16	16	16
Philadelphia	13	13	13	13	13	13	13	13	13	13	13	13
Pittsburgh	15	14	14	13	13	13	13	14	14	15	15	15
Cleveland	13½	14	13	14	14	14	14	14	14	14	14	14
Indianapolis	12	12	12	12	12	12	12	12	12	12	12½	13
Chicago	14	14	14	14	14	14	14	14	14	14	14	14
Detroit			14	14		14		14	14	14	14	14
Milwaukee	11	11	11	11	11	11	11	11	11	11	11	11
Minneapolis	12	12	12	12	12	12	12	12	12	12	12	12
St. Louis	13	13	13	13	13	13	13	13	13	13	13	13
Kansas City, Mo	13	14	13	14	13	14	14	13	14	13	13	13
Washington, D. C	15	15	15	15	15	15	15	15	15	15	14½	14½
Jacksonville	18½	18½	18½	18½	18½	18½	18½	19	18½	19	19	18½
Louisville	13	13	13	12	12	12	12	12	13	13	13	13
Birmingham	18	18	18	18	18	18	18	18	18	18	18	18
New Orleans	14	14	14	14	14	14	14	14	14	14	14	14
Dallas	12	12	12	12	12½	12½	12	12½	13	12	13	12
Butte	13	13	13	13	13		13		13	13	13	13
Denver	12			12	12	12	12	12	12	12	12	12
Salt Lake City	10						10	10	10	10	10	
Seattle		12	12	12	12	11½		11	12	11	12	
Portland, Oreg	11½	12		12	12	12	12	12½				
Los Angeles	15	15	15	15	15			15	15	15	15	15
San Francisco	14	14	14	14	14	14	14	14	14	14	14	14

Bureau of Agricultural Economics. Compiled from reports of the bureau secured through the cooperation of milk distributors, producers' associations, and municipal officers.

TABLE 459.—*Creamery butter production in factories in the United States, by States, 1918–1927*

State	1918	1919	1920	1921	1922	1923	1924	1925	1926	1927
	1,000 lbs.	*1,000 lbs.*	*1,000 lbs.*	*1,000 lbs.*	*1,000 lbs.*	*1,000 lbs.*	*1,000 lbs.*	*1,000 lbs.*	*1,000 lbs.*	*1,000 lbs.*
Me	1,453	1,141	727	719	596	402	568	479	547	517
N. H	459	397	300	305	309	424	271	137	90	72
Vt	10,858	10,677	13,253	14,919	12,289	11,935	12,294	9,372	8,305	6,732
Mass	2,439	2,849	3,198	3,895	2,999	1,844	1,790	2,026	2,150	2,514
R. I	70	65	58	77	76	76	105	68	75	100
Conn	813	930	877	1,165	986	753	820	675	617	550
N. England	16,092	16,059	18,413	21,080	17,255	15,434	15,848	12,757	11,784	10,485
N. Y	13,898	13,716	16,949	24,298	25,474	18,893	25,974	16,960	14,222	12,864
N. J	133	179	143	214	261	437	642	170	49	101
Pa	10,977	12,446	11,422	14,629	12,803	13,142	12,444	11,476	11,808	11,709
Middle Atlantic	25,008	26,341	28,514	39,141	38,538	32,472	39,060	28,606	26,079	24,674
Ohio	54,555	60,573	65,594	78,724	84,193	79,195	80,932	77,566	79,386	79,603
Ind	40,624	44,659	39,223	47,854	48,158	51,484	54,355	54,362	57,592	62,436
Ill	39,855	44,621	41,051	48,866	47,249	51,359	58,225	56,872	62,544	59,875
Mich	42,582	45,207	45,404	55,011	59,954	64,818	70,676	70,729	72,040	69,368
Wis	82,860	85,054	97,355	124,504	142,235	139,895	153,335	161,369	159,733	153,545
E. North Central	260,476	280,114	288,627	354,959	381,789	386,751	417,523	420,898	431,295	424,827
Minn	124,816	130,786	120,297	154,268	170,463	199,926	229,474	245,669	268,437	274,860
Iowa	86,943	87,915	84,290	106,516	129,778	141,407	159,378	156,361	168,827	177,224
Mo	30,175	38,411	35,228	42,422	46,565	51,818	56,801	55,953	66,861	62,549
N. Dak	12,050	14,697	13,419	16,177	21,675	23,355	28,515	31,500	34,898	32,462
S. Dak	18,536	17,479	14,071	18,886	21,146	27,447	24,643	29,193	29,814	32,843
Nebr	62,477	60,467	56,661	66,653	74,809	76,748	81,423	83,930	90,882	95,004
Kans	36,660	35,642	32,899	37,000	40,204	42,674	46,844	47,768	50,998	50,667
W. North Central	371,657	385,397	356,865	441,922	504,640	563,375	627,078	650,374	710,717	725,609
Del	270	253	350	395	203	154	150	80	67	50
Md	297	315	440	620	542	382	500	339	266	229
D. C	6	5	503	577	475	10	____	461	52	____
Va	1,372	1,597	2,210	2,833	3,118	4,231	4,614	3,842	4,378	5,881
W. Va	180	328	867	530	420	276	466	533	487	287
N. C	678	829	832	1,263	1,549	1,718	1,683	1,556	1,680	2,032
S. C	17	27	16	19	165	537	527	429	364	432
Ga	4	6	7	85	979	1,868	1,826	1,836	1,982	3,044
Fla	39	17	____	11	81	99	20	22	105	129
So. Atlantic	2,863	3,377	5,225	6,333	7,532	9,275	9,786	9,098	9,381	12,084
Ky	3,177	5,321	7,875	10,746	12,010	12,244	12,942	14,087	16,975	19,364
Tenn	2,068	3,735	5,903	8,707	9,164	11,463	12,762	11,286	11,826	17,190
Ala	912	696	398	742	917	831	889	1,086	991	1,237
Miss	2,274	2,477	2,626	4,286	5,778	5,715	5,648	4,895	6,896	7,920
E. South Central	8,431	12,229	16,802	24,481	27,869	30,253	32,191	31,354	36,688	45,711
Ark	427	363	345	586	731	996	1,259	1,174	1,325	1,710
La	70	46	55	160	87	185	125	90	92	324
Okla	8,167	10,481	9,596	10,427	11,142	14,065	14,421	15,841	19,664	23,617
Tex	4,982	8,289	9,125	11,257	10,179	10,956	11,997	10,866	14,594	24,276
W. South Central	13,646	19,179	19,121	22,430	22,139	26,202	27,802	27,971	35,675	49,927
Wyo	1,286	1,140	875	1,277	1,403	1,894	1,941	1,999	2,289	2,009
Colo	12,652	13,144	12,979	15,290	16,410	18,625	18,130	18,794	18,255	20,871
N. Mex	10	6	6	29	129	185	251	326	455	447
Idaho	4,330	4,514	4,660	4,935	7,582	9,883	13,431	15,101	18,456	20,918
Ariz	1,416	1,000	828	1,358	623	600	2,107	1,034	1,489	2,150
Utah	4,174	3,796	3,567	4,549	5,913	7,500	8,585	7,034	8,037	9,909
Nev	1,496	1,726	2,018	2,388	2,642	2,361	2,640	2,593	2,432	2,187
Mont	4,581	5,389	5,168	7,439	7,713	10,667	13,874	13,968	15,549	16,759
Mountain	29,945	30,715	30,101	37,265	42,415	51,715	60,959	60,849	66,962	75,250
Wash	16,407	18,487	23,751	23,228	24,239	26,666	29,331	25,673	28,914	29,870
Oreg	15,357	14,432	14,288	15,289	17,158	18,128	20,993	21,575	22,570	22,831
Calif	58,293	61,795	61,870	68,810	69,941	81,943	75,509	72,371	71,701	75,227
Pacific	90,057	94,714	99,909	107,327	111,338	126,737	125,833	119,619	123,185	127,928
Total	818,175	868,125	863,577	1,054,938	1,153,515	1,242,214	1,356,080	1,361,526	1,451,766	1,496,495

Bureau of Agricultural Economics. The compilations are made from reports of factories to the bureau.

TABLE 460.—*Creamery butter: Receipts, gross weight, at five markets, 1927–1928*

NEW YORK

Year	Jan.	Feb.	Mar.	Apr.	May	June	July	Aug.	Sept.	Oct.	Nov.	Dec.	Total
	1,000 lbs.	1,000 lbs.	1,000 lbs.	1,000 lbs.	1,000 lbs.	1,000 lbs.	1,000 lbs.	1,000 lbs.	1,000 lbs.	1,000 lbs.	1,000 lbs.	1,000 lbs.	1,000 lbs.
Av. 1921–1925	16,355	15,026	17,766	16,842	22,666	30,062	27,548	22,710	20,237	18,234	15,276	15,516	238,240
1927	17,345	17,878	20,455	20,528	26,579	32,262	28,782	26,606	20,344	19,013	16,041	15,489	261,322
1928	18,945	18,474	20,506	19,264	22,539	27,412	26,559	23,722	21,103	19,702	17,067	15,300	250,593

CHICAGO

Year	Jan.	Feb.	Mar.	Apr.	May	June	July	Aug.	Sept.	Oct.	Nov.	Dec.	Total
Av. 1921–1925	14,524	13,887	15,970	16,439	24,649	32,434	28,251	22,842	16,896	15,885	12,872	14,347	228,995
1927	14,885	14,810	18,412	21,084	26,918	32,140	27,780	22,380	16,037	14,513	13,004	13,237	235,200
1928	17,052	15,928	19,232	17,881	22,649	29,784	25,654	21,357	16,418	15,295	14,036	15,228	230,514

PHILADELPHIA

Year	Jan.	Feb.	Mar.	Apr.	May	June	July	Aug.	Sept.	Oct.	Nov.	Dec.	Total
Av. 1921–1925	4,762	4,350	5,136	4,986	6,425	9,210	7,523	6,295	5,173	5,058	4,472	4,696	68,086
1927	6,053	5,763	6,517	6,487	8,970	9,936	8,257	7,595	5,828	5,325	5,447	5,549	81,727
1928	6,716	6,343	6,725	6,429	7,578	10,077	8,640	7,735	6,690	6,404	5,532	5,626	84,495

BOSTON

Year	Jan.	Feb.	Mar.	Apr.	May	June	July	Aug.	Sept.	Oct.	Nov.	Dec.	Total
	1,000 lbs.	1,000 lbs.	1,000 lbs.	1,000 lbs.	1,000 lbs.	1,000 lbs.	1,000 lbs.	1,000 lbs.	1,000 lbs.	1,000 lbs.	1,000 lbs.	1,000 lbs.	1,000 lbs.
Av. 1921–1925	4,441	4,653	5,099	5,074	8,683	13,764	11,905	8,762	6,632	5,216	3,774	3,412	81,413
1927	4,590	5,366	6,129	6,558	10,143	12,245	11,932	8,847	5,949	4,636	3,865	4,357	84,617
1928	5,874	5,619	5,985	6,768	8,658	11,454	12,562	9,389	6,331	5,501	4,292	4,891	87,324

SAN FRANCISCO

Year	Jan.	Feb.	Mar.	Apr.	May	June	July	Aug.	Sept.	Oct.	Nov.	Dec.	Total
Av. 1921–1925	1,858	1,564	2,006	2,554	2,773	2,694	2,507	2,481	1,992	2,146	1,910	1,945	26,431
1927	1,883	1,685	2,120	2,641	2,925	3,190	2,919	2,627	1,897	1,938	1,538	1,346	26,709
1928	1,508	1,433	1,852	1,816	2,158	2,591	2,486	2,328	1,939	2,005	1,869	2,047	24,032

TOTAL, 1918–1928

Year	Jan.	Feb.	Mar.	Apr.	May	June	July	Aug.	Sept.	Oct.	Nov.	Dec.	Total
Av. 1921–1925	41,940	39,479	45,978	45,895	65,196	88,165	77,734	63,090	50,930	46,539	38,304	39,916	643,166
1918			49,308	45,048	50,851	83,058	79,149	60,456	46,708	51,169	38,277	35,797	[1] 539,821
1919	37,867	34,846	36,592	41,287	63,669	84,993	68,926	55,246	43,282	35,573	30,731	25,910	558,922
1920	29,827	29,009	35,314	28,002	43,571	66,043	71,167	53,714	43,551	33,378	26,917	26,050	486,543
1921	30,779	28,935	35,154	39,088	59,563	78,449	61,464	62,734	50,216	45,350	36,421	37,257	565,410
1922	41,775	39,041	45,101	40,716	67,063	92,632	76,918	60,172	45,577	40,595	37,372	38,401	625,363
1923	47,843	39,877	48,955	47,947	64,328	89,976	75,336	56,243	49,307	45,393	39,759	41,460	646,424
1924	44,476	47,756	52,328	51,690	67,572	91,742	92,036	67,959	56,247	49,760	35,868	39,471	696,905
1925	44,825	41,785	48,351	50,035	67,454	88,024	82,918	68,341	53,303	51,599	42,099	42,993	681,727
1926	46,809	46,809	54,646	53,990	64,653	89,993	81,053	59,849	52,985	45,280	40,588	42,825	679,480
1927	44,756	45,502	53,633	57,298	75,535	89,773	79,670	68,055	50,055	45,425	39,895	39,978	689,575
1928	50,095	47,797	54,300	52,158	63,582	81,318	75,901	64,531	52,481	48,907	42,796	43,092	676,958

Bureau of Agricultural Economics. Compiled from reports of bureau representatives in the various markets.

[1] 10-months' total, March to December, inclusive.

TABLE 461.—*Creamery butter: Production reported by factories, United States, 1917–1927*

Year	Jan.	Feb.	Mar.	Apr.	May	June	July	Aug.	Sept.	Oct.	Nov.	Dec.	Total
	1,000 lbs.	1,000 lbs.	1,000 lbs.	1,000 lbs.	1,000 lbs.	1,000 lbs.	1,000 lbs.	1,000 lbs.	1,000 lbs.	1,000 lbs.	1,000 lbs.	1,000 lbs.	1,000 lbs.
1917	43,997	38,459	47,371	53,809	75,108	98,898	94,151	83,936	76,744	56,176	42,705	48,157	759,511
1918	46,432	44,464	51,161	59,407	87,639	106,460	99,515	87,223	74,462	65,961	47,816	47,635	818,175
1919	53,604	45,748	56,227	68,892	105,346	120,762	106,156	86,245	70,508	60,128	46,446	48,063	868,125
1920	49,044	46,355	56,303	60,622	86,845	114,695	110,844	90,669	77,106	65,129	53,570	52,395	863,577
1921	58,906	56,556	67,677	82,763	119,077	130,633	111,898	111,638	89,932	84,374	70,024	71,460	1,054,938
1922	73,505	67,405	79,532	86,623	132,351	150,034	135,231	114,160	92,359	83,070	68,628	70,617	1,153,515
1923	83,688	74,134	88,311	100,547	134,350	158,371	138,278	120,802	102,273	89,297	74,909	77,254	1,242,214
1924	87,468	86,731	95,760	106,012	139,954	161,992	164,443	137,836	115,102	100,536	77,282	82,964	1,356,080
1925	87,121	80,218	92,302	107,023	145,478	164,253	158,920	136,738	108,325	104,520	85,492	91,136	1,361,526
1926	97,893	94,222	112,432	121,049	155,912	178,276	159,554	133,294	116,732	103,068	88,481	90,853	1,451,766
1927	97,965	95,522	111,451	126,415	168,808	188,792	170,484	146,808	113,546	102,399	86,058	88,247	1,496,495

Bureau of Agricultural Economics.

TABLE 462.—*Creamery butter:* [1] *Cold-storage holdings, United States, 1915–1928*

Year	Jan. 1	Feb. 1	Mar. 1	Apr. 1	May 1	June 1	July 1	Aug. 1	Sept. 1	Oct. 1	Nov. 1	Dec. 1
	1,000 pounds	1,000 pounds	1,000 pounds	1,000 pounds	1,000 pounds	1,000 pounds	1,000 pounds	1,000 pounds	1,000 pounds	1,000 pounds	1,000 pounds	1,000 pounds
Average: 1916–1920	48,697	32,673	19,510	9,849	6,288	14,395	59,134	100,967	112,059	106,552	93,700	73,147
1921–1925	45,981	30,730	19,446	9,477	5,488	16,076	66,008	106,191	118,381	110,116	91,649	67,999
1915								68,578	101,662	99,450	92,719	71,849
1916	48,977	31,139	15,033	3,346	1,082	7,017	53,863	102,537	105,836	100,522	85,260	67,292
1917	46,134	30,474	16,952	6,805	3,607	9,953	49,982	88,992	108,179	109,154	100,115	79,928
1918	50,726	26,618	18,808	14,629	9,536	12,698	49,140	88,305	99,334	87,883	80,874	65,111
1919	43,910	36,777	24,191	11,909	9,659	29,435	90,158	123,546	131,388	121,816	100,474	73,654
1920	53,737	38,359	22,568	12,555	7,554	12,872	52,526	101,455	115,558	113,385	101,778	79,750
1921	58,682	41,486	27,103	14,732	7,712	21,682	61,991	82,838	92,292	90,116	77,983	65,129
1922	48,412	35,047	22,582	9,113	3,830	13,202	67,410	103,151	112,039	96,680	73,857	47,773
1923	26,819	16,122	8,910	4,824	3,248	10,112	62,768	101,774	102,731	96,117	76,472	51,508
1924	30,299	15,246	9,847	7,842	8,913	22,348	74,184	134,118	156,440	153,494	135,018	100,832
1925	65,694	45,748	28,789	10,875	3,739	13,036	63,687	109,075	128,403	114,172	94,916	74,754
1926	52,785	39,381	26,313	17,392	17,527	30,561	86,897	131,152	138,151	125,342	100,871	64,381
1927	34,347	17,952	7,952	3,044	3,436	25,404	89,996	145,147	163,701	147,396	118,679	83,224
1928	46,289	28,273	14,404	5,716	5,109	15,952	69,750	120,437	136,175	128,071	105,811	70,985

Bureau of Agricultural Economics. Compiled from reports from cold-storage establishments.

[1] Quantities given are net weights.

33023°—29——63

TABLE 463.—Butter: Receipts, gross weight at five markets, by State of origin, 1922–1928

NEW YORK

[All figures in 1,000 pounds]

State of origin	1922	1923	1924	1925	1926	1927	1928 Total	Jan.	Feb.	Mar.	Apr.	May	June	July	Aug.	Sept.	Oct.	Nov.	Dec.
Minnesota	80,589	84,944	74,166	57,206	57,038	57,081	44,654	3,532	3,297	4,399	3,823	3,578	4,396	4,116	4,349	3,584	3,425	2,658	3,497
Iowa	43,489	48,440	57,781	56,833	62,093	56,935	68,676	4,242	4,811	5,020	4,988	6,022	7,728	8,281	6,800	5,961	6,238	4,784	3,801
Illinois	33,538	33,830	35,039	39,440	40,037	37,954	35,816	3,864	3,263	3,426	3,179	3,363	3,554	2,946	3,072	2,316	2,070	2,477	2,286
Nebraska	24,074	20,359	24,811	25,088	27,157	28,457	28,138	1,695	2,142	2,457	2,384	3,037	3,093	3,118	2,456	2,326	2,132	1,824	1,474
Ohio	10,631	9,834	7,350	7,121	6,674	7,565	7,498	398	474	341	314	511	950	1,036	975	733	661	779	326
Wisconsin	12,803	11,771	13,730	16,903	17,792	17,615	15,459	1,598	1,491	1,763	1,804	1,432	1,327	975	1,067	854	1,063	842	1,243
New York	9,598	6,130	8,185	16,974	6,177	5,385	5,978	242	243	316	251	425	839	958	592	778	584	448	302
Michigan	7,213	7,075	11,265	15,498	13,669	13,566	15,227	1,088	1,047	954	899	1,373	2,090	1,814	1,474	1,682	1,064	1,074	668
Indiana	5,991	5,222	3,930	5,958	5,209	5,417	5,150	312	216	182	209	425	986	613	491	587	487	347	313
Missouri	3,674	4,649	3,988	5,396	6,045	6,540	6,182	563	325	439	344	547	704	408	404	765	646	382	455
Pennsylvania	2,349	1,279	859	525	1,176	1,025	1,074	94	77	176	4	31	22	124	115	125	66	121	119
Tennessee	1,185	1,132	87	1,034	1,881	2,369	2,305	237	192	244	176	181	176	175	302	174	280	96	92
California	364	288	----	102	2,065	161	223	78	95	45	----	----	2	3	(¹)	(¹)	(¹)	(¹)	(¹)
Kansas	429	1,294	1,064	847	204	3,808	4,797	388	445	392	376	548	429	527	423	471	315	251	232
Massachusetts	417	259	647	345	417	223	66	1	17	11	12	(¹)	(¹)	3	(¹)	1	2	13	1
Virginia	652	417	684	432	1,218	473	535	13	16	11	4	66	74	132	38	35	66	48	24
South Dakota	353	260	270	279	710	1,129	1,290	120	61	13	2	88	200	303	229	122	58	24	111
Kentucky	701	517	954	463	109	978	884	22	29	3	(¹)	(¹)	182	140	152	136	76	31	23
North Dakota	246	134	397	193	22	573	2,397	211	106	89	132	211	281	344	200	191	263	209	160
Vermont	27	46	----	58	104	52	48	----	----	----	----	----	30	7	1	10	----	----	----
Maryland	380	151	132	276	104	131	283	4	4	25	50	38	44	8	15	40	59	24	25
North Carolina	195	358	198	193	52	340	415	42	12	25	26	38	46	47	67	39	35	18	20
Georgia	95	98	97	178	171	38	86	12	1	----	34	----	2	2	1	(¹)	(¹)	2	9
Alabama	124	234	70	138	224	220	370	40	29	30	34	56	54	33	48	16	7	6	17
Washington	29	194	----	27	466	310	26	2	(¹)	----	1	----	(¹)	(¹)	(¹)	1	----	----	----
New Jersey	80	129	----	22	663	256	812	63	32	54	8	143	71	72	125	46	31	57	(¹)
Mississippi	54	142	----	203	535	1,251	502	----	----	----	23	94	92	46	76	90	21	147	30
Oklahoma	----	261	----	327	19	363	296	28	5	----	26	----	----	48	24	20	31	29	21
Montana	----	----	465	37	513	288	1,222	50	26	----	134	83	40	283	225	(¹)	40	82	51
Other States	496	686	852	181	146	730	403	6	20	45	24	238	----	(¹)	(¹)	----	----	70	----
Canada	1,828	3,631	950	1,850	----	89	74	----	----	----	----	----	----	----	----	----	----	24	----
Total	241,604	243,764	248,759	244,127	252,742	261,322	250,593	18,945	18,474	20,506	19,264	22,539	27,412	26,559	23,722	21,103	19,702	17,067	15,300

(¹) Less than 500 pounds.

Wisconsin	74,773	70,588	79,928	75,941	72,200	64,611	58,108	4,055	3,807	4,430	4,615	6,071	8,098	6,824	5,685	4,359	3,996	3,198	2,970
Minnesota	37,483	39,611	46,767	54,859	43,569	48,057	50,230	3,704	3,642	4,860	3,882	4,085	5,427	4,745	4,412	3,680	3,434	3,806	4,553
Iowa	40,735	42,108	46,896	46,150	41,092	39,347	39,948	2,682	2,979	3,417	3,442	4,265	5,147	4,641	3,793	2,778	2,511	2,313	1,980
Nebraska	16,958	17,433	20,054	19,361	22,505	17,090	19,498	1,598	1,341	1,564	1,449	1,786	2,752	2,332	1,597	1,079	1,188	1,204	1,608
South Dakota	9,639	14,249	15,971	18,151	16,402	16,513	18,270	1,368	1,291	1,776	1,638	1,627	2,492	2,188	1,676	1,345	1,054	844	971
Kansas	5,935	10,300	11,098	7,864	8,036	9,989	12,981	1,468	879	821	963	1,364	1,668	1,431	1,066	848	650	970	853
Illinois	7,465	7,392	8,870	5,819	6,632	8,057	6,371	222	216	355	198	646	1,371	1,168	863	474	431	242	185
Missouri	8,959	11,188	11,975	9,678	10,411	13,484	11,508	774	597	629	582	1,202	1,013	1,033	1,278	1,047	1,106	943	1,304
North Dakota	3,049	3,418	6,301	8,511	6,114	4,181	2,919	105	311	290	249	227	289	263	232	146	395	192	220
Oklahoma	1,733	1,894	2,144	2,735	4,392	4,510	2,329	413	379	164	210	253	271	182	201	104	61	13	78
Colorado	1,317	1,239	1,829	430	828	678	1,315	146	104	163	85	150	181	200	111	86	43		46
Ohio	874	425	360	619	417	194	128	3	1	4	2	5	(1)	22	6	26	29	5	25
Michigan	1,609	1,966	1,761	1,474	1,297	1,024	923	99	47	50	28	45	177	72	48	97	133	99	28
Indiana	1,027	1,109	1,102	805	867	749	943	88	89	121	31	20	175	129	59	14	45	54	118
Kentucky	291	871	560	539	957	1,888	1,894	109	107	127	65	201	287	225	140	274	162	72	125
Texas	35	216	102	78	212	3,680	2,322	193	113	127	349	594	397	173	120	34	54	55	113
Montana	299	643	1,077	343	107	194	165		3	28	76	48	8	2					
Tennessee	34	112	35	137	126	438	113	11	13	5	7	12	(1)	3	36	23	(1)	1	2
Mississippi	298	144	198	66	44	31	49	3			5	15	13	5	1				7
California	192	319	77		(1)	76	26		2	24									
Pennsylvania	19	36	103	55		2	15					(1)							15
Idaho	34	233	202		64		7						7						
New York	49	25	153	69	35	31	275	1		274	(1)								(1)
Other States	218	158	520	154	196	376	177	10	7	3	5	26	18	16	33	4	3	25	27
Canada	47	215		470															
Total	[2]213,101	225,892	258,083	254,308	236,546	235,200	230,514	17,052	15,928	19,232	17,881	22,649	29,784	25,654	21,357	16,418	15,295	14,036	15,228

[1] Not over 500 pounds.
[2] Includes 29,000 pounds from New Zealand.

TABLE 463.—Butter: Receipts, gross weight at five markets, by State of origin, 1922–1928—Continued

PHILADELPHIA

[All figures in 1,000 pounds.]

State of origin	1922	1923	1924	1925	1926	1927	1928												
							Total	Jan.	Feb.	Mar.	April	May	June	July	Aug.	Sept.	Oct.	Nov.	Dec.
Minnesota	24,594	27,194	34,753	32,168	40,936	45,478	54,427	3,974	4,158	4,710	4,290	5,021	5,927	5,242	5,133	4,293	4,170	3,718	3,791
Illinois	9,973	11,753	10,874	11,156	7,766	4,807	3,811	581	218	316	306	310	415	205	279	294	342	304	241
Ohio	4,309	3,437	3,437	3,224	3,505	3,162	2,665	297	218	174	135	236	363	297	190	156	244	217	138
Pennsylvania	3,697	2,571	2,392	1,735	1,268	1,097	731	49	35	52	80	55	80	64	80	64	87	24	61
Indiana	4,447	3,757	2,297	1,688	1,848	1,736	1,502	215	138	149	192	111	61	103	115	141	98	96	83
Wisconsin	4,710	4,119	3,446	2,963	4,305	6,313	3,307	256	289	233	241	178	660	394	208	238	190	120	300
Michigan	1,605	1,812	1,926	6,415	3,418	1,835	1,356	104	69	56	67	96	341	444	21	54	18	29	57
New York	2,275	5,673	2,221	2,221	1,262	596	690	173	186	22	—	24	135	—	36	70	—	44	—
Iowa	1,391	1,314	1,677	2,313	4,288	5,244	4,808	224	308	304	420	446	509	458	461	389	492	437	360
Missouri	483	942	722	637	1,490	1,444	1,921	134	93	165	105	153	196	184	214	201	140	169	167
Tennessee	1,754	915	915	722	1,101	1,101	1,742	104	39	46	21	169	311	301	266	191	149	72	73
Virginia	1,145	1,247	1,638	1,196	1,027	935	881	36	23	21	28	27	173	104	128	141	58	71	71
California	357	285	224	245	287	243	4	—	—	—	—	—	—	—	—	—	—	—	—
New Jersey	57	42	19	24	44	38	101	4	16	5	25	46	2	—	(1)	—	—	—	—
North Dakota	253	71	44	—	40	—	—	—	—	—	—	—	—	—	—	—	—	—	—
Delaware	258	—	21	189	1	6	1	—	1	5	(1)	—	—	—	—	—	—	—	—
Nebraska	1,677	1,757	2,409	3,510	4,957	4,341	4,271	454	395	366	379	418	414	536	409	276	267	173	184
Maryland	453	1,057	137	138	242	205	98	16	16	16	22	76	(1)	3	2	2	13	12	—
South Dakota	6	11	110	76	158	263	418	3	49	27	77	—	92	3	24	2	7	8	8
Kentucky	159	119	187	57	221	313	212	—	7	3	2	102	66	63	(1)	64	3	2	50
Kansas	86	223	320	628	127	370	384	4	5	3	5	1	84	2	20	61	77	—	21
North Carolina	1	14	7	26	87	33	5	—	(1)	—	—	—	1	1	2	(1)	—	—	—
West Virginia	93	160	145	146	197	277	225	17	20	19	13	20	40	21	16	17	21	15	6
Mississippi	346	401	311	115	276	493	695	47	57	9	—	61	180	204	117	20	28	—	15
Other States	140	151	588	299	444	460	205	24	3	3	21	28	27	6	13	16	—	21	—
Canada	—	252	391	173	—	—	—	—	—	—	—	—	—	—	—	—	—	—	—
Total	64,269	68,598	76,731	72,064	79,345	81,727	84,495	6,716	6,343	6,725	6,429	7,578	10,077	8,640	7,735	6,690	6,404	5,532	5,626

BOSTON

State of origin	1922	1923	1924	1925	1926	1927	1928												
							Total	Jan.	Feb.	Mar.	April	May	June	July	Aug.	Sept.	Oct.	Nov.	Dec.
Illinois	33,273	33,517	25,384	13,555	11,766	13,557	12,251	1,572	913	1,057	1,098	1,266	1,264	1,383	852	706	808	634	698
Minnesota	11,213	15,880	22,744	26,975	30,948	30,830	33,652	1,596	2,161	2,330	2,708	3,034	4,079	4,661	3,865	3,044	2,315	1,716	2,143
Vermont	6,339	5,854	5,923	4,071	3,075	1,974	1,974	155	139	211	319	259	300	167	115	64	101	72	73
New York	5,776	5,578	5,468	5,769	3,327	2,607	1,626	206	113	167	52	172	154	243	206	55	91	72	95
Iowa	3,982	3,023	5,361	4,360	4,616	3,969	4,261	164	151	220	294	490	495	672	749	387	323	163	153
Ohio	4,041	3,064	3,282	2,661	2,046	2,751	2,879	170	141	93	75	287	392	401	391	296	289	166	178

Receipts at markets, by States of origin — Continued.

State																		
Indiana	2,554	2,722	2,436	1,434	1,122	1,576	1,805	194	74	33	10	114	292	402	197	116	106	107	163
Nebraska	2,152	3,274	6,378	8,086	8,860	10,335	12,159	762	738	901	963	1,287	1,627	2,082	1,087	633	703	679	697
Michigan	2,533	1,555	2,394	1,867	1,928	1,675	1,737	109	9	47	71	125	637	680	197	51	35	27	1
South Dakota	2,133	1,891	2,450	3,070	2,940	3,151	2,985	140	200	165	159	295	445	494	512	144	93	45	107
Missouri	884	646	1,404	3,170	3,151	3,526	3,959	195	236	126	306	425	672	494	465	334	182	265	289
Wisconsin	2,215	1,813	1,983	989	735	346	168	180	68	50	225	235	450	385	221	103	75	116	84
Massachusetts	870	702	723	19	22	14	94	20	(¹)	3	3	6	29	3	3	(¹)	(¹)	2	23
New Hampshire	467	263	143	143	119	240	95	137	(¹)	2	5	1	2	3	(¹)	1	(¹)	(¹)	2
Pennsylvania	303	188	26	46	30	228	298	21	20	(¹)	2	1	1	1	(¹)	1	21	53	(¹)
Kentucky	132	72	91				14	137					174	120	65	119	103	38	65
Kansas	404	402	507	1,048	1,705	1,532	1,801	202	96	248	381	174	218	6	1	2	1		
Maine	197	87	196	192	116	167	86	30	21	2	3	2	3	120		3	7	(¹)	(¹)
Oklahoma	319	166	288	151	463	664	575	6	23	21	15	100	67	80	67	30	60	67	41
North Dakota	302	1,345	1,230	2,167	1,871	1,871	1,227	203	63	120	67	22	49	131	49	161	106	46	79
Montana	23	49	220	39	183	183	14		14										
Other States	361	231	261	201	754	211	1,616	112	236	90	196	317	170	170	130	64	89	25	
Canada		137	29		5	1	2												
Total	80,473	82,659	86,921	82,476	83,243	84,617	87,324	5,874	5,619	5,985	6,768	8,658	11,454	12,562	9,389	6,331	5,501	4,292	4,891

SAN FRANCISCO

State																		
California	23,352	21,805	22,984	21,587	20,701	18,976	17,732	1,150	1,217	1,721	1,704	1,692	1,701	1,454	1,439	1,242	1,439	1,499	1,474
Oregon	585	1,177	948	1,195	2,306	2,253	1,796	44	8	6	51	195	379	399	275	103	104	84	148
Washington	332	682	606	469	327	300	182				2	13	49	43	75	7	7		6
Nevada	388	293	258	252	63	113	74	118	63	58	134	19	20	11	7	19		
Idaho	402	502	490	1,043	1,191	1,722	1,255	147	97	73	2	83	224	135	141	99	141	59	187
Montana	155	361	700	1,895	2,331	2,173	2,150	21	21	49	58	52	294	135	273	340	254	192	197
Utah	136	179	158	98	95	223	384	23					84	294	79	79	53	35	35
Illinois	118		1	204					27	1	1				57				
Colorado	120	30	21	545	192	406	260	27		2		(¹)	20	44	86	57			
Nebraska	46	25	47	349	55	77	33						7		24				
Minnesota	74		172	298	339	441	165	24						96	69				
Iowa	51	24		237															
Other States	157	117	26	284	4	25	1							1					6
Canada		316		326															
Total	25,016	25,511	26,411	28,752	27,604	26,709	24,032	1,508	1,433	1,852	1,816	2,158	2,591	2,486	2,328	1,939	2,005	1,869	2,047

Bureau of Agricultural Economics. Compiled from reports of bureau representatives in the various markets.

¹ Not over 500 pounds.

TABLE 464—*Butter: International trade, average 1909-1913, annual 1924-1927*

Country	Average 1909-1913		1924		1925		1926		1927, preliminary	
	Imports	Exports	Imports	Exports	Imports	Exports	Imports	Exports	Imports	Exports
PRINCIPAL EXPORTING COUNTRIES	*1,000 pounds*	*1,000 pounds*	*1,000 pounds*	*1,000 pounds*	*1,000 pounds*	*1,000 pounds*	*1,000 pounds*	*1,000 pounds*	*1,000 pounds*	*1,000 pounds*
Denmark	6,241	195,530	2,049	272,033	1,744	270,674	2,816	292,115	2,241	315,721
New Zealand	47	38,761	1	142,179	13	139,476	16	130,820	0	163,020
Australia	46	77,859	1 2,368	111,086	1 13	128,494	1 3,726	83,016	1 10,935	75,089
Netherlands	4,987	75,133	3,613	76,570	5,757	87,598	3,347	100,428	4,042	105,714
Argentina	113	6,934	3	65,437	6	59,282	15	64,234	3	46,808
Irish Free State	0	0	8,757	51,187	9,381	44,975	6,501	56,099	4,836	65,576
Russia	2,202	150,294	1 339	149,456	1 191	155,476	1 263	59,408	1 428	1 71,777
Finland	2,370	26,337	14	18,184	4	29,081	196	29,127	2	33,238
Canada	3,388	3,973	1,174	22,344	100	26,647	9,152	9,814	11,209	2,696
Sweden	330	45,870	1,234	11,827	406	20,333	79	33,353	63	40,707
Latvia 1	0	0	2	8,084	10	15,772	32	22,343	28	23,724
Estonia	0	0	0	7,025	0	14,208	0	19,161	0	21,839
Italy	972	7,870	1,002	6,436	259	8,009	153	5,679	2,084	2,805
Spain	939	259	344	423	295	583	309	408	1 337	1 303
PRINCIPAL IMPORTING COUNTRIES										
United Kingdom	455,489	1,179	570,761	2,239	616,300	1,445	626,325	1,688	626,003	1,703
Germany	111,441	498	117,896	59	212,993	304	215,584	264	238,683	190
France	13,713	40,769	6,176	7,997	6,655	8,211	1,499	11,040	12,078	23,501
Belgium	14,024	3,125	10,322	543	9,191	871	5,013	1,899	2,549	2,966
Switzerland	11,106	44	19,993	252	19,092	177	17,818	131	18,727	159
United States	1,647	4,125	19,405	8,257	7,212	5,343	8,029	5,483	8,460	4,343
Dutch East Indies	4,152	0	7,092	0	7,321	0	10,115	0	2 7,289	0
Greece	206	8	10,727	0	1 914	0	1,009	0	1,625	0
Czechoslovakia	0	0	3,637	58	1,203	310	1,160	334	1,682	370
Norway	976	3,137	1,276	419	1,467	468	2,369	338	2,513	25
Austria	3 6,281	3 4,267	3,864	1 10	2,856	1 334	4,648	583	4,230	440
Cuba	1,459	0	2,443	0	2,655	0	2,169	0	------	------
Egypt	2,350	4 166	2,354	57	2,384	56	2,839	44	2,575	67
China	5 1,677	0	1,551	0	1,697	0	1,762	0	1,530	0
Peru	462	20	1,814	10	1,653	9	1,844	6	1,441	9
Algeria	1,946	9	1,553	36	1,830	32	1,507	53	1 2,124	1 48
Philippine Islands	1,665	0	1,298	0	991	0	1,188	0	1,072	0
Trinidad and Tobago	847	0	1,049	0	918	0	1,038	0	1,344	0
Union of South Africa	3,913	26	1,579	411	705	793	48	262	1,244	242
Total 33 countries	654,989	686,193	805,690	862,619	916,216	918,961	932,569	928,130	971,377	1,003,080

Division of Statistical and Historical Research. Official sources, except where otherwise noted. Butter includes all butter made from milk, melted and renovated butter, but does not include margarine, cocoa butter, or ghee.

1 International Yearbook of Agricultural Statistics.
2 Java and Madura only.
3 Average for Austria-Hungary.
4 2-year average.
5 4-year average.

TABLE 465.—*Butterfat: Estimated price per pound, received by producers, in the United States, 1920-1928*

Year	Jan.	Feb.	Mar.	Apr.	May	June	July	Aug.	Sept.	Oct.	Nov.	Dec.
	Cents	Cents	Cents	Cents	Cents	Cents	Cents	Cents	Cents	Cents	Cents	Cents
1920									55.3	56.3	56.5	49.4
1921	48.4	42.8	44.9	41.8	29.7	27.6	31.6	36.8	36.2	40.0	40.6	39.9
1922	33.4	34.0	34.5	33.4	33.4	33.9	34.8	32.8	35.5	39.2	44.2	50.3
1923	47.0	44.9	44.9	46.0	40.3	36.9	36.7	38.7	42.2	44.1	47.8	49.2
1924	50.6	48.5	46.4	40.8	37.6	37.1	37.8	35.8	36.6	36.6	37.0	41.1
1925	40.6	37.9	41.5	40.5	40.3	39.9	40.5	41.3	42.6	47.1	47.8	47.6
1926	45.2	43.1	42.9	40.4	39.1	39.3	38.6	38.6	40.5	42.4	44.8	47.9
1927	46.9	46.8	48.0	47.1	43.6	40.8	40.3	39.4	41.6	44.4	45.8	47.8
1928	48.5	46.0	46.5	45.4	44.4	43.5	43.3	44.3	46.5	47.0	47.6	49.2

Bureau of Agricultural Economics. Based on returns from special price reporters. Quotations cover butterfat for all uses.

TABLE 466.—*Butter, 92-score creamery: Average wholesale price, at five leading markets, 1927–1928*

NEW YORK

Year	Jan.	Feb.	Mar.	Apr.	May	June	July	Aug.	Sept.	Oct.	Nov.	Dec.	Average
	Cents	Cents	Cents	Cents	Cents	Cents	Cents	Cents	Cents	Cents	Cents	Cents	Cents
Average: 1910–1914	33	31	31	29	27	27	27	28	30	31	34	35	30
1921–1925	47	45	46	43	39	38	40	41	43	46	49	49	44
1927	49	52	50	50	43	43	42	42	46	48	50	52	47
1928	49	47	49	45	45	44	45	47	49	48	51	50	47

CHICAGO

Year	Jan.	Feb.	Mar.	Apr.	May	June	July	Aug.	Sept.	Oct.	Nov.	Dec.	Average
Av. 1921–1925	45	45	46	41	36	38	38	39	42	44	48	48	42
1927	48	50	49	48	41	40	40	41	45	46	48	51	46
1928	47	46	48	44	43	43	44	46	47	46	49	49	46

SAN FRANCISCO

Year	Jan.	Feb.	Mar.	Apr.	May	June	July	Aug.	Sept.	Oct.	Nov.	Dec.	Average
Av. 1921–1925	43	44	40	37	37	40	41	43	46	47	46	46	42
1927	47	48	45	42	41	42	42	44	47	48	49	48	45
1928	46	45	43	40	42	43	46	48	50	51	49	50	46

PHILADELPHIA

Year	Jan.	Feb.	Mar.	Apr.	May	June	July	Aug.	Sept.	Oct.	Nov.	Dec.	Average
1927	50	52	51	51	44	43	43	43	47	49	51	53	48
1928	50	48	50	46	46	45	46	48	50	49	52	51	48

BOSTON

Year	Jan.	Feb.	Mar.	Apr.	May	June	July	Aug.	Sept.	Oct.	Nov.	Dec.	Average
1927	50	52	51	51	44	43	42	42	46	48	48	50	47
1928	49	47	50	46	45	44	45	47	49	48	50	50	48

Bureau of Agricultural Economics. Compiled from Urner-Barry reports, 1910–1917 (New York), average of daily range; subsequently from reports of bureau representatives in the markets. Earlier data available in 1925 Yearbook, p. 1094, Table 501, and 1927 Yearbook, p. 1082.

TABLE 467.—*Butter: Average export price per pound in Copenhagen, Denmark, 1914–1928*

Year	Jan.	Feb.	Mar.	Apr.	May	June	July	Aug.	Sept.	Oct.	Nov.	Dec.	Av.
	Cents	Cents	Cents	Cents	Cents	Cents	Cents	Cents	Cents	Cents	Cents	Cents	Cents
Average: 1910–1914	25.8	26.2	26.4	24.7	23.3	23.7	24.6	25.0	26.1	27.2	26.5	27.2	25.6
1921–1925	39.2	39.3	39.5	36.8	34.0	34.3	37.3	40.0	41.2	42.1	41.6	39.5	38.7
1914	26.1	25.6	25.6	24.1	23.4	23.9	25.9	24.4	25.0	27.8	27.3	29.9	25.8
1915	29.6	26.9	28.0	27.6	29.6	29.1	31.0	32.6	34.7	41.6	40.5	36.6	32.3
1916	33.8	35.4	37.8	36.8	36.3	35.7	36.7	40.1	42.1	42.6	44.3	44.9	38.9
1917	45.3	39.6	38.4	37.2	38.6	40.5	45.0	49.7	54.6	65.4	68.4	65.5	49.0
1918	64.2	63.7	64.0	65.0	65.3	64.7	65.1	65.0	62.0	58.3	75.6	76.0	65.7
1919	75.8	73.8	72.4	71.1	58.2	50.8	48.4	46.5	54.7	53.8	59.5	52.1	59.8
1920	48.9	42.1	49.2	49.8	44.2	44.8	42.4	42.9	43.6	45.7	44.7	44.0	45.2
1921	42.4	39.3	40.4	43.9	33.5	32.4	38.3	41.1	36.4	38.3	39.9	31.8	38.1
1922	31.1	31.0	32.9	33.8	33.5	37.0	39.4	39.1	41.1	40.7	39.9	39.7	36.6
1923	40.5	41.3	41.0	34.5	29.5	29.3	30.7	34.7	40.3	38.9	39.4	41.4	36.8
1924	40.0	39.5	36.9	31.3	36.4	33.4	37.8	41.1	42.3	46.1	44.2	46.8	39.6
1925	42.0	45.4	46.1	40.6	36.9	39.4	40.5	44.2	45.7	46.5	44.6	37.8	42.5
1926	36.5	40.2	38.8	36.2	34.8	35.7	35.4	36.1	36.6	36.3	34.9	37.1	36.6
1927	36.4	39.3	36.8	35.2	32.9	33.2	32.2	35.0	39.6	39.4	41.2	33.0	36.6
1928	35.4	37.5	40.0	36.8	35.4	34.9	36.4	38.0	40.2	39.5	40.6	42.4	38.1

Bureau of Agricultural Economics. Danish Butter Journal (Smør Tidende) official quotations. For earlier years, 1882–1913, see the United States Department of Agriculture Yearbook, 1923, p. 923.

Conversion from Danish quotations in øre per pound (1.1023 pounds) at par of exchange (100 øre = 26.8 cents) to July, 1914; beginning July, 1914, to December, 1926, inclusive, from weekly quotations in kroner per 100 kg., at average monthly exchange rate as quoted by Federal Reserve Board. Beginning January, 1927, to date at par of exchange.

TABLE 468.—*Cheese, whole milk American Cheddar: Production in the United States, 1917–1927*

Year	Jan.	Feb.	Mar.	Apr.	May	June	July	Aug.	Sept.	Oct.	Nov.	Dec.	Total
	1,000 lbs.	1,000 lbs.	1,000 lbs.	1,000 lbs.	1,000 lbs.	1,000 lbs.	1,000 lbs.	1,000 lbs.	1,000 lbs.	1,000 lbs.	1,000 lbs.	1,000 lbs.	1,000 lbs.
1917	8,519	9,415	11,918	17,577	28,932	38,796	35,296	32,248	37,613	22,303	14,262	8,070	264,949
1918	8,143	7,860	11,992	17,931	31,285	40,184	34,332	29,996	25,424	18,862	12,172	9,097	247,278
1919	12,065	12,964	20,118	22,751	35,958	45,708	36,574	32,049	27,366	24,223	14,216	11,152	295,144
1920	10,457	11,509	14,954	18,856	29,832	41,376	34,313	26,787	22,935	20,054	13,308	10,303	254,684
1921	11,889	12,857	17,678	23,521	34,556	36,444	26,977	27,652	23,612	21,496	13,426	11,618	261,726
1922	12,837	13,927	18,774	21,740	31,349	36,254	33,265	29,496	25,581	25,785	18,382	15,416	282,806
1923	15,092	15,326	20,184	24,014	32,942	41,382	38,288	31,822	28,648	25,566	18,236	16,608	308,108
1924	17,718	18,886	22,955	24,597	33,657	43,517	40,716	33,602	30,539	26,210	17,252	15,046	324,695
1925	16,834	17,991	21,598	26,889	38,012	45,782	43,706	37,659	31,548	28,253	20,349	18,619	347,240
1926	19,519	19,984	25,216	29,221	38,598	46,320	40,164	33,239	28,809	23,164	16,386	15,295	335,915
1927	16,660	17,085	21,318	24,533	34,704	41,489	38,195	31,944	25,783	23,012	16,717	16,337	307,777

Bureau of Agricultural Economics.

TABLE 469.—*Cheese, whole-milk American Cheddar: Production, United States, by States, 1919–1927*

State	1919	1920	1921	1922	1923	1924	1925	1926	1927
	1,000 pounds	1,000 pounds	1,000 pounds	1,000 pounds	1,000 pounds	1,000 pounds	1,000 pounds	1,000 pounds	1,000 pounds
Vermont	2,960	1,382	1,380	954	1,200	1,755	1,120	1,114	629
Other New England States	12	3	79	----	----	34	6	128	96
New England	2,972	1,385	1,459	954	1,200	1,789	1,126	1,242	725
New York	46,510	30,829	37,970	47,726	37,448	36,608	38,401	31,663	24,931
New Jersey	446	130		634	196	155			
Pennsylvania	2,928	2,673	3,208	2,209	2,497	1,750	1,349	1,681	1,750
Middle Atlantic	49,884	33,632	41,178	50,569	40,141	38,513	39,750	33,344	26,681
Ohio	963	659	654	195	128	366	253	269	303
Indiana	70	42	117	62	78	306	198	234	701
Illinois	2,538	999	1,751	2,401	2,875	2,498	2,444	2,902	2,836
Michigan	5,188	4,032	5,064	3,657	4,342	5,867	5,844	6,827	5,906
Wisconsin	201,836	188,548	182,777	193,376	226,916	235,186	258,684	248,059	227,447
East North Central	210,595	194,280	190,363	199,691	234,339	244,223	267,423	258,291	237,193
Minnesota	8,998	5,502	5,693	5,291	7,229	9,790	8,419	8,984	7,556
Iowa	859	545	313	344	361	530	501	383	410
Missouri	302	380	382	96	224	105	252	312	484
Others	97	31	141	190	186	354	477	912	1,301
West North Central	10,256	6,458	6,529	5,921	8,000	10,779	9,649	10,591	9,751
South Atlantic	387	220	184	226	277	276	155	110	164
Tennessee	51	26	50	71	284	398	321	172	154
Others			29		51		37		15
East South Central	51	26	79	71	335	398	358	172	169
West South Central	3	----	15	51	----	37	----	5	----
Wyoming	1,612	1,180	1,543	3,416	1,791	1,883	1,923	2,118	2,067
Idaho	2,578	1,722	2,117	3,368	5,311	7,343	7,320	7,986	7,434
Utah	907	849	1,027	3,219	2,139	2,162	1,753	1,809	2,205
Montana	269	233	113	259	641	792	1,296	1,484	1,435
Others	476	231	529	187	318	701	482	650	1,390
Mountain	5,842	4,215	5,329	10,449	10,200	12,881	12,774	14,047	14,531
Washington	1,745	1,143	1,910	2,928	2,762	2,998	3,076	3,130	2,924
Oregon	8,348	8,282	8,777	8,720	7,678	9,951	9,903	11,517	11,435
California	5,661	5,043	5,904	3,226	3,082	2,850	3,026	3,466	4,204
Pacific	15,154	14,468	16,591	14,874	13,522	15,799	16,005	18,113	18,563
Total	295,144	254,684	261,727	282,806	308,014	324,695	347,240	335,915	307,777

Bureau of Agricultural Economics. The compilations are made from reports of factories to the bureau.

TABLE 470.—*Cheese: Receipts, gross weight, at five markets, 1927–1928*

NEW YORK

Year	Jan.	Feb.	Mar.	Apr.	May	June	July	Aug.	Sept.	Oct.	Nov.	Dec.	Total
	1,000 lbs.	*1,000 lbs.*	*1,000 lbs.*	*1,000 lbs.*	*1,000 lbs.*	*1,000 lbs.*	*1,000 lbs.*	*1,000 lbs.*	*1,000 lbs.*	*1,000 lbs.*	*1,000 lbs.*	*1,000 lbs.*	*1,000 lbs.*
Av. 1921–1925	3,064	2,954	3,531	3,772	4,480	5,346	5,821	4,441	4,052	4,015	3,689	2,962	48,127
1927	2,847	2,844	3,284	3,505	3,502	4,814	5,228	4,824	5,108	4,398	3,367	3,216	46,937
1928	3,695	3,403	3,944	4,017	4,158	4,865	4,495	4,326	4,085	4,476	3,408	3,400	48,272

CHICAGO

Year	Jan.	Feb.	Mar.	Apr.	May	June	July	Aug.	Sept.	Oct.	Nov.	Dec.	Total
Av. 1921–1925	7,398	7,512	8,629	8,822	10,699	12,525	11,833	11,293	9,915	10,599	8,480	7,970	115,674
1927	7,170	9,104	9,145	10,210	13,263	11,940	13,139	12,557	11,915	9,918	7,487	7,785	123,633
1928	7,713	7,184	7,401	7,615	7,626	9,152	10,792	9,450	9,108	8,639	6,930	5,654	97,264

PHILADELPHIA

Year	Jan.	Feb.	Mar.	Apr.	May	June	July	Aug.	Sept.	Oct.	Nov.	Dec.	Total
Av. 1921–1925	1,093	1,052	1,255	1,216	1,655	2,166	2,179	1,945	1,888	2,013	1,393	1,065	18,920
1927	1,140	1,409	1,047	1,290	2,041	2,357	2,409	1,899	2,027	2,183	1,362	1,232	20,396
1928	1,295	1,261	1,343	1,312	1,796	2,092	2,821	1,752	2,096	2,405	1,693	1,173	21,039

BOSTON

Year	Jan.	Feb.	Mar.	Apr.	May	June	July	Aug.	Sept.	Oct.	Nov.	Dec.	Total
Av. 1921–1925	641	587	735	925	1,187	2,057	2,056	1,452	1,368	1,470	1,097	762	14,336
1927	834	857	694	796	1,211	1,654	1,736	1,919	1,347	1,466	1,162	912	14,588
1928	898	1,031	991	1,113	1,587	1,884	1,950	2,048	1,607	2,154	1,281	818	17,362

SAN FRANCISCO

Year	Jan.	Feb.	Mar.	Apr.	May	June	July	Aug.	Sept.	Oct.	Nov.	Dec.	Total
Av. 1921–1925	682	714	717	777	985	1,090	1,364	1,201	853	865	827	688	10,763
1927	716	702	786	1,121	1,284	1,369	1,622	1,357	1,125	1,031	900	681	12,694
1928	808	836	975	1,082	1,086	1,223	1,683	1,152	1,326	991	867	647	12,676

TOTAL, 1918–1928

Year	Jan.	Feb.	Mar.	Apr.	May	June	July	Aug.	Sept.	Oct.	Nov.	Dec.	Total
Av. 1921–1925	12,877	12,819	14,868	15,512	19,006	23,184	23,253	20,331	18,076	18,962	15,485	13,447	207,821
1918								20,536	16,112	12,383	13,796	10,398	11,292
1919	10,988	10,271	13,386	15,362	20,069	22,648	22,267	18,417	18,519	18,491	14,650	12,199	197,267
1920	11,094	9,655	13,918	8,583	16,140	21,874	19,797	16,416	12,831	12,924	13,802	11,633	168,667
1921	11,488	11,283	12,758	13,952	19,361	21,680	19,324	15,999	14,923	16,653	13,228	10,973	181,622
1922	10,734	11,258	14,789	15,565	19,146	22,770	20,211	19,806	17,463	18,323	15,699	14,071	199,835
1923	13,063	12,617	15,354	16,433	18,963	25,406	25,764	21,680	18,619	21,325	16,557	13,256	219,037
1924	13,899	16,092	16,540	16,175	19,030	22,041	25,143	19,996	18,855	17,479	14,884	14,922	215,056
1925	15,202	12,845	14,898	15,436	18,529	24,025	25,825	24,176	20,520	21,029	17,059	14,012	223,556
1926	14,853	13,568	15,055	15,531	14,972	21,777	21,973	20,736	18,784	18,699	15,954	15,986	207,888
1927	12,707	14,916	14,956	16,922	21,301	22,134	24,134	22,556	21,522	18,996	14,278	13,826	218,248
1928	14,409	13,715	14,654	15,139	16,253	19,216	21,741	18,728	18,222	18,665	14,179	11,692	196,613

Bureau of Agricultural Economics. Compiled from reports of bureau representatives in the various markets. See 1927 Yearbook, p. 1084, for data for earlier years.

TABLE 471.—*Cheese: Receipts, gross weight, at five markets, by State of origin, 1921–1928*

NEW YORK

State of origin	1921	1922	1923	1924	1925	1926	1927	1928
	1,000 pounds	*1,000 pounds*	*1,000 pounds*	*1,000 pounds*	*1,000 pounds*	*1,000 pounds*	*1,000 pounds*	*1,000 pounds*
New York	22,413	21,770	16,909	14,478	14,107	11,180	11,867	13,390
Wisconsin	17,044	16,100	19,758	16,339	18,978	17,587	19,258	23,002
Illinois	7,061	6,997	8,535	8,382	7,211	7,406	7,231	5,132
Pennsylvania	1,623	1,181	955	618	1,105	745	434	745
Michigan	787	506	619	644	472	301	440	837
Ohio	773	632	321	136	374	363	587	646
Massachusetts	420	189	228	235	248	244	189	64
Indiana	187	182	277	581	2,075	5,653	3,833	1,923
Nebraska	144	23	4	240	48	76	150	42
Missouri	131	315	170	48	98	158	287	123
Minnesota	112	494	249	352	118	551	279	179
New Jersey	97	46	40	48	16	18	204	186
Iowa	57	94	206	295	777	346	421	178
Virginia	24	5	4	49	23	12	3	24
Tennessee	15	74	3	8	15	13	1	34
Vermont	14	97	305	79	273	47	3	16
Other States	625	215	414	172	85	78	279	214
Canada	454	1,189	428	255	140	585	1,471	1,537
Total	51,981	50,109	49,425	42,959	46,163	45,363	46,937	48,272

BOSTON

	1921	1922	1923	1924	1925	1926	1927	1928
New York	5,868	6,527	7,402	5,209	4,546	4,328	2,831	3,787
Wisconsin	3,294	3,091	3,392	4,317	7,787	6,229	7,170	9,953
Illinois	1,782	2,091	3,881	2,931	1,782	3,622	3,261	1,845
Vermont	1,444	471	623	736	432	413	124	47
Pennsylvania	132	136	183	181	206	152	197	56
Ohio	71	35	23	137	201	162	196	110
New Hampshire	55	75	50	41	6	5	2	2
Massachusetts	39	32	27	13	8	5	41	65
Indiana	36	66	28	1	47	60	170	388
Maine	35	17	38	5	4	114	143	147
Michigan	31	296	191	74	198	184	200	422
Other States	142	475	71	23	97	162	221	353
Canada	279	209	5	56	--------	1	32	187
Total	13,208	13,521	15,914	13,724	15,314	15,437	14,588	17,362

CHICAGO

	1921	1922	1923	1924	1925	1926	1927	1928
Wisconsin	76,706	95,656	110,648	117,439	119,244	100,676	109,504	82,954
Illinois	3,102	4,011	4,497	3,965	4,592	3,293	2,996	2,900
Minnesota	2,687	1,960	3,177	2,733	3,108	3,265	2,503	2,979
Michigan	1,687	1,415	729	1,241	118	238	550	137
Montana	313	26	203	311	81	--------	66	--------
Iowa	287	810	705	620	606	457	263	296
New York	221	2,391	2,429	1,667	1,282	2,218	3,489	4,246
Kansas	166	3	51	30	45	72	26	36
Pennsylvania	163	308	289	158	115	112	532	479
California	113	57	--------	--------	9	94	3	45
Ohio	99	301	147	91	745	315	532	176
South Dakota	78	17	16	64	2	106	138	9
Missouri	56	222	83	188	65	43	122	583
Texas	32	9	15	2	38	35	12	15
Colorado	27	104	16	34	192	42	31	58
Indiana	16	22	66	50	49	93	43	255
Utah	11	8	14	7	8	2	36	1
New Jersey	--------	45	24	95	32	--------	41	445
Idaho	--------	19	168	675	337	534	88	26
Other States	85	90	122	281	81	250	916	1,057
Canada	--------	250	246	373	380	3,259	1,742	567
Total	85,849	107,724	123,645	130,024	131,129	115,104	123,633	97,264

TABLE 471.—*Cheese: Receipts, gross weight, at five markets, by State of origin, 1921–1928*—Continued

PHILADELPHIA

State of origin	1921	1922	1923	1924	1925	1926	1927	1928
	1,000 pounds	*1,000 pounds*	*1,000 pounds*	*1,000 pounds*	*1,000 pounds*	*1,000 pounds*	*1,000 pounds*	*1,000 pounds*
Wisconsin	8,487	10,638	8,884	8,003	10,850	11,428	12,723	14,735
New York	7,068	4,660	4,538	3,655	3,627	2,630	2,462	2,201
Illinois	2,557	2,955	4,126	4,333	4,073	4,636	3,704	2,701
Pennsylvania	2,041	517	245	240	84	63	41	4
Ohio	205	223	136	26	11	133	86	82
New Jersey	121	14	36	3	3	--------	9	74
Indiana	100	95	142	95	201	122	115	110
Michigan	45	115	131	199	111	188	634	499
Minnesota	41	1	54	-------	68	184	416	343
Iowa	3	25	44	164	37	1	3	2
Other States	284	73	27	148	30	69	77	122
Canada	--------	8	(¹)	(¹)	-------	-------	126	166
Total	20,952	19,324	18,363	16,866	19,095	19,454	20,396	21,039

SAN FRANCISCO

State of origin	1921	1922	1923	1924	1925	1926	1927	1928
California	4,800	3,416	3,650	2,603	2,316	2,123	2,515	3,508
Oregon	2,245	2,448	2,557	2,710	3,029	3,148	3,273	2,877
Wisconsin	1,064	1,353	1,979	2,216	1,987	2,694	2,198	1,820
Illinois	505	855	1,441	821	463	222	192	91
New York	388	314	249	310	307	529	596	572
Colorado	176	322	222	256	323	294	241	225
Washington	145	108	112	58	120	50	91	17
Idaho	139	222	1,039	2,262	2,835	2,858	3,331	3,334
Utah	24	10	17	76	164	387	199	30
Montana	-----	56	338	5	64	79	1	160
Minnesota	-----	-----	63	152	154	94	24	-------
Other States	146	53	23	13	93	52	33	42
Total	9,632	9,157	11,690	11,482	11,855	12,530	12,694	12,676

Bureau of Agricultural Economics. Compiled from reports of bureau representatives in the various markets.

¹ Not over 500 pounds.

TABLE 472—*American cheese:* [1] *Cold-storage holdings, United States, 1915–1928* [2]

Year	Jan. 1	Feb. 1	Mar. 1	Apr. 1	May 1	June 1	July 1	Aug. 1	Sept. 1	Oct. 1	Nov. 1	Dec. 1
	1,000 lbs.	*1,000 lbs.*	*1,000 lbs.*	*1,000 lbs.*	*1,000 lbs.*	*1,000 lbs.*	*1,000 lbs.*	*1,000 lbs.*	*1,000 lbs.*	*1,000 lbs.*	*1,000 lbs.*	*1,000 lbs.*
Average: 1916–1920	40,038	31,287	22,110	15,286	11,040	13,060	29,545	52,425	66,219	63,736	55,731	48,060
1921–1925	38,835	31,016	24,597	19,103	18,152	21,505	39,324	55,240	63,428	61,751	56,313	50,330
1915									28,575	24,144	32,428	31,271
1916	28,558	18,908	13,373	8,443	6,546	7,301	16,357	31,569	46,776	49,579	45,713	37,080
1917	31,855	22,113	15,560	9,842	7,928	11,626	34,159	67,595	91,545	90,671	78,087	75,166
1918	66,784	56,298	37,743	27,965	17,736	20,395	30,054	48,804	55,742	42,065	33,402	25,625
1919	19,823	15,486	9,837	6,750	6,027	12,478	37,501	62,645	76,661	81,359	72,889	62,508
1920	53,168	43,631	34,039	23,431	16,963	13,502	29,654	51,512	60,372	55,007	48,566	39,921
1921	34,115	25,000	17,477	14,294	13,466	17,814	34,948	41,284	46,635	45,163	42,969	34,055
1922	27,691	21,430	15,006	10,745	10,868	15,481	33,130	46,580	53,625	49,473	40,852	37,291
1923	33,617	26,593	20,693	14,465	14,077	17,507	36,834	55,839	63,960	62,384	57,927	55,105
1924	49,566	40,506	35,160	28,294	26,202	27,172	45,239	65,864	76,406	73,153	67,905	58,705
1925	49,187	41,552	34,647	27,716	26,147	29,550	46,468	66,634	76,512	78,582	71,913	66,495
1926	58,457	50,339	42,587	38,041	35,597	39,346	54,069	73,681	81,297	77,646	72,491	63,881
1927	54,596	46,026	39,382	35,193	32,487	35,826	49,999	67,091	69,749	65,453	59,035	53,447
1928	47,765	41,793	36,710	31,887	30,207	36,716	53,646	73,088	83,906	81,833	82,318	74,325

Bureau of Agricultural Economics. Compiled from reports from cold-storage establishments.

[1] Quantities given are net weight.
[2] The term "American cheese" is intended to cover only those varieties known as twins, flats, daisies, Cheddars, longhorns, and square prints. It does not, therefore, include all kinds of cheese made in America.

TABLE 473.—*Cheese: International trade, average 1909–1913, annual 1924–1927*

Country	Year ended Dec. 31									
	Average, 1909–1913		1924		1925		1926		1927, preliminary	
	Imports	Exports	Imports	Exports	Imports	Exports	Imports	Exports	Imports	Exports
PRINCIPAL EXPORTING COUNTRIES	*1,000 pounds*	*1,000 pounds*	*1,000 pounds*	*1,000 pounds*	*1,000 pounds*	*1,000 pounds*	*1,000 pounds*	*1,000 pounds*	*1,000 pounds*	*1,000 pounds*
Netherlands	522	127,379	889	170,353	1,163	175,711	1,081	185,706	1,284	214,565
New Zealand	3	55,561	19	178,582	2	154,196	1	163,693	7	167, 193
Canada	1,054	167,260	909	121,466	10,274	150,743	1,219	134,657	1,721	110,533
Italy	13,308	60,560	4,157	74,148	3,868	86,228	7,920	72,947	13,126	70,078
Switzerland	7,150	70,075	4,163	43,776	3,765	51,726	3,456	61,972	3,638	75,058
Denmark	1,414	527	673	19,480	819	18,783	1,427	15,345	1,105	11,644
Australia	360	799	[1] 471	[1] 6,605	[1] 550	[1] 9,609	[1] 1,859	[1] 4,803	[1] 2,097	[1] 2,338
Argentina	10,447	[2] 6	2,546	3,461	3,402	657	3,341	866	3,228	1,224
Yugoslavia	0	0	[1] 191	7,439	[1] 265	4,856	[1] 342	4,170	[1] 3	5,807
Finland	478	2,086	36	5,613	33	8,421	62	6,364	34	6,502
Czechoslovakia	0	0	1,671	5,431	1,777	8,048	1,964	7,732	2,533	8,463
Hungary	0	0	1	1,344	1,923	1,769	1,626	1,834	1,733	2,609
Bulgaria	[3] 52	[2] 5,972	16	258	0	199	[1] 42	186	[1] 19	5,740
Russia	3,911	7,011	[1] 58	[1] 303	[1] 289	[1] 14	[1] 130	[1] 72	[1] 133	[1] 1,847
PRINCIPAL IMPORTING COUNTRIES										
United Kingdom	257,407	950	318,041	843	331,500	1,950	333,187	2,994	325,898	5,363
Germany	48,687	1,967	96,702	1,239	162,940	2,491	141,345	2,320	158,740	3,160
United States	46,346	5,142	59,176	4,299	62,403	9,190	78,417	3,903	79,796	3,410
France	49,056	26,880	32,792	28,891	34,064	29,978	34,673	31,481	43,902	30,481
Belgium	31,771	354	37,388	1,633	38,275	1,817	33,187	1,239	36,495	1,004
Austria	[4] 12,298	[4] 966	10,142	1,189	7,970	681	7,665	1,376	7,553	1,387
Algeria	6,592	138	7,547	174	7,897	278	5,464	234	6,849	[1] 210
Egypt	8,182	[5] 48	5,960	117	7,157	155	6,842	79	6,740	176
Spain	5,032	53	6,599	87	5,307	133	7,023	79	[1] 7,576	[1] 447
Cuba	0	7	5,619	8	5,499	3	4,463	2		
Irish Free State	0	0	2,590	542	2,823	483	2,740	403	2,414	212
Sweden	946	41	2,210	266	1,214	730	1,375	656	1,522	574
Dutch East Indies	757	0	1,383	0	1,362	0	1,763	0	[6] 1,677	
Norway	663	377	1,106	737	1,301	702	1,266	757	1,452	894
British India	1,314	0	1,046	[1] 4	1,157	0	1,190	[1] 5	1,332	[1] 4
Tunis	1,382	19	1,073	48	1,185	10	1,125	22	1,314	14
Brazil	4,178	[2] 1	646	1	1,101	0	1,545	0		
Union of South Africa	4,991	3	552	127	256	190	344	114	483	239
Total, 32 countries	522,821	534,182	606,372	678,464	701,541	719,751	688,174	706,011	714,404	731,176

Division of Statistical and Historical Research. Official sources except where otherwise noted. All cheese made from milk, including cottage cheese.

[1] International Yearbook of Agricultural Statistics.
[2] 4-year average.
[3] 3-year average.
[4] Average for Austria-Hungary.
[5] 1 year only.
[6] Java and Madura only.

TABLE 474.—*Cheese, No. 1 American fresh flats: Average wholesale price per pound, New York, 1910–1928*

Year	Jan.	Feb.	Mar.	Apr.	May	June	July	Aug.	Sept.	Oct.	Nov.	Dec.	Average
Average:	*Cents*	*Cents*	*Cents*	*Cents*	*Cents*	*Cents*	*Cents*	*Cents*	*Cents*	*Cents*	*Cents*	*Cents*	*Cents*
1910–1914	16	16	16	16	13	14	14	15	15	16	16	16	15
1921–1925	24	23	23	21	19	20	22	23	23				
1924	22	22	21	17	17	20	21	21	22	20	21	23	21
1925	24	24	24	23	21	23	24	25	26	27	27		24
1926		24	23	21	20	22	23	23	24	25			
1927			23		23	24	25	26	27	28			
1928	27	24	23	22	23	25	26	26	27		26	26	

Bureau of Agricultural Economics. January, 1910–February, 1919, compiled from Urner-Barry reports; subsequently from reports of bureau representatives in the market.

TABLE 475.—*Oleomargarine: Production and consumption in the United States, 1924–1927*

Year beginning July	Production			Stocks beginning of year	Exports	Stocks end of year	Consumption	
	Colored	Uncolored	Total				Total	Per capita
	1,000 lbs.	*1,000 lbs.*	*1,000 lbs.*	*1,000 lbs.*	*1,000 lbs.*	*1,000 lbs.*	*1,000 lbs.*	*Lbs.*
1924	11,280	204,123	215,403	2,607	887	2,720	214,403	1.87
1925	13,181	234,866	248,047	2,720	1,256	2,942	246,569	2.12
1926	14,502	2x2,655	257,157	2,942	942	3,299	255,858	2.17
1927	15,351	279,348	294,699	3,299	732	3,187	294,079	2.46

Bureau of Agricultural Economics. Production and stocks from reports of the Bureau of Internal Revenue. Exports from reports of the Bureau of Foreign and Domestic Commerce. See 1927 Yearbook, p. 1088, for data for earlier years.

TABLE 476.—*Oleomargarine: Materials used in manufacture, 1917–1927*

Material	Year beginning July—										
	1917	1918	1919	1920	1921	1922	1923	1924	1925	1926	1927
	1,000 pounds	*1,000 pounds*	*1,000 pounds*	*1,000 pounds*	*1,000 pounds*	*1,000 pounds*	*1,000 pounds*	*1,000 pounds*	*1,000 pounds*	*1,000 pounds*	*1,000 pounds*
Oleo oil	96,378	97,464	89,842	49,676	40,980	46,645	52,265	44,102	47,418	48,741	45,477
Coconut oil	61,773	69,640	80,784	103,112	57,394	65,656	83,059	79,449	98,307	107,654	141,000
Cottonseed oil	36,454	37,846	39,450	18,533	15,420	18,757	20,640	20,966	25,608	23,372	24,801
Milk	61,128	68,000	76,000	79,716	53,939	59,835	69,090	61,924	72,662	73,700	83,115
Peanut oil	21,593	38,764	48,346	16,332	11,625	6,922	5,656	4,392	5,257	4,872	5,459
Salt	18,279	21,432	24,864	25,365	16,262	17,998	20,593	18,725	20,593	21,683	25,024
Oleo stearine	3,427	2,456	2,132	4,858	4,574	4,815	5,317	5,250	5,314	5,145	5,532
Neutral lard	45,702	45,764	38,456	29,268	27,057	29,568	32,210	25,674	25,172	24,872	25,036
Oleo stock	7,526	6,342	5,804	2,065	2,143	2,322	2,756	3,183	3,082	2,552	1,738
Butter	4,548	5,680	6,845	1,499	1,107	1,576	1,900	1,509	2,330	2,070	2,484
Corn oil	60	40	35	926			457	196	174	183	38
Soy-bean oil				461					1	33	
Edible tallow				233			24	111	93	219	70
Mustard-seed oil				110			38	27	34	53	56
Coloring				26	11	11	26	38	41	18	19
Miscellaneous	14	11	14	9,776	3,417	2,918	432	688	1,374	918	1,220
Total	356,882	393,439	412,572	341,956	233,929	257,023	294,463	266,234	307,460	316,085	361,069

Bureau of Agricultural Economics. 1917–1919, Institute of Margarin Manufacturers; 1920–1927, annual reports of the Bureau of Internal Revenue.

TABLE 477.—*Oleomargarine, standard, uncolored: Monthly average wholesale price per pound, Chicago, 1914–1928*

Year	Jan.	Feb.	Mar.	Apr.	May	June	July	Aug.	Sept.	Oct.	Nov.	Dec.	Average
	Cents	*Cents*	*Cents*	*Cents*	*Cents*	*Cents*	*Cents*	*Cents*	*Cents*	*Cents*	*Cents*	*Cents*	*Cents*
Average: 1914–1920	24.6	24.4	24.1	24.4	25.0	25.0	24.9	24.9	25.3	25.4	26.1	26.1	25.0
1921–1925	22.3	21.7	21.3	20.7	20.4	20.1	20.5	21.3	21.4	21.6	22.0	22.3	21.3
1914	18.0	18.0	18.0	17.0	17.0	17.0	17.0	17.0	18.0	18.0	18.0	18.0	17.6
1915	18.0	18.0	18.0	18.0	17.0	17.0	17.0	17.0	17.0	17.0	17.0	17.0	17.3
1916	17.0	17.0	17.0	18.0	19.0	19.0	19.0	19.0	19.0	20.0	22.0	24.0	19.2
1917	22.5	22.5	22.5	24.5	25.5	25.5	25.5	25.5	26.5	28.5	28.5	28.5	25.5
1918	28.5	28.5	28.5	28.5	28.5	28.5	28.5	29.5	29.5	30.5	32.5	32.5	29.5
1919	32.5	32.5	31.5	31.5	34.5	35.5	35.5	35.5	36.5	34.5	35.5	35.5	34.3
1920	35.5	34.4	33.5	33.5	33.5	32.6	31.7	30.5	30.5	29.5	29.5	27.0	31.8
1921	24.9	23.6	22.2	20.5	19.8	18.5	18.9	20.5	20.5	20.5	20.1	19.5	20.8
1922	19.0	17.5	17.5	17.5	17.5	17.5	18.2	18.5	18.5	18.5	19.2	20.5	18.3
1923	20.5	20.5	20.5	20.5	20.5	20.5	20.5	20.5	21.0	21.5	22.2	22.5	20.9
1924	22.5	22.5	21.9	20.5	20.5	20.5	21.2	22.5	22.5	23.0	24.0	24.5	22.2
1925	24.5	24.5	24.5	24.5	24.5	23.5	23.7	24.5	24.5	24.5	24.5	24.5	24.3
1926	24.5	24.3	23.5	23.3	22.5	22.5	22.5	22.5	22.5	21.8	21.5	22.8	
1927	21.5	21.5	21.5	21.5	21.5	21.5	21.5	21.5	23.9	24.5	23.5	23.5	22.3
1928	23.5	23.5	23.5	21.5	21.5	21.5	21.5	21.5	22.0	23.5	23.5	23.5	22.5

Bureau of Agricultural Economics. Compiled from Bureau of Labor Statistics Wholesale Price Bulletins.

TABLE 478.—*Poultry, live: Freight receipts, by States, at New York, 1927, 1928, and monthly, 1928*

State	1927	1928	1928											
			Jan.	Feb.	Mar.	Apr.	May	June	July	Aug.	Sept.	Oct.	Nov.	Dec.
	Car-loads	Car-loads	Car-loads	Car-loads	Car-loads	Car-loads	Car-loads	Car-loads	Car-loads	Car-loads	Car-loads	Car-loads	Car-loads	Car-loads
Ala	82	176	3	10	34	42	31	9	7	9	6	4	14	7
Ark	420	410	31	41	74	50	43	38	37	24	15	13	21	23
Colo	52	89	4	14	10	5	6	7	9	4	3	9	10	8
Ga	45	151	4	12	23	28	35	23	8	3	1	1	5	8
Ill	1,227	874	75	53	45	54	54	62	67	87	92	106	99	80
Ind	1,267	842	81	49	32	29	44	55	47	71	83	111	119	121
Iowa	856	586	32	8	8	3	12	60	69	70	98	95	70	61
Kans	661	474	77	49	28	26	37	37	25	32	61	44	25	33
Ky	739	741	56	75	105	112	100	40	45	51	37	41	40	39
La		1						1						
Mass		1							1					
Mich		6								1	5			
Minn	223	164	7	1				7	12	13	24	43	40	17
Miss	154	188	12	42	46	24	21	9	11	8	4		5	6
Mo	2,147	1,896	132	132	158	141	148	165	158	195	198	158	149	162
Nebr	996	1,078	72	54	40	22	38	64	61	106	134	172	174	141
N. Mex	1	4	3											1
N. Y		1	1											
N. C	91	158	3	20	21	31	26	17	7	4	8	2	10	9
N. Dak		33									4	9	17	3
Ohio	429	343	12	5	2	2	7	22	34	26	33	58	74	68
Okla	751	873	119	133	125	94	78	56	42	69	53	28	34	42
Pa	58	36			1	1	2	4		3	6	1	8	10
S. C	29	41		8	2	5	14	7					3	2
S. Dak	187	313	12	9	8	4	4	11	12	21	36	79	69	48
Tenn	975	1,060	82	124	143	205	150	61	54	53	46	33	55	54
Tex	365	436	74	101	94	43	47	27	17	10	1	1	10	11
Va	56	68	1	7	7	10	13	5	3	5	3	1	5	8
Wis	253	219	1				2	14	28	39	37	47	39	12
Wyo	2	5	2					1			1			1
Other States	38													
Total	12,104	11,267	896	947	1,006	931	913	801	754	904	989	1,056	1,095	975

Bureau of Agricultural Economics.

TABLE 479.—*Poultry, live: Freight receipts, make-up by classes of cars unloaded, at New York, 1927 and 1928*

Class	1927	1928												
		Total	Jan.	Feb.	Mar.	Apr.	May	June	July	Aug.	Sept.	Oct.	Nov.	Dec.
	Per cent	Per cent	Per cent	Per cent	Per cent	Per cent	Per cent	Per cent	Per cent	Per cent	Per cent	Per cent	Per cent	Per cent
Fowls	66.2	68.9	77.2	87.9	92.3	93.0	87.3	79.2	55.5	52.8	50.2	50.7	49.7	62.4
Broilers	5.9	4.9	0.6	0.4	0.4	1.0	7.8	16.1	23.0	13.3	0.9	0.2	0.2	0.4
Chickens	22.4	20.0	16.7	7.6	3.0	1.0	0.2	0.5	6.7	30.4	45.6	45.0	34.0	25.1
Stags	0.2	0.2	0.0	0.0	0.5	2.3	0.8	0.1	0.0	0.0	0.0	0.0	0.0	0.0
Cocks	2.3	2.3	1.5	1.9	2.1	0.8	3.3	3.5	2.8	2.7	2.2	1.6	1.4	1.4
Capons	0.3	0.3	1.2	1.0	0.4	0.4	0.0	0.0	0.0	0.0	0.0	0.0	0.1	0.3
Ducks	1.7	1.3	1.3	0.5	0.5	0.4	0.3	0.4	0.5	0.7	1.0	1.9	3.3	2.7
Geese	1.0	1.0	1.4	0.5	0.4	0.4	0.2	0.1	0.0	0.1	0.1	0.6	3.8	3.8
Turkeys	0.9	1.1	0.1	0.2	0.4	0.1	0.1	0.1	0.0	0.0	0.0	0.0	7.5	3.9

Bureau of Agricultural Economics.

TABLE 480.—*Poultry, dressed: Receipts, gross weight, at four markets, 1920–1928*

BOSTON

Year	Jan.	Feb.	Mar.	Apr.	May	June	July	Aug.	Sept.	Oct.	Nov.	Dec.	Total
	1,000 lbs.	1,000 lbs.	1,000 lbs.	1,000 lbs.	1,000 lbs.	1,000 lbs.	1,000 lbs.	1,000 lbs.	1,000 lbs.	1,000 lbs.	1,000 lbs.	1,000 lbs.	1,000 lbs.
Av. 1921–1925	5,130	3,328	2,526	1,955	2,394	2,718	2,480	2,588	2,692	4,009	9,092	10,785	49,696
1920	3,934	1,749	1,597	1,037	1,464	2,221	1,858	1,696	2,096	2,628	5,911	7,895	34,086
1921	3,377	2,229	1,465	1,707	1,795	2,086	1,499	2,437	2,482	3,581	7,472	9,791	39,921
1922	4,175	2,765	2,478	1,705	2,551	2,883	2,091	2,198	2,479	3,306	7,488	10,444	44,563
1923	7,690	3,785	2,917	1,946	2,439	2,778	2,427	2,661	2,674	4,418	10,752	11,526	56,013
1924	6,210	4,607	3,072	2,235	2,602	2,952	3,492	2,856	3,270	4,402	11,842	13,724	61,264
1925	4,200	3,252	2,697	2,181	2,582	2,893	2,893	2,786	2,554	4,336	7,907	8,439	46,720
1926	3,778	2,981	2,837	2,052	2,598	3,196	3,161	3,677	3,960	4,089	8,891	11,942	53,162
1927	4,318	3,610	2,440	2,398	3,653	3,455	2,996	3,612	3,404	4,663	8,511	10,245	53,305
1928	4,591	3,756	4,137	2,877	3,285	3,290	3,899	3,468	3,355	4,680	7,716	10,329	55,583

NEW YORK

Year	Jan.	Feb.	Mar.	Apr.	May	June	July	Aug.	Sept.	Oct.	Nov.	Dec.	Total
Av. 1921–1925	14,791	9,810	7,559	6,765	8,000	8,887	8,737	9,574	10.887	14,720	25,594	29,943	155,266
1920	11,217	7,557	5,480	1,367	5,480	5,292	6,129	4,428	6,273	8,053	17,651	23,718	101,093
1921	11,441	7,006	5,190	5,021	4,883	6,150	5,314	8,992	10,277	11,887	21,182	27,208	124,551
1922	10,783	6,909	6,371	6,399	7,896	8,822	6,785	7,768	9,115	12,594	22,232	32,538	138,212
1923	21,730	12,335	8,390	6,916	6,804	8,589	9,414	9,497	9,653	16,509	26,822	27,289	163,948
1924	15,603	11,927	9,893	7,368	10,172	10,157	10,502	10,504	12,981	15,916	28,875	35,464	179,362
1925	14,400	10,871	7,949	8,119	10,245	10,717	11,668	11,110	12,409	16,696	28,857	27,216	170,257
1926	13,078	10,646	9,921	8,248	10,594	14,041	13,555	14,609	15,068	18,129	31,924	33,082	192,895
1927	12,954	8,957	8,722	7,770	11,633	13,635	12,168	14,589	15,470	17,682	31,740	32,797	188,117
1928	14,999	11,064	9,322	9,703	10,628	11,127	13,252	13,850	14,332	21,799	31,846	32,454	194,376

PHILADELPHIA

Year	Jan.	Feb.	Mar.	Apr.	May	June	July	Aug.	Sept.	Oct.	Nov.	Dec.	Total
Av. 1921–1925	2,217	1,648	1,553	1,071	1,223	1,495	1,416	1,545	1,429	1,784	3,514	6,257	25,151
1920	1,553	1,881	1,906	918	1,466	1,286	1,019	1,215	1,044	1,588	2,348	5,382	21,606
1921	1,498	1,071	1,411	1,005	1,303	1,565	1,226	1,419	1,587	2,020	2,882	5,905	22,892
1922	1,947	1,790	1,077	664	1,182	1,304	1,237	1,217	1,237	1,356	2,653	5,655	21,319
1923	2,206	1,530	1,388	1,042	1,055	1,509	1,343	1,618	1,348	1,749	3,281	6,542	24,611
1924	2,614	1,818	1,704	1,194	1,234	1,458	1,536	1,660	1,421	1,873	4,053	7,075	27,640
1925	2,818	2,030	2,183	1,450	1,343	1,638	1,739	1,810	1,552	1,924	4,702	6,106	29,295
1926	2,906	1,791	2,203	1,717	1,374	1,758	1,853	2,039	2,352	2,123	4,916	7,094	32,126
1927	2,885	2,006	2,005	1,769	1,695	1,668	1,398	1,918	2,530	2,613	4,432	6,903	31,822
1928	2,373	1,601	1,885	1,359	1,558	2,177	1,931	1,763	2,097	2,965	4,925	7,210	31,844

CHICAGO

Year	Jan.	Feb.	Mar.	Apr.	May	June	July	Aug.	Sept.	Oct.	Nov.	Dec.	Total
Av. 1921–1925	8,415	4,570	3,628	2,668	2,677	2,997	2,957	3,033	3,436	4,568	15,950	22,997	77,895
1920	6,646	2,687	980	816	1,512	2,369	2,379	2,659	3,370	4,001	10,752	19,153	57,324
1921	6,343	3,328	2,794	2,104	2,421	2,524	2,097	2,615	3,804	4,157	15,723	17,082	64,992
1922	5,345	3,042	3,394	2,744	2,744	3,597	3,590	4,250	4,290	4,178	13,167	23,320	73,661
1923	11,497	5,208	4,057	2,532	2,912	3,329	3,679	4,018	4,724	5,411	15,163	27,743	90,273
1924	12,723	8,043	5,675	4,385	3,311	3,295	4,042	2,523	2,196	4,791	15,675	21,805	88,464
1925	6,167	3,230	2,219	1,573	1,996	2,239	1,376	1,760	2,168	4,303	20,022	25,033	72,086
1926	6,360	3,159	2,383	1,792	1,805	2,105	2,154	2,607	2,897	6,397	22,863	23,110	77,632
1927	6,495	3,546	2,195	1,835	2,872	2,257	1,227	2,257	2,531	3,752	15,739	19,029	63,735
1928	6,639	3,591	2,216	1,876	2,137	1,977	2,771	2,829	3,580	5,719	15,301	18,544	67,180

TOTAL

Year	Jan.	Feb.	Mar.	Apr.	May	June	July	Aug.	Sept.	Oct.	Nov.	Dec.	Total
Av. 1921–1925	30,553	19,355	15,265	12,458	14,294	16,097	15,590	16,740	18,444	25,081	54,150	69,981	308,009
1920	23,350	13,874	8,411	4,138	9,922	11,168	11,385	9,998	12,783	16,270	36,662	56,148	214,109
1921	22,659	13,634	10,860	9,837	10,402	12,325	10,136	15,463	18,150	21,645	47,259	59,986	252,356
1922	22,250	14,506	13,320	11,512	14,373	16,606	13,703	15,433	17,121	21,434	45,540	71,957	277,755
1923	43,123	22,858	16,752	12,436	13,210	16,205	16,863	17,794	18,399	28,087	56,018	73,100	334,845
1924	37,150	26,395	20,344	15,182	17,319	17,862	19,572	17,543	19,868	26,982	60,445	78,068	356,730
1925	27,585	19,383	15,048	13,323	16,166	17,487	17,676	17,466	18,683	27,259	61,488	66,794	318,358
1926	26,122	18,576	17,344	13,809	16,371	21,099	20,724	22,932	24,278	30,738	68,594	75,228	355,815
1927	26,652	18,119	15,362	13,772	19,853	21,015	17,789	22,376	23,935	28,710	60,422	68,974	336,979
1928	28,602	20,012	17,560	15,815	17,608	18,571	21,853	21,910	23,564	35,163	59,788	68,537	348,983

Bureau of Agricultural Economics. Compiled from reports of bureau representatives in the various markets.

TABLE 481.—Poultry, dressed: Receipts, gross weight, at four markets, by States of origin, 1922–1928

[Units: 1,000 pounds]

BOSTON

State	1922	1923	1924	1925	1926	1927	Total 1928	January	February	March	April	May	June	July	August	September	October	November	December
Illinois	19,618	23,308	20,155	12,292	14,768	14,203	11,719	1,401	959	867	393	998	745	925	716	484	1,041	1,309	1,781
Indiana	5,939	6,558	7,382	6,524	4,884	5,225	5,368	605	424	490	283	302	419	336	384	435	403	531	756
Iowa	4,422	7,131	6,834	6,957	8,141	7,003	6,648	826	421	303	262	202	399	554	574	720	637	680	1,070
Ohio	1,708	1,141	1,216	255	300	533	390	22	37		27		22	27	53	60	86	56	(¹)
Kansas	1,454	1,850	2,864	3,566	4,027	3,592	4,557	380	280	317	255	317	480	513	371	373	324	578	389
New York	1,454	1,043	1,111	1,045	1,251	1,467	1,709	4	207	245	252	135	44	23	47	96	315	182	159
Oklahoma	1,253	2,222	1,737	1,699	1,571	2,066	2,662	190	268	452	391	355	140	146	104	136	42	224	214
Minnesota	1,076	527	878	1,737	5,076	5,886	6,677	460	151	183	74	30	140	497	453	591	1,015	1,148	1,935
Michigan	1,015	911	834	929	524	970	888	36	29	26	173	188	22	1	69	23	53	116	155
Kentucky	1,005	1,330	854	822	970	524	855	4	3	4	3	73	165	150	88	45	133	94	93
Missouri	774	1,086	2,540	1,822	1,944	453	1,881	169	195	337	239	168	83	81	72	81	168	99	183
Wisconsin	680	291	612	375	1,236	1,509	932	44	5	5		6	12	18	32	70	102	165	63
Maine	647	791	706	709	438	690	509		32	15	7	212	232	302	346	260	246	108	432
Nebraska	471	682	1,336	1,707	2,297	1,930	3,298	216	337	281	118	3	1	1	29			316	21
Massachusetts	413	357	344	205	260	495	85	8	2	6	3	1	1	1	1	1	1	12	6
Vermont	200	149	105	74	34	26	204	3	(¹)	1	1		42					12	57
Tennessee	65	39	73	118	234	160	330	15	41	77		46	1	2	1	2	2	52	1
New Hampshire	53	47	50	41	29	62	28	1	1	1		(¹)	1	11			1	5	
Pennsylvania	49	72	114	180	47	260	17	3										11	
Maryland	39	59	92	11	24	2	104									(¹)			
North Dakota	14	294	314	237	553	469	478	42	42	30	55		42	10	122	9	87	68	289
South Dakota	3	121	101	92	131	46	114				7		1		6	3	1	44	45
Texas	(²)	(²)		2,797	3,703		5,034	91	247	309	270	214	128	219		67		1,600	1,680
Other States	2,189	4,681	6,185	467	555	5,110	1,761	25	95	139	64	35	30	64	6			306	993
Canada	22	120	1,750	174	165	72	7										1		7
Total	44,563	56,013	61,264	46,720	53,162	53,305	55,583	4,591	3,756	4,137	2,877	3,285	3,290	3,899	3,468	3,555	4,680	7,716	10,329

CHICAGO

State	1922	1923	1924	1925	1926	1927	Total 1928	January	February	March	April	May	June	July	August	September	October	November	December
Iowa	19,001	18,654	21,023	21,538	21,420	14,719	13,117	1,837	612	265	345	253	260	346	349	538	1,430	2,888	3,994
Illinois	18,720	17,497	13,184	4,517	5,920	3,893	2,581	299	119	17	42	17	100	203	111	162	231	583	646
Wisconsin	7,555	7,372	11,771	10,267	5,701	3,982	3,409	303	195	86	48	52	68	144	149	114	254	1,067	929
Minnesota	7,310	10,764	11,425	10,267	12,586	10,541	7,829	980	463	267	93	41	160	246	179	231	443	2,077	2,649
Missouri	3,952	4,509	4,621	5,954	7,388	4,812	6,379	402	164	108	264	740	536	547	483	688	900	830	717
South Dakota	3,348	7,594	5,984	5,714	6,041	4,769	5,371	375	369	312	85	173	167	377	219	392	754	1,033	1,964
North Dakota	3,292	3,602	3,252	3,411	4,110	4,769	5,933	375	317	122	38	126	12	24	4	17	150	2,418	2,448
Kansas	2,499	1,813	1,690	2,149	2,632	2,915	4,315	465	303	80	167	218	156	307	520	457	536	606	592
Nebraska	1,959	818	849	2,731	411	3,247	4,295	551	356	147	283	218	186	240	280	389	410	429	806
Indiana	1,347	937	508	80	107	536	4,559	64	23	12	14	9	22	108	54	55	62	48	88
Kentucky	849					208	32	1	2	1	(¹)	(¹)	1	(¹)		2	1	14	9

Oklahoma	439	424	72	202	105	73	149	231	204	275	351	187	2,712	2,250	1,998	2,476	2,164	2,217	801
Texas	1,669	696	75	61	132	42	(²)	80	110	118	83	236	3,302	2,577	1,378	1,802	4,077	4,507	709
Tennessee	28	59	113	25	24	1	45	2	4	35	6	66	361	66	371	186	564	810	694
Michigan	40	87	1	(²)	24	2		89	(²)	88	(²)	23	379	66	40	82	186	276	332
Montana	822	487	37	100	109	47	17	21	4	21	68	92	1,530	1,022	1,773	1,738	2,095	1,500	271
Arkansas	105	94	120	93	64	43	63	53	16	23	20	16	688	238	177	117	315	335	256
New York	4	61	101					1	81	92	4	2	661	715	837	385	339	94	247
Mississippi	2	3				(²)	(²)		(²)	(²)	1		7	6	3	12	49	40	169
Idaho	103	47	2	100	109	47	6	3	(²)	49	15	6	171	120	26	131	75	94	69
Colorado	139	60		93	64	43		53	78	7	26	7	293	228	222	390	169	80	63
Wyoming	113	103								40	25	11	260	133	98	81	109	39	17
Other States	238	232	26	54	46	21	27	20	78	40	69	90	941	312	194	179	260	182	173
Canada		55											55		371	141		30	28
Total	18,544	15,301	5,719	3,580	2,829	2,771	1,977	2,137	1,876	2,216	3,591	6,639	67,180	63,735	77,632	72,086	88,464	90,273	73,661

NEW YORK

Illinois	4,013	3,062	2,401	1,439	1,226	1,382	1,484	1,849	2,174	1,879	1,864	2,091	24,864	28,356	32,890	45,861	57,246	48,267	40,911
Indiana	1,747	1,278	1,188	745	709	1,083	725	383	1,074	850	775	1,067	11,624	11,385	12,918	15,215	14,886	15,814	17,021
Iowa	5,473	4,932	4,875	1,992	1,268	1,386	894	482	685	667	1,151	2,519	26,324	25,226	25,840	18,775	18,775	19,520	15,854
Missouri	3,271	2,643	2,611	2,216	1,824	1,434	1,283	921	703	571	696	1,644	19,817	19,231	19,146	17,148	18,429	14,630	10,522
Kansas	2,467	2,989	2,946	2,403	2,230	1,199	732	922	583	1,097	1,519	1,983	21,070	20,725	20,757	11,379	8,429	15,115	10,174
Texas	4,374	5,342	156	278	637	933	721	740	469	774	849	908	16,181	13,192	10,059	6,665	12,108	7,206	5,296
Ohio	270	412	459	80	197	143	167	27	82	31	108	330	2,306	3,920	3,298	4,352	4,337	4,131	5,113
Minnesota	3,440	3,319	2,236	864	700	951	430	102	245	232	589	829	13,937	10,820	11,840	9,372	4,070	6,382	4,412
Tennessee	481	423	418	459	531	296	232	486	171	180	277	588	4,542	4,507	3,531	2,773	9,143	3,445	3,964
Kentucky	384	437	424	260	343	279	392	634	671	611	487	312	5,234	4,700	4,497	4,361	5,082	5,524	3,873
New York	144	578	903	1,301	2,500	2,671	2,399	1,925	1,096	209	178	63	14,167	16,438	12,966	11,459	4,361	3,062	3,572
Nebraska	1,195	1,446	1,094	865	516	558	418	312	465	713	628	847	7,041	7,314	6,979	4,610	3,036	3,062	2,515
Oklahoma	808	1,318	372	319	322	216	377	432	109	349	544	7,057	9,057	7,229	6,336	4,288	2,704	3,036	2,254
Virginia	240	399	279	339	309	270	194	26	13	12	25	52	5,478	2,229	2,299	3,105	2,553	2,704	1,904
Michigan	97	4	42	56	27	23	108	775	863	239	281	46	2,561	2,158	952	1,899	1,399	1,956	1,901
Wisconsin	333	389	214	138	83	23	23	37	19	72	102	136	659	659	702	3,058	2,588	1,683	1,503
New Jersey	52	70	18	12	15	34	14	46	9	35	101	233	1,551	1,843	2,787	1,303	2,862	1,552	1,395
Maryland	93	61	13	28	24	19	28	15	19	11	18	27	649	1,022	1,298	1,021	2,364	860	1,226
Pennsylvania	69	83	79	38	51	48	66	72	72	40	20	22	346	757	896	922	1,661	1,140	1,220
South Dakota	647	656	636	358	195	185	86	99	120	149	149	315	3,595	1,332	2,970	1,795	959	1,408	848
Massachusetts	26	58	37	5	8	4	25	151	20				660	757	911	1,146	1,299	632	649
California	100	101	133	5	1	(²)	4	68	14	555	68	68	1,117	425	461	459	528	709	165
North Dakota	518	295	144	20	1	2	26	32	23	7	60	136	1,236	318	605	1,056	760	515	326
Arkansas	(¹)	4	3		6	6	6	4	4	3		10	40	78	788	668	(²)	326	100
Delaware	6	423		5				37	1	1	3	4	54	56	65	91	84	64	(²)
Colorado	681		27	20		24	38				55	19	1,180	315	600	434	530	(²)	(²)
Washington	68	595	24					37	(²)	27			190	248	673	205	173	238	(²)
Idaho	546	5		89	127	83	55	47	17	30	95	372	1,656	244	416	176	242	(²)	(²)
Montana	253	520	67					4		3	179	31	1,471	202	120	123	203	814	503
Other States	658		24					47	17	30	243	35	1,928	846	843	462	601	532	203
Canada													47	47	98	279	175		
Total	32,454	31,846	21,799	14,332	13,850	13,252	11,127	10,628	9,703	9,322	11,064	14,999	194,376	188,117	192,895	170,257	179,362	163,948	138,212

¹ Not over 500 pounds.   ² Included in "Other States."

TABLE 481.—*Poultry, dressed; Receipts, gross weight, at four markets, by States of origin, 1922–1928*—Continued

PHILADELPHIA

State	1922	1923	1924	1925	1926	1927	1928 Total	January	February	March	April	May	June	July	August	September	October	November	December
	1,000 pounds	*1,000 pounds*	*1,000 pounds*	*1,000 pounds*	*1,000 pounds*	*1,000 pounds*	*1,000 pounds*	*1,000 pounds*	*1,000 pounds*	*1,000 pounds*	*1,000 pounds*	*1,000 pounds*	*1,000 pounds*	*1,000 pounds*	*1,000 pounds*	*1,000 pounds*	*1,000 pounds*	*1,000 pounds*	*1,000 pounds*
Illinois	7,165	9,497	9,456	8,728	5,505	4,232	1,940	249	147	103	139	141	133	18	167	137	135	205	366
Virginia	2,241	2,588	2,448	2,331	1,745	1,458	1,097	74	62	52	35	37	37	51	39	38	46	278	348
Indiana	1,907	1,762	1,231	1,750	3,659	4,135	3,263	300	173	175	151	220	217	206	271	339	382	426	403
Pennsylvania	1,372	1,260	919	901	805	824	245	10	34	5	9	23	70	6		2	3	14	68
Minnesota	1,274	2,389	2,252	2,732	3,796	4,475	3,062	345	128		26	9	150	347	147	165	242	521	991
Ohio	1,153	820	1,206	741	507	696	491	71	24	19	24		39	31	28	28	66	70	64
Missouri	1,088	522	1,002	2,315	2,035	1,168	1,249	107	90	137	50	89	55	107	121	64	106	73	250
Iowa	1,017	1,124	1,883	2,700	3,536	4,179	4,962	381	160	124	118	77	230	442	265	352	796	818	1,199
West Virginia	985	957	982	1,034	797	410	291	8	2		(¹)						(¹)	121	160
Kansas	660	655	932	910	885	1,615	4,901	226	207	485	151	182	370	349	372	634	537	769	619
New York	424	368	1,047	676	852	759	683	55	21	71	25	153	203			26	63		66
Wisconsin	396	406	268	697	787	544	570	26	33				27		10	34	139	155	146
Oklahoma	321	446	880	1,302	2,474	2,067	2,710	261	205	203	277	235	278	188	188	153	215	262	245
Delaware	262	138	77	77	47	10	1			1									1
Texas	213	130	798	303	1,208	1,829	1,745	9	86	170	142	136	130	(¹)	17	42		461	540
Maryland	201	256	162	233	181	84	106		5	7	8	4	4	21	2	5	5	5	49
Nebraska	167	298	453	377	1,354	673	1,089	132	107	144	61	84	122	91	51	49	70	96	82
Michigan	142	36	39	256	36	102	47	29						3			18		
Kentucky	81	68	459	171	105	504	542		24	131	128	72	62	43	23	1	27	2	6
New Jersey	63	71	227	15	107	113	306	23	49	46		20			21		80	50	39
South Dakota	45	16	17	321	88	132	150	22	1		9							51	66
North Dakota	4	650	595	436	427	445	620	22	31	9	(¹)							199	359
Other States	138	154	307	289	1,190	1,368	1,774	23	12	3	6	76	50	28	21	29	35	349	1,143
Total	21,319	24,611	27,640	29,295	32,126	31,822	31,844	2,373	1,601	1,885	1,359	1,558	2,177	1,931	1,763	2,097	2,965	4,925	7,210

Bureau of Agricultural Economics. Compiled from reports of bureau representatives in the various markets.

¹ Not over 500 pounds.

TABLE 482.—*Frozen poultry:* [1] *Cold-storage holdings, United States, 1916–1928*

Year	Jan. 1	Feb. 1	Mar. 1	Apr. 1	May 1	June 1	July 1	Aug. 1	Sept. 1	Oct. 1	Nov. 1	Dec. 1
	1,000 lbs.	1,000 lbs.	1,000 lbs.	1,000 lbs.	1,000 lbs.	1,000 lb.s	1,000 lbs.	1,000 lbs.	1,000 lbs.	1,000 lbs.	1,000 lbs.	1,000 lbs.
Average:												
1916–1920					44,660	35,186	31,613	28,572	28,451	30,003	38,313	50,346
1921–1925	102,063	108,750	101,045	82,066	61,570	47,742	40,930	36,051	32,730	33,829	42,881	70,979
1916					17,847	6,559	6,216	7,032	8,882	20,041	31,175	27,139
1917	32,184	35,601	27,796	25,988	67,242	64,286	60,194	54,132	56,093	46,737	51,743	49,561
1918	64,557	68,238	56,950	44,115	26,523	18,929	17,652	18,756	23,034	29,798	44,433	71,238
1919	108,722	119,675	109,627	92,897	71,162	55,616	49,212	40,573	32,918	30,492	33,139	54,749
1920	87,512	92,253	78,421	61,436	40,525	30,535	24,790	22,364	21,331	22,953	31,070	49,046
1921	79,025	81,096	79,001	62,315	47,651	35,408	27,268	21,188	20,064	25,602	34,876	65,167
1922	103,697	103,350	88,709	68,471	50,840	38,602	34,837	30,659	27,671	25,984	30,238	51,781
1923	100,170	121,632	113,503	94,872	74,562	57,274	49,100	41,250	34,131	33,142	40,363	63,274
1924	93,434	99,486	93,497	76,067	52,068	39,299	34,886	33,604	33,837	40,070	55,139	87,939
1925	133,990	138,189	130,513	108,608	82,732	68,126	58,562	53,558	47,946	44,345	53,787	86,733
1926	111,501	108,512	95,397	73,124	52,783	42,808	36,730	35,793	38,634	44,771	64,842	106,854
1927	144,497	145,076	129,510	104,697	77,282	61,525	50,064	42,293	39,711	43,201	52,315	85,030
1928	117,490	118,154	103,494	83,169	56,832	43,872	38,230	40,395	40,749	43,578	58,093	79,173

Bureau of Agricultural Economics. Compiled from reports from cold-storage establishments.

[1] Quantities given net weight.

TABLE 483.—*Chickens: Estimated price per pound, received by producers, United States, 1910–1928*

Year beginning July—	July 15	Aug. 15	Sept. 15	Oct. 15	Nov. 15	Dec. 15	Jan. 15	Feb. 15	Mar. 15	Apr. 15	May 15	June 15	Weighted av.
	Cents	Cents	Cents	Cents	Cents	Cents	Cents	Cents	Cents	Cents	Cents	Cents	Cents
Average:													
1910–1913	11.9	11.8	11.7	11.6	10.8	10.6	10.7	11.0	11.3	11.6	11.7	11.8	11.2
1914–1920	19.4	18.9	19.0	18.1	17.2	16.9	17.4	18.4	19.0	19.9	20.0	20.1	18.1
1921–1925	20.9	20.2	19.7	19.1	18.2	17.9	18.6	19.3	19.8	20.6	21.3	21.4	19.1
1910	12.2	12.0	11.8	11.4	11.0	10.6	10.6	10.6	10.7	10.9	11.0	11.1	11.0
1911	11.2	11.2	11.0	10.6	10.0	9.7	10.0	10.4	10.6	11.0	11.1	11.0	10.4
1912	11.2	11.3	11.4	11.4	11.0	10.8	11.0	11.4	11.7	11.9	12.0	11.2	11.2
1913	13.0	12.8	12.7	13.0	11.4	11.3	11.5	12.0	12.4	13.0	12.7	13.1	12.0
1914	13.4	13.1	12.8	12.0	11.1	10.7	10.9	11.3	11.7	11.9	12.0	12.2	11.5
1915	12.2	12.2	12.0	11.8	11.5	11.2	11.5	12.1	12.5	13.1	13.6	14.0	12.0
1916	14.1	14.1	14.2	14.4	13.9	13.6	14.1	15.1	15.7	17.3	17.5	17.7	14.6
1917	17.4	16.7	18.4	18.5	17.0	17.5	18.4	20.3	20.2	20.7	20.6	21.3	18.4
1918	23.2	23.4	23.6	22.2	21.7	22.4	22.1	21.8	23.4	25.7	26.7	26.4	23.0
1919	26.8	26.1	25.0	23.3	22.0	22.0	23.3	25.7	26.9	28.4	28.0	27.4	24.2
1920	28.4	26.6	26.9	24.6	22.9	20.6	21.7	22.3	22.8	22.2	21.8	21.5	22.8
1921	21.7	21.4	20.2	19.1	18.6	18.2	18.9	19.0	19.4	20.0	20.2	20.6	19.3
1922	20.7	18.9	18.6	18.1	17.2	17.2	17.3	18.6	18.8	19.4	20.1	20.3	18.2
1923	20.6	19.8	19.7	19.0	17.7	16.6	17.5	18.2	18.9	19.4	20.3	20.5	18.3
1924	20.2	20.0	19.8	19.4	18.5	17.9	18.5	19.1	20.0	21.1	22.0	21.6	19.2
1925	21.4	20.8	20.4	20.0	19.2	19.5	20.9	21.5	21.9	23.1	23.7	23.9	20.7
1926	23.6	22.1	21.4	20.8	20.0	19.8	20.1	21.1	21.3	21.8	21.7	20.2	20.7
1927	19.9	19.7	19.4	19.7	19.4	19.2	19.6	20.1	20.1	20.8	21.5	21.5	19.8
1928	21.9	21.6	22.3	22.0	21.5	21.2							

Bureau of Agricultural Economics. Based on returns from special price reporters. Average price of chickens (live weight) of all ages as reported.

TABLE 484.—*Turkeys: Estimated price per pound, received by producers, United States, 1912–1928*

Year beginning October—	Oct. 15	Nov. 15	Dec. 15	Jan. 15	Year beginning October—	Oct. 15	Nov. 15	Dec. 15	Jan. 15
	Cents	Cents	Cents	Cents		Cents	Cents	Cents	Cents
1912	13.6	14.4	14.8	14.9	1921	25.7	28.2	32.5	30.7
1913	14.6	15.2	15.5	15.5	1922	25.1	29.5	32.3	29.7
1914	14.1	14.1	14.5	14.5	1923	26.6	27.9	24.5	23.1
1915	13.7	14.8	15.5	15.6	1924	23.3	24.2	25.8	26.2
1916	17.0	18.6	19.6	19.5	1925	24.0	28.3	31.1	31.7
1917	20.0	21.0	23.0	22.9	1926	26.6	29.8	32.8	31.6
1918	23.9	25.7	27.0	27.3	1927	26.4	30.8	32.3	29.8
1919	26.6	28.3	31.1	32.0	1928	27.2	31.2	30.5	28.2
1920	30.0	31.8	33.1	33.0					

Bureau of Agricultural Economics. Based on returns from special price reporters.

TABLE 485.—*Eggs: Receipts at five markets, 1927–1928*[1]

BOSTON

Year	Jan.	Feb.	Mar.	Apr.	May	June	July	Aug.	Sept.	Oct.	Nov.	Dec.	Total
Av. 1921–1925	*1,000 cases* 87	*1,000 cases* 121	*1,000 cases* 214	*1,000 cases* 326	*1,000 cases* 327	*1,000 cases* 209	*1,000 cases* 148	*1,000 cases* 123	*1,000 cases* 95	*1,000 cases* 101	*1,000 cases* 64	*1,000 cases* 65	*1,000 cases* 1,880
1927	120	153	245	307	270	234	155	128	109	92	65	82	1,960
1928	102	145	229	211	258	200	158	112	96	96	78	72	1,757

NEW YORK

Year	Jan.	Feb.	Mar.	Apr.	May	June	July	Aug.	Sept.	Oct.	Nov.	Dec.	Total
Av. 1921–1925	332	461	898	1,062	948	778	569	478	414	353	235	271	6,799
1927	458	542	863	1,094	1,038	716	521	441	386	355	319	315	7,048
1928	412	613	931	1,052	1,089	767	591	494	407	392	268	272	7,288

PHILADELPHIA

Year	Jan.	Feb.	Mar.	Apr.	May	June	July	Aug.	Sept.	Oct.	Nov.	Dec.	Total
Av. 1921–1925	88	112	177	258	246	168	127	123	120	91	63	74	1,648
1927	96	100	183	244	211	158	119	114	117	80	68	59	1,549
1928	97	133	176	210	246	175	168	117	140	103	75	95	1,735

CHICAGO

Year	Jan.	Feb.	Mar.	Apr.	May	June	July	Aug.	Sept.	Oct.	Nov.	Dec.	Total
Av. 1921–1925	164	327	571	803	836	654	395	307	224	153	77	93	4,605
1927	243	326	628	1,002	935	594	363	255	231	127	101	96	4,901
1928	200	366	592	813	849	562	356	284	241	150	75	113	4,601

SAN FRANCISCO

Year	Jan.	Feb.	Mar.	Apr.	May	June	July	Aug.	Sept.	Oct.	Nov.	Dec.	Total
Av. 1921–1925	58	59	96	98	88	81	70	60	51	48	44	49	801
1927	54	57	78	83	69	65	68	66	54	50	50	56	750
1928	52	63	106	75	61	59	61	69	54	52	49	55	756

TOTAL, 1919–1928

Year	Jan.	Feb.	Mar.	Apr.	May	June	July	Aug.	Sept.	Oct.	Nov.	Dec.	Total
Av. 1921–1925	729	1,080	1,956	2,548	2,445	1,890	1,308	1,091	904	746	483	552	15,733
1919	494	1,014	1,556	2,761	2,424	1,890	1,276	1,018	826	691	394	341	14,686
1920	508	815	1,447	1,934	2,203	1,805	1,143	911	806	594	398	382	12,946
1921	653	1,161	2,209	2,467	2,055	1,561	1,142	1,107	909	727	488	531	15,010
1922	809	1,025	1,952	2,902	2,583	1,926	1,304	1,019	816	704	484	492	16,016
1923	852	1,032	2,118	2,268	2,852	2,066	1,349	1,180	988	844	555	587	16,691
1924	714	1,006	1,654	2,539	2,544	1,871	1,431	1,042	876	748	457	524	15,406
1925	618	1,176	1,846	2,563	2,193	2,025	1,315	1,106	930	709	433	626	15,540
1926	906	1,070	1,741	2,086	2,261	2,015	1,386	1,081	933	699	581	752	15,511
1927	971	1,178	1,997	2,730	2,523	1,767	1,226	1,004	897	704	603	608	16,208
1928	863	1,320	2,034	2,361	2,503	1,763	1,334	1,076	938	793	545	607	16,137

Bureau of Agricultural Economics. Compiled from reports of bureau representatives in the various markets. See 1927 Yearbook, p. 1098, for data for earlier years.

[1] In cases of 30 dozen.

TABLE 486.—*Eggs: Receipts at six markets, by States of origin, 1922-1928* [1]

BOSTON

State	1922	1923	1924	1925	1926	1927	1928 Total	Jan.	Feb.	Mar.	Apr.	May	June	July	Aug.	Sept.	Oct.	Nov.	Dec.
	1,000 cases	*1,000 cases*	*1,000 cases*	*1,000 cases*	*1,000 cases*	*1,000 cases*	*1,000 cases*	*1,000 cases*	*1,000 cases*	*1,000 cases*	*1,000 cases*	*1,000 cases*	*1,000 cases*	*1,000 cases*	*1,000 cases*	*1,000 cases*	*1,000 cases*	*1,000 cases*	*1,000 cases*
Illinois	710	845	691	390	327	319	251	25	8	27	39	50	21	16	10	9	16	17	13
Indiana	320	233	185	156	163	211	152	4	4	13	29	32	24	16	10	8	3	3	3
Iowa	142	146	186	259	270	307	194	3	6	20	19	22	26	30	20	17	16	10	5
Minnesota	108	109	191	250	229	219	236	1	2	12	36	50	41	35	20	16	7	6	4
Ohio	108	87	75	39	52	115	53	2	1	3	5	7	6	8	2	7	4	2	1
Missouri	100	78	80	158	134	131	106	9	15	27	15	15	8	4	4	1	4	2	4
Maine	99	122	99	100	82	76	84	10	8	11	10	11	9	5	15	4	3	3	6
Kansas	83	61	57	174	182	206	244	12	39	40	19	21	18	14	3	3	20	14	15
Michigan	42	43	37	40	41	41	36	1	(²)	1	5	7	6	5	2	1	3	2	6
New York	40	36	37	28	31	41	32	5	1	1	2	4	3	(²)	1	1	1	4	3
New Hampshire	38	44	28	32	22	25	31	5	3	4	4	4	2	1	1	1		2	1
Vermont	37	36	25	27	18	17	22	2	2	2	3	3	3	2	1	(²)	1	1	1
Massachusetts	24	21	16	12	7	16	7	2	(²)	1	1	(²)	(²)	(²)	1				
Nebraska	19	19	31	61	91	87	94	3	21	18	5	9	11	9	3	5	5	3	2
Other States	100	64	80	107	159	149	215	18	35	49	19	23	22	13	7	6	8	8	7
Total	1,970	1,944	1,829	1,833	1,808	1,960	1,757	102	145	229	211	258	200	158	112	96	96	78	72

CHICAGO

State	1922	1923	1924	1925	1926	1927	1928 Total	Jan.	Feb.	Mar.	Apr.	May	June	July	Aug.	Sept.	Oct.	Nov.	Dec.
Missouri	1,045	880	661	604	655	832	674	25	53	96	133	133	80	43	36	27	24	10	14
Iowa	843	996	892	888	875	927	826	40	71	72	155	156	90	69	55	54	30	15	19
Kansas	532	501	433	439	403	477	446	37	57	68	53	72	48	35	29	17	12	9	9
Wisconsin	474	584	592	473	485	503	427	19	19	34	72	96	66	38	29	22	9	6	17
Minnesota	462	610	644	573	618	583	545	13	23	43	98	112	73	41	48	39	25	9	21
South Dakota	405	551	595	564	514	445	467	8	25	53	87	87	66	46	36	32	21	3	3
Nebraska	352	359	465	511	464	420	438	23	52	51	54	61	62	49	30	33	12	4	7
Illinois	310	256	194	87	148	152	120	4	8	12	36	27	15	7	3	3	3	4	2
Oklahoma	103	101	72	42	70	82	96	3	16	39	22	9	4	1	1	1	1	1	(²)
North Dakota	23	33	46	14	53	27	38	(²)	1	6	8	6	7	6	2	1	(²)	(²)	(²)
Texas	22	49	25	14	13	36	97	1	10	39	25	20	10		(²)	4	2	1	2
Michigan	18	18	20	15	13	37	57	5	4	4	6	6	1	5	(²)	(²)	(²)	1	(²)
Arkansas	14	20	3		23	48	32	(²)	9	13	3			(²)					
Other States	81	51	37	104	241	332	338	22	18	62	61	54	39	16	11	8	12	16	19
Total	4,684	5,009	4,679	4,498	4,575	4,901	4,601	200	366	592	813	849	562	356	284	241	150	75	113

[1] In cases of 30 dozen.   ² Not over 500 cases.

TABLE 486.—*Eggs: Receipts at six markets, by States of origin, 1922–1928*—Continued

NEW YORK

State	1922	1923	1924	1925	1926	1927	1928 Total	Jan.	Feb.	Mar.	Apr.	May	June	July	Aug.	Sept.	Oct.	Nov.	Dec.
	1,000 cases	*1,000 cases*	*1,000 cases*	*1,000 cases*	*1,000 cases*	*1,000 cases*	*1,000 cases*	*1,000 cases*	*1,000 cases*	*1,000 cases*	*1,000 cases*	*1,000 cases*	*1,000 cases*	*1,000 cases*	*1,000 cases*	*1,000 cases*	*1,000 cases*	*1,000 cases*	*1,000 cases*
Illinois	1,379	1,342	1,223	1,258	939	950	869	80	50	114	150	132	99	60	43	38	45	38	20
Iowa	921	934	942	924	1,102	1,038	1,071	8	29	106	190	217	150	119	91	74	66	14	7
Indiana	726	575	526	568	542	566	468	19	11	55	95	98	67	42	28	19	15	4	4
Ohio	514	436	327	324	394	356	276	5	11	23	58	74	41	28	11	10	8	4	3
New York	491	645	615	688	637	605	666	54	42	58	95	108	85	61	44	36	24	28	31
Missouri	438	453	415	364	351	342	349	20	43	69	59	50	24	20	19	10	14	9	12
California	354	430	331	456	439	502	589	47	73	54	34	49	34	40	54	46	62	48	48
Pennsylvania	265	238	274	244	240	212	191	13	11	18	24	32	24	20	15	10	7	9	8
Tennessee	251	249	141	189	120	195	186	7	26	66	39	30	6	3	5	2	1	2	8
Kansas	222	242	181	197	237	214	280	13	58	43	29	23	25	24	21	16	14	6	8
Minnesota	217	264	261	246	201	178	204	1	5	15	25	37	29	26	16	22	11	7	10
Washington	143	271	254	375	543	655	661	66	77	47	39	44	45	43	59	53	64	56	68
Kentucky	143	103	61	74	69	97	63	1	6	15	19	6	6	1	4	1	(²)	(²)	11
New Jersey	134	199	222	216	213	194	180	10	10	14	14	27	24	20	14	11	14	11	11
Michigan	100	107	97	70	56	36	46	1	1	2	9	15	6	2	3	4	3	3	1
Maryland	84	124	124	118	118	141	131	9	10	23	25	20	12	10	8	5	3	3	3
Virginia	65	99	104	92	80	111	102	5	5	23	20	16	8	7	6	4	3	2	3
Wisconsin	54	54	68	90	78	54	54	4	4	4	11	12	8	3	1	(²)	1	2	4
Delaware	52	63	82	80	80	87	72	6	6	12	13	12	8	6	6	2	2	1	1
Nebraska	38	55	57	56	55	64	132	5	21	20	19	12	12	13	10	9	5	1	1
Other States	230	273	238	265	324	451	798	42	106	150	85	68	54	43	39	35	32	19	25
Total	6,821	7,156	6,543	6,894	6,818	7,048	7,288	412	613	931	1,052	1,089	767	591	494	407	392	268	272

PHILADELPHIA

State	1922	1923	1924	1925	1926	1927	1928 Total	Jan.	Feb.	Mar.	Apr.	May	June	July	Aug.	Sept.	Oct.	Nov.	Dec.
Illinois	274	312	304	254	189	110	124	24	3	7	13	22	11	10	6	7	5	6	10
Missouri	152	147	134	131	260	221	183	9	17	24	12	16	19	26	19	16	15	5	5
Indiana	149	125	103	98	113	129	60	2	2	1	13	12	11	7	4	4	1	1	2
Ohio	149	100	103	129	100	96	54	(²)	1	4	4	13	8	6	4	4	1	2	7
Pennsylvania	147	174	155	133	109	97	273	16	19	36	41	49	36	23	15	11	7	8	12
Michigan	145	163	148	123	113	95	61	---	---	1	11	16	9	7	5	9	2	1	---
Virginia	144	149	153	120	99	129	125	6	6	24	24	27	14	8	8	9	2	2	2
Iowa	71	80	106	109	105	127	128	(²)	3	8	15	22	15	23	13	13	1	1	1
Maryland	68	66	58	55	38	35	38	2	3	7	8	6	3	2	2	2	1	1	1

Minnesota	10	11	26	34	20	31	22	13	12	9	6	2	196	151	104	113	84	75	63
Tennessee	(²)	(²)	1	(²)	(²)	7	1	4	1	8	5	2	22	59	15	27	12	25	61
Kansas	5	4	6	9	8	3	4	5	7	14	19	3	91	60	68	43	45	70	48
Delaware	2	1	1	1	2	5	5	10	9	8	4	3	49	16	23	35	46	53	46
Wisconsin	2	1	4	4	3	5	4	7	8	1	1	3	38	46	53	37	34	34	29
West Virginia	1	(²)	(²)	(²)	(²)	(²)	1	1	1	1	1	1	6	13	9	17	21	26	27
New York	(²)	(²)	3	1	1	1	1	4	2	1	1	5	24	6	19	29	26	35	17
Nebraska	(²)	3	2	3	8	3	1	4	1	3	9	2	29	30	46	17	15	36	15
Other States	5	29	15	17	8	6	10	18	29	19	34	19	234	129	103	92	48	57	98
Total	95	75	103	140	117	168	175	246	210	176	133	97	1,735	1,549	1,566	1,572	1,595	1,727	1,703

SAN FRANCISCO

California	50	45	51	50	63	53	57	56	71	102	62	50	710	705	710	686	737	825	824
Oregon	2	3	1	4	5	2	(²)	1	1	1	(²)	(²)	23	19	16	37	10	13	7
Washington	2	1	(²)	(²)	1	1	(²)	(²)	(²)	1	(²)	1	6	17	6	11	6	10	6
Idaho	(²)	(²)	(²)	(²)	1	1	1	4	3	3	(²)	1	13	6	10	6	3	6	1
Other States	1	(²)	(²)	(²)	1	1	1	(²)	(²)	1	1	(²)	4	3	2	3	4	1	1
Total	55	49	52	54	69	61	59	61	75	106	63	52	756	750	744	743	760	855	838

LOS ANGELES

California	31	26	27	26	38	36	58	74	87	93	68	40	604	409	446	456			
Idaho	(²)	(²)	(²)	1	2	1	1	3	3	1	(²)	(²)	10	22	56	62			
Oregon	3	(²)	2	1	1	(²)	1	1	1	1	1	(²)	7	19	19	24			
Utah	7	1	(²)	2	(²)	(²)	1	1	(²)	1	(²)	(²)	4	6	26	16			
Other States	1	1	1	(²)	1	(²)	1	1	(²)	1	(²)	(²)	8	4	13	17			
Total	41	27	29	27	41	37	60	78	90	95	68	40	633	460	560	575			

Bureau of Agricultural Economics. Compiled from reports of bureau representatives in the various markets.

² Not over 500 cases.

TABLE 487.—*Eggs: Quarterly receipts at New York by regions of origin, 1921–1928*

JANUARY, FEBRUARY, MARCH

Year	Quantity	East [1]	Mid-West [2]	South [3]	Mountain [4]	Pacific [5]	Miscellaneous [6]
	1,000 cases	*Per cent*	*Per cent*	*Per cent*	*Per cent*	*Per cent*	*Per cent*
1921	1,791	9.2	62.3	11.4	_____	12.1	5.0
1922	1,679	14.3	71.1	12.3	_____	11.5	.8
1923	1,814	18.2	54.2	11.3	0.2	15.0	1.1
1924	1,428	25.0	48.0	7.2	1.5	16.8	1.5
1925	1,748	21.5	49.3	9.5	1.2	17.8	.7
1926	1,678	20.2	50.4	6.8	2.5	19.4	.7
1927	1,863	19.3	47.5	10.0	2.5	19.8	.9
1928	1,956	17.2	45.6	11.7	4.5	20.1	.9

APRIL, MAY, JUNE

Year	Quantity	East	Mid-West	South	Mountain	Pacific	Miscellaneous
1921	2,436	14.0	77.5	3.0	_____	4.1	1.4
1922	2,938	16.6	76.1	3.7	_____	3.0	.6
1923	2,884	21.1	69.6	3.6	0.2	4.4	1.1
1924	2,841	21.4	72.4	1.7	.6	3.0	.9
1925	2,825	21.4	69.8	2.7	.3	5.2	.6
1926	2,599	21.5	69.5	1.8	.6	6.0	.6
1927	2,847	19.7	67.9	3.3	1.3	7.1	.7
1928	2,907	19.7	63.6	4.4	2.8	8.7	.8

JULY, AUGUST, SEPTEMBER

Year	Quantity	East	Mid-West	South	Mountain	Pacific	Miscellaneous
1921	1,482	12.3	77.4	1.0	_____	8.0	1.3
1922	1,400	18.2	73.2	.9	_____	6.3	1.4
1923	1,540	18.2	69.1	.6	0.3	10.9	.9
1924	1,434	21.9	69.4	.8	.4	6.5	1.0
1925	1,467	21.6	66.1	.5	.7	10.4	.7
1926	1,513	20.1	65.8	.8	.5	12.2	.6
1927	1,348	20.6	59.3	.6	1.2	17.5	.8
1928	1,492	19.3	54.6	1.0	3.4	20.9	.8

OCTOBER, NOVEMBER, DECEMBER

Year	Quantity	East	Mid-West	South	Mountain	Pacific	Miscellaneous
1921	883	12.0	67.3	7.9	_____	11.0	1.8
1922	805	16.4	61.4	3.9	_____	17.5	.8
1923	919	18.9	58.2	2.6	0.6	18.1	1.6
1924	840	19.3	52.6	1.7	.8	24.4	1.2
1925	855	19.2	45.1	1.2	1.8	32.0	.7
1926	1,028	18.0	41.1	2.4	1.7	36.1	.7
1927	990	16.7	35.4	2.1	2.9	42.0	.9
1928	932	17.8	37.3	.9	4.1	39.1	.8

Bureau of Agricultural Economics.

[1] East—Maine, New Hampshire, Vermont, Massachusetts, Rhode Island, Connecticut, New York, New Jersey, Pennsylvania, Delaware, Maryland, West Virginia, and Virginia.
[2] Mid-West—Ohio, Indiana, Kentucky, Illinois, Missouri, Kansas, Nebraska, Iowa, South Dakota, North Dakota, Minnesota, Wisconsin, and Michigan.
[3] South—North Carolina, Tennessee, South Carolina, Georgia, Florida, Alabama, Louisiana, Oklahoma, Texas, Mississippi, and Arkansas.
[4] Mountain—Montana, Idaho, Wyoming, Colorado, Utah, Nevada, Arizona, and New Mexico.
[5] Pacific—Washington, Oregon, and California.
[6] Miscellaneous—Parcel post and Canada.

Table 488.—*Case eggs:*[1] *Cold-storage holdings, United States, 1915–1928*

Year	Jan. 1	Feb. 1	Mar. 1	Apr. 1	May 1	June 1	July 1	Aug. 1	Sept. 1	Oct. 1	Nov. 1	Dec. 1
	1,000 cases	1,000 cases	1,000 cases	1,000 cases	1,000 cases	1,000 cases	1,000 cases	1,000 cases	1,000 cases	1,000 cases	1,000 cases	1,000 cases
Average:												
1916–1920	1,202	256	23	248	2,560	5,251	6,630	6,849	6,472	5,645	4,272	2,466
1921–1925	1,117	203	27	1,030	4,346	7,475	9,147	9,513	9,070	7,790	5,668	3,315
1915								5,029	5,683	5,019	3,687	2,788
1916	1,508	458	35	264	2,327	4,593	5,574	6,060	5,600	4,868	3,985	2,146
1917	920	149	7	190	2,105	4,922	6,617	6,895	6,436	5,837	4,638	2,948
1918	1,300	200	20	344	2,957	5,499	6,554	6,568	6,265	5,369	3,812	2,071
1919	740	130	26	320	3,278	6,098	7,659	7,850	7,685	6,858	5,087	3,341
1920	1,542	342	29	122	2,135	5,143	6,747	6,872	6,372	5,295	3,838	1,824
1921	408	43	43	1,926	4,909	6,844	7,534	7,605	7,210	6,269	4,380	2,403
1922	889	179	13	950	4,648	8,056	9,811	10,161	9,608	7,924	5,726	3,257
1923	1,311	213	13	453	3,737	7,890	10,222	10,509	9,883	8,737	6,645	4,028
1924	1,927	500	44	579	3,563	6,875	8,685	9,267	8,778	7,409	5,267	3,102
1925	1,050	81	21	1,240	4,872	7,712	9,482	10,024	9,873	8,612	6,322	3,786
1926	1,683	578	77	872	3,735	7,236	9,133	9,845	9,573	8,048	5,888	3,215
1927	1,096	253	92	1,868	5,501	8,962	10,565	10,746	9,650	7,960	5,485	2,956
1928	882	26	66	1,087	4,515	8,168	10,002	10,496	9,944	8,542	6,247	3,542

Bureau of Agricultural Economics. Compiled from reports from cold-storage establishments.

[1] 30-dozen cases.

Table 489.—*Frozen eggs:*[1] *Cold-storage holdings, United States, 1916–1928*

Year	Jan. 1	Feb. 1	Mar.1	Apr. 1	May 1	June 1	July 1	Aug. 1	Sept. 1	Oct. 1	Nov. 1	Dec. 1
	1,000 lbs.	1,000 lbs.	1,000 lbs.	1,000 lbs.	1,000 lbs.	1,000 lbs.	1,000 lbs.	1,000 lbs.	1,000 lbs.	1,000 lbs.	1,000 lbs.	1,000 lbs.
Average:												
1917–1921	14,586	12,602	10,842	9,859	10,624	14,288	17,578	19,531	21,188	20,654	19,051	20,269
1921–1925	24,552	20,725	16,926	14,749	18,418	25,065	30,579	34,008	36,086	35,868	33,802	29,314
1916					3,133	4,176	5,410	5,822	5,223	6,457	6,307	5,104
1917	2,737	1,724	1,334	2,394	3,329	7,558	13,398	15,384	19,741	17,585	16,424	13,979
1918	14,603	12,207	9,746	9,001	9,488	11,555	12,895	15,240	15,871	14,757	13,281	11,832
1919	8,980	7,760	6,931	5,989	8,046	11,568	16,472	19,024	21,017	20,687	18,976	22,690
1920	19,286	16,394	13,836	11,039	10,529	13,939	17,388	20,055	21,901	23,584	20,461	29,945
1921	27,325	24,927	22,363	20,873	21,730	26,822	27,737	27,952	27,408	26,656	26,114	22,899
1922	19,260	16,209	13,193	10,473	14,154	18,273	23,528	27,855	34,516	33,545	30,523	26,233
1923	22,787	18,517	14,603	10,311	12,921	20,730	29,686	36,192	37,280	43,836	40,424	36,004
1924	32,087	27,682	23,106	20,736	23,707	29,956	33,565	35,184	34,128	31,006	26,633	22,100
1925	21,303	16,292	11,364	11,353	19,579	29,544	38,379	42,855	47,099	44,299	45,314	39,336
1926	33,905	29,256	24,167	21,849	25,739	34,815	45,688	51,810	52,634	51,062	44,966	38,620
1927	33,593	31,207	26,053	33,272	52,053	71,605	81,263	81,418	77,508	71,208	62,066	54,703
1928	47,020	38,575	31,362	34,411	51,532	67,941	77,744	81,670	89,196	82,255	73,327	64,201

Bureau of Agricultural Economics.

[1] Quantities given are net weight.

TABLE 490.—*Eggs in the shell: International trade, average 1909–1913, annual 1924–1927*

Country	Year ended Dec. 31									
	Average, 1909–1913		1924		1925		1926		1927, preliminary	
	Imports	Exports	Imports	Exports	Imports	Exports	Imports	Exports	Imports	Exports
PRINCIPAL EXPORTING COUNTRIES	*1,000 dozen*	*1,000 dozen*	*1,000 dozen*	*1,000 dozen*	*1,000 dozen*	*1,000 dozen*	*1,000 dozen*	*1,000 dozen*	*1,000 dozen*	*1,000 dozen*
China	270	25,542	847	78,688	0	65,376	0	63,230	0	50,235
Denmark	2,243	34,340	1,215	69,374	473	67,225	192	69,351	283	70,404
Netherlands	19,542	29,360	7,982	52,426	8,447	71,063	9,620	86,414	10,502	103,614
Irish Free State	0	0	628	42,728	611	43,592	440	43,662	372	49,462
Poland	0	0	820	15,317	1,302	39,787	82	86,076	184	96,400
United States	[1] 1,701	12,108	383	28,117	609	24,999	298	26,634	* 250	28,707
Italy	4,104	33,482	4,055	38,356	6,872	44,612	10,226	31,535	22,379	20,700
Morocco		[2] 5,653	0	15,785	0	15,654	0	15,614	0	
Belgium	19,148	11,521	2,689	13,837	2,909	18,003	790	32,969	990	40,260
Egypt	[1] 101	9,690	14	17,140	11	13,174	1	8,939		9,197
Hungary	[3] 91,561	[3] 177,163	16	8,825	310	21,010	234	24,749	302	20,933
Bulgaria	55	16,512	3	13,605	0	16,219	0	17,391	0	18,335
Rumania	18	12,323	0	11,757	0	15,891	1	16,683		
Lithuania	0	0	0	7,060	0	5,415	0	5,787	0	5,349
Union of South Africa	1,382	[4] 90	71	2,401	184	2,592	62	2,609	126	3,446
Estonia	0	0	13	943	0	1,426	0	1,036	0	1,340
Finland	2,899	3	113	58	54	114	23	83	17	26
Russia	18,081	274,891								
PRINCIPAL IMPORTING COUNTRIES										
United Kingdom	190,015	0	200,079	628	216,828	713	220,741	500	243,475	
Germany	228,279	675	104,471	705	203,045	1,547	196,852	182	225,118	286
Japan	6,867	0	38,157	0	28,822	0	25,462	0	21,700	0
Spain	7,404	618	22,706	3	19,048	15	25,318	20		
Switzerland	19,747	48	16,874	12	17,337	10	17,198	10	16,159	12
France	37,215	8,920	9,498	4,494	7,382	5,168	7,337	17,020	12,085	20,253
Austria	0	0	17,203	0	16,460	0	22,315	1,732	24,780	2,002
Cuba	4,732	0	13,019	0	11,937	0	11,774	0		0
Philippine Islands	4,315	0	5,108	0	5,754	0	4,942			0
Canada	6,341	148	4,981	2,717	2,722	2,466	3,560	1,777	3,227	448
Argentina	2,351	0	3,003	4,555	6,321	3,585	8,477	1,475	10,976	977
Sweden	4,207	3,781	2,861	1,057	933	1,153	1,560	2,619	215	5,485
Czechoslovakia	0	0	1,779	10	1,944	495	4,032	1,437	4,287	3,286
Norway	387	4	92	1,092	127	1,129	126	452	84	98
Total 31 countries	672,965	656,872	458,680	431,690	560,442	482,433	571,663	559,986	597,511	551,255

Bureau of Agricultural Economics.   Official sources.

[1] 1 year only.
[2] 2-year average.
[3] Average for Austria-Hungary.
[4] 4-year average.

TABLE 491.—*Eggs not in the shell: International trade, average 1909–1913, annual 1924–1927*

Country	Average 1909-1913		1924		1925		1926		1927 preliminary	
	Imports	Exports	Imports	Exports	Imports	Exports	Imports	Exports	Imports	Exports
	1,000 pounds	*1,000 pounds*	*1,000 pounds*	*1,000 pounds*	*1,000 pounds*	*1,000 pounds*	*1,000 pounds*	*1,000 pounds*	*1,000 pounds*	*1,000 pounds*
PRINCIPAL EXPORTING COUNTRIES										
China	0	17,217	0	94,712	0	133,895	0	132,471	0	100,856
PRINCIPAL IMPORTING COUNTRIES										
United Kingdom	------	------	48,461	653	53,599	913	65,235	613	71,683	------
United States	¹ 394	(²)	19,722	505	33,987	301	25,738	522	15,341	661
Germany	11,214	3,225	10,254	1,606	13,958	1,989	14,559	2,157	17,836	1,544
France	1,967	426	4,752	83	3,821	68	4,237	54	4,055	119
Netherlands	0	0	3,773	1,033	4,304	917	3,882	665	3,970	862
Italy	381	4	1,348	12	1,291	19	1,318	0	953	27
Canada	(²)	(²)	741	0	1,507	0	1,379	0	2,025	0
Irish Free State	------	------	1,006	88	1,091	19	1,022	22	1,090	37
Belgium	------	------	220	27	980	100	795	112	1,123	85
Sweden	³ 255	0	560	7	804	2	758	20	674	------
Denmark	526	⁴ 6	782	20	780	16	569	3	------	------
Total 12 countries	14,737	20,878	91,619	98,746	116,122	138,239	119,492	136,639	118,750	104,191

Bureau of Agricultural Economics. Compiled from official sources.

¹ 4-year average.
² Stated in value only.
³ 2-year average.
⁴ 3-year average.

TABLE 492.—*Eggs: Estimated price per dozen, received by producers, United States, 1910–1928*

Year beginning April	Apr. 15	May 15	June 15	July 15	Aug. 15	Sept. 15	Oct. 15	Nov. 15	Dec. 15	Jan. 15	Feb. 15	Mar. 15	Weighted av.
	Cents	*Cents*	*Cents*	*Cents*	*Cents*	*Cents*	*Cents*	*Cents*	*Cents*	*Cents*	*Cents*	*Cents*	*Cents*
Average:													
1910–1913	16.7	16.6	16.5	16.5	17.7	20.4	23.9	28.1	30.0	27.5	23.1	19.2	19.0
1914–1920	26.0	27.0	26.2	27.3	29.5	33.6	38.2	43.9	49.0	45.5	34.8	27.4	30.1
1921–1925	21.1	21.3	21.7	23.3	25.8	30.2	36.9	46.4	48.4	38.0	31.9	22.7	25.9
1910	18.6	18.4	18.2	17.9	18.5	20.9	23.8	27.2	29.7	26.2	19.3	15.7	19.3
1911	14.8	14.6	14.4	14.8	16.4	18.7	21.8	26.1	29.1	29.3	26.8	21.2	18.2
1912	17.4	16.9	16.7	17.0	18.2	20.6	24.0	27.8	28.2	24.8	21.1	17.9	18.9
1913	15.9	16.5	16.8	16.4	17.7	21.3	26.0	31.3	32.9	29.8	25.3	22.2	19.8
1914	16.4	16.9	17.2	17.5	19.1	22.5	23.7	28.2	31.9	31.7	23.7	16.5	19.3
1915	16.6	16.5	16.1	16.3	17.3	20.6	24.6	29.4	31.1	28.8	24.2	18.2	19.0
1916	17.7	18.5	18.9	19.9	21.6	25.3	30.4	34.9	38.3	38.1	35.7	25.3	23.3
1917	28.5	30.2	29.9	29.0	30.5	35.8	38.5	41.2	45.9	48.9	45.8	30.9	33.0
1918	30.4	30.6	29.5	33.0	35.2	39.1	44.9	51.7	59.3	55.3	34.8	33.9	34.9
1919	36.0	38.9	36.1	37.9	40.6	43.1	51.0	59.1	69.6	60.9	48.5	40.5	41.8
1920	36.6	37.5	35.9	37.8	42.5	48.6	54.6	62.9	67.1	54.5	31.0	26.8	39.3
1921	20.5	19.4	20.1	24.3	28.9	30.9	39.4	50.0	51.1	31.7	31.4	19.5	25.3
1922	20.0	20.9	20.2	20.3	20.6	27.3	34.6	43.6	47.2	37.8	29.9	25.4	24.7
1923	21.6	21.8	20.9	21.3	23.6	29.8	34.6	45.5	45.5	35.4	33.6	20.4	25.2
1924	19.1	19.8	21.1	22.8	26.1	31.8	38.2	45.8	49.9	48.6	35.7	23.9	26.1
1925	24.2	24.8	26.1	27.9	30.0	31.1	37.7	46.8	48.1	36.3	28.9	24.1	28.3
1926	24.8	25.2	25.7	25.7	26.4	31.5	36.8	44.9	47.6	36.9	29.0	20.8	27.5
1927	20.3	19.8	17.8	20.7	23.4	29.4	35.6	41.6	43.3	38.2	29.1	23.4	24.2
1928	22.8	24.2	23.9	25.6	27.4	31.4	34.9	39.6	42.9	33.0	31.9	28.0	27.4

Bureau of Agricultural Economics. Based on returns from special price reporters.

TABLE 493.—*Eggs: Average price per dozen at specified cities, 1926–1928*

FRESH FIRSTS AT NEW YORK

Year	Jan.	Feb.	Mar.	Apr.	May	June	July	Aug.	Sept.	Oct.	Nov.	Dec.	Average
	Cents	Cents	Cents	Cents	Cents	Cents	Cents	Cents	Cents	Cents	Cents	Cents	Cents
Average:													
1914–1920	49	41	33	31	32	31	33	36	40	44	53	57	40
1921–1925	50	40	28	27	27	27	29	31	38	44	54	52	37
1926	38	31	29	32	31	30	29	31	38	40	50	48	36
1927	42	32	25	26	23	23	25	28	34	40	44	45	32
1928	45	32	29	28	30	29	30	31	33	32	37	37	33

FRESH FIRSTS AT CHICAGO

Year	Jan.	Feb.	Mar.	Apr.	May	June	July	Aug.	Sept.	Oct.	Nov.	Dec.	Average
Average:													
1914–1920	45	37	29	29	30	28	30	32	36	40	47	51	36
1921–1925	46	35	25	24	25	25	26	28	33	39	50	47	34
1926	36	29	27	29	29	28	27	29	36	40	48	44	34
1927	38	27	24	23	22	22	23	26	33	37	42	43	30
1928	43	29	27	27	28	28	28	30	32	34	41	39	32

WESTERN FIRSTS AT BOSTON

Year	Jan.	Feb.	Mar.	Apr.	May	June	July	Aug.	Sept.	Oct.	Nov.	Dec.	Average
1926	39	31	29	31	31	30	29	30	37	40	50	50	36
1927	41	31	26	25	24	23	25	28	34	39	44	44	32
1928	46	35	29	29	30	30	30	32	34	36	44	43	35

WESTERN EXTRA FIRSTS AT PHILADELPHIA

Year	Jan.	Feb.	Mar.	Apr.	May	June	July	Aug.	Sept.	Oct.	Nov.	Dec.	Average
1926	41	36	30	32	33	34	32	34	42	47	60	52	39
1927	43	33	27	26	26	25	28	33	40	48	55	50	36
1928	50	37	30	30	32	32	33	36	39	42	50	45	38

FRESH EXTRAS AT SAN FRANCISCO

Year	Jan.	Feb.	Mar.	Apr.	May	June	July	Aug.	Sept.	Oct.	Nov.	Dec.	Average
1926 [1]	34	27	26	29	28	31	33	37	43	50	49	44	36
1927 [2]	33	25	23	24	24	24	26	32	39	47	44	38	32
1928	33	24	25	25	26	29	30	33	39	44	45	38	35

Bureau of Agricultural Economics. Prices 1910–1922 are averages of daily prices in New York Journal of Commerce, Price Current and Chicago Dairy Produce, Philadelphia Commercial List; average of weekly prices quoted in Boston Chamber of Commerce and Pacific Dairy Review. Beginning 1923, monthly prices from the Bureau of Labor Statistics, except San Francisco, which is from the Pacific Dairy Review. Earlier data are available in 1925 Yearbook, p. 1224, Table 636, and 1927 Yearbook, p. 1105.

[1] Year 1926 are prices as quoted by the San Francisco Mercantile Exchange in the Pacific Dairy Review not subject to discount.
[2] Beginning January, 1927, prices furnished by the Bureau of Agricultural Economics to the Pacific Dairy Review, for United States No. 1 extras.

FOREIGN TRADE OF THE UNITED STATES IN AGRICULTURAL PRODUCTS

TABLE 494.—*Foreign trade of the United States in agricultural products, summary, 1909–1928*

Year ended June 30	Agricultural exports[1] — Total exports (1,000 dollars)	Domestic (1,000 dollars)	Percentage of total	Reexports (1,000 dollars)	Total imports (1,000 dollars)	Agricultural imports[1] (1,000 dollars)	Percentage of total	Excess of agricultural exports (1,000 dollars)	Forest products — Exports Domestic (1,000 dollars)	Reexports (1,000 dollars)	Imports (1,000 dollars)	Excess of imports (1,000 dollars)
1909	1,638,356	903,238	55.1	9,585	1,311,920	701,780	53.5	211,043	72,442	4,983	60,753	[3]16,672
1910	1,710,084	871,158	50.9	14,470	1,556,947	791,372	50.8	94,256	85,030	9,802	75,009	[3]19,823
1911	2,013,549	1,030,794	51.2	14,665	1,527,226	770,781	50.5	274,678	103,039	7,587	71,736	[3]38,890
1912	2,170,320	1,050,627	48.4	12,108	1,653,265	886,399	53.6	176,336	108,122	6,413	69,581	[3]44,954
1913	2,428,506	1,123,652	46.3	15,029	1,813,008	912,925	50.4	225,756	124,836	7,432	82,878	[3]49,390
1914	2,329,684	1,113,974	47.8	17,729	1,893,926	908,346	52.7	223,357	106,979	4,518	81,162	[3]30,335
1915	2,716,178	1,475,938	54.3	34,420	1,674,170	997,184	59.6	513,174	52,554	5,089	79,451	21,808
1916	4,272,178	1,518,071	35.5	42,088	2,197,884	1,348,291	61.3	211,868	68,155	4,364	94,265	21,746
1917	6,227,164	1,968,253	31.6	37,640	2,659,355	1,598,091	60.1	407,802	68,919	11,172	129,380	49,489
1918	5,838,652	2,280,466	39.1	39,553	2,945,655	1,825,417	62.0	494,602	87,181	6,066	128,490	35,243
1919	7,081,462	3,579,918	50.6	103,530	3,095,720	1,929,384	62.3	1,754,064	113,275	6,004	132,588	13,309
1920	7,949,309	3,861,511	48.6	122,598	5,238,352	3,408,977	65.1	575,132	190,049	11,026	229,092	28,017
1921	6,385,884	2,607,641	40.8	87,019	3,654,459	2,059,816	56.4	634,844	141,876	7,805	225,162	75,481
1922	3,699,900	1,915,866	51.8	40,783	2,608,079	1,371,510	52.6	585,139	94,115	5,120	156,844	57,609
1923	3,886,682	1,799,168	46.3	43,359	3,780,959	2,076,371	54.9	[2]233,844	129,981	6,989	234,599	97,629
1924	4,223,973	1,867,098	44.7	57,640	3,554,037	1,874,622	52.7	50,116	162,374	6,642	216,711	47,695
1925	4,778,155	2,280,381	47.7	53,826	3,824,128	2,056,619	53.8	277,588	156,187	11,633	227,423	59,603
1926	4,653,148	1,891,739	40.7	48,440	4,464,872	2,528,213	56.6	[2]588,034	162,731	28,172	238,545	47,642
1927	4,867,346	1,907,864	39.2	50,534	4,252,024	2,280,340	53.6	[2]321,942	171,970	23,053	238,247	43,224
1928, preliminary	4,772,836	1,815,504	38.0	50,232	4,145,951	2,192,404	52.9	[2]326,668	175,352	24,687	215,766	15,727

Bureau of Agricultural Economics. This table supersedes Table No. 472 in the Yearbook of Agriculture, 1927; the value of total imports and exports has been given and the imports of "rubber and similar gums" have been deducted from "imports of forest products" and added to "imports, agricultural."

[1] Does not include forest products.
[2] Excess of agricultural imports.
[3] Excess of exports.

TABLE 495.—*Agricultural products: Value of principal groups exported from and imported into the United States, 1926–1928*

Article	Domestic exports			Imports		
	1926	1927	1928, preliminary	1926	1927	1928, preliminary
ANIMALS AND ANIMAL PRODUCTS	*1,000 dollars*	*1,000 dollars*	*1,000 dollars*	*1,000 dollars*	*1,000 dollars*	*1,000 dollars*
Animals, live	6,975	5,949	6,701	12,191	17,630	26,208
Dairy products	20,766	17,523	17,043	31,456	42,100	37,754
Eggs and egg products	8,236	7,901	6,534	9,369	7,592	3,710
Hides and skins, raw (except fur)	10,629	11,754	11,242	94,286	95,052	146,423
Meats and meat products	254,038	203,431	178,779	11,411	17,636	23,027
Silk, unmanufactured				412,913	421,393	383,214
Wool and mohair, unmanufactured	118	146	172	125,494	83,683	79,451
Animal products, miscellaneous	14,054	13,927	13,609	45,347	38,090	36,961
Total animals and animal products	314,816	260,631	234,080	742,467	723,176	736,748
VEGETABLE PRODUCTS						
Chocolate and cocoa	573	596	596	42,727	52,268	57,397
Coffee	9,147	7,863	4,537	313,225	293,429	297,838
Cotton, unmanufactured:						
Long staple				23,375	12,461	18,137
Sea-island	342	411	176			
Other	165,925	129,085	121,056			
Short staple	747,922	730,583	692,169	26,835	24,745	26,666
Linters	3,530	6,845	7,136			
Total cotton, unmanufactured	917,719	866,924	820,537	50,210	37,206	44,803
Fruits	105,115	128,053	112,023	55,229	54,141	55,871
Grains and grain products	264,204	406,382	404,041	35,444	28,480	34,616
Nuts	1,289	1,667	1,524	31,408	33,079	29,472
Oilseeds and oilseed products	40,377	40,882	42,116	148,684	158,163	143,952
Rubber and similar gums				609,947	374,907	312,300
Seeds, except oilseeds	3,419	3,714	3,498	13,196	10,351	8,516
Spices	207	220	248	17,278	18,906	19,019
Sugar, molasses, and sirups	22,798	10,367	9,527	232,206	265,285	245,538
Tea				30,874	30,959	29,006
Tobacco, unmanufactured	167,251	136,075	135,971	60,144	76,672	58,804
Vegetables	18,986	20,324	21,255	39,568	38,709	39,185
Vegetable products, miscellaneous	25,838	24,166	25,551	105,606	84,609	79,339
Total vegetable products	1,576,923	1,647,233	1,581,424	1,785,746	1,557,164	1,455,656
Total animal and vegetable products	1,891,739	1,907,864	1,815,504	2,528,213	2,280,340	2,192,404
FOREST PRODUCTS						
Dyeing and tanning materials	1,782	1,939	2,714	8,150	8,967	9,633
Gums, resins, and balsams	33,478	38,279	29,685	34,170	31,878	31,584
Wood	120,921	125,955	136,690	108,040	103,613	87,529
Forest products, miscellaneous	6,550	5,797	6,263	88,185	93,789	87,020
Total forest products	162,731	171,970	175,352	238,545	238,247	215,766
Total agricultural products	2,054,470	2,079,834	1,990,856	2,766,758	2,518,587	2,408,170

Bureau of Agricultural Economics. Compiled from Monthly Summary of Foreign Commerce of the United States, June issues, 1927 and 1928.

In the statistics of foreign commerce of the United States, the Philippine Islands are treated as a foreign country.

The statistics of foreign commerce include the trade of the customs districts of Alaska, Hawaii, and Porto Rico with foreign countries, but do not include the trade of these Territories with the United States.

TABLE 496.—*Agricultural products: Value of trade between Continental United States and noncontiguous Territories, 1922–1928*

Year ended June 30—	Porto Rico		Hawaii		Alaska	
	Shipments to	Shipments from	Shipments to	Shipments from	Shipments to	Shipments from
	1,000 dollars	*1,000 dollars*	*1,000 dollars*	*1,000 dollars*	*1,000 dollars*	*1,000 dollars*
1922	21,926	53,892	12,734	66,292	7,123	13
1923	24,080	61,801	15,976	93,313	8,297	190
1924	28,819	66,581	17,539	104,267	9,016	365
1925	29,710	70,190	17,954	97,430	9,774	415
1926	32,212	70,385	17,806	105,470	9,539	516
1927	32,603	84,061	18,019	98,600	8,735	592
1928, preliminary	27,976	82,326	18,995	110,338	9,435	175

Bureau of Agricultural Economics. Compiled from Monthly Summary of Foreign Commerce of the United States, June issues, 1923–1928.

TABLE 497.—*Exports and imports of selected forest products, 1909–1928*

Year ended June 30—	Domestic exports						Imports			
	Lumber		Rosin	Spirits of turpentine	Timber, hewn and sawed	Camphor, crude	Lumber		Shellac	Wood pulp
	Boards, deals, and planks	Staves					Boards, deals, planks, and other sawed	Shingles		
	1,000 M feet	*Thousands*	*1,000 barrels*	*1,000 gallons*	*1,000 M feet*	*1,000 pounds*	*1,000 M feet*	*1,000 M*	*1,000 pounds*	*1,000 L. tons*
1909	1,358	52,583	2,170	17,502	419	1,990	846	1,058	19,185	274
1910	1,684	49,784	2,144	15,588	491	3,007	1,054	763	29,402	378
1911	2,032	65,726	2,190	14,818	532	3,726	872	643	15,495	492
1912	2,307	64,163	2,474	19,599	438	2,155	905	515	18,746	478
1913	2,550	89,006	2,806	21,094	512	3,709	1,091	560	21,912	502
1914	2,405	77,151	2,418	18,901	441	3,477	929	895	16,720	508
1915	1,129	39,297	1,372	9,464	174	3,729	939	1,487	24,153	588
1916	1,177	57,538	1,571	9,310	201	4,574	1,218	1,769	25,818	507
1917	1,042	61,469	1,639	8,842	184	6,885	1,175	1,924	32,540	699
1918	1,068	63,207	1,071	5,095	106	3,638	1,283	1,878	22,913	504
1919	1,073	62,753	882	8,065	92	2,623	977	1,757	14,269	475
1920	1,518	80,791	1,322	7,461	234	4,026	1,492	2,152	34,151	727
1921	1,269	65,710	877	9,742	123	2,093	920	1,831	23,872	624
1922	1,543	35,162	786	10,786	268	1,592	1,124	2,190	30,768	902
1923	1,549	57,466	1,040	9,012	383	3,498	1,958	2,695	32,773	1,293
1924	1,867	60,868	1,205	11,194	815	1,955	1,786	2,417	28,512	1,188
1925	1,929	79,922	1,412	12,308	586	1,904	1,732	2,551	21,436	1,529
1926	1,985	75,534	1,073	10,254	652	2,616	1,869	2,482	26,188	1,469
1927	2,013	74,826	1,229	13,820	707	2,175	1,861	2,275	28,707	1,509
1928, preliminary	2,313	78,256	1,300	14,322	825	2,704	1,529	2,034	23,012	1,519

Bureau of Agricultural Economics. Compiled from Foreign Commerce and Navigation of the United States, 1909–1918, and Monthly Summary of Foreign Commerce of the United States, June issues, 1920–1928.

TABLE 498.—*Exports of selected domestic agricultural products, averages 1900–1926, annual 1909–1928*

Year ended June 30—	Butter	Cheese	Milk, condensed and evaporated	Eggs in the shell	Pork and its products, total [1]	Pork, fresh	Pork, pickled	Bacon, including Cumberland sides	Hams and shoulders, including Wiltshire sides	Lard
	1,000 pounds	*1,000 pounds*	*1,000 pounds*	*1,000 pounds*	*1,000 pounds*	*1,000 pounds*	*1,000 pounds*	*1,000 pounds*	*1,000 pounds*	*1,000 pounds*
Average:										
1900–1904	15, 425	31, 552	(2)	3, 125	1, 305, 217	28, 090	119, 050	361, 686	209, 954	576, 414
1905–1909	12, 484	11, 849	(2)	5, 439	1, 248, 682	13, 157	125, 799	271, 929	208, 230	622, 299
1910–1914	4, 278	4, 916	15, 774	13, 170	913, 025	2, 024	48, 275	182, 474	166, 813	474, 355
1915–1921	19, 519	37, 015	383, 512	26, 392	1, 678, 917	34, 669	42, 252	705, 741	326, 692	542, 567
1922–1926	7, 202	6, 676	191, 475	30, 783	1, 563, 645	32, 453	33, 553	320, 960	296, 941	853, 620
1909	5, 981	6, 823	(2)	5, 207	1, 053, 142	9, 555	52, 355	244, 579	212, 170	528, 723
1910	3, 141	2, 847	13, 311	5, 326	707, 110	1, 040	40, 032	152, 163	146, 885	362, 928
1911	4, 878	10, 367	12, 180	8, 559	879, 455	1, 355	45, 729	156, 675	57, 709	476, 108
1912	6, 092	6, 338	20, 643	15, 406	1, 071, 952	2, 598	56, 321	208, 574	204, 044	532, 256
1913	3, 586	2, 599	16, 526	20, 409	984, 697	2, 458	53, 749	200, 994	159, 545	519, 025
1914	3, 694	2, 428	16, 209	16, 149	921, 913	2, 668	45, 543	193, 964	165, 882	481, 458
1915	9, 851	55, 363	37, 236	20, 784	1, 106, 180	3, 908	45, 656	346, 718	203, 701	475, 532
1916	13, 487	44, 394	159, 578	26, 396	1, 462, 697	63, 006	63, 461	579, 809	282, 209	427, 011
1917	26, 835	66, 050	259, 141	24, 926	1, 501, 948	50, 436	46, 993	667, 152	266, 657	444, 770
1918	17, 736	44, 303	528, 759	18, 969	1, 692, 124	21, 390	33, 222	815, 294	419, 572	392, 506
1919	33, 740	18, 792	728, 741	28, 385	2, 704, 694	19, 644	31, 504	1, 238, 247	667, 240	724, 771
1920	27, 156	19, 378	708, 463	38, 327	1, 762, 611	27, 225	41, 643	803, 667	275, 456	587, 225
1921	7, 829	10, 826	262, 668	26, 960	1, 522, 162	57, 075	33, 286	489, 298	172, 012	746, 157
1922	7, 512	7, 471	277, 311	33, 762	1, 516, 320	25, 911	33, 510	350, 549	271, 642	812, 379
1923	9, 410	8, 446	157, 038	34, 284	1, 794, 880	43, 772	40, 934	408, 334	319, 269	952, 642
1924	5, 425	3, 938	213, 613	32, 832	1, 934, 189	49, 113	37, 469	423, 500	381, 564	1, 014, 898
1925	8, 384	9, 432	173, 547	25, 107	1, 400, 149	27, 603	26, 726	236, 263	292, 214	792, 735
1926	5, 280	4, 094	135, 865	27, 931	1, 172, 685	15, 867	29, 126	186, 153	220, 014	695, 445
1927	5, 048	3, 773	108, 942	27, 962	1, 012, 668	10, 881	27, 962	127, 576	143, 649	675, 812
1928, preliminary	3, 965	2, 873	108, 943	22, 940	1, 046, 279	11, 059	31, 650	126, 977	127, 819	716, 361

Year ended June 30—	Beef and its products, total [3]	Oleo oil	Cotton lint [4]	Linters [4]	Cottonseed oil, crude and refined	Cottonseed cake and meal	Linseed cake and meal	Prunes	Raisins	Apples, fresh	Oranges	Sugar, raw and refined [5]
	1,000 pounds	*1,000 pounds*	*1,000 bales*	*1,000 bales*	*1,000 gallons*	*1,000 pounds*	*1,000 pounds*	*1,000 pounds*	*1,000 pounds*	*1,000 barrels*	*1,000 boxes*	*1,000 sh. tons*
Average:												
1900–1904	636, 969	147, 626	6, 669		38, 792	1, 074, 720	552, 190	39, 767	3, 314	1, 109	(2)	6
1905–1909	599, 332	188, 550	8, 303		45, 863	1, 173, 349	684, 450	35, 003	6, 856	1, 239	(2)	16
1910–1914	221, 513	116, 225	8, 840		36, 192	933, 288	661, 819	80, 428	18, 004	1, 551	1, 186	35
1915–1921	434, 209	78, 154	6, 290		27, 923	706, 718	397, 783	60, 582	57, 477	1, 641	1, 635	510
1922–1926	188, 223	102, 130	6, 904		8, 203	567, 863	579, 815	129, 650	91, 513	2, 764	2, 096	412
1909	418, 844	179, 985	8, 896		51, 087	1, 233, 750	682, 765	22, 602	7, 880	896	867	40
1910	286, 296	126, 092	6, 413		29, 861	640, 089	652, 317	89, 015	8, 526	922	932	63
1911	265, 924	138, 697	8, 068		30, 069	804, 597	559, 675	51, 031	18, 660	1, 721	1, 179	28
1912	233, 925	126, 467	11, 070		53, 263	1, 293, 690	596, 115	74, 328	19, 949	1, 456	1, 197	40
1913	170, 208	92, 850	9, 125		42, 031	1, 128, 092	838, 120	117, 951	28, 121	2, 150	1, 063	22
1914	151, 212	97, 017	9, 522		25, 738	799, 974	662, 869	69, 814	14, 766	1, 507	1, 559	26
1915	394, 981	80, 482	8, 581	226	42, 449	1, 479, 065	524, 794	43, 479	24, 845	2, 352	1, 759	275
1916	457, 556	102, 646	5, 917	251	35, 535	1, 057, 222	640, 916	57, 423	75, 015	1, 466	1, 575	815
1917	423, 674	67, 110	5, 702	474	21, 188	1, 150, 160	536, 984	59, 645	51, 993	1, 740	1, 850	625
1918	600, 132	56, 603	4, 455	186	13, 437	44, 681	151, 400	32, 927	54, 988	635	1, 240	288
1919	591, 302	59, 292	5, 442	84	23, 828	311, 624	202, 788	59, 072	84, 150	1, 576	1, 402	558
1920	368, 002	74, 529	7, 035	52	21, 253	449, 573	336, 336	114, 066	86, 857	1, 051	1, 619	722
1921	203, 815	106, 415	5, 570	53	37, 769	454, 701	391, 264	57, 461	24, 492	2, 665	2, 001	292
1922	222, 462	117, 174	6, 592	126	12, 215	532, 721	484, 059	109, 398	49, 639	1, 094	1, 641	1, 001
1923	194, 912	104, 956	5, 205	48	8, 572	454, 350	574, 612	79, 229	93, 962	1, 756	1, 799	375
1924	185, 372	92, 965	5, 784	115	5, 256	250, 366	560, 114	136, 448	88, 152	4, 098	2, 592	135
1925	190, 211	105, 145	8, 239	200	7, 101	885, 375	691, 126	171, 771	90, 783	3, 201	2, 197	251
1926	152, 320	90, 410	8, 110	102	7, 869	716, 505	589, 166	151, 405	135, 027	3, 672	2, 253	300
1927	151, 531	92, 720	11, 281	278	7, 677	990, 516	625, 121	175, 544	152, 337	7, 098	3, 340	114
1928, preliminary	106, 807	64, 851	7, 890	231	8, 196	664, 523	606, 304	260, 625	193, 099	3, 144	2, 988	106

Footnotes at end of table.

TABLE 498.—*Exports of selected domestic agricultural products, averages 1900–1926, annual 1909–1928*—Continued

Year ended June 30—	Barley, including flour and malt [6]	Corn, including corn-meal	Oats, including oat-meal	Rice, including flour, meal, and broken rice	Rye, including flour	Wheat, including flour	To-bacco, un-manu-fac-tured [7]	Glu-cose and grape sugar	Hops	Starch
	1,000 bushels	*1,000 bushels*	*1,000 bushels*	*1,000 pounds*	*1,000 bushels*	*1,000 bushels*	*1,000 pounds*	*1,000 pounds*	*1,000 pounds*	*1,000 pounds*
Average:										
1900–1904	11,931	111,484	22,188	3,511	2,734	196,690	328,321	167,108	11,420	68,173
1905–1909	9,907	77,857	13,614	17,009	1,186	116,181	321,197	151,690	15,613	52,143
1910–1914	8,087	41,409	9,655	18,489	888	107,103	392,183	180,524	15,548	96,206
1915–1921	28,197	45,292	83,085	241,607	26,357	257,030	468,037	168,735	15,342	150,613
1922–1926	24,471	66,759	22,382	260,030	32,880	207,237	496,665	178,889	16,920	269,865
1909	6,729	37,665	2,334	1,567	1,296	116,373	287,901	112,225	10,447	33,228
1910	4,454	38,128	2,549	7,050	242	89,173	357,196	149,820	10,589	51,536
1911	9,507	65,615	3,846	15,575	40	71,338	355,327	181,963	13,105	158,239
1912	1,655	41,797	2,678	26,798	31	81,891	379,845	171,156	12,191	83,645
1913	17,874	50,780	36,455	24,801	1,855	145,159	418,797	200,149	17,591	110,898
1914	6,945	10,726	2,749	18,223	2,273	147,955	449,750	199,531	24,263	76,714
1915	28,712	50,668	100,609	75,449	13,027	335,702	348,346	158,463	16,210	107,037
1916	30,821	39,897	98,960	120,695	15,250	246,221	443,293	186,406	22,410	210,185
1917	20,319	66,753	95,106	181,372	13,703	205,962	411,599	214,973	4,825	146,424
1918	28,717	49,073	125,091	196,363	17,186	132,579	289,171	97,858	3,495	73,883
1919	26,997	23,019	109,005	193,128	36,467	287,402	629,288	136,230	7,467	143,788
1920	34,555	16,729	43,436	483,385	41,531	222,030	648,038	245,264	30,780	237,609
1921	27,255	70,906	9,391	440,855	47,337	369,313	506,526	141,954	22,206	135,365
1922	27,543	179,490	21,237	541,509	29,944	282,566	463,389	273,982	19,522	386,873
1923	21,909	96,596	25,413	370,670	51,663	224,900	454,364	162,693	13,497	260,796
1924	13,913	23,135	8,796	227,757	19,902	159,880	597,630	148,051	20,461	262,842
1925	28,543	9,791	16,777	112,037	50,242	260,803	430,702	139,577	16,122	214,247
1926	30,449	24,783	39,687	48,175	12,647	108,035	537,240	170,142	14,998	224,569
1927	19,655	19,819	15,041	304,358	21,697	219,160	516,401	148,789	13,369	233,111
1928, preliminary	39,275	19,410	9,822	309,808	26,326	206,729	489,982	145,951	11,812	281,388

Year ended June 30—	Corn-starch [8]	Corn oil	Apples, dried	Apricots, dried	Apricots, canned [9]	Pears, canned [9]	Peaches, canned [9]	Pine-apples, canned [9]
	1,000 pounds	*1,000 pounds*	*1,000 pounds*	*1,000 pounds*	*1,000 pounds*	*1,000 pounds*	*1,000 pounds*	*1,000 pounds*
1913		19,839	41,575	35,017				
1914		18,282	33,566	17,402				
1915		17,790	42,589	23,764				
1916		8,968	16,219	23,940				
1917		8,780	10,358	9,841				
1918	38,659	1,831	2,603	5,230				
1919	105,727	1,095	18,909	20,975				
1920	163,315	12,483	11,819	26,768				
1921	110,514	6,919	18,053	8,332				
1922	348,940	5,280	12,431	16,736				
1923	254,060	5,224	12,817	11,193	[10] 13,809	49,358	54,624	21,848
1924	255,135	4,196	30,323	38,777	26,576	38,431	50,374	25,238
1925	209,865	3,586	19,225	13,292	31,360	53,851	57,390	26,252
1926	208,463	2,927	24,833	18,132	29,547	75,876	83,160	37,543
1927	212,375	405	32,670	17,901	35,896	66,104	81,896	37,426
1928, preliminary	275,921	329	21,704	23,684	29,013	52,671	86,634	51,227

Bureau of Agricultural Economics. Compiled from Foreign Commerce and Navigation of the United States, 1900–1918, and Monthly Summary of Foreign Commerce of the United States, June issues 1921–1928.

Conversion factors used: Corn meal, 1 barrel=4 bushels corn; oatmeal, 18 pounds=1 bushel oats; rye flour, 1 barrel=6 bushels rye; malt, 1.1 bushels=1 bushel barley; wheat flour, 1 barrel=1900–1908, 4.75 bushels grain; 1909–1917, 4.7 bushels; 1918 and 1919, 4.5 bushels; 1920, 4.6 bushels; 1921–1928, 4.7 bushels; apples, 3 boxes=1 barrel; cottonseed oil, 7.5 pounds=1 gallon.

[1] Includes canned, fresh, salted, or pickled pork, lard, neutral lard, lard oil, bacon, and hams.
[2] Reported in value only.
[3] Includes canned, cured, and fresh beef, oleo oil, oleo stock, oleomargarine, tallow, and stearin from animal fats.
[4] Bales of 500 pounds gross; lint cotton and linters not separately reported prior to 1915.
[5] Includes maple sugar, 1915–1928.
[6] Includes barley flour 1919–1922. Barley flour not separately reported prior to 1919 nor since 1922.
[7] Includes "Stems, trimmings, and scrap tobacco."
[8] Included with "Starch" prior to 1918.
[9] Given in value only prior to 1923.
[10] Jan. 1 to June 30.

33023°—29——65

TABLE 499.—*Imports of selected agricultural products, averages 1900–1926, annual 1909–1928*

Year ended June 30—	Butter	Cheese	Cattle hides	Goatskins	Total hides and skins except furs	Silk [1]	Cotton, unmanufactured	Wool, unmanufactured, including mohair, etc.	Total tobacco, unmanufactured
	1,000 pounds	1,000 pounds	1,000 pounds	1,000 pounds	1,000 pounds	1,000 pounds	1,000 pounds	1,000 pounds	1,000 pounds
Average:									
1900–1904	192	17,846	131,736	83,047	309,360	13,942	67,292	155,394	28,216
1905–1909	532	30,462	138,922	95,555	372,292	20,061	78,771	209,413	38,688
1910–1914	2,480	49,220	253,430	95,822	530,909	28,671	110,957	207,584	55,790
1915–1921	9,445	20,213	332,076	85,358	573,359	42,895	177,606	394,663	66,695
1922–1926	13,684	55,865	228,236	78,251	436,741	64,866	175,609	329,968	68,470
1909	646	35,548	192,252	104,048	444,554	25,188	86,518	266,409	43,123
1910	1,360	40,818	318,004	115,845	608,619	23,457	86,038	263,928	46,853
1911	1,008	45,569	150,128	86,914	374,891	26,666	113,768	137,648	48,203
1912	1,026	46,542	251,012	95,341	537,768	26,585	109,780	193,401	54,740
1913	1,162	49,388	268,042	96,250	572,197	32,101	121,852	195,293	67,977
1914	7,842	63,784	279,963	84,759	561,071	34,546	123,347	247,649	61,175
1915	3,828	50,139	344,341	66,547	538,218	31,053	185,205	308,083	45,809
1916	713	30,088	434,178	100,657	743,670	41,925	232,801	534,828	48,078
1917	524	14,482	386,600	105,640	700,207	40,351	147,062	372,372	49,105
1918	1,806	9,839	267,500	66,933	432,517	43,681	103,326	379,130	86,991
1919	4,131	2,442	253,877	89,005	448,142	50,069	103,592	422,415	83,951
1920	20,771	17,914	439,461	126,996	798,569	58,410	345,314	427,578	94,005
1921	34,344	16,585	204,936	41,728	352,193	34,778	125,939	318,236	58,923
1922	9,551	34,271	204,936	83,535	392,904	57,437	179,165	255,087	65,225
1923	15,772	54,555	405,383	89,401	682,893	63,188	236,092	525,473	75,786
1924	29,466	66,597	176,475	65,881	365,194	56,595	146,024	239,122	54,497
1925	7,189	61,489	199,310	65,956	387,447	70,270	155,092	284,706	76,870
1926	6,440	62,412	155,587	86,484	355,266	76,838	161,454	345,512	69,974
1927	10,710	89,782	156,938	83,571	368,876	85,162	190,963	271,128	92,983
1928, preliminary	4,955	75,423	307,362	84,751	532,436	87,221	175,450	248,033	81,105

Year ended June 30—	Rubber and similar gums, crude, total	Coffee	Tea	Cocoa or cacao beans	Bananas	Olives	Almonds in terms of shelled [2]	Peanuts in terms of shelled [2]	Walnuts in terms of shelled [2]	Coconut meat [3]
	1,000 pounds	1,000 pounds	1,000 pounds	1,000 pounds	1,000 bunches	1,000 Gallons	1,000 pounds	1,000 pounds	1,000 pounds	1,000 pounds
Average:										
1900–1904	66,973	928,799	94,342	54,936	(4)	(4)	7,862	(5)	6 18,017	(5)
1905–1909	95,054	965,058	98,353	91,774	6 36,988	7 2,796	13,832	(5)	26,849	7 15,010
1910–1914	161,771	899,339	95,108	141,800	43,684	4,388	16,039	22,615	28,497	45,128
1915–1921	390,618	1,227,534	105,675	319,103	37,157	4,335	19,857	49,659	19,748	252,370
1922–1926	759,824	1,337,950	96,089	376,247	48,924	7 6,247	23,755	46,918	31,179	358,772
1909	114,599	1,049,869	114,917	129,855	36,974	2,969	11,029	(5)	26,158	23,843
1910	154,621	871,470	85,626	108,668	38,157	4,555	18,556	29,276	33,641	21,306
1911	145,744	875,367	102,564	138,058	44,699	3,045	15,523	18,834	33,619	37,817
1912	175,966	885,201	101,407	145,969	44,521	5,077	17,231	11,248	37,214	69,912
1913	170,747	863,131	94,813	140,039	42,357	3,946	13,856	14,989	17,213	40,870
1914	161,777	1,001,528	91,131	176,268	48,684	5,316	15,027	38,726	20,800	55,735
1915	196,122	1,118,691	96,988	192,307	41,092	3,622	13,679	19,338	20,490	96,485
1916	304,183	1,201,104	109,866	243,232	36,755	5,938	14,546	25,407	23,733	118,613
1917	364,914	1,319,871	103,364	338,654	34,661	5,642	19,916	32,385	23,839	256,801
1918	414,984	1,143,891	151,315	399,040	34,550	2,385	20,845	75,463	16,252	507,576
1919	422,215	1,046,029	108,172	313,037	35,382	3,501	25,615	20,425	9,057	315,749
1920	660,610	1,414,228	97,826	420,331	36,848	5,206	28,533	128,390	28,961	258,229
1921	371,300	1,348,926	72,196	327,123	40,808	4,054	15,861	46,202	15,902	213,134
1922	578,512	1,238,012	86,142	317,124	46,120	(4)	28,036	9,678	35,174	294,104
1923	810,028	1,305,188	96,669	381,508	44,504	(4)	24,345	45,013	25,970	338,597
1924	633,489	1,429,617	105,443	382,971	44,935	6,848	24,207	50,683	26,428	344,920
1925	824,434	1,279,570	92,779	382,570	50,513	5,901	22,503	93,191	36,623	371,961
1926	952,659	1,437,364	99,411	417,060	58,550	5,992	19,686	36,026	31,698	444,278
1927	993,272	1,444,847	97,402	425,184	57,102	5,212	15,890	49,792	31,776	507,136
1928 preliminary	959,242	1,535,393	90,099	411,543	64,029	6,458	18,496	63,783	20,347	518,173

Footnotes at end of table.

TABLE 499.—*Imports of selected agricultural products, averages 1900-1926, annual 1909-1928*—Continued

Year ended June 30—	Coconut oil	Olive oil, edible and inedible	Chinese wood oil or Chinese nut oil	Flax-seed	Lin-seed oil	Sugar, raw and refined	Mo-lasses	Jute and jute butts, un-man-ufac-tured	Mani-la or abaca	Sisal and hene-quen
	1,000 pounds	*1,000 pounds*	*1,000 pounds*	*1,000 bushels*	*1,000 gals.*	*1,000 short tons*	*1,000 gallons*	*1,000 long tons*	*1,000 long tons*	*1,000 long tons*
Average:										
1900-1904	(8)	9,746	(8)	504	(9)	1,894	13,788	102	54	87
1905-1909	7 44,486	32,541	(9)	218	(9)	1,961	20,221	114	58	98
1910-1914	54,145	41,736	39,242	7,258	368	2,194	33,859	93	72	140
1915-1921	179,674	45,472	45,920	14,156	1,183	2,981	113,669	86	70	171
1922-1926	215,049	113,967	81,084	18,198	7,563	4,225	179,021	72	75	108
1909	52,491	33,746	(9)	594	(9)	2,095	22,093	157	62	91
1910	48,346	34,089	(9)	5,002	(9)	2,047	31,292	68	93	100
1911	51,118	37,382	(9)	10,499	(9)	1,969	23,838	65	74	118
1912	46,371	41,044	35,757	6,842	737	2,052	28,828	101	69	114
1913	50,504	43,803	44,975	5,294	174	2,370	33,927	125	74	154
1914	74,386	52,361	36,993	8,653	192	2,533	51,410	106	50	216
1915	63,135	55,230	37,052	10,666	535	2,710	70,840	83	51	186
1916	66,008	60,820	37,262	14,679	50	2,817	85,717	108	79	229
1917	79,223	61,381	51,481	12,394	111	2,666	110,238	113	77	143
1918	259,195	19,889	36,118	13,367	51	2,452	130,731	78	86	150
1919	344,728	32,983	46,625	8,427	990	2,918	130,075	53	68	153
1920	271,540	52,716	79,602	23,392	4,550	3,798	154,670	77	77	176
1921	173,889	35,288	33,300	16,170	1,997	3,506	113,414	90	52	159
1922	230,236	83,337	55,572	13,632	22,494	4,232	87,908	62	44	72
1923	212,573	117,262	89,392	25,006	7,568	4,367	161,135	85	98	98
1924	181,230	113,409	80,898	19,577	2,379	3,765	174,037	84	98	97
1925	250,121	118,071	94,695	13,419	3,145	4,337	215,778	56	73	146
1926	10 200,878	137,757	84,861	19,354	2,231	4,420	256,246	71	62	126
1927	286,776	134,729	102,428	24,224	177	4,420	260,259	89	61	116
1928, preliminary	273,309	118,056	89,012	18,112	46	4,045	246,895	81	48	124

Year ended June 30—	Milk and cream fresh [11]	Cream, fresh	Eggs, whole, in the shell	Eggs and egg yolks, dried, frozen, or pre-pared	Whole eggs, dried [12]	Whole eggs, frozen [12]	Yolks, dried [12]	Yolks, frozen [12]	Egg albu-men, dried [13]	Egg al-bumen, frozen, pre-pared and pre-served [12]	Hair of the Angora (mo-hair) [13]
	1,000 gallons	*1,000 gallons*	*1,000 dozen*	*1,000 pounds*	*1,000 pounds*	*1,000 pounds*	*1,000 pounds*	*1,000 pounds*	*1,000 pounds*	*1,000 pounds*	*1,000 pounds*
1913		1,247	1,367	228							
1914		1,773	6,015	3,420							
1915		2,077	3,047	8,572							
1916		1,194	733	6,022							
1917		744	1,110	10,318							
1918		712	1,619	14,598							
1919	2,592	(14)	848	9,085							
1920	3,989	(14)	1,348	24,091							
1921	4,391	(14)	3,316	28,768							
1922	4,536	(14)	1,224	16,540					7,388		15 7,220
1923	5,148	(14)	535	14,821					3,213		
1924	6,623	16 1,646	426	17 14,830	16 544	16 1,106	16 522	16 1,210	6,642	16 636	3,583
1925	6,418	4,765	682		1,884	8,751	4,281	4,151	3,257	1,106	2,404
1926	7,479	4,798	276		1,365	12,647	6,004	5,662	4,490	5,119	6,463
1927	6,106	5,273	296		1,132	8,114	4,468	4,601	3,859	3,967	6,547
1928, preliminary	5,425	4,819	256		575	611	3,486	1,229	2,361	553	2,204

Bureau of Agricultural Economics. Complied from Commerce and Navigation of the United States. 1900-1918, and Monthly Summary of Foreign Commerce, June issue, 1919-1928.

1 Includes "Silk, raw or as reeled from cocoon," "Silk waste," and "Silk cocoons."
2 Conversion factors used: Almonds, 30 per cent unshelled equals shelled. Peanuts, 3 pounds unshelled equals 2 pounds shelled. Walnuts, 42 per cent unshelled equals shelled.
3 Includes broken, or shredded, desiccated and prepared copra.
4 Reported in value only.
5 Included with "All other nuts."
6 2-year average.
7 3-year average.
8 Included with "All other, fixed or expressed" vegetable oils.

9 Included with "All other, fixed or expressed" vegetable oils, 1905-1906, and "Nut oil, or oil of nuts." 1907-1911.
10 Does not include "duitable" coconut oil.
11 Not separately classified prior to 1919.
12 Not separately classified prior to January, 1924.
13 Not separately classified prior to 1922.
14 Not separately classified.
15 Beginning Sept. 22, 1922.
16 Beginning Jan. 1, 1924.
17 July 1-Dec. 31, 1923.

TABLE 500.—*Principal agricultural products exported from the United States, by countries, 1925–1928*

Article and country to which exported	Year ended June 30—							
	1925	1926	1927	1928	1925	1926	1927	1928
ANIMALS AND ANIMAL PRODUCTS	*Thou-sands*	*Thou-sands*	*Thou-sands*	*Thou-sands*	*Per cent*	*Per cent*	*Per cent*	*Per cent*
Cattle:								
Total	106	36	21	16	100.0	100.0	100.0	100.0
Mexico	99	30	16	14	93.4	83.3	76.2	87.5
Cuba	3	3	3	1	2.8	8.3	14.3	6.2
Other countries	4	3	2	1	3.8	8.4	9.5	6.3
	1,000 pounds	*1,000 pounds*	*1,000 pounds*	*1,000 pounds*				
Butter:								
Total	8,384	5,280	5,048	3,965	100.0	100.0	100.0	100.0
United Kingdom	2,354	0	0	20	28.1	.0	.0	.5
Mexico	1,109	1,015	859	724	13.2	19.2	17.0	18.3
Cuba	870	782	734	479	10.4	14.8	14.5	12.1
Panama	806	719	582	311	9.6	13.6	11.5	7.8
Haitian Republic	565	585	498	479	6.7	11.1	9.9	12.1
Other West Indies [1]	805	479	550	391	9.6	9.1	10.9	9.9
Peru	455	424	356	358	5.4	8.0	7.1	9.0
Other South America	325	384	605	390	3.9	7.3	12.0	9.8
Philippine Islands	181	230	187	190	2.2	4.4	3.7	4.8
Other countries	914	662	677	623	10.9	12.5	13.4	15.7
Cheese:								
Total	9,432	4,094	3,773	2,873	100.0	100.0	100.0	100.0
Germany	3,601	13	0	0	38.2	.3	.0	.0
Canada	1,334	216	350	259	14.1	5.3	9.3	9.0
Cuba	1,063	910	832	359	11.3	22.2	22.1	12.5
Other West Indies [1]	566	600	479	331	6.0	14.7	12.7	11.5
Mexico	983	940	670	581	10.4	23.0	17.8	20.2
Panama	408	403	434	432	4.3	9.8	11.5	15.0
Other Central America	276	278	284	293	2.9	6.8	7.5	10.2
China	144	233	252	145	1.5	5.7	6.7	5.0
Other countries	1,057	501	472	473	11.3	12.2	12.4	16.6
Milk:								
Condensed—								
Total	49,297	42,656	35,799	36,975	100.0	100.0	100.0	100.0
Total Europe	973	479	424	151	2.0	1.1	1.2	.4
Cuba	21,226	16,337	12,843	11,462	43.1	38.3	35.9	31.0
Philippine Islands	6,961	7,767	6,471	7,575	14.1	18.2	18.1	20.5
Japan, including Chosen	5,873	4,744	4,029	5,385	11.9	11.1	11.3	14.6
China	2,668	3,811	3,621	2,513	5.4	8.9	10.1	6.8
Hong Kong	2,409	1,992	2,065	3,764	4.9	4.7	5.8	10.2
Mexico	1,404	1,285	1,308	985	2.8	3.0	3.7	2.7
Other countries	7,783	6,241	5,038	5,140	15.8	14.7	13.9	13.8
Evaporated—								
Total	124,250	93,210	73,143	71,968	100.0	100.0	100.0	100.0
Total Europe	85,891	52,147	30,527	24,401	69.1	55.9	41.7	33.9
Germany	43,355	19,306	1,851	16	34.9	20.7	2.5	.0
United Kingdom	28,662	29,181	27,418	23,805	23.1	31.3	37.5	33.1
Netherlands	7,328	1,743	202	0	5.9	1.9	.3	.0
France	3,765	1,011	410	0	3.0	1.1	.6	.0
Other Europe	2,781	906	646	580	2.2	.9	.8	.8
Philippine Islands	10,067	12,902	12,806	15,563	8.1	13.8	17.5	21.6
Peru	5,013	3,737	4,215	3,569	4.0	4.0	5.8	5.0
Panama	3,742	3,597	4,127	3,589	3.0	3.9	5.6	5.0
Cuba	3,121	2,942	2,958	2,647	2.5	3.2	4.0	3.7
China	2,608	3,227	3,025	3,035	2.1	3.5	4.1	4.2
Mexico	2,589	3,293	2,714	2,157	2.1	3.5	3.7	3.0
British Malaya	1,338	1,853	1,932	2,817	1.1	2.0	2.6	3.9
Other countries	9,881	9,512	10,839	14,190	8.0	10.2	15.0	19.7
Powdered—								
Total	5,623	3,270	3,007	3,289	100.0	100.0	100.0	100.0
Total Europe	4,059	1,124	504	595	72.2	34.4	16.8	18.1
Germany	1,036	205	56	54	18.4	6.3	1.9	1.6
United Kingdom	702	191	131	45	12.5	5.8	4.4	1.4
France	276	165	149	166	4.9	5.0	5.0	5.0
Other Europe	2,045	563	168	330	36.4	17.3	5.5	10.1

[1] Excludes Bermuda.

TABLE 500.—*Principal agricultural products exported from the United States, by countries, 1925–1928*—Continued

Article and country to which exported	Year ended June 30—							
	1925	1926	1927	1928	1925	1926	1927	1928
ANIMALS AND ANIMAL PRODUCTS—con.								
Milk—Continued.	1,000 pounds	1,000 pounds	1,000 pounds	1,000 pounds	Per cent	Per cent	Per cent	Per cent
Powdered—Continued.								
Japan, including Chosen	414	468	338	372	7.4	14.3	11.2	11.3
Cuba	237	162	214	265	4.2	5.0	7.1	8.1
Mexico	140	143	304	230	2.5	4.4	10.1	7.0
Canada	130	112	85	48	2.3	3.4	2.8	1.5
Panama	128	199	227	217	2.3	6.1	7.5	6.6
China	87	432	408	355	1.5	13.2	13.6	10.8
Peru	86	129	168	119	1.5	3.9	5.6	3.6
Venezuela	55	105	170	225	1.0	3.2	5.7	6.8
Other South America	107	185	335	471	3.2	5.7	11.1	14.3
Other countries	180	211	254	392	1.9	6.4	8.5	11.9
Eggs, in the shell:	1,000 dozen	1,000 dozen	1,000 dozen	1,000 dozen				
Total	25,107	27,931	27,962	22,940	100.0	100.0	100.0	100.0
Total Europe	777	1,419	304	756	3.1	5.1	1.1	3.3
United Kingdom	777	1,418	303	748	3.1	5.1	1.1	3.3
Other Europe	0	1	1	2	.0	.0	.0	.0
Cuba	11,958	12,235	11,903	8,372	47.6	43.8	42.6	36.5
Mexico	4,719	4,039	3,899	3,697	18.8	14.5	13.9	16.1
Argentina	3,568	4,960	6,763	6,451	14.2	17.8	24.2	28.1
Canada	2,681	3,425	3,162	1,136	10.7	12.3	11.3	5.0
Other countries	1,404	1,853	1,931	2,534	5.6	6.5	6.9	11.0
Beef, canned:	1,000 pounds	1,000 pounds	1,000 pounds	1,000 pounds				
Total	1,835	2,350	2,996	2,215	100.0	100.0	100.0	100.0
Total Europe	753	1,472	1,729	1,424	41.0	62.6	57.7	64.3
United Kingdom	692	1,419	1,680	1,316	37.7	60.4	56.1	59.4
Germany	29	9	2	0	1.6	.4	.1	.0
Netherlands	0	1	0	18	.0	.0	.0	.8
Other Europe	32	43	47	90	1.7	1.8	1.5	4.1
Philippine Islands	213	105	99	95	11.6	4.5	3.3	4.3
Cuba	163	155	334	95	8.9	6.6	11.1	4.3
Canada	142	50	47	40	7.7	2.1	1.6	1.8
Other West Indies [1]	125	217	118	176	6.8	9.2	3.8	7.9
Mexico	95	100	80	60	5.2	4.3	2.7	2.7
Newfoundland and Labrador	67	45	77	30	3.7	1.9	2.6	1.4
Honduras	42	36	26	23	2.3	1.5	.9	1.0
Panama	34	42	25	24	1.9	1.8	.8	1.1
Other countries	201	128	461	248	10.9	5.5	15.5	11.2
Beef, pickled and other cured:								
Total	22,407	19,279	18,834	11,417	100.0	100.0	100.0	100.0
Total Europe	4,192	3,130	2,788	2,209	18.7	16.2	14.8	19.3
United Kingdom	1,944	952	801	516	8.7	4.9	4.3	4.5
Norway	1,264	1,120	977	829	5.6	5.8	5.2	7.3
Other Europe	984	1,058	1,010	864	4.4	5.5	5.3	7.5
Newfoundland and Labrador	7,841	6,501	6,689	4,709	35.0	33.7	35.5	41.2
West Indies [1]	5,011	4,684	4,999	2,134	22.4	24.3	26.5	18.7
Dutch Guiana	1,109	1,062	987	479	4.9	5.5	5.2	4.2
Other South America	1,925	1,536	734	260	8.6	8.0	3.9	2.3
British West Africa	868	927	881	444	3.9	4.8	4.7	3.9
Other countries	1,461	1,439	1,756	1,182	6.5	7.5	9.4	10.4
Bacon:								
Total	211,706	165,229	118,347	118,896	100.0	100.0	100.0	100.0
Total Europe	177,909	136,397	89,656	91,768	84.0	82.6	75.8	77.2
United Kingdom	104,626	86,557	59,353	42,405	49.4	52.4	50.2	35.7
Germany	25,972	14,043	6,818	9,838	12.3	8.5	5.8	8.3
Norway	8,775	7,050	2,422	3,236	4.1	4.3	2.0	2.7
Netherlands	7,995	6,379	2,480	632	3.8	3.9	2.1	.5
Italy	7,357	3,264	1,439	8,113	3.5	2.0	1.2	6.8
Other Europe	23,184	19,104	17,144	27,544	10.9	11.5	14.5	23.2
Cuba	27,330	22,085	21,007	19,107	12.9	13.4	17.8	16.1
Other countries	6,467	6,747	7,684	8,021	3.1	4.0	6.4	6.7

[1] Excludes Bermuda.

TABLE 500.—*Principal agricultural products exported from the United States, by countries, 1925–1928*—Continued

Article and country to which exported	Year ended June 30—							
	1925	1926	1927	1928	1925	1926	1927	1928
ANIMALS AND ANIMAL PRODUCTS—con.	*1,000 pounds*	*1,000 pounds*	*1,000 pounds*	*1,000 pounds*	*Per cent*	*Per cent*	*Per cent*	*Per cent*
Cumberland sides:								
Total	24, 557	20, 924	9, 229	8, 071	100. 0	100. 0	100. 0	100. 0
Total Europe	24, 323	20, 420	8, 905	7, 706	99. 0	97. 6	96. 5	95. 5
United Kingdom	23, 979	20, 352	8, 866	7, 642	97. 6	97. 3	96. 1	94. 7
Other Europe	344	68	39	64	1. 4	. 3	. 4	. 8
Other countries	234	504	324	365	1. 0	2. 4	3. 5	4. 5
Hams and shoulders, cured:								
Total	277, 567	208, 446	142, 742	127, 013	100. 0	100. 0	100. 0	100. 0
Total Europe	248, 900	187, 035	125, 441	105, 801	89. 7	89. 9	87. 9	83. 3
United Kingdom	229, 125	180, 611	123, 565	103, 321	82. 5	86. 6	86. 6	81. 3
Belgium	13, 400	3, 929	451	660	4. 8	1. 9	. 3	. 5
Other Europe	6, 375	2, 495	1, 425	1, 820	2. 4	1. 3	1. 0	1. 5
Cuba	15, 725	10, 553	6, 548	8, 161	5. 7	5. 1	4. 6	6. 4
Other countries	12, 942	10, 858	10, 753	13, 051	4. 6	5. 1	7. 5	10. 3
Wiltshire sides:								
Total	14, 647	11, 569	907	806	100. 0	100. 0	100. 0	100. 0
Total Europe	12, 025	9, 557	826	724	82. 1	82. 6	91. 1	89. 8
United Kingdom	12, 025	9, 525	826	699	82. 1	82. 3	91. 1	86. 7
Other Europe	0	32	0	25	. 0	. 3	. 0	3. 1
Canada	2, 573	2, 011	79	73	17. 6	17. 4	8. 7	9. 1
Other countries	49	1	2	9	. 3	. 0	. 2	1. 1
Pork:								
Canned—								
Total	4, 185	5, 947	6, 731	8, 614	100. 0	100. 0	100. 0	100. 0
Total Europe	4, 018	5, 242	5, 675	7, 729	96. 0	88. 1	84. 3	89. 7
United Kingdom	4, 003	5, 196	5, 595	7, 632	95. 7	87. 4	83. 1	88. 6
Other Europe	15	46	●80	97	. 3	. 7	1. 2	1. 1
Other countries	167	705	1, 056	885	4. 0	11. 9	15. 7	10. 3
Fresh—								
Total	27, 603	15, 868	10, 881	11, 059	100. 0	100. 0	100. 0	100. 0
Total Europe	22, 033	11, 660	7, 388	7, 420	79. 8	73. 5	67. 9	67. 1
United Kingdom	19, 016	10, 686	7, 128	6, 418	68. 9	67. 3	65. 5	58. 0
Other Europe	3, 017	974	260	1, 002	10. 9	6. 2	2. 4	9. 1
Cuba	2, 045	2, 138	1, 763	1, 557	7. 4	13. 5	16. 2	14. 1
Canada	1, 755	1, 194	590	798	6. 4	7. 5	5. 4	7. 2
Other countries	1, 770	876	1, 140	1, 284	6. 4	5. 5	10. 5	11. 6
Pickled—								
Total	26, 726	29, 126	27, 962	31, 650	100. 0	100. 0	100. 0	100. 0
Total Europe	6, 411	5, 871	4, 801	7, 016	24. 0	20. 2	17. 2	22. 2
United Kingdom	3, 281	2, 972	3, 857	5, 184	12. 3	10. 2	13. 8	16. 4
Norway	1, 814	1, 469	394	722	6. 8	5. 0	1. 4	2. 3
Germany	492	476	134	289	1. 8	1. 6	. 5	. 9
Other Europe	824	954	416	821	3. 1	3. 4	1. 5	2. 6
Canada	5, 392	7, 889	5, 800	7, 056	20. 2	27. 1	20. 7	22. 3
Newfoundland and Labrador	4, 206	3, 580	3, 532	3, 734	15. 7	12. 3	12. 6	11. 8
Cuba	3, 909	5, 935	7, 760	7, 626	14. 6	20. 4	27. 8	24. 1
British West Indies and Bermudas	2, 672	2, 457	2, 730	2, 851	10. 0	8. 4	9. 8	9. 0
Haitian Republic	1, 014	972	917	1, 055	3. 8	3. 3	3. 3	3. 3
Other countries	3, 122	2, 422	2, 422	2, 312	11. 7	8. 3	8. 6	7. 3

Table 500.—*Principal agricultural products exported from the United States, by countries, 1925–1928*—Continued

Article and country to which exported	Year ended June 30—							
	1925	1926	1927	1928	1925	1926	1927	1928
ANIMALS AND ANIMAL PRODUCTS—con.								
Lard:	*1,000 pounds*	*1,000 pounds*	*1,000 pounds*	*1,000 pounds*	*Per cent*	*Per cent*	*Per cent*	*Per cent*
Total	792,735	695,445	675,812	716,361	100.0	100.0	100.0	100.0
Total Europe	623,875	518,691	489,376	519,188	78.7	74.6	72.4	72.5
Germany	251,983	208,541	174,621	176,771	31.8	30.0	25.8	24.7
United Kingdom	223,011	218,146	222,086	233,564	28.1	31.4	32.9	32.6
Netherlands	50,369	41,479	46,071	35,784	6.4	6.0	6.8	5.0
Italy	41,145	13,891	7,642	20,384	5.2	2.0	1.1	2.8
Belgium	22,538	14,092	12,718	14,541	2.8	2.0	1.9	2.0
Other Europe	34,829	22,542	26,238	38,144	4.4	3.2	3.9	5.4
Cuba	86,480	77,377	79,599	78,469	10.9	11.1	11.8	11.0
Other countries	82,380	99,377	106,837	118,704	10.4	14.3	15.8	16.5
Lard compounds, containing animal fats:								
Total	8,922	14,958	10,548	5,654	100.0	100.0	100.0	100.0
Cuba	2,750	7,691	3,649	1,594	30.8	51.4	34.6	28.2
Haitian Republic	1,528	1,458	564	154	17.1	9.7	5.3	2.7
Mexico	1,252	1,020	542	585	14.0	6.8	5.1	10.3
United Kingdom	657	423	1,868	389	7.4	2.8	17.7	6.9
Central America	598	815	492	638	6.7	5.4	4.7	11.3
British West Indies and Bermudas	294	264	327	299	3.3	1.8	3.1	5.3
South America	274	1,226	665	310	3.1	8.2	6.3	5.5
Virgin Islands	253	276	233	264	2.8	1.8	2.2	4.7
Philippine Islands	19	37	177	274	.2	.2	1.7	4.8
Other countries	1,297	1,748	2,031	1,147	14.6	11.9	19.3	20.3
Lard, neutral:								
Total	20,421	20,132	20,057	23,799	100.0	100.0	100.0	100.0
Total Europe	18,670	18,641	18,283	21,809	91.4	92.6	91.2	91.6
Netherlands	6,141	4,645	5,260	6,784	30.1	23.1	26.2	28.5
Germany	4,706	5,519	5,895	5,623	23.0	27.4	29.4	23.6
United Kingdom	2,702	4,039	3,530	5,096	13.2	20.1	17.6	21.4
Norway	1,891	1,315	1,039	1,228	9.3	6.5	5.2	5.2
Sweden	1,227	904	912	696	6.0	4.5	4.5	2.9
Denmark	1,027	1,001	726	1,176	5.0	5.0	3.6	4.9
Other Europe	976	1,218	921	1,206	4.8	6.0	4.7	5.1
Other countries	1,751	1,491	1,774	1,990	8.6	7.4	8.8	8.4
Oleo oil:								
Total	105,145	90,410	92,720	64,851	100.0	100.0	100.0	· 100.0
Total Europe	102,135	87,177	88,128	61,611	97.1	96.4	95.0	95.0
Netherlands	46,207	26,271	27,270	17,608	43.9	29.1	29.4	27.2
Germany	18,869	24,005	25,443	18,267	17.9	26.6	27.4	28.2
United Kingdom	12,453	17,611	18,691	16,092	11.8	19.5	20.2	24.8
Norway	8,918	5,541	5,460	3,596	8.5	6.1	5.9	5.5
Greece	6,661	5,735	3,972	454	6.3	6.3	4.3	.7
Other Europe	9,027	8,014	7,292	5,594	8.7	8.8	7.8	8.6
Other countries	3,010	3,233	4,592	3,240	2.9	3.6	5.0	5.0
VEGETABLE PRODUCTS								
Cotton, excluding linters:	*1,000 bales [2]*	*1,000 bales [2]*	*1,000 bales [2]*	*1,000 bales [2]*				
Total	8,239	8,110	11,281	7,889	100.0	100.0	100.0	100.0
Total Europe	7,141	6,624	8,813	6,427	86.7	81.7	78.1	81.5
United Kingdom	2,605	2,278	2,623	1,442	31.6	28.1	23.3	18.3
Germany	1,766	1,657	2,829	2,090	21.4	20.4	25.1	26.5
France	933	927	1,063	904	11.3	11.4	9.4	11.5
Italy	748	743	841	708	9.1	9.2	7.5	9.0
Other Europe	1,089	1,019	1,457	1,283	13.3	12.6	12.8	16.2
Japan	850	1,118	1,644	1,007	10.3	13.8	14.6	12.8
Other countries	248	368	824	455	3.0	4.5	7.3	5.7

[2] Bales of 500 pounds.

TABLE 500.—*Principal agricultural products exported from the United States, by countries, 1925–1928*—Continued

Article and country to which exported	Year ended June 30—							
	1925	1926	1927	1928	1925	1926	1927	1928
VEGETABLE PRODUCTS—continued	*1,000 bales* [2]	*1,000 bales* [2]	*1,000 bales* [2]	*1,000 bales* [2]	*Per cent*	*Per cent*	*Per cent*	*Per cent*
Linters:								
Total	200	102	278	231	100.0	100.0	100.0	100.0
Total Europe	191	88	258	212	95.5	86.3	92.8	91.8
Germany	126	33	154	132	63.0	32.4	55.4	57.1
France	19	16	26	36	9.5	15.7	9.4	15.6
United Kingdom	18	19	51	22	9.0	18.6	18.3	9.5
Belgium	9	4	12	7	4.5	3.9	4.3	3.0
Other Europe	19	16	15	15	9.5	15.7	5.4	6.6
Canada	9	14	20	18	4.5	13.7	7.2	7.8
Other countries	0	0	0	1	.0	.0	.0	.4
Fruits:								
Dried—								
Apples—	*1,000 pounds*	*1,000 pounds*	*1,000 pounds*	*1,000 pounds*				
Total	19,225	24,833	32,670	21,704	100.0	100.0	100.0	100.0
Total Europe	18,552	23,840	31,313	20,735	96.5	96.0	95.8	95.5
Germany	6,632	8,864	12,158	10,877	34.5	35.7	37.2	50.1
Netherlands	4,714	7,871	9,568	3,315	24.5	31.7	29.3	15.3
United Kingdom	2,577	1,902	2,282	1,018	13.4	7.7	7.0	4.7
Sweden	2,169	1,975	2,278	2,524	11.3	8.0	7.0	11.6
Denmark	911	1,053	1,371	1,384	4.7	4.2	4.2	6.4
Other Europe	1,549	2,175	3,656	1,617	8.1	8.7	11.1	7.4
Other countries	673	993	1,357	969	3.5	4.0	4.2	4.5
Apricots—								
Total	13,292	18,132	17,901	23,684	100.0	100.0	100.0	100.0
Total Europe	10,699	16,221	15,776	21,158	80.5	89.5	88.1	89.3
Germany	3,082	3,946	4,593	6,512	23.2	21.8	25.7	27.5
United Kingdom	1,994	2,654	2,084	1,964	15.0	14.6	11.6	8.3
Netherlands	1,426	4,063	3,316	4,651	10.7	22.4	18.5	19.6
France	1,018	931	409	1,273	7.7	5.1	2.3	5.4
Denmark	836	1,707	1,962	2,469	6.3	9.4	11.0	10.4
Sweden	749	776	952	994	5.6	4.3	5.3	4.2
Other Europe	1,594	2,144	2,460	3,295	12.0	11.9	13.7	13.9
Canada	1,664	1,132	1,257	1,920	12.5	6.2	7.0	8.1
Other countries	929	779	868	606	7.0	4.3	4.9	2.6
Prunes—								
Total	171,771	151,405	175,544	260,625	100.0	100.0	100.0	100.0
Total Europe	150,541	125,278	145,710	223,574	87.6	82.7	83.0	85.8
Germany	55,000	18,893	38,553	79,732	32.0	12.5	22.0	30.6
United Kingdom	31,633	37,096	40,173	45,601	18.4	24.5	22.9	17.5
France	20,240	39,146	27,217	27,390	11.8	25.9	15.5	10.5
Netherlands	15,565	8,943	10,242	23,140	9.1	5.9	5.8	8.9
Sweden	5,465	4,871	6,854	7,047	3.2	3.2	3.9	2.7
Other Europe	22,638	16,329	22,671	40,664	13.1	10.7	12.9	15.6
Canada	14,776	17,723	20,454	23,272	8.6	11.7	11.7	8.9
Other countries	6,454	8,404	9,380	13,779	3.8	5.6	5.3	5.3
Raisins—								
Total	90,783	135,027	152,337	193,099	100.0	100.0	100.0	100.0
Total Europe	39,287	83,706	97,714	131,925	43.3	62.0	64.1	68.3
United Kingdom	23,675	43,185	49,991	70,034	26.1	32.0	32.8	36.3
Germany	5,100	18,738	16,039	18,733	5.6	13.9	10.5	9.7
Netherlands	4,266	13,802	13,857	18,598	4.7	10.2	9.1	9.6
Denmark	3,802	2,107	1,994	1,593	4.2	1.6	1.3	.8
Other Europe	2,444	5,874	15,833	22,967	2.7	4.3	10.4	11.9
Canada	38,040	32,914	37,400	40,148	41.9	24.4	24.6	20.8
China	3,485	4,406	3,549	4,144	3.8	3.3	2.3	2.1
Japan	1,919	2,513	2,801	3,086	2.1	1.9	1.8	1.6
Other countries	8,052	11,488	10,873	13,796	8.9	8.4	7.2	7.2

[2] Bales of 500 pounds.

TABLE 500.—*Principal agricultural products exported from the United States, by countries, 1925–1928*—Continued

Article and country to which exported	Year ended June 30—							
	1925	1926	1927	1928	1925	1926	1927	1928
VEGETABLE PRODUCTS—continued								
Fruits—Continued.								
Fresh—	*1,000 barrels*	*1,000 barrels*	*1,000 barrels*	*1,000 barrels*	*Per cent*	*Per cent*	*Per cent*	*Per cent*
Apples— Total	1,505	1,851	4,483	1,349	100.0	100.0	100.0	100.0
Total Europe	1,384	1,678	4,154	1,184	92.0	90.7	92.7	87.8
United Kingdom	1,255	1,477	3,305	1,004	83.4	79.8	73.7	74.4
Other Europe	129	201	849	180	8.6	10.9	19.0	13.4
Other countries	121	173	329	165	8.0	9.3	7.3	12.2
Apples—	*1,000 boxes*	*1,000 boxes*	*1,000 boxes*	*1,000 boxes*				
Total	5,088	5,464	7,844	5,384	100.0	100.0	100.0	100.0
Total Europe	3,973	3,993	6,142	4,025	78.1	73.1	78.3	74.8
United Kingdom	3,354	2,717	3,723	2,709	65.9	49.7	47.5	50.3
Germany	291	577	1,237	737	5.7	10.6	15.8	13.7
Other Europe	328	699	1,182	579	6.5	12.8	15.0	10.8
Canada	443	631	730	542	8.7	11.5	9.3	10.1
Other countries	672	840	972	817	13.2	15.4	12.4	15.1
Oranges— Total	2,197	2,241	3,340	2,988	100.0	100.0	100.0	100.0
Canada	1,980	1,995	2,636	2,346	90.1	89.0	78.9	78.5
United Kingdom	81	114	403	402	3.7	5.1	12.1	13.5
Other countries	136	132	301	240	6.2	5.9	9.0	8.0
Canned—	*1,000 pounds*	*1,000 pounds*	*1,000 pounds*	*1,000 pounds*				
Total	201,233	266,673	270,370	255,876	100.0	100.0	100.0	100.0
Total Europe	172,367	233,545	232,707	215,795	85.7	87.6	86.1	84.3
United Kingdom	156,798	207,702	203,016	177,256	77.9	77.9	75.1	69.3
Other Europe	15,569	25,843	29,691	38,539	7.8	9.7	11.0	15.0
Canada	9,412	11,149	15,491	17,993	4.7	4.2	5.7	7.0
Other countries	19,454	21,979	22,172	22,088	9.6	8.2	8.2	8.7
Glucose: Total	136,823	165,589	138,347	139,183	100.0	100.0	100.0	100.0
Total Europe	106,450	131,194	102,195	104,004	77.8	79.2	73.9	74.7
United Kingdom	82,751	101,898	74,079	73,334	60.5	61.5	53.5	52.7
Sweden	5,489	5,414	3,640	4,930	4.0	3.3	2.6	3.5
Belgium	3,906	4,270	4,943	4,931	2.9	2.6	3.6	3.5
Italy	3,014	3,585	4,680	6,242	2.2	2.2	3.4	4.5
Other Europe	11,290	16,027	14,853	14,567	8.2	9.6	10.8	10.5
Egypt	4,708	3,291	4,823	3,283	3.4	2.0	3.5	2.4
British South Africa	3,794	4,565	4,553	5,117	2.8	2.8	3.3	3.7
Argentina	2,415	3,162	3,170	3,103	1.8	1.9	2.3	2.2
Other countries	19,456	23,377	23,606	23,676	14.2	14.1	17.0	17.0
Grains and grain products: Barley—	*1,000 bushels*	*1,000 bushels*	*1,000 bushels*	*1,000 bushels*				
Total	23,653	27,181	17,044	36,580	100.0	100.0	100.0	10.00
Total Europe	22,412	21,175	14,254	25,607	94.8	77.9	83.6	70.0
United Kingdom	8,578	13,223	8,981	10,151	36.3	48.6	52.7	27.8
Germany	7,775	3,883	2,066	11,599	32.9	14.3	12.1	31.7
Netherlands	2,526	922	815	2,581	10.7	3.4	4.8	7.1
Belgium	2,225	1,727	1,576	642	9.4	6.4	9.2	1.8
Other Europe	1,308	1,420	816	634	5.5	5.2	4.8	1.6
Canada	709	5,755	2,184	10,453	3.0	21.2	12.8	28.6
Other countries	532	251	606	520	2.2	.9	3.6	1.4

TABLE 500.—*Principal agricultural products exported from the United States, by countries, 1925–1928*—Continued

Article and country to which exported	Year ended June 30—							
	1925	1926	1927	1928	1925	1926	1927	1928
VEGETABLE PRODUCTS—continued								
Grains and grain products—Contd.	*1,000 bushels*	*1,000 bushels*	*1,000 bushels*	*1,000 bushels*	*Per cent*	*Per cent*	*Per cent*	*Per cent*
Corn— Total	8,460	23,137	17,563	18,374	100.0	100.0	100.0	100.0
Canada	4,239	8,071	10,536	6,454	50.1	34.9	60.0	35.1
Cuba	2,267	2,097	2,016	1,021	26.8	9.1	11.5	5.6
Mexico	1,366	4,453	2,124	323	16.1	19.2	12.0	1.8
United Kingdom	141	2,378	1,268	1,885	1.7	10.3	7.2	10.3
Netherlands	77	3,510	560	4,311	.9	15.2	3.2	23.5
Germany	26	742	2	2,520	.3	3.2	.0	13.7
Denmark	0	999	553	845	0	4.3	3.1	4.6
Other countries	344	887	504	1,015	4.1	3.8	3.0	5.4
Oats— Total	10,874	30,975	9,245	6,034	100.0	100.0	100.0	100.0
Total Europe	5,596	16,119	2,532	1,243	51.5	52.0	27.4	20.6
Germany	1,302	2,632	297	115	12.0	8.5	3.2	1.9
United Kingdom	1,168	4,563	1,259	645	10.7	14.7	13.6	10.7
Belgium	829	2,540	352	123	7.6	8.2	3.8	2.0
France	474	4,287	239	44	4.4	13.8	2.6	.7
Other Europe	1,823	2,097	385	316	16.8	6.8	4.2	5.3
Canada	3,751	13,351	5,198	3,426	34.5	43.1	56.2	56.8
Cuba	1,264	1,093	1,170	1,028	11.6	3.5	12.7	17.0
Mexico	99	127	132	98	.9	.4	1.4	1.6
Other countries	164	285	213	239	1.5	1.0	2.3	4.0
Oatmeal— Total	*1,000 pounds* 106,256	*1,000 pounds* 156,805	*1,000 pounds* 104,334	*1,000 pounds* 68,192	100.0	100.0	100.0	100.0
Total Europe	87,511	130,684	74,806	39,749	82.4	83.3	71.7	58.3
United Kingdom	32,467	46,526	18,885	14,447	30.6	29.7	18.1	21.2
Netherlands	21,179	31,843	25,930	7,485	19.9	20.3	24.9	11.0
Finland	11,308	17,532	13,219	9,471	10.6	11.2	12.7	13.9
Belgium	5,738	7,057	4,736	2,890	5.4	4.5	4.5	4.2
Other Europe	16,819	27,726	12,036	5,456	15.9	17.6	11.5	8.0
South America	5,304	3,768	1,164	9,757	5.0	2.4	1.1	14.3
Mexico	3,365	3,993	4,027	3,739	3.2	2.5	3.9	5.5
British India	1,344	804	850	1,770	1.3	.5	.8	2.6
Canada	1,238	3,265	1,913	3,582	1.2	2.1	1.8	5.3
Other countries	7,494	14,291	21,574	9,595	6.9	9.2	20.7	14.0
Rice— Total	74,602	27,588	234,548	230,432	100.0	100.0	100.0	100.0
Total Europe	43,667	16,467	121,914	133,819	58.5	59.7	52.0	58.1
United Kingdom	21,017	8,071	33,675	35,459	28.2	29.3	14.4	15.4
Belgium	8,398	2,452	18,764	12,778	11.3	8.9	8.0	5.5
Germany	3,622	3,417	36,917	35,851	4.9	12.4	15.7	15.6
France	3,409	273	5,169	12,388	4.6	1.0	2.2	5.4
Other Europe	7,221	2,254	27,389	37,343	9.5	8.1	11.7	16.2
South America	16,980	3,315	24,847	41,205	22.8	12.0	10.6	17.9
Canada	7,030	918	7,525	14,227	9.4	3.3	3.2	6.2
Central America	3,423	2,302	3,468	5,888	4.6	8.3	1.5	2.6
Japan	565	436	68,518	2,020	.8	1.6	29.2	.9
Other countries	2,937	4,150	8,276	33,273	3.9	15.1	3.5	14.3
Rye— Total	*1,000 bushels* 49,909	*1,000 bushels* 12,505	*1,000 bushels* 21,613	*1,000 bushels* 26,044	100.0	100.0	100.0	100.0
Total Europe	25,381	5,466	7,485	5,955	50.9	43.7	34.6	22.9
Germany	8,344	1,179	1,577	1,245	16.7	9.4	7.3	4.8
Netherlands	5,127	1,234	1,768	1,388	10.3	9.9	8.2	5.3
Norway	2,933	1,499	489	298	5.9	12.0	2.3	1.1
United Kingdom	327	330	2,345	1,710	.7	2.6	10.8	6.6
Other Europe	8,650	1,224	1,306	1,314	17.3	9.8	6.0	5.1
Canada	24,524	7,017	14,118	20,080	49.1	56.1	65.3	77.1
Other countries	4	22	10	9	.0	.2	.1	.0

Table 500.—*Principal agricultural products exported from the United States, by countries, 1925–1928*—Continued

Article and country to which exported	Year ended June 30—							
	1925	1926	1927	1928	1925	1926	1927	1928
VEGETABLE PRODUCTS—continued								
Grains and grain products—Contd. Rye flour—	*1,000 barrels*	*1,000 barrels*	*1,000 barrels*	*1,000 barrels*	*Per cent*	*Per cent*	*Per cent*	*Per cent*
Total	55	24	14	47	100.0	100.0	100.0	100.0
Total Europe	48	8	6	38	87.3	33.3	42.9	80.9
Sweden	16	2	0	7	29.1	8.3	.0	14.9
Germany	14	0	0	0	25.5	.0	.0	.0
Netherlands	8	1	0	1	14.5	4.2	.0	2.1
Denmark	3	1	0	1	5.5	4.2	.0	2.1
France	1	0	0	0	1.8	.0	.0	.0
Finland	1	1	0	0	1.8	.0	.0	.0
Norway	0	0	4	28	.0	4.2	28.6	59.6
Other Europe	5	3	2	1	9.1	12.4	14.3	2.2
Canada	4	4	5	4	7.3	16.7	35.7	8.5
Philippine Islands	0	7	0	0	.0	29.2	.0	.0
Other countries	3	5	3	5	5.4	20.8	21.4	10.6
Wheat—								
Total	195,490	63,189	156,250	145,999	100.0	100.0	100.0	100.0
Total Europe	130,939	33,893	111,198	89,203	67.0	53.6	71.2	61.1
United Kingdom	40,274	16,335	39,341	36,574	20.6	25.9	25.2	25.1
Italy	25,727	2,877	10,407	10,450	13.2	4.6	6.7	7.2
Netherlands	16,727	3,720	17,131	11,559	8.6	5.9	11.0	7.9
Belgium	15,178	4,302	8,926	8,797	7.8	6.8	5.7	6.0
France	14,290	613	16,079	5,127	7.3	1.0	10.3	3.5
Germany	7,960	1,704	7,287	5,582	4.1	2.7	4.7	3.8
Other Europe	10,783	4,342	12,027	11,114	5.4	6.7	7.6	7.6
Canada	55,597	20,638	26,793	45,563	28.4	32.7	17.1	31.2
Japan, including Chosen	4,100	5,178	7,336	6,304	2.1	8.2	4.7	4.3
China	374	17	1,099	0	.2	.0	.7	.0
Other countries	4,480	3,463	9,824	4,929	2.3	5.5	6.3	3.4
Wheat, flour—								
Total	13,896	9,542	13,385	12,821	100.0	100.0	100.0	100.0
Total Europe	8,204	3,121	6,063	5,093	59.0	32.7	45.3	39.7
United Kingdom	2,105	860	1,733	1,224	15.1	9.0	12.9	9.5
Germany	1,995	340	834	534	14.4	3.6	6.2	4.2
Netherlands	1,781	774	1,565	1,530	12.8	8.1	11.7	11.9
Greece	582	249	282	113	4.2	2.6	2.1	.9
Other Europe	1,741	898	1,646	1,692	12.5	9.4	12.4	13.2
Cuba	1,233	1,144	1,199	1,216	8.9	12.0	9.0	9.5
Other West Indies [1]	728	607	747	676	5.2	6.4	5.6	5.3
Brazil	688	864	904	873	5.0	9.1	6.8	6.8
Philippine Islands	589	596	666	727	4.2	6.2	5.0	5.7
Central America	576	561	2,356	697	4.1	5.9	17.6	5.4
Honk Kong	450	371	618	929	3.2	3.9	4.6	7.2
China	129	489	418	790	.9	5.1	3.1	6.2
Kwantung	43	266	189	136	.3	2.8	1.4	1.1
Other countries	1,256	1,523	225	1,684	9.2	15.9	1.6	13.1
Hops—	*1,000 pounds*	*1,000 pounds*	*1,000 pounds*	*1,000 pounds*				
Total	16,122	14,998	13,369	11,812	100.0	100.0	100.0	100.0
Total Europe	11,301	10,537	9,378	7,718	70.1	70.3	70.1	65.3
United Kingdom	5,758	4,115	4,559	6,121	35.7	27.4	34.1	51.8
Belgium	4,768	3,791	1,892	255	29.6	25.3	14.2	2.2
Other Europe	775	2,631	2,927	1,342	4.8	17.6	21.8	11.3
Canada	3,318	2,937	2,772	3,168	20.6	19.6	20.7	26.8
Other countries	1,503	1,524	1,219	926	9.3	10.1	9.2	7.9

[1] Excludes Bermuda.

TABLE 500.—*Principal agricultural products exported from the United States, by countries, 1925–1928*—Continued

Article and country to which exported	Year ended June 30—							
	1925	1926	1927	1928	1925	1926	1927	1928
VEGETABLE PRODUCTS—continued								
Grains and grain products—Contd. Oil cake and oil-cake meal— Cottonseed cake—	*1,000 pounds*	*1,000 pounds*	*1,000 pounds*	*1,000 pounds*	*Per cent*	*Per cent*	*Per cent*	*Per cent*
Total	593, 663	506, 582	599, 448	520, 079	100. 0	100. 0	100. 0	100. 0
Total Europe	593, 610	505, 701	585, 526	519, 969	100. 0	99. 8	97. 7	100. 0
Denmark	434, 530	408, 114	345, 747	443, 579	73. 2	80. 6	57. 7	85. 3
Germany	100, 911	73, 489	215, 887	58, 781	17. 0	14. 5	36. 0	11. 3
Other Europe	58, 169	24, 098	23, 892	17, 609	9. 8	4. 7	4. 0	3. 4
Other countries	53	881	13, 922	110	. 0	. 2	2. 3	. 0
Cottonseed meal— Total	291, 711	209, 922	391, 068	144, 444	100. 0	100. 0	100. 0	100. 0
Total Europe	281, 122	191, 216	360, 620	126, 757	96. 4	91. 1	92. 2	87. 8
United Kingdom	134, 855	91, 867	150, 699	45, 842	46. 2	43. 8	38. 5	31. 7
Germany	89, 502	47, 013	127, 687	39, 157	30. 7	22. 4	32. 7	27. 1
Norway	21, 194	17, 768	28, 746	11, 656	7. 3	8. 5	7. 4	8. 1
Other Europe	35, 571	34, 568	53, 488	30, 102	12. 2	16. 4	13. 6	20. 9
Other countries	10, 589	18, 706	30, 448	17, 687	3. 6	8. 9	7. 8	12. 2
Linseed or flaxseed cake— Total	671, 460	577, 908	609, 520	589, 173	100. 0	100. 0	100. 0	100. 0
Total Europe	671, 390	577, 891	609, 394	589, 055	100. 0	100. 0	100. 0	100. 0
Netherlands	395, 439	416, 202	381, 104	305, 322	58. 9	72: 0	62. 5	51. 8
Belgium	187, 904	125, 301	171, 487	235, 883	28. 0	21. 7	28. 1	40. 0
United Kingdom	71, 038	26, 513	45, 522	38, 700	10. 6	4. 6	7. 5	6. 6
Other Europe	17, 009	9, 875	11, 281	9, 150	2. 5	1. 7	1. 9	1. 6
Other countries	70	17	126	118	. 0	. 0	. 0	. 0
Oils, vegetable: Cottonseed— Total	53, 261	59, 016	57, 580	61, 470	100. 0	100. 0	100. 0	100. 0
Canada	23, 714	36, 387	37, 683	49, 407	44. 5	61. 7	65. 4	80. 4
Netherlands	9, 252	2, 445	350	0	17. 4	4. 1	. 6	. 0
Cuba	3, 914	4, 869	2, 770	2, 033	7. 3	8. 3	4. 8	3. 3
Mexico	3, 809	4, 362	3, 868	5, 318	7. 2	7. 4	6. 7	8. 7
Germany	2, 405	288	747	42	4. 5	. 5	1. 3	. 1
Norway	2, 079	1, 565	2, 325	131	3. 9	2. 7	4. 0	. 2
Argentina	1, 573	1, 536	2, 160	1, 108	3. 0	2. 6	3. 8	1. 8
Other countries	6, 515	7, 564	7, 677	3, 431	12. 2	12. 7	13. 4	5. 5
Starch: Total	214, 247	224, 570	233, 112	281, 388	100. 0	100. 0	100. 0	100. 0
Total Europe	195, 477	201, 191	210, 390	212, 982	91. 2	89. 6	90. 3	75. 7
United Kingdom	161, 928	162, 051	166, 399	169, 483	75. 6	72. 2	71. 4	60. 2
Netherlands	14, 939	19, 511	18, 021	16, 415	7. 0	8. 7	7. 7	5. 8
Germany	128	0	1, 455	1, 274	. 1	. 0	. 6	. 5
Other Europe	18, 482	19, 629	24, 515	25, 810	8. 5	8. 7	10. 6	9. 2
Japan	2, 038	4, 764	1, 791	17, 702	1. 0	2. 1	. 8	6. 3
Other countries	16, 732	18, 615	20, 931	50, 704	7. 8	8. 3	8. 9	18. 0

TABLE 500.—*Principal agricultural products exported from the United States, by countries, 1925–1928*—Continued

Article and country to which exported	Year ended June 30—							
	1925	1926	1927	1928	1925	1926	1927	1928
VEGETABLE PRODUCTS—continued								
Sugar, refined:	*1,000 short tons*	*1,000 short tons*	*1,000 short tons*	*1,000 short tons*	*Per cent*	*Per cent*	*Per cent*	*Per cent*
Total	251	300	114	106	100.0	100.0	100.0	100.0
Total Europe	167	217	67	61	66.5	72.3	58.8	57.5
United Kingdom	88	131	37	35	35.1	43.7	32.5	33.0
France	12	12	5	1	4.8	4.0	4.4	.9
Greece	12	7	3	2	4.8	2.3	2.6	1.9
Norway	12	27	15	13	4.8	9.0	13.2	12.3
Other Europe	43	40	7	10	17.0	13.3	6.1	9.4
Uruguay	22	33	19	13	8.8	11.0	16.7	12.3
Canada	9	5	2	4	3.6	1.7	1.8	3.8
Newfoundland and Labrador	5	4	1	1	2.0	1.3	.9	.9
Cuba	4	1	0	0	1.6	.3	.0	.0
British Africa	2	4	5	5	.8	1.3	4.4	4.7
Mexico	1	2	4	2	.4	.7	3.5	1.9
Other countries	41	34	16	20	16.3	11.4	13.9	18.9
Tobacco, leaf:	*1,000 pounds*	*1,000 pounds*	*1,000 pounds*	*1,000 pounds*				
Total	420,223	528,131	510,186	483,185	100.0	100.0	100.0	100.0
Total Europe	287,352	343,880	346,444	315,740	68.4	65.1	67.9	65.3
United Kingdom	140,772	185,431	154,038	170,873	33.5	35.1	30.2	35.4
Spain	32,746	10	20,774	15,017	7.8	.0	4.1	3.1
France	30,277	54,497	41,834	23,675	7.2	10.3	8.2	4.9
Germany	19,126	24,300	31,171	27,411	4.6	4.6	6.1	5.7
Netherlands	15,873	24,155	31,576	26,941	3.8	4.6	6.2	5.6
Belgium	15,203	15,448	31,368	17,447	3.6	2.9	6.1	3.6
Italy	9,421	10,314	3,408	3,510	2.2	2.0	.7	.7
Other Europe	23,934	29,725	32,275	30,866	5.7	5.6	6.3	6.3
China	53,933	98,142	77,216	68,447	12.8	18.6	15.1	14.2
Australia	20,532	22,728	21,821	23,449	4.9	4.3	4.3	4.9
Canada	11,659	13,519	14,541	16,496	2.8	2.6	2.9	3.4
Other countries	46,747	49,862	50,164	59,053	11.1	9.4	9.8	12.2
Potatoes:	*1,000 bushels*	*1,000 bushels*	*1,000 bushels*	*1,000 bushels*				
Total	3,653	1,824	2,092	2,424	100.0	100.0	100.0	100.0
Cuba	1,869	920	950	1,412	51.2	50.4	45.4	58.3
Canada	1,038	343	594	444	28.4	18.8	28.4	18.3
Panama	195	151	123	147	5.3	8.3	5.9	6.1
Mexico	168	178	139	71	4.6	9.8	6.6	2.9
Other countries	383	232	286	350	10.5	12.7	13.7	14.4

Bureau of Agricultural Economics. Compiled from Monthly Summary of Foreign Commerce of the United States, June issues, 1926–1928, and official records of the Bureau of Foreign and Domestic Commerce.

TABLE 501.—*Bananas: United States imports, by months, 1910–1929*

Year ended June 30	July	August	September	October	November	December	January
	Bunches	Bunches	Bunches	Bunches	Bunches	Bunches	Bunches
1910	4,766	4,510	3,868	2,850	2,383	2,056	1,489
1911	4,735	4,894	4,003	3,406	2,814	2,618	2,126
1912	5,513	4,797	3,688	3,687	2,851	2,629	2,447
1913	5,049	4,222	3,111	3,306	2,444	2,363	2,530
1914	5,735	4,380	4,255	3,625	2,994	3,207	2,637
1915	6,092	4,311	3,704	3,212	2,599	2,236	1,886
1916	4,528	4,066	3,164	2,494	2,616	2,424	1,867
1917	3,868	4,327	2,718	2,629	2,298	2,082	2,255
1918	4,110	3,961	3,330	2,574	2,541	2,025	1,745
1919	3,430	3,571	2,670	2,759	2,077	1,732	2,256
1920	4,151	2,824	3,177	2,942	2,547	2,209	1,976
1921	4,568	4,791	2,884	2,725	2,969	2,384	1,939
1922	4,662	4,572	3,983	3,561	3,442	2,660	2,632
1923	4,836	4,573	2,698	4,302	2,776	2,669	2,594
1924	4,737	3,871	3,363	3,389	3,053	2,895	2,767
1925	5,195	5,192	4,129	3,672	2,904	2,664	3,123
1926	6,231	5,841	5,530	4,363	3,558	3,205	3,602
1927	5,403	5,047	3,355	4,979	4,050	3,594	3,131
1928	5,987	6,332	4,903	4,744	4,412	3,957	3,472
1929	6,632	6,592	4,672	4,839	4,336	3,533	---------

Year ended June 30	February	March	April	May	June	Total
	Bunches	Bunches	Bunches	Bunches	Bunches	Bunches
1910	1,767	2,575	3,211	4,193	4,489	38,157
1911	2,253	3,249	3,768	5,219	5,614	44,699
1912	2,555	3,108	4,177	4,525	4,544	44,521
1913	2,600	2,904	3,815	4,795	5,218	42,357
1914	2,803	3,640	4,736	4,952	5,720	48,684
1915	1,832	2,813	3,208	4,081	5,118	41,092
1916	1,746	2,391	2,858	3,993	4,608	36,755
1917	1,802	2,547	2,977	3,258	3,900	34,661
1918	2,005	2,652	3,037	3,350	3,220	34,550
1919	2,153	2,819	2,824	4,512	4,579	35,382
1920	1,799	3,225	3,912	3,655	4,431	36,848
1921	2,186	3,229	4,172	3,770	5,191	40,808
1922	2,515	3,885	3,882	4,948	5,378	46,120
1923	2,403	3,377	4,449	4,912	4,915	44,504
1924	2,239	3,420	4,788	5,397	5,016	44,935
1925	2,029	4,041	4,007	6,159	7,398	50,513
1926	3,184	4,401	6,320	5,420	6,895	58,550
1927	3,504	5,309	5,636	6,240	6,854	57,102
1928	4,139	5,626	6,031	7,172	7,254	64,029

Bureau of Agricultural Economics. Compiled from Monthly Summary of Foreign Commerce of the United States.

TABLE 502.—*Oil cake and oil-cake meal: International trade, average 1909–1913, annual 1925–1927*

Country	Average 1909–1913		1925		1926		1927, preliminary	
	Imports	Exports	Imports	Exports	Imports	Exports	Imports	Exports
PRINCIPAL EXPORTING COUNTRIES	*1,000 pounds*	*1,000 pounds*	*1,000 pounds*	*1,000 pounds*	*1,000 pounds*	*1,000 pounds*	*1,000 pounds*	*1,000 pounds*
United States	0	1,704,124	88,535	1,487,756	120,555	1,449,758	188,884	1,569,969
Russia	0	1,453,413	0	808,927	0	[1] 882,060		
Germany	1,686,416	525,108	749,836	718,287	971,767	835,906	1,231,000	697,136
British India	1,262	268,648	[2] 157	[2] 2,437,179	[2] 305	[2] 2,499,052	[2] 220	[2] 581,860
France	288,968	476,863	52,701	252,003	55,132	304,737	89,750	322,201
Egypt	0	161,624	3	287,698	11	355,684	2	401,257
China	[3] 174	147,468	0	259,092	0	284,486	0	230,257
Italy	10,550	55,115	1,085	180,815	631	140,812	632	264,403
Argentina	0	42,587	0	98,270	0	134,037	0	173,438
Dutch East Indies	2,509	13,242	0	76,303	0	105,788	0	[4] 137,112
Peru	0	10,930	0	51,657	0	66,656	0	88,428
Brazil	0	[5] 6,574	0	70,586	0	61,720		
Czechoslovakia	0	0	46,706	48,801	57,251	61,046	72,818	54,879
Canada	7,752	51,370	8,774	46,397	19,192	39,323	15,486	46,147
Spain	0	2,164	3,504	29,904	1,493	44,445		
Australia	148	1,347	[6] 33	[6] 16,857	[6] 15	[6] 902	[6] 4,772	[6] 926
Hungary	[7] 53,673	[7] 124,873	636	9,853	8,591	14,233	15,911	15,966
PRINCIPAL IMPORTING COUNTRIES								
Denmark	1,002,329	15,777	1,627,436	16,238	1,532,525	33,434	1,616,389	
United Kingdom	790,865	161,798	1,013,179	131,006	1,105,848	193,265	1,091,700	144,243
Netherlands	707,116	219,819	572,491	98,920	731,235	117,686	592,427	130,177
Japan	189,868	0	356,821	20,083	392,675	29,894	314,853	29,436
Belgium	543,648	155,373	324,512	60,065	280,276	79,031	346,573	81,035
Sweden	346,755	1,535	207,877	12,203	372,952	6,262	278,728	15,346
Irish Free State	0	0	126,521	0	104,666	0	111,835	0
Finland	25,333	2,125	147,192	0	216,906	0	163,078	0
Switzerland	69,352	1,413	91,071	7,117	83,944	13,653	56,064	18,536
Norway	55,112	2,889	69,822	128	71,900	56	77,686	
Ceylon	[8] 40,494	[8] 28,509	44,720	18,918	42,851	17,953	42,990	19,393
Austria			18,988	2,002	20,293	1,812	33,204	745
Total 29 countries	5,822,324	5,634,688	5,552,600	5,247,065	6,191,014	5,773,691	6,345,002	5,022,890

Bureau of Agricultural Economics. Official sources except as otherwise noted.

The class called here "Oil cake and oil-cake meal" includes the edible cake and meal remaining after making oil from such products as cottonseed, flaxseed, peanuts, corn, etc. Soy-bean cake is not included in this table.

[1] Economic Review, the Soviet Union of Jan. 1, 1928.
[2] Sea trade only.
[3] 3-year average.
[4] Java and Madura only.
[5] 4-year average.
[6] Year ended June 30.
[7] Average for Austria-Hungary.
[8] 1 year only.

TABLE 503.—*Rubber: International trade, average 1909–1913, annual 1925–1927*

Country	Year ended Dec. 31							
	Average 1909–1913		1925		1926		1927, preliminary	
	Imports	Exports	Imports	Exports	Imports	Exports	Imports	Exports
PRINCIPAL EXPORTING COUNTRIES	*1,000 pounds*	*1,000 pounds*	*1,000 pounds*	*1,000 pounds*	*1,000 pounds*	*1,000 pounds*	*1,000 pounds*	*1,000 pounds*
British Malaya	[1] 53,472	[1] 85,435	357,171	710,025	340,890	883,119	411,472	832,030
Dutch East Indies	[2] 1	7,679	0	533,752	0	538,986	0	[3] 627,934
Ceylon	[4] 1,299	10,953	8,809	102,206	10,944	131,876	11,119	125,063
Brazil	0	84,938	[1] 49	50,486	0	48,954	0	57,730
British India	0	[4] 1,504	104	22,583	18	22,118	72	25,363
French-Indo China	1	398	[1] 13	17,653	[1] 25	19,350	[1] 31	21,225
British North Borneo	0	[1] 331	0	12,152	0	[1] 13,656	0	[1] 14,788
Bolivia	0	8,395	0	7,480	0	6,845		
Mexico	0	[1] 13,462	214	9,971	[1] 259	[1] 11,080	[1] 313	[1] 10,946
French Guinea	[1] 241	3,937	[1] 49	2,967	[1] 81	[1] 2,773	[1] 4	[1] 2,060
French Equatorial Africa	[1] 10	[1] 3,775	0	3,768	[1] 389	[1] 3,483	[1] 454	[1] 3,332
Kamerun	0	6,409	0	[1] 1,832	0	[1] 2,286	[1] 7	[1] 1,970
Ecuador	0	[*] 1,040	0	2,949	0	2,400		
Belgian Congo	0	7,755	0	1,696	3	2,489	0	[1] 3,307
Nigeria	0	3,054	0	2,128	0	[1] 3,571	0	[1] 4,474
Switzerland	391	725	1,036	1,347	914	1,750	1,093	1,694
Gold Coast	0	2,393	0	[1] 1,098	0	[1] 1,418	0	[1] 711
Peru	0	5,030	0	16	0	463	0	2
Angola	0	5,620	0	[1] 67	0	[1] 1,836	0	[1] 962
PRINCIPAL IMPORTING COUNTRIES								
United States	100,180	0	888,478	0	925,878	0	954,750	0
France	32,704	21,615	88,718	14,897	107,361	20,222	108,373	21,130
Germany	42,004	9,844	79,579	3,571	55,201	4,185	93,836	6,721
Japan	1,917	0	28,793	0	40,923	0	46,997	0
Canada	3,945	0	44,548	0	45,367	0	59,146	0
Italy	5,381	225	26,381	817	23,087	596	25,494	204
United Kingdom	43,141	0	11,043	0	190,251	0	134,955	0
Netherlands	10,822	7,172	6,909	4,949	11,925	5,943	10,813	9,389
Russia	19,131	0	14,192	0	[1] 16,395	0	[1] 22,857	0
Belgium	25,891	20,749	8,486	1,969	8,112	2,665	16,610	2,073
Spain	1,067	0	7,487	0	8,804	0		
Austria	[5] 6,696	[5] 1,619	5,401	913	5,008	1,019	2,924	62
Sweden	1,695	1	3,705	109	4,701	167	4,951	168
Czechoslovakia [1]	0	0	773	20	1,122	32	6,568	489
Hungary	0	0	997	134	1,327	68	2,424	78
Denmark	250	0	1,082	1	1,291	4	1,300	[1] 7
Total 35 countries	350,239	314,058	1,584,017	1,511,556	1,800,276	1,733,354	1,916,563	1,773,912

Division of Statistical and Historical Research. Official sources except where otherwise noted.

Figures for rubber include "India rubber," so-called, caoutchouc, caucho, jebe (Peru), hule (Mexico), borracha, massarandubà, mangabeira, manicoba, sorva, and seringa (Brazil), gumelastiek (Dutch East Indies), caura, ser nambi (Venezuela).

[1] International Yearbook of Agricultural Statistics.
[2] 1-year only.
[3] Java and Madura from official source. Other Dutch East Indies from International Yearbook of Agricultural Statistics.
[4] 3-year average.
[5] Average for Austria-Hungary.

TABLE 504.—*Vegetable oils: Exports from the United States, 1910–1928*

Year ended June 30—	Corn	Cotton-seed	Linseed	Cocoa butter or but-terine	Coconut	Peanut	Soy bean
	1,000 lbs.	1,000 lbs.	1,000 gals.	1,000 lbs.	1,000 lbs.	1,000 lbs.	1,000 lbs.
1910	11,299	223,955	228				
1911	25,317	225,521	175				
1912	23,866	399,471	247				
1913	19,839	315,233	1,734				
1914	18,282	192,963	239				
1915	17,790	318,367	1,212				
1916	8,968	266,512	714				
1917	8,780	158,912	1,202				
1918	1,831	100,780	1,188				
1919	1,095	178,709	1,096				
1920	12,483	159,400	1,136	11,048	141,088	4,922	67,782
1921	6,919	283,268	561	3,171	6,639	1,595	5,118
1922	5,280	91,615	366	1,856	10,185	1,802	537
1923	5,224	64,292	414	957	12,993	188	2,495
1924	4,196	39,418	350	888	19,423	168	2,892
1925	3,586	53,261	320	1,577	17,890	(1)	579
1926	2,927	59,015	311	1,766	15,444	(1)	623
1927	405	57,580	365	290	19,826	(1)	3,104
1928 [2]	329	61,470	296	1,897	22,358	(1)	7,514

Bureau of Agricultural Economics. Compiled from Foreign Commerce and Navigation of the United States, 1910–1918; Monthly Summary of Foreign Commerce of the United States, June issues, 1919–1928.

[1] Included with "other vegetable oils and fats."
[2] Preliminary.

TABLE 505.—*Vegetable oils: Imports into the United States, 1910–1928*

Year ended June 30—	Castor [1]	Chinese nut	Cocoa butter or but-terine	Coco-nut	Cot-ton-seed [1]	Lin-seed	Olive	Palm	Palm ker-nel	Pea-nut	Rape-seed	Soy bean
	1,000 gals.	1,000 gals.	1,000 lbs.	1,000 lbs.	1,000 lbs.	1,000 gals.	1,000 gals.	1,000 lbs.	1,000 lbs.	1,000 gals.	1,000 gals.	1,000 lbs.
1910	7	[2] 5,760	3,370	48,346	(3)	(3)	4,545	92,772	(3)	(4)	[5] 1,083	(3)
1911	7	[2] 7,042	4,279	51,118	(3)	(3)	4,984	57,100	(3)	(4)	[5] 1,363	(3)
1912	8	4,768	6,075	46,371	1,513	737	5,473	47,159	25,393	896	1,183	28,021
1913	5	5,997	3,603	50,504	3,384	174	5,840	50,229	23,569	1,196	1,550	12,340
1914	189	4,932	2,839	74,386	17,293	192	6,981	58,040	34,328	1,337	1,464	16,360
1915	63	4,940	150	63,135	15,162	535	7,364	31,486	4,906	853	1,499	19,207
1916	253	4,968	400	66,008	17,181	50	8,109	40,497	6,761	1,475	2,561	98,120
1917	324	6,864	150	79,223	13,703	111	8,184	36,074	1,857	3,026	1,085	162,690
1918	1,175	4,816	(6)	259,195	14,291	51	2,652	27,405	19	8,289	3,056	336,825
1919	472	6,217	3	344,728	20,410	990	4,398	19,281	1,945	11,393	2,091	236,805
1920	271	10,614	42	271,540	24,165	4,550	7,029	50,165	54	22,064	1,230	195,774
1921	99	4,440	915	173,889	1,315	1,997	4,705	31,076	2,769	2,422	1,172	49,331
1922	46	7,410	7,123	230,236	(6)	22,494	11,112	39,159		384	1,352	8,283
1923	185	11,919	3,010	212,573	45	7,568	15,635	118,816		1,007	1,770	38,635
1924	36	10,786	1,169	181,230	(6)	2,379	15,121	86,784	1,126	2,008	2,068	17,631
1925	41	12,626	733	250,121	0	3,145	15,743	114,387	37,364	468	1,959	20,434
1926	66	11,315	14	200,878	283	2,231	18,368	152,254	85,074	450	2,088	17,401
1927	22	13,657	256	286,776	6,396	177	17,964	110,184	14,760	1,061	2,731	23,553
1928 [7]	125	11,868	18	273,309	1	46	15,741	186,123	56,021	648	2,604	13,562

Bureau of Agricultural Economics. Compiled from Foreign Commerce and Navigation of the United States 1910–1918: Monthly Summary of Foreign Commerce of the United States, June issues, 1919–1928.

[1] Imports for consumption.
[2] Includes peanut oil.
[3] Included in all other fixed or expressed.
[4] Included in Chinese nut oil.
[5] Includes hempseed.
[6] Less than 500 pounds.
[7] Preliminary.

GENERAL NOTE.—International trade tables not appearing here are to be found with the other tables of the various commodities.

33023°—29——66

MISCELLANEOUS AGRICULTURAL STATISTICS

TABLE 506.—*Crop summary: Acreage, production, and yield per acre, 1926–1928*

Crop	Acreage 1926	Acreage 1927	Acreage 1928	Unit	Production 1926	Production 1927	Production 1928	Yield per acre 1926	Yield per acre 1927	Yield per acre 1928
	1,000 acres	*1,000 acres*	*1,000 acres*		*Thousands*	*Thousands*	*Thousands*			
Corn	99,713	98,393	100,761	Bushel	2,692,217	2,763,093	2,839,959	27.0	28.1	28.2
Winter wheat	36,987	37,723	36,179	___do	627,433	552,747	578,964	17.0	14.7	16.0
Durum wheat, 4 States.	4,774	5,484	6,711	___do	43,981	79,100	92,770	9.2	14.4	13.8
Other spring wheat	14,576	15,577	14,834	___do	159,626	246,527	231,015	11.0	15.8	15.6
All wheat	56,337	58,784	57,724	___do	831,040	878,374	902,749	14.8	14.9	15.6
Oats	44,177	41,941	41,733	___do	1,246,848	1,182,594	1,449,531	28.2	28.2	34.7
Barley	7,970	9,476	12,539	___do	184,905	265,882	356,868	23.2	28.1	28.5
Rye	3,578	3,648	3,444	___do	40,795	58,164	41,766	11.4	15.9	12.1
Buckwheat	694	810	750	___do	12,676	15,755	13,163	18.3	19.5	17.6
Flaxseed	2,907	2,837	2,721	___do	19,335	25,847	19,321	6.7	9.1	7.1
Rice	1,034	1,012	965	___do	41,730	44,774	41,881	40.4	44.2	43.4
Grain sorghums [1]	6,690	6,723	6,497	___do	137,515	137,358	142,533	20.6	20.4	21.9
Cotton	47,087	40,138	45,326	Bale	17,977	12,955	14,373	[2]182.6	[2]154.5	[2]151.8
Cottonseed				Ton	7,982	5,759	6,390			
Hay, tame	58,558	60,885	57,775	___do	86,144	106,001	93,031	1.47	1.74	1.61
Hay, wild	12,911	14,813	13,144	___do	9,568	17,326	12,922	.74	1.17	.98
All hay	71,469	75,698	70,919	___do	95,712	123,327	105,953	1.34	1.63	1.49
Cloverseed (red and alsike).	530	1,214	713	Bushel	728	1,727	1,106	1.37	1.42	1.55
Beans, dry, edible [1]	1,649	1,571	1,577	___do	17,396	16,181	16,598	10.5	10.3	10.5
Soy beans [3]	920	1,162	1,122	___do	11,219	15,770	16,305	12.2	13.6	14.5
Peanuts [3]	1,315	1,785	1,910	Pound	879,923	1,311,793	1,231,190	669.1	734.9	644.6
Cowpeas [3]	1,336	1,826	1,388	Bushel	13,009	19,644	13,395	9.7	10.8	9.6
Velvet beans [3]	1,353	1,534	1,541	Ton	571	726	705	[2]844.1	[2]946.6	[2]915.0
Potatoes	3,122	3,476	3,825	Bushel	354,328	402,741	462,943	113.5	115.9	121.0
Sweet potatoes	819	933	810	___do	82,703	94,112	77,661	101.0	100.9	95.9
Tobacco	1,656	1,585	1,912	Pound	1,297,889	1,211,909	1,373,501	783.6	764.7	718.3
Sugar cane, except for sirup (La.).	163	90	157	Ton	1,105	1,178	2,540	6.8	13.2	16.1
Cane sirup	132	114	113	Gallon	22,172	20,839	21,783	168.0	182.8	192.8
Sugar beets	677	721	646	Ton	7,223	7,753	7,040	10.7	10.8	10.9
Sorghum sirup	387	366	348	Gallon	34,538	30,268	26,972	89.2	82.7	77.5
Maple sugar and sirup (as sugar).	[4]14,712	[4]14,603	[4]14,388	Pound	33,465	32,612	26,492	[5]2.27	[5]2.23	[5]1.84
Broomcorn [1]	306	230	252	Ton	54	39	46	[2]355.6	[2]335.6	[2]361.2
Hops [1]	21	25	26	Pound	31,522	30,658	32,742	1,516.0	1,246.0	1,254.0
Fruit crops:										
Apples, total				Bushel	246,524	123,693	184,920			
Apples, commercial.				Barrel	39,119	26,017	35,308			
Peaches				Bushel	[6]69,865	[6]45,463	[6]68,374			
Pears				___do	25,249	18,373	23,783			
Grapes				Ton	[7]2,438	[7]2,605	[7]2,636			
Oranges (2 States)				Box	38,867	31,200	44,000			
Grapefruit (Fla.)				___do	7,800	7,200	9,000			
Lemons (Calif.)				___do	7,712	6,000	7,100			
Cranberries	28	28	29	Barrel	744	496	531	26.1	17.4	18.6
Commercial truck crops:										
Asparagus	85	90	95	Crate	7,813	7,877	9,235	92.0	87.0	97.0
Beans, snap	98	111	135	Ton	117	125	147	1.2	1.1	1.1
Cabbage	129	144	137	___do	1,034	1,205	976	8.0	8.4	7.1
Cantaloupes	102	106	100	Crate	14,393	15,014	15,521	142.0	142.0	155.0
Carrots	19	26	24	Bushel	5,523	7,763	6,628	291.0	295.0	281.0
Cauliflower	23	18	21	Crate	5,538	4,096	4,987	246.0	231.0	242.0
Celery	22	25	26	___do	5,767	7,585	7,173	264.0	309.0	272.0
Corn, sweet (canning).	317	215	289	Ton	816	399	536	2.6	1.9	1.9
Cucumbers	112	94	112	Bushel	9,224	8,256	8,535	82.0	88.0	76.0
Eggplant	3	3	4	___do	791	782	896	243.0	262.0	230.0
Lettuce	106	122	127	Crate	17,150	19,383	18,589	162.0	159.0	147.0
Onions	74	77	77	Bushel	21,119	23,595	19,025	285.0	308.0	246.0
Peas, green	262	221	268	Ton	261	239	277	1.0	1.1	1.0
Peppers	15	15	19	Bushel	3,890	3,502	4,418	254.0	240.0	239.0
Potatoes, early [8]	324	348	401	___do	36,624	44,825	55,368	113.0	129.0	138.0
Spinach	52	55	63	Ton	124	141	138	2.4	2.6	2.2

[1] Principal producing States.
[2] Pounds.
[3] Includes total crop gathered, hogged off, and otherwise utilized except where harvested for hay only.
[4] Trees tapped.
[5] Per tree.
[6] The production of peaches shown includes some estimated quantities not harvested or not utilized as follows: 1926, 1,462,000 bushels; 1927, 2,708,000 bushels; 1928, 2,917,000 bushels.
[7] The production of grapes includes 15,000 tons not harvested in 1926; 142,000 tons not harvested in 1927; and 153,000 tons not harvested in 1928.
[8] Included in "Potatoes."

1036

TABLE 506.—*Crop summary: Acreage, production, and yield per acre, 1926–1928—*
Continued

Corn	Acreage			Unit	Production			Yield per acre		
	1926	1927	1928		1926	1927	1928	1926	1927	1928
Commercial truck crops—Continued.	*1,000 acres*	*1,000 acres*	*1,000 acres*		*Thousands*	*Thousands*	*Thousands*			
Strawberries_____	152	189	204	Quart___	277,940	319,519	325,045	1,823.0	1,691.0	1,596.0
Tomatoes_____	372	397	401	Ton_____	1,376	1,641	1,402	3.7	4.1	3.5
Watermelons_____	199	183	210	Number	69,698	57,682	61,773	350.0	316.0	294.0
Total with duplications eliminated.	357,451	357,190	360,982							

Bureau of Agricultural Economics. Estimates of the crop-reporting board.

TABLE 507.—*Acreage of 19 crops, 1924–1928, value of 22 crops, 1926–1928, and computed value of all crops, 1927 and 1928, by States*

State	Acreage of 19 crops [1]					Value of 22 crops [2]			Computed value of all crops [3]	
	1924	1925	1926	1927	1928	1926	1927	1928	1927	1928
	1,000 acres	*1,000 acres*	*1,000 acres*	*1,000 acres*	*1,000 acres*	*1,000 dollars*	*1,000 dollars*	*1,000 dollars*	*1,000 dollars*	*1,000 dollars*
Maine_____	1,592	1,592	1,591	1,587	1,580	74,648	58,059	39,222	63,108	42,633
New Hampshire____	523	523	523	519	511	15,444	14,670	12,632	18,570	15,990
Vermont_____	1,141	1,141	1,141	1,136	1,121	32,440	28,209	27,027	36,635	35,100
Massachusetts_____	573	573	575	568	560	30,811	30,222	29,436	44,444	43,288
Rhode Island_____	61	61	62	60	59	3,170	2,608	2,587	3,780	3,749
Connecticut_____	480	481	479	479	476	30,240	29,526	29,239	36,452	36,098
New York_____	7,868	7,841	7,621	7,638	7,396	219,355	199,650	177,726	259,286	230,813
New Jersey_____	720	708	686	684	682	37,184	35,020	29,370	50,029	41,957
Pennsylvania_____	7,186	7,314	7,150	7,129	7,007	223,854	214,532	189,016	249,456	219,786
Ohio_____	10,541	10,751	10,651	10,402	10,284	261,612	232,931	230,122	267,737	264,508
Indiana_____	10,694	10,878	10,641	10,223	10,125	202,495	192,159	202,819	213,510	225,354
Illinois_____	19,721	20,131	19,774	19,201	19,742	360,048	356,513	432,514	387,514	470,124
Michigan_____	8,344	8,322	8,255	8,282	8,195	205,951	185,764	194,621	226,541	237,343
Wisconsin_____	9,452	9,534	9,502	9,507	9,447	243,992	247,132	240,936	305,101	297,452
Minnesota_____	17,899	17,923	17,868	17,682	17,609	290,122	287,756	290,407	323,321	326,300
Iowa_____	21,170	21,489	21,574	21,368	21,631	405,744	447,970	501,712	486,924	545,339
Missouri_____	13,981	14,525	13,997	13,137	13,425	245,995	238,282	249,140	267,733	279,933
North Dakota_____	20,192	20,452	19,453	20,140	20,315	176,920	256,588	223,507	278,900	242,942
South Dakota_____	15,762	15,918	13,629	16,383	15,597	113,245	225,326	156,859	242,286	168,666
Nebraska_____	19,649	19,674	19,486	20,306	20,280	241,683	359,878	315,419	378,819	332,020
Kansas_____	21,740	21,594	21,573	21,924	22,877	303,382	328,286	371,290	360,754	408,011
Delaware_____	341	344	346	339	344	10,456	11,674	11,633	16,214	16,157
Maryland_____	1,618	1,637	1,640	1,654	1,670	55,818	57,462	49,829	71,828	62,286
Virginia_____	4,036	4,208	4,232	4,104	4,140	143,646	153,964	145,576	181,134	171,266
West Virginia_____	1,633	1,794	1,744	1,742	1,727	59,962	57,142	56,545	70,546	69,809
North Carolina_____	6,668	6,821	6,960	6,692	6,722	278,798	299,895	264,568	344,707	304,101
South Carolina_____	5,011	5,076	4,982	5,027	4,862	115,082	136,897	117,744	166,948	143,590
Georgia_____	8,737	9,009	9,318	9,235	9,092	169,443	208,261	185,744	260,326	232,180
Florida_____	890	876	851	954	1,024	53,205	58,126	55,328	93,752	89,239
Kentucky_____	5,227	5,354	5,323	5,151	5,268	154,934	153,500	169,220	172,472	190,135
Tennessee_____	6,261	6,388	6,726	6,278	6,228	149,879	154,126	165,733	185,694	199,678
Alabama_____	7,091	7,287	7,369	6,974	7,273	140,343	182,629	159,649	225,468	197,098
Mississippi_____	5,777	6,046	6,232	5,923	6,365	156,215	189,197	176,896	227,948	213,128
Arkansas_____	6,473	6,994	7,073	6,257	6,792	154,526	163,629	168,926	197,143	203,525
Louisiana_____	3,711	3,943	4,014	3,681	4,191	96,292	106,514	114,716	150,020	161,572
Oklahoma_____	14,829	15,210	15,900	14,719	15,636	263,789	243,750	263,942	280,172	303,382
Texas_____	27,737	26,546	30,257	29,344	30,072	516,787	612,154	649,827	737,535	782,924
Montana_____	6,501	6,662	6,772	7,457	7,602	96,947	137,051	117,526	159,362	136,658
Idaho_____	2,472	2,579	2,616	2,824	2,843	82,611	95,272	84,675	108,264	96,222
Wyoming_____	1,562	1,638	1,670	1,763	1,784	26,647	27,660	28,488	31,432	32,373
Colorado_____	5,709	5,608	5,934	5,688	5,885	82,717	87,691	86,356	115,383	113,626
New Mexico_____	1,269	904	1,287	972	1,193	26,800	22,696	26,198	29,475	34,023
Arizona_____	485	480	519	543	574	22,253	28,077	34,226	33,425	40,745
Utah_____	911	992	987	1,012	1,037	25,796	26,011	29,561	37,159	42,230
Nevada_____	361	421	402	405	407	8,685	7,797	10,144	8,122	10,567
Washington_____	3,198	3,486	3,475	3,611	3,599	120,853	144,469	121,674	176,182	148,383
Oregon_____	2,428	2,674	2,702	2,758	2,735	67,017	80,311	77,066	107,081	102,755
California_____	3,966	4,467	4,587	4,610	4,657	244,275	259,080	285,206	479,778	528,159
United States___	344,191	348,869	350,149	348,072	352,641	7,042,111	7,676,116	7,602,597	9,168,470	9,093,217

Bureau of Agricultural Economics. Estimates of the crop-reporting board.

[1] Includes corn, wheat, oats, barley, rye, buckwheat, potatoes, sweet potatoes, tobacco, flax, rice, all hay, cotton, peanuts, grain sorghums, beans, broomcorn, hops, and cranberries.
[2] Includes the 19 crops listed in Note 1 and also cloverseed, oranges, and apples.
[3] Value of 22 crops shown in preceding columns adjusted basis relation all crops (not including nursery, greenhouse, and forest products), and 22 crops, 1919 Census.

TABLE 508.—*Farm returns, 1927, with comparisons*

[Averages of reports of owner-operators for their own farms for calendar year]

		United States						North Atlantic		East North Central		West North Central		South Atlantic		South Central		Western	
		1922	1923	1924	1925	1926	1927	1926	1927	1926	1927	1926	1927	1926	1927	1926	1927	1926	1927
Number of reports		6,094	16,183	15,103	15,330	13,475	13,859	1,436	1,477	2,591	2,560	2,969	3,129	1,764	1,837	3,269	3,418	1,446	1,438
Size of farm	acres	252	298	303	304	315	275	138	139	152	148	353	355	203	189	421	249	599	643
Value of farm real estate, Jan. 1	dollars	13,586	14,530	14,323	14,157	13,379	12,543	9,385	9,405	13,827	13,002	19,879	19,082	9,252	8,231	9,904	8,905	16,091	14,982
Value of farm personality, Jan. 1	dollars	2,844	2,960	2,937	2,965	2,929	2,893	3,203	3,395	2,846	2,889	4,188	4,068	1,634	1,563	1,949	1,817	4,012	4,087
Receipts:																			
Crop sales		816	850	1,012	993	926	978	1,020	983	614	605	735	825	939	1,005	975	1,068	1,654	1,721
Sales of livestock		660	760	780	897	894	851	418	448	953	966	1,775	1,562	363	364	488	488	1,020	1,104
Sales of livestock products		454	550	570	585	589	638	1,442	1,709	770	845	516	540	291	343	253	249	690	684
Miscellaneous other		42	80	72	76	39	38	79	68	35	35	38	42	33	30	24	21	50	50
Total		1,972	2,240	2,434	2,551	2,448	2,505	2,959	3,208	2,372	2,452	3,064	2,970	1,626	1,742	1,740	1,782	3,414	3,559
Cash outlay:																			
Hired labor		331	350	384	386	386	387	514	568	292	287	328	357	386	367	338	355	653	635
Livestock bought		204	240	222	242	242	238	180	210	231	279	401	358	121	137	180	150	284	275
Feed bought		175	210	248	244	232	243	498	596	206	258	314	292	124	125	114	98	245	240
Fertilizer		57	60	66	69	73	64	131	135	50	55	10	11	234	181	62	46	17	18
Seed		43	40	47	47	48	49	70	78	50	51	53	58	39	33	34	34	52	53
Taxes on farm property		174	190	192	191	183	180	171	169	208	213	245	235	122	111	121	119	240	245
Machinery and tools		123	110	103	119	130	129	130	141	122	131	191	190	65	57	91	94	187	204
Miscellaneous other		150	150	151	179	179	157	210	217	176	156	201	173	95	78	110	76	361	312
Total		1,257	1,350	1,410	1,477	1,473	1,457	1,904	2,114	1,337	1,430	1,743	1,674	1,186	1,089	1,050	972	2,039	1,982
Receipts less cash outlay		715	890	1,024	1,074	975	1,048	1,055	1,094	1,035	1,022	1,321	1,296	440	653	690	810	1,375	1,577
Increase in inventory of personal property		202	130	181	223	158	242	111	239	134	66	4	346	129	165	283	170	319	602
Net result		917	1,020	1,205	1,297	1,133	1,290	1,166	1,333	1,169	1,088	1,325	1,642	569	818	973	980	1,694	2,179
Interest paid		(¹)	230	230	225	215	201	111	109	179	171	371	359	101	84	157	133	340	313
Spent for farm improvements		(¹)	140	133	131	128	141	159	168	129	142	154	169	96	114	99	119	148	142
NONCASH (ESTIMATED) ITEMS																			
Value of food produced and used on the farm ²	dollars	294	265	266	274	282	273	292	286	288	266	292	284	306	307	263	256	251	247
Value of family labor, including owner ²	do	716	870	789	793	779	768	944	941	873	842	950	919	492	489	523	505	977	1,024
Change in value of real estate during the year	do	-52	-66	+145	+173	+2	+49	+140	+66	+14	-23	-92	+71	-73	+74	-44	+58	+227	+183

Bureau of Agricultural Economics. Computed from reports of individual farms operated by their owners. Tables for 1922 in Agriculture Yearbook, 1924, pp. 1131–1132; tables for 1923–24 in Agriculture Yearbook, 1925, pp. 1342–1343; tables for 1925–26 in Agriculture Yearbook, 1927, pp. 1132–1133.

¹ Not reported for 1922. ² Averages of farms for which the item was reported.

TABLE 509.—*Farm returns, 1927, with comparisons: Proportion of farmers obtaining net results within specified ranges, 1922–1927*

	United States						North Atlantic		East North Central		West North Central		South Atlantic		South Central		Western	
	1922	1923	1924	1925	1926	1927	1926	1927	1926	1927	1926	1927	1926	1927	1926	1927	1926	1927
Number of reports	6,094	16,183	15,103	15,330	13,475	13,859	1,436	1,477	2,591	2,560	2,969	3,129	1,764	1,837	3,269	3,418	1,446	1,438
Size of farm ___acres	252	298	303	304	315	275	138	139	152	148	353	355	203	189	421	249	599	643
Value of farm property Jan. 1 per farm ___dollars	16,430	17,490	17,260	17,122	16,308	15,445	12,558	12,800	16,673	15,891	24,067	23,150	10,886	9,794	11,853	10,712	20,103	19,069
Net result per farm ___do	917	1,020	1,205	1,297	1,133	1,290	1,166	1,333	1,169	1,088	1,325	1,642	569	818	973	980	1,694	2,179
Proportion obtaining—	*Per cent*	*Per cent*	*Per cent*	*Per cent*	*Per cent*	*Per cent*	*Per cent*	*Per cent*	*Per cent*	*Per cent*	*Per cent*	*Per cent*	*Per cent*	*Per cent*	*Per cent*	*Per cent*	*Per cent*	*Per cent*
$5,000 or more	1.77	1.88	2.69	3.00	2.29	3.19	2.16	2.91	1.12	1.25	3.13	4.67	0.51	1.20	1.65	1.90	6.43	9.32
$3,000 to $4,999	3.89	4.67	6.10	6.82	5.49	6.42	5.78	4.87	5.48	4.49	7.88	10.00	2.15	2.78	3.82	4.33	8.09	10.64
$2,500 to $2,999	2.51	2.88	3.61	4.03	3.59	3.86	3.48	4.67	4.32	3.40	5.09	5.94	1.98	2.07	2.26	2.34	4.29	5.21
$2,000 to $2,499	4.33	5.13	5.99	6.26	5.46	6.53	6.69	7.52	7.45	7.07	7.41	8.82	2.44	3.86	2.78	4.50	6.43	7.79
$1,500 to $1,999	7.78	8.91	9.30	9.92	9.05	9.58	9.61	11.04	11.38	10.08	11.01	12.05	4.42	6.59	7.13	7.26	10.30	11.20
$1,000 to $1,499	14.39	14.49	15.13	15.44	14.09	15.46	15.53	16.66	17.02	17.42	14.96	16.23	9.18	13.55	12.02	13.63	16.25	15.85
$500 to $999	22.82	23.07	21.86	21.79	22.10	22.07	21.87	20.11	23.74	23.87	19.43	19.34	20.07	23.79	25.06	25.25	20.68	17.11
$0 to $499	27.98	26.09	24.68	22.32	26.43	23.98	24.30	19.90	22.35	23.01	16.94	15.79	39.63	34.40	36.34	31.77	16.80	15.92
$0 to —$499	9.89	9.10	7.85	7.81	8.56	6.68	8.29	7.51	5.48	7.07	8.76	4.38	15.36	9.74	7.68	7.11	7.68	5.15
—$500 to —$999	2.36	2.07	1.57	1.54	1.69	1.28	1.53	1.35	1.08	1.48	2.63	1.50	2.44	1.31	.89	.97	1.87	1.11
—$1,000 or more	2.28	1.71	1.22	1.07	1.25	.95	.76	.95	.58	.86	2.76	1.28	1.82	.71	.37	.94	1.18	.70
	100.00	100.00	100.00	100.00	100.00	100.00	100.00	100.00	100.00	100.00	100.00	100.00	100.00	100.00	100.00	100.00	100.00	100.00

Bureau of Agricultural Economics. See Table 476, Yearbook, 1927, for distribution by geographical divisions, 1925. The reports are those tabulated in Table 508.

TABLE 510.—*Wheat: Cost of production, by States, 1927*

State	Reports	Average acreage in wheat per farm	Average yield per acre	Gross cost per acre to—										Credit per acre (straw)	Net cost	
				Prepare and plant	Harvest and thresh	Market	Miscellaneous labor[1]	Commercial fertilizer	Manure	Seed	Land rent	Miscellaneous costs[2]	Total		Per acre	Per bushel
	Number	Acres	Bushels	Dollars	Dollars	Dollars	Dollars	Dollars	Dollars	Dollars	Dollars	Dollars	Dollars	Dollars	Dollars	Dollars
New York	73	14	26	7.52	6.89	1.61	.27	3.31	2.84	3.10	6.74	3.83	36.11	4.51	31.60	1.22
New Jersey	24	15	24	5.44	7.44	1.73	.19	3.37	4.96	2.88	6.05	2.79	34.85	6.42	28.43	1.18
Pennsylvania	180	15	21	6.01	5.40	1.27	.15	3.43	3.47	2.88	6.01	3.53	32.10	4.95	27.15	1.29
Maryland	26	32	20	4.94	6.26	1.84	.23	4.05	1.49	2.38	6.90	3.24	31.33	4.58	26.75	1.34
Virginia	85	20	16	4.83	4.35	1.14	.22	2.93	1.43	2.15	6.54	2.58	26.17	2.98	23.19	1.45
West Virginia	37	14	16	4.79	5.14	1.72	.24	2.43	1.47	2.69	6.17	1.68	26.33	2.79	23.54	1.47
North Carolina	53	12	15	4.80	4.38	1.22	.24	3.52	.97	2.03	6.00	2.60	25.76	2.66	23.10	1.54
South Carolina	24	7	11	2.47	4.06	1.30	.25	2.38	.21	1.57	7.35	2.01	21.60	1.52	20.08	1.83
Georgia	31	8	11	2.36	4.28	.90	.10	1.50	.47	1.67	3.86	2.09	17.23	.42	16.81	1.53
Ohio	190	18	21	4.85	4.89	1.12	.09	2.79	1.29	2.58	6.01	3.01	26.78	2.41	24.37	1.16
Indiana	252	26	20	3.92	4.26	.99	.11	2.36	1.19	2.19	6.11	2.31	23.42	1.66	21.76	1.09
Illinois	152	37	16	3.50	3.75	.77	.16	.69	.82	2.01	6.28	2.14	20.07	1.03	19.04	1.19
Michigan	101	15	23	6.26	5.06	1.00	.16	2.32	2.97	2.36	5.53	2.83	29.09	2.76	26.33	1.14
Wisconsin	67	7	21	3.93	4.32	1.88	.15	.26	1.65	2.39	7.54	2.91	25.04	2.39	22.65	1.08
Minnesota	224	29	15	3.50	3.74	1.04	.29	.06	.79	2.16	8.69	2.44	19.15	.96	18.19	1.21
Iowa	60	27	20	2.85	4.23	1.03	.18	.09	.89	2.05	8.70	1.98	22.46	1.21	21.25	1.06
Missouri	111	32	12	3.87	3.60	1.02	.12	.96	.84	1.80	4.90	2.02	18.95	1.07	17.88	1.49
North Dakota	96	186	14	3.54	3.90	.82	.13		.21	1.75	2.90	1.98	15.26	.24	15.02	1.07
South Dakota	103	94	15	2.29	3.51	1.05	.16		.33	1.70	3.02	2.02	13.95	.37	13.58	.91
Nebraska	213	78	21	3.03	3.86	.94	.09	.01	.38	1.49	5.44	1.92	18.07	.37	17.70	.84
Kansas	361	137	13	3.16	4.01	.68	.22	.14	.40	1.46	4.33	2.36	16.08	.26	15.82	1.22
Kentucky	49	25	14	3.23	3.76	1.18	.54	2.27	1.53	1.89	6.16	2.94	21.18	1.64	19.54	1.40
Tennessee	50	18	9	4.01	3.65	1.02	.09	1.66	.01	1.73	6.56	1.77	23.43	1.21	22.22	2.47
Texas	50	83	12	2.68	3.45	.77	.22		.25	1.37	4.57	1.87	15.21	.37	14.84	1.24
Oklahoma	68	123	11	3.08	3.50	.71	.52	.05	.27	1.38	4.14	2.39	15.22	.14	15.08	1.37
Montana	105	135	20	4.21	5.22	2.05	.57		.78	1.26	4.96	1.67	18.09	.55	17.54	.88
Wyoming	26	52	19	3.36	3.14	2.38	1.63	.01	1.15	1.29	3.16	3.09	16.20	.57	15.63	.82
Colorado	70	84	21	4.40	5.22	1.60	2.79			1.73	6.79	1.68	25.25	.80	24.45	1.16
New Mexico	13	77	9	4.54	5.63	1.05	3.61		3.19	2.18	5.63	3.68	22.16	.46	21.70	2.41
Utah	18	45	31	6.95	8.15	2.11	2.60	.01		2.02	14.00	3.96	43.99	1.35	42.64	1.38
Idaho	43	60	33	4.39	6.42	1.77		.14	.19	1.71	11.71	3.24	32.17	1.04	31.13	.94

State	Reports	Average acreage in wheat per farm	Average yield per acre	Prepare and plant	Harvest and thresh	Market	Miscellaneous labor		Fertilizer and manure	Seed	Land rent	Miscellaneous costs	Total	Credit per acre (straw)	Per acre	Per bushel
Washington	53	227	24	4.35	5.12	1.16	.76	.08	.33	1.50	10.93	3.12	27.35	.59	28.76	1.12
Oregon	43	83	24	4.24	5.05	1.36	.69	---	.33	2.22	10.29	2.87	27.05	.80	26.25	1.09
California	48	170	20	4.31	4.10	1.22	.60	---	.08	1.97	7.60	2.87	22.75	.82	21.93	1.10
Total or average [3]	3,119	63	18	4.03	4.40	1.13	.30	1.15	1.05	1.98	6.28	2.48	22.80	1.50	21.30	1.18

Bureau of Agricultural Economics. From returns to mail inquiry sent to crop reporters. For figures for 1923, 1924, 1925, and 1926 see Agriculture Yearbooks, 1924, p. 1134; 1925, p. 1326; 1926, p. 1209; and 1927, p. 1135.

[1] Includes miscellaneous labor, irrigating and water, seed treatment, and material.
[2] Sacks and twine, crop insurance, use of implements, use of storage buildings, and overhead.
[3] The total includes 20 reports from the following States in which there were not enough reports to show State averages: Maine, Delaware, Alabama, Mississippi, Arkansas, and Nevada.

TABLE 511.—*Wheat: Cost of production, by yield groups, 1927*

Yield group (bushels per acre)	Reports	Average acreage in wheat per farm	Average yield per acre	Gross cost per acre to—									Credit per acre (straw)	Net cost	
				Prepare and plant	Harvest and thresh	Market	Miscellaneous labor [1]	Fertilizer and manure	Seed	Land rent	Miscellaneous costs [2]	Total		Per acre	Per bushel
	Number	*Acres*	*Bushels*	*Dollars*	*Dollars*	*Dollars*	*Dollar*	*Dollars*	*Dollars*	*Dollars*	*Dollars*	*Dollars*	*Dollar*	*Dollars*	*Dollars*
Winter-wheat belt: [3]															
6 and under	105	188	4	2.73	2.25	0.36	0.03	0.31	1.29	3.16	1.47	11.60	0.31	11.29	2.82
7 to 12	202	106	10	3.14	3.27	.66	.13	.77	1.51	3.85	1.79	15.12	.44	14.68	1.47
13 to 18	192	93	16	3.26	4.00	.85	.15	.77	1.55	4.62	2.21	17.41	.41	17.00	1.06
19 to 24	162	83	21	3.57	4.83	1.00	.14	.66	1.54	5.51	2.43	19.68	.38	19.30	.92
25 and over	92	52	28	3.20	5.38	1.16	.14	.59	1.63	6.34	2.36	20.80	.42	20.38	.73
Total or average	753	103	15	3.22	3.91	.80	.13	.66	1.51	4.72	2.06	17.01	.40	16.61	1.11
Spring-wheat belt: [4]															
6 and under	9	65	5	4.18	2.86	.52	.14	1.12	1.83	2.96	2.42	16.03	.83	15.20	3.04
7 to 12	119	87	10	3.14	3.32	.73	.16	.29	1.95	3.58	1.82	14.99	.24	14.75	1.48
13 to 18	123	123	15	3.31	3.96	1.04	.17	.59	1.80	3.68	2.16	16.71	.39	16.32	1.09
19 and over	76	120	23	3.17	4.55	1.89	.21	.47	1.60	3.94	2.35	18.18	.72	17.46	.76
Total or average	327	108	15	3.24	3.83	1.11	.17	.47	1.81	3.69	2.08	16.40	.42	15.98	1.07

Bureau of Agricultural Economics. From returns to mail inquiry sent to crop reporters. For figures for 1923, 1924, 1925, and 1926 see Agriculture Yearbooks, 1924, p. 1133; 1925, p. 1328; 1926, p. 1210; and 1927, p. 1136.

[1] Includes miscellaneous labor, irrigating and water, seed treatment, and material.
[2] Includes sacks and twine, crop insurance, use of implements, use of storage buildings, and overhead.
[3] Winter-wheat belt as used here includes Kansas, Nebraska, Missouri, and Oklahoma.
[4] Spring-wheat belt as used here includes western Minnesota, North Dakota, eastern South Dakota, and eastern Montana

TABLE 512.—Wheat: Production costs and yields, by States, 1923-1927

State	Averages for farms reporting										Yield per acre						State yields[2] average 1923–1927
	Net cost per bushel					Net cost per acre										Average, 1923–1927[1]	
	1923	1924	1925	1926	1927	1923	1924	1925	1926	1927	1923	1924	1925	1926	1927		
	Dollars	Dollars	Dollars	Dollars	Dollars	Dollars	Dollars	Dollars	Dollars	Dollars	Bushels	Bushels	Bushels	Bushels	Bushels	Bushels	Bushels
New York	1.21	1.27	1.36	1.44	1.22	30.26	27.93	32.75	31.77	31.60	25	22	24	22	26	24	20
New Jersey	1.22	1.43	1.14	1.14	1.18	29.22	31.52	27.79	31.93	28.43	24	22	25	28	24	25	21
Pennsylvania	1.24	1.41	1.36	1.20	1.29	27.28	28.23	29.81	27.53	27.15	22	20	22	23	21	22	19
Maryland	1.28	1.42	1.21	1.05	1.34	25.53	26.93	27.91	28.34	26.75	20	19	23	27	20	22	19
Virginia	1.50	1.62	1.54	1.34	1.45	23.53	24.23	26.26	23.50	23.19	15	15	18	20	16	17	14
West Virginia	1.57	1.58	1.44	1.47	1.47	23.60	25.28	25.90	26.84	23.54	15	16	18	17	16	17	14
North Carolina	1.79	1.82	1.89	1.47	1.83	23.32	23.28	25.90	25.07	23.10	13	13	15	17	11	14	12
South Carolina	1.67	1.74	1.82	1.20	1.20	23.32	23.65	21.83	25.26	20.08	13	12	12	16	11	13	12
Georgia	1.92	1.71	1.65	.95	1.16	21.68	20.91	21.41	25.26	16.81	10	11	13	17	11	12	11
Ohio	1.13	1.18	1.37	1.04	1.09	23.74	24.74	24.63	24.72	24.37	21	21	18	26	21	21	18
Indiana	1.10	1.16	1.35	1.00	1.19	21.96	22.03	21.54	22.89	21.76	20	19	16	22	20	19	17
Illinois	.96	1.13	1.16	1.03	1.14	19.16	20.30	20.84	20.94	19.04	20	18	18	21	16	19	18
Michigan	1.18	1.01	1.25	1.10	1.08	23.66	26.22	26.28	24.25	26.33	17	26	21	22	23	21	16
Wisconsin	1.23	1.00	1.14	1.03	1.21	20.86	23.07	23.84	24.79	22.65	15	23	21	24	15	21	20
Minnesota	1.19	.88	1.16	.97	1.06	17.85	19.42	18.61	18.21	18.19	19	22	16	15	15	17	15
Iowa	1.03	.95	1.19	1.19	1.49	19.65	20.97	22.55	22.65	21.25	15	22	19	21	20	20	19
Missouri	1.24	1.30	1.29	1.11	1.07	18.66	19.43	19.36	18.88	17.88	15	15	15	17	12	15	13
North Dakota	1.41	.90	1.08	1.35	1.07	12.66	14.37	13.05	13.46	15.02	9	16	14	10	14	13	11
South Dakota	1.13	.96	1.13	1.72	.91	13.57	14.45	14.74	12.05	13.58	12	15	13	7	15	12	12
Nebraska	1.27	.90	1.13	1.13	.84	16.55	18.96	16.67	16.95	17.70	13	21	15	15	21	17	15
Kansas	1.21	.99	1.40	1.00	1.22	15.69	16.79	15.37	16.06	15.82	13	17	11	16	14	14	13
Kentucky	1.37	1.65	1.50	.98	1.40	20.57	19.77	21.56	21.57	19.54	15	12	14	22	15	15	13
Tennessee	1.48	1.56	1.51	1.36	2.47	19.26	21.09	22.09	21.68	22.22	13	13	14	16	9	13	13
Texas	1.28	.88	1.56	.89	1.24	15.35	16.70	12.44	16.93	14.84	12	19	8	19	12	14	12
Oklahoma	1.13	.92	1.39	.90	1.37	13.53	15.58	13.90	17.18	15.08	12	17	10	19	11	13	12
Arkansas	1.61	1.09	1.65	1.13		19.31	14.11	19.83	18.11		12	13	12	16		13	15
Montana	1.09	1.05	1.15	1.29	.88	17.48	16.73	16.16	16.73	17.54	16	16	14	13	20	16	17
Wyoming	.98	1.04	.87		.82	17.59	17.31	16.16		15.63	17	17	23		19	19	13
Colorado	1.07	1.01	1.23	1.04	1.16		21.31	22.19	23.85	24.45	18	21	18	23	21	19	16
New Mexico	.97	1.28		.99	2.41	16.45	20.53		24.47	21.70	17	16		25	9	17	19
Utah	1.19	1.52	1.25	1.29	1.38	38.10	42.48	41.18	42.43	42.64	32	28	33	33	31	31	23
Idaho	1.04	1.24	1.00	1.15	.94	29.12	28.46	32.14	31.08	31.13	28	23	32	27	33	29	26
Washington	.97	1.38	1.23	1.22	1.12	27.06	26.17	29.45	24.30	26.76	28	19	24	20	24	23	21
Oregon	1.12	1.26	1.26	1.27	1.09	26.94	26.54	26.46	26.64	26.25	24	21	21	21	24	22	21

Bureau of Agricultural Economics. From returns to mail inquiry sent to crop reporters.

[1] 4-year average yields for the States of Arkansas, Wyoming, and New Mexico.

[2] State average yields, obtained by the Division of Crop and Livestock Estimates, carried to nearest whole number.

TABLE 513.—*Corn: Cost of production, by States, 1927*

State	Reports	Average acreage in corn per farm	Average yield per acre	Prepare and plant	Cultivate	Harvest	Market	Miscellaneous labor[1]	Commercial fertilizer	Manure	Seed	Land rent	Miscellaneous costs[2]	Total	Credit per acre (stover and fodder)	Net cost Per acre	Net cost Per bushel
	Number	*Acres*	*Bushels*	*Dollars*	*Dollars*	*Dollars*	*Dollars*	*Dollars*	*Dollars*	*Dollars*	*Dollars*	*Dollars*	*Dollars*	*Dollars*	*Dollars*	*Dollars*	*Dollars*
New York	84	6	43	8.13	4.84	7.95	2.37	0.18	3.35	7.11	0.99	7.28	4.08	46.28	6.71	39.57	0.92
New Jersey	33	13	53	5.93	3.62	10.29	2.49	.11	3.10	6.92	.37	6.29	3.18	42.36	5.21	37.15	.70
Pennsylvania	184	12	45	6.54	3.96	7.67	2.56	.11	2.10	6.56	.61	6.12	3.45	39.68	4.35	35.33	.79
Delaware	10	20	43	5.22	4.80	8.46	2.04		1.49	5.50	.42	4.79	3.45	36.17	3.35	32.82	.76
Maryland	36	19	52	5.83	3.20	7.38	3.02	.12	1.79	5.48	.45	4.77	2.81	36.80	6.20	30.60	.59
Virginia	94	17	40	5.61	3.97	5.26	2.11		1.86	2.73	.40	6.69	2.51	31.41	3.62	27.79	.69
West Virginia	80	9	36	6.63	5.46	5.11	2.55		1.86	2.18	.50	6.95	2.53	33.77	3.64	30.13	.84
North Carolina	115	20	29	4.82	3.98	3.24	2.12	.18	4.21	1.14	.37	6.90	2.53	29.49	3.95	25.54	.88
South Carolina	62	27	24	3.72	3.79	1.84	2.43	.12	4.21	.29	.36	6.45	2.40	25.60	1.77	23.83	.99
Georgia	97	36	20	3.21	3.47	1.49	1.44	.04	2.24	.60	.35	4.45	2.59	19.88	1.22	18.66	.93
Ohio	239	24	43	5.54	3.47	6.41	1.99	.09	1.44	4.44	.43	6.41	2.83	33.05	3.19	29.86	.69
Indiana	322	37	39	4.35	2.84	3.59	1.73	.04	.65	2.30	.42	6.33	2.05	24.30	.89	23.41	.60
Illinois	250	61	34	3.71	2.38	2.71	1.31	.03	.24	1.08	.51	6.58	2.62	21.17	.68	20.49	.60
Michigan	118	20	32	6.21	3.84	5.37	2.21		.19	4.98	.61	5.33	3.38	32.12	3.71	28.41	.89
Wisconsin	181	14	37	4.90	3.61	5.22	2.89	.04	.61	6.89	.88	6.93	3.38	35.35	4.07	31.28	.85
Minnesota	312	33	32	4.06	3.13	3.60	1.74	.05	.10	3.52	.80	5.27	2.21	24.48	2.11	22.37	.70
Iowa	273	79	43	3.84	2.67	3.40	1.94	.11	.16	2.32	.57	9.13	2.38	26.52	.93	25.59	.60
Missouri	258	42	33	3.75	2.99	2.82	2.11	.11	.24	1.38	.36	5.69	1.89	21.34	1.22	20.12	.61
North Dakota	36	30	25	3.89	2.71	3.53	1.38	.02	.02	.88	.84	2.20	1.73	17.20	3.38	13.82	.55
South Dakota	146	80	29	3.21	2.00	2.92	1.83	.09	.01	.85	.50	1.95	1.79	16.95	.85	16.10	.56
Nebraska	321	89	34	2.79	2.01	2.91	1.59	.13	.04	.87	.30	5.31	1.76	17.71	.43	17.28	.51
Kansas	395	54	30	2.46	2.00	2.45	1.64	.04	.02	.68	.29	4.42	1.36	15.38	.51	14.87	.45
Kentucky	144	24	31	4.49	3.89	3.02	2.32	.10	1.36	1.55	.41	6.77	2.35	26.26	1.56	24.70	.82
Tennessee	119	27	22	4.49	3.64	2.62	2.61	.05	2.04	.65	.38	7.17	1.94	25.59	1.25	24.34	.79
Alabama	80	29	22	3.79	4.45	2.05	2.33	.03	2.94	.73	.36	4.75	1.91	23.34	1.13	22.21	1.01
Mississippi	217	36	22	3.93	4.40	1.99	1.83	.12	2.04	.85	.46	5.37	2.51	23.50	1.03	22.47	1.02
Louisiana	33	41	21	3.73	3.96	1.56	1.77	.15	2.94	.93	.38	5.05	3.14	23.61	.67	22.94	1.09
Texas	179	27	25	3.07	2.67	1.58	1.75	.13	.30	.62	.38	5.13	1.88	17.51	.37	17.14	.69
Oklahoma	100	28	28	2.89	2.64	1.92	2.10	.03	.13	.47	.30	3.84	1.36	15.68	.38	15.30	.55
Arkansas	73	23	22	3.96	3.43	1.73	1.99	.11	.84	.75	.39	5.54	1.99	20.73	1.01	19.72	.90
Montana	23	29	29	4.27	1.98	2.73	2.80	.25		.27	.73	1.00	1.55	15.58	1.94	13.64	.62
Wyoming	14	37	23	2.75	1.53	3.29	3.09	.16		.96	.52	1.75	1.05	15.10	.53	14.57	.63
Colorado	57	74	21	3.21	2.24	2.26	1.60	.99		1.62	.33	4.88	1.70	18.83	.93	17.90	.85
New Mexico	30	21	23	4.05	2.39	2.65	1.69	2.54		2.48	.49	7.21	1.85	25.35	1.38	23.97	1.04
Total or average[3]	4,778	40	33	4.21	3.13	3.63	1.95	.14	.95	2.39	.48	5.91	2.26	25.05	1.84	23.21	.70

Bureau of Agricultural Economics. From returns to mail inquiry sent to crop reporters. For figures for 1923, 1924, 1925, and 1926 see Agriculture Yearbooks, 1924, p. 1136; 1925; p. 1380; 1926, p. 1212; and 1927, p. 1138.

[1] Includes miscellaneous labor, irrigating, and water. [2] Sacks and twine, crop insurance, use of implements, use of storage buildings, and overhead. [3] The total includes 63 reports from the following States, in which there were not enough reports to show State averages: Maine, Vermont, Massachusetts, Rhode Island, Connecticut, Florida, Utah, Idaho, Washington, Oregon, and California.

Table 514.—Corn: Cost of production, by yield groups, 1927

| Yield group (bushels per acre) | Reports | Average acreage in corn per farm | Average yield per acre | Gross cost per acre to— | | | | | | | | | | Credit per acre (stover and fodder) | Net cost | |
				Prepare and plant	Cultivate	Harvest	Market	Miscellaneous labor [1]	Fertilizer and manure	Seed	Land rent	Miscellaneous costs [2]	Total		Per acre	Per bushel
	Number	*Acres*	*Bushels*	*Dollars*	*Dollars*	*Dollars*	*Dollars*	*Dollar*	*Dollars*	*Dollars*	*Dollars*	*Dollars*	*Dollars*	*Dollars*	*Dollars*	*Dollars*
All States:																
7 and under	97	33	3	4.12	2.58	1.80	0.38	0.07	3.20	0.56	3.75	2.02	18.48	2.49	15.99	5.33
8 to 17	467	33	13	3.65	3.11	2.10	1.17	.07	2.44	.41	4.13	2.14	19.22	1.32	17.90	1.38
18 to 27	1,163	34	22	3.93	3.14	2.70	1.68	.14	2.55	.46	4.81	2.05	21.46	1.45	20.01	.91
28 to 37	1,245	38	32	3.94	2.90	3.32	1.86	.10	2.54	.45	5.72	2.13	22.96	1.67	21.29	.67
38 to 47	989	45	41	4.30	3.08	4.09	2.19	.15	3.36	.48	6.67	2.24	26.56	1.75	24.81	.61
48 to 57	502	39	51	4.90	3.37	5.28	2.55	.17	5.33	.56	7.58	2.78	32.52	2.34	30.18	.59
58 and over	315	20	68	5.79	3.91	6.88	3.12	.26	7.67	.57	8.87	3.21	40.28	3.99	36.29	.53
United States	4,778	40	33	4.21	3.13	3.63	1.95	.14	3.34	.48	5.91	2.26	25.05	1.84	23.21	.70
Corn Belt: [3]																
17 and under	45	36	11	4.07	2.53	2.32	.78	.12	2.52	.39	4.41	2.26	19.40	.96	18.44	1.68
18 to 27	200	51	23	3.60	2.31	2.68	1.40	.09	1.72	.41	4.99	1.75	18.95	.92	18.03	.78
28 to 37	404	60	32	3.67	2.49	3.00	1.55	.05	1.88	.41	6.10	2.01	21.16	.96	20.20	.63
38 to 47	489	63	41	3.78	2.61	3.45	1.92	.10	2.28	.43	7.19	1.96	23.72	1.05	22.67	.55
48 to 57	240	59	51	3.85	2.57	3.86	2.06	.05	2.72	.48	8.33	2.36	26.28	1.05	25.23	.49
58 and over	94	49	63	4.64	3.11	4.65	2.51	.14	4.03	.48	8.92	2.82	31.30	1.86	29.44	.47
Total or average	1,472	58	38	3.80	2.56	3.34	1.79	.07	2.28	.43	6.82	2.08	23.17	1.06	22.11	.58

Bureau of Agricultural Economics. From returns to mail inquiry sent to crop reporters. For figures for 1923, 1924, 1925, and 1926 see Agriculture Yearbooks, 1924, p. 1135; 1925, p. 1332; 1926, p. 1213; and 1927, p. 1139.

[1] Includes miscellaneous labor, irrigating, and water.
[2] Includes sacks and twine, use of implements, use of storage buildings, and overhead.
[3] Corn Belt as used here includes Indiana, Illinois, Iowa, western Ohio, eastern Nebraska, northeast corner of Kansas, and the northern three-fourths of Missouri.

TABLE 515.—Corn: Production costs and yields, by States, 1923–1927

State	Net cost per bushel					Net cost per acre					Yield per acre						State yield average[2] 1923–1927
	1923	1924	1925	1926	1927	1923	1924	1925	1926	1927	1923	1924	1925	1926	1927	Average 1923–1927[1]	
	Dollars	Dollars	Dollars	Dollars	Dollars	Dollars	Dollars	Dollars	Dollars	Dollars	Bushels	Bushels	Bushels	Bushels	Bushels	Bushels	Bushels
New York	0.91	0.95	0.95	1.02	0.92	35.43	38.18	41.64	45.07	39.57	39	40	44	44	43	42	34
New Jersey	.79	1.07	.87	.89	.70	41.31	44.01	48.66	50.99	37.15	52	41	56	57	53	52	42
Pennsylvania	.78	.91	.71	.72	.79	38.03	35.39	38.24	32.90	35.33	49	39	54	46	45	47	42
Delaware	.73	.95	.82	.85	.76	31.51	32.19	40.87	30.45	32.82	43	34	50	36	43	41	33
Maryland	.69	.80	.61	.64	.59	31.80	32.08	32.08	27.12	30.60	47	41	53	46	52	48	40
Virginia	.79	.83	.83	.71	.69	27.01	27.53	29.20	31.73	27.79	39	33	35	38	40	37	26
West Virginia	.79	.91	1.08	.79	.84	33.28	30.91	35.78	29.93	30.13	42	34	45	40	36	39	33
North Carolina	.95	1.18	1.56	1.00	.88	30.91	29.52	29.27	23.55	25.54	31	25	27	30	29	28	21
South Carolina	1.01	1.17	1.39	1.24	.99	24.58	24.58	20.86	18.25	23.83	23	21	16	19	24	21	15
Georgia	1.05	1.02	.99	.96	.93	23.22	18.45	19.86	23.37	18.66	18	18	15	19	20	18	13
Florida	1.12	1.04	.57	.83		21.37	25.00	30.74	23.37		19	24	20	28		23	14
Ohio	.64	.84	.49	.62	.69	31.45	25.00	30.74	30.19	29.86	49	36	54	49	43	46	38
Indiana	.55	.74	.51	.53	.60	24.57	24.35	24.10	24.04	23.41	45	33	49	45	39	42	36
Illinois	.52	.58	.68	.54	.60	21.38	21.88	23.29	22.10	20.49	41	38	46	41	34	40	36
Michigan	.74	.90	.62	.71	.89	28.99	27.12	30.00	28.32	28.41	39	30	44	40	32	37	33
Wisconsin	.71	1.04	.55	.73	.85	29.03	27.04	28.55	31.11	31.28	41	26	48	40	37	38	35
Minnesota	.57	.78	.60	.60	.70	22.18	22.49	23.55	22.84	22.37	39	29	38	38	32	35	33
Iowa	.52	.75	.66	.56	.60	24.09	22.49	26.18	25.40	25.59	46	33	48	45	33	43	37
Missouri	.61	.68	.78	.62	.61	20.21	20.51	20.40	19.37	20.12	33	30	34	31	33	32	28
North Dakota	.42	.73	.55	.86	.55	13.40	11.70	14.44	12.92	13.82	32	16	22	15	25	22	25
South Dakota	.50	.71	.59	.76	.56	17.54	16.36	16.36	15.25	16.10	35	23	21	20	29	26	24
Nebraska	.49	.68	.76	.79	.51	17.10	17.06	16.62	15.08	17.28	35	25	30	19	34	29	26
Kansas	.53	.54	.87	.88	.45	13.71	13.99	13.68	24.52	14.87	26	26	23	15	33	25	20
Kentucky	.80	.80	1.14	.68	.82	28.01	25.50	26.44	24.31	24.70	35	32	35	36	30	34	28
Tennessee	.77	.81	1.07	.81	.79	24.77	24.41	24.41	22.25	24.34	32	31	28	30	31	30	24
Alabama	.99	.87	1.25	1.01	1.01	19.83	21.57	21.59	25.48	24.70	20	19	19	22	22	20	14
Mississippi	1.17	1.14	1.95	1.02	1.02	23.38	22.29	24.70	23.42	22.21	20	19	23	25	22	22	16
Louisiana	1.15	1.17	.99	.98	1.09	21.86	24.32	25.09	18.00	22.47	19	18	20	24	21	22	16
Texas	.81	1.35	.95	.62	.79	17.76	18.02	13.84	15.05	22.94	22	21	9	29	28	20	18
Oklahoma	.86	.86	.83	.56	.55	13.71	14.79	20.89	21.12	15.30	16	21	14	27	28	21	17
Arkansas	1.06	.70	.83	.92	.90	22.30	20.43	11.65	12.42	19.72	21	22	22	23	22	22	19
Montana	.65	.93	.69	1.13	.62	15.49	13.45	20.84	13.13	13.64	24	15	14	11	23	17	19
Wyoming	.49	.90	.80	.77	.63	14.15	14.38	15.28	13.13	14.57	29	17	25	17	25	22	20
Colorado	.57	.85	.69	.84	.85	15.83	15.50	15.50	13.13	17.90	28	18	22	21	21	22	15
New Mexico	.85	.78	.80	.93	1.04	18.61	12.43	13.65	21.50	23.97	22	16	17	23	23	20	17

Bureau of Agricultural Economics. From returns to mail inquiry sent to crop reporters.

[1] 4-year average yield for the State of Florida.

[2] State average yields, obtained by the Division of Crop and Livestock Estimates, carried to nearest whole number.

TABLE 516.—Oats: Cost of production, by States, 1927

State	Reports	Average acreage in oats per farm	Average yield per acre	Gross cost per acre to— Prepare and plant	Harvest and thresh	Market	Miscellaneous labor [1]	Commercial fertilizer	Manure	Seed	Land rent	Miscellaneous costs [2]	Total	Credit per acre (straw)	Net cost Per acre	Net cost Per bushel
	Number	Acres	Bushels	Dollars	Dollars	Dollars	Dollars	Dollars	Dollars	Dollars	Dollars	Dollars	Dollars	Dollars	Dollars	Dollars
Maine	35	15	39	6.86	7.68	1.90	0.16	1.72	3.64	3.49	7.42	5.08	37.95	2.87	35.08	0.90
New York	135	12	40	6.78	6.75	1.49	.19	2.65	1.35	2.12	6.07	3.51	30.91	4.37	26.54	.66
New Jersey	21	11	43	6.09	7.06	1.72	.18	1.83	1.52	1.62	5.42	2.84	26.78	4.90	21.88	.51
Pennsylvania	184	12	40	5.59	5.05	1.58	.15	2.03	.67	1.76	5.19	2.99	25.01	3.96	21.06	.53
Maryland	15	10	38	4.81	5.45	1.39	.20	3.12	.13	1.55	7.75	2.44	26.84	4.63	22.21	.58
Virginia	32	10	23	4.36	4.14	1.30	.26	2.60	.44	1.70	5.43	2.14	22.37	2.55	19.82	.86
West Virginia	49	8	25	4.23	4.77	1.21	.31	2.01	.98	1.99	5.39	2.13	23.97	1.99	21.98	.81
North Carolina	49	8	28	4.23	4.34	1.32	.20	2.81	.41	1.89	6.07	2.55	23.82	2.13	21.98	.75
South Carolina	45	16	33	2.67	5.23	1.65	.26	2.67	.11	2.04	6.32	2.63	23.58	2.91	20.91	.63
Georgia	45	16	24	2.25	3.96	1.01	.20	1.26	.12	1.53	4.22	2.31	16.86	2.63	20.95	.67
Ohio	199	18	42	4.22	4.87	1.32	.20	1.30	.34	1.30	5.81	3.01	22.37	.85	16.01	.48
Indiana	210	24	30	2.69	3.72	.87	.07	.46	.37	1.20	5.78	2.07	17.23	2.31	20.06	.53
Illinois	181	37	39	1.97	3.13	.75	.12	.10	.22	1.36	6.43	1.90	15.98	1.45	15.78	.50
Michigan	131	14	42	5.34	5.17	1.73	.20	1.24	1.47	1.32	5.40	2.84	24.71	1.11	14.87	.57
Wisconsin	252	25	34	3.92	4.81	2.00	.15	.20	.39	1.56	6.75	2.99	23.77	2.51	22.20	.51
Minnesota	384	35	39	3.37	4.01	1.18	.13	.05	.70	1.45	5.08	2.39	18.26	2.49	21.28	.50
Iowa	247	47	20	1.84	3.83	1.21	.22	.11	.42	1.51	8.48	2.39	20.01	1.19	17.07	.47
Missouri	125	18	27	2.44	2.99	1.02	.11	.41	.38	1.38	4.20	1.70	14.62	1.49	18.52	.69
North Dakota	84	54	33	3.44	3.77	1.05	.11		.08	1.09	2.50	1.97	14.01	.90	13.72	.50
South Dakota	147	47	32	2.18	3.53	1.45	.19		.30	1.23	3.62	2.50	14.53	.57	13.44	.42
Nebraska	251	34	27	2.18	3.71	1.18	.15		.29	1.17	5.27	2.03	16.11	.51	14.02	.48
Kansas	226	21	23	2.51	3.18	.98	.07		.31	1.25	4.30	2.16	15.37	.86	15.25	.54
Kentucky	29	9	22	3.35	3.65	1.36	.19	.05	.16	1.05	6.19	1.72	18.48	.68	14.69	.75
Tennessee	27	12	24	3.08	3.89	1.29	.20	1.03	1.24	1.32	6.17	1.50	21.06	1.18	17.30	.91
Mississippi	27	20	27	2.28	4.23	1.24	.28	1.23	1.13	1.13	5.64	2.35	21.70	.98	20.08	.84
Texas	87	33	21	2.69	3.71	1.00	.22	1.44	.05	1.13	4.49	2.73	21.70	1.56	20.14	.67
Oklahoma	64	26	39	4.18	3.76	1.05	.06	.06	.18	1.24	1.99	1.99	14.93	.44	14.32	.53
Montana	67	28	40	3.28	4.68	2.21	.67	.02	.15	1.12	3.58	1.89	14.47	.61	14.03	.43
Wyoming	24	34	37	4.41	4.57	2.79	.55		.40	1.70	2.81	2.29	17.65	.92	16.73	.42
Colorado	48	30	55	4.84	5.54	1.61	1.72		1.17	1.73	2.35	2.05	17.64	.77	16.87	.31
Idaho	24	19	54	4.41	6.48	1.69	1.65	.14	.24	2.00	6.59	3.15	26.05	1.52	24.53	.45
Washington	19	20	50	4.84	6.39	1.44	.89	.35	.62	1.68	8.32	4.00	28.20	1.21	26.99	.54
Oregon	33	22	35	4.57	4.70	1.36	.08		.52	1.68	6.10	2.70	21.71	.98	20.73	.59
Total or average [3]	3,590	26	34	3.49	4.37	1.31	.22	.64	.63	1.47	5.61	2.45	20.19	1.72	18.47	.54

Bureau of Agricultural Economics. From returns to mail inquiry sent to crop reporters. For figures for 1923, 1924, 1925, and 1926 see Agriculture Yearbooks, 1924, p. 1138; 1925, p. 1334; 1926, p. 1215; and 1927, p. 1141.

[1] Includes miscellaneous labor, irrigating and water, seed treatment, and material. [2] Sacks and twine, crop insurance, use of implements, use of storage buildings, and overhead. [3] The total includes 74 reports from the following States in which there were not enough reports to show State averages: New Hampshire, Vermont, Connecticut, Delaware, Florida, Alabama, Arkansas, New Mexico, Utah, Nevada, and California.

TABLE 517.—Oats: Production costs and yields, by States, 1923–1927

Average for farms reporting

State	Net cost per bushel					Net cost per acre					Yield per acre					Average, 1923–1927 [1]	State yield [2] average, 1923–1927
	1923	1924	1925	1926	1927	1923	1924	1925	1926	1927	1923	1924	1925	1926	1927		
	Dollar	Dollar	Dollar	Dollar	Dollar	Dollars	Dollars	Dollars	Dollars	Dollars	Bushels	Bushels	Bushels	Bushels	Bushels	Bushels	Bushels
Maine	0.82	0.95	0.69	0.84	0.90	39.20	39.73	37.12	36.88	35.08	48	42	54	44	39	45	39
New York	.63	.63	.62	.69	.66	25.23	25.69	27.49	28.12	26.54	40	41	44	41	40	41	35
New Jersey	.65	.65	.59	.56	.51	20.04	22.92	18.27	21.69	21.88	31	35	31	39	43	36	31
Pennsylvania	.65	.55	.58	.54	.53	22.20	22.70	23.37	22.14	21.05	34	41	40	41	40	39	34
Maryland	.58	.62	.65	.61	.58	20.38	22.28	22.64	21.85	22.21	35	36	35	36	38	36	31
Virginia	.70	.66	.79	.76	.86	19.62	18.60	22.07	21.37	21.98	28	28	28	28	23	27	23
West Virginia	.83	.73	.69	.79	.81	23.28	22.52	24.19	22.52	20.91	28	31	35	33	27	31	25
North Carolina	.79	.87	.81	.68	.75	21.28	20.97	21.90	21.04	21.04	27	24	27	27	28	27	25
South Carolina	.68	.76	.82	.71	.63	19.79	21.21	22.12	21.21	20.95	27	28	27	30	33	29	22
Georgia	.72	.76	.78	.71	.67	19.95	20.22	17.83	21.21	16.01	29	22	23	22	24	24	19
Ohio	.51	.42	.42	.42	.48	16.04	17.07	19.86	16.90	20.06	39	48	47	48	42	45	37
Indiana	.49	.42	.46	.47	.53	15.88	16.83	15.78	20.05	15.78	33	41	34	38	30	35	30
Illinois	.41	.40	.45	.47	.50	19.68	20.82	16.54	16.42	14.87	39	42	37	34	30	36	32
Michigan	.50	.45	.55	.49	.57	19.99	20.49	20.78	15.91	22.20	39	46	38	39	39	40	34
Wisconsin	.51	.49	.45	.46	.51	17.14	18.26	21.91	19.90	21.28	39	42	49	42	42	43	40
Minnesota	.42	.40	.38	.46	.50	17.23	18.77	17.73	20.69	17.07	41	46	47	37	34	41	35
Iowa	.43	.43	.43	.46	.47	14.84	15.48	18.84	17.15	18.52	44	44	44	39	39	41	36
Missouri	.55	.55	.52	.59	.69	11.55	13.67	15.00	17.81	13.72	27	28	29	24	20	26	23
North Dakota	.44	.38	.43	.59	.50	15.01	14.37	13.66	14.11	13.44	26	36	32	20	27	28	25
South Dakota	.41	.50	.53	.79	.42	14.90	16.12	14.76	11.84	14.02	37	38	36	15	33	32	29
Nebraska	.41	.54	.54	.72	.48	14.57	15.65	14.75	11.79	14.39	36	32	28	20	32	30	28
Kansas	.47	.54	.54	.60	.54	17.90	17.57	14.51	14.39	14.69	31	29	27	24	27	28	24
Kentucky	.81	.70	.83	---	.75	17.21	18.61	21.69	---	17.30	22	25	26	---	23	24	22
Tennessee	.69	.61	.87	.69	.91	15.84	16.41	19.04	17.92	20.08	23	27	22	26	22	24	21
Texas	.48	.50	.79	.39	.53	13.12	14.55	14.20	18.89	14.32	33	33	18	49	27	32	28
Oklahoma	.57	.48	.55	.47	.67	16.44	15.75	13.71	15.87	14.03	23	30	25	34	21	27	23
Montana	.51	.57	.63	.63	.43	16.32	17.74	15.15	14.47	16.73	32	31	24	23	39	30	30
Wyoming	.48	.59	.60	---	.42	17.76	17.74	19.33	---	16.87	37	30	32	---	40	35	34
Colorado	.57	.67	.74	.64	.61	22.68	22.04	25.05	25.70	24.53	40	33	34	40	40	37	27
Utah	.74	.80	.78	.71	---	37.11	35.78	41.23	39.12	---	50	45	53	55	---	51	40
Idaho	.56	.68	.58	.56	.49	28.07	24.98	25.48	27.54	26.99	50	37	44	49	55	47	44

Bureau of Agricultural Economics. From returns to mail inquiry sent to crop reporters.

[1] 4-year average yields for the States of Kentucky, Wyoming, and Utah.

[2] State average yields, obtained by the Division of Crop and Livestock Estimates, carried to nearest whole number.

TABLE 518.—*Oats: Cost of production, by yield groups, 1927*

Yield group (bushels per acre)	Reports	Average acreage in oats per farm	Average yield per acre	Gross cost per acre to—									Credit per acre (straw)	Net cost	
				Prepare and plant	Harvest[1]	Market	Miscellaneous labor[2]	Fertilizer and manure	Seed	Land rent	Miscellaneous costs[3]	Total		Per acre	Per bushel
	No.	Acres	Bu.	Doll.	Doll.	Doll.	Doll.	Doll.	Doll.	Doll.	Doll.	Doll.	Doll.	Doll.	Doll.
All States															
17 and under	416	25	11	2.78	2.67	0.58	0.20	0.68	1.36	4.06	1.83	14.16	0.74	13.42	1.22
18 to 22	416	26	20	3.05	3.69	.97	.16	1.33	1.41	4.62	2.11	17.34	1.23	16.11	.81
23 to 27	329	28	25	3.28	3.92	1.07	.18	1.08	1.36	4.84	2.22	17.95	1.27	16.68	.67
28 to 32	583	30	30	3.27	4.09	1.21	.14	1.15	1.42	5.39	2.32	18.99	1.47	17.52	.58
33 to 37	391	31	35	3.40	4.44	1.30	.18	1.15	1.51	5.62	2.40	20.00	1.86	18.14	.52
38 to 42	613	27	40	3.70	4.66	1.50	.21	1.42	1.52	5.90	2.56	21.47	2.06	19.41	.49
43 to 47	200	24	45	4.22	5.02	1.74	.14	1.46	1.50	6.41	2.64	23.13	2.27	20.86	.46
48 to 52	359	21	50	4.02	5.69	1.75	.28	1.59	1.55	6.81	2.95	24.64	2.37	22.27	.45
53 to 57	71	21	55	4.19	5.09	2.04	.36	1.59	1.57	6.36	3.14	24.34	3.72	20.62	.37
58 to 62	115	20	60	4.34	5.90	1.93	.41	2.02	1.59	7.28	2.98	26.45	2.53	23.92	.40
63 and over	97	19	73	4.47	6.68	2.28	1.09	1.77	1.82	10.16	3.73	32.00	2.49	29.51	.40

Bureau of Agricultural Economics. From returns to mail inquiry sent to crop reporters. For figures for 1923, 1924, 1925, and 1926 see Agriculture Yearbooks, 1924, p. 1137; 1925, p. 1335; 1926 p. 1217; and 1927, p. 1143.

[1] Threshing is included under harvesting.
[2] Includes miscellaneous labor, irrigating and water, seed treatment, and material.
[3] Sacks and twine, crop insurance, use of implements, use of storage buildings, and overhead.

TABLE 519.—*Potatoes: Cost of production, 1927*

State groups	Reports	Average acreage in potatoes per farm	Average yield per acre	Gross cost per acre to—										Credit per acre (culls)	Net cost	
				Prepare and plant	Cultivate	Harvest	Market	Miscellaneous labor[1]	Fertilizer and manure	Seed	Land rent	Miscellaneous costs[2]	Total		Per acre	Per bushel
	No.	Acres	Bu.	Doll.	Doll.	Doll.	Doll.	Doll.	Doll.	Doll.	Doll.	Doll.	Doll.	Doll.	Doll.	Doll.
Northeastern[3]	276	10	165	12.77	6.81	15.44	11.18	6.91	25.85	22.46	10.35	8.31	120.08	0.41	119.67	0.73
Eastern[4]	98	5	108	9.13	4.98	9.90	8.09	1.75	14.17	15.82	8.87	4.99	77.70	.15	77.55	.72
Central[5]	206	6	109	7.54	3.76	8.78	7.24	1.74	5.68	17.13	7.43	3.84	63.14	.06	63.08	.58
North Central[6]	396	7	112	7.50	4.32	9.79	7.47	2.35	7.03	11.72	5.99	3.91	60.08	.31	59.77	.53
Western[7]	129	12	187	9.30	5.44	15.72	13.73	3.48	4.82	17.10	11.93	11.04	92.56	1.14	91.42	.49

Bureau of Agricultural Economics. From returns to mail inquiry sent to crop reporters.

[1] Includes miscellaneous labor, irrigating and water, spraying, and spray material.
[2] Sacks and twine, crop insurance, use of implements, use of storage buildings, and overhead.
[3] Maine, New Hampshire, Vermont, Massachusetts, Rhode Island, Connecticut, New York, New Jersey, and Pennsylvania.
[4] Delaware, Maryland, Virginia, West Virginia, North Carolina, Kentucky, and Tennessee.
[5] Ohio, Indiana, Illinois, Iowa, Missouri, Kansas, and Nebraska.
[6] Michigan, Wisconsin, Minnesota, North Dakota, and South Dakota.
[7] Montana, Wyoming, Colorado, New Mexico, Utah, Nevada, Idaho, Washington, Oregon, and California.

Table 520.—*Potatoes: Production costs, by State groups, 1924–1927*

State groups	Number of reports				Net cost per acre				Net cost per bushel				Yield per acre			
	1924	1925	1926	1927	1924	1925	1926	1927	1924	1925	1926	1927	1924	1925	1926	1927
					Doll.	Doll.	Doll.	Doll.	Doll.	Doll.	Doll.	Doll.	Bu.	Bu.	Bu.	Bu.
Northeastern [1]	431	328	260	276	99.54	107.88	123.08	119.67	0.58	0.72	0.74	0.73	171	149	167	165
Eastern [2]	167	130	94	98	82.06	78.51	84.34	77.55	.67	.79	.73	.72	123	100	115	108
Central [3]	212	251	226	206	56.09	58.00	66.94	63.08	.51	.60	.64	.58	111	96	105	109
North Central [4]	508	423	396	396	47.10	54.76	62.40	59.77	.38	.52	.52	.53	125	106	121	112
Western [5]	181	101	116	129	67.83	90.57	82.36	91.42	.47	.58	.56	.49	144	156	146	187

Bureau of Agricultural Economics. From returns to mail inquiry sent to crop reporters.

[1] Maine, New Hampshire, Vermont, Massachusetts, Rhode Island, Connecticut, New York, New Jersey, and Pennsylvania.
[2] Delaware, Maryland, Virginia, West Virginia, North Carolina, Kentucky, and Tennessee.
[3] Ohio, Indiana, Illinois, Iowa, Missouri, Kansas, and Nebraska.
[4] Michigan, Wisconsin, Minnesota, North Dakota, and South Dakota.
[5] Montana, Wyoming, Colorado, New Mexico, Utah, Nevada, Idaho, Washington, Oregon, and California.

Table 521.—*Cotton: Cost of production, by yield groups, 1927*

Yield group (pounds of lint per acre)	Reports	Average acreage in cotton per farm	Average yield of lint per acre	Gross cost per acre to—										Credit per acre (cotton-seed)	Net cost of lint	
				Prepare and plant	Cultivate	Harvest and market	Miscellaneous labor [1]	Fertilizer and manure	Seed	Ginning	Land rent	Miscellaneous costs [2]	Total		Per acre	Per pound
	No.	Acres	Lbs.	Doll.	Doll.	Doll.	Doll.	Doll.	Doll.	Doll.	Doll.	Doll.	Doll.	Doll.	Doll.	Doll.
60 and under	45	30	37	3.95	5.36	2.21	0.33	2.80	1.02	0.62	4.00	2.66	22.95	1.30	21.65	0.59
61 to 100	72	36	87	3.61	4.88	4.78	.28	2.62	1.05	1.18	4.40	2.23	25.03	2.65	22.38	.26
101 to 140	90	67	126	3.79	5.07	5.95	.68	3.78	1.07	1.56	4.90	2.60	29.40	3.89	25.51	.20
141 to 180	135	60	164	3.77	5.57	6.80	.39	2.95	1.09	1.89	5.17	2.34	29.97	4.95	25.02	.15
181 to 220	117	47	202	4.24	5.83	8.29	.65	3.91	1.10	2.30	6.11	3.02	35.45	6.73	28.72	.14
221 to 260	197	69	245	4.30	6.49	9.47	.53	4.27	1.10	2.69	6.73	2.64	38.22	7.56	30.66	.13
261 to 300	102	95	291	4.76	7.11	11.58	.76	6.23	1.17	3.33	7.01	3.48	45.43	9.72	35.71	.12
301 to 340	32	52	325	4.53	6.92	11.82	.57	5.09	1.27	3.65	6.86	2.92	43.63	10.64	32.99	.10
341 to 380	54	42	361	5.10	7.22	12.05	.91	6.82	1.13	3.85	7.59	3.44	48.11	10.47	37.64	.10
381 to 420	52	26	401	5.35	7.18	13.84	.97	7.31	1.25	4.31	9.88	3.95	54.04	11.85	42.19	.11
421 to 460	26	15	443	5.73	8.87	14.41	.61	7.87	1.04	4.61	8.20	3.72	55.06	13.23	41.83	.09
461 to 500	47	42	496	5.70	7.09	16.01	1.80	9.06	1.29	5.37	9.82	4.59	60.73	15.02	45.71	.09
501 and over	23	24	609	4.82	5.46	21.07	3.28	5.72	1.44	6.81	13.14	3.61	65.35	17.99	47.36	.08

Bureau of Agricultural Economics. From returns to mail inquiry sent to crop reporters.

[1] Includes miscellaneous labor, irrigating and water, dusting, and dusting material.
[2] Includes picking sacks and sheets, crop insurance, use of implements, use of storage buildngs, and overhead.

TABLE 522.—*Cotton: Production costs, by yield groups, 1923–1927*

Yield group (pounds of lint per acre)[1]	Farms reporting					Average yield of lint per acre					Net cost of lint per pound[2]				
	1923	1924	1925	1926	1927	1923	1924	1925	1926	1927	1923	1924	1925	1926	1927
	No.	No.	No.	No.	No.	Lbs.	Lbs.	Lbs.	Lbs.	Lbs.	Cts.	Cts.	Cts.	Cts.	Cts.
60 and under	281	24	47	32	45	40	36	34	41	37	61	51	71	47	59
61 to 100	451	107	79	91	72	89	93	89	89	87	30	27	31	25	26
101 to 140	407	186	112	114	90	124	125	126	126	126	22	20	21	20	20
141 to 180	394	284	207	166	135	161	161	162	164	164	17	18	18	16	15
181 to 220	279	221	187	130	117	200	200	202	200	202	16	16	16	15	14
221 to 260	257	288	277	200	197	245	246	246	246	245	13	13	13	13	13
261 to 300	165	156	158	106	102	290	293	292	292	291	12	13	12	12	12
301 to 340	34	39	54	48	32	324	324	325	326	325	14	11	12	12	10
341 to 380	54	46	70	46	54	356	361	360	360	361	12	11	12	10	10
381 to 420	94	60	79	56	52	401	400	400	400	401	11	10	10	12	11
421 to 460	27	21	39	19	26	444	448	446	447	443	11	10	11	10	9
461 to 500	60	33	65	41	47	495	493	496	493	496	10	8	9	9	9
501 and over	16	6	31	21	23	618	637	600	582	609	9	7	8	9	8

Bureau of Agricultural Economics. From returns to mail inquiry sent to crop reporters.

[1] The average yield per acre of lint cotton in the United States has been as follows: 1923, 130.6 pounds; 1924, 157.4 pounds; 1925, 167.2 pounds; 1926, 182.6 pounds; 1927, 154.5 pounds.
[2] The average cost per pound for the yield groups which closely approximated the average yields for the United States are as follows: 1923, 22 cents; 1924, 18 cents; 1925, 18 cents; 1926, 15.5 cents; 1927, 17 cents. At least a part of the yearly variations in costs in some of the upper and lower yield groups may be due to the small number of reports and to the relative number of reports received each year from various sections of the Cotton Belt.

TABLE 523.—*Indexes of the volume of net agricultural production* [1]

[1919–1927 = 100]

Year	Grains	Fruits and vegetables	Truck crops	Meat animals	Dairy products	Poultry products	Cotton and cottonseed	Total
1919	101	82	71	96	81	81	91	90
1920	116	101	86	92	80	81	105	96
1921	100	76	74	91	91	93	64	87
1922	100	109	101	97	95	97	77	96
1923	97	108	99	107	103	108	80	100
1924	100	106	111	108	108	105	108	106
1925	95	97	115	102	111	105	128	106
1926	93	116	114	103	114	112	143	111
1927	99	105	129	103	117	118	103	107
1928			124	107	117	118		

Bureau of Agricultural Economics.

[1] These indexes are based on estimates of production for sale and for consumption in the farm home. Production fed to livestock or used for seed is not included. For example, instead of total production, only the amounts of corn and oats shipped out of county where grown and only a small percentage of the hay crops are included. The index of dairy products represents total milk production for all purposes. Production of meat animals is represented by total slaughter, including slaughter for farm use. Calendar-year production of livestock and livestock products are here compared with crop production of the same year. Each group index, as well as the total, is obtained by multiplying the yearly quantities by a 1919–1927 average price for each of the commodities, and the sum of these yearly values or average prices, divided by the corresponding average sum for the period 1919–1927, taken as 100. Commodities included: Grains—wheat, corn, oats, barley, rye, buckwheat, kafir, rice; fruits and vegetables—grapes, apples, apricots, peaches, pears, cranberries, strawberries, figs, grapefruit, lemons, olives, oranges, potatoes, sweet potatoes, dry edible beans; meat animals—cattle, calves, sheep, lambs, hogs; cotton and cottonseed; dairy products—total milk production; poultry products—chickens and eggs; truck crops—asparagus, snap beans, cabbage, cantaloupes, cauliflower, celery, cucumbers, lettuce, onions, peas, spinach, strawberries, tomatoes, watermelons; total includes also wool and hay. These commodities constitute about 90 per cent of the gross income from agricultural production

TABLE 524.—*Current value of capital invested, rates earned on agricultural and nonagricultural capital, and income per farm available for capital, labor, and management, 1919–1927*

Year beginning July	Current value of all capital invested in agricultural production [1]	Current value of operator's net investment in agricultural production [2]	Rates earned for capital and management on—			Income per farm available for—	
			Total capital investment	Operator's net capital investment	All nonagricultural corporations [3]	Capital, labor, and management [4]	Labor and management [5]
	1,000,000 dollars	*1,000,000 dollars*	*Per cent*	*Per cent*	*Per cent*	*Dollars*	*Dollars*
1919	79,449	47,065	6.3	5.7	----------	1,246	917
1920	73,139	41,172	.5	−4.2	----------	684	397
1921	63,811	34,711	1.2	−2.3	4.5	514	270
1922	62,549	34,321	3.2	1.2	11.1	682	440
1923	60,472	33,046	3.5	1.6	13.0	766	533
1924	59,743	32,574	4.4	3.2	12.0	854	624
1925	59,712	32,727	5.2	4.3	13.0	922	690
1926	58,299	31,856	4.3	2.9	(6)	862	636
1927	58,431	32,191	4.6	3.4	----------	886	657

Bureau of Agricultural Economics.

[1] As of Jan. 1 in the period indicated. Values include land, buildings (dwellings and other), livestock, implements, machinery, motor vehicles, and an allowance for cash working capital.
[2] Total capital investment less property rented from nonoperators and debts owed to nonoperators.
[3] Calendar year net profits including compensation to officers (after deducting depreciation) as percentages of "fair" (market) value of capital stock of all corporations estimated by the United States Treasury Department at 75.4 billion dollars in 1921, 75.8 in 1922, 81.8 in 1924, and 95.2 in 1925.
[4] Net income available for operators' capital, labor, and management calculated on the basis of the number of farmers interpolated between 6,448,000 in 1920 and 6,372,000 in 1925.
[5] After allowing 4½ per cent on operators' net capital investment.
[6] Available data indicate that at least the same percentage was earned in 1926 as in 1925.

TABLE 525.—*Gross value of farm production and gross income, 1919–1927*

Year beginning July	Gross value of all farm production [1]	Deductions for products fed, used for seed, and waste [2]	Gross income from farm production						
			Total	Grains	Meat animals	Fruits and vegetables	Cotton and cottonseed	Dairy and poultry products	All other
	1,000,000 dollars	*1,000,000 dollars*	*1,000,000 dollars*	*1,000,000 dollars*	*1,000,000 dollars*	*1,000,000 dollars*	*1,000,000 dollars*	*1,000,000 dollars*	*1,000,000 dollars*
1919	24,025	8,306	15,719	3,005	3,346	1,747	2,271	3,598	1,752
1920	17,800	5,132	12,668	2,246	2,328	1,705	1,272	3,502	1,615
1921	12,894	3,680	9,214	1,266	1,932	1,379	760	2,877	1,000
1922	14,909	4,543	10,366	1,393	2,180	1,410	1,251	2,957	1,175
1923	16,249	4,961	11,288	1,393	2,167	1,526	1,608	3,315	1,279
1924	17,086	5,083	12,003	1,842	2,619	1,333	1,719	3,258	1,232
1925	16,995	4,325	12,670	1,594	2,848	1,686	1,749	3,589	1,204
1926	16,487	4,360	12,127	1,455	2,883	1,585	1,260	3,775	1,169
1927	17,033	4,780	12,253	1,636	2,842	1,453	1,458	3,628	1,236

Bureau of Agricultural Economics.

[1] These gross values of all farm production are here evaluated in terms of crop year (practically July–June) production and weighted average farm prices.
[2] These deductions, to obtain gross income, cover portions of crops and dairy products fed to livestock, used for seed in further crop production, and waste. For the industry as a whole these deductions constitute raw materials, the income from which is derived from the finished products sold or consumed in the farm home.

33023°—29——67

TABLE 526.—*Distribution of gross income from agricultural production, 1919–1927*

Year beginning July	Gross income	Value of food and fuel consumed on farms	Cash income from sales	Distribution of cash income					
				Wages to hired labor[1]	Operating costs	Taxes on operator-owned investment	Rent on property rented from nonoperators	Interest on debts to nonoperators	Balance available for living expenses, etc.
	1,000,000 dollars	*1,000,000 dollars*	*1,000,000 dollars*	*1,000,000 dollars*	*1,000,000 dollars*	*1,000,000 dollars*	*1,000,000 dollars*	*1,000,000 dollars*	*1,000,000 dollars*
1919	15,719	2,887	12,832	1,492	3,306	388	1,712	787	5,147
1920	12,668	2,645	10,023	1,732	3,689	545	1,399	897	1,761
1921	9,214	2,129	7,085	1,088	2,448	582	959	840	1,168
1922	10,366	2,168	8,198	1,061	2,501	617	1,014	809	2,196
1923	11,288	2,360	8,928	1,204	2,760	626	1,034	774	2,530
1924	12,003	2,327	9,676	1,207	2,865	635	1,094	758	3,117
1925	12,670	2,535	10,135	1,216	3,053	654	1,127	758	3,327
1926	12,127	2,590	9,537	1,238	2,980	654	1,042	750	2,873
1927	12,253	2,437	9,816	1,231	2,970	654	1,043	750	3,168

Bureau of Agricultural Economics.

[1] Includes value of board as well as cash.

TABLE 527.—*Index numbers of farm prices, United States, 1910–1928*

[August, 1909–July, 1914=100]

GRAIN

Year	Jan.	Feb.	Mar.	Apr.	May	June	July	Aug.	Sept.	Oct.	Nov.	Dec.	Average
1910	110	112	112	109	107	106	107	106	102	97	92	90	104
1911	91	90	88	89	92	94	97	99	101	104	103	102	96
1912	104	107	110	116	123	122	115	106	100	95	87	82	106
1913	84	86	86	88	91	94	93	95	98	97	96	97	92
1914	97	98	99	100	101	100	97	104	111	110	108	111	103
1915	123	134	136	138	139	127	118	115	106	101	99	102	120
1916	112	115	111	111	113	110	113	127	138	147	158	157	126
1917	161	169	179	217	251	246	250	248	233	223	213	213	217
1918	218	227	234	235	231	227	228	230	229	222	216	217	226
1919	217	214	220	234	245	245	248	246	233	222	220	229	231
1920	241	242	246	261	277	283	266	252	222	193	157	138	231
1921	138	136	131	118	116	117	109	103	100	94	88	88	112
1922	91	102	111	114	115	111	105	100	97	101	106	111	105
1923	113	114	117	121	123	119	112	109	111	113	110	108	114
1924	110	113	114	113	114	116	130	141	140	150	147	155	129
1925	172	178	172	152	159	164	152	157	148	135	138	140	156
1926[1]	143	140	133	131	131	130	125	128	121	123	121	120	129
1927[1]	120	122	121	119	127	140	139	138	134	128	120	123	128
1928[1]	125	128	136	144	160	152	142	120	117	116	110	112	130

FRUITS AND VEGETABLES

Year	Jan.	Feb.	Mar.	Apr.	May	June	July	Aug.	Sept.	Oct.	Nov.	Dec.	Average
1910	90	93	92	92	96	93	90	94	94	88	84	87	91
1911	92	94	97	106	108	121	129	125	109	94	93	102	106
1912	109	118	130	144	150	135	116	104	86	74	73	78	110
1913	79	81	81	83	92	99	103	102	96	97	96	97	92
1914	101	106	110	115	117	119	113	102	92	79	71	72	100
1915	75	78	77	82	90	91	89	85	76	79	84	89	83
1916	99	108	112	114	117	124	125	123	121	129	147	156	123
1917	167	208	241	265	283	270	219	165	146	150	155	156	202
1918	158	162	157	156	160	160	172	177	166	160	158	155	162
1919	154	156	167	179	197	205	216	219	194	186	187	206	189
1920	226	252	279	323	373	366	314	239	180	150	141	144	249
1921	136	127	125	124	132	140	156	178	171	162	162	165	148
1922	159	173	181	190	206	197	174	129	109	101	101	104	152
1923	117	122	130	146	157	161	165	151	131	123	114	114	136
1924	118	123	123	128	132	146	142	138	113	109	108	110	124
1925	122	131	138	146	162	184	178	178	142	152	194	194	160
1926[2]	214	218	220	253	240	216	195	166	136	136	142	137	189
1927[2]	140	142	140	147	158	201	195	172	145	138	136	141	155
1928[2]	144	153	174	179	181	168	156	137	127	114	109	108	146

[1] Kafir omitted.   [2] Onions and cabbage omitted.

TABLE 527.—*Index numbers of farm prices, United States, 1910-1928*—Continued

MEAT ANIMALS

Year	Jan.	Feb.	Mar.	Apr.	May	June	July	Aug.	Sept.	Oct.	Nov.	Dec.	Average
1910	99	100	109	115	110	109	103	98	102	101	96	93	103
1911	96	93	92	88	84	82	83	88	88	84	83	82	87
1912	83	85	87	96	98	96	95	100	103	104	99	99	95
1913	99	103	109	113	109	110	111	110	109	110	108	107	108
1914	109	112	114	114	113	112	114	118	117	111	106	104	112
1915	103	101	101	103	106	107	106	105	106	108	101	98	104
1916	101	108	116	121	123	124	124	123	127	122	123	125	120
1917	131	144	162	177	179	177	173	178	190	194	186	190	173
1918	187	188	194	204	210	207	205	211	214	204	198	199	202
1919	201	204	211	224	227	221	228	227	197	185	177	173	206
1920	181	184	184	186	181	182	181	177	177	169	150	124	173
1921	123	119	125	114	111	105	109	112	101	98	92	91	108
1922	95	108	118	117	119	121	120	114	112	113	108	107	113
1923	110	110	110	110	108	103	105	104	112	106	100	98	106
1924	101	102	104	106	107	105	103	116	115	121	115	113	109
1925	123	126	145	146	139	139	148	149	143	141	136	136	139
1926	140	146	147	146	148	154	152	144	148	148	142	140	146
1927	140	143	144	143	137	129	131	136	142	145	141	138	139
1928	138	139	139	142	151	150	157	162	174	160	150	143	150

DAIRY PRODUCTS

Year	Jan.	Feb.	Mar.	Apr.	May	June	July	Aug.	Sept.	Oct.	Nov.	Dec.	Average
1910	106	103	98	101	97	96	95	97	100	102	103	105	100
1911	104	99	96	94	92	90	92	95	97	97	101	104	97
1912	107	108	106	103	102	99	99	100	102	105	103	103	103
1913	102	100	100	99	98	96	96	102	106	100	104	104	100
1914	105	102	100	98	96	95	96	99	101	101	103	102	100
1915	102	101	98	97	97	94	93	95	96	98	100	102	98
1916	102	99	100	99	99	97	96	100	101	106	112	116	102
1917	115	117	116	119	123	120	119	123	129	138	142	146	125
1918	149	150	148	144	142	142	141	146	152	163	169	172	152
1919	173	165	164	166	166	166	167	170	175	181	190	197	173
1920	196	194	189	192	187	182	181	185	186	190	189	182	188
1921	172	165	160	154	141	132	133	138	140	146	148	147	148
1922	140	134	133	131	126	128	127	129	133	136	140	147	134
1923	151	151	148	147	142	142	143	139	142	145	153	157	148
1924	152	150	146	134	128	126	123	120	126	130	132	137	134
1925	134	134	137	132	132	130	131	135	137	146	146	146	137
1926	147	143	141	133	130	128	129	128	133	134	141	144	136
1927	144	143	139	140	136	132	130	129	135	139	141	145	138
1928	145	145	142	139	136	134	134	135	141	143	144	146	140

POULTRY PRODUCTS

Year	Jan.	Feb.	Mar.	Apr.	May	June	July	Aug.	Sept.	Oct.	Nov.	Dec.	Average
1910	130	116	98	91	90	89	88	90	98	109	120	129	104
1911	116	90	77	74	74	73	75	81	89	100	115	125	91
1912	127	118	97	84	82	81	83	88	97	109	123	124	101
1913	111	98	87	81	82	84	85	90	101	116	133	138	101
1914	130	119	99	86	85	87	89	95	105	112	123	133	105
1915	133	114	91	84	84	84	84	88	97	111	126	134	103
1916	127	110	95	90	93	96	99	106	120	137	156	166	116
1917	162	156	139	134	145	141	138	147	162	174	185	198	157
1918	210	201	168	150	148	149	160	172	185	205	229	247	185
1919	234	190	165	175	185	185	186	195	203	225	255	275	206
1920	267	236	205	189	186	185	191	204	222	243	267	272	222
1921	243	185	131	114	111	114	128	143	156	180	210	211	161
1922	176	140	118	110	114	113	111	114	132	159	187	198	139
1923	175	151	130	117	117	114	116	126	144	165	191	198	145
1924	162	157	109	105	109	115	121	132	153	176	203	217	147
1925	213	166	124	127	131	135	141	148	152	175	208	213	161
1926	172	145	128	133	135	138	137	137	155	173	202	212	156
1927	173	145	115	114	112	102	112	122	143	167	189	195	141
1928	177	144	122	121	.128	127	134	140	156	168	185	197	150

TABLE 527.—*Index numbers of farm prices, United States, 1910–1928*—Continued

COTTON AND COTTONSEED

Year	Jan.	Feb.	Mar.	Apr.	May	June	July	Aug.	Sept.	Oct.	Nov.	Dec.	Average
1910	116	113	113	113	114	113	113	115	112	111	113	115	113
1911	117	114	113	114	116	116	110	100	88	77	72	70	101
1912	71	76	81	85	89	89	93	92	89	88	91	97	87
1913	97	96	95	95	94	94	94	93	101	106	102	98	97
1914	96	99	99	98	100	101	100	86	66	58	54	57	85
1915	60	65	67	73	74	72	70	70	81	99	99	100	78
1916	100	100	99	102	104	107	109	115	128	144	163	160	119
1917	148	144	149	160	169	189	204	199	197	214	232	237	187
1918	244	249	257	251	235	234	235	246	264	253	236	235	245
1919	225	208	206	213	232	249	260	259	252	277	295	292	247
1920	293	295	298	304	303	301	297	266	218	175	132	101	248
1921	93	89	80	76	78	78	79	91	130	150	137	131	101
1922	129	128	131	135	144	160	166	166	160	168	186	195	156
1923	203	215	224	222	211	207	199	190	204	221	238	253	216
1924	255	247	219	226	222	219	215	219	175	182	179	176	211
1925	182	183	195	189	184	183	186	186	178	171	144	139	177
1926	138	142	133	135	130	132	126	130	134	94	88	81	122
1927	85	94	102	101	113	119	125	136	179	169	162	153	128
1928	152	141	147	154	166	162	170	153	142	147	146	148	152

ALL GROUPS

Year	Jan.	Feb.	Mar.	Apr.	May	June	July	Aug.	Sept.	Oct.	Nov.	Dec.	Average
1910	106	105	107	108	105	104	102	102	102	101	99	99	103
1911	100	97	95	94	94	95	95	96	95	92	92	92	95
1912	94	97	99	104	107	104	101	100	98	97	95	95	99
1913	95	96	97	98	98	99	99	101	103	104	104	103	100
1914	104	105	104	104	104	104	103	104	102	98	96	97	102
1915	100	101	100	102	104	101	99	97	97	101	99	100	100
1916	104	106	108	110	111	112	113	117	123	128	137	139	117
1917	140	148	159	176	188	188	185	183	184	187	187	191	176
1918	194	197	199	200	198	196	197	203	207	204	200	201	200
1919	200	194	197	207	215	216	222	222	208	206	209	212	209
1920	219	221	222	230	235	234	224	209	194	178	158	140	205
1921	135	128	123	115	112	110	111	116	118	120	116	115	116
1922	114	118	123	123	127	128	126	120	119	123	126	131	124
1923	134	136	136	137	135	133	130	128	132	134	136	137	135
1924	137	136	131	130	129	130	132	139	132	138	137	139	134
1925	146	146	151	147	146	148	149	152	144	143	144	143	147
1926 [3]	143	143	140	140	139	139	136	133	134	130	130	127	136
1927 [3]	126	127	126	125	126	130	130	132	140	139	137	137	131
1928 [3]	137	135	137	140	148	145	145	139	141	137	134	134	139

Bureau of Agricultural Economics. Prices of farm production received by producers collected monthly from a list of about 12,000 special price reporters. This list is made up almost entirely of country-town dealers, elevator managers, buyers, and merchants.

The commodities by groups are as follows: Grains—wheat, corn, oats, barley, rye, kafir; fruits and vegetables—apples, oranges, grapefruit, potatoes, sweet potatoes, beans, onions, cabbage; meat animals—beef cattle, calves, hogs, sheep, lambs; dairy products—butter (represents butter, butterfat, and cream), milk; poultry products—chickens, eggs; cotton and cottonseed; all groups includes also horses (represents horses and mules), hay, flax, tobacco, and wool.

[3] Kafir, onions, and cabbage omitted.

TABLE 528.—*Index numbers of farm prices, 1910–1928: By groups, crop-year averages*

[August, 1909–July, 1914=100]

Year beginning July	Grains	Fruits and vegetables	Meat animals	Dairy products	Poultry products	Cotton and cottonseed	All groups
1910	95	96	94	98	95	114	98
1911	107	120	88	101	98	84	97
1912	93	87	104	101	97	93	97
1913	98	105	111	101	106	99	103
1914	120	85	108	99	104	69	101
1915	109	98	110	98	104	94	104
1916	172	186	143	112	138	148	146
1917	229	162	192	139	169	229	192
1918	226	170	210	162	364	234	203
1919	246	252	190	185	217	286	220
1920	164	163	140	170	191	140	152
1921	102	175	107	137	150	129	119
1922	111	129	110	141	142	194	130
1923	112	131	104	144	141	224	132
1924	155	134	125	131	158	188	142
1925	140	200	144	139	157	151	143
1926	124	153	142	137	148	106	129
1927	136	160	141	138	146	154	138

Bureau of Agricultural Economics.
See footnotes, Table 527.
GENERAL NOTE.—Tables similar to Tables 495–501, 1927 Yearbook, index numbers of wholesale prices, are omitted.

TABLE 529.—*Index numbers of general trend of prices and wages*

[1910–1914=100]

Year and month	Wholesale prices of all commodities [1]	Industrial wages [2]	Prices paid by farmers for commodities used in— Living	Prices paid by farmers for commodities used in— Production	Prices paid by farmers for commodities used in— Living production	Farm wages	Taxes [3]
1910	103		98	98	98	97	
1911	95		100	103	101	97	
1912	101		101	98	100	101	
1913	102		100	102	100	104	
1914	100		102	99	101	101	100
1915	103	101	107	103	106	102	102
1916	129	114	125	121	123	112	104
1917	180	129	148	152	150	140	106
1918	198	160	180	176	178	176	118
1919	210	185	214	192	205	206	130
1920	230	222	227	175	206	239	155
1921	150	203	165	142	156	150	217
1922	152	197	160	140	152	146	232
1923	156	214	161	142	153	166	246
1924	152	218	162	143	154	166	249
1925	162	223	165	149	159	168	250
1926	154	229	164	144	156	171	253
1927	149	231	161	144	154	170	
1928	153	232				169	
1928							
January	151	230				161	
February	151	230					
March	150	233	162	145	155		
April	152	227				166	
May	154	230					
June	153	232	163	148	157		
July	154	230				170	
August	155	231					
September	157	234	163	144	156		
October	153	234				175	
November	151	233					
December	151	237					

Bureau of Agricultural Economics.

[1] Bureau of Labor Statistics. Index for 1928 obtained by multiplying new series by 156.6.
[2] Average weekly earnings, New York State factories. June, 1914=100.
[3] Index of estimate of total taxes paid on all farm property. 1914=100.

TABLE 530.—*Index numbers of prices paid by farmers, 1910–1928*

[Base 1910–1914=100]

Year or date	Commodities used in production							Wages paid to hired labor	Commodities bought for use in production plus wages paid to hired labor	Commodities bought for family maintenance[2]	Taxes on farm property[3]
	Feed	Machinery	Fertilizer	Building materials for other than house	Equipment and supplies	Seed[1]	All commodities bought for use in production				
1910	92	101	97	100	101	------	98	97	98	98	------
1911	108	103	97	102	100	------	103	97	101	100	------
1912	90	100	102	103	100	105	98	101	99	101	------
1913	108	98	104	101	100	94	102	104	102	99	------
1914	103	98	101	93	99	101	99	101	100	102	100
1915	98	101	113	102	106	117	103	102	103	107	102
1916	129	111	122	118	129	112	121	112	119	125	104
1917	186	132	139	137	156	141	152	140	149	148	106
1918	196	160	173	161	180	188	176	176	176	180	118
1919	208	178	185	189	179	264	192	206	196	214	130
1920	133	188	189	205	188	149	175	239	189	227	155
1921	91	175	159	156	151	125	142	150	144	165	217
1922	118	156	131	159	139	133	140	146	142	160	232
1923	128	151	128	160	138	142	142	166	147	161	246
1924	135	155	122	159	131	148	143	166	148	162	249
1925	145	158	131	163	136	170	149	168	154	165	250
1926	120	156	129	163	142	190	144	171	150	164	253
1927	124	157	123	164	134	192	144	170	150	161	258
1923:											
Jan. 15	121	149	123	158	137	138	138	137	138	158	------
Apr. 15	129	150	127	160	143	143	142	148	144	163	------
July 15	132	153	130	163	141	139	144	169	150	163	------
Oct. 15	131	153	130	161	130	146	142	174	149	162	------
1924:											
Jan. 15	127	154	127	160	130	142	141	159	145	163	------
Apr. 15	128	154	117	160	137	155	142	163	147	162	------
July 15	138	155	119	158	132	148	143	168	149	159	------
Oct. 15	148	155	125	159	125	148	145	171	151	161	------
1925:											
Jan. 15	154	157	127	161	126	163	149	156	150	164	------
Apr. 15	146	158	130	161	138	178	150	163	153	166	------
July 15	147	157	132	165	141	178	152	169	156	166	------
Oct. 15	134	157	134	164	140	159	147	173	153	165	------
1926:											
Jan. 15	126	155	130	162	140	183	145	159	148	165	------
Apr. 15	119	156	128	163	143	191	144	166	149	164	------
June 15	119	156	132	163	146	196	145	174	152	165	------
Sept. 15	122	156	127	162	144	188	145	176	152	163	------
Dec. 15	115	156	128	162	140	192	143	162	147	163	------
1927:											
Mar. 15	117	157	121	164	137	202	143	166	148	161	------
June 15	128	157	121	164	133	202	145	172	151	161	------
Sept. 15	130	157	125	164	133	181	145	175	152	161	------
Dec. 15	123	157	125	161	132	181	142	161	146	161	------
1928:											
March	130	156	133	160	132	181	145	166	149	162	------
June	143	156	133	161	130	181	148	170	153	163	------
September	131	156	132	162	131	177	144	175	151	163	------
December	------	------	------	------	------	------	------	------	------	------	------

Bureau of Agricultural Economics. Compiled from prices reported to the Department of Agriculture by retail dealers throughout the United States. The index numbers include only commodities bought by farmers; the commodities being weighted according to purchases reported by actual farmers in farm management and rural-life studies from 1920 to 1925.

[1] 1912–1914=100.
[2] Includes food clothing, household operating expenses, furniture and furnishings, and building material for house.
[3] 1914=100.

GENERAL NOTE.—Tables similar to Tables 504–507, 1927 Yearbook, pertaining to farm business and farm family living in certain localities, and Table 508, Average prevailing farm wage rates, by geographic divisions, are omitted.

TABLE 531.—*Farm wage rates and index numbers, 1866–1928*

[1910–1914=100]

Year	Average yearly farm wage¹ Per month— With board	Per month— Without board	Per day— With board	Per day— Without board	Weighted average wage rate per month²	Index numbers of farm wages
	Doll.	*Doll.*	*Doll.*	*Doll.*	*Doll.*	*Doll.*
1866³	10.09	15.50	0.64	0.90	13.14	55
1869	9.97	15.50	.63	.87	12.93	54
1874 or 1875	11.16	17.10	.68	.94	14.19	59
1877 or 1879⁴	10.86	16.79	.61	.84	13.34	56
1879 or 1880	11.70	17.53	.64	.89	14.14	59
1880 or 1881	12.32	18.52	.67	.92	14.82	62
1881 or 1882	12.88	19.11	.70	.97	15.48	65
1884 or 1885	13.08	19.22	.71	.96	15.58	65
1887 or 1888	13.29	19.67	.72	.98	15.87	66
1889 or 1890	13.29	19.45	.72	.97	15.79	66
1891 or 1892	13.48	20.02	.73	.98	16.06	67
1893	13.85	19.97	.72	.92	15.93	67
1894	12.70	18.57	.65	.84	14.60	61
1895	12.75	18.74	.65	.85	14.69	62
1898	13.29	19.16	.71	.94	15.58	65
1899	13.90	19.97	.75	.99	16.34	68
1902	15.51	22.12	.83	1.09	18.12	76
1906	18.73	26.19	1.03	1.32	21.92	92
1909	20.48	28.09	1.04	1.31	23.00	96
1910	19.58	28.04	1.07	1.40	23.08	97
1911	19.85	28.33	1.07	1.40	23.25	97
1912	20.46	29.14	1.12	1.44	24.01	101
1913	21.27	30.21	1.15	1.48	24.83	104
1914	20.90	29.72	1.11	1.44	24.26	101
1915	21.08	29.97	1.12	1.45	24.46	102
1916	23.04	32.58	1.24	1.60	26.83	112
1917	28.64	40.19	1.56	2.00	33.42	140
1918	35.12	49.13	2.05	2.61	42.12	176
1919	40.14	56.77	2.44	3.10	49.11	206
1920	47.24	65.05	2.84	3.56	57.01	239
1921	30.25	43.58	1.66	2.17	35.77	150
1922	29.31	42.09	1.64	2.14	34.91	146
1923	33.09	46.74	1.91	2.45	39.64	166
1924⁵	33.34	47.22	1.88	2.44	39.67	166
1925⁵	33.88	47.80	1.89	2.46	40.12	168
1926⁵	34.86	48.86	1.91	2.49	40.92	171
1927⁵	34.58	48.63	1.90	2.46	40.60	170
1928⁵	34.66	48.65	1.88	2.43	40.44	169
1923—January	27.87	40.50	1.46	1.97	32.61	137
April	30.90	44.41	1.55	2.09	35.42	148
July	34.64	48.61	1.84	2.44	40.30	169
October	34.56	48.42	2.02	2.58	41.52	174
1924—January	31.55	45.53	1.79	2.38	38.01	159
April	33.57	47.38	1.77	2.34	38.95	163
July	34.34	48.02	1.87	2.43	40.15	168
October	34.38	48.46	1.93	2.51	40.81	171
1925—January	31.07	45.04	1.74	2.31	37.24	156
April	33.86	47.40	1.77	2.33	39.04	163
July	34.94	48.55	1.89	2.44	40.62	170
October	34.91	48.99	1.95	2.53	41.28	173
1926—January	31.82	46.26	1.76	2.33	37.94	159
April	34.38	48.40	1.78	2.35	39.56	166
July	36.10	49.89	1.91	2.48	41.59	174
October	36.00	50.10	1.97	2.55	42.10	176
1927—January	32.94	47.07	1.79	2.36	38.79	162
April	34.53	48.47	1.78	2.37	39.71	166
July	35.59	49.52	1.89	2.44	41.07	172
October	35.68	49.77	1.96	2.51	41.71	175
1928—January	32.50	46.75	1.76	2.34	38.35	161
April	34.46	48.44	1.78	2.34	39.56	166
July	35.39	49.32	1.84	2.39	40.55	170
October	35.75	49.60	1.96	2.51	41.71	175
1929—January	33.04	47.24	1.78	2.34	38.75	162

Bureau of Agricultural Economics.

¹ Yearly averages are from reports by crop reporters, giving average wages for the year in their localities.
² This column has significance only as an essential step in computing the wage index.
³ Years 1866 to 1878 in gold.
⁴ 1877 or 1878, 1878 or 1879 (combined).
⁵ Weighted average of quarterly reports, April (weight 1), July (weight 5), October (weight 5), and January of the following year (weight 1).

TABLE 532.—*Wages: Male farm labor, by States, quarterly, 1928*

State and division	Per month, with board				Per month, without board				Per day, with board [1]				Per day, without board			
	Jan.	Apr.	July	Oct.	Jan.	Apr.	July	Oct.	Jan.	Apr.	July	Oct.	Jan.	Apr.	July	Oct.
	Doll.	Doll.	Doll.	Doll.	Doll.	Doll.	Doll.	Doll.	Doll.	Doll.	Doll.	Doll.	Doll.	Doll.	Doll.	Doll.
Maine	43.00	45.00	47.00	47.00	62.00	64.00	66.00	65.00	2.40	2.40	2.50	2.60	3.00	3.10	3.10	3.30
New Hampshire	45.00	45.00	48.00	49.00	70.00	73.00	72.00	74.00	2.50	2.50	2.50	2.55	3.30	3.40	3.35	3.65
Vermont	45.00	49.00	50.00	48.00	68.00	71.00	70.00	72.00	2.40	2.50	2.55	2.60	3.15	3.20	3.25	3.40
Massachusetts	50.00	50.00	50.00	49.00	81.00	80.00	81.00	80.00	2.70	2.80	3.05	2.90	3.50	3.60	3.70	3.75
Rhode Island	50.00	55.00	53.00	54.00	83.00	85.00	85.00	80.00	2.60	2.80	3.00	3.00	3.60	3.70	3.80	3.80
Connecticut	52.00	53.00	54.00	53.00	83.00	82.00	81.00	81.00	2.80	2.75	3.00	2.80	3.60	3.60	3.80	3.75
New York	43.75	48.00	49.50	49.75	66.00	69.25	70.00	70.75	2.75	2.85	2.85	3.00	3.60	3.60	3.65	3.80
New Jersey	46.00	45.00	49.00	47.00	70.00	70.00	75.00	70.00	2.75	2.80	2.85	2.85	3.50	3.40	3.55	3.55
Pennsylvania	38.00	37.50	39.25	39.75	58.50	57.25	58.75	59.75	2.45	2.40	2.45	2.55	3.25	3.15	3.25	3.30
North Atlantic	43.33	45.05	46.71	46.58	66.36	67.43	68.60	68.71	2.62	2.65	2.71	2.78	3.42	3.40	3.48	3.58
Ohio	36.00	39.00	39.00	38.75	50.00	55.00	54.50	53.75	2.50	2.45	2.40	2.45	3.05	3.10	3.05	3.10
Indiana	35.00	36.25	37.00	37.00	47.00	48.50	49.00	49.00	2.00	2.00	2.00	2.20	2.65	2.60	2.60	2.75
Illinois	40.50	42.00	42.75	43.25	53.00	54.00	53.50	55.00	2.20	2.10	2.25	2.30	2.80	2.70	2.85	2.95
Michigan	38.25	41.75	43.00	43.00	54.25	58.75	60.00	60.00	2.45	2.50	2.60	2.75	3.15	3.20	3.30	3.40
Wisconsin	38.00	46.75	48.50	48.75	56.75	64.00	65.75	65.25	2.10	2.25	2.45	2.50	2.85	2.95	3.10	3.10
Minnesota	31.25	45.00	45.50	47.00	48.50	50.60	61.25	63.75	1.80	2.20	2.25	2.80	2.70	2.95	3.05	3.55
Iowa	41.00	48.25	48.25	47.75	53.50	58.00	58.50	58.50	2.25	2.40	2.45	2.55	3.00	3.05	3.10	3.20
Missouri	33.00	33.50	33.50	33.00	44.00	44.50	45.00	44.00	1.60	1.60	1.60	1.70	2.15	2.15	2.15	2.20
North Dakota	26.25	40.00	47.25	54.25	43.75	60.00	65.00	75.75	1.75	2.20	2.35	4.15	2.65	3.20	3.30	5.05
South Dakota	36.75	46.75	48.00	48.25	53.25	63.75	65.25	66.00	2.35	2.40	2.40	3.00	3.15	3.20	3.30	3.80
Nebraska	40.25	43.25	43.75	43.00	55.00	59.50	57.50	58.00	2.45	2.35	2.40	2.45	3.20	3.10	3.10	3.30
Kansas	35.50	36.00	37.50	39.25	51.00	51.50	52.25	54.25	2.25	2.05	2.40	2.50	2.95	2.80	3.05	3.20
North Central	36.38	41.38	42.29	42.73	50.81	55.66	56.18	56.96	2.12	2.18	2.26	2.48	2.81	2.85	2.93	3.14
Delaware	30.00	31.00	34.50	32.00	45.00	45.00	50.00	46.00	2.25	2.00	2.30	2.35	2.80	2.50	2.75	3.05
Maryland	34.00	36.00	36.00	36.00	49.00	49.75	52.75	52.50	1.95	1.95	2.00	2.30	2.65	2.60	2.65	2.90
Virginia	30.00	29.00	29.00	30.00	40.00	43.00	41.00	41.25	1.60	1.60	1.55	1.65	2.05	2.10	2.20	2.15
West Virginia	35.50	33.50	33.25	33.25	49.50	47.00	47.75	48.00	1.75	1.70	1.70	1.75	2.30	2.30	2.30	2.45
North Carolina	28.25	27.00	27.50	27.75	40.50	37.00	39.00	39.25	1.50	1.40	1.45	1.50	1.90	1.85	1.85	1.90
South Carolina	20.00	20.00	20.75	21.00	29.00	27.75	28.50	28.00	.95	1.00	1.00	1.00	1.30	1.35	1.25	1.25
Georgia	19.75	19.75	20.50	19.50	27.75	28.00	29.00	27.25	1.00	1.05	1.05	1.05	1.35	1.30	1.35	1.35
Florida	24.00	22.00	22.75	24.00	35.00	34.50	36.25	37.00	1.10	1.15	1.25	1.25	1.60	1.55	1.70	1.70
South Atlantic	25.40	24.89	25.38	25.43	36.36	35.20	36.22	35.78	1.31	1.31	1.33	1.38	1.74	1.72	1.75	1.78
Kentucky	25.50	26.25	28.25	27.25	35.50	36.50	39.25	38.00	1.25	1.25	1.40	1.40	1.65	1.65	1.80	1.80
Tennessee	24.00	23.00	24.50	24.50	31.00	33.00	34.00	33.25	1.10	1.10	1.15	1.20	1.45	1.50	1.50	1.50
Alabama	20.00	21.00	22.00	21.00	27.50	29.00	31.00	30.00	1.10	1.15	1.10	1.15	1.40	1.50	1.40	1.50
Mississippi	22.00	22.25	23.00	21.75	31.25	31.50	31.75	31.25	1.15	1.15	1.20	1.15	1.55	1.55	1.60	1.55
Arkansas	24.50	23.75	25.00	26.00	36.00	34.50	35.00	35.75	1.15	1.20	1.20	1.20	1.60	1.55	1.50	1.60
Louisiana	22.50	22.75	23.50	25.75	34.25	34.75	34.50	35.25	1.15	1.15	1.15	1.25	1.55	1.50	1.45	1.55
Oklahoma	28.00	29.50	30.00	31.25	41.25	42.50	43.00	42.25	1.60	1.50	1.80	1.80	2.15	1.95	2.20	2.25
Texas	28.00	28.00	29.00	31.25	41.00	40.00	42.00	42.50	1.45	1.40	1.40	1.60	1.85	1.80	1.85	2.00
South Central	24.68	24.88	25.99	26.57	35.25	35.58	36.86	36.74	1.26	1.25	1.30	1.37	1.66	1.64	1.68	1.74
Montana	45.00	55.25	58.00	60.50	69.75	74.50	78.50	83.25	2.65	2.70	2.75	3.70	3.50	3.65	3.60	4.35
Idaho	48.00	55.00	55.75	55.50	68.50	77.00	75.75	77.75	2.35	2.50	2.65	3.00	3.25	3.20	3.45	3.75
Wyoming	44.25	49.25	51.25	53.00	64.00	73.75	70.75	77.00	2.35	2.35	2.40	2.65	3.30	3.45	3.20	3.55
Colorado	38.50	39.25	41.00	40.50	60.65	59.25	62.00	60.50	2.20	2.10	2.20	2.35	2.95	2.95	3.00	3.15
New Mexico	34.50	35.00	35.00	36.25	49.00	51.00	51.00	49.25	1.65	1.70	1.60	1.85	2.10	2.15	2.20	2.30
Arizona	48.00	45.00	45.00	52.00	70.00	70.00	65.00	72.00	2.00	2.00	1.95	2.20	2.50	2.50	2.50	2.70
Utah	58.25	56.25	57.50	53.50	77.75	78.40	76.00	74.00	2.45	2.45	2.50	2.40	3.05	3.00	3.20	3.15
Nevada	62.00	59.00	64.00	62.00	83.00	76.00	80.00	80.00	2.65	2.35	2.15	2.65	3.40	3.10	3.00	3.50
Washington	42.75	51.50	50.75	52.75	68.00	75.25	74.00	78.00	2.20	2.50	2.60	2.85	3.25	3.30	3.40	3.70
Oregon	42.00	48.00	48.50	49.00	65.60	68.00	69.50	69.75	2.25	2.40	2.50	2.75	3.00	3.15	3.20	3.25
California	59.00	62.00	62.00	62.00	86.00	88.00	88.00	90.00	2.60	2.50	2.60	2.70	3.50	3.50	3.60	3.65
Far Western	49.57	53.10	53.64	54.21	73.18	75.94	75.99	77.68	2.36	2.37	2.44	2.66	3.18	3.20	3.28	3.44
United States	32.50	34.46	35.39	35.75	46.75	48.44	49.32	49.60	1.76	1.78	1.84	1.96	2.34	2.34	2.39	2.51

Bureau of Agricultural Economics. As reported by field-aid crop reporters.

[1] Includes piece work.

TABLE 533.—*Estimated average monthly wages and value of perquisites of non-casual hired farm laborers, by States, 1925*

State	All laborers		Laborers boarded by their employers		Laborers not boarded by their employers		Unmarried laborers		Married laborers	
	Wages (cash)	Perquisites [1]	Wages (cash)	Perquisites [1]	Wages (cash)	Perquisites [1]	Wages (cash)	Perquisites [1]	Wages (cash)	Perquisites [1]
	Dolls.	Dolls.	Dolls.	Dolls.	Dolls.	Dolls.	Dolls.	Dolls.	Dolls.	Dolls.
Maine	53.75	26.38	44.91	28.99	65.88	22.24	41.64	27.36	62.07	25.42
New Hampshire	63.39	28.91	45.28	38.79	73.96	23.14	42.93	31.21	75.66	27.56
Vermont	49.14	34.45	48.86	33.28	58.84	33.49	39.42	35.98	59.48	32.49
Massachusetts	77.45	15.84	49.63	34.75	83.31	12.67	57.80	18.62	84.24	15.52
Rhode Island	65.33	29.74	60.00	35.20	96.00	27.62	20.00	30.80	32.70	27.60
Connecticut	66.06	22.97	40.20	33.40	80.60	16.56	48.64	23.86	80.42	20.69
New York	56.26	32.19	47.79	37.18	65.63	25.55	46.41	33.68	63.54	30.61
New Jersey	70.31	25.58	48.75	35.75	80.03	22.23	52.33	23.83	73.96	26.54
Pennsylvania	48.26	32.48	41.22	35.06	57.26	28.76	42.47	30.16	53.76	35.41
Ohio	43.67	29.90	39.32	31.74	47.52	28.28	37.65	29.07	49.19	31.24
Indiana	41.62	33.61	39.66	30.11	43.78	37.41	38.71	28.90	42.03	39.12
Illinois	49.16	34.06	47.04	34.03	51.24	34.03	45.84	30.47	51.87	37.12
Michigan	48.10	31.79	41.69	35.30	54.87	28.79	40.98	32.90	55.13	30.97
Wisconsin	48.16	30.82	46.20	35.71	54.17	17.00	46.02	28.99	56.72	38.32
Minnesota	48.08	29.12	46.93	31.81	51.78	18.91	46.28	28.81	55.05	30.29
Iowa	50.44	32.45	49.69	33.09	52.17	31.36	49.13	30.51	52.38	35.86
Missouri	38.24	28.16	35.50	28.02	41.90	28.88	33.82	25.18	43.07	30.91
North Dakota	49.49	32.75	48.02	35.36	57.67	18.31	46.68	32.13	61.94	37.40
South Dakota	50.05	30.76	56.00	34.29	45.42	10.92	49.49	29.43	47.34	44.57
Nebraska	46.99	30.14	44.56	33.18	55.31	19.68	44.35	30.10	56.22	30.24
Kansas	44.24	33.36	41.99	35.12	48.78	29.54	40.41	32.91	51.68	34.11
Maryland	38.20	32.27	33.00	38.88	42.78	26.45	30.96	25.39	40.29	36.01
Delaware	51.58	25.18	43.33	30.50	55.11	22.91	36.67	22.00	53.80	25.53
Virginia	33.83	27.96	30.08	29.67	36.97	26.53	26.08	24.92	35.02	28.69
West Virginia	41.52	30.91	32.63	36.76	51.69	24.22	29.33	24.88	44.70	33.12
North Carolina	35.12	22.79	28.36	29.01	41.09	17.30	30.84	19.20	36.45	23.58
South Carolina	22.55	24.30	20.64	31.58	24.33	17.51	21.80	25.88	26.19	23.73
Georgia	24.97	26.33	20.77	26.49	28.57	26.20	21.45	22.66	28.41	29.16
Florida	46.50	23.06	25.00	31.00	67.67	15.44	33.83	27.50	52.38	20.82
Kentucky	33.21	27.35	32.06	26.50	34.22	28.08	28.78	26.71	36.19	27.74
Tennessee	31.03	20.67	26.50	23.98	33.23	19.05	27.83	22.22	30.96	20.08
Alabama	25.83	24.82	23.84	30.81	28.54	16.66	25.47	27.94	30.17	22.43
Mississippi	33.00	30.58	28.55	35.52	39.39	26.27	26.79	25.11	35.72	35.07
Arkansas	34.14	22.46	30.20	23.23	40.00	21.63	29.30	23.18	39.91	22.16
Louisiana	33.64	19.25	21.50	24.50	35.66	18.38	29.94	14.70	33.82	21.07
Oklahoma	35.46	30.23	33.42	30.59	41.50	28.27	32.45	30.20	40.90	30.29
Texas	38.51	32.92	33.80	34.34	41.46	32.03	31.41	25.44	41.07	37.02
Montana	56.94	36.36	53.73	40.10	77.50	16.26	52.20	39.98	72.25	24.76
Idaho	62.38	38.13	55.64	41.41	80.25	31.16	55.63	40.46	74.50	31.18
Wyoming	53.20	39.71	50.47	41.06	75.00	28.90	47.41	41.63	71.05	33.00
Colorado	52.52	29.47	44.85	33.11	62.29	25.01	44.24	31.89	61.21	26.85
New Mexico	38.00	26.57	35.00	37.20	45.50	(2)	36.67	37.20	47.00	(2)
Arizona	72.50								72.50	
Utah	63.00	30.90	58.33	41.17	70.00	15.50	59.00	30.88	66.67	31.00
Nevada	73.75	64.88	65.00	76.50			68.00	68.00	67.50	61.75
Washington	62.22	33.04	54.37	35.37	91.50	24.79	53.43	36.61	85.45	21.75
Oregon	62.39	33.54	58.58	38.68	75.33	16.09	60.41	34.05	65.84	31.82
California	82.81	32.70	62.89	55.34	93.87	20.12	67.17	34.61	92.99	31.63
New England	63.07	25.08	46.07	33.28	76.41	19.18	46.70	27.89	74.40	23.31
Middle Atlantic	53.36	31.84	44.28	35.98	63.43	26.65	44.89	31.34	60.29	32.40
East North Central	46.23	32.37	43.51	33.33	49.44	31.23	42.71	29.72	49.66	35.71
West North Central	47.06	31.15	45.96	33.01	49.73	26.74	45.11	30.08	51.01	33.52
South Atlantic	32.81	26.97	27.39	30.99	37.50	23.51	26.48	23.71	35.57	28.27
East South Central	31.01	24.71	27.93	28.18	33.55	22.06	27.36	25.26	33.24	24.42
West South Central	35.83	27.63	32.07	28.90	39.94	26.14	31.18	25.86	39.70	29.40
Mountain	55.80	35.13	50.95	40.59	66.96	22.22	50.31	38.48	68.21	28.21
Pacific	71.98	33.00	58.28	42.34	91.05	20.21	59.93	35.17	88.21	30.09
United States	46.44	30.34	42.62	33.51	51.44	26.05	42.29	29.87	49.81	30.93

Bureau of Agricultural Economics. The data above are calculated from the reports of over 3,500 voluntary correspondents of the Department of Agriculture.
Total earnings may be found by adding wages and perquisite values.

[1] Farm values.　　　　　　　　[2] No perquisites reported.

TABLE 534.—*Estimated earnings per day of casual hired farm laborers, by States, 1926*

| State | All laborers | | | | | | | | Laborers boarded by their employers | | Laborers not boarded by their employers | |
| | Wages (cash) | | | Perquisites[1] | | | Total (cash plus perquisites)[2] | | | | | |
	Average	Highest	Lowest	Average	Highest[3]	Average	Highest	Lowest	Perquisites	Total earnings	Perquisites[1]	Total earnings
	Dolls.	Dolls.	Dolls.	Dolls.	Dolls.	Dolls.	Dolls.	Dolls.	Dolls.	Dolls.	Dolls.	Dolls.
Maine	4.01	8.00	2.00	.71	3.74	4.98	9.83	3.00	1.30	4.97	0.22	5.06
New Hampshire	3.59	5.00	2.00	.44	2.00	4.15	7.00	3.00	1.17	4.80	.11	3.86
Vermont	3.14	4.50	2.00	1.03	2.18	4.12	5.45	3.00	1.32	4.24	-----	3.67
Massachusetts	3.89	5.00	3.00	.21	2.81	4.13	6.81	3.20	2.70	6.44	-----	3.93
Rhode Island	3.63	4.50	3.00	.29	1.34	3.93	5.84	3.20	----	----	.29	3.93
Connecticut	3.68	4.50	2.50	.51	2.33	4.20	5.74	3.24	1.83	5.02	.07	3.93
New York	4.00	12.00	2.00	.93	2.67	4.96	12.00	2.70	1.35	5.19	.11	4.46
New Jersey	4.51	7.00	2.80	.64	2.33	5.22	7.83	3.25	2.33	7.83	.04	4.69
Pennsylvania	3.15	6.00	1.50	.94	3.05	4.16	6.50	2.00	1.25	4.34	.01	3.64
Ohio	3.52	10.00	1.50	.76	3.16	4.45	10.00	1.50	1.19	4.56	.30	4.33
Indiana	3.37	6.50	1.50	.91	2.50	4.38	8.45	2.40	1.20	4.59	.26	4.00
Illinois	3.81	8.00	1.00	1.18	3.16	5.10	9.25	1.90	1.43	5.35	.30	4.16
Michigan	3.28	8.00	1.50	.75	2.35	4.04	8.00	2.50	1.15	3.13	.17	3.77
Wisconsin	2.99	5.00	1.50	1.09	2.50	4.08	6.78	1.75	1.28	4.25	.12	3.25
Minnesota	3.38	7.00	1.50	1.35	3.66	4.73	8.92	2.83	1.49	4.89	.14	3.08
Iowa	4.00	7.00	1.50	1.34	2.99	5.42	8.69	2.00	1.47	5.61	.55	4.26
Missouri	2.55	6.00	1.00	.87	2.39	3.48	6.37	1.08	1.15	3.76	.38	2.99
North Dakota	4.11	11.00	1.50	1.55	2.63	5.58	12.80	1.50	1.61	5.65	-----	3.25
South Dakota	3.64	11.00	1.50	1.52	2.84	5.23	12.25	2.38	1.61	5.32	.10	3.51
Nebraska	3.74	7.20	1.70	1.40	2.78	5.19	9.79	2.75	1.52	5.29	.22	4.14
Kansas	3.74	7.00	1.25	1.44	3.00	5.21	9.00	2.50	1.50	5.27	.10	3.80
Maryland	3.23	5.00	1.75	.67	1.90	4.04	5.99	2.50	1.01	4.09	.18	3.96
Delaware	3.27	4.00	2.50	.46	1.50	3.88	5.00	3.00	1.25	4.50	.06	3.56
Virginia	2.31	4.50	1.00	.63	2.24	2.99	5.25	1.50	1.01	3.81	.19	2.65
West Virginia	2.21	4.00	1.00	.95	2.67	3.25	5.17	2.00	1.23	3.35	.25	2.98
North Carolina	2.01	4.00	1.00	.54	1.72	2.54	5.25	1.00	.88	2.96	.33	2.28
South Carolina	1.60	5.00	1.00	.43	1.75	1.97	3.30	1.00	1.03	2.56	.20	1.73
Georgia	1.58	2.75	.88	.50	2.16	2.09	4.33	.90	1.02	2.70	.31	1.86
Florida	2.55	6.00	.90	.23	1.09	2.66	6.00	1.00	.73	2.67	.14	2.66
Kentucky	2.25	5.00	.75	.61	2.12	2.90	5.00	1.00	.94	3.16	.29	2.64
Tennessee	1.85	3.00	1.00	.39	2.04	2.19	4.54	1.00	.80	2.58	.12	1.92
Alabama	1.67	2.75	.60	.57	2.57	2.26	4.16	1.00	1.18	2.85	.20	1.85
Mississippi	2.02	5.00	1.00	.56	2.08	2.59	5.00	1.00	.93	2.97	.33	2.34
Arkansas	1.88	4.00	.75	.54	3.00	2.41	5.57	.75	1.13	2.92	.20	2.10
Louisiana	1.79	3.00	1.00	.48	1.50	2.33	3.62	1.12	1.04	2.98	.25	2.06
Oklahoma	3.15	6.00	.75	1.07	2.82	4.16	7.00	1.25	1.51	4.98	.27	2.69
Texas	2.45	5.25	1.25	.84	2.25	3.26	6.00	1.25	1.18	3.51	.55	3.08
Montana	3.45	12.00	2.00	1.58	2.90	4.97	7.17	3.29	1.62	4.94	.91	5.43
Idaho	3.32	9.00	2.25	1.29	2.00	4.67	10.00	2.95	1.37	4.46	.50	6.76
Wyoming	2.72	4.00	1.50	1.56	2.19	4.24	5.33	3.00	1.56	4.24	-----	-----
Colorado	3.62	10.00	1.75	1.42	3.50	5.21	11.50	3.42	1.65	5.25	.50	4.93
New Mexico	2.64	5.00	1.50	.81	1.95	3.42	6.17	1.50	1.32	3.95	.22	2.85
Arizona	2.02	2.50	1.50	.79	1.67	3.00	4.00	2.00	1.36	3.40	.31	2.49
Utah	3.31	5.50	2.00	.72	2.33	4.09	6.83	2.00	1.42	4.67	.17	3.65
Nevada	3.00	3.50	2.50	1.58	1.58	4.58	4.58	4.58	1.58	4.58	-----	-----
Washington	3.69	12.00	2.00	1.07	2.42	4.85	13.35	2.85	1.35	4.95	.35	4.41
Oregon	2.98	4.50	2.00	1.06	2.50	3.95	5.58	2.50	1.36	4.21	.11	3.19
California	3.86	12.00	2.00	.70	2.49	4.56	12.00	3.00	1.47	5.01	.22	4.28
New England	3.74	8.00	2.00	.61	3.74	4.44	9.83	3.00	1.37	4.74	.12	4.26
Middle Atlantic	3.57	12.00	1.50	.93	3.05	4.60	12.00	2.00	1.31	4.78	.07	4.16
East North Central	3.47	10.00	1.00	.98	3.16	4.54	10.00	1.50	1.29	4.75	.26	4.05
West North Central	3.57	11.00	1.00	1.32	3.66	4.95	12.80	1.08	1.48	5.16	.35	3.48
South Atlantic	2.17	6.00	.88	.59	2.67	2.76	6.00	.90	1.03	3.24	.25	2.38
East South Central	1.96	5.00	.60	.54	2.57	2.50	5.00	1.00	.97	2.92	.23	2.17
West South Central	2.43	6.00	.75	.76	3.00	3.13	7.00	.75	1.29	3.19	.31	2.46
Mountain	3.29	12.00	1.50	1.30	2.50	4.60	11.50	1.50	1.55	4.74	.34	4.02
Pacific	3.66	12.00	2.00	.88	2.50	4.53	13.35	2.50	1.40	4.78	.23	4.19
United States	3.18	12.00	.60	.97	3.74	4.20	13.35	.75	1.35	4.66	.24	3.27

Bureau of Agricultural Economics. The data above are calculated from the reports of over 5,300 voluntary correspondents of the Department of Agriculture.

[1] Farm values.
[2] The total values of wages and perquisites here given are not the sums of average wages and of perquisite values as reported to the left. Many of the correspondents' reports were incomplete, some as to wages, some as to perquisites. Their data were included in the separate respective tabulations of cash wages and of perquisites if complete in the one, even though not in the other. The reports used in calculating total earnings were complete in both respects, permitting totaling their values for tabulation.
[3] The lowest values are of course zero, as some laborers get no perquisites.

TABLE 535.—*Percentages of total remuneration of noncasual hired farm laborers formed by certain perquisites and by wages, by geographic divisions, 1925*

Geographic divisions	Board (board, room, washing)	Shelter (house rent, fuel, electricity)	Dairy and poultry products (milk, butter, eggs, chickens for meat)	Meats or meat products (pork, lard, beef, other meats, etc.)	Flour (wheat, corn meal)	Vegetables and fruit (mostly potatoes and apples)	Miscellaneous food	For livestock allowed kept by laborers (chickens, cows, pigs, horses, or mules)		Use of employers'—		Miscellaneous perquisites	Wages
								Feed	Pasture or range	Horses or mules	Tools or vehicles		
	P. ct.	*P. ct.*	*P. ct.*	*P. ct.*	*P. ct.*	*P. ct.*	*P. ct.*	*P. ct.*	*P. ct.*	*P. ct.*	*P. ct.*	*P. ct.*	*P. ct.*
New England	14.3	5.9	2.4	0.1	0.1	1.2		0.4	0.1	1.6	1.9	0.4	71.6
Middle Atlantic	19.5	7.0	2.5	.4	.1	1.9	0.1	1.0	.3	1.3	1.6	1.7	62.6
East North Central	19.8	6.2	4.3	1.5		1.2	.1	3.1	.9	1.3	1.9	.9	58.8
West North Central	26.3	3.9	2.3	.4		.5		1.5	.7	1.2	2.0	1.0	60.2
South Atlantic	14.2	9.6	2.3	1.3	1.0	1.6	.3	2.7	2.5	3.5	4.2	1.9	54.9
East South Central	13.8	7.3	2.5	1.2	.5	1.2	.3	3.2	3.8	4.8	4.1	1.6	55.7
West South Central	17.8	6.8	2.3	.3	.1	.7	.4	2.8	2.2	3.9	4.8	1.4	56.5
Mountain	26.6	3.2	1.4	.1		.4	.1	1.2	.4	1.7	2.7	.8	61.4
Pacific	19.0	5.2	1.1	.1		.3		.4	.4	.9	1.5	2.5	68.6
United States	20.7	5.8	2.7	.8	.1	1.0	.1	2.0	1.0	1.8	2.3	1.2	60.5

Bureau of Agricultural Economics. Compiled from reports of over 3,500 voluntary correspondents of the Department of Agriculture.

TABLE 536.—*Percentages of total remuneration of casual hired farm laborers formed by certain perquisites and by wages, by geographic divisions, 1926*

Geographic division	Lodging		Fuel	Light	Washing	Food			Transportation to and from work	Other use of farm horses and vehicles	Miscellaneous	Wages
	Unfurnished	Furnished				Produced on the farm	Not produced on the farm	Board				
	P. ct.	*P. ct.*	*P. ct.*	*P. ct.*	*P. ct.*	*P. ct.*	*P. ct.*	*P. ct.*	*P. ct.*	*P. ct.*	*P. ct.*	*P. ct.*
New England	0.4	2.5	0.6	0.2	0.4	0.5	0.1	8.3	0.2	0.5	0.2	86.1
Middle Atlantic	.6	3.4	.4	.2	.6	.5	(1)	13.6	.2	.3	.4	79.8
East North Central	.8	4.6	.4	.2	.6	.7	(1)	13.4	.2	.4	.2	78.5
West North Central	1.0	6.3	.4	.3	.8	.4	.2	16.6	.3	.6	.1	73.0
South Atlantic	2.7	2.3	1.4	.1	.2	1.3	.1	11.0	1.0	1.0	(1)	78.9
East South Central	2.6	2.8	1.4	.2	.3	1.4	.2	9.2	1.7	1.9	.2	78.1
West South Central	2.9	4.1	1.1	.1	.5	1.0	.1	11.9	1.0	1.2	.2	75.6
Mountain	1.2	6.0	1.1	.3	.4	.4	(1)	17.5	.5	.7	.2	71.7
Pacific	1.9	2.8	.8	.2	.1	.4	.1	12.3	.3	.4	.1	80.6
United States	1.3	4.7	.6	.2	.6	.6	.1	14.1	.4	.6	.2	76.6

Bureau of Agricultural Economics. Compiled from reports of over 5,300 voluntary correspondents of the U. S. Department of Agriculture.

1 Less than 0.1 per cent.

TABLE 537.—Number of farms per 1,000 changing ownership by various methods, by States and geographic divisions, 12 months ended March 15, 1926–1928

Geographic division and State	Voluntary sales and trades[1]			Delinquent taxes			Foreclosure of mortgage, bankruptcy, etc.[2]			Total			Inheritance and gift			Administrators' and executors' sales[3]		Miscellaneous and unclassified			Total all classes — Excluding administrators' and executors' sales			Total all classes — Including administrators' and executors' sales	
	1926	1927	1928	1926	1927	1928	1926	1927	1928	1926	1927	1928	1926	1927	1928	1927	1928	1926	1927	1928	1926	1927	1928	1927	1928
United States	29.6	28.3	26.3	4.2	5.1	5.2	17.4	18.2	17.6	21.6	23.3	22.8	8.0	8.8	8.8	7.0	6.7	2.2	1.1	1.3	61.4	61.5	59.3	68.5	66.0
New England	34.0	32.4	34.9	4.5	3.8	3.0	9.3	8.6	7.7	13.8	12.4	10.7	8.4	9.0	10.4	7.5	7.1	1.9	.7	1.0	58.1	55.4	57.0	62.9	64.1
Middle Atlantic	35.4	37.0	33.7	3.0	3.0	3.4	8.8	8.8	8.4	11.8	11.8	11.8	8.3	8.8	8.6	8.7	8.2	2.5	1.5	1.8	58.0	59.1	55.5	67.8	64.1
East North Central	25.8	25.8	24.0	3.8	3.7	4.2	15.1	16.7	16.5	18.9	20.4	20.7	8.5	9.8	9.7	8.2	8.3	1.4	1.4	1.1	55.2	57.4	55.6	66.5	63.9
West North Central	23.0	24.3	24.3	4.3	4.7	5.1	26.5	27.3	27.3	30.8	32.0	32.4	8.0	8.1	8.4	6.5	6.5	2.5	1.3	1.5	64.3	65.7	66.2	72.2	72.7
South Atlantic	28.0	24.2	20.0	5.5	6.9	5.4	14.0	14.1	17.9	19.5	21.0	23.3	9.7	10.2	10.6	7.7	7.9	1.8	.9	1.1	59.1	56.3	55.0	64.0	62.9
East South Central	33.5	29.3	27.5	4.0	6.0	5.4	17.1	15.7	14.6	21.1	21.7	20.0	8.1	9.8	9.2	7.5	6.6	1.8	.8	1.1	59.8	61.1	58.6	68.6	64.4
West South Central	34.7	31.1	27.9	3.8	3.8	4.7	14.9	16.1	14.8	18.7	19.9	19.5	6.7	7.8	7.8	4.4	4.2	2.2	.7	1.2	62.3	59.5	55.4	63.9	59.6
Mountain	32.0	33.7	34.8	9.4	8.0	12.0	40.8	37.3	27.4	50.2	45.3	39.4	6.7	7.0	5.6	4.4	3.7	3.5	2.3	1.9	90.7	87.1	81.7	91.5	85.4
Pacific	35.6	36.3	34.3	3.3	4.5	4.2	17.3	15.6	14.8	20.6	20.1	19.0	6.2	6.9	7.1	4.0	4.4	3.3	1.4	1.4	65.7	64.7	62.7	68.7	67.1
New England:																									
Maine	31.7	32.8	33.2	6.7	6.0	5.2	11.1	10.5	8.8	17.8	16.5	14.0	8.3	11.8	11.5	6.5	5.7	2.5	.6	1.0	60.3	61.7	59.7	68.2	65.4
New Hampshire	34.4	33.5	37.8	6.1	5.0	5.1	6.9	8.8	9.0	13.0	13.8	14.1	7.4	8.4	7.9	6.0	5.0	1.9	.4	.5	56.7	56.1	60.3	62.1	65.3
Vermont	46.3	42.6	40.6	1.3	1.7	1.2	11.9	10.8	8.8	13.2	12.5	10.0	8.8	10.3	10.9	9.8	10.2	1.6	1.1	1.5	69.9	66.5	63.0	76.3	73.2
Massachusetts	28.0	28.0	35.0	2.1	1.4	1.3	5.7	4.4	5.7	7.8	5.8	7.0	8.6	10.4	9.5	8.0	6.0	1.4	.3	1.0	45.8	44.5	52.5	52.5	58.5
Rhode Island	39.6	35.0	30.0	6.9	4.0	1.2	9.3	6.5	2.5	16.2	10.5	3.7	9.9	9.0	8.9	8.0	5.0	4.2	0	.8	69.8	54.5	43.1	62.5	48.1
Connecticut	27.1	23.9	29.7	6.5	3.0	1.0	8.6	3.0	3.0	15.1	6.0	4.0	8.2	9.0	11.0	9.1	10.5	1.0	1.5	.8	51.4	43.4	45.5	52.5	56.0
Middle Atlantic:																									
New York	33.4	37.5	35.6	4.1	3.9	5.2	10.8	12.7	12.2	14.9	16.6	17.4	8.7	10.4	9.2	8.0	7.5	2.7	1.8	1.9	59.7	66.3	64.1	74.3	71.6
New Jersey	59.4	54.4	44.4	2.8	3.4	4.0	7.8	6.0	6.9	10.6	9.4	10.9	7.5	8.0	7.2	6.8	9.3	.6	.6	.9	78.1	71.2	63.4	78.0	72.7
Pennsylvania	33.7	34.0	30.2	1.9	2.1	1.7	7.0	5.6	5.5	8.9	7.7	7.2	8.0	7.6	8.2	9.6	8.6	2.5	1.3	1.9	53.1	50.6	47.5	60.2	56.1
East North Central:																									
Ohio	29.8	30.8	27.3	1.6	2.1	1.8	11.2	11.5	11.4	12.8	13.6	13.2	8.1	8.1	9.1	9.7	9.2	2.3	1.2	1.2	53.0	54.6	50.6	64.3	59.8
Indiana	26.8	25.8	23.6	4.2	4.2	6.3	14.0	16.9	16.8	18.2	18.9	23.0	9.0	10.5	9.9	10.5	9.5	2.3	1.4	1.4	56.2	59.6	57.9	70.1	67.7
Illinois	20.8	21.7	20.0	1.4	1.8	3.5	15.7	16.8	17.0	17.1	18.6	20.5	10.5	12.4	12.7	11.0	9.5	1.2	1.1	1.0	51.1	54.1	54.7	65.1	64.2
Michigan	22.3	30.5	30.5	4.6	4.6	7.0	16.6	16.7	18.8	21.2	21.3	25.8	8.9	6.9	10.0	7.9	6.4	1.7	1.2	1.2	62.6	66.1	67.0	74.6	73.9
Wisconsin	18.9	19.8	18.2	4.8	4.0	3.7	22.4	20.5	19.0	27.2	24.5	22.7	5.7	6.9	6.2	5.8	5.4	2.7	2.0	1.8	54.5	53.2	48.9	59.0	54.3

	1	2	3	4	5	6	7	8	9	10	11	12	13	14	15	16	17	18	19	20	21	22	23	24	25
West North Central:																									
Minnesota	18.0	18.5	18.4	3.8	4.5	5.5	26.8	24.7	26.8	30.6	29.2	31.9	6.7	6.7	6.3	5.3	4.3	2.6	1.7	1.5	57.9	56.1	58.1	61.4	62.4
Iowa	15.5	18.7	17.2	2.6	2.5	2.3	26.4	27.3	28.1	29.5	29.8	30.4	7.7	8.5	7.4	7.0	7.8	2.1	1.1	1.4	54.7	58.2	57.6	65.2	65.2
Missouri	29.9	23.9	27.2	2.4	3.7	3.7	21.4	24.1	24.1	28.1	28.7	30.4	8.5	10.6	8.6	7.0	7.2	3.1	1.1	1.8	66.2	67.2	67.6	67.6	73.7
North Dakota	23.7	23.9	28.6	12.7	18.1	16.5	46.3	43.0	51.1	59.0	61.1	57.9	8.7	13.3	8.1	8.1	6.2	2.2	1.3	0.8	91.8	93.0	93.3	97.6	98.5
South Dakota	16.7	20.8	26.9	13.6	15.0	11.1	52.5	51.1	52.9	66.1	66.1	55.9	8.0	11.9	8.0	7.8	9.2	1.6	1.4	1.5	93.0	96.2	94.4	101.7	99.6
Nebraska	23.4	26.2	26.4	2.2	3.6	3.4	21.9	25.0	24.9	24.1	28.5	28.3	7.3	8.0	8.4	9.0	6.8	2.6	1.4	1.0	57.4	57.4	57.6	71.9	74.3
Kansas	29.7	29.6	27.3	3.0	2.9	3.6	15.8	16.0	15.8	18.8	18.9	23.0	8.3	8.1	8.1	7.2	6.5	2.5	1.2	1.2	59.3	60.6	65.1	67.1	67.1
South Atlantic:																									
Delaware	22.7	20.9	17.9	2.5	2.0	2.0	10.3	10.0	8.2	8.0	12.5	10.0	9.5	9.5	9.6	7.7	7.8	0	0.9	0.9	43.0	43.4	38.8	53.4	48.1
Maryland	32.3	30.0	28.5	4.7	3.8	3.6	12.2	13.6	13.4	14.2	17.2	17.4	9.4	9.4	8.1	7.7	7.8	1.4	0.6	0.8	55.7	57.2	54.8	66.4	62.6
Virginia	23.2	19.3	17.3	3.2	2.6	2.5	13.8	11.8	12.0	17.0	14.3	14.6	10.2	11.1	11.0	7.2	7.2	2.2	0.3	1.0	52.8	44.1	43.9	50.9	51.1
West Virginia	30.1	28.2	22.5	7.0	10.2	9.4	8.4	11.5	7.6	7.6	17.8	17.8	13.2	11.1	13.0	8.8	8.8	2.3	1.1	1.1	58.2	60.8	67.6	67.6	59.4
North Carolina	25.0	21.3	19.1	5.9	8.6	8.6	8.7	11.5	14.0	14.6	20.1	22.4	10.1	11.1	10.1	8.9	9.2	2.3	0.4	1.0	50.7	54.1	52.7	62.9	61.5
South Carolina	18.0	14.1	14.1	5.2	8.6	8.1	21.5	22.6	27.6	26.7	30.7	36.2	11.5	11.7	11.9	9.2	9.2	2.0	1.0	1.0	57.4	53.8	62.8	60.8	72.0
Georgia	25.3	24.0	21.7	6.6	8.2	8.2	22.3	19.3	23.7	28.9	27.9	29.7	10.7	10.7	11.9	9.9	9.9	2.5	0.8	1.5	67.7	63.4	64.4	72.4	74.3
Florida	81.0	63.5	31.7	7.2	6.6	11.7	8.9	8.5	12.4	16.1	15.1	24.1	4.3	4.3	4.2	2.7	3.0	2.5	0	0	101.7	83.4	60.6	86.4	62.7
East South Central:																									
Kentucky	35.3	31.0	30.5	7.5	5.0	5.7	12.2	16.1	17.2	17.2	24.1	24.1	9.3	9.5	8.4	7.7	7.7	2.1	1.0	1.2	63.0	65.3	72.9	72.9	73.0
Tennessee	29.1	25.3	21.3	4.5	2.0	2.7	13.5	13.5	13.6	16.0	19.8	24.1	9.4	9.4	8.7	7.7	7.7	1.9	0.8	1.1	55.9	49.0	63.0	63.0	56.0
Alabama	35.5	30.3	27.8	1.5	8.2	1.8	11.2	14.2	13.5	13.0	15.7	14.3	9.3	9.9	8.0	5.9	5.0	1.0	0.3	0.9	56.6	52.1	55.5	62.1	58.0
Mississippi	34.6	30.9	31.7	8.3	7.1	10.4	15.9	18.7	12.9	20.0	24.2	24.2	9.3	10.7	8.7	2.7	7.4	2.2	0	0.9	64.8	70.2	72.6	77.6	70.3
West South Central:																									
Arkansas	42.6	38.2	45.5	2.9	3.0	5.8	17.8	19.9	15.1	20.7	22.9	20.9	7.4	7.4	8.1	3.6	5.0	2.8	0.6	1.4	73.1	64.7	69.1	72.6	68.3
Louisiana	31.7	29.4	34.5	5.3	4.8	17.5	17.5	16.1	18.4	22.8	22.0	23.7	9.1	9.1	9.5	8.8	9.3	3.4	0.9	1.5	66.1	64.7	69.3	69.3	73.5
Oklahoma	33.7	29.4	38.4	6.6	8.8	24.1	24.1	24.2	21.6	32.4	32.4	36.2	10.7	10.6	4.5	4.1	4.5	3.9	0.9	1.3	71.8	60.2	71.9	71.9	65.1
Texas	32.4	29.4	26.3	1.6	2.0	1.4	8.9	10.5	9.5	10.9	12.3	12.3	8.7	8.7	6.5	3.0	3.8	2.0	0.6	1.0	51.8	51.0	54.8	54.8	49.5
Mountain:																									
Montana	30.1	35.2	45.2	10.1	13.0	15.5	60.8	56.0	40.9	70.9	69.0	56.4	5.7	5.1	4.7	5.0	5.2	2.8	2.5	2.0	108.5	112.4	109.0	117.6	114.0
Idaho	27.7	26.5	34.5	7.8	5.6	14.5	39.6	32.6	28.3	47.4	60.7	43.0	7.0	7.0	5.6	3.5	4.3	3.4	2.3	2.3	83.3	74.6	86.8	77.8	91.7
Wyoming	28.2	38.4	38.4	14.5	6.4	12.9	25.6	25.0	19.3	42.4	39.3	38.1	6.8	6.0	5.8	4.5	4.3	3.9	1.8	1.9	80.5	78.5	84.8	82.0	82.0
Colorado	33.9	35.7	30.0	13.7	5.9	12.0	43.3	36.3	26.1	57.0	46.5	38.1	6.8	6.6	6.8	5.6	5.3	6.4	1.6	1.6	100.6	95.0	76.0	78.8	78.8
New Mexico	49.2	30.0	33.9	10.2	5.4	12.0	30.3	30.3	30.6	37.8	39.5	26.0	6.8	5.8	4.6	3.9	4.6	4.1	2.2	1.3	98.0	95.3	99.2	71.6	71.6
Arizona	26.9	39.3	35.9	4.5	8.8	5.4	48.1	40.3	38.7	53.9	45.8	43.8	5.8	5.8	3.9	4.0	4.5	5.1	3.2	2.4	90.5	89.9	88.6	92.3	92.3
Utah	20.8	23.0	23.0	10.9	5.0	5.1	30.9	30.9	18.3	23.4	25.6	19.7	3.5	3.5	4.9	3.0	3.0	3.7	1.0	0.7	52.4	56.0	58.0	58.0	59.1
Nevada	20.8	23.8	26.3	0	2.0	1.4	30.9	24.6	18.3	30.9	26.6	19.7	3.5	3.5	4.1	3.0	3.0	3.7	1.7	0.8	59.5	48.3	57.9	57.7	52.3
Pacific:																									
Washington	34.8	35.7	35.5	7.5	8.7	7.0	21.0	20.3	15.3	28.5	29.0	23.3	7.0	7.4	6.4	4.2	3.8	2.5	1.5	1.6	72.2	67.4	73.6	77.8	71.2
Oregon	29.7	34.1	37.4	3.5	5.2	7.1	17.2	16.0	17.9	20.7	21.2	23.9	7.9	7.9	6.5	4.6	5.3	3.0	1.8	1.8	59.9	64.5	70.5	70.5	76.1
California	38.5	34.5	35.1	2.1	2.0	1.5	14.2	13.0	15.0	30.9	15.0	23.0	6.3	6.3	5.9	3.3	3.2	3.9	1.2	1.4	64.6	57.1	57.1	61.3	61.3

Bureau of Agricultural Economics. Based upon returns from crop reporters. Revised figures. Supersedes Table 513, 1927 Yearbook. The farm bankruptcy statistics included with Table 513 of the 1927 Yearbook appear separately as Table 539.

[1] Including contracts to purchase (but not options)
[2] Including loss of title by default of contract, sales to avoid foreclosure, and surrender of title or other transfers to avoid foreclosure.
[3] Including all other sales in settlement of estates.

TABLE 538.—*Farm real estate: Index numbers of estimated value per acre, by geographic divisions and States, 1912–1928* [1]

[1912–1914=100 per cent]

Geographic division and State	1912	1913	1914	1915	1916	1917	1918	1919	1920	1921	1922	1923	1924	1925	1926	1927	1928
United States	97	100	103	103	108	117	129	140	170	157	139	135	130	127	124	119	117
Geographic divisions:																	
New England	99	101	100	99	102	112	117	123	140	135	134	130	128	127	128	127	127
Middle Atlantic	98	100	102	100	104	112	117	121	136	127	118	116	114	114	113	111	110
East North Central	97	100	103	103	110	116	127	135	161	151	132	128	121	116	111	104	101
West North Central	97	100	103	105	114	122	134	147	184	174	150	142	132	126	121	115	113
South Atlantic	98	100	103	98	108	119	135	161	198	174	146	152	151	148	149	137	134
East South Central	97	100	103	99	109	120	140	162	199	163	149	149	142	141	139	133	130
West South Central	96	100	104	100	103	116	134	143	177	159	136	132	136	144	144	139	137
Mountain	98	102	100	98	98	106	117	130	151	133	122	115	110	105	103	101	101
Pacific	94	99	106	107	111	122	129	134	156	155	151	148	147	146	144	143	142
New England:																	
Maine	100	102	98	96	98	110	115	124	142	132	127	129	127	124	126	124	124
New Hampshire	97	101	102	101	98	103	111	116	129	123	126	111	109	111	113	112	112
Vermont	101	101	98	104	115	127	133	136	150	150	145	134	130	125	126	125	123
Massachusetts	98	100	102	98	100	110	114	119	140	134	134	132	131	132	134	131	131
Rhode Island	100	101	100	102	106	112	118	123	130	130	127	124	126	128	130	133	134
Connecticut	98	100	102	100	102	110	116	121	137	134	140	137	140	137	137	138	139
Middle Atlantic:																	
New York	98	100	102	100	103	109	115	118	133	123	116	115	112	111	109	108	106
New Jersey	98	100	102	100	102	111	115	119	130	130	121	115	120	124	129	128	127
Pennsylvania	98	100	102	100	105	114	119	124	140	131	120	118	116	114	114	112	111
East North Central:																	
Ohio	98	100	102	107	113	119	131	135	159	134	124	122	118	110	105	99	96
Indiana	98	100	102	101	110	116	128	135	161	147	119	115	108	102	95	87	84
Illinois	97	100	103	102	105	111	119	130	160	153	126	123	116	115	109	99	96
Michigan	98	99	103	105	111	120	134	137	154	152	148	145	138	133	129	127	125
Wisconsin	97	100	103	104	117	124	133	143	171	168	154	147	139	130	125	122	120
West North Central:																	
Minnesota	95	100	105	107	122	138	155	167	213	212	187	177	170	159	155	145	140
Iowa	96	99	104	112	128	134	145	160	213	197	162	156	143	136	130	121	117
Missouri	97	100	103	102	108	115	125	137	167	156	133	127	117	112	104	99	96
North Dakota	97	100	103	103	112	118	124	130	145	141	136	128	114	109	105	100	99
South Dakota	96	101	103	101	108	116	126	145	181	173	146	126	117	115	107	97	96
Nebraska	98	100	102	101	104	110	127	145	179	166	144	139	128	123	123	119	117
Kansas	101	99	99	103	109	115	122	132	151	149	130	127	118	115	113	113	113
South Atlantic:																	
Delaware	100	101	99	100	105	115	124	129	139	129	119	119	107	112	114	111	111
Maryland	97	100	103	104	109	118	129	136	166	146	141	136	133	131	130	126	124
Virginia	97	100	103	97	117	125	142	167	189	180	157	170	162	154	148	138	137
West Virginia	97	100	103	101	104	112	122	135	154	141	125	127	125	120	116	110	109
North Carolina	97	99	104	102	114	130	152	176	223	196	166	195	192	187	185	178	174
South Carolina	101	98	101	94	98	107	122	162	230	186	126	128	136	138	128	113	110
Georgia	98	101	101	94	105	116	131	172	217	172	136	125	123	116	112	104	102
Florida	96	99	105	97	103	109	126	143	178	176	157	155	163	172	223	183	176
East South Central:																	
Kentucky	97	100	103	100	111	127	146	170	200	172	151	147	141	140	139	134	130
Tennessee	96	100	104	100	110	121	145	168	200	169	154	158	148	137	134	130	127
Alabama	98	98	103	98	98	103	128	143	177	147	135	143	144	154	154	145	145
Mississippi	97	102	102	97	111	121	131	155	218	150	148	143	134	136	134	126	123
West South Central:																	
Arkansas	98	101	101	95	109	129	149	169	222	186	174	170	160	160	153	150	147
Louisiana	99	102	99	95	106	112	143	157	198	163	140	144	137	141	143	135	132
Oklahoma	98	101	101	95	104	114	130	140	166	160	139	133	125	131	130	128	127
Texas	95	100	105	103	103	115	133	141	174	156	133	128	137	146	146	141	139
Mountain:																	
Montana	97	100	103	100	94	100	106	114	126	105	96	87	81	75	72	70	71
Idaho	100	101	99	96	99	114	130	146	172	162	136	133	129	123	119	117	116
Wyoming	97	103	100	103	94	97	121	147	176	146	131	121	112	100	95	94	95
Colorado	98	103	98	93	102	107	110	118	141	132	123	113	98	92	89	82	82
New Mexico	100	104	96	100	96	111	118	127	144	125	115	110	110	108	106	108	108
Arizona	95	100	105	97	95	105	125	140	165	148	135	124	128	121	125	123	122
Utah	100	102	98	98	104	117	122	144	167	137	133	133	131	130	129	128	127
Nevada	96	100	103	102	99	96	103	117	135	123	119	112	108	102	99	99	99
Pacific:																	
Washington	98	100	103	100	102	112	118	122	140	132	124	117	115	113	112	111	110
Oregon	97	100	103	99	100	104	112	118	130	130	122	115	113	110	107	106	106
California	93	99	108	111	116	130	136	142	167	168	166	165	164	164	163	162	161

Bureau of Agricultural Economics. Based on values as reported by crop reporters. Values as reported by the census for 1910, 1920, and 1925 will be found in Table 511 of the 1927 Yearbook.

[1] All farm land with improvements, as of Mar. 1. Corrections for certain years have been made in earlier figures published for Wisconsin and Georgia, the East North Central, South Atlantic and East South Central divisions, and the United States. Owing to rounding of figures, 1912–1914 will not always equal exactly 100 per cent.

NOTE.—A table similar to Table 511, 1927 Yearbook, census figures on value of farm lands and buildings, is omitted.

TABLE 539.—*Bankruptcies among farmers and per cent the farmer cases are of all bankruptcies, years ended June 30, 1924-1928*

Geographic division and State	1924 Total	1924 Farmers Number	1924 Farmers Per cent of all cases	1925 Total	1925 Farmers Number	1925 Farmers Per cent of all cases	1926 Total	1926 Farmers Number	1926 Farmers Per cent of all cases	1927 Total	1927 Farmers Number	1927 Farmers Per cent of all cases	1928 Total	1928 Farmers Number	1928 Farmers Per cent of all cases
United States	41,524	7,772	18.7	44,236	7,872	17.8	47,049	7,769	16.5	48,066	6,296	13.1	53,444	5,679	10.6
New England	3,394	196	5.8	3,272	169	5.2	3,165	145	4.6	3,412	105	3.1	4,666	162	3.5
Maine	904	136	15.0	871	103	11.8	853	101	11.8	810	51	6.3	837	77	9.2
New Hampshire	130	6	4.6	86	5	5.8	108	7	6.5	105	7	6.7	110	7	6.4
Vermont	101	27	26.7	205	39	19.0	197	17	8.6	125	21	16.8	195	29	14.9
Massachusetts	1,476	11	.7	1,378	7	.5	1,438	12	.8	1,646	10	.6	2,468	18	.7
Rhode Island	123	1	.8	132	2	1.5	111	0	0	195	2	1.0	208	0	0
Connecticut	660	15	2.3	600	13	2.2	458	8	1.7	531	14	2.6	848	31	3.7
Middle Atlantic	5,386	171	3.2	7,348	190	2.6	6,508	224	3.4	7,189	224	3.1	7,878	274	3.5
New York	3,633	105	2.9	5,376	104	1.9	4,410	122	2.8	4,758	145	3.0	5,548	152	2.7
New Jersey	535	14	2.6	719	16	2.2	802	33	4.1	846	16	1.9	576	12	2.1
Pennsylvania	1,218	52	4.3	1,253	70	5.6	1,296	69	5.3	1,585	63	4.0	1,754	110	6.3
East North Central	5,585	684	12.2	5,692	760	13.4	7,470	844	11.3	7,842	719	9.2	9,354	874	9.3
Ohio	1,531	209	13.7	1,813	214	11.8	2,171	188	8.7	2,396	137	5.7	2,802	157	5.6
Indiana	403	101	25.1	360	97	26.9	471	112	23.8	413	76	18.4	547	114	20.9
Illinois	1,923	194	10.1	1,596	190	11.9	2,590	234	9.0	2,943	257	8.7	3,143	374	11.9
Michigan	814	44	5.4	868	46	5.3	930	50	5.4	818	34	4.2	1,192	41	3.4
Wisconsin	914	136	14.9	1,055	213	20.2	1,308	260	19.9	1,272	215	16.9	1,670	188	11.3
West North Central	6,547	2,785	42.5	7,363	2,889	39.2	7,953	2,813	35.4	7,944	2,404	30.3	7,149	1,729	24.2
Minnesota	1,452	430	29.6	1,586	369	23.3	1,962	419	21.4	1,840	294	16.0	2,104	266	12.6
Iowa	1,317	663	50.3	1,707	861	50.4	1,759	791	45.0	1,593	656	41.2	1,297	534	41.2
Missouri	1,106	238	21.5	1,482	287	19.4	1,530	301	19.7	1,614	314	19.5	1,741	288	16.5
North Dakota	1,047	782	74.7	837	629	75.1	773	536	69.3	567	376	66.3	258	153	59.3
South Dakota	373	236	63.3	556	352	63.3	623	368	59.1	626	352	56.2	478	239	50.0
Nebraska	515	172	33.4	525	178	33.9	658	238	36.2	689	181	26.3	578	135	23.4
Kansas	737	264	35.8	670	213	31.8	648	160	24.7	1,015	231	22.8	693	114	16.5
South Atlantic	6,426	1085	16.9	5,884	1037	17.6	5,889	747	12.7	5,874	585	10.0	6,895	685	9.9
Delaware	46	6	13.0	40	8	20.0	44	5	11.4	30	4	13.3	35	10	28.6
Maryland	307	42	13.7	175	38	21.7	315	54	17.1	267	35	13.1	317	49	15.5
District of Columbia	72	0	.0	83	0	.0	112	0	.0	131	0	.0	147	1	.7
Virginia	1,167	84	7.2	1,407	95	6.8	1,689	111	6.6	1,844	97	5.3	1,976	109	5.5
West Virginia	348	11	3.2	414	19	4.6	482	10	2.1	657	16	2.4	794	25	3.1
North Carolina	319	36	11.3	308	45	14.6	319	37	11.6	389	50	12.9	377	38	10.1
South Carolina	416	36	8.7	230	26	11.3	275	53	19.3	280	47	16.8	289	46	15.9
Georgia	3,386	843	25.0	3,041	798	26.2	2,502	467	18.7	1,973	327	16.6	2,380	394	16.6
Florida	365	22	6.0	186	8	4.3	151	10	6.6	303	9	3.0	580	13	2.2
East South Central	4,981	483	9.7	5,316	517	9.7	6,119	579	9.5	6,364	615	9.7	7,562	521	6.9
Kentucky	605	104	17.2	682	108	15.8	1,027	117	11.4	1,209	164	13.6	1,748	191	10.9
Tennessee	1,669	112	6.7	1,844	109	5.9	2,052	134	6.5	2,132	101	4.7	2,376	102	4.3
Alabama	2,125	218	10.3	2,248	242	10.8	2,670	295	11.0	2,600	318	12.2	2,622	211	8.0
Mississippi	582	49	8.4	542	58	10.7	370	33	8.9	423	32	7.6	816	17	2.1
West South Central	3,527	788	22.3	2,750	650	23.6	2,979	764	25.6	2,741	567	20.7	2,870	561	19.5
Arkansas	560	104	18.6	338	85	25.1	448	101	22.5	416	94	22.6	379	89	23.5
Louisiana	488	171	35.0	362	77	21.3	473	159	33.6	471	119	25.3	481	93	19.3
Oklahoma	956	138	14.4	921	145	15.7	844	170	20.1	782	145	18.5	820	108	13.2
Texas	1,523	375	24.6	1,129	343	30.4	1,214	334	27.5	1,072	209	19.5	1,190	271	22.8
Mountain	2,245	1040	46.3	2,563	1071	41.8	2,677	1142	42.7	1,915	609	31.8	1,747	420	24.0
Montana	855	551	64.4	703	460	65.4	1,052	624	59.3	536	245	45.7	346	126	36.4
Idaho	414	231	55.8	468	260	55.6	433	223	51.5	337	161	47.8	284	101	35.6
Wyoming	102	36	35.3	143	48	33.6	117	38	32.5	114	31	27.2	148	44	29.7
Colorado	341	128	37.5	686	220	32.1	479	143	29.9	400	90	22.5	387	63	16.3
New Mexico	144	28	19.4	95	27	28.4	141	50	35.5	67	22	32.8	98	27	27.6
Arizona	82	31	37.8	62	19	30.6	84	29	34.5	114	30	26.3	86	23	26.7
Utah	302	35	11.6	382	32	8.4	358	33	9.2	325	26	8.0	380	34	8.9
Nevada	5	0	.0	24	2	8.3	13	2	15.4	22	4	18.2	18	2	11.1
Pacific	3,433	540	15.7	4,048	589	14.6	4,289	511	11.9	4,785	468	10.0	5,323	453	8.5
Washington	874	213	24.4	824	196	23.8	951	182	19.1	1,097	160	14.6	1,143	144	12.6
Oregon	799	91	11.4	928	100	10.8	1,085	109	10.0	1,044	72	6.9	1,213	67	5.5
California	1,760	236	13.4	2,296	293	12.8	2,253	220	9.8	2,644	236	8.9	2,967	242	8.2

Bureau of Agricultural Economics. Compiled from annual reports of the Attorney General.

TABLE 540.—*Farms and farm land, 1920 and 1925*

State and division	Number of farms			Land in farms					
				Acreage			Acres per farm		
	1920	1925	Change	1920	1925	Change	1920	1925	Change
			Per cent			*Per cent*			*Per cent*
Maine	48,227	50,033	+3.7	5,425,968	5,161,428	-4.9	112	103	-8.0
New Hampshire	20,523	21,065	+2.6	2,603,806	2,262,064	-13.1	127	107	-15.7
Vermont	29,075	27,786	-4.4	4,235,811	3,925,683	-7.3	146	141	-3.4
Massachusetts	32,001	33,454	+4.5	2,494,477	2,367,629	-5.1	78	71	-9.0
Rhode Island	4,083	3,911	-4.2	331,600	309,013	-6.8	81	79	-2.5
Connecticut	22,655	23,240	+2.6	1,898,980	1,832,110	-3.5	84	79	-6.0
New England	156,564	159,489	+1.9	16,990,642	15,857,927	-6.7	109	99	-9.2
New York	193,195	188,754	-2.3	20,632,803	19,269,926	-6.6	107	102	-4.7
New Jersey	29,702	29,671	-.1	2,282,585	1,924,545	-15.7	77	65	-15.6
Pennsylvania	202,250	200,443	-.9	17,657,513	16,296,468	-7.7	87	81	-6.9
Middle Atlantic	425,147	418,868	-1.5	40,572,901	37,490,939	-7.6	95	90	-5.3
Ohio	256,695	244,703	-4.7	23,515,888	22,219,248	-5.5	92	91	-1.1
Indiana	205,126	195,786	-4.6	21,063,332	19,915,120	-5.5	103	102	-1.0
Illinois	237,181	225,601	-4.9	31,974,775	30,731,947	-3.9	135	136	+.7
Michigan	196,447	192,327	-2.1	19,032,961	18,035,290	-5.2	97	94	-3.1
Wisconsin	189,295	193,155	+2.0	22,148,223	21,850,853	-1.3	117	113	-3.4
East North Central	1,084,744	1,051,572	-3.1	117,735,179	112,752,458	-4.2	109	107	-1.8
Minnesota	178,478	188,231	+5.5	30,221,758	30,059,137	-.5	169	160	-5.3
Iowa	213,439	213,490	(¹)	33,474,896	33,280,813	-.6	157	156	-.6
Missouri	263,004	260,473	-1.0	34,774,679	32,641,893	-6.1	132	125	-5.3
North Dakota	77,690	75,970	-2.2	36,214,751	34,327,410	-5.2	466	452	-3.0
South Dakota	74,637	79,537	+6.6	34,636,491	32,017,986	-7.6	464	403	-13.1
Nebraska	124,417	127,734	+2.7	42,225,475	42,024,775	-.5	339	329	-2.9
Kansas	165,286	165,879	+.4	45,425,179	43,729,129	-3.7	275	264	-4.0
West North Central	1,096,951	1,111,314	+1.3	256,973,229	248,081,143	-3.5	234	223	-4.7
Delaware	10,140	10,257	+1.2	944,511	899,641	-4.8	93	88	-5.4
Maryland	47,908	49,001	+2.3	4,757,999	4,433,398	-6.8	99	90	-9.1
District of Columbia	204	139	-31.9	5,668	3,813	-32.7	28	27	-3.6
Virginia	186,242	193,723	+4.0	18,561,112	17,210,174	-7.3	100	89	-11.0
West Virginia	87,289	90,380	+3.5	9,569,790	8,979,847	-6.2	110	99	-10.0
North Carolina	269,763	283,482	+5.1	20,021,736	18,593,670	-7.1	74	66	-10.8
South Carolina	192,693	172,767	-10.3	12,426,675	10,638,900	-14.4	64	62	-3.1
Georgia	310,732	249,095	-19.8	25,441,061	21,945,496	-13.7	82	88	+7.3
Florida	54,005	59,217	+9.7	6,046,691	5,864,519	-3.0	112	99	-11.6
South Atlantic	1,158,976	1,108,061	-4.4	97,775,243	88,569,458	-9.4	84	80	-4.8
Kentucky	270,626	258,524	-4.5	21,612,772	19,913,104	-7.9	80	77	-3.8
Tennessee	252,774	252,669	(¹)	19,510,856	17,901,139	-8.3	77	71	-7.8
Alabama	256,099	237,631	-7.2	19,576,856	16,739,139	-14.5	76	70	-7.9
Mississippi	272,101	257,228	-5.5	18,196,979	16,053,243	-11.8	67	62	-7.5
East South Central	1,051,600	1,006,052	-4.3	78,897,463	70,606,625	-10.5	75	70	-6.7
Arkansas	232,604	221,991	-4.6	17,456,750	15,632,439	-10.5	75	70	-6.7
Louisiana	135,463	132,450	-2.2	10,019,822	8,837,502	-11.8	74	67	-9.5
Oklahoma	191,988	197,218	+2.7	31,951,934	30,868,965	-3.4	166	157	-5.4
Texas	436,033	465,646	+6.8	114,020,621	109,674,410	-3.8	261	236	-9.6
West South Central	996,088	1,017,305	+2.1	173,449,127	165,013,316	-4.9	174	162	-6.9
Montana	57,677	46,904	-18.7	35,070,656	32,735,723	-6.7	608	698	+14.8
Idaho	42,106	40,592	-3.6	8,375,873	8,116,147	-3.1	199	200	+.5
Wyoming	15,748	15,512	-1.5	11,809,351	18,663,308	+58.0	750	1,203	+60.4
Colorado	59,934	58,020	-3.2	24,462,014	24,167,270	-1.2	408	417	+2.2
New Mexico	29,844	31,687	+6.2	24,409,633	27,850,325	+14.1	818	879	+7.5
Arizona	9,975	10,802	+8.3	5,802,126	11,065,291	+90.7	582	1,024	+75.9
Utah	25,662	25,992	+1.3	5,050,410	5,000,724	-1.0	197	192	-2.5
Nevada	3,163	3,883	+22.8	2,357,163	4,090,586	+73.5	745	1,053	+41.3
Mountain	244,109	233,392	-4.4	117,337,226	131,689,374	+12.2	481	564	+17.3
Washington	66,288	73,267	+10.5	13,244,720	12,610,310	-4.8	200	172	-14.0
Oregon	50,206	55,911	+11.4	13,542,318	14,130,847	+4.3	270	253	-6.3
California	117,670	136,409	+15.9	29,365,667	27,516,955	-6.3	250	202	-19.2
Pacific	234,164	265,587	+13.4	56,152,705	54,258,112	-3.4	240	204	-15.0
United States	6,448,343	6,371,640	-1.2	955,883,715	924,319,352	-3.3	148	145	-2.0

Bureau of Agricultural Economics. Compiled from the Bureau of the Census reports; based on final figures.

¹ Less than 0.1 per cent.

TABLE 541.—*Pasture land: Acreage in farms, 1924*

State and division	Total pasture		Pasture land suitable for crops		Woodland pasture		Other pasture	
	Acreage	Acres per farm	Acreage	Acres per farm	Acreage	Acres per farm	Acreage	Acres per farm
Maine	1,751,785	35	195,768	4	980,645	20	575,372	11
New Hampshire	1,087,385	52	89,673	4	779,501	37	218,211	10
Vermont	2,175,508	78	252,220	9	1,031,310	37	891,978	32
Massachusetts	876,892	26	95,162	3	482,453	14	299,277	9
Rhode Island	110,985	28	33,599	9	50,093	13	27,293	7
Connecticut	784,779	34	104,987	5	356,652	15	323,140	14
New England	6,787,334	43	771,409	5	3,680,654	23	2,335,271	15
New York	7,403,503	39	2,080,544	11	2,025,249	11	3,297,710	17
New Jersey	335,057	11	185,477	6	43,610	1	105,970	4
Pennsylvania	4,573,383	23	1,697,457	8	1,391,193	7	1,484,733	7
Middle Atlantic	12,311,943	29	3,963,478	9	3,460,052	8	4,888,413	12
Ohio	8,137,800	33	3,997,407	16	1,854,403	8	2,285,990	9
Indiana	5,720,492	29	2,731,771	14	1,878,949	10	1,109,772	6
Illinois	7,281,963	32	4,007,856	18	1,896,966	8	1,377,141	6
Michigan	5,722,569	30	1,756,387	9	2,407,150	13	1,559,032	8
Wisconsin	8,671,556	45	1,703,243	9	4,431,416	23	2,536,897	13
East North Central	35,534,380	34	14,196,664	13	12,468,884	12	8,868,832	8
Minnesota	7,903,217	42	2,163,341	11	3,556,303	19	2,183,573	12
Iowa	9,476,720	44	5,149,742	24	1,970,145	9	2,356,833	11
Missouri	13,298,822	51	6,858,678	26	4,780,176	18	1,659,968	6
North Dakota	8,940,886	118	3,110,925	41	337,240	4	5,492,721	72
South Dakota	13,797,123	173	6,148,511	77	287,661	4	7,360,951	93
Nebraska	19,493,945	153	4,381,148	34	657,020	5	14,455,777	113
Kansas	17,889,753	108	7,797,601	47	651,057	4	9,441,095	57
West North Central	90,800,466	82	35,609,946	32	12,239,602	11	42,950,918	39
Delaware	101,633	10	78,868	8	10,386	1	12,379	1
Maryland	892,910	18	525,523	11	187,183	4	180,204	4
District of Columbia	503	4	262	2	96	1	145	1
Virginia	5,287,994	27	2,964,815	15	1,331,719	7	919,460	5
West Virginia	4,288,452	47	1,726,130	19	905,058	10	1,657,264	18
North Carolina	2,817,046	10	881,893	3	1,386,759	5	548,394	2
South Carolina	1,637,431	9	310,566	2	1,008,359	6	318,506	2
Georgia	3,848,939	15	811,562	3	2,324,250	9	713,127	3
Florida	1,489,070	25	257,788	4	793,782	13	437,500	7
South Atlantic	20,363,978	18	7,557,407	7	7,947,592	7	4,858,979	4
Kentucky	7,746,432	30	5,500,897	21	1,207,516	5	1,038,019	4
Tennessee	4,697,449	19	2,588,462	10	1,364,386	5	744,601	3
Alabama	3,544,354	15	1,129,151	5	1,928,087	8	487,116	2
Mississippi	4,291,459	17	1,412,430	5	2,027,611	8	851,418	3
East South Central	20,279,694	20	10,630,940	11	6,527,600	6	3,121,154	3
Arkansas	3,064,063	14	956,359	4	1,675,575	8	432,129	2
Louisiana	1,709,231	13	784,503	6	674,327	5	250,401	2
Oklahoma	13,015,006	66	3,878,644	20	2,971,895	15	6,164,467	31
Texas	75,067,862	161	13,617,251	29	11,230,062	24	50,220,549	108
West South Central	92,856,162	91	19,236,757	19	16,551,859	16	57,067,546	56
Montana	22,714,811	484	4,124,050	88	1,311,615	28	17,279,146	368
Idaho	3,553,774	88	363,740	9	646,139	16	2,543,895	63
Wyoming	16,313,347	1,052	2,200,974	142	370,749	24	13,741,624	886
Colorado	15,350,783	265	5,113,819	88	1,114,461	19	9,122,503	157
New Mexico	24,049,460	759	5,358,041	169	2,144,857	68	16,546,562	522
Arizona	10,101,361	935	143,440	13	389,389	36	9,568,532	886
Utah	3,067,251	118	138,512	5	97,357	4	2,831,382	109
Nevada	2,973,821	766	81,882	21	63,069	16	2,828,870	729
Mountain	98,124,608	420	17,524,458	75	6,137,636	26	74,462,514	319
Washington	5,202,358	71	444,156	6	1,317,170	18	3,441,032	47
Oregon	8,803,000	157	598,869	11	2,144,963	38	6,059,168	108
California	16,871,635	124	3,033,414	22	4,227,934	31	9,610,287	70
Pacific	30,876,993	116	4,076,439	15	7,690,067	29	19,110,487	72
United States	407,935,558	64	113,567,498	18	76,703,946	12	217,664,114	34

Bureau of Agricultural Economics. Compiled from the Bureau of the Census reports; based on final figures.

TABLE 542.—*Land utilization: Cultivable land, crop land, and plowland lying idle or fallow, in stated years*

State and division	Cultivable land[1] Acreage, 1924	Cultivable land[1] Acres per farm	Harvested crops Acreage 1919[2]	Harvested crops Acreage 1924[1]	Harvested crops Acreage 1928, 47 crops only[3]	Harvested crops Per cent change 1919–1924	Harvested crops Per cent change 1924–1928, 47 crops only	Harvested crops Acres per farm 1919	Harvested crops Acres per farm 1924	Crop failure Acreage, 1924	Crop failure Acres per farm	Idle or fallow plowland Acreage, 1924	Idle or fallow plowland Acres per farm
Maine	1,839,283	37	1,648,521	1,699,221	1,593,000	+3.1	−0.9	34	33	7,355	(³)	30,584	1
New Hampshire	632,519	30	541,495	553,058	512,000	+2.1	−2.3	26	26	1,683	(³)	17,777	1
Vermont	1,401,876	50	1,189,020	1,151,948	1,123,000	−3.1	−1.7	41	41	5,851	(³)	16,801	1
Massachusetts	772,519	23	657,082	689,688	564,000	+5.0	−2.1	21	21	4,793	(³)	47,496	1
Rhode Island	109,602	28	74,316	75,061	59,000	+1.0	−3.3	18	19	407	(³)	6,228	2
Connecticut	639,341	28	511,848	528,155	476,000	+3.2	−.8	23	23	5,140	(³)	31,779	1
New England	5,395,140	34	4,622,282	4,697,131	4,327,000	1.6	−1.5	30	29	25,229	(³)	150,665	1
New York	11,168,207	59	8,788,658	8,474,188	7,548,000	−3.6	−6.0	45	45	91,041	(³)	706,287	4
New Jersey	1,311,528	44	1,093,174	949,599	795,000	−13.1	−3.3	37	32	20,994	1	197,303	7
Pennsylvania	10,128,506	51	8,398,144	7,523,342	7,032,000	−10.4	−2.5	42	38	102,129	1	1,045,409	5
Middle Atlantic	22,608,241	54	18,279,976	16,947,129	15,375,000	−7.3	−4.3	43	40	214,164	1	1,948,999	5
Ohio	15,692,363	64	12,448,866	10,894,200	10,486,000	−12.5	−2.8	48	45	286,514	1	705,400	3
Indiana	14,712,850	75	12,325,426	10,620,561	10,392,000	−13.8	−5.5	60	54	380,900	2	1,004,435	5
Illinois	25,332,693	112	20,943,321	19,675,482	20,153,000	−6.1	(⁴)	88	87	646,600	3	912,790	4
Michigan	11,427,768	59	9,632,720	8,670,458	8,330,000	−10.0	−2.7	49	45	173,930	1	995,548	5
Wisconsin	11,831,157	61	9,790,136	9,603,491	9,610,000	−1.9	−.4	52	50	268,404	1	321,487	2
East North Central	78,986,831	75	65,140,469	59,464,282	58,971,000	−8.7	−2.0	60	57	1,736,348	2	3,939,660	4
Minnesota	20,814,531	111	16,781,770	17,989,094	17,731,000	+7.2	−1.5	94	96	195,681	1	525,805	3
Iowa	27,147,417	127	21,216,389	21,515,827	21,855,000	+1.4	+1.4	99	101	422,694	2	108,631	1
Missouri	22,137,114	85	15,983,353	13,758,796	13,721,000	−13.9	+4.0	61	53	686,054	3	871,808	3
North Dakota	24,975,326	329	19,649,375	19,971,302	20,359,000	+1.6	+.5	253	263	322,499	3	1,664,670	22
South Dakota	22,589,257	284	15,092,743	15,794,809	15,684,000	+4.7	−1.1	202	199	346,721	4	301,038	4
Nebraska	25,079,246	196	19,295,288	19,820,790	20,445,000	+2.7	+3.4	155	155	591,378	5	296,358	2
Kansas	31,694,108	191	22,279,272	22,435,013	22,922,000	+.7	+5.0	135	135	916,324	6	598,565	4
West North Central	174,436,999	157	130,298,190	131,285,631	132,717,000	.8	+.9	119	118	3,481,351	3	4,366,875	4
Delaware	597,727	58	494,901	400,977	395,000	−19.0	+1.0	49	39	6,615	1	108,035	1
Maryland	2,753,088	56	2,110,741	1,801,178	1,784,000	−14.7	+.8	44	37	36,982	1	413,020	8

District of Columbia	2,633	2,288	2,279	—	-.4	—	11	16	34	(5)	140	1
Virginia	8,333,003	5,033,571	4,185,646	4,290,000	-16.8	+2.3	27	22	113,562	1	1,286,036	7
West Virginia	3,647,269	2,131,903	1,767,358	1,736,000	-17.1	+5.5	24	20	27,754	1	216,815	2
North Carolina	7,738,826	6,173,532	5,836,303	6,030,000	-5.5	+1.3	23	21	145,338	1	1,136,674	4
South Carolina	5,346,522	5,572,558	4,682,110	4,940,000	-17.0	+4.4	29	27	92,450	1	632,370	4
Georgia	11,507,379	11,415,550	9,305,046	9,525,000	-18.5	+8.7	37	27	111,992	1	2,456,248	10
Florida	2,280,072	1,553,615	1,473,058	1,182,000	-5.2	+11.6	29	25	35,443	1	617,791	10
South Atlantic	42,206,469	34,493,659	29,453,955	30,512,000	-14.6	+1.7	30	27	570,170	1	6,867,149	6
Kentucky	12,328,270	6,773,958	5,351,907	5,347,000	-21.0	+1.0	25	21	131,553	1	1,512,118	6
Tennessee	10,176,968	7,153,509	6,382,547	6,392,000	-10.8	+.4	25	25	110,907	1	1,268,171	5
Alabama	8,820,864	7,836,064	7,233,122	7,358,000	-7.7	+2.1	31	30	101,649	1	948,709	4
Mississippi	8,121,322	6,603,072	5,802,981	6,456,000	-12.1	+9.9	30	23	157,782	1	889,439	3
East South Central	39,447,424	28,366,603	24,770,557	25,553,000	-12.7	+3.3	27	25	501,891	1	4,618,437	5
Arkansas	8,279,558	6,715,048	6,337,059	6,922,000	-5.6	+5.3	29	29	174,210	1	922,159	4
Louisiana	5,004,031	4,022,244	3,683,671	4,355,000	-8.3	+9.9	30	28	216,038	2	578,787	4
Oklahoma	19,716,379	15,339,040	14,711,444	15,690,000	-4.1	+5.5	80	75	761,527	4	527,525	3
Texas	42,985,967	25,467,351	27,225,026	30,331,000	+6.9	+8.6	58	53	1,229,460	3	1,064,387	2
West South Central	76,045,935	51,543,683	51,962,200	57,298,000	+.8	+7.4	52	51	2,381,235	2	3,092,808	3
Montana	12,598,274	3,911,989	6,425,457	7,654,000	+64.3	+16.8	68	137	307,874	7	1,750,015	37
Idaho	4,078,076	2,784,908	2,602,610	2,886,000	-6.5	+14.0	66	64	371,980	9	763,557	19
Wyoming	4,078,853	1,193,225	1,574,970	1,832,000	+32.0	+15.2	76	102	150,981	10	154,273	10
Colorado	12,313,119	5,327,378	5,909,923	6,117,000	+10.9	+10.2	89	102	832,274	14	418,589	7
New Mexico	7,142,892	1,179,193	1,338,074	1,202,000	-6.0	-6.0	40	43	249,730	8	189,416	6
Arizona	721,686	458,572	468,998	636,000	+23.3	+28.3	46	43	28,320	3	91,978	9
Utah	1,563,198	1,069,729	1,034,988	1,183,000	-2.3	+10.6	41	40	100,645	3	299,475	12
Nevada	615,496	392,327	384,932	407,000	-7.0	+12.4	124	94	131,491	34	39,571	10
Mountain	43,111,594	16,307,321	19,739,952	21,917,000	+21.0	+10.3	67	85	2,174,295	9	3,706,874	16
Washington	6,527,805	4,228,636	3,355,785	3,618,000	-20.6	+12.6	64	46	491,268	7	2,329,557	32
Oregon	4,826,206	2,968,458	2,627,690	2,753,000	-11.5	+12.8	59	47	457,098	8	1,178,020	21
California	11,434,756	6,840,656	5,291,151	5,052,000	-22.7	+18.2	58	39	984,900	7	1,693,642	12
Pacific	22,788,767	14,037,750	11,274,626	11,423,000	-19.7	+15.1	60	42	1,933,266	7	5,201,219	20
United States	505,027,400	363,089,933	349,595,463	358,098,000	-3.7	+2.3	56	55	13,017,949	2	33,892,686	5

Bureau of Agricultural Economics.   Compiled from the Bureau of the Census reports, except acreage of 47 harvested crops for 1928, which are estimates of the crop-reporting board.

1 Includes acreage of land from which crops were harvested, plus crop failure, plus plowland lying idle or fallow, plus plowable pasture.
2 Includes acreage of crops harvested, which is over 3,000,000 acres greater than land from which crops were harvested because of double cropping, mostly in the Carolinas, Georgia, and Florida; also an estimated acreage of farm gardens, and of fruit orchards.
3 The 47 crops do not include fruits, and are the preliminary estimates of the Bureau of Agricultural Economics.
4 Less than 0.1 per cent.
5 Less than one-half acre.

TABLE 543.—*Woodland and other land in farms, 1919 and 1924*

State and division	Woodland (including that pastured) Acreage 1919	1924	Change	Acres per farm 1919	1924	Per cent pastured, 1924	Land, other than crop, pasture, or forest land (farmsteads, lanes, waste land, etc.) Acreage, 1924	Acres per farm, 1924	Woodland cleared and made suitable for crops, 1920–1924, inclusive Acreage	Acres per farm reporting
			Per cent							
Maine	2,447,597	2,489,037	+1.7	51	50	39.4	257,736	5	15,844	8
New Hampshire	1,299,838	1,316,244	+1.3	63	62	59.2	95,090	5	607	4
Vermont	1,428,309	1,549,034	+8.5	49	56	66.6	82,795	3	2,135	7
Massachusetts	1,030,386	1,119,922	+8.7	32	33	43.1	175,911	5	3,181	4
Rhode Island	130,462	144,924	+11.1	32	37	34.6	27,194	7	416	4
Connecticut	683,719	729,923	+6.8	30	31	48.9	139,706	6	5,580	6
New England	7,020,311	7,349,084	+4.7	45	46	50.1	778,432	5	27,763	7
New York	4,160,567	3,805,629	−8.5	22	20	53.2	998,380	5	10,929	5
New Jersey	454,768	297,152	−34.7	15	10	14.7	209,895	7	2,944	5
Pennsylvania	4,043,902	3,530,189	−12.7	20	18	39.4	1,153,040	6	12,432	5
Middle Atlantic	8,659,237	7,632,970	11.9	20	18	45.3	2,361,315	6	26,305	5
Ohio	3,198,929	2,827,493	−11.6	12	12	65.6	1,413,402	6	33,859	6
Indiana	3,141,042	2,716,962	−13.5	15	14	69.2	1,375,536	7	44,632	6
Illinois	3,102,579	2,635,608	−15.1	13	12	72.0	1,396,505	6	44,412	7
Michigan	3,217,000	3,301,781	+2.6	16	17	72.9	1,746,709	9	159,514	8
Wisconsin	5,401,910	5,648,127	+4.6	29	29	78.5	1,834,672	9	343,472	7
East North Central	18,061,460	17,129,971	−5.2	16	17	72.8	7,766,824	7	625,889	7
Minnesota	4,482,656	4,749,811	+6.0	25	25	74.9	2,331,222	12	363,341	10
Iowa	2,295,274	2,212,940	−3.6	11	10	89.0	1,563,623	7	46,946	8
Missouri	8,553,857	7,405,843	−13.4	33	28	64.5	1,438,968	6	285,867	10
North Dakota	679,836	510,762	−24.9	9	7	66.0	3,348,601	44	7,356	14
South Dakota	536,183	400,054	−25.4	7	5	71.9	1,667,724	21	1,464	8
Nebraska	900,933	883,268	−2.0	7	7	74.4	1,606,484	13	6,830	7
Kansas	1,316,093	994,396	−24.3	8	6	65.5	1,599,530	10	11,188	6
West North Central	18,761,832	17,157,074	−8.6	17	15	71.3	13,536,152	12	722,992	10
Delaware	222,658	198,566	−10.8	22	19	5.2	90,969	9	845	5
Maryland	1,327,221	1,132,943	−14.6	28	23	16.5	367,213	7	9,946	5
District of Columbia	828	276	−66.7	4	2	34.8	759	5	2	2
Virginia	7,907,352	6,855,232	−13.3	42	35	19.4	1,030,479	5	167,376	6
West Virginia	3,469,444	3,168,623	−8.7	40	35	28.6	506,691	6	67,693	6
North Carolina	10,299,547	8,456,483	−17.9	38	30	16.4	1,849,967	7	210,009	5
South Carolina	5,302,575	3,570,365	−32.7	28	21	28.2	1,403,507	8	66,830	7
Georgia	10,491,848	7,045,813	−32.8	34	28	33.0	2,679,177	11	148,538	9
Florida	2,780,790	2,292,083	−17.6	51	39	34.6	854,864	14	126,052	13
South Atlantic	41,802,263	32,720,384	−21.7	36	30	24.3	8,783,626	8	797,291	7
Kentucky	6,018,280	4,835,418	−19.7	22	19	25.0	1,711,397	7	154,563	6
Tennessee	7,080,169	5,562,497	−21.4	28	22	24.5	1,417,073	6	181,314	7
Alabama	8,301,177	5,784,045	−30.3	32	24	33.3	1,647,114	7	231,764	7
Mississippi	7,014,898	5,447,097	−22.3	26	21	37.2	1,633,406	6	175,937	8
East South Central	28,414,524	21,629,057	−23.9	27	22	30.2	6,408,990	6	743,578	7
Arkansas	7,396,028	5,392,900	−27.1	32	24	31.1	1,527,852	7	363,712	9
Louisiana	3,614,040	2,406,219	−33.4	27	18	28.0	1,116,851	8	86,180	9
Oklahoma	4,206,171	3,429,973	−18.5	22	17	86.6	1,558,146	8	119,811	11
Texas	14,532,913	12,690,824	−12.7	33	27	88.5	3,777,070	8	435,851	14
West South Central	29,749,152	23,919,916	−19.6	30	24	69.2	7,979,919	8	1,005,554	11
Montana	1,646,462	1,545,773	−6.1	29	33	84.9	1,312,530	28	18,153	11
Idaho	820,876	743,561	−9.4	19	18	86.9	750,615	18	27,536	10
Wyoming	421,806	445,161	+5.5	27	29	83.3	397,670	26	1,948	11
Colorado	1,415,420	1,352,967	−4.4	24	23	82.4	1,378,681	24	10,499	11
New Mexico	1,817,460	2,314,995	+27.4	61	73	92.7	1,845,876	58	16,483	27
Arizona	523,648	436,786	−16.6	52	40	89.1	338,287	31	4,477	23
Utah	212,762	161,228	−24.2	8	6	60.4	444,916	17	2,082	14
Nevada	28,637	69,622	+143.1	9	18	90.6	576,598	148	747	53
Mountain	6,887,071	7,070,093	+2.7	28	30	86.8	7,045,173	30	81,925	13
Washington	1,813,061	1,855,583	+2.3	27	25	71.0	785,890	11	66,922	4
Oregon	2,309,596	2,664,637	+15.4	46	48	80.5	580,836	10	49,042	6
California	4,252,287	4,665,423	+9.7	36	34	90.6	1,806,489	13	51,683	14
Pacific	8,374,944	9,185,643	+9.7	36	35	83.7	3,173,215	12	167,647	6
United States	167,730,794	143,794,192	−14.3	26	23	53.3	57,833,646	9	4,198,944	8

Bureau of Agricultural Economics. Compiled from the Bureau of the Census reports; based on final figures.

TABLE 544.—*Size of farm, by tenure, 1925*

Acres	United States	New England	Middle Atlantic	East North Central	West North Central	South Atlantic	East South Central	West South Central	Mountain	Pacific
	Number	*Number*	*Number*	*Number*	*Number*	*Number*	*Number*	*Number*	*Number*	*Number*
All farms	6,371,640	159,489	418,868	1,051,572	1,111,314	1,108,061	1,006,052	1,017,305	233,392	265,587
Under 20	966,584	30,385	74,437	96,958	59,990	233,729	224,494	135,318	26,678	84,595
20 to 49	1,450,643	29,271	71,373	168,002	89,827	354,421	346,230	297,911	26,892	66,716
50 to 99	1,421,078	38,368	117,598	319,425	170,617	255,439	222,577	235,016	27,522	34,516
100 to 174	1,383,777	36,799	108,546	311,568	351,199	160,805	138,159	205,986	40,306	30,409
175 to 499	942,378	22,744	45,213	150,504	363,535	90,252	66,571	112,675	62,076	28,808
500 to 999	143,852	1,544	1,413	4,472	58,840	10,076	6,077	18,063	31,877	11,490
1,000 and over	63,328	378	288	643	17,306	3,339	1,944	12,336	18,041	9,053
Owned farms	3,868,332	148,159	348,179	771,876	685,797	609,304	497,825	412,064	179,198	215,930
Under 20	508,561	28,274	66,284	82,438	44,425	105,155	54,004	29,660	22,801	75,520
20 to 49	714,795	27,679	64,036	142,056	59,689	149,684	117,495	76,997	20,878	56,281
50 to 99	972,915	36,104	98,808	246,980	114,817	164,781	156,822	108,532	19,410	26,661
100 to 174	907,689	34,138	83,843	207,116	202,060	113,652	108,956	105,864	28,975	23,085
175 to 499	613,064	20,405	34,025	90,280	211,463	66,315	54,122	69,697	46,443	20,314
500 to 999	103,894	1,273	1,014	2,677	40,387	7,434	4,940	12,475	25,810	7,884
1,000 and over	47,414	286	169	329	12,956	2,283	1,486	8,839	14,881	6,185
Managed farms	40,700	2,462	4,465	6,606	5,569	6,137	1,731	3,058	2,410	8,262
Under 20	2,723	170	187	169	85	371	127	98	111	1,405
20 to 49	4,538	260	377	387	168	674	178	194	176	2,124
50 to 99	5,937	452	933	1,144	518	854	238	277	216	1,305
100 to 174	9,084	607	1,416	2,136	1,630	1,141	293	476	338	1,047
175 to 499	10,964	715	1,279	2,210	2,136	1,864	470	638	460	1,192
500 to 999	3,323	179	182	365	574	665	215	380	316	447
1,000 and over	4,131	79	91	195	458	568	210	995	793	742
Tenant farms	2,462,608	8,868	66,224	273,090	419,948	492,620	506,496	602,183	51,784	41,395
Under 20	455,300	1,941	7,966	14,351	15,480	128,203	170,363	105,560	3,766	7,670
20 to 49	731,310	1,332	6,960	25,559	29,970	204,063	228,557	220,720	5,838	8,311
50 to 99	442,226	1,812	17,857	71,301	55,282	89,804	65,517	126,207	7,896	6,550
100 to 174	467,004	2,054	23,287	102,316	147,509	46,012	28,910	99,646	10,993	6,277
175 to 499	318,350	1,624	9,909	58,014	149,936	22,073	11,979	42,340	15,173	7,302
500 to 999	36,635	92	217	1,430	17,879	1,977	922	5,208	5,751	3,159
1,000 and over	11,783	13	28	119	3,892	488	248	2,502	2,367	2,126

Bureau of Agricultural Economics.

TABLE 545.—*Number of farms, per cent of farms and per cent of acreage, by tenure, 1925*

Geographic division and State	Farms operated by—						Acreage operated by—		
	Owners	Managers	Tenants	Owners	Managers	Tenants	Owners	Managers	Tenants
	Number	Number	Number	Per cent	Per cent	Per cent	Per cent	Per cent	Per cent
United States	3,868,332	40,700	2,462,608	60.7	0.7	38.6	66.6	4.7	28.7
New England	148,159	2,462	8,868	92.8	1.6	5.6	90.4	3.7	5.9
Maine	47,984	350	1,699	95.9	.7	3.4	95.6	1.4	3.0
New Hampshire	19,895	156	1,014	94.4	.8	4.8	93.2	2.6	4.2
Vermont	24,889	307	2,590	89.6	.1	9.3	86.8	2.5	10.7
Massachusetts	30,870	979	1,605	92.2	3.0	4.8	86.6	9.0	4.4
Rhode Island	3,263	176	472	83.4	4.5	12.1	80.1	7.8	12.1
Connecticut	21,258	494	1,488	91.5	2.1	6.4	87.0	6.3	6.7
Middle Atlantic	348,179	4,465	66,224	83.1	1.1	15.8	78.6	2.4	19.0
New York	159,949	2,261	26,544	84.7	1.2	14.1	80.2	2.6	17.2
New Jersey	24,535	413	4,723	82.7	1.4	15.9	73.0	3.5	23.5
Pennsylvania	163,695	1,791	34,957	81.7	.9	17.4	77.3	2.1	20.6
East North Central	771,876	6,606	273,090	73.4	.6	26.0	67.0	1.5	31.5
Ohio	181,347	1,060	62,296	74.1	.4	25.5	67.9	1.2	30.9
Indiana	137,429	1,268	57,089	70.2	.6	29.2	63.6	1.4	35.0
Illinois	129,074	1,877	94,650	57.2	.8	42.0	51.4	1.5	47.1
Michigan	161,974	1,234	29,119	84.2	.7	15.1	80.2	2.0	17.7
Wisconsin	162,052	1,167	29,936	83.9	.6	15.5	80.4	1.3	18.3
West North Central	685,797	5,569	419,948	61.7	.5	37.8	62.8	1.4	35.8
Minnesota	136,382	766	51,083	.725	.4	27.1	67.2	.7	32.1
Iowa	116,444	1,650	95,396	.545	.8	44.7	51.4	1.2	47.4
Missouri	174,383	1,063	85,027	66.9	.5	32.6	69.6	1.1	29.3
North Dakota	49,513	361	26,096	65.2	.4	34.4	68.5	.8	30.7
South Dakota	46,160	331	33,046	58.0	.5	41.5	65.4	2.4	32.2
Nebraska	67,766	669	59,299	53.1	.5	46.4	60.8	1.8	37.4
Kansas	95,149	729	70,001	57.4	.4	42.2	58.9	1.6	39.5
South Atlantic	609,304	6,137	492,620	55.0	.5	44.5	65.8	4.0	30.2
Delaware	6,515	74	3,668	63.5	.7	35.8	51.7	1.8	46.5
Maryland	35,138	936	12,927	71.7	1.9	26.4	60.3	4.1	35.6
Dist. Columbia	81	19	39	58.2	13.7	28.1	33.1	45.7	21.2
Virginia	143,587	1,238	48,898	74.1	.7	25.2	77.3	3.0	19.7
West Virginia	74,943	662	14,775	82.9	.8	16.3	83.3	2.4	14.3
North Carolina	154,805	423	128,254	54.6	.2	45.2	67.4	1.3	31.3
South Carolina	59,969	368	112,430	34.7	.2	65.1	56.3	2.7	41.0
Georgia	88,680	1,407	159,008	35.6	.6	63.8	54.2	3.6	42.2
Florida	45,586	1,010	12,621	77.0	1.7	21.3	67.5	21.5	11.0
East South Central	497,825	1,731	506,496	49.5	.2	50.3	69.5	1.3	29.2
Kentucky	175,442	281	82,801	67.9	.1	32.0	79.5	.7	19.8
Tennessee	148,627	324	103,718	58.8	.2	41.0	72.8	.7	26.5
Alabama	92,948	448	144,235	39.1	.2	60.7	60.2	1.5	38.3
Mississippi	80,808	678	175,742	31.4	.3	68.3	63.0	2.6	34.4
West South Central	412,064	3,058	602,183	40.5	.3	59.2	59.2	7.3	33.5
Arkansas	95,476	616	125,899	43.0	.3	56.7	64.1	2.0	33.8
Louisiana	52,386	503	79,561	39.5	.4	60.1	63.6	6.7	29.7
Oklahoma	81,226	494	115,498	41.1	.3	58.6	50.6	4.3	45.1
Texas	182,976	1,445	281,225	39.3	.3	60.4	60.6	8.9	30.5
Mountain	179,198	2,410	51,784	76.8	1.0	22.2	74.8	10.7	14.5
Montana	36,281	367	10,256	77.3	77.8	21.9	77.5	5.8	16.7
Idaho	30,195	511	9,886	74.4	1.2	24.4	76.2	3.3	20.5
Wyoming	12,545	191	2,776	80.9	1.2	17.9	80.7	10.4	8.9
Colorado	39,517	585	17,918	68.1	1.0	30.9	72.0	5.3	22.7
New Mexico	26,005	256	5,426	82.1	.8	17.1	71.1	17.0	11.9
Arizona	8,179	296	2,327	75.7	2.8	21.5	68.5	22.7	8.8
Utah	23,013	90	2,889	88.5	.4	11.1	89.4	3.7	6.9
Nevada	3,463	114	306	89.1	3.0	7.9	65.8	29.5	4.7
Pacific	215,930	8,262	41,395	81.3	3.1	15.6	69.2	11.0	19.8
Washington	60,389	935	11,943	82.4	1.3	16.3	71.7	2.9	25.4
Oregon	45,887	618	9,406	82.0	1.2	16.8	76.8	6.4	16.8
California	109,654	6,709	20,046	80.4	4.9	14.7	64.2	17.2	18.6

Bureau of Agricultural Economics.

TABLE 546.—Livestock: Total and number per farm, by tenure, 1925

Item	United States	New England	Middle Atlantic	East North Central	West North Central	South Atlantic	East South Central	West South Central	Mountain	Pacific
	Number	Number	Number	Number	Number	Number	Number	Number	Number	Number
All farms:										
Horses and mules	22,081,520	262,368	972,066	3,617,652	6,859,570	1,828,551	2,045,019	3,652,225	1,962,502	881,567
Horses and mules per farm	4	2	3	4	7	7	9	4	4	5
Beef cattle	35,057,156	45,695	228,901	2,588,447	13,476,258	2,302,760	1,630,622	6,652,159	6,434,534	1,747,780
Beef cattle per farm	17	5	5	11	21	9	5	18	18	52
Dairy cattle	25,703,210	1,073,313	3,080,347	7,117,990	5,728,221	1,832,410	2,005,518	2,357,249	971,280	1,536,882
Dairy cattle per farm	7	9	9	9	10	10	10	5	9	10
Swine	60,853,526	193,240	1,049,508	11,774,248	24,600,317	4,175,886	3,432,941	3,451,290	1,310,798	845,298
Swine per farm	14	4	6	18	29	6	6	7	12	13
Owned farms:										
Horses and mules	13,894,416	238,593	757,745	2,376,985	4,197,224	1,124,603	1,271,202	1,863,167	1,446,709	618,188
Horses and mules per farm	4	2	3	4	7	7	9	5	5	5
Beef cattle	24,541,008	41,811	173,694	1,686,410	8,879,165	1,802,178	1,211,513	4,508,554	4,990,411	1,247,272
Beef cattle per farm	19	4	5	10	23	9	6	23	57	45
Dairy Cattle	17,959,115	955,474	2,410,821	5,208,325	3,770,549	1,211,841	1,208,996	1,360,767	720,018	1,022,324
Dairy cattle per farm	7	8	9	9	11	11	11	6	9	9
Swine	31,796,105	159,665	770,660	7,188,483	15,167,980	2,664,329	2,226,954	2,113,614	949,788	553,622
Swine per farm	14	4	6	16	30	7	7	8	11	11
Managed farms:										
Horses and mules	429,307	8,253	18,422	40,035	53,416	30,833	15,124	56,307	146,340	60,577
Horses and mules per farm	13	4	5	7	11	11	11	21	70	11
Beef cattle	2,218,904	1,868	8,923	59,950	238,483	127,595	27,176	631,172	813,391	310,346
Beef cattle per farm	176	11	16	30	68	61	41	416	701	342
Dairy cattle	349,126	36,481	59,823	75,656	35,983	35,864	11,826	19,776	16,509	57,208
Dairy cattle per farm	15	18	17	15	14	11	12	14	15	19
Swine	790,545	23,381	35,148	186,061	242,986	87,425	24,900	41,981	44,219	104,444
Swine per farm	41	24	19	44	60	24	26	28	44	80
Tenant farms:										
Horses and mules	7,757,797	15,522	195,899	1,200,632	2,608,930	673,115	758,693	1,732,751	369,453	202,802
Horses and mules per farm	4	4	4	5	7	7	7	4	8	6
Beef cattle	8,297,244	2,016	46,284	792,087	4,358,610	372,987	391,933	1,512,433	630,732	190,162
Beef cattle per farm	11	5	5	7	17	4	3	9	33	36
Dairy cattle	7,304,969	81,358	609,703	1,834,009	1,921,689	584,705	694,696	976,706	234,763	457,350
Dairy cattle per farm	6	13	11	10	10	10	10	4	9	18
Swine	18,267,876	10,194	243,700	4,399,704	9,189,341	1,424,132	1,291,087	1,295,695	316,791	187,292
Swine per farm	13	4	8	22	28	5	5	5	12	13

TABLE 547.—*Value of land and buildings, and expenditure per farm, by tenure, 1925*

Geographic division	Value of land and buildings per farm				Expenditure per farm											
					All farmers			Owners			Managers			Tenants		
	All farmers	Owners	Managers	Tenants	Feed	Fertilizer	Labor	Feed	Fertilizer	Labor	Feed	Fertilizer	Labor	Feed	Fertilizer	Labor
	Doll.	Doll.	Doll.	Doll.	Doll.	Doll.	Doll.	Doll.	Doll.	Doll.	Doll.	Doll.	Doll.	Doll.	Doll.	Doll.
United States__	7,764	8,018	39,335	6,842	235	106	341	251	106	340	1,148	616	2,644	181	97	267
New England__	5,678	5,321	27,139	5,687	495	220	533	476	205	458	1,557	816	3,273	516	240	482
Mid. Atlantic__	6,637	6,177	26,270	8,029	381	125	376	371	119	349	1,224	317	2,278	380	145	329
E. N. Central__	10,483	8,806	31,438	14,716	197	70	268	192	67	252	793	231	1,810	200	74	258
W. N. Central__	14,875	14,155	31,051	15,836	289	70	307	308	68	324	1,317	221	1,231	245	75	270
South Atlantic__	3,699	4,771	31,730	2,395	124	131	239	132	133	251	745	752	1,978	90	122	142
E. S. Central__	2,466	3,244	23,567	1,630	97	58	135	107	56	150	1,064	454	1,489	76	59	99
W. S. Central__	4,875	8,125	54,059	3,770	150	64	310	168	68	340	1,480	1,074	2,875	124	53	261
Mountain_____	9,310	3,133	48,073	9,573	295	93	530	280	82	499	1,922	364	3,415	266	127	470
Pacific_____	16,926	14,580	62,884	29,993	481	343	953	438	399	758	1,059	1,098	4,265	617	273	1,029

TABLE 548.—*Length of time on farm, by tenure, 1925*

Period	United States	New England	Middle Atlantic	East North Central	West North Central	South Atlantic	East South Central	West South Central	Mountain	Pacific
	Number	Number	Number	Number	Number	Number	Number	Number	Number	Number
All farmers reporting__	6,218,479	155,940	407,899	1,030,640	1,094,603	1,069,860	977,634	994,925	228,113	258,865
Less than 1 year__	1,150,056	10,285	38,551	109,566	151,041	226,621	237,021	314,532	31,482	30,957
1 year_____	539,034	8,522	26,995	70,519	90,840	93,384	101,260	109,895	16,694	20,925
2 years_____	443,571	8,992	27,956	64,903	74,490	78,143	76,983	77,908	13,983	20,213
3 years_____	366,859	9,291	26,424	59,413	63,520	60,415	56,632	59,184	12,644	19,336
4 years_____	485,040	10,369	30,735	79,333	92,478	82,291	77,980	70,377	16,128	25,349
5 to 6 years____	539,342	13,241	35,484	95,806	108,997	82,666	76,935	72,420	23,775	30,018
7 to 8 years____	342,462	9,154	23,857	64,442	67,833	49,832	43,568	45,814	20,995	16,967
9 to 10 years___	333,487	10,273	25,873	63,695	62,839	55,652	43,449	38,497	17,812	15,397
11 to 14 years__	529,741	16,454	41,046	106,191	103,396	82,807	64,769	56,956	29,523	28,139
15 and over____	1,488,887	59,359	130,518	316,772	279,169	258,049	199,037	149,342	45,077	51,564
All owners reporting__	3,779,761	144,918	339,052	755,882	675,053	589,333	487,135	403,022	174,776	210,610
Less than 1 year__	233,990	7,538	20,431	38,632	30,671	36,155	35,470	40,054	9,676	15,363
1 year_____	166,622	6,864	16,957	30,705	24,975	24,221	23,043	20,034	7,380	12,443
2 years_____	181,403	7,780	20,041	34,115	25,964	27,238	24,683	19,146	7,900	14,536
3 years_____	187,000	8,405	20,560	36,368	27,450	27,473	23,364	19,489	8,670	15,221
4 years_____	295,544	9,530	25,005	55,507	52,634	45,389	40,938	32,145	12,809	21,587
5 to 6 years____	378,399	12,361	29,807	71,910	71,770	53,254	50,324	42,203	20,587	26,183
7 to 8 years____	254,816	8,589	20,305	49,495	47,489	34,552	29,929	30,202	19,208	15,047
9 to 10 years___	260,825	9,809	22,947	51,338	47,618	41,070	31,168	26,151	16,682	14,042
11 to 14 years__	446,588	15,781	37,728	90,344	85,584	67,059	51,821	43,828	28,029	26,414
15 and over____	1,374,574	58,261	125,251	297,468	260,898	232,922	176,395	129,770	43,835	49,774
All managers reporting__	39,197	2,363	4,336	6,385	5,440	5,923	1,663	2,974	2,262	7,851
Less than 1 year__	11,673	389	1,061	2,036	2,183	1,508	420	1,048	790	2,238
1 year_____	5,794	280	609	1,051	909	811	224	410	296	1,204
2 years_____	4,127	222	431	728	566	622	202	266	223	867
3 years_____	2,889	191	297	433	331	490	121	220	145	661
4 years_____	3,021	192	344	443	311	529	142	231	161	668
5 to 6 years____	3,123	221	375	454	339	550	143	216	147	678
7 to 8 years____	1,787	148	229	273	173	289	80	126	116	353
9 to 10 years___	1,509	116	214	258	131	281	74	91	70	274
11 to 14 years__	2,148	218	308	275	212	350	109	129	118	429
15 and over____	3,126	386	468	434	285	493	148	237	196	479
All tenants reporting__	2,399,521	8,659	64,531	268,373	414,110	474,604	488,836	588,929	51,075	40,404
Less than 1 year__	904,393	2,358	17,059	68,898	118,187	188,958	201,131	273,430	21,016	13,356
1 year_____	366,618	1,378	9,429	38,763	64,956	68,352	77,993	89,451	9,018	7,278
2 years_____	258,041	990	7,484	30,060	47,960	50,283	52,098	58,496	5,860	4,810
3 years_____	176,970	695	5,567	22,612	35,739	32,452	33,147	39,475	3,829	3,454
4 years_____	186,475	647	5,386	23,383	39,533	36,373	36,900	38,001	3,158	3,094
5 to 6 years____	157,820	659	5,302	23,442	36,888	28,862	26,468	30,001	3,041	3,157
7 to 8 years____	85,859	417	3,323	14,674	20,171	14,991	13,559	15,486	1,671	1,567
9 to 10 years___	71,153	348	2,712	12,099	15,090	14,301	12,307	12,255	1,060	1,081
11 to 14 years__	81,005	455	3,470	15,572	17,600	15,398	12,839	12,999	1,376	1,296
15 and over____	111,187	712	4,799	18,870	17,986	24,634	22,494	19,335	1,046	1,311

Bureau of Agricultural Economics.

TABLE 549.—*Acreage per farm reporting of the principal crops harvested, by tenure,*
1925

Geographic division	Tenant farms reporting—					Owned farms reporting—				
	Corn for grain, average per farm	Wheat, average per farm	Oats, average per farm	Cotton, average per farm	To- bacco, average per farm	Corn for grain, average per farm	Wheat, average per farm	Oats, average per farm	Cotton, average per farm	To- bacco, average per farm
	Acres	*Acres*	*Acres*	*Acres*	*Acres*	*Acres*	*Acres*	*Acres*	*Acres*	*Acres*
New England	2.8	3.2	9.4	--------	9.5	2.3	3.0	7.5	--------	7.5
Middle Atlantic	11.4	16.5	10.6	--------	5.0	6.3	8.9	7.8	--------	3.9
East North Central	34.3	24.4	24.9	16.4	4.0	18.0	15.6	15.5	12.7	2.8
West North Central	49.4	73.6	35.7	23.9	3.4	37.4	65.6	29.1	15.1	1.6
South Atlantic	11.1	12.5	5.8	12.8	4.4	10.5	9.4	5.8	10.5	3.8
East South Central	11.4	13.3	9.3	14.2	4.2	13.1	11.8	8.6	11.2	3.2
West South Central	12.4	71.0	24.1	30.5	0.5	14.6	76.8	25.6	28.6	1.0
Mountain	38.0	62.6	18.7	43.4	--------	26.3	54.3	16.7	30.2	--------
Pacific	14.7	119.8	31.6	70.5	--------	4.8	68.7	19.7	41.9	--------
United States	21.2	47.6	28.2	21.0	4.3	18.2	35.0	18.7	18.7	3.5

Geographic division	Managed farms reporting—					All farms reporting—				
	Corn for grain, aver- age per farm	Wheat, aver- age per farm	Oats, aver- age per farm	Cotton, aver- age per farm	To- bacco, aver- age per farm	Corn for grain, aver- age per farm	Wheat, aver- age per farm	Oats, aver- age per farm	Cotton, aver- age per farm	To- bacco, aver- age per farm
	Acres	*Acres*	*Acres*	*Acres*	*Acres*	*Acres*	*Acres*	*Acres*	*Acres*	*Acres*
New England	4.1	5.0	13.1	--------	58.4	2.4	3.1	7.7	--------	8.6
Middle Atlantic	13.7	18.2	14.7	--------	7.4	7.3	10.6	8.4	--------	4.4
East North Central	40.5	31.4	29.6	45.2	4.8	23.4	18.4	18.4	15.2	3.2
West North Central	61.5	96.6	43.8	66.9	4.9	42.5	68.8	31.8	21.8	2.2
South Atlantic	38.0	29.0	19.6	45.2	11.9	10.9	10.4	6.0	12.0	4.2
East South Central	48.5	34.7	46.9	59.4	8.0	12.3	12.3	9.1	13.3	3.6
West South Central	80.9	109.6	75.9	93.0	7.0	13.5	74.5	25.1	30.0	0.9
Mountain	97.3	110.0	49.3	250.8	--------	29.8	56.6	17.5	38.2	--------
Pacific	39.7	242.4	66.0	140.1	--------	7.1	84.3	22.8	61.1	--------
United States	45.3	59.8	32.5	74.3	15.9	19.6	39.1	21.8	20.3	3.9

Bureau of Agriculture Economics. Compiled from Census Bureau reports.

TABLE 550.—*Rural and farm population, percentage of total population gainfully*
employed in agriculture, and percentage of total

Census year	Percentage of population			Percentage gainfully employed in agricul- ture
	"Rural" outside of places 8,000 or more	"Rural" outside of places 2,500 or more	On farms	
1820	95.1	--------	--------	83.1
1830	93.3	--------	--------	
1840	91.5	--------	--------	77.5
1850	87.5	--------	--------	
1860	83.9	--------	--------	
1870	79.1	--------	--------	47.5
1880	77.4	70.5	--------	44.3
1890	71.0	63.9	--------	39.2
1900	67.1	60.0	--------	35.7
1910	61.3	54.2	34.7	33.2
1920	56.2	48.6	29.5	26.3
1925	--------	--------	25.3	--------

Bureau of Agricultural Economics. Compiled from reports of Bureau of the Census.

TABLE 551.—Number of marketing and purchasing associations, estimated membership, and estimated amount of business, by geographic divisions and States, 1927–28

Geographic division and State	Cotton and cotton products			Dairy products			Forage			Fruits and vegetables			Grain			Livestock			Nuts		
	Listed	Estimated membership	Estimated business	Listed	Estimated membership	Estimated business	Listed	Estimated membership	Estimated business	Listed	Estimated membership	Estimated business	Listed	Estimated membership	Estimated business	Listed	Estimated membership	Estimated business	Listed	Estimated membership	Estimated business
	Number		1,000 dollars	Number		1,000 dollars	Number		1,000 dollars	Number		1,000 dollars	Number		1,000 dollars	Number		1,000 dollars	Number		1,000 dollars
United States	125	140,000	97,000	2,419	600,000	620,000	15	2,000	1,400	1,259	215,000	300,000	3,455	900,000	680,000	2,012	450,000	320,000	40	15,000	14,600
New England				75	35,800	64,640				30	2,150	3,470	3	600	150						
Maine				5	2,400	8,000				21	1,100	880									
New Hampshire				3	200	380							1	300	140						
Vermont				43	6,600	11,000							1	200							
Massachusetts				15	22,800	32,000				5	650	2,570	1	100	10						
Rhode Island				2	100	260															
Connecticut				7	3,700	13,000				3	350	10									
Middle Atlantic				143	109,100	165,000	2	200	100	107	16,000	18,510	7	2,200	2,920	3	1,400	3,030			
New York				92	65,200	120,000	2	200	100	82	10,700	11,160	4	1,000	2,340	2	1,000	2,660			
New Jersey										8	3,200	5,350									
Pennsylvania				51	43,900	45,000				17	2,100	2,000	3	1,200	580	1	400	370			
East North Central	1			1,111	183,300	162,140				143	22,500	10,960	945	305,000	165,080	755	200,000	133,380			
Ohio				37	32,800	21,000				20	5,100	3,530	210	70,000	38,750	70	33,000	20,500			
Indiana				26	7,400	5,140				25	2,000	200	133	65,000	22,950	90	26,000	18,330			
Illinois	1			43	30,400	7,000				23	2,000	640	440	112,000	76,900	330	78,000	64,810			
Michigan				97	40,100	37,000				59	9,800	3,760	102	34,000	19,480	93	25,000	13,250			
Wisconsin				908	73,000	92,000				26	3,600	2,830	60	24,000	7,000	172	38,000	16,430			
West North Central	5	800		966	211,600	154,120	1	250	10	141	23,250	8,980	2,183	522,000	419,240	1,175	227,000	165,080			
Minnesota				654	103,000	100,000				47	5,600	2,770	308	100,000	46,600	359	70,000	49,730			
Iowa	5	800	150	230	51,200	40,000				3	450	270	377	100,000	65,000	430	80,000	77,800			
Missouri				12	11,600	3,500	1	250	10	68	13,700	5,140	160	48,000	20,970	151	41,000	21,280			
North Dakota				22	1,800	1,000				11	1,200	430	394	62,000	73,220	69	9,000	2,490			
South Dakota				26	6,900	2,700				4	500		242	66,000	48,100	95	12,000	5,830			
Nebraska				17	35,500	6,000				6	1,600	350	354	70,000	79,750	43	10,000	6,280			
Kansas				5	1,700	920				2	200	20	348	82,000	85,100	28	5,000	1,650			

	301	16,500	10,600	10,500	24	10,200	15,780	4			159	28,000	49,520	7	2,100	1,110	28	600	1,530	4	4,500	920
South Atlantic	15	51,100	35,750		36	6,600	2,240	2	400	10	90	14,800	4,660	4	900	250	19	3,500	1,430	2	300	
Delaware	7	5,000	4,700				200	130					350	530	3	1,300	980	1	200	80		
Maryland	3	2,500	3,200		3	3,900	8,000				10	1,750	3,580									
District of Columbia					11	1,000	4,700	1	200		14	7,400	13,800	1	300	100	10	5,000	1,000	1	3,000	500
Virginia					11	2,500	1,900	1	200		10	300	970				17	3,400	300			
West Virginia			4,700		7	2,400	130				16	4,000	5,120									
North Carolina			3,200				920				9	3,000	5,000									
South Carolina	3	2,500									8	4,000	1,370									
Georgia	8	9,000	2,700								86	7,200	19,150	3	500	30						
Florida	20	9,000																200	50		1,500	420
East South Central	15	51,100	35,750		36	6,600	2,240	2	400	10	90	14,800	4,660	4	900	250	19	3,500	1,430	2	300	
Kentucky	4	6,100	2,350		6	700	310	1	200		13	2,000	1,640	2	800	220	3	300	1,100	1	200	
Tennessee	9	28,000	9,000		26	5,200	1,100	1	200		46	5,400	950	2	100	30	8	1,100	70	1	100	
Alabama	9	17,000	24,400		2	200	290				19	4,400	1,320				7	2,000	250			
Mississippi	2	17,000			2	500	570				12	3,000	750				1		10			
West South Central	68	69,600	45,100		7	4,600	780	2	200	200	141	18,600	8,870	101	27,300	25,250	7	700	3,820	1	50	30
Arkansas	6	17,800	1,400				130				76	8,000	2,710	2	900	2,740	1	100				
Louisiana	1	7,800	3,000		1	200	130				23	5,000	3,940	4	1,000	3,910			50			
Oklahoma	13	14,000	18,500		2	300	260				12	1,800	630	81	18,400	14,520	4	400	20			
Texas	48	30,000	22,200		4	4,100	380	2	200	200	30	3,800	1,590	14	7,000	3,780	2	200	3,750	1	50	30
Mountain	5	1,700	4,700		30	11,000	6,750	4	550	650	78	19,500	28,830	139	31,100	35,970	20	3,700	2,950		50	
Montana					5	700	830				3	200	160	65	13,200	18,920	12	2,400	440			
Idaho					10	9,000	4,800				13	1,900	2,900	13	2,300	5,420						
Wyoming					1	100	130		50		1	100		6	1,000	1,310						
Colorado					6	600	770	2	400		42	8,900	19,230	47	13,000	9,520	6	1,100	2,510			
New Mexico	2	700	2,000		1	100	140	1	100		3	300	100	5	800	620	1	100				
Arizona	3	1,000	2,700								4	100	670									
Utah					7	500	80				12	8,000	5,770	2	400	50	1	100				50
Nevada														1	400	130						
Pacific	1	300	700		87	27,800	48,550	4	400	430	380	70,200	166,200	66	8,800	30,030	5	5,100	2,950	33	10,150	13,650
Washington					23	11,500	15,000	1	200		60	7,900	12,700	47	6,300	17,700	1			1		100
Oregon	1	300	700		44	6,600	6,550	3	200	20	35	4,700	6,320	9	700	1,120	4	100	20	4	150	
California					20	9,700	27,000			410	285	57,600	147,180	10	1,800	11,210	4	5,000	8,780	29	10,000	13,550

TABLE 551.—*Number of marketing and purchasing associations, estimated membership, and estimated amount of business, by geographic divisions and States, 1927–28*—Continued

Geographic division and State	Poultry and poultry products			Tobacco			Wool and mohair			Miscellaneous selling			Miscellaneous buying			Total		
	Listed	Estimated membership	Estimated business	Listed	Estimated membership	Estimated business	Listed	Estimated membership	Estimated business	Listed	Estimated membership	Estimated business	Listed	Estimated membership	Estimated business	Listed	Estimated membership	Estimated business
	Number		*1,000 dollars*	*Number*		*1,000 dollars*	*Number*		*1,000 dollars*	*Number*		*1,000 dollars*	*Number*		*1,000 dollars*	*Number*		*1,000 dollars*
United States	90	50,000	40,000	16	15,000	22,000	99	25,000	7,000	595	190,000	70,000	1,205	398,000	128,000	11,400	3,000,000	2,300,000
New England	2	300	460				4	950	60	17	5,200	1,950	82	37,900	16,010	213	82,900	86,740
Maine							1	700	30	3	1,400	440	26	5,400	3,180	56	11,000	12,480
New Hampshire										1	900	200	8	2,700	1,800	13	4,100	2,580
Vermont										11	2,500	1,220	4	1,350	720	60	10,700	13,000
Massachusetts							2	150	20	2	400	90	12	25,000	7,800	37	49,100	42,480
Rhode Island													4	300	310	6	400	570
Connecticut							1	100	10				28	3,150	2,140	41	7,600	15,620
Middle Atlantic	4	800	500	5	700	130	39	2,400	190	37	7,500	4,240	161	77,400	22,870	508	217,700	217,490
New York	3	500	500				28	700	90	12	1,900	330	65	46,000	16,000	291	127,500	153,260
New Jersey				1	300	80				3	1,600	480	11	2,900	2,750	22	7,700	8,580
Pennsylvania	1	300		4	400	50	11	1,700	100	22	4,000	3,430	85	28,500	4,120	195	82,500	55,650
East North Central	6	3,500	740	5	5,100	2,660	7	9,000	1,094	168	56,000	18,330	217	72,200	27,526	3,358	866,600	521,910
Ohio	1	1,800	500				1	7,000	800	15	6,000	1,170	20	14,500	5,170	375	170,300	91,420
Indiana	1	200	40	1	100	1	3	1,100	130	14	5,300	2,050	29	8,800	7,600	309	115,400	56,500
Illinois	2	600	100				1	200	20	18	8,300	1,520	40	12,400	3,160	900	243,900	154,150
Michigan							1	200	86	71	22,800	6,900	41	9,000	5,544	464	141,200	86,020
Wisconsin	2	900	100	4	5,000	2,660	1	200	58	50	13,600	6,690	87	27,500	6,052	1,310	185,800	133,820
West North Central	28	19,000	12,930				15	5,050	569	193	77,700	27,340	521	144,350	34,381	5,228	1,231,000	822,780
Minnesota	15	8,000	1,000				4	2,500	260	20	5,100	1,380	140	44,800	8,200	1,547	339,000	209,940
Iowa	2	2,500	30				2	650	82	13	4,800	4,270	104	27,300	5,748	1,161	264,900	193,700
Missouri	8	8,000	11,800				2	300	30	130	58,800	17,900	87	21,150	7,000	624	203,500	87,780
North Dakota							2	800	90	9	1,800	1,190	27	5,500	1,150	534	82,100	79,570
South Dakota	1	300					2	500	75	3	1,300	350	24	4,800	1,015	397	86,300	58,070
Nebraska	2	2,200	100				1	100	32	11	2,700	1,370	67	23,800	7,098	501	145,900	100,980
Kansas							2	200		7	3,200	880	72	17,000	4,170	464	109,300	92,740

South Atlantic	4	200	20	2	5,100	2	2,150	4	1,400	120	38	10,000	4,570	63	21,000	9,430	363	107,600	95,750
Delaware				1							1	300	90	1	150	10	9	1,000	760
Maryland					5,000	1	2,150	2	100		2	400	230	10	5,450	1,480	32	18,100	16,500
District of Columbia						1											1	1,000	4,700
Virginia								2	1,300	120	9	4,100	1,710	22	6,500	5,750	68	28,800	24,850
West Virginia											5	1,800	760	7	3,300	640	42	10,300	3,400
North Carolina	1	100	10	1	100						10	1,100	1,170	15	4,100	70	58	17,100	12,580
South Carolina		100	10								2	500	130	1	1,100	100	15	6,100	8,400
Georgia	1										8	1,600	360	4	1,000	100	45	17,300	4,960
Florida	3										1	200	120	3	400	320	93	7,900	19,600
East South Central	8	1,200	65	3	4,000		17,000	13	2,000	205	59	13,500	4,150	24	6,300	1,210	275	104,600	66,970
Kentucky	2	100	25	1	1,000		15,000	4	500	25	17	1,200	810	7	2,400	350	45	9,000	19,480
Tennessee	5	800	40	2	3,000		2,000	7	1,400	100	17	3,500	700	7	2,100	380	126	29,100	7,730
Alabama	1							2	100	80	14	2,600	1,820	8	1,700	380	63	39,300	13,110
Mississippi		300									21	6,200	820	2	100	100	41	27,200	26,650
West South Central	14	1,800	330	1	100		60	2	200	140	39	9,400	3,290	45	11,450	2,250	428	144,000	90,120
Arkansas	2	500						2			5	1,200	580	12	2,300	680	104	30,800	8,160
Louisiana	1	100	10	1	100						5	2,200	710	2	200	70	40	16,600	11,830
Oklahoma		1,200	320				60				7	3,000	700	14	4,000	860	133	41,900	35,790
Texas	11								200	140	20	3,000	1,300	17	4,950	640	151	54,700	34,340
Mountain	10	6,700	3,055					13	1,700	2,772	30	8,100	4,210	33	9,750	2,993	362	93,800	92,880
Montana	2	400	40					2	700	1,000	4	300	350	9	2,700	600	102	20,600	22,340
Idaho	2	3,000	1,180					3	300	72	6	2,500	1,550	7	2,600	528	54	21,600	16,450
Wyoming	1	200	60					1	100	600	3	1,900	680	3	1,200	320	16	4,600	3,100
Colorado	1	400						2	300	360	7	1,500	680	7	650	410	116	26,500	33,480
New Mexico	1	300									3	600	140	3	400	540	21	3,500	4,190
Arizona	1	100	35								4	900	460	3	200	135	15	2,600	4,000
Utah	2	2,300	1,740					4	200	500	3	400	350	5	2,000	460	36	13,900	8,950
Nevada								1	100	240							2	500	370
Pacific	14	16,500	21,900					2	2,300	1,850	14	2,600	1,920	59	17,650	11,330	665	161,800	305,360
Washington	6	8,500	10,000					1	2,200	1,750	5	700	580	36	9,400	3,920	177	44,300	59,900
Oregon	2	2,000	1,900					1	100	100	4	700	850	8	2,050	510	109	19,400	19,140
California	6	6,000	10,00								5	1,200	490	15	6,200	6,900	379	98,100	226,320

Bureau of Agricultural Economics.

NOTE.—Tables similar to Tables 520 and 521, 1927 Yearbook, farms reporting sales and purchases through cooperative associations, by States, and by tenure, are omitted.

TABLE 552.—*Farm population*[1] *of the United States, 1910, 1920–1928, by years*

Year	Number	Year	Number
1910 (estimated)	31, 400, 000	1924 (estimated)	29, 400, 000
1920 (estimated)	31, 000, 000	1925 (Census of 1925)	28, 981, 668
1921 (estimated)	30, 600, 000	1926 (estimated)	28, 502, 000
1922 (estimated)	30, 200, 000	1927 (estimated)	27, 853, 000
1923 (estimated)	29, 800, 000	1928 (estimated)	27, 699, 000

Bureau of the Census.

[1] Farm population, as here used, is in accord with the definition in the 1925 Census of Agriculture—namely "all persons living on farms."

TABLE 553.—*Estimated population, January 1 of 1925, 1926, 1927, and 1928*

	1925	1926	1927	1928
United States	114, 553, 000	116, 257, 000	117, 882, 000	119, 320, 000
Alabama	2, 484, 000	2, 512, 000	2, 538, 000	2, 562, 000
Arizona	419, 000	436, 000	452, 000	468, 000
Arkansas	1, 869, 000	1, 891, 000	1, 913, 000	1, 935, 000
California	4, 112, 000	4, 248, 000	4, 375, 000	4, 501, 000
Colorado	1, 032, 000	1, 050, 000	1, 066, 000	1, 083, 000
Connecticut	1, 555, 000	1, 589, 000	1, 621, 000	1, 653, 000
Delaware	236, 000	239, 000	241, 000	243, 000
District of Columbia	507, 000	521, 000	534, 000	546, 000
Florida	1, 256, 000	1, 290, 000	1, 340, 000	1, 389, 000
Georgia	3, 083, 000	3, 120, 000	3, 155, 000	3, 188, 000
Idaho	502, 000	515, 000	528, 000	541, 000
Illinois	7, 037, 000	7, 148, 000	7, 250, 000	7, 351, 000
Indiana	3, 079, 000	3, 110, 000	3, 137, 000	3, 164, 000
Iowa	2, 420, 000	2, 421, 000	2, 424, 000	2, 427, 000
Kansas	1, 812, 000	1, 817, 000	1, 824, 000	1, 832, 000
Kentucky	2, 499, 000	2, 516, 000	2, 531, 000	2, 546, 000
Louisiana	1, 891, 000	1, 909, 000	1, 926, 000	1, 943, 000
Maine	785, 000	788, 000	791, 000	794, 000
Maryland	1, 551, 000	1, 570, 000	1, 589, 000	1, 608, 000
Massachusetts	4, 130, 000	4, 171, 000	4, 220, 000	4, 269, 000
Michigan	4, 228, 000	4, 340, 000	4, 443, 000	4, 547, 000
Minnesota	2, 590, 000	2, 631, 000	2, 669, 000	2, 706, 000
Mississippi	[1] 1, 790, 618	[1] 1, 790, 618	[1] 1, 790, 618	[1] 1, 790, 618
Missouri	3, 476, 000	3, 491, 000	3, 504, 000	3, 517, 000
Montana	662, 000	684, 000	705, 000	[1] 548, 889
Nebraska	1, 365, 000	1, 378, 000	1, 390, 000	1, 403, 000
Nevada	[1] 77, 407	[1] 77, 407	[1] 77, 407	[1] 77, 407
New Hampshire	451, 000	453, 000	454, 000	455, 000
New Jersey	3, 560, 000	3, 640, 000	3, 715, 000	3, 789, 000
New Mexico	382, 000	386, 000	390, 000	394, 000
New York	11, 102, 000	11, 233, 000	11, 364, 000	11, 493, 000
North Carolina	2, 789, 000	2, 835, 000	2, 877, 000	2, 920, 000
North Dakota	641, 000	[2] 641, 192	[2] 641, 192	[2] 641, 192
Ohio	6, 406, 000	6, 535, 000	6, 655, 000	6, 774, 000
Oklahoma	2, 271, 000	2, 318, 000	2, 363, 000	2, 407, 000
Oregon	856, 000	870, 000	884, 000	896, 000
Pennsylvania	9, 406, 000	9, 545, 000	9, 672, 000	9, 798, 000
Rhode Island	675, 000	686, 000	699, 000	711, 000
South Carolina	1, 794, 000	1, 815, 000	1, 835, 000	1, 855, 000
South Dakota	678, 000	685, 000	693, 000	701, 000
Tennessee	2, 438, 000	2, 458, 000	2, 476, 000	2, 494, 000
Texas	5, 163, 000	5, 263, 000	5, 355, 000	5, 447, 000
Utah	499, 000	509, 000	518, 000	527, 000
Vermont	[1] 352, 428	[1] 352, 428	[1] 352, 428	[1] 352, 428
Virginia	2, 470, 000	2, 503, 000	2, 532, 000	2, 562, 000
Washington	1, 497, 000	1, 524, 000	1, 550, 000	1, 576, 000
West Virginia	1, 623, 000	1, 654, 000	1, 683, 000	1, 712, 000
Wisconsin	2, 826, 000	2, 865, 000	2, 901, 000	2, 937, 000
Wyoming	226, 000	233, 000	238, 000	245, 000

Bureau of the Census.

[1] Population Jan. 1, 1920; decrease 1910 to 1920; no estimate made.
[2] Population State census, 1925. No estimate made.

GENERAL NOTE.—Tables similar to Table 514, farm population, by age, etc.; Table 516, farm population, by States, and Table 517, rural population, by States, 1927 Yearbook, are omitted.

Table 554.—*Refrigerated space, United States: All cold storages and meat-packing establishments reporting to the Bureau of Agricultural Economics, October 1, 1927*

Division and State	Concerns	Space held at temperatures of—				Total space
		10° F. and below	11° to 29° F. inclusive	30° to 44° F. inclusive	45° F. and above	
New England:		*Cubic feet*	*Cubic feet*	*Cubic feet*	*Cubic feet*	*Cubic feet*
Maine	8	437, 380	5, 950	934, 097	4, 907	1, 382, 334
New Hampshire and Vermont	5	7, 494	58, 876	349, 325	30, 000	445, 695
Massachusetts	36	7, 071, 400	1, 378, 438	14, 413, 193	388, 025	23, 251, 056
Rhode Island	5	338, 178	409, 080	834, 928		1, 582, 186
Connecticut	8	152, 890	267, 750	1, 356, 069	12, 000	1, 788, 709
Total	62	8, 007, 342	2, 120, 094	17, 887, 612	434, 932	28, 449, 980
Middle Atlantic:						
New York	190	13, 310, 733	5, 758, 461	61, 627, 262	2, 699, 040	83, 395, 496
New Jersey	37	3, 810, 765	1, 044, 526	13, 997, 773	510, 823	19, 363, 887
Pennsylvania	101	3, 636, 285	2, 995, 263	19, 979, 209	768, 400	27, 379, 157
Total	328	20, 757, 783	9, 798, 250	95, 604, 244	3, 978, 263	130, 138, 540
East North Central:						
Ohio	90	2, 739, 054	2, 135, 406	20, 892, 574	1, 339, 268	27, 106, 302
Indiana	46	964, 682	1, 331, 049	14, 644, 943	1, 008, 832	17, 949, 506
Illinois	80	22, 417, 636	26, 459, 515	72, 475, 887	7, 637, 523	128, 990, 561
Michigan	35	1, 808, 234	1, 135, 551	8, 696, 147	106, 193	11, 746, 125
Wisconsin	68	787, 368	872, 994	11, 516, 062	1, 452, 890	14, 629, 314
Total	319	28, 716, 974	31, 934, 515	128, 225, 613	11, 544, 706	200, 421, 808
West North Central:						
Minnesota	28	2, 941, 741	2, 390, 103	14, 721, 805	2, 774, 384	22, 828, 033
Iowa	36	2, 290, 548	2, 029, 409	18, 470, 333	1, 526, 484	24, 316, 774
Missouri	48	3, 745, 917	2, 189, 569	27, 702, 869	1, 245, 788	34, 884, 143
North and South Dakota	9	246, 208	662, 954	5, 219, 403	465, 030	6, 593, 595
Nebraska	21	3, 081, 996	1, 848, 765	16, 171, 528	1, 540, 075	22, 642, 364
Kansas	29	2, 803, 803	3, 877, 349	28, 571, 200	6, 598, 958	41, 851, 310
Total	171	15, 110, 213	12, 998, 149	110, 857, 138	14, 150, 719	153, 116, 219
South Atlantic:						
Delaware and Maryland	19	546, 132	366, 431	3, 071, 085	258, 668	4, 242, 316
District of Columbia	4	306, 000	1, 500	3, 493, 750	618, 750	4, 420, 000
Virginia	26	230, 960	809, 492	11, 357, 504	1, 396, 350	13, 794, 306
West Virginia	18	6, 979	112, 507	4, 386, 658	394, 221	4, 900, 365
North and South Carolina	9	18, 000	30, 500	525, 376	31, 500	605, 376
Georgia	19	220, 022	293, 946	3, 456, 923	27, 351	3, 998, 242
Florida	11	60, 817	193, 970	625, 047	57, 822	937, 656
Total	106	1, 388, 910	1, 808, 346	26, 916, 343	2, 784, 662	32, 898, 261
East South Central:						
Kentucky	14	345, 546	341, 498	4, 297, 788	43, 814	5, 028, 646
Tennessee	19	467, 882	471, 804	5, 110, 677	284, 094	6, 334, 457
Alabama and Mississippi	8	120, 653	54, 648	1, 160, 696	85, 972	1, 421, 969
Total	41	934, 081	867, 950	10, 569, 161	413, 880	12, 785, 072
West South Central:						
Arkansas	5		5, 000	1, 132, 440		1, 137, 440
Louisiana	7	267, 812	95, 249	2, 530, 852	100, 000	2, 993, 913
Oklahoma	14	413, 065	1, 208, 397	5, 885, 414	971, 772	8, 478, 648
Texas	54	963, 002	1, 489, 738	10, 929, 239	2, 039, 345	15, 421, 324
Total	80	1, 643, 879	2, 798, 384	20, 477, 945	3, 111, 117	28, 031, 325
Mountain:						
Montana	6	36, 227	43, 848	186, 545	18, 968	285, 588
Idaho	11	43, 835	73, 023	639, 746	6, 870	763, 474
Colorado	21	1, 136, 877	889, 262	5, 139, 606	422, 396	7, 588, 141
Utah	6	99, 760	273, 091	725, 908	38, 400	1, 137, 159
Arizona	3	11, 000		480, 778		491, 778
Wyoming, New Mexico, and Nevada	5	8, 262	12, 144	270, 709	7, 675	298, 790
Total	52	1, 335, 961	1, 291, 368	7, 443, 292	494, 309	10, 564, 930
Pacific:						
Washington	100	997, 079	3, 951, 423	30, 796, 590	753, 422	36, 498, 514
Oregon	29	1, 216, 503	1, 567, 112	4, 493, 282	178, 547	7, 455, 444
California	70	1, 701, 060	1, 761, 839	22, 406, 013	207, 944	26, 076, 856
Alaska	5	77, 152	1, 300, 388	30, 084	2, 000	1, 409, 624
Total	204	3, 991, 794	8, 580, 762	57, 725, 969	1, 141, 913	71, 440, 438
Total for the United States	1, 363	81, 886, 937	72, 197, 818	475, 707, 317	38, 054, 501	667, 846, 573

TABLE 554.—*Refrigerated space, United States: All cold storages and meat-packing establishments reporting to the Bureau of Agricultural Economics, October 1, 1927—* Continued

SUMMARY BY CLASS OF BUSINESS

Class of business	Con- cerns	Space held at temperatures of—				Total space
		10° F. and below	11° to 29° F., inclusive	30° to 44° F., inclusive	45° F. and above	
		Cubic feet	Cubic feet	Cubic feet	Cubic feet	Cubic feet
Meat-packing establishments	378	13, 394, 307	33, 361, 006	176, 862, 508	21, 937, 083	245, 554, 904
Private cold storages	273	3, 885, 602	2, 780, 340	17, 301, 828	838, 097	24, 805, 867
Public cold storages	462	47, 736, 413	21, 179, 386	197, 890, 545	7, 089, 977	273, 896, 321
Combined public and private cold storages	219	8, 932, 017	9, 978, 798	37, 073, 157	1, 291, 138	57, 275, 110
Packing establishments doing public cold-storage business	31	7, 938, 598	4, 898, 288	46, 579, 279	6, 898, 206	66, 314, 371
Total	1, 363	81, 886, 937	72, 197, 818	475, 707, 317	38, 054, 501	667, 846, 573

Bureau of Agricultural Economics.

TABLE 555.—*Freight tonnage originating on railways in the United States, 1922–1927* [1]

Commodity	Calendar year					
	1922	1923	1924	1925	1926	1927
FARM PRODUCTS						
Animals and animal products:	*1,000 short tons*	*1,000 short tons*	*1,000 short tons*	*1,000 short tons*	*1,000 short tons*	*1,000 short tons*
Animals, live—						
Horses and mules	491	603	531	544	513	541
Cattle and calves	9,567	9,400	9,316	9,330	9,241	8,636
Sheep and goats	1,159	1,159	1,215	1,224	1,270	1,296
Hogs	5,795	6,944	6,707	5,502	5,271	5,369
Packing-house products—						
Fresh meats	2,614	3,023	3,001	2,904	2,996	2,986
Hides and leather	1,081	1,090	1,025	1,026	984	1,010
Other packing-house products	2,049	2,397	2,395	2,140	2,023	1,957
Total packing-house products	5,744	6,510	6,421	6,070	6,003	5,953
Eggs	565	597	572	591	644	651
Butter and cheese	507	571	649	686	725	747
Poultry	292	366	376	357	408	407
Wool	360	291	294	263	281	356
Other animals and products	1,750	1,814	1,668	1,758	1,888	2,054
Total animals and animal products	26,230	28,255	27,749	26,325	26,244	26,010
Vegetable products:						
Cotton	3,074	2,887	3,261	4,127	4,482	4,182
Fruits and vegetables	9,683	10,398	10,868	11,634	12,223	12,029
Potatoes	4,829	4,698	4,590	4,614	4,339	4,728
Grain and grain products—						
Grain—						
Wheat	24,805	23,091	27,442	21,548	24,379	26,237
Corn	19,275	15,151	14,883	12,680	13,924	13,162
Oats	7,646	8,332	8,507	8,450	6,496	5,518
Other grain	5,245	4,739	5,616	4,564	4,014	5,216
Grain products—						
Flour and meal	10,694	10,518	10,330	9,901	10,137	10,027
Other mill products	9,000	10,002	10,083	9,578	9,768	10,179
Total grain and grain products	76,665	71,833	76,861	66,721	68,718	70,339
Hay, straw, and alfalfa	5,723	5,965	5,802	5,506	5,028	4,468
Sugar, sirup glucose, and molasses	5,091	4,891	5,356	5,700	5,744	5,584
Tobacco	882	1,099	1,069	1,038	1,010	1,053
Other vegetable products	11,868	13,406	15,277	17,118	17,609	18,469
Total vegetable products	117,815	115,177	123,084	116,458	119,153	120,852
Canned goods (food products)	3,106	3,435	3,731	4,144	4,070	4,204
Total farm products	147,151	146,867	154,564	146,927	149,467	151,066
OTHER FREIGHT						
Products of mines	532,998	713,735	638,520	678,336	758,064	713,731
Products of forests	89,059	115,618	108,090	107,391	104,859	99,391
Manufactures	211,308	258,471	246,432	274,001	284,640	279,407
Merchandise, all l. c. l. freight	43,229	44,339	40,551	40,587	39,498	38,432
Total tonnage	1,023,745	1,279,030	1,188,157	1,247,242	1,336,528	1,282,027

Bureau of Agricultural Economics. Compiled from reports of the Interstate Commerce Commission. Figures for earlier years appear in previous issues of the Yearbook.

[1] Freight tonnage as delivered at original shipping point.

TABLE 556.—*Index numbers of freight rates on livestock, wheat, and cotton,*
1913–1928

Year beginning July 1	Livestock						
	Cattle				Hogs		
	Western district	Eastern district	Southern district	United States	Western district	Eastern district	United States
1913	100	100	100	100	100	100	100
1914	100	104	100	100	99	102	100
1915	100	108	99	101	99	107	101
1916	100	113	98	102	99	116	102
1917	101	116	98	103	100	122	104
1918	126	158	120	129	124	169	132
1919	128	157	120	131	124	169	132
1920	166	207	148	170	161	222	172
1921	165	211	147	170	160	230	173
1922	156	197	137	160	153	218	164
1923	155	201	136	160	153	217	164
1924	153	199	136	159	151	214	163
1925	153	199	136	158	150	214	161
1926	153	199	136	158	150	214	161
1927	152	199	136	157	150	214	161
1928 [1]	152	198	136	157	150	211	161

Year beginning July 1	Livestock—Continued				Wheat				Cotton
	Sheep			Total	Spring	Western	Winter	All wheat [2]	
	Western district	Eastern district	United States						
1913	100	100	100	100	100	100	100	100	100
1914	99	102	99	100	100	100	101	101	100
1915	98	105	99	101	101	100	100	100	100
1916	98	112	100	102	101	100	101	101	100
1917	99	129	103	103	101	100	101	101	103
1918	118	167	126	130	127	126	129	128	133
1919	119	167	127	131	127	126	128	128	136
1920	152	225	164	170	164	154	166	164	172
1921	148	226	160	170	160	148	162	160	176
1922	137	199	147	160	149	140	152	150	164
1923	137	200	147	160	149	140	152	150	164
1924	137	200	146	158	149	140	152	150	166
1925	135	200	145	157	148	140	152	150	166
1926	134	200	144	157	148	140	152	150	166
1927	134	200	144	157	148	140	151	149	165
1928 [1]	134	196	144	157	148	140	149	148	164

Bureau of Agricultural Economics. These relatives are based on the average of the monthly rates in effect during the crop year. Rates in effect in 1913=100. For points of origin and destination, see Yearbook, 1926, pp. 1248–1249.

[1] Based on rates in effect to Dec. 31, 1928.
[2] Index for spring, western, and winter wheat weighted respectively 2, 1, and 5. Weight based on average production, 1923–1927.

GENERAL NOTE.—Tables similar to Table 523, 1927 yearbook, index numbers of cotton freight rates, by origin and destination, and Table 525, ocean freight rates, are omitted.

TABLE 557.—*Fertilizer and fertilizer materials: Production and value in the United States, 1925–1927*

Item	Quantity			Value		
	1925	1926	1927	1925	1926	1927
	Short tons	*Short tons*	*Short tons*	*Dollars*	*Dollars*	*Dollars*
Fish scrap, dried and acidulated		46,992	44,403			
Lime sold for agricultural purposes [1]	298,976	297,010	322,893	2,129,169	2,153,233	2,237,871
Lime, calcareous marl and peat for fertilizer:						
Calcareous marl, sold	68,670	55,060	52,962	187,839	146,094	180,166
Hydrated lime, sold	166,965	184,293	215,027	1,384,651	1,465,572	1,622,082
Limestone, pulverized, sold	1,954,480	1,850,620	2,206,470	2,880,589	3,064,235	3,360,704
Peat, produced [2]	72,436	61,936		452,898	364,413	
Total	2,262,551	2,151,909		4,905,977	5,040,314	
Phosphate rock, sold or used:						
Florida—	*Long tons*	*Long tons*	*Long tons*			
Hard rock	171,649	116,264	131,254	707,933	465,308	525,016
Land pebble	2,758,315	2,591,943	2,506,166	8,081,137	8,218,200	8,121,146
Total	2,929,964	2,708,207	2,637,420	8,789,070	8,683,508	8,646,162
South Carolina—						
Land rock	2,147			8,051		
Tennessee and Kentucky—						
Brown and blue rock	477,077	464,192	[3] 477,172	2,429,059	2,048,272	[3] 2,300,296
Other States	72,631	37,577	51,510	319,498	162,020	288,405
Total phosphate rock	3,481,819	3,209,976	3,166,102	11,545,678	10,893,800	11,234,863
Pyrites produced	170,081	166,559	215,786	650,448	616,668	804,006

Bureau of Agricultural Economics. Compiled from annual reports of the American Fertilizer Handbook, Bureau of Mines, and the Geological Survey. Figures for earlier years appear in previous issues of the Yearbook.

[1] Porto Rico and Hawaii included.   [2] Production for all purposes.   [3] Tennessee only.

TABLE 558.—*Fertilizers and fertilizer materials: Production, consumption, imports, and exports, United States, 1923–1927*

Item	1923	1924	1925	1926	1927 [1]
Sulphate of ammonia:	*Short tons*	*Short tons*	*Short tons*	*Short tons*	*Short tons*
Production [2]	575,363	544,622	639,019	690,976	683,000
Sales [2]	558,196	660,996	604,457	682,967	
Imports for consumption	3,967	6,720	26,613	9,392	19,211
Exports	172,118	132,571	137,918	202,860	155,335
Nitrate of soda, imports for consumption	998,680	1,105,035	1,245,693	1,024,009	838,636
Sulphuric acid:					
Production (50° Baumé) [3]	1,631,216	1,576,544	1,979,292	1,745,759	1,656,871
Imports for consumption [4]	11,754	7,734	18,191	27,969	17,434
Exports	4,122	5,636	3,769	4,612	3,756
Made and consumed [3]	1,365,883	1,782,816	1,316,316	2,058,683	1,897,721
Acid phosphate:					
Production [3]	3,367,220	3,250,498	3,846,401	3,799,054	3,466,738
Sales [3] [5]	3,037,393	3,381,202	3,550,762	3,536,552	3,446,519
Potash:					
Production, domestic	39,029	43,719	51,565	46,324	76,819
Sales, domestic	35,164	37,492	52,823	51,369	94,722
Imports for consumption—					
Kainit	187,833	175,513	204,767	203,702	115,345
Manure salts	301,721	258,998	430,340	354,413	311,357
Muriate of potash	151,757	144,623	180,351	223,049	183,475
Sulphate of potash	71,390	84,780	77,226	78,258	77,172
Other potash-bearing substances [6]	32,228	46,946	29,002	52,357	10,531
Total imports for consumption	744,929	710,860	921,686	911,779	697,880

Bureau of Agricultural Economics. Compiled from annual reports of the Bureau of the Census, Bureau of Mines, Bureau of Foreign and Domestic Commerce, Geological Survey, and the American Fertilizer Handbook. Figures for earlier years appear in previous issues of the Yearbook.

[1] Subject to revision.
[2] By-products of coke ovens. The quantity produced from other sources (coal gas, bone carbonizing, etc.), was estimated to be 28,000 short tons in 1923 and 25,000 short tons in 1924–1927.
[3] Fertilizer establishments only.
[4] Imports for all purposes.
[5] Quantity sold as acid phosphate or used in the manufacture of other fertilizers.
[6] Includes ashes (wood), beet root, other potash-bearing substances (alunite, leucite, etc.) used for fertilizer.

NOTE.—A table similar to Table 527, 1927 Yearbook, farm expenditures for fertilizers, by States, is omitted.

TABLE 559.—*Fertilizer, commercial: Sold in cotton States, 1922–1928*

COMMERCIAL FERTILIZER

State	Year ended	1922	1923	1924	1925	1926	1927 [1]	1928 [1]
		Short tons	Short tons	Short tons	Short tons	Short tons	Short tons	Short tons
Virginia	Dec. 31	449,942	422,350	441,895	451,656	435,223	301,153	336,173
North Carolina	June 30	924,536	1,081,813	1,189,316	1,217,468	1,213,178	1,144,019	1,378,348
South Carolina	...do....	505,768	678,795	897,093	866,377	840,955	720,396	817,548
Georgia	...do....	525,579	677,040	688,783	770,889	760,643	705,053	897,964
Florida	May 31	323,087	378,885	386,521	361,849	355,373	402,842	456,455
Alabama	Sept. 30	295,429	436,786	472,260	580,000	603,444	461,000	690,267
Mississippi	...do....	130,648	215,854	213,516	257,763	280,890	210,602	316,893
Louisiana	Aug. 31	66,470	108,712	129,288	103,989	116,049	90,090	132,684
Texas	...do....	34,316	76,223	126,592	103,416	123,900	79,560	139,477
Arkansas	Sept. 30	40,325	74,774	89,112	122,742	103,931	63,562	103,880
Tennessee	May 31	112,656	105,417	135,270	155,248	135,257	115,973	156,956
Total		3,408,756	4,256,649	4,769,646	4,991,397	4,968,843	4,294,250	5,426,645

COTTONSEED MEAL USED AS FERTILIZER [2]

North Carolina	June 30	110,899	108,772	117,626	109,029	150,377	176,476	112,165
Mississippi	Sept. 30	39,290	41,867	49,923	62,090	71,937	81,075	51,015

Bureau of Agricultural Economics. Based on sales of fertilizer tags. Figures for earlier years appear in previous issues of the Yearbook.

[1] For 1927 and 1928 sales are reported to the following dates: June 1, Mississippi, Louisiana, and Arkansas; July 1, Virginia and Alabama; and 1928, July 1 for Texas. Sales after these dates do not usually exceed 1 or 2 per cent of the United States total for the year.

[2] Not separately reported except for North Carolina and Mississippi.

TABLE 560.—*Insecticides and fungicides: Average wholesale price per pound, New York, 1919–1927* [1]

Year	Arsenic white	Calcium arsenate	Lead arsenate		Paris green	Bordeaux mixture		Lime-sulphur solution per gallon
			Powder	Paste		Powder	Paste	
	Cents	Cents	Cents	Cents	Cents	Cents	Cents	Cents
1919	9.9		29.9	14.9	35.8	16.5	12.4	19.1
1920	13.8		26.3	13.3	36.2	19.3	13.2	18.8
1921	7.9	19.1	19.4	11.6	27.0	17.2	10.9	16.6
1922	8.9	13.7	14.8	11.1	22.6	16.8	10.8	16.5
1923	14.2	16.4	22.2	15.7	30.4	22.0	16.3	16.5
1924	9.4	10.6	20.9	13.1	28.8	16.3	12.5	16.5
1925	5.1	7.8	15.6	11.0	21.5	13.2	11.0	16.5
1926	3.8	8.0	14.6	11.0	18.4	11.5	11.0	14.7
1927	4.0	7.5	13.8		19.2	11.5	11.0	15.5

Bureau of Agricultural Economics. Compiled from the Oil, Paint, and Drug Reporter.

[1] Average of monthly range.

TABLE 561.—*Insecticides and fungicides: Production of certain arsenic compounds, and quantity of arsenic used in their manufacture, specified years*

Year ended	Calcium arsenate	Lead arsenate		Paris green	Arsenic (99 per cent prime white) used in the manufacture of—		
		Powder	Paste		Calcium arsenate	Lead arsenate	Paris green
	Pounds	Pounds	Pounds	Pounds	Pounds	Pounds	Pounds
Dec. 31:							
1919	1,191,868	11,465,788					
1921	2,419,684	9,229,701					
1923	13,261,233	10,755,137					
June 30:							
1925	19,911,262	13,523,902	341,580	3,544,887	7,702,069	3,932,644	2,441,540
1926	5,363,320	16,573,784	324,430	2,863,691	2,111,782	5,384,193	2,255,069
Aug. 31, 1927	18,715,563	18,359,122	368,932	5,743,048	7,012,219	5,153,103	4,195,693

Bureau of Agricultural Economics. Compiled from reports of the Bureau of the Census.

TABLE 562.—*Fertilizer used on cotton, 1926–1928*

State	Acreage in cotton					
	July 1			Fertilized		
	1926 [1]	1927 [1]	1928	1926	1927	1928
	1,000 acres	*1,000 acres*	*1,000 acres*	*1,000 acres*	*1,000 acres*	*1,000 acres*
Missouri	472	305	371	24	15	19
Virginia	95	65	81	89	62	79
North Carolina	2,015	1,749	1,919	1,955	1,679	1,900
South Carolina	2,716	2,454	2,479	2,553	2,258	2,330
Georgia	4,025	3,501	3,874	3,864	3,291	3,719
Florida	108	67	101	98	56	87
Tennessee	1,178	985	1,120	589	473	683
Alabama	3,699	3,214	3,706	3,366	2,828	3,447
Mississippi	3,809	3,408	4,139	1,828	1,329	2,028
Arkansas	3,867	3,142	3,760	1,469	943	1,504
Louisiana	2,019	1,585	2,046	848	634	880
Oklahoma	5,083	4,187	4,426	36	21	44
Texas	19,140	16,850	18,353	766	421	1,101
New Mexico	125	100	114	1	1	
Arizona	168	140	202			
California	167	130	223			
All other	44	23	29			
United States	48,730	41,905	46,943	17,486	14,011	17,821

State	Fertilizer used					
	Average per acre			Total		
	1926	1927	1928	1926	1927	1928
	Pounds	*Pounds*	*Pounds*	*Short tons*	*Short tons*	*Short tons*
Missouri	125	125	125	1,500	938	1,188
Virginia	390	375	375	17,355	11,625	14,812
North Carolina	440	420	440	430,100	352,590	418,000
South Carolina	325	315	325	414,862	355,635	378,625
Georgia	257	247	260	496,524	406,438	483,470
Florida	245	215	255	12,005	6,020	11,092
Tennessee	220	206	216	64,790	48,719	73,764
Alabama	255	243	262	429,165	343,602	451,557
Mississippi	222	216	220	202,908	143,532	223,080
Arkansas	185	173	187	135,882	81,570	140,624
Louisiana	190	175	185	80,560	55,475	81,400
Oklahoma	175	145	190	3,150	1,522	4,180
Texas	185	185	197	70,855	38,942	108,448
New Mexico	190	165		95	82	
Arizona						
California						
All other						
United States	270	264	268	2,359,751	1,846,690	2,390,240

State	Value								
	Average price per ton			Total			Average per acre		
	1926	1927	1928	1926	1927	1928	1926	1927	1928
	Dollars	*Dollars*	*Dollars*	*1,000 dollars*	*1,000 dollars*	*1,000 dollars*	*Dollars*	*Dollars*	*Dollars*
Missouri	35.00	35.50	34.40	52	33	41	2.17	2.20	2.16
Virginia	30.50	24.00	28.30	529	279	419	5.94	4.50	5.30
North Carolina	30.10	24.00	29.00	12,946	8,462	12,122	6.62	5.04	6.38
South Carolina	29.20	22.00	27.30	12,114	7,824	10,336	4.75	3.47	4.44
Georgia	31.10	23.00	29.70	15,442	9,348	14,359	4.00	2.84	3.86
Florida	30.50	27.50	30.80	366	166	342	3.73	2.96	3.93
Tennessee	36.20	28.30	33.20	2,345	1,379	2,449	3.98	2.92	3.59
Alabama	33.20	26.00	32.20	14,248	8,934	14,540	4.23	3.16	4.22
Mississippi	37.50	32.30	36.50	7,609	4,636	8,142	4.16	3.49	4.01
Arkansas	38.40	31.50	37.00	5,218	2,569	5,203	3.55	2.72	3.46
Louisiana	38.60	34.00	39.30	3,110	1,886	3,199	3.67	2.97	3.64
Oklahoma	31.00	32.00	32.00	98	49	134	2.72	2.33	3.05
Texas	37.20	33.20	38.50	2,636	1,293	4,175	3.44	3.07	3.79
New Mexico	35.00	32.50		3	3		3.00	3.00	
Arizona									
California									
All other									
United States	32.51	25.38	31.57	76,716	46,861	75,461	4.39	3.34	4.23

Bureau of Agricultural Economics. Based on returns from crop correspondents. Figures for earlier years appear in previous issues of the Yearbook.

[1] Acreage in cotton June 25.

TABLE 563.—*Coffee: International trade, averages 1909–1913, annual 1924–1927*

Country	Average 1909–1913		1925		1926		1927, preliminary	
	Imports	Exports	Imports	Exports	Imports	Exports	Imports	Exports
PRINCIPAL EXPORTING COUNTRIES	*1,000 pounds*	*1,000 pounds*	*1,000 pounds*	*1,000 pounds*	*1,000 pounds*	*1,000 pounds*	*1,000 pounds*	*1,000 pounds*
Brazil	0	1,672,282	0	1,783,367	0	1,818,999	0	1,999,352
Colombia	0	104,398	0	257,506	[1] 0	[1] 324,639		
Dutch East Indies	4,227	54,149	3,474	153,725	2,439	164,070	[2] 62	[2] 74,385
Venezuela	0	111,326	0	118,254	0	133,946	0	112,579
Guatemala	0	85,951	[1] 0	[1] 98,434	[1] 0	[1] 94,823	[1] 0	[1] 116,311
Salvador	[3] 1,593	62,830	0	70,689	0	111,611	0	79,813
Haiti	0	61,943	0	72,495	0	73,675	0	68,290
Mexico	[4] 167	48,991	1,012	53,151	[1] 153	[1] 46,836	[1] 220	[1] 57,522
Costa Rica	0	27,515	0	[5] 33,906	0	[5] 40,248	[1] 0	[1] 35,613
Nicaragua	[6] 138	19,033	[1] 67	23,859	[1] 99	38,959	[1] 0	[1] 25,152
British India	[4] 605	27,780	2,540	29,003	4,746	12,247	4,664	31,329
Jamaica	0	8,263	0	[1] 11,650	0	[1] 7,439	[1] 0	[1] 9,153
PRINCIPAL IMPORTING COUNTRIES								
United States	907,899	[7] 44,251	1,283,695	25,207	1,493,316	29,433	1,433,340	18,459
France	245,752	41	370,673	369	340,023	293	350,668	174
Germany	399,965	1,757	200,329	359	232,364	267	274,337	241
Netherlands	283,633	189,288	133,716	45,767	114,262	44,984	111,358	36,861
Italy	58,278	458	93,070	10	96,417	3	100,851	3
Sweden	74,486	24	80,592	3	92,519	31	95,034	23
Belgium	111,738	33,627	87,706	545	88,011	412	91,648	848
Spain	29,317	9	42,846	1	44,680	3	[1] 54,689	[1] 2
Argentina	28,125	0	44,286	0	51,312	0	54,069	0
Denmark	33,102	152	45,249	183	55,996	535	54,445	631
United Kingdom	28,581	241	49,559	216	25,189	221	45,490	212
Finland	28,624	0	41,712	0	29,167	0	33,678	0
Norway	29,309	0	32,015	0	37,293	0	37,818	0
Cuba	24,906	4	28,202	1	15,671	2		
Union of South Africa	26,458	36	29,001	8	27,829	13	29,532	10
Switzerland	25,029	62	24,054	91	29,144	150	29,250	201
Czechoslovakia	0	0	28,168	4	29,200	1	29,590	4
Canada	13,378	55	21,185	55	24,747	41	26,513	58
Egypt	15,654	0	17,179	24	20,815	10	21,925	4
Yugoslavia [1]	0	0	22,054	19	20,506	2	20,679	1
British Malaya	[7] 7,524	[7] 7,137	18,912	11,825	18,581	10,234	18,870	10,364
Austria	[8] 128,304	[8] 8	14,891	0	18,873	4	18,190	5
Poland	0	0	15,644	1	13,990	1	15,398	2
Hungary			5,895	0	6,934	0	8,043	0
Russia	26,073	0	[1] 2,958	[1] 0	[1] 650	[1] 0	[1] 1,911	[1] 0
Total 37 countries	2,532,865	2,561,611	2,740,684	2,790,727	2,934,926	2,954,132	2,962,272	2,677,602

Division of Statistical and Historical Research. Compiled from official sources except where otherwise noted. The item, coffee, comprises unhulled and hulled, ground or otherwise prepared, but imitation or "surrogate" coffee and chicory are excluded.

[1] International Yearbook of Agricultural Statistics.   [5] Fiscal year, presumably a crop year ended Sept. 30.
[2] Java and Madura only.   [6] 3-year average.
[3] 1-year only.   [7] Chiefly from Porto Rico.
[4] 4-year average.   [8] Average for Austria-Hungary.

TABLE 564.—*Coffee, Rio, No. 7: Average wholesale price per pound, New York, 1920–1928*

Year	Jan.	Feb.	Mar.	Apr.	May	June	July	Aug.	Sept.	Oct.	Nov.	Dec.	Average [1]
	Cents	*Cents*	*Cents*	*Cents*	*Cents*	*Cents*	*Cents*	*Cents*	*Cents*	*Cents*	*Cents*	*Cents*	*Cents*
Av. 1921–1925	12.5	13.1	13.2	12.8	12.4	13.1	12.8	13.0	13.5	13.9	14.3	14.2	13.2
1920	16.3	14.8	15.0	15.1	15.6	15.0	13.1	9.4	8.2	7.6	7.5	6.6	12.0
1921	6.7	6.7	6.4	6.0	6.2	6.7	6.5	7.0	7.9	8.1	8.8	9.3	7.2
1922	9.6	9.0	9.6	10.8	11.0	11.0	10.4	10.0	10.2	10.2	10.8	11.1	10.3
1923	11.9	13.0	13.0	11.5	11.6	11.7	10.9	10.7	10.7	11.4	11.0	10.9	11.5
1924	10.9	14.2	15.6	15.3	14.8	14.6	16.5	16.6	17.7	20.7	22.6	22.6	16.8
1925	23.4	22.4	21.2	20.2	18.6	21.6	19.7	20.7	21.2	19.5	18.5	17.1	20.3
1926	18.5	19.1	18.2	18.3	19.8	20.1	19.8	19.2	17.7	16.1	16.3	15.3	18.2
1927	15.3	14.9	15.8	16.2	15.4	14.8	14.2	13.9	13.5	14.7	14.5	14.2	14.8
1928	14.8	15.7	16.8	15.4	15.7	15.7	16.5	17.3	17.3	17.8	18.1	18.1	16.4

Bureau of Agricultural Economics. Compiled from Bureau of Labor Statistics reports. Data for 1890–1919 are available in 1924 Yearbook, p. 832, Table 426.

[1] Derived from the figures upon which the monthly averages are based.

TABLE 565.—*Tea: International trade, average 1909–1913, annual 1924–1927*

Country	Average 1909–1913		1925		1926		1927, preliminary	
	Imports	Exports	Imports	Exports	Imports	Exports	Imports	Exports
PRINCIPAL EXPORTING COUNTRIES	1,000 pounds	1,000 pounds	1,000 pounds	1,000 pounds	1,000 pounds	1,000 pounds	1,000 pounds	1,000 pounds
British India [1]	[2] 8,002	[2] 267,887	7,536	336,276	7,297	339,087	7,839	366,561
Ceylon	[3] 1	189,016	1	209,791	0	217,184	[4] 2	[4] 227,034
Dutch East Indies	6,742	46,675	7,983	102,281	7,778	120,174	[5] 7,268	[5] 111,790
China	18,890	197,997	3,211	108,875	11,011	109,129	8,809	114,651
Japan	590	35,823	777	28,041	1,115	23,965	882	23,487
Formosa	68	23,640	29	21,028	57	22,412	84	22,817
PRINCIPAL IMPORTING COUNTRIES								
United Kingdom	293,045	0	402,156	0	410,986	0	451,415	0
United States	98,897	0	100,962	0	95,930	0	89,169	0
Australia	35,442	0	[4] 49,935	0	[4] 46,949	0	[4] 49,672	0
Canada	37,927	0	37,392	0	37,630	0	38,117	0
Netherlands	11,383	45	19,949	26	26,177	25	27,694	28
Irish Free State	0	0	22,611	0	23,596	0	23,667	0
Russia	157,704	866	[4] 37,174	[4] 1,769	[4] 43,804	[4] 1,300	[4] 51,286	[4] 395
Persia [6]	9,446	125	14,449	2,135	15,146	438		
New Zealand	7,542	0	10,835	0	10,928	0	10,825	0
Morocco	6,696	0	12,020	0	11,184	0	[4] 11,333	0
Union of South Africa	5,192	61	9,815	8	10,303	6	11,812	9
British Malaya	[4] 11,983	[4] 5,318	9,127	1,301	11,198	1,533	10,778	1,238
Egypt	1,950	0	9,644	221	8,408	300	8,605	233
Germany	8,964	23	9,153	1	10,116	0	11,409	0
Chile	3,505	0	5,233	0	5,168	0	5,392	0
Poland	0	0	3,717	3	3,938	1	4,621	0
Argentina	3,890	0	4,071	0	2,739	0	4,101	0
French Indo-China	3,295	1,145	4,060	2,281	5,592	2,530	5,095	1,711
France	2,806	61	3,841	125	3,570	108	3,022	47
Czechoslovakia	0	0	1,351	0	1,449	9	1,457	2
Austria	[7] 3,424	[7] 3	875	0	1,231	0	1,278	0
Hungary			621	1	646	23	884	0
Total 28 countries	737,384	768,685	788,478	814,163	813,946	838,224	846,516	870,003

Bureau of Agricultural Economics. Official sources except where otherwise noted.

[1] Sea-borne trade only.
[2] Includes some land trade.
[3] 2-year average.
[4] International Yearbook of Agricultural Statistics.
[5] Java and Madura only.
[6] Fiscal year ended Mar. 21.
[7] Average for Austria-Hungary.

TABLE 566.—*Tea, Formosa, fine: Average wholesale price per pound, New York, 1920–1928*

Year	Jan.	Feb.	Mar.	Apr.	May	June	July	Aug.	Sept.	Oct.	Nov.	Dec.	Average [1]
	Cts.	Cts.	Cts.	Cts.	Cts.	Cts.	Cts.	Cts.	Cts.	Cts.	Cts.	Cts.	Cts.
Av. 1921–1925	30.3	30.3	30.3	30.2	29.9	29.8	29.8	29.8	30.0	30.4	31.6	32.3	30.4
1920	36.5	36.5	36.5	36.5	36.5	36.5	36.5	34.3	31.0	31.0	28.6	23.8	33.7
1921	24.5	24.5	24.5	24.1	22.4	22.0	22.0	22.0	22.3	23.0	28.0	29.0	24.0
1922	30.0	30.0	30.0	30.0	30.0	30.0	30.0	30.0	30.5	30.5	31.0	31.0	30.2
1923	31.0	31.0	31.0	31.0	31.0	31.0	31.0	31.0	31.0	31.0	31.0	31.0	31.0
1924	31.0	31.0	31.0	31.0	31.0	31.0	31.0	31.0	31.3	32.5	32.9	35.0	31.7
1925	35.0	35.0	35.0	35.0	35.0	35.0	35.0	35.0	35.0	35.0	35.3	35.0	35.0
1926	35.5	35.5	35.5	35.5	35.5	35.5	35.5	35.5	35.5	35.5	35.5	35.5	35.5
1927	34.5	34.5	34.5	34.5	34.5	34.5	34.5	34.5	34.5	34.5	32.9	32.5	34.2
1928	32.5	32.5	32.5	32.5	32.5	32.5	32.5	32.5	32.5	31.0	31.0	31.0	32.1

Bureau of Agricultural Economics. Compiled from Bureau of Labor Statistics reports. Data for 1890–1919 are available in 1924 Yearbook, p. 834, Table 427.

[1] Derived from the figures upon which the monthly averages are based.

TABLE 567.—*Copra: International trade, years 1923–1927*

Country	Year ended Dec. 31—					
	1923		1924		1925	
	Imports	Exports	Imports	Exports	Imports	Exports
	1,000 pounds	*1,000 pounds*	*1,000 pounds*	*1,000 pounds*	*1,000 pounds*	*1,000 pounds*
Principal exporting countries:						
British India	1,055	8,913	3,817	1,042	7,025	231
British Malaya	141,458	344,336	150,784	356,269	149,666	343,248
Ceylon	141	113,732	292	198,149	640	254,656
Dutch East Indies	103	706,270	[1] 2	757,687	0	773,837
Philippine Islands	0	456,642	0	345,597	0	323,434
Principal importing countries:						
Australia [1]	81,559	0	68,989	0	71,871	0
Belgium	[2] 17,654	[2] 19	[2] 25,233	[2] 41	19,140	260
Denmark	147,982	0	118,435	0	108,142	0
France [3]	308,255	194	318,615	285	344,392	25
Germany	317,204	0	323,539	473	379,511	578
Netherlands	325,277	72	327,696	315	293,075	156
Italy	28,971	6	34,455	0	56,743	16
Sweden	27,076	0	29,637	2	31,129	0
United Kingdom	155,543	0	158,576	0	174,830	0
United States	332,974	0	291,064	0	364,076	0
Total	1,885,252	1,630,184	1,851,134	1,659,860	2,000,240	1,696,441

Country	Year ended Dec. 31—			
	1926		1927	
	Imports	Exports	Imports	Exports
	1,000 pounds	*1,000 pounds*	*1,000 pounds*	*1,000 pounds*
Principal exporting countries:				
British India	663	3,662	2,867	2,032
British Malaya	181,461	415,306	126,645	320,414
Ceylon	641	270,973	[1] 224	[1] 221,997
Dutch East Indies	0	830,873	0	[1] 868,107
Philippine Islands	549	383,647	290	439,419
Principal importing countries:				
Australia [1]	78,659	0	79,772	0
Belgium	21,684	30	12,390	121
Denmark	107,000	0	111,336	0
France [3]	304,725	17	345,355	19
Germany	438,087	1,434	413,295	310
Netherlands	340,257	936	297,870	554
Italy	51,709	7	61,779	12
Sweden	35,957	0	22,015	0
United Kingdom	130,859	0	79,596	0
United States	457,599	0	450,995	0
Total	2,149,850	1,906,885	2,004,429	1,852,985

Bureau of Agricultural Economics.　Compiled from official sources.

[1] From International Yearbook of Agricultural Statistics.
[2] Includes fragments of dried coconuts.
[3] Includes some coconut.

TABLE 568.—*Coconut oil: International trade, 1923–1927*

Country	Year ended Dec. 31—									
	1923		1924		1925		1926		1927	
	Im-ports	Ex-ports	Im-ports	Ex-ports	Im-ports	Ex-ports	Im-ports	Ex-ports	Im-ports	Ex-ports
	1,000 pounds	*1,000 pounds*	*1,000 pounds*	*1,000 pounds*	*1,000 pounds*	*1,000 pounds*	*1,000 pounds*	*1,000 pounds*	*1,000 pounds*	*1,000 pounds*
Principal exporting countries:										
Australia [1]	487	2,059	173	421	382	413	232	450	255	398
British Malaya	10	13,495	20	13,649	27	17,214	184	19,233	56	23,072
Ceylon	0	53,821	1	61,895	18	69,095	9	63,892	[1] 11	[1] 75,392
Dutch East Indies	8,528	2,916	7,042	15,773	9,632	20,606	10,376	32,812	[2] 764	[2] 19,374
France [3]	9,227	5,850	11,008	23,837	12,566	23,498	10,199	29,512	10,417	34,795
Germany	43,059	5,348	19,192	5,817	•12,812	17,512	4,139	15,076	2,355	27,305
Netherlands	3,344	145,100	3,545	110,902	11,460	115,689	10,717	117,981	13,147	115,792
Philippine Islands	0	196,613	0	246,097	0	229,560	0	258,579	0	319,232
Principal importing countries:										
Belgium [3]	27,277	4,865	26,455	7,218	25,533	6,196	32,118	5,561	38,761	3,631
British India	23	2,248	4,606	1,064	10,601	948	1,892	1,766	9,903	948
Denmark	15,405	16,398	24,466	17,176	38,321	10,836	32,533	17,859	19,126	22,132
Egypt	9,334	1	10,882	0	12,067	0	10,200	1	10,905	2
Italy [3]	4,380	69	11,485	56	6,807	245	5,450	42	7,633	55
New Zealand	621	0	331	0	720	0	778	0	981	0
Sweden	16,294	4,630	19,037	4,743	24,363	3,503	27,184	5,209	28,162	4,203
United Kingdom	56,022	6,160	52,886	7,074	68,723	5,914	82,510	6,068	91,349	5,535
United States	181,882	16,562	224,763	17,961	233,174	17,901	245,129	15,952	293,370	20,418
Total	375,893	476,135	415,892	533,683	467,206	539,130	473,650	589,993	527,195	672,284

Bureau of Agricultural Economics. Compiled from official sources.

[1] International Yearbook of Agricultural Statistics.
[2] Java and Madura only.
[3] Includes some other oils.

TABLE 569.—*Copra, South-Sea Island: Average price per pound, in bags, f. o. b.*
New York, 1917–1928

Year	Jan.	Feb.	Mar.	Apr.	May	June	July	Aug.	Sept.	Oct.	Nov.	Dec.	Average
	Cents	*Cents*	*Cents*	*Cents*	*Cents*	*Cents*	*Cents*	*Cents*	*Cents*	*Cents*	*Cents*	*Cents*	*Cents*
1917	8.2	8.2	8.1	8.5	9.1	9.3	8.6	9.4	9.3	9.2	9.8	9.5	8.9
1918	9.6	9.6	9.4	9.5	9.3	8.8	9.2	9.2	9.6	9.4	9.2	8.8	9.3
1919	8.8	7.5	6.6	7.5	9.5	10.6	10.9	10.8	10.2	9.9	(1)	(1)	
1920	11.9	10.9	10.2	(1)	10.5	9.6	9.2	7.9	8.1	9.2	8.0	6.6	
1921	5.8	5.0	4.5	4.6	5.1	5.0	4.6	4.6	5.0	4.7	4.2	4.4	5.0
1922	4.5	4.4	4.9	4.5	4.6	4.6	4.5	4.5	4.4	4.4	4.6	4.8	4.6
1923	5.1	5.2	5.8	6.0	5.5	4.9	4.6	4.6	4.8	5.2	5.2	5.4	5.2
1924	5.6	5.8	5.6	5.3	5.1	5.1	5.2	5.6	5.9	5.9	6.0	6.1	5.6
1925	6.1	6.0	5.9	5.9	5.9	5.9	5.9	6.2	6.2	6.2	6.2	6.2	6.0
1926	6.1	6.1	6.1	6.1	6.0	6.1	6.0	5.6	5.6	5.6	5.2	5.1	5.8
1927	5.0	5.3	5.1	5.1	5.2	5.2	5.2	5.2	5.2	5.2	5.2	5.3	5.2
1928	5.4	5.5	5.4	5.4	5.4	5.3	5.0	4.9	4.8	4.8			

Bureau of Agricultural Economics. Compiled from Oil, Paint, and Drug Reporter, 1917–1927; subsequently from Bureau of Labor Statistics Wholesale Price Bulletin.

[1] Nominal.

TABLE 570.—*Coconut oil, Cochin: Average price per pound, in barrels, New York, 1909–1928*

Year	Jan.	Feb.	Mar.	Apr.	May	June	July	Aug.	Sept.	Oct.	Nov.	Dec.	Average
Average:	Cents	Cents	Cents	Cents	Cents	Cents	Cents	Cents	Cents	Cents	Cents	Cents	Cents
1909–1913	9.64	9.31	9.11	9.19	9.36	9.64	9.97	10.48	-----	11.64	11.31	10.53	-----
1914–1920	16.68	16.48	16.40	16.25	16.18	16.13	15.75	16.08	15.99	16.29	16.27	16.62	16.26
1921–1925	11.14	10.73	10.50	10.44	10.74	10.50	10.35	10.77	10.79	10.97	11.12	11.10	10.76
1909	7.58	7.14	6.94	6.90	6.96	7.32	7.86	7.91	8.30	9.06	9.81	9.82	7.97
1910	10.14	9.61	9.73	10.28	10.64	10.19	10.14	10.78	11.16	11.50	10.81	10.32	10.44
1911	9.94	9.31	8.34	8.00	8.54	8.81	9.32	9.75	-----	13.00	11.48	9.38	-----
1912	9.80	9.66	9.68	9.89	9.92	9.89	9.78	10.00	10.69	10.91	10.82	10.62	10.14
1913	10.72	10.83	10.88	10.88	10.74	12.00	12.75	13.98	13.71	13.71	13.62	12.50	12.19
1914	11.92	11.41	10.95	10.55	10.75	10.81	11.00	14.50	15.69	15.15	14.00	14.94	12.64
1915	14.70	14.84	14.50	13.19	11.40	10.69	10.70	10.75	10.75	11.15	13.28	15.65	12.63
1916	15.44	15.56	17.25	18.00	16.81	16.00	14.85	13.56	13.85	14.81	15.12	15.75	15.58
1917	16.62	16.75	16.45	17.75	18.66	18.20	17.22	16.94	17.34	17.67	18.00	18.41	17.50
1918	19.00	19.44	19.14	19.16	18.44	18.20	18.62	18.35	18.50	19.09	18.40	18.50	18.74
1919	18.00	17.19	16.38	15.94	17.38	19.95	21.06	21.45	19.53	19.69	20.10	19.44	18.84
1920	21.08	20.19	20.12	19.19	19.83	19.08	16.83	17.00	16.25	16.50	15.00	13.66	17.89
1921	12.95	11.12	10.12	10.00	11.31	11.12	10.60	11.25	11.00	10.85	10.34	10.20	10.90
1922	10.08	9.91	10.06	9.78	9.75	9.47	9.38	9.38	9.17	9.12	9.25	9.62	9.58
1923	10.25	10.25	10.48	10.75	11.03	10.65	10.25	10.16	10.08	10.12	10.25	10.38	10.39
1924	10.42	10.50	10.35	10.19	10.09	9.78	9.88	10.80	10.75	11.25	11.75	11.81	10.63
1925	12.00	11.88	11.50	11.50	11.50	11.50	11.64	12.25	12.94	13.50	14.00	13.50	12.31
1926	12.81	12.25	12.00	12.00	12.00	12.15	12.25	11.75	11.55	11.00	(1)	(1)	(1)
1927	(1)	(1)	(1)	(1)	(1)	(1)	(1)	(1)	(1)	(1)	(1)	10.20	-----
1928	10.20	10.20	10.20	10.20	10.20	9.60	9.60	9.50	9.50	9.50	9.60	9.80	9.80

Bureau of Agricultural Economics. Compiled from weekly quotations in the Oil, Paint, and Drug Reporter.

[1] No quotations.

TABLE 571.—*Raw silk: Production in specified countries, average 1909–1913, 1921–1925, annual 1925–1927*

Country	Average, 1909–1913	Average, 1921–1925	1925	1926	1927
WESTERN EUROPE	1,000 pounds	1,000 pounds	1,000 pounds	1,000 pounds	1,000 pounds
Italy	8,524	9,487	9,656	8,499	10,201
France	992	548	573	529	650
Spain	182	177	221	187	183
Total	9,698	10,212	10,450	9,215	11,034
Eastern Europe, Levant, and Central Asia [1]	6,611	1,874	2,524	2,359	2,293
FAR EAST					
China:					
Exports from Shanghai	12,576	10,456	12,599	12,225	13,283
Exports from Canton	5,146	6,418	6,923	7,055	5,809
Japan:					
Exports from Yokohama and Kobe [2]	21,898	46,336	56,978	66,193	68,839
British India:					
Exports from Bengal and Cashmere	428	121	66	121	176
Indo-China:					
Exports from Saigon, Haipong, etc	[3] 32	84	132	143	132
Total	40,680	63,415	76,698	85,737	88,239
Grand total	56,389	75,501	89,672	97,311	101,566

Bureau of Agricultural Economics. Compiled from Statistique de la Production de la Soie, Silk Merchants Union, Lyon, France.

[1] Includes Hungary, Czechoslovakia, Yugoslavia, Rumania, Bulgaria, Greece, Salonika, Adrianopole Crete, the Caucasus, Turkestan, Central Asia, and Persia.
[2] Previous to 1923 only exports from Yokohama are included.
[3] For years 1911–1913.

TABLE 572.—*Federal-aid highway system: Mileage, Federal-aid apportionment for fiscal year 1930, and total apportionment for years 1917 to 1930, inclusive*

State	Mileage in approved system, Dec. 31, 1928	Apportionment for fiscal year 1930	Aggregate of apportionment for fiscal years 1917 to 1930, inclusive	State	Mileage in approved system, Dec. 31, 1928	Apportionment for fiscal year 1930	Aggregate of apportionment for fiscal years 1917 to 1930, inclusive
		Dollars	Dollars			Dollars	Dollars
Alabama	3,884.00	1,554,221	18,998,379	New Hampshire	980.91	365,625	4,266,367
Arizona	1,498.00	1,061,111	12,794,435	New Jersey	1,181.70	937,434	11,274,587
Arkansas	5,021.13	1,284,382	15,449,867	New Mexico	3,298.00	1,189,085	14,537,595
California	4,777.40	2,495,345	29,538,012	New York	5,451.00	3,617,748	44,928,039
Colorado	3,332.00	1,388,755	16,474,488	North Carolina	4,002.70	1,716,919	20,863,391
Connecticut	835.43	477,110	5,757,689	North Dakota	7,214.00	1,197,586	14,334,636
Delaware	435.62	365,625	3,570,933	Ohio	5,899.30	2,754,446	34,006,415
Florida	1,926.00	909,235	10,794,951	Oklahoma	5,594.30	1,748,857	21,309,601
Georgia	5,576.70	1,980,443	24,371,620	Oregon	2,891.50	1,191,989	14,443,245
Idaho	2,770.00	933,902	11,361,684	Pennsylvania	5,017.97	3,325,854	41,334,156
Illinois	6,618.48	3,118,949	39,240,801	Rhode Island	362.36	365,625	3,764,444
Indiana	4,701.50	1,917,036	23,969,626	South Carolina	3,230.00	1,061,447	12,977,492
Iowa	7,212.00	2,020,861	25,586,714	South Dakota	5,956.00	1,229,282	14,840,117
Kansas	7,925.00	2,058,305	25,653,444	Tennessee	3,252.80	1,609,662	20,117,031
Kentucky	3,700.00	1,417,634	17,469,419	Texas	11,690.95	4,531,162	54,137,441
Louisiana	2,712.93	1,026,696	12,331,694	Utah	1,677.33	848,592	10,362,370
Maine	1,428.86	678,501	8,505,554	Vermont	1,043.00	365,625	4,365,382
Maryland	1,527.72	633,615	7,828,697	Virginia	3,251.70	1,433,405	17,815,181
Massachusetts	1,308.00	1,090,077	13,376,711	Washington	2,927.50	1,149.489	13,570,023
Michigan	5,243.00	2,204,966	26,971,618	West Virginia	2,094.87	796,408	9,736,351
Minnesota	6,849.60	2,108,104	25,933,220	Wisconsin	5,493.36	1,854,580	23,028,062
Mississippi	3,632.10	1,311,391	16,057,017	Wyoming	3,097.00	939,536.	11,379,726
Missouri	7,530.00	2,392,021	29,987,979	Hawaii	174.60	365,625	2,197,028
Montana	4,673.50	1,554,060	18,083,020				
Nebraska	5,574.85	1,586,299	19,391,653	Total	188,016.67	73,125,000	890,750,000
Nevada	1,540.00	960,375	11,662,095				

Bureau of Public Roads.

TABLE 573.—*Current status of Federal-aid road construction, as of June 30, 1928*

State	Completed mileage	Under construction — Estimated total cost	Under construction — Federal aid allotted	Under construction — Mileage Original	Stage	Total	Approved for construction — Estimated total cost	Approved for construction — Federal aid allotted	Approved — Mileage Original	Stage	Total	Balance of Federal-aid funds available for new projects
		Dollars	Dollars				Dollars	Dollars				Dollars
Alabama	1,748.0	5,195,635.95	2,583,180.18	270.5	55.9	326.4	717,945.71	358,972.83	48.7	12.4	61.1	1,645,844.81
Arizona	851.4	1,795,361.35	1,577,922.94	86.0	0.6	86.6	122,094.33	42,024.80		4.2	4.2	2,896,024.65
Arkansas	1,678.2	4,906,901.45	2,174,942.33	180.7		180.7	250,474.55	102,444.55	9.9	6.2	16.1	1,766,771.75
California	1,455.6	6,122,281.76	2,929,250.54	120.7	8.2	128.9	1,573,168.56	703,031.15	43.7		43.7	3,363,012.39
Colorado	979.3	5,134,698.11	2,627,641.63	189.4	9.2	198.5	287,928.34	159,230.93	12.7	14.5	27.2	2,573,202.04
Connecticut	206.5	3,289,777.06	831,098.01	34.4		34.4	285,289.67	66,951.17	3.6		3.6	566,752.61
Delaware	195.7	470,022.22	95,739.75	5.7	3.9	9.6	310,591.60	155,295.80	12.9		12.9	190,680.44
Florida	385.8	4,185,912.27	1,773,093.63	99.7	5.4	105.1	905,396.31	333,505.44	30.7		30.7	1,210,489.75
Georgia	2,457.5	3,701,359.50	1,805,098.52	168.2	30.7	198.9	2,934,550.18	1,239,573.27	102.3	50.1	152.4	17,567.82
Idaho	937.1	2,067,804.47	1,235,873.81	116.5	56.8	173.3	1,100,504.72	653,836.57	101.6	1.8	103.4	138,890.41
Illinois	1,685.4	19,966,945.33	9,204,790.58	620.1		620.1	3,896,721.88	1,942,068.60	148.0		148.0	114,597.22
Indiana	1,060.1	10,285,596.57	4,915,301.36	314.2	3.5	317.7	1,671,729.13	807,135.04	61.3		61.3	267,083.14
Iowa	2,831.5	7,006,259.73	2,993,700.52	145.2	137.3	282.5	1,827,757.31	778,011.52	10.2	71.4	81.6	171,307.77
Kansas	2,024.4	4,812,182.97	1,907,366.82	242.8		242.8	1,348,337.76	598,232.45	106.3		106.3	1,284,552.84
Kentucky	1,148.9	4,924,557.22	2,488,415.88	227.4		227.4	1,159,696.00	579,848.00	62.7		62.7	529,296.09
Louisiana	1,276.0	4,161,328.09	2,072,905.40	193.0		193.0	724,325.88	239,803.83	8.8		8.8	317,573.20
Maine	428.7	1,294,982.17	528,952.60	39.7		39.7	586,603.30	200,682.36	14.2		14.2	1,380,996.50
Maryland	557.5		353,730.00	30.0		30.0	858,534.80	416,900.00	38.6	7.2	45.8	143,816.23
Massachusetts	501.1	3,785,205.01	1,133,667.82	71.4		71.4	361,296.54	84,345.00	5.6		5.6	2,151,418.10
Michigan	1,337.3	13,340,940.37	5,616,223.08	328.5	54.7	383.2	1,150,043.70	525,885.00	29.4	6.5	35.9	627,344.95
Minnesota	3,823.8	6,287,137.00	2,088,100.00	305.0	30.9	335.9	1,201,168.35	291,000.00	49.8	20.6	70.4	398,471.43
Mississippi	1,533.6	4,361,785.79	2,149,654.95	228.3	39.0	267.3	201,358.23	100,459.53	11.5	0.6	12.1	892,222.08
Missouri	2,210.1	4,630,264.01	1,900,212.49	132.8		132.8	1,511,404.60	602,718.59	46.3	13.7	60.0	1,550,939.55
Montana	1,299.3	3,526,790.69	2,385,241.58	275.6	4.1	279.7	2,345,539.14	1,308,589.18	235.1	10.7	245.8	4,353,988.31
Nebraska	3,032.3	6,436,612.14	3,206,959.06	644.1	197.4	841.5	75,620.57	37,768.83		23.2	23.2	65,727.25
Nevada	305.6	1,156,011.48	1,012,597.47	137.3	28.4	165.7	59,079.34	51,419.58		23.7	23.7	595,556.89
New Hampshire	418.3	661,935.44	272,455.16	19.0		19.0	490,414.66	190,235.78	9.2		9.2	253,177.00
New Jersey	1,740.3	5,847,748.19	1,089,947.35	155.2		155.2	777,265.15	492,343.74	56.1	0.5	56.6	894,813.28
New Mexico	864.8	2,414,979.86	602,034.50	460.7		460.7						3,910,462.81
New York	582.4	30,549,500.00	7,164,693.95	89.7	13.0	102.7	8,328,900.00	1,806,847.50	116.9	8.6	125.5	1,141,531.23
North Carolina	3,155.1	3,660,655.06	981,951.81	626.3	165.4	791.7	534,495.97	259,500.00	5.0	19.5	24.5	637,992.37
North Dakota	1,805.9		1,740,332.78	250.2	6.0	256.2	1,240,836.16	502,502.23	192.4	121.7	314.1	2,591,001.85
Ohio	1,589.7	11,260,370.37	4,150,846.38	171.0	6.4	177.4	4,757,780.00	1,340,636.26	88.6	6.7	95.3	387,602.49
Oklahoma	1,104.9	3,367,788.78	1,617,074.66	40.7		40.7	1,871,838.77	837,936.01	109.7	15.5	125.2	1,207,098.47
Oregon	1,387.0	1,517,571.16	847,554.19	240.7		240.7	278,334.10	146,673.72	6.7		6.7	1,999,143.13
Pennsylvania		13,745,519.18	3,983,882.84	26.8		26.8	4,414,639.79	1,318,026.22	82.4		82.4	1,850,129.27
Rhode Island	136.2	1,723,452.42	431,049.92				311,081.95	80,919.55	4.0		4.0	576,046.16
South Carolina	1,631.6	8,499,229.16	1,887,138.22	205.5	120.7	326.2	394,006.44	69,700.00	10.4	8.1	18.5	64,396.43

South Dakota	2,584.4	3,458,251.40	1,855,200.66	584.0	73.3	657.3	655,789.73	360,684.24	107.0	39.2	146.2	514,514.16
Tennessee	1,075.6	4,524,754.78	1,939,405.06	138.9		138.9	4,267,517.00	1,363,324.58	25.6	94.3	119.9	284,777.15
Texas	5,965.9	8,914,648.60	3,494,782.06	224.8	125.1	349.9	6,241,573.47	2,627,108.00	161.9	156.0	317.9	3,975,468.70
Utah	806.5	1,996,561.57	1,364,004.82	112.2	12.3	124.5	328,886.36	240,095.90	19.4	1.5	20.9	220,749.79
Vermont	201.3	2,345,384.25	884,978.39	51.2		51.2	584,323.08	147,454.36	11.9		11.9	25,473.81
Virginia	1,266.9	4,221,703.93	1,337,952.75	99.3	21.6	120.9	884,718.69	156,605.91	31.6		31.6	237,853.61
Washington	777.7	4,144,458.77	1,437,000.00	105.4	18.1	123.5	1,142,840.68	440,236.89	21.2	5.0	26.2	481,843.46
West Virginia	606.9	2,789,397.94	1,244,328.22	105.6		105.6	617,098.44	294,283.84	25.3		25.3	478,763.16
Wisconsin	2,046.9	7,931,130.44	3,251,570.37	277.2	25.2	302.4	1,400,034.42	433,988.43	36.5	15.7	52.2	1,435,440.82
Wyoming	1,442.5	2,260,697.90	1,417,612.15	227.0	32.1	259.1	296,051.33	190,064.91	41.8		41.8	167,116.50
Hawaii	36.2	301,973.75	60,383.43	3.2		3.2	175,931.99	57,501.20	1.8		1.8	1,064,241.58
Total	71,074.3	261,754,800.99	105,297,930.62	9,493.9	1,285.2	10,779.0	67,461,518.09	25,741,403.29	2,359.3	759.1	3,118.4	53,643,770.45

Bureau of Public Roads.

NOTE.—A table similar to Table 540, 1927 Yearbook, Federal highways completed and under construction, is omitted.

TABLE 574.—*Mileage of roads in State highway systems at end of 1927, as reported by State highway departments*

State	Grand total mileage	Earth, non-surfaced		Total surfaced mileage	Surfaced roads, by types							
		Unimproved	Improved to grade		Sand-clay, topsoil	Gravel, chert, etc.	Water-bound macadam (treated and untreated)	Bituminous macadam	Sheet asphalt	Bituminous concrete	Portland cement concrete	Brick and block
Alabama	3,919	1,366	169	2,384	739	1,349	37	45	6	101	107	
Arizona	2,041	326	249	1,466		1,252		23	15	40	136	
Arkansas	8,506	2,534	1,546	4,426		3,617	144	156		271	238	
California	6,573	2,352	532	3,689		1,152	61	339	357	109	1,671	
Colorado	9,095	4,549	776	3,770	98	3,397				13	262	
Connecticut	1,966		115	1,851		363	765	243		148	330	2
Delaware	629			629		23	5	23	6	3	563	6
Florida	6,339	2,878	243	3,218	789	8	1,376	150	238	35	306	316
Georgia	6,380	2,596	279	3,505	1,947	632	90	229	75	9	522	1
Idaho	4,219	1,569	491	2,159	54	1,902		16	5	131	51	
Illinois	9,890	4,735	86	5,069			1	4	1	9	4,967	87
Indiana	4,364		15	4,349		1,530	1,093	269		28	1,348	81
Iowa	7,078	1,200	1,436	4,442		3,434					975	33
Kansas	7,922	4,313	1,626	1,983	762	359		151		3	555	153
Kentucky	9,647	4,428	694	4,525		1,745	2,175	329		14	236	26
Louisiana	7,979	2,723	31	5,225		5,103		20	1	49	37	15
Maine	1,788	293		1,495	4	1,171	8	224			88	
Maryland	2,519			2,519		384	1,106		42	40	947	
Massachusetts	1,590	11	14	1,565		110	285	711		214	242	3
Michigan	7,144	975	62	6,107	91	3,233	571	130		236	1,835	11
Minnesota	6,936		393	6,543	279	5,330				70	839	25
Mississippi	6,723	2,040	554	4,129	5	3,744	11	51	7	14	277	20
Missouri	7,482	2,138	1,431	3,913		2,205		94			1,593	21
Montana	7,957	6,568	314	1,075		1,032		6		4	33	
Nebraska	6,167	2,202	625	3,340	132	3,096			3	11	79	19
Nevada	3,552	2,214	19	1,319	10	1,230		13		16	50	
New Hampshire	2,310	143	97	2,070		1,699	117	159		71	24	
New Jersey	1,821	26	136	1,659		310	132	60	92	279	737	49
New Mexico	9,253	6,936	524	1,793		1,720				1	72	
New York	13,929	3,676	49	10,204		126	2,107	3,869		248	3,577	277
North Carolina	7,083		857	6,226	1,765	1,110	191	370	66	809	1,858	57
North Dakota	7,185	3,862	1,595	1,728		1,718			1		9	
Ohio	11,000	298	806	9,896		3,438	1,450	1,613	39	226	1,652	1,478
Oklahoma	6,142	3,133	1,175	1,834		949	32		20	103	694	36
Oregon	4,393	764	219	3,410		2,506		7		689	208	
Pennsylvania	12,167		3,340	8,827		1,294	2,224	403	193	314	4,029	370
Rhode Island	867	210	178	479		23	118	134	8	120	76	
South Carolina	5,592	984	86	4,522	3,484	543	38	11	75	118	253	
South Dakota	6,015	1,137	1,982	2,896	21	2,872					3	
Tennessee	5,033	1,011	313	3,709		1,533	1,090	588	35	80	383	
Texas	18,728	7,703	1,754	9,271	297	5,713	691	1,528	17	223	720	82
Utah	3,436	628	1,420	1,388		1,085	28	5	12	52	206	
Vermont	4,226	124	858	3,244	1,000	2,033	48	63			100	
Virginia	5,245	789	300	4,156	1,057	756	1,114	631	10	3	585	
Washington	3,300	461	169	2,670		1,983		31	3	38	601	14
West Virginia	3,820	781	829	2,210		646	114	675	1	87	541	146
Wisconsin	10,280	675	959	8,646	47	5,643	530	123	4	10	2,288	1
Wyoming	3,123	1,466		624	1,033		994				27	12
Total, 1927	293,353	86,817	29,970	176,566	12,581	86,095	17,752	13,496	1,332	5,066	36,915	3,329
Total, 1926	287,928	96,413	28,456	163,059	11,396	79,286	18,428	12,927	890	4,815	31,936	3,381
Total, 1925	274,911	103,271	26,786	144,854	11,025	68,771	16,709	12,105	853	4,561	27,645	3,185
Total, 1924	261,216	94,651	34,456	132,109	10,446	63,158	17,033	10,346	784	4,427	22,825	3,090
Total, 1923	251,611	103,843	36,368	111,400	8,875	52,917	15,422	8,847	651	3,907	17,916	2,865
Total, 1921	209,242	102,963	21,421	¹84,858	8,622	36,458	16,978	6,749	396	2,444	10,114	2,089

Bureau of Public Roads.

¹ Includes 1,008 miles of miscellaneous surfacing not allocated to types.

TABLE 575.—*Total State highway income and funds available, 1927, as reported by State authorities*

State	Total funds available	Balances at first of year	State highway bonds sold	State taxes and appropriations	Motor-vehicle fees	Gasoline-tax receipts	From counties and miscellaneous	Federal-aid road funds used
	1,000 dollars	*1,000 dollars*	*1,000 dollars*	*1,000 dollars*	*1,000 dollars*	*1,000 dollars*	*1,000 dollars*	*1,000 dollars*
Alabama	12,697	1,896	5,091		2,383	1,854	222	1,251
Arizona	2,435	-138		891	477	474	10	721
Arkansas	22,164	140	13,236		3,662	4,339	282	505
California	27,547	4,230		5,886	4,038	10,600	364	2,429
Colorado	6,919	1,879		1,242	729	1,741	180	1,148
Connecticut	22,998	8,286		3,166	6,838	2,887	1,207	614
Delaware	3,731	606	773		846	632	363	511
Florida	24,149	4,677		149	4,524	8,244	4,867	1,688
Georgia	15,364	1,266			3,600	4,993	2,759	2,746
Idaho	4,558	736		347	193	1,669	546	1,067
Illinois	36,641	1,711	12,176	16	15,589	3,953	198	2,998
Indiana	17,213	2,921			5,147	6,461	608	2,076
Iowa	29,523	6,021	492		9,272	2,866	8,299	2,573
Kansas	16,509	377		150	3,934	3,851	4,731	3,466
Kentucky	12,142	-2,322		877	4,205	5,283	2,679	1,420
Louisiana	13,027	563	2,034		4,129	2,979	2,249	1,073
Maine	9,928	1,517	506	1,074	2,678	1,898	1,623	632
Maryland	12,524	1,724	1,863	2,922	2,206	1,687	1,402	720
Massachusetts	19,049	725	1,150	1,132	12,458		2,700	884
Michigan	29,842	3,815			10,404	10,618	2,341	2,664
Minnesota	26,740	6,829		1,936	10,222	5,036	661	2,056
Mississippi	7,560	1,991			208	2,270	1,146	1,945
Missouri	30,839	7,061	5,157		8,193	6,353	607	3,468
Montana	1,790	107				531	257	895
Nebraska	9,755	2,400		100	1,089	3,657	84	2,425
Nevada	2,156	-67	100	42	230	233	622	996
New Hampshire	4,884	1,130			1,840	1,259	201	454
New Jersey	37,809	7,978	9,000	5,818	10,200	3,379	452	1,072
New Mexico	5,087	5	1,226	564	229	1,171	110	1,782
New York	103,384	49,961	3,675	19,770	18,000		8,331	3,647
North Carolina	53,961	17,110	20,000		5,894	8,121	1,123	1,713
North Dakota	5,343	799			977	929	88	2,550
Ohio	34,080	2,738		143	25,191	3,640		2,368
Oklahoma	13,288	1,534			2,550	4,798	3,199	1,207
Oregon	11,287	870			4,620	3,888	797	1,112
Pennsylvania	74,211	24,982		24	27,745	11,821	6,070	3,569
Rhode Island	7,605	652	3,500	197	2,096	730		430
South Carolina	22,604	253			2,132	3,019	16,077	1,123
South Dakota	7,395	1,337		474	1,291	2,075	1,501	717
Tennessee	15,837	933	2,500	38	3,640	3,626	3,288	1,812
Texas	25,879	366			11,170	7,464	1,914	4,965
Utah	4,498	628		29	631	1,305	756	1,149
Vermont	4,486	250		478	1,759	905	392	702
Virginia	15,689	1,221		2,005	5,124	3,910	1,560	1,869
Washington	8,628				3,900	3,799	230	699
West Virginia	23,835	6,605	8,500		3,732	3,676	60	1,262
Wisconsin	21,551	4,361			9,344	4,438	1,051	2,357
Wyoming	3,268	50		94	536	756	902	930
Total	922,499	182,714	90,979	49,564	259,855	169,818	89,109	80,460

Bureau of Public Roads.

TABLE 576.—*Total State highway road and bridge disbursements, 1927, as reported by State authorities*

State	Total disbursements	Construction	Maintenance	Miscellaneous expenses	Retirement of bonds	Interest on bonds	Equipment material, etc.	County funds, right of way, traffic, etc.
	1,000 dollars	*1,000 dollars*	*1,000 dollars*	*1,000 dollars*	*1,000 dollars*	*1,000 dollars*	*1,000 dollars*	*1,000 dollars*
Alabama	10, 765	6, 860	810	830	652	896	717	
Arizona	2, 608	1, 323	1, 040	119			126	
Arkansas	14, 532	4, 412	1, 917	641	5, 372	318	553	1, 319
California	20, 559	8, 573	5, 218	1, 575	1, 775	3, 031	41	346
Colorado	5, 232	2, 896	843	369	600	467	25	32
Connecticut	12, 784	7, 886	4, 336	562				
Delaware	3, 480	1, 982	148	486	263	437	11	153
Florida	23, 557	19, 707	2, 579	1, 258			13	
Georgia	15, 114	11, 966	1, 573	1, 115			317	143
Idaho	3, 847	2, 520	676	426			196	29
Illinois	30, 270	24, 257	1, 943	2, 487	399	151	95	938
Indiana	14, 798	4, 583	2, 629	661	2, 000	3, 606	1, 125	194
Iowa	24, 077	15, 034	3, 567	4, 778				698
Kansas	16, 509	15, 357	1, 000	152				
Kentucky	11, 485	7, 412	1, 895	823			888	467
Louisiana	10, 753	6, 511	2, 737	597	30	26	657	195
Maine	8, 684	5, 134	1, 570	462	446	568	355	149
Maryland	10, 598	3, 651	3, 953		2, 003	991		
Massachusetts	18, 380	10, 804	2, 754	3, 575	1, 048		199	
Michigan	25, 883	14, 039	5, 121	1, 409	529	2, 239	522	2, 024
Minnesota	17, 837	10, 540	4, 235	144	189	1, 596	668	465
Mississippi	6, 481	4, 074	1, 747	555			63	42
Missouri	25, 997	15, 734	3, 234	1, 893	2, 995	2, 141		
Montana	1, 541	1, 034	158	209			132	8
Nebraska	8, 004	5, 144	1, 848	423			488	101
Nevada	2, 199	1, 479	331	204	100	30	41	14
New Hampshire	3, 565	1, 411	1, 645	464			45	
New Jersey	27, 763	15, 300	1, 760	1, 642	2, 872		43	6, 146
New Mexico	5, 089	2, 977	1, 003	213	445	28	417	6
New York	58, 798	37, 305	7, 069	3, 447	400	4, 220	972	5, 385
North Carolina	33, 145	17, 089	2, 798	1, 928		3, 825	111	7, 394
North Dakota	4, 567	3, 435	428	511			170	23
Ohio	18, 214	3, 641	13, 842	731				
Oklahoma	12, 816	9, 745	2, 193	660				218
Oregon	10, 263	3, 168	2, 984	748	1, 600	1, 663		100
Pennsylvania	50, 064	17, 598	15, 044	5, 657	3, 509	4, 291	1, 191	2, 774
Rhode Island	4, 242	1, 363	1, 868	449	118	186	155	103
South Carolina	13, 410	9, 163	1, 923	489			424	1, 411
South Dakota	4, 862	2, 446	1, 165	315	450	269	38	179
Tennessee	16, 003	8, 395	3, 708	1, 562	1, 000	94	1, 244	
Texas	20, 018	11, 365	8, 085	395			173	
Utah	3, 929	2, 080	796	81	413	325	217	17
Vermont	4, 080	2, 421	1, 319	161			179	
Virginia	14, 714	9, 375	3, 980	603			450	306
Washington	8, 628	5, 634	2, 243	751				
West Virginia	19, 311	11, 945	2, 172	590	2, 320	2, 053	231	
Wisconsin	17, 547	9, 473	4, 175	544			25	3, 330
Wyoming	2, 873	1, 797	721	188			73	
Total	699, 875	400, 038	138, 783	47, 882	31, 528	33, 545	13, 390	34, 709

Bureau of Public Roads.

TABLE 577.—*Mileage of county and local roads at end of 1927, from records and reports of local authorities*

State	Total mileage	Earth, nonsurfaced	Surfaced roads, by types								
			Total surfaced	Sand-clay, topsoil	Gravel, chert, etc.	Water-bound macadam (treated and untreated)	Bituminous macadam	Sheet asphalt	Bituminous concrete	Portland cement concrete	Brick and block
Alabama	59,787	43,967	15,820	8,282	7,111	259	44	2	47	70	5
Arizona	19,625	17,941	1,684	250	1,079	25	-----	54	13	263	-----
Arkansas	66,039	64,196	1,843	210	1,574	46	7	1	-----	5	-----
California	78,583	58,607	19,976	1,607	11,992	1,114	2,152	9	1,044	2,058	-----
Colorado	59,184	56,571	2,613	1,315	1,292	-----	-----	-----	2	4	-----
Connecticut	12,021	10,493	1,528	-----	986	378	74	7	-----	83	-----
Delaware	3,167	2,869	298	-----	79	160	21	-----	30	7	1
Florida	23,244	12,727	10,517	3,417	988	4,652	175	635	68	78	504
Georgia	92,082	82,572	9,510	7,692	1,289	73	228	38	-----	188	2
Idaho	33,130	27,349	5,781	2,112	3,552	-----	71	-----	41	5	-----
Illinois	87,730	74,681	13,049	-----	11,206	439	78	23	-----	1,186	117
Indiana	69,245	23,310	45,935	-----	42,675	1,523	297	16	177	1,093	154
Iowa	96,556	89,187	7,369	-----	7,363	-----	-----	-----	-----	6	-----
Kansas	121,324	119,698	1,626	580	887	75	35	7	1	39	2
Kentucky	51,614	40,521	11,093	159	3,966	6,886	55	2	5	20	-----
Louisiana	25,141	20,865	4,276	22	4,224	19	5	-----	5	1	-----
Maine	19,214	15,877	3,337	9	3,298	13	14	-----	-----	3	-----
Maryland	12,192	9,404	2,788	143	1,647	896	7	4	-----	91	-----
Massachusetts	17,758	10,838	6,920	19	4,362	975	1,077	4	409	57	17
Michigan	73,872	57,487	16,385	19	13,758	1,312	139	7	70	1,075	5
Minnesota	103,313	77,458	25,855	5,578	20,084	72	-----	11	18	92	-----
Mississippi	50,052	41,594	8,458	204	8,010	32	50	7	71	79	5
Missouri	103,065	95,239	7,826	1,462	4,955	1,210	92	-----	51	56	-----
Montana	58,924	57,200	1,724	120	1,600	2	2	-----	-----	-----	-----
Nebraska	87,736	87,097	639	196	401	4	2	-----	9	24	3
Nevada	20,107	19,630	477	16	461	-----	-----	-----	-----	-----	-----
New Hampshire	9,715	9,394	321	23	265	22	10	-----	1	-----	-----
New Jersey	14,856	8,458	6,398	74	3,446	1,022	398	354	465	575	64
New Mexico	38,964	38,613	351	86	265	-----	-----	-----	-----	-----	-----
New York	65,560	46,283	19,277	-----	6,693	7,084	4,658	-----	-----	842	-----
North Carolina	64,447	42,862	21,585	17,950	2,730	250	260	90	30	250	25
North Dakota	99,609	98,971	638	-----	638	-----	-----	-----	-----	-----	-----
Ohio	73,753	39,672	34,081	-----	25,012	5,926	2,145	49	47	634	268
Oklahoma	117,485	116,019	1,466	219	1,124	2	11	8	6	96	-----
Oregon	47,265	38,860	8,406	234	6,594	1,050	9	-----	362	156	-----
Pennsylvania	79,074	63,368	15,706	-----	11,878	1,855	518	67	430	530	428
Rhode Island	1,671	1,297	374	-----	174	101	55	20	20	1	3
South Carolina	50,537	41,218	9,319	9,062	189	7	-----	-----	46	12	3
South Dakota	114,250	113,059	1,191	-----	1,191	-----	-----	-----	-----	-----	-----
Tennessee	59,457	50,645	8,812	234	4,800	3,662	38	6	7	64	1
Texas	169,836	155,990	13,846	2,634	10,490	467	40	26	20	169	-----
Utah	19,980	18,367	1,613	25	1,514	-----	9	-----	24	41	-----
Vermont	10,810	9,363	1,447	143	1,300	-----	1	3	-----	-----	-----
Virginia	52,290	45,254	7,036	3,710	1,591	1,280	330	-----	-----	125	-----
Washington	43,535	29,550	13,985	993	10,348	1,654	44	-----	124	780	42
West Virginia	30,979	29,476	1,503	-----	601	214	374	4	37	222	51
Wisconsin	69,248	52,102	17,146	2,874	13,175	739	-----	-----	-----	358	-----
Wyoming	42,205	41,877	328	97	231	-----	-----	-----	-----	-----	-----
Total, 1927	2,720,231	2,308,076	412,156	71,770	263,088	45,500	13,525	1,454	3,680	11,438	1,700
Total, 1926	2,712,262	2,325,257	387,005	69,711	245,524	42,732	11,651	1,548	3,607	10,405	1,827
Total, 1925	2,731,172	2,354,766	376,406	58,211	224,036	65,604	10,490	1,921	3,420	10,106	2,059
Total, 1924	2,743,195	2,403,637	[3]339,558	53,638	193,465	60,139	7,853	1,489	2,991	8,363	1,624
Total, 1923	2,744,116	2,416,175	[3]327,941	52,425	186,314	59,200	6,950	1,395	2,824	7,289	1,569
Total, 1921	2,732,052	2,429,150	[4]302,902	54,717	163,441	60,367	3,515	1,205	2,534	5,497	1,331

Bureau of Public Roads.

[1] Includes 559 miles miscellaneous types.
[2] Includes 9,996 miles miscellaneous types.
[3] Includes 9,975 miles miscellaneous types.
[4] Includes 10,295 miles miscellaneous types.

33023°—29——70

TABLE 578.—*Local road income and funds available, 1927, compiled from records of local authorities*

State	Total funds available	Balance at first of year	Local road-bond sales	Local road taxes and appropriations	Motor-vehicle fees	Gasoline-tax receipts	Funds from State for local roads	Miscellaneous income
	1,000 dollars	*1,000 dollars*	*1,000 dollars*	*1,000 dollars*	*1,000 dollars*	*1,000 dollars*	*1,000 dollars*	*1,000 dollars*
Alabama	12,347	1,240	122	5,448	42	3,228		2,267
Arizona	1,786	126		741	163	530	94	132
Arkansas	9,686	426		2,399			6,661	200
California	45,285	14,454	1,723	17,340	2,901	7,821	135	911
Colorado	5,594	269		2,882	495	1,173	552	223
Connecticut	2,881	82		2,799				
Delaware	2,174	266	310	1,311			284	3
Florida	93,329	33,226	37,763	14,040	1,108	3,105		4,087
Georgia	19,172	2,483	1,566	11,982		2,079		1,062
Idaho	6,907	2,079	66	3,073	1,223		153	313
Illinois	29,313		1,166	27,505				642
Indiana	48,039	9,428	10,824	25,937		1,848		2
Iowa	27,154	4,501	782	13,652		3,629	722	3,868
Kansas	32,175	8,594	2,708	13,319		7,054		500
Kentucky	10,290		3,462	6,102	464			262
Louisiana	16,811	6,342	820	8,408			102	1,139
Maine	2,661	D.—85	40	2,606				100
Maryland	4,916		1,310	3,277				329
Massachusetts	15,209	149	140	8,100			6,475	345
Michigan	54,938	10,452	7,424	26,481	7,021		2,024	1,536
Minnesota	23,452	873	1,020	18,410			1,673	1,476
Mississippi	37,073	9,477	9,112	12,908	2,085	2,164		1,327
Missouri	12,676	1,003	456	9,947			10	1,260
Montana	5,835	1,200	120	2,970	1,250		75	220
Nebraska	10,251	878		6,356	2,540		52	425
Nevada	1,589	510	35	744	5	235	2	58
New Hampshire	3,787			3,720			67	
New Jersey	29,572	1,125	16,222	8,536	2,852		837	
New Mexico	732	70	221	277	151		4	9
New York	44,291	4,291		29,967	4,743		5,290	
North Carolina	35,364	1,158	9,642	13,586				10,978
North Dakota	5,999	1,350		4,000	648		1	
Ohio	86,170	13,198	17,680	44,122	2,400	3,520	5,250	
Oklahoma	17,288	2,050	1,500	7,950	2,589	2,399		800
Oregon	14,430	1,500	4,000	5,300	1,450	180	1,150	850
Pennsylvania	77,610	17,241	10,832	36,597		2,494	1,502	8,944
Rhode Island	959	28	50	822			12	47
South Carolina	20,667	720	13,658	2,934		1,903		1,452
South Dakota	5,565			4,058	1,187		162	158
Tennessee	23,760	8,180	5,341	7,245		111		2,883
Texas	41,355	8,312	10,500	17,300	4,143		150	950
Utah	2,054	575		1,412				67
Vermont	1,200	15		885			300	
Virginia	14,312	4,110	1,558	4,058		1,882		2,704
Washington	10,450	750	95	7,120	780	115	780	810
West Virginia	16,870	3,600	3,500	9,680				90
Wisconsin	34,017	1,861	5,313	19,021		1,390	3,456	2,976
Wyoming	727	1		586			9	131
Total	1,018,722	178,108	181,081	477,913	40,240	46,860	37,984	56,536

Bureau of Public Roads.

TABLE 579.—*Local road disbursements, 1927, compiled from records of local authorities*

State	Total local disbursements	Construction	Maintenance	Miscellaneous and overhead [1]	Bond payments		County-fund transfers to State [2]	Unexpended balances end of year
					Interest	Retirements and sinking funds		
	1,000 dollars	*1,000 dollars*	*1,000 dollars*	*1,000 dollars*	*1,000 dollars*	*1,000 dollars*	*1,000 dollars*	*1,000 dollars*
Alabama	10,506	1,367	6,032	220	1,541	1,346	34	1,807
Arizona	1,610	279	978	214	76	63	----------	176
Arkansas	8,900	750	2,175	75	3,250	2,650	----------	786
California	30,737	9,963	12,936	2,692	2,521	2,625	1,481	13,067
Colorado	5,041	1,096	3,324	603	3	15	99	454
Connecticut	2,961	635	2,326	----------	----------	----------	----------	-80
Delaware	1,669	421	474	40	468	266	338	167
Florida	53,792	31,991	7,989	5,023	6,853	1,936	3,614	35,923
Georgia	14,337	5,035	6,386	593	1,575	748	2,683	2,152
Idaho	4,470	820	1,252	629	959	810	520	1,917
Illinois	27,661	8,018	15,932	825	1,055	1,831	----------	1,652
Indiana	37,225	10,217	11,036	736	3,709	11,527	39	10,775
Iowa	24,275	9,194	11,805	1,161	975	1,140	----------	2,879
Kansas	17,687	8,003	5,496	1,679	917	1,592	7,182	7,306
Kentucky	6,898	1,076	3,478	448	920	976	2,202	1,190
Louisiana	11,806	3,066	2,865	527	2,784	2,564	554	4,451
Maine	2,700	350	2,100	128	60	62	----------	-39
Maryland	3,968	1,284	1,869	173	384	258	1,020	-72
Massachusetts	14,882	7,934	6,491	85	32	340	103	224
Michigan	40,693	18,496	12,981	----------	2,673	6,543	----------	14,245
Minnesota	23,447	14,701	4,716	2,000	1,140	890	----------	5
Mississippi	18,130	2,247	8,733	253	3,703	3,194	5,790	13,153
Missouri	11,176	3,200	5,365	965	825	821	----------	1,500
Montana	4,765	1,000	2,200	275	540	750	65	1,005
Nebraska	8,904	4,603	3,382	631	190	98	85	1,262
Nevada	679	91	338	81	72	97	386	524
New Hampshire	2,207	215	1,706	286	----------	----------	1,580	----------
New Jersey	27,188	8,811	4,918	475	2,677	10,307	----------	2,384
New Mexico	492	123	281	58	22	8	28	212
New York	40,000	29,000	4,000	2,800	2,700	1,500	----------	4,291
North Carolina	25,721	6,306	5,121	1,244	5,202	7,848	5,996	3,647
North Dakota	4,230	3,643	496	91	----------	----------	----------	1,769
Ohio	62,366	22,191	13,553	2,240	5,517	18,865	11,713	12,091
Oklahoma	12,725	2,675	7,200	800	1,100	950	3,132	1,431
Oregon	12,710	7,200	2,750	410	1,100	1,250	----------	1,720
Pennsylvania	54,715	22,025	12,794	6,305	5,134	8,457	8,894	14,001
Rhode Island	954	283	527	35	34	75	----------	5
South Carolina	6,357	1,909	2,041	131	1,386	890	11,373	2,937
South Dakota	6,223	3,252	2,778	157	7	29	555	-1,213
Tennessee	11,150	3,723	3,570	360	2,271	1,226	4,756	7,854
Texas	28,170	6,225	9,320	1,065	6,360	5,200	1,817	11,368
Utah	1,277	357	608	87	156	69	222	555
Vermont	1,000	400	600	----------	----------	----------	200	----------
Virginia	10,654	2,124	5,664	----------	1,307	1,559	----------	3,658
Washington	9,694	3,800	3,900	400	794	800	----------	756
West Virginia	13,370	7,220	3,000	200	1,300	1,650	----------	3,500
Wisconsin	27,388	11,599	10,119	4,041	683	946	4,464	2,165
Wyoming	736	262	366	42	41	25	7	-16
Total	748,246	289,180	237,971	41,283	75,016	104,796	80,932	189,544

Bureau of Public Roads.

[1] Administration and engineering.
[2] Not applicable to local road and bridge disbursements.

TABLE 580.—*Motor-vehicle registration, 1927, as reported by State authorities*

State	Registered motor vehicles (private and commercial)			Registered motor cycles	Tax-exempt motor cars	Number licenses and permits		Year's increase in registration	
	All motor cars and trucks	Passenger autos, taxis and busses	Motor trucks and road tractors			Dealers' licenses	Operators and chauffeurs	Number	Per cent
Alabama	243,539	211,633	31,906	420	167	3,919	1,630	17,609	7.8
Arizona	81,047	68,597	12,450	271	991	212	801	7,365	10.0
Arkansas	206,568	174,524	32,044	303	775	479	4,932	—(2,851)	—1.4
California	1,693,195	1,479,411	213,784	9,444	24,431	3,270	240,985	92,720	5.8
Colorado	268,492	245,107	23,385	1,362	283			19,879	8.0
Connecticut	281,521	238,509	43,012	3,083	2,530	5,600	323,881	18,286	6.9
Delaware	47,124	38,037	9,087	313	44	438	51,945	2,290	5.1
Florida	394,734	332,979	61,755	1,243	3,526	2,547	4,949	—(6,828)	—1.7
Georgia	300,635	262,630	38,005	909	934	792	2,553	23,167	8.4
Idaho	101,336	91,306	10,030	440	1,313	406	476	6,576	6.9
Illinois	1,438,985	1,254,421	184,564	6,135	979	4,594	100,393	68,482	5.0
Indiana	813,637	697,359	116,278	3,501	7,267	2,584	39,212	41,311	5.3
Iowa	704,203	649,309	54,894	1,787	2,871	2,531	2,964	5,205	.7
Kansas	501,901	447,273	54,628	1,218	2,552	2,525		10,625	2.2
Kentucky	285,621	255,892	29,729	693	1,832	1,051	8,410	4,064	1.4
Louisiana	255,000	216,000	39,000	510	209	1,297	14,177	15,500	6.5
Maine	163,623	132,927	30,696	1,245	1,237	1,297	196,284	12,137	8.0
Maryland	276,863	265,768	11,095	2,415	2,919	6,788	74,493	24,011	9.5
Massachusetts	694,107	614,359	79,748	7,245	1,356	2,048	102,285	3,917	.6
Michigan	1,154,773	998,781	155,992	3,585	371	2,128	297,437	35,988	3.2
Minnesota	646,682	565,401	81,281	2,295	2,702	2,087	17,988	16,397	2.6
Mississippi	218,043	196,239	21,804	83	74	656		12,843	6.2
Missouri	682,419	610,303	72,116	1,835	1,739	2,387	31,499	27,865	4.2
Montana	112,735	94,733	18,002	156	1,387	481	338	8,777	8.4
Nebraska	373,912	342,357	31,555	1,109	1,255	3,052		7,139	1.9
Nevada	25,776	20,414	5,362	99	42	533		1,762	7.3
New Hampshire	96,009	83,415	12,594	1,387	22	541	116,716	7,008	7.9
New Jersey	712,396	586,510	125,886	6,857	7,002	2,917	821,015	60,981	9.4
New Mexico	59,291	57,643	1,648	170	786	170		4,295	7.8
New York	1,937,918	1,624,535	313,383	16,347	13,782	4,482	2,317,408	122,484	5.7
North Carolina	430,499	390,223	40,276	1,194	5,848	6,330		45,452	11.8
North Dakota	160,701	144,830	15,871	277	3			2,879	1.8
Ohio	1,570,734	1,374,402	196,332	7,749	11,429	26,997		90,488	6.1
Oklahoma	503,126	437,776	65,350	1,200	530			3,188	.6
Oregon	244,572	223,582	20,990	2,030	1,273	604	55,124	11,004	4.7
Pennsylvania	1,554,915	1,354,548	200,367	14,267	2,325	28,347	1,564,161	99,731	6.9
Rhode Island	118,014	98,861	19,153	1,250	727	300	136,860	7,268	6.6
South Carolina	199,635	179,571	20,064	325	91	508		18,446	10.2
South Dakota	169,552	153,019	16,533	229	1,104			1,322	.8
Tennessee	294,567	269,086	25,481	904	3,046	632		14,928	5.3
Texas	1,111,407	996,397	115,010	3,081	2,505	3,323	53,265	61,538	5.9
Utah	93,974	80,730	13,244	531	173			8,594	10.1
Vermont	79,527	73,308	6,219	601	28	658		5,464	7.4
Virginia	337,607	288,666	48,941	2,025	1,141	2,950	8,450	14,993	4.6
Washington	384,583	326,667	57,916	2,501	5,319	4,879	397,975	21,304	5.9
West Virginia	245,819	217,689	28,130	1,431	1,895	13,701	86,800	17,983	7.9
Wisconsin	698,289	609,795	88,494	2,963	760	2,949		36,007	5.4
Wyoming	51,955	45,539	6,416	134	466	306		2,072	4.2
District of Columbia	111,680	98,162	13,518	1,151	2,968	1,958	58,595	183	.2
Total	23,133,241	20,219,223	2,914,018	120,303	¹127,009	155,444	7,134,001	1,131,848	5.1

Bureau of Public Roads.

¹ Includes 7,859 United States cars at large not allocated to States.

TABLE 581.—*Motor-vehicle revenues, 1927, as reported by State authorities*

State	Gross receipts	Motor-car registration receipts			Miscellaneous receipts	Disposition of gross receipts [1]			
		All motor cars	Passenger cars and busses	Trucks, etc.		Collection costs	State highways	Local roads	On road bonds and miscellaneous
	1,000 dollars	*1,000 dollars*	*1,000 dollars*	*1,000 dollars*	*1,000 dollars*	*1,000 dollars*	*1,000 dollars*	*1,000 dollars*	*1,000 dollars*
Alabama	3,127	3,110			17	126	844	610	1,547
Arizona	455	443			12		455		
Arkansas	3,662	3,619			43	73	806	476	2,307
California	8,796	7,492	4,852	2,640	1304	1,244	3,775	3,775	2
Colorado	1,600	1,500	1,248	252	100	80	760	760	
Connecticut	6,806	5,197	3,895	1,302	1,609		6,806		
Delaware	846	674	489	185	172		846		
Florida	5,692	5,601	4,077	1,524	91	584	3,829	1,277	2
Georgia	3,713	3,659	3,039	620	54	115	3,598		
Idaho	1,502	1,459	1,211	248	43		156	1,346	
Illinois	14,840	13,929	10,635	3,294	911		9,191		5,649
Indiana	5,431	5,069	3,915	1,154	362	251	5,180		
Iowa	10,372	9,743	8,786	957	629	414	9,605	353	
Kansas	6,519					253	3,935	2,331	
Kentucky	4,365	4,304	3,375	929	61	224	3,677	464	
Louisiana	4,199						4,199		
Maine	2,559	1,981	1,535	446	578	202	1,371		986
Maryland	2,988	2,347	2,071	276	641	299	2,151		538
Massachusetts	13,137	10,558	7,319	3,239	2,579	1,267	10,822		1,048
Michigan	17,984	16,528	12,465	4,063	1,456	1,117	9,785	6,000	1,082
Minnesota	10,234	10,111	8,211	1,900	123		6,451		3,783
Mississippi	2,557	2,221			336	126	202	2,229	
Missouri	8,253					402	2,715		5,136
Montana	1,136	1,039	855	184	97	31		1,105	
Nebraska	3,740	3,575	3,017	558	165	112	1,088	2,540	
Nevada	230	229			1	10	90		130
New Hampshire	1,915	1,537			378	156	1,759		
New Jersey	12,964	9,294	5,680	3,614	3,670	533	7,900	4,531	
New Mexico	528	502	444	58	26	54	316	158	
New York	31,758	28,375	20,141	8,234	3,383	1,922	22,073	4,743	3,020
North Carolina	3,247					150	2,332		765
North Dakota	1,595	1,570	1,339	231	25	170	777	648	
Ohio	10,745	10,399			346	367	5,128	5,250	
Oklahoma	5,754						2,302	3,452	
Oregon	6,527	6,326	5,408	918	201	367	1,357		4,803
Pennsylvania	26,017	19,694	13,734	5,960	6,323	1,566	15,048	1,501	7,902
Rhode Island	2,093	1,694	1,265	429	399	179	1,914		
South Carolina	2,187	2,078	1,772	306	109		2,178	9	
South Dakota	2,492	2,473	2,142	331	19	67	1,237	1,188	
Tennessee	3,766					93	3,673		
Texas	15,627	15,046	12,584	2,462	581	599	10,884	4,144	
Utah	672					132			540
Vermont	1,879	1,611	1,385	226	268	120	1,759		
Virginia	5,236	4,840	4,143	697	396	258	4,978		
Washington	6,482	5,930	4,607	1,323	552	248	4,941	893	400
West Virginia	4,004	3,605	3,084	521	399	257	1,390		2,357
Wisconsin	9,773	9,518	7,872	1,646	255	550	5,428	3,795	
Wyoming	526	515	404	111	11		274		252
District of Columbia	531	120	99	21	411	159			372
Total	301,061					14,877	189,985	53,578	42,621

Bureau of Public Roads.

[1] These figures do not always agree with those shown on highway-income tables because of time of disposition and use of fiscal years.

TABLE 582.—*Gasoline taxes, 1927, as reported by State authorities*

State	Total tax earnings, with refunds deducted	Collection costs	Construction, etc.		State and county road-bond payments	Miscellaneous uses	Gasoline consumed by motor vehicles	Tax rates per gallon
			State highways[1]	Local roads[1]				
	1,000 dollars	*1,000 dollars*	*1,000 dollars*	*1,000 dollars*	*1,000 dollars*	*1,000 dollars*	*1,000 gallons*	*Cents*
Alabama	5,909	24	2,619	2,962	304		149,620	4
Arizona	1,389		621	768			40,217	4
Arkansas	4,339		1,042	564	2,733		94,346	5
California	22,467	42	13,159	9,266			928,749	3
Colorado	3,140	21	2,161	958			122,493	3
Connecticut	3,097		3,097				152,745	2
Delaware	662		662				23,487	3
Florida	11,009	3	7,552	2,514		940	251,410	5
Georgia	7,078	4	4,800	1,920		354	192,103	4
Idaho	1,572	12	1,436			124	40,877	4
Illinois[2]	6,199	25	3,087	3,087			[2]690,000	2
Indiana	10,134	15	6,746	2,530		843	337,769	3
Iowa	7,248	58	1,833	3,666		1,691	288,620	3
Kansas	4,595		3,851	744			229,732	2
Kentucky	5,913	12	5,901				118,268	5
Louisiana	3,034		3,034				151,703	2
Maine	2,289	13	2,276				72,007	4
Maryland	4,169	2	2,973			1,194	118,335	4
Massachusetts[3]							[4]310,000	0
Michigan	14,261	44	8,410	2,807	3,000		561,144	3
Minnesota	5,175		5,175				258,744	2
Mississippi	4,891	4	2,302	2,378	207		119,343	4
Missouri	6,331	48	6,283				316,549	2
Montana	1,436		1,436				47,880	3
Nebraska	3,665	8	3,657				183,246	2
Nevada	472		236		236		11,791	4
New Hampshire	1,269		1,269				44,898	3
New Jersey[5]	4,098	25	3,983			90	[5]356,000	2
New Mexico	1,432	31	1,295		106		30,117	5
New York[3]							[4]920,000	0
North Carolina	8,787	47	6,445		2,295		219,667	4
North Dakota	1,276	25	1,210			41	63,778	2
Ohio	19,910		11,998	7,912			752,028	3
Oklahoma	7,198		4,799	2,399			239,932	3
Oregon	3,643	8	3,635				122,823	3
Pennsylvania	17,296		13,838	3,458			691,562	3
Rhode Island	916		737		179		56,145	2
South Carolina	5,080	5	3,045	1,523	507		101,608	5
South Dakota	2,394	5	2,075		242	72	65,965	4
Tennessee	4,476		4,476				149,206	3
Texas	15,651		11,738			3,913	594,592	3
Utah	1,462	5	944		513		41,774	3½
Vermont	905		905				33,167	3
Virginia	7,140		4,760	2,380			158,424	4½
Washington	3,821		3,821				191,072	2
West Virginia	3,807		3,807				99,918	4
Wisconsin	6,027	10	2,215	3,368		434	301,356	2
Wyoming	756	4	752				25,884	3
District of Columbia	1,149					1,149	57,440	2
Total or average	258,967	500	182,096	55,440	10,086	10,845	11,128,534	2.76

Bureau of Public Roads.

[1] These figures do not always agree with those shown on highway-income tables because of time of disposition and use of fiscal years.
[2] Tax assessed only last 5 months, but consumption estimated for full year.
[3] State assessed no gasoline tax during year.
[4] Estimated consumption.
[5] Tax assessed only last 6 months, but consumption estimated for full year.

TABLE 583.—*Quarterly and annual average rate in cents per hour, by geographic divisions, for common labor employed on Federal-aid projects, 1922–1928*

Year and quarter ending—	New England	Middle Atlantic	East North Central	West North Central	South Atlantic	East South Central	West South Central	Mountain	Pacific	United States
1922										
March	30	-------	26	30	18	19	24	34	47	28
June	37	33	30	30	21	20	24	36	48	31
September	41	37	33	32	23	21	25	39	50	34
December	43	41	35	32	21	20	23	40	49	34
Average	40	37	33	32	21	20	24	38	49	33
1923										
March	45	41	32	29	19	20	23	38	47	33
June	53	46	40	35	29	23	24	41	52	38
September	53	48	42	37	28	23	25	40	56	40
December	54	48	42	37	29	24	26	43	59	40
Average	53	47	41	36	27	23	25	41	54	39
1924										
March	53	50	41	35	29	23	26	39	51	39
June	51	47	40	35	28	25	26	42	53	39
September	49	42	40	38	28	24	28	41	53	38
December	47	41	40	37	29	24	28	39	53	38
Average	49	43	40	36	28	24	27	40	53	38
1925										
March	46	40	36	39	24	24	28	40	52	37
June	46	43	37	38	29	25	25	45	53	38
September	47	43	37	36	28	25	26	45	52	38
December	46	46	36	37	26	25	28	45	52	38
Average	46	43	37	37	27	25	26	44	52	38
1926										
March	50	45	38	36	28	26	26	43	52	36
June	48	45	38	36	28	25	27	45	53	38
September	48	47	37	36	30	25	27	44	52	39
December	50	48	40	36	30	24	28	42	52	39
Average	49	47	38	36	29	25	27	44	52	38
1927										
March	47	48	40	37	29	24	27	42	52	38
June	50	46	38	38	27	25	31	44	52	40
September	49	47	38	37	28	25	30	46	53	40
December	49	46	40	37	27	25	31	47	54	40
Average	49	47	39	37	28	25	30	45	53	40
1928										
March	52	48	41	38	22	26	27	42	52	38
June	49	43	38	36	26	26	29	46	52	40
September	48	42	38	38	26	25	27	49	53	42
December	51	42	40	39	28	26	30	45	52	41
Average	49	43	39	38	26	26	28	46	52	41

Bureau of Public Roads.

TABLE 584.—*Hunters' licenses issued by States, with total money returns, for the seasons 1925–26 and 1926–27*

State	Resident		Nonresident and alien		Total		Money returns [1]	
	1925–26	1926–27	1925–26	1926–27	1925–26	1926–27	1925–26	1926–27
							Dollars	*Dollars*
Alaska [2]			137	182	137	182	9, 210. 00	12, 860. 00
Alabama	[3] 52, 000	54, 635	[3] 120	131	[3] 52, 120	54, 766	[3] 72, 000. 00	83, 484. 24
Arizona	29, 738	38, 134	388	631	30, 126	38, 765	44, 312. 50	52, 449. 35
Arkansas	3, 624	[3] 90, 000	565		4, 189	90, 000	12, 217. 00	90, 000. 00
California	229, 266	250, 891	1, 973	2, 641	231, 239	253, 532	251, 951. 30	279, 701. 00
Colorado	[4] 97, 217	[4] 90, 999	371	365	97, 588	91, 364	224, 373. 00	205, 237. 45
Connecticut	34, 688	37, 521	399	599	35, 087	38, 120	38, 678. 00	111, 070. 50
Delaware	[4] 2, 109	[4] 2, 115	390	356	2, 499	2, 471	6, 414. 90	6, 064. 50
Florida	[3] 56, 561	59, 679	[3] 861	709	[3] 57, 422	60, 388	[3] 144, 704. 00	163, 105. 00
Georgia	65, 862	64, 755	190	226	66, 052	64, 981	78, 825. 80	79, 155. 00
Idaho	[4] 66, 169	[4] 70, 500	669	568	66, 838	71, 068	126, 604. 45	143, 357. 75
Illinois	295, 440	286, 908	2, 050	1, 691	297, 490	288, 599	242, 080. 00	231, 196. 02
Indiana	[4] 197, 078	[4] 251, 226	355	449	197, 433	251, 675	182, 750. 70	232, 930. 20
Iowa	155, 889	[4] 161, 008	277	290	156, 166	161, 298	158, 659. 00	163, 908. 00
Kansas	114, 910	113, 526	118	129	115, 028	113, 655	116, 680. 00	115, 461. 00
Kentucky	88, 654	90, 954	458	62	89, 112	91, 016	78, 790. 90	78, 850. 00
Louisiana	91, 334	106, 210	320	262	91, 654	106, 472	99, 334. 00	126, 097. 00
Maine	[4] 36, 122	[4] 37, 241	3, 436	54	39, 558	37, 295	46, 002. 40	62, 913. 35
Maryland	65, 773	62, 869	2, 147	2, 117	67, 920	64, 986	121, 073. 82	117, 420. 55
Massachusetts	107, 453	108, 746	1, 357	2, 621	108, 810	111, 367	219, 098. 30	234, 556. 00
Michigan	288, 090	293, 084	2, 190	2, 385	290, 280	295, 469	355, 306. 57·	379, 003. 20
Minnesota	171, 893	172, 000	417	400	172, 310	172, 400	239, 365. 75	240, 000. 00
Mississippi [5]								
Missouri	[4] 237, 590	[4] 255, 426	2, 230	3, 998	239, 820	259, 424	269, 216. 50	313, 265. 48
Montana	71, 249	[4] 67, 078	205	[4] 3, 578	71, 454	70, 656	146, 628. 00	145, 104. 30
Nebraska	[4] 139, 282	[4] 146, 246	[4] 452	[4] 474	139, 734	146, 720	143, 805. 00	150, 995. 25
Nevada	[3] 5, 300	5, 506	[3] 50	60	[3] 5, 350	5, 566	[3] 7, 500. 00	8, 259. 00
New Hampshire	[4] 52, 000	[4] 52, 647	[3] 2, 200	[4] 2, 305	[3] 54, 200	54, 952	[3] 104, 800. 00	105, 648. 45
New Jersey	[4] 153, 960	[4] 167, 415	[4] 1, 607	[4] 1, 787	155, 567	169, 202	270, 907. 50	232, 093. 25
New Mexico	14, 847	16, 399	625	723	15, 472	17, 122	45, 642. 00	49, 388. 45
New York	335, 913	615, 344	3, 234	5, 070	339, 147	620, 414	454, 849. 25	822, 415. 00
North Carolina	([5])	137, 099	([5])	876	([5])	137, 975	([5])	203, 000. 00
North Dakota	35, 983	34, 238	178	160	36, 161	34, 398	54, 791. 00	51, 943. 70
Ohio	361, 030	363, 000	68		361, 098	363, 000	362, 050. 00	453, 750. 00
Oklahoma	[4] 91, 900	[4] 80, 169	275	154	92, 175	80, 323	96, 025. 00	82, 416. 50
Oregon	53, 353	54, 922	715	748	54, 068	55, 670	199, 916. 50	202, 395. 00
Pennsylvania	521, 855	520, 574	3, 190	3, 505	525, 045	524, 079	646, 467. 25	649, 549. 10
Rhode Island	10, 659	13, 213	254	274	10, 913	13, 487	13, 070. 00	16, 313. 00
South Carolina	75, 810	68, 048	1, 024	1, 065	76, 834	69, 113	117, 142. 00	116, 466. 05
South Dakota	84, 241	91, 924	1, 141	1, 464	85, 382	93, 388	119, 052. 00	133, 136. 00
Tennessee	44, 089	45, 000	218	200	44, 307	45, 200	62, 055. 00	63, 000. 00
Texas	71, 745	83, 707	325	397	72, 070	84, 104	139, 877. 25	163, 540. 95
Utah	[4] 52, 223	[4] 52, 942	129	[4] 98	52, 352	53, 040	87, 734. 47	116, 944. 73
Vermont	[4] 38, 387	[4] 37, 049	[4] 1, 109	[4] 1, 128	39, 496	38, 177	54, 275. 45	53, 454. 15
Virginia	91, 483	95, 054	2, 005	2, 194	93, 488	97, 248	147, 438. 45	154, 242. 60
Washington	[4] 181, 814	[4] 196, 213	[4] 3, 336	[4] 729	185, 150	196, 942	339, 046. 50	358, 656. 00
West Virginia	123, 551	[4] 127, 305	105	235	123, 656	127, 540	125, 130. 00	130, 830. 00
Wisconsin	164, 488	155, 843	396	231	164, 884	156, 074	184, 288. 00	146, 046. 10
Wyoming	[4] 24, 572	[4] 23, 885	922	592	25, 494	24, 477	69, 962. 00	63, 000. 00
Total	5, 287, 194	5, 949, 247	45, 181	48, 913	5, 332, 375	5, 998, 160	7, 130, 101. 51	8, 194, 673. 17

Bureau of Biological Survey.

[1] Includes amounts received from combined hunting and fishing licenses, but not from licenses to fish only.

[2] No resident license required.

[3] Estimated.

[4] Combined hunting and fishing license.

[5] Figures not available.

TABLE 585.—*National forests: Net areas and grazing receipts, by forests and districts, calendar year 1928*

District and forest	Net areas [1]	Receipts from grazing [2]	District and forest	Net areas [1]	Receipts from grazing [2]
District 1:	*Acres*	*Dollars*	**District 4:**	*Acres*	*Dollars*
Absaroka	856, 679	7, 417. 69	Ashley	986, 789	12, 442. 32
Beartooth	660, 544	4, 888. 90	Boise	1, 063, 313	13, 727. 80
Beaverhead	1, 339, 292	17, 714. 21	Cache	778, 092	26, 323. 34
Bitterroot	1, 050, 912	2, 649. 65	Caribou	710, 782	30, 589. 16
Blackfeet	832, 886	204. 32	Challis	1, 344, 764	9, 009. 65
Cabinet	834, 004	1, 040. 65	Dixie	852, 372	16, 928. 17
Clearwater	793, 178	2, 487. 69	Fishlake	1, 386, 459	28, 736. 81
Coeur d'Alene	666, 763	426. 63	Humboldt	1, 322, 215	58, 017. 45
Custer	590, 666	21, 392. 52	Idaho	1, 734, 182	11, 184. 16
Deerlodge	828, 653	11, 655. 13	Kaibab	723, 411	1, 355. 44
Flathead	1, 719, 112	96. 51	La Sal	530, 922	11, 715. 16
Gallatin	580, 922	7, 425. 87	Lemhi	1, 358, 792	23, 029. 03
Helena	685, 136	12, 909. 60	Manti	724, 715	29, 919. 20
Jefferson	1, 040, 859	17, 265. 88	Minidoka	591, 184	25, 647. 36
Kaniksu	465, 482	256. 93	Nevada	1, 175, 128	5, 378. 22
Kootenai	1, 360, 942	718. 69	Payette	1, 308, 311	18, 130. 53
Lewis and Clark	810, 731	4, 205. 34	Powell	1, 051, 716	16, 639. 03
Lolo	878, 469	2, 055. 39	Salmon	1, 708, 015	11, 953. 07
Madison	953, 922	18, 560. 47	Sawtooth	1, 166, 729	27, 825. 61
Missoula	1, 246, 786	4, 940. 88	Targhee	1, 376, 941	33, 862. 93
Nezperce	1, 661, 107	11, 016. 57	Teton	1, 881, 212	9, 550. 94
Pend Oreille	676, 424	745. 35	Toiyabe	1, 883, 661	7, 676. 96
Selway	1, 689, 157	2, 308. 63	Uinta	1, 078, 782	39, 640. 25
St. Joe	599, 842	842. 67	Wasatch	609, 866	12, 062. 00
			Weiser	565, 945	15, 045. 50
Total	22, 822, 468	153, 226. 17	Wyoming	1, 668, 048	37, 842. 52
District 2:			Total	29, 582, 346	534, 232. 61
Arapaho	637, 106	5, 420. 37			
Bellevue-Savanna	10, 710		**District 5:**		
Bighorn	1, 125, 632	28, 085. 65	Angeles	644, 130	1, 273. 88
Black Hills	623, 901	8, 548. 75	California	823, 712	5, 749. 59
Cochetopa	908, 787	11, 449. 33	Cleveland	380, 589	1, 585. 70
Colorado	830, 343	10, 730. 18	Eldorado	551, 798	7, 666. 24
Grand Mesa	659, 584	22, 503. 85	Inyo	1, 585, 634	10, 494. 67
Gunnison	911, 629	19, 779. 07	Klamath	1, 533, 380	3, 120. 97
Harney	508, 902	5, 945. 21	Lassen	945, 957	10, 074. 85
Hayden	394, 844	15, 759. 78	Modoc	1, 492, 264	32, 954. 36
Holy Cross	1, 124, 318	23, 649. 64	Mono	1, 261, 048	20,-192. 70
Leadville	929, 033	13, 962. 02	Plumas	1, 111, 935	16, 471. 36
Medicine Bow	552, 275	9, 435. 55	San Bernardino	596, 959	2, 278. 21
Michigan	178, 885		Santa Barbara	1, 775, 098	12, 449. 40
Chippewa	191, 785		Sequoia	1, 329, 926	13, 949. 10
Montezuma	719, 412	21, 850. 84	Shasta	890, 175	8, 263. 92
Nebraska	205, 946	10, 275. 84	Sierra	1, 493, 473	14, 680. 32
Pike	1, 087, 473	9, 377. 88	Stanislaus	821, 438	10, 535. 44
Rio Grande	1, 136, 757	25, 008. 67	Tahoe	532, 030	10, 725. 80
Routt	750, 334	17, 707. 01	Trinity	1, 410, 636	7, 048. 65
San Isabel	600, 216	7, 996. 92			
San Juan	1, 248, 657	36, 644. 17	Total	19, 180, 182	189, 515. 16
Shoshone	1, 619, 657	13, 774. 42			
Superior	813, 466		**District 6:**		
Uncompahgre	756, 310	20, 795. 67	Cascade	1, 026, 800	1, 888. 15
Washakie	868, 135	7, 402. 32	Chelan	1, 809, 072	7, 512. 18
White River	884, 873	28, 883. 99	Columbia	759, 103	2, 181. 83
Wichita	61, 480	3, 394. 86	Colville	747, 188	8, 749. 10
			Crater	862, 518	5, 302. 47
Total	20, 340, 450	378, 381. 99	Deschutes	1, 297, 909	4, 656. 94
			Fremont	849, 286	16, 752. 73
District 3:			Malheur	1, 049, 110	20, 773. 87
Apache	1, 564, 439	21, 561. 03	Mount Baker	1, 460, 611	567. 17
Carson	1, 094, 344	14, 996. 03	Mount Hood	1, 062, 869	4, 223. 28
Coconino	1, 717, 697	24, 891. 63	Ochoco	719, 273	17, 843. 48
Coronado	1, 481, 812	27, 981. 74	Olympic	1, 529, 530	220. 47
Crook	1, 424, 546	21, 899. 95	Rainier	1, 261, 530	7, 937. 90
Datil	1, 748, 648	18, 727. 43	Santiam	610, 923	1, 706. 95
Gila	1, 596, 234	18, 576. 46	Siskiyou	1, 362, 636	850. 38
Lincoln	1, 113, 975	13, 344. 19	Siuslaw	553, 503	95. 81
Manzano	679, 448	6, 212. 73	Snoqualmie	619, 651	304. 39
Prescott	1, 208, 270	24, 018. 29	Umatilla	1, 249, 936	26, 530. 71
Santa Fe	1, 270, 394	9, 241. 45	Umpqua	1, 014, 374	1, 842. 16
Sitgreaves	686, 671	5, 794. 90	Wallowa	969, 137	30, 788. 29
Tonto	2, 261, 792	42, 320. 21	Wenatchee	860, 718	6, 075. 27
Tusayan	1, 293, 271	14, 182. 73	Whitman	1, 341, 830	25, 158. 44
Total	19, 141, 541	263, 748. 77	Total	23, 017, 507	191, 961. 97

[1] Net areas as of June 30, 1928.
[2] Fiscal year ended June 30, 1928 (preliminary).

TABLE 585.—*National forests: Net areas and grazing receipts, by forests and districts, calendar year 1928*—Continued

District and forest	Net areas	Receipts from grazing	District and forest	Net areas	Receipts from grazing
District 7:	*Acres*	*Dollars*	District 7—Continued.	*Acres*	*Dollars*
Alabama	109, 625	35. 58	Tobyhanna	23, 259	
Allegheny	251, 568		Unaka	184, 250	81. 82
Cherokee	312, 698	120. 15	White Mountain	484, 020	214. 84
Choctawhatchee	184, 449	108. 00			
Humphreys	3, 184	64. 80	Total	4, 049, 265	[3] 2, 663. 48
Luquillo	12, 443				
Monongahela	188, 220	325. 45	District 8:		
Nantahala	250, 198	358. 51	Chugach	4, 799, 803	
Natural Bridge	161, 117	168. 44	Tongass	16, 547, 294	
Ocala	158, 731	394. 44			
Ouachita	672, 298	29. 28	Total	21, 347, 097	
Ozark	334, 937	177. 66			
Pisgah	289, 652	217. 56	Total, 151 national		
Shenandoah	428, 616	285. 45	forests	159, 480, 856	1, 713, 730. 15

Forest Service.

[3] Includes receipts of $81.50 from the Dix National Forest and the McClellan National Forest, both of which have been abolished.

TABLE 586.—*Crossties: Number purchased, by kinds of wood, and average cost per tie, 1905, 1909, 1923, 1925, and 1927*

Kind of wood	Crossties purchased					Average cost per tie			
	1905	1909	1923	1925	1927 [1]	1905	1909	1923	1925
	Thousands	*Thousands*	*Thousands*	*Thousands*	*Thousands*	*Cents*	*Cents*	*Cents*	*Cents*
Oak	34, 677	57, 132	62, 915	47, 256	31, 091	55	51	103	96
Pine [2]	18, 351	28, 669	24, 338	20, 421	21, 059	42	52	90	90
Douglas fir	3, 633	9, 067	15, 317	12, 709	11, 065	33	41	86	65
Gum		378	3, 051	3, 731	4, 337		52	73	65
Cypress	3, 484	4, 589	5, 244	5, 100	3, 793	33	41	104	110
Hemlock	1, 713	2, 642	3, 478	1, 971	2, 768	33	33	80	77
Cedar	6, 963	6, 777	3, 676	3, 432	2, 540	44	46	86	83
Chestnut	4, 718	6, 629	4, 420	3, 070	1, 941	48	44	95	93
Maple	25	158	3, 035	3, 111	1, 792	40	45	95	95
Beech	34	195	2, 279	1, 619	1, 156	40	36	96	102
Tamarack and larch	3, 371	3, 311	4, 220	2, 447	1, 150	37	41	64	74
Birch	36		369	1, 803	900	40		83	102
Redwood	591	2, 088	2, 493	1, 203	755	20	53	95	71
All others	385	2, 116	1, 141	3, 469	19, 091	43	45		
Total	[3] 77,981	123, 751	135, 976	111, 342	103, 438	47	49	95	88

Bureau of the Census in cooperation with the Forest Service.

[1] Preliminary figures.
[2] Includes southern pine, western yellow pine, and lodge-pole pine. In 1909 the total number was composed of southern pine, 21,385,000 (at 52 cents); lodge-pole pine, 487,000 (at 46 cents); and western yellow pine, 6,797,000 (at 53 cents). In 1923 the total was composed of: southern pine, 22,049,000 (at 91 cents); lodge-pole pine, 949,000 (at 82 cents); and western yellow pine, 1,340,000 (at 82 cents).
[3] Steam railroads only.

TABLE 587.—*Production of lumber, by States, 1899, 1909, 1919, 1925–1927*

State	1899	1909	1919	1925	1926	1927 (Preliminary)
	M ft. b. m.	*M ft. b. m.*	*M ft. b. m.*	*M ft. b. m.*	*M ft. b. m.*	*M ft. b. m.*
Alabama	1,101,386	1,691,001	1,798,746	2,235,738	2,105,122	2,171,687
Arizona	36,182	62,731	73,655	145,609	115,232	169,085
Arkansas	1,623,987	2,111,300	1,772,157	1,597,130	1,441,018	1,229,481
California	737,035	1,143,507	1,259,363	[1] 2,042,991	[1] 2,187,959	[1] 2,070,811
Colorado	133,746	141,710	64,864	71,069	75,278	67,321
Connecticut	108,093	168,371	86,708	41,650	47,367	55,949
Delaware	35,955	55,440	27,437	7,324	9,433	16,824
Florida	790,373	1,201,734	1,137,432	1,063,876	920,585	907,128
Georgia	1,311,917	1,342,249	893,965	1,365,174	1,145,489	1,201,008
Idaho	65,363	645,800	765,388	1,140,575	947,471	923,986
Illinois	388,469	170,181	64,628	29,456	38,357	28,663
Indiana	1,036,999	556,418	282,487	178,560	139,472	148,492
Iowa	352,411	132,021	18,493	(2)	(2)	(2)
Kansas	10,665	4,716	2,840	(2)	(2)	(2)
Kentucky	774,651	860,712	512,078	207,278	216,759	197,618
Louisiana	1,115,366	3,551,918	3,163,871	3,293,091	2,889,530	2,385,724
Maine	784,647	1,111,565	596,116	330,103	340,893	263,818
Maryland	183,711	267,939	113,362	88,963	68,444	67,541
Massachusetts	344,190	361,200	166,841	109,625	86,168	88,298
Michigan	3,018,338	1,889,724	875,891	797,610	663,344	578,254
Minnesota	2,342,338	1,561,508	699,639	578,703	471,090	396,891
Mississippi	1,206,265	2,572,669	2,390,135	3,127,678	2,894,994	2,556,612
Missouri	723,754	660,159	321,383	186,789	178,568	189,136
Montana	255,685	308,582	287,378	388,854	378,698	396,267
Nebraska	4,655	(2)	505	---------	---------	---------
Nevada	725	(2)	20,335	(4)	(4)	(4)
New Hampshire	572,447	649,606	338,777	260,680	243,007	215,912
New Jersey	74,118	61,620	36,888	9,816	6,953	5,044
New Mexico	30,880	91,987	86,808	152,330	127,110	172,517
New York	878,448	681,440	357,764	197,654	170,963	142,505
North Carolina	1,286,638	2,177,715	1,654,435	1,040,735	970,965	1,055,222
Ohio	990,497	542,904	280,076	140,736	141,499	127,880
Oklahoma	22,104	225,730	168,403	157,580	149,929	169,943
Oregon	734,538	1,898,995	2,577,403	4,216,383	4,454,735	3,992,852
Pennsylvania	2,333,278	1,462,771	630,471	330,822	318,797	277,722
Rhode Island	18,528	25,489	11,030	3,686	5,426	6,815
South Carolina	466,429	897,660	621,679	980,289	920,825	817,016
South Dakota	[5] 33,734	31,057	42,970	46,779	49,281	46,909
Tennessee	950,958	1,223,849	792,132	642,359	683,323	595,297
Texas	1,232,402	2,099,130	1,379,774	1,578,008	1,456,121	1,446,460
Utah	17,548	12,638	11,917	5,861	6,479	6,152
Vermont	375,809	351,571	218,479	126,433	111,638	90,880
Virginia	959,119	2,101,716	1,098,038	709,180	676,663	535,616
Washington	1,429,032	3,862,916	4,961,220	7,027,325	7,546,239	7,325,862
West Virginia	778,051	1,472,942	763,103	583,353	588,788	541,879
Wisconsin	3,389,166	2,025,038	1,116,338	1,068,612	912,524	819,507
Wyoming	16,963	28,602	8,674	16,105	19,392	12,863
All other	[6] 6,571	[7] 11,230	---------	16,069	14,002	14,012
United States	[8] 35,084,166	44,509,761	[8][9] 34,552,076	[10][11] 38,338,641	[10][11] 36,935,930	[10][11] 34,529,450

SUMMARY BY LUMBER PRODUCING REGIONS

REGIONS						
Northeastern	5,709,224	5,197,012	2,583,873	1,506,756	1,409,089	1,231,308
Lake	8,749,842	5,476,270	2,691,868	2,444,925	2,046,958	1,794,652
Central	5,643,379	5,487,165	3,015,887	1,968,531	1,986,766	1,828,956
North Carolina pine	2,712,186	5,177,091	3,374,152	2,730,204	2,568,453	2,407,854
Southern pine	8,403,802	14,795,731	12,704,483	14,418,275	13,002,788	12,068,043
Pacific (north)	2,163,570	5,761,911	7,538,623	11,243,708	12,000,974	11,318,714
Pacific (south)	737,760	1,143,507	1,279,698	2,042,991	2,187,959	2,070,811
Rocky Mountain (north)	321,048	954,382	1,052,766	1,529,429	1,326,169	1,320,253
Rocky Mountain (south)	235,319	337,668	245,918	390,974	343,491	427,933
Prairie	[12] 408,036	[12] 179,024	64,808	[12] 62,848	[12] 63,283	[13] 60,921

Forest Service in cooperation with Bureau of the Census.

[1] Includes cut of Nevada.
[2] Included in "All other."
[3] Includes cut of Nebraska.
[4] Included with California.
[5] Includes cut of North Dakota.
[6] Reported as cut of Alaska.
[7] Includes cut of Nebraska and Nevada.
[8] Includes both merchant and custom sawing.
[9] Includes 2,655 mills cutting less than 50,000 feet each per year
[10] Mills cutting less than 50,000 feet each year excluded.
[11] Excludes custom mills.
[12] Includes "All other."

TABLE 588.—*Lumber consumption: Apparent quantity and per capita, by States and regions, 1926* [1]

[Preliminary figures]

SOFTWOODS AND HARDWOODS

State	Derived within State	Derived externally—			Apparent consumption [2]	
		From other States	From foreign imports [2]	Total	Total quantity	Per capita
	M feet b. m.	*M feet b. m.*	*M feet b. m.*	*M feet b. m.*	*M feet b. m.*	*Feet b. m.*
Alabama	701, 189	146, 207	405	146, 612	847, 801	336
Arizona	44, 251	35, 008	402	35, 410	79, 661	179
Arkansas	336, 867	136, 364		136, 364	473, 231	249
California	1, 247, 749	2, 263, 733	62, 079	2, 325, 812	3, 573, 561	828
Colorado	47, 012	184, 630		184, 630	231, 642	219
Connecticut	39, 414	206, 023	130, 610	336, 633	376, 047	234
Delaware	9, 433	71, 892	500	72, 392	81, 825	341
District of Columbia		90, 176		90, 176	90, 176	171
Florida	448, 290	234, 555	45, 995	280, 550	728, 840	553
Georgia	317, 492	72, 330		72, 330	389, 822	124
Idaho	157, 707	67, 141	1, 509	68, 650	226, 357	434
Illinois	21, 864	2, 303, 330	145, 778	2, 449, 108	2, 470, 972	343
Indiana	90, 146	726, 024	43, 012	769, 036	859, 182	275
Iowa	2, 312	542, 258	22, 729	564, 987	567, 299	234
Kansas	823	375, 409		375, 409	376, 232	207
Kentucky	98, 970	352, 490	28	352, 518	451, 488	179
Louisiana	545, 225	146, 064	451	146, 515	691, 740	360
Maine	121, 668	46, 740	35, 806	82, 546	204, 214	258
Maryland	40, 479	304, 031	1, 473	305, 504	345, 983	219
Massachusetts	69, 324	640, 950	312, 841	953, 791	1, 023, 115	244
Michigan	463, 139	1, 150, 547	59, 255	1, 209, 802	1, 672, 941	381
Minnesota	172, 332	598, 370	43, 000	641, 370	813, 702	307
Mississippi	456, 540	34, 593		34, 593	491, 133	274
Missouri	88, 746	669, 926		669, 926	758, 672	217
Montana	184, 207	57, 801	8, 323	66, 124	250, 331	360
Nebraska		263, 712	14, 000	277, 712	277, 712	201
Nevada	1, 034	48, 551	503	49, 054	50, 088	647
New Hampshire	143, 058	49, 940	24, 350	74, 290	217, 348	479
New Jersey	6, 849	695, 222	82, 940	778, 162	785, 011	213
New Mexico	46, 268	31, 881		31, 881	78, 149	201
New York	125, 562	2, 706, 689	495, 482	3, 202, 171	3, 327, 733	294
North Carolina	422, 214	253, 484		253, 484	675, 698	236
North Dakota		129, 970	18, 068	148, 038	148, 038	231
Ohio	109, 350	1, 379, 795	46, 615	1, 426, 410	1, 535, 760	233
Oklahoma	71, 310	376, 005		376, 005	447, 315	191
Oregon	983, 818	80, 967	16, 040	97, 007	1, 080, 825	1, 232
Pennsylvania	217, 183	1, 754, 025	176, 831	1, 930, 856	2, 148, 039	223
Rhode Island	3, 544	126, 667	40, 295	166, 962	170, 506	246
South Carolina	134, 777	43, 333		43, 333	178, 110	98
South Dakota	24, 411	113, 312	17, 000	130, 312	154, 723	225
Tennessee	221, 214	430, 097		430, 097	651, 311	264
Texas	687, 260	770, 994	3, 336	774, 330	1, 461, 590	275
Utah	6, 479	121, 750	500	122, 250	128, 729	250
Vermont	68, 416	28, 183	14, 800	42, 983	111, 399	316
Virginia	192, 291	364, 324		364, 324	556, 615	221
Washington	1, 427, 153	113, 607	30, 906	144, 513	1, 571, 666	1, 022
West Virginia	125, 855	165, 100		165, 100	290, 955	174
Wisconsin	474, 965	528, 051	37, 000	565, 051	1, 040, 016	360
Wyoming	15, 241	85, 210		85, 210	100, 451	426
Total	11, 213, 431	22, 117, 461	1, 932, 862	24, 050, 323	35, 263, 754	301

[1] The term "apparent consumption" is used because these figures are compiled from figures showing the quantities of domestic lumber retained in and distributed into each State, plus the foreign lumber which apparently enters that State. The results by regions are considered approximately correct. The State figures are subject to greater discrepancies on account of transfers which can not readily be traced.

[2] Lumber imports are deemed to include boards, planks and deals, railway ties, and sawed cabinet woods. In distributing imports the sources and the ports of entry are used as the primary guides, but in some instances it has seemed proper to pass suitable quantities on through one State to another in order to harmonize per capita consumption between neighboring States in similar circumstances. The population figures used are the estimates of the Bureau of the Census, dated Mar. 14, 1928.

TABLE 588.—*Lumber consumption: Apparent quantity and per capita, by States and regions, 1926*—Continued

SUMMARY, BY REGIONS

Region	Derived within region	Derived externally—			Apparent consumption [2]	
		From other regions	From foreign imports [2]	Total	Total quantity	Per capita
	M feet b. m.	*M feet b. m.*	*M feet b. m.*	*M feet b. m.*	*M feet b. m.*	*Feet b. m.*
Northeastern	1,332,603	6,232,865	1,315,928	7,548,793	8,881,396	253
Lake	1,470,009	1,917,395	139,255	2,056,650	3,526,659	355
Central	1,201,436	5,581,471	235,433	5,816,904	7,018,340	259
North Carolina pine	952,645	457,778	----------	457,778	1,410,423	196
Southern pine	5,065,648	415,637	50,187	465,824	5,531,472	273
Pacific (north)	2,506,437	99,108	46,946	146,054	2,652,491	1,098
Pacific (south)	1,269,078	2,291,989	62,582	2,354,571	3,623,649	825
Rocky Mountain (north)	361,777	105,079	9,832	114,911	476,688	392
Rocky Mountain (south)	194,270	423,460	902	424,362	618,632	234
Prairie	44,718	1,407,489	71,797	1,479,286	1,524,004	219
Total	14,398,621	18,932,271	1,932,862	24,050,323	35,263,754	301
Special regions:						
New England	721,931	821,996	558,702	1,380,698	2,102,629	260
Industrial	3,140,624	11,672,055	1,647,588	13,319,643	16,460,267	278

Forest Service, in cooperation with the Bureau of the Census.

[2] See footnote 2, p. 1110.

TABLE 589.—*Lumber prices: Average values per thousand feet, f. o. b. mill, Douglas fir and southern yellow pine*

Year and month	Douglas fir Price	Price index 1913=100	Southern yellow pine Price	Price index 1913=100
	Dollars		*Dollars*	
1913	11.44	100.0	14.77	100.0
1914	10.58	92.5	13.68	92.6
1915	9.80	85.5	13.02	88.2
1916	11.63	101.7	16.12	109.2
1917	16.93	147.9	21.13	143.1
1918	21.21	186.3	26.45	179.1
1919	25.83	225.9	33.94	229.8
1920	36.78	323.3	44.74	302.9
1921	19.98	174.7	21.18	143.4
1922	23.90	208.9	26.44	179.0
1923	28.93	252.9	30.81	208.6
1924	23.14	202.3	28.16	190.7
1925	21.63	189.1	28.31	191.7
1926	21.13	184.7	1 26.83	181.7
1927	20.42	178.5	25.62	173.5
1928	20.01	174.9	25.32	171.4
1921				
January	20.20	176.6	21.35	144.6
February	18.85	164.7	21.18	143.4
March	17.59	153.2	20.92	141.7
April	16.87	147.3	20.36	137.9
May	16.42	143.2	20.82	140.9
June	15.90	143.5	22.32	151.1
July	15.28	133.4	20.75	140.5
August	14.98	130.8	20.40	138.1
September	14.86	129.8	20.61	139.5
October	15.97	139.6	21.59	146.2
November	17.07	149.2	23.14	156.7
December	17.75	155.1	21.77	147.4
1922				
January	18.73	163.7	22.68	153.6
February	22.75	198.9	22.61	153.1
March	22.40	195.8	22.27	151.5
April	20.44	178.7	22.78	154.2
May	21.10	184.4	24.85	168.2
June	23.24	203.1	29.07	196.8
July	24.18	211.3	27.19	184.2
August	24.83	217.0	28.47	192.8
September	27.13	237.2	31.24	211.5
October	27.97	244.5	31.71	214.7
November	25.82	225.7	30.61	207.2
December	26.49	231.6	30.61	207.2
1923				
January	28.54	249.5	30.42	205.9
February	29.42	257.2	32.81	222.1
March	30.22	264.2	33.71	228.2
April	31.46	275.0	33.38	226.0
May	31.02	271.2	33.85	229.2
June	30.36	265.4	32.40	219.4
July	27.68	242.9	31.14	210.8
August	26.97	235.7	30.82	208.6
September	27.18	237.5	27.53	186.4
October	27.24	238.1	28.77	194.7
November	28.97	253.2	27.83	188.4
December	26.94	235.5	26.56	179.8
1924				
January	28.30	247.4	29.40	199.1
February	26.33	230.2	30.16	204.1
March	24.69	215.8	29.83	202.0
April	24.39	213.2	29.14	197.3
1924				
May	22.40	195.8	27.55	186.2
June	22.99	201.0	27.36	185.5
July	21.93	191.7	25.91	175.4
August	22.42	196.0	27.77	188.0
September	21.58	188.6	29.46	199.5
October	21.10	184.5	26.71	180.8
November	21.48	187.7	25.81	174.7
December	21.82	190.7	30.13	204.0
1925				
January	22.52	196.9	29.43	199.3
February	22.19	194.0	29.66	200.8
March	21.99	192.2	29.02	196.5
April	21.60	188.8	28.29	191.5
May	21.70	189.7	27.07	183.3
June	21.24	185.7	26.58	180.0
July	21.18	185.1	27.55	186.5
August	22.25	194.5	28.56	193.4
September	21.39	187.0	30.50	206.5
October	21.28	186.0	28.17	190.7
November	21.33	186.5	27.14	183.8
December	21.05	184.0	29.01	196.4
1926				
January	22.29	194.8	27.66	187.3
February	21.41	187.2	28.29	191.5
March	21.70	189.7	27.14	183.8
April	21.62	189.0	26.33	178.3
May	21.19	185.2	26.04	176.3
June	21.34	186.5	26.93	182.3
July	21.25	185.8	26.80	181.4
August	21.04	183.9	26.58	180.0
September	20.73	181.2	25.78	174.5
October	20.68	180.8	--------	--------
November	20.44	178.7	24.88	168.4
December	19.93	174.2	27.15	183.8
1927				
January	19.72	172.4	27.08	183.3
February	19.73	172.5	26.85	181.8
March	19.82	173.3	26.08	176.6
April	20.50	179.2	26.11	176.8
May	20.47	178.9	25.92	175.5
June	20.36	178.0	26.04	176.3
July	20.29	177.4	26.33	178.3
August	20.30	177.4	24.12	163.3
September	19.89	173.9	23.77	160.9
October	20.09	175.6	24.00	162.5
November	19.53	170.7	22.78	154.2
December	19.24	168.2	22.15	150.0
1928				
January	18.66	163.1	23.39	158.4
February	19.13	167.2	24.88	168.4
March	19.15	167.4	24.35	164.9
April	19.11	167.0	25.90	175.4
May	19.14	167.3	24.72	167.4
June	19.79	173.0	25.09	169.9
July	20.27	177.2	26.07	176.5
August	20.65	180.5	25.41	172.0
September	20.67	180.7	25.47	172.4
October	20.49	179.1	26.99	182.7
November	20.42	178.5	26.01	176.1
December	20.76	181.5	25.84	174.9

Forest Service. Compiled from reports of actual sales.

¹ Based on prices for 11 months.

NOTE.—Tables 553, pulpwood consumption, and 554, woodland on farms, 1927 Yearbook, omitted.

Table 590.—*State appropriations for forestry, 1925, and Federal allotments to States, 1929*

State	Total State appropriations, 1925	Allotment of Federal funds under Clark-McNary law, 1929 — Forest-fire cooperation	Cooperation in distribution of forest-planting stock to farmers	State	Total State appropriations, 1925	Allotment of Federal funds under Clark-McNary law, 1929 — Forest-fire cooperation	Cooperation in distribution of forest-planting stock to farmers
	Dollars	Dollars	Dollars		Dollars	Dollars	Dollars
Alabama	55,843	43,070	2,000	North Carolina	23,730	41,438	2,000
California	98,720	53,595	687	North Dakota	3,100	----------	2,000
Colorado	5,000	----------	2,000	Ohio	188,950	3,903	2,000
Connecticut	180,581	7,620	2,000	Oklahoma	5,000	15,630	2,000
Delaware	----------	765	2,000	Oregon	42,500	65,012	2,000
Florida	----------	25,000	555	Pennsylvania	630,482	43,298	2,000
Georgia	10,000	38,380	2,000	Rhode Island	6,300	1,374	----------
Idaho	126,900	50,671	1,240	South Carolina	----------	11,810	----------
Illinois	59,000	850	----------	South Dakota	6,420	375	----------
Indiana	13,025	1,700	2,000	Tennessee	23,100	21,260	1,000
Iowa	----------	----------	2,000	Texas	48,980	30,722	----------
Kansas	----------	----------	2,000	Vermont	37,117	7,448	2,000
Kentucky	15,000	14,609	2,000	Virginia	20,000	30,991	2,000
Louisiana	60,000	39,937	2,000	Washington	91,000	69,155	2,000
Maine	202,000	49,450	1,500	West Virginia	45,000	20,762	1,000
Maryland	32,175	7,210	2,000	Wisconsin	64,000	32,636	1,533
Massachusetts	352,000	22,210	2,000	Wyoming	----------	----------	1,656
Michigan	401,000	74,594	2,000				
Minnnesota	176,200	71,623	----------	Total	5,571,020	1,045,800	64,671
Mississippi	----------	33,415	----------				
Missouri	2,000	8,000	1,500	Hawaii	----------	----------	2,000
Montana	37,320	19,928	2,000	Porto Rico	36,166	----------	2,000
Nebraska	2,500	----------	2,000	Administration and contingent	----------	154,200	6,329
New Hampshire	94,164	14,746	2,000				
New Jersey	234,765	16,564	2,000	Total	5,607,180	1,200,000	75,000
New Mexico	2,762	1,916	----------				
New York	2,174,386	54,142	2,000				

Forest Service.

TABLE 591.—*Temperature: Normal [1] and 1928, by months, at selected points in the United States*

Station	January Normal	January 1928	February Normal	February 1928	March Normal	March 1928	April Normal	April 1928	May Normal	May 1928	June Normal	June 1928	July Normal	July 1928	August Normal	August 1928	September Normal	September 1928	October Normal	October 1928	November Normal	November 1928	December Normal	December 1928	Annual Normal	Annual 1928
	°F.	°F.	°F.	°F.	°F.	°F.	°F.	°F.	°F.	°F.	°F.	°F.	°F.	°F.	°F.	°F.	°F.	°F.	°F.	°F.	°F.	°F.	°F.	°F.	°F.	°F.
Greenville, Me.	12.8	14.0	12.4	13.6	23.5	23.5	36.4	35.1	49.5	49.5	58.5	57.6	65.4	65.4	62.5	64.4	55.0	51.3	45.6	43.6	30.7	30.7	18.0	24.0	39.2	39.4
Boston, Mass.	27.9	23.0	28.3	29.6	35.4	35.5	46.4	46.8	57.1	55.4	66.5	65.0	71.7	73.2	69.9	73.6	63.2	62.4	53.6	56.6	42.0	44.8	32.5	32.5	49.6	51.3
Buffalo, N.Y.	24.6	26.2	24.3	28.8	31.1	30.3	42.5	39.4	52.0	52.0	64.4	64.5	69.8	69.0	68.6	68.0	62.4	62.4	53.2	53.9	39.4	41.1	29.8	33.5	47.0	46.9
Canton, N.Y.	16.3	18.2	18.0	16.9	27.7	26.0	42.5	39.4	56.2	53.2	65.1	61.4	68.9	69.0	66.0	69.6	59.3	54.8	47.2	48.6	33.9	36.0	22.7	28.6	44.0	43.5
Trenton, N.J.	30.5	30.8	30.7	30.7	39.1	39.1	49.8	49.6	61.1	53.8	70.7	67.8	74.6	73.4	72.9	75.5	66.4	61.2	55.1	56.6	44.4	44.6	34.4	35.8	52.5	53.1
Pittsburgh, Pa.	30.8	30.8	32.3	32.4	39.6	38.6	51.2	46.6	62.4	59.4	70.7	67.0	74.5	73.4	72.9	74.4	66.4	61.2	55.7	57.0	43.2	43.8	34.2	35.2	52.8	51.6
Scranton, Pa.	26.6	29.9	27.3	27.3	35.7	34.8	48.1	45.2	59.4	57.9	68.0	65.0	72.8	71.2	69.8	71.8	63.9	60.0	53.1	53.8	40.5	43.0	30.7	35.2	49.4	50.0
Cincinnati, Ohio	29.9	31.2	32.8	33.2	40.9	40.6	52.4	49.6	63.1	61.8	71.2	67.0	75.1	75.4	73.0	75.6	67.1	63.8	55.7	59.4	42.5	44.0	33.4	36.8	53.2	53.3
Cleveland, Ohio	26.9	30.3	27.4	29.2	34.6	38.6	46.2	49.4	57.9	61.8	67.9	67.0	71.4	71.0	70.0	72.8	63.9	61.6	53.6	59.8	41.0	44.0	31.7	36.8	49.9	49.9
Evansville, Ind.	34.1	34.1	36.1	37.2	45.0	45.0	56.1	52.5	66.7	65.5	75.4	69.8	78.9	79.5	77.7	79.0	70.7	67.0	59.4	62.8	46.6	46.8	37.1	39.8	57.0	56.6
Indianapolis, Ind.	27.4	28.9	31.1	30.2	40.0	39.2	52.1	47.8	62.9	61.4	71.9	65.4	75.7	75.3	73.6	74.2	66.9	63.0	55.5	58.8	42.3	42.2	32.2	32.2	52.7	52.7
Chicago, Ill.	23.7	23.7	26.3	30.3	35.3	35.3	47.3	44.7	58.2	58.3	67.3	61.4	72.5	72.6	71.6	71.3	66.2	62.3	54.0	57.0	40.1	42.2	28.1	32.0	49.2	49.6
Peoria, Ill.	24.5	25.5	25.9	27.0	37.0	40.4	50.9	47.6	61.7	63.3	70.9	66.0	75.2	75.6	73.7	74.8	66.7	61.2	55.5	57.0	37.5	41.7	28.1	32.0	49.9	51.5
Grand Rapids, Mich.	24.5	26.0	23.7	27.0	31.5	28.5	47.0	47.8	58.0	58.0	67.8	61.1	72.3	72.3	69.7	71.1	62.7	54.2	51.2	51.8	38.4	40.8	28.5	31.7	48.3	48.3
Marquette, Mich.	16.3	16.3	16.3	18.3	24.8	26.5	37.8	34.8	49.0	49.0	59.2	55.2	64.2	63.4	64.0	64.2	57.5	53.2	46.7	47.7	33.3	35.3	22.6	27.0	41.0	41.3
Madison, Wis.	19.9	19.9	19.1	25.0	30.6	30.6	45.4	45.8	57.6	60.0	67.2	62.5	71.9	71.9	69.8	70.2	62.9	59.0	50.3	50.3	35.2	35.0	22.8	27.0	46.0	46.8
Duluth, Minn.	7.9	10.8	11.4	14.4	23.7	25.0	37.0	33.0	49.0	48.2	57.2	55.6	63.9	63.0	62.6	63.6	55.1	51.6	44.1	44.0	30.0	33.4	15.9	20.2	38.0	38.9
St. Paul, Minn.	12.6	12.6	15.5	16.8	29.1	29.1	45.0	45.5	57.9	57.9	67.1	61.8	72.1	71.4	69.4	69.4	61.3	57.0	48.5	49.8	32.5	35.3	19.0	25.0	44.2	45.0
Des Moines, Iowa	19.1	28.0	22.2	23.7	35.0	40.8	50.1	50.1	61.3	64.2	70.6	66.5	75.4	75.4	73.1	73.8	65.6	62.0	53.4	55.5	38.4	40.4	26.0	29.8	49.8	51.0
Dubuque, Iowa	20.1	19.1	22.3	23.7	34.0	37.4	48.6	48.4	60.3	60.4	69.4	64.5	73.9	73.6	71.6	73.8	65.0	59.8	53.9	53.8	38.4	39.2	24.9	31.0	48.1	49.0
St. Louis, Mo.	31.1	31.1	34.8	38.7	44.1	46.6	56.1	52.4	66.1	66.6	75.0	68.8	78.9	79.9	77.5	77.9	70.5	67.4	58.8	58.8	45.4	45.6	34.3	38.0	56.5	56.2
Springfield, Mo.	37.0	37.0	35.2	38.2	45.2	45.2	56.0	51.8	64.5	66.1	72.5	66.8	78.8	76.6	77.4	75.9	68.1	66.3	58.2	62.7	45.7	45.4	36.2	38.0	55.7	55.0
Bismarck, N. Dak.	7.8	7.8	10.3	15.2	24.2	22.0	42.1	42.1	54.4	55.0	62.8	59.4	69.8	69.0	67.3	66.7	55.8	52.8	44.9	44.9	28.5	32.6	14.7	22.5	40.5	43.2
Devils Lake, N. Dak.	.3	.3	4.5	16.8	18.5	22.7	38.2	33.8	52.7	54.0	62.6	63.8	68.1	66.0	66.5	63.8	55.5	52.8	41.4	41.4	22.6	30.0	8.0	19.0	36.4	39.3
Pierre, S. Dak.	16.0	16.0	18.6	26.6	31.5	28.0	48.6	46.6	58.7	63.0	68.1	68.6	75.0	75.0	72.8	74.0	60.6	60.0	49.8	50.4	32.6	32.6	21.8	19.0	46.4	48.6
North Platte, Nebr.	22.9	22.9	26.6	31.7	36.6	40.3	48.4	47.4	58.7	62.5	67.5	62.2	73.0	73.9	72.0	72.9	62.1	62.4	49.7	52.2	36.6	37.0	26.7	28.3	48.3	50.1
Omaha, Nebr.	21.9	21.9	25.5	29.6	37.0	37.0	51.2	47.4	62.4	65.1	71.6	66.5	77.6	77.1	74.4	76.5	66.1	63.8	53.4	56.2	38.5	40.6	26.4	28.3	50.6	52.4
Concordia, Kans.	26.4	26.4	29.8	32.9	41.0	46.4	53.5	50.8	63.5	65.0	73.0	67.0	78.4	78.1	76.5	76.3	68.3	67.1	56.1	57.5	41.4	42.2	30.7	30.7	53.1	54.4
Dodge City, Kans.	29.8	29.8	33.2	36.6	42.8	45.3	53.6	50.2	62.9	62.9	72.5	66.5	78.2	78.0	76.5	75.8	69.4	68.5	56.1	57.5	42.6	42.6	32.6	35.7	54.3	54.7
Iola, Kans.	34.2	34.2	38.0	40.3	44.5	48.4	55.3	52.6	67.2	63.9	71.0	69.5	79.0	79.0	77.0	77.4	69.0	68.0	58.5	57.8	44.1	44.1	33.9	36.0	55.6	55.6
Washington, D.C.	35.9	35.9	35.3	37.6	42.6	42.4	53.3	51.9	63.7	64.1	72.1	71.0	78.1	78.1	75.6	77.4	69.0	64.9	57.4	59.9	45.2	49.4	36.6	39.0	55.0	57.3
Lynchburg, Va.	37.5	37.5	39.2	40.3	47.3	47.4	57.3	53.3	64.1	64.8	71.8	71.1	78.7	79.0	76.3	76.3	67.3	64.5	58.5	58.5	47.2	49.8	39.5	40.6	57.6	57.6
Norfolk, Va.	40.6	40.6	42.7	43.6	48.2	48.1	56.8	56.1	66.2	66.3	74.4	73.8	78.7	78.0	79.4	79.4	71.6	69.8	62.5	64.6	51.4	52.3	43.1	44.6	59.9	59.9
Parkersburg, W. Va.	32.5	32.5	34.2	34.3	42.8	41.6	53.2	54.0	63.8	61.2	71.5	68.2	74.6	76.0	73.9	76.3	67.3	63.8	56.1	57.3	43.0	45.2	34.2	44.3	54.2	54.0
Charlotte, N.C.	41.2	41.2	42.5	43.9	50.4	50.9	59.8	57.4	68.3	67.6	75.4	75.4	78.1	80.0	78.1	79.8	71.5	68.8	61.0	64.6	50.6	51.4	43.0	44.3	60.2	60.5
Charleston, S.C.	49.9	49.8	48.8	52.4	57.4	57.1	64.0	64.5	72.7	71.0	79.9	78.9	81.4	81.0	82.0	82.0	77.8	70.4	67.6	70.6	58.1	57.6	51.7	52.3	66.0	66.0
Atlanta, Ga.	42.6	42.6	45.3	43.7	52.0	51.8	61.0	57.9	69.0	67.4	76.0	74.1	78.1	80.6	79.8	78.7	71.5	71.4	61.7	65.3	52.1	51.4	44.7	45.2	61.2	60.7
Thomasville, Ga.	51.0	51.0	52.4	54.3	60.2	60.2	66.0	64.5	74.0	71.6	78.0	78.0	81.0	81.1	81.0	80.6	76.3	76.3	68.0	65.3	58.5	58.5	52.3	52.5	67.1	66.7
Jacksonville, Fla.	55.4	52.5	58.0	57.0	62.6	63.8	68.7	66.6	75.0	71.6	79.9	79.0	82.1	81.5	81.7	81.0	78.3	77.5	71.1	72.7	62.2	61.0	56.3	55.6	69.3	68.3

Station	Jan.	Feb.	Mar.	Apr.	May	June	July	Aug.	Sept.	Oct.	Nov.	Dec.	Annual
Miami, Fla.	67.1	67.3	69.4	72.8	76.4	78.2	80.1	80.4	80.1	77.0	71.8	68.0	74.4
Memphis, Tenn.	44.3	44.8	51.7	61.3	69.4	77.4	80.7	79.8	73.2	63.3	52.3	44.5	61.3
Nashville, Tenn.	41.6	43.6	49.6	59.3	68.2	76.7	79.9	79.0	72.6	61.1	48.5	43.0	53.8
Birmingham, Ala.	48.0	49.6	55.4	63.6	71.1	78.1	79.9	79.3	74.9	64.8	53.3	49.2	62.5
Mobile, Ala.	54.7	57.3	62.0	68.2	74.4	81.0	82.8	82.3	78.4	69.3	58.6	55.2	67.0
New Orleans, La.	57.3	50.8	62.8	69.2	75.4	77.2	82.0	81.4	77.2	69.3	58.6	49.1	69.2
Shreveport, La.	50.9	54.5	61.5	67.6	74.5	81.4	84.8	82.0	78.2	67.3	54.2	49.3	67.0
Amarillo, Tex.	38.1	41.4	46.9	57.2	64.1	73.0	76.9	75.7	70.4	54.7	44.2	40.6	69.3
Brownsville, Tex.	58.5	62.0	68.2	71.6	76.5	78.8	82.6	84.4	82.6	74.9	67.8	60.0	65.9
El Paso, Tex.	44.6	48.5	55.5	62.4	71.5	82.6	84.0	81.3	79.8	67.8	54.4	44.9	57.6
Fort Worth, Tex.	46.4	51.4	58.2	62.2	71.8	82.6	83.3	84.1	78.9	67.9	54.8	47.5	73.0
Galveston, Tex.	49.2	52.0	55.7	63.8	72.2	83.6	83.8	80.3	79.9	74.9	63.5	56.4	64.2
San Antonio, Tex.	52.0	56.3	62.8	68.1	76.1	80.6	84.3	83.0	80.3	63.5	54.8	53.7	66.1
Oklahoma City, Okla.	55.4	55.4	63.3	63.0	81.0	80.9	88.6	83.4	81.8	66.7	54.4	56.6	69.0
Little Rock, Ark.	39.6	44.9	50.0	65.6	74.8	78.0	86.6	88.8	80.6	72.1	59.4	53.7	69.4
Havre, Mont.	44.9	48.3	53.0	69.1	47.8	81.0	77.4	80.9	74.1	70.5	44.2	39.3	60.8
Kalispell, Mont.	43.8	44.2	53.9	59.8	39.3	72.8	74.1	81.4	69.8	63.6	36.8	44.2	61.9
Havre	23.3	20.8	27.1	62.1	52.1	52.1	69.5	63.6	57.0	43.5	23.9	23.0	44.5
Kalispell	13.6	23.3	31.2	43.7	33.1	53.8	65.6	62.8	56.4	43.1	26.8	20.4	43.3
Cheyenne, Wyo.	27.8	27.2	33.3	41.0	34.4	57.5	65.8	64.0	56.5	44.5	28.5	28.6	44.4
Sheridan, Wyo.	22.4	22.2	34.8	40.9	32.2	57.2	67.3	65.6	56.7	43.0	22.1	21.6	43.6
Pueblo, Colo.	32.9	33.6	36.9	50.4	37.4	74.2	74.2	67.4	65.8	52.0	31.5	30.7	49.3
Santa Fe, N. Mex.	55.1	53.2	41.4	67.0	60.2	65.4	72.4	69.8	69.6	50.4	30.7	30.0	71.2
Phoenix, Ariz.	31.0	33.8	36.0	67.0	59.7	88.5	65.4	88.8	89.8	52.0	52.0	52.0	48.5
Modena, Utah	33.8	34.5	45.7	45.5	60.2	40.5	74.5	74.2	70.6	43.1	28.1	31.9	52.5
Salt Lake City, Utah	30.2	34.5	46.0	41.7	37.3	74.1	75.7	72.0	65.6	52.5	31.1	30.0	49.1
Winnemucca, Nev.	29.2	36.0	41.4	45.2	30.0	68.5	71.6	72.5	61.1	48.3	27.8	32.1	51.6
Boise, Idaho	29.8	34.8	42.7	45.4	41.8	63.0	73.0	61.9	63.1	51.0	28.3	28.1	52.2
Seattle, Wash.	39.5	42.3	46.1	49.4	45.3	72.7	67.5	55.9	64.0	54.1	34.0	41.7	54.0
Walla Walla, Wash.	32.7	29.7	37.1	48.5	44.0	74.0	65.5	62.8	66.1	54.2	40.0	40.6	54.1
Portland, Oreg.	39.4	38.6	43.4	50.8	40.0	63.8	63.9	66.7	62.5	53.4	40.8	41.5	54.3
Roseburg, Oreg.	43.1	43.1	47.1	51.1	47.1	60.1	65.4	66.4	60.0	53.5	40.8	47.6	52.4
Eureka, Calif.	50.0	48.2	52.4	54.2	48.3	55.5	54.2	54.2	52.0	52.8	44.1	48.2	64.0
Fresno, Calif.	61.4	52.4	49.4	60.0	57.5	62.2	70.2	72.9	64.7	54.2	58.8	46.2	64.2
Los Angeles, Calif.	46.6	48.5	52.0	57.5	60.0	62.9	63.9	73.0	69.2	63.7	58.8	46.0	64.7
Sacramento, Calif.	46.0	51.1	51.4	60.9	59.4	63.6	73.0	72.0	69.4	63.0	43.2	46.1	59.8
San Diego, Calif.	57.8	55.1	54.8	56.7	58.5	60.2	68.7	68.7	64.9	59.6	59.0	56.1	61.6
San Francisco, Calif.	50.4	52.2	55.1	54.2	55.0	59.6	61.4	59.1	58.5	57.8	49.6	57.1	57.1

Weather Bureau.

1 Normals are based on records of 30 or more years of observations.

TABLE 592.—*Precipitation: Normal [1] and 1928, by months, at selected points in the United States*

Station	Jan. Normal	Jan. 1928	Feb. Normal	Feb. 1928	Mar. Normal	Mar. 1928	Apr. Normal	Apr. 1928	May Normal	May 1928	June Normal	June 1928	July Normal	July 1928	Aug. Normal	Aug. 1928	Sept. Normal	Sept. 1928	Oct. Normal	Oct. 1928	Nov. Normal	Nov. 1928	Dec. Normal	Dec. 1928	Annual Normal	Annual 1928
	Ins.	*Ins.*	*Ins.*	*Ins.*	*Ins.*	*Ins.*	*Ins.*	*Ins.*	*Ins.*	*Ins.*	*Ins.*	*Ins.*	*Ins.*	*Ins.*	*Ins.*	*Ins.*	*Ins.*	*Ins.*	*Ins.*	*Ins.*	*Ins.*	*Ins.*	*Ins.*	*Ins.*	*Ins.*	*Ins.*
Greenville, Me.	2.83	4.01	2.97	1.69	3.16	2.55	2.93	3.87	3.31	4.63	3.81	3.58	4.93	3.86	3.55	4.52	3.83	4.02	3.28	3.84	2.99	2.71	3.27	3.29	40.88	42.55
Boston, Mass.	3.61	1.66	3.50	2.66	3.57	1.56	3.34	4.68	3.18	3.08	2.89	5.56	3.49	4.14	3.62	2.45	3.14	4.47	3.15	2.88	3.33	1.85	3.45	2.61	40.27	37.60
Buffalo, N. Y.	3.30	3.14	3.14	2.00	2.57	1.76	2.10	2.10	3.10	3.18	2.82	2.82	3.03	3.03	3.08	1.84	3.07	3.07	3.29	2.39	2.67	2.67	3.36	1.87	36.08	34.38
Canton, N. Y.	2.50	2.67	2.37	2.45	2.50	3.00	2.18	2.80	3.00	1.51	3.29	4.21	3.50	3.30	3.65	3.23	2.35	1.02	3.03	2.39	3.16	2.67	3.29	1.22	35.22	33.47
Trenton, N. J.	3.11	1.74	2.70	4.09	3.03	2.19	2.92	2.67	3.08	2.45	3.09	4.21	3.94	3.30	4.75	3.23	3.40	1.02	2.52	2.52	3.16	2.29	2.73	1.91	35.24	34.47
Pittsburgh, Pa.	3.05	1.30	2.70	2.16	3.03	4.25	2.92	4.05	3.21	1.09	3.81	7.73	4.05	4.93	3.23	3.23	2.58	1.02	2.53	1.22	2.29	1.91	2.69	1.1	35.24	34.85
Scranton, Pa.	3.03	1.40	3.07	3.20	3.03	2.05	3.12	5.03	3.27	1.63	3.67	6.76	4.03	4.03	3.69	3.10	2.65	1.82	2.52	.66	2.77	1.91	2.80	1.18	39.40	16.39
Cincinnati, Ohio	3.48	1.65	3.23	2.16	3.89	1.31	3.12	3.66	3.70	.76	3.66	6.76	3.31	8.57	3.41	6.04	2.65	1.27	2.51	2.3.18	2.64	2.29	2.98	.49	38.63	37.49
Cleveland, Ohio	3.48	2.03	3.07	2.36	3.89	2.08	3.12	2.15	3.12	2.04	3.12	4.69	3.45	2.07	3.21	2.85	3.33	1.27	2.78	2.51	2.64	2.77	3.02	1.41	35.63	39.49
Evansville, Ind.	3.74	1.42	2.58	2.59	3.89	1.04	3.90	5.23	3.86	2.04	3.04	4.04	3.42	1.91	2.77	1.15	3.31	1.25	2.78	2.59	2.64	2.64	2.44	1.41	38.89	32.56
Indianapolis, Ind.	2.95	1.74	2.83	2.83	3.93	1.50	3.62	2.76	3.89	3.04	3.30	8.77	3.34	1.82	3.36	1.41	3.31	.87	2.78	2.93	3.35	2.64	2.98	1.41	40.00	33.82
Chicago, Ill.	1.90	.73	2.07	1.57	2.73	2.44	3.38	2.84	3.54	1.48	3.77	8.77	3.33	3.07	3.31	5.03	3.40	1.87	2.53	2.74	3.35	4.00	2.04	2.19	40.00	91.33
Peoria, Ill.	1.78	.36	2.07	1.73	2.73	.96	3.38	2.34	4.06	3.21	3.77	6.60	3.58	4.35	3.12	3.46	4.03	3.18	2.29	2.53	2.37	3.97	1.77	2.53	34.95	37.01
Grand Rapids, Mich.	2.95	1.32	1.97	1.54	2.26	2.04	2.43	2.66	3.44	3.09	3.48	8.03	2.92	2.07	2.61	3.62	4.03	3.14	2.81	3.27	2.91	4.47	2.81	2.67	34.04	37.62
Marquette, Mich.	2.38	1.83	1.97	1.92	2.26	1.67	2.43	4.08	2.96	1.94	3.22	8.48	3.12	1.32	2.67	4.49	3.25	4.31	2.76	5.10	2.91	1.93	2.63	2.66	32.54	40.10
Madison, Wis.	1.48	.40	1.56	1.76	2.26	2.91	2.57	2.57	2.85	2.97	3.76	8.13	2.76	2.63	3.21	4.03	3.72	1.78	2.43	2.76	1.45	1.86	1.13	1.15	32.44	35.89
Duluth, Minn.	.97	.70	.95	1.09	1.54	.83	2.06	2.90	3.25	2.95	3.91	5.22	2.57	7.08	3.18	6.10	3.67	3.86	2.63	3.34	1.30	.30	1.05	1.64	32.08	29.99
St. Paul, Minn.	.92	.31	.93	1.63	1.43	.80	2.91	2.45	3.25	2.16	3.76	5.72	3.50	3.63	3.01	7.75	4.16	3.67	2.43	2.16	1.45	.21	1.16	1.15	32.08	40.15
Des Moines, Iowa	1.07	.11	1.43	3.10	2.03	1.71	2.85	1.95	4.22	2.16	5.68	3.88	3.94	3.68	3.24	9.38	4.41	1.87	2.20	2.46	1.30	4.62	1.08	1.44	32.06	34.47
Dubuque, Iowa	1.30	.20	1.43	1.69	2.03	2.14	2.85	1.71	4.34	1.55	5.68	8.87	3.22	3.94	3.24	4.03	3.46	1.70	2.48	2.24	1.70	4.88	1.44	1.10	32.08	32.80
St. Louis, Mo.	2.34	1.91	2.43	2.43	3.39	2.27	3.86	3.02	4.38	2.18	4.76	8.82	2.98	6.16	2.99	6.10	3.42	1.70	2.05	2.21	2.50	1.90	2.21	1.03	41.27	27.24
Springfield, Mo.	2.34	.72	2.43	1.09	3.39	2.36	3.86	6.62	5.19	3.97	4.14	12.27	4.21	3.01	3.27	7.81	4.11	1.70	3.05	1.69	2.79	2.08	2.31	2.31	41.98	42.80
Bismarck, N. Dak.	.45	.28	.51	.11	.78	.89	1.52	1.08	2.32	2.44	3.56	5.17	2.24	3.27	1.82	3.34	1.63	1.15	1.25	.19	2.72	.57	.57	2.70	16.36	16.02
Devils Lake, N. Dak.	.47	.10	.47	.08	.78	.67	1.63	1.33	2.03	1.30	3.08	6.68	2.57	3.22	2.48	2.41	1.63	1.15	1.25	.19	.72	.07	.57	.31	16.30	18.06
Pierre, S. Dak.	.46	.14	.47	.08	.86	.97	1.82	.99	2.13	1.43	3.08	4.64	2.35	2.07	2.01	1.11	1.43	.27	1.07	.07	.43	.62	.54	.30	18.41	16.45
North Platte, Nebr.	.39	.13	.55	.17	.86	1.40	2.06	.04	2.78	3.62	3.22	2.15	2.74	5.04	2.39	2.99	1.35	.96	1.07	.29	.47	.50	.63	.19	18.41	14.09
Omaha, Nebr.	.70	.01	.92	.93	1.37	.97	2.36	1.51	3.77	1.97	4.41	4.56	3.54	5.20	3.05	3.12	3.21	2.73	2.17	2.61	1.07	2.87	.93	.68	27.80	19.79
Concordia, Kans.	.61	.11	.92	.92	1.23	.47	2.36	1.25	3.77	4.18	4.41	10.58	3.78	7.03	2.91	5.47	2.60	1.97	1.97	3.01	1.07	.99	.93	.30	29.09	30.09
Dodge City, Kans.	.41	.63	.81	.60	1.23	1.84	1.94	2.64	2.59	8.85	3.30	5.30	3.14	2.34	2.67	2.78	1.90	1.13	1.30	3.19	.73	2.35	.57	.82	20.55	28.85
Iola, Kans.	1.32	.20	1.78	2.22	2.62	2.17	4.49	4.49	4.70	4.00	5.47	2.66	3.31	2.17	3.49	2.52	4.93	1.06	2.99	4.87	2.37	9.01	1.39	2.23	37.72	27.77
Washington, D. C.	3.55	2.63	3.37	2.69	3.75	1.93	3.27	4.55	3.63	4.00	3.79	2.98	4.71	3.31	4.01	4.14	3.24	6.01	2.84	.67	2.37	2.01	3.32	1.21	42.40	46.36
Lynchburg, Va.	3.43	2.53	3.26	2.40	3.77	2.63	3.25	3.05	2.98	1.63	3.79	4.21	4.21	2.17	4.78	4.75	3.15	9.79	3.15	2.33	2.37	.79	3.25	1.02	42.64	43.40
Norfolk, Va.	3.10	1.51	3.33	2.85	3.77	2.73	3.23	4.24	3.38	2.14	7.84	7.84	5.75	4.41	5.22	4.70	3.23	1.67	2.16	1.24	2.16	3.79	3.44	3.35	44.51	44.94
Parkersburg, W. Va.	3.58	1.46	2.73	2.73	3.54	1.89	3.31	4.24	3.63	1.84	4.00	8.63	4.29	4.29	3.51	4.75	2.76	11.13	2.48	2.18	2.57	2.88	3.34	3.34	39.39	50.44
Charlotte, N. C.	4.00	1.77	4.30	3.57	4.17	3.53	3.31	5.87	3.31	4.05	4.22	4.49	5.10	1.76	5.07	13.14	2.99	11.13	2.95	1.13	2.14	2.52	3.86	1.07	46.17	37.03
Charleston, S. C.	4.95	.43	4.94	7.44	3.32	3.08	2.63	2.64	4.59	1.05	4.59	2.75	6.89	5.16	6.53	2.01	2.99	4.53	3.27	1.18	2.14	1.03	2.72	1.09	51.84	42.76
Atlanta, Ga.	4.10	2.83	4.61	2.50	5.30	5.69	3.61	3.60	3.47	2.08	3.74	2.75	4.82	6.89	4.82	4.01	2.99	8.16	3.27	2.19	2.14	1.21	2.70	1.70	45.32	42.76
Thomasville, Ga.	4.10	.94	4.61	5.41	5.03	9.77	3.63	7.92	3.47	6.97	3.74	5.45	6.71	6.70	5.75	3.75	4.88	8.02	2.96	1.66	2.68	1.10	4.31	1.84	52.50	44.15
Jacksonville, Fla.	2.80	.68	3.09	3.54	2.91	4.38	2.38	8.19	4.02	2.33	5.53	4.10	6.71	8.96	5.81	5.85	7.35	9.25	4.46	2.33	1.98	.67	3.02	1.34	49.86	51.62

Station																									
Miami, Fla.	2.52	.42	1.87	2.02	2.17	.45	3.09	.42	6.22	10.67	6.86	6.14	5.42	3.65	6.17	9.75	8.34	17.00	8.44	3.63	2.91	.42	1.69	.74	55.70	55.31
Memphis, Tenn.	4.81	1.65	4.51	2.42	5.26	3.14	4.78	6.70	4.19	2.51	3.55	3.96	3.18	1.36	3.36	3.91	2.80	2.06	2.68	5.15	4.24	4.06	4.51	4.13	47.87	39.05
Nashville, Tenn.	4.76	2.55	4.27	2.64	5.70	3.26	4.13	3.22	3.87	2.89	4.00	8.84	3.88	3.62	2.49	6.82	3.42	2.49	3.71	6.82	3.30	2.63	4.30	1.38	47.34	45.95
Birmingham, Ala.	5.52	1.91	5.23	1.77	5.70	7.71	4.81	3.95	3.84	3.84	4.46	8.84	5.17	2.16	3.62	5.10	3.38	2.20	4.26	5.46	3.64	2.20	5.02	.91	53.35	51.14
Mobile, Ala.	4.85	.91	5.52	8.52	5.98	5.47	4.63	6.86	3.95	3.57	5.43	5.13	6.89	3.33	5.81	5.74	5.00	4.65	6.92	6.61	3.14	1.61	4.79	5.82	61.80	57.07
New Orleans, La.	4.34	2.29	4.38	2.93	4.72	4.08	5.24	7.47	4.60	6.48	5.88	4.42	6.37	5.81	12.68	6.80	5.03	4.30	6.88	5.30	3.65	5.10	4.79	6.06	57.39	72.76
Shreveport, La.	3.93	1.19	3.40	1.73	4.11	4.08	4.63	5.11	4.22	2.57	3.50	2.84	3.56	3.46	12.66	4.08	2.80	3.31	2.70	2.70	3.14	2.87	4.29	4.86	43.48	36.97
Amarillo, Tex.	.51	T.	1.24	1.73	1.71	.74	1.43	1.70	2.79	6.48	2.87	2.68	1.96	5.89	2.84	1.70	2.30	1.31	2.55	.92	.92	3.54	.92	.51	21.01	32.34
Brownsville, Tex.	1.50	1.33	1.73	.71	1.26	.05	1.43	1.70	2.27	6.48	2.87	2.68	1.96	.71	2.87	1.15	2.30	8.91	3.08	2.93	1.98	4.88	1.56	1.64	27.43	33.66
El Paso, Tex.	.46	T.	.42	.73	.36	.05	.28	.22	.33	.48	.58	.58	.96	.39	.87	.80	8.91	1.31	3.08	1.47	1.99	.79	.52	.13	9.17	8.21
Fort Worth, Tex.	2.05	.46	1.83	3.53	2.32	1.10	4.02	5.70	4.65	3.77	3.35	T.	2.61	4.24	3.81	4.15	2.49	.04	1.70	2.58	2.58	1.97	1.87	5.50	33.20	44.58
Galveston, Tex.	3.41	.41	3.53	5.85	2.78	.54	3.02	5.43	4.33	1.54	11.58	4.36	3.14	4.23	3.82	4.20	4.36	7.20	2.52	3.33	3.33	2.52	1.61	2.04	44.87	39.19
San Antonio, Tex.	1.46	.65	2.93	6.45	1.84	2.34	3.19	3.20	4.20	3.90	4.37	3.20	2.86	3.29	2.46	1.69	2.23	6.30	1.20	1.90	1.90	2.29	1.50	2.95	27.28	30.20
Oklahoma City, Okla.	1.19	.51	1.14	1.33	1.98	1.75	3.19	3.68	4.78	1.92	3.67	4.88	2.86	3.29	3.67	2.74	2.86	.61	1.87	1.87	1.87	2.88	1.50	2.01	31.18	27.48
Little Rock, Ark.	4.73	1.18	4.00	4.62	1.70	1.70	5.19	7.01	4.78	3.86	6.72	4.21	3.50	2.79	2.76	4.19	2.71	.52	3.17	4.70	4.19	2.59	4.14	5.68	48.54	42.38
Havre, Mont.	.73	.14	.52	.23	.51	.34	.99	.64	1.80	.45	2.86	4.32	1.87	1.49	2.86	.16	.67	.42	1.29	.16	.61	.02	.61	.85	13.42	10.89
Kalispell, Mont.	1.57	.15	1.14	.14	.95	.74	1.50	1.80	1.46	.45	2.51	1.10	1.10	.87	1.06	1.27	1.29	.04	1.06	1.27	1.35	.50	.55	1.00	15.05	11.94
Cheyenne, Wyo.	.42	.33	.67	1.28	1.02	.74	.80	.83	2.43	2.67	1.61	2.51	2.10	.95	1.61	2.32	1.20	.08	.96	.52	.52	1.19	.64	.17	15.02	14.67
Sheridan, Wyo.	.85	1.36	1.28	.66	1.16	1.52	1.99	1.70	2.65	1.62	2.04	2.85	2.22	1.49	2.04	2.02	1.27	.29	1.07	1.15	1.15	1.12	.50	.36	15.69	17.04
Pueblo, Colo.	.31	.01	.51	.51	.59	1.41	1.31	.29	1.60	1.62	1.94	1.47	1.94	1.06	1.36	2.15	.75	.12	.75	.36	.36	1.19	.50	.58	11.69	10.47
Santa Fe, N. Mex.	.67	.01	.66	.80	.80	1.31	1.31	.63	1.26	2.80	1.36	2.38	1.07	.65	1.38	.58	.18	.13	.45	.70	.70	1.00	.74	.23	14.30	13.08
Phoenix, Ariz.	.80	.18	.51	.98	.68	.13	.40	.07	.12	2.03	.07	.00	1.07	2.80	.07	1.81	1.44	.44	.44	.70	.70	1.00	1.00	1.01	.780	6.19
Modena, Utah.	.85	.81	.79	.57	1.03	1.01	2.05	1.55	.79	1.76	.32	.26	.52	.95	.32	1.51	.47	.19	.75	.59	.59	.16	.55	.52	10.17	6.95
Salt Lake City, Utah.	1.31	.45	.98	.28	1.03	.81	2.09	1.92	1.43	.80	.72	.00	1.21	.17	.80	1.86	1.83	.16	.78	1.12	1.35	.22	1.43	.54	16.19	12.10
Winnemucca, Nev.	1.03	.45	.94	.96	1.90	.84	1.18	.88	.06	.01	.92	.43	.24	.20	.72	.58	.58	.10	.41	.68	.68	.64	1.08	.35	8.57	5.52
Boise, Idaho.	1.73	.96	1.48	.82	2.46	1.18	1.43	1.51	1.87	.31	1.33	.11	.63	.11	1.33	.78	.41	.25	.53	.28	1.28	.76	1.57	1.11	13.14	9.53
Seattle, Wash.	4.94	2.88	3.98	2.51	3.05	2.59	2.87	2.60	1.61	.31	1.32	1.32	1.53	.42	1.53	2.84	1.77	.53	.49	3.19	5.03	2.29	5.00	3.49	34.12	12.44
Walla Walla, Wash.	1.96	5.11	2.88	.91	2.59	5.87	2.27	4.47	1.61	.74	1.52	2.44	2.61	.63	1.52	3.12	.95	.86	.64	1.04	6.10	5.30	6.72	3.17	17.06	12.44
Portland, Oreg.	6.60	5.11	5.52	1.19	3.91	7.21	2.87	4.57	2.19	.74	1.09	.39	.44	.33	1.65	3.12	1.27	.65	.34	1.65	6.10	2.54	5.34	7.51	41.78	34.69
Roseburg, Oreg.	5.31	4.64	4.01	2.01	7.21	7.01	3.33	5.86	1.98	.12	1.72	.32	.32	.42	1.50	2.61	.58	.84	.58	4.66	6.28	4.90	3.08	4.46	33.06	24.77
Eureka, Calif.	7.11	6.67	2.78	2.78	5.01	5.23	3.65	5.29	1.80	.12	.08	.11	.11	1.02	.02	2.21	2.33	.58	.18	5.18	4.90	6.28	6.28	7.82	39.95	35.25
Fresno, Calif.	1.73	.08	1.43	.81	1.58	1.99	1.04	.29	.44	.08	.15	.01	.00	.00	T.	.21	.57	.00	.21	.29	.93	1.57	1.67	1.47	9.43	5.54
Los Angeles, Calif.	3.10	1.02	2.63	1.67	1.78	2.78	1.97	.45	.18	.29	.08	.04	.01	.00	.08	T.	.17	.00	.17	.02	1.67	.63	2.70	2.70	15.31	8.69
Sacramento, Calif.	3.72	1.17	1.38	3.09	2.78	3.39	1.77	.77	.35	.02	.15	.01	.01	T.	.15	.14	.38	.00	.38	.15	1.88	.98	3.03	2.66	18.02	12.57
San Diego, Calif.	2.06	1.21	.79	1.97	2.57	2.69	.77	.14	.80	.03	.05	T.	.03	.00	.05	.13	.54	.03	.45	.13	.63	.63	2.63	2.42	10.36	5.50
San Francisco, Calif.	4.54	2.40	3.93	3.14	4.65	1.61	1.61	1.31	.80	.26	.18	T.	.02	T.	.18	1.12	.45	T.	T.	2.35	2.35	3.35	3.95	4.89	22.10	18.99

Weather Bureau.

T. = Trace, indicates an amount too small to measure.

[1] Normals are based on records of 20 or more years of observations.

TABLE 593.—*Frost: Dates of killing frosts, with length of growing season*

Station	Date of last killing frost in spring, 1928	Date of first killing frost in fall, 1928	Spring frosts — Latest date of killing frost	Spring frosts — Average date of last killing frost	Fall frosts — Earliest date of killing frost	Fall frosts — Average date of first killing frost	Length of growing season between average dates of killing frosts
							Days
Greenville, Me	May 17¹	Sept. 10¹	June 23	May 30	Aug. 26	Sept. 14	107
Portland, Me	Apr. 16	Sept. 27	June 20	May 14	Sept. 11	Oct. 18	157
Concord, N. H	May 10¹	...do....	June 5	May 7	Sept. 6	Sept. 30	146
Northfield, Vt	May 15	Sept. 24	June 20	May 22	Aug. 27	Sept. 19	120
Boston, Mass	Apr. 17	Oct. 27	May 16	Apr. 14	Sept. 26	Oct. 24	193
Hartford, Conn	Apr. 21¹	...do....	May 22	Apr. 23	Sept. 16	Oct. 13	173
Albany, N. Y	Apr. 11	Oct. 15	May 30	...do....	Sept. 15	Oct. 16	176
Buffalo, N. Y	Apr. 27	Oct. 26	May 21	Apr. 28	Oct. 3	Oct. 21	176
Canton, N. Y	May 14	Oct. 1	June 2	May 8	Sept. 11	Sept. 28	143
Setauket, N. Y	Apr. 17¹	Nov. 24	May 17	Apr. 16	Oct. 22	Nov. 10	208
Syracuse, N. Y	Apr. 21	Oct. 27	May 5	Apr. 24	Oct. 1	Oct. 22	181
Atlantic City, N. J	Apr. 18	Oct. 30	Apr. 30	Apr. 11	...do....	Nov. 5	208
Trenton, N. J	...do....	Oct. 27	May 17	Apr. 20	Sept. 22	Oct. 19	182
Erie, Pa	Apr. 25¹	...do....	...do....	...do....	Oct. 9	Nov. 2	196
Harrisburg, Pa	Apr. 16	...do....	May 12	Apr. 10	Oct. 3	Oct. 27	200
Pittsburgh, Pa	Apr. 28	Oct. 30	May 29	Apr. 21	Sept. 25	Oct. 22	184
Scranton, Pa	Apr. 18	Oct. 15	May 10	Apr. 20	Sept. 14	Oct. 13	176
Cincinnati, Ohio	Apr. 16	Oct. 29	Apr. 26	Apr. 14	Sept. 30	Oct. 25	194
Cleveland, Ohio	Apr. 20¹	Nov. 21	May 21	Apr. 15	Oct. 2	Nov. 2	201
Columbus, Ohio	Apr. 26	Oct. 30	May 17	Apr. 17	Sept. 21	Oct. 18	184
Dayton, Ohio	Apr. 16	...do....	May 11	Apr. 15	Oct. 9	Oct. 27	195
Toledo, Ohio	Apr. 25	Oct. 26	May 29	Apr. 22	Sept. 9	Oct. 18	179
Evansville, Ind	Apr. 15¹	Nov. 11	Apr. 26	Apr. 6	Sept. 30	Oct. 27	204
Fort Wayne, Ind	Apr. 28	Sept. 26	May 28	Apr. 25	Sept. 14	Oct. 13	171
Indianapolis, Ind	Apr. 20	Oct. 26	May 25	Apr. 16	Sept. 21	Oct. 19	186
Cairo, Ill	Apr. 28	Oct. 31	Apr. 30	Mar. 31	Sept. 30	Oct. 29	212
Chicago, Ill	...do....	Sept. 26	May 23	Apr. 18	Sept. 20	Oct. 18	183
Peoria, Ill	Apr. 28	...do....	May 11	Apr. 15	Sept. 26	Oct. 19	187
Springfield, Ill	Apr. 15	...do....	May 25	...do....	Sept. 25	...do....	187
Alpena, Mich	May 7	Sept. 28	June 9	May 13	Sept. 6	Sept. 30	140
Detroit, Mich	Apr. 16	Oct. 29	May 31	Apr. 30	Sept. 21	Oct. 14	167
Grand Haven, Mich	Apr. 27	Oct. 30	May 28	May 1	Sept. 23	Oct. 17	169
Grand Rapids, Mich	Apr. 28	Oct. 26	...do....	Apr. 28	...do....	...do....	172
Ludington, Mich	May 7	Oct. 30	June 17	May 2	Sept. 4	Oct. 21	172
Marquette, Mich	Apr. 27¹	Oct. 20	June 6	May 13	Aug. 23	Oct. 9	149
Green Bay, Wis	...do.¹...	Oct. 26	May 30	May 5	Sept. 16	...do....	157
La Crosse, Wis	Apr. 28¹	Sept. 26	May 24	Apr. 28	Sept. 10	Oct. 10	165
Madison, Wis	Apr. 27	...do....	May 25	Apr. 25	Sept. 16	Oct. 17	175
Milwaukee, Wis	Apr. 20	Oct. 29	May 29	Apr. 28	Sept. 25	Oct. 16	171
Duluth, Minn	Apr. 27¹	Sept. 23	June 14	May 7	Sept. 10	Oct. 4	150
Minneapolis, Minn	Apr. 25	Oct. 29	May 20	Apr. 26	Sept. 13	Oct. 10	167
Moorhead, Minn	May 5	Sept. 23	June 8	May 13	Aug. 25	Sept. 24	134
Charles City, Iowa	Apr. 28	Sept. 27	May 21	Apr. 30	Sept. 12	Oct. 7	160
Des Moines, Iowa	Apr. 27	Sept. 26	May 31	Apr. 21	Sept. 13	Oct. 10	172
Dubuque, Iowa	Apr. 20	Oct. 26	May 21	Apr. 20	Sept. 21	Oct. 15	178
Keokuk, Iowa	Apr. 15	Oct. 29	May 4	Apr. 14	Sept. 18	Oct. 13	182
Columbia, Mo	...do....	Nov. 4	May 9	Apr. 12	...do....	Oct. 14	185
St. Joseph, Mo	Apr. 19¹	Oct. 31	Apr. 28	Apr. 11	Sept. 26	...do....	186
St. Louis, Mo	Apr. 15	Nov. 20	May 22	Apr. 4	Sept. 30	Oct. 28	207
Springfield, Mo	...do....	Nov. 3	May 19	Apr. 14	...do....	Oct. 21	190
Bismarck, N. Dak	Apr. 24	Sept. 23	June 7	May 11	Aug. 23	Sept. 20	132
Devils Lake, N. Dak	May 22	...do....	...do....	May 16	Aug. 8	Sept. 19	126
Williston, N. Dak	May 11	Sept. 17	June 16	May 15	Aug. 22	Sept. 20	128
Huron, S. Dak	Apr. 27	Sept. 25	June 21	May 10	Aug. 23	Sept. 23	136
Pierre, S. Dak	Apr. 24¹	...do....	May 19	Apr. 30	Sept. 12	Oct. 5	158
Rapid City, S. Dak	...do....	Sept. 27¹	May 21	May 4	Sept. 13	Sept. 29	148
Yankton, S. Dak	Apr. 27	Sept. 25	May 27	May 1	Sept. 14	Oct. 6	158
North Platte, Nebr	Apr. 22	Sept. 27	May 24	...do....	Sept. 10	Sept. 30	152
Omaha, Nebr	Apr. 19¹	Oct. 29	May 19	Apr. 15	Sept. 18	Oct. 13	181
Valentine, Nebr	Apr. 27¹	Sept. 27	June 21	May 6	Sept. 12	Oct. 1	148
Concordia, Kans	Apr. 15	Oct. 30	May 19	Apr. 17	Sept. 20	Oct. 17	183
Dodge City, Kans	Apr. 14	Nov. 1	May 27	Apr. 21	Sept. 23	Oct. 21	183
Iola, Kans	Apr. 15	Nov. 3	May 4	Apr. 7	Sept. 26	Oct. 23	199
Wichita, Kans	...do....	Nov. 2	May 15	Apr. 10	Sept. 23	Oct. 25	198
Washington, D. C	Apr. 18	Oct. 30	May 12	Apr. 8	Oct. 2	Oct. 20	195
Lynchburg, Va	Apr. 17	Oct. 27	May 7	Apr. 28	...do....	Oct. 27	182
Norfolk, Va	Mar. 20	Nov. 24	Apr. 26	Mar. 25	Oct. 11	Nov. 17	237
Richmond, Va	Apr. 17¹	Nov. 12	...do....	Apr. 7	Oct. 12	Oct. 31	207
Wytheville, Va	...do....	Oct. 27	May 15	Apr. 15	Sept. 19	Oct. 13	181
Elkins, W. Va	Apr. 26	...do....	May 26	May 8	Sept. 20	Oct. 8	153
Parkersburg, W. Va	...do....	Oct. 26	May 22	Apr. 16	Oct. 1	Oct. 16	183
Asheville, N. C	Apr. 17	Nov. 5	May 10	Apr. 15	Oct. 3	Oct. 20	188
Charlotte, N. C	Mar. 20	Nov. 21	Apr. 26	Mar. 28	Oct. 8	Nov. 5	222
Raleigh, N. C	...do....	...do....	...do....	Mar. 29	...do....	...do....	221
Wilmington, N. C	Mar. 19	Nov. 24	May 1	Mar. 23	Oct. 16	Nov. 13	235
Charleston, S. C	Feb. 19¹	Nov. 26¹	Apr. 2	Feb. 20	Nov. 8	Dec. 10	293
Columbia, S. C	Mar. 19	Nov. 21	Apr. 17	Mar. 18	Oct. 30	Nov. 18	245

¹ Temperature 32° F. or below.

TABLE 593.—*Frost: Dates of killing frosts, with length of growing season*—Continued

Station	Date of last killing frost in spring, 1928	Date of first killing frost in fall, 1928	Spring frosts — Latest date of killing frost	Spring frosts — Average date of last killing frost	Fall frosts — Earliest date of killing frost	Fall frosts — Average date of first killing frost	Length of growing season between average dates of killing frosts
							Days
Greenville, S. C	Mar. 20[1]	Nov. 21	Apr. 24	Apr. 3	Oct. 10	Nov. 2	213
Atlanta, Ga	do	do	Apr. 17	Mar. 31	Oct. 11	Nov. 7	221
Augusta, Ga	Feb. 26[1]	Nov. 24	do	Mar. 22	Oct. 21	Nov. 10	233
Macon, Ga	Mar. 3	do	Apr. 18	Mar. 23	Oct. 11	Nov. 7	229
Savannah, Ga	Feb. 20	Nov. 27	Apr. 13	Feb. 26	Oct. 25	Nov. 24	271
Thomasville, Ga	do	Nov. 21	Apr. 26	Mar. 14	Oct. 21	Nov. 15	246
Apalachicola, Fla	Feb. 19	Dec. 9	Mar. 23	Feb. 14	Nov. 13	Dec. 7	296
Avon Park, Fla	Jan. 29		Feb. 25	Jan. 12	Nov. 14	Dec. 26	348
Jacksonville, Fla	Feb. 19	Nov. 27	Apr. 10	Feb. 16	Nov. 12	Dec. 6	293
Miami, Fla	Jan. 29	None	Feb. 19	(²)	Dec. 26	(²)	(²)
Tampa, Fla	do	do	Apr. 7	Jan. 26	Nov. 21	Jan. 3[3]	342
Chattanooga, Tenn	Mar. 20	Nov. 21	May 14	Apr. 2	Sept. 30	Oct. 26	207
Knoxville, Tenn	do	Nov. 9	Apr. 26	do	Oct. 1	Oct. 28	209
Memphis, Tenn	Mar. 18	Nov. 20	Apr. 25	Mar. 22	Oct. 2	Nov. 3	226
Nashville, Tenn	Mar. 19	Nov. 11	Apr. 24	Apr. 2	Oct. 8	Oct. 27	208
Birmingham, Ala	Mar. 18	Nov. 17	Apr. 17	Mar. 16	Oct. 21	Nov. 9	238
Mobile, Ala	Feb. 19	Nov. 26	Apr. 6	Feb. 17	Oct. 31	Dec. 5	291
Montgomery, Ala	Mar. 18	do	Apr. 5	Mar. 10	Oct. 21	Nov. 11	246
New Orleans, La	Feb. 19	Dec. 9	Mar. 27	Jan. 25	Nov. 11	Dec. 16	325
Shreveport, La	Feb. 26[1]	Nov. 20	Apr. 9	Mar. 6	Oct. 20	Nov. 10	249
Abilene, Tex	Apr. 15	Nov. 19	Apr. 23	Mar. 21	Oct. 19	do	234
Amarillo, Tex	Apr. 10	Nov. 2	May 23	Apr. 17	Sept. 22	Oct. 29	195
Brownsville, Tex	Jan. 2[1]	None	Mar. 8	Jan. 28	Nov. 15	Dec. 22	328
Corpus Christi, Tex	do	do	Mar. 19	Jan. 21	Nov. 29	Dec. 28	341
Del Rio, Tex	Jan. 4[1]	Dec. 19	Mar. 27	Feb. 28	Oct. 27	Nov. 17	262
El Paso, Tex	Apr. 10	Nov. 18	Apr. 26	Mar. 14	do	Nov. 15	246
Fort Worth, Tex	Feb. 25[1]	Dec. 5	Apr. 9	Mar. 11	Oct. 22	Nov. 12	246
Galveston, Tex	Jan. 4[1]	None	Mar. 1	Jan. 19	Nov. 16	Dec. 26	341
Palestine, Tex	Feb. 26[1]	Nov.30[1]	Apr. 5	Mar. 13	Oct. 20	Nov. 13	245
San Antonio, Tex	Mar. 17	Dec. 20	do	Feb. 24	Oct. 30	Nov. 28	277
Taylor, Tex	Feb. 26[1]	Dec. 8	do	Mar. 13	do	Nov. 22	254
Oklahoma City, Okla	Apr. 15[1]	Nov. 3	Apr. 30	Mar. 31	Oct. 7	Nov. 2	216
Fort Smith, Ark	do	Nov. 20	Apr. 17	Mar. 21	Oct. 9	Nov. 6	230
Little Rock, Ark	Feb. 26	do	Apr. 26	Mar. 18	Oct. 22	Nov. 14	241
Havre, Mont	Apr. 23[1]	Sept. 24	June 6	May 16	Aug. 25	Sept. 19	126
Helena, Mont	Apr. 13	Oct. 4	June 9	May 9	do	Sept. 28	142
Kalispell, Mont	May 3	do	June 7	May 5	Sept. 10	Oct. 2	150
Miles City, Mont	Apr. 21	Sept. 25	May 31	do	Sept. 7	do	150
Cheyenne, Wyo	May 4	Oct. 12	June 13	May 20	Aug. 25	Sept. 19	122
Lander, Wyo	May 5[1]	Sept. 10	June 18	May 19	Aug. 23	Sept. 18	122
Sheridan, Wyo	May 4	Sept. 6	June 6	May 20	Aug. 25	Sept. 26	123
Yellowstone Park, Wyo	June 10	Aug. 29	June 22	May 21	do	Sept. 16	118
Denver, Colo	Apr. 26[1]	Oct. 17	June 6	May 4	Sept. 12	Oct. 8	157
Grand Junction, Colo	Apr. 9	Nov. 3	May 14	Apr. 19	Sept. 14	Oct. 19	183
Pueblo, Colo	Apr. 14	Oct. 22	June 2	Apr. 27	Sept. 12	Oct. 8	164
Roswell, N. Mex	Apr. 10	Nov. 3	May 7	Apr. 12	Oct. 10	Oct. 27	198
Santa Fe, N. Mex	Apr. 22	Oct. 17	May 18	Apr. 25	Sept. 25	Oct. 18	176
Flagstaff, Ariz	June 13[1]	Oct. 23	June 17	May 31	Sept. 12	Sept. 24	116
Phoenix, Ariz	Jan. 26	Dec. 17	Mar. 31	Feb. 16	Nov. 5	Dec. 3	290
Tucson, Ariz	Apr. 6	None	Apr. 6	Mar. 11	Oct. 22	Nov. 9	243
Yuma, Ariz	None	do	Feb. 18	Jan. 2	Nov. 30	Dec. 25	357
Modena, Utah	May 5[1]	Sept. 13[1]	July 3	May 23	Sept. 5	Sept. 26	126
Salt Lake City, Utah	Apr. 9	Oct. 22	June 18	Apr. 20	Sept. 22	Oct. 20	183
Reno, Nev	May 3	Oct. 14	June 18	May 13	Sept. 6	Oct. 3	143
Winnemucca, Nev	May 4[1]	Sept. 13	June 22	May 16	Aug. 22	Sept. 26	133
Boise, Idaho	May 3	Oct. 21	June 16	Apr. 27	Sept. 11	Oct. 12	168
Lewiston, Idaho	Apr. 8	Oct. 12	May 10	Apr. 5	Sept. 21	Oct. 25	203
Pocatello, Idaho	May 3	Oct. 11	June 1	May 1	Sept. 12	Oct. 6	158
Seattle, Wash	Mar. 14	Dec. 3	May 10	Mar. 17	Oct. 18	Nov. 21	249
Spokane, Wash	Apr. 20	Oct. 12	June 8	Apr. 14	Sept. 7	Oct. 13	182
Walla Walla, Wash	Apr. 8	do	Apr. 28	Mar. 30	Sept. 28	Nov. 5	220
Baker, Oreg	May 3	do	June 23	May 8	Aug. 30	Sept. 30	145
Portland, Oreg	Mar. 14[1]	Nov. 18	May 2	Mar. 18	Oct. 13	Nov. 19	246
Roseburg, Oreg	Feb. 20[1]	Oct. 13	May 24	Apr. 14	Sept. 24	Nov. 12	212
Eureka, Calif	Jan. 16	Dec. 17	Apr. 7	Feb. 8	Nov. 11	Nov. 26	291
Fresno, Calif	Feb. 16	Dec. 15	Apr. 14	Feb. 22	Oct. 31	Dec. 2	283
Independence, Calif	Apr. 9[1]	Oct. 12	May 24	Apr. 6	Sept. 24	Oct. 28	205
Los Angeles, Calif	None	None	Feb. 17	(²)	Nov. 2	(²)	(²)
Red Bluff, Calif	Feb. 22	Dec. 11	May 9	Mar. 10	Nov. 8	Dec. 6	271
Sacramento, Calif	Jan. 16	Dec. 15	May 7	Feb. 19	Nov. 11	Nov. 29	283
San Bernardino, Calif	Jan. 25[1]		Apr. 18	Mar. 8	Oct. 23	Nov. 22	259
San Diego, Calif	None	None	Jan. 20	(²)	Dec. 26	(²)	(²)
San Francisco, Calif	do	Dec. 16	Mar. 27	Jan. 25	Dec. 4	Dec. 10	319

Weather Bureau.

[1] Temperature 32° F. or below.   [2] Frosts do not occur every year.   [3] Of year following.

INDEX TO ARTICLES[1]

Abortion—
disease, loss to livestock industry. John R. Mohler_____ 433–434
infectious, control investigations_____ 61

Agriculture—
conditions in Appalachians_____ 132–134
Department—
housing situation, discussion by Secretary_ 50–52
reorganization, discussion by Secretary___ 46–50

Agents, county—
help from local volunteer leaders. F. A. Merrill_____ 274–276
training of local extension leaders_____ 275–276

"Agricultural—
Economics Literature," monthly review, aid to extension worker. Mary G. Lacy_____ 266–267
experiment stations. *See* Experiment stations.
maps. O. E. Baker_____ 640–665
products, demand, effects of World War___ 635

Agriculture—
gross income, discussion by Secretary_____ 6
post-war depression, cause_____ 7
report for year by Secretary_____ 1–116
world conditions, results of war. O. C. Stine_____ 632–635

Airplane dusting, cotton fields, effectiveness and economy. B. R. Coad_____ 117–120

Airplanes, aid in forest-fire control. Howard R. Flint_____ 312–313

Alaska—
forests, source of paper supply. B. F. Heintzleman_____ 120–122
timber consumption, control by Federal Government_____ 121–122

Alfalfa—
corn rotation, value in dairying_____ 252–253
seed—
and red-clover seed, imported, coloring. E. Brown_____ 122–123
imported, coloring_____ 122–123
yellowing from leaf-hopper attack_____ 123–125

Allard, H. A.: "Chrysanthemum flowering season varies according to daily exposure to light."_____ 194

Allen—
L. J.: "Cattle tick passes from Oklahoma after battle of 22 years"_____ 184–185
R. S.: "Livestock improvement greatly influenced by educational exhibits"_____ 430–433

Allison, F. E.—
"Nitrogen loss from soil by leaching is largely preventable"_____ 479–480
"Organic materials may hurt crops if applied undecayed"_____ 482–483

Aluminum sulphate, effectiveness in control of damping-off of forest seedlings_____ 333, 334

Ammonium sulphate, aid to lawn grass and check to weeds. B. E. Brown_____ 411–413

Animal—
casings, export requirements_____ 460
husbandry, research, yields in dividends. E. W. Sheets_____ 125–128
industry problems, discussion by Secretary_ 57–62

Animals—
domestic, improvement work_____ 61
wild, effect on forest production. W. B. Bell_____ 608–610
See also Calves; Cattle; Hogs; Horses; Lambs; Livestock; Poultry; Sheep.

Ants—
house invaders, poisoning. E. A. Back and R. T. Cotton_____ 131–132
poisoning, directions_____ 131–132

Aphids, life history. P. W. Mason_____ 128–131

Aphis maidis, carrier of sugar-cane mosaic_____ 567

Appalachians, land utilization and resources. Millard Peck_____ 132–134

Apple—
orchards, regions and acreage, 1924_____ 657
trees, spraying against Japanese beetle_____ 399

Apples, spray-residue removal—
by washes_____ 389–390
methods_____ 553–555

Appropriations, Federal, for research work__ 94–96

Argentina—
competition in corn markets_____ 4
crop yields, relation to weather_____ 606–607

Arizona, dourine eradication, methods and progress_____ 370–374

Arsenical-spray residues, removal from fruits—
by washing_____ 389–390
methods_____ 68, 553–555

Ashbrook, Frank G.: "Muskrat farming in marsh areas becomes a profitable industry"_____ 469–470

Ashe, W. W.—
"Forest purchases by United States help solve farm problem in the East"_____ 329–331
"Trees of small size unprofitable to cut for making lumber"_____ 587–590

"Aunt Sammy," aid to farm women_____ 513–514

Australia, wheat yields, relation to weather__ 607

Automobiles. *See* Motor vehicles.

Avocado—
culls, source of oil and livestock feed. G. S. Jamieson_____ 134
industry, development in Florida and California. T. Ralph Robinson_____ 135–137
oil, utilization_____ 134

Avocados, varieties for planting in California and Florida_____ 135, 136–137

Back, E. A.—
"Ants that invade houses are easily killed by poison" (With R. T. Cotton)_____ 131–132
"Bedbugs, extermination by fumigation, method" (with R. T. Cotton)_____ 138
"Cockroaches can be quickly eradicated by sodium fluoride" (with R. T. Cotton)___ 205

Bacteria—
dissemination by nemas, methods_____ 478–479
soil, usefulness to farmers, and multiplication. Lewis T. Leonard_____ 543–544

Bagasse—
from sugar cane, value in industry. Sidney F. Sherwood_____ 137–138
production and uses_____ 137–138

Baker, O. E.: "Agricultural maps"_____ 640–665

Baldwin, H. T.: "Exhibits that talk prove an effective educational device"_____ 269–273

Bankruptcies, farm, numbers, 1927–28_____ 309–311

Banks, intermediate-credit, aid to farmers__ 37–38

Barberries, relation to stem-rust epidemic. L. D. Hutton_____ 535–537

Barley—
growing, regions and acreage, 1924_____ 647
stem-rust epidemics, cause_____ 535–537

Barleys, foreign introductions, value_____ 380

Barnett, Claribel R.: "Bibliographical aids to the use of recent agricultural bulletins"_____ 156–159

Barns, tobacco, for flue curing, fireproof construction. E. G. Moss_____ 577–578

Baskets—
making of pine needles, 4–H club profits___ 617
standard sizes under container act. H. A. Spilman_____ 213–214

Bates, E. N.—
"Rice dried on farm by use of machinery imported from Italy" (with others)____ 526–528
"Smut on Pacific coast wheat can profitably be removed by washing" (with G. P. Bodnar)_____ 542–543

Bats, value as insect killers_____ 608

Bean beetle, Mexican—
control methods_____ 462

[1] See p. 1139 for Index to Statistics.

Bean beetle, Mexican—Continued. Page
spread in eastern United States. Neale F.
Howard_____ 460–462
Beans—
field, growing regions, production and acreage, 1924_____ 652
velvet. See Velvet beans.
Bear River Migratory Bird Refuge, appropriation for, and value_____ 90
BECKER, JOSEPH A.: "Crop-yield forecasts demand study of many complex relationships"_____ 245–247
Bedbugs, extermination by fumigation, method. E. A. Back and R. T. Cotton___ 138
Beef—
cuts, purchasing, considerations_____ 146–147
grade stamp, advantages_____ 145–146
grading and stamping, protection of consumer's interest. W. C. Davis_____ 144–146
production on grass, research work_____ 128
quality and cut, considerations for buying and cooking. H. K. Warner_____ 146–148
Beekeeping, studies in South in field laboratory. James I. Hambleton_____ 141–142
Bees—
breeding, experiments_____ 138–141
insemination, artificial, in breeding experiments. James I. Hambleton_____ 138–141
package, production in South_____ 141
queen, rearing in South_____ 141–142
Beeswax, candle making and other uses. Harold J. Clay_____ 142–144
Beetle—
Japanese. See Japanese beetle.
Mexican bean. See Bean beetle, Mexican.
Beets, sugar. See Sugar beets.
BELL, W. B.: "Wild animals affect forest production in many important ways"___ 608–610
Belt failure, cause and prevention. R. W. Frey and F. P. Veitch_____ 151–154
Belts, engine, cutting, installation and care_ 151–154
BENNETT, HUGH H.: "Soil deterioration by sheet erosion lowers fertility of vast area"_ 544–547
BENSON, A. O.: "Wood-selection rules help but should not be followed blindly"_____ 626–627
Bermuda grass—
characteristics for pasture grass_____ 154
pastures, improvement methods. H. N. Vinall and W. T. Cobb_____ 154–156
Bibliographies, aid to use of recent agricultural bulletins. Claribel R. Barnett_____ 156–159
Bird refuges, necessity in saving wild life. Ernest P. Walker_____ 159–162
Birds—
attraction to wood lots, methods and practices. W. L. McAtee_____ 162–164
economic value, studies_____ 90
food supply, provisions for_____ 162–163
migratory—
conservation, discussion by Secretary____ 90–91
protection_____ 159–160
See also Game; Waterfowl; Wild life.
BISHOPP, F. C.—
"Cattle-grub damage reduced by various methods of control"_____ 181–182
"Fleas controlled by creosote oil sprays and other insecticides"_____ 297
"House-fly control is best accomplished by preventing breeding"_____ 377
BLACK—
R. H.—
"Combined wheat may be cleaned for safe storage in two ways"_____ 210–211
"Dockage removal at thresher is aided by self-cleaning screen"_____ 259–260
W. H.: "Beef steers produced on range should show maximum weight for age"_ 148–150
Black Prairie, cotton production, 1924_____ 643
Black stem rust, evidence of barberries' presence. L. D. Hutton_____ 535–537
Blackberries—
English varieties, introduction into United States. George M. Darrow_____ 164–165
importations, description and growth____ 164–165
Blight, early, of tomatoes, cause, growth, and control_____ 583–585
Blister rust, white-pine, control—
feasible in Eastern States. J. F. Martin_ 167–169
natural, in Western States. Stephen N. Wyckoff_____ 166–167

Bluegrass, Kentucky— Page
seed setting detrimental to turf making____ 414
treatment for lawns_____ 412
Boar, selection for herd improvement_____ 367–368
BODNAR, G. P.—
"Rice dried on farm by use of machinery imported from Italy" (with others)____ 526–528
"Smut on Pacific coast wheat can profitably be removed by washing" (with E. N. Bates)_____ 542–543
Boll weevil, cotton—
activity, relation to yield forecasts_____ 246–247
control—
by airplane dusting, advantages___ 117, 119–120
study_____ 77–78
Bollworm, pink, eradication_____ 104–105
Boophilus annulatus. See Tick, cattle.
BOOTH, J. F.: "Cooperative handling of grain on large scale is now making headway" (with W. J. Kuhrt)_____ 215–217
BOREE, B. C.: "Produce clearing house operation necessitates full market information"_ 506
Borer, corn. See Corn borer.
BOYD, GEORGE R.: "Tree poisoning tried for clearing land is found effective"_____ 592–594
BRANDES, E. W.: "Sugar industry saved in Louisiana by using disease-resistant varieties of cane"_____ 565–567
BRANDON, MARY J.: "Wool yields can be increased by rigid culling and selection"_ 630–632
Breeding—
bees, by artificial insemination, experiments. Jas. I. Hambleton_____ 138–141
cabbages, yellows-resistant strains. J. C. Walker_____ 635–636
corn, for cold resistance, results. J. R. Holbert and W. L. Burlison_____ 227–229
dairy cows, studies. J. C. McDowell____ 255–256
ewes, experiments with feed_____ 411
hogs, selection of foundation animals_____ 365–368
livestock—
factors in improvement_____ 428–430
improvement throughout world_____ 420–422
prunes, in California_____ 507–508
velvet beans, bush variety, for distinguishable seeds, results_____ 598–600
waterfowl, necessity for protection. W. L. McAtee_____ 601–602
See also Crossbreeding.
BRIERLEY, PHILIP: "Tulip 'breaking' is proved to be caused by mosaic infection" (with others)_____ 596–597
BRIGGS, C. A.: "Livestock weighed under improved conditions at many public stockyards"_____ 434–438
BROOKS, CHARLES: "Peach rots and how temperature affects their development"____ 485
Broomcorn—
brush—
production, effect of harvesting time____ 169–171
value at different stages of development__ 171
harvesting at milk stage, effect on quality of brush. J. B. Sieglinger_____ 169–171
BROWN—
B. E.: "Lawn grass aided, weeds checked by ammonium sulphate"_____ 411–413
E.—
"Alfalfa and red-clover seed, if imported, are colored artificially"_____ 122–123
"Seed law forbids the interstate shipment of misbranded seed"_____ 538
HYLTON R.: "Fire risk in country grain elevators not recognized enough"_____ 295–296
Brown-tail moth, infestation and control___ 344, 345
BROWNE, C. A.: "Food spoilage, which causes heavy losses due to many causes"_ 305–308
Buckwheat growing, regions and acreage, 1924_____ 649
Bud variations, prune, varietal and trade significance. A. D. Shamel_____ 507–508
Budget—
county and township, study for tax reduction_____ 570–572
family, planning and results_____ 556–557
farm family, study in Maryland homes___ 283–284
Budgeting, farm resources, benefits_____ 212–213
Buildings—
Department, needs and appropriations_____ 50–52
farm, lumber grades suitable. C. V. Sweet_____ 439–441

Page

Bulbs, narcissus, fumigation for flies.
Charles F. Doucette_____ 470–474
Bulletins, agricultural—
Department and State, value to farmers.
M. C. Wilson_____ 171–174
distribution_____ 508–511
recent, bibliographical aids for use.
Claribel R. Barnett_____ 156–159
Bulls, proving for milk and butterfat inheritance_____ 82
BURCH, D. S.: "Livestock betterment registers advancement throughout the world".. 420–422
BURGESS, A. F.: "Gipsy-moth and browntail moth, campaign status"_____ 342–345
BURKE, H. E.: "Insect control in national parks is many-sided problem"_____ 382–385
BURLISON, W. L.: "Corn breeding for resistance to cold yields good results" (with J. R. Holbert)_____ 227–229
BURRUS, RUSSELL L.: "Wool carelessly packed fails to realize its full value in market" (with John P. Roberts)_____ 629–630
Business men, demand for agricultural information. C. B. Sherman_____ 174
Butter—
imports and exports, discussion by Secretary_____ 22–24
quality certification, profit to buyer. Roy C. Potts_____ 175–176
Butterfat—
production, relation to size of cow, studies_ 255–256
sales in Corn Belt, 1919–1924_____ 255
By-products, milk, utilization, discussion by Secretary_____ 84–85

Cabbages, yellows-resistant—
development by plant breeding J. C. Walker_____ 635–636
varieties_____ 636
Cakes—
flour requirements for different kinds. J. A. Le Clerc_____ 176–177
home-made and bakery, ingredients, comparison_____ 176–177
Calcium cyanide, use—
as rat poison_____ 518, 521
for fumigation of narcissus bulbs_____ 471–473
Calendar—
history and aid to agriculture. C. F. Marvin_____ 177–180
proposed modification_____ 179–180
California—
avocado industry, development_____ 135–137
eggs, marketing by grades_____ 217–218
rice, drying by Italian machine_____ 526–528
water conservation by forest litter. W. C. Lowdermilk_____ 326–327
CALLANDER, W. F.: "Crop reports lessen price swings; assist farmer to plan work"_ 242–245
Calves—
feeding on range, recommendation_____ 150
numbers on farms, 1925_____ 661
See also Cattle.
Canada, wheat yields, relation to weather_ 606, 607
Candles, manufacture, description of process_____ 142–143
Cane—
sirup. See Sirups.
sugar. See Sugar cane.
Canned goods, 4–H brand, standardization and marketing_____ 615
Canning, vegetables, by new steam process, retention of flavors. Lawrence H. James_ 180–181
Capital, farm, values, readjustment_____ 9–11
Capper-Ketcham Act, provisions for extension work_____ 110
CARTER, WALTER: "Sugar-beet leaf hopper studies afford basis for damage forecasts"_____ 559–560
Cattle—
beef, cost of fattening in Corn Belt_____ 424
dairy, profits on Nevada Reclamation Project. L. E. Cline_____ 247–248
grubs—
damage, reduction by various control methods. F. C. Bishopp_____ 181–182
losses from_____ 89
migration and control_____ 181–182

Cattle—Continued.
Page
Johne's disease, symptoms and control.
L. B. Ernest_____ 183
numbers on farms, 1925_____ 661
production and prices, discussion by Secretary_____ 18–20
sterility, prevention by rations_____ 81–82
tick. See Tick, cattle.
tuberculosis, reduction of 50 per cent, result of testing campaign. A. E. Wight. 186–187
See also Bulls: Calves; Cows; Steers..
Cemeteries, care and upkeep, discussion___ 187–190
Cemetery, neatness and beauty, enhancement by parklike arrangement. Furman Lloyd Mulford_____ 187–190
Cereals—
foreign introductions, value_____ 379–380
seed-borne diseases, control by dust fungicides. R. W. Leukel_____ 537–538
CHACE, E. M.: "Coloring of mature fruit by ethylene gas unobjectionable"_____ 205–206
CHATFIELD, CHARLOTTE: "Fruits' composition given in tables for reckoning nutrients"_____ 340–341
Cheese—
imports and exports, discussion by Secretary_____ 22–24
making, investigations, discussion by Secretary_____ 84
Chemistry—
and Soils Bureau—
functions_____ 47
service to farmers_____ 76–81
value to agriculture, discussion by Secretary_____ 80
Cherries—
Higan. See Cherries, Japanese.
Japanese—
flowering, varieties, description, and propagation_____ 401–403
Higan, use in adornment of parks. Paul Russell_____ 401–403
Chicken, for canning, inspection_____ 499–500
Chickens—
growth, increase by protein feeds_____ 500–502
mineral requirements, study_____ 502–504
production areas, numbers and value, 1925. 665
tuberculosis, extent, symptoms, and control_____ 594–595
See also Fowls; Poultry.
Chicks, rearing methods, improvement by extension campaigns. H. L. Shrader____ 190–191
Children, sun suits for, benefits in health and play. Ruth O'Brien_____ 191–193
Chimneys, cleaning. T. A. H. Miller_____ 193–194
Cholera, hog. See Hog cholera.
CHRISTENSEN, CHRIS L.: "Cooperative associations practice pooling to cut costs and spread risks"_____ 214–215
Chrysanthemums, flowering season, variation with light exposure. H. A. Allard____ 194
Cicada, periodical, brood emergence records_____ 196–200
Cicadas, 17-year and 13-year races, harmlessness. J. A. Hyslop_____ 196–200
Citrus fruits—
decay prevention. H. R. Fulton_____ 200–201
propagation—
discussion by Secretary_____ 67–68
methods. Walter T. Swingle and T. Ralph Robinson_____ 201–204
Clarke-McNary law, encouragement to forestry_____ 98
CLAY, HAROLD J.: "Beeswax goes largely into candles but has numerous other uses"___ 142–144
Clearing houses, operation, necessity for market information. B. C. Boree_____ 506
CLEMENT, C. E.: "Milk stations for cooling product help maintain its quality"_____ 462–464
CLINE, L. E.: "Dairy cows help in developing Nevada Reclamation Project"_____ 247–248
Clothing, for children, benefits from sun suits_____ 191–193
Clover—
red—
cross-pollination, factors affecting_____ 524–525
hairiness in American types due to leaf hopper. A. J. Pieters_____ 521–524
origin and introduction_____ 521–523

Clover—Continued.
 red—Continued. Page
  seed, and alfalfa seed, imported, coloring.
   E. Brown_____ 122–123
  seed, imported, coloring_____ 122–123
  seed production, factors. E. A. Hollo-
   well_____ 524–525
  yellowing from leaf-hopper attack_____ 123–125
 sweet. *See* Sweet clover.
Clubs, 4–H, products—
 marketing by women. Ola Powell Mal-
  colm_____ 614–620
 standardization_____ 614–616
Coad, B. R.: "Airplane dusting of cotton
 fields proves effective, economical"_____ 117–120
Cobb, W. T.: "Bermuda-grass pastures can
 be made profitable by the proper methods"
 (with H. N. Vinall)_____ 154–156
Cockroaches, habits and eradication. E. A.
 Back and R. T. Cotton_____ 204–205
Cod-liver oil, in feeds, vitamin preservation.
 E. M. Nelson_____ 205
Coffee standards, use and benefits_____ 573
Coffman, F. A.: "Oat varieties that resist
 smut grown by experimentation" (with
 others)_____ 481–482
College students, diet, analysis. Edith Haw-
 ley_____ 258
Collier, George W.: "Corn-stover shred-
 ding pays if supply of hay and straw is
 short"_____ 231–232
Color measurement, factor in grading farm
 products. Dorothy Nickerson_____ 206–208
Coloring, fruit, by ethylene gas, harmlessness.
 E. M. Chace_____ 205–206
Colors, food, certified, harmlessness and
 purity. H. T. Herrick_____ 302–303
Colts, numbers on farms, 1925_____ 660
Combine, improvement by invention of new
 attachments. W. M. Hurst_____ 208–210
Concrete, use for irrigation pipes. Samuel
 Fortier_____ 395–396
Conifers, seeds, scatter-distance, study_____ 587
Containers, standards, establishment. H. A.
 Spilman_____ 213–214
Cook, O. F.: "Cotton progress in irrigated
 valleys a community problem."_____ 238–240
Coombs, Whitney: "Tax relief sought
 through controlling expenditures."_____ 570–572
Coons, George H.—
 "Sugar-beet disease control progressing
  toward solution."_____ 557–559
 "Sugar-beet leaf spot controlled by dusting
  from an auto truck" (with Dewey
  Stewart)_____ 560–561
Cooper—
 J. M.: "Sheep of the Columbia type well
  adapted to intermountain region."____ 540–541
 M. R.: "Machinery plays vital rôle in
  making agriculture efficient"_____ 441–443
Cooperation—
 advantages in turkey marketing_____ 218–220
 aid to farmers, discussion by Secretary_29–31, 38–43
 grain marketing, progress. J. F. Booth
  and W. J. Kuhrt_____ 215–217
 livestock marketing, study. Kelsey B.
  Gardner_____ 422–423
 success in growing irrigated cotton_____ 238–240
 tobacco growers', failure, causes. J. J.
  Scanlan_____ 578–580
Cooperative—
 associations—
  pooling to cut costs and spread risks.
   Chris L. Christensen_____ 214–215
  services to cotton growers and spinners_ 237–238
 marketing. *See* Marketing, cooperative.
Corn—
 alfalfa rotation, value in dairying_____ 252–253
 Belt—
  chickens, numbers and value, 1925_____ 665
  eastern, dairying, growth. H. A.
   Miller_____ 254–255
  hogs, numbers on farms, 1925_____ 663
  horses, mules, and colts, numbers on
   farms, 1925_____ 660
  location, and acreage, 1924_____ 644
  milk cows, numbers on farms, 1924_____ 662
  tractors, use, statistics, 1925_____ 659
 binder, attachments for borer control____ 223–224

Corn—Continued.
 borer, European—
  control by mechanica means. R. B. Page
   Gray_____ 222–224
  control, discussion by Secretary____ 87, 107–108
  introduction and control work, general
   review_____ 224–227
  research, foundation for control of pest.
   W. R. Walton_____ 224–227
 breeding for cold resistance, results. J. R.
  Holbert and W. L. Burlison_____ 227–229
 fodder. *See* Corn stover.
 frost-resistant strains, studies_____ 227–229
 mill feeds, production and consumption,
  1925–1927_____ 287
 plants, effect of potash deficiency in soil.
  John F. Trost_____ 229–230
 production and marketing, discussion by
  Secretary_____ 4
 silo filling, experiments_____ 541–542
 stover, shredded, substitute for hay and
  straw. George W. Collier_____ 231–232
 yields, relation to weather, study_____ 607
Cotton, R. T.—
 "Ants that invade houses are easily killed
  by poison" (with E. A. Back)_____ 131–132
 "Bedbugs, extermination by fumigation
  method" (with E. A. Back)_____ 138
 "Cockroaches can be quickly eradicated by
  sodium fluoride" (with E. A. Back)_____ 205
Cotton—
 area, fertilizer consumption, relation to crop
  returns. Lawrence Myers_____ 292–293
 Belt—
  hogs, numbers on farms, 1925_____ 663
  horses, mules, and colts, numbers on
   farms, 1925_____ 660
  location, acreage, and production_____ 643
 boll weevil. *See* Boll weevil.
 bollworm, pink, eradication_____ 104–105
 classification service under standards act.
  C. L. Finch_____ 233
 community production in irrigated valleys.
  O. F. Cook_____ 238–240
 cooperative marketing—
  advantages_____ 39–40
  associations, contracts and services.
   J. S. Hathcock_____ 237–238
 crop—
  forecasts, relation to boll-weevil activ-
   ity_____ 246–247
  loans, stabilization, effect of airplane
   dusting_____ 120
 exports, decline, discussion by Secretary___ 5
 fabrics, favor for clothing and household
  use. Ruth O'Brien_____ 233–235
 fiber research, aid to marketing. Arthur
  W. Palmer_____ 235–236
 fibers, properties_____ 236
 fields, dusting by airplane, effectiveness
  and economy. B. R. Coad_____ 117–120
 futures market, use for hedging_____ 237
 irrigated, marketing problems_____ 239–240
 prices—
  discussion by Secretary_____ 11–14
  relation to staple length_____ 240–241
 production and marketing, discussion by
  Secretary_____ 2, 11–16, 67
 standards—
  basis_____ 223
  extension through research_____ 236
 staple—
  length, effect on demand_____ 13–15
  production, adjustment to market. B.
   Youngblood_____ 240–241
 uses, discussion by Secretary_____ 14–16, 114
 varieties, foreign introductions, value_____ 381
 yields, relation to fertilizer consumption_ 292–293
Cottonseed—
 feed products, output 1918–1927_____ 286–287
 grading by kernel content and components.
  G. S. Meloy_____ 241–242
 kernel content and components, basis for
  grading. G. S. Meloy_____ 241–242
 oil—
  and protein content, determination_____ 242
  refining process, value_____ 77
Cover crops, study in South, report by Secre-
 tary_____ 70

Page

Cow, "talking," value as educational exhibit_____ 270-271
Cows—
  dairy—
    feeding costs, studies_____ 255-256
    persistency in milk production, studies.
      M. H. Fohrman_____ 249-251
    size, relation to production and income.
      J. C. McDowell_____ 255-256
  milk—
    and butterfat production, average in 43
      States_____ 82
    numbers on farms, 1924_____ 662
  See also Cattle.
Credit, facilities, discussion by Secretary____ 36-38
Creosote oil sprays, use for flea control_____ 297
Crop—
  land, acreage and location, map_____ 642
  reports, benefits to farmers. W. F. Callander_____ 242-245
  yield forecasts, relationships, study. Joseph
    A. Becker_____ 245-247
Crops—
  acreage, determination by intentions-toplant reports_____ 391-392
  distribution within United States, maps_ 640-665
  injury by application of undecayed organic
    material. F. E. Allison_____ 482-483
  intentions-to-plant reports, benefits to
    farmers_____ 391-392
  production and marketing, discussion by
    Secretary_____ 1-5, 11-18, 74-75
Cross-pollination, red clover, factors_____ 524-525
Crossbreeding—
  sheep, for western range conditions_____ 540-541
  See also Breeding.
Cultivators, sizes for corn and cotton_____ 442-443
Curly top, in sugar beets—
  control progress_____ 88-89
  occurrence and control_____ 557,558
Currants, wild, eradication—
  in East_____ 167-169
  natural, in West_____ 166-167
Cut-over lands, grazing, benefits_____ 260-263
Cyclone insurance, importance_____ 612-614
Cyclones, damage to farm property_____ 612-613

Dairy—
  herd improvement associations, numbers in
    22 countries. Joseph B. Parker_____ 253-254
  industry, discussion by Secretary_____ 22-24
  products, cooperative marketing, progress_ 40-41
  sanitation, studies, discussion by Secretary_ 83
Dairying—
  crop rotation at Beltsville. T. E. Woodward_____ 252-253
  in eastern Corn Belt, growth. H. A.
    Miller_____ 254-255
  labor-saving equipment. T. E. Woodward_____ 251
  research work, discussion by Secretary_____ 81-85
  success on Nevada reclamation project.
    L. E. Cline_____ 247-248
Damping-off—
  in sugar beets, occurrence and control_____ 557
  of forest-tree seedlings, prevention. Carl
    Hartley_____ 332-334
DANTZIG, TOBIAS: "Fabrics' stiffness is measurable by device made for the purpose"
  (with Esther C. Peterson)_____ 279-280
DARROW, GEORGE M.: "Blackberries of four
  English varieties are introduced into United
  States"_____ 164-165
Date—
  palms, pollination experiments, duscussion
    by Secretary_____ 66
  varieties—
    fruit characters, studies_____ 256-257
    identification by vegetative characters.
      Silas C. Mason_____ 256-257
DAVIS, W. C.: "Beef grading and stamping
  protects consumer's interest"_____ 144-146
DAWSON, O. L.: "Weather relationship to
  yields studied in Canada and Argentina"_____ 606-607
DAY, P. C.: "Hail-occurrence data for the
  United States gathered and analyzed"__ 350-352
Daylight, length, effect on—
  flowering season of chrysanthemums_____ 194

Page

Daylight, length, effect on—Continued.
  plant growth and flowering_____ 71
  See also Light.
Dennis plant, toxicity to fish and insects____ 388
DEWEY, LYSTER H.: "Kapok and like fibers
  used for pillows, life preservers, insulation"_____ 403-404
Diet, college students, analysis. Edith
  Hawley_____ 258
Dietaries, study by Home Economics Bureau_____ 113-114
DILLMAN, A. C.: "Flax resistant to wilt developed at experiment stations"_____ 296-297
Dockage—
  feeding value_____ 259
  removal—
    at thresher, aid by self-cleaning screen.
      R. H. Black_____ 259-260
    from wheat, methods_____ 210-211
DOUCETTE, CHARLES F.: "Narcissus bulbs
  attacked by flies may be fumigated"_____ 470-474
Douglas fir. See Fir, Douglas.
Dourine—
  characteristics and spread_____ 371, 372-373
  eradication in Arizona_____ 370-374
  samples, methods of obtaining_____ 371-374
Drainage investigations, discussion by Secretary_____ 108
Drugs—
  act. See Food and drugs act.
  adulteration and misbranding, instances___ 304
Dry farming—
  discussion by Secretary_____ 65
  sweet clover growing, recommendations__ 567-569
DUNNING, DUNCAN: "Woodland thinning by
  preserving better trees often profitable"____ 624
Dust—
  explosion hazards in manufacturing plants.
    David J. Price_____ 263-265
  layers, for roads, kinds and application____ 531
Dusting—
  airplane, for cotton boll weevil, advantages
    and limitations_____ 118-120
  cotton fields, by airplane, effectiveness and
    economy. B. R. Coad_____ 117-120
  sugar beets, for leaf-spot control. George
    H. Coons and Dewey Stewart_____ 560-561
Dusts, fungicidal, use against seed-borne
  diseases of cereals_____ 537-538
Dyes—
  food, certified, harmlessness and purity.
    H. T. Herrick_____ 302-303
  importance in disease diagnosis and as
    medicinal agents. W. C. Holmes_____ 265-266
DYKSTRA, T. P.: "Tulip 'breaking' is proved
  to be caused by mosaic infection" (with
  others)_____ 596-597
Dysentery, chronic bacterial, diagnosis_____ 183

Eastern States, agricultural features_____ 640
Economics, services, discussion by Secretary_ 71-76
Economists, demand for agricultural information_____ 174
Education, work of radio service_____ 514-515
Egg—
  prices, relation to standardization_____ 267-269
  production—
    factors influencing returns_____ 494-495
    increase by protein feeds_____ 500-502
    research work_____ 127
  standardization, value in recognition of
    quality in prices. George H. Powers__ 267-269
Eggs—
  California, grading, aid in cooperative marketing. A. V. Swarthout_____ 217-218
  quality, basis of standardization_____ 267-269
Elevators, farmers', volume of business_____ 215
Elk, conservation, discussion by Secretary__ 91-92
Employees, salaries, retirements, and annuities_____ 49
Energy, solar, radiant, receipt and effects____ 551
Engines, belts, cutting, installation and
  care_____ 151-154
Enteritis, chronic bacterial, diagnosis_____ 183
Entomology, economic investigations, discussion by Secretary_____ 86-89
Enzymes, cause of food spoilage, discussion_ 305-306
ERNEST, L. B.: "Cattle malady called
  Johne's disease to be fought cooperatively"_ 183

Erosion—   Page
    control by terracing_____ 575
    damage and control measures_____ 544–547
    sheet, cause of soil deterioration of vast area.
        Hugh H. Bennett_____ 544–547
Ethylene gas, harmlessness as fruit coloring.
    E. M. Chace_____ 205–206
Eumerus sp., injury to narcissus bulbs and
    control_____ 470–474
Europe, agricultural changes due to World
    War_____ 632–634
EVANS—
    RAYMOND: "Movie audiences in many
        countries see Department's films" (with
        H. B. McClure)_____ 465–467
    W. L.: "Produce agency act protects con-
        signor in interstate trade" (with H. A.
        Spillman)_____ 504–506
Ewes—
    feeding experiments in breeding_____ 411
    Rambouillet, clean wool averages_____ 631–632
Exhibits—
    educational, influence on livestock improve-
        ment. R. S. Allen_____ 430–433
    livestock, value to Department and com-
        mercial concerns_____ 430–433
    "talking", effectiveness as educational
        device. H. T. Baldwin_____ 269–273
    use of motion pictures_____ 110–111
Expenditures, farm family—
    for living_____ 283–284
    under budget system_____ 555–557
Experiment stations—
    endowments for research work_____ 95–96
    work, discussion by Secretary_____ 109
Exports—
    agricultural products, effects of World
        War_____ 632–633
    farm products, discussion by Secretary____ 5–6,
                                            22–24, 74
    meat, supervision requirements. Wm. H.
        Smith, jr_____ 458–460
Extension—
    chick campaigns, benefits to poultrymen.
        H. L. Shrader_____ 190–191
    leaders, volunteer, aid to county agents.
        F. A. Merrill_____ 274–276
    Service—
        aid by Department and State publica-
            tions_____ 171–174
        appropriations and work, discussion by
            Secretary_____ 109–112
    work—
        among negroes, promotion by local organ-
            izations. J. B. Pierce_____ 474–477
        in economics, value to farmers_____ 76
    workers—
        aid by "Agricultural Economics Litera-
            ture." Mary G. Lacy_____ 266–267
        need of general and vocational training.
            E. H. Shinn_____ 276–279
        requirements_____ 278

Fabrics, stiffness, measurement by special
    device. Esther C. Peterson and Tobias
    Dantzig_____ 279–280
FAIRBANK, H. S.: "Highway needs are in-
    dicated by taking censuses of traffic"_____ 358–361
Family living—
    needs, relation to income of farms, study.
        Eugene Merritt_____ 280–282
    value of farm products, study in Maryland
        homes. Chase G. Woodhouse_____ 283–284
Farm—
    bankruptcies, numbers, 1927–28_____ 309–311
    hands, wages and perquisites_____ 600–601
    income—
        increase by combining enterprises. R. S.
            Kifer_____ 212–213
        relation to family living needs, study.
            Eugene Merritt_____ 280–282
        relation to topography_____ 132–134
    labor. *See* Labor.
    land—
        marginal, in East, purchase for reforesta-
            tion_____ 329–331
        quality, relation to living standards___ 284–286
        living supply for families, study in Mary-
            land homes. Chase G. Woodhouse____ 283–284
    management work, reorganization, discus-
        sion by Secretary_____ 73–75

Farm—Continued.   Page
    owners, investments and total assets in four
        States_____ 392
    prices. *See* Prices, farm.
    products—
        exports, discussion by Secretary__ 5–6, 22–24, 74
        freight-rate reduction under Hoch-Smith
            law_____ 334–336
        grading by color measurement. Dorothy
            Nickerson_____ 206–208
        money value as source of farm living__ 283–284
        surplus, utilization by 4-H clubs_____ 616–617
    relief—
        discussion by Secretary_____ 27–32
        results of freight-rate reduction under
            Hoch-Smith law. Thor Hultgren___ 334–336
        woods, profit source. W. R. Mattoon___ 628–629
Farmers—
    benefits from intentions-to-plant reports_ 391–392
    cooperative marketing schools_____ 221–222
    investments of savings, diversity need.
        David L. Wickens_____ 392–394
    living standards—
        divergence on good and poor farms. C.
            J. Galpin_____ 284–286
        improvement by budget system_____ 555–557
        use of agricultural publications_____ 171–174
Farming, tenant, opportunities for begin-
    ners. Howard A. Turner_____ 574–575
Farms—
    foreclosure rate, 1927–28. E. H. Wiecking_ 309–311
    tenancy changes, discussion by Secretary___ 9–10
Farrowing time, effect on mortality of pigs_ 364–365
Feed, livestock, from avocado culls, produc-
    tion_____ 134
Feeding—
    cattle, on range, recommendations_____ 148–150
    ewes, experiments in breeding_____ 411
    range steers for weight_____ 148–150
Feeds—
    adulteration and misbranding, instances_ 303–304
    chemical analyses_____ 426–427, 428
    cod-liver-oil, vitamin preservation. E. M.
        Nelson_____ 205
    commercial, distribution in United States.
        Floyd J. Hosking_____ 286–288
    protein, value to poultry_____ 500–502
Fence posts, treatment for—
    increased durability. George M. Hunt____ 290
    timber economy in Custer Forest. C. N.
        Whitney_____ 288–289
Fencing, forest ranges, progress in Arizona
    and New Mexico. E. G. Miller_____ 331–332
Fertilizer—
    double phosphate, useful properties. K.
        D. Jacob_____ 294
    nitrogen, manufacture and value of urea.
        Edmund C. Shorey_____ 597–598
Fertilizers—
    concentrated, danger of burning plants, pre-
        vention. William H. Ross and Albert
        R. Merz_____ 291–292
    consumption in cotton area, relation to crop
        returns. Lawrence Myers_____ 292–293
    for pecan orchards, formulas_____ 488–490
    production and concentration, discussion
        by Secretary_____ 79–80
    use on lawns_____ 411–413, 415–417
Fever tick, cattle. *See* Tick, cattle.
Fibers, Bombax group, kinds, origin, value,
    and uses_____ 403–404
Films, motion-picture, loan to foreign coun-
    tries. Raymond Evans and H. B. Mc-
    Clure_____ 465–467
Finance. *See* Credit.
FINCH, C. L.: "Cotton classification service
    is maintained under standards act"_____ 233
Fir, Douglas—
    cut-over land, fire hazard minimized by
        grazing. D. C. Ingram_____ 260–263
    lumber prices_____ 1112
Fire risk, in country grain elevators, import-
    ance. Hylton R. Brown_____ 295–296
Fires—
    causes in country elevators_____ 295
    farm, losses, annual_____ 78
    forest. *See* Forest fires.
    in peat deposits, survey_____ 486
FISHER, D. F.: "Fruit washes and their re-
    lation to storage diseases"_____ 338–340

Page

Flavors, vegetable, retention in steam-process
canning. Lawrence H. James_____ 180–181
Flax—
growing, regions and acreage, 1924_____ 650
wilt—
causal organism_____ 296
resistant, development at experiment
stations. A. C. Dillman_____ 296–297
Fleas, control by creosote oil sprays and other
insecticides. F. C. Bishopp_____ 297
Fleeces—
falsification in packing_____ 630
Rambouillet ewes, clean wool averages__ 631–632
FLEMING, WALTER E.: "Quarantined nursery stock may be shipped if infestation removed"_____ 512–513
Flies—
control—
methods_____ 377
on dairy farms, methods. R. P. Hotis_ 300–302
injury to narcissus bulbs, and control____ 470–474
species troublesome to dairy farmer_____ 300
FLINT—
HOWARD R.: "Forest-fire patrol by airplane greatly helps ground force"_____ 312–313
L. H.: "Paper-mulch trials center about
three lines of usefulness"_____ 483–484
Flood, Mississippi Valley, rehabilitation
work_____ 111
Floods, New England, damage_____ 112
Florida, avocado industry, development___ 135–137
Flour—
insects, control, discussion by Secretary___ 87–88
requirements for cakes of different kinds.
J. A. Le Clerc_____ 176–177
Flowering time, in plants, effect of day length_ 71
Flowers—
diseases, description and control_____ 297–299
fungous diseases, necessity for control.
Freeman Weiss_____ 297–299
Flues, soot removal, directions_____ 193–194
Fly traps, directions for use_____ 300–301
Fodder—
corn. See Corn stover.
uses of sorghums, area in 1924_____ 649
FOHRMAN, M. H.: "Dairy cows' persistency
in production of milk is subject of studies" 249–251
FOLSOM, J. C.: "Wages of farm hands augmented by many important perquisites"_ 600–601
Food—
and drugs act, protection to farmer_____ 303–304
colors, certified, harmlessness and purity.
H. T. Herrick_____ 302–303
constituents, minor, survey plans. E. T.
Wherry_____ 394–395
Drug, and Insecticide Administration—
functions_____ 47
protection to farmer. George P. Lar-
rick_____ 303–305
spoilage—
causes and losses from. C. A. Browne_ 305–308
prevention_____ 306–307, 308
Foodstuffs, labels on packages, significance_ 405–408
Foot-and-mouth disease, eradication, methods,
cost, and importance. H. W. Schoening_ 308–309
Foot rot, disease of vegetables_____ 605–606
Forage—
crops, foreign introductions, value_____ 381
plants, injury by early grazing_____ 348–349
sorghum acreage, 1924_____ 649
Forest—
fires—
control in Oregon by aid of settlers. John
D. Guthrie_____ 317–319
destruction of wild life. R. H. Rut-
ledge_____ 315–316
fighting with power pump. C. R. Tillot-
son_____ 311–312
patrol by airplane, aid in control work.
Howard R. Flint_____ 312–313
prevention, individual and social responsibility. Evan W. Kelley_____ 314–315
prevention on cut-over lands by grazing 260–263
lands, purchase in Lake States. E. W.
Tinker_____ 321–323
lecture tour of schools conducted in Pacific
Northwest. John D. Guthrie_____ 323–325
litter—
conservation of water for California farms.
W. C. Lowdermilk_____ 326–327

Page

Forest—Continued.
fires—Continued.
value as fertilizer for farm crops. W. R.
Mattoon_____ 325–326
planting, Huron National Forest, efficiency
and cost. Fred R. Johnson_____ 328–329
production, effect of wild animals on. W.
B. Bell_____ 608–610
purchases, aid in solution of farm problem
in East. W. W. Ashe_____ 329–331
ranges. See Ranges.
Forestry, relation to agriculture, discussion
by Secretary_____ 96–102, 110
Forests—
Alaskan, source of paper supply. B. F.
Heintzleman_____ 120–122
grazing permits, factors affecting. John H.
Hatton_____ 320–321
national—
Alaskan, timber consumption, control_ 121–122
lambing experiments_____ 409–410
preservation of wilderness areas. E. W.
Tinker_____ 610–612
repayment for administration cost_____ 102
relation to wild animals, studies_____ 608–610
scatter-distance of seeds, study_____ 586–587
FORTIER, SAMUEL: "Irrigation pipes of concrete economical under some conditions"_ 395–396
Four-H brand, value to club women_____ 614–616
Fowls, tuberculosis, and eradication measures. Elmer Lash_____ 594–595
FOX, HENRY: "Japanese beetle in narrow
range meets variety of conditions"_____ 396–398
Freight rates, reduction under Hoch-Smith
law, aid in farm relief. Thor Hultgren__ 334–336
FREY, R. W.—
"Belt failure often caused by neglect or
faulty installation" (with F. P. Veitch) 151–154
"Harness life can be doubled or trebled by
cleaning and repair" (with F. P. Veitch)_ 352–
354
Fruit—
growing, districts and acreage, 1924_____ 656
mature, coloring by ethylene gas. E. M.
Chace_____ 205–206
production, discussion by Secretary__ 25, 26, 67–69
trees, aphid infestation, description__ 128–129, 131
washers, tests_____ 554
washes, relation to storage diseases. D. F.
Fisher_____ 338–340
washing for spray residue removal_____ 389–390
worm, Mexican, eradication_____ 103–104
Fruits—
and vegetables—
for canning, grading service extension.
R. R. Pailthorp_____ 337–338
inspection at shipping points, extension.
F. G. Robb_____ 336–337
composition, determination from diet
tables. Charlotte Chatfield_____ 340–341
cooperative marketing, advantages_____ 41
dry-cleaning methods, success_____ 553
exports, discussion by Secretary_____ 6
foreign introductions, numbers_____ 381
spray residue, removal, methods_____ 553–555
storage rots, result of washing for market.
D. F. Fisher_____ 338–340
wiping for removal of spray residue_____ 553
FRY, W. H.: "Soil particles that glitter are
often mistaken for gold"_____ 547
FULTON, H. R.: "Citrus decay less if care
used by grower, dealer, and consumer"__ 200–201
Fumigant, new, discovery_____ 77
Fumigation—
calcium cyanide, effectiveness against rats_ 521
method of exterminating bedbugs. E. A.
Back and R. T. Cotton_____ 138
Fungi, spread by nemas_____ 478–479
Fungicides—
liquid, use, disadvantages_____ 537
use against seed-borne diseases of cereals.
R. W. Leukel_____ 537–538
Fungous diseases, of flowers, control meas-
ures_____ 298–299
Fur—
bearers—
disease research, aid to fur farmers. J. E.
Shillinger_____ 341–342
raising in captivity, discussion by Secre-
tary_____ 92

Fur—Continued.   **Page**

farmers, aid by research in combating outbreaks of disease. J. E. Shillinger_____ 341–342
muskrat, increase in demand and value____ 470

GALLOWAY, B. T.: "Immigrant plants hold
large place among United States crops"_ 379–381
GALPIN, C. J.—
"Farm living standards widely divergent
on good and on poor United States
farms"_____ 284–286
"Standard of living may be improved by
use of family budget"_____ 555–557
Game. See Birds, migratory; Waterfowl;
Wild life.
GARDNER, KELSEY B.: "Livestock cooperative association efficient, intensive study
shows"_____ 422–423
GEHL, R. M.: "Rice dried on farm by use of
machinery imported from Italy" (with
others)_____ 526–528
Gipsy-moth—
and brown-tail moth, campaign status.
A. F. Burgess_____ 342–345
control, discussion by Secretary_____ 88
infestation areas in New England____ 342, 343–344
Gooseberries, wild, eradication—
in East_____ 167–169
natural, in West_____ 166–167
Grades—
dressed poultry, description_____ 496–498
eggs, standards of quality_____ 267–269
fruits and vegetables for canning, extension
of service. R. R. Pailthorp_____ 337–338
grain, under standards act, discussion by
Secretary_____ 52–54
Grading—
beef, necessity and advantages_____ 144–146
eggs, in California, aid in cooperative marketing. A. V. Swarthout_____ 217–218
farm products, importance of color factor.
Dorothy Nickerson_____ 206–208
Grafting, citrus fruits, new methods_____ 201–204
Grain—
cleaning devices_____ 210–211
cooperative handling on large scale, progress.
J. F. Booth and W. J. Kuhrt_____ 215–217
dockage removal at thresher_____ 259–260
drying equipment, need on farms. W. M.
Hurst_____ 345–346
dust explosions, prevention studies_____ 263–265
elevators, country, fire risk, importance.
Hylton R. Brown_____ 295–296
futures act, enforcement, advantages from_ 54–56
harvesting—
machinery, improvement_____ 208–210
time, effect on quality_____ 346–347
marketing associations, volume of business_ 215–217
quality, effect of time of harvesting with
combine machine. B. E. Rothgeb____ 346–347
standards act, enforcement, advantages
from_____ 52–54
test weight per bushel, effect of drying
methods_____ 346
See also Oats; Rye; Wheat.
Grape districts, location and acreage, 1924____ 658
Grapefruit. See Citrus fruits.
Grapevines, spraying against Japanese
beetle_____ 399–400
Grass—
Bermuda. See Bermuda grass.
lawn. See Lawns.
utilization in beef production_____ 128
GRAY, R. B.: "Corn-borer control by mechanical means is advanced a stage"____ 222–224
Grazing—
early, injury to livestock and range. Arnold
R. Standing and Ernest Winkler_____ 348–349
permits, on national forests, factors affecting. John H. Hatton_____ 320–321
value in minimizing fire hazard on Douglas
fir cut-over lands. D. C. Ingram_____ 260–263
Great Plains—
northern, hog production, profits. R. E.
Hutton_____ 368–369
winter-wheat seeding date, variation with
locality. A. F. Swanson_____ 614
Green manure, effect on soil organisms_____ 544

GRIFFITHS, DAVID: "Lily breeding is fertile   **Page**
field for plant improvement."_____ 418–420
Grubs, cattle. See Cattle grubs.
GUTHRIE, JOHN D.—
"Forest fires fought in Oregon by settlers
aiding U. S. Foresters."_____ 317–319
"Forest-lecture tour of schools conducted in
Pacific Northwest."_____ 323–325

Hailstorms, average distribution for 12-year
period. P. C. Day_____ 350–352
HAMBLETON, JAS. I.—
"Bee breeding by artificial insemination
done experimentally."_____ 138–141
"Beekeeping studies to be made in South in
field laboratory."_____ 141–142
Hampers, standard sizes under container act.
H. A. Spilman_____ 213–214
Harness, preservation by cleaning and repair-
ing. F. V. Veitch and R. W. Frey_____ 352–354
HARTLEY, CARL: "Forest tree seedlings kept
from damping-off by aluminum sulphate."_ 332–334
HARTMAN, WILLIAM A.: "Grubstake stage of
settlers in northern Lake States meas-
ured"_____ 349–350
Harvester, combine, improvement by inven-
tion of new attachments. W. M. Hurst_ 208–210
Harvesters, grain and cotton, improvement__ 108
HATHCOCK, J. S.: "Cotton cooperatives liberalize contracts and extend services"_____ 237–238
HATTON, JOHN H.—
"Forest grazing permits largely influenced
by proximity of ranches"_____ 320–321
"Lambing loss declines in the national forests as shelter is provided"_____ 409–410
HAWKINS, LON A.: "Spray-residue removal
by mechanical methods is extensively
tested"_____ 553–555
HAWLEY, EDITH: "Diet of college students
ample, analysis shows"_____ 258
Hay—
marketing, improvement by Federal inspection. K. B. Seeds_____ 354–356
production, regions and acreage, 1924_____ 651
Heat, solar, radiation study_____ 549–551
Heel flies, attack on cattle, and control_____ 181, 182
HEINTZLEMAN, B. F.: "Alaskan forests to
supply paper while maintaining growth"_ 120–122
HEITZ, THOMAS W.: "Poultry (dressed) is
covered in tentative grades and standards"_____ 496–498
Hemp growing, regions and acreage, 1924____ 654
HEMPHILL, JOSEPHINE F.: "Radio audience
gets housekeepers' chats five days each
week"_____ 513–514
HENRY, ALFRED J.: "Rainfall distribution is
compared at near-by measurement stations"_____ 516–518
Hens, egg production, research work_____ 127
HERRICK, H. T.—
"Food colors certified by the Department
are both harmless and pure"_____ 302–303
"Molds pressed into service in utilizing
some farm products" (with O. E. May)_ 464–465
Hides and skins, Federal standards, necessity. M. C. Romberger_____ 356–357
Highways—
needs, indication by traffic census. H. S.
Fairbank_____ 358–361
research work, value_____ 107
traffic censuses, aid in improvement pro-
gram_____ 358–359
See also Roads.
Hoch-Smith law, reduction of freight rates___ 334
Hog cholera—
losses, reduction by sanitation. U. G.
Houck_____ 361–363
prevention, progress_____ 57–58
similarity to other diseases_____ 362–363
Hogs—
breeders, selection for herd profits. J. H.
Zeller_____ 365–368
disease prevention by sanitation_____ 361–363
numbers on farms, 1925_____ 663
production—
and prices, discussion by Secretary_ 18–19, 20–21
profits in northern Great Plains. R. E.
Hutton_____ 368–369

Hogs—Continued. Page
raising and fattening, study _____ 423–424
sanitation, prevention of cholera and other
diseases. U. G. Houck_____ 361–363
See also Pigs; Sow; Swine.
HOLBERT, J. R.: "Corn breeding for resistance to cold yields good results (with W. L.
Burlison)_____ 227–229
HOLLOWELL, E. A.—
"Alfalfa and red clover yellowed by leaf-
hopper attack" (with John Monteith,
jr.)_____ 123–125
"Red-clover seed production depends on
many factors"_____ 524–525
HOLMES, W. C.: "Dyes important both in
diagnosis of disease and as medicinal
agents"_____ 265–266
Home Economics Bureau, work, discussion
by Secretary_____ 113–114
Homemakers, apportionment of time over
tasks_____ 621–622
Homes—
equipment, relation to time requirements
for tasks_____ 622
farm, equipment, census figures_____ 46
Honey, food value and vitamin deficiency.
Hazel E. Munsell_____ 369–370
Honeycomb foundations, making from bees-
wax_____ 142
Hops, production, regions and acreage, 1919__ 654
Horse meat, foreign demand and American
production. R. P. Steddom_____ 374–377
Horses—
dourine, eradication in Arizona. F. L.
Schneider and H. E. Kemper_____ 370–374
Morgan, improvement work_____ 60
numbers on farms, 1925_____ 660
HOSKING, FLOYD J.: "Feeds commercially
produced have wide distribution in
U. S."_____ 286–288
HOTIS, R. P.—
"Fly-control methods in use at Beltsville
can be used on all dairy farms"_____ 300–302
"Milk transportation in tanks coming into
use widely in United States"_____ 446–449
HOUCK, U. G.: "Hog-cholera losses can be
much reduced by sanitary measures"____ 361–363
House fly—
breeding places, treatment_____ 377
control by prevention of breeding. F. C.
Bishopp_____ 377
Housekeepers' chats, preparation and broad-
casting. Josephine F. Hemphill_____ 513–514
HOWARD—
NEALE F.: "Mexican bean beetle continues
destructive spread in eastern United
States"_____ 460–462
P. E.: "Nitrogen supply of United States
much dependent on imports"_____ 480–481
HOWE, PAUL E.: "Meat combines high nu-
tritive value with great palatability"____ 449–450
HULBERT, L. S.: "Cooperative marketing
contracts established on a firm legal basis"_ 218
HUNT, GEORGE M.—
"Fence posts properly treated have greatly
increased durability"_____ 290
"Wood of native trees compared regarding
resistance to decay"_____ 625–626
Huron National Forest, reforestation, effi-
ciency and cost. Fred R. Johnson_____ 328–329
HURST—
LEWIS A.: "Sugar cane requires nitrogen
as chief plant-food element"_____ 563–564
W. M.—
"Combine harvester is improved by in-
vention of new attachments"_____ 208–210
"Grain drying on farm awaits develop-
ment of suitable equipment"_____ 345–346
HUTTON—
L. D.: "Rust epidemics of local areas be-
tray barberries' presence"_____ 535–537
R. E.: "Hogs can be produced profitably
in parts of northern Great Plains"____ 368–369
Hybrids, rose, development for hardiness__ 532–534
Hydrochloric acid, use in cleaning fruits__ 389–390,
553–555
HYSLOP, J. A.—
"Cicada appearing at 17-year and 13-year
intervals is not a serious pest"_____ 196–200

HYSLOP, J. A.—Continued. Page
"Insect-pest survey assembles data from
all parts of country"_____ 385–388
Ice box construction. T. A. H. Miller_____ 378
Imports, seed, samples, exhibit in Depart-
ment_____ 538–540
Income, farm. See Farm income.
Index, farm prices, interpretation_____ 7–9
INGRAM, D. C.: "Douglas fir cut-over land's
fire hazard is minimized by grazing"____ 260–263
Inoculation, tulips, with mosaic infection,
methods_____ 596–597
Insect pests—
losses from, annual_____ 86
survey, purpose and extent. J. A. Hyslop_ 385–
388
Insecticide act, protection to farmers_____ 305
Insecticides—
and fungicides, research investigations_____ 77–78
Japanese-beetle, effectiveness_____ 86–87
neonicotine, characteristics and use_____ 389
residues—
removal from fruit_____ 553–555
removal from fruit by washes. R. C.
Roark_____ 389–390
rotenone, toxicity and use_____ 388
use—
against bedbugs_____ 138
against house ants_____ 131–132
for flea control_____ 297
Insects—
control—
in national parks, problem. H. E.
Burke_____ 382–385
investigations, discussion by Secretary__ 86–89
damage in national parks_____ 382–383
plant pests, control, discussion by Secre-
tary_____ 102–105
Insemination, artificial, of bees, in breeding
experiments. Jas. I. Hambleton_____ 138–141
Inspection—
dressed poultry, establishment of Federal
service. Rob R. Slocum_____ 498–500
Federal, of hay, aid in marketing. K. B.
Seeds_____ 354–356
fruits and vegetables, extension at shipping
points. F. G. Robb_____ 336–337
grain, under standards act, discussion by
Secretary_____ 52–54
horse meat, extent_____ 374–377
meat and livestock, extent of service_____ 58–59
Insurance—
against minor losses, wastefulness. V. N.
Valgren_____ 390
windstorm, importance for farm property.
V. N. Valgren_____ 612–614
Intentions-to-plant reports, aid to farmers in
planning production. John B. Shepard_ 391–392
Iodine, in foods, content and function, sur-
vey_____ 394
Irrigation—
investigations, discussion by Secretary_____ 109
pipes, concrete, substitution for earth
ditches. Samuel Fortier_____ 395–396
problems, discussion by Secretary_____ 64–65

JACKSON, WILLIAM: "Livestock farmers can
obtain better profits with better husbandry"_____ 423–425
JACOB, K. D.: "Fertilizer known as double
superphosphate has useful properties"____ 294
JAMES, LAWRENCE H.: "Canning of vegetables by new steam process holds flavors
better."_____ 180–181
JAMIESON, G. S.: "Avocado culls may prove
source of oil and livestock feed"_____ 134
Japanese beetle—
control—
investigations_____ 86–87
methods. Loren B. Smith_____ 398–401
increase and spread. Henry Fox_____ 396–398
spread, prevention methods_____ 512–513
JARDINE, Secretary: Report on "The year in
agriculture"_____ 1–116
Johne's disease, diagnosis_____ 183
JOHNSON—
FRED R.—
"Forest planting on Huron forest both
efficient and cheap."_____ 328–329

Johnson—Continued.
FRED R.—Continued.   Page
"Tree planting goes ahead in Nebraska
with Federal help"_____ 590–592
JAMES: "Tobacco wildfire is less serious
menace than it once seemed"_____ 581–583
JONES, LEWIS A.: "Terracing to control
erosion if well done is paying investment"_____ 575–577
JULL, M. A.: "Poultry breeders can increase
profits by controlling production"_____ 494–496

Kapok and similar fibers, description, uses,
etc. Lyster H. Dewey_____ 403–404
KELLEY, EVAN W.: "Forest-fire prevention is
an individual and social responsibility"_ 314–315
KEMPER, H. E.: "Horse malady called dourine yielding to eradication program"
(with F. L. Schneider)_____ 370–374
KEPHART, L. W.: "Sweet clover in dry-
farming belt, once started, rarely fails"__ 567–569
KERR, ROBERT H.: "Meat-packing plants
under Federal control use pure water
supply"_____ 456–458
KIFER, R. S.: "Combining enterprises properly may increase income from farm"____ 212–213
KIMBALL, HERBERT H.: "Solar-radiation
study reveals facts highly important to
farmers"_____ 549–551
KNEELAND, HILDEGARDE: "Women on
farms average 63 hours' work weekly in
survey of 700 homes"_____ 620–622
KUHRT, W. J.: "Cooperative handling of
grain on large scale is now making headway" (with J. F. Booth)_____ 215–217
KUNSMAN, C. H.: "Light rays a factor in
helping to solve many farm problems"__ 417–418

Labels—
foodstuffs packages, meaning to alert
buyer, Katharine A. Smith_____ 405–408
4-H brand on various products, value___ 615–616
meat, requirements. F. W. Meyst_____ 452–453
Labor—
dairy-farm, saving by equipment_____ 251
farm, wages and perquisites_____ 600–601
Laborers, farm, wages and perquisites_____ 600–601
Lactation. See Milk production.
LACY, MARY G.: "Economics literature
monthly review aids the extension
worker"_____ 266–267
LA FORGE, F. B.: "Insect poison called rote-
none highly toxic but costly at present"___ 388
Lake States, forest lands, purchase. E. W.
Tinker_____ 321–323
LAMBERT, E. B.: "Mushroom culture in the
United States is a growing industry"____ 468–469
Lambing, losses, decline in national forests.
J. H. Hatton_____ 409–410
Lambs—
numbers on farms, 1925_____ 664
twinning, increase by extra feed at breeding
season. C. G. Potts_____ 410–411
Land—
Appalachian, utilization and resources.
Millard Peck_____ 132–134
clearing by poisoning trees, effectiveness.
George R. Boyd_____ 592–594
cultivated areas, expansion_____ 10–11
settlement in northern Wisconsin, grubstake stage, duration_____ 349–350
LARRICK, GEORGE P.: "Food, drug, insecticide administration protects farmer in
many ways"_____ 303–305
LASH, ELMER: "Tuberculosis of fowls can be
eradicated by using simple measures"___ 594–595
Lawn grass. See Lawns.
Lawns—
growing requirements. Russel A. Oak-
ley_____ 413–417
improvement—
by use of ammonium sulphate_ 411–413, 416–417
methods_____ 415–417
Leaching, soil, prevention_____ 479–480
Leaf—
hopper—
attack on alfalfa and red clover, cause of
yellowing. John Monteith, jr., and E.
A. Hollowell_____ 123–125

Leaf—Continued.
hopper—Continued.   Page
potato. See Potato leaf hopper.
sugar-beet. See Sugar-beet leaf hopper.
spot—
Cercospora, in sugar beets, occurrence and
control_____ 557, 558, 559
Septoria, of tomatoes, cause, growth, and
control_____ 583–585
sugar-beet, control by dusting from auto
truck. George H. Coons and Dewey
Stewart_____ 560–561
Leather—
goods, losses in curing and tanning_____ 77
quality and care for machine belts_____ 151–154
Leave, annual and sick, regulations_____ 49–50
LE CLERC, J. A.: "Cake of different kinds
needs flour of different kinds"_____ 176–177
LEE, A. R.: "Poultry need protein for their
best growth and egg production"_____ 500–502
Legislation, farm-relief, discussion by Secre-
tary_____ 29–32
Legumes, hairy, freedom from leaf-hopper
attack_____ 124
Lemons. See Citrus fruits.
LEONARD, LEWIS T.: "Soil bacteria useful to
farmers may be caused to multiply"_____ 543–544
LEUKEL, R. W.: "Seed-borne diseases of ce-
reals succumb to dust fungicides"_____ 537–538
Library accessions, numbers_____ 116
Lice, plant. See Aphids.
Light—
exposure, effect on flowering season of chrys-
anthemums_____ 194
rays, factor in solving farm problems. Russel A. Oakley_____ 417–418
See also Daylight.
Lilium spp., hybridization experiments___ 419–420
Lily breeding, fertile field for plant improvement. David Griffiths_____ 418–420
Linseed, feed products, production and consumption, annual_____ 287
Livestock—
abortion disease, losses to industry. John
R. Mohler_____ 433–434
cooperative marketing, advantages_____ 40
disease control, discussion by Secretary_ 57–59, 61
farmers, profits, increase with better husbandry. William Jackson_____ 423–425
feeding, cost reduction. Arthur T. Sem-
ple_____ 426–428
gains on Bermuda-grass pasture_____ 156
improvement—
advancement throughout world. D. S.
Burch_____ 420–422
by selective breeding. Hugh C. McPhee 428–
430
influence of educational exhibits. R. S.
Allen_____ 430–433
investigations, discussion by Secretary__ 60–61
industry, discussion by Secretary_____ 18–22
losses from foot-and-mouth disease in Eu-
rope_____ 309
marketing, cooperative association, efficiency. Kelsey B. Gardner_____ 422–423
poisoning as result of early grazing_____ 349
production, aid by market reports_____ 453–455
weighing, improved conditions at public
stockyards. C. A. Briggs_____ 434–436
See also Boar; Bulls; Calves; Cattle; Colts;
Horses; Sheep; Sow; Steers.
Living—
farm family—
home supply in Maryland, study.
Chase G. Woodhouse_____ 283–284
needs, relation to income, study. Eugene
Merritt_____ 230–282
standards—
farm, divergence on good and poor farms.
C. J. Galpin_____ 284–286
improvement by use of family budget.
C. J. Galpin_____ 555–557
Locust, 17-year, misnomer for periodical
cicada_____ 196
Logging—
advantages of tractor over older methods.
Quincy Randles_____ 438–439
farm woodlands, profits from large and
small trees_____ 587–590

Page

Logs, cutting and sawing, waste from small trees_____ 588–590
Louisiana, sugar industry, salvation by use of resistant sugar cane. E. W. Brandes_ 565–567
LOWDERMILK, W. C.: "Forest litter aids in conserving water for California farms"__ 326–327
Lumber—
cutting on farm, value of large and small trees_____ 587–590
grades suitable for farm buildings. C. V. Sweet_____ 439–441

McATEE, W. L.—
"Birds can be attracted to wood lots by various measures and practices"_____ 162–164
"Waterfowl breeding a necessary adjunct to protective measures"_____ 601–602
McCALL, A. G.: "Soil survey in 25 years maps more than half our arable land"____ 548
McCARTHY, B. F.: "Meat market reports help cattle men to suit consumer demand"_ 453–455
McCLURE, H. B.: "Movie audiences in many countries see Department's films" (with Raymond Evans)_____ 465–467
McDOWELL, J. C.: "Dairy studies show that within breeds the bigger cows win"_____ 255–256
Machinery—
agricultural, effects upon production____ 634–635
belts, cutting, installation, and care_____ 151–154
corn-borer control, improvement. R. B. Gray_____ 222–224
harvesting, improvement_____ 108, 208–210
rôle in making agriculture efficient. M. R. Cooper_____ 441–443
McKAY—
A. W.: "Cooperative-marketing schools for farmers held in three States_____ 221–222
M. B.: "Tulip 'breaking' is proved to be caused by mosaic infection" (with others)_____ 596–597
McPHEE, HUGH C.: "Livestock improvement can be accomplished by selective breeding_____ 428–430
McSWEENEY-McNARY law, encouragement to forestry_____ 98, 101
MALCOLM, OLA POWELL: "Women market 4-H brand products in increasing volume"_____ 614–620
Manikins, "talking," value as educational exhibit_____ 269–273
MANNY, T. B.: "Cooperative marketing hampered by lapses into former practices"_ 220–221
Manure, addition of organisms to soil_____ 544
Maps, agricultural. O. E. Baker_____ 640–665
Market—
information, use by clearing houses_____ 506
news, circulation and demand_____ 72–73
quotations, issue by Department_____ 504
Marketing—
associations, cooperative, maintenance difficulties. T. B. Manny_____ 220–221
cooperative—
advantages of pooling. Chris L. Christensen_____ 214–215
benefits, discussion by Secretary___ 29–31, 38–43
contracts, legal basis. L. S. Hulbert____ 218
cotton associations, contracts and services. J. S. Hathcock_____ 237–238
of dressed turkeys, means of added profit. D. H. Propps_____ 218–220
of eggs in California, grading practice__ 217–218
of tobacco, failure, causes_____ 578–580
schools for farmers in three States. A. W. McKay_____ 221–222
dressed poultry, grades, establishment___ 496–498
4-H brand products by women. Ola Powell Malcolm_____ 614–620
hay, improvement by Federal inspection. K. B. Seeds_____ 354–356
hides and skins, necessity for standards__ 356–357
wheat, discussion by Secretary____ 2–4, 17–18
wool, price decrease through careless packing. Russell L. Burrus and John P. Roberts_____ 629–630
Markets—
European, effects of World War_____ 633, 635
4-H club, organization in North Carolina_ 617–618

Page

Marshes, utilization for muskrat farming__ 469–470
MARTIN, J. F.: "Blister-rust control proves feasible in the Eastern States"_____ 167–169
MARVIN, C. F.: "Calendar has played great part in history and success of farming"__ 177–180
MASON—
O. W.: "Aphids' life history differs greatly from that of most insects"_____ 128–131
SILAS C.: "Date varieties at all growth stages shown by vegetative characters"_ 256–257
MATTOON, W. R.—
"Forest litter a good fertilizer of farm as well as tree crops"_____ 325–326
"Woods on the farm like saving account if rightly handled"_____ 628, 629
MAY, O. E.: "Molds pressed into service in utilizing some farm products" (with H. T. Herrick)_____ 464–465
Meat—
consumption, study, aid to livestock producer_____ 453–455
handling, need for constant cleanliness. A. J. Pistor_____ 451–452
horse, demand, production, and inspection_____ 374–377
inspection service, extent_____ 58–59
labels, requirements. F. W. Meyst_____ 452–453
market reports, aid to cattle men. B. F. McCarthy_____ 453–455
nutritive value and palatability, study. Paul E. Howe_____ 449–450
packing plants, Federal, use of pure water supply. Robert H. Kerr_____ 456–458
quality indications_____ 146–148
Meats—
exports, supervision requirements. Wm. H. Smith, jr_____ 458–460
production and prices, discussion by Secretary_____ 18–21
Medicines, use of biological stains_____ 265–266
MELOY, G. S.: "Cottonseed's kernel content and components are basis for grading"___ 241–242
MERRILL—
F. A.: "Extension agents get invaluable help from local volunteer leaders"_____ 274–276
M. C.: "Publications for farmers distributed in millions by Federal Government"_____ 508–511
MERRITT, EUGENE: "Family living needs studied in relation to income of farms"__ 280–282
MERZ, ALBERT R.: "Fertilizer concentration need not increase the risk of burning plants" (with William H. Ross)_____ 291–292
Mexican—
bean beetle. See Bean beetle, Mexican.
fruit worm, eradication_____ 103–104
MEYERS, LAWRENCE: Fertilizer consumption in cotton area varies with return from crop"_____ 292–293
MEYST, F. W.: "Meat labels must be informative and not false or misleading"_____ 452–453
Mica, presence and characteristics in soils___ 547
Microorganisms, cause of food spoilage, discussion_____ 306–307
Milk—
by-products, utilization, discussion by Secretary_____ 84–85
cooling stations, aid to maintenance of quality. C. E. Clement_____ 462–464
cows. See Cattle, dairy; Cows, dairy; Cows, milk.
evaporation studies, discussion by Secretary_____ 84–85
goat's, food value, research work_____ 127–128
imports and exports, discussion by Secretary_____ 22–24
production—
persistency of dairy cows, studies. M. H. Fohrman_____ 249–251
relation to size of cow_____ 255–256
secretion studies, discussion by Secretary__ 81
shipments, methods_____ 463–464
transportation tanks for, use in United States. R. P. Hotis_____ 446–449
viscosity studies, discussion by Secretary_ 84
MILLER—
E. G.: "Forest-range fencing is proceeding rapidly in Arizona and New Mexico"__ 331–332

MILLER—Continued.   **Page**
 H. A.: "Dairying in eastern Corn Belt
  has field for continued growth"_____ 254–255
T. A. H.—
 "Chimney cleaning without sweep's aid
  requires only salt"_____ 193–194
 "Ice chest for small family may be of
  simple construction"_____ 378
Mineral requirements, poultry, variation
 with age. H. W. Titus_____ 502–504
MITCHELL, G. F.: "Tea, coffee standards
 save on purchases by Government agen-
 cies"_____ 573
MOHLER, JOHN R.: "Livestock industry
 suffers heavy loss by abortion disease"____433–434
Molds—
 reactions, study_____ 464–465
 utilization in farm products. H. T. Herrick and O. E. May_____ 464–465
Monilia rot, development, temperature range 485
MONTEITH, JOHN, Jr.: "Alfalfa and red clover
 yellowed by leaf-hopper attacks" (with
 E. A. Hollowell, jr.)_____ 123–125
MORRISON, B. Y.: "Roses developed for
 dooryard are still far from well known"__ 532–534
MORSE, W. J.: "Velvet beans of a bush
 variety developed with distinguishable
 seed"_____ 598–600
Mortgages, farm, desirability as investments. 393
Mosaic—
 diseases, control work, report by Secretary_ 69
 sugar-cane—
  cause, infection, and spread_____ 566–567
  resistance studies, results_____ 564–566
 tulip, cause of "breaking." M. B. Mc-
  Kay and others_____ 596–597
Moss, E. G.: "Tobacco barns for flue curing
 best if made fireproof."_____ 577–578
Moth—
 brown-tail, infestation and control_____ 344, 345
 gipsy. See Gipsy moth.
Motion pictures—
 distribution, by States_____ 466–467
 films, number and circulation_____ 110–111
Motor vehicles, operation costs, relation to
 road building_____ 359–361
Mulch, paper, usefulness, trials. L. H.
 Flint_____ 483–484
Mules, numbers on farms, 1925_____ 660
MULFORD, FURMAN LLOYD: "Cemetery
 neatness and beauty are enhanced by park-
 like arrangement"_____ 187–190
MUNSEL, HAZEL E.: "Honey has valuable
 food properties but is low in vitamins"___ 369–370
Mushroom culture, increase in United States.
 E. B. Lambert_____ 468–469
Mushrooms, imports for 1924_____ 469
Muskrat farming, development of industry.
 Frank G. Ashbrook_____ 469–470

Narcissus bulbs, fumigation for flies. Charles
 F. Doucette_____ 470–474
Naval stores, experiment station, rosin strain-
 ing, study_____ 534–535
Nebraska, tree planting, progress with Fed-
 eral aid. Fred R. Johnson_____ 590–592
Negro extension work, promotion by local
 organizations. J. B. Pierce_____ 474–477
NELSON, E. M.: "Cod-liver oil in feeds
 requires care to preserve vitamin"_____ 205
Nemas, carriers of bacterial and fungous diseases from plant to plant. G. Steiner___ 477–479
Nematodes. See Nemas.
Neonicotine, substitute for nicotine as insect-
 icide_____ 388–389
Newsprint, paper pulp, sources and produc-
 tion_____ 120–122
NICKERSON, DOROTHY: "Color measurement of farm products is a factor in grading"_____ 206–208
Nicotine, insecticidal substitute for, development. C. R. Smith_____ 388–389
Nitrogen—
 consumption in United States_____ 480
 loss in soil by leaching, prevention. F. E.
  Allison_____ 479–480
 requirement of sugar cane. Lewis A.
  Hurst_____ 563–564
 supply, dependence on imports. P. E.
  Howard_____ 480–481

Nitrogen—Continued.   **Page**
 urea, fertilizer value. Edmund C. Shorey_ 597–
                598
Nursery stock, quarantined, disinfection for
 shipment. Walter E. Fleming_____ 512–513
Nutrition—
 animal, factors essential_____ 427
 value of fruits, tables for determining____ 340–341

OAKLEY, RUSSEL A.: "Lawn growing requires
 good seed, fertilizer and persistent work. 413–417
Oat belt, location and acreage, 1924_____ 646
Oats—
 black-stem-rust epidemics, cause_____ 535–537
 foreign introductions, value_____ 380
 smut-resistant varieties, experiments.
  T. R. Stanton and others_____ 481–482
O'BRIEN, RUTH—
 "Children's sun suits benefit health and
  promote happy play"_____ 191–193
 "Cotton fabrics again in fashion's favor for
  women's summer wear"_____ 233–235
Odors, water, cause and removal_____ 604
Oklahoma, cattle-tick eradication. L. J.
 Allen_____ 184–185
OLSON, OTTO: "Tobacco growth much af-
 fected by care and condition of seed bed"_ 580–581
Oranges. See Citrus fruits.
Orchards—
 apple, regions and acreage, 1924_____ 657
 peach, regions and acreage, 1924_____ 658
Oregon, forest-fire control by aid of settlers.
 John D. Guthrie_____ 317–319
OVERPECK, JOHN C.: "Sugar-beet seed in
 New Mexico grown by rapid method"____ 562
Ox warbles. See Cattle grubs.

Pacific Northwest, forest-lecture tour of
 schools. John D. Guthrie_____ 323–325
Packers and stockyards—
 act, enforcement, discussion by Secretary_ 56–57
 Administration, abolition_____ 47
Packing, wool, methods and results_____ 630
PAILTHORP, R. R.: "Fruits and vegetables for
 canning are sold increasingly by grade"_ 337–338
PAINE, H. S.: "Sweet potatoes as possible
 source of starch investigated"_____ 569–570
Paint, prevention of checking and weathering
 of wood. Rolf Thelen_____ 623
PALMER, ARTHUR W.: "Cotton-fiber research points way to better marketing
 practices"_____ 235–236
Paper—
 mulch, usefulness, trials. L. H. Flint___ 483–484
 newsprint, pulp sources and production_ 120–122
 supply in Alaskan forests. B. F. Heintzle-
  man_____ 120–122
Parasites—
 animal, control investigations_____ 58
 intestinal, control in fur bearers_____ 342
PARKER—
 JOHN H.: "Sorgo known as Atlas yields well
  and resists lodging"_____ 551–553
 JOSEPH B.: "Dairy-herd improvement associations formed in all leading coun-
  tries_____ 253–254
Parks, national, insect control, problem.
 H. E. Burke_____ 382–385
Pastures, Bermuda-grass, improvement
 methods. H. N. Vinall and W. T. Cobb_ 154–156
Pavement, road, types, wearing qualities____ 359,
                360–361
Peach—
 orchards, regions and acreage, 1924_____ 658
 rots, development, effect of temperature.
  Charles Brooks_____ 485
 trees, spraying against Japanese beetle____ 399
Peaches, "phony" disease, control work,
 report by Secretary_____ 68–69
Peanut growing, regions and acreage, 1924__ 652
Peat deposits as fire hazard, survey. Harry
 E. Roethe_____ 486
Pecan shelling plants, increase with demand
 for cracked kernels. C. A. Reed_____ 486–487
Pecans—
 fertilizer experiments. J. J. Skinner_____ 488–490
 production, 1924–1926_____ 487
PECK, MILLARD: "Appalachian land uses
 affected by aftermath of war"_____ 132–134
Perquisites, value to farm laborers_____ 600–601

Page

Personnel—
and Business Administration Office, functions_____ 47
numbers and turnover_____ 48
PETERSON, ESTHER C.: "Fabrics' stiffness is measurable by device made for the purpose" (with Tobias Dantzig)_____ 279–280
"Phony" disease, of peaches, control work, report by Secretary_____ 68–69
PIERCE, J. B.: "Negro extension work promoted by local organization activity"___ 474–477
PIETERS, A. J.: "Red clover's hairiness in American types is due to the leaf hopper"_____ 521–524
Pigs—
death rates, data. Oscar Steanson_____ 364–365
farrowing time, effect on mortality_____ 364–365
spring and fall farrowing death rates, comparison_____ 365
See also Hogs; Swine.
Pine—
western yellow, treatment for fence posts_ 288–289
white, blister-rust control—
in East_____ 167–169
in West_____ 166–167
Pipe, concrete, use in irrigation_____ 395–396
PISTOR, A. J.: "Meat handling needs to be safeguarded by constant cleanliness"____ 451–452
Plant—
diseases, transmission by nemas_____ 477–479
industries, research work, discussion by Secretary_____ 62–71
introduction gardens, location_____ 491–492
introductions, tests before establishment. Knowles A. Ryerson_____ 490–493
lice. See Aphids.
quarantine—
act, enforcement, discussion by Secretary_____ 102–105
and Control Administration, functions_ 47
Planting-intentions reports, benefits to farmers_____ 391–392
Plants—
burning by fertilizer concentration, prevention. William H. Ross and Albert R. Merz_____ 291–292
foreign, introduction—
and importance. B. T. Galloway____ 379–381
discussion by Secretary_____ 63
quarantined, disinfection for shipment, methods_____ 512–513
Poison baits, preparation and use against house ants_____ 132
Poisons—
rat, development and efficacy. James Silver_____ 518–521
tree, effectiveness in clearing land. George R. Boyd_____ 592–594
Pooling, advantages in cooperative marketing. Chris L. Christensen_____ 214–215
Population, movement to and from farms, discussion by Secretary_____ 43–46
Pork—
exports, requirements for Great Britain and Netherlands_____ 459
products, exports, discussion by Secretary_ 6
PORTE, W. S.: "Tomato-blight control effected by destroying remains of the crop" (with Fred J. Pritchard)_____ 583–585
Posts, fence. See Fence posts.
Potash—
deficiency in soil, effect on corn plants. John F. Trost_____ 229–230
importations, 1927_____ 493
production, increase in U. S. J. W. Turrentine_____ 493
Potato leaf hopper—
cause of hairiness in red clover of American type. A. J. Pieters_____ 521–524
infestation of legumes, control_____ 125
Potatoes—
growing, regions and acreage, 1924_____ 654
intentions-to-plant reports, reliability____ 391, 392
POTTS, C. G.: "Lamb twinning can be increased by extra feed at breeding season"_____ 411
ROY C.: "Butter certified as to quality brings profit, pleases buyer"_____ 175–176

Page

Poultry—
banding, advantages_____ 495–496
breeding, profits, increase by production control. M. A. Jull_____ 494–496
dressed—
inclusion in Federal inspection service. Rob R. Slocum_____ 498–500
tentative grades and standards. Thomas W. Heitz_____ 496–498
industry, discussion by Secretary_____ 24
mineral requirements at different ages. H. W. Titus_____ 502–504
production, investigations, report_____ 60
protein needs for growth and egg production. A. R. Lee_____ 500–502
raising, benefits from extension campaigns 190–191
tuberculosis, extent, symptoms, and control_____ 594–595
See also Chickens; Fowls; Turkeys.
POWERS, GEORGE H.: "Egg standardization facilitates recognition of quality in prices" 267–269
Precipitation. See Rainfall.
Predatory animals, losses from, and control__ 92–93
Press Service, work, discussion by Secretary_ 114
PRICE, DAVID J.: "Dust-explosion hazard exists in nearly all manufacturing plants" 263–265
Prices—
cattle and hogs, effect of tuberculosis eradication_____ 187
changes, measurement of those paid and received by farmers. C. M. Purves and C. F. Sarle_____ 444–446
cotton, discussion by Secretary_____ 11–14
depression, effect on cooperative associations_____ 220
farm—
changes, measurement_____ 444–446
products, discussion by Secretary_____ 2–4, 7–9
index numbers, interpretation_____ 7–9
livestock and meat, discussion by Secretary_____ 19–22
variation, control by crop reporting_____ 243, 244
wheat, relation to protein content, discussion_____ 17–18
PRITCHARD, FRED J.: "Tomato-blight control effected by destroying remains of the crop" (with W. S. Porte)_____ 583–585
Produce agency act, protection to consignor in interstate trade. H. A. Spillman and W. L. Evans_____ 504–506
Property, insurance against windstorms, importance_____ 612–614
PROPPS, D. H.: "Cooperative marketing of dressed turkeys is means of added profit"_ 218–220
Protein—
content of wheat, price factor, discussion___ 17–18
need by chickens, study_____ 500–502
Prune bud variations, varietal and trade significance. A. D. Shamel_____ 507–508
Prunus subhirtella. See Cherries.
Publications—
agricultural—
bibliographical aids, discussion_____ 156–159
Department and State, use by farmers__ 171–174
State, lists, description_____ 158
Department, list_____ 637–639
for farmers, distribution by Federal Government. M. C. Merrill_____ 508–511
numbers and distribution_____ 115–116
preparation by Department_____ 511
purchase, instructions_____ 509–510
Pulp, newsprint, sources and production____ 120–122
Pumps, motor, effectiveness in fighting forest fires. C. R. Tillotson_____ 311–312
Purnell Act, provisions for research work_____ 95–96
PURVES, C. M.: "Measuring changes in prices paid and prices received by farmers" (with C. F. Sarle)_____ 444–446
Radio—
broadcasting of housekeeper's chats. Josephine F. Hemphill_____ 513–514
Service—
educational programs, expansion. Morse Salisbury_____ 514–515
expansion, discussion by Secretary_____ 114–115
Rainfall—
distribution, comparison at nearby measurement stations. Alfred J. Henry____ 516–518
gauges, proximity, discussion_____ 516–518
measurement stations, work_____ 516–518

Raisin districts, location and acreage, 1924____ 658
RAMSEY, G. B.: "Watery soft rot is very
  serious market disease of vegetables"_____ 605–606
RANDLES, QUINCY: "Logging with tractors
  has many advantages over older methods". 438–
                                            439
Range, feed requirements of livestock and
  converting factors_____ 321
Ranges—
  forest, fencing, progress in Arizona and New
    Mexico. E. G. Miller_____ 331–332
  injury by early grazing_____ 348–349
Raspberries, breeding, discussion by Secre-
  tary_____ 68
Rats—
  control by poisoning_____ 518–521
  poisons, new, development and efficacy.
    James Silver_____ 518–521
Real estate—
  farm, forced sales, 1927–28_____ 309–311
  values, readjustment_____ 9–11
Recreation areas, provision by Forest Service 610–
Red clover. See Clover, red.   612
Red squill, use as rat poison_____ 518–519
REED, C. A.: "Pecan shelling plants increase with demand for cracked kernels". 486–487
Reforestation, progress in Nebraska_____ 590–592
Refrigerator, small, construction_____ 378
Reindeer, protection and breeding, discussion
  by Secretary_____ 93–94
Research—
  agricultural, bibliographical aids, discus-
    sion_____ 156–159
  animal husbandry, yields in dividends.
    E. W. Sheets_____ 125–128
  corn-borer, foundation for control of pest.
    W. R. Walton_____ 224–227
  cotton-fiber, aid to marketing. Arthur W.
    Palmer_____ 235–236
  Federal expenditure for_____ 94–96
  fur-bearer diseases, aid to fur farmer. J. E.
    Shillinger_____ 341–342
  importance to progress of mankind. A. F.
    Woods_____ 525–526
Rhizopus rot, development, temperature
  range_____ 485
Ribes spp. See Currants; Gooseberries.
Rice—
  drying on farm by use of Italian machinery.
    E. N. Bates and others_____ 526–528
  growing, regions and acreage, 1924_____ 650
  quality, effects of climate_____ 526–528
Roaches, habits and eradication_____ 204–205
Road—
  drags, types, construction, and use on the
    farm_____ 528–531
  work, farm outlets, need for skill and equip-
    ment. R. E. Royall_____ 528–531
Roads—
  dust layers for_____ 531
  Federal-aid, construction, 1928 and previous
    years_____ 105–107
  improvement, effect on operating costs of
    vehicles_____ 359–361
  maintenance, equipment needed by
    farmer_____ 528–531
  national-forest, mileage improvement____ 106–107
  See also Highways.
ROARK, R. C.: "Insecticide residues removed
  from fruit by various washes"_____ 389–390
ROBB, F. G.: "Fruit and vegetable inspec-
  tion at shipping points is increasing"____ 336–337
ROBERTS, JOHN P.: "Wool carelessly
  packed fails to realize its full value in market" (with Russell L. Burrus)_____ 629–630
ROBINSON, T. RALPH—
  "Avocado industry is rapidly developing
    in Florida and California"_____ 135–137
  "Citrus specialists find new methods of
    propagation" (with Walter T. Swin-
    gle)_____ 201–204
Rodents—
  effect upon forest production_____ 608
  See also Rats.
ROETHE, HARRY E.: "Peat deposits under
  some conditions are serious fire hazard____ 486
ROMBERGER, M. C.: "Hides and skins to be
  classed and graded under U. S. stand-
  ards"_____ 356–357

Root rot in sugar beets, occurrence and
  control_____ 557, 559
Roses—
  climbing hybrids, description and habits. 532–534
  development for dooryard. B. Y. Morri-
    son_____ 532–534
Rosin—
  quality reduction by poor straining. F. P.
    Veitch_____ 534–535
  straining, improvement needs_____ 534–535
ROSS, WILLIAM H.: "Fertilizer concentration
  need not increase the risk of burning
  plants" (with Albert R. Merz)_____ 291–292
Rot, Monilia, development, temperature
  range_____ 485
Rotenone, toxicity and use as insecticide.
  F. B. La Forge_____ 388
ROTHGEB, B. E.: "Grain quality affected by
  time of harvesting with combine ma-
  chine"_____ 346–347
Rots, citrus, prevention methods_____ 200–201
Roundworms. See Nemas.
ROYALL, R. E.: "Road work on farm outlets
  needs skill and right equipment"_____ 528–531
Rubber, production in United States, discus-
  sion by Secretary_____ 66–67
Rural life, improvement needs, discussion by
  Secretary_____ 45–46
RUSSELL, PAUL: "Japanese Higan cherries
  gain in favor for the adornment of parks". 401–403
Rust—
  blister. See Blister rust.
  stem, evidence of barberries' presence___ 535–537
RUTLEDGE, R. H.: "Forest fires destroy deer,
  grouse, bear, and other wild life"_____ 315–316
Rye—
  growing, regions and acreage, 1924_____ 648
  stem-rust epidemics, cause_____ 535–537
RYERSON, KNOWLES A.: "Plant immigrants
  pass numerous tests before becoming established"_____ 490–493

Salaries, average, for Department_____ 49
SALE, J. W.: "Water supply of rural communities frequently requires purification"__ 603–604
SALISBURY, MORSE: "Radio service of the
  department expands educational program"_____ 514–515
Sanitation, hogs, prevention of cholera and
  other diseases. U. G. Houck_____ 361–363
SARLE, C. F.: "Measuring changes in prices
  paid and prices received by farmers"
  (with C. M. Purves)_____ 444–446
Scales, arrangement and tests at stock-
  yards_____ 435–437
SCANLAN, J. J.: "Tobacco cooperative's failure attributed to numerous difficulties". 578–580
SCHNEIDER, F. L.: "Horse malady called
  dourine yielding to eradication program"
  (with H. E. Kemper)_____ 370–374
SCHOENING, H. W.: "Foot-and-mouth disease
  eradication by slaughter proved cheapest
  for U. S."_____ 308–309
Schools, cooperative marketing, for farmers. 221–222
Sclerotinia, cause of watery soft rot of vege-
  tables_____ 605–606
Screens, self-cleaning, use in dockage removal.
  R. H. Black_____ 259–260
Secretary, report of year in agriculture_____ 1–116
Seed—
  act, Federal prosecutions_____ 538
  alfalfa. See Alfalfa seed.
  cotton. See Cottonseed.
  imported, coloring, need and regulations. 122–123
  imports, samples, exhibit in department. 538–540
  misbranded, interstate shipment forbidden
    by law. E. Brown_____ 538
  red-clover. See Clover, red, seed.
  samples of introduced plants, collection.
    H. C. Skeels_____ 538–540
Seeding, winter wheat in Great Plains_____ 614
Seedlings, forest-tree, damping-off, prevention. Carl Hartley_____ 332–334
SEEDS, K. B.: "Hay marketing is much
  improved by Federal inspection"_____ 354–356
Seeds—
  foreign, removal from wheat, methods___ 210–211
  imported plants, descriptions_____ 539–540
  tree, scatter-distance, study_____ 586–587

Page

SEMPLE, ARTHUR T.: "Livestock feeder who knows feed nutrients can cut down costs" 426–428
Settlers, northern Lake States, grubstake stage, duration. William A. Hartman.. 349–350
Shade, tomato plants, aid in control of yellows. 586
SHAMEL, A. D.: "Prune bud variations have varietal and trade significance" 507–508
SHAPOVALOV, MICHAEL: "Tomato yellows due to virus that causes curly top in beets".. 585–586
Sheep—
    Columbia type—
        adaptation to intermountain region. J. M. Cooper 540–541
        origin and characteristics 540–541
    crossbreeding for western range conditions 540–541
    culling for flock improvement 631
    grazing on cut-over lands, benefits 261–262
    investigations, discussion by Secretary 60
    production and prices, discussion by Secretary 18–19, 21–22
    raising, areas, and numbers on farms, 1925.. 664
    wool production, research work 126–127
SHEETS, E. W.: "Animal husbandry research yields dividends to all" 125–128
SHEPHARD, JOHN B.: "Intentions-to-plant reports aid farmer to plan production".. 391–392
SHERMAN, C. B.: "Business men demand and get increasing fund of agricultural information" 174
SHERWOOD, SIDNEY F.: "Bagasse from sugar cane, once waste now is valuable in industry" 137–138
SHILLINGER, J. E.: "Fur farmers aided by research in combating outbreaks of disease" 341–342
SHINN, E. H.: "Extension workers need general and vocational training" 276–279
SHOREY, EDMUND C.: "Urea demonstrated to be valuable as nitrogen fertilizer" 597–598
SHRADER, H. L.: "Chick-rearing methods often greatly improved by extension campaigns" 190–191
SIEGLINGER, J. B.: "Broomcorn harvesting at the milk stage produces best brush".. 169–171
SIGGINS, H. W.: "Tree crops may be wind sown at distance from the seed trees" 586–587
Silage, use of sorghums, area in 1924 649
Silo filling, experiments. T. E. Woodward. 541–542
SILVER, JAMES: "Rat control aided by development of effective new poisons" 518–521
Sires—
    dairy, proving for milk and butterfat inheritance 82
    purebred, use in foreign countries 421
    selection, important factors 429–430
Sirup production, sugar-cane varieties for, study. P. A. Yoder 564–565
Sirups, cane and sorghum, standardization, benefits 77
SKEELS, H. C.: "Seed samples of introduced plants make big collection" 538–540
SKINNER, J. J.: "Pecans respond to commercial fertilizer when rightly applied" 488–490
Skins and hides, Federal standards, necessity. M. C. Romberger 356–357
SLOCUM, ROB R.: "Poultry (dressed) now included in the Federal inspection service". 498–500
SMITH—
    C. R.: "Insecticide research develops a promising substitute for nicotine" 388–389
    KATHARINE A.: "Labels on packages of foodstuffs mean much to alert buyer".. 405–408
    LOREN B.: "Japanese beetle is controlled on some trees by spraying" 398–401
    WM. H., jr.: "Meats for export are required to undergo special supervision" 458–460
Smith-Lever appropriation, increase 110
Smut, wheat, removal on Pacific coast. E. N. Bates and G. P. Bodnar 542–543
Soil—
    bacteria, usefulness to farmers, and multiplication. Lewis T. Leonard 543–544
    deterioration by sheet erosion, effect on fertility of vast area. Hugh H. Bennett. 544–547
    erosion. See Erosion.
    farm woodland, depletion by logging methods 590

Soil—Continued.
    glittering particles, resemblance to gold. W. H. Fry 547
    leaching, prevention 479–480
    nitrates, loss by leaching, prevention. F. E. Allison 479–480
    potash deficiency, effect on corn plants. John F. Trost 229–230
    surveys—
        extent and usefulness in 25 years. A. G. McCall 548
        work, extent and value, discussion by Secretary 78–79
Solar radiation—
    importance to farmers. Herbert H. Kimball 549–551
    measurements 550
Soot, removal from chimneys, directions 193–194
Sorghum—
    grain, growing, regions and acreage, 1924 649
    growing for cane sirup, regions and acreage, 1924 653
    sirup. See Sirups.
Sorghums—
    forage, regions and acreage, 1924 649
    See also Sorgo.
Sorgo—
    Atlas, yields and lodging resistance. John H. Parker 551–553
    Kansas Orange, comparison with Atlas sorgo 552
South Dakota, tax levies, purposes, for 8-year period 571
Sow—
    selection for herd improvement 366, 368
    "talking," value as educational exhibit 271–273
Spectrum, solar, characteristics 549
SPILMAN, H. A.—
    "Container act sets standard sizes for hampers and baskets" 213–214
    "Produce agency act protects consignor in interstate trade" (with W. L. Evans).. 504–506
Spoilage, prevention, research work 81
Spray residue, removal from fruits—
    by mechanical methods, tests. Lon A. Hawkins 553–555
    by washes 389–390
    hazards 338–340
Spraying, flies on dairy farm, directions 301–302
Sprays, Japanese beetle, directions for use. 398–401
Squill, red, use as rat poison 518–519
Stains, biological, importance in medicine 265–266
Standard container act, provisions. H. A. Spilman 213–214
Standardization, butter, benefits 175–176
Standards—
    cotton—
        basis of classification service. C. L. Finch 233
        extension through research 236
        egg, relation to prices. George H. Powers. 267–269
    farm living, divergence on good and poor farms. C. J. Galpin 284–286
    Federal, for hides and skins, necessity. M. C. Romberger 356–357
    tea and coffee, use by Government purchasing agencies. G. F. Mitchell 573
STANDING, ARNOLD R.: "Grazing too early in season is harmful to livestock and range" (with Ernest Winkler) 348–349
STANTON, T. R.: "Oat varieties that resist smut grown by experimentation" (with others) 481–482
Starch, recovery from sweet potatoes. H. S. Paine 569–570
Statistics. See Index to Statistics, p. 1139.
Steam-process canning, vegetables, retention of flavors. Lawrence H. James 180–181
STEANSON, OSCAR: "Hog profits greatly affected by heavy death rate of pigs" 364–365
STEDDOM, R. P.: "Horses of United States supply foreign demand for edible horse meat" 374–377
Steers, beef, on range, feeding for maximum weight for age. W. H. Black 148–150
STEINER, G.: "Nemas carry bacterial and fungous diseases from plant to plant" 477–479
Stem rust, black, evidence of barberries' presence. L. D. Hutton 535–537

Page

Sterility, in cattle, prevention by rations____ 81–82
STEWART, DEWEY: "Sugar-beet leaf spot
controlled by dusting from an auto truck"
(with George H. Coons)_____ 560–561
Stiffness, of fabrics, definition and measure-
ment_____ 279–280
STINE, O. C.: "World's agriculture much
changed by the war and its results"_____ 632–635
Stock—
medicines, adulteration and misbranding,
instances_____ 304
See also Livestock.
Storage rots, of fruits, result of washing for
market. D. F. Fisher_____ 338–340
Stover, corn, shredded, substitute for hay and
straw. George W. Collier_____ 231–232
Strawberries—
breeding, discussion by Secretary_____ 68
production regions and acreage, 1924_____ 659
Sugar—
crops, kinds, growing regions, and acreage__ 653
industry, Louisiana, salvation by use of disease-resistant cane. E. W. Brandes___ 565–567
Sugar-beet—
leaf hopper—
cause of tomato yellows_____ 585–586
control progress_____ 88–89
study and damage forecasts. Walter
Carter_____ 559–560
leaf spot, control by dusting from auto truck.
George H. Coons and Dewey Stewart___ 560–561
seed, growing in New Mexico. John C.
Overpeck_____ 562
Sugar beets—
crop adaptation to leaf-hopper attack____ 559–560
disease—
control, progress. G. H. Coons_____ 557–559
resistant varieties, development_____ 70
dusting for leaf-spot control. George H.
Coons and Dewey Stewart_____ 560–561
growing regions and acreage, 1924_____ 653
one-seed, study. A. F. Woods_____ 563
Sugar cane—
bagasse as valuable product. Sidney F.
Sherwood_____ 137–138
Cayana, sirup production and disadvan-
tages_____ 564–565
disease-resistant varieties, development____ 70
growing, regions and acreage, 1924_____ 653
mosaic—
resistant varieties, extension_____ 565–566
See also Mosaic.
nitrogen requirement. Lewis A. Hurst__ 563–564
varieties for sirup production, study. P.
A. Yoder_____ 564–565
Sugars, honey, character and digestibility_ 369–370
Sulphur requirements for chickens, study____ 504
Sun—
radiation, importance to farmers. Herbert
H. Kimball_____ 549–551
suits, for children, benefits in health and
play. Ruth O'Brien_____ 191–193
Sunburn, red clover, cause and description_ 123, 124
Sunlight, effect on growth, studies_____ 417–418
Superintendent of Documents, duties_____ 510
Superphosphate, double—
directions for mixture_____ 294
useful properties as fertilizer. K. D. Jacob 294
SWANSON, A. F.: "Winter-wheat seeding
date in the Great Plains varies with
locality"_____ 614
SWARTHOUT, A. V.: "Cooperative marketing
of California eggs is promoted by grading"__ 217–218
SWEET, C. V.: "Lumber grades suited for
various kinds of buildings on the farm"___ 439–441
Sweet clover—
growing in dry-farming belt_____ 567–569
hardiness in dry-farming belt. L. W.
Kephart_____ 567–569
Sweet potatoes—
growing, regions and acreage, 1924_____ 654
starch recovery, investigations. H. S.
Paine_____ 569
Swine—
sanitation exhibit, McLean County
system_____ 431–432
See also Boar; Hogs; Pigs; Sow.

Page

SWINGLE, WALTER T.: "Citrus specialists
find new methods of propagation" (with
T. Ralph Robinson)_____ 201–204
Tanks, milk transportation, increase in use_ 446–449
TAPKE, V. F.: "Oat varieties that resist smut
grown by experimentation" (with others)__ 481–482
Tariff, relation to agriculture, discussion by
Secretary_____ 32–35
Taxation, farm, discussion by Secretary_____ 35–36
Taxes—
farm, reduction by control of local expendi-
tures. Whitney Coombs_____ 570–572
local, percentage of total tax levy_____ 571–572
Tea standards, use and benefits_____ 573
Temperature changes, effects of solar radia-
tion_____ 550, 551
Tenancy, farm changes, discussion by Secre-
tary_____ 9–10
Tenant farming, opportunities for beginners.
Howard A. Turner_____ 574–575
Terraces, construction and use in erosion
control. Lewis A. Jones_____ 575–577
Texas fever tick. See Tick, cattle.
Thallium sulphate, use as rat poison_____ 518, 520
THELEN, ROLF—
"Wood checking and weathering can be
prevented by paint"_____ 623
"Wood for different uses needs different
degrees of dryness"_____ 623–624
THOR HULTGREN: "Freight-rate charges un-
der Hoch-Smith law help in farm relief"__ 334–336
Threadworms. See Nemas.
Tick, cattle, eradication—
in Oklahoma. L. J. Allen_____ 184–185
methods_____ 184
progress_____ 58
TILLOTSON, C. R.: "Forest fire fighting with a
power pump is found effective"_____ 311–312
Timber—
consumption, Alaska, control by Federal
Government_____ 121–122
growing on farms, possibilities_____ 97–99
production on farm, value of large and small
trees_____ 587–590
treatment, for fence posts, Custer National
Forest_____ 288–289
Time, farm women, apportionment over
tasks_____ 621–622
TINKER, E. W.—
"Forest lands in Lake States to be bought
by U. S. Government"_____ 321–323
"Wilderness areas in the national forests are
to be preserved"_____ 610–612
TITUS, H. W.: "Poultry's mineral requirements vary at different ages"_____ 502–504
Tobacco—
barns, for flue-curing, fireproof construction. E. G. Moss_____ 577–578
cooperative marketing, difficulties_____ 578–580
exports, increase, discussion by Secretary___ 5
growers—
benefits from intentions-to-plant reports_ 391–392
cooperative association, failure, causes.
J. J. Scanlan_____ 578–580
growing, regions and acreage, 1924_____ 650
growth, effects of care of seed bed. Otto
Olson_____ 580–581
seed bed, care, recommendations_____ 580–581
shade cloth, improvement_____ 77
wildfire, occurrence and prevention. James
Johnson_____ 581–583
Tomato—
blight, control by destruction of crop remains. W. S. Porte and Fred J. Pritch-
ard_____ 583–585
yellows, cause and prevention. Michael
Shapovalov_____ 585–586
Topography, farm, relation to income_____ 132–134
Tornadoes, damage to farm property_____ 612–613
Tractors—
advantages in logging operations. Quincy
Randles_____ 438–439
numbers in agricultural regions, 1925_____ 659
Traffic censuses, indication of highway needs.
H. S. Fairbank_____ 358–360

Page

Training, vocational, need by extension workers. E. H. Shinn_____ 276–279
Transportation. *See* Freight.
Traps, Japanese-beetle, use_____ 401
Tree—
  crops, wind sowing, distance study. H. W. Siggins_____ 586–587
  seeds, scatter-distance, factors affecting__ 586–587
Trees—
  forest—
    destruction by insects in national parks_____ 382–384
    seedling, damping-off prevention. Carl Hartley_____ 332–334
  native, decay resistance, comparisons. George M. Hunt_____ 625–626
  planting in Nebraska, progress with Federal aid. Fred R. Johnson_____ 590–592
  poisoning in clearing land, effectiveness. George R. Boyd_____ 592–594
  size, factor in lumber profits. W. W. Ashe_____ 587–590
  thinning methods_____ 625
Trost, John F.: "Corn plants dying early may reveal potash lack in soil"_____ 229–230
Trucks, milk transportation, increase in use_____ 446–449
Tuberculin testing, financial benefits_____ 187
Tuberculosis—
• eradication progress_____ 57
  in cattle, eradication progress_____ 186–187
  of fowls, and eradication measures. Elmer Lash_____ 594–595
Tulip "breaking," cause and prevention. M. B. McKay and others_____ 596–597
Tulips, inoculation with mosaic disease, methods_____ 597
Turf, growing requirements_____ 413, 414
Turkeys—
  cooperative marketing as means of added profit. D. H. Propps_____ 218–220
  loss of weight in dressing_____ 219
Turner, Howard A.: "Tenant farming on share basis usually best for beginners"___ 574–575
Turpentine and rosin industry, benefits from research_____ 77
Turrentine, J. W.: "Potash production in U. S. increasing though still far below needs"_____ 493

Ultra-violet rays, effect on physical development_____ 549
Urea, manufacture and value as nitrogen fertilizer. Edmund C. Shorey_____ 597–598

Valgren, V. N.—
  "Insurance against trifling losses is wasteful generally"_____ 390
  "Windstorm insurance on farm property is highly important"_____ 612–614
Vegetables—
  canning by new steam process, retention of flavors. Lawrence H. James_____ 180–181
  cooperative marketing, advantages_____ 41
  flavor, preservation by steam-process canning. Lawrence H. James_____ 180–181
  production—
    areas and acreage, 1924_____ 655
    discussion by Secretary_____ 26–27, 69
  watery soft rot, damage and losses_____ 605–606
  See also Fruits and vegetables.
Veitch, F. P.—
  "Belt failure often caused by neglect or faulty installation" (with R. W. Frey)_ 151–154
  "Harness life can be doubled or trebled by cleaning and repair" (with R. W. Frey)_____ 352–354
  "Rosin when poorly strained is much reduced in quality"_____ 534–535
Velvet beans—
  bush variety—
    advantages_____ 598–599
    with distinguishable seed, development. W. J. Morse_____ 598–600
  growing, regions and acreage, 1924_____ 649
Veterinarians, need for greater number_____ 61–62
Vinall, H. N.: "Bermuda-grass pastures can be made profitable by the proper methods" (with W. T. Cobb)_____ 154–156

Page

Vitamins—
  cod-liver oil, preservation in feeds. E. M. Nelson_____ 205
  deficiency in honey_____ 370
  source in meat_____ 450

Wages, farm labor, addition of perquisites. J. C. Folsom_____ 600–601
Walker—
  Ernest P.: "Bird refuges play indispensable part in saving wild life"_____ 159–162
  J. C.: "Yellows-resistant cabbages developed by plant breeding"_____ 635–636
Walton, W. R.: "Corn-borer research lays foundation for control of the pest"_____ 224–227
War, World, effects on agriculture. O. C. Stine_____ 632–635
Warbles, ox. *See* Cattle grubs.
Warner, H. K.: "Beef should be bought and cooked according to both quality and cut"_____ 146–148
Water—
  conservation by forest litter, for California farms. W. C. Lowdermilk_____ 326–327
  hardness, cause and remedy_____ 603
  pure, need in meat-packing industry_____ 456–457
  supply, rural communities, purification. J. W. Sale_____ 603–604
Waterfowl—
  conservation, discussion by Secretary_____ 90–91
  propagation, necessity in conservation. W. L. McAtee_____ 601–602
  protection, necessity of breeding places__ 601–602
  refuges_____ 160–161
  See also Wild life.
Watery soft rot, disease of vegetables. G. B. Ramsey_____ 605–606
Weather—
  Bureau—
    collection of hailstorm data_____ 350–352
    work, discussion by Secretary_____ 112–113
  effect on aphid infestation_____ 131
  relationship to yields, studies. O. L. Dawson_____ 606–607
  See also Rainfall.
Weathering, wood, prevention by painting__ 625
Weeds—
  control by use of ammonium sulphate_____ 412
  seeds, removal from wheat, methods_____ 210–211
Weiss, Freeman: "Flowers may disappoint unless effort made to check fungous disease"_____ 297–299
Western States, agricultural features_____ 640
Wheat—
  black stem-rust epidemics, cause_____ 535–537
  combine-harvested, cleaning for storage, methods. R. H. Black_____ 210–211
  exports, decline, discussion by Secretary___ 5
  harvesting time, effect on quality_____ 346–347
  mill feeds, output and distribution_____ 286
  production and marketing, discussion by Secretary_____ 2–4, 17–18
  protein content, price factor, discussion____ 17–18
  regions, location and acreage, 1924_____ 645
  smut—
    removal on Pacific coast. E. N. Bates and G. P. Bodnar_____ 542–543
    resistant strains, development_____ 65–66
  washing for smut removal, on Pacific coast. E. N. Bates and G. P. Bodnar____ 542–543
  winter—
    Great Plains, seeding date variation with locality. A. F. Swanson_____ 614
    seeding date in Great Plains. A. F. Swanson_____ 614
    yields, relation to weather, study_____ 606–607
Wheats, foreign introductions, value_____ 379–380
Wherry, E. T.: "Iodine survey planned in studies of minor constituents of food"_____ 394–395
White pine. *See* Pine, white.
Whitney, C. N.: "Fence-post treatment economizes timber from Custer Forest"__ 288–289
Wickens, David L.: "Investment of farm savings not diverse enough, records show"_____ 392–394
Wiecking, E. H.: "Foreclosure rate in farm reality still heavy in 1927–28"_____ 309–311
Wight, A. E.: "Cattle tuberculosis reduced 50 per cent by testing campaign"_____ 186–187

Wild life—

 conservation—

  discussion by Secretary_____ 89–94

  through bird refuges. Earnest P. Walker_____ 159–162

 destruction by forest fires. R. H. Rutledge_____ 315–316

Wilderness areas, preservation in national forests. E. W. Tinker_____ 610–612

Wildfire, tobacco, occurrence and prevention. James Johnson_____ 581–583

WILSON, M. C.: "Bulletins from U. S. and State agencies valued by farmers"_____ 171–174

Windbreaks, tree species adapted for_____ 592

Windstorm insurance, farm property, importance. V. N. Valgren_____ 612–614

Windstorms, damage to farm property____ 612–613

WINKLER, ERNEST: "Grazing too early in season is harmful to livestock and range" (with Arnold R. Standing)_____ 348–349

Women—

 farm—

  apportionment of time over tasks_____ 621–622

  average working week. Hildegarde Kneeland_____ 620–622

  4–H, profits from club projects_____ 614–620

Wood—

 condition of dryness for different uses. Rolf Thelen_____ 623–624

 description, use of common terms_____ 626

 lots—

  attraction of birds, methods and practices. W. L. McAtee_____ 162–164

  farm, management for profit_____ 587–590

  farm, sources of profit_____ 628–629

 native trees—

  classification as to decay resistance_____ 626

  comparative decay resistance. George M. Hunt_____ 625–626

 painting for prevention of checking and weathering. Rolf Thelen_____ 623

 preservatives, use on fence posts_____ 288–290

 seasoning, rules_____ 627

 selection, general rules. A. O. Benson___ 626–627

 value as farm crop, discussion by Secretary_ 96–98, 110

WOODHOUSE, CHASE G.: "Family living supplied by farm recorded in Maryland home study"_____ 283–284

Woodlands—

 farm, acreage increase, necessity_____ 97–99

 thinning, methods and benefits. Rolf Thelen_____ 624

WOODS, A. F.—

 "Research in every field important to progress of mankind"_____ 525–526

 "Sugar beets with only one viable seed would reduce costs greatly"_____ 563

Woods—

 farm, source of profit. W. R. Mattoon__ 628–629

 litter, value as fertilizer for farm crops____ 325–326

WOODWARD, T. E.—

 "Dairy experiments at Beltsville find corn and alfalfa most profitable"_____ 252–253

 "Dairy-farm labor saved by utilizing latest implements"_____ 251

 "Silo filling without a man in the silo gives good results"_____ 541–542

Wool—

 improvement, factors affecting quantity and quality_____ 631

 market, price decrease through careless packing. Russell L. Burrus and John P. Roberts_____ 629–630

 packing methods, importance_____ 629–630

 production—

  and prices, discussion by Secretary_____ 18–19, 21–22

  research work, benefits_____ 125–127

  variations, cause and control_____ 126

 scoured, types and prices_____ 630

 yields, increase by culling and selection. Mary J. Brandon_____ 630–632

WYCKOFF, STEPHEN N.: "Blister-rust control in western States is aided by nature"____ 166–167

Yellow—

 blight, of tomatoes, cause and control____ 585–586

 top, alfalfa, cause and description_____ 123, 124

Yellowing, alfalfa and red clover, from leafhopper attack. John Monteith, jr., and E. A. Hollowell_____ 123–125

Yellows, in cabbages, prevalence in Central States_____ 635

YODER, P. A.: "Sugar-cane varieties for sirup production now being tried out"_____ 564–565

YOUNGBLOOD, B.: "Cotton quality studies show opportunities to adjust staple production"_____ 240–241

ZELLER, J. H.: "Hog profits increased by proper selection of foundation animals"_ 365–368

Agricultural— Page
general_____ 666-1035
miscellaneous_____ 1036-1119
products—
  domestic, exports 1900-1928_____ 1018-1019
  exports and imports, value_____ 1016-1017
  foreign trade, 1909-1928_____ 1015-1035
  selected, imports, 1900-1928_____ 1020-1021
Alfalfa—
meal, prices at Kansas City, 1920-1928_____ 866
hay. *See* Hay.
seed, acreage, production, etc_____ 888-889
Almonds, production and value, 1919-1928___ 788
Animal products—
and farm animals_____ 902-972
exports, destination 1925-1928_____ 1022-1025
See also Dairy and Poultry.
Animals—
exports, destination 1925-1928_____ 1022
farm, and animal products_____ 902-972
  See also Calves; Cattle; Hogs; Horses;
    Lambs; Livestock; Poultry; Sheep.
Apple trees, numbers in orchards, by age and
variety_____ 759-763
Apples—
cold-storage holdings, 1916-1928_____ 767
exports, destination, 1925-1928_____ 1026, 1027
prices, 1889-1928_____ 764, 768-769
production, annual and by States____ 764-765
shipments, car-lot, 1927-28_____ 766
trade—
  foreign, 1889-1928_____ 764
  international, 1909-1913, 1924-1927_____ 767
Apricots—
dried, exports, destination, 1925-1928_____ 1026
production and value, 1919-1928_____ 787
Arsenic, use in insecticides and fungicides___ 1086
Asparagus—
acreage and production, 1925-1928_____ 789-790
prices, 1925-1928_____ 789-790
shipments, car-lot, 1920-1928_____ 790
Automobiles. *See also* Motor vehicles.

Bacon—
exports, destination, 1925-1928_____ 1023-1024
prices at Bristol, 1909-1928_____ 937
Bananas, imports, 1910-1929_____ 1032
Bankruptcies, farmers, 1924-1928_____ 1065
Barley—
acreage, production, etc., 1900-1928___ 728-731, 733
exports, destination, 1925-1928_____ 1027
inspection for classification_____ 735
marketings and stocks on hand_____ 733-734
prices, 1900-1928_____ 728, 732, 737
receipts at markets, 1909-1927_____ 735
trade, international, 1910-1914, 1925-1928____ 736
world acreage, yield, and production_ 730-731, 733
yields by States, 1914-1928_____ 732
Beans—
dry—
  acreage, production etc_____ 828-829
  prices, 1899, 1909, 1914-1928_____ 828, 830
  shipments, car-lot, 1920-1928_____ 830
Lima, imports, 1925-1928_____ 826
snap—
  acreage, production, and prices_____ 790-791
  shipments, car-lot, 1920-1928_____ 791
soy. *See* Soy beans.
string, imports, 1925-1928_____ 826
velvet, acreage, yield, and production_____ 835
Beef—
canned, exports, destination, 1925-1928_____ 1023
pickled, exports, destination, 1925-1928_____ 1023
cattle. *See* Cattle, beef.
cured, stocks in storage, 1916-1928_____ 918
frozen, stocks in storage, 1916-1928_____ 917
prices—
  at Chicago and New York, 1927-28_____ 964
  at leading cities, 1913-1928_____ 919

Beef—Continued. Page
products, trade, international, 1911-1913,
  1924-1927_____ 918
stocks on hand, 1916-1928_____ 917-918
trade, international, 1911-1913 and 1924-1927_ 918
See also Meats.
Beeswax, prices at Chicago, 1920-1928_____ 971
Beets, imports, 1925-1928_____ 826
Boston, wool prices, monthly, 1900-1928____ 958-959
Bread, prices in leading cities, 1913-1928_____ 690
Bridges, State disbursements for, 1927_____ 1098
Bristol, prices of bacon, 1909-1928_____ 937
Broomcorn, acreage, production, and prices__ 836
Buckwheat—
acreage, production, etc., 1909-1928_____ 753, 754
prices, 1909-1928_____ 755
yields by States_____ 754, 755
Buenos Aires, corn prices, spot, 1912-1928____ 715
Buildings, farm and land, value, 1925_____ 1074
Butter—
creamery, production, 1917-1927_____ 985, 987
exports, destination, 1925-1928_____ 1022
market receipts, 1918-1928_____ 986, 988-991
prices at six markets, 1910-1928_____ 993
trade, international, 1909-1913 and 1924-1927_ 992
Butterfat, prices received by producers, 1920-
1928_____ 992

Calves—
livestock and meat situation, 1923-1928_____ 920
market receipts, 1909-1928_____ 906-907, 909
number on farms—
  1927, 1928, 1929_____ 975
  and value, 1925-1929_____ 903
prices, 1900-1928_____ 912, 913-914
shipments from stockyards, 1925-1928_____ 909
slaughter, U. S., 1907-1928_____ 909, 915-916
Cabbage—
acreage, production, and prices_____ 792-793
imports, 1925-1928_____ 826
shipments, car-lot, 1920-1927_____ 793
Cantaloupes—
acreage, production, and prices_____ 794
shipments, car-lot, 1920-1928_____ 795
Carrots—
acreage, production, and prices_____ 795
imports, 1925-1928_____ 826
shipments, car-lot, 1920-1928_____ 796
Cattle—
beef—
  number and value, 1840, 1850, 1860, 1867-
    1929_____ 902
  prices, 1909-1928_____ 911, 912-914
dairy—
  number and value, 1850, 1860, 1867-1929_ 973-976
  purebred, number registered, 1900-1928__ 976
  See also Dairy herd.
exports, destination, 1925-1928_____ 1022
feeder, shipments from stockyards, 1920-
  1928_____ 910-911
inspected, shipments from stockyards, 1920-
  1928_____ 910-911
livestock and meat situation, 1923-1928____ 920
market receipts, 1909-1928_____ 906-909
number—
  and value, 1840, 1850, 1860, 1867-1929___ 902-903
  in foreign countries_____ 904-905
shipments from stockyards, 1920-1928___ 908-911
slaughter in—
  specified countries, 1914-1927_____ 917
  U. S., 1907-1928_____ 908, 915-916
ticks. *See* Ticks, cattle.
tuberculin testing, 1917-1928_____ 976
tuberculosis eradication, status, 1928_____ 977
See also Calves; Cows.
Cauliflower—
acreage, production, and prices_____ 796
shipments, car-lot, 1920-1927_____ 797

Celery— Page
acreage, production, and prices_____ 797
imports, 1925–1928_____ 826
shipments, car-lot, 1920–1927_____ 798
Cheese—
American—
cold-storage holdings, 1915–1928_____ 997
prices at New York, 1910–1928_____ 998
Cheddar, production, 1917–1927_____ 994
exports, destination, 1925–1928_____ 1022
receipts at five markets, 1918–1928_____ 995–997
trade, international, 1909–1913, 1924–1927__ 998
Cherries—
imports and exports, 1923–1928_____ 773
production and value, 1919–1928_____ 786, 787
Chicago, prices of—
beef, 1913–1928_____ 919
beeswax, 1920–1928_____ 971
cattle and calves, 1900–1928_____ 913–914
hides, 1894–1928_____ 966–967
hogs, 1901–1928_____ 930–931
lard, 1920–1928_____ 936
meats, 1927–28_____ 964–966
oleomargarine, 1914–1928_____ 999
sheep and lambs, 1905–1928_____ 948–949
Chickens—
prices, 1910–1928_____ 1005
See also Poultry.
Cholera, hog. See Hog cholera.
Citrus fruits—
prices, 1919–1928_____ 772–773
production, 1899, 1909, 1919–1928__ 769, 786, 787, 788
shipments, car-lot, 1920–1927_____ 770
Clover—
hay. See Hay.
seed—
acreage, production, etc_____ 886–887
prices, 1910–1928_____ 886–887, 890, 891
receipts at Chicago, 1909–1928_____ 886
Coconut oil—
prices at New York, 1909–1928_____ 1092
trade, international, 1923–1927_____ 1091
Coffee—
prices at New York, 1920–1928_____ 1088
trade, international, 1909–1913 and 1924–1927_ 1088
Cold storage, space, 1927_____ 1081–1082
Commodities, measuring equivalents, tables_ 668
Copenhagen, prices of butter, 1914–1928_____ 993
Copra—
prices at New York, 1917–1928_____ 1091
trade, international, 1923–1927_____ 1090
Corn—
acreage, production, etc., 1890–1928_____ 702–703, 706–708
canned, pack in U. S., 1917–1928_____ 798
cost of production—
by States, 1923–1927_____ 1043, 1045
by yield groups, 1927_____ 1044
exports, destination, 1925–1928_____ 1028
farm stocks, 1909–1928_____ 709
futures trading, 1924–25 and 1927–28_____ 716
inspection for classification_____ 710
marketings by farmers, 1917–1927_____ 708–709
prices—
1890–1928_____ 702, 705, 714–716
spot at Buenos Aires, 1912–1928_____ 715
spot at Liverpool, 1912–1928_____ 716
receipts at primary markets, 1909–1925 and
1921–1927_____ 709
sweet, acreage, production, and prices_____ 798
stocks on hand, 1926–1929_____ 712–713
trade, international, 1910–1914, 1925–1928___ 711
utilization, by States, 1927–28_____ 704
visible supply, 1909–1928_____ 712
world acreage, yield, and production_____ 706–708
yields by States—
1914–1928_____ 705
1923–1927_____ 1045
Cotton—
acreage—
abandoned, 1918–1928_____ 839
production, etc_____ 836–838
carry-over, July 31, 1928_____ 844–846
consumption, 1927–28_____ 846–847
exports, destination, 1925–1928_____ 1025–1026
fertilizers, use and value, 1926–1928_____ 1087
freight rates, index numbers, 1913–1928_____ 1084
ginned—
1909–1928, by seasons_____ 840
1928–29, grade and staple_____ 847–848

Cotton—Continued. Page
lint, acreage and production, 1909–1928_____ 839, 840–843
linters, production, 1917–1928_____ 839
marketings by farmers, monthly, 1916–1927_ 843
middling, prices, spot, 1909–1928_____ 851
mill consumption, 1918–1928_____ 849
premiums for staple lengths, 1920–1928_____ 852
prices, 1849, 1859, 1866–1928_____ 836, 837, 838, 850–851, 853
production costs by yield groups, 1923–1927_____ 1049–1050
supply and distribution, 1913–1928_____ 844
trade, international, 1910–1914, 1925–1928_ 849
Cottonseed—
cake, exports, destination, 1925–1928_____ 1030
meal—
exports, destination, 1925–1928_____ 1030
prices, 1920–1928_____ 855, 857
oil—
exports, destination, 1925–1928_____ 1030
prices, 1909–1928_____ 855, 856
trade, international_____ 856
prices, 1910–1928_____ 854, 855
production, annual and by States_____ 854
products, production, 1909–1928_____ 854
Cowpeas—
acreage, production, etc., 1927 and 1928____ 834
prices, 1915–1928_____ 834, 835
Cows—
dairy. See Cattle, dairy; Cows, milk.
milk—
numbers and value, 1850, 1860, 1867–1929_____ 973–974
prices received by producers, 1910–1928_ 979
numbers on farms and value, 1925–1929____ 903
See also Cattle.
Cranberries—
production and prices, 1914–1928_____ 774
shipments, car-lot, 1920–1927_____ 774
Cream, receipts at New York, 1927 and 1928_ 982
Crops, acreage, production and yield, 1926–1928_____ 1036–1037
Crossties, wood, number and cost_____ 1108
Cucumbers—
acreage, production, and prices_____ 799
imports, 1925–1928_____ 826
shipments, car-lot, 1920–1928_____ 800
Dairy—
cattle. See Cattle, dairy; Diary herd.
cows. See Cows, dairy.
herd, improvement associations, 1906–1929_ 978
herds—
tuberculin testing, 1917–1928_____ 976
tuberculosis eradication, status, 1928_____ 977
products—
production, 1922–1927_____ 980–981
receipts, prices, etc_____ 980–999
Eggplant—
acreage, production, and prices_____ 800
imports, 1925–1928_____ 826
Eggs—
cold-storage holdings, 1915–1928_____ 1011
exports, destination, 1925–1928_____ 1023
market receipts, 1917–1928_____ 1006–1010
prices, 1910–1928_____ 1013–1014
trade, international, 1909–1913 and 1924–1927_____ 1012–1013
Endive, imports, 1925–1928_____ 826
Exports—
agricultural—
destination, 1925–1928_____ 1022–1031
products, 1900–1928_____ 1015–1019, 1022–1031, 1033–1035
See also Foreign trade.
Farm—
animals and animal products_____ 902–972
buildings and land, values, 1925_____ 1074
income, value, etc., 1919–1927_____ 1051–1052
land—
acreage, 1920 and 1925_____ 1066, 1071–1072
and buildings, value, 1925_____ 1074
lands, idle, acreage, 1919 and 1924_____ 1068–1069
population, 1910 and 1920–1928_____ 1080
prices, index numbers, 1910–1928_____ 1052–1055
products, index numbers, 1919–1928_____ 1050
returns, 1927_____ 1038–1039

Farms—Continued. Page
wage rates, 1866–1928_____ 1057–1061
woodland, acreage, 1919 and 1924_____ 1070
Farmers, bankruptcies, 1924–1928_____ 1065
Farms—
acreage in principal crops, 1925_____ 1075
numbers and acreage, 1920 and 1925_____ 1066,
1071–1072
ownership changes, 1926–1928_____ 1062–1063
size, by tenure, 1925_____ 1071
tenure, length, 1925_____ 1074
value, index numbers, 1912–1928_____ 1064
Federal-aid projects, average wage, 1922–1928_ 1105
Fertilizer—
commercial, sale in cotton States_____ 1086
materials, production, value, etc_____ 1085
Fertilizers—
production, value, etc_____ 1085
use on cotton, and value, 1926–1928 _____ 1087
Figs, production and value, 1919–1928_____ 786, 788
Filberts, production and value, 1927 and 1928 _ 786
Flax—
world acreage and production_____ 740–741
See also Flaxseed.
Flaxseed—
acreage, production, etc., 1909–1928_____ 738–739
cake, exports, destination, 1925–1928_____ 1030
for oil production, 1919–1928_____ 743
marketings and stocks in store_____ 742, 744
oil. *See* Linseed oil.
prices, 1909–1928_____ 738, 739, 744
receipts at Minneapolis, 1909–1928_____ 742
trade, international, 1911–1913, 1924–1927_ 743
See also Flax.
Flour—
rye, exports, destination, 1925–1928_____ 1029
spring patents, prices at Minneapolis, 1909–
1928_____ 690
wheat—
exports, destination, 1925–1928_____ 1029
trade, international, 1910–1914 and 1925–
1928_____ 685
Foreign trade, agricultural products, 1909–
1928_____ 1015–1035
Forest products, selected, foreign trade, 1909–
1928_____ 1017
Forestry, appropriations, Federal and State_ 1113
Forests, national—
areas by States, 1928_____ 1107–1108
grazing receipts, by States, 1928_____ 1107–1108
Freight—
rates, agricultural products, index numbers, 1913–1928_____ 1084
tonnage, railways, 1922–1928_____ 1083
Frost, killing dates with length of growing
season_____ 1118–1119
Fruits—
canned, exports, destination, 1925–1928____ 1027
dried, exports, destination, 1925–1928_____ 1026
fresh, exports, destination, 1925–1928_____ 1027
production, marketing, prices, etc___ 759–788, 827
unloads at 11 markets, 1926–1928_____ 827
Fungicides—
manufacture, stated years_____ 1086
prices in New York, 1919–1927_____ 1086

Gasoline taxes, by States, 1927_____ 1104
Glucose, exports, destination, 1925–1928_____ 1027
Goats, numbers clipped, and average clip,
1920–1928_____ 960
Grain products, exports, destination, 1925–
1928_____ 1027–1030
Grains—
exports, destination, 1925–1928_____ 1027–1030
principal crops_____ 669–758
Grapefruit—
prices, 1919–1928_____ 772, 786
production, 1899, 1909, 1919–1928_____ 769, 786, 787
shipments, car-lot, 1920–1927_____ 770
Grapes—
California, sales in 11 markets_____ 776
prices, 1924–1928_____ 776
production, 1919–1928_____ 775, 787
shipments, car-lot, 1920–1928_____ 775
Grazing receipts, national forests, by States,
1928_____ 1107–1108

Hams and shoulders, exports, destination,
1925–1928_____ 1024
Hawaii, sugar production, 1914–1928_____ 877

Hay— Page
alfalfa—
acreage and production, 1919–1928_____ 861
prices, 1910–1928_____ 864, 865
clover—
acreage and production, 1919–1928_____ 861
prices, 1910–1928_____ 864
prairie, prices, 1910–1928_____ 865
receipts at 11 markets, 1908–1927_____ 862
stocks on farms, May 1, 1910–1928_____ 862
tame—
acreage, production, etc., 1909–1928_____ 857,
858, 860–862
exports and imports, 1909–1928_____ 857
prices, 1909–1928_____ 857, 862, 863–866
timothy—
acreage and production, 1919–1928_____ 861
prices, 1910–1928_____ 864, 866
wild, acreage, production, etc., 1909–1928___ 857,
859–862
yield per acre, 1919–1928_____ 860–861
Heifers, numbers on farms, 1927–1929_____ 975
Hides, prices at Chicago, 1894–1928_____ 966–967
Highways—
federal-aid, mileage and apportionment,
1917–1930_____ 1093
mileage by States, 1927_____ 1096
See also Roads.
Hog—
cholera, control work of Department,
1919–1928_____ 938
products, prices, 1913–1928_____ 936–937
Hogs—
inspected shipments from stockyards,
1920–1928_____ 928–929
live weight at Chicago, 1909–1928_____ 928
livestock and meat situation, 1921–1928_____ 933
market receipts, 1909–1928_____ 926–927
numbers—
and values, 1840, 1850, 1860, 1867–1929__ 921–922
in foreign countries_____ 923–924
prices, 1901–1928_____ 930–931
slaughter, 1907–1928_____ 927, 931–932
surveys, results, 1923–1928_____ 924–925
See also Pigs.
Honey, prices, 1920–1928_____ 972
Hops—
acreage, production, prices, etc_____ 868
consumption in U. S., 1910–1928_____ 868
exports, destination, 1925–1928_____ 1029
trade, international, 1909–1913 and 1924–1927_ 870
world acreage, yield, and production_____ 869
Horse-radish, imports, 1925–1928_____ 826
Horses—
market receipts, 1916–1928_____ 971
numbers on farms and value, 1910–1929____ 967–
968, 970
prices received by producers, 1910–1928_____ 970
See also Mules.
Hunters' licenses, returns by States, 1925–
1927_____ 1106

Imports—
agricultural products, 1900–1928_____ 1015–1017,
1020–1021, 1032, 1033–1034, 1035
See also Foreign trade.
Income, farm, value, etc., 1919–1927_____ 1051–1052
Index numbers—
farm prices, 1910–1928_____ 1052–1055
farm products, 1919–1928_____ 1050
farm values, 1912–1928_____ 1064
farm wage rates, 1866–1928_____ 1057
freight rates, agricultural products, 1913–
1928_____ 1084
prices paid by farmers, 1910–1928_____ 1056
Insecticides—
manufacture, stated years_____ 1086
prices in New York, 1919–1927_____ 1086

Kale, imports from Bermuda, 1925–1928_____ 826
Kansas City—
prices of—
alfalfa meal, 1920–1928_____ 866
cattle and calves, 1928_____ 914
receipts and prices of grain sorghums_____ 757
Kid hair, production, 1920–1928_____ 960
Labor, wage rate on Federal-aid projects,
1922–1928_____ 1105
Lamb—
frozen, cold-storage holdings, 1916–1928____ 951
prices at Chicago and New York, 1927–28__ 966

Lamb—Continued.   Page
   situation, 1921–1928_____ 951
   trade, international, 1911–1913 and 1924–1927_ 952
   See also Meats; Mutton.
Lambs—
   livestock and meat situation, 1921–1928____ 951
   numbers and value, 1925–1929_____ 940
   prices, 1905–1928_____ 948–949
   slaughter, 1907–1928_____ 950
   See also Sheep.
Land—
   farm, acreage, 1920 and 1925_____ 1066, 1071–1072
   pasture, acreage, 1924_____ 1067
   utilization, stated years_____ 1066–1072
Lard—
   compounds, exports, destination, 1925–1928_ 1025
   exports, destination, 1925–1928_____ 1025
   prices, 1909–1928_____ 936–937
   rendered, situation, 1921–1928_____ 933
   stocks on hand—
     1900–1928_____ 961–962
     1916–1928_____ 934
Lemons—
   California, farm value, 1919–1928_____ 788
   prices at New York, 1919–1928_____ 772
   production, 1899, 1909, 1919–1928_____ 769, 788
   shipments, car-lot, 1920–1927_____ 770
   trade, international, 1911–1913 and 1924–1927_ 771
Lespedeza seed, acreage, production, etc_____ 887
Lettuce—
   acreage, production, and prices_____ 801
   shipments, car-lot, 1920–1928_____ 801
Lima beans, imports, 1925–1928_____ 826
Limes, production and value, 1927–1928_____ 786
Linseed—
   meal, prices at Minneapolis, 1909–1928_____ 746
   oil—
     prices at New York, 1910–1918_____ 746
     trade, international, 1909–1913, 1924–1927_ 745
Lint, cotton, acreage and production, 1909–
   1928_____ 839, 840–843
Linters, cotton—
   exports, destination, 1925–1928_____ 1026
   production, 1917–1928_____ 839
Liverpool, prices of—
   corn, 1912–1928_____ 716
   cotton, 1912–1928_____ 853
   lard, 1909–1928_____ 937
   wheat, 1914–1928_____ 689
Livestock—
   freight rates, index numbers_____ 1084
   numbers—
     on farms, 1925_____ 1073
     slaughtered and condemned, 1907–1928___ 960
     situation, 1921–1928_____ 920, 933, 951
Louisiana, sugar production, 1914–1928_____ 876
Lumber—
   consumption, by States and regions, 1926__ 1110–
                            1111
   prices, 1913–1928_____ 1112
   production by States and regions_____ 1109
London, prices of wool, monthly, 1921–1928__ 959

Marketing associations, membership and
   business_____ 1076–1079
Meal. *See under specific name.*
Measures, equivalent weights_____ 668
Meat—
   products—
     inspection, Federal, 1907–1928_____ 962
     trade, international, 1911–1913, 1924–1927_ 963
     situation, 1921–1928_____ 920, 933, 951
Meats—
   inspection, Federal, 1907–1928_____ 962
   prices at Chicago and New York, 1927–28__ 964–
                            966
   stocks on hand, 1900–1928_____ 961–962
   trade, international, 1911–1913, 1924–1927___ 963
Middlings, flour, prices at Minneapolis, 1909–
   1928_____ 691
Milk, condensed—
   exports, destination, 1925–1928_____ 1022
   trade, international, 1909–1913 and 1924–1927_ 983
Milk—
   cows. *See* Cattle, dairy; Cows, milk.
   evaporated, exports, destination, 1925–1928_ 1022
   fluid, receipts at New York, 1927 and 1928__ 981
   powdered, exports, destination, 1925–1928__ 1022–
                            1023
   prices, 1920–1928_____ 983–984

Minneapolis, prices of—   Page
   bran and middlings, 1909–1928_____ 691
   flour, spring patents, 1909–1928_____ 690
   rye, weighted average, 1909–1928_____ 701
   wheat, weighted average, 1909–1928_____ 687
Mohair, production by States, 1920–1928_____ 960
Motor vehicles—
   registration, by States, 1927_____ 1102
   revenues, 1927, by States_____ 1103
Mules—
   market receipts, 1916–1928_____ 971
   number on farms and value, 1910–1929_____ 967,
                            969–970
   See also Horses.
Mutton—
   frozen, cold-storage holdings, 1916–1928____ 951
   prices at Chicago and New York, 1927–28___ 966
   situation, 1921–1928_____ 951
   trade, international, 1911–1913 and 1924–1927_ 952
   See also Meats.

New Orleans, prices of rice, 1909–1928_____ 751, 753
New York, prices of—
   American cheese, 1910–1928_____ 998
   beef, 1913–1928_____ 919
   coconut oil, 1909–1928_____ 1092
   coffee, 1920–1928_____ 1088
   copra, 1917–1928_____ 1091
   meats, 1927–28_____ 964–966
   peanut oil, 1916–1928_____ 874
   tea, 1920–1928_____ 1089
Nuts, production and value, 1919–1928_____ 786–789

Oatmeal—
   exports, destination, 1925–1928_____ 1028
   trade, international, 1910–1914, 1925–1928___ 726
Oats—
   acreage, production, etc., 1900–1928_____ 717–718
   cost of production—
     by States, 1923–1927_____ 1046–1047
     by yield groups, 1927_____ 1048
   exports, destination, 1925–1928_____ 1028
   inspection for classification_____ 724
   marketings, farm stocks and shipments____ 722–723
   prices, 1900–1928_____ 717, 719, 727
   receipts at primary markets, 1900–1927____ 723
   stocks in store, 1926–1929_____ 724
   trade, international, 1910–1914, 1925–1928___ 726
   visible supply, 1909–1928_____ 725
   world acreage, yield, and production_____ 720–722
   yield by States—
     1914–1928_____ 719
     1923–1927_____ 1047
Oil—
   cake—
     exports, destination, 1925–1928_____ 1030
     meal, exports, destination, 1925–1928___ 1030
     meal, trade international_____ 1033
     trade, international, 1909–1913, 1924–1927_ 1033
   coconut. *See* Coconut oil.
   cottonseed. *See* Cottonseed oil.
   flaxseed. *See* Linseed oil.
   olive, trade, international, 1909–1913 and
     1924–1927_____ 777
   peanut. *See* Peanut oil.
Oils, vegetable—
   exports—
     1910–1928_____ 1035
     destination, 1925–1928_____ 1030
   imports, 1910–1928_____ 1035
Okra, imports, 1925–1928_____ 826
Oleo oil, exports, destination, 1925–1928_____ 1025
Oleomargarine—
   manufacture, materials used, 1917–1927____ 999
   prices at Chicago, 1914–1928_____ 999
   production and consumption, 1908–1927____ 999
Olive oil, trade, international, 1909–1913 and
   1924–1927_____ 777
Olives, production and value, 1919–1928_____ 788
Omaha, prices of—
   hogs, 1927–28_____ 931
   sheep and lambs, 1927–28_____ 949
Onions—
   acreage, production, and prices_____ 802, 804
   imports, origin, 1920–1928_____ 803
   shipments, car-lot, 1920–1927_____ 803
Oranges—
   exports, destination, 1925–1928_____ 1027
   prices, 1919–1928_____ 772–773, 786
   production, 1899, 1909, 1919–1928_____ 769, 786, 787

Oranges—Continued. Page
shipments, car-lot, 1920–1927_____ 770
trade, international, 1911–1913 and 1924–1927_ 771

Parsley, imports, 1925–1928_____ 826
Pasture—
condition, 1st of month, 1909–1928_____ 866–867
lands, acreage, 1924_____ 1067
Peaches—
foreign trade, 1913–1928_____ 778
prices, 1913–1928_____ 778, 781
production, annual and by States_____ 778, 779
shipments, car-lot, 1927–1928_____ 780
Peanut oil—
prices at New York, 1916–1928_____ 874
trade, international, 1909–1913 and 1924–1927_ 874
Peanuts—
acreage, production, etc., 1916–1928_____ 870–871
for oil, production, 1919–1928_____ 872
prices, 1910–1928_____ 870–872
trade, international, 1909–1913, 1925–1927___ 873
Pears—
prices, 1910–1928_____ 781, 783
production, annual and by States_____ 781–782
shipments, car-lot, 1920–1927_____ 783
trade, foreign, 1913–1928_____ 781
Peas—
acreage, production, and prices_____ 804–805
canned, pack in U. S., 1917–1928_____ 805
imports, 1925–1928_____* 826
shipments, car-lot, 1925–1928_____ 805
Pecans—
prices, 1925–1928_____ 789
production and value, 1925–1928_____ 788–789
Peppers—
acreage, production, and prices_____ 806
imports, 1925–1928_____ 826
Pigs—
numbers and values, 1925–1929_____ 922
surveys, results, 1923–1928_____ 924–925
See also Hogs.
Pine, southern yellow, lumber prices_____ 1112
**Pineapples, production and value, 1927 and
1928**_____ 786
Plums, production and value, 1919–1928_____ 787
Population—
farm, 1910 and 1920–1928_____ 1080
percentage employed in agriculture, 1820–
1925_____ 1075
Pork—
canned, exports, destination, 1925–1928____ 1024
carcasses, prices in Great Britain, 1909–1928_ 938
fresh, exports, destination, 1925–1928_____ 1024
pickled, exports, destination, 1925–1928____ 1024
prices at Chicago and New York, 1927–28__ 965
situation, 1921–1928_____ 933
stocks on hand, 1916–1928_____ 934–935
trade, international, 1909–1913 and 1924–1927_ 935
See also Meats.
Potatoes—
acreage and production, 1909–1928_____ 806–808,
810–811
exports—
1909–1928_____ 806, 814
destination, 1925–1928_____ 1031
imports, 1909–1928_____ 806, 814
prices, 1909–1928_____ 806–807, 809, 815–816
production costs by States, 1924–1927__ 1048–1049
shipments, car-lot, 1920–1928_____ 812–814
trade, international, 1911–1913, 1924–1927___ 814
world crop, acreage, yield, and production__ 810–
811
yield—
by States, 1914–1928_____ 809
per acre, 1909–1928_____ 818, 819
Poultry—
frozen, cold-storage holdings, 1916–1928____ 1005
live and dressed_____ 1000–1005
market receipts, 1920–1928_____ 1000–1004
See also Chickens; Turkeys.
**Precipitation, selected points by months,
1928**_____ 1116–1117
Prices—
alfalfa—
meal, at Kansas City, 1920–1928_____ 866
seed, 1912–1928_____ 888, 889, 891
apples, 1889–1928_____ 764, 768–769
asparagus, 1925–1928_____ 789–790
barley, 1900–1928_____ 728, 732, 737

Prices—Continued. Page
beans—
dry, 1899, 1909, 1914–1928_____ 828, 830
snap, 1925–1928_____ 790–791
beef—
at leading cities, 1913–1928_____ 919
cattle, 1909–1928_____ 911, 912–914
beeswax, at Chicago, 1920–1928_____ 971
bran and middlings, at Minneapolis, 1909–
1928_____ 691
broomcorn, 1915–1928_____ 836
buckwheat, 1909–1928_____ 755
butter, at six markets, 1910–1928_____ 993
butterfat, 1920–1928_____ 992
cabbage, 1925–1928_____ 792–793, 794
cantaloupes, by States, 1925–1928_____ 794
carrots, by States, 1925–1928_____ 795
cauliflower, by States, 1925–1928_____ 796
celery, by States, 1925–1928_____ 797
cheese, American, at New York, 1910–1928_ 998
chickens, 1910–1928_____ 1005
citrus fruits, 1919–1928_____ 772–773, 786
clover seed, 1910–1928_____ 886–887, 890, 891
cocoanut oil, New York, 1900–1928_____ 1092
coffee, New York, 1920–1928_____ 1088
corn—
1890–1928_____ 702, 705, 714–716
by States, 1925–1928_____ 798
cotton, 1849, 1859, 1866–1928_____ 836–837,
838, 850–851, 853
cottonseed—
1910–1928_____ 854, 855
meal, 1920–1928_____ 855, 857
oil, 1909–1928_____ 855, 856
cowpeas, 1915–1928_____ 834, 835
cranberries, by States, 1924–1928_____ 771
cucumbers, by States, 1925–1928_____ 799
eggplant, by States, 1925–1928_____ 800
eggs, 1910–1928_____ 1013–1014
farm, index numbers, 1910–1928_____ 1052–1055
flaxseed, 1909–1928_____ 738, 739, 744
grapefruit, 1919–1928_____ 772, 786
grapes, 1924–1928_____ 776
hay—
1910–1928_____ 864–866
tame, 1909–1928_____ 857, 862, 863–866
hides, at Chicago, 1894–1928_____ 966–967
hog products, 1913–1928_____ 936–937
hogs, 1901–1928_____ 930–931
honey, 1920–1928_____ 972
hops, December 1, 1910–1928_____ 868
horses, 1910–1928_____ 970
insecticides and fungicides, 1919–1927_____ 1086
lambs, 1905–1928_____ 948–949
lemons, at New York, 1919–1928_____ 772
lespedeza seed, 1925–1928_____ 887
lettuce, by States, 1925–1928_____ 801
linseed—
meal at Minneapolis, 1909–1928_____ 746
oil at New York, 1910–1928_____ 746
lumber, 1913–1928_____ 1112
meats, at Chicago and New York, 1927–28_ 964–966
milk, 1920–1928_____ 983–984
milk cows, 1910–1928_____ 979
oats, 1890–1928_____ 717, 719, 727
oleomargarine, at Chicago, 1914–1928_____ 999
onions, 1925–1928_____ 802, 804
oranges, 1919–1928_____ 772–773, 786
paid by farmers, index numbers, 1910–1928_ 1056
peaches, 1913–1928_____ 778, 781
peanuts, 1910–1928_____ 870–872
pears, 1910–1928_____ 781, 783
peas, by States, 1925–1928_____ 804–805
pecans, 1925–1928_____ 789
peppers, by States, 1925–1928_____ 806
pork carcasses in Great Britain, 1909–1928__ 938
potatoes, 1909–1928_____ 806–807, 809, 815–816
rice, 1909–1928_____ 750, 751, 753
rye, 1909–1928_____ 693, 695, 701
sirup—
sorgo, 1925–1928_____ 884
sugar-cane, 1925–1928_____ 885
sorghums, 1909–1928_____ 757, 758
soy-bean oil, crude, 1910–1928_____ 833
soy beans, 1913–1928_____ 831, 833
spinach, by States, 1925–1928_____ 817
strawberries, 1925–1928_____ 784, 785
sweet potatoes, 1909–1928_____ 818, 819, 820
tea, at New York, 1920–1928_____ 1089
timothy seed, 1910–1928_____ 888, 890, 892

Prices—Continued. Page
tobacco, 1890-1928_____ 893-895, 898
tomatoes, by States, 1925-1928_____ 821
turkeys, 1912-1928_____ 1005
watermelons, 1924-1928_____ 823, 824
wheat, 1849, 1859, 1866-1928_____ 669-670,
675-676, 686-689
wool, by month and grade, 1900-1928_ ___ 957-959
Prunes—
exports, destination, 1925-1928_____ 1026
production and value, 1919-1928_____ 786, 787
Purchasing associations, membership and
business_____ 1076-1079

Raisins—
exports, destination, 1925-1928_____ 1026
production and value, 1919-1928_____ 787
Rice—
acreage, production, etc., 1909-1928_____ 747
exports, destination, 1925-1928_____ 1028
prices, 1909-1928_____ 750, 751, 753
receipts at New Orleans, 1909-1928_____ 751
trade, international, 1909-1913 and 1924-1927 752
world acreage, yield and production__ 748-749, 750
Roads—
county, mileage, 1927_____ 1099
Federal aid, construction, 1928_____ 1094-1095
local—
disbursements, 1927_____ 1101
income and funds available, 1927_____ 1100
mileage, 1927_____ 1099
State—
disbursements for 1927_____ 1098
funds available, 1927_____ 1097
mileage, 1927_____ 1096
See also Highways.
Rubber, trade international, 1909-1913 and
1924-1927_____ 1034
Rye—
acreage, production, etc., 1909-1928_____ 693-694
exports, destination, 1925-1928_____ 1028
marketing receipts, 1909-1927_____ 699
prices, 1909-1928_____ 693, 695, 701
stocks in store, 1926-1929_____ 700
trade—
foreign, 1909-1928_____ 693
international, 1910-1914, 1925-1928_____ 700
world acreage, yield and production_____ 696-698
yields by State, 1914-1928_____ 695

Seed, alfalfa, prices, 1912-1928_____ 888, 889, 891
Sheep—
inspected, shipments from stockyards,
1920-1928_____ 945-946
livestock and meat situation, 1921-1928___ 951
market receipts, 1909-1928_____ 943-944
numbers—
and value, 1840, 1850, 1860, 1867-1929___ 939-940
in foreign countries_____ 941-942
prices, 1905-1929_____ 946-949
slaughter—
1907-1928_____ 944, 950
1923-1928_____ 950
See also Lambs.
Silk, raw, production by countries, 1909-1913
and 1921-1927_____ 1092
Sirup—
maple, production, 1917-1928_____ 885
sorgo, acreage, production, and prices_____ 884
sugar-cane, acreage, production, etc_____ 885
Skins. See Hides.
Sorghums—
acreage, production, and value_____ 756
inspection for classification_____ 758
prices, 1909-1928_____ 757, 758
receipts and prices at Kansas City_____ 757
yields by States, 1921-1928_____ 757
Sorgo sirup, acreage, production, and prices_ 884
Soy-bean oil—
crude, prices, 1910-1928_____ 833
trade, international, 1923-1927_____ 832
Soy beans—
acreage, production, etc., 1927 and 1928____ 831
prices, 1913-1928_____ 831, 833
trade, international, 1923-1927_____ 832
Spinach—
acreage, production, and prices_____ 817
shipments, car-lot, 1920-1928_____ 817
Starch, exports, destination, 1925-1928_____ 1030
Stock. See Livestock.

Strawberries— Page
acreage and production, 1925-1928_____ 784
prices, 1925-1928_____ 784, 785
shipments, car-lot, 1920-1928_____ 785
Sugar—
cane, production, 1909-1928_____ 876-877
granulated, prices, 1913-1928_____ 884
maple, production, 1917-1928_____ 885
prices, 1909-1928_____ 883-884
production, 1909-1928_____ 876-877, 881
refined, exports, destination, 1925-1928_____ 1031
trade, international, 1909-1913, 1924-1927___ 882
world production, 1909-1929_____ 879, 880, 883
Sugar beets—
acreage, production, etc_____ 875
prices, by States, 1924-1928_____ 875
production, 1909-1928_____ 876, 877
world acreage, production, etc_____ 878
Sweet potatoes—
acreage and production, 1909-1928_____ 818
prices, 1909-1928_____ 818, 819, 820
shipments, car-lot, 1920-1927_____ 819
Swine. See Hogs.

Taxes, gasoline, by States, 1927_____ 1104
Tea—
prices at New York, 1920-1928_____ 1089
trade, international, 1909-1913, 1924-1927___ 1089
Temperature, selected points, by months,
1928_____ 1114-1115
Ticks, cattle, eradication progress and status,
1928_____ 919
Timothy—
hay. See Hay.
seed—
acreage, production, etc_____ 888
prices, 1910-1928_____ 888, 890, 892
receipts at Chicago, 1909-1928_____ 889
Tobacco—
acreage, production, etc_____ 893-895, 898
exports—
annual and by classes_____ 893, 899-900
destination, 1925-1928_____ 1031
prices, 1890-1928_____ 893-895, 898
trade, international, 1909-1913, 1925-1927___ 901
world acreage, production, and yield_____ 896-897
Tomatoes—
acreage, production, and prices_____ 821
canned, pack in U. S., 1917-1928_____ 823
exports, 1923-1928_____ 822
imports, 1923-1928_____ 822
shipment, car-lot, 1920-1928_____ 822
Trade, foreign. See Foreign trade.
Transportation. See Freight.
Truck crops, acreage and production, 1922-
1928_____ 825
Tuberculosis, eradication work in dairy
herds, 1917-1928_____ 976-977
Turkeys, prices, 1912-1928_____ 1005

Veal, prices at Chicago and New York, 1927-
1928_____ 964
Vegetable—
oils. See Oils, vegetable.
products, exports, destination, 1925-1928___ 1025-
1031
Vegetables—
imports, 1925-1928_____ 826
production, shipments, prices, etc_____ 789-827
unloads at 11 markets, 1926-1928_____ 827
Velvet beans, acreage, yield, and production_ 835

Wages, farm, rates, 1866-1928_____ 1057-1061
Walnuts, English, production and value,
1919-1928_____ 786, 788
Watermelons—
acreage and production, 1925-1928_____ 823
prices, 1924-1928_____ 823, 824
shipments, car-lot, 1927-1928_____ 824
Weights, equivalent measures_____ 668
Wheat—
acreage, production, etc_____ 669-674, 676, 677-679
cost of production—
by States, 1923-1927_____ 1040-1041, 1042
by yield groups, 1927_____ 1041
durum, acreage, production, etc_____ 674
exports—
1849, 1859, 1866-1928_____ 669-670
destination, 1925-1928_____ 1029
freight rates, index numbers, 1913-1928_____ 1084

Wheat—Continued.	Page
futures trading, 1924–25 and 1927–28	692
imports, 1849, 1859, 1866–1928	669–670
inspection for exports, 1921–1928	684
marketings by farmers, 1917–1927	682
mill stocks, reports, 1879–1927	690
prices—
1849, 1859, 1866–1928	669–670, 675–676, 686–689
1909–1928	686–689
spot, at Liverpool, 1914–1928	689
production by classes, 1921–1928	686
receipts—
at markets, 1917–1927	681
inspected, by classes, 1925–1927	683
stocks—
and shipments, 1909–1928	681
in store, 1926–1929	684
supply and distribution, 1899–1928	682

Wheat—Continued.	Page
trade, international, 1910–1914 and 1925–1928	685
visible supply, 1909–1928	683
winter, acreage abandoned, 1914–1928	676
world acreage, yields, and production	677–680
yields by States, 1914–1928	674, 675, 1045
Winnipeg, wheat prices, 1909–1928	689
Woodland, farm, acreage, 1919 and 1924	1070
Wool—
consumption, annual and by classes, 1910–1928	952, 956
fleece, production, by States, 1925–1928	953
prices, by month and grade, 1900–1928	957–959
raw, production, foreign trade, etc., 1909–1928	952, 957
stocks on hand, 1920–1928	954
trade, international, 1909–1913, 1925–1927	955

ADDITIONAL COPIES

OF THIS PUBLICATION MAY BE PROCURED FROM
THE SUPERINTENDENT OF DOCUMENTS
U.S.GOVERNMENT PRINTING OFFICE
WASHINGTON, D. C.
AT

$1.50 PER COPY

▽